The Top 6000 Companies in The East of England

Companies with assets exceeding £8,000,000

John D Blackburn
Editor

dp

First Edition

Spring 2019

ISBN-13: 978-1-912736-21-8

ISBN-10: 1-912736-21-7

Printed in 8pt Nimbus Sans L

Designed by URW++ Design and Development GmbH

Dellam Publishing Limited

2 Heath Drive, Sutton, Surrey, SM2 5RP

Fax: 020 8770 7478 email: enquiries@dellam.com

SAN: 0177881 EAN/GLN: 5030670177882

Table of Contents

Acknowledgements

This is a long and detailed publication containing thousands of facts and figures. It is only to be expected, despite continuous and repeated editing and checking, that errors may occur. In such cases, once we are aware of any, we publish a correction on our website.

Readers are encouraged to check regularly at www.dellam.com/books for any corrections and updates.

Although we take extreme care to ensure accuracy and being up-to-date, we cannot accept responsibility for any errors or omissions.

We appreciate your interest in our publications, and your comments and suggestions are always welcome. Please contact us at enquiries@dellam.com.

Scotland
Northern Ireland
North East
(England)
North West
(England)
Yorkshire and
The Humber
East Midlands
(England)
West Midlands
(England)
Wales
East of
England
See London
Inset
South East
(England)
South West
(England)

Scotland
North East (England)
North West (England)
Yorkshire and The Humber
East Midlands (England)
West Midlands (England)
Wales
East of England
London
South East (England)
South West (England)

Introduction

This study looks at all companies registered in the East of England and where their total assets are more than £8,000,000.

The region has a population of 6.3 million in 2017 with the UK being 66 million.

The region comprises the counties of Bedfordshire, Cambridgeshire, Essex, Hertfordshire, Norfolk and Suffolk. The main towns are Bedford, Luton, Basildon, Peterborough, Southend-on-Sea, Norwich, Ipswich, Colchester, Chelmsford and Cambridge.

The aim of this study is to provide an overview of the key movers and shakers in the East of England corporate sector. Only key data has been isolated, particularly the company's net worth and total assets, but also its full name, date incorporated, registered office, activities, shareholders, directors (with date of birth, occupation and nationality) and number of employees.

Two indicators of size are used: net worth and total assets. These are preferable to turnover which is influenced by profit margins and whether the companies are capital or labour intensive.

A short summary of the corporate sector in the East of England:

The region is largely rural and coastal with many market towns and a few medium sized cities such as Peterborough, Norwich, Luton and Cambridge. The southern part lies in the London commuter belt. The regional economy is heavily reliant on services, with a strong financial services sector, but also automotive and pharmaceutical sectors.

Total regional output (GVA) in 2016 was £147 billion (UK £1,748 billion) with total output (GVA) per head being £24,041 (UK £26,621). Economic growth (GVA), 2010-2016, was 1.9%, the same as the UK.

From May-July 2018, employment was 3,075,000 (UK being 32,397,000) with employment level at 78.4% (UK 75.5%). Unemployment rate in 2018 was 3.1% with the UK being 4%.

Manufacturing jobs in 2018 was 7.7% of all jobs and public sector jobs was 15%.

The region makes up 8.3% of total UK output, the third largest of any region. Manufacturing accounts for 11.6% of that output, just below the UK average.

There were 14,040 manufacturing businesses in the region in 2017, an increase of 1.9% from previous year. The region's largest manufacturing sectors are food and drink, transport equipment and metals.

The region had 565,000 enterprises in 2018 (down 1% on 2017) and 138,000 employers. Some 75% were made up of single employee businesses.

There were 36,935 new businesses in 2017 (up 13%) and 37,770 businesses ceased trading (up 13%).

Standard cataloguing guidelines for company names in the profile section have been used, but there will be occurrences when the name may not be strictly alphabetical. A certain licence was adopted where it was felt that strictly alphabetical could lead to improper cataloguing. Some company names have been shortened in the league tables for aesthetic reasons.

John D Blackburn
Editor

This page is intentionally left blank

Total Assets League Table

Company	Value	Company	Value
Astrazeneca PLC	£63,353,999,360	Greene King Retailing Limited	£2,168,999,936
BFC Finance Limited	£56,129,875,968	Greene King Retailing Parent Limited	£2,145,500,032
Astrazeneca Treasury Limited	£52,575,326,208	AZENCO4 Limited	£2,066,287,360
HFC Finance Limited	£48,204,828,672	Premier Foods Group Services Limited	£2,043,000,064
Tesco PLC	£44,884,000,768	Spirit Pubs Debenture Holdings Limited	£2,010,210,048
Astrazeneca Intermediate Holdings Limited	£36,037,722,112	Intertek Finance PLC	£1,983,534,976
Canada Life Limited	£31,149,299,712	Taylor Wimpey Holdings Limited	£1,941,644,032
Tesco Stores Limited	£26,563,000,320	Thomas Cook UK Limited	£1,917,830,016
Mylan Holdings Ltd.	£20,996,255,744	Signet Group Limited	£1,798,029,184
FCE Bank PLC	£19,598,000,128	Cardtronics Holdings Limited	£1,769,944,064
Astrazeneca Sweden Investments Limited	£15,696,541,696	Affinity Water Holdco Finance Limited	£1,732,210,048
Tesco Holdings Limited	£14,917,999,616	De Lage Landen Leasing Limited	£1,721,616,000
Astrazeneca UK Limited	£14,558,000,128	Affinity Water Limited	£1,713,879,040
Osprey Holdco Limited	£11,413,799,936	Hilton Finance (UK) Limited	£1,676,255,104
Osprey Acquisitions Limited	£11,306,300,416	Britvic PLC	£1,664,099,968
Anglian Water Services Limited	£10,790,700,032	Ford VH Limited	£1,662,572,288
Aldermore Bank PLC	£10,467,399,680	Premier Financing Limited	£1,658,599,936
Tesco Corporate Treasury Services PLC	£8,073,999,872	Memec Group Holdings Limited	£1,636,634,240
Anglian Water Services Financing PLC	£7,506,400,256	Premier Inn Hotels Limited	£1,612,189,056
Tesco Overseas Investments Limited	£7,190,000,128	Anglian Water Services Holdings Limited	£1,609,092,992
EE Limited	£7,143,000,064	Spirit Managed Funding Limited	£1,595,494,016
Easyjet PLC	£6,994,999,808	Sandbrook Overseas Investments Limited	£1,577,538,688
Equitable Life Assurance Society,(The)	£6,791,000,064	Hilton HHC Limited	£1,552,382,464
Easyjet Airline Company Limited	£6,672,999,936	GE Money Home Lending Holdings Limited	£1,547,659,136
Tesco Property Holdings Limited	£6,563,639,808	Biffa Waste Services Limited	£1,547,399,936
Rexam Limited	£6,200,710,656	Kudos Pharmaceuticals Limited	£1,517,933,056
Thomas Cook Group Treasury Limited	£5,947,229,184	Randstad Group UK	£1,516,844,032
Shawbrook Group PLC	£5,758,700,032	Greene King Pubs Limited	£1,511,479,040
Shawbrook Bank Limited	£5,752,000,000	TUI Travel Holdings Limited	£1,510,323,968
AWG Parent Co Limited	£5,573,062,144	Hilton International Hotels (UK) Limited	£1,487,772,288
RCI Financial Services Limited	£5,533,118,976	TUI Travel Aviation Finance Limited	£1,479,454,848
Greene King PLC	£5,221,199,872	J D Wetherspoon PLC	£1,476,313,984
Taylor Wimpey PLC	£4,966,099,968	Connect Plus (M25) Limited	£1,469,575,040
Whitbread Group PLC	£4,904,000,000	Connect Plus (M25) Holdings Limited	£1,469,575,040
Whitbread PLC	£4,892,400,128	Bourne Leisure Holdings Limited	£1,465,027,968
Ford Motor Company Limited	£4,653,000,192	Hospital Topco Limited	£1,451,212,032
Taylor Wimpey UK Limited	£4,373,367,808	Computacenter PLC	£1,449,507,968
First Choice Holidays Finance Limited	£4,349,268,992	Halma Public Limited Company	£1,446,855,936
Greene King Brewing and Retailing Limited	£3,969,999,872	Stansted Airport Limited	£1,443,810,048
TUI UK Limited	£3,931,000,064	Britvic Soft Drinks Limited	£1,437,943,040
Premier Foods Investments Limited	£3,851,200,000	MBDA UK Limited	£1,418,300,032
Leonardo MW Ltd	£3,811,793,920	TUI UK Transport Limited	£1,414,221,952
Mylan Holdings Acquisition Limited	£3,811,553,024	Cardtronics PLC	£1,403,024,000
Thomas Cook Investments (2) Limited	£3,789,469,184	RHM Group Holding Limited	£1,402,599,936
Suffolk Life Annuities Limited	£3,663,960,064	CSR Limited	£1,395,337,856
Rexam Group Holdings Limited	£3,550,648,320	Hilton UK Hotels Limited	£1,338,172,928
Qualcomm Technologies International, Ltd.	£3,480,067,840	3DS Financial Services Ltd	£1,304,574,848
Kier Limited	£3,475,500,032	Airbus Defence and Space Limited	£1,294,900,992
Tesco Overseas ULC	£3,233,027,072	MRH (GB) Limited	£1,289,891,968
Hilton International IP Holding Limited	£3,080,324,096	Countryside Properties PLC	£1,244,099,968
The Canada Life Group (U.K.) Limited	£3,079,300,096	TJX UK	£1,234,300,032
Igroup 8 Limited	£3,009,617,920	Signet Holdings Limited	£1,202,115,712
Hilton Worldwide Holding LLP	£2,958,253,056	Biffa Group Limited	£1,201,200,000
ARM Limited	£2,909,374,976	Synthomer PLC	£1,200,700,032
Taylor Wimpey Developments Limited	£2,906,313,984	Rexam UK Holdings Limited	£1,195,672,320
TUI Airways Limited	£2,847,000,064	David Lloyd Leisure Limited	£1,191,868,032
Wildcat Acquisition Holdings (UK) Limited	£2,814,381,056	Merck Sharp & Dohme Finance Europe Limited	£1,183,533,696
Kier Group PLC	£2,809,400,064	Spirit Group Retail Limited	£1,182,068,992
Rexam Overseas Holdings Limited	£2,762,554,112	Ball UK Holdco Limited	£1,168,871,168
Premier Foods Group Limited	£2,759,600,128	Cambridge Silicon Radio Holdings Limited	£1,163,511,808
BUUK Infrastructure No 2 Limited	£2,706,832,896	Safestore Holdings PLC	£1,156,600,064
George Wimpey Limited	£2,676,461,056	Scira Offshore Energy Limited	£1,154,504,960
Daiwater Investment Limited	£2,604,868,096	Thomas Cook Group Hedging Limited	£1,137,655,040
Hilton Worldwide Manage Limited	£2,571,142,144	Axalta Coating Systems UK Holding Limited	£1,117,739,648
AWG Group Limited	£2,566,819,072	BUUK Infrastructure Issuer PLC	£1,113,814,272
Cummins Generator Technologies Limited	£2,536,200,960	Thomas Cook Airlines Limited	£1,104,685,952
Hilton International IP Holding 2 Limited	£2,523,724,800	Aveva Solutions Limited	£1,104,462,976
Hilton Worldwide Holding 2 Limited	£2,394,284,288	Impellam Group PLC	£1,101,500,032
Aveva Group PLC	£2,371,713,024	Spirit Pub Company (Managed) Limited	£1,094,790,016
Cambridge Antibody Technology Group Limited	£2,339,109,120	Blue Sea Overseas Investments Limited	£1,090,800,000
Premier Foods PLC	£2,188,499,968	MC Treasury Limited	£1,086,730,624
Mytravel Group Limited	£2,188,100,096	Randstad Luxembourg UK Limited	£1,077,890,048

Thomas Cook Continental Holdings Limited	£1,061,576,128
Rexam European Holdings Limited	£1,055,580,032
Biffa PLC	£1,054,300,032
Intertek Testing Services Holdings Limited.	£1,042,019,968
Yazaki Europe Limited	£1,034,148,224
Memec Holdings Limited	£1,025,385,088
Senior Engineering Investments Limited	£1,019,582,976
Raytheon Systems Limited	£1,008,046,016
Spirit Group Parent Limited	£1,003,294,976
Ford International Liquidity Management Limited	£988,768,704
EE Finance PLC	£986,796,992
Hilton Worldwide FS Treasury Limited	£986,574,848
European Tyre Enterprise Limited	£971,427,008
Northgate Information Solutions Holdings Ltd	£965,958,016
Medimmune Limited	£963,582,976
Thomas Cook Group UK Limited	£962,800,000
Speedy 1 Limited	£951,678,976
Senior PLC	£950,800,000
Britannia Soft Drinks Limited	£950,691,968
Moto Investments Limited	£944,910,016
Moto Ventures Limited	£942,611,008
Moto Holdings Limited	£941,016,000
Marshall of Cambridge (Holdings) Limited	£939,100,032
GE Healthcare Limited	£932,070,016
Moto Hospitality Limited	£915,643,008
H.L. Foods Limited	£915,600,000
Hutchison Ports Europe Limited	£912,062,016
Countryside Properties (UK) Limited	£906,195,008
Costco Wholesale UK Limited	£895,956,992
Ocado Group PLC	£894,499,968
Costco UK Holdings Limited	£893,710,016
Accord Healthcare Limited	£891,985,984
Skanska UK PLC	£891,872,000
Illumina Cambridge Limited	£890,447,296
B/E Aerospace (UK) Limited	£886,112,832
Halma International Limited	£884,907,008
Sir Robert McAlpine (Holdings) Limited	£880,270,976
AB InBev UK Limited	£858,534,016
Tesco Treasury Services PLC	£852,000,000
Kier Construction Limited	£849,164,032
Intertek USD Finance Ltd	£848,457,408
Eisai Europe Limited	£847,257,024
Atlantis Equityco Limited	£842,520,000
Atlantis Midco Limited	£842,342,336
Seajacks International Limited	£842,342,336
Atlantis Investorco Limited	£842,293,120
Vauxhall Motors Limited	£839,100,032
Sir Robert McAlpine Limited	£833,086,016
Avnet Bidco Limited	£828,454,976
Albanwise Limited	£821,648,000
Haven Leisure Limited	£818,675,968
Halma Overseas Funding Limited	£817,015,616
Essity Holding UK Limited	£816,427,008
Premier Lotteries Capital UK Limited	£815,200,000
Premier Lotteries UK Limited	£814,899,968
Tesco Distribution Limited	£813,977,024
Tesco (Overseas) Limited	£811,825,024
HBVB	£810,892,032
Ocado Holdings Limited	£796,200,000
Onix Investments UK Ltd	£795,908,160
Northgate UK Holdings 4 Limited	£790,800,000
PPD International Investments Limited	£789,945,984
Newarthill Limited	£781,009,984
PPD Global Ltd	£777,835,008
Skanska Construction UK Limited	£774,459,008
Carestream Dental Technology Parent Limited	£770,097,920
Nissan Motor (GB) Limited	£767,649,024
Marshall Motor Holdings PLC	£765,670,976
CP Holdings Limited	£762,854,976
TUI UK Retail Limited	£755,000,000
Deuce Holdco Limited	£753,836,992
Deuce Acquisitions Limited	£752,817,984
Perkins Engines Company Limited	£748,249,984
GE Healthcare UK Limited	£748,172,032
Hutchison Ports (UK) Limited	£746,881,984
LSF9 Robin Investments Limited	£745,630,976
Solai Holdings Limited	£745,441,984
BHL (UK) Holdings Ltd	£741,400,000
Galliard Group Limited	£741,121,024
United Church Schools Foundation Ltd	£739,315,008
Aviva Central Services UK Limited	£734,000,000
Halma Financing Limited	£729,502,336
Greene King Investments Limited	£719,790,976
Computacenter (UK) Limited	£719,790,016
Wimpey Overseas Holdings Limited	£719,470,976
Acco Brands Europe Limited	£715,107,456
Port of Tilbury London Limited	£711,844,992
Essity UK Limited	£709,411,968
Synthomer Holdings Limited	£698,342,976
Countrywide PLC	£697,339,008
Premier Foods Investments No.1 Limited	£697,100,032
Costa Limited	£695,470,016
GE Medical Systems Limited	£695,057,984
NIS Acquisitions Limited	£687,932,032
Bluestone Consolidated Holdings Limited	£687,120,640
Chelmer Housing Partnership Limited	£685,174,976
Football Association Limited	£675,270,016
The Rothschild Foundation	£673,321,664
Martin McColl Limited	£672,665,024
Inexus Connections Limited	£670,928,576
Ocado Operating Limited	£663,800,000
Camelot UK Lotteries Limited	£651,699,968
Wimpey Dormant Investments Limited	£651,478,976
BGL (Holdings) Limited	£648,499,968
M Group Services Limited	£647,417,984
Sopra Steria Limited	£646,472,000
TJX Europe Limited	£643,612,992
Copthorn Holdings Limited	£634,208,000
International Flavours & Fragrances (GB) Holdings	£627,436,992
Biffa Holdings Limited	£622,896,000
Halma Investment Holdings Limited	£621,440,256
Renewable Energy Systems Holdings Limited	£620,592,000
Intralot Finance UK Limited	£618,260,544
BISL Limited	£616,499,968
Thor Topco Limited	£615,545,024
Scimitar Topco Limited	£613,473,024
London Luton Airport Limited	£611,750,016
Merck Sharp & Dohme Limited	£607,619,008
Bourne Leisure Limited	£606,860,032
David Lloyd Leisure Group Limited	£603,902,976
Motor Fuel Limited	£600,638,016
Stonegate Pub Company Financing PLC	£595,761,024
Splendid Hospitality Group LLP	£593,888,832
Wembley National Stadium Limited	£589,750,976
Amshold Group Limited	£587,838,016
Safestore Acquisition Limited	£576,177,024
Elysium Healthcare Holdings 2 Limited	£575,473,024
Pharmathen Holding 4 Ltd	£572,464,256
CD & R Firefly Bidco Limited	£571,460,992
Senior Five Limited	£570,557,504
Care UK Health & Social Care PLC	£568,059,008
Sopra Steria Holdings Limited	£567,552,000
Countrywide Group PLC	£567,011,968
Hyundai Motor UK Limited	£566,403,968
Acteon Group Limited	£565,715,008
Biffa Corporate Holdings Limited	£565,246,016
Old English Inns Limited	£562,993,024
TUI Travel Limited	£560,000,000
London Luton Airport Holdings III Limited	£558,387,968
London Luton Airport Holdings I Limited	£558,017,984
Vinci PLC	£556,436,992
G.K. Holdings No.1 Limited	£555,361,984
Jardine Motors Group UK Limited	£552,494,976
United Learning Trust	£550,627,968

Company	Value
Stock Spirits Group PLC	£548,683,712
Biffa Group Holdings (UK) Limited	£547,592,576
Thomas Cook Tour Operations Limited	£546,156,992
Vinci Construction UK Limited	£546,112,000
Lancaster Public Limited Company	£545,438,976
Tesco Blue (GP) Limited	£543,312,000
Safestore Group Limited	£543,182,976
Tesco Property Finance 1 PLC	£543,115,200
Port of Felixstowe Limited	£542,270,016
Manpower Holdings Limited	£532,308,992
Intertek Holdings Limited	£529,723,008
Premier Foods Finance PLC	£529,000,000
Ball Beverage Packaging Europe Limited	£526,601,248
Ford Retail Limited	£521,963,008
Hardwicke Investments Limited	£521,184,992
International Transport Limited	£519,320,000
3DS Financial Services EMEA Ltd	£515,662,784
Bakkavor Finance Limited	£514,768,000
HIC Treasury Limited	£514,079,584
Parker Hannifin Manufacturing Limited	£512,844,000
Network Treasury Services Limited	£506,721,056
Affinity Water Acquisitions (Midco) Limited	£505,950,016
Oxley Wharf Property 1 Limited	£505,461,952
LSF9 Robin Newco 1 Limited	£504,305,984
Acco Europe Limited	£503,971,008
Rhodia Holdings Limited	£501,308,992
HIC Racing (Chiswick) Limited	£499,137,952
TGA UK Omega Limited	£498,702,016
Whitbread (Condor) Holdings Limited	£498,235,008
Schering-Plough Holdings Limited	£498,076,992
BFSL Limited	£496,343,008
RMPA Holdings Limited	£492,438,016
RMPA Services PLC	£492,438,016
Spirit Group Equity Limited	£491,040,000
Perkins Holdings Limited	£490,375,008
David Lloyd Leisure GR Limited	£489,438,016
BAM Construct UK Limited	£489,200,000
Greene King Neighbourhood Estate Pubs Limited	£487,143,008
Willmott Dixon Holdings Limited	£486,071,008
Accolade Topco Limited	£485,166,016
Ocado Innovation Limited	£484,800,000
McColl's Retail Group PLC	£483,860,000
Affinity Water Acquisitions Limited	£483,198,016
Care UK Health & Social Care Holdings Limited	£481,000,000
Ocado Retail Limited	£476,100,000
Smiths Interconnect Group Limited	£474,943,008
Roche Products Limited	£474,462,016
Consort Medical PLC	£472,100,000
CNH Industrial Capital Europe Limited	£471,639,008
TGA UK Alpha Limited	£470,486,016
Care UK Health & Social Care Investments Ltd	£467,300,000
GPL Investments Limited	£456,754,112
Merck Sharp & Dohme (Holdings) Limited	£455,840,992
Anglian Water (Osprey) Financing PLC	£455,227,008
Eisai Manufacturing Limited	£454,234,976
Burton's Foods Limited	£450,767,008
Safestore Limited	£447,948,000
Astrazeneca US Investments Limited	£447,838,688
GDL Holdco Limited	£445,380,064
Kier Living Limited	£443,208,000
Caterpillar UK Engines Company Limited	£441,944,992
ASCO Acquisitions Limited	£440,761,984
BGL Group Limited	£439,000,000
Mylan Holdings Acquisition 2 Limited	£438,799,488
Axalta Coating Systems U.K. (2) Limited	£437,250,048
Bio Products Laboratory Holdings Limited	£434,364,000
Hilton Food Group PLC	£433,360,000
Northgate Public Services (UK) Limited	£431,332,000
Pitney Bowes Global Ltd.	£428,969,984
Iveco Limited	£428,003,008
Telford Homes PLC	£427,688,000
BUUK Infrastructure Limited	£422,461,856

Company	Value
Ball UK Holdings, Ltd	£421,335,584
Huntleigh Technology Limited	£418,406,784
Lanber Properties LLP	£418,378,048
Janssen-Cilag Limited	£415,416,992
Caretech Holdings PLC	£411,977,984
Libra (Longhurst Group) Treasury PLC	£411,956,992
Wallace Partnership Group Limited	£410,841,984
Naga UK Topco Limited	£409,176,992
Kodak International Finance Limited	£408,733,472
Spirit Pub Company (Holdco) Limited	£408,715,008
Tati Company Limited	£407,121,664
DFKA Ltd	£406,983,200
AGCO Finance Limited	£404,260,000
IMO Car Wash Group Limited	£400,265,984
TCGH Holdings Limited	£400,000,000
Hexcel Composites Limited	£399,604,000
Spirit Pub Company (Leased) Limited	£398,808,000
Forth Ports Finance PLC	£395,316,000
McCormick International Holdings	£394,406,016
BUUK Infrastructure No 1 Limited	£394,047,968
Affinity Water Acquisitions (Investments) Limited	£389,361,984
Ocado Central Services Limited	£387,900,000
Boing Acquisitions Limited	£386,828,000
Spirit Pub Company (SGE) Limited	£386,057,984
Bauer Radio Limited	£384,135,008
Rose Midco Limited	£383,684,992
Brighthouse Limited	£383,449,984
Elliott Group Limited	£383,399,008
Countryside Properties (Holdings) Limited	£382,449,984
Morrison Utility Services Limited	£382,244,000
Lupo Limited	£381,716,000
TGA UK Finance Limited	£380,143,872
Palm Paper Limited	£380,070,784
Thomas Cook Retail Limited	£379,560,992
GTC Pipelines Limited	£379,185,600
Affinity Water Capital Funds Limited	£378,851,008
Elysium Healthcare Holdings 3 Limited	£377,808,992
Lotus Cars Limited	£377,296,000
Mentmore Limited	£376,945,984
Accolade Midco Limited	£376,896,000
Hill Holdings Limited	£376,777,984
Affinity Water Acquisitions (Holdco) Limited	£375,929,984
Intertek Capital Resources Limited	£375,728,736
Robinsons Soft Drinks Limited	£371,625,984
Signet Trading Limited	£369,443,008
Kier Holdings Limited	£365,131,008
Naga UK Bidco Limited	£364,713,984
TGA Industries Limited	£364,696,992
Kwik-Fit Group Limited	£364,127,008
Impellam Holdings Limited	£363,576,000
Sorbon Homes Limited	£362,632,832
Kodak Alaris Holdings Limited	£361,712,192
Thomas Cook Finance PLC	£361,270,912
GE Money Servicing Limited	£359,737,984
Oldeurope Limited	£359,551,008
Spirit Pub Company Limited	£358,660,992
Fairview Holdings Limited	£356,788,992
Volkerwessels UK Limited	£351,801,984
BAM Construction Limited	£351,600,000
Turners (Soham) Holdings Limited	£350,580,000
Tesco Mobile Limited	£349,728,992
NPS (Holdings) Limited	£346,600,000
Argon NPS Limited	£346,600,000
Turners (Soham) Limited	£344,785,984
Runwood Homes Limited	£344,548,032
Cardif Pinnacle Insurance Holdings PLC	£344,260,000
Frontier Bidco Limited	£343,931,008
Gresham Insurance Company Limited	£342,000,000
Whirlpool UK Appliances Limited	£341,740,000
Regis Group (Holdings) Limited	£339,087,360
Marshall Motor Group Limited	£337,616,992
Renewable Energy Systems Limited	£336,766,016

Company	Amount
Access UK Ltd	£336,664,000
Britvic Overseas Limited	£336,556,992
MSX International Limited	£334,536,992
Caversham Finance Limited	£333,688,000
GW Pharmaceuticals PLC	£332,915,008
Pinnacle Insurance PLC	£332,326,016
Dimex Limited	£332,260,992
Thomas Cook West Investments Limited	£327,123,232
Hospital Company (QAH Portsmouth) Limited	£325,800,000
Hospital Company (QAH Portsmouth) Holdings Ltd	£325,800,000
Access Technology Group Limited	£324,291,008
Kier Property Developments Limited	£324,087,008
Anduff Car Wash Limited	£324,005,056
Care UK Limited	£323,600,000
Global Marine Systems Limited	£322,786,080
Caterpillar UK Group Limited	£322,132,992
CVS Group PLC	£319,000,000
BUUK Infrastructure Holdings Limited	£316,759,168
ACI Worldwide (EMEA) Limited	£316,646,016
Harman Automotive UK Limited	£316,307,360
Global Marine Holdings Limited	£315,619,040
Chelmsford Diocesan Board of Finance (The)	£314,894,016
Skanska Construction Holdings UK Limited	£314,691,008
Gannett International Finance LLP	£313,151,264
Elliott Group Holdings (UK) Limited	£311,284,000
Vale of Aylesbury Housing Trust Limited	£310,596,000
McCormick Europe Limited	£309,884,000
Fairview New Homes Limited	£309,481,984
Caterpillar Overseas Limited	£308,056,992
Amsprop Investments Limited	£308,055,968
Signet UK Finance PLC	£306,881,696
OPW Holdco Limited	£305,996,000
Aspect Ventures Limited	£305,964,000
Hill Residential Limited	£305,825,984
Napp Pharmaceutical Holdings Limited	£304,665,984
Kier Integrated Services Limited	£303,859,008
Cardtronics UK Limited	£303,830,016
Stapleton's (Tyre Services) Limited	£303,412,000
Bio Products Laboratory Limited	£302,643,008
Renault U.K. Limited	£300,583,008
Meritcape Limited	£300,435,936
Galliard Holdings Limited	£299,718,112
Inland Homes PLC	£299,600,000
Archant Holdings Limited	£297,553,696
Martin-Brower UK Ltd	£297,467,008
Baxter Healthcare Limited	£296,004,992
Robinsons (Finance) No.2 Limited	£295,481,984
Northgate Information Solutions Limited	£295,300,000
MSXI UK Limited	£294,891,008
Kwik-Fit (GB) Limited	£294,072,000
Union Maritime Limited	£292,708,416
DST Financial Services International Limited	£292,230,016
Indesit Company UK Holdings Limited	£291,823,264
Best Holdings (UK) Limited	£291,121,248
BPH Finance Number 1 Limited	£289,932,000
Affinity Water Holdings Limited	£287,670,016
Sorbon Investments Limited	£287,305,344
Swift Hotels Limited	£287,163,008
Sopra Steria Services Limited	£286,088,000
Group Lotus Limited	£283,384,000
Canada Life Finance (U.K.) Limited	£281,772,992
Du Pont (U.K.) Limited	£280,651,008
Keymed (Medical & Industrial Equipment) Limited	£279,856,992
Amersham Biosciences	£278,908,224
G's Group Holdings Limited	£278,699,008
Mothercare PLC.	£276,700,000
Willmott Dixon Construction Limited	£275,884,160
Rose Holdco Limited	£273,116,992
Arthur Topco Limited	£272,017,984
Henkel Limited	£270,438,016
Weston Homes PLC	£270,049,984
South Central Property Limited	£268,950,304

Company	Amount
Parker Hannifin 2007 LLP	£268,478,016
International Car Wash Group Financing PLC	£268,332,992
Bluecastle Enterprises Limited	£267,046,032
Parker Hannifin (GB) Limited	£266,548,992
Pitney Bowes Holdco Limited	£266,402,000
Weston Group PLC	£265,880,992
First Data Europe Limited	£265,202,000
Affinity Water Finance (2004) PLC	£264,904,000
Tesco Property Holdings (No.2) Limited	£264,796,080
LSF9 Robin Midco Limited	£263,548,992
UNEX Group Holdings Limited	£263,355,712
ASCO Group Limited	£263,300,000
Raytheon United Kingdom Limited	£263,128,992
Newsquest Media Group Limited	£262,886,000
Abbey Developments Limited	£262,689,568
Paypoint PLC	£262,524,000
Forfarmers UK Limited	£262,495,008
GE Money Home Finance Limited	£262,042,608
Hexcel Holdings (UK) Limited	£260,003,072
Galliard Homes Limited	£257,703,344
LSF9 Robin Newco 2 Limited	£257,162,000
Camelot Holdco Limited	£256,728,000
Kodak Limited	£255,500,000
Ball Beverage Packaging UK Ltd	£255,106,000
Brighthouse Holdings Limited	£254,842,000
Impellam UK Limited	£254,456,992
Kier Services Limited	£253,762,000
Coveris Flexibles (Gainsborough) UK Limited	£252,456,992
Majestic Wine PLC	£251,967,008
Camelot Topco Limited	£250,944,992
CVS (UK) Limited	£250,786,000
Atalian Servest Group Holdings Limited	£247,700,000
Montanaro UK Smaller Co's Investment Trust PLC	£247,676,992
Spirit Managed Holdings Limited	£247,378,000
TCCT Retail Limited	£247,055,008
Care UK Health & Social Care Finance Limited	£246,902,000
Gyron Internet Limited	£246,318,000
Aesica Pharmaceuticals Limited	£246,000,000
TCCT Holdings UK Limited	£245,396,992
JRL Group Holdings Limited	£244,142,128
Malthurst Limited	£243,398,000
F. Perkins Limited	£241,420,992
Tesco TLB Properties Limited	£241,308,480
Walstead Holdings Limited	£237,936,160
Hamsard 3352 Limited	£237,866,800
CNH Industrial Capital Limited	£236,037,680
Spirit (SGL) Limited	£234,996,000
Hovis Limited	£234,578,000
Atalian Servest Limited	£234,400,000
Aura Finance Limited	£234,196,032
Brighthouse Group Limited	£233,292,000
Northgate UK Holdings 2 Limited	£232,900,000
Dhamecha Holdings Limited	£232,784,000
Northgate UK Holdings 3 Limited	£232,000,000
Northgate UK Holdings 1 Limited	£232,000,000
Mothercare UK Limited	£231,000,000
London Luton Airport Group Limited	£230,424,000
Connect Plus (M25) Intermediate Limited	£230,339,008
JRL Group Limited	£229,338,288
Domino Printing Sciences Public Limited Company	£229,044,000
Shogun Finance Limited	£227,207,008
Adda Hotels	£226,913,728
London Luton Airport Operations Limited	£225,952,992
Avnet Holdings UK Limited	£225,816,336
Tradex Insurance Holdings Limited	£224,988,992
Tradex Insurance Company Limited	£224,964,000
Safran Electrical & Power UK Ltd	£224,582,000
Hill Partnerships Limited	£224,531,008
Wallace Estates Limited	£224,355,008
Safestore Properties Limited	£223,668,992
Hopkins and Moore (Developments) Limited	£223,499,008
R. G. Carter Holdings Limited	£223,375,008

Steria UK Corporate Limited	£222,722,000	Blackbuck Topco Limited	£192,817,216
Itron Development UK Ltd	£222,199,360	Kier Highways Limited	£192,764,992
Pitney Bowes Holdings Limited	£221,423,008	Greene King Acquisitions No.2 Limited	£192,723,008
Synthomer (UK) Limited	£221,330,000	Envigo CRS Limited	£192,271,008
Computerlinks (UK) Limited	£221,203,920	Roche Holding (UK) Limited	£190,786,000
Kwik-Fit Euro Limited	£220,903,008	Pitney Bowes Limited	£190,344,000
Hovis Holdings Limited	£220,691,008	Aura Holdings (Newcastle) Limited	£190,340,992
W.E.Black Limited	£220,541,120	Kier Infrastructure and Overseas Limited	£190,048,000
SKF (U.K) Limited	£219,952,000	Sir Robert McAlpine Enterprises Limited	£189,664,992
Oxley Wharf Property 2 Limited	£219,689,360	The Capital Pub Company Limited	£189,635,008
Myriad Capital PLC	£219,074,000	Morrison Utility Services Holdings Limited	£189,391,008
Newsquest Capital Limited	£219,000,000	UK Real Estate Limited	£189,299,520
Sealed Air Limited	£218,580,992	Dhamecha Foods Limited	£188,968,992
OPW Topco Limited	£217,980,000	IBC Vehicles Limited	£188,624,000
Lancaster Motor Company Limited	£217,504,992	Crane Limited	£188,136,288
Caretech Community Services Limited	£216,876,000	Inland Homes 2013 Limited	£187,183,264
Thistledove Limited	£216,868,000	GHG 37 (Alexandra Hospital) Limited	£187,176,992
Stock Spirits (UK) Limited	£216,776,992	Sogea Holdings (UK) Limited	£186,660,992
Shanly Homes Limited	£213,357,648	Tuskerdirect Limited	£185,849,040
Medtronic Limited	£212,692,992	PPG Industries (UK) Limited	£185,780,992
Carestream Dental Technology Topco Limited	£212,537,744	The Babraham Institute	£185,104,000
Malthurst Petroleum Limited	£212,475,008	P G S International Limited	£184,642,336
PPD CT Investments LLP	£212,380,416	Kestrel Loans No. 4 Limited	£184,448,000
Panther Securities P L C	£211,962,000	Barnardo's	£184,364,000
Rhodia Limited	£211,896,000	Britvic Brands LLP	£184,016,000
Zara UK Topco Limited	£211,290,000	Ventus Investments Limited	£183,856,448
Volkerwessels Limited	£211,092,992	Senior Finance Four Limited	£183,024,992
Tesco Food Sourcing Limited	£210,518,000	Sir Robert McAlpine Capital Ventures Limited	£182,715,392
Swan Housing Capital PLC	£210,447,008	Hexcel (U.K.) Limited	£182,416,512
Bairds Malt Limited	£209,660,000	Kestrel Holdings Limited	£182,340,992
Twentieth Century Fox Television Distribution (UK)	£209,570,784	Bauer Consumer Media Limited	£182,107,008
Navigator Terminals Midco Limited	£209,240,000	Bourne Holidays Limited	£181,990,000
Woodford Holdings Limited	£209,200,000	Thompson Investments (London) Limited	£180,576,736
Care UK Community Partnerships Ltd	£209,184,992	VolkerFitzpatrick Limited	£179,503,008
Oxley Wharf Limited	£208,570,912	St.Albans Diocesan Board of Finance (The)	£179,470,000
Be Living Holdings Ltd	£208,207,008	Elysium Healthcare No. 2 Limited	£179,348,992
Whitbread Hotel Company Limited	£207,151,008	Beko PLC	£179,327,008
Midwich Group PLC	£207,031,008	The Active Learning Trust Limited	£178,816,000
Solvay Solutions UK Limited	£207,010,000	TM Group Holdings Limited	£178,732,000
Volac International Limited	£206,500,000	AMPY Holdings Limited	£178,723,760
Basinghall Mortgage Finance No.1 Limited	£206,357,536	Seajacks 2 Limited	£178,079,824
Hopkins Homes Limited	£206,300,992	Abbeyfield Society (The)	£177,806,000
McLaren Construction Limited	£205,860,512	Spen Hill Developments Limited	£177,520,000
Costco Limited	£205,079,008	Kingsway Asset Co Limited	£177,003,936
Camelot Bidco Limited	£205,054,000	Domino UK Limited	£176,591,008
Genzyme Limited	£205,024,992	Sorbon Estates Limited	£175,584,336
Atlas Copco UK Holdings Limited	£204,647,008	Norse Group Limited	£175,304,000
Pacific (BC) Topco 3 Limited	£203,882,384	Independent Pipelines Limited	£174,732,416
TLC Group Limited	£203,683,040	Dow Agrosciences Limited	£174,562,000
Skanska Rashleigh Weatherfoil Limited	£202,738,000	Wilson Connolly Holdings Limited	£173,555,008
PPD UK Holdings Limited	£202,576,000	BBA Aviation Lynton Group Limited	£173,122,000
CATM Australasia Holdings Limited	£202,451,776	Memec Group Limited	£173,006,208
Seajacks 5 Limited	£202,436,176	Malthurst Retail Limited	£172,567,008
Inexus Group (Holdings) Limited	£201,603,168	Fluxys UK Limited	£172,487,536
Blackbuck Acquisitions Limited	£201,193,792	Platinum Topco Limited	£171,971,168
Blackbuck Midco Limited	£201,193,792	McMullen & Sons, Limited	£171,648,000
Wren Topco Limited	£200,296,992	Lundbeck UK LLP	£171,163,008
Blue Arrow Ltd.	£199,786,000	Sherrygreen Limited	£171,018,000
Higgins Group PLC	£199,340,000	Rexam Finance Sweden Limited	£170,789,856
EResearchTechnology UK 1 Limited	£199,326,000	Britvic International Investments Limited	£170,228,000
Rights and Issues Investment Trust PLC	£198,870,000	Ragleth Limited	£170,010,000
Countryside Zest (Beaulieu Park) LLP	£198,711,696	Carlisle Staffing PLC	£169,970,000
UK Waste Management Limited	£198,639,008	Unity Schools Partnership	£169,808,000
Ball Europe Limited	£198,525,648	Xaar PLC	£169,750,000
Zellis UK Limited	£198,071,008	Yang Ming (UK) Ltd	£169,668,224
Pacific (BC) Topco 5 Limited	£196,817,488	Inland Limited	£169,394,176
Pacific (BC) Topco 4 Limited	£196,308,000	Watford Association Football Club Limited (The)	£168,852,896
Retail Charity Bonds PLC	£193,619,008	Norfolk Capital Limited	£168,826,000
RC Bond Holdings Limited	£193,568,992	Welding Institute (The)	£168,782,000
London Luton Airport Holdings II Limited	£193,224,992	Smart Meter Assets 1 Ltd	£168,669,520
Kier Finance Limited	£193,208,992	Butlins Skyline Limited	£168,567,008
Horizon Discovery Group PLC	£193,164,992	Burton's Foods (Holdings) Limited	£168,338,000

Company	Value
MJT Securities Limited	£167,686,224
Anglia Maltings (Holdings) Limited	£167,528,992
Victory Housing Trust	£167,332,992
CNH Industrial Oldco Capital Limited	£167,024,544
GDSK Limited	£166,474,480
Kidde Products Limited	£166,066,000
Hydac Limited	£165,738,576
Kier Cross Keys Dev LLP	£165,480,000
Aeroflex Limited	£165,408,000
DFKA UK Holdings Limited	£164,295,024
Seajacks 1 Limited	£163,129,808
GDL (Millharbour) Limited	£162,070,064
NHS Professionals Limited	£162,048,992
Peerglow Asset Limited	£161,026,672
Spearhead International Limited	£160,636,000
Electrolux PLC	£159,998,000
Camelot Interco Limited	£158,732,000
GE Bio-Sciences Investments Limited	£157,712,000
Bayard Metering (UK)	£157,576,000
Ridgeway Garages (Newbury) Limited	£157,060,000
Hospital Company (Oxford John Radcliffe) Holdings	£156,732,992
Hospital Company (Oxford John Radcliffe) Ltd	£156,732,992
Maritime Group Limited	£156,342,000
Inhealth Group Limited	£156,195,008
Myriad Healthcare Holdings Limited	£155,879,008
MHL Holdco Limited	£155,523,360
Bespak Europe Limited	£155,496,992
Bayer Cropscience Limited	£155,350,000
NEC Capital (UK) PLC	£154,100,000
MRBL Limited	£154,090,000
Seajacks 3 Limited	£154,071,056
Randstad UK Holding Limited	£154,052,000
Hollywood Bowl Group PLC	£153,584,000
International Car Wash Group Ltd.	£153,356,000
Coveris Flexibles UK Limited	£153,338,000
Galliard Developments Limited	£153,230,640
Compare The Market Limited	£153,200,000
The Lindsell Train Investment Trust PLC	£152,376,000
EUSA Pharma (UK) Limited	£152,351,008
Inhealth Group Holdings PLC	£152,156,992
Xaarjet Limited	£151,696,000
NEC Europe Ltd	£151,679,792
Ely Diocesan Board of Finance (The)	£151,627,008
Norwich Diocesan Board of Finance Limited (The)	£150,900,000
Shared Services Connected Ltd	£150,602,000
Mytravel Pioneer Limited	£150,000,000
Safestore Investments Limited	£150,000,000
Platinum Acquisition Limited	£149,896,496
RR Donnelley UK Limited	£149,876,992
Beckman Holdings Limited	£149,832,992
Senior UK Limited	£149,584,000
Inhealth UK Holdings Limited	£149,200,992
Paypoint Collections Limited	£148,905,184
Spirit Pub Company (Services) Limited	£148,659,008
EResearchTechnology Limited	£148,514,112
Optionis Limited	£148,430,544
Clarke International Limited	£148,342,096
Bespak Holdings Limited	£148,196,992
RANC Holdings Limited	£148,106,368
Mustard Global Limited	£147,909,088
Hexcel Europe Limited	£147,885,440
Moto Finance PLC	£147,866,000
Cardpoint Limited	£147,822,000
UNEX Finance Limited	£147,775,664
Essity Operations Manchester Limited	£147,176,000
General Domestic Appliances Holdings Limited	£146,974,000
Forextra Developments Limited	£146,904,336
Peterborough Diocesan Board of Finance (The)	£146,862,800
Rexam Finance Company Limited	£146,840,592
ABSL1 Limited	£146,092,176
Rexam Beverage Can (India Holdings) Limited	£146,070,464
Intertek Overseas Holdings Limited	£145,764,000
Inhealth Limited	£145,763,008
Lotus Group International Limited	£145,638,000
Cambridge Innovation Capital PLC	£145,322,288
UNEX Investment Properties Limited	£143,787,232
Maritime Transport Limited	£143,298,000
UNEX Holdings Limited	£143,235,408
Countrywide Estate Agents	£143,219,008
Parker Hannifin Limited	£143,076,000
Arrow Electronics (UK) Limited	£142,663,008
Durkan Holdings Limited	£142,434,064
Kwik-Fit Finance Limited	£142,388,992
Sepura PLC	£142,070,320
Druid Group Limited	£141,682,000
Harman International Industries Limited	£141,404,992
Pacific (BC) Topco 2 Limited	£141,320,560
Consensus Support Services Limited	£141,296,992
Acteon US Financing Limited	£140,689,792
GVS Prepaid Limited	£139,968,496
Autolink Concessionaires (M6) PLC	£139,007,008
TUI Travel Group Solutions Limited	£138,948,096
Stantec Europe Limited	£138,834,000
EResearchTechnology UK 2 Limited	£138,743,920
ITS Testing Services (UK) Limited	£138,723,008
Majestic Wine Warehouses Limited	£138,679,008
Camelot Midco Limited	£138,330,000
Care UK Healthcare Holdings Limited	£138,112,992
Elysium Healthcare LC Limited	£137,518,000
Brookgate Limited	£137,155,808
Macarthys Laboratories Limited	£137,148,992
Chamberlain Holdings Public Limited Company	£136,760,208
Hampden Holdings Limited	£136,648,496
Fairview Hotels Limited	£136,622,640
Thrive Homes Finance PLC	£135,878,000
TUI Group Fleet Finance Limited	£135,841,088
David Lloyd Leisure Properties No.2 Limited	£135,176,992
Porcelanosa U.K. Limited	£134,772,000
Stefanini International Holdings Ltd	£134,697,600
Arthur Pikco Limited	£134,348,992
Arthur Midco 2 Limited	£134,282,000
Costa Express Limited	£133,937,000
Biffa Municipal Limited	£133,547,000
Papa Topco Limited	£133,039,000
Papa Midco Limited	£133,035,000
Archant Community Media Limited	£132,899,000
Be Living Limited	£132,793,184
Consort Medical Finance Limited	£132,617,608
Taylor Woodrow Construction	£132,612,000
International Flavours & Fragrances I.F.F.(GB) Ltd	£132,164,000
Kingsway Mezz Hold Co Limited	£131,986,816
CQS Natural Resources Growth and Income PLC	£131,823,000
James Latham Public Limited Company	£131,763,000
TUI Travel Overseas Holdings Limited	£131,721,000
John Innes Centre	£131,468,000
Aprite (GB) Limited	£131,193,000
Matthew Homes Limited	£131,039,160
Balanus Limited	£131,015,000
Senior Finance Six Limited	£130,925,520
Imagination Technologies Group Limited	£130,912,000
Kier International Limited	£130,469,000
Oxford Cambridge and RSA Examinations	£130,200,000
CATM North America Holdings Limited	£129,756,576
Overture Bidco Limited	£129,579,000
St Albans Operating Company Limited	£129,475,000
Graincorp UK Limited	£129,298,000
Caring Homes Healthcare Group Limited	£129,171,000
Buzzard Leisure Limited	£129,000,000
Mick George Limited	£128,930,000
Marshall of Cambridge Aerospace Limited	£128,769,000
Saffron Housing Finance PLC	£128,359,000
Housing Gateway Limited	£128,319,832
Autolink Concessionaires (A19) Limited	£128,286,992
Medivet Group Limited	£128,100,616

Company	Value
Porvair PLC	£127,947,000
BV PMT Holdings Ltd	£127,540,856
THR Number One PLC	£127,210,000
Autolink Holdings (M6) Ltd	£127,078,000
Foray 989 Limited	£126,810,000
Konica Minolta Business Solutions (UK) Limited	£126,706,000
Northgate Public Services Limited	£126,600,000
Origin UK Operations Limited	£126,524,000
Eisai Limited	£126,478,576
Australian Pacific Touring (U.K.) Limited	£126,385,120
Hutchison Ports (UK) Holding Limited	£126,277,000
Lathams Limited	£125,868,000
Cambridge Meridian Academies Trust	£125,650,000
Granitte Investments (UK) Limited	£125,554,400
Platinum Newco II Limited	£125,000,000
P.J. Carey (Contractors) Limited	£124,872,688
Acco-Rexel Group Services Limited	£124,768,000
Kier Developments Limited	£124,506,000
Shure Europe Holdings Limited	£124,386,464
Treatt PLC	£124,265,000
Linx Printing Technologies Limited	£124,090,000
GHG 2 (Clementine Churchill Hospital) Limited	£124,077,000
Malthurst South East Limited	£124,077,000
David Lloyd Leisure Properties No.4 Limited	£123,962,000
ASCO (DC4) Limited	£123,841,000
Newincco 1270 Limited	£123,700,328
Five Arrows Investments Limited	£123,690,912
Flamingo Horticulture Investments Limited	£123,647,000
Morrison Utility Services Investments Limited	£123,531,000
Triangle Aviation (UK) Holdings Limited	£123,488,112
Triplerose Limited	£123,471,992
Process Sensing Technologies Ltd.	£123,401,472
Boing Midco Limited	£123,128,000
Overture Topco Limited	£122,598,000
Apperly Estates Limited	£122,557,816
Tesco Freetime Limited	£122,312,000
Retro Properties Limited	£122,175,000
Avingtrans PLC	£121,749,000
Arkarius Bidco Limited	£121,735,624
Aesica BC Limited	£121,700,000
Industrial Chemicals Group Limited	£121,617,424
3D European Holdings Limited	£121,134,000
Lundbeck Group Limited	£121,013,320
Willoughby (880) Limited	£120,908,000
Atlas Copco Limited	£120,718,000
Higgins Construction PLC	£120,509,000
Anglian Windows Limited	£120,272,000
Henry Moore Foundation (The)	£119,924,160
Taylor Wimpey Property Company Limited	£119,677,000
Premier Inn Ochre Limited	£119,652,000
David Lloyd Leisure Operations Holdings Limited	£119,509,000
Malthurst Estates Limited	£119,496,000
Trelanoak Limited	£119,140,000
Early Learning Centre Limited	£119,100,000
PPG Holdings (U.K.) Limited	£118,706,000
Taylor Wimpey 2007 Limited	£118,685,000
Reliance Infra Projects (UK) Limited	£118,668,744
Corona Energy Retail 4 Limited	£118,481,440
CH Old Co Limited	£118,400,000
Frontier Midco Limited	£118,117,000
Teaching Personnel Limited	£117,922,000
TGA UK Holdings Limited	£117,714,096
Chaplin Group Limited	£117,549,480
Shiva Kingsway Limited	£117,024,896
Hill Group Services Limited	£117,019,000
Tattersalls Limited	£117,009,000
Uniserve Holdings Limited	£116,781,000
Teledyne E2V Limited	£116,781,000
Acteon UK Financing Limited	£116,712,552
LDH (La Doria) Limited	£116,552,000
The Cam Academy Trust	£116,442,000
Taylor Wimpey SH Capital Limited	£116,364,000
EUSA Pharma Holdco 1 (UK) Limited	£116,354,376
EUSA Pharma Holdco 2 (UK) Limited	£116,352,608
Howard Investment Company Limited	£116,120,264
Midwich Limited	£116,061,000
Perkins Group Limited	£116,042,000
Hallmark Care Homes Group Holdings Limited	£115,878,248
Spen Hill Regeneration Limited	£115,346,424
Anglian Group Limited	£115,093,000
Skanska Project Developments Limited	£115,084,000
Produce Investments Limited	£114,788,000
P. Flannery Plant Hire (Oval) Limited	£114,142,808
Hutchinson Group Limited	£114,041,000
Seachill UK Limited	£113,339,000
Amgen Limited	£112,766,000
GHG 3 (Ross Hall Hospital) Limited	£112,766,000
Flying Trade Group PLC	£112,340,544
The Gala Film Partners, LLP	£112,058,120
Education Management Corporation Limited	£111,891,240
Mastercard Prepaid Management Services Limited	£111,878,000
RO Trading Limited	£111,794,000
Xaar Technology Limited	£111,631,000
SME Group PLC	£111,588,000
Vindis Group Limited	£111,467,584
Norwich City Football Club PLC	£111,391,000
Selex Elsag Limited	£111,179,000
Thor Midco Limited	£110,966,000
Lorien Resourcing Limited	£110,621,000
Thor Holdco Limited	£110,385,000
Iveco Holdings Limited	£109,994,000
Archant Community Media Holdings Limited	£109,663,936
Swan New Homes Limited	£109,661,000
Laxmi BNS Holdings Limited	£109,609,696
Wernick Hire Limited	£109,399,168
AFE Group Limited	£108,945,000
B & M Care Group Limited	£108,836,704
Morrisroe Group Limited	£108,799,408
Countryside Properties (WGL) Limited	£108,540,000
Altro Group PLC (The)	£108,345,000
Aura (Newcastle) Project Company Limited	£108,321,000
Melesey Limited	£108,172,000
Peak Securities Limited	£108,068,072
Arrow Electronics UK Holding Limited	£107,973,000
Mulalley & Co. Limited	£107,964,000
Town and City Pub Group Limited	£106,963,000
David Lloyd Leisure Properties No.3 Limited	£106,861,000
City & Country Group PLC	£106,828,824
Refined Holdings Limited	£106,678,000
Higgins Homes PLC	£106,665,000
Pitney Bowes Software Europe Limited	£106,453,000
Sika Limited	£106,345,200
Volkerrail Group Limited	£106,023,000
Bryant Park Hospitality UK Limited	£105,830,000
Corona Gas Management Limited	£105,769,296
MHE JVCO Limited	£105,500,000
UNEX Corporation Limited	£105,272,592
Capital Pub Company Trading Limited	£105,237,000
Motus Group (UK) Limited	£105,122,000
Diligenta Limited	£105,087,000
RCG-Moody International Limited	£104,807,000
Amsprop London Limited	£104,494,552
Corporate Associates Limited	£104,283,760
Amsprop Bishopsgate Limited	£103,946,048
Gallagher Holdings Limited	£103,837,488
Jarrold & Sons Limited	£103,712,000
Greenyard Frozen UK Limited	£103,519,000
Spirit Pub Company (Trent) Limited	£103,507,000
Flamingo Horticulture Ltd	£103,454,000
Alternative Bridging Corporation Limited	£103,020,976
Aviva Health UK Limited	£102,872,000
TWI Limited	£102,772,000
Frontier Holdco Limited	£102,742,000
GS Acquisitions Limited	£102,444,000

Company	Amount
Farmland Reserve UK Limited	£102,399,000
Mid Holding Co UK Limited	£102,321,984
International Industrial Metals Limited	£102,287,560
Matchroom Sport Limited	£101,950,608
Sorbon Finance Limited	£101,949,224
SLR Management Limited	£101,139,400
O-I Glass Limited	£100,909,000
Liebherr - Great Britain Limited	£100,768,560
Lancaster Cars Limited	£100,647,000
Wren Midco Limited	£100,600,096
Spreadex.Com Limited	£100,599,856
Spreadex Limited	£100,599,856
The Original Bowling Company Limited	£100,523,000
Ardex Holdings UK Limited	£100,100,000
Ardex Investments UK Limited	£100,063,000
Bard Pharmaceuticals Limited	£100,001,000
R.G. Carter Construction Limited	£99,933,000
TTP Group PLC	£99,588,000
Triangle Regional Aircraft Leasing Limited	£99,569,944
Action for Children	£99,481,000
Polyco Healthline Limited	£99,279,000
The Invicta Film Partnership No.23, LLP	£99,070,112
Besana UK Limited	£98,957,624
Kelvin Hughes Limited	£98,847,000
Ridgeon Holdings Limited	£98,714,000
Hagondale Limited	£98,650,648
Hawk Incentives Limited	£98,199,000
H.L. Hutchinson Limited	£97,800,000
The Invicta Film Partnership No.37, LLP	£97,431,904
Skanska J.V. Projects Ltd	£97,344,000
Pizza Hut (U.K.) Limited	£97,308,000
Strutt and Parker (Farms),Limited	£97,179,000
Anglian Venture Holdings Limited	£97,138,000
Metaswitch Networks Ltd	£97,042,192
Space Truust UK Ltd	£96,950,280
Cambridge Education Group Limited	£96,736,000
Rexam Finance Netherlands Limited	£96,665,768
Laindon Holdings Limited	£96,455,984
Grigny (UK) Limited	£96,418,048
Care UK Clinical Services Limited	£96,340,000
THR Number 12 PLC	£96,257,000
Selex ES International Ltd	£95,750,000
Kodak Alaris Limited	£95,606,152
David Lloyd Clubs Holdings Limited	£95,138,000
Bush Boake Allen Enterprises Limited	£94,925,000
Dencora 2000 Limited	£94,873,824
David Lloyd Clubs Limited	£94,857,000
Mylan UK Healthcare Limited	£94,587,000
Mediterranean Shipping Company (UK) Limited	£94,421,000
Dreams Topco Limited	£94,250,000
Dreams Limited	£94,250,000
Signature Flight Support London Luton Limited	£94,052,920
J O Sims Holdings Limited	£94,023,232
Wren Buyerco Limited	£94,009,480
CGN Global Uranium Limited	£93,845,576
Acushnet Europe Ltd	£93,835,000
Inspiration Trust	£93,723,832
Regis Group Services Limited	£93,702,584
J O Sims Holdings (1896) Limited	£93,618,784
Cergold Limited	£93,224,952
Hamsard 3353 Limited	£93,007,432
Seajacks 4 Limited	£92,655,336
Network Homes Investments Limited	£92,629,920
John Sisk & Son Limited	£92,521,000
Shaneel Enterprises Limited	£92,480,160
Biffa GS UK Holdings Limited	£92,156,000
Gardline Shipping Limited	£92,055,000
Carraig Gheal Wind Farm Limited	£91,991,248
Cosco Shipping (UK) Company Limited	£91,660,536
Stantec UK Limited	£91,520,000
Skanska Infrastructure Investment UK Limited	£91,503,000
Balton CP Limited	£91,419,928
Oxley Wharf Property 3 Limited	£91,353,488
Rabbah Bloodstock Limited	£91,309,224
Charles Wilson Engineers Limited	£91,267,480
Pentagon Limited	£91,099,000
R O Ventures Limited	£91,076,080
Claas UK Limited	£91,041,000
Takeda UK Limited	£91,023,712
Toro Principal Manufacturing Limited	£91,008,752
Cambridge Colleges Funding PLC	£90,848,096
Kerneos Holding Northern Europe Limited	£90,405,000
Platinum Midco Limited	£90,332,704
Platinum Midco 2 Limited	£90,332,704
Juddmonte Farms Limited	£90,121,096
Countrywide Surveyors Limited	£90,116,000
Colleycare Limited	£89,918,456
Avnet EMG Ltd.	£89,700,000
Signature Flight Support Limited	£89,625,048
GHG 34 (Priory Hospital) Limited	£89,559,000
Amshold Securities Limited	£89,152,768
Biffa Waste Management Limited	£88,983,000
Loxford School Trust Limited	£88,856,584
Microlease Limited	£88,697,000
Martin McColl Retail Limited	£88,414,000
Gardline Holdings Limited	£88,261,000
Rockley Dene Homes Limited	£88,143,448
Fulton Maritime Limited	£88,097,576
Anderson Construction Limited	£88,019,768
Napp Pharmaceutical Group Limited	£87,942,000
Fulton Maritime Holdings Limited	£87,923,608
Thoratec Europe Limited	£87,681,592
DSV Air & Sea Limited	£87,552,000
Skanska TAM Limited	£87,536,000
Halma Euro Trading Limited	£87,525,712
PHH 1 Limited	£87,468,000
Ground Control Holdings Limited	£87,304,584
Galliard Construction Limited	£87,221,768
Lancaster Luxury Vehicles Limited	£87,158,000
Pro Cam Europe Limited	£87,089,000
Wandale Limited	£86,751,960
Signet Direct Diamond Sourcing Limited	£86,724,216
Richard Shuttleworth Trustees	£86,653,000
Central Trust Syndicate Number One Limited	£86,607,000
Garreg Lwyd Energy Limited	£86,383,000
Teledyne E2V (UK) Limited	£86,287,000
Castledon Ltd	£86,284,000
Ipeco Holdings Limited	£86,283,000
Bosch Rexroth Limited	£86,185,000
Services Machinery & Trucks Ltd	£85,918,000
Blue Anchor Leisure Holdings Limited	£85,864,000
Blue Anchor Leisure Limited	£85,860,000
Slug and Lettuce Company Limited	£85,570,000
Caversham Trading Limited	£85,510,000
Generics (U.K.) Limited	£85,286,000
Away Resorts Limited	£85,240,272
Cambridge Consultants Limited	£85,147,424
J. Reddington Ltd	£85,098,440
Larkfleet Homes Limited	£85,049,576
Polar Speed Distribution Limited	£85,041,064
Volkerrail Limited	£84,958,000
Amshold International Limited	£84,816,392
Muntons (Holdings) PLC	£84,695,000
MTK Wireless Limited	£84,693,952
GW Pharma Limited	£84,644,096
Kreutzer Touristik GB Limited	£84,572,904
Macron Safety Systems (UK) Limited	£84,565,000
The Mossbourne Federation	£84,459,000
Brook Street (UK) Limited	£84,448,000
Imagination Technologies Limited	£84,409,000
Mansley Group Holdings Limited	£84,375,952
Swan Investments Group Limited	£84,370,776
J J Food Service Holdings Limited	£83,924,080
Newmarston Ltd	£83,866,736

Tilda Limited	£83,850,000
Edgewell Personal Care Holdings UK Ltd.	£83,820,000
Muntons PLC	£83,778,000
Carlisle Group Limited	£83,748,000
DC Management Services Limited	£83,639,000
Carlson Wagonlit UK Ltd	£83,417,200
A.J. Morrisroe & Sons Limited	£83,417,040
Greene King Properties Limited	£83,318,560
Blancco Technology Group PLC	£83,201,000
Anglian Home Improvements Group Limited	£83,131,000
Selecta UK Holding Limited	£83,043,000
Greenvale AP Limited	£83,000,000
TUI Northern Europe Limited	£83,000,000
Samsung Cambridge Solution Centre Limited	£82,883,376
Overture Midco Limited	£82,830,000
Overture Midco II Limited	£82,830,000
Lumesse Holdings Limited	£82,672,792
Immobiliare Cardi Marmi Limited	£82,481,720
Voicevale Limited	£82,394,624
Prometic Pharma SMT Limited	£82,372,512
The Entertainer (Amersham) Limited	£82,294,000
Ideal Shopping Direct Limited	£82,227,000
The Childwick Trust	£82,194,424
Lakehouse Contracts Limited	£82,165,000
Tapesilver Limited	£82,094,000
Perkinelmer (UK) Holdings Limited	£82,093,000
Costa International Limited	£82,091,000
Trans-Siberian Gold PLC	£82,058,000
Aurora Limited	£81,670,392
Portugal Finco Limited	£81,490,000
Durkan Limited	£81,418,736
Notcutts Limited	£81,382,808
DSV Road Limited	£81,376,000
Rothamsted Research Limited	£81,311,000
QI Partners	£81,193,000
Boortmalt UK Limited	£81,184,200
University of Suffolk Ltd	£80,952,000
Aura (Newcastle) Project Company Phase 2 Ltd	£80,853,000
Cashflows Europe Limited	£80,789,000
ADM Arkady Limited	£80,653,456
Riva Topco Limited	£80,563,944
TM Vending Limited	£80,395,000
TUI Ireland Limited	£80,144,000
Guia Limited	£80,000,096
Wilson Properties (London) Ltd	£79,949,496
Local Car and Van Rental Limited	£79,721,456
Landis + Gyr Limited	£79,693,000
United Church Schools Trust	£79,497,000
Countryside Properties (WPL) Limited	£79,453,000
Intertek UK Holdings Limited	£79,448,000
Kier Property Limited	£79,416,000
Kendallco Limited	£79,369,000
De Lage Landen Limited	£79,230,000
Ralph Lauren UK Limited	£79,218,344
Masterson Holdings Limited	£78,976,696
Country Court Care Homes 3 Propco Limited	£78,951,128
Spirit Group Holdings Limited	£78,843,000
SSL Group (UK) Limited	£78,824,912
Kier Facilities Services Limited	£78,801,000
Aurora Group Holdings (UK) Limited	£78,621,088
St.Edmundsbury & Ipswich Diocesan Board of Finance	£78,526,000
RES UK & Ireland Limited	£78,506,000
Norse Commercial Services Limited	£78,416,576
Leica Microsystems Cambridge Limited	£78,326,000
Saint Vincent Holdings Limited	£78,216,000
Volkerstevin Group Limited	£78,214,000
CDK U.K. Limited	£78,097,000
Notcutts Group Limited	£78,049,856
Carpetright of London Limited	£77,989,000
Solo Cup Finance Limited	£77,963,000
One Group Construction Limited	£77,921,280
Sir Robert McAlpine Road Holdings Limited	£77,887,336
Rhone Products (UK) Limited	£77,570,408
Jagex Limited	£77,512,520
Blancco (Software) Services Limited	£77,475,976
City North (Telford Homes) Limited	£77,221,000
Gilmore Jacobs Limited	£77,194,880
PXP Financial Limited	£77,055,944
Next Generation Clubs Limited	£77,038,000
Softbox (Topco) Limited	£76,984,640
RG Carter Group Limited	£76,867,872
Ethypharm Holdings UK Ltd	£76,845,232
Comensura Limited	£76,838,000
Rexam Finance Germany Limited	£76,747,352
Larkfleet Limited	£76,677,024
Science Group PLC	£76,609,000
Acco UK Limited	£76,585,000
Temple Fields 514 Limited	£76,585,000
Walsworth Limited	£76,470,080
Ridgeons Limited	£76,379,000
Heptares Therapeutics Limited	£76,371,416
George Thurlow and Sons (Holdings) Limited	£76,301,000
Comland Group Limited	£76,224,000
GHG 7 (Chiltern Hospital) Limited	£76,218,000
DFKA Intermediate Limited	£76,214,000
Moralis Group Limited	£76,208,752
VWS (UK) Ltd	£76,190,000
Nexus Infrastructure PLC	£76,042,000
Pauls Malt Limited	£75,864,000
MBH Finco. Limited	£75,860,288
Cummins Cogeneration Limited	£75,777,608
Kestrel Acquisitions Limited	£75,718,000
GHG 4 (Princess Margaret Hospital) Limited	£75,675,000
Kelly Communications Group Limited	£75,496,664
Mundibiopharma Limited	£75,442,888
WO & PO Jolly Holdings Limited	£75,387,776
Countryside Properties (Joint Ventures) Limited	£75,265,104
Kenninghall Holdings Limited	£75,251,056
Sealey (UK) Limited	£75,251,000
Jack Sealey Limited	£75,250,000
Riva Holdco 1 Limited	£75,228,032
Laxmico Limited	£75,175,608
NIS Receivables No.1 Limited	£75,000,000
Harwich International (Holdings) Limited	£74,942,000
Bafin Holdings	£74,928,000
Gravity Media Group Holdings Limited	£74,647,000
Greenwich Millennium Village Limited	£74,629,264
Osborne Co-operative Academy Trust	£74,568,000
MM (UK) Limited	£74,536,256
Multimatic Ltd.	£74,386,488
Amino Technologies PLC	£74,288,000
Kettle Foods Ltd.	£73,952,000
HCT Portland Limited	£73,717,096
Hudson Chemical Tankers Limited	£73,716,288
Kathleen and Michael Connolly Foundation (UK) Ltd	£73,627,760
Wilkinson Sword Limited	£73,601,000
Selecta U.K. Limited	£73,467,000
Burghley House Preservation Trust Limited	£73,427,192
Benefit Cosmetics Limited	£73,419,360
Ensign Holdco 1 Limited	£73,359,000
Ulgrave Limited	£73,215,000
Ridgeland Properties Limited	£73,175,928
Thurlow Nunn (Holdings) Limited	£73,166,000
Five Star Inns Limited	£72,991,000
Kier Partnership Homes Limited	£72,971,000
The Shared Learning Trust	£72,919,000
Cresta Estates Limited	£72,809,952
Countryside Properties (WHL) Limited	£72,726,000
Dhamecha Property Limited	£72,533,000
Seetec Business Technology Centre Limited	£72,501,000
Medivet Partnership LLP	£72,368,000
Hi-Tec Sports Public Limited Company	£72,359,424
Durkan Estates Limited	£72,139,800
Swift Advances PLC	£72,088,000

Company	Value
Lawsons Holdings Limited	£72,056,328
Perkinelmer Life Sciences International Holdings	£72,018,000
Sharksfin Holdings Limited	£72,016,672
SME Investments Limited	£71,963,288
Dart Products Europe Ltd.	£71,869,000
Kebbell Holdings Limited	£71,795,368
Monsanto UK Limited	£71,629,000
Kier Ventures Limited	£71,587,000
Education Personnel Bidco Limited	£71,569,000
Malthurst (UK) Limited	£71,500,000
Heathpatch Limited	£71,413,920
Doe Holdings Limited	£71,406,672
Royal Docks Property LLP	£71,380,480
Altro Limited	£71,364,000
Hughes Electrical Limited	£71,319,464
Sir Robert McAlpine (A19) Limited	£71,256,816
Hincroft Limited	£71,227,072
Spirit Pub Company (Supply) Limited	£71,181,000
Nemo (UK) Holdco, Ltd.	£71,130,000
Midgard Ltd	£71,057,872
Avnet (Holdings) Ltd	£70,979,000
The Against Malaria Foundation	£70,883,608
Edgewell Personal Care UK Limited	£70,825,568
Tesco Red (3LP) Limited	£70,755,168
Kebbell Development Limited	£70,591,016
Lenta Properties Limited	£70,508,912
Aviva Consumer Products UK Limited	£70,402,000
Halamar (Chancery Lane) Limited	£70,298,448
GHG 5 (London Independent Hospital) Limited	£70,235,000
Cosco Maritime (UK) Limited	£70,223,720
Benacre Properties Company	£70,222,600
Ransome's Trading Holding Company Limited	£70,168,304
Vanderbilt Homes Limited	£70,113,000
Luxottica North Europe Limited	£70,059,000
Hanover Housing Developments Limited	£70,036,000
Mothercare Group Limited (The)	£70,013,000
Kwik-Fit (NL) Limited	£69,987,000
Kenwake Limited	£69,879,800
Vanderbilt Topco Ltd	£69,853,000
Waverley House Hotel Limited	£69,639,704
European Investments (Crook Hill) Limited	£69,570,696
National Football Centre Limited	£69,510,000
Origin Holdings (UK) Limited	£69,451,488
Bristol Laboratories Limited	£69,361,760
Lifehealth Limited	£69,330,896
Agri-Chemicals Limited	£69,286,584
The Electricity Network Company Limited	£69,103,256
Roselead Limited	£68,582,288
Smiths Industries Industrial Group Limited	£68,211,000
Affinity Water Southeast Limited	£68,113,000
ABVR Holdings Limited	£67,983,000
ABVR Finance Limited	£67,983,000
Transforming Education in Norfolk	£67,895,000
Kier Overseas (Nine) Limited	£67,820,752
CW Lamley & Co Limited	£67,733,312
FPS 1995 Limited	£67,660,536
Carlson Wagonlit New Holdco Limited	£67,607,120
Quickdrop Limited	£67,552,240
Sue Ryder	£67,543,000
Rightforsuccess Trust	£67,436,608
Affinity Water East Limited	£67,421,000
Diamond Corporation Limited	£67,295,496
Elysium Healthcare No. 3 Limited	£67,242,000
Luxottica Retail UK Ltd	£66,817,000
VMS (Holdings) Limited	£66,764,032
Amino Communications Limited	£66,722,776
The Gap Partnership Group Limited	£66,720,896
Vanderbilt Thames Valley Limited	£66,667,000
Jawaby Property Investment Limited	£66,645,216
Ipswich Borough Assets Limited	£66,532,344
Racal Acoustics Limited	£66,500,000
Metsa Wood UK Limited	£66,394,000
Tour Partner Group Midco Limited	£66,387,204
Chelverton UK Dividend Trust PLC	£66,386,000
Britvic Finance Partnership LLP	£66,350,000
Diomed Developments Limited	£66,227,728
VMS (Fleet Management) Limited	£66,223,952
Randstad Solutions Limited	£66,218,000
FIH Group PLC	£66,202,000
Don Construction Holdings Limited	£66,104,872
Kier Fleet Services Limited	£65,921,000
Centus Biotherapeutics Limited	£65,846,048
Acteon UK Financing II (NOK) Limited	£65,813,304
Maltco 3 Limited	£65,776,000
Lorne Stewart PLC	£65,703,000
The Holmes Care (Group) Limited	£65,683,720
Hallam Meat Company Limited	£65,665,856
Frontier Developments PLC	£65,543,000
Goldstar Transport Limited	£65,369,708
J O Sims Limited	£65,364,976
Abbey Total Care Group Limited	£65,309,764
VRS Investments Limited	£65,282,000
The Invicta Film Partnership No.20, LLP	£65,264,124
Betex LLP	£65,017,936
Omar Group Finance Limited	£64,971,980
Omar Group Holdings Limited	£64,971,976
McNicholas Construction Services Limited	£64,961,000
First Wave Housing Limited	£64,824,000
Tower Bridge Homes Care Limited	£64,816,460
Qatar Bloodstock Limited	£64,815,956
Fieldrose Limited	£64,728,000
Adnams PLC	£64,708,000
Gates Group Limited	£64,662,576
John Grose Group Limited	£64,323,000
Galldris Services Ltd	£64,286,348
Agricola Group Limited	£64,265,000
Ransomes Jacobsen Limited	£64,194,000
Beckman Coulter United Kingdom Limited	£64,166,000
Hill of Towie Limited	£64,152,000
Bedfordshire Schools Trust Limited	£63,985,000
Arjo UK Limited	£63,871,000
Signature Senior Lifestyle Finance Limited	£63,823,416
SME Holdings Limited	£63,635,392
Netcracker Technology EMEA Limited	£63,528,000
GHG 8 (Park Hospital) Limited	£63,514,000
Camfaud Group Limited	£63,478,664
ENRA Group Limited	£63,454,864
Topgolf Limited	£63,387,980
The Benacre Company	£63,222,216
Direct Table Foods Limited	£63,072,032
OPW Midco Limited	£63,051,000
Regentsmead Limited	£63,029,272
J.B Shropshire & Sons Limited	£62,983,860
Sapientia Education Trust	£62,967,000
JRL Plant and Logistics Limited	£62,889,348
Eastern Multi-Academy Trust	£62,657,000
TPH (UK) Limited	£62,613,000
Carestream Health UK, Limited	£62,592,000
Progress Rail Services UK Limited	£62,417,000
Arthur Midco 1 Limited	£62,415,000
OEC International Limited	£62,348,000
Bullen Properties Limited	£62,331,304
Scholars' Education Trust	£62,194,000
Flamingo Flowers Ltd.	£62,093,000
Laridge Investments Limited	£62,087,812
Oikos Storage Limited	£62,062,652
Proquest European Holdings Limited	£61,985,740
New Ladderswood LLP	£61,847,616
NPS (UK2) Limited	£61,786,000
Pretoria Energy Company (Mepal) Limited	£61,717,656
Signature Flatbreads (UK) Ltd	£61,579,000
Acteon US Holdings Limited	£61,553,368
MN Fox Topco Limited	£61,494,680
A H Worth and Company Limited	£61,458,000

Company	Value
Archant Limited	£61,441,000
Anglian Learning	£61,307,276
Ball Beverage Packaging Holdings UK Limited	£61,228,240
Parker Hannifin Manufacturing (UK) Limited	£61,215,000
Bridge Road Southall Limited	£61,180,600
R P Valves Limited	£61,078,300
Altair (UK) Ltd	£61,074,296
Glenchamber Wind Energy Limited	£61,071,000
Girls' Education Company,Limited	£61,070,000
Marylebone Finco Limited	£61,022,936
Cambridge Colleges Funding II PLC	£60,835,704
Medacs Healthcare PLC	£60,833,000
Frontline Limited	£60,731,000
S & B Commercials Limited	£60,623,000
Camelot Global Lottery Solutions Limited	£60,554,000
ILB Investments Limited	£60,520,232
Harris Holdings (Grays) Limited	£60,435,548
G's Fresh Limited	£60,424,000
The MTL Instruments Group Limited	£60,413,000
Coloplast Limited	£60,367,000
Property Finance Capital Limited	£60,334,692
Hotel Chocolat Group PLC	£60,220,024
Covidien UK Limited	£60,209,000
Willmott Dixon Public & Commercial Limited	£60,193,952
Barley Pub Company Limited	£60,171,000
Dillons Stores Limited	£60,160,000
Perkinelmer Limited	£60,081,000
Mundipharma Research Limited	£59,977,000
Fifty Shades Ltd	£59,905,328
American Can Holdings (U.K.) Limited	£59,882,000
Careys New Homes Limited	£59,838,172
Leidos Limited	£59,838,000
Mountcharm Limited	£59,818,216
RO Property Management Limited	£59,752,972
Olympus Keymed Group Limited	£59,692,000
Fairview Homes Limited	£59,639,000
Uniserve Limited	£59,599,056
Dunsfold Airport Limited	£59,573,812
Ensign Holdco 4 Limited	£59,430,000
NHS Shared Business Services Limited	£59,393,000
Pitney Bowes Finance Limited	£59,288,000
West Norfolk Academies Trust	£59,114,756
Inspectorate International Limited	£59,093,000
Booking.Com Limited	£59,021,036
Randstad CPE Limited	£58,950,000
Empower Learning Academy Trust	£58,780,768
Volkerstevin Limited	£58,728,000
Gray's Inn Capital 2 Limited	£58,627,048
Vinci UK Developments Limited	£58,511,000
Beacon Multi-Academy Trust Limited	£58,470,000
Rexam Property Developments Limited	£58,462,436
Axalta Powder Coating Systems UK Limited	£58,454,000
Ernest Doe & Sons Limited	£58,442,136
CSR Imaging UK Ltd.	£58,438,680
Anglian Group (Investments) Limited	£58,375,000
Morrison Data Services Limited	£58,320,000
Chrysalis Multi Academy Trust	£58,293,000
Anthony Nicholas (UK) Limited	£58,186,260
Sarena House LLP	£58,106,640
Marriott Holdings Limited	£58,072,360
Blue Arrow Holdings Limited	£58,053,000
S.Wernick & Sons (Holdings) Limited	£57,941,668
Harwich International Port Limited	£57,908,000
The Federation of European Biochemical Societies	£57,838,208
Kier Cross Keys Holdco 1 LLP	£57,818,000
Clinimed (Holdings) Limited	£57,811,084
Wellmode Limited	£57,800,000
HEB Real Estate Limited	£57,800,000
Erith Hills LLP	£57,766,896
The Perse School	£57,740,000
Industrial and Financial Systems, IFS UK Ltd	£57,601,820
UH Holdings Limited	£57,600,556
Property Finance Nominees (No.3) Limited	£57,545,068
Galldris Holdings Limited	£57,328,408
Marriott Motor Group Limited	£57,265,016
Peterborough Keys Academies Trust	£57,105,000
Takeda Cambridge Limited	£57,073,000
NPS Property Consultants Limited	£56,866,000
Kier Finance & Treasury Holdings Limited	£56,800,000
Aesica Queenborough Limited	£56,800,000
Churchill Contract Services Group Holdings Limited	£56,729,320
Stephen James (Automotive) Limited	£56,729,000
ADB Construction Limited	£56,682,264
CATM Europe Holdings Limited	£56,670,000
BP INV2 Holdco Ltd	£56,647,000
Targetfollow Group Limited	£56,629,000
Mettler-Toledo Safeline X-Ray Limited	£56,543,816
Deutsche Telekom (UK) Limited	£56,534,000
A.J.N. Steelstock Ltd.	£56,484,324
Wrist Holding UK Limited	£56,484,000
Specialist Cars Holdings Limited	£56,435,476
European Investments (Cornwall) Limited	£56,410,928
Chiltern Learning Trust	£56,348,000
Edgewell Personal Care Investments UK Ltd.	£56,288,000
Albon Engineering and Manufacturing PLC	£56,286,808
The Gap Partnership Bidco Limited	£56,270,084
Avanti Schools Trust	£56,126,000
Titan Airways Limited	£56,083,504
Paypoint Network Limited	£56,049,036
Rhodia International Holdings Limited	£55,991,000
Panther (VAT) Properties Limited	£55,986,056
Spirit Pub Company (Investments) Limited	£55,986,000
The Company of Biologists, Limited	£55,975,576
Gray's Inn Capital Limited	£55,939,044
Bounty (UK) Limited	£55,808,000
Snap-On Equipment Limited	£55,747,728
L. Lynch (Plant Hire & Haulage) Limited	£55,744,604
Quixant PLC	£55,619,584
McLaren Construction (London) Limited	£55,406,156
Phoenix Advance Limited	£55,333,000
F. Vindis & Sons (Bedford) Limited	£55,199,932
Countryside L & Q (Oaks Village) LLP	£55,110,628
R.C.Treatt & Co.Limited	£55,100,000
The Papworth Trust	£55,098,000
TJX Europe Buying Limited	£55,088,000
H. G. Construction (Holdings) Limited	£55,033,000
Millennium Investments 2000 Ltd	£54,958,592
Dhamecha Group Limited	£54,941,000
Focusrite PLC	£54,926,000
L.H.D.Limited	£54,914,556
D-Link (Europe) Limited	£54,911,244
A P P Wholesale PLC	£54,911,108
Pioneer DJ Europe Limited	£54,872,156
Trinity (D) Limited	£54,845,432
McGrath Brothers (Holdings) Limited	£54,844,800
Victoria Docks Hotel Company (Number Two) Ltd	£54,760,104
One GE Healthcare UK	£54,736,000
Bathstore.Com Limited	£54,720,000
Aryzta Bakeries UK Ltd	£54,715,000
JBS Global (UK) Limited	£54,645,752
AG Retail Cards Limited	£54,537,000
Ground Control Limited	£54,382,528
Polyfield Property Limited	£54,363,792
Abzena (UK) Limited	£54,314,000
Abzena Limited	£54,289,000
Shamrock Topco Limited	£54,167,856
Azelis UK Life Sciences Limited	£54,160,000
Hitchin Property Trust Limited (The)	£54,147,968
Kingsway Mezz Co Limited	£54,069,952
Woodland Group Limited	£53,996,000
Leica Microsystems (UK) Limited	£53,985,000
Rebus Group Limited	£53,963,000
Legra Academy Trust	£53,961,176
E - Leather Limited	£53,823,740

Company	Amount	Company	Amount
Syngenta UK Limited	£53,780,000	Fairacres Group Limited	£50,470,680
McNicholas Construction (Holdings) Limited	£53,749,000	Inland Finance Ltd	£50,457,752
Millennium Cash & Carry Limited	£53,710,732	JJ Food Service Limited	£50,369,880
CCW 600 Limited	£53,708,168	KH Holdco Limited	£50,366,000
Downing Strategic Micro-Cap Investment Trust PLC	£53,679,000	Cobb Europe Limited	£50,261,680
Albea UK Limited	£53,621,000	Vanderbilt Development Finance Ltd	£50,253,000
Hotels4U.Com Limited	£53,600,000	Shelfside Group LLP	£50,248,940
CML Microsystems PLC	£53,507,000	Amazon Acquisitions Limited	£50,067,000
Realpubs II Limited	£53,473,000	The Meller Educational Trust	£50,062,852
Reyhold Limited	£53,438,000	Howard Hunt (City) Limited	£49,997,000
MacDonald Humfrey (Automation) Limited	£53,419,000	Tamdown Group Limited	£49,973,000
National Institute of Agricultural Botany Trust	£53,406,000	Wheat Quarter Limited	£49,967,944
Buyagift PLC	£53,391,976	Good Harvest Group Limited	£49,967,744
Reynolds Catering Supplies Limited	£53,377,000	Essex Group Holdings Limited	£49,911,736
MN Fox Bidco Limited	£53,329,552	NPS (UK5) Limited	£49,887,000
COFCO International UK Ltd	£53,293,328	Koei Tecmo Europe Limited	£49,884,272
Merloni Domestic Appliances Limited	£53,276,000	Carbon60 Limited	£49,787,000
Spaces Personal Storage Limited	£53,262,000	Softbox Systems Limited	£49,647,188
Ravensale Limited	£53,164,788	GHG 31 (Blackheath Hospital) Limited	£49,633,000
Bay Restaurant Group Limited	£53,117,000	Intertek International Limited	£49,566,000
Robinsons Autoservices Limited	£53,065,276	Itron Metering Solutions UK Limited	£49,543,000
Openarch Properties Limited	£53,053,384	Brayford Hotels Holdings Ltd	£49,497,020
Mytravel North America Limited	£53,028,248	Ingrebourne Valley Limited	£49,465,152
Kingsway Senior Hold Co Limited	£53,024,576	Al Jazeera International Limited	£49,428,116
Rebus Holdings Limited	£53,017,000	Kymab Group Limited	£49,372,000
Boral (UK) Limited	£53,009,000	Brookgate Property Limited	£49,366,316
Norton Way Motors Limited	£52,995,000	Bertram Trading Limited	£49,364,000
London Inn Hotels (Stratford) Limited	£52,877,656	The Thrive Partnership Academy Trust	£49,335,416
Norwood Ravenswood	£52,817,000	Mouskos LLP	£49,201,652
S-P RIL Limited	£52,808,000	Navigator Terminals Seal Sands Limited	£49,185,000
Desiman Limited	£52,780,984	The Injured Jockeys Fund	£49,120,868
Grundfos Pumps Limited	£52,742,000	NIS Receivables No. 2 Limited	£49,100,000
Kier National Limited	£52,719,000	Generations Multi Academy Trust	£49,084,224
Spring Petroleum Company Ltd	£52,695,000	Marshall of Cambridge (Garage Properties) Limited	£48,992,000
KH Finance Limited	£52,648,000	Du Pont (U.K.) Industrial Limited	£48,982,000
Cementation Skanska Limited	£52,347,000	Breheny Group Limited	£48,970,960
The Seckford Foundation	£52,260,000	TCR New Limited	£48,970,824
Rank Hovis Milling Limited	£52,255,000	Envigo International Limited	£48,956,000
Optoma Europe Ltd	£52,228,000	Golf Entertainment International Limited	£48,893,816
Ingrebourne Valley Holdings Ltd	£52,131,416	Alex Brands Rocket Holdings Limited	£48,893,388
A.C. Lighting (Holdings) Limited	£52,121,268	David Lloyd Leisure Properties No.1 Limited	£48,891,000
Walstead Group Limited	£52,118,000	Woods Holdings Limited	£48,876,000
Wilson James Group Limited	£51,979,000	Fiat Chrysler Automobiles Services UK Limited	£48,838,000
UKLS Acquisitions Limited	£51,828,000	Industrial Chemicals Limited	£48,816,096
Burnt Mill Academy Trust	£51,801,000	Frank G. Gates Limited	£48,764,520
GPP Langstone LLP	£51,733,540	Regulus Bidco Limited	£48,721,544
Displaylink (UK) Limited	£51,606,760	Park Air Systems Limited	£48,685,000
The Chelmsford Learning Partnership	£51,600,000	Smiths Detection-Watford Limited	£48,547,000
J.S.T. (U.K.) Limited	£51,579,028	Gladstone Court Developments Limited	£48,541,488
The Leys and St Faith's Schools Foundation	£51,478,000	OTV Birwelco Limited	£48,530,000
Three Rivers Property Investments Limited	£51,317,440	GHG 6 (Thornbury Hospital) Limited	£48,506,000
Elysium Healthcare (Lighthouse) Limited	£51,317,000	Strides Arcolab International Ltd	£48,504,460
Nicholls & Clarke Limited	£51,268,684	Bush Boake Allen Limited	£48,495,000
Toomey Leasing Group Limited	£51,202,128	Pinnacle Schools (Gateshead) Limited	£48,456,844
Microsoft Research Limited	£51,162,000	Pitney Bowes Software Holdings Limited	£48,438,000
Temple Fields 522 Limited	£51,146,000	A D Bly Construction Limited	£48,401,884
Kingsway Hall Hotel Limited	£51,120,312	The Automation Partnership (Cambridge) Limited	£48,373,000
ABVR Group Limited	£51,100,000	K U H Limited	£48,324,208
Sheikh Holdings Group (Investments) Limited	£51,078,424	European Investments (Cornwall) Holdings Limited	£48,295,900
Leicester Citybus Limited	£51,021,000	Be Living Group Limited	£48,292,448
Intertek Testing Management Ltd	£51,020,000	Newman Street Hotel Limited	£48,265,764
McLaren Construction (South) Limited	£50,998,824	ASCO (DC3) Limited	£48,259,000
Grosvenor Park 2002 Film LLP	£50,934,048	McGee Group (Holdings) Limited	£48,231,040
Central Tyre (Commercial) Limited	£50,730,000	CWT Holdco Limited	£48,218,652
Glenmark Pharmaceuticals Europe Limited	£50,697,828	Global Education Management Systems Limited	£48,202,720
HG Construction Limited	£50,590,000	Graincorp (Canada) Holdings UK Limited	£48,116,000
Omar Group Investments Limited	£50,569,632	Amsprop Portland Limited	£48,103,136
Thomas Cook UK Travel Limited	£50,550,000	MCF Commercial Limited	£48,084,928
Sabre Retail Fashion Limited	£50,532,000	GHG 12 (Hampshire Clinic) Limited	£48,009,000
Flying Trade Limited	£50,511,628	Walstead Finance Limited	£47,963,000
Acheson Industries (Europe) Limited	£50,488,000	Elizabeth Holdings PLC	£47,948,596
Leisure Parks Real Estate (Holdings) Limited	£50,471,672	ITC Enterprises Limited	£47,797,640

Company	Value
Staples Brothers Limited	£47,718,688
Walstead Press Group Limited	£47,717,000
Gateway Learning Community	£47,700,860
Consensus Holdco Limited	£47,657,416
Churchill Contract Services Limited	£47,620,276
Wadlow Energy Limited	£47,619,000
Peter Colby Commercials Limited	£47,606,064
Cambridge University Press (Holdings) Limited	£47,562,000
Crocus Home Loans Limited	£47,509,992
Elektron Technology UK Limited	£47,376,000
The Hoddesdon School Trust	£47,362,856
Tour Partner Group Limited	£47,284,208
Country Court Care Homes 3 SB Limited	£47,278,724
Hemnall Limited	£47,236,056
CP Regents Park Two Limited	£47,227,640
Tradewise Group of Companies Limited	£47,179,276
Zenith Hygiene Group Limited	£47,140,000
Ssangyong Motor UK Limited	£47,100,000
NDC Technologies Limited	£46,868,000
Grosvenor Park 2005 Film Partnership No.1 LLP	£46,802,520
Air Works UK Engineering Limited	£46,795,796
RO Financing Company Limited	£46,587,744
Mapeley Steps Contractor Limited	£46,538,000
Aim Academies Trust	£46,473,104
SintecMedia LON Ltd	£46,466,108
I4B Holdings Limited	£46,464,000
Green Label Foods Ltd.	£46,437,396
Cambridge Academic Partnership	£46,436,000
London Tower Crane Hire & Sales Limited	£46,363,016
The Invicta Film Partnership No.10, LLP	£46,335,496
GHG 17 (Ridgeway Hospital) Limited	£46,269,000
The Harrodian School Limited	£46,261,300
Assetsteady Limited	£46,190,052
Turners Britannia Parks Limited	£46,165,736
Cheshunt Lakeside Developments Limited	£46,140,764
Gilead Sciences International Ltd.	£46,055,000
HaskoningDHV UK Limited	£46,037,972
Aspire (CRP) Limited	£46,037,000
The Invicta Film Partnership No.14, LLP	£46,030,152
MTCE Limited	£46,017,740
G's Growers Limited	£45,887,000
Connolly Homes PLC	£45,881,904
Casemasters Limited	£45,880,908
Abbey Group Limited	£45,860,296
Kimbolton School	£45,850,828
R.Robinson & Co.(Motor Services) Limited	£45,826,848
Thomas Deacon Education Trust	£45,750,000
Norse Care Limited	£45,711,972
Kier Business Services Limited	£45,610,000
SLR Consulting Limited	£45,580,956
Bowman Ingredients Limited	£45,541,000
Bell Educational Trust Limited (The)	£45,494,000
Motor Parts Direct Limited	£45,425,640
Medlock Electrical Distributors Limited	£45,418,612
QED (Slough) Limited	£45,413,172
Essex Community Foundation	£45,355,232
Inland Property Limited	£45,341,128
Share PLC	£45,286,000
Lighthouse Healthcare Group Limited	£45,142,000
J. Coffey Construction Limited	£45,137,436
The Wensum Trust	£45,096,384
Arena Event Services Group Limited	£45,085,000
E.W.Pepper Limited	£45,070,812
Malt U.K. Holdco Limited	£45,052,000
Five Arrows Limited	£45,047,000
Brookstream Properties Limited	£45,009,612
Green Hill Energy Limited	£45,007,000
Oakfield (Foods) Limited	£44,994,880
Netcall PLC	£44,958,000
Greenyard Fresh UK Ltd	£44,951,624
Cantab Capital Partners LLP	£44,949,000
Cooper Roller Bearings Company Limited	£44,938,000
First Essex Buses Limited	£44,921,000
Denland Limited	£44,881,004
Mingold Limited	£44,881,000
Granta Park Estates Limited	£44,871,264
John F Hunt Group Ltd	£44,868,924
Dow Properties Limited	£44,860,032
Chilton Home Farms Ltd	£44,841,792
The St Paul's Walden Bury Estate Company Ltd	£44,783,732
Marshall Group Properties Limited	£44,776,512
Spicerhaart Group Limited	£44,756,000
Ascott Farms Limited	£44,735,912
Perkins Small Engines Limited	£44,683,000
The Royal Air Force Central Fund	£44,561,656
Mylan Pharma UK Limited	£44,497,000
Nellsar Limited	£44,493,512
Brentwood Academies Trust	£44,454,524
Harris (Belmont) Charity	£44,451,272
Sagentia Limited	£44,449,000
Shamrock Bidco Limited	£44,416,624
John Innes Foundation	£44,336,944
Livingston Ltd	£44,311,000
John Henry Group Limited	£44,252,884
Coveris Flexibles Holdings UK Limited	£44,130,000
Acton Gardens LLP	£44,104,536
Cheveley Park Stud Limited	£44,098,652
Levantera Developments Limited	£44,040,472
Smile Stores Limited	£44,032,000
KSEYE Group Limited	£44,022,188
Hawk Incentives Holdings Limited	£44,010,000
Prefect Software LLP	£43,967,152
Sequence (UK) Limited	£43,965,000
Country Court Care Homes 2 Limited	£43,948,052
Elysium Healthcare (Ultimate Care) Limited	£43,884,684
Willmott Partnership Homes Limited	£43,801,500
Timeboard Investments LLP	£43,800,520
Hertswood Academy	£43,777,864
Chobham Manor LLP	£43,774,000
Sen Trust Southend	£43,739,704
Hoopers Limited	£43,706,348
Cannon Kirk Property Limited	£43,696,788
G S Shropshire Holdings Limited	£43,635,592
Squibb Group Limited	£43,628,464
Bush Boake Allen Holdings (U.K.) Limited	£43,604,000
Smiths Metal Centres Limited	£43,564,832
The Coaching Inn Group Ltd	£43,564,464
Maritime Transport Services Limited	£43,561,000
Dai Europe Ltd	£43,542,000
Babraham Bioscience Technologies Limited	£43,520,000
BWI UK Limited	£43,517,000
KCH (UK) Holdings Limited	£43,489,848
MTS (Holdings) Limited	£43,478,000
City Link (Cardiff) Limited	£43,447,000
The Yare Education Trust	£43,439,720
Jack Richards Holdings Limited	£43,423,372
Unisurge International Limited	£43,406,000
Goldstar Transport Holdings Limited	£43,354,924
Cantel Medical (UK) Limited	£43,315,000
South West Essex Community Education Trust Ltd	£43,314,000
Romeo Midco Limited	£43,309,000
Imperial Pharmaceuticals Limited	£43,295,732
Sumitomo Electric Europe Limited	£43,287,000
A.A.Fisher (Properties) Limited	£43,273,648
The Abbey Group Cambridgeshire Limited	£43,206,404
Russell Burgess Limited	£43,137,000
Gatetrade Limited	£43,130,088
Churchgate Estates Limited	£43,095,528
BRE Trust	£43,026,000
Essex Group Holdings International Limited	£42,993,160
Electrolux Investments	£42,966,000
The Invicta Film Partnership No.22, LLP	£42,851,436
Doncaster School Solutions Limited	£42,817,000
Doncaster School Solutions (Holdings) Limited	£42,817,000

Gog Magog Partnership LLP	£42,817,000
Gentian Partnerships Limited	£42,814,832
OP UK Bidco Limited	£42,779,068
New Anglia Local Enterprise Partnership Limited	£42,756,584
Central Trust Limited	£42,709,000
KSEYE Capital Holdings Limited	£42,678,068
Ransome's Dock Limited	£42,670,700
Motus Holdings (UK) Limited	£42,667,856
Cleanland Limited	£42,653,320
Bakkavor Central Finance Limited	£42,641,000
Produce World Investments Ltd	£42,609,000
8x8 UK Investments Limited	£42,604,680
Rittal Holdings Limited	£42,555,000
Kier Hammersmith Limited	£42,532,000
Kier Commercial Investments Limited	£42,511,000
Regis Group (UBK) Limited	£42,504,644
Ballast Phoenix Limited	£42,484,000
Climax Molybdenum U.K. Limited	£42,449,000
Kier Project Investment Limited	£42,445,000
Jockey Club Estates Limited	£42,437,000
Ground Construction Limited	£42,434,328
Warrant Investments PLC	£42,415,112
Electron House (Overseas) Limited	£42,412,000
Merritts Properties Limited	£42,388,588
Bosch Lawn and Garden Limited	£42,236,000
Pro Cam CP Limited	£42,218,000
Bathstore Group Limited	£42,208,000
Registration Transfers Limited	£42,187,484
ESRI Holdings Limited	£42,185,500
Wryde Croft Wind Farm Limited	£42,107,000
Marshall North West Limited	£42,052,000
Blessville Limited	£42,040,620
Faerch Plast UK Limited	£42,025,412
Dashtag	£42,025,000
Southend East Community Academy Trust	£41,973,168
L & L Inc Limited	£41,962,976
Bio-Rad Laboratories Limited	£41,961,000
Volkerhighways Limited	£41,902,000
Incorporated Bishop's Stortford College Association	£41,871,000
Joseph Gallagher Group Limited	£41,862,936
Elite Mobile (Holdings) Limited	£41,816,000
Berkhamsted Schools Group	£41,814,000
K.J. Shortis Limited	£41,775,000
City Lifting Limited	£41,766,104
Kier Homes Caledonia Limited	£41,733,000
Epson (U.K.) Limited	£41,722,000
Wickford Development Company Limited	£41,692,656
Solo Cup (UK) Limited	£41,692,000
International Society for Krishna Consciousness Ltd	£41,681,696
Essex Services Group Limited	£41,670,440
Napp Pharmaceuticals Limited	£41,612,000
R.V.L. Properties Limited	£41,608,816
Global Metcorp Limited	£41,590,520
Queens' School (Bushey)	£41,587,780
RANC Care Homes Limited	£41,548,828
Hoole Hall Country Club Limited	£41,544,000
S H Pratt Holdings Limited	£41,530,084
Science Recruitment Group Ltd	£41,527,000
Mack-Brooks Exhibitions Limited	£41,500,960
Grange Management (Holdings) Limited	£41,500,924
GHG 11 (Mount Alvernia Hospital) Limited	£41,477,000
Erindale Limited	£41,399,480
S H Pratt Group Limited	£41,329,732
Shamrock Midco Limited	£41,308,772
SLV Group Holding UK Limited	£41,304,756
Hull Propco Limited	£41,279,000
Enterprise Residential Development Limited	£41,230,000
Portcrest Limited	£41,222,624
Wilton Park Developments Limited	£41,221,760
Aesica M2 Limited	£41,200,000
Aesica M1 Limited	£41,200,000
Coastfields Leisure Limited	£41,152,764
Anglia Components Limited	£41,085,144
Morley Finco Limited	£40,970,660
Quadram Institute Bioscience	£40,941,000
Cokenach Limited	£40,893,108
Brooks Events Limited	£40,874,968
Darktrace Limited	£40,862,000
Bussey & Sabberton Bros.Limited	£40,820,216
Dermal Laboratories Limited	£40,770,980
Costa China Holdings Limited	£40,748,000
Descram Holdings Limited	£40,742,104
Lumesse Limited	£40,739,432
Arnold White Estates Limited	£40,617,808
The Harrogate International Hotel Limited	£40,575,000
P & O Ferrymasters Holdings Limited	£40,558,996
Brogan Group Holdings Ltd	£40,528,576
Interquest Group (UK) Limited	£40,527,684
The Recruit Venture Group Ltd	£40,511,532
Ridgeon Properties Limited	£40,472,460
NEC (UK) Ltd.	£40,467,000
Sumatra Copper & Gold PLC	£40,463,276
Drapers' Multi-Academy Trust	£40,456,000
Anglian Water Facilities Management Hldgs UK Ltd	£40,454,000
Hughes TV and Audio Limited	£40,402,320
Emerald Topco Limited	£40,401,000
Roys (Wroxham),Limited	£40,307,512
FDR U.K. Limited	£40,302,000
Glasswells Limited	£40,298,344
Intertek Inspection Services UK Limited	£40,266,000
Black Swan International Limited	£40,257,028
Betts Limited	£40,203,000
Amazon Spring Waters Investment Limited	£40,174,640
SRM (Redcar & Cleveland) Limited	£40,153,800
Staploe Education Trust	£40,127,688
Bluestone APAC Holdings Limited	£40,121,288
Trafalgar Leisure Ltd	£40,114,984
EV Holdings Limited	£40,110,000
Brooks Bros. (UK) Limited	£40,082,352
Fluke Precision Measurement Limited	£40,073,000
Norwich Airport Limited	£40,069,680
South Suffolk Learning Trust	£40,066,000
Ransomes Limited	£40,062,000
The Jewish Community Secondary School Trust	£40,056,592
South East Essex Academy Trust	£39,979,948
Primagraphics Limited	£39,947,688
Anglo-Dutch Property (UK) Holding Limited	£39,928,000
CAE Technology Services Limited	£39,802,160
Test Equipment Asset Management Limited	£39,761,000
The North London Collegiate School	£39,737,320
E. Hobbs (Farms) Limited	£39,735,652
The Freedom Travel Group Limited	£39,729,000
Jarvis Group Limited	£39,724,920
Agria Pet Insurance Limited	£39,673,584
Breheny Civil Engineering Limited	£39,666,392
Merchant Taylors' School	£39,653,028
Flynn Pharma (Holdings) Limited	£39,612,872
Wind Farm Holdings Limited	£39,600,000
Turners Parks Group Limited	£39,590,648
Westgate House Developments Limited	£39,558,556
National Adhesives Holding Ltd.	£39,540,000
DSV Solutions Limited	£39,532,000
Hops Pub Company Limited	£39,525,000
Nene Park Trust	£39,504,000
Merton Acquisitions Limited	£39,461,368
ABM Technical Solutions Limited	£39,368,328
PJHP Limited	£39,342,392
Charles River Discovery Research Services UK Ltd	£39,314,000
Regal Healthcare Holdings Limited	£39,255,436
First Choice Holidays Limited	£39,251,000
Ipswich Town Finance Company Limited	£39,209,000
Willmott Dixon Interiors Limited	£39,203,756
G.R.Wright & Sons Limited	£39,198,168
Oldrid & Co.,Limited	£39,196,568

Company	Value
George A. Sherriff Limited	£39,190,160
GHG 19 (Albyn Hospital) Limited	£39,160,000
Total Produce Limited	£39,150,000
Snowmountain Enterprises Limited	£39,137,432
Wilkin & Sons Limited	£39,123,000
Everbuild Building Products Limited	£39,071,000
Manor (2016) Holdings Limited	£39,028,252
Toppesfield Limited	£39,023,788
Yum! III (UK) Limited	£38,921,000
Peter Sowerby Foundation	£38,917,536
OOCL (Europe) Limited	£38,896,160
Fluke (UK) Limited	£38,849,000
Staples UK Limited	£38,789,000
Astex Therapeutics Limited	£38,704,152
Dyer and Butler Limited	£38,692,000
Hotel Chocolat Limited	£38,670,712
Grimsthorpe & Drummond Castle Trust Limited	£38,646,920
Chevalier (2015) Ltd	£38,618,736
City & Country Residential Ltd	£38,515,748
Greene King Developments Limited	£38,514,772
Staples (Vegetables) Limited	£38,513,044
Caretech Estates (No 7) Limited	£38,475,000
Flightsafety International U.K. Limited	£38,474,648
Jackson Civil Engineering Group Limited	£38,469,624
Citygate Developments 2005 Limited	£38,460,020
Toureen Group Limited	£38,441,624
Hampton Academies Trust	£38,401,788
Connells Residential	£38,349,000
Jack Richards & Son Limited	£38,321,272
Kelling Estate LLP	£38,293,188
Proquest UK Holdings Ltd	£38,280,296
Cathedral Holdings Limited	£38,227,716
Intertain (Bars) Limited	£38,221,000
The Share Centre Limited	£38,213,000
Parkdale Investments Limited	£38,207,036
Tesco Maintenance Limited	£38,186,000
RO Properties Limited	£38,183,000
Huntleigh Healthcare Limited	£38,141,000
Norwood Schools Ltd.	£38,106,000
S A Designer Parfums Limited	£38,092,696
Kelly Communications Limited	£38,074,008
Bakkavor Estates Limited	£38,042,000
AMT Fruit Limited	£38,018,400
Hockerill College Academy Trust	£37,989,000
Baik Agency Limited	£37,987,656
Produce World Group Ltd	£37,972,000
Hillary Bidco Limited	£37,972,000
Focus Tankers Limited	£37,956,832
Jaysam Contractors Limited	£37,892,284
Ellesmere Property Investment Company Limited	£37,889,332
OPD Group Limited	£37,850,904
Jollyes Retail Group Limited	£37,843,816
Horizon Discovery Limited	£37,828,000
Frederick Hiam,Limited	£37,692,032
Red Gate Software Limited	£37,652,364
Ridgeway Bavarian Limited	£37,651,000
National Film and Television School (The)	£37,639,464
New Demipower Limited	£37,636,804
Alperton Community School	£37,629,564
Dame Alice Owen's School	£37,629,000
Netherhall Gardens Ltd	£37,621,308
Arnold White Group Limited	£37,614,328
Shelfside (Holdings) Limited	£37,585,772
Intertek Nominees Limited	£37,580,000
McLaren Construction (Midlands & North) Limited	£37,570,376
Damco UK Limited	£37,533,000
Scimitar Care Hotels PLC	£37,530,288
Eagle 456 Limited	£37,521,620
Special New Fruit Licensing Limited	£37,458,324
Powergas Africa Limited	£37,415,864
Vernalis Limited	£37,409,000
CATM Africa Holdings Limited	£37,396,192
User Friendly Properties (No. 2) Limited	£37,342,124
Dage Precision Industries Limited	£37,294,408
41/43 Maddox St. Limited	£37,245,172
Halsbury Strategic Limited	£37,050,132
Axalta Coating Systems UK Limited	£37,046,000
Lincolnshire Field Products Limited	£37,033,788
Gapsun Properties Limited	£36,992,648
Aston Barclay Holdings Limited	£36,912,000
Porvair Filtration Group Limited	£36,905,000
Premier Euro Hotels Limited	£36,904,408
Diocese of Norwich Education and Academies Trust	£36,898,188
National Pharmacy Association Limited	£36,872,000
Redwings Horse Sanctuary	£36,801,868
Northwood Paper Sales Limited	£36,769,968
Apatech Limited	£36,755,124
Baker Perkins Holdings Limited	£36,686,000
Johnson & Johnson Innovation Limited	£36,677,000
Habendum Limited	£36,671,224
Randstad Sourceright Limited	£36,655,000
Aurient Investments Limited	£36,616,536
HPC Healthline UK Limited	£36,579,000
Connells Survey & Valuation Limited	£36,504,000
NPS (UK4) Limited	£36,500,000
TJX Germany Ltd.	£36,500,000
Carl Zeiss Microscopy Limited	£36,463,000
Santray Limited	£36,447,964
Bennett PLC	£36,419,904
Edward Le Bas Properties Limited	£36,403,928
Swan Commercial Services Limited	£36,372,000
Deanplan Limited	£36,345,976
Elveden Farms Limited	£36,334,328
Olivegate Properties Limited	£36,333,076
Hilton UK Manage Limited	£36,292,152
Emcure Pharma UK Ltd	£36,279,172
Bucks Developments Limited	£36,256,732
Waters Limited	£36,251,000
Emerald Midco 1 Limited	£36,238,000
Amino Holdings Limited	£36,234,396
Emerald Midco 2 Limited	£36,219,000
Volac Renewable Energy Limited	£36,200,000
Walstead Roche Limited	£36,188,000
Navigator Terminals UK Limited	£36,138,000
The European Film Partners III LLP	£36,126,636
AFP 2015-1 Limited	£36,101,164
Prime Place (Millbrook) LLP	£36,097,628
Howard Lewisham Limited	£36,078,172
Triangle (Funding One) Limited	£36,065,204
Flakt Woods Limited	£36,053,000
Intertain Limited	£36,027,000
Crystal Windows & Doors Limited	£35,993,184
Thomas Bates & Son Limited	£35,982,312
Associated Lead Mills Ltd.	£35,974,448
H.Young & Co.,Limited	£35,964,352
G.B.N. Services Limited	£35,935,224
The Abington Group Limited	£35,931,504
Global Self Drive Limited	£35,909,784
Earlham Institute	£35,906,000
Rectory Homes Limited	£35,903,320
PMS International Holdings PLC	£35,895,000
BAM Properties Limited	£35,893,000
B.M. Polyco Limited	£35,886,000
Epay Limited	£35,870,000
Caterpillar Logistics (UK) Limited	£35,869,000
GW Research Limited	£35,856,184
Optima Investments Limited	£35,816,160
Chester International Hotel Limited	£35,808,000
Wembley Multi Academy Trust	£35,774,840
3VS UK Limited	£35,726,692
MSHA International Ltd.	£35,705,724
Villa Plus Limited	£35,678,952
Toy Brokers Holdings Limited	£35,664,852
New Sparta Holdings Limited	£35,658,912

Company	Amount
Optima Contracting Limited	£35,641,144
Imerys Aluminates Limited	£35,623,000
Palacath Limited	£35,614,168
Clearview Homes Limited	£35,594,368
Alzheimer's Research UK	£35,557,940
Electrolux Professional Limited	£35,556,000
Wycombe High School Academies Trust	£35,518,004
Chelmsford Cars and Commercials Limited	£35,515,080
Alconbury Packing Solutions Limited	£35,466,480
Patek Philippe Salon Limited	£35,443,052
Cambridge Arts & Sciences Limited	£35,442,000
Lawson Partners Limited	£35,412,956
Anglia Ruskin Development Ltd	£35,400,000
Gowrie Laxmico Limited	£35,392,188
Ipswich Town Stadium Company Limited	£35,385,000
Girton Town Charity	£35,382,000
Knowles (Transport) Limited	£35,372,984
Science, Engineering and Mfg Technologies Alliance	£35,358,000
Empress Garland Limited	£35,354,432
Total Worldfresh Limited	£35,346,000
The Stephen Perse Foundation	£35,345,776
EV Finco Limited	£35,338,000
Aquila MB3 Limited	£35,317,248
Aquila MB2 Limited	£35,316,752
Skechers USA Ltd.	£35,301,000
Camelot Business Solutions Limited	£35,300,000
The Barnes Group Limited	£35,295,000
Starbridge Property Investment Limited	£35,278,976
Winfresh (UK) Limited	£35,262,428
Carl Zeiss Ltd	£35,221,000
Power on Connections Ltd	£35,199,272
Hayter Holdings Limited	£35,180,000
Telford Homes City North Limited	£35,179,000
Hayward Tyler Limited	£35,148,000
PFE Express Limited	£35,138,688
Domnick Hunter Group Limited	£35,116,000
Net Pay (EUR) Limited	£35,109,772
London Pharma & Chemicals Holdings Ltd	£35,091,484
THR Number Two Limited	£35,086,000
Dorma UK Limited	£35,074,032
Blackhawk Network (UK) Ltd.	£35,073,000
Ontex Retail UK Limited	£35,052,964
Softbox (Bidco) Limited	£35,043,948
Building Research Establishment Limited	£35,017,000
CSSC Properties Limited	£34,992,000
Sema Lease UK Limited	£34,949,944
Clays Ltd.	£34,938,392
Chartman Limited	£34,930,000
Eckoh PLC	£34,918,000
Leena Plaza Limited	£34,866,832
Foreign Currency Direct PLC	£34,767,336
Badger Building (E.Anglia) Limited	£34,747,636
Hoo Hing Holdings Limited	£34,708,916
CAE Technology Holdings Limited	£34,676,052
Royston Holdings Limited	£34,668,704
CTV Outside Broadcasts Limited	£34,603,000
TTP PLC	£34,569,000
Station Road Developments (Cambridge) Limited	£34,554,668
IT Luggage Limited	£34,542,608
Elite Mobile Limited	£34,514,000
NPA Insurance Limited	£34,502,848
Metier Healthcare Limited	£34,452,380
Metier Holdings Limited	£34,452,380
The Bentley Wood Trust	£34,422,152
Amsprop Central Limited	£34,407,408
CEG Administrative Services Limited	£34,402,000
Bury St Edmunds Academy Trust	£34,336,588
Truckeast Limited	£34,319,724
Saffron Academy Trust	£34,285,536
Tower Crane Asset Management Holdings Limited	£34,274,960
Marchase Limited	£34,260,184
Jelmac Properties	£34,260,152
Corona Energy Retail 1 Limited	£34,249,204
Citygate Holdings Limited	£34,243,736
Lumesse Corporate Limited	£34,194,132
MoveWithUs Conveyancing Limited	£34,170,176
H (Lincs) Limited	£34,164,976
Anexhold Limited	£34,162,740
New River Holdings Limited	£34,151,528
Adilsons Properties Limited	£34,103,272
British Limbless Ex-Service Men's Association	£34,064,508
Comline Holdings Limited	£34,061,712
Focusrite Audio Engineering Limited	£34,002,000
BBC Studioworks Limited	£33,958,312
East Barnet School	£33,897,964
Aquila Estates Limited	£33,881,256
Partners in Property (U.K.) Limited	£33,841,200
Lawsons (Whetstone) Limited	£33,820,152
The Invicta Film Partnership No.25, LLP	£33,805,844
Dominion Hospitality Limited	£33,749,000
Dominion Hospitality Topco Limited	£33,749,000
Chargemaster Limited	£33,741,000
Softbox (Midco) Limited	£33,731,464
Kier Parkman Servigroup Limited	£33,647,000
Heythrop Park Limited	£33,644,216
Cooperscroft Care Home Limited	£33,605,224
Aquaterra Energy Group Limited	£33,568,000
GHG 9 (Bath Clinic) Limited	£33,564,000
Travel Choice Limited	£33,545,954
Coyle Personnel PLC	£33,545,504
Comparex UK Limited	£33,477,328
McCormick Kutas Food Service Limited	£33,466,626
Uniserve (Air Freight) Limited	£33,466,564
Solus (London) Limited	£33,452,000
ACM ULR Limited	£33,378,000
Tanglewood (Lincolnshire) Limited	£33,331,404
Silver Street Automotive Limited	£33,324,000
Pharmaceuticals Direct Limited	£33,313,492
Roos Energy Limited	£33,296,000
Clarence Estates (London) Limited	£33,288,554
Newsells Park Stud Limited	£33,275,000
A-Roads Investments Limited	£33,247,534
Skanska Cementation International Limited	£33,210,000
The Boxford Group Ltd.	£33,207,212
Dyer & Butler 2014 Limited	£33,206,000
Evergreen Finance Limited	£33,140,000
Total Produce Holdings (UK) Limited	£33,135,000
Tasmar Limited	£33,117,756
Seabrook Holdings Limited	£33,100,808
Citygate Automotive Limited	£33,090,256
Victoria Docks Hotel Company Limited	£33,074,908
Bloom Engineering Holdings Limited	£33,021,120
CLFIS (U.K.) Limited	£32,976,000
DST Financial Services Europe Limited	£32,960,000
Haydon School	£32,915,100
Greenstone Oxford Limited	£32,909,552
Hemnall Investments Limited	£32,862,030
Chesterhill Investments Limited	£32,855,708
Intertek Finance No. 2 Ltd	£32,798,308
Peter Brett Associates LLP	£32,766,530
Ordan UK Limited	£32,745,952
West End Homes Limited	£32,745,056
DCI Group Limited	£32,740,788
Beaconsfield High School	£32,735,524
Mervyn Lambert Plant Limited	£32,723,292
Snape Maltings	£32,713,000
The Boston Witham Academies Federation	£32,713,000
Alan Boswell Group Limited	£32,699,260
Astute Electronics Limited	£32,676,324
Inland Homes Developments Limited	£32,649,186
Result Clothing Limited	£32,560,452
Navigator Terminals North Tees Limited	£32,549,000
Annodata Limited	£32,548,760
Redsky IT Holdings Limited	£32,542,000

Company	Amount
AST Group Holdings Limited	£32,536,224
MN Sports Bidco Limited	£32,489,954
Zenith Hygiene Systems Limited	£32,489,000
Orchard Funding Group PLC	£32,489,000
Baker Perkins Limited	£32,418,000
Lawrence David Limited	£32,392,168
Proquest Information and Learning Limited	£32,391,066
Sunwin Services Group (2010) Limited	£32,358,000
Alfreds Way Investments (No. 2) Limited	£32,326,216
Zenith Multi Academy Trust	£32,310,996
Suffolk Academies Trust	£32,306,888
Exlservice (UK) Limited	£32,245,568
Whitehouse Leisure International Limited	£32,217,508
Nikon X-Tek Systems Limited	£32,208,000
Anderson Design & Build Limited	£32,197,072
University of Essex Knowledge Gateway Holdings Ltd	£32,182,892
Land Charter (Harlow) Ltd	£32,171,076
Carlisle Staffing Services Limited	£32,144,000
GHG 15 (Highfield Hospital) Limited	£32,127,000
Amshold Trading Limited	£32,109,412
GHG 14 (Shirley Oaks Hospital) Limited	£32,080,000
Gardline Limited	£32,058,864
John Hanlon & Co. Limited	£32,050,052
DB Investments Limited	£32,046,208
Hayes Point (Sully) Limited	£32,034,484
The Passmores Co-operative Learning Community	£31,966,984
Star Cargo PLC	£31,941,142
Tesco Family Dining Limited	£31,887,000
Hotel Chocolat Retail Ltd	£31,846,558
O'Neill Investments Limited	£31,838,832
Metro Global Holdings Limited	£31,833,718
Regis Group (Nationwide) Limited	£31,826,976
Mass Consultants Limited	£31,821,000
Gracewell Healthcare Limited	£31,813,000
Paul Rackham Limited	£31,795,774
Eversleigh Investment and Property Company Ltd	£31,795,298
St Mary's CE Academy, Cheshunt	£31,793,000
Tanglewood Care Homes Limited	£31,727,570
Forfarmers UK Holdings Limited	£31,717,000
Fairview Ventures Limited	£31,698,000
Terex Cranes UK Limited	£31,691,000
Preston Manor Academy Trust	£31,668,798
PMS International Group PLC	£31,663,000
Co-op Group Travel 2 Holdings Limited	£31,587,000
GHG 16 (Chelsfield Park Hospital) Limited	£31,572,000
The Harlow Health Centres Trust Limited	£31,567,586
Spire Bricks and Mortar Limited	£31,562,448
Sunrise UK Holdco Limited	£31,534,000
Inca Digital Printers Limited	£31,495,000
Danfoss Limited	£31,494,000
Yavneh College Academy Trust	£31,446,916
Bugler Group Limited	£31,377,884
Xtera Topco Limited	£31,366,754
McLaren Construction (UK) Limited	£31,339,948
M & D Silk Properties Ltd	£31,327,848
Consort Medical Finance 2010 Limited	£31,327,000
BEW Electrical Distributors Limited	£31,321,718
Southwater Property Promotion Limited	£31,320,696
Compass Education Trust Ltd	£31,301,000
V.B. Investments Limited	£31,251,000
Aquila EHS Limited	£31,217,220
Sinclair International Limited	£31,210,000
Alan Bartlett & Sons (Chatteris) Limited	£31,194,474
Omar Park Homes Limited	£31,190,724
Lancaster Sports Cars Limited	£31,183,000
UK Credit Limited	£31,181,000
John Henry and Sons (Developments) Ltd	£31,168,772
Grovemere Property Limited	£31,147,182
Joseph King Holdings Limited	£31,143,144
Norfolk Free Range Limited	£31,133,952
MDM Timber Limited	£31,131,984
P2P Mailing Ltd	£31,127,270

Company	Amount
Pregis Europe Limited	£31,071,240
Leisure Parks Real Estate Limited	£31,056,944
William Blythe Limited	£31,042,000
BP INV2 Pledgeco Ltd	£31,034,000
Dentex Healthcare Group Limited	£31,000,684
Whitehouse Leisure International Holdings Limited	£30,991,480
Sinek Global Finance & Trading LLP	£30,981,460
The Forum Trust Limited	£30,978,092
Autoprotect (MBI) Ltd	£30,969,302
Trinity College (CSP) Limited	£30,960,812
EC English London Limited	£30,937,344
Jobserve Limited	£30,930,700
Bidwells LLP	£30,876,064
Fairview Estates (Housing) Limited	£30,832,000
Kier Dormant Holdings Limited	£30,826,000
Arinso People Services Limited	£30,823,936
ESCO UK Holding Company I Ltd	£30,798,602
Union Investcorp Limited	£30,790,780
Combat Medical Holdings Ltd	£30,785,776
South Lincolnshire Academies Trust	£30,782,958
GHG 13 (Chaucer Hospital) Limited	£30,781,000
Metropolitan Infrastructure Limited	£30,776,924
Kendon Packaging Group Public Limited Company	£30,774,174
Saxonchart Limited	£30,768,108
Andrew Weir & Company Limited	£30,743,000
MEL Aviation Limited	£30,741,658
Stockplace Investments Limited	£30,712,906
Openarch Towerview Limited	£30,706,960
Etcetera Construction Services Limited	£30,702,602
Diaverum Facilities Management Limited	£30,700,578
Domino Investments Limited	£30,686,856
S Elvin Limited	£30,662,140
Cambridge Enterprise Limited	£30,637,396
Carter Accommodation Group Limited	£30,601,708
Orwell Trucks Limited	£30,579,000
St.Albans High School for Girls	£30,539,000
Keepstem Limited	£30,536,480
ESRI (UK) Limited	£30,528,396
Racing Welfare	£30,493,000
Avery Dennison U.K. Limited	£30,487,000
TAM International North Sea Limited	£30,466,048
QED Luton (Challney) Holdings Limited	£30,447,000
QED Luton (Challney) Limited	£30,447,000
Invordan Britannia Limited	£30,445,110
Westfield Academy	£30,417,196
Kier (NR) Limited	£30,405,000
R.G. Carter Farms Limited	£30,359,628
Esselte Limited	£30,358,000
Padwicks Travel (Wembley) Limited	£30,341,244
Pretoria Energy Company (Chittering) Limited	£30,328,772
Agricola Holdings Limited	£30,297,000
ACR Investments Limited	£30,292,428
Spiral Partnership Trust	£30,279,000
GHG 18 (Saxon Clinic) Limited	£30,262,000
Bugler Developments Limited	£30,251,396
Smith and Holbourne (Holdings) Limited	£30,192,784
J & A (International) Holdings Limited	£30,188,420
New Hall School Trust	£30,183,080
PCL Transport Limited	£30,098,416
SPD Moorgate Limited	£30,092,000
Beaumont School	£30,084,808
Harbour Club Limited	£30,071,000
Chartco Limited	£30,067,000
Elysium Healthcare Property 2 Limited	£30,056,000
Exagris Limited	£30,044,408
ASG2 Limited	£30,043,000
Shawcor UK Limited	£30,019,000
Fluxys Interconnector Limited	£30,003,936
Crystal Home Improvements Holdings Limited	£29,984,880
CSS Computer Security Solutions Limited	£29,956,776
GPS Food Group (UK) Limited	£29,946,258
Techaid Facilities Limited	£29,912,552

Company	Amount
Electro-Motive Diesel Limited	£29,892,000
Layher Limited	£29,869,548
Trimble UK Limited	£29,865,000
Breyer Holdings Limited	£29,830,864
Broadgate Builders (Spalding) Limited	£29,816,798
Speciality Stores Limited	£29,800,000
Cambridge Commodities Limited	£29,750,216
KPIT Technologies (UK) Limited	£29,745,258
Saxton Limited	£29,712,904
Saxton 4x4 Limited	£29,712,520
Agricultural Central Trading Limited	£29,703,392
The Morley Agricultural Foundation	£29,651,606
ML Accessories Group Limited	£29,631,966
Premier Topco Limited	£29,625,332
Instalcom Limited	£29,624,182
PGR Enterprises Ltd	£29,564,568
Life Education Trust	£29,559,000
KGM Underwriting Services Limited	£29,555,680
Silverson Machines Holdings Limited	£29,534,494
Seneca Environmental Solutions Ltd	£29,532,112
Videojet Technologies Limited	£29,508,000
Gearhouse Broadcast Limited	£29,481,000
Sunlight PV Ltd	£29,480,514
GHG 32 (Goring Hall Hospital) Limited	£29,452,000
J W D Holdings Limited	£29,450,662
Angel Care PLC	£29,445,680
Kwik-Fit Holdings Limited	£29,419,000
Everest Limited	£29,419,000
Tesco Blue (3LP) Limited	£29,399,260
Towers & Co.,Limited	£29,375,000
Defaqto Group Limited	£29,360,876
Gresham's School	£29,330,988
R Stanton-Gleaves UK Limited	£29,330,048
Stevenage Bioscience Catalyst	£29,295,452
R.H.Topham & Sons Limited	£29,288,316
Atalian Servest Food Co Limited	£29,283,000
Fraser Capital Management Limited	£29,278,020
Commercial Freeholds & Investments Ltd	£29,262,552
Dupont (UK) Electronic Materials Limited	£29,255,614
Acteon UK Financing III (EUR) Ltd	£29,237,044
Probe Oil Tools Limited	£29,237,000
JRL Property Holdings Limited	£29,217,624
Goodwill SIP Limited	£29,198,068
Q V Foods Limited	£29,194,000
E.M. Chamberlain Estates Limited	£29,185,836
P. Tuckwell Limited	£29,179,760
Freshlinc Group Limited	£29,158,818
Conduit Street Holdings Limited	£29,147,776
Warners (Midlands) Public Limited Company	£29,143,580
The Invicta Film Partnership No.27, LLP	£29,141,476
Grant & Stone Limited	£29,137,628
Ridley Godfrey (Holdings) Limited	£29,120,916
Sanwalton Limited	£29,112,644
Abrahams Consolidated Limited	£29,106,552
The Hart Schools Trust Ltd	£29,082,856
F.J. Church & Sons Limited	£29,058,780
Wilton House Limited	£29,044,988
Greenyard Flowers UK Ltd	£29,020,288
Breyer Group Public Limited Company	£29,019,344
Seajacks UK Limited	£29,017,994
Emerald Bidco Limited	£29,002,000
Explorer Holdings UK Limited	£29,000,000
SPC Holdings Limited	£28,996,648
Jaysam Developments Borehamwood Limited	£28,973,820
Rex Partners LLP	£28,973,348
Visteon Engineering Services Limited	£28,963,000
Tesco Fuchsia (3LP) Limited	£28,947,276
ATB Group UK Limited	£28,894,516
Michael Broughton Limited	£28,890,798
Spirit (Faith) Limited	£28,865,000
Spurdown Limited	£28,823,032
TES Enterprise Solutions Ltd	£28,815,054
H.R. Philpot & Son (Barleylands) Limited	£28,809,888
MTALX Limited	£28,795,316
Gita Properties Limited	£28,789,296
The Evelyn Trust	£28,766,678
Industrial Water Jetting Systems Limited	£28,761,624
2020 Holdings (England) Limited	£28,757,052
Saba Infra Holdings UK Limited	£28,750,320
Desira Holdings PLC	£28,745,720
Stock Finance (Koruna) Limited	£28,645,654
Joseph Gallagher Limited	£28,537,716
Fairview New Homes (Properties) Limited	£28,527,000
Takely Education Trust	£28,520,000
Blitzfair Limited	£28,516,492
Ensign Holdco 3 Limited	£28,515,000
Pharmadent Holdings Limited	£28,510,594
Parkway Hellas Holdings Limited	£28,500,000
Seax Trust	£28,476,304
Riva Holdco 2 Limited	£28,474,828
Countryside Four Limited	£28,433,140
PX Manufacturing Ltd	£28,387,940
Tradewise Insurance Services Limited	£28,386,768
Freshlinc Limited	£28,383,608
Troston Farms Limited	£28,381,980
Wood Hall Land & Properties Limited	£28,376,944
Bruel & Kjaer VTS Limited	£28,370,000
ACI Global Limited	£28,367,000
James Taylor Homes Group Limited	£28,359,404
Medacs Global Group Limited	£28,353,000
Longford Securities & Equities (K & T) Limited	£28,351,580
The Mathworks Limited	£28,340,612
South Essex Stockholders Limited	£28,336,720
ORTU Federation Ltd	£28,315,000
Newell Properties Developments Limited	£28,293,432
Formula One Auto Centres Limited	£28,280,052
Birketts LLP	£28,262,352
Pasta Foods Limited	£28,254,192
Truck-Lite Europe Limited	£28,167,000
Perry Ellis Europe Limited	£28,153,460
Lea Bridge Hill LLP	£28,153,000
Specialist Cars Limited	£28,076,506
Volkerrail Specialist Businesses Limited	£28,070,000
Digica Group Finance Limited	£28,069,000
John Adams Leisure Limited	£28,062,388
Biofocus DPI (Holdings) Ltd	£28,060,000
EVI Technologies Limited	£28,059,880
Inspectorate Holdings PLC	£28,058,984
Nicholas King Developments PLC	£28,041,000
Community Reinsurance Corporation Limited	£28,039,992
Care UK Health & Rehabilitation Services Limited	£28,033,000
Fox International Group Limited	£28,032,884
Thorlabs Limited	£28,030,180
Arcus Solutions (Holdings) Limited	£28,027,000
Broadway Travel Service (Wimbledon) Limited	£27,996,404
Milpharm Limited	£27,974,948
The Knights Templar School	£27,963,070
ITAB UK Ltd	£27,955,988
Fairview New Homes (Charlton) Limited	£27,937,000
Readie Construction Limited	£27,932,864
MBI MBO Limited	£27,927,000
Gibbons (Holdings) Limited	£27,881,952
Pepkor UK Retail Limited	£27,856,412
SFAET Ltd	£27,800,000
Stantec Treatment Group Limited	£27,792,000
Simon Elvin Holdings Limited	£27,777,356
Shenfield High School	£27,761,460
L. Lynch (Holdings) Limited	£27,694,116
Peacock Holdings (2015) Limited	£27,645,786
PMQUE Limited	£27,638,876
Tattershall Lakes Limited	£27,634,676
Reesink Turfcare UK Limited	£27,616,120
DDD Investments Limited	£27,611,426
Abbey College, Ramsey	£27,607,926

Kelly Property Company Limited	£27,588,656
Biffa Environmental Municipal Services Limited	£27,585,000
Wood Green Animal Shelters	£27,560,376
Panther Investment Properties Limited	£27,539,376
Cwind Ltd	£27,538,000
AK Retail Holdings Limited	£27,529,558
Serruys Property Company Limited	£27,517,096
Epic Staunton LLP	£27,515,298
R.D.Trading Limited	£27,504,084
Ipswich Town Football Club Company Limited	£27,443,000
The Hill Company Limited	£27,435,568
RL Retail Services Limited	£27,429,290
Roe Bros. & Co Ltd.	£27,416,088
The Original Cottage Company Limited	£27,320,876
Mouskos Holdings Limited	£27,300,036
Opal Bay Limited	£27,281,920
Rose Group Limited	£27,264,040
The Invicta Film Partnership No.8, LLP	£27,248,724
Centre for Engineering and Manufacturing Excellence	£27,218,968
Fishpools Holdings Limited	£27,214,488
Industrial Water Jetting Systems Group Limited	£27,162,302
M. & J. Engineers Limited	£27,153,640
Hartismere Family of Schools	£27,139,760
D.D.D. Limited	£27,138,234
Fengrain Limited	£27,137,816
3D Systems Europe Limited	£27,130,000
Soul Coffee House Limited	£27,126,388
John E.Fells & Sons Limited	£27,073,200
Lee Chapel Multi Academy Trust	£27,055,000
Hoo Hing Limited	£27,048,712
Seven Asset Limited	£27,036,750
Openarch Estates Limited	£27,036,236
Toureen Contractors Limited	£27,035,496
CCP Management LLP	£27,030,534
Bridge Academy Trust	£27,009,968
Kelly Comms Limited	£27,006,284
Regulus Topco Limited	£27,001,328
Regulus Midco Limited	£26,996,276
Ensign Bus Company Limited	£26,987,252
Twinmar Investments Limited	£26,985,058
Transeur Properties Limited	£26,975,800
Excellence in Education Trust	£26,965,340
Inland Homes (Essex) Limited	£26,959,236
Jensten Group Limited	£26,954,544
Archaylen Property Limited	£26,938,988
Framingham House Investments Limited	£26,916,964
Sherrygreen Homes Ltd	£26,906,754
Melbourn Science Park Limited	£26,897,000
OAG Aviation Worldwide Limited	£26,871,000
Rooff Holdings Limited	£26,858,154
Sewells Reservoir Construction Limited	£26,855,104
Evolution Academy Trust	£26,854,236
The St Neots Learning Partnership	£26,849,380
HaskoningDHV UK Holdings Limited	£26,844,944
Aspire Academies Trust	£26,840,500
Velji Bhovan & Sons (Trading) Limited	£26,832,736
Yours Clothing Limited	£26,820,168
Chigwell School	£26,811,000
2020 Developments (Luton) Limited	£26,803,900
E & J Properties Limited	£26,794,584
Boston Limited	£26,768,804
Kings Langley School	£26,733,576
RG Securities (No.2) Limited	£26,723,616
Lanber Nursing Homes LLP	£26,723,600
Alami International Limited	£26,703,044
The King Edmund School	£26,687,660
R.G. Carter Projects Limited	£26,657,956
Mission Therapeutics Limited	£26,634,878
Lawes Agricultural Trust	£26,624,868
The Horse Trust	£26,617,376
Queen Elizabeth's School Barnet	£26,613,764
Howard Ventures Limited	£26,599,556
Bauer Technologies Limited	£26,593,588
VGC Group Limited	£26,583,700
Lymington Precision Engineering (LPE) Limited	£26,579,000
SEH Group Limited	£26,563,954
Caskade Caterers Limited	£26,553,772
Roots Hall Limited	£26,523,532
United Therapeutics Europe, Ltd.	£26,513,814
Ryan Elizabeth Holdings Public Limited Company	£26,457,876
Carter Accommodation Holdings Limited	£26,450,444
Paradigm Commercial PLC	£26,445,000
Lamb-Weston/Meijer UK Limited	£26,444,370
Kidney Research UK	£26,428,000
Miriad Property Investments Limited	£26,427,208
Jollyes Group Limited	£26,417,982
Warehouse Express Limited	£26,400,000
Careprogress Limited	£26,391,724
London Care Partnership Limited	£26,390,636
Melton House Investments Limited	£26,362,588
GHG 36 (Winterbourne Hospital) Limited	£26,355,000
Britten-Pears Foundation (The)	£26,352,872
JF Hillebrand UK Limited	£26,352,304
Katrin Properties Limited	£26,322,198
Falcon Tower Crane Services Ltd	£26,301,750
Grosvenor Park 2004 Film Partnership No.1 LLP	£26,292,000
NEEB Holdings Ltd.	£26,273,942
Horsforth Holdings Limited	£26,262,000
Perkinelmer LAS (UK) Limited	£26,261,000
Advanced Lighting Technologies Europe Limited	£26,249,848
Towers Thompson Holdings Limited	£26,248,000
Kingsley Care Homes Limited	£26,228,764
Kirkmore Capital Limited	£26,217,256
McGrath Bros. (Environmental) Ltd.	£26,192,572
Raspberry Pi Foundation	£26,148,986
Bespoke Foods Group Limited	£26,142,942
Volkerservices Limited	£26,081,000
Grange Renewable Energy Limited	£26,079,000
Milburn Productions Limited	£26,073,310
Carter and Ward of Wickford Limited	£26,069,764
SJR Farming Limited	£26,053,000
Nordson (U.K.) Limited	£26,051,878
M L Accessories Limited	£26,038,210
TRAD Properties LLP	£26,020,592
Hatch End High School	£26,020,154
J.L. Knight Roadworks Limited	£26,005,224
Plume School	£26,001,436
Stephen Austin (Holdings) Limited	£25,994,000
Navitas Petroleum Limited	£25,953,000
Aquila BTE 1 Limited	£25,938,068
Apertio Limited	£25,936,000
Lakeside Food Group Limited	£25,919,416
Walstead UK Holdings Limited	£25,912,000
Commodity Centre (Group) Limited	£25,900,236
Envirowales Limited	£25,897,028
George Bateman & Son Limited	£25,884,940
Athena Care Homes (UK) Limited	£25,884,150
St Albans School	£25,872,000
Deards Services Limited	£25,868,690
Herts & Essex Multi Academy Trust	£25,844,080
Meldire Limited	£25,837,640
Taliesin Management Limited	£25,825,456
Rowlandson Investments Limited	£25,810,204
Barking Power Limited	£25,810,000
Safe Computing Limited	£25,791,000
Wheatley (Buntingford) Limited	£25,767,456
ARJ Construction Holdings Limited	£25,759,548
Alphasense Limited	£25,754,936
Berlesduna Academy Trust	£25,748,876
Carnarvon Hotels Limited	£25,728,970
Chivgate Limited	£25,710,050
Chicken Cabins Limited	£25,707,024
WTS Media Group Limited	£25,686,730
North Essex Multi-Academy Trust	£25,669,688

Gredley House Investments Limited	£25,669,238
Ocean Holidays Limited	£25,649,200
Rockley Sands (Estates) Limited	£25,649,000
Nower Hill High School	£25,637,360
Super Toughened Glass Limited	£25,631,762
Healthcare (Barts) Limited	£25,617,806
TCMC Furniture Limited	£25,608,000
WEL (No 1) Ltd	£25,577,424
Richard Long Group Limited	£25,548,540
Synergy Flavours Limited	£25,516,324
Bath Road Properties Limited	£25,498,034
Aston Barclay Holdings Group Limited	£25,497,000
Eckoh UK Limited	£25,491,000
Lancaster Specialist Cars Limited	£25,487,000
Quartix Holdings PLC	£25,436,000
The Hotel Folk Limited	£25,424,332
Essex & Herts Air Ambulance Trust	£25,420,800
Bourne Leisure Group Limited	£25,413,000
Esselte Holdings Limited	£25,404,000
Marlborough Information Services Limited	£25,400,120
Optionis Group Limited	£25,394,012
Lifeplus Europe Limited	£25,389,920
Turners Regency Parks Limited	£25,354,924
Hadleigh Holdings Limited	£25,341,416
Fork Rent Limited	£25,332,156
First Eastern Counties Buses Limited	£25,294,000
Wheatley Group Developments Limited	£25,292,056
Lousin Holdings Limited	£25,285,380
Kirly Limited	£25,276,404
Providence Marian Company	£25,274,174
Metis Homes Limited	£25,263,516
ARJ Construction Limited	£25,260,292
Curtis Medical Investments Limited	£25,231,250
J W Grant Co	£25,227,008
SintecMedia WEM Ltd	£25,215,930
The Ockendon Academy	£25,208,908
Townhold Limited	£25,175,964
Aspire Media Group Limited	£25,166,184
Chase (Palace Wharf) Limited	£25,149,852
W Lamb Limited	£25,146,604
A. F. Machinery Limited	£25,142,550
Enrich Learning Trust	£25,124,722
Audio Network Limited	£25,119,788
Harlow Agricultural Merchants Limited	£25,117,320
Tappenden & Co. Limited	£25,087,848
Polyco (Group) Limited	£25,086,000
Agreserves Limited	£25,076,988
Watford Health Campus Partnership LLP	£25,073,000
KH Finance No.2 Limited	£25,071,000
Healthcare Homes Holdings Limited	£25,066,880
Ammeraal Beltech UK Holding Limited	£25,050,192
Kier Foley Street Holdco 1 LLP	£25,034,000
OEConnection Limited	£25,020,248
Brown Brothers Distribution Limited	£24,996,752
Global Graphics Software Limited	£24,995,400
Lumendi Limited	£24,993,696
Cardiff Gate Business Park Limited	£24,927,388
The Invicta Film Partnership No.26, LLP	£24,924,640
St.Helen's School Northwood	£24,897,000
Pineridge Investments Limited	£24,892,824
Zara UK Midco Limited	£24,890,000
Alternative Bridging (UK 1) Limited	£24,886,840
RMR Capital Limited	£24,877,212
Safegold Properties Limited	£24,876,724
Lantern Services (Holdings) Ltd	£24,863,076
Klyne Aviation Limited	£24,853,164
Cottis House Limited	£24,853,140
Motherwell Holdings Limited	£24,807,754
Worldwide Fruit Limited	£24,804,000
Comland Commercial Limited	£24,775,468
Blenheim Property Management Limited	£24,772,198
Tex Holdings PLC	£24,767,000
Richardsons Leisure Limited	£24,743,276
Fesa (UK) Limited	£24,704,206
Triconnex Ltd	£24,702,000
Cheergrey Properties Limited	£24,686,116
Estates and Lets 2 LLP	£24,684,110
Knowles (UK) Limited	£24,675,106
Countryside Properties (Uberior) Limited	£24,675,000
Churchmanor Holdings Limited	£24,650,726
Joseph King (Norfolk) Co-ordination Limited	£24,650,144
One Stop Private Doctors Limited	£24,633,720
Arcofina LLP	£24,628,286
Inflite Engineering Services Limited	£24,626,656
Paragon Land & Estates Ltd	£24,622,824
Spar (UK) Limited	£24,605,934
Spar Food Distributors Limited	£24,605,884
Tilia Properties Limited	£24,605,560
Chemilines Group Holdings Limited	£24,584,000
The Invicta Film Partnership No.13, LLP	£24,578,374
IQGeo Group PLC	£24,572,000
Clerks Well Properties Limited	£24,570,936
Sansbury Bailey Holdings Limited	£24,553,000
Power On Investments Limited	£24,551,076
Bouygues E & S Infrastructure UK Limited	£24,544,000
Hitchin Girls' School	£24,518,878
HL Display UK Holding Limited	£24,489,000
Countryside Properties (Springhead) Limited	£24,480,658
Ethypharm UK Limited	£24,475,888
EBM - Papst UK Limited	£24,465,800
Bushey St James Trust	£24,446,866
Swift Brickwork Contractors Limited	£24,444,694
Simon Elvin Limited	£24,422,124
Ascend Global Intermediate Holdings, Ltd.	£24,409,136
Exheat Group Limited	£24,356,926
Broadgate Homes Limited	£24,337,748
Peli Biothermal Limited	£24,329,584
Air Business Limited	£24,324,104
Community Foods Limited	£24,323,060
Kluman and Balter Holdings Limited	£24,322,160
Lapid Developments Limited	£24,292,516
Synergy Multi Academy Trust	£24,285,980
SJD Accountancy Limited	£24,285,448
Dry Drayton Estate Limited	£24,282,824
Arrhenius Holdings Limited	£24,216,760
Broadland Wineries Limited	£24,202,070
Pilgrim Foodservice Limited	£24,178,890
Aston Barclay Limited	£24,158,000
EMG Holdings Limited	£24,155,764
Be at One Holdings Limited	£24,154,556
Coffeeheaven International Limited	£24,144,000
Jeesal Akman Holdings Limited	£24,132,036
Bullen Developments Limited	£24,113,224
Beeson Wright Limited	£24,100,966
Draeger Medical UK Limited	£24,080,000
Camfaud Concrete Pumps Limited	£24,072,484
Biochrom Limited	£24,066,976
Kier Integrated Services (Holdings) Limited	£24,048,000
E.G.L. Homecare Limited	£24,045,456
City & Country Bristol Limited	£24,045,074
Gibson Propco Limited	£24,043,000
Openview Security Solutions Limited	£24,037,484
Elsoms (Spalding) Limited	£24,026,982
Ubisense Limited	£24,025,000
Woolpit Business Parks Limited	£24,020,712
Fairview Enfield Limited	£24,004,000
St. Mary's School Cambridge	£23,997,420
Porvair Filtration Limited	£23,997,000
Mouskos Capital Limited	£23,990,352
Www.Nakedwines.Com Limited	£23,975,000
Princebuild Holdings Limited	£23,969,410
Norfolk Farm Produce Limited	£23,956,256
Sardar Properties (U.K.) Limited	£23,952,000
Chelmer Foods Limited	£23,947,330

Company	Value
Project Helix Holdco Ltd	£23,940,140
Fine Foods International (Manufacturing) Limited	£23,932,704
Hayman Group Limited	£23,930,704
Raynham Farm Company Limited (The)	£23,923,140
Westcliff High School for Boys Limited	£23,913,304
Day Webster Limited	£23,895,506
Demipower Limited	£23,874,314
Prinhold Limited	£23,869,468
Alenco (Holdings) Limited	£23,867,000
Lundbeck Limited	£23,865,264
R.G. Carter Cambridge Limited	£23,852,200
Alban Academies Trust	£23,835,900
Sonnet Care Homes Finance Limited	£23,822,758
European Coffee Corporation Limited	£23,818,008
AMI Corporations Ltd	£23,816,296
Fairfield Limited	£23,815,196
Danes Educational Trust	£23,811,000
Global Graphics PLC	£23,807,400
Commodore Kitchens Limited	£23,798,642
Jarrold (St. James) D1/D2 Limited	£23,796,932
Telespazio Vega UK Limited	£23,795,000
Fairfield Garage (Leigh-on-Sea) Limited	£23,789,480
Alfred Homes Limited	£23,769,700
BWP (Cambridge) Limited	£23,661,184
Hilborough Farms Limited	£23,654,136
Phelan Construction Limited	£23,631,652
Norish Limited	£23,631,248
SJO Enterprises Limited	£23,605,686
Aquinna Homes PLC	£23,573,548
Kelly Fleet Services Limited	£23,571,540
Park High School	£23,561,744
Telegenic Limited	£23,560,308
Cyberscience PLC	£23,559,432
EC English Cambridge Limited	£23,539,772
Prentice Aircraft and Cars Limited	£23,539,168
Queenswood School Limited	£23,533,380
Canada Life (U.K.) Limited	£23,519,000
Medway Fundco Limited	£23,485,214
Jackson Frameworks Limited	£23,483,726
Euro-Matic (Brazil) Limited	£23,480,654
Walstead Peterborough Limited	£23,477,000
N & C Building Products Limited	£23,468,466
Freiberger (UK) Limited	£23,464,196
O-I Sales and Distribution UK Limited	£23,462,000
Wadlow Energy Holdings Limited	£23,460,000
Linkage Community Trust	£23,459,206
Kanta Enterprises Limited	£23,451,408
Chicken Villas Limited	£23,448,416
Canons High School	£23,441,502
Lysander Student Properties Operations Limited	£23,441,000
Chaldean Properties Limited	£23,416,676
OAT 2012 Limited	£23,404,640
Walsingham College Trust Association Limited	£23,400,682
C J Bourne (Asset Management) Limited	£23,396,024
St. Margaret's School Bushey	£23,384,684
Salmon Management and Finance Limited	£23,369,664
Heathland Whitefriars Federation	£23,349,020
Ridgeons Land LLP	£23,332,000
J C A Engineering Ltd	£23,321,000
Property Recycling Group PLC	£23,319,254
Micross UK Solutions Limited	£23,309,576
Hemel Snowcentre Limited	£23,288,000
Marblelane Limited	£23,281,300
Snowcentres Limited	£23,279,000
Flamingo Produce Ltd.	£23,271,000
Cargobull Finance Limited	£23,251,000
F. Brazil Reinforcements Limited	£23,249,700
Goodman Family Investments Limited	£23,247,308
Norfolk Academies	£23,246,000
Moorepay Limited	£23,245,000
O.A.Taylor & Sons Bulbs Limited	£23,232,678
Martin Mathew & Co. Limited	£23,228,284
SF11 Limited	£23,219,880
Invesco Capita Holdings Limited	£23,217,878
ISN Europe Limited	£23,214,898
Premier Bidco Limited	£23,187,088
Walsingham Estate Properties Limited	£23,180,184
Grosvenor Park 2007 S48 Film LLP	£23,177,000
Mercury Land Holdings Limited	£23,169,784
Heritage Care Limited	£23,166,000
Norfolk Community Foundation	£23,163,000
Highway Stops Retail Limited	£23,157,496
Global Marine Systems (Vessels) Limited	£23,147,494
Myatt's Field Development LLP	£23,142,160
Wilson Connolly Limited	£23,140,000
Barsham Securities Limited	£23,128,712
The King's School, Ely	£23,124,940
Central G H Trust	£23,115,232
Jark Ventures PLC	£23,114,560
Seckford Education Trust	£23,083,000
TFX Group Limited	£23,063,000
Rivers Multi Academy Trust	£23,059,332
Comland Holdings Limited	£23,055,412
Cambridgeshire Educational Trust	£23,042,760
Bishop's Hatfield Girls' School	£23,018,768
Karsten UK Limited	£23,012,368
Fishpools Limited	£22,924,174
Dunward Properties Limited	£22,902,012
Heritage Developments Limited	£22,887,240
John Milton Academy Trust	£22,886,282
Fairline Yachts Limited	£22,886,000
Countryside Properties (Bicester) Limited	£22,878,528
WCM Investments Ltd	£22,858,166
Open Fibre Networks Limited	£22,853,760
B.P. Mitchell Haulage Contractors Limited	£22,840,176
Salisbury Holdings Limited	£22,835,000
RWF Health and Community Developers (Tranche 1)	£22,827,822
Skanska Major Projects Limited	£22,816,000
P.J. Carey Plant Hire (Oval) Limited	£22,805,350
Satco Investments Limited	£22,797,708
Sonnet Care Homes Midco Limited	£22,779,628
Iris Insurance Brokers Limited	£22,769,232
George Tanner (Shalford) Limited	£22,768,240
Fujichem Sonneborn Limited	£22,759,570
Bow Village Limited	£22,758,864
Denny Bros Holdings Limited	£22,743,674
Country Court Care Homes 3 MB Limited	£22,722,986
M.J.S. Holdings (March) Limited	£22,720,636
Parkstone Limited	£22,716,966
Media 10 Holdings Limited	£22,715,204
Network New Build Limited	£22,708,172
Eastwood Park Academy Trust	£22,697,932
Adcock Refrigeration and Air Conditioning Limited	£22,693,344
Islam Channel Limited	£22,683,580
McGrath Bros. (Waste Control) Limited	£22,663,392
Gentec Energy PLC	£22,644,030
ACES Academies Trust	£22,643,336
Country Court Care Homes 3 SB Holdco Limited	£22,641,746
Cricklewood Developments Limited	£22,632,000
Opecprime Properties Limited	£22,600,000
Thurlow Nunn Limited	£22,595,000
Seymour Distribution Limited	£22,586,000
Metals & Materials Limited	£22,585,000
Micross Foods Holdings Limited	£22,578,652
Demipower (1991) Limited	£22,569,406
Targetfollow (Development) Limited	£22,564,344
Concurrent Technologies PLC	£22,543,204
Tristel PLC	£22,540,000
Moody Homes Limited	£22,531,148
W.H.Palmer & Co.(Industries) Limited	£22,525,120
Munnelly Group PLC	£22,497,000
Dyer & Butler Holdings Limited	£22,491,000
Ashe Group Holdings Limited	£22,486,904
Peppercorn Property Investments Limited	£22,478,208

Company	Amount	Company	Amount
Openview Group Limited	£22,470,132	IFCO Systems UK Ltd	£21,765,852
JCA Head Co Limited	£22,464,000	Sir William Ramsay School Academy Trust	£21,760,852
Twinmar Group Limited	£22,460,782	Vix Technology UK Limited	£21,746,000
Country Court Care Homes Limited	£22,454,608	KSEYE Capital No.1 Limited	£21,745,690
Ecotherm Insulation (UK) Ltd	£22,447,292	Contact Technologies UK Limited	£21,736,164
Rowlands 2014 Limited	£22,445,204	Poste Hotels Limited	£21,733,034
OEC Europe Holdings Limited	£22,444,252	Hilton Properties Limited	£21,732,836
Aixtron Limited	£22,442,788	Citizen Machinery UK Ltd	£21,732,640
Bancroft's School	£22,429,332	R.& J.M.Place Limited	£21,720,984
John Banks Limited	£22,424,232	Zip Heaters (UK) Ltd	£21,717,238
Stephen Austin & Sons Limited	£22,414,000	Hamelin Brands Limited	£21,712,000
Spirit Pub Company (Derwent) Limited	£22,410,000	Storm Technologies Limited	£21,701,044
Site Sales Marketing Limited	£22,387,996	Sopra Steria Recruitment Limited	£21,681,000
Twinmar Limited	£22,381,960	Bexhill UK Limited	£21,669,884
Swift Group Holdings Limited	£22,380,266	Parametric Investments Limited	£21,635,436
Silverwell Technology Limited	£22,375,742	Sussex Gardens Hotels Limited	£21,618,956
Stockvale Limited	£22,371,544	Intelek Limited	£21,614,000
Wrest Park Limited	£22,351,964	Premonition Analytics Limited	£21,600,000
Hitchin Boys' School	£22,343,014	J.L.G.Investments Limited	£21,596,648
Skanska Infrastructure Development UK Limited	£22,338,000	East Anglian Air Ambulance	£21,593,548
D.C.K. Concessions Limited	£22,324,000	Robert Deards Limited	£21,579,480
Flocklynn Limited	£22,303,452	Com Dev Europe Limited	£21,578,000
Alliance Asset Management Limited	£22,277,954	Anzco Foods UK Limited	£21,575,996
Mundipharma International Limited	£22,263,000	Salisbury Workplace Services Limited	£21,566,000
New Landmark Investment Limited	£22,262,130	Cogels Investments Ltd	£21,554,420
East of England Agricultural Society	£22,252,378	Crystal Home Improvements Group Limited	£21,546,712
Goymour Properties Limited	£22,249,016	Shamir UK Limited	£21,544,656
Acclaim DMW Holdings Limited	£22,241,580	Residential Land Holdings Limited	£21,526,836
DCK Group Limited	£22,238,000	BMS Limited	£21,526,000
Parker Hannifin (Holdings) Limited	£22,234,000	Motorclean Limited	£21,524,038
Lignacite Limited	£22,220,824	Appleyard Group Limited	£21,521,000
Borras Construction Ltd.	£22,216,240	British Pipeline Agency Limited	£21,511,444
Falck UK Limited	£22,175,792	Astro Lighting Holdings Limited	£21,509,184
Greens of Soham Limited	£22,175,000	Knighton Foods Limited	£21,500,000
Asset Education	£22,165,416	Iliffe Media Limited	£21,469,556
Union Carriers Limited	£22,164,462	AVL Powertrain UK Limited	£21,461,362
Grosvenor Park (Harris & Trotter) 2002 Film LLP	£22,162,680	Desira Group PLC	£21,459,128
Dhollandia U.K. Limited	£22,155,434	European Investments (Lancashire) Limited	£21,454,676
Kier Overseas (Seventeen) Limited	£22,145,916	Bauder Limited	£21,446,036
Greystead Properties Limited	£22,134,078	Manufacturing Services Investment Limited	£21,423,330
Tesco Property Partner (No.1) Limited	£22,106,228	Blue Square Marketing Limited	£21,420,340
Phlexglobal Limited	£22,103,000	Spencers Property Investments Limited	£21,419,826
GHG 35 (Droitwich Spa Hospital) Limited	£22,101,000	Grimme (U.K.) Limited	£21,413,880
Firstan Limited	£22,094,060	Broadleaf Park LLP	£21,410,000
Borras Group Holdings Limited	£22,079,048	Reald Europe Limited	£21,406,884
Edmonton Academy Trust	£22,072,404	Red Tree (2004) LLP	£21,403,640
Corona Energy Limited	£22,062,484	Rotamead Limited	£21,396,398
East Anglian Property Limited	£22,052,218	R3 Polygon UK Ltd.	£21,393,000
LB Enterprises Limited	£22,029,252	Cornelius Vermuyden School	£21,363,280
Lasted Limited	£22,026,456	Saybest Limited	£21,355,000
Maurice Crouch (Growers) Limited	£22,013,528	The Invicta Film Partnership No.9, LLP	£21,354,288
SBH Gatwick Limited	£21,996,404	Hawkes Limited	£21,351,756
Yparho Investments Limited	£21,981,840	The Aldenham Foundation	£21,350,544
Alboro Holdings Limited	£21,966,168	Wildlife Trust for Beds, Cambs and Northants	£21,345,990
Pheasant Eye Limited	£21,962,856	WWW Sunoptic Com UK Limited	£21,345,202
Vinayak Properties Limited	£21,953,264	Countryside Maritime Limited	£21,331,328
Bourne Leisure (Hopton) Limited	£21,937,000	Micronclean Limited	£21,314,632
254 Kilburn HR LLP	£21,930,924	Anglia Autoflow Limited	£21,308,762
Lituanica UK Ltd	£21,924,308	Tithe Academy	£21,301,552
Intermune Holdings Limited	£21,910,400	Kigass Limited	£21,296,502
DSV Road Holding Limited	£21,904,000	Community Health Services Limited	£21,296,000
Green Label Poultry Limited	£21,890,184	Fortem Solutions Limited	£21,291,008
Clarenco LLP	£21,870,000	Resham PLC	£21,289,094
Princebuild Limited.	£21,868,492	Qatar Racing Limited	£21,275,036
Rowan International Limited	£21,866,686	Aspire Learning Trust (Whittlesey)	£21,265,452
Lindal Valve Company Limited	£21,855,000	Ercol (Holdings) Limited	£21,239,000
Orion Media Limited	£21,853,000	Bamrose Enterprises Limited	£21,195,012
Kier Reading LLP	£21,832,000	Duncan Lewis Solicitors Ltd	£21,194,938
Bluestone Mortgage Finance No.2 Limited	£21,830,904	Astle Limited	£21,188,000
Lindal Holdings Limited	£21,799,000	Olive Business Solutions Limited	£21,160,996
Kent, Surrey & Sussex Community Rehabilitation Co	£21,794,000	AER Rents Limited	£21,152,090
Barnack Estates UK Limited	£21,779,844	Simon Balle Academies Trust	£21,149,000

Company	Value	Company	Value
Alterium Limited	£21,144,684	ARM UK Holdings Limited	£20,502,910
Cunningham Holdings (London) Limited	£21,143,368	H.& G.Car Parks Limited	£20,502,416
Mayday Healthcare PLC	£21,135,084	AMS Care Limited	£20,491,914
T F S Loans Limited	£21,130,558	Sandy Balls Estate Limited	£20,488,504
The Finance Store Limited	£21,109,796	Woodland Global Ltd	£20,482,866
Four CS MAT	£21,109,614	Leda Investments Limited	£20,473,632
The Union of Evangelical Churches	£21,088,468	Arinso UK Limited	£20,461,006
Sopress Investments Limited	£21,077,000	Sunnen Products Limited	£20,447,320
Digital House Group Ltd	£21,071,540	RSS Jet Centre Limited	£20,442,050
Johnson Care Limited	£21,071,216	SCCS Survey Equipment Limited	£20,437,000
Myddleton London Limited	£21,065,404	Sines Parks Ltd	£20,432,996
Hexcel Overseas	£21,061,278	H & D Support Services (Holdings) Limited	£20,426,000
Bourn Hall Limited	£21,058,040	H & D Support Services Limited	£20,426,000
H L C (Wood Products) Limited	£21,056,724	Orwell Multi Academy Trust	£20,423,148
Muraspec Decorative Solutions Limited	£21,036,000	J.A. Phillips Holdings Limited	£20,419,454
Schneider Electric Software GB Limited	£21,025,080	Shields Environmental Group (Holdings) Ltd.	£20,411,000
I Go 4 Ltd.	£21,012,030	Thomas Sinden Limited	£20,384,588
Norfolk Wildlife Trust	£20,993,532	Independent Meters Limited	£20,383,076
Villachase Limited	£20,990,900	Arcus FM Limited	£20,379,000
C. J. H. Farming Limited	£20,980,712	Keystone Developments (LG) Limited	£20,349,000
KSEYE Capital No.2 Limited	£20,979,084	Strides Pharma Global (UK) Ltd	£20,348,244
York House (Meat Products) Limited	£20,976,072	Amneal Pharma UK Holdings Limited	£20,340,656
Garden City (Scotfield) LLP	£20,969,870	Vida Wood UK Limited	£20,334,064
Herts Insurance Consultants Limited	£20,964,260	Biffa Polymers Limited	£20,331,000
Port of Boston Limited	£20,960,000	Ford JL Limited	£20,319,110
The Invicta Film Partnership No.15, LLP	£20,950,716	Seaside Leisure Parks Limited	£20,313,196
Stockvale Investments Limited	£20,948,290	T.E.Scudder Limited	£20,308,644
Titon Holdings PLC	£20,930,000	Aerospares 2000 Limited	£20,302,044
The King's (The Cathedral) School, Peterborough	£20,919,308	London Distribution Park LLP	£20,301,448
Lochailort Fairfield Limited	£20,909,460	IMBOLC Limited	£20,299,934
Ingram Micro Services Holdings Ltd	£20,903,000	Bauer Golden Square Limited	£20,293,000
P.F. Ahern & Sons Limited	£20,893,946	Washbrook Capital Limited	£20,285,024
Ardex UK Limited	£20,875,000	Huntleigh International Holdings Limited	£20,284,438
Anritsu EMEA Limited	£20,866,786	The Eden Academy	£20,257,000
Zest Living Limited	£20,862,288	Thames Reinforcements Limited	£20,254,036
Kier Reading Holdco 1 LLP	£20,851,000	PRGX UK Ltd	£20,247,620
Adil Catering Limited	£20,837,032	A1 Pharmaceuticals Holdings Limited	£20,243,268
The Practice (Group) Limited	£20,820,000	Fairview New Homes (South East) Limited	£20,231,000
Pasta Foods Investments Limited	£20,813,194	EMG Anglia Limited	£20,228,764
St Bede's Inter Church School	£20,812,368	Environmental Group Limited	£20,226,580
The Countryside Restoration Trust	£20,805,672	Fleximize Capital Limited	£20,216,784
Werner UK Sales & Distribution Ltd.	£20,798,000	Bellman Property Group Limited	£20,216,372
Verulam School	£20,791,232	T.H.Clements & Son Limited	£20,214,000
Watford Grammar School for Boys	£20,789,344	Bauer AR Holdings Limited	£20,200,000
Isuzu Truck (UK) Limited	£20,784,428	Paradigm Development Services Limited	£20,196,000
Colchester Zoo Holdings Limited	£20,777,640	Travelpack Marketing & Leisure Services Limited	£20,189,584
Gardline Marine Sciences Limited	£20,774,840	Grant Family Holdings Limited	£20,179,292
Thurlow Nunn Standen Limited	£20,765,000	Grant Family Investments Limited	£20,179,292
Newhall Land Limited	£20,760,996	Red Kite Schools Trust	£20,175,320
Asiatic Carpets Holdings Limited	£20,743,478	K L Technologies Limited	£20,173,406
Aquila Chelmsford Limited	£20,735,054	Friargate Coventry Development Limited	£20,164,530
The Swiss Laundry,Limited	£20,721,048	Haras Investments Limited	£20,151,376
Harvest Investments Solutions Limited	£20,705,364	Rattlerow Properties Limited	£20,115,896
Astro Lighting Limited	£20,685,228	Cardel Group Limited	£20,100,000
Pangbourne Developments Limited	£20,678,000	Britvic EMEA Limited	£20,076,000
Landex Limited	£20,665,156	Dalton Resources Limited	£20,066,192
Countryside Sigma Limited	£20,654,072	Direct Insurance Group PLC	£20,066,124
J H & A J King Farms Limited	£20,645,944	Stema Shipping (UK) Limited	£20,056,992
Moulton Bulb Company Limited	£20,634,594	Fengrain (Services) Limited	£20,043,212
Gentian Investments Limited	£20,633,750	Fresh Wharf Estates Limited	£20,026,982
Belchim Crop Protection Limited	£20,629,048	Elysium Healthcare No. 4 Limited	£20,008,000
Dencora Estates Limited	£20,625,876	John F Hunt Power Limited	£20,003,154
SHOO 802AA Limited	£20,611,000	Redbridge Produce & Flowers Limited	£19,995,000
CloudFM Integrated Services Limited	£20,588,512	Erba Diagnostics UK Limited	£19,985,104
Whitehill & Bordon Development Company Phase 1A	£20,580,000	Carlson Vehicle Transfer Ltd	£19,983,736
Southbank UK Limited	£20,554,700	Blue Tree Limited	£19,974,350
Historic House Hotels Limited	£20,545,322	Openarch Greenside Limited	£19,970,492
Tallentire Energy Limited	£20,532,000	Hydac Technology Limited	£19,970,478
Glorious Solutions Limited	£20,526,442	Long Term Reversions (Torquay) Limited	£19,960,864
Avocado Developments Limited	£20,517,598	Cambridge Primary Education Trust	£19,958,256
Eastleaf Ltd	£20,515,848	Majestic Property & Estates Limited	£19,955,034
Katsouris Brothers Limited	£20,508,800	Thomas Ridley and Son,Limited	£19,910,284

Company	Amount
SIP Group Limited	£19,897,728
Smithfield Foods Limited	£19,888,000
Brownlow Enterprises Limited	£19,872,860
WPA Support Services Limited	£19,869,000
Riverstone Pictures (Show Dogs) Limited	£19,864,386
Cliffords Limited	£19,864,160
Bucyrus UK Limited	£19,857,000
G.S. Shropshire & Sons Limited	£19,851,734
Quixant UK Limited	£19,843,388
Fairview Hotels Investments (2) Limited	£19,836,746
The Solihull Hotel Company Limited	£19,835,000
Optima Chemical Ltd	£19,829,948
Durite Limited	£19,827,032
RQ Capital Limited	£19,815,660
Life Fitness (UK) Limited	£19,815,374
Elektron Technology PLC	£19,800,000
Mersea Homes Limited	£19,774,444
Fulton St James Limited	£19,762,148
Atlas Multi Academy Trust	£19,753,760
Alpha Schools (Holdings) Limited	£19,740,234
East Anglia's Childrens Hospices	£19,739,388
Konings Juices & Drinks UK Limited	£19,725,720
Walstead United Kingdom Limited	£19,717,000
The Bartrum Group Limited	£19,714,440
Contechs Holdings Limited	£19,691,052
M.P.I. (Herts) Limited	£19,687,272
M.P.I. Limited	£19,684,456
Desilu Group Limited	£19,674,460
Business & Communications Limited	£19,673,224
L V Shipping Limited	£19,670,016
E.D. & A.D. Cooke, Bourne (Farms) Limited	£19,668,346
Keen & Toms Holdings Limited	£19,667,552
Ashe Construction Limited	£19,663,114
F.P.Smith (Holdings) Limited	£19,659,640
Forebury Estates Limited	£19,652,080
Padfield (Hayleys) Limited	£19,640,844
Roger Skinner Limited	£19,635,860
Ball Company	£19,628,154
Falkland Islands Company Limited	£19,627,000
George Brown's Implements (Holdings) Limited	£19,625,980
Jarvis Homes Limited	£19,621,248
Labvantage Solutions Limited	£19,619,416
Icknield High School	£19,599,454
ACO Technologies PLC	£19,590,186
Vindis Developments Limited	£19,585,020
Sanctuary Personnel Limited	£19,584,872
Horta Properties Limited	£19,575,724
J.E.Piccaver & Co. (Gedney Marsh)	£19,566,324
Poste Holdings Limited	£19,559,456
Fauna & Flora International	£19,551,206
Beacon Educational Trust Limited (The)	£19,536,838
Grant & Bowman International Limited	£19,532,718
Sunsave 25 (Wix Lodge Farm) Limited	£19,526,000
Pipers Corner School	£19,523,812
The Holmes Care Limited	£19,503,908
Kier Trade City LLP	£19,496,000
J. Walker & Son (Investments) Limited	£19,493,572
Derby School Solutions (Holdings) Limited	£19,464,000
Derby School Solutions Limited	£19,464,000
Marwin Securities Limited	£19,456,530
Usborne PLC	£19,433,000
Jepco Limited	£19,430,632
S. Dad Limited	£19,428,012
Wimpey Corporate Services Limited	£19,428,000
Constable Homes Limited	£19,423,994
Emmett UK Limited	£19,421,000
Facet Capital Limited	£19,419,258
Showcard Print Limited	£19,416,000
Welland Medical Limited	£19,405,456
Q.N. Hotels Limited	£19,404,120
DJM 88 Limited	£19,402,752
Twinmar Investments Holdings Limited	£19,399,046
User Friendly Properties Limited	£19,398,370
JSA Services Limited	£19,393,340
Sparquote Limited	£19,368,620
Ritelite (Systems) Limited	£19,349,188
Delbanco Meyer & Company Limited	£19,346,000
Boxford (Suffolk) Holdings Limited	£19,320,700
Hayter Limited	£19,320,000
Stratton Education Trust	£19,305,306
Swanlea Limited	£19,301,774
Virgin Wine Online Limited	£19,298,000
Keystone 2 Limited	£19,282,810
The Marlborough Science Academy Limited	£19,276,802
Ortona Limited	£19,276,264
Denecroft Estates Limited	£19,275,098
Chalcroft Limited	£19,274,662
Nine Heathrow Ventures Limited	£19,260,404
R.G. Carter Limited	£19,259,434
Media 10 Limited	£19,237,392
Sandfields Farms Limited	£19,236,968
Homeguard Properties Limited	£19,216,532
Shields Environmental Investment (Holdings) Ltd	£19,212,000
Warrant Properties Limited	£19,209,212
Key Developments (Godalming) LLP	£19,195,320
Porcelanosa (South East) Limited	£19,179,000
SHOO 803AA Limited	£19,160,000
Kent Blaxill Group Limited	£19,149,880
Hearing Dogs for Deaf People	£19,148,224
Quinn Investment Holdings (London) Limited	£19,140,008
Simarco Holdings Limited	£19,120,640
Milbank Ventures Limited	£19,102,024
T & B (Contractors) Limited	£19,100,484
T & B (Contractors) Holdings Limited	£19,100,484
European Investments (Earlseat) Limited	£19,100,000
Brogan Group Ltd	£19,099,396
Dominion Pubs and Bars Limited	£19,099,000
Swarco UK Limited	£19,096,000
Arisen Chef Ltd	£19,091,982
GDL (Slough Developments) Limited	£19,077,416
YMCA Trinity Group	£19,060,000
Ratcliff Group Limited (The)	£19,052,848
I.M.O. Precision Controls Limited	£19,038,160
N.R.C. Plant Limited	£19,035,140
Omavale Limited	£19,027,584
Wickland (Holdings) Limited	£19,022,956
Timber Connection Limited	£19,019,700
Flamborough Holidays Limited	£19,017,000
Jackson Mechanical Services (UK) Limited	£19,010,232
SintecMedia Global Ltd	£19,009,208
Friars 716 Limited	£19,001,000
Mothers Ltd	£18,980,012
Southern Cement Ltd	£18,976,804
Macquarie Corona Energy Holdings Limited	£18,975,828
Archigen Biotech Limited	£18,974,144
A.J. Bush Limited	£18,972,558
Saba Park Services UK Limited	£18,971,592
Be at One Limited	£18,970,004
Queen Elizabeth's Girls' School (Barnet)	£18,958,656
SOP International Limited	£18,958,460
Ebberod Capital Ltd	£18,954,268
1spatial PLC	£18,954,000
Chelmer Valley High School	£18,951,836
Ilot Investments UK Ltd	£18,942,062
LPA Group PLC	£18,937,000
Suez Water Technologies & Solutions Services UK	£18,932,000
Sotherby LLP	£18,917,582
Norfolk Capital Group Limited	£18,913,000
MRB Holdings Ltd	£18,909,664
The Fitzwimarc School Academy Trust	£18,907,334
Brown & Carroll (London) Limited	£18,904,998
Tritton Farming Partnership LLP	£18,903,956
John W. Doubleday Limited	£18,903,896
Ilot Capital UK Ltd	£18,871,134

Company	Value
PHH 2 Limited	£18,859,400
Business Control Solutions Group Limited	£18,851,000
Thumbzup UK Limited	£18,839,764
Smiths Business Information Services Limited	£18,836,000
Chadwell Heath Academy	£18,834,648
Camfed International	£18,817,672
The Helena Romanes School	£18,815,024
NET Academies Trust	£18,812,000
Hilary Russell Group Ltd	£18,810,644
Mistras Group Limited	£18,807,000
Elliot Leigh Property Investments 2 Ltd	£18,802,786
Moody Venture Capital LLP	£18,801,380
Cheale Group Limited	£18,799,536
Rickmansworth School	£18,782,918
Garrets Bidco Limited	£18,780,188
SCB Holdings (Sandy) Limited	£18,779,712
Elvin Investments Limited	£18,776,366
MN Sports Holdings Limited	£18,767,960
European Investments (Lancashire 2) Limited	£18,713,342
European Investments (Reaps Moss) Limited	£18,713,342
Luminescence Holdings Ltd	£18,707,136
Betcrown Limited	£18,706,236
Stirling Civil Engineering Limited	£18,700,000
C.I. Industries Limited	£18,688,746
Independent Power Networks Limited	£18,686,192
Leisuregrow Holdings Limited	£18,682,000
Geodis United Kingdom Limited	£18,675,016
GHG 24 (Sloane Hospital) Limited	£18,675,000
Edward Le Bas Limited	£18,668,884
Stanton Holding Limited	£18,660,364
Pirin Ltd	£18,658,932
Elizabeth Estates (NWB) Limited	£18,648,896
King Street Manchester Property LLP	£18,640,838
Brayleys Cars Limited	£18,639,416
Countrywide Electrical Distributors Limited	£18,634,840
Indo European Foods Limited	£18,626,150
Skanska Cementation International Holdings Limited	£18,610,000
Whitehall Resources Limited	£18,607,244
Daarasp LLP	£18,595,234
J.Browne Construction Company Limited	£18,558,708
Trumpf Limited	£18,550,284
Earlseat Wind Farm Ltd	£18,545,000
Kampa UK Ltd	£18,537,160
Kitchen Range Foods Limited	£18,533,000
Holden & Holden Limited	£18,530,000
Rational UK Limited	£18,518,472
Welch's Group Holdings Limited	£18,516,196
Fold Hill Foods Limited	£18,500,264
Amsprop City Properties Limited	£18,491,500
Vinepost Limited	£18,481,164
Double A Group Services Limited	£18,480,432
Turnhold Properties Limited	£18,473,580
S N B Holdings Limited	£18,470,068
Lint Group Limited	£18,456,874
FIC Grand Plaza Ltd	£18,441,596
CATS Canterbury Limited	£18,416,000
Ransome's Trading Limited	£18,415,952
Churton Property Developments Limited	£18,413,018
Tican Process Holdings Limited	£18,412,088
Easy Cleaning Solutions Limited	£18,408,270
Spalding Grammar School	£18,386,160
Webb Investments Ltd.	£18,380,896
Learning Pathways Academy	£18,359,500
Cytocell Limited	£18,351,782
Wheatley PLC	£18,351,416
Sines Parks Holdings Limited	£18,351,088
Claxton Engineering Services Limited	£18,342,000
H.Stain Limited	£18,329,352
Alan Boswell Insurance Brokers Limited	£18,327,354
M.W. Beer & Co. Limited	£18,323,732
Right Choice Insurance Brokers Limited	£18,314,632
Selecta Holding Limited	£18,314,000
European Investments (SCEL) Limited	£18,296,544
Northfield Avenue (Holdings) Limited	£18,292,048
Amalgamated Berkshire Properties Limited	£18,287,200
Express Freight Services (U.K.) Limited	£18,283,578
Abbey View Produce Limited	£18,282,696
United Reformed Church (Eastern Province) Trust	£18,281,024
Kefco Sales Limited	£18,256,392
Asino Limited	£18,243,436
Newfields Agricultural Holdings Limited	£18,242,404
Comline Auto Parts Limited	£18,240,080
Edstrom UK Holdings PLC	£18,239,662
M.Price Limited	£18,238,488
Freeline Therapeutics Limited	£18,233,322
Ashley Wilde Group Limited	£18,226,848
Hatfield Trading Limited	£18,215,704
Wood Farm (Stanmore) Limited	£18,215,322
Business Control Solutions Public Limited Company	£18,195,678
Rigel Capital Partners Limited	£18,180,716
MY Construction & Carpentry Limited	£18,180,600
Friar's Pride Limited	£18,178,222
Korda Developments Limited	£18,174,750
Map Media Limited	£18,166,048
Datapaq Limited	£18,165,000
L.C.F.Arthey & Sons Limited	£18,161,340
Naked Wines International Limited	£18,161,000
Flo-Mech Holdings Limited	£18,153,820
Gray & Sons (Chelmsford) Limited	£18,147,604
Winstanley and York Road Regeneration LLP	£18,146,000
Reichmann Properties PLC	£18,139,238
W.& H.Marriage & Sons Limited	£18,132,350
Mr. Fothergill's Seeds Limited	£18,125,452
Bellcoin Holdings Limited	£18,123,984
Jessica House Developments Limited	£18,121,020
Ovenden Papers Limited	£18,115,964
Cromwell Community College	£18,111,240
Yelcon Limited	£18,109,448
Hapag-Lloyd (U.K.) Limited	£18,103,140
Wood Hall Investments Limited	£18,096,462
Dabasia Estates LLP	£18,089,284
CloudFM Group Limited	£18,078,180
Fastglobe (Mastics) Limited	£18,062,200
Cornelius Group PLC	£18,054,144
Brington North LLP	£18,038,368
Quanta Consultancy Services Group Ltd	£18,037,472
SLR Holdings Limited	£18,029,672
Le Bas Investment Trust Limited	£18,025,536
Cheale Meats Limited	£18,022,880
ASL Technology Holdings Ltd.	£18,019,000
A.E. Lenton (Holdings) Limited	£18,018,910
J.W. Suckling Transport Limited	£18,013,616
A1 Pharmaceuticals Public Limited Company	£18,008,192
Scotsdale Nursery and Garden Centre Limited	£18,003,356
Ortona Properties Limited	£17,989,976
John F Hunt Limited	£17,978,696
Property and Commercial Enterprises Limited	£17,964,918
Speycrest Limited	£17,964,598
RQ Capital Loans Limited	£17,963,524
Bithia Limited	£17,960,416
Bespoke Foods Holding Limited	£17,945,468
Catco Kids LLP	£17,944,464
Davroc Limited	£17,936,524
GHG 33 (Beaumont Hospital) Limited	£17,927,000
Kershaw Group Limited	£17,925,080
A. T. Cross Limited	£17,919,740
Angel Property Investments Limited	£17,917,088
Greenbrook Industries Limited	£17,893,746
Applied Satellite Technology Limited	£17,891,290
Castlestone Investments Limited	£17,873,204
Healthcare Homes Group Limited	£17,872,780
The Practice Surgeries Limited	£17,858,000
Charterhouse Simon Limited	£17,854,982
GHG 20 (Sarum Road Hospital) Limited	£17,853,000

Company	Amount
Comtec Group (International) Limited	£17,835,000
O.W. Wortley & Sons Limited	£17,831,720
Colchester Zoo Limited	£17,824,566
Stainless Metalcraft (Chatteris) Limited	£17,824,544
Tobar Group Trading Limited	£17,817,164
Telegenic Holdings Limited	£17,815,356
Richard Johnston Limited	£17,812,262
Fairview New Homes (Chase Road) Limited	£17,800,000
Excelredstone Converged Solutions Limited	£17,792,348
Vokera Limited	£17,788,000
Richard Hale School	£17,787,580
Mercantile Trust Limited	£17,774,000
Twilight Real Estate Limited	£17,772,256
Kendric Ash Limited	£17,753,196
Telensa Ltd	£17,741,052
Calpri Ltd	£17,727,750
Kiln Park Estates Limited	£17,714,000
Kymab Limited	£17,714,000
Robert Lee Distribution Limited	£17,693,266
Lynxvale Limited	£17,691,848
KMG Systems Limited	£17,691,124
Minhoco 20 Limited	£17,688,000
Regis Group (Barclays) Limited	£17,686,348
Cygnet Care Limited	£17,667,356
Ellgia Holdings Limited	£17,667,214
Oakburn European Properties Limited	£17,665,056
Alcohols Limited	£17,664,496
Beds with Ease Limited	£17,662,488
Crispin & Borst Limited	£17,656,000
Levy Associates Limited	£17,654,000
Trailer Resources Limited	£17,652,592
Azurie Blue Limited	£17,652,464
Birch Farms (C & N) LLP	£17,649,324
SWP Group Limited	£17,644,882
Gray's Inn 10 Limited	£17,638,348
Ruislip High School	£17,633,988
M. Anderson Construction Limited	£17,631,444
F & R Cawley Limited	£17,599,710
Fairview New Homes (Developments) Limited	£17,592,000
Premier Midco Limited	£17,584,038
The Invicta Film Partnership No. 17, LLP	£17,576,724
Hypro EU Limited	£17,574,000
London and Hertfordshire Limited	£17,566,748
Ammeraal Beltech Limited	£17,563,440
Hascombe & Valiant Stud Limited	£17,552,200
Dage Holdings Limited	£17,540,268
Bluegnome Limited	£17,538,988
Antec International Limited	£17,536,000
Berry Recruitment Limited	£17,534,026
MCSA Group Limited	£17,531,404
Soul Foods Limited	£17,520,264
P.J. Duffy & Son (Farms) Limited	£17,515,656
Scientific Digital Imaging PLC	£17,513,000
H. Smith Food Group PLC	£17,509,352
Signet Group Services Limited	£17,505,000
KCG Holdings Ltd	£17,500,100
Cranfield Technology Park Investments Limited	£17,481,700
Crown Holdings Limited	£17,480,976
Unity Education Trust	£17,476,628
Everguard Limited	£17,474,784
BAM Monk Bridge Limited	£17,454,000
Investment Company PLC (The)	£17,451,180
Exploration Electronics Limited	£17,450,164
Painesend Farm LLP	£17,446,600
Hallgarten Wines,Limited	£17,434,252
Arthenella Limited	£17,429,196
Fulton Central Limited	£17,405,402
Industrial Tool Supplies (London) Limited	£17,399,344
Insignis Academy Trust	£17,393,248
Gippeswyk Community Educational Trust	£17,385,916
Kesgrave High School	£17,379,164
Howard Sawston Ltd	£17,377,340
The Brand Machine Limited	£17,374,024
Former Reichmann Properties PLC	£17,363,948
S Chaplin Holdings Limited	£17,362,248
Countrywide Developments (UK) PLC	£17,355,384
Gough Hotels Limited	£17,352,792
Roadside Group Ltd	£17,351,000
Cantay Estates Limited	£17,345,136
Woodford Heating Holdings Limited	£17,343,320
Thurstable School Sports College & Sixth Form Centre	£17,331,808
E.G.T. Finance Limited	£17,331,720
Maldon Electric Securities,Limited	£17,316,856
The Parkes LLP	£17,316,784
Hugh Crane Holdings Limited	£17,316,304
Altenmark Limited	£17,303,840
John Saul Limited	£17,299,194
Pantheon Hotels and Leisure Limited	£17,291,444
Suffolk Life Pensions Limited	£17,288,000
Simarco International Limited	£17,272,356
Suffolk Wildlife Trust Limited	£17,258,000
Offsite Archive Storage and Integrated Services UK	£17,257,258
John Hampden Grammar School	£17,252,404
Baby Network Limited	£17,236,060
DSJ Homes Limited	£17,235,500
Penlaw & Company Limited	£17,231,378
Richard Wright Music Limited	£17,229,790
Tillomed Laboratories Limited	£17,229,562
Lorien Limited	£17,225,000
Offley Chase Estates Limited	£17,192,640
Nicholas King Homes PLC	£17,183,000
Manor Service Stations Limited	£17,179,000
Kings Leisure Limited	£17,175,358
Ventress Group Limited	£17,164,816
Alternative Bridging (UK 2) Limited	£17,161,092
NVSM Limited	£17,151,288
Regis 2000 Limited	£17,150,980
Camstar Herbs Limited	£17,149,070
Truman Securities Limited	£17,147,800
G.H. Parker (North Cotes) Limited	£17,146,736
Oakman Inns and Restaurants Limited	£17,146,456
London City Bond Limited	£17,133,680
Hamton Environmental Services Limited	£17,124,328
Les Residence Falcon Wharf Limited	£17,120,400
MSCM Limited	£17,119,856
Plymouth (Notte Street) Limited	£17,104,904
Reads Property Developments Ltd	£17,103,278
Tri-Continental Limited	£17,101,246
S.T.C.Plumbing & Heating Merchants Limited	£17,098,472
St Georges School (Harpenden) Limited	£17,096,652
L & M (Heating) Supplies Limited	£17,089,968
Tican (Chilled) Limited	£17,086,000
Radical Investments Limited	£17,080,976
Cyanconnode Holdings PLC	£17,071,012
T F Bowman & Son Limited	£17,070,040
Charter Projects (Developments) Limited	£17,063,354
R.H.Amar & Co Limited	£17,062,040
R.A. Latta (Farms) Limited	£17,036,968
Tenmill Limited	£17,036,908
Roman Investments Limited	£17,029,512
Aura Finance (Holdco) Limited	£17,024,372
De Soutter Medical Limited	£17,021,444
Skylight Investments Limited	£17,019,638
Fulton Hyde Limited	£16,997,012
Provide Community Interest Company	£16,994,058
Dr Challoner's Grammar School	£16,988,000
O'Brien Waste Recycling Solutions Ltd	£16,987,000
Sonnet Care Homes Holdco Limited	£16,984,258
Incodia International Ltd	£16,982,000
Jacklin Properties Limited	£16,981,492
Quanta Consultancy Services Limited	£16,980,568
Hawkins & Associates Limited	£16,970,284
The AES Tring Park School Trust	£16,963,774
The Foremost Currency Group Ltd	£16,955,046

Finer Limited	£16,949,120
CQK Limited	£16,949,028
The Harrow Academies Trust	£16,948,598
Hull Holdings Limited	£16,944,852
Galderma (U.K.) Limited	£16,943,000
Connect Access Group Ltd	£16,941,962
Fitzmaurice Holdings Limited	£16,928,040
GDL (Luton) Developments Limited	£16,923,480
New Sparta Film Distribution Limited	£16,922,080
Falck EMS UK Limited	£16,907,368
Arpo Global Limited	£16,907,318
Wise Trading Limited	£16,904,696
McGee Civil Engineering Limited	£16,900,368
N W Brown Group Limited	£16,890,068
Birdlife International	£16,884,820
Metro Partners LLP	£16,880,308
UNEX Limited	£16,878,644
Aspect Contracts Limited	£16,875,372
Chassis-Cab Limited	£16,869,506
Into UEA LLP	£16,856,000
Go Homes Ltd	£16,853,836
Price Bailey Group Limited	£16,839,000
Van Hage & Company (Holdings) Limited	£16,836,390
Family Amusements Limited	£16,821,682
Martlane Limited	£16,817,976
MJC Properties (Essex) Limited	£16,813,306
Bentwaters Parks Limited	£16,799,960
Emico Limited	£16,787,244
P.C. Howard Limited	£16,779,960
Elgon (Enfield) Limited	£16,779,368
Cambridgeshire Industrial Properties Limited	£16,767,480
Rose Film Partnership LLP	£16,761,960
Grangebrook Estates Limited	£16,751,529
London Pharma & Chemicals Group Ltd	£16,735,017
Ball. Roller & Transmission Bearings Limited	£16,730,120
Premier Inn International Development Limited	£16,714,270
Hamamatsu Photonics UK Limited	£16,714,114
Institute of Grocery Distribution (The)	£16,713,299
Seymour International Limited	£16,707,000
Lay & Wheeler Limited	£16,707,000
Corporate Investments Limited	£16,705,100
Excitech Limited	£16,704,616
Harouni Group of Companies Limited	£16,696,130
Fairview New Homes (Willow Way) Limited	£16,690,000
Thomson Sawmills Holdings Limited	£16,677,180
Optimum Group Services PLC	£16,675,437
Hills Group Enterprises Limited	£16,674,323
Renault Group U.K. Limited	£16,671,500
Startling Music Limited	£16,666,777
Enfield Fancy Goods Limited	£16,664,887
MA Securities London Limited	£16,654,916
Thule Holding Limited	£16,652,151
Creightons PLC	£16,646,000
JSM Construction Limited	£16,643,443
JSM Group Holdings Limited	£16,643,443
Fluorocarbon Group Limited	£16,641,542
Thames Valley Air Ambulance	£16,635,763
Coryton Advanced Fuels Limited	£16,633,164
Askham Village Community Limited	£16,619,195
Countryside Annington (Mill Hill) Limited	£16,601,500
Ziegler UK Limited	£16,594,064
Cambridge Broadband Networks Limited	£16,589,359
Lexitron Limited	£16,584,190
KWS UK Limited	£16,579,000
Denville Hall 2012	£16,574,064
Country Retirement & Nursing Homes Ltd	£16,571,283
Abbotsley Farms Limited	£16,570,914
Flo-Mech. Limited	£16,568,132
Cokenach Property Limited	£16,558,619
McCutcheon Norveil Consultancy Limited	£16,556,840
Grace Foods UK Limited	£16,555,000
BDL Group Public Limited Company (The)	£16,541,557
E.W.Ballard Holdings Limited	£16,537,662
Panther Trading Limited	£16,531,522
The Claxton Trust	£16,529,449
Altomart Limited	£16,528,765
Rivers Finance Group PLC	£16,517,509
Silverson Machines Limited	£16,510,545
SG Technologies Limited	£16,504,000
Silnat Holdings Limited	£16,500,291
Rivers Leasing PLC	£16,499,837
George Browns Limited	£16,497,736
Change Schools Partnership	£16,488,100
Stamford Property Company Limited	£16,482,476
Morris Education Trust	£16,478,094
Chalcroft Holdings Limited	£16,477,751
Forest Commercial Services Limited	£16,475,931
Brent Housing Ltd	£16,469,177
Mentmore Gransden Limited	£16,466,602
Vandyke Upper School	£16,466,549
Eurobase Systems Limited	£16,466,334
R C Tinsley 2012 Limited	£16,466,076
Alpha 3 Manufacturing Limited	£16,459,000
Collease Truck and Trailer Rentals Limited	£16,449,799
Westlake Estates Limited	£16,449,147
Farecla Products Limited	£16,444,479
Commercial Body Fittings Limited	£16,442,860
Garrets International Limited	£16,437,936
Propshop Limited	£16,431,915
Sifcon International PLC	£16,430,931
Rowe Farming Limited	£16,421,000
Hampden Insurance Holdings Limited	£16,417,032
Tobar International Limited	£16,403,248
Amersham School	£16,401,055
Rannerlow Limited	£16,395,316
Gilbertson & Page Limited	£16,385,766
D.H.Sanderson and Son Limited	£16,384,989
Kier Integrated Services Group Limited	£16,377,000
Republic Technologies (UK) Limited	£16,375,000
The APM Group Limited	£16,374,439
B.A.T.S. Ilford Limited	£16,373,346
Rollins & Sons (London) Limited	£16,373,052
Cavenham Estates Limited	£16,372,992
Sandhill Homes Limited	£16,372,683
Make Believe Ideas Ltd	£16,366,366
Caretech Estates Limited	£16,363,000
Starbones Limited	£16,362,519
Geo. E. Gittus & Sons Limited	£16,359,677
Werner Access Products UK Holdings Limited	£16,346,000
Netscientific PLC	£16,346,000
Velfac Limited	£16,340,000
F.H. Nash Limited	£16,339,382
Barstone Limited	£16,331,224
Stonebond Properties Limited	£16,312,428
Herma UK Limited	£16,311,131
Elysium Healthcare Property 3 Limited	£16,310,000
Pico Technology (Holdings) Limited	£16,307,159
Geoghegan Bros. Limited	£16,305,339
TJX UK Property Limited	£16,295,000
Monarock Limited	£16,269,961
Alcedo Shipping Limited	£16,269,907
Kubach & Sambrook (Metals) Limited	£16,255,821
Napp Laboratories Limited	£16,254,000
Littleberries LLP	£16,251,027
Go Interiors Limited	£16,250,010
Heraeus Noblelight Limited	£16,245,000
R.H.Claydon Limited	£16,242,017
Home Counties Estates Limited	£16,229,434
Milltrust BLA LLP	£16,225,272
T.S.G. Building Services PLC	£16,224,464
Ramco (Harlow) Limited	£16,202,669
Glastry Advisory Partners Limited	£16,196,895
Jelmac (Primary Care) Properties Limited	£16,186,455
Caretech Estates (No. 5) Limited	£16,166,000

Company	Value
C.U. Phosco Limited	£16,165,517
Saw Property Company Limited	£16,162,275
Supreme Hotels LLP	£16,153,491
Castle View School Academy Trust	£16,146,449
Chauncy School	£16,143,711
Premiair Aerospace Limited	£16,138,727
Flamingo Holdings Limited	£16,133,000
C.E. Davidson Farms Ltd.	£16,130,224
GEMS Schools Limited	£16,124,856
Chiltern Way Academy Trust	£16,124,637
Earl Estates Limited	£16,114,566
Jarvis Contracting Limited	£16,112,338
SME Properties Limited	£16,102,450
4 BG Group Ltd	£16,101,068
Tetra Pak Processing UK Limited	£16,092,751
Elysium Healthcare (Farndon) Limited	£16,087,000
Local Boy'z Group Holding Limited	£16,085,824
Grant & Boyd Limited	£16,081,908
TJX Europe Buying (Deutschland) Limited	£16,075,000
St. Elizabeth Hospice (Suffolk)	£16,067,109
Genie Topco Limited	£16,063,000
Timewell Properties Limited	£16,060,228
St Ivo School	£16,058,093
THR Number 5 Limited	£16,048,269
Kromachem Holdings Limited	£16,031,411
Aquatronic Group Management PLC	£16,031,349
Havens Christian Hospice	£16,029,000
Marlborough Highways Group Limited	£16,001,876
Frelene Limited	£16,000,356
Stevenage Road Residential Developments Limited	£15,998,236
WJ Management Limited	£15,991,835
ADC Holdings Limited	£15,989,031
Shelbourne Reynolds Engineering Limited	£15,986,637
Regal Healthcare Properties Limited	£15,984,177
Balvraid Properties Limited	£15,982,739
Euston Biogas Limited	£15,976,121
1LIFE Management Solutions Limited	£15,968,000
J Alston & Sons Limited	£15,962,887
Bungay High School	£15,957,542
Sunray Estates Limited	£15,948,466
Air Works Empire UK Limited	£15,946,796
Callcott Holdings Limited	£15,945,234
Kier Stoke Limited	£15,945,000
Ortona Management Limited	£15,938,720
Beaconsfield School	£15,935,924
MLS (Overseas) Limited	£15,935,551
Grants of Shoreditch Limited	£15,935,510
Abel Homes Limited	£15,935,002
Thomson Sawmills Limited	£15,907,542
North Norfolk Academy Trust	£15,903,000
Morelli Group Limited	£15,901,264
Dawson Books Limited	£15,899,000
Residential Land Management 2 Ltd	£15,896,826
Gee Group Ltd	£15,895,332
Haas Automation Limited	£15,893,589
Rannoch Food Group Limited	£15,890,600
Anglo European Academy Trust	£15,887,779
NDEMIC Creations Ltd	£15,878,876
Vanneck Residential LLP	£15,878,174
Granta Design Limited	£15,869,667
Tazaki Foods Limited	£15,858,909
Haas 2007 Limited	£15,853,689
Viners Capital Properties Limited	£15,850,952
Coventry Foundationcampus Limited	£15,841,000
Rican Securities Limited	£15,836,983
Suffolk Community Foundation	£15,811,808
Stonemanor Limited	£15,797,151
Walter John Cook and Sons Limited	£15,791,169
Ceragon (UK) Limited	£15,776,645
Celador Radio Broadcasting Limited	£15,774,442
Hadleigh Bakery Limited	£15,772,858
Orley Farm School Trust	£15,772,453
Smartcomms SC Limited	£15,767,000
Whitfield Finance Limited	£15,756,673
Precision Printing Co. Limited	£15,753,570
W & L Investments LLP	£15,752,335
Mapeley Columbus II Limited	£15,750,000
Strauss Logistics Limited	£15,744,729
Gade Property Developments Limited	£15,730,458
AWG Land Holdings Limited	£15,729,000
CEVA Animal Health Limited	£15,709,163
Bourne Grammar School	£15,707,177
Classic Management Services Limited	£15,698,553
The Church of Pentecost - UK	£15,687,379
Elsoms Seeds Limited	£15,677,365
Robinson Young Limited	£15,671,505
Knight Roadworks (2010) Limited	£15,670,964
The Dispute Service Limited	£15,670,269
Country House Weddings Limited	£15,669,194
Greenseed International Limited	£15,661,782
Hildo Limited	£15,655,811
Personnel Holdings Limited	£15,655,000
Teaching Personnel Holdings Limited	£15,655,000
S & T Audio Limited	£15,651,796
Watford Grammar School for Girls	£15,644,219
Central Property Investments Limited	£15,641,023
API Microelectronics Limited	£15,630,000
Chemtest Limited	£15,589,624
Wood International Agency Limited	£15,587,165
Frith's Flexible Packaging Limited	£15,586,405
RWH Travel Limited	£15,583,813
Ramblers Holidays Group Limited	£15,583,555
A. & E. G. Heading Limited	£15,581,271
R.F. West Limited	£15,579,216
Marshall Land Systems Ltd	£15,575,617
F. Vindis & Sons (Sawston) Limited	£15,575,142
Ingleby (1884) Limited	£15,573,000
Advante Limited	£15,571,409
Leitrim Properties Limited	£15,569,435
Dominion Hospitality Midco Limited	£15,569,000
O'Hara Property Investment Holding Company Ltd	£15,568,922
Multitrust Property Investments Limited	£15,567,156
Stanley Dock Properties Limited	£15,561,307
Maldon Crystal Salt Company Limited	£15,561,000
London Executive Aviation Limited	£15,557,000
Silverbridge Properties Limited	£15,552,931
P.I.P. Electrics Limited	£15,552,661
Kingfisher (EU) Limited	£15,549,479
Aquaterra Energy Limited	£15,544,000
Marylebone Square Holdings Ltd	£15,528,017
Firstan Holdings Limited	£15,523,632
Dencora Dereham Retail Partnership LLP	£15,517,410
Barlow Tyrie Limited	£15,515,728
Pure Recycling Warwick Limited	£15,515,000
Waddesdon Church of England School	£15,508,692
SD Underwriting Limited	£15,501,952
Molecular Products Limited	£15,500,573
A. & B. Glass Company Limited	£15,499,528
Jabac Finances Limited	£15,498,803
Capespan International Limited	£15,494,000
Big Easy Restaurants Limited	£15,493,501
Cappagh Browne Utilities Limited	£15,484,426
The Stoke By Nayland Club Ltd.	£15,482,543
Roselead (Wattisham) Limited	£15,474,613
Kitewood (Creekside) Limited	£15,473,662
C.John Norris (Cars & Caravans) Limited	£15,464,725
Rowan International Topco Limited	£15,457,829
Churchmanor Limited	£15,447,206
Elysium Healthcare (St Mary's) Limited	£15,445,244
Starke Industries Limited	£15,439,765
Sapphire Food South East No.4 Limited	£15,432,386
Telensa Holdings Limited	£15,431,291
NPS (UK6) Limited	£15,425,000
Kenford Developments Limited	£15,424,357

Company	Value
Taylor Properties Trading Ltd	£15,415,743
Grantol Investments Limited	£15,415,446
MNS Care PLC	£15,414,494
Berwen Limited	£15,401,277
T. Rippon Estates Limited	£15,393,681
Ward Farming Limited	£15,393,552
Talbot House Business Centre Limited	£15,386,373
R Group Holdings Limited	£15,374,000
Blenheim Estates Limited	£15,362,492
Belsize Garages Project Limited	£15,362,346
Plumbcity Limited	£15,348,757
County Care Homes Limited	£15,347,158
Buffaload Logistics Limited	£15,337,059
Optimise Media Group Limited	£15,326,013
Landex Holdings Limited	£15,324,004
Laxkan Holdings Ltd	£15,322,764
GB Ingredients Limited	£15,319,000
Vetex Limited	£15,314,148
Eternit UK Limited	£15,314,000
Kotecha Ltd	£15,312,185
Parker Hannifin Industries Limited	£15,311,000
WJ Groundwater Limited	£15,310,471
Mallard Leasing Limited	£15,307,777
Permastore Group Limited	£15,304,000
JW Froehlich UK Limited	£15,302,396
Alan Day Investments LLP	£15,300,143
Minhoco 26 Limited	£15,297,341
Permastore Limited	£15,293,000
Point Pedro Property Holdings Limited	£15,288,470
O'Brien Waste Recycling Solutions Holdings Limited	£15,288,000
Origin Frames Limited	£15,283,468
Chappell Estates Limited	£15,274,624
Wymondham Property Management Company Limited	£15,272,892
CEG Properties Limited	£15,270,000
Osem U.K. Limited	£15,267,264
Allaway Group Limited	£15,260,275
Canada Life Asset Management Limited	£15,254,000
CML Microcircuits (UK) Limited	£15,249,581
Kier Minerals Limited	£15,247,000
MM Flowers Limited	£15,242,891
West Hatch High School Academy Trust	£15,242,000
Hudson Lisse Limited	£15,234,200
Flamingo Plants Ltd	£15,227,000
Marden Homes Limited	£15,226,653
Oakray Limited	£15,224,925
Alcatel IP Networks Limited	£15,216,826
Theatre Royal (Norwich) Trust Limited	£15,215,966
Clement Clarke (Holdings) Limited	£15,209,229
Orlight Limited	£15,203,643
Caretech Community Services (No.2) Limited	£15,198,000
VSL Group Holdings Limited	£15,197,883
MC Power Limited	£15,195,000
Viglen Limited	£15,187,131
Princes Risborough School	£15,184,344
UNEX Gredley (Holdings) Limited	£15,184,085
Hutton East Limited	£15,182,505
Treebond Limited	£15,179,623
Ocourage Limited	£15,176,342
Abzena Holdings Limited	£15,175,000
NHV Helicopters Ltd	£15,174,545
Haileybury Academy Trust	£15,172,721
Chaldean Estate Limited	£15,170,424
Banks Mills Limited	£15,170,277
Munnelly Support Services Limited	£15,170,000
Vahnea Marolda Investments LLP	£15,168,396
Fibron BX Limited	£15,165,722
Alpi UK Limited	£15,153,209
V.G.Clements (Contractors) Limited	£15,146,263
Oyster Properties Limited	£15,145,685
Whitecliff Bay Holiday Park Limited	£15,145,498
SCH 2014 Limited	£15,143,761
R. & I. Grant & Co. Limited	£15,115,267
Pickering Interfaces Limited	£15,112,178
Kent,Blaxill & Co,Limited	£15,106,639
The Construction Workers Guild Limited	£15,103,765
Regency Homes Limited	£15,092,611
Palmhall Limited	£15,091,000
Betting Shop Services Limited	£15,085,530
G.W. Daniels and Son Limited	£15,080,943
Dialgreen Estates Limited	£15,080,637
Salperton Park Estate Limited	£15,077,502
NQA Certification Limited	£15,076,540
Cornwall	£15,073,055
Southend High School for Boys Academy Trust	£15,065,219
Z Hotel Poland Street Property LLP	£15,058,413
BR Pharma International Limited	£15,056,712
Wernick Buildings Limited	£15,053,596
Kingspan Timber Solutions Limited	£15,050,853
Burney Realty Limited	£15,034,011
Rosper Estates Limited	£15,031,205
Timeboard Industrial Properties LLP	£15,028,699
Et Ceteris Limited	£15,022,091
Belgrave Land (Sheffield) Limited	£15,021,822
Randstad HR Solutions Limited	£15,021,000
RPSD2 Limited	£15,011,804
UML Marylebone Limited	£15,011,344
R.G. Carter Engineering Limited	£15,008,276
William Vere (Holdings) Limited	£14,993,621
The Paddocks Care Home Ltd	£14,987,614
Rigby Taylor Limited	£14,985,000
TTP Labtech Limited	£14,975,000
Vinci Environment UK Limited	£14,973,000
Bluestar Enterprise Limited	£14,963,473
Knight Build Limited	£14,961,662
Fairview New Homes (Colindale) Limited	£14,953,000
Palm Recycling Limited	£14,946,428
452 Finchley Road LLP	£14,943,261
Searles (Camping Ground) Limited	£14,942,513
BS Project Services Limited	£14,931,000
Gerald McDonald & Company Limited	£14,922,663
Metrosold Limited	£14,919,094
Pizza Gogo Ltd	£14,916,840
Property & Investment Management Limited	£14,908,334
Fineraid Limited	£14,906,744
Carlisle Staffing Services Holdings Limited	£14,902,000
Enco Products Limited	£14,898,000
Tesco Pension Investment Limited	£14,896,000
St Columba's College and Preparatory School	£14,891,098
The Land Group (Suffolk) Limited	£14,885,395
Abacus Hotels Limited	£14,878,855
The Olive Tree Limited	£14,876,810
Long Term Reversions (Harrogate) Limited	£14,875,668
GHG 26 (Beardwood Hospital) Limited	£14,874,000
HRS Investments Limited	£14,872,608
H. Erben Holdings Limited	£14,858,951
Ashley King (Developments) Limited	£14,858,661
JMBC Properties Ltd	£14,850,377
Potter & Moore Innovations Limited	£14,846,000
Selborne Care Limited	£14,845,953
Natures Menu Limited	£14,840,652
Hexagon Investment Holdings Limited	£14,830,570
Donald Moody Investments and Developments Ltd	£14,824,668
SG Technologies Group Limited	£14,823,000
Interaction Recruitment PLC	£14,820,169
Liebherr-Rental Limited	£14,808,942
Tompsett Holdings Limited	£14,804,657
Hudson Almere Limited	£14,802,959
Dengie Crops Limited	£14,795,695
Thurne-Middleby Ltd	£14,790,000
NBC Europe Ltd.	£14,784,000
Waveney Valley Academies Trust	£14,782,000
L Bennett & Son Holdings Limited	£14,781,277
Masterlord Estates Limited	£14,780,794
Joyce Frankland Academy, Newport	£14,777,702

Company	Amount
No Climb Products Limited	£14,774,944
Quinta Raddison Limited	£14,771,891
CATMJ Limited	£14,770,266
Avocet Capital Limited	£14,770,126
Arthur's Partners LLP	£14,767,284
Bioline Agrosciences Limited	£14,761,932
Benfleet Schools Trust	£14,751,000
Construct Holdings Limited	£14,748,920
South Eastern Leisure UK Limited	£14,738,644
Lamesta Limited	£14,738,456
Coversure Insurance Services Limited	£14,732,386
Levolux Limited	£14,732,000
Surya Hotels Limited	£14,728,591
Bartrum's Road Services Limited	£14,725,129
Ironmongerydirect Limited	£14,691,625
Denso Automotive UK Ltd.	£14,688,000
Gamit Limited	£14,683,744
Exclusive Contract Services Limited	£14,679,518
Select Enterprises (Holdings) Limited	£14,678,742
Deltech Europe Limited	£14,673,403
Al Asayl Bloodstock Ltd	£14,666,714
Centurion Safety Products Ltd	£14,666,665
South Bristol (Ashton Park) Limited	£14,666,000
French & Jupps Limited	£14,657,962
Summerhill Birmingham Limited	£14,644,183
FJC Topco Limited	£14,633,877
Good Harvest Properties (Southwark) Limited	£14,631,545
The Giles Academy	£14,631,260
Sherrygold No.1 Limited	£14,630,546
Deben Group Industries Limited	£14,629,955
Sterndale Systems Limited	£14,628,791
Omniport Norwich Limited	£14,622,938
Micropress Printers Limited	£14,605,279
Stonewater Enterprises Limited	£14,599,352
Clarksteel Holdings Limited	£14,595,698
BRT (Wisbech) Limited	£14,590,516
Venture Lighting Europe Limited	£14,589,358
Evangelical Lutheran Church of England Trust Ltd	£14,589,172
Swift 1st Limited	£14,577,000
B Emerald Limited	£14,568,722
Purcell School (The)	£14,567,751
Amsik Limited	£14,564,792
Gardiner Real Estate PLC	£14,560,000
Euroview Manufacturing Limited	£14,556,602
Volkerlaser Ltd	£14,555,000
Alpha Trust	£14,547,794
Automated Systems Group Limited	£14,542,000
Express Vending Group Limited	£14,538,369
A.W. & D. Hammond Limited	£14,535,519
Brooklands Helix Developments Limited	£14,530,922
Boxford (Suffolk) Farms Limited	£14,516,884
Meadow Holdings Limited	£14,514,291
Mono Holdings Limited	£14,510,316
Agetur (U.K.) Limited	£14,509,239
Hutton Construction Limited	£14,502,867
Lodwick Homes Limited	£14,500,062
Pledge Office Chairs Limited	£14,494,900
Veritas Educational Trust	£14,484,234
S. Sacker (Claydon) Limited	£14,481,174
Norfolk and Waveney Enterprise Services	£14,477,050
Passportcard Limited	£14,473,239
Davis and Dann Limited	£14,469,876
Connectix Limited	£14,468,799
Frimstone Limited	£14,466,948
Trustonic Limited	£14,463,869
The Practice Corporate Management Limited	£14,463,000
Weir Waste Services Limited	£14,458,736
Bristol Fruit Sales (Market) Limited	£14,458,000
Valley Trucks Holdings Limited	£14,455,042
Thames Industrial Estate Limited	£14,454,908
Rosemary & Thyme Limited	£14,450,627
Grant & Bowman Limited	£14,443,814
HLT Stakis Operator Limited	£14,441,632
Rooff Ltd	£14,435,934
Landchief Limited	£14,434,618
Price Bailey LLP	£14,421,000
SDJ Enterprises Limited	£14,420,452
Anglia Aircraft Restorations Limited	£14,418,854
Premier PLC	£14,417,769
Kingshott School Trust Limited	£14,414,740
SDV 2025 ZDP PLC	£14,413,000
Transmec Properties Limited	£14,407,471
Durman Stearn Holdings Limited	£14,402,476
Masteroast Holdings Limited	£14,395,083
Freshtime UK Limited	£14,393,080
Redsky IT (Hemel) Limited	£14,391,736
Sitecrest Limited	£14,391,378
Langley School (1960) Limited	£14,387,005
Bowlplex Limited	£14,385,000
Caretech Estates (No 2) Limited	£14,383,000
Latimer Hill LLP	£14,366,000
Eastern Credit Limited	£14,362,199
JDM Technology Group Limited	£14,360,296
Stonewater Capital Limited	£14,356,649
Francis Associates (43) LLP	£14,355,587
Routebuy Limited	£14,339,306
Natural Balance Foods Limited	£14,336,937
Defender No.1 Production LLP	£14,335,035
The C. Alma Baker Trust	£14,331,364
Eurobase International Limited	£14,328,032
Seabourne Group Limited	£14,315,059
Baldwin Filters Limited	£14,314,776
David Black & Son Limited	£14,313,516
West One Technology Ltd	£14,308,900
Cambridge Medipark Limited	£14,308,664
Clearsprings (Management) Limited	£14,308,389
Rapid Electronics Holdings Limited	£14,298,119
Newport School Solutions Limited	£14,298,000
Newport School Solutions (Holdings) Limited	£14,298,000
H.Erben Limited	£14,291,031
KLM UK Engineering Limited	£14,290,000
Crop's Foods Ltd.	£14,288,526
FAI Automotive PLC	£14,284,172
Schottlander Limited	£14,279,057
Interguide Group Limited	£14,276,818
Silverton Property Investments Limited	£14,273,929
Contracting Made Easy Ltd	£14,269,625
Rattlerow Farms Limited	£14,265,120
Colts Cabs Limited	£14,243,478
Element Energy Limited	£14,234,085
Enfield Innovations Ltd	£14,227,513
Futuresource Holdings Limited	£14,223,611
The Diamond Learning Partnership Trust	£14,222,307
Henbrandt Limited	£14,219,180
F.H. Hale & Sons (Builders) Limited	£14,184,136
The Activity Superstore Limited	£14,181,681
Insignia Investments Limited	£14,180,130
Aurient Investments N16 Ltd	£14,177,548
Alchemie GRP Limited	£14,172,339
London Internet Exchange Limited	£14,157,472
Foregain Limited	£14,143,351
Cadastra Limited	£14,132,905
Lima Orthopaedics UK Limited	£14,129,957
Investment Properties (Luton) Limited	£14,128,222
Global Resale, Ltd	£14,125,037
NIAB.	£14,125,000
Stuart Group Limited	£14,114,177
Orchid Drinks Limited	£14,113,000
Vernalis (R & D) Limited	£14,107,000
The UK Holiday Group Limited	£14,103,925
ASM Metal Recycling Ltd.	£14,079,676
Verco Office Furniture Limited	£14,057,772
C.W. & J. Cargill Limited	£14,051,263
Start-Rite Shoes Limited	£14,050,000

Marine Point Property LLP	£14,048,415	I & C Holdings Limited	£13,721,347
Henley Group Holdings Limited	£14,042,932	Vantage Volante Limited	£13,718,099
Amersham (Holdings) Ltd.	£14,039,869	Cloud Topco Limited	£13,715,934
Express Vending Limited	£14,036,931	Horizon Land Limited	£13,711,959
Riverstone Solutions 2 Limited	£14,035,968	W.D.King Limited	£13,699,625
Laxkan Ltd	£14,028,788	Palmers (St Albans) Limited	£13,698,190
Webster Estates Ltd	£14,026,737	I & C Limited	£13,688,336
Fulton Grand Limited	£14,022,891	Comtec Cable Accessories Limited	£13,674,000
Inhealth Molecular Imaging Limited	£14,021,000	L & M Holding Ltd	£13,660,850
Spiritualists' National Union (The)	£14,015,770	Kier Trade City Holdco 1 LLP	£13,659,000
Grimston Trust Limited	£14,012,352	Abbey Mills Properties Ltd	£13,656,690
The Shoe Quarter Limited	£14,008,924	Youngman Group Limited	£13,653,707
BRE Global Limited	£14,007,000	E.F.G. Housewares Limited	£13,650,907
Oak Tree Schools Holdings Limited	£14,004,221	Ad Meliora Academy Trust	£13,642,772
Southgate Packaging Limited	£13,991,731	KM Estates Limited	£13,638,141
Virbac Limited	£13,986,033	Reliance Entertainment Productions 7 Ltd	£13,636,532
Acteon Group Properties Limited	£13,984,000	Paul Strickland Scanner Centre	£13,635,338
Rakon UK Holdings Limited	£13,980,000	Mirrorstoke Limited	£13,632,225
Welney Farms Property Limited	£13,978,730	Martin Dawn PLC	£13,624,930
Central Lending Funding Number One Limited	£13,972,000	Roundwood Park School Academy Trust	£13,617,675
Bango PLC	£13,968,559	Rex Trade Associates Limited	£13,606,803
The Derbyshire Hotel Derby Limited	£13,964,061	RA Securities London Limited	£13,602,942
Aurora Distribution Limited	£13,962,589	Clarke Property Partner Limited	£13,600,487
Triplehigh Limited	£13,952,020	Vinci Fleet Services Limited	£13,580,000
The Big Prawn Co. Ltd.	£13,945,287	Select Enterprises Limited	£13,570,220
Lismire LLP	£13,944,123	Trentpeak Limited	£13,564,798
Wisdom Toothbrushes Limited	£13,932,000	Moody International (Russia) Limited	£13,562,750
Clarion Academy Trust	£13,931,491	Longmill Realty Limited	£13,562,213
Saint Francis Hospice	£13,928,000	Franke Coffee Systems UK Limited	£13,562,108
DBD Distribution Limited	£13,918,050	James Southall & Company Limited	£13,560,000
Artisan (UK) PLC	£13,917,463	Beamglow Limited	£13,558,577
Nationwide Metal Recycling Limited	£13,915,019	The Keswick Enterprises Group Limited	£13,552,875
Cosco Shipping Lines (UK) Limited	£13,908,348	Abbey Properties Cambridgeshire Limited	£13,544,637
A.G.Wright & Son,(Farms) Limited	£13,907,674	PPG Kansai Automotive Finishes UK LLP	£13,543,955
Defender No.1 Sale & Leaseback LLP	£13,907,090	Farcet Fen Limited	£13,541,480
Waste Recycling Environmental Limited	£13,903,600	MAS (Holdings) Limited	£13,536,307
Early Learning Holdings Limited	£13,900,000	GHG 22 (Garden Hospital) Limited	£13,530,000
Chelsea Stores Holdings Limited	£13,900,000	Rolec Services Limited	£13,523,962
Career Teachers Limited	£13,898,000	Arthur Branwell & Co. Limited	£13,522,801
Fitzjohns Avenue Ltd	£13,891,572	Waldersey Farms Limited	£13,519,531
Harrow High School	£13,889,414	Crownfield Holdings Limited	£13,503,106
Baruch Investments Limited	£13,884,581	Dr Challoner's High School	£13,496,036
Shedmead Limited	£13,875,975	Waystone Limited	£13,491,168
Butchers and Drovers Charitable Institution	£13,873,957	Taylor Made Holdings UK Limited	£13,481,622
Sato UK Limited	£13,872,000	Cripps Developments Limited	£13,472,245
Netcall Telecom Limited	£13,866,000	Neville Trust Limited	£13,459,802
Essex County Care Limited	£13,853,347	Nicholls Limited	£13,458,243
Carrain Limited	£13,853,009	Murfitts Industries Limited	£13,456,248
Pledream Properties Limited	£13,850,547	Lemon Groundwork Solutions Ltd	£13,436,697
JPJ Installations Limited	£13,850,398	The Cavity Insulation Guarantee Agency	£13,433,049
King Edward VI Grammar School, Chelmsford	£13,848,000	M & D Developments Limited	£13,431,778
Slush Puppie Limited	£13,844,823	Howard Hunt Mail Limited	£13,418,588
T.Rippon & Sons (Holdings) Limited	£13,839,137	Ralph Peters & Sons Limited	£13,414,859
Trust Estates (Clarence Street) Limited	£13,832,904	Dron & Dickson Limited	£13,414,604
Bourne Court Properties Limited	£13,832,547	HCL Insurance BPO Services Limited	£13,412,000
E.E. & A. Tee Limited	£13,828,376	Kingsmead School	£13,411,465
Saba Infra Cambridgeshire Limited	£13,827,983	Wright Medical UK Ltd	£13,407,556
Shearer Property C Limited	£13,824,684	Green Spark Renewable Energy (UK) Ltd	£13,400,612
CRK Finance Limited	£13,820,178	Marz Limited	£13,388,672
Integrated Microwave Technology Ltd	£13,817,817	Prime Place (Woking Island Site) LLP	£13,387,849
The Gap Partnership Limited	£13,806,309	Adonia Medical Group Limited	£13,384,936
Charles Wharton Limited	£13,804,503	Pregis Limited	£13,380,024
Anglia Innovation Partnership LLP	£13,798,000	Thomas Lipton Ltd	£13,378,481
Halsbury Homes (South East) Limited	£13,795,717	Moog Fernau Limited	£13,377,836
Fullfield Limited	£13,795,072	Hedgemans Limited	£13,375,961
Higgins Investments PLC	£13,784,537	Chalk Farm Marine LLP	£13,372,217
Astwood Securities Limited	£13,780,052	Adventure Forest Group Limited	£13,371,000
Neopost Technologies Limited	£13,761,000	Thursford Collection (The)	£13,369,253
Farrington Care Homes Limited	£13,752,100	Cocksedge Building Contractors Limited	£13,365,475
R. Maskell Limited	£13,745,360	Walsingham Estate Management Limited	£13,362,742
Inntel Group Limited	£13,731,509	Naked Wines Prepayments Trustee Company Ltd	£13,361,000
East Midlands Training Limited	£13,727,504	London School of Theology	£13,359,058

Company	Value
E.V. Offshore Limited	£13,356,000
Blowplast Limited	£13,355,391
Zian Hi-Tech (U.K.) Limited	£13,352,515
Corporate Express UK Holding Limited	£13,351,000
Coherent (UK) Holdings Limited	£13,347,000
TLC Care Homes Limited	£13,344,789
Tharros Limited	£13,336,089
The Elstree UTC	£13,336,000
South Essex Academy Trust	£13,330,038
Corporate Express (Holdings) Limited	£13,327,000
Workout Limited	£13,325,661
KNM Project Services Limited	£13,322,356
Charles Gallagher Limited	£13,316,507
Hill's Garages (Woodford) Limited	£13,312,039
Mid Norfolk Academy Trust	£13,307,961
Punjab House Associated Ltd	£13,301,499
Ellis Bros (Contractors) Limited	£13,295,898
Robert Gibbs (Contracting) Company Limited	£13,294,702
Ocean Gateway LLP	£13,291,004
Rocket Medical Group PLC	£13,290,275
Garrets Bidco 2 Limited	£13,286,820
Rapidrop Global Limited	£13,277,743
Autumn Foods Holdings Limited	£13,268,194
Michell Instruments Limited	£13,266,787
Marsdens Caterers of Sheffield Limited	£13,265,836
Kelly Rail Group Ltd	£13,264,636
The Enterprise Department Limited	£13,261,326
The Guild of Construction Workers Limited	£13,253,820
M.& R.Bowman Limited	£13,250,904
DBD Enterprises Limited	£13,241,074
K.M. Packaging Services Limited	£13,225,403
R. S. Baker & Sons Limited	£13,225,074
Booking.Com Customer Service Center (UK) Limited	£13,223,796
Galapagos Biotech Limited	£13,221,579
Twenty 1 Construction Limited	£13,219,799
Blue 8 Technologies Limited	£13,217,752
Phoenix Datacom Limited	£13,216,794
Ascend Global Holdings, Ltd.	£13,216,702
Sick (UK) Ltd.	£13,214,000
Rylston Road Limited	£13,203,523
Reilly Concrete Pumping Limited	£13,202,001
Kier Hammersmith Holdco Limited	£13,200,000
Tanners Wharf Limited	£13,197,287
Quinto Crane & Plant Limited	£13,196,822
Digital Copier Systems Eastern Limited	£13,196,040
Poole Investments Limited	£13,190,435
St.Lawrence Hall Farms Limited	£13,184,902
Trieste Group LLP	£13,177,274
Contamac Holdings Limited	£13,170,719
Monitor Audio Limited	£13,170,543
Jarrold (St. James) Limited	£13,168,514
Rocket Medical PLC	£13,167,504
Creo Pharma Limited	£13,160,766
Chivers Farms Limited	£13,160,365
De Sangosse Ltd.	£13,159,320
Thule Outdoor Limited	£13,157,285
Cambridge Pharma Limited	£13,155,185
Pemberton Farms Limited	£13,144,839
Kier Integrated Services (Estates) Limited	£13,142,000
Traditional Norfolk Poultry Limited	£13,132,753
Shropshire Energy (UK) Limited	£13,132,561
SDSDAB Limited	£13,122,368
Marchanson Limited	£13,118,397
Prior Scientific Instruments Limited	£13,114,236
St.Martins' (Northwood) Preparatory School Trust	£13,108,400
J & J Restaurants Limited	£13,098,473
Henlow Church of England Academy	£13,097,991
Local Generation Limited	£13,092,000
Kelly Rail U.K. Ltd	£13,083,854
Island Waste Services Limited	£13,078,739
Westway Services Holdings (2010) Ltd.	£13,072,953
R. Maskell (Holdings) Limited	£13,072,307
A. & A. 2000 Limited	£13,066,475
A & A Woodford Limited	£13,066,474
Presdales School Academy Trust	£13,057,244
Motorclean Group Limited	£13,056,928
Central Park Enterprises Limited	£13,056,013
Oakburn Properties Limited	£13,053,889
Alderforce North Limited	£13,052,243
Birmingham Resi Property LLP	£13,043,578
James Taylor Group Limited	£13,037,748
Life Build Solutions Ltd	£13,032,305
Ivor Holmes Limited	£13,031,888
Epoch RJK Limited	£13,028,976
NWES Property Services Limited	£13,028,604
Murkett Brothers (Holdings) Limited	£13,016,665
Howard Cambridge Limited	£13,013,268
Keech Hospice Care	£13,013,000
CN Group Limited	£13,011,000
Frisco (U.K.) Sales Limited	£13,002,582
Deekay Investments Limited	£12,999,221
MVM Holdings Limited	£12,993,000
E.M. Chamberlain Group Limited	£12,978,610
Gozzett Holdings Limited	£12,978,038
Encocam Limited	£12,972,333
Fishnet Properties Limited	£12,971,217
Emerson Crane Hire Limited	£12,959,049
Colchester Royal Grammar School	£12,953,564
Tangent International Group PLC	£12,952,195
Air Livery Limited	£12,950,391
Hedingham School and Sixth Form	£12,947,634
Global Group (UK) Ltd	£12,943,000
Pengethley Potatoes Limited	£12,938,748
Avon Freeholds Limited	£12,934,297
Roberto Bucci (U.K.) Limited	£12,934,021
E.G.T. Bridging Finance Limited	£12,921,594
Longmill Rickbost Ltd	£12,921,310
Gada Limited	£12,918,597
Sunsave 12 (Derriton Fields) Ltd	£12,917,000
Turpin Distribution Services Limited	£12,916,129
Interlink Direct Limited	£12,912,190
The Invicta Film Partnership No.34, LLP	£12,911,442
GK Foods (UK) Limited	£12,909,000
Eastern Counties Laundries Limited	£12,903,000
Van Hage & Company Limited	£12,901,151
Taylors Service Garages (Boston) Limited	£12,896,352
Airflow Developments Limited	£12,894,293
V.U.K. Holdings Limited	£12,882,639
Valiant Holdings Limited	£12,875,541
IGD Services Limited	£12,871,688
Anglian Community Enterprise (ACE) CIC	£12,871,402
Carlisle Security Services Limited	£12,868,000
Akhter Group Limited	£12,864,000
Halstead Securities Limited	£12,863,214
Cambridge Display Technology Limited	£12,851,000
Fulton Clover Limited	£12,850,465
Beckhithe Farms Limited	£12,843,080
Harber Properties Limited	£12,842,437
P.F.K. Ling Limited	£12,834,476
Eastmarket Grain LLP	£12,828,413
Swanbrae Limited	£12,828,343
Galileo Homes Limited	£12,817,154
OYO Developments Limited	£12,816,066
Heley Holdings Limited	£12,813,648
Sapphire Rural Destination No. 5 Limited	£12,813,208
Ashworth Homes Limited	£12,811,055
Import Services Limited	£12,805,501
Noble Foods (We) Limited	£12,804,017
The John Apthorp Charity	£12,803,858
Leonard F.Jollye (Brookmans Park) Limited	£12,799,988
Perrin Group Holdings Limited	£12,789,620
Gateway Reversions Limited	£12,789,421
Newsells Park Estates Limited	£12,789,000
Signature Lessee Limited	£12,788,826

Slingsby Advanced Composites Limited	£12,784,845
Lester Hotels Group Limited	£12,769,418
Rothamsted Enterprises Limited	£12,768,342
A.C. Entertainment Technologies Limited	£12,762,417
K.M. Packaging Holdings Limited	£12,754,119
Ikarim Business Services Ltd	£12,753,014
Planshore Limited	£12,753,003
Fiveways Municipal Vehicle Hire Limited	£12,742,331
Mount Grace School	£12,742,163
Bracco UK Limited	£12,741,000
Southend High School for Girls Academy Trust	£12,739,329
Grangewood Builders Limited	£12,724,654
Senior Finance Seven Limited	£12,720,575
M.J.S. Construction (March) Limited	£12,717,433
UML Wembley Limited	£12,715,205
Excelredstone Services Limited	£12,712,179
Thomas Dane Limited	£12,709,585
Anglo-Norden Forest Products Limited	£12,708,651
Purple Surgical Holdings Limited	£12,701,356
Senju Manufacturing (Europe) Limited	£12,698,394
Hypnos Limited	£12,696,132
Suffolk Agricultural Association	£12,688,146
Aspin Construction Group Limited	£12,683,000
Pure International Limited	£12,681,089
Thorney Bay Park Limited	£12,679,404
Aula Limited	£12,674,346
Ashley House PLC.	£12,669,000
Realpubs Limited	£12,668,125
Ashwicken Sporting LLP	£12,664,013
TRB Technology Group Limited	£12,663,954
Chester Greyhound Retail Park LLP	£12,659,511
Underwoods Garage (Tiptree) Limited	£12,658,231
Manor Crest Homes Limited	£12,657,548
Lynton Homes (3) Limited	£12,656,336
Oleoland Hotel Company Limited	£12,656,068
St. Helena Hospice Limited	£12,655,362
Bondgrip Limited	£12,643,251
S.C.W.S. (Holdings) Limited	£12,642,381
Inntel Limited	£12,639,540
Tangent International Limited	£12,639,202
Apollo Property Investment Limited	£12,639,118
Spicerhaart Corporate Sales Limited	£12,634,000
Farleigh Hospice	£12,633,000
Elastomer Trading Limited	£12,626,629
Drayton Building Services Limited	£12,624,000
Jaltek Systems Limited	£12,623,971
NPMA Ltd	£12,622,000
Tilia Trading Group Limited	£12,617,108
St George Healthcare Limited	£12,615,239
Kier (Newcastle) Investment Ltd	£12,602,751
RP2 Holdings Limited	£12,601,265
G.& J.Peck Limited	£12,599,288
Lord Rayleigh's Farms Limited	£12,598,131
Camden Development Company Limited	£12,590,037
Dernford Holdings Limited	£12,588,449
Jark Industrial Limited	£12,583,139
Abbot's Hill Limited	£12,574,897
Homepines Investments Limited	£12,574,484
Campion Willcocks Limited	£12,571,443
CDT Holdings Limited	£12,570,000
AMP GM006 Limited	£12,565,271
Apem Components Limited	£12,564,560
Musco (St Albans Place) Ltd	£12,563,735
Ariyan Hotels Limited	£12,561,352
Apical Limited	£12,549,325
Aspin Group Limited	£12,547,000
Sigma Imaging (UK) Limited	£12,546,896
Gago Invest Limited	£12,525,304
Icandy World Limited	£12,520,670
Fidion Limited	£12,518,187
Manor Fresh Limited	£12,508,413
Toomey Motor Group Limited	£12,508,058
Signature Lessee I Limited	£12,507,380
Rexam Finance Poland Limited	£12,503,138
Coulson Group Limited	£12,501,105
Arnold Family Holdings Limited	£12,500,293
Aesica Holdco Limited	£12,500,000
Claas Eastern Ltd	£12,490,000
Genesis Pharmaceuticals Limited	£12,483,941
Simat Properties Limited	£12,479,319
Chartridge PLC	£12,479,161
Paytemp Limited	£12,476,315
NGB Construction Limited	£12,472,619
R. Bratley (Quadring) Limited	£12,471,111
Chelmsford County High School for Girls	£12,465,123
Keelings Fresh International Limited	£12,463,365
Fred Hartley (Estates) Limited	£12,460,526
Days of Your Life Limited	£12,458,953
Mando Corporation Limited	£12,457,688
A.R. Craven Farms Limited	£12,453,849
David Watson Transport Limited	£12,450,602
St. Christopher School (Letchworth) Limited	£12,449,324
Stafford House Study Holidays Limited	£12,445,000
Duff Morgan & Vermont (Holdings) Limited	£12,442,991
Chartridge Developments Limited	£12,441,293
Thurlow Estate Farms Limited	£12,436,883
Sherfield School Limited	£12,436,704
K K Investment Ltd	£12,435,536
Acclaim Handling Limited	£12,431,751
Radio Developments Ltd	£12,430,948
Jewers Doors Limited	£12,422,484
Abbey Cross Trading Limited	£12,419,587
Gerrard International Limited	£12,418,943
Balcraft Properties Limited	£12,418,675
Duff Morgan & Vermont Limited	£12,416,422
Harrington (Properties) Limited	£12,405,532
Group Tyre Wholesale Limited	£12,405,432
AMP GM001 Limited	£12,405,297
Vision Group (Holdings) Limited	£12,402,173
Maylands Green Limited	£12,394,912
Luminescence International Ltd	£12,394,648
The Tabor Group Ltd	£12,393,842
Richards Dry Dock and Engineering Limited	£12,390,600
Wilcox Holdings Limited	£12,389,194
Stat Marine Limited	£12,380,829
UTM Limited	£12,369,484
Sofis Limited	£12,364,706
UNEX Smithfield Limited	£12,362,361
Greenswan Consultants Limited	£12,355,968
Midland Chilled Foods Limited	£12,348,820
Armour Home Electronics Limited	£12,341,896
C.M. Cadman Group Limited (The)	£12,338,106
The Good Shepherd Catholic Trust	£12,335,773
Iliffe Print Cambridge Limited	£12,335,000
Subex (UK) Limited	£12,333,000
Bourn Bioscience Limited	£12,326,381
Norfolk Environmental Waste Services Limited	£12,326,008
Rose Builders Ltd	£12,323,222
F. Copson Limited	£12,321,717
Westleigh Properties Limited	£12,320,530
Rainham Industrial Services Limited	£12,320,000
The Professional Darts Corporation Limited	£12,316,423
Laindon Trading LLP	£12,315,570
NW3 Capital Ltd	£12,304,672
Galldris Construction Limited	£12,304,427
Gunpowder Mill Developments Limited	£12,296,000
Wheatley Properties Limited	£12,295,192
A.E. Lenton Limited	£12,291,994
Securon Holdings Limited	£12,291,989
Luvata Welwyn Garden Ltd	£12,289,000
Honywood Community Science School	£12,283,731
HTG Trading Limited	£12,281,000
Omex Agrifluids Limited	£12,278,895
Kailas Hotel Finance Company Limited	£12,270,350

Company	Amount
Mitcham Earthmoving Limited	£12,266,373
Satco Plastics Limited	£12,255,343
Colchester Catalyst Charity	£12,253,983
A.G.E. Nursing Homes Limited	£12,253,589
D.H. Industries Limited	£12,252,316
Green Mountain Estates Ltd	£12,238,257
Redeemed Christian Church of God	£12,237,841
St James Media LLP	£12,236,442
Playmobil (U.K.) Limited	£12,219,283
Sembmarine SLP Ltd	£12,219,000
Continental Datagraphics Limited	£12,214,557
Robinson Young Holdings Limited	£12,214,360
T. Visaman & Sons Limited	£12,199,468
Carbery (UK) Limited	£12,191,704
Hilands Property Partners LLP	£12,190,634
Walters Holdings Limited	£12,189,385
Longford Securities & Equities Limited	£12,183,284
UIDUK Ltd	£12,182,200
Simmons (Bakers) Limited	£12,178,610
Ikarus Engineering Limited	£12,166,363
Motocaddy Holdings Limited	£12,157,212
One Broker Limited	£12,155,480
Stourgarden Limited	£12,150,241
Inpra UK Limited	£12,144,319
Tutis Properties Limited	£12,140,165
Tristel Solutions Limited	£12,128,000
R.B. Securities Limited	£12,118,672
Elysium Healthcare (Healthlinc) Limited	£12,118,000
Greentech Distribution PLC	£12,112,316
Danzer UK Limited	£12,107,000
European Flavours & Fragrances PLC	£12,096,720
Tetworth Farms LLP	£12,095,974
DPA Support Services Limited	£12,091,000
Motocaddy Limited	£12,088,785
Solopark Limited	£12,082,575
R.G. Boyce Limited	£12,081,909
Angel Care (Orchid Care Homes) Ltd	£12,071,952
AS24 Fuel Card Ltd	£12,063,256
The Charis Trust	£12,060,992
Wilton & Bain Group Limited	£12,059,723
AMP GM 003 Limited	£12,059,148
Totes Isotoner (UK) Limited	£12,056,711
P.J. Thory Limited	£12,055,756
Seasons Hotels Limited	£12,051,679
Park Securities Limited	£12,041,426
Sines LLP	£12,040,737
TTKW Limited	£12,036,129
Windcrest (U.K.) Limited	£12,035,480
Gibson Developments Limited	£12,027,817
S.Hille & Co.(Holdings) Limited	£12,025,737
Turner Properties Limited	£12,023,430
LGS Holdings Limited	£12,022,776
Soda Studios Limited	£12,020,679
Instrumel Ltd	£12,019,719
Memorial Gardens Limited	£12,004,784
M. Gaze & Co. Limited	£12,003,954
Aequitas Estates (Poyle) Limited	£12,003,844
Intermay Management Ltd	£12,002,911
Dippy Ridge Limited	£12,001,912
Kane Group Limited	£11,999,000
Agrofarm London Limited	£11,998,731
Barconn Group Limited	£11,997,160
Flahive Developments Limited	£11,993,425
Costa Express Holdings Limited	£11,984,000
Respivert Ltd.	£11,975,000
Aylesbury Grammar School	£11,958,914
Godstowe Preparatory School Company Limited (The)	£11,947,864
Harringtons Builders PLC	£11,947,578
Knott Park One LLP	£11,944,262
Certsure LLP	£11,943,000
Masteroast Coffee Co. Limited	£11,942,184
Beechwood Park School Limited	£11,940,903
Astor Lodge Holdings Limited	£11,938,191
Daly Holdings Limited	£11,936,437
Poplars Resource Management Company Limited	£11,928,000
C.T. Baker Limited	£11,924,895
M & W Newco Limited	£11,919,091
Saba Infra Gloucestershire Limited	£11,914,174
Milton Hall Estates Limited	£11,910,715
Mountcharm (S.E.) Limited	£11,910,514
E.M.Chamberlain Limited	£11,905,425
Monumart Limited	£11,903,880
The Produce Connection Limited	£11,902,403
Peter Brotherhood Limited	£11,896,619
Anglia Ruskin Enterprise Ltd	£11,891,000
RG Reversions 2014 Limited	£11,889,146
Skanska Construction (Regions) Limited	£11,881,000
Turnstone Estates Limited	£11,880,798
George Tufts and Son Limited	£11,880,696
Pro Cam UK Limited	£11,878,000
Specialist Cars Property (Stevenage) Limited	£11,870,000
Thomas Cook Aircraft Engineering Limited	£11,865,000
St. Nicholas Hospice (Suffolk)	£11,863,814
Crendon Timber Engineering Limited	£11,861,781
HTS Estates Limited	£11,861,277
C. U. Lighting Limited	£11,859,919
Boniface Engineering Limited	£11,854,880
Rangemist Limited	£11,854,180
Network Homes Investments (Stockwell) Limited	£11,853,693
Green Energy Options Ltd	£11,850,639
Future Travel Limited	£11,843,000
AMP GM007 Limited	£11,842,658
Thomson Travel Group (Holdings) Limited	£11,842,000
Lantern Recovery Specialists PLC	£11,841,107
Albion Bunker and Trading LLP	£11,832,822
Jean-Luc Developments Ltd	£11,829,471
EMS-FP & S Limited	£11,823,361
Dr Michael Prager Holdings Limited	£11,820,336
Maurice Mason Limited	£11,815,013
A.E.Bullock Limited	£11,813,649
RealVNC Limited	£11,812,564
VNC Group Limited	£11,812,564
Sharan Properties Limited	£11,806,635
Aprirose Trading Limited	£11,799,484
Alto (UK) Ltd	£11,798,471
Acacia Homes Limited	£11,795,027
Harbour Shipping Limited	£11,785,648
James Taylor Homes (Lincolns Inn) Limited	£11,783,210
Grangewood Brentwood Limited	£11,779,108
Newstraid Benevolent Fund	£11,778,210
NeilMed Holding Company Limited	£11,773,630
Garnham Management Services Limited	£11,771,305
Policyfast Limited	£11,766,191
Defender No.2 Production LLP	£11,763,425
Stephensons of Essex Limited	£11,763,189
A.E. & W.A.Farr Limited	£11,761,223
B Crystal Limited	£11,756,635
G's Fresh Beetroot Limited	£11,755,000
KDM Timber Limited	£11,752,581
Beale's Limited	£11,751,299
Delamode PLC	£11,749,829
Balgores Motors (1982) Limited	£11,746,194
Kirkmore HT Limited	£11,742,264
Charlie Properties Limited	£11,733,035
Pearl Properties Limited	£11,731,613
David Phillip (Investments) Limited	£11,723,731
Kingswood Village Limited	£11,718,365
McGinley Aviation Holdings Limited	£11,717,253
Crowland Cranes Limited	£11,713,837
Rooff Property LLP	£11,712,768
Noble Gift Packaging Limited	£11,711,019
Dencora (Watford) LLP	£11,708,090
Marshall of Scunthorpe Limited	£11,708,000
Majestic Bingo Limited	£11,707,000

Company	Amount
Big Sky Developments Ltd	£11,705,938
Chilford Hundred Education Trust	£11,702,057
Kier North Tyneside Limited	£11,702,000
Belgrave Land (Perth) Limited	£11,700,486
Stable Lads Welfare Trust Housing Association Ltd	£11,696,000
The Chartridge Conference Company Limited	£11,693,407
MacIntyre Transport Limited	£11,687,246
Sapphire Food North East No.1 Limited	£11,669,363
Birchwood High School	£11,660,566
Optimise Media (UK) Limited	£11,654,392
Cloverton Property Ltd	£11,653,989
Pant y Wal Investments Limited	£11,646,300
Norfolk Truck & Van Limited	£11,625,560
FFEI Holdings Limited	£11,625,000
Absolute Radio Limited	£11,621,000
J. Van Vliet London Cash & Carry Limited	£11,620,717
Broadfields Academy Trust	£11,617,000
SBG Holding International Ltd	£11,611,418
GBST Limited	£11,609,151
S.F. Williams (Foils) Limited	£11,608,287
Churchtown Estates Limited	£11,608,272
Chapman Ventilation Group Limited	£11,607,523
Charles Kalms, Henry Ronson Immanuel College	£11,606,515
Fujitsu General Air Conditioning (UK) Limited	£11,606,000
Halfen Limited	£11,601,000
Sisk Consolidated Investments Limited	£11,598,033
Orthene Holdings Limited	£11,594,368
Lymington Precision Engineers Co. Limited	£11,594,000
Calumet Wex International Limited	£11,593,000
Badger BC Investments Limited	£11,586,682
Trevester Limited	£11,581,366
Basetek (Holdings) Limited	£11,580,636
Alterra Farms Limited	£11,579,649
Basetek Limited	£11,579,098
Marshall Thermo King Limited	£11,576,450
Milton Hall Cambridge Limited	£11,575,671
Howard Stansted Limited	£11,574,031
Abacus Group Limited	£11,567,000
Branded Stocks (UK) Ltd	£11,563,443
Wheatland Cheese Co. Limited	£11,550,367
Burrough Court Estate Limited	£11,548,832
The Gap Partnership Holdings Limited	£11,542,918
Sara (London) Limited	£11,542,600
Brick Projects (Marland) Limited	£11,541,019
ITAB Holdings UK Ltd	£11,539,123
Kara Designs Ltd	£11,538,804
Jamestown Industries Limited	£11,534,398
TBS G.B. Telematic & Biomedical Services Limited	£11,527,463
Bango. Net Limited	£11,526,325
Streamadvice Limited	£11,524,590
Graysons Hospitality Limited	£11,518,000
Tun Abdul Razak Research Centre	£11,516,181
Maybury Media LLP	£11,514,990
Energypro Asset Management Limited	£11,500,334
Crane Investments Ltd	£11,493,055
F-Star Delta Limited	£11,490,492
West Herts Community Free School Trust	£11,487,138
Castle Point Gas & Heating Co. Limited	£11,486,657
Moller Institute Limited	£11,482,398
Resolute Corporate Holdings Limited	£11,478,855
Arihant Limited	£11,477,931
Peachey Basildon Group Limited (The)	£11,475,234
Biomarsh Environmental Ltd	£11,462,998
Coherent (UK) Limited	£11,461,000
Dynamic Cassette International Limited	£11,458,331
Laurence Homes (Eastern) Limited	£11,456,866
Manor Farm Solar Limited	£11,456,423
Bondmason Client Ltd	£11,454,215
Fooks Property Company Limited	£11,445,773
Manormaker (Nominee No. 1) Limited	£11,445,329
Bucyrus Europe Limited	£11,444,000
The Cambridge Union Society	£11,441,977
Caretech Estates (No.4) Limited	£11,441,000
Ebrex Business Solutions Limited	£11,435,763
H.C.Moss (Builders) Limited	£11,434,513
Purslow Investments Limited	£11,433,935
Willis Dawson Property Limited	£11,433,607
Bartrums Haulage and Storage Limited	£11,430,892
Rogerson Holdings Limited	£11,427,661
Hurco Europe Limited	£11,422,529
Jet Investments Limited	£11,420,842
Unifruit Limited	£11,420,123
Robus Multi Academy Trust	£11,417,043
CED Limited	£11,415,241
Mountfield Group PLC	£11,414,190
D.J.Fisher (Farms) Limited	£11,413,270
Appetite Holdings Limited	£11,407,620
Unifruit Group Limited	£11,405,024
GHL (Kilmorie) Limited	£11,403,809
Ariston Thermo UK Ltd	£11,403,000
Radia Estates Limited	£11,398,139
Clark-Drain Limited	£11,395,618
Harlequin Direct Limited	£11,393,563
Tustin Properties Ltd	£11,390,600
Orion Alloys Limited	£11,383,459
Mortgage Guarantee Limited	£11,380,622
Specialist Cars Tring Limited	£11,377,725
A.M.P. Air Conditioning Limited	£11,372,225
DDW Holdings Limited	£11,371,000
Netsupport Ltd.	£11,369,666
Doctors on Call Limited	£11,368,000
Premier Holidays Limited	£11,365,323
Snellings Limited	£11,360,836
Peppercorn Investments Limited	£11,360,579
The Invicta Film Partnership No.11, LLP	£11,357,982
KFG Quickserve Limited	£11,356,000
Automotive Lighting UK Limited	£11,346,000
Forest Freight Limited	£11,339,004
Knight Strip Metals Limited	£11,338,008
Q Acoustics Limited	£11,336,041
Castledon School Academy Trust	£11,334,799
Rammamere House Limited	£11,334,457
Essex Motor Company Limited	£11,332,361
Camfield Estate Company Limited	£11,330,886
Smith Farms (Clacton) Limited	£11,322,960
Getech Limited	£11,317,000
F-Star Alpha Limited	£11,315,629
Watts Industries UK Limited	£11,307,419
J.E. & V.M. Dalton Limited	£11,306,765
Screen Subtitling Systems Limited	£11,300,446
Ercol Furniture Limited	£11,300,000
Roythornes Limited	£11,299,595
Adventure Forest Limited	£11,295,000
Greenfields Family Investment Company Limited	£11,286,136
Hy-Pro International Limited	£11,285,000
Filross Securities Limited	£11,264,200
The United Healthcare Land Company Limited	£11,263,950
Agriturf Holdings Limited	£11,263,723
Land Management Limited	£11,257,629
Caps Cases Limited	£11,256,583
Howard Bedford Limited	£11,255,967
KDM International Limited	£11,253,666
Lanswood Limited	£11,249,099
GAIAE Limited	£11,240,534
Inexus (Services) Limited	£11,235,683
Wenta	£11,234,375
Metro Properties Limited	£11,234,227
Ziji Productions Limited	£11,230,180
Hewitsons LLP	£11,215,645
Arcese Real Estate UK Limited	£11,212,517
Vega Industries Limited	£11,210,557
David Barke (Holdings) Limited	£11,194,091
Knight Noise Limited	£11,193,108
Environ Freshford Mill Limited	£11,190,815

Company	Value
Clearview Homes (Western Avenue) Ltd	£11,188,561
Harris Family Finance Company Limited	£11,186,659
Proctor Bros. (Long Sutton) Limited	£11,185,980
Stafford House School of English Limited	£11,184,000
Pass J. Holdings Limited	£11,181,216
Hamden Homes Limited	£11,166,515
Warners Group Publications PLC	£11,162,679
TK Maxx	£11,160,000
Kestates Limited	£11,154,944
Jeesal Holdings Limited	£11,152,477
Angelica Estates Limited	£11,145,977
Jarrold (St. James) 3 SJC Limited	£11,145,356
Wisbech Grammar School	£11,139,702
EPG Development IV LLP	£11,138,334
Riverway Investments Limited	£11,138,222
Crown House Homes (North Station) Limited	£11,133,644
Tradelink Direct Limited	£11,133,583
LC Bet Limited	£11,133,000
Newell Properties Limited	£11,132,191
Camvac Limited	£11,132,038
D & B Scaffolding Limited	£11,123,651
D & B Scaffolding Holdings Ltd	£11,123,267
Care UK (Urgent Care) Limited	£11,121,000
The Highcrest Academy	£11,119,521
Luna Estates Limited	£11,116,017
OSG U.K. Limited	£11,113,925
Saffie Investments Limited	£11,110,722
South Coast Furnishing Company Limited	£11,110,070
Intertek Testing & Certification Limited	£11,108,000
LC Packaging UK Ltd	£11,107,196
66 Queen Square Limited	£11,106,000
Cousins Holdings Limited	£11,104,184
Glenageary Estates LLP	£11,102,064
Aquasium Technology Limited	£11,101,347
Letchworth Housing Investments Limited	£11,100,612
Geoffrey Mason Limited	£11,099,426
Dagless Limited	£11,098,141
Beaconsfield Educational Trust Limited	£11,097,913
Goodkind Estates Limited	£11,093,533
R.T.Rate Limited	£11,092,069
Knight Precision Metals Limited	£11,088,492
Orchard Funding Limited	£11,088,239
Paypoint Retail Solutions Limited	£11,082,752
Connected Learning	£11,081,906
AOC (UK) Ltd	£11,081,126
Eurocity Properties (Central) Limited	£11,077,806
Carlton Group Developments Ltd	£11,074,216
Freedom Destinations Limited	£11,073,008
Antas Limited	£11,068,894
Transmec UK Limited	£11,061,722
Nine Reading Hotel Limited	£11,058,695
Transporter Sales & Hire Limited	£11,049,455
LDC (Boston) Limited	£11,046,398
Ascott Properties Limited	£11,046,111
I Hennig & Co Limited	£11,044,106
Laen Limited	£11,042,900
Tulip Properties & Real Estate Ltd	£11,042,356
RRD GDS Limited	£11,042,000
Plotplan Limited	£11,041,436
Stewards Academy Trust	£11,041,368
Wesley House, Cambridge	£11,038,986
Lumesse Holdings UK Limited	£11,036,322
C & K Meats Limited	£11,036,139
Beaufort House Limited	£11,034,758
Allway Connections Limited	£11,033,198
G.Holmes White (Properties) Limited	£11,026,583
Hoddesdon Developments Ltd	£11,024,788
Rysa Lodge Residential Properties Limited	£11,021,501
Vision (Office Automation) Limited	£11,019,820
Ramon Holdings Limited	£11,013,729
OBM Properties Limited	£11,013,415
Churchtown Farm Solar Limited	£11,001,576

Company	Value
Tesco Mobile Services Limited	£11,001,000
Matrix Networks Limited	£10,998,472
East Langford Solar Limited	£10,998,135
Countryside 28 Limited	£10,997,263
Turners (East Anglia) Limited	£10,995,202
Benchmark Leisure Limited	£10,994,773
Birchwood Capital Limited	£10,993,089
Ivor Crowson Developments (Stamford) Limited	£10,990,456
Architectural Glazing Limited	£10,988,029
Dassault Systemes Biovia Limited	£10,988,000
The Fremantle Trust	£10,988,000
Ridgeon Estate Company Limited	£10,986,132
Global Chair Components Limited	£10,985,535
Connect Scaffolding Limited	£10,985,383
Minton Holdings Limited	£10,979,686
Boulters Meadow Limited	£10,975,960
The Harlow Education Trust	£10,974,151
T. Bro Investment Limited	£10,973,910
Boss Cabins Limited	£10,955,566
Church of God in Christ (Calvary) Limited	£10,955,311
M & J Charters LLP	£10,951,856
Rolling Components Limited	£10,948,669
Mayfair Carpet Gallery Limited	£10,941,125
Loughton Care Centre Limited	£10,939,000
Rateneed Limited	£10,935,814
The Yonder Digital Group Limited	£10,934,350
Buildvantage Limited	£10,928,216
Gardar Property Co Limited	£10,927,883
Jarvis Commercial Properties Limited	£10,925,077
Munro Holdings (Cambridge) Limited	£10,924,094
St. Luke's Hospice (Harrow & Brent) Ltd.	£10,918,000
The Brickfields Trust	£10,916,899
Micross Components Limited	£10,916,706
Trurating Limited	£10,915,411
St Andrew's Tutorial Services Limited	£10,914,313
Cremer (UK) Manufacturing Co. Ltd	£10,913,476
Direktek Ltd	£10,910,667
Flyers CNV Limited	£10,903,344
Culham Limited	£10,894,474
Edinburgh Sainsbury Holdings LLP	£10,892,010
WHTC Ltd	£10,884,137
Plastic Extruders Limited	£10,880,418
Grove & Dean (Holdings) Limited	£10,878,883
Elegant Electronics Limited	£10,876,214
Aspire Schools	£10,875,851
Hanmere Polythene Limited	£10,874,486
Claydon Securities Limited	£10,870,228
Performance Timber Products Group Limited	£10,869,843
John Tinney & Co Limited	£10,867,970
Gleneden Plant Sales Limited	£10,867,942
The Cambridge Crystallographic Data Centre	£10,864,714
Grove & Dean Limited	£10,859,063
Moores Refrigeration Controlled Transport Limited	£10,857,401
Sapphire Food North West No. 3 Limited	£10,854,095
HP Solar Limited	£10,853,181
Chelsea Portfolio Limited	£10,853,024
Norfolk Broads Direct Limited	£10,850,555
Norfolk Broads Holdings Limited	£10,850,552
Sawston Farms (Cambs) Limited	£10,839,513
Butlins Operations Limited	£10,827,000
Ares Properties Ltd	£10,815,564
Jack Brand Limited	£10,809,012
Astonpalm Limited	£10,804,680
Hindu Education Authority Ltd	£10,800,594
Hel Group Limited	£10,800,524
Devantier Group Limited	£10,798,694
Premier Decorations Limited	£10,791,078
Greenheath Farming Company Limited	£10,785,384
Monk's Walk School	£10,784,000
Essex Cares Limited	£10,782,089
Farsound Aviation Limited	£10,781,000
Marcantonio Foods Limited	£10,779,802

Company	Amount
Pitchset Limited	£10,778,681
DBCN Limited	£10,778,467
Defender No.2 Sale & Leaseback LLP	£10,773,785
Dock and Let Limited	£10,770,755
UK Livelines Limited	£10,769,800
Avocet Academy Trust	£10,764,575
William de Ferrers School	£10,763,226
Sensient Colors UK Ltd	£10,762,310
Welding Alloys Limited	£10,761,293
Autism Anglia	£10,761,000
API Microwave Limited	£10,761,000
Dawe Estates Limited	£10,760,215
Alstons (Upholstery) Limited	£10,750,000
Crystal Group Limited	£10,749,148
Goodfellow Cambridge Limited	£10,748,000
O'Malley Haulage Limited	£10,745,246
Keystone 1 Limited	£10,738,972
Pampisford Properties Limited	£10,738,799
Hazlemere Holdings Limited	£10,729,429
T.J.Evers Limited	£10,727,255
Hales Group Limited	£10,724,789
St Joseph's College Limited	£10,724,256
Festool UK Limited	£10,723,078
British Gaskets Limited	£10,719,914
N.P.K. Holdings Limited	£10,719,184
Claas Manns Ltd	£10,717,000
Good for Food Limited	£10,715,997
Innovative Design Systems Limited	£10,714,940
Subway Realty Limited	£10,713,355
Rayfern Holdings Limited	£10,709,147
Offerco Limited	£10,707,692
Ace Investments Limited	£10,704,509
Cambrionix Holdings Limited	£10,703,365
OOCL Logistics (Europe) Limited	£10,702,000
Regaltags Global Limited	£10,701,417
RP2 Limited	£10,700,064
Tesco International Services Limited	£10,698,000
I S & G (Holdings) Limited	£10,694,187
Quanticate Limited	£10,692,478
Eurosalamis Enterprises Ltd.	£10,690,461
York Apartments Limited	£10,688,985
Chiltern Distribution Ltd	£10,685,822
Business Management Software Limited	£10,684,255
Bauer Digital Radio Limited	£10,683,000
Blackwater Partners Limited	£10,680,402
S & W Design & Build (Group) Limited	£10,672,160
H. Butterfield Limited	£10,669,637
Twinglobe Limited	£10,668,499
Fortis Property Investment LLP	£10,665,583
Aldwickbury School Trust Limited	£10,662,670
Camstead Limited	£10,658,368
City Link (Cardiff) Holdings Limited	£10,653,000
Norfolk Capital Hotels Limited	£10,649,000
Market Field Learning Community	£10,648,381
Farlingaye High School	£10,646,972
Gratnells Limited	£10,635,009
Hudson Camden Limited	£10,631,425
Brianco Services Limited	£10,631,070
Hauck Heat Treatment Limited	£10,627,000
St Albans Diocesan Property Company Limited	£10,625,620
Ticketgrange Limited	£10,623,406
MLM Consulting Engineers Limited	£10,622,410
Letchworth Hall Hotel (Trading) Limited	£10,612,703
C.W.Parker (Wainfleet) Limited	£10,608,598
Fresh Linen Limited	£10,608,290
VHC Sub-Holdings (UK)	£10,600,000
K.C.Y. Limited	£10,596,495
Saba Infra Hertfordshire Limited	£10,594,414
Hamlin Electronics Europe Limited	£10,587,000
Bold-Rock Management and Investments Ltd	£10,582,725
Pet and Aquatics Properties Limited	£10,580,000
Care Providers Recruitment Limited	£10,569,541
Grindley Biogas Limited	£10,562,677
Sonnet Care Homes (Essex) Limited	£10,557,253
Averys (Radnage) Limited	£10,556,071
GDL (Aylesbury) Limited	£10,556,005
Chiltern Cold Storage Group Limited	£10,554,841
Pride Care Homes Peterborough Limited	£10,553,846
Taylor Made Joinery Interiors Limited	£10,550,596
Dagless Holdings Limited	£10,527,657
Bucci Freight Services Limited	£10,526,289
Bricks St Property Group Ltd	£10,520,352
Aylesbury High School	£10,510,000
Dayla Holdings Limited	£10,505,968
F.H.Easton Limited	£10,505,778
Alba Broadcasting Corporation Limited	£10,496,773
Amadeus IG Limited	£10,493,825
KFM Holdings Limited	£10,487,314
Bluestone Mortgage Holdings Limited	£10,485,629
Hall Contracts (Lakenheath) Limited	£10,485,211
Magdalene Limited	£10,484,000
DOT100 Limited	£10,483,857
Istec Services Limited	£10,483,850
R. C. Tinsley Limited	£10,482,164
Finecare Homes (Stevenage) Limited	£10,474,520
C.J.C. Lee (Saxthorpe) Limited	£10,471,551
Novum Holdings UK Limited	£10,470,726
Novum Structures UK Limited	£10,468,736
Hand Laundry (Bury) Limited (The)	£10,466,038
Keelings UK Group Limited	£10,465,914
A.E.Hewison Limited	£10,463,817
DW Windsor Group Limited	£10,463,567
Alicat Workboats Limited	£10,461,809
Precon Products Ltd	£10,461,211
Reids of Norwich Limited	£10,460,726
Hudson Richmond Limited	£10,457,273
Hildon House Limited	£10,454,791
Heathrow Aviation Engineering UTC	£10,451,370
Devitt Insurance Services Limited	£10,450,637
Mill Hill Properties Limited	£10,449,145
Skeltools Limited	£10,443,987
Buckingham Hotels Group Limited	£10,440,906
Clinimed Limited	£10,438,991
Wenta Business Centres Limited	£10,438,055
Lint (Redington Road) Limited	£10,437,188
The Royston Schools Academy Trust	£10,436,495
Grosvenor Park 2005 S42 Film LLP	£10,430,548
Megnum Limited	£10,416,754
Hudson Arnhem Limited	£10,414,724
Lipman Properties Limited	£10,387,718
Haydon Holdings Limited	£10,374,261
Conamar Building Services Limited	£10,370,541
Werner UK Operations Limited	£10,370,000
Ellis Timber (Holdings) Limited	£10,368,728
Trinity View Homes Limited	£10,365,423
BAM Glory Mill Limited	£10,353,000
A 1 Bacon Company Limited	£10,351,159
Hera Primary Academy Trust	£10,347,522
Castle Green Kendal Limited	£10,346,048
Thomas Brooker & Sons Limited	£10,343,006
CMS Developments Limited	£10,339,015
Microlights Limited	£10,337,502
Frederic Smart & Son Limited	£10,335,910
GHL (Summerstown) Limited	£10,332,428
K & R Projects Company Limited	£10,329,996
Wholesale Welding Supplies Limited	£10,329,870
CASP	£10,329,564
Sedum Limited	£10,325,868
Saba Infra Cardiff Limited	£10,321,327
Klyne Air Limited	£10,311,751
Opus Bestpay Limited	£10,308,810
Helmet Integrated Systems Limited	£10,302,487
Meridian Audio Limited	£10,298,243
Ufford Park Limited	£10,295,885

Hudson Brent Limited	£10,286,558
Kromachem Limited	£10,286,504
Thorney Leys Developments Limited	£10,282,169
W.D. Coe Limited	£10,282,000
Top 100 Limited	£10,281,437
Pinnacle Foods Limited	£10,280,604
1spatial Group Limited	£10,280,107
Gascoigne Halman Group Limited	£10,280,000
Childs Property Limited	£10,276,015
S. Franses Limited	£10,273,747
Freman College	£10,273,000
Amsprop Estates Limited	£10,272,408
M R Scott Limited	£10,268,870
Jojo's Mojo Limited	£10,268,139
SOM Restaurants Ltd	£10,267,467
The I.S. Group Limited	£10,265,530
Queensgate Finco Ltd	£10,264,102
Shopfittings Direct Limited	£10,263,358
Place UK Limited	£10,255,596
Greens Farming Limited	£10,254,904
Coex Properties LLP	£10,249,546
Anness Publishing Limited	£10,239,593
Mumford's Mill Rentals Limited	£10,236,803
Shenley Park Trust	£10,235,764
F.W. Hipkin Limited	£10,233,493
Cathard Investments Limited	£10,231,407
Plutus Estates Limited	£10,229,884
Seatrax (U.K.) Limited	£10,229,627
Oakbridge Homes (Group) Ltd	£10,227,017
Town Close House Educational Trust Limited	£10,223,458
H. Morrell Property Investments Limited	£10,222,718
Oakbridge Homes Limited	£10,222,191
Titano Real Estate Limited	£10,220,638
Grant Farming Limited	£10,220,038
Skewbald Limited	£10,219,899
Kingsgate Community Church	£10,217,656
Defaqto Ltd	£10,212,446
TCL Manufacturing Limited	£10,205,224
Manor Lodge School	£10,201,621
Seabrook Warehousing Limited	£10,200,498
M G 111 Ltd	£10,195,050
Gibson Bidco Limited	£10,194,000
Rimex Metals (U.K.) Limited	£10,193,596
P J M Farms Limited	£10,187,853
Albendan Limited	£10,185,047
Oni PLC	£10,183,827
Fulton Lincoln Limited	£10,182,852
Dalin Limited	£10,182,163
Devantier Properties Limited	£10,180,069
Fluorocarbon Company Limited	£10,179,217
Paradine Holdings Limited	£10,175,627
Densitron Technologies Limited	£10,169,522
Tropical Marine Centre Limited	£10,168,000
Trust Tees Limited	£10,165,131
Plastique Holdings Limited	£10,158,776
Cambustion Limited	£10,154,215
Corbus Europe Limited	£10,153,909
BW Foundation	£10,148,786
Gardline Maritime Limited	£10,143,781
Contechs Consulting Limited	£10,142,994
Carmelite House (Jarrold) Limited	£10,137,974
Gainsborough's House Society	£10,136,767
Baruch Holdings Limited	£10,136,729
Fulton Regent Limited	£10,135,039
Nigel Skinner Financial Advisers Limited	£10,129,492
Contamac Limited	£10,128,423
AMS Care Wiltshire Limited	£10,127,908
Antoniou Investments Limited	£10,114,621
Henfield Hire Limited	£10,114,325
Chemilines Limited	£10,114,000
Positive Entertainment Ltd	£10,110,334
John Huntingdon's Charity	£10,110,274
Carl F Groupco Limited	£10,107,000
Automotive UK No.1	£10,100,000
Geoffrey Mayhew Farms Limited	£10,099,397
Landmark Aviation (UK) Limited	£10,099,046
Trend Marine Products Limited	£10,098,777
Letting International Limited	£10,095,509
Wintertime Properties Limited	£10,091,992
Haag-Streit UK Limited	£10,090,963
Pinewood School Academy Trust	£10,087,884
Cambridge Realty Limited	£10,086,681
Fowler Smith & Jones Trust	£10,085,867
Trend Machinery & Cutting Tools Limited	£10,083,295
Stebbings Car Centre Limited	£10,072,947
M-Ship Limited	£10,065,852
Armored Auto UK Limited	£10,065,709
ABL (Holding) Limited	£10,062,947
Agrifac UK Ltd	£10,059,294
Leisuregrow Products Limited	£10,058,143
Robsons of Spalding Limited	£10,055,982
Direct Consolidated Limited	£10,053,131
Hardall International Limited	£10,052,168
Loppingdale Plant Limited	£10,049,394
Hudson Kensington Limited	£10,048,801
Andgrove Property Investments Limited	£10,048,160
Cummins ESB Nigeria Limited	£10,045,365
Pratt & Whitney Canada (UK) Limited	£10,042,931
Mainline Communications Group Limited	£10,042,000
Water Incorporated	£10,041,309
UML Eagle Limited	£10,039,261
Camflats Limited	£10,037,507
Donatantonio Limited	£10,037,156
MDS Civil Engineering Limited	£10,032,659
Jaltek Holdings Limited	£10,027,652
Rogers Rental Limited	£10,026,678
Chart Forte Holdings Ltd	£10,022,515
Marton Geotechnical Services Limited	£10,018,815
WHL Investments Limited	£10,018,473
The Property Warehouse Limited	£10,018,453
St. Vincent's Charitable Trust	£10,010,634
Greenshoots Limited	£10,009,976
M.J. Worth Limited	£10,008,585
M.Baker Produce Limited	£10,007,478
East Anglian Installations Limited	£10,007,223
Axcorp Limited	£10,005,154
The Watford UTC	£10,003,247
PJG Developments Limited	£10,000,778
Kelly Communications Enterprises Limited	£10,000,001
ASCO (DC2) Limited	£10,000,000
Holdings U.K. No.3 Limited	£10,000,000
Tendring Farms Limited	£9,998,594
SAFL British Hotels Limited	£9,996,787
BPC Interiors Limited	£9,986,314
The Sele School	£9,982,146
The Book Trade Charity (BTBS)	£9,978,932
Aveva Finance Limited	£9,977,620
Hardys Farm Limited	£9,975,530
Jackson Civils Limited	£9,965,656
Mayflower High School	£9,965,367
Windsor Integrated Services Group Limited	£9,963,176
KFG Restaurants Limited	£9,961,000
Richardson & Cock Limited	£9,954,495
Brandbank Limited	£9,947,499
Caskade Properties Limited	£9,944,650
Treelane Limited	£9,944,000
Tudor Court Primary Academy Trust	£9,942,944
Clark Construction (South East) Ltd	£9,941,884
Helgor Trading Limited	£9,927,330
CATS College London Limited	£9,927,000
Caudwell Farms	£9,926,341
North West Steel Limited	£9,922,967
Treehouse Group Limited	£9,920,000
Denbourne Investments Limited	£9,918,081

Cannon Kirk (UK) Limited	£9,916,904
Landlink Ltd	£9,908,202
William Robinson Gravetye Charity	£9,904,080
James Taylor Construction Limited	£9,902,033
Micross Components Holdings Ltd	£9,901,345
SystemsAccountants Holdings Limited	£9,900,127
Ramsgate Development Company Limited	£9,895,806
Central Developments (UK) Limited	£9,892,160
Emerson Park Academy	£9,891,558
Exaclair Limited	£9,891,042
Alderforce Limited	£9,890,436
Trox UK Limited	£9,890,000
Uniserve (Europe) Limited	£9,889,359
Gentian (Newcastle) Limited	£9,885,537
City Brewery Limited	£9,884,925
Roger Warnes Transport Limited	£9,884,686
Scotline Limited	£9,884,397
Glazewing Limited	£9,882,679
DMC Contracts Limited	£9,877,729
Spence Refit Ltd	£9,874,049
Movac Group Limited	£9,872,440
Coward Asset Limited	£9,869,744
Atlantic Healthcare PLC	£9,868,513
Prime Estates Limited	£9,864,104
Hall & Watts Holdings Limited	£9,858,509
Birch's Park Homes Limited	£9,858,340
Craft & Sons Limited	£9,853,613
Sines Parks (S.E.) Limited	£9,846,920
Miller & Miller (Chemicals) Limited	£9,843,544
I F E Global Holdings Limited	£9,841,866
N.E.M. Co. Limited	£9,832,953
Arugula Spruce Limited	£9,832,582
Onslow Inc. Ltd	£9,831,311
Thornhill Estates Limited	£9,829,936
Maritzcx Limited	£9,826,336
Winter & Co. UK Limited	£9,825,453
Horsham Properties Limited	£9,821,486
Goodmayes Properties Ltd	£9,820,061
GHG 25 (Werndale Hospital) Limited	£9,820,000
Flegg Education Academy Trust	£9,819,368
Residential Management Group Limited	£9,818,000
BHW Automotive Limited	£9,814,509
BC Legal Limited	£9,811,543
Loose Hall Farm Limited	£9,803,768
Riverstone Europe LLP	£9,803,717
S and J Investments (Delivery Office Southall) Limited	£9,803,563
T Gilmartin Holdings Limited	£9,800,848
Keswick European Holdings Limited	£9,794,534
Broadham Care Limited	£9,789,000
Jenny Moody Properties Limited	£9,785,297
Quadro Epsom Limited	£9,785,000
Europlants (UK) Limited	£9,783,909
Mouskos & Sons Co. Limited	£9,782,518
Derek Hales (Plumbing Contractors) Limited	£9,780,453
London Hoist Limited	£9,780,384
Radical Sportscars Limited	£9,776,224
South Mimms Services Limited	£9,763,739
Cardif Pinnacle Insurance Management Services	£9,760,000
Wilcox Commercial Vehicles Limited	£9,755,909
Erinastar Limited	£9,754,188
Pajef Limited	£9,752,659
Construct Reason Limited	£9,743,577
P.H. Betts (Holdings) Limited	£9,741,988
Hugh Crane Limited	£9,739,247
Hunnable Holdings Limited	£9,731,600
Purebond Limited	£9,725,268
Burgess Properties Limited	£9,714,823
Green Label Farms LLP	£9,714,011
The Burdens Group Limited	£9,713,896
DB Broadcast Ltd	£9,712,746
James Taylor Homes (Harrow) Limited	£9,704,903
Ventress Property Developments Limited	£9,693,127
London Fluid System Technologies Limited	£9,684,841
Monument Group Limited	£9,683,589
MacLeans (Foils) Limited	£9,676,976
Power Adhesives Limited	£9,676,196
Griffin Davy Saffron Estates LLP	£9,675,555
Gravity Media Group Limited	£9,672,000
Oakeve Limited	£9,666,006
Manor Crest Construction Limited	£9,659,841
Murkett Brothers Limited	£9,655,599
Rapid Electronics Limited	£9,654,326
AAG UK Parent Limited	£9,653,373
Tesco International Internet Retailing Limited	£9,651,000
Esin Cash & Carry Limited	£9,649,767
Access Platform Sales Limited	£9,647,870
Amalgamated Berkshire Estates Limited	£9,646,738
Association for Cultural Exchange Limited (The)	£9,644,771
Beechfield Estates Limited	£9,641,629
Aston Heating Limited	£9,641,046
Hendrie Estates Limited	£9,640,564
Noahs Ark Chemicals Limited	£9,640,393
BICL Limited	£9,637,162
Caretech Estates (No 3) Limited	£9,634,000
Rusant Limited	£9,633,257
Biffa Leicester Limited	£9,626,163
Playags UK Limited	£9,624,531
Harlow and District Sports Trust	£9,622,407
Spitalfields Works Limited	£9,622,018
Institute of Advanced Motorists Limited (The)	£9,621,000
S & J Padfield Estates LLP	£9,619,884
Chipperfield Land Company Limited	£9,617,214
Kara Management Ltd	£9,607,503
Durkin and Sons Limited	£9,601,057
Foulger Transport Limited	£9,592,695
Rex Venture Resources Limited	£9,591,554
Leywood Estates Limited	£9,588,801
Holywells Residential Lettings Limited	£9,588,030
Sovereign Recovery (UK) Limited	£9,582,107
Manichem Limited	£9,575,481
O.B.C. (Europe) Limited	£9,564,465
Lawford & Sons Limited	£9,563,350
FBSE Finance Limited	£9,559,271
Norpap Property (Telford) Ltd	£9,556,848
The Mill Hotel Limited	£9,555,213
Mowbray Indigo Limited	£9,554,123
Consolidated Equities Limited	£9,551,268
Millharbour Developments Limited	£9,549,624
Heulwen Solar Limited	£9,544,876
Mumford & Wood Limited	£9,543,218
LRW Engineering Limited	£9,541,693
European Independent Purchasing Company Ltd	£9,541,228
Retreat East Limited	£9,539,649
Flamingo Plants Group Ltd	£9,535,000
Britvic Asset Company No.2 Limited	£9,535,000
Agellus Hotels Limited	£9,533,000
The London Outpost Limited	£9,531,085
Colwyn Developments Limited	£9,529,454
Yorkshire Dales Country Park Limited	£9,524,737
Capital Cash Limited	£9,524,672
RDL1 Limited	£9,522,393
Popsoda Limited	£9,522,041
D.N. Grady & Sons Limited	£9,518,366
Mono Properties Limited	£9,513,597
Skylord Travel PLC	£9,513,370
Worstead Farms Limited	£9,510,763
Vertical Group Limited	£9,509,582
The Invicta Film Partnership No.12, LLP	£9,506,957
Tompsett Burgess Growers Limited	£9,506,076
Action for Children Services Limited	£9,506,013
J.A.C. Computer Services Limited	£9,504,991
Kier Management Consulting Limited	£9,504,000
Unit Export Limited	£9,498,871
Quebec Court Freehold Limited	£9,496,658

Randstad Middle East Limited	£9,496,000	Symbio Energy Limited	£9,278,916
C P Timber Limited	£9,495,771	Plaut International Limited	£9,271,291
Chesside Homes Limited	£9,484,207	Specflue Limited	£9,269,537
Jenga (UK) Limited	£9,483,444	Farmwealth Limited	£9,269,000
Clarucci Industry Limited	£9,480,432	Lors Homes Limited	£9,252,404
International Fertilizer Association Limited	£9,477,764	Transam Trucking Limited	£9,251,935
Omniport Limited	£9,472,469	Buyanovsky Property Management Limited	£9,248,971
North Herts Hospice Care Association	£9,472,188	Tom Blackwell (Contractors & Plant Hire) Limited	£9,244,759
Winpost Limited	£9,470,990	SW1 Management Limited	£9,244,449
Blenheim Consultancy Services Limited	£9,469,599	Mason Pearson Bros. Limited	£9,241,883
E. Feldman Limited	£9,467,060	MacDuffy (Holdings) Limited	£9,238,074
Shakoor Capital Limited	£9,465,524	Noodle Properties Limited	£9,237,281
First Potteries Limited	£9,462,000	HFIS PLC	£9,232,645
J. Isaacs Management Limited	£9,451,799	Amalgamated Berkshire Holdings Limited	£9,231,178
Kimberley Capital Limited	£9,447,750	Akira Financial Limited	£9,209,521
Movac Holdings Limited	£9,444,879	P J Southgate Limited	£9,206,998
Plaza Investments Limited	£9,433,733	Aeropak (Chemical Products) Limited	£9,202,702
Sapphire Food South West No. 2 Limited	£9,432,150	British Board of Agrement	£9,198,000
Smith Bros Timber (East Anglia) Limited	£9,429,034	Rayleigh Schools Trust	£9,197,546
J & A (International) Limited	£9,419,233	Althea Healthcare (Holdings) Limited	£9,193,297
Dallas Burston Ashbourne Holdings Limited	£9,415,455	Chai-Lifeline Cancer Care	£9,185,151
Kristall Real Estate Limited	£9,415,099	PS Construction Investments Ltd	£9,185,047
Displayplan Limited	£9,413,746	TC Project Management Limited	£9,178,041
Close Homes Limited	£9,406,609	Meg Trading Limited	£9,171,223
Kings Hedges Investments Limited	£9,403,726	Derrick Services (UK) Limited	£9,169,629
Strongholding Limited	£9,400,342	Stace LLP	£9,168,929
Quest Motor Group Limited	£9,396,238	K.E.M. Property Services Limited	£9,165,317
Wm.Kerr (Farms) Limited	£9,395,973	GH London Ground Handling Services Limited	£9,162,851
Megaman (UK) Limited	£9,394,464	Exheat Limited	£9,161,591
Vigeland Properties Ltd	£9,391,358	Perfect Practices Group Limited	£9,160,334
Duoview Properties Limited	£9,389,861	Symology Limited	£9,155,261
Wivenhoe House Hotel Limited	£9,388,912	Killiney UK Limited	£9,155,209
The Chocolate Tasting Club PLC	£9,387,935	TJM (London) LLP	£9,151,179
Telephonetics Limited	£9,387,000	Abbey Investments Limited	£9,148,889
Beauty Wholesale Limited	£9,373,346	The Chesterford Group Limited	£9,148,577
Global Medics Limited	£9,373,000	Norse Eastern Limited	£9,143,978
J E Investments Limited	£9,368,510	G.J.W.Titmuss Limited	£9,142,991
Elysium Healthcare (Acorn Care) Limited	£9,367,000	Topfib Limited	£9,139,298
Turnlet Films (JN) Limited	£9,366,773	Steiner UK Limited	£9,136,322
Perrywood Garden Centre & Nurseries Limited	£9,364,987	Ripmax Limited	£9,129,936
Namu Limited	£9,363,888	Rega Research Limited	£9,128,473
Hall of Fame Stud Limited	£9,362,927	HTG Investments Limited	£9,121,000
Casterton College Rutland	£9,360,293	Essafinaat UK Limited	£9,119,296
Anglia Restaurants Ltd	£9,358,073	S & J Padfield & Partners LLP	£9,118,094
Enterprise Finance Limited	£9,350,643	UML Wigmore Limited	£9,117,172
Sinai (Antiques) Limited	£9,345,633	APT-Skidata Limited	£9,115,000
Porter and Makins Limited	£9,343,976	Guarding UK Ltd	£9,113,401
Bowes Farms Limited	£9,339,275	Aesthetic Medical Corporation Limited	£9,109,867
Beta Pharmaceuticals Limited	£9,334,672	Clavering Care Limited	£9,105,500
Amsair Aircraft Limited	£9,332,958	Abbots Ripton Farming Company Limited	£9,104,121
Upminster Academies Trust	£9,326,000	KCK Peterborough Devco LLP	£9,097,000
Radical Motorsport Limited	£9,324,192	Fricor Limited	£9,089,048
Sunrose Property Limited	£9,322,711	Lincoln's Farm & Investments Limited	£9,085,295
Geo Management Limited	£9,321,333	Acteon Middle East and Far East Investments Limited	£9,075,000
Rijac Properties Limited	£9,321,262	Gibbs Denley Holdings Limited	£9,069,830
Tallington Holdings Limited	£9,320,761	UML Westminster Limited	£9,067,016
Tunnelcraft Limited	£9,319,844	Visiongroup (GB) Limited	£9,065,733
RSA Island Village Limited	£9,314,666	Fulca Limited	£9,060,190
Valens Resources Group PLC	£9,314,632	Ambury Developments Limited	£9,060,000
Residential Loans Ltd.	£9,312,835	John Burgess & Co. Limited	£9,058,938
CRU Sturton Street Limited	£9,311,308	Choice Discount Stores Limited	£9,057,000
Fifty Six Investments Limited	£9,308,961	Winocap Holding Limited	£9,055,529
The Churchmanor Estates Company PLC	£9,303,997	WD1A Limited	£9,054,424
Aebi Schmidt UK Limited	£9,302,000	Assetbridge Finance Limited	£9,051,600
Kaykem Fast Foods Limited	£9,301,802	Thomas Gibson Fine Art Limited	£9,049,142
The Ursuline Academy Ilford	£9,295,986	Maison Moti Limited	£9,041,150
Oranmore Precast Limited	£9,291,420	Kier Overseas (Twenty-Three) Limited	£9,036,413
Ventureforth 2000 Limited	£9,290,629	Peter Green Haulage Limited	£9,033,584
Land Finance & Mortgage Corporation Limited (The)	£9,289,210	George East (Housewares) Limited	£9,028,359
Walstead Southernprint Limited	£9,288,000	UML Chiltern Limited	£9,020,699
Fitzwilliam Information Services Trust Limited	£9,287,005	Hevingham Development Company Limited	£9,019,179
Morplan Limited	£9,280,863	Green Space London Limited	£9,016,640

Company	Value
Wentworth Holdings Limited	£9,013,501
Willow Securities Limited	£9,007,788
GHL (Crescent Lane) Limited	£9,001,030
St. Aubyn's (Woodford Green) School Trust	£9,000,073
Nobo Group Limited	£9,000,000
Poggenpohl Group UK Limited	£8,996,083
Ezra Attia Limited	£8,991,860
Cygnet Street Developments Limited	£8,983,481
Hallmark Care Homes (Brighton) Ltd	£8,983,063
Allandale Investments Limited	£8,978,322
Long Term Reversions No 1 Limited	£8,974,374
Reach Active Group Limited	£8,969,035
R B Emerson Limited	£8,964,391
Highfield Park Trust	£8,963,462
Jalaram Limited	£8,962,572
R K Property Investments Ltd.	£8,951,534
Didsbury Engineering Co.Limited	£8,946,877
Stody Estate Limited	£8,944,074
Crossco (820) Limited	£8,942,397
Inero Limited	£8,936,755
Amadeus Capital Partners Limited	£8,931,660
Palatial Leisure Limited	£8,929,539
Redbridge Sports Centre Trust Limited	£8,929,152
Pertwee & Back,Limited	£8,928,536
MacKenzie Taylor Holdings Limited	£8,928,267
Newcome-Baker Farms Limited	£8,925,846
Yomans (London) Limited	£8,925,338
Titon Hardware Limited	£8,925,000
East Coast Community Healthcare C.I.C.	£8,924,366
Amadeus Partners Limited	£8,907,078
Wentworth Hotel Limited	£8,906,850
Cambridge Construction Limited	£8,901,514
Leonard F Jollye (Holdings) Limited	£8,900,390
Claas Western Ltd	£8,899,000
Hubbard Products Limited	£8,898,400
Buckinghamshire UTC.	£8,898,000
Anacreonte Properties Limited	£8,891,334
Creative Car Park Ltd	£8,881,248
UME PFI Investments Holding Limited	£8,877,455
Distribution Supplies Limited	£8,874,530
Hydraquip Hose & Hydraulics Limited	£8,871,910
Fleximize Limited	£8,871,602
Union of UEA Students Limited	£8,862,000
Tican (UK) Holdings Limited	£8,861,939
Atalian Servest Security Limited	£8,860,000
Fristling Hall Farm Limited	£8,859,298
Team Consulting Limited	£8,858,934
Springfield Holdings Limited	£8,848,820
Askew & Barrett (Pulses) Limited	£8,843,015
Latif International Limited	£8,841,004
Hospice of St. Francis (Berkhamsted) Limited	£8,838,000
Direct Boot and Shoe Supplies Limited	£8,836,903
Beale's Hotels Limited	£8,832,589
The Partnership in Care Limited	£8,830,949
Archway Apartments Limited	£8,830,916
St Edmundsbury and Ipswich Diocesan Multi-Academy	£8,829,444
Manford Securities & Investments Limited	£8,829,439
Blumarble Capital Limited	£8,825,088
Stellison Limited	£8,811,118
J P & S Servicess Ltd	£8,810,590
Diss High School	£8,807,957
Stane Park Ltd.	£8,807,172
Gonville Hotels Limited	£8,806,158
Kudos Catering (UK) Limited	£8,801,063
Thames Card Technology Limited	£8,799,751
Blanco UK Limited	£8,799,211
Westpoint Property Limited	£8,798,897
HJP Media LLP	£8,792,276
Austin (GB) Limited	£8,778,846
QOTD Film Investment Limited	£8,769,251
ITAB Shop Products UK Ltd	£8,754,000
Olivewood Limited	£8,748,244

Company	Value
MEL Aviation Components Limited	£8,746,572
Fardaar LLP	£8,746,325
Motivair Compressors Limited	£8,746,272
Kimberley Property Investments Limited	£8,743,523
Ridgepoint Homes Limited	£8,741,330
Stortford Interiors (UK) Limited	£8,736,838
UK Salads Limited	£8,729,347
Grosvenor Park 2006 S48 Film LLP	£8,726,160
Chard Robinson Usten Ltd	£8,725,935
PIL Membranes Limited	£8,723,631
G.B. Kent & Sons PLC	£8,718,532
Ancient House Press PLC	£8,717,941
Ancient House Printing Group Limited	£8,717,941
Genie Bidco Limited	£8,712,453
Investland Limited	£8,706,044
Stratton Hall Farms Limited	£8,704,966
Dilawar Property Ltd.	£8,687,118
RCT Construction Limited	£8,681,129
Premier Quilting Company Limited	£8,675,334
Global Graphics (UK) Limited	£8,673,429
Scimitar House (Holdings) Limited	£8,663,172
Step 6 Ltd	£8,658,125
Countryside 26 Limited	£8,648,898
Kilmorie Investments LLP	£8,648,531
Barnardiston Hall Preparatory School Limited	£8,647,581
Soho Loop Limited	£8,645,959
Kout Food Group Restaurants UK Limited	£8,641,000
S.A. (300) Limited	£8,638,000
Chemtest Holdings Limited	£8,633,780
Gower Acres Limited	£8,633,592
Unique Forwarding Limited	£8,620,816
Manu Ventures LLP	£8,611,226
Seymour House Residential Care Homes Limited	£8,594,592
St.Michael's Manor Limited	£8,589,856
Parthings Farm - Management and Promotion Limited	£8,586,173
F & S Energy Limited	£8,583,598
Harris Commercial Repairs Limited	£8,581,317
Metro Investments (Stevenage) LLP	£8,568,294
Littlebury Developments Limited	£8,567,834
Taylors Legal Limited	£8,566,699
Mulcroft Limited	£8,559,722
M. S. Oakes Securities Limited	£8,556,476
Pioneering Foods Group Limited	£8,543,003
Huxley Global Limited	£8,538,746
Larkspur Investments Limited	£8,533,528
Landex Commercial Property Limited	£8,533,218
Food Processing Holding Ltd	£8,529,726
Kristall Realty Investments Limited	£8,526,193
Morrison Data Services (Water) Limited	£8,523,000
GDL (Romford) Limited	£8,516,545
Pareto Law Limited	£8,516,000
The Taxassist Direct Group Limited	£8,512,037
Cardtronics Creative UK Limited	£8,507,000
Teknomek Limited	£8,500,207
Broadrich Limited	£8,500,139
Fotolec Technologies Holdings Limited	£8,498,769
Gentian (Mid-Essex) Limited	£8,497,281
UCL Frognal Limited	£8,496,399
Cook's Delights Limited	£8,493,234
Marshall of Stevenage Limited	£8,490,000
Matthews International Transport Limited	£8,486,223
Aura (Newcastle) Holding Company Limited	£8,486,000
SBH Tamworth Limited	£8,485,613
Interiors with Art Limited	£8,479,317
International Tin Association Ltd	£8,474,704
Rhiannon Properties Limited	£8,473,616
Fraserfort Limited	£8,472,000
Alboro Developments Limited	£8,470,462
Structural Holdings and Consultancy Limited	£8,468,009
Gristwood and Toms Limited	£8,466,469
Donatantonio Group Limited	£8,466,016
Martin Audio Limited	£8,464,731

Company	Value
Silk Industries Limited	£8,462,408
SW1 Trading Limited	£8,460,992
TSI Instruments Ltd	£8,456,275
Stockplace Hartford Ltd	£8,451,924
Applepeach Limited	£8,451,681
R.B.R. (Crops) Limited	£8,446,081
Kent Leisure Parks Limited	£8,439,404
Cossam Investment Co Ltd	£8,438,694
Ranplan Holdings Limited	£8,437,738
Geoffrey Mayhew Farms (Holdings) Limited	£8,437,602
Rockford Components Limited	£8,437,227
Thomas Mills High School	£8,433,917
Renaissance Global Investment Ltd	£8,427,574
1LMS (Holdings) Limited	£8,425,000
Cambridge Centre for Sixth Form Studies	£8,424,185
Inhealth Properties Limited	£8,417,000
Borno Chemists Limited	£8,416,165
Chelsteen Homes Limited	£8,414,945
Oblue Limited	£8,407,542
Betts International Limited	£8,406,000
Kenwyn Solar Limited	£8,403,000
PQW Brenley Corner Limited	£8,399,154
Ashcoe Holdings Limited	£8,396,189
Bunting Magnetics Europe Limited	£8,396,000
A Russell (Farmers) Limited	£8,393,092
Starglade Parks Limited	£8,391,390
Cadena AM Limited	£8,390,976
Simm Tronic Limited	£8,387,818
White Lodge (Norwich) Limited	£8,385,525
Samson Materials Handling Limited	£8,382,472
Abington Farms Limited	£8,374,123
Stanmore Implants Worldwide Limited	£8,373,000
Edwardian Care Homes Limited	£8,370,665
Tilsworth Developments Limited	£8,370,648
Highrak Limited	£8,368,730
Gray's of Norwich Limited	£8,362,398
H. W. Group Ltd.	£8,355,054
Sahara Care Limited	£8,354,130
Hay Farming Limited	£8,352,721
Road Tech Computer Systems Limited	£8,350,735
Road Tech Holdings Limited	£8,350,735
SEH (Property and Administration) Limited	£8,350,237
Glazing Vision Limited	£8,346,891
Brandon House Limited	£8,344,554
Canna (B) Investors LLP	£8,344,391
SVK Capital Management Limited	£8,336,550
Anglia Home Furnishings Holdings Ltd	£8,333,566
Global Resources Investment Trust PLC	£8,333,000
Unicourt Properties Limited	£8,332,172
Bucknalls Developments Limited	£8,327,124
Ellgia Recycling Ltd	£8,326,036
Trollope & Colls Limited	£8,326,000
Peerless Europe Ltd.	£8,325,214
GHG 28 (Manor Hospital) Limited	£8,315,000
Wensum Valley Hotel Golf & Country Club Limited	£8,313,706
Audbern Limited	£8,311,586
Angloflora Farms Limited	£8,294,573
The Pero Investments Limited	£8,288,811
J.L. Ashby & Company Limited	£8,288,655
Sabres Educational Trust	£8,283,485
Chard Properties (UK) Limited	£8,280,931
Willis Gambier (UK) Limited	£8,279,756
Woodledge Limited	£8,275,650
Orbit Investment Securities Services PLC	£8,273,677
Survey Roofing Group Limited	£8,273,365
UML Mayfair Limited	£8,264,092
John A.Taylor & Sons Limited	£8,263,199
Chestnut Inns Limited	£8,261,295
Pear Tree Mead Academy	£8,258,817
English Architectural Glazing Limited	£8,253,875
Greater Peterborough UTC	£8,252,830
Saffron Insurance Holdings Limited	£8,251,955
Highassets Limited	£8,245,822
Salavera Trading Limited	£8,245,438
C.F.Anderson & Son Limited	£8,242,549
1 Big Data Management Limited	£8,240,972
Wood Green Investments Limited	£8,237,548
PPA Group Limited	£8,237,172
CKH Developments Limited	£8,236,000
Cloud Possibilities Limited	£8,233,487
Calchan Holdings Limited	£8,232,410
Canfield House Limited	£8,227,754
Meldongreen Limited	£8,220,038
Bowler Group Limited	£8,217,296
Global Ridgeway Holdings Limited	£8,216,143
Premier 1983 Limited	£8,213,219
Car World (Cambs) Ltd	£8,208,640
Active Education Academy Trust	£8,199,739
Pamina Estates Limited	£8,188,296
Aitch Demolition Co. Ltd	£8,186,222
Long Term Reversions (Dulwich) Limited	£8,180,588
Salient Investments Ltd.	£8,179,708
The Gorhambury Estates Company Limited	£8,167,348
Whitestone Property Services Limited	£8,164,258
Allpress Farms Limited	£8,162,244
Tex Plastics (Derby) Limited	£8,160,821
Holdcare Limited	£8,160,756
Adil Property Investment Limited	£8,156,480
Azuri Technologies Ltd	£8,152,740
Harrod UK Limited	£8,149,635
Agri Business Limited	£8,147,929
RJM Metal Consultancy Limited	£8,145,859
Teen Spirit Limited	£8,143,551
Daylighting Power Limited	£8,141,984
Stanley Tee LLP	£8,141,335
Heli Properties LLP	£8,140,383
Abbey Ravenscroft Park Limited	£8,138,937
Displayplan Holdings Limited	£8,130,274
Hi-Tec Europe Limited	£8,129,508
H.Stern (Jewellery) Limited	£8,128,656
NMSIM Group Limited	£8,127,476
Rapleys Limited Liability Partnership	£8,118,729
Kirkmore Rhino 1 Limited	£8,115,622
Transporter Engineering Limited	£8,114,486
Hats Group Ltd	£8,106,915
Linkhaven Estates Ltd	£8,105,050
Viewrose Limited	£8,103,932
Eastern Attachments Limited	£8,102,738
Thomas,Arthur & Gordon,Limited	£8,091,394
City & Westminster Developments Limited	£8,084,778
94 Camlet Way LLP	£8,084,432
ADR Care Homes Limited	£8,084,016
Klipspringer Limited	£8,082,018
Lyndon Hurst Limited	£8,081,361
Pemberton Farms (Holdings) Limited	£8,081,007
Beacon (Mimms) Limited	£8,075,082
SA.GI.MA. Limited	£8,068,944
Narada Europe (UK) Ltd	£8,068,727
Connect Utilities Limited	£8,059,324
Hi-Tec Sports UK Limited	£8,056,063
Kiss FM Radio Limited	£8,056,000
Atalian Servest Group Limited	£8,055,000
Le Vack Estates Limited	£8,053,605
McCann Family LLP	£8,050,408
Rooff Group Limited (The)	£8,047,577
Telida Limited	£8,044,808
Harwood Hutton Limited	£8,042,977
Nacropolis (Langley) Ltd	£8,042,739
Sandhill Park Limited	£8,041,243
Benacre Investments Limited	£8,034,587
Table Bay Services LLP	£8,033,374
Alexander Fraser & Son,Limited	£8,030,567
Henley Group Finance Limited	£8,026,161
First Midland Red Buses Limited	£8,025,000

Dalebrook Supplies Limited	£8,023,302	Himelight Limited	£8,014,373
Intrasales (Lye Lane) Limited	£8,022,078	Davis Schottlander & Davis Limited	£8,004,182
RBR Property Investments Limited	£8,021,086	Gracechurch Sports Management Limited	£8,001,742
Saniflo Limited	£8,017,655	TN (UK) Consultancy Ltd	£8,001,449
Artillery Properties Limited	£8,017,093	Coopers Investments Limited	£8,000,254

Age of Companies

1800s [36]
Adnams PLC
Albea UK Limited
Anglia Maltings (Holdings) Ltd
Archant Community Media Ltd
Barnardo's
Beale's Limited
Britannia Soft Drinks Limited
Bush Boake Allen Limited
Centurion Safety Products Ltd
Equitable Life Assurance Society,(The)
First Choice Holidays Limited
Five Arrows Limited
Fooks Property Co Ltd
Forfarmers UK Limited
Gilbertson & Page Limited
Girls' Education Co Ltd
Greene King PLC
Halma PLC
Investment Company PLC
Kodak Limited
McMullen & Sons, Limited
N & C Building Products Ltd
N.P.K. Holdings Limited
NPA Insurance Limited
Queenswood School Limited
Ransomes Limited
Rhodia International Holdings Ltd
Solvay Solutions UK Limited
Swift Hotels Limited
Tesco International Internet Retailing
Towers & Co.,Limited
United Church Schools Foundation Ltd
Whitbread Group PLC
Wilkin & Sons Limited
Wilkinson Sword Limited
H.Young & Co.,Limited

1900-1909 [34]
C.T. Baker Limited
Arthur Branwell & Co. Limited
Thomas Brooker & Sons Limited
Thomas Cook Retail Limited
Crane Limited
Dashtag
Early Learning Centre Limited
Falkland Islands Co Ltd
Football Association Limited
Alexander Fraser & Son,Limited
Godstowe Preparatory School Co Ltd
Grace Foods UK Limited
Hilton UK Hotels Limited
Incorporated Bishop's Stortford College Association
Institute of Grocery Distribution
Intertek International Limited
Jarrold & Sons Limited
G.B. Kent & Sons PLC
Kent,Blaxill & Co Ltd
James Latham PLC
Nicholls & Clarke Limited
Norwich Diocesan Board of Finance
Pauls Malt Limited
Renault U.K. Limited
Rexam Overseas Holdings Ltd
Roche Products Limited
James Southall & Co Ltd
Spiritualists' National Union
Synthomer PLC
George Thurlow and Sons (Holdings)
Trollope & Colls Limited
United Reformed Church (Eastern Province) Trust
Watford Association Football Club
Whirlpool UK Appliances Ltd

1910-1919 [28]
Altro Limited
Apperly Estates Limited
Atlas Copco Limited
Chelmsford Diocesan Board of Finance
Costa China Holdings Limited
D.D.D. Limited
Elliott Group Limited
Ely Diocesan Board of Finance
Exaclair Limited
Gardiner Real Estate PLC
Gresham Insurance Co Ltd
Grimston Trust Limited
Lancaster Motor Co Ltd
Lawford & Sons Limited
Norwich City Football Club PLC
Papworth Trust
G.& J.Peck Limited
Thomas Ridley and Son,Limited
Rigby Taylor Limited
SKF (U.K) Limited
St.Albans Diocesan Board of Finance
St.Edmundsbury and Ipswich Diocesan Board of Finance
Start-Rite Shoes Limited
Strutt and Parker (Farms),Limited
Tati Co Ltd
R.C.Treatt & Co.Limited
Vauxhall Motors Limited
G.R.Wright & Sons Limited

1920-1929 [60]
Acco UK Limited
C.F.Anderson & Son Limited
Appleyard Group Limited
Ball Beverage Packaging UK Ltd
George Bateman & Son Limited
Thomas Bates & Son Limited
Bayer Cropscience Limited
Bowman Ingredients Limited
Bussey & Sabberton Bros.Limited
COFCO International UK Ltd
Coulson Group Limited
Dron & Dickson Limited
Duff Morgan & Vermont (Holdings) Ltd
Ercol Furniture Limited
Eternit UK Limited
Evelyn Trust
John E.Fells & Sons Limited
Filross Securities Limited
Flakt Woods Limited
Ford Motor Co Ltd
Ford Retail Limited
French & Jupps Limited
Fresh Wharf Estates Limited
Gorhambury Estates Co Ltd
Goymour Properties Limited
Henkel Limited
Frederick Hiam,Limited
Hoopers Limited
Hypnos Limited
Iliffe Print Cambridge Limited
International Flavours & Fragrances
I.F.F.(Great Britain)
Kier Integrated Services (Estates)
Kigass Limited
Land Management Limited
Maldon Crystal Salt Co Ltd
Merck Sharp & Dohme (Holdings) Ltd
Micronclean Limited
Mothercare Group Limited
Muntons PLC
Napp Laboratories Limited
Norfolk Capital Hotels Limited
Norfolk Wildlife Trust
Pertwee & Back,Limited
Peterborough Diocesan Board of Finance
Pitney Bowes Limited
Rexam Limited
Rhodia Limited
Rollins & Sons (London) Ltd
Rooff Group Limited
S.A. (300) Limited
Selecta UK Holding Limited
Sika Limited
Skanska Construction (Regions) Ltd
Skanska Construction UK Ltd
Swiss Laundry,Limited
Tesco Holdings Limited
Truck-Lite Europe Limited
Warners (Midlands) PLC
Whitbread Hotel Co Ltd
Willmott Dixon Holdings Ltd

1930-1939 [71]
Abbey Developments Limited
Abrahams Consolidated Limited
Aeroflex Limited
Amersham (Holdings) Ltd.
Averys (Radnage) Limited
Beacon (Mimms) Limited
George Browns Limited
H. Butterfield Limited
R.G. Carter Limited
F.J. Church & Sons Limited
Churchtown Estates Limited
Clays Ltd.
Covidien UK Limited
Robert Deards Limited
Deards Services Limited
Delbanco Meyer & Co Ltd
Eastern Counties Laundries Ltd
First Eastern Counties Buses Ltd
Fishpools Limited
Frontline Limited
GB Ingredients Limited
GE Medical Systems Limited
Frank G. Gates Limited
Grant & Boyd Limited
Hand Laundry (Bury) Limited
Hapag-Lloyd (U.K.) Limited
Haras Investments Limited
F.W. Hipkin Limited
Hitchin Property Trust Limited
Horse Trust
Icandy World Limited
Ipswich Town Football Club Co Ltd
Kendon Packaging Group PLC
W.D.King Limited
Laindon Holdings Limited
Land Finance & Mortgage Corporation
Le Bas Investment Trust Ltd
Lord Rayleigh's Farms Limited
Maldon Electric Securities,Limited
Marsdens Caterers of Sheffield Ltd
Marshall Motor Group Limited
Marshall North West Limited
Marshall of Cambridge Aerospace Ltd

Martin McColl Limited
Gerald McDonald & Co Ltd
Mentmore Limited
C.John Norris (Cars & Caravans) Ltd
Oikos Storage Limited
Oldrid & Co.,Limited
Panther Securities P L C
F. Perkins Limited
Permastore Limited
Premier Foods Group Limited
Prentice Aircraft and Cars Ltd
RCG-Moody International Ltd
Raytheon United Kingdom Ltd
Rexam UK Holdings Limited
Roys (Wroxham),Limited
Senior PLC
St Paul's Walden Bury Estate Co Ltd
St.Albans High School for Girls
Stapleton's (Tyre Services) Ltd
Taylor Wimpey PLC
Thornhill Estates Limited
Toomey Motor Group Limited
Tun Abdul Razak Research Centre
VWS (UK) Ltd
Volkerstevin Limited
Walsingham College Trust Association
Arnold White Estates Limited
Wilson Connolly Limited

1940-1949 [104]

Abington Farms Limited
Acheson Industries (Europe) Ltd
J Alston & Sons Limited
Ancient House Press PLC
J.L. Ashby & Co Ltd
Baldwin Filters Limited
Baxter Healthcare Limited
Berwen Limited
W.E.Black Limited
Boxford (Suffolk) Holdings Ltd
Brianco Services Limited
British Gaskets Limited
Broadway Travel Service (Wimbledon)
Brook Street (UK) Limited
John Burgess & Co. Limited
Burrough Court Estate Limited
Claas UK Limited
Climax Molybdenum U.K. Limited
Consort Medical PLC
F. Copson Limited
Corporate Express UK Holding Ltd
Maurice Crouch (Growers) Ltd
Cummins Generator Technologies Ltd
Dagless Limited
G.W. Daniels and Son Limited
Denecroft Estates Limited
Didsbury Engineering Co.Limited
Ernest Doe & Sons Limited
Durite Limited
Elektron Technology PLC
Elsoms (Spalding) Limited
Enco Products Limited
T.J.Evers Limited
Forebury Estates Limited
Fujichem Sonneborn Limited
Gratnells Limited
Hallgarten Wines,Limited
Fred Hartley (Estates) Ltd
Hill's Garages (Woodford) Ltd
Hughes Electrical Limited
H.L. Hutchinson Limited
Intelek Limited
Intertek UK Holdings Limited
Investment Properties (Luton) Ltd
J.L.G.Investments Limited
K U H Limited
Knight Strip Metals Limited
Knowles (Transport) Limited
Kwik-Fit Holdings Limited
L.H.D.Limited
W Lamb Limited
Leica Microsystems (UK) Ltd
A.E. Lenton Limited
Lignacite Limited
London School of Theology
Marcantonio Foods Limited
Maurice Mason Limited
Medlock Electrical Distributors Ltd
H. Morrell Property Investments Ltd
Norfolk Capital Group Limited
Notcutts Limited
OEC Europe Holdings Limited
Ovenden Papers Limited
Parker Hannifin (GB) Limited
E.W.Pepper Limited
Prior Scientific Instruments Ltd
Proctor Bros. (Long Sutton) Ltd
R3 Polygon UK Ltd.
Raytheon Systems Limited
Rexam Property Developments Ltd
Rhone Products (UK) Limited
Ridgeon Properties Limited
Ripmax Limited
Robinsons Autoservices Limited
Salmon Management and Finance Ltd
Shawbrook Bank Limited
Sifcon International PLC
Silverson Machines Limited
Simmons (Bakers) Limited
Skanska Cementation International
Slush Puppie Limited
F.P.Smith (Holdings) Limited
Smith Farms (Clacton) Limited
Smith and Holbourne (Holdings) Ltd
St Georges School (Harpenden) Ltd
St.Helen's School Northwood
H.Stain Limited
Stody Estate Limited
TUI Airways Limited
Taylor Wimpey Holdings Limited
E.E. & A. Tee Limited
Teledyne E2V (UK) Limited
Tesco PLC
Tex Holdings PLC
Thomas,Arthur & Gordon,Limited
Turners (Soham) Limited
Verco Office Furniture Limited
Webb Investments Ltd.
Andrew Weir & Co Ltd
Welding Institute
Wentworth Hotel Limited
Wernick Buildings Limited
G.Holmes White (Properties) Ltd
A H Worth and Co Ltd

1950-1959 [172]

Abbey Group Limited
Abbey Investments Limited
Abbeyfield Society
Abbot's Hill Limited
Abbots Ripton Farming Co Ltd
Acco-Rexel Group Services Ltd
Aebi Schmidt UK Limited
Airflow Developments Limited
Alcohols Limited
Alenco (Holdings) Limited
Alstons (Upholstery) Limited
Amalgamated Berkshire Estates Ltd
Amalgamated Berkshire Holdings Ltd
R.H.Amar & Co Limited
Association for Cultural Exchange
Sandy Balls Estate Limited
Banks Mills Limited
Barlow Tyrie Limited
Bartrum's Road Services Ltd
Beckman Coulter United Kingdom Ltd
Berkhamsted Schools Group
David Black & Son Limited
Blue Arrow Ltd.
Bounty (UK) Limited
Britvic Soft Drinks Limited
Russell Burgess Limited
Burgess Properties Limited
CED Limited
CP Holdings Limited
Carlisle Group Limited
Carter and Ward of Wickford Ltd
Caudwell Farms
E.M.Chamberlain Limited
Claas Western Ltd
Claydon Securities Limited
Colchester Catalyst Charity
Company of Biologists, Limited
Consolidated Equities Limited
E.D. & A.D. Cooke, Bourne (Farms)
Cossam Investment Co Ltd
Countryside Properties (UK) Ltd
Hugh Crane Limited
Cresta Estates Limited
Crownfield Holdings Limited
J.E. & V.M. Dalton Limited
Davis Schottlander & Davis Ltd
F.H.Easton Limited
Easy Cleaning Solutions Ltd
Electrolux Professional Ltd
R B Emerson Limited
Envigo International Limited
H. Erben Holdings Limited
H.Erben Limited
Evangelical Lutheran Church of England Trust
Eversleigh Investment and Property Co
A.E. & W.A.Farr Limited
S. Franses Limited
Fraserfort Limited
GE Money Home Finance Limited
General Domestic Appliances Holdings
Geo. E. Gittus & Sons Limited
Glasswells Limited
J W Grant Co
Group Lotus Limited
Grovemere Property Limited
F.H. Hale & Sons (Builders) Ltd
Harlow and District Sports Trust
Hawkes Limited
A. & E. G. Heading Limited
I Hennig & Co Limited
E. Hobbs (Farms) Limited
Ivor Holmes Limited
P.C. Howard Limited
Impellam Holdings Limited
John Innes Centre
Inspectorate International Ltd
Institute of Advanced Motorists Ltd
Intertek Overseas Holdings Ltd
J. Isaacs Management Limited

Kebbell Development Limited
Wm.Kerr (Farms) Limited
Kiln Park Estates Limited
Kings Leisure Limited
Lancaster Cars Limited
Lancaster Luxury Vehicles Ltd
Edward Le Bas Properties Ltd
C.J.C. Lee (Saxthorpe) Ltd
Leywood Estates Limited
Lindal Valve Co Ltd
Loose Hall Farm Limited
M. & J. Engineers Limited
Macarthys Laboratories Limited
Marwin Securities Limited
Geoffrey Mason Limited
Sir Robert McAlpine Limited
Meadow Holdings Limited
Merloni Domestic Appliances Ltd
Minton Holdings Limited
Mothercare UK Limited
NDC Technologies Limited
NEEB Holdings Ltd.
New River Holdings Limited
Newcome-Baker Farms Limited
Norwood Schools Ltd.
O-I Glass Limited
Oakburn Properties Limited
Orley Farm School Trust
Osem U.K. Limited
Padfield (Hayleys) Limited
G.H. Parker (North Cotes) Ltd
C.W.Parker (Wainfleet) Ltd
Pasta Foods Limited
Perkins Holdings Limited
J.E.Piccaver & Co. (Gedney Marsh)
Pipers Corner School
R.& J.M.Place Limited
Porter and Makins Limited
S H Pratt Group Limited
Premier Quilting Co Ltd
M.Price Limited
RWH Travel Limited
R.T.Rate Limited
Raynham Farm Co Ltd
Rexam Finance Co Ltd
Richardson & Cock Limited
Ridgeon Estate Co Ltd
Rimex Metals (U.K.) Limited
T.Rippon & Sons (Holdings) Ltd
T. Rippon Estates Limited
R.Robinson & Co.(Motor Services)
Rockley Sands (Estates) Ltd
A Russell (Farmers) Limited
SWP Group Limited
D.H.Sanderson and Son Limited
Sato UK Limited
Sawston Farms (Cambs) Limited
T.E.Scudder Limited
Seachill UK Limited
Searles (Camping Ground) Ltd
G.S. Shropshire & Sons Ltd
Signet Group Limited
J O Sims Holdings Limited
Skeltools Limited
Smile Stores Limited
Smiths Detection-Watford Ltd
South Coast Furnishing Co Ltd
South Mimms Services Limited
Spar (UK) Limited
St. Christopher School (Letchworth)
Staples (Vegetables) Limited
Staples Brothers Limited
John A.Taylor & Sons Limited
Taylor Properties Trading Ltd
Taylor Wimpey Developments Ltd
Tesco Stores Limited
Thurlow Nunn (Holdings) Ltd
R. C. Tinsley Limited
G.J.W.Titmuss Limited
V.U.K. Holdings Limited
Van Hage & Company (Holdings) Ltd
Ventress Property Developments Ltd
Volkerhighways Limited
J. Walker & Son (Investments) Ltd
Wernick Hire Limited
Charles Wharton Limited
Whitecliff Bay Holiday Park Ltd
Ashley Wilde Group Limited
S.F. Williams (Foils) Limited
Wimpey Dormant Investments Ltd
Worstead Farms Limited
A.G.Wright & Son,(Farms) Ltd
Carl Zeiss Ltd

1960-1969 [250]

41/43 Maddox St. Limited
A.J.N. Steelstock Ltd.
ADM Arkady Limited
ASM Metal Recycling Ltd.
Adda Hotels
Advante Limited
Agricultural Central Trading Ltd
Alboro Developments Limited
Aldermore Bank PLC
Aldwickbury School Trust Ltd
Allpress Farms Limited
Alto (UK) Ltd
American Can Holdings (U.K.) Ltd
Anglia Autoflow Limited
Antec International Limited
Ardex UK Limited
L.C.F.Arthey & Sons Limited
Assetsteady Limited
Aston Heating Limited
Astor Lodge Holdings Limited
Avery Dennison U.K. Limited
Aveva Solutions Limited
Azelis UK Life Sciences Ltd
R. S. Baker & Sons Limited
Ball. Roller & Transmission Bearings
E.W.Ballard Holdings Limited
Beaconsfield Educational Trust Ltd
Beamglow Limited
Beechwood Park School Limited
Biffa Environmental Municipal Services
Biffa Waste Services Limited
Bosch Rexroth Limited
Bourne Leisure Group Limited
Bouygues E & S Infrastructure UK Ltd
M.& R.Bowman Limited
R. Bratley (Quadring) Limited
Breheny Civil Engineering Ltd
Breyer Group PLC
British Board of Agrement
Broadland Wineries Limited
George Brown's Implements (Holdings)
A.E.Bullock Limited
Bunting Magnetics Europe Ltd
Burghley House Preservation Trust
CML Microsystems PLC
CQK Limited
Callcott Holdings Limited
Cambridgeshire Industrial Properties
Camden Development Co Ltd
Camfield Estate Co Ltd
Campion Willcocks Limited
P.J. Carey Plant Hire (Oval) Ltd
C.W. & J. Cargill Limited
Carnarvon Hotels Limited
RG Carter Group Limited
Casemasters Limited
Castle Green Kendal Limited
Castlestone Investments Ltd
Caversham Finance Limited
Cementation Skanska Limited
Chappell Estates Limited
Chelsteen Homes Limited
Chicken Cabins Limited
Church of God in Christ (Calvary)
City & Country Residential Ltd
R.H.Claydon Limited
T.H.Clements & Son Limited
V.G.Clements (Contractors) Ltd
W.D. Coe Limited
Connolly Homes PLC
Coopers Investments Limited
Countrywide Estate Agents
Cousins Holdings Limited
Crispin & Borst Limited
Davis and Dann Limited
Dayla Holdings Limited
Deanplan Limited
Diomed Developments Limited
Duff Morgan & Vermont Limited
Ellis Bros (Contractors) Ltd
Elsoms Seeds Limited
FAI Automotive PLC
FCE Bank PLC
Fairfield Garage (Leigh-on-Sea) Ltd
Fairview Estates (Housing) Ltd
D.J.Fisher (Farms) Limited
A.A.Fisher (Properties) Ltd
Five Star Inns Limited
Flamborough Holidays Limited
Fluke (UK) Limited
Fluorocarbon Co Ltd
Frith's Flexible Packaging Ltd
GBST Limited
Galderma (U.K.) Limited
Gardline Shipping Limited
M. Gaze & Co. Limited
Gita Properties Limited
Gonville Hotels Limited
Gough Hotels Limited
Grant & Bowman Limited
Greystead Properties Limited
Grundfos Pumps Limited
Hadleigh Bakery Limited
Hamlin Electronics Europe Ltd
Hanmere Polythene Limited
Harrod UK Limited
Hauck Heat Treatment Limited
Hevingham Development Co Ltd
Higgins Construction PLC
Higgins Homes PLC
S.Hille & Co.(Holdings) Ltd
Hilton International Hotels (UK) Ltd
Hughes TV and Audio Limited
Huntleigh Healthcare Limited
I.M.O. Precision Controls Ltd
International Fertilizer Association
International Society for Krishna
Consciousness
Intertek Inspection Services UK Ltd
Intertek Testing Management Ltd
Ipeco Holdings Limited

Iveco Holdings Limited
Jabac Finances Limited
Jockey Club Estates Limited
Katsouris Brothers Limited
Kebbell Holdings Limited
Keymed (Medical & Industrial Equipment)
Kidney Research UK
Kier Integrated Services Ltd
Kier International Limited
Kier Living Limited
Kier Property Developments Ltd
LDC (Boston) Limited
LPA Group PLC
Lancaster Specialist Cars Ltd
Langley School (1960) Limited
Lathams Limited
Edward Le Bas Limited
A.E. Lenton (Holdings) Ltd
Liebherr - Great Britain Ltd
P.F.K. Ling Limited
Livingston Ltd
Lotus Cars Limited
MEL Aviation Limited
Mack-Brooks Exhibitions Ltd
Malthurst Petroleum Limited
W.& H.Marriage & Sons Limited
Marshall Thermo King Limited
McGee Civil Engineering Ltd
McGee Group (Holdings) Limited
Meldire Limited
Merck Sharp & Dohme Limited
Merritts Properties Limited
Moorepay Limited
H.C.Moss (Builders) Limited
Motivair Compressors Limited
Moto Hospitality Limited
Motus Group (UK) Limited
Moulton Bulb Co Ltd
Mouskos & Sons Co. Limited
Mumford & Wood Limited
Mytravel Group Limited
Napp Pharmaceutical Group Ltd
F.H. Nash Limited
Navigator Terminals Seal Sands Ltd
Neopost Technologies Limited
No Climb Products Limited
Norfolk Broads Direct Limited
Northgate Public Services (UK) Ltd
Norton Way Motors Limited
OSG U.K. Limited
P.I.P. Electrics Limited
Palm Paper Limited
W.H.Palmer & Co.(Industries) Ltd
Parkdale Investments Limited
Peachey Basildon Group Limited
Peak Securities Limited
Pemberton Farms Limited
H.R. Philpot & Son (Barleylands)
Pitney Bowes Finance Limited
Plastic Extruders Limited
Porvair Filtration Group Ltd
Poste Hotels Limited
Proquest UK Holdings Ltd
Purcell School
Quinto Crane & Plant Limited
R O Ventures Limited
R.B.R. (Crops) Limited
RO Property Management Limited
RSS Jet Centre Limited
Ratcliff Group Limited
Republic Technologies (UK) Ltd
Richardsons Leisure Limited
Rights and Issues Investment Trust PLC
Rowlandson Investments Limited
Runwood Homes Limited
Sue Ryder
S-P RIL Limited
S.C.W.S. (Holdings) Limited
Scotsdale Nursery and Garden Centre
Selex ES International Ltd
Selex Elsag Limited
Senior Engineering Investments Ltd
Sensient Colors UK Ltd
Silver Street Automotive Ltd
Simat Properties Limited
Skanska Cementation International Holdings
Skanska Rashleigh Weatherfoil Ltd
Skanska UK PLC
Frederic Smart & Son Limited
Smiths Industries Industrial Group
Snowmountain Enterprises Ltd
Spurdown Limited
St.Lawrence Hall Farms Limited
St.Martins' (Northwood) Preparatory School Trust
St.Michael's Manor Limited
Stafford House School of English Ltd
Startling Music Limited
Stellison Limited
H.Stern (Jewellery) Limited
Stirling Civil Engineering Ltd
Suffolk Wildlife Trust Limited
Syngenta UK Limited
Synthomer (UK) Limited
Tattersalls Limited
Taylor Wimpey Property Co Ltd
Tilia Properties Limited
Timewell Properties Limited
Toomey Leasing Group Limited
R.H.Topham & Sons Limited
Town Close House Educational Trust
Troston Farms Limited
Trox UK Limited
Twinmar Limited
UNEX Gredley (Holdings) Ltd
Usborne PLC
Vinci PLC
Vinci UK Developments Limited
Walstead Press Group Limited
Walstead Roche Limited
Welding Alloys Limited
Werner UK Sales & Distribution Ltd.
S.Wernick & Sons (Holdings) Ltd
Wheatley Group Developments Ltd
Wheatley PLC
Wheatley Properties Limited
Wickford Development Co Ltd
Willmott Dixon Construction Ltd
Wilson Connolly Holdings Ltd
Yelcon Limited
Yomans (London) Limited

1970-1979 [379]

A 1 Bacon Co Ltd
Abbey Cross Trading Limited
Abbey View Produce Limited
Acushnet Europe Ltd
Adcock Refrigeration and Air Conditioning
P.F. Ahern & Sons Limited
Akhter Group Limited
Alami International Limited
Albanwise Limited
Albon Engineering and Manufacturing PLC
Alfreds Way Investments (No. 2) Ltd
Alpha 3 Manufacturing Limited
Ammeraal Beltech Limited
Ancient House Printing Group Ltd
Andgrove Property Investments Ltd
Anduff Car Wash Limited
Anglo-Norden Forest Products Ltd
Angloflora Farms Limited
Ascott Farms Limited
Ashe Group Holdings Limited
Ashworth Homes Limited
Astle Limited
Atlas Copco UK Holdings Ltd
Axalta Powder Coating Systems UK Ltd
B.M. Polyco Limited
BDL Group PLC
M.Baker Produce Limited
Balton CP Limited
Bard Pharmaceuticals Limited
Barnes Group Limited
Bartrums Haulage and Storage Ltd
Bauder Limited
Bauer Consumer Media Limited
Bauer Radio Limited
Beacon Educational Trust Ltd
Bell Educational Trust Limited
Bennett PLC
P.H. Betts (Holdings) Limited
Biffa Holdings Limited
Biffa Waste Management Limited
Biomarsh Environmental Ltd
Blue Anchor Leisure Limited
Boral (UK) Limited
Borno Chemists Limited
Bourne Leisure (Hopton) Ltd
Bowlplex Limited
R.G. Boyce Limited
Bristol Fruit Sales (Market) Ltd
British Pipeline Agency Ltd
Broadgate Builders (Spalding) Ltd
Michael Broughton Limited
Brown Brothers Distribution Ltd
J.Browne Construction Co Ltd
Bullen Developments Limited
C.M. Cadman Group Limited
Calumet Wex International Ltd
Cambridge Construction Limited
Cambridge Consultants Limited
Cambridge Enterprise Limited
Camstar Herbs Limited
Canada Life (U.K.) Limited
Canada Life Limited
P.J. Carey (Contractors) Ltd
Careys New Homes Limited
Chalcroft Limited
E.M. Chamberlain Estates Ltd
E.M. Chamberlain Group Ltd
Charterhouse Simon Limited
Chesterhill Investments Ltd
Cheveley Park Stud Limited
Citizen Machinery UK Ltd
Clark-Drain Limited
Clarke International Limited
Clarksteel Holdings Limited
Cliffords Limited
Coastfields Leisure Limited
Cobb Europe Limited
Coherent (UK) Limited
Peter Colby Commercials Ltd
Colchester Zoo Limited
Collease Truck and Trailer Rentals
Coloplast Limited
Commodore Kitchens Limited

Community Foods Limited
Community Reinsurance Corporation
Comtec Cable Accessories Ltd
Thomas Cook UK Travel Limited
Walter John Cook and Sons Ltd
Costa International Limited
Costa Limited
Cottis House Limited
Creightons PLC
A. T. Cross Limited
Ivor Crowson Developments (Stamford)
Cyberscience PLC
Danzer UK Limited
Dart Products Europe Ltd.
Lawrence David Limited
Deekay Investments Limited
Desilu Group Limited
Dhamecha Foods Limited
Domino Printing Sciences PLC
Dorma UK Limited
Durkan Holdings Limited
Durkan Limited
Dyer and Butler Limited
E.G.L. Homecare Limited
EBM - Papst UK Limited
EMG Anglia Limited
ESRI (UK) Limited
Simon Elvin Limited
Elysium Healthcare (Healthlinc) Ltd
Enfield Fancy Goods Limited
Epson (U.K.) Limited
Erinastar Limited
Esselte Holdings Limited
Esselte Limited
Essex Services Group Limited
Express Freight Services (U.K.) Ltd
Faerch Plast UK Limited
Farecla Products Limited
Farmland Reserve UK Limited
Farmwealth Limited
E. Feldman Limited
Fengrain (Services) Limited
Fengrain Limited
Firstan Limited
Fitzmaurice Holdings Limited
Flamingo Plants Ltd
P. Flannery Plant Hire (Oval) Ltd
Flo-Mech. Limited
Fluke Precision Measurement Ltd
Fold Hill Foods Limited
Forest Freight Limited
Formula One Auto Centres Ltd
Fox International Group Ltd
Friar's Pride Limited
Frimstone Limited
JW Froehlich UK Limited
GE Healthcare Limited
Gade Property Developments Ltd
Charles Gallagher Limited
Geoghegan Bros. Limited
Gibson Developments Limited
Thomas Gibson Fine Art Ltd
Goodfellow Cambridge Limited
R. & I. Grant & Co. Limited
Gray & Sons (Chelmsford) Ltd
Peter Green Haulage Limited
Greenseed International Ltd
Grigny (UK) Limited
Grimsthorpe & Drummond Castle Trust
Grove & Dean Limited
H (Lincs) Limited
H.& G.Car Parks Limited

HTS Estates Limited
Derek Hales (Plumbing Contractors)
Hallam Meat Co Ltd
Halma International Limited
A.W. & D. Hammond Limited
Hampden Insurance Holdings Ltd
Hamton Environmental Services Ltd
John Hanlon & Co. Limited
Harber Properties Limited
Harris Commercial Repairs Ltd
Harris Holdings (Grays) Ltd
HaskoningDHV UK Limited
Henbrandt Limited
Heraeus Noblelight Limited
A.E.Hewison Limited
Hexcel (U.K.) Limited
Hi-Tec Sports PLC
Historic House Hotels Limited
Holden & Holden Limited
Home Counties Estates Limited
Hoo Hing Holdings Limited
Hunnable Holdings Limited
Hydac Technology Limited
I.S. Group Limited
ITS Testing Services (UK) Ltd
Imagination Technologies Ltd
Incodia International Ltd
Industrial Chemicals Group Ltd
Industrial Tool Supplies (London)
Industrial Water Jetting Systems Ltd
Jalaram Limited
Janssen-Cilag Limited
Jarvis Homes Limited
Leonard F.Jollye (Brookmans Park)
KDM International Limited
KMG Systems Limited
Keelings UK Group Limited
Kefco Sales Limited
Kelvin Hughes Limited
Kenford Developments Limited
Kier Infrastructure and Overseas Ltd
Kier Overseas (Seventeen) Ltd
Kier Ventures Limited
Joseph King (Norfolk) Co-ordination
Joseph King Holdings Limited
Kirly Limited
Kitchen Range Foods Limited
J.L. Knight Roadworks Limited
Konica Minolta Business Solutions (UK)
Kubach & Sambrook (Metals) Ltd
Kwik-Fit (GB) Limited
L & M (Heating) Supplies Ltd
Landchief Limited
Landis + Gyr Limited
Lapid Developments Limited
R.A. Latta (Farms) Limited
Lemon Groundwork Solutions Ltd
Letchworth Hall Hotel (Trading) Ltd
Lexitron Limited
Linkage Community Trust
Lorien Resourcing Limited
Lorne Stewart PLC
Lundbeck Limited
MBI MBO Limited
MCSA Group Limited
Macron Safety Systems (UK) Ltd
Majestic Property & Estates Ltd
Mando Corporation Limited
Marchanson Limited
Maritime Transport Limited
Marshall of Scunthorpe Limited
Martin Mathew & Co. Limited

R. Maskell Limited
Mason Pearson Bros. Limited
Matthew Homes Limited
Matthews International Transport Ltd
Sir Robert McAlpine Enterprises Ltd
McNicholas Construction (Holdings)
Mediterranean Shipping Company (UK)
Medtronic Limited
Meldongreen Limited
Michell Instruments Limited
Microlease Limited
Micropress Printers Limited
Midland Chilled Foods Limited
Midwich Limited
Milburn Productions Limited
Miller & Miller (Chemicals) Ltd
Mirrorstoke Limited
Mitcham Earthmoving Limited
Moody International (Russia) Ltd
Donald Moody Investments and Developments
Moog Fernau Limited
Henry Moore Foundation
Moores Refrigeration Controlled Transport
A.J. Morrisroe & Sons Limited
Movac Group Limited
Muntons (Holdings) PLC
Murkett Brothers Limited
NEC (UK) Ltd.
National Film and Television School
National Pharmacy Association Ltd
Navigator Terminals UK Limited
Newarthill Limited
Nordson (U.K.) Limited
Norfolk Farm Produce Limited
Norish Limited
M. S. Oakes Securities Ltd
Oakray Limited
Olympus Keymed Group Limited
Omavale Limited
PMS International Group PLC
Palacath Limited
Panther Investment Properties Ltd
Panther Trading Limited
Penlaw & Co Ltd
Perry Ellis Europe Limited
David Phillip (Investments) Ltd
Pickering Interfaces Limited
Pinnacle Insurance PLC
Pirin Ltd
Pitney Bowes Holdings Limited
Pizza Hut (U.K.) Limited
Pledge Office Chairs Limited
Pledream Properties Limited
Poggenpohl Group UK Limited
Power Adhesives Limited
Precision Printing Co. Limited
Princebuild Limited.
Pro Cam CP Limited
Probe Oil Tools Limited
Proquest Information and Learning
Purple Surgical Holdings Ltd
R K Property Investments Ltd.
R.V.L. Properties Limited
Randstad CPE Limited
Ransomes Jacobsen Limited
Redbridge Sports Centre Trust Ltd
Redsky IT (Hemel) Limited
Rega Research Limited
Jack Richards & Son Limited
Rijac Properties Limited
Robinson Young Limited

Rooff Ltd
Rotamead Limited
Ryan Elizabeth Holdings PLC
S.T.C.Plumbing & Heating Merchants
SEH (Property and Administration)
Safe Computing Limited
Saint Francis Hospice
Samson Materials Handling Ltd
Saniflo Limited
Scimitar Care Hotels PLC
Seabourne Group Limited
Jack Sealey Limited
Seaside Leisure Parks Limited
Serruys Property Co Ltd
Shelbourne Reynolds Engineering Ltd
K.J. Shortis Limited
Sick (UK) Ltd.
Sinai (Antiques) Limited
Skanska Major Projects Limited
Roger Skinner Limited
Snape Maltings
Solopark Limited
Sopra Steria Recruitment Ltd
Sopress Investments Limited
Sorbon Estates Limited
South Essex Stockholders Ltd
Spar Food Distributors Limited
Spearhead International Ltd
Speycrest Limited
Squibb Group Limited
St. Aubyn's (Woodford Green) School Trust
Stantec UK Limited
Steria UK Corporate Limited
Stockvale Limited
Stoke By Nayland Club Ltd.
J.W. Suckling Transport Ltd
Suffolk Life Annuities Limited
Suffolk Life Pensions Limited
Sussex Gardens Hotels Limited
Swanbrae Limited
TUI UK Retail Limited
TUI UK Transport Limited
Tamdown Group Limited
O.A.Taylor & Sons Bulbs Ltd
Taylor Wimpey UK Limited
Taylors Service Garages (Boston) Ltd
Tazaki Foods Limited
Techaid Facilities Limited
Tex Plastics (Derby) Limited
Theatre Royal (Norwich) Trust Ltd
P.J. Thory Limited
Thursford Collection
Tilda Limited
Titon Hardware Limited
Trans-Siberian Gold PLC
Transam Trucking Limited
Trend Machinery & Cutting Tools Ltd
Trend Marine Products Limited
Trentpeak Limited
Trumpf Limited
P. Tuckwell Limited
Turpin Distribution Services Ltd
UK Waste Management Limited
UNEX Corporation Limited
UNEX Finance Limited
UNEX Investment Properties Ltd
UNEX Smithfield Limited
Unit Export Limited
Viglen Limited
Virbac Limited
Vokera Limited
Volkerwessels UK Limited
Walstead Southernprint Limited
Willmott Partnership Homes Ltd
Charles Wilson Engineers Ltd
George Wimpey Limited
Winter & Co. UK Limited
M.J. Worth Limited
O.W. Wortley & Sons Limited
Richard Wright Music Limited
York House (Meat Products) Ltd

1980-1989 [647]

A. & B. Glass Co Ltd
A.C. Entertainment Technologies Ltd
A.M.P. Air Conditioning Ltd
ABL (Holding) Limited
ACI Worldwide (EMEA) Limited
ACO Technologies PLC
AOC (UK) Ltd
AS24 Fuel Card Ltd
AWG Group Limited
Abacus Group Limited
Abbey Group Cambridgeshire Ltd
Abel Homes Limited
Access Platform Sales Limited
Access UK Ltd
Acclaim Handling Limited
Acco Europe Limited
Action for Children Services Ltd
John Adams Leisure Limited
Adil Catering Limited
Aeropak (Chemical Products) Ltd
Agri-Chemicals Limited
Air Business Limited
Airbus Defence and Space Ltd
Aldenham Foundation
Allway Connections Limited
Altro Group PLC
Amgen Limited
Amsik Limited
Amsprop London Limited
M. Anderson Construction Ltd
Anglia Ruskin Enterprise Ltd
Anglian Water Services Limited
Anglo-Dutch Property (UK) Holding
Anness Publishing Limited
Annodata Limited
Apem Components Limited
Applied Satellite Technology Ltd
Ariston Thermo UK Ltd
Armored Auto UK Limited
Armour Home Electronics Ltd
Ashe Construction Limited
Askew & Barrett (Pulses) Ltd
Askham Village Community Ltd
Aston Barclay Limited
Astute Electronics Limited
Australian Pacific Touring (U.K.)
Avingtrans PLC
Avnet (Holdings) Ltd
Avnet EMG Ltd.
Axalta Coating Systems UK Ltd
B & M Care Group Limited
BAM Construction Limited
BBA Aviation Lynton Group Ltd
BEW Electrical Distributors Ltd
BS Project Services Limited
Badger Building (E.Anglia) Ltd
Bafin Holdings
Balanus Limited
Balgores Motors (1982) Limited
Ball Beverage Packaging Holdings UK
Bamrose Enterprises Limited
John Banks Limited
David Barke (Holdings) Ltd
Barking Power Limited
Barnack Estates UK Limited
Barsham Securities Limited
Bathstore.Com Limited
Bauer Digital Radio Limited
Bauer Technologies Limited
Beaufort House Limited
Beckman Holdings Limited
M.W. Beer & Co. Limited
Beko PLC
Bellcoin Holdings Limited
Bentwaters Parks Limited
Bioline Agrosciences Limited
Tom Blackwell (Contractors & Plant Hire)
Blitzfair Limited
Blowplast Limited
Bold-Rock Management and Investments Ltd
Boniface Engineering Limited
Borras Construction Ltd.
Alan Boswell Group Limited
Bourn Hall Limited
Bourne Holidays Limited
Jack Brand Limited
Britten-Pears Foundation
Britvic EMEA Limited
Britvic International Investments
Brooks Bros. (UK) Limited
Bruel & Kjaer VTS Limited
Bryant Park Hospitality UK Ltd
Roberto Bucci (U.K.) Limited
Bucyrus Europe Limited
Bugler Developments Limited
Burdens Group Limited
Burton's Foods Limited
Bush Boake Allen Holdings (U.K.) Ltd
A.J. Bush Limited
Business Control Solutions Group Ltd
C. U. Lighting Limited
CASP
CDK U.K. Limited
CEG Properties Limited
CH Old Co Limited
CML Microcircuits (UK) Limited
CN Group Limited
Cadastra Limited
Cambridge Crystallographic Data Centre
Cambustion Limited
Camflats Limited
Camstead Limited
Canada Life Group (U.K.) Ltd
Caps Cases Limited
Carbon60 Limited
Care UK Limited
Carl F Groupco Limited
Carrain Limited
R.G. Carter Projects Limited
Caskade Caterers Limited
Castle Point Gas & Heating Co. Ltd
Central Property Investments Ltd
Chamberlain Holdings PLC
Charlie Properties Limited
Charter Projects (Developments) Ltd
Chartman Limited
Chassis-Cab Limited
Cheale Meats Limited
Chemilines Limited
Chester International Hotel Ltd
Chicken Villas Limited
Chilton Home Farms Ltd
Chipperfield Land Co Ltd

Chivgate Limited
Choice Discount Stores Limited
Churchmanor Estates Company PLC
Churchmanor Limited
Clarence Estates (London) Ltd
Classic Management Services Ltd
Claxton Engineering Services Ltd
Clement Clarke (Holdings) Ltd
Clinimed Limited
Colleycare Limited
Colwyn Developments Limited
Com Dev Europe Limited
Comline Auto Parts Limited
Commercial Body Fittings Ltd
Community Health Services Ltd
Computacenter (UK) Limited
Concurrent Technologies PLC
Connells Residential
Construct Holdings Limited
Construct Reason Limited
Thomas Cook Airlines Limited
Thomas Cook Group UK Limited
Cooper Roller Bearings Co Ltd
Cornelius Group PLC
Corporate Associates Limited
Cosco Shipping (UK) Co Ltd
Countrywide Surveyors Limited
Coversure Insurance Services Ltd
Coyle Personnel PLC
Crendon Timber Engineering Ltd
Crop's Foods Ltd.
Culham Limited
D.H. Industries Limited
DC Management Services Limited
DSV Road Holding Limited
Dagless Holdings Limited
Dai Europe Ltd
Damco UK Limited
Dassault Systemes Biovia Ltd
Datapaq Limited
Davroc Limited
Martin Dawn PLC
De Lage Landen Leasing Limited
Demipower Limited
Denbourne Investments Limited
Dengie Crops Limited
Densitron Technologies Limited
Denso Automotive UK Ltd.
Dermal Laboratories Limited
Descram Holdings Limited
Devantier Properties Limited
Devitt Insurance Services Ltd
Dimex Limited
Direct Table Foods Limited
Displayplan Limited
Domino UK Limited
Dow Agrosciences Limited
Dow Properties Limited
P.J. Duffy & Son (Farms) Ltd
Duoview Properties Limited
Durkan Estates Limited
Durkin and Sons Limited
Dynamic Cassette International Ltd
EE Limited
EResearchTechnology Limited
East Anglian Property Limited
East of England Agricultural Society
Ecotherm Insulation (UK) Ltd
Eisai Limited
Electrolux PLC
Electron House (Overseas) Ltd
Elegant Electronics Limited
Elgon (Enfield) Limited
Emmett UK Limited
Encocam Limited
Entertainer (Amersham) Limited
Envigo CRS Limited
Ercol (Holdings) Limited
Etcetera Construction Services Ltd
Eurobase Systems Limited
European Flavours & Fragrances PLC
Excelredstone Converged Solutions
Excitech Limited
Exclusive Contract Services Ltd
Exploration Electronics Ltd
FDR U.K. Limited
Fairview Enfield Limited
Family Amusements Limited
Farleigh Hospice
Farsound Aviation Limited
Fastglobe (Mastics) Limited
Fesa (UK) Limited
Festool UK Limited
Fibron BX Limited
First Data Europe Limited
First Essex Buses Limited
First Midland Red Buses Ltd
First Potteries Limited
Five Arrows Investments Ltd
Flahive Developments Limited
Flying Trade Group PLC
Flying Trade Limited
Focusrite Audio Engineering Ltd
Ford JL Limited
Forextra Developments Limited
Framingham House Investments Ltd
Freiberger (UK) Limited
Frelene Limited
Frisco (U.K.) Sales Limited
G's Group Holdings Limited
G's Growers Limited
G.B.N. Services Limited
GEMS Schools Limited
Gallagher Holdings Limited
Joseph Gallagher Limited
Galliard Homes Limited
Gee Group Ltd
Generics (U.K.) Limited
Genzyme Limited
Geodis United Kingdom Limited
Mick George Limited
Getech Limited
Robert Gibbs (Contracting) Co Ltd
Glazewing Limited
Global Graphics Software Ltd
Global Marine Systems Limited
Grange Management (Holdings) Ltd
Grangebrook Estates Limited
Grant & Stone Limited
Greenbrook Industries Limited
Greens Farming Limited
Greenyard Fresh UK Ltd
John Grose Group Limited
Ground Control Limited
H L C (Wood Products) Limited
HG Construction Limited
HIC Racing (Chiswick) Limited
HIC Treasury Limited
HPC Healthline UK Limited
HTG Trading Limited
Haag-Streit UK Limited
Haas Automation Limited
Halfen Limited
Halstead Securities Limited
Hamamatsu Photonics UK Limited
Harbour Shipping Limited
Hardall International Limited
Harlow Agricultural Merchants Ltd
Harman International Industries Ltd
Harrington (Properties) Ltd
Harrogate International Hotel Ltd
Haven Leisure Limited
Hawk Incentives Holdings Ltd
Hay Farming Limited
Haydon Holdings Limited
Hayman Group Limited
Hearing Dogs for Deaf People
Hedgemans Limited
Hi-Tec Sports UK Limited
Higgins Group PLC
Higgins Investments PLC
Highrak Limited
Hildon House Limited
JF Hillebrand UK Limited
Homepines Investments Limited
Hopkins and Moore (Developments) Ltd
Horta Properties Limited
Hospice of St. Francis (Berkhamsted)
John F Hunt Limited
Domnick Hunter Group Limited
Huntleigh Technology Limited
Hurco Europe Limited
Hutton Construction Limited
IBC Vehicles Limited
IT Luggage Limited
Ideal Shopping Direct Limited
Imerys Aluminates Limited
Inflite Engineering Services Ltd
Inntel Limited
Interaction Recruitment PLC
Island Waste Services Limited
Istec Services Limited
Iveco Limited
J & A (International) Limited
J.A.C. Computer Services Ltd
J.S.T. (U.K.) Limited
JJ Food Service Limited
JSA Services Limited
Jaltek Systems Limited
Jawaby Property Investment Ltd
Jaysam Contractors Limited
Jewers Doors Limited
Richard Johnston Limited
Juddmonte Farms Limited
K.M. Packaging Services Ltd
KWS UK Limited
Kanta Enterprises Limited
Kaykem Fast Foods Limited
Kelly Communications Limited
Kenwake Limited
Kettle Foods Ltd.
Kier Construction Limited
Kier Fleet Services Limited
Kier Homes Caledonia Limited
Kier Integrated Services Group Ltd
Kier Limited
Kier Minerals Limited
Kier National Limited
Kier Overseas (Nine) Limited
Kier Overseas (Twenty-Three) Ltd
Kier Project Investment Ltd
King's School, Ely
Kingshott School Trust Limited
Kiss FM Radio Limited
Knowles (UK) Limited
Kodak International Finance Ltd

Kromachem Holdings Limited
Kromachem Limited
L V Shipping Limited
LC Packaging UK Ltd
Lakeside Food Group Limited
Mervyn Lambert Plant Limited
Lancaster PLC
Landlink Ltd
Lantern Recovery Specialists PLC
Laurence Homes (Eastern) Ltd
Layher Limited
Robert Lee Distribution Ltd
Leicester Citybus Limited
Lenta Properties Limited
Leonardo MW Ltd
Levolux Limited
Lincolnshire Field Products Ltd
Linx Printing Technologies Ltd
David Lloyd Leisure Limited
London City Bond Limited
London Hoist Limited
London Luton Airport Limited
London Outpost Limited
Long Term Reversions (Harrogate) Ltd
Longmill Realty Limited
Luxottica North Europe Limited
Lymington Precision Engineers Co.
Lyndon Hurst Limited
Lynxvale Limited
M & D Developments Limited
MDM Timber Limited
MSX International Limited
MTL Instruments Group Limited
MacDonald Humfrey (Automation) Ltd
Majestic Wine PLC
Majestic Wine Warehouses Ltd
Maltco 3 Limited
Manford Securities & Investments Ltd
Manor Service Stations Limited
Maritime Transport Services Ltd
Maritzcx Limited
Marshall Group Properties Ltd
Marshall Motor Holdings PLC
Marshall of Cambridge (Garage Properties)
Marshall of Cambridge (Holdings) Ltd
Martin-Brower UK Ltd
Mass Consultants Limited
Masteroast Coffee Co. Limited
Matchroom Sport Limited
Mayfair Carpet Gallery Limited
McGrath Bros. (Waste Control) Ltd
McGrath Brothers (Holdings) Ltd
McNicholas Construction Services Ltd
Medimmune Limited
Meritcape Limited
Metaswitch Networks Ltd
Microlights Limited
Micross Components Limited
Mistras Group Limited
Jenny Moody Properties Ltd
Mortgage Guarantee Limited
Mothercare PLC.
Motorclean Limited
Mr. Fothergill's Seeds Limited
Mulalley & Co. Limited
Mulcroft Limited
Munnelly Support Services Ltd
N.E.M. Co. Limited
NEC Capital (UK) PLC
NPMA Ltd
NPS (UK4) Limited
Natures Menu Limited
Nene Park Trust
Netcall PLC
Netcracker Technology EMEA Ltd
Netsupport Ltd.
Neville Trust Limited
Newsquest Media Group Limited
Nikon X-Tek Systems Limited
Nobo Group Limited
Norfolk Truck & Van Limited
Norfolk and Waveney Enterprise Services
North Herts Hospice Care Association
North West Steel Limited
Norwich Airport Limited
O'Hara Property Investment Holding Co
OEConnection Limited
OOCL Logistics (Europe) Ltd
OTV Birwelco Limited
Oakbridge Homes (Group) Ltd
Oakfield (Foods) Limited
Offley Chase Estates Limited
Ontex Retail UK Limited
Opecprime Properties Limited
Optima Contracting Limited
Optimum Group Services PLC
Ortona Limited
PFE Express Limited
PMS International Holdings PLC
PPD Global Ltd
PPG Holdings (U.K.) Limited
PPG Industries (UK) Limited
PRGX UK Ltd
Padwicks Travel (Wembley) Ltd
Palmhall Limited
Pantheon Hotels and Leisure Ltd
Park Air Systems Limited
Parkstone Limited
Partnership in Care Limited
Pass J. Holdings Limited
Pengethley Potatoes Limited
Pentagon Limited
Peppercorn Property Investments Ltd
Perkins Engines Co Ltd
Perkins Group Limited
Ralph Peters & Sons Limited
Phelan Construction Limited
Phoenix Datacom Limited
Pitney Bowes Software Europe Ltd
Planshore Limited
Plaut International Limited
Playmobil (U.K.) Limited
Poole Investments Limited
Port of Boston Limited
Porvair PLC
Premier Decorations Limited
Premier Holidays Limited
Premier PLC
Primagraphics Limited
Prime Estates Limited
Princebuild Holdings Limited
Pro Cam UK Limited
Property and Commercial Enterprises
Q V Foods Limited
Quinta Raddison Limited
R.B. Securities Limited
RANC Care Homes Limited
RCT Construction Limited
RG Securities (No.2) Limited
Rabbah Bloodstock Limited
Paul Rackham Limited
Randstad Solutions Limited
Randstad UK Holding Limited
Ransome's Dock Limited
Rapid Electronics Limited
Rateneed Limited
Ravensale Limited
Reads Property Developments Ltd
Renewable Energy Systems Ltd
Resham PLC
Residential Management Group Ltd
Rexam European Holdings Ltd
Rhiannon Properties Limited
Ridgeons Limited
Ritelite (Systems) Limited
Rittal Holdings Limited
Road Tech Computer Systems Ltd
Rockford Components Limited
Rockley Dene Homes Limited
Roe Bros. & Co Ltd.
Rogers Rental Limited
Rolec Services Limited
Rolling Components Limited
Roman Investments Limited
Rothamsted Research Limited
S & B Commercials Limited
SG Technologies Limited
SME Group PLC
SOP International Limited
Saba Park Services UK Limited
S. Sacker (Claydon) Limited
Safegold Properties Limited
Sagentia Limited
Sara (London) Limited
Satco Investments Limited
John Saul Limited
Schering-Plough Holdings Ltd
Science, Engineering and Manufacturing Technologies Alliance
Scotline Limited
Seabrook Holdings Limited
Seetec Business Technology Centre
Senior UK Limited
Sewells Reservoir Construction Ltd
Shamir UK Limited
Shaneel Enterprises Limited
Sharan Properties Limited
Sherrygreen Limited
Shogun Finance Limited
Signature Flight Support London Luton
J O Sims Limited
John Sisk & Son Limited
Sisk Consolidated Investments Ltd
Site Sales Marketing Limited
Sitecrest Limited
Skylord Travel PLC
Slingsby Advanced Composites Ltd
Sofis Limited
Solai Holdings Limited
Solihull Hotel Co Ltd
Sonnet Care Homes (Essex) Ltd
Sparquote Limited
Specialist Cars Limited
St Andrew's Tutorial Services Ltd
St. Elizabeth Hospice (Suffolk)
St. Helena Hospice Limited
St. Luke's Hospice (Harrow & Brent) Ltd.
St. Mary's School Cambridge
St. Nicholas Hospice (Suffolk)
Stafford House Study Holidays Ltd
Stansted Airport Limited
Stantec Europe Limited
Star Cargo PLC
Stephensons of Essex Limited
Paul Strickland Scanner Centre
Stuart Group Limited

Suffolk Agricultural Association
Swan Investments Group Limited
Swift Advances PLC
Symology Limited
Synergy Flavours Limited
T & B (Contractors) Limited
TAM International North Sea Ltd
TM Vending Limited
TTP Group PLC
TUI Ireland Limited
Tangent International Group PLC
Tangent International Limited
Tanglewood (Lincolnshire) Ltd
George Tanner (Shalford) Ltd
Taylor Made Joinery Interiors Ltd
Team Consulting Limited
Teknomek Limited
Telegenic Limited
Tesco (Overseas) Limited
Tesco Property Holdings Ltd
Thompson Investments (London) Ltd
Three Rivers Property Investments
Ticketgrange Limited
John Tinney & Co Limited
Titan Airways Limited
Titon Holdings PLC
Total Worldfresh Limited
Totes Isotoner (UK) Limited
Travelpack Marketing & Leisure Services
Treatt PLC
Tri-Continental Limited
Turner Properties Limited
Turnstone Estates Limited
Twinglobe Limited
UK Holiday Group Limited
UK Real Estate Limited
Underwoods Garage (Tiptree) Ltd
Unifruit Limited
Uniserve (Air Freight) Limited
Uniserve (Europe) Limited
Uniserve Holdings Limited
Uniserve Limited
Unisurge International Limited
Velfac Limited
William Vere (Holdings) Ltd
Vernalis (R & D) Limited
Vernalis Limited
Vida Wood UK Limited
Villa Plus Limited
Villachase Limited
Vinci Construction UK Limited
Vinci Fleet Services Limited
F. Vindis & Sons (Sawston) Ltd
Vindis Developments Limited
Vindis Group Limited
Vision (Office Automation) Ltd
Voicevale Limited
VolkerFitzpatrick Limited
Volkerwessels Limited
WJ Groundwater Limited
Waldersey Farms Limited
Walstead Peterborough Limited
Roger Warnes Transport Ltd
Waystone Limited
Webster Estates Ltd
Welch's Group Holdings Limited
Welland Medical Limited
Wenta
Weston Homes PLC
J D Wetherspoon PLC
Wheatland Cheese Co. Limited
Wholesale Welding Supplies Ltd
Wickland (Holdings) Limited
Wilton House Limited
Winpost Limited
Wise Trading Limited
Wood Green Animal Shelters
Wood International Agency Ltd
A & A Woodford Limited
Woodland Global Ltd
Yazaki Europe Limited
Zellis UK Limited
Zest Living Limited

1990-1994 [415]

1 Big Data Management Limited
1LIFE Management Solutions Ltd
3D European Holdings Limited
A. F. Machinery Limited
A.G.E. Nursing Homes Limited
A1 Pharmaceuticals PLC
AES Tring Park School Trust
AGCO Finance Limited
API Microelectronics Limited
APM Group Limited
ARM Limited
Absolute Radio Limited
Affinity Water Capital Funds Ltd
Affinity Water East Limited
Affinity Water Limited
Affinity Water Southeast Ltd
Agreserves Limited
Agrifac UK Ltd
Air Livery Limited
Alba Broadcasting Corporation Ltd
Allaway Group Limited
Alpi UK Limited
Altenmark Limited
Altomart Limited
Amsprop Estates Limited
Amsprop Investments Limited
Anderson Construction Limited
Anglia Ruskin Development Ltd
Anglian Group Limited
Anglian Windows Limited
Arrow Electronics (UK) Limited
Arthenella Limited
Ashley House PLC.
Aspect Ventures Limited
Astrazeneca PLC
Astrazeneca Treasury Limited
Atalian Servest Food Co Ltd
Automated Systems Group Ltd
Automation Partnership (Cambridge)
Aveva Group PLC
Aviva Consumer Products UK Ltd
Aviva Health UK Limited
BFSL Limited
BGL Group Limited
BICL Limited
Ball Beverage Packaging Europe Ltd
Bartrum Group Limited
Baruch Holdings Limited
Benacre Investments Limited
Besana UK Limited
Biffa Polymers Limited
Big Easy Restaurants Limited
Birdlife International
Black Swan International Ltd
Blanco UK Limited
Blue Arrow Holdings Limited
Blue Sea Overseas Investments Ltd
William Blythe Limited
Boston Limited
Alan Boswell Insurance Brokers Ltd
Boxford (Suffolk) Farms Ltd
Branded Stocks (UK) Ltd
Brown & Carroll (London) Ltd
Bucyrus UK Limited
Business Management Software Ltd
C & K Meats Limited
CAE Technology Services Ltd
CQS Natural Resources Growth and Income
Cambridge Display Technology Ltd
Camelot UK Lotteries Limited
Camfaud Concrete Pumps Limited
Camfed International
Cantel Medical (UK) Limited
Capespan International Limited
Cardif Pinnacle Insurance Holdings PLC
Cardif Pinnacle Insurance Management Services
Cardiff Gate Business Park Ltd
Care UK Community Partnerships Ltd
Caretech Community Services Ltd
Carlisle Security Services Ltd
Carlisle Staffing PLC
Carlisle Staffing Services Ltd
Carlson Wagonlit UK Ltd
Carpetright of London Limited
Charles Kalms, Henry Ronson Immanuel College
Chelmer Foods Limited
Chelmsford Cars and Commercials Ltd
Churton Property Developments Ltd
Claas Eastern Ltd
Clavering Care Limited
Cleanland Limited
Clearview Homes Limited
Clinimed (Holdings) Limited
J. Coffey Construction Ltd
Colts Cabs Limited
Comparex UK Limited
Conamar Building Services Ltd
Conduit Street Holdings Ltd
Connectix Limited
Contamac Limited
Thomas Cook UK Limited
Cornwall
Corona Energy Retail 4 Limited
Corona Gas Management Limited
Costco Limited
Costco Wholesale UK Limited
Countryside Maritime Limited
Countrywide Electrical Distributors
Coveris Flexibles UK Limited
Crocus Home Loans Limited
D & B Scaffolding Limited
D.C.K. Concessions Limited
DB Broadcast Ltd
DBD Distribution Limited
DST Financial Services Europe Ltd
DST Financial Services International
Dage Precision Industries Ltd
Dalebrook Supplies Limited
Thomas Dane Limited
Danfoss Limited
De Lage Landen Limited
De Sangosse Ltd.
Deben Group Industries Limited
Defaqto Ltd
Demipower (1991) Limited
Desira Group PLC
Dippy Ridge Limited
Direct Boot and Shoe Supplies Ltd
Direktek Ltd

Distribution Supplies Limited
Dominion Pubs and Bars Limited
Domino Investments Limited
John W. Doubleday Limited
Druid Group Limited
E.G.T. Finance Limited
ESRI Holdings Limited
Earl Estates Limited
East Anglian Installations Ltd
Eckoh UK Limited
Elite Mobile Limited
Elizabeth Estates (NWB) Ltd
Elveden Farms Limited
Elysium Healthcare No. 3 Ltd
Emerson Crane Hire Limited
Ensign Bus Co Ltd
Enterprise Department Limited
Enterprise Residential Development
Eurobase International Limited
Europlants (UK) Limited
Euroview Manufacturing Limited
Everbuild Building Products Ltd
Evergreen Finance Limited
Exheat Limited
Express Vending Limited
Ezra Attia Limited
Fauna & Flora International
Fieldrose Limited
Fine Foods International (Manufacturing)
Flamingo Flowers Ltd.
Flamingo Produce Ltd.
Flocklynn Limited
Foulger Transport Limited
Fremantle Trust
Frontier Developments PLC
G's Fresh Beetroot Limited
GE Bio-Sciences Investments Ltd
Gada Limited
Gamit Limited
Gardline Marine Sciences Ltd
Garrets International Limited
Gatetrade Limited
Gearhouse Broadcast Limited
Gerrard International Limited
Glazing Vision Limited
Global Graphics (UK) Limited
Goldstar Transport Limited
Grangewood Builders Limited
Granta Design Limited
Granta Park Estates Limited
Grants of Shoreditch Limited
Greenswan Consultants Limited
Grimme (U.K.) Limited
Gristwood and Toms Limited
H. W. Group Ltd.
H.L. Foods Limited
Hagondale Limited
Harbour Club Limited
Harlow Health Centres Trust Ltd
Harrodian School Limited
Harwich International Port Ltd
HaskoningDHV UK Holdings Ltd
Havens Christian Hospice
Helmet Integrated Systems Ltd
John Henry Group Limited
Herma UK Limited
Hill Partnerships Limited
Hilton Properties Limited
Holmes Care Limited
Hoo Hing Limited
Hopkins Homes Limited
Hotel Chocolat Limited
Howard Hunt (City) Limited
Huntleigh International Holdings Ltd
Hutchison Ports (UK) Holding Ltd
Hy-Pro International Limited
Hydac Limited
Hypro EU Limited
IFCO Systems UK Ltd
Imagination Technologies Group Ltd
Import Services Limited
Independent Pipelines Limited
Inexus (Services) Limited
Ingrebourne Valley Limited
Inspectorate Holdings PLC
International Tin Association Ltd
International Transport Ltd
Jardine Motors Group UK Ltd
Jarvis Contracting Limited
Jobserve Limited
WO & PO Jolly Holdings Ltd
KLM UK Engineering Limited
Kane Group Limited
Keech Hospice Care
Kier Facilities Services Ltd
Kier Group PLC
Kier Management Consulting Ltd
Kier Services Limited
Nicholas King Homes PLC
Knight Build Limited
Lakehouse Contracts Limited
Lamb-Weston/Meijer UK Limited
Lancaster Sports Cars Limited
Ralph Lauren UK Limited
Lawsons (Whetstone) Limited
Leica Microsystems Cambridge Ltd
Life Fitness (UK) Limited
Longford Securities & Equities Ltd
Loppingdale Plant Limited
Lotus Group International Ltd
Lundbeck Group Limited
Luvata Welwyn Garden Ltd
Luxottica Retail UK Ltd
L. Lynch (Holdings) Limited
L. Lynch (Plant Hire & Haulage) Ltd
M.P.I. Limited
MJT Securities Limited
MSHA International Ltd.
MTCE Limited
Mainline Communications Group Ltd
Mallard Leasing Limited
Manor Lodge School
Marden Homes Limited
Marshall Land Systems Ltd
Marton Geotechnical Services Ltd
Maylands Green Limited
Sir Robert McAlpine (Holdings) Ltd
Medacs Healthcare PLC
Merck Sharp & Dohme Finance Europe
Meridian Audio Limited
Mersea Homes Limited
Molecular Products Limited
Moller Institute Limited
Montanaro UK Smaller Companies
Investment Trust
Moody Homes Limited
Morelli Group Limited
Mountcharm Limited
Multitrust Property Investments Ltd
Mundipharma International Ltd
NEC Europe Ltd
NPS Property Consultants Ltd
National Football Centre Ltd
Netcall Telecom Limited
Nissan Motor (GB) Limited
Noble Foods (We) Limited
Noble Gift Packaging Limited
Norfolk Environmental Waste Services
Norse Commercial Services Ltd
North London Collegiate School
Northgate Information Solutions Holdings
Oakbridge Homes Limited
Oleoland Hotel Co Ltd
Olive Tree Limited
Omex Agrifluids Limited
Oni PLC
Orchid Drinks Limited
Origin UK Operations Limited
Orwell Trucks Limited
PJG Developments Limited
PX Manufacturing Ltd
Pajef Limited
Palatial Leisure Limited
Paradigm Commercial PLC
Park Securities Limited
Paypoint Network Limited
Pearl Properties Limited
Peerless Europe Ltd.
Perkins Small Engines Limited
J.A. Phillips Holdings Ltd
Pineridge Investments Limited
Polyfield Property Limited
Poplars Resource Management Co Ltd
Port of Felixstowe Limited
Port of Tilbury London Limited
Poste Holdings Limited
Pregis Limited
Property & Investment Management Ltd
Propshop Limited
Purebond Limited
Q.N. Hotels Limited
Quanta Consultancy Services Ltd
R P Valves Limited
R.D.Trading Limited
RP2 Limited
Ramco (Harlow) Limited
Randstad HR Solutions Limited
Randstad Middle East Limited
Rannerlow Limited
Rational UK Limited
Rebus Holdings Limited
Rectory Homes Limited
Regentsmead Limited
Reilly Concrete Pumping Ltd
Renault Group U.K. Limited
Reynolds Catering Supplies Ltd
Rican Securities Limited
Richards Dry Dock and Engineering
Robinsons Soft Drinks Limited
Rogerson Holdings Limited
Rowan International Limited
Rysa Lodge Residential Properties
SPC Holdings Limited
Saba Infra Holdings UK Limited
Salient Investments Ltd.
Sandhill Park Limited
Sardar Properties (U.K.) Ltd
Schottlander Limited
Science Recruitment Group Ltd
Screen Subtitling Systems Ltd
Sealey (UK) Limited
Seatrax (U.K.) Limited
Selecta U.K. Limited
Seymour Distribution Limited
Seymour International Limited
Shanly Homes Limited

Share Centre Limited
Share PLC
Shawcor UK Limited
Shenley Park Trust
G S Shropshire Holdings Ltd
Richard Shuttleworth Trustees
Simm Tronic Limited
Sinclair International Limited
Smith Bros Timber (East Anglia) Ltd
H. Smith Food Group PLC
Smithfield Foods Limited
Sopra Steria Services Limited
South Central Property Limited
Specflue Limited
St. Vincent's Charitable Trust
Stainless Metalcraft (Chatteris) Ltd
Staples UK Limited
Stat Marine Limited
Sterndale Systems Limited
Stortford Interiors (UK) Ltd
Structural Holdings and Consultancy
Sunnen Products Limited
Swanlea Limited
Swarco UK Limited
Swift Brickwork Contractors Ltd
Swift Group Holdings Limited
TCL Manufacturing Limited
TFX Group Limited
TK Maxx
TUI UK Limited
Tappenden & Co. Limited
James Taylor Construction Ltd
Terex Cranes UK Limited
Tesco Distribution Limited
Thames Card Technology Limited
Tharros Limited
Tican Process Holdings Limited
Tillomed Laboratories Limited
Timber Connection Limited
Topfib Limited
Toureen Contractors Limited
Tradelink Direct Limited
Tradex Insurance Co Ltd
Trailer Resources Limited
Transmec UK Limited
Trelanoak Limited
Triplehigh Limited
Truckeast Limited
Tunnelcraft Limited
Turnhold Properties Limited
Ufford Park Limited
United Church Schools Trust
VHC Sub-Holdings (UK)
F. Vindis & Sons (Bedford) Ltd
J. Van Vliet London Cash & Carry
Volac International Limited
Warners Group Publications PLC
Warrant Investments PLC
Waters Limited
Watts Industries UK Limited
Wenta Business Centres Limited
West End Homes Limited
Westleigh Properties Limited
Arnold White Group Limited
Wildlife Trust for Bedfordshire, Cambridgeshire and Northamptonshire
Willow Securities Limited
Winfresh (UK) Limited
Wisdom Toothbrushes Limited
Xaar Technology Limited
Yours Clothing Limited
Zip Heaters (UK) Ltd

1995 [116]

Abacus Hotels Limited
Abbey Properties Cambridgeshire Ltd
Advanced Lighting Technologies Europe
Alliance Asset Management Ltd
Antas Limited
Aryzta Bakeries UK Ltd
Ascott Properties Limited
Babraham Institute
Barnardiston Hall Preparatory School
Benchmark Leisure Limited
Bio-Rad Laboratories Limited
Bosch Lawn and Garden Limited
Broadgate Homes Limited
Brookstream Properties Limited
Bucci Freight Services Limited
C. J. H. Farming Limited
CDT Holdings Limited
CEVA Animal Health Limited
Cavity Insulation Guarantee Agency
Chiltern Cold Storage Group Ltd
Chivers Farms Limited
City Lifting Limited
Computacenter PLC
Comtec Group (International) Ltd
Corporate Express (Holdings) Ltd
Cosco Shipping Lines (UK) Ltd
A.R. Craven Farms Limited
Crowland Cranes Limited
Crystal Windows & Doors Ltd
Curtis Medical Investments Ltd
D-Link (Europe) Limited
DB Investments Limited
DSV Air & Sea Limited
Denny Bros Holdings Limited
Dhollandia U.K. Limited
E - Leather Limited
Easyjet Airline Co Ltd
Essex Community Foundation
FPS 1995 Limited
Fairacres Group Limited
Fairview Hotels Limited
Flightsafety International U.K. Ltd
Former Reichmann Properties PLC
GTC Pipelines Limited
GW Research Limited
Gates Group Limited
Global Self Drive Limited
Greenyard Flowers UK Ltd
Hamden Homes Limited
Hampden Holdings Limited
Hats Group Ltd
Henley Group Holdings Limited
Hexcel Composites Limited
Hotel Folk Limited
Hutchison Ports Europe Limited
Ironmongerydirect Limited
Lifehealth Limited
London Executive Aviation Ltd
London Internet Exchange Ltd
M.J.S. Construction (March) Ltd
MLM Consulting Engineers Ltd
MTS (Holdings) Limited
MVM Holdings Limited
Sir Robert McAlpine Capital Ventures
McCormick Europe Limited
Metsa Wood UK Limited
Mill Hotel Limited
Morrison Data Services Limited
Newsquest Capital Limited
OOCL (Europe) Limited
Oak Tree Schools Holdings Ltd
Olivewood Limited
Opal Bay Limited
Pareto Law Limited
Pizza Gogo Ltd
Porcelanosa (South East) Ltd
Porcelanosa U.K. Limited
Porvair Filtration Limited
Produce Connection Limited
Produce World Group Ltd
Produce World Investments Ltd
Quadram Institute Bioscience
Rebus Group Limited
Redbridge Produce & Flowers Ltd
Result Clothing Limited
Rexam Beverage Can (India Holdings)
Rhodia Holdings Limited
Roadside Group Ltd
Rose Builders Ltd
Salperton Park Estate Limited
Saybest Limited
Seabrook Warehousing Limited
Skanska Infrastructure Development UK
Softbox Systems Limited
Solus (London) Limited
St Joseph's College Limited
Stamford Property Co Ltd
Stema Shipping (UK) Limited
Stourgarden Limited
T. Bro Investment Limited
TJX Europe Buying (Deutschland) Ltd
TJX Europe Limited
TJX UK
Teen Spirit Limited
Thoratec Europe Limited
User Friendly Properties Ltd
Van Hage & Co Ltd
Ventureforth 2000 Limited
Vigeland Properties Ltd
Vix Technology UK Limited
WTS Media Group Limited
Waverley House Hotel Limited
Wimpey Corporate Services Ltd
Windcrest (U.K.) Limited
Woodledge Limited
Carl Zeiss Microscopy Limited

1996 [121]

AMPY Holdings Limited
Alphasense Limited
Amalgamated Berkshire Properties Ltd
Amino Holdings Limited
Angel Care PLC
Aprite (GB) Limited
Arrow Electronics UK Holding Ltd
Aula Limited
Autolink Concessionaires (M6) PLC
Aviva Central Services UK Ltd
BAM Properties Limited
BISL Limited
BRE Trust
Babraham Bioscience Technologies Ltd
Ballast Phoenix Limited
Biofocus DPI (Holdings) Ltd
Blessville Limited
Brownlow Enterprises Limited
Bush Boake Allen Enterprises Ltd
Buzzard Leisure Limited
Cambridge Antibody Technology Group
R.G. Carter Construction Ltd
Chartridge Conference Co Ltd
Cheergrey Properties Limited
Chelsea Portfolio Limited

Chesside Homes Limited
Childs Property Limited
Churchgate Estates Limited
City & Westminster Developments Ltd
Coaching Inn Group Ltd
Computerlinks (UK) Limited
Cook's Delights Limited
Corona Energy Limited
Corona Energy Retail 1 Limited
Costa Express Limited
Country Court Care Homes Ltd
DPA Support Services Limited
DSV Solutions Limited
Dawe Estates Limited
De Soutter Medical Limited
Direct Insurance Group PLC
Drayton Building Services Ltd
EC English Cambridge Limited
Eastern Attachments Limited
Edwardian Care Homes Limited
Elysium Healthcare (Acorn Care) Ltd
Elysium Healthcare No. 4 Ltd
Essity UK Limited
Eurosalamis Enterprises Ltd.
Foray 989 Limited
Forest Commercial Services Ltd
Fricor Limited
Future Travel Limited
Galliard Construction Limited
Gentec Energy PLC
Gibbons (Holdings) Limited
Gilead Sciences International Ltd.
Global Chair Components Ltd
Good Harvest Group Limited
Goodman Family Investments Ltd
D.N. Grady & Sons Limited
Greenvale AP Limited
HFIS PLC
Habendum Limited
Harlequin Direct Limited
Highfield Park Trust
Imperial Pharmaceuticals Ltd
Industrial and Financial Systems, IFS UK
Intertek Finance PLC
Intertek Testing & Certification Ltd
Intertek Testing Services Holdings Limited.
Jark Ventures PLC
KPIT Technologies (UK) Limited
Kelly Communications Group Ltd
Kelly Fleet Services Limited
LDH (La Doria) Limited
Lifeplus Europe Limited
Lindal Holdings Limited
MBDA UK Limited
Magdalene Limited
Maison Moti Limited
McCormick Kutas Food Service Ltd
Multimatic Ltd.
Next Generation Clubs Limited
Norwood Ravenswood
OPD Group Limited
Openarch Greenside Limited
PPD UK Holdings Limited
Panther (VAT) Properties Ltd
Polar Speed Distribution Ltd
Property Finance Nominees (No.3) Ltd
J. Reddington Ltd
Ridgeway Garages (Newbury) Ltd
Rocket Medical PLC
Rosemary & Thyme Limited
Routebuy Limited
Saba Infra Cardiff Limited
Safestore Properties Limited
Sedum Limited
Senju Manufacturing (Europe) Ltd
Smiths Business Information Services
Spencers Property Investments Ltd
St. Margaret's School Bushey
Stanmore Implants Worldwide Ltd
Sumitomo Electric Europe Ltd
TLC Care Homes Limited
Taylor Woodrow Construction
Teaching Personnel Limited
Tesco International Services Ltd
Tesco Overseas Investments Ltd
Tesco TLB Properties Limited
Thomson Sawmills Limited
Thomson Travel Group (Holdings) Ltd
Thule Outdoor Limited
Tower Bridge Homes Care Ltd
Triplerose Limited
Ulgrave Limited
Volkerrail Limited
WWW Sunoptic Com UK Limited
Wright Medical UK Ltd
Zenith Hygiene Systems Limited

1997 [136]

AMI Corporations Ltd
Activity Superstore Limited
Agri Business Limited
Amadeus Capital Partners Ltd
Amersham Biosciences
Amshold Securities Limited
Aquatronic Group Management PLC
Arihant Limited
Associated Lead Mills Ltd.
Astonpalm Limited
Astro Lighting Limited
Autism Anglia
Autolink Holdings (M6) Ltd
BAM Construct UK Limited
Bauer AR Holdings Limited
Beckhithe Farms Limited
Birch's Park Homes Limited
Blenheim Estates Limited
Blenheim Property Management Ltd
Boxford Group Ltd.
Bristol Laboratories Limited
Building Research Establishment Ltd
Burney Realty Limited
CNH Industrial Capital Europe Ltd
CWT Holdco Limited
Cambridge Arts & Sciences Ltd
Cannon Kirk (UK) Limited
Care UK Clinical Services Ltd
Carlson Vehicle Transfer Ltd
Castledon Ltd
Chaldean Estate Limited
Claas Manns Ltd
Coherent (UK) Holdings Limited
Comland Commercial Limited
Construction Workers Guild Ltd
Contechs Consulting Limited
Continental Datagraphics Ltd
Craft & Sons Limited
Dage Holdings Limited
C.E. Davidson Farms Ltd.
Desiman Limited
Dry Drayton Estate Limited
EC English London Limited
Eckoh PLC
Emico Limited
Eurocity Properties (Central) Ltd
European Coffee Corporation Ltd
FIH Group PLC
Fairview Homes Limited
Fairview New Homes (Chase Road) Ltd
Fairview New Homes (South East) Ltd
Fifty Six Investments Limited
Forum Trust Limited
GE Healthcare UK Limited
Galapagos Biotech Limited
Galliard Holdings Limited
Gap Partnership Limited
Gowrie Laxmico Limited
Gray's of Norwich Limited
Greene King Brewing and Retailing
Ground Construction Limited
Harwich International (Holdings) Ltd
Hayward Tyler Limited
Heathpatch Limited
Hutchison Ports (UK) Limited
IGD Services Limited
ITAB UK Ltd
Ikarus Engineering Limited
Instalcom Limited
Instrumel Ltd
Intrasales (Lye Lane) Limited
JPJ Installations Limited
Jamestown Industries Limited
Jepco Limited
Keepstem Limited
Kings Hedges Investments Ltd
Kudos Pharmaceuticals Limited
Labvantage Solutions Limited
Leitrim Properties Limited
Letting International Limited
Lodwick Homes Limited
MNS Care PLC
Malthurst (UK) Limited
Malthurst Limited
Malthurst Retail Limited
Mathworks Limited
McCutcheon Norveil Consultancy Ltd
Medivet Group Limited
Merchant Taylors' School
Metier Healthcare Limited
Microsoft Research Limited
Milpharm Limited
N.R.C. Plant Limited
NIAB.
Napp Pharmaceutical Holdings Ltd
Newell Properties Limited
Openview Security Solutions Ltd
Optoma Europe Ltd
Orlight Limited
Oxford Cambridge and RSA Examinations
Palmers (St Albans) Limited
Partners in Property (U.K.) Ltd
Perrin Group Holdings Limited
Pitney Bowes Software Holdings Ltd
Pratt & Whitney Canada (UK) Ltd
Professional Darts Corporation Ltd
RCI Financial Services Limited
RSA Island Village Limited
Radical Motorsport Limited
Ridgeland Properties Limited
Roche Holding (UK) Limited
Sealed Air Limited
Seven Asset Limited
Sharksfin Holdings Limited
Silverton Property Investments Ltd
Simarco International Limited
Thomas Sinden Limited
Smiths Metal Centres Limited

Sogea Holdings (UK) Limited
Stonewater Capital Limited
TM Group Holdings Limited
TTP Labtech Limited
TTP PLC
Takeda UK Limited
Towers Thompson Holdings Ltd
Trinity College (CSP) Limited
Venture Lighting Europe Ltd
Ventus Investments Limited
WJ Management Limited
Walsworth Limited
Warehouse Express Limited
Waste Recycling Environmental Ltd
Wembley National Stadium Ltd
Xaar PLC
Xaarjet Limited
Yang Ming (UK) Ltd

1998 [130]

ACI Global Limited
APT-Skidata Limited
Adilsons Properties Limited
Agricola Holdings Limited
Alzheimer's Research UK
Amadeus Partners Limited
Amino Communications Limited
Anglia Restaurants Ltd
Arinso UK Limited
Artillery Properties Limited
Artisan (UK) PLC
Astrazeneca UK Limited
Aurient Investments Limited
Automotive Lighting UK Limited
B/E Aerospace (UK) Limited
BBC Studioworks Limited
BMS Limited
BR Pharma International Ltd
Bairds Malt Limited
Balcraft Properties Limited
Bancroft's School
Bespak Europe Limited
Betts International Limited
Betts Limited
Big Prawn Co. Ltd.
Biochrom Limited
Booking.Com Limited
C J Bourne (Asset Management) Ltd
Bowler Group Limited
Brandbank Limited
Business & Communications Ltd
C P Timber Limited
Cambridge Commodities Limited
Cannon Kirk Property Limited
Cantay Estates Limited
Carbery (UK) Limited
Cardtronics UK Limited
Chai-Lifeline Cancer Care
Chartco Limited
Chartridge Developments Ltd
City Link (Cardiff) Limited
Contracting Made Easy Ltd
Country House Weddings Limited
Dillons Stores Limited
E.F.G. Housewares Limited
E.G.T. Bridging Finance Ltd
EMS-FP & S Limited
East Anglia's Childrens Hospices
Elizabeth Holdings PLC
Essity Holding UK Limited
Everguard Limited
Fairfield Limited
Farrington Care Homes Limited
Fiveways Municipal Vehicle Hire Ltd
Friargate Coventry Development Ltd
Galldris Construction Limited
Gleneden Plant Sales Limited
Goodkind Estates Limited
Greenwich Millennium Village Ltd
Hall Contracts (Lakenheath) Ltd
Helgor Trading Limited
Hilborough Farms Limited
Homeguard Properties Limited
Illumina Cambridge Limited
JSM Construction Limited
Kelly Comms Limited
Kendric Ash Limited
Kenninghall Holdings Limited
Kier Business Services Limited
Kwik-Fit Euro Limited
LB Enterprises Limited
Larkfleet Limited
Latif International Limited
Lawson Partners Limited
London Luton Airport Group Ltd
London Luton Airport Operations Ltd
M L Accessories Limited
MJC Properties (Essex) Limited
Metier Holdings Limited
Mill Hill Properties Limited
Millennium Investments 2000 Ltd
Milton Hall Estates Limited
Motor Parts Direct Limited
Muraspec Decorative Solutions Ltd
NPS (UK5) Limited
Napp Pharmaceuticals Limited
Northwood Paper Sales Limited
O.B.C. (Europe) Limited
Oakburn European Properties Ltd
Orion Alloys Limited
Parker Hannifin Manufacturing (UK)
Paypoint Collections Limited
Paypoint PLC
Phlexglobal Limited
Qualcomm Technologies International, Ltd.
Rattlerow Farms Limited
Rattlerow Properties Limited
Redsky IT Holdings Limited
Redwings Horse Sanctuary
Reichmann Properties PLC
Residential Loans Ltd.
Robsons of Spalding Limited
Rooff Holdings Limited
Rosper Estates Limited
Schneider Electric Software GB Ltd
Shakoor Capital Limited
Shedmead Limited
Shopfittings Direct Limited
J.B Shropshire & Sons Limited
Skanska J.V. Projects Ltd
Sorbon Homes Limited
Sorbon Investments Limited
South Eastern Leisure UK Ltd
Spaces Personal Storage Ltd
Spreadex.Com Limited
Super Toughened Glass Limited
TUI Northern Europe Limited
Takeda Cambridge Limited
Tesco Overseas ULC
Thistledove Limited
Triangle (Funding One) Limited
Tristel Solutions Limited
UNEX Holdings Limited
Unicourt Properties Limited
West One Technology Ltd
Westlake Estates Limited
Whitehouse Leisure International Ltd
Wymondham Property Management Co Ltd
YMCA Trinity Group
Zian Hi-Tech (U.K.) Limited

1999 [144]

1LMS (Holdings) Limited
A. & A. 2000 Limited
ACM ULR Limited
AFE Group Limited
Agetur (U.K.) Limited
Agriturf Holdings Limited
Aixtron Limited
Amshold International Limited
Anacreonte Properties Limited
Apical Limited
Astex Therapeutics Limited
Astwood Securities Limited
Atalian Servest Group Holdings Ltd
Aurora Limited
Automotive UK No.1
Bango. Net Limited
Beauty Wholesale Limited
Brookgate Property Limited
Buyagift PLC
CSR Imaging UK Ltd.
CSSC Properties Limited
CVS (UK) Limited
Cambridge Broadband Networks Ltd
Canada Life Asset Management Ltd
Careprogress Limited
Caretech Community Services (No.2)
Carter Accommodation Holdings Ltd
R.G. Carter Cambridge Limited
Cavenham Estates Limited
Chelverton UK Dividend Trust PLC
Churchill Contract Services Ltd
Clark Construction (South East) Ltd
Clearsprings (Management) Ltd
Connect Scaffolding Limited
Thomas Cook Tour Operations Ltd
Country Retirement & Nursing Homes Ltd
DSV Road Limited
S. Dad Limited
Delamode PLC
Dialgreen Estates Limited
Dock and Let Limited
Duncan Lewis Solicitors Ltd
EMG Holdings Limited
George East (Housewares) Ltd
Epay Limited
Euro-Matic (Brazil) Limited
Fairview New Homes (Colindale) Ltd
Fairview New Homes (Developments)
Firstan Holdings Limited
Foregain Limited
Freedom Travel Group Limited
Freshtime UK Limited
GE Money Servicing Limited
GW Pharma Limited
Joseph Gallagher Group Ltd
Genesis Pharmaceuticals Ltd
Geo Management Limited
Grangewood Brentwood Limited
Gravity Media Group Limited
Green Label Foods Ltd.
HRS Investments Limited
Hales Group Limited
Hawkins & Associates Limited
Herts Insurance Consultants Ltd

Hexcel Overseas
Heythrop Park Limited
Hilton Finance (UK) Limited
Himelight Limited
Igroup 8 Limited
Industrial Chemicals Limited
Intertek Capital Resources Ltd
K.C.Y. Limited
Kara Designs Ltd
Lanswood Limited
Leisuregrow Products Limited
Lester Hotels Group Limited
Levy Associates Limited
Long Term Reversions (Dulwich) Ltd
Long Term Reversions (Torquay) Ltd
Lumesse Limited
Luminescence International Ltd
MLS (Overseas) Limited
MSCM Limited
Marriott Motor Group Limited
Melbourn Science Park Limited
Metro Properties Limited
Metrosold Limited
Millennium Cash & Carry Ltd
B.P. Mitchell Haulage Contractors
Mono Holdings Limited
Mono Properties Limited
Morplan Limited
NPS (UK6) Limited
Nellsar Limited
Ocado Retail Limited
Old English Inns Limited
Openarch Estates Limited
Perkinelmer (UK) Holdings Ltd
Perkinelmer LAS (UK) Limited
Perkinelmer Limited
Perrywood Garden Centre & Nurseries
Pharmaceuticals Direct Limited
Premier Financing Limited
RL Retail Services Limited
Randstad Group UK
Randstad Sourceright Limited
Red Gate Software Limited
Regis Group (Barclays) Limited
Regis Group (Nationwide) Ltd
Regis Group (UBK) Limited
Regis Group Services Limited
Roots Hall Limited
Roselead Limited
Rothamsted Enterprises Limited
S & T Audio Limited
SLR Consulting Limited
Sandhill Homes Limited
Sanwalton Limited
Signet Group Services Limited
Signet Holdings Limited
Signet Trading Limited
SintecMedia WEM Ltd
Spirit (Faith) Limited
Spirit Group Retail Limited
Spreadex Limited
St George Healthcare Limited
TLC Group Limited
TUI Travel Group Solutions Ltd
TWI Limited
Talbot House Business Centre Ltd
Topgolf Limited
Townhold Limited
Trafalgar Leisure Ltd
George Tufts and Son Limited
Tuskerdirect Limited
Vantage Volante Limited
Vega Industries Limited
Virgin Wine Online Limited
Volkerlaser Ltd
Weir Waste Services Limited
Welney Farms Property Limited
Wood Hall Investments Limited
Woodford Holdings Limited
Worldwide Fruit Limited

2000 [160]

AB InBev UK Limited
ABM Technical Solutions Ltd
AWG Parent Co Limited
Aerospares 2000 Limited
Agricola Group Limited
Alcatel IP Networks Limited
Anglian Water Facilities Management Holdings (UK)
Anzco Foods UK Limited
Archant Holdings Limited
Archant Limited
Arena Event Services Group Ltd
Arisen Chef Ltd
Aspin Group Limited
Aspire Media Group Limited
Autolink Concessionaires (A19) Ltd
Basetek Limited
Be at One Limited
Benefit Cosmetics Limited
Bespak Holdings Limited
Bexhill UK Limited
Biffa Group Holdings (UK) Ltd
Blue 8 Technologies Limited
Bluecastle Enterprises Limited
Bourne Leisure Holdings Ltd
Bourne Leisure Limited
Bracco UK Limited
British Limbless Ex-Service Men's Association
N W Brown Group Limited
Burton's Foods (Holdings) Ltd
Butlins Skyline Limited
CNH Industrial Oldco Capital Ltd
Cambridge Centre for Sixth Form Studies
Capital Pub Co Ltd
Cardpoint Limited
Cargobull Finance Limited
Cathedral Holdings Limited
Chartridge PLC
Chelmer Housing Partnership Ltd
Cocksedge Building Contractors Ltd
Comensura Limited
Comland Holdings Limited
Connells Survey & Valuation Ltd
Consensus Support Services Ltd
Constable Homes Limited
Cosco Maritime (UK) Limited
Costco UK Holdings Limited
Cripps Developments Limited
Crown Holdings Limited
Deltech Europe Limited
Dencora 2000 Limited
Deutsche Telekom (UK) Limited
Du Pont (U.K.) Industrial Ltd
Dunward Properties Limited
E.V. Offshore Limited
Eagle 456 Limited
East Anglian Air Ambulance
Easyjet PLC
Edgewell Personal Care Holdings UK Ltd.
English Architectural Glazing Ltd
Essity Operations Manchester Ltd
Fairview Holdings Limited
Fairview New Homes (Willow Way) Ltd
Fairview New Homes Limited
First Choice Holidays Finance Ltd
Flamingo Holdings Limited
Freshlinc Limited
Gilmore Jacobs Limited
Goodmayes Properties Ltd
Greens of Soham Limited
H. G. Construction (Holdings) Ltd
Hexcel Holdings (UK) Limited
Horizon Land Limited
Howard Lewisham Limited
Inca Digital Printers Limited
Indo European Foods Limited
Ingram Micro Services Holdings Ltd
Innovative Design Systems Ltd
Interlink Direct Limited
International Flavours & Fragrances (GB) Holdings
Interquest Group (UK) Limited
Iris Insurance Brokers Limited
J J Food Service Holdings Ltd
J W D Holdings Limited
Jackson Mechanical Services (UK) Ltd
Jagex Limited
Jarvis Commercial Properties Ltd
Johnson & Johnson Innovation Ltd
Kier Commercial Investments Ltd
Kier Dormant Holdings Limited
Kudos Catering (UK) Limited
LC Bet Limited
Leisuregrow Holdings Limited
Lindsell Train Investment Trust PLC
London Fluid System Technologies Ltd
MDS Civil Engineering Limited
MacIntyre Transport Limited
MacLeans (Foils) Limited
Mapeley Columbus II Limited
Mapeley Steps Contractor Ltd
Marblelane Limited
Marriott Holdings Limited
McCormick International Holdings
Megaman (UK) Limited
Melesey Limited
Memec Group Holdings Limited
Memec Group Limited
Memec Holdings Limited
Mettler-Toledo Safeline X-Ray Ltd
Monsanto UK Limited
Mountcharm (S.E.) Limited
Murfitts Industries Limited
Network New Build Limited
Newsells Park Estates Limited
Newsells Park Stud Limited
Omniport Limited
Openarch Towerview Limited
Orbit Investment Securities Services PLC
Paddocks Care Home Ltd
Pampisford Properties Limited
Parker Hannifin (Holdings) Ltd
Personnel Holdings Limited
Pitney Bowes Global Ltd.
Premier Foods Group Services Ltd
Racing Welfare
Redeemed Christian Church of God
Regis 2000 Limited
Registration Transfers Limited
Rylston Road Limited
SCB Holdings (Sandy) Limited
Sahara Care Limited
Shelfside (Holdings) Limited

Sigma Imaging (UK) Limited
Silverwell Technology Limited
SintecMedia Global Ltd
Skanska Construction Holdings UK Ltd
Skechers USA Ltd.
Solo Cup (UK) Limited
Sopra Steria Limited
Spicerhaart Group Limited
Spirit (SGL) Limited
Storm Technologies Limited
T.S.G. Building Services PLC
Tabor Group Ltd
Telford Homes PLC
Thames Valley Air Ambulance
Thorney Bay Park Limited
Tican (Chilled) Limited
Tompsett Burgess Growers Ltd
Traditional Norfolk Poultry Ltd
Treelane Limited
Trimble UK Limited
UTM Limited
United Therapeutics Europe, Ltd.
Volkerservices Limited
Westpoint Property Limited
Whitbread PLC
Wilcox Commercial Vehicles Ltd
Willmott Dixon Interiors Ltd
Wilson Properties (London) Ltd
Ziji Productions Limited

2001 [143]

3D Systems Europe Limited
Abzena (UK) Limited
Acteon Group Limited
Adventure Forest Limited
Agria Pet Insurance Limited
Aitch Demolition Co. Ltd
Ambury Developments Limited
Amsprop Central Limited
Amsprop City Properties Ltd
Anglia Components Limited
Anglian Group (Investments) Ltd
Anglian Water Services Financing PLC
Anglian Water Services Holdings Ltd
Apatech Limited
Aprirose Trading Limited
Aquasium Technology Limited
Aquila Chelmsford Limited
Archant Community Media Holdings Ltd
Ardex Holdings UK Limited
Aspin Construction Group Ltd
Audio Network Limited
Stephen Austin (Holdings) Ltd
Baruch Investments Limited
Be Living Holdings Ltd
Beds with Ease Limited
Biffa Municipal Limited
Blue Tree Limited
Bluegnome Limited
Brent Housing Ltd
Bugler Group Limited
C.I. Industries Limited
CCW 600 Limited
CSR Limited
Carlisle Staffing Services Holdings
F & R Cawley Limited
Central Developments (UK) Ltd
Centre for Engineering and Manufacturing Excellence
Chaldean Properties Limited
Chemilines Group Holdings Ltd
Coffeeheaven International Ltd
Thomas Cook Aircraft Engineering
Countryside Properties (Bicester)
Cytocell Limited
Dencora Estates Limited
Digital Copier Systems Eastern Ltd
Dilawar Property Ltd.
Double A Group Services Ltd
Draeger Medical UK Limited
Early Learning Holdings Ltd
East Midlands Training Limited
Eastern Credit Limited
Envirowales Limited
Epoch RJK Limited
Essex County Care Limited
European Film Partners III LLP
European Independent Purchasing Co Ltd
Fairview Ventures Limited
Fiat Chrysler Automobiles Services UK
Finer Limited
Freedom Destinations Limited
GW Pharmaceuticals PLC
Global Metcorp Limited
Go Interiors Limited
Gredley House Investments Ltd
Grosvenor Park (Harris & Trotter) 2002 Film LLP
Grosvenor Park 2002 Film LLP
Guild of Construction Workers Ltd
Gyron Internet Limited
Harringtons Builders PLC
Hawk Incentives Limited
Heley Holdings Limited
Hill Holdings Limited
Hill Residential Limited
Howard Stansted Limited
ITAB Holdings UK Ltd
Inexus Group (Holdings) Ltd
Ipswich Town Finance Co Ltd
Ipswich Town Stadium Co Ltd
Itron Metering Solutions UK Ltd
JBS Global (UK) Limited
Jarvis Group Limited
Keystone Developments (LG) Ltd
Kier Integrated Services (Holdings)
Kier Partnership Homes Limited
Kimberley Property Investments Ltd
Ashley King (Developments) Ltd
Kingsway Hall Hotel Limited
Korda Developments Limited
Leda Investments Limited
London Inn Hotels (Stratford) Ltd
Lumesse Corporate Limited
Manor Crest Construction Ltd
Maritime Group Limited
Martlane Limited
Masterson Holdings Limited
McLaren Construction (UK) Ltd
Monarock Limited
Monument Group Limited
Movac Holdings Limited
MoveWithUs Conveyancing Ltd
Mytravel North America Limited
NVSM Limited
Newmarston Ltd
Noahs Ark Chemicals Limited
Optimise Media Group Limited
Paytemp Limited
Permastore Group Limited
Place UK Limited
Quixant PLC
Radia Estates Limited
S A Designer Parfums Limited
SME Holdings Limited
Sansbury Bailey Holdings Ltd
Sequence (UK) Limited
Skewbald Limited
Smartcomms SC Limited
Snap-On Equipment Limited
Sopra Steria Holdings Limited
Southern Cement Ltd
Spirit Group Equity Limited
Spirit Managed Holdings Ltd
Spirit Pub Company (Supply) Ltd
Spring Petroleum Co Ltd
St Columba's College and Preparatory School
Stane Park Ltd.
Subex (UK) Limited
Subway Realty Limited
Tesco Freetime Limited
Tetra Pak Processing UK Ltd
Thames Industrial Estate Ltd
Triangle Regional Aircraft Leasing
Unique Forwarding Limited
University of Essex Knowledge Gateway Holdings
Victoria Docks Hotel Co Ltd
Volkerrail Specialist Businesses Ltd
Wallace Estates Limited
Wellmode Limited
Weston Group PLC
Wilcox Holdings Limited
Wimpey Overseas Holdings Ltd
Wisbech Grammar School
Woods Holdings Limited
York Apartments Limited

2002 [142]

A.C. Lighting (Holdings) Ltd
ADR Care Homes Limited
AWG Land Holdings Limited
Accord Healthcare Limited
Aim Academies Trust
Angel Property Investments Ltd
Apertio Limited
Aquila EHS Limited
Aquila Estates Limited
Ardex Investments UK Limited
Aston Barclay Holdings Limited
Astrazeneca US Investments Ltd
Atalian Servest Security Ltd
Stephen Austin & Sons Limited
Ball Company
Ball Europe Limited
Ball UK Holdings, Ltd
Belchim Crop Protection Ltd
Velji Bhovan & Sons (Trading) Ltd
Biffa Leicester Limited
Bio Products Laboratory Holdings Ltd
Breheny Group Limited
CLFIS (U.K.) Limited
Cambridge Medipark Limited
Cambridge University Press (Holdings)
Canada Life Finance (U.K.) Ltd
Caretech Holdings PLC
Charles River Discovery Research Services UK
City & Country Group PLC
Cokenach Limited
Countryside Four Limited
Countrywide Developments (UK) PLC
Crystal Home Improvements Group Ltd
Cyanconnode Holdings PLC
Dallas Burston Ashbourne Holdings

Desira Holdings PLC
Dhamecha Group Limited
Diamond Corporation Limited
Digica Group Finance Limited
Du Pont (U.K.) Limited
Electrolux Investments
Enterprise Finance Limited
Everest Limited
Fairview New Homes (Properties) Ltd
First Wave Housing Limited
Gardline Limited
Gentian Partnerships Limited
Global Marine Holdings Limited
Global Medics Limited
Gracechurch Sports Management Ltd
Greenyard Frozen UK Limited
Gunpowder Mill Developments Ltd
Hexcel Europe Limited
Hills Group Enterprises Ltd
Indesit Company UK Holdings Ltd
Inhealth Group Limited
Interiors with Art Limited
Intermay Management Ltd
Intertek Holdings Limited
Invicta Film Partnership No.10, LLP
Invicta Film Partnership No.11, LLP
Invicta Film Partnership No.12, LLP
Invicta Film Partnership No.13, LLP
Invicta Film Partnership No.14, LLP
Invicta Film Partnership No.15, LLP
Invicta Film Partnership No.8, LLP
Invicta Film Partnership No.9, LLP
J C A Engineering Ltd
K & R Projects Co Ltd
Kelly Rail U.K. Ltd
Kidde Products Limited
Kier Developments Limited
Kier Property Limited
Kingsley Care Homes Limited
Koei Tecmo Europe Limited
Kwik-Fit Finance Limited
Kwik-Fit Group Limited
L & L Inc Limited
LRW Engineering Limited
Laen Limited
Laridge Investments Limited
Long Term Reversions No 1 Ltd
MM (UK) Limited
Media 10 Limited
Morrison Data Services (Water) Ltd
Morrison Utility Services Ltd
Mossbourne Federation
Mundipharma Research Limited
Murkett Brothers (Holdings) Ltd
Mytravel Pioneer Limited
New Demipower Limited
Newport School Solutions Ltd
O'Neill Investments Limited
Olivegate Properties Limited
Optimise Media (UK) Limited
Origin Frames Limited
P & O Ferrymasters Holdings Ltd
PCL Transport Limited
Paypoint Retail Solutions Ltd
Perkinelmer Life Sciences International Holdings
Pioneering Foods Group Limited
Plastique Holdings Limited
Plaza Investments Limited
Plumbcity Limited
Premier Foods Investments Ltd
Price Bailey Group Limited
Rainham Industrial Services Ltd
Rannoch Food Group Limited
RealVNC Limited
Realpubs Limited
Rivers Finance Group PLC
Rose Group Limited
S N B Holdings Limited
Sapphire Food North East No.1 Ltd
Sapphire Food North West No. 3 Ltd
Sapphire Food South East No.4 Ltd
Sapphire Food South West No. 2 Ltd
Sapphire Rural Destination No. 5 Ltd
Sepura PLC
Sherrygold No.1 Limited
Silverbridge Properties Ltd
Skanska Infrastructure Investment UK
Soul Foods Limited
P J Southgate Limited
St Albans School
St James Media LLP
Stonemanor Limited
Synthomer Holdings Limited
TSI Instruments Ltd
Teledyne E2V Limited
Telensa Ltd
Temple Fields 514 Limited
Tendring Farms Limited
Tompsett Holdings Limited
Tradewise Insurance Services Ltd
Transeur Properties Limited
Transporter Engineering Ltd
Trinity (D) Limited
Ubisense Limited
United Learning Trust
VMS (Fleet Management) Limited
Yparho Investments Limited

2003 [153]

1spatial Group Limited
Abbey Total Care Group Limited
Action for Children
Alchemie GRP Limited
Alderforce Limited
Anderson Design & Build Ltd
The John Apthorp Charity
Arinso People Services Limited
Asiatic Carpets Holdings Ltd
Astrazeneca Sweden Investments Ltd
Aurora Distribution Limited
Baik Agency Limited
Bayard Metering (UK)
Be Living Limited
L Bennett & Son Holdings Ltd
Beta Pharmaceuticals Limited
Biffa GS UK Holdings Limited
A D Bly Construction Limited
Bow Village Limited
Brayleys Cars Limited
Business Control Solutions PLC
CMS Developments Limited
Capital Cash Limited
R.G. Carter Farms Limited
Chocolate Tasting Club PLC
City Link (Cardiff) Holdings Ltd
Cloverton Property Ltd
Corbus Europe Limited
Countryside Properties (Uberior) Ltd
Countrywide Group PLC
County Care Homes Limited
Coveris Flexibles (Gainsborough) UK
Coward Asset Limited
Crystal Home Improvements Holdings
DSJ Homes Limited
Defender No.1 Production Limited Liability Partnership
Defender No.1 Sale & Leaseback Limited Liability Partnership
Defender No.2 Production Limited Liability Partnership
Defender No.2 Sale & Leaseback Limited Liability Partnership
Displaylink (UK) Limited
Dispute Service Limited
Donatantonio Limited
Dyer & Butler Holdings Limited
EVI Technologies Limited
Edgewell Personal Care Investments UK Ltd.
Elektron Technology UK Limited
Element Energy Limited
Elliot Leigh Property Investments 2 Ltd
Empress Garland Limited
Exlservice (UK) Limited
Express Vending Group Limited
Finance Store Limited
Fineraid Limited
Ford International Liquidity Management
Fortem Solutions Limited
Gala Film Partners, LLP
Gentian (Newcastle) Limited
Global Education Management Systems
Golf Entertainment International Ltd
Greenshoots Limited
Grosvenor Park 2004 Film Partnership No.1 LLP
Guarding UK Ltd
Hayes Point (Sully) Limited
Hazlemere Holdings Limited
Henfield Hire Limited
Heritage Developments Limited
Highassets Limited
Hill Co Ltd
Hospital Company (Oxford John Radcliffe) Holdings
Hospital Company (Oxford John Radcliffe)
Hotels4U.Com Limited
Hutchinson Group Limited
Hydraquip Hose & Hydraulics Ltd
Independent Power Networks Ltd
Intertek Nominees Limited
Invicta Film Partnership No. 17, LLP
Islam Channel Limited
Isuzu Truck (UK) Limited
J & J Restaurants Limited
JRL Plant and Logistics Ltd
Jackson Civils Limited
K.E.M. Property Services Ltd
Kara Management Ltd
Karsten UK Limited
Katrin Properties Limited
Kelly Property Co Ltd
Kershaw Group Limited
Kier Parkman Servigroup Ltd
Kimbolton School
Kingspan Timber Solutions Ltd
Lawsons Holdings Limited
Lipman Properties Limited
Lituanica UK Ltd
London Pharma & Chemicals Group Ltd
London Tower Crane Hire & Sales Ltd
Longford Securities & Equities (K & T)
M.P.I. (Herts) Limited
Macquarie Corona Energy Holdings Ltd
Manpower Holdings Limited
Martin Audio Limited

Maybury Media LLP
Mayday Healthcare PLC
Megnum Limited
Morley Agricultural Foundation
Motherwell Holdings Limited
Newport School Solutions (Holdings)
Norfolk Broads Holdings Ltd
Norfolk Free Range Limited
Olive Business Solutions Ltd
Ordan UK Limited
PIL Membranes Limited
Parker Hannifin Manufacturing Ltd
Parkes LLP
Popsoda Limited
Potter & Moore Innovations Ltd
Power on Connections Ltd
Property Warehouse Limited
Quickdrop Limited
RES UK & Ireland Limited
RMPA Holdings Limited
RMPA Services PLC
Regal Healthcare Properties Ltd
Renewable Energy Systems Holdings
Safestore Acquisition Limited
Safestore Group Limited
Safestore Holdings PLC
Saxton 4x4 Limited
Seymour House Residential Care Homes
Sherfield School Limited
Signature Flight Support Ltd
Silk Industries Limited
Sines Parks Ltd
Spen Hill Developments Limited
Spirit Group Holdings Limited
Spirit Group Parent Limited
Stantec Treatment Group Ltd
Stebbings Car Centre Limited
Streamadvice Limited
TUI Travel Overseas Holdings Ltd
Tesco Mobile Limited
Tesco Mobile Services Limited
Tesco Property Partner (No.1) Ltd
Tilia Trading Group Limited
Treebond Limited
Tristel PLC
UK Livelines Limited
V.B. Investments Limited
Volkerrail Group Limited
WPA Support Services Limited
Walters Holdings Limited
Warrant Properties Limited
Wind Farm Holdings Limited
Workout Limited

2004 [158]

3VS UK Limited
AK Retail Holdings Limited
Adil Property Investment Ltd
Aesica Pharmaceuticals Limited
Aesthetic Medical Corporation Ltd
Affinity Water Finance (2004) PLC
Against Malaria Foundation
Agellus Hotels Limited
Al Jazeera International Ltd
Amino Technologies PLC
Applepeach Limited
Autoprotect (MBI) Ltd
BHW Automotive Limited
Barconn Group Limited
Betting Shop Services Limited
Blancco Technology Group PLC
Buckingham Hotels Group Ltd
CP Regents Park Two Limited
Care UK (Urgent Care) Limited
Caterpillar Overseas Limited
Celador Radio Broadcasting Ltd
Cheale Group Limited
Chelsea Stores Holdings Ltd
Citygate Developments 2005 Ltd
Kathleen and Michael Connolly Foundation (UK)
Copthorn Holdings Limited
Crossco (820) Limited
DDD Investments Limited
DMC Contracts Limited
Daarasp LLP
Thomas Deacon Education Trust
Dencora Dereham Retail Partnership LLP
Derby School Solutions (Holdings)
Derby School Solutions Limited
Eisai Europe Limited
Elysium Healthcare (Farndon) Ltd
Elysium Healthcare (St Mary's) Ltd
Fardaar LLP
Foreign Currency Direct PLC
Fraser Capital Management Ltd
GE Money Home Lending Holdings Ltd
Glenmark Pharmaceuticals Europe Ltd
Good Harvest Properties (Southwark)
Goodwill SIP Limited
Gozzett Holdings Limited
Greene King Neighbourhood Estate Pubs
Greene King Retailing Limited
Greene King Retailing Parent Ltd
Gresham's School
Grosvenor Park 2005 Film Partnership No.1 LLP
Grosvenor Park 2005 S42 Film LLP
Ground Control Holdings Ltd
H & D Support Services (Holdings)
H & D Support Services Limited
HCL Insurance BPO Services Ltd
Halma Financing Limited
Halma Investment Holdings Ltd
Hayter Holdings Limited
Hayter Limited
Hindu Education Authority Ltd
I Go 4 Ltd.
Independent Meters Limited
Inhealth Limited
Inhealth Properties Limited
Injured Jockeys Fund
Invesco Capita Holdings Ltd
Invicta Film Partnership No.20, LLP
Invicta Film Partnership No.22, LLP
Invicta Film Partnership No.23, LLP
Invicta Film Partnership No.25, LLP
Invicta Film Partnership No.26, LLP
Invicta Film Partnership No.27, LLP
J E Investments Limited
J P & S Servicess Ltd
Jewish Community Secondary School Trust
K K Investment Ltd
Kestrel Acquisitions Limited
Kestrel Holdings Limited
Keswick Enterprises Group Ltd
Kingsgate Community Church
Linkhaven Estates Ltd
Lupo Limited
MRB Holdings Ltd
Make Believe Ideas Ltd
Masterlord Estates Limited
Medway Fundco Limited
Motocaddy Limited
Motor Fuel Limited
NHS Shared Business Services Ltd
Natural Balance Foods Limited
Net Pay (EUR) Limited
Newell Properties Developments Ltd
Norfolk Community Foundation
Northfield Avenue (Holdings) Ltd
Oakeve Limited
Omniport Norwich Limited
Openview Group Limited
Original Bowling Co Ltd
PPG Kansai Automotive Finishes UK LLP
Parametric Investments Limited
Parkway Hellas Holdings Ltd
Peppercorn Investments Limited
Pero Investments Limited
Pico Technology (Holdings) Ltd
Prefect Software LLP
Premier Foods Investments No.1 Ltd
Premier Foods PLC
Premier Inn Hotels Limited
Price Bailey LLP
Quest Motor Group Limited
RO Properties Limited
RO Trading Limited
RWF Health and Community Developers (Tranche 1)
Racal Acoustics Limited
Rapleys Limited Liability Partnership
Red Tree (2004) LLP
Refined Holdings Limited
Retreat East Limited
Retro Properties Limited
Rowe Farming Limited
SIP Group Limited
SLR Holdings Limited
Scira Offshore Energy Limited
Sema Lease UK Limited
Special New Fruit Licensing Ltd
Spirit Managed Funding Limited
Spirit Pub Company (Managed) Ltd
Spirit Pub Company (Services) Ltd
Spirit Pubs Debenture Holdings Ltd
Stockplace Investments Limited
Strides Arcolab International Ltd
Suez Water Technologies & Solutions Services UK
Sunray Estates Limited
Swan New Homes Limited
Swift 1st Limited
TBS G.B. Telematic & Biomedical Services
THR Number 5 Limited
Tallington Holdings Limited
Tapesilver Limited
Tasmar Limited
Taylor Made Holdings UK Ltd
Telegenic Holdings Limited
Telephonetics Limited
Thorlabs Limited
Thule Holding Limited
Thurlow Nunn Standen Limited
Tilsworth Developments Limited
Toppesfield Limited
Travel Choice Limited
UK Salads Limited
UNEX Group Holdings Limited
United Healthcare Land Co Ltd
University of Suffolk Ltd
Vanderbilt Homes Limited
Victory Housing Trust
Visiongroup (GB) Limited
Wintertime Properties Limited

Wryde Croft Wind Farm Limited

2005 [165]

1spatial PLC
ARJ Construction Limited
ARM UK Holdings Limited
AVL Powertrain UK Limited
Abbey Ravenscroft Park Limited
Access Technology Group Ltd
Acco Brands Europe Limited
Aquaterra Energy Limited
Aquinna Homes PLC
Architectural Glazing Limited
Arcofina LLP
Austin (GB) Limited
Avnet Holdings UK Limited
BAM Monk Bridge Limited
BPH Finance Number 1 Limited
BUUK Infrastructure Limited
Baby Network Limited
Bango PLC
Belgrave Land (Perth) Limited
Belsize Garages Project Ltd
Betex LLP
Biffa Corporate Holdings Ltd
Bourn Bioscience Limited
Britvic PLC
Broadham Care Limited
Buffaload Logistics Limited
CTV Outside Broadcasts Limited
Calpri Ltd
Car World (Cambs) Ltd
Carmelite House (Jarrold) Ltd
Cashflows Europe Limited
Caterpillar Logistics (UK) Ltd
Caterpillar UK Engines Co Ltd
Caterpillar UK Group Limited
Caversham Trading Limited
Central Lending Funding Number One
Chard Properties (UK) Limited
M & J Charters LLP
Citygate Automotive Limited
Citygate Holdings Limited
Connect Utilities Limited
Countryside Properties (Holdings)
Creative Car Park Ltd
Crystal Group Limited
Cygnet Care Limited
DCK Group Limited
Defaqto Group Limited
Dernford Holdings Limited
Diligenta Limited
Doctors on Call Limited
Electricity Network Co Ltd
Elysium Healthcare Property 2 Ltd
Elysium Healthcare Property 3 Ltd
Essex & Herts Air Ambulance Trust
Essex Motor Co Ltd
Fishnet Properties Limited
Fishpools Holdings Limited
Foremost Currency Group Ltd
Fortis Property Investment LLP
Fristling Hall Farm Limited
G's Fresh Limited
Gentian Investments Limited
Greene King Acquisitions No.2 Ltd
Grosvenor Park 2006 S48 Film LLP
Grosvenor Park 2007 S48 Film LLP
Hadleigh Holdings Limited
Healthcare (Barts) Limited
Healthcare Homes Group Limited
Hexagon Investment Holdings Ltd
Horizon Discovery Limited
Hospital Company (QAH Portsmouth) Holdings
Hospital Company (QAH Portsmouth)
Howard Investment Co Ltd
John F Hunt Power Limited
Hyundai Motor UK Limited
IQGeo Group PLC
Inexus Connections Limited
Inhealth Group Holdings PLC
Inland Homes PLC
Inland Limited
John Innes Foundation
Invicta Film Partnership No.34, LLP
Invicta Film Partnership No.37, LLP
Jarrold (St. James) 3 SJC Ltd
Leonard F Jollye (Holdings) Ltd
KFG Quickserve Limited
Kent Leisure Parks Limited
Kier Highways Limited
Killiney UK Limited
Life Build Solutions Ltd
Lint (Redington Road) Limited
Lint Group Limited
Richard Long Group Limited
Lumesse Holdings UK Limited
M-Ship Limited
MY Construction & Carpentry Ltd
Manor Fresh Limited
Marchase Limited
Marlborough Information Services Ltd
Marz Limited
Mastercard Prepaid Management Services
Martin McColl Retail Limited
McGrath Bros. (Environmental) Ltd.
McLaren Construction Limited
Millharbour Developments Ltd
Mothers Ltd
Motorclean Group Limited
Motus Holdings (UK) Limited
Mumford's Mill Rentals Limited
Munnelly Group PLC
NWES Property Services Limited
New Hall School Trust
Nexus Infrastructure PLC
O'Malley Haulage Limited
OYO Developments Limited
Oakman Inns and Restaurants Ltd
Open Fibre Networks Limited
PXP Financial Limited
Painesend Farm LLP
Patek Philippe Salon Limited
Pilgrim Foodservice Limited
Pinnacle Schools (Gateshead) Ltd
Policyfast Limited
Produce Investments Limited
Property Recycling Group PLC
QED (Slough) Limited
RG Reversions 2014 Limited
RHM Group Holding Limited
RRD GDS Limited
Ragleth Limited
Rapidrop Global Limited
Reach Active Group Limited
Rexam Group Holdings Limited
SCCS Survey Equipment Limited
SME Investments Limited
SME Properties Limited
Safestore Limited
Satco Plastics Limited
Seckford Foundation
Selborne Care Limited
Select Enterprises Limited
Signature Senior Lifestyle Finance
SintecMedia LON Ltd
Southbank UK Limited
Speedy 1 Limited
Spence Refit Ltd
Stace LLP
Stanton Holding Limited
Starglade Parks Limited
Station Road Developments (Cambridge)
Stonebond Properties Limited
Strauss Logistics Limited
Suffolk Community Foundation
Sunrose Property Limited
Taliesin Management Limited
Temple Fields 522 Limited
Thurlow Nunn Limited
Trinity View Homes Limited
Turners (East Anglia) Limited
UNEX Limited
Vale of Aylesbury Housing Trust Ltd
Wood Green Investments Limited
Woodland Group Limited
Youngman Group Limited
Ziegler UK Limited

2006 [192]

A-Roads Investments Limited
AMS Care Limited
ASCO (DC2) Limited
ASCO (DC3) Limited
ASCO (DC4) Limited
ASG2 Limited
Ace Investments Limited
Adventure Forest Group Limited
Akira Financial Limited
Amsair Aircraft Limited
Amsprop Bishopsgate Limited
Amsprop Portland Limited
Anritsu EMEA Limited
Arcese Real Estate UK Limited
Atlantic Healthcare PLC
Aura Holdings (Newcastle) Ltd
B.A.T.S. Ilford Limited
BAM Glory Mill Limited
BPC Interiors Limited
Baker Perkins Limited
The C. Alma Baker Trust
Barstone Limited
Be Living Group Limited
Birketts LLP
Blackhawk Network (UK) Ltd.
Blenheim Consultancy Services Ltd
Brogan Group Ltd
Bullen Properties Limited
Cambridge Education Group Ltd
Cantab Capital Partners LLP
Career Teachers Limited
Carestream Health UK, Limited
Caretech Estates Limited
Carlson Wagonlit New Holdco Ltd
R. G. Carter Holdings Limited
Catco Kids LLP
Chigwell School
Chiltern Distribution Ltd
Contact Technologies UK Ltd
Contechs Holdings Limited
Countryside Annington (Mill Hill)
Countryside Properties (Joint Ventures)
Countryside Properties (Springhead)
Countryside Sigma Limited
DFKA Intermediate Limited

Days of Your Life Limited
Doncaster School Solutions (Holdings)
Doncaster School Solutions Ltd
Eastleaf Ltd
Education Management Corporation Ltd
Elastomer Trading Limited
Electro-Motive Diesel Limited
Elysium Healthcare (Lighthouse) Ltd
Elysium Healthcare (Ultimate Care)
Explorer Holdings UK Limited
FFEI Holdings Limited
Fluorocarbon Group Limited
Flynn Pharma (Holdings) Ltd
GHG 11 (Mount Alvernia Hospital) Ltd
GHG 12 (Hampshire Clinic) Ltd
GHG 13 (Chaucer Hospital) Ltd
GHG 14 (Shirley Oaks Hospital) Ltd
GHG 15 (Highfield Hospital) Ltd
GHG 16 (Chelsfield Park Hospital)
GHG 17 (Ridgeway Hospital) Ltd
GHG 18 (Saxon Clinic) Limited
GHG 19 (Albyn Hospital) Ltd
GHG 2 (Clementine Churchill Hospital)
GHG 20 (Sarum Road Hospital) Ltd
GHG 22 (Garden Hospital) Ltd
GHG 24 (Sloane Hospital) Ltd
GHG 25 (Werndale Hospital) Ltd
GHG 26 (Beardwood Hospital) Ltd
GHG 28 (Manor Hospital) Ltd
GHG 3 (Ross Hall Hospital) Ltd
GHG 31 (Blackheath Hospital) Ltd
GHG 32 (Goring Hall Hospital) Ltd
GHG 33 (Beaumont Hospital) Ltd
GHG 34 (Priory Hospital) Ltd
GHG 35 (Droitwich Spa Hospital) Ltd
GHG 36 (Winterbourne Hospital) Ltd
GHG 37 (Alexandra Hospital) Ltd
GHG 4 (Princess Margaret Hospital)
GHG 5 (London Independent Hospital)
GHG 6 (Thornbury Hospital) Ltd
GHG 7 (Chiltern Hospital) Ltd
GHG 8 (Park Hospital) Limited
GHG 9 (Bath Clinic) Limited
GPL Investments Limited
Gateway Learning Community
Global Group (UK) Ltd
Go Homes Ltd
Grantol Investments Limited
Green Energy Options Ltd
Hamelin Brands Limited
Hatfield Trading Limited
Hilton HHC Limited
Hoddesdon Developments Ltd
Holmes Care (Group) Limited
Hoole Hall Country Club Ltd
Howard Ventures Limited
John F Hunt Group Ltd
ITAB Shop Products UK Ltd
JDM Technology Group Limited
Jarrold (St. James) D1/D2 Ltd
Jarrold (St. James) Limited
Kampa UK Ltd
Keelings Fresh International Ltd
Kier Finance & Treasury Holdings Ltd
Kier Finance Limited
Kier Holdings Limited
Kilmorie Investments LLP
Knight Noise Limited
Kwik-Fit (NL) Limited
Land Group (Suffolk) Limited
Landex Limited
Lay & Wheeler Limited
Leena Plaza Limited
Local Car and Van Rental Ltd
MM Flowers Limited
Malt U.K. Holdco Limited
Manor Crest Homes Limited
Matrix Networks Limited
McCann Family LLP
Metropolitan Infrastructure Ltd
Micross Components Holdings Ltd
Midgard Ltd
Monitor Audio Limited
Morrisroe Group Limited
Moto Holdings Limited
Moto Investments Limited
Moto Ventures Limited
Newstraid Benevolent Fund
Norse Group Limited
O-I Sales and Distribution UK Ltd
OBM Properties Limited
Osprey Acquisitions Limited
Osprey Holdco Limited
Oyster Properties Limited
P G S International Limited
Perse School
Practice (Group) Limited
Quadro Epsom Limited
R Group Holdings Limited
RBR Property Investments Ltd
RP2 Holdings Limited
Rakon UK Holdings Limited
Ramon Holdings Limited
Reids of Norwich Limited
Residential Land Holdings Ltd
Respivert Ltd.
Rex Partners LLP
Jack Richards Holdings Ltd
Ridgepoint Homes Limited
Rooff Property LLP
Roselead (Wattisham) Limited
Rusant Limited
SJR Farming Limited
Safestore Investments Limited
Sanctuary Personnel Limited
Shared Learning Trust
Sherrygreen Homes Ltd
Skanska Project Developments Ltd
Southgate Packaging Limited
Sovereign Recovery (UK) Ltd
Spirit Pub Company (Leased) Ltd
Spirit Pub Company (Trent) Ltd
Sumatra Copper & Gold PLC
TGA Industries Limited
TPH (UK) Limited
Targetfollow Group Limited
Tesco Blue (GP) Limited
Tesco Maintenance Limited
Tesco Property Finance 1 PLC
Tesco Property Holdings (No.2) Ltd
Test Equipment Asset Management Ltd
Thames Reinforcements Limited
Top 100 Limited
Total Produce Holdings (UK) Ltd
Total Produce Limited
Toureen Group Limited
Tower Crane Asset Management Holdings
Union Maritime Limited
VGC Group Limited
VNC Group Limited
Victoria Docks Hotel Company (Number Two)
Videojet Technologies Limited
T. Visaman & Sons Limited
Water Incorporated
Whitehall Resources Limited
Willmott Dixon Public & Commercial
Windsor Integrated Services Group

2007 [180]

ASL Technology Holdings Ltd.
ATB Group UK Limited
Acteon Middle East and Far East Investments
Acteon US Financing Limited
Acteon US Holdings Limited
Aesica Queenborough Limited
Alboro Holdings Limited
Anglian Venture Holdings Ltd
Aquila BTE 1 Limited
Aspect Contracts Limited
Astrazeneca Intermediate Holdings
Atalian Servest Limited
Aura (Newcastle) Holding Co Ltd
Aura (Newcastle) Project Co Ltd
Avocado Developments Limited
Away Resorts Limited
BW Foundation
Barley Pub Co Ltd
Bay Restaurant Group Limited
Beechfield Estates Limited
Biffa Group Limited
F. Brazil Reinforcements Ltd
Brighthouse Group Limited
Brighthouse Holdings Limited
Brighthouse Limited
CATS Canterbury Limited
CEG Administrative Services Ltd
CKH Developments Limited
CVS Group PLC
Caring Homes Healthcare Group Ltd
Chalcroft Holdings Limited
Clarucci Industry Limited
Comland Group Limited
Thomas Cook Finance PLC
Thomas Cook Investments (2) Ltd
Countryside 26 Limited
Countryside 28 Limited
Coventry Foundationcampus Ltd
Creo Pharma Limited
DCI Group Limited
Derbyshire Hotel Derby Limited
Derrick Services (UK) Limited
Donatantonio Group Limited
Eisai Manufacturing Limited
Elliott Group Holdings (UK) Ltd
Elysium Healthcare No. 2 Ltd
Essex Group Holdings Limited
Exagris Limited
Finecare Homes (Stevenage) Ltd
Flamingo Plants Group Ltd
Franke Coffee Systems UK Ltd
Fujitsu General Air Conditioning (UK)
GK Foods (UK) Limited
Garnham Management Services Ltd
Global Marine Systems (Vessels) Ltd
Gray's Inn 10 Limited
Green Space London Limited
HLT Stakis Operator Limited
Haas 2007 Limited
Hallmark Care Homes Group Holdings
Hardwicke Investments Limited
Hemel Snowcentre Limited
Heptares Therapeutics Limited
Hilands Property Partners LLP
Hilton Food Group PLC
Hilton UK Manage Limited

Hops Pub Co Ltd
Hubbard Products Limited
John Huntingdon's Charity
I S & G (Holdings) Limited
Inhealth Molecular Imaging Ltd
Insignia Investments Limited
Interguide Group Limited
Into UEA LLP
Intralot Finance UK Limited
Itron Development UK Ltd
Jackson Frameworks Limited
Jark Industrial Limited
Jollyes Group Limited
K L Technologies Limited
K.M. Packaging Holdings Ltd
KFG Restaurants Limited
KH Finance Limited
KH Holdco Limited
Kerneos Holding Northern Europe Ltd
Kier Stoke Limited
Klyne Air Limited
Kotecha Ltd
Leisure Parks Real Estate Ltd
Les Residence Falcon Wharf Ltd
Liebherr-Rental Limited
David Lloyd Leisure Group Ltd
David Lloyd Leisure Properties No.1
London Care Partnership Ltd
MC Treasury Limited
MCF Commercial Limited
MRH (GB) Limited
MSXI UK Limited
MTK Wireless Limited
Manichem Limited
Marshall of Stevenage Limited
Metis Homes Limited
Mountfield Group PLC
NIS Acquisitions Limited
NIS Receivables No. 2 Limited
Narada Europe (UK) Ltd
Nationwide Metal Recycling Ltd
Network Homes Investments (Stockwell)
Network Homes Investments Ltd
Network Treasury Services Ltd
Anthony Nicholas (UK) Limited
Northgate Information Solutions Ltd
Novum Holdings UK Limited
Novum Structures UK Limited
Origin Holdings (UK) Limited
PQW Brenley Corner Limited
Parker Hannifin 2007 LLP
Parker Hannifin Industries Ltd
Pheasant Eye Limited
Pinnacle Foods Limited
Plotplan Limited
Precon Products Ltd
Premier 1983 Limited
Pro Cam Europe Limited
Pure Recycling Warwick Limited
Quanticate Limited
Quartix Holdings PLC
Ransome's Trading Limited
Readle Construction Limited
Realpubs II Limited
Resolute Corporate Holdings Ltd
Rex Trade Associates Limited
Rex Venture Resources Limited
Rexam Finance Germany Limited
Rexam Finance Netherlands Ltd
Rexam Finance Poland Limited
Rexam Finance Sweden Limited
Right Choice Insurance Brokers Ltd
Riverstone Europe LLP
Rose Film Partnership LLP
SJD Accountancy Limited
SRM (Redcar & Cleveland) Ltd
Sandbrook Overseas Investments Ltd
Sandfields Farms Limited
Santray Limited
Saxonchart Limited
Scientific Digital Imaging PLC
Seajacks UK Limited
Selecta Holding Limited
George A. Sherriff Limited
Sines Parks (S.E.) Limited
Slug and Lettuce Co Ltd
Snowcentres Limited
Soda Studios Limited
Specialist Cars Holdings Ltd
Specialist Cars Property (Stevenage)
Spen Hill Regeneration Limited
Splendid Hospitality Group LLP
Ssangyong Motor UK Limited
Stanley Tee LLP
Starbones Limited
Stephen Perse Foundation
Stock Spirits (UK) Limited
Sunlight PV Ltd
Swan Commercial Services Ltd
TJM (London) LLP
TRB Technology Group Limited
TUI Travel Limited
Targetfollow (Development) Ltd
Taylor Wimpey 2007 Limited
Teaching Personnel Holdings Ltd
Tican (UK) Holdings Limited
Town and City Pub Group Ltd
Transmec Properties Limited
UH Holdings Limited
UME PFI Investments Holding Ltd
Vinci Environment UK Limited
Vinepost Limited
Visteon Engineering Services Ltd
Ward Farming Limited

2008 [132]

A P P Wholesale PLC
API Microwave Limited
Abbotsley Farms Limited
Acteon Group Properties Ltd
Amazon Acquisitions Limited
Arcus FM Limited
Bakkavor Central Finance Ltd
Bakkavor Estates Limited
Bakkavor Finance Limited
Basetek (Holdings) Limited
Bauer Golden Square Limited
Belgrave Land (Sheffield) Ltd
Book Trade Charity (BTBS)
Bowes Farms Limited
Peter Brett Associates LLP
Breyer Holdings Limited
Cadena AM Limited
Camvac Limited
Canna (B) Investors LLP
Caretech Estates (No 2) Ltd
Caretech Estates (No 3) Ltd
Caretech Estates (No.4) Ltd
Central G H Trust
Chargemaster Limited
Chemtest Holdings Limited
Chemtest Limited
Church of Pentecost - UK
Connect Plus (M25) Holdings Ltd
Connect Plus (M25) Intermediate Ltd
Connect Plus (M25) Limited
Thomas Cook Continental Holdings
Thomas Cook Group Treasury Ltd
Costa Express Holdings Limited
Countryside Zest (Beaulieu Park) LLP
Crane Investments Ltd
Devantier Group Limited
Dhamecha Holdings Limited
Dhamecha Property Limited
Diaverum Facilities Management Ltd
RR Donnelley UK Limited
Ebberod Capital Ltd
Erindale Limited
Essex Cares Limited
Excelredstone Services Limited
Falck UK Limited
Falcon Tower Crane Services Ltd
Fitzwilliam Information Services Trust
Freshlinc Group Limited
Fullfield Limited
GPS Food Group (UK) Limited
Garden City (Scotfield) LLP
Glenageary Estates LLP
Halma Overseas Funding Limited
Healthcare Homes Holdings Ltd
Hewitsons LLP
Holdcare Limited
ILB Investments Limited
Impellam Group PLC
Inland Finance Ltd
Investland Limited
JRL Group Limited
Jackson Civil Engineering Group Ltd
Jelmac (Primary Care) Properties Ltd
Jelmac Properties
KFM Holdings Limited
Kelling Estate LLP
Kier (NR) Limited
Nicholas King Developments PLC
Klyne Aviation Limited
Lanber Nursing Homes LLP
Lanber Properties LLP
David Lloyd Leisure Operations Holdings
David Lloyd Leisure Properties No.2
David Lloyd Leisure Properties No.3
David Lloyd Leisure Properties No.4
Local Generation Limited
Masteroast Holdings Limited
Metro Partners LLP
Morrison Utility Services Holdings
Morrison Utility Services Investments
Mowbray Indigo Limited
NHS Professionals Limited
NIS Receivables No.1 Limited
NPS (UK2) Limited
Naked Wines Prepayments Trustee Co Ltd
National Adhesives Holding Ltd.
Offsite Archive Storage and Integrated Services (UK)
Optima Investments Limited
Orchard Funding Limited
P2P Mailing Ltd
Portcrest Limited
Power On Investments Limited
Practice Surgeries Limited
RJM Metal Consultancy Limited
Rangemist Limited
Raspberry Pi Foundation
Reald Europe Limited
Regis Group (Holdings) Limited
Reliance Infra Projects (UK) Ltd

Robinson Young Holdings Ltd
Roythornes Limited
SD Underwriting Limited
SEH Group Limited
SLR Management Limited
Science Group PLC
Seasons Hotels Limited
Seneca Environmental Solutions Ltd
Sinek Global Finance & Trading LLP
Smiths Interconnect Group Ltd
Specialist Cars Tring Limited
Spicerhaart Corporate Sales Ltd
Stable Lads Welfare Trust Housing Association
Stockvale Investments Limited
T F S Loans Limited
TUI Travel Holdings Limited
Tetworth Farms LLP
Trevester Limited
Union Investcorp Limited
Union of Evangelical Churches
Valens Resources Group PLC
Valiant Holdings Limited
Walstead United Kingdom Ltd
David Watson Transport Ltd
R.F. West Limited
Westway Services Holdings (2010) Ltd.
Willis Dawson Property Limited
Willis Gambier (UK) Limited
Wilson James Group Limited
Winocap Holding Limited
Wrest Park Limited
Www.Nakedwines.Com Limited
Zenith Hygiene Group Limited

2009 [133]

AMT Fruit Limited
Acton Gardens LLP
Air Works UK Engineering Ltd
Alfred Homes Limited
Alicat Workboats Limited
Amazon Spring Waters Investment Ltd
Audbern Limited
Aura (Newcastle) Project Company Phase 2
Aurient Investments N16 Ltd
BWI UK Limited
Balvraid Properties Limited
Alan Bartlett & Sons (Chatteris)
Berry Recruitment Limited
Bertram Trading Limited
Bidwells LLP
Blue Square Marketing Limited
Boortmalt UK Limited
Boss Cabins Limited
Brookgate Limited
CSS Computer Security Solutions Ltd
Cambridge Union Society
Canfield House Limited
Care UK Health & Social Care PLC
Caretech Estates (No. 5) Ltd
Central Park Enterprises Ltd
Central Trust Limited
Central Trust Syndicate Number One
Clarenco LLP
Clerks Well Properties Limited
Close Homes Limited
Coex Properties LLP
Contamac Holdings Limited
Cummins Cogeneration Limited
Cummins ESB Nigeria Limited
Dawson Books Limited
Day Webster Limited
Displayplan Holdings Limited
Drapers' Multi-Academy Trust
Earlham Institute
Earlseat Wind Farm Ltd
Ebrex Business Solutions Ltd
Elite Mobile (Holdings) Ltd
Estates and Lets 2 LLP
FBSE Finance Limited
Ford VH Limited
Fowler Smith & Jones Trust
Fresh Linen Limited
G.K. Holdings No.1 Limited
Girton Town Charity
Glorious Solutions Limited
Graincorp (Canada) Holdings UK Ltd
Graincorp UK Limited
Green Hill Energy Limited
Green Label Farms LLP
HL Display UK Holding Limited
Halma Euro Trading Limited
Hanover Housing Developments Ltd
Harvest Investments Solutions Ltd
Hill Group Services Limited
Hill of Towie Limited
Hotel Chocolat Retail Ltd
Howard Hunt Mail Limited
IMO Car Wash Group Limited
Impellam UK Limited
Inhealth UK Holdings Limited
Intertain (Bars) Limited
Intertain Limited
JRL Group Holdings Limited
Jean-Luc Developments Ltd
Keen & Toms Holdings Limited
Kier North Tyneside Limited
Kymab Limited
Laxmico Limited
Lima Orthopaedics UK Limited
Lincoln's Farm & Investments Ltd
Local Boy'z Group Holding Ltd
London Pharma & Chemicals Holdings Ltd
Lorien Limited
Lumesse Holdings Limited
Lundbeck UK LLP
Map Media Limited
Media 10 Holdings Limited
Medivet Partnership LLP
Meller Educational Trust
Mercantile Trust Limited
OPW Topco Limited
Ocado Group PLC
Ocean Gateway LLP
Offerco Limited
Omar Park Homes Limited
One Broker Limited
Original Cottage Co Ltd
Orion Media Limited
PPD CT Investments LLP
Paradigm Development Services Ltd
Performance Timber Products Group
Pet and Aquatics Properties Ltd
Providence Marian Company
QED Luton (Challney) Holdings Ltd
QED Luton (Challney) Limited
Ransome's Trading Holding Co Ltd
Recruit Venture Group Ltd
William Robinson Gravetye Charity
Romeo Midco Limited
Rose Holdco Limited
Rose Midco Limited
SDJ Enterprises Limited
Saba Infra Gloucestershire Ltd
Saffron Insurance Holdings Ltd
Saxton Limited
Senior Finance Four Limited
Sines LLP
Nigel Skinner Financial Advisers
Spirit Pub Company (Investments) Ltd
Stanley Dock Properties Ltd
Stefanini International Holdings Ltd
Steiner UK Limited
TUI Travel Aviation Finance Ltd
Tattershall Lakes Limited
Thurlow Estate Farms Limited
Toy Brokers Holdings Limited
Transporter Sales & Hire Ltd
Treehouse Group Limited
Tropical Marine Centre Limited
Turners Britannia Parks Ltd
Turners Regency Parks Limited
UK Credit Limited
User Friendly Properties (No. 2) Ltd
Valley Trucks Holdings Limited
Vinayak Properties Limited
Walstead UK Holdings Limited
Wivenhoe House Hotel Limited
Yorkshire Dales Country Park Ltd

January-June 2010 [55]

4 BG Group Ltd
Alderforce North Limited
Alternative Bridging Corporation Ltd
Althea Healthcare (Holdings) Ltd
Beale's Hotels Limited
Bithia Limited
Brayford Hotels Holdings Ltd
CAE Technology Holdings Ltd
Care UK Health & Social Care Finance
Care UK Health & Social Care Holdings
Care UK Health & Social Care Investments
Churchmanor Holdings Limited
Colchester Zoo Holdings Ltd
Consort Medical Finance 2010 Ltd
Coryton Advanced Fuels Limited
Cwind Ltd
DFKA Ltd
DFKA UK Holdings Limited
Alan Day Investments LLP
EResearchTechnology UK 1 Ltd
EResearchTechnology UK 2 Ltd
Falck EMS UK Limited
Fleximize Limited
GS Acquisitions Limited
Galldris Services Ltd
Gentian (Mid-Essex) Limited
Greentech Distribution PLC
Harwood Hutton Limited
Hendrie Estates Limited
Heritage Care Limited
Knight Roadworks (2010) Ltd
Laxmi BNS Holdings Limited
Letchworth Housing Investments Ltd
MTALX Limited
Motocaddy Holdings Limited
OPW Holdco Limited
Ocado Holdings Limited
Oldeurope Limited
Palm Recycling Limited
Parthings Farm - Management and Promotion
Pharmadent Holdings Limited
Pitchset Limited
Premier Lotteries Capital UK Ltd
Premier Lotteries UK Limited

Quebec Court Freehold Limited
Residential Land Management 2 Ltd
SJO Enterprises Limited
SW1 Management Limited
Saba Infra Hertfordshire Ltd
Shawbrook Group PLC
Stevenage Bioscience Catalyst
Surya Hotels Limited
Tustin Properties Ltd
VSL Group Holdings Limited
Werner Access Products UK Holdings

July-December 2010 [86]

AAG UK Parent Limited
AMS Care Wiltshire Limited
Abbey Mills Properties Ltd
Acacia Homes Limited
Alpha Schools (Holdings) Ltd
Anglian Community Enterprise (ACE) CIC
Anglian Water (Osprey) Financing PLC
Arcus Solutions (Holdings) Ltd
Arrhenius Holdings Limited
Ashwicken Sporting LLP
Asino Limited
Avon Freeholds Limited
Bio Products Laboratory Ltd
Bluestar Enterprise Limited
Britvic Overseas Limited
CATS College London Limited
Carlton Group Developments Ltd
Ceragon (UK) Limited
Chadwell Heath Academy
Charis Trust
Chelmsford County High School for Girls
Churchill Contract Services Group Holdings
CloudFM Integrated Services Ltd
Co-op Group Travel 2 Holdings Ltd
Countryside Restoration Trust
Dr Challoner's Grammar School
Eastern Multi-Academy Trust
Education Personnel Bidco Ltd
Flyers CNV Limited
Four CS MAT
Galileo Homes Limited
Giles Academy
Gracewell Healthcare Limited
Graysons Hospitality Limited
Greene King Developments Ltd
Greene King Investments Ltd
Greene King Pubs Limited
Group Tyre Wholesale Limited
Hall & Watts Holdings Limited
Harlow Education Trust
Hartismere Family of Schools
Hemnall Limited
Hilton Worldwide Manage Ltd
Howard Sawston Ltd
ITC Enterprises Limited
Industrial Water Jetting Systems Group
King's (The Cathedral) School, Peterborough
Kingsmead School
Laindon Trading LLP
Geoffrey Mayhew Farms Limited
Metro Global Holdings Limited
Norse Care Limited
Norse Eastern Limited
OPW Midco Limited
Ockendon Academy
One GE Healthcare UK
Opus Bestpay Limited
Orthene Holdings Limited
P J M Farms Limited
PGR Enterprises Ltd
Property Finance Capital Ltd
Provide CIC
Qatar Bloodstock Limited
Queen Elizabeth's School Barnet
Rapid Electronics Holdings Ltd
Regal Healthcare Holdings Ltd
Rivers Leasing PLC
Robinsons (Finance) No.2 Ltd
Rothschild Foundation
SOM Restaurants Ltd
Sabres Educational Trust
Sapientia Education Trust
Sembmarine SLP Ltd
Shure Europe Holdings Limited
M & D Silk Properties Ltd
Solo Cup Finance Limited
Stratton Hall Farms Limited
TCCT Retail Limited
Telespazio Vega UK Limited
Triconnex Ltd
Unity Schools Partnership
VMS (Holdings) Limited
Wadlow Energy Limited
Watford Grammar School for Boys
Watford Grammar School for Girls
Westcliff High School for Boys Ltd

January-June 2011 [139]

66 Queen Square Limited
Active Education Academy Trust
Alban Academies Trust
Albion Bunker and Trading LLP
Alterra Farms Limited
Amersham School
Anglian Learning
Avanti Schools Trust
Aylesbury Grammar School
Aylesbury High School
Bedfordshire Schools Trust Ltd
Beeson Wright Limited
Bellman Property Group Limited
Benfleet Schools Trust
Brentwood Academies Trust
Bridge Academy Trust
Britvic Finance Partnership LLP
Buckinghamshire UTC.
Calchan Holdings Limited
Cam Academy Trust
Cambridge Academic Partnership
Cambridge Meridian Academies Trust
Cambridge Silicon Radio Holdings Ltd
Cambridgeshire Educational Trust
Camelot Business Solutions Ltd
Camelot Global Lottery Solutions Ltd
Capital Pub Company Trading Ltd
Chart Forte Holdings Ltd
Chilford Hundred Education Trust
Chiltern Learning Trust
Chrysalis Multi Academy Trust
Churchtown Farm Solar Limited
City & Country Bristol Limited
Compass Education Trust Ltd
Corporate Investments Limited
DBD Enterprises Limited
Dame Alice Owen's School
Danes Educational Trust
East Barnet School
East Coast Community Healthcare C.I.C.
East Langford Solar Limited
Ellgia Recycling Ltd
European Tyre Enterprise Ltd
F & S Energy Limited
Farlingaye High School
Freman College
Gap Partnership Holdings Ltd
Gippeswyk Community Educational Trust
Grange Renewable Energy Ltd
Gray's Inn Capital Limited
Greene King Properties Limited
Griffin Davy Saffron Estates LLP
Guia Limited
Hallmark Care Homes (Brighton) Ltd
John Hampden Grammar School
Haydon School
Heathrow Aviation Engineering UTC
Highcrest Academy
Hockerill College Academy Trust
Hoddesdon School Trust
Holdings U.K. No.3 Limited
Honywood Community Science School
Ikarim Business Services Ltd
Insignis Academy Trust
Intertek USD Finance Ltd
Jollyes Retail Group Limited
KNM Project Services Limited
Kelly Rail Group Ltd
Kesgrave High School
King Edmund School
King Edward VI Grammar School, Chelmsford
Kingfisher (EU) Limited
Klipspringer Limited
Knights Templar School
Lee Chapel Multi Academy Trust
Leidos Limited
Lymington Precision Engineering (LPE)
Manor Farm Solar Limited
Meg Trading Limited
Melton House Investments Ltd
Thomas Mills High School
Mission Therapeutics Limited
Moto Finance PLC
New Anglia Local Enterprise Partnership
New Ladderswood LLP
North Essex Multi-Academy Trust
Notcutts Group Limited
ORTU Federation Ltd
Parker Hannifin Limited
Practice Corporate Management Ltd
Progress Rail Services UK Ltd
Queens' School (Bushey)
RO Financing Co Ltd
Radical Sportscars Limited
Rickmansworth School
Robus Multi Academy Trust
Roos Energy Limited
Saffron Academy Trust
Select Enterprises (Holdings) Ltd
Sheikh Holdings Group (Investments)
Signet Direct Diamond Sourcing Ltd
Skylight Investments Limited
Snellings Limited
South East Essex Academy Trust
South Essex Academy Trust
South Lincolnshire Academies Trust
South Suffolk Learning Trust
Southend High School for Boys Academy Trust
Southend High School for Girls Academy Trust
Space Truust UK Ltd
Spirit Pub Company (Holdco) Ltd
Spirit Pub Company (SGE) Ltd

Spirit Pub Co Ltd
Staploe Education Trust
TJX Europe Buying Limited
TN (UK) Consultancy Ltd
Tanners Wharf Limited
Tesco Food Sourcing Limited
Tesco Treasury Services PLC
Tithe Academy
Triangle Aviation (UK) Holdings Ltd
Trust Tees Limited
Unifruit Group Limited
Viewrose Limited
Vision Group (Holdings) Ltd
WEL (No 1) Ltd
Wadlow Energy Holdings Limited
Walsingham Estate Management Ltd
Walsingham Estate Properties Ltd
Waveney Valley Academies Trust
West Hatch High School Academy Trust
West Norfolk Academies Trust
William de Ferrers School
Wood Farm (Stanmore) Limited
Wrist Holding UK Limited
Wycombe High School Academies Trust
Yavneh College Academy Trust
Yonder Digital Group Limited
Zenith Multi Academy Trust

July-December 2011 [144]

ACES Academies Trust
ASCO Acquisitions Limited
ASCO Group Limited
Abbey College, Ramsey
Aesica BC Limited
Aesica Holdco Limited
Aesica M1 Limited
Aesica M2 Limited
Allandale Investments Limited
Alpha Trust
Anglia Home Furnishings Holdings Ltd
Anglo European Academy Trust
Archaylen Property Limited
Atlas Multi Academy Trust
Azurie Blue Limited
BRT (Wisbech) Limited
Be at One Holdings Limited
Beacon Multi-Academy Trust Ltd
Bentley Wood Trust
Birchwood High School
Bishop's Hatfield Girls' School
Bourne Grammar School
Brand Machine Limited
Britvic Asset Company No.2 Ltd
Britvic Brands LLP
Bungay High School
Burnt Mill Academy Trust
Bury St Edmunds Academy Trust
CRK Finance Limited
Canons High School
Care Providers Recruitment Ltd
Carraig Gheal Wind Farm Ltd
Casterton College Rutland
Central Tyre (Commercial) Ltd
Chauncy School
Chelmer Valley High School
City Brewery Limited
City North (Telford Homes) Ltd
Colchester Royal Grammar School
Dalton Resources Limited
Diss High School
Don Construction Holdings Ltd
Dr Challoner's High School
Dunsfold Airport Limited
EE Finance PLC
Eastwood Park Academy Trust
Emerson Park Academy
Empower Learning Academy Trust
Enrich Learning Trust
Generations Multi Academy Trust
Global Ridgeway Holdings Ltd
Good Shepherd Catholic Trust
Harouni Group of Companies Ltd
Harrow High School
Hart Schools Trust Ltd
Hatch End High School
Highway Stops Retail Limited
Hitchin Girls' School
Horsforth Holdings Limited
Icknield High School
Inland Homes (Essex) Limited
Inntel Group Limited
Inpra UK Limited
Knight Precision Metals Ltd
Knott Park One LLP
Lasted Limited
Leys and St Faith's Schools Foundation
Loughton Care Centre Limited
MC Power Limited
R. Maskell (Holdings) Limited
Mayflower High School
Geoffrey Mayhew Farms (Holdings)
Medacs Global Group Limited
Mentmore Gransden Limited
Mount Grace School
Myddleton London Limited
Mylan Pharma UK Limited
NBC Europe Ltd.
NMSIM Group Limited
Naked Wines International Ltd
National Institute of Agricultural Botany Trust
North Norfolk Academy Trust
Nower Hill High School
Oranmore Precast Limited
Osborne Co-operative Academy Trust
PJHP Limited
Pangbourne Developments Ltd
Pant y Wal Investments Limited
Park High School
Passmores Co-operative Learning Community
Plume School
Dr Michael Prager Holdings Ltd
Princes Risborough School
Prinhold Limited
Punjab House Associated Ltd
Queen Elizabeth's Girls' School (Barnet)
Ramblers Holidays Group Ltd
Sir William Ramsay School Academy Trust
Red Kite Schools Trust
Reliance Entertainment Productions 7 Ltd
Rivers Multi Academy Trust
Roundwood Park School Academy Trust
Royston Schools Academy Trust
S and J Investments (Delivery Office Southall)
SF11 Limited
SFAET Ltd
SG Technologies Group Limited
Saint Vincent Holdings Limited
Scholars' Education Trust
Scimitar Topco Limited
Seax Trust
Senior Finance Six Limited
Senior Five Limited
Showcard Print Limited
South West Essex Community Education Trust
Southend East Community Academy Trust
St Ivo School
St Neots Learning Partnership
Stevenage Road Residential Developments
Stewards Academy Trust
Stratton Education Trust
Supreme Hotels LLP
TCCT Holdings UK Limited
TRAD Properties LLP
Table Bay Services LLP
Tanglewood Care Homes Limited
Tesco Pension Investment Ltd
Thrive Partnership Academy Trust
Thurstable School Sports College and Sixth Form Centre
Tobar Group Trading Limited
Trustonic Limited
Turners (Soham) Holdings Ltd
Turners Parks Group Limited
UIDUK Ltd
Ursuline Academy Ilford
Vandyke Upper School
Veritas Educational Trust
Verulam School
Volkerstevin Group Limited
Waddesdon Church of England School
Wallace Partnership Group Ltd
Wensum Valley Hotel Golf & Country Club
White Lodge (Norwich) Limited
Wildcat Acquisition Holdings (UK)

January-March 2012 [78]

ACR Investments Limited
Active Learning Trust Limited
Anexhold Limited
Anglia Innovation Partnership LLP
Apollo Property Investment Ltd
Aspire Learning Trust (Whittlesey)
Atlantis Equityco Limited
Atlantis Investorco Limited
Atlantis Midco Limited
BWP (Cambridge) Limited
Bushey St James Trust
Butlins Operations Limited
Chelmsford Learning Partnership
Chestnut Inns Limited
Clarke Property Partner Ltd
Cogels Investments Ltd
Cromwell Community College
Cunningham Holdings (London) Ltd
Daylighting Power Limited
Elstree UTC
Fifty Shades Ltd
Forfarmers UK Holdings Limited
Galliard Group Limited
Garrets Bidco 2 Limited
Garrets Bidco Limited
Gog Magog Partnership LLP
Henlow Church of England Academy
Hertswood Academy
Hildo Limited
Hillary Bidco Limited
Horsham Properties Limited
Ingleby (1884) Limited
Inland Homes Developments Ltd
Jojo's Mojo Limited
Kluman and Balter Holdings Ltd
Learning Pathways Academy
Longmill Rickbost Ltd

Lors Homes Limited
Marlborough Science Academy Ltd
Milbank Ventures Limited
Morris Education Trust
Myatt's Field Development LLP
NDEMIC Creations Ltd
Norfolk Academies
OAT 2012 Limited
Oblue Limited
Ortona Management Limited
Ortona Properties Limited
Presdales School Academy Trust
Pretoria Energy Company (Chittering)
Qatar Racing Limited
RQ Capital Limited
Ridgeway Bavarian Limited
The Helena Romanes School
SDSDAB Limited
Sabre Retail Fashion Limited
Salavera Trading Limited
Salisbury Workplace Services Ltd
Seajacks 1 Limited
Seajacks 2 Limited
Seajacks 3 Limited
Seajacks International Limited
Sen Trust Southend
Shenfield High School
St Bede's Inter Church School
St Mary's CE Academy, Cheshunt
Sunwin Services Group (2010) Ltd
Symbio Energy Limited
Tallentire Energy Limited
Timeboard Investments LLP
R C Tinsley 2012 Limited
Tradex Insurance Holdings Ltd
Trieste Group LLP
Tutis Properties Limited
Wandale Limited
Wensum Trust
Woolpit Business Parks Limited
Yum! III (UK) Limited

April-June 2012 [42]

AG Retail Cards Limited
Affinity Water Acquisitions (Holdco)
Affinity Water Acquisitions (Investments)
Affinity Water Acquisitions (Midco)
Affinity Water Acquisitions Ltd
Bathstore Group Limited
Beaumont School
Boulters Meadow Limited
Broadrich Limited
Buildvantage Limited
Chobham Manor LLP
Thomas Cook Group Hedging Ltd
Dalin Limited
Diamond Learning Partnership Trust
Eden Academy
Ellesmere Property Investment Co Ltd
S Elvin Limited
European Investments (Cornwall) Ltd
European Investments (SCEL) Ltd
Fulca Limited
GH London Ground Handling Services
Gladstone Court Developments Ltd
Gower Acres Limited
Hincroft Limited
Intermune Holdings Limited
Intertek Finance No. 2 Ltd
Kout Food Group Restaurants UK Ltd
Legra Academy Trust
Libra (Longhurst Group) Treasury PLC
Life Education Trust
Lismire LLP
Netscientific PLC
PPD International Investments Ltd
Purslow Investments Limited
Rayfern Holdings Limited
Regency Homes Limited
Seajacks 4 Limited
Seckford Education Trust
Sele School
Shropshire Energy (UK) Limited
Spiral Partnership Trust
Transforming Education in Norfolk

July-September 2012 [42]

Alperton Community School
Angel Care (Orchid Care Homes) Ltd
Aspire Academies Trust
Azuri Technologies Ltd
Boston Witham Academies Federation
Brooks Events Limited
C.U. Phosco Limited
CNH Industrial Capital Limited
Change Schools Partnership
Chesterford Group Limited
Childwick Trust
Thomas Cook West Investments Ltd
Denville Hall 2012
Esin Cash & Carry Limited
Evolution Academy Trust
Flegg Education Academy Trust
Francis Associates (43) LLP
Joyce Frankland Academy, Newport
Granitte Investments (UK) Ltd
Grant Farming Limited
Greenfields Family Investment Co Ltd
Harris (Belmont) Charity
Inspiration Trust
Larkspur Investments Limited
MRBL Limited
Minhoco 20 Limited
Monk's Walk School
NET Academies Trust
Optima Chemical Ltd
Pitney Bowes Holdco Limited
Premier Inn Ochre Limited
Samsung Cambridge Solution Centre
South Bristol (Ashton Park) Ltd
Epic Staunton LLP
Step 6 Ltd
Sunsave 12 (Derriton Fields) Ltd
Synergy Multi Academy Trust
Tenmill Limited
Upminster Academies Trust
WHTC Ltd
Wembley Multi Academy Trust
Wood Hall Land & Properties Ltd

October-December 2012 [71]

Adonia Medical Group Limited
Air Works Empire UK Limited
Al Asayl Bloodstock Ltd
Aura Finance Limited
Axalta Coating Systems UK Holding
BUUK Infrastructure Holdings Ltd
BUUK Infrastructure Issuer PLC
BUUK Infrastructure No 1 Ltd
BUUK Infrastructure No 2 Ltd
Beaconsfield School
Blue Anchor Leisure Holdings Ltd
Blumarble Capital Limited
Bricks St Property Group Ltd
CATMJ Limited
Cambridge Innovation Capital PLC
Cambridge Primary Education Trust
Cardtronics Creative UK Ltd
R.G. Carter Engineering Ltd
Certsure LLP
Commodity Centre (Group) Ltd
Cooperscroft Care Home Limited
Countrywide PLC
Coveris Flexibles Holdings UK Ltd
EPG Development IV LLP
Eastmarket Grain LLP
Emcure Pharma UK Ltd
Federation of European Biochemical Societies
Flamingo Horticulture Investments
GPP Langstone LLP
Garreg Lwyd Energy Limited
Glastry Advisory Partners Ltd
Global Resources Investment Trust PLC
Greater Peterborough UTC
Hall of Fame Stud Limited
Harman Automotive UK Limited
Hedingham School and Sixth Form
Hitchin Boys' School
Ingrebourne Valley Holdings Ltd
Jensten Group Limited
Johnson Care Limited
KDM Timber Limited
Kailas Hotel Finance Co Ltd
Kelly Communications Enterprises Ltd
Kings Langley School
Levantera Developments Limited
London Distribution Park LLP
Lousin Holdings Limited
Malthurst Estates Limited
Micross Foods Holdings Limited
Mouskos LLP
NW3 Capital Ltd
Namu Limited
Ocourage Limited
PHH 1 Limited
PHH 2 Limited
PMQUE Limited
Polyco (Group) Limited
Portugal Finco Limited
Rightforsuccess Trust
SW1 Trading Limited
Saba Infra Cambridgeshire Ltd
Safran Electrical & Power UK Ltd
Saw Property Co Ltd
Signature Lessee Limited
J O Sims Holdings (1896) Ltd
Sines Parks Holdings Limited
TES Enterprise Solutions Ltd
Thomson Sawmills Holdings Ltd
Trurating Limited
Twenty 1 Construction Limited
West Herts Community Free School Trust

January-March 2013 [36]

ARJ Construction Holdings Ltd
Affinity Water Holdings Ltd
Agrofarm London Limited
Arpo Global Limited
Aveva Finance Limited
Avocet Capital Limited
B Crystal Limited
B Emerald Limited
Best Holdings (UK) Limited
Bondgrip Limited

Clarion Academy Trust
Direct Consolidated Limited
Dreams Limited
Dreams Topco Limited
Et Ceteris Limited
Green Spark Renewable Energy (UK) Ltd
HBVB
Key Developments (Godalming) LLP
Lantern Services (Holdings) Ltd
Leisure Parks Real Estate (Holdings)
Micross UK Solutions Limited
Musco (St Albans Place) Ltd
Navitas Petroleum Limited
OAG Aviation Worldwide Limited
Openarch Properties Limited
S & J Padfield & Partners LLP
S & J Padfield Estates LLP
Preston Manor Academy Trust
Quixant UK Limited
RMR Capital Limited
Rayleigh Schools Trust
Ridgeons Land LLP
Shared Services Connected Ltd
Skanska TAM Limited
Spalding Grammar School
Taylor Wimpey SH Capital Ltd

April-June 2013 [41]

A1 Pharmaceuticals Holdings Ltd
Amneal Pharma UK Holdings Ltd
Amshold Group Limited
Amshold Trading Limited
Blackwater Partners Limited
Booking.Com Customer Service Center (UK)
Cambridge Colleges Funding PLC
Cergold Limited
Connected Learning
Consensus Holdco Limited
Countryside Properties (WPL) Ltd
Darktrace Limited
Ethypharm UK Limited
Focus Tankers Limited
HTG Investments Limited
Richard Hale School
Kodak Alaris Holdings Limited
Kodak Alaris Limited
MEL Aviation Components Ltd
MHE JVCO Limited
MHL Holdco Limited
Marlborough Highways Group Ltd
Milton Hall Cambridge Limited
Naga UK Bidco Limited
Naga UK Topco Limited
New Landmark Investment Ltd
Ocean Holidays Limited
One Group Construction Limited
Proquest European Holdings Ltd
Royal Air Force Central Fund
SBG Holding International Ltd
Saffron Housing Finance PLC
Seajacks 5 Limited
Peter Sowerby Foundation
Sunsave 25 (Wix Lodge Farm) Ltd
TC Project Management Limited
TCGH Holdings Limited
Telida Limited
Tesco Family Dining Limited
Watford Health Campus Partnership LLP
Westfield Academy

July-September 2013 [48]

AMP GM 003 Limited
Alterium Limited
BHL (UK) Holdings Ltd
Simon Balle Academies Trust
Beaconsfield High School
Big Sky Developments Ltd
Broadfields Academy Trust
Bucks Developments Limited
Camelot Bidco Limited
Caretech Estates (No 7) Ltd
Cornelius Vermuyden School
Deuce Acquisitions Limited
Deuce Holdco Limited
European Investments (Crook Hill)
European Investments (Earlseat) Ltd
European Investments (Lancashire)
F-Star Alpha Limited
FIC Grand Plaza Ltd
FJC Topco Limited
Facet Capital Limited
Good for Food Limited
Greenheath Farming Co Ltd
HP Solar Limited
Henley Group Finance Limited
John Henry and Sons (Developments) Ltd
Herts & Essex Multi Academy Trust
Hotel Chocolat Group PLC
KH Finance No.2 Limited
Kenwyn Solar Limited
Kestrel Loans No. 4 Limited
Metals & Materials Limited
New Sparta Film Distribution Ltd
New Sparta Holdings Limited
Radio Developments Ltd
Ridley Godfrey (Holdings) Ltd
Simarco Holdings Limited
Sonnet Care Homes Finance Ltd
Sonnet Care Homes Holdco Ltd
Stock Spirits Group PLC
TJX Germany Ltd.
Tesco Corporate Treasury Services PLC
Timeboard Industrial Properties LLP
Tritton Farming Partnership LLP
Vanderbilt Development Finance Ltd
Vanderbilt Thames Valley Ltd
Washbrook Capital Limited
Watford UTC
Woodford Heating Holdings Ltd

October-December 2013 [61]

8x8 UK Investments Limited
AMP GM001 Limited
Altair (UK) Ltd
Axalta Coating Systems U.K. (2) Ltd
Badger BC Investments Limited
Bluestone APAC Holdings Ltd
Bluestone Consolidated Holdings Ltd
Borras Group Holdings Limited
Cambridge Colleges Funding II PLC
Camelot Holdco Limited
Camelot Interco Limited
Camelot Midco Limited
Camelot Topco Limited
Carter Accommodation Group Ltd
Chard Robinson Usten Ltd
Chase (Palace Wharf) Limited
Diocese of Norwich Education and Academies Trust
ENRA Group Limited
EV Holdings Limited
Forth Ports Finance PLC
Frontier Bidco Limited
Frontier Holdco Limited
Frontier Midco Limited
Global Graphics PLC
Grove & Dean (Holdings) Ltd
Inland Homes 2013 Limited
Kent, Surrey and Sussex Community Rehabilitation Co
Keswick European Holdings Ltd
Kier Hammersmith Limited
London Luton Airport Holdings I Ltd
London Luton Airport Holdings II Ltd
London Luton Airport Holdings III
Loxford School Trust Limited
MAS (Holdings) Limited
MBH Finco. Limited
Majestic Bingo Limited
McColl's Retail Group PLC
Midwich Group PLC
Myriad Capital PLC
Newincco 1270 Limited
Ocado Innovation Limited
Oxley Wharf Limited
Oxley Wharf Property 1 Limited
Oxley Wharf Property 2 Limited
Oxley Wharf Property 3 Limited
PS Construction Investments Ltd
Peli Biothermal Limited
Pemberton Farms (Holdings) Ltd
Positive Entertainment Ltd
Premiair Aerospace Limited
QOTD Film Investment Limited
Quinn Investment Holdings (London)
Randstad Luxembourg UK Limited
SVK Capital Management Limited
Sonnet Care Homes Midco Ltd
Spirit Pub Company (Derwent) Ltd
Stock Finance (Koruna) Limited
T & B (Contractors) Holdings Ltd
THR Number Two Limited
Toro Principal Manufacturing Ltd
Tradewise Group of Companies Ltd

January-March 2014 [59]

Abzena Limited
Arthur Midco 1 Limited
Arthur Midco 2 Limited
Arthur Pikco Limited
Arthur Topco Limited
Aura Finance (Holdco) Limited
BC Legal Limited
BRE Global Limited
Blancco (Software) Services Ltd
Butchers and Drovers Charitable Institution
Cokenach Property Limited
DW Windsor Group Limited
EV Finco Limited
European Investments (Lancashire 2)
European Investments (Reaps Moss)
Euston Biogas Limited
Exheat Group Limited
GAIAE Limited
GDSK Limited
Gapsun Properties Limited
Green Label Poultry Limited
Green Mountain Estates Ltd
Heulwen Solar Limited
Hilton Worldwide FS Treasury Ltd
Hilton Worldwide Holding 2 Ltd
Horizon Discovery Group PLC
Housing Gateway Limited
Hovis Holdings Limited
Hovis Limited
Jeesal Akman Holdings Limited

Jeesal Holdings Limited
Jenga (UK) Limited
Knighton Foods Limited
Landmark Aviation (UK) Limited
Lawes Agricultural Trust
Le Vack Estates Limited
Lighthouse Healthcare Group Ltd
Manufacturing Services Investment
Moody Venture Capital LLP
Moralis Group Limited
NGB Construction Limited
One Stop Private Doctors Ltd
Premier Foods Finance PLC
RC Bond Holdings Limited
Regaltags Global Limited
Retail Charity Bonds PLC
Ruislip High School
Salisbury Holdings Limited
Senior Finance Seven Limited
Smart Meter Assets 1 Ltd
St Albans Diocesan Property Co Ltd
Stockplace Hartford Ltd
Stonegate Pub Company Financing PLC
Telford Homes City North Ltd
Thrive Homes Finance PLC
Trust Estates (Clarence Street) Ltd
Vahnea Marolda Investments LLP
WD1A Limited
Werner UK Operations Limited

April-June 2014 [59]

Archigen Biotech Limited
Ascend Global Holdings, Ltd.
Ascend Global Intermediate Holdings, Ltd.
Atalian Servest Group Limited
Boing Acquisitions Limited
Boing Midco Limited
CRU Sturton Street Limited
CloudFM Group Limited
Country Court Care Homes 2 Ltd
DOT100 Limited
Durman Stearn Holdings Limited
Emerald Bidco Limited
Emerald Midco 1 Limited
Emerald Midco 2 Limited
Emerald Topco Limited
Fotolec Technologies Holdings Ltd
GHL (Crescent Lane) Limited
Gardline Maritime Limited
Glenchamber Wind Energy Ltd
Harrow Academies Trust
Heathland Whitefriars Federation
Hilton Worldwide Holding LLP
Howard Bedford Limited
International Car Wash Group Financing
International Car Wash Group Ltd.
JMBC Properties Ltd
Jet Investments Limited
Kent Blaxill Group Limited
Kier Hammersmith Holdco Ltd
Kier Trade City Holdco 1 LLP
Kier Trade City LLP
Luminescence Holdings Ltd
Lysander Student Properties Operations
M & W Newco Limited
MN Sports Bidco Limited
MN Sports Holdings Limited
Mid Holding Co UK Limited
Monumart Limited
Morley Finco Limited
Ocado Central Services Limited
Ocado Operating Limited
Phoenix Advance Limited
Plutus Estates Limited
Q Acoustics Limited
RANC Holdings Limited
Riverway Investments Limited
Signet UK Finance PLC
Silnat Holdings Limited
Silverson Machines Holdings Ltd
Softbox (Bidco) Limited
Softbox (Midco) Limited
Softbox (Topco) Limited
THR Number One PLC
Titano Real Estate Limited
Tudor Court Primary Academy Trust
UML Eagle Limited
Vanderbilt Topco Ltd
Viners Capital Properties Ltd
Wilton Park Developments Ltd

July-September 2014 [60]

ABSL1 Limited
Aquila MB2 Limited
Aquila MB3 Limited
Archway Apartments Limited
Arnold Family Holdings Limited
Athena Care Homes (UK) Limited
Bluestone Mortgage Holdings Ltd
Brick Projects (Marland) Ltd
CGN Global Uranium Limited
Cambrionix Holdings Limited
Castle View School Academy Trust
Cricklewood Developments Ltd
Cygnet Street Developments Ltd
Dencora (Watford) LLP
Dentex Healthcare Group Ltd
Environ Freshford Mill Limited
Ethypharm Holdings UK Ltd
Flo-Mech Holdings Limited
GVS Prepaid Limited
Galliard Developments Limited
HEB Real Estate Limited
Hampton Academies Trust
International Industrial Metals Ltd
Jaysam Developments Borehamwood Ltd
KCH (UK) Holdings Limited
Kendallco Limited
Kingsway Asset Co Limited
Kingsway Mezz Co Limited
Kingsway Mezz Hold Co Limited
Kingsway Senior Hold Co Ltd
CW Lamley & Co Limited
Mylan UK Healthcare Limited
Netherhall Gardens Ltd
OEC International Limited
Optionis Group Limited
Optionis Limited
Pear Tree Mead Academy
Peerglow Asset Limited
Pinewood School Academy Trust
Pioneer DJ Europe Limited
Powergas Africa Limited
Premier Inn International Development
Renaissance Global Investment Ltd
Rigel Capital Partners Limited
Rowlands 2014 Limited
SA.GI.MA. Limited
SCH 2014 Limited
Shearer Property C Limited
Shiva Kingsway Limited
Speciality Stores Limited
St Albans Operating Co Ltd
Sunrise UK Holdco Limited
Taxassist Direct Group Limited
James Taylor Homes (Harrow) Ltd
UKLS Acquisitions Limited
VRS Investments Limited
Vanneck Residential LLP
Volac Renewable Energy Limited
Wesley House, Cambridge
Wheatley (Buntingford) Limited

October-December 2014 [58]

94 Camlet Way LLP
AER Rents Limited
AMP GM006 Limited
Accolade Midco Limited
Accolade Topco Limited
Acteon UK Financing Limited
Alternative Bridging (UK 1) Ltd
Angelica Estates Limited
Antoniou Investments Limited
Ares Properties Ltd
Argon NPS Limited
Avocet Academy Trust
Basinghall Mortgage Finance No.1 Ltd
Cappagh Browne Utilities Ltd
Consort Medical Finance Ltd
Daly Holdings Limited
Dyer & Butler 2014 Limited
EUSA Pharma (UK) Limited
Ellgia Holdings Limited
Enfield Innovations Ltd
Focusrite PLC
GDL (Millharbour) Limited
Gago Invest Limited
Gardline Holdings Limited
Gateway Reversions Limited
Hamsard 3352 Limited
Hamsard 3353 Limited
Hospital Topco Limited
I F E Global Holdings Limited
Jaltek Holdings Limited
Kier Reading Holdco 1 LLP
Kier Reading LLP
L & M Holding Ltd
Lea Bridge Hill LLP
Lumendi Limited
MacKenzie Taylor Holdings Ltd
Mansley Group Holdings Limited
Mundibiopharma Limited
NPS (Holdings) Limited
NQA Certification Limited
Nine Heathrow Ventures Limited
Northgate Public Services Ltd
O'Brien Waste Recycling Solutions Ltd
Papa Midco Limited
Papa Topco Limited
Paragon Land & Estates Ltd
Passportcard Limited
Pepkor UK Retail Limited
Project Helix Holdco Ltd
Rank Hovis Milling Limited
Ranplan Holdings Limited
SPD Moorgate Limited
Sarena House LLP
Signature Flatbreads (UK) Ltd
Southwater Property Promotion Ltd
Survey Roofing Group Limited
Swan Housing Capital PLC
James Taylor Homes (Lincolns Inn)

January 2015 [11]
AFP 2015-1 Limited
AMP GM007 Limited
Autumn Foods Holdings Limited
Commercial Freeholds & Investments Ltd
Countryside L & Q (Oaks Village) LLP
EUSA Pharma Holdco 1 (UK) Ltd
EUSA Pharma Holdco 2 (UK) Ltd
Halsbury Strategic Limited
Pretoria Energy Company (Mepal) Ltd
SSL Group (UK) Limited
Soul Coffee House Limited

February 2015 [18]
Asset Education
Castledon School Academy Trust
Chevalier (2015) Ltd
Fitzwimarc School Academy Trust
Food Processing Holding Ltd
Halsbury Homes (South East) Ltd
Inero Limited
Luna Estates Limited
Munro Holdings (Cambridge) Ltd
Mylan Holdings Ltd.
Norfolk Capital Limited
Pamina Estates Limited
Point Pedro Property Holdings Ltd
Premonition Analytics Limited
Ramsgate Development Co Ltd
TCMC Furniture Limited
Takely Education Trust
Thurne-Middleby Ltd

March 2015 [23]
3DS Financial Services Ltd
Alex Brands Rocket Holdings Ltd
Baker Perkins Holdings Limited
Fleximize Capital Limited
Freeline Therapeutics Limited
HJP Media LLP
Harris Family Finance Co Ltd
Inland Property Limited
Lamesta Limited
Malthurst South East Limited
Noodle Properties Limited
PPA Group Limited
Peacock Holdings (2015) Ltd
Regulus Bidco Limited
Regulus Midco Limited
Regulus Topco Limited
Springfield Holdings Limited
St Edmundsbury and Ipswich Diocesan Multi-Academy Trust
Stonewater Enterprises Limited
Thumbzup UK Limited
UML Wigmore Limited
Whitfield Finance Limited
Willoughby (880) Limited

April 2015 [12]
AST Group Holdings Limited
Ariyan Hotels Limited
Cambridge Realty Limited
Edinburgh Sainsbury Holdings LLP
Minhoco 26 Limited
Nicholls Limited
O'Brien Waste Recycling Solutions Holdings
Pharmathen Holding 4 Ltd
Premier Euro Hotels Limited
SBH Gatwick Limited
UML Chiltern Limited
Vertical Group Limited

May 2015 [18]
CD & R Firefly Bidco Limited
Cloud Topco Limited
Edgewell Personal Care UK Ltd
Fork Rent Limited
I & C Holdings Limited
I & C Limited
Ilot Capital UK Ltd
Ilot Investments UK Ltd
Larkfleet Homes Limited
Pasta Foods Investments Ltd
QI Partners
Shields Environmental Group (Holdings) Ltd.
Shields Environmental Investment (Holdings)
UML Marylebone Limited
Wentworth Holdings Limited
Wren Buyerco Limited
Wren Midco Limited
Wren Topco Limited

June 2015 [17]
Abzena Holdings Limited
Astro Lighting Holdings Ltd
Buyanovsky Property Management Ltd
Cloud Possibilities Limited
Dupont (UK) Electronic Materials Ltd
Erba Diagnostics UK Limited
Grant Family Holdings Limited
Grant Family Investments Ltd
Haileybury Academy Trust
Halamar (Chancery Lane) Ltd
J H & A J King Farms Limited
Sir Robert McAlpine (A19) Ltd
Sir Robert McAlpine Road Holdings
Orchard Funding Group PLC
Playags UK Limited
Truman Securities Limited
Union of UEA Students Limited

July 2015 [15]
3DS Financial Services EMEA Ltd
Acteon UK Financing II (NOK) Ltd
Alconbury Packing Solutions Ltd
Brooklands Helix Developments Ltd
Peter Brotherhood Limited
Centus Biotherapeutics Limited
Flamingo Horticulture Ltd
Kier Foley Street Holdco 1 LLP
M.J.S. Holdings (March) Ltd
Norpap Property (Telford) Ltd
Strides Pharma Global (UK) Ltd
Suffolk Academies Trust
Tulip Properties & Real Estate Ltd
Whitehouse Leisure International Holdings
Zara UK Topco Limited

August 2015 [15]
Ashcoe Holdings Limited
Bluestone Mortgage Finance No.2 Ltd
Hardys Farm Limited
Howard Cambridge Limited
Hutton East Limited
Stephen James (Automotive) Ltd
David Lloyd Leisure GR Ltd
Memorial Gardens Limited
Paradine Holdings Limited
Premier Bidco Limited
Premier Midco Limited
Premier Topco Limited
Shoe Quarter Limited
R Stanton-Gleaves UK Limited
TTKW Limited

September 2015 [17]
2020 Holdings (England) Ltd
Bloom Engineering Holdings Ltd
Cheshunt Lakeside Developments Ltd
Gascoigne Halman Group Limited
Hascombe & Valiant Stud Ltd
Hull Propco Limited
Invordan Britannia Limited
JSM Group Holdings Limited
Keystone 1 Limited
Keystone 2 Limited
LSF9 Robin Investments Limited
LSF9 Robin Midco Limited
ML Accessories Group Limited
MN Fox Bidco Limited
MN Fox Topco Limited
Sorbon Finance Limited
Zara UK Midco Limited

October 2015 [26]
2020 Developments (Luton) Ltd
Bondmason Client Ltd
Connect Access Group Ltd
Country Court Care Homes 3 MB Ltd
Country Court Care Homes 3 Propco
Country Court Care Homes 3 SB Holdco
Country Court Care Homes 3 SB Ltd
Fluxys Interconnector Limited
Fluxys UK Limited
JCA Head Co Limited
KM Estates Limited
King Street Manchester Property LLP
McLaren Construction (London) Ltd
McLaren Construction (Midlands & North)
McLaren Construction (South) Ltd
Mustard Global Limited
S H Pratt Holdings Limited
Prime Place (Millbrook) LLP
Prime Place (Woking Island Site) LLP
Radical Investments Limited
Sotherby LLP
Spire Bricks and Mortar Ltd
James Taylor Group Limited
Telensa Holdings Limited
Tour Partner Group Limited
Tour Partner Group Midco Ltd

November 2015 [18]
Anglia Aircraft Restorations Ltd
BFC Finance Limited
Betcrown Limited
Birchwood Capital Limited
Brogan Group Holdings Ltd
Countryside Properties PLC
Denland Limited
HFC Finance Limited
Kestates Limited
Land Charter (Harlow) Ltd
Mercury Land Holdings Limited
Myriad Healthcare Holdings Ltd
Navigator Terminals Midco Ltd
Navigator Terminals North Tees Ltd
Nemo (UK) Holdco, Ltd.
Reesink Turfcare UK Limited
Reyhold Limited
TJX UK Property Limited

December 2015 [19]

Anglian Home Improvements Group Ltd
Appetite Holdings Limited
Axcorp Limited
Bucknalls Developments Limited
DJM 88 Limited
GDL (Slough Developments) Ltd
Grindley Biogas Limited
Jessica House Developments Ltd
Manormaker (Nominee No. 1) Ltd
Mingold Limited
NHV Helicopters Ltd
Prometic Pharma SMT Limited
Queensgate Finco Ltd
SystemsAccountants Holdings Ltd
Tobar International Limited
UML Wembley Limited
Walstead Finance Limited
Walstead Group Limited
Walstead Holdings Limited

January 2016 [19]

AZENCO4 Limited
Acteon UK Financing III (EUR) Ltd
Benacre Company
Benacre Properties Company
Birch Farms (C & N) LLP
Brington North LLP
ESCO UK Holding Company I Ltd
Erith Hills LLP
Fairline Yachts Limited
GDL (Luton) Developments Ltd
Iliffe Media Limited
Jacklin Properties Limited
Kier (Newcastle) Investment Ltd
Kreutzer Touristik GB Limited
Polyco Healthline Limited
Saffie Investments Limited
Taylors Legal Limited
UML Mayfair Limited
UML Westminster Limited

February 2016 [29]

452 Finchley Road LLP
Assetbridge Finance Limited
Chiltern Way Academy Trust
Clearview Homes (Western Avenue) Ltd
Doe Holdings Limited
E & J Properties Limited
Gannett International Finance LLP
Genie Bidco Limited
Genie Topco Limited
Global Resale, Ltd
ISN Europe Limited
Marylebone Finco Limited
Mouskos Capital Limited
Mouskos Holdings Limited
Newman Street Hotel Limited
Northgate UK Holdings 1 Ltd
Northgate UK Holdings 2 Ltd
Northgate UK Holdings 3 Ltd
Northgate UK Holdings 4 Ltd
Pregis Europe Limited
Riva Topco Limited
Road Tech Holdings Limited
Rocket Medical Group PLC
Spitalfields Works Limited
TGA UK Alpha Limited
TGA UK Finance Limited
TGA UK Holdings Limited
TGA UK Omega Limited
Vetex Limited

March 2016 [18]

BP INV2 Holdco Ltd
BP INV2 Pledgeco Ltd
T F Bowman & Son Limited
Cardtronics PLC
Dabasia Estates LLP
Excellence in Education Trust
Goldstar Transport Holdings Ltd
Grant & Bowman International Ltd
Hemnall Investments Limited
Littlebury Developments Ltd
Lochailort Fairfield Limited
Manor (2016) Holdings Limited
Newfields Agricultural Holdings Ltd
Plymouth (Notte Street) Ltd
Pride Care Homes Peterborough Ltd
Strongholding Limited
WCM Investments Ltd
Westgate House Developments Ltd

April 2016 [24]

Aequitas Estates (Poyle) Ltd
Alternative Bridging (UK 2) Ltd
BV PMT Holdings Ltd
Countryside Properties (WGL) Ltd
Countryside Properties (WHL) Ltd
Fitzjohns Avenue Ltd
GDL Holdco Limited
Galldris Holdings Limited
Gap Partnership Bidco Limited
Gap Partnership Group Limited
Gibson Bidco Limited
Gibson Propco Limited
Gray's Inn Capital 2 Limited
Ipswich Borough Assets Limited
KSEYE Capital Holdings Limited
KSEYE Capital No.1 Limited
KSEYE Capital No.2 Limited
KSEYE Group Limited
Kristall Real Estate Limited
London and Hertfordshire Ltd
Tesco Blue (3LP) Limited
Tesco Fuchsia (3LP) Limited
Tesco Red (3LP) Limited
W & L Investments LLP

May 2016 [13]

Ball UK Holdco Limited
Cardtronics Holdings Limited
Digital House Group Ltd
Ensign Holdco 1 Limited
Ensign Holdco 3 Limited
Ensign Holdco 4 Limited
Gravity Media Group Holdings Ltd
Littleberries LLP
Riverstone Pictures (Show Dogs) Ltd
Riverstone Solutions 2 Limited
Shamrock Bidco Limited
Shamrock Midco Limited
Shamrock Topco Limited

June 2016 [21]

ADB Construction Limited
Ammeraal Beltech UK Holding Ltd
Bath Road Properties Limited
Birmingham Resi Property LLP
CCP Management LLP
Chester Greyhound Retail Park LLP
Comline Holdings Limited
DBCN Limited
Simon Elvin Holdings Limited
Elvin Investments Limited
Essex Group Holdings International
GDL (Romford) Limited
Hollywood Bowl Group PLC
KCG Holdings Ltd
Konings Juices & Drinks UK Ltd
Marine Point Property LLP
NeilMed Holding Co Ltd
Royston Holdings Limited
Scimitar House (Holdings) Ltd
Twentieth Century Fox Television Distribution (U.K.), Ltd.
Union Carriers Limited

July 2016 [26]

ADC Holdings Limited
Ad Meliora Academy Trust
Amadeus IG Limited
Berlesduna Academy Trust
CATM Europe Holdings Limited
Hugh Crane Holdings Limited
Friars 716 Limited
Gardar Property Co Limited
Hilton International IP Holding Ltd
IMBOLC Limited
M Group Services Limited
Metro Investments (Stevenage) LLP
John Milton Academy Trust
Ridgeon Holdings Limited
Riva Holdco 1 Limited
Riva Holdco 2 Limited
Starbridge Property Investment Ltd
Starke Industries Limited
Thor Holdco Limited
Thor Midco Limited
Thor Topco Limited
Twinmar Group Limited
Twinmar Investments Holdings Ltd
Twinmar Investments Limited
Yare Education Trust
Z Hotel Poland Street Property LLP

August 2016 [24]

Alcedo Shipping Limited
Arugula Spruce Limited
Avnet Bidco Limited
Biffa PLC
D & B Scaffolding Holdings Ltd
Dominion Hospitality Limited
Edmonton Academy Trust
Hi-Tec Europe Limited
Holywells Residential Lettings Ltd
Kirkmore Rhino 1 Limited
LGS Holdings Limited
Landex Commercial Property Ltd
MacDuffy (Holdings) Limited
Manu Ventures LLP
Milltrust BLA LLP
Miriad Property Investments Ltd
Mylan Holdings Acquisition 2 Ltd
Mylan Holdings Acquisition Ltd
Platinum Acquisition Limited
Platinum Midco Limited
Platinum Newco II Limited
Platinum Topco Limited
RPSD2 Limited
Shelfside Group LLP

September 2016 [18]

Acclaim DMW Holdings Limited
Aspire Schools
Bespoke Foods Group Limited
Crown House Homes (North Station)
Dominion Hospitality Midco Ltd
Dominion Hospitality Topco Ltd
T Gilmartin Holdings Limited
Hull Holdings Limited
Kirkmore Capital Limited
Kristall Realty Investments Ltd
Landex Holdings Limited
Lynton Homes (3) Limited
Market Field Learning Community
McGinley Aviation Holdings Ltd
Platinum Midco 2 Limited
Pure International Limited
SBH Tamworth Limited
WHL Investments Limited

October 2016 [26]

BGL (Holdings) Limited
Bespoke Foods Holding Limited
CATM Africa Holdings Limited
CATM Australasia Holdings Ltd
CATM North America Holdings Ltd
Cambridge Pharma Limited
Chaplin Group Limited
Elysium Healthcare Holdings 2 Ltd
Elysium Healthcare Holdings 3 Ltd
Environmental Group Limited
Essafinaat UK Limited
Fidion Limited
Fulton Maritime Holdings Ltd
Fulton Maritime Limited
Gainsborough's House Society
Heli Properties LLP
Kymab Group Limited
Nacropolis (Langley) Ltd
Overture Bidco Limited
Overture Midco II Limited
Overture Midco Limited
Overture Topco Limited
Pacific (BC) Topco 5 Limited
Process Sensing Technologies Ltd.
Royal Docks Property LLP
James Taylor Homes Group Ltd

November 2016 [28]

254 Kilburn HR LLP
Abington Group Limited
Arthur's Partners LLP
Camfaud Group Limited
Care UK Health & Rehabilitation Services
Cathard Investments Limited
S Chaplin Holdings Limited
Claxton Trust
Elysium Healthcare LC Limited
Fairview New Homes (Charlton) Ltd
Farcet Fen Limited
KCK Peterborough Devco LLP
LSF9 Robin Newco 1 Limited
LSF9 Robin Newco 2 Limited
Laxkan Holdings Ltd
Laxkan Ltd
M G 111 Ltd
MA Securities London Limited
Nine Reading Hotel Limited
Pacific (BC) Topco 2 Limited
Pacific (BC) Topco 3 Limited
Pacific (BC) Topco 4 Limited
RA Securities London Limited
RDL1 Limited
Hilary Russell Group Ltd
Signature Lessee I Limited
Ventress Group Limited
Whitbread (Condor) Holdings Ltd

December 2016 [14]

Arkarius Bidco Limited
Aspire (CRP) Limited
Aurora Group Holdings (UK) Ltd
Brickfields Trust
F-Star Delta Limited
Greenstone Oxford Limited
Hilton International IP Holding 2
I4B Holdings Limited
Immobiliare Cardi Marmi Ltd
Integrated Microwave Technology Ltd
Kitewood (Creekside) Limited
Merton Acquisitions Limited
Newhall Land Limited
Wheat Quarter Limited

January 2017 [31]

Albendan Limited
Blackbuck Acquisitions Limited
Blackbuck Midco Limited
Blackbuck Topco Limited
Chapman Ventilation Group Ltd
Ellis Timber (Holdings) Ltd
Energypro Asset Management Ltd
Fairview Hotels Investments (2) Ltd
GDL (Aylesbury) Limited
HCT Portland Limited
Hera Primary Academy Trust
Hudson Almere Limited
Hudson Arnhem Limited
Hudson Brent Limited
Hudson Camden Limited
Hudson Chemical Tankers Ltd
Hudson Kensington Limited
Hudson Lisse Limited
Hudson Richmond Limited
J & A (International) Holdings Ltd
KGM Underwriting Services Ltd
Kier Cross Keys Dev LLP
Kier Cross Keys Holdco 1 LLP
David Lloyd Clubs Holdings Ltd
David Lloyd Clubs Limited
Marylebone Square Holdings Ltd
Onslow Inc. Ltd
Rammamere House Limited
M R Scott Limited
Unity Education Trust
Xtera Topco Limited

February 2017 [16]

ABVR Finance Limited
ABVR Group Limited
ABVR Holdings Limited
Brandon House Limited
Bridge Road Southall Limited
Chalk Farm Marine LLP
Compare The Market Limited
Cremer (UK) Manufacturing Co. Ltd
Downing Strategic Micro-Cap Investment Trust
Fulton Lincoln Limited
Fulton Regent Limited
JRL Property Holdings Limited
Latimer Hill LLP
Mid Norfolk Academy Trust
OP UK Bidco Limited
TCR New Limited

March 2017 [11]

Aston Barclay Holdings Group Ltd
Fulton Clover Limited
Fulton Hyde Limited
Omar Group Finance Limited
Omar Group Holdings Limited
Omar Group Investments Limited
Orwell Multi Academy Trust
SAFL British Hotels Limited
TUI Group Fleet Finance Ltd
Twilight Real Estate Limited
Whitehill & Bordon Development Company Phase 1A

April 2017 [11]

Carestream Dental Technology Parent
Carestream Dental Technology Topco
Combat Medical Holdings Ltd
Daiwater Investment Limited
European Investments (Cornwall) Holdings
Kingswood Village Limited
Perfect Practices Group Ltd
S & W Design & Build (Group) Ltd
SHOO 802AA Limited
UCL Frognal Limited
Whitestone Property Services Ltd

May 2017 [15]

Bourne Court Properties Ltd
Cardel Group Limited
Care UK Healthcare Holdings Ltd
Cranfield Technology Park Investments
DDW Holdings Limited
Fulton Central Limited
Gibbs Denley Holdings Limited
Kirkmore HT Limited
RQ Capital Loans Limited
SHOO 803AA Limited
Soho Loop Limited
THR Number 12 PLC
Thorney Leys Developments Ltd
Turnlet Films (JN) Limited
Wilton & Bain Group Limited

June 2017 [9]

Aquaterra Energy Group Limited
Arjo UK Limited
Futuresource Holdings Limited
Kimberley Capital Limited
Thomas Lipton Ltd
Quanta Consultancy Services Group Ltd
Rowan International Topco Ltd
Services Machinery & Trucks Ltd
Winstanley and York Road Regeneration LLP

July 2017 [6]

Broadleaf Park LLP
Caskade Properties Limited
Fulton Grand Limited
Fulton St James Limited
GHL (Kilmorie) Limited
SLV Group Holding UK Limited

August 2017

Onix Investments UK Ltd
Securon Holdings Limited

September 2017

Affinity Water Holdco Finance Ltd
Edstrom UK Holdings PLC
Huxley Global Limited
Summerhill Birmingham Limited

October 2017

Hel Group Limited
SDV 2025 ZDP PLC

November 2017

GHL (Summerstown) Limited

December 2017

Peterborough Keys Academies Trust

This page is intentionally left blank

Company Profiles

1 Big Data Management Limited
Incorporated: 16 May 1994 *Employees:* 18
Net Worth: £4,407,770 *Total Assets:* £8,240,972
Registered Office: 1st Floor, Sheraton House, Lower Road, Chorleywood, Rickmansworth, Herts, WD3 5LH
Activities: Other letting and operating of own or leased real estate
Parent: Melsom Holdings Limited
Officers: David John Ridler, Secretary/Director; Clare Elizabeth Ridler [1969] Director; David John Ridler [1963] Director

1LIFE Management Solutions Limited
Incorporated: 7 December 1990 *Employees:* 313
Net Worth: £5,684,000 *Total Assets:* £15,968,000
Registered Office: LDH House, St Ives Business Park, Parsons Green, St Ives, Cambs, PE27 4AA
Activities: Operation of sports facilities
Officers: Ian Arthur Hendrie, Secretary; Mark Braithwaite [1978] Managing Director [British/South African]; Keith Hamill [1952] Director/Vice Chairman; Ian Arthur Hendrie [1970] Director; Julian Frederick Nicholls [1951] Director

1LMS (Holdings) Limited
Incorporated: 26 October 1999
Net Worth Deficit: £875,000 *Total Assets:* £8,425,000
Registered Office: LDH House, St Ives Business Park, Parsons Green, St Ives, Cambs, PE27 4AA
Activities: Activities of other holding companies n.e.c.
Officers: Ian Arthur Hendrie, Secretary; Mark Braithwaite [1978] Managing Director [British/South African]; Keith Hamill [1952] Director/Vice Chairman; Ian Arthur Hendrie [1970] Director; Julian Frederick Nicholls [1951] Director

1spatial Group Limited
Incorporated: 3 June 2003 *Employees:* 68
Net Worth: £1,862,275 *Total Assets:* £10,280,107
Registered Office: Tennyson House, Cambridge Business Park, Cowley Road, Cambridge, CB4 0WZ
Activities: Information technology consultancy activities
Parent: 1spatial Holdings Limited
Officers: Susan Margaret Wallace, Secretary; Duncan James Guthrie [1972] Sales Director; Claire Milverton [1974] Director

1spatial PLC
Incorporated: 20 April 2005 *Employees:* 206
Net Worth: £6,790,000 *Total Assets:* £18,954,000
Registered Office: Tennyson House, Cambridge Business Park, Cowley Road, Cambridge, CB4 0WZ
Activities: Other information technology service activities
Officers: Susan Margaret Wallace, Secretary; Peter John Massey [1962] Director; Claire Milverton [1974] Director; Nicole Payne [1980] Director; Andrew Henry Roberts [1952] Director/Chairman; Francis David Small [1958] Director

2020 Developments (Luton) Limited
Incorporated: 1 October 2015 *Employees:* 1
Net Worth Deficit: £490,118 *Total Assets:* £26,803,900
Registered Office: Kenilworth Stadium, 1 Maple Road East, Luton, Beds, LU4 8AW
Activities: Development of building projects
Parent: 2020 Holdings (England) Limited
Officers: Dr Paul Dean Ballantyne [1964] Director; Stephen Paul Browne [1968] Director; Robert James Curson [1951] Director; Simon James Mark Gibb [1962] Finance Director; Michael Brian Herrick [1948] Director; Gary Peter Sweet [1964] Director; David Charles Wilkinson [1947] Director/Consultant

2020 Holdings (England) Limited
Incorporated: 30 September 2015 *Employees:* 360
Net Worth Deficit: £1,443,075 *Total Assets:* £28,757,052
Registered Office: Kenilworth Stadium, 1 Maple Road East, Luton, Beds, LU4 8AW
Activities: Activities of other holding companies n.e.c.
Major Shareholder: Paul Dean Ballantyne
Officers: Dr Paul Dean Ballantyne [1964] Director; Stephen Paul Browne [1968] Director; Robert James Curson [1951] Director; Simon James Mark Gibb [1962] Finance Director; Michael Brian Herrick [1948] Director; Gary Peter Sweet [1964] Director; David Charles Wilkinson [1947] Director/Consultant

254 Kilburn HR LLP
Incorporated: 22 November 2016
Net Worth: £8,299,500 *Total Assets:* £21,930,924
Registered Office: Suite 2, Fountain House, 1a Elm Park, Stanmore, Middlesex, HA7 4AU

3D European Holdings Limited
Incorporated: 18 September 1990
Net Worth: £90,965,000 *Total Assets:* £121,134,000
Registered Office: Mark House, Mark Road, Hemel Hempstead, Herts, HP2 7UA
Activities: Activities of head offices
Parent: 3D Systems Corporation
Officers: David James Langfield, Secretary; Andrew Johnson [1974] Director/Legal [American]; David James Langfield [1974] Finance Director

3D Systems Europe Limited
Incorporated: 2 April 2001 *Employees:* 119
Net Worth: £17,942,000 *Total Assets:* £27,130,000
Registered Office: Mark House, Mark Road, Hemel Hempstead, Herts, HP2 7UA
Activities: Wholesale of other machinery and equipment
Officers: David James Langfield, Secretary; Andrew Johnson [1974] Director/Legal [American]; David James Langfield [1974] Finance Director

3DS Financial Services EMEA Ltd
Incorporated: 2 July 2015
Net Worth: £514,924,288 *Total Assets:* £515,662,784
Registered Office: Unit 334 Cambridge Science Park, Milton Road, Cambridge, CB4 0WN
Activities: Activities of financial services holding companies
Parent: Dassault Systemes UK Limited
Officers: John Cyril Christian Colleemallay [1969] Senior Director Group Treasury & Financing [French]; Jane Jenkins [1969] Finance Director

3DS Financial Services Ltd
Incorporated: 4 March 2015
Net Worth: £37,281,764 *Total Assets:* £1,304,574,848
Registered Office: Unit 334 Cambridge Science Park, Milton Road, Cambridge, CB4 0WN
Activities: Activities of financial services holding companies
Parent: Dassault Systemes UK Limited
Officers: John Cyril Christian Colleemallay [1969] Senior Director Group Treasury & Financing [French]; Jane Jenkins [1969] Finance Director

3VS UK Limited
Incorporated: 31 March 2004 *Employees:* 101
Net Worth: £6,089,738 *Total Assets:* £35,726,692
Registered Office: 39a Joel Street, Northwood Hills, Northwood, Middlesex, HA6 1NZ
Activities: Activities of head offices
Major Shareholder: Anuj Somchand Shah
Officers: Anuj Somchand Shah [1966] Director/Actuary

4 BG Group Ltd
Incorporated: 7 January 2010 *Employees:* 173
Net Worth: £3,086,978 *Total Assets:* £16,101,068
Registered Office: BG Office, 7 Brundon Lane, Sudbury, Suffolk, CO10 1XR
Activities: Activities of head offices
Major Shareholder: Roy David Jones
Officers: Joanne White, Secretary; Roy David Jones [1957] Director; Andrew Thurlbourn [1961] Director

41/43 Maddox St. Limited
Incorporated: 30 August 1960 *Employees:* 32
Net Worth: £35,873,912 *Total Assets:* £37,245,172
Registered Office: Unit 96 The Maltings Business Centre, The Maltings, Stanstead Abbotts, Herts, SG12 8HG
Activities: Buying and selling of own real estate
Officers: William Arthur Henry Lascelles Lucas, Secretary/Director; Annabel Barbara Lucas [1958] Director; James Christopher Lascelles Lucas [1961] Director/Property Manager; William Arthur Henry Lascelles Lucas [1965] Director; Caroline Sarah Vallance [1959] Director

452 Finchley Road LLP
Incorporated: 1 February 2016
Net Worth: £4,041,383 *Total Assets:* £14,943,261
Registered Office: Grenville House, 4 Grenville Avenue, Broxbourne, Herts, EN10 7DH

66 Queen Square Limited
Incorporated: 7 March 2011
Net Worth: £11,024,000 *Total Assets:* £11,106,000
Registered Office: Maple Cross House, Denham Way, Maple Cross, Rickmansworth, Herts, WD3 9SW
Activities: Development of building projects
Parent: Skanska Project Developments Limited
Officers: Steven Leven, Secretary; Culdip Kelly Kaur Gangotra [1970] Director/Accountant; Helen Katherine Martin [1975] Director/Civil Engineer; Martin George Neeson [1968] Director/Manager

8x8 UK Investments Limited
Incorporated: 6 November 2013
Net Worth: £42,589,416 *Total Assets:* £42,604,680
Registered Office: Oxford House, Bell Business Park, Aylesbury, Bucks, HP19 8JR
Activities: Activities of other holding companies n.e.c.
Parent: 8x8, Inc
Officers: Edward Alec Kemp, Secretary; Mary Ellen Genovese [1959] Director/Chief Financial Officer [American]; Bryan R Martin [1967] Director/Chief Technology Officer [American]; Vikram Verma [1964] Director/Chief Executive Officer [American]

94 Camlet Way LLP
Incorporated: 16 December 2014
Net Worth: £1,679,477 *Total Assets:* £8,084,432
Registered Office: Grenville House, 4 Grenville Avenue, Broxbourne, Herts, EN10 7DH

A 1 Bacon Company Limited
Incorporated: 19 November 1979 *Employees:* 68
Net Worth: £4,056,175 *Total Assets:* £10,351,159
Registered Office: Brook House, Lovet Road, Harlow, Essex, CM19 5TB
Activities: Processing and preserving of meat
Major Shareholder: Robert James Cannon
Officers: Richard James Shrosbree, Secretary/Administrator; Mark Nicholas Canon [1962] Director/General Manager; Robert James Canon [1964] Director/Company Administrator; Peter Graham Dawson [1956] Sales Director; Steven Hind [1960] Operations Director; Richard James Shrosbree [1969] Director/Administrator

A P P Wholesale PLC
Incorporated: 2 April 2008 *Employees:* 159
Net Worth: £24,937,112 *Total Assets:* £54,911,108
Registered Office: Units 12-14 Sterling Industrial Estate, Rainham Road South, Dagenham, Essex, RM10 8TX
Activities: Wholesale of hardware, plumbing and heating equipment and supplies
Major Shareholder: Allan Paul Pierce
Officers: Michael John Brockman, Secretary; Michael John Brockman [1978] Director; David Fulton [1953] Director; Allan Paul Pierce [1947] Director; Matthew Pierce [1974] Director; Stuart Brian Snell [1961] Director

A-Roads Investments Limited
Incorporated: 19 December 2006
Net Worth: £26,386,576 *Total Assets:* £33,247,534
Registered Office: 36 James Bedford Close, Pinner, Middlesex, HA5 3TD
Activities: Activities of head offices
Parent: BIIF Bidco Limited
Officers: John Ivor Cavill [1972] Director; Matthew James Edwards [1985] Associate Director

A. & A. 2000 Limited
Incorporated: 29 October 1999 *Employees:* 57
Net Worth: £10,472,359 *Total Assets:* £13,066,475
Registered Office: 3rd Floor, Crown House, 151 High Road, Loughton, Essex, IG10 4LG
Activities: Activities of head offices
Shareholders: Ann Kathleen Warren; Alan Michael Warren
Officers: Alan Michael Warren, Secretary; Alan Michael Warren [1957] Director/Electrical Engineer; Ann Kathleen Warren [1956] Director/Sales Consultant

A. & B. Glass Company Limited
Incorporated: 6 February 1981 *Employees:* 439
Net Worth: £4,531,650 *Total Assets:* £15,499,528
Registered Office: Addison Road, Chilton Industrial Estate, Sudbury, Suffolk, CO10 2YW
Activities: Glazing
Parent: A & B Glass Holding Company Limited
Officers: David Frank Barrett [1957] Director; Paul Brian McManus [1967] Director; Stephen Derek Stone [1963] Director

A. F. Machinery Limited
Incorporated: 23 November 1990 *Employees:* 85
Net Worth: £16,287,208 *Total Assets:* £25,142,550
Registered Office: The Estate Office, Larkshall, East Wretham, Thetford, Norfolk, IP24 1QY
Activities: Support activities for crop production
Officers: Richard Symon Abrey, Secretary; Christopher Peter Abrey [1950] Director/Farmer; Giles Matthew Richard Abrey [1973] Director/Farmer; Matthew Robert Abrey [1983] Director/Farmer; Richard Symon Abrey [1947] Director/Farmer; Robert Abrey [1955] Director/Farmer; Thomas Russell William Abrey [1979] Director/Farmer

A.C. Entertainment Technologies Limited
Incorporated: 2 April 1982 *Employees:* 120
Net Worth: £6,879,397 *Total Assets:* £12,762,417
Registered Office: Centauri House, Hillbottom Road, Sands Industrial Estate, High Wycombe, Bucks, HP12 4HQ
Activities: Non-specialised wholesale trade
Parent: A.C. Lighting (Holdings) Ltd
Officers: Derri Anthony Gordon, Secretary; Lance Newton Bromhead [1968] Director; Peter Joseph Butler [1968] Audio & Visual Director; Phillip Robert Capstick [1965] Managing Director; Derri Anthony Gordon [1981] Financial Director; David Arthur Leggett [1953] Director; Christopher John Millard [1960] Director; Mark Graham Tonks [1963] Director; Jonathan Bevis Walters [1967] UK Sales Director

A.C. Lighting (Holdings) Limited
Incorporated: 16 August 2002 *Employees:* 280
Net Worth: £32,245,020 *Total Assets:* £52,121,268
Registered Office: Centauri House, Hillbottom Road, Sands Industrial Estate, High Wycombe, Bucks, HP12 4HQ
Activities: Activities of head offices
Major Shareholder: David Arthur Leggett
Officers: Phillip Robert Capstick, Secretary; David Arthur Leggett [1953] Director

A.G.E. Nursing Homes Limited
Incorporated: 5 December 1990 *Employees:* 254
Net Worth: £5,231,714 *Total Assets:* £12,253,589
Registered Office: 249 Cranbrook Road, Ilford, Essex, IG1 4TG
Activities: Residential nursing care facilities
Shareholders: Julia Rosalyn Hainsworth-Adams; Stewart Andrew Hainswoth
Officers: Julia Rosalyn Hainsworth-Adams, Secretary; Stewart Andrew Hainsworth [1969] Finance Director; Julia Rosalyn Hainsworth-Adams [1965] Managing Director

A.J.N. Steelstock Ltd.
Incorporated: 13 April 1961 *Employees:* 344
Net Worth: £18,386,852 *Total Assets:* £56,484,324
Registered Office: Icknield Way, Kentford, Newmarket, Suffolk, CB8 7QT
Activities: Wholesale of metals and metal ores
Shareholders: Jean Boyden; Alan Boyden; Neil Robert Boyden
Officers: Jean Mary Boyden, Secretary; Courtney Bell [1969] Director/Company Accountant; Alan John Boyden [1965] Director/Manager; Jean Mary Boyden [1936] Director; Neil Robert Boyden [1970] Director/Steel Stockholders; Neil Cressall [1969] Director/Sales Representative; Clare McGall [1973] Operations Director; Shaun Nolan [1974] Operations Director; Christopher Sage [1980] Operations Director

A.M.P. Air Conditioning Limited
Incorporated: 13 April 1989 *Employees:* 45
Net Worth: £7,921,601 *Total Assets:* £11,372,225
Registered Office: Blenheim House, Blenhiem Court, Brown Fields, Welwyn Garden City, Herts, AL7 1AD
Activities: Steam and air conditioning supply
Officers: Timothy Francis Young, Secretary; Alfredos Marios Armaos [1964] Director/Country Manager [Greek]; Yuji Hirota [1962] Director [Japanese]; Pollyanne McConachie [1962] Director; Tsuguo Takano [1971] Director/Office Worker [Japanese]; Enrique Vilamitjana Perez [1968] Managing Director [Spanish]; Timothy Francis Young [1970] Commercial Director

A1 Pharmaceuticals Holdings Limited
Incorporated: 30 April 2013 *Employees:* 37
Net Worth: £14,493,644 *Total Assets:* £20,243,268
Registered Office: Unit 20 & 21 Easter Industrial Park, Ferry Lane South, Rainham, Essex, RM13 9BP
Activities: Manufacture of basic pharmaceutical products
Officers: Carmen Lewis [1965] Director/Secretary Administrator; Gary Stephen Lewis [1960] Director/Pharmacist

A1 Pharmaceuticals Public Limited Company
Incorporated: 24 February 1992 *Employees:* 37
Net Worth: £14,392,724 *Total Assets:* £18,008,192
Registered Office: Unit 20 & 21 Easter Industrial Park, Ferry Lane South, Rainham, Essex, RM13 9BP
Activities: Wholesale of pharmaceutical goods
Shareholders: Gary Stephen Lewis; Carmen Lewis
Officers: Carmen Lewis, Secretary/Administrator; Carmen Lewis [1965] Director/Secretary Administrator; Gary Stephen Lewis [1960] Director/Pharmacist

AAG UK Parent Limited
Incorporated: 11 October 2010
Net Worth: £9,653,373 *Total Assets:* £9,653,373
Registered Office: Sword House, Totteridge Road, High Wycombe, Bucks, HP13 6DG
Activities: Activities of head offices
Parent: Armored Auto (UK) Limited
Officers: Emily Kellum Boss [1962] Director [American]; Timothy W Gorman [1960] Director [American]; Mark S Lavigne [1971] Director/Business Executive [American]

AB InBev UK Limited
Incorporated: 27 April 2000 *Employees:* 991
Net Worth: £111,152,000 *Total Assets:* £858,534,016
Registered Office: Porter Tun House, 500 Capability Green, Luton, Beds, LU1 3LS
Activities: Manufacture of beer
Parent: Nimbuspath Limited
Officers: Kayleigh Anne Wilshaw, Secretary; Oliver James Devon [1989] Finance Director; Jens Hoffmann [1975] Supply Director Germany & UK [German]; Martin Evert Ijntema [1981] Sales Director [Dutch]; Paula Nogueira Lindenberg [1975] Director/President BU West [Brazilian]; Rory McLellan [1978] Commercial Director; Claire Louise Richardson [1983] People Director; James Malcom Rowe [1978] UK Operations Director; Tatiana Stadukhina [1982] Marketing Director [American]; Andrew George Whiting [1982] Legal Director

Abacus Group Limited
Incorporated: 19 July 1988 *Employees:* 3
Net Worth: £11,487,000 *Total Assets:* £11,567,000
Registered Office: Avnet House, Rutherford Close, Meadwy, Stevenage, Herts, SG1 2EF
Activities: Activities of head offices
Parent: Electron House (Overseas) Limited
Officers: Thomas Ludaescher [1961] Director [German]; Mark McKrell [1966] Finance Director; Harvey Woodford [1963] Director/VP Corporate Secretary [American]

Abacus Hotels Limited
Incorporated: 13 September 1995 *Employees:* 295
Net Worth: £7,434,182 *Total Assets:* £14,878,855
Registered Office: White Lion House, 20 Station Street, Swaffham, Norfolk, PE37 7LH
Activities: Hotels and similar accommodation
Officers: Michael James Halls, Secretary/Director; Howard James Darking [1953] Director; Thomas Frederick Franke [1929] Director/Property Developer [American]; Michael James Halls [1947] Director

Abbey College, Ramsey
Incorporated: 15 August 2011 *Employees:* 161
Net Worth: £26,613,448 *Total Assets:* £27,607,926
Registered Office: Abbey College, Abbey Road, Ramsey, Cambs, PE26 1DG
Activities: General secondary education
Officers: John Alexander Rodney Chrisp [1945] Director; Andrew Christoforou [1971] Director/Headmaster; Helen Clarke [1967] Director/Homemaker; Alan John Dods [1956] Director/IT Consultant; Esmond James Edwards [1949] Director/Chartered Accountant; Madeleine Ann Jackson [1950] Director/Retired; Gareth Idwal Jones [1952] Director/Design and Technology Technician; Neil Robinson [1961] Director/Teacher; Ian Rout [1970] Director/Support Worker - Adults with Disabilities; Stephen Roy Smith [1958] Director; John Francis Stevens [1959] Director/Surveyor; Lisa Jane Williamson [1969] Director/Administrator

Abbey Cross Trading Limited
Incorporated: 4 July 1974 *Employees:* 75
Net Worth: £6,393,376 *Total Assets:* £12,419,587
Registered Office: Unit 2, 40 Comet Way, Eastwoodbury Lane, Southend on Sea, Essex, SS2 6XW
Activities: Manufacture of basic iron and steel and of ferro-alloys
Major Shareholder: Alan Leslie Moore
Officers: Ben Patrick Moore, Secretary; Alan Leslie Moore [1950] Director [Irish]; Ben Patrick Moore [1983] Managing Director [Irish]; Gary Andrew Wiley [1964] Director/General Manager

Abbey Developments Limited
Incorporated: 25 January 1939 *Employees:* 70
Net Worth: £181,635,776 *Total Assets:* £262,689,568
Registered Office: Abbey House, 2 Southgate Road, Potters Bar, Herts, EN6 5DU
Activities: Construction of domestic buildings
Parent: Abbey Group Limited
Officers: Jordan Lee Collison, Secretary; David John Dawson, Secretary; William Patrick Joseph Callinan [1958] Director; Edward John Costello [1959] Director [Irish]; Stuart David Critchell [1966] Director; David John Dawson [1964] Director; Lorenzo Guiseppe Fraquelli [1958] Director; Charles Hubert Gallagher [1959] Director [Irish]

The Abbey Group Cambridgeshire Limited
Incorporated: 24 November 1987 *Employees:* 20
Net Worth: £22,393,772 *Total Assets:* £43,206,404
Registered Office: Nene Lodge, Funthams Lane, Whittlesey, Peterborough, PE7 2PB
Activities: Activities of head offices
Major Shareholder: David Clifford Sutton
Officers: Tracey Jayne Salisbury, Secretary; Carl David Sutton [1975] Director; David Clifford Sutton [1950] Director; Nicholas Robert Sutton [1977] Director

Abbey Group Limited
Incorporated: 10 November 1954 *Employees:* 4
Net Worth: £27,561,040 *Total Assets:* £45,860,296
Registered Office: Abbey House, 2 Southgate Road, Potters Bar, Herts, EN6 5DU
Activities: Activities of head offices
Parent: Abbey Public Limited Company
Officers: David John Dawson, Secretary; David John Dawson [1964] Director/Accountant; Lorenzo Guiseppe Fraquelli [1958] Director; Charles Hubert Gallagher [1959] Director [Irish]

Abbey Investments Limited
Incorporated: 21 January 1955
Net Worth: £8,983,964 *Total Assets:* £9,148,889
Registered Office: Abbey House, 2 Southgate Road, Potters Bar, Herts, EN6 5DU
Activities: Other letting and operating of own or leased real estate
Parent: Abbe Group Limited
Officers: David John Dawson, Secretary; David John Dawson [1964] Director/Accountant; Lorenzo Guiseppe Fraquelli [1958] Director; Charles Hubert Gallagher [1959] Director [Irish]

Abbey Mills Properties Ltd
Incorporated: 10 August 2010
Net Worth: £9,517,519 *Total Assets:* £13,656,690
Registered Office: Unicorn House, Station Close, Potters Bar, Herts, EN6 1TL
Activities: Buying and selling of own real estate
Parent: Panther Securities PLC
Officers: Simon Jeffrey Peters, Secretary; Andrew Stewart Perloff [1944] Director; John Henry Perloff [1968] Director; Simon Jeffrey Peters [1977] Director

Abbey Properties Cambridgeshire Limited
Incorporated: 18 December 1995 *Employees:* 4
Net Worth: £11,274,060 *Total Assets:* £13,544,637
Registered Office: Nene Lodge, Funthams Lane, Whittlesey, Peterborough, Cambs, PE7 2PB
Activities: Development of building projects
Shareholders: Carl David Sutton; Nicholas Robert Sutton
Officers: Tracey Jayne Salisbury, Secretary; Carl David Sutton [1975] Director; David Clifford Sutton [1950] Director; Nicholas Robert Sutton [1977] Director

Abbey Ravenscroft Park Limited
Incorporated: 7 July 2005 *Employees:* 88
Net Worth: £1,816,617 *Total Assets:* £8,138,937
Registered Office: 9 Spareleaze Hill, Loughton, Essex, IG10 1BS
Activities: Residential nursing care facilities
Officers: Devyani Jayanti Patel, Company Secretary; Devyani Jayanti Patel [1953] Director/Secretary; Jayanti Mohanlal Patel [1949] Director/Businessman

Abbey Total Care Group Limited
Incorporated: 28 April 2003 *Employees:* 542
Net Worth: £34,179,184 *Total Assets:* £65,309,764
Registered Office: 9 Spareleaze Hill, Loughton, Essex, IG10 1BS
Activities: Activities of head offices
Officers: Devyani Jayanti Patel, Secretary/Director; Devyani Jayanti Patel [1953] Director/Secretary; Jayanti Mohanlal Patel [1949] Director

Abbey View Produce Limited
Incorporated: 14 September 1972 *Employees:* 132
Net Worth: £13,202,802 *Total Assets:* £18,282,696
Registered Office: Abbey View Nursery, Galley Hill Road, Waltham Abbey, Essex, EN9 2AG
Activities: Growing of other non-perennial crops
Major Shareholder: Brian John Hibberd
Officers: William James Worwood, Secretary/Accountant; Brian John Hibberd [1950] Director; Luke Hibberd [1984] Director; Scott Wilkinson [1974] Director

Abbeyfield Society (The)
Incorporated: 27 November 1956 *Employees:* 1,141
Net Worth: £143,220,992 *Total Assets:* £177,806,000
Registered Office: St Peter's House, 2 Bricket Road, St Albans, Herts, AL1 3JW
Activities: Residential care activities for the elderly and disabled
Officers: Jonathan William Edward Sweet, Secretary; Sara Jayne Beamand [1966] Director; Andrew Lionel Dudley de Hochepied Larpent [1951] Director; Andre Maurice Decraene [1946] Director [Belgian]; Norman Alistair Greville [1957] Director; Elizabeth Amanda Houlihan [1950] Director; Jennifer Ann Lawrence [1966] Director/Accountant; Jeffrey Medlock [1940] Director/Retired; Cedric Meiring [1958] Director/Retired [South African]; William Ian David Plaistowe [1942] Director/Chartered Accountant; Christopher John Addison Smith [1949] Director; Kenneth Staveley [1938] Director/Retired; Stephen Venner [1944] Director; Professor Brian Owen Williams [1947] Director/Medical Member Tribunals Service MoJ

Abbot's Hill Limited
Incorporated: 6 January 1956 *Employees:* 184
Net Worth: £7,110,488 *Total Assets:* £12,574,897
Registered Office: Bunkers Lane, Hemel Hempstead, Herts, HP3 8RP
Activities: Pre-primary education
Parent: Abbot's Hill School
Officers: Caroline Korniczky, Secretary; Nigel John Chadwick [1960] Director; Jonathan William Gillespie [1966] Director/Headmaster; Martin Hart [1966] Assistant Director; Robert Neil James [1962] Director/Solicitor; Janet Mary Mark [1946] Director/Headteacher Retired; Jason Vidal Roberts McCaldin [1966] Director/Bursar; Jill Lesley Myers [1962] Director/Housewife; Jean Ross [1954] Director/Retired; Dr Linda Summerton [1962] Director; Dr Shori Thakur [1973] Director/Lecturer; David Walters [1964] Director/Chartered Accountant

Abbots Ripton Farming Company Limited
Incorporated: 28 January 1959 *Employees:* 42
Net Worth: £2,998,632 *Total Assets:* £9,104,121
Registered Office: The Estate Office, Grange Farm, Abbots Ripton, Huntingdon, Cambs, PE28 2PH
Activities: Growing of cereals (except rice), leguminous crops and oil seeds
Shareholders: Archibald Hugh Duberly; Hugo Edward Stainton Jackson; John Ailwyn de Ramsey
Officers: Lee Benjamin Halling, Secretary; Lady Alison Mary de Ramsey [1954] Director; The Right Honourable Lord de Ramsey [1942] Director/Farmer; The Hon Andrew Edward Fellowes [1950] Director/Farmer; The Hon Freddie John Fellowes [1978] Director; Jennifer Julia Fellowes [1940] Director

Abbotsley Farms Limited
Incorporated: 11 January 2008 *Employees:* 6
Net Worth: £8,412,428 *Total Assets:* £16,570,914
Registered Office: Suite C, Unex House, Bourges Boulevard, Peterborough, Cambs, PE1 1NG
Activities: Growing of cereals (except rice), leguminous crops and oil seeds
Shareholders: Michael Raymond Topham; Janice Mary Topham
Officers: Janice Topham, Secretary; Louise Margaret Santry [1986] Director; Janice Mary Topham [1955] Director; Michael Raymond Topham [1953] Director/Accountant; Samuel Peter Topham [1987] Director

Abel Homes Limited
Incorporated: 6 January 1987 *Employees:* 34
Net Worth: £6,120,136 *Total Assets:* £15,935,002
Registered Office: Neaton Business Park (North), Norwich Road, Watton, Thetford, Norfolk, IP25 6JB
Activities: Construction of domestic buildings
Shareholders: Anthony Noel Abel; Margaret Gwyneth Abel; Christopher Anthony Abel
Officers: Paul Matthew Legrice, Secretary; Anthony Noel Abel [1953] Director; Christopher Anthony Abel [1983] Director/Builder; Margaret Gwyneth Abel [1957] Director; Noel Frederick Bartram [1952] Director; Paul Matthew Legrice [1979] Finance and Operations Director

Abington Farms Limited
Incorporated: 19 June 1948 *Employees:* 7
Net Worth: £6,954,089 *Total Assets:* £8,374,123
Registered Office: Abington Park Farm, Great Abington, Cambs, CB21 6AX
Activities: Growing of cereals (except rice), leguminous crops and oil seeds
Shareholders: Simon Robert Frank Chaplin; Hilary Ann Russell; David John Harold Chaplin
Officers: Hilary Ann Russell, Secretary/Director; David John Harold Chaplin [1963] Director; Simon Robert Frank Chaplin [1967] Director/Farmer; Hilary Ann Russell [1965] Director

The Abington Group Limited
Incorporated: 11 November 2016 *Employees:* 3
Net Worth: £35,867,104 *Total Assets:* £35,931,504
Registered Office: Abington Park Farm, Great Abington, Cambs, CB21 6AX
Activities: Mixed farming
Parent: Chaplin Group Limited
Officers: David John Harold Chaplin [1963] Director/General Manager; Simon Robert Frank Chaplin [1967] Director/General Manager; Hilary Ann Russell [1965] Director

ABL (Holding) Limited
Incorporated: 2 July 1982 *Employees:* 4
Net Worth: £9,176,830 *Total Assets:* £10,062,947
Registered Office: 16 Hillbottom Road, Sands Industrial Estate, High Wycombe, Bucks, HP12 4HJ
Activities: Non-trading company
Parent: PSV Glass & Glazing Limited
Officers: Philip Iain Powell, Secretary; John Wright, Secretary; Nicholas Paul Andrews [1976] Director; Paul Marcus Andrews [1949] Director; Suzanne Kathryn Andrews [1976] Director; Philip Iain Powell [1966] Finance Director

ABM Technical Solutions Limited
Incorporated: 25 July 2000 *Employees:* 652
Previous: Westway Services Limited
Net Worth: £28,928,600 *Total Assets:* £39,368,328
Registered Office: Artemis Building, Odyssey Business Park, West End Road, South Ruislip, Middlesex, HA4 6QE
Activities: Other service activities n.e.c.
Parent: Westway Services Holdings (2010) Ltd
Officers: Mike Bindeman [1958] Director [American]; Jason Robert Pease [1970] Director; Colin Andrew Stevenson [1963] Finance Director

Abrahams Consolidated Limited
Incorporated: 7 September 1931 *Employees:* 5
Net Worth: £24,990,806 *Total Assets:* £29,106,552
Registered Office: Ground Floor, 4 Victoria Square, St Albans, Herts, AL1 3TF
Activities: Buying and selling of own real estate
Shareholders: Linda Joy Abrahams; Peter David Abrahams
Officers: Darren Glyn Jordan, Secretary; Peter David Abrahams [1943] Director; Roy Neil Arthur [1948] Director/Chartered Accountant; Gordon Everard Wood [1952] Director/Chartered Surveyor; David Philip Wray [1948] Director/Retired Solicitor

ABSL1 Limited
Incorporated: 30 September 2014
Net Worth: £48,274,500 *Total Assets:* £146,092,176
Registered Office: 22 Barn Rise, Wembley, Middlesex, HA9 9NQ
Activities: Other letting and operating of own or leased real estate
Parent: ABSL Holdings Limited
Officers: Paul Gary Hirst, Secretary; Anthony David Chambers [1955] Director/Property Consultant; Daniel Freedman [1971] Director/Lawyer; Paul Gary Hirst [1961] Director/Property Consultant

Absolute Radio Limited
Incorporated: 24 December 1991 *Employees:* 26
Net Worth: £8,454,000 *Total Assets:* £11,621,000
Registered Office: Media House, Peterborough Business Park, Lynch Wood, Peterborough, Cambs, PE2 6EA
Activities: Radio broadcasting
Parent: Bauer AR Holdings Limited
Officers: Deidre Ann Ford [1960] Managing Director; Paul Anthony Keenan [1963] Director/Publisher; Sarah Jane Vickery [1963] Finance Director

ABVR Finance Limited
Incorporated: 2 February 2017
Net Worth Deficit: £2,429,000 *Total Assets:* £67,983,000
Registered Office: The Car Auction, Drovers Way, Chelmsford, Essex, CM2 5PP
Activities: Activities of other holding companies n.e.c.
Parent: ABVR Holdings Limited
Officers: Alexander Tristan Craddock [1979] Director; John Leslie Crichton [1970] Director/Accountant; Neil Thomas Hodson [1963] Director; Oliver John Tudor Jones [1976] Director; Martin Andrew Potter [1968] Director; David Martin James Scarborough [1966] Director; Glenn David Paul Scarborough [1963] Director; Laurence Edward William Vaughan [1963] Director/Chairman

ABVR Group Limited
Incorporated: 2 February 2017
Net Worth Deficit: £1,211,000 *Total Assets:* £51,100,000
Registered Office: The Car Auction, Drovers Way, Chelmsford, Essex, CM2 5PP
Activities: Activities of other holding companies n.e.c.
Parent: ABVR Finance Limited
Officers: Alexander Tristan Craddock [1979] Director; John Leslie Crichton [1970] Director/Accountant; Neil Thomas Hodson [1963] Director; Oliver John Tudor Jones [1976] Director; Martin Andrew Potter [1968] Director; David Martin James Scarborough [1966] Director; Glenn David Paul Scarborough [1963] Director; Laurence Edward William Vaughan [1963] Director/Chairman

ABVR Holdings Limited
Incorporated: 2 February 2017 *Employees:* 268
Net Worth Deficit: £959,000 *Total Assets:* £67,983,000
Registered Office: The Car Auction, Drovers Way, Chelmsford, Essex, CM2 5PP
Activities: Sale of used cars and light motor vehicles
Parent: Rutland Registrations Limited
Officers: Alexander Tristan Craddock [1979] Director; John Leslie Crichton [1970] Director/Accountant; Neil Thomas Hodson [1963] Director; Oliver John Tudor Jones [1976] Director; Martin Andrew Potter [1968] Director; David Martin James Scarborough [1966] Director; Glenn David Paul Scarborough [1963] Director; Laurence Edward William Vaughan [1963] Director/Chairman

Abzena (UK) Limited
Incorporated: 28 September 2001 *Employees:* 49
Previous: Polytherics Limited
Net Worth Deficit: £8,572,000 *Total Assets:* £54,314,000
Registered Office: Babraham Research Campus, Babraham, Cambridge, CB22 3AT
Activities: Research and experimental development on biotechnology
Parent: Abzena Limited
Officers: Michelle Dawn Neaves, Secretary; Dr Campbell Bunce [1970] Director/SVP Scientific Operations; Jonathan Howard Goldman [1965] Director/Investment Professional [American]; Richard Henry John Milbank [1964] Director/Chief Financial Officer; Michelle Dawn Neaves [1976] Director/Chartered Accountant; Nicholas O'Leary [1983] Director/Investment Professional [American]

Abzena Holdings Limited
Incorporated: 26 June 2015 *Employees:* 3
Net Worth: £811,000 *Total Assets:* £15,175,000
Registered Office: Babraham Research Campus, Babraham, Cambridge, CB22 3AT
Activities: Activities of other holding companies n.e.c.
Parent: Abzena Limited
Officers: Michelle Dawn Neaves, Secretary; Dr Campbell Bunce [1970] Director/SVP Scientific Operations; Richard Henry John Milbank [1964] Director/Chief Financial Officer; Michelle Dawn Neaves [1976] Director/Chartered Accountant

Abzena Limited
Incorporated: 25 March 2014 *Employees:* 236
Previous: Abzena PLC
Net Worth: £43,689,000 *Total Assets:* £54,289,000
Registered Office: Babraham Research Campus, Babraham, Cambridge, CB22 3AT
Activities: Research and experimental development on biotechnology
Parent: Astro Bidco Limited
Officers: Michelle Dawn Neaves, Secretary; Jonathan Goldman [1965] Director/Investment Professional [American]; Richard Henry John Milbank [1964] Director/Chief Financial Officer; Nicholas O'Leary [1983] Director/Investment Professional [American]; Brian Regan [1977] Director/Investment Professional [American]

Acacia Homes Limited
Incorporated: 6 August 2010
Net Worth: £6,535,208 *Total Assets:* £11,795,027
Registered Office: Sorbon, Aylesbury End, Beaconsfield, Bucks, HP9 1LW
Activities: Development of building projects
Shareholders: Sorbon Homes Limited; Michael James Shanly
Officers: Nicholas Mark Trott, Secretary; Michael James Shanly [1945] Director; Nicholas Mark Trott [1964] Director/Chartered Accountant

Access Platform Sales Limited
Incorporated: 10 February 1987 *Employees:* 24
Net Worth: £325,979 *Total Assets:* £9,647,870
Registered Office: Leewood Business Park, Upton, Huntingdon, Cambs, PE28 5YQ
Activities: Other specialised construction activities n.e.c.
Parent: Access Platform Sales Holdings Limited
Officers: Kian Golestani, Secretary; Christopher William Banks [1967] Director/Technical Engineering Manager; Stephen Robert Couling [1957] Director; James Ian Daintith [1958] Director; Anthony David Jennings [1959] Director and Accountant; Lee Malcolm Louder [1962] Sales Director; Shane Paver [1968] Director/General Manager (Scotland); Kevin Brian John Shadbolt [1963] Director

Access Technology Group Limited
Incorporated: 27 September 2005 *Employees:* 1,332
Net Worth: £69,211,000 *Total Assets:* £324,291,008
Registered Office: The Old School, School Lane, Stratford St Mary, Colchester, Essex, CO7 6LZ
Activities: Activities of head offices
Parent: Ingleby (1861) Limited
Officers: Michael James Audis [1971] Director; Christopher Andrew Armstrong Bayne [1971] Director; Stephen James Blundell [1970] Director; Paul Francis Bosson [1962] Director; Adam John Witherow Brown [1963] Director; David Michael England [1962] Director; Jonathan Robert Jorgensen [1978] Director

Access UK Ltd
Incorporated: 6 February 1989 *Employees:* 1,156
Net Worth: £73,075,000 *Total Assets:* £336,664,000
Registered Office: The Old School, School Lane, Stratford St Mary, Colchester, Essex, CO7 6LZ
Activities: Other information technology service activities
Parent: Access Technology Group
Officers: Michael James Audis [1971] Director; Christopher Andrew Armstrong Bayne [1971] Director; Stephen James Blundell [1970] Director; Adam John Witherow Brown [1963] Director; Jonathan Robert Jorgensen [1978] Director

Acclaim DMW Holdings Limited
Incorporated: 22 September 2016 *Employees:* 103
Net Worth: £18,669,704 *Total Assets:* £22,241,580
Registered Office: Ellisam House, Purfleet Industrial Park, Purfleet, Essex, RM15 4YD
Activities: Other service activities n.e.c.
Major Shareholder: Carmel Frances Swift
Officers: Carmel Frances Swift [1959] Director; Samuel David Woods [1982] Director

Acclaim Handling Limited
Incorporated: 26 October 1988 *Employees:* 108
Net Worth: £3,490,044 *Total Assets:* £12,431,751
Registered Office: Ellisam House, Purfleet Industrial Park, A13, Purfleet, Essex, RM15 4YD
Activities: Renting and leasing of other machinery, equipment and tangible goods n.e.c.
Officers: Ian Raymond Foxall, Secretary; Richard David Bonser [1961] Operations Director; Stephen Kenneth Frost [1962] Regional Director; Philip Neil Hyslop [1955] Director/Sales & Marketing; Carmel Frances Swift [1959] Director/Secretary; Samuel David Woods [1982] Director

Acco Brands Europe Limited
Incorporated: 10 August 2005
Net Worth: £393,598,592 *Total Assets:* £715,107,456
Registered Office: Oxford House, Oxford Road, Aylesbury, Bucks, HP21 8SZ
Activities: Activities of head offices
Officers: Richard Mark Geddie, Secretary; Neal Vernon Fenwick [1961] Director; Christopher Neil Hopkinson [1969] Director; Dr. Walter Joe Thomas [1966] Director/Solicitor

Acco Europe Limited
Incorporated: 23 June 1987
Net Worth: £214,523,008 *Total Assets:* £503,971,008
Registered Office: Oxford House, Oxford Road, Aylesbury, Bucks, HP21 8SZ
Activities: Activities of head offices
Officers: Richard Mark Geddie, Secretary; Neal Vernon Fenwick [1961] Director; Christopher Neil Hopkinson [1969] Director; Pamela Rolnick Schneider [1959] Director/Legal Counsel [American]; Dr. Walter Joe Thomas [1966] Director/Solicitor

Acco UK Limited
Incorporated: 6 May 1924 *Employees:* 332
Net Worth: £12,903,000 *Total Assets:* £76,585,000
Registered Office: Oxford House, Oxford Road, Aylesbury, Bucks, HP21 8SZ
Activities: Manufacture of paper stationery
Officers: Richard Mark Geddie, Secretary; George Lee Foot [1972] Director; Christopher Neil Hopkinson [1969] Director; Michael Howard O'Connell Stranders [1975] Director/VP, EMEA Marketing; Marc Alphons Temmerman [1966] Director/VP Operations and Logistics [Belgian]; Dr. Walter Joe Thomas [1966] Director/Solicitor; Mark George Wilkinson [1972] Director/Marketing and Business Development Manager

Acco-Rexel Group Services Limited
Incorporated: 11 March 1950
Net Worth: £124,767,000 *Total Assets:* £124,768,000
Registered Office: Oxford House, Oxford Road, Aylesbury, Bucks, HP21 8SZ
Activities: Activities of head offices
Officers: Richard Mark Geddie, Secretary; Richard Mark Geddie [1970] Director/Accountant; Christopher Neil Hopkinson [1969] Director; Dr. Walter Joe Thomas [1966] Director/Solicitor

Accolade Midco Limited
Incorporated: 16 December 2014 *Employees:* 1
Net Worth Deficit: £11,516,000 *Total Assets:* £376,896,000
Registered Office: The Old School, School Lane, Stratford St Mary, Colchester, Essex, CO7 6LZ
Activities: Activities of head offices
Parent: Accolade PFSCO Limited
Officers: Michael James Audis [1971] Director/Chief Operating Officer

Accolade Topco Limited
Incorporated: 16 December 2014 *Employees:* 1,332
Net Worth Deficit: £91,545,000 *Total Assets:* £485,166,016
Registered Office: The Old School, School Lane, Stratford St Mary, Colchester, Essex, CO7 6LZ
Activities: Activities of head offices
Parent: Armstrong Bidco Limited
Officers: Michael James Audis [1971] Director/Chief Operating Officer; Stephen James Blundell [1970] Director; Jonathan Robert Jorgensen [1978] Group Sales Director

Accord Healthcare Limited
Incorporated: 21 November 2002 *Employees:* 1,197
Net Worth: £7,378,000 *Total Assets:* £891,985,984
Registered Office: Sage House, 319 Pinner Road, North Harrow, Middlesex, HA1 4HF
Activities: Manufacture of pharmaceutical preparations
Officers: Pradeep Bhagia, Secretary; Dr James Burt [1974] Director/Chemical Engineer; Binish Hasmukhbhai Chudgar [1963] Director/Businessman [Indian]; Anthony Leonard Cordrey [1961] Senior Director - EU Strategic Operations; Lord Jitesh Kishorekumar Gadhia [1970] Director; John Geoffrey Goddard [1951] Director; Roger Marquilles Escola [1975] Director/Head of Legal Affairs - Europe [Spanish]; Nilesh Parmar [1968] Director; Phillip Semmens [1971] Director/Vice President Hospitals - Europe

Ace Investments Limited
Incorporated: 14 August 2006 *Employees:* 15
Net Worth: £22,689 *Total Assets:* £10,704,509
Registered Office: Jubilee House, 7-9 The Oaks, Ruislip, Middlesex, HA4 7LF
Activities: Hotels and similar accommodation
Officers: Alim Amirali Janmohamed, Company Secretary; Alim Amirali Janmohamed [1981] Director; Amirali Hassanali Moledina Janmohamed [1952] Director/Hotelier

ACES Academies Trust
Incorporated: 8 August 2011 *Employees:* 239
Previous: Hinchingbrooke School
Net Worth: £20,510,594 *Total Assets:* £22,643,336
Registered Office: Hinchingbrooke School, Brampton Road, Huntingdon, Cambs, PE29 3BN
Activities: General secondary education
Officers: Beverley John Frederick Curtis [1945] Director/Retired; Paul Francis Fenney [1951] Director/Retired; Clifford Gary Fluet [1971] Director/Solicitor; Robin McGowan Gildersleeve [1949] Director/School Improvement Specialist; Andrew Ernest Goulding [1959] Director/Headmaster; Brian John Message [1965] Director/Business Owner; Gary James Weston [1973] Commercial Director

Acheson Industries (Europe) Limited
Incorporated: 26 June 1947
Net Worth: £32,774,000 *Total Assets:* £50,488,000
Registered Office: Henkel Limited, Wood Lane End, Hemel Hempstead, Herts, HP2 4RQ
Activities: Non-trading company
Parent: Henkel of America Inc.
Officers: Sutinder Bhandal, Secretary; Sutinder Singh Bhandal [1968] Director/Legal Counsel; Peter David Budden [1963] Director/Accountant; Eamonn Gallagher [1960] Director

ACI Global Limited
Incorporated: 11 September 1998 *Employees:* 193
Net Worth: £27,120,000 *Total Assets:* £28,367,000
Registered Office: 55-57 Clarendon Road, Watford, Herts, WD17 1FQ
Activities: Business and domestic software development
Parent: ACI Worldwide (EMEA) Limited
Officers: Dennis P. Byrnes, Secretary; Scott William Behrens [1971] Director/Accountant [American]; Dennis P. Byrnes [1963] Director/Attorney [American]; David Graham King [1966] Director/Businessman; Simon Paul Stokes [1965] Director/Corporate Executive

ACI Worldwide (EMEA) Limited
Incorporated: 28 October 1988 *Employees:* 340
Net Worth: £267,070,000 *Total Assets:* £316,646,016
Registered Office: 55-57 Clarendon Road, Watford, Herts, WD17 1FQ
Activities: Information technology consultancy activities
Parent: Applied Communications Inc. U.K. Holding Limited
Officers: Bryan Peterson, Secretary; Scott William Behrens [1971] Director/Accountant [American]; David Graham King [1966] Director/Businessman; Bryan Anthony Peterson [1962] Director/Certified Public Accountant [American]; Simon Paul Stokes [1965] Director/Corporate Executive

ACM ULR Limited
Incorporated: 27 August 1999
Net Worth: £14,149,000 *Total Assets:* £33,378,000
Registered Office: Pegasus House, Bakewell Road, Orton Southgate, Peterborough, Cambs, PE2 6YS
Activities: Other business support service activities n.e.c.
Parent: BISL Limited
Officers: Julian Charles Brown, Secretary; Matthew Oliver Donaldson [1973] Director; Duncan Alistair Finch [1965] Director/Chartered Accountant; Seamus Declan Keating [1963] Director [Irish]; Dominic James Platt [1969] Director/Chief Financial Officer; Peter Thompson [1970] Group Director

ACO Technologies PLC
Incorporated: 10 October 1984 *Employees:* 238
Net Worth: £13,870,088 *Total Assets:* £19,590,186
Registered Office: Hitchin Road, Meppershall, Shefford, Beds, SG17 5TE
Activities: Manufacture of other articles of concrete, plaster and cement
Major Shareholder: Thomas Iver Ahlmann
Officers: Kevin John Skipper, Secretary; Hans Julius Ahlmann [1952] Director/Engineer [German]; Richard William Hill [1952] Director/Accountant

ACR Investments Limited
Incorporated: 29 February 2012
Net Worth: £11,645,533 *Total Assets:* £30,292,428
Registered Office: Ground Floor, 4 Churchill Court, 58 Station Road, North Harrow, Middlesex, HA2 7SA
Activities: Other letting and operating of own or leased real estate
Shareholder: Bharat Mohanial Popat
Officers: Kishorkumar Mohanlal Ramji Popat, Secretary; Mohammad Akhtar [1962] Director/Property Investor; Bharat Mohanlal Popat [1962] Director/Consultant; Kishorkumar Mohanlal Ramji Popat [1959] Director/Estate Agent; Paul Stuart Weldon [1960] Director/Estate Agent

Acteon Group Limited
Incorporated: 8 June 2001 *Employees:* 1,567
Net Worth: £233,080,992 *Total Assets:* £565,715,008
Registered Office: Ferryside, Ferry Road, Norwich, NR1 1SW
Activities: Activities of head offices
Officers: Rolf Althen, Secretary; Richard Charles Higham [1958] Director; Kevin Francis Ovenden [1961] Director/Chartered Accountant

Acteon Group Properties Limited
Incorporated: 15 March 2008 *Employees:* 2
Net Worth: £2,357,000 *Total Assets:* £13,984,000
Registered Office: Ferryside, Ferry Road, Norwich, NR1 1SW
Activities: Other letting and operating of own or leased real estate
Parent: Acteon Group Limited
Officers: Paul Lionel Alcock [1967] Director; Kevin Francis Ovenden [1961] Director/Chartered Accountant

Acteon Middle East and Far East Investments Limited
Incorporated: 23 November 2007 *Employees:* 2
Net Worth: £9,030,000 *Total Assets:* £9,075,000
Registered Office: Ferryside, Ferry Road, Norwich, NR1 1SW
Activities: Other business support service activities n.e.c.
Parent: Acteon Group Limited
Officers: Kevin Francis Ovenden, Secretary; Matthew William Alan Grant [1973] Director; Kevin Francis Ovenden [1961] Director

Acteon UK Financing II (NOK) Limited
Incorporated: 10 July 2015
Net Worth: £3,513,853 *Total Assets:* £65,813,304
Registered Office: Ferryside, Ferry Road, Norwich, NR1 1SW
Activities: Other business support service activities n.e.c.
Parent: Acteon Group Limited
Officers: Matthew William Alan Grant [1973] Director/Group Financial Controller; Sandeep Uppal [1973] Tax Director

Acteon UK Financing III (EUR) Ltd
Incorporated: 18 January 2016
Net Worth: £1,432,670 *Total Assets:* £29,237,044
Registered Office: Ferryside, Ferry Road, Norwich, NR1 1SW
Activities: Other business support service activities n.e.c.
Parent: Acteon Group Limited
Officers: Matthew William Alan Grant [1973] Director/Group Financial Controller; Sandeep Uppal [1973] Tax Director

Acteon UK Financing Limited
Incorporated: 7 November 2014 *Employees:* 2
Net Worth: £1,220,394 *Total Assets:* £116,712,552
Registered Office: Ferryside, Ferry Road, Norwich, NR1 1SW
Activities: Other business support service activities n.e.c.
Parent: Acteon Group Limited
Officers: Matthew William Alan Grant [1973] Director; Sandeep Uppal [1973] Director

Acteon US Financing Limited
Incorporated: 30 November 2007
Net Worth: £140,366,816 *Total Assets:* £140,689,792
Registered Office: Ferryside, Ferry Road, Norwich, NR1 1SW
Activities: Other business support service activities n.e.c.
Parent: Acteon US Holdings Limited
Officers: Kevin Francis Ovenden, Secretary; Matthew William Alan Grant [1973] Director/Chartered Accountant

Acteon US Holdings Limited
Incorporated: 30 November 2007 *Employees:* 1
Net Worth: £52,576,900 *Total Assets:* £61,553,368
Registered Office: Ferry Side, Ferry Road, Norwich, NR1 1SW
Activities: Other business support service activities n.e.c.
Parent: Acteon Group Limited
Officers: Kevin Francis Ovenden, Secretary; Matthew William Alan Grant [1973] Director/Chartered Accountant

Action for Children
Incorporated: 14 May 2003 *Employees:* 3,283
Net Worth: £78,775,000 *Total Assets:* £99,481,000
Registered Office: 3 The Boulevard, Ascot Road, Watford, Herts, WD18 8AG
Activities: Child day-care activities
Officers: Richard Hood, Secretary; Sheryl Milanda Anderson [1953] Director/Methodist Minister; Leslie Clifford [1962] Director/Chartered Accountant; Richard Anthony Cryer [1947] Director/Retired; Gillian Ellis [1958] Director/Retired; Evelyn Patricia Gordon [1956] Charity Director and Non-Executive Director; Tracy Ann Griffin [1962] Director; Kate Guthrie [1963] HR Director; Josephine Audrey Larbie [1956] Director/Management Consultant & Executive Coach; Deborah Jayne Morgan [1961] Director/Retired; Daleep Satyanand Mukarji [1946] Retired Director of Christian Aid; Sarika Bijendra Patel [1965] Director; Markus Hardy Ruetimann [1958] Director [British/Swiss]; Fiona Talitha Flora Thorne [1969] Director/Communications Advisor

Action for Children Services Limited
Incorporated: 3 January 1989 *Employees:* 5
Net Worth: £2,788,113 *Total Assets:* £9,506,013
Registered Office: 3 The Boulevard, Ascot Road, Watford, Herts, WD18 8AG
Activities: Other residential care activities n.e.c.
Parent: Action for Children
Officers: Richard Hood, Secretary; Julie Sandra Bentley [1969] Director/Chief Executive; Catherine Anne Guthrie [1963] HR Professional/Director; Carol Ann Iddon [1957] Managing Director of a Charity; Deborah Jayne Morgan [1961] Director/Retired

Active Education Academy Trust
Incorporated: 27 May 2011 *Employees:* 73
Net Worth: £7,539,877 *Total Assets:* £8,199,739
Registered Office: Wigmore Hall, Eaton Green Road, Luton, Beds, LU2 9JB
Activities: Primary education
Officers: Katie Carolyne Paxton-Doggett, Secretary; Helen Gail Barnett [1963] Director/Charity Chief Executive; Toni Emma Chivers [1971] Director/Active Education Manager; Ruhena Mahmood [1980] Director/Project Manager [Bangladeshi]; Shajel Panchal Soora [1980] Director/Regulatory Affairs Specialist; Dr Muhammad Yasin Rehman [1972] Director/Education and Management Consultant; David Michael Sansom [1978] Director/Headteacher; Sarah Alison Sobye Smart [1963] Director/Teaching Assistant; Jonathan David Williets [1969] Director

The Active Learning Trust Limited
Incorporated: 9 January 2012 *Employees:* 1,040
Net Worth: £159,968,000 *Total Assets:* £178,816,000
Registered Office: Isle of Ely Primary School, School Road, off Cam Drive, Ely, Cambs, CB6 2FG
Activities: Pre-primary education
Officers: Karen Jarvis, Secretary; Lesley Patricia Adams [1955] Director/Retired; David John Bateson [1955] Director/Executive Principal Ashfield Academy; Jeremy Beswick [1958] Director/Consultant; Dr Adam David Boddison [1981] Director; Clive Robert James Bush [1951] Director/Chief Executive, The Active Learning Trust; Helen Clare Capron [1981] Director/Teacher; Jacqueline Cutchey [1950] Director/Retired; Robert Douglas Dool [1952] Director/Retired; Richard Gregory Hely Hutchinson [1980] Director and Company Secretary; Mark Andrew Kerr [1968] Director/Bank Manager; Marion Lloyd [1951] Director/Education Consultant; Gary Patrick Peile [1956] Director/Chief Executive Officer; Simon Anthony Staite [1956] Director/Partner

The Activity Superstore Limited
Incorporated: 18 February 1997 *Employees:* 48
Net Worth: £2,941,270 *Total Assets:* £14,181,681
Registered Office: 1st Floor, 41-45 High Street, Saffron Walden, Essex, CB10 1AR
Activities: Retail sale via mail order houses or via Internet
Shareholders: Shaun Powell; Vicki Anne Foster
Officers: Stuart Neilege Miller, Secretary/Accountant [Irish]; Vicki Anne Foster [1978] Director; Stuart Neilege Miller [1968] Director/Accountant [Irish]; Shaun Powell [1963] Director

Acton Gardens LLP
Incorporated: 23 December 2009
Net Worth: £6,114,350 *Total Assets:* £44,104,536
Registered Office: Countryside House, The Drive, Brentwood, Essex, CM13 3AT

Acushnet Europe Ltd
Incorporated: 29 January 1975 *Employees:* 296
Net Worth: £55,146,000 *Total Assets:* £93,835,000
Registered Office: Caxton Road, St Ives Industrial Estate, St Ives, Cambs, PE27 3LU
Activities: Manufacture of sports goods
Officers: Robin Maurice Newbery, Secretary; Matthew Christian Johnson [1973] Director/General Manager; Robin Maurice Newbery [1970] Financial Director; Thomas Pacheco [1968] Director/Executive VP CFO & Treasurer [American]; George Eugene Sine [1962] Director/Vice President Asia Pacific & EMEA [American]

Ad Meliora Academy Trust
Incorporated: 8 July 2016 *Employees:* 107
Net Worth: £12,343,274 *Total Assets:* £13,642,772
Registered Office: St Edmund's Academy, Kilhams Way, Kings Lynn, Norfolk, PE30 2HU
Activities: Other business support service activities n.e.c.
Officers: Barbara Jane Kimpton, Secretary; Lisa Cook [1972] Director/Headteacher; Karl Jermyn [1972] Director/Financial Consultant; William Brannan Mollison [1954] Director; Dorothy Ann Pulsford-Harris [1944] Director/Retired; Andrew James Walder [1959] Director/Retired

John Adams Leisure Limited
Incorporated: 13 October 1983 *Employees:* 36
Net Worth: £16,977,142 *Total Assets:* £28,062,388
Registered Office: Hercules House, Pierson Road, Alconbury Weald, Huntingdon, Cambs, PE28 4YA
Activities: Non-specialised wholesale trade
Officers: Anthony Carson Shepherd, Secretary/Director; Michael Richard Moody [1953] Director; Simon Richard Pilkington [1967] Managing Director; Anthony Carson Shepherd [1948] Director

ADB Construction Limited
Incorporated: 29 June 2016 *Employees:* 261
Net Worth: £4,066,191 *Total Assets:* £56,682,264
Registered Office: Unit 4d Nup End Business Centre, Old Knebworth, Herts, SG3 6QJ
Activities: Activities of other holding companies n.e.c.
Major Shareholder: Paul Anthony Helliar
Officers: Paul Anthony Helliar [1970] Director

ADC Holdings Limited
Incorporated: 14 July 2016 *Employees:* 95
Net Worth: £3,621,475 *Total Assets:* £15,989,031
Registered Office: 2nd Floor, Unit 9 Gateway, 1000 Whittle Way, Arlington Business Park, Stevenage, Herts, SG1 2FP
Activities: Non-trading company
Major Shareholder: Anshul Pangotra
Officers: Dr Anshul Pangotra [1976] Director/Dental Surgeon

Adcock Refrigeration and Air Conditioning Limited
Incorporated: 7 April 1977 *Employees:* 227
Net Worth: £16,956,104 *Total Assets:* £22,693,344
Registered Office: The Maltings, Station Road, Great Shelford, Cambridge, CB22 5LR
Activities: Repair of other equipment
Shareholders: Beryl Irene Adcock; John Richard Adcock
Officers: Beryl Irene Adcock, Secretary; Beryl Irene Adcock [1932] Director/Office Manager; John Richard Adcock [1933] Director/Chairman & Chief Executive; Paul John Brant [1963] Divisional Director; Nigel Martin Claydon [1957] Divisional Director; Phillip John Prior [1961] Managing Director; Sandra Jane Prior [1963] Director/Beauty Therapist

Adda Hotels
Incorporated: 17 May 1966
Net Worth Deficit: £73,370,872 *Total Assets:* £226,913,728
Registered Office: Maple Court, Central Park, Reeds Crescent, Watford, Herts, WD24 4QQ
Activities: Hotels and similar accommodation
Parent: Hilton Worldwide Limited
Officers: Stuart Beasley [1971] Director/Financial Controller; Richard Geoffrey Beeston [1982] Director/Chartered Accountant; Stephen Patrick Cassidy [1968] Director/SVP Operations UK & Ireland; Michelle Momdjian [1976] Director/Attorney; George Christopher Ogle [1974] Director/Attorney; James Owen Percival [1968] Director/Accountant; Brian McKay Wilson [1962] Director/Company Secretary

Adil Catering Limited
Incorporated: 17 May 1983 *Employees:* 210
Net Worth: £12,802,922 *Total Assets:* £20,837,032
Registered Office: 34-36 London Road, Wembley, Middlesex, HA9 7EX
Activities: Unlicenced restaurants and cafes
Parent: Adil Restaurants Limited
Officers: Irshad Adil, Secretary; Irshad Adil [1950] Director/Housewife; Mohammed Adil [1945] Director/Caterer

Adil Property Investment Limited
Incorporated: 19 February 2004
Net Worth: £3,208,502 *Total Assets:* £8,156,480
Registered Office: 91 Wellesley Road, Ilford, Essex, IG1 4LJ
Activities: Other letting and operating of own or leased real estate
Major Shareholder: Syed Adil Hussain Shah
Officers: Shazia Batool Shah, Secretary; Mumtaz Begum Shah [1954] Director; Shahzia Batool Shah [1982] Director/Secretary; Syed Adil Hussain Shah [1955] Director

Adilsons Properties Limited
Incorporated: 3 February 1998 *Employees:* 5
Net Worth: £17,684,168 *Total Assets:* £34,103,272
Registered Office: 34-36 London Road, Wembley, Middlesex, HA9 7EX
Activities: Other letting and operating of own or leased real estate
Parent: Adilson Limited
Officers: Zahair Adil [1976] Director

ADM Arkady Limited
Incorporated: 1 May 1967 *Employees:* 24
Net Worth: £48,857,644 *Total Assets:* £80,653,456
Registered Office: 5 Hercules Way, Leavesden Park, Watford, Herts, WD25 7GS
Activities: Wholesale of grain, unmanufactured tobacco, seeds and animal feeds
Parent: Archer Daniels Midland Company
Officers: Paul William Briggs, Secretary; Graham Lawrence Atkinson [1960] Director/Commodity Trader; Paul William Briggs [1958] Director

Adnams PLC
Incorporated: 24 March 1890 *Employees:* 203
Net Worth: £28,642,000 *Total Assets:* £64,708,000
Registered Office: East Green, Southwold, Suffolk, IP18 6JW
Activities: Distilling, rectifying and blending of spirits
Officers: Elizabeth Sarah Cantwell, Secretary; Jonathan Adnams [1956] Director; Nicola Joy Dulieu [1963] Director; Michael Guy Hilliard Heald [1950] Director; Karen Hester [1962] Director; Bridget Fiona McIntyre [1961] Director; Stephen Crommelin Pugh [1958] Director; Dr Steven Michael Sharp [1950] Marketing Director; Andrew Charles Wood [1960] Director

Adonia Medical Group Limited
Incorporated: 2 October 2012 *Employees:* 163
Net Worth: £9,708,360 *Total Assets:* £13,384,936
Registered Office: The Pavilion, Josselin Road, Basildon, Essex, SS13 1QB
Activities: Non-trading company
Shareholders: Gay Goudsmit; Patrick James Bowler; Ronald Thomas Sullivan
Officers: Paul William Wilkinson, Secretary; Patrick James Bowler [1950] Director; Gay Goudsmit [1973] Director/Engineer [Dutch]; Ronald Thomas Sullivan [1953] Director; Paul William Wilkinson [1965] Director

ADR Care Homes Limited
Incorporated: 31 October 2002 *Employees:* 106
Net Worth: £3,456,244 *Total Assets:* £8,084,016
Registered Office: Bethany Francis House, 106 Cambridge Street, St Neots, Cambs, PE19 1PL
Activities: Residential care activities for the elderly and disabled
Officers: Anthony David Rudd, Secretary/Director; Anthony David Rudd [1956] Director/Accountant; Shelina Rudd [1963] Director/Administrator

Advanced Lighting Technologies Europe Limited
Incorporated: 20 June 1995 *Employees:* 61
Net Worth: £7,515,482 *Total Assets:* £26,249,848
Registered Office: c/o Venture Lighting Europe Ltd, Trinity Court, Batchworth Island, Church Street, Rickmansworth, Herts, WD3 1RT
Activities: Activities of head offices
Officers: Philip Colin Croker [1978] Managing Director; Sabu Krishnan [1958] Director/Engineer [American]; Richard John Morris [1963] Managing Director

Advante Limited
Incorporated: 18 March 1960 *Employees:* 46
Net Worth: £9,826,062 *Total Assets:* £15,571,409
Registered Office: 10-11 Argent Court, Sylvan Way, Southfields Business Park, Basildon, Essex, SS15 6TH
Activities: Renting and leasing of other machinery, equipment and tangible goods n.e.c.
Parent: Gee Group Ltd
Officers: Carl Adrian Brian [1965] Director/Chartered Accountant; Francis Stanley Chapman [1950] Director/Plant Manager; Julie Ann Devenish [1964] Finance Director; Wilhelmina Francisca Henrica Messenger [1968] Director/Marketing Manager [Dutch]

Adventure Forest Group Limited
Incorporated: 21 March 2006 *Employees:* 993
Net Worth: £2,448,000 *Total Assets:* £13,371,000
Registered Office: Unit 6 Fornham Business Court, The Drift, Fornham St Martin, Bury St Edmunds, Suffolk, IP31 1SL
Activities: Other amusement and recreation activities n.e.c.
Shareholders: Tristram Thomas Burke Mayhew; Rebecca Kathleen Sarah Mayhew
Officers: Rebecca Kathleen Sarah Mayhew, Secretary/Director; William James Kennedy Galbraith [1970] Operations Director; Nicholas Hall [1971] Director; The Honourable Jerome Patrick Burke Mayhew [1970] Director; Rebecca Kathleen Sarah Mayhew [1968] Director; Tristram Thomas Burke Mayhew [1968] Managing Director; Jon Noakes [1978] Managing Director

Adventure Forest Limited
Incorporated: 21 December 2001 *Employees:* 763
Net Worth: £3,060,000 *Total Assets:* £11,295,000
Registered Office: Unit 6 Fornham Business Court, The Drift, Fornham St Martin, Bury St Edmunds, Suffolk, IP31 1SL
Activities: Other amusement and recreation activities n.e.c.
Shareholders: Tristram Thomas Burke Mayhew; Rebecca Kathleen Sarah Mayhew; Adventure Forest Group Limited
Officers: Nicholas Hall, Secretary; Andrew Mark Davies [1973] Director; William James Kennedy Galbraith [1970] Operations Director; Nicholas Hall [1971] Director; The Honourable Jerome Patrick Burke Mayhew [1970] Director; Rebecca Kathleen Sarah Mayhew [1968] Director; Tristram Thomas Burke Mayhew [1968] Director/Chairman; Jon Noakes [1978] Managing Director

Aebi Schmidt UK Limited
Incorporated: 24 November 1955 *Employees:* 58
Net Worth: £2,939,000 *Total Assets:* £9,302,000
Registered Office: Southgate Way, Orton Southgate, Peterborough, Cambs, PE2 6GP
Activities: Sale of other motor vehicles
Parent: Aebi Schmidt Holding AG
Officers: Paul Martin Squires, Secretary; Richard John Bryant [1966] Director; Gerhard Neudorfer [1966] Commercial Director [Austrian]; Thomas Schenkirsch [1975] Director/Finance Controller [German]

Aequitas Estates (Poyle) Limited
Incorporated: 12 April 2016
Net Worth Deficit: £29,571 *Total Assets:* £12,003,844
Registered Office: 3rd Floor, Sterling House, Langston Road, Loughton, Essex, IG10 3TS
Activities: Other business support service activities n.e.c.
Parent: GDL (Aylesbury) Limited
Officers: Allan William Porter, Secretary; John Cole [1971] Director; Stephen Stuart Solomon Conway [1948] Director; Jonathan Simon Goldstein [1966] Director; Donagh O'Sullivan [1968] Director [Irish]

AER Rents Limited
Incorporated: 26 November 2014 *Employees:* 66
Net Worth: £2,141,526 *Total Assets:* £21,152,090
Registered Office: Lynwood House, 373-375 Station Road, Harrow, Middlesex, HA1 2AW
Activities: Activities of other holding companies n.e.c.
Parent: Hailstone Holdings Limited
Officers: Siobhan Shaw, Secretary; Ciaran Mahon [1967] Director [Irish]; Stephen O'Flaherty [1961] Director [Irish]

Aeroflex Limited
Incorporated: 6 August 1936 *Employees:* 263
Net Worth: £70,154,000 *Total Assets:* £165,408,000
Registered Office: Longacres House, Six Hills Way, Stevenage, Herts, SG1 2AN
Activities: Manufacture of electronic measuring, testing etc. equipment, not for industrial process control
Parent: Viavi Solutions Inc.
Officers: Kevin Ian David Brown, Secretary; Ian Phillip Langley [1967] Director/Engineer; Amar Mandanna Maletira [1969] Director/Chief Financial Officer [American]; Kevin Christopher Siebert [1968] Director/General Counsel [American]

Aeropak (Chemical Products) Limited
Incorporated: 28 August 1980 *Employees:* 92
Net Worth: £5,716,137 *Total Assets:* £9,202,702
Registered Office: Haslers, Old Station Road, Loughton, Essex, IG10 4PL
Activities: Manufacture of other chemical products n.e.c.
Parent: Diomed Developments Limited
Officers: Andrew James Head, Secretary; Elizabeth Kennedy [1947] Director/Head of Purchasing and Supply; Michael Jonathan Yarrow [1947] Director

Aerospares 2000 Limited
Incorporated: 26 June 2000 *Employees:* 16
Net Worth: £15,022,468 *Total Assets:* £20,302,044
Registered Office: 3 Caxton Way, Watford Business Park, Watford, Herts, WD18 8UA
Activities: Service activities incidental to air transportation
Parent: Nextgen Limited
Officers: Adam Meir Nemenyi, Secretary; Adam Meir Nemenyi [1981] Director/Aviator

The AES Tring Park School Trust
Incorporated: 19 August 1994 *Employees:* 143
Net Worth: £12,446,107 *Total Assets:* £16,963,774
Registered Office: The Mansion, Tring Park, Tring, Herts, HP23 5LX
Activities: General secondary education
Officers: Stephen Paul Robinson, Secretary; Mary Patricia Bonar [1947] Director/Solicitor; Alice Camilla Cave [1983] Director/Solicitor; David John Clark [1958] Director/Retired Headteacher; Michael Dawson Geddes [1944] Director/Retired; John Michael Harper [1945] Director; Mark Andrew Hewitt [1964] Director; Janet Rosalind Mitchell [1953] Director/Retired; Angela Elizabeth Odell [1955] Director/Healthcare Manager; Eric Gilbert Pillinger [1944] Director; June Marian Taylor [1943] Director/Retired Headmistress; Mark Reynell Taylor [1962] Director/School Bursar; Daniel Joseph Zammit [1955] Director

Aesica BC Limited
Incorporated: 15 July 2011
Net Worth Deficit: £8,300,000 *Total Assets:* £121,700,000
Registered Office: Suite B Breakspear Park, Breakspear Way, Hemel Hempstead, Herts, HP2 4TZ
Activities: Manufacture of basic pharmaceutical products
Parent: Aesica M2 Limited
Officers: Andrew Leonard Jackson, Secretary; Jonathan Martin Glenn [1968] Director; Paul Andrew Hayes [1966] Director

Aesica Holdco Limited
Incorporated: 23 August 2011
Net Worth: £9,200,000 *Total Assets:* £12,500,000
Registered Office: Suite B Breakspear Park, Breakspear Way, Hemel Hempstead, Herts, HP2 4TZ
Activities: Manufacture of basic pharmaceutical products
Parent: Consort Medical PLC
Officers: Andrew Leonard Jackson, Secretary; Dr Manja Hermina Elisabeth Maria Boerman [1966] Director [Dutch]; Jonathan Martin Glenn [1968] Director; Paul Andrew Hayes [1966] Director

Aesica M1 Limited
Incorporated: 10 August 2011
Net Worth: £2,300,000 *Total Assets:* £41,200,000
Registered Office: Suite B Breakspear Park, Breakspear Way, Hemel Hempstead, Herts, HP2 4TZ
Activities: Manufacture of basic pharmaceutical products
Parent: Aesica Holdco Limited
Officers: Andrew Leonard Jackson, Secretary; Jonathan Martin Glenn [1968] Director; Paul Andrew Hayes [1966] Director

Aesica M2 Limited
Incorporated: 10 August 2011
Net Worth: £10,400,000 *Total Assets:* £41,200,000
Registered Office: Suite B Breakspear Park, Breakspear Way, Hemel Hempstead, Herts, HP2 4TZ
Activities: Manufacture of basic pharmaceutical products
Parent: Aesica M1 Limited
Officers: Andrew Leonard Jackson, Secretary; Jonathan Martin Glenn [1968] Director; Paul Andrew Hayes [1966] Director

Aesica Pharmaceuticals Limited
Incorporated: 23 July 2004 *Employees:* 191
Net Worth: £133,800,000 *Total Assets:* £246,000,000
Registered Office: Suite B Breakspear Park, Breakspear Way, Hemel Hempstead, Herts, HP2 4TZ
Activities: Manufacture of basic pharmaceutical products
Parent: Aesica BC Limited
Officers: Andrew Leonard Jackson, Secretary; Dr Manja Hermina Elisabeth Maria Boerman [1966] Director [Dutch]; Jonathan Martin Glenn [1968] Director; Paul Andrew Hayes [1966] Director

Aesica Queenborough Limited
Incorporated: 22 August 2007 *Employees:* 457
Net Worth: £9,200,000 *Total Assets:* £56,800,000
Registered Office: Suite B Breakspear Park, Breakspear Way, Hemel Hempstead, Herts, HP2 4TZ
Activities: Manufacture of basic pharmaceutical products
Parent: Aesica Pharmaceuticals Limited
Officers: Andrew Leonard Jackson, Secretary; Dr Manja Hermina Elisabeth Maria Boerman [1966] Director [Dutch]; Jonathan Martin Glenn [1968] Director; Paul Andrew Hayes [1966] Director

Aesthetic Medical Corporation Limited
Incorporated: 13 September 2004
Net Worth: £9,091,807 *Total Assets:* £9,109,867
Registered Office: 1 Royal Terrace, Southend on Sea, Essex, SS1 1EA
Activities: Other human health activities
Officers: Angela Maria Curtis [1951] Director [Irish]

AFE Group Limited
Incorporated: 8 November 1999 *Employees:* 1,233
Net Worth: £77,219,000 *Total Assets:* £108,945,000
Registered Office: 9 Bryggen Road, North Lynn Industrial Estate, King's Lynn, Norfolk, PE30 2HZ
Activities: Other manufacturing n.e.c.
Parent: ALI UK Limited
Officers: Timothy Simon Smith, Secretary/Director; Maurizio Anastasia [1970] Director/Chief Financial Officer [Italian]; Timothy Simon Smith [1966] Director

Affinity Water Acquisitions (Holdco) Limited
Incorporated: 12 June 2012
Net Worth: £375,929,984 *Total Assets:* £375,929,984
Registered Office: The Hub, Tamblin Way, Hatfield, Herts, AL10 9EZ
Activities: Activities of other holding companies n.e.c.
Parent: Affinity Water Acquisitions (Investments) Limited
Officers: Timothy John William Monod, Secretary; Tom Goossens [1981] Director [Dutch]; Jaroslava Korpancova [1974] Director [Czech]; Anthony Charles Roper [1960] Investment Director; Angela Louise Roshier [1975] Director; Scott Springett [1968] Director/Investment Management

Affinity Water Acquisitions (Investments) Limited
Incorporated: 12 June 2012
Net Worth: £389,168,992 *Total Assets:* £389,361,984
Registered Office: The Hub, Tamblin Way, Hatfield, Herts, AL10 9EZ
Activities: Activities of other holding companies n.e.c.
Parent: Daiwater Investment Limited
Officers: Timothy John William Monod, Secretary; Tom Goossens [1981] Director [Dutch]; Jaroslava Korpancova [1974] Director [Czech]; Anthony Charles Roper [1960] Investment Director; Angela Louise Roshier [1975] Director; Scott Springett [1968] Director/Investment Management

Affinity Water Acquisitions (Midco) Limited
Incorporated: 12 June 2012
Net Worth: £375,644,000 *Total Assets:* £505,950,016
Registered Office: The Hub, Tamblin Way, Hatfield, Herts, AL10 9EZ
Activities: Activities of other holding companies n.e.c.
Parent: Affinity Water Acquisitions (Holdco) Limited
Officers: Timothy John William Monod, Secretary; Tom Goossens [1981] Director [Dutch]; Jaroslava Korpancova [1974] Director [Czech]; Anthony Charles Roper [1960] Investment Director; Angela Louise Roshier [1975] Director; Scott Springett [1968] Director/Investment Management

Affinity Water Acquisitions Limited
Incorporated: 31 May 2012
Net Worth: £352,972,992 *Total Assets:* £483,198,016
Registered Office: The Hub, Tamblin Way, Hatfield, Herts, AL10 9EZ
Activities: Activities of other holding companies n.e.c.
Parent: Affinity Water Acquisitions (Midco) Limited
Officers: Timothy John William Monod, Secretary; Tom Goossens [1981] Director [Dutch]; Jaroslava Korpancova [1974] Director [Czech]; Anthony Charles Roper [1960] Investment Director; Angela Louise Roshier [1975] Director; Scott Springett [1968] Director/Investment Management

Affinity Water Capital Funds Limited
Incorporated: 17 July 1991
Net Worth: £202,308,992 *Total Assets:* £378,851,008
Registered Office: The Hub, Tamblin Way, Hatfield, Herts, AL10 9EZ
Activities: Activities of other holding companies n.e.c.
Parent: Affinity Water Acquisitions Limited
Officers: Timothy John William Monod, Secretary; Tom Goossens [1981] Director [Dutch]; Jaroslava Korpancova [1974] Director [Czech]; Anthony Charles Roper [1960] Investment Director; Angela Louise Roshier [1975] Director; Scott Springett [1968] Director/Investment Management

Affinity Water East Limited
Incorporated: 1 December 1991
Net Worth: £65,602,000 *Total Assets:* £67,421,000
Registered Office: The Hub, Tamblin Way, Hatfield, Herts, AL10 9EZ
Activities: Activities of other holding companies n.e.c.
Parent: Affinity Water Capital Funds Limited
Officers: Timothy John William Monod, Secretary; Michael Patrick Calabrese [1969] Director/Chartered Accountant [Italian]; Stuart Neil Ledger [1976] Director

Affinity Water Finance (2004) PLC
Incorporated: 27 May 2004
Net Worth: £55,000 *Total Assets:* £264,904,000
Registered Office: The Hub, Tamblin Way, Hatfield, Herts, AL10 9EZ
Activities: Financial intermediation not elsewhere classified
Parent: Affinity Water Limited
Officers: Timothy John William Monod, Secretary; Jaroslava Korpancova [1974] Director [Czech]; Stuart Neil Ledger [1976] Director/Chief Financial Officer; Anthony Charles Roper [1960] Investment Director; Angela Louise Roshier [1975] Director; Pauline Mary Walsh [1967] Director [Irish]

Affinity Water Holdco Finance Limited
Incorporated: 8 September 2017 *Employees:* 1,357
Net Worth: £206,488,000 *Total Assets:* £1,732,210,048
Registered Office: Tamblin Way, Hatfield, Herts, AL10 9EZ
Activities: Activities of other holding companies n.e.c.
Parent: Affinity Water Capital Funds Limited
Officers: Tim John William Monod, Secretary; Tom Goossens [1981] Investment Director [Dutch]; Jaroslava Korpancova [1974] Managing Director [Czech]; Anthony Charles Roper [1960] Investment Director; Angela Louise Roshier [1975] Director/Asset Manager; Scott Springett [1968] Director/Investment Management

Affinity Water Holdings Limited
Incorporated: 7 January 2013
Net Worth: £287,670,016 *Total Assets:* £287,670,016
Registered Office: Tamblin Way, Hatfield, Herts, AL10 9EZ
Activities: Activities of other holding companies n.e.c.
Parent: Affinity Water Holdco Finance Limited
Officers: Tim John William Monod, Secretary; Tom Goossens [1981] Director [Dutch]; Jaroslava Korpancova [1974] Director [Czech]; Stuart Neil Ledger [1976] Director/Chief Financial Officer; Anthony Charles Roper [1960] Investment Director; Angela Louise Roshier [1975] Director; Scott Springett [1968] Director/Investment Management; Pauline Mary Walsh [1967] Director [Irish]

Affinity Water Limited
Incorporated: 17 October 1990 *Employees:* 1,357
Net Worth: £211,916,000 *Total Assets:* £1,713,879,040
Registered Office: Tamblin Way, Hatfield, Herts, AL10 9EZ
Activities: Water collection, treatment and supply
Parent: Affinity Water Holdings Limited
Officers: Timothy John William Monod, Secretary; Christopher Wesley Bolt [1953] Director/Consultant; Anthony David Cocker [1959] Director; Trevor John Didcock [1963] Director; Susan Mary Hooper [1960] Director; Jaroslava Korpancova [1974] Director [Czech]; Stuart Neil Ledger [1976] Director; David Newsome [1957] Director/Civil Engineer; Patrick Francis John O'Donnell Bourke [1957] Finance Director; Anthony Charles Roper [1960] Investment Director; Angela Louise Roshier [1975] Director; Pauline Mary Walsh [1967] Director [Irish]

Affinity Water Southeast Limited
Incorporated: 23 June 1992
Net Worth: £66,940,000 *Total Assets:* £68,113,000
Registered Office: The Hub, Tamblin Way, Hatfield, Herts, AL10 9EZ
Activities: Non-trading company
Parent: Affinity Water Capital Funds Limited
Officers: Timothy John William Monod, Secretary; Michael Patrick Calabrese [1969] Director/Chartered Accountant [Italian]; Stuart Neil Ledger [1976] Director

AFP 2015-1 Limited
Incorporated: 28 January 2015
Net Worth: £20 *Total Assets:* £36,101,164
Registered Office: Denmark House, St Thomas Place, Ely, Cambs, CB7 4EX
Activities: Other business support service activities n.e.c.
Parent: Asset Finance Partners Limited
Officers: Christoph Widmer [1967] Director [Swiss]

AG Retail Cards Limited
Incorporated: 29 May 2012 *Employees:* 3,405
Net Worth Deficit: £51,977,000 *Total Assets:* £54,537,000
Registered Office: The Crystal Building, Langston Road, Loughton, Essex, IG10 3TH
Activities: Other retail sale of new goods in specialised stores (not commercial art galleries and opticians)
Parent: Lakeshore Lending Limited
Officers: Edward Michael Shepherd [1971] Director/Chief Executive Officer; Jeff Weiss [1963] Director [American]; Morry Weiss [1940] Director [American]; Zev Weiss [1966] Director/CEO of American Greetings Corporation [American]

The Against Malaria Foundation
Incorporated: 9 July 2004
Net Worth: £50,637,692 *Total Assets:* £70,883,608
Registered Office: 10 Bricket Road, St Albans, Herts, AL1 3JX
Activities: Other human health activities
Officers: Robert Mather, Secretary; Arthur William Boler [1958] Director Underserved Markets [American]; Jonathan Paul Benedict Calascione [1961] Director/Partner Management Consultancy; Dr. Stephanie Jayne Cook [1972] Director/Doctor; Guy Savaric Scott Davis [1959] Director Insolvency Management; Professor Richard Paul Lane [1951] Director/Retired; Robert Mather [1964] Director/CEO, AMF; Jeremy Schwartz [1963] Director/CEO, The Body Shop; Peter Robert Sherratt [1961] Managing Director

AGCO Finance Limited
Incorporated: 11 July 1990 *Employees:* 35
Net Worth: £30,421,000 *Total Assets:* £404,260,000
Registered Office: Building 7, Croxley Park, Hatters Lane, Watford, Herts, WD18 8YN
Activities: Financial intermediation not elsewhere classified
Shareholders: De Lage Landen Leasing Limited; AGCO International Limited
Officers: Julia Laura Kortz, Secretary; Mark Albert Casement [1965] Director; Duncan John Hullis [1963] Director; Saul Brendan Jones [1974] Director

Agellus Hotels Limited
Incorporated: 29 November 2004 *Employees:* 145
Net Worth: £6,837,000 *Total Assets:* £9,533,000
Registered Office: The Forge, Lower Green, Higham, Bury St Edmunds, Suffolk, IP28 6NL
Activities: Hotels and similar accommodation
Shareholders: Chestnut Inns Limited; Holdings Three Limited
Officers: David James Minchin [1963] Director; Philip Hugh Geoffrey Turner [1968] Director/Banking

Agetur (U.K.) Limited
Incorporated: 3 March 1999 *Employees:* 159
Net Worth: £5,052,056 *Total Assets:* £14,509,239
Registered Office: 2 Crossways Business Centre, Bicester Road, Kingswood, Aylesbury, Bucks, HP18 0RA
Activities: Construction of other civil engineering projects n.e.c.
Major Shareholder: Robert John Rexton
Officers: Nicola Blair Rexton, Secretary; Christopher David Dickens [1974] Director/Quantity Surveyor; James Richard Phillips [1972] Director; Robert John Rexton [1948] Director [Australian]

Agreserves Limited
Incorporated: 8 July 1994 *Employees:* 15
Net Worth: £19,902,004 *Total Assets:* £25,076,988
Registered Office: Manor Farm, Church End, Woodwalton, Huntingdon, Cambs, PE28 5YU
Activities: Growing of cereals (except rice), leguminous crops and oil seeds
Parent: Farmland Reserve UK Limited
Officers: Paul Allen, Secretary; Benjamin Michael Conway [1980] Director/General Manager; Todd Nelson Jones [1962] Director/Vice President [American]; Don M Sleight [1955] Director/Vice President [American]

Agri Business Limited
Incorporated: 18 June 1997 *Employees:* 91
Net Worth: £4,386,154 *Total Assets:* £8,147,929
Registered Office: 70 High Street, Haverhill, Suffolk, CB9 8AR
Activities: Freight transport by road
Major Shareholder: Lennard Arthur Barrett
Officers: Paul Donno Donno, Secretary; Lennard Arthur Barrett [1942] Director/Manager

Agri-Chemicals Limited
Incorporated: 23 July 1982
Net Worth: £20,984,856 *Total Assets:* £69,286,584
Registered Office: Portland House, 69-71 Wembley Hill Road, Wembley, Middlesex, HA9 8BU
Activities: Wholesale of agricultural machinery, equipment and supplies
Parent: Solai Holdings Limited
Officers: Bhupendra Shantilal Kansagra, Secretary; Bhupendra Shantilal Kansagra [1956] Director; Ramesh Shantilal Kansagra [1950] Director

Agria Pet Insurance Limited
Incorporated: 25 July 2001 *Employees:* 103
Net Worth: £11,683,386 *Total Assets:* £39,673,584
Registered Office: First Floor, Blue Leanie, Walton Street, Aylesbury, Bucks, HP21 7QW
Activities: Financial intermediation not elsewhere classified
Officers: Stuart Clarke [1973] Finance Director; Monica Dreijer [1961] Director/Deputy CEO Agria Forsakringsaktiebolaget [Swedish]; Agnes Fabricius [1972] Director/Chief Executive Officer [Swedish]; Baharan Hellstrom [1979] Director/BA Manager Europe at Agria [Swedish]; Simon Wheeler [1960] Managing Director

Agricola Group Limited
Incorporated: 28 June 2000
Net Worth Deficit: £1,277,000 *Total Assets:* £64,265,000
Registered Office: Horizon House, Fred Castle Way, Rougham Industrial Estate, Rougham, Bury St Edmunds, Suffolk, IP30 9ND
Activities: Manufacture of prepared feeds for farm animals
Officers: Anna Lindsay Stoodley Mortenson, Secretary; Yoram Maurits Knoop [1969] Director/Chief Executive [Dutch]; Steven Richard Read [1963] Director/Chief Operating Officer; Stijn Anton Steendijk [1969] Director [Dutch]; Arnout Engelbert Traas [1959] Director [Dutch]

Agricola Holdings Limited
Incorporated: 16 September 1998 *Employees:* 4
Net Worth: £1,713,000 *Total Assets:* £30,297,000
Registered Office: Horizon House, Fred Castle Way, Rougham Industrial Estate, Rougham, Bury St Edmunds, Suffolk, IP30 9ND
Activities: Manufacture of prepared feeds for farm animals
Officers: Anna Lindsay Stoodley Mortenson, Secretary; Yoram Maurits Knoop [1969] Director/Chief Executive [Dutch]; Steven Richard Read [1963] Director/Chief Operating Officer; Stijn Anton Steendijk [1969] Director [Dutch]; Arnout Engelbert Traas [1959] Director [Dutch]

Agricultural Central Trading Limited
Incorporated: 24 January 1962 *Employees:* 97
Net Worth: £14,101,143 *Total Assets:* £29,703,392
Registered Office: 90 The Broadway, Chesham, Bucks, HP5 1EG
Activities: Agents selling agricultural raw materials, livestock, textile raw materials and semi-finished goods
Officers: Helen Mary Isabel Fellows, Secretary; Andrew John Sidney Beaty [1970] Director/Farmer; Malcolm George Corfield [1953] Director/Farmer; Ian Richard Davey [1965] Director/Farmer; John Dursley Hamilton [1954] Director/Chief Executive; John Lewis Rowlands [1949] Director/Accountant

Agrifac UK Ltd
Incorporated: 6 October 1994
Net Worth: £817,219 *Total Assets:* £10,059,294
Registered Office: 4 Thorby Avenue, March, Cambs, PE15 0AZ
Activities: Wholesale of other machinery and equipment
Parent: Agrifac Machinery BV
Officers: Andrew Carse [1986] Director

Agriturf Holdings Limited
Incorporated: 27 October 1999 *Employees:* 71
Net Worth: £2,216,974 *Total Assets:* £11,263,723
Registered Office: Spalding Road, Sutterton, Boston, Lincs, PE20 2ET
Activities: Activities of head offices
Shareholders: Joseph Robert Ferris Lulham; Nigel Edward Wates
Officers: John Southern, Secretary; John Southern [1961] Finance Director; John William Wates [1957] Director/CS; Nigel Edward Wates [1956] Director

Agrofarm London Limited
Incorporated: 8 March 2013
Net Worth: £4,863,967 *Total Assets:* £11,998,731
Registered Office: Finance House, Aviation Way, Southend Airport, Southend on Sea, Essex, SS2 6UN
Activities: Activities of head offices
Officers: Andrew Keith Murray, Secretary; Jorg Rolf Buhlmann [1958] Director/Lawyer [Swiss]

P.F. Ahern & Sons Limited
Incorporated: 7 October 1975 *Employees:* 65
Net Worth: £16,409,204 *Total Assets:* £20,893,946
Registered Office: 106 Charter Avenue, Ilford, Essex, IG2 7AD
Activities: Activities of head offices
Shareholders: Patrick Brian Ahern; Lilian Beatrice Scott
Officers: Lilian Beatrice Scott, Secretary; Patrick Brian Ahern [1947] Director; Lilian Beatrice Scott [1948] Director; Peter Ryan Scott [1978] Director/Chief Executive

Aim Academies Trust
Incorporated: 7 March 2002 *Employees:* 241
Previous: Barnet City Academy
Net Worth: £42,662,272 *Total Assets:* £46,473,104
Registered Office: London Academy, Spur Road, Edgware, Middlesex, HA8 8DE
Activities: General secondary education
Officers: Jeremy Menell, Secretary; Lord Howard Darryl Leigh [1959] Director/Investment Banker; Paddy McGrath [1977] Director/Teacher; Jeremy Menell [1970] Director/Chartered Accountant; Philip O'Hear [1949] Director/Education Consultant; Dr Michael Harris Platt [1935] Director/Dental Surgeon; Simon Joseph Pollins [1964] Finance Director; Neville John Portelli [1959] Creative Director; Michael Brian Shalson [1943] Director; Peter Shalson [1957] Director; Michael Henry Van Praagh [1961] Director/Chartered Accountant

Air Business Limited
Incorporated: 14 January 1986 *Employees:* 379
Net Worth: £12,502,815 *Total Assets:* £24,324,104
Registered Office: The Beacon, Mosquito Way, Hatfield, Herts, AL10 9WN
Activities: Unlicensed carriers
Parent: An Post (NI) Ltd
Officers: Philip John Ions, Secretary/Financial Controller; Patrick Laurence Knight [1954] HR Director [Irish]; Peter Quinn [1959] Director [Irish]; Adam Peter Sherman [1965] Managing Director

Air Livery Limited
Incorporated: 29 August 1991 *Employees:* 159
Net Worth: £8,297,350 *Total Assets:* £12,950,391
Registered Office: Southern House, Liberator Road, Norwich International Airport, Norwich, NR6 6EU
Activities: Repair and maintenance of aircraft and spacecraft
Parent: Satys UK Holdings Ltd
Officers: Mark Thomas, Secretary; Christophe Jean Lucien Cador [1965] Director [French]; Muriel Christianne Monique Helye [1970] Director [French]; Thierry Jean Patrick Melet [1965] Director [French]; Mark Wynne Thomas [1977] Director/Chartered Accountant

Air Works Empire UK Limited
Incorporated: 21 December 2012 *Employees:* 3
Net Worth: £15,945,351 *Total Assets:* £15,946,796
Registered Office: King Street House, 15 Upper King Street, Norwich, NR3 1RB
Activities: Painting
Parent: Air Works UK Engineering Ltd
Officers: Anand Bhaskar Dhanyamraju [1965] Director/Employment with a Private Sector Company [Indian]; Michael Peter Schulhof [1942] Director/Private Investor [American]; Suresh Kumar Soni [1963] Director/Investment Banker [American]

Air Works UK Engineering Limited
Incorporated: 5 December 2009 *Employees:* 6
Net Worth: £10,960,641 *Total Assets:* £46,795,796
Registered Office: King Street House, 15 Upper King Street, Norwich, NR3 1RB
Activities: Painting
Officers: Michael Peter Schulhof [1942] Director/Private Investor [American]; Suresh Kumar Soni [1963] Director/Investment Banker [American]

Airbus Defence and Space Limited
Incorporated: 5 December 1989 *Employees:* 2,921
Net Worth: £233,058,000 *Total Assets:* £1,294,900,992
Registered Office: Gunnels Wood Road, Stevenage, Herts, SG1 2AS
Activities: Other manufacturing n.e.c.
Parent: Airbus SE
Officers: Alan Shaw, Secretary; Nigel Ramon Ede [1963] Director/Chartered Accountant; Colin Paynter [1958] Managing Director Astrium UK; Julian Bruce Whitehead [1962] Director/Executive Vice President Finance

Airflow Developments Limited
Incorporated: 8 June 1955 *Employees:* 99
Net Worth: £9,382,342 *Total Assets:* £12,894,293
Registered Office: Lancaster Road, Cressex Business Park, High Wycombe, Bucks, HP12 3QP
Activities: Manufacture of other electrical equipment
Shareholder: Herr Jurgen Mueller
Officers: Gunther Mueller, Secretary; Gunther Mueller [1968] Director [Austrian]; Juergen Mueller [1967] Director [Austrian]; Alan Siggins [1965] Director

Aitch Demolition Co. Ltd
Incorporated: 20 September 2001 *Employees:* 8
Net Worth: £5,238,288 *Total Assets:* £8,186,222
Registered Office: First Floor, Radius House, 51 Clarendon Road, Watford, Herts, WD17 1HP
Activities: Site preparation
Parent: Aitch Plant and Equipment Limited
Officers: Rennee Allen, Secretary; Harold Talbot John Allen [1962] Director/Demolition Contractor

Aixtron Limited
Incorporated: 17 August 1999 *Employees:* 71
Net Worth: £16,895,492 *Total Assets:* £22,442,788
Registered Office: Aixtron Limited, Anderson Road, Swavesey, Cambridge, CB24 4FQ
Activities: Manufacture of other machine tools
Parent: Aixtron SE
Officers: Dr Felix Jan Grawert [1975] Director [German]; Dr Bernd Schulte [1962] Director [German]

AK Retail Holdings Limited
Incorporated: 10 June 2004 *Employees:* 1,107
Net Worth: £10,133,386 *Total Assets:* £27,529,558
Registered Office: Newcombe House, Bakewell Road, Orton Southgate, Peterborough, Cambs, PE2 6XU
Activities: Retail sale of clothing in specialised stores
Major Shareholder: Andrew Robert Killingsworth
Officers: David James Preece, Secretary; Andrew Robert Killingsworth [1962] Director; David James Preece [1956] Director; Richard James Thurlow [1955] Director/Chartered Accountant

Akhter Group Limited
Incorporated: 9 July 1979 *Employees:* 41
Net Worth: £9,037,000 *Total Assets:* £12,864,000
Registered Office: Akhter House, Perry Road, Harlow, Essex, CM18 7PN
Activities: Activities of head offices
Officers: Alan Laffoley [1954] Technical Director; Professor Humayun Akhter Mughal [1953] Managing Director

Akira Financial Limited
Incorporated: 30 November 2006
Net Worth: £4,966,995 *Total Assets:* £9,209,521
Registered Office: 9 Northgate Street, Ipswich, Suffolk, IP1 3BX
Activities: Financial leasing
Shareholders: Jonathan Enver Emin; Carmen Adele Suling Emin; Jonathan Enver Emin
Officers: Michael John Flatman, Secretary; Carmen Adele Suling Emin [1971] Director; Jonathan Enver Emin [1971] Director

Al Asayl Bloodstock Ltd
Incorporated: 26 October 2012
Net Worth Deficit: £11,333,738 *Total Assets:* £14,666,714
Registered Office: Lushington House, 119 High Street, Newmarket, Suffolk, CB8 9AE
Activities: Activities of racehorse owners
Major Shareholder: Sheikha Alyasia Alnahyan
Officers: Isobel Hoblyn [1965] Director/Consultant; Johnny Peter Hoblyn [1968] Director/Consultant

Al Jazeera International Limited
Incorporated: 16 September 2004 *Employees:* 136
Net Worth: £33,798,856 *Total Assets:* £49,428,116
Registered Office: Premier Suite, 4 Churchill Court, 58 Station Road, North Harrow, Middlesex, HA2 7ST
Activities: Television programming and broadcasting activities
Officers: Jankhana Jaydeep Desai, Secretary; Mandan Safdari, Secretary; Muftah Al Suwaidan [1959] Director [Qatari]; Khalid Abdulla M Al-Mulla [1967] Director [Qatari]

Alami International Limited
Incorporated: 4 December 1973 *Employees:* 11
Net Worth: £15,710,513 *Total Assets:* £26,703,044
Registered Office: 7 Bridgefields, Welwyn Garden City, Herts, AL7 1RX
Activities: Wholesale of textiles
Officers: Bharat Vora, Secretary; Ashwin Kumar Vora [1956] Director/Businessman; Bharat Vora [1961] Director/Businessman; Hasmukh Jayantilal Vora [1953] Director/Businessman; Satishkumar Jayantilal Vora [1949] Director/Businessman [Canadian]

Alba Broadcasting Corporation Limited
Incorporated: 13 July 1990 *Employees:* 11
Net Worth Deficit: £35,162,268 *Total Assets:* £10,496,773
Registered Office: Suite 105a, Citibase Watford, 42-44 Clarendon Road, Watford, Herts, WD17 1JJ
Activities: Wholesale of radio, television goods & electrical household appliances (other than records, tapes, CDs)
Parent: Harvard International Limited
Officers: Lei Li [1978] Director [Chinese]; Zhuoyan Xu [1985] Director [Chinese]; Xuhui Zhou [1968] Director/Chairman [Chinese]

Alban Academies Trust
Incorporated: 9 February 2011 *Employees:* 216
Previous: Sandringham School Academy Trust
Net Worth: £21,938,350 *Total Assets:* £23,835,900
Registered Office: Sandringham School, The Ridgeway, St Albans, Herts, AL4 9NX
Activities: General secondary education
Officers: Julia Suzanne Shaw, Secretary; Naresh Chouhan [1964] Director/Risk, Compliance & Assurance Consultant; Gregory James Comninos [1949] Director/Retired; Nicholas Joseph Daymond [1962] Director/Headteacher; Duncan Alan Hugh Gibbons [1961] Director; Alan Kirby Gray [1958] Director/Headteacher; Ann Elizabeth Irwin [1952] Director; Linda Marion Keen [1953] Director; David George Richard Kennedy [1959] Director/Key Customer Manager; Norman Kennedy Leinster [1965] Director/Civil Servant; Jeremy Paul Loukes [1967] Director/School Improvement Adviser; Richard Kelvin Springall [1957] Technical Director; Deborah Jane Strazza [1965] Director; Penelope Ann Thei [1948] Director; James Robert Wright [1944] Retired HR Director

Albanwise Limited
Incorporated: 22 March 1978 *Employees:* 91
Net Worth: £300,067,008 *Total Assets:* £821,648,000
Registered Office: Old School House, Fincham Road, Barton Bendish, King's Lynn, Norfolk, PE33 9DL
Activities: Growing of cereals (except rice), leguminous crops and oil seeds
Officers: Janine Grant, Secretary; Luca Rinaldo Contardo Padulli [1955] Director [Italian]

Albea UK Limited
Incorporated: 21 April 1899 *Employees:* 232
Net Worth: £32,187,000 *Total Assets:* £53,621,000
Registered Office: De Novo House, Newcomen Way, Colchester, Essex, CO4 9AE
Activities: Manufacture of plastic packing goods
Parent: Betts Limited
Officers: Derek James Eaton [1968] Director/Group Financial Controller; Karl Graves [1972] Director/General Manager; Arnaud Schuh [1969] Director/Executive VP, Tubes [French]

Albendan Limited
Incorporated: 30 January 2017 *Employees:* 1
Net Worth: £214,562 *Total Assets:* £10,185,047
Registered Office: 298 Hills Road, Cambridge, CB2 0QG
Activities: Activities of investment trusts
Shareholders: Alexander Watts; Benjamin Watts; Daniel Meitrie Watts
Officers: Derek Colin Watts [1953] Director

Albion Bunker and Trading LLP
Incorporated: 19 April 2011
Net Worth: £11,734,288 *Total Assets:* £11,832,822
Registered Office: Suite 1, The Studio, St Nicholas Close, Elstree, Herts, WD6 3EW

Albon Engineering and Manufacturing PLC
Incorporated: 14 May 1973 *Employees:* 430
Net Worth: £26,335,950 *Total Assets:* £56,286,808
Registered Office: Rochehall Way, Purdeys Industrial Estate, Rochford, Essex, SS4 1JU
Activities: Machining
Major Shareholder: Laurence John Albon
Officers: Brenda Rose Albon, Secretary; Brenda Rose Albon [1945] Director/Secretary; Mark James Albon [1969] Director/Engineer; Stephen William Dawson [1967] Sales Director

Alboro Developments Limited
Incorporated: 1 September 1960 *Employees:* 2
Net Worth: £2,215,180 *Total Assets:* £8,470,462
Registered Office: Alboro Developments Ltd, Ely Road, Waterbeach, Cambridge, CB25 9PG
Activities: Other letting and operating of own or leased real estate
Parent: Alboro Holdings Ltd
Officers: Rachel Marie Lucas, Secretary; Mark Edward Davenport [1967] Director

Alboro Holdings Limited
Incorporated: 23 November 2007 *Employees:* 105
Net Worth: £8,089,236 *Total Assets:* £21,966,168
Registered Office: Alboro Developments Ltd, Ely Road, Waterbeach, Cambridge, CB25 9PG
Activities: Activities of construction holding companies
Shareholders: Mark Edward Davenport; Rachel Davenport
Officers: Ann Boutwood, Secretary; Mark Edward Davenport [1967] Director; Rachel Letitia Davenport [1967] Director

Alcatel IP Networks Limited
Incorporated: 28 February 2000 *Employees:* 21
Net Worth: £6,036,277 *Total Assets:* £15,216,826
Registered Office: The Old Studio, High Street, West Wycombe, Bucks, HP14 3AB
Activities: Other telecommunications activities
Parent: Nokia Corporation
Officers: Sally Ann Knapp, Secretary; Mark Alexander Leith Smallwood [1966] Director/Engineer; Ioli Tassopoulou [1984] Director/Solicitor [Greek]

Alcedo Shipping Limited
Incorporated: 18 August 2016 *Employees:* 13
Net Worth: £10,910,627 *Total Assets:* £16,269,907
Registered Office: Long Reach House, London Road, Purfleet, Essex, RM19 1PD
Activities: Sea and coastal freight water transport
Parent: Priveq Limited
Officers: Michael Gray Esq [1948] Director; Karel Van Bellingen [1984] Director [Belgian]

Alchemie GRP Limited
Incorporated: 4 September 2003
Net Worth: £5,114,390 *Total Assets:* £14,172,339
Registered Office: St Andrews Castle, 33 St Andrews Street South, Bury St Edmunds, Suffolk, IP33 3PH
Activities: Activities of head offices
Officers: Haslen Matthew Back [1967] Director

Alcohols Limited
Incorporated: 5 April 1955 *Employees:* 54
Net Worth: £12,355,989 *Total Assets:* £17,664,496
Registered Office: Charringtons House, The Causeway, Bishop's Stortford, Herts, CM23 2ER
Activities: Distilling, rectifying and blending of spirits
Parent: W.H.Palmer & Co. (Industries) Limited
Officers: Richard Charles Evans [1964] Director/Chartered Accountant; Robert Harry Ling [1952] Director/Accountant; Adam John Wallis [1960] Director

Alconbury Packing Solutions Limited
Incorporated: 24 July 2015 *Employees:* 3
Net Worth: £11,665 *Total Assets:* £35,466,480
Registered Office: Alconbury Packing Solutions Limited, Enterprise Campus, Alconbury Weald, Huntingdon, Cambs, PE28 4YA
Activities: Other letting and operating of own or leased real estate
Parent: MM Flowers Ltd
Officers: Amalio Fuster Fernandez-Delgado [1980] Director/Lawyer [Spanish]; Andrew James Kirkham [1968] Director; Philip Scott Whelan [1974] Managing Director

The Aldenham Foundation
Incorporated: 10 September 1984 *Employees:* 255
Net Worth: £13,741,699 *Total Assets:* £21,350,544
Registered Office: Aldenham School, Aldenham Road, Elstree, Borehamwood, Herts, WD6 3AJ
Activities: Pre-primary education
Officers: Karl Mahon, Secretary; Sarah Elizabeth Altman [1967] Finance & Operations Director; Joseph Trevor Barton [1957] Director; Anthony John Bingham [1950] Director/Chartered Accountant; Andrew Js Cox [1960] Director/Chartered Surveyor; Fiona Cuttell [1970] Director/Assistant Company Secretary; Alan Charles Day [1956] Director/Chartered Surveyor; Ian Andrew Dewar [1957] Director/Chartered Accountant; Anthony Graham Hellman [1958] Director/Investment Manager; David Stephen Lambert [1945] Director/Herts County Councillor; Retired University Lecturer; Ronak Mashru [1978] Sales Director; Michael O'Dwyer [1967] Director; Dr Deborah Anne Price-Williams [1957] Director/Doctor; Vandana Mayank Shah [1960] Director/Solicitor; Harriet Simmons [1961] Director/Food Law Consultant; Torquil Charles Fflorance Barrow Sligo-Young [1959] Director; The Venerable Jonathan Peter Smith [1955] Director/Archdeacon; David Thomas Tidmarsh [1962] Director/Headmaster; Thomas Franey Wells [1951] Director

Alderforce Limited
Incorporated: 20 November 2003 *Employees:* 388
Net Worth: £5,876,899 *Total Assets:* £9,890,436
Registered Office: 34-36 London Road, Wembley, Middlesex, HA9 7EX
Activities: Unlicenced restaurants and cafes
Major Shareholder: Raja Jameel Adil
Officers: Mohammed Adil, Secretary; Raja Jameel Adil [1971] Director/Solicitor

Alderforce North Limited
Incorporated: 17 February 2010 *Employees:* 695
Net Worth: £779,735 *Total Assets:* £13,052,243
Registered Office: 34-36 London Road, Wembley, Middlesex, HA9 7EX
Activities: Unlicenced restaurants and cafes
Major Shareholder: Raja Jameel Adil
Officers: Mohammed Adil, Secretary; Raja Jameel Adil [1971] Director/Solicitor

Aldermore Bank PLC
Incorporated: 10 February 1969 *Employees:* 936
Net Worth: £766,700,032 *Total Assets:* £10,467,399,680
Registered Office: 1st Floor, Block B, Western House, Lynch Wood, Peterborough, Cambs, PE2 6FZ
Activities: Banks
Parent: Aldermore Group PLC
Officers: Marius Van Niekerk, Secretary; Patrick Noel Butler [1960] Director [Irish]; Danuta Gray [1958] Director; John Charles Fortescue Hitchins [1955] Director; Hetash Surendrakumar Kellan [1971] Director [South African]; Christopher James Mack [1971] Director; Phillip Monks [1960] Director; Christine Joan Palmer [1966] Director/Chief Risk Officer; Alan Patrick Pullinger [1965] Director [South African]; Peter Anderson Shaw [1959] Director; Christopher Paul Stamper [1955] Director; Catherine Lucy Turner [1963] Director

Aldwickbury School Trust Limited
Incorporated: 20 March 1969 *Employees:* 95
Net Worth: £7,787,951 *Total Assets:* £10,662,670
Registered Office: Aldwickbury School, Wheathampstead Road, Harpenden, Herts, AL5 1AD
Activities: Primary education
Officers: Jennifer Hill, Secretary; Dr Roger Leonard Axworthy [1956] Director/Deputy Bursar and Clerk to the Court; Phillip Barr [1959] Director/Retired Vice Principal & Ofsted Inspector; Alexandra Virginia Louise Beaty [1964] Director/Solicitor; Edward Richard Leslie Bond [1976] Director/Teacher; Christopher Simon Boothby [1960] Media Director; Jeremy Graham Bromfield [1950] Director/Semi-Retired School Archivist; Judith Anne Bryant [1963] Director/Barrister; John Cavanagh [1960] Director/Queens Counsel; Andrew Coley [1961] Director/Project Manager/QS; Rachel Kate Cooke [1981] Operations Director; Christian Mark Dinwoodie [1959] Director/Consultant; Catherine Thea Dugmore [1967] Director; Andrew Charles Hine [1966] Director/Consultant; James Simon Hodgson [1969] Director/Teacher

Alenco (Holdings) Limited
Incorporated: 30 June 1950
Net Worth: £18,488,000 *Total Assets:* £23,867,000
Registered Office: Parker House, 55 Maylands Avenue, Hemel Hempstead Industrial Estate, Hemel Hempstead, Herts, HP2 4SJ
Activities: Non-trading company
Parent: Parker Hannifin (Holdings) Limited
Officers: Graham Mark Ellinor, Secretary; Graham Mark Ellinor [1964] Director/Accountant; James Alan David Elsey [1970] HR Director

Alex Brands Rocket Holdings Limited
Incorporated: 20 March 2015
Net Worth: £40,770,104 *Total Assets:* £48,893,388
Registered Office: 22 Wycombe End, Beaconsfield, Bucks, HP9 1NB
Activities: Retail sale of games and toys in specialised stores
Parent: Poof-Alex Holdings LLC
Officers: Kenneth Dunaj [1966] Director/President and COO [American]

Alfred Homes Limited
Incorporated: 11 May 2009 *Employees:* 29
Net Worth Deficit: £8,239,881 *Total Assets:* £23,769,700
Registered Office: Lunar House, Mercury Park, Wooburn Green, High Wycombe, Bucks, HP10 0HH
Activities: Construction of domestic buildings
Parent: Comland Wessex Limited
Officers: Christopher Giles Martin, Secretary/Director; Stuart James Crossley [1944] Director; Gregg Clifford Joslin [1976] Director; Christopher Giles Martin [1968] Director

Alfreds Way Investments (No. 2) Limited
Incorporated: 1 November 1972
Net Worth: £24,610,448 *Total Assets:* £32,326,216
Registered Office: Atlas House, 28 Great Cambridge Road, Enfield, Middlesex, EN1 1UU
Activities: Development of building projects
Officers: Judith Erlich, Secretary; Baruch Erlich [1962] Director/Solicitor; Judith Erlich [1960] Director/Secretary

Alicat Workboats Limited
Incorporated: 29 April 2009 *Employees:* 106
Net Worth: £3,419,651 *Total Assets:* £10,461,809
Registered Office: Alicat Workboats Limited, Southtown Road, Great Yarmouth, Norfolk, NR31 0JJ
Activities: Building of ships and floating structures
Parent: Richards Dry Dock and Engineering Limited
Officers: Simon Coote [1973] Director; Stephen Frederick Thacker [1965] Director

Allandale Investments Limited
Incorporated: 8 August 2011
Net Worth Deficit: £587,394 *Total Assets:* £8,978,322
Registered Office: 54 The Enterprise Centre, Cranborne Road, Potters Bar, Herts, EN6 3DQ
Activities: Financial intermediation not elsewhere classified
Major Shareholder: Aleksei Bazhenov
Officers: Nigel David Rowlinson, Secretary; Patrick Joseph Albert Hansen [1972] Director [Luxembourger]

Allaway Group Limited
Incorporated: 15 November 1990 *Employees:* 77
Net Worth: £12,821,263 *Total Assets:* £15,260,275
Registered Office: 1 Queens Road, Hertford, SG14 1EN
Activities: Other letting and operating of own or leased real estate
Officers: Catherine Alison Wade [1990] Director; Rosemary Grace Wade [1992] Director; Victoria Rose Wade [1986] Director; William Charles Wade [1988] Director

Alliance Asset Management Limited
Incorporated: 28 September 1995 *Employees:* 44
Net Worth: £3,906,374 *Total Assets:* £22,277,954
Registered Office: 3 Eaton Court, Colmworth Business Park, Eaton Socon, Cambs, PE19 8ER
Activities: Other business support service activities n.e.c.
Major Shareholder: Jeremy Wayne Lavallin
Officers: Catherine Jane Werrett, Secretary; Kevin Joseph Finn [1960] Director; Jeremy Wayne Lavallin [1958] Director; Colin Mather [1963] Director; Catherine Jane Werrett [1972] Director/Accountant

Allpress Farms Limited
Incorporated: 9 March 1965 *Employees:* 76
Net Worth: £4,095,988 *Total Assets:* £8,162,244
Registered Office: Hollyhouse Farm, Horseway, Chatteris, Cambridge, PE16 6XQ
Activities: Growing of vegetables and melons, roots and tubers
Parent: Horseway Holdings Limited
Officers: Terry Neil Warby, Secretary; Jeremy Benjamin Allpress [1961] Director; Nicholas Lenton Allpress [1961] Director/Farmer; Patrick William Allpress [1964] Director/Farmer; Lyndon John Mills [1945] Director/Chartered Accountant; Terry Neil Warby [1968] Director/Accountant

Allway Connections Limited
Incorporated: 26 April 1988 *Employees:* 3
Net Worth: £10,012,283 *Total Assets:* £11,033,198
Registered Office: c/o APS Accountancy Limited, 4 Cromwell Court, New Street, Aylesbury, Bucks, HP20 2PB
Activities: Other professional, scientific and technical activities n.e.c.
Shareholders: Richard Charles Smith; Caroline Smith
Officers: Caroline Smith, Secretary/Accountant; Caroline Smith [1959] Director/Accountant; Richard Charles Smith [1956] Director/Engineer

Alperton Community School
Incorporated: 31 July 2012 *Employees:* 187
Net Worth: £32,979,520 *Total Assets:* £37,629,564
Registered Office: Alperton Community School, Stanley Avenue, Wembley, Middlesex, HA0 4JE
Activities: General secondary education
Officers: Suresh Chandra Jatla, Secretary; Safoora Ahmed [1980] Director/Homemaker; Frances Jeanne Edwards [1981] Director/Teacher; Maureen Griffith [1945] Director/Retired; Michael Jonathan Heiser [1957] Director/Senior Adviser (Finance); Nevia Johnson [1981] Director/Councillor; Sujatha Jothi [1971] Director/Software Engineer [Indian]; Gerard Patrick McKenna [1961] Director/Headteacher; Vijesh Patel [1972] Director/Senior Manager - Business Intelligence; Mona Shah [1963] Director/Legal Department Co-ordinator; Ian Spencer Slade [1967] Director/Teacher; Vimalkumar Tailor [1970] Director/Bank Manager; Daksha Mahendrarai Thanki [1965] Director

Alpha 3 Manufacturing Limited
Incorporated: 15 August 1972 *Employees:* 195
Net Worth: £12,660,000 *Total Assets:* £16,459,000
Registered Office: Avnet House, Rutherford Close, Meadway, Stevenage, Herts, SG1 2EF
Activities: Wholesale of radio, television goods & electrical household appliances (other than records, tapes, CDs)
Shareholders: Memec Group Holdings Limited; Avnet Holdings UK Limited
Officers: Stephen Lawson [1961] Managing Director; Thomas Ludaescher [1961] Director [German]; Harvey Woodford [1963] Director/VP Corporate Secretary [American]

Alpha Schools (Holdings) Limited
Incorporated: 29 September 2010 *Employees:* 404
Net Worth: £3,620,512 *Total Assets:* £19,740,234
Registered Office: 19 London Road, High Wycombe, Bucks, HP11 1BJ
Activities: Primary education
Officers: Paul Matthew Buss, Secretary; Paul Matthew Buss [1979] Finance Director; Ali Khan [1965] Director; Robin John Stattersfield [1978] Director

Alpha Trust
Incorporated: 30 August 2011 *Employees:* 87
Previous: Colchester County High School for Girls
Net Worth: £11,757,948 *Total Assets:* £14,547,794
Registered Office: Colchester County High School for Girls, Norman Way, Colchester, Essex, CO3 3US
Activities: General secondary education
Officers: Lyndon John Hopkins, Secretary; Allan Godfrey Blundell [1936] Director; Alan Charnock [1954] Director/Retired; Roger Terence Cooke [1947] Director/Retired Teacher; Deborah Ann Emm [1968] Director/Learning Support Assistant; Linda Ann Gous [1954] Director; Laurence Clifford Jones [1948] Director; Andrew Keeble [1962] Director; Gillian Elizabeth Marshall [1960] Director/Headteacher; Ian James Mosley [1955] Director/Architect; Gregory John Simpson [1961] Director/Retired

Alphasense Limited
Incorporated: 16 October 1996 *Employees:* 77
Net Worth: £22,020,792 *Total Assets:* £25,754,936
Registered Office: Sensor Technology House, 300 Avenue West, Skyline 120, Great Notley, Braintree, Essex, CM77 7AA
Activities: Manufacture of electronic measuring, testing etc. equipment, not for industrial process control
Major Shareholder: Rose Gotley
Officers: Dr Arthur Wallace Burnley [1951] Sales & Marketing Director; Dean Curran [1976] Director; Andrea Caroline Gotley [1953] Director/Chief Executive Officer; Simon Francis Ramsdale [1969] Finance Director; Dr John Robert Saffell [1953] Technical Director

Alpi UK Limited
Incorporated: 1 June 1990 *Employees:* 124
Net Worth: £2,202,869 *Total Assets:* £15,153,209
Registered Office: Alpi House, Miles Gray Road, Basildon, Essex, SS14 3HJ
Activities: Other transportation support activities
Shareholder: Piero Albini
Officers: Lorenzo Albini [1975] Director/Freight Forwarder [Italian]; Piero Albini [1939] Director [Italian]

J Alston & Sons Limited
Incorporated: 7 October 1948 *Employees:* 4
Net Worth: £4,500,855 *Total Assets:* £15,962,887
Registered Office: Park Farm, Silfield, Wymondham, Norfolk, NR18 9NQ
Activities: Growing of cereals (except rice), leguminous crops and oil seeds
Shareholders: Alan Lang Alston; James Alan Alston
Officers: Lisa Alston, Secretary; Alan Lang Alston [1935] Director/Farmer; James Alan Alston [1969] Director; Lisa Alston [1970] Director/Company Secretary

Alstons (Upholstery) Limited
Incorporated: 2 February 1951 *Employees:* 222
Net Worth: £7,662,000 *Total Assets:* £10,750,000
Registered Office: Albro Works, Gosbecks Road, Colchester, Essex, CO2 9JU
Activities: Manufacture of other furniture
Shareholders: TCMC Furniture Limited; Thailand Carpet Manufacturing PCL
Officers: Terence Henry Cramphorn, Secretary; Terence Henry Cramphorn [1956] Director/Accountant; Zoe Caroline Dickens [1973] Director; Philip Grindrod [1953] Director; Andrew Simon Kennaugh [1969] Commercial Director; Chaiyut Srivikorn [1966] Director/Business Owner [Thai]; Pimol Srivikorn [1964] Director/Business Owner [Thai]; Walliwan Varavarn [1957] Director [Thai]

Altair (UK) Ltd
Incorporated: 13 November 2013 *Employees:* 95
Net Worth: £53,878,824 *Total Assets:* £61,074,296
Registered Office: Parker House, 55 Maylands Avenue, Hemel Hempstead Industrial Estate, Hemel Hempstead, Herts, HP2 4SJ
Activities: Manufacture of other special-purpose machinery n.e.c.
Parent: Parker Hannifin Corporation
Officers: Graham Mark Ellinor [1964] Finance Director; James Alan David Elsey [1970] Human Resources Director; Javaid Riaz [1967] Director/Division Operations Manager

Altenmark Limited
Incorporated: 18 October 1994
Net Worth: £12,959,973 *Total Assets:* £17,303,840
Registered Office: Prospero House, 46-48 Rothesay Road, Luton, Beds, LU1 1QZ
Activities: Other letting and operating of own or leased real estate
Shareholders: Graham Blakesley; Shimshon Torn-Hibler
Officers: Graham Blakesley, Secretary; Shimshon Tom-Hibler, Secretary; Graham Blakesley [1961] Property Investment Director; Shimshon Tom-Hibler [1953] Director/Property Investor

Alterium Limited
Incorporated: 24 July 2013
Net Worth: £1,221,158 *Total Assets:* £21,144,684
Registered Office: Holbrook House, 51 John Street, Ipswich, Suffolk, IP3 0AH
Activities: Activities of financial services holding companies
Officers: Navjyot Singh Dhillon [1968] Director; Nimesh Raghavendra Kamath [1975] Director; Adam Digby Knight [1974] Director; Daniel Andre McPherson [1972] Director; Peter John Tuvey [1979] Director

Alternative Bridging (UK 1) Limited
Incorporated: 15 October 2014
Net Worth: £109,388 *Total Assets:* £24,886,840
Registered Office: 1st Floor, Healthaid House, Marlborough Hill, Harrow, Middlesex, HA1 1UD
Activities: Financial intermediation not elsewhere classified
Parent: Alternative Bridging Corporation Limited
Officers: Robert Jeffrey Piper, Secretary; Stephen Daniel Meller [1967] Director; Brian Leslie Rubins [1939] Director; Jonathan Rubins [1967] Director

Alternative Bridging (UK 2) Limited
Incorporated: 8 April 2016
Net Worth: £15,945 *Total Assets:* £17,161,092
Registered Office: 1st Floor, Healthaid House, Marlborough Hill, Harrow, Middlesex, HA1 1UD
Activities: Financial intermediation not elsewhere classified
Parent: Alternative Bridging Corporation Limited
Officers: Robert Jeffrey Piper, Secretary; Stephen Daniel Meller [1967] Director; Brian Leslie Rubins [1939] Director; Jonathan Rubins [1967] Director

Alternative Bridging Corporation Limited
Incorporated: 18 March 2010 *Employees:* 2
Net Worth: £488,333 *Total Assets:* £103,020,976
Registered Office: 1st Floor, Healthaid House, Marlborough Hill, Harrow, Middlesex, HA1 1UD
Activities: Financial intermediation not elsewhere classified
Parent: Southern Group Limited
Officers: Robert Jeffrey Piper, Secretary; Allan Howard Kay [1963] Director/Chief Operating Officer; Stephen Daniel Meller [1967] Director; Brian Leslie Rubins [1939] Director; Jonathan Rubins [1967] Director; Steven Sharpe [1967] Director

Alterra Farms Limited
Incorporated: 7 February 2011 *Employees:* 2
Net Worth: £5,955,797 *Total Assets:* £11,579,649
Registered Office: Office Farm, Letheringham, Woodbridge, Suffolk, IP13 7RA
Activities: Mixed farming
Major Shareholder: Alastair John Kerr
Officers: Alastair John Kerr [1973] Director/Farmer

Althea Healthcare (Holdings) Limited
Incorporated: 24 June 2010 *Employees:* 92
Net Worth: £2,197,948 *Total Assets:* £9,193,297
Registered Office: Kingsley House, Clapham Road South, Lowestoft, Suffolk, NR32 1QS
Activities: Residential care activities for the elderly and disabled
Shareholders: Sumithra Chandrakanthi Thayanandarajah; Velummayilum Thayanandarajah
Officers: Ian Stuart Jarvis, Secretary; Ian Stuart Jarvis [1966] Director/Business Executive; Cameron Dyer Thayan [1995] Director/Trainee Accountant; Ewan Dyer Thayan [1997] Director/Trainee Accountant; Sumithra Chandrakanthi Thayanandarajah [1959] Director/Business Executive; Velummayilum Thayanandarajah [1961] Director/Business Executive

Alto (UK) Ltd
Incorporated: 24 October 1962
Previous: David Group Limited
Net Worth: £2,390,159 *Total Assets:* £11,798,471
Registered Office: Blunts Chase, Coopersale Lane, Theydon Bois, Essex, CM16 7NT
Activities: Activities of other holding companies n.e.c.
Shareholder: Keith David Tuson
Officers: Darren John Brockway [1972] Director/Chartered Accountant; Olivia Toni Brockway [1975] Director

Altomart Limited
Incorporated: 31 December 1991 *Employees:* 3
Net Worth: £12,654,108 *Total Assets:* £16,528,765
Registered Office: Suite 2, Rama Apartments, 17 St Anns Road, Harrow, Middlesex, HA1 1JU
Activities: Sale of new cars and light motor vehicles
Officers: Rekha Soni, Secretary; Raajnish Mahendra Soni [1971] Director

Altro Group PLC (The)
Incorporated: 24 April 1980 *Employees:* 811
Net Worth: £85,417,000 *Total Assets:* £108,345,000
Registered Office: Works Road, Letchworth Garden City, Herts, SG6 1NW
Activities: Activities of head offices
Shareholder: David Joseph Kahn
Officers: Edmond Patrick Boyle, Secretary [Irish]; Edmond Patrick Boyle [1951] Director [Irish]; Paul Lawrence Caller [1963] Divisional Director; Michael Peter Fincham [1937] Director; David Joseph Kahn [1931] Director; Richard Julian Kahn [1961] Director; James Forbes Henderson Park [1941] Director

Altro Limited
Incorporated: 7 April 1919 *Employees:* 533
Net Worth: £54,935,000 *Total Assets:* £71,364,000
Registered Office: Works Road, Letchworth Garden City, Herts, SG6 1NW
Activities: Manufacture of other chemical products n.e.c.
Parent: The Altro Group PLC
Officers: Edmond Patrick Boyle, Secretary [Irish]; Edmond Patrick Boyle [1951] Director [Irish]; Paul Lawrence Caller [1963] Divisional Director; Michael Peter Fincham [1937] Director; David Joseph Kahn [1931] Managing Director; Richard Julian Kahn [1961] Director; James Forbes Henderson Park [1941] Director

Alzheimer's Research UK
Incorporated: 10 December 1998 *Employees:* 130
Net Worth: £4,183,431 *Total Assets:* £35,557,940
Registered Office: 3 Riverside, Granta Park, Cambridge, CB21 6AD
Activities: Other human health activities
Officers: Philip Dunn, Secretary; Nicholas Paul Antill [1957] Director/Financial Consultant; Christopher Carter [1949] Director/Banker [Canadian]; Michael John Cooper [1960] Director/Worldwide CEO, PhD Media; Shirley Christine Cramer [1955] Director/Voluntary Sector Manager; Giles Thomas Peter Dennison [1970] Director/Solicitor; Dr Rupert William Evenett [1963] Director/Social Investor; Professor Rob John Howard [1961] Director/Psychiatrist; David Mayhew [1940] Director/Banker; Dr Ruth McKernan [1958] Director/Scientist; Caroline Van Den Brul [1954] Director/Management Consultant/Trainer

Amadeus Capital Partners Limited
Incorporated: 26 June 1997 *Employees:* 28
Net Worth: £3,304,080 *Total Assets:* £8,931,660
Registered Office: Suite 1, 2nd Floor, 2 Quayside, Cambridge, CB5 8AB
Activities: Activities of venture and development capital companies
Parent: Amadeus Partners Limited
Officers: Carl Irving Dickinson, Secretary; Anne Margaret Glover [1954] Director/Venture Capitalist; Hermann Maria Hauser [1948] Director [Austrian]; Andrea Traversone [1970] Director/Venture Capitalist [Italian]; Alex Rupert Van Someren [1965] Director/Partner Venture Capital

Amadeus IG Limited
Incorporated: 27 July 2016
Net Worth: £10,493,825 *Total Assets:* £10,493,825
Registered Office: Suite 1, 2nd Floor, 2 Quayside, Cambridge, CB5 8AB
Activities: Fund management activities
Parent: Amadeus EIII General Partner LP
Officers: Carl Dickinson [1979] Director/General Counsel; Andrea Traversone [1970] Director [Italian]

Amadeus Partners Limited
Incorporated: 23 October 1998 *Employees:* 28
Net Worth: £8,331,641 *Total Assets:* £8,907,078
Registered Office: Suite 1, 2nd Floor, 2 Quayside, Cambridge, CB5 8AB
Activities: Activities of venture and development capital companies
Shareholders: Anne Margaret Glover; Hermann Maria Hauser
Officers: Carl Irving Dickinson, Secretary; Anne Margaret Glover [1954] Director/Venture Capitalist; Hermann Maria Hauser [1948] Director [Austrian]

Amalgamated Berkshire Estates Limited
Incorporated: 11 July 1958 *Employees:* 2
Net Worth: £7,798,666 *Total Assets:* £9,646,738
Registered Office: Bridge House, One Station Road, Amersham, Bucks, HP7 0BQ
Activities: Other letting and operating of own or leased real estate
Parent: Amalgamated Berkshire Holdings Limited
Officers: Daphne Yaffa Barber, Secretary; Daphne Yaffa Barber [1952] Director/Company Secretary; Neill Hugo Simon Barber [1976] Director

Amalgamated Berkshire Holdings Limited
Incorporated: 29 April 1958 *Employees:* 5
Net Worth: £9,076,164 *Total Assets:* £9,231,178
Registered Office: Bridge House, One Station Road, Amersham, Bucks, HP7 0BQ
Activities: Buying and selling of own real estate
Major Shareholder: Geoffrey David Barber
Officers: Daphne Yaffa Barber, Secretary; Daphne Yaffa Barber [1952] Director/Company Secretary; Neill Hugo Simon Barber [1976] Director

Amalgamated Berkshire Properties Limited
Incorporated: 28 February 1996 *Employees:* 2
Net Worth: £1,913,281 *Total Assets:* £18,287,200
Registered Office: Bridge House, One Station Road, Amersham, Bucks, HP7 0BQ
Activities: Other letting and operating of own or leased real estate
Parent: Amalgamated Berkshire Holdings Limited
Officers: Daphne Yaffa Barber, Secretary; Daphne Yaffa Barber [1952] Director/Company Secretary; Neill Hugo Simon Barber [1976] Director

R.H.Amar & Co Limited
Incorporated: 17 July 1951 *Employees:* 83
Net Worth: £6,304,235 *Total Assets:* £17,062,040
Registered Office: Turnpike Way, High Wycombe, Bucks, HP12 3TF
Activities: Other business support service activities n.e.c.
Shareholders: Henry Raoul Amar; Ruth Amar
Officers: Ruth Amar, Secretary; Henry Raoul Amar [1938] Director/Chairman; Robert Edward Sam Amar [1976] Managing Director; Timothy John Brady [1967] Director/Operations; Simon Douglas Stewart Fry [1964] Marketing Director; John Heynen [1967] Commercial Director; Paul Martin Tuhrim [1959] Finance Director

Amazon Acquisitions Limited
Incorporated: 10 June 2008
Net Worth: £14,078,000 *Total Assets:* £50,067,000
Registered Office: 1 Gateshead Close, Sunderland Road, Sandy, Beds, SG19 1RS
Activities: Renting and leasing of other machinery, equipment and tangible goods n.e.c.
Parent: BP INV2 Pledgeco Ltd
Officers: Richard Andrew Hehir, Secretary; Joseph Adam Connolly [1978] Director; Richard Andrew Hehir [1983] Director/Chartered Accountant; Allan William Pirie [1973] Director

Amazon Spring Waters Investment Limited
Incorporated: 2 September 2009
Net Worth: £39,686,940 *Total Assets:* £40,174,640
Registered Office: 19 London End, Beaconsfield, Bucks, HP9 2HN
Activities: Other professional, scientific and technical activities n.e.c.
Major Shareholder: Lawrence Phillips
Officers: Michael Baines, Secretary; Lawrence Phillips [1971] Director/Businessman [New Zealander]; Timothy Ashley Sparks [1956] Director

Ambury Developments Limited
Incorporated: 6 March 2001
Net Worth: £6,105,000 *Total Assets:* £9,060,000
Registered Office: Lancaster House, Lancaster Way, Ermine Business Park, Huntingdon, Cambs, PE29 6XU
Activities: Development of building projects
Parent: AWG Property Limited
Officers: Elizabeth Ann Horlock Clarke, Secretary; John Francis Cormie [1958] Director; James Raymond Tilbrook [1973] Director/Surveyor

American Can Holdings (U.K.) Limited
Incorporated: 6 August 1968
Net Worth Deficit: £15,005,000 *Total Assets:* £59,882,000
Registered Office: 100 Capability Green, Luton, Beds, LU1 3LG
Activities: Activities of head offices
Parent: Ball Beverage Packaging Holdings UK Limited
Officers: John Peters, Secretary; Colin Gillis [1954] Managing Director [Canadian]; Philip James Hocken [1977] Director/Accountant; Richard John Peachey [1965] Director/Solicitor

Amersham (Holdings) Ltd.
Incorporated: 14 June 1932 *Employees:* 1
Net Worth: £13,749,366 *Total Assets:* £14,039,869
Registered Office: Whyte Posts, 66 High Street, Old Amersham, Bucks, HP7 0DS
Activities: Activities of open-ended investment companies
Officers: Parveen Kapila, Secretary; Parveen Kapila [1951] Director/Accountant; Sheena Jane Owen [1959] Director; Anne Patricia Smillie [1958] Director; Elizabeth Dawn Smillie [1963] Director; James Smillie [1929] Director/Chairman; Susan Carole Smillile [1965] Director

Amersham Biosciences
Incorporated: 10 June 1997
Net Worth: £254,633,136 *Total Assets:* £278,908,224
Registered Office: Pollards Wood, Nightingales Lane, Chalfont St Giles, Bucks, HP8 4SP
Activities: Activities of head offices
Parent: Amersham NMP China Limited
Officers: Julia Elizabeth Casey [1980] Managing Director, Business Development; Katherine Ann Jones [1976] Director/Financial Controller

Amersham School
Incorporated: 8 June 2011 *Employees:* 96
Net Worth: £14,791,281 *Total Assets:* £16,401,055
Registered Office: Amersham School, Stanley Hill, Amersham, Bucks, HP7 9HH
Activities: General secondary education
Officers: Peter George Edward Ashman, Secretary; Shaun David Aherne [1963] Director; David Hollinghurst Bridges [1952] Director/Retired School Teacher; Graham John Burke [1946] Director; William Edward Charters [1967] Director/Bank Manager; Graeme John Coles [1970] Bank Director; Nigel Peter Davies [1963] Director/Bank Official; Samantha Claire Huxley [1985] Director/Exams Officer/Data Manager; James Ivory [1973] Director/School Teacher; Sharon Elizabeth Jarrett [1961] Director/Headteacher; Charlotte Clair McCoy [1955] Director/Retired; Cecilia Payton [1978] Director/Teacher; Elizabeth Patricia Wright [1988] Director/Teacher

Amgen Limited
Incorporated: 1 March 1989 *Employees:* 504
Net Worth: £2,788,000 *Total Assets:* £112,766,000
Registered Office: 240 Cambridge Science Park, Milton Road, Cambridge, CB4 0WD
Activities: Research and experimental development on biotechnology
Parent: Amgen Inc.
Officers: Sophie Jane Hodges, Secretary; Justin Gary Claeys [1972] Executive Director Finance [American]; Christine Lee Fox [1968] General Manager, Director [American]; Christopher Paul Walker [1970] Director/Regulatory Affairs Professional

AMI Corporations Ltd
Incorporated: 28 January 1997 *Employees:* 26
Previous: Ukay Fuels Ltd
Net Worth: £4,124,553 *Total Assets:* £23,816,296
Registered Office: Knight House, Threshelfords Business Park, Inworth Road, Feering, Colchester, Essex, CO5 9SE
Activities: Wholesale of petroleum and petroleum products
Major Shareholder: Anthony Iameo
Officers: Antonio Iameo, Secretary; Antonio Iameo [1967] Director/Businessman

Amino Communications Limited
Incorporated: 8 January 1998 *Employees:* 62
Net Worth: £22,599,112 *Total Assets:* £66,722,776
Registered Office: Prospect House, Buckingway Business Park, Anderson Road, Swavesey, Cambs, CB24 4UQ
Activities: Television programming and broadcasting activities
Parent: Amino Holdings Limited
Officers: Stephanie Lord, Secretary; Mark Andrew Russell Carlisle [1977] Director/Chief Financial Officer; Donald Kevin McGarva [1965] Director/Chief Executive Officer

Amino Holdings Limited
Incorporated: 23 December 1996
Net Worth: £13,229,287 *Total Assets:* £36,234,396
Registered Office: Prospect House, Buckingway Business Park, Anderson Road, Swavesey, Cambs, CB24 4UQ
Activities: Television programming and broadcasting activities
Parent: Amino Technologies PLC
Officers: Stephanie Lord, Secretary; Mark Andrew Russell Carlisle [1977] Director/Chief Financial Officer; Donald Kevin McGarva [1965] Director/Chief Executive Officer

Amino Technologies PLC
Incorporated: 24 March 2004 *Employees:* 197
Net Worth: £54,558,000 *Total Assets:* £74,288,000
Registered Office: Prospect House, Buckingway Business Park, Anderson Road, Swavesey, Cambs, CB24 4UQ
Activities: Television programming and broadcasting activities
Officers: Stephanie Lord, Secretary; Karen Bach [1970] Director; Mark Andrew Russell Carlisle [1977] Director/Chief Financial Officer; Michael Clegg [1960] Director [American]; Donald Kevin McGarva [1965] Director; Steven McKay [1963] Director [American]; Thomas Keith Todd [1953] Director

Ammeraal Beltech Limited
Incorporated: 18 March 1974 *Employees:* 109
Net Worth: £4,541,596 *Total Assets:* £17,563,440
Registered Office: Foxholes Business Park, John Tate Road, Hertford, SG13 7QE
Activities: Manufacture of other plastic products
Parent: Ammeraal Beltech UK Holding Limited
Officers: Susan Farley, Secretary; Jorge Crusafon Comerma [1971] Director [Spanish]; Charles John Edmund Haynes [1971] Managing Director; Max Granger Weller [1971] Director

Ammeraal Beltech UK Holding Limited
Incorporated: 21 June 2016 *Employees:* 2
Net Worth: £402,811 *Total Assets:* £25,050,192
Registered Office: Ammeraal Beltech UK Holding Limited, Foxholes Business Park, John Tate Road, Hertford, SG13 7QE
Activities: Activities of production holding companies
Parent: Ammeraal Beltech International Beheer BV
Officers: Prakash Krishnaswamy Iyengar [1968] Director/Corporate Executive Officer [American]; Cornelis Gerardus Maria Van Der Drift [1961] Director/Chief Financial Officer [Dutch]

Amneal Pharma UK Holdings Limited
Incorporated: 19 April 2013 *Employees:* 17
Net Worth: £11,836,409 *Total Assets:* £20,340,656
Registered Office: Felsted Business Centre, Cock Green, Felsted, Essex, CM6 3LY
Activities: Manufacture of pharmaceutical preparations
Officers: Chirag Patel [1966] Director/Business Executive [American]

AMP GM 003 Limited
Incorporated: 19 September 2013
Net Worth Deficit: £3,487,886 *Total Assets:* £12,059,148
Registered Office: Unit 8 Peerglow Centre, Marsh Lane, Ware, Herts, SG12 9QL
Activities: Production of electricity
Parent: Solarplicity Debt Funding Limited
Officers: Stephen Campbell Joseph Ellis [1959] Director; Saira Jane Johnston [1976] Director; Ronan Niall Kierans [1978] Director [Irish]; Nicholas Simon Parker [1969] Director; Rollo Andrew Johnstone Wright [1976] Director

AMP GM001 Limited
Incorporated: 12 November 2013
Net Worth Deficit: £3,270,419 *Total Assets:* £12,405,297
Registered Office: Unit 8 Peerglow Centre, Marsh Lane, Ware, Herts, SG12 9QL
Activities: Production of electricity
Parent: Solarplicity Debt Funding Limited
Officers: Stephen Campbell Joseph Ellis [1959] Director; Saira Jane Johnston [1976] Director; Ronan Niall Kierans [1978] Director [Irish]; Nicholas Simon Parker [1969] Director; Rollo Andrew Johnstone Wright [1976] Director

AMP GM006 Limited
Incorporated: 14 October 2014
Net Worth Deficit: £2,983,221 *Total Assets:* £12,565,271
Registered Office: Unit 8 Peerglow Centre, Marsh Lane, Ware, Herts, SG12 9QL
Activities: Production of electricity
Parent: Solarplicity Debt Funding Limited
Officers: Stephen Campbell Joseph Ellis [1959] Director; Saira Jane Johnston [1976] Director; Ronan Niall Kierans [1978] Director [Irish]; Nicholas Simon Parker [1969] Director; Rollo Andrew Johnstone Wright [1976] Director

AMP GM007 Limited
Incorporated: 7 January 2015
Net Worth Deficit: £1,816,026 *Total Assets:* £11,842,658
Registered Office: Unit 8 Peerglow Centre, Marsh Lane, Ware, Herts, SG12 9QL
Activities: Production of electricity
Parent: Solarplicity Debt Funding Limited
Officers: Stephen Campbell Joseph Ellis [1959] Director; Saira Jane Johnston [1976] Director; Ronan Niall Kierans [1978] Director [Irish]; Nicholas Simon Parker [1969] Director; Rollo Andrew Johnstone Wright [1976] Director

AMPY Holdings Limited
Incorporated: 6 June 1996
Net Worth: £178,717,872 *Total Assets:* £178,723,760
Registered Office: 1 Lysander Drive, Northfields Industrial Estate, Market Deeping, Peterborough, PE6 8FB
Activities: Non-trading company
Parent: Landis + Gyr Holdco 2 LLC
Officers: Stephen George Cunningham [1966] Director/Chief Executive Officer; Charles Philip Walker [1972] Director/Chief Financial Officer

AMS Care Limited
Incorporated: 8 March 2006 *Employees:* 123
Net Worth: £10,735,931 *Total Assets:* £20,491,914
Registered Office: 2 Ambassador House, Wolseley Road, Harrow, Middlesex, HA3 5RT
Activities: Residential nursing care facilities
Major Shareholder: Saloni Chotai
Officers: Saloni Chotai, Secretary/Lawyer; Manish Chotai [1961] Director/Chartered Accountant; Saloni Chotai [1963] Director/Lawyer

AMS Care Wiltshire Limited
Incorporated: 6 September 2010 *Employees:* 62
Net Worth: £4,897,600 *Total Assets:* £10,127,908
Registered Office: 2 Ambassador House, Wolseley Road, Harrow, Middlesex, HA3 5RT
Activities: Residential care activities for the elderly and disabled
Major Shareholder: Saloni Chotai
Officers: Saloni Chotai, Secretary; Manish Chotai [1961] Director/Chartered Accountant; Saloni Chotai [1963] Director/Lawyer

Amsair Aircraft Limited
Incorporated: 13 June 2006
Net Worth Deficit: £4,513,165 *Total Assets:* £9,332,958
Registered Office: Amshold House, Goldings Hill, Loughton, Essex, IG10 2RW
Activities: Non-scheduled passenger air transport
Parent: Amshold Trading Limited
Officers: Michael Edward Ray, Secretary; Roger George Adams [1950] Director/Certified Accountant; Claude Manuel Littner [1949] Director [British/American]; Michael Edward Ray [1963] Director/Chartered Accountant; Daniel Paul Sugar [1971] Director; Simon Sugar [1969] Director

Amshold Group Limited
Incorporated: 5 June 2013 *Employees:* 23
Net Worth: £535,119,008 *Total Assets:* £587,838,016
Registered Office: Amshold House, Goldings Hill, Loughton, Essex, IG10 2RW
Activities: Buying and selling of own real estate
Major Shareholder: Alan Michael Sugar
Officers: Michael Edward Ray, Secretary; Roger George Adams [1950] Director/Certified Accountant; Michael Edward Ray [1963] Director/Certified Accountant; Lord Alan Michael Sugar [1947] Director/Chairman; Daniel Paul Sugar [1971] Director; Simon Sugar [1969] Director

Amshold International Limited
Incorporated: 10 February 1999
Net Worth: £4,156,491 *Total Assets:* £84,816,392
Registered Office: Amshold House, Goldings Hill, Loughton, Essex, IG10 2RW
Activities: Buying and selling of own real estate
Parent: Amsprop London Limited
Officers: Michael Edward Ray, Secretary; Roger George Adams [1950] Director/Certified Accountant; Louise Jane Baron [1974] Director; Andrew Norman Cohen [1961] Director/Chartered Surveyor; Claude Manuel Littner [1949] Director [British/American]; Michael Edward Ray [1963] Director/Chartered Accountant; Lord Alan Michael Sugar [1947] Chairman and Managing Director; Daniel Paul Sugar [1971] Director; Simon Sugar [1969] Director

Amshold Securities Limited
Incorporated: 21 March 1997
Net Worth: £188,758 *Total Assets:* £89,152,768
Registered Office: Amshold House, Goldings Hill, Loughton, Essex, IG10 2RW
Activities: Activities of other holding companies n.e.c.
Parent: Amshold Group Limited
Officers: Michael Edward Ray, Secretary; Claude Manuel Littner [1949] Director [British/American]; Michael Edward Ray [1963] Director/Chartered Accountant

Amshold Trading Limited
Incorporated: 5 June 2013 *Employees:* 58
Net Worth: £4,769,068 *Total Assets:* £32,109,412
Registered Office: Amshold House, Goldings Hill, Loughton, Essex, IG10 2RW
Activities: Activities of head offices
Major Shareholder: Alan Michael Sugar
Officers: Michael Edward Ray, Secretary; Roger George Adams [1950] Director/Certified Accountant; Michael Edward Ray [1963] Director/Certified Accountant; Lord Alan Michael Sugar [1947] Director/Chairman; Daniel Paul Sugar [1971] Director; Simon Sugar [1969] Director

Amsik Limited
Incorporated: 15 May 1989
Net Worth: £6,546,743 *Total Assets:* £14,564,792
Registered Office: 79 College Road, Harrow, Middlesex, HA1 1BD
Activities: Buying and selling of own real estate
Major Shareholder: Sandeep Singh Sahni
Officers: Priyaneet Sahni, Secretary; Sandeep Singh Sahni [1972] Director/Property Dealer

Amsprop Bishopsgate Limited
Incorporated: 1 August 2006
Net Worth: £53,309,284 *Total Assets:* £103,946,048
Registered Office: Amshold House, Goldings Hill, Loughton, Essex, IG10 2RW
Activities: Buying and selling of own real estate
Parent: Amsprop Limited
Officers: Michael Edward Ray, Secretary; Roger George Adams [1950] Director/Certified Accountant; Andrew Norman Cohen [1961] Director/Chartered Surveyor; James Hughes [1963] Estates Director; Claude Manuel Littner [1949] Director [British/American]; Michael Edward Ray [1963] Director/Chartered Accountant; Daniel Paul Sugar [1971] Director; Simon Sugar [1969] Director

Amsprop Central Limited
Incorporated: 26 September 2001
Net Worth: £18,543,966 *Total Assets:* £34,407,408
Registered Office: Amshold House, Goldings Hill, Loughton, Essex, IG10 2RW
Activities: Buying and selling of own real estate
Parent: Amsprop Limited
Officers: Michael Edward Ray, Secretary; Roger George Adams [1950] Director/Certified Accountant; Louise Jane Baron [1974] Director; Andrew Norman Cohen [1961] Director/Chartered Surveyor; James Hughes [1963] Estates Director; Claude Manuel Littner [1949] Director [British/American]; Michael Edward Ray [1963] Director/Chartered Accountant; Daniel Paul Sugar [1971] Director; Simon Sugar [1969] Director

Amsprop City Properties Limited
Incorporated: 23 April 2001
Net Worth: £13,232,221 *Total Assets:* £18,491,500
Registered Office: Amshold House, Goldings Hill, Loughton, Essex, IG10 2RW
Activities: Buying and selling of own real estate
Parent: Amsprop Limited
Officers: Michael Edward Ray, Secretary; Roger George Adams [1950] Director/Certified Accountant; Louise Jane Baron [1974] Director; Andrew Norman Cohen [1961] Director/Chartered Surveyor; James Hughes [1963] Estates Director; Claude Manuel Littner [1949] Director [British/American]; Michael Edward Ray [1963] Director/Chartered Accountant; Daniel Paul Sugar [1971] Director; Simon Sugar [1969] Director

Amsprop Estates Limited
Incorporated: 19 March 1993
Net Worth: £9,796,504 *Total Assets:* £10,272,408
Registered Office: Amshold House, Goldings Hill, Loughton, Essex, IG10 2RW
Activities: Buying and selling of own real estate
Parent: Amsprop Limited
Officers: Michael Edward Ray, Secretary; Roger George Adams [1950] Director/Certified Accountant; Louise Jane Baron [1974] Director; Andrew Norman Cohen [1961] Director/Chartered Surveyor; James Hughes [1963] Estates Director; Claude Manuel Littner [1949] Director [British/American]; Michael Edward Ray [1963] Director/Chartered Accountant; Daniel Paul Sugar [1971] Director; Simon Sugar [1969] Director

Amsprop Investments Limited
Incorporated: 5 March 1990
Net Worth: £199,924,304 *Total Assets:* £308,055,968
Registered Office: Amshold House, Goldings Hill, Loughton, Essex, IG10 2RW
Activities: Buying and selling of own real estate
Parent: Amsprop Limited
Officers: Michael Edward Ray, Secretary; Roger George Adams [1950] Director/Certified Accountant; Louise Jane Baron [1974] Director; Andrew Norman Cohen [1961] Director/Chartered Surveyor; James Hughes [1963] Estates Director; Claude Manuel Littner [1949] Director [British/American]; Michael Edward Ray [1963] Director/Chartered Accountant; Daniel Paul Sugar [1971] Director; Simon Sugar [1969] Director

Amsprop London Limited
Incorporated: 8 February 1989
Net Worth: £97,547,224 *Total Assets:* £104,494,552
Registered Office: Amshold House, Goldings Hill, Loughton, Essex, IG10 2RW
Activities: Buying and selling of own real estate
Parent: Amshold Group Limited
Officers: Michael Edward Ray, Secretary; Roger George Adams [1950] Director/Certified Accountant; Louise Jane Baron [1974] Director; Andrew Norman Cohen [1961] Director/Chartered Surveyor; James Hughes [1963] Estates Director; Claude Manuel Littner [1949] Director [British/American]; Michael Edward Ray [1963] Director/Chartered Accountant; Lord Alan Michael Sugar [1947] Chairman and Managing Director; Daniel Paul Sugar [1971] Director; Simon Sugar [1969] Director

Amsprop Portland Limited
Incorporated: 1 August 2006
Net Worth: £20,478,624 *Total Assets:* £48,103,136
Registered Office: Amshold House, Goldings Hill, Loughton, Essex, IG10 2RW
Activities: Buying and selling of own real estate
Parent: Amsprop Limited
Officers: Michael Edward Ray, Secretary; Roger George Adams [1950] Director/Certified Accountant; Andrew Norman Cohen [1961] Director/Chartered Surveyor; James Hughes [1963] Estates Director; Claude Manuel Littner [1949] Director [British/American]; Michael Edward Ray [1963] Director/Chartered Accountant; Daniel Paul Sugar [1971] Director; Simon Sugar [1969] Director

AMT Fruit Limited
Incorporated: 3 March 2009
Net Worth: £7,873,851 *Total Assets:* £38,018,400
Registered Office: Frans House, Fenton Way, Chatteris, Cambs, PE16 6UP
Activities: Wholesale of fruit and vegetables
Parent: Munoz Group Ltd
Officers: Fernando Juan de Lucas Lopez [1973] Director [Spanish]; Jonathan Michael Hedge [1964] Director

Anacreonte Properties Limited
Incorporated: 20 September 1999 *Employees:* 3
Net Worth: £6,513,914 *Total Assets:* £8,891,334
Registered Office: 45 Shortmead Street, Biggleswade, Beds, SG18 0AT
Activities: Buying and selling of own real estate
Shareholders: Antonio Anacreonte; Angela Anacreonte
Officers: Antonio Anacreonte, Secretary; Angela Anacreonte [1950] Director; Antonio Anacreonte [1945] Director/Property Developer

Ancient House Press PLC
Incorporated: 13 May 1946 *Employees:* 88
Net Worth: £2,695,748 *Total Assets:* £8,717,941
Registered Office: 8 Whittle Road, Hadleigh Road Industrial Estate, Ipswich, Suffolk, IP2 0HA
Activities: Printing n.e.c.
Parent: Ancient House Printing Group Ltd
Officers: Micheal John Underdown, Secretary; Allison Berry [1964] Director; Paul Sadler [1958] Operations Director; Michael John Underdown [1965] Director

Ancient House Printing Group Limited
Incorporated: 19 January 1971 *Employees:* 88
Net Worth: £2,713,183 *Total Assets:* £8,717,941
Registered Office: 8 Whittle Road, Hadleigh Road Industrial Estate, Ipswich, Suffolk, IP2 0HA
Activities: Printing n.e.c.
Shareholders: June Sylvia Underdown; Peter John Underdown Discretionary Settlement
Officers: Micheal John Underdown, Secretary; Allison Berry [1964] Director; Michael John Underdown [1965] Director

C.F.Anderson & Son Limited
Incorporated: 1 January 1925 *Employees:* 3
Net Worth: £2,388,238 *Total Assets:* £8,242,549
Registered Office: 228 Old London Road, Marks Tey, Colchester, Essex, CO6 1HD
Activities: Other letting and operating of own or leased real estate
Officers: Suzanne Eliane Anderson, Secretary; Jonathan James Hunter Anderson [1938] Director/Timber Importer; Suzanne Eliane Anderson [1946] Director; Adam Christopher Kemeny [1985] Director

Anderson Construction Limited
Incorporated: 25 April 1991 *Employees:* 271
Net Worth: £31,805,812 *Total Assets:* £88,019,768
Registered Office: Springfield Lodge, Colchester Road, Springfield, Chelmsford, Essex, CM2 5PW
Activities: Management consultancy activities other than financial management
Officers: Andrew Christopher Short, Secretary; Mark Jonathan Anderson [1961] Director

M. Anderson Construction Limited
Incorporated: 21 December 1987 *Employees:* 153
Net Worth: £8,719,424 *Total Assets:* £17,631,444
Registered Office: Springfield Lodge, Colchester Road, Springfield, Chelmsford, Essex, CM2 5PW
Activities: Development of building projects
Officers: Andrew Christopher Short, Secretary; Mark Jonathan Anderson [1961] Director

Anderson Design & Build Limited
Incorporated: 10 March 2003
Net Worth: £19,398,720 *Total Assets:* £32,197,072
Registered Office: Springfield Lodge, Colchester Road, Springfield, Chelmsford, Essex, CM2 5PW
Activities: Buying and selling of own real estate
Officers: Andrew Christopher Short, Secretary; Mark Jonathan Anderson [1961] Director

Andgrove Property Investments Limited
Incorporated: 20 July 1977 *Employees:* 1
Net Worth: £8,625,170 *Total Assets:* £10,048,160
Registered Office: 2nd Floor, Hygeia House, 66 College Road, Harrow, Middlesex, HA1 1BE
Activities: Development of building projects
Shareholders: Anthony David Gross; Helena Gross
Officers: Anthony David Gross [1938] Director; Helena Gross [1939] Director; Robert Lawrence Gross [1963] Director

Anduff Car Wash Limited
Incorporated: 17 March 1970 *Employees:* 56
Net Worth: £280,204,128 *Total Assets:* £324,005,056
Registered Office: 35-37 Amersham Hill, High Wycombe, Bucks, HP13 6NU
Activities: Other service activities n.e.c.
Officers: Peter James Davies [1978] Director; Stewart Malcolm Greenhalgh [1949] Technical Director; Nazim Ilyas [1982] Finance Director; Tim Neil Walton [1973] Managing Director

Anexhold Limited
Incorporated: 30 March 2012 *Employees:* 212
Net Worth: £10,576,574 *Total Assets:* £34,162,740
Registered Office: 22-26 King Street, King's Lynn, Norfolk, PE30 1HJ
Activities: Activities of production holding companies
Shareholders: Predict S.L.U.; Craig Richard Taylor
Officers: Gonzalo Raspall Coromina, Secretary; Gonzalo Raspall Coromina [1972] Director [Spanish]; Ramon Andreu Ferrando [1964] Director [Spanish]; Jeffrey John Halliwell [1954] Director; Craig Richard Taylor [1966] Director

Angel Care (Orchid Care Homes) Ltd
Incorporated: 12 September 2012 *Employees:* 93
Net Worth: £5,992,633 *Total Assets:* £12,071,952
Registered Office: 116 Headstone Drive, Harrow, Middlesex, HA1 4UH
Activities: Residential nursing care facilities
Major Shareholder: Sandip Ruparelia
Officers: Sandip Ruparelia [1963] Director

Angel Care PLC
Incorporated: 16 January 1996 *Employees:* 245
Net Worth: £16,481,334 *Total Assets:* £29,445,680
Registered Office: 116 Headstone Drive, Harrow, Middlesex, HA1 4UH
Activities: Residential nursing care facilities
Shareholders: Sandip Ruparelia; Priti Ruparelia
Officers: Priti Ruparelia, Secretary/Care Home Operator; Priti Ruparelia [1963] Director/Care Home Operator; Sandip Ruparelia [1963] Director/Care Home Operator

Angel Property Investments Limited
Incorporated: 19 September 2002 *Employees:* 3
Net Worth: £9,680,686 *Total Assets:* £17,917,088
Registered Office: Churchill House, Stirling Way, Borehamwood, Herts, WD6 2HP
Activities: Other letting and operating of own or leased real estate
Officers: Richard Ian Basch, Secretary; Richard Ian Basch [1978] Director/Accountant; Adam James Margolis [1979] Director/Self Employed; Laura Margolis [1978] Director/Administrator

Angelica Estates Limited
Incorporated: 30 December 2014
Net Worth: £5,202,693 *Total Assets:* £11,145,977
Registered Office: 50 Lancaster Road, Enfield, Middlesex, EN2 0BY
Activities: Other letting and operating of own or leased real estate
Shareholders: Gerald Anthony Malton; Annabel Susan Malton
Officers: Annabel Susan Malton [1960] Director; Generald Anthony Malton [1960] Director

Anglia Aircraft Restorations Limited
Incorporated: 25 November 2015
Net Worth Deficit: £884,312 *Total Assets:* £14,418,854
Registered Office: 3 Twyford Court, High Street, Dunmow, Essex, CM6 1AE
Activities: Repair and maintenance of aircraft and spacecraft
Major Shareholder: Graham Frederick Peacock
Officers: Graham Frederick Peacock [1950] Director

Anglia Autoflow Limited
Incorporated: 12 February 1969 *Employees:* 28
Net Worth: £19,149,958 *Total Assets:* £21,308,762
Registered Office: The Homestead, Wortham Ling, Diss, Norfolk, IP22 1SR
Activities: Manufacture of lifting and handling equipment
Major Shareholder: Robert William Wills
Officers: Robert Wills, Secretary/Director; Barry Landymore [1956] Director/Engineer; Robert Wills [1976] Director

Anglia Components Limited
Incorporated: 13 June 2001 *Employees:* 133
Net Worth: £11,497,853 *Total Assets:* £41,085,144
Registered Office: Anglia Components Limited, Sandall Road, Wisbech, Cambs, PE13 2PS
Activities: Wholesale of electronic and telecommunications equipment and parts
Parent: Anglia Components Investments Limited
Officers: Malcolm John Fry, Secretary; John Bowman [1968] Director

Anglia Home Furnishings Holdings Ltd
Incorporated: 2 September 2011 *Employees:* 228
Net Worth Deficit: £80,421 *Total Assets:* £8,333,566
Registered Office: Burch House, Saville Road, Peterborough, PE3 7PR
Activities: Retail of furniture, lighting, and similar (not musical instruments or scores) in specialised store
Officers: John Edwin Chillcott [1958] Director; Christopher Roy Stafford [1974] Finance Director

Anglia Innovation Partnership LLP
Incorporated: 5 March 2012 *Employees:* 8
Previous: Norwich Research Partners LLP
Net Worth: £2,303,000 *Total Assets:* £13,798,000
Registered Office: Centrum, Norwich Research Park, Colney, Norwich, NR4 7UG

Anglia Maltings (Holdings) Limited
Incorporated: 26 June 1890 *Employees:* 359
Net Worth: £85,792,000 *Total Assets:* £167,528,992
Registered Office: Great Ryburgh, Fakenham, Norfolk, NR21 7AS
Activities: Manufacture of other food products n.e.c.
Parent: Ragleth Ltd
Officers: Alan William Clark, Secretary; Alan William Clark [1960] Director/Accountant; Adrian Cordy Dyter [1968] Director; Richard William Farrar [1958] Managing Director; The Honourable Edward Richard Iliffe [1968] Director/Businessman; Christopher Guy Johnson [1964] Director/Businessman; Stella Helen Morse [1967] Director/Chartered Accountant; David George Fossett Thompson [1954] Director/Chief Executive; Edward John Whitley [1961] Director/Businessman

Anglia Restaurants Ltd
Incorporated: 15 December 1998 *Employees:* 261
Net Worth: £2,713,425 *Total Assets:* £9,358,073
Registered Office: 107 Salhouse Road, Norwich, NR7 9AW
Activities: Licenced restaurants
Shareholders: Michelle Ann Williams; Arthur Elias Williams
Officers: Michelle Ann Williams, Secretary; Arthur Elias Williams [1962] Director/Restaurateur; Michelle Ann Williams [1965] Director

Anglia Ruskin Development Ltd
Incorporated: 18 August 1992 *Employees:* 4
Net Worth: £32,400,000 *Total Assets:* £35,400,000
Registered Office: Bishop Hall Lane, Chelmsford, Essex, CM1 1SQ
Activities: Buying and selling of own real estate
Parent: Anglia Ruskin University Higher Education Corporation
Officers: Paul Wakefield Bogle, Secretary; Paul Wakefield Bogle [1972] Director/Secretary & Clerk; Michael Alan Frost [1965] Director of Finance; Timothy Charles Matthews [1954] Director/Chartered Surveyor; James Rolfe [1967] Director/Professional Services in Higher Education

Anglia Ruskin Enterprise Ltd
Incorporated: 3 April 1989 *Employees:* 124
Net Worth: £11,319,000 *Total Assets:* £11,891,000
Registered Office: Bishop Hall Lane, Chelmsford, Essex, CM1 1SQ
Activities: Other education n.e.c.
Parent: Anglia Ruskin University Higher Education Corporation
Officers: Paul Wakefield Bogle, Secretary; Paul Wakefield Bogle [1972] Director/Secretary & Clerk; Stuart David Powell [1974] Director/Accountant; James Rolfe [1967] Director/Professional Services in Higher Education; Professor Roderick Evan Watkins [1964] Director/Deputy Vice Chancellor

Anglian Community Enterprise (ACE) Community Interest Company
Incorporated: 15 September 2010 *Employees:* 925
Net Worth: £3,549,798 *Total Assets:* £12,871,402
Registered Office: 659-662 The Crescent, Colchester Business Park, Colchester, Essex, CO4 9YQ
Activities: Hospital activities
Officers: Sharon Jane Charlton [1963] Director; David John Harrison [1963] Director/Accountant; Jayne Hiley [1961] Director of Clinical and Corporate Governance; Lawrence Payne [1954] Director; Anne Elizabeth Thain [1962] Director/Healthcare; Richard Tierney [1961] Director/Business Consultant; Lynne Woodcock [1956] Director

Anglian Group (Investments) Limited
Incorporated: 1 March 2001
Net Worth: £11,129,000 *Total Assets:* £58,375,000
Registered Office: Liberator Road, Norwich, NR6 6EU
Activities: Financial management
Parent: Anglian Home Improvements Group Limited
Officers: Nicholas Andrew Roberts [1961] Director

Anglian Group Limited
Incorporated: 25 February 1991
Net Worth: £52,229,000 *Total Assets:* £115,093,000
Registered Office: Liberator Road, Norwich, NR6 6EU
Activities: Non-trading company
Parent: Anglian Group (Investments) Limited
Officers: Nicholas Andrew Roberts [1961] Director

Anglian Home Improvements Group Limited
Incorporated: 7 December 2015 *Employees:* 1,586
Net Worth Deficit: £11,810,000 *Total Assets:* £83,131,000
Registered Office: Liberator Road, Norwich, NR6 6EU
Activities: Activities of head offices
Officers: Matthias Gradischnig [1983] Director/Investment Analyst [Austrian]; Alexander Leicester [1979] Director/Investment Manager; Peter David Leigh Mottershead [1964] Director; Nicholas Andrew Roberts [1961] Director; Jesse Guy Watts [1955] Director; Jennifer Ann Zaremba [1971] Director

Anglian Learning
Incorporated: 15 March 2011 *Employees:* 556
Previous: Bottisham Multi Academy Trust
Net Worth: £53,871,300 *Total Assets:* £61,307,276
Registered Office: Bottisham Village College, Lode Road, Bottisham, Cambridge, CB25 9DL
Activities: General secondary education
Officers: Richard Charles Cowling [1952] Director; Jonathan Mark Culpin [1969] Director/Chief Executive; David Robert Lamkin [1954] Director/Software Consultant; Dr Claire Alison Lawton [1952] Director/Psychiatrist; Kenneth Joseph Murphy [1961] Director; Sue Clare Speller [1956] Director R&D IT

Anglian Venture Holdings Limited
Incorporated: 13 November 2007
Net Worth: £64,845,000 *Total Assets:* £97,138,000
Registered Office: Lancaster House, Lancaster Way, Ermine Business Park, Huntingdon, Cambs, PE29 6XU
Activities: Activities of head offices
Parent: Osprey Holdco Limited
Officers: Claire Tytherleigh Russell, Secretary; Anthony Donnelly [1964] Director; Scott Robert James Longhurst [1967] Finance Director; Claire Tytherleigh Russell [1964] Director/Lawyer; Peter John Simpson [1967] Director; Wayne Paul Young [1976] Director/Chartered Accountant

Anglian Water (Osprey) Financing PLC
Incorporated: 22 December 2010
Net Worth: £163,000 *Total Assets:* £455,227,008
Registered Office: Lancaster House, Lancaster Way, Ermine Business Park, Huntingdon, Cambs, PE29 6XU
Activities: Other business support service activities n.e.c.
Parent: Osprey Acqusitions Limited
Officers: Claire Tytherleigh Russell, Secretary; Dr Stephen Robert Billingham [1948] Director; Scott Robert James Longhurst [1967] Director; Peter John Simpson [1967] Director

Anglian Water Facilities Management Holdings (UK) Limited
Incorporated: 3 October 2000
Net Worth: £40,449,000 *Total Assets:* £40,454,000
Registered Office: Lancaster House, Lancaster Way, Ermine Business Park, Huntingdon, Cambs, PE29 6XU
Activities: Non-trading company
Parent: AWG Group Limited
Officers: Elizabeth Ann Horlock Clarke, Secretary; Alan Gladston [1970] Director/Accountant; Gerard Mackin Morgan [1957] Director/Head of Finance and Performance

Anglian Water Services Financing PLC
Incorporated: 28 November 2001
Net Worth: £48,000,000 *Total Assets:* £7,506,400,256
Registered Office: Lancaster House, Lancaster Way, Ermine Business Park, Huntingdon, Cambs, PE29 6XU
Activities: Other business support service activities n.e.c.
Parent: Anglian Water Services Limited
Officers: Claire Tytherleigh Russell, Secretary; Dr Stephen Robert Billingham [1948] Director; Natalie Ceeney [1971] Director; Dame Veronica Anne Courtice [1952] Director, University of Cambridge; John Raymond Hirst [1952] Director; Scott Robert James Longhurst [1967] Finance Director; Zarin Homi Patel [1961] Independent Director; Jane Elizabeth Pilcher [1962] Director; Alexander Charles Plant [1969] Director; Peter John Simpson [1967] Director; Paul Frederick Garry Whittaker [1960] Director

Anglian Water Services Holdings Limited
Incorporated: 28 November 2001
Net Worth: £1,609,092,992 *Total Assets:* £1,609,092,992
Registered Office: Lancaster House, Lancaster Way, Ermine Business Park, Huntingdon, Cambs, PE29 6XU
Activities: Activities of head offices
Parent: AWG Group Limited
Officers: Claire Tytherleigh Russell, Secretary; Dr Stephen Robert Billingham [1948] Director; Natalie Ceeney [1971] Director; Dame Veronica Anne Courtice [1952] Director, University of Cambridge; John Raymond Hirst [1952] Director; Scott Robert James Longhurst [1967] Finance Director; Zarin Homi Patel [1961] Independent Director; Jane Elizabeth Pilcher [1962] Director; Alexander Charles Plant [1969] Director; Peter John Simpson [1967] Director; Paul Frederick Garry Whittaker [1960] Director

Anglian Water Services Limited
Incorporated: 1 April 1989 *Employees:* 4,600
Net Worth: £1,217,400,064 *Total Assets:* £10,790,700,032
Registered Office: Lancaster House, Lancaster Way, Ermine Business Park, Huntingdon, Cambs, PE29 6XU
Activities: Water collection, treatment and supply
Parent: Anglian Water Services UK Parent Co Limited
Officers: Claire Tytherleigh Russell, Secretary; Dr Stephen Robert Billingham [1948] Director; James Alexander Bryce [1974] Director/Senior Principal; Natalie Ceeney [1971] Director; Dame Veronica Anne Courtice [1952] Director, University of Cambridge; John Raymond Hirst [1952] Director; Scott Robert James Longhurst [1967] Finance Director; Niall Patrick Mills [1968] Director/Chartered Engineer; Zarin Homi Patel [1961] Independent Director; Peter John Simpson [1967] Director/Chief Executive Officer; Duncan John Symonds [1973] Director/Civil Engineer; Paul Frederick Garry Whittaker [1960] Director

Anglian Windows Limited
Incorporated: 17 September 1990 *Employees:* 1,586
Net Worth: £46,577,000 *Total Assets:* £120,272,000
Registered Office: Liberator Road, Norwich, NR6 6EU
Activities: Glazing
Parent: Anglian Group Ltd
Officers: Nicholas Andrew Roberts [1961] Director; Martin James Rutter [1972] Sales Director

Anglo European Academy Trust
Incorporated: 14 November 2011 *Employees:* 176
Net Worth: £12,053,354 *Total Assets:* £15,887,779
Registered Office: Willow Green, Ingatestone, Essex, CM4 0DJ
Activities: General secondary education
Officers: David Anthony Barrs [1955] Director; Nikki Chatha [1979] Director; Peter Clark [1968] Director; Marina Fairfield [1969] Director; Roger William Franklin [1934] Director/Retired; Donald Frank Frost [1935] Director; Michael Frost [1965] Director of Finance; Jody Marie Gee [1972] Director/Headmistress; Helle Gulowsen [1967] Director/Translator [Norwegian]; Kenneth Hoyle [1948] Director/Retired Lecturer; Claire Jones [1984] Director; Nicola Jane Maher [1966] Director/Teacher; Paul Anthony Mason [1956] Director/Solicitor; Claire Maureen Penn [1958] Director; Neil Richards [1981] Director; Alys Rowland [1983] Director; Neil Wanags Livingstone [1972] Director/Computer Programmer; Michael Frederick Reginald Whalley [1940] Director; Amanda Jane Willis [1972] Director/Teacher

Anglo-Dutch Property (UK) Holding Limited
Incorporated: 3 June 1985
Net Worth: £4,312,000 *Total Assets:* £39,928,000
Registered Office: Etel House, Avenue One, Letchworth Garden City, Herts, SG6 2HU
Activities: Dormant company
Parent: Kwik Fit (NL) Ltd
Officers: Ian Vincent Ellis, Secretary; Simon Ashley Paul King [1969] Director; Guy Thomas Wheeler [1962] Director

Anglo-Norden Forest Products Limited
Incorporated: 3 March 1971 *Employees:* 32
Net Worth: £3,186,838 *Total Assets:* £12,708,651
Registered Office: Eagle Wharf, Helena Road, Ipswich, Suffolk, IP3 0BT
Activities: Agents involved in the sale of timber and building materials
Officers: Anthony Louis O'Brien, Secretary; Anders Wedel [1971] Director [Danish]

Angloflora Farms Limited
Incorporated: 5 June 1979 *Employees:* 2
Net Worth: £7,433,749 *Total Assets:* £8,294,573
Registered Office: 1-4 London Road, Spalding, Lincs, PE11 2TA
Activities: Growing of cereals (except rice), leguminous crops and oil seeds
Parent: Angloflora (Holdings) Limited
Officers: Ronald John James Rusman, Company Secretary [Dutch]; Astrid Rusman [1966] Director [German]; Ronald John James Rusman [1964] Director/Company Secretary [Dutch]

Anness Publishing Limited
Incorporated: 24 April 1989 *Employees:* 7
Net Worth: £9,716,071 *Total Assets:* £10,239,593
Registered Office: 3 Warners Mill, Silks Way, Braintree, Essex, CM7 3GB
Activities: Book publishing
Major Shareholder: Paul Leonard Anness
Officers: Joanna Lorenz, Secretary/Publisher; Paul Leonard Anness [1955] Director/Publisher; Joanna Lorenz [1962] Director/Publisher; Helen Sudell [1961] Director/Publishing; Benjamin James Worley [1969] Director/Print Professional

Annodata Limited
Incorporated: 20 April 1988 *Employees:* 291
Net Worth: £11,171,027 *Total Assets:* £32,548,760
Registered Office: The Maylands Building, Maylands Avenue, Hemel Hempstead Industrial Estate, Hemel Hempstead, Herts, HP2 7TG
Activities: Other information technology service activities
Parent: Kyocera Document Solutions Inc
Officers: Richard McClure, Secretary; Graham Cox [1959] Director; Norihiko Ina [1963] Director [Japanese]; Hironao Katsukura [1965] Director [Japanese]; Takuya Marubayashi [1967] Director [Japanese]; Rod Tonna-Barthet [1968] Sales Director

Anritsu EMEA Limited
Incorporated: 15 March 2006 *Employees:* 80
Net Worth: £4,932,504 *Total Assets:* £20,866,786
Registered Office: 200 Capability Green, Luton, Beds, LU1 3LU
Activities: Other service activities n.e.c.
Parent: Anritsu Corporation
Officers: Eisuke Matsuo, Secretary; Osamu Nagata [1959] Director [Japanese]; Riccardo Rossetti [1967] Director [Italian]; Takeshi Shima [1964] Director [Japanese]

Antas Limited
Incorporated: 8 September 1995
Net Worth: £9,452,763 *Total Assets:* £11,068,894
Registered Office: Botanic House, 100 Hills Road, Cambridge, CB2 1PH
Activities: Growing of cereals (except rice), leguminous crops and oil seeds
Officers: Michael John Aubrey, Secretary/Solicitor; Doctor Francesco Saverio Amman [1957] Director [Italian]; Simon Neil Fowler [1967] Director/Land Agent; Christoph Gruninger [1943] Director/Banker [German]

Antec International Limited
Incorporated: 19 April 1961 *Employees:* 56
Net Worth: £13,765,000 *Total Assets:* £17,536,000
Registered Office: Windham Road, Chilton Industrial Estate, Sudbury, Suffolk, CO10 2XD
Activities: Manufacture of other chemical products n.e.c.
Parent: Lanxess AG
Officers: Christopher James Flett [1969] Director/Accountant; Dr Juan Gonzalez-Blanco [1965] Director/Chemist/Head of Global Production for MPP-ACD [German]; Jacques Louis Albert Perez [1962] Managing Director and Country Representative [French]

Antoniou Investments Limited
Incorporated: 9 December 2014
Net Worth: £497,695 *Total Assets:* £10,114,621
Registered Office: Toronto Suite, Maple House, High Street, Potters Bar, Herts, EN6 5BS
Activities: Other letting and operating of own or leased real estate
Shareholders: Demetrios Antoniou; Harry Zenonos Antoniou; Maria Zenonos Polycarpou
Officers: Demetrios Antoniou [1976] Director; Harry Zenonos Antoniou [1983] Director; Maria Zenonos Polycarpou [1978] Director

Anzco Foods UK Limited
Incorporated: 10 August 2000 *Employees:* 16
Net Worth: £7,475,652 *Total Assets:* £21,575,996
Registered Office: Unit 7 Bates Industrial Estate, Church Road, Harold Wood, Romford, Essex, RM3 0HU
Activities: Wholesale of meat and meat products
Officers: Peter William Conley [1967] Director/COO Sales and Marketing [New Zealander]; Poh Ying Loke [1955] Director/General Manager Finance [New Zealander]; Richard William Walker [1972] Director/General Manager of Marketing [New Zealander]

AOC (UK) Ltd
Incorporated: 16 January 1987 *Employees:* 31
Net Worth: £4,474,153 *Total Assets:* £11,081,126
Registered Office: Factory Lane, Brantham, Manningtree, Essex, CO11 1NT
Activities: Agents specialised in the sale of other particular products
Officers: Albert Jan Bakker [1969] Director/CEO EU/Asia [Dutch]; Peter Stephen Cheshire [1955] Sales Director; Michel Joseph Pierre Govaert [1963] Director [Dutch]

Apatech Limited
Incorporated: 1 March 2001 *Employees:* 65
Net Worth: £34,201,144 *Total Assets:* £36,755,124
Registered Office: 370 Centennial Avenue, Centennial Park, Elstree, Herts, WD6 3TJ
Activities: Manufacture of other chemical products n.e.c.
Parent: Baxter Holding BV
Officers: Andrew Neil Goldney [1968] Director/General Manager; Brian Keith Morgan [1969] Director/Business Executive [American]

Apem Components Limited
Incorporated: 9 June 1983 *Employees:* 175
Net Worth: £8,118,370 *Total Assets:* £12,564,560
Registered Office: Drakes Drive, Long Crendon, Aylesbury, Bucks, HP18 9BA
Activities: Manufacture of other electrical equipment
Officers: Joel Rene Gerard Becquet [1957] Director/Chief Financial Officer [French]; James Peter Minton Cooper [1975] Managing Director; Marc Francois Jean-Marie Enjalbert [1962] Director/President [French]

Apertio Limited
Incorporated: 10 May 2002
Net Worth: £25,062,000 *Total Assets:* £25,936,000
Registered Office: The Forum, Lancaster Way, Ermine Business Park, Huntingdon, Cambs, PE29 6XU
Activities: Other information technology service activities
Parent: Nokia UK Limited
Officers: Hans-Joerg Daub [1963] Director/Chief Financial Officer [German]; Trevor Dryden Foster [1970] Director/Accountant; Cormac Vincent Whelan [1964] Director [Irish]

API Microelectronics Limited
Incorporated: 8 June 1992 *Employees:* 157
Net Worth: £8,319,000 *Total Assets:* £15,630,000
Registered Office: Fenner Road, South Denes, Great Yarmouth, Norfolk, NR30 3PX
Activities: Manufacture of electronic components
Officers: Richard John Farrington [1956] Director/Certified Chartered Accountant; Matthew John Howchin [1964] Director/Operations Manager; Robert Edward Tavares [1961] Director [American]

API Microwave Limited
Incorporated: 27 June 2008 *Employees:* 69
Net Worth: £7,010,000 *Total Assets:* £10,761,000
Registered Office: Fenner Road, South Denes, Great Yarmouth, Norfolk, NR30 3PX
Activities: Manufacture of electronic components
Officers: Richard John Farrington [1956] Director/Certified Chartered Accountant; Matthew John Howchin [1964] Director/Operations Manager; Robert Edward Tavares [1961] Director [American]

Apical Limited
Incorporated: 26 January 1999 *Employees:* 124
Net Worth Deficit: £632,113 *Total Assets:* £12,549,325
Registered Office: 110 Fulbourn Road, Cambridge, CB1 9NJ
Activities: Manufacture of electronic components
Parent: ARM Limited
Officers: Graham Stephen Budd [1968] Director; Jeremy Piers Davies [1960] Director/VP and General Manager MPG; Andrew Mark Smith [1966] Director/Chief Information Officer

The APM Group Limited
Incorporated: 13 October 1993 *Employees:* 104
Net Worth: £12,816,245 *Total Assets:* £16,374,439
Registered Office: 6th Floor, Sword House, Totteridge Road, High Wycombe, Bucks, HP13 6DG
Activities: Management consultancy activities other than financial management
Major Shareholder: Richard Charles Pharro
Officers: Rodney John Baker [1942] Director/Management Consultant; Michael Fraser Dallas [1943] Director/Project Manager; Adrian John Dooley [1956] Director; Nicholas Richard Houlton [1963] Operations and Marketing Director; Richard Charles Pharro [1952] Director

Apollo Property Investment Limited
Incorporated: 14 February 2012 *Employees:* 1
Net Worth: £106,599 *Total Assets:* £12,639,118
Registered Office: 188 High Road, Loughton, Essex, IG10 1DN
Activities: Development of building projects
Major Shareholder: Gary Patrick Couch
Officers: Gary Patrick Couch [1962] Director

Apperly Estates Limited
Incorporated: 25 July 1919
Net Worth: £88,995,448 *Total Assets:* £122,557,816
Registered Office: Bourbon Court, Nightingales Corner, Little Chalfont, Bucks, HP7 9QS
Activities: Other letting and operating of own or leased real estate
Officers: Rachel Claire Azcona, Secretary; David Robert Apperly [1956] Director/Chartered Surveyor; Rachel Claire Azcona [1966] Director/Commercial Strategy Consultant; Jonathan Charles Bennett Houlton [1961] Finance Director; Richard Henry Faber Merriam [1957] Director/Chartered Surveyor; Arthur Peter MacLean Mullineux [1981] Director/Investment Manager; Jonathan Vivian Richard Stevenson [1981] Director/Head of Acquisitions & Development; Alison Charlotte Winkfield [1962] Director/Travel Consultant

Appetite Holdings Limited
Incorporated: 7 December 2015 *Employees:* 131
Net Worth: £3,601,851 *Total Assets:* £11,407,620
Registered Office: 1 Hertsmere Industrial Park, Warwick Road, Borehamwood, Herts, WD6 1GT
Activities: Manufacture of other food products n.e.c.
Major Shareholder: Paul Luigi Ugo
Officers: Paul Luigi Ugo [1966] Director

Applepeach Limited
Incorporated: 19 March 2004 *Employees:* 9
Net Worth: £4,407,042 *Total Assets:* £8,451,681
Registered Office: CP House, Otterspool Way, Watford Bypass, Watford, Herts, WD25 8JJ
Activities: Management of real estate on a fee or contract basis
Shareholders: Lenta Properties Limited; Searchgrade Limited
Officers: Eric Lewis, Secretary; Paul Andrew Filer [1957] Director; Mark Gibbor [1988] Director; Michael Robert Goldberger [1956] Director; David Alan Pearlman [1945] Director

Appleyard Group Limited
Incorporated: 31 August 1923
Net Worth: £6,294,000 *Total Assets:* £21,521,000
Registered Office: 770 The Crescent, Colchester Business Park, Colchester, Essex, CO4 9YQ
Activities: Activities of head offices
Parent: Jardine Motors Group UK Limited
Officers: Mark Finch, Secretary; Mark Charles Finch [1967] Director/Company Secretary; David John Muir [1980] Director

Applied Satellite Technology Limited
Incorporated: 6 August 1987 *Employees:* 67
Net Worth: £10,556,274 *Total Assets:* £17,891,290
Registered Office: Satellite House, Bessemer Way, Harfrey's Industrial Estate, Great Yarmouth, Norfolk, NR31 0LX
Activities: Satellite telecommunications activities
Major Shareholder: Gregory Stuart Darling
Officers: Christopher John Binnie, Secretary; Christopher John Binnie [1966] Finance Director; Stuart James Castell [1967] ASBB Director; Gregory Stuart Darling [1953] Director; Susan Margaret Darling [1956] Director/Administrator [New Zealander]; David Charles Davies [1963] Director; Alexandra Mary Johnson [1955] Director; Andrew John Smith [1972] Group Technical Director; Mark Andrew Peter Sykes [1964] Director

Aprirose Trading Limited
Incorporated: 3 September 2001 *Employees:* 7
Net Worth: £7,771,837 *Total Assets:* £11,799,484
Registered Office: Aprirose House, 48a High Street, Edgware, Middlesex, HA8 7EQ
Activities: Agents specialised in the sale of other particular products
Parent: Aprirose Trading Holding Limited
Officers: Mansukhlal Gosar Gudka, Secretary; Manish Mansukhlal Gudka [1970] Director; Mansukhlal Gosar Gudka [1941] Director; Parag Mansukhlal Gudka [1971] Director/Export Manager

Aprite (GB) Limited
Incorporated: 10 October 1996 *Employees:* 586
Net Worth: £13,363,000 *Total Assets:* £131,193,000
Registered Office: The Rivers Office Park, Denham Way, Rickmansworth, Herts, WD3 9YS
Activities: Sale of new cars and light motor vehicles
Parent: Nissan Motor (GB) Limited
Officers: Steven Neil Tiffin, Secretary; Laurent Frank Christian David [1971] Director [French]; Gareth John Main [1967] Director/General Manager; Jordi Vila Onses [1963] Director/Vice President Sales [Spanish]

APT-Skidata Limited
Incorporated: 14 July 1998 *Employees:* 80
Net Worth: £510,000 *Total Assets:* £9,115,000
Registered Office: 1 Maxted Corner, Maxted Road, Hemel Hempstead Industrial Estate, Hemel Hempstead, Herts, HP2 7RA
Activities: Manufacture of other special-purpose machinery n.e.c.
Parent: Swarco AG
Officers: Steffan John Evans, Secretary; Wilhelmus Johannes Balk [1969] Managing Director [Dutch]; Peter Anthony Brown [1967] Managing Director; Jeremy Peter Cowling [1967] Director; Steffan John Evans [1978] Finance Director; James Toal [1965] Director/Management [American]

The John Apthorp Charity
Incorporated: 30 December 2003
Net Worth: £12,800,648 *Total Assets:* £12,803,858
Registered Office: Egale 1, 80 St Albans Road, Watford, Herts, WD17 1DL
Activities: Other education n.e.c.
Officers: Kate Arnold, Secretary; Duncan Mark Apthorp [1960] Director/Engineer; John Dorrington Apthorp [1935] Director; Justin James Apthorp [1962] Director; Kate Arnold [1967] Director/Service Resource Administrator

Aquasium Technology Limited
Incorporated: 26 June 2001 *Employees:* 61
Net Worth: £6,536,009 *Total Assets:* £11,101,347
Registered Office: 43 Pembroke Avenue, Denny Industrial Estate, Waterbeach, Cambridge, CB25 9QX
Activities: Manufacture of other special-purpose machinery n.e.c.
Shareholder: Foresight VCT PLC
Officers: Gavin Crick [1958] Director; John Peter Cumberland [1943] Director; Russell George Healey [1970] Director/Corporate Financier; Robert Leonard Nicolson [1955] Director

Aquaterra Energy Group Limited
Incorporated: 12 June 2017 *Employees:* 70
Net Worth: £2,301,000 *Total Assets:* £33,568,000
Registered Office: Innovation House, 2 Alkmaar Way, Norwich, NR6 6BF
Activities: Activities of other holding companies n.e.c.
Officers: Nicholas Paul Hawkes, Secretary; Mark Boyd [1956] Director; Per Arne Jensen [1964] Director [Norwegian]; George Graham Morrison [1971] Director; Gavin Jonathon Prise [1962] Board Director; Alan James Stark Wilson [1957] Director

Aquaterra Energy Limited
Incorporated: 29 July 2005 *Employees:* 63
Net Worth: £8,146,000 *Total Assets:* £15,544,000
Registered Office: Innovation House, 2 Alkmaar Way, Norwich, NR6 6BF
Activities: Manufacture of machinery for mining
Parent: Aquaterra Energy Group Limited
Officers: Nicholas Paul Hawkes, Secretary; Mark Boyd [1956] Director; Per Arne Jensen [1964] Director [Norwegian]; James Robert Larnder [1978] Director; Stewart David Maxwell [1967] Director/Engineer; George Graham Morrison [1971] Director/Engineer; Gavin Jonathon Prise [1962] Director; Alan Wilson [1957] Director

Aquatronic Group Management PLC
Incorporated: 29 August 1997 *Employees:* 145
Net Worth: £8,946,152 *Total Assets:* £16,031,349
Registered Office: AGM House, London Road, Copford, Colchester, Essex, CO6 1GT
Activities: Manufacture of pumps
Major Shareholder: David Victor Taylor
Officers: Minerva Sharry, Secretary; Paul Michael Keyes [1955] Director; Claire Georgina Larkins [1980] Director; Timothy Lister [1980] Service Director; Konstantinos Manousakis [1961] Products Director [Greek]; Minerva Sharry [1973] Finance Director; David Victor Taylor [1936] Director/Chairman; Ian David Taylor [1965] Technical Director; Mark Andrew Taylor [1962] Director/Chief Executive Officer

Aquila BTE 1 Limited
Incorporated: 2 May 2007
Net Worth: £7,755,020 *Total Assets:* £25,938,068
Registered Office: 22 Barn Rise, Wembley, Middlesex, HA9 9NQ
Activities: Other letting and operating of own or leased real estate
Parent: Aquila House Property Limited
Officers: Paul Gary Hirst, Secretary/Surveyor; Anthony David Chambers [1955] Director/Surveyor; Daniel Freedman [1971] Director/Lawyer; Paul Gary Hirst [1961] Director/Surveyor

Aquila Chelmsford Limited
Incorporated: 21 February 2001
Net Worth: £12,027,747 *Total Assets:* £20,735,054
Registered Office: 22 Barn Rise, Wembley, Middlesex, HA9 9NQ
Activities: Other letting and operating of own or leased real estate
Parent: Aquila House Property Limited
Officers: Anne Shirley Chambers, Secretary; Anthony David Chambers [1955] Director/Chartered Surveyor; Daniel Freedman [1971] Director/Lawyer; Paul Gary Hirst [1961] Director

Aquila EHS Limited
Incorporated: 23 January 2002 *Employees:* 3
Net Worth: £5,168,227 *Total Assets:* £31,217,220
Registered Office: 22 Barn Rise, Wembley, Middlesex, HA9 9NQ
Activities: Other letting and operating of own or leased real estate
Parent: Aquila House Property Limited
Officers: Anne Shirley Chambers, Secretary; Anthony David Chambers [1955] Director/Surveyor; Daniel Freedman [1971] Director/Lawyer; Paul Gary Hirst [1961] Director

Aquila Estates Limited
Incorporated: 3 December 2002 *Employees:* 3
Net Worth Deficit: £3,367,769 *Total Assets:* £33,881,256
Registered Office: 22 Barn Rise, Wembley, Middlesex, HA9 9NQ
Activities: Other letting and operating of own or leased real estate
Parent: Aquila House Property Limited
Officers: Paul Gary Hirst, Secretary/Director; Anthony David Chambers [1955] Director/Chartered Surveyor; Daniel Freedman [1971] Director/Lawyer; Paul Gary Hirst [1961] Director

Aquila MB2 Limited
Incorporated: 30 September 2014 *Employees:* 3
Previous: ABSL2 Limited
Net Worth Deficit: £118 *Total Assets:* £35,316,752
Registered Office: 22 Barn Rise, Wembley, Middlesex, HA9 9NQ
Activities: Activities of other holding companies n.e.c.
Parent: Aquila MB3 Limited
Officers: Paul Gary Hirst, Secretary; Anthony David Chambers [1955] Director/Property Consultant; Daniel Freedman [1971] Director/Lawyer; Paul Gary Hirst [1961] Director/Property Consultant

Aquila MB3 Limited
Incorporated: 30 September 2014
Previous: ABSL3 Limited
Net Worth Deficit: £1,184,910 *Total Assets:* £35,317,248
Registered Office: 22 Barn Rise, Wembley, Middlesex, HA9 9NQ
Activities: Activities of other holding companies n.e.c.
Parent: Aquila House Holdings Limited
Officers: Paul Gary Hirst, Secretary; Anthony David Chambers [1955] Director/Property Consultant; Daniel Freedman [1971] Director/Lawyer; Paul Gary Hirst [1961] Director/Property Consultant

Aquinna Homes PLC
Incorporated: 5 February 2005 *Employees:* 20
Net Worth: £8,895,664 *Total Assets:* £23,573,548
Registered Office: Highway House, 17 London End, Beaconsfield, Bucks, HP9 2HN
Activities: Construction of domestic buildings
Major Shareholder: Stephen Harvey Brazier
Officers: Stephen Harvey Brazier, Secretary; Stephen Harvey Brazier [1963] Director; Simon Richard Seymour [1969] Director

Arcese Real Estate UK Limited
Incorporated: 6 June 2006
Net Worth: £6,729,259 *Total Assets:* £11,212,517
Registered Office: Thurrock Parkway, Thurrock Park Industrial Estate, Tilbury, Essex, RM18 7HY
Activities: Other letting and operating of own or leased real estate
Parent: Arcese Immobiliare SpA
Officers: Alberto Dejana [1959] Director/Chief Executive [Italian]; Michele Nascetti [1969] Managing Director [Italian]

Archant Community Media Holdings Limited
Incorporated: 28 June 2001
Net Worth: £21,981,912 *Total Assets:* £109,663,936
Registered Office: Prospect House, Rouen Road, Norwich, NR1 1RE
Activities: Publishing of newspapers
Shareholders: Archant Holdings Limited; Archant BHGC Limited
Officers: Tara Cross [1971] Director/Deputy Company Secretary; Brian Gerard McCarthy [1962] Finance Director

Archant Community Media Limited
Incorporated: 15 January 1884 *Employees:* 1,415
Net Worth: £82,003,000 *Total Assets:* £132,899,000
Registered Office: Prospect House, Rouen Road, Norwich, NR1 1RE
Activities: Publishing of newspapers
Parent: Archant Community Media Holdings Limited
Officers: Jeffrey Lawrence Henry [1961] Director; Matthew James Kelly [1969] Director/Chief Content Officer; Brian Gerard McCarthy [1962] Finance Director; Craig Nigel Nayman [1959] Commercial Director; Deirdre Annuncia Willmott [1964] Group HR Director [Irish]

Archant Holdings Limited
Incorporated: 25 July 2000
Net Worth: £296,445,664 *Total Assets:* £297,553,696
Registered Office: Prospect House, Rouen Road, Norwich, NR1 1RE
Activities: Dormant company
Parent: Archant Limited
Officers: Tara Cross [1971] Director/Deputy Company Secretary; Brian Gerard McCarthy [1962] Finance Director

Archant Limited
Incorporated: 18 December 2000 *Employees:* 1,262
Net Worth: £12,722,000 *Total Assets:* £61,441,000
Registered Office: Prospect House, Rouen Road, Norwich, NR1 1RE
Activities: Activities of head offices
Officers: Simon Tristan Bax [1959] Director; Simon Charles Copeman [1966] Director; Alison Jane Hastings [1965] Director; Jeffrey Lawrence Henry [1961] Director/Chief Executive Officer; David John McLeavy Hill [1957] Director; Brian Gerard McCarthy [1962] Finance Director; Michael Jeffrey Walsh [1949] Director

Archaylen Property Limited
Incorporated: 14 September 2011 *Employees:* 2
Net Worth: £6,832,227 *Total Assets:* £26,938,988
Registered Office: Beeches Farm, Icknield Way, Tring, Herts, HP23 4LA
Activities: Development of building projects
Shareholders: Peter Donald Dean; Andrew Frederick Screech; Susan Jane Dean; Sarah Lois Dean; Stephen Douglas John Marshall; Gubblecote Properties Limited
Officers: Andrew Frederick Screech, Secretary; Peter Donald Dean [1944] Director; Sarah Lois Dean [1971] Director; Stephen Douglas John Marshall [1955] Director; Andrew Frederick Screech [1975] Director/Property Manager

Archigen Biotech Limited
Incorporated: 15 April 2014 *Employees:* 35
Net Worth: £5,950,887 *Total Assets:* £18,974,144
Registered Office: 1 Francis Crick Avenue, Cambridge Biomedical Campus, Cambridge, CB2 0AA
Activities: Other business support service activities n.e.c.
Shareholder: AstraZeneca UK Limited
Officers: Matthew Ian Conacher, Secretary; Karl David Bradshaw [1974] Evaluation Director; Dr Tae Han Kim [1957] Director [South Korean]; Noreen Parsons [1965] Director/Franchise Head [Irish]; Patrick Yuhmin Yang [1948] Director [American]; Hoyeol Yoon [1963] Director [South Korean]

Architectural Glazing Limited
Incorporated: 3 February 2005 *Employees:* 134
Net Worth: £5,531,210 *Total Assets:* £10,988,029
Registered Office: Chiswick Avenue, Mildenhall, Bury St Edmunds, Suffolk, IP28 7AY
Activities: Activities of head offices
Shareholders: Edward Charles Whipp; Jeremy Mark Cocks; Simon Edward Gladwin
Officers: Jeremy Mark Cocks, Director and Secretary; Jeremy Mark Cocks [1962] Director and Secretary; Simon Edward Gladwin [1963] Director; Edward Charles Whipp [1964] Director

Archway Apartments Limited
Incorporated: 19 August 2014
Net Worth Deficit: £1,630,570 *Total Assets:* £8,830,916
Registered Office: 42 Lytton Road, Barnet, Herts, EN5 5BY
Activities: Buying and selling of own real estate
Officers: Joseph Peter Gerrard [1954] Director; Michael Gerrard [1957] Director

Arcofina LLP
Incorporated: 8 February 2005
Net Worth Deficit: £14,976 *Total Assets:* £24,628,286
Registered Office: Suite 105, Viglen House, Alperton Lane, Wembley, Middlesex, HA0 1HD
Officers: Jerome Joliat [1935] Member; Mohamed Abdelouahab Rahim [1952] Member

Arcus FM Limited
Incorporated: 17 January 2008 *Employees:* 693
Net Worth: £5,185,000 *Total Assets:* £20,379,000
Registered Office: Enterprise House, 168-170 Upminster Road, Upminster, Essex, RM14 2RB
Activities: Management of real estate on a fee or contract basis
Officers: Paul Duckels [1977] Director; Ian David Ellis [1955] Director; David Furness [1966] Director; Christopher Mark Green [1965] Managing Director; Joanne Hall [1981] Director/Regional Manager; Samantha Holmes [1971] HSQE Director; Samantha Lambton [1966] HR Director; Danny Malyon [1969] Director/Head of FM Sainsbury's Supermarkets Ltd; Anthony Benedict Mars [1968] Director/Head of Design Construction and Delivery, Property; Neil Pearce [1967] Director; Stephen Terence Patrick Willis [1965] Director

Arcus Solutions (Holdings) Limited
Incorporated: 25 October 2010 *Employees:* 1,664
Net Worth: £8,873,000 *Total Assets:* £28,027,000
Registered Office: Enterprise House, 168-170 Upminster Road, Upminster, Essex, RM14 2RB
Activities: Activities of head offices
Officers: Terry Douglas [1966] Director; Ian David Ellis [1955] Director; Richard John Fabian [1956] Director; Christopher Mark Green [1965] Director; Neil Pearce [1967] Director; Stephen Terence Patrick Willis [1965] Director

Ardex Holdings UK Limited
Incorporated: 3 October 2001 *Employees:* 2
Net Worth: £97,178,000 *Total Assets:* £100,100,000
Registered Office: Homefield Road, Haverhill, Suffolk, CB9 8QP
Activities: Other manufacturing n.e.c.
Officers: Darren Paul Carty, Secretary; Peter Richard Bell [1957] Director; Mark Eslamlooy [1966] Director [German]

Ardex Investments UK Limited
Incorporated: 1 March 2002
Net Worth: £100,063,000 *Total Assets:* £100,063,000
Registered Office: c/o Ardex UK Limited, Homefield Road, Haverhill, Suffolk, CB9 8QP
Activities: Non-trading company
Officers: Darren Paul Carty, Secretary; Peter Richard Bell [1957] Director; Mark Eslamlooy [1966] Director [German]

Ardex UK Limited
Incorporated: 23 August 1960 *Employees:* 110
Net Worth: £14,357,000 *Total Assets:* £20,875,000
Registered Office: Homefield Road, Haverhill, Suffolk, CB9 8QP
Activities: Manufacture of paints, varnishes and similar coatings, mastics and sealants
Officers: Darren Paul Carty, Secretary; Peter Richard Bell [1957] Director; Mark Eslamlooy [1966] Director [German]

Arena Event Services Group Limited
Incorporated: 11 September 2000 *Employees:* 511
Net Worth: £16,151,000 *Total Assets:* £45,085,000
Registered Office: Needingworth Industrial Estate, Needingworth Road, St Ives, Cambs, PE27 4NB
Activities: Other sports activities
Parent: WB Co (1403) Limited
Officers: Gregory Malcolm Lawless [1960] Director [Irish]; Christopher James Piggott [1967] Director; Piers Leigh Stuart Wilson [1967] Director/Chartered Accountant; David John Withey [1957] Sales Director

Ares Properties Ltd
Incorporated: 13 November 2014
Net Worth: £3,884,290 *Total Assets:* £10,815,564
Registered Office: Floor 2, 555-557 Cranbrook Road, Ilford, Essex, IG2 6HE
Activities: Buying and selling of own real estate
Parent: Albrox Limited
Officers: Ghulam Asghar Alahi [1970] Director

Argon NPS Limited
Incorporated: 3 December 2014 *Employees:* 7
Net Worth: £48,000,000 *Total Assets:* £346,600,000
Registered Office: Peoplebuilding 2, Peoplebuilding Estate, Maylands Avenue, Hemel Hempstead Industrial Estate, Hemel Hempstead, Herts, HP2 4NW
Activities: Other information technology service activities
Parent: Argon NPS (Holdings) Limited
Officers: Stephen James Callaghan [1960] Director; Alan George O'Reilly [1961] Director [Irish]

Arihant Limited
Incorporated: 15 December 1997 *Employees:* 9
Net Worth: £5,839,376 *Total Assets:* £11,477,931
Registered Office: 18 Parkfield Gardens, North Harrow, Middlesex, HA2 6JR
Activities: Other letting and operating of own or leased real estate
Officers: Himanshu Anantrai Shah, Secretary; Himanshu Anantrai Shah [1966] Director/Self Employed & Lettings; Sejal Himanshu Shah [1971] Director/Employed and Lettings

Arinso People Services Limited
Incorporated: 3 July 2003
Net Worth: £30,823,936 *Total Assets:* £30,823,936
Registered Office: Peoplebuilding 2, Peoplebuilding Estate, Maylands Avenue, Hemel Hempstead Industrial Estate, Hemel Hempstead, Herts, HP2 4NW
Activities: Information technology consultancy activities
Parent: Northgate Information Solutions Holdings Limited
Officers: Malcolm Robert Bennett, Secretary; Steven James Chalker [1974] Chief Financial Director; Andrew Phillip Monshaw [1962] Director [American]

Arinso UK Limited
Incorporated: 2 January 1998
Net Worth: £20,461,006 *Total Assets:* £20,461,006
Registered Office: Peoplebuilding 2, Peoplebuilding Estate, Maylands Avenue, Hemel Hempstead Industrial Estate, Hemel Hempstead, Herts, HP2 4NW
Activities: Other information technology service activities
Parent: Northgate Information Solutions Holdings Limited
Officers: Malcolm Robert Bennett, Secretary; Steven James Chalker [1974] Chief Financial Director; Andrew Phillip Monshaw [1962] Director [American]

Arisen Chef Ltd
Incorporated: 21 February 2000 *Employees:* 755
Net Worth: £1,179,926 *Total Assets:* £19,091,982
Registered Office: 21-23 Town Square, Stevenage, Herts, SG1 1BP
Activities: Unlicenced restaurants and cafes
Major Shareholder: Michael Garo Ghazarian
Officers: Karen Tracey Ghazarian, Secretary; Michael Garo Ghazarian [1964] Director/Restaurateur

Ariston Thermo UK Ltd
Incorporated: 24 February 1986 *Employees:* 49
Net Worth: £597,000 *Total Assets:* £11,403,000
Registered Office: 3 Juniper West, Fenton Way, Southfields Business Park, Basildon, Essex, SS15 6SJ
Activities: Non-specialised wholesale trade
Major Shareholder: Francesco Merloni
Officers: Mustafa Findik [1964] Director; Giacomo Guerrieri [1969] Director/Thermic Comfort Controlling [Italian]; Laurent Alexis Michel Henri Jacquemin [1969] ELCO Division Director [Belgian]

Ariyan Hotels Limited
Incorporated: 23 April 2015 *Employees:* 20
Net Worth: £95,206 *Total Assets:* £12,561,352
Registered Office: Jubilee House, 7-9 The Oaks, Ruislip, Middlesex, HA4 7LF
Activities: Hotels and similar accommodation
Officers: Alim Amirali Janmohamed, Secretary; Alim Amirali Janmohamed [1981] Director; Amirali Hassanali Moledina Janmohamed [1952] Director/Hotelier

ARJ Construction Holdings Limited
Incorporated: 7 February 2013 *Employees:* 91
Net Worth: £5,121,800 *Total Assets:* £25,759,548
Registered Office: Bedford House, Rutherford Close, Meadway Technology Park, Stevenage, Herts, SG1 2EF
Activities: Activities of construction holding companies
Shareholders: ADH Professional Services Limited; SWK Management Services Limited; SJD Professional Services Limited
Officers: Stephen John Doherty [1977] Director; Andrew David Holt [1971] Director; Sean William Kneller [1977] Director

ARJ Construction Limited
Incorporated: 16 August 2005 *Employees:* 91
Net Worth: £5,017,236 *Total Assets:* £25,260,292
Registered Office: Bedford House, Rutherford Close, Meadway Technology Park, Stevenage, Herts, SG1 2EF
Activities: Construction of commercial buildings
Parent: ARJ Construction Holdings Limited
Officers: Stephen John Doherty, Secretary; Stephen John Doherty [1977] Director; Andrew David Holt [1971] Director; Sean William Kneller [1977] Director

Arjo UK Limited
Incorporated: 29 June 2017 *Employees:* 647
Net Worth: £41,012,000 *Total Assets:* £63,871,000
Registered Office: ArjoHuntleigh House, Houghton Hall Business Park, Houghton Regis, Dunstable, Beds, LU5 5XF
Activities: Manufacture of medical and dental instruments and supplies
Officers: Sukraj Singh Gill, Secretary; Bettina Tudor Fitt [1962] Director/President UKI; Sukraj Singh Gill [1984] Finance Director; Khizer Ismail Ibrahim [1973] Director; Karl Joacim Claesson Lindoff [1973] Director/Group CEO [Swedish]; Sven Jonas Lindqvist [1962] Director/Group CFO [Swedish]; Paul Gerard Lyon [1962] Director/President Global Sales & Service [Australian]

Arkarius Bidco Limited
Incorporated: 19 December 2016 *Employees:* 4
Net Worth Deficit: £7,953,684 *Total Assets:* £121,735,624
Registered Office: KD Tower, Cotterells, Hemel Hempstead, Herts, HP1 1FW
Activities: Activities of head offices
Parent: Arkarius Midco Limited
Officers: Kevin John Budge [1961] Director; Derek Andrew Kelly [1972] Director; Jeremy Steven Newman [1959] Director

ARM Limited
Incorporated: 12 November 1990 *Employees:* 5,434
Net Worth: £2,336,134,912 *Total Assets:* £2,909,374,976
Registered Office: 110 Fulbourn Road, Cambridge, CB1 9NJ
Activities: Other business support service activities n.e.c.
Parent: ARM Finance UK Limited
Officers: Carolyn Herzog, Secretary; Yasir Othman Al-Rumayyan [1970] Director/Business Executive [Saudi Arabian]; Graham Stephen Budd [1968] Director; Marcelo Claure [1970] Director/Company Executive [American]; Ronald D Fisher [1947] Director/Company Executive [American]; Michael Peter Muller [1959] Director; Alok Sama [1962] Director/Company Executive; Simon Anthony Segars [1967] Director; Masayoshi Son [1957] Director/Company Executive [Japanese]

ARM UK Holdings Limited
Incorporated: 25 February 2005 *Employees:* 2
Net Worth: £20,502,410 *Total Assets:* £20,502,910
Registered Office: 110 Fulbourn Road, Cambridge, CB1 9NJ
Activities: Activities of other holding companies n.e.c.
Parent: ARM Limited
Officers: Graham Stephen Budd [1968] Director; Andrew Mark Smith [1966] Director/Chief Information Officer

Armored Auto UK Limited
Incorporated: 17 March 1989 *Employees:* 53
Net Worth: £5,952,406 *Total Assets:* £10,065,709
Registered Office: Sword House, Totteridge Road, High Wycombe, Bucks, HP13 6DG
Activities: Manufacture of other chemical products n.e.c.
Parent: Energizer UK Limited
Officers: Emily Kellum Boss [1962] Director [American]; Timothy William Gorman [1960] Director/Business Executive [American]; Mark S Lavigne [1971] Director/Business Executive [American]

Armour Home Electronics Limited
Incorporated: 28 November 1980 *Employees:* 85
Net Worth: £1,206,758 *Total Assets:* £12,341,896
Registered Office: Stortford Hall Industrial Park, Dunmow Road, Bishop's Stortford, Herts, CM23 5GZ
Activities: Wholesale of radio, television goods & electrical household appliances (other than records, tapes, CDs)
Shareholder: George Leonard Dexter
Officers: Nicola Ann Spence, Secretary; George Leonard Dexter [1962] Director; Chris William Emerson [1957] Sales & Marketing Director; Nicola Ann Spence [1962] Director/Accountant

Arnold Family Holdings Limited
Incorporated: 26 September 2014 *Employees:* 108
Net Worth: £2,653,781 *Total Assets:* £12,500,293
Registered Office: Anson Road, Norwich Airport, Norwich, NR6 6EH
Activities: Non-trading company
Major Shareholder: Oliver William Arnold
Officers: Oliver William Arnold [1975] Director

Arpo Global Limited
Incorporated: 27 February 2013 *Employees:* 45
Net Worth: £10,855,620 *Total Assets:* £16,907,318
Registered Office: Sterling House, Hamlin Way, Harwick Narrows Industrial Estate, Kings Lynn, Norfolk, PE30 4NG
Activities: Wholesale of other intermediate products
Officers: Charles David McIntyre [1974] Commercial Director; Clive Russell Turner [1977] Sales Director; Marcus James Turner [1970] Managing Director; Stephen Richard Turner [1972] Director/Merchant

Arrhenius Holdings Limited
Incorporated: 20 August 2010 *Employees:* 137
Net Worth: £7,521,620 *Total Assets:* £24,216,760
Registered Office: 74 The Close, Norwich, NR1 4DR
Activities: Activities of head offices
Major Shareholder: Jonathon Mark Lansley
Officers: Robert Bell [1979] Director/Chartered Accountant; Jonathon Mark Lansley [1962] Director/Business Manager

Arrow Electronics (UK) Limited
Incorporated: 14 February 1991 *Employees:* 450
Net Worth: £66,705,000 *Total Assets:* £142,663,008
Registered Office: Kao 1, Kao Park, Hockham Way, Harlow, Essex, CM17 9NA
Activities: Wholesale of electronic and telecommunications equipment and parts
Parent: Arrow Electronics, Inc
Officers: Paul Ewing, Secretary; Dean Hassell [1968] Sales Director; Christopher David Stansbury [1965] Director [American]; Gregory Paul Tarpinian [1962] Director [American]

Arrow Electronics UK Holding Limited
Incorporated: 31 October 1996
Net Worth: £26,443,000 *Total Assets:* £107,973,000
Registered Office: Kao 1, Kao Park, Hockham Way, Harlow, Essex, CM17 9NA
Activities: Activities of other holding companies n.e.c.
Parent: Arrow Electronics, Inc
Officers: Paul Ewing, Secretary; Dean Hassell [1968] Sales Director; Christopher David Stansbury [1965] Director [American]; Gregory Paul Tarpinian [1962] Director [American]

Arthenella Limited
Incorporated: 17 February 1993 *Employees:* 57
Net Worth: £16,156,849 *Total Assets:* £17,429,196
Registered Office: Electro House, Edinburgh Way, Harlow, Essex, CM20 2EG
Activities: Installation of industrial machinery and equipment
Major Shareholder: Anthony John Rogers
Officers: Janet Anne Rogers, Secretary; Anthony John Rogers [1939] Director

L.C.F.Arthey & Sons Limited
Incorporated: 3 April 1964 *Employees:* 5
Net Worth: £16,879,608 *Total Assets:* £18,161,340
Registered Office: The Priory, Kersey, Suffolk, IP7 6DU
Activities: Growing of cereals (except rice), leguminous crops and oil seeds
Shareholders: Philip Nicholson; Michael Rundle
Officers: Clive William Arthey [1959] Director/Farmer; Elaine Foster Arthey [1951] Director; Lancelot John Spalding Arthey [1953] Director/Farmer

Arthur Midco 1 Limited
Incorporated: 11 February 2014
Net Worth Deficit: £49,448,000 *Total Assets:* £62,415,000
Registered Office: 99 Bridge Road East, Welwyn Garden City, Herts, AL7 1GL
Activities: Activities of head offices
Parent: Arthur Topco Limited
Officers: John Vincent Bowman [1963] Director; Jonathan Nicholas Roback [1969] Director

Arthur Midco 2 Limited
Incorporated: 11 February 2014
Net Worth: £500,000 *Total Assets:* £134,282,000
Registered Office: 99 Bridge Road East, Welwyn Garden City, Herts, AL7 1GL
Activities: Activities of head offices
Parent: Arthur Pikco Limited
Officers: John Vincent Bowman [1963] Director; Jonathan Nicholas Roback [1969] Director

Arthur Pikco Limited
Incorporated: 3 March 2014
Net Worth Deficit: £40,444,000 *Total Assets:* £134,348,992
Registered Office: 99 Bridge Road East, Welwyn Garden City, Herts, AL7 1GL
Activities: Activities of head offices
Parent: Arthur Midco 1 Limited
Officers: John Vincent Bowman [1963] Director; Jonathan Nicholas Roback [1969] Director

Arthur Topco Limited
Incorporated: 4 February 2014 *Employees:* 536
Net Worth Deficit: £91,009,000 *Total Assets:* £272,017,984
Registered Office: 99 Bridge Road East, Welwyn Garden City, Herts, AL7 1GL
Activities: Activities of head offices
Officers: John Vincent Bowman [1963] Director; Jonathan Nicholas Roback [1969] Director; Matthew James Robinson [1974] Director/Investment Professional; Simon James Edward Roddis [1968] Director/Investment Professional

Arthur's Partners LLP
Incorporated: 3 November 2016
Net Worth: £14,713,362 *Total Assets:* £14,767,284
Registered Office: 55 Station Road, Beaconsfield, Bucks, HP9 1QL
Officers: Francesca Byng [1949] Member; Fiona Elizabeth Livingstone-Learmonth [1956] Member; Elizabeth Cecily Stewart-Liberty [1930] Member; Oliver James Stewart-Liberty [1947] Member; Richard Justin Stewart-Liberty [1946] Member; Tatiana Atalanta Wilde [1976] Member

Artillery Properties Limited
Incorporated: 15 May 1998
Net Worth: £2,512,356 *Total Assets:* £8,017,093
Registered Office: 1 Beauchamp Court, 10 Victors Way, Barnet, Herts, EN5 5TZ
Activities: Development of building projects
Major Shareholder: Selwyn Howard David Tarn
Officers: Selwyn Howard David Tarn [1961] Director

Artisan (UK) PLC
Incorporated: 8 September 1998 *Employees:* 49
Net Worth: £6,187,662 *Total Assets:* £13,917,463
Registered Office: 2b Vantage Park, Washingley Road, Huntingdon, Cambs, PE29 6SR
Activities: Activities of head offices
Parent: Aspen Finance Limited
Officers: Philip Richard Speer, Secretary; Ian David Dyke [1959] Director; Michael John Eyres [1956] Director/Surveyor; Geoffrey James Lawler [1969] Director/Chartered Accountant; Geoffrey Hugh Melamet [1958] Director

Arugula Spruce Limited
Incorporated: 17 August 2016 *Employees:* 1
Net Worth Deficit: £158,938 *Total Assets:* £9,832,582
Registered Office: Suite 2, Viscount House, 6a Love Lane, Pinner, Middlesex, HA5 3EF
Activities: Buying and selling of own real estate
Major Shareholder: Zareen Syed Habib
Officers: Zareen Syed Habib, Secretary; Zareen Syed Habib [1971] Director [Canadian]

Aryzta Bakeries UK Ltd
Incorporated: 16 January 1995 *Employees:* 446
Net Worth: £10,838,000 *Total Assets:* £54,715,000
Registered Office: Unit 12 Humphrys Road, Woodside Estate, Dunstable, Beds, LU5 4TP
Activities: Manufacture of bread; manufacture of fresh pastry goods and cakes
Officers: Thierry Cacaly, Secretary; Thierry Cacaly [1971] Director/Head of Aryzta Foods Solutions UK [French]; Sean Timothy Murphy [1969] Director/Accountant [Irish]; James Anthony Proctor [1972] Director [Irish]

AS24 Fuel Card Ltd
Incorporated: 14 March 1985 *Employees:* 10
Net Worth: £611,079 *Total Assets:* £12,063,256
Registered Office: Millhouse, 32-38 East Street, Rochford, Essex, SS4 1DB
Activities: Retail sale of automotive fuel in specialised stores
Officers: Roland Maxime Saunion, Secretary; Bruno Claude Sylvain Leroy [1971] Director [French]; Raphael Manuel Oliver [1958] Director [French]; Roland Maxime Saunion [1978] Director [French]

Ascend Global Holdings, Ltd.
Incorporated: 27 June 2014 *Employees:* 187
Net Worth Deficit: £23,291,388 *Total Assets:* £13,216,702
Registered Office: Dryden House, St Johns Street, Huntingdon, Cambs, PE29 3NU
Activities: Activities of other holding companies n.e.c.
Parent: Ascend Learning LLC
Officers: Tracey Gough, Secretary; Lawrence Adam Gold [1967] Director/Attorney [American]; Nicolas William Harding [1983] Director/Accountant; Mandeep Singh Johar [1971] Director/Chief Financial Officer [Indian]; Greg Sebasky [1958] Director [American]

Ascend Global Intermediate Holdings, Ltd.
Incorporated: 30 June 2014
Net Worth: £20,702,004 *Total Assets:* £24,409,136
Registered Office: Dryden House, St Johns Street, Huntingdon, Cambs, PE29 3NU
Activities: Activities of other holding companies n.e.c.
Parent: Ascend Global Holdings Ltd
Officers: Tracey Gough, Secretary; Lawrence Adam Gold [1967] Director/Attorney [American]; Nicolas William Harding [1983] Director/Accountant; Mandeep Singh Johar [1971] Director/Chief Financial Officer [Indian]; Greg Sebasky [1958] Director [American]

ASCO (DC2) Limited
Incorporated: 7 August 2006
Net Worth: £1,344,000 *Total Assets:* £10,000,000
Registered Office: Great Yarmouth Offshore Supply Base, South Denes Road, Great Yarmouth, Norfolk, NR30 3LX
Activities: Operation of warehousing and storage facilities for water transport activities
Parent: ASCO Acquisitions Limited
Officers: Fraser Nicol McIntyre, Secretary; Peter Ian France [1968] Director; John Gilbert Gemmell [1971] Director/Private Equity Executive; Richard Peter Hanson [1956] Director; John Joseph Leahy [1957] Director [Irish]; Mark Johnstone Walker [1968] Director/Accountant

ASCO (DC3) Limited
Incorporated: 24 August 2006
Net Worth Deficit: £51,819,000 *Total Assets:* £48,259,000
Registered Office: Great Yarmouth Offshore Supply Base, South Denes Road, Great Yarmouth, Norfolk, NR30 3LX
Activities: Other business support service activities n.e.c.
Parent: ASCO (DC2) Limited
Officers: Fraser Nicol McIntyre, Secretary; Peter Ian France [1968] Director; Mark Johnstone Walker [1968] Director/Accountant

ASCO (DC4) Limited
Incorporated: 7 August 2006
Net Worth Deficit: £125,962,000 *Total Assets:* £123,841,000
Registered Office: Great Yarmouth Offshore Supply Base, South Denes Road, Great Yarmouth, Norfolk, NR30 3LX
Activities: Operation of warehousing and storage facilities for water transport activities
Parent: ASCO (DC3) Limited
Officers: Fraser Nicol McIntyre, Secretary; Peter Ian France [1968] Director; Mark Johnstone Walker [1968] Director/Accountant

ASCO Acquisitions Limited
Incorporated: 9 November 2011
Net Worth: £185,884,992 *Total Assets:* £440,761,984
Registered Office: Great Yarmouth Offshore Supply Base, South Denes Road, Great Yarmouth, Norfolk, NR30 3LX
Activities: Activities of other holding companies n.e.c.
Parent: ASCO Group Limited
Officers: Fraser Nicol McIntyre, Secretary; Peter Ian France [1968] Director; John Gilbert Gemmell [1971] Director/Private Equity Executive; Richard Peter Hanson [1956] Director; John Joseph Leahy [1957] Director [Irish]

ASCO Group Limited
Incorporated: 18 November 2011 *Employees:* 1,578
Net Worth Deficit: £110,241,000 *Total Assets:* £263,300,000
Registered Office: Great Yarmouth Offshore Supply Base, South Denes Road, Great Yarmouth, Norfolk, NR30 3LX
Activities: Activities of other holding companies n.e.c.
Parent: Doughty Hanson & Co V Limited
Officers: Fraser Nicol McIntyre, Secretary; Stephen John Bucksey [1956] Director; Peter Ian France [1968] Director; John Gilbert Gemmell [1971] Director/Private Equity Executive; Richard Peter Hanson [1956] Director; John Joseph Leahy [1957] Director [Irish]; Michael Straughen [1950] Director

Ascott Farms Limited
Incorporated: 11 June 1973 *Employees:* 19
Net Worth: £28,798,592 *Total Assets:* £44,735,912
Registered Office: Ascott Estate Office, Wing, Leighton Buzzard, Beds, LU7 0PS
Activities: Growing of cereals (except rice), leguminous crops and oil seeds
Shareholders: Paul David Hunston; Evelyn de Rothschild; Graham James Hearne
Officers: Anthony James de Rothschild, Secretary; Anthony James de Rothschild [1977] Director; Jessica de Rothschild [1974] Production Director

Ascott Properties Limited
Incorporated: 28 March 1995 *Employees:* 1
Net Worth: £9,572,191 *Total Assets:* £11,046,111
Registered Office: Ascott Estate Office, Ascott Wing, Leighton Buzzard, Beds, LU7 0PS
Activities: Other letting and operating of own or leased real estate
Parent: Ascott Farms Limited
Officers: Sir Evelyn de Rothschild [1931] Director/Merchant Banker; Jessica de Rothschild [1974] Production Director; Paul Hunston [1960] Director/Solicitor

ASG2 Limited
Incorporated: 20 December 2006 *Employees:* 33
Net Worth: £6,635,000 *Total Assets:* £30,043,000
Registered Office: The Courtyard, Ketteringham Hall, Church Road, Ketteringham, Wymondham, Norwich, NR18 9RS
Activities: Wholesale of meat and meat products
Officers: Graham Mark Edwards, Secretary/Director; Graham Mark Edwards [1970] Director; Gary Irvine [1966] Director

J.L. Ashby & Company Limited
Incorporated: 13 August 1942 *Employees:* 4
Net Worth: £4,775,795 *Total Assets:* £8,288,655
Registered Office: 2 Liscombe West, Liscombe Park, Soulbury, Leighton Buzzard, Beds, LU7 0JL
Activities: Growing of cereals (except rice), leguminous crops and oil seeds
Officers: Elizabeth Anne Ashby, Secretary; Michael James Ashby [1971] Director/Farmer; Richard John Ashby [1945] Director/Farmer

Ashcoe Holdings Limited
Incorporated: 19 August 2015 *Employees:* 14
Net Worth: £217,866 *Total Assets:* £8,396,189
Registered Office: 53-63 Redbridge Lane East, Ilford, Essex, IG4 5EY
Activities: Activities of other holding companies n.e.c.
Major Shareholder: John Maitland Coe
Officers: Ashley Katherine Coe [1986] Director/Wine and Spirit Merchant; Jacqueline Coe [1957] Director; John Maitland Coe [1955] Director/Wine and Spirit Merchant

Ashe Construction Limited
Incorporated: 18 April 1989 *Employees:* 109
Net Worth: £3,776,758 *Total Assets:* £19,663,114
Registered Office: Ashe House, Cooks Way, Hitchin, Herts, SG4 0JE
Activities: Construction of other civil engineering projects n.e.c.
Shareholder: Robert Stephen Blake
Officers: Daniel Armes [1976] Technical Director; Neil Robert Blake [1971] Director; Robin Alexander Blake [1968] Managing Director; Richard John Clay [1964] Finance Director; Justin Lee Howard [1972] Regional Director; Andrew Robert Morris [1967] Commercial Director; Martin John Petts [1963] Director/Chartered Builder; Ian Curnow Robbins [1973] Special Works Director

Ashe Group Holdings Limited
Incorporated: 30 August 1972 *Employees:* 116
Net Worth: £5,876,500 *Total Assets:* £22,486,904
Registered Office: Ashe House, Cooks Way, Hitchin, Herts, SG4 0JE
Activities: Development of building projects
Shareholder: Robert Stephen Blake
Officers: Louise Blake, Secretary; Neil Robert Blake [1971] Director; Robert Stephen Blake [1938] Director/Chartered Surveyor; Robin Alexander Blake [1968] Director/Civil Engineer

Ashley House PLC.
Incorporated: 29 November 1990 *Employees:* 85
Net Worth: £5,792,000 *Total Assets:* £12,669,000
Registered Office: Unit 1 Barnes Wallis Court, Wellington Road, Cressex Business Park, High Wycombe, Bucks, HP12 3PS
Activities: Development of building projects
Officers: James Andrew John Hathaway, Secretary; James Andrew John Hathaway [1977] Finance Director; Jonathan Holmes [1968] Commercial Director; Christopher Peter Lyons [1951] Director/Chairman; Stephen Gregory Minion [1946] Director; Antony John Walters [1967] Director; Andrew John Willetts [1963] Director

Ashwicken Sporting LLP
Incorporated: 7 July 2010 *Employees:* 10
Net Worth: £8,737,820 *Total Assets:* £12,664,013
Registered Office: 22-26 King Street, King's Lynn, Norfolk, PE30 1HJ
Officers: David James Flux [1968] Member; Lisa Jane Flux [1972] Member; Oliver James Flux [1997] Member

Ashworth Homes Limited
Incorporated: 17 October 1973 *Employees:* 3
Net Worth: £10,498,443 *Total Assets:* £12,811,055
Registered Office: 278a High Street, Berkhamsted, Herts, HP4 1AH
Activities: Buying and selling of own real estate
Major Shareholder: Peter John Windus
Officers: Peter John Windus [1947] Director/Chartered Surveyor

Asiatic Carpets Holdings Limited
Incorporated: 25 March 2003 *Employees:* 36
Net Worth: £15,014,914 *Total Assets:* £20,743,478
Registered Office: 42 Lytton Road, Barnet, Herts, EN5 5BY
Activities: Retail sale of textiles in specialised stores
Shareholders: Sharon Mozell Kelaty; Frederick Sion Kelaty
Officers: Frederick Sion Kelaty, Secretary; Frederick Sion Kelaty [1968] Director; Sharon Mozell Kelaty [1964] Director

Asino Limited
Incorporated: 14 December 2010
Net Worth Deficit: £4,856,154 *Total Assets:* £18,243,436
Registered Office: Hill House, Lowlands Road, Harrow, Middlesex, HA1 3EQ
Activities: Development of building projects
Major Shareholder: Donovan Gijsbertus Wijsmuller
Officers: Brian Martin Comer [1960] Director [Irish]; Luke Andrew Comer [1957] Director [Irish]

Askew & Barrett (Pulses) Limited
Incorporated: 1 September 1982 *Employees:* 32
Net Worth: £3,804,700 *Total Assets:* £8,843,015
Registered Office: 108 Smeeth Road, Marshland St James, Wisbech, Cambs, PE14 8JF
Activities: Agents selling agricultural raw materials, livestock, textile raw materials and semi-finished goods
Shareholders: Darryl Evan Askew; Patrick Edward Barrett
Officers: Patrick Edward Barrett, Secretary; Christopher Askew [1985] Director; Darryl Evan Askew [1950] Director/Produce Merchant; Justin Lee Barrett [1977] Director; Patrick Edward Barrett [1947] Director/Produce Merchant

Askham Village Community Limited
Incorporated: 23 August 1988 *Employees:* 156
Net Worth: £6,522,597 *Total Assets:* £16,619,195
Registered Office: Suite 2B, 4th Floor, Congress House, 14 Lyon Road, Harrow, Middlesex, HA1 2EN
Activities: Residential nursing care facilities
Shareholders: Salim Kamrudin Punjani Giga; Salma Salim Giga
Officers: Salma Salim Giga, Secretary; Salim Kamrudin Punjani Giga [1949] Director; Salma Salim Giga [1954] Director; Aliyyah-Begum Nasser [1983] Director/Consultant; Rabiyyah-Begum Raval [1981] Director/Optometrist

ASL Technology Holdings Ltd.
Incorporated: 18 October 2007 *Employees:* 108
Net Worth Deficit: £2,827,000 *Total Assets:* £18,019,000
Registered Office: Technology House, 20 Trafalgar Way, Bar Hill, Cambridge, CB23 8SQ
Activities: Activities of head offices
Shareholders: Mobeus Income & Growth VCT PLC; The Income & Growth VCT PLC
Officers: Paul Derry, Secretary; David Campbell [1969] Director/Accountant; Paul Bruce Derry [1964] Sales Director; Mark Garius [1957] Director [Swiss]; Edward Aston Wass [1971] Director/Fund Manager; Simon Whapshott [1973] Operations Director

ASM Metal Recycling Ltd.
Incorporated: 8 December 1967 *Employees:* 85
Net Worth: £6,179,590 *Total Assets:* £14,079,676
Registered Office: 55 Station Road, Beaconsfield, Bucks, HP9 1QL
Activities: Recovery of sorted materials
Shareholders: Tasmar Limited; Paul Valentine McDonald; Christopher Anthony McDonagh; Paul Martin McDonagh
Officers: Paul Martin McDonagh [1971] Director; Paul Valentine McDonald [1965] Managing Director; Christopher James Morgan [1963] Director

Aspect Contracts Limited
Incorporated: 21 December 2007 *Employees:* 236
Net Worth: £6,771,374 *Total Assets:* £16,875,372
Registered Office: Aspect House, Honywood Road, Basildon, Essex, SS14 3DS
Activities: Remediation activities and other waste management services
Shareholder: Antony Paul Smith
Officers: Gavin James Lawrence, Secretary; Grant Martin Eugene Beglan [1964] Director; Craig Henry John Foster [1961] Operations Director; Ian Rodney Gooden [1971] Director/Manager; Gavin James Lawrence [1971] Finance Director; Philip Brendan Mullins [1980] Commercial Director; Darren Paul Senior [1971] Director/Manager; Antony Paul Smith [1970] Director

Aspect Ventures Limited
Incorporated: 8 February 1990
Net Worth: £58,031,000 *Total Assets:* £305,964,000
Registered Office: Westgate Brewery, Bury St Edmunds, Suffolk, IP33 1QT
Activities: Non-trading company
Parent: Spirit Retail Bidco Limited
Officers: Lindsay Anne Keswick, Secretary; Richard Smothers [1967] Director

Aspin Construction Group Limited
Incorporated: 25 September 2001 *Employees:* 255
Previous: Aspin Group Limited
Net Worth Deficit: £1,213,000 *Total Assets:* £12,683,000
Registered Office: Nexus House, Boundary Way, Hemel Hempstead Industrial Estate, Hemel Hempstead, Herts, HP2 7SJ
Activities: Activities of head offices
Shareholders: Thomas Hutton Wood; Rael Nurick
Officers: Dimitri Korvyakov [1975] Director [American]; Matt Michael Meehan [1957] Director [American]; Thomas Wood [1971] Director [American]

Aspin Group Limited
Incorporated: 10 February 2000 *Employees:* 215
Previous: Aspin Foundations Limited
Net Worth Deficit: £3,490,000 *Total Assets:* £12,547,000
Registered Office: Nexus House, Boundary Way, Hemel Hempstead Industrial Estate, Hemel Hempstead, Herts, HP2 7SJ
Activities: Construction of commercial buildings
Parent: Aspin Construction Group Limited
Officers: Dimitri Korvyakov [1975] Director [American]; Matt Michael Meehan [1957] Director [American]; Graham Gregory Rusling [1955] Director; Iain Duncan Sale [1966] Director; Thomas Hutton Wood [1971] Director [American]

Aspire (CRP) Limited
Incorporated: 7 December 2016
Net Worth Deficit: £3,256,000 *Total Assets:* £46,037,000
Registered Office: Council Offices, London Road, Saffron Walden, Essex, CB11 4ER
Activities: Other letting and operating of own or leased real estate
Parent: Uttlesford District Council
Officers: Richard Peter Auty [1976] Local Authority Director; Alan Bryn Jones [1949] Director/Business Owner; Mary Lines [1955] Director/Retired; Adrian Stephen Webb [1966] Local Authority Director; Nicola Anne Wittman [1968] Local Authority Director

Aspire Academies Trust
Incorporated: 21 August 2012 *Employees:* 350
Net Worth: £23,237,754 *Total Assets:* £26,840,500
Registered Office: Bovingdon Primary Academy, High Street, Bovingdon, Herts, HP3 0HL
Activities: Primary education
Officers: Graham Frederick Barrett [1956] Director; Christopher John Canfield [1953] Director/Retired; Carole Ann Connelly [1958] Director/Education Advisor; Ross Paul Hayward [1985] Director/Solicitor; Vicky Parsey [1967] Director/Executive Principal; Prasad Nagnath Pitale [1971] Director/Financial Planning and Analysis; David Geoffrey Stent [1949] Managing Director

Aspire Learning Trust (Whittlesey)
Incorporated: 26 March 2012 *Employees:* 258
Previous: Sir Harry Smith Academy Trust
Net Worth: £17,328,248 *Total Assets:* £21,265,452
Registered Office: Sir Harry Smith Academy, Eastrea Road, Whittlesey, Cambs, PE7 1XB
Activities: General secondary education
Officers: Susan Munns, Secretary; Stephen Ackerman [1964] Director/Operations Manager; Timothy John Beebe [1966] Director/Bank Manager; Jonathan Digby [1965] Director/College Principal; John Hall Donnachie [1945] Director/Retired; John King [1947] Director/Architect; John Michael Mullen [1950] Director/Retired; Joanna Phillips [1966] Director/Civil Servant; Jed Roberts [1955] Director/Retired

Aspire Media Group Limited
Incorporated: 13 March 2000 *Employees:* 391
Net Worth: £15,097,664 *Total Assets:* £25,166,184
Registered Office: Tower Business Park, Kelvedon Road, Tiptree, Colchester, Essex, CO5 0LX
Activities: Activities of head offices
Major Shareholder: Robert Arthur Cowling
Officers: Robert Arthur Cowling, Secretary/Director; Cheryl Suzanne Cowling [1966] Director; Robert Arthur Cowling [1960] Director

Aspire Schools
Incorporated: 20 September 2016
Net Worth: £8,957,051 *Total Assets:* £10,875,851
Registered Office: The Wycombe Grange, 56 Amersham Hill, Coventon Road, High Wycombe, Bucks, HP13 6PQ
Activities: General secondary education
Officers: Martin John Keen, Secretary; Fiona Mary Bowers [1972] Director; Jonathan Charles Fletcher [1969] Director/Headteacher; Elizabeth Ann Hutton [1942] Director/Retired Magistrate; Debra Rutley [1965] Director/Aspire Executive Principal; Mark Wayne Shaw [1968] Director/Councillor; Generalyn Wilson [1954] Director/Retired Headteacher

Asset Education
Incorporated: 11 February 2015 *Employees:* 354
Net Worth: £19,473,760 *Total Assets:* £22,165,416
Registered Office: St Helen's School, Woodbridge Road, Ipswich, Suffolk, IP4 2LT
Activities: Primary education
Officers: Edna Casey [1949] Director/Retired; George Hamilton Clarke [1939] Director/Retired; Nick Denny [1968] Director/Chief Executive; Clare Elizabeth Flintoff [1963] Director/Headteacher; Dr Clare Elizabeth Gartland [1971] Director/Senior Lecturer; Barry David Gostling [1971] Director/Certified Chartered Accountant; Michael Christopher Barrow Mattinson [1948] Director/Retired but serving as a Justice of the Peace; Jeremy James Pentreath [1968] Director/Headteacher; Gareth Robert Stevens [1980] Director/Solicitor; John Haydn West-Burnham [1946] Director/Professor

Assetbridge Finance Limited
Incorporated: 20 February 2016 *Employees:* 2
Net Worth: £247,813 *Total Assets:* £9,051,600
Registered Office: Jasmine House, 8 Parkway, Welwyn Garden City, Herts, AL8 6HG
Activities: Credit granting by non-deposit taking finance houses and other specialist consumer credit grantors
Shareholders: Charlie Jack Wilson; Paul John Wilson
Officers: Charlie Jack Wilson [1990] Director; Paul John Wilson [1959] Director

Assetsteady Limited
Incorporated: 20 October 1967
Net Worth: £25,704,264 *Total Assets:* £46,190,052
Registered Office: 100 Capability Green, Luton, Beds, LU1 3LG
Activities: Activities of head offices
Parent: Ball Beverage Packaging Holdings UK Limited
Officers: John Peters, Secretary; Colin Gillis [1954] Managing Director [Canadian]; Philip James Hocken [1977] Director/Vice President; Richard John Peachey [1965] Director/Solicitor

Associated Lead Mills Ltd.
Incorporated: 6 June 1997 *Employees:* 51
Net Worth: £10,360,480 *Total Assets:* £35,974,448
Registered Office: Unit B, Bingley Road, Hoddesdon, Herts, EN11 0NX
Activities: Wholesale of metals and metal ores
Parent: Envirolead Distribution Limited
Officers: Maurice Elliot Sherling [1949] Director [Irish]; Barry Howard Smith [1956] Director/General Manager

Association for Cultural Exchange Limited (The)
Incorporated: 19 May 1958 *Employees:* 23
Net Worth: £8,058,127 *Total Assets:* £9,644,771
Registered Office: Stapleford Granary, Bury Road, Stapleford, Cambridge, CB22 5BP
Activities: Cultural education
Officers: Dr Paul Brooke Barnes, Secretary; Prof Ann Barrett [1943] Director/Retired Doctor; John Bryden [1947] Director/Musician; Richard Burge [1935] Director/Retired; Sally Hickling [1961] Director/Lawyer; Dr Roland Ernest Randall [1943] Director/Lecturer; Mark Sanders [1955] Director/Retired; Allan Thomas Treacy [1947] Director/Retired

AST Group Holdings Limited
Incorporated: 20 April 2015
Net Worth: £16,031,137 *Total Assets:* £32,536,224
Registered Office: Satellite House, Bessemer Way, Haffrey's Industrial Estate, Great Yarmouth, Norfolk, NR31 0LX
Activities: Activities of head offices
Major Shareholder: Gregory Stuart Darling
Officers: Christopher John Binnie, Secretary; Gregory Stuart Darling [1953] Director

Astex Therapeutics Limited
Incorporated: 14 April 1999 *Employees:* 117
Net Worth: £33,570,140 *Total Assets:* £38,704,152
Registered Office: 436 Cambridge Science Park, Milton Road, Cambridge, CB4 0QA
Activities: Research and experimental development on biotechnology
Parent: Otsuka America Inc
Officers: Neil Steven Jones, Secretary; Dr. Mohammad Azab [1955] Director/President and CMO [Canadian/French]; Sir Thomas Leon Blundell [1942] Director; Dr Andrew Bodnar [1948] Director/Physician [American]; Harren Jhoti [1962] Director; Dr. Robert Dwyer McQuade [1957] Director/EVP/Chief Strategic Officer [American]; Toshiki Sudo [1968] Director [Japanese]

Astle Limited
Incorporated: 22 May 1973 *Employees:* 85
Net Worth: £58,000 *Total Assets:* £21,188,000
Registered Office: Airport House, The Airport, Cambridge, CB5 8RY
Activities: Sale of new cars and light motor vehicles
Parent: CMG 2007 Limited
Officers: Stephen Robert Jones, Secretary; Richard John Blumberger [1975] Director; Daksh Gupta [1970] Director

Aston Barclay Holdings Group Limited
Incorporated: 24 March 2017
Net Worth: £25,497,000 *Total Assets:* £25,497,000
Registered Office: The Car Auction, Drovers Way, Chelmsford, Essex, CM2 5PP
Activities: Sale of used cars and light motor vehicles
Parent: ABVR Group Limited
Officers: John Leslie Crichton [1970] Director/Accountant; Neil Thomas Hodson [1963] Director; Martin Andrew Potter [1968] Director

Aston Barclay Holdings Limited
Incorporated: 5 September 2002 *Employees:* 268
Net Worth: £15,608,000 *Total Assets:* £36,912,000
Registered Office: The Car Auction, Drovers Way, Chelmsford, Essex, CM2 5PP
Activities: Sale of used cars and light motor vehicles
Parent: Aston Barclay Holdings Group Limited
Officers: John Leslie Crichton [1970] Director/Accountant; Neil Thomas Hodson [1963] Director; Martin Andrew Potter [1968] Director

Aston Barclay Limited
Incorporated: 18 June 1982 *Employees:* 268
Previous: Aston Barclay PLC
Net Worth: £7,341,000 *Total Assets:* £24,158,000
Registered Office: The Car Auction, Drovers Way, Chelmsford, Essex, CM2 5PP
Activities: Sale of used cars and light motor vehicles
Parent: Aston Barclay Holdings Limited
Officers: John Leslie Crichton [1970] Director/Accountant; Neil Thomas Hodson [1963] Director; Martin Andrew Potter [1968] Director

Aston Heating Limited
Incorporated: 18 March 1964
Net Worth: £3,860,757 *Total Assets:* £9,641,046
Registered Office: Moss Lodge, Moss Lane, Romford, Essex, RM1 2PT
Activities: Plumbing, heat and air-conditioning installation
Shareholders: Evan Charles Ivey; Lyn Dalton
Officers: Michael William John Thomas, Secretary; Evan Charles Ivey [1959] Director; Alan Thomas [1960] Director/Heating Engineer; Michael William John Thomas [1951] Director/Plumbing Engineer

Astonpalm Limited
Incorporated: 20 October 1997
Net Worth: £6,482,390 *Total Assets:* £10,804,680
Registered Office: Alton House, 66-68 High Street, Northwood, Middlesex, HA6 1BL
Activities: Development of building projects
Major Shareholder: Barry Attarzadeh
Officers: Peter William Johnson, Secretary; Barry Attarzadeh [1956] Director [Canadian]

Astor Lodge Holdings Limited
Incorporated: 19 December 1962 *Employees:* 2
Net Worth: £9,986,970 *Total Assets:* £11,938,191
Registered Office: York House, Empire Way, Wembley, Middlesex, HA9 0FQ
Activities: Other letting and operating of own or leased real estate
Parent: Hydecourt Developments Limited
Officers: David Lessman, Secretary/Director; Julia Ruth Bekhor [1960] Director; David Lessman [1925] Director

Astrazeneca Intermediate Holdings Limited
Incorporated: 30 November 2007
Net Worth: £36,037,722,112 *Total Assets:* £36,037,722,112
Registered Office: 1 Francis Crick Avenue, Cambridge Biomedical Campus, Cambridge, CB2 0AA
Activities: Other business support service activities n.e.c.
Parent: AstraZeneca PLC
Officers: Katie Louise Jackson-Turner, Secretary; Iain Alistair Collins [1970] Director; Marc Pierre Jean Dunoyer [1952] Director/Chief Financial Officer [French]; Adrian Charles Noel Kemp [1966] Director; Jonathan Thomas Charles Slade [1965] Director/Group Treasurer

Astrazeneca PLC
Incorporated: 17 June 1992 *Employees:* 60,000
Net Worth: £14,960,000,000 *Total Assets:* £63,353,999,360
Registered Office: 1 Francis Crick Avenue, Cambridge Biomedical Campus, Cambridge, CB2 0AA
Activities: Manufacture of basic pharmaceutical products
Officers: Adrian Charles Noel Kemp, Secretary/Company Official; Professor Genevieve Bernadette Berger [1955] Director/Chief Research and Development Officer [Swiss]; Philip Arthur John Broadley [1961] Director; Graham Chipchase [1963] Director/Chief Executive; Marc Pierre Jean Dunoyer [1952] Director/Chief Financial Officer [French]; Deborah Disanzo Eldracher [1960] Board Director [American]; Leif Valdemar Johansson [1951] Director/Chairman [Swedish]; Rudolph Harold Peter Markham [1946] Director; Sherilyn Dawn McCoy [1958] Director [American]; Tony Shu Kam Mok [1960] Director/Professor [Canadian]; Sabera Nazneen Rahman [1967] Director; Pascal Claude Roland Soriot [1959] Director/Chief Executive Officer [French]; Marcus Wallenberg [1956] Director [Swedish]

Astrazeneca Sweden Investments Limited
Incorporated: 8 April 2003
Net Worth: £15,213,524,992 *Total Assets:* £15,696,541,696
Registered Office: 1 Francis Crick Avenue, Cambridge Biomedical Campus, Cambridge, CB2 0AA
Activities: Other business support service activities n.e.c.
Parent: AstraZeneca Treasury Limited
Officers: Katie Louise Jackson-Turner, Secretary; Yvonne Louise Bertlin [1964] Director/Head of Tax Sweden [Swedish]; Iain Alistair Collins [1970] Director; Jonathan Thomas Charles Slade [1965] Director/Group Treasurer

Astrazeneca Treasury Limited
Incorporated: 18 March 1994
Net Worth: £11,631,526,912 *Total Assets:* £52,575,326,208
Registered Office: 1 Francis Crick Avenue, Cambridge Biomedical Campus, Cambridge, CB2 0AA
Activities: Activities of head offices
Parent: AstraZeneca UK Limited
Officers: Katie Louise Jackson-Turner, Secretary; Iain Alistair Collins [1970] Director; Adrian Charles Noel Kemp [1966] Director; Jonathan Thomas Charles Slade [1965] Director/Group Treasurer

Astrazeneca UK Limited
Incorporated: 26 November 1998 *Employees:* 6,195
Net Worth: £8,481,999,872 *Total Assets:* £14,558,000,128
Registered Office: 1 Francis Crick Avenue, Cambridge Biomedical Campus, Cambridge, CB2 0AA
Activities: Activities of head offices
Parent: AstraZeneca Intermediate Holdings Limited
Officers: Adrian Charles Noel Kemp, Secretary/Company Official; Iain Alistair Collins [1970] Director; Marc Pierre Jean Dunoyer [1952] Director/Chief Financial Officer [French]; Pascal Claude Roland Soriot [1959] Director/Chief Executive Officer [French]

Astrazeneca US Investments Limited
Incorporated: 3 July 2002
Net Worth: £446,657,216 *Total Assets:* £447,838,688
Registered Office: 1 Francis Crick Avenue, Cambridge Biomedical Campus, Cambridge, CB2 0AA
Activities: Other business support service activities n.e.c.
Parent: AstraZeneca PLC
Officers: Katie Louise Jackson-Turner [1966] Director; Adrian Charles Noel Kemp [1966] Director; Jonathan Thomas Charles Slade [1965] Director/Group Treasurer

Astro Lighting Holdings Limited
Incorporated: 8 June 2015 *Employees:* 102
Net Worth: £12,644,432 *Total Assets:* £21,509,184
Registered Office: The Astro Building, Midas, River Way, Harlow, Essex, CM20 2GJ
Activities: Other retail sale not in stores, stalls or markets
Shareholders: Clare Louise Fearon; Penelope Jane Bassant; John Turner Fearon; James Edward Bassant
Officers: Penelope Jane Bassant, Secretary; Clare Louise Fearon, Secretary; James Edward Bassant [1966] Design Director; John Turner Fearon [1950] Director/Chairman; Marc Yves Alexandre Gilbert [1970] Sales Director [French]; Stuart Spencer Grant [1967] Director/Chief Executive Officer; Donna Louise Howard [1971] Marketing Director; Nicholas Charles Edward Land [1948] Director; Rachel Elizabeth Prince [1981] Director/Chief Financial Officer

Astro Lighting Limited
Incorporated: 7 February 1997 *Employees:* 82
Net Worth: £11,682,277 *Total Assets:* £20,685,228
Registered Office: The Astro Building, Midas, River Way, Harlow, Essex, CM20 2GJ
Activities: Wholesale of radio, television goods & electrical household appliances (other than records, tapes, CDs)
Parent: Astro Lighting Holdings Limited
Officers: James Edward Bassant, Secretary; James Edward Bassant [1966] Design Director; John Turner Fearon [1950] Director/Chairman; Marc Yves Alexandre Gilbert [1970] Sales Director [French]; Stuart Spencer Grant [1967] Managing Director; Donna Louise Howard [1971] Marketing Director; Rachel Elizabeth Prince [1981] Director/Chief Financial Officer

Astute Electronics Limited
Incorporated: 7 December 1988 *Employees:* 128
Net Worth: £5,916,580 *Total Assets:* £32,676,324
Registered Office: Astute House, Rutherford Close, Meadway Technology Park, Stevenage, Herts, SG1 2EF
Activities: Wholesale of electronic and telecommunications equipment and parts
Major Shareholder: Geoffrey Ian Hill
Officers: Ian Fantham, Secretary; Ian Fantham [1964] Sales Director; Geoffrey Ian Hill [1963] Director/Sales Consultant

Astwood Securities Limited
Incorporated: 20 October 1999
Net Worth Deficit: £2,188,802 *Total Assets:* £13,780,052
Registered Office: York House, Empire Way, Wembley, Middlesex, HA9 0FQ
Activities: Other letting and operating of own or leased real estate
Officers: Lilly Bordon, Secretary; David Bordon [1958] Director; Lilly Bordon [1928] Director; Marcel Bordon [1954] Director; Michael Bordon [1958] Director; Christopher Collins [1956] Director

Atalian Servest Food Co Limited
Incorporated: 17 December 1990 *Employees:* 1,762
Previous: Servest Food Co Limited
Net Worth: £1,162,000 *Total Assets:* £29,283,000
Registered Office: Servest House, Heath Farm Business Centre, Tut Hill, Fornham All Saints, Bury St Edmunds, Suffolk, IP28 6LG
Activities: Other food services
Parent: Servest Group Limited
Officers: Laura Clare Ryan, Secretary; Thomas Edward Evans [1987] Director; Sean Fisher [1978] Director [British/South African]; Philip Henry Watts [1964] Director

Atalian Servest Group Holdings Limited
Incorporated: 10 June 1999 *Employees:* 22,339
Previous: Servest Limited
Net Worth: £1,900,000 *Total Assets:* £247,700,000
Registered Office: Servest House, Heath Farm Business Centre, Tut Hill, Fornham All Saints, Bury St Edmunds, Suffolk, IP28 6LG
Activities: Other business support service activities n.e.c.
Parent: Atalian Global Services UK 2 Limited
Officers: Laura Clare Ryan, Secretary; Daniel Grant Dickson [1985] Director; Kenton James Fine [1968] Director/Businessman; Robert Andrew Legge [1968] Director; Dennis Christopher Zietsman [1958] Director/Accountant [South African]

Atalian Servest Group Limited
Incorporated: 1 May 2014 *Employees:* 6
Previous: Servest Group Holdings Limited
Net Worth: £3,134,000 *Total Assets:* £8,055,000
Registered Office: Servest House, Heath Farm Business Centre, Tut Hill, Fornham All Saints, Bury St Edmunds, Suffolk, IP28 6LG
Activities: Combined facilities support activities
Parent: Servest Limited
Officers: Laura Clare Ryan, Secretary; Daniel Grant Dickson [1985] Director; Kenton James Fine [1968] Director; Robert Legge [1968] Director; Andrew Sugars [1970] Director; Dennis Christopher Zietsman [1958] Director [South African]

Atalian Servest Limited
Incorporated: 29 August 2007 *Employees:* 22,339
Previous: Servest Group Limited
Net Worth: £5,400,000 *Total Assets:* £234,400,000
Registered Office: Servest House, Heath Farm Business Centre, Tut Hill, Fornham All Saints, Bury St Edmunds, Suffolk, IP28 6LG
Activities: Combined facilities support activities
Parent: Servest Group Holdings Limited
Officers: Laura Clare Ryan, Secretary; Daniel Grant Dickson [1985] Director; Thomas Edward Evans [1987] Director; Kenton James Fine [1968] Director; Sean Fisher [1978] Director [British/South African]; Robert Legge [1968] Director; Andrew Sugars [1970] Director; Johan Andrew Venter [1962] Director; Dennis Christopher Zietsman [1958] Director [South African]

Atalian Servest Security Limited
Incorporated: 19 February 2002 *Employees:* 1,148
Previous: Servest Security Services Limited
Net Worth: £853,000 *Total Assets:* £8,860,000
Registered Office: Servest House, Heath Farm Business Centre, Tut Hill, Fornham All Saints, Bury St Edmunds, Suffolk, IP28 6LG
Activities: Private security activities
Parent: Servest Group Limited
Officers: Laura Clare Ryan, Secretary; Thomas Edward Evans [1987] Director; Sean Fisher [1978] Director [British/South African]; Steven Scott Moore [1983] Director

ATB Group UK Limited
Incorporated: 9 May 2007 *Employees:* 305
Previous: ATB Laurence Scott Limited
Net Worth: £13,387,413 *Total Assets:* £28,894,516
Registered Office: Hardy Road, Norwich, NR1 1JN
Activities: Manufacture of electric motors, generators and transformers
Parent: ATB Morley Limited
Officers: Stephen Kolowiecki, Secretary; Zhaohui Han [1974] Director [Chinese/British]; Stephen Kolowiecki [1958] Director

Athena Care Homes (UK) Limited
Incorporated: 3 September 2014 *Employees:* 443
Net Worth: £8,222,314 *Total Assets:* £25,884,150
Registered Office: Unit 2 Rima House, A13 Approach, Ripple Road, Barking, Essex, IG11 0RH
Activities: Activities of head offices
Shareholders: Udayan Agarwal; Mala Agarwal
Officers: Mala Agarwal, Secretary; Mala Agarwal [1969] Director; Udayan Agarwal [1969] Director

Atlantic Healthcare PLC
Incorporated: 17 July 2006 *Employees:* 17
Net Worth: £6,652,241 *Total Assets:* £9,868,513
Registered Office: Atlantic House, 10 Rose & Crown Walk, Saffron Walden, Essex, CB10 1JH
Activities: Activities of head offices
Shareholders: Fiona Mary Wilson Waterworth; Tobias Adam Wilson Waterworth; Thesis Nominees Ltd
Officers: James Hansord, Secretary; Andrew Richard Boyce [1962] Director/Chief Executive Officer; William Ringo [1945] Director [American]; Thomas Wellner [1965] Director/Chief Executive Officer [Canadian]; Tobias Adam Wilson Waterworth [1964] Director/Chartered Accountant; Charles Woler [1949] Director [French]

Atlantis Equityco Limited
Incorporated: 24 February 2012 *Employees:* 239
Net Worth: £497,911,424 *Total Assets:* £842,520,000
Registered Office: South Denes Business Park, South Beach Parade, Great Yarmouth, Norfolk, NR30 3QR
Activities: Activities of other holding companies n.e.c.
Parent: Atlantis Investorco Limited
Officers: William Burton Blair Ainslie [1963] Managing Director; Satoru Harada [1967] Director/Management [Japanese]; Satoru Nakagawa [1965] Director [Japanese]; Peter Niklai [1973] Director/Financial Investor [Hungarian]; Ikumori Osuka [1988] Director [Japanese]; Kosuke Tashiro [1976] Director/Management [Japanese]; Tetsuro Toyoda [1962] Director/Private Equity Fund Manager [Japanese]

Atlantis Investorco Limited
Incorporated: 24 February 2012 *Employees:* 239
Net Worth: £497,765,312 *Total Assets:* £842,293,120
Registered Office: South Denes Business Park, South Beach Parade, Great Yarmouth, Norfolk, NR30 3QR
Activities: Activities of other holding companies n.e.c.
Parent: Marubeni Corporation
Officers: Satoru Harada [1967] Director/Management [Japanese]; Satoru Nakagawa [1965] Director [Japanese]; Hiroyuki Nakano [1963] Director [Japanese]; Peter Niklai [1973] Director/Financial Investor [Hungarian]; Ikumori Osuka [1988] Director [Japanese]; Kosuke Tashiro [1976] Director/Management [Japanese]; Tetsuro Toyoda [1962] Director/Private Equity Fund Manager [Japanese]

Atlantis Midco Limited
Incorporated: 24 February 2012 *Employees:* 239
Net Worth: £503,137,504 *Total Assets:* £842,342,336
Registered Office: South Denes Business Park, South Beach Parade, Great Yarmouth, Norfolk, NR30 3QR
Activities: Activities of other holding companies n.e.c.
Parent: Atlantis Equityco Limited
Officers: William Burton Blair Ainslie [1963] Managing Director; Satoru Harada [1967] Director/Management [Japanese]; Satoru Nakagawa [1965] Director [Japanese]; Peter Niklai [1973] Director/Financial Investor [Hungarian]; Ikumori Osuka [1988] Director [Japanese]; Kosuke Tashiro [1976] Director/Management [Japanese]; Tetsuro Toyoda [1962] Director/Private Equity Fund Manager [Japanese]

Atlas Copco Limited
Incorporated: 21 October 1919 *Employees:* 532
Net Worth: £34,502,000 *Total Assets:* £120,718,000
Registered Office: Swallowdale Lane, Hemel Hempstead, Herts, HP2 7EA
Activities: Other business support service activities n.e.c.
Parent: Atlas Copco UK Holdings Limited
Officers: Alex Christiaan Jan Bongaerts, Secretary; Alex Christiaan Jan Bongaerts [1960] Director/Holding Manager [Belgian]; Geert Henri Follens [1959] Director [Belgian]; Kevin George Prince [1961] Director; Andrew Walker [1961] Director [Irish]

Atlas Copco UK Holdings Limited
Incorporated: 23 December 1974 *Employees:* 22
Net Worth: £165,663,008 *Total Assets:* £204,647,008
Registered Office: Swallowdale Lane, Hemel Hempstead, Herts, HP2 7EA
Activities: Activities of head offices
Parent: Atlas Copco Airpower N.V.
Officers: Alex Christiaan Jan Bongaerts, Secretary; Alex Christiaan Jan Bongaerts [1960] Director/Holding Manager [Belgian]; Geert Henri Follens [1959] Director [Belgian]

Atlas Multi Academy Trust
Incorporated: 26 July 2011 *Employees:* 128
Previous: St Albans Girls' School
Net Worth: £17,976,620 *Total Assets:* £19,753,760
Registered Office: St Albans Girls' School, Sandridgebury Lane, St Albans, Herts, AL3 6DB
Activities: Pre-primary education
Officers: Sally Jane Molloy, Secretary; Claire Frances Ruth Barnard [1960] Director/Teacher/Housewife; Margaret Catherine Chapman [1966] Director/Headteacher; Robert Anthony Foster [1949] Director; Rachael Patricia Kenningham [1971] Director/Freelance Communications Specialist; Paul Andrew Lerwill [1955] Director/Retired; Peter Edward Loach [1953] Director/Retired Headteacher; Mary Elizabeth Newman [1958] Director/Retired; Claire Elizabeth Robins [1967] Director/Headteacher; Anthony Paul Snook [1955] Director/Consultant; Paul Oliver Webster [1952] Director/Accountant; Alan Westcott [1946] Director/Retired

Audbern Limited
Incorporated: 15 December 2009 *Employees:* 2
Net Worth: £2,139,716 *Total Assets:* £8,311,586
Registered Office: Old Bishops' College, Churchgate, Cheshunt, Herts, EN8 9XP
Activities: Activities of other holding companies n.e.c.
Shareholder: Wayne Christopher Rolfe
Officers: Audrey Helen Rolfe [1933] Director; Wayne Christopher Rolfe [1966] Director

Audio Network Limited
Incorporated: 23 July 2001 *Employees:* 131
Net Worth: £16,954,494 *Total Assets:* £25,119,788
Registered Office: School Farm Studios, Gestingthorpe Road, Little Maplestead, Halstead, Essex, CO9 2SN
Activities: Sound recording and music publishing activities
Officers: Kim Laura Clarke, Secretary; Robert Ashley Hurst [1964] Director; Dan Marriott [1968] Director/Investment Professional [American]; Miles William John Ruffell [1960] Director/Private Investor; James Robert Smith [1969] Director/Chief Executive Officer [American]; Andrew Borradaile Sunnucks [1965] Director

Aula Limited
Incorporated: 11 September 1996
Net Worth: £11,763,909 *Total Assets:* £12,674,346
Registered Office: Trinity Hall, Cambridge, CB2 1TJ
Activities: Buying and selling of own real estate
Parent: Trinity Hall
Officers: Paul Ffolkes Davis, Secretary; Paul Ffolkes Davis [1954] Director/College Bursar; Dr Simon David Guest [1968] Director/University Teaching Officer; Dr Cristiano Andrea Ristuccia [1964] Director/College Teaching Officer [Italian]

Aura (Newcastle) Holding Company Limited
Incorporated: 23 January 2007
Net Worth: £50,000 *Total Assets:* £8,486,000
Registered Office: Eaton Court, Maylands Avenue, Hemel Hempstead Industrial Estate, Hemel Hempstead, Herts, HP2 7TR
Activities: Activities of head offices
Parent: Aura Holdings (Newcastle) Limited
Officers: Kevin John Pearson, Secretary; John Stephen Gordon [1962] Director; Peter Kenneth Johnstone [1965] Finance Director; John McDonagh [1969] Director; Kirsty Jane Thirwell [1971] Director

Aura (Newcastle) Project Company Limited
Incorporated: 24 January 2007
Net Worth Deficit: £12,812,000 *Total Assets:* £108,321,000
Registered Office: Eaton Court, Maylands Avenue, Hemel Hempstead Industrial Estate, Hemel Hempstead, Herts, HP2 7TR
Activities: Construction of commercial buildings
Parent: Aura (Newcastle) Holding Company Limited
Officers: Kevin John Pearson, Secretary; John Stephen Gordon [1962] Director; Peter Kenneth Johnstone [1965] Finance Director; John McDonagh [1969] Director; Kirsty Jane Thirwell [1971] Director

Aura (Newcastle) Project Company Phase 2 Ltd
Incorporated: 29 September 2009
Net Worth Deficit: £7,797,000 *Total Assets:* £80,853,000
Registered Office: Eaton Court, Maylands Avenue, Hemel Hempstead Industrial Estate, Hemel Hempstead, Herts, HP2 7TR
Activities: Activities of head offices
Parent: Aura (Newcastle) Holding Company Phase 2 Limited
Officers: Kevin John Pearson, Secretary; John Stephen Gordon [1962] Director; Peter Kenneth Johnstone [1965] Finance Director; John McDonagh [1969] Director; Kirsty Jane Thirlwell [1971] Director

Aura Finance (Holdco) Limited
Incorporated: 11 February 2014 *Employees:* 3
Net Worth: £3,274,523 *Total Assets:* £17,024,372
Registered Office: 3rd Floor, Premiere House, Elstree Way, Borehamwood, Herts, WD6 1JH
Activities: Credit granting by non-deposit taking finance houses and other specialist consumer credit grantors
Parent: January Loan Services Limited
Officers: Emily Henrietta Gestetner [1967] Director; Harry Leon Landy [1978] Director; Danny Stephen Waters [1984] Director

Aura Finance Limited
Incorporated: 11 December 2012 *Employees:* 4
Net Worth: £29,113,396 *Total Assets:* £234,196,032
Registered Office: 3rd Floor, Premiere House, Elstree Way, Borehamwood, Herts, WD6 1JH
Activities: Other business support service activities n.e.c.
Parent: Aura Finance (Holdco) Limited
Officers: Emily Henrietta Gestetner [1967] Director; David Stewart [1965] Director; Stephen Bryan Wasserman [1984] Director; Danny Stephen Waters [1984] Director

Aura Holdings (Newcastle) Limited
Incorporated: 20 December 2006
Net Worth Deficit: £20,514,000 *Total Assets:* £190,340,992
Registered Office: Eaton Court, Maylands Avenue, Hemel Hempstead Industrial Estate, Hemel Hempstead, Herts, HP2 7TR
Activities: Activities of head offices
Shareholders: Dalmore Capital (Aura) Limited; Elgin BSF Limited
Officers: Kevin John Pearson, Secretary; John Stephen Gordon [1962] Director; Peter Kenneth Johnstone [1965] Finance Director; Robert John William Wotherspoon [1967] Director/Accountant

Aurient Investments Limited
Incorporated: 16 June 1998
Net Worth: £19,288,732 *Total Assets:* £36,616,536
Registered Office: 1st Floor, Argyle House, South Entrance, Joel Street, Northwood Hills, Northwood, Middlesex, HA6 1NW
Activities: Buying and selling of own real estate
Parent: Milestone Properties UK Limited
Officers: Menal Mahendra Mehta, Secretary; Menal Mahendra Mehta [1972] Director/Businessman; Richard Lewis Whitehorn [1950] Director/Property Consultant

Aurient Investments N16 Ltd
Incorporated: 4 February 2009
Net Worth: £3,740,346 *Total Assets:* £14,177,548
Registered Office: 1st Floor, Argyle House, South Entrance, Joel Street, Northwood Hills, Northwood, Middlesex, HA6 1NW
Activities: Other letting and operating of own or leased real estate
Parent: Aurient Investments Ltd
Officers: Menal Mahendra Mehta [1972] Director; Richard Lewis Whitehorn [1950] Director/Surveyor

Aurora Distribution Limited
Incorporated: 29 April 2003 *Employees:* 24
Net Worth: £1,057,718 *Total Assets:* £13,962,589
Registered Office: Apex Park, 6 Little Burrow, Welwyn Garden City, Herts, AL7 4SW
Activities: Manufacture of electric lighting equipment
Parent: Aurora Limited
Officers: Kevin Ronald Bell [1951] Managing Director

Aurora Group Holdings (UK) Limited
Incorporated: 21 December 2016 *Employees:* 466
Net Worth: £16,531,579 *Total Assets:* £78,621,088
Registered Office: 6 Little Burrow, Welwyn Garden City, Herts, AL7 4SW
Activities: Activities of other holding companies n.e.c.
Parent: Aurora Group Holdings Ltd
Officers: Kevin Ronald Bell [1951] Director

Aurora Limited
Incorporated: 15 June 1999 *Employees:* 347
Net Worth: £27,356,520 *Total Assets:* £81,670,392
Registered Office: 6 Little Burrow, Welwyn Garden City, Herts, AL7 4SW
Activities: Manufacture of electric lighting equipment
Parent: Aurora Lighting BV
Officers: Kevin Ronald Bell [1951] Managing Director

Stephen Austin & Sons Limited
Incorporated: 26 February 2002 *Employees:* 143
Net Worth: £6,193,000 *Total Assets:* £22,414,000
Registered Office: Caxton Hill, Ware Road, Hertford, SG13 7LU
Activities: Printing n.e.c.
Parent: Stephen Austin (Holdings) Limited
Officers: Michael Chitson [1958] Director/Printer; Peter Granville Fowler [1938] Director; Rory James Fowler [1971] Director/Printer

Austin (GB) Limited
Incorporated: 15 December 2005 *Employees:* 37
Net Worth: £2,413,422 *Total Assets:* £8,778,846
Registered Office: Cardinal Point, Park Road, Rickmansworth, Herts, WD3 1RE
Activities: Construction of commercial buildings
Major Shareholder: Sunita Davda
Officers: Prakash Chandra Jayantilal Davda [1960] Director; Adrian Thomas Ward [1963] Director/Senior Project Construction Manager

Stephen Austin (Holdings) Limited
Incorporated: 18 December 2001 *Employees:* 151
Net Worth: £7,309,000 *Total Assets:* £25,994,000
Registered Office: Caxton Hill, Ware Road, Hertford, SG13 7LU
Activities: Activities of production holding companies
Parent: S A Printing Group Limited
Officers: Michael Chitson [1958] Director/Printer; Peter Granville Fowler [1938] Director; Rory James Fowler [1971] Director/Printer

Australian Pacific Touring (U.K.) Limited
Incorporated: 7 September 1982 *Employees:* 25
Net Worth: £104,260,104 *Total Assets:* £126,385,120
Registered Office: 1st Floor, Chalfont Court, 5 Hill Avenue, Amersham, Bucks, HP6 5BD
Activities: Travel agency activities
Shareholder: Geoffrey William McGeary
Officers: Ross Kemp, Secretary; Christopher Phillips Hall [1967] Director [Australian]; Ross Malcolm Kemp [1964] Finance Director [Australian]; Robert Howard McGeary [1968] Director [Australian]

Autism Anglia
Incorporated: 23 July 1997 *Employees:* 235
Net Worth: £7,544,000 *Total Assets:* £10,761,000
Registered Office: Century House, Riverside Office Centre, North Station Road, Colchester, Essex, CO1 1RE
Activities: Primary education
Officers: David Holmes, Secretary; Janet Barker [1957] Director; Andrew Charles Edwin Beevers [1951] Director/Senior Sales Manager; David George Burrage [1948] Director/Headteacher (Retired); Corinna Nancy Cranch [1965] Director/Private Landlord; Angela Eley [1954] Director/Retired Teacher; James Brian McElhinney [1952] Director/Accountant; Stephen Jonathan Pittuck [1964] Director/Bank Official; Judith Winward [1960] Director/Solicitor

Autolink Concessionaires (A19) Limited
Incorporated: 23 June 2000
Net Worth: £14,450,725 *Total Assets:* £128,286,992
Registered Office: Eaton Court, Maylands Avenue, Hemel Hempstead Industrial Estate, Hemel Hempstead, Herts, HP2 7TR
Activities: Construction of roads and motorways
Parent: Autolink Holdings (A19) Limited
Officers: Kevin John Pearson, Secretary; Antony Richard Gates [1967] Managing Director; Robert John William Wotherspoon [1967] Director/Accountant

Autolink Concessionaires (M6) PLC
Incorporated: 21 May 1996
Net Worth: £2,122,000 *Total Assets:* £139,007,008
Registered Office: Eaton Court, Maylands Avenue, Hemel Hempstead Industrial Estate, Hemel Hempstead, Herts, HP2 7TR
Activities: Construction of commercial buildings
Parent: Autolink Holdings (M6) Limited
Officers: Kevin John Pearson, Secretary; David Richard Bradbury [1969] Director/Senior Investment Manager; Benjamin Christopher Jacob Dean [1979] Investment Director; Antony Richard Gates [1967] Managing Director; David Honeyman [1967] Director/Financial Controller; Christopher James [1968] Investment Director; Robert John William Wotherspoon [1967] Director/Accountant

Autolink Holdings (M6) Ltd
Incorporated: 17 February 1997
Net Worth: £3,820,000 *Total Assets:* £127,078,000
Registered Office: Eaton Court, Maylands Avenue, Hemel Hempstead, Herts, HP2 7TR
Activities: Construction of roads and motorways
Parent: Innisfree Nominees Limited (Acting in its Capacity as Nominee of Innisfree M & G PPP LP)
Officers: Kevin John Pearson, Secretary; David Richard Bradbury [1969] Director/Senior Investment Manager; Benjamin Christopher Jacob Dean [1979] Investment Director; Antony Richard Gates [1967] Managing Director; Christopher James [1968] Investment Director; Robert John William Wotherspoon [1967] Director/Accountant

Automated Systems Group Limited
Incorporated: 19 May 1994 *Employees:* 108
Net Worth: £5,813,000 *Total Assets:* £14,542,000
Registered Office: 20 Trafalgar Way, Bar Hill, Cambridge, CB23 8SQ
Activities: Photocopying, document preparation and other specialised office support activities
Parent: ASL Technology Holdings Ltd
Officers: David Campbell [1969] Director/Accountant; Paul Bruce Derry [1964] Sales Director; Mark Garius [1957] Director [Swiss]; Simon Whapshott [1973] Operations Director

The Automation Partnership (Cambridge) Limited
Incorporated: 2 June 1993 *Employees:* 177
Net Worth: £35,572,000 *Total Assets:* £48,373,000
Registered Office: Automation Partnership, Grantham Close, Royston, Herts, SG8 5WY
Activities: Other manufacturing n.e.c.
Parent: TAP Biosystems Group Limited
Officers: David Campbell, Secretary; David Campbell [1967] Director/Accountant; Nicholas Vandeleur Cooke [1964] Director/Accountant; Dr Thorsten Peuker [1973] Director [German]

Automotive Lighting UK Limited
Incorporated: 3 September 1998 *Employees:* 5
Net Worth Deficit: £38,683,000 *Total Assets:* £11,346,000
Registered Office: Red Lion Farm, 119 Coxtie Green Road, Brentwood, Essex, CM14 5PT
Activities: Manufacture of electric lighting equipment
Shareholders: Fiat Chrysler Automobiles N.V.; Magneti Marelli SpA
Officers: Charles Rohan Ravindra de Alwis, Secretary; Anna Carla Carniato [1959] Director/Company Executive [Italian]; Riccardo Codecasa [1962] Director/Manager [Italian]; Charles Rohan Ravindra de Alwis [1959] Director/Solicitor

Automotive UK No.1
Incorporated: 9 June 1999
Previous: GM Automotive UK
Net Worth Deficit: £6,400,000 *Total Assets:* £10,100,000
Registered Office: Griffin House, UK1-101-135 Osborne Road, Luton, Beds, LU1 3YT
Activities: Other business support service activities n.e.c.
Parent: Peugeot S.A.
Officers: Rabiya Sultana Nagi, Secretary; James Charles Highnam [1969] Director of Finance; Peter Thomas Hope [1966] Director; Stephen Norman [1954] Director [French]; Michael Wright [1963] Director

Autoprotect (MBI) Ltd
Incorporated: 31 March 2004 *Employees:* 161
Net Worth: £1,175,742 *Total Assets:* £30,969,302
Registered Office: Warwick House, Roydon Road, Harlow, Essex, CM19 5DY
Activities: Activities of insurance agents and brokers
Parent: Correlation Three Investments Limited
Officers: Nisha Manaktala, Secretary; William Paul Beaumont [1962] Director; Michael McVeigh [1971] Director; Graeme Nieman [1985] Director [Dutch]

Autumn Foods Holdings Limited
Incorporated: 26 January 2015 *Employees:* 22
Net Worth: £1,681,412 *Total Assets:* £13,268,194
Registered Office: Loomswood Farms, Hasketon, Woodbridge, Suffolk, IP13 6JW
Activities: Wholesale of meat and meat products
Shareholders: Geoffrey Maurice Buchanan; William Edwin Buchanan
Officers: Geoffrey Maurice Buchanan [1970] Director; William Edwin Buchanan [1968] Director; Stephen Andrew Harley [1963] Director/Chief Financial Officer; John Michael Reid [1964] Director

Avanti Schools Trust
Incorporated: 26 January 2011 *Employees:* 323
Net Worth: £51,890,000 *Total Assets:* £56,126,000
Registered Office: Avanti House Secondary School, Wemborough Road, Stanmore, Middlesex, HA7 2EQ
Activities: Pre-primary education
Officers: Shamita Kumar, Secretary; Dr James William Biddulph [1976] Director/Headteacher; Gerard Vincent Irwin Davis [1948] Director/Retired (Local Government Officer); Vijay Doshi [1967] Director of Finance; Nitesh Bipinchandra Gor [1975] Director/Consultant; Mayurkumar Parsuram Manibhai Patel [1959] Director/Solicitor; Dr Krutika Pau [1961] Director/Children's Services Consultant; Kumar Sureshchandra Raval [1971] Director and Founder, Faith in Leadership; Bavaani Vadivale-Nanthabalan [1957] Director/Executive Headteacher [Singaporean]; Dr Molly Jane Warrington [1949] Director/Retired University Lecturer; Michael Robert Younger [1948] Director/Retired University Professor

Avery Dennison U.K. Limited
Incorporated: 12 November 1963 *Employees:* 25
Net Worth: £9,448,000 *Total Assets:* £30,487,000
Registered Office: 1 Thomas Road, Wooburn Industrial Park, Wooburn Green, High Wycombe, Bucks, HP10 0PE
Activities: Manufacture of other articles of paper and paperboard n.e.c.
Parent: Avery Dennison Holding Limited
Officers: Michael Collins [1967] Director European Finance Shared Services [Irish]; Huibert Nicolaas Van Gijn [1962] Finance Director [Dutch]; Christopher Russell Johnson [1975] Director [American]

Averys (Radnage) Limited
Incorporated: 25 March 1938 *Employees:* 3
Net Worth: £2,878,676 *Total Assets:* £10,556,071
Registered Office: Eastfield House, Eastfield Farm, Mavis Enderby, Spilsby, Lincs, PE23 4EJ
Activities: Mixed farming
Major Shareholder: Penelope Ruth Avery
Officers: Penelope Ruth Avery, Secretary; Penelope Ruth Avery [1950] Director/Farmer; Roderick James Avery [1977] Director/Farmer

Aveva Finance Limited
Incorporated: 12 March 2013
Net Worth: £9,892,002 *Total Assets:* £9,977,620
Registered Office: High Cross, Madingley Road, Cambridge, CB3 0HB
Activities: Business and domestic software development
Officers: Claire Denton, Secretary; James Singer Kidd [1970] Director/Accountant; David Mathew Ward [1976] Director/Chief Financial Officer

Aveva Group PLC
Incorporated: 9 June 1994 *Employees:* 2,867
Net Worth: £1,926,221,056 *Total Assets:* £2,371,713,024
Registered Office: High Cross, Madingley Road, Cambridge, CB3 0HB
Activities: Manufacture of communication equipment other than telegraph, and telephone apparatus and equipment
Officers: David Mathew Ward, Secretary; Philip Stanley Aiken [1949] Director [Australian]; Jennifer Margaret Allerton [1951] Director; Emmanuel Andre Marie Babeau [1967] Director/Deputy CEO and CFO, Schneider Electric [French]; Paula Lynn Dowdy [1965] Director [American]; Craig Barry Hayman [1963] Director/Chief Executive Officer; Peter Walter Herweck [1966] Director/EVP Industry Business, Schneider Electric [German]; Christopher John Humphrey [1957] Director; James Singer Kidd [1970] Director/Deputy Chief Executive and CFO; Rohinton Mobed [1959] Director

Aveva Solutions Limited
Incorporated: 4 May 1964 *Employees:* 452
Net Worth: £971,617,024 *Total Assets:* £1,104,462,976
Registered Office: High Cross, Madingley Road, Cambridge, CB3 0HB
Activities: Other software publishing
Parent: Aveva Group PLC
Officers: David Mathew Ward, Secretary; Philip Stanley Aiken [1949] Director [Australian]; Jennifer Margaret Allerton [1951] Director; Emmanuel Andre Marie Babeau [1967] Director/Deputy CEO and CFO, Schneider Electric [French]; Craig Barry Hayman [1963] Director/Chief Executive Officer; Peter Walter Herweck [1966] Director/EVP Industry Business, Schneider Electric [German]; Christopher John Humphrey [1957] Director; James Singer Kidd [1970] Director/Deputy Chief Executive and CFO; Rohinton Mobed [1959] Director

Avingtrans PLC
Incorporated: 4 December 1985 *Employees:* 656
Net Worth: £69,076,000 *Total Assets:* £121,749,000
Registered Office: Chatteris Business Park, Honeysome Road, Chatteris, Cambs, PE16 6SA
Activities: Activities of head offices
Officers: Stephen Michael King, Secretary; John Simon Clarke [1959] Director; Stephen Michael King [1966] Director; Roger Steven McDowell [1955] Director; Stephen McQuillan [1961] Director; Leslie James Thomas [1957] Director; Dr Graham Kenneth Thornton [1948] Director

Aviva Central Services UK Limited
Incorporated: 7 October 1996
Net Worth: £102,000,000 *Total Assets:* £734,000,000
Registered Office: 8 Surrey Street, Norwich, NR1 3NG
Activities: Other service activities n.e.c.
Parent: Aviva Group Holdings Limited
Officers: Nitinbhai Babubhai Maganbhai Amin [1956] Director; Julian Charles Baddeley [1981] Director/Solicitor; Arlene Cairns [1978] Director [British/Australian]; Stuart Edmund Robinson [1972] Director; David Frederick Swiffen Rogers [1956] Director/Insurance Company Official

Aviva Consumer Products UK Limited
Incorporated: 24 June 1992
Net Worth: £65,419,000 *Total Assets:* £70,402,000
Registered Office: 8 Surrey Street, Norwich, NR1 3NG
Activities: Other business support service activities n.e.c.
Parent: Aviva Insurance Limited
Officers: Adam Beckett [1976] Director; Andrew James Morrish [1968] Director; Stephen Forder Pond [1969] Director/Chartered Accountant

Aviva Health UK Limited
Incorporated: 26 January 1990
Net Worth: £13,194,000 *Total Assets:* £102,872,000
Registered Office: 8 Surrey Street, Norwich, NR1 3NG
Activities: Administration of financial markets
Parent: Aviva Insurance Limited
Officers: Adam Beckett [1976] Director; Paul Carey Brencher [1971] Director; Mark Andrew Noble [1972] Director; Adrian Leslie Nye [1974] Director

AVL Powertrain UK Limited
Incorporated: 4 May 2005 *Employees:* 222
Net Worth: £3,823,109 *Total Assets:* £21,461,362
Registered Office: Langdale House, Sable Way, Southfields Business Park, Laindon, Basildon, Essex, SS15 6LN
Activities: Engineering related scientific and technical consulting activities
Parent: AVL UK Holdings Limited
Officers: Nicole Russell, Secretary; Martin Panzitt [1967] Director [Austrian]; Matthias Hans Wellers [1967] Managing Director [German]

Avnet (Holdings) Ltd
Incorporated: 30 January 1989 *Employees:* 3
Net Worth: £63,460,000 *Total Assets:* £70,979,000
Registered Office: Avnet House, Rutherford Close, Stevenage, Herts, SG1 2EF
Activities: Activities of head offices
Officers: Thomas Ludaescher [1961] Director [German]; Mark McKrell [1966] Finance Director; Harvey Woodford [1963] Director/VP Corporate Secretary [American]

Avnet Bidco Limited
Incorporated: 10 August 2016 *Employees:* 1
Net Worth: £677,510,976 *Total Assets:* £828,454,976
Registered Office: Avnet House, Rutherford Close, Stevenage, Herts, SG1 2EF
Activities: Non-trading company
Parent: Avnet Holdings Europe Limited
Officers: Harvey Woodford [1963] Director/VP Corporate Secretary [American]

Avnet EMG Ltd.
Incorporated: 18 March 1980 *Employees:* 276
Net Worth: £48,203,000 *Total Assets:* £89,700,000
Registered Office: Avnet House, Rutherford Close, Meadway, Stevenage, Herts, SG1 2EF
Activities: Non-specialised wholesale trade
Parent: Avnet (Holdings) Ltd
Officers: Thomas Ludaescher [1961] Director [German]; Mark McKrell [1966] Finance Director; Harvey Woodford [1963] Director/VP Corporate Secretary [American]

Avnet Holdings UK Limited
Incorporated: 5 August 2005 *Employees:* 3
Net Worth: £221,969,216 *Total Assets:* £225,816,336
Registered Office: Avnet House, Rutherford Close, Stevenage, Herts, SG1 2EF
Activities: Other business support service activities n.e.c.
Parent: Avnet, Inc
Officers: Steven Bosmans [1969] Tax Director [Belgian]; Mark McKrell [1966] Finance Director; Harvey Woodford [1963] Director/VP Corporate Secretary [American]

Avocado Developments Limited
Incorporated: 6 February 2007
Net Worth: £6,088,453 *Total Assets:* £20,517,598
Registered Office: Kimberley House, 31 Burnt Oak Broadway, Edgware, Middlesex, HA8 5LD
Activities: Development of building projects
Officers: Harish Keshra Halai [1971] Director; Shital Mansukhlal Haria [1971] Director; Bipin Mohanlal Shah [1958] Director/Certified Chartered Accountant; Hiren Hasmukh Shah [1979] Director/Certified Chartered Accountant

Avocet Academy Trust
Incorporated: 8 October 2014 *Employees:* 114
Net Worth: £9,656,271 *Total Assets:* £10,764,575
Registered Office: c/o Wickham Market Primary School, Dallinghoo Road, Wickham Market, Woodbridge, Suffolk, IP13 0RP
Activities: Primary education
Officers: Anthony Melvin Cooper [1946] Director/H&S Consultant; Marie-Claire Delbrouque [1979] Director Flagship Homes; Jonathan Duggan [1950] Director/Landowner; Jonathan Railton Legh-Smith [1966] Director/Head of Partnerships & Strategic Research; Dr Jeremy Mead [1958] Director; Cheryl Singleton [1975] Director/Headteacher; Roger Theobald [1949] Director/Retired Senior Adviser - Education

Avocet Capital Limited
Incorporated: 18 March 2013 *Employees:* 41
Net Worth: £11,315,825 *Total Assets:* £14,770,126
Registered Office: Avocet House, Wilford Bridge Road, Melton, Woodbridge, Suffolk, IP12 1RB
Activities: Manufacture of optical precision instruments
Officers: Ashley Paul Walker [1973] Director; Paul Howard Walker [1949] Director; Stephanie Ruth Walker [1947] Director; Stephen Andrew Walker [1975] Director

Avon Freeholds Limited
Incorporated: 7 October 2010
Net Worth: £6,977,019 *Total Assets:* £12,934,297
Registered Office: 88 Edgware Way, Edgware, Middlesex, HA8 8JS
Activities: Other letting and operating of own or leased real estate
Officers: Chavi Moskovitz, Secretary; Israel Moskovitz [1964] Director [Canadian]

Away Resorts Limited
Incorporated: 21 December 2007 *Employees:* 32
Net Worth Deficit: £20,601,112 *Total Assets:* £85,240,272
Registered Office: IMEX, 575-599 Maxted Road, Hemel Hempstead, Herts, HP2 7DX
Activities: Holiday centres and villages
Parent: Away Resorts Holdings Ltd
Officers: Neill Timothy Ryder, Secretary; Carl Anthony Castledine [1969] Director; Greg Lashley [1964] Director; Neill Timothy Ryder [1976] Director

AWG Group Limited
Incorporated: 1 April 1989 *Employees:* 121
Net Worth: £2,326,373,888 *Total Assets:* £2,566,819,072
Registered Office: Lancaster House, Lancaster Way, Ermine Business Park, Huntingdon, Cambs, PE29 6XU
Activities: Activities of head offices
Parent: AWG (UK) Holdings Limited
Officers: Elizabeth Ann Horlock Clarke, Secretary; Claire Tytherleigh Russell, Secretary; Scott Robert James Longhurst [1967] Finance Director; Claire Tytherleigh Russell [1964] Director/Lawyer; Peter John Simpson [1967] Director

AWG Land Holdings Limited
Incorporated: 10 September 2002
Net Worth Deficit: £2,912,000 *Total Assets:* £15,729,000
Registered Office: Lancaster House, Lancaster Way, Ermine Business Park, Huntingdon, Cambs, PE29 6XU
Activities: Other letting and operating of own or leased real estate
Parent: AWG Property Limited
Officers: Elizabeth Ann Horlock Clarke, Secretary; John Francis Cormie [1958] Director; James Raymond Tilbrook [1973] Director/Surveyor

AWG Parent Co Limited
Incorporated: 29 February 2000
Net Worth: £3,471,886,080 *Total Assets:* £5,573,062,144
Registered Office: Lancaster House, Lancaster Way, Ermine Business Park, Huntingdon, Cambs, PE29 6XU
Activities: Activities of head offices
Parent: Osprey Acquisitions Limited
Officers: Claire Tytherleigh Russell, Secretary; Projesh Banerjea [1986] Director/Financier [Indian]; John Richard Barry [1968] Director/Investor; Dr Stephen Robert Billingham [1948] Director; James Alexander Bryce [1974] Director/Senior Principal; Mamoun Jamai [1981] Director/Senior Portfolio Manager [Moroccan]; Scott Robert James Longhurst [1967] Finance Director; Manoj Mehta [1970] Investment Director; Niall Patrick Mills [1968] Director/Chartered Engineer; Robert Stewart Napier [1947] Director/Chief Executive; Alexandros Nassuphis [1969] Director/Investment Professional [German]; Peter John Simpson [1967] Director; Duncan John Symonds [1973] Director/Civil Engineer

Axalta Coating Systems U.K. (2) Limited
Incorporated: 12 December 2013 *Employees:* 1
Net Worth: £437,227,264 *Total Assets:* £437,250,048
Registered Office: Unit 1 Quadrant Park, Mundells, Welwyn Garden City, Herts, AL7 1FS
Activities: Activities of other holding companies n.e.c.
Parent: Axalta Coating Systems UK Holding Limited
Officers: James Ian Blenkinsopp [1957] Director/Business Analyst; Michael Keith Davis [1962] Director

Axalta Coating Systems UK Holding Limited
Incorporated: 13 December 2012
Net Worth: £713,165,376 *Total Assets:* £1,117,739,648
Registered Office: Unit 1 Quadrant Park, Mundells, Welwyn Garden City, Herts, AL7 1FS
Activities: Activities of other holding companies n.e.c.
Parent: Axalta Coating Systems Limited
Officers: James Ian Blenkinsopp [1957] Director; Michael Keith Davis [1962] Director

Axalta Coating Systems UK Limited
Incorporated: 31 March 1988 *Employees:* 55
Net Worth: £25,503,000 *Total Assets:* £37,046,000
Registered Office: Unit 1 Quadrant Park, Mundells, Welwyn Garden City, Herts, AL7 1FS
Activities: Manufacture of paints, varnishes and similar coatings, mastics and sealants
Parent: Axalta Coating Systems UK Holding Limited
Officers: James Ian Blenkinsopp, Secretary; James Ian Blenkinsopp [1957] Director/Business Analyst/Controller; Michael Keith Davis [1962] Director/Sales Manager

Axalta Powder Coating Systems UK Limited
Incorporated: 28 September 1972 *Employees:* 61
Net Worth: £41,233,000 *Total Assets:* £58,454,000
Registered Office: Unit 1 Quadrant Park, Mundells, Welwyn Garden City, Herts, AL7 1FS
Activities: Manufacture of paints, varnishes and similar coatings, mastics and sealants
Parent: Axalta Coating Systems UK Holding Limited
Officers: James Ian Blenkinsopp, Secretary; James Ian Blenkinsopp [1957] Director/Business Analyst/Controller; John Ridgeway [1959] Director/Site Manager

Axcorp Limited
Incorporated: 30 December 2015
Net Worth Deficit: £3,989 *Total Assets:* £10,005,154
Registered Office: 36 South Approach, Northwood, Middlesex, HA6 2ET
Activities: Management consultancy activities other than financial management
Major Shareholder: Derrick Williams
Officers: Derrick Alexander Williams [1963] Director

Aylesbury Grammar School
Incorporated: 22 February 2011 *Employees:* 153
Net Worth: £9,062,349 *Total Assets:* £11,958,914
Registered Office: Aylesbury Grammar School, Walton Road, Aylesbury, Bucks, HP21 7RP
Activities: General secondary education
Officers: Caroline Cobb, Secretary; Kevin Martin Amor [1961] Director/Chartered Accountant; Paul Anthony Bown [1951] Director; Michael John Brock [1954] Director/Consultant; Lee William George Cobley [1958] Director/RAF Officer; James Richard Collins [1957] Director; Josephine Ann Dennis [1941] Director; Louise-Emma Fabre [1975] Director/Teacher; Kevin Bruce Hardern [1949] Director; Christopher King [1956] Director/School Data Manager; Narendra Laljani [1958] Director/Dean of Graduate Studies; Keith Lavery [1967] Director/Health & Safety & Environmental Advisor; Abayomi Adebola Odukoya [1967] Director/Software Engineer; Mark Sturgeon [1972] Director/Teacher; Andrea Christiane Ward [1967] Director/Consultant [German]; Richard Duncan Williams [1959] Director/Solicitor; Simon Winman [1962] Director/Head of Club Development

Aylesbury High School
Incorporated: 13 May 2011 *Employees:* 106
Net Worth: £7,725,000 *Total Assets:* £10,510,000
Registered Office: Aylesbury High School, Walton Road, Aylesbury, Bucks, HP21 7SX
Activities: General secondary education
Officers: Keith Andrew Marshall, Secretary; Helen Margaret Bush [1971] Director/Freelance Editing; James Chandler [1974] Finance Director; Arfan Bashir Chaudhry [1967] Director/Civil Servant; John Francis Clarke [1963] Director; Gladden Jonathan Mark Cook [1974] Director/Teacher; James Edward Mark Davis [1967] Director/Solicitor; Christina Reid Elliot [1965] Director/Royal Air Force; Neil Alexander Esslemont [1976] Director/Engineering Geologist; Mark Joseph Francas [1954] Director/Retired [British/Australian]; Dr Alexandra Kate Johnston [1961] Director/Lawyer; Alison Elaine Pexton [1961] School Development Director; Dennis John Phillips [1935] Director/Retired; Alan Peter Rosen [1955] Director/Headteacher; Gillian Kathleen Sharman [1964] Director/Exams Officer; Lisa Joanne Westcott [1966] Director/Education - Student Welfare Co-ordinator; Antony John Woods [1970] Director/Head of Corporate Development

Azelis UK Life Sciences Limited
Incorporated: 20 June 1968 *Employees:* 98
Net Worth: £42,075,000 *Total Assets:* £54,160,000
Registered Office: Foxholes Business Park, John Tate Road, Hertford, SG13 7YH
Activities: Wholesale of chemical products
Parent: Azelis UK Holdings Limited
Officers: Thijs Bakker [1974] Director; Anna Bertona [1967] Director [Italian]; Stephen Edward Roberts [1964] Director/Chartered Accountant; Joan Teresa Traynor [1959] Managing Director

AZENCO4 Limited
Incorporated: 22 January 2016
Net Worth: £2,053,214,336 *Total Assets:* £2,066,287,360
Registered Office: 1 Francis Crick Avenue, Cambridge Biomedical Campus, Cambridge, CB2 0AA
Activities: Other business support service activities n.e.c.
Parent: AstraZeneca Treasury Limited
Officers: Matthew Ian Conacher, Secretary; Iain Alistair Collins [1970] Director; Katie Louise Jackson-Turner [1966] Director/Solicitor; Adrian Charles Noel Kemp [1966] Director

Azuri Technologies Ltd
Incorporated: 10 July 2012 *Employees:* 23
Net Worth: £5,664,023 *Total Assets:* £8,152,740
Registered Office: St John's Innovation Centre, Cowley Road, Cambridge, CB4 0WS
Activities: Manufacture of consumer electronics
Shareholder: IP2IPO Portfolio L.P.
Officers: Liam Hickey, Secretary; Simon Cj Bransfield-Garth [1960] Director; Alan Paul Harper [1956] Director; Liam Hickey [1966] Director/Chartered Accountant [Irish]; Javier Muller [1967] Director/Manager [Spanish]; Peter Alexander Reinartz [1961] Director [Belgian]

Azurie Blue Limited
Incorporated: 26 October 2011 *Employees:* 4
Net Worth: £4,714,171 *Total Assets:* £17,652,464
Registered Office: Enterprise House, Beesons Yard, Bury Lane, Rickmansworth, Herts, WD3 1DS
Activities: Other business support service activities n.e.c.
Officers: Dominique Elisabeth Jacqueline Sharpe [1953] Director [French]; Edward Adrian Sharpe [1975] Director/Solicitor; Georgina Alexandra Sharpe [1978] Director; William John Ashdown Sharpe [1947] Director

B & M Care Group Limited
Incorporated: 23 April 1986 *Employees:* 1,348
Net Worth: £67,901,384 *Total Assets:* £108,836,704
Registered Office: Old Town Court, 70 Queensway, Hemel Hempstead, Herts, HP2 5HD
Activities: Activities of head offices
Major Shareholder: William John Hughes
Officers: Trinna Ann Bruton, Secretary; Trinna Ann Bruton [1967] Director; William John Hughes [1941] Director [Irish]; Rachel Ann Rodgers [1964] Director; Ian Sloan [1959] Director/Quantity Surveyor; Dr Colleen Mary Wood [1977] Director/Clinical Advisor

B Crystal Limited
Incorporated: 13 March 2013
Net Worth: £4,528,279 *Total Assets:* £11,756,635
Registered Office: Portland House, 69-71 Wembley Hill Road, Wembley, Middlesex, HA9 8BU
Activities: Sea and coastal freight water transport
Parent: Union Maritime Limited
Officers: Bhupendra Shantilal Kansagra, Secretary; Laurent Elie Cadji [1977] Director/Businessman; Lewis Levy Cadji [1938] Director/Businessman; Bhupendra Shantilal Kansagra [1956] Director/Businessman; Ramesh Shantilal Kansagra [1950] Director/Businessman

B Emerald Limited
Incorporated: 13 March 2013
Net Worth: £5,434,628 *Total Assets:* £14,568,722
Registered Office: Portland House, 69-71 Wembley Hill Road, Wembley, Middlesex, HA9 8BU
Activities: Sea and coastal freight water transport
Parent: Union Maritime Limited
Officers: Bhupendra Shantilal Kansagra, Secretary; Laurent Elie Cadji [1977] Director/Businessman; Lewis Levy Cadji [1938] Director/Businessman; Bhupendra Shantilal Kansagra [1956] Director/Businessman; Ramesh Shantilal Kansagra [1950] Director/Businessman

B.A.T.S. Ilford Limited
Incorporated: 1 September 2006 *Employees:* 2
Net Worth: £10,762,027 *Total Assets:* £16,373,346
Registered Office: 48 Westmoreland Avenue, Hornchurch, Essex, RM11 2EE
Activities: Other letting and operating of own or leased real estate
Parent: BATS Holdings Limited
Officers: Maria Bernadette Seaton, Secretary; Spencer Brian Seaton [1962] Director

B.M. Polyco Limited
Incorporated: 12 May 1978 *Employees:* 96
Net Worth: £10,637,000 *Total Assets:* £35,886,000
Registered Office: Polyco Healthline, South Fen Road, Bourne, Lincs, PE10 0DN
Activities: Other manufacturing n.e.c.
Officers: David Greenwood [1955] Director; Jason Prichard [1969] Director/Company Secretary; Neil Antony Wilson [1976] Director

B/E Aerospace (UK) Limited
Incorporated: 16 July 1998 *Employees:* 1,598
Net Worth: £655,614,208 *Total Assets:* £886,112,832
Registered Office: Nissen House, Grovebury Road, Leighton Buzzard, Beds, LU7 4TB
Activities: Other service activities n.e.c.
Parent: BE Aerospace Holdings (UK) Limited
Officers: Steven Jon Buesing [1974] Director/Vice President & Controller [American]; Keith Stephen Delderfield [1962] Managing Director; Andrew Davis Moore [1976] Director/General Counsel, Interior Systems [American]; David J Nieuwsma [1964] Director/Chief Operating Officer [American]

Babraham Bioscience Technologies Limited
Incorporated: 23 August 1996 *Employees:* 41
Net Worth: £23,561,000 *Total Assets:* £43,520,000
Registered Office: Babraham Hall, Babraham, Cambridge, CB22 3AT
Activities: Letting and operating of conference and exhibition centres
Parent: The Babraham Institute
Officers: Derek Thomas Edward Jones [1961] Director/Chief Executive; Dr Karen Jane Lewis [1963] Executive Director, Public Sector; Dr Jane Katharine Osbourn [1966] Director/VP R&D and Site Leader; Professor Clive Page [1958] Director/Professor & Biomedical Consultant; Joanne Parfrey [1972] Non-Executive Director/Business Advisor; Rebecca Louise Paxton [1980] Director/Chief Financial Officer; Dr Andrew John McGlashan Richards [1960] Director

The Babraham Institute
Incorporated: 19 January 1995 *Employees:* 352
Net Worth: £155,054,000 *Total Assets:* £185,104,000
Registered Office: Babraham Hall, Babraham, Cambridge, CB22 3AT
Activities: Other research and experimental development on natural sciences and engineering
Officers: Simon John Jones, Secretary; Graham Peter Allen [1958] Director/Vice President; Geoffrey Ernest Braham [1961] Director/Accountant; Professor Doreen Ann Cantrell [1957] Director/Vice Principal, University of Dundee; Anthony James Clare [1970] Director/Law Firm Partner; Professor Anne Carla Ferguson Smith [1961] Director/Professor of Genetics and Head of Dept of Genetics; Dr Lynne Christine Gailey [1954] Director/Justice of The Peace; Professor Nicholas Clwyd Jones [1950] Director/Scientist; Professor David Glyn Kipling [1964] Director/University Professor; Professor Clive Page [1958] Director/Scientist and Biomedical Consultant; Professor Peter William Jack Rigby [1947] Director/Scientist

Baby Network Limited
Incorporated: 28 February 2005 *Employees:* 15
Net Worth: £11,470,030 *Total Assets:* £17,236,060
Registered Office: 5 Elstree Gate, Elstree Way, Borehamwood, Herts, WD6 1JD
Activities: Video production activities
Parent: Twenty-First Century Fox, Inc.
Officers: Kathryn Frances Fink [1966] Director [Australian]; Jan Koeppen [1970] Executive Director [Dutch]; Diego Fernando Londono [1970] Executive Director [Colombian]

Badger BC Investments Limited
Incorporated: 8 November 2013
Net Worth: £1,632,146 *Total Assets:* £11,586,682
Registered Office: Borough Offices, Churchgate, Cheshunt, Herts, EN8 9XJ
Activities: Other letting and operating of own or leased real estate
Parent: Broxbourne Borough Council
Officers: Nathalie Loretta Boateng, Secretary; Sandra Lesley Beck [1966] Director/Head of Financial Services; Nathalie Loretta Boateng [1969] Director/Solicitor; Jeffrey Thomas Stack [1961] Director/Local Government Officer

Badger Building (E.Anglia) Limited
Incorporated: 21 July 1989 *Employees:* 46
Net Worth: £28,233,458 *Total Assets:* £34,747,636
Registered Office: Stanley House, Stanley Street, Lowestoft, Suffolk, NR32 2DZ
Activities: Construction of domestic buildings
Major Shareholder: Stephen Derek George
Officers: Stephen Derek George, Secretary; Stephen Derek George [1957] Director/Builder; Robert John Lockhart [1972] Director; Simon John Muirhead [1978] Director

Bafin Holdings
Incorporated: 2 March 1982 *Employees:* 1
Net Worth: £74,923,000 *Total Assets:* £74,928,000
Registered Office: The Old Dairy, Griffin Farm, Conger Lane, Toddington, Beds, LU5 6BT
Activities: Activities of head offices
Parent: Manpower Holdings Limited
Officers: Andrew Lewis Windmill, Secretary; Mark Anthony Cahill [1958] Director; Andrew Lewis Windmill [1956] Director

Baik Agency Limited
Incorporated: 28 July 2003 *Employees:* 97
Net Worth: £4,776,542 *Total Assets:* £37,987,656
Registered Office: 19-20 Bourne Court, Southend Road, Woodford Green, Essex, IG8 8HD
Activities: Activities of head offices
Major Shareholder: Thierry Andre Victor Cohen
Officers: Nathalie Izumi Cohen [1970] Director [Italian]

Bairds Malt Limited
Incorporated: 12 June 1998 *Employees:* 222
Net Worth: £77,085,000 *Total Assets:* £209,660,000
Registered Office: Station Maltings, Witham, Essex, CM8 2DU
Activities: Manufacture of malt
Parent: Maltco 3 Limited
Officers: Brett Alan Weimann, Secretary; Alistair Garrard Bell [1961] Director/Chief Financial Officer [Australian]; Darren Smith [1968] Director/President [Canadian]; Roger Graham Woodley [1958] Director/Maltster (CEO)

R. S. Baker & Sons Limited
Incorporated: 2 May 1963 *Employees:* 18
Net Worth: £12,420,306 *Total Assets:* £13,225,074
Registered Office: The Abattoir, Elsing, Dereham, Norfolk, NR20 3EW
Activities: Development of building projects
Shareholders: Carl Andrew Baker; David John Baker
Officers: Carl Andrew Baker, Secretary; Carl Andrew Baker [1965] Director; David John Baker [1967] Director; Margaret Baker [1939] Director

C.T. Baker Limited
Incorporated: 22 November 1900 *Employees:* 285
Net Worth: £5,987,707 *Total Assets:* £11,924,895
Registered Office: 8 Market Place, Holt, Norfolk, NR25 6BW
Activities: Retail sale in non-specialised stores with food, beverages or tobacco predominating
Shareholders: Michael John Morton Baker; Richard James Malcolm Baker
Officers: Michael John Morton Baker, Secretary; Duncan Charles Baker [1979] Finance Director; Michael John Morton Baker [1946] Director; Nicholas Miles Custance Morton Baker [1963] Director/Sales Manager; Richard James Malcolm Baker [1961] Chartered Accountant Director; Jane Heather Ruth Gurney-Read [1958] Director

Baker Perkins Holdings Limited
Incorporated: 10 March 2015 *Employees:* 378
Net Worth: £14,870,000 *Total Assets:* £36,686,000
Registered Office: Manor Drive, Paston Parkway, Peterborough, PE4 7AP
Activities: Activities of production holding companies
Major Shareholder: John Embleton Cowx
Officers: John Embleton Cowx [1946] Director

Baker Perkins Limited
Incorporated: 14 February 2006 *Employees:* 377
Net Worth: £10,640,000 *Total Assets:* £32,418,000
Registered Office: Manor Drive, Paston Parkway, Peterborough, PE4 7AP
Activities: Manufacture of machinery for food, beverage and tobacco processing
Officers: John Embleton Cowx [1946] Director

M.Baker Produce Limited
Incorporated: 1 March 1971 *Employees:* 16
Net Worth: £9,378,126 *Total Assets:* £10,007,478
Registered Office: Wyberton House, Main Road, Old Leake, Boston, Lincs, PE22 9HT
Activities: Growing of cereals (except rice), leguminous crops and oil seeds
Parent: The Trustees of M Baker Settlement
Officers: Edith Alice Baker, Secretary; Edith Alice Baker [1942] Director; Ian Michael Baker [1969] Director

The C. Alma Baker Trust
Incorporated: 16 March 2006 *Employees:* 11
Net Worth: £8,070,116 *Total Assets:* £14,331,364
Registered Office: Roythornes Solicitors, Enterprise Campus, Alconbury Weald, Huntingdon, Cambs, PE28 4XA
Activities: Mixed farming
Officers: Charles Robin Boyes [1939] Director/Retired Solicitor; Simon Fred Boyton Taylor [1945] Director/Farmer; Edward Francis Patrick Valletta [1962] Director/Bursar; David Heneage Wynne-Finch [1970] Director/Farmer

Bakkavor Central Finance Limited
Incorporated: 28 July 2008
Net Worth Deficit: £1,145,000 *Total Assets:* £42,641,000
Registered Office: Bakkavor, West Marsh Road, Spalding, Lincs, PE11 2BB
Activities: Accounting and auditing activities
Parent: Bakkavor Foods Limited
Officers: Simon Witham, Secretary; Marc Stephen Archer [1963] Director; Agust Gudmundsson [1964] Director [Icelander]

Bakkavor Estates Limited
Incorporated: 5 August 2008
Net Worth Deficit: £2,347,000 *Total Assets:* £38,042,000
Registered Office: Bakkavor, West Marsh Road, Spalding, Lincs, PE11 2BB
Activities: Activities of other holding companies n.e.c.
Parent: Bakkavor Foods Limited
Officers: Simon Witham, Secretary; Marc Stephen Archer [1963] Director; Agust Gudmundsson [1964] Director [Icelander]

Bakkavor Finance Limited
Incorporated: 28 July 2008
Net Worth: £456,792,000 *Total Assets:* £514,768,000
Registered Office: Bakkavor, West Marsh Road, Spalding, Lincs, PE11 2BB
Activities: Accounting and auditing activities
Parent: Bakkavor (London) Limited
Officers: Simon Witham, Secretary; Agust Gudmundsson [1964] Director [Icelander]

Balanus Limited
Incorporated: 1 August 1984
Net Worth: £113,667,000 *Total Assets:* £131,015,000
Registered Office: Ground Floor, County House, 100 New London Road, Chelmsford, Essex, CM2 0RG
Activities: Financial intermediation not elsewhere classified
Parent: Countrywide Group PLC
Officers: Himanshu Haridas Raja [1965] Director/Financial Officer; Gareth Rhys Williams [1964] Director/Solicitor

Balcraft Properties Limited
Incorporated: 18 June 1998
Net Worth: £8,526,763 *Total Assets:* £12,418,675
Registered Office: Hill House, Lowlands Road, Harrow, Middlesex, HA1 3EQ
Activities: Development of building projects
Major Shareholder: Donovan Gijsbertus Wijsmuller
Officers: Brian Martin Comer [1960] Director [Irish]; Luke Andrew Comer [1957] Director [Irish]; Thomas Donnellan [1960] Director [Irish]

Baldwin Filters Limited
Incorporated: 31 August 1949 *Employees:* 109
Net Worth: £1,252,094 *Total Assets:* £14,314,776
Registered Office: Parker House, 55 Maylands Avenue, Hemel Hempstead Industrial Estate, Hemel Hempstead, Herts, HP2 4SJ
Activities: Other manufacturing n.e.c.
Parent: Parker Hannifin Corporation
Officers: Graham Mark Ellinor [1964] Finance Director; James Alan David Elsey [1970] Human Resources Director

Balgores Motors (1982) Limited
Incorporated: 14 July 1982 *Employees:* 242
Net Worth: £7,580,233 *Total Assets:* £11,746,194
Registered Office: 1 Bryant Avenue, Gallows Corner, Romford, Essex, RM3 0AP
Activities: Other service activities incidental to land transportation, n.e.c.
Major Shareholder: Paul Alfred Austin
Officers: Paul Alfred Austin, Secretary; Paul Alfred Austin [1952] Director/Engineer; Steven Arthur Austin [1957] Director/Engineer

Ball Beverage Packaging Europe Limited
Incorporated: 1 November 1990 *Employees:* 178
Previous: Rexam Beverage Can Europe Limited
Net Worth: £84,044,408 *Total Assets:* £526,601,248
Registered Office: 100 Capability Green, Luton, Beds, LU1 3LG
Activities: Other service activities n.e.c.
Parent: Rexam UK Holdings Limited
Officers: John Peters, Secretary; Colin Gillis [1954] Managing Director [Canadian]; Philip James Hocken [1977] Director/Vice President; Richard John Peachey [1965] Director/Solicitor

Ball Beverage Packaging Holdings UK Limited
Incorporated: 17 March 1987
Previous: Rexam Beverage Can Holdings UK Ltd
Net Worth Deficit: £18,130,552 *Total Assets:* £61,228,240
Registered Office: 100 Capability Green, Luton, Beds, LU1 3LG
Activities: Activities of head offices
Parent: Rexam Overseas Holdings Limited
Officers: John Peters, Secretary; Colin Gillis [1954] Managing Director [Canadian]; Philip James Hocken [1977] Director/Vice President; Richard John Peachey [1965] Director/Solicitor

Ball Beverage Packaging UK Ltd
Incorporated: 25 April 1924 *Employees:* 305
Previous: Rexam Beverage Can UK Ltd
Net Worth: £139,931,008 *Total Assets:* £255,106,000
Registered Office: 100 Capability Green, Luton, Beds, LU1 3LG
Activities: Manufacture of light metal packaging
Parent: Assetsteady Limited
Officers: John Peters, Secretary; Colin Gillis [1954] Managing Director [Canadian]; Philip James Hocken [1977] Director/Accountant; Richard John Peachey [1965] Director/Solicitor

Ball Company
Incorporated: 28 November 2002
Net Worth Deficit: £3,401,058 *Total Assets:* £19,628,154
Registered Office: 100 Capability Green, Luton, Beds, LU1 3LG
Activities: Non-trading company
Parent: Ball UK Holdings, Ltd
Officers: Charles Ernest Baker, Secretary/Associate General Counsel [American]; Philip James Hocken [1977] Director/Vice President; Richard John Peachey [1965] Director/Lawyer

Ball Europe Limited
Incorporated: 28 November 2002
Net Worth: £143,113,552 *Total Assets:* £198,525,648
Registered Office: 100 Capability Green, Luton, Beds, LU1 3LG
Activities: Non-trading company
Parent: Ball UK Holdings, Ltd
Officers: Charles Ernest Baker, Secretary/Associate General Counsel [American]; Philip James Hocken [1977] Director/Vice President; Richard John Peachey [1965] Director/Lawyer

Ball UK Holdco Limited
Incorporated: 18 May 2016
Net Worth Deficit: £25,872,040 *Total Assets:* £1,168,871,168
Registered Office: 100 Capability Green, Luton, Beds, LU1 3LG
Activities: Activities of head offices
Parent: Ball Corporation
Officers: Charles Ernest Baker [1957] Director/VP, General Counsel and Corporate Secretary [American]; John Wells [1968] Director/Vice President Global Taxes [American]

Ball UK Holdings, Ltd
Incorporated: 8 November 2002
Net Worth: £188,567,040 *Total Assets:* £421,335,584
Registered Office: 100 Capability Green, Luton, Beds, LU1 3LG
Activities: Non-trading company
Parent: Ball European Holdings S.A.R.L.
Officers: Charles Ernest Baker, Secretary/USA [American]; Philip James Hocken [1977] Director/Vice President; Richard John Peachey [1965] Director/Lawyer

Ball. Roller & Transmission Bearings Limited
Incorporated: 2 August 1967 *Employees:* 141
Net Worth: £7,662,792 *Total Assets:* £16,730,120
Registered Office: 21-24 Regal Road, Wisbech, Cambs, PE13 2RQ
Activities: Non-specialised wholesale trade
Parent: BRT (Wisbech) Ltd
Officers: Grahame Allen [1966] Director; Anthony George Clarke [1946] Director; Phillip David Clarke [1970] Director/Salesman; Simon David Clarke [1973] Director; Lindsey Jane Lowery [1961] Director

E.W.Ballard Holdings Limited
Incorporated: 17 June 1964 *Employees:* 2
Net Worth: £14,893,681 *Total Assets:* £16,537,662
Registered Office: Paternoster Farm, Sporehams Lane, Danbury, Essex, CM3 4AQ
Activities: Other letting and operating of own or leased real estate
Officers: Matthew William Okendon, Secretary; Margaret Ockendon [1944] Director; Matthew William Ockendon [1977] Director/Farmer; Sally Trussler [1973] Director/Banker

Ballast Phoenix Limited
Incorporated: 5 December 1996 *Employees:* 124
Net Worth: £15,017,000 *Total Assets:* £42,484,000
Registered Office: 1 Victoria Stables, Essex Way, Bourne, Lincs, PE10 9JZ
Activities: Manufacture of other non-metallic mineral products n.e.c.
Parent: Phoenix Advance Limited
Officers: Paul Christian Lee Knight [1971] Managing Director; Matthew Lloyd Turner [1966] Financial Director; David Michael York [1949] Director/Chairman

Simon Balle Academies Trust
Incorporated: 22 August 2013 *Employees:* 196
Net Worth: £18,936,000 *Total Assets:* £21,149,000
Registered Office: Simon Balle School, Mangrove Road, Hertford, SG13 8AJ
Activities: General secondary education
Officers: Jayne Abery [1969] Director; Sandie Abery [1947] Director/Retired; Hannah Louise Ahmet [1988] Director/Teacher; Clare Bishop [1977] Director/HR; Joanna Susan Brown [1979] Director/Accountant; Tara June Bullworthy [1964] Director; Paul Raymond Cable [1979] Director/Marketing; Paul Christopher Connolly [1959] Research Director; Emma Louise Davies [1971] Director/Events Planner; William John Davies [1968] Director/IT Consultant; Joanna Elizabeth Ennis [1972] Director; Roy Jeffery Hardcastle [1949] Director/Retired; Rachel Kirk [1981] Director/Local Government Officer; Christian Mark Lafferty [1967] Director/Researcher; Alison Louise Mackie [1969] Director/Consultant; Sally Crystal Mason [1979] Director/Accountant; Ann Eluned Orpin [1962] Director; Andrew James Robert Porrer [1975] Director/Software Engineer; Alison Jennifer Saunders [1959] Director; John Wigget [1973] Director/Architect

Sandy Balls Estate Limited
Incorporated: 1 July 1959 *Employees:* 205
Net Worth: £18,011,456 *Total Assets:* £20,488,504
Registered Office: IMEX, 575-599 Maxted Road, Hemel Hempstead Industrial Estate, Hemel Hempstead, Herts, HP2 7DX
Activities: Holiday centres and villages
Parent: Away Resorts Ltd
Officers: Carl Anthony Castledine [1969] Director; Greg Lashley [1964] Director; Neill Timothy Ryder [1976] Director

Balton CP Limited
Incorporated: 22 December 1976 *Employees:* 1,209
Net Worth: £21,451,602 *Total Assets:* £91,419,928
Registered Office: CP House, Otterspool Way, Watford, Herts, WD25 8HU
Activities: Non-specialised wholesale trade
Parent: Premier Telecommunication International Limited
Officers: Eric Lewis, Secretary; Andrew Joseph Baker [1965] Director/Chief Executive Officer; Paul Andrew Filer [1957] Director/Chartered Accountant; Alexei James Schreier [1976] Director; Kevin Edgar Torlage [1964] Director/Chief Finance Officer

Balvraid Properties Limited
Incorporated: 25 March 2009 *Employees:* 2
Net Worth: £5,710,873 *Total Assets:* £15,982,739
Registered Office: Bankside, 300 Peachman Way, Broadland Business Park, Norwich, NR7 0LB
Activities: Development of building projects
Shareholders: Simon Richard Commercial; Simon John Hashim
Officers: Simon Richard Commercial [1962] Director/Chartered Surveyor; Simon John Hashim [1953] Director

BAM Construct UK Limited
Incorporated: 3 February 1997 *Employees:* 2,297
Net Worth: £155,400,000 *Total Assets:* £489,200,000
Registered Office: Breakspear Park, Breakspear Way, Hemel Hempstead, Herts, HP2 4FL
Activities: Construction of commercial buildings
Parent: BAM Group (UK) Limited
Officers: Frazer Hamilton Wardhaugh, Secretary; Douglas Walker Keillor [1969] Director; James William Robert Wimpenny [1964] Executive Director

BAM Construction Limited
Incorporated: 4 May 1989
Net Worth: £69,400,000 *Total Assets:* £351,600,000
Registered Office: Breakspear Park, Breakspear Way, Hemel Hempstead, Herts, HP2 4FL
Activities: Construction of commercial buildings
Parent: BAM Construct UK Limited
Officers: Frazer Hamilton Wardhaugh, Secretary; Timothy George Chell [1968] Director; David Bruce Dickson [1966] Director; David Richard Ellis [1961] Director; Ian Edward Fleming [1961] Director; Adam Charles Harding [1972] Director; Douglas Walker Keillor [1969] Regional Director; John Eric Phillips [1961] Director; Roderic Stiles [1963] Regional Director; James William Robert Wimpenny [1964] Regional Director

BAM Glory Mill Limited
Incorporated: 27 June 2006
Net Worth Deficit: £5,259,000 *Total Assets:* £10,353,000
Registered Office: Breakspear Park, Breakspear Way, Hemel Hempstead, Herts, HP2 4FL
Activities: Buying and selling of own real estate
Officers: Euan James Miller, Secretary; Douglas Peters [1967] Director

BAM Monk Bridge Limited
Incorporated: 28 September 2005
Net Worth: £894,000 *Total Assets:* £17,454,000
Registered Office: Breakspear Park, Breakspear Way, Hemel Hempstead, Herts, HP2 4FL
Activities: Buying and selling of own real estate
Officers: Euan James Miller, Secretary; Douglas Peters [1967] Director/Accountant

BAM Properties Limited
Incorporated: 19 November 1996
Net Worth: £27,883,000 *Total Assets:* £35,893,000
Registered Office: Breakspear Park, Breakspear Way, Hemel Hempstead, Herts, HP2 4FL
Activities: Buying and selling of own real estate
Officers: Euan Miller, Secretary; Douglas Peters [1967] Director/Accountant; James William Robert Wimpenny [1964] Director

Bamrose Enterprises Limited
Incorporated: 22 May 1985 *Employees:* 2
Net Worth: £19,232,510 *Total Assets:* £21,195,012
Registered Office: 34 West Drive, Harrow Weald, Middlesex, HA3 6TS
Activities: Administration of financial markets
Officers: Chandrabala Dalia, Secretary; Chandrabala Dalia [1946] Director; Sheetal Dalia-Patel [1972] Director; Heena Rajiv Sodha [1969] Director

Bancroft's School
Incorporated: 19 February 1998 *Employees:* 228
Net Worth: £16,635,126 *Total Assets:* £22,429,332
Registered Office: High Road, Woodford Green, Essex, IG8 0RF
Activities: Primary education
Officers: Lionel Green, Secretary; Rejpaul Singh Bhumbra [1973] Director/Surgeon; Bernadette Sarah Conroy [1966] Director; Raymond John Gooding [1950] Director/Councillor; Professor Peter Graham Kopelman [1951] Director/University Principal; James Michael Rose [1971] Director/Stockbroker; Ed Sautter [1958] Director/Solicitor; Saheeda Begum Siddiqui [1956] Director/Solicitor; Councillor Michael John Stark [1942] Director/Councillor; Richard Van Maanen [1960] Director/Chartered Surveyor; Richard Williamson [1972] Strategy Director; Lizzie Wingham [1978] Director/TV Production

Bango PLC
Incorporated: 8 March 2005 *Employees:* 78
Net Worth: £10,723,438 *Total Assets:* £13,968,559
Registered Office: 5 Westbrook Centre, Milton Road, Cambridge, CB4 1YG
Activities: Other telecommunications activities
Officers: Rachel Greenhalgh, Secretary; Raymond Anderson [1958] Director; Nancy Cruickshank [1970] Director; Gianluca Cristian D'Agostino [1969] Investor and Director [Italian]; Anil Malhotra [1962] Director/Software Marketing; Carolyn Ann Rand [1964] Director/Chartered Accountant; Martin Paul Rigby [1955] Director/Fund Manager; David Valentine James Sear [1964] Managing Director, Financial Services

Bango. Net Limited
Incorporated: 7 October 1999 *Employees:* 74
Net Worth Deficit: £5,796,050 *Total Assets:* £11,526,325
Registered Office: 5 Westbrook Centre, Milton Road, Cambridge, CB4 1YG
Activities: Other telecommunications activities
Parent: Bango PLC
Officers: Rachel Christine Greenhalgh, Secretary; Raymond Anderson [1958] Director/Manager; Anil Malhotra [1962] Director/Software Marketing; Carolyn Ann Rand [1964] Director/Chartered Accountant; David Valentine James Sear [1964] Managing Director, Financial Services

John Banks Limited
Incorporated: 11 July 1984 *Employees:* 164
Net Worth: £3,526,207 *Total Assets:* £22,424,232
Registered Office: Kempson Way, Moreton Hall, Bury St Edmunds, Suffolk, IP32 7AR
Activities: Sale of new cars and light motor vehicles
Major Shareholder: John Eric Banks
Officers: Melanie Koren Hayley Banks-Browne, Secretary; John Eric Banks [1944] Director; Justin Carl Banks [1970] Director; Mark John Banks [1967] Director; Mary Carol Lynn Banks [1943] Director; Melanie Koren Hayley Banks-Browne [1965] Director; Mark Evans [1974] Sales Director; Christopher Hepton [1963] Director; Andrew James Smith [1979] Finance Director

Banks Mills Limited
Incorporated: 19 July 1955 *Employees:* 2
Net Worth: £9,827,976 *Total Assets:* £15,170,277
Registered Office: 29 St Neots Road, Sandy, Beds, SG19 1LE
Activities: Other letting and operating of own or leased real estate
Parent: SCB Holdings (Sandy) Limited
Officers: Gary Leon Carney, Secretary; Richard Lewin Banks [1942] Director

Barconn Group Limited
Incorporated: 9 August 2004 *Employees:* 159
Net Worth: £3,888,684 *Total Assets:* £11,997,160
Registered Office: Ingram House, Meridian Way, Norwich, NR7 0TA
Activities: Activities of construction holding companies
Shareholders: Spencer Nathan Connett; Antony John Barker
Officers: Anthony John Barker [1953] Director; Spencer Nathan Connett [1971] Director

Bard Pharmaceuticals Limited
Incorporated: 21 August 1970 *Employees:* 426
Net Worth: £73,193,000 *Total Assets:* £100,001,000
Registered Office: Unit 191 Cambridge Science Park, Milton Road, Cambridge, CB4 0AB
Activities: Manufacture of pharmaceutical preparations
Parent: Napp Pharmaceutical Group Limited
Officers: Stuart David Baker [1935] Director/Attorney [American]; Colm Joseph Moody [1965] Director of Production and Supply Chain [Irish]; Ake Gunnar Wikstrom [1951] Director/Advisor [Swedish]

David Barke (Holdings) Limited
Incorporated: 11 March 1981
Net Worth: £5,174,037 *Total Assets:* £11,194,091
Registered Office: 10 Towerfield Road, Shoeburyness, Essex, SS3 9QE
Activities: Activities of other holding companies n.e.c.
Officers: Oliver David Barke, Secretary/Director; David Allen Barke [1984] Director; Guy John Barke [1979] Director; James Frank David Barke [1942] Director; James Christian Barke [1974] Director; Oliver David Barke [1975] Director

Barking Power Limited
Incorporated: 2 March 1989
Net Worth: £14,213,000 *Total Assets:* £25,810,000
Registered Office: Barking Power Station, Chequers Lane, Dagenham, Essex, RM9 6PF
Activities: Production of electricity
Parent: The Mayor and Commonalty and Citizens of The City of London
Officers: Philip Gregory [1980] Director; Paul Graham Wilkinson [1962] Director/Surveyor; Peter Derek Young [1966] Director/Chartered Surveyor

Barley Pub Company Limited
Incorporated: 19 December 2007 *Employees:* 1,094
Net Worth: £6,575,000 *Total Assets:* £60,171,000
Registered Office: Porter Tun House, 500 Capability Green, Luton, Beds, LU1 3LS
Activities: Public houses and bars
Parent: Town and City Pub Group Limited
Officers: Suzanne Louise Baker [1963] Director; Simon David Longbottom [1971] Director/Chief Executive Officer; David Andrew Ross [1973] Director/Chief Financial Officer

Barlow Tyrie Limited
Incorporated: 23 October 1956 *Employees:* 28
Net Worth: £12,733,285 *Total Assets:* £15,515,728
Registered Office: 19 Springwood Drive, Braintree, Essex, CM7 2RN
Activities: Manufacture of other furniture
Shareholders: Peter Tyrie; Daniel Carter
Officers: James Robert Tyrie [1971] Sales Director; Mark Thomas Tyrie [1970] Director/Furniture Designer; Peter Thomas Tyrie [1944] Director/Garden Furniture Manufacturer

Barnack Estates UK Limited
Incorporated: 14 April 1987 *Employees:* 69
Previous: Barnack UK Limited
Net Worth: £8,745,932 *Total Assets:* £21,779,844
Registered Office: Barnack House, Southgate Way, Orton Southgate, Peterborough, Cambs, PE2 6GP
Activities: Non-specialised wholesale of food, beverages and tobacco
Shareholders: Robert Peter Turnbull Facer; Helen Margaret Facer
Officers: Helen Margaret Facer, Secretary; Helen Margaret Facer [1965] Director; Robert Peter Turnbull Facer [1962] Director

Barnardiston Hall Preparatory School Limited
Incorporated: 3 January 1995 *Employees:* 156
Net Worth: £3,943,863 *Total Assets:* £8,647,581
Registered Office: Greenwood House, Greenwood Court, Bury St Edmunds, Suffolk, IP32 7GY
Activities: Primary education
Major Shareholder: Lt Col Keith Anthony Boulter
Officers: Rebecca Alice Richardson, Secretary; Keith Anthony Boulter [1950] Director; Rebecca Alice Richardson [1976] Director/Teacher

Barnardo's
Incorporated: 20 April 1899 *Employees:* 8,128
Net Worth: £2,038,000 *Total Assets:* £184,364,000
Registered Office: Barnardo House, Tanners Lane, Barkingside, Ilford, Essex, IG6 1QG
Activities: Other social work activities without accommodation n.e.c.
Officers: David Mark Cunningham, Secretary; John Harold Bartlett [1953] Director/Head of Tax; Neil Braithwaite [1959] Managing Director; Alexis Jane Cleveland [1954] Director/Retired Cabinet Officer; Amanda Ellingworth [1957] Director; Zoe Elizabeth Harris [1975] Marketing Director; Dennis Vincent Hone [1958] Finance Director; Sheikh Mansurah Tal-At Mannings [1963] Director/Lawyer; Darra Singh [1959] Director/Partner; Colin James Walsh [1955] Director/Chief Executive

The Barnes Group Limited
Incorporated: 23 March 1978 *Employees:* 208
Net Worth: £8,371,000 *Total Assets:* £35,295,000
Registered Office: 6 Bermuda Road, Ransomes Europark, Ipswich, Suffolk, IP3 9RU
Activities: Development of building projects
Shareholder: William David Barnes
Officers: John Robert Goosen, Secretary; Mark Nicholas Bailey [1966] Divisional Director; William David Barnes [1955] Director/Chartered Accountant; Christopher Mark Bruce [1963] Divisional Director; Colin Simon Clements [1966] Director; Mark Anthony Hart [1964] Divisional Director; John Leonard Stevens [1973] Director; Robert Frank Steward [1963] Divisional Director

Barsham Securities Limited
Incorporated: 29 June 1987 *Employees:* 5
Net Worth: £16,275,321 *Total Assets:* £23,128,712
Registered Office: Branford House, 8a Hungate, Beccles, Suffolk, NR34 9TL
Activities: Other letting and operating of own or leased real estate
Shareholders: Colin Robert Holmes; Stuart Robert Holmes
Officers: Marion Ann Easey, Secretary; Maria Madeline Cripps [1965] Director/Hairdresser; Colin Robert Holmes [1933] Director/Surveyor; Stuart Robert Holmes [1960] Director/Surveyor

Barstone Limited
Incorporated: 14 March 2006 *Employees:* 130
Net Worth: £3,982,199 *Total Assets:* £16,331,224
Registered Office: St John's Court, Easton Street, High Wycombe, Bucks, HP11 1JX
Activities: Activities of head offices
Shareholders: Russell Graham Barley; Gregory Hamlin Stone
Officers: Gregory Hamlin Stone, Secretary/Director; Natalie Anne Barley [1969] Director; Russell Graham Barley [1961] Director; Caroline Billing [1965] Finance Director; Elizabeth Louise Stone [1962] Director/General Medical Practitioner; Gregory Hamlin Stone [1961] Director

Alan Bartlett & Sons (Chatteris) Limited
Incorporated: 29 April 2009 *Employees:* 281
Net Worth: £12,529,731 *Total Assets:* £31,194,474
Registered Office: Great Acre Fen, Chatteris, Cambs, PE16 6EG
Activities: Growing of vegetables and melons, roots and tubers
Major Shareholder: Alan Bartlett
Officers: Pamela Jane Bartlett, Secretary; Alan Bartlett [1956] Director; Oliver Bartlett [1991] Director; Toby Bartlett [1991] Director; Terry Hawthorn [1964] Director

The Bartrum Group Limited
Incorporated: 22 June 1993 *Employees:* 293
Net Worth: £10,978,002 *Total Assets:* £19,714,440
Registered Office: Langton Green, Eye, Suffolk, IP23 7HN
Activities: Activities of head offices
Shareholder: Robert Philip Bartrum
Officers: Karen Loretta Bambury, Secretary; Robert Philip Bartrum [1965] Director; Shaun Alan Bartrum [1964] Director; Stephen John Potter [1958] Director

Bartrum's Road Services Limited
Incorporated: 10 March 1955 *Employees:* 106
Net Worth: £10,305,188 *Total Assets:* £14,725,129
Registered Office: Langton Green, Eye, Suffolk, IP23 7HN
Activities: Freight transport by road
Parent: The Bartrum Group Limited
Officers: Karen Loretta Bambury, Secretary; Robert Philip Bartrum [1965] Director; Shaun Alan Bartrum [1964] Director; Stephen John Potter [1958] Director

Bartrums Haulage and Storage Limited
Incorporated: 25 May 1978 *Employees:* 170
Net Worth: £1,557,936 *Total Assets:* £11,430,892
Registered Office: Langton Green, Eye, Suffolk, IP23 7HN
Activities: Freight transport by road
Parent: The Bartrum Group Limited
Officers: Karen Loretta Bambury, Secretary; Robert Philip Bartrum [1965] Director; Shaun Alan Bartrum [1964] Director/Traffic Manager; Stephen John Potter [1958] Director/Traffic Manager

Baruch Holdings Limited
Incorporated: 5 October 1993
Net Worth: £3,257,529 *Total Assets:* £10,136,729
Registered Office: York House, Empire Way, Wembley, Middlesex, HA9 0FQ
Activities: Other letting and operating of own or leased real estate
Parent: Baruch Investments Limited
Officers: Emil Baruch, Secretary/Director; Emil Baruch [1960] Director; Robert Baruch [1963] Director

Baruch Investments Limited
Incorporated: 28 March 2001 *Employees:* 36
Net Worth: £10,163,017 *Total Assets:* £13,884,581
Registered Office: York House, Empire Way, Wembley, Middlesex, HA9 0FQ
Activities: Activities of head offices
Shareholders: Emil Baruch; Robert Baruch
Officers: Emil Baruch, Secretary/Director; Emil Baruch [1960] Director; Robert Baruch [1963] Director

Basetek (Holdings) Limited
Incorporated: 17 June 2008 *Employees:* 33
Net Worth: £8,136,725 *Total Assets:* £11,580,636
Registered Office: Unit 16 Bath Street, Ipswich, Suffolk, IP2 8SD
Activities: Activities of other holding companies n.e.c.
Major Shareholder: Jamie Philip Ashfield
Officers: Jamie Philip Ashfield [1956] Director

Basetek Limited
Incorporated: 18 January 2000 *Employees:* 33
Net Worth: £8,135,858 *Total Assets:* £11,579,098
Registered Office: Unit 16 Bath Street, Ipswich, Suffolk, IP2 8SD
Activities: Support activities for petroleum and natural gas mining
Officers: Francoise Anne Ashfield, Secretary/Director [French]; Francoise Anne Ashfield [1953] Director [French]; Jamie Philip Ashfield [1956] Director; Pierre Jamie Luke Ashfield [1989] Director; Lorna Mary Fraser [1979] Finance Director

Basinghall Mortgage Finance No.1 Limited
Incorporated: 9 October 2014
Net Worth: £2,497,545 *Total Assets:* £206,357,536
Registered Office: 1 Station Square, Cambridge, CB1 2GA
Activities: Activities of mortgage finance companies
Parent: Bluestone Mortgages Limited
Officers: Peter Timothy McGuinness [1969] Director/Banker; Andrew James Voss [1976] Director/Chief Financial Officer

George Bateman & Son Limited
Incorporated: 23 July 1928 *Employees:* 101
Net Worth: £18,917,072 *Total Assets:* £25,884,940
Registered Office: Salem Bridge Brewery, Mill Lane, Wainfleet, Lincs, PE24 4JE
Activities: Manufacture of beer
Officers: Jaclyn Carol Bateman [1957] Marketing Director; Stuart George Carson Bateman [1960] Managing Director (Trading); Haydn Biddle [1946] Director/Chairman; John Derek Else [1944] Director/Consultant; Ian William Furniss [1962] Finance Director; Jeffrey Philip Moore [1954] Director; Stephen John Oliver [1958] Director

Thomas Bates & Son Limited
Incorporated: 3 January 1927 *Employees:* 15
Net Worth: £28,555,750 *Total Assets:* £35,982,312
Registered Office: The Old Brickworks, Church Road, Harold Wood, Romford, Essex, RM3 0JA
Activities: Buying and selling of own real estate
Shareholders: Michael Bates; Joshua James Bates
Officers: James David Clark, Secretary; Joshua James Bates [1969] Director/Farmer; Michael Bates [1936] Director/Farmer; James David Clark [1983] Finance Director; Joseph Jackson [1982] Director

Bath Road Properties Limited
Incorporated: 7 June 2016
Net Worth Deficit: £1,159,321 *Total Assets:* £25,498,034
Registered Office: 3rd Floor, Sterling House, Langston Road, Loughton, Essex, IG10 3TS
Activities: Development of building projects
Parent: Galliard Developments Limited
Officers: Allan William Porter, Secretary; John Cole [1971] Director; Stephen Stuart Solomon Conway [1948] Director; Rory Anthony O'Connor [1959] Director [Irish]; Donagh O'Sullivan [1968] Director [Irish]

Bathstore Group Limited
Incorporated: 4 May 2012 *Employees:* 741
Net Worth Deficit: £24,047,000 *Total Assets:* £42,208,000
Registered Office: Home House, 3 Albany Place, Hydeway, Welwyn Garden City, Herts, AL7 3UQ
Activities: Other retail sale of new goods in specialised stores (not commercial art galleries and opticians)
Parent: Bathstore Holdings LLC
Officers: Geoffrey Brian Battersby [1960] Director

Bathstore.Com Limited
Incorporated: 6 April 1988 *Employees:* 741
Net Worth Deficit: £11,535,000 *Total Assets:* £54,720,000
Registered Office: 3 Albany Place, Hydeway, Welwyn Garden City, Herts, AL7 3UQ
Activities: Other retail sale of new goods in specialised stores (not commercial art galleries and opticians)
Parent: Bathstore Group Limited
Officers: Geoffrey Brian Battersby [1960] Director; Ian James Herrett [1971] Director/Chief Executive Officer

Bauder Limited
Incorporated: 11 December 1979 *Employees:* 144
Net Worth: £12,507,656 *Total Assets:* £21,446,036
Registered Office: King Street House, 15 Upper King Street, Norwich, NR3 1RB
Activities: Agents involved in the sale of timber and building materials
Parent: Bauder GmbH
Officers: Ian Barry Mundford, Secretary; Jan Bauder [1982] Director [German]; Tim Bauder [1986] Director [German]; Andrew Allan Hartley MacKenzie [1966] Managing Director

Bauer AR Holdings Limited
Incorporated: 21 April 1997 *Employees:* 3
Net Worth: £20,200,000 *Total Assets:* £20,200,000
Registered Office: Media House, Peterborough Business Park, Lynch Wood, Peterborough, Cambs, PE2 6EA
Activities: Radio broadcasting
Parent: Bauer Golden Square Limited
Officers: Deidre Ann Ford [1960] Managing Director; Paul Anthony Keenan [1963] Director/Publisher; Sarah Jane Vickery [1963] Finance Director

Bauer Consumer Media Limited
Incorporated: 3 July 1974 *Employees:* 653
Net Worth: £165,030,000 *Total Assets:* £182,107,008
Registered Office: Media House, Peterborough Business Park, Lynch Wood, Peterborough, Cambs, PE2 6EA
Activities: Activities of head offices
Parent: HBVB
Officers: Paul Anthony Keenan [1963] Director/Publisher; Robert James Munro-Hall [1966] Group Managing Director; Sarah Jane Vickery [1963] Finance Director

Bauer Digital Radio Limited
Incorporated: 7 January 1985 *Employees:* 3
Net Worth: £7,828,000 *Total Assets:* £10,683,000
Registered Office: Media House, Peterborough Business Park, Lynch Wood, Peterborough, Cambs, PE2 6EA
Activities: Television programme production activities
Parent: Bauer Radio Limited
Officers: Graeme Maxwell Allan [1956] Director/Chartered Engineer; Richard Jackson [1969] Director/Head of Finance - Bauer Radio; Susan Ruth Tattum [1969] Director/Chartered Accountant

Bauer Golden Square Limited
Incorporated: 22 May 2008 *Employees:* 3
Net Worth: £20,293,000 *Total Assets:* £20,293,000
Registered Office: Media House, Peterborough Business Park, Lynch Wood, Peterborough, Cambs, PE2 6EA
Activities: Activities of head offices
Parent: Bauer Radio Limited
Officers: Deidre Ann Ford [1960] Managing Director; Paul Anthony Keenan [1963] Director/Publisher; Sarah Jane Vickery [1963] Finance Director

Bauer Radio Limited
Incorporated: 16 October 1978 *Employees:* 112
Net Worth: £311,529,984 *Total Assets:* £384,135,008
Registered Office: Media House, Peterborough Business Park, Lynch Wood, Peterborough, Cambs, PE2 6EA
Activities: Activities of head offices
Parent: HBVB
Officers: Deidre Ann Ford [1960] Managing Director; Paul Anthony Keenan [1963] Director/Publisher; Sarah Jane Vickery [1963] Finance Director

Bauer Technologies Limited
Incorporated: 24 May 1989 *Employees:* 72
Net Worth: £3,856,601 *Total Assets:* £26,593,588
Registered Office: Millers Three, Southmill Road, Bishop's Stortford, Herts, CM23 3DH
Activities: Construction of commercial buildings
Parent: Bauer Spezialtiefbau GmbH
Officers: Martin Robert Blower, Secretary; Hans Joachim Bliss [1955] Director [German]; Martin Robert Blower [1956] Director; Michael Dennis Jones [1968] Managing Director

Baxter Healthcare Limited
Incorporated: 18 November 1948 *Employees:* 1,157
Net Worth: £101,793,000 *Total Assets:* £296,004,992
Registered Office: Caxton Way, Thetford, Norfolk, IP24 3SE
Activities: Manufacture of basic pharmaceutical products
Parent: Baxter Europe Holdings Ltd
Officers: Jon Garay [1973] Finance Director [Spanish]; Andrew Neil Goldney [1968] Director/General Manager; Bo Anders Caspersson Tarras-Wahlberg [1975] Director/Legal Adviser [Swedish]

Bay Restaurant Group Limited
Incorporated: 19 December 2007 *Employees:* 743
Net Worth Deficit: £20,783,000 *Total Assets:* £53,117,000
Registered Office: Porter Tun House, 500 Capability Green, Luton, Beds, LU1 3LS
Activities: Public houses and bars
Parent: TDR Capital LLP
Officers: Suzanne Louise Baker [1963] Director; Simon David Longbottom [1971] Director/Chief Executive Officer; David Andrew Ross [1973] Director/Chief Financial Officer

Bayard Metering (UK)
Incorporated: 5 August 2003
Net Worth: £52,814,000 *Total Assets:* £157,576,000
Registered Office: 1 Lysander Drive, Northfields Industrial Estate, Market Deeping, Peterborough, PE6 8FB
Activities: Activities of head offices
Parent: Landis + Gyr AG
Officers: Stephen George Cunningham [1966] Director/Chief Financial Officer; Charles Philip Walker [1972] Director/Chief Financial Officer

Bayer Cropscience Limited
Incorporated: 8 January 1927 *Employees:* 134
Net Worth: £39,586,000 *Total Assets:* £155,350,000
Registered Office: 230 Cambridge Science Park, Milton Road, Cambridge, CB4 0WB
Activities: Wholesale of chemical products
Parent: Bayer PLC
Officers: Colin Andrew Barker, Secretary; Lars Friedrich Bruening [1963] Director [German]; Louise Jane Hemingway [1971] Director/Head of Development & Regulatory Affairs; Sreeparna Arun Kurdikar [1969] Director/Chief Financial Officer [American]; Michael Simon Muncey [1962] Director

BBA Aviation Lynton Group Limited
Incorporated: 22 September 1983
Net Worth: £172,354,000 *Total Assets:* £173,122,000
Registered Office: Voyager House, 142 Prospect Way, Luton, Beds, LU2 9QH
Activities: Activities of head offices
Parent: BBA Overseas Holdings Limited
Officers: Michael Friedrich Lange [1964] Director/Managing Partner ME Business Solutions SaRL [German]; Iain Fraser MacLeod [1955] Director; Daniel Vincent Marcinik [1964] Finance Director [American]

BBC Studioworks Limited
Incorporated: 1 July 1998 *Employees:* 94
Previous: BBC Studios and Post Production Limited
Net Worth: £24,250,308 *Total Assets:* £33,958,312
Registered Office: Room N101, Neptune House, BBC Elstree Centre, Eldon Avenue, Borehamwood, Herts, WD6 1NL
Activities: Television programme production activities
Parent: BBC Commercial Holdings Limited
Officers: Peter John Ranyard, Secretary; David Conway [1976] Managing Director; Robert Glyn Isherwood [1968] Group Finance and Operations Director

BC Legal Limited
Incorporated: 27 March 2014 *Employees:* 94
Net Worth: £7,673,815 *Total Assets:* £9,811,543
Registered Office: 9 & 11 Nelson Street, Southend on Sea, Essex, SS1 1EF
Activities: Solicitors
Shareholders: Charlotte Emily Owen; Alexander George Boris Cetnik
Officers: Alexander George Boris Cetnik [1968] Director; Charlotte Emily Owen [1978] Director

BDL Group Public Limited Company (The)
Incorporated: 8 November 1977 *Employees:* 128
Net Worth: £7,892,398 *Total Assets:* £16,541,557
Registered Office: Carey House, Great Central Way, Wembley, Middlesex, HA9 0HR
Activities: Construction of commercial buildings
Parent: Carey Group PLC
Officers: Fiona Mary O'Donnell, Secretary; Timothy Joseph Barnes [1954] Director; John Carey [1941] Director [Irish]; Denis Patrick Deacy [1965] Group Managing Director

Be at One Holdings Limited
Incorporated: 3 October 2011 *Employees:* 414
Net Worth Deficit: £1,022,868 *Total Assets:* £24,154,556
Registered Office: Porter Tun House, 500 Capability Green, Luton, Beds, LU1 3LS
Activities: Public houses and bars
Parent: TDR Capital LLP
Officers: Toby John Rolph, Secretary; Simon David Longbottom [1971] Director; David Andrew Ross [1973] Director

Be at One Limited
Incorporated: 19 October 2000 *Employees:* 414
Net Worth: £1,897,674 *Total Assets:* £18,970,004
Registered Office: Porter Tun House, 500 Capability Green, Luton, Beds, LU1 3LS
Activities: Public houses and bars
Parent: Be at One Holdings Limited
Officers: Simon David Longbottom [1971] Director; David Andrew Ross [1973] Director

Be Living Group Limited
Incorporated: 1 September 2006
Previous: Willmott Regeneration Limited
Net Worth: £48,286,040 *Total Assets:* £48,292,448
Registered Office: Spirella, 2 Icknield Way, Letchworth Garden City, Herts, SG6 4GY
Activities: Development of building projects
Parent: Be Living Holdings Limited
Officers: Wendy Jane McWilliams, Secretary; Graham Mark Dundas [1979] Director/Accountant; Colin Enticknap [1958] Director/Chartered Surveyor; Michael Leonard Hart [1955] Director/Chartered Builder; Wendy Jane McWilliams [1958] Director/Solicitor; Richard John Willmott [1963] Director/Chartered Builder

Be Living Holdings Ltd
Incorporated: 1 May 2001 *Employees:* 104
Previous: Willmott Residential Limited
Net Worth: £61,459,000 *Total Assets:* £208,207,008
Registered Office: Spirella, 2 Icknield Way, Letchworth Garden City, Herts, SG6 4GY
Activities: Development of building projects
Shareholders: Walsworth Limited; Hardwicke Investments Limited
Officers: Wendy Jane McWilliams, Secretary; Graham Mark Dundas [1979] Director/Chartered Accountant; Christopher Simon Durkin [1963] Director/Chartered Builder; Colin Enticknap [1958] Director/Chartered Surveyor; Michael Leonard Hart [1955] Director/Chartered Builder; Wendy Jane McWilliams [1958] Director/Solicitor; Richard John Willmott [1963] Director/Chartered Builder

Be Living Limited
Incorporated: 29 January 2003 *Employees:* 77
Previous: Prime Place Developments Limited
Net Worth: £2,896,230 *Total Assets:* £132,793,184
Registered Office: Spirella 2, Icknield Way, Letchworth Garden City, Herts, SG6 4GY
Activities: Buying and selling of own real estate
Parent: Be Living Group Limited
Officers: Wendy Jane McWilliams, Secretary; Graham Mark Dundas [1979] Director/Chartered Accountant; Colin Enticknap [1958] Director/Chartered Surveyor; Wendy Jane McWilliams [1958] Director/Solicitor; Richard John Willmott [1963] Director/Chartered Builder

Beacon (Mimms) Limited
Incorporated: 7 January 1938 *Employees:* 1
Net Worth: £7,031,778 *Total Assets:* £8,075,082
Registered Office: Plantagenet House, 4 Plantagenet Road, New Barnet, Herts, EN5 5JQ
Activities: Other letting and operating of own or leased real estate
Major Shareholder: Christopher Edward Scarfe
Officers: Nicholas James Scarfe, Secretary; Nicholas James Scarfe [1992] Director

Beacon Educational Trust Limited (The)
Incorporated: 25 August 1972 *Employees:* 124
Net Worth: £13,004,383 *Total Assets:* £19,536,838
Registered Office: The Beacon, Amersham Road, Chesham Bois, Amersham, Bucks, HP6 5PF
Activities: Primary education
Officers: Francis Charles Muzika, Secretary; Simon James Allcock [1980] Director/Housemaster; Michael Bond [1972] Director/Headmaster; Rosalind Josephine Garrett-Bowes [1957] Director/Chartered Accountant; Sarah Jane Gillam [1958] Director/Headteacher; Justin David Robert Hardman [1968] Technology Director; Richard David Standish Herbert [1954] Director/Chartered Surveyor; David Mark Hollander [1959] Managing Director; Stephanie Horrocks [1949] Director/Retired; Philippa Jane Kirkbride [1957] Director/Senior Product Developer; Fiona Elizabeth McCallum Mayhew [1970] Director; Deborah Ann McGregor [1959] Director; Nilesh Kundanlal Pandya [1971] Finance Director; Joanna Ruth Pardon [1962] Director/Headmistress; Marcus Thompson [1972] Director/Lawyer; Alison Mary Sherwood Thomson [1958] Director/Doctor; Antony Crispin Tomlinson [1958] Director/Solicitor

Beacon Multi-Academy Trust Limited
Incorporated: 4 November 2011 *Employees:* 502
Previous: Beal Multi-Academy Trust Limited
Net Worth: £53,741,000 *Total Assets:* £58,470,000
Registered Office: Beal High School, Woodford Bridge Road, Ilford, Essex, IG4 5LP
Activities: General secondary education
Officers: Suda Ratnam, Secretary; Nadjie Carol Butler [1960] Director; Michelle Fuller [1970] Director; Dr Simon James Gibbons [1970] Director; Balbinder Ranbir Singh Panesar [1952] Director/Retired; Shona Ramsay [1958] Director; Suda Ratnam [1968] Director; Jatinder Saini [1954] Director; Dr Elizabeth Sidwell [1949] Director; Elizabeth Slattery [1958] Director/Lawyer; Michael Roderick Stokes [1969] Director/Manager; Alan Edward Weinberg [1946] Director/Councillor

Beaconsfield Educational Trust Limited
Incorporated: 21 February 1962 *Employees:* 65
Net Worth: £5,733,784 *Total Assets:* £11,097,913
Registered Office: Davenies School, Station Road, Beaconsfield, Bucks, HP9 1AA
Activities: Primary education
Officers: Guy Cornelius, Secretary; Susan Jane Clifford [1959] Director/Headmistress; Antonia Kate St Aubyn Dalmahoy [1973] Managing Director; Andrew Gregory Simon Davies [1960] Director/Headmaster; Nicholas Guy Edwards [1963] Director/Accountant; Neil Gallagher [1973] Director/Chief Financial Officer; Christopher Michael Hilditch [1968] Director/Solicitor; Karen Elaine Janse Van Vuuren [1960] Director; Thomas William Jenkin [1977] Director/Teacher; Siobhan Lowrey [1971] Director/Marketing/Creative Consultant [British/Australian]; Michael John Reyner [1963] Director/Partner, Executive Search Firm; Jamie Robert Shuttle [1972] Director/Consultant

Beaconsfield High School
Incorporated: 5 September 2013 *Employees:* 107
Net Worth: £30,235,520 *Total Assets:* £32,735,524
Registered Office: Beaconsfield High School, Wattleton Road, Beaconsfield, Bucks, HP9 1RR
Activities: General secondary education
Officers: Zoe Arabella Barrows [1966] Director/Teacher; Dr Lorraine Diane Couves [1964] Director; Gemma Davies [1993] Director/Teacher; Sara Louise Davies [1969] Director/Architect; Janet Mary Dixon [1959] Director/Teacher; Christopher Thomas Edmonds [1969] Director; Michael James Edwards [1970] Director/Management Consultant; Sanjiv Bhimji Gohil [1973] Director/Police Officer; Gaby Clare Heppner-Logan [1969] Communications Director; Alison Mary Hood [1965] Director/Solicitor; Kate Joanna Ing [1968] Director/School Administration Manager [British/German]; Clare Louise Lewis [1966] Director/Housewife; James Nicholas Robert Morton [1981] Director/Head of Strategy; Bhupendra Manibhai Patel [1955] Director/Executive Coach & Strategy Consultant; Charles Richard Pybus [1965] Director/Chartered Accountant; Rachel Ann Smith [1964] Director/Headteacher; Deborah Maria Starrs [1966] Director/Teaching Assistant

Beaconsfield School
Incorporated: 17 October 2012 *Employees:* 79
Net Worth: £13,791,225 *Total Assets:* £15,935,924
Registered Office: The Beaconsfield School, Wattleton Road, Beaconsfield, Bucks, HP9 1SJ
Activities: General secondary education
Officers: Claire Rawlinson, Secretary; Jean-Marc Brannon [1979] Director/Teacher; Richard Cook [1966] Director; Susan Elizabeth Cook [1966] Director/Teaching Assistant; Jane Valerie D'Agostino [1964] Director/Accountant; John Fletcher [1969] Director/Headteacher; Anthony Matthew Harrison [1981] Director/Barrister; Andrew David Hodson [1965] Director/Chartered Surveyor; Narlep Kaur [1974] Director/Airline Cabin Crew; James Anthony McEvoy [1968] Director/Police Officer; Tamara Marie McMillen [1968] Director/Executive [Irish]; Joseph Steven McNally [1968] Director/Teacher; Amanda Rayner [1960] Director/Event Manager; Graham Geofrey Smith [1952] Director/Professional Coach; Bronwen Rose Zeun [1954] Director/Retired

Beale's Hotels Limited
Incorporated: 11 February 2010 *Employees:* 158
Net Worth: £3,563,816 *Total Assets:* £8,832,589
Registered Office: West Lodge Park, Cockfosters Road, Barnet, Herts, EN4 0PY
Activities: Hotels and similar accommodation
Shareholder: Beale Trust
Officers: Michael George Pettit, Secretary; Andrew Edward Beale [1963] Director; Nicholas Henderson Beale [1969] Director/Surveyor; Antony Peter King [1953] Director

Beale's Limited
Incorporated: 15 February 1895 *Employees:* 158
Net Worth: £6,482,426 *Total Assets:* £11,751,299
Registered Office: Beales Ltd, West Lodge Park, Cockfosters Road, Barnet, Herts, EN4 0PY
Activities: Hotels and similar accommodation
Parent: Beales Hotels Limited
Officers: Michael George Pettit, Secretary; Andrew Edward Beale [1963] Director/Hotelier; Nicholas Henderson Beale [1969] Director/Surveyor

Beamglow Limited
Incorporated: 6 October 1966 *Employees:* 151
Net Worth: £5,657,228 *Total Assets:* £13,558,577
Registered Office: Somersham Road, St Ives, Huntingdon, Cambs, PE27 3LP
Activities: Other manufacturing n.e.c.
Shareholder: Moira Griffin
Officers: Adrian Philip Brown, Secretary; Wayne Bellchamber [1958] Technical Director; Adrian Philip Brown [1968] Finance Director; Brian Griffin [1947] Director; Moira Griffin [1947] Managing Director; Huw Roberts [1963] Sales Director

Beaufort House Limited
Incorporated: 19 August 1986 *Employees:* 2
Net Worth: £4,281,263 *Total Assets:* £11,034,758
Registered Office: Tennyson House, Cambridge Business Park, Cambridge, CB4 0WZ
Activities: Development of building projects
Major Shareholder: Michael John Osborne
Officers: Michael John Osborne [1952] Director/Economist

Beaumont School
Incorporated: 13 June 2012 *Employees:* 167
Net Worth: £28,221,080 *Total Assets:* £30,084,808
Registered Office: Beaumont School, Oakwood Drive, St Albans, Herts, AL4 0XB
Activities: General secondary education
Officers: Sharon Lucille Banks, Secretary; Martin James Atkinson [1970] Director/Deputy Headteacher; Brenda Austin [1970] Director/Teacher [Irish]; Anna Aurora Battaglia [1962] Director/Senior Lecturer [Italian]; Mike Reginald Cameron [1960] Director/Education Consultant; Catherine Inez Davies [1980] Director/Teacher; Andrew James Gray [1992] Director/Teacher; Alexander Neal Hall [1979] Director/Solicitor; William Ian Johnston [1968] Human Resources Director; Gary Keith Kellett [1972] Director/Chartered Civil Engineer; Simone Sonia Kilka-Green [1969] Director/Solicitor; Prof David Alan Lee [1966] Director/University Professor; Dr Michele Lloyd [1968] Director/Senior Lecturer in Education; Peter Joseph Mayne [1975] Director/Self Employed Consultant; Jonathan Mountstevens [1979] Director/Deputy Headteacher; Yvonne Paula Powdrell [1967] Director/Deputy Headteacher; Lisanne Jane Sherwood [1964] Director/Teaching Assistant; Victoria Mary Stewart [1967] Director/Teaching Assistant; Alison Wallis [1960] Director/Human Resources Professional

Beauty Wholesale Limited
Incorporated: 8 June 1999 *Employees:* 29
Net Worth: £1,738,514 *Total Assets:* £9,373,346
Registered Office: 3 George Street, Watford, Herts, WD18 0BX
Activities: Wholesale of perfume and cosmetics
Parent: KMS Holdings Limited
Officers: Gulam Nasser [1965] Director

Beckhithe Farms Limited
Incorporated: 25 November 1997 *Employees:* 16
Net Worth: £10,899,641 *Total Assets:* £12,843,080
Registered Office: Hall Farm, Reedham, Norwich, NR13 3HW
Activities: Mixed farming
Shareholders: Barry Ernest Brooks; Sadie Ann Brooks
Officers: Sadie Ann Brooks, Secretary/Director; Barry Ernest Brooks [1946] Director; Sadie Ann Brooks [1947] Director; Bethany Kerry Ann Gray [1995] Director; Gary Martin Gray [1969] Director/Farms Manager; Kerry Ann Gray [1972] Director/Beauty Therapist; Sarah Jane Haistead [1976] Director

Beckman Coulter United Kingdom Limited
Incorporated: 2 November 1959 *Employees:* 197
Net Worth: £34,242,000 *Total Assets:* £64,166,000
Registered Office: Oakley Court, Kingsmead Business Park, London Road, High Wycombe, Bucks, HP11 1JU
Activities: Non-specialised wholesale trade
Parent: VJ Holdco UK Limited
Officers: Jan Pospisil [1959] Director/VP Commercial Operations Europe [Czech]; Keith Graham Ward [1953] Director; Robert Todd Young [1972] Director

Beckman Holdings Limited
Incorporated: 10 October 1988
Net Worth: £101,891,000 *Total Assets:* £149,832,992
Registered Office: Oakley Court, Kingsmead Business Park, London Road, High Wycombe, Bucks, HP11 1JU
Activities: Non-trading company
Parent: Launchchange Limited
Officers: Jan Pospisil [1959] Director/VP Commercial Operations Europe [Czech]; Keith Graham Ward [1953] Director; Robert Todd Young [1972] Director

Bedfordshire Schools Trust Limited
Incorporated: 28 February 2011 *Employees:* 494
Previous: Bedfordshire East Multi-Academy Trust
Net Worth: £59,654,000 *Total Assets:* £63,985,000
Registered Office: Best House, Shefford Road, Clifton, Shefford, Beds, SG17 5QS
Activities: Primary education
Officers: Ilona Bond [1955] Director/Retired [Irish]; Dr Alan Lee [1964] Director/Chief Executive; Claire Mycock [1957] Deputy Director; Anthony John Sanderson [1955] Director/Management Consultant; David Shelvey [1957] Director/Financial Consultant; Paul Adrian Walker [1950] Director/Head of Commercial Development

Beds with Ease Limited
Incorporated: 7 June 2001
Net Worth: £619,398 *Total Assets:* £17,662,488
Registered Office: 5th Floor, Jansel House, Hitchin Road, Luton, Beds, LU2 7XH
Activities: Travel agency activities
Major Shareholder: Hussein Gulamali Rajan
Officers: Adam Trevor Pardini, Secretary; Jill Louise Mitchell [1971] Director/Accountant; Adam Trevor Pardini [1969] Director; Hussein Gulamali Rajan [1956] Director/Travel Agent

Beechfield Estates Limited
Incorporated: 12 July 2007 *Employees:* 3
Net Worth: £5,355 *Total Assets:* £9,641,629
Registered Office: 19 King Street, King's Lynn, Norfolk, PE30 1HB
Activities: Development of building projects
Shareholders: Rui Pan; Qinqin Song; Chengrun He
Officers: Weipeng Gu, Secretary; Weipeng Gu [1989] Director [Chinese]; Andrew David Auldio Jamieson [1956] Director

Beechwood Park School Limited
Incorporated: 23 September 1964 *Employees:* 166
Net Worth: £8,971,751 *Total Assets:* £11,940,903
Registered Office: Beechwood Park School, Markyate, Herts, AL3 8AW
Activities: Primary education
Officers: Timothy John Blad, Secretary; Andrew Mark Briscoe [1960] Director/Retired; Clare Elizabeth Cutler [1972] Director/Career Break; Gary John Freer [1961] Director/Solicitor; Jonathan William James Gillespie [1966] Director/Headmaster; Mark Hammond [1968] Director/Financial Consultant; Rosalind Kate Hardy [1970] Director/Headmistress; James Simon Hodgson [1969] Director/Headmaster; Gavin Eric Mairs [1972] Director/Journalist; Dr Richard James Maloney [1971] Director/Headmaster; Yvonne Mary Mercer [1957] Director/Retired; Linda Christine Roberts [1946] Director/Retired; Katharine Elizabeth Swaine [1970] Human Resources Director; Simon James Thompson [1967] Director/Retired; Dr Russell Mardon Viner [1963] Director/Doctor [Australian]

M.W. Beer & Co. Limited
Incorporated: 13 March 1981 *Employees:* 16
Net Worth: £9,898,061 *Total Assets:* £18,323,732
Registered Office: 6-7 Grange Court, The Limes, Ingatestone, Essex, CM4 0GB
Activities: Non-specialised wholesale trade
Parent: M W Beer Holdings Limited
Officers: Clifford Holmes, Secretary; Martin Beer [1963] Director; Michael William Beer [1939] Director/Commodity Dealer; Clifford Holmes [1969] Director

Beeson Wright Limited
Incorporated: 28 June 2011 *Employees:* 8
Net Worth: £8,713,585 *Total Assets:* £24,100,966
Registered Office: 4 Office Village, Forder Way, Hampton, Peterborough, Cambs, PE7 8GX
Activities: Construction of commercial buildings
Shareholders: Andrew Beeson; Neville David Wright; Joanne Beeson; Marilyn Jane Wright
Officers: Andrew Beeson [1976] Director; Joanne Beeson [1982] Director; Marilyn Jane Wright [1951] Director; Neville David Wright [1950] Director

Beko PLC
Incorporated: 22 August 1989 *Employees:* 238
Net Worth: £30,350,000 *Total Assets:* £179,327,008
Registered Office: Beko House, 1 Greenhill Crescent, Watford, Herts, WD18 8QU
Activities: Manufacture of electric domestic appliances
Parent: Arcelik A.S.
Officers: Gul Arslanoglu, Secretary; Mehmet Ragip Balcioglu [1967] Director; Hakan Hamdi Bulgurlu [1972] Director/Mechanical Engineer [Turkish]; Levent Cakiroglu [1967] Director [Turkish]; Fatih Kemal Ebiclioglu [1967] Director [Turkish]; Mustafa Rahmi Koc [1930] Director [Turkish]; Sir David Norman Reddaway [1953] Director; Polat SEN [1976] Director [Turkish]

Belchim Crop Protection Limited
Incorporated: 26 November 2002 *Employees:* 16
Net Worth: £12,570,761 *Total Assets:* £20,629,048
Registered Office: 1b Fenice Court, Eaton Socon, St Neots, Cambs, PE19 8EP
Activities: Wholesale of chemical products
Officers: Herbert Peumans [1968] Managing Director [Belgian]

Belgrave Land (Perth) Limited
Incorporated: 13 June 2005 *Employees:* 3
Net Worth: £3,928,176 *Total Assets:* £11,700,486
Registered Office: First Floor, Radius House, 51 Clarendon Road, Watford, Herts, WD17 1HP
Activities: Development of building projects
Shareholders: John Hoyle; Richard Swaine; Jonathan Willoughby
Officers: Richard David Swaine, Secretary; John Fearnley Hoyle [1947] Director; Richard David Swaine [1962] Director; Jonathan James Willoughby [1966] Director

Belgrave Land (Sheffield) Limited
Incorporated: 28 March 2008 *Employees:* 3
Net Worth: £4,771,292 *Total Assets:* £15,021,822
Registered Office: First Floor, Radius House, 51 Clarendon Road, Watford, Herts, WD17 1HP
Activities: Other letting and operating of own or leased real estate
Shareholders: John Fearnley Hoyle; Richard David Swaine; Jonathan James Willoughby
Officers: Richard David Swaine, Secretary; John Fearnley Hoyle [1947] Director; Richard David Swaine [1962] Director; Jonathan James Willoughby [1966] Director

Bell Educational Trust Limited (The)
Incorporated: 5 April 1972 *Employees:* 223
Net Worth: £38,513,000 *Total Assets:* £45,494,000
Registered Office: 1 Red Cross Lane, Cambridge, CB2 0QU
Activities: Other education n.e.c.
Officers: Reshard Sheik Mahmad Auladin [1954] Director/Self Employed; Toni Elizabeth Fazaeli [1955] Director/Educational Consultant; John Gandy [1952] Chartered Surveyor/Director; Elizabeth Jan King [1961] Director/Management Consultant; Mike Milanovic [1954] Director/Retired; Russell Charles Prior [1964] Director/Banker; Alexander John Scott-Barrett [1955] Director; Geoffrey Spink [1949] Director; Sarah Laetitia Squire [1949] Director/Retired (University Administrator); Anthony Laurence Tomei [1949] Director/Retired

Bellcoin Holdings Limited
Incorporated: 18 February 1985 *Employees:* 30
Net Worth: £10,089,830 *Total Assets:* £18,123,984
Registered Office: Plaza, off Edinburgh Avenue, Skegness, Lincs, PE25 2UG
Activities: Public houses and bars
Major Shareholder: Brian William Bell
Officers: Brian William Bell, Secretary; Brian William Bell [1940] Director/Amusement Caterer; Lyn Mary Bell [1952] Director/Amusement Caterer

Bellman Property Group Limited
Incorporated: 10 February 2011 *Employees:* 2
Net Worth: £8,559,297 *Total Assets:* £20,216,372
Registered Office: Ground Floor, Unit 501 Centennial Park, Centennial Avenue, Elstree, Borehamwood, Herts, WD6 3FG
Activities: Other service activities n.e.c.
Shareholder: Laurence Alan Bellman
Officers: Sarah Jane Bellman, Secretary; Laurence Alan Bellman [1956] Director, Surveyor and Property Manager; Neil Andrew Evans [1954] Director/Solicitor

Belsize Garages Project Limited
Incorporated: 11 July 2005
Net Worth Deficit: £275,618 *Total Assets:* £15,362,346
Registered Office: Suite 2, Fountain House, 1a Elm Park, Stanmore, Middlesex, HA7 4AU
Activities: Construction of domestic buildings
Parent: Belsize Ltd
Officers: Paul Simon Godfrey [1980] Director; Tal Orly [1963] Director [Israeli]

The Benacre Company
Incorporated: 19 January 2016 *Employees:* 23
Net Worth: £4,754,835 *Total Assets:* £63,222,216
Registered Office: The Estate & Farms Office, Hall Farm, Benacre, Beccles, Suffolk, NR34 7LJ
Activities: Growing of cereals (except rice), leguminous crops and oil seeds
Parent: Benacre (Holding) Limited
Officers: Hugh Murray Charles Coghill [1950] Director/Chartered Surveyor; Lady Susan Barbara Christie Gooch [1938] Director/Landowner; Lucinda Hutson [1970] Director/Landowner; Victoria Vere Nicoll [1974] Director

Benacre Investments Limited
Incorporated: 6 March 1992
Net Worth: £5,704,188 *Total Assets:* £8,034,587
Registered Office: 1 Tower House, Tower Centre, Hoddesdon, Herts, EN11 8UR
Activities: Other letting and operating of own or leased real estate
Major Shareholder: Steven John Dale
Officers: Steven John Dale [1957] Director/Travel Consultant

Benacre Properties Company
Incorporated: 19 January 2016 *Employees:* 5
Net Worth: £29,853,728 *Total Assets:* £70,222,600
Registered Office: The Estate & Farms Office, Hall Farm, Benacre, Beccles, Suffolk, NR34 7LJ
Activities: Other letting and operating of own or leased real estate
Parent: Benacre Properties (Holding) Limited
Officers: Hugh Murray Charles Coghill [1950] Director/Chartered Surveyor; Lady Susan Barbara Christie Gooch [1938] Director/Landowner; Lucinda Hutson [1970] Director/Landowner; Victoria Vere Nicoll [1974] Director

Benchmark Leisure Limited
Incorporated: 10 March 1995
Net Worth Deficit: £137,190 *Total Assets:* £10,994,773
Registered Office: Rock House, Scotgate, Stamford, Lincs, PE9 2YQ
Activities: Buying and selling of own real estate
Parent: BLL Investments Limited
Officers: Alex John Charles Duce [1980] Director; Roland John Bernard Duce [1948] Director; Brian Dryden Foord [1938] Director; Jonathan Dryden Foord [1967] Director

Benefit Cosmetics Limited
Incorporated: 9 February 2000 *Employees:* 523
Net Worth: £50,226,812 *Total Assets:* £73,419,360
Registered Office: Marconi Building, New Street, Chelmsford, Essex, CM1 1PH
Activities: Wholesale of perfume and cosmetics
Parent: LVMH Moet Hennessy Louis Vuitton
Officers: Hugues Philippe Dusseaux [1954] Director/President [French]; Sarah Anne Harbon [1975] Sales Director; Andrea Dawn Lansbury [1964] Director; Jean Andre Rougeot [1958] Managing Director [French]

Benfleet Schools Trust
Incorporated: 11 March 2011 *Employees:* 209
Net Worth: £11,182,000 *Total Assets:* £14,751,000
Registered Office: The Appleton School, Croft Road, Benfleet, Essex, SS7 5RN
Activities: General secondary education
Officers: Ian Kenneth Clark, Secretary; Sarah Elizabeth Dignasse [1957] Director/Educational Consultant; Jonathan David Fryer [1975] Director/Information & Communication Manager; Reverend Peter Hillman [1969] Director/Clerk in Holy Orders; Sandra Mary Johnson [1953] Director/Self Employed Consultant; Karen Kerridge [1963] Director/Headteacher; Rachel Nolan [1976] Director/Civil Servant; Clive Robert Purdy [1959] Director/Chartered Accountant; Terry Anthony Reynolds [1947] Director

L Bennett & Son Holdings Limited
Incorporated: 19 June 2003 *Employees:* 234
Net Worth: £4,046,983 *Total Assets:* £14,781,277
Registered Office: 3 Prime Point, Bessemer Road, Welwyn Garden City, Herts, AL7 1HU
Activities: Wholesale trade of motor vehicle parts and accessories
Shareholders: John Leonard Bennett; Mark Amos Bennett
Officers: John Leonard Bennett [1968] Managing Director; Mark Amos Bennett [1971] Sales Director

Bennett PLC
Incorporated: 18 November 1971 *Employees:* 43
Net Worth: £28,737,434 *Total Assets:* £36,419,904
Registered Office: Low Green Barn, Nowton, Bury St Edmunds, Suffolk, IP29 5ND
Activities: Development of building projects
Officers: Karina Parker, Secretary; Adam John Bell [1967] Director/Chartered Surveyor; Andrew David Horsburgh [1964] Director/Accountant; Christine Mary Parker [1943] Director; Edward George Parker [1972] Director; Karina Parker [1976] Director; Nigel James Parker [1939] Director

The Bentley Wood Trust
Incorporated: 5 July 2011 *Employees:* 256
Net Worth: £30,126,728 *Total Assets:* £34,422,152
Registered Office: Bentley Wood High School, Bridges Road, Stanmore, Middlesex, HA7 3NA
Activities: Pre-primary education
Officers: Marcello Borgese [1966] Director/House Husband; Calvin Niklaus Hardy [1969] Director; Dr Janice Karen Howkins [1955] Director; Andrew McLeod Lewis [1959] Director/Government Service; Raakhi Patel [1978] Director/Accountant; Iram Qazi [1967] Director/Homemaker; Clive Westall [1965] Director/Headteacher

Bentwaters Parks Limited
Incorporated: 4 July 1984 *Employees:* 13
Net Worth: £13,672,448 *Total Assets:* £16,799,960
Registered Office: The Control Tower, Rendlesham, Woodbridge, Suffolk, IP12 2TW
Activities: Management of real estate on a fee or contract basis
Shareholders: William John Kemball; Jane Elizabeth Kemball
Officers: Jane Elizabeth Kemball, Secretary; Sarah Jane Brown [1965] Director/Manager; John William Kemball [1972] Director/Estate Manager; William John Kemball [1939] Farmer and Director

Berkhamsted Schools Group
Incorporated: 5 March 1959 *Employees:* 317
Net Worth: £34,173,000 *Total Assets:* £41,814,000
Registered Office: 6 Chesham Road, Berkhamsted, Herts, HP4 3AA
Activities: Pre-primary education
Officers: Stephen Robert Elliff, Secretary; David John Atkins [1966] Director/Chartered Surveyor; Professor Sarah-Jayne Blakemore [1974] Director/Neuroscientist; Anne Kathleen Fahy [1960] Director/Chief Financial Officer [Irish]; Dr Mark Alexander Fenton [1965] Director/Headmaster; Andrew Russell Hart [1962] Director/Solicitor; Gavin Crawford Laws [1957] Director; Kerry Musgrave [1968] Director/Legal Trainer; Christopher Nicholls [1954] Director/Retired; Stuart Stacy Rolland [1964] Managing Director; Sarah Ann Shields [1973] Director/VP and General Manager; Samantha Jeanne Tidey [1965] Director; Sandra Turner [1952] Director; Andrew John Wilcock [1955] Director/Headmaster; Jonathan David Williams [1966] Director/Partner

Berlesduna Academy Trust
Incorporated: 7 July 2016 *Employees:* 201
Net Worth: £21,636,650 *Total Assets:* £25,748,876
Registered Office: School House, Church Road, Basildon, Essex, SS14 2EX
Activities: Primary education
Officers: Eileen Margaret Patching [1956] Director; Susan Pauline Segger [1951] Director; Robin Taverner [1954] Director/Education Adviser; Sean Terence Tobin [1971] Director; Steven Peter West [1965] Director

Berry Recruitment Limited
Incorporated: 5 October 2009 *Employees:* 167
Net Worth: £2,967,850 *Total Assets:* £17,534,026
Registered Office: Porters House, 4 Porters Wood, St Albans, Herts, AL3 6PQ
Activities: Temporary employment agency activities
Parent: Berry Recruitment Group Limited
Officers: Michael Robert Sarson, Secretary; Antony George Berry [1940] Director; Spencer Morgan Berry [1971] Director; Christopher Chown [1975] Director; Susan Marie Folds [1940] HR Director; Lee James Gamble [1971] Director; Ian David Haddock [1959] Director/Management Consultant; Ian Michael Langley [1962] Director/Executive Chairman; Michael Robert Sarson [1956] Director; Michelle Stewart [1974] Managing Director

Bertram Trading Limited
Incorporated: 17 March 2009 *Employees:* 360
Net Worth Deficit: £7,908,000 *Total Assets:* £49,364,000
Registered Office: 1 Broadland Business Park, Norwich, NR7 0WF
Activities: Non-specialised wholesale trade
Parent: Aurelius Omega Limited
Officers: Nicholas David Goodwin [1963] Director/Chief Finance Officer; Stephen Edward Moon [1970] Director

Berwen Limited
Incorporated: 11 February 1946 *Employees:* 4
Net Worth: £13,141,085 *Total Assets:* £15,401,277
Registered Office: Estate House, Marsh Way, Fairview Industrial Park, Rainham, Essex, RM13 8UH
Activities: Buying and selling of own real estate
Officers: Elizabeth Mary Berry, Secretary; John Berry [1943] Director; Simon John Berry [1969] Director

Besana UK Limited
Incorporated: 31 May 1990 *Employees:* 469
Net Worth: £13,148,088 *Total Assets:* £98,957,624
Registered Office: Bluestem Road, Ransomes Industrial Estate, Ipswich, Suffolk, IP3 9RR
Activities: Non-specialised wholesale trade
Parent: Uncle Vincent Limited
Officers: Simon Mark Albert Melik, Secretary; Giuseppe Calcagni [1940] Director [Italian]; Simon Mark Albert Melik [1963] Director

Bespak Europe Limited
Incorporated: 24 February 1998 *Employees:* 734
Net Worth: £107,336,000 *Total Assets:* £155,496,992
Registered Office: Suite B Breakspear Park, Breakspear Way, Hemel Hempstead, Herts, HP2 4TZ
Activities: Manufacture of basic pharmaceutical products
Parent: Consort Medical PLC
Officers: Andrew Leonard Jackson, Secretary; Dr Keyvan Djamarani [1961] Director; Jonathan Martin Glenn [1968] Company Director; Paul Andrew Hayes [1966] Director

Bespak Holdings Limited
Incorporated: 14 April 2000
Net Worth: £108,031,000 *Total Assets:* £148,196,992
Registered Office: Suite B Breakspear Park, Breakspear Way, Hemel Hempstead, Herts, HP2 4TZ
Activities: Activities of head offices
Parent: Consort Medical PLC
Officers: Andrew Leonard Jackson, Secretary; Jonathan Martin Glenn [1968] Director; Paul Andrew Hayes [1966] Director

Bespoke Foods Group Limited
Incorporated: 30 September 2016 *Employees:* 86
Net Worth: £2,465,904 *Total Assets:* £26,142,942
Registered Office: Shannon Place, Shannon Road, Potton, Beds, SG19 2YH
Activities: Activities of open-ended investment companies
Major Shareholder: Ian James Affleck
Officers: Ian James Affleck [1961] Director; Duncan Marsh [1971] Commercial Director

Bespoke Foods Holding Limited
Incorporated: 17 October 2016 *Employees:* 6
Net Worth: £2,335,008 *Total Assets:* £17,945,468
Registered Office: Shannon Place, Shannon Road, Potton, Beds, SG19 2YH
Activities: Activities of other holding companies n.e.c.
Parent: Bespoke Foods Group Limited
Officers: Ian James Affleck [1961] Director; Duncan Marsh [1971] Commercial Director

Best Holdings (UK) Limited
Incorporated: 31 January 2013 *Employees:* 123
Net Worth: £143,520,192 *Total Assets:* £291,121,248
Registered Office: 166 College Road, Harrow, Middlesex, HA1 1RA
Activities: Activities of other holding companies n.e.c.
Major Shareholder: Alfred William Best
Officers: Ian Michael Farr, Secretary; Alfred William Best [1970] Director; Waseem Hanif [1967] Director

Beta Pharmaceuticals Limited
Incorporated: 23 October 2003 *Employees:* 80
Net Worth: £5,926,742 *Total Assets:* £9,334,672
Registered Office: Unit 7 & 8 Swanbridge Industrial Park, Black Croft Road, Witham, Essex, CM8 3YN
Activities: Wholesale of pharmaceutical goods
Major Shareholder: Naseen Mohamed Valji
Officers: Mohamed Raza Kanji, Secretary; Mohamed Raza Kanji [1971] Director/Pharmacist; Naseen Valji [1959] Director/Chemist

Betcrown Limited
Incorporated: 25 November 2015
Net Worth Deficit: £1,082,391 *Total Assets:* £18,706,236
Registered Office: Hill House, Lowlands Road, Harrow, Middlesex, HA1 3EQ
Activities: Development of building projects
Major Shareholder: Donovan Gijsbertus Wijsmuller
Officers: Brian Martin Comer [1960] Director [Irish]; Luke Andrew Comer [1957] Director [Irish]

Betex LLP
Incorporated: 19 February 2005
Net Worth: £26,000,100 *Total Assets:* £65,017,936
Registered Office: 166 College Road, Harrow, Middlesex, HA1 1RA
Officers: Tom Bennet [1966] LLP Member; Warrick Richard Booth [1964] LLP Member; Samuel Brodovcky [1978] LLP Member; Nicholas Exarchos [1964] LLP Member; Vittorio Fazio [1969] LLP Member; Alastair Keith MacKeith [1958] LLP Member; Edward Maravanyika [1975] LLP Member; Janardan Nedyam Menon [1967] LLP Member; Nilesh Ambalal Patel [1961] LLP Member; Matthieu Prevot [1978] LLP Member; Suresh Sadasivan [1968] LLP Member; Alexander Michael Trojanow [1976] LLP Member; Julian Max Rupert Trott [1964] LLP Member; Daniel Paul Wray [1976] LLP Member; Oleksandr Zakharchenko [1968] LLP Member

Betting Shop Services Limited
Incorporated: 10 December 2004 *Employees:* 443
Net Worth Deficit: £68,917,552 *Total Assets:* £15,085,530
Registered Office: 4 Simon Campion Court, 232-234 High Street, Epping, Essex, CM16 4AU
Activities: Gambling and betting activities
Officers: Julian Knight, Secretary; Gregory Roy Knight [1964] Director; Julian William Knight [1970] Director

P.H. Betts (Holdings) Limited
Incorporated: 21 January 1974 *Employees:* 206
Net Worth: £5,362,598 *Total Assets:* £9,741,988
Registered Office: Broadwater Road, Framlingham, Suffolk, IP13 9LL
Activities: Activities of production holding companies
Shareholders: Judith Irene Grace Betts; Patrick Hugh Betts
Officers: Judith Irene Grace Betts, Secretary; Judith Irene Grace Betts [1937] Director; Patrick Hugh Betts [1933] Director; Isobel Judith McGovern [1972] Director/Secretary; Juliet Anne Nash [1960] Director/Housewife; Joshua George Simpkin Betts [1982] Director/Executive; Suzy Aprile Sledmere [1976] Director/Housewife

Betts International Limited
Incorporated: 25 June 1998
Net Worth: £3,273,000 *Total Assets:* £8,406,000
Registered Office: De Novo House, Newcomen Way, Colchester, Essex, CO4 9AE
Activities: Manufacture of plastic packing goods
Parent: Betts Limited
Officers: Derek James Eaton [1968] Director/Group Financial Controller; Charles-Antoine Jean Marie Roucayrol [1971] Director/General Counsel [French]

Betts Limited
Incorporated: 25 June 1998 *Employees:* 2
Net Worth: £12,117,000 *Total Assets:* £40,203,000
Registered Office: De Novo House, Newcomen Way, Colchester, Essex, CO4 9AE
Activities: Manufacture of plastic packing goods
Parent: Twist Beauty Packaging UK Limited
Officers: Derek James Eaton [1968] Director/Group Financial Controller; Charles-Antoine Jean Marie Roucayrol [1971] Director/General Counsel [French]

BEW Electrical Distributors Limited
Incorporated: 1 March 1983 *Employees:* 281
Net Worth: £6,469,876 *Total Assets:* £31,321,718
Registered Office: Unit 5 Northumberland Court, Dukes Park Industrial Estate, Chelmsford, Essex, CM2 6UW
Activities: Non-specialised wholesale trade
Shareholders: Philip Randall Webb; Ronald William Locker
Officers: Philip Randall Webb, Secretary; Neil Andrew Godfrey [1965] Director/Financial Accountant; Dominic Christopher Groves [1975] Director; Darren Locker [1972] Director; Ronald William Locker [1951] Director; David John Shirt [1963] Director; Philip Randall Webb [1950] Director

Bexhill UK Limited
Incorporated: 8 May 2000 *Employees:* 7
Net Worth: £3,663,811 *Total Assets:* £21,669,884
Registered Office: 721 Capability Green, Luton, Beds, LU1 3LU
Activities: Credit granting by non-deposit taking finance houses and other specialist consumer credit grantors
Parent: Orchard Funding Group PLC
Officers: Liam Leo McShane, Secretary; Tatiana Korenkova [1972] Director/Financial Controller; Emmia Louise Stratford [1982] Director/System Manager; Rabinder Singh Takhar [1965] Solicitor Director

BFC Finance Limited
Incorporated: 2 November 2015
Net Worth: £56,129,875,968 *Total Assets:* £56,129,875,968
Registered Office: Porter Tun House, 500 Capability Green, Luton, Beds, LU1 3LS
Activities: Activities of production holding companies
Officers: Yannick Bomans [1983] Director Control Parent Companies [Belgian]; Gert Boulange [1977] Director/Employee [Belgian]

BFSL Limited
Incorporated: 13 April 1992
Net Worth: £21,837,000 *Total Assets:* £496,343,008
Registered Office: Pegasus House, Bakewell Road, Orton Southgate, Peterborough, Cambs, PE2 6YS
Activities: Activities of financial services holding companies
Parent: BISL Limited
Officers: Julian Charles Brown, Secretary; Matthew Oliver Donaldson [1973] Director; Duncan Alistair Finch [1965] Director/Chartered Accountant; Seamus Declan Keating [1963] Director [Irish]; Dominic James Platt [1969] Director/Chief Financial Officer; Peter Thompson [1970] Group Director

BGL (Holdings) Limited
Incorporated: 18 October 2016 *Employees:* 2,684
Net Worth: £6,600,000 *Total Assets:* £648,499,968
Registered Office: Pegasus House, Southgate Park, Bakewell Road, Orton Southgate, Peterborough, Cambs, PE2 6YS
Activities: Activities of financial services holding companies
Parent: BHL (UK) Holdings Limited
Officers: Julian Charles Brown, Secretary; Katherine Hae-Eun Chung [1976] Director/Private Equity Investor [American]; Matthew Oliver Donaldson [1973] Director/Chief Executive Officer; Inaki Echave [1972] Director/Private Equity Investor [Spanish]; Lord Jitesh Kishorekumar Gadhia [1970] Director; Alison Deborah Hewitt [1963] Director; Patricia Doreen Jackson [1952] Director; Seamus Declan Keating [1963] Director [Irish]; Stephen Klinkert [1953] Director [British/Australian]; Dominic James Platt [1969] Director/Chief Financial Officer; Stephen John Van Rooyen [1973] Director/Chief Executive

BGL Group Limited
Incorporated: 21 March 1991 *Employees:* 2,608
Net Worth: £9,100,000 *Total Assets:* £439,000,000
Registered Office: Pegasus House, Bakewell Road, Orton Southgate, Peterborough, Cambs, PE2 6YS
Activities: Activities of financial services holding companies
Parent: BGL (Holdings) Limited
Officers: Julian Charles Brown, Secretary; Matthew Oliver Donaldson [1973] Director; Dominic James Platt [1969] Director/Chief Financial Officer

BHL (UK) Holdings Ltd
Incorporated: 10 July 2013 *Employees:* 3,321
Net Worth: £55,700,000 *Total Assets:* £741,400,000
Registered Office: Bath House, 16 Bath Row, Stamford, Lincs, PE9 2QU
Activities: Activities of other holding companies n.e.c.
Officers: Lucy Sinfield, Secretary; Simon Andrew James [1970] Director; Stephen Klinkert [1953] Director [South African/British/Australian]; Ian Robert Leech [1960] Director/Chartered Accountant

Velji Bhovan & Sons (Trading) Limited
Incorporated: 22 November 2002 *Employees:* 187
Net Worth: £19,431,612 *Total Assets:* £26,832,736
Registered Office: VB House, Woodside End, Alperton, Wembley, Middlesex, HA0 1UR
Activities: Non-specialised wholesale of food, beverages and tobacco
Officers: Chunilal Velji Nathwani, Secretary; Chandulal Velji Nathwani [1938] Director/Sales Executive; Chunilal Velji Nathwani [1936] Director/Sales Executive; Mahendra Velji Nathwani [1946] Director/Sales Executive; Manharlal Velji Nathwani [1949] Director/Sales Executive; Natwarlal Velji Nathwani [1940] Director/Sales Executive

BHW Automotive Limited
Incorporated: 10 December 2004 *Employees:* 266
Net Worth: £1,292,683 *Total Assets:* £9,814,509
Registered Office: Ground Floor, Swift House, 18 Hoffmanns Way, Chelmsford, Essex, CM1 1GU
Activities: Maintenance and repair of motor vehicles
Parent: Enzo Automotive Limited
Officers: Karamjot Singh Aujla [1982] Director; Kashmir Singh [1960] Director

BICL Limited
Incorporated: 21 March 1991
Previous: Budget Insurance Company Limited
Net Worth: £9,579,563 *Total Assets:* £9,637,162
Registered Office: Bath House, 16 Bath Row, Stamford, Lincs, PE9 2QU
Activities: Non-life insurance
Parent: BHL (UK) Holdings Limited
Officers: Lucy Sinfield, Secretary; Stephen Klinkert [1953] Director [South African/British/Australian]; Ian Robert Leech [1960] Director

Bidwells LLP
Incorporated: 31 March 2009 *Employees:* 489
Net Worth: £1,455,106 *Total Assets:* £30,876,064
Registered Office: Bidwell House, Trumpington Road, Cambridge, CB2 9LD
Officers: Generald Peter Leslie Collins [1957] Member; Patrick Leo McMahon [1965] Member; Richard John Pilsworth [1964] Member; James Vernon Abraham [1965] LLP Member; Jonathan Armitage [1966] LLP Member; David Gareth Bainbridge [1974] LLP Member; David Bentley [1966] LLP Member; James Edward Spencer Brooke [1966] LLP Member; Brian Steven Buckingham [1962] LLP Member; Mark Richard Buddle [1973] LLP Member; Roland Bull [1983] LLP Member; Finlay Campbell Clark [1966] LLP Member; Rosalind Anne Clifford [1973] LLP Member; Neil Cole [1972] LLP Member; Robert Coote [1975] LLP Member; Robert Couch [1968] LLP Member; Eilzabeth Fiona Craig [1962] LLP Member; Michael John Derbyshire [1964] LLP Member; Giles Alexander Lee Dobson [1979] LLP Member; Derek Graham Farrow [1964] LLP Member; Andrew Richard Flood [1973] LLP Member; Ian William Gatiss [1964] LLP Member; Andrew Jonathan Groves [1975] LLP Member; William Heigham [1976] LLP Member; Raymond Henderson [1961] LLP Member; Daniel Edward Jones [1969] LLP Member; Philip Kentish [1975] LLP Member; James Frank Churton Keys [1968] LLP Member; James Andrew Terry Lankfer [1965] LLP Member; Andrew Christopher James Long [1966] LLP Member; Steven Paul McLaughlin [1967] LLP Member; Mark Meeson [1968] LLP Member; Ian George Peck [1957] LLP Member; Ralph William Peters [1975] LLP Member; Nicholas Roy Pettit [1967] LLP Member; Jonathan Phillips [1966] LLP Member; Matthew Stephen Richards [1982] LLP Member; Richard James Skeates [1963] LLP Member; Catherine Anne Spitzer [1972] LLP Member; James Westwood Squier [1953] LLP Member; Patrick Stanton [1983] LLP Member; Darryl Alexander Stevenson [1965] LLP Member; Colin Jonathan Summers [1978] LLP Member; Christopher Surfleet [1971] LLP Member; Simon Regan Thomas [1966] LLP Member; Richard Stephen Todd [1983] LLP Member; John Vartan Tweddle [1946] LLP Member; Ian Thomas Wakeling [1975] LLP Member; Saul Rafe Western [1970] LLP Member; David Bowen Williams [1968] LLP Member; Paul Willmott [1962] LLP Member; Andrew Thallon Wood [1963] LLP Member

Biffa Corporate Holdings Limited
Incorporated: 16 December 2005
Net Worth Deficit: £704,572,032 *Total Assets:* £565,246,016
Registered Office: Coronation Road, Cressex, High Wycombe, Bucks, HP12 3TZ
Activities: Collection of non-hazardous waste
Parent: Biffa Group Holdings (UK) Ltd
Officers: Richard Neil Pike [1969] Director/Chief Financial Officer; Michael Robert Mason Topham [1972] Director/Chief Executive Officer

Biffa Environmental Municipal Services Limited
Incorporated: 10 May 1967 *Employees:* 717
Previous: Cory Environmental Municipal Services Limited
Net Worth: £7,868,000 *Total Assets:* £27,585,000
Registered Office: Coronation Road, Cressex Business Park, High Wycombe, Bucks, HP12 3TZ
Activities: Collection of non-hazardous waste
Parent: Biffa Waste Services Limited
Officers: Rachael Hambrook, Secretary; Richard Neil Pike [1969] Director/Chief Financial Officer; Michael Robert Mason Topham [1972] Director/Chief Executive Officer

Biffa Group Holdings (UK) Limited
Incorporated: 2 October 2000
Previous: Biffa Limited
Net Worth: £511,986,304 *Total Assets:* £547,592,576
Registered Office: Coronation Road, Cressex, High Wycombe, Bucks, HP12 3TZ
Activities: Activities of head offices
Parent: Biffa Group Limited
Officers: Richard Neil Pike [1969] Director/Chief Financial Officer; Michael Robert Mason Topham [1972] Director/Chief Executive Officer

Biffa Group Limited
Incorporated: 25 October 2007
Net Worth: £859,400,000 *Total Assets:* £1,201,200,000
Registered Office: Coronation Road, Cressex, High Wycombe, Bucks, HP12 3TZ
Activities: Activities of head offices
Parent: Biffa Group Holdings Ltd
Officers: Rachael Hambrook, Secretary; Richard Neil Pike [1969] Director/Chief Financial Officer; Michael Robert Mason Topham [1972] Director/Chief Executive Officer

Biffa GS UK Holdings Limited
Incorporated: 9 January 2003
Previous: Greenstar UK Holdings Limited
Net Worth: £10,497,000 *Total Assets:* £92,156,000
Registered Office: Coronation Road, Cressex, High Wycombe, Bucks, HP12 3TZ
Activities: Collection of non-hazardous waste
Parent: Biffa GS Holdings Limited
Officers: Richard Neil Pike [1969] Director/Chief Financial Officer; Michael Robert Mason Topham [1972] Director/Chief Executive Officer

Biffa Holdings Limited
Incorporated: 22 November 1971
Net Worth: £378,456,992 *Total Assets:* £622,896,000
Registered Office: Coronation Road, Cressex, High Wycombe, Bucks, HP12 3TZ
Activities: Collection of non-hazardous waste
Parent: Reclamation & Disposal Ltd
Officers: Richard Neil Pike [1969] Director/Chief Financial Officer; Michael Robert Mason Topham [1972] Director/Chief Executive Officer

Biffa Leicester Limited
Incorporated: 27 November 2002 *Employees:* 179
Net Worth Deficit: £23,837,906 *Total Assets:* £9,626,163
Registered Office: Biffa, Coronation Road, Cressex Business Park, High Wycombe, Bucks, HP12 3TZ
Activities: Collection of non-hazardous waste
Parent: Biffa Corporate Holdings Ltd
Officers: Dr. John Kieran Casey [1967] Director [Irish]; Richard Neil Pike [1969] Director/Chief Financial Officer; Michael Robert Mason Topham [1972] Director/Chief Executive Officer

Biffa Municipal Limited
Incorporated: 12 November 2001 *Employees:* 2,314
Net Worth: £58,177,000 *Total Assets:* £133,547,000
Registered Office: Coronation Road, Cressex, High Wycombe, Bucks, HP12 3TZ
Activities: Collection of non-hazardous waste
Parent: Biffa GS UK Holdings Limited
Officers: Rachael Hambrook, Secretary; Stephen Cole [1972] Finance Director; Simon Crook [1961] Business Director; Peter Barnaby Dickson [1973] Development Director; Roger John Edwards [1969] Managing Director; David Simon Maidman [1963] Operation Director; Michael Robert Mason Topham [1972] Director/Chief Executive Officer

Biffa PLC
Incorporated: 18 August 2016 *Employees:* 7,773
Net Worth: £341,200,000 *Total Assets:* £1,054,300,032
Registered Office: Coronation Road, Cressex, High Wycombe, Bucks, HP12 3TZ
Activities: Activities of other holding companies n.e.c.
Officers: Rachael Hambrook, Secretary; Michael Charles Edward Averill [1951] Director; Gab Saturnio Barbaro [1971] Managing Director [Italian/Australian]; Carol Tredway Chesney [1962] Director [American]; Kenneth Lever [1953] Director; David Robert Martin [1951] Director; Richard Neil Pike [1969] Director/Chief Financial Officer; Michael Robert Mason Topham [1972] Director/Chief Financial Officer

Biffa Polymers Limited
Incorporated: 8 July 1992 *Employees:* 118
Net Worth Deficit: £3,521,000 *Total Assets:* £20,331,000
Registered Office: Coronation Road, Cressex, High Wycombe, Bucks, HP12 3TZ
Activities: Recovery of sorted materials
Parent: Biffa GS UK Holdings Limited
Officers: Rachael Hambrook, Secretary; Richard Neil Pike [1969] Director/Chief Financial Officer; Michael Robert Mason Topham [1972] Director/Chief Executive Officer

Biffa Waste Management Limited
Incorporated: 4 October 1973
Net Worth: £60,486,000 *Total Assets:* £88,983,000
Registered Office: Coronation Road, Cressex, High Wycombe, Bucks, HP12 3TZ
Activities: Collection of non-hazardous waste
Parent: UK Waste Management Holdings Limited
Officers: Richard Neil Pike [1969] Director/Chief Financial Officer; Michael Robert Mason Topham [1972] Director/Chief Executive Officer

Biffa Waste Services Limited
Incorporated: 16 January 1969 *Employees:* 4,469
Net Worth: £427,800,000 *Total Assets:* £1,547,399,936
Registered Office: Coronation Road, Cressex, High Wycombe, Bucks, HP12 3TZ
Activities: Collection of non-hazardous waste
Parent: Biffa Holdings Ltd
Officers: Rachael Hambrook, Secretary; Richard Neil Pike [1969] Director/Chief Financial Officer; Michael Robert Mason Topham [1972] Director/Chief Executive Officer

Big Easy Restaurants Limited
Incorporated: 5 November 1993 *Employees:* 361
Previous: Corrett Restaurants Limited
Net Worth Deficit: £308,477 *Total Assets:* £15,493,501
Registered Office: Eden House, Reynolds Road, Beaconsfield, Bucks, HP9 2FL
Activities: Licenced restaurants
Major Shareholder: Paul Corrett
Officers: Jennifer Philcox, Secretary; Paul Corrett [1952] Director

The Big Prawn Co. Ltd.
Incorporated: 23 October 1998 *Employees:* 89
Net Worth: £6,248,974 *Total Assets:* £13,945,287
Registered Office: 1a Marriott Way, Melton Constable, Norfolk, NR24 2BT
Activities: Processing and preserving of fish, crustaceans and molluscs
Parent: The Big Prawn Co. (Holdings) Ltd
Officers: Vincent James Gotts, Secretary; St John Colin Kenneth Agnew [1964] Director; Craig Andrew Harrison [1970] Sales Director; Lisa Claire O'Hanlon [1965] Director; Sean Dennis O'Hanlon [1964] Director; William David Rash [1969] Director

Big Sky Developments Ltd
Incorporated: 14 August 2013
Net Worth: £3,980,029 *Total Assets:* £11,705,938
Registered Office: South Norfolk House, Cygnet Court, Long Stratton, Norwich, NR15 2XE
Activities: Development of building projects
Parent: Big Sky Ventures
Officers: Julie Ann Brown, Secretary; Stuart Michael Bizley [1961] Director/Chartered Surveyor; Spencer Charles Burrell [1973] Development Director; Peter Brian Catchpole [1963] Assistant Director - Resources; Sandra Caroline Dinneen [1964] Director/Chief Executive

Bio Products Laboratory Holdings Limited
Incorporated: 16 October 2002 *Employees:* 2,893
Net Worth: £149,928,000 *Total Assets:* £434,364,000
Registered Office: Bio Products Laboratory, Dagger Lane, Elstree, Herts, WD6 3BX
Activities: Other human health activities
Shareholders: Naga UK Bidco Limited; Naga UK Bidco Limited
Officers: Kieu Hoang [1944] Director [American]; Kevin Lane [1961] Director/President [American]; Xu Wu [1967] Director [Chinese]

Bio Products Laboratory Limited
Incorporated: 11 August 2010
Net Worth: £74,935,000 *Total Assets:* £302,643,008
Registered Office: c/o Bio Products Laboratory, Dagger Lane, Elstree, Herts, WD6 3BX
Activities: Other business support service activities n.e.c.
Parent: Bio Products Laboratory Holdings Limited
Officers: Kieu Hoang [1944] Director [American]; Kevin Lane [1961] Director/President [American]; Xu Wu [1967] Director [Chinese]

Bio-Rad Laboratories Limited
Incorporated: 11 April 1995 *Employees:* 146
Net Worth: £21,641,000 *Total Assets:* £41,961,000
Registered Office: 3rd and 4th Floor, The Junction, Station Road, Watford, Herts, WD17 1ET
Activities: Non-specialised wholesale trade
Parent: Bio-Metrics (U.K.) Limited
Officers: Philip Howard [1957] Director/Regional Sales Manager; Norman David Schwartz [1950] Director/C.E.O. & President [American]

Biochrom Limited
Incorporated: 13 March 1998 *Employees:* 49
Net Worth: £18,007,030 *Total Assets:* £24,066,976
Registered Office: Building 1020, Cambourne Business Park, Cambourne, Cambridge, CB23 6DW
Activities: Other manufacturing n.e.c.
Officers: Joe Joseph Eyles, Secretary; Jeffrey Duchemin [1965] Director/Chief Executive [American]; Joe Joseph Eyles [1972] Director/Certified Chartered Accountant; Kamalam Unninayar [1967] Director/Chief Financial Officer [American]

Biofocus DPI (Holdings) Ltd
Incorporated: 23 September 1996
Net Worth: £28,045,000 *Total Assets:* £28,060,000
Registered Office: Robinson Building, Chesterford Research Park, Little Chesterford, Saffron Walden, Essex, CB10 1XL
Activities: Activities of head offices
Parent: Charles River Laboratories Holdings Limited
Officers: Sarah Margaret Price, Secretary; Birgit Girshick [1970] Director/Manager [American/German]; David P Johst [1961] Director [American]; Dr Jacqueline Anne MacRitchie [1966] Director/Scientist; David Ross Smith [1965] Director

Bioline Agrosciences Limited
Incorporated: 14 October 1988 *Employees:* 85
Previous: Syngenta Bioline Limited
Net Worth: £11,753,952 *Total Assets:* £14,761,932
Registered Office: Telstar Nursery, Holland Road, Little Clacton, Clacton-on-Sea, Essex, CO16 9QG
Activities: Raising of other animals
Officers: Maha Fournier [1969] Director [French]; Laurent Martel [1966] Director [French]; Ludwik Pokorny [1966] Director [French]

Biomarsh Environmental Ltd
Incorporated: 25 July 1973 *Employees:* 110
Net Worth: £2,656,213 *Total Assets:* £11,462,998
Registered Office: Biomarsh House, Fountain Drive, Mead Lane, Hertford, SG13 7UB
Activities: Sewerage
Parent: Biomarsh Holdings Limited
Officers: Martin Kevin Travers, Secretary; Malcolm John Travers [1975] Director/General Manager; Margaret Travers [1954] Director; M Martin Kevin Travers [1977] Director; Michelle Kathleen Travers [1978] Director/Office Manager; Roderick Ernest Travers [1945] Director/Transport Contractor

Birch Farms (C & N) LLP
Incorporated: 7 January 2016 *Employees:* 1
Net Worth: £16,186,516 *Total Assets:* £17,649,324
Registered Office: Hellens, Hardys Green, Birch, Colchester, Essex, CO2 0NY
Officers: Claire Cottrell [1947] Member; Nicholas Rupert Round Cottrell [1970] Member; James Edward Keith [1960] Member; Maxwell Colin Bernard Ward [1949] Member

Birch's Park Homes Limited
Incorporated: 1 August 1997 *Employees:* 9
Net Worth: £4,644,508 *Total Assets:* £9,858,340
Registered Office: Bluebell Woods, Ely Road, Waterbeach, Cambridge, CB25 9NW
Activities: Recreational vehicle parks, trailer parks and camping grounds
Parent: Birch's Group Limited
Officers: Carol Anne Birch, Secretary/Land Management; Carol Anne Birch [1953] Director; Charles Edward Birch [1978] Director; Charles Frederick Birch [1953] Director/Land Management; James Michael Birch [1983] Director

Birchwood Capital Limited
Incorporated: 19 November 2015 *Employees:* 2
Net Worth: £721,073 *Total Assets:* £10,993,089
Registered Office: 3 Warners Mill, Silks Way, Braintree, Essex, CM7 3GB
Activities: Fund management activities
Major Shareholder: Nigel Anthony Brooks
Officers: Nigel Anthony Brooks [1969] Investment Director

Birchwood High School
Incorporated: 29 September 2011 *Employees:* 174
Net Worth: £9,757,843 *Total Assets:* £11,660,566
Registered Office: Birchwood High School, Parsonage Lane, Bishop's Stortford, Herts, CM23 5BD
Activities: General secondary education
Officers: Nicola Coop, Secretary; Lee Elizabeth Bothwell [1958] Director/Senior Administration Manager; Nicole Brown [1967] Director/Soft Services Manager; Ruth Helen Crowland [1974] Director/Specialist Teacher; Catherine Gater [1971] Director/Gender Project Officer; John Dylan Frederic Gray [1971] Executive Director; Sally Joanne Gubb [1970] Director/Operational Manager; Alan Thomas Hazell [1959] Director; Dr Chris John Ingate [1961] Director/Headteacher; Ross Noblett [1989] Director/Teacher; Michael Phillips [1976] Director/Teacher; Dr Neville Douglas Prior [1960] Director; Hilary Scotcher [1971] Director/Store Assistant; Andrew David Paul Sheriff [1966] Director/Accountant; Mark Anthony Stocker [1962] Director/Actuary; Dr Annie Swanepoel [1969] Director/Psychiatrist [German]; Gillian Turner [1976] Director/Accountant; Liza Margaret Watkins [1971] Director/Head of Automation; Emma Louise White [1968] Director/Music Teacher; James Neville Winter [1960] Director/Head of Field Sales

Birdlife International
Incorporated: 2 November 1994 *Employees:* 206
Net Worth: £14,474,485 *Total Assets:* £16,884,820
Registered Office: David Attenborough Building, Pembroke Street, Cambridge, CB2 3QZ
Activities: Other professional, scientific and technical activities n.e.c.
Officers: Sara Patricia Zurita Serrano, Secretary; Mark David Anderson [1964] Director/Chief Executive Officer [South African]; Achilles Brunnel Byaruhanga [1968] Director [Ugandan]; Dr Michael John Clarke [1960] Director/Chief Executive RSPB; Claudia Christina Feltrup-Azafzaf [1964] Executive Director [German]; Dr Braulio Ferreia de Souza Dias [1953] Director/University Professor [Brazilian]; Philippe Marcel Alfred Funcken [1969] Managing Director, Natagora ASBL [Belgian]; Kevin Grant Hague [1960] Director/Chief Executive Officer [New Zealander]; Dr Gergo Denes Halmos [1976] Executive Director [Hungarian]; Professor Sarath Wimalabandara Kotagama [1950] Director [Sri Lankan]; Dr Shawn Kaihekulani Lum [1963] Director [American]; Rosabel Miro Rodriguez [1967] Executive Director [Panamanian]; David O'Neill [1970] Director/Chief Conservation Officer [American]; Nicholas John Prentice [1956] Director/Chartered Accountant; Simon Rye [1963] Policy Director [Norwegian]; Assad Adel Serhal [1958] Director [Lebanese]; Yehya Shehadeh [1972] Director [Jordanian]; Paul Darren Sullivan [1965] Director/Conservation [Australian]; Vera Voronova [1987] Director/CEO - ACBK [Kazakh]; Dr Angel Alberto Yanosky Farran [1962] Director/Biology Environmental Advisor [Argentinian]

Birketts LLP
Incorporated: 31 January 2006 *Employees:* 542
Net Worth: £16,889,720 *Total Assets:* £28,262,352
Registered Office: Providence House, 141-145 Princes Street, Ipswich, Suffolk, IP1 1QJ
Officers: Gavin John Acheson [1965] Member; Henry Norris Adams [1974] Member; Gregory Sanderson Allan [1980] Member; James Alexander Allen [1967] Member; Matthew Michael Charlton Atkins [1963] Member; James St John Austin [1960] Member; Christopher John Barker [1957] Member; Vicki Leanne Barnard-Chilton [1977] Member; Katie Jane Beaven [1981] Member; Nicholas John Burnett [1954] Member; Christopher Samuel Roy Coupland [1978] Member; Oliver Peter Crichton [1975] Member; Alexander Charles Robert Davey [1972] Member; James Maynard Dinwiddy [1972] Member; Richard John Eaton [1967] Member; Nigel Charles Farthing [1955] Member; Timothy William Galloway [1970] Member; Robert Victor Gibbs [1954] Member; Mark Edward Gipson [1969] Member; Peter Goddard [1956] Member; Quentin Robert Golder [1962] Member; Oliver Timothy Gravell [1959] Member; Stefan John Harris-Wright [1979] Member; Mark Andrew Henry [1969] Member; Katherine Julie Herbert [1961] Member; Daden Henry Edward Hunt [1974] Member; Catherine Jennifer Johnson [1968] Member; Adam Mark Jones [1976] Member; Steven Russell Kay [1972] Member; Grace Elizabeth Kerr [1965] Member; Louise Mary Long [1966] Member; Melissa Anne Loucas [1972] Member; Paul Nigel Matthews [1953] Member; Rachel Mary McKillop-Wilkin [1971] Member; Ruth Morris [1972] Member; Thomas James Newcombe [1977] Member; Matthew Timothy Newnham [1976] Member; Kevin Jeffrey Palmer [1959] Member; Karl David Pocock [1978] Member; Adrian Marcus Possener [1964] Member; Stuart James Raven [1977] Member; James Robinson [1980] Member; Max Roessler [1956] Member; Jack Hain Royall [1975] Member; Rafael Jonathan Ruiz [1970] Member; Andrew Graham Rush [1970] Member; John Scannell [1958] Member; Christopher Peter Schwer [1964] Member; Adrian Charles Seagers [1964] Member; Neil Geoffrey Sparrow [1953] Member; Lorna Natalie Spear [1974] Member; Paul Leslie Squire [1977] Member; Caroline Jane Stenner [1959] Member; Ruth Elizabeth Sunaway [1981] Member; Laura Elizabeth Thomas [1979] Member; Nigel Howard Thompson [1958] Member; Abigail Nellie Trencher [1972] Member; Bhargav Madhukar Trivedi [1982] Member; Walter Douglas Robinson Turner [1960] Member; Laurence Christopher Weeks [1969] Member; Sophia Olivia Wesley-Kay [1983] Member; Jeanette Deborah Wheeler [1970] Member; Nicholas Woo [1963] Member; Lisa Ann Wortley [1959] Member

Birmingham Resi Property LLP
Incorporated: 22 June 2016
Net Worth: £13,043,578 *Total Assets:* £13,043,578
Registered Office: Aprirose House, 48a High Street, Edgware, Middlesex, HA8 7EQ
Officers: Manish Mansukhlal Gudka [1970] Member; Gareth Jones [1973] Member; Suraj Rashmikant Shah [1982] LLP Member

Bishop's Hatfield Girls' School
Incorporated: 1 November 2011 *Employees:* 106
Net Worth: £21,781,796 *Total Assets:* £23,018,768
Registered Office: Bishop's Hatfield Girls' School, Woods Avenue, Hatfield, Herts, AL10 8NL
Activities: General secondary education
Officers: Deborah Louise Daniel, Secretary; Dr Osama Ahmed Aswania [1967] Director/Business Operations Manager; Caroline Jane Banwell [1965] Director/HR and Legal; Jane Hilary Bennett [1948] Director/Retired; Professor Adrian Boswood [1964] Director/Veterinary Surgeon; Dr Alison Bune [1970] Director/Teacher; Deborah Louise Daniel [1964] Director/School Business Manager; Jaimie Juliette Grossman [1989] Director/Teacher; Susan Elizabeth Jones [1952] Director/Retired Teacher; Ian Lennox [1955] Finance Director; Rupert Titus Beauchamp Lyons [1964] Director/Chief Executive; Theodora Nickson [1956] Director/Headteacher; Andrew David North [1974] Sales Director; Rosemary Ramsdale [1959] Director/Hotel Owner; Professor Peter Edward Richardson [1966] Director/University Professor; Juliana Balaceanu Stirbu [1976] Director [Romanian]; Saul Underwood [1970] Director/Caretaker; Alfred Wood [1967] Director/Co-Headteacher

BISL Limited
Incorporated: 30 July 1996
Net Worth: £183,900,000 *Total Assets:* £616,499,968
Registered Office: Pegasus House, Bakewell Road, Orton Southgate, Peterborough, Cambs, PE2 6YS
Activities: Other business support service activities n.e.c.
Parent: BGL Group Limited
Officers: Julian Charles Brown, Secretary; Matthew Oliver Donaldson [1973] Director; Duncan Alistair Finch [1965] Director/Chartered Accountant; Seamus Declan Keating [1963] Director [Irish]; Dominic James Platt [1969] Director/Chief Financial Officer; Peter Thompson [1970] Group Director

Bithia Limited
Incorporated: 24 February 2010
Net Worth: £7,577,203 *Total Assets:* £17,960,416
Registered Office: 100 Hills Road, Cambridge, CB2 1PH
Activities: Growing of cereals (except rice), leguminous crops and oil seeds
Officers: Michael John Aubrey, Secretary; Doctor Francesco Saverio Amman [1957] Director [Italian]; Simon Neil Fowler [1967] Director/Land Agent; Christoph Gruninger [1943] Director/Banker [German]

David Black & Son Limited
Incorporated: 17 March 1956 *Employees:* 15
Net Worth: £11,405,341 *Total Assets:* £14,313,516
Registered Office: Red House Farm, Bacton, Stowmarket, Suffolk, IP14 4SB
Activities: Mixed farming
Officers: Emma Louise Sheppard, Secretary; David Black [1932] Director; Ian David Black [1962] Director/Project Manager; James Thomas Black [1958] Director

W.E.Black Limited
Incorporated: 7 December 1946 *Employees:* 23
Net Worth: £208,373,440 *Total Assets:* £220,541,120
Registered Office: Hawridge Place, Hawridge Common, Hawridge, Chesham, Bucks, HP5 2ZD
Activities: Construction of domestic buildings
Major Shareholder: Eric John Spencer Gadsden
Officers: Judith Long, Secretary; Eric John Spencer Gadsden [1944] Director; Sarah Louise Gadsden [1985] Planning Director; Judith Elizabeth Long [1955] Finance Director; James Ian Lyons [1963] Construction Director

Black Swan International Limited
Incorporated: 18 June 1991 *Employees:* 544
Net Worth: £15,825,221 *Total Assets:* £40,257,028
Registered Office: Chiswick House, 3 Christchurch Road, Norwich, NR2 2AD
Activities: Residential care activities for the elderly and disabled
Officers: Brett William Burton, Secretary/Director; Brett William Burton [1966] Secretary/Director; Clive Robert Hill [1956] Director; Thomas Bruce Lyons [1980] Managing Director; Steve Winfield [1955] Director

Blackbuck Acquisitions Limited
Incorporated: 25 January 2017 *Employees:* 140
Net Worth: £87,903,896 *Total Assets:* £201,193,792
Registered Office: 1 Capability Green, Luton, Beds, LU1 3LU
Activities: Activities of production holding companies
Parent: Blackburn Midco Limited
Officers: Philip Giles Callow [1972] Director; Matthew Paul Plose [1973] Director

Blackbuck Midco Limited
Incorporated: 30 January 2017 *Employees:* 140
Net Worth: £87,897,872 *Total Assets:* £201,193,792
Registered Office: 1 Capability Green, Luton, Beds, LU1 3LU
Activities: Activities of production holding companies
Parent: Blackbuck Topco Limited
Officers: Philip Giles Callow [1972] Director; Matthew Paul Plose [1973] Director

Blackbuck Topco Limited
Incorporated: 30 January 2017 *Employees:* 140
Net Worth Deficit: £16,124,419 *Total Assets:* £192,817,216
Registered Office: 1 Capability Green, Luton, Beds, LU1 3LU
Activities: Activities of production holding companies
Officers: Philip Giles Callow [1972] Director; Matthew Paul Plose [1973] Director; Gehan Talwatte [1964] Director/Entrepreneur

Blackhawk Network (UK) Ltd.
Incorporated: 2 May 2006 *Employees:* 52
Net Worth: £2,974,000 *Total Assets:* £35,073,000
Registered Office: Westside, London Road, Hemel Hempstead, Herts, HP3 9TD
Activities: Other professional, scientific and technical activities n.e.c.
Parent: Blackhawk Network, Inc.
Officers: Michelle Josephine Wainhouse, Secretary; Patrick Philip Gurney [1970] Finance Director; Matthew David Howe [1971] Managing Director; Mabel Francis Wilson [1959] Director/Compliance Officer [Ghanaian]

Blackwater Partners Limited
Incorporated: 15 April 2013 *Employees:* 228
Net Worth: £3,910,983 *Total Assets:* £10,680,402
Registered Office: Seymour House, 140 Broomfield Road, Chelmsford, Essex, CM1 1RN
Activities: Dormant company
Shareholders: Julie Marie Player; John Kevin Player
Officers: Julie Marie Player, Secretary; John Kevin Player [1961] Director

Tom Blackwell (Contractors & Plant Hire) Limited
Incorporated: 18 November 1985 *Employees:* 36
Net Worth: £6,305,569 *Total Assets:* £9,244,759
Registered Office: Woodcot Place, White Ash Green, Halstead, Essex, CO9 1PB
Activities: Other specialised construction activities n.e.c.
Shareholders: Albert Ernest Blackwell; Anne Norwood Blackwell
Officers: Anne Norwood Blackwell, Secretary; Albert Ernest Blackwell [1941] Director/Businessman; Anne Norwood Blackwell [1948] Director/Bookkeeper

Blancco (Software) Services Limited
Incorporated: 5 March 2014
Previous: Blancco Technology Group Ltd
Net Worth: £11,350,195 *Total Assets:* £77,475,976
Registered Office: Unit 6b Vantage Park, Washingley Road, Huntingdon, Cambs, PE29 6SR
Activities: Activities of other holding companies n.e.c.
Parent: Blancco Technology Group PLC
Officers: Adam Paul Moloney [1969] Director

Blancco Technology Group PLC
Incorporated: 27 April 2004 *Employees:* 258
Previous: Regenersis PLC
Net Worth: £54,103,000 *Total Assets:* £83,201,000
Registered Office: Unit 6b Vantage Park, Washingley Road, Huntingdon, Cambs, PE29 6SR
Activities: Other telecommunications activities
Officers: Frank Blin [1954] Director; Matthew Craig Jones [1960] Director [American]; Adam Paul Moloney [1969] Director; Philip Graham Rogerson [1945] Director; Thomas Kevin Skelton [1960] Director/Chief Executive Officer [American]; Robert Stanley Lawrence Woodward [1959] Director/Chief Executive Officer

Blanco UK Limited
Incorporated: 24 December 1991 *Employees:* 64
Net Worth: £3,686,270 *Total Assets:* £8,799,211
Registered Office: 1 Victor Way, Radlett Road, Colney Street, St Albans, Herts, AL2 2FL
Activities: Wholesale of hardware, plumbing and heating equipment and supplies
Officers: Simon John Hart [1961] Managing Director; Stuart Jonathan Ridge [1958] Director - Chartered Certified Accountant

Blenheim Consultancy Services Limited
Incorporated: 28 March 2006 *Employees:* 4
Net Worth: £6,559,293 *Total Assets:* £9,469,599
Registered Office: 22 Barn Rise, Wembley, Middlesex, HA9 9NQ
Activities: Management of real estate on a fee or contract basis
Major Shareholder: Anthony David Chambers
Officers: Paul Gary Hirst, Secretary; Anthony David Chambers [1955] Director; Daniel Freedman [1971] Director/Lawyer; Paul Gary Hirst [1961] Director

Blenheim Estates Limited
Incorporated: 1 October 1997
Net Worth: £8,066,735 *Total Assets:* £15,362,492
Registered Office: 28 Church Road, Stanmore, Middlesex, HA7 4XR
Activities: Other letting and operating of own or leased real estate
Parent: Blenheim Property Management Ltd
Officers: Jacqueline Smith, Secretary; Dennis Isaac Warwick [1952] Director

Blenheim Property Management Limited
Incorporated: 1 October 1997
Net Worth: £16,120,106 *Total Assets:* £24,772,198
Registered Office: 28 Church Road, Stanmore, Middlesex, HA7 4XR
Activities: Other letting and operating of own or leased real estate
Shareholders: Alan Harold Warwick; Sheldon Andrew Cordell
Officers: Jacqueline Smith, Secretary; Dennis Isaac Warwick [1952] Director

Blessville Limited
Incorporated: 22 October 1996
Net Worth Deficit: £3,622,067 *Total Assets:* £42,040,620
Registered Office: Hill House, Lowlands Road, Harrow, Middlesex, HA1 3EQ
Activities: Development of building projects
Major Shareholder: Donovan Gijsbertus Wijsmuller
Officers: Brian Martin Comer [1960] Director [Irish]; Luke Andrew Comer [1957] Director [Irish]

Blitzfair Limited
Incorporated: 28 January 1985 *Employees:* 3
Net Worth: £13,044,592 *Total Assets:* £28,516,492
Registered Office: c/o Messrs Elliot Woolfe & Rose, 1st Floor, Equity House, 128-136 High Street, Edgware, Middlesex, HA8 7TT
Activities: Development of building projects
Major Shareholder: Geoffrey Harvey Toms
Officers: Benjamin George Harvey Toms, Secretary; Geoffrey Harvey Toms [1946] Director/Property Executive; Stephen Nathaniel Toms [1966] Director/Chartered Surveyor

Bloom Engineering Holdings Limited
Incorporated: 15 September 2015 *Employees:* 164
Previous: Sterling Bloom Holdings Limited
Net Worth: £6,547,853 *Total Assets:* £33,021,120
Registered Office: Kings Head House, 15 London End, Beaconsfield, Bucks, HP9 2HN
Activities: Activities of other holding companies n.e.c.
Parent: Caledonia Sterling Industries LLP
Officers: Kathryn Elizabeth Tackley, Secretary; Mark Daniel Blair [1963] Director/Chief Finance Officer [American]; David Walter Boyce [1977] Director/Chief Executive Officer [American]; Thomas William Leader [1964] Director

Blowplast Limited
Incorporated: 9 September 1988 *Employees:* 65
Net Worth: £8,060,413 *Total Assets:* £13,355,391
Registered Office: Unit 1 Sands Industrial Estate, Hillbottom Road, High Wycombe, Bucks, HP12 4HJ
Activities: Manufacture of other plastic products
Shareholders: Jaimini Rajendra Patel; Rajendra Kanubhai Patel
Officers: Jaimini Patel, Secretary; Rajendra Kanubhai Patel [1953] Director/Businessman

Blue 8 Technologies Limited
Incorporated: 29 December 2000
Net Worth: £13,217,752 *Total Assets:* £13,217,752
Registered Office: Peoplebuilding 2, Peoplebuilding Estate, Maylands Avenue, Hemel Hempstead Industrial Estate, Hemel Hempstead, Herts, HP2 4NW
Activities: Other information technology service activities
Parent: Northgate Public Services (UK) Limited
Officers: Stephen James Callaghan [1960] Director

Blue Anchor Leisure Holdings Limited
Incorporated: 6 December 2012 *Employees:* 201
Net Worth: £58,505,000 *Total Assets:* £85,864,000
Registered Office: Robin Hood Park, South Road, Chapel St Leonards, Skegness, Lincs, PE24 5TR
Activities: Buying and selling of own real estate
Officers: Peter Raymond Franciscus Holmes [1948] Director/Certified Accountant; Jonathan Scott Moses [1974] Director/Caravan Park Manager; Sally-Ann Woodward [1967] Director

Blue Anchor Leisure Limited
Incorporated: 22 January 1973 *Employees:* 201
Net Worth: £58,504,000 *Total Assets:* £85,860,000
Registered Office: Robin Hood Park, South Road, Chapel St Leonards, Skegness, Lincs, PE24 5TR
Activities: Recreational vehicle parks, trailer parks and camping grounds
Parent: Blue Anchor Leisure Holdings Limited
Officers: Peter Raymond Fransiscus Holmes [1948] Director/Certified Accountant; Jonathan Scott Moses [1974] Director/Caravan Park Manager; Sally-Ann Woodward [1967] Director

Blue Arrow Holdings Limited
Incorporated: 27 February 1991 *Employees:* 3
Net Worth: £41,130,000 *Total Assets:* £58,053,000
Registered Office: 800 The Boulevard, Capability Green, Luton, Beds, LU1 3BA
Activities: Activities of head offices
Parent: Impellam Holdings Limited
Officers: Rebecca Jane Watson, Secretary; Julia Robertson [1958] Director; Rebecca Jane Watson [1969] Director/Solicitor

Blue Arrow Ltd.
Incorporated: 10 November 1959 *Employees:* 655
Net Worth: £65,444,000 *Total Assets:* £199,786,000
Registered Office: 800 The Boulevard, Capability Green, Luton, Beds, LU1 3BA
Activities: Temporary employment agency activities
Parent: Blue Arrow Holdings Limited
Officers: Rebecca Jane Watson, Secretary; Julia Robertson [1958] Director; Rebecca Jane Watson [1969] Director/Solicitor

Blue Sea Overseas Investments Limited
Incorporated: 19 July 1994
Net Worth: £113,900,000 *Total Assets:* £1,090,800,000
Registered Office: Westpoint, Peterborough Business Park, Lynch Wood, Peterborough, Cambs, PE2 6FZ
Activities: Other business support service activities n.e.c.
Parent: Mytravel Group Limited
Officers: Shirley Bradley, Secretary; Alan Charles Donald [1963] Director

Blue Square Marketing Limited
Incorporated: 21 January 2009 *Employees:* 917
Net Worth: £14,007,220 *Total Assets:* £21,420,340
Registered Office: Tate House, Watermark Way, Hertford, SG13 7TZ
Activities: Advertising agencies
Major Shareholder: Neil Graham Avery
Officers: David Robert Piechulla, Secretary; Neil Graham Avery [1964] Director; David Robert Piechulla [1980] Finance Director; Parin Shah [1972] Operations Director

Blue Tree Limited
Incorporated: 19 July 2001 *Employees:* 10
Net Worth: £2,627,925 *Total Assets:* £19,974,350
Registered Office: Beech House, Melbourn Science Park, Melbourn, Herts, SG8 6HB
Activities: Wholesale of wine, beer, spirits and other alcoholic beverages
Shareholders: Victoria Katharine Fowkes Bolt; Benjamin James Bolt
Officers: Nigel Anthony Watson, Secretary; Benjamin James Bolt [1971] Director/Commercial Manager; Victoria Katharine Fowkes Bolt [1970] Director/Marketing

Bluecastle Enterprises Limited
Incorporated: 20 December 2000
Net Worth Deficit: £29,417,268 *Total Assets:* £267,046,032
Registered Office: Suite No 2, First Floor, Kenwood House, 77a Shenley Road, Borehamwood, Herts, WD6 1AG
Activities: Tax consultancy
Major Shareholder: Vadim Giner
Officers: Jennifer Elizabeth Westmoreland [1967] Director/Financial Controller

Bluegnome Limited
Incorporated: 15 October 2001 *Employees:* 62
Net Worth: £15,834,157 *Total Assets:* £17,538,988
Registered Office: 19 Granta Park, Great Abington, Cambridge, CB21 6DF
Activities: Research and experimental development on biotechnology
Officers: Charles Dadswell, Secretary; Paula Lynn Dowdy [1965] Director [American]; Andre Jacques Nel [1972] Finance Director [South African]

Bluestar Enterprise Limited
Incorporated: 27 September 2010
Net Worth: £1,260,832 *Total Assets:* £14,963,473
Registered Office: Unit 4 Imperial Park, Stonefield Way, South Ruislip, Middlesex, HA4 0JW
Activities: Wholesale of perfume and cosmetics
Major Shareholder: Manisha Thakrar
Officers: Nayan Thakrar [1960] Director

Bluestone APAC Holdings Limited
Incorporated: 30 October 2013
Previous: Bluestone Consolidated Holdings II (UK) Limited
Net Worth: £40,120,896 *Total Assets:* £40,121,288
Registered Office: 1 Station Square, Cambridge, CB1 2GA
Activities: Activities of financial services holding companies
Parent: Bluestone Consolidated Holdings Limited
Officers: Peter Timothy McGuinness [1969] Director; Andrew James Voss [1976] Director/Chief Financial Officer

Bluestone Consolidated Holdings Limited
Incorporated: 29 October 2013 *Employees:* 270
Net Worth: £42,197,604 *Total Assets:* £687,120,640
Registered Office: 1 Station Square, Cambridge, CB1 2GA
Activities: Activities of financial services holding companies
Major Shareholder: Henry Evan Rees
Officers: Alan Cameron [1960] Director/Banker [Australian]; Andrew John Cumming [1954] Director; Alistair James Jeffery [1966] Director/Businessman; Pardip Khroud [1981] Director/Chartered Accountant; Peter Timothy McGuinness [1969] Director

Bluestone Mortgage Finance No.2 Limited
Incorporated: 3 August 2015
Net Worth: £3,659,683 *Total Assets:* £21,830,904
Registered Office: 1 Station Square, Cambridge, CB1 2GA
Activities: Activities of mortgage finance companies
Parent: Bluestone Mortgages Limited
Officers: Peter Timothy McGuinness [1969] Director/Banker; Andrew James Voss [1976] Director/Chief Financial Officer

Bluestone Mortgage Holdings Limited
Incorporated: 6 August 2014
Previous: Bluestone Mortgages Investment Limited
Net Worth: £3,042,555 *Total Assets:* £10,485,629
Registered Office: 1 Station Square, Cambridge, CB1 2GA
Activities: Activities of financial services holding companies
Parent: Bluestone Consolidated Holdings Limited
Officers: Emily Bourke, Secretary; Alistair James Jeffery [1966] Director/Businessman; Peter Timothy McGuinness [1969] Director; Andrew James Voss [1976] Director/Chief Financial Officer

Blumarble Capital Limited
Incorporated: 12 November 2012 *Employees:* 2
Net Worth: £4,248,616 *Total Assets:* £8,825,088
Registered Office: First Floor, 39 High Street, Billericay, Essex, CM12 9BA
Activities: Financial intermediation not elsewhere classified
Shareholders: Stuart Peter Wilson; Michael Edward Henson
Officers: Michael Edward Henson [1974] Director; Stuart Peter Wilson [1974] Director

A D Bly Construction Limited
Incorporated: 21 January 2003 *Employees:* 252
Previous: A D Bly Holdings Limited
Net Worth: £5,098,966 *Total Assets:* £48,401,884
Registered Office: Unit 4d Nup End Business Centre, Old Knebworth, Herts, SG3 6QJ
Activities: Construction of other civil engineering projects n.e.c.
Officers: Antony David Bly, Secretary/Director; Antony David Bly [1962] Director; Paul Anthony Helliar [1970] Director; Stuart Anthony Hirst [1969] Director/Quantity Surveyor; Aaron Bruce William McSkimming [1969] Director; Robert John O'Connor [1955] Director; Michael Paul Pringle [1958] Director; Mark John Thompson [1961] Director

William Blythe Limited
Incorporated: 10 July 1991 *Employees:* 9
Net Worth: £18,870,000 *Total Assets:* £31,042,000
Registered Office: Synthomer Building, Temple Fields, Harlow, Essex, CM20 2BH
Activities: Manufacture of other inorganic basic chemicals
Parent: Synthomer Holdings Limited
Officers: Richard Atkinson, Secretary; Teresa Christina Pepper, Secretary/Accountant [Irish]; David Crossley [1980] Director; Pauline Hale [1965] Director; Kevin Charles Hudson [1964] Director; Teresa Christina Pepper [1957] Director [Irish]

BMS Limited
Incorporated: 16 October 1998 *Employees:* 3
Net Worth: £11,819,000 *Total Assets:* £21,526,000
Registered Office: 800 The Boulevard, Capability Green, Luton, Beds, LU1 3BA
Activities: Activities of head offices
Parent: Carlisle Group Limited
Officers: Rebecca Jane Watson, Secretary; Julia Robertson [1958] Director; Rebecca Jane Watson [1969] Director/Solicitor

Boing Acquisitions Limited
Incorporated: 9 June 2014
Net Worth: £63,425,000 *Total Assets:* £386,828,000
Registered Office: 35-37 Amersham Hill, High Wycombe, Bucks, HP13 6NU
Activities: Other retail sale in non-specialised stores
Parent: Boing Midco Limited
Officers: Jonathan Samuel Booth [1961] Director; Thomas Bruce Mangas [1967] Director/Chief Executive Officer [American]; Nilesh Kundanlal Pandya [1971] Director; Michael Andrew James Smith [1962] Director

Boing Midco Limited
Incorporated: 9 June 2014 *Employees:* 4
Net Worth: £116,122,000 *Total Assets:* £123,128,000
Registered Office: 35-37 Amersham Hill, High Wycombe, Bucks, HP13 6NU
Activities: Other retail sale in non-specialised stores
Parent: Boing Topco Limited
Officers: Jonathan Samuel Booth [1961] Director; Thomas Bruce Mangas [1967] Director/Chief Executive Officer [American]; Nilesh Kundanlal Pandya [1971] Director; Michael Andrew James Smith [1962] Director

Bold-Rock Management and Investments Ltd
Incorporated: 26 October 1987 *Employees:* 2
Net Worth: £2,510,200 *Total Assets:* £10,582,725
Registered Office: Ground Floor, Elizabeth House, 54-58 High Street, Edgware, Middlesex, HA8 7EJ
Activities: Other business support service activities n.e.c.
Major Shareholder: Corinne Lena Davin Evens
Officers: Alon Bar [1980] Director [Israeli]; Corinne Evens [1955] Director [Belgian]

Bondgrip Limited
Incorporated: 14 March 2013 *Employees:* 1
Net Worth: £10,013,523 *Total Assets:* £12,643,251
Registered Office: Cart Lodge, Bigods Lane, Church End, Great Dunmow, Essex, CM6 3BE
Activities: Mixed farming
Major Shareholder: Peter Dulvey Stonham
Officers: Helen Stonham, Secretary; Peter Dulvey Stonham [1963] Director/Civil Engineer

Bondmason Client Ltd
Incorporated: 3 October 2015 *Employees:* 2
Net Worth: £3 *Total Assets:* £11,454,215
Registered Office: 4 Kinsbourne Court, 96-100 Luton Road, Harpenden, Herts, AL5 3BL
Activities: Activities auxiliary to financial intermediation n.e.c.
Major Shareholder: Stephen William Findlay
Officers: Stephen William Findlay [1980] Director/Accountant

Boniface Engineering Limited
Incorporated: 23 October 1987 *Employees:* 55
Net Worth: £5,164,777 *Total Assets:* £11,854,880
Registered Office: Yare House, 62-64 Thorpe Road, Norwich, NR1 1RY
Activities: Manufacture of other transport equipment n.e.c.
Parent: Miller Industries Inc
Officers: Frank Madonia, Secretary; Jeffrey Iisley Badgley [1952] Director [American]; Michael John Boniface [1955] Managing Director

The Book Trade Charity (BTBS)
Incorporated: 15 October 2008 *Employees:* 6
Net Worth: £9,896,463 *Total Assets:* £9,978,932
Registered Office: The Foyle Centre, The Retreat, Kings Langley, Herts, WD4 8LT
Activities: Other service activities n.e.c.
Officers: David Hicks, Secretary; Elise Burns [1974] Sales Director; Isobel Margaret Dixon [1969] Director/Literary Agent [British/South African]; David Warwick Graham [1960] Managing Director; Kate Patricia McFarlan [1957] Director/Business Operations; David Edward Henry Neale [1943] Director/Retired; Jonathan Charles Peter Nowell [1958] Director; Peter Fraser Tanner [1952] Director; Emily-Jane Taylor [1980] Finance Director; Ann Veronica Woodhall [1951] HR/Facilities Director; Gemma Leigh Woodward [1972] Director/Investment Manager

Booking.Com Customer Service Center (UK) Limited
Incorporated: 3 May 2013 *Employees:* 1,208
Net Worth: £7,381,142 *Total Assets:* £13,223,796
Registered Office: Block 3 & 4 Westbrook Centre, Milton Road, Cambridge, CB4 1YG
Activities: Other business support service activities n.e.c.
Parent: Priceline.Com Bookings Acquisition Company Limited
Officers: Klaus Jurgen Dietrich Mollat [1964] Director of Finance Operations [German]; Alessandro Rotelli [1976] Customer Service Director EMEA [Italian]; James Robert Waters [1985] Global Director Customer Service

Booking.Com Limited
Incorporated: 18 February 1998 *Employees:* 170
Net Worth: £50,517,140 *Total Assets:* £59,021,036
Registered Office: Block 3, Westbrook Centre, Milton Road, Cambridge, CB4 1YG
Activities: Other business support service activities n.e.c.
Parent: Priceline.Com International Limited
Officers: Andrea D'Amico [1975] Director [Italian]; Klaus Jurgen Dietrich Mollat [1964] Director of Finance Operations [German]

Boortmalt UK Limited
Incorporated: 23 December 2009 *Employees:* 2
Net Worth: £11,615,220 *Total Assets:* £81,184,200
Registered Office: 24-25 Eastern Way, Bury St Edmunds, Suffolk, IP32 7AD
Activities: Activities of head offices
Officers: Yvan Schaepman [1974] Director [Belgian]; Charles Nicholas George Tozer [1971] Director

Boral (UK) Limited
Incorporated: 19 March 1971 *Employees:* 2
Net Worth: £51,861,000 *Total Assets:* £53,009,000
Registered Office: Wayside, Rushmere Lane, Orchard Leigh, Chesham, Bucks, HP5 3QY
Activities: Other specialised construction activities n.e.c.
Officers: Alice Sophie Stoker, Secretary; Graham Charles Froebel [1955] Director/Accountant [Australian]; Stephen John Morrison [1962] Managing Director

Borno Chemists Limited
Incorporated: 5 October 1972 *Employees:* 133
Net Worth: £5,927,696 *Total Assets:* £8,416,165
Registered Office: 124 Newland Street, Witham, Essex, CM8 1BA
Activities: Dispensing chemist in specialised stores
Major Shareholder: Emad Hashim Borno
Officers: Emad Hashim Borno [1941] Director/Pharmacist; Hamish Borno [1976] Director/Pharmacist

Borras Construction Ltd.
Incorporated: 2 October 1980 *Employees:* 123
Net Worth: £10,354,537 *Total Assets:* £22,216,240
Registered Office: 1 Salar House, Campfield Road, St Albans, Herts, AL1 5HT
Activities: Construction of commercial buildings
Parent: Borras Group Holdings Limited
Officers: Carol Ann Borras, Secretary; Carol Ann Borras [1953] Director/Secretary; Raymond Duncan Borras [1947] Director/Builder; Robert Broadfield [1968] Director/Surveyor; Michael George Howlett [1955] Director/Chartered Builder; Mark Lennard [1967] Director/Purchasing Manager; Paul Pickering [1970] Director/Surveyor

Borras Group Holdings Limited
Incorporated: 12 December 2013 *Employees:* 123
Previous: B.G.H Limited
Net Worth: £10,386,410 *Total Assets:* £22,079,048
Registered Office: 1 Salar House, Campfield Road, St Albans, Herts, AL1 5HT
Activities: Activities of construction holding companies
Shareholders: Rae Borras; Carol Ann Borras; The Borras Family Trust
Officers: Carol Ann Borras [1954] Director/Company Secretary; Raymond Duncan Borras [1947] Director

Bosch Lawn and Garden Limited
Incorporated: 28 June 1995 *Employees:* 327
Net Worth: £8,786,000 *Total Assets:* £42,236,000
Registered Office: Suffolk Works, Stowmarket, Suffolk, IP14 1EY
Activities: Manufacture of other electrical equipment
Parent: Bosch Power Tools Holding AG (Scintilla AG)
Officers: Stephen John Blackwell, Secretary; Dr Annette Vicky Becker [1971] Director/Senior Vice President Business Unit Home & Garden [German]; Stephen John Blackwell [1969] Director/Certified Chartered Accountant; Stuart Briscoe [1970] Managing Director

Bosch Rexroth Limited
Incorporated: 22 July 1963 *Employees:* 688
Net Worth: £44,213,000 *Total Assets:* £86,185,000
Registered Office: 15 Cromwell Road, St Neots, Cambs, PE19 2ES
Activities: Manufacture of other special-purpose machinery n.e.c.
Parent: Robert Bosch Holdings Limited
Officers: Jonathan Burton, Secretary; Paul Anthony Bowden [1963] Director; Dr Steffen Tobias Hoffmann [1965] Director [German]; Alastair John Johnstone [1959] Manufacturing Director; Karl Frederik Nilner [1972] Director [Swedish]

Boss Cabins Limited
Incorporated: 1 December 2009 *Employees:* 96
Net Worth: £6,408,367 *Total Assets:* £10,955,566
Registered Office: BCS House, Pinfold Road, Bourne, Lincs, PE10 9HT
Activities: Manufacture of trailers and semi-trailers
Major Shareholder: Judith Wordsworth
Officers: Timothy Mark McBain Allan, Secretary; Timothy Mark McBain Allan [1963] Director; Graham Ian Stansfield [1969] Director; Harold Duncan Wordsworth [1940] Director; Judith Wordsworth [1962] Director; Matthew Jason Wordsworth [1973] Director; Niall Duncan Wordsworth [1968] Director

Boston Limited
Incorporated: 8 December 1992 *Employees:* 154
Net Worth: £4,792,572 *Total Assets:* £26,768,804
Registered Office: 5 Theobald Court, Theobald Street, Elstree, Herts, WD6 4RN
Activities: Other information technology service activities
Officers: Ashok Uttamlal Chauhan, Secretary; Manojkumar Nayee [1963] Director/Computer Sales

The Boston Witham Academies Federation
Incorporated: 26 July 2012 *Employees:* 450
Net Worth: £26,633,000 *Total Assets:* £32,713,000
Registered Office: Marian Campus, Marian Road, Boston, Lincs, PE21 9HB
Activities: Pre-primary education
Officers: Daniel Mark Cowburn Elkington [1985] Director/Independent Financial Advisor; Tony Elmer [1939] Director/Retired Businessman; Jessica Gale [1950] Director/Retired; John Arthur McGarel [1945] Director; Christopher John Penney [1961] Director; Carole Shepheard [1947] Director/Retired Deputy Headteacher; Jodie Wrigglesworth [1988] Director/Lawyer

Alan Boswell Group Limited
Incorporated: 6 January 1989 *Employees:* 322
Net Worth: £11,869,734 *Total Assets:* £32,699,260
Registered Office: Harbour House, 126 Thorpe Road, Norwich, NR1 1UL
Activities: Activities of head offices
Major Shareholder: Alan Charles Boswell
Officers: Alan Charles Boswell [1948] Director/Insurance Broker; Christopher John Gibbs [1966] Director/Insurance Broker

Alan Boswell Insurance Brokers Limited
Incorporated: 13 March 1991 *Employees:* 172
Net Worth: £6,874,734 *Total Assets:* £18,327,354
Registered Office: Harbour House, 126 Thorpe Road, Norwich, NR1 1UL
Activities: Activities of insurance agents and brokers
Parent: Alan Boswell Group Ltd
Officers: Heath Douglas Alexander-Bew [1972] Director/Insurance Broker; Gillian Suzanne Anderson Brown [1962] HR Director; Alan Charles Boswell [1948] Director/Insurance Broker; Andrew James Dowler [1969] Director/Insurance Broker; Alastair Fitzroy Drew [1985] Director/Chartered Accountant; Christopher John Gibbs [1966] Director/Insurance Broker; Adrian Mark Rayner [1965] Director/Insurance Broker

Boulters Meadow Limited
Incorporated: 18 June 2012 *Employees:* 4
Net Worth: £7,193,356 *Total Assets:* £10,975,960
Registered Office: Sorbon, Aylesbury End, Beaconsfield, Bucks, HP9 1LW
Activities: Development of building projects
Parent: Sorbon Homes Limited
Officers: Nicholas Mark Trott, Secretary; Tamra Michelle Booth [1974] Director; Michael James Shanly [1945] Director; Nicholas Mark Trott [1964] Director/Accountant

Bounty (UK) Limited
Incorporated: 29 June 1959 *Employees:* 585
Net Worth: £52,685,000 *Total Assets:* £55,808,000
Registered Office: 29 Broadwater Road, Welwyn Garden City, Herts, AL7 3BQ
Activities: Other professional, scientific and technical activities n.e.c.
Parent: Romeo Bidco Limited
Officers: James Coleman Kelleher [1959] Director [Irish]; Richard Price [1963] Director

Bourn Bioscience Limited
Incorporated: 15 June 2005 *Employees:* 135
Net Worth: £5,716,294 *Total Assets:* £12,326,381
Registered Office: Bourn Hall, Bourn, Cambridge, CB23 2TN
Activities: Specialists medical practice activities
Major Shareholder: Michael Charles MacNamee
Officers: Simon Mark Barton, Secretary; Simon Mark Barton [1965] Finance Director; Dawn Course [1969] Director/Head of Core Services; Alan Michael Dexter [1942] Director; Danielle Patricia Garland [1986] Director/Investment Manager; Nicola Charlotte Graver [1962] HR Director; Dr Michael Charles MacNamee [1958] Director

Bourn Hall Limited
Incorporated: 19 March 1985 *Employees:* 135
Net Worth: £11,104,330 *Total Assets:* £21,058,040
Registered Office: Bourn Hall Clinic, Bourn, Cambridge, CB23 2TN
Activities: Specialists medical practice activities
Major Shareholder: Michael Charles MacNamee
Officers: Simon Mark Barton, Secretary; Simon Mark Barton [1965] Finance Director; Dawn Course [1969] Director/Head of Core Services; Nicola Charlotte Graver [1962] HR Director; Dr Michael Charles MacNamee [1958] Director/Chief Executive

C J Bourne (Asset Management) Limited
Incorporated: 23 December 1998 *Employees:* 426
Net Worth: £11,491,303 *Total Assets:* £23,396,024
Registered Office: Gardiner House, 6b Hemnall Street, Epping, Essex, CM16 4LW
Activities: Activities of head offices
Officers: Donald Hayes, Secretary; Lady Joy Hilary Bourne [1946] Director; Katie Luan Cohen [1970] Director; Merryl Hayley Flitterman [1967] Director; Lucy Sarah Furman [1972] Director; Donald Hayes [1934] Director/Chartered Secretary; Claire Rebecca Lefton [1980] Director

Bourne Court Properties Limited
Incorporated: 3 May 2017
Net Worth: £140,715 *Total Assets:* £13,832,547
Registered Office: 3rd Floor, Sterling House, Langston Road, Loughton, Essex, IG10 3TS
Activities: Development of building projects
Parent: Galliard Holdings
Officers: Allan William Porter, Secretary; David Edward Conway [1976] Director; Stephen Stuart Solomon Conway [1948] Director; Jonathan Michael Morgan [1978] Director; Donagh O'Sullivan [1968] Construction Director [Irish]

Bourne Grammar School
Incorporated: 16 November 2011 *Employees:* 128
Net Worth: £12,941,521 *Total Assets:* £15,707,177
Registered Office: Bourne Grammar School, South Road, Bourne, Lincs, PE10 9JE
Activities: General secondary education
Officers: Fiona Hill, Secretary; Chris Atkinson [1957] Director; James Allen Barker [1992] Director/Systems Administrator; Stuart Brett [1971] Director; Robert Brown [1947] Director; Joyce Burrows [1944] Director; Clinton Delport [1978] Director/Teacher; Stephen Dharamraj [1967] Director; Ian Michael Fytche [1964] Director/Chief Executive; Geoffrey Richard Greatwood [1948] Director; Claire Fiona Hawkins [1972] Director/Chartered Accountant; Jonathan Mark Kendrew [1973] Director; Jonathan Paul Maddox [1965] Director/Headteacher; Ian John George Mears [1955] Director; Christopher Moon [1974] Director; Stephen Nightingale [1957] Director/Turf Accountant; Robert James Parker [1964] Director; Suneetha Venkata Vijaya Durga Siddabattuni [1978] Director/Doctor; Lincoln Scott Taylor [1969] Director; Sue Woolley [1958] Director/Councillor

Bourne Holidays Limited
Incorporated: 12 October 1984 *Employees:* 2,573
Net Worth: £55,252,000 *Total Assets:* £181,990,000
Registered Office: No 1 Park Lane, Hemel Hempstead, Herts, HP2 4YL
Activities: Development of building projects
Parent: Bourne Leisure Limited
Officers: Jane Elizabeth Bentall [1970] Director/Accountant; Paul Charles Flaum [1970] Director; Iain Stuart Macmillan [1976] Director; Simon Thompson [1971] Director

Bourne Leisure (Hopton) Limited
Incorporated: 19 January 1973 *Employees:* 185
Net Worth: £8,971,000 *Total Assets:* £21,937,000
Registered Office: 1 Park Lane, Hemel Hempstead, Herts, HP2 4YL
Activities: Recreational vehicle parks, trailer parks and camping grounds
Parent: Bourne Leisure Group Limited
Officers: Jane Elizabeth Bentall [1970] Director/Accountant; Paul Charles Flaum [1970] Director; Iain Stuart Macmillan [1976] Director

Bourne Leisure Group Limited
Incorporated: 13 June 1969
Net Worth: £54,000 *Total Assets:* £25,413,000
Registered Office: 1 Park Lane, Hemel Hempstead, Herts, HP2 4YL
Activities: Recreational vehicle parks, trailer parks and camping grounds
Parent: Colaingrove Limited
Officers: Jane Elizabeth Bentall [1970] Director/Accountant; Paul Charles Flaum [1970] Director; Iain Stuart Macmillan [1976] Director

Bourne Leisure Holdings Limited
Incorporated: 9 June 2000 *Employees:* 13,721
Net Worth: £437,088,992 *Total Assets:* £1,465,027,968
Registered Office: No 1 Park Lane, Hemel Hempstead, Herts, HP2 4YL
Activities: Recreational vehicle parks, trailer parks and camping grounds
Officers: Colin David Russell Allen [1960] Director; Jane Elizabeth Bentall [1970] Director/Accountant; Richard John Cook [1972] Director; Geoffrey Ian Cooper [1954] Director; Roisin Jane Catherine Donnelly [1961] Director; Paul Charles Flaum [1970] Director; Paul Edward Woodstock Harris [1969] Director; Iain Stuart Macmillan [1976] Director; Simon Thompson [1971] Director

Bourne Leisure Limited
Incorporated: 9 June 2000 *Employees:* 3
Net Worth: £6,439,000 *Total Assets:* £606,860,032
Registered Office: No 1 Park Lane, Hemel Hempstead, Herts, HP2 4YL
Activities: Recreational vehicle parks, trailer parks and camping grounds
Parent: Foray 989 Limited
Officers: Jane Elizabeth Bentall [1970] Director/Accountant; Paul Charles Flaum [1970] Director; Iain Stuart Macmillan [1976] Director

Bouygues E & S Infrastructure UK Limited
Incorporated: 13 November 1961 *Employees:* 212
Net Worth: £1,614,000 *Total Assets:* £24,544,000
Registered Office: Belgrave House, Hatfield Business Park, Frobisher Way, Hatfield, Herts, AL10 9TQ
Activities: Other specialised construction activities n.e.c.
Parent: Bouygues Energies & Services SAS
Officers: Brian Clayton, Secretary; Paul Andrew Cadman [1962] Director; David John Carr [1969] Director; Timothy Nicholas Grier [1962] Director; Jean-Luc Luc Midena [1969] Director [French]; Keith Pedder [1965] Director; Fabienne Paula Viala [1962] Director [French]

Bow Village Limited
Incorporated: 17 April 2003
Net Worth: £15,514,571 *Total Assets:* £22,758,864
Registered Office: 1 Beauchamp Court, 10 Victors Way, Barnet, Herts, EN5 5TZ
Activities: Management of real estate on a fee or contract basis
Major Shareholder: Santokh Singh Chima
Officers: Mohinder Kaur Chima, Secretary; Santokh Singh Chima [1959] Director/Solicitor

Bowes Farms Limited
Incorporated: 10 July 2008 *Employees:* 13
Net Worth: £7,019,387 *Total Assets:* £9,339,275
Registered Office: Saham Hall Farm, Threxton Road, Saham Toney, Thetford, Norfolk, IP25 7AB
Activities: Raising of dairy cattle
Shareholders: Kevin Dudley Bowes; Jane Mary Bowes; Sally Heather Dowling; Mary Jane Bowes
Officers: Kevin Dudley Bowes [1944] Director

Bowler Group Limited
Incorporated: 8 December 1998 *Employees:* 17
Net Worth: £5,118,713 *Total Assets:* £8,217,296
Registered Office: Bowler House, Harvey Road, Basildon, Essex, SS13 1DD
Activities: Operation of warehousing and storage facilities for land transport activities
Major Shareholder: Jonathan Paul Bowler
Officers: Ian Cooke, Secretary; Jonathan Paul Bowler [1980] Director/Property Manager; Ian Cooke [1954] Director/Accountant; Ricardo Weatherall [1960] Director/Freight Forwarder

Bowlplex Limited
Incorporated: 22 March 1976 *Employees:* 150
Net Worth: £14,385,000 *Total Assets:* £14,385,000
Registered Office: Focus 31 West Wing, Cleveland Road, Hemel Hempstead Industrial Estate, Hemel Hempstead, Herts, HP2 7BW
Activities: Other sports activities
Parent: Kendallco Limited
Officers: Stephen Burns [1976] Managing Director; Laurence Brian Keen [1976] Finance Director

T F Bowman & Son Limited
Incorporated: 11 March 2016 *Employees:* 2
Net Worth: £1,049,258 *Total Assets:* £17,070,040
Registered Office: 1-4 London Road, Spalding, Lincs, PE11 2TA
Activities: Other service activities n.e.c.
Officers: Peter Andrew Bowman [1954] Director; Rita Bowman [1953] Director

Bowman Ingredients Limited
Incorporated: 3 May 1923 *Employees:* 183
Previous: Jas Bowman & Sons Limited
Net Worth: £30,392,000 *Total Assets:* £45,541,000
Registered Office: Ickleford Mill, Hitchin, Herts, SG5 3UN
Activities: Manufacture of other food products n.e.c.
Shareholders: Anthony Guy Bowman; Rory Peter Bowman
Officers: Lorraine Muller, Secretary; Tessa Patricia Bartlett [1977] Director; Anthony Guy Bowman [1946] Miller & Director; Rory Peter Bowman [1960] Director; Philippa Margaret Pelly [1949] Director/Medical Practice Manager

M.& R.Bowman Limited
Incorporated: 4 March 1963 *Employees:* 7
Net Worth: £8,027,363 *Total Assets:* £13,250,904
Registered Office: 1st Floor, Sheraton House, Lower Road, Chorleywood, Rickmansworth, Herts, WD3 5LH
Activities: Construction of commercial buildings
Major Shareholder: Raymond Valentine Mawhood
Officers: Lisa Jane Ashton-Jones, Secretary; Lisa Jane Ashton-Jones [1966] Director/Landlord & Property Developer; Philip Ashton-Jones [1964] Director/Barrister; Barbara Ann Mawhood [1943] Director; Raymond Valentine Mawhood [1942] Director

Boxford (Suffolk) Farms Limited
Incorporated: 23 February 1993 *Employees:* 124
Net Worth: £1,295,222 *Total Assets:* £14,516,884
Registered Office: The Stoke by Nayland Club, Keepers Lane, Leavenheath, Colchester, Essex, CO6 4PZ
Activities: Growing of pome fruits and stone fruits
Officers: Jonathan Loshak, Secretary; Robert Michael Alexander England [1965] Director/Farming; Jonathan Loshak [1944] Director; Carmella Jane Peake Meyer [1957] Director; Robert Rendall [1977] Director; Susanna Peake Rendall [1954] Director

Boxford (Suffolk) Holdings Limited
Incorporated: 29 March 1949 *Employees:* 24
Net Worth: £6,490,422 *Total Assets:* £19,320,700
Registered Office: The Stoke by Nayland Club, Keepers Lane, Leavenheath, Colchester, Essex, CO6 4PZ
Activities: Activities of head offices
Officers: Jonathan Loshak, Secretary; Iain Kenneth John Clarke [1969] Financial Director; Jonathan Loshak [1944] Director; Carmella Jane Peake Meyer [1957] Director/Special Projects Manager; Sir William Eric Peacock [1944] Director; Robert Peake Rendall [1977] Director; Susanna Peake Rendall [1954] Director; Tamara Clare Unwin [1956] Director

The Boxford Group Ltd.
Incorporated: 21 November 1997 *Employees:* 455
Net Worth: £13,426,447 *Total Assets:* £33,207,212
Registered Office: The Stoke by Nayland Club, Keepers Lane, Leavenheath, Colchester, Essex, CO6 4PZ
Activities: Activities of head offices
Officers: Jonathan Loshak, Secretary; Jonathan Loshak [1944] Director; Carmella Jane Peake Meyer [1957] Director/Special Projects Manager; Susanna Peake Rendall [1954] Managing Director; Tamara Clare Unwin [1956] Director

R.G. Boyce Limited
Incorporated: 13 December 1973 *Employees:* 3
Net Worth: £410,154 *Total Assets:* £12,081,909
Registered Office: Suite One, Beacon House, Kempson Way, Bury St Edmunds, Suffolk, IP32 7AR
Activities: Raising of poultry
Officers: Andrew Richard Boyce, Secretary/Director; Andrew Richard Boyce [1962] Director; Robert Generald Boyce [1937] Director

BP INV2 Holdco Ltd
Incorporated: 3 March 2016 *Employees:* 81
Net Worth: £19,613,000 *Total Assets:* £56,647,000
Registered Office: 1 Gateshead Close, Sunderland Road, Sandy, Beds, SG19 1RS
Activities: Other service activities n.e.c.
Shareholder: Buckthorn Partners LLP
Officers: Richard Andrew Hehir, Secretary; Christiaan Bennie Burger [1965] Director [South African]; Mark Ramin Chaichian [1977] Director; Nicholas Wilding Gee [1963] Director; Allan William Pirie [1973] Director

BP INV2 Pledgeco Ltd
Incorporated: 3 March 2016
Net Worth: £31,034,000 *Total Assets:* £31,034,000
Registered Office: 1 Gateshead Close, Sunderland Road, Sandy, Beds, SG19 1RS
Activities: Other service activities n.e.c.
Shareholders: BP INV2 Newco Ltd; FET Global Holdings Limited
Officers: Richard Andrew Hehir, Secretary; Mark Brookes [1975] Director [Irish]; Christiaan Bennie Burger [1965] Director [South African]; Mark Ramin Chaichian [1977] Director; Joseph Adam Connolly [1978] Director; Nicholas Wilding Gee [1963] Director; John Ivascu [1977] Director [American]; Mark Steven Traylor [1961] Director/Investor Relations and Finance [American]

BPC Interiors Limited
Incorporated: 24 July 2006 *Employees:* 14
Net Worth: £1,348,551 *Total Assets:* £9,986,314
Registered Office: 19-20 Bourne Court, Southend Road, Woodford Green, Essex, IG8 8HD
Activities: Other business support service activities n.e.c.
Parent: BPC Interiors Holdings Limited
Officers: Anne Knight, Secretary; Nicola Parmenter, Secretary; Paul John Johnson [1965] Director; Barry Knight [1960] Director/Chartered Surveyor

BPH Finance Number 1 Limited
Incorporated: 18 January 2005 *Employees:* 939
Net Worth: £192,563,008 *Total Assets:* £289,932,000
Registered Office: Queens Court, 9-17 Eastern Road, Romford, Essex, RM1 3NG
Activities: Activities of head offices
Parent: BPH Subholdco Limited
Officers: Jonathan Patrick Braidley [1965] Director/Investment Professional; Christopher Andre Kula [1983] Director/Chartered Accountant [German/Canadian]

BR Pharma International Limited
Incorporated: 1 July 1998 *Employees:* 36
Net Worth: £12,410,152 *Total Assets:* £15,056,712
Registered Office: Haslers, Old Station Road, Loughton, Essex, IG10 4PL
Activities: Wholesale of pharmaceutical goods
Shareholders: Joel Rabin; Rebecca Eleanor Blinston-Jones; Fabienne Rabin
Officers: Fabienne Rabin, Secretary; Sheryl Anne Glanvill [1970] Operations Director [New Zealander]; Joel Rabin [1974] Director; Christina White [1967] Finance Director

Bracco UK Limited
Incorporated: 10 October 2000 *Employees:* 19
Net Worth: £10,088,000 *Total Assets:* £12,741,000
Registered Office: Unit 15 Valley Business Centre, Gordon Road, High Wycombe, Bucks, HP13 6EQ
Activities: Wholesale of pharmaceutical goods
Shareholder: Diana Bracco
Officers: Sauro Orlandi, Secretary; Luca di Palma [1971] Director of Bracco UK Ltd [Italian]; Steven Kennedy [1955] Director; Frederic Tridon [1971] Director [French]

Jack Brand Limited
Incorporated: 9 June 1986 *Employees:* 89
Net Worth: £7,418,889 *Total Assets:* £10,809,012
Registered Office: Bridge House Buildings, Claydon, Ipswich, Suffolk, IP6 0HX
Activities: Production of meat and poultry meat products
Parent: Jack Brand Holdings Limited
Officers: Alison Jane Brand, Secretary; Paul Nicholas Adams [1964] Director; Alison Jane Brand [1975] Director; Graham John Charles Brand [1946] Director/Poultry Processing Packing

The Brand Machine Limited
Incorporated: 1 December 2011 *Employees:* 68
Net Worth: £1,882,424 *Total Assets:* £17,374,024
Registered Office: Unit 1 Windsor Industrial Estate, 424 Ware Road, Hertford, SG13 7EW
Activities: Wholesale of clothing and footwear
Officers: Jacqueline Anne Jalil, Secretary; Abu Talib Jalil [1965] Director; Jacqueline Anne Jalil [1963] Director

Brandbank Limited
Incorporated: 15 October 1998 *Employees:* 224
Net Worth: £3,200,570 *Total Assets:* £9,947,499
Registered Office: 35b Barnard Road, Norwich, NR5 9JB
Activities: Data processing, hosting and related activities
Parent: Nielsen Holdings PLC
Officers: Christopher Graham Head [1980] Director/Chartered Accountant; Peter Michael Nickituk [1967] Managing Director

Branded Stocks (UK) Ltd
Incorporated: 1 November 1993 *Employees:* 5
Net Worth: £6,406,972 *Total Assets:* £11,563,443
Registered Office: Unit 9 Hemmells, Laindon, Basildon, Essex, SS15 6GF
Activities: Agents involved in the sale of textiles, clothing, fur, footwear and leather goods
Major Shareholder: John Henry Sharp
Officers: John Henry Sharp [1955] Director

Brandon House Limited
Incorporated: 9 February 2017
Net Worth Deficit: £27,305 *Total Assets:* £8,344,554
Registered Office: 104 College Road, Harrow, Middlesex, HA1 1BQ
Activities: Letting and operating of conference and exhibition centres
Officers: Kishorkant Bhattessa [1941] Director/Hotelier; Jitendrakumar Maganbhai Patel [1952] Director; Vinodrai Harmanbhai Patel [1938] Director/Retired; Yogesh Patel [1956] Director; Dr Mayank Ramanlal Shah [1958] Director/Doctor

Arthur Branwell & Co. Limited
Incorporated: 3 February 1904 *Employees:* 45
Net Worth: £5,603,860 *Total Assets:* £13,522,801
Registered Office: Bronte House, 58-62 High Street, Epping, Essex, CM16 4AE
Activities: Other business support service activities n.e.c.
Shareholder: Christopher James Bolton
Officers: Nigel Day, Secretary; Christopher James Bolton [1947] Director; Colin Lindsay Cooper [1957] Director; William Henry Denyer [1949] Director; Richard James Kenny [1961] Director; William James Kenny [1931] Director

R. Bratley (Quadring) Limited
Incorporated: 5 February 1962 *Employees:* 28
Net Worth: £4,568,046 *Total Assets:* £12,471,111
Registered Office: Quadring Eaudyke, Spalding, Lincs, PE11 4QB
Activities: Growing of cereals (except rice), leguminous crops and oil seeds
Shareholders: Carolyn Margaret Bratley; John Morris Bratley; Charlotte Emily Bratley
Officers: Carolyn Margaret Bratley, Secretary; Carolyn Margaret Bratley [1946] Director/Housewife; Charlotte Emily Bratley [1974] Director; John Morris Bratley [1943] Director/Farmer; Joseph Oliver Bratley [1973] Director/Farmer

Brayford Hotels Holdings Ltd
Incorporated: 7 April 2010 *Employees:* 139
Net Worth: £7,653,155 *Total Assets:* £49,497,020
Registered Office: 27-29 Lumley Avenue, Skegness, Lincs, PE25 2AT
Activities: Activities of head offices
Shareholders: Leigh Morris Hall; Dean Anthony Wann
Officers: Leigh Morris Hall, Secretary; Leigh Morris Hall [1969] Director; Dean Anthony Wann [1971] Director

Brayleys Cars Limited
Incorporated: 8 January 2003 *Employees:* 230
Net Worth: £5,862,981 *Total Assets:* £18,639,416
Registered Office: Lyon Way, Hatfield Road, St Albans, Herts, AL4 0QU
Activities: Sale of new cars and light motor vehicles
Parent: AWR Holdings UK Limited
Officers: Richard Geoffrey Lipscombe, Secretary; Paul Stuart Brayley [1962] Director

F. Brazil Reinforcements Limited
Incorporated: 7 June 2007 *Employees:* 92
Net Worth: £6,122,049 *Total Assets:* £23,249,700
Registered Office: Romainville Way, Charfleets Industrial Estate, Canvey Island, Essex, SS8 0RB
Activities: Manufacture of other fabricated metal products n.e.c.
Major Shareholder: Francis Brazil
Officers: John FitzGenerald, Secretary; Francis Joseph Brazil [1962] Director [Irish]; John FitzGenerald [1978] Director [Irish]

BRE Global Limited
Incorporated: 26 March 2014 *Employees:* 292
Net Worth: £8,788,000 *Total Assets:* £14,007,000
Registered Office: Bucknalls Lane, Garston, Watford, Herts, WD25 9XX
Activities: Technical testing and analysis
Parent: BRE Group Ltd
Officers: Anthony Richard Tanner, Secretary; Nicholas Brian Farrimond [1965] Director/Chief Finance Officer; Dr Deborah Anita Smith [1960] Director/Scientist

BRE Trust
Incorporated: 22 November 1996 *Employees:* 638
Net Worth Deficit: £17,176,000 *Total Assets:* £43,026,000
Registered Office: Bucknalls Lane, Garston, Watford, Herts, WD25 9XX
Activities: Other research and experimental development on natural sciences and engineering
Officers: Anthony Richard Tanner, Secretary; June Mary Barnes [1954] Non-Executive Director of Urban and Civic PLC; Julia Bernadette Barrett [1966] Director of Sustainability; Francesca Anne Howard Berriman [1964] Director/Chief Executive; Professor Nicholas Robert Jennings [1966] Director/Academic; Peter William MacDonald Lobban [1947] Director/Chief Executive; James Garwood Michael Wates [1960] Director; Philip George Wilbraham [1960] Expansion Programme Director; Gary Wingrove [1960] Projects and Construction Director

Breheny Civil Engineering Limited
Incorporated: 19 March 1963 *Employees:* 483
Previous: J.Breheny Contractors Limited
Net Worth: £12,643,955 *Total Assets:* £39,666,392
Registered Office: Flordon Road, Creeting St Mary, Needham Market, Ipswich, Suffolk, IP6 8NH
Activities: Other construction installation
Shareholders: John Nicholas Edward Breheny; Heather Jewell (formerly Aldous); Sandra Marie Jones Dec'd
Officers: Shums Aziz, Secretary; Betty Irene Breheny [1929] Director; John Nicholas Edward Breheny [1964] Director/Chairman; Trevor Alan Stiff [1962] Director/Civil Engineer

Breheny Group Limited
Incorporated: 4 January 2002 *Employees:* 501
Net Worth: £17,758,764 *Total Assets:* £48,970,960
Registered Office: Flordon Road, Creeting St Mary, Ipswich, Suffolk, IP6 8NH
Activities: Other specialised construction activities n.e.c.
Shareholders: John Nicholas Edward Breheny; Heather Jewell Formerly Aldous; Sandra Marie Jones Dec'd
Officers: Shums Aziz, Secretary; Betty Irene Breheny [1929] Director; John Nicholas Edward Breheny [1964] Director/Chairman

Brent Housing Ltd
Incorporated: 20 November 2001
Net Worth: £10,209,922 *Total Assets:* £16,469,177
Registered Office: c/o Dattani Chartered Accountants, Scottish Provident House, 76-80 College Road, Harrow, Middlesex, HA1 1BQ
Activities: Other letting and operating of own or leased real estate
Officers: Brendan Michael Monaghan [1951] Director/Builder [Irish]

Brentwood Academies Trust
Incorporated: 18 May 2011 *Employees:* 384
Net Worth: £37,194,168 *Total Assets:* £44,454,524
Registered Office: St Martin's School Brentwood, Hanging Hill Lane, Hutton, Brentwood, Essex, CM13 2HG
Activities: General secondary education
Officers: Ann Pessell, Secretary; John Duffy [1960] Director/Engineer; William Haynes [1989] Director/Founder, Miru 3D; Christopher Paul Hearn [1965] Director/Accountant; Christopher Robert Holme [1978] Director/Solicitor; Anthony Dominic McGarel [1975] Director/Deputy Principal & Chief Executive South Essex College; Michael John O'Sullivan [1966] Director/Headteacher; Stuart Palmer [1963] Director/Retired; Anita Astrid Pratten [1965] Director/Business Manager; Kanta Wild-Smith [1948] Director/Retired Local Government Officer

Peter Brett Associates LLP
Incorporated: 28 January 2008 *Employees:* 640
Net Worth: £15,772,019 *Total Assets:* £32,766,530
Registered Office: Buckingham Court, Kingsmead Business Park, London Road, High Wycombe, Bucks, HP11 1JU

Breyer Group Public Limited Company
Incorporated: 2 December 1963 *Employees:* 300
Net Worth: £6,235,903 *Total Assets:* £29,019,344
Registered Office: Faringdon Avenue, Harold Hill, Romford, Essex, RM3 8ST
Activities: Construction of domestic buildings
Parent: Breyer Holdings Limited
Officers: Hilda May Breyer, Secretary; Timothy Breyer [1961] Director; Anne Sarah Dyer [1962] HR Director; Neil Ian Fisher [1963] Finance Director; Warren Michael Sean Hand [1966] Director/Quantity Surveyor; John Andrew Patrick Walsh [1962] Construction Director

Breyer Holdings Limited
Incorporated: 29 July 2008 *Employees:* 300
Net Worth: £7,044,296 *Total Assets:* £29,830,864
Registered Office: Faringdon Avenue, Harold Hill, Romford, Essex, RM3 8ST
Activities: Activities of construction holding companies
Major Shareholder: Timothy Breyer
Officers: Timothy Breyer [1961] Director; Neil Ian Fisher [1963] Finance Director; Warren Michael Sean Hand [1966] Director

Brianco Services Limited
Incorporated: 23 November 1943 *Employees:* 4
Net Worth: £8,706,179 *Total Assets:* £10,631,070
Registered Office: Newmans House, Queens Road, Barnet, Herts, EN5 4DL
Activities: Other letting and operating of own or leased real estate
Parent: Nufrend Limited
Officers: Derek Robert Newman [1984] Director; Janice Newman [1986] Director; Martha Newman [1952] Director

Brick Projects (Marland) Limited
Incorporated: 21 July 2014
Net Worth: £1,638,174 *Total Assets:* £11,541,019
Registered Office: Kimberley House, 31 Burnt Oak Broadway, Edgware, Middlesex, HA8 5LD
Activities: Other letting and operating of own or leased real estate
Parent: St Katherine Investment Group Limited
Officers: Sunil Premchand Hemraj Shah [1960] Director/Chartered Accountant; Terence John Williams [1947] Director

The Brickfields Trust
Incorporated: 23 December 2016 *Employees:* 97
Net Worth: £9,811,212 *Total Assets:* £10,916,899
Registered Office: Great Wakering Primary School, High Street, Great Wakering, Southend on Sea, Essex, SS3 0EJ
Activities: Other education n.e.c.
Officers: Joanne Lyn Dabbs [1968] Director/School Finance Officer; Andrew Dennis Knight [1978] Director/Head of Commissioning; Marianne Louise Norman [1967] Director/Education Officer; Hayley O'Dea [1972] Director/Headteacher; Daniel Smith [1989] Director/Senior Bank Manager; Anna Eileen Stokes [1974] Director/Receptionist

Bricks St Property Group Ltd
Incorporated: 21 November 2012
Previous: Fowe Developments Limited
Net Worth: £3,870,147 *Total Assets:* £10,520,352
Registered Office: Second Floor, Kestrel House, Falconry Court, Bakers Lane, Epping, Essex, CM16 5BD
Activities: Other business support service activities n.e.c.
Shareholders: Raymond Peter Wells; Keriane Wells
Officers: Scott McArthur [1978] Director; Stephen Charles Reid [1958] Director; Keriane Wells [1963] Director; Raymond Peter Wells [1958] Director; Anthony John Wood [1958] Director

Bridge Academy Trust
Incorporated: 9 June 2011 *Employees:* 239
Previous: Moulsham High School
Net Worth: £22,907,748 *Total Assets:* £27,009,968
Registered Office: Moulsham High School, Brian Close, Chelmsford, Essex, CM2 9ES
Activities: General secondary education
Officers: Lisa Doreen Willams, Secretary; Damian Paul Barrett [1971] Director/Company Secretary; Stephen George Bennett [1948] Director/Chartered Secretary; Dr Trevor Bolton [1958] Director/Pro Vice Chancellor (Partnerships); Nicola Helen Dunn [1967] Director/HM Inspector of Health & Safety; Mark Farmer [1972] Director/Teacher; Paul John Kitson [1971] Development Director/Civil Servant; Keith John Mogford [1957] Development Director; Stuart Andrew Moore [1968] Director; Brian Robert Payne [1950] Director/Retired; Karen Dawn Salmons [1965] Director/Business Manager

Bridge Road Southall Limited
Incorporated: 7 February 2017
Net Worth Deficit: £542,148 *Total Assets:* £61,180,600
Registered Office: 3rd Floor, Sterling House, Langston Road, Loughton, Essex, IG10 3TS
Activities: Development of building projects
Parent: Galliard Developments Limited
Officers: Allan William Porter, Secretary; John Cole [1971] Director; Stephen Stuart Solomon Conway [1948] Director; Jonathan Simon Goldstein [1966] Director; Rory Anthony O'Connor [1959] Director [Irish]; Donagh O'Sullivan [1968] Construction Director [Irish]

Brighthouse Group Limited
Incorporated: 16 May 2007 *Employees:* 2,526
Previous: Brighthouse Group PLC
Net Worth: £71,324,000 *Total Assets:* £233,292,000
Registered Office: 5 Hercules Way, Leavesden, Watford, Herts, WD25 7GS
Activities: Retail sale of audio and video equipment in specialised stores
Officers: David John Harwood, Secretary; Graeme James Campbell [1972] Finance Director; Hamish Stewart Paton [1976] Director

Brighthouse Holdings Limited
Incorporated: 17 May 2007
Net Worth: £196,879,008 *Total Assets:* £254,842,000
Registered Office: 5 Hercules Way, Leavesden, Watford, Herts, WD25 7GS
Activities: Retail sale of audio and video equipment in specialised stores
Parent: Brighthouse Group PLC
Officers: David John Harwood, Secretary; Graeme James Campbell [1972] Finance Director; Hamish Stewart Paton [1976] Director

Brighthouse Limited
Incorporated: 30 January 2007 *Employees:* 2,526
Net Worth: £222,264,000 *Total Assets:* £383,449,984
Registered Office: 5 Hercules Way, Leavesden, Watford, Herts, WD25 7GS
Activities: Retail sale of electrical household appliances in specialised stores
Parent: Brighthouse Holdings Ltd
Officers: David John Harwood, Secretary; Graeme James Campbell [1972] Finance Director; Hamish Stewart Paton [1976] Director

Brington North LLP
Incorporated: 29 January 2016
Net Worth: £7,570,768 *Total Assets:* £18,038,368
Registered Office: James Hall, Parsons Green, St Ives, Cambs, PE27 4AA

Bristol Fruit Sales (Market) Limited
Incorporated: 30 June 1971 *Employees:* 339
Net Worth: £6,155,000 *Total Assets:* £14,458,000
Registered Office: Total Produce, Enterprise Way, Pinchbeck, Spalding, Lincs, PE11 3YR
Activities: Wholesale of fruit and vegetables
Parent: Total Produce Limited
Officers: Mark Christopher Owen, Secretary; Andrew Roger Allmond [1944] Director; Jacinta Frances Devine [1972] Director [Irish]; Nicholas George Matthews [1970] Managing Director; Francis Gerard McKernan [1962] Director; Mark Christopher Owen [1965] Director; Denis Leslie Punter [1953] Director

Bristol Laboratories Limited
Incorporated: 27 June 1997 *Employees:* 335
Net Worth: £44,480,316 *Total Assets:* £69,361,760
Registered Office: Unit 3 Canalside, North Bridge Road, Berkhamsted, Herts, HP4 1EG
Activities: Wholesale of pharmaceutical goods
Parent: Bristol Laboratories Group Limited
Officers: Sreekumar Nair Kodupurath, Secretary; Sanjay Shrikishan Pashine [1975] Director; Raju Puthenvilayil Mathaikutty [1956] Director; Priti Ramachandran [1982] Director; Thembalath Ramachandran [1949] Director

Britannia Soft Drinks Limited
Incorporated: 5 March 1896
Net Worth: £163,152,000 *Total Assets:* £950,691,968
Registered Office: Breakspear Park, Breakspear Way, Hemel Hempstead, Herts, HP2 4TZ
Activities: Manufacture of soft drinks; production of mineral waters and other bottled waters
Parent: Britvic PLC
Officers: Judith Moore, Secretary; Mathew James Dunn [1974] Director/Chief Financial Officer; Peter Simon Litherland [1964] Director/Chief Executive; Alexandra Clare Thomas [1974] Director/General Counsel and Company Secretary

British Board of Agrement
Incorporated: 2 May 1966 *Employees:* 153
Net Worth Deficit: £944,000 *Total Assets:* £9,198,000
Registered Office: Bucknalls Lane, Garston, Watford, Herts, WD25 9BA
Activities: Other professional, scientific and technical activities n.e.c.
Officers: Claire Curtis-Thomas [1958] Director/Chief Executive; Richard Vincent Gunning [1953] Director; Neil Roberts Hannah [1955] Director; Valerie Ellen Le Vaillant [1957] Director; Professor Robert John Lowe [1955] Director/Professor of Energy & Building Science; Brian Desmond Patrick Moore [1959] Operations Director; Helen Rachael Wylde [1968] Director

British Gaskets Limited
Incorporated: 25 March 1947 *Employees:* 102
Net Worth: £6,153,594 *Total Assets:* £10,719,914
Registered Office: BG Group Office, 7 Brundon Lane, Sudbury, Suffolk, CO10 1XR
Activities: Manufacture of other plastic products
Shareholders: Roy David Jones; 4 BG Group Limited
Officers: Joanne White, Secretary; Roy David Jones [1957] Director/Manager; Yuko Jones [1962] Director [Japanese]; Gregory Edward Mazurkewicz [1957] Operations Director [American]; Andrew Thurlbourn [1961] Director

British Limbless Ex-Service Men's Association
Incorporated: 6 November 2000 *Employees:* 34
Net Worth: £33,258,056 *Total Assets:* £34,064,508
Registered Office: Frankland Moore House, 185-187 High Road, Chadwell Heath, Romford, Essex, RM6 6NA
Activities: Activities of other membership organisations n.e.c.
Officers: Barry John Le Grys, Secretary; Miles Courtenay Ambler [1960] Director/Financial Consultant; Adrian John Bradshaw [1958] Director/Army Officer; William Lloyd Dixon [1984] Director/Banker; Alison Laura Grant [1968] Director/Retired; Anthony John Harris [1981] Director/Leadership and Development Consultant; Rebecca Charlotte Maciejewska [1967] Director/Trust Secretary; Philip David Monkhouse [1968] Director/Factory Operative; Andrew Kenneth Mudd [1956] Director/Retired; Mark Nicholas Pillans [1971] Director/Communications Consultant; Colin Rouse [1957] Director/Retired; Robert John Watts [1952] Director/Retired

British Pipeline Agency Limited
Incorporated: 30 September 1975 *Employees:* 141
Net Worth: £1,290,850 *Total Assets:* £21,511,444
Registered Office: 5-7 Alexandra Road, Hemel Hempstead, Herts, HP2 5BS
Activities: Transport via pipeline
Shareholders: BP Oil UK Limited; Shell U.K. Limited
Officers: Julian Coyne, Secretary; Stephen Brown [1969] Director/Oil Company Executive; Peter Malcolm Davis [1961] Director/General Manager; Paul Jerzy Dubenski [1963] Director/Oil Company Executive; Neil Emmett [1970] Director/Oil Company Executive; Emmanuelle Tucci [1983] Director/Oil Company Executive [French]

Britten-Pears Foundation (The)
Incorporated: 5 November 1986 *Employees:* 16
Net Worth: £25,623,634 *Total Assets:* £26,352,872
Registered Office: The Red House, Golf Lane, Aldeburgh, Suffolk, IP15 5PZ
Activities: Archives activities
Officers: Keith Arthur Nicholls, Secretary; Caroline Brazier [1958] Director/Librarian; Sir Vernon James Ellis [1947] Director/Company Chairman; Sarah Mary Faulder [1957] Director/Chief Executive; Jane Scott Hay [1960] International Managing Director; Penelope Chloe Heath [1955] Director/Art Conservator; Professor Christopher Francis Higgins [1955] Director/Retired; Sir Christopher Kingston Howes [1942] Director and Adviser; Angela Marie Christine Mallinson [1960] Director/Music Agent; Colin Herbert Matthews [1946] Director/Composer; Oliver Max Rivers [1966] Finance Director; Janis Elizabeth Susskind [1952] Music Publishing Director [American/British]

Britvic Asset Company No.2 Limited
Incorporated: 23 August 2011
Net Worth: £467,000 *Total Assets:* £9,535,000
Registered Office: Breakspear Park, Breakspear Way, Hemel Hempstead, Herts, HP2 4TZ
Activities: Manufacture of soft drinks; production of mineral waters and other bottled waters
Parent: Britannia Soft Drinks Limited
Officers: Judith Moore, Secretary; Mathew James Dunn [1974] Director/Chief Financial Officer; Peter Simon Litherland [1964] Director/Chief Executive; Alexandra Clare Thomas [1974] Director/General Counsel and Company Secretary

Britvic Brands LLP
Incorporated: 27 October 2011
Net Worth: £183,176,000 *Total Assets:* £184,016,000
Registered Office: Breakspear Park, Breakspear Way, Hemel Hempstead, Herts, HP2 4TZ
Officers: Mathew James Dunn [1974] LLP Member; Alexandra Clare Thomas [1974] LLP Member

Britvic EMEA Limited
Incorporated: 13 October 1986 *Employees:* 42
Net Worth Deficit: £52,337,000 *Total Assets:* £20,076,000
Registered Office: Breakspear Park, Breakspear Way, Hemel Hempstead, Herts, HP2 4TZ
Activities: Manufacture of soft drinks; production of mineral waters and other bottled waters
Parent: Britannia Soft Drinks Limited
Officers: Judith Moore, Secretary; Christophe Garcia [1975] Director [French]; Hessel Douwe de Jong [1969] International Managing Director [Dutch]; Stephen Andrew Smith [1972] Director

Britvic Finance Partnership LLP
Incorporated: 22 February 2011
Net Worth: £66,307,000 *Total Assets:* £66,350,000
Registered Office: Breakspear Park, Breakspear Way, Hemel Hempstead, Herts, HP2 4TZ

Britvic International Investments Limited
Incorporated: 13 October 1986
Net Worth: £169,670,000 *Total Assets:* £170,228,000
Registered Office: Breakspear Park, Breakspear Way, Hemel Hempstead, Herts, HP2 4TZ
Activities: Manufacture of soft drinks; production of mineral waters and other bottled waters
Parent: Britannia Soft Drinks Limited
Officers: Judith Moore, Secretary; Mathew James Dunn [1974] Director/Chief Financial Officer; Peter Simon Litherland [1964] Director/Chief Executive; Alexandra Clare Thomas [1974] Director/General Counsel and Company Secretary

Britvic Overseas Limited
Incorporated: 17 August 2010
Net Worth: £74,459,000 *Total Assets:* £336,556,992
Registered Office: Breakspear Park, Breakspear Way, Hemel Hempstead, Herts, HP2 4TZ
Activities: Manufacture of soft drinks; production of mineral waters and other bottled waters
Parent: Britannia Soft Drinks Limited
Officers: Judith Moore, Secretary; Mathew James Dunn [1974] Director/Chief Financial Officer; Peter Simon Litherland [1964] Director/Chief Executive; Alexandra Clare Thomas [1974] Director/General Counsel and Company Secretary

Britvic PLC
Incorporated: 27 October 2005 *Employees:* 4,781
Net Worth: £377,300,000 *Total Assets:* £1,664,099,968
Registered Office: Breakspear Park, Breakspear Way, Hemel Hempstead, Herts, HP2 4TZ
Activities: Manufacture of soft drinks; production of mineral waters and other bottled waters
Officers: Jonathan Mark Adelman, Secretary; Suniti Kiransinh Chauhan [1974] Director/Finance [American]; Susan Michelle Clark [1964] Director; John Patrick Daly [1956] Director [Irish]; Mathew James Dunn [1974] Director/Chief Financial Officer; Christopher William Eccleshare [1955] Director; Peter Simon Litherland [1964] Director/Chief Executive; Ian Philip McHoul [1960] Director/Chief Financial Officer; Euan Angus Sutherland [1969] Director

Britvic Soft Drinks Limited
Incorporated: 16 March 1953 *Employees:* 1,903
Net Worth: £768,606,016 *Total Assets:* £1,437,943,040
Registered Office: Breakspear Park, Breakspear Way, Hemel Hempstead, Herts, HP2 4TZ
Activities: Manufacture of soft drinks; production of mineral waters and other bottled waters
Parent: Britannia Soft Drinks Limited
Officers: Alexandra Clare Thomas, Secretary; Matthew Robert Barwell [1966] Strategic Marketing & Innovation Director; Mathew James Dunn [1974] Director/Chief Financial Officer; Richard Paul Graham [1968] Director/General Manager; Clive Alastair Hooper [1964] Director; Peter Simon Litherland [1964] Director/Chief Executive

Broadfields Academy Trust
Incorporated: 6 August 2013 *Employees:* 148
Net Worth: £9,898,000 *Total Assets:* £11,617,000
Registered Office: Broadfields Primary School, Roseberry Drive, Edgware, Middlesex, HA8 8JP
Activities: Primary education
Officers: Robin Archibald [1964] Director/Headteacher; Manoj Parmar [1970] Director/Regional Finance Manager; Kajal Shah [1973] Director

Broadgate Builders (Spalding) Limited
Incorporated: 2 February 1976 *Employees:* 80
Net Worth: £15,572,112 *Total Assets:* £29,816,798
Registered Office: Broadgate House, Broadgate, Weston Hills, Spalding, Lincs, PE12 6DB
Activities: Construction of domestic buildings
Major Shareholder: The Estate of the late David Deas Bissett-Clarke
Officers: Susan Jane Foreman, Secretary; Ian John Canham [1965] Director/Accountant

Broadgate Homes Limited
Incorporated: 3 January 1995 *Employees:* 57
Net Worth: £16,108,030 *Total Assets:* £24,337,748
Registered Office: Broadgate House, Broadgate, Weston Hills, Spalding, Lincs, PE12 6DB
Activities: Development of building projects
Shareholder: The Estate of the late David Deas Bissett-Clarke
Officers: Susan Jane Foreman, Secretary; Ian John Canham [1965] Director/Accountant

Broadham Care Limited
Incorporated: 3 May 2005 *Employees:* 112
Net Worth: £5,170,000 *Total Assets:* £9,789,000
Registered Office: c/o Elysium Healthcare, 2 Imperial Place, Maxwell Road, Borehamwood, Herts, WD6 1JN
Activities: Residential care activities for the elderly and disabled
Parent: Elysium Healthcare Holdings 3 Limited
Officers: Sarah Juliette Livingston, Secretary; Lesley Joy Chamberlain [1963] Director/Group Chief Executive; Dr Quazi Shams Mahfooz Haque [1968] Executive Medical Director; Steven John Woolgar [1955] Director of Policy and Regulation

Broadland Wineries Limited
Incorporated: 15 September 1965 *Employees:* 135
Net Worth: £7,524,194 *Total Assets:* £24,202,070
Registered Office: Chapel Street, Cawston, Norwich, NR10 4BG
Activities: Manufacture of wine from grape
Parent: Arrhenius Holdings Ltd
Officers: Robert Bell [1979] Director/Chartered Accountant; Hew Richard Hamilton Dalrymple BT [1955] Director; Jonathon Mark Lansley [1962] Director/Chairman

Broadleaf Park LLP
Incorporated: 10 July 2017
Net Worth: £8,029,000 *Total Assets:* £21,410,000
Registered Office: Gate House, Turnpike Road, High Wycombe, Bucks, HP12 3NR

Broadrich Limited
Incorporated: 13 April 2012 *Employees:* 3
Net Worth: £4,147,333 *Total Assets:* £8,500,139
Registered Office: Northside House, Mount Pleasant, Barnet, Herts, EN4 9EE
Activities: Other letting and operating of own or leased real estate
Parent: Mountcharm Group Limited
Officers: Jason Robert Cooper, Secretary; Adam Cooper [1971] Director; Jason Robert Cooper [1947] Director; Melvyn Frank Cooper [1941] Director

Broadway Travel Service (Wimbledon) Limited
Incorporated: 22 August 1949 *Employees:* 170
Net Worth: £3,930,320 *Total Assets:* £27,996,404
Registered Office: 5th Floor, Jansel House, Hitchin Road, Luton, Beds, LU2 7XH
Activities: Travel agency activities
Officers: Hussein Gulamali Rajan, Secretary; Claire Loscombe [1976] Finance Director; Jill Louise Mitchell [1971] Finance Director; Adam Trevor Pardini [1969] Director/Travel Agent; Hasnen Gulamali Rajan [1949] Director/Accountant; Mustapha Gulamali Rajan [1947] Director/Technician; Lynn Smith [1973] HR Director; Philip Turner [1981] Product Director; Steve Tyler [1983] Director/Travel Agent

Brogan Group Holdings Ltd
Incorporated: 19 November 2015 *Employees:* 445
Net Worth: £26,378,320 *Total Assets:* £40,528,576
Registered Office: 4 Falcon Gate, Falcon Way, Shire Park, Welwyn Garden City, Herts, AL7 1TW
Activities: Activities of head offices
Major Shareholder: James Christopher Brogan
Officers: James Christopher Brogan [1957] Director; Giles Williamson [1969] Director

Brogan Group Ltd
Incorporated: 7 March 2006 *Employees:* 160
Net Worth: £7,970,709 *Total Assets:* £19,099,396
Registered Office: 4 Falcon Gate, Falcon Way, Shire Park, Welwyn Garden City, Herts, AL7 1TW
Activities: Construction of commercial buildings
Parent: Brogan Group Holdings Ltd
Officers: Giles Williamson, Secretary; James Christopher Brogan [1957] Director; Wayne Karl Smith [1981] Director; Giles Williamson [1969] Director

Brook Street (UK) Limited
Incorporated: 6 October 1948 *Employees:* 533
Net Worth: £42,909,000 *Total Assets:* £84,448,000
Registered Office: 34 George Street, Luton, Beds, LU1 2AZ
Activities: Temporary employment agency activities
Parent: Brook Street Bureau PLC
Officers: Damian Paul Whitham, Secretary; Mark Joseph Donnelly [1968] Finance Director; John Karl Kinderman [1961] Director; Leigh Emma Passingham [1972] Director; Damian Paul Whitham [1967] Director

Thomas Brooker & Sons Limited
Incorporated: 25 February 1909 *Employees:* 70
Net Worth: £8,940,132 *Total Assets:* £10,343,006
Registered Office: Unit 7 Bilton Road, Cadwell Lane, Hitchin, Herts, SG4 0SB
Activities: Retail sale of hardware, paints and glass in specialised stores
Officers: Thomas Andrew Brooker, Secretary; David John Brooker [1938] Director; Douglas William Brooker [1962] Marketing Director; Thomas Andrew Brooker [1961] Managing Director; Thomas Paul Brooker [1935] Director

Brookgate Limited
Incorporated: 27 October 2009 *Employees:* 10
Net Worth: £57,050,884 *Total Assets:* £137,155,808
Registered Office: Two Station Place, Cambridge, CB1 2FP
Activities: Other business support service activities n.e.c.
Officers: Jonathan Christian Wooles, Secretary; Roderick Carnan [1956] Director; Colin Rutherford [1959] Director; Sven Jurgen Topel [1966] Director; Jonathan Christian Wooles [1963] Director

Brookgate Property Limited
Incorporated: 10 December 1999
Previous: Brookgate CB1 Limited
Net Worth: £40,011,024 *Total Assets:* £49,366,316
Registered Office: Two Station Place, Cambridge, CB1 2FP
Activities: Buying and selling of own real estate
Parent: Brookgate Limited
Officers: Jonathan Christian Wooles, Secretary; Sven Jurgen Topel [1966] Director; Jonathan Christian Wooles [1963] Director/Chartered Accountant

Brooklands Helix Developments Limited
Incorporated: 14 July 2015 *Employees:* 5
Net Worth Deficit: £8,697 *Total Assets:* £14,530,922
Registered Office: Decimal Place, Chiltern Avenue, Amersham, Bucks, HP6 5FG
Activities: Buying and selling of own real estate
Parent: Inland Homes 2013
Officers: Nishith Malde [1958] Director; Gary John Skinner [1968] Managing Director; Stephen Desmond Wicks [1951] Director

Brooks Bros. (UK) Limited
Incorporated: 17 June 1982 *Employees:* 306
Net Worth: £19,044,854 *Total Assets:* £40,082,352
Registered Office: Blackwater Place, Blackwater Trading Estate, The Causeway, Maldon, Essex, CM9 4GG
Activities: Agents involved in the sale of timber and building materials
Major Shareholder: George Albert Sherriff
Officers: Richard William Dawkes, Secretary; Mark Fleming [1965] Director; Simon John Shaw Greig [1971] Director; Matthew John Hall [1979] Director; Darren Patrick McCarthy [1979] Director; George Albert Sheriff [1937] Director/Timber Merchant; Mark Sheriff [1961] Director/Timber Merchant

Brooks Events Limited
Incorporated: 29 August 2012 *Employees:* 117
Net Worth: £24,404,952 *Total Assets:* £40,874,968
Registered Office: Romeland House, Romeland Hill, St Albans, Herts, AL3 4ET
Activities: Activities of exhibition and fair organisers
Officers: Sally Ann Brooks [1962] Director; Stephen Charles Brooks [1962] Director/Exhibition Organiser

Brookstream Properties Limited
Incorporated: 14 July 1995
Net Worth: £15,940,611 *Total Assets:* £45,009,612
Registered Office: Hill House, Lowlands Road, Harrow, Middlesex, HA1 3EQ
Activities: Development of building projects
Shareholders: Luke Andrew Comer; Brian Martin Comer
Officers: Brian Martin Comer [1960] Director [Irish]; Luke Andrew Comer [1957] Director [Irish]

Peter Brotherhood Limited
Incorporated: 27 July 2015 *Employees:* 160
Net Worth: £1,253,424 *Total Assets:* £11,896,619
Registered Office: 1 Kimpton Road, Luton, Beds, LU1 3LD
Activities: Manufacture of engines and turbines, except aircraft, vehicle and cycle engines
Parent: Hayward Tyler Group PLC
Officers: Stephen Michael King [1966] Director; Stephen McQuillan [1961] Director

Michael Broughton Limited
Incorporated: 30 April 1973 *Employees:* 128
Net Worth: £24,280,818 *Total Assets:* £28,890,798
Registered Office: 16 The Havens, Ransomes Europark, Ipswich, Suffolk, IP3 9SJ
Activities: Development of building projects
Major Shareholder: Michael Edward Broughton
Officers: Carol Joan Broughton, Secretary/Director; Carol Joan Broughton [1943] Director; Matthew Edward Broughton [1968] Director/Projects Manager; Michael Arthur Broughton [1967] Director/Plant Hire Manager; Michael Edward Broughton [1944] Director

Brown & Carroll (London) Limited
Incorporated: 6 January 1994 *Employees:* 139
Net Worth: £10,718,735 *Total Assets:* £18,904,998
Registered Office: The Brown & Carroll Works, Honywood Road, Basildon, Essex, SS14 3DT
Activities: Joinery installation
Shareholders: Paul James Carroll; Stephen Brown
Officers: Stephen Dennis Brown, Secretary; Stephen Dennis Brown [1959] Director; Paul James Carroll [1962] Director; Gordon John Emm [1966] Operations Director; Stephen Pierce Perkins [1969] Commercial Director

Brown Brothers Distribution Limited
Incorporated: 19 July 1979 *Employees:* 190
Net Worth: £16,791,728 *Total Assets:* £24,996,752
Registered Office: P O Box 162, Needham Road, Stowmarket, Suffolk, IP14 2ZR
Activities: Manufacture of paints, varnishes and similar coatings, mastics and sealants
Parent: PPG Industries (UK) Limited
Officers: David Heal [1976] Regional Protective Coatings Director - Western Europe; Ruth Stewart [1976] Finance Director; Jennifer Victoria Summers [1979] Finance Director

N W Brown Group Limited
Incorporated: 27 January 2000 *Employees:* 73
Net Worth: £14,128,410 *Total Assets:* £16,890,068
Registered Office: Richmond House, 16-20 Regent Street, Cambridge, CB2 1DB
Activities: Other business support service activities n.e.c.
Shareholders: Marcus Walter Johnson; Margaret Ann Johnson; Kirly Limited
Officers: Michael James Tolond, Secretary; Charlotte Grundy [1984] Director/Chartered Accountant; Richard Mark Jeffries [1957] Director/Solicitor; Marcus Walter Johnson [1951] Director; Colin David Robert Manktelow [1965] Director/Investment Manager; Kathryn Jane Miller [1972] Director; Oliver William Phillips [1977] Director/Investment Manager; Lynda Jane Turner [1955] Director/Financial Adviser

George Brown's Implements (Holdings) Limited
Incorporated: 26 January 1968 *Employees:* 157
Net Worth: £14,584,578 *Total Assets:* £19,625,980
Registered Office: Grovebury Road, Leighton Buzzard, Beds, LU7 4UX
Activities: Activities of head offices
Officers: Andrew Peter Brown, Secretary; Andrew Peter Brown [1954] Parts Director; Christopher Bernard William Brown [1953] Director/Agricultural Engineer; Richard William Gray Brown [1959] Director/Farm Manager

J.Browne Construction Company Limited
Incorporated: 21 January 1971 *Employees:* 176
Net Worth: £10,557,858 *Total Assets:* £18,558,708
Registered Office: Meelin House, Unit 2 Pavilion Business Centre, 6 Kinetic Crescent, Enfield, Middlesex, EN3 7FJ
Activities: Construction of water projects
Parent: J. Browne Group Holdings Limited
Officers: Norah Carmel Browne, Secretary; Jeremy Browne [1971] Director [Irish]; Jonathan Mark Dodd [1973] Director; Paul Denis McMahon [1966] Managing Director

Brownlow Enterprises Limited
Incorporated: 27 November 1996 *Employees:* 129
Net Worth: £14,629,377 *Total Assets:* £19,872,860
Registered Office: Salisbury House, 81 High Street, Potters Bar, Herts, EN6 5AS
Activities: Residential care activities for the elderly and disabled
Shareholders: William Heneghan; Margaret Heneghan
Officers: Damien Heneghan [1975] Director [Irish]; David Heneghan [1979] Director [Irish]; Liam James Heneghan [1975] Director; Margaret Heneghan [1945] Director/Nurse [Irish]; William Heneghan [1945] Director [Irish]

George Browns Limited
Incorporated: 24 May 1938 *Employees:* 129
Net Worth: £11,046,314 *Total Assets:* £16,497,736
Registered Office: Grovebury Road, Leighton Buzzard, Beds, LU7 4UX
Activities: Agents involved in the sale of machinery, industrial equipment, ships and aircraft
Parent: George Brown's Implements (Holdings) Limited
Officers: Christopher Bernard William Brown, Secretary; Andrew Peter Brown [1954] Parts Director; Christopher Bernard William Brown [1953] Director/Agricultural Engineer; Richard William Gray Brown [1959] Director/Farm Manager; Peter Martin Doe [1956] Director/Accountant; Peter Stephen Hopkinson [1955] Director/Salesman; Stephen Lee [1966] Director/Salesman

BRT (Wisbech) Limited
Incorporated: 8 July 2011 *Employees:* 141
Net Worth: £4,180,425 *Total Assets:* £14,590,516
Registered Office: 21-24 Regal Road, Wisbech, Cambs, PE13 2RQ
Activities: Non-specialised wholesale trade
Shareholders: Phillip David Clarke; Simon David Clarke
Officers: Grahame Allen [1966] Director; Anthony George Clarke [1946] Director; Phillip David Clarke [1970] Director; Simon David Clarke [1973] Director; Lindsey Jane Lowery [1961] Director

Bruel & Kjaer VTS Limited
Incorporated: 15 January 1981 *Employees:* 94
Net Worth: £25,556,000 *Total Assets:* £28,370,000
Registered Office: Jarman Way, Royston, Herts, SG8 5BQ
Activities: Manufacture of other special-purpose machinery n.e.c.
Parent: Spectris Group Holdings Limited
Officers: Susan Janet Street, Secretary; Bjarne Grolsted Kristensen [1967] Finance Director [Danish]; John Nicholl Sawford [1959] Director/General Manager; Joseph Michael Vorih [1967] Director [American]

Bryant Park Hospitality UK Limited
Incorporated: 13 November 1985
Net Worth: £17,027,000 *Total Assets:* £105,830,000
Registered Office: Queens Court, 9-17 Eastern Road, Romford, Essex, RM1 3NG
Activities: Hotels and similar accommodation
Parent: BPH Finance Number 1 Limited
Officers: Jonathan Patrick Braidley [1965] Director/Investment Professional; Christopher Andre Kula [1983] Director/Chartered Accountant [German/Canadian]

BS Project Services Limited
Incorporated: 28 March 1980 *Employees:* 85
Net Worth: £14,931,000 *Total Assets:* £14,931,000
Registered Office: 34 George Street, Luton, Beds, LU1 2AZ
Activities: Temporary employment agency activities
Parent: Brook Street Bureau PLC
Officers: Damian Paul Whitham, Secretary; Mark Joseph Donnelly [1968] Finance Director; John Karl Kinderman [1961] Director; Damian Paul Whitham [1967] Director

Roberto Bucci (U.K.) Limited
Incorporated: 22 March 1982 *Employees:* 13
Net Worth: £9,721,387 *Total Assets:* £12,934,021
Registered Office: 1 Town Quay Wharf, Abbey Road, Barking, Essex, IG11 7BZ
Activities: Other transportation support activities
Officers: Gebhard Boito [1944] Director [Italian]; Roberto Bucci [1936] Director [Italian]; Davide Gnerre [1994] Director [Italian]

Bucci Freight Services Limited
Incorporated: 27 November 1995 *Employees:* 10
Net Worth: £8,069,141 *Total Assets:* £10,526,289
Registered Office: 1 Town Quay Wharf, Abbey Road, Barking, Essex, IG11 7BZ
Activities: Other service activities incidental to land transportation, n.e.c.
Officers: Gebhard Boito [1944] Director [Italian]; Roberto Bucci [1936] Director [Italian]; Davide Gnerre [1994] Director [Italian]

Buckingham Hotels Group Limited
Incorporated: 12 January 2004 *Employees:* 24
Net Worth: £5,177,685 *Total Assets:* £10,440,906
Registered Office: 156 West Wycombe Road, High Wycombe, Bucks, HP12 3AE
Activities: Hotels and similar accommodation
Officers: Frieda Dad, Secretary; Shafqat Dad [1969] Director

Buckinghamshire UTC.
Incorporated: 26 May 2011 *Employees:* 30
Net Worth: £8,511,000 *Total Assets:* £8,898,000
Registered Office: Bucks UTC, Oxford Road, Aylesbury, Bucks, HP21 8PB
Activities: Technical and vocational secondary education
Officers: Robert William Carvey, Secretary; Michael Charles Appleyard [1942] Director/Councillor; Russell Brittain [1969] HR Director; Timothy Coole [1957] Director/Academic; Baljit Dhillon [1950] Director/Business Consultant; John McGrath [1971] Business Director; Karen Elizabeth Mitchell [1963] Director/Vice Principal; Fiona Morag Morey [1964] Director/Senior Academic; Matthew James Richards [1987] Director/IT Manager; Alan Neale Sherwell [1950] Director/Retired; Eric Sisi [1962] Director/Vice President [Canadian]; Sarah Valentine [1973] Director/School Principal

Bucknalls Developments Limited
Incorporated: 23 December 2015
Net Worth Deficit: £116,170 *Total Assets:* £8,327,124
Registered Office: Decimal Place, Chiltern Avenue, Amersham, Bucks, HP6 5FG
Activities: Development of building projects
Shareholder: Inland Ltd
Officers: Shaun Lyne [1957] Director/Retired; Nishith Malde [1958] Finance Director; Timothy Francis O'Sullivan [1963] Director [Irish]; Desmond Richard Wicks [1989] Director/Senior Land Manager

Bucks Developments Limited
Incorporated: 20 September 2013 *Employees:* 2
Net Worth Deficit: £191,385 *Total Assets:* £36,256,732
Registered Office: Decimal Place, Chiltern Avenue, Amersham, Bucks, HP6 5FG
Activities: Development of building projects
Parent: Inland Homes PLC
Officers: Nishith Malde, Secretary; Nishith Malde [1958] Director; Gary John Skinner [1968] Managing Director; Stephen Desmond Wicks [1951] Director

Bucyrus Europe Limited
Incorporated: 30 April 1985
Net Worth: £9,256,000 *Total Assets:* £11,444,000
Registered Office: Legal Services, Frank Perkins Way, Eastfield, Peterborough, Cambs, PE1 5FQ
Activities: Engineering design activities for industrial process and production
Parent: Bucyrus Europe Holdings Limited
Officers: Johanna Elizabeth Deason, Secretary; Nigel John Burroughs [1964] Director/Tax Accountant; Martin Daldrup [1964] Director [German]

Bucyrus UK Limited
Incorporated: 24 October 1994 *Employees:* 3
Net Worth: £19,802,000 *Total Assets:* £19,857,000
Registered Office: Legal Services, Frank Perkins Way, Eastfield, Peterborough, Cambs, PE1 5FQ
Activities: Engineering design activities for industrial process and production
Parent: Caterpillar Global Mining Europe GmbH
Officers: Johanna Elizabeth Deason, Secretary; Nigel John Burroughs [1964] Director/Tax Accountant; Martin Daldrup [1964] Managing Director [German]

Buffaload Logistics Limited
Incorporated: 3 March 2005 *Employees:* 218
Net Worth: £1,371,268 *Total Assets:* £15,337,059
Registered Office: Grove Parc, Grove Lane, Ellington, Huntingdon, Cambs, PE28 0AA
Activities: Non-specialised wholesale trade
Shareholders: Ranjit Singh Boparan; Bajinder Kaur Boparan; Ross John Taylor; Invest 1 Co Limited
Officers: Julie Feltwell, Secretary; Graham Mark Edwards [1970] Director; Julie Ann Feltwell [1968] Director/Transport Manager; Ian David Perks [1968] Business Development Director; Edward Samuel Power [1946] Director/Chairman [Irish]

Bugler Developments Limited
Incorporated: 30 July 1981 *Employees:* 66
Net Worth: £10,335,437 *Total Assets:* £30,251,396
Registered Office: Bugler House, 25 High Street, Rickmansworth, Herts, WD3 1ET
Activities: Development of building projects
Parent: Bugler Group Limited
Officers: Andrew Philip Hawkins, Secretary; Andrew Thomas Bugler [1968] Director/Solicitor; Denis Patrick Bugler [1961] Director/Builder; Kieran Thomas Bugler [1963] Director; Jeremy Graham [1969] Construction Director; Steven James Tough [1973] Surveying Director

Bugler Group Limited
Incorporated: 22 March 2001 *Employees:* 66
Previous: Bugler Holdings Limited
Net Worth: £11,384,305 *Total Assets:* £31,377,884
Registered Office: Bugler House, 25 High Street, Rickmansworth, Herts, WD3 1ET
Activities: Development of building projects
Shareholders: Andrew Thomas Bugler; Denis Patrick Bugler; Kieran Thomas Bugler
Officers: Andrew Philip Hawkins, Secretary; Andrew Thomas Bugler [1968] Director/Solicitor; Denis Patrick Bugler [1961] Director/Builder; Kieran Thomas Bugler [1963] Director/Builder; Steven James Tough [1973] Commercial Director

Building Research Establishment Limited
Incorporated: 17 February 1997 *Employees:* 339
Net Worth Deficit: £29,692,000 *Total Assets:* £35,017,000
Registered Office: Bucknalls Lane, Garston, Watford, Herts, WD25 9XX
Activities: Other research and experimental development on natural sciences and engineering
Parent: BRE Group Ltd
Officers: Anthony Richard Tanner, Secretary; Nicholas Brian Farrimond [1965] Director/Chief Finance Officer; Niall Gerard Trafford [1962] Director/Chief Operating Officer

Buildvantage Limited
Incorporated: 1 May 2012
Net Worth: £1,103,756 *Total Assets:* £10,928,216
Registered Office: Orion House, 104-106 Cranbrook Road, Ilford, Essex, IG1 4LZ
Activities: Development of building projects
Officers: Ravi Kumar [1966] Director

Bullen Developments Limited
Incorporated: 25 March 1971 *Employees:* 10
Net Worth: £8,101,838 *Total Assets:* £24,113,224
Registered Office: The Lowlands, Costessey Lane, Drayton, Norwich, NR8 6HA
Activities: Other building completion and finishing
Parent: RG Carter Group Limited
Officers: Jonathan Martin Gibbins, Secretary; Robert George Russell Carter [1953] Director; Anna Maria Dugdale [1966] Director; Nigel Charles Handley Howorth [1967] Director/Chartered Surveyor; Ginny Alice Seaman [1987] Director

Bullen Properties Limited
Incorporated: 15 August 2006 *Employees:* 5
Previous: Bullen Investments Limited
Net Worth: £50,852,492 *Total Assets:* £62,331,304
Registered Office: The Lowlands, Drayton, Norwich, NR8 6HA
Activities: Buying and selling of own real estate
Shareholders: Robert George Russell Carter; Robert George Russell Carter
Officers: Generald William Victor Daniels, Secretary; Robert George Russell Carter [1953] Director/Builder; Nigel Charles Handley Howorth [1967] Director/Chartered Surveyor; David Richard White [1952] Director

A.E.Bullock Limited
Incorporated: 6 June 1966 *Employees:* 2
Net Worth: £11,135,086 *Total Assets:* £11,813,649
Registered Office: 29 Mill Lane, Welwyn, Herts, AL6 9EU
Activities: Development of building projects
Shareholders: Derek Brian Bullock; Patricia Ann Bullock; Richard Norman Taylor
Officers: Patricia Ann Bullock, Secretary; Christopher Brian Bullock [1971] Director/Building Contractor; Derek Brian Bullock [1929] Director/Master Builder; Patricia Ann Bullock [1944] Director/Secretary

Bungay High School
Incorporated: 8 July 2011 *Employees:* 108
Net Worth: £14,966,865 *Total Assets:* £15,957,542
Registered Office: Queens Road, Bungay, Suffolk, NR35 1RW
Activities: General secondary education
Officers: Lynda Jacqueline Eldrett, Secretary; Roger Allens [1944] Director/Solicitor; Nathan Brunsden [1980] Director/Teacher; Jayne Capps-Jenner [1957] Director/Personal Assistant; Maureen Davies [1934] Director/Retired; Andrea Dunford [1967] Director/Teacher; Angelo Goduti [1977] Director/Headteacher; Christine Johnson [1957] Director/Retired; Sylvia Knights [1948] Director/Retired; Simon Linger [1959] Director/IT Systems Architect; Stella MacKenzie [1956] Director/Semi-Retired Teacher; Ian Newton [1960] Director/Teacher; Michael James Osborn [1948] Director/Charity Worker; Anne Rickwood [1951] Director/Retired Headteacher; Linda Scott [1953] Director/Retired; Zoe Buchanan Sprake [1953] Director; Aidan Taylor [1968] Business Development Director

Bunting Magnetics Europe Limited
Incorporated: 3 February 1964 *Employees:* 43
Net Worth: £1,968,000 *Total Assets:* £8,396,000
Registered Office: Northbridge Road, Berkhamsted, Herts, HP4 1EH
Activities: Manufacture of other fabricated metal products n.e.c.
Parent: Bunting Magnetics Co
Officers: Sarah Gilling, Secretary; Simon Adrian Ayling [1970] Managing Director; Robert John Bunting [1949] Director [American]; Sarah Gilling [1970] Director/Accountant

The Burdens Group Limited
Incorporated: 31 August 1982 *Employees:* 57
Net Worth: £2,068,387 *Total Assets:* £9,713,896
Registered Office: Spalding Road, Sutterton, Boston, Lincs, PE20 2ET
Activities: Agents involved in the sale of machinery, industrial equipment, ships and aircraft
Parent: Agriturf Limited
Officers: John Southern, Secretary; Kevin Richard Bell [1970] Sales Director; John Southern [1961] Finance Director; Shaun Richard Taylor [1964] Group Sales Director; John William Wates [1957] Director

John Burgess & Co. Limited
Incorporated: 22 September 1948 *Employees:* 14
Net Worth: £7,411,887 *Total Assets:* £9,058,938
Registered Office: Burgess Building, Wratten Road East, Hitchin, Herts, SG5 2AP
Activities: Construction of commercial buildings
Officers: Anne Elizabeth Burgess, Secretary; Anne Elizabeth Burgess [1954] Director/Secretary; Christopher John Burgess [1950] Director/Builder; David John Christopher Burgess [1977] Director

Russell Burgess Limited
Incorporated: 17 November 1955 *Employees:* 613
Net Worth: £2,715,000 *Total Assets:* £43,137,000
Registered Office: Stanley's Farm, Great Drove, Yaxley, Peterborough, PE7 3TW
Activities: Activities of other holding companies n.e.c.
Shareholder: David William Ashley Burgess
Officers: David William Ashley Burgess, Secretary; Henry Zaccheus Brown [1957] Director; Andrew Stanley Burgess [1965] Director; David William Ashley Burgess [1968] Director; David Stanley Lambert Burgess [1939] Director; Jason Charles Burgess [1966] Director

Burgess Properties Limited
Incorporated: 11 December 1958 *Employees:* 4
Net Worth: £9,064,424 *Total Assets:* £9,714,823
Registered Office: Burgess Building, Wratten Road East, Hitchin, Herts, SG5 2AP
Activities: Development of building projects
Shareholder: Anne Elizabeth Burgess
Officers: Anne Elizabeth Burgess, Secretary; Anne Elizabeth Burgess [1954] Director; Christopher John Burgess [1950] Director

Burghley House Preservation Trust Limited
Incorporated: 3 April 1969 *Employees:* 105
Net Worth: £68,039,648 *Total Assets:* £73,427,192
Registered Office: Burghley Estate Office, 61 St Martins, Stamford, Lincs, PE9 2LQ
Activities: Other letting and operating of own or leased real estate
Officers: Joshua Fitch, Secretary; Jonathan Charles Chenevix-Trench [1961] Director/Banker; Edward George Clive [1968] Director/Fine Art Auctioneer; Andrew James Feilden [1941] Director/Chartered Surveyor; Sir Giles Henry Charles Floyd [1932] Director/Farmer; Edward Mortimer Harley [1960] Director/Stockbroker; The Honorable Edward Douglas Leigh-Pemberton [1959] Director/Surveyor; Sir John Grenfell Nutting [1942] Director/Barrister; William Alexander Michael Oswald [1962] Director; William Henry Marcello Parente [1951] Director; Stuart John Richmond-Watson [1951] Director; Brian Turnbull Julius Stevens [1938] Director/Solicitor; Jane Tufnell [1964] Director/Investment Professional

Burney Realty Limited
Incorporated: 12 May 1997 *Employees:* 4
Net Worth: £7,305,370 *Total Assets:* £15,034,011
Registered Office: 249 Cranbrook Road, Ilford, Essex, IG1 4TG
Activities: Other business support service activities n.e.c.
Shareholders: Daren Mark Burney; Paula Tracey Burney
Officers: Paula Tracey Burney, Secretary; Daren Mark Burney [1964] Director; Paula Tracey Burney [1963] Director/Company Secretary; Sarah Mellissa Burney [1993] Director/Business Executive

Burnt Mill Academy Trust
Incorporated: 10 November 2011 *Employees:* 549
Net Worth: £39,988,000 *Total Assets:* £51,801,000
Registered Office: Stem Academy, Velizy Avenue, Harlow, Essex, CM20 3EZ
Activities: General secondary education
Officers: Angela Alabi, Secretary; Paul Wakefield Bogle [1972] Director/Secretary and Clerk; Rod Bristow [1958] Director/President, UK and Core, Pearson; Martin Anthony Richard Collier [1963] Director/The Master; Joanne Lisa Coton [1972] Director; Paul Drayton [1960] Director/Retired; Daniel Joseph Kolinsky [1971] Director/Barrister; Andrew Philip Lee [1961] Director; Helena Christine Mills [1967] Director/Academy CEO; Ashley Charles Reid [1965] Director/Head of UK Multi-Asset Portfolio Management, HSBC; Professor Roy Sanders [1937] Director/Retired Consultant Surgeon

Burrough Court Estate Limited
Incorporated: 12 January 1944 *Employees:* 7
Net Worth: £9,834,173 *Total Assets:* £11,548,832
Registered Office: 14 All Saints Street, Stamford, Lincs, PE9 2PA
Activities: Growing of cereals (except rice), leguminous crops and oil seeds
Shareholders: Dawn Elizabeth Wilson; Anthony Crawford Keene
Officers: Dawn Elizabeth Wilson, Secretary; Anthony Crawford Keene [1933] Director/Farmer; Dawn Elizabeth Wilson [1964] Director; Rebecca Alice Wilson [1992] Director; Richard Ian Wilson [1963] Director; Toby Richard Keene Wilson [1994] Director

Burton's Foods (Holdings) Limited
Incorporated: 15 September 2000
Net Worth: £126,214,000 *Total Assets:* £168,338,000
Registered Office: 74-78 Victoria Street, St Albans, Herts, AL1 3XH
Activities: Dormant company
Parent: Ontario Teachers Pension Plan Board
Officers: Simon Leon Browne [1970] Director; Nicholas Peter Field [1978] Director

Burton's Foods Limited
Incorporated: 2 January 1987 *Employees:* 1,771
Net Worth: £224,620,992 *Total Assets:* £450,767,008
Registered Office: 74-78 Victoria Street, St Albans, Herts, AL1 3XH
Activities: Manufacture of rusks and biscuits; manufacture of preserved pastry goods and cakes
Parent: Ontario Teachers Pension Plan Board
Officers: Sarah Ann Spittle, Secretary; Simon Leon Browne [1970] Director; Nicholas Peter Field [1978] Director; Sarah Ann Spittle [1969] Director/Accountant

Bury St Edmunds Academy Trust
Incorporated: 7 July 2011 *Employees:* 298
Net Worth: £32,106,212 *Total Assets:* £34,336,588
Registered Office: Beetons Way, Bury St Edmunds, Suffolk, IP32 6RF
Activities: General secondary education
Officers: Stephen Reginald Boor [1957] Director/Retired Highways Manager; Ian Cox [1957] Director/Retired Bank Manager; Vicky Dorothy Neale [1955] Director/Headteacher; Christopher Francis Pamplin [1964] Director/Publisher; Elana White [1970] Director/Heads PA; Ellie White [1970] Director/Administrator; Michael Owen Wilcock [1963] Director; Adam Archer Wilkinson [1969] Director/Engineering

Bush Boake Allen Enterprises Limited
Incorporated: 16 September 1996
Net Worth: £67,874,000 *Total Assets:* £94,925,000
Registered Office: Duddery Hill, Haverhill, Suffolk, CB9 8LG
Activities: Activities of head offices
Officers: Robert Anderson [1965] Director/VP Finance EAME [American]; Keith John Hammond [1958] Finance Director; Jeroen Henricus Maria Van Noorden [1960] Director/Lawyer [Dutch]

Bush Boake Allen Holdings (U.K.) Limited
Incorporated: 5 July 1982
Net Worth: £43,601,000 *Total Assets:* £43,604,000
Registered Office: Duddery Hill, Haverhill, Suffolk, CB9 8LG
Activities: Activities of head offices
Officers: Keith John Hammond [1958] Finance Director; Jeroen Henricus Maria Van Noorden [1960] Director/Lawyer [Dutch]

Bush Boake Allen Limited
Incorporated: 17 March 1897
Net Worth: £42,550,000 *Total Assets:* £48,495,000
Registered Office: Duddery Hill, Haverhill, Suffolk, CB9 8LG
Activities: Activities of head offices
Officers: Keith John Hammond [1958] Finance Director; Susanne Jane Olive [1973] Director/HR Manager UK; Jeroen Henricus Maria Van Noorden [1960] Director/Lawyer [Dutch]

A.J. Bush Limited
Incorporated: 13 January 1981 *Employees:* 6
Net Worth: £14,623,728 *Total Assets:* £18,972,558
Registered Office: 361 Rayleigh Road, Eastwood, Leigh on Sea, Essex, SS9 5PS
Activities: Other letting and operating of own or leased real estate
Shareholders: Alan Joseph Bush; Brenda May Bush
Officers: Brenda May Bush, Secretary; Alan Joseph Bush [1946] Director; Brenda May Bush [1946] Director

Bushey St James Trust
Incorporated: 3 January 2012 *Employees:* 227
Net Worth: £21,397,720 *Total Assets:* £24,446,866
Registered Office: c/o Bushey Meads School, Coldharbour Lane, Bushey, Herts, WD23 4PA
Activities: Primary education
Officers: Imelda Dempsey, Secretary; Richard Daryl Abrahams [1965] Director/Regional Manager; Dinah Foster Hoeksma [1945] Director; Janet Elspeth Buchanan McNulty [1948] Director/Retired; Samuel Charles Russell [1984] Director; Nicholas Adam Smith [1978] Director/Chief Financial Officer; Sir Alan William Steer [1948] Director/Education; Jeremy William Turner [1965] Director/Executive Principal

Business & Communications Limited
Incorporated: 3 September 1998
Net Worth: £19,673,224 *Total Assets:* £19,673,224
Registered Office: The Mount, The Sidings, Station Road, Longstanton, Cambridge, CB24 3DS
Activities: Other telecommunications activities
Parent: Communications Trading House Limited
Officers: James Henry, Secretary/Director; James Henry [1965] Director; John Gerard Henry [1970] Director/Civil Engineer; Stephen James Henry [1969] Operations Director

Business Control Solutions Group Limited
Incorporated: 14 January 1987 *Employees:* 191
Net Worth: £10,751,000 *Total Assets:* £18,851,000
Registered Office: Ground Floor, Churchgate, New Road, Peterborough, Cambs, PE1 1TT
Activities: Information technology consultancy activities
Parent: Business Control Solutions Group Trustees Ltd
Officers: Roger Alan Shepherd, Secretary; Alexander Campbell Anderson [1954] Director; Paul David Brock [1967] Director; Steve Russell [1945] Director; Roger Alan Shepherd [1966] Director/Accountant; Nigel David Walder [1963] Director

Business Control Solutions Public Limited Company
Incorporated: 28 July 2003 *Employees:* 178
Net Worth: £8,553,678 *Total Assets:* £18,195,678
Registered Office: Ground Floor, Churchgate, New Road, Peterborough, Cambs, PE1 1TT
Activities: Information technology consultancy activities
Parent: Business Control Solutions Group Limited
Officers: Roger Alan Shepherd, Secretary; Paul David Brock [1967] Director; Roger Alan Shepherd [1966] Finance Director

Business Management Software Limited
Incorporated: 31 October 1990 *Employees:* 65
Net Worth: £9,195,491 *Total Assets:* £10,684,255
Registered Office: 2 Peterborough Business Park, Lynch Wood, Peterborough, Cambs, PE2 6FZ
Activities: Information technology consultancy activities
Parent: Automatic Data Processing Inc.
Officers: Richard Anderson [1972] Director

Bussey & Sabberton Bros.Limited
Incorporated: 2 October 1922 *Employees:* 238
Net Worth: £25,293,244 *Total Assets:* £40,820,216
Registered Office: 95 Whiffler Road, Norwich, NR3 2EU
Activities: Sale of new cars and light motor vehicles
Shareholders: Charles Bussey; David Charles Bussey; Paul Charles Bussey
Officers: Charles Bussey [1939] Director; David Charles Bussey [1967] Director; Paul Charles Bussey [1965] Marketing Director; Philip James Collins [1965] Aftersales Director; Scott Matthew Slater [1981] Finance Director

Butchers and Drovers Charitable Institution
Incorporated: 6 February 2014
Net Worth: £13,820,071 *Total Assets:* £13,873,957
Registered Office: Ground Floor, 4 Victoria Square, St Albans, Herts, AL1 3TF
Activities: Other service activities n.e.c.
Officers: Michael Peter Attwood [1958] Purchasing & Supply Chain Director - IPC Europe; Dennis Leslie Clark [1945] Director/Retired; Andrew Robert Garvey [1946] Director/Retired; Edward Frederick Hoefling [1952] Director/Corporate Treasurer; Susan Elizabeth Hoefling [1964] Director/Clerk; Tina Louisa Houlihan [1976] Director/Chief Executive; Ian Kelly [1943] Director/Retired; Graham John Sharp [1938] Director/Retired; James Ian Sydenham [1967] Managing Director

Butlins Operations Limited
Incorporated: 10 February 2012
Net Worth: £2,991,000 *Total Assets:* £10,827,000
Registered Office: 1 Park Lane, Hemel Hempstead, Herts, HP2 4YL
Activities: Hotels and similar accommodation
Parent: Butlins Skyline Limited
Officers: Jane Elizabeth Bentall [1970] Director/Accountant; Paul Charles Flaum [1970] Director; Iain Stuart Macmillan [1976] Director

Butlins Skyline Limited
Incorporated: 9 June 2000 *Employees:* 3,843
Net Worth: £53,970,000 *Total Assets:* £168,567,008
Registered Office: No 1 Park Lane, Hemel Hempstead, Herts, HP2 4YL
Activities: Recreational vehicle parks, trailer parks and camping grounds
Parent: Bourne Leisure Limited
Officers: Jane Elizabeth Bentall [1970] Director/Accountant; Paul Charles Flaum [1970] Director; Iain Stuart Macmillan [1976] Director

H. Butterfield Limited
Incorporated: 17 August 1936 *Employees:* 73
Net Worth: £8,332,148 *Total Assets:* £10,669,637
Registered Office: Selbourne Road, Luton, Beds, LU4 8QF
Activities: Agents involved in the sale of timber and building materials
Shareholders: Simon Anthony Worboys; Peter John Worboys
Officers: Anthony Ivor Hunt, Secretary; Anthony Ivor Hunt [1945] Director; Peter John Worboys [1967] Director; Simon Anthony Worboys [1964] Director/Chartered Accountant

BUUK Infrastructure Holdings Limited
Incorporated: 26 November 2012
Previous: Brookfield Utilities UK Holdings Limited
Net Worth: £152,074,832 *Total Assets:* £316,759,168
Registered Office: Energy House, Woolpit Business Park, Woolpit, Bury St Edmunds, Suffolk, IP30 9UP
Activities: Activities of head offices
Parent: BUUK Infrastructure Limited
Officers: Paul Lucas Sim, Secretary; Jonathan Grant Kelly [1982] Director/Managing Partner [Canadian]; Gabriele Montesi [1981] Director [Italian]; Paul Lucas Sim [1974] Director/Lawyer [Australian]

BUUK Infrastructure Issuer PLC
Incorporated: 1 November 2012
Previous: Brookfield Utilities Issuer UK PLC
Net Worth Deficit: £8,289,113 *Total Assets:* £1,113,814,272
Registered Office: Energy House, Woolpit Business Park, Woolpit, Bury St Edmunds, Suffolk, IP30 9UP
Activities: Activities of head offices
Parent: BUUK Infrastructure No 2 Limited
Officers: Paul Lucas Sim, Secretary; Darryl John Corney [1960] Director; Jonathan Grant Kelly [1982] Director/Managing Partner [Canadian]; Clive Eric Linsdell [1962] Director; Gabriele Montesi [1981] Director [Italian]; Paul Lucas Sim [1974] Director [Australian]

BUUK Infrastructure Limited
Incorporated: 1 April 2005
Previous: IEG Infrastructure Limited
Net Worth: £210,702,832 *Total Assets:* £422,461,856
Registered Office: Energy House, Woolpit Business Park, Woolpit, Bury St Edmunds, Suffolk, IP30 9UP
Activities: Activities of other holding companies n.e.c.
Parent: Prime Ieg Australia No 2 Pty Ltd
Officers: Darryl John Corney [1960] Director; Clive Eric Linsdell [1962] Director; Neil Edward Shaw [1962] Managing Director

BUUK Infrastructure No 1 Limited
Incorporated: 9 October 2012
Previous: Brookfield Utilities UK No 1 Limited
Net Worth: £235,508,768 *Total Assets:* £394,047,968
Registered Office: Energy House, Woolpit Business Park, Woolpit, Bury St Edmunds, Suffolk, IP30 9UP
Activities: Activities of head offices
Parent: BUUK Infrastructure Holdings Limited
Officers: Christopher Mumford, Secretary; Jonathan Grant Kelly [1982] Director/Managing Partner [Canadian]; Clive Eric Linsdell [1962] Director; Gabriele Montesi [1981] Director [Italian]; Neil Edward Shaw [1962] Director; Paul Lucas Sim [1974] Director/Lawyer [Australian]; Sjoerd Van Krimpen [1982] Director [Dutch]

BUUK Infrastructure No 2 Limited
Incorporated: 9 October 2012 *Employees:* 1,049
Previous: Brookfield Utilities UK No 2 Limited
Net Worth: £820,768,000 *Total Assets:* £2,706,832,896
Registered Office: Energy House, Woolpit Business Park, Woolpit, Bury St Edmunds, Suffolk, IP30 9UP
Activities: Activities of head offices
Parent: BUUK Infrastructure No 1 Limited
Officers: Christopher Mumford, Secretary; Darryl John Corney [1960] Director; Jonathan Grant Kelly [1982] Director/Managing Partner [Canadian]; Clive Eric Linsdell [1962] Director; Gabriele Montesi [1981] Director [Italian]; Neil Edward Shaw [1962] Director; Paul Lucas Sim [1974] Director/Lawyer [Australian]

Buyagift PLC
Incorporated: 25 November 1999 *Employees:* 125
Net Worth: £7,119,070 *Total Assets:* £53,391,976
Registered Office: 4 Imperial Place, Maxwell Road, Borehamwood, Herts, WD6 1JN
Activities: Retail sale via mail order houses or via Internet
Major Shareholder: Pierre-Edouard Robert Raymond Marie-Joseph Sterin
Officers: Daniel Jeremy Mountain, Secretary; Syed Kashif Abbas [1979] Director [Pakistani]; Pierre Charles Boccon-Liaudet [1969] Director [French]; Daniel Jeremy Mountain [1974] Managing Director; John Richard Perkins [1964] Director

Buyanovsky Property Management Limited
Incorporated: 9 June 2015 *Employees:* 4
Net Worth: £287,794 *Total Assets:* £9,248,971
Registered Office: 724 Capability Green, Luton, Beds, LU1 3LU
Activities: Other service activities n.e.c.
Officers: Ludmila Buyanovsky, Secretary; Dmitry Buyanovsky [1997] Director/Student; Ilia Buyanovsky [1995] Director/Student; Valentin Buyanovsky [1964] Director/Manager

Buzzard Leisure Limited
Incorporated: 23 July 1996
Net Worth: £54,300,000 *Total Assets:* £129,000,000
Registered Office: Westpoint, Peterborough Business Park, Lynch Wood, Peterborough, Cambs, PE2 6FZ
Activities: Other business support service activities n.e.c.
Parent: Mytravel North America Limited
Officers: Shirley Bradley, Secretary; Paul Andrew Hemingway [1971] Director

BV PMT Holdings Ltd
Incorporated: 2 April 2016 *Employees:* 454
Net Worth Deficit: £15,855,185 *Total Assets:* £127,540,856
Registered Office: 48 Lancaster Way Business Park, Ely, Cambs, CB6 3NW
Activities: Activities of other holding companies n.e.c.
Officers: Jesse Ross Feldman [1977] Director/Private Equity Investor [American]

BW Foundation
Incorporated: 25 July 2007
Net Worth: £8,897,445 *Total Assets:* £10,148,786
Registered Office: 336 Pinner Road, Harrow, Middlesex, HA1 4LB
Activities: Activities of religious organisations
Officers: Mohamed Iqbal Asaria [1950] Director/Economist; Riazali Esmail [1957] Director/Pharmacist; Sabira Mohamed Kanji [1957] Director/Accountant; Mukhtar Manji [1965] Director/Pharmacist; Murtaza Versi [1952] Director/Engineer

BWI UK Limited
Incorporated: 16 June 2009 *Employees:* 182
Net Worth: £18,124,000 *Total Assets:* £43,517,000
Registered Office: Windmill Road, Luton, Beds, LU1 3XL
Activities: Manufacture of other parts and accessories for motor vehicles
Shareholder: Shougang Group
Officers: Li Daoshan [1983] Director/Legal Manager [Chinese]; Christopher Brian Haynes [1965] Director/Plant Manager BWI Group; Huang Yan [1978] Global Director: Capital Operation/Legal Affairs [Chinese]; Chen Zhouping [1966] Managing Director [Chinese]

BWP (Cambridge) Limited
Incorporated: 14 February 2012 *Employees:* 310
Net Worth: £617,351 *Total Assets:* £23,661,184
Registered Office: Reardon & Co Ltd, Breckenwood Road, Fulbourn, Cambridge, CB21 5DQ
Activities: Other business support service activities n.e.c.
Major Shareholder: Bernard William Plumb
Officers: Nicholas John Diss [1958] Director/Chartered Accountant; Bernard William Plumb [1946] Director

C & K Meats Limited
Incorporated: 4 December 1992 *Employees:* 161
Net Worth: £3,168,354 *Total Assets:* £11,036,139
Registered Office: 8 Hopper Way, Diss Business Park, Diss, Norfolk, IP22 4GT
Activities: Wholesale of meat and meat products
Shareholders: Christopher Joseph Burrows; Kevin James Burrows
Officers: Paula Marie Burrows, Secretary; Christopher Joseph Burrows [1959] Director/Catering Butcher; Craig John Burrows [1985] Operations Director; Kevin James Burrows [1964] Director/Wholesale Meat Trader

C P Timber Limited
Incorporated: 14 April 1998 *Employees:* 17
Net Worth: £1,627,134 *Total Assets:* £9,495,771
Registered Office: 5 Yeomans Court, Ware Road, Hertford, SG13 7HJ
Activities: Wholesale of wood, construction materials and sanitary equipment
Shareholders: Christopher Jonathan Powell; Virginia Ruth Powell
Officers: Maurice Powell, Secretary; Christopher Jonathan Powell [1962] Director/Timber Trader; Virginia Ruth Powell [1964] Director

C. J. H. Farming Limited
Incorporated: 20 December 1995 *Employees:* 18
Net Worth: £5,881,780 *Total Assets:* £20,980,712
Registered Office: Boyton Hall Farmhouse, Boyton Cross, Chelmsford, Essex, CM1 4LN
Activities: Growing of cereals (except rice), leguminous crops and oil seeds
Major Shareholder: Christopher James Harold Philpot
Officers: Annette Caroline Philpot, Secretary; Christopher James Harold Philpot [1969] Director; Peter John Harold Philpot [1943] Director; Simon Andrew Thorneycroft [1980] Director

C. U. Lighting Limited
Incorporated: 20 November 1987 *Employees:* 198
Net Worth: £3,045,699 *Total Assets:* £11,859,919
Registered Office: Charles House, Lower Road, Great Amwell, Ware, Herts, SG12 9TA
Activities: Other specialised construction activities n.e.c.
Parent: CU Phosco Limited
Officers: David Frain, Secretary; Charles James William Marques [1954] Director; Nicholas David Robin Marques [1959] Managing Director; Philip David Marques [1966] Director

C.I. Industries Limited
Incorporated: 21 May 2001
Net Worth: £6,476,827 *Total Assets:* £18,688,746
Registered Office: Whitegate Farm Bungalow, Witcham Road, Mepal, Ely, Cambs, CB6 2AF
Activities: Other letting and operating of own or leased real estate
Shareholder: Vanessa Pinfold
Officers: Robin David Currey, Secretary/Director; Georgina Ottilie Kathe Currey [1936] Director; James Duncan Currey [1972] Director/Graphic Designer; Robin David Currey [1939] Director

C.U. Phosco Limited
Incorporated: 24 September 2012 *Employees:* 206
Net Worth: £8,912,878 *Total Assets:* £16,165,517
Registered Office: Charles House, Lower Road, Great Amwell, Ware, Herts, SG12 9TA
Activities: Activities of head offices
Officers: David Frain, Secretary; Charles James William Marques [1954] Director; Jason Lewis Bradwell Marques [1970] Director; Nicholas David Robin Marques [1959] Director; Philip David Marques [1966] Director

Cadastra Limited
Incorporated: 20 March 1987
Net Worth: £13,566,757 *Total Assets:* £14,132,905
Registered Office: The Balsams Barn, Balsams Lane, Standon, Ware, Herts, SG11 1NS
Activities: Activities of financial services holding companies
Shareholders: John Howard Williamson; Pamela Jeannette Williamson
Officers: Pamela Jeannette Williamson, Secretary; John Howard Williamson [1944] Director

Cadena AM Limited
Incorporated: 1 July 2008
Net Worth: £8,388,379 *Total Assets:* £8,390,976
Registered Office: 1-3 High Street, Dunmow, Essex, CM6 1UU
Activities: Activities of head offices
Shareholders: Gillian Ann Whight; Paul James Whight
Officers: Gillian Whight, Secretary; Barrie James Whight [1977] Director; Leigh Whight [1976] Director; Paul James Whight [1951] Director

C.M. Cadman Group Limited (The)
Incorporated: 1 July 1975 *Employees:* 68
Net Worth: £4,068,439 *Total Assets:* £12,338,106
Registered Office: Cadman House, Maurice Way, Stanway, Colchester, Essex, CO3 0NW
Activities: Construction of commercial buildings
Shareholders: Alan Maurice Cadman; Linda Violet Williams; Violet Elizabeth Cadman
Officers: Matthew Robert Kett, Secretary; Alan Maurice Cadman [1954] Director/Builder; Stuart Nigel James Cadman [1964] Director/Construction Manager; Violet Elizabeth Cadman [1929] Director/Secretary; Linda Violet Williams [1959] Director/Accounts Assistant

CAE Technology Holdings Limited
Incorporated: 18 May 2010 *Employees:* 242
Net Worth: £4,650,611 *Total Assets:* £34,676,052
Registered Office: CAE House, Colonial Way, Watford, Herts, WD24 4PT
Activities: Activities of other holding companies n.e.c.
Parent: Caerus Assets Limited
Officers: Richard Behan [1978] Director; Justin Matthew Harling [1973] Director

CAE Technology Services Limited
Incorporated: 7 February 1992 *Employees:* 242
Net Worth: £9,711,106 *Total Assets:* £39,802,160
Registered Office: CAE House, Colonial Way, Watford, Herts, WD24 4PT
Activities: Other information technology service activities
Parent: Seckloe 194 Limited
Officers: Richard Behan [1978] Director; Umesh Chauhan [1965] Finance Director; Justin Matthew Harling [1973] Managing Director

Calchan Holdings Limited
Incorporated: 25 February 2011
Net Worth: £5,379,585 *Total Assets:* £8,232,410
Registered Office: Warwick House, Spitfire Close, Ermine Business Park, Huntingdon, Cambs, PE29 6XY
Activities: Research and experimental development on biotechnology
Officers: Brenda Elizabeth Reynolds, Secretary; Catherine Elizabeth Bingham [1965] Managing Director; Allan Patrick Marchington [1966] Director/Investor; Dr Liam Thomas Ratcliffe [1963] Director/Venture Partner; Brenda Elizabeth Reynolds [1955] Director; Simon Nicholas Tate [1966] Director/Chief Scientific Officer

Callcott Holdings Limited
Incorporated: 18 February 1964 *Employees:* 2
Net Worth: £13,735,288 *Total Assets:* £15,945,234
Registered Office: Bell Lane Office Village, Bell Lane, Little Chalfont, Amersham, Bucks, HP6 6FA
Activities: Development of building projects
Shareholders: David Ian Brasier; Michael Allen Brasier
Officers: Josephine Paula Brasier, Secretary; David Ian Brasier [1942] Director/Estate Agent; Michael Allen Brasier [1947] Director/Chartered Surveyor

Calpri Ltd
Incorporated: 8 December 2005
Net Worth Deficit: £153,584 *Total Assets:* £17,727,750
Registered Office: Second Floor, De Burgh House, Market Road, Wickford, Essex, SS12 0FD
Activities: Other business support service activities n.e.c.
Major Shareholder: Marco Andrea Pagotto
Officers: Yvano Dandrea [1966] Director [Swiss]

Calumet Wex International Limited
Incorporated: 20 April 1976
Previous: Calumet International Limited
Net Worth Deficit: £659,000 *Total Assets:* £11,593,000
Registered Office: 13 Frensham Road, Norwich, NR3 2BT
Activities: Activities of distribution holding companies
Parent: Calumet Wex Holding GmbH
Officers: Eric Marie Karl Rene Blumenthal [1968] Director/Executive Board Member [German]; Dr Joerg Dockendorf [1978] Managing Director [German]; Richard Glatzel [1983] Director [German]; Bernard Charles Hewitt [1952] Director/Business Executive; Louis Wahl [1968] Director/Chief Executive

The Cam Academy Trust
Incorporated: 13 January 2011 *Employees:* 800
Previous: Comberton Academy Trust
Net Worth: £108,243,000 *Total Assets:* £116,442,000
Registered Office: Comberton Village College, West Street, Comberton, Cambridge, CB23 7DU
Activities: Primary education
Officers: Mark Andrew Norman, Secretary; David Graham Daniels [1962] General Director; Jonathan Mark Goodridge [1950] Director; Colin Ayton Greenhalgh [1941] Director/Retired; John Hartley [1955] Director/Headmaster; Patricia Mary Kelleher [1962] Director/School Principal; Symeon Krintas [1972] Director; Stephen Charles Richard Munday [1964] Director/Chief Executive Officer; George Alexander Pearson [1957] Director; Andrew James Read [1968] Director of Education; Kris Stutchbury [1959] Director/Lecturer; Dr Nicola Hannah Walshe [1975] Director/Lecturer; Roderick Warsap [1964] Director/Executive Headteacher; Sue Williamson [1951] Director/Chief Executive

Cambridge Academic Partnership
Incorporated: 9 March 2011 *Employees:* 269
Previous: Parkside Federation Academies
Net Worth: £44,223,000 *Total Assets:* £46,436,000
Registered Office: Parkside Community College, Parkside, Cambridge, CB1 1EH
Activities: General secondary education
Officers: Tracy Jayne Piesse, Secretary; Julius Carrington [1971] Director/COO Global Client Management/Corporate Governance; Baroness Janet Cohen [1940] Director; Richard Geoffrey Meade Conway [1960] Director/Insurance Company Executive; Sara Elizabeth Garnham [1960] Director; Phineas Richard Hodson [1984] Director/Consultant; Andrew Charles Hutchinson [1959] Director/Executive Principal; Helen Margaret Murley [1961] HR Director; Janet Diana Swadling [1961] Director; Stephen Watts [1952] Director/College Lecturer

Cambridge Antibody Technology Group Limited
Incorporated: 5 August 1996
Net Worth: £2,339,109,120 *Total Assets:* £2,339,109,120
Registered Office: 1 Francis Crick Avenue, Cambridge Biomedical Campus, Cambridge, CB2 0AA
Activities: Other research and experimental development on natural sciences and engineering
Parent: AstraZeneca Treasury Limited
Officers: Matthew Ian Conacher, Secretary; Iain Alistair Collins [1970] Director; Katie Louise Jackson-Turner [1966] Director/Solicitor; Adrian Charles Noel Kemp [1966] Director/Solicitor

Cambridge Arts & Sciences Limited
Incorporated: 23 October 1997 *Employees:* 295
Net Worth: £12,056,000 *Total Assets:* £35,442,000
Registered Office: Kett House, Station Road, Cambridge, CB1 2JH
Activities: General secondary education
Parent: CEG Colleges Limited
Officers: Michael Ioakimides [1965] Director; Philip Leslie Symes [1962] Director/Chief Financial Officer; Brendan Grant Webb [1969] Director; Stuart Alan White [1967] Managing Director

Cambridge Broadband Networks Limited
Incorporated: 18 November 1999 *Employees:* 82
Net Worth Deficit: £6,690,245 *Total Assets:* £16,589,359
Registered Office: Byron House, Cambridge Business Park, Cowley Road, Cambridge, CB4 0WZ
Activities: Other telecommunications activities
Officers: Sarah Jean Gowing, Secretary; Lionel Chmilewsky [1961] Director [French]; Martin Charles Gibson [1970] Director/Investment Advisor; Hermann Maria Hauser [1948] Director/Venture Capitalist [Austrian]; Achim Michael Lederle [1967] Director [German]; Jonathan McKay [1955] Director; John Benedict Philbin Naylon [1973] Director/Engineer

Cambridge Centre for Sixth Form Studies
Incorporated: 29 March 2000 *Employees:* 60
Net Worth: £3,117,562 *Total Assets:* £8,424,185
Registered Office: 4-5 Benet Place, Cambridge, CB2 1EL
Activities: General secondary education
Officers: Jennifer Susanne Neild, Secretary; John Tannatt Dix [1961] Director/Bursar; Graeme Alexander Lockhart [1954] Director/Architect; Duncan Edward Walker [1968] Director/Bursar

Cambridge Colleges Funding II PLC
Incorporated: 27 November 2013 *Employees:* 3
Net Worth: £89,010 *Total Assets:* £60,835,704
Registered Office: Mills & Reeve LLP, Botanic House, 100 Hills Road, Cambridge, CB2 1PH
Activities: Other credit granting n.e.c.
Officers: Claire Margaret Clarke, Secretary; Nicholas Graham Allen [1952] Director/Bursar; Donald Peter Hearn [1947] Director; Simon Peter Summers [1956] Director/Bursar

Cambridge Colleges Funding PLC
Incorporated: 27 June 2013
Net Worth: £94,010 *Total Assets:* £90,848,096
Registered Office: Mills & Reeve LLP, Botanic House, 100 Hills Road, Cambridge, CB2 1PH
Activities: Other credit granting n.e.c.
Officers: Claire Margaret Clarke, Secretary; Nicholas Graham Allen [1952] Director/Bursar; Donald Peter Hearn [1947] Director; Simon Peter Summers [1956] Director/Bursar

Cambridge Commodities Limited
Incorporated: 1 July 1998 *Employees:* 107
Net Worth: £11,870,130 *Total Assets:* £29,750,216
Registered Office: 203 Lancaster Way Business Park, Ely, Cambs, CB6 3NX
Activities: Wholesale of chemical products
Parent: Cambridge Commodities Holdings Limited
Officers: Linda Susan Stevens, Secretary; Neil William Stanley Hammill [1981] Commercial Director; Ian Alexander Mitchell [1982] Director/Chartered Accountant; James Stevens [1976] Director/Commodity Trader; Tom Stevens [1965] Director; Ian York [1959] Sales Director

Cambridge Construction Limited
Incorporated: 1 June 1973 *Employees:* 3
Net Worth: £7,188,935 *Total Assets:* £8,901,514
Registered Office: c/o Eastern Counties Leather, Langford Arch, London Road, Sawston, Cambs, CB2 4EG
Activities: Other letting and operating of own or leased real estate
Shareholder: Jacinta Louise Dean
Officers: Jacinta Louise Byrne, Secretary; Susan Annabel Ward [1965] Director/Administrator

Cambridge Consultants Limited
Incorporated: 24 December 1971 *Employees:* 531
Net Worth: £61,417,148 *Total Assets:* £85,147,424
Registered Office: Unit 29 Science Park, Milton Road, Cambridge, CB4 0DW
Activities: Other research and experimental development on natural sciences and engineering
Parent: Altran UK Holding Limited
Officers: Mammen Eapen, Secretary/Chartered Accountant [British/Australian]; Dominique Cerutti [1961] Director [French]; Mammen Eapen [1958] Director/Chartered Accountant [British/Australian]; Raymond Anthony Edgson [1962] Director; Richard Newland Hall [1968] Director/Chief Operations Officer; Albin Jacquemont [1965] Director/Chief Financial Officer [French]; Richard Thomas Traherne [1970] Director/Chief Commercial Officer; Eric Wilkinson [1963] Director/Chief Operations Officer

The Cambridge Crystallographic Data Centre
Incorporated: 18 August 1987 *Employees:* 60
Net Worth: £6,890,343 *Total Assets:* £10,864,714
Registered Office: 12 Union Road, Cambridge, CB2 1EZ
Activities: Other professional, scientific and technical activities n.e.c.
Officers: Christopher Harrington Knight, Secretary; Professor Alessia Bacchi [1966] Director/Professor [Italian]; Judith Nancy Currano [1976] Director/Librarian [American]; Dr David Martinsen [1951] Director/Publisher [American]; Dr John Overington [1965] Director of Bioinformatics; Prof Paul Robert Raithby [1951] Director/Professor; Dr Christoph Martin Stahl [1969] Director/Head of Molecular Design and Chemical Biology [German]

Cambridge Display Technology Limited
Incorporated: 2 January 1992 *Employees:* 106
Net Worth: £4,643,000 *Total Assets:* £12,851,000
Registered Office: Unit 12 Cardinal Park, Cardinal Way, Godmanchester, Cambs, PE29 2XG
Activities: Other research and experimental development on natural sciences and engineering
Parent: CDT Holdings Limited
Officers: Hilary Charles, Secretary; Yoshiaki Oda [1961] Director/Company Executive [Japanese]; Hiroshi Ueda [1956] Director/Company Executive [Japanese]; Jim Veninger [1962] Director/VP Technology Development [American]; Takeshi Yamada [1967] Director/Office Worker [Japanese]

Cambridge Education Group Limited
Incorporated: 6 December 2006 *Employees:* 1,497
Net Worth: £11,950,000 *Total Assets:* £96,736,000
Registered Office: Kett House, Station Road, Cambridge, CB1 2JH
Activities: Activities of head offices
Parent: Camelot Bidco Limited
Officers: Michael Ioakimides [1965] Director; Philip Leslie Symes [1962] Director/Chief Financial Officer; Brendan Grant Webb [1969] Director

Cambridge Enterprise Limited
Incorporated: 5 September 1972 *Employees:* 59
Net Worth: £24,422,724 *Total Assets:* £30,637,396
Registered Office: The Old Schools, Trinity Lane, Cambridge, CB2 1TN
Activities: Management consultancy activities other than financial management
Officers: Emma Rampton, Secretary; Prof Alan Frank Blackwell [1962] Director/Academic [New Zealander]; Charles William Alfred Cotton [1947] Director; Professor Andrew David Neely [1967] Director/Academic; Professor Sir Keith O'Nions [1944] Director/Academic; Anthony Louis Odgers [1967] Director/Chief Financial Officer; Dr Jane Osbourn [1966] Director/Scientist; Debapriya Purkayastha [1967] Director/Investments; Dr Anthony Raven [1954] Director/Academic; Dr Paul James Seabright [1966] Deputy Director

Cambridge Innovation Capital PLC
Incorporated: 8 October 2012 *Employees:* 9
Net Worth: £143,993,040 *Total Assets:* £145,322,288
Registered Office: Hauser Forum, 3 Charles Babbage Road, Cambridge, CB3 0GT
Activities: Activities of other holding companies n.e.c.
Officers: Robert Timothy Sprawson, Secretary; Dr Dipti Mahendra Amin [1964] Director; Humphrey William Battcock [1955] Director/Private Equity Investor; Edward Anfrid Pringle Benthall [1963] Director; Clive Hedley William Birch [1953] Director/Retired Chartered Accountant; Dr Victor Christou [1966] Senior Investment Director; Adam Martin Glinsman [1965] Director/Asset Management Executive; Professor Ian Malcolm Leslie [1955] Director/Professor; Michael Peter Muller [1959] Director/Chief Technology Officer; Professor Andrew David Neely [1967] Director/Professor; Robert Timothy Sprawson [1970] Director/Chartered Accountant

Cambridge Medipark Limited
Incorporated: 18 December 2002
Net Worth: £4,562,631 *Total Assets:* £14,308,664
Registered Office: Countryside House, The Drive, Great Warley, Brentwood, Essex, CM13 3AT
Activities: Development of building projects
Shareholders: Countryside Properties (Joint Ventures) Limited; Liberty Property Trust
Officers: Tracy Marina Warren, Secretary; Andrew Joseph Blevins [1964] Managing Director; Andrew Mark Carrington [1975] Commercial Director; Graham Stewart Cherry [1959] Director/Chief Executive; Michael Thomas Hagan [1957] Director/Chief Investment Officer [American]; Elizabeth Susan Roche [1973] Director

Cambridge Meridian Academies Trust
Incorporated: 4 March 2011 *Employees:* 983
Net Worth: £115,281,000 *Total Assets:* £125,650,000
Registered Office: Swavesey Village College, Gibraltar Lane, Swavesey, Cambridge, CB24 4RS
Activities: Pre-primary education
Officers: Helen Louise Anderson, Secretary; Lesley Christine Birch [1962] Director/Headteacher; John Hall [1950] Director/Head of Operations & Logistics; Alan John Hardy [1954] Director/Accountant; Shirley Marie Jamieson [1952] Director/Head of Marketing; James William Kennedy [1963] Director/HR Executive Leader; Roger Moore [1945] Director/Education Adviser and Consultant; Paul Steven Phillipson [1960] Director/Retired; David Robert Ruddy [1957] Director/Consultant; Mark Richard Squires [1960] Communications Director; Mark Edward Woods [1972] Director/Principal

Cambridge Pharma Limited
Incorporated: 26 October 2016
Net Worth: £5,472,058 *Total Assets:* £13,155,185
Registered Office: c/o Hewitsons LLP, Shakespeare House, 42 Newmarket Road, Cambridge, CB5 8EP
Activities: Research and experimental development on social sciences and humanities
Officers: Jawad Nunes [1950] Director [American]; Chetan Narendra Patel [1959] Director [American]; Michael Schick [1958] Director [American]

Cambridge Primary Education Trust
Incorporated: 22 November 2012 *Employees:* 148
Net Worth: £18,241,852 *Total Assets:* £19,958,256
Registered Office: Histon and Impington Junior School, The Green, Histon, Cambridge, CB24 9JA
Activities: Primary education
Officers: Linda Jane Doyle, Secretary; Lesley Christine Birch [1962] Director/Headteacher; John Alfred Frost [1945] Director/Retired; Paul Douglas Larbey [1973] Director/Telecoms Executive; Robert Stuart Plumbly [1961] Director/VAT Consultant; Kieran John Reynolds [1977] Director/Chief Operating Officer; Penelope Rose Todman [1949] Director/Retired Headteacher; John-Mark Winstanley [1986] Primary PGCE Course Director; Mark Edward Woods [1972] Director/Teacher

Cambridge Realty Limited
Incorporated: 14 April 2015
Net Worth: £310,684 *Total Assets:* £10,086,681
Registered Office: The Station House, 15 Station Road, St Ives, Cambs, PE27 5BH
Activities: Buying and selling of own real estate
Major Shareholder: John Edward Story
Officers: Simon Matthew Grice [1964] Director/Trader; John Edward Story [1951] Director; Regina Clara Wrench [1963] Director [American]; Spencer Frank Wrench [1961] Director

Cambridge Silicon Radio Holdings Limited
Incorporated: 6 May 2011
Net Worth: £938,434,624 *Total Assets:* £1,163,511,808
Registered Office: Churchill House, Cambridge Business Park, Cowley Road, Cambridge, CB4 0WZ
Activities: Activities of other holding companies n.e.c.
Parent: CSR Limited
Officers: Gordon Thomas Rowe [1965] Senior Director, Finance [Canadian]

The Cambridge Union Society
Incorporated: 30 November 2009 *Employees:* 14
Net Worth: £10,895,471 *Total Assets:* £11,441,977
Registered Office: 9a Bridge Street, Cambridge, CB2 1UB
Activities: Cultural education
Officers: William Alexander Bailey, Secretary; David Henry Branch [1973] Director/Management Consultant; Rachel Green [1977] Finance and Operations Director; John Nicholas Heath [1956] Director/Chartered Surveyor; Imran Mateo Firoz Hussein [1997] Director/Student [Malaysian]; The Honorable Daniel Janner QC [1957] Director/QC; David Nicholas Robinson [1958] Director/Accountant; William Edward Smart [1997] Director/Student; Lord Christopher Robert Smith [1951] Director/Master of Pembroke College, Cambridge; Araba Arba Kurankyiwa Taylor [1961] Director/Barrister, Deputy District Judge; Nigel Wooldridge Brown [1945] Director/Banker; Nigel John Yandell [1961] Director/Academic (Writer & Teacher)

Cambridge University Press (Holdings) Limited
Incorporated: 3 December 2002 *Employees:* 124
Net Worth: £28,920,000 *Total Assets:* £47,562,000
Registered Office: University Printing House, Shaftesbury Road, Cambridge, CB2 8BS
Activities: Activities of other holding companies n.e.c.
Officers: Sally-Anne Muddiman, Secretary; Catriona Ann Sheret, Secretary; Andrew Philip Chandler [1957] Director/Chief Financial Officer; Paul Joseph Colbert [1967] Sales Director [Irish]; Peter Andrew Jestyn Phillips [1962] Director/Chief Executive; Catriona Ann Sheret [1970] Director/Solicitor

Cambridgeshire Educational Trust
Incorporated: 10 June 2011 *Employees:* 144
Previous: Chesterton Community College
Net Worth: £21,663,322 *Total Assets:* £23,042,760
Registered Office: Chesterton Community College, Gilbert Road, Cambridge, CB4 3NY
Activities: General secondary education
Officers: Anne Constantine [1952] Director/Retired; Paul Garnet George Goodridge [1965] Finance Director; Dr Morag Grace Morrison-Helme [1959] Director/University Lecturer [British/Australian]; Mary Sanders [1946] Director/Freelance Science Editor; Lucy Miriam Scott [1973] Director/Headteacher; David James Warwick [1965] Director

Cambridgeshire Industrial Properties Limited
Incorporated: 21 February 1967 *Employees:* 4
Net Worth: £7,711,201 *Total Assets:* £16,767,480
Registered Office: 115c Milton Road, Cambridge, CB4 1XE
Activities: Development of building projects
Shareholders: Estate of Mr Alan Walter Bullen; Rachel Ruth Kindred; Alan Bullen Discretionary Settlement
Officers: Steven William Beach, Secretary; Rachel Ruth Kindred [1983] Director/Administrator

Cambrionix Holdings Limited
Incorporated: 30 September 2014
Net Worth: £1,649,790 *Total Assets:* £10,703,365
Registered Office: St Johns Innovation Centre, Cowley Road, Cambridge, CB4 0WS
Activities: Other business support service activities n.e.c.
Major Shareholder: Dominic Plunkett
Officers: Kevin O'Hara, Secretary; Dominic Plunkett [1973] Director/Electronics Engineer; Steven Tyson [1976] Director; Victoria Tyson [1978] Director

Cambustion Limited
Incorporated: 1 May 1987 *Employees:* 62
Net Worth: £9,348,471 *Total Assets:* £10,154,215
Registered Office: Unit J6, The Paddocks, 347 Cherry Hinton Road, Cambridge, CB1 8DH
Activities: Manufacture of other special-purpose machinery n.e.c.
Parent: Fidion Ltd.
Officers: Colin Dailly, Secretary/Software Engineer; Bruce William Glover Campbell [1971] Director/Engineering; Colin Dailly [1961] Director/Engineer; Gregory David Inman [1969] Director/Engineer; Christopher David Nickolaus [1980] Products Director; Dr. Mark Simon Peckham [1968] Director/Engineer; Kingsley St John Reavell [1973] Director/Engineering; Dr Jonathan Philip Robert Symonds [1976] R&D Director

Camden Development Company Limited
Incorporated: 7 May 1963 *Employees:* 5
Net Worth: £10,419,700 *Total Assets:* £12,590,037
Registered Office: 1 Beauchamp Court, Victors Way, Barnet, Herts, EN5 5TZ
Activities: Development of building projects
Parent: Embleton Trust Corporation Limited
Officers: Olive May Herman, Secretary; Julia Deborah Burton [1962] Director; Rosalind Carol Gelbart [1958] Director; Charles Robert Herman [1956] Director/Investment Manager; Olive May Herman [1931] Director; Paul Philip Herman [1968] Director

Camelot Bidco Limited
Incorporated: 19 July 2013
Net Worth Deficit: £11,552,000 *Total Assets:* £205,054,000
Registered Office: Kett House, Station Road, Cambridge, CB1 2JH
Activities: Activities of head offices
Parent: Camelot Holdco Limited
Officers: Michael Ioakimides [1965] Director; Philip Leslie Symes [1962] Director/Chief Financial Officer; Brendan Grant Webb [1969] Director

Camelot Business Solutions Limited
Incorporated: 7 March 2011 *Employees:* 87
Net Worth: £2,900,000 *Total Assets:* £35,300,000
Registered Office: Magdalen House, Tolpits Lane, Watford, Herts, WD18 9RN
Activities: Gambling and betting activities
Parent: Premier Lotteries UK Limited
Officers: John Edward Michael Dillon, Secretary; John Edward Michael Dillon [1963] Legal Director and Company Secretary; Ilya Kachko [1979] Director/Portfolio Manager [Canadian]; Andrew Jonathan Mark Taylor [1961] Director/Private Equity Investor

Camelot Global Lottery Solutions Limited
Incorporated: 7 March 2011 *Employees:* 209
Previous: Camelot Strategic Solutions Limited
Net Worth Deficit: £11,544,000 *Total Assets:* £60,554,000
Registered Office: Magdalen House, Tolpits Lane, Watford, Herts, WD18 9RN
Activities: Gambling and betting activities
Parent: Premier Lotteries UK Limited
Officers: John Edward Michael Dillon, Secretary; Bogdan Cenanovic [1976] Director/Vice President, Technology, Media & Telecom [Canadian]; Ilya Kachko [1979] Director/Portfolio Manager [Canadian]; Dr David Thomas Kelly [1963] Non-Executive Director; Michael Charles Lightman [1963] Director [American]; John Henderson McNeil [1968] Director [American]; Wayne Lawrence Pickup [1976] Director/Chief Executive [New Zealander]; Jane Sarah Rowe [1959] Director/Senior Vice President [Canadian]; Robert Oscar Rowley [1949] Director

Camelot Holdco Limited
Incorporated: 18 November 2013 *Employees:* 1,497
Net Worth Deficit: £32,299,000 *Total Assets:* £256,728,000
Registered Office: Kett House, Station Road, Cambridge, CB1 2JH
Activities: Activities of other holding companies n.e.c.
Parent: Camelot Interco Limited
Officers: Michael Ioakimides [1965] Director; Philip Leslie Symes [1962] Director/Chief Financial Officer; Brendan Grant Webb [1969] Director

Camelot Interco Limited
Incorporated: 18 November 2013
Net Worth: £43,814,000 *Total Assets:* £158,732,000
Registered Office: Kett House, Station Road, Cambridge, CB1 2JH
Activities: Activities of other holding companies n.e.c.
Parent: Camelot Midco Limited
Officers: Michael Ioakimides [1965] Director; Philip Leslie Symes [1962] Director/Chief Financial Officer; Brendan Grant Webb [1969] Director

Camelot Midco Limited
Incorporated: 18 November 2013 *Employees:* 2
Net Worth: £41,615,000 *Total Assets:* £138,330,000
Registered Office: Kett House, Station Road, Cambridge, CB1 2JH
Activities: Activities of other holding companies n.e.c.
Parent: Camelot Topco Limited
Officers: Michael Ioakimides [1965] Director; Philip Leslie Symes [1962] Director/Chief Financial Officer; Brendan Grant Webb [1969] Director

Camelot Topco Limited
Incorporated: 18 November 2013 *Employees:* 1,518
Net Worth Deficit: £94,854,000 *Total Assets:* £250,944,992
Registered Office: Kett House, Station Road, Cambridge, CB1 2JH
Activities: Activities of other holding companies n.e.c.
Shareholders: Bridgepoint Advisers Limited; Bridgepoint Europe (SGP) Limited
Officers: Christopher David Gairdner Bell [1973] Director; Alan Bowkett [1951] Director; Christopher John Busby [1972] Director; Michael Ioakimides [1965] Director; Philip Leslie Symes [1962] Director/Chief Financial Officer; Brendan Grant Webb [1969] Director

Camelot UK Lotteries Limited
Incorporated: 27 May 1993 *Employees:* 667
Net Worth: £33,600,000 *Total Assets:* £651,699,968
Registered Office: Tolpits Lane, Watford, Herts, WD18 9RN
Activities: Gambling and betting activities
Parent: Premier Lotteries UK Limited
Officers: John Edward Michael Dillon, Secretary; Ilya Kachko [1979] Director/Portfolio Manager [Canadian]; David Thomas Kelly [1963] Non-Executive Director; Nigel Railton [1967] Director/Chief Executive; Sir Hugh Michael Robertson [1962] Director/Chairman; Sarah Jane Rowe [1959] Director/Senior Vice President [Canadian]; Robert Oscar Rowley [1949] Director; Andrew Jonathan Mark Taylor [1961] Regional Managing Director; Jennelle Lisa Tilling [1969] Director [Australian/British]; Robert Malcolm Walker [1945] Director/Deputy Chairman

Camfaud Concrete Pumps Limited
Incorporated: 6 August 1991 *Employees:* 114
Net Worth: £8,971,779 *Total Assets:* £24,072,484
Registered Office: High Road, Thornwood Common, Epping, Essex, CM16 6LU
Activities: Construction of commercial buildings
Parent: Oxford Pumping Holdings Ltd.
Officers: David Anthony Faud [1966] Director

Camfaud Group Limited
Incorporated: 10 November 2016 *Employees:* 278
Net Worth Deficit: £577,504 *Total Assets:* £63,478,664
Registered Office: High Road, Thornwood Common, Epping, Essex, CM16 6LU
Activities: Activities of other holding companies n.e.c.
Officers: David Anthony Faud [1966] Director; Bruce Franklin Young [1959] Director/President and Chief Executive Officer [American]

Camfed International
Incorporated: 18 November 1993 *Employees:* 261
Net Worth: £9,126,494 *Total Assets:* £18,817,672
Registered Office: 24 Castle Street, St Giles Court, Cambridge, CB3 0AJ
Activities: Activities of extraterritorial organisations and bodies
Officers: Luxon Shumba, Secretary; Dr Valerie Caton [1952] Director/Retired Diplomat; Ann Lesley Cotton [1949] Charity Director; Miranda Theresa Claire Curtis [1955] Director; Lucy Ann Ariel Lake [1972] Director/Charity; Rosemary O'Mahony [1954] Director/Consultant [Irish]; Grace Yaa Duodua Owen [1969] Director/Leadership Consultant; Robert Daniell Sansom [1959] Director/Business Executive/Entrepreneur; Nicholas Swift [1964] Director

Camfield Estate Company Limited
Incorporated: 18 August 1964 *Employees:* 5
Net Worth: £6,389,403 *Total Assets:* £11,330,886
Registered Office: Camfield Place, Hatfield, Herts, AL9 6JE
Activities: Growing of cereals (except rice), leguminous crops and oil seeds
Shareholder: Ian Hamilton McCorquodale
Officers: Glen McCorquodale [1939] Director/Stockbroker; Ian Hamilton McCorquodale [1937] Director/Publisher

Camflats Limited
Incorporated: 19 May 1986 *Employees:* 2
Net Worth: £7,337,471 *Total Assets:* £10,037,507
Registered Office: 2 Primes Corner, Histon, Cambridge, CB24 9AG
Activities: Other letting and operating of own or leased real estate
Major Shareholder: Christopher Robert Dyason
Officers: Christopher Robert Dyason [1948] Director

Campion Willcocks Limited
Incorporated: 7 November 1968 *Employees:* 38
Net Worth: £749,799 *Total Assets:* £12,571,443
Registered Office: Oakfield House, 59 Hill Avenue, Amersham, Bucks, HP6 5ED
Activities: Management consultancy activities other than financial management
Major Shareholder: David Mark Campion
Officers: Neil Frederick Jowitt, Secretary; Brenda Campion [1937] Director; David Mark Campion [1964] Director; David Malcolm Campion [1937] Director; Richard Alan Clifford [1978] Director; Neil Frederick Jowitt [1961] Director; David Lawton Roberts [1962] Director

Camstar Herbs Limited
Incorporated: 6 February 1979 *Employees:* 40
Net Worth: £9,648,513 *Total Assets:* £17,149,070
Registered Office: Chestnuts Farm, Langton Green, Eye, Suffolk, IP23 7HL
Activities: Other processing and preserving of fruit and vegetables
Parent: Starke Industries Limited
Officers: Tracey Clark, Secretary; Tracey Clark [1972] Director; Martin Thomas Hoxworth [1967] Director; Edward James Bruce Starke [1971] Director

Camstead Limited
Incorporated: 23 April 1986 *Employees:* 5
Net Worth: £4,429,192 *Total Assets:* £10,658,368
Registered Office: 1 St Mary's Court, Main Street, Hardwick, Cambridge, CB23 7QS
Activities: Buying and selling of own real estate
Parent: Yelcon Limited
Officers: Terence Joseph Padian, Secretary; Stephen Kenneth Holman [1957] Director/Chartered Surveyor; Terence Joseph Padian [1950] Director/Management Accountant; Martin Rapley [1957] Director/Property Developer

Camvac Limited
Incorporated: 1 May 2008 *Employees:* 133
Net Worth: £5,200,958 *Total Assets:* £11,132,038
Registered Office: Burrell Way, Thetford, Norfolk, IP24 3QY
Activities: Manufacture of plastic plates, sheets, tubes and profiles
Shareholder: David Grove Discretionary Will Trust
Officers: Alistair Pearce, Secretary; Keith Anthony Chapman [1955] Director/Consultant; Steve Jackson [1965] Director; Leszek Richard Litwinowicz [1958] Director; Peter Francis Lombardi [1945] Director; Alistair Pearce [1970] Director; Simon Smith [1967] Director

Canada Life (U.K.) Limited
Incorporated: 4 April 1974
Net Worth: £23,515,000 *Total Assets:* £23,519,000
Registered Office: Canada Life Place, Potters Bar, Herts, EN6 5BA
Activities: Activities of head offices
Parent: Canada Life Limited
Officers: Kathryn Louise Bateman [1964] Director/Chief Financial Officer; Douglas Allan Brown [1971] Director; Ashleigh Martin Kewney [1966] Director/Head of Tax

Canada Life Asset Management Limited
Incorporated: 23 September 1999
Net Worth: £12,384,000 *Total Assets:* £15,254,000
Registered Office: Canada Life Place, High Street, Potters Bar, Herts, EN6 5BA
Activities: Security and commodity contracts dealing activities
Parent: The Canada Life Group (U.K.) Limited
Officers: Narmadha Dharshini Riley, Secretary; Douglas Allan Brown [1971] Director/Chief Executive; Alan Henry Clifton [1946] Director; Ian Gilmour [1952] Director; David John Marchant [1964] Director

Canada Life Finance (U.K.) Limited
Incorporated: 24 July 2002
Net Worth: £39,058,000 *Total Assets:* £281,772,992
Registered Office: Canada Life Place, Potters Bar, Herts, EN6 5BA
Activities: Financial intermediation not elsewhere classified
Shareholders: Sophie Desmarais; Paul Desmarais, Jr; Andre Desmarais; Michael Plessis-Belair; Guy Fortin
Officers: Kathryn Louise Bateman [1964] Director; Douglas Allan Brown [1971] Director; Ashleigh Martin Kewney [1966] Director/Head of Taxation

The Canada Life Group (U.K.) Limited
Incorporated: 9 March 1988
Net Worth: £2,751,300,096 *Total Assets:* £3,079,300,096
Registered Office: Canada Life Place, Potters Bar, Herts, EN6 5BA
Activities: Other business support service activities n.e.c.
Shareholders: Sophie Desmarais; Paul Desmarais, Jr; Andre Desmarais; Michel Plessis-Belair; Guy Fortin
Officers: Lisa Annette Rodriguez, Secretary; Marcia Dominic Campbell [1959] Director; Cecil Hayes [1956] Director [Irish]; Arshil Jamal [1967] Director [Canadian]; Paul Anthony Mahon [1963] Director [Canadian]; Susan Jane McArthur [1963] Director [Canadian]; Nathan Moss [1955] Director; Derek Nigel Donald Netherton [1945] Director; Robert Jeffrey Orr [1958] Director [Canadian]; Siim Alden Vanaselja [1956] Director [Canadian]

Canada Life Limited
Incorporated: 25 February 1970
Net Worth: £2,854,799,872 *Total Assets:* £31,149,299,712
Registered Office: Canada Life Place, Potters Bar, Herts, EN6 5BA
Activities: Life insurance
Parent: The Canada Life Group (U.K.) Limited
Officers: Lisa Annette Rodriguez, Secretary; Keith William Abercromby [1964] Director; Douglas Allan Brown [1971] Director/Chief Executive; Marcia Dominic Campbell [1959] Director; Arshil Jamal [1967] Director [Canadian]; Paul Anthony Mahon [1963] Director [Canadian]; Susan Jane McArthur [1963] Director [Canadian]; Mary-Anne Bridget McIntyre [1961] Director; Derek Nigel Donald Netherton [1945] Director; Siim Alden Vanaselja [1956] Director [Canadian]

Canfield House Limited
Incorporated: 1 September 2009 *Employees:* 4
Net Worth: £2,127,180 *Total Assets:* £8,227,754
Registered Office: 3 Twyford Court, High Street, Dunmow, Essex, CM6 1AE
Activities: Other letting and operating of own or leased real estate
Major Shareholder: Graham Frederick Peacock
Officers: James Christopher Peacock, Secretary; Adam Thomas Peacock [1983] Director/Consultant; Graham Frederick Peacock [1950] Director; James Christopher Peacock [1980] Director/Actuary

Canna (B) Investors LLP
Incorporated: 5 August 2008
Net Worth: £8,344,391 *Total Assets:* £8,344,391
Registered Office: c/o William Heard, 8c Kings Parade, Cambridge, CB2 1SJ

Cannon Kirk (UK) Limited
Incorporated: 11 July 1997
Net Worth Deficit: £5,180,353 *Total Assets:* £9,916,904
Registered Office: Lupins Close, Littleport, Ely, Cambs, CB6 1FN
Activities: Construction of domestic buildings
Parent: Aledo Holdco (UK) Limited
Officers: Michael Canon, Secretary; Cathal Canon [1953] Director/Builder [Irish]; Michael Canon [1956] Director/Builder [Irish]; David Cortese [1983] Director/Finance Professional; Owen Kirk [1952] Director/Builder [Irish]

Cannon Kirk Property Limited
Incorporated: 13 March 1998
Net Worth Deficit: £3,203,108 *Total Assets:* £43,696,788
Registered Office: Lupins Close, Littleport, Ely, Cambs, CB6 1FN
Activities: Development of building projects
Parent: Aledo Holdco (UK) Limited
Officers: Michael Canon, Secretary; Cathal Canon [1953] Director [Irish]; Michael Canon [1956] Director [Irish]; David Cortese [1983] Director/Finance Professional; Owen Kirk [1952] Director [Irish]

Canons High School
Incorporated: 5 July 2011 *Employees:* 143
Net Worth: £21,116,816 *Total Assets:* £23,441,502
Registered Office: Shaldon Road, Edgware, Middlesex, HA8 6AN
Activities: General secondary education
Officers: Kevin Andrew Bartle [1972] Director/Teacher; Jacqueline Brennan [1969] Director/PA; Audrey Anne Brightwell [1937] Director; Natalie Cain [1979] Director/Assistant Facilities Manager; Jennifer Hart [1982] Director/Teacher; Anthony Bernard Richard Hickin [1957] Director; David Esseh Inyang [1953] Director/Engineering/Management Consultant; Dimple Khagram [1972] Managing Director; George Kynaston [1988] Director/Education Professional; Alexandra Joanne Mawson [1983] Director/Teacher [Australian]; Heni Patel [1978] Director/Neurophysiology Medical Secretary; Athena Pitsillis [1988] Director/Teacher; Keith Edward Rutter [1948] Director/Retired; Ronald Derrick Warshaw [1926] Director; Stephen John Leete Wright [1946] Director/Councillor

Cantab Capital Partners LLP
Incorporated: 31 January 2006
Net Worth: £21,447,000 *Total Assets:* £44,949,000
Registered Office: City House, Hills Road, Cambridge, CB2 1RE

Cantay Estates Limited
Incorporated: 20 February 1998 *Employees:* 2
Net Worth: £14,156,821 *Total Assets:* £17,345,136
Registered Office: Hawridge Place, Hawridge, Chesham, Bucks, HP5 2UG
Activities: Development of building projects
Officers: Carys Gadsden, Secretary; Eric John Spencer Gadsden [1944] Director; Sarah Louise Gadsden [1985] Director/Chartered Surveyor; Tony Nolan [1962] Director; Tony Norman Tompkins [1947] Director

Cantel Medical (UK) Limited
Incorporated: 10 March 1992 *Employees:* 9
Net Worth: £39,960,000 *Total Assets:* £43,315,000
Registered Office: Cantel UK, Campfield Road, Shoeburyness, Southend on Sea, Essex, SS3 9BX
Activities: Other professional, scientific and technical activities n.e.c.
Parent: Cantel Medical International BV
Officers: Neil Thomas Blewitt [1960] Senior VP Endoscopy & Clean Air & UK Managing Director; Jorgen Hansen [1967] Director [Danish]; Michael James Pollard [1972] Director/Accountant

Capespan International Limited
Incorporated: 2 February 1994 *Employees:* 36
Net Worth: £8,798,000 *Total Assets:* £15,494,000
Registered Office: Unit 3a, Burkes Lodge, 20 London End, Beaconsfield, Bucks, HP9 2JH
Activities: Wholesale of fruit and vegetables
Officers: Graham Linney, Secretary; Geoffrey Ian Green [1961] Group Procurement & New Business Development Director; Graham Linney [1964] Director/Accountant

Capital Cash Limited
Incorporated: 19 March 2003 *Employees:* 288
Net Worth: £2,338,312 *Total Assets:* £9,524,672
Registered Office: Artisan, Hillbottom Road, Sands Industrial Estate, High Wycombe, Bucks, HP12 4HJ
Activities: Retail sale of other second-hand goods in stores (not incl. antiques)
Major Shareholder: Mark Sands
Officers: Paul Jefferson Graham, Secretary; Paul Jefferson Graham [1971] Director/Certified Accountant; William John Murphy [1962] Operations Director; Carl Murray [1962] Director; Colin George Sanders [1964] Director; Derrick Stephen Woolf [1947] Director/Accountant

The Capital Pub Company Limited
Incorporated: 4 December 2000
Net Worth: £48,273,000 *Total Assets:* £189,635,008
Registered Office: Westgate Brewery, Bury St Edmunds, Suffolk, IP33 1QT
Activities: Public houses and bars
Parent: Greene King PLC
Officers: Lindsay Anne Keswick, Secretary; Richard Smothers [1967] Director

Capital Pub Company Trading Limited
Incorporated: 14 February 2011
Net Worth: £104,939,000 *Total Assets:* £105,237,000
Registered Office: Westgate Brewery, Bury St Edmunds, Suffolk, IP33 1QT
Activities: Public houses and bars
Shareholder: The Capital Pub Company Limited
Officers: Lindsay Keswick, Secretary; Richard Smothers [1967] Director

Cappagh Browne Utilities Limited
Incorporated: 3 November 2014 *Employees:* 201
Net Worth Deficit: £1,831,947 *Total Assets:* £15,484,426
Registered Office: Meelin House, Unit 2 Pavilion Business Centre, 6 Kinetic Crescent, Enfield, Middlesex, EN3 7FJ
Activities: Other business support service activities n.e.c.
Shareholders: Cappagh Contractors Construction (London) Limited; J.Brown Construction Company Limited
Officers: Jeffrey Paul Birtwhistle [1963] Director/Civil Engineer; Jeremy Browne [1971] Director [Irish]; Jonathan Mark Dodd [1973] Director; Michael John Ferncombe [1967] Director; Thomas Augustine Ferncombe [1942] Director [Irish]; Matthew Simon Guest [1972] Director; Paul Denis McMahon [1966] Director

Caps Cases Limited
Incorporated: 19 May 1982 *Employees:* 219
Net Worth: £3,253,273 *Total Assets:* £11,256,583
Registered Office: Caps Cases Ltd, Studlands Park Industrial Estate, Newmarket, Suffolk, CB8 7AU
Activities: Manufacture of other paper and paperboard containers
Parent: Tradegreat Limited
Officers: Nicholas James Drewry, Secretary; Angela Brenda Bissett [1955] Director/Secretary; Charles Henry Bissett [1952] Director/Chairman; James Thomas Bissett [1987] Director; Mark Henry Bissett [1978] Production Director; Trevor Charles Bissett [1976] Managing Director; Nicholas James Drewry [1988] Director/Chartered Accountant

Car World (Cambs) Ltd
Incorporated: 13 January 2005 *Employees:* 42
Net Worth: £3,681,259 *Total Assets:* £8,208,640
Registered Office: Ivatt Way, Westwood, Peterborough, Cambs, PE3 7PN
Activities: Sale of used cars and light motor vehicles
Major Shareholder: Mahmood Fazal
Officers: Mahmood Fazal, Secretary; Mahmood Fazal [1967] Director/Motor Trader; Tariq Fazal [1976] Director/Manager

Carbery (UK) Limited
Incorporated: 7 October 1998
Net Worth Deficit: £4,629,313 *Total Assets:* £12,191,704
Registered Office: Synergy House, 2 Hillbottom Road, Sands Industrial Estate, High Wycombe, Bucks, HP12 4HJ
Activities: Activities of head offices
Officers: Colm Anthony Leen, Secretary; Gerard Brickley [1972] Director [Irish]; Peter Fleming [1953] Director [Irish]; Jason Mathew Hawkins [1972] Director/Chief Executive [Irish]; Colm Anthony Leen [1962] Director/Accountant [Irish]; Pat Moriarity [1959] Director/Chief Executive [Irish]; Peader Murphy [1964] Director [Irish]; Dermot O'Leary [1958] Director [Irish]; Jerome O'Mahony [1965] Director/Farmer [Irish]; Joe O'Sullivan [1955] Director [Irish]; Patrick Joseph Ryan [1962] Director/Farmer [Irish]; Timothy John Sullivan [1977] Director/Farmer [Irish]

Carbon60 Limited
Incorporated: 5 January 1988 *Employees:* 142
Net Worth: £18,739,000 *Total Assets:* £49,787,000
Registered Office: 800 The Boulevard, Capability Green, Luton, Beds, LU1 3BA
Activities: Other activities of employment placement agencies
Parent: Impellam UK Limited
Officers: Rebecca Jane Watson, Secretary; Julia Robertson [1958] Director; Rebecca Jane Watson [1969] Director/Solicitor

Cardel Group Limited
Incorporated: 16 May 2017 *Employees:* 5
Net Worth Deficit: £759,083 *Total Assets:* £20,100,000
Registered Office: 5 The Marquis Centre, Royston Road, Baldock, Herts, SG7 6XL
Activities: Activities of production holding companies
Officers: Gary Andrew Kennedy, Secretary; Jonathan Howard Ford [1962] Director; Marshall Thomas Haldane [1962] Director; David Owen Hughes [1959] Director; Gary Andrew Kennedy [1965] Director/Chartered Accountant; Richard Peter Whitwell [1964] Director

Cardif Pinnacle Insurance Holdings PLC
Incorporated: 5 May 1992 *Employees:* 245
Net Worth: £142,234,000 *Total Assets:* £344,260,000
Registered Office: Pinnacle House, A1 Barnet Way, Borehamwood, Herts, WD6 2XX
Activities: Life insurance
Parent: BNP Paribas Cardif
Officers: Matthew Justin Lorimer, Secretary; Gerard Binet [1953] Development and Strategy Director [French]; Peter John Box [1952] Director; Stanislas Louis Paul Francois Chevalet [1961] Director [French]; Marie Haderer [1979] Director/Actuary [French]; Matthew Justin Lorimer [1967] Director/Solicitor; Nicholas Dutfield Rochez [1954] Director; Andrew Miles Wigg [1972] Director

Cardif Pinnacle Insurance Management Services PLC
Incorporated: 2 July 1992 *Employees:* 188
Net Worth: £2,184,000 *Total Assets:* £9,760,000
Registered Office: Pinnacle House, A1 Barnet Way, Borehamwood, Herts, WD6 2XX
Activities: Other business support service activities n.e.c.
Parent: Cardif Pinnacle Insurance Holdings PLC
Officers: Matthew Justin Lorimer, Secretary; Gerard Binet [1953] Development and Strategy Director [French]; Peter John Box [1952] Director; Stanislas Louis Paul Francois Chevalet [1961] Director/Exco Member COO BNPPC [French]; Marie Haderer [1979] Director/Actuary [French]; Matthew Justin Lorimer [1967] Director/Solicitor; Nicholas Dutfield Rochez [1954] Director; Andrew Miles Wigg [1972] Director

Cardiff Gate Business Park Limited
Incorporated: 6 June 1991
Net Worth: £2,983,065 *Total Assets:* £24,927,388
Registered Office: Eaton Court, Maylands Avenue, Hemel Hempstead Industrial Estate, Hemel Hempstead, Herts, HP2 7TR
Activities: Construction of commercial buildings
Parent: Robert McAlpine Enterprises Limited
Officers: Kevin John Pearson, Secretary; Andrew Reginald Bolt [1957] Director/Construction & Property; Robert John William Wotherspoon [1967] Director/Chartered Accountant

Cardpoint Limited
Incorporated: 27 October 2000
Net Worth: £147,822,000 *Total Assets:* £147,822,000
Registered Office: 1st Floor, Building 4, Trident Place, Mosquito Way, Hatfield, Herts, AL10 9UL
Activities: Other business support service activities n.e.c.
Parent: Cardtronics Holdings Limited
Officers: Jana Hile [1976] Director [Australian]; Marc Christopher Terry [1961] Managing Director

Cardtronics Creative UK Limited
Incorporated: 24 October 2012
Net Worth: £8,417,000 *Total Assets:* £8,507,000
Registered Office: 1st Floor, Building 4, Trident Place, Mosquito Way, Hatfield, Herts, AL10 9UL
Activities: Other business support service activities n.e.c.
Officers: Marc Christopher Terry [1961] Managing Director

Cardtronics Holdings Limited
Incorporated: 18 May 2016
Net Worth: £1,575,544,320 *Total Assets:* £1,769,944,064
Registered Office: 1st Floor, Building 4, Trident Place, Mosquito Way, Hatfield, Herts, AL10 9UL
Activities: Other business support service activities n.e.c.
Parent: Cardtronics PLC
Officers: Paul Carbonelli [1983] Director [American]; Erich Brad Conrad [1972] Director/Business Executive [American]; Paul Gullo [1966] Director [American]; Angela Weinstein [1973] Director [American]

Cardtronics PLC
Incorporated: 11 March 2016 *Employees:* 2,244
Net Worth: £294,096,544 *Total Assets:* £1,403,024,000
Registered Office: 1st Floor, Building 4, Trident Place, Hatfield, Herts, AL10 9UL
Activities: Other business support service activities n.e.c.
Officers: Aimie Marie Killeen, Secretary; John Timothy Arnoult [1949] Director [American]; Douglas Lee Braunstein [1961] Director [American]; Jorge Mario Diaz [1964] Director [American]; Julie Gardner [1958] Director [American]; Warren Calvin Jenson [1956] Director [American]; George Patrick Phillips [1950] Director [American]; Mark Rossi [1956] Director [American]; Juli Christina Spottiswood [1966] Director [American]; Edward Hamilton West [1966] Director/Business Executive [American]

Cardtronics UK Limited
Incorporated: 30 July 1998 *Employees:* 39
Net Worth: £174,751,008 *Total Assets:* £303,830,016
Registered Office: First Floor, Building 4, Trident House, Mosquito Way, Hatfield, Herts, AL10 9UL
Activities: Other business support service activities n.e.c.
Parent: Cardpoint Limited
Officers: Jana Hile [1976] Director [Australian]; Marc Christopher Terry [1961] Managing Director

Care Providers Recruitment Limited
Incorporated: 5 July 2011 *Employees:* 3
Net Worth: £2,302,823 *Total Assets:* £10,569,541
Registered Office: Treviot House, 186-192 High Road, Ilford, Essex, IG1 1LR
Activities: Other residential care activities n.e.c.
Parent: Day Webster Limited
Officers: Hugh Woods Ballard, Secretary; Wayne Arthur St John [1974] Director; Daniel Jonathan Wise [1982] Director; Hugh William Woods Ballard [1968] Director

Care UK (Urgent Care) Limited
Incorporated: 16 September 2004 *Employees:* 1,649
Net Worth Deficit: £11,634,000 *Total Assets:* £11,121,000
Registered Office: Connaught House, 850 The Crescent, Colchester Business Park, Colchester, Essex, CO4 9QB
Activities: General medical practice activities
Parent: Care UK (Urgent Care) Holdings Limited
Officers: Jonathan David Calow, Secretary; James William Easton [1964] Director; Michael Robert Parish [1959] Director; Andrew James MacKenzie Prosser [1965] Director/Chartered Accountant; Philip James Whitecross [1963] Director

Care UK Clinical Services Limited
Incorporated: 10 November 1997 *Employees:* 3,494
Net Worth: £69,260,000 *Total Assets:* £96,340,000
Registered Office: Connaught House, 850 The Crescent, Colchester Business Park, Colchester, Essex, CO4 9QB
Activities: Other human health activities
Parent: Care UK Healthcare Holdings Limited
Officers: Jonathan David Calow, Secretary; James William Easton [1964] Director; Michael Robert Parish [1959] Director; Andrew James MacKenzie Prosser [1965] Director/Chartered Accountant; Philip James Whitecross [1963] Director

Care UK Community Partnerships Ltd
Incorporated: 11 September 1991 *Employees:* 8,831
Net Worth: £121,526,000 *Total Assets:* £209,184,992
Registered Office: Connaught House, 850 The Crescent, Colchester Business Park, Colchester, Essex, CO4 9QB
Activities: Residential care activities for the elderly and disabled
Parent: Care UK Limited
Officers: Jonathan David Calow, Secretary; Andrew Ronald Knight [1967] Director; Michael Robert Parish [1959] Director; Richard Charles Pearman [1975] Director; Matthew Alexander Rosenberg [1977] Director; Philip James Whitecross [1963] Director

Care UK Health & Rehabilitation Services Limited
Incorporated: 28 November 2016 *Employees:* 226
Net Worth: £3,170,000 *Total Assets:* £28,033,000
Registered Office: Connaught House, 850 The Crescent, Colchester Business Park, Colchester, Essex, CO4 9QB
Activities: Other human health activities
Parent: Care UK Healthcare Holdings Limited
Officers: Jonathan David Calow, Secretary; James William Easton [1964] Director; Michael Robert Parish [1959] Director; Andrew James MacKenzie Prosser [1965] Director/Accountant; Philip James Whitecross [1963] Director

Care UK Health & Social Care Finance Limited
Incorporated: 16 February 2010
Net Worth: £91,649,000 *Total Assets:* £246,902,000
Registered Office: Connaught House, 850 The Crescent, Colchester Business Park, Colchester, Essex, CO4 9QB
Activities: Activities of head offices
Parent: Care UK Health & Social Care Holdings Limited
Officers: Jonathan David Calow, Secretary; Jonathan David Calow [1969] Director/Lawyer; Michael Robert Parish [1959] Director; Philip James Whitecross [1963] Director

Care UK Health & Social Care Holdings Limited
Incorporated: 16 February 2010 *Employees:* 15,148
Net Worth Deficit: £472,500,000 *Total Assets:* £481,000,000
Registered Office: Connaught House, 850 The Crescent, Colchester Business Park, Colchester, Essex, CO4 9QB
Activities: Activities of head offices
Shareholders: Bridgepoint Europe (SGP) Limited; Bridgepoint Advisers Limited
Officers: Jonathan David Calow, Secretary; Jonathan Raoul Hughes [1965] Director/Investment Banker; Robert Patrick Moores [1962] Director/Investment Banker; Michael Robert Parish [1959] Director; Philip James Whitecross [1963] Director

Care UK Health & Social Care Investments Limited
Incorporated: 16 February 2010 *Employees:* 15,148
Net Worth Deficit: £4,600,000 *Total Assets:* £467,300,000
Registered Office: Connaught House, 850 The Crescent, Colchester Business Park, Colchester, Essex, CO4 9QB
Activities: Activities of head offices
Parent: Care UK Health & Social Care Finance Limited
Officers: Jonathan David Calow, Secretary; Jonathan David Calow [1969] Director/Lawyer; Michael Robert Parish [1959] Director; Philip James Whitecross [1963] Director

Care UK Health & Social Care PLC
Incorporated: 6 November 2009
Net Worth: £293,491,008 *Total Assets:* £568,059,008
Registered Office: Connaught House, 850 The Crescent, Colchester Business Park, Colchester, Essex, CO4 9QB
Activities: Activities of other holding companies n.e.c.
Parent: Care UK Health & Social Care Investments Limited
Officers: Jonathan David Calow, Secretary; Jonathan David Calow [1969] Director/Lawyer; Michael Robert Parish [1959] Director; Philip James Whitecross [1963] Director

Care UK Healthcare Holdings Limited
Incorporated: 24 May 2017 *Employees:* 54
Net Worth: £118,285,000 *Total Assets:* £138,112,992
Registered Office: Connaught House, 850 The Crescent, Colchester Business Park, Colchester, Essex, CO4 9QB
Activities: Other human health activities
Parent: Care UK Limited
Officers: Jonathan David Calow, Secretary; Jonathan David Calow [1969] Director/Lawyer; James William Easton [1964] Director; Michael Robert Parish [1959] Director; Andrew James MacKenzie Prosser [1965] Director/Chartered Accountant; Philip James Whitecross [1963] Director

Care UK Limited
Incorporated: 29 September 1982 *Employees:* 33
Net Worth Deficit: £131,900,000 *Total Assets:* £323,600,000
Registered Office: Connaught House, 850 The Crescent, Colchester Business Park, Colchester, Essex, CO4 9QB
Activities: Activities of head offices
Parent: Care UK Health & Social Care PLC
Officers: Jonathan David Calow, Secretary/Group Director of Legal Services; Jonathan David Calow [1969] Director/Lawyer; Michael Robert Parish [1959] Director; Philip James Whitecross [1963] Director

Career Teachers Limited
Incorporated: 20 March 2006 *Employees:* 42
Net Worth: £9,428,000 *Total Assets:* £13,898,000
Registered Office: 800 The Boulevard, Capability Green, Luton, Beds, LU1 3BA
Activities: Temporary employment agency activities
Parent: Impellam Holdings Limited
Officers: Rebecca Jane Watson, Secretary; Julia Robertson [1958] Director; Rebecca Jane Watson [1969] Director/Solicitor

Careprogress Limited
Incorporated: 26 October 1999 *Employees:* 207
Net Worth: £13,218,546 *Total Assets:* £26,391,724
Registered Office: c/o Elysium Healthcare, 2 Imperial Place, Maxwell Road, Borehamwood, Herts, WD6 1JN
Activities: Residential care activities for the elderly and disabled
Parent: Elysium Healthcare Holdings 3 Limited
Officers: Sarah Juliette Livingston, Secretary; Lesley Joy Chamberlain [1963] Director/Group Chief Executive; Dr Quazi Shams Mahfooz Haque [1968] Executive Medical Director; Steven John Woolgar [1955] Director of Policy and Regulation

Carestream Dental Technology Parent Limited
Incorporated: 3 April 2017 *Employees:* 1,135
Net Worth: £214,190,688 *Total Assets:* £770,097,920
Registered Office: Wiltron House, Rutherford Close, Stevenage, Herts, SG1 2EF
Activities: Activities of head offices
Parent: Carestream Dental Technology Holdings 2 Limited
Officers: Nicola Gizzi [1966] Director [Italian]; Jane Louise Guinn [1959] Director; Philippe Louis Denis Maillet [1960] Director [French]

Carestream Dental Technology Topco Limited
Incorporated: 21 April 2017 *Employees:* 4
Net Worth: £166,544,128 *Total Assets:* £212,537,744
Registered Office: Wiltron House, Rutherford Close, Stevenage, Herts, SG1 2EF
Activities: Manufacture of medical and dental instruments and supplies
Parent: Carestream Dental Technology Parent Limited
Officers: Nicola Gizzi [1966] Director [Italian]; Jane Louise Guinn [1959] Director; Philippe Louis Denis Maillet [1960] Director [French]

Carestream Health UK, Limited
Incorporated: 21 September 2006 *Employees:* 114
Net Worth: £44,108,000 *Total Assets:* £62,592,000
Registered Office: One Park Lane, Hemel Hempstead, Herts, HP2 4YJ
Activities: Manufacture of medical and dental instruments and supplies
Parent: Carestream Health Netherlands BV
Officers: Orsolya Corr, Secretary; Charles McCaffrey [1964] Director; Jane Victoria Moverley [1973] Director/Chartered Accountant; Mandy Diane Parsons [1966] Director/HR Manager

Caretech Community Services (No.2) Limited
Incorporated: 15 December 1999 *Employees:* 436
Net Worth: £229,000 *Total Assets:* £15,198,000
Registered Office: 5th Floor, Metropolitan House, 3 Darkes Lane, Potters Bar, Herts, EN6 1AG
Activities: Other human health activities
Officers: Gareth Dufton, Secretary; Gareth Dufton [1976] Director/Chartered Accountant; Farouq Rashid Sheikh [1958] Director; Haroon Rashid Sheikh [1956] Director

Caretech Community Services Limited
Incorporated: 29 March 1993 *Employees:* 969
Net Worth: £6,922,000 *Total Assets:* £216,876,000
Registered Office: 5th Floor, Metropolitan House, 3 Darkes Lane, Potters Bar, Herts, EN6 1AG
Activities: Other human health activities
Parent: Caretech Holdings PLC
Officers: Gareth Dufton, Secretary; Gareth Dufton [1976] Director/Chartered Accountant; Farouq Rashid Sheikh [1958] Director; Haroon Rashid Sheikh [1956] Director

Caretech Estates (No 2) Limited
Incorporated: 29 February 2008
Net Worth: £656,000 *Total Assets:* £14,383,000
Registered Office: 5th Floor, Metropolitan Houe, 3 Darkes Lane, Potters Bar, Herts, EN6 1AG
Activities: Other letting and operating of own or leased real estate
Parent: Caretech Holdings PLC
Officers: Gareth Dufton, Secretary; Gareth Dufton [1976] Director/Chartered Accountant; Farouq Rashid Sheikh [1958] Director

Caretech Estates (No 3) Limited
Incorporated: 29 February 2008
Net Worth: £400,000 *Total Assets:* £9,634,000
Registered Office: 5th Floor, Metropolitan House, 3 Darkes Lane, Potters Bar, Herts, EN6 1AG
Activities: Other letting and operating of own or leased real estate
Parent: Caretech Holdings PLC
Officers: Gareth Dufton, Secretary; Gareth Dufton [1976] Director/Chartered Accountant; Farouq Rashid Sheikh [1958] Director

Caretech Estates (No 7) Limited
Incorporated: 29 July 2013
Net Worth: £3,480,000 *Total Assets:* £38,475,000
Registered Office: 5th Floor, Metropolitan House, 3 Darkes Lane, Potters Bar, Herts, EN6 1AG
Activities: Other letting and operating of own or leased real estate
Parent: Caretech Holdings PLC
Officers: Gareth Dufton, Secretary; Gareth Dufton [1976] Director/Chartered Accountant; Farouq Rashid Sheikh [1958] Director; Haroon Rashid Sheikh [1956] Director

Caretech Estates (No. 5) Limited
Incorporated: 23 September 2009
Net Worth: £786,000 *Total Assets:* £16,166,000
Registered Office: 5th Floor, Metropolitan House, Darkes Lane, Potters Bar, Herts, EN6 1AG
Activities: Other letting and operating of own or leased real estate
Parent: Caretech Holdings PLC
Officers: Gareth Dufton, Secretary; Gareth Dufton [1976] Director/Chartered Accountant; Farouq Rashid Sheikh [1958] Director; Haroon Rashid Sheikh [1956] Director

Caretech Estates (No.4) Limited
Incorporated: 26 March 2008
Net Worth: £420,000 *Total Assets:* £11,441,000
Registered Office: 5th Floor, Metropolitan House, 3 Darkes Lane, Potters Bar, Herts, EN6 1AG
Activities: Other letting and operating of own or leased real estate
Parent: Caretech Holdings PLC
Officers: Gareth Dufton, Secretary; Gareth Dufton [1976] Director/Chartered Accountant; Farouq Rashid Sheikh [1958] Director

Caretech Estates Limited
Incorporated: 12 October 2006
Net Worth: £1,337,000 *Total Assets:* £16,363,000
Registered Office: 5th Floor, Metropolitan House, 3 Darkes Lane, Potters Bar, Herts, EN6 1AG
Activities: Other letting and operating of own or leased real estate
Parent: Caretech Holdings PLC
Officers: Gareth Dufton, Secretary; Gareth Dufton [1976] Director/Chartered Accountant; Farouq Rashid Sheikh [1958] Director; Haroon Rashid Sheikh [1956] Director

Caretech Holdings PLC
Incorporated: 10 June 2002 *Employees:* 4,744
Net Worth: £204,200,992 *Total Assets:* £411,977,984
Registered Office: 5th Floor, Metropolitan House, 3 Darkes Lane, Potters Bar, Herts, EN6 1AG
Activities: Activities of head offices
Officers: Gareth Dufton, Secretary; Michael John Adams [1971] Director; James Stuart Cumming [1950] Director; Gareth Dufton [1976] Director/Chartered Accountant; Karl Upton Monaghan [1962] Director [Irish]; Farouq Rashid Sheikh [1958] Director; Haroon Rashid Sheikh [1956] Director

P.J. Carey (Contractors) Limited
Incorporated: 9 November 1979 *Employees:* 982
Net Worth: £56,466,940 *Total Assets:* £124,872,688
Registered Office: Carey House, Great Central Way, Wembley, Middlesex, HA9 0HR
Activities: Construction of commercial buildings
Parent: Carey Group PLC
Officers: Fiona Mary O'Donnell, Secretary; Bjourn Bigley [1979] Director [Irish]; Jason Anthony Carey [1975] Director [Irish]; John Anthony Carey [1964] Director [Irish]; John Carey [1941] Director [Irish]; Patrick Joseph Carey [1945] Director [Irish]; Thomas Noel Carey [1973] Director; Thomas Carey [1943] Director [Irish]; Denis Patrick Deacy [1965] Director; Paul Albert Johnson [1970] Director/Health & Safety Officer; Martin James McGuire [1972] Director; Joe O'Hagan [1967] Director; Paul Quigley [1958] Estimating Director [Irish]; Steven John Regan [1974] Director; Stephen Peter Smith [1957] Director

P.J. Carey Plant Hire (Oval) Limited
Incorporated: 29 October 1968 *Employees:* 61
Net Worth: £3,621,148 *Total Assets:* £22,805,350
Registered Office: Carey House, Great Central Way, Wembley, Middlesex, HA9 0HR
Activities: Renting and leasing of cars and light motor vehicles
Parent: Carey Group PLC
Officers: Fiona Mary O'Donnell, Secretary; John Carey [1941] Director [Irish]; Patrick Joseph Carey [1945] Director [Irish]; Thomas Noel Carey [1973] Director; Thomas Carey [1943] Director [Irish]; Gary Condon [1961] Managing Director

Careys New Homes Limited
Incorporated: 5 December 1975 *Employees:* 4
Previous: Maxplan Properties Limited
Net Worth: £9,953,778 *Total Assets:* £59,838,172
Registered Office: Carey House, Great Central Way, Wembley, Middlesex, HA9 0HR
Activities: Development of building projects
Parent: Carey Group PLC
Officers: Fiona Mary O'Donnell, Secretary; John Carey [1941] Director [Irish]; Thomas Carey [1943] Director [Irish]; Denis Patrick Deacy [1965] Group Managing Director; Gregory Charles Ketteridge [1958] Director

C.W. & J. Cargill Limited
Incorporated: 14 September 1960 *Employees:* 14
Net Worth: £9,931,308 *Total Assets:* £14,051,263
Registered Office: The Dairy House, High Street, Dunwich, Saxmundham, Suffolk, IP17 3DN
Activities: Growing of cereals (except rice), leguminous crops and oil seeds
Shareholder: David Ross Bowser Cargill
Officers: Penelope Margaret Mead, Secretary; Christina Pamela Cargill [1950] Director; David Ross Bowser Cargill [1949] Director/Farmer; Maureen Cargill [1952] Director; Peter James David Cargill [1955] Director/Farmer; Penelope Margaret Mead [1954] Director; Claire Elizabeth Owen [1981] Director; Diana Margaret Willis [1953] Director

Cargobull Finance Limited
Incorporated: 11 December 2000 *Employees:* 1
Net Worth: £9,228,000 *Total Assets:* £23,251,000
Registered Office: Building 7, Croxley Park, Hatters Lane, Watford, Herts, WD18 8YN
Activities: Renting and leasing of cars and light motor vehicles
Officers: Thies Johannes Philipp Engering [1974] Director [German]; Duncan John Hullis [1963] Director/General Manager; Simon John Trudgeon [1968] Director/Credit Risk Officer

Caring Homes Healthcare Group Limited
Incorporated: 11 September 2007 *Employees:* 3,201
Net Worth: £50,708,000 *Total Assets:* £129,171,000
Registered Office: Bradbury House, 830 The Crescent, Colchester Business Park, Colchester, Essex, CO4 9YQ
Activities: Residential nursing care facilities
Parent: MHL Holdco Limited
Officers: Nigel Bennett Schofield, Secretary; Craig Griffin [1967] Director; Peter Martin Hill [1968] Director; Paul Anthony Keith Jeffery [1966] Director/Accountant; Michael Geoffrey Medlicott [1943] Director; Nigel Bennett Schofield [1950] Director/Solicitor

Carl F Groupco Limited
Incorporated: 14 July 1988 *Employees:* 40
Net Worth: £6,452,000 *Total Assets:* £10,107,000
Registered Office: Culley Court, Orton Southgate, Peterborough, Cambs, PE2 6WA
Activities: Wholesale of hardware, plumbing and heating equipment and supplies
Major Shareholder: Geoffrey David Gahan
Officers: David Peacefull Wakeley, Secretary; John Crittenden [1959] Managing Director; Geoffery David Gahan [1944] Director; John Martin King [1960] Sales Director; David Peacefull Wakeley [1955] Finance Director

Carlisle Group Limited
Incorporated: 27 September 1952 *Employees:* 3
Net Worth: £23,296,000 *Total Assets:* £83,748,000
Registered Office: 800 The Boulevard, Capability Green, Luton, Beds, LU1 3BA
Activities: Activities of head offices
Parent: Impellam UK Limited
Officers: Rebecca Jane Watson, Secretary; Julia Robertson [1958] Director; Rebecca Jane Watson [1969] Director/Solicitor

Carlisle Security Services Limited
Incorporated: 15 October 1991 *Employees:* 1,388
Net Worth: £1,297,000 *Total Assets:* £12,868,000
Registered Office: 800 The Boulevard, Capability Green, Luton, Beds, LU1 3BA
Activities: Other business support service activities n.e.c.
Parent: Carlisle Support Services Group Limited
Officers: Rebecca Jane Watson, Secretary; Julia Robertson [1958] Director; Rebecca Jane Watson [1969] Director/Solicitor

Carlisle Staffing PLC
Incorporated: 18 November 1993 *Employees:* 436
Net Worth: £11,850,000 *Total Assets:* £169,970,000
Registered Office: 800 The Boulevard, Capability Green, Luton, Beds, LU1 3BA
Activities: Temporary employment agency activities
Parent: Carlisle Staffing Services Limited
Officers: Rebecca Jane Watson, Secretary; Julia Robertson [1958] Director; Rebecca Jane Watson [1969] Director/Solicitor

Carlisle Staffing Services Holdings Limited
Incorporated: 26 February 2001 *Employees:* 3
Net Worth: £11,925,000 *Total Assets:* £14,902,000
Registered Office: 800 The Boulevard, Capability Green, Luton, Beds, LU1 3BA
Activities: Temporary employment agency activities
Parent: BMS Limited
Officers: Rebecca Jane Watson, Secretary; Julia Robertson [1958] Director; Rebecca Jane Watson [1969] Director/Solicitor

Carlisle Staffing Services Limited
Incorporated: 1 September 1993 *Employees:* 3
Net Worth: £598,000 *Total Assets:* £32,144,000
Registered Office: 800 The Boulevard, Capability Green, Luton, Beds, LU1 3BA
Activities: Temporary employment agency activities
Parent: Carlisle Staffing Services Holdings Limited
Officers: Rebecca Jane Watson, Secretary; Julia Robertson [1958] Director; Rebecca Jane Watson [1969] Director/Solicitor

Carlson Vehicle Transfer Ltd
Incorporated: 28 August 1997 *Employees:* 187
Net Worth: £9,373,759 *Total Assets:* £19,983,736
Registered Office: Carlson House, Bradfield Road, Wix, Manningtree, Essex, CO11 2SP
Activities: Freight transport by road
Major Shareholder: Manuel Antelo
Officers: Edoardo Cumino [1965] Sales Director (LV) [Italian]; Patrice Grosset [1964] Director/Chairman [French]; Steven Reynolds [1966] Director/Operations; Stuart Martin Warren [1958] Managing Director

Carlson Wagonlit New Holdco Limited
Incorporated: 23 May 2006
Net Worth: £31,605,128 *Total Assets:* £67,607,120
Registered Office: Maple House, High Street, Potters Bar, Herts, EN6 5RF
Activities: Travel agency activities
Shareholders: Marilyn Arleen Nelson; Barbara Ann Carlson Gage
Officers: Narinder Sanotra, Secretary; Christopher Bowen [1960] Director; Denise Harman [1970] Director [Irish]; Sanjay Kapoor [1967] Director [British/Australian]; Rhodri Llewelyn Hollister Turner [1977] Director/Chief Financial Officer

Carlson Wagonlit UK Ltd
Incorporated: 12 May 1994 *Employees:* 944
Net Worth: £20,163,888 *Total Assets:* £83,417,200
Registered Office: Maple House, High Street, Potters Bar, Herts, EN6 5RF
Activities: Travel agency activities
Parent: CWT Holdco Limited
Officers: Narinder Sanotra, Secretary; Christopher Bowen [1960] Director; Denise Harman [1970] Commercial Director [Irish]; Sanjay Kapoor [1967] Director [British/Australian]; Rhodri Llewelyn Hollister Turner [1977] Director/Chief Financial Officer

Carlton Group Developments Ltd
Incorporated: 8 July 2010
Net Worth Deficit: £56,393 *Total Assets:* £11,074,216
Registered Office: 501 High Road, Ilford, Essex, IG1 1TZ
Activities: Management of real estate on a fee or contract basis
Major Shareholder: Paul Waraich
Officers: Amar Waraich, Secretary; Swinder Paul Waraich [1952] Director

Carmelite House (Jarrold) Limited
Incorporated: 27 July 2005 *Employees:* 2
Net Worth: £7,020,451 *Total Assets:* £10,137,974
Registered Office: St James Mill, Whitefriars, Norwich, NR3 1SH
Activities: Other letting and operating of own or leased real estate
Officers: Christopher John Doggett, Secretary/Director; Christopher John Doggett [1960] Director; David John McLeavy Hill [1957] Director

Carnarvon Hotels Limited
Incorporated: 24 November 1967 *Employees:* 171
Net Worth: £10,346,123 *Total Assets:* £25,728,970
Registered Office: 17 Bourne Court, Southend Road, Woodford Green, Essex, IG8 8HD
Activities: Hotels and similar accommodation
Shareholders: Michael Anthony Harris; Albert Harris
Officers: Robert Phaidonos Aristotelous, Secretary; Albert Harris [1922] Director/Hotelier; Daniel Harris [1984] Director/Hotelier; Gregory Lewis Ralph Harris [1947] Director/Hotelier; Michael Anthony Harris [1954] Director/Hotelier

Carpetright of London Limited
Incorporated: 17 December 1992
Net Worth: £35,068,000 *Total Assets:* £77,989,000
Registered Office: Purfleet By Pass, Purfleet, Essex, RM19 1TT
Activities: Activities of other holding companies n.e.c.
Parent: Carpetright PLC
Officers: Neil Lloyd Page [1963] Director/Accountant; Jeremy Andrew Sampson [1968] Director/Solicitor

Carraig Gheal Wind Farm Limited
Incorporated: 14 July 2011
Net Worth: £7,275,483 *Total Assets:* £91,991,248
Registered Office: Beeston Lodge, Beeston Lane, Spixworth, Norwich, NR10 3TN
Activities: Production of electricity
Shareholders: Pacific Shelf 1678 Limited; Ampere UK Wind On-Shore S.L.
Officers: Robert John Forrest [1964] Director; John Andrew Morgan [1964] Director; Angela Louise Roshier [1975] Director/Head of Asset Management; Adam George Waddington [1974] Investment Director

Carrain Limited
Incorporated: 19 August 1982 *Employees:* 5
Net Worth: £9,210,941 *Total Assets:* £13,853,009
Registered Office: 1 Beauchamp Court, Victors Way, Barnet, Herts, EN5 5TZ
Activities: Development of building projects
Officers: Olive May Herman, Secretary; Julia Deborah Burton [1962] Director; Rosalind Carol Gelbart [1958] Director; Charles Robert Herman [1956] Director; Olive May Herman [1931] Director; Paul Philip Herman [1968] Director

Carter Accommodation Group Limited
Incorporated: 13 December 2013 *Employees:* 114
Previous: Ensco 1036 Limited
Net Worth: £439,043 *Total Assets:* £30,601,708
Registered Office: Garage Lane, Setchey, King's Lynn, Norfolk, PE33 0BE
Activities: Dormant company
Parent: Connection Capital LLP
Officers: Darren Anthony Arnold [1962] Director; Bernard John Dale [1964] Director; Carl Fisher [1968] Director; Jonathan Scott Smith [1970] Director

Carter Accommodation Holdings Limited
Incorporated: 13 December 1999
Previous: Carter (F.C.) Holdings Limited
Net Worth: £6,609,389 *Total Assets:* £26,450,444
Registered Office: Garage Lane, Setchey, King's Lynn, Norfolk, PE33 0BE
Activities: Activities of head offices
Parent: Carter Accommodation Group Limited
Officers: Darren Anthony Arnold [1962] Director; David Horkan [1967] Operations Director; Jonathan Scott Smith [1970] Director; Tzigane Abigail Woolner [1973] Finance Director

Carter and Ward of Wickford Limited
Incorporated: 26 November 1954 *Employees:* 23
Net Worth: £23,995,928 *Total Assets:* £26,069,764
Registered Office: Construction House, Runwell Road, Wickford, Essex, SS11 7HJ
Activities: Development of building projects
Shareholder: Peter Brian Carter
Officers: Peter Brian Carter, Secretary; Graham Peter Carter [1966] Director; Lee David Carter [1962] Director; Peter Brian Carter [1939] Director; Jane Marie Wickham [1967] Director

R.G. Carter Cambridge Limited
Incorporated: 18 November 1999 *Employees:* 131
Net Worth: £4,438,561 *Total Assets:* £23,852,200
Registered Office: 9-11 High Road, Drayton, Norwich, NR8 6AH
Activities: Construction of commercial buildings
Parent: R.G. Carter Construction Limited
Officers: Robert John Alflatt, Secretary; Robert Edward Russell Carter [1982] Director; Robin William Carter [1963] Director/Surveyor; Richard Stephen Clark [1963] Director; John Richard Ford [1966] Director; Robert Wallis Halfyard [1974] Director; Dean Peter Hall [1965] Director; Timothy John Leggett [1970] Director

R.G. Carter Construction Limited
Incorporated: 27 November 1996 *Employees:* 606
Net Worth: £34,429,000 *Total Assets:* £99,933,000
Registered Office: 9-11 Drayton High Road, Drayton, Norwich, NR8 6AH
Activities: Construction of commercial buildings
Parent: RGCC Limited
Officers: Jonathan Martin Gibbins, Secretary; Robert John Alflatt [1977] Director; James George Stratton Carter [1985] Director; Robert Edward Russell Carter [1982] Director; Stephen Anthony Clarke [1971] Director; Anna Maria Dugdale [1966] Director; Grant John Keys [1981] Director; Michael Turner [1972] Director; Emily Clare Vintners [1978] Director

R.G. Carter Engineering Limited
Incorporated: 29 October 2012 *Employees:* 95
Net Worth: £2,211,251 *Total Assets:* £15,008,276
Registered Office: 9-11 Drayton High Road, Drayton, Norwich, NR8 6AH
Activities: Non-trading company
Parent: R.G. Carter Technical Services Limited
Officers: Robert John Alflatt, Secretary; Ivan Richard Groom [1970] Director; Joseph McDermottroe [1974] Director; Michael Turner [1972] Director

R.G. Carter Farms Limited
Incorporated: 21 August 2003 *Employees:* 4
Net Worth: £15,522,873 *Total Assets:* £30,359,628
Registered Office: The Lowlands, Costessey Lane, Drayton, Norwich, NR8 6HA
Activities: Growing of cereals (except rice), leguminous crops and oil seeds
Parent: RG Carter Group Limited
Officers: Jonathan Martin Gibbins, Secretary; Robert George Russell Carter [1953] Director; Anna Maria Dugdale [1966] Director; Nigel Charles Handley Howorth [1967] Director/Chartered Surveyor

RG Carter Group Limited
Incorporated: 22 December 1967 *Employees:* 20
Previous: R. G. Carter Holdings Limited
Net Worth: £50,871,196 *Total Assets:* £76,867,872
Registered Office: Drayton, Norwich, NR8 6AH
Activities: Activities of head offices
Parent: R. G. Carter Holdings Limited
Officers: Jonathan Martin Gibbins, Secretary; Donald Carter [1949] Director; James George Stratton Carter [1985] Director; Robert Edward Russell Carter [1982] Director; Robert George Russell Carter [1953] Director/Builder; Anna Maria Dugdale [1966] Director; Sir Anthony John Habgood [1946] Director/Deputy Chairman; Richard Mark Jeffries [1957] Director; Emily Clare Vintners [1978] Finance Director

R. G. Carter Holdings Limited
Incorporated: 15 August 2006 *Employees:* 1,076
Previous: RG Carter Group Limited
Net Worth: £123,734,000 *Total Assets:* £223,375,008
Registered Office: Drayton, Norwich, NR8 6AH
Activities: Activities of construction holding companies
Shareholders: Robert George Russell Carter; Robert George Russell Carter; Robert George Russell Carter; Robert George Russell Carter
Officers: Jonathan Martin Gibbins, Secretary; Donald Carter [1949] Director; James George Stratton Carter [1985] Director; Robert Edward Russell Carter [1982] Director; Robert George Russell Carter [1953] Director/Builder; Anna Maria Dugdale [1966] Director; Sir Anthony John Habgood [1946] Director/Deputy Chairman; Richard Mark Jeffries [1957] Director; Emily Clare Vintners [1978] Finance Director

R.G. Carter Limited
Incorporated: 16 November 1932 *Employees:* 118
Net Worth: £6,510,065 *Total Assets:* £19,259,434
Registered Office: 9 Drayton High Road, Drayton, Norwich, NR8 6AH
Activities: Construction of commercial buildings
Parent: R.G. Carter Construction Limited
Officers: Robert John Alflatt, Secretary; Paul Cushing [1977] Director; Jonathan James Dicks [1981] Director; Grant John Keys [1981] Director; Alexander Craig MacKay [1987] Director; Mario Daniel Rackham [1973] Director

R.G. Carter Projects Limited
Incorporated: 24 May 1985 *Employees:* 97
Net Worth: £7,171,215 *Total Assets:* £26,657,956
Registered Office: Drayton, Norwich, NR8 6AH
Activities: Construction of commercial buildings
Parent: R.G. Carter Construction Limited
Officers: Robert John Alflatt, Secretary; James George Stratton Carter [1985] Director; Steven John Duke [1957] Director; David Roy Sutton [1963] Director; Michael Turner [1972] Director

Casemasters Limited
Incorporated: 8 December 1965
Net Worth: £42,165,208 *Total Assets:* £45,880,908
Registered Office: Inflite House, Stansted Airport, Stansted, Essex, CM24 1RY
Activities: Other letting and operating of own or leased real estate
Parent: Swan Investments Group Ltd.
Officers: Linda Vera Ellis, Secretary; Pauline May Monksfield [1982] Director/Customer Liaison; Penny Annette Stephens [1952] Director/Administration; Raymond Aubrey Stephens [1937] Director/Engineer; William Charles Stephens [1985] Director/Estimating Engineer

Cashflows Europe Limited
Incorporated: 19 April 2005 *Employees:* 133
Previous: Voice Commerce Limited
Net Worth: £10,520,000 *Total Assets:* £80,789,000
Registered Office: CPC1, Capital Park, Fulbourn, Cambridge, CB21 5XE
Activities: Financial intermediation not elsewhere classified
Parent: RGB Holding Limited
Officers: Martin David Belsham [1960] Director/Chief Executive Officer; Ian Matthew Charles Gascoigne [1981] Director/Banker; Julian Grant Beresford Leigh [1974] Director/Chief Financial Officer; Lindsey Villon McMurray [1971] Director

Caskade Caterers Limited
Incorporated: 16 October 1984 *Employees:* 788
Net Worth: £6,578,674 *Total Assets:* £26,553,772
Registered Office: The Pavilion, 56 Rosslyn Crescent, Harrow, Middlesex, HA1 2SZ
Activities: Licenced restaurants
Parent: MSHA International Limited
Officers: Hamid Ali [1956] Director

Caskade Properties Limited
Incorporated: 24 July 2017
Net Worth: £4,389,597 *Total Assets:* £9,944,650
Registered Office: The Pavilion, Rosslyn Crescent, Harrow, Middlesex, HA1 2SZ
Activities: Buying and selling of own real estate
Major Shareholder: Hamid Ali
Officers: Hamid Ali [1956] Director

CASP
Incorporated: 13 January 1988 *Employees:* 23
Net Worth: £9,551,931 *Total Assets:* £10,329,564
Registered Office: Raleigh House, 14c Compass Point Business Park, Stocks Bridge Way, St Ives, Cambs, PE27 5JL
Activities: Other research and experimental development on natural sciences and engineering
Officers: Dr John Robert Parker, Secretary; Dr Andrew Buckley [1958] Director/Administrator; Dr Peter Friend [1934] Director/Retired; Sally Anne Gibson [1963] Director/Lecturer; Dr James Philip Parkinson Hirst [1958] Director/Geologist; David Murray Dennis James [1941] Director/Retired; Dr Stephanie Jane Kape [1971] Director/Chartered Geologist; Dr Bruce Levell [1954] Director/Professor; Professor John Edward Alan Marshall [1954] Director/Geologist; Dr Gary John Nichols [1957] Director/Technical Manager; Dr John Robert Parker [1942] Director/Retired; Clive Anthony Graham Pickton [1952] Director/Petroleum Consultant; Dr Martin John Whiteley [1955] Director/University Lecturer

Casterton College Rutland
Incorporated: 26 July 2011 *Employees:* 120
Previous: Casterton Business and Enterprise College Academy Trust
Net Worth: £6,709,986 *Total Assets:* £9,360,293
Registered Office: Casterton Business and Enterprise College, Ryhall Road, Great Casterton, Stamford, Lincs, PE9 4AT
Activities: General secondary education
Officers: Helen Cook, Secretary; Susan Ball [1960] Director/Teacher; Victoria Isabella Brown [1976] Director/HR Manager; Bejamin George Foster Callaghan [1960] Director; David Chapman [1963] Director/Regional Safety Adviser; Stephen Henderson Craig [1953] Director/Retired Business Manager; Steve Cutler [1990] Director/Corporation Tax Assistant Manager; Sian Dwyer [1958] Director; Robin Jones [1976] Director/Retail Manager; Kevin John Norris [1958] Director/Self Employed; Matt Shough [1973] Director/Head of Higher Education; Robert Slack [1972] Director/Engineer; Carl Smith [1965] Director/Principal; Andrew Tindall [1962] Director/IT Manager; Mary Elizabeth Town [1964] Director/Business Manager; Alan Stewart Walters [1955] Director/Councillor

Castle Green Kendal Limited
Incorporated: 22 December 1964 *Employees:* 112
Net Worth: £2,526,520 *Total Assets:* £10,346,048
Registered Office: Kirkland House, 11-15 Peterborough Road, Harrow, Middlesex, HA1 2AX
Activities: Hotels and similar accommodation
Officers: Haider Ladhu Jaffer [1940] Director; Dr Manoj Raman [1960] Director; Hassanali Amirali Dawood Suleman [1954] Director

Castle Point Gas & Heating Co. Limited
Incorporated: 27 October 1983 *Employees:* 51
Net Worth: £8,922,247 *Total Assets:* £11,486,657
Registered Office: 21-25 Hart Road, Benfleet, Essex, SS7 3PB
Activities: Other service activities n.e.c.
Shareholders: Keith Wells; Rhiannan Falkus; Katherine Ward
Officers: Keith Wells, Secretary; Christopher Falkus [1973] Director; Keith Wells [1978] Director/Contracts Manager

Castle View School Academy Trust
Incorporated: 24 July 2014 *Employees:* 102
Net Worth: £14,185,532 *Total Assets:* £16,146,449
Registered Office: Castle View School, Foksville Road, Canvey Island, Essex, SS8 7FH
Activities: General secondary education
Officers: Clair Tilley, Secretary; Stephen James Durkin [1975] Director/Headteacher; David Brian Kreyling [1981] Director/Executive Manager; Nichola Mann [1976] Director/Human Resources Consultant; Tony Theobald [1966] Director/Operations Manager; Clair Tilley [1973] Director/Business Manager; Dean Andrew Trotter [1965] Director/Foster Carer; Michaela Christine White [1969] Director/Charity Manager

Castledon Ltd
Incorporated: 11 June 1997 *Employees:* 771
Net Worth: £70,716,000 *Total Assets:* £86,284,000
Registered Office: Aviation Way, Southend on Sea, Essex, SS2 6UN
Activities: Activities of head offices
Shareholders: Steven John Johnson; Ian Johnson; Richard James Johnson
Officers: Bernadette Clare Barber, Secretary; Christopher Johnson [1947] Director; Elizabeth Johnson [1947] Director; Steven John Johnson [1969] Director; Sarah Jane Nash [1967] Director/Accountant

Castledon School Academy Trust
Incorporated: 5 February 2015 *Employees:* 79
Net Worth: £9,995,166 *Total Assets:* £11,334,799
Registered Office: Castledon School, Bromfords Drive, Wickford, Essex, SS12 0PW
Activities: Other education n.e.c.
Officers: Oluyemi Adeeko [1965] Director/Doctor; Nicole Blom [1983] Director of D & N Blom Ltd; Jonathan Brewer [1971] Director/Headteacher; Philip Chambers [1960] Director/HR and Payroll Consultant; Jane Freeman [1992] Director/Reverend; Helen Gray [1971] Director/Nurse; Simon Holliday [1980] Director/Headteacher; Sandra Mary Tucker [1954] Director; Kerry Wallace [1986] Director

Castlestone Investments Limited
Incorporated: 3 December 1965 *Employees:* 4
Net Worth: £15,964,458 *Total Assets:* £17,873,204
Registered Office: Enterprise House, Beesons Yard, Bury Lane, Rickmansworth, Herts, WD3 1DS
Activities: Development of building projects
Parent: Miaglen Limited
Officers: Sandra Estella Lask, Secretary; Ronald John Joseph Lask [1939] Director/Surveyor; Sandra Estella Lask [1943] Director

Catco Kids LLP
Incorporated: 4 January 2006
Net Worth: £7,173,211 *Total Assets:* £17,944,464
Registered Office: 166 College Road, Harrow, Middlesex, HA1 1RA
Officers: Simon Marcus Bottle [1973] LLP Member; Johnny Byrne [1935] LLP Member; Sandy Rivera [1971] LLP Member; Doctor Vishwas Murlidhar Sapatnekar [1947] LLP Member

Caterpillar Logistics (UK) Limited
Incorporated: 7 June 2005 *Employees:* 192
Net Worth Deficit: £1,286,000 *Total Assets:* £35,869,000
Registered Office: Eastfield, Frank Perkins Way, Peterborough, Cambs, PE1 5FQ
Activities: Wholesale trade of motor vehicle parts and accessories
Parent: Caterpillar (U.K.) Limited
Officers: Johanna Elizabeth Deason, Secretary; Nigel John Burroughs [1964] Director/Tax Accountant; Sandeep Virmani [1972] Director/Business Resource Manager

Caterpillar Overseas Limited
Incorporated: 27 July 2004
Net Worth: £307,575,008 *Total Assets:* £308,056,992
Registered Office: Eastfield, Frank Perkins Way, Peterborough, Cambs, PE1 5FQ
Activities: Other business support service activities n.e.c.
Parent: Caterpillar Overseas Credit Corporation SARL
Officers: Johanna Elizabeth Deason, Secretary; Nigel John Burroughs [1964] Director/Tax Accountant; Sandeep Virmani [1972] Director/Business Resource Manager

Caterpillar UK Engines Company Limited
Incorporated: 29 September 2005
Net Worth: £441,944,992 *Total Assets:* £441,944,992
Registered Office: Eastfield, Frank Perkins Way, Peterborough, Cambs, PE1 5FQ
Activities: Activities of head offices
Parent: Caterpillar Luxembourg S.A.R.L.
Officers: Johanna Elizabeth Deason, Secretary; Nigel John Burroughs [1964] Director/Taxation Accountant; David John Goldspink [1966] Director/General Manager; Paul David Thompson [1980] Director/Business Resource Manager [American]

Caterpillar UK Group Limited
Incorporated: 15 November 2005
Net Worth: £322,132,992 *Total Assets:* £322,132,992
Registered Office: Eastfield, Frank Perkins Way, Peterborough, Cambs, PE1 5FQ
Activities: Activities of head offices
Parent: Caterpillar UK Acquisition Partners LP
Officers: Nigel John Burroughs [1964] Director/Taxation Accountant; Sandeep Virmani [1972] Director/Business Resource Manager

Cathard Investments Limited
Incorporated: 23 November 2016 *Employees:* 3
Net Worth: £6,655,322 *Total Assets:* £10,231,407
Registered Office: Howard House, 66 Hutton Road, Shenfield, Brentwood, Essex, CM15 8NB
Activities: Other letting and operating of own or leased real estate
Major Shareholder: John Carroll
Officers: John Carroll [1923] Director/Builder; Mark Andrew Carroll [1955] Director

Cathedral Holdings Limited
Incorporated: 14 April 2000 *Employees:* 2
Net Worth: £35,525,804 *Total Assets:* £38,227,716
Registered Office: 22 Barn Rise, Wembley, Middlesex, HA9 9NQ
Activities: Development of building projects
Parent: Monument Assets Limited
Officers: Anthony David Chambers, Secretary/Director; Anthony David Chambers [1955] Director; Sarah Davies [1976] Director/Chartered Accountant

CATM Africa Holdings Limited
Incorporated: 10 October 2016
Net Worth: £5,300,446 *Total Assets:* £37,396,192
Registered Office: 1st Floor, Building 4, Trident Place, Mosquito Way, Hatfield, Herts, AL10 9UL
Activities: Activities of other holding companies n.e.c.
Parent: Cardtronics Holdings Limited
Officers: Paul Carbonelli [1983] Director [American]; Erich Brad Conrad [1972] Director/Business Executive [American]; Paul Gullo [1966] Director [American]; Jana Hile [1976] Director [Australian]; Marc Christopher Terry [1961] Managing Director; Angela Weinstein [1973] Director [American]

CATM Australasia Holdings Limited
Incorporated: 12 October 2016
Net Worth: £202,451,776 *Total Assets:* £202,451,776
Registered Office: 1st Floor, Building 4, Trident Place, Mosquito Way, Hatfield, Herts, AL10 9UL
Activities: Activities of other holding companies n.e.c.
Parent: Cardtronics Holdings Limited
Officers: Paul Carbonelli [1983] Director [American]; Erich Brad Conrad [1972] Director/Business Executive [American]; Paul Gallo [1966] Director [American]; Jana Hile [1976] Director [Australian]; Marc Christopher Terry [1961] Managing Director; Angela Weinstein [1973] Director [American]

CATM Europe Holdings Limited
Incorporated: 21 July 2016 *Employees:* 6
Net Worth Deficit: £316,000 *Total Assets:* £56,670,000
Registered Office: Cardtronics UK Limited, First Floor, Building 4, Trident House, Mosquito Way, Hatfield, Herts, AL10 9UL
Activities: Other business support service activities n.e.c.
Parent: Cardtronics Holdings Limited
Officers: Jana Hile [1976] Director [Australian]; Marc Christopher Terry [1961] Managing Director

CATM North America Holdings Limited
Incorporated: 10 October 2016
Net Worth: £31,901,802 *Total Assets:* £129,756,576
Registered Office: 1st Floor, Building 4, Trident Place, Mosquito Way, Hatfield, Herts, AL10 9UL
Activities: Activities of other holding companies n.e.c.
Parent: Cardtronics Holdings Limited
Officers: Paul Carbonelli [1983] Director [American]; Erich Brad Conrad [1972] Director/Business Executive [American]; Paul Gullo [1966] Director [American]; Angela Weinstein [1973] Director [American]

CATMJ Limited
Incorporated: 4 December 2012 *Employees:* 219
Net Worth: £3,218,051 *Total Assets:* £14,770,266
Registered Office: Studlands Park Industrial Estate, Newmarket, Suffolk, CB8 7AU
Activities: Dormant company
Major Shareholder: Charles Henry Bissett
Officers: Angela Brenda Bissett [1955] Director; Charles Henry Bissett [1952] Director; Trevor Charles Bissett [1976] Director

CATS Canterbury Limited
Incorporated: 29 August 2007 *Employees:* 170
Net Worth: £5,191,000 *Total Assets:* £18,416,000
Registered Office: Kett House, Station Road, Cambridge, CB1 2JH
Activities: General secondary education
Shareholders: CEG Colleges Limited; CEG Colleges Limited
Officers: Michael Ioakimides [1965] Director; Philip Leslie Symes [1962] Director/Chief Financial Officer; Brendan Grant Webb [1969] Director; Stuart Alan White [1967] Managing Director

CATS College London Limited
Incorporated: 17 November 2010 *Employees:* 97
Net Worth Deficit: £3,029,000 *Total Assets:* £9,927,000
Registered Office: Kett House, Station Road, Cambridge, CB1 2JH
Activities: General secondary education
Parent: CEG Colleges Limited
Officers: Michael Ioakimides [1965] Director; Philip Leslie Symes [1962] Director/Chief Financial Officer; Brendan Grant Webb [1969] Director; Stuart Alan White [1967] Managing Director

Caudwell Farms
Incorporated: 15 May 1951 *Employees:* 10
Net Worth: £1,953,059 *Total Assets:* £9,926,341
Registered Office: The Estate Office, Hartley House, Holbeach St Matthews, Spalding, Lincs, PE12 8EW
Activities: Growing of cereals (except rice), leguminous crops and oil seeds
Parent: George Hay Company Limited
Officers: Leslie Nicola Hay, Secretary; Andrew George Hay [1964] Director

Cavenham Estates Limited
Incorporated: 23 April 1999 *Employees:* 6
Net Worth: £9,204,406 *Total Assets:* £16,372,992
Registered Office: Langham Hall, Langham, Colchester, Essex, CO4 5PS
Activities: Buying and selling of own real estate
Shareholders: Katherine Henrietta Warburton; Julian Alexander Tolhurst; Elisabeth Ann Tolhurst
Officers: Katherine Henrietta Warburton, Secretary; Elisabeth Ann Tolhurst [1945] Director/Speech Therapist; Julian Alexander Tolhurst [1972] Director/Property Manager; Katherine Henrietta Warburton [1970] Director/Property Manager

Caversham Finance Limited
Incorporated: 24 December 1963 *Employees:* 1,868
Net Worth: £134,201,000 *Total Assets:* £333,688,000
Registered Office: 5 Hercules Way, Leavesden, Watford, Herts, WD25 7GS
Activities: Retail sale of electrical household appliances in specialised stores
Parent: Brighthouse Limited
Officers: David John Harwood, Secretary; Brian Edward Brodie [1965] Director; Graeme James Campbell [1972] Director; Stuart John Deane [1965] Director; Lysa Maria Hardy [1970] Director; Hugh John Harvey [1959] Director; Ian David Larkin [1968] Director [Irish]; Lars Magnus Mattsson [1973] Director [Swedish]; Hamish Stewart Paton [1976] Commercial Director; David Anthony Poole [1969] Director

Caversham Trading Limited
Incorporated: 17 March 2005 *Employees:* 658
Net Worth: £73,485,000 *Total Assets:* £85,510,000
Registered Office: 5 Hercules Way, Leavesden, Watford, Herts, WD25 7GS
Activities: Retail sale of electrical household appliances in specialised stores
Parent: Caversham Finance Ltd
Officers: David John Harwood, Secretary; Graeme James Campbell [1972] Finance Director; Hamish Stewart Paton [1976] Director

The Cavity Insulation Guarantee Agency
Incorporated: 5 April 1995 *Employees:* 27
Net Worth Deficit: £5,815,519 *Total Assets:* £13,433,049
Registered Office: CIGA House, 3 Vimy Court, Vimy Road, Leighton Buzzard, Beds, LU7 1FG
Activities: Other specialised construction activities n.e.c.
Officers: Nigel Donohue, Secretary; Danielle Louise Belton [1985] Director; David John Burton [1957] Director/Key Account Manager; Philip Dickin [1961] Director; Michael John Dyson [1945] Director; Sarah Louise Greensitt [1974] Director; Marc Lawson [1970] Sales Director; Michael Ian Morrall [1983] Director; Nicholas Ralph [1962] Director; David Fairfax Robson [1978] Director; Ian Rodney Tebb [1947] Director

F & R Cawley Limited
Incorporated: 28 February 2001 *Employees:* 215
Net Worth: £5,500,312 *Total Assets:* £17,599,710
Registered Office: 1 Covent Garden Close, Luton, Beds, LU4 8QB
Activities: Collection of non-hazardous waste
Shareholders: Jonathan Cawley; Brian Cawley
Officers: Simon Platt, Secretary; Brian Cawley [1951] Director; Jonathan Cawley [1949] Director; Anthony Thomas Goodman [1957] Sales Director; Philip John Gudgeon [1976] Director of Waste Collection and Logistics; Stephen Esmond Kimbell [1953] Director; Anna Louise Pegg [1978] Director of Customer Service; Simon Peter Platt [1965] Finance Director

CCP Management LLP
Incorporated: 7 June 2016
Net Worth: £27,028,534 *Total Assets:* £27,030,534
Registered Office: CCP Management LLP, City House, Hills Road, Cambridge, CB2 1RE
Officers: Dr Ewan McKinnon Kirk [1961] Member; Fraser Robert McIntyre [1969] Member; Dr Genia Diamond [1976] LLP Member; Adam Martin Glinsman [1965] LLP Member; Dr Tom James Howat [1981] LLP Member; Dr Matthew Killeya [1979] LLP Member; Erich Pitkin Schlaikjer [1959] LLP Member

CCW 600 Limited
Incorporated: 12 February 2001 *Employees:* 49
Net Worth: £8,897,553 *Total Assets:* £53,708,168
Registered Office: Global House, Saville Road, Peterborough, PE3 7PR
Activities: Renting and leasing of cars and light motor vehicles
Major Shareholder: Christopher Charles Webb
Officers: Fraser Alexander Winchester Morrison, Secretary; Christopher Charles Webb [1971] Director

CD & R Firefly Bidco Limited
Incorporated: 8 May 2015 *Employees:* 4
Net Worth: £42,974,000 *Total Assets:* £571,460,992
Registered Office: Gladstone Place, 36-38 Upper Marlborough Road, St Albans, Herts, AL1 3UU
Activities: Activities of head offices
Parent: CD & R Firefly 4 Limited
Officers: William Bahlsen Bannister [1967] Director/Chief Executive; Thomas McKenzie Biggart [1966] Director/Surveyor; Jeremy Clarke [1963] Managing Director; Simon Lane [1963] Director/Accountant

CDK U.K. Limited
Incorporated: 5 August 1988
Net Worth: £77,989,000 *Total Assets:* £78,097,000
Registered Office: Building 9, Croxley Park, Hatters Lane, Watford, Herts, WD18 8WW
Activities: Activities of head offices
Officers: Joanne Pascucci, Secretary; Oliver Ellis [1972] Sales & Marketing Director; Mark Justin Elsey [1967] Finance Director; Jacqueline Fielding [1964] Vice President (Director)

CDT Holdings Limited
Incorporated: 20 June 1995 *Employees:* 106
Net Worth: £7,107,000 *Total Assets:* £12,570,000
Registered Office: Unit 12 Cardinal Park, Cardinal Way, Godmanchester, Cambs, PE29 2XG
Activities: Other professional, scientific and technical activities n.e.c.
Parent: Sumitomo Chemical Co., Limited
Officers: Hilary Charles, Secretary; Yoshiaki Oda [1961] Director/Company Executive [Japanese]; Hiroshi Ueda [1956] Director/Company Executive [Japanese]; Jim Veninger [1962] Director/VP Technology Development [American]; Takeshi Yamada [1967] Director/Office Worker [Japanese]

CED Limited
Incorporated: 3 April 1959 *Employees:* 111
Net Worth: £2,532,364 *Total Assets:* £11,415,241
Registered Office: 728 London Road, West Thurrock, Grays, Essex, RM20 3LU
Activities: Agents involved in the sale of timber and building materials
Major Shareholder: Michael Elliott Walley Heap
Officers: Richard Robert Davies, Secretary; Ian John Burridge [1970] Director; Richard Robert Davies [1950] Director; Gary Ewing [1965] Director/Manager; Calum Stuart Fraser [1961] Director/Manager; Giles Elliott James Walley Heap [1972] Director; Michael Elliott Walley Heap [1946] Director; Patrick Robert Courtney Parker [1942] Director; Antony Richard Spink [1970] Director/Company Accountant; Howard White [1964] Director/Operations Manager

CEG Administrative Services Limited
Incorporated: 29 August 2007 *Employees:* 163
Net Worth Deficit: £514,000 *Total Assets:* £34,402,000
Registered Office: Kett House, Station Road, Cambridge, CB1 2JH
Activities: General secondary education
Parent: Cambridge Education Group Limited
Officers: Michael Ioakimides [1965] Director; Philip Leslie Symes [1962] Director/Chief Financial Officer; Brendan Grant Webb [1969] Director

CEG Properties Limited
Incorporated: 3 March 1989
Net Worth: £2,611,000 *Total Assets:* £15,270,000
Registered Office: Kett House, Station Road, Cambridge, CB1 2JH
Activities: Other letting and operating of own or leased real estate
Parent: Cambridge Education Group Limited
Officers: Elizabeth Ruth Armstrong [1956] Director/Educationalist; Michael Ioakimides [1965] Director; Philip Leslie Symes [1962] Director/Chief Financial Officer; Brendan Grant Webb [1969] Director

Celador Radio Broadcasting Limited
Incorporated: 12 July 2004
Net Worth Deficit: £10,330,972 *Total Assets:* £15,774,442
Registered Office: Media House, Peterborough Business Park, Lynch Wood, Peterborough, Cambs, PE2 6EA
Activities: Radio broadcasting
Parent: Bauer Radio Limited
Officers: Diedre Ann Ford [1960] Managing Director; Paul Anthony Keenan [1963] Director/Publisher; Sarah Jane Vickery [1963] Finance Director

Cementation Skanska Limited
Incorporated: 21 August 1968 *Employees:* 378
Net Worth: £25,968,000 *Total Assets:* £52,347,000
Registered Office: Maple Cross House, Denham Way, Maple Cross, Rickmansworth, Herts, WD3 9SW
Activities: Construction of commercial buildings
Parent: Skanska Construction UK Limited
Officers: Steven Leven, Secretary; James Maxwell Dunbar [1964] Director; Dr Jonathan David Morris [1973] Director

Central Developments (UK) Limited
Incorporated: 19 March 2001 *Employees:* 3
Net Worth: £2,715,733 *Total Assets:* £9,892,160
Registered Office: 20 Greenhill Park, New Barnet, Barnet, Herts, EN5 1HP
Activities: Development of building projects
Shareholders: John Andreou Papadouris; Servas Developments Ltd
Officers: Joseph Servas, Secretary; John Andrea Papadouris [1945] Director/Civil Engineer; Joseph Servas [1941] Director/Civil Engineer; Stavros Servas [1981] Director/Office Administrator

Central G H Trust
Incorporated: 25 July 2008
Net Worth: £22,558,140 *Total Assets:* £23,115,232
Registered Office: Noble House, Eaton Road, Hemel Hempstead Industrial Estate, Hemel Hempstead, Herts, HP2 7UB
Activities: Other business support service activities n.e.c.
Officers: Christopher Edward Stedman, Secretary; Colin Paul Barnes [1971] Director/Partner; Philip James Hutchinson [1945] Director/Manager; Laurie Roy Pollard [1979] Director; Oliver Muckle Whiley [1955] Director

Central Lending Funding Number One Limited
Incorporated: 12 May 2005
Net Worth: £6,041,000 *Total Assets:* £13,972,000
Registered Office: St Crispins House, Duke Street, Norwich, NR3 1PD
Activities: Activities of mortgage finance companies
Parent: Central Homeloans Limited
Officers: Anthony Richardson, Secretary; Debbie Carol Burton [1971] Director/Chief Executive; Paul Joseph Hollander [1980] Director/Chartered Accountant; Warren Anthony Travis [1965] Director/Accountant; Andrew Clive Turner [1958] Director

Central Park Enterprises Limited
Incorporated: 27 January 2009 *Employees:* 73
Net Worth: £5,193,985 *Total Assets:* £13,056,013
Registered Office: Rawden Enterprise Park, Sixth Avenue, Bluebridge Industrial Estate, Halstead, Essex, CO9 2FL
Activities: Activities of construction holding companies
Shareholder: Steven Paul Hadley
Officers: Roger Bryan Cox [1967] Director; Steven Paul Hadley [1977] Director

Central Property Investments Limited
Incorporated: 29 September 1987 *Employees:* 7
Net Worth: £9,386,067 *Total Assets:* £15,641,023
Registered Office: Northside House, Mount Pleasant, Barnet, Herts, EN4 9EE
Activities: Other letting and operating of own or leased real estate
Shareholders: Michael Christopher Moniatis; Nicos Christopher Moniatis
Officers: Louise Anne Moniatis [1981] Director; Michael Christopher Moniatis [1950] Director; Nicos Christopher Moniatis [1952] Director

Central Trust Limited
Incorporated: 16 September 2009 *Employees:* 43
Net Worth: £42,481,000 *Total Assets:* £42,709,000
Registered Office: St Crispins House, Duke Street, Norwich, NR3 1PD
Activities: Activities of mortgage finance companies
Parent: Norfolk Capital Limited
Officers: Anthony Richardson, Secretary; Stephen Paul Baker [1956] Director/Financial Services Consultant; Debbie Carol Burton [1971] Director/Chief Executive; Paul Joseph Hollander [1980] Director/Chartered Accountant; Jane Elizabeth McMahon [1954] Director/Regulatory Consultant; Warren Anthony Travis [1965] Director/Accountant; Andrew Clive Turner [1958] Director/Accountant

Central Trust Syndicate Number One Limited
Incorporated: 16 September 2009
Net Worth: £36,932,000 *Total Assets:* £86,607,000
Registered Office: St Crispins House, Duke Street, Norwich, NR3 1PD
Activities: Activities of mortgage finance companies
Parent: Central Trust Limited
Officers: Anthony Richardson, Secretary; Stephen Paul Baker [1956] Director/Financial Services Consultant; Debbie Carol Burton [1971] Director/Chief Executive; Paul Joseph Hollander [1980] Director/Chartered Accountant; Jane Elizabeth McMahon [1954] Director/Regulatory Consultant; Warren Anthony Travis [1965] Director/Accountant; Andrew Clive Turner [1958] Director/Accountant

Central Tyre (Commercial) Limited
Incorporated: 2 September 2011 *Employees:* 171
Previous: Stapleton's (Retail) Limited
Net Worth Deficit: £803,000 *Total Assets:* £50,730,000
Registered Office: Etel House, Avenue One, Letchworth Garden City, Herts, SG6 2HU
Activities: Maintenance and repair of motor vehicles
Parent: Kwik Fit (GB) Limited
Officers: Ian Ellis, Secretary; Mark Lynott [1975] Director; Masaya Ogura [1980] Director [Japanese]; Mark Richard Slade [1975] Director

Centre for Engineering and Manufacturing Excellence Ltd
Incorporated: 21 June 2001 *Employees:* 23
Net Worth: £24,749,272 *Total Assets:* £27,218,968
Registered Office: CEME Campus, Marsh Way, Rainham, Essex, RM13 8EU
Activities: Other letting and operating of own or leased real estate
Officers: Harjeet Singh Sadheura, Secretary; Judith Jane Armitt [1953] Director/Civil Servant; Martin Tilston Broadhurst [1953] Director; Dr Keyvan Mehdi Djamarani [1961] Director/General Manager; Rachel Hadley [1975] Director/HR Manager; Yvonne Kelly [1964] Director/Principal & CEO; Findlay Cameron MacAlpine [1964] Director/Chartered Surveyor; Barak Maoz [1957] Director/Management Consultant; Geoffrey Simon Richman [1966] Director/Finance Manager Ford Motor Co; Harjeet Singh Sadheura [1959] Director/Chief Financial Officer; Mark Peter Williams [1964] Director/Chief Executive

Centurion Safety Products Ltd
Incorporated: 16 May 1879 *Employees:* 131
Net Worth: £11,914,741 *Total Assets:* £14,666,665
Registered Office: Howlett Way, Fisons Way Industrial Estate, Thetford, Norfolk, IP24 1HZ
Activities: Manufacture of other plastic products
Officers: Chris John Zanone, Secretary; Nigel John Bewley Atkinson [1953] Director; Robert Iain Cameron Brown [1966] Director; James Edward Coleman Davis [1965] Director; Andrew Mark Gordon [1977] Marketing Director; Stephen John Hall [1953] Director; Steve Neumann [1978] Sales Director; Jeffrey Graham Ward [1978] Director [American]; Chris John Zanone [1972] Director/Finance & IT

Centus Biotherapeutics Limited
Incorporated: 9 July 2015
Net Worth: £52,504,792 *Total Assets:* £65,846,048
Registered Office: 1 Francis Crick Avenue, Cambridge Biomedical Campus, Cambridge, CB2 0AA
Activities: Other business support service activities n.e.c.
Shareholder: AstraZeneca UK Limited
Officers: Matthew Ian Conacher, Secretary; Karl David Bradshaw [1974] Evaluation Director; Noreen Parsons [1965] Director/Franchise Head [Irish]; Mitsuhiro Sato [1960] Director/Executive Vice President & COO [Japanese]; Yoshifumi Torii [1967] Director [Japanese]

Ceragon (UK) Limited
Incorporated: 31 December 2010
Net Worth: £15,776,645 *Total Assets:* £15,776,645
Registered Office: Egale 1, 80 St Albans Road, Watford, Herts, WD17 1DL
Activities: Non-trading company
Parent: Ceragon Networks (UK) Limited
Officers: Doron Ovadia Arazi [1963] Director/Deputy CEO & CFO [Israeli]; Ira Palti [1957] Director/CEO & President [Israeli]

Cergold Limited
Incorporated: 2 April 2013
Net Worth: £8,888,329 *Total Assets:* £93,224,952
Registered Office: Hill House, Lowlands Road, Harrow, Middlesex, HA1 3EQ
Activities: Buying and selling of own real estate
Major Shareholder: Donovan Gijsbertus Wijsmuller
Officers: Brian Martin Comer [1960] Director [Irish]; Luke Andrew Comer [1957] Director [Irish]

Certsure LLP
Incorporated: 5 November 2012 *Employees:* 327
Net Worth: £3,718,000 *Total Assets:* £11,943,000
Registered Office: Warwick House, Houghton Hall Park, Houghton Regis, Dunstable, Beds, LU5 5ZX

CEVA Animal Health Limited
Incorporated: 31 July 1995 *Employees:* 79
Net Worth: £4,813,618 *Total Assets:* £15,709,163
Registered Office: Unit 3 Anglo Office Park, White Lion Road, Amersham, Bucks, HP7 9FB
Activities: Veterinary activities
Officers: Yan Pierre Francois Gabe, Secretary; Valerie Mazeaud [1964] Director [French]; Marc Dominique Prikazsky [1959] Director [French]; Cuneyt Seckin [1970] Managing Director [Turkish]

CGN Global Uranium Limited
Incorporated: 22 July 2014 *Employees:* 5
Net Worth: £3,043,315 *Total Assets:* £93,845,576
Registered Office: First Floor, 50 St Andrew's Street, Cambridge, CB2 3AH
Activities: Agents involved in the sale of fuels, ores, metals and industrial chemicals
Officers: Fei HE [1977] Director [Chinese]; Jian Huang [1965] Director/General Manager [Chinese]; Zhihuai Xu [1965] Director [Chinese]

CH Old Co Limited
Incorporated: 8 December 1986
Net Worth: £106,500,000 *Total Assets:* £118,400,000
Registered Office: Premier House, Centrium Business Park, Griffiths Way, St Albans, Herts, AL1 2RE
Activities: Other processing and preserving of fruit and vegetables
Parent: Premier Financing Limited
Officers: Simon Nicholas Wilbraham, Secretary; Duncan Neil Leggett [1979] Director; Simon Alan Rose [1966] Director/Solicitor; Simon Nicholas Wilbraham [1969] Director/Company Secretary

Chadwell Heath Academy
Incorporated: 16 August 2010 *Employees:* 135
Net Worth: £18,014,352 *Total Assets:* £18,834,648
Registered Office: Christie Gardens, Chadwell Heath, Romford, Essex, RM6 4RS
Activities: General secondary education
Officers: Norman Ernest Abbott [1936] Director; Teresa Ann Banks [1958] Director/School Manager; Peter Michael Brewster [1951] Director/Civil Engineer; Stephen Nicholas Bull [1957] Director/Headmaster; Farzana Chowdhury [1976] Director/Solicitor; Abdus Samad Hamid [1973] Director/Network Security Analyst; Nicola Dionne Merry [1972] Director/Production Manager; Yasmeen Sattar [1980] Director/Secretary; Dhirajlal Velji Shah [1951] Director/Business Owner (Retail); Paul Southcott [1958] Director/Design Technology Technician; Philip Terry [1954] Director/Clerical Officer; Keith Edward Wilkinson [1947] Director/Retired

Chai-Lifeline Cancer Care
Incorporated: 24 September 1998 *Employees:* 25
Net Worth: £8,954,543 *Total Assets:* £9,185,151
Registered Office: York House, Empire Way, Wembley, Middlesex, HA9 0FQ
Activities: Other human health activities
Officers: Louise Hager [1955] Director; Jonathan Andrew Hodes [1968] Director/Chartered Accountant and Chartered Tax Adviser; Lady Pamela Audrey Kalms [1931] Director; Richard Lawrence Segal [1963] Director/Company Chairman; Susan Lesley Shipman [1948] Director; Dr Adrian Tookman [1953] Director/Doctor of Medicine; Philip David Weinstein [1953] Director; Lord Lord of Graffham David Young [1932] Director

Chalcroft Holdings Limited
Incorporated: 5 March 2007 *Employees:* 87
Net Worth: £474,660 *Total Assets:* £16,477,751
Registered Office: 2 Campbells Business Park, Campbells Meadow, King's Lynn, Norfolk, PE30 4YR
Activities: Activities of construction holding companies
Shareholders: Mark Andrew Reeve; David Reeve
Officers: Todd Clinton Hallam [1976] EHS Director [New Zealander]; Paul Morley [1969] Director; David Reeve [1970] Director; Mark Andrew Reeve [1966] Director

Chalcroft Limited
Incorporated: 9 July 1979
Net Worth: £3,554,910 *Total Assets:* £19,274,662
Registered Office: 4 Campbells Business Park, Campbells Meadow, King's Lynn, Norfolk, PE30 4YR
Activities: Construction of commercial buildings
Parent: Chalcroft Holdings Ltd
Officers: Todd Clinton Hallam [1976] Environmental, Health & Safety Director [New Zealander]; Paul Morley [1969] Construction Director; David Reeve [1970] Financial Director; Mark Andrew Reeve [1966] Director/Construction Engineer

Chaldean Estate Limited
Incorporated: 13 October 1997 *Employees:* 8
Net Worth: £7,606,496 *Total Assets:* £15,170,424
Registered Office: The Old Grain Store, Bromley Lane, Much Hadham, Herts, SG10 6HU
Activities: Growing of cereals (except rice), leguminous crops and oil seeds
Major Shareholder: Gordon Morrison
Officers: Morag Broom, Secretary; David Ian Alexander Morrison [1976] Director; Mary Scott Morrison [1951] Director

Chaldean Properties Limited
Incorporated: 11 December 2001
Net Worth: £7,749,547 *Total Assets:* £23,416,676
Registered Office: The Old Grain Store, Bromley Lane, Much Hadham, Herts, SG10 6HU
Activities: Buying and selling of own real estate
Shareholders: David Ian Alexander Morrison; Morag Elizabeth Broom
Officers: Morag Broom, Secretary; Morag Elizabeth Broom [1979] Director/Sales Consultant; David Ian Alexander Morrison [1976] Director; Mary Scott Morrison [1951] Director

Chalk Farm Marine LLP
Incorporated: 10 February 2017
Net Worth: £4,745,914 *Total Assets:* £13,372,217
Registered Office: Grenville House, 4 Grenville Avenue, Broxbourne, Herts, EN10 7DH

E.M. Chamberlain Estates Limited
Incorporated: 29 June 1973
Net Worth: £15,315,583 *Total Assets:* £29,185,836
Registered Office: Houghton Hall, The Green, Houghton Regis, Dunstable, Beds, LU5 5DY
Activities: Other letting and operating of own or leased real estate
Parent: Chamberlain Holdings PLC
Officers: Vena Chambury, Secretary; Christopher Paul Bugden [1966] Finance Director; John Maxwell Chamberlain [1942] Director; Vena Chambury [1955] Director/Estate Management; Stefan Mucha [1957] Director; Peter Bernard Wayte [1949] Director/Solicitor

E.M. Chamberlain Group Limited
Incorporated: 1 December 1972
Net Worth: £9,827,498 *Total Assets:* £12,978,610
Registered Office: Houghton Hall, The Green, Houghton Regis, Dunstable, Beds, LU5 5DY
Activities: Other letting and operating of own or leased real estate
Parent: Chamberlain Holdings PLC
Officers: Vena Chambury, Secretary; Christopher Paul Bugden [1966] Finance Director; John Maxwell Chamberlain [1942] Director; Vena Chambury [1955] Director/Estate Management; Stefan Mucha [1957] Director; Peter Bernard Wayte [1949] Director/Solicitor

Chamberlain Holdings Public Limited Company
Incorporated: 12 May 1983 *Employees:* 32
Net Worth: £81,428,648 *Total Assets:* £136,760,208
Registered Office: Houghton Hall, The Green, Houghton Regis, Dunstable, Beds, LU5 5DY
Activities: Activities of other holding companies n.e.c.
Major Shareholder: John Maxwell Chamberlain
Officers: Christopher Paul Bugden, Secretary; Christopher Paul Bugden [1966] Finance Director; John Maxwell Chamberlain [1942] Director; Vena Chambury [1955] Director/Estate Management; Stefan Mucha [1957] Director; Peter Bernard Wayte [1949] Director/Solicitor

E.M.Chamberlain Limited
Incorporated: 28 February 1957
Net Worth: £4,679,668 *Total Assets:* £11,905,425
Registered Office: Houghton Hall, The Green, Houghton Regis, Dunstable, Beds, LU5 5DY
Activities: Construction of commercial buildings
Parent: Chamberlain Holdings PLC
Officers: Vena Chambury, Secretary; Christopher Paul Bugden [1966] Finance Director; John Maxwell Chamberlain [1942] Director; Vena Chambury [1955] Director/Estate Management; Stefan Mucha [1957] Director; Peter Bernard Wayte [1949] Director/Solicitor

Change Schools Partnership
Incorporated: 16 August 2012 *Employees:* 198
Net Worth: £12,209,419 *Total Assets:* £16,488,100
Registered Office: Notley Green Primary School, Blickling Road, Great Notley, Braintree, Essex, CM77 7ZJ
Activities: Primary education
Officers: Michael George Baker [1946] Director/Member; Jonathan Dancy [1950] Director; Stuart Ellis [1966] Director/Lead Headteacher; Alison Ann Fiala [1957] Director/Lead Commissioner Primary; Sarah Elizabeth Garner [1972] Director/Chief Financial Officer; Malachy Bruce Hanley [1965] Director; Philip Edward Heady [1952] Director; Paul Heavers [1943] Finance Director; James Lawrence Saunders [1975] Director; Steven Vanderheide [1972] Director; Robin Boissonnat Whitworth [1954] Director

Chaplin Group Limited
Incorporated: 14 October 2016 *Employees:* 169
Net Worth: £94,931,232 *Total Assets:* £117,549,480
Registered Office: Abington Park Farm, Great Abington, Cambs, CB21 6AX
Activities: Activities of other holding companies n.e.c.
Shareholders: Simon Robert Frank Chaplin; Hilary Ann Russell; David John Harold Chaplin
Officers: David John Harold Chaplin [1963] Director/General Manager; Simon Robert Frank Chaplin [1967] Director/General Manager; Hilary Ann Russell [1965] Director

S Chaplin Holdings Limited
Incorporated: 28 November 2016
Net Worth: £16,822,440 *Total Assets:* £17,362,248
Registered Office: Argents Chartered Accountants, 15 Palace Street, Norwich, NR3 1RT
Activities: Mixed farming
Parent: Chaplin Group Limited
Officers: Simon Robert Frank Chaplin [1967] Director/General Manager

Chapman Ventilation Group Limited
Incorporated: 25 January 2017 *Employees:* 137
Net Worth: £4,735,010 *Total Assets:* £11,607,523
Registered Office: 15-20 Woodfield Road, Welwyn Garden City, Herts, AL7 1JQ
Activities: Other business support service activities n.e.c.
Shareholders: David Theodorus Chapman; Anthony Chapman
Officers: Anthony Chapman [1965] Director; David Chapman [1972] Director; Simon Andrew Hyams [1983] Director

Chappell Estates Limited
Incorporated: 14 September 1964 *Employees:* 2
Net Worth: £13,614,949 *Total Assets:* £15,274,624
Registered Office: Aquila House, Waterloo Lane, Chelmsford, Essex, CM1 1BN
Activities: Buying and selling of own real estate
Shareholder: Robert William Chappell OBE
Officers: Sarah Frances Peeters, Secretary/Personal Assistant; Robert William Chappell OBE [1942] Director/Optometrist; Janet Edith Handley [1949] Director/Lecturer

Chard Properties (UK) Limited
Incorporated: 20 May 2005 *Employees:* 10
Net Worth: £5,584,038 *Total Assets:* £8,280,931
Registered Office: 35a High Street, Ruislip, Middlesex, HA4 7AU
Activities: Retail of furniture, lighting, and similar (not musical instruments or scores) in specialised store
Shareholders: Amarjit Singh Chard; Narinder Kaur Chard
Officers: Balraj Chard, Secretary; Amarjit Singh Chard [1949] Director [Indian]; Narinder Kaur Chard [1948] Director

Chard Robinson Usten Ltd
Incorporated: 21 November 2013
Net Worth: £899,168 *Total Assets:* £8,725,935
Registered Office: 2 Hills Road, Cambridge, CB2 1JP
Activities: Activities of other holding companies n.e.c.
Shareholders: Neil Adam Robinson; Stephen Michael Chard
Officers: James Robert Peace, Secretary; Stephen Michael Chard [1971] Director [New Zealander]; Francisco Javier Farres Quesada [1967] Director [Spanish]; Juan Miguel Pascual Rodriguez [1967] Director [Spanish]; Neil Adam Robinson [1972] Director

Chargemaster Limited
Incorporated: 9 October 2008 *Employees:* 272
Previous: Chargemaster PLC
Net Worth: £23,864,000 *Total Assets:* £33,741,000
Registered Office: 500 Capability Green, Luton, Beds, LU1 3LS
Activities: Manufacture of other transport equipment n.e.c.
Shareholder: David Kenneth Martell
Officers: David Kenneth Martell [1948] Director; Terence Michael Thornton [1963] Director/Oil Company Executive; Roy Eric Williamson [1963] Director/Oil Company Executive

The Charis Trust
Incorporated: 11 November 2010
Net Worth: £12,028,581 *Total Assets:* £12,060,992
Registered Office: Woodham View, Little Baddow Road, Woodham Walter, Maldon, Essex, CM9 6RP
Activities: Non-trading company
Officers: Andrew James Barker [1961] Director; Andrew Charles Green [1946] Director/Fund Manager; Jane Mary Green [1953] Director/Fund Manager; Riichard John Green [1949] Director; Jonathan Paul Boniface Harris [1949] Director/Chartered Accountant

The Charles Kalms, Henry Ronson Immanuel College
Incorporated: 12 April 1990 *Employees:* 157
Net Worth: £6,817,146 *Total Assets:* £11,606,515
Registered Office: 87-91 Elstree Road, Bushey, Herts, WD23 4EB
Activities: Primary education
Officers: Antony Berkin, Secretary; Dr Daphna Regina Atar [1972] Director/Scientist [British/Swiss]; Keith Philip Barnett [1961] Director/Solicitor; Hannah Ruth Boyden [1977] Director; Lynda Gail Dullop [1962] Director; Valerie Helen Eppel [1968] Director/Chartered Accountant; Annette Hilary Deborah Koslover [1964] Director/Solicitor; Erica Marks [1964] Operations Director; Lucy Gabrielle Marks [1971] Director/Solicitor; Neal Menashe [1972] Director [Italian]; Edward Misrahi [1969] Director/Fund Management; Michelle Laura Sint [1965] Director/Teacher; Professor Anthony Nigel Warrens [1959] Director/University Professor; Eliezer Zobin [1975] Director/Rabbi

Charles River Discovery Research Services UK Limited
Incorporated: 19 December 2002 *Employees:* 313
Previous: Biofocus DPI Ltd
Net Worth: £21,670,000 *Total Assets:* £39,314,000
Registered Office: Robinson Building, Chesterford Research Park, Little Chesterford, Saffron Walden, Essex, CB10 1XL
Activities: Research and experimental development on biotechnology
Parent: Biofocus DPI Holdings Limited
Officers: Sarah Margaret Price, Secretary; Birgit Girshick [1970] Director/Manager [American/German]; David P Johst [1961] Director [American]; Dr Jacqueline Anne MacRitchie [1966] Director/Scientist; David Ross Smith [1965] Director

Charlie Properties Limited
Incorporated: 1 October 1982 *Employees:* 4
Net Worth: £9,901,579 *Total Assets:* £11,733,035
Registered Office: Old Station Road, Loughton, Essex, IG10 4PL
Activities: Development of building projects
Officers: Christina Hilliard, Secretary; Philipos Andrea [1967] Director/Solicitor; Christina Hilliard [1962] Director/Company Secretary; Laura McManus Andrea [1969] Director

Chart Forte Holdings Ltd
Incorporated: 14 June 2011
Net Worth: £5,937,296 *Total Assets:* £10,022,515
Registered Office: Cervantes House, 5-9 Headstone Road, Harrow, Middlesex, HA1 1PD
Activities: Other service activities n.e.c.
Shareholders: Jalaluddin Kajani; Mawash Kajani
Officers: Mawash Kajani, Secretary; Jalaluddin Kajani [1957] Director [Irish]; Mawash Kajani [1966] Director [Irish]

Chartco Limited
Incorporated: 14 October 1998 *Employees:* 130
Net Worth: £18,133,000 *Total Assets:* £30,067,000
Registered Office: Unit 4 Voltage, Mollison Avenue, Enfield, Middlesex, EN3 7XQ
Activities: Non-specialised wholesale trade
Parent: Ensign Holdco 4 Limited
Officers: Sukhjeevan Singh Samra [1976] Finance Director; Martin Stuart Taylor [1967] Director, KH Charts

Charter Projects (Developments) Limited
Incorporated: 16 November 1982 *Employees:* 1
Net Worth: £6,463,543 *Total Assets:* £17,063,354
Registered Office: 203 London Road, Hadleigh, Benfleet, Essex, SS7 2RD
Activities: Development of building projects
Officers: Nigel Baylis, Secretary; Lucia Elizabeth Baylis [1948] Director/Secretary [Italian]; Nigel Baylis [1945] Managing Director; Margaret Maria Jones [1954] Director

Charterhouse Simon Limited
Incorporated: 12 September 1973 *Employees:* 2
Net Worth: £14,463,325 *Total Assets:* £17,854,982
Registered Office: 52 Alston Road, Barnet, Herts, EN5 4EY
Activities: Other letting and operating of own or leased real estate
Major Shareholder: Richard Stephen Leslie
Officers: Kim Mulvey, Secretary; Claudia Ruth Leslie [1955] Director/Consultant; Richard Stephen Leslie [1943] Director/Chartered Accountant

M & J Charters LLP
Incorporated: 23 March 2005 *Employees:* 2
Net Worth: £7,600,000 *Total Assets:* £10,951,856
Registered Office: Watergate, Broxhill Road, Havering-Atte-Bower, Romford, Essex, RM4 1QH
Officers: Lawrence Jefferson Gilbert [1948] Member; Richard Henry Maskell [1943] Member

Chartman Limited
Incorporated: 11 November 1987 *Employees:* 149
Net Worth: £27,139,000 *Total Assets:* £34,930,000
Registered Office: Gladstone Place, 36-38 Upper Marlborough Road, St Albans, Herts, AL1 3UU
Activities: Retail sale of automotive fuel in specialised stores
Parent: Chartman Holdings Limited
Officers: David Hathaway, Secretary; William Bahlsen Bannister [1967] Director/Chief Executive; Jeremy Clarke [1963] Director/Chief Operating Officer; Simon Paul Lane [1963] Director/Chief Financial Officer

The Chartridge Conference Company Limited
Incorporated: 20 November 1996 *Employees:* 158
Net Worth: £289,334 *Total Assets:* £11,693,407
Registered Office: 6 Hunting Gate, Hitchin, Herts, SG4 0TY
Activities: Hotels and similar accommodation
Major Shareholder: Mohd Zamri Bin Muda
Officers: Graham Barrie Cantillion [1965] Director; Zulkifli Bin Jafar [1972] Director [Malaysian]; Mohd Zamri Bin Muda [1951] Director [Malaysian]

Chartridge Developments Limited
Incorporated: 11 September 1998
Net Worth: £1,314,510 *Total Assets:* £12,441,293
Registered Office: Chartridge House, 30 Shepherds Lane, Beaconsfield, Bucks, HP9 2DT
Activities: Construction of domestic buildings
Parent: Chartridge PLC
Officers: Lesley Anne Farrer, Secretary/Director; Ann Lesley Brown [1960] Director/Certified Accountant; Lesley Anne Farrer [1959] Commercial Director; Karl McKenzie [1962] Director/Construction Manager; Edgar Graham Thomson [1955] Director/Chairman

Chartridge PLC
Incorporated: 30 March 2000 *Employees:* 8
Net Worth: £1,382,094 *Total Assets:* £12,479,161
Registered Office: Chartridge House, 30 Shepherds Lane, Beaconsfield, Bucks, HP9 2DT
Activities: Construction of domestic buildings
Shareholders: Lesley Anne Farrer; Edgar Graham Thomson
Officers: Lesley Anne Farrer, Secretary/Director; Lesley Anne Farrer [1959] Director; Edgar Graham Thomson [1955] Director

Chase (Palace Wharf) Limited
Incorporated: 10 October 2013 *Employees:* 4
Net Worth: £1,155,592 *Total Assets:* £25,149,852
Registered Office: Jasmine House, 8 Parkway, Welwyn Garden City, Herts, AL8 6HG
Activities: Construction of domestic buildings
Shareholders: Michael Jaffray de Hauteville Bell; Christopher Guthrie Little
Officers: Tony Carey [1972] Director/Accountant; Michael Jaffray de Hauteville Bell [1941] Director; Christopher Guthrie Little [1947] Director/Investment Banker; Nicolas Sean Warren [1961] Director/Surveyor

Chassis-Cab Limited
Incorporated: 28 May 1982 *Employees:* 150
Net Worth: £5,593,341 *Total Assets:* £16,869,506
Registered Office: Daf House, Addison Way, Great Blakenham, Ipswich, Suffolk, IP6 0RL
Activities: Sale of other motor vehicles
Shareholders: Sally Anne Ruffles; Jane Elizabeth Allum
Officers: Steven Rodney Goodwin, Finance Director; Jane Elizabeth Allum [1968] Director/Housewife; Robert Baxter [1962] Managing Director; Steven Rodney Goodwin [1968] Finance Director; Anne Esther Ruffles [1939] Director/Secretary; Sally Anne Ruffles [1966] IT Director

Chauncy School
Incorporated: 5 July 2011 *Employees:* 203
Net Worth: £14,858,085 *Total Assets:* £16,143,711
Registered Office: Chauncy School, Park Road, Ware, Herts, SG12 0DP
Activities: General secondary education
Officers: Fiona Louise Martin [1974] Director/Financial Consultant; Robert Stuart Watson [1962] Director/Production Co-ordinator; Mark Andrew Wilkinson [1967] Director/IT Consultant

Cheale Group Limited
Incorporated: 21 April 2004 *Employees:* 154
Net Worth: £12,455,882 *Total Assets:* £18,799,536
Registered Office: Orchard Farm, Little Warley, Brentwood, Essex, CM13 3EN
Activities: Activities of head offices
Shareholders: Paul Cheale; Joseph Thomas Cheale; Marcus Andrew Cheale
Officers: Paul Cheale, Secretary/Director; Marcus Andrew Cheale [1971] Director; Paul Cheale [1938] Director/Meat Wholesaler; Priscilla Cheale [1942] Director/Company Secretary

Cheale Meats Limited
Incorporated: 11 August 1980 *Employees:* 6
Net Worth: £12,571,589 *Total Assets:* £18,022,880
Registered Office: Orchard Farm, Little Warley, Brentwood, Essex, CM13 3EN
Activities: Production of meat and poultry meat products
Parent: Cheale Group Limited
Officers: Paul Cheale, Secretary; Michael Charlwood [1954] Director/Accountant; Adam Harry Joseph Cheale [1974] Director/General Manager; Marcus Andrew Cheale [1971] Director; Paul Cheale [1938] Director/Meat Wholesaler; Priscilla Cheale [1942] Director/Company Secretary

Cheergrey Properties Limited
Incorporated: 5 February 1996 *Employees:* 1
Net Worth: £17,782,424 *Total Assets:* £24,686,116
Registered Office: Water Circle, City Meadows, Stansted, Essex, CM22 6DR
Activities: Other letting and operating of own or leased real estate
Parent: Cheergrey Limited
Officers: Iain Edward Anderson, Secretary; Michael Robert Johnstone [1945] Director/Investor

Chelmer Foods Limited
Incorporated: 6 April 1992 *Employees:* 21
Net Worth: £18,153,100 *Total Assets:* £23,947,330
Registered Office: 1st Floor, Upminster Library, 26 Corbets Tey Road, Upminster, Essex, RM14 2BB
Activities: Other processing and preserving of fruit and vegetables
Major Shareholder: Roger Arthur Weaire
Officers: Paul William Pleasant, Secretary; Simon John Heather [1986] Sales Director; Paul William Pleasant [1979] Financial Director; Anthony Julian Smith [1965] Director; James Weaire [1978] Director/Manager; Roger Arthur Weaire [1945] Director; Christopher Edward Wilding [1986] Sales Director

Chelmer Housing Partnership Limited
Incorporated: 7 November 2000 *Employees:* 275
Net Worth: £149,102,000 *Total Assets:* £685,174,976
Registered Office: Myriad House, 33 Springfield Lyons Approach, Springfield, Chelmsford, Essex, CM2 5LB
Activities: Renting and operating of Housing Association real estate
Officers: Jeremy John Jacobs, Secretary; Stephen George Bennett [1948] Director/Chartered Secretary; Rosemary Elisabeth Braithwaite [1964] Director/Financial Controller; Peter John Cogan [1972] Retail Customer Operations Director, Thames Water; Neil Ian Fisher [1963] Finance Director; Anthony Charles Goymour [1956] Director/Social Housing Treasury Consultant; Karen Angela Mayhew [1956] Director/Chief Executive Housing Association; Marc Noaro [1968] Director/Chief Customer Officer, Eurostar International; Nicola Mary Sawford [1965] Director; Joanna Rebecca Wanmer [1972] Director/Local Government Officer

Chelmer Valley High School
Incorporated: 6 July 2011 *Employees:* 158
Net Worth: £16,168,827 *Total Assets:* £18,951,836
Registered Office: Chelmer Valley High School, Court Road, Broomfield, Chelmsford, Essex, CM1 7ER
Activities: General secondary education
Officers: Neil Peter Barnes [1962] Director/Risk Management; Christopher Kenneth Davidson [1957] Director/Civil Servant; Elizabeth Claire Goodchild [1962] Director/Headteacher; Samantha Hill [1983] Director/Teacher; Colin Linnell [1955] Director/Sales Manager; Richard Stephen Lock [1965] Director/Accountant; Geoffrey Mark Lockwood [1961] Director/Technical Manager; Francesca Luke [1955] Director/Retired; Clifford Douglas Mann [1960] Director/Caretaker; Suzanne Yvonne Mycock [1964] Director/Teacher; Nigel Perks [1957] Director/Housing Manager; John Salmon [1943] Director/Retired; Adrian James Shaw [1964] Director; Ross Spacey [1979] Director; Dr Gillian Mary Sturman [1943] Director/Retired University Lecturer; Melva Whybrow [1952] Director/Retired

Chelmsford Cars and Commercials Limited
Incorporated: 1 April 1993 *Employees:* 7
Net Worth: £30,431,570 *Total Assets:* £35,515,080
Registered Office: 144 New London Road, Chelmsford, Essex, CM2 0AW
Activities: Other letting and operating of own or leased real estate
Shareholders: Gary Paul Sharp; Julie Sharp
Officers: Julie Sharp, Secretary; Gary Paul Sharp [1961] Director/Car Dealer

Chelmsford County High School for Girls
Incorporated: 19 November 2010 *Employees:* 89
Net Worth: £9,927,488 *Total Assets:* £12,465,123
Registered Office: Chelmsford County High School for Girls, Broomfield Road, Chelmsford, Essex, CM1 1RW
Activities: General secondary education
Officers: Wendy Jayne Newton, Secretary; Richard Simon Brown [1966] Director/Accountant; Nicole Monique Chapman [1951] Director/Teacher; Sarah Elizabeth Clements [1980] Director/Teacher; Peter Dennis Cook [1949] Director/Construction Consultant; Rosalind Elizabeth Cornish [1949] Director/Retired; Stephen Kenneth Simpson Miles [1960] Director/Engineering Manager; Ruth Russet Neave [1965] Director/Solicitor; Jason Laurence Oster [1970] Director/Head of Sales & Marketing; Mark Stephen Rowell [1974] Director/Teacher; Lauren Marie Smith [1975] Director/Teacher; Duncan John Stevens [1959] Director; Richard Leslie Vass [1967] Director/Chartered Accountant; Yvonne Wickers [1961] Director/Teacher; Michael Roy Worboys [1960] Director/Head of Advanced Technology

Chelmsford Diocesan Board of Finance (The)
Incorporated: 16 July 1914 *Employees:* 128
Net Worth: £292,860,000 *Total Assets:* £314,894,016
Registered Office: Guy Harlings, 53 New Street, Chelmsford, Essex, CM1 1AT
Activities: Activities of religious organisations
Officers: Margaret Constance Essery, Secretary; Isabel Adcock [1949] Director/Retired; The Venerable Elwin Wesley Cockett [1959] Director/Minister of Religion; The Venerable Annette Joy Cooper [1953] Director/Archdeacon; Stephen Geoffrey Cottrell [1958] Director/Bishop; Vevet Norine Deer [1954] Director/Civil Servant; Mary Caroline Durlacher [1951] Director/Housewife; Canon Roger James Ennals [1948] Director/Retired; Richard Ford Freeman [1947] Director/Retired; Canon Dean Gillespie [1991] Director/Marketing - International Development; Robert Ian Hammond [1966] Director/Civil Servant; Frank Hawkins [1948] Director/Retired; Nicholas James Henshall [1962] Director/Priest Dean of Chelmsford; The Ven Vanessa Anne Herrick [1958] Director/Minister of Religion; Peter Hill [1950] Director/Bishop; Christine Gladys Horton [1947] Director; Canon Jillian Sarah Leonard [1950] Director/Retired; The Ven Michael John Lodge [1953] Director/Minister of Religion; Percy William Cecil Lomax [1944] Director; Ronald Victor James McLernon [1943] Director; Mary Elizabeth Moore [1946] Director; Roger Anthony Brett Morris [1968] Director/Bishop; Peter Warren Morriss [1942] Director; John Perumbalath [1966] Director/Minister of Religion; The Revd David Philip Ritchie [1960] Director/Minister; The Revd Canon Marie Segal [1957] Director/Priest; Roger Iain Shilling [1943] Director; The Venerable Elizabeth Snowden [1958] Director/Minister; Louise Margaret Williams [1966] Director/Priest; John Harold Winterbotham [1945] Director/Retired

The Chelmsford Learning Partnership
Incorporated: 12 January 2012 *Employees:* 532
Previous: The Boswells Academy Trust
Net Worth: £42,751,000 *Total Assets:* £51,600,000
Registered Office: The Boswells School, Burnham Road, Chelmsford, Essex, CM1 6LY
Activities: General secondary education
Officers: Ruth Lesley Sheridan, Secretary; Russell Ayling [1947] Director/Retired; Paul Banks [1974] Director/Headteacher; Ruth Ann Bird [1947] Director/Retired; Roger Karl Blundell [1978] Director/Manager; Gillian Susan Box [1958] Director/HR Consultant; Anthony Gerard Brookes [1959] Director; Ken Cocksedge [1957] Director/Retired; Paul Leslie Edwards [1978] Director; Shelley Margaret Jones [1962] Director/Headteacher; Nicola Jane Kershaw [1952] Director/Librarian; Gemma Rogers [1981] Director; Lindsay Whitehouse [1954] Director/Retired; Janet Agnes Wood [1967] Director/Chartered Accountant

Chelsea Portfolio Limited
Incorporated: 7 March 1996
Net Worth: £5,639,082 *Total Assets:* £10,853,024
Registered Office: Fremnells, Hawkswood Road, Downham, Billericay, Essex, CM11 1JT
Activities: Other letting and operating of own or leased real estate
Parent: Frasertown Limited
Officers: Shobha Sharma, Secretary/Sub Postmaster; Sanjay Ashok Sharma [1965] Director

Chelsea Stores Holdings Limited
Incorporated: 11 March 2004
Net Worth Deficit: £24,500,000 *Total Assets:* £13,900,000
Registered Office: Cherry Tree Road, Watford, Herts, WD24 6SH
Activities: Activities of head offices
Parent: Mothercare PLC
Officers: Lynne Samatha Medini, Secretary; Darren Wayne Clark [1979] Director/Accountant; Kirsty Rowena Homer [1974] HR Director

Chelsteen Homes Limited
Incorporated: 1 November 1968 *Employees:* 11
Net Worth: £6,005,911 *Total Assets:* £8,414,945
Registered Office: 14 Wells Street, Chelmsford, Essex, CM1 1HZ
Activities: Development of building projects
Major Shareholder: William Alexander Poulton
Officers: Nicola Louise Poulton, Secretary; Alan John Poulton [1933] Director; William Alexander Poulton [1963] Director

Chelverton UK Dividend Trust PLC
Incorporated: 6 April 1999
Previous: Chelverton Small Companies Dividend Trust PLC
Net Worth: £51,794,000 *Total Assets:* £66,386,000
Registered Office: Hamilton Centre, Rodney Way, Chelmsford, Essex, CM1 3BY
Activities: Activities of investment trusts
Officers: Norman Stewart Hughson Lamont [1942] Director; Howard Vivian Peter Myles [1949] Director; William Alexander Van Heesewijk [1959] Director/Investment Trust Management [Brazilian]; Andrew Keith Watkins [1952] Director

Chemilines Group Holdings Limited
Incorporated: 30 November 2001 *Employees:* 113
Net Worth: £18,482,000 *Total Assets:* £24,584,000
Registered Office: Chemilines House, Alperton Lane, Wembley, Middlesex, HA0 1DX
Activities: Wholesale of pharmaceutical goods
Shareholders: Ravindra Prabhudas Karia; Jagdish Prabhudas Karia
Officers: Ravindra Prabhudas Karia, Secretary; Jagdish Prabhudas Karia [1958] Director; Ravindra Prabhudas Karia [1953] Director

Chemilines Limited
Incorporated: 28 July 1987 *Employees:* 84
Net Worth: £6,462,000 *Total Assets:* £10,114,000
Registered Office: Chemilines House, Alperton Lane, Wembley, Middlesex, HA0 1DX
Activities: Wholesale of pharmaceutical goods
Parent: Chemilines Group Holdings Limited
Officers: Ravindra Prabhudas Karia, Secretary; Sadhana Ravindra Karia, Secretary; Jagdish Prabhudas Karia [1958] Director; Ravindra Prabhudas Karia [1953] Director

Chemtest Holdings Limited
Incorporated: 18 February 2008 *Employees:* 160
Net Worth: £1,865,231 *Total Assets:* £8,633,780
Registered Office: 11 Depot Road, Newmarket, Suffolk, CB8 0AL
Activities: Activities of head offices
Major Shareholder: Peter James Noone
Officers: Kevin Alan Hempson, Secretary; Kevin Alan Hempson [1962] Director; Peter James Noone [1970] Director

Chemtest Limited
Incorporated: 21 February 2008 *Employees:* 139
Net Worth: £12,892,357 *Total Assets:* £15,589,624
Registered Office: 11 Depot Road, Newmarket, Suffolk, CB8 0AL
Activities: Other professional, scientific and technical activities n.e.c.
Officers: Kevin Alan Hempson, Secretary; David Paul Clarke [1974] Sales Director; Darrell Stuart Hall [1967] Director; Kevin Alan Hempson [1962] Director; Peter James Noone [1970] BD Director

Cheshunt Lakeside Developments Limited
Incorporated: 25 September 2015 *Employees:* 4
Net Worth: £252,634 *Total Assets:* £46,140,764
Registered Office: Decimal Place, Chiltern Avenue, Amersham, Bucks, HP6 5FG
Activities: Development of building projects
Shareholder: Inland Homes PLC
Officers: Andrew John Chrysostomou [1984] Director; Benjamin George Anker David [1977] Director; Nishith Malde [1958] Director; Gary John Skinner [1968] Managing Director

Chesside Homes Limited
Incorporated: 4 June 1996 *Employees:* 2
Net Worth: £4,206,233 *Total Assets:* £9,484,207
Registered Office: Enterprise House, Beesons Yard, Bury Lane, Rickmansworth, Herts, WD3 1DS
Activities: Development of building projects
Shareholders: Edward John Costello; Ann Patricia Costello
Officers: Ann Patricia Costello, Secretary/Director; Ann Patricia Costello [1941] Director; Edward John Costello [1937] Director [Irish]

Chester Greyhound Retail Park LLP
Incorporated: 22 June 2016
Net Worth: £12,659,511 *Total Assets:* £12,659,511
Registered Office: Aprirose House, 48a High Street, Edgware, Middlesex, HA8 7EQ
Officers: Manish Mansukhlal Gudka [1970] Member; Gareth Jones [1973] Member; Suraj Rashmikant Shah [1982] LLP Member

Chester International Hotel Limited
Incorporated: 13 March 1986 *Employees:* 71
Net Worth: £30,993,000 *Total Assets:* £35,808,000
Registered Office: Queens Court, 9-17 Eastern Road, Romford, Essex, RM1 3NG
Activities: Hotels and similar accommodation
Parent: BPH Finance Number 1 Limited
Officers: Jonathan Patrick Braidley [1965] Director/Investment Professional; Christopher Andre Kula [1983] Director/Chartered Accountant [German/Canadian]

The Chesterford Group Limited
Incorporated: 27 September 2012 *Employees:* 485
Previous: Eastgate Foods Limited
Net Worth: £2,275,884 *Total Assets:* £9,148,577
Registered Office: Chesterford House, 14 Stansted Distribution Centre, Start Hill, Great Hallingbury, Bishop's Stortford, Herts, CM22 7DG
Activities: Activities of other holding companies n.e.c.
Shareholders: Hugh Robert Lipscombe; Hugh Robert Lipscombe; Brian Peter Homent; James Scott Lipscombe
Officers: Emma Louise Fulcher, Secretary; Emma-Louise Louise Fulcher [1977] Finance Director; Paul John Goodgame [1975] Director; Hugh Robert Lipscombe [1952] Director; James Scott Lipscombe [1980] Director

Chesterhill Investments Limited
Incorporated: 26 January 1972 *Employees:* 7
Net Worth: £19,187,268 *Total Assets:* £32,855,708
Registered Office: Albany House, 10 Wood Street, Barnet, Herts, EN5 4BW
Activities: Buying and selling of own real estate
Major Shareholder: Brian Alan Binstock
Officers: Stephen David Cole, Secretary; Brian Alan Binstock [1947] Director/Accountant; Pauline Elizabeth Binstock [1947] Director/Secretary; Stephen David Cole [1959] Director/Property Consultant

Chestnut Inns Limited
Incorporated: 14 February 2012 *Employees:* 10
Net Worth: £6,234,894 *Total Assets:* £8,261,295
Registered Office: The Forge, Lower Green, Higham, Bury St Edmunds, Suffolk, IP28 6NL
Activities: Public houses and bars
Officers: David James Minchin [1963] Director; Philip Hugh Geoffrey Turner [1968] Director/Banking

Chevalier (2015) Ltd
Incorporated: 12 February 2015 *Employees:* 167
Net Worth: £8,046,605 *Total Assets:* £38,618,736
Registered Office: 1 Gainsborough Road, Felixstowe, Suffolk, IP11 7HT
Activities: Activities of head offices
Shareholders: Guy Barker; Dean Anthony Braybrook
Officers: Guy Barker [1974] Commercial Director; Dean Anthony Braybrook [1971] Managing Director; Gary James Spicer [1965] Finance Director; Richard James Stannard [1982] Estimating Director

Cheveley Park Stud Limited
Incorporated: 13 August 1975 *Employees:* 49
Net Worth: £35,440,900 *Total Assets:* £44,098,652
Registered Office: The Office, Cheveley Park Stud, Duchess Drive, Newmarket, Suffolk, CB8 9DD
Activities: Raising of horses and other equines
Parent: Hallam Meat Company Limited
Officers: Christopher James Dant, Secretary; Christopher James Dant [1969] Director/Chartered Accountant; Christopher James Richardson [1959] Director/Stud Manager; Sir Michael Ronald Stoute [1945] Director/Racehorse Trainer; David Brian Thompson [1936] Director; Patricia Thompson [1940] Director; Richard Charles Thompson [1964] Director; Katharine Patricia Woodward [1968] Director

Chicken Cabins Limited
Incorporated: 8 December 1965 *Employees:* 690
Net Worth: £12,908,308 *Total Assets:* £25,707,024
Registered Office: 64 Wolsey Road, Northwood, Middlesex, HA6 2EH
Activities: Unlicenced restaurants and cafes
Major Shareholder: Aly Hassanali Moleaina Janmohamed
Officers: Samirah Janmohamed, Secretary; Aly Hassanali Moleaina Janmohamed [1957] Director; Shehzad Janmohamed [1984] Director

Chicken Villas Limited
Incorporated: 16 December 1982 *Employees:* 2
Net Worth: £1,996,626 *Total Assets:* £23,448,416
Registered Office: First Floor, Kirkland House, 11-15 Peterborough Road, Harrow, Middlesex, HA1 2AX
Activities: Other letting and operating of own or leased real estate
Parent: Mulcroft Limited
Officers: Maya Bharat Patel, Secretary; Bharat Chandubhai Patel [1964] Director/Businessman; Maya Bharat Patel [1965] Director/Secretary

Chigwell School
Incorporated: 14 June 2006 *Employees:* 190
Net Worth: £24,517,000 *Total Assets:* £26,811,000
Registered Office: Chigwell School, High Road, Chigwell, Essex, IG7 6QF
Activities: Primary education
Officers: Claire Jones, Secretary; Susannah Louise Aliker [1966] Director/Accountant; Emma Brett [1970] Director/Chartered Accountant; John Frederick Cullis [1941] Director/University Tutor; Rev Christopher Mark Davies [1976] Director/Clerk in Holy Orders; Dr Graham Peter Dixon [1956] Director/Head of Radio EBU; Nicholas Antony Garnish [1965] Director; Jennifer Mary Gwinn [1950] Director/Retired; Martin James Higgins [1960] Director; Robin William John Howard [1959] Director/Barrister; Andrew Neil Howat [1959] Director/Group Treasurer; Melody Jones [1975] Director/Teacher; Reverend Benjamin William King [1976] Director/Minister of Religion; David Morriss [1942] Director/Consultant; Isobel Peck [1968] Marketing Director; Meera Ragha [1990] Director/Solicitor; Purmima SEN [1971] Director; Roseanne Serrelli [1968] Director/Solicitor

Childs Property Limited
Incorporated: 26 March 1996 *Employees:* 3
Net Worth: £4,195,169 *Total Assets:* £10,276,015
Registered Office: c/o W B Lemon & Co Limited, Russell Gardens, Wickford, Essex, SS11 8BL
Activities: Management of real estate on a fee or contract basis
Major Shareholder: Kevin Roy Childs
Officers: Kevin Roy Childs [1954] Director/Steel Reinforcement

The Childwick Trust
Incorporated: 21 September 2012 *Employees:* 2
Net Worth: £81,951,744 *Total Assets:* £82,194,424
Registered Office: 9 The Green, Childwickbury, St Albans, Herts, AL3 6JJ
Activities: Other service activities n.e.c.
Officers: Peter David Anwyl-Harris [1949] Investment Director; Mark Philip Farmar [1951] Director/Accountant; Michael John Alexander Fiddes [1959] Director/Chartered Surveyor; Clare Mary Maurice [1954] Director/Solicitor; Dr Alan Patrick O'Connell Stranders [1947] Director/Retired General Practitioner; John Dudley Wood [1944] Director/Retired

Chilford Hundred Education Trust
Incorporated: 5 January 2011 *Employees:* 210
Net Worth: £10,676,818 *Total Assets:* £11,702,057
Registered Office: Linton Village College, Cambridge Road, Linton, Cambs, CB21 4JB
Activities: Primary education
Officers: Magdalena Agnieszka Syposz, Secretary; Julie Bidwell [1959] Director; Gillian May Carter [1954] Director/Teacher; Linda Gillian Fisher [1964] Director/Lecturer; Anna Elisabeth Harvey [1978] Director/Lawyer; Dr Robert William James Loe [1979] Director/Education Research and Consultancy; Helena Marsh [1981] Director/Executive Principal; Tom Paul Meeks [1983] Director/Accountant; Mark Stephen Slater [1968] Director/Company Secretary

Chiltern Cold Storage Group Limited
Incorporated: 3 February 1995 *Employees:* 242
Net Worth: £1,200,831 *Total Assets:* £10,554,841
Registered Office: Shrewsbury Avenue, Woodston Industrial Estate, Peterborough, Cambs, PE2 7LB
Activities: Operation of warehousing and storage facilities for land transport activities
Parent: Chiltern Storage Holdings Limited
Officers: John Selwyn Davidson [1970] Director/Cold Storage Manager; Thomas Edward Lewis [1989] Director

Chiltern Distribution Ltd
Incorporated: 5 April 2006 *Employees:* 243
Previous: Chiltern Cold Storage Group Holdings Limited
Net Worth: £1,660,534 *Total Assets:* £10,685,822
Registered Office: Building 3, Funthams Lane, Whittlesey, Peterborough, PE7 2PB
Activities: Activities of head offices
Major Shareholder: Paul Anthony Jackson
Officers: Paul Anthony Jackson [1962] Director

Chiltern Learning Trust
Incorporated: 10 March 2011 *Employees:* 823
Net Worth: £44,959,000 *Total Assets:* £56,348,000
Registered Office: c/o Denbigh High School, Alexandra Avenue, Luton, Beds, LU3 1HE
Activities: General secondary education
Officers: Teresa Catherine Kelly, Secretary; Tracy Roberta Margaret Cowan [1966] Director/Administrator; Simon Foster [1966] Director/Business Executive; Brian Alan Howseman [1944] Director; Shahed Ahmed Koyes [1980] Director; Andrew Lewin [1974] Director/Operations Manager; Stewart John Parfitt [1967] Engineering Director; Graham John Pryor [1955] Director/Project Manager; Suzanne Spicer [1968] Director/Certified Chartered Accountant; Felicity Rose Ann Tasker [1947] Director/Retired; Lorraine Nicola Thomas [1956] Director/Bank Manager

Chiltern Way Academy Trust
Incorporated: 15 February 2016 *Employees:* 107
Net Worth: £13,770,289 *Total Assets:* £16,124,637
Registered Office: Wendover Campus, Church Lane, Wendover, Aylesbury, Bucks, HP22 6NL
Activities: General secondary education
Officers: Linda Barbara Duncan Switzer, Secretary; Tracey Hughes [1967] Director/Head of Marketing and Public Engagement; Michael William Hugh Jones [1963] Director/Headmaster; Ian Patrick McCaul [1968] Director/Principal [Irish]; Marian Edith Millward [1952] Director/Retired; David James Mortimer [1953] Director/Retired; Rodney Munday [1972] Director/Warrant Officer; Reine Pryce-Jones [1946] Director/Retired School Teacher; Tabitha Rowe [1990] Director/Teacher; Sophie Shepherd [1972] Director/Academy Governor; Dary Sweeney [1960] Director/Entrepreneur [Irish]; John Mason Twining [1961] Director/Teacher; Colin James Tyler [1958] Director/Retired

Chilton Home Farms Ltd
Incorporated: 10 October 1980 *Employees:* 89
Net Worth: £39,325,256 *Total Assets:* £44,841,792
Registered Office: Estate Office, Dorton Road, Chilton, Aylesbury, Bucks, HP18 9NA
Activities: Growing of cereals (except rice), leguminous crops and oil seeds
Officers: Lady Sara Roberta Aubrey-Fletcher, Secretary; Sir Henry Egerton Aubrey Fletcher [1945] Director/Farmer; Harry Buchanan Aubrey-Fletcher [1982] Director/Property Promotion & Development; Lady Sara Roberta Aubrey-Fletcher [1950] Director

Chipperfield Land Company Limited
Incorporated: 24 June 1987 *Employees:* 2
Net Worth: £8,913,481 *Total Assets:* £9,617,214
Registered Office: The Cottage, Ashlyns Hall, Chesham Road, Berkhamsted, Herts, HP4 2ST
Activities: Construction of domestic buildings
Parent: CLCH 1 Limited
Officers: Michael John Waterhouse [1936] Director; Robert John Waterhouse [1971] Director

Chivers Farms Limited
Incorporated: 22 March 1995 *Employees:* 8
Net Worth: £8,973,695 *Total Assets:* £13,160,365
Registered Office: Victoria Farm, Main Street, Hardwick, Cambridge, CB23 7QS
Activities: Growing of cereals (except rice), leguminous crops and oil seeds
Shareholders: John Benjamin Chivers; Caroline Elizabeth Chivers
Officers: John Benjamin Chivers, Secretary; Caroline Elizabeth Chivers [1964] Director; John Benjamin Chivers [1970] Director; Judith Chivers [1941] Director; Valerie Walton Chivers [1932] Director

Chivgate Limited
Incorporated: 10 December 1986 *Employees:* 46
Net Worth: £6,643,029 *Total Assets:* £25,710,050
Registered Office: 40 Thorby Avenue, March, Cambs, PE15 0AZ
Activities: Activities of head offices
Officers: Rafal Tetnowski, Secretary; Elzbieta Tetnowska [1966] Director [Polish]; Dr Pawel Tomil Tetnowski [1970] Director; Rafal Tetnowski [1971] Director; Stanislaw Frank Tetnowski [1943] Director [Polish]

Chobham Manor LLP
Incorporated: 13 June 2012
Net Worth: £35,502,000 *Total Assets:* £43,774,000
Registered Office: Gate House, Turnpike Road, High Wycombe, Bucks, HP12 3NR

The Chocolate Tasting Club PLC
Incorporated: 28 April 2003 *Employees:* 7
Net Worth: £4,923,539 *Total Assets:* £9,387,935
Registered Office: Mint House, Newark Close, Royston, Herts, SG8 5HL
Activities: Retail sale via mail order houses or via Internet
Parent: Hotel Chocolat Group PLC
Officers: Peter Mark Harris, Secretary; Peter Mark Harris [1955] Director; Matthew Paul Margereson [1970] Director; Matthew Robert Phillip Pritchard [1974] Director; Angus Thirlwell [1963] Director

Choice Discount Stores Limited
Incorporated: 7 April 1983 *Employees:* 507
Net Worth: £3,604,000 *Total Assets:* £9,057,000
Registered Office: 14-14a Rectory Road, Hadleigh, Benfleet, Essex, SS7 2ND
Activities: Retail of furniture, lighting, and similar (not musical instruments or scores) in specialised store
Officers: William George Prentice, Secretary; Paul Jonathan Britton [1966] Director/Retailer; Cornelius Andrew Donovan [1970] Director; Mark Donovan [1961] Director/Retailer

Chrysalis Multi Academy Trust
Incorporated: 9 March 2011 *Employees:* 267
Previous: Claremont High School Academy Trust
Net Worth: £54,264,000 *Total Assets:* £58,293,000
Registered Office: Claremont High School, Claremont Avenue, Kenton, Harrow, Middlesex, HA3 0UH
Activities: General secondary education
Officers: Steven Raphael Brunswick [1954] Director/Structural Engineer; Raxita Kapashi [1964] Director/Chartered Accountant; Shyamal Kishan Kataria [1984] Director/Chartered Accountant; Olivia Louisy [1988] Director/Recruitment Consultant; Reverend Grenville Thomas [1966] Director/Vicar

F.J. Church & Sons Limited
Incorporated: 4 January 1937 *Employees:* 55
Net Worth: £20,493,550 *Total Assets:* £29,058,780
Registered Office: Centenary Works, Manor Way, Rainham, Essex, RM13 8RH
Activities: Recovery of sorted materials
Parent: FJC Topco Ltd
Officers: Patrick John Church [1957] Director; Ian Simon Magson [1967] Managing Director

Church of God in Christ (Calvary) Limited
Incorporated: 25 September 1969
Net Worth: £10,371,812 *Total Assets:* £10,955,311
Registered Office: 127 Dunstable Road, Luton, Beds, LU1 1BW
Activities: Activities of religious organisations
Officers: Clevere Athelstan Fenty, Secretary; Clevere Athelstan Fenty, Secretary; Rev Alvin Blake [1935] Director/Minister of Religion; Rev Clevere Athelstan Fenty [1949] Director/Minister of Religion; Geoffrey Folkes [1959] Director/Minister of Religion; Michael Emanuel Gardner [1958] Director/Minister of Religion; Herald Horace Grant [1958] Director; Rev David Henry [1970] Director/Bus Driver; Revd Elroy Calvert Patrick [1955] Director/Minister of Religion; Revd Dave Robinson [1959] Director/Builder; Winston George Spencer [1957] Director/Electrician [Jamaican]; Rev Gladstone Thompson [1949] Director/Minister of Religion; Rev Cleveland Theodore Wallace [1932] Director/Minister of Religion [Jamaican]; Rev Michael Emanuel Williams [1932] Director/Minister of Religion [Jamaican]

The Church of Pentecost - UK
Incorporated: 31 March 2008 *Employees:* 54
Net Worth: £11,204,913 *Total Assets:* £15,687,379
Registered Office: 746 Green Lane, Dagenham, Essex, RM8 1YX
Activities: Activities of religious organisations
Officers: Reverend James Kofi Sam, Secretary; Kwaku Joe Adomako [1962] Director/Lecturer; Revd Osei Owusu Afriyie [1955] Director/Minister of Religion; Reverend Kwame Twumasi Appiah [1955] Director/Minister of Religion [Ghanaian]; Alex Appenteng Boateng [1978] Director/Pharmacist [Ghanaian]; Reverend Emmanuel Danso [1963] Director/Minister of Religion; Reverend George Kwaku Korankye [1968] Director/Minister of Religion; Reverend James Kofi Sam [1957] Director/Minister of Religion

Churchgate Estates Limited
Incorporated: 6 November 1996
Net Worth: £43,075,132 *Total Assets:* £43,095,528
Registered Office: 227 London Road, Romford, Essex, RM7 9BQ
Activities: Activities of head offices
Officers: Ameet Kotecha, Secretary; Ameet Kotecha [1973] Director; Ranjan Madhusudan Kotecha [1947] Director/Business Consultant

Churchill Contract Services Group Holdings Limited
Incorporated: 16 July 2010 *Employees:* 10,877
Net Worth: £26,871,478 *Total Assets:* £56,729,320
Registered Office: Unit 1, 40 Coldharbour Lane, Harpenden, Herts, AL5 4UN
Activities: Combined facilities support activities
Shareholders: Joel Matthew Briggs; Philip John Moxom
Officers: Caroline Briggs, Secretary; Joel Matthew Briggs [1961] Director; Philip John Moxom [1960] Director

Churchill Contract Services Limited
Incorporated: 20 April 1999 *Employees:* 9,382
Net Worth: £21,657,852 *Total Assets:* £47,620,276
Registered Office: Unit 1, 40 Coldharbour Lane, Harpenden, Herts, AL5 4UN
Activities: Other cleaning services
Parent: Churchill Contract Services Group Holdings Limited
Officers: Joel Matthew Briggs, Secretary; Joel Matthew Briggs [1961] Director/Businessman; Philip John Moxom [1960] Director/Businessman

The Churchmanor Estates Company PLC
Incorporated: 1 July 1980 *Employees:* 9
Net Worth: £1,936,892 *Total Assets:* £9,303,997
Registered Office: 11 Black Horse Lane, Ipswich, Suffolk, IP1 2EF
Activities: Buying and selling of own real estate
Officers: Stephen Montague Clark, Secretary; Felicity Amanda Clark [1960] Director/Manager; Stephen Montague Clark [1956] Director/Chartered Surveyor; Alan David Rosten [1975] Finance Director

Churchmanor Holdings Limited
Incorporated: 24 February 2010 *Employees:* 9
Net Worth: £9,183,083 *Total Assets:* £24,650,726
Registered Office: 11 Black Horse Lane, Ipswich, Suffolk, IP1 2EF
Activities: Buying and selling of own real estate
Major Shareholder: Stephen Montague Clark
Officers: Stephen Montague Clark, Secretary; Felicity Amanda Clark [1960] Director; Stephen Montague Clark [1956] Director/Chartered Surveyor

Churchmanor Limited
Incorporated: 4 July 1985 *Employees:* 3
Net Worth: £7,246,292 *Total Assets:* £15,447,206
Registered Office: 11 Black Horse Lane, Ipswich, Suffolk, IP1 2EF
Activities: Other letting and operating of own or leased real estate
Officers: Stephen Montague Clark, Secretary; Felicity Amanda Clark [1960] Director; Stephen Montague Clark [1956] Director/Chartered Surveyor

Churchtown Estates Limited
Incorporated: 22 January 1937
Net Worth: £11,275,468 *Total Assets:* £11,608,272
Registered Office: 400 Capability Green, Luton, Beds, LU1 3AE
Activities: Other letting and operating of own or leased real estate
Shareholders: Catherine Ingrid Hesketh; Henry Channon; Hugh William Inge-Innes-Lillingston
Officers: Pamela Jane Whelan, Secretary; Catherine Ingrid Hesketh [1952] Director/Secretary; Hugh William Ing-Innes-Lillingston [1956] Director

Churchtown Farm Solar Limited
Incorporated: 20 April 2011
Net Worth Deficit: £2,278,562 *Total Assets:* £11,001,576
Registered Office: Beaufort Court, Egg Farm Lane, off Station Road, Kings Langley, Herts, WD4 8LR
Activities: Production of electricity
Parent: European Investments (Cornwall) Limited
Officers: Dominic Hearth, Secretary; Steven William Hughes [1972] Global Support Services Director, UK&I - Commercial; Mitesh Raj Patel [1982] Director/Chartered Accountant; Tracy Jane Scott [1976] Director/Delivery Project Manager; Mark Christopher Wayment [1958] Director

Churton Property Developments Limited
Incorporated: 16 August 1994
Net Worth: £11,037,154 *Total Assets:* £18,413,018
Registered Office: 47 Canons Drive, Edgware, Harrow, Middlesex, HA8 7RG
Activities: Other letting and operating of own or leased real estate
Shareholders: John O'Connor; Patrick Thomas Osullivan
Officers: Patrick Thomas O'Sullivan, Secretary/Management Consultant; John O'Connor [1951] Director; Patrick Thomas O'Sullivan [1950] Director

Citizen Machinery UK Ltd
Incorporated: 24 June 1974 *Employees:* 48
Net Worth: £10,542,794 *Total Assets:* £21,732,640
Registered Office: 1 Park Avenue, Bushey, Herts, WD23 2DA
Activities: Agents involved in the sale of machinery, industrial equipment, ships and aircraft
Parent: Citizen Machinery Co., Ltd.
Officers: Jonathan Matthew Hart [1979] Director; Edward Harry James [1969] Managing Director; Hiromitsu Kamata [1963] Director/Financial Manager [Japanese]; Toshiyuki Nagasawa [1957] Director/General Manager [Japanese]; Darren Michael John Wilkins [1965] Deputy Managing Director

City & Country Bristol Limited
Incorporated: 15 June 2011
Net Worth Deficit: £2,861,303 *Total Assets:* £24,045,074
Registered Office: Bentfield Place, Bentfield Road, Stansted, Essex, CM24 8HL
Activities: Development of building projects
Parent: City & Country Residential Ltd
Officers: Andrew Ian Sargeant, Secretary; Suzanne Michele Aplin [1973] Director; Mark Townshend Fowler [1970] Director; Helen Margaret Moore [1965] Director; Andrew Ian Sargeant [1971] Director; David Richard Sargeant [1967] Director; Timothy Robert Sargeant [1965] Director; Simon Vernon-Harcourt [1969] Director

City & Country Group PLC
Incorporated: 6 February 2002 *Employees:* 148
Net Worth: £37,850,580 *Total Assets:* £106,828,824
Registered Office: Bentfield Place, Bentfield Road, Stansted, Essex, CM24 8HL
Activities: Activities of head offices
Officers: Andrew Ian Sargeant, Secretary; Mark Townshend Fowler [1970] Director; Helen Margaret Moore [1965] Director/Sales and Marketing Consultant; Andrew Ian Sargeant [1971] Director/Property Developer; David Richard Sargeant [1967] Director; Neil Edward Sargeant [1959] Director/Builder Developer [Australian/British]; Timothy Robert Sargeant [1965] Director; Simon Vernon-Harcourt [1969] Director

City & Country Residential Ltd
Incorporated: 12 March 1962 *Employees:* 67
Net Worth: £28,704,522 *Total Assets:* £38,515,748
Registered Office: Bentfield Place, Bentfield Road, Stansted, Essex, CM24 8HL
Activities: Development of building projects
Parent: City & Country Group PLC
Officers: Andrew Ian Sargeant, Secretary; Suzanne Michele Aplin [1973] Director; Mark Townshend Fowler [1970] Director; Helen Margaret Moore [1965] Director/Sales and Marketing Consultant; Andrew Ian Sargeant [1971] Director/Developer; David Richard Sargeant [1967] Director; Timothy Robert Sargeant [1965] Director; Simon Vernon-Harcourt [1969] Director

City & Westminster Developments Limited
Incorporated: 1 August 1996 *Employees:* 4
Net Worth: £5,005,607 *Total Assets:* £8,084,778
Registered Office: Handel House, 95 High Street, Edgware, Middlesex, HA8 7DB
Activities: Development of building projects
Shareholders: Francis Henry Jones; Shaida Nagsh-Jones
Officers: Shaida Nagsh-Jones, Secretary; Francis Henry Jones [1948] Director

City Brewery Limited
Incorporated: 21 September 2011 *Employees:* 80
Net Worth: £85,252 *Total Assets:* £9,884,925
Registered Office: Wellington House, 90-92 Butt Road, Colchester, Essex, CO3 3DA
Activities: Activities of head offices
Major Shareholder: Paul Rupert Lewin
Officers: Colin Richard Arthurs [1954] Director/Chief Executive; Paul Rupert Lewin [1955] Director/Business Consultant

City Lifting Limited
Incorporated: 15 May 1995 *Employees:* 175
Net Worth: £10,816,432 *Total Assets:* £41,766,104
Registered Office: 9 Juliette Way, Purfleet Industrial Park, South Ockendon, Essex, RM15 4YD
Activities: Other specialised construction activities n.e.c.
Shareholders: Trevor Mark Jepson; Clare Gillian Jepson
Officers: Clare Gillian Jepson [1959] Director; Trevor Mark Jepson [1958] Director; Robert John Jones [1963] Director/Crane Hire Manager

City Link (Cardiff) Holdings Limited
Incorporated: 29 January 2003
Net Worth: £3,313,000 *Total Assets:* £10,653,000
Registered Office: Astral House, Imperial Way, Watford, Herts, WD24 4WW
Activities: Activities of head offices
Parent: Vinci Pensions Limited
Officers: Ian David Hudson [1964] Director/Chartered Accountant; Rory John Murphy [1969] Director/Chartered Surveyor

City Link (Cardiff) Limited
Incorporated: 22 April 1998
Net Worth Deficit: £104,000 *Total Assets:* £43,447,000
Registered Office: Astral House, Imperial Way, Watford, Herts, WD24 4WW
Activities: Activities of head offices
Parent: City Link (Cardiff) Holdings Limited
Officers: Ian David Hudson [1964] Director/Chartered Accountant; Rory John Murphy [1969] Director/Chartered Surveyor

City North (Telford Homes) Limited
Incorporated: 23 November 2011
Previous: United House City North Limited
Net Worth: £36,055,000 *Total Assets:* £77,221,000
Registered Office: Telford House, Britannia Road, Queensgate, Waltham Cross, Herts, EN8 7TF
Activities: Activities of construction holding companies
Shareholders: City North Islington Holdings Limited; Telford Homes City North Limited
Officers: Joseph Mullee, Secretary; David Myles Campbell [1965] Group Sales and Marketing Director; Jonathan Graham Di-Stefano [1974] Director/Chief Executive; John Anthony FitzGenerald [1971] Group Managing Director; Dominic Richard Albert Ismael Jones [1967] Director; Jack Anthony Morris [1956] Director; Joseph Mullee [1978] Director/Accountant; Katie Rogers [1981] Finance Director

Citygate Automotive Limited
Incorporated: 8 November 2005 *Employees:* 456
Net Worth: £4,156,558 *Total Assets:* £33,090,256
Registered Office: 664 Victoria Road, Ruislip, Middlesex, HA4 0LN
Activities: Sale of new cars and light motor vehicles
Parent: Citygate Holdings Limited
Officers: Peter Dickey, Secretary; Peter Dickey [1956] Company Secretary/Director; Jonathan Kevin Smith [1965] Director

Citygate Developments 2005 Limited
Incorporated: 17 November 2004 *Employees:* 3
Net Worth: £3,589,006 *Total Assets:* £38,460,020
Registered Office: 16 Queen Street, Norwich, NR2 4SG
Activities: Other letting and operating of own or leased real estate
Parent: Citygate Developments Limited
Officers: Phillip Arthur Thorpe, Secretary; Alan Jones [1958] Director; Iain Reid [1966] Director; Phillip Arthur Thorpe [1960] Director/Accountant

Citygate Holdings Limited
Incorporated: 8 November 2005 *Employees:* 496
Net Worth: £4,581,340 *Total Assets:* £34,243,736
Registered Office: 664 Victoria Road, Ruislip, Middlesex, HA4 0LN
Activities: Activities of head offices
Major Shareholder: Jonathan Kevin Smith
Officers: Peter Dickey, Secretary; Peter Dickey [1956] Director; Stephen Paul Shepherd [1954] Director/Management Consultant; Jonathan Kevin Smith [1965] Director; Timothy John Worrall [1946] Director

CKH Developments Limited
Incorporated: 17 January 2007 *Employees:* 7
Net Worth: £76,000 *Total Assets:* £8,236,000
Registered Office: Cross Keys Homes, Shrewsbury Avenue, Woodston, Peterborough, Cambs, PE2 7BZ
Activities: Other accommodation
Parent: Cross Keys Homes
Officers: Claire Patricia Higgins, Secretary; Donald James Bell [1944] Director/Retired; Michael Joseph Heekin [1966] Executive Director of Finance; Claire Patricia Higgins [1963] Director/Chief Executive; Suzanne O'Brien [1970] Director/Finance & Marketing [Irish]; Andrew Robert Orrey [1962] Director/Retired

Claas Eastern Ltd
Incorporated: 12 April 1994 *Employees:* 95
Previous: Eastern Harvesters Ltd
Net Worth: £4,802,000 *Total Assets:* £12,490,000
Registered Office: Saxham, Bury St Edmunds, Suffolk, IP28 6QZ
Activities: Other retail sale not in stores, stalls or markets
Parent: Claas UK Ltd
Officers: Colin William Blow [1962] After Sales Director; Edmund Grant Dennis [1981] Director/Retail Controller; Jeremy Brian Preece [1967] Sales Director; Mark Pryce [1960] Commercial Director; Richard Andrew Vaughan [1964] Director/General Manager Retail Operations

Claas Manns Ltd
Incorporated: 16 October 1997 *Employees:* 79
Previous: Anglia Harvesters Ltd
Net Worth: £3,020,000 *Total Assets:* £10,717,000
Registered Office: Saxham, Bury St Edmunds, Suffolk, IP28 6QZ
Activities: Other retail sale not in stores, stalls or markets
Parent: Claas UK Ltd
Officers: Edmund Grant Dennis [1981] Director/Retail Controller; Thomas James Hancock [1983] Business Director; Richard David Holliday [1970] Sales Director; Paul Francis Moss [1961] Director/General Sales Manager; Richard Andrew Vaughan [1964] Director/General Manager Retail Operations

Claas UK Limited
Incorporated: 19 April 1949 *Employees:* 87
Net Worth: £52,530,000 *Total Assets:* £91,041,000
Registered Office: Saxham Business Park, Saxham, Bury St Edmunds, Suffolk, IP28 6QZ
Activities: Agents involved in the sale of machinery, industrial equipment, ships and aircraft
Parent: Claas Holdings Ltd
Officers: Christian Radons [1976] Regional Director [German]; Thomas Spiering [1980] Director/Chief Financial Officer [German]; Arthur Trevor Tyrrell [1967] Director/Chief Executive; Richard Andrew Vaughan [1964] Director/General Manager; Brian Keith Wain [1975] Director/Customer Service Manager; Jeremy Mark Wiggins [1973] Director/National Sales & Marketing Manager

Claas Western Ltd
Incorporated: 27 August 1955 *Employees:* 79
Previous: Western Harvesters Limited
Net Worth: £2,375,000 *Total Assets:* £8,899,000
Registered Office: Saxham Business Park, Saxham, Bury St Edmunds, Suffolk, IP28 6QZ
Activities: Other retail sale not in stores, stalls or markets
Parent: Claas UK Ltd
Officers: Edmund Grant Dennis [1981] Director/Retail Controller; William Paul Clark Greenway [1980] Sales Director; Steven David McCahill [1967] Director/Commercial Manager; Richard Andrew Vaughan [1964] Director/General Manager

Clarence Estates (London) Limited
Incorporated: 1 March 1984 *Employees:* 5
Net Worth: £20,902,912 *Total Assets:* £33,288,554
Registered Office: Lynwood House, 373-375 Station Road, Harrow, Middlesex, HA1 2AW
Activities: Development of building projects
Major Shareholder: Ali Tekin Atalar
Officers: Kerem Benjamin Atalar, Secretary; Dr Ali Tekin Atalar [1947] Director; Kerem Benjamin Atalar [1981] Director; Sara Elisabeth Atalar [1986] Director

Clarenco LLP
Incorporated: 5 February 2009 *Employees:* 188
Net Worth: £20,796,000 *Total Assets:* £21,870,000
Registered Office: Unit 6 Lancaster Court, Coronation Road, Cressex Business Park, High Wycombe, Bucks, HP12 3TD
Officers: Carol Ann Clare [1958] Member; Michael George Clare [1955] Member

Clarion Academy Trust
Incorporated: 4 January 2013 *Employees:* 122
Previous: Hobart High School (Academy Trust) Limited
Net Worth: £12,613,019 *Total Assets:* £13,931,491
Registered Office: Hobart High School, Kittens Lane, Loddon, Norwich, NR14 6JU
Activities: General secondary education
Officers: James Adams [1969] Director/Headteacher; Patricia Elizabeth Bell [1946] Director; Peter Ian Fraser [1951] Director; Shirley Jane Gates [1970] Director; Steven Derek Gray [1967] Project Director; Donna Clare Harris [1958] Director/Solicitor; John Organ [1964] Director/Retired; James Philip Wright [1960] Director/Farmer

Clark Construction (South East) Ltd
Incorporated: 11 October 1999 *Employees:* 2
Net Worth: £4,781,063 *Total Assets:* £9,941,884
Registered Office: Brentford Grange Farm, Beaconsfield Road, Coleshill, Amersham, Bucks, HP7 0JU
Activities: Other building completion and finishing
Shareholders: Timothy Richard Clark; Angela Felice Clark
Officers: Angela Felice Clark, Secretary; Angela Felice Clark [1956] Director/Company Secretary; Timothy Richard Clark [1961] Director/Builder

Clark-Drain Limited
Incorporated: 2 November 1978 *Employees:* 199
Net Worth: £5,907,272 *Total Assets:* £11,395,618
Registered Office: Station Road, Yaxley, Peterborough, PE7 3EQ
Activities: Manufacture of other chemical products n.e.c.
Parent: Clarksteel Holdings Limited
Officers: Ronald Francis Clark [1949] Director/Engineer; Rebecca Louise Hardy [1982] Director; Darren John Hughes [1972] Director; Sarah Jayne Hughes [1973] Director; Pamela May Spencer [1960] Director; Rachel Ellen Stuffins [1976] Director

Clarke International Limited
Incorporated: 18 February 1970 *Employees:* 156
Net Worth: £30,386,856 *Total Assets:* £148,342,096
Registered Office: Sealand House, Hemnall Street, Epping, Essex, CM16 4LG
Activities: Other retail sale in non-specialised stores
Parent: Clarke Group International Limited
Officers: Sandra Elaine Clarke, Secretary; John Alan Clarke [1943] Director; Sandra Elaine Clarke [1943] Director

Clarke Property Partner Limited
Incorporated: 6 February 2012
Net Worth Deficit: £18,324 *Total Assets:* £13,600,487
Registered Office: Sealand House, Hemnall Street, Epping, Essex, CM16 4LG
Activities: Other retail sale in non-specialised stores
Parent: Majestic Property & Estates Limited
Officers: John Alan Clarke [1943] Director

Clarksteel Holdings Limited
Incorporated: 20 May 1971 *Employees:* 199
Net Worth: £7,642,263 *Total Assets:* £14,595,698
Registered Office: Station Road, Yaxley, Peterborough, Cambs, PE7 3EQ
Activities: Manufacture of other fabricated metal products n.e.c.
Shareholders: Ronald Francis Clark; Graham Clive Holdich Smith; Pamela May Spencer
Officers: Ronald Francis Clark [1949] Director/Engineer; Pamela May Spencer [1960] Director

Clarucci Industry Limited
Incorporated: 5 February 2007 *Employees:* 3
Net Worth: £9,284,409 *Total Assets:* £9,480,432
Registered Office: Bedmond Hill House, Bedmond Hill, Hemel Hempstead, Herts, HP3 8SF
Activities: Financial management
Major Shareholder: Claudio Raffaele Guglielmucci
Officers: Sheila Margaret Donovan, Secretary; Sheila Margaret Donovan [1940] Director; Claudio Raffaele Guglielmucci [1940] Director [Italian]; Nicolantonio Guglielmucci [1964] Director

Classic Management Services Limited
Incorporated: 18 February 1980 *Employees:* 2
Net Worth: £11,643,258 *Total Assets:* £15,698,553
Registered Office: Unit 6 Penn Street Works, Penn Street, Amersham, Bucks, HP7 0PX
Activities: Buying and selling of own real estate
Officers: Amanda Louise Tanith Buckles, Secretary; Neil Anthony Aldred [1947] Director; Peter Alexander Buckles [1946] Director

Clavering Care Limited
Incorporated: 27 January 1993
Net Worth: £6,390,325 *Total Assets:* £9,105,500
Registered Office: 36 Railway Approach, Harrow, Middlesex, HA3 5AA
Activities: Residential nursing care facilities
Parent: TLC Group Ltd
Officers: Gagan Puri, Secretary; William Charles Neal [1986] Director; Paavan Popat [1985] Managing Director; Honourable Shivaan Shillin Popat [1988] Director; Gagan Puri [1978] Finance Director

Claxton Engineering Services Limited
Incorporated: 1 July 1985 *Employees:* 113
Net Worth: £5,379,000 *Total Assets:* £18,342,000
Registered Office: Ferryside, Ferry Road, Norwich, NR1 1SW
Activities: Support activities for petroleum and natural gas mining
Parent: Acteon Group Limited
Officers: Dr Bernhard Bruggaier [1961] Director [German]; Dannie Michael Claxton [1968] Director/Project Engineer; Laura Anne Claxton [1973] Director

The Claxton Trust
Incorporated: 3 November 2016 *Employees:* 202
Net Worth: £14,680,405 *Total Assets:* £16,529,449
Registered Office: The Claxton Trust, Fairlands Primary School, Pound Avenue, Stevenage, Herts, SG1 3JA
Activities: Pre-primary education
Officers: Joanna Louise Wibberley-Young, Secretary; Emma Elizabeth Flawn [1977] Director/Headteacher; Claire Louise Kemp [1973] Director/Access to Education Officer; Generaldine Nina Louch [1948] Director/Education Consultant; Deborah Karen Pepe [1974] Director/Employee Relations Manager; Gordon James Rumsey [1971] Director/Financial Adviser; Robert Patrick Charles Staples [1972] Director/Headteacher; Jocelyn Claudette Claire Wolfe [1943] Director/Teacher (Retired); Hayley Yendell [1975] Director/Early Years Adviser

R.H.Claydon Limited
Incorporated: 13 December 1968 *Employees:* 86
Net Worth: £8,028,163 *Total Assets:* £16,242,017
Registered Office: Saxham Industrial Estate, Saxham, Bury St Edmunds, Suffolk, IP28 6RZ
Activities: Wholesale trade of motor vehicle parts and accessories
Shareholders: Michael Hugh Claydon; Elizabeth Ina Beck
Officers: Clive Raymond Maskell, Secretary; Elizabeth Ina Beck [1953] Director; Doreen Alice Claydon [1929] Director; Michael Hugh Claydon [1957] Managing Director; Ruby Louella Claydon [1992] Director; Clive Raymond Maskell [1970] Finance Director

Claydon Securities Limited
Incorporated: 6 September 1956 *Employees:* 3
Net Worth: £8,797,029 *Total Assets:* £10,870,228
Registered Office: Sunningdale Court, Birchen Grove, Luton, Beds, LU2 7TR
Activities: Other letting and operating of own or leased real estate
Parent: C.G. Claydon Limited
Officers: Margot Jacqueline Bramley, Secretary; Margot Jacqueline Bramley [1935] Director; Shirley Irene Cooke [1932] Director; Simon Richard Cooke [1962] Director

Clays Ltd.
Incorporated: 14 July 1938 *Employees:* 888
Net Worth: £19,985,124 *Total Assets:* £34,938,392
Registered Office: Clays Printing Works, Popson Street, Bungay, Suffolk, NR35 1ED
Activities: Printing n.e.c.
Major Shareholder: Mario Pozzoni
Officers: John Paul Hulley, Secretary; John Paul Hulley [1963] Director; Kate Patricia McFarlan [1957] Director; Jonathan Charles Peter Nowell [1958] Director; Mario Francesco Pozzoni [1958] Director [Italian]; Maurizio Luca Vercelli Dequarti [1967] Director [Italian]

Cleanland Limited
Incorporated: 1 March 1991
Net Worth: £42,399,896 *Total Assets:* £42,653,320
Registered Office: 35-37 Amersham Hill, High Wycombe, Bucks, HP13 6NU
Activities: Buying and selling of own real estate
Officers: Peter James Davies [1978] Director; Nazim Ilyas [1982] Finance Director; Tim Neil Walton [1973] Managing Director

Clearsprings (Management) Limited
Incorporated: 30 September 1999 *Employees:* 133
Net Worth: £5,452,194 *Total Assets:* £14,308,389
Registered Office: 26 Brook Road, Brook Road Business Park, Rayleigh, Essex, SS6 7XJ
Activities: Activities of head offices
Shareholder: Graham Ian King
Officers: Randle James Slatter, Secretary; Graham Ian King [1967] Director; Randle James Slatter [1956] Finance Director; James Courtenay Vyvyan Robinson [1958] Managing Director

Clearview Homes (Western Avenue) Ltd
Incorporated: 10 February 2016
Net Worth: £2 *Total Assets:* £11,188,561
Registered Office: 201 Clearview House, Pinner Road, Northwood, Middlesex, HA6 1BX
Activities: Buying and selling of own real estate
Officers: Ramon Juan Dias [1962] Director; Stephen John Murphy [1960] Director

Clearview Homes Limited
Incorporated: 2 April 1991 *Employees:* 36
Net Worth: £15,867,783 *Total Assets:* £35,594,368
Registered Office: Clearview House, 201 Pinner Road, Northwood, Middlesex, HA6 1BX
Activities: Development of building projects
Officers: Donna Murphy, Secretary; Ramon Juan Dias [1962] Director; Stephen John Murphy [1960] Director

Clement Clarke (Holdings) Limited
Incorporated: 25 July 1989 *Employees:* 170
Net Worth Deficit: £64,821 *Total Assets:* £15,209,229
Registered Office: Edinburgh Way, Harlow, Essex, CM20 2TT
Activities: Activities of head offices
Parent: Metall Zug AG
Officers: Stephen David Jacobs, Secretary; Peter Demarmels [1977] Director/Head of Corporate Development [Swiss]; Guerino Ostacchini [1964] Director/General Manager; Rene Ott [1956] Director [Swiss]

T.H.Clements & Son Limited
Incorporated: 21 January 1966 *Employees:* 301
Net Worth: £7,532,000 *Total Assets:* £20,214,000
Registered Office: West End, Benington, Boston, Lincs, PE22 0EJ
Activities: Growing of vegetables and melons, roots and tubers
Parent: NG25 Limited
Officers: Simon John Lingard, Secretary; Christopher Ashley Clements [1981] Director/Business Manager; Christopher Terence Gedney [1959] Director; Richard James Mowbray [1974] Commercial Director

V.G.Clements (Contractors) Limited
Incorporated: 1 March 1960 *Employees:* 1,153
Net Worth: £7,737,540 *Total Assets:* £15,146,263
Registered Office: Cardinal House, Bury Street, Ruislip, Middlesex, HA4 7GD
Activities: Construction of commercial buildings
Parent: VGC Group Limited
Officers: Olivia Fitzpatrick, Secretary; Matthew John Fitzpatrick [1945] Director [Irish]; Laurence Richard McKidd [1955] Director; Ciara Melanie Pryce [1979] Director; Christopher Edward Ryan [1979] Director

Clerks Well Properties Limited
Incorporated: 6 November 2009
Net Worth: £7,871,933 *Total Assets:* £24,570,936
Registered Office: 290 High Street, Aldeburgh, Suffolk, IP15 5DQ
Activities: Other letting and operating of own or leased real estate
Officers: Julie Buss [1981] Director/Property Manager; Anna Canty [1975] Director/Property Manager; Blake Nicholas Gorst [1945] Director/Chartered Surveyor; Vanessa Jean Gorst [1944] Director

CLFIS (U.K.) Limited
Incorporated: 18 January 2002 *Employees:* 1,024
Net Worth Deficit: £95,076,000 *Total Assets:* £32,976,000
Registered Office: Canada Life Place, High Street, Potters Bar, Herts, EN6 5BA
Activities: Other business support service activities n.e.c.
Parent: The Canada Life Group (U.K.) Limited
Officers: Lisa Annette Rodriguez, Secretary; Kathryn Louise Bateman [1964] Director; Douglas Allan Brown [1971] Director/Chief Operating Officer; Robert Craig Fazzini-Jones [1974] Director; David John Marchant [1964] Director; Karen Helen Pengelly [1973] Director; Richard Paul Priestley [1971] Director; Timothy James Stoves [1980] Director

Cliffords Limited
Incorporated: 12 April 1972 *Employees:* 126
Net Worth: £11,397,538 *Total Assets:* £19,864,160
Registered Office: Aquila House, Waterloo Lane, Chelmsford, Essex, CM1 1BN
Activities: Activities of head offices
Shareholder: Clifford Anthony Peter Stubbings
Officers: Stuart Wesley Orrin, Secretary; Jason Livens [1969] Director; Stuart Wesley Orrin [1978] Director; Clifford Anthony Peter Stubbings [1930] Director; Richard James Clifford Stubbings [1958] Director

Climax Molybdenum U.K. Limited
Incorporated: 28 February 1940 *Employees:* 74
Net Worth: £34,537,000 *Total Assets:* £42,449,000
Registered Office: Needham Road, Stowmarket, Suffolk, IP14 2AE
Activities: Manufacture of other inorganic basic chemicals
Parent: Ametalco Limited
Officers: Dr Alan Armour [1948] Director/Manager Chemical Sales & Development; Michael Jeffrey Kendrick [1960] Director/Executive Officer [American]

Clinimed (Holdings) Limited
Incorporated: 23 August 1991 *Employees:* 643
Net Worth: £38,254,960 *Total Assets:* £57,811,084
Registered Office: Cavell House, Knaves Beech Way, Loudwater, High Wycombe, Bucks, HP10 9QY
Activities: Activities of head offices
Shareholders: Nigel Denis Piercey; Julian Mark Piercey; Daniel Jared Piercey
Officers: Suzanne Bryden, Secretary; Dr Daniel Jared Piercey [1963] Director; Julian Mark Piercey [1959] Managing Director; Nigel Denis Piercey [1954] Managing Director

Clinimed Limited
Incorporated: 28 June 1982 *Employees:* 115
Net Worth: £1,354,202 *Total Assets:* £10,438,991
Registered Office: Cavell House, Knaves Beech Way, Loudwater, High Wycombe, Bucks, HP10 9QY
Activities: Wholesale of pharmaceutical goods
Parent: Clinimed (Holdings) Limited
Officers: Suzanne Bryden, Secretary; Sean LEA Farbrother [1967] Director/Group Chief Executive

Close Homes Limited
Incorporated: 17 September 2009
Net Worth: £7,184,091 *Total Assets:* £9,406,609
Registered Office: Dovedale House, Hurricane Way, Wickford, Essex, SS11 8YB
Activities: Residents property management
Shareholders: Martin Close; Anthony John Close
Officers: Kelly Close, Secretary; Anthony John Close [1972] Director; Martin Close [1970] Director

Cloud Possibilities Limited
Incorporated: 2 June 2015
Net Worth: £5,984,021 *Total Assets:* £8,233,487
Registered Office: 506 Centennial Park, Centennial Avenue, Elstree, Herts, WD6 3FG
Activities: Activities of other holding companies n.e.c.
Major Shareholder: Mehool Harshadray Sanghrajka
Officers: Professor Stephen John Heppell [1950] Director; David Leonard Prais [1964] Director; Mehool Harshadray Sanghrajka [1966] Director/IT Consultant; Vijay Narendra Shah [1981] Director; Vishaal Narendra Shah [1984] Director/Entrepreneur

Cloud Topco Limited
Incorporated: 27 May 2015 *Employees:* 69
Net Worth Deficit: £1,919,401 *Total Assets:* £13,715,934
Registered Office: 7 Marchmont Gate, Boundary Way, Hemel Hempstead, Herts, HP2 7BF
Activities: Other human health activities
Parent: Caliornia Bidco Limited
Officers: Richard Holland, Secretary; Ajay Bhuneswarlal Chadha [1964] Director [German]; Richard Holland [1966] Director

CloudFM Group Limited
Incorporated: 20 June 2014 *Employees:* 306
Net Worth: £3,170,823 *Total Assets:* £18,078,180
Registered Office: CloudFM House, 3 Charter Court, Newcomen Way, Colchester, Essex, CO4 9YA
Activities: Combined facilities support activities
Officers: Peter Brumby [1964] Director; Adam Clayfield [1970] Director; Steven John Corbett [1977] Director; John Terry Cotton [1971] Director; Jeffrey Peter Dewing [1964] Director; Christopher Edward Gallop [1961] Managing Director; Derrick Alan Hidden [1972] Director of Technical Consultancy; David May [1980] Finance Director; Helen Marie Tidswell [1977] Communications Director

CloudFM Integrated Services Limited
Incorporated: 8 July 2010 *Employees:* 164
Previous: Technical Facilities Solutions Ltd
Net Worth: £2,950,529 *Total Assets:* £20,588,512
Registered Office: CloudFM House, 3 Charter Court, Newcomen Way, Colchester, Essex, CO4 9YA
Activities: Combined facilities support activities
Parent: CloudFM Group Limited
Officers: Peter Brumby [1964] Director; Adam Clayfield [1970] Commercial Director; Steven John Corbett [1977] Director; John Terry Cotton [1971] Director; Jeffrey Peter Dewing [1964] Director; Christopher Edward Gallop [1961] Director/Business Consultant; Derrick Alan Hidden [1972] Director/MD Engineering; David May [1980] Finance Director; Helen Marie Tidswell [1977] Communications Director

Cloverton Property Ltd
Incorporated: 4 February 2003
Net Worth: £1,998,166 *Total Assets:* £11,653,989
Registered Office: 10 Broadfield Way, Buckhurst Hill, Essex, IG9 5AG
Activities: Other letting and operating of own or leased real estate
Officers: George Somogyi, Secretary/Director; George Somogyi [1953] Director; Thomas David Somogyi [1983] Director

CML Microcircuits (UK) Limited
Incorporated: 30 March 1982 *Employees:* 98
Net Worth: £12,756,767 *Total Assets:* £15,249,581
Registered Office: Oval Park, Hatfield Road, Langford, Maldon, Essex, CM9 6WG
Activities: Manufacture of telegraph and telephone apparatus and equipment
Parent: CML Microsystems PLC
Officers: Roger Michael Driver, Secretary; Christopher Arthur Gurry [1963] Director/Business Development; Michael Ian Gurry [1960] Manufacturing Director; Mark John McCabe [1969] Managing Director CML Microcircuits (UK) Ltd; Neil Bartley Pritchard [1971] Director; Leslie Watson [1959] Director/Engineer; Christopher Nigel Wilson [1967] Director/Engineer

CML Microsystems PLC
Incorporated: 12 December 1968 *Employees:* 220
Net Worth: £41,770,000 *Total Assets:* £53,507,000
Registered Office: Oval Park, Hatfield Road, Langford, Maldon, Essex, CM9 6WG
Activities: Manufacture of electronic components
Officers: Neil Bartley Pritchard, Secretary; Geoffrey Frederick Barnes [1945] Director/Chartered Accountant; Nigel Graham Clark [1954] Director; Christopher Arthur Gurry [1963] Director; James Andrew Lindop [1957] Director; Neil Bartley Pritchard [1971] Director; Hugh Francis Rudden [1959] Director

CMS Developments Limited
Incorporated: 2 July 2003 *Employees:* 4
Net Worth: £1,011,912 *Total Assets:* £10,339,015
Registered Office: Unit 6 Penn Street Works, Penn Street, Amersham, Bucks, HP7 0PX
Activities: Development of building projects
Officers: Amanda Louise Tanith Buckles, Secretary; Neil Anthony Aldred [1947] Director; Amanda Louise Tanith Buckles [1975] Director; Peter Alexander Buckles [1946] Director; Jonathan Paul Yendell [1969] Director

CN Group Limited
Incorporated: 17 July 1985 *Employees:* 370
Net Worth: £5,682,000 *Total Assets:* £13,011,000
Registered Office: Loudwater Mill, Station Road, Loudwater, High Wycombe, Bucks, HP10 9TY
Activities: Activities of head offices
Officers: Neil Edward Carpenter, Secretary; Simon Alton Westrop, Secretary; Henry Kennedy Faure Walker [1972] Director; Paul Anthony Hunter [1964] Director

CNH Industrial Capital Europe Limited
Incorporated: 12 August 1997
Net Worth: £47,751,000 *Total Assets:* £471,639,008
Registered Office: Room 32-521, Cranes Farm Road, Basildon, Essex, SS14 3AD
Activities: Financial leasing
Shareholders: BNP Paribas SA; CNH Industrial NV
Officers: Nicholas David James, Secretary; Jean-Michel Robert Boyer [1963] Director/CEO, Country Manager [French]; Jonathan Mark Cooper [1962] Director/Head of Sales; David Robert Humphreys [1961] Director/Country Retail Finance Sales Manager; Pierre-Thomas Alexandre Jean Joire [1977] Director/Chief Accounting Officer CNH Industrial Financial [French]; Philippe Lambert [1967] Director/Global Head of Transport [French]; Francois Thierry Millot [1961] Director/Head of Retail Finance [French]

CNH Industrial Capital Limited
Incorporated: 27 July 2012 *Employees:* 16
Previous: Iveco FS Holdings Limited
Net Worth: £107,202,456 *Total Assets:* £236,037,680
Registered Office: Cranes Farm Road, Basildon, Essex, SS14 3AD
Activities: Activities of head offices
Parent: CNH Industrial NV
Officers: Simon Marc McCarthy, Secretary; Enrico Bretto [1961] Director/Manager [Italian]; Mario Bruni [1974] Director [Italian]; Simon Marc McCarthy [1971] Director/Solicitor [Australian]

CNH Industrial Oldco Capital Limited
Incorporated: 25 February 2000
Previous: CNH Industrial Capital UK Limited
Net Worth: £520,595 *Total Assets:* £167,024,544
Registered Office: Cranes Farm Road, Basildon, Essex, SS14 3AD
Activities: Other business support service activities n.e.c.
Parent: CNH Industrial NV
Officers: Simon Marc McCarthy, Secretary; John Edwin Chick [1959] Director/Country Portfolio Manager; Simon Marc McCarthy [1971] Director/Solicitor [British/Australian]

Co-op Group Travel 2 Holdings Limited
Incorporated: 20 October 2010 *Employees:* 1
Net Worth: £1,609,000 *Total Assets:* £31,587,000
Registered Office: Westpoint, Peterborough Business Park, Lynch Wood, Peterborough, Cambs, PE2 6FZ
Activities: Other business support service activities n.e.c.
Parent: TCCT Holdings UK Limited
Officers: Shirley Bradley, Secretary; Alan Charles Donald [1963] Director

The Coaching Inn Group Ltd
Incorporated: 22 May 1996 *Employees:* 616
Previous: Bulldog Hotel Group Ltd.
Net Worth: £10,108,641 *Total Assets:* £43,564,464
Registered Office: Friars House, Quaker Lane, Boston, Lincs, PE21 6BZ
Activities: Other amusement and recreation activities n.e.c.
Shareholder: Business Growth Fund PLC
Officers: Mark William Porcher, Secretary; Kevin Charity [1965] Director; Lilian Margaret Charity [1958] Director; Mark Stephen Freer [1964] Director; Andrew Graham Guy [1948] Director/Chief Executive; Mark William Porcher [1964] Director; Edward Walsh [1986] Director

Coastfields Leisure Limited
Incorporated: 20 December 1972 *Employees:* 179
Net Worth: £12,102,961 *Total Assets:* £41,152,764
Registered Office: 4 Cyrus Way, Cygnet Park, Hampton, Peterborough, Cambs, PE7 8HP
Activities: Recreational vehicle parks, trailer parks and camping grounds
Shareholders: Lynda Joyce Silvester; Lloyd Bennet Silvester
Officers: Lloyd Bennet Silvester, Secretary; Lloyd Bennet Silvester [1972] Sales Director; Lynda Joyce Silvester [1947] Director/Caravan Site Proprietor

Cobb Europe Limited
Incorporated: 16 September 1974 *Employees:* 166
Net Worth: £33,106,806 *Total Assets:* £50,261,680
Registered Office: The Oaks, Apex 12, Old Ipswich Road, Ardleigh, Colchester, Essex, CO7 7QR
Activities: Raising of poultry
Officers: Neil Cross, Secretary; Stuart Burrell [1973] Director; Neil Cross [1980] Director/Chartered Accountant; Tore Mercan [1968] Sales Director; Mark Andrew Sams [1969] Director/Accountant; John Charles Vincent [1959] Production Director; Richard Weatherley [1980] Production Director; Gabrielle Olivia Zeter [1981] Director

Cocksedge Building Contractors Limited
Incorporated: 5 June 2000 *Employees:* 116
Net Worth: £6,638,271 *Total Assets:* £13,365,475
Registered Office: 25 Hampstead Avenue, Mildenhall, Bury St Edmunds, Suffolk, IP28 7AS
Activities: Development of building projects
Parent: Cocksedge (Holdings) Limited
Officers: Timothy Andrew Grant, Secretary; Justin Peter Buckingham [1971] Contract Director; Timothy Andrew Grant [1962] Director/Chartered Accountant; Stephen Christopher Nugent [1977] Director/Quantity Surveyor Contracts Manager

W.D. Coe Limited
Incorporated: 30 September 1960 *Employees:* 225
Net Worth: £5,535,000 *Total Assets:* £10,282,000
Registered Office: 20-28 Norwich Road, Ipswich, Suffolk, IP1 2NH
Activities: Retail sale of clothing in specialised stores
Officers: Bridget Jane Coe [1967] Director; David John Coe [1938] Director; William David Coe [1969] Director; Peter Paul Hubka [1959] Director; Matthew Steven Rawlings [1977] Director Menswear Retailer

Coex Properties LLP
Incorporated: 5 May 2009 *Employees:* 2
Net Worth: £6,002,571 *Total Assets:* £10,249,546
Registered Office: c/o Haslers, Old Station Road, Loughton, Essex, IG10 4PL
Officers: Lovisa Elina Elisabet Pelosi [1990] Member; Andrew John Sheen [1959] Member; Karola Elisabet Sheen [1957] Member; Lukas Wilhelm Sheen [1985] Member

COFCO International UK Ltd
Incorporated: 27 March 1920 *Employees:* 98
Previous: Nidera UK Limited
Net Worth: £13,900,914 *Total Assets:* £53,293,328
Registered Office: The Havens, Ransomes Europark, Ipswich, Suffolk, IP3 9SJ
Activities: Support activities for crop production
Officers: Nicholas Adam Kerridge, Secretary; Timothy Edward Capey [1979] Director; Dennis Dewsbery [1949] Director/Business Consultant; Mark Stuart Dordery [1967] Director/Chief Executive; Andrew Eccles [1973] Director; Nicholas Adam Kerridge [1973] Director/Accountant; Stuart Shiells [1976] Director/Trader; Martin Vine [1957] Director

Coffeeheaven International Limited
Incorporated: 31 August 2001
Net Worth: £22,262,000 *Total Assets:* £24,144,000
Registered Office: Costa House, Houghton Hall Business Park, Porz Avenue, Houghton Regis, Dunstable, Beds, LU5 5YG
Activities: Production of coffee and coffee substitutes
Parent: Costa Limited
Officers: Russell William Fairhurst, Secretary; Sarah Louise Highfield [1978] Finance Director; Dominic James Paul [1971] Managing Director; Katherine Joanna Seljeflot [1972] Group HR Director-Costa

J. Coffey Construction Limited
Incorporated: 10 June 1994 *Employees:* 105
Net Worth: £16,315,123 *Total Assets:* £45,137,436
Registered Office: 93-95 Greenford Road, Harrow, Middlesex, HA1 3QF
Activities: Other specialised construction activities n.e.c.
Major Shareholder: James Anthony Coffey
Officers: Edward Generald Barrett [1965] Director/Surveyor [Irish]; James Anthony Coffey [1954] Director/Building Contractor [Irish]; Mary Teresa Coffey [1957] Director/Secretary [Irish]; Thomas Patrick Mitchell [1958] Director [Irish]

Cogels Investments Ltd
Incorporated: 27 January 2012
Net Worth: £19,949,570 *Total Assets:* £21,554,420
Registered Office: Courtlands, Station Road, Felsted, Essex, CM6 3HB
Activities: Activities of head offices
Officers: Lucia Blyth, Secretary; Claudia Rose Emily Blyth [1991] Director; Emilia Alice Barbara Blyth [1997] Director/Student; Lucia Blyth [1958] Director/Housewife; Olivia Marie Isabelle Blyth [1994] Director; Stephen William Blyth [1955] Director/Retired

Coherent (UK) Holdings Limited
Incorporated: 7 April 1997 *Employees:* 4
Net Worth: £13,253,000 *Total Assets:* £13,347,000
Registered Office: St Thomas Place, Cambridgeshire Business Park, Ely, Cambs, CB7 4EX
Activities: Non-trading company
Parent: Coherent Inc
Officers: Lynne Dowell, Secretary; Bret Dimarco [1968] Director/General Counsel [American]; Richard Gerard Gleeson [1961] Director/VP Sales EMEA; Daniel Allen Hunter [1959] Director/Vice President, Corporate Controller [American]; Mitchell Arnold McPeek [1960] Director/Vice President, Tax & Treasury - Coherent Inc [American]

Coherent (UK) Limited
Incorporated: 15 December 1970 *Employees:* 12
Net Worth: £11,289,000 *Total Assets:* £11,461,000
Registered Office: St Thomas' Place, Cambridgeshire Business Park, Ely, Cambs, CB7 4EX
Activities: Other professional, scientific and technical activities n.e.c.
Parent: Coherent (UK) Holdings Ltd
Officers: Roger Alan Beaman, Secretary; Bret Dimarco [1968] Director/EVP General Councils Secretary [American]; Richard Gerard Gleeson [1961] Director/VP European Operations; Daniel Allen Hunter [1959] Director/Corporate Controller [American]; Mitchell Arnold McPeek [1960] Director/VP Tax & Treasury [American]

Cokenach Limited
Incorporated: 9 May 2002 *Employees:* 13
Net Worth: £38,552,128 *Total Assets:* £40,893,108
Registered Office: Estate Office, Cokenach, Barkway, Royston, Herts, SG8 8DL
Activities: Growing of cereals (except rice), leguminous crops and oil seeds
Major Shareholder: Niels Holch Povlsen
Officers: Soren From, Secretary; Kenneth Grant [1977] Director; Niels Holch Povlsen [1977] Director/IT Consultant [Danish]; Troels Holch Povlsen [1949] Director [Danish]

Cokenach Property Limited
Incorporated: 28 February 2014
Net Worth: £2,325,924 *Total Assets:* £16,558,619
Registered Office: The Estate Office, Cokenach, Barkway, Herts, SG8 8DL
Activities: Activities of other holding companies n.e.c.
Major Shareholder: Niels Holch Povlsen
Officers: Kenneth Grant [1977] Director; Jessica Polvsen [1978] Director [Danish]; Niels Holch Polvsen [1977] Director [Danish]

Peter Colby Commercials Limited
Incorporated: 8 April 1974 *Employees:* 36
Net Worth: £14,061,109 *Total Assets:* £47,606,064
Registered Office: School Lane, Sprowston, Norwich, NR7 8TL
Activities: Other letting and operating of own or leased real estate
Parent: Saint Vincent Holdings Limited
Officers: Emma Jane Colby, Secretary; Michael John Sutton, Secretary; Simon William Beckett [1964] Director/Accountant; Peter George Colby [1942] Director

Colchester Catalyst Charity
Incorporated: 7 August 1959 *Employees:* 3
Net Worth: £11,944,532 *Total Assets:* £12,253,983
Registered Office: 14 Dedham Vale Business Centre, Manningtree Road, Dedham, Colchester, Essex, CO7 6BL
Activities: Other human health activities
Officers: Peter Wilfrid Edgar Fitt, Secretary; Professor Naomi Joan Busfield [1940] Director; Peter Wilfrid Edgar Fitt [1946] Director/Chartered Accountant; Christine Hayward [1953] Director/Teacher; Dr Max Peter Hickman [1963] Director/General Practitioner; Mark Ferens Pertwee [1962] Director; Dr Thilaka Prakash Rudra [1951] Director/Consultant Physician; Keith Songhurst [1975] Director/Solicitor; Elizabeth Thrower [1962] Director/NHS Occupational Therapist

Colchester Royal Grammar School
Incorporated: 9 September 2011 *Employees:* 172
Net Worth: £10,263,178 *Total Assets:* £12,953,564
Registered Office: Colchester Royal Grammar School, 6 Lexden Road, Colchester, Essex, CO3 3ND
Activities: General secondary education
Officers: Emmanuelle Anning [1973] Director/Teacher [French]; Salome Azarmi [1967] Director/Solicitor; Glynis Ann Barritt [1951] Director; James Michael Carter [1973] Director; Professor George Anthony Constantinides [1975] Director/University Professor in Digital Computation; Richard Andrew Crayston [1947] Director/Retired Chartered Surveyor; Mike John Elliff [1970] Managing Director; Philip Michael Hoddell [1964] Director/Solicitor; Deborah Mary Hoy [1966] Director/Retired; John Christopher Johnston [1953] Director/Bank Manager; Ross Thomas Neale [1991] Director/Teacher; Judith Anne Owens [1955] Director/Retired Chartered Surveyor; Janet Perry [1960] Director/NHS Chief Financial Controller Chartered Management; David James Ratcliffe [1990] Director/IT Technician; Philip Michael Roberts [1949] Director; Dr Iain Alexander Ross [1975] Director/Teacher; John Richard Russell [1966] Director/Headmaster; Dr John Graham Tillett [1933] Director; Iain Stewart Turner [1965] Director/Banker

Colchester Zoo Holdings Limited
Incorporated: 5 March 2010 *Employees:* 385
Net Worth: £17,909,248 *Total Assets:* £20,777,640
Registered Office: Stanway Hall, Maldon Road, Stanway, Colchester, Essex, CO3 0SL
Activities: Other business support service activities n.e.c.
Major Shareholder: Dominique Ange Tropeano
Officers: Anthony Pascal Tropeano, Secretary; Sarah Dominique Knuckley [1972] Director; Anthony Steven Pascal Tropeano [1969] Director; Dr Dominique Ange Tropeano [1945] Director [French]

Colchester Zoo Limited
Incorporated: 30 July 1976 *Employees:* 385
Net Worth: £15,426,393 *Total Assets:* £17,824,566
Registered Office: Stanway Hall, Maldon Road, Stanway, Colchester, Essex, CO3 0SL
Activities: Botanical and zoological gardens and nature reserves activities
Major Shareholder: Dominique Ange Tropeano
Officers: Anthony Pascal Tropeano, Secretary; Sarah Dominique Knuckey [1972] Director/Secretary; Anthony Steven Pascal Tropeano [1969] Director/Zoo Curator; Dr Dominique Ange Tropeano [1945] Zoo Director [French]

Collease Truck and Trailer Rentals Limited
Incorporated: 14 April 1975 *Employees:* 41
Net Worth: £4,639,036 *Total Assets:* £16,449,799
Registered Office: School Lane, Sprowston, Norwich, NR7 8TL
Activities: Renting and leasing of trucks and other heavy vehicles
Parent: Saint Vincent Holdings Limited
Officers: Emma Jane Colby, Secretary; Michael John Sutton, Secretary; Simon William Beckett [1964] Director/Accountant; Peter George Colby [1942] Director

Colleycare Limited
Incorporated: 16 March 1988 *Employees:* 867
Net Worth: £58,875,964 *Total Assets:* £89,918,456
Registered Office: Old Town Court, 70 Queensway, Hemel Hempstead, Herts, HP2 5HD
Activities: Residential nursing care facilities
Parent: B & M Care Group Limited
Officers: Trinna Ann Bruton, Secretary; Trinna Ann Bruton [1967] Director; William John Hughes [1941] Director [Irish]; Rachel Ann Rodgers [1964] Director; Ian Sloan [1959] Director/Quantity Surveyor; Dr Colleen Mary Wood [1977] Director/Clinical Advisor

Coloplast Limited
Incorporated: 5 February 1973 *Employees:* 474
Net Worth: £28,085,000 *Total Assets:* £60,367,000
Registered Office: Nene Hall, Lynchwood Park, Peterborough Business Park, Peterborough, Cambs, PE2 6FX
Activities: Non-specialised wholesale trade
Parent: Coloplast A/S
Officers: Myles Davies [1972] Business Support Director; Henrik Deneke [1967] Director/Vice President [Danish]; Generaldine Anne Harkins [1961] Business Unit Director; Ashley Alexander Julian Knight [1969] Marketing Director; Alain Michel Herve Morvan [1962] Director [French]; Annemarie Van Neck [1975] Director/General Manager [Dutch]; Peter Volkers [1959] Director [Danish]

Colts Cabs Limited
Incorporated: 26 July 1991
Net Worth: £5,593,067 *Total Assets:* £14,243,478
Registered Office: 5 Elstree Gate, Elstree Way, Borehamwood, Herts, WD6 1JD
Activities: Taxi operation
Major Shareholder: Michael Glassman
Officers: Michael Glassman [1963] Director/Taxi Fleet Operator

Colwyn Developments Limited
Incorporated: 30 May 1985 *Employees:* 3
Net Worth: £6,317,355 *Total Assets:* £9,529,454
Registered Office: 10 Neale Street, Ipswich, Suffolk, IP1 3JB
Activities: Buying and selling of own real estate
Shareholder: Kevin Paul Cattermole
Officers: Jeremy William Goddard, Secretary; Kevin Paul Cattermole [1957] Property Director; Jeremy William Goddard [1953] Director/Estate Agent

Com Dev Europe Limited
Incorporated: 15 November 1984 *Employees:* 167
Net Worth: £2,751,000 *Total Assets:* £21,578,000
Registered Office: Unit 10 Triangle Business Park, Quilters Way, Stoke Mandeville, Aylesbury, Bucks, HP22 5SX
Activities: Satellite telecommunications activities
Parent: Com Dev Investments Limited
Officers: Anthony Richard Vaughan Hutchings [1956] Finance Director; John Cain Little [1960] Director; Victor Jay Miller [1966] Director/Vice President and General Counsel, Defense/Space [American]; Sarah Ransome Wallis [1970] Director

Combat Medical Holdings Ltd
Incorporated: 27 April 2017
Net Worth: £30,784,280 *Total Assets:* £30,785,776
Registered Office: Lamer House, Lamer Lane, Wheathampstead, St Albans, Herts, AL4 8RL
Activities: Activities of other holding companies n.e.c.
Major Shareholder: Alberto Martinez
Officers: Edward Alexander Bruce-White, Secretary; Edward Alexander Bruce-White [1975] Director; Alberto Martinez [1974] Director - Medical Devices [Spanish]; Ronnie Potel [1975] Director/Financial Consultant

Comensura Limited
Incorporated: 9 October 2000 *Employees:* 67
Net Worth: £29,784,000 *Total Assets:* £76,838,000
Registered Office: 800 The Boulevard, Capability Green, Luton, Beds, LU1 3BA
Activities: Management consultancy activities other than financial management
Parent: Impellam Holdings Limited
Officers: Rebecca Jane Watson, Secretary; Simon Ian Moore [1978] Director/Accountant; Julia Robertson [1958] Director; Rebecca Jane Watson [1969] Director/Solicitor

Comland Commercial Limited
Incorporated: 4 November 1997 *Employees:* 10
Net Worth: £20,337,672 *Total Assets:* £24,775,468
Registered Office: Lunar House, Mercury Park, Wooburn Green, High Wycombe, Bucks, HP10 0HH
Activities: Management of real estate on a fee or contract basis
Parent: MCF Commercial Limited
Officers: Christopher Giles Martin, Secretary/Chartered Accountant; Christopher Robert Ayres [1982] Director; Stuart James Crossley [1944] Director; Christopher Giles Martin [1968] Director/Chartered Accountant

Comland Group Limited
Incorporated: 13 June 2007 *Employees:* 55
Previous: Comland Group PLC
Net Worth: £64,596,000 *Total Assets:* £76,224,000
Registered Office: Lunar House, Wooburn Green, High Wycombe, Bucks, HP10 0HH
Activities: Activities of head offices
Shareholders: Stuart James Crossley; Christopher Giles Martin
Officers: Christopher Giles Martin, Secretary/Director; Christopher Robert Ayres [1982] Director; Stuart James Crossley [1944] Director; Christopher Giles Martin [1968] Director

Comland Holdings Limited
Incorporated: 10 August 2000 *Employees:* 3
Net Worth: £12,862,180 *Total Assets:* £23,055,412
Registered Office: Lunar House, Mercury Park, Wooburn Green, High Wycombe, Bucks, HP10 0HH
Activities: Non-trading company
Parent: Comland Commercial Limited
Officers: Christopher Giles Martin, Secretary/Chartered Accountant; Christopher Robert Ayres [1982] Director; Stuart James Crossley [1944] Director; Christopher Giles Martin [1968] Director/Chartered Accountant

Comline Auto Parts Limited
Incorporated: 3 March 1988 *Employees:* 131
Net Worth: £5,834,961 *Total Assets:* £18,240,080
Registered Office: Unit B1, Luton Enterprise Park, Sundon Park Road, Luton, Beds, LU3 3GU
Activities: Wholesale trade of motor vehicle parts and accessories
Officers: Divyesh Mansukhlal Kamdar, Secretary; Mansukhlal Chandulal Kamdar [1936] Director [Kenyan]; Anita Divyesh Kamdar [1962] Marketing Director; Divyesh Mansukhlal Kamdar [1961] Director/Chartered Accountant; Ishan Divyesh Kamdar [1988] Director/Business Development; Nilesh Kanti Popat [1964] Director/General Manager

Comline Holdings Limited
Incorporated: 14 June 2016 *Employees:* 210
Net Worth: £5,217,654 *Total Assets:* £34,061,712
Registered Office: Unit B1, Luton Enterprise Park, Sundon Park Road, Luton, Beds, LU3 3GU
Activities: Activities of distribution holding companies
Shareholders: Divyesh Mansukhlal Kamdar; Nilesh Kanti Popat
Officers: Divyesh Mansukhlal Kamdar, Secretary; Anita Divyesh Kamdar [1962] Director; Divyesh Mansukhlal Kamdar [1961] Director; Ishan Divyesh Kamdar [1988] Director; Nilesh Kanti Popat [1964] Director

Commercial Body Fittings Limited
Incorporated: 19 September 1984 *Employees:* 64
Net Worth: £14,499,075 *Total Assets:* £16,442,860
Registered Office: 80 Bridge Road East, Welwyn Garden City, Herts, AL7 1JY
Activities: Wholesale trade of motor vehicle parts and accessories
Major Shareholder: Giovanni Marco Negri
Officers: Giovanni Marco Negri [1938] Managing Director; Mark Negri [1966] Director; Louisa Angelina Elizabeth Traversi [1964] Director

Commercial Freeholds & Investments Ltd
Incorporated: 12 January 2015 *Employees:* 5
Net Worth: £1,743,297 *Total Assets:* £29,262,552
Registered Office: 5 Elstree Gate, Elstree Way, Borehamwood, Herts, WD6 1JD
Activities: Development of building projects
Major Shareholder: Christopher Richard Cradock
Officers: Samantha Bolton [1972] Director; Christopher Richard Cradock [1942] Director; Francis Christoper Richard Cradock [1962] Director; Susan Margret Drake Cradock [1942] Director; Tracy Margaret Jeannie MacDonald [1964] Director

Commodity Centre (Group) Limited
Incorporated: 5 December 2012 *Employees:* 88
Net Worth: £8,947,134 *Total Assets:* £25,900,236
Registered Office: Commodity House, Braxted Park Road, Great Braxted, Witham, Essex, CM8 3EW
Activities: Activities of other holding companies n.e.c.
Major Shareholder: Alec Gunn
Officers: Alec Gunn [1953] Director; Andrew Derek Jordan [1983] Finance Director; Dean Warriner [1984] Director

Commodore Kitchens Limited
Incorporated: 9 May 1979 *Employees:* 152
Net Worth: £9,970,740 *Total Assets:* £23,798,642
Registered Office: Acorn House, Gumley Road, Grays, Essex, RM20 4XP
Activities: Manufacture of kitchen furniture
Parent: Nobia Holdings UK Limited
Officers: Nicola Jane Hardcastle, Secretary; Antony Lawrence Amodio [1965] Director; Daniel Arthur Edward Carr [1975] Finance Director; Peter Kane [1965] Managing Director; Kristoffer Ljungfelt [1977] Director [Swedish]; Darren James Mahoney [1966] Design Director; Jasdip Nijjar [1986] Director

Community Foods Limited
Incorporated: 1 September 1977 *Employees:* 108
Net Worth: £3,465,746 *Total Assets:* £24,323,060
Registered Office: Community House, 29-31 Eastways, Witham, Essex, CM8 3YQ
Activities: Non-specialised wholesale trade
Parent: Community Foods (Holdings) Ltd
Officers: Vince Leo Andrew [1956] Operations Director; Jamie Andrew Chambers [1966] Technical Director; Joseph Erskine [1957] Ingredients Director; David Andrew Gray [1967] Director/Chartered Accountant; Tracy Kane [1974] Brands Director; David Alan Graham Lewis [1969] Director; Martin Leslie Rome [1961] Director

Community Health Services Limited
Incorporated: 16 July 1987 *Employees:* 708
Net Worth: £3,222,000 *Total Assets:* £21,296,000
Registered Office: Connaught House, 850 The Crescent, Colchester Business Park, Colchester, Essex, CO4 9QB
Activities: Other service activities n.e.c.
Parent: CHS Healthcare Limited
Officers: Jonathan David Calow, Secretary; Andrew Ronald Knight [1967] Director; Michael Robert Parish [1959] Director; Richard Charles Pearman [1975] Director; Matthew Alexander Rosenberg [1977] Director; Philip James Whitecross [1963] Director

Community Reinsurance Corporation Limited
Incorporated: 15 November 1972 *Employees:* 5
Net Worth: £4,638,412 *Total Assets:* £28,039,992
Registered Office: Hampden House, Great Hampden, Great Missenden, Bucks, HP16 9RD
Activities: Non-life insurance
Parent: Hampden Insurance Group Limited
Officers: Charles Guy Camroux-Oliver [1970] Director/Solicitor; Stephen Leonard Carter [1955] Director/Solicitor; Francis William Johnston [1952] Director/Chartered Accountant; Christopher John Ridgwell [1945] Executive Director; Heather Susan Russell [1961] Director/Reinsurance Manager

The Company of Biologists, Limited
Incorporated: 31 December 1952 *Employees:* 51
Net Worth: £50,997,432 *Total Assets:* £55,975,576
Registered Office: Bidder Building, Station Road, Cambridge, CB24 9LF
Activities: Pre-press and pre-media services
Officers: Kay Anita Richmond, Secretary; Professor Sarah Jane Bray [1958] Director/Professor of Developmental Biology; Prof Julian Francis Burke [1953] Director/University Lecturer/Chief Scientific Officer; Alastair Downie [1964] Director/IT Manager; Professor Matthew Freeman [1961] Director/Scientist; Professor Clare Margaret Isacke [1957] Director/Scientist; Professor Jane Alison Langdale [1960] Director/University Research Professor; Professor Laura Marie Machesky [1965] Director/Professor of Cell Biology [American]; Professor Simon Hugh Piper Maddrell [1937] Director/Retired; Dr Bruce Sean Munro [1961] Director/Research Scientist; Professor Goran Erik Nilsson [1959] Director/University Professor [Swedish]; Professor Peter William Jack Rigby [1947] Director/Scientist; Dr Stephen John Royle [1977] Director/Scientist; Dr Holly Shiels [1971] Director/Scientist [British/Canadian]; Professor Robert Daniel St Johnston [1960] Director/Research Scientist; Professor Kate Gillian Storey [1960] Director/Research Biologist; Professor Parsh Vyas [1961] Director/Medical Academic; Professor Alan Martin Wilson [1964] Director/University Professor

Compare The Market Limited
Incorporated: 23 February 2017
Net Worth: £104,500,000 *Total Assets:* £153,200,000
Registered Office: Pegasus House, Southgate Park, Bakewell Road, Orton Southgate, Peterborough, Cambs, PE2 6YS
Activities: Other business support service activities n.e.c.
Parent: BGL Group Limited
Officers: Julian Charles Brown, Secretary; Mark Andrew Allan [1981] Director/Chief Financial Officer; Jonathon Iain Carlton Brown [1971] Director/Chief Executive; Matthew Oliver Donaldson [1973] Director/Chief Executive Officer; Lord Jitesh Kishorekumar Gadhia [1970] Director/Banker; David John Osborne [1966] Global Director; Dominic James Platt [1969] Director/Chief Financial Officer

Comparex UK Limited
Incorporated: 5 October 1994 *Employees:* 48
Net Worth: £1,480,642 *Total Assets:* £33,477,328
Registered Office: OneSixSix, 166 College Road, Harrow, Middlesex, HA1 1BH
Activities: Information technology consultancy activities
Officers: Richard Best [1973] Managing Director; Marcel Kloeppner [1977] Finance Director [German]

Compass Education Trust Ltd
Incorporated: 10 June 2011
Previous: The Billericay School
Net Worth: £22,322,000 *Total Assets:* £31,301,000
Registered Office: The Billericay School, School Road, Billericay, Essex, CM12 9LH
Activities: General secondary education
Officers: Jennifer Ann Moore, Secretary; Colin John Breathwick [1943] Director/Management Consultant; Martin Clark [1961] Director/Senior Risk Manager at HSBC; David Neil Franklin [1954] Director/Retired; Sandra Elizabeth Hillier [1947] Director/Retired; Jane Helen Lyon [1954] Director/Primary School Finance/Personnel Manager; Stewart Paul Martin [1963] Director/Chartered Accountant; Ian Miller [1958] Director/Engineering Manager; Ahson Mohammed [1966] Director/Headteacher

Computacenter (UK) Limited
Incorporated: 9 September 1981 *Employees:* 4,210
Net Worth: £83,038,000 *Total Assets:* £719,790,016
Registered Office: Computacenter, Hatfield Avenue, Hatfield, Herts, AL10 9TW
Activities: Information technology consultancy activities
Parent: Computacenter PLC
Officers: Raymond John Gray, Secretary; Francis Anthony Conophy [1958] Finance Director [Irish]; Kevin John James [1964] Director/Group Chief Commercial Officer; Michael John Norris [1961] Director/Chief Executive

Computacenter PLC
Incorporated: 2 October 1995 *Employees:* 14,026
Net Worth: £488,846,016 *Total Assets:* £1,449,507,968
Registered Office: Hatfield Avenue, Hatfield, Herts, AL10 9TW
Activities: Activities of head offices
Officers: Raymond John Gray, Secretary; Francis Anthony Conophy [1958] Director [Irish]; Philip William Hulme [1948] Director; Gregory Hugh Lock [1947] Director; Michael John Norris [1961] Director/Chief Executive; Sir Peter James Ogden [1947] Director; Timothy Martin Powell [1954] Director; Dr Ros Catherine Rivaz [1955] Director; Peter Ryan [1961] Director/Consultant; Regine Stachelhaus [1955] Director [German]

Computerlinks (UK) Limited
Incorporated: 20 November 1996 *Employees:* 72
Net Worth: £221,203,920 *Total Assets:* £221,203,920
Registered Office: Suffolk House, Fordham Road, Newmarket, Suffolk, CB8 7AA
Activities: Non-trading company
Parent: Arrow Electronics Inc
Officers: Kieran Cooper, Secretary; Kieran David Cooper [1969] Director; Paul Hayhurst [1962] Operations Director; Mark McHale [1965] Managing Director; Christopher David Stansbury [1965] Director/Senior VP and CFO [American]

Comtec Cable Accessories Limited
Incorporated: 19 January 1978 *Employees:* 88
Net Worth: £3,229,000 *Total Assets:* £13,674,000
Registered Office: 2 Cardinal Distribution Park, Godmanchester, Huntingdon, Cambs, PE29 2XJ
Activities: Wired telecommunications activities
Major Shareholder: John Thomas Archer
Officers: John Thomas Archer [1955] Director; John Stuart Buck [1962] Director; Daniel Conway [1968] Director; Steven Paul Doddington [1972] Sales Director

Comtec Group (International) Limited
Incorporated: 2 June 1995 *Employees:* 159
Previous: Tayvin 40 Limited
Net Worth: £5,167,000 *Total Assets:* £17,835,000
Registered Office: Cardinal Way, Cardinal Distribution Park, Godmanchester, Huntingdon, Cambs, PE29 2XN
Activities: Wired telecommunications activities
Major Shareholder: John Thomas Archer
Officers: John Thomas Archer [1955] Director; John Stuart Buck [1962] Director; Daniel Conway [1968] Director

Conamar Building Services Limited
Incorporated: 15 February 1994 *Employees:* 46
Net Worth: £2,422,459 *Total Assets:* £10,370,541
Registered Office: 29-31 Orchard Road, Stevenage, Herts, SG1 3HE
Activities: Development of building projects
Shareholders: Cornelius Joseph Dower; Paul Elliott Cornelius Dower; Neil Michael Dower
Officers: Cornelius Joseph Dower, Secretary; Cornelius Joseph Dower [1949] Director; Neil Michael Dower [1976] Director; Paul Elliot Cornelius Dower [1984] Director/Certified Chartered Accountant

Concurrent Technologies PLC
Incorporated: 6 June 1985 *Employees:* 109
Net Worth: £18,716,050 *Total Assets:* £22,543,204
Registered Office: 4 Gilberd Court, Newcomen Way, Colchester, Essex, CO4 9WN
Activities: Manufacture of loaded electronic boards
Officers: Jean Barbara Annear [1954] Director; Michael Collins [1946] Director/Solicitor; David Evans-Hughes [1955] Director/Software Engineer; Glen Andrew Fawcett [1955] Director/Engineer; Clive Mannering Thomson [1948] Director

Conduit Street Holdings Limited
Incorporated: 11 January 1991 *Employees:* 6
Net Worth: £17,028,648 *Total Assets:* £29,147,776
Registered Office: Gardiner House, 6b Hemnall Street, Epping, Essex, CM16 4LW
Activities: Other letting and operating of own or leased real estate
Officers: Donald Hayes, Secretary; Lady Joy Hilary Bourne [1946] Director; Katie Luan Cohen [1970] Director; Merryl Hayley Flitterman [1967] Director; Lucy Sarah Furman [1972] Director; Donald Hayes [1934] Director; Claire Rebecca Lefton [1980] Director

Connect Access Group Ltd
Incorporated: 15 October 2015 *Employees:* 198
Net Worth: £13,115,460 *Total Assets:* £16,941,962
Registered Office: Hadham Park, Hadham Road, Bishop's Stortford, Herts, CM23 1JH
Activities: Scaffold erection
Major Shareholder: Oliver Cave
Officers: Oliver James Robert Aylwin Cave [1967] Director

Connect Plus (M25) Holdings Limited
Incorporated: 29 August 2008
Net Worth Deficit: £175,590,000 *Total Assets:* £1,469,575,040
Registered Office: Connect Plus House, St Albans Road, South Mimms, Herts, EN6 3NP
Activities: Activities of construction holding companies
Shareholders: BBDE Orbital Holdings LLP; Edge Orbital Holdings Ltd
Officers: Alastair John Campbell, Secretary; Sofia Athanassiou [1977] Director/Civil Engineer [British/Greek]; Abdellha Benhatta [1956] Director [French]; Philip Michael Bentley [1972] Assurance Director; Alastair John Campbell [1969] Director/Chartered Accountant; Andrew Maxwell Dean [1967] Director; Jane Elizabeth Guyett [1959] Director/Banker; Richard Daniel Knight [1974] Director; Barry Paul Millsom [1974] Director; Brian Roland Walker [1955] Director

Connect Plus (M25) Intermediate Limited
Incorporated: 3 October 2008
Total Assets: £230,339,008
Registered Office: Connect Plus House, St Albans Road, South Mimms, Herts, EN6 3NP
Activities: Financial intermediation not elsewhere classified
Shareholders: BBDE Orbital Holdings LLP; Edge Orbital Holdings Ltd
Officers: Alastair John Campbell, Secretary; Sofia Athanassiou [1977] Director/Civil Engineer [British/Greek]; Abdellah Benhatta [1968] Director [French]; Philip Michael Bentley [1972] Assurance Director; Alastair John Campbell [1969] Director/Chartered Accountant; Andrew Maxwell Dean [1967] Director; Jane Elizabeth Guyett [1959] Director/Banker; Richard Daniel Knight [1974] Director; Barry Paul Millsom [1974] Director; Brian Roland Walker [1955] Director

Connect Plus (M25) Limited
Incorporated: 29 August 2008
Net Worth Deficit: £175,590,000 *Total Assets:* £1,469,575,040
Registered Office: Connect Plus House, St Albans Road, South Mimms, Herts, EN6 3NP
Activities: Construction of roads and motorways
Parent: Connect Plus (M25) Holdings Limited
Officers: Alastair John Campbell, Secretary; Sofia Athanassiou [1977] Director/Civil Engineer [British/Greek]; Abdellah Benhatta [1968] Director [French]; Philip Michael Bentley [1972] Assurance Director; Alastair John Campbell [1969] Director/Chartered Accountant; Andrew Maxwell Dean [1967] Director; Jane Elizabeth Guyett [1959] Director/Banker; Richard Daniel Knight [1974] Director; Barry Paul Millsom [1974] Director; Brian Roland Walker [1955] Director

Connect Scaffolding Limited
Incorporated: 13 December 1999
Net Worth: £8,597,463 *Total Assets:* £10,985,383
Registered Office: Hadham Park, Hadham Road, Bishop's Stortford, Herts, CM23 1JH
Activities: Scaffold erection
Major Shareholder: Oliver James Robert Aylwin Cave
Officers: Oliver James Robert Aylwin Cave [1967] Director/Scaffolding Contractor

Connect Utilities Limited
Incorporated: 7 February 2005
Net Worth Deficit: £9,515,400 *Total Assets:* £8,059,324
Registered Office: Energy House, Woolpit Business Park, Windmill Avenue, Woolpit, Bury St Edmunds, Suffolk, IP30 9UP
Activities: Other business support service activities n.e.c.
Parent: Inexus Group (Holdings) Limited
Officers: Christopher Paul Mumford, Company Secretary; Darryl John Corney [1960] Director; Clive Eric Linsdell [1962] Director

Connected Learning
Incorporated: 21 June 2013 *Employees:* 281
Net Worth: £7,584,432 *Total Assets:* £11,081,906
Registered Office: Powers Hall Academy, Spa Road, Witham, Essex, CM8 1NA
Activities: Primary education
Officers: Jane Bass [1954] Director/Headteacher; Claire Elizabeth Brazier [1968] Director/School Business Manager; Donald Graham Burton [1945] Director/Retired; Rowland Graham Joseph Costin [1961] Director/Computer Analyst; Nicholas Charles Redfern [1959] Director/Retired; Susan Sings [1946] Director/Retired; Bruce John Tuxford [1955] Director/Retired; Simon Noel Webb [1954] Director/Academy Chief Learning Officer

Connectix Limited
Incorporated: 4 May 1993 *Employees:* 95
Net Worth: £1,855,417 *Total Assets:* £14,468,799
Registered Office: 500 Avenue West, Skyline 120, Braintree, Essex, CM77 7AA
Activities: Manufacture of communication equipment other than telegraph, and telephone apparatus and equipment
Major Shareholder: Kevin Arthur Hancock
Officers: Sarah Jane Hancock, Secretary; Timothy Roland Brown [1969] Marketing & Development Director; Kevin Arthur Hancock [1968] Managing Director; Mark Hancock [1966] Director; Steven John Hancock [1964] Director

Connells Residential
Incorporated: 8 April 1980 *Employees:* 2,052
Net Worth: £18,617,000 *Total Assets:* £38,349,000
Registered Office: Cumbria House, 16-20 Hockliffe Street, Leighton Buzzard, Beds, LU7 1GN
Activities: Activities of insurance agents and brokers
Parent: Connells Limited
Officers: Richard John Twigg, Secretary; David Christopher Livesey [1959] Director/Mortgage Services; David Kerry Plumtree [1969] Director; Reginald Stephen Shipperley [1958] Director/Estate Agent; Richard John Twigg [1965] Director

Connells Survey & Valuation Limited
Incorporated: 4 August 2000 *Employees:* 460
Net Worth: £21,395,000 *Total Assets:* £36,504,000
Registered Office: Cumbria House, 16-20 Hockliffe Street, Leighton Buzzard, Beds, LU7 1GN
Activities: Other professional, scientific and technical activities n.e.c.
Parent: Connells Limited
Officers: Richard John Twigg, Secretary; Ross Tobias Benjamin Bowen [1970] Managing Director; Warren James Wright [1958] Director/Chartered Surveyor

Kathleen and Michael Connolly Foundation (UK) Limited
Incorporated: 16 December 2004 *Employees:* 16
Net Worth: £63,764,392 *Total Assets:* £73,627,760
Registered Office: Manor Farm Court, Lower Sundon, Beds, LU3 3UZ
Activities: Other business support service activities n.e.c.
Officers: Kathryn Anne Watts, Secretary/Accountant; Shyam Sunder Ashoka [1954] Director/Solicitor; Michael Andrew Callanan [1959] Managing Director; Vanessa Susan Connolly [1955] Director/Trustee; Nigel Kevin Croft [1958] Director/Headteacher; Andrew Sutherland Rowe [1936] Director/Chartered Accountant

Connolly Homes PLC
Incorporated: 20 May 1963 *Employees:* 15
Net Worth: £40,926,960 *Total Assets:* £45,881,904
Registered Office: Manor Farm Court, Lower Sundon, Luton, Beds, LU3 3NZ
Activities: Construction of domestic buildings
Parent: Connolly Holdings PLC
Officers: Kathryn Anne Watts, Secretary/Accountant; Michael Andrew Callanan [1959] Building Director; Michael Christopher Mulchinock [1954] Technical Director

Consensus Holdco Limited
Incorporated: 27 June 2013
Net Worth: £1 *Total Assets:* £47,657,416
Registered Office: Bradbury House, 830 The Crescent, Colchester Business Park, Colchester, Essex, CO4 9YQ
Activities: Residential nursing care facilities
Parent: MHL Holdco Limited
Officers: Nigel Bennett Schofield, Secretary; Derek George Cormack [1959] Director [Irish]; Peter Martin Hill [1968] Director; Helena Jeffery [1945] Director; Paul Anthony Keith Jeffery [1966] Director; Nigel Bennett Schofield [1950] Director

Consensus Support Services Limited
Incorporated: 2 October 2000 *Employees:* 1,496
Net Worth: £26,128,000 *Total Assets:* £141,296,992
Registered Office: Bradbury House, 830 The Crescent, Colchester Business Park, Colchester, Essex, CO4 9YQ
Activities: Residential care activities for the elderly and disabled
Parent: Consensus Holdco Limited
Officers: Nigel Bennett Schofield, Secretary; Peter Martin Hill [1968] Director/Accountant; Paul Anthony Keith Jeffery [1966] Director/Accountant; Nigel Bennett Schofield [1950] Director/Solicitor

Consolidated Equities Limited
Incorporated: 1 April 1954 *Employees:* 2
Net Worth: £9,139,145 *Total Assets:* £9,551,268
Registered Office: 173 Hempstead Road, Watford, Herts, WD17 3HG
Activities: Other letting and operating of own or leased real estate
Shareholder: Telford Thomas Rice
Officers: Margaret Jamieson Rice, Secretary; Margaret Jamieson Rice [1940] Director; Telford Thomas Rice [1960] Director/Building Manager

Consort Medical Finance 2010 Limited
Incorporated: 1 April 2010
Net Worth Deficit: £6,570,000 *Total Assets:* £31,327,000
Registered Office: Suite B Breakspear Park, Breakspear Way, Hemel Hempstead, Herts, HP2 4TZ
Activities: Financial intermediation not elsewhere classified
Parent: Consort Medical PLC
Officers: Andrew Leonard Jackson, Secretary; Jonathan Martin Glenn [1968] Director; Paul Andrew Hayes [1966] Director

Consort Medical Finance Limited
Incorporated: 23 December 2014
Net Worth: £23,422,132 *Total Assets:* £132,617,608
Registered Office: Suite B Breakspear Park, Breakspear Way, Hemel Hempstead, Herts, HP2 4TZ
Activities: Financial intermediation not elsewhere classified
Parent: Bespak Holdings Limited
Officers: Andrew Leonard Jackson, Secretary; Jonathan Martin Glenn [1968] Director; Paul Andrew Hayes [1966] Director

Consort Medical PLC
Incorporated: 22 March 1946 *Employees:* 2,018
Net Worth: £246,300,000 *Total Assets:* £472,100,000
Registered Office: Suite B Breakspear Park, Breakspear Way, Hemel Hempstead, Herts, HP2 4TZ
Activities: Manufacture of medical and dental instruments and supplies
Officers: Andrew Leonard Jackson, Secretary; Christopher David Brinsmead [1959] Director; Stephen Paul Crummett [1965] Director; Dr Peter John Fellner [1943] Director; Maria Charlotta Ginman [1965] Director [Finnish]; Jonathan Martin Glenn [1968] Director/Chief Executive Officer; Paul Andrew Hayes [1966] Director; Dr Andrew Joseph Hosty [1965] Director; Dr William John Jenkins [1947] Director; Ian James Nicholson [1960] Director

Constable Homes Limited
Incorporated: 9 March 2000
Net Worth Deficit: £2,631,974 *Total Assets:* £19,423,994
Registered Office: Springfield Lodge, Colchester Road, Springfield, Chelmsford, Essex, CM2 5PW
Activities: Buying and selling of own real estate
Major Shareholder: Mark Jonathan Anderson
Officers: Andrew Christopher Short, Secretary; Mark Jonathan Anderson [1961] Director

Construct Holdings Limited
Incorporated: 30 April 1986
Net Worth: £2,935,987 *Total Assets:* £14,748,920
Registered Office: 1 Nelson Street, Southend on Sea, Essex, SS1 1EG
Activities: Other service activities n.e.c.
Shareholders: Brian Ernest Edward Burrett; Lorna Anne Sara Burrett
Officers: David Christian Wyatt, Secretary/Sales Manager; Brian Ernest Edward Burrett [1939] Director/Solicitor; Russell Bruce Reason [1963] Director/Plant Hirer; David Christian Wyatt [1951] Director/Sales Manager

Construct Reason Limited
Incorporated: 3 October 1980 *Employees:* 12
Net Worth: £373,036 *Total Assets:* £9,743,577
Registered Office: Beaver House, Northern Road, Sudbury, Suffolk, CO10 6XQ
Activities: Development of building projects
Shareholders: Brian Ernest Edward Burrett; Lorna Anne Sara Burrett
Officers: Janet Lord, Secretary; David Christian Wyatt, Secretary; Russell Bruce Reason [1963] Director/Plant Hirer; David Christian Wyatt [1951] Sales Director

The Construction Workers Guild Limited
Incorporated: 22 April 1997
Net Worth: £577,913 *Total Assets:* £15,103,765
Registered Office: 2 Mountside, Stanmore, Middlesex, HA7 2DT
Activities: Other business support service activities n.e.c.
Parent: Guild Corporate Services Group Limited
Officers: Derek Stephen Reynolds [1959] Managing Director

Contact Technologies UK Limited
Incorporated: 17 November 2006
Net Worth: £15,817,375 *Total Assets:* £21,736,164
Registered Office: c/o APEM Components Ltd, Drakes Drive, Long Crendon, Bucks, HP18 9BA
Activities: Activities of head offices
Officers: Joel Rene Gerard Becquet [1957] Director/Chief Financial Officer [French]; James Peter Minton Cooper [1975] Managing Director; Marc Francois Jean-Marie Enjalbert [1962] Director/President [French]

Contamac Holdings Limited
Incorporated: 13 October 2009 *Employees:* 76
Net Worth: £8,019,075 *Total Assets:* £13,170,719
Registered Office: Carlton House, Shire Hill, Saffron Walden, Essex, CB11 3AU
Activities: Activities of head offices
Parent: Haohai Healthcare Holdings (BVI) Co. Ltd
Officers: Linda Clark, Secretary; Wu Jianying [1964] Director [Chinese]; Robert John McGregor [1971] Director; Huang Ming [1975] Director [Chinese]; Minjie Tang [1975] Director [Chinese]; Simon David Wyatt [1960] Director/Chartered Accountant

Contamac Limited
Incorporated: 10 May 1991 *Employees:* 76
Net Worth: £7,475,666 *Total Assets:* £10,128,423
Registered Office: Carlton House, Shire Hill, Saffron Walden, Essex, CB11 3AU
Activities: Manufacture of other plastic products
Parent: Contamac Holdings Ltd
Officers: Linda Clark, Secretary; Martin Dalsing [1959] Director [American]; Robert Edward Lewis [1969] Director; Cheung Kwai Anthony Mak [1947] Director [Hong Kong]; John Alexander McGregor [1945] Director; Robert John McGregor [1971] Director; Simon David Wyatt [1960] Director/Chartered Accountant

Contechs Consulting Limited
Incorporated: 8 October 1997 *Employees:* 51
Net Worth: £2,110,347 *Total Assets:* £10,142,994
Registered Office: 2 Sable Court, Sylvan Way, Southfields Business Park, Basildon, Essex, SS15 6SR
Activities: Other information technology service activities
Parent: Contechs Holdings Limited
Officers: Ian Keith Brookes, Secretary/Director; Ian Keith Brookes [1969] Director; Yogendra Carpenter [1961] Director; Peter Richard Jarvis [1965] Director/Engineer; Robert Simon Wakefield [1957] Director

Contechs Holdings Limited
Incorporated: 15 December 2006 *Employees:* 169
Net Worth: £4,237,159 *Total Assets:* £19,691,052
Registered Office: 2 Sable Court, Sylvan Way, Southfields Business Park, Basildon, Essex, SS15 6SR
Activities: Activities of head offices
Shareholders: Peter Richard Jarvis; Ian Keith Brookes
Officers: Ian Keith Brookes, Secretary/Director; Ian Keith Brookes [1969] Director; Peter Richard Jarvis [1965] Director/Engineer; Robert Simon Wakefield [1957] Director

Continental Datagraphics Limited
Incorporated: 27 August 1997 *Employees:* 178
Net Worth: £9,283,071 *Total Assets:* £12,214,557
Registered Office: 1st Floor, Building 1, Albany Place, Welwyn Garden City, Herts, AL7 3BG
Activities: Other engineering activities
Parent: Boeing United Kingdom Limited
Officers: Simon Howard Jones, Secretary; Sir Michael Anthony Arthur [1950] Director/Businessman; David Lawrence Malmo [1958] Director/President & CEO [American]; Andrew Timothy Masson [1979] Director; John Norman Palmer [1962] Director; David John Pitchforth [1965] Director/Engineer

Contracting Made Easy Ltd
Incorporated: 11 February 1998
Net Worth: £756,860 *Total Assets:* £14,269,625
Registered Office: Anglo Dal House, 5 Spring Villa Park, Edgware, Middlesex, HA8 7EB
Activities: Other business support service activities n.e.c.
Shareholders: Victor Korman; Denise Korman
Officers: Denise Korman, Secretary; Eli Korman [1982] Director; Victor Korman [1958] Director/Accountant

Thomas Cook Aircraft Engineering Limited
Incorporated: 12 December 2001 *Employees:* 468
Net Worth Deficit: £5,929,000 *Total Assets:* £11,865,000
Registered Office: Westpoint, Peterborough Business Park, Lynch Wood, Peterborough, Cambs, PE2 6FZ
Activities: Other business support service activities n.e.c.
Parent: Thomas Cook Airlines Limited
Officers: Emma Louise Langford, Secretary; John Mark Boler [1970] Director; Christoph Debus [1971] Director [German]; Paul William Hutchings [1966] Director

Thomas Cook Airlines Limited
Incorporated: 21 April 1986 *Employees:* 2,430
Net Worth: £405,780,000 *Total Assets:* £1,104,685,952
Registered Office: Westpoint, Peterborough Business Park, Lynch Wood, Peterborough, Cambs, PE2 6FZ
Activities: Scheduled passenger air transport
Parent: Thomas Cook Group Airlines Limited
Officers: Shirley Bradley, Secretary; John Mark Boler [1970] Director; Christoph Debus [1971] Director [German]; Paul William Hutchings [1966] Director

Walter John Cook and Sons Limited
Incorporated: 28 September 1976 *Employees:* 60
Net Worth: £10,620,473 *Total Assets:* £15,791,169
Registered Office: Richmond Holiday Centre, Richmond Drive, Skegness, Lincs, PE25 3TQ
Activities: Holiday centres and villages
Major Shareholder: Mark Robert Williams
Officers: Mark Robert Williams, Secretary; Andrew William Downing [1964] Managing Director; Stephen John Parish [1965] Financial Director; Mark Robert Williams [1968] Director/Caravan Park Manager

Thomas Cook Continental Holdings Limited
Incorporated: 9 June 2008
Net Worth: £597,218,560 *Total Assets:* £1,061,576,128
Registered Office: Westpoint, Peterborough Business Park, Lynch Wood, Peterborough, Cambs, PE2 6FZ
Activities: Other business support service activities n.e.c.
Parent: Thomas Cook Investments (2) Limited
Officers: Shirley Bradley, Secretary/Deputy Company Secretary; Alan Charles Donald [1963] Director

Thomas Cook Finance PLC
Incorporated: 23 October 2007
Net Worth: £6,018,232 *Total Assets:* £361,270,912
Registered Office: Westpoint, Peterborough Business Park, Lynch Wood, Peterborough, Cambs, PE2 6FZ
Activities: Other business support service activities n.e.c.
Parent: Thomas Cook Group Tour Operations Limited
Officers: Rebecca Ann Symondson-Powell, Secretary; Christopher James Corner [1974] Director

Thomas Cook Group Hedging Limited
Incorporated: 10 April 2012
Net Worth: £990,998,016 *Total Assets:* £1,137,655,040
Registered Office: Westpoint, Peterborough Business Park, Lynch Wood, Peterborough, Cambs, PE2 6FZ
Activities: Other business support service activities n.e.c.
Parent: TCGH Holdings Limited
Officers: Shirley Bradley, Secretary; Christopher James Corner [1974] Director

Thomas Cook Group Treasury Limited
Incorporated: 24 April 2008
Net Worth Deficit: £84,319,000 *Total Assets:* £5,947,229,184
Registered Office: Westpoint, Peterborough Business Park, Lynch Wood, Peterborough, Cambs, PE2 6FZ
Activities: Other business support service activities n.e.c.
Parent: Thomas Cook Investments (2) Limited
Officers: Shirley Bradley, Company Secretary; Christopher James Corner [1974] Director

Thomas Cook Group UK Limited
Incorporated: 21 November 1988
Net Worth: £894,899,968 *Total Assets:* £962,800,000
Registered Office: Westpoint, Peterborough Business Park, Lynch Wood, Peterborough, Cambs, PE2 6FZ
Activities: Activities of head offices
Parent: Mytravel Group Limited
Officers: Shirley Bradley, Secretary; Alan Charles Donald [1963] Director

Thomas Cook Investments (2) Limited
Incorporated: 23 January 2007
Net Worth: £904,574,464 *Total Assets:* £3,789,469,184
Registered Office: Westpoint, Peterborough Business Park, Lynch Wood, Peterborough, Cambs, PE2 6FZ
Activities: Other business support service activities n.e.c.
Parent: Thomas Cook Group Tour Operations Limited
Officers: Shirley Bradley, Secretary; Alan Charles Donald [1963] Director

Thomas Cook Retail Limited
Incorporated: 22 April 1909 *Employees:* 24
Net Worth: £158,612,992 *Total Assets:* £379,560,992
Registered Office: Westpoint, Peterborough Business Park, Lynch Wood, Peterborough, Cambs, PE2 6FZ
Activities: Travel agency activities
Parent: Thomas Cook Group UK Limited
Officers: Shirley Bradley, Company Secretary & Legal Adviser; Alan Charles Donald [1963] Director

Thomas Cook Tour Operations Limited
Incorporated: 18 May 1999 *Employees:* 270
Net Worth Deficit: £1,898,072,064 *Total Assets:* £546,156,992
Registered Office: Westpoint, Peterborough Business Park, Lynch Wood, Peterborough, Cambs, PE2 6FZ
Activities: Travel agency activities
Parent: Thomas Cook Group UK Limited
Officers: Shirley Bradley, Company Secretary & Legal Adviser; Alan Charles Donald [1963] Director

Thomas Cook UK Limited
Incorporated: 22 July 1991 *Employees:* 1,189
Net Worth Deficit: £58,580,000 *Total Assets:* £1,917,830,016
Registered Office: Westpoint, Peterborough Business Park, Lynch Wood, Peterborough, Cambs, PE2 6FZ
Activities: Other business support service activities n.e.c.
Parent: Sandbrook UK Investments Limited
Officers: Shirley Bradley, Secretary; Alan Charles Donald [1963] Director

Thomas Cook UK Travel Limited
Incorporated: 7 April 1978 *Employees:* 1,510
Net Worth: £50,546,000 *Total Assets:* £50,550,000
Registered Office: Westpoint, Peterborough Business Park, Lynch Wood, Peterborough, Cambs, PE2 6FZ
Activities: Other business support service activities n.e.c.
Parent: Thomas Cook UK Limited
Officers: Shirley Bradley, Secretary; Paul Andrew Hemingway [1971] Director

Thomas Cook West Investments Limited
Incorporated: 26 July 2012
Net Worth: £292,836,512 *Total Assets:* £327,123,232
Registered Office: Westpoint, Peterborough Business Park, Lynch Wood, Peterborough, Cambs, PE2 6FZ
Activities: Other business support service activities n.e.c.
Parent: Sandbrook Overseas Investments Limited
Officers: Shirley Bradley, Secretary; Alice Hannah Marsden [1983] Director

Cook's Delights Limited
Incorporated: 5 June 1996 *Employees:* 90
Net Worth: £891,160 *Total Assets:* £8,493,234
Registered Office: Lynwood House, 373-375 Station Road, Harrow, Middlesex, HA1 2AW
Activities: Wholesale of meat and meat products
Parent: Catering 328 Limited
Officers: Sue Shuk Yin Liu, Secretary; Ronny Wai Kin Liu [1960] Director; Sue Shuk Yin Liu [1961] Director; Andrew Pao [1964] Director

E.D. & A.D. Cooke, Bourne (Farms) Limited
Incorporated: 10 May 1951 *Employees:* 2
Net Worth: £16,440,375 *Total Assets:* £19,668,346
Registered Office: Larkfleet House, Falcon Way, Bourne, Lincs, PE10 0FF
Activities: Growing of cereals (except rice), leguminous crops and oil seeds
Shareholders: Adam George Andrew Cooke; Peter Edward Delanoix Cooke; Mark Thomas Hindmarch; Jarred Thomas Wright
Officers: Adam George Andrew Cooke, Secretary; Adam George Andrew Cooke [1962] Director/Farmer; Peter Edward Delanoix Cooke [1956] Director/Farmer

Cooper Roller Bearings Company Limited
Incorporated: 16 June 1982 *Employees:* 176
Net Worth: £41,256,000 *Total Assets:* £44,938,000
Registered Office: Wisbech Road, Kings Lynn, Norfolk, PE30 5JX
Activities: Manufacture of bearings, gears, gearing and driving elements
Parent: Kaydon Europa BV
Officers: Paula Jane Owen, Secretary; Ian Lindsay Bloxham [1960] Director/General Manager; Sharon Linda Smith [1962] Managing Director; Bo Peter Torpman [1973] Director/Business Area Controller [Swedish]

Coopers Investments Limited
Incorporated: 16 December 1968 *Employees:* 5
Net Worth: £6,555,192 *Total Assets:* £8,000,254
Registered Office: 10 Union Street, Barnet, Herts, EN5 4HZ
Activities: Other letting and operating of own or leased real estate
Shareholder: Simon Ashley Cooper
Officers: Vanessa Jane Wennell, Secretary; Simon Ashley Cooper [1960] Director/Surveyor; Stanley Cooper [1929] Director/Building Surveyor

Cooperscroft Care Home Limited
Incorporated: 13 November 2012 *Employees:* 153
Net Worth: £20,119,264 *Total Assets:* £33,605,224
Registered Office: 36 Railway Approach, Harrow, Middlesex, HA3 5AA
Activities: Residential nursing care facilities
Parent: TLC Group Ltd
Officers: Gagan Puri, Secretary; William Charles Neal [1986] Director; Paavan Popat [1985] Managing Director; Honourable Shivaan Shillin Popat [1988] Director; Gagan Puri [1978] Finance Director

F. Copson Limited
Incorporated: 26 April 1947
Net Worth: £11,597,960 *Total Assets:* £12,321,717
Registered Office: Kanta House, Victoria Road, South Ruislip, Middlesex, HA4 0JQ
Activities: Other letting and operating of own or leased real estate
Officers: Bhasker Tailor, Secretary; Jawahar Jamnadas Chatwani [1948] Director; Rashmi Jamnadas Chatwani [1954] Director; Satish Jamnadas Chatwani [1953] Director

Copthorn Holdings Limited
Incorporated: 25 May 2004
Net Worth: £428,582,016 *Total Assets:* £634,208,000
Registered Office: Countryside House, The Drive, Great Warley, Brentwood, Essex, CM13 3AT
Activities: Activities of head offices
Parent: Countryside Properties PLC
Officers: Gary Whitaker, Secretary; Graham Stewart Cherry [1959] Director/Chief Executive; Ian Russell Kelley [1961] Director/Chief Executive - Partnerships North Division; Phillip Victor Lyons [1964] Director/Chief Executive - Housebuilding; Iain Duncan McPherson [1973] Director; Michael Ian Scott [1977] Director/Chief Financial Officer; Ian Calvert Sutcliffe [1959] Director/Executive Chairman; Rebecca Jane Worthington [1971] Director/Accountant

Corbus Europe Limited
Incorporated: 15 July 2003
Net Worth Deficit: £258,093 *Total Assets:* £10,153,909
Registered Office: 66 Montpelier Rise, Wembley, Middlesex, HA9 8RQ
Activities: Information technology consultancy activities
Parent: Corbus LLC
Officers: Rajesh Kumar Soin [1947] Director [American]; Vishal Soin [1973] Director [American]

Cornelius Group PLC
Incorporated: 6 August 1985 *Employees:* 150
Net Worth: £4,835,255 *Total Assets:* £18,054,144
Registered Office: Cornelius House, Woodside, Dunmow Road, Bishop's Stortford, Herts, CM23 5RG
Activities: Wholesale of chemical products
Major Shareholder: Neville Prior
Officers: Phillip Timothy Gibbons, Secretary; Richard John Herring, Secretary; David William Ian Brown [1960] Director; Gary Eric Fisher [1954] Director; Phillip Timonthy Gibbons [1969] Finance Director; Dr Neville Douglas Prior [1960] Director; Sheila Prior [1935] Director; Darren Spiby [1968] Sales Director; Joanne Marie Stephenson [1970] Director/Marketing Consultant

Cornelius Vermuyden School
Incorporated: 28 August 2013 *Employees:* 96
Net Worth: £19,679,984 *Total Assets:* £21,363,280
Registered Office: Cornelius Vermuyden School, Dinant Avenue, Canvey Island, Essex, SS8 9QS
Activities: General secondary education
Officers: Alan Leslie Wilson, Secretary; Nicola Jane Bainbridge [1971] Director/Pastoral Manager; Beatrice Louisa Binks [1940] Director/Retired; Christine Ann Bonham [1969] Director; Daniel Joseph Coleman [1972] Director/Electrician; Reginald Paul Fuller [1957] Director/Financial Adviser; Ian Hockey [1981] Director/Headteacher; Danny Michael McCartney [1974] Director/Chartered Accountant; Nadia Ounzain [1986] Director/Teacher; Jeffrey Alan Stanley [1955] Director; Reverend Marion Gladys Walford [1954] Director/Priest

Cornwall
Incorporated: 27 August 1994
Net Worth: £15,035,106 *Total Assets:* £15,073,055
Registered Office: 5 Elstree Gate, Elstree Way, Borehamwood, Herts, WD6 1JD
Activities: Activities of other holding companies n.e.c.
Officers: Graham David Hill, Secretary; Bruce Victor Grakal [1940] Director [American]; John Gwilym Hemingway [1931] Director; Graham David Hill [1946] Director/Accountant

Corona Energy Limited
Incorporated: 22 August 1996
Net Worth: £15,665,727 *Total Assets:* £22,062,484
Registered Office: Building 2, Level 2, Croxley Park, Watford, Herts, WD18 8YA
Activities: Activities of head offices
Parent: Macquarie Corona Energy Holdings Limited
Officers: Shaheda Begum Thomas, Secretary; Neil Trevor Mitchell [1974] Commercial Director; Philip Morton [1968] Finance Director; Paul Christian Plewman [1972] Director/Banker [Irish]

Corona Energy Retail 1 Limited
Incorporated: 22 August 1996 *Employees:* 212
Net Worth: £11,361,115 *Total Assets:* £34,249,204
Registered Office: Building 2, Level 2, Croxley Park, Watford, Herts, WD18 8YA
Activities: Trade of gas through mains
Parent: Corona Energy Limited
Officers: Shaheda Begum Thomas, Secretary; Neil Trevor Mitchell [1974] Commercial Director; Philip Morton [1968] Finance Director; Paul Christian Plewman [1972] Director/Banker [Irish]

Corona Energy Retail 4 Limited
Incorporated: 11 March 1993
Net Worth: £7,582,111 *Total Assets:* £118,481,440
Registered Office: Building 2, Level 2, Croxley Park, Watford, Herts, WD18 8YA
Activities: Trade of electricity
Parent: Corona Energy Limited
Officers: Shaheda Begum Thomas, Secretary; Neil Trevor Mitchell [1974] Commercial Director; Philip Morton [1968] Finance Director; Paul Christian Plewman [1972] Director/Banker [Irish]

Corona Gas Management Limited
Incorporated: 10 December 1993
Net Worth: £1,048,717 *Total Assets:* £105,769,296
Registered Office: Building 2, Level 2, Croxley Park, Watford, Herts, WD18 8YA
Activities: Wholesale of other fuels and related products
Parent: Corona Energy Retail 1 Limited
Officers: Shaheda Begum Thomas, Secretary; Neil Trevor Mitchell [1974] Commercial Director; Philip Morton [1968] Finance Director; Paul Christian Plewman [1972] Director/Banker [Irish]

Corporate Associates Limited
Incorporated: 24 December 1987
Net Worth: £96,932,088 *Total Assets:* £104,283,760
Registered Office: Tollgate Barn, Tollgate West, Stanway, Colchester, Essex, CO3 8RJ
Activities: Financial intermediation not elsewhere classified
Shareholders: Carole Ann Watts; Jayne Catherine Watts; Daniel John Watts; Jason James Watts
Officers: Jayne Catherine Gee [1967] Director; Daniel John Watts [1975] Director; Jason James Watts [1970] Director

Corporate Express (Holdings) Limited
Incorporated: 30 November 1995
Net Worth: £13,327,000 *Total Assets:* £13,327,000
Registered Office: Hampden Court, Kingsmead Business Park, Frederick Place, High Wycombe, Bucks, HP11 1JU
Activities: Other business support service activities n.e.c.
Parent: Corporate Express UK Holding Limited
Officers: Steven Mayes, Secretary; Michael Celina Herman Henckaers [1983] Director [Belgian]; Steven Paul Mayes [1982] Finance Director

Corporate Express UK Holding Limited
Incorporated: 12 April 1948
Net Worth: £13,351,000 *Total Assets:* £13,351,000
Registered Office: Hampden Court, Kingsmead Business Park, Frederick Place, High Wycombe, Bucks, HP11 1JU
Activities: Activities of head offices
Officers: Steven Mayes, Secretary; Michael Celina Herman Henckaers [1983] Director [Belgian]; Steven Paul Mayes [1982] Finance Director

Corporate Investments Limited
Incorporated: 1 June 2011
Net Worth Deficit: £820,691 *Total Assets:* £16,705,100
Registered Office: Tollgate Barn, Tollgate West, Colchester, Essex, CO3 8RJ
Activities: Development of building projects
Shareholders: Jayne Catherine Gee; Daniel John Watts; Jason James Watts
Officers: Jayne Catherine Gee [1967] Director; Daniel John Watts [1975] Director; Jason James Watts [1970] Director

Coryton Advanced Fuels Limited
Incorporated: 22 April 2010 *Employees:* 42
Net Worth: £13,144,067 *Total Assets:* £16,633,164
Registered Office: The Manorway, Coryton, Stanford-le-Hope, Essex, SS17 9LN
Activities: Other treatment of petroleum products (excluding petrochemicals manufacture)
Parent: Premier Bidco Limited
Officers: Andrew David Willson, Secretary; Nicholas Brian Pye [1974] Director/Chief Executive Officer; Andrew David Willson [1964] Director

Cosco Maritime (UK) Limited
Incorporated: 13 June 2000 *Employees:* 15
Net Worth: £16,433,450 *Total Assets:* £70,223,720
Registered Office: Cosco House, Vicarage Drive, Barking, Essex, IG11 7NA
Activities: Sea and coastal freight water transport
Parent: Cosco Shipholdings (UK) Limited
Officers: Romeo Abenes Mendoza, Secretary; Li Sun [1975] Director/Accounting Manager [Chinese]; Gang Wang [1971] Director [Chinese]

Cosco Shipping (UK) Company Limited
Incorporated: 2 February 1988 *Employees:* 54
Previous: Cosco (UK) Limited
Net Worth: £34,897,472 *Total Assets:* £91,660,536
Registered Office: Cosco House, Vicarage Drive, Barking, Essex, IG11 7NA
Activities: Other transportation support activities
Parent: State-Owned Assets Supervision and Administration Commission of The State Council (SASAC)
Officers: Romeo Abenes Mendoza, Secretary; Jing Guo [1961] Director/Shipping [Chinese]; Ji Lin [1970] Director [Chinese]; Li Sun [1975] Director/Accounting Manager [Chinese]; Gang Wang [1971] Director [Chinese]; Haihua Yu [1963] Director [Chinese]

Cosco Shipping Lines (UK) Limited
Incorporated: 3 March 1995 *Employees:* 63
Previous: Coscon (UK) Ltd
Net Worth: £6,572,329 *Total Assets:* £13,908,348
Registered Office: Cosco House, Vicarage Drive, Barking, Essex, IG11 7NA
Activities: Sea and coastal freight water transport
Parent: Cosco Container Lines Europe GmbH
Officers: Thambyah Wignarajah, Secretary; Dongxiang Li [1977] Director [Chinese]; Ji Lin [1970] Director/Chairman [Chinese]; Jun Shi [1976] Director [Chinese]; Yong Wang [1973] Director [Chinese]; Zhendong Zhang [1968] Managing Director [Chinese]

Cossam Investment Co Ltd
Incorporated: 26 June 1958 *Employees:* 5
Previous: Cossam Investment Co.,Limited
Net Worth: £5,014,541 *Total Assets:* £8,438,694
Registered Office: 141 Stanmore Hill, Stanmore, Middlesex, HA7 3ED
Activities: Other letting and operating of own or leased real estate
Officers: Stephen Samuel, Secretary; Babara Ruth Cohen [1960] Director/Speech Therapist; Gideon Elisha Cohen [1985] Director/Student; Simon Charles Cohen [1962] Director/Solicitor; Judith Samuel [1950] Director; Stephen Samuel [1948] Director/Chartered Accountant; Stephen Samuel [1948] Director/Chartered Accountant

Costa China Holdings Limited
Incorporated: 15 November 1919 *Employees:* 3
Net Worth: £10,716,000 *Total Assets:* £40,748,000
Registered Office: Costa House, Houghton Hall Business Park, Porz Avenue, Houghton Regis, Dunstable, Beds, LU5 5YG
Activities: Non-trading company
Parent: Costa International Limited
Officers: Russell William Fairhurst, Secretary; Sarah Louise Highfield [1978] Finance Director; Dominic James Paul [1971] Managing Director; Katherine Joanna Seljeflot [1972] Director

Costa Express Holdings Limited
Incorporated: 25 March 2008 *Employees:* 3
Previous: Coffee Nation Holdings Limited
Net Worth Deficit: £22,630,000 *Total Assets:* £11,984,000
Registered Office: 3 Knaves Beech Business Centre, Davies Way, Loudwater, High Wycombe, Bucks, HP10 9QR
Activities: Activities of head offices
Parent: Costa Limited
Officers: Russell William Fairhurst, Secretary; Sarah Louise Highfield [1978] Finance Director; Scott Martin [1969] Director/Chief Executive; Nicholas Clive Orrin [1966] Director

Costa Express Limited
Incorporated: 11 January 1996
Previous: Coffee Nation Limited
Net Worth: £115,413,000 *Total Assets:* £133,937,000
Registered Office: 3 Knaves Beech, Loudwater, High Wycombe, Bucks, HP10 9QR
Activities: Other business support service activities n.e.c.
Parent: Costa Express Holdings Limited
Officers: Russell William Fairhurst, Secretary; Sarah Louise Highfield [1978] Finance Director; Scott Martin [1969] Managing Director; Nicholas Clive Orrin [1966] Director

Costa International Limited
Incorporated: 23 February 1979
Net Worth: £79,488,000 *Total Assets:* £82,091,000
Registered Office: Costa House, Houghton Hall Business Park, Porz Avenue, Houghton Regis, Dunstable, Beds, LU5 5YG
Activities: Non-trading company
Parent: Costa Limited
Officers: Russell William Fiarhurst, Secretary; Jason Cotta [1970] Director; Sarah Louise Highfield [1978] Finance Director; Dominic James Paul [1971] Managing Director; Katherine Joanna Seljeflot [1972] Group HR Director - Costa

Costa Limited
Incorporated: 28 July 1976 *Employees:* 11,052
Net Worth: £538,300,032 *Total Assets:* £695,470,016
Registered Office: Costa House, Houghton Hall Business Park, Porz Avenue, Houghton Regis, Dunstable, Beds, LU5 5YG
Activities: Production of coffee and coffee substitutes
Parent: The Coca-Cola Company
Officers: Russell William Fairhurst, Secretary; Jason Cotta [1970] Director; Sarah Louise Highfield [1978] Finance Director; Dominic James Paul [1971] Managing Director; Katherine Joanna Seljeflot [1972] Group HR Director Costa

Costco Limited
Incorporated: 23 December 1992
Net Worth: £203,444,000 *Total Assets:* £205,079,008
Registered Office: Hartspring Lane, Watford, Herts, WD25 8JS
Activities: Other letting and operating of own or leased real estate
Parent: Costco Wholesale UK Limited
Officers: Magan Khushalbhai Chauhan, Secretary; Magan Khushalbhai Chauhan [1951] Director; James Patrick Murphy [1952] Managing Director [American]; Stephen Michael Pappas [1954] Director [American]

Costco UK Holdings Limited
Incorporated: 28 February 2000 *Employees:* 6,628
Net Worth: £590,630,976 *Total Assets:* £893,710,016
Registered Office: UK Home Office, Hartspring Lane, Watford, Herts, WD25 8JS
Activities: Non-specialised wholesale trade
Parent: Costco Wholesale Corporation
Officers: Magan Khushalbhai Chauhan, Secretary; Richard Galanti [1956] Director/Chief Financial Officer [American]; James Patrick Murphy [1952] Director/Senior Vice President - Europe [American]

Costco Wholesale UK Limited
Incorporated: 6 August 1991 *Employees:* 6,556
Net Worth: £595,078,016 *Total Assets:* £895,956,992
Registered Office: UK Home Office, 213 Hartspring Lane, Watford, Herts, WD25 8JS
Activities: Non-specialised wholesale trade
Parent: Costco UK Holdings Limited
Officers: Magan Khushalbhai Chauhan, Secretary; Walter Craig Jelinek [1952] Director [American]; James Patrick Murphy [1952] Director [American]; Stephen Michael Pappas [1954] Director [American]

Cottis House Limited
Incorporated: 7 August 1973 *Employees:* 2
Net Worth: £16,446,516 *Total Assets:* £24,853,140
Registered Office: Millhouse, 32-38 East Street, Rochford, Essex, SS4 1DB
Activities: Renting and operating of Housing Association real estate
Parent: Cottis Property Holdings Ltd
Officers: Stephen Peter Johnson, Secretary; Janice Eileen Johnson [1953] Director/Secretary; Stephen Peter Johnson [1953] Director/Builder

Coulson Group Limited
Incorporated: 4 December 1920 *Employees:* 87
Net Worth: £7,535,935 *Total Assets:* £12,501,105
Registered Office: William James House, Cowley Road, Cambridge, CB4 0WX
Activities: Activities of head offices
Officers: Paul Charles Glover, Secretary; Paul Charles Glover [1971] Director/Management Accountant; Christopher William James [1955] Director/Builder; Philip Robert James [1959] Director/Builder; Stephen Terrell [1954] Director/Builder; Graham Peter Watts [1959] Director

Country Court Care Homes 2 Limited
Incorporated: 1 May 2014 *Employees:* 462
Net Worth: £20,322,836 *Total Assets:* £43,948,052
Registered Office: c/o Duncan & Toplis Limited, Enterprise Way, Pinchbeck, Spalding, Lincs, PE11 3YR
Activities: Residential nursing care facilities
Parent: Country Court Care Group Limited
Officers: Abdul Aziz Kachra [1952] Director; Al-Karim Kachra [1988] Finance Director; Alykhan Kachra [1986] Director

Country Court Care Homes 3 MB Limited
Incorporated: 7 October 2015
Net Worth: £1 *Total Assets:* £22,722,986
Registered Office: c/o Duncan & Toplis Limited, Enterprise Way, Pinchbeck, Spalding, Lincs, PE11 3YR
Activities: Activities of other holding companies n.e.c.
Parent: Country Court Care Homes 3 MB Holdco Limited
Officers: Abdul Aziz Kachra [1952] Director; Al-Karim Kachra [1988] Director; Alykhan Kachra [1986] Director/Operations

Country Court Care Homes 3 Propco Limited
Incorporated: 7 October 2015
Net Worth: £23,821,500 *Total Assets:* £78,951,128
Registered Office: c/o Duncan & Toplis Limited, Enterprise Way, Pinchbeck, Spalding, Lincs, PE11 3YR
Activities: Other letting and operating of own or leased real estate
Parent: Country Court Care Homes 3 SB Limited
Officers: Abdul Aziz Kachra [1952] Director; Al-Karim Kachra [1988] Director; Alykhan Kachra [1986] Director/Operations

Country Court Care Homes 3 SB Holdco Limited
Incorporated: 7 October 2015
Net Worth: £1 *Total Assets:* £22,641,746
Registered Office: c/o Duncan & Toplis Limited, Enterprise Way, Pinchbeck, Spalding, Lincs, PE11 3YR
Activities: Activities of other holding companies n.e.c.
Parent: Country Court Care Homes 3 MB Limited
Officers: Abdul Aziz Kachra [1952] Director; Al-Karim Kachra [1988] Director; Alykhan Kachra [1986] Director/Operations

Country Court Care Homes 3 SB Limited
Incorporated: 7 October 2015
Net Worth: £1 *Total Assets:* £47,278,724
Registered Office: c/o Duncan & Toplis Limited, Enterprise Way, Pinchbeck, Spalding, Lincs, PE11 3YR
Activities: Activities of other holding companies n.e.c.
Parent: Country Court Care Homes 3 SB Holdco Limited
Officers: Abdul Aziz Kachra [1952] Director; Al-Karim Kachra [1988] Director; Alykhan Kachra [1986] Director/Operations

Country Court Care Homes Limited
Incorporated: 23 September 1996 *Employees:* 477
Net Worth: £8,129,344 *Total Assets:* £22,454,608
Registered Office: c/o Duncan & Toplis Limited, Enterprise Way, Pinchbeck, Spalding, Lincs, PE11 3YR
Activities: Residential nursing care facilities
Parent: Country Court Care Group Limited
Officers: Al-Karim Kachra, Secretary; Abdulaziz Kachra [1952] Director; Al-Karim Kachra [1988] Financial Director; Alykhan Kachra [1986] Director/Operations

Country House Weddings Limited
Incorporated: 12 August 1998 *Employees:* 248
Net Worth: £9,225,184 *Total Assets:* £15,669,194
Registered Office: Regency House, 33 Wood Street, Barnet, Herts, EN5 4BE
Activities: Other business support service activities n.e.c.
Parent: Country House Weddings Holdings Ltd
Officers: Harry Bramer, Secretary/Director; Harry Bramer [1949] Director; Nicholas Bramer [1983] Director

Country Retirement & Nursing Homes Ltd
Incorporated: 17 June 1999 *Employees:* 158
Net Worth: £10,675,414 *Total Assets:* £16,571,283
Registered Office: Kingsley House, Clapham Road South, Lowestoft, Suffolk, NR32 1QS
Activities: Residential care activities for the elderly and disabled
Officers: Velummayilum Thayanandarajah, Secretary; Wasantha Darshana [1978] Director/Business Executive; Deborah Ann Edwards [1974] Director/Business Executive; Sarah Louise Ferguson [1966] Director/Business Executive; Ian Stuart Jarvis [1966] Director/Business Executive; Cameron Dyer Thayan [1995] Director/Trainee Accountant; Ewan Dyer Thayan [1997] Director/Trainee Accountant; Sumithra Chandrakanthi Thayanandarajah [1959] Director/Business Executive; Velummayilum Thayanandarajah [1961] Director/Company Executive

Countryside 26 Limited
Incorporated: 29 March 2007
Net Worth: £256,628 *Total Assets:* £8,648,898
Registered Office: Countryside House, The Drive, Great Warley, Brentwood, Essex, CM13 3AT
Activities: Development of building projects
Parent: Countryside Properties (UK) Limited
Officers: Tracy Marina Warren, Secretary; Graham Stewart Cherry [1959] Director/Chief Executive; Ian Russell Kelley [1961] Director/Chief Executive - Partnerships North; Gary Neville Whitaker [1963] Director/General Counsel

Countryside 28 Limited
Incorporated: 23 February 2007
Net Worth Deficit: £4,563,554 *Total Assets:* £10,997,263
Registered Office: Countryside House, The Drive, Great Warley, Brentwood, Essex, CM13 3AT
Activities: Construction of domestic buildings
Parent: Countryside Properties (UK) Limited
Officers: Tracy Marina Warren, Secretary; Graham Stewart Cherry [1959] Director/Chief Executive; Ian Russell Kelley [1961] Director; Gary Neville Whitaker [1963] Director/General Counsel

Countryside Annington (Mill Hill) Limited
Incorporated: 8 December 2006
Net Worth Deficit: £2,389,118 *Total Assets:* £16,601,500
Registered Office: Countryside House, The Drive, Brentwood, Essex, CM13 3AT
Activities: Development of building projects
Shareholders: Annington Developments Limited; Countryside Properties (Joint Ventures) Limited
Officers: Tracy Marina Warren, Secretary; Catherine Brooking [1966] Development Director; Andrew Peter Chadd [1964] Director; Graham Stewart Cherry [1959] Director/Chief Executive; David Everett [1957] Director; James Christian Hopkins [1959] Director; Nicholas Peter Vaughan [1962] Director

Countryside Four Limited
Incorporated: 23 April 2002
Net Worth Deficit: £1,354,789 *Total Assets:* £28,433,140
Registered Office: Countryside House, The Drive, Great Warley, Brentwood, Essex, CM13 3AT
Activities: Development of building projects
Parent: Countryside Properties (UK) Limited
Officers: Tracy Marina Warren, Secretary; Michael Ian Scott [1977] Director/Financial Controller; Gary Neville Whitaker [1963] Director/General Counsel

Countryside L & Q (Oaks Village) LLP
Incorporated: 26 January 2015
Net Worth: £52,101,088 *Total Assets:* £55,110,628
Registered Office: Countryside House, The Drive, Great Warley, Brentwood, Essex, CM13 3AT

Countryside Maritime Limited
Incorporated: 17 October 1990
Net Worth: £636,295 *Total Assets:* £21,331,328
Registered Office: Countryside House, The Drive, Brentwood, Essex, CM13 3AT
Activities: Development of building projects
Officers: Tracy Marina Warren, Secretary; Matthew David Brown [1980] Director/Surveyor; Michael Goulding [1964] Director/Senior Area Manager; Paul John Kitson [1971] Project Director; Darren Paul David Ottley [1979] Director/Accountant; Thomas Andrew Sheriff [1973] Director; Andrew Usher [1980] Director

Countryside Properties (Bicester) Limited
Incorporated: 22 February 2001
Net Worth: £6,836,509 *Total Assets:* £22,878,528
Registered Office: Countryside House, The Drive, Brentwood, Essex, CM13 3AT
Activities: Buying and selling of own real estate
Shareholders: Bicester Lane Limited; Countryside Properties (Joint Ventures) Limited
Officers: Tracy Marina Warren, Secretary; Lord Geoffrey Robert James Borwick [1955] Director; Thomas James Robert Borwick [1987] Director; Andrew Mark Carrington [1975] Commercial Director; Christopher Martin Hobden [1949] Director; Phillip Victor Lyons [1964] Director/Chief Executive - Housebuilding; Rupert James Stephens [1976] Director/Chartered Surveyor

Countryside Properties (Holdings) Limited
Incorporated: 6 September 2005
Previous: Countryside Properties Limited
Net Worth: £382,449,984 *Total Assets:* £382,449,984
Registered Office: Countryside House, The Drive, Brentwood, Essex, CM13 3AT
Activities: Activities of construction holding companies
Parent: Copthorn Holdings Limited
Officers: Gary Whitaker, Secretary; Graham Stewart Cherry [1959] Director/Chief Executive; Ian Russell Kelley [1961] Director/Chief Executive - Partnerships North Division; Phillip Victor Lyons [1964] Director/Chief Executive - Housebuilding; Iain Duncan McPherson [1973] Director; Michael Ian Scott [1977] Director/Chief Financial Officer; Ian Calvert Sutcliffe [1959] Director/Executive Chairman; Rebecca Jane Worthington [1971] Director/Accountant

Countryside Properties (Joint Ventures) Limited
Incorporated: 27 February 2006
Net Worth Deficit: £6,760,325 *Total Assets:* £75,265,104
Registered Office: Countryside House, The Drive, Great Warley, Brentwood, Essex, CM13 3AT
Activities: Activities of construction holding companies
Parent: Countryside Properties (UK) Limited
Officers: Tracy Marina Warren, Secretary; Graham Stewart Cherry [1959] Director/Chief Executive; Michael Ian Scott [1977] Director/Financial Controller; Gary Neville Whitaker [1963] Director/General Counsel; Rebecca Jane Worthington [1971] Director/Accountant

Countryside Properties (Springhead) Limited
Incorporated: 20 June 2006
Previous: Countryside Land Securities (Springhead) Limited
Net Worth: £10,002,299 *Total Assets:* £24,480,658
Registered Office: Countryside House, The Drive, Great Warley, Brentwood, Essex, CM13 3AT
Activities: Development of building projects
Parent: Countryside Properties (UK) Limited
Officers: Tracy Marina Warren, Secretary; Graham Stewart Cherry [1959] Director/Chief Executive; Iain Duncan McPherson [1973] Regional Managing Director; Rebecca Jane Worthington [1971] Director/Accountant

Countryside Properties (Uberior) Limited
Incorporated: 30 June 2003
Net Worth: £5,766,000 *Total Assets:* £24,675,000
Registered Office: Countryside House, The Drive, Brentwood, Essex, CM13 3AT
Activities: Development of building projects
Parent: Countryside Properties (UK) Limited
Officers: Tracy Marina Warren, Secretary; Catherine Brooking [1966] Development Director; David Everett [1957] Director

Countryside Properties (UK) Limited
Incorporated: 14 November 1958 *Employees:* 1,085
Net Worth: £379,871,008 *Total Assets:* £906,195,008
Registered Office: Countryside House, The Drive, Brentwood, Essex, CM13 3AT
Activities: Development of building projects
Parent: Countryside Properties (Holdings) Limited
Officers: Gary Whitaker, Secretary; Graham Stewart Cherry [1959] Director/Chief Executive; Ian Russell Kelley [1961] Director/Chief Executive - Partnerships North Division; Phillip Victor Lyons [1964] Director/Chief Executive - Housebuilding; Iain Duncan McPherson [1973] Director; Michael Ian Scott [1977] Director/Chief Financial Officer; Ian Calvert Sutcliffe [1959] Director/Executive Chairman; Rebecca Jane Worthington [1971] Director/Accountant

Countryside Properties (WGL) Limited
Incorporated: 4 April 2016 *Employees:* 431
Previous: Westleigh Group Limited
Net Worth: £3,374,000 *Total Assets:* £108,540,000
Registered Office: Countryside House, The Drive, Great Warley, Brentwood, Essex, CM13 3AT
Activities: Development of building projects
Parent: Countryside Properties (UK) Limited
Officers: Tracy Marina Warren, Secretary; Gary Stephen Belcher [1968] Director; Kathryn Louise Facey [1964] Finance Director; Ian Russell Kelley [1961] Director; Daniel Jonathan Lang [1981] Technical Director; Glyn Mabey [1965] Director; Matthew Neil Moore [1975] Director; Simon Haywood Preston [1974] Director; Mark Robert Jason Rockley [1967] Director

Countryside Properties (WHL) Limited
Incorporated: 9 April 2016 *Employees:* 6
Previous: Westleigh Holdings Limited
Net Worth: £445,000 *Total Assets:* £72,726,000
Registered Office: Countryside House, The Drive, Great Warley, Brentwood, Essex, CM13 3AT
Activities: Development of building projects
Parent: Westleigh Group Limited
Officers: Tracy Marina Warren, Secretary; Gary Stephen Belcher [1968] Director; Kathryn Louise Facey [1964] Finance Director; Ian Russell Kelley [1961] Director; Glyn Mabey [1965] Director; Matthew Neil Moore [1975] Director

Countryside Properties (WPL) Limited
Incorporated: 18 June 2013 *Employees:* 430
Previous: Westleigh Partnerships Limited
Net Worth: £37,374,000 *Total Assets:* £79,453,000
Registered Office: Countryside House, The Drive, Great Warley, Brentwood, Essex, CM13 3AT
Activities: Development of building projects
Parent: Westleigh Holdings Limited
Officers: Tracy Marina Warren, Secretary; Gary Stephen Belcher [1968] Director; Kathryn Louise Facey [1964] Finance Director; Ian Russell Kelley [1961] Director; Daniel Jonathan Lang [1981] Technical Director; Glyn Mabey [1965] Director; Matthew Neil Moore [1975] Director; Simon Haywood Preston [1974] Business Development Director; Mark Robert Jason Rockley [1967] Director

Countryside Properties PLC
Incorporated: 18 November 2015 *Employees:* 1,557
Net Worth: £792,099,968 *Total Assets:* £1,244,099,968
Registered Office: Countryside House, The Drive, Brentwood, Essex, CM13 3AT
Activities: Activities of other holding companies n.e.c.
Officers: Gary Neville Whitaker, Secretary; Amanda Jane Burton [1959] Non-Executive Director and Chair; David Howell [1949] Director/Chairman; Douglas Malcolm Hurt [1956] Director; Sally Morgan [1957] Charity Adviser and Non-Executive Director; Michael Ian Scott [1977] Director/Chief Financial Officer; Ian Calvert Sutcliffe [1959] Director/Chief Executive Officer; Rebecca Jane Worthington [1971] Director/Chief Financial Officer

The Countryside Restoration Trust
Incorporated: 20 July 2010 *Employees:* 11
Net Worth: £19,822,604 *Total Assets:* £20,805,672
Registered Office: Birds Farm, Haslingfield Road, Barton, Cambs, CB23 7AG
Activities: Mixed farming
Officers: William John Cross [1951] Director/Farmer; Annabelle Evans [1969] Director/Solicitor; Graham Charles Girling [1949] Director/Retired; Frank Zacharias Robin Goldsmith [1975] Director/Member of Parliament; Christopher Robin Knights [1939] Director/Farmer; David Francis Mills [1943] Director/Owner of British Wildlife Centre; Robin Page [1943] Director/Farmer and Writer; Mark Raymond Rose [1954] Director; Philip Nicholas Watts [1943] Director/Farmer

Countryside Sigma Limited
Incorporated: 20 June 2006
Net Worth: £3,185,885 *Total Assets:* £20,654,072
Registered Office: Countryside House, The Drive, Great Warley, Brentwood, Essex, CM13 3AT
Activities: Development of building projects
Shareholders: Countryside Properties (UK) Limited; Liverpool Inpartnership 2007 Limited
Officers: Tracy Marina Warren, Secretary; Graeme Ronald Rae Hogg [1965] Director; Ian Russell Kelley [1961] Director; Ian Simpson [1963] Land and New Business Director; Gwynn Galloway Thomson [1967] Director

Countryside Zest (Beaulieu Park) LLP
Incorporated: 24 September 2008
Net Worth: £152,263,584 *Total Assets:* £198,711,696
Registered Office: Countryside House, The Drive, Great Warley, Brentwood, Essex, CM13 3AT

Countrywide Developments (UK) PLC
Incorporated: 28 January 2002 *Employees:* 4
Net Worth: £9,213,167 *Total Assets:* £17,355,384
Registered Office: 416 Green Lane, Ilford, Essex, IG3 9JX
Activities: Buying and selling of own real estate
Major Shareholder: Glenn Howard Cohen
Officers: Laurence Melvin Cohen, Secretary; Glenn Howard Cohen [1970] Director; Laurence Melvyn Cohen [1939] Director

Countrywide Electrical Distributors Limited
Incorporated: 5 January 1994 *Employees:* 47
Net Worth: £13,813,023 *Total Assets:* £18,634,840
Registered Office: 44-48 Freshwater Road, Dagenham, Essex, RM8 1RX
Activities: Wholesale of household goods (other than musical instruments) n.e.c
Major Shareholder: Ravinder Kumar Sood
Officers: Ravinder Kumar Sood, Secretary; Ravinder Kumar Sood [1947] Managing Director; Jayantilal Velani [1958] Director

Countrywide Estate Agents
Incorporated: 27 January 1964 *Employees:* 5,982
Net Worth Deficit: £1,574,000 *Total Assets:* £143,219,008
Registered Office: Ground Floor, County House, 100 New London Road, Chelmsford, Essex, CM2 0RG
Activities: Real estate agencies
Parent: Balanus Limited
Officers: Gareth Rhys Williams, Secretary; Paul Lewis Creffield [1954] Director; Himanshu Haridas Raja [1965] Director/Financial Officer; Gareth Rhys Williams [1964] Director/Solicitor

Countrywide Group PLC
Incorporated: 29 October 2003 *Employees:* 270
Net Worth: £160,574,000 *Total Assets:* £567,011,968
Registered Office: Ground Floor, County House, 100 New London Road, Chelmsford, Essex, CM2 0RG
Activities: Financial intermediation not elsewhere classified
Parent: Countrywide PLC
Officers: Gareth Rhys Williams, Secretary; Paul Lewis Creffield [1954] Director; Himanshu Haridas Raja [1965] Director/Financial Officer

Countrywide PLC
Incorporated: 21 December 2012 *Employees:* 9,463
Net Worth: £309,136,992 *Total Assets:* £697,339,008
Registered Office: Ground Floor, County House, 100 New London Road, Chelmsford, Essex, CM2 0RG
Activities: Activities of head offices
Officers: Gareth Williams, Secretary; Natalie Anna Ceeney [1971] Director; Paul Lewis Creffield [1954] Director; Alexander Rupert Gavin [1954] Director; Caleb Samuel Kramer [1969] Director; Jane Elizabeth Stuart Lighting [1956] Non-Executive Director and Business Mentor; Peter James Long [1952] Director; Himanshu Haridas Raja [1965] Director/Financial Officer; David Mark Shuttleworth [1963] Director; Catherine Lucy Turner [1963] Director; David Kenneth Watson [1959] Director

Countrywide Surveyors Limited
Incorporated: 4 November 1985 *Employees:* 639
Net Worth: £68,066,000 *Total Assets:* £90,116,000
Registered Office: Ground Floor, County House, 100 New London Road, Chelmsford, Essex, CM2 0RG
Activities: Other business support service activities n.e.c.
Parent: Balanus Limited
Officers: Gareth Rhys Williams, Secretary; Matthew Cumber [1969] Director/Surveying; Matthew Emblem [1983] Finance Director; James McAllister Gibson [1960] Director/Surveyor; Paul Anthony Wareham [1965] Director of Field Operations

County Care Homes Limited
Incorporated: 2 March 2003 *Employees:* 171
Net Worth: £5,670,939 *Total Assets:* £15,347,158
Registered Office: Oak House, Morris Green, Sible Hedingham, Essex, CO9 3LU
Activities: Residential nursing care facilities
Shareholders: Gareth James Nixon-Moss; Enid Mary Nixon-Moss
Officers: Enid Mary Nixon Moss, Secretary; Enid Mary Nixon Moss [1960] Director; Gareth James Nixon Moss [1957] Director/Barrister

Cousins Holdings Limited
Incorporated: 19 March 1964
Net Worth: £9,606,975 *Total Assets:* £11,104,184
Registered Office: Five Ways, 57-59 Hatfield Road, Potters Bar, Herts, EN6 1HS
Activities: Activities of head offices
Shareholder: Alexander Eric Gordon Cousins
Officers: Rory Alexander John Cousins [1981] Director

Coventry Foundationcampus Limited
Incorporated: 29 August 2007 *Employees:* 65
Net Worth: £6,225,000 *Total Assets:* £15,841,000
Registered Office: Kett House, Station Road, Cambridge, CB1 2JH
Activities: First-degree level higher education
Parent: CEG UFP Limited
Officers: Michael Ioakimides [1965] Director; Philip Leslie Symes [1962] Director/Chief Financial Officer; Brendan Grant Webb [1969] Director

Coveris Flexibles (Gainsborough) UK Limited
Incorporated: 4 June 2003 *Employees:* 1,075
Net Worth: £19,734,000 *Total Assets:* £252,456,992
Registered Office: Holland Place, Wardentree Park, Pinchbeck, Spalding, Lincs, PE11 3ZN
Activities: Manufacture of plastic packing goods
Officers: Trace Lee Norton [1963] Sales Director; Jonathan Pallas [1962] Director; Gary Edward Rehwinkel [1961] Director [American]

Coveris Flexibles Holdings UK Limited
Incorporated: 21 December 2012 *Employees:* 5
Previous: Portugal Topco Limited
Net Worth: £37,164,000 *Total Assets:* £44,130,000
Registered Office: Holland Place, Wardentree Park, Pinchbeck, Spalding, Lincs, PE11 3ZN
Activities: Activities of other holding companies n.e.c.
Officers: Sarah Gooding [1979] Director; Andreas Heigl [1977] Director/Group Treasurer [Austrian]; Jonathan Pallas [1962] Director; Gary Edward Rehwinkel [1961] Director [American]

Coveris Flexibles UK Limited
Incorporated: 4 May 1994 *Employees:* 1,303
Net Worth: £44,968,000 *Total Assets:* £153,338,000
Registered Office: Holland Place, Wardentree Park, Pinchbeck, Spalding, Lincs, PE11 3ZN
Activities: Printing n.e.c.
Officers: Trace Lee Norton [1963] Sales Director; Jonathan Pallas [1962] Director; Dennis Patterson [1959] Director/Operations Manager; Gary Edward Rehwinkel [1961] Director [American]

Coversure Insurance Services Limited
Incorporated: 10 May 1989 *Employees:* 83
Net Worth: £1,818,844 *Total Assets:* £14,732,386
Registered Office: Coversure House, Vantage Park, Washingley Road, Huntingdon, Cambs, PE29 6SR
Activities: Activities of insurance agents and brokers
Parent: C I S G Ltd
Officers: Georgina Elizabeth Bourner, Secretary; Carl Anthony Ashton [1980] Risk and Compliance Director; Cheryl Dawn Astley [1962] Director/Chief Technology Officer; Robert Michael Darling [1963] Finance Director; Sarah Darling [1969] Managing Director; Edward George FitzGenerald Hannan [1978] Director/Chief Financial Officer; Stephen Guy Parker [1965] Group Commercial Director; Christopher James Woosnam [1981] Mergers and Acquisitions Director

Covidien UK Limited
Incorporated: 29 January 1937
Net Worth: £2,376,000 *Total Assets:* £60,209,000
Registered Office: Building 9, Croxley Park, Hatters Lane, Watford, Herts, WD18 8WW
Activities: Manufacture of knitted and crocheted hosiery
Parent: CDK U.K. Limited
Officers: Joanne Pascucci, Senior Corporate Secretary; Mark Justin Elsey [1967] Finance Director; Jacqueline Fielding [1964] Vice President (Director)

Coward Asset Limited
Incorporated: 11 June 2003
Net Worth: £7,509,729 *Total Assets:* £9,869,744
Registered Office: Swiss House, Beckingham Street, Tolleshunt Major, Essex, CM9 8LZ
Activities: Other letting and operating of own or leased real estate
Parent: CBE Group Limited
Officers: Beverley Coward, Secretary; Paul Victor Coward [1956] Director/Warehouse Manager

Coyle Personnel PLC
Incorporated: 27 July 1988 *Employees:* 156
Net Worth: £16,604,924 *Total Assets:* £33,545,504
Registered Office: Hygeia, 66-68 College Road, Harrow, Middlesex, HA1 1BE
Activities: Temporary employment agency activities
Major Shareholder: Kevin Michael Coyle
Officers: Howard Pepperdine, Secretary; Richard James Button [1973] Director/Operations Manager; Anna Louise Cooper [1978] Director; Ashling Michelle Coyle [1989] Director; Christopher John Coyle [1984] Director; Kevin Michael Coyle [1956] Chairman and Managing Director; Noreen Patricia Coyle [1959] Director [Irish]; Roger Andrew Stewart [1965] Director/Consultant

CP Holdings Limited
Incorporated: 22 March 1957 *Employees:* 7,059
Net Worth: £395,296,000 *Total Assets:* £762,854,976
Registered Office: CP House, Otterspool Way, Watford, Herts, WD25 8JJ
Activities: Activities of head offices
Shareholders: Lady Lilly Schreier; Iris Gibbor; Mark Gibbor; Robert Glatter; Michael Montague Wreschner; Alexei James Schreier
Officers: Eric Lewis, Secretary; Paul Andrew Filer [1957] Director/Chartered Accountant; Iris Gibbor [1951] Director; Mark Gibbor [1988] Director; Robert Glatter [1937] Director; Mark Hennebry [1966] Director [Irish]; Michael Barry Hirst OBE [1943] Director; Philip Hoffbrand [1967] Director/Solicitor; Eric Lewis [1927] Director/Solicitor; Alexei James Schreier [1976] Director/Executive; Lady Lilly Schreier [1924] Director; John Ernest Smith [1949] Director

CP Regents Park Two Limited
Incorporated: 8 December 2004 *Employees:* 124
Net Worth: £1,011,530 *Total Assets:* £47,227,640
Registered Office: CP House, Otterspool Way, Watford, Herts, WD25 8JJ
Activities: Hotels and similar accommodation
Parent: CP Holdings Limited
Officers: Eric Lewis, Secretary; Paul Andrew Filer [1957] Director/Chartered Accountant; Iris Gibbor [1951] Director; Mark Gibbor [1988] Director; Mark Hennebry [1966] Director [Irish]; Eric Lewis [1927] Director/Solicitor; Alexei James Schreier [1976] Director

CQK Limited
Incorporated: 19 April 1960 *Employees:* 175
Net Worth: £11,389,841 *Total Assets:* £16,949,028
Registered Office: Ground Floor, Cambridge House, Cambridge Road, Harlow, Essex, CM20 2EQ
Activities: Hotels and similar accommodation
Officers: Alex Simon Layer, Secretary; Geoffrey Peter Goddard [1959] Director; Miriam Catherine Goddard [1964] Director [Irish]

CQS Natural Resources Growth and Income PLC
Incorporated: 7 October 1994
Previous: City Natural Resources High Yield Trust PLC
Net Worth: £95,217,000 *Total Assets:* £131,823,000
Registered Office: Springfield Lodge, Colchester Road, Springfield, Chelmsford, Essex, CM2 5PW
Activities: Activities of investment trusts
Officers: Carole Cable [1961] Director; Christopher Casey [1955] Director; Alun Grant Evans [1955] Director/Business Development; Helen Foster Green [1963] Director/Chartered Accountant; Richard Other Prickett [1951] Director

Craft & Sons Limited
Incorporated: 19 February 1997 *Employees:* 4
Net Worth: £6,253,654 *Total Assets:* £9,853,613
Registered Office: 1 James Way, Stevenage, Herts, SG1 3HA
Activities: Renting and operating of Housing Association real estate
Shareholders: Helen Madeleine Craft; Paul Duncan Alexander Craft
Officers: Benedict Joshua Craft, Secretary; Benedict Joshua Craft [1995] Director; Helen Madeleine Craft [1967] Director; Isaac Alexander Craft [1995] Director/Student; Paul Duncan Alexander Craft [1964] Director

Hugh Crane Holdings Limited
Incorporated: 25 July 2016 *Employees:* 85
Net Worth: £8,454,376 *Total Assets:* £17,316,304
Registered Office: King Street House, 15 Upper King Street, Norwich, NR3 1RB
Activities: Activities of other holding companies n.e.c.
Shareholders: Nicholas Jeremy Edgar Crane; Robert Henry Edward Crane; Philip William Hugh Crane
Officers: Nicholas Jeremy Edgar Crane [1955] Director/Farmer; Philip William Hugh Crane [1952] Director; Robert Henry Edward Crane [1961] Director

Crane Investments Ltd
Incorporated: 24 October 2008 *Employees:* 1
Net Worth: £6,038,894 *Total Assets:* £11,493,055
Registered Office: 10 Durham Avenue, Gidea Park, Romford, Essex, RM2 6JS
Activities: Other letting and operating of own or leased real estate
Major Shareholder: Ashok Kumar Patel
Officers: Aprajay Patel [1984] Director; Ashok Kumar Patel [1950] Director/Solicitor

Crane Limited
Incorporated: 3 July 1908 *Employees:* 509
Net Worth: £110,809,960 *Total Assets:* £188,136,288
Registered Office: Crane House, Epsilon Terrace, West Road, Ipswich, Suffolk, IP3 9FJ
Activities: Manufacture of taps and valves
Parent: Crane S C Holdings Limited
Officers: Jason Charles Locke, Secretary; Robert Sheldon Evans [1944] Director/Chief Executive [American]; Mark Royston Hopes [1962] Director; Max Homer Mitchell [1963] Director [American]; Richard Clive Tuck [1960] Director/President

Hugh Crane Limited
Incorporated: 12 October 1959 *Employees:* 13
Net Worth: £2,363,980 *Total Assets:* £9,739,247
Registered Office: Cedars Farm, Upton, Norwich, NR13 6AW
Activities: Growing of cereals (except rice), leguminous crops and oil seeds
Parent: Hugh Crane Holdings Limited
Officers: Nicholas Jeremy Edgar Crane, Secretary; Nicholas Jeremy Edgar Crane [1955] Director/Farmer; Philip William Hugh Crane [1952] Director; Robert Henry Edward Crane [1961] Director

Cranfield Technology Park Investments Limited
Incorporated: 4 May 2017 *Employees:* 4
Net Worth: £2,231,357 *Total Assets:* £17,481,700
Registered Office: 7th Floor, Metropolitan House, 3 Darkes Lane, Potters Bar, Herts, EN6 1AG
Activities: Buying and selling of own real estate
Parent: Sheikh Holdings Group (Investments) Limited
Officers: Gareth Norman Dufton [1976] Director/Chartered Accountant; Akbar Sheikh [1989] Director; Farouq Rashid Sheikh [1958] Director; Yusuf Sheikh [1992] Director

A.R. Craven Farms Limited
Incorporated: 19 October 1995 *Employees:* 14
Net Worth: £5,578,680 *Total Assets:* £12,453,849
Registered Office: Poplar Farm, Main Road, Stickford, Boston, Lincs, PE22 8EL
Activities: Mixed farming
Major Shareholder: Andrew Robert Craven
Officers: Judith Mary Craven, Secretary; Andrew Robert Craven [1961] Director/Farmer; Judith Mary Craven [1962] Director

Creative Car Park Ltd
Incorporated: 22 September 2005 *Employees:* 58
Net Worth: £3,604,534 *Total Assets:* £8,881,248
Registered Office: The Studio, St Nicholas Close, Elstree, Borehamwood, Herts, WD6 3EW
Activities: Other business support service activities n.e.c.
Parent: Creative Technologies and Systems Limited
Officers: Willem Marthinus de Beer [1967] Director/Consultant [South African]

Creightons PLC
Incorporated: 29 September 1975 *Employees:* 365
Net Worth: £9,605,000 *Total Assets:* £16,646,000
Registered Office: 1210 Lincoln Road, Werrington, Peterborough, Cambs, PE4 6ND
Activities: Manufacture of perfumes and toilet preparations
Shareholder: William Oliver McIlroy
Officers: Nicholas Desmond John O'Shea, Secretary; Mary Teresa Carney [1953] Director/Tax Consultant; Philippa Clark [1969] Sales & Marketing Director; Paul Forster [1958] Director/Chartered Accountant; William Torrance Glencross [1946] Director/Marketing Consultant; Bernard James Mary Johnson [1945] Director/Management Consultant; William Oliver McIlroy [1945] Director/Company Investor; Nicholas Desmond John O'Shea [1954] Director/Chartered Management Accountant; Martin Stevens [1961] Technical Director

Cremer (UK) Manufacturing Co. Ltd
Incorporated: 24 February 2017 *Employees:* 26
Net Worth: £2,444,303 *Total Assets:* £10,913,476
Registered Office: c/o Procter & Gamble, London Plant West Office, Hedley Avenue, West Thurrock, Essex, RM20 4AL
Activities: Other manufacturing n.e.c.
Parent: Cremer Oleo Management GmbH
Officers: Mr Andrew Brian Aylwin [1969] Director/Chief Production Officer; Ullrich Wegner [1964] Director/Chief Executive Officer [German]

Crendon Timber Engineering Limited
Incorporated: 24 February 1986 *Employees:* 332
Net Worth: £3,931,250 *Total Assets:* £11,861,781
Registered Office: Crendon Timber Engineering Limited, Drakes Drive, Long Crendon, Aylesbury, Bucks, HP18 9BA
Activities: Sawmilling and planing of wood
Officers: Peter Lisnalea Johnston [1960] Director; Stephen Trevor Thompstone [1960] Director

Creo Pharma Limited
Incorporated: 5 February 2007 *Employees:* 17
Net Worth: £7,760,969 *Total Assets:* £13,160,766
Registered Office: Felsted Business Centre, Cock Green, Felsted, Essex, CM6 3LY
Activities: Wholesale of pharmaceutical goods
Parent: Creo Pharma Holdings Limited
Officers: Sharon Ingmire Hart, Secretary; Luke Ingmire Hart [1972] Director/Executive; Sharon Ingmire Hart [1967] Director/Executive; Chintu Patel [1966] Director/Business Executive [American]; Chirag Patel [1966] Director/CEOA Chairman [American]; Gautam Patel [1972] Director/Investor [American]; Janos Vaczi [1967] Managing Director [Hungarian]

Cresta Estates Limited
Incorporated: 7 June 1952
Net Worth: £10,876,705 *Total Assets:* £72,809,952
Registered Office: Atlas House, 28 Great Cambridge Road, Enfield, Middlesex, EN1 1UU
Activities: Other letting and operating of own or leased real estate
Shareholder: Baruch Erlich
Officers: Judith Erlich, Secretary; Baruch Erlich [1962] Director/Solicitor

Cricklewood Developments Limited
Incorporated: 25 July 2014 *Employees:* 7
Net Worth Deficit: £605,000 *Total Assets:* £22,632,000
Registered Office: 50 Lancaster Road, Enfield, Middlesex, EN2 0BY
Activities: Development of building projects
Parent: Fairview New Homes Limited
Officers: Jonathan Mark Baxter, Secretary; Michael Blakey [1963] Director; Nicholas Martin Dulcken [1967] Director; Generald Anthony Malton [1960] Director; Darren Lee McCormack [1982] Sales Director; Richard James Paterson [1957] Director; Jonathan Andrew Spring [1972] Land Buying Director; Michael Raymond Walker [1958] Director; Robert Kenneth Williams [1964] Director

Cripps Developments Limited
Incorporated: 2 October 2000 *Employees:* 27
Net Worth: £6,109,051 *Total Assets:* £13,472,245
Registered Office: Dencora House, Blyburgate, Beccles, Suffolk, NR34 9TY
Activities: Construction of domestic buildings
Shareholders: Edmund Daniel Cripps; Richard Charles Youngs
Officers: Paul Andrew Leach, Secretary/Accountant; Edmund Daniel Cripps [1967] Director/Property Developer; Paul Andrew Leach [1961] Director/Accountant; Richard Charles Youngs [1936] Property Director

Crispin & Borst Limited
Incorporated: 23 January 1964
Net Worth: £15,801,000 *Total Assets:* £17,656,000
Registered Office: Astral House, Imperial Way, Watford, Herts, WD24 4WW
Activities: Construction of commercial buildings
Parent: C & B Holdings Limited
Officers: Barry John Boxall [1957] Director/Construction Manager; Christopher Carl Brennan [1969] Director/Accountant; Generald James Smith [1956] Director/Chartered Builder

CRK Finance Limited
Incorporated: 4 November 2011
Net Worth: £13,746,638 *Total Assets:* £13,820,178
Registered Office: 116 Goodmayes Road, Ilford, Essex, IG3 9UZ
Activities: Other credit granting n.e.c.
Officers: Sundesh Kudhail, Secretary; Sundesh Kumar Kudhail [1959] Director; Surinder Kudhail [1960] Director

Crocus Home Loans Limited
Incorporated: 11 April 1990
Net Worth: £1,737,858 *Total Assets:* £47,509,992
Registered Office: Saffron House, 1a Market Street, Saffron Walden, Essex, CB10 1HX
Activities: Financial intermediation not elsewhere classified
Parent: Saffron Building Society
Officers: Thomas Gary Barr [1962] Director; Geoffrey Richard Dunn [1949] Director; Colin Howard Field [1973] Finance Director; Darren Lee Garner [1971] Director/Chief Financial Officer; Neil Jonathan Holden [1959] Director; Elizabeth Janet Kelly [1965] Director; Nicholas John Treble [1959] Director; Jennifer Ann Zaremba [1971] Director

Cromwell Community College
Incorporated: 16 March 2012 *Employees:* 167
Net Worth: £14,672,426 *Total Assets:* £18,111,240
Registered Office: Cromwell Community College, Wenny Road, Chatteris, Cambs, PE16 6UU
Activities: General secondary education
Officers: Karen Jarvis, Secretary; Lesley Patricia Adams [1955] Director/Retired; David John Bateson [1955] Director/Executive Principal; Jeremy Beswick [1958] Director/Consultant; Dr Adam David Boddison [1981] Director; Clive Robert James Bush [1951] Director/Retired; Jacqueline Cutchey [1950] Director/Retired; The Hon Richard Gregory Hely-Hutchinson [1980] Director and Company Secretary; Mark Andrew Kerr [1968] Director/Bank Manager; Marion Lloyd [1951] Director/Education Consultant; Gary Patrick Peile [1956] Director

Crop's Foods Ltd.
Incorporated: 6 April 1989 *Employees:* 26
Previous: M D C Foods Limited
Net Worth: £1,906,713 *Total Assets:* £14,288,526
Registered Office: 254 Capability Green, Luton, Beds, LU1 3LU
Activities: Wholesale of fruit and vegetables
Parent: Crop's & Partners UK Limited
Officers: Michael Dennis Cullinane, Secretary; Michael Dennis Cullinane [1948] Director; Michel Delbaere [1953] Director [Belgian]; Pieter Anthony Delbaere [1979] Director/Business Unit Manager [Belgian]; Paul Andrew Weatherby [1973] Managing Director

A. T. Cross Limited
Incorporated: 22 January 1979 *Employees:* 79
Net Worth: £7,310,055 *Total Assets:* £17,919,740
Registered Office: Cross House, Unit 14 Windmill Trading Estate, Thistle Road, Luton, Beds, LU1 3XJ
Activities: Agents specialised in the sale of other particular products
Parent: At Cross Europe Limited
Officers: Mark Ernest Luthringshauser [1961] Director/Chief Financial Officer [American]; Karl Henry Pearson III [1969] Director/Chief Executive Officer [American]; Russ William Roenick [1977] Director [American]; Clive Aiden Roger Seabrook [1967] Managing Director

Crossco (820) Limited
Incorporated: 13 August 2004 *Employees:* 1
Net Worth: £1,521,151 *Total Assets:* £8,942,397
Registered Office: c/o Envirotec Ltd, Desborough Park Road, High Wycombe, Bucks, HP12 3BX
Activities: Activities of head offices
Major Shareholder: Christopher Lister
Officers: Christopher Lister [1951] Director; Alexander Ernest Watson [1937] Director

Maurice Crouch (Growers) Limited
Incorporated: 24 October 1944 *Employees:* 18
Net Worth: £17,717,880 *Total Assets:* £22,013,528
Registered Office: 12-13 The Crescent, Wisbech, Cambs, PE13 1EH
Activities: Growing of cereals (except rice), leguminous crops and oil seeds
Major Shareholder: Judith Anne Fairey
Officers: Peter Donald Cornwell, Secretary; Judith Anne Fairey [1944] Director; Michael David Richardson Fairey [1968] Director/Farmer; Nigel Verden Miller Walker [1947] Farm Director

Crowland Cranes Limited
Incorporated: 5 May 1995 *Employees:* 54
Net Worth: £7,402,271 *Total Assets:* £11,713,837
Registered Office: Crease Drove, Crowland, Peterborough, PE6 0BN
Activities: Other specialised construction activities n.e.c.
Parent: Crowland Cranes (Holdings) Limited
Officers: Jennifer Margaret Issitt, Secretary; Jennifer Margaret Issitt [1971] Director/Secretary; Peter James Issitt [1972] Director/Crane Engineer

Crown Holdings Limited
Incorporated: 4 September 2000 *Employees:* 751
Net Worth: £7,490,740 *Total Assets:* £17,480,976
Registered Office: Crown House, 855 London Road, Grays, Essex, RM20 3LG
Activities: Activities of head offices
Major Shareholder: Russell Lee Christopher Morgan
Officers: Javed Taher, Secretary; Charles Nicholas Beer [1971] Managing Director; Deirdre Morgan [1952] Director; Russell Lee Christopher Morgan [1952] Director/Chairman; Christopher John Sullivan [1956] Director

Crown House Homes (North Station) Limited
Incorporated: 11 September 2016
Net Worth Deficit: £864,343 *Total Assets:* £11,133,644
Registered Office: Ground Floor, Swift House, 18 Hoffmanns Way, Chelmsford, Essex, CM1 1GU
Activities: Construction of domestic buildings
Parent: Crown House Homes (Colchester) Limited
Officers: Ian Michael Monks [1969] Director; Andrew Paul Perillo [1967] Director

Crownfield Holdings Limited
Incorporated: 2 January 1951 *Employees:* 100
Net Worth: £5,269,498 *Total Assets:* £13,503,106
Registered Office: Thurston Building, Hallsford Bridge Industrial Estate, Ongar, Essex, CM5 9RB
Activities: Activities of head offices
Shareholders: Ian Harry Terry; Jean Iris Terry
Officers: Jean Iris Terry, Secretary; Ian Harry Terry [1940] Director; Jean Iris Terry [1940] Director/Company Secretary; Simon Harry Terry [1963] Director

Ivor Crowson Developments (Stamford) Limited
Incorporated: 10 January 1975 *Employees:* 4
Net Worth: £6,394,913 *Total Assets:* £10,990,456
Registered Office: Manor Stone House, Barnack, Stamford, Lincs, PE9 3DW
Activities: Development of building projects
Shareholders: Ivor Crowson; Marion Rose Crowson
Officers: Marion Rose Crowson, Secretary; Ivor Crowson [1946] Director; Julia Honey Crowson [1975] Director; Marion Rose Crowson [1946] Director; Nicholas Ivor Crowson [1972] Director

CRU Sturton Street Limited
Incorporated: 22 May 2014
Net Worth Deficit: £32,414 *Total Assets:* £9,311,308
Registered Office: 2 Hills Road, Cambridge, CB2 1JP
Activities: Development of building projects
Shareholders: Neil Adam Robinson; Stephen Michael Chard
Officers: James Robert Peace, Secretary; Stephen Michael Chard [1971] Director [New Zealander]; Francisco Javier Farres Quesada [1957] Director [Spanish]; Juan Miguel Pascual Rodriguez [1967] Director [Spanish]; Neil Adam Robinson [1972] Director

Crystal Group Limited
Incorporated: 2 September 2005 *Employees:* 251
Net Worth: £3,975,662 *Total Assets:* £10,749,148
Registered Office: Crystal House, Unit 1 King George Close, Romford, Essex, RM7 7PN
Activities: Other manufacturing n.e.c.
Shareholder: John Ettore Antonio Oddi
Officers: Michael Brian Ballard [1965] Director/Accountant; Agostina Boland [1965] Director

Crystal Home Improvements Group Limited
Incorporated: 6 February 2002
Net Worth Deficit: £227,441 *Total Assets:* £21,546,712
Registered Office: Crystal House, Unit 1 King George Close, Romford, Essex, RM7 7PN
Activities: Other manufacturing n.e.c.
Parent: Crystal Home Improvements Holdings Ltd
Officers: Michael Brian Ballard [1965] Director/Accountant; Agostina Boland [1965] Director

Crystal Home Improvements Holdings Limited
Incorporated: 2 December 2003
Net Worth: £4,561,855 *Total Assets:* £29,984,880
Registered Office: Crystal House, Unit 1 King George Close, Romford, Essex, RM7 7PN
Activities: Other manufacturing n.e.c.
Parent: Crystal Group Ltd
Officers: Michael Brian Ballard [1965] Director/Accountant; Agostina Boland [1965] Director

Crystal Windows & Doors Limited
Incorporated: 2 August 1995 *Employees:* 251
Net Worth: £16,671,328 *Total Assets:* £35,993,184
Registered Office: Crystal House, Unit 1 King George Close, Eastern Avenue, Romford, Essex, RM7 7PN
Activities: Other manufacturing n.e.c.
Parent: Crystal Home Improvement Group Ltd
Officers: Michael Brian Ballard [1965] Finance Director; Agostina Boland [1965] Director; Michael Charles Farley [1976] Director; Mark Raynor [1962] Director

CSR Imaging UK Ltd.
Incorporated: 22 October 1999
Net Worth: £58,438,680 *Total Assets:* £58,438,680
Registered Office: Churchill House, Cowley Road, Cambridge Business Park, Cambridge, CB4 0WZ
Activities: Other professional, scientific and technical activities n.e.c.
Parent: Qualcomm Incorporated
Officers: Gordon Thomas Rowe [1965] Senior Director, Finance [Canadian]

CSR Limited
Incorporated: 26 March 2001
Previous: CSR PLC
Net Worth: £1,368,641,792 *Total Assets:* £1,395,337,856
Registered Office: Churchill House, Cambridge Business Park, Cowley Road, Cambridge, CB4 0WZ
Activities: Activities of other holding companies n.e.c.
Parent: Qualcomm Incorporated
Officers: Kevin John Cadieux [1961] Director [American]; Gordon Thomas Rowe [1965] Senior Director, Finance [Canadian]

CSS Computer Security Solutions Limited
Incorporated: 16 December 2009
Net Worth: £6,102,941 *Total Assets:* £29,956,776
Registered Office: Suffolk House, Fordham Road, Newmarket, Suffolk, CB8 7AA
Activities: Activities of head offices
Parent: Arrow Electronics Inc
Officers: Kieran Cooper, Secretary; Kieran David Cooper [1969] Director; Mark McHale [1965] Director

CSSC Properties Limited
Incorporated: 7 December 1999
Net Worth: £33,419,000 *Total Assets:* £34,992,000
Registered Office: Compton Court, 20-24 Temple End, High Wycombe, Bucks, HP13 5DR
Activities: Buying and selling of own real estate
Officers: Simon Norris Lee, Secretary; Wendy Eley [1976] Director; Raymond John Peter Haskell [1960] Director/Estate Manager; Marian Holmes [1952] Director/Civil Servant; Simon Norris Lee [1961] Director/Chief Executive

CTV Outside Broadcasts Limited
Incorporated: 23 March 2005 *Employees:* 142
Net Worth: £16,621,000 *Total Assets:* £34,603,000
Registered Office: Unit 3 The Merlin Centre, Lancaster Road, Cressex Business Park, High Wycombe, Bucks, HP12 3QL
Activities: Television programme production activities
Officers: Andrew David Maries, Secretary; Hamish Francis Alexander Greig [1957] Director/Engineer; Barry Gibson Johnstone [1945] Managing Director [New Zealander]; Andrew David Maries [1965] Director/Accountant

Culham Limited
Incorporated: 21 January 1983
Net Worth: £5,482,296 *Total Assets:* £10,894,474
Registered Office: 7 Coombehurst Close, Hadley Wood, Herts, EN4 0JU
Activities: Other letting and operating of own or leased real estate
Shareholders: Twinglobe 2008 Ltd; Twinglobe Holdings Limited
Officers: Mihir Kantilal Thakerar, Secretary; Dipak Thakerar [1965] Director/Accountant; Mihir Kantilal Thakerar [1963] Director

Cummins Cogeneration Limited
Incorporated: 13 July 2009 *Employees:* 29
Net Worth Deficit: £42,491,624 *Total Assets:* £75,777,608
Registered Office: Unit 7 Chancery Gate Close, Stonefield Way, South Ruislip, Middlesex, HA4 0JS
Activities: Production of electricity
Officers: Navaratnarajah Navendrha, Secretary; Gino Butera [1963] Director [Australian]; Aditya Khilnani [1990] Director; Asha Khilnani [1959] Director; Deepak Khilnani [1959] Director/Company Secretary; Alexandre Savelli [1968] Executive Director [American]

Cummins ESB Nigeria Limited
Incorporated: 13 July 2009 *Employees:* 4
Net Worth: £7,454,613 *Total Assets:* £10,045,365
Registered Office: Unit 7 Chancery Gate Business Park, Stonefield Way, South Ruislip, Middlesex, HA4 0JS
Activities: Trade of electricity
Officers: Navaratnarajah Navendrha, Secretary; Alok Joshi [1970] Director [Indian]; Aditya Khilnani [1990] Director; Deepak Khilnani [1959] Director/Company Secretary; Chris Oberholster [1962] Director/Company Executive [South African]

Cummins Generator Technologies Limited
Incorporated: 27 August 1947 *Employees:* 607
Net Worth: £2,401,757,952 *Total Assets:* £2,536,200,960
Registered Office: Fountain Court, Lynch Wood, Peterborough, Cambs, PE2 6FZ
Activities: Manufacture of electric motors, generators and transformers
Parent: Cummins EMEA Holdings Limited
Officers: Joseph Morgan Rigler, Secretary; John McCormack Barrowman [1952] Director/VP Operations; Rafael Villaneva Hernandez [1963] Director/Manager [Mexican]; Antonio Leitao [1964] Director [French]; Desmond Joseph McMenamin [1978] Director/General Manager; Joseph Morgan Rigler [1980] Director/Lawyer; Edward David Smith [1976] Director/Chartered Accountant; Alexey Ustinov [1970] Managing Director [Russian]

Cunningham Holdings (London) Limited
Incorporated: 1 February 2012 *Employees:* 47
Net Worth: £15,136,327 *Total Assets:* £21,143,368
Registered Office: 46-54 High Street, Ingatestone, Essex, CM4 9DW
Activities: Construction of commercial buildings
Major Shareholder: James Joseph Cunningham
Officers: Sarah Cunningham, Secretary; James Joseph Cunningham [1976] Director [Irish]

Curtis Medical Investments Limited
Incorporated: 8 December 1995 *Employees:* 5
Net Worth: £15,805,850 *Total Assets:* £25,231,250
Registered Office: First Floor Offices, 99 Bancroft, Hitchin, Herts, SG5 1NQ
Activities: Other letting and operating of own or leased real estate
Shareholder: Michael Hill
Officers: Anthony George Bunker [1944] Director/Consultant; Jeremy John Hill [1974] Director; Kate Monica Adelaide Hill [1974] Director; Michael Hill [1936] Director/Chartered Surveyor; Mark Wilfrid Seaman-Hill [1957] Director

CVS (UK) Limited
Incorporated: 17 May 1999 *Employees:* 3,469
Net Worth: £45,035,000 *Total Assets:* £250,786,000
Registered Office: CVS House, Owen Road, Diss, Norfolk, IP22 4ER
Activities: Veterinary activities
Parent: CVS Group PLC
Officers: Richard Aidan John Gilligan, Secretary; Richard Fairman [1967] Director; Simon Campbell Innes [1960] Director/Chief Executive

CVS Group PLC
Incorporated: 13 July 2007 *Employees:* 5,642
Net Worth: £157,700,000 *Total Assets:* £319,000,000
Registered Office: CVS House, Owen Road, Diss, Norfolk, IP22 4ER
Activities: Veterinary activities
Officers: Richard Aidan John Gilligan, Secretary; Richard Andrew Connell [1955] Director; Richard Fairman [1967] Director; Simon Campbell Innes [1960] Director/Chief Executive; Deborah Jane Kemp [1961] Director; Michael Kinloch McCollum [1967] Director

Cwind Ltd
Incorporated: 8 June 2010 *Employees:* 74
Net Worth: £4,714,000 *Total Assets:* £27,538,000
Registered Office: Ocean House, 1 Winsford Way, Boreham Interchange, Chelmsford, Essex, CM2 5PD
Activities: Other business support service activities n.e.c.
Parent: Global Marine Systems Limited
Officers: Jaime Violet Cable, Secretary; Ian Peter Bryan [1960] Director; Ian David Douglas [1968] Director/Chief Executive; Richard Fraser-Smith [1964] Director/Accountant; Bruce Neilson-Watts [1970] Director

CWT Holdco Limited
Incorporated: 7 May 1997
Net Worth: £44,286,420 *Total Assets:* £48,218,652
Registered Office: Maple House, High Street, Potters Bar, Herts, EN6 5RF
Activities: Travel agency activities
Parent: Carlson Wagonlit New Holdco Limited
Officers: Narinder Sanotra, Secretary; Christopher Bowen [1960] Director; Denise Harman [1970] Director [Irish]; Sanjay Kapoor [1967] Director [British/Australian]; Rhodri Llewelyn Hollister Turner [1977] Director/Chief Financial Officer

Cyanconnode Holdings PLC
Incorporated: 7 October 2002 *Employees:* 54
Previous: Cyan Holdings PLC
Net Worth: £13,963,967 *Total Assets:* £17,071,012
Registered Office: Merlin Place, Milton Road, Cambridge, CB4 0DP
Activities: Wireless telecommunications activities
Officers: Heather Marie Peacock, Secretary; Henry James Berry [1947] Director; John James Cronin [1955] Director/Chairman; William David Johns-Powell [1957] Director; Heather Marie Peacock [1967] Financial Director; Paul Graham Ratcliff [1955] Director

Cyberscience PLC
Incorporated: 28 December 1977 *Employees:* 45
Net Worth: £16,976,632 *Total Assets:* £23,559,432
Registered Office: Rawdon House, High Street, Hoddesdon, Herts, EN11 8BD
Activities: Business and domestic software development
Major Shareholder: Paul John Rogers
Officers: Simon Mathew Foden, Secretary; Simon Mathew Foden [1972] Operations Director; Julia Sarah Pyper [1958] Director/Consultant

Cygnet Care Limited
Incorporated: 9 December 2005 *Employees:* 173
Net Worth: £4,603,832 *Total Assets:* £17,667,356
Registered Office: Pen House, Church Road, Earsham, Norfolk, NR35 2TJ
Activities: Other human health activities
Shareholders: Robert James Blackham; Sally Ann Crawford
Officers: Sally Ann Crawford, Secretary; Robert James Blackham [1971] Director/Residential Care Provider; Suzanne Mary Blackham [1940] Director/Residential Care Provider; Sally Ann Crawford [1967] Director/Residential Care Provider

Cygnet Street Developments Limited
Incorporated: 2 September 2014
Net Worth: £5,075,405 *Total Assets:* £8,983,481
Registered Office: 3rd Floor, Sterling House, Langston Road, Loughton, Essex, IG10 3TS
Activities: Development of building projects
Parent: Galliard Holdings Limited
Officers: Allan William Porter, Secretary; David Edward Conway [1976] Director; Stephen Stuart Solomon Conway [1948] Director

Cytocell Limited
Incorporated: 8 June 2001 *Employees:* 39
Net Worth: £13,971,724 *Total Assets:* £18,351,782
Registered Office: Unit 4 Technopark, Newmarket Road, Cambridge, CB5 8PB
Activities: Other human health activities
Parent: Oxford Gene Technology IP Limited
Officers: Anthony John Lenhardt, Secretary; Dr John George Anson [1960] Director; Dr Michael Robert Evans [1958] Director; Dr David Andrew Arlwydd Owen [1944] Director; David Oxlade [1949] Director; Kenji Tsujimoto [1971] Director/Business Executive [Japanese]; Gregory Alun Williams [1980] Director

D & B Scaffolding Holdings Ltd
Incorporated: 25 August 2016 *Employees:* 40
Net Worth: £8,660,032 *Total Assets:* £11,123,267
Registered Office: 10-12 Mulberry Green, Harlow, Essex, CM17 0ET
Activities: Activities of other holding companies n.e.c.
Shareholders: Gerald Alan Dobbs; Naomi Patricia Gowers
Officers: Bellman Bird [1959] Director; Generald Alan Dobbs [1960] Director

D & B Scaffolding Limited
Incorporated: 28 February 1994 *Employees:* 40
Net Worth: £8,660,415 *Total Assets:* £11,123,651
Registered Office: 10-12 Mulberry Green, Old Harlow, Essex, CM17 0ET
Activities: Other specialised construction activities n.e.c.
Parent: D & B Scaffolding Holdings Ltd
Officers: Generald Alan Dobbs, Secretary; Bellman Bird [1959] Director/Scaffolding Contractor; Generald Alan Dobbs [1960] Director/Scaffolding Contractor

D-Link (Europe) Limited
Incorporated: 30 May 1995 *Employees:* 258
Net Worth: £29,288,148 *Total Assets:* £54,911,244
Registered Office: First Floor, Artemis Building, Odyssey Business Park, West End Road, South Ruislip, Middlesex, HA4 6QE
Activities: Other information technology service activities
Parent: D-Link Corporation
Officers: Rick Ching Yei Chen, Secretary; Gen-Kwo Lee [1958] Director [Taiwanese]; Kevin Wen Huang Wen [1961] Director/Businessman [Australian]; Shu-Chen Yu [1971] Director [Taiwanese]

D.C.K. Concessions Limited
Incorporated: 19 May 1992 *Employees:* 1,414
Net Worth: £11,502,000 *Total Assets:* £22,324,000
Registered Office: DCK House, Station Court, Radford Way, Billericay, Essex, CM12 0DZ
Activities: Retail sale of watches and jewellery in specialised stores
Major Shareholder: Alan Richard Witzenfeld
Officers: Ian Matthew Byrne, Secretary; Lorraine Bottomley [1967] Retail Director; Ian Matthew Byrne [1962] Director/Chartered Accountant; Daniel John Colyer [1980] Director; Mark Mullens [1965] Director; Catherine Wallwork [1961] Retail Operations Director; Alan Richard Witzenfeld [1954] Director; Mark Joseph Witzenfeld [1982] Business Development Director

D.D.D. Limited
Incorporated: 16 May 1912 *Employees:* 304
Net Worth: £4,715,009 *Total Assets:* £27,138,234
Registered Office: 94 Rickmansworth Road, Watford, Herts, WD18 7JJ
Activities: Manufacture of basic pharmaceutical products
Parent: DDD Investments Limited
Officers: Carl Atkinson [1974] Director; Hanna Joy Coonagh [1972] Director; Digby Lawrence Spence Halsby [1976] Non Executive Director; Roger Harrison [1969] Managing Director; Simon Morris [1973] HR Director; Charles Philip Wadsworth [1962] Finance Director

D.H. Industries Limited
Incorporated: 17 March 1980 *Employees:* 60
Net Worth: £5,909,520 *Total Assets:* £12,252,316
Registered Office: Sullivan House, Fenton Way, Laindon, Essex, SS15 6TD
Activities: Machining
Shareholders: Howard Michael Sullivan; Pamasol Willi Maeder AG
Officers: Andrew Philip Snell Sheard, Secretary; Corinne Ruoss-Maeder [1965] Director; Marcel Ruoss-Maeder [1965] Director [Swiss]; Howard Michael Sullivan [1943] Director/Chemical Engineer; Paul Patrick Sullivan [1970] Director/Project Engineer

Daarasp LLP
Incorporated: 17 February 2004
Net Worth: £18,337,988 *Total Assets:* £18,595,234
Registered Office: 166 College Road, Harrow, Middlesex, HA1 1RA
Officers: John Alan Hall [1949] LLP Member; Niresh Patel [1956] LLP Member

Dabasia Estates LLP
Incorporated: 10 March 2016
Net Worth: £13,283,921 *Total Assets:* £18,089,284
Registered Office: c/o Albury Associates Limited, 79 College Road, Harrow, Middlesex, HA1 1BD
Officers: Davendra Laxmidas Dabasia [1979] Member; Laxmidas Premji Dabasia [1954] Member; Rama Laxmidas Dabasia [1957] Member; Sima Dabasia [1979] Member

S. Dad Limited
Incorporated: 4 June 1999
Net Worth: £9,056,960 *Total Assets:* £19,428,012
Registered Office: 3 Shelley Road, High Wycombe, Bucks, HP11 2UP
Activities: Other letting and operating of own or leased real estate
Shareholder: Safdar Dad
Officers: Safdar Dad, Secretary/Engineer; Tahira Dad, Secretary; Safdar Dad [1971] Director/Engineer

Dage Holdings Limited
Incorporated: 12 June 1997
Net Worth: £16,762,716 *Total Assets:* £17,540,268
Registered Office: 25 Faraday Road, Rabans Lane Industrial Area, Aylesbury, Bucks, HP19 8RY
Activities: Activities of head offices
Officers: Gina Anne Beredo [1974] Director/Laywer [American]; Liaqat Ali Sadiq [1961] Finance Director; Joseph Stockunas [1960] Director/Businessman [American]; Philip Vere [1956] Director/President

Dage Precision Industries Limited
Incorporated: 27 February 1992 *Employees:* 138
Net Worth: £26,065,836 *Total Assets:* £37,294,408
Registered Office: 25 Faraday Road, Rabans Lane Industrial Estate, Aylesbury, Bucks, HP19 8RY
Activities: Other manufacturing n.e.c.
Officers: Gina Anne Beredo [1974] Director/Laywer [American]; Liaqat Ali Sadiq [1961] Finance Director; Philip Vere [1956] Director/President

Dagless Holdings Limited
Incorporated: 8 February 1983 *Employees:* 213
Net Worth: £5,719,390 *Total Assets:* £10,527,657
Registered Office: Brigstock Road, Wisbech, Cambs, PE13 3JJ
Activities: Activities of head offices
Shareholders: Richard William Pennington; Simon Victor Smeeth
Officers: Carolyn Jane Smeeth, Secretary; Edmund Oliver Smeeth [1985] Director; Sam Peter Smeeth [1982] Director; Simon Victor Smeeth [1955] Director

Dagless Limited
Incorporated: 11 October 1945 *Employees:* 197
Net Worth: £5,533,326 *Total Assets:* £11,098,141
Registered Office: Brigstock Road, Wisbech, Cambs, PE13 3JJ
Activities: Manufacture of other products of wood; manufacture of articles of cork, straw and plaiting materials
Parent: Dagless Holdings Limited
Officers: Carolyn Jane Smeeth, Secretary; Carolyn Jane Smeeth [1958] Director/Secretary; Edmund Oliver Smeeth [1985] Director/Manager; Sam Peter Smeeth [1982] Director; Simon Victor Smeeth [1955] Director/Timber Importer

Dai Europe Ltd
Incorporated: 26 October 1984 *Employees:* 156
Net Worth: £4,299,000 *Total Assets:* £43,542,000
Registered Office: 3rd Floor, Block C, Westside, London Road, Apsley, Hemel Hempstead, Herts, HP3 9TD
Activities: Management consultancy activities other than financial management
Parent: DAI Global LLC
Officers: Erin Cerpa, Secretary; James John Boomgard [1954] Director [American]; Michael James Jakobowski [1960] Director [American]; Christopher Lockett [1963] Managing Director

Daiwater Investment Limited
Incorporated: 24 April 2017 *Employees:* 1,418
Net Worth: £734,065,024 *Total Assets:* £2,604,868,096
Registered Office: The Hub, Tamblin Way, Hatfield, Herts, AL10 9EZ
Activities: Activities of other holding companies n.e.c.
Shareholders: DIF Tamblin Limited; Infrastructure Investments (Affinity) Limited; Allianz SE
Officers: Timothy John William Monod, Secretary; Tom Goossens [1981] Investment Director [Dutch]; Jaroslava Korpancova [1974] Managing Director [Czech]; Anthony Charles Roper [1960] Investment Director; Angela Louise Roshier [1975] Director/Asset Manager; Scott Springett [1968] Director/Investment Management

Dalebrook Supplies Limited
Incorporated: 2 December 1992 *Employees:* 54
Net Worth: £6,830,121 *Total Assets:* £8,023,302
Registered Office: Aquila House, Waterloo Lane, Chelmsford, Essex, CM1 1BN
Activities: Manufacture of other plastic products
Parent: Tey Holdings Limited
Officers: Gillian Ruth Beresford, Secretary; Jennie Lee Knott [1967] Director; Leslie Spencer Linch [1943] Director

Dalin Limited
Incorporated: 8 June 2012
Net Worth Deficit: £10,614,570 *Total Assets:* £10,182,163
Registered Office: Hill House, Lowlands Road, Harrow, Middlesex, HA1 3EQ
Activities: Development of building projects
Major Shareholder: Donovan Gijsbertus Wijsmuller
Officers: Brian Martin Comer [1960] Director [Irish]; Luke Andrew Comer [1957] Director [Irish]

Dallas Burston Ashbourne Holdings Limited
Incorporated: 13 May 2002
Net Worth: £8,691,742 *Total Assets:* £9,415,455
Registered Office: Bampton Road, Harold Hill, Romford, Essex, RM3 8UG
Activities: Wholesale of pharmaceutical goods
Parent: Ethypharm Holdings UK Ltd
Officers: Roseline Georgette Joannesse [1959] Director/Vice President Legal Affairs [French]; Jean-Hugues Louis Marie Lecat [1956] Director [French]

J.E. & V.M. Dalton Limited
Incorporated: 22 April 1952 *Employees:* 44
Net Worth: £7,309,468 *Total Assets:* £11,306,765
Registered Office: Dalmark House, Eye, Peterborough, Cambs, PE6 7UD
Activities: Other manufacturing n.e.c.
Shareholders: Anthony John Dalton; Peter Duncan Fox
Officers: Matthew John Dalton, Secretary; Anthony John Dalton [1946] Director/Seed Representative; Linda Joyce Dalton [1950] Director/Secretary; Matthew John Dalton [1980] Director; Patrick Owen Dalton [1982] Director; Peter Duncan Fox [1962] Director/Production Manager; Ronald Francis Fox [1934] Director/Seed Representative; Emma Louise Windsor [1965] Director

Dalton Resources Limited
Incorporated: 26 October 2011
Net Worth Deficit: £647,768 *Total Assets:* £20,066,192
Registered Office: Suite 1, The Studio, St Nicholas Close, Elstree, Herts, WD6 3EW
Activities: Construction of commercial buildings
Major Shareholder: Iryna Simonchuk
Officers: Christiana Savva [1974] Director/Private Employee [Cypriot]; Iryna Simonchuk [1968] Deputy Director [Ukrainian]

Daly Holdings Limited
Incorporated: 23 December 2014 *Employees:* 86
Previous: Sky Holdings (UK) Limited
Net Worth: £5,350,709 *Total Assets:* £11,936,437
Registered Office: 167 Turners Hill, Cheshunt, Herts, EN8 9BH
Activities: Activities of insurance agents and brokers
Major Shareholder: Michael James Daly
Officers: Michael James Daly [1955] Director; Scott Forrester [1980] Director/Insurance Broker; Jae LEA Pearse [1975] Director/Insurance Broker

Damco UK Limited
Incorporated: 12 September 1984
Net Worth: £11,135,000 *Total Assets:* £37,533,000
Registered Office: Suffolk Place, Parker Avenue, Felixstowe, Suffolk, IP11 4BB
Activities: Sea and coastal freight water transport
Parent: A P Moller-Maersk A/S
Officers: Danielle Crawford, Secretary; Anthony Alan Akerman [1968] Managing Director; Dev Dhingra [1986] Finance Director [Indian]; Brian Godsafe [1957] Managing Director

Dame Alice Owen's School
Incorporated: 10 March 2011 *Employees:* 194
Net Worth: £35,776,000 *Total Assets:* £37,629,000
Registered Office: Dame Alice Owen's School, Dugdale Hill Lane, Potters Bar, Herts, EN6 2DU
Activities: General secondary education
Officers: Lona Hennigan, Secretary; Lucy Amelia Bailie [1972] Director/School Administrator; Nicholas Matthew Barnes [1974] Director; Timothy Eric Bonham [1952] Director; David John Barrington Burrowes [1969] Director/Lawyer; Monique Choudhuri [1961] Director/Management Consultant; Richard Hamilton Fleetwood Fuller [1960] Sales and Personnel Director, Fuller's; Seamus Joseph Gillen [1959] Director; Stephen Frederick Goodyear [1955] Director/CEO Youngs Brewery; Gary Kenneth Haigh [1964] Director/Retired; Sandra Dawn Huckle [1964] Director/Chartered Accountant; Peter Frederick John Knell [1945] Director/Hertsmere Borough Councillor; Daniel Latham [1993] Director/Teacher; Peter James Martin [1952] Director; Hannah Nemko [1975] Director/Headteacher; Andrew James Porter [1972] Director/Partner at Communications Agency; Jonathan Robinson [1975] Director/Teacher; Sally Louise Tanner [1964] Director/IBM Employee; Glenn Taylor [1967] Director; Charles Mortimer Tracy [1962] Director/Education Manager; Jacqueline Tyler [1971] Director/Administrator; Paul Richard Wells [1958] Director

Thomas Dane Limited
Incorporated: 12 January 1994 *Employees:* 17
Net Worth: £8,584,285 *Total Assets:* £12,709,585
Registered Office: 38 Market Square, Toddington, Dunstable, Beds, LU5 6BS
Activities: Retail sale of other second-hand goods in stores (not incl. antiques)
Major Shareholder: Thomas Kevin Surrey Dane
Officers: Thomas Kevin Surrey Dane [1961] Director/Art Dealer

Danes Educational Trust
Incorporated: 16 June 2011 *Employees:* 135
Previous: St. Clement Danes School
Net Worth: £22,237,000 *Total Assets:* £23,811,000
Registered Office: St Clement Danes School, Chenies Road, Chorleywood, Herts, WD3 6EW
Activities: General secondary education
Officers: Nils Michael Blythe [1956] Director/Communications Consultant; Rosemary Faunch [1954] Director/Management Consultant; Darren Franklin [1971] Contract Director; Rachel Gauke [1972] Director/Lawyer; Doctor Malcolm Frederick Green [1951] Director/Retired; Rosemary Elizabeth Hadfield [1946] Director; Rachel Althea Rodney Hatfield [1963] Director/Lawyer; Louise Marcelle Victoria Soden [1952] Director/Educational Consultant; Kathleen Maeve Unger [1956] Director/HR Manager; Dr Josephine Anne Valentine [1958] Director/Headteacher

Danfoss Limited
Incorporated: 29 April 1991 *Employees:* 227
Net Worth: £16,437,000 *Total Assets:* £31,494,000
Registered Office: 22 Wycombe End, Beaconsfield, Bucks, HP9 1NB
Activities: Other manufacturing n.e.c.
Officers: Torben Christensen [1966] Director [Danish]; Jens Garde Gad [1964] Director [Danish]; Marcus Postings [1962] Director; Anders Stahlschmidt [1967] Director/Lawyer [Danish]; Nick Andrew Wanless [1968] Director/Accountant

G.W. Daniels and Son Limited
Incorporated: 1 April 1946 *Employees:* 7
Net Worth: £12,332,956 *Total Assets:* £15,080,943
Registered Office: Home Farm, Hemsby, Great Yarmouth, Norfolk, NR29 4LE
Activities: Growing of cereals (except rice), leguminous crops and oil seeds
Major Shareholder: Felicity Daniels
Officers: Felicity Daniels, Secretary; Felicity Daniels [1948] Director/Housewife; Helen Mary Daniels [1926] Director/Housewife; Robert Daniels [1982] Director; Simon George Daniels [1952] Managing Director; William Daniels [1980] Director

Danzer UK Limited
Incorporated: 6 September 1978 *Employees:* 16
Net Worth: £6,120,000 *Total Assets:* £12,107,000
Registered Office: 46 Market Hill, Maldon, Essex, CM9 4QA
Activities: Agents involved in the sale of timber and building materials
Officers: Leigh Sarah Hawes, Secretary; James Robert Angel [1966] Commercial Director; Hans Joachim Danzer [1970] Director/General Manager [German]; Michael Evans [1958] Director/Salesman; Markus Pfister [1960] Director/General Manager [Swiss]; Kenneth Anthony Walsh [1960] Managing Director

Darktrace Limited
Incorporated: 10 June 2013 *Employees:* 362
Net Worth: £13,952,000 *Total Assets:* £40,862,000
Registered Office: Maurice Wilkes Building, St John's Innovation Park, Cowley Road, Cambridge, CB4 0DS
Activities: Business and domestic software development
Officers: Richard Eaton, Secretary; Vanessa Colomar [1973] Director; Nicole Eagan [1964] Director [American]; Andrew Mark Kanter [1969] Director/Attorney [American]; Philip Michael Pearson [1973] Director/Partner; Stephen Robert Shanley [1986] Director/Investor [American]; Johannes Kornelius Jan Sikkens [1978] Director [Dutch]; Robert Webb QC [1948] Director/Chairman

Dart Products Europe Ltd.
Incorporated: 12 May 1970 *Employees:* 496
Previous: Solo Cup Europe Limited
Net Worth: £56,706,000 *Total Assets:* £71,869,000
Registered Office: 3 Flaxley Road, Kingston Park, Peterborough, Cambs, PE2 9EN
Activities: Manufacture of other plastic products
Parent: Solo Cup (UK) Limited
Officers: Claire Theresa Dart [1929] Director/Businesswomen [American]; Robert Charles Dart [1958] Director/Businessman [Irish]; Thomas Lynn Jewell [1967] Director/Businessman [American]; James Donald Lammers [1959] Director/Businessman [American]

Dashtag
Incorporated: 31 October 1906
Net Worth: £15,005,000 *Total Assets:* £42,025,000
Registered Office: West Hill, Hertford Road, Hoddesdon, Herts, EN11 9BU
Activities: Activities of head offices
Parent: Schering-Plough Holdings Limited
Officers: Richard Robinski, Secretary; Louise Jane Houson [1976] Director; Simon Nicholson [1975] Director; Ebru Can Temucin [1972] Director [Turkish]

Dassault Systemes Biovia Limited
Incorporated: 7 December 1988 *Employees:* 104
Net Worth Deficit: £4,544,000 *Total Assets:* £10,988,000
Registered Office: Unit 334 Cambridge Science Park, Milton Road, Cambridge, CB4 0WN
Activities: Other research and experimental development on natural sciences and engineering
Parent: Dassault Systemes UK Limited
Officers: Jane Jenkins [1969] Finance Director; John Howard Kitchingman [1966] Managing Director; Leif Erik Pedersen [1964] Director [Danish]

Datapaq Limited
Incorporated: 13 December 1983 *Employees:* 25
Net Worth: £16,571,000 *Total Assets:* £18,165,000
Registered Office: 52 Hurricane Way, Norwich, NR6 6JB
Activities: Manufacture of other electrical equipment
Parent: TGA Industries Ltd
Officers: Vincent Gosling [1971] Site Director; Jeroen Van de Wiel [1974] Director/CFO EMEA [Dutch]; Herman Warnshuis [1964] Director/Business Executive [Dutch]

Lawrence David Limited
Incorporated: 26 April 1973 *Employees:* 258
Net Worth: £9,468,443 *Total Assets:* £32,392,168
Registered Office: Woodston Point, Shrewsbury Avenue, Peterborough, Cambs, PE2 7LB
Activities: Other engineering activities
Parent: Wielton S.A.
Officers: Paul Yallop, Secretary; Andrew Robert Dodge [1968] Director; Laurence David Marshall [1966] Managing Director; Jonathan Todd [1972] Director/Chief Financial Officer

C.E. Davidson Farms Ltd.
Incorporated: 12 May 1997
Net Worth: £6,590,070 *Total Assets:* £16,130,224
Registered Office: South View, Fressingfield, Eye, Suffolk, IP21 5PJ
Activities: Growing of cereals (except rice), leguminous crops and oil seeds
Major Shareholder: Peter Geoffrey Davidson
Officers: Peter Geoffrey Davidson, Secretary/Builders/Farmers; Bridget Ann Davidson [1956] Director/Builders/Farmers; Charles Peter Davidson [1986] Director; Nathan James Davidson [1983] Director; Peter Geoffrey Davidson [1955] Director/Builders/Farmers

Davis and Dann Limited
Incorporated: 26 March 1965 *Employees:* 9
Net Worth: £5,725,378 *Total Assets:* £14,469,876
Registered Office: Kanta House, Victoria Road, South Ruislip, Middlesex, HA4 0JQ
Activities: Wholesale of pharmaceutical goods
Officers: Satish Jamnadas Chatwani, Secretary; Jawahar Jamnadas Chatwani [1948] Director; Rashmi Jamnadas Chatwani [1954] Director; Satish Jamnadas Chatwani [1953] Director

Davis Schottlander & Davis Limited
Incorporated: 14 March 1952 *Employees:* 54
Net Worth: £5,905,310 *Total Assets:* £8,004,182
Registered Office: Fifth Avenue, Letchworth Garden City, Letchworth, Herts, SG6 2WD
Activities: Dental practice activities
Officers: Mark Seaman, Secretary; Dr Brian Dennis Schottlander [1943] Director/Dental Manufacturer; Ian James Schottlander [1974] Director; Susan Ann Schottlander [1947] Director/Dental Manufacturer

Davroc Limited
Incorporated: 7 February 1980 *Employees:* 186
Net Worth: £14,847,193 *Total Assets:* £17,936,524
Registered Office: Ibroc House, Essex Road, Hoddesdon, Herts, EN11 0QS
Activities: Agents involved in the sale of timber and building materials
Shareholders: Pietro Corbisiero; Giuseppe Corbisiero
Officers: Pietro Corbisiero, Secretary [Italian]; Giuseppe Corbisiero [1955] Director [Italian]; Pietro Corbisiero [1953] Director [Italian]

Dawe Estates Limited
Incorporated: 3 December 1996 *Employees:* 4
Net Worth: £7,541,234 *Total Assets:* £10,760,215
Registered Office: Fen View, 17a Broad Street, Ely, Cambs, CB7 4AJ
Activities: Growing of cereals (except rice), leguminous crops and oil seeds
Major Shareholder: Peter John Dawe
Officers: Dr Peter John Dawe [1954] Director/Entrepreneur; Susan Jane Dawe [1955] Director/Counsellor

Martin Dawn PLC
Incorporated: 3 November 1983 *Employees:* 3
Net Worth: £1,973,218 *Total Assets:* £13,624,930
Registered Office: Roots Hall Stadium, Southend on Sea, Essex, SS2 6NQ
Activities: Buying and selling of own real estate
Major Shareholder: Ronald Martin
Officers: Julie Dawn Martin, Secretary; Julie Dawn Martin [1961] Director/Secretary; Ronald Martin [1953] Director/Property Developer; Simon Patrick Wainwright [1957] Director/Chartered Surveyor

Dawson Books Limited
Incorporated: 20 April 2009 *Employees:* 98
Net Worth Deficit: £892,000 *Total Assets:* £15,899,000
Registered Office: 1 Broadland Business Park, Norwich, NR7 0WF
Activities: Non-specialised wholesale trade
Parent: Bertram Trading Limited
Officers: Nicholas David Goodwin [1963] Director/Chief Financial Officer; Stephen Edward Moon [1970] Director

Alan Day Investments LLP
Incorporated: 5 March 2010
Net Worth: £15,134,329 *Total Assets:* £15,300,143
Registered Office: Green Close Cottage, The Green, Sarratt, Rickmansworth, Herts, WD3 6AY
Officers: Alan Christian Day [1973] Member; Alan Edwin Day [1933] Member; Michael John Day [1963] Member; Stephen Robert Day [1958] Member

Day Webster Limited
Incorporated: 29 October 2009 *Employees:* 205
Net Worth: £3,710,449 *Total Assets:* £23,895,506
Registered Office: Treviot House, 186-192 High Road, Ilford, Essex, IG1 1LR
Activities: Other activities of employment placement agencies
Officers: Rebecca Louisa Woods Ballard, Secretary; Wayne Arthur St John [1974] Director; Daniel Jonathan Wise [1982] Director; Hugh William Woods Ballard [1968] Director

Dayla Holdings Limited
Incorporated: 26 January 1961 *Employees:* 93
Net Worth: £6,414,306 *Total Assets:* £10,505,968
Registered Office: Unit 2, 50 Aylesbury Road, Aston Clinton, Aylesbury, Bucks, HP22 5AH
Activities: Manufacture of soft drinks; production of mineral waters and other bottled waters
Shareholders: Timothy John Cooper; Susan Frances Lapham
Officers: Timothy John Cooper, Secretary; Timothy John Cooper [1957] Director/Soft Drinks Factor - Manufacturer

Daylighting Power Limited
Incorporated: 20 January 2012
Net Worth Deficit: £2,208,875 *Total Assets:* £8,141,984
Registered Office: 57 Belmont Lane, Stanmore, Middlesex, HA7 2PU
Activities: Other manufacturing n.e.c.
Officers: Alka Jasooja, Secretary; Alka Jasooja [1977] Director/Employee [Indian]

Days of Your Life Limited
Incorporated: 28 November 2006 *Employees:* 49
Net Worth: £1,145,741 *Total Assets:* £12,458,953
Registered Office: 1st Floor, 41-45 High Street, Saffron Walden, Essex, CB10 1AR
Activities: Agents involved in the sale of a variety of goods
Shareholders: Vicki Anne Foster; Shaun Powell
Officers: Stuart Neilege Miller, Secretary/Accountant [Irish]; Vicki Anne Foster [1978] Director; Martin Neal Leppard [1957] Director; Stuart Neilege Miller [1968] Director/Accountant [Irish]; Shaun Powell [1963] Director

DB Broadcast Ltd
Incorporated: 27 April 1992 *Employees:* 42
Net Worth: £4,954,744 *Total Assets:* £9,712,746
Registered Office: Kestrel House, Sedgeway Business Park, Witchford, Ely, Cambs, CB6 2HY
Activities: Other telecommunications activities
Parent: DB Broadcast Holdings Limited
Officers: Ross Amory [1982] Finance Director; David Jonathan Bird [1962] Managing Director; Graham Melvin Pearl [1961] Engineering Director; Thomas Edward Swan [1958] Director/Sales Manager

DB Investments Limited
Incorporated: 23 November 1995 *Employees:* 3
Net Worth: £24,287,684 *Total Assets:* £32,046,208
Registered Office: Haslers, Old Station Road, Loughton, Essex, IG10 4PL
Activities: Other business support service activities n.e.c.
Shareholders: David Howard Sanders; Barry Roy Peterson
Officers: David Howard Sanders, Secretary; Barry Roy Peterson [1953] Director; David Howard Sanders [1958] Director

DBCN Limited
Incorporated: 16 June 2016
Net Worth: £808,541 *Total Assets:* £10,778,467
Registered Office: Ground Floor, Unit 501 Centennial Park, Centennial Avenue, Elstree, Borehamwood, Herts, WD6 3FG
Activities: Fund management activities
Major Shareholder: Nicola Scott Knight
Officers: Nathaniel Julian Scott Knight [1973] Director/Media Consultant; Adrian Jeremy Scott Knight [1940] Director/Retired; Benedict John Scott Knight [1969] Director; Nicola Scott Knight [1945] Director/Retired

DBD Distribution Limited
Incorporated: 30 January 1990 *Employees:* 175
Net Worth: £2,813,304 *Total Assets:* £13,918,050
Registered Office: Boundary Park, Boundary Way, Hemel Hempstead, Herts, HP2 7GE
Activities: Other specialised construction activities n.e.c.
Parent: DBD Enterprises Ltd
Officers: Michael Geoffrey Taylor, Secretary; John Martin Appleyard [1961] Operations Director; Dr Samuel David Firth-Bernard [1981] Managing Director; Neil Harvey [1965] Financial Director; Michael Geoffrey Taylor [1954] Director/Chairman

DBD Enterprises Limited
Incorporated: 2 June 2011 *Employees:* 175
Net Worth: £1,119,836 *Total Assets:* £13,241,074
Registered Office: Boundary Park, Boundary Way, Hemel Hempstead, Herts, HP2 7GE
Activities: Non-trading company
Major Shareholder: Samuel David Firth-Bernard
Officers: Dr Samuel David Firth-Bernard [1981] Director; Neil Harvey [1965] Financial Director

DC Management Services Limited
Incorporated: 3 September 1986 *Employees:* 413
Net Worth: £23,249,000 *Total Assets:* £83,639,000
Registered Office: Unit 1 Martinbridge Estate, Lincoln Road, Enfield, Middlesex, EN1 1SP
Activities: Other letting and operating of own or leased real estate
Parent: DCMS Holdings Limited
Officers: Benjamin James Collins [1977] Managing Director; Jodie Collins [1980] Director; Megan Sarah Collins [1986] Director; Nicholas John Davis [1978] Director; Richard Ennis [1975] Director; Patrick James O'Donnell [1949] Director; Peter David Williams [1971] Director/Accountant [Australian]

DCI Group Limited
Incorporated: 31 January 2007 *Employees:* 356
Net Worth: £3,603,714 *Total Assets:* £32,740,788
Registered Office: Violet Hill Road, Stowmarket, Suffolk, IP14 1NN
Activities: Activities of head offices
Parent: DCI Group Holdings Limited
Officers: Simon Eric Hobson, Secretary; Debra Biggin [1962] Director; John Antony William Biggin [1961] Managing Director; Lisa Caroline Hobson [1968] Director; Simon Eric Hobson [1966] Finance Director

DCK Group Limited
Incorporated: 15 March 2005 *Employees:* 1,414
Net Worth: £4,799,000 *Total Assets:* £22,238,000
Registered Office: Porters House, Station Court, Radford Way, Billericay, Essex, CM12 0DZ
Activities: Activities of head offices
Shareholders: Alan Richard Witzenfeld; Lyetta Witzenfeld
Officers: Ian Matthew Byrne, Secretary/Director; Ian Matthew Byrne [1962] Director; Alan Richard Witzenfeld [1954] Director

DDD Investments Limited
Incorporated: 1 June 2004 *Employees:* 304
Net Worth: £5,322,656 *Total Assets:* £27,611,426
Registered Office: 94 Rickmansworth Road, Watford, Herts, WD18 7JJ
Activities: Activities of head offices
Officers: Carl Atkinson [1974] Director; Hanna Joy Coonagh [1972] Director; Digby Lawrence Spence Halsby [1976] Director; Roger Harrison [1969] Managing Director; Simon Morris [1973] HR Director; Charles Philip Wadsworth [1962] Finance Director

DDW Holdings Limited
Incorporated: 23 May 2017 *Employees:* 508
Net Worth: £3,783,000 *Total Assets:* £11,371,000
Registered Office: 14-14a Rectory Road, Benfleet, Essex, SS7 2ND
Activities: Activities of head offices
Shareholders: Cornelius Andrew Donovan; Mark Donovan; Frances Ann Watkins
Officers: Frances Ann Watkins, Secretary; Cornelius Andrew Donovan [1970] Director; Mark Donovan [1961] Director

De Lage Landen Leasing Limited
Incorporated: 4 May 1989 *Employees:* 176
Net Worth: £153,748,992 *Total Assets:* £1,721,616,000
Registered Office: Building 7, Croxley Park, Hatters Lane, Watford, Herts, WD18 8YN
Activities: Financial leasing
Parent: De Lage Landen Limited
Officers: Duncan John Hullis [1963] Director/General Manager; Vijay Chandulal Shah [1969] Director/Country Finance Manager; Simon John Trudgeon [1968] Director/Credit Risk Officer

De Lage Landen Limited
Incorporated: 17 December 1992
Net Worth: £78,956,000 *Total Assets:* £79,230,000
Registered Office: Building 7, Croxley Park, Hatters Lane, Watford, Herts, WD18 8YN
Activities: Activities of head offices
Parent: De Lage Landen International B.V.
Officers: Duncan John Hullis [1963] Director/General Manager; Simon John Trudgeon [1968] Director/Credit Risk Officer; Bas Van Asseldonk [1977] Director/Executive Vice President [Dutch]

De Sangosse Ltd.
Incorporated: 11 November 1993 *Employees:* 10
Net Worth: £9,681,441 *Total Assets:* £13,159,320
Registered Office: Hillside Mill, Quarry Lane, Swaffham Bulbeck, Cambridge, CB25 0LU
Activities: Wholesale of chemical products
Officers: Keith French, Secretary; Doctor David George Cameron [1957] Managing Director; Christophe Maquin [1963] Marketing Director [French]; Jean Michel Maurer [1965] Director/Financial and Administrative [French]

De Soutter Medical Limited
Incorporated: 26 February 1996 *Employees:* 124
Net Worth: £12,595,548 *Total Assets:* £17,021,444
Registered Office: 1 Halton Brook Business Park, Weston Road, Aston Clinton, Aylesbury, Bucks, HP22 5WF
Activities: Manufacture of medical and dental instruments and supplies
Parent: Descram Limited
Officers: Clare Dovey, Secretary; Anna Maria Desoutter [1954] Director [German]; Charles Robert Desoutter [1954] Director/Engineer; George Charles Desoutter [1978] Director/Engineer; Max Roger Desoutter [1980] Director; Roger Charles Desoutter [1923] Director; Alexandra Rose Wansbrough [1977] Director

Thomas Deacon Education Trust
Incorporated: 1 April 2004 *Employees:* 482
Previous: TDA Education Trust
Net Worth: £37,048,000 *Total Assets:* £45,750,000
Registered Office: The Thomas Deacon Academy, Queens Gardens, Peterborough, Cambs, PE1 2UW
Activities: Pre-primary education
Officers: Simon John Smith, Secretary; Dr Richard Barnes [1946] Director/Senior Tutor; Paul Antony Clegg [1959] Director/Manager; Mohamedraza Yusufali Mavani [1976] Director/Accountant; Kelly Peck [1976] Director/Solicitor; Mark James Potter [1974] Director/Headmaster; Saqib Rehman [1978] Director; Simon John Smith [1973] Director of Resources; Julie Ann Taylor [1961] Director/Principal; Eric William Winstone [1951] Director/Retired

Deanplan Limited
Incorporated: 3 April 1969
Net Worth: £2,945,082 *Total Assets:* £36,345,976
Registered Office: Atlas House, 28 Great Cambridge Road, Enfield, Middlesex, EN1 1UU
Activities: Other letting and operating of own or leased real estate
Officers: Judith Erlich, Secretary; Baruch Erlich [1962] Director/Solicitor; Judith Erlich [1960] Director/Secretary

Robert Deards Limited
Incorporated: 4 June 1931 *Employees:* 3
Net Worth: £20,599,876 *Total Assets:* £21,579,480
Registered Office: Plantagenet House, 4 Plantagenet Road, New Barnet, Herts, EN5 5JQ
Activities: Other letting and operating of own or leased real estate
Major Shareholder: Christopher Edward Scarfe
Officers: Nicholas James Scarfe, Secretary; Nicholas James Scarfe [1992] Director

Deards Services Limited
Incorporated: 6 March 1937 *Employees:* 1
Net Worth: £22,508,088 *Total Assets:* £25,868,690
Registered Office: Plantagenet House, 4 Plantagenet Road, New Barnet, Herts, EN5 5JQ
Activities: Other letting and operating of own or leased real estate
Major Shareholder: Christopher Edward Scarfe
Officers: Nicholas James Scarfe, Secretary; Nicholas James Scarfe [1992] Director

Deben Group Industries Limited
Incorporated: 29 April 1993 *Employees:* 41
Net Worth: £11,360,591 *Total Assets:* £14,629,955
Registered Office: Avocet House, Wilford Bridge Road, Melton, Woodbridge, Suffolk, IP12 1RB
Activities: Wholesale of household goods (other than musical instruments) n.e.c
Parent: Avocet Capital Ltd
Officers: Stephanie Ruth Walker, Secretary; Ashley Paul Walker [1973] Director; Paul Howard Walker [1949] Director; Stephanie Ruth Walker [1947] Director; Stephen Andrew Walker [1975] Director Procurement

Deekay Investments Limited
Incorporated: 27 June 1972 *Employees:* 4
Net Worth: £7,491,810 *Total Assets:* £12,999,221
Registered Office: Kimberley House, 31 Burnt Oak Broadway, Edgware, Middlesex, HA8 5LD
Activities: Other letting and operating of own or leased real estate
Parent: Paru Limited
Officers: Neel Mahendra Shah, Secretary; Khimchand Hansraj Chandaria [1935] Director; Nirmala Khimcand Chandaria [1937] Director; Bindi Holding [1956] Director; Neel Mahendra Shah [1974] Director

Defaqto Group Limited
Incorporated: 4 May 2005 *Employees:* 3
Net Worth: £26,865,056 *Total Assets:* £29,360,876
Registered Office: Financial Research Centre, Haddenham Business Park, Pegasus Way, Haddenham, Aylesbury, Bucks, HP17 8LJ
Activities: Activities of head offices
Parent: Regulus Bidco Limited
Officers: Remko Peter Bijtjes [1971] Director/Sales Executive [Dutch]; Syed Zahid Hussain Bilgrami [1971] Director/Executive; Alastair Colin Gillies Brown [1974] Director/Accountant

Defaqto Ltd
Incorporated: 9 November 1993 *Employees:* 120
Net Worth: £6,020,540 *Total Assets:* £10,212,446
Registered Office: Financial Research Centre, Pegasus Way, Haddenham, Aylesbury, Bucks, HP17 8LJ
Activities: Market research and public opinion polling
Parent: Regulus Bidco Limited
Officers: Remko Peter Bijtjes [1971] Director/Sales Executive [Dutch]; Syed Zahid Hussain Bilgrami [1971] Director/Executive; Alastair Colin Gillies Brown [1974] Director/Accountant

Defender No.1 Production Limited Liability Partnership
Incorporated: 25 September 2003
Net Worth: £11,651,940 *Total Assets:* £14,335,035
Registered Office: 99 Kenton Road, Harrow, London, HA3 0AN
Officers: Joerg Birkholz [1964] LLP Member; Nicholas Mark Brown [1962] LLP Member; Neil John Campbell [1970] LLP Member; Stephen Brian Dainton [1967] LLP Member; David Michael Gorton [1963] LLP Member; Tahir Roland Khan Gandapur [1961] LLP Member; John Robert King [1960] LLP Member; Luigi La Vecchia [1967] LLP Member; Vittorio Martino [1965] LLP Member; Ian James McBride [1961] LLP Member; Adrian Mutu [1979] LLP Member; Michael Alexander Northeast Roffey [1966] LLP Member; Angus John Drennan Wink [1967] LLP Member

Defender No.1 Sale & Leaseback Limited Liability Partnership
Incorporated: 25 September 2003
Net Worth: £13,889,142 *Total Assets:* £13,907,090
Registered Office: 99 Kenton Road, Harrow, London, HA3 0AN
Officers: Joerg Birkholz [1964] LLP Member; Nicholas Mark Brown [1962] LLP Member; Neil John Campbell [1970] LLP Member; Stephen Brian Dainton [1967] LLP Member; David Michael Gorton [1963] LLP Member; Tahir Roland Khan-Gandapur [1961] LLP Member; John Robert King [1960] LLP Member; Luigi La Vecchia [1967] LLP Member; Vittorio Martino [1965] LLP Member; Ian James McBride [1961] LLP Member; Adrian Mutu [1979] LLP Member; Michael Alexander Northeast Roffey [1966] LLP Member; Angus John Drennan Wink [1967] LLP Member

Defender No.2 Production Limited Liability Partnership
Incorporated: 25 September 2003
Net Worth: £9,593,878 *Total Assets:* £11,763,425
Registered Office: 99 Kenton Road, Harrow, London, HA3 0AN
Officers: Martin Jeffrey Stewart Bates [1970] LLP Member; Stuart Andrew Clark [1971] LLP Member; Bobby Console-Verma [1966] LLP Member; Jevin John Davis [1970] LLP Member; Thomas Stefan Duetoft [1964] LLP Member; Justin Garth Excell [1965] LLP Member; Kevin Lindsay Fordham [1954] LLP Member; Matthew Haigh [1972] LLP Member; John Hitchcox [1961] LLP Member; Trevor Neil Hubner [1968] LLP Member; Jeremy Griffith Hughes [1962] LLP Member; Stephanie Judith Jerron-Quarshie [1965] LLP Member; Tom Martin Johannessen [1970] LLP Member; David Michael Kingham [1967] LLP Member; Timothy John Peat [1961] LLP Member; Margaret Robertson [1962] LLP Member; Darren John Sharp [1967] LLP Member

Defender No.2 Sale & Leaseback Limited Liability Partnership
Incorporated: 25 September 2003
Net Worth: £10,766,310 *Total Assets:* £10,773,785
Registered Office: 99 Kenton Road, Harrow, London, HA3 0AN
Officers: Martin Jeffrey Stewart Bates [1970] LLP Member; Bobby Console-Verma [1966] LLP Member; Jevin John Davis [1970] LLP Member; Thomas Stefan Duetoft [1964] LLP Member; Justin Garth Excell [1965] LLP Member; Kevin Lindsay Fordham [1954] LLP Member; Matthew Haigh [1972] LLP Member; John Hitchcox [1961] LLP Member; Trevor Neil Hubner [1968] LLP Member; Jeremy Griffith Hughes [1962] LLP Member; Tom Martin Johannessen [1970] LLP Member; Timothy John Peat [1961] LLP Member; Margaret Robertson [1962] LLP Member; Darren John Sharp [1967] LLP Member

Delamode PLC
Incorporated: 19 February 1999 *Employees:* 99
Net Worth: £1,518,580 *Total Assets:* £11,749,829
Registered Office: 700 Avenue West, Skyline 120, Braintree, Essex, CM77 7AA
Activities: Freight transport by road
Officers: Shaun Roy Godfrey [1966] Director; Danor Ionescu [1969] Director/CEO of Logistics [Romanian]

Delbanco Meyer & Company Limited
Incorporated: 27 August 1936 *Employees:* 2
Net Worth: £18,656,000 *Total Assets:* £19,346,000
Registered Office: P O Box 772, 8 Beechwood Avenue, Chorleywood, Rickmansworth, Herts, WD3 5RL
Activities: Development of building projects
Shareholder: Jonathan Hugh Rose
Officers: Edmund Anthony William Kramers, Secretary; Edmund Anthony William Kramers [1953] Director; Jonathan Hugh Rose [1958] Director/Chairman

Deltech Europe Limited
Incorporated: 19 June 2000 *Employees:* 33
Net Worth: £11,991,451 *Total Assets:* £14,673,403
Registered Office: Piperell Way, Haverhill, Suffolk, CB9 8PH
Activities: Manufacture of plastics in primary forms
Officers: Robert Elefante [1949] Director [American]

Demipower (1991) Limited
Incorporated: 7 November 1991 *Employees:* 609
Net Worth: £1,107,776 *Total Assets:* £22,569,406
Registered Office: Jubilee House, 7-9 The Oaks, Ruislip, Middlesex, HA4 7LF
Activities: Unlicenced restaurants and cafes
Shareholders: Amirali Hassanali Moledina Janmohamed; Alim Amirali Janmohamed
Officers: Alim Amirali Janmohamed, Company Secretary; Alim Amirali Janmohamed [1981] Director; Amirali Hassanali Moledina Janmohamed [1952] Director

Demipower Limited
Incorporated: 31 January 1989 *Employees:* 776
Net Worth: £3,531,754 *Total Assets:* £23,874,314
Registered Office: Jubilee House, 7-9 The Oaks, Ruislip, Middlesex, HA4 7LF
Activities: Unlicenced restaurants and cafes
Shareholders: Amirali Hassanali Moledina Janmohamed; Alim Amirali Janmohamed
Officers: Alim Amirali Janmohamed, Company Secretary; Alim Amirali Janmohamed [1981] Director; Amirali Hassanali Moledina Janmohamed [1952] Director/Fast Food Catering

Denbourne Investments Limited
Incorporated: 20 November 1980 *Employees:* 4
Net Worth: £7,013,955 *Total Assets:* £9,918,081
Registered Office: Salisbury House, 81 High Street, Potters Bar, Herts, EN6 5AS
Activities: Buying and selling of own real estate
Shareholders: Kyriacos Neocleous; Keti Neocleous
Officers: Keti Neocleous, Company Secretary; Kyriacos Neocleous [1955] Director

Dencora (Watford) LLP
Incorporated: 1 August 2014
Net Worth: £9,402,367 *Total Assets:* £11,708,090
Registered Office: Dencora Court, 2 Meridian Way, Norwich, NR7 0TA

Dencora 2000 Limited
Incorporated: 15 September 2000 *Employees:* 12
Net Worth: £48,861,712 *Total Assets:* £94,873,824
Registered Office: Dencora Court, 2 Meridian Way, Norwich, NR7 0TA
Activities: Buying and selling of own real estate
Shareholder: Joseph King
Officers: Oliver Burnett Chipperfield, Secretary/Director; Christopher Hugh Bradley-Watson [1957] Director/Chartered Surveyor; Oliver Burnett Chipperfield [1957] Director; Andrew William King [1980] Director/Chartered Surveyor; Edward Joseph King [1976] Director

Dencora Dereham Retail Partnership LLP
Incorporated: 16 February 2004
Net Worth: £8,150,074 *Total Assets:* £15,517,410
Registered Office: Dencora Court, Meridian Way, Norwich, NR7 0TA

Dencora Estates Limited
Incorporated: 11 January 2001
Net Worth: £16,825,342 *Total Assets:* £20,625,876
Registered Office: Dencora Court, 2 Meridian Way, Norwich, NR7 0TA
Activities: Other letting and operating of own or leased real estate
Parent: Dencora 2000 Limited
Officers: Oliver Burnett Chipperfield, Secretary/Director; Christopher Hugh Bradley-Watson [1957] Director; Oliver Burnett Chipperfield [1957] Director/Accountant; Andrew William King [1980] Director/Chartered Surveyor; Edward Joseph King [1976] Director

Denecroft Estates Limited
Incorporated: 31 July 1947 *Employees:* 4
Net Worth: £14,240,615 *Total Assets:* £19,275,098
Registered Office: York House, Empire Way, Wembley, Middlesex, HA9 0FQ
Activities: Development of building projects
Parent: UK Real Estate Limited
Officers: Jeremy Louis Landau, Secretary; Nicholas John Capstick-Dale [1962] Director

Dengie Crops Limited
Incorporated: 14 December 1988 *Employees:* 86
Net Worth: £9,340,915 *Total Assets:* £14,795,695
Registered Office: Hall Road, Asheldham, Southminster, Essex, CM0 7JF
Activities: Other manufacturing n.e.c.
Officers: Angela Downs, Secretary; John David Fisher [1954] Director/Farmer; Ian Robert Hassard [1957] Director; Simon Alfred Hollington [1960] Director/Farmer; Peter John Lodge [1941] Director/Retired; Robert Charles Malden [1955] Director; Christopher John Mee [1958] Director/Farmer; Nicholas Peter Mee [1960] Director/Farmer; Robert Lincoln Procter [1945] Director/Farmer; Michael Lawrence Austin Pudney [1945] Director; Martin Antony Smith [1962] Director/Farmer

Denland Limited
Incorporated: 25 November 2015
Net Worth: £3 *Total Assets:* £44,881,004
Registered Office: Hill House, Lowlands Road, Harrow, Middlesex, HA1 3EQ
Activities: Development of building projects
Major Shareholder: Donovan Gijsbertus Wijsmuller
Officers: Brian Martin Comer [1960] Director [Irish]; Luke Andrew Comer [1957] Director [Irish]

Denny Bros Holdings Limited
Incorporated: 26 January 1995 *Employees:* 107
Net Worth: £21,673,254 *Total Assets:* £22,743,674
Registered Office: Kempson Way, Bury St Edmunds, Suffolk, IP32 7AR
Activities: Other letting and operating of own or leased real estate
Shareholder: Barry Douglas Denny
Officers: Andrew Haig Denny, Secretary; Andrew Haig Denny [1969] Director/Chartered Accountant; Barry Douglas Denny [1949] Director/Printer; Graham Dennis Denny [1962] Director/Print Manager

Densitron Technologies Limited
Incorporated: 21 November 1985 *Employees:* 5
Previous: Densitron Technologies PLC
Net Worth: £6,870,363 *Total Assets:* £10,169,522
Registered Office: Aisle Barn, 100 High Street, Balsham, Cambridge, CB21 4EP
Activities: Activities of head offices
Parent: Quixant PLC
Officers: Woon Hing Allen Chong [1969] Director; Heather Jane Hall [1974] Finance Director; Nicholas Charles Leopold Jarmany [1961] Chief Executive Director; Jonathan Francis Jayal [1982] Director; Gary Paul Mullins [1971] Director

Denso Automotive UK Ltd.
Incorporated: 1 January 1984 *Employees:* 197
Previous: Denso Sales UK Ltd.
Net Worth: £8,366,000 *Total Assets:* £14,688,000
Registered Office: Breakspear Place, Breakspear Park, Hemel Hempstead, Herts, HP2 4TZ
Activities: Wholesale trade of motor vehicle parts and accessories
Parent: Denso International UK Ltd
Officers: Gerko Bernard Dekker, Secretary; Richard John Henson [1953] Director/Business Executive; Yuji Ishizuka [1961] Director/Head of OE Sales EU [Japanese]; Alan William Richards [1962] Managing Director

Dentex Healthcare Group Limited
Incorporated: 3 July 2014 *Employees:* 16
Net Worth: £25,708,708 *Total Assets:* £31,000,684
Registered Office: Nicholas House, River Front, Enfield, Middlesex, EN1 3FG
Activities: Dental practice activities
Officers: Mark Frederick Bonar Cockburn [1956] Director; Barry Koors Lanesman [1959] Director [South African]; Justin Colin Rodrigues [1987] Director; Eben Andries Van Heerden [1970] Director [South African]; David Allan Vinokur [1979] Director/Private Equity [South African]; Michael Brent Zurowski [1965] Director/Chief Financial Officer

Denville Hall 2012
Incorporated: 9 August 2012 *Employees:* 63
Net Worth: £16,390,921 *Total Assets:* £16,574,064
Registered Office: Denville Hall, 62 Ducks Hill Road, Northwood, Middlesex, HA6 2SB
Activities: Residential care activities for the elderly and disabled
Officers: Richard Langley Berry [1950] Director/Retired; Hemlata Bountra [1960] Director/Accountant; Joanna David [1940] Director/Actress; Generaldine James Blatchley OBE [1950] Director/Actress; Derek Lamden [1949] Director/Front of House Manager; Louisa MacGregor Rix [1955] Director/Interior Designer; The Honourable Sarah Jill Ward [1951] Director/Actor and Artist

Derby School Solutions (Holdings) Limited
Incorporated: 10 March 2004
Net Worth Deficit: £2,788,000 *Total Assets:* £19,464,000
Registered Office: Astral House, Imperial Way, Watford, Herts, WD24 4WW
Activities: Activities of head offices
Parent: Infrastructure Investments Holdings Limited
Officers: Ian Hudson, Secretary; David Wyn Davies [1968] Director/Accountant; Hannah Holman [1980] Director

Derby School Solutions Limited
Incorporated: 12 March 2004
Net Worth Deficit: £2,788,000 *Total Assets:* £19,464,000
Registered Office: Astral House, Imperial Way, Watford, Herts, WD24 4WW
Activities: Combined facilities support activities
Parent: Derby School Solutions (Holdings) Limited
Officers: Ian Hudson, Secretary; David Wyn Davies [1968] Director/Accountant; Hannah Holman [1980] Director

The Derbyshire Hotel Derby Limited
Incorporated: 25 June 2007
Previous: Venice Regal Derby Limited
Net Worth: £456,969 *Total Assets:* £13,964,061
Registered Office: 1st Floor, Monument House, 215 Marsh Road, Pinner, Middlesex, HA5 5NE
Activities: Hotels and similar accommodation
Parent: Serani Hotels Ltd
Officers: Rajiv Dhirendra Nathwani [1988] Director/Financier

Dermal Laboratories Limited
Incorporated: 2 November 1981 *Employees:* 146
Net Worth: £30,581,380 *Total Assets:* £40,770,980
Registered Office: Haslers, Old Station Road, Loughton, Essex, IG10 4PL
Activities: Manufacture of pharmaceutical preparations
Parent: Diomed Developments Limited
Officers: Andrew James Head, Secretary; Michael Jonathan Yarrow [1947] Director

Dernford Holdings Limited
Incorporated: 28 September 2005 *Employees:* 5
Net Worth: £9,419,753 *Total Assets:* £12,588,449
Registered Office: 3 Trust Court, Vision Park, Histon, Cambridge, CB24 9PW
Activities: Activities of head offices
Officers: Derek Arthur Dazeley [1932] Director/Chartered Surveyor; Simon James Dazeley [1958] Director/Chartered Surveyor; David James Foord [1961] Director; Elizabeth Mary January [1944] Director/Artist

Derrick Services (UK) Limited
Incorporated: 6 December 2007 *Employees:* 67
Net Worth: £4,337,250 *Total Assets:* £9,169,629
Registered Office: Falcongate House, Faraday Road, Harfreys Industrial Estate, Great Yarmouth, Norfolk, NR31 0NF
Activities: Repair of other equipment
Officers: Mark Chandler [1968] Director/Chief Operating Officer; Amit Jain [1980] Director [Indian]; John Ivan Knights [1955] Director/Chief Financial Officer; Abhishek Kumar [1978] Director/Chairman [Indian]; Mark Thomas Michael Prendergast [1965] Director

Descram Holdings Limited
Incorporated: 23 November 1988 *Employees:* 193
Net Worth: £35,068,336 *Total Assets:* £40,742,104
Registered Office: 1 Halton Brook Business Park, Weston Road, Aston Clinton, Aylesbury, Bucks, HP22 5WF
Activities: Activities of head offices
Shareholder: Charles Robert Desoutter
Officers: Clare Dovey, Secretary; Charles Robert Desoutter [1954] Director/Engineer; George Charles Desoutter [1978] Director/Engineer; Maximillian Roger Desoutter [1980] Director; Roger Charles Desoutter [1923] Director; William Paul Desoutter [1982] Director; Alexandra Rose Wansbrough [1977] Director

Desilu Group Limited
Incorporated: 19 April 1971
Net Worth: £16,563,979 *Total Assets:* £19,674,460
Registered Office: First Floor, Woodgate Studios, 2-8 Games Road, Cockfosters, Barnet, Herts, EN4 9HN
Activities: Buying and selling of own real estate
Shareholder: Christopher Joseph
Officers: Eleanor Joseph, Secretary; George Josife [1962] Director

Desiman Limited
Incorporated: 21 January 1997 *Employees:* 7
Net Worth: £25,283,052 *Total Assets:* £52,780,984
Registered Office: Kingsbridge House, 601 London Road, Westcliff on Sea, Essex, SS0 9PE
Activities: Other letting and operating of own or leased real estate
Shareholders: Hilary Corder; Paul Fellows
Officers: Marc Ormerod Atkinson, Secretary; Marc Ormerod Atkinson [1964] Director/Solicitor; Paul Terence Fellows [1969] Director/Developer

Desira Group PLC
Incorporated: 19 March 1990 *Employees:* 249
Net Worth: £3,639,555 *Total Assets:* £21,459,128
Registered Office: Victoria Road, Diss, Norfolk, IP22 4GS
Activities: Sale of new cars and light motor vehicles
Parent: Desira Holdings PLC
Officers: Michelle Suzanne Gant, Secretary/Director; John Paul Desira [1948] Director/Garage Proprietor; Susan Margaret Desira [1949] Director; Michelle Suzanne Gant [1974] Marketing Director; Stuart Peter Stone [1969] Managing Director

Desira Holdings PLC
Incorporated: 4 October 2002 *Employees:* 249
Net Worth: £8,312,094 *Total Assets:* £28,745,720
Registered Office: Victoria Road, Diss, Norfolk, IP22 4GS
Activities: Sale of new cars and light motor vehicles
Major Shareholder: John Paul Desira
Officers: Michelle Suzanne Gant, Secretary; John Paul Desira [1948] Director; Paul Andrew James Desira [1983] Director; Susan Margaret Desira [1949] Director; Michelle Suzanne Gant [1974] Marketing Director; Charlotte Marie Garvey [1978] Director/Home Maker; Stuart Peter Stone [1969] Managing Director; Juliette Louise Taylor [1976] Director/Home Maker

Deuce Acquisitions Limited
Incorporated: 19 August 2013 *Employees:* 4,611
Net Worth Deficit: £58,326,000 *Total Assets:* £752,817,984
Registered Office: The Hangar, Mosquito Way, Hatfield Business Park, Hatfield, Herts, AL10 9AX
Activities: Activities of head offices
Parent: Deuce Midco Limited
Officers: Patrick James Burrows [1967] Director/Chartered Accountant; Manjit Dale [1965] Director/Investment Professional; Donald Glenn Earlam [1965] Director; Scott Anthony Lloyd [1975] Director; Brian Jonathan Magnus [1966] Director/Partner, Private Equity; Peter William Phillipson [1954] Director [Irish]; Mark Andrew Stephens [1982] Director/Investment Professional [Irish]

Deuce Holdco Limited
Incorporated: 19 August 2013 *Employees:* 4,611
Net Worth Deficit: £51,150,000 *Total Assets:* £753,836,992
Registered Office: The Hangar, Mosquito Way, Hatfield Business Park, Hatfield, Herts, AL10 9AX
Activities: Activities of head offices
Parent: Deuce Topco Limited
Officers: Brian Jonathan Magnus [1966] Director/Partner, Private Equity; Mark Andrew Stephens [1982] Director/Investment Professional [Irish]

Deutsche Telekom (UK) Limited
Incorporated: 15 March 2000 *Employees:* 22
Net Worth: £32,518,000 *Total Assets:* £56,534,000
Registered Office: Alchemy Building, Bessemer Road, Welwyn Garden City, Herts, AL7 1HE
Activities: Other telecommunications activities
Parent: Deutsche Telekom AG
Officers: Sasha Marchant, Secretary; Claire Sandra Hilton [1958] Director/Telecommunications; Michaela Klitsch [1968] Director [German]; Uli Kuhbacher [1961] Director/General Counsel [German]; Daniel Meredith [1973] Director; Thorsten Mueller [1973] Director [German]; James Timothy Rowe [1967] Director

Devantier Group Limited
Incorporated: 14 May 2008 *Employees:* 3
Net Worth: £8,857,494 *Total Assets:* £10,798,694
Registered Office: 2 Primes Corner, Histon, Cambridge, CB24 9AG
Activities: Activities of head offices
Major Shareholder: Christopher Robert Dyason
Officers: Christopher Robert Dyason [1948] Director

Devantier Properties Limited
Incorporated: 3 May 1988
Net Worth: £4,740,328 *Total Assets:* £10,180,069
Registered Office: 2 Primes Corner, Histon, Cambridge, CB24 9AG
Activities: Other letting and operating of own or leased real estate
Major Shareholder: Christopher Robert Dyason
Officers: Christopher Robert Dyason, Secretary; Christopher Robert Dyason [1948] Director

Devitt Insurance Services Limited
Incorporated: 2 November 1989 *Employees:* 138
Net Worth: £3,010,486 *Total Assets:* £10,450,637
Registered Office: North House, St Edwards Way, Romford, Essex, RM1 3PP
Activities: Activities of insurance agents and brokers
Parent: CKH Limited
Officers: Anthony Edward Chapman [1962] Director/Accountant; William James Hughes [1971] Managing Director

DFKA Intermediate Limited
Incorporated: 25 August 2006
Net Worth: £76,214,000 *Total Assets:* £76,214,000
Registered Office: 38 Barnard Road, Bowthorpe Employment Area, Norwich, NR5 9JP
Activities: Activities of head offices
Parent: Campbell Soup Company
Officers: Katherine Susan Atkinson, Secretary; Carlos Arturo Abrams-Rivera [1967] Director [American]; Ashley James Hicks [1974] Managing Director; Thomas Smith [1955] Director [American]

DFKA Ltd
Incorporated: 22 January 2010 *Employees:* 3
Net Worth: £136,385,856 *Total Assets:* £406,983,200
Registered Office: 38 Barnard Road, Bowthorpe Employment Area, Norwich, NR5 9JP
Activities: Activities of head offices
Parent: Campbell Soup Company
Officers: Katherine Susan Atkinson, Secretary; Carlos Arturo Abrams-Rivera [1967] Director [American]; Ashley James Hicks [1974] Managing Director; Thomas Smith [1955] Director [American]

DFKA UK Holdings Limited
Incorporated: 26 April 2010 *Employees:* 3
Net Worth: £132,999,312 *Total Assets:* £164,295,024
Registered Office: 38 Barnard Road, Bowthorpe Employment Area, Norwich, NR5 9JP
Activities: Activities of head offices
Parent: DFKA Intermediate Limited
Officers: Katherine Susan Atkinson, Secretary; Carlos Arturo Abrams-Rivera [1967] Director [American]; Ashley James Hicks [1974] Managing Director; Thomas Smith [1955] Director [American]

Dhamecha Foods Limited
Incorporated: 20 March 1974 *Employees:* 628
Net Worth: £76,463,000 *Total Assets:* £188,968,992
Registered Office: 2 Hathaway Close, Stanmore, Middlesex, HA7 3NR
Activities: Wholesale of wine, beer, spirits and other alcoholic beverages
Parent: Dhamecha Group Limited
Officers: Mukesh Manilal Vithlani, Secretary; Khodidas Ratanshi Dhamecha [1930] Director; Shantilal Ratanshi Dhamecha [1931] Director; Jitendra Patel [1959] Director

Dhamecha Group Limited
Incorporated: 4 March 2002
Net Worth: £41,816,000 *Total Assets:* £54,941,000
Registered Office: 2 Hathaway Close, Stanmore, Middlesex, HA7 3NR
Activities: Activities of head offices
Parent: Dhamecha Holdings Limited
Officers: Mukesh Manilal Vithlani, Secretary; Khodidas Ratanshi Dhamecha [1930] Director; Shantilal Ratanshi Dhamecha [1931] Director

Dhamecha Holdings Limited
Incorporated: 1 March 2008 *Employees:* 628
Net Worth: £100,586,000 *Total Assets:* £232,784,000
Registered Office: 2 Hathaway Close, Stanmore, Middlesex, HA7 3NR
Activities: Activities of head offices
Shareholders: Khodidas Ratanshi Dhamecha; Shantilal Ratanshi Dhamecha
Officers: Mukesh Manilal Vithlani, Secretary; Khodidas Ratanshi Dhamecha [1930] Director; Shantilal Ratanshi Dhamecha [1931] Director; Jitendra Patel [1959] Director/Accountant

Dhamecha Property Limited
Incorporated: 3 March 2008
Net Worth: £14,927,000 *Total Assets:* £72,533,000
Registered Office: 2 Hathaway Close, Stanmore, Middlesex, HA7 3NR
Activities: Renting and operating of Housing Association real estate
Parent: Dhamecha Group Limited
Officers: Mukesh Manilal Vithlani, Secretary; Khodidas Ratanshi Dhamecha [1930] Director; Shantilal Ratanshi Dhamecha [1931] Director; Jitendra Patel [1959] Director/Accountant

Dhollandia U.K. Limited
Incorporated: 17 November 1995 *Employees:* 24
Net Worth: £13,235,641 *Total Assets:* £22,155,434
Registered Office: Dhollandia UK, Latham Road, Huntingdon, Cambs, PE29 6YG
Activities: Manufacture of other transport equipment n.e.c.
Major Shareholder: Nancy Alois Dhollander
Officers: Nancy Dhollander, Secretary; Nancy Dhollander [1968] Director [Belgian]; Christopher Mark Lay [1975] Director/Sales Manager

Dialgreen Estates Limited
Incorporated: 14 July 1999 *Employees:* 2
Net Worth: £9,724,599 *Total Assets:* £15,080,637
Registered Office: 5 Beauchamp Court, Victors Way, Barnet, Herts, EN5 5TZ
Activities: Other letting and operating of own or leased real estate
Major Shareholder: Francis Jarlath Burke
Officers: Francis Jarlath Burke [1946] Director [Irish]

Diamond Corporation Limited
Incorporated: 19 March 2002 *Employees:* 2
Net Worth: £29,463,552 *Total Assets:* £67,295,496
Registered Office: Toronto Suite, Maple House, High Street, Potters Bar, Herts, EN6 5BS
Activities: Other letting and operating of own or leased real estate
Shareholders: Demetrios Zenonos Antoniou; Harry Zenonos Antoniou
Officers: Demetrios Antoniou [1976] Director/Administrator; Harry Antoniou [1983] Director/Administrator

The Diamond Learning Partnership Trust
Incorporated: 9 May 2012 *Employees:* 279
Net Worth: £13,009,831 *Total Assets:* £14,222,307
Registered Office: Andrew Road, Eynsbury, St Neots, Cambs, PE19 2QE
Activities: Primary education
Officers: Tracy Joanne Bryden, Secretary; Alan Edward Ball [1947] Director/Retired; Hazel Bell [1975] Director/Engineer; Tracy Joanne Bryden [1963] Director/Headteacher; Alexander David Chambers [1975] Finance and IT Director; Susannah Clare Connell [1970] Director; Sandra Denise Gill [1966] Director/Civil Servant; David Alan Lowndes [1953] Director/Freelance Press Photographer; Godfrey Brian Smith [1944] Director/Retired; Gregor Stanley Watson [1965] Director/Chief Executive; Mark David Young [1973] Director/Engineer

Diaverum Facilities Management Limited
Incorporated: 9 June 2008
Net Worth: £3,747,639 *Total Assets:* £30,700,578
Registered Office: Blenheim Gate, 22-24 Upper Marlborough Road, St Albans, Herts, AL1 3AL
Activities: Other business support service activities n.e.c.
Parent: Diaverum Holding UK Limited
Officers: Dag Olov Andersson Tilk [1961] Director [Swedish]; Michael Thomas Hartnett [1968] Director/Business Manager Healthcare; Magnus Anders Olof Sjoholm [1968] Director [Swedish]

Didsbury Engineering Co.Limited
Incorporated: 11 December 1941 *Employees:* 33
Net Worth: £7,766,031 *Total Assets:* £8,946,877
Registered Office: Lawrence Walter House, Addison Road, Chilton Industrial Estate, Sudbury, Suffolk, CO10 2YW
Activities: Manufacture of lifting and handling equipment
Parent: HBS Electronics (Holdings) Limited
Officers: John Keith Bedford, Secretary; Gary Walter Harvey [1957] Director; Nicholas Gary Harvey [1987] Director; Nicholas Francis Smith [1958] Director

Digica Group Finance Limited
Incorporated: 19 November 2002 *Employees:* 2
Net Worth: £24,543,000 *Total Assets:* £28,069,000
Registered Office: Computacenter, Hatfield Avenue, Hatfield, Herts, AL10 9TW
Activities: Activities of head offices
Parent: Computacenter (UK) Limited
Officers: Raymond John Gray, Secretary; Francis Anthony Conophy [1958] Finance Director [Irish]; Raymond John Gray [1976] Director/Accountant

Digital Copier Systems Eastern Limited
Incorporated: 15 February 2001
Net Worth: £9,575,481 *Total Assets:* £13,196,040
Registered Office: Fitzroy House, Crown Street, Ipswich, Suffolk, IP1 3LG
Activities: Other business support service activities n.e.c.
Major Shareholder: Nigel Wallis
Officers: Nigel Wallis [1965] Director/Salesperson

Digital House Group Ltd
Incorporated: 13 May 2016
Net Worth: £21,003,152 *Total Assets:* £21,071,540
Registered Office: 4 Gransden Business Park, Potton Road, Abbotsley, St Neots, Cambs, PE19 6TY
Activities: Activities of financial services holding companies
Shareholder: Nelson Damian Duboscq
Officers: Eduardo Bruchou [1954] Director [Argentinian]; Nelson Damian Duboscq [1962] Director [Argentinian]; Hernan Jorge Kazah [1970] Director [Argentinian]; John Mark Rogers [1967] Director [American]; Luis Maria Julio Saguier [1966] Director [Argentinian]; Angel Jose Uribe [1975] Director/Investor [Argentinian]

Dilawar Property Ltd.
Incorporated: 13 June 2001
Net Worth: £3,370,270 *Total Assets:* £8,687,118
Registered Office: 416 Green Lane, Ilford, Essex, IG3 9JX
Activities: Other letting and operating of own or leased real estate
Officers: Krishan Kaur, Secretary; Dilawar Singh [1945] Director/Property Consultant

Diligenta Limited
Incorporated: 12 August 2005 *Employees:* 2,686
Net Worth: £64,716,000 *Total Assets:* £105,087,000
Registered Office: Lynch Wood, Peterborough, Cambs, PE2 6FY
Activities: Financial intermediation not elsewhere classified
Officers: Alan Peter Jackson, Secretary; Sir Michael Anthony Arthur [1950] Director; Suresh Muthuswami [1963] Director/President & Global Head [Indian]; Ganapathy Subramaniam Natarajan [1959] Director/TCS Chief Operating Officer [Indian]; Sir Robert Paul Reid [1934] Director; Daniel Praveen Sundaradas [1972] Director/Chief Executive [Indian]

Dillons Stores Limited
Incorporated: 20 January 1998 *Employees:* 1,288
Net Worth: £49,900,000 *Total Assets:* £60,160,000
Registered Office: McColl's House, Ashwells Road, Brentwood, Essex, CM15 9ST
Activities: Retail sale of tobacco products in specialised stores
Parent: Martin McColl Limited
Officers: Rachel Peat, Secretary; Robbie Ian Bell [1973] Director/Chief Financial Officer; Simon Jeremy Ian Fuller [1977] Director; Steven Green [1981] Director; Simon Jonathan Miller [1963] Director

Dimex Limited
Incorporated: 20 October 1983
Net Worth: £332,260,992 *Total Assets:* £332,260,992
Registered Office: Yule Catto Building, Temple Fields, Harlow, Essex, CM20 2BH
Activities: Manufacture of soap and detergents
Parent: Synthomer Holdings Limited
Officers: Richard Atkinson, Secretary; Richard Atkinson [1962] Director/Company Secretary; Stephen Guy Bennett [1964] Director

The Diocese of Norwich Education and Academies Trust
Incorporated: 17 October 2013 *Employees:* 952
Previous: The Diocese of Norwich Multi-Academy Trust
Net Worth: £28,316,988 *Total Assets:* £36,898,188
Registered Office: Diocesan House, 109 Dereham Road, Easton, Norwich, NR9 5ES
Activities: Primary education
Officers: Mark Edward Allbrook [1954] Director; Jane Margaret Bourne [1956] Director/Retired; Susan Elaine Bunting [1972] Finance Director; Simon John Cox [1976] Director/Chief Information Officer; William John Julian Crawshay [1960] Director/Retired; Paul Nicholas Dunning [1962] Diocesan Director of Education; Christopher Hedges [1958] Director/Teacher; Daphne Mary King [1957] Director/Retired College Principal; Neil Patrick Loveday [1965] Director/Accountant; Linda Parker [1949] Director/Retired; Pamela Elizabeth Wells [1955] Director/Independent Education Consultant; David Wright [1942] Director/Retired

Diomed Developments Limited
Incorporated: 2 January 1963 *Employees:* 238
Net Worth: £54,324,936 *Total Assets:* £66,227,728
Registered Office: Haslers, Old Station Road, Loughton, Essex, IG10 4PL
Activities: Manufacture of basic pharmaceutical products
Major Shareholder: Michael Jonathan Yarrow
Officers: Heather Jennifer Yarrow, Secretary; Heather Jennifer Yarrow [1949] Director; Michael Jonathan Yarrow [1947] Director; Nicola Irene Yarrow [1987] Director

Dippy Ridge Limited
Incorporated: 24 July 1992 *Employees:* 1
Net Worth: £2,319,347 *Total Assets:* £12,001,912
Registered Office: Pudding Lane, Pinchbeck, Spalding, Lincs, PE11 3TJ
Activities: Activities of head offices
Parent: J O Sims Holdings Limited
Officers: Andrew James Bell, Secretary; Christopher Oliver Sims [1959] Director

Direct Boot and Shoe Supplies Limited
Incorporated: 2 December 1994 *Employees:* 29
Net Worth: £4,806,379 *Total Assets:* £8,836,903
Registered Office: 1-3 Woodford Avenue, Gants Hill, Ilford, Essex, IG2 6UF
Activities: Wholesale of clothing and footwear
Major Shareholder: Mark Redvers Cooper
Officers: Ann Cooper, Secretary; Mark Redvers Cooper [1953] Director/Shoe Retailer and Embroiderer

Direct Consolidated Limited
Incorporated: 11 January 2013 *Employees:* 160
Net Worth: £912,408 *Total Assets:* £10,053,131
Registered Office: Dickens House, Guithavon Street, Witham, Essex, CM8 1BJ
Activities: Activities of other holding companies n.e.c.
Major Shareholder: Martin Patrick Blackwell
Officers: Linda Blackwell [1967] Director; Martin Patrick Blackwell [1970] Director

Direct Insurance Group PLC
Incorporated: 23 January 1996 *Employees:* 49
Net Worth: £2,193,095 *Total Assets:* £20,066,124
Registered Office: Cumberland House, 129 High Street, Billericay, Essex, CM12 9AH
Activities: Non-life insurance
Shareholders: David Paul Bearman; Pauline Mary Bearman
Officers: Canan Oral, Secretary; David Paul Bearman [1978] Director/Insurance Broker; Pauline Mary Bearman [1953] Director; Neil Robert Milner [1978] Director/Insurance Broker; Canan Oral [1972] Director/Insurance Broker; Simon Piggott [1977] Director/Insurance Intermediary; James Richard Potter [1979] Director/Insurance Underwriter

Direct Table Foods Limited
Incorporated: 17 May 1984 *Employees:* 485
Net Worth: £42,421,820 *Total Assets:* £63,072,032
Registered Office: Saxham Business Park, Little Saxham, Bury St Edmunds, Suffolk, IP28 6RX
Activities: Processing and preserving of meat
Shareholders: Clemens Tonnies; Robert Tonnies
Officers: Anthony Michael Stanton, Secretary; Carsten Svejgaard Jakobsen [1945] Director/Chairman [Danish]; Robert James Nugent [1965] Operations Director; Colin Perry [1959] Financial Director; Anthony Michael Stanton [1957] Director

Direktek Ltd
Incorporated: 22 October 1991 *Employees:* 37
Previous: Direktek Distribution Limited
Net Worth: £9,599,636 *Total Assets:* £10,910,667
Registered Office: 5 Century Point, Halifax Road, High Wycombe, Bucks, HP12 3SL
Activities: Wholesale of computers, computer peripheral equipment and software
Major Shareholder: Trevor Robert Marshall
Officers: Janette Marshall, Secretary; Trevor Robert Marshall [1960] Managing Director

Displaylink (UK) Limited
Incorporated: 25 June 2003 *Employees:* 149
Net Worth: £43,496,656 *Total Assets:* £51,606,760
Registered Office: 140 Science Park, Milton Road, Cambridge, CB4 0GF
Activities: Other research and experimental development on natural sciences and engineering
Officers: John Lee, Secretary; Alan George Duncan [1948] Director/Venture Partner Draper Esprit; William Mark Evans [1957] Director/General Partner Balderton Capital [Canadian]; Henry Howard Happel III [1945] Director/Businessman [American]; Martin Kirk Jackson [1959] Director/Engineer; Dr Hans-Dieter Otto Koch [1953] Director/Venture Capitalist [German]; David Mooring [1958] Director/Technology Entrepreneur [American]; Graham William O'Keeffe [1963] Director/Company CEO

Displayplan Holdings Limited
Incorporated: 4 December 2009 *Employees:* 65
Net Worth: £6,252,303 *Total Assets:* £8,130,274
Registered Office: Clare House, High Street, Baldock, Herts, SG7 6BE
Activities: Activities of other holding companies n.e.c.
Shareholders: Scott Morris; Neil Patrick Campbell
Officers: Neil Campbell, Secretary; Neil Patrick Campbell [1963] Director [Irish]; Scott Morris [1975] Director; Alan Frank Smith [1946] Director

Displayplan Limited
Incorporated: 9 April 1984 *Employees:* 65
Net Worth: £7,694,695 *Total Assets:* £9,413,746
Registered Office: Clare House, High Street, Baldock, Herts, SG7 6BE
Activities: Non-specialised wholesale trade
Parent: Displayplan Holdings Limited
Officers: Neil Patrick Campbell, Secretary; Neil Patrick Campbell [1963] Managing Director [Irish]; Scott Morris [1975] Managing Director; Alan Frank Smith [1946] Director

The Dispute Service Limited
Incorporated: 31 July 2003 *Employees:* 127
Net Worth: £7,045,285 *Total Assets:* £15,670,269
Registered Office: 1 The Progression Centre, 42 Mark Road, Hemel Hempstead, Herts, HP2 7DW
Activities: Activities of other membership organisations n.e.c.
Officers: Nicholas Hankey, Secretary; Mark Lee Allan [1973] Director/Insurance Executive; Jodi Berg [1956] Director/Lawyer; David Jonathan Richard Cox [1983] Managing Director; Nicholas Hankey [1961] Director/Chartered Accountant; Stephen Harriott [1959] Director; Prof Thomas Martin Partington [1944] Director/Retired

Diss High School
Incorporated: 4 July 2011 *Employees:* 133
Net Worth: £7,681,615 *Total Assets:* £8,807,957
Registered Office: Walcot Road, Diss, Norfolk, IP22 4DH
Activities: General secondary education
Officers: Valerie Ann Attenborough [1947] Director/Retired; Julie Michaela Botwright [1967] Director; Chris Brown [1977] Director/Headteacher; Sonia Browne [1970] Director; Jennifer Dennis [1938] Director; Stephen Kenneth Drake [1958] Director/Solicitor; Lisa Jane Hamill [1972] Director/Head of Learning & Development; Dr Janet Joy Hunt [1958] Director; Clare Louise Jacobs [1970] Director/Science Technician; Kim Jarocki [1988] Director/Teacher; Derek Johnson [1971] Director/Education Manager; Keith Walter Kiddie [1953] Director/Retired Army Officer; Jessamyn Earl Read [1994] Director/Teacher; Joy Shawcross [1956] Director/Retired Teacher; Stephen Thomas Wells [1951] Director/Retired Teacher

Distribution Supplies Limited
Incorporated: 22 March 1994 *Employees:* 39
Net Worth: £6,110,586 *Total Assets:* £8,874,530
Registered Office: 10 Jesus Lane, Cambridge, CB5 8BA
Activities: Wholesale of wood, construction materials and sanitary equipment
Parent: Signature Tiles Ltd
Officers: Carol Rosalind Miller, Company Secretary; Carol Rosalind Miller [1959] Director/Company Secretary; Simon David Miller [1961] Director

DJM 88 Limited
Incorporated: 30 December 2015
Net Worth Deficit: £2,136 *Total Assets:* £19,402,752
Registered Office: Second Floor, De Burgh House, Market Road, Wickford, Essex, SS12 0FD
Activities: Activities of other holding companies n.e.c.
Officers: Dejan Markovic [1955] Director [Serbian]; Rebecca Ann White [1990] Director

DMC Contracts Limited
Incorporated: 8 July 2004 *Employees:* 23
Net Worth: £4,712,255 *Total Assets:* £9,877,729
Registered Office: Unit 17 The Capstan Centre, Tilbury, Essex, RM18 7HH
Activities: Floor and wall covering
Shareholders: David Andrew McCartney; Michelle McCartney
Officers: Michelle McCartney, Secretary; Lee Bird [1973] Director; Edward Conor McCann [1970] Director [Irish]; David Andrew McCartney [1971] Director; Alexander Eugene Morrissey [1975] Director

Dock and Let Limited
Incorporated: 2 March 1999 *Employees:* 3
Net Worth: £848,528 *Total Assets:* £10,770,755
Registered Office: 166 College Road, Harrow, Middlesex, HA1 1RA
Activities: Development of building projects
Major Shareholder: Michael Spencer Docker
Officers: Michele Docker, Secretary; Michael Spencer Docker [1963] Director/Property Developer

Doctors on Call Limited
Incorporated: 7 October 2005
Net Worth: £7,631,000 *Total Assets:* £11,368,000
Registered Office: 800 The Boulevard, Capability Green, Luton, Beds, LU1 3BA
Activities: Temporary employment agency activities
Parent: Global Medics Limited
Officers: Rebecca Jane Watson, Secretary; Nigel Marsh [1962] Director; Julia Robertson [1958] Director; Rebecca Jane Watson [1969] Director/Solicitor

Ernest Doe & Sons Limited
Incorporated: 15 March 1947 *Employees:* 513
Previous: Ernest Doe & Sons,Limited
Net Worth: £8,342,223 *Total Assets:* £58,442,136
Registered Office: Ulting, Maldon, Essex, CM9 6QH
Activities: Sale of other motor vehicles
Officers: Angus Ernest Doe [1985] Director/Manager; Colin Ernest Doe [1956] Director/Agricultural Engineer; Graham Charles Kendrick Parker [1968] Director/Sales Manager

Doe Holdings Limited
Incorporated: 4 February 2016 *Employees:* 525
Net Worth: £25,476,684 *Total Assets:* £71,406,672
Registered Office: Ulting, Maldon, Essex, CM9 6QH
Activities: Activities of head offices
Officers: Angus Ernest Doe [1985] Director; Colin Ernest Doe [1956] Director/Agricultural Engineer

Dominion Hospitality Limited
Incorporated: 23 August 2016
Net Worth Deficit: £2,294,000 *Total Assets:* £33,749,000
Registered Office: 31 Haverscroft Industrial Estate, New Road, Attleborough, Norfolk, NR17 1YE
Activities: Management consultancy activities other than financial management
Parent: Dominion Hospitality Midco Limited
Officers: Karthik Bhaskar Achar [1971] Director [French]; William Arthur Neil Buchanan [1965] Director; Samuel Edward Kennedy [1960] Director; Michael Terry Livanos [1982] Director [American]; Michael David Stewart [1968] Director [American]

Dominion Hospitality Midco Limited
Incorporated: 20 September 2016
Net Worth: £3,984,000 *Total Assets:* £15,569,000
Registered Office: 31 Haverscroft Industrial Estate, New Road, Attleborough, Norfolk, NR17 1YE
Activities: Dormant company
Parent: Dominion Hospitality Topco Limited
Officers: Karthik Bhaskar Achar [1971] Director [French]; William Arthur Neil Buchanan [1965] Director; Samuel Edward Kennedy [1960] Director; Michael Terry Livanos [1982] Director [American]; Michael David Stewart [1968] Director [American]

Dominion Hospitality Topco Limited
Incorporated: 20 September 2016
Net Worth: £3,990,000 *Total Assets:* £33,749,000
Registered Office: 31 Haverscroft Industrial Estate, New Road, Attleborough, Norfolk, NR17 1YE
Activities: Dormant company
Parent: Stellex Capital Partners LP
Officers: Karthik Bhaskar Achar [1971] Director [French]; William Arthur Neil Buchanan [1965] Director; Samuel Edward Kennedy [1960] Director; Michael Terry Livanos [1982] Director [American]; Michael David Stewart [1968] Director [American]

Dominion Pubs and Bars Limited
Incorporated: 10 December 1992
Previous: The Chapman Group Limited
Net Worth: £7,416,000 *Total Assets:* £19,099,000
Registered Office: 31 Haverscroft Industrial Estate, New Road, Attleborough, Norfolk, NR17 1YE
Activities: Public houses and bars
Parent: Dominion Hospitality Limited
Officers: Karthik Bhaskar Achar [1971] Director [French]; William Arthur Neil Buchanan [1965] Director; Samuel Edward Kennedy [1960] Director; Michael Terry Livanos [1982] Director [American]; Michael David Stewart [1968] Director [American]

Domino Investments Limited
Incorporated: 12 February 1993 *Employees:* 138
Net Worth: £18,046,308 *Total Assets:* £30,686,856
Registered Office: 17 Aden Road, Enfield, Middlesex, EN3 7SU
Activities: Activities of production holding companies
Major Shareholder: Keith Childs
Officers: Timothy John Childs, Secretary; Brenda Ann Childs [1941] Director; Keith Childs [1941] Director; Timothy John Childs [1966] Director; Georgina Elizabeth Hofer [1969] Director; Jacquiline Louise Squire [1969] Director

Domino Printing Sciences Public Limited Company
Incorporated: 17 April 1978 *Employees:* 28
Net Worth: £152,918,000 *Total Assets:* £229,044,000
Registered Office: Domino Printing Sciences PLC, Trafalgar Way, Bar Hill, Cambridge, CB23 8TU
Activities: Manufacture of other general-purpose machinery n.e.c.
Parent: Brother Industries Ltd
Officers: John-Paul Martin, Secretary; Nigel Robert Bond [1957] Managing Director; Rachel Catherine Hurst [1971] Group Operations Director; Tetsuro Koide [1962] Director [Japanese]; Toshikazu Koike [1955] Director [Japanese]; Harumi Okuyama [1965] Director [Japanese]; Robert Pulford [1964] Managing Director; Ichiro Sasaki [1957] Director [Japanese]

Domino UK Limited
Incorporated: 5 September 1983 *Employees:* 844
Net Worth: £41,372,000 *Total Assets:* £176,591,008
Registered Office: Domino UK, Trafalgar Way, Bar Hill, Cambridge, CB23 8TU
Activities: Manufacture of other electrical equipment
Parent: Domino Printing Sciences PLC
Officers: John-Paul Martin, Secretary; Nigel Robert Bond [1957] Director/Chartered Accountant; Joseph Graham Harrison [1972] Director/Chief Financial Officer; Rachel Catherine Hurst [1971] Group Operations Director

Don Construction Holdings Limited
Incorporated: 18 October 2011 *Employees:* 754
Net Worth: £28,684,584 *Total Assets:* £66,104,872
Registered Office: Hawthorn House, Helions Bumpstead Road, Haverhill, Suffolk, CB9 7AA
Activities: Activities of other holding companies n.e.c.
Officers: Hakam Abu Risheh [1960] Director [French]; Mamoun Alshanteer [1962] Director [Jordanian]; Ruba Ghandour [1993] Director [Canadian]; Tawfic Ghandour [1961] Director/Chief Executive Officer [Canadian]; James Francis Igoe [1957] Director; Akef Malhas [1955] Director [Jordanian]; Majda Mishlawi [1955] Director [Jordanian]

Donatantonio Group Limited
Incorporated: 6 November 2007 *Employees:* 33
Net Worth: £521,596 *Total Assets:* £8,466,016
Registered Office: Lupa House, York Way, Borehamwood, Herts, WD6 1PX
Activities: Activities of other holding companies n.e.c.
Shareholders: Proven VCT PLC; Proven Growth and Income VCT PLC
Officers: Manish Mandavia, Secretary; Simon Bell [1964] Director; Peter Maurice Crystal [1948] Director/Lawyer; Manish Jayant Mandavia [1972] Director; Malcolm Kennedy Hunt Moss [1959] Director/Venture Fund Manager; Elizabeth Catherine Scarborough [1968] Director; Timothy Ross Scarborough [1968] Commercial Director

Donatantonio Limited
Incorporated: 16 October 2003 *Employees:* 33
Net Worth: £4,294,745 *Total Assets:* £10,037,156
Registered Office: Lupa House, York Way, Borehamwood, Herts, WD6 1PX
Activities: Non-specialised wholesale of food, beverages and tobacco
Parent: Donatantonio Group Ltd
Officers: Manish Mandavia, Secretary; Simon Bell [1964] Director; Peter Maurice Crystal [1948] Director/Solicitor; Manish Jayant Mandavia [1972] Director; Malcolm Kennedy Hunt Moss [1959] Director/Founding Partner; Elizabeth Catherine Scarborough [1968] Director; Timothy Ross Scarborough [1968] Commercial Director

Doncaster School Solutions (Holdings) Limited
Incorporated: 28 November 2006
Net Worth Deficit: £11,247,000 *Total Assets:* £42,817,000
Registered Office: Astral House, Imperial Way, Watford, Herts, WD24 4WW
Activities: Activities of head offices
Parent: Vinci Pensions Limited
Officers: Ian David Hudson [1964] Director/Chartered Accountant; Rory John Murphy [1969] Director/Chartered Surveyor

Doncaster School Solutions Limited
Incorporated: 28 November 2006
Net Worth Deficit: £11,247,000 *Total Assets:* £42,817,000
Registered Office: Astral House, Imperial Way, Watford, Herts, WD24 4WW
Activities: Development of building projects
Parent: Doncaster School Solutions (Holdings) Limited
Officers: Ian David Hudson [1964] Director/Chartered Accountant; Rory John Murphy [1969] Director/Chartered Surveyor

RR Donnelley UK Limited
Incorporated: 30 September 2008 *Employees:* 1,654
Previous: RR Donnelley Global Document Solutions Group Limited
Net Worth: £104,949,000 *Total Assets:* £149,876,992
Registered Office: Tower Close, Huntingdon, Cambs, PE29 7YD
Activities: Other business support service activities n.e.c.
Officers: Jonathan Simon Richard Dally, Secretary; John Samuel Farmer [1960] Director; Michael Stuart Gordon [1961] Director/Business Executive; Kevin Trevor Woor [1965] Director/Business Executive

Dorma UK Limited
Incorporated: 5 April 1978 *Employees:* 442
Net Worth: £8,607,841 *Total Assets:* £35,074,032
Registered Office: Wilbury Way, Hitchin, Herts, SG4 0AB
Activities: Other building completion and finishing
Officers: Shane Antony Christie, Secretary; Stephen Alfred Bewick [1966] Director; Bernhard Brinker [1965] Director [German]; Shane Antony Christie [1975] Finance Director; Roberto Gaspari [1959] Director [Italian]

DOT100 Limited
Incorporated: 30 April 2014 *Employees:* 4,929
Net Worth Deficit: £190,018 *Total Assets:* £10,483,857
Registered Office: Kingfisher House, No 11 Hoffmanns Way, Chelmsford, Essex, CM1 1GU
Activities: Take-away food shops and mobile food stands
Officers: Gurprit Dhaliwal [1982] Director; Surinderjit Singh Kandola [1965] Director

Double A Group Services Limited
Incorporated: 26 March 2001
Previous: U2013 Limited
Net Worth: £11,339,020 *Total Assets:* £18,480,432
Registered Office: The Hive, Camrose Avenue, London, HA8 6AG
Activities: Operation of sports facilities
Parent: Double A Group Ltd
Officers: Mahendra Patel, Secretary; Anthony Andrew Kleanthous [1966] Director

John W. Doubleday Limited
Incorporated: 10 January 1992 *Employees:* 48
Net Worth: £9,668,622 *Total Assets:* £18,903,896
Registered Office: Holbeach St Johns, Spalding, Lincs, PE12 8SQ
Activities: Wholesale of agricultural machinery, equipment and supplies
Parent: J W D Holdings Limited
Officers: Graham Collishaw [1958] Director; Ian James Doubleday-Collishaw [1981] Director; Jayne Elizabeth Doubleday-Collishaw [1958] Director; Zoe Spencer [1985] Director

Dow Agrosciences Limited
Incorporated: 9 May 1989 *Employees:* 137
Net Worth: £112,655,000 *Total Assets:* £174,562,000
Registered Office: CPC2, Capital Park, Fulbourn, Cambridge, CB21 5XE
Activities: Manufacture of other inorganic basic chemicals
Parent: The Dow Chemical Company
Officers: Cathrine Anne Jenkins, Secretary; Andrew Michael Jones [1966] Commercial Director; Richard Anthony McCormack [1966] Director/Financial Controller

Dow Properties Limited
Incorporated: 13 November 1987 *Employees:* 6
Net Worth: £20,748,246 *Total Assets:* £44,860,032
Registered Office: 195 Hale Lane, Edgware, Middlesex, HA8 9QN
Activities: Buying and selling of own real estate
Shareholders: Kazi Mohammed Morad Arefin; Dimitra Arefin
Officers: Dr Kazi Mohammed Morad Arefin, Secretary; Dimitra Arefin [1942] Director

Downing Strategic Micro-Cap Investment Trust PLC
Incorporated: 17 February 2017
Net Worth: £51,744,000 *Total Assets:* £53,679,000
Registered Office: Hamilton Centre, Rodney Way, Chelmsford, Essex, CM1 3BY
Activities: Activities of investment trusts
Officers: Hugh Graham Cazalet Aldous [1944] Director; Dr Linda Kathryn Bell [1957] Director/Chief Executive; Andrew Thomas Griffiths [1962] Director; Stephen Yapp [1957] Director

DPA Support Services Limited
Incorporated: 17 September 1996
Net Worth Deficit: £1,544,000 *Total Assets:* £12,091,000
Registered Office: Astral House, Imperial Way, Watford, Herts, WD24 4WW
Activities: Activities of head offices
Parent: DPASS Holdings Limited
Officers: Ian David Hudson [1964] Director/Chartered Accountant; Rory John Murphy [1969] Director/Chartered Surveyor

Dr Challoner's Grammar School
Incorporated: 25 November 2010 *Employees:* 175
Net Worth: £12,956,000 *Total Assets:* £16,988,000
Registered Office: Dr Challoner's Grammar School, Chesham Road, Amersham, Bucks, HP6 5HA
Activities: General secondary education
Officers: Sean Gerrard Kennedy, Secretary; David Alastair Atkinson [1973] Director; Gareth Cadman [1985] Director/Teacher; Joseph Henry Cronly [1971] Director/Investment Manager; Isobel Anne Darby [1957] Director/Accountant; George Randal Davies [1988] Director/Teacher; Alison Davis [1963] Director/Chief Information Officer; Giri Fox [1975] Director/Chief Commercial Officer; Leon Joel Glenister [1988] Director/Barrister; Shaun Malcolm Kennedy [1952] Director/Retired; Matthew John Lawrence [1974] Director/Consultant; Dr David Stewart Mackintosh [1947] Director/Retired Chief Executive; Stephen Anthony Nokes [1952] Director/Headmaster; Dr Mark William Pegg [1953] Director; Jane Susan Penton-Hauchard [1960] Director/Human Resources Consultant; Susan Elizabeth Tanner [1954] Director/Education Consultant; Michael Tingey [1967] Group Commercial Director; Emma Westcott [1966] Director/Leadership and Education Consultant

Dr Challoner's High School
Incorporated: 5 July 2011 *Employees:* 139
Net Worth: £11,187,906 *Total Assets:* £13,496,036
Registered Office: Dr Challoner's High School, Cokes Lane, Little Chalfont, Amersham, Bucks, HP7 9QB
Activities: General secondary education
Officers: Caroline Cobb, Secretary; Nicola Jane Astbury [1964] Director/Consultant Haematologist; Tymon Piers Broadhead [1966] Director/Chartered Accountant; Katherine Anne Brown [1989] Director/Teacher; Nicholas Milton Canney [1971] Managing Director; Nisha de Alwis [1981] Director/Teacher; Khorshed Dinshaw [1954] Director; Simon Paul Graylen Eggleton [1967] Director; Dr Reza Gholami [1979] Director/Senior Lecturer [Danish]; Janet John [1950] Director/Retired; Victoria Jane Martin [1972] Director/Chartered Accountant; Christine Mary Preston [1954] Director/Teacher; Jeremy Alistair St John Rhodes [1959] Director/Petroleum Reservoir Engineer; Alan Peter Roe [1973] Director/Headmaster; Anurag Sekhri [1970] Director/Management Consultant; Rosamund Elizabeth Shield [1969] Director/Lawyer; Sheena Singla [1975] Director/Solicitor; Graham Peter Stubbs [1971] Director/Banker; Pauline Elizabeth Wood [1964] Corporate Communication Director

Draeger Medical UK Limited
Incorporated: 24 October 2001 *Employees:* 154
Net Worth: £6,265,000 *Total Assets:* £24,080,000
Registered Office: The Willows, Mark Road, Hemel Hempstead, Herts, HP2 7BW
Activities: Repair of other equipment
Parent: Dragerwerk AG & Co. KGaA
Officers: Matthew Bedford, Secretary; Michael Allan Norris [1957] Director [American]

Drapers' Multi-Academy Trust
Incorporated: 30 September 2009 *Employees:* 311
Net Worth: £35,643,000 *Total Assets:* £40,456,000
Registered Office: Drapers' Academy, Settle Road, Harold Hill, Romford, Essex, RM3 9XR
Activities: Primary education
Officers: Philip Norman, Secretary; Patrick Beddows [1961] Director/Partner, Land Management; Professor Alison Mary Blunt [1969] Director/Professor of Geography; Professor Virginia Grace Davis [1958] Director/Professor of Medieval History [Irish]; Stephen Peter Foakes [1950] Director/Retired; Gillian Kemp [1972] Director of Education; Jonathan David Morgan [1972] Director/Academic Registrar and Council Secretary; Timothy Gerard Orchard [1963] Director; Professor Kim Mary Piper [1967] Director/Professor of Pathology; Professor Morag Elizabeth Shiach [1958] Director/Professor; David Michael Sumner [1971] Finance Director

Drayton Building Services Limited
Incorporated: 16 December 1996 *Employees:* 238
Net Worth: £3,623,000 *Total Assets:* £12,624,000
Registered Office: 9-11 High Road, Drayton, Norwich, NR8 6AH
Activities: Other specialised construction activities n.e.c.
Parent: RGCC Limited
Officers: Robert John Alflatt, Secretary; James George Stratton Carter [1985] Director; Emily Clare Vintners [1978] Director

Dreams Limited
Incorporated: 4 March 2013 *Employees:* 1,837
Net Worth: £33,143,000 *Total Assets:* £94,250,000
Registered Office: Knaves Beech Business Centre, 14 Davies Way, Loudwater, High Wycombe, Bucks, HP10 9YU
Activities: Retail of furniture, lighting, and similar (not musical instruments or scores) in specialised store
Parent: Dreams Holdco Limited
Officers: Kim Suhail Zaheer, Secretary; Michael Francis Logue [1972] Director/Chief Executive Officer; Kim Suhail Zaheer [1971] Director

Dreams Topco Limited
Incorporated: 4 March 2013 *Employees:* 1,837
Net Worth: £32,043,000 *Total Assets:* £94,250,000
Registered Office: 14 Knaves Beech Business Centre, Davies Way, Loudwater, High Wycombe, Bucks, HP10 9YU
Activities: Activities of other holding companies n.e.c.
Officers: Paul David Daccus [1972] Managing Director

Dron & Dickson Limited
Incorporated: 22 April 1927 *Employees:* 102
Net Worth: £8,004,850 *Total Assets:* £13,414,604
Registered Office: Dron & Dickson House, Cumberland Place, Whapload Road, Lowestoft, Suffolk, NR32 1UQ
Activities: Repair of electrical equipment
Parent: Dron & Dickson Group Limited
Officers: Colin Michael Rowley, Secretary; Leonard Peter Collins [1979] Strategic Growth Director; Thomas William Redmond Irwin [1979] Sales & Marketing Director; Bruce McHattie [1973] Operations Director; Colin Michael Rowley [1972] Managing Director

Druid Group Limited
Incorporated: 27 October 1993
Net Worth: £123,891,000 *Total Assets:* £141,682,000
Registered Office: Three Cherry Trees Lane, Hemel Hempstead, Herts, HP2 7AH
Activities: Activities of head offices
Parent: Sopra Steria Holdings Limited
Officers: Peter Atherton Cashmore, Secretary; Davinder Singh Ahluwalia [1952] Director; John Powell Torrie [1954] Director

Dry Drayton Estate Limited
Incorporated: 1 August 1997 *Employees:* 3
Net Worth: £9,854,597 *Total Assets:* £24,282,824
Registered Office: Scotland Farm, Dry Drayton, Cambridge, CB23 8AU
Activities: Growing of cereals (except rice), leguminous crops and oil seeds
Major Shareholder: Adrian Michael Peck
Officers: Cherry Mary Stamford, Secretary; Adrian Michael Peck [1950] Director/Farmer

DSJ Homes Limited
Incorporated: 6 November 2003
Net Worth: £3,035,303 *Total Assets:* £17,235,500
Registered Office: 555-557 Cranbrook Road, Gants Hill, Ilford, Essex, IG2 6HE
Activities: Buying and selling of own real estate
Shareholders: Jasbir Singh Jhumat; Pardeep Singh Jhumat
Officers: Pardeep Singh Jhumat, Secretary; Jasbir Singh Jhumat [1968] Director; Pardeep Singh Jhumat [1971] Director

DST Financial Services Europe Limited
Incorporated: 10 December 1991
Previous: International Financial Data Services (UK) Limited
Net Worth: £32,249,000 *Total Assets:* £32,960,000
Registered Office: DST House, St Nicholas Lane, Basildon, Essex, SS15 5FS
Activities: Financial intermediation not elsewhere classified
Parent: DST Financial Services International Limited
Officers: Richard David Barrett [1963] Director; Andrew Charles Hume [1963] Director; William Slattery [1955] Director [Irish]; Brian Edward Sweeney [1967] Director [Irish]; Nicholas Paul Wright [1967] Director

DST Financial Services International Limited
Incorporated: 11 November 1992 *Employees:* 3,630
Previous: International Financial Data Services Limited
Net Worth: £184,152,992 *Total Assets:* £292,230,016
Registered Office: DST House, St Nicholas Lane, Basildon, Essex, SS15 5FS
Activities: Other information technology service activities
Shareholders: DSTI Holdings Limited; DST Systems, Inc.
Officers: Richard David Barrett [1963] Director; Andrew Charles Hume [1963] Director; William Slattery [1955] Director [Irish]; Brian Edward Sweeney [1967] Director [Irish]; Nicholas Paul Wright [1967] Director

DSV Air & Sea Limited
Incorporated: 16 October 1995 *Employees:* 356
Net Worth: £29,952,000 *Total Assets:* £87,552,000
Registered Office: Scandinavia House, Refinery Road, Parkeston, Harwich, Essex, CO12 4QG
Activities: Other transportation support activities
Parent: DSV A/S
Officers: Gary Maurice Ridsdale, Secretary; Jens Bjorn Andersen [1966] Director/Chief Executive [Danish]; Michael Dyhre Hansen [1958] Director [Danish]; Morten Landry [1980] Managing Director [Danish]; Jens Hesselberg Lund [1969] Finance Director [Danish]; Carsten Elmdal Trolle [1965] Managing Director [Danish]

DSV Road Holding Limited
Incorporated: 3 August 1982
Net Worth: £21,897,000 *Total Assets:* £21,904,000
Registered Office: Scandinavia House, Refinery Road, Parkeston, Harwich, Essex, CO12 4QG
Activities: Other transportation support activities
Parent: DSV A/S
Officers: Gary Maurice Ridsdale, Secretary; Jesper Kenneth Hansen [1974] Managing Director [Danish]; Jens Hesselberg Lund [1969] Director/Chief Finance Officer [Danish]; Soren Schmidt [1972] Operations Director [Danish]

DSV Road Limited
Incorporated: 10 November 1999 *Employees:* 757
Net Worth: £23,552,000 *Total Assets:* £81,376,000
Registered Office: Scandinavia House, Refinery Road, Parkeston, Harwich, Essex, CO12 4QG
Activities: Freight transport by road
Parent: DSV A/S
Officers: Gary Maurice Ridsdale, Secretary; Jesper Kenneth Hansen [1974] Managing Director [Danish]; Jens Hesselberg Lund [1969] Director/Chief Finance Officer [Danish]; Soren Schmidt [1972] Operations Director [Danish]

DSV Solutions Limited
Incorporated: 13 December 1996 *Employees:* 789
Net Worth: £1,062,000 *Total Assets:* £39,532,000
Registered Office: Scandinavia House, Parkeston, Harwich, Essex, CO12 4QG
Activities: Other transportation support activities
Parent: DSV A/S
Officers: Gary Maurice Ridsdale, Secretary; Brian Skovgaard Ejsing [1966] Director [Danish]; Jens Hesselberg Lund [1969] Director/Chief Finance Officer [Danish]; John Ellis McCafferty [1957] Managing Director; Jens Peter Pinstrup Nielsen [1954] Director [Danish]

Du Pont (U.K.) Industrial Limited
Incorporated: 18 January 2000 *Employees:* 161
Net Worth: £38,507,000 *Total Assets:* £48,982,000
Registered Office: 4th Floor, Kings Court, London Road, Stevenage, Herts, SG1 2NG
Activities: Other manufacturing n.e.c.
Parent: Du Pont (U.K.) Limited
Officers: Stephen Reeve, Secretary; Adrian Paul Gough [1958] Director; Stephen Reeve [1963] Director/Accountant

Du Pont (U.K.) Limited
Incorporated: 8 October 2002 *Employees:* 123
Net Worth: £17,543,000 *Total Assets:* £280,651,008
Registered Office: 4th Floor, Kings Court, London Road, Stevenage, Herts, SG1 2NG
Activities: Manufacture of plastics in primary forms
Parent: DowDupont Inc.
Officers: Stephen Reeve, Secretary; Adrian Paul Gough [1958] Director; Stephen Reeve [1963] Director/Accountant; Patrick Stephan Schriber [1960] Director Legal EMEA of Dupont de Nemours International

Duff Morgan & Vermont (Holdings) Limited
Incorporated: 27 September 1923 *Employees:* 111
Net Worth: £4,619,939 *Total Assets:* £12,442,991
Registered Office: 34 Whiffler Road, Norwich, NR3 2AN
Activities: Activities of head offices
Shareholders: David John Barratt; Penelope Constance Isabel Barratt
Officers: Jason Paul Curtis, Secretary; David John Barratt [1947] Director; Frederick David Nicholas Barratt [1987] Director of Aftersales; Penelope Constance Isabel Barratt [1954] Director/Personal Assistant

Duff Morgan & Vermont Limited
Incorporated: 5 September 1969 *Employees:* 111
Net Worth: £4,596,870 *Total Assets:* £12,416,422
Registered Office: 34 Whiffler Road, Norwich, NR3 2AN
Activities: Sale of new cars and light motor vehicles
Parent: Duff Morgan & Vermont (Holdings) Limited
Officers: Jason Paul Curtis, Secretary; David John Barratt [1947] Director; Frederick David Nicholas Barratt [1987] Director of Aftersales; Penelope Constance Isabel Barratt [1954] Director/Personal Assistant; Jeremy Charles Trett [1970] Director/General Sales Manager; Danny Camiel Paula Verhulst [1967] Director/Certified Accountant [Belgian]

P.J. Duffy & Son (Farms) Limited
Incorporated: 9 September 1986 *Employees:* 5
Net Worth: £14,046,387 *Total Assets:* £17,515,656
Registered Office: Lynway Nurseries, Stimpsons Cross, Algarkirk, Boston, Lincs, PE20 2BE
Activities: Growing of cereals (except rice), leguminous crops and oil seeds
Major Shareholder: Philip John Duffy
Officers: Philip John Duffy, Secretary; Karen Marina Duffy [1951] Director/Housewife; Philip John Duffy [1950] Director

Duncan Lewis Solicitors Ltd
Incorporated: 23 February 1999 *Employees:* 462
Previous: Duncan Lewis (Solicitors) Limited
Net Worth: £6,761,083 *Total Assets:* £21,194,938
Registered Office: Spencer House, 29 Grove Hill Road, Harrow on the Hill, Harrow, Middlesex, HA1 3BN
Activities: Solicitors
Major Shareholder: Amarpal Singh Gupta
Officers: Vinia Majaba, Secretary; Bernadette Adusei [1980] Director/Solicitor; Vanketaramana Appalakondiah [1950] Director/Solicitor; Bahar Ata [1980] Director/Chartered Legal Executive; Manjinder Kaur Atwal [1982] Director/Solicitor; Ahmed Hassan Aydeed [1987] Director/Solicitor; Tamana Aziz [1976] Director/Solicitor; Lail Bhunndoo [1969] Director/Solicitor; Jason Charles Bruce [1978] Director/Solicitor; Rachel Caswell [1981] Director/Solicitor; Bernadette Chikwe [1971] Director/Solicitor; Dianne Cowie [1976] Director/Solicitor; Nicholas de Freitas [1981] Director/Solicitor; Sobashni de Silva [1973] Director/Solicitor; James de Vere Moss [1974] Director/Solicitor; Hardeep Singh Dhaliwal [1970] Director/Solicitor; Sheena Donlon [1984] Director/Solicitor; Sara Dowie [1979] Director/Solicitor; Zofia Eugenia Duszynska [1964] Director/Solicitor; Sophie Vivienne Fretten [1983] Director/Solicitor; Richard Gray [1968] Director/Solicitor; Amarpal Singh Gupta [1973] Director/Solicitor; Forida Hakim [1978] Director/Solicitor; Trevor James Hatton [1974] Director/Solicitor; David Mark Head [1963] Director/Solicitor; Toufique Hossain [1979] Director/Solicitor; Heather Iqbal Rayner [1972] Director/Solicitor; Rubin Italia [1971] Director/Solicitor; Nina Joshi [1971] Director/Solicitor; Meeta Kumari [1977] Director/Solicitor; Julie Margaret Leslie [1961] Director/Solicitor; Alia Lewis [1980] Director/Solicitor; Ravi Mahey [1978] Director/Solicitor; Abbid Majeed [1983] Director/Solicitor; Jenna McKinney [1978] Director/Solicitor; Emine Mehmet [1976] Director/Solicitor; Gabor Nagy [1979] Director/Solicitor; Adeeba Naseem [1978] Director/Solicitor; Anthony Okumah [1977] Director/Solicitor; Chinedu Orogbu [1974] Director/Solicitor; James Richard Packer [1969] Director/Solicitor; Krina Parmar [1983] Director; Alexander Peebles [1980] Director/Solicitor; Satya Sridhar Ponnada [1969] Director/IT Manager; Syed Talha Hamad Rafique [1940] Director/Solicitor; Vicash Ramkissoon [1974] Director/Solicitor; Caroline Roche [1984] Director/Solicitor; Sangita Shah [1971] Director/Solicitor; Subbiah Kandasamy Sivapunniyam [1960] Director/Solicitor [Indian]; Vinita Templeton [1975] Director/Solicitor; Rebecca Thomas [1965] Director/Solicitor; Randolph Anthony Thompson [1963] Director/Solicitor; Kathy Katholiki Walker [1977] Director/Solicitor; Rohena Wallace [1983] Director/Solicitor; Lorick Winarskie [1965] Director/Solicitor; Ayan Yalchin [1974] Director/Solicitor

Dunsfold Airport Limited
Incorporated: 10 November 2011
Net Worth: £38,654,592 *Total Assets:* £59,573,812
Registered Office: Bidwell House, Trumpington Road, Cambridge, CB2 9LD
Activities: Other letting and operating of own or leased real estate
Officers: Robert Coote, Secretary; Rory Buchanan Landman [1961] Director/Senior Bursar; John Vartan Tweddle [1946] Director

Dunward Properties Limited
Incorporated: 15 December 2000 *Employees:* 2
Net Worth: £6,383,713 *Total Assets:* £22,902,012
Registered Office: Langford Hall Barn, Witham Road, Langford, Maldon, Essex, CM9 4ST
Activities: Buying and selling of own real estate
Major Shareholder: Duncan Clemson Watson
Officers: Margaret Anne Watson, Secretary; Duncan Clemson Watson [1974] Director/Property Consultant

Duoview Properties Limited
Incorporated: 1 June 1982
Net Worth: £8,152,891 *Total Assets:* £9,389,861
Registered Office: 55 Crown Street, Brentwood, Essex, CM14 4BD
Activities: Development of building projects
Parent: Flashlock Limited
Officers: Julia Lorraine Hatcher, Secretary; David Robert Horn [1962] Director; Duncan James Horn [1930] Director

Dupont (UK) Electronic Materials Limited
Incorporated: 4 June 2015
Net Worth: £15,318,364 *Total Assets:* £29,255,614
Registered Office: 4th Floor, Kings Court, London Road, Stevenage, Herts, SG1 2NG
Activities: Other service activities n.e.c.
Parent: Du Pont (U.K.) Limited
Officers: Stephen Reeve, Secretary; Adrian Paul Gough [1958] Director/Business Development Manager; Stephen Reeve [1963] Director/Accountant

Durite Limited
Incorporated: 31 March 1942 *Employees:* 74
Previous: Gordon Equipments Limited
Net Worth: £13,547,973 *Total Assets:* £19,827,032
Registered Office: Durite Works, Valley Road, Dovercourt, Essex, CO12 4RX
Activities: Wholesale trade of motor vehicle parts and accessories
Parent: Spring Bidco Limited
Officers: Steven Grant Fobel [1964] Director/Investor; Jean Charles Julien [1951] Director [French]; Pierre Nadeau [1962] Director

Durkan Estates Limited
Incorporated: 19 May 1987 *Employees:* 9
Net Worth: £12,984,717 *Total Assets:* £72,139,800
Registered Office: 4 Elstree Gate, Elstree Way, Borehamwood, Herts, WD6 1JD
Activities: Development of building projects
Officers: Ronan Patrick Murphy, Secretary; Daniel Gerard Durkan [1964] Director - Sales [Irish]; Ronan Patrick Murphy [1969] Director/Chartered Accountant [Irish]

Durkan Holdings Limited
Incorporated: 9 June 1977 *Employees:* 175
Net Worth: £58,871,960 *Total Assets:* £142,434,064
Registered Office: 4 Elstree Gate, Elstree Way, Borehamwood, Herts, WD6 1JD
Activities: Development of building projects
Officers: Ronan Patrick Murphy, Secretary; Daniel Gerard Durkan [1964] Director/Chief Executive [Irish]; Ronan Patrick Murphy [1969] Director/Chartered Accountant [Irish]

Durkan Limited
Incorporated: 15 December 1970 *Employees:* 171
Net Worth: £37,842,612 *Total Assets:* £81,418,736
Registered Office: 4 Elstree Gate, Elstree Way, Borehamwood, Herts, WD6 1JD
Activities: Development of building projects
Officers: Ronan Patrick Murphy, Secretary; James Philip Briggs [1960] Managing Director; Ian Philip Cresswell [1965] Health & Safety Director; Daniel Gerard Durkan [1964] Director/Chief Executive [Irish]; Dean Martin [1968] Construction Director; Ronan Patrick Murphy [1969] Director/Chartered Accountant [Irish]; Shane Rooney [1965] Commercial Director [Irish]

Durkin and Sons Limited
Incorporated: 6 June 1983 *Employees:* 71
Net Worth: £7,758,808 *Total Assets:* £9,601,057
Registered Office: Suite 10, Second Floor, Alperton House, Bridgewater Road, Wembley, Middlesex, HA0 1EH
Activities: Construction of other civil engineering projects n.e.c.
Major Shareholder: Michael Edward Durkin
Officers: Edward Durkin, Secretary; Edward Durkin [1956] Director/Company Secretary; Michael Durkin [1954] Director; Monica Durkin [1935] Director [Irish]

Durman Stearn Holdings Limited
Incorporated: 4 April 2014 *Employees:* 147
Net Worth: £9,746,153 *Total Assets:* £14,402,476
Registered Office: 264 High Street, Cottenham, Cambridge, CB24 8RZ
Activities: Activities of construction holding companies
Shareholders: Allan Edgar Stearn; John Arthur Durman
Officers: Nicholas Graham Robert Barrett, Secretary; John Arthur Durman [1940] Director/Quantity Surveyor; Richard John Durman [1966] Director/Manager; Allan Edgar Stearn [1966] Construction Director

DW Windsor Group Limited
Incorporated: 16 January 2014 *Employees:* 126
Net Worth: £6,368,523 *Total Assets:* £10,463,567
Registered Office: DW Windsor, Pindar Road, Hoddesdon, Herts, EN11 0DX
Activities: Other business support service activities n.e.c.
Shareholders: Nikola Susan Thompson; Thomas Walter David Webster
Officers: Terence Albert Dean [1959] Director; Nikola Susan Thompson [1962] Director; Thomas Walter David Webster [1961] Director

Dyer & Butler 2014 Limited
Incorporated: 29 October 2014
Net Worth: £4,217,000 *Total Assets:* £33,206,000
Registered Office: Abel Smith House, Gunnels Wood Road, Stevenage, Herts, SG1 2ST
Activities: Construction of other civil engineering projects n.e.c.
Parent: M Group Services Limited
Officers: Ian Cusden, Secretary; James Michael Arnold [1965] Director; Martin Geoffrey Beesley [1966] Director/Accountant; John Harold Davies [1969] Financial Director; James Neil Edwards [1962] Managing Director; James Robert Winnicott [1968] Director

Dyer & Butler Holdings Limited
Incorporated: 23 June 2003 *Employees:* 4
Net Worth: £9,079,000 *Total Assets:* £22,491,000
Registered Office: Abel Smith House, Gunnels Wood Road, Stevenage, Herts, SG1 2ST
Activities: Construction of other civil engineering projects n.e.c.
Parent: Dyer and Butler 2014 Limited
Officers: Ian Cusden, Secretary; John Harold Davies [1969] Director; James Neil Edwards [1962] Commercial Director

Dyer and Butler Limited
Incorporated: 25 September 1979 *Employees:* 536
Net Worth: £17,504,000 *Total Assets:* £38,692,000
Registered Office: Abel Smith House, Gunnels Wood Road, Stevenage, Herts, SG1 2ST
Activities: Construction of other civil engineering projects n.e.c.
Parent: Dyer and Butler Holdings Limited
Officers: Ian Cusden, Secretary; Steven David Broom [1974] Director; John Harold Davies [1969] Director/Accountant; Richard Denyer [1960] Director; James Neil Edwards [1962] Commercial Director; Mark Stewart Foster [1972] Divisional Director; Anthony John Steer [1972] Commercial Director; Craig Iain Watt [1971] Director

Dynamic Cassette International Limited
Incorporated: 29 September 1983 *Employees:* 183
Net Worth: £8,025,256 *Total Assets:* £11,458,331
Registered Office: Marsh Lane Industrial Estate, Boston, Lincs, PE21 7TX
Activities: Manufacture of plastics in primary forms
Major Shareholder: John William Studholme
Officers: John William Studholme [1943] Director/Engineer; Tammy Nicola Studholme [1968] Director/General Manager

E & J Properties Limited
Incorporated: 25 February 2016 *Employees:* 2
Net Worth: £23,081,994 *Total Assets:* £26,794,584
Registered Office: Treviot House, 186-192 High Road, Ilford, Essex, IG1 1LR
Activities: Renting and operating of Housing Association real estate
Shareholders: Intertrust Trustee 2 (Guernsey) Ltd as Trustee for The Heaven Scent QNUPS; Intertrust Trustee 2 (Guernsey) Ltd as Trustee for The Kleg QNUPS
Officers: Barry Albert Elvidge [1949] Director; Howard Victor Jones [1950] Director

E - Leather Limited
Incorporated: 31 January 1995 *Employees:* 169
Net Worth: £46,604,312 *Total Assets:* £53,823,740
Registered Office: Kingsbridge Centre, Sturrock Way, Peterborough, PE3 8TZ
Activities: Other manufacturing n.e.c.
Officers: John Kennedy, Secretary; Ian Duncan Boyce [1944] Director; Andrew Clifford Winawer Brandler [1956] Director; John Patrick Kennedy [1969] Director; Ilias Korosis [1979] Director/Partner [Greek]; James Lindsay Lewis [1975] Director [Australian]; Christopher James McBean [1958] Director; Arne Claudio Morteani [1974] Director/Principal, ETF Manager LLP [German]; Patrick Gerard Sheehan [1960] Director/Managing Partner

E.F.G. Housewares Limited
Incorporated: 13 March 1998 *Employees:* 78
Net Worth: £8,588,254 *Total Assets:* £13,650,907
Registered Office: 55 High Street, Hoddesdon, Herts, EN11 8TQ
Activities: Wholesale of china and glassware and cleaning materials
Parent: Enfield Fancy Goods Limited
Officers: Alan Brian Shipton, Secretary/Wholesaler; Alan Brian Shipton [1938] Director/Wholesaler; Daren Shipton [1968] Director/Manager; Mark William Shipton [1973] Director/Manager; Trevor Roderick Shipton [1943] Director/Wholesaler

E.G.L. Homecare Limited
Incorporated: 21 February 1979 *Employees:* 281
Net Worth: £13,815,526 *Total Assets:* £24,045,456
Registered Office: Campfield Road, Shoeburyness, Essex, SS3 9FL
Activities: Other manufacturing n.e.c.
Shareholders: Roger William Walters; Teresa Walters
Officers: Trevor Andrew Ballard, Secretary; Trevor Andrew Ballard [1956] Finance Director; Terence David Dearlove [1953] Managing Director; Roger William Walters [1945] Director/Chairman CEO; Stuart Treston Walters [1976] Commercial Director; Teresa Walters [1947] Director

E.G.T. Bridging Finance Limited
Incorporated: 1 September 1998 *Employees:* 3
Net Worth: £12,019 *Total Assets:* £12,921,594
Registered Office: 35 Glanleam Road, Stanmore, Middlesex, HA7 4NW
Activities: Credit granting by non-deposit taking finance houses and other specialist consumer credit grantors
Parent: E.G.T. Finance Limited
Officers: Dana Houri [1997] Director; Leanne Houri [1996] Director/Trainee; Shaoul Houri [1957] Director; Talia Houri [1990] Director/Teacher

E.G.T. Finance Limited
Incorporated: 27 January 1993 *Employees:* 5
Net Worth: £5,171,496 *Total Assets:* £17,331,720
Registered Office: 35 Glanleam Road, Stanmore, Middlesex, HA7 4NW
Activities: Other credit granting n.e.c.
Shareholder: Shaoul Houri
Officers: Shaoul Houri [1957] Director

E.V. Offshore Limited
Incorporated: 1 March 2000 *Employees:* 57
Net Worth: £5,344,000 *Total Assets:* £13,356,000
Registered Office: EV Technology Centre, 19 Frensham Road, Norwich, NR3 2BT
Activities: Support activities for petroleum and natural gas mining
Parent: EV Finco Limited
Officers: John Joseph Houston, Secretary; John Joseph Houston [1964] Finance Director; Fraser Louden [1965] Director; Jonathan James Renton Thursby [1968] Director

Eagle 456 Limited
Incorporated: 18 April 2000 *Employees:* 3
Net Worth: £14,599,464 *Total Assets:* £37,521,620
Registered Office: 22 Barn Rise, Wembley, Middlesex, HA9 9NQ
Activities: Other letting and operating of own or leased real estate
Parent: Aquila House Property Limited
Officers: Paul Gary Hirst, Secretary/Director; Anthony David Chambers [1955] Director; Daniel Freedman [1971] Director/Lawyer; Paul Gary Hirst [1961] Director

Earl Estates Limited
Incorporated: 29 June 1994 *Employees:* 3
Net Worth: £10,248,005 *Total Assets:* £16,114,566
Registered Office: c/o Tees Law, Cathedral Place, Brentwood, Essex, CM14 4ES
Activities: Development of building projects
Shareholder: Michael John Christmas
Officers: Michael John Christmas [1954] Director/Chartered Surveyor; Martin Thomas Harrison [1954] Director/Chartered Surveyor

Earlham Institute
Incorporated: 23 March 2009 *Employees:* 105
Previous: The Genome Analysis Centre
Net Worth: £25,217,000 *Total Assets:* £35,906,000
Registered Office: Earlham Institute, Norwich Research Park, Colney Lane, Norwich, NR4 7UZ
Activities: Other research and experimental development on natural sciences and engineering
Officers: Professor Jean Duthie Beggs [1950] Director/Professor; Andrea Finegan [1969] Director/Lecturer [German]; Terence John Gould [1952] Director/Solicitor; Professor Edward John Louis [1959] Director/Professor [American]; Dr Alasdair James MacNab [1954] Executive Director; Amanda Jane Tagg [1973] Director/Solicitor; Dame Janet Maureen Thornton [1949] Director/Research Scientist; Professor Veronica Van Heyningen [1946] Director/Research Scientist, Emeritus Professor; Professor Robbie Waugh [1959] Director/Scientist

Earlseat Wind Farm Ltd
Incorporated: 9 April 2009
Net Worth: £1,089,000 *Total Assets:* £18,545,000
Registered Office: Beaufort Court, Egg Farm Lane, Kings Langley, Herts, WD4 8LR
Activities: Production of electricity
Parent: European Investments (Earlseat) Limited
Officers: Dominic James Hearth, Secretary; Steven William Hughes [1972] Generation and Asset Management Director; Fraser Stephen Merry [1968] Director/Chartered Surveyor; Mitesh Raj Patel [1982] Director/Group Financial Controller

Early Learning Centre Limited
Incorporated: 25 March 1909 *Employees:* 24
Net Worth Deficit: £114,600,000 *Total Assets:* £119,100,000
Registered Office: Cherry Tree Road, Watford, Herts, WD24 6SH
Activities: Other retail sale of new goods in specialised stores (not commercial art galleries and opticians)
Parent: Early Learning Holdings Limited
Officers: Lynne Samatha Medini, Secretary; Kirsty Rowena Homer [1974] HR Director; William Glyn Lawrence Hughes [1976] Director/Chief Financial Officer; Mark Newton-Jones [1967] Director; Kevin Jonathan Rusling [1977] Managing Director, International

Early Learning Holdings Limited
Incorporated: 29 March 2001
Net Worth Deficit: £4,800,000 *Total Assets:* £13,900,000
Registered Office: Cherry Tree Road, Watford, Herts, WD24 6SH
Activities: Non-trading company
Parent: Chelsea Stores Holdings Limited
Officers: Lynne Samatha Medini, Secretary; Darren Wayne Clark [1979] Director/Accountant; Kirsty Rowena Homer [1974] HR Director

George East (Housewares) Limited
Incorporated: 6 May 1999 *Employees:* 76
Net Worth: £3,790,094 *Total Assets:* £9,028,359
Registered Office: 1-5 Masterlord Industrial Estate, Station Road, Leiston, Suffolk, IP16 4JD
Activities: Wholesale of household goods (other than musical instruments) n.e.c
Officers: Wouter Beremd Jan Meijerink [1969] Director/Board Member [Dutch]; Ward Marc Willem Poppelaars [1974] Director [Dutch]; Nicholas Squire [1963] Director

East Anglia's Childrens Hospices
Incorporated: 16 April 1998 *Employees:* 315
Net Worth: £18,562,756 *Total Assets:* £19,739,388
Registered Office: 42 High Street, Milton, Cambridge, CB24 6DF
Activities: Other human health activities
Officers: Graham Butland, Secretary/Hospice Chief Executive; Lily Jeanette Bacon [1966] Director; Sheila Jean Childerhouse [1951] Director/Businesswoman; Roger Cobley [1942] Director/Consultant; Nicholas Davies [1969] Director/Barrister; Robert Michael Dawson [1954] Director/Consultant; Emma Sophia Deterding [1964] Director/Interior Designer; Paul Green [1963] Director/Commodity Trader; Judi Ingram [1963] Director/Nurse; Annmarie Lloyd-Jones [1951] Director/Retired; Bradley Kenneth Duncan McLean [1977] Director/General Manager; Ann Monks [1960] Marketing Director; John Pickering [1957] Director/Chartered Accountant; William Arthur Self [1982] Director; Dr Virginia Jane Warren [1955] Director/Doctor

East Anglian Air Ambulance
Incorporated: 6 September 2000 *Employees:* 55
Net Worth: £20,579,058 *Total Assets:* £21,593,548
Registered Office: Hangar E, Gambling Close, Norwich Airport, Norwich, NR6 6EG
Activities: Other human health activities
Officers: Christopher Hamilton Dicker, Secretary; Duncan John Astill [1972] Director/Solicitor; Stephanie Bourne [1952] Director; William George Cubitt [1959] Director; Roger Steven Holden [1952] Director/Partner; Lord Arthur Edward Rory Iveagh [1969] Director/Landowner [Irish]; Nigel Rudolph Savory [1953] Director/Chartered Accountant; Penelope Anne Walkinshaw [1959] Director; Thomas Franey Wells [1951] Director

East Anglian Installations Limited
Incorporated: 26 November 1992 *Employees:* 40
Net Worth: £8,596,253 *Total Assets:* £10,007,223
Registered Office: 22-26 King Street, King's Lynn, Norfolk, PE30 1HJ
Activities: Manufacture of other fabricated metal products n.e.c.
Shareholder: Neil John Williamson
Officers: Melvyn Edward George Harbour, Secretary; Daniel Paul Boore [1974] Director/Salesman; Neil John Williamson [1966] Director

East Anglian Property Limited
Incorporated: 11 February 1987 *Employees:* 3
Net Worth: £20,014,540 *Total Assets:* £22,052,218
Registered Office: Lakeside, Roman Drive, Brundall, Norfolk, NR13 5LU
Activities: Development of building projects
Parent: East Anglian Property Preservation Limited
Officers: Alan Jones, Secretary; Alan Jones [1958] Director/Builder; Linda Mary Jones [1961] Director; Phillip Arthur Thorpe [1960] Director/Accountant

East Barnet School
Incorporated: 4 March 2011 *Employees:* 173
Net Worth: £31,794,992 *Total Assets:* £33,897,964
Registered Office: East Barnet School, 5 Chestnut Grove, Barnet, Herts, EN4 8PU
Activities: General secondary education
Officers: Susan Waters, Secretary; Deborah Ann Brazier [1967] Director/Accountant; Debbie Jane Cuthbert [1951] Director/Educational Consultant; Theodoulos Lakis Diamandis [1971] Director/Learning & Development Manager; Stuart Morrison Gates [1959] Director/Self Employed, Sole Trader; Scott Michael Harrison [1949] Director/Education Consultant; Dr Angela Marie Hind [1964] Charity Director; Major John Bernard Ireton [1957] Director/Head of Department Veolia Water Central; Susan Patricia McDonald [1968] Charity Director; Nicholas John Mottershead [1958] Director/Dubbing Mixer; Caroline Roncarati [1971] Director/Teacher; Joanna Ray Tambourides [1948] Director/Councillor and P.A; Claire Elizabeth Thomas [1963] Deputy Director of Charity; Timothy John Beech Williamson [1960] Director/Civil Servant; Mariam Zaman [1989] Director/Teacher; Ingrid Zanchetta [1972] Director/Programme Development Manager [Italian]

East Coast Community Healthcare C.I.C.
Incorporated: 22 March 2011 *Employees:* 848
Net Worth: £3,286,159 *Total Assets:* £8,924,366
Registered Office: Hamilton House, Battery Green Road, Lowestoft, Suffolk, NR32 1DE
Activities: Hospital activities
Officers: Peter Francis Gosling, Secretary; Simon Bragg [1965] Director; Noreen Cushen [1962] Director of Quality and Development [Irish]; Dr Andrew Robert Emerson [1960] Director/Doctor; Elizabeth Marie Goddard [1968] Director/Triage Team Lead; Lisa Jane Judge [1979] Director/Senior District Nursing Sister; Sean Mark Toms Kent [1965] Director; Rachel Lilley [1964] Director; Adele Madin [1971] Director; Anna Kathleen McCreadie [1961] Director; Ian Grant Morrison [1965] Director; Anthony Osmanski [1953] Director/Chairman; Jonathan Huw Williams [1961] Director/Health Executive

East Langford Solar Limited
Incorporated: 20 April 2011
Net Worth Deficit: £1,851,968 *Total Assets:* £10,998,135
Registered Office: Beaufort Court, Egg Farm Lane, off Station Road, Kings Langley, Herts, WD4 8LR
Activities: Production of electricity
Parent: European Investments (Cornwall) Limited
Officers: Dominic Hearth, Secretary; Steven William Hughes [1972] Global Support Services Director, UK&I - Commercial; Mitesh Raj Patel [1982] Director/Chartered Accountant; Tracy Jane Scott [1976] Director/Delivery Project Manager; Mark Christopher Wayment [1958] Director

East Midlands Training Limited
Incorporated: 9 March 2001 *Employees:* 27
Net Worth Deficit: £2,900,823 *Total Assets:* £13,727,504
Registered Office: c/o Ryanair Limited, Enterprise House, Stanstead Airport, Stanstead, Essex, CM24 1QW
Activities: Other transportation support activities
Parent: Ryanair DAC
Officers: Peter Brendan Bellew [1965] Director/Chief Operations Officer, Ryanair [Irish]; Tracey McCann [1973] Director of Finance [Irish]

East of England Agricultural Society
Incorporated: 7 October 1981 *Employees:* 31
Net Worth: £20,768,404 *Total Assets:* £22,252,378
Registered Office: East of England Showground, Alwalton, Peterborough, Cambs, PE2 6XE
Activities: Activities of other membership organisations n.e.c.
Officers: Hedley Richard Quentin Arnold, Secretary; Thomas Benjamin White Beazley [1963] Director/Farmer; Richard Cranmer Bramley [1958] Director/Retired; Robert William Dalgliesh [1954] Director/Chartered Surveyor; Geoffrey John Dodgson [1951] Director; Benjamin Mark John Harris [1978] Director/Farmer; James Robert Parrish [1968] Director/Farm Partner; John Stuart Greer Paton [1946] Director/Chartered Surveyor; Charles David Reynolds [1969] Director/Consultant; Andrew Henry Riddington [1965] Director; Nigel Peter Rome [1961] Director/Farmer

Eastern Attachments Limited
Incorporated: 20 May 1996 *Employees:* 43
Net Worth: £5,898,811 *Total Assets:* £8,102,738
Registered Office: Eastern House, Maurice Gaymer Road, Attleborough, Norfolk, NR17 2QZ
Activities: Manufacture of other fabricated metal products n.e.c.
Officers: Simon Paul Leslie, Secretary; Christopher Andrew Leslie [1962] Director/Technical Manager; Daniel James Leslie [1977] Director/Technical Manager; Philip Matthew Leslie [1974] Director/Agricultural Technician; Simon Paul Leslie [1975] Director/Production Manager

Eastern Counties Laundries Limited
Incorporated: 5 August 1930 *Employees:* 314
Net Worth: £8,296,414 *Total Assets:* £12,903,000
Registered Office: 28 Robjohns Road, Widford Industrial Estate, Chelmsford, Essex, CM1 3AF
Activities: Washing and (dry-)cleaning of textile and fur products
Officers: Malcolm Robert Clarke, Secretary; Malcolm Robert Clarke [1955] Director/Accountant; Jeremy Croyden Moore [1958] Director/Manager; Oliver Moore [1989] Operations Director; Timothy William Moore [1959] Director/Manager; Wendy Maureen Dalton Moore [1933] Director/Secretary

Eastern Credit Limited
Incorporated: 10 August 2001 *Employees:* 7
Net Worth: £6,396,168 *Total Assets:* £14,362,199
Registered Office: Sandbanks, 69 Marine Parade, Gorleston, Great Yarmouth, Norfolk, NR31 6EZ
Activities: Financial leasing
Shareholders: Derek Ivan Needham; Paul Needham
Officers: David Raymond King, Secretary; Derek Ivan Needham [1949] Director; Paul Needham [1976] Director/Manager

Eastern Multi-Academy Trust
Incorporated: 6 August 2010 *Employees:* 862
Previous: CWA Academy Trust
Net Worth: £53,622,000 *Total Assets:* £62,657,000
Registered Office: Trust Offices, Queen Mary Road, King's Lynn, Norfolk, PE30 4QG
Activities: Primary education
Officers: David Alan Evans, Secretary; Lady Karen Jean Fisher [1951] Director; Wendy Jayne Fisher [1965] Director/Freelance Consumer Researcher; Deborah Gates [1961] Local Authority Director; Jason William Hall [1972] Director/Chartered Accountant; Graham John Pearson [1958] Director/Account General Manager; Julie Perry [1972] Director/Global Risk Management; Dr Duncan Ramsey [1967] Director/Chief Executive; James Rowney [1967] Director; Derek Edward Stringer [1945] Director/Retired Management Consultant; Julie Ann Taylor [1961] Director/Chief Executive; David Malcolm Wilde [1966] Director

Eastleaf Ltd
Incorporated: 21 June 2006 *Employees:* 3
Net Worth Deficit: £238,507 *Total Assets:* £20,515,848
Registered Office: Suite 7 & 8 Broomfield Business Centre, 80-82 Broomfield Road, Chelmsford, Essex, CM1 1SS
Activities: Buying and selling of own real estate
Parent: Chancellor Management Limited
Officers: Ashok Gupta, Secretary; Alison Claire Khattar [1969] Director; Navin Khattar [1972] Director [Singaporean]

Eastmarket Grain LLP
Incorporated: 30 October 2012
Total Assets: £12,828,413
Registered Office: Office 11, 6-8 Dartford Road, March, Cambs, PE15 8AQ

F.H.Easton Limited
Incorporated: 28 January 1956 *Employees:* 6
Net Worth: £4,433,242 *Total Assets:* £10,505,778
Registered Office: The Villa, The Old Turnpike, Bunwell, Norwich, NR16 1SN
Activities: Growing of cereals (except rice), leguminous crops and oil seeds
Shareholders: Mark George Easton; Andrew John Easton; William Frank Easton
Officers: Mark George Easton, Secretary; Andrew John Easton [1959] Director/Depot Manager; Charles Henry Easton [1986] Director/Accounts & HR Manager; George Miles Easton [1988] Director/Farm Foreman; George Peter Easton [1939] Director/Farmer; Mark George Easton [1960] Director/Depot Manager; William Frank Easton [1965] Director/Farmer

Eastwood Park Academy Trust
Incorporated: 11 July 2011 *Employees:* 166
Previous: Eastwood Park Academy Trust Ltd.
Net Worth: £19,924,304 *Total Assets:* £22,697,932
Registered Office: The Eastwood Academy, Rayleigh Road, Leigh on Sea, Southend on Sea, Essex, SS9 5UU
Activities: General secondary education
Officers: Katherine Elaine Toms, Secretary; David Arthur Allen [1956] Director/Retired; Adeela Hassan Fethi [1979] Director/Florist; Karen Heath [1963] Director/Civil Servant; Neil Houchen [1977] Director/Headteacher; Lee Whittick [1967] Director/Bank Manager

Easy Cleaning Solutions Limited
Incorporated: 20 October 1950 *Employees:* 253
Previous: Jeyes Limited
Net Worth Deficit: £428,147 *Total Assets:* £18,408,270
Registered Office: Easy Cleaning, Brunel Way, Thetford, Norfolk, IP24 1HF
Activities: Manufacture of other chemical products n.e.c.
Major Shareholder: David James Pearce
Officers: Darren James Mosley [1966] Director/Chief Executive Officer; David Pearce [1966] Director

Easyjet Airline Company Limited
Incorporated: 17 March 1995 *Employees:* 12,139
Net Worth: £2,012,000,000 *Total Assets:* £6,672,999,936
Registered Office: Hangar 89, London Luton Airport, Luton, Beds, LU2 9PF
Activities: Scheduled passenger air transport
Parent: Easyjet PLC
Officers: Daud Khan, Secretary; Margaret Christine Browne [1960] Director; Robert Etienne Carey [1979] Director [French]; Andrew Robert Findlay [1969] Director; Johan Peter Lundgren [1966] Director [Swedish]

Easyjet PLC
Incorporated: 24 March 2000 *Employees:* 13,104
Net Worth: £3,259,000,064 *Total Assets:* £6,994,999,808
Registered Office: Hangar 89, London Luton Airport, Luton, Beds, LU2 9PF
Activities: Activities of head offices
Officers: Daud Khan, Secretary; Robert John Orr Barton [1944] Director; Dr. Andreas Bierwirth [1971] Director [German]; Andrew Robert Findlay [1969] Director; Moya Marguerite Greene [1954] Director [Canadian]; Charles Mark Gurassa [1956] Director; Anastassia Lauterbach [1972] Director [German]; Nicholas Leeder [1969] Director [Australian/French]; Johan Peter Lundgren [1966] Director [Swedish]; Andrew David Martin [1960] Director; Julie Helen Southern [1959] Director

Ebberod Capital Ltd
Incorporated: 25 September 2008
Net Worth: £378,758 *Total Assets:* £18,954,268
Registered Office: First Floor, Water Circle, City Meadows, Stansted, Essex, CM22 6DR
Activities: Financial intermediation not elsewhere classified
Parent: Sectra AB
Officers: Shelley Louise Binns, Secretary; Mats Franzen [1969] Director/Chief Financial Officer [Swedish]; Jane Sarah Rendall [1973] Managing Director

EBM - Papst UK Limited
Incorporated: 13 May 1975 *Employees:* 86
Net Worth: £17,794,676 *Total Assets:* £24,465,800
Registered Office: Chelmsford Business Park, Chelmsford, Essex, CM2 5EZ
Activities: Manufacture of electric motors, generators and transformers
Parent: EBM Beteiligungs GmbH
Officers: Stefan Robert Brandl, Secretary; Stefan Robert Brandl [1968] Director/Chief Executive [German]; David John Jarvis [1957] Director/Manager; Sandra Jarvis [1956] Director/Commercial; Raymond Lionel Ladyman [1960] Director/Operations; Geoffrey Mark Lockwood [1961] Director/Technical

Ebrex Business Solutions Limited
Incorporated: 23 July 2009 *Employees:* 176
Net Worth: £6,100,684 *Total Assets:* £11,435,763
Registered Office: Ferry House, South Denes Road, Great Yarmouth, Norfolk, NR30 3PJ
Activities: Freight transport by road
Shareholders: Josef de Waal; Arvid Rolf Edouard Meijer; Antonius Matheus Maria Cuppens; Heinrich Josef de Waal
Officers: Derek John Ward, Secretary; Antonius Matheus Maria Cuppens [1948] Director [Dutch]; Josef de Waal [1946] Director/Forwarding Agent [German]; Arvid Rolf Edouard Meijer [1962] Director [Dutch]

EC English Cambridge Limited
Incorporated: 12 June 1996 *Employees:* 57
Net Worth Deficit: £4,191,565 *Total Assets:* £23,539,772
Registered Office: Tennyson House, Cambridge Business Park, Cambridge, CB4 0WZ
Activities: Non-trading company
Officers: Michael William Giffin [1967] Director/Chief Financial Officer; Andrew Mangion [1970] Director [Maltese]; Michael Xuereb [1972] Director/Chief Executive [Maltese]

EC English London Limited
Incorporated: 17 December 1997 *Employees:* 64
Net Worth: £1,790,498 *Total Assets:* £30,937,344
Registered Office: Tennyson House, Cambridge Business Park, Cambridge, CB4 0WZ
Activities: Technical and vocational secondary education
Officers: Michael William Giffin [1967] Director/Chief Financial Officer; Andrew Mangion [1970] Director [Maltese]; Michael Xuereb [1972] Director/Chief Executive [Maltese]

Eckoh PLC
Incorporated: 12 September 1997 *Employees:* 214
Net Worth: £21,809,000 *Total Assets:* £34,918,000
Registered Office: Telford House, Corner Hall, Hemel Hempstead, Herts, HP3 9HN
Activities: Other telecommunications activities
Officers: Christine Gillian Herbert, Secretary; David John Coghlan [1954] Director [British/Australian]; Christine Gillian Herbert [1970] Director; Christopher John Humphrey [1957] Director; Guy Leighton Millward [1965] Director; Nicholas Barnaby Philpot [1964] Director/Chief Executive Officer

Eckoh UK Limited
Incorporated: 5 March 1993 *Employees:* 167
Net Worth: £21,922,000 *Total Assets:* £25,491,000
Registered Office: Telford House, Corner Hall, Hemel Hempstead, Herts, HP3 9HN
Activities: Other telecommunications activities
Parent: Eckoh PLC
Officers: Christine Gillian Herbert, Secretary; Christine Gillian Herbert [1970] Director; Nicholas Barnaby Philpot [1964] Director/Chief Operating Officer

Ecotherm Insulation (UK) Ltd
Incorporated: 21 December 1984 *Employees:* 17
Net Worth Deficit: £187,623 *Total Assets:* £22,447,292
Registered Office: Harvey Road, Burnt Mills Estate, Basildon, Essex, SS13 1QJ
Activities: Other construction installation
Shareholders: Kingspan Insulation Limited; Kingspan Insulation Limited
Officers: Patrick Alan Lawlor [1970] Director [Irish]; Ralph Mannion [1971] Director [Irish]; Lwana Quarrell [1972] Director/Accountant; Peter Charles Wilson [1956] Managing Director [Irish]

The Eden Academy
Incorporated: 18 April 2012 *Employees:* 330
Net Worth: £14,639,000 *Total Assets:* £20,257,000
Registered Office: Grangewood School, Fore Street, Eastcote, Pinner, Middlesex, HA5 2JQ
Activities: Primary education
Officers: Keith James Holroyd, Secretary; Hardip Singh Begol [1971] Director/Senior Civil Servant; James Kempe Clarke [1963] Director/Retired; Victoria Collis [1970] Director/Consultant; Karen Deacon [1960] Director of Education and Social Care; Susan Frances Douglas [1970] Director/Educational Consultant; Brian David Eaton [1957] Director/University Lecturer; Helen Marion Susan Milner [1957] Director/Project Manager; Barry Joseph Nolan [1968] Director/Banker; Angela St John [1959] Director; Collette Gwendoline Stone [1956] Director/Civil Servant

Edgewell Personal Care Holdings UK Ltd.
Incorporated: 25 February 2000 *Employees:* 5
Previous: Energizer Holdings UK Company Limited
Net Worth: £47,179,000 *Total Assets:* £83,820,000
Registered Office: Sword House, Totteridge Road, High Wycombe, Bucks, HP13 6DG
Activities: Non-trading company
Parent: Edgewell Personal Care Investments UK Ltd
Officers: David Paul Hatfield [1960] Director/Executive Officer [American]; Colin Anthony Hutchison [1958] Director/Chief Operating Officer; Rod Ryan Little [1969] Director/Chief Financial Officer [American]

Edgewell Personal Care Investments UK Ltd.
Incorporated: 14 March 2003
Previous: Energizer Investments UK Limited
Net Worth: £56,288,000 *Total Assets:* £56,288,000
Registered Office: Sword House, Totteridge Road, High Wycombe, Bucks, HP13 6DG
Activities: Non-trading company
Parent: Edgewell Personal Care Company
Officers: David Paul Hatfield [1960] Director/Executive Officer [American]; Colin Anthony Hutchison [1958] Director/Chief Operating Officer; Rod Ryan Little [1969] Director/Chief Financial Officer [American]

Edgewell Personal Care UK Limited
Incorporated: 13 May 2015
Net Worth: £59,372,320 *Total Assets:* £70,825,568
Registered Office: Sword House, Totteridge Road, High Wycombe, Bucks, HP13 6DG
Activities: Non-trading company
Parent: Wilkinson Sword Limited
Officers: David Paul Hatfield [1960] Director/Executive [American]; Colin Anthony Hutchison [1958] Director/Chief Operating Officer; Rod Ryan Little [1969] Director/Chief Financial Officer [American]

Edinburgh Sainsbury Holdings LLP
Incorporated: 27 April 2015 *Employees:* 5
Net Worth: £10,892,010 *Total Assets:* £10,892,010
Registered Office: Aprirose House, 48a High Street, Edgware, Middlesex, HA8 7EQ
Officers: Manish Mansukhlal Gudka [1970] Member; Gareth Jones [1973] Member; Suraj Rashmikant Shah [1982] LLP Member

Edmonton Academy Trust
Incorporated: 4 August 2016 *Employees:* 240
Net Worth: £19,442,016 *Total Assets:* £22,072,404
Registered Office: Edmonton County School, Great Cambridge Road, Enfield, Middlesex, EN1 1HQ
Activities: Primary education
Officers: Peter Quentin Blane [1969] Finance Sales Director; Konrad Hogarth Halls [1961] Director/Facilities Management; Rob Leak [1951] Director/Retired; Dr Christine Maria Martin [1965] Director/Software Engineer [British/American]; Salih Suavi [1960] Director/IT Manager; Dr Susan Mary Tranter [1963] Director/Executive Headteacher; Elizabeth Nicola Whale [1980] Director/Merchandiser

Edstrom UK Holdings PLC
Incorporated: 11 September 2017 *Employees:* 60
Net Worth: £6,625,259 *Total Assets:* £18,239,662
Registered Office: Unit D4, Drakes Drive, Long Crendon Industrial Estate, Long Crendon, Bucks, HP18 9BA
Activities: Other professional, scientific and technical activities n.e.c.
Officers: Scott Gage, Secretary; Scott Gage [1969] Director [American]; Brett Charles Habstritt [1975] Director [American]

Education Management Corporation Limited
Incorporated: 21 December 2006 *Employees:* 1,725
Net Worth Deficit: £13,604,114 *Total Assets:* £111,891,240
Registered Office: 2nd Floor, Hygeia Building, 66 College Road, Harrow, Middlesex, HA1 1BE
Activities: Activities of other holding companies n.e.c.
Officers: Derek Russell Smith [1962] Director

Education Personnel Bidco Limited
Incorporated: 14 July 2010
Net Worth Deficit: £21,588,000 *Total Assets:* £71,569,000
Registered Office: 99 Bridge Road East, Welwyn Garden City, Herts, AL7 1GL
Activities: Activities of head offices
Parent: Education Personnel Holdco Limited
Officers: John Vincent Bowman [1963] Director; Jonathan Nicholas Roback [1969] Director

Edwardian Care Homes Limited
Incorporated: 15 July 1996 *Employees:* 28
Net Worth: £4,406,915 *Total Assets:* £8,370,665
Registered Office: Victoria House, 14-26 Victoria Street, Luton, Beds, LU1 2UA
Activities: Residential nursing care facilities
Shareholders: Sheikh Mubashir Hussain; Nadia Care Centre Limited
Officers: Nadiya Hussain, Secretary; Sheikh Mubashir Hussain [1950] Director/General Manager Residential Homes

EE Finance PLC
Incorporated: 11 November 2011
Net Worth: £12,000 *Total Assets:* £986,796,992
Registered Office: Trident Place, Mosquito Way, Hatfield, Herts, AL10 9BW
Activities: Financial management
Parent: EE Limited
Officers: Marc David Allera [1972] Director/Chief Executive Officer; Stephen Christopher Harris [1970] Director

EE Limited
Incorporated: 10 May 1989 *Employees:* 12,176
Net Worth: £3,502,000,128 *Total Assets:* £7,143,000,064
Registered Office: Trident Place, Mosquito Way, Hatfield, Herts, AL10 9BW
Activities: Other telecommunications activities
Parent: British Telecommunications PLC
Officers: Marc David Allera [1972] Director/Chief Executive Officer; Stephen John Best [1966] Managing Director; Stephen Christopher Harris [1970] Director; Jeffrey Neil Langlands [1976] Director/Lawyer; Mark Gareth Tipton [1971] Group Director; John Howard Watson [1963] Director/Chief Executive Officer

Eisai Europe Limited
Incorporated: 25 October 2004 *Employees:* 1,012
Net Worth: £414,406,016 *Total Assets:* £847,257,024
Registered Office: European Knowledge Centre, Mosquito Way, Hatfield, Herts, AL10 9SN
Activities: Activities of head offices
Parent: Eisai Co.Ltd
Officers: Simon Gerard Thomas, Secretary; Elaine Louise Archer [1970] Director/CFO EMEA; Toshitaka Asano [1966] Director [Japanese]; Nicholas Conrad Burgin [1959] Director; Gary Bryan Hendler [1966] Director/President and CEO; Kazuhiko Masano [1971] Director [Japanese]

Eisai Limited
Incorporated: 11 April 1988 *Employees:* 182
Net Worth: £105,982,944 *Total Assets:* £126,478,576
Registered Office: European Knowledge Centre, Mosquito Way, Hatfield, Herts, AL10 9SN
Activities: Wholesale of pharmaceutical goods
Parent: Eisai Europe Limited
Officers: Simon Gerard Thomas, Secretary; Nicholas Conrad Burgin [1959] Director; Gary Bryan Hendler [1966] Director/President and CEO; Teiji Kimura [1963] Director [Japanese]; Kazuhiko Masano [1971] Director [Japanese]

Eisai Manufacturing Limited
Incorporated: 1 March 2007 *Employees:* 105
Net Worth: £74,089,208 *Total Assets:* £454,234,976
Registered Office: European Knowledge Centre, Mosquito Way, Hatfield, Herts, AL10 9SN
Activities: Manufacture of basic pharmaceutical products
Parent: Eisai Europe Limited
Officers: Simon Gerard Thomas, Secretary; Nicholas Conrad Burgin [1959] Director; Alex John Felthouse [1973] Director; Yoshiteru Kato [1960] Director [Japanese]; Shin Ujiie [1980] Director [Japanese]; Tatsuyuki Yasuno [1968] Director/Corporate Officer, VP [Japanese]

Elastomer Trading Limited
Incorporated: 30 March 2006 *Employees:* 3
Net Worth: £12,301,307 *Total Assets:* £12,626,629
Registered Office: 3 Pugh Place, Stanford-le-Hope, Essex, SS17 8BL
Activities: Other professional, scientific and technical activities n.e.c.
Officers: David George Dyer, Secretary; Igor Golberg [1951] Managing Director

The Electricity Network Company Limited
Incorporated: 4 October 2005
Net Worth: £6,453,628 *Total Assets:* £69,103,256
Registered Office: Energy House, Woolpit Business Park, Woolpit, Bury St Edmunds, Suffolk, IP30 9UP
Activities: Transmission of electricity
Parent: BUUK Infrastructure No 2 Limited
Officers: Christopher Mumford, Secretary; Susan Lisa Standring, Secretary; Darryl John Corney [1960] Director; Clive Eric Linsdell [1962] Managing Director; David Walter Overman [1961] Director/Electricity Networks Manager; John Trounson [1966] Director

Electro-Motive Diesel Limited
Incorporated: 18 August 2006 *Employees:* 158
Net Worth: £8,247,000 *Total Assets:* £29,892,000
Registered Office: c/o Perkins Engines Company Limited, Eastfield, Frank Perkins Way, Peterborough, Cambs, PE1 5FQ
Activities: Maintenance and repair of motor vehicles
Parent: Caterpillar International Holdings S.A.R.L
Officers: Johanna Elizabeth Deason, Secretary; Nigel John Burroughs [1961] Director/Tax Accountant; Jonathan Mark Caen [1967] Sales Director; Martin Albert Haycraft [1969] Director/Senior Vice President [American]; Colin Murphy [1962] Director/Chartered Accountant, Head of Finance

Electrolux Investments
Incorporated: 6 September 2002 *Employees:* 5
Net Worth: £42,907,000 *Total Assets:* £42,966,000
Registered Office: Electrolux, Addington Way, Luton, Beds, LU4 9QQ
Activities: Activities of head offices
Parent: Electrolux AB
Officers: Erik Martin Bendixen [1968] Director [Swedish]; Guillaume Durey de Noinville [1960] Director [French]; Friberg Maria Therese [1975] Director [Swedish]; Hanna Nilsson [1977] Director/Head of Global Tax and Accounting [Swedish]; Lars Anders Tarnholm [1968] Director/Business Controller [Swedish]

Electrolux PLC
Incorporated: 29 December 1988 *Employees:* 338
Net Worth: £39,009,000 *Total Assets:* £159,998,000
Registered Office: Electrolux, Addington Way, Luton, Beds, LU4 9QQ
Activities: Manufacture of electric domestic appliances
Parent: Electrolux Investments
Officers: John Alistair Bissill Heycock, Secretary; Cornelius Braam [1969] Director [Dutch]; Guillaume Durey de Noinville [1960] Director [French]; Ola Nilsson [1969] Director/CEO Electrolux Small Appliances [Swedish]

Electrolux Professional Limited
Incorporated: 17 September 1959 *Employees:* 70
Net Worth: £22,435,000 *Total Assets:* £35,556,000
Registered Office: Electrolux, Addington Way, Luton, Beds, LU4 9QQ
Activities: Manufacture of other electrical equipment
Parent: Electrolux PLC
Officers: John Alistair Bissill Heycock, Secretary; Fabio Zarpellon [1967] Director [Italian]

Electron House (Overseas) Limited
Incorporated: 20 November 1985 *Employees:* 3
Net Worth: £42,231,000 *Total Assets:* £42,412,000
Registered Office: Avnet House, Rutherford Close, Stevenage, Herts, SG1 2EF
Activities: Activities of head offices
Parent: Avnet, Inc
Officers: Thomas Ludaescher [1961] Director [German]; Mark McKrell [1966] Finance Director; Harvey Woodford [1963] Director/VP Corporate Secretary [American]

Elegant Electronics Limited
Incorporated: 7 February 1984 *Employees:* 4
Net Worth: £4,652,565 *Total Assets:* £10,876,214
Registered Office: 16 Astons Road, Northwood, Middlesex, HA6 2LD
Activities: Retail sale of computers, peripheral units and software in specialised stores
Shareholders: Deepak Kumar; Niranjana Kumar
Officers: Deepak Kumar, Secretary; Deepak Kumar [1961] Director; Niranjana Kumar [1956] Director; Sham Kumar [1990] Director/Editorial Assistant

Elektron Technology PLC
Incorporated: 20 January 1948 *Employees:* 986
Net Worth: £12,900,000 *Total Assets:* £19,800,000
Registered Office: Broers Building, 21 J J Thomson Avenue, Cambridge, CB3 0FA
Activities: Activities of production holding companies
Officers: Andrew Paul Weatherstone, Secretary; Giovanni Maria Ciuccio [1981] Director [Italian/South African]; Keith Anthony Daley [1955] Director; Richard John Piper [1952] Director; Andrew Paul Weatherstone [1964] Finance Director; John Frederick Wilson [1976] Director

Elektron Technology UK Limited
Incorporated: 31 October 2003 *Employees:* 200
Net Worth: £15,311,000 *Total Assets:* £47,376,000
Registered Office: c/o Elektron Technology PLC, Broers Building, 21 J J Thomson Avenue, Cambridge, CB3 0FA
Activities: Manufacture of electronic components
Parent: Elektron Technology PLC
Officers: Andrew Paul Weatherstone, Secretary; German Casillas [1971] Director/Vice President [American]; Andrew Paul Weatherstone [1964] Finance Director; John Frederick Wilson [1976] Director

Element Energy Limited
Incorporated: 23 January 2003 *Employees:* 32
Net Worth: £1,503,766 *Total Assets:* £14,234,085
Registered Office: Suite 1, Bishop Bateman Court, Thompson's Lane, Cambridge, CB5 8AQ
Activities: Engineering related scientific and technical consulting activities
Parent: Element Energy Holdings Limited
Officers: Julie Lorraine Taylor, Secretary; Celine Stephanie Cluzel [1980] Director/Low Carbon Energy Consultant [French]; Dr Mark Hughes [1975] Director; Ben Andrew Madden [1977] Director/Engineer; Dr Shane Anthony Slater [1973] Director/Consulting Engineer [Irish]; Alexander Henry Stewart [1985] Director of Low Energy Consultancy Company; Dr Ian Thomas Walker [1976] Director/Energy Consultant

Elgon (Enfield) Limited
Incorporated: 1 November 1984
Net Worth: £9,634,732 *Total Assets:* £16,779,368
Registered Office: Eagle House Surgery, 291 High Street, Enfield, Middlesex, EN3 4DN
Activities: Dispensing chemist in specialised stores
Major Shareholder: Jayesh Jayantilal Lakhani
Officers: Anil Jayantilal Lakhani, Secretary; Anil Jayantilal Lakhani [1957] Director/Pharmacist; Jayesh Jayantilal Lakhani [1959] Director/Pharmacist

Elite Mobile (Holdings) Limited
Incorporated: 9 March 2009 *Employees:* 203
Net Worth: £29,723,000 *Total Assets:* £41,816,000
Registered Office: Kings Suite, 4th Floor, Amba House, 15 College Road, Harrow, Middlesex, HA1 1BA
Activities: Activities of other holding companies n.e.c.
Shareholder: Ketan Chandulal Gokani
Officers: Ketan Chandulal Gokani [1974] Director

Elite Mobile Limited
Incorporated: 7 November 1994 *Employees:* 93
Net Worth: £23,572,000 *Total Assets:* £34,514,000
Registered Office: Wembley Stadium Industrial Estate, First Way, Wembley, Middlesex, HA9 0TU
Activities: Non-specialised wholesale trade
Parent: Elite Mobile (Holdings) Limited
Officers: Ketan Gokani, Secretary; Amit Kumar Shantilal Dhamecha [1969] Director; Ketan Chandulal Gokani [1974] Director

Elizabeth Estates (NWB) Limited
Incorporated: 2 December 1991 *Employees:* 1
Net Worth: £6,003,628 *Total Assets:* £18,648,896
Registered Office: Merchant House, 33 Fore Street, Ipswich, Suffolk, IP4 1JL
Activities: Other letting and operating of own or leased real estate
Shareholders: Richard William Cattermole; Richard William Cattermole
Officers: Abigail Louise Cattermole [1977] Estate Director

Elizabeth Holdings PLC
Incorporated: 27 March 1998 *Employees:* 16
Net Worth: £34,873,792 *Total Assets:* £47,948,596
Registered Office: Merchant House, 33 Fore Street, Ipswich, Suffolk, IP4 1JL
Activities: Other letting and operating of own or leased real estate
Major Shareholder: Richard William Cattermole
Officers: Abigail Louise Cattermole, Secretary; Philip Thomas Barden [1961] Director/Solicitor; Abigail Louise Cattermole [1977] Estate Director

Ellesmere Property Investment Company Limited
Incorporated: 8 June 2012
Net Worth: £13,470,301 *Total Assets:* £37,889,332
Registered Office: Ley Farm, Stetchworth Ley, Stetchworth, Newmarket, Suffolk, CB8 9TX
Activities: Buying and selling of own real estate
Shareholders: The Marquis of James Granville Stafford; Henry Alexander Egerton
Officers: Lord Henry Alexander Egerton [1977] Director/Property and Renewable Energy; James Granville Stafford [1975] Director/Property and Farming

Ellgia Holdings Limited
Incorporated: 31 December 2014 *Employees:* 140
Net Worth: £3,057,380 *Total Assets:* £17,667,214
Registered Office: Unit 7 Lancaster Way Business Park, Ely, Cambs, CB6 3NW
Activities: Dormant company
Shareholders: Steven Robert Crook; La Vallette Investment Management Limited
Officers: Steven Robert Crook [1965] Managing Director; Joseph Edward Hemsley-Rudd [1981] Sales Director; John Richard Lavington [1971] Director; Cameron Murdoch [1967] Director

Ellgia Recycling Ltd
Incorporated: 10 June 2011 *Employees:* 2
Net Worth Deficit: £411,829 *Total Assets:* £8,326,036
Registered Office: Unit 7 Lancaster Way Business Park, Ely, Cambs, CB6 3NW
Activities: Collection of non-hazardous waste
Shareholders: Steven Robert Crook; Ellgia Holdings Limited; La Vallette Investment Management Company
Officers: Steven Robert Crook [1965] Managing Director; Joseph Edward Hemsley-Rudd [1981] Sales Director; Cameron Murdoch [1967] Director/Engineering Consultant

Elliot Leigh Property Investments 2 Ltd
Incorporated: 21 July 2003 *Employees:* 16
Previous: Elliot Leigh Property Management Limited
Net Worth: £8,901,201 *Total Assets:* £18,802,786
Registered Office: 19-20 Bourne Court, Southend Road, Woodford Green, Essex, IG8 8HD
Activities: Management of real estate on a fee or contract basis
Parent: EL Property Holdings Limited
Officers: Elliot James Altman, Secretary; Elliot James Altman [1976] Director/Property Consultant; Leigh Ryce Young [1972] Director/Self Employed

Elliott Group Holdings (UK) Limited
Incorporated: 15 August 2007
Net Worth Deficit: £255,444,000 *Total Assets:* £311,284,000
Registered Office: Manor Drive, Peterborough, Cambs, PE4 7AP
Activities: Renting and leasing of other machinery, equipment and tangible goods n.e.c.
Parent: TDR Capital General Partner II Limited
Officers: James O'Malley, Secretary; James O'Malley [1977] Director/Lawyer [American]; Sundip Thakrar [1965] Director/Chief Financial Officer; Dr Andrew Oliver Tyler [1967] Director/Chief Executive; Lee Andrew Young [1972] Director

Elliott Group Limited
Incorporated: 21 April 1917 *Employees:* 1,028
Net Worth: £202,162,000 *Total Assets:* £383,399,008
Registered Office: Manor Drive, Peterborough, PE4 7AP
Activities: Other manufacturing n.e.c.
Parent: Elliott Group Holdings (UK) Limited
Officers: James O'Malley, Secretary; James O'Malley [1977] Director/Lawyer [American]; Sundip Thakrar [1965] Director/Chief Financial Officer; Dr Andrew Tyler [1976] Director/Chief Executive; Lee Andrew Young [1972] Director

Ellis Bros (Contractors) Limited
Incorporated: 10 January 1963 *Employees:* 96
Net Worth: £10,766,016 *Total Assets:* £13,295,898
Registered Office: 7 Lansdowne Road, Skegness, Lincs, PE25 2DJ
Activities: Growing of cereals (except rice), leguminous crops and oil seeds
Major Shareholder: Frederick William John Ellis
Officers: Frederick William John Ellis [1948] Director/Builder; Ian Frederick Ellis [1974] Director/Surveyor

Ellis Timber (Holdings) Limited
Incorporated: 5 January 2017
Net Worth: £10,354,145 *Total Assets:* £10,368,728
Registered Office: The Sawmill, Main Road, Hevingham, Norwich, NR10 5LX
Activities: Sawmilling and planing of wood
Officers: Edna Mary Ellis [1938] Director; Mark Ellis [1966] Director/Sawmill Manager; Mervyn Roy Ellis [1937] Director; Paul Ellis [1962] Director/Sawmill Manager

Elsoms (Spalding) Limited
Incorporated: 4 December 1943 *Employees:* 98
Net Worth: £18,912,944 *Total Assets:* £24,026,982
Registered Office: Pinchbeck Road, Spalding, Lincs, PE11 1QG
Activities: Agents selling agricultural raw materials, livestock, textile raw materials and semi-finished goods
Shareholder: Roger Anthony Luke Keeling
Officers: Andrew Peter Davis, Secretary; John Michael Bloomer [1965] Director/Consultant; David James Sharples Coop [1970] Director; Andrew Peter Davis [1974] Finance Director; Andrew Piers Symons Keeling [1973] Director; Rachel Petronella Keeling [1972] Director; Roger Anthony Luke Keeling [1977] Director; Nicholas Waterman [1965] Director; Robin Laurie Wood [1961] Director/Seedsman

Elsoms Seeds Limited
Incorporated: 13 April 1960 *Employees:* 94
Net Worth: £9,459,536 *Total Assets:* £15,677,365
Registered Office: Pinchbeck Road, Spalding, Lincs, PE11 1QG
Activities: Agents selling agricultural raw materials, livestock, textile raw materials and semi-finished goods
Parent: Elsoms (Spalding) Limited
Officers: Andrew Peter Davis, Secretary; David James Sharples Coop [1970] Director; Andrew Peter Davis [1974] Finance Director; Roger Anthony Luke Keeling [1977] Director; Robin Laurie Wood [1961] Director/Seedsman

The Elstree UTC
Incorporated: 11 January 2012 *Employees:* 8
Net Worth: £12,199,000 *Total Assets:* £13,336,000
Registered Office: Elstree UTC, Studio Way, Borehamwood, Herts, WD6 5NN
Activities: General secondary education
Officers: Alexander Hall, Secretary; Geoffrey Keith Butler [1951] Director/Retired/Part Time Educational Consultant; Geoffrey Dominic Bygate [1961] Director/University Lecturer; Claire Charles [1973] Director/Professional Coach; Judy Glasman [1957] Director/University Academic Manager; Brian Gunner Larholm [1974] Director/Entrepreneur [Danish]; Anne Elisabeth Lean [1960] Director/Projects and Partnerships Manager; Christopher William Mitchell [1979] Director/Headteacher; Roger William Morris [1949] Managing Director; Dalia Smith [1970] Director/Landlord and Author; David Zerafa [1987] Director/Company Member of Staff

Elveden Farms Limited
Incorporated: 25 February 1991 *Employees:* 200
Net Worth: £14,382,901 *Total Assets:* £36,334,328
Registered Office: The Estate Office, Elveden, Thetford, Norfolk, IP24 3TQ
Activities: Mixed farming
Officers: Michael John Douglas, Secretary; Lisa Jane Bowman [1973] Finance & Services Director; Michael John Douglas [1960] Director/Chartered Surveyor; Arthur Edward Rory Guinness [1969] Director/Farmer [Irish]; Robin Ivan Howard [1955] Business Consultant & Director; Ian Mighell Monks [1960] Director/Chartered Surveyor

Simon Elvin Holdings Limited
Incorporated: 1 June 2016 *Employees:* 172
Net Worth: £24,467,816 *Total Assets:* £27,777,356
Registered Office: c/o Simon Elvin Limited, Thomas Road, Wooburn Industrial Park, Wooburn Green, High Wycombe, Bucks, HP10 0PE
Activities: Activities of head offices
Shareholder: Simon Peel Elvin
Officers: Janet Elizabeth Elvin [1940] Director; Jonathan Charles Elvin [1971] Director/Property Developer; Julian Peel Elvin [1968] Director/Advertising Manager; Simon Peel Elvin [1941] Director

Elvin Investments Limited
Incorporated: 1 June 2016 *Employees:* 1
Net Worth: £18,682,604 *Total Assets:* £18,776,366
Registered Office: c/o Simon Elvin Limited, Thomas Road, Wooburn Industrial Park, Wooburn Green, High Wycombe, Bucks, HP10 0PE
Activities: Activities of open-ended investment companies
Shareholder: Simon Peel Elvin
Officers: Janet Elizabeth Elvin [1940] Director; Jonathan Charles Elvin [1971] Director/Property Developer; Julian Peel Elvin [1968] Director/Advertising Manager; Simon Peel Elvin [1941] Director

S Elvin Limited
Incorporated: 13 June 2012 *Employees:* 5
Previous: Simon Elvin Holdings Limited
Net Worth: £21,728,240 *Total Assets:* £30,662,140
Registered Office: c/o Simon Elvin Ltd, Thomas Road, Woodburn Industrial Park, Woodburn Green, Bucks, HP10 0PE
Activities: Activities of head offices
Officers: Mark Stuart Blundell, Secretary; Janet Elizabeth Elvin [1940] Director; Jonathan Charles Elvin [1971] Director; Julian Peel Elvin [1968] Director; Simon Peel Elvin [1941] Director; Stuart McKay [1946] Director

Simon Elvin Limited
Incorporated: 16 August 1977 *Employees:* 69
Net Worth: £23,718,536 *Total Assets:* £24,422,124
Registered Office: Wooburn Industrial Park, Wooburn Green, Bucks, HP10 0PE
Activities: Other publishing activities
Officers: Mark Stuart Blundell, Secretary; Janet Elizabeth Elvin [1940] Director; Jonathan Charles Elvin [1971] Director/Property Developer; Julian Peel Elvin [1968] Director/Advertising Manager; Simon Peel Elvin [1941] Director; Ian Kenneth Alexander Jackson [1959] Director; Stuart McKay [1946] Director; David Malcolm Orr [1950] Operations Director

Ely Diocesan Board of Finance (The)
Incorporated: 19 November 1915 *Employees:* 40
Net Worth: £145,160,992 *Total Assets:* £151,627,008
Registered Office: Diocesan Office, Bishop Woodford House, Barton Road, Ely, Cambs, CB7 4DX
Activities: Activities of religious organisations
Officers: Paul Lawson Evans, Secretary; Frances Godden, Secretary; Donald Arthur Ashmore [1946] Director/Purchasing Manager; The Revd Canon Edwood Brian Benedict Atling [1946] Director/Clerk in Holy Orders; Mark Philip John Bonney [1957] Director/Clerk in Holy Orders; Francis William Miles Burkitt [1964] Director/Banker; Stephen David Conway [1957] Director/Clerk in Holy Orders; Adrian Mark Daffern [1968] Director/Clerk in Holy Orders; Rev Martin Nicholas Dale [1955] Director/Clerk in Holy Orders [British/Swiss]; Susan Elizabeth Freestone [1955] Director/School Principal; Rev Dr Alexander James Hughes [1975] Director/Clerk in Holy Orders; Simon Kershaw [1959] Director/Software Consultant; Elaine Margaret Levitt [1945] Director/Retired; Diana Mary Lucas [1940] Director/Retired; George Lynn [1955] Director; Rev Anna Ruth Matthews [1978] Director/Clerk in Holy Orders; Peter Benson Maxwell [1950] Director; The Venerable Hugh Kyle McCurdy [1958] Director/Clerk in Holy Orders; Martin McFarlane [1978] Director/Manager; Rev Nicholas Ian Moir [1961] Director/Clerk in Holy Orders; Rev Alison Margaret Myers [1966] Director/Clerk in Holy Orders; Robert Paul Needle [1959] Director/Shop Manager; Carol Ann Nicholas-Letch [1946] Director/Retired; Janet Rosemary Perrett [1942] Director/Retired; Dr Arvan David Pritchard [1962] Director/Software Engineer; Sarah Margaret Robinson [1962] Director/Pastoral Worker; Malcolm John Shreeve [1945] Director/Retired; The Revd Simon Talbott [1957] Director/Clerk in Holy Orders; Elizabeth Lawes Taylor [1961] Director/Consultant [British/Australian]; The Revd Jason Taylor [1971] Director/Clerk in Holy Orders; Stephen Edgar Tooke [1946] Director/Area Organiser; Tim Walters [1964] Director

Elysium Healthcare (Acorn Care) Limited
Incorporated: 17 January 1996 *Employees:* 240
Previous: Acorn Care Limited
Net Worth: £6,373,000 *Total Assets:* £9,367,000
Registered Office: 2 Imperial Place, Maxwell Road, Borehamwood, Herts, WD6 1JN
Activities: Specialists medical practice activities
Parent: Elysium Healthcare (Lighthouse) Limited
Officers: Sarah Juliette Livingston, Secretary; Lesley Joy Chamberlain [1963] Director/Group Chief Executive; Dr Quazi Shams Mahfooz Haque [1968] Executive Medical Director; Steven John Woolgar [1955] Director of Policy and Regulation

Elysium Healthcare (Farndon) Limited
Incorporated: 11 October 2004 *Employees:* 126
Previous: Raphael Health Care Ltd
Net Worth: £7,518,000 *Total Assets:* £16,087,000
Registered Office: c/o Elysium Healthcare, 2 Imperial Place, Maxwell Road, Borehamwood, Herts, WD6 1JN
Activities: Other human health activities
Parent: Elysium Healthcare Holdings 3 Limited
Officers: Sarah Juliette Livingston, Secretary; Lesley Joy Chamberlain [1963] Director/Group Chief Executive; Dr Quazi Shams Mahfooz Haque [1968] Group Medical Director; Steven John Woolgar [1955] Director of Policy and Regulation

Elysium Healthcare (Healthlinc) Limited
Incorporated: 30 July 1979 *Employees:* 324
Previous: Healthlinc Individual Care Limited
Net Worth: £9,581,000 *Total Assets:* £12,118,000
Registered Office: 2 Imperial Place, Maxwell Road, Borehamwood, Herts, WD6 1JN
Activities: Specialists medical practice activities
Parent: Elysium Healthcare (Lighthouse) Limited
Officers: Sarah Juliette Livingston, Secretary; Lesley Joy Chamberlain [1963] Director/Group Chief Executive; Dr Quazi Shams Mahfooz Haque [1968] Executive Medical Director; Steven John Woolgar [1955] Director of Policy and Regulation

Elysium Healthcare (Lighthouse) Limited
Incorporated: 18 May 2006 *Employees:* 15
Previous: Lighthouse Healthcare Limited
Net Worth: £48,078,000 *Total Assets:* £51,317,000
Registered Office: 2 Imperial Place, Maxwell Road, Borehamwood, Herts, WD6 1JN
Activities: Activities of head offices
Parent: Lighthouse Healthcare Group Limited
Officers: Sarah Juliette Livingston, Secretary; Lesley Joy Chamberlain [1963] Director/Group Chief Executive; Dr Quazi Shams Mahfooz Haque [1968] Executive Medical Director; Steven John Woolgar [1955] Director of Policy and Regulation

Elysium Healthcare (St Mary's) Limited
Incorporated: 18 May 2004 *Employees:* 377
Previous: St Mary's Hospitals Limited
Net Worth: £2,297,465 *Total Assets:* £15,445,244
Registered Office: c/o Elysium Healthcare, 2 Imperial Place, Maxwell Road, Borehamwood, Herts, WD6 1JN
Activities: Hospital activities
Parent: Elysium Healthcare (Ultimate Care) Limited
Officers: Sarah Juliette Livingston, Secretary; Lesley Joy Chamberlain [1963] Director/Group Chief Executive; Dr Quazi Shams Mahfooz Haque [1968] Executive Medical Director; Steven John Woolgar [1955] Director of Policy and Regulation

Elysium Healthcare (Ultimate Care) Limited
Incorporated: 20 February 2006 *Employees:* 654
Previous: St George Ultimate Care Limited
Net Worth: £4,425,032 *Total Assets:* £43,884,684
Registered Office: c/o Elysium Healthcare, 2 Imperial Place, Maxwell Road, Borehamwood, Herts, WD6 1JN
Activities: Other human health activities
Parent: Elysium Healthcare Holdings 3 Limited
Officers: Sarah Juliette Livingston, Secretary; Lesley Joy Chamberlain [1963] Director/Group Chief Executive; Dr Quazi Shams Mahfooz Haque [1968] Executive Medical Director; Steven John Woolgar [1955] Director of Policy and Regulation

Elysium Healthcare Holdings 2 Limited
Incorporated: 10 October 2016 *Employees:* 3,290
Net Worth: £63,930,000 *Total Assets:* £575,473,024
Registered Office: 2 Imperial Place, Maxwell Road, Borehamwood, Herts, WD6 1JN
Activities: Non-trading company
Parent: Elysium Healthcare Holdings 1 Limited
Officers: Sarah Juliette Livingston, Secretary; Lesley Joy Chamberlain [1963] Director/Chief Executive Officer; Dr Quazi Shams Mahfooz Haque [1968] Executive Medical Director; Steven John Woolgar [1955] Director of Policy and Regulation

Elysium Healthcare Holdings 3 Limited
Incorporated: 10 October 2016 *Employees:* 11
Net Worth: £54,745,000 *Total Assets:* £377,808,992
Registered Office: 2 Imperial Place, Maxwell Road, Borehamwood, Herts, WD6 1JN
Activities: Non-trading company
Parent: Elysium Healthcare Holdings 2 Limited
Officers: Sarah Juliette Livingston, Secretary; Lesley Joy Chamberlain [1963] Director/Chief Executive Officer; Dr Quazi Shams Mahfooz Haque [1968] Executive Medical Director; Steven John Woolgar [1955] Director of Policy and Regulation

Elysium Healthcare LC Limited
Incorporated: 22 November 2016
Net Worth: £134,075,000 *Total Assets:* £137,518,000
Registered Office: 2 Imperial Place, Maxwell Road, Borehamwood, Herts, WD6 1JN
Activities: Non-trading company
Parent: Elysium Healthcare Holdings 3 Limited
Officers: Sarah Juliette Livingston, Secretary; Lesley Joy Chamberlain [1963] Director/Chief Executive Officer; Dr Quazi Shams Mahfooz Haque [1968] Executive Medical Director

Elysium Healthcare No. 2 Limited
Incorporated: 11 May 2007 *Employees:* 1,356
Previous: Priory Secure Services Limited
Net Worth: £23,858,000 *Total Assets:* £179,348,992
Registered Office: 2 Imperial Place, Maxwell Road, Borehamwood, Herts, WD6 1JN
Activities: Hospital activities
Parent: Elysium Healthcare Holdings 3 Limited
Officers: Sarah Juliette Livingston, Secretary; Lesley Joy Chamberlain [1963] Director/Chief Executive Officer; Dr Quazi Shams Mahfooz Haque [1968] Executive Medical Director; Steven John Woolgar [1955] Director of Policy and Regulation

Elysium Healthcare No. 3 Limited
Incorporated: 14 November 1994 *Employees:* 176
Previous: Craegmoor Hospitals Limited
Net Worth: £24,619,000 *Total Assets:* £67,242,000
Registered Office: 2 Imperial Place, Maxwell Road, Borehamwood, Herts, WD6 1JN
Activities: Other human health activities
Parent: Elysium Healthcare Holdings 3 Limited
Officers: Sarah Juliette Livingston, Secretary; Lesley Joy Chamberlain [1963] Director/Chief Executive Officer; Dr Quazi Shams Mahfooz Haque [1968] Executive Medical Director; Steven John Woolgar [1955] Director of Policy and Regulation

Elysium Healthcare No. 4 Limited
Incorporated: 26 September 1996 *Employees:* 107
Previous: Speciality Care (Care Homes) Limited
Net Worth: £7,037,000 *Total Assets:* £20,008,000
Registered Office: 2 Imperial Place, Maxwell Road, Borehamwood, Herts, WD6 1JN
Activities: Other human health activities
Parent: Elysium Healthcare No. 3 Limited
Officers: Sarah Juliette Livingston, Secretary; Lesley Joy Chamberlain [1963] Director/Chief Executive Officer; Dr Quazi Shams Mahfooz Haque [1968] Executive Medical Director; Steven John Woolgar [1955] Director of Policy and Regulation

Elysium Healthcare Property 2 Limited
Incorporated: 29 March 2005
Previous: Partnerships in Care Property 13 Limited
Net Worth: £9,098,000 *Total Assets:* £30,056,000
Registered Office: 2 Imperial Place, Maxwell Road, Borehamwood, Herts, WD6 1JN
Activities: Hospital activities
Parent: Elysium Healthcare Limited
Officers: Sarah Juliette Livingston, Secretary; Lesley Joy Chamberlain [1963] Director/Chartered Accountant; Dr Quazi Shams Mahfooz Haque [1968] Group Medical Director

Elysium Healthcare Property 3 Limited
Incorporated: 4 November 2005
Previous: Partnerships in Care Property 18 Limited
Net Worth: £6,687,000 *Total Assets:* £16,310,000
Registered Office: 2 Imperial Place, Maxwell Road, Borehamwood, Herts, WD6 1JN
Activities: Hospital activities
Parent: Elysium Healthcare Limited
Officers: Sarah Juliette Livingston, Secretary; Lesley Joy Chamberlain [1963] Director/Chartered Accountant; Dr Quazi Shams Mahfooz Haque [1968] Group Medical Director

Emcure Pharma UK Ltd
Incorporated: 6 November 2012 *Employees:* 6
Net Worth: £8,047,284 *Total Assets:* £36,279,172
Registered Office: 220 Butterfield, Great Marlings, Luton, Beds, LU2 8DL
Activities: Wholesale of pharmaceutical goods
Officers: Zarir Jal Cama [1947] Director; William Steven Marth [1954] Director/Business Executive [American]; Samit Satish Mehta [1980] Director [Indian]; Tajuddin Shaikh [1974] Director/Accountant [Indian]; Ajit Chand Srimal [1958] Director/Chief Executive

Emerald Bidco Limited
Incorporated: 12 June 2014
Net Worth: £10,352,000 *Total Assets:* £29,002,000
Registered Office: Mandeville House, 62 The Broadway, Amersham, Bucks, HP7 0HJ
Activities: Activities of head offices
Parent: Emerald Midco 2 Limited
Officers: Richard James Riegel [1963] Director [American]; Karen Jane Roy [1966] Director; Jacqueline Susan Veness [1960] Director/Chartered Accountant

Emerald Midco 1 Limited
Incorporated: 30 April 2014
Net Worth: £33,235,000 *Total Assets:* £36,238,000
Registered Office: Mandeville House, 62 The Broadway, Amersham, Bucks, HP7 0HJ
Activities: Activities of head offices
Parent: Overture Topco Limited
Officers: Richard James Riegel [1963] Director [American]; Karen Jane Roy [1966] Director; Jacqueline Susan Veness [1960] Director/Chartered Accountant

Emerald Midco 2 Limited
Incorporated: 30 April 2014
Net Worth: £27,668,000 *Total Assets:* £36,219,000
Registered Office: Mandeville House, 62 The Broadway, Amersham, Bucks, HP7 0HJ
Activities: Activities of head offices
Parent: Emerald Midco 1 Limited
Officers: Richard James Riegel [1963] Director [American]; Karen Jane Roy [1966] Director; Jacqueline Susan Veness [1960] Director/Chartered Accountant

Emerald Topco Limited
Incorporated: 30 April 2014 *Employees:* 3
Net Worth: £36,191,000 *Total Assets:* £40,401,000
Registered Office: Mandeville House, 62 The Broadway, Amersham, Bucks, HP7 0HJ
Activities: Activities of head offices
Parent: Overture Bidco Limited
Officers: Richard James Riegel [1963] Director [American]; Karen Jane Roy [1966] Director; Jacqueline Susan Veness [1960] Director/Chartered Accountant

Emerson Crane Hire Limited
Incorporated: 18 April 1991 *Employees:* 115
Net Worth: £4,710,834 *Total Assets:* £12,959,049
Registered Office: Emerson House, Freshwater Road, Dagenham, Essex, RM8 1RX
Activities: Renting and leasing of construction and civil engineering machinery and equipment
Major Shareholder: Edward Clancy
Officers: Liam Clancy [1981] Director/Manager; Paul Clancy [1962] Director/Crane Hire; Robert Thomas Jackson [1971] Director/Crane Hire Technical Representative

R B Emerson Limited
Incorporated: 3 October 1957 *Employees:* 110
Net Worth: £5,730,283 *Total Assets:* £8,964,391
Registered Office: 8a Coopers Way, Temple Farm Industrial Estate, Southend on Sea, Essex, SS2 5TE
Activities: Electrical installation
Parent: R B Emerson Group Limited
Officers: Andrew Casey, Secretary; Michael Frederick Adams [1964] Director/Executive; Andrew Casey [1970] Director/Executive; Michael Herbert Maddocks [1956] Director/Executive

Emerson Park Academy
Incorporated: 2 August 2011 *Employees:* 98
Net Worth: £8,294,083 *Total Assets:* £9,891,558
Registered Office: Wych Elm Road, Hornchurch, Essex, RM11 3AD
Activities: General secondary education
Officers: Ian Richard Buckmaster, Secretary; Veedoula Kumarl Bharaj [1973] Director/Civil Servant; Terrence Lee Huff [1968] Director/Health Service Official; John Peter Luff [1962] Director/Management Consultant; Scott McGuinness [1972] Director/Headteacher; Sarah Jane Meacher [1971] Director/Headteacher; Carol Jane Newton [1961] Director/Teacher; Victoria Anne O'Connor [1967] Director; Neil Robert Rebeugeot-Smith [1969] Director/Architect; Martin Tilbury [1955] Director/Retired

EMG Anglia Limited
Incorporated: 7 January 1974 *Employees:* 231
Net Worth: £308,434 *Total Assets:* £20,228,764
Registered Office: 5 Fornham Road, Bury St Edmunds, Suffolk, IP32 6AL
Activities: Sale of new cars and light motor vehicles
Parent: EMG Holdings Limited
Officers: Matthew Neil Stockdale, Secretary; James Coad [1977] Group Aftersales Director; Kevin James Driscoll [1965] Group Sales Director; Roy Brian Jakes [1969] Director; Karen Jane Kenny [1965] Corporate Affairs Director; Gregory Peter O'Gorman [1968] Director; Matthew Neil Stockdale [1985] Director; Nicholas Storey [1961] Director

EMG Holdings Limited
Incorporated: 14 June 1999 *Employees:* 3
Net Worth: £14,470,000 *Total Assets:* £24,155,764
Registered Office: 5 Fornham Road, Bury St Edmunds, Suffolk, IP32 6AL
Activities: Activities of head offices
Parent: Portcrest Limited
Officers: Matthew Neil Stockdale, Secretary; Matthew Neil Stockdale [1985] Financial Director; Nicholas Storey [1961] Director; Paula Storey [1966] Director

Emico Limited
Incorporated: 11 June 1997 *Employees:* 88
Net Worth: £5,597,381 *Total Assets:* £16,787,244
Registered Office: 1st Floor, Forsyth House, 39 Mark Road, Hemel Hempstead, Herts, HP2 7DN
Activities: Electrical installation
Parent: Emico Holdings Limited
Officers: David Perrotton, Secretary/Director; John Anthony Barry [1962] Director/Electrical Engineer [Irish]; Matthew Thomas Cunningham [1967] Director; David George Perrotton [1966] Director

Emmett UK Limited
Incorporated: 22 November 1988 *Employees:* 241
Net Worth: £4,300,000 *Total Assets:* £19,421,000
Registered Office: Washway Road, Fosdyke, Spalding, Lincs, PE12 6LQ
Activities: Growing of vegetables and melons, roots and tubers
Parent: Sansbury Bailey Holdings Limited
Officers: Lisa Jayne Alcock, Secretary; Lisa Jayne Alcock [1984] Director; Colin Sansbury Bailey [1969] Director; Alexander Boughton [1987] Sales Director; David Alan Trumble [1980] Finance Director

Empower Learning Academy Trust
Incorporated: 12 July 2011 *Employees:* 442
Previous: Hall Mead School
Net Worth: £51,636,392 *Total Assets:* £58,780,768
Registered Office: Hall Mead School, Marlborough Gardens, Upminster, Essex, RM14 1SF
Activities: General secondary education
Officers: Paula Garner, Secretary; James Brooks [1952] Director/Retired; Keith Butcher [1972] Director/Chartered Surveyor; Anthony Farrow [1975] Director/Business Manager; David Nicholas Harries [1960] Director; Simon London [1970] Director/Headteacher; Keith James Stewart [1961] Director/Shipping Manager; Stuart Mark Walton [1970] Director/Operations Manager

Empress Garland Limited
Incorporated: 29 August 2003 *Employees:* 417
Net Worth: £18,218,344 *Total Assets:* £35,354,432
Registered Office: Campfield Road, Shoeburyness, Essex, SS3 9FL
Activities: Other manufacturing n.e.c.
Shareholders: Roger William Walters; Teresa Walters
Officers: Trevor Andrew Ballard, Secretary; Terence David Dearlove [1953] Director; Roger William Walters [1945] Director; Teresa Walters [1947] Director

EMS-FP & S Limited
Incorporated: 26 March 1998 *Employees:* 142
Previous: FP & S Parts and Service Limited
Net Worth: £765,911 *Total Assets:* £11,823,361
Registered Office: 11 Rash's Green, Toftwood, Dereham, Norfolk, NR19 1JG
Activities: Wholesale trade of motor vehicle parts and accessories
Parent: BPW Limited
Officers: David John Smith, Secretary; Neill Robert Groves [1970] Director; Hans-Peter Tapio Henry Kraatz [1955] Director [Finnish]; Stephen Brian Turton [1958] Director; Thorsten Winterberg [1969] Director/Chairman [Danish]

Enco Products Limited
Incorporated: 12 June 1946
Net Worth: £2,876,000 *Total Assets:* £14,898,000
Registered Office: Grace House, Bessemer Road, Welwyn Garden City, Herts, AL7 1HW
Activities: Other food services
Parent: Grace Foods UK Limited
Officers: Khine Oo, Secretary; Andrea Denise Lewis-Coy [1970] Director/CEO Gracekennedy Foods International [Jamaican]; Brian Anthony Mitchell [1983] Director/Chief Financial Officer [Jamaican]

Encocam Limited
Incorporated: 5 September 1985 *Employees:* 191
Net Worth: £8,726,336 *Total Assets:* £12,972,333
Registered Office: 5 Stukeley Business Centre, Blackstone Road, Huntingdon, Cambs, PE18 6EF
Activities: Other manufacturing n.e.c.
Major Shareholder: Mike Mehrdad Ashmead
Officers: Dr Mike Mehrdad Ashmead, Secretary; Dr Mike Mehrdad Ashmead [1949] Director/Founder & Chairman

Energypro Asset Management Limited
Incorporated: 17 January 2017 *Employees:* 4
Net Worth: £5,947,750 *Total Assets:* £11,500,334
Registered Office: Nicholas House, River Front, Enfield, Middlesex, EN1 3FG
Activities: Other business support service activities n.e.c.
Shareholder: Steven Derrick Fawkes
Officers: David Anderson [1953] Director; Dr Steven Derrick Fawkes [1959] Director; Delvin Martin Lane [1974] Director; Stephen Michael Packer [1968] Director; Matthew William Pumfrey [1971] Director; Michael Anthony Tivey [1970] Director

Enfield Fancy Goods Limited
Incorporated: 2 March 1978 *Employees:* 82
Net Worth: £9,762,571 *Total Assets:* £16,664,887
Registered Office: 55 High Street, Hoddesdon, Herts, EN11 8TQ
Activities: Activities of head offices
Parent: EFG SIP
Officers: Alan Brian Shipton, Secretary; Alan Brian Shipton [1938] Director; Daren Shipton [1968] Director; Mark William Shipton [1973] Director; Trevor Roderick Shipton [1943] Director

Enfield Innovations Ltd
Incorporated: 3 October 2014 *Employees:* 2
Net Worth: £686,418 *Total Assets:* £14,227,513
Registered Office: 50 Civic Centre, Silver Street, Enfield, Middlesex, EN1 3XA
Activities: Buying and selling of own real estate
Parent: London Borough of Enfield
Officers: Matthew Bowmer [1965] Director/Accountant; Mark Timothy Bradbury [1961] Director/Chartered Surveyor; Joanna Michelle Embling [1949] Director; Sally Ann McTernan [1963] Director; Jayne Middleton-Albooye [1963] Director/Solicitor; Peter Chukuaduom Madako Nwosu [1965] Director/Chartered Accountant; Sabri Ozaydin [1968] Director/Manufacturer

English Architectural Glazing Limited
Incorporated: 20 April 2000 *Employees:* 73
Net Worth: £3,275,265 *Total Assets:* £8,253,875
Registered Office: Chiswick Avenue, Mildenhall, Suffolk, IP28 7AY
Activities: Other construction installation
Shareholders: Jeremy Mark Cocks; Edward Charles Whipp; Simon Edward Gladwin
Officers: Jeremy Mark Cocks, Secretary/Director; Jeremy Mark Cocks [1962] Director; Simon Edward Gladwin [1963] Managing Director; Edward Charles Whipp [1964] Director

ENRA Group Limited
Incorporated: 13 November 2013 *Employees:* 2
Previous: ENRA Group Ltd
Net Worth Deficit: £358,797 *Total Assets:* £63,454,864
Registered Office: 3rd Floor, Premiere House, Elstree Way, Borehamwood, Herts, WD6 1JH
Activities: Other business support service activities n.e.c.
Parent: Newincco 1270 Limited
Officers: Emily Henrietta Gestetner [1967] Director; Harry Leon Landy [1978] Director; Danny Stephen Waters [1984] Director

Enrich Learning Trust
Incorporated: 2 August 2011 *Employees:* 320
Previous: Enrich Learning Trust Ltd
Net Worth: £21,420,376 *Total Assets:* £25,124,722
Registered Office: Wymondham High Academy, Folly Road, Wymondham, Norfolk, NR18 0QT
Activities: Primary education
Officers: Peter William Jordan, Secretary; Michael Bolger [1951] Director Recruitment; Neil James Collins [1969] Director; Steve Frost [1963] Director/Sales and Business Development; Jeffrey Stephen Lansdell [1970] Director/Business Design Architect; Robert Michael Linnell [1949] Director/Consultant; Andrew Duncan Rowley [1954] Director/Chartered Accountant; Leda Carol Ann Tarabay [1960] Director/Accountant

Ensign Bus Company Limited
Incorporated: 23 October 1991 *Employees:* 213
Net Worth: £21,773,740 *Total Assets:* £26,987,252
Registered Office: The Rifle Range, Juliette Close, Purfleet Industrial Park, Aveley, South Ockendon, Essex, RM15 4YF
Activities: Other passenger land transport
Major Shareholder: Peter Ivor Newman
Officers: Louise Amy Pirie, Secretary; Roger Frederick Jackson [1958] Engineering Director; Peter Ivor Newman [1940] Director; Ross Christopher Newman [1970] Operations Director; Stephen Philip Newman [1972] Director/Operations Manager

Ensign Holdco 1 Limited
Incorporated: 10 May 2016 *Employees:* 202
Net Worth Deficit: £7,514,000 *Total Assets:* £73,359,000
Registered Office: Unit 4 Voltage, Mollison Avenue, Enfield, Middlesex, EN3 7XQ
Activities: Activities of head offices
Shareholders: Equistone General Partner V LLP; Equistone Partners Europe Limited
Officers: Christopher Nicholas Sebastian Jehan Candfield [1985] Investment Director [British/German]; Sukhjeevan Singh Samra [1976] Director; Tim Allan Swales [1978] Director; Martin Stuart Taylor [1967] Director

Ensign Holdco 3 Limited
Incorporated: 10 May 2016
Net Worth: £88,000 *Total Assets:* £28,515,000
Registered Office: Unit 4 Voltage, Mollison Avenue, Enfield, Middlesex, EN3 7XQ
Activities: Activities of head offices
Parent: Ensign Holdco 2 Limited
Officers: Sukhjeevan Singh Samra [1976] Commercial Director; Martin Stuart Taylor [1967] Director

Ensign Holdco 4 Limited
Incorporated: 10 May 2016
Net Worth: £22,320,000 *Total Assets:* £59,430,000
Registered Office: Unit 4 Voltage, Mollison Avenue, Enfield, Middlesex, EN3 7XQ
Activities: Activities of head offices
Parent: Ensign Holdco 3 Limited
Officers: Sukhjeevan Singh Samra [1976] Director; Martin Stuart Taylor [1967] Commercial Director

The Enterprise Department Limited
Incorporated: 11 April 1994 *Employees:* 149
Net Worth: £7,029,634 *Total Assets:* £13,261,326
Registered Office: 11 Bridge Street, Bishop's Stortford, Herts, CM23 2JU
Activities: Other business support service activities n.e.c.
Parent: Damartex
Officers: George Henry Cook [1974] Logistics Director; Stuart Creeley [1962] Finance Director; Victoria Jayne Laws [1971] Managing Director; Andrew Ross McDermott [1966] Commercial Director; Andrea Smith [1967] Finance Director

Enterprise Finance Limited
Incorporated: 16 May 2002 *Employees:* 60
Net Worth: £8,228,437 *Total Assets:* £9,350,643
Registered Office: 3rd Floor, Premiere House, Elstree Way, Borehamwood, Herts, WD6 1JH
Activities: Banks
Parent: ENRA Group Limited
Officers: Emily Henrietta Gestetner [1967] Director; Harry Leon Landy [1978] Director; David Stewart [1965] Director; Danny Stephen Waters [1984] Director

Enterprise Residential Development Limited
Incorporated: 11 April 1994 *Employees:* 29
Previous: Enterprise Property Group Limited
Net Worth: £2,015,000 *Total Assets:* £41,230,000
Registered Office: Scutches Barn, 17 High Street, Whittlesford, Cambridge, CB22 4LT
Activities: Development of building projects
Officers: Marilyn Ann Gibb-Rice, Secretary; Simon John Brown [1968] Director; Neil John Davison [1962] Director/Construction Manager; Robert James Morell Keatley [1965] Director; Christopher Charles Micklethwaite [1958] Director; Peter Robert Stocking [1961] Director; Ian Richard Watson [1960] Director; Dominic Henry Johnstone White [1969] Director

The Entertainer (Amersham) Limited
Incorporated: 24 September 1986 *Employees:* 1,704
Net Worth: £32,360,000 *Total Assets:* £82,294,000
Registered Office: Boughton Business Park, Bell Lane, Little Chalfont, Bucks, HP6 6GL
Activities: Retail sale of games and toys in specialised stores
Major Shareholder: Gary Peter Grant
Officers: Catherine Ann Grant, Secretary; Mark James Campbell [1974] Director; Catherine Ann Grant [1954] Director/Secretary; Duncan Peter Grant [1982] Director; Gary Peter Grant [1958] Director/Toy Retailer; Stuart James Grant [1984] Director

Envigo CRS Limited
Incorporated: 14 May 1984 *Employees:* 1,174
Previous: Huntingdon Life Sciences Limited
Net Worth Deficit: £27,962,000 *Total Assets:* £192,271,008
Registered Office: Woolley Road, Alconbury, Huntingdon, Cambs, PE28 4HS
Activities: Other research and experimental development on natural sciences and engineering
Parent: Envigo International Limited
Officers: Michael Gregory O'Reilly, Secretary; Michael Gregory O'Reilly [1966] Director/SVP Legal; Stephen Daniel Symonds [1974] Director/Financial Controller

Envigo International Limited
Incorporated: 14 December 1951
Previous: Life Sciences Research Limited
Net Worth: £34,537,000 *Total Assets:* £48,956,000
Registered Office: Woolley Road, Alconbury, Huntingdon, Cambs, PE28 4HS
Activities: Other professional, scientific and technical activities n.e.c.
Major Shareholder: Andrew Baker
Officers: Michael Gregory O'Reilly, Secretary; Michael Gregory O'Reilly [1966] Director/SVP Legal; Stephen Daniel Symonds [1974] Director/Financial Controller

Environ Freshford Mill Limited
Incorporated: 28 August 2014 *Employees:* 1
Net Worth Deficit: £255,364 *Total Assets:* £11,190,815
Registered Office: 1st Floor, Bridge House, 25 Fiddlebridge Lane, Hatfield, Herts, AL10 0SP
Activities: Construction of domestic buildings
Shareholders: Environ Coastal Homes (South Devon) Limited; Berrypink Limited
Officers: David John Vetters Boden [1957] Director; Lawrence Stanier Pinkney [1957] Director

Environmental Group Limited
Incorporated: 20 October 2016
Net Worth Deficit: £1,286,370 *Total Assets:* £20,226,580
Registered Office: Aspect House, Honywood Road, Basildon, Essex, SS14 3DS
Activities: Activities of other holding companies n.e.c.
Major Shareholder: Antony Paul Smith
Officers: Grant Martin Eugene Beglan [1964] Director; Craig Henry John Foster [1961] Operations Director; Gavin James Lawrence [1971] Finance Director; Philip Brendan Mullins [1980] Commercial Director; Antony Paul Smith [1970] Director

Envirowales Limited
Incorporated: 1 October 2001 *Employees:* 140
Net Worth Deficit: £10,077,512 *Total Assets:* £25,897,028
Registered Office: Faulkner House, Victoria Street, St Albans, Herts, AL1 3SE
Activities: Other business support service activities n.e.c.
Parent: Envirolead Recycling Limited
Officers: Conor Gerard Murphy, Secretary; James Flood [1954] Director/Engineer [Irish]; Carl Phillip Green [1964] Director; Stephen Brian Kelly [1957] Environmental Director; Doctor Anthony Patrick Mullins [1947] Director/Engineer [Irish]; Conor Gerard Murphy [1964] Director [Irish]; Maurice Elliot Sherling [1949] Director [Irish]

Epay Limited
Incorporated: 14 January 1999 *Employees:* 91
Net Worth: £4,026,000 *Total Assets:* £35,870,000
Registered Office: Kingfisher House, 2 Woodbrook Crescent, Billericay, Essex, CM12 0EQ
Activities: Other telecommunications activities
Officers: Jonathan Allen Fricker [1971] I T Director; Nigel Robert Stephenson [1974] Director/Head of Finance [British/South African]; Rick Weller [1957] Director/Financial Management [American]

EPG Development IV LLP
Incorporated: 15 October 2012
Net Worth: £11,133,119 *Total Assets:* £11,138,334
Registered Office: Scutches Barn, 17 High Street, Whittlesford, Cambs, CB22 4LT
Officers: Mary Ballantyne [1944] LLP Member; Jacqueline Avril Sharon Burfitt [1953] LLP Member; Nicola Mary Corkill [1955] LLP Member; James Ralph Griffith [1954] LLP Member; Susan Griffith [1955] LLP Member; Helen Christine Hutchinson [1946] LLP Member; Dr Peter Hutchinson [1944] LLP Member; Morgan Lewis Jones [1957] LLP Member; John Robert Latham [1964] LLP Member; Janet Love [1955] LLP Member; Timothy John Marks [1958] LLP Member; Laura Isabel McNair [1951] LLP Member; Ian Richard Watson [1960] LLP Member; Jacqueline Anne Watson [1959] LLP Member; Mark William Wood [1943] LLP Member

Epoch RJK Limited
Incorporated: 15 November 2001
Net Worth: £11,033,645 *Total Assets:* £13,028,976
Registered Office: Chemilines House, Alperton Lane, Wembley, Middlesex, HA0 1DX
Activities: Other letting and operating of own or leased real estate
Parent: Chemilines Group Holdings Limited
Officers: Ravindra Prabhudas Karia, Secretary; Jagdish Prabhudas Karia [1958] Director; Ravindra Prabhudas Karia [1953] Director

Epson (U.K.) Limited
Incorporated: 16 November 1979 *Employees:* 139
Net Worth Deficit: £3,378,000 *Total Assets:* £41,722,000
Registered Office: Westside, London Road, Hemel Hempstead, Herts, HP3 9TD
Activities: Wholesale of computers, computer peripheral equipment and software
Parent: Seiko Epson Corporation
Officers: Sian Faru Eva Wilkie Nath, Secretary; Andrew Duncan Campbell-Ferguson [1968] Managing Director; Hideki Kitamura [1960] Director [Japanese]; Kazuyoshi Yamamoto [1960] Director/President, Epson Europe B.V [Japanese]

Equitable Life Assurance Society,(The)
Incorporated: 18 August 1892 *Employees:* 237
Total Assets: £6,791,000,064
Registered Office: The Equitable Life Assurance Society, Walton Street, Aylesbury, Bucks, HP21 7QW
Activities: Life insurance
Officers: Jean Florence Fleet, Secretary; Penelope Jane Avis [1968] Director; Ian Brimecome [1953] Director/Investment Banker; Lord Daniel William Finkelstein [1962] Director/Journalist; Ian Andrew Gibson [1949] Director; Keith Nicholson [1949] Director; Cathryn Elizabeth Riley [1962] Director; Martin Wayne Sinkinson [1967] Director/Actuary; Simon Antony Small [1961] Director

Erba Diagnostics UK Limited
Incorporated: 16 June 2015 *Employees:* 19
Net Worth: £2,763,464 *Total Assets:* £19,985,104
Registered Office: 4 Bartholemews Walk, Ely, Cambs, CB7 4EA
Activities: Activities of other holding companies n.e.c.
Officers: Dr Laurence Carlo Tisi [1968] Director/Service; Nikhil Kumar Suresh Vazirani [1991] Director/Service [Indian]; Suresh Hassanand Vazirani [1949] Director [Indian]

H. Erben Holdings Limited
Incorporated: 25 July 1951 *Employees:* 62
Net Worth: £6,470,229 *Total Assets:* £14,858,951
Registered Office: Lady Lane, Hadleigh, Ipswich, Suffolk, IP7 6AS
Activities: Agents specialised in the sale of other particular products
Parent: B. G. Holding S. P. A.
Officers: Jannine Marie Erben, Secretary; Andrew Berlin [1960] Director [American]; Rick Brandt [1964] Director/Executive Vice President of Sales [American]; Roberto Del Bon [1960] Director [Italian]; Alexander Erben [1976] Director/Business Manager; Robert Goldberg [1972] Director/General Counsel [American]; Jeremy Lagomarsino [1970] Director/Executive Vice President of Business Development [American]; Steven Spiegel [1962] Director [American]

H.Erben Limited
Incorporated: 1 October 1954 *Employees:* 55
Net Worth: £6,037,274 *Total Assets:* £14,291,031
Registered Office: Lady Lane, Hadleigh, Ipswich, Suffolk, IP7 6AS
Activities: Agents involved in the sale of a variety of goods
Parent: H Erben Holdings Ltd
Officers: Jannine Marie Erben, Secretary; Andrew Berlin [1960] Director [American]; Roberto Del Bon [1960] Director [Italian]; Alexander Erben [1976] Director; Robert Goldberg [1972] Director/General Counsel [American]; Jeremy Lagomarsino [1970] Director/Executive Vice President of BD and Strategy [American]; Sandra Shand-Brown [1967] Director/Departmental Manager; Steven Spiegel [1962] Director [American]; Michal Szczygiel [1981] Sales Director; Allan White [1962] Director/Business Development Manager

Ercol (Holdings) Limited
Incorporated: 1 December 1983 *Employees:* 164
Net Worth: £18,102,000 *Total Assets:* £21,239,000
Registered Office: Summerleys Road, Prince Risborough, Bucks, HP27 9PX
Activities: Activities of head offices
Major Shareholder: Edward Randolph Tadros
Officers: Edward Randolph Tadros, Secretary; Sophie Mirman [1956] Director [British/French]; Edward William Tadros [1980] Director; Edward Randolph Tadros [1949] Chairman/Director

Ercol Furniture Limited
Incorporated: 26 January 1920 *Employees:* 161
Net Worth: £4,800,000 *Total Assets:* £11,300,000
Registered Office: Summerleys Road, Princes Risborough, Bucks, HP27 9PX
Activities: Manufacture of other furniture
Parent: Ercol (Holdings) Limited
Officers: David Matthew Finch [1982] Finance Director; Rachel Lydia Galbraith [1971] Creative Director; Antony Charles Maskrey [1970] Director/Chief Operating Officer; Ian Peers [1968] Operations Director; Daniel Christopher Sugrue [1971] Sales & Marketing Director; Edward Randolph Tadros [1949] Chairman Director; Henry Tadros [1987] International & Contract Sales Director

EResearchTechnology Limited
Incorporated: 28 April 1987 *Employees:* 122
Net Worth: £30,136,936 *Total Assets:* £148,514,112
Registered Office: Pearl House, Peterborough Business Park, Lynch Wood, Peterborough, Cambs, PE2 6FZ
Activities: Other professional, scientific and technical activities n.e.c.
Officers: Andrew Fitzgibbon, Secretary; James Corrigan [1963] Director [American]; Gary Mitcheltree [1963] Director/VP Finance [American]; Waqar Nasim [1966] Director [American]

EResearchTechnology UK 1 Limited
Incorporated: 17 May 2010 *Employees:* 611
Net Worth: £60,871,000 *Total Assets:* £199,326,000
Registered Office: Pearl House, Peterborough Business Park, Lynch Wood, Peterborough, Cambs, PE2 6FZ
Activities: Non-trading company
Officers: Andrew Fitzgibbon, Secretary; James Corrigan [1963] Director [American]; Gary Mitcheltree [1963] Director/VP Finance [American]; Waqar Nasim [1966] Director [American]

EResearchTechnology UK 2 Limited
Incorporated: 17 May 2010
Net Worth: £103,968,736 *Total Assets:* £138,743,920
Registered Office: Pearl House, Peterborough Business Park, Lynch Wood, Peterborough, Cambs, PE2 6FZ
Activities: Non-trading company
Officers: Andrew Fitzgibbon, Secretary; James Corrigan [1963] Director [American]; Gary Mitcheltree [1963] Director/VP Finance [American]; Waqar Nasim [1966] Director [American]

Erinastar Limited
Incorporated: 2 January 1976 *Employees:* 4
Net Worth: £9,692,969 *Total Assets:* £9,754,188
Registered Office: Cavendish House, 369 Burnt Oak Broadway, Edgware, Middlesex, HA8 5AW
Activities: Activities of religious organisations
Officers: Dov Cohen [1981] Director/Property Manager; Richard Simon Lewis [1949] Director; David Reichmann [1962] Director; Dov Reichmann [1930] Director

Erindale Limited
Incorporated: 30 April 2008 *Employees:* 1
Net Worth: £13,443,007 *Total Assets:* £41,399,480
Registered Office: 34-36 London Road, Wembley, Middlesex, HA9 7EX
Activities: Other letting and operating of own or leased real estate
Major Shareholder: Raja Jameel Adil
Officers: Mohammed Adil, Secretary; Raja Jameel Adil [1971] Director/Solicitor

Erith Hills LLP
Incorporated: 27 January 2016
Net Worth: £55,222,000 *Total Assets:* £57,766,896
Registered Office: Springfield Lodge, Colchester Road, Chelmsford, Essex, CM2 5PW

ESCO UK Holding Company I Ltd
Incorporated: 21 January 2016
Net Worth: £6,418,477 *Total Assets:* £30,798,602
Registered Office: c/o Wagstaffs Chartered Accountants, Richmond House, Walkern Road, Stevenage, Herts, SG1 3QP
Activities: Activities of other holding companies n.e.c.
Parent: ESCO Technologies Inc
Officers: Mark Dunger [1962] Director [American]; Alyson Schlinger Barclay [1959] Director [American]

Esin Cash & Carry Limited
Incorporated: 12 September 2012 *Employees:* 2
Net Worth: £2,256,122 *Total Assets:* £9,649,767
Registered Office: Unit 1-8 Centenary Industrial Estate, Jeffreys Road, Enfield, Middlesex, EN3 7UF
Activities: Retail sale in non-specialised stores with food, beverages or tobacco predominating
Parent: TFC Holdings London Limited
Officers: Ercan Ucur [1970] Director; Huseyin Ucur [1945] Director

ESRI (UK) Limited
Incorporated: 29 November 1976 *Employees:* 263
Net Worth: £5,359,947 *Total Assets:* £30,528,396
Registered Office: Millennium House, 65 Walton Street, Aylesbury, Bucks, HP21 7QG
Activities: Business and domestic software development
Parent: ESRI Holdings Limited
Officers: Stuart Richard Bonthrone [1965] Sales Director; Gareth Huw Davies [1967] Director/Chartered Accountant; Charles Joseph Kennelly [1965] Director/Chief Technology Officer; Timothy Luke Welch [1965] Sales Director

ESRI Holdings Limited
Incorporated: 7 May 1991 *Employees:* 368
Net Worth: £13,732,945 *Total Assets:* £42,185,500
Registered Office: Millennium House, 65 Walton Street, Aylesbury, Bucks, HP21 7QG
Activities: Other business support service activities n.e.c.
Shareholders: IMBOLC Limited; Laura Catherine Dangermond; Paul Jacob Dangermond
Officers: Stuart Richard Bonthrone [1965] Director; Charles Joseph Kennelly [1965] Director

Essafinaat UK Limited
Incorporated: 19 October 2016
Net Worth Deficit: £1,090,983 *Total Assets:* £9,119,296
Registered Office: 16 Hillside Meadow, Fordham, Ely, Cambs, CB7 5PJ
Activities: Raising of horses and other equines
Officers: Sandra Gillian Miller, Secretary; Jennifer Marie Hennessy [1974] Director/UK Lawyer and Trust Manager

Esselte Holdings Limited
Incorporated: 13 November 1978
Net Worth: £25,404,000 *Total Assets:* £25,404,000
Registered Office: Oxford House, Oxford Road, Aylesbury, Bucks, HP21 8SZ
Activities: Activities of head offices
Officers: Robert Michael Grimes, Secretary; Robert Michael Grimes [1980] Director/Barrister [Irish]; Katherine Alexandra Spence [1982] Director/Company Secretary

Esselte Limited
Incorporated: 27 September 1979 *Employees:* 15
Net Worth Deficit: £51,812,000 *Total Assets:* £30,358,000
Registered Office: Oxford House, Oxford Road, Aylesbury, Bucks, HP21 8SZ
Activities: Activities of head offices
Officers: Robert Michael Grimes, Secretary; Robert Michael Grimes [1980] Director/Barrister [Irish]; Katherine Alexandra Spence [1982] Director/Company Secretary

Essex & Herts Air Ambulance Trust
Incorporated: 18 March 2005 *Employees:* 55
Net Worth: £24,105,684 *Total Assets:* £25,420,800
Registered Office: The Business Centre, Earls Colne Business Park, Earls Colne, Colchester, Essex, CO6 2NS
Activities: Other human health activities
Officers: Brenda Patricia Playford, Secretary; Philip Christopher Caborn [1969] Director/Head of Sales; Dr Ramzi Mounir Freij [1963] Director/Consultant; Clive Martin Gilham [1959] Financial Director; Darren Mark Hayward [1971] Director/Solicitor; Roy John Marfleet [1957] Director; Annalisa Ridsdill Smith [1966] Director/Training Provider; Claire Smith [1978] Director; Jonathan Charles Gosselin Trower [1958] Director; Andrew Tunningly [1967] Commercial Director

Essex Cares Limited
Incorporated: 14 October 2008 *Employees:* 859
Net Worth: £3,918,178 *Total Assets:* £10,782,089
Registered Office: Seax House, Victoria Road South, Chelmsford, Essex, CM1 1QH
Activities: Other social work activities without accommodation n.e.c.
Parent: Essex County Council
Officers: Geoffrey Richard Benn [1954] Managing Director; Penelope Ann Channer [1956] Director/Councillor; Joseph Terence Coogan [1976] Director/Social Care Professional; Philip William George [1961] Director; Keir Lynch [1967] Executive Director Local Government; Peter James Martin [1944] Director/Businessman; Wendy Thomas [1960] Nurse, Director of Quality

Essex Community Foundation
Incorporated: 30 May 1995 *Employees:* 11
Net Worth: £44,561,012 *Total Assets:* £45,355,232
Registered Office: 121 New London Road, Chelmsford, Essex, CM2 0QT
Activities: Other social work activities without accommodation n.e.c.
Officers: Claire Louise Zita Read, Secretary; Nicholas Kenneth Alston [1952] Non-Executive Director and Advisor; Clare Jocelyn Ball [1960] Executive Director Portigon AG; Dame Katharine Mary Barker [1957] Director/Economist; Charles Richard Maurice Bishop [1960] Director/Investor; Lee Blissett [1967] Director/Wealth Manager; Charles Nicholas Cryer [1972] Director/Business Consultant; Russell Philip Edey [1942] Director/Retired; Simon Andrew Dalton Hall [1955] Director/Retired; Sandra Pennington Hollis [1956] Director/Retired; Peter James Martin [1944] Director/Retired; Claire Louise Zita Read [1974] Director/Solicitor; Rosemary McCarty Turner [1939] Director/Retired [American]; Joanna Katherine Wells [1971] Charity Trust Director; Vivienne Carole Wiggins [1960] Director/Chief Executive Officer

Essex County Care Limited
Incorporated: 27 June 2001 *Employees:* 313
Previous: Southend Care Limited
Net Worth: £5,546,960 *Total Assets:* £13,853,347
Registered Office: 57-59 Avenue Road, Westcliff on Sea, Essex, SS0 7PJ
Activities: Residential care activities for the elderly and disabled
Parent: Johnson Care Limited
Officers: Natalie-Jane Elizabeth Vive-Kananda, Secretary; Dr Davie Seeniapen Vive Kananda [1951] Director/Care Home Proprietor; Stuart John Mohan Vive-Kananda [1982] Director

Essex Group Holdings International Limited
Incorporated: 7 June 2016 *Employees:* 199
Net Worth: £2,422,013 *Total Assets:* £42,993,160
Registered Office: Millhouse, 32-38 East Street, Rochford, Essex, SS4 1DB
Activities: Electrical installation
Shareholders: James Hansford; John Sylvester Sampson; Mark Sampson
Officers: James Hansford [1978] Director; John Sylvester Sampson [1944] Director; Mark Peter Sampson [1978] Director

Essex Group Holdings Limited
Incorporated: 6 December 2007 *Employees:* 199
Net Worth: £14,336,014 *Total Assets:* £49,911,736
Registered Office: Unit 22a West Station Yard, Spital Road, Maldon, Essex, CM9 6TS
Activities: Electrical installation
Parent: Essex Group Holdings International Limited
Officers: Mark Sampson, Secretary/Director; James Hansford [1978] Director/Accountant; John Sylvester Sampson [1944] Director/Electrical Contractor; Mark Peter Sampson [1978] Director/Electrical Contractor; Michael John Ventham [1951] Director/Chartered Accountant

Essex Motor Company Limited
Incorporated: 26 April 2005 *Employees:* 67
Net Worth: £3,264,296 *Total Assets:* £11,332,361
Registered Office: 54 Sun Street, Waltham Abbey, Essex, EN9 1EJ
Activities: Sale of new cars and light motor vehicles
Shareholders: William Gary Cook; Darren Lowe; Karen Cook
Officers: William Gary Cook, Secretary; William Gary Cook [1957] Director; Darren Lowe [1969] Director; Simon Nicholas Ross [1966] Director/Accountant

Essex Services Group Limited
Incorporated: 1 September 1975 *Employees:* 194
Previous: Essex Services Group PLC
Net Worth: £9,849,633 *Total Assets:* £41,670,440
Registered Office: Viking Business Centre, Danes Road, Romford, Essex, RM7 0HL
Activities: Electrical installation
Parent: Essex Group Holdings Limited
Officers: James Hansford, Secretary; James Hansford [1978] Director/Accountant; John Sylvester Sampson [1944] Director/Electrical Contractor; Mark Peter Sampson [1978] Director; Michael John Ventham [1951] Director/Chartered Accountant

Essity Holding UK Limited
Incorporated: 5 November 1998 *Employees:* 9
Previous: SCA UK Holdings Limited
Net Worth: £62,368,000 *Total Assets:* £816,427,008
Registered Office: Southfields Road, Dunstable, Beds, LU6 3EJ
Activities: Activities of head offices
Officers: Paul Andrew Bailey, Secretary; Paul Andrew Bailey [1963] Director/Accountant; Daniel Paul Richard Minney [1967] Director/Vice President Sales & Marketing; Kevin John Starr [1965] Director/Vice President

Essity Operations Manchester Limited
Incorporated: 29 November 2000 *Employees:* 168
Previous: SCA Hygiene Products Manchester Limited
Net Worth: £22,815,000 *Total Assets:* £147,176,000
Registered Office: Southfields Road, Dunstable, Beds, LU6 3EJ
Activities: Manufacture of paper and paperboard
Officers: Paul Andrew Bailey, Secretary/Accountant; Paul Andrew Bailey [1963] Director/Accountant; Daniel Paul Richard Minney [1967] Director/Vice President Sales & Marketing; Kevin John Starr [1965] Director/Vice President

Essity UK Limited
Incorporated: 12 July 1996 *Employees:* 1,310
Previous: SCA Hygiene Products UK Limited
Net Worth: £465,104,000 *Total Assets:* £709,411,968
Registered Office: Southfields Road, Dunstable, Beds, LU6 3EJ
Activities: Manufacture of paper and paperboard
Officers: Paul Andrew Bailey, Secretary/Accountant; Paul Andrew Bailey [1963] Director/Accountant; Antony Richards [1966] UK Regional Supply Chain Director; Christina Maria Rydebrink [1966] Regional Director [Swedish]; Kevin John Starr [1965] Director/Vice President

Estates and Lets 2 LLP
Incorporated: 10 March 2009
Net Worth: £13,385,354 *Total Assets:* £24,684,110
Registered Office: 166 College Road, Harrow, Middlesex, HA1 1RA
Officers: Michael Docker [1963] Member; Michele Docker [1965] Member; Charles Sedgwick Pear [1983] LLP Member

Et Ceteris Limited
Incorporated: 6 March 2013 *Employees:* 110
Net Worth: £10,953,324 *Total Assets:* £15,022,091
Registered Office: Edison House, 163 Dixons Hill Road, Welham Green, Herts, AL9 7JE
Activities: Other professional, scientific and technical activities n.e.c.
Shareholders: Tamsin Kate Bennis Rossiter; William Jonathan Rossiter
Officers: Tamsin Kate Bennis Rossiter, Secretary; Tamsin Kate Bennis Rossiter [1968] Director; William Jonathan Rossiter [1965] Director

Etcetera Construction Services Limited
Incorporated: 17 April 1986 *Employees:* 6
Net Worth: £28,465,444 *Total Assets:* £30,702,602
Registered Office: Riverside House, 1-5 Como Street, Romford, Essex, RM7 7DN
Activities: Construction of other civil engineering projects n.e.c.
Shareholder: Michael Harkins
Officers: Janet Margaret Harkins, Secretary; Darren Michael Harkins [1972] Director; Janet Margaret Harkins [1954] Director

Eternit UK Limited
Incorporated: 26 November 1926
Net Worth Deficit: £44,627,000 *Total Assets:* £15,314,000
Registered Office: Whaddon Road, Meldreth, Royston, Herts, SG8 5RL
Activities: Other letting and operating of own or leased real estate
Officers: Jayne Arkell [1974] Director/Country Manager UK; Xavier Georges Roger Janin [1969] Director/General Manager [French]

Ethypharm Holdings UK Ltd
Incorporated: 4 July 2014 *Employees:* 1
Net Worth: £24,243,340 *Total Assets:* £76,845,232
Registered Office: Bampton Road, Harold Hill, Romford, Essex, RM3 8UG
Activities: Dormant company
Parent: Ethypharm S.A.
Officers: Roseline Georgette Joannesse [1959] Director/Vice President Legal Affairs [French]; Jean-Hugues Louis Marie Lecat [1956] Director [French]

Ethypharm UK Limited
Incorporated: 11 June 2013 *Employees:* 17
Previous: DB Ashbourne Limited
Net Worth: £5,230,574 *Total Assets:* £24,475,888
Registered Office: Bampton Road, Harold Hill, Romford, Essex, RM3 8UG
Activities: Wholesale of pharmaceutical goods
Parent: Dallas Burston Ashbourne Holdings Limited
Officers: Roseline Georgette Joannesse [1959] Director/Vice President Legal Affairs [French]; Jean-Hugues Louis Marie Lecat [1956] Director [French]; Lisa Elaine Tomkins [1978] Finance Director

Euro-Matic (Brazil) Limited
Incorporated: 30 September 1999
Net Worth Deficit: £1,367,904 *Total Assets:* £23,480,654
Registered Office: c/o Plasticum Norwich Ltd, Stanford Tuck Road, North Walsham, Norfolk, NR28 0TY
Activities: Activities of production holding companies
Officers: Adrian Geoffrey Wilkes, Secretary; Adrian Geoffrey Wilkes [1964] Director; Roel Zeevat [1968] Director/Chief Executive Officer [Dutch]

Eurobase International Limited
Incorporated: 1 October 1991 *Employees:* 89
Net Worth: £10,232,862 *Total Assets:* £14,328,032
Registered Office: Essex House, County Place, Chelmsford, Essex, CM2 0RE
Activities: Dormant company
Major Shareholder: John Wilson
Officers: Jonathan Grahame Moon, Secretary; Jonas Paul Locke [1975] Director; Jonathan Grahame Moon [1969] Finance Director; John Wilson [1947] Managing Director; Matthew Wilson [1986] Director/Marketing

Eurobase Systems Limited
Incorporated: 4 May 1988 *Employees:* 89
Net Worth: £5,898,056 *Total Assets:* £16,466,334
Registered Office: Essex House, County Place, Chelmsford, Essex, CM2 0RE
Activities: Business and domestic software development
Parent: Eurobase International Ltd
Officers: Jonathan Grahame Moon, Secretary; Jonas Paul Locke [1975] Director; Jonathan Grahame Moon [1969] Finance Director; Peter Ian Morgan Hare [1955] Director; John Wilson [1947] Director

Eurocity Properties (Central) Limited
Incorporated: 3 September 1997
Net Worth: £131,547 *Total Assets:* £11,077,806
Registered Office: Unicorn House, Station Close, Potters Bar, Herts, EN6 1TL
Activities: Buying and selling of own real estate
Parent: Panther Securities PLC
Officers: Simon Jeffrey Peters, Company Secretary; Andrew Stewart Perloff [1944] Director; John Henry Perloff [1968] Director; Simon Jeffrey Peters [1977] Director

European Coffee Corporation Limited
Incorporated: 22 August 1997 *Employees:* 60
Net Worth: £13,807,752 *Total Assets:* £23,818,008
Registered Office: Unit B, Chiltern Park Industrial Estate, Boscombe Road, Dunstable, Beds, LU5 4LT
Activities: Activities of other holding companies n.e.c.
Major Shareholder: Anne Kathrin Rothfos
Officers: Generald John Annetts, Secretary; Generald John Annetts [1952] Director; Holger Bebensee [1958] Director [German]

The European Film Partners III LLP
Incorporated: 14 December 2001
Net Worth: £32,776,124 *Total Assets:* £36,126,636
Registered Office: 99 Kenton Road, Harrow, Middlesex, HA3 0AN
Officers: Andrew Iain Bennett [1966] LLP Member; Paul St John Brine [1950] LLP Member; Daniel William Deschamps Chamier [1964] LLP Member; Stephen Trevor Din [1964] LLP Member; Jeremy Ryton Drax [1960] LLP Member; Gavin Colunba Dredge [1973] LLP Member; Michael John Thornton Dudley [1957] LLP Member; Gavin Rhys Eddy [1967] LLP Member; Richard Oliver Fagan [1945] LLP Member; Benjamin James Ernest Guest [1973] LLP Member; Gerrard Leslie Henry [1953] LLP Member; John Edward Inglis [1961] LLP Member; John Anthony Maloney [1964] LLP Member; Christopher Ator Potts [1967] LLP Member; Martin Vincent Quinn [1964] LLP Member; Manfred Johan Schepers [1960] LLP Member; Tariq Shaikh [1969] LLP Member; Peter Skinner [1930] LLP Member; Rupert Peregrine Austin Tyer [1963] LLP Member; Thomas Henry Wiggin [1969] LLP Member

European Flavours & Fragrances PLC
Incorporated: 20 March 1981 *Employees:* 174
Net Worth: £6,779,742 *Total Assets:* £12,096,720
Registered Office: 9 Peerglow Estate, Marshlane, Ware, Herts, SG12 9QL
Activities: Other manufacturing n.e.c.
Major Shareholder: Clive Edward Kersey
Officers: Jason James Blackman, Secretary; Clive Edward Kersey [1952] Group Managing Director; Gary Peter Kersey [1958] Director/Purchasing; Spencer Andrew Kersey [1982] Sales Director; Marc Leon Smith [1958] Operations Director

European Independent Purchasing Company Ltd
Incorporated: 8 August 2001 *Employees:* 129
Net Worth: £252,078 *Total Assets:* £9,541,228
Registered Office: Rapid House, 40 Oxford Road, High Wycombe, Bucks, HP11 2EE
Activities: Other food services
Officers: Neil Marshal Black, Secretary; Neil Marshal Black [1970] Director/Accountant; Neil Christopher Denny [1971] Managing Director; Bryan David Griffiths [1966] Managing Director; Paula Marketta Heikkila [1973] Director/Subway Franchisor [Finnish]; Sascha Hoerig [1974] Director/Entrepreneur [German]; Andre Loeffler [1974] Director/Business Development Manager [German]; Rachana Pancholi [1970] Director; Jitendra Jayanand Patel [1969] Director/Business Owner; Vimal Patel [1979] Director; Michael Igor Piasecki [1980] Director/Development Agent, Franchisee Subway Group [Polish/American]; Fabien Petorin [1983] Director/Franchisee Subway [French]

European Investments (Cornwall) Holdings Limited
Incorporated: 7 April 2017
Net Worth Deficit: £6,142,855 *Total Assets:* £48,295,900
Registered Office: Beaufort Court, Egg Farm Lane, off Station Road, Kings Langley, Herts, WD4 8LR
Activities: Financial intermediation not elsewhere classified
Parent: The Renewables Infrastructure Group (UK) Investments Limited
Officers: Dominic James Hearth, Secretary; Steven William Hughes [1972] Global Support Services Director, UK&I - Commercial; Mitesh Raj Patel [1982] Director/Chartered Accountant; Tracy Jane Scott [1976] Director/Delivery Project Manager; Mark Christopher Wayment [1958] Director

European Investments (Cornwall) Limited
Incorporated: 13 April 2012
Net Worth: £2,565,519 *Total Assets:* £56,410,928
Registered Office: Beaufort Court, Egg Farm Lane, off Station Road, Kings Langley, Herts, WD4 8LR
Activities: Other business support service activities n.e.c.
Parent: European Investments (SCEL) Limited
Officers: Dominic Hearth, Secretary; Steven William Hughes [1972] Global Support Services Director, UK&I - Commercial; Mitesh Raj Patel [1982] Director/Chartered Accountant; Tracy Jane Scott [1976] Director/Delivery Project Manager; Mark Christopher Wayment [1958] Director

European Investments (Crook Hill) Limited
Incorporated: 27 September 2013
Net Worth: £2,491,793 *Total Assets:* £69,570,696
Registered Office: 2 Hunting Gate, Hitchin, Herts, SG4 0TJ
Activities: Other business support service activities n.e.c.
Parent: Ventus Investments Limited
Officers: Valeria Rosati [1975] Director/Fund Manager [Italian]; Marissa Ann Szczepaniak [1980] Associate Director

European Investments (Earlseat) Limited
Incorporated: 9 September 2013
Net Worth: £1,595,000 *Total Assets:* £19,100,000
Registered Office: Beaufort Court, Egg Farm Lane, Kings Langley, Herts, WD4 8LR
Activities: Other business support service activities n.e.c.
Parent: European Investments Solar Holdings Limited
Officers: Dominic James Hearth, Secretary; Steven William Hughes [1972] Generation & Asset Management Director; Fraser Stephen Merry [1968] Director/Chartered Surveyor; Mitesh Raj Patel [1982] Director/Group Financial Controller

European Investments (Lancashire 2) Limited
Incorporated: 10 February 2014
Net Worth: £2,050,000 *Total Assets:* £18,713,342
Registered Office: 2 Hunting Gate, Hitchin, Herts, SG4 0TJ
Activities: Other business support service activities n.e.c.
Parent: Ventus Investments Ltd
Officers: Valeria Rosati [1975] Director/Fund Manager [Italian]; Marissa Ann Szczepaniak [1980] Associate Director

European Investments (Lancashire) Limited
Incorporated: 27 September 2013
Net Worth: £7,700,310 *Total Assets:* £21,454,676
Registered Office: 2 Hunting Gate, Hitchin, Herts, SG4 0TJ
Activities: Other business support service activities n.e.c.
Parent: Ventus Investments Ltd
Officers: Anne-Noelle Noelle Le Gal [1983] Director/Senior Associate [French]; Valeria Rosati [1975] Director/Fund Manager [Italian]; Marissa Ann Szczepaniak [1980] Associate Director

European Investments (Reaps Moss) Limited
Incorporated: 11 February 2014
Net Worth: £2,050,000 *Total Assets:* £18,713,342
Registered Office: 2 Hunting Gate, Hitchin, Herts, SG4 0TJ
Activities: Other business support service activities n.e.c.
Parent: European Investments (Lancashire 2) Limited
Officers: Valeria Rosati [1975] Director/Fund Manager [Italian]; Marissa Ann Szczepaniak [1980] Associate Director

European Investments (SCEL) Limited
Incorporated: 5 April 2012
Net Worth: £7,893,309 *Total Assets:* £18,296,544
Registered Office: Beaufort Court, Egg Farm Lane, off Station Road, Kings Langley, Herts, WD4 8LR
Activities: Other business support service activities n.e.c.
Parent: The Renewables Infrastructure Group (UK) Investments Limited
Officers: Dominic Hearth, Secretary; Steven William Hughes [1972] Global Support Services Director, UK&I; Mitesh Raj Patel [1982] Director/Chartered Accountant; Tracy Jane Scott [1976] Director/Delivery Project Manager

European Tyre Enterprise Limited
Incorporated: 28 February 2011 *Employees:* 235
Net Worth: £393,198,016 *Total Assets:* £971,427,008
Registered Office: Etel House, Avenue One, Letchworth Garden City, Herts, SG6 2HU
Activities: Activities of head offices
Shareholders: Itochu Europe PLC; Itochu Corporation PLC
Officers: Ian Vincent Ellis, Secretary; Stephen Mark Childs [1973] Director; Takeshi Fukuda [1974] Director [Japanese]; Wataru Goroku [1974] Director [Japanese]; Yasuyuki Harada [1959] Director [Japanese]; Mitsutaka Ishida [1968] Director [Japanese]; Tetsuji Kawakami [1964] Director [Japanese]; Yutaka Kimbara [1970] Director [Japanese]; Mark Lynott [1975] Director; Kenji Murai [1966] Director [Japanese]; Mark Richard Slade [1975] Director

Europlants (UK) Limited
Incorporated: 21 December 1990
Net Worth: £6,335,735 *Total Assets:* £9,783,909
Registered Office: Great North Road A1000, Bell Bar, Hatfield, Herts, AL9 6DA
Activities: Other business support service activities n.e.c.
Major Shareholder: Renato Antonio Carlo Canale
Officers: Valeria Magdalena Lucie Canale, Secretary; Renato Antonio Carlo Canale [1942] Director/Horticulturist

Eurosalamis Enterprises Ltd.
Incorporated: 16 February 1996 *Employees:* 1
Net Worth: £4,115,895 *Total Assets:* £10,690,461
Registered Office: Cuckmans Farm, 67 Ragged Hall Lane, St Albans, Herts, AL2 3NP
Activities: Other letting and operating of own or leased real estate
Major Shareholder: Pantelis Christoforou
Officers: Pantelis Christoforou, Secretary; Pantelis Christoforou [1970] Director; Theodoula Christoforou [1970] Director

Euroview Manufacturing Limited
Incorporated: 17 December 1992 *Employees:* 129
Net Worth Deficit: £3,180,124 *Total Assets:* £14,556,602
Registered Office: Kingfisher House, 11 Hoffmanns Way, Chelmsford, Essex, CM1 1GU
Activities: Shaping and processing of flat glass
Parent: Hubco Ltd
Officers: Perry John Hubble, Secretary; Lorraine Ellen Hubble [1961] Director/Caterer; Perry John Hubble [1960] Director/Joiner

EUSA Pharma (UK) Limited
Incorporated: 26 November 2014 *Employees:* 51
Net Worth: £103,497,744 *Total Assets:* £152,351,008
Registered Office: Breakspear Park, Breakspear Way, Hemel Hempstead, Herts, HP2 4TZ
Activities: Wholesale of pharmaceutical goods
Parent: EUSA Pharma Holdco 2 (UK) Limited
Officers: Emma Jane Johnson [1981] Director; Dr. Dev Kumar [1974] Director/Head of Legal and Compliance; Lee Scot Morley [1970] Director; Bryan Geoffrey Morton [1955] Director

EUSA Pharma Holdco 1 (UK) Limited
Incorporated: 28 January 2015
Net Worth: £90,787,216 *Total Assets:* £116,354,376
Registered Office: Ground Floor, Breakspear Park, Breakspear Way, Hemel Hempstead, Herts, HP2 4TZ
Activities: Management consultancy activities other than financial management
Officers: Evis Hursever [1975] Director/Principal; Emma Jane Johnson [1981] Director; Lee Scot Morley [1970] Director; Petri Tapani Vainio [1959] Managing Director [Finnish]

EUSA Pharma Holdco 2 (UK) Limited
Incorporated: 29 January 2015
Net Worth: £116,352,608 *Total Assets:* £116,352,608
Registered Office: Ground Floor, Breakspear Park, Breakspear Way, Hemel Hempstead, Herts, HP2 4TZ
Activities: Management consultancy activities other than financial management
Officers: Emma Jane Johnson [1981] Director; Lee Scot Morley [1970] Director

Euston Biogas Limited
Incorporated: 11 February 2014 *Employees:* 2
Net Worth Deficit: £1,586,512 *Total Assets:* £15,976,121
Registered Office: 1 Whitbreads Business Centre, Whitbreads Farm Lane, Chatham Green, Chelmsford, Essex, CM3 3FE
Activities: Manufacture of gas
Parent: Strutt and Parker (Farms) Limited
Officers: Charles Oswald Fillingham [1960] Director; Stuart Richard Wallis [1980] Director/Chartered Accountant

EV Finco Limited
Incorporated: 6 March 2014
Net Worth Deficit: £53,160,000 *Total Assets:* £35,338,000
Registered Office: EV Technology Centre, 19 Frensham Road, Sweet Briar Industrial Estate, Norwich, NR3 2BT
Activities: Activities of head offices
Parent: EV Holdings Limited
Officers: John Joseph Houston, Secretary; Andrew James Davidson [1985] Director/Investment Manager; John Joseph Houston [1964] Finance Director; Fraser Louden [1965] Director; Shaun Norman Skene Middleton [1968] Director/Managing Partner; Christopher Milburn [1966] Director; Jonathan James Renton Thursby [1968] Director

EV Holdings Limited
Incorporated: 20 December 2013 *Employees:* 16
Net Worth Deficit: £50,555,000 *Total Assets:* £40,110,000
Registered Office: EV Technology Centre, 19 Frensham Road, Sweet Briar Industrial Estate, Norwich, NR3 2BT
Activities: Activities of head offices
Officers: John Joseph Houston, Secretary; Andrew James Davidson [1985] Director/Investment Manager; John Joseph Houston [1964] Finance Director; Fraser Louden [1965] Director; Shaun Norman Skene Middleton [1968] Director/Managing Partner; Christopher Milburn [1966] Director; Jonathan James Renton Thursby [1968] Director

The Evangelical Lutheran Church of England Trust Limited
Incorporated: 5 March 1957
Net Worth: £14,582,921 *Total Assets:* £14,589,172
Registered Office: 28 Huntingdon Road, Cambridge, CB3 0HH
Activities: Other service activities n.e.c.
Officers: Doreen Muriel Rosser, Secretary; Jon Jay Ehlers [1962] Director/Church Minister [American]; The Reverend Jaime Rone Kriger [1970] Director; Cynthia Estelle Lumley [1956] Director/Principal [Canadian/British]; Doreen Muriel Rosser [1948] Director/Assistant Registrar London School of Theology; Reverend George Stanley Samiec [1957] Director/Minister of Religion [Australian]; Reiner Thoelke [1940] Director/Retired

The Evelyn Trust
Incorporated: 1 May 1920
Net Worth: £25,612,814 *Total Assets:* £28,766,678
Registered Office: Shakespeare House, 42 Newmarket Road, Cambridge, CB5 8EP
Activities: Financial intermediation not elsewhere classified
Officers: William Pike, Secretary; Amy Agnew [1979] Director/Charity; Trevor Patrick Baglin [1958] Director; William Mark Ransford Dawkins [1956] Director/Consultant; Professor Rebecca Clare FitzGenerald [1968] Director/Academic Medical Researcher; Adrian Charles Frost [1957] Director/Investment Manager; Jeremy Henry Moore Newsum [1955] Director; Jeremy Wingate Pemberton [1977] Director; William Pike [1953] Director/Trustee; Julia Elizabeth Offord Squier [1954] Director/Chartered Physiotherapist; Catherine Peta Thomas [1953] Director/Retired Teacher

Everbuild Building Products Limited
Incorporated: 24 January 1994 *Employees:* 335
Net Worth: £10,843,000 *Total Assets:* £39,071,000
Registered Office: The Sika Building, Watchmead, Welwyn Garden City, Herts, AL7 1BQ
Activities: Manufacture of other chemical products n.e.c.
Officers: Daniel Emil Lang [1971] Director [Swiss]; Paul Schuler [1955] Director [Swiss]

Everest Limited
Incorporated: 18 October 2002 *Employees:* 661
Net Worth Deficit: £5,593,000 *Total Assets:* £29,419,000
Registered Office: Everest House, Sopers Road, Cuffley, Potters Bar, Herts, EN6 4SG
Activities: Glazing
Parent: Hillary Bidco Ltd
Officers: Robert Alexander Asplin [1979] Director; Joanne Maria Holland [1960] Director [Australian]; Karl Sean Munns [1970] Director

Evergreen Finance Limited
Incorporated: 8 March 1991 *Employees:* 7
Net Worth: £32,159,000 *Total Assets:* £33,140,000
Registered Office: No 1 Park Lane, Hemel Hempstead, Herts, HP2 4YL
Activities: Financial intermediation not elsewhere classified
Parent: Colaingrove Limited
Officers: Jane Elizabeth Bentall [1970] Director/Accountant; Paul Charles Flaum [1970] Director; Iain Stuart Macmillan [1976] Director

Everguard Limited
Incorporated: 25 June 1998 *Employees:* 4
Net Worth: £14,457,477 *Total Assets:* £17,474,784
Registered Office: 2nd Floor, Katherine House, 11 Wyllyotts Place, Potters Bar, Herts, EN6 2JD
Activities: Other letting and operating of own or leased real estate
Shareholders: Chrysanthos Zacharia; Andreas Zacharia; Paraskevou Pamela Gumuskaya
Officers: Paraskevou Pamela Gumuskaya [1980] Director/Senior Manager; Andreas Zacharia [1976] Director/Property Manager; Chrysanthos Zacharia [1974] Director/Property Manager

T.J.Evers Limited
Incorporated: 26 October 1943 *Employees:* 100
Net Worth: £3,687,374 *Total Assets:* £10,727,255
Registered Office: New Road, Tiptree, Essex, CO5 0HQ
Activities: Construction of commercial buildings
Parent: Trevester Limited
Officers: Marie Paveley, Secretary; Mervyn John Denney [1961] Director/Contracts Manager; Alan Michael Evers [1969] Director/Buyer; Stephen Michael Ewers [1965] Director/Contracts Manager; Kevin Philip Howell [1971] Director/Quantity Surveyor

Eversleigh Investment and Property Company Limited
Incorporated: 22 May 1956 *Employees:* 7
Net Worth: £24,980,772 *Total Assets:* £31,795,298
Registered Office: Marquis House, 68 Great North Road, Hatfield, Herts, AL9 5ER
Activities: Development of building projects
Shareholders: Malcolm James Geoffrey King; Jeffrey Stuart King; Caroline Francis Yannaghas
Officers: Jeffrey Stuart King, Secretary; Jeffrey Stuart King [1947] Director/Site Representative; Malcolm James Geoffrey King [1945] Director/Chartered Surveyor; Caroline Francis Yannaghas [1942] Director/Femme Sole

EVI Technologies Limited
Incorporated: 10 February 2003 *Employees:* 247
Net Worth: £20,785,554 *Total Assets:* £28,059,880
Registered Office: Poseidon House, Castle Park, Cambridge, CB3 0RD
Activities: Other information technology service activities
Parent: Amazon.Com, Inc.
Officers: Phaedra Ann Andrews [1975] Finance Director [American]; David William Hardcastle [1972] Director; John Bradford Stone [1971] Director [American]

Evolution Academy Trust
Incorporated: 26 July 2012 *Employees:* 401
Net Worth: £23,184,032 *Total Assets:* £26,854,236
Registered Office: Suite 1, Keswick Hall, Norwich, NR4 6TJ
Activities: Primary education
Officers: Steve Bramble [1984] Director/Charity Worker; Sheila Anne Greenacre [1954] Director/Retired Headteacher; Mark Jeffries [1957] Director/Solicitor; Victoria Jane Newrick [1973] Director/Headteacher; David Michael Rich [1967] Director/Financial Consultant; Drew Whitehead [1965] Director/Consultant

Exaclair Limited
Incorporated: 18 October 1911 *Employees:* 78
Net Worth: £4,129,577 *Total Assets:* £9,891,042
Registered Office: Guildhall House, Old Medow Road, Hardwick Industrial Estate, Kings Lynn, Norfolk, PE30 4LW
Activities: Other manufacturing n.e.c.
Parent: Exaclair Holdings Ltd
Officers: Mark Anthony Daisley [1965] Managing Director; Charles Nusse [1972] Director/Chairman [French]; Francois Nusse [1935] Director [French]

Exagris Limited
Incorporated: 25 June 2007 *Employees:* 473
Net Worth Deficit: £30,325,998 *Total Assets:* £30,044,408
Registered Office: Amersham Court, 154 Station Road, Amersham, Bucks, HP6 5DW
Activities: Growing of cereals (except rice), leguminous crops and oil seeds
Major Shareholder: Carolyn Sian Lilley
Officers: Timothy John Deborde, Secretary; Timothy John de Borde [1966] Director/Accountant; Dr Carolyn Sian Lilley [1967] Director/Housewife; David George Plumer Lilley [1966] Director/Investment Manager

Excellence in Education Trust
Incorporated: 1 March 2016 *Employees:* 180
Net Worth: £24,017,226 *Total Assets:* £26,965,340
Registered Office: c/o Oakington Manor Primary School, Oakington Manor Drive, Wembley, Middlesex, HA9 6NF
Activities: Primary education
Officers: Sheila Ann Campbell, Secretary; Cyril Copitch [1947] Director/Facilities Manager; Ivan Deshumkh [1942] Director/Retired; Jo Jhally [1949] Director/Retired; Sylvia Libson OBE [1948] Director/Executive Headteacher; Narinder Nathan [1948] Director/Retired [Malaysian]; Waleed Shamki [1962] Director/Office Manager; Everton Sharpe [1957] Director/Headteacher; Darren David Singer [1969] Director/Accountant; Uwem Utip [1960] Director/Lawyer

Excelredstone Converged Solutions Limited
Incorporated: 11 June 1986 *Employees:* 273
Previous: Redstone Converged Solutions Limited
Net Worth: £8,383,835 *Total Assets:* £17,792,348
Registered Office: Trafalgar House, 712 London Road, Grays, Essex, RM20 3JT
Activities: Information technology consultancy activities
Parent: Excelredstone Comunica Limited
Officers: Barry John Horgan [1971] Director [Irish]; Brendan Loughrey [1961] Managing Director; Jakob Moeller-Jensen [1973] Director [Danish]; Matthew Salter [1971] Operations Director [New Zealander]; Steven Williams [1979] Finance Director

Excelredstone Services Limited
Incorporated: 9 January 2008 *Employees:* 140
Previous: Excel I.T Services Limited
Net Worth: £7,283,940 *Total Assets:* £12,712,179
Registered Office: Trafalgar House, 712 London Road, Grays, Essex, RM20 3JT
Activities: Other information technology service activities
Officers: Barry John Horgan, Secretary; Barry John Horgan [1971] Director [Irish]; Jakob Moeller-Jensen [1973] Director [Danish]; Simon Hobart Charles Morrish [1974] Director; Matthew Porter [1960] Director [Irish]

Excitech Limited
Incorporated: 11 March 1985 *Employees:* 118
Net Worth: £8,271,259 *Total Assets:* £16,704,616
Registered Office: Design Technology Centre, 8 Kinetic Crescent, Innova Business Park, Enfield, Middlesex, EN3 7XH
Activities: Business and domestic software development
Major Shareholder: Adrian Robert Atkinson
Officers: Peter Blake, Secretary; Adrian Robert Atkinson [1956] Director/Chairman; Leigh Atkinson [1958] Strategic Director; Peter Blake [1976] Director/Accountant; David Aled Hughes [1965] Managing Director

Exclusive Contract Services Limited
Incorporated: 6 November 1987 *Employees:* 3,689
Net Worth: £4,333,110 *Total Assets:* £14,679,518
Registered Office: Ground Floor, Prospect Place, 85 Great North Road, Hatfield, Herts, AL9 5DA
Activities: General cleaning of buildings
Parent: The Exclusive Services Group Limited
Officers: Janet Katherine Sheridan, Secretary/Director; Amanda Jane Evans [1972] Director; Gary Martin Evans [1960] Director; Debbie Lancaster [1956] Director; James Patrick Melvin [1957] Director; Dr Nileshbhai Jayantilal Sachdev [1958] Director; Janet Katherine Sheridan [1945] Director

Exheat Group Limited
Incorporated: 7 January 2014 *Employees:* 226
Net Worth: £13,252,681 *Total Assets:* £24,356,926
Registered Office: 17 Old Millers Wharf, Fishergate, Norwich, NR3 1GS
Activities: Activities of head offices
Major Shareholder: Peter Brookes Smithers
Officers: Zek Meadows, Secretary; Robert John Coss [1973] Technical Director; Zek Meadows [1979] Finance Director; Peter Brookes Smithers [1951] Director/Group Chairman; Robert Vincent Smithers [1985] Director/Group Chief Executive

Exheat Limited
Incorporated: 28 June 1991 *Employees:* 84
Net Worth: £6,860,325 *Total Assets:* £9,161,591
Registered Office: 17 Old Millers Wharf, Fishergate, Norwich, NR3 1GS
Activities: Manufacture of other electrical equipment
Parent: Exheat Group Limited
Officers: Zek Meadows, Secretary; Robert John Coss [1973] Technical Director; Mark Edward Jenner [1981] Sales and Engineering Director; Zek Meadows [1979] Finance Director; Peter Brookes Smithers [1951] Director/Group Chairman; Robert Vincent Smithers [1985] Director/Group Chief Executive

Exlservice (UK) Limited
Incorporated: 21 October 2003 *Employees:* 124
Net Worth: £21,017,790 *Total Assets:* £32,245,568
Registered Office: Vaughan Chambers, Vaughan Road, Harpenden, Herts, AL5 4EE
Activities: Other business support service activities n.e.c.
Parent: Exlservice Holdings Inc
Officers: Vishal Chhibbar [1968] Director/Executive [Indian]; Rohit Kapoor [1964] Director/Company Executive [American]

Exploration Electronics Limited
Incorporated: 10 May 1982 *Employees:* 18
Net Worth: £17,237,278 *Total Assets:* £17,450,164
Registered Office: London Road, Beccles, Suffolk, NR34 8TS
Activities: Other engineering activities
Officers: Kathryn Ellen Allen, Secretary; Susan Ellen Allen, Secretary; Bruce Harry Allen [1950] Director/Engineer; Susan Ellen Allen [1955] Director

Explorer Holdings UK Limited
Incorporated: 7 December 2006
Net Worth: £27,000,000 *Total Assets:* £29,000,000
Registered Office: Breakspear Park, Breakspear Way, Hemel Hempstead, Herts, HP2 4TZ
Activities: Other information technology service activities
Parent: JDM Technology Group Limited
Officers: James Douglas McFarlane [1950] Director [Canadian]

Express Freight Services (U.K.) Limited
Incorporated: 29 August 1979 *Employees:* 68
Net Worth: £14,225,159 *Total Assets:* £18,283,578
Registered Office: Armada House, Tilbury Freeport, Tilbury, Essex, RM18 7ET
Activities: Freight transport by road
Parent: R Swain & Sons Limited
Officers: Andrew John Baxter [1966] Director; Matthew Deer [1975] Director; Stuart James Rigby [1963] Director

Express Vending Group Limited
Incorporated: 4 June 2003 *Employees:* 255
Net Worth: £7,166,589 *Total Assets:* £14,538,369
Registered Office: 1 Finway Road, Hemel Hempstead, Herts, HP2 7PT
Activities: Activities of head offices
Officers: Daniel Henry Abrahams [1973] Finance Director; Wesley Mulligan [1963] Managing Director [Irish]

Express Vending Limited
Incorporated: 17 July 1992 *Employees:* 252
Net Worth: £5,797,632 *Total Assets:* £14,036,931
Registered Office: 1 Finway Road, Hemel Hempstead, Herts, HP2 7PT
Activities: Other food services
Parent: Express Vending Group Limited
Officers: Paul Nathaniel Ian Hearne [1975] Sales Director; Anthony Michael Leon [1979] Director

Ezra Attia Limited
Incorporated: 21 January 1993
Net Worth: £5,338,538 *Total Assets:* £8,991,860
Registered Office: Ground Floor, Elizabeth House, 54-58 High Street, Edgware, Middlesex, HA8 7EJ
Activities: Other business support service activities n.e.c.
Officers: Lee Maurice Gold [1987] Director

F & S Energy Limited
Incorporated: 10 February 2011 *Employees:* 9
Net Worth: £2,234,249 *Total Assets:* £8,583,598
Registered Office: 23 Hall Street, Chelmsford, Essex, CM2 0HG
Activities: Trade of electricity
Shareholders: Steven Nicholas Funnell; Imtiaaz Sali
Officers: Steven Nicholas Funnell [1970] Director/Utilities; Imtiaaz Sali [1981] Director/Utilities

F-Star Alpha Limited
Incorporated: 4 September 2013
Net Worth: £11,267,180 *Total Assets:* £11,315,629
Registered Office: Eddeva B920, Babraham Research Campus, Cambridge, CB22 3AT
Activities: Research and experimental development on biotechnology
Officers: Tolga Hassan, Secretary; Nessan Anthony Bermingham [1972] Director/Venture Partner and Board Chairman [Irish]; John Blodgett Edwards [1961] Director [American]; Dr Jean-Francois Formela [1956] Director/Venture Capital Partner [French]; Dr Eliot Richard Forster [1966] Director; Dr Deborah Harland [1960] Director/Venture Capital Investor; Tolga Hassan [1971] Director/Chief Financial Officer and Chartered Accountant; Patrick Johan Hendrik Krol [1963] Director/Managing Partner [Dutch]; Dr Florian Ruker [1957] Director [Austrian]; Helmut Schuehsler [1959] Managing Partner, Director [Austrian]

F-Star Delta Limited
Incorporated: 30 December 2016
Net Worth: £1,342,466 *Total Assets:* £11,490,492
Registered Office: Eddeva B920, Babraham Research Campus, Cambridge, CB22 3AT
Activities: Other business support service activities n.e.c.
Officers: Nessan Anthony Bermingham [1972] Director/Venture Partner and Board Chairman [Irish]; John Blodgett Edwards [1961] Director [American]; Dr Jean-Francois Formela [1956] Director/Venture Capital Partner [French]; Dr Eliot Richard Forster [1966] Director; Dr Deborah Harland [1960] Director/Venture Capital Investor; Tolga Hassan [1971] Director/Chief Financial Officer and Chartered Accountant; Patrick Johan Hendrik Krol [1963] Director/Managing Partner [Dutch]; Dr Florian Ruker [1957] Director [Austrian]; Helmut Schuehsler [1959] Managing Partner, Director [Austrian]

Facet Capital Limited
Incorporated: 9 July 2013
Net Worth: £4,842,911 *Total Assets:* £19,419,258
Registered Office: Suite 1, Staple House, Eleanors Cross, Dunstable, Beds, LU6 1SU
Activities: Fund management activities
Parent: LJ Capital Limited
Officers: Richard Eugene Hutchinson [1952] Director

Faerch Plast UK Limited
Incorporated: 17 June 1971 *Employees:* 269
Previous: Anson Packaging Limited
Net Worth: £24,997,600 *Total Assets:* £42,025,412
Registered Office: 78 Lancaster Way Business Park, Ely, Cambs, CB6 3NW
Activities: Manufacture of other plastic products
Parent: Avro Holdings Limited
Officers: Lars Gade Hansen [1968] Director/Chief Executive Officer [Danish]; James Andrew Osborne-Smith [1964] Operations Director; Tom Sand-Kristensen [1971] Director/Group CFO [Danish]

FAI Automotive PLC
Incorporated: 8 May 1969 *Employees:* 108
Net Worth: £10,336,142 *Total Assets:* £14,284,172
Registered Office: F A I Automotive PLC, Chiltern Trading Estate, Grovebury Road, Leighton Buzzard, Beds, LU7 4TU
Activities: Wholesale trade of motor vehicle parts and accessories
Shareholders: Kevin Grant Walker; Sean Scott Walker
Officers: Peter Charles Guinn, Secretary; Jonathan Paul Alexander [1977] Director; Ted Cooper [1951] Director; Peter Charles Guinn [1969] Finance Director; Sean Scott Walker [1958] Director

Fairacres Group Limited
Incorporated: 13 February 1995 *Employees:* 238
Net Worth: £35,132,228 *Total Assets:* £50,470,680
Registered Office: Fairacres, Stock Lane, Ingatestone, Essex, CM4 9QL
Activities: Activities of head offices
Shareholder: George Rodney Kean
Officers: Tracy Ann Nicol, Secretary; Michael Phillip Rodney Kean [1971] Director; Susan Elizabeth Seager [1962] Director

Fairfield Garage (Leigh-on-Sea) Limited
Incorporated: 21 September 1967 *Employees:* 147
Net Worth: £10,166,285 *Total Assets:* £23,789,480
Registered Office: Arterial Road, Eastwood, Leigh on Sea, Essex, SS9 4XX
Activities: Sale of new cars and light motor vehicles
Officers: Simon Neal Goldring, Secretary/Accountant; Simon Neal Goldring [1961] Director/Accountant; Michael Andrew Kent Styles [1959] Director

Fairfield Limited
Incorporated: 31 July 1998 *Employees:* 147
Net Worth: £10,192,000 *Total Assets:* £23,815,196
Registered Office: Arterial Road, Eastwood, Leigh on Sea, Essex, SS9 4XX
Activities: Activities of head offices
Officers: Simon Neal Goldring, Secretary/Financial Director; Simon Neal Goldring [1961] Financial Director; Michael Andrew Kent Styles [1959] Director

Fairline Yachts Limited
Incorporated: 6 January 2016 *Employees:* 302
Net Worth Deficit: £8,344,000 *Total Assets:* £22,886,000
Registered Office: Nene Valley Business Park, Oundle, Peterborough, Cambs, PE8 4HN
Activities: Building of pleasure and sporting boats
Shareholders: Igor Glyanenko; Alexander Volov
Officers: Larisa Bondareva [1964] Finance Director; Karl Tristan Gilding [1959] Director; Igor Glyanenko [1972] Director [Russian]; Martyn John Hicks [1976] Director; Andrey Lomakin [1968] Director [Russian]; David Rolfe Tydeman [1955] Director; Alexander Volov [1972] Director [Russian]

Fairview Enfield Limited
Incorporated: 17 February 1984
Net Worth: £23,333,000 *Total Assets:* £24,004,000
Registered Office: 50 Lancaster Road, Enfield, Middlesex, EN2 0BY
Activities: Development of building projects
Parent: Fairview New Homes Limited
Officers: Jonathan Mark Baxter, Secretary; Michael Blakey [1963] Director; Nicholas Martin Dulcken [1967] Director; Generald Anthony Malton [1960] Director; Darren Lee McCormack [1982] Sales Director; Richard James Paterson [1957] Director; Jonathan Andrew Spring [1972] Land Buying Director; Michael Raymond Walker [1958] Director; Robert Kenneth Williams [1964] Finance Director

Fairview Estates (Housing) Limited
Incorporated: 6 August 1963 *Employees:* 219
Net Worth: £9,068,000 *Total Assets:* £30,832,000
Registered Office: 50 Lancaster Road, Enfield, Middlesex, EN2 0BY
Activities: Construction of domestic buildings
Parent: Fairview New Homes Limited
Officers: Jonathan Mark Baxter, Secretary; Daniel John Carroll [1980] Director; Rhys Bernard Davies [1982] Director/Land Buyer; Steven Eastwood [1967] Commercial Director; Mark John Jackson [1971] Planning Director; Generald Anthony Malton [1960] Director; Vasos Ptohopoulos [1975] Director [Greek]; John Andrew Barker Reid [1966] Design Director; Timothy Simon Sellens [1959] Director/Head of Affordable Housing; Martin Richard Smith [1955] Director; Robert Kenneth Williams [1964] Finance Director; John Wood [1958] Director

Fairview Holdings Limited
Incorporated: 2 October 2000 *Employees:* 226
Net Worth: £252,863,008 *Total Assets:* £356,788,992
Registered Office: 50 Lancaster Road, Enfield, Middlesex, EN2 0BY
Activities: Activities of construction holding companies
Shareholders: Michael Raymond Walker; Robert Kenneth Williams; Michael Blakey; Nicholas Martin Dulcken; Gerald Anthony Malton; Richard James Paterson
Officers: Jonathan Mark Baxter, Secretary; Michael Blakey [1963] Director; Dennis John Cope [1933] Director; Nicholas Martin Dulcken [1967] Director; Generald Anthony Malton [1960] Director; Darren Lee McCormack [1982] Sales Director; Richard James Paterson [1957] Director; Jonathan Andrew Spring [1972] Land Buying Director; Michael Raymond Walker [1958] Director; Robert Kenneth Williams [1964] Finance Director

Fairview Homes Limited
Incorporated: 22 April 1997 *Employees:* 9
Net Worth Deficit: £266,000 *Total Assets:* £59,639,000
Registered Office: 50 Lancaster Road, Enfield, Middlesex, EN2 0BY
Activities: Development of building projects
Parent: Fairview New Homes Limited
Officers: Jonathan Mark Baxter, Secretary; Michael Blakey [1963] Director; Nicholas Martin Dulcken [1967] Director; Generald Anthony Malton [1960] Director; Darren Lee McCormack [1982] Sales Director; Richard James Paterson [1957] Director; Martin Richard Smith [1955] Director; Jonathan Andrew Spring [1972] Land Buying Director; Michael Raymond Walker [1958] Director; Robert Kenneth Williams [1964] Finance Director

Fairview Hotels Investments (2) Limited
Incorporated: 26 January 2017
Net Worth: £1,518,115 *Total Assets:* £19,836,746
Registered Office: Kanta House, Victoria Road, South Ruislip, Middlesex, HA4 0JQ
Activities: Activities of real estate investment trusts
Parent: Fairview Hotels Limited
Officers: Bhasker Tailor, Secretary; Jawahar Jamnadas Chatwani [1948] Director; Rashmi Jamnadas Chatwani [1954] Director; Satish Jamnadas Chatwani [1953] Director

Fairview Hotels Limited
Incorporated: 4 July 1995 *Employees:* 534
Previous: Fairview Hotels & Healthcare Limited
Net Worth: £53,232,356 *Total Assets:* £136,622,640
Registered Office: Kanta House, Victoria Road, South Ruislip, Middlesex, HA4 0JQ
Activities: Hotels and similar accommodation
Officers: Bhasker Tailor, Secretary; Jawahar Jamnadas Chatwani [1948] Director; Rashmi Jamnadas Chatwani [1954] Director; Satish Jamnadas Chatwani [1953] Director

Fairview New Homes (Charlton) Limited
Incorporated: 18 November 2016
Net Worth: £405,000 *Total Assets:* £27,937,000
Registered Office: 50 Lancaster Road, Enfield, Middlesex, EN2 0BY
Activities: Development of building projects
Parent: Fairview New Homes Limited
Officers: Jonathan Mark Baxter, Secretary; Michael Blakey [1963] Director; Nicholas Martin Dulcken [1967] Director; Generald Anthony Malton [1960] Director; Darren Lee McCormack [1982] Sales Director; Richard James Paterson [1957] Director; Jonathan Andrew Spring [1972] Land Buying Director; Michael Raymond Walker [1958] Director; Robert Kenneth Williams [1964] Director

Fairview New Homes (Chase Road) Limited
Incorporated: 5 December 1997 *Employees:* 9
Net Worth: £573,000 *Total Assets:* £17,800,000
Registered Office: 50 Lancaster Road, Enfield, Middlesex, EN2 0BY
Activities: Development of building projects
Parent: Fairview New Homes Limited
Officers: Jonathan Mark Baxter, Secretary; Michael Blakey [1963] Director; Nicholas Martin Dulcken [1967] Director; Generald Anthony Malton [1960] Director; Darren Lee McCormack [1982] Sales Director; Richard James Paterson [1957] Director; Martin Richard Smith [1955] Director; Jonathan Andrew Spring [1972] Land Buying Director; Michael Raymond Walker [1958] Director; Robert Kenneth Williams [1964] Finance Director

Fairview New Homes (Colindale) Limited
Incorporated: 10 May 1999 *Employees:* 9
Net Worth: £4,478,000 *Total Assets:* £14,953,000
Registered Office: 50 Lancaster Road, Enfield, Middlesex, EN2 0BY
Activities: Development of building projects
Parent: Fairview New Homes Limited
Officers: Jonathan Mark Baxter, Secretary; Michael Blakey [1963] Director; Nicholas Martin Dulcken [1967] Director; Generald Anthony Malton [1960] Director; Darren Lee McCormack [1982] Sales Director; Richard James Paterson [1957] Director; Martin Richard Smith [1955] Director; Jonathan Andrew Spring [1972] Land Buying Director; Michael Raymond Walker [1958] Director; Robert Kenneth Williams [1964] Finance Director

Fairview New Homes (Developments) Limited
Incorporated: 2 November 1999
Net Worth: £2,358,000 *Total Assets:* £17,592,000
Registered Office: 50 Lancaster Road, Enfield, Middlesex, EN2 0BY
Activities: Development of building projects
Parent: Fairview New Homes Limited
Officers: Jonathan Mark Baxter, Secretary; Michael Blakey [1963] Director; Nicholas Martin Dulcken [1967] Director; Generald Anthony Malton [1960] Director; Darren Lee McCormack [1982] Sales Director; Richard James Paterson [1957] Director; Jonathan Andrew Spring [1972] Land Buying Director; Michael Raymond Walker [1958] Director; Robert Kenneth Williams [1964] Finance Director

Fairview New Homes (Properties) Limited
Incorporated: 19 December 2002 *Employees:* 9
Net Worth: £1,264,000 *Total Assets:* £28,527,000
Registered Office: 50 Lancaster Road, Enfield, Middlesex, EN2 0BY
Activities: Development of building projects
Parent: Fairview New Homes Limited
Officers: Jonathan Mark Baxter, Secretary; Michael Blakey [1963] Director; Nicholas Martin Dulcken [1967] Director; Generald Anthony Malton [1960] Director; Darren Lee McCormack [1982] Sales Director; Richard James Paterson [1957] Director; Martin Richard Smith [1955] Director; Jonathan Andrew Spring [1972] Land Buying Director; Michael Raymond Walker [1958] Director; Robert Kenneth Williams [1964] Finance Director

Fairview New Homes (South East) Limited
Incorporated: 2 September 1997
Net Worth: £19,954,000 *Total Assets:* £20,231,000
Registered Office: 50 Lancaster Road, Enfield, Middlesex, EN2 0BY
Activities: Development of building projects
Parent: Fairview Enfield Limited
Officers: Jonathan Mark Baxter, Secretary; Michael Blakey [1963] Director; Nicholas Martin Dulcken [1967] Director; Generald Anthony Malton [1960] Director; Darren Lee McCormack [1982] Sales Director; Richard James Paterson [1957] Director; Jonathan Andrew Spring [1972] Land Buying Director; Michael Raymond Walker [1958] Director; Robert Kenneth Williams [1964] Finance Director

Fairview New Homes (Willow Way) Limited
Incorporated: 8 March 2000
Net Worth: £1,058,000 *Total Assets:* £16,690,000
Registered Office: 50 Lancaster Road, Enfield, Middlesex, EN2 0BY
Activities: Development of building projects
Parent: Fairview New Homes Limited
Officers: Jonathan Mark Baxter, Secretary; Michael Blakey [1963] Director; Nicholas Martin Dulcken [1967] Director; Generald Anthony Malton [1960] Director; Darren Lee McCormack [1982] Sales Director; Richard James Paterson [1957] Director; Martin Richard Smith [1955] Director; Jonathan Andrew Spring [1972] Land Buying Director; Michael Raymond Walker [1958] Director; Robert Kenneth Williams [1964] Finance Director

Fairview New Homes Limited
Incorporated: 2 October 2000 *Employees:* 9
Net Worth: £238,704,992 *Total Assets:* £309,481,984
Registered Office: 50 Lancaster Road, Enfield, Middlesex, EN2 0BY
Activities: Activities of construction holding companies
Parent: Fairview Holdings Limited
Officers: Jonathan Mark Baxter, Secretary; Michael Blakey [1963] Director; Dennis John Cope [1933] Director; Nicholas Martin Dulcken [1967] Director; Generald Anthony Malton [1960] Director; Darren Lee McCormack [1982] Sales Director; Richard James Paterson [1957] Director; Jonathan Andrew Spring [1972] Land Buying Director; Michael Raymond Walker [1958] Development Director; Robert Kenneth Williams [1964] Finance Director

Fairview Ventures Limited
Incorporated: 11 September 2001 *Employees:* 8
Net Worth: £1,247,000 *Total Assets:* £31,698,000
Registered Office: 50 Lancaster Road, Enfield, Middlesex, EN2 0BY
Activities: Development of building projects
Parent: Fairview New Homes Limited
Officers: Jonathan Mark Baxter, Secretary; Michael Blakey [1963] Director; Nicholas Martin Dulcken [1967] Director; Generald Anthony Malton [1960] Director/Accountant; Darren Lee McCormack [1982] Sales Director; Richard James Paterson [1957] Director; Jonathan Andrew Spring [1972] Land Buying Director; Michael Raymond Walker [1958] Director; Robert Kenneth Williams [1964] Finance Director

Falck EMS UK Limited
Incorporated: 9 March 2010
Net Worth: £16,390,520 *Total Assets:* £16,907,368
Registered Office: Walker House, George Street, Aylesbury, Bucks, HP20 2HU
Activities: Other service activities n.e.c.
Parent: Falck UK Limited
Officers: Jens Beck [1975] Director [Danish]; Lars Bjorn Heineke [1968] Director/Vice President Finance [Danish]; Jacob Just-Bomholt [1974] Director [Danish]; Mark Raisbeck [1965] Director [Danish]

Falck UK Limited
Incorporated: 23 January 2008
Net Worth: £17,251,576 *Total Assets:* £22,175,792
Registered Office: Walker House, George Street, Aylesbury, Bucks, HP20 2HU
Activities: Other human health activities
Parent: Falck Holding A/S
Officers: Jesper Aunbol [1970] Director [Danish]; Jakob Just Bomholt [1974] Director [Danish]; Stig Tiedemann [1959] Director [Danish]

Falcon Tower Crane Services Ltd
Incorporated: 16 January 2008 *Employees:* 417
Net Worth: £13,630,570 *Total Assets:* £26,301,750
Registered Office: Shipdham Airfield Industrial Estate, Shipdham, Thetford, Norfolk, IP25 7SD
Activities: Other specialised construction activities n.e.c.
Officers: Andrew Brown, Secretary; Andrew Brown [1985] Director/Accountant; Barbara Ivy Brown [1957] Director; Philip Gale [1969] Director/Service Manager; Ian Gray [1966] Director/Sales Manager; Steve Paxman [1963] Director/Sales Manager

Falkland Islands Company Limited
Incorporated: 9 July 1902 *Employees:* 146
Net Worth: £1,167,000 *Total Assets:* £19,627,000
Registered Office: Kenburgh Court, 133-137 South Street, Bishop's Stortford, Herts, CM23 3HX
Activities: Development of building projects
Parent: FIH Group PLC
Officers: David Antony Casey [1966] Finance Director; John Laurence Foster [1958] Managing Director; Tara Francis [1973] Retail Director; Kevin John Ironside [1970] Retail Director; Susan Jane Helena Knipe [1971] Procurement Director [St Helenian]; Richard Sawle [1954] Director; Roy Alan Smith [1965] Construction Director

Family Amusements Limited
Incorporated: 23 January 1981 *Employees:* 151
Net Worth: £9,703,746 *Total Assets:* £16,821,682
Registered Office: Regal House, Manwick Road, Felixstowe, Suffolk, IP11 2DQ
Activities: Other amusement and recreation activities n.e.c.
Major Shareholder: James Stanley George Threadwell
Officers: Deborah Jean Woodmansee, Secretary; Darren John Threadwell [1966] Director/Amusement Caterer; James Stanley George Threadwell [1958] Director/Amusement Caterer; Sarah Threadwell [1965] Director

Farcet Fen Limited
Incorporated: 21 November 2016 *Employees:* 2
Net Worth: £13,087,517 *Total Assets:* £13,541,480
Registered Office: Heydon Lodge, Flint Cross, Newmarket Road, Heydon, Royston, Herts, SG8 7PN
Activities: Mixed farming
Officers: Jon Santa Cruz Azcabide [1977] Director/Lawyer [Spanish]; Mikel Santa Cruz Azcabide [1980] Director/Engineer [Spanish]

Fardaar LLP
Incorporated: 27 March 2004 *Employees:* 6
Net Worth: £8,739,090 *Total Assets:* £8,746,325
Registered Office: 166 College Road, Harrow, Middlesex, HA1 1RA
Officers: Naishad Patel [1963] LLP Member; Meera Nalin Shah [1973] LLP Member; Priya Nalin Kantilal Shah [1972] LLP Member; Edward Watson [1971] LLP Member

Farecla Products Limited
Incorporated: 24 November 1971 *Employees:* 62
Net Worth: £12,925,181 *Total Assets:* £16,444,479
Registered Office: Broadmeads, Ware, Herts, SG12 9HS
Activities: Manufacture of other chemical products n.e.c.
Shareholder: Benita Alexandra Freedman
Officers: Alun Roy Oxenham, Secretary; Marie-Armelle Chupin [1957] Director [French]; Michael Strickland Chaldecott [1960] Managing Director; Sung Hun Yu [1969] Director [American]

Farleigh Hospice
Incorporated: 4 March 1982 *Employees:* 262
Net Worth: £10,741,000 *Total Assets:* £12,633,000
Registered Office: Farleigh Hospice, North Court Road, Broomfield, Chelmsford, Essex, CM1 7FH
Activities: Other human health activities
Officers: Sharon Amanda Ellingham, Secretary; Lesley Carol Baliga [1956] Finance Director; Hilary Mary Bebb [1943] Director/Retired; Dr Andrew David Blainey [1950] Director; Joanna Louise Pittman [1977] Director/Chartered Accountant; Suzanne Riches [1969] Director/Safety and Compliance Manager; Emma Sayers [1970] Director/HR Manager; Richard Shail [1943] Director/Chartered Accountant; Keith Charles Spiller [1962] Director/Retired Banker

Farlingaye High School
Incorporated: 13 June 2011 *Employees:* 286
Net Worth: £9,216,953 *Total Assets:* £10,646,972
Registered Office: Farlingaye High School, Ransom Road, Woodbridge, Suffolk, IP12 4JX
Activities: General secondary education
Officers: Mandy Rozier, Secretary; June Hilda Cowles [1962] Director; Elizabeth Crookall [1971] Director/Learning Support Assistant; Andrew Dalby [1955] Director/Engineer; Nigel Edge [1968] Director/Teacher; Dr Louise Karen Franks [1965] Director; Dr Louise Karen Franks [1965] Director; Sarah Harris [1970] Director; Neville Howe [1960] Director; Belinda Jarvis [1964] Director; Beverley Rogers [1970] Director; Dr Andrew Sievewright [1965] Director/Headteacher; Jeremy William Raymond Steventon-Barnes [1970] Director/Information Technology; Katharina Thomas [1964] Director [German]; Alex Van Marle [1973] Director; Nicholas Daniel Webb [1973] Director/Teacher

Farmland Reserve UK Limited
Incorporated: 4 October 1977 *Employees:* 15
Net Worth: £101,516,000 *Total Assets:* £102,399,000
Registered Office: Manor Farm, Church End, Woodwalton, Huntingdon, Cambs, PE28 5YU
Activities: Buying and selling of own real estate
Parent: Farmland Reserve, Inc.
Officers: Brent J Garlic, Secretary; Benjamin Michael Conway [1980] Director/Financial Controller; Don M Sleight [1955] Director/Company President [American]

Farmwealth Limited
Incorporated: 10 March 1978
Net Worth: £8,862,000 *Total Assets:* £9,269,000
Registered Office: Beaufort House, 136 High Street, Newmarket, Suffolk, CB8 8JP
Activities: Activities of agricultural holding companies
Parent: Spearhead International Limited
Officers: Charles Delmar Morgan, Secretary; Jane Louise Perkins [1980] Finance Director; Tomasz Jacek Zdziebkowski [1962] Director [Polish]

A.E. & W.A.Farr Limited
Incorporated: 30 May 1958 *Employees:* 19
Net Worth: £2,950,940 *Total Assets:* £11,761,223
Registered Office: Newnham Manor, Newnham, Baldock, Herts, SG7 5LA
Activities: Growing of cereals (except rice), leguminous crops and oil seeds
Shareholders: Timothy Mark Alexander Farr; Nicholas John Arthur Farr
Officers: Timothy Mark Alexander Farr, Secretary; Alexander Farr [1986] Director/Farmer; Annabelle Jane Durance Farr [1947] Director/Secretary; Nicholas John Arthur Farr [1950] Director/Farmer; Patricia Elizabeth Catherine Mary Farr [1954] Director/Farmer; Timothy Mark Alexander Farr [1958] Director/Engineer/Farmer; Edward Wainright-Lee [1978] Director/Farmer; Lucinda Jane Barbara Wainright-Lee [1952] Director; Richard Anthony Herbert Wainright-Lee [1947] Director

Farrington Care Homes Limited
Incorporated: 18 February 1998 *Employees:* 368
Net Worth: £8,953,928 *Total Assets:* £13,752,100
Registered Office: Sai Villa, 1 Farrington Place, Northwood, Middlesex, HA6 3SW
Activities: Residential nursing care facilities
Officers: Paren Chuni Nathwani, Secretary; Kiran Chuni Nathwani [1962] Director; Paren Chuni Nathwani [1965] Director

Farsound Aviation Limited
Incorporated: 17 February 1986 *Employees:* 35
Net Worth: £8,269,000 *Total Assets:* £10,781,000
Registered Office: 15 Ashton Gate, Ashton Road, Romford, Essex, RM3 8UF
Activities: Agents involved in the sale of a variety of goods
Parent: Farsound Investments Limited
Officers: Jonathan Charles Richardson, Secretary; Joseph Boucher [1983] Director/Chartered Accountant; Andrew Olaf Fischer [1964] Director [German]; Ian Fisher [1950] Director; Lee Kelsey [1976] Sales Director; Christopher Terence Knott [1979] Director/Accountant; Jonathan Mark Medhurst [1973] Procurement Director; Philip Charles Northfield [1952] Technical Director; Daniel O'Neill [1983] Director [Irish]; Jonathan Charles Richardson [1960] Director; Kevin Stephen Sargent [1961] Director; David Skinner [1962] Director

Fastglobe (Mastics) Limited
Incorporated: 17 December 1985 *Employees:* 86
Net Worth: £13,965,879 *Total Assets:* £18,062,200
Registered Office: Grovedell House, 15 Knightswick Road, Canvey Island, Essex, SS8 9PA
Activities: Other specialised construction activities n.e.c.
Shareholders: Christopher Ivan Pugh; Karen Pugh
Officers: Karen Pugh, Secretary; Christopher Ivan Pugh [1962] Director; Craig Pugh [1989] Director/Construction/Surveying; Emma Lisa Pugh [1991] Director; Michael Ward [1972] Director/Regional Manager

Fauna & Flora International
Incorporated: 13 January 1992 *Employees:* 328
Net Worth: £15,580,713 *Total Assets:* £19,551,206
Registered Office: The David Attenborough Building, Pembroke Street, Cambridge, CB2 3QZ
Activities: Activities of other membership organisations n.e.c.
Officers: Svetlana Ignatieva, Secretary; Paul Michael Baldwin [1965] Director/Retired; David William Gibson [1962] Lawyer, Director; Dr Charlotte Anne Grezo [1956] Director/Sustainability Adviser; Andrew Neville Joy [1957] Director/Investment Management; Dr Sandra Knapp [1956] Director/Scientist [British/American]; Annette Elizabeth Lanjouw [1961] Director/Biologist and Conservationist [Dutch]; Professor Nigel Leader-Williams [1949] Director/Academic; Dr Michael Maunder [1963] Director; Richard Mark Plackett [1963] Director/Retired Investment Manager; Sir Gareth Arthur Ludovic Emrys Rhys Williams [1961] Director; Andrew Francis Sykes [1957] Director; Edward Van Cutsem [1973] Director/Asset Management; Diana Van de Kamp [1963] Director, Charity [American]; Hugo Henri Carel Van Vredenburch [1965] Director [Dutch]; Dr Bhaskar Vira [1967] Director/University Lecturer [Indian]; Richard Malcolm Walker [1980] Director; John Prier Wotton [1954] Director/Solicitor

FBSE Finance Limited
Incorporated: 20 March 2009 *Employees:* 7
Net Worth: £1,823,379 *Total Assets:* £9,559,271
Registered Office: Ground Floor, Regent House, Theobald Street, Borehamwood, Herts, WD6 4RS
Activities: Activities of mortgage finance companies
Major Shareholder: Dorian Grant Nineberg
Officers: Rosalind Caroline Nineberg, Secretary; Dorian Grant Nineberg [1958] Director/Financier; Hayley Nineberg [1985] Director; Rosalind Caroline Nineberg [1958] Director/Administrator

FCE Bank PLC
Incorporated: 3 September 1963 *Employees:* 1,746
Net Worth: £2,408,000,000 *Total Assets:* £19,598,000,128
Registered Office: Central Office, Eagle Way, Brentwood, Essex, CM13 3AR
Activities: Financial leasing
Officers: Howard Paul Cohen, Secretary; Michael David Lavender, Secretary; Charles Alan Bilyeu [1963] Director/Chief Executive Officer [American]; John Dalrymple Callender [1950] Director; John Coffey [1959] Director/Chief Risk Officer; Talita Ferreira [1971] Director; Paul Roger Kiernan [1965] Finance Director; John Reed [1959] Director; Thomas Charles Schneider [1964] Director [American]; Suzanna Taverne [1960] Director

FDR U.K. Limited
Incorporated: 27 May 1987
Net Worth: £38,148,000 *Total Assets:* £40,302,000
Registered Office: Janus House, Endeavour Drive, Basildon, Essex, SS14 3WF
Activities: Financial intermediation not elsewhere classified
Parent: First Data Corporation
Officers: Craig William Gurney [1973] Director/Accountant; Gregory Arnold Piel [1962] Director/Associate General Counsel [American]; Keith Peter Rowling [1963] Managing Director

The Federation of European Biochemical Societies
Incorporated: 3 October 2012 *Employees:* 9
Net Worth: £55,802,332 *Total Assets:* £57,838,208
Registered Office: 98 Regent Street, Cambridge, CB2 1DP
Activities: Publishing of learned journals
Officers: Professor Vaclav Paces, Secretary; Prof Dr Cecilia Maria Paisde Faroa de Andrade Arraiano [1959] Director/Coordinating Investigator Full Professor [Portuguese]; Prof Dr Miguel Angel de La Rosa [1955] Director/University Professor [Spanish]; Dr Irene Diaz Moreno [1977] Director/Professor of Biochemistry and Molecular Biology [Spanish]; Professor Jerka Dumic [1969] Director/Professor [Croatian]; Professor Emmanouil Fragkoulis [1947] Director [Greek]; Professor Laszlo Fesus [1947] Director/Professor of Biochemistry [Hungarian]; Professor Alain Krol [1947] Director of Research Emeritus at The CNRS [French]; Professor Francesco Michaelangeli [1961] Director/University Lecturer; Professor Vaclav Paces [1942] Director [Czech]; Prof. Ferhan Girgin Sagin [1964] Director [Turkish]; Prof. Joel Leonard Sussman [1943] Director/Professor Emeritus [Israeli]; Professor Beata Vertessy [1961] Director [Hungarian]; Prof. Tomas Zima [1966] Director/Professor of Biochemistry, Rector of University [Czech]

E. Feldman Limited
Incorporated: 25 September 1978 *Employees:* 12
Net Worth: £9,207,161 *Total Assets:* £9,467,060
Registered Office: Unit 6 Barking Industrial Estate, Alfreds Way, Barking, Essex, IG11 0TJ
Activities: Wholesale of clothing and footwear
Shareholders: Emanuel Feldman; Thelma Feldman
Officers: Thelma Feldman, Secretary; Emanuel Feldman [1936] Director/Merchant; Thelma Feldman [1939] Director

John E.Fells & Sons Limited
Incorporated: 1 May 1920 *Employees:* 50
Net Worth: £10,591,224 *Total Assets:* £27,073,200
Registered Office: Fells House, Station Road, Kings Langley, Herts, WD4 8LH
Activities: Wholesale of wine, beer, spirits and other alcoholic beverages
Parent: Atlantis Wine Holdings Ltd
Officers: Louise Catherine Rimes, Secretary; Alan Robert Campbell [1962] Sales Director; Nicholas John Gurney [1970] Director/Certified Chartered Accountant; Robert Wyndham Hill-Smith [1951] Managing Director [Australian]; Stephen Antony Moody [1960] Managing Director; John Andrew Douglas Symington [1960] Director/Port Producer; Paul Douglas Symington [1953] Director/Port Producer; Edward Jared MacLeod Thornton [1965] Development Director; Simon William Michael Thorpe [1966] Commercial Director; Miguel Torres Maczassek [1974] Director [Spanish]

Fengrain (Services) Limited
Incorporated: 1 August 1972
Net Worth: £582,561 *Total Assets:* £20,043,212
Registered Office: Fengrain, Hook Lane, Wimblington, March, Cambs, PE15 0QN
Activities: Wholesale of grain, unmanufactured tobacco, seeds and animal feeds
Parent: Fengrain Ltd
Officers: Kevin Peter Cooper, Secretary/Company Accountant; Kevin Peter Cooper [1962] Director/Accountant; Sarah Elizabeth Easton [1966] Director/Farmer & Chartered Accountant; Donald James McGowan [1963] Director/Farmer; Richard Means [1977] Director/Chartered Surveyor; Michael James Mottram [1958] Director/Farmer; Robert Hugh Munro [1966] Marketing Director; Nigel Raymond Russell [1952] Director/Farmer; Michael Harold Speed Sly [1968] Director/Farmer; John Robert Wall [1949] Director/Accountant; Harold Miles Warnick [1956] Director/Chartered Engineer; Paul Nigel Wilkinson [1945] Director

Fengrain Limited
Incorporated: 1 September 1972 *Employees:* 47
Net Worth: £1,648,013 *Total Assets:* £27,137,816
Registered Office: Hook Lane, Wimblington, Cambs, PE15 0QN
Activities: Agents selling agricultural raw materials, livestock, textile raw materials and semi-finished goods
Officers: Kevin Peter Cooper, Secretary/Company Accountant; Kevin Peter Cooper [1962] Director/Accountant; Sarah Elizabeth Easton [1966] Director/Farmer & Chartered Accountant; Donald James McGowan [1963] Director/Farmer; Richard Means [1977] Director/Chartered Surveyor; Michael James Mottram [1958] Director/Farmer; Robert Hugh Munro [1966] Marketing Director; Nigel Raymond Russell [1952] Director/Farmer; Michael Harold Speed Sly [1968] Director/Farmer; John Robert Wall [1949] Director/Accountant; Harold Miles Warnick [1956] Director/Chartered Engineer; Paul Nigel Wilkinson [1945] Director

Fesa (UK) Limited
Incorporated: 18 October 1984 *Employees:* 104
Net Worth: £7,753,724 *Total Assets:* £24,704,206
Registered Office: Claylake, Spalding, Lincs, PE12 6BL
Activities: Wholesale of fruit and vegetables
Shareholders: James Frank Rogers; Jose Ortiz-Carrillo; Anecoop
Officers: Hakim Elmouaffaq, Secretary; Hakim El Mouaffaq [1967] Deputy Managing Director [French]; Joan Mir Piqueras [1958] Director [Spanish]; Maria Del Carmen Morales Abad [1967] Director [Spanish]; Jose Ortiz Carrillo [1926] Director/Chairman [Spanish]; Jose Ortiz Pintor [1957] Director [Spanish]; James Frank Rogers [1947] Director/Vice-Chairman; Justin Szymborski [1970] Managing Director; Francisco Tello-Espinosa [1975] Commercial Director [Spanish]

Festool UK Limited
Incorporated: 11 December 1985 *Employees:* 54
Previous: TTS Tooltechnic Systems GB Limited
Net Worth: £5,199,066 *Total Assets:* £10,723,078
Registered Office: Saxham Business Park, Saxham, Bury St Edmunds, Suffolk, IP28 6RX
Activities: Non-specialised wholesale trade
Officers: Bjorn Ole Held [1975] Director/Cluster Manager [German]

FFEI Holdings Limited
Incorporated: 4 August 2006 *Employees:* 77
Net Worth: £6,861,000 *Total Assets:* £11,625,000
Registered Office: The Cube, Maylands Avenue, Hemel Hempstead Industrial Estate, Hemel Hempstead, Herts, HP2 7DF
Activities: Other manufacturing n.e.c.
Major Shareholder: Andrew Michael Cook
Officers: Julian Christopher Payne, Secretary; Andrew Michael Cook [1965] Director/Manager; Julian Christopher Payne [1960] Director/Manager; Robert Charles Wilson [1958] Director/Research & Development

Fiat Chrysler Automobiles Services UK Limited
Incorporated: 1 March 2001 *Employees:* 51
Previous: Fiat U.K. Limited
Net Worth: £2,171,000 *Total Assets:* £48,838,000
Registered Office: Cranes Farm Road, Basildon, Essex, SS14 3XX
Activities: Accounting and auditing activities
Shareholders: FCA Partecipazioni S.P.A.; FCA Italy S.P.A.; Fiat Chrysler Automobiles NV
Officers: Giorgio Giulio Maria Barberis [1973] Director [Italian]; Charles Rohan Ravindra de Alwis [1959] Director/Solicitor; Diego Pistone [1950] Director [Italian]; Tiziana Spinetta [1971] Director/Manager [Italian]

Fibron BX Limited
Incorporated: 28 January 1987 *Employees:* 90
Previous: Cortland Fibron BX Limited
Net Worth: £8,668,543 *Total Assets:* £15,165,722
Registered Office: Unit 2 R D Park, Stephenson Close, Hoddesdon, Herts, EN11 0BW
Activities: Other manufacturing n.e.c.
Parent: Cortland U.K. Holdings Limited
Officers: Andrew James Finch, Secretary; Bruno Cianfini [1970] Commercial Director; Andrew Olaf Fischer [1964] Director [German]; Balraj Singh Virdi [1986] Director

FIC Grand Plaza Ltd
Incorporated: 31 July 2013 *Employees:* 47
Net Worth: £2,959,539 *Total Assets:* £18,441,596
Registered Office: Delson Suite, 2nd Floor, Amba House, 15 College Road, Harrow, Middlesex, HA1 1BA
Activities: Hotels and similar accommodation
Parent: BHD
Officers: Mohammed Jeffri [1962] Director/Manager [Malaysian]; AB Ghani Mohd Ali [1957] Director/Admin Officer [Malaysian]; Mohd Shahrin Mohd Ali [1969] Director [Malaysian]; Bin Mohd Nor Muzzammil [1971] Director [Malaysian]

Fidion Limited
Incorporated: 11 October 2016 *Employees:* 62
Net Worth: £11,712,443 *Total Assets:* £12,518,187
Registered Office: Unit J6, The Paddocks, 347 Cherry Hinton Road, Cambridge, CB1 8DH
Activities: Activities of production holding companies
Officers: Bruce William Glover Campbell [1971] Director/Engineer; Dr Colin Dailly [1961] Director/Engineer; Gregory David Inman [1969] Director/Engineer; Christopher David Nickolaus [1980] Products Director; Dr. Mark Simon Peckham [1968] Director/Engineer; Kingsley St John Reavell [1973] Director/Engineer; Dr Jonathan Philip Robert Symonds [1976] R&D Director

Fieldrose Limited
Incorporated: 7 July 1992 *Employees:* 1,510
Net Worth: £11,166,164 *Total Assets:* £64,728,000
Registered Office: First Floor, Kirkland House, 11-15 Peterborough Road, Harrow, Middlesex, HA1 2AX
Activities: Unlicenced restaurants and cafes
Shareholders: Bharat Chandubhai Patel; Maya Bharat Patel
Officers: Maya Bharat Patel, Secretary; Bharat Chandubhai Patel [1964] Director/Businessman; Maya Bharat Patel [1965] Director/Secretary

Fifty Shades Ltd
Incorporated: 3 February 2012 *Employees:* 2
Net Worth: £58,444,604 *Total Assets:* £59,905,328
Registered Office: Russell House, 140 High Street, Edgware, Middlesex, HA8 7LW
Activities: Artistic creation
Major Shareholder: Erika Lena Mitchell
Officers: Niall Patrick Leonard, Secretary; Erika Mitchell [1963] Director

Fifty Six Investments Limited
Incorporated: 3 June 1997
Net Worth: £6,628,978 *Total Assets:* £9,308,961
Registered Office: Unex House, Church Lane, Stetchworth, Cambs, CB8 9TN
Activities: Other letting and operating of own or leased real estate
Shareholders: Timothy Casey Oscar Gredley; Pollyanna Georgina Gredley
Officers: Andrew John Page, Secretary; Timothy Casey Oscar Gredley [1986] Director; William Jerome Gredley [1933] Director; Andrew John Page [1976] Director/Certified Chartered Accountant

FIH Group PLC
Incorporated: 7 August 1997 *Employees:* 335
Previous: Falkland Islands Holdings PLC
Net Worth: £41,733,000 *Total Assets:* £66,202,000
Registered Office: Kenburgh Court, 133-137 South Street, Bishop's Stortford, Herts, CM23 3HX
Activities: Activities of head offices
Shareholder: Anita Goldberg Zucker
Officers: Carol Claire Bishop, Secretary; Jeremy James Brade [1961] Director/Business Executive; John Laurence Foster [1958] Director; Robert Bruce Johnston [1965] Non-Executive Director and Investment Professional [Canadian]; Robin George Walton Williams [1957] Director

Filross Securities Limited
Incorporated: 20 September 1927
Net Worth: £7,843,940 *Total Assets:* £11,264,200
Registered Office: 28 Church Road, Stanmore, Middlesex, HA7 4XR
Activities: Development of building projects
Major Shareholder: Lawrence Michael Alkin
Officers: Kim Min Chong, Secretary; Lawrence Michael Alkin [1939] Director

The Finance Store Limited
Incorporated: 20 May 2003 *Employees:* 55
Net Worth: £189,947 *Total Assets:* £21,109,796
Registered Office: Broom House, 39-43 London Road, Hadleigh, Benfleet, Essex, SS7 2QL
Activities: Financial intermediation not elsewhere classified
Officers: Paul James Auger [1963] Director/Finance Broker; Martin Paul Graham [1962] Director/Administrator; Ranjit Narwal [1962] Director/Finance Broker; Howard Peter Snell [1955] Director/Financial Executive

Fine Foods International (Manufacturing) Limited
Incorporated: 6 October 1994 *Employees:* 60
Net Worth: £6,495,608 *Total Assets:* £23,932,704
Registered Office: Unit B, Chiltern Park Industrial Estate, Boscombe Road, Dunstable, Beds, LU5 4LT
Activities: Production of coffee and coffee substitutes
Parent: European Coffee Corporation Limited
Officers: Generald John Annetts, Secretary; Generald John Annetts [1952] Director; Austin Lewis Sugarman [1959] Director

Finecare Homes (Stevenage) Limited
Incorporated: 26 September 2007 *Employees:* 54
Previous: Tanzanite Nursing Homes Limited
Net Worth: £6,353,527 *Total Assets:* £10,474,520
Registered Office: Best Western Roebuck Inn, London Road, Stevenage, Herts, SG2 8DS
Activities: Other business support service activities n.e.c.
Parent: Somani Holdings Ltd
Officers: Hassanali Karmali Alibhai Somani, Secretary; Hassanali Karmali Alibhai Somani [1961] Director; Nilufa Hassan Somani [1961] Director

Finer Limited
Incorporated: 17 December 2001
Net Worth: £11,016,095 *Total Assets:* £16,949,120
Registered Office: 35a High Street, Ruislip, Middlesex, HA4 7AU
Activities: Other letting and operating of own or leased real estate
Shareholders: Jaswir Singh Malhi; Inderjit Kaur Malhi
Officers: Amandeep Malhi, Secretary; Amandeep Malhi [1980] Director; Baljinder Kaur Malhi [1982] Director; Inderjit Kaur Malhi [1957] Director; Jaswir Singh Malhi [1953] Marketing Director [Indian]

Fineraid Limited
Incorporated: 5 December 2003 *Employees:* 3
Net Worth: £9,543,034 *Total Assets:* £14,906,744
Registered Office: Northside House, Mount Pleasant, Barnet, Herts, EN4 9EE
Activities: Other service activities n.e.c.
Shareholder: Melvyn Frank Cooper
Officers: Jason Robert Cooper, Secretary; Adam Cooper [1971] Director; Jason Robert Cooper [1967] Director; Melvyn Frank Cooper [1941] Director

First Choice Holidays Finance Limited
Incorporated: 23 October 2000
Net Worth: £214,099,008 *Total Assets:* £4,349,268,992
Registered Office: Wigmore House, Wigmore Lane, Luton, Beds, LU2 9TN
Activities: Financial intermediation not elsewhere classified
Parent: First Choice Holidays Limited
Officers: Dr Bernd Kaiser [1967] Director [German]; Nicholas James Overton-Smith [1974] Director/Accountant

First Choice Holidays Limited
Incorporated: 28 July 1896
Net Worth: £39,251,000 *Total Assets:* £39,251,000
Registered Office: Wigmore House, Wigmore Lane, Luton, Beds, LU2 9TN
Activities: Non-scheduled passenger air transport
Parent: TUI Travel Holdings Limited
Officers: Simon Kenneth Arnold [1977] Director; David John Burling [1968] Director

First Data Europe Limited
Incorporated: 22 April 1986 *Employees:* 8
Net Worth: £24,946,000 *Total Assets:* £265,202,000
Registered Office: Janus House, Endeavour Drive, Basildon, Essex, SS14 3WF
Activities: Financial intermediation not elsewhere classified
Parent: FDR UK Limited
Officers: Geoffrey Peter James Crang [1961] Director/Payment Relations for EMEA; Michael David Earnshaw [1972] Finance Director; Nigel Motyer [1966] Director/General Manager [Irish]; Gert Werner Vido [1964] Director/Head of Corporate Institutional Clients, FD, EMEA [Austrian]

First Eastern Counties Buses Limited
Incorporated: 14 July 1931 *Employees:* 739
Net Worth Deficit: £2,066,000 *Total Assets:* £25,294,000
Registered Office: Bus Depot, Westway, Chelmsford, Essex, CM1 3AR
Activities: Other urban, suburban or metropolitan passenger land transport (not underground, metro or similar)
Parent: Firstbus (South) Limited
Officers: Michael Hampson, Secretary; David Brian Alexander [1965] Regional Managing Director; Stephen Anthony Wickers [1970] Director; Michael James Henry Wilson [1958] Director/Bus Driver

First Essex Buses Limited
Incorporated: 19 November 1985 *Employees:* 1,002
Net Worth Deficit: £6,568,000 *Total Assets:* £44,921,000
Registered Office: Bus Depot, Westway, Chelmsford, Essex, CM1 3AR
Activities: Other urban, suburban or metropolitan passenger land transport (not underground, metro or similar)
Parent: Firstbus (South) Limited
Officers: Michael Hampson, Secretary; David Brian Alexander [1965] Regional Managing Director; Anthony Charles Green [1969] Employee Director; Stephen Anthony Wickers [1970] Director

First Midland Red Buses Limited
Incorporated: 15 April 1981 *Employees:* 168
Net Worth Deficit: £176,000 *Total Assets:* £8,025,000
Registered Office: Bus Depot, Westway, Chelmsford, Essex, CM1 3AR
Activities: Other urban, suburban or metropolitan passenger land transport (not underground, metro or similar)
Parent: Firstbus (South) Limited
Officers: Michael Hampson, Secretary; David Brian Alexander [1965] Regional Managing Director; Simon Chadfield [1971] Director/Driver; Nigel Wilfrid Eggleton [1958] Managing Director

First Potteries Limited
Incorporated: 31 August 1988 *Employees:* 350
Net Worth Deficit: £4,335,000 *Total Assets:* £9,462,000
Registered Office: Bus Depot, Westway, Chelmsford, Essex, CM1 3AR
Activities: Other urban, suburban or metropolitan passenger land transport (not underground, metro or similar)
Parent: Firstbus (South) Limited
Officers: Michael Hampson, Secretary; David Brian Alexander [1965] Regional Managing Director; Simon Chadfield [1971] Director/Driver; Nigel Wilfrid Eggleton [1958] Managing Director

First Wave Housing Limited
Incorporated: 12 September 2002 *Employees:* 118
Previous: Brent Housing Partnership Limited
Net Worth: £24,790,000 *Total Assets:* £64,824,000
Registered Office: Brent Civic Centre, Engineers Way, Wembley, Middlesex, HA9 0FJ
Activities: Management of real estate on a fee or contract basis
Parent: London Borough of Brent
Officers: Peter Gadsdon, Secretary; George Crane [1949] Director/Councillor; Akintoye Mobolaji Durowoju [1969] Director/Chartered Surveyor; Peter Gadsdon [1962] Director; Martin Frank Smith [1960] Director; Gail Elizabeth Tolley [1957] Director

Firstan Holdings Limited
Incorporated: 28 October 1999 *Employees:* 152
Net Worth: £7,874,565 *Total Assets:* £15,523,632
Registered Office: The Packaging Centre, Cardinal Way, Godmanchester, Huntingdon, Cambs, PE29 2XN
Activities: Manufacture of other paper and paperboard containers
Major Shareholder: Andrew Thomas Hartwig
Officers: Dawn Mutter, Secretary; Andrew Thomas Hartwig [1954] Director; Lynn Hartwig [1964] Director; Paul Terence Hartwig [1965] Production Director; Sally Hartwig [1962] Director

Firstan Limited
Incorporated: 27 April 1976 *Employees:* 152
Net Worth: £14,444,992 *Total Assets:* £22,094,060
Registered Office: The Packaging Centre, Cardinal Way, Godmanchester, Huntingdon, Cambs, PE29 2XN
Activities: Manufacture of paper and paperboard
Parent: Firstan Holding Ltd
Officers: Dawn Mutter, Secretary; Andrew Thomas Hartwig [1954] Director; Paul Terence Hartwig [1965] Director; Sally Hartwig [1962] Director; Simon Lacey [1969] Commercial Director; Dawn Mutter [1965] Finance Director

D.J.Fisher (Farms) Limited
Incorporated: 19 February 1964 *Employees:* 11
Net Worth: £8,523,105 *Total Assets:* £11,413,270
Registered Office: Hall Road, Southminster, Essex, CM0 7EH
Activities: Growing of cereals (except rice), leguminous crops and oil seeds
Shareholder: John David Fisher
Officers: Benjamin David Fisher, Secretary; Benjamin David Fisher [1980] Managing Director; John David Fisher [1954] Director

A.A.Fisher (Properties) Limited
Incorporated: 20 March 1962 *Employees:* 2
Net Worth: £31,120,048 *Total Assets:* £43,273,648
Registered Office: Unit 3 Fisher's Industrial Estate, Wiggenhall Road, Watford, Herts, WD18 0FE
Activities: Renting and operating of Housing Association real estate
Parent: A A Fisher Limited
Officers: Pamela Ann Saunders, Secretary; William Moorton Fisher [1951] Director; Pamela Jill Ryman [1954] Director

Fishnet Properties Limited
Incorporated: 25 April 2005 *Employees:* 1
Net Worth: £4,284,997 *Total Assets:* £12,971,217
Registered Office: 3a Chestnut House, Farm Close, Shenley, Herts, WD7 9AD
Activities: Buying and selling of own real estate
Shareholders: Lawrence Marcel Albonico; Heather Elizabeth Scanlan
Officers: Lawrence Marcel Albonico, Secretary; Lawrence Marcel Albonico [1964] Director/Property; Heather Elizabeth Scanlan [1968] Director/Media Consultant

Fishpools Holdings Limited
Incorporated: 28 April 2005 *Employees:* 199
Net Worth: £19,692,528 *Total Assets:* £27,214,488
Registered Office: 107-115 High Street, Waltham Cross, Herts, EN8 7AL
Activities: Activities of head offices
Shareholders: Ian Carson; John Ernest Fishpool
Officers: Edward Duggan, Secretary; Ian Carson [1938] Director; John Ernest Fishpool [1938] Director; Simon John Fishpool [1963] Director

Fishpools Limited
Incorporated: 10 July 1935 *Employees:* 197
Net Worth: £12,352,475 *Total Assets:* £22,924,174
Registered Office: 107-115 High Street, Waltham Cross, Herts, EN8 7AL
Activities: Retail of furniture, lighting, and similar (not musical instruments or scores) in specialised store
Parent: Fishpools Holdings Limited
Officers: Edward Duggan, Secretary; Ian Carson [1938] Director/Solicitor; John Ernest Fishpool [1938] Director/Home Furnisher; Simon John Fishpool [1963] Director/Home Furnisher

Fitzjohns Avenue Ltd
Incorporated: 25 April 2016
Net Worth: £3 *Total Assets:* £13,891,572
Registered Office: Suite 2, Fountain House, 1a Elm Park, Stanmore, Middlesex, HA7 4AU
Activities: Development of building projects
Officers: Paul Simon Godfrey [1980] Director/Property Developer

Fitzmaurice Holdings Limited
Incorporated: 1 August 1973 *Employees:* 61
Net Worth: £16,147,399 *Total Assets:* £16,928,040
Registered Office: Avian Way, Salhouse Road, Norwich, NR7 9AJ
Activities: Freight transport by road
Shareholders: Timothy Patrick Bernard Fitzmaurice; Dominic Kevin Fitzmaurice
Officers: Dominic Kevin Fitzmaurice, Secretary; Dominic Kevin Fitzmaurice [1961] Director/Transport Manager; Kevin James Fitzmaurice [1927] Director/Transport Manager; Timothy Patrick Bernard Fitzmaurice [1952] Director/Transport Manager

Fitzwilliam Information Services Trust Limited
Incorporated: 30 June 2008
Net Worth: £6,033,679 *Total Assets:* £9,287,005
Registered Office: Fitzwilliam College, Storey's Way, Cambridge, CB3 0DG
Activities: Library activities
Officers: Valter Duarte Ramalho Monteiro, Secretary; The Venerable John Stuart Beer [1944] Director/Archdeacon of The Church of England; Dr John Richard Adrian Cleaver [1947] Director/University Researcher; Valter Duarte Ramalho Monteiro [1962] Director/Accountant [Portuguese]; Sir Kenneth Aphunezi Olisa [1951] Director

The Fitzwimarc School Academy Trust
Incorporated: 11 February 2015 *Employees:* 196
Net Worth: £15,398,772 *Total Assets:* £18,907,334
Registered Office: The Fitzwimarc School, Hockley Road, Rayleigh, Essex, SS6 8EB
Activities: General secondary education
Officers: Guy Blakesley [1967] Director/Househusband; Martin Timothy Chantree [1968] Director/Foreign Exchange Trader, Lloyds Banking Group; Steven James Cooper [1961] Director/Careers Advisor; Paul Christopher Dudmish [1951] Director/Part Time Schools Transport Driver; Peggy Eileen Findlay [1932] Director/Retired; Simon Granville Gosden [1956] Director; Robert Alexander Harris [1972] Director/Headteacher; Sofia Ribeiro Mitchell [1966] Director/Housewife; Robert Edward Pigram [1950] Director/Retired; Lisa Sloan [1972] Director/Accountant; Emma Whitehouse [1970] Director/Lawyer

Five Arrows Investments Limited
Incorporated: 9 April 1986
Net Worth: £123,614,072 *Total Assets:* £123,690,912
Registered Office: Windmill Hill, Silk Street, Waddesdon, Aylesbury, Bucks, HP18 0JZ
Activities: Security and commodity contracts dealing activities
Parent: Five Arrows Securities Limited
Officers: Craig Christian Armstrong [1971] Director; Magnus James Goodlad [1972] Director

Five Arrows Limited
Incorporated: 17 July 1899
Net Worth: £25,342,000 *Total Assets:* £45,047,000
Registered Office: Windmill Hill, Silk Street, Waddesdon, Aylesbury, Bucks, HP18 0JZ
Activities: Other professional, scientific and technical activities n.e.c.
Shareholder: Nathaniel Charles Jacob Rothschild
Officers: Craig Christian Armstrong [1971] Director/Investment Manager; Magnus James Goodlad [1972] Director; The Hon Hannah Mary Rothschild [1962] Director; Lord Nathaniel Charles Jacob Rothschild [1936] Director

Five Star Inns Limited
Incorporated: 2 April 1964 *Employees:* 300
Net Worth: £35,015,000 *Total Assets:* £72,991,000
Registered Office: Queens Court, 9-17 Eastern Road, Romford, Essex, RM1 3NG
Activities: Hotels and similar accommodation
Parent: BPH Finance Number 1 Limited
Officers: Jonathan Patrick Braidley [1965] Director/Investment Professional; Christopher Andre Kula [1983] Director/Chartered Accountant [German/Canadian]

Fiveways Municipal Vehicle Hire Limited
Incorporated: 18 February 1998 *Employees:* 20
Net Worth: £4,786,879 *Total Assets:* £12,742,331
Registered Office: 10-12 Mulberry Green, Old Harlow, Essex, CM17 0ET
Activities: Renting and leasing of other machinery, equipment and tangible goods n.e.c.
Parent: Fiveways Holdings Ltd
Officers: Anthony Scott Martin [1972] Director

FJC Topco Limited
Incorporated: 31 July 2013 *Employees:* 55
Net Worth: £1,164,568 *Total Assets:* £14,633,877
Registered Office: Centenary Works, Manor Way, New Road, Rainham, Essex, RM13 8RH
Activities: Remediation activities and other waste management services
Shareholder: Patrick John Church
Officers: Patrick John Church [1957] Director; Ian Magson [1967] Director

Flahive Developments Limited
Incorporated: 23 February 1981 *Employees:* 4
Net Worth: £10,746,826 *Total Assets:* £11,993,425
Registered Office: Unit 28 Orbital 25 Business Park, Dwight Road, Watford, Herts, WD18 9DA
Activities: Other letting and operating of own or leased real estate
Officers: Kevin Flahive [1975] Director/Surveyor; Patricia Flahive [1948] Director; Karen Heffer [1977] Director/Advertising Account Co-ordinator; Joanna Wallace [1974] Director/Accounts Clerk; Catherine Ann Wright [1971] Director/Accounts Clerk

Flakt Woods Limited
Incorporated: 3 October 1928 *Employees:* 333
Net Worth: £15,337,000 *Total Assets:* £36,053,000
Registered Office: Axial Way, Cuckoo Farm Business Park, Colchester, Essex, CO4 5ZD
Activities: Manufacture of non-domestic cooling and ventilation equipment
Parent: Woods Holdings Limited
Officers: Paul Hickford, Secretary; Steve Chesney [1978] Plant Director

Flamborough Holidays Limited
Incorporated: 10 February 1965 *Employees:* 153
Net Worth: £11,868,000 *Total Assets:* £19,017,000
Registered Office: 1 Park Lane, Hemel Hempstead, Herts, HP2 4YL
Activities: Holiday centres and villages
Parent: Haven Leisure Limited
Officers: Jane Elizabeth Bentall [1970] Director/Accountant; Paul Charles Flaum [1970] Director; Iain Stuart Macmillan [1976] Director

Flamingo Flowers Ltd.
Incorporated: 21 April 1994 *Employees:* 821
Previous: Finlay Flowers UK Limited
Net Worth: £1,522,000 *Total Assets:* £62,093,000
Registered Office: Flamingo House, Cockerell Close, Stevenage, Herts, SG1 2NB
Activities: Wholesale of flowers and plants
Parent: Flamingo Horticulture Investments Ltd
Officers: David Richard Brown [1971] Operations Director; Richard Capaldi [1960] Director/Accountant; Martin John Hudson [1957] Director; Peter Matthew Mason [1971] Finance Director

Flamingo Holdings Limited
Incorporated: 2 October 2000 *Employees:* 3
Previous: Finlays Horticulture Holdings Limited
Net Worth: £16,133,000 *Total Assets:* £16,133,000
Registered Office: Flamingo House, Unit D, Cockerell Close, Stevenage, Herts, SG1 2NB
Activities: Wholesale of flowers and plants
Parent: Flamingo Horticulture Ltd
Officers: David Richard Brown [1971] Operations Director; Richard Capaldi [1960] Director/Accountant; Martin John Hudson [1957] Director

Flamingo Horticulture Investments Limited
Incorporated: 31 October 2012 *Employees:* 16
Previous: Finlays Horticulture Investments Limited
Net Worth: £95,383,000 *Total Assets:* £123,647,000
Registered Office: Flamingo House, Unit D, Cockerell Close, Stevenage, Herts, SG1 2NB
Activities: Wholesale of flowers and plants
Parent: Flamingo Horticulture Ltd
Officers: David Richard Brown [1971] Director; Richard Capaldi [1960] Director/Accountant; Martin John Hudson [1957] Director/Chief Executive Officer

Flamingo Horticulture Ltd
Incorporated: 29 July 2015
Net Worth Deficit: £747,000 *Total Assets:* £103,454,000
Registered Office: Flamingo House, Cockerell Close, Stevenage, Herts, SG1 2NB
Activities: Wholesale of flowers and plants
Parent: Zara UK Midco 2 Ltd
Officers: Richard Capaldi [1960] Director/Accountant; Martin John Hudson [1957] Director

Flamingo Plants Group Ltd
Incorporated: 17 January 2007 *Employees:* 6
Previous: Butters Group Limited
Net Worth: £5,486,000 *Total Assets:* £9,535,000
Registered Office: Flamingo House, Cockerell Close, Stevenage, Herts, SG1 2NB
Activities: Other manufacturing n.e.c.
Major Shareholder: Flamingo Flowers Limited
Officers: David Richard Brown [1971] Director; Richard Capaldi [1960] Director; Martin John Hudson [1957] Director; Peter Matthew Mason [1971] Finance Director

Flamingo Plants Ltd
Incorporated: 25 June 1973 *Employees:* 239
Previous: Keith Butters Limited
Net Worth: £2,417,000 *Total Assets:* £15,227,000
Registered Office: Flamingo House, Cockerell Close, Stevenage, Herts, SG1 2NB
Activities: Other manufacturing n.e.c.
Parent: Castlegate 363 Limited
Officers: David Richard Brown [1971] Director; Peter Matthew Mason [1971] Finance Director

Flamingo Produce Ltd.
Incorporated: 14 June 1994 *Employees:* 165
Previous: Finlays Fresh Produce UK Limited
Net Worth: £299,000 *Total Assets:* £23,271,000
Registered Office: Flamingo House, Unit D Cockerell Close, Stevenage, Herts, SG1 2NB
Activities: Wholesale of fruit and vegetables
Parent: Flamingo Horticulture Investments Ltd
Officers: David Richard Brown [1971] Operations Director; Richard Capaldi [1960] Director/Accountant; James Dale [1979] Director/General Manager; Lorraine Dalton [1973] Finance Director; Martin John Hudson [1957] Director; Ian Stuart Michell [1973] Managing Director

P. Flannery Plant Hire (Oval) Limited
Incorporated: 16 June 1972 *Employees:* 107
Net Worth: £60,040,660 *Total Assets:* £114,142,808
Registered Office: 27a Maxwell Road, Northwood, Middlesex, HA6 2XY
Activities: Other specialised construction activities n.e.c.
Major Shareholder: Patrick Flannery
Officers: Gareth Austin Corbett [1979] Director [Irish]; Martin Christopher Flannery [1978] Director; Patrick Flannery [1980] Director; Patrick Flannery [1950] Director/Plant Hire Contractor [Irish]; John Anthony Moran [1961] Director

Flegg Education Academy Trust
Incorporated: 13 July 2012 *Employees:* 128
Net Worth: £7,869,085 *Total Assets:* £9,819,368
Registered Office: Somerton Road, Martham, Great Yarmouth, Norfolk, NR29 4QD
Activities: General secondary education
Officers: Catherine Alice Bates [1993] Director/Trainee Solicitor; Steve Guratsky [1958] Director/Retired; Joanne Elizabeth Hand [1971] Director/Higher Education Champion; Andrew James Moore [1979] Director/ICT Systems Manager; Peter Grant Spencer [1947] Director/Retired; Stephen Paul Wiggins [1966] Director/Software Design Engineer; Stephen Paul Wiggins [1966] Director/IT Consultant

Fleximize Capital Limited
Incorporated: 12 March 2015 *Employees:* 4
Net Worth: £555,256 *Total Assets:* £20,216,784
Registered Office: Holbrook House, 51 John Street, Ipswich, Suffolk, IP3 0AH
Activities: Credit granting by non-deposit taking finance houses and other specialist consumer credit grantors
Parent: Alterium Limited
Officers: Daniel O'Sullivan [1986] Finance Director; Peter John Tuvey [1979] Director

Fleximize Limited
Incorporated: 6 January 2010 *Employees:* 4
Net Worth: £3,598,743 *Total Assets:* £8,871,602
Registered Office: Holbrook House, 51 John Street, Ipswich, Suffolk, IP3 0AH
Activities: Credit granting by non-deposit taking finance houses and other specialist consumer credit grantors
Parent: Alterium Limited
Officers: Daniel O'Sullivan [1986] Finance Director; Peter John Tuvey [1979] Director

Flightsafety International U.K. Limited
Incorporated: 10 November 1995 *Employees:* 133
Net Worth: £30,493,920 *Total Assets:* £38,474,648
Registered Office: Christchurch House, Upper George Street, Luton, Beds, LU1 2RS
Activities: Other service activities n.e.c.
Parent: Flightsafety International Inc.
Officers: David Dudley Davenport [1960] Director [American]; Kenneth Motschwiller [1956] Director/Executive [American]

Flo-Mech Holdings Limited
Incorporated: 29 September 2014 *Employees:* 44
Net Worth: £5,375,959 *Total Assets:* £18,153,820
Registered Office: 1 The Forum, Minerva Business Park, Lynch Wood, Peterborough, Cambs, PE2 6FT
Activities: Other business support service activities n.e.c.
Major Shareholder: Alan John Elderkin
Officers: Alan John Elderkin [1945] Director/Engineer; Patricia Mary Elderkin [1948] Director

Flo-Mech. Limited
Incorporated: 11 November 1974 *Employees:* 44
Net Worth: £5,833,334 *Total Assets:* £16,568,132
Registered Office: Flo-Mech House, Paxton Road, Orton Goldhay, Peterborough, Cambs, PE2 5YA
Activities: Manufacture of machinery for food, beverage and tobacco processing
Parent: Flo-Mech Holdings Ltd
Officers: Colin William Hill, Secretary; Robin Alec Cattermole [1976] Director; Simon Andrew Richard Dealtrey [1972] Director; Alan John Elderkin [1945] Director; Andrew James Elderkin [1978] Director; Patricia Mary Elderkin [1948] Director; Stuart John Elderkin [1972] Director; Christopher Graham Ellis [1968] Director/Systems and Controls Specialist; Colin William Hill [1957] Director

Flocklynn Limited
Incorporated: 4 June 1991 *Employees:* 166
Net Worth: £12,408,475 *Total Assets:* £22,303,452
Registered Office: Marley Road, St Ives, Huntingdon, Cambs, PE27 3EX
Activities: Activities of head offices
Officers: Michael Andrew Smith, Secretary; Michael Andrew Smith [1962] Director; Stephen James Smith [1960] Director

Fluke (UK) Limited
Incorporated: 5 September 1960 *Employees:* 72
Net Worth: £6,106,000 *Total Assets:* £38,849,000
Registered Office: 52 Hurricane Way, Norwich, NR6 6JB
Activities: Wholesale of electronic and telecommunications equipment and parts
Parent: TGA Industries Ltd
Officers: Ankush Malhotra [1977] Director/Vice President, Fluke EMEA [Indian]; Robertus Meijs [1979] Director/Fluke EMEA Controller [Dutch]; Jeroen Van de Wiel [1974] Director/Finance Associate [Dutch]

Fluke Precision Measurement Limited
Incorporated: 18 January 1979 *Employees:* 98
Net Worth: £19,360,000 *Total Assets:* £40,073,000
Registered Office: 52 Hurricane Way, Norwich Airport, Norwich, NR6 6JB
Activities: Manufacture of electronic measuring, testing etc. equipment, not for industrial process control
Parent: TGA Industries Ltd
Officers: Vincent Gosling, Secretary; Vincent Gosling [1971] Director/Site Manager; Ankush Malhotra [1977] Director/Vice President, Fluke EMEA [Indian]; Herman Warnshuis [1964] Director/Vice President [Dutch]

Fluorocarbon Company Limited
Incorporated: 3 September 1962 *Employees:* 70
Net Worth: £2,053,558 *Total Assets:* £10,179,217
Registered Office: Fluorocarbon House, Caxton Hill, Hertford, SG13 7NH
Activities: Manufacture of other plastic products
Parent: Fluorocarbon Group Ltd
Officers: Fergus Wells, Secretary; Fergus John Wells [1978] Director; Trevor Jesse Wells [1943] Director

Fluorocarbon Group Limited
Incorporated: 15 June 2006 *Employees:* 369
Net Worth: £7,153,594 *Total Assets:* £16,641,542
Registered Office: Fluorocarbon House, Caxton Hill, Hertford, SG13 7NH
Activities: Activities of head offices
Major Shareholder: Trevor Jesse Wells
Officers: Fergus John Wells, Secretary; Richard Gareth Griffiths [1946] Director/Notary Public; Fergus Wells [1978] Finance Director; Trevor Jesse Wells [1943] Director

Fluxys Interconnector Limited
Incorporated: 16 October 2015 *Employees:* 2
Net Worth: £29,992,570 *Total Assets:* £30,003,936
Registered Office: Clarendon House, Clarendon Road, Cambridge, CB2 8FH
Activities: Activities of other holding companies n.e.c.
Parent: Fluxys UK Limited
Officers: Nicolas Christian Robert Daubies [1971] Director/Employee (Legal Manager) [Belgian]; Ben de Waele [1979] Director/Employee (International Business) [Belgian]

Fluxys UK Limited
Incorporated: 16 October 2015 *Employees:* 2
Net Worth: £60,424,208 *Total Assets:* £172,487,536
Registered Office: Clarendon House, Clarendon Road, Cambridge, CB2 8FH
Activities: Activities of other holding companies n.e.c.
Parent: Fluxys Europe BV
Officers: Nicolas Christian Robert Daubies [1971] Director/Employee (Legal Manager) [Belgian]; Ben de Waele [1979] Director/Employee (International Business) [Belgian]

Flyers CNV Limited
Incorporated: 3 September 2010 *Employees:* 3
Previous: Haddad Europe Limited
Net Worth: £579,131 *Total Assets:* £10,903,344
Registered Office: Unit 1 Windsor Industrial Estate, 424 Ware Road, Hertford, SG13 7EW
Activities: Wholesale of clothing and footwear
Major Shareholder: Abu Talib Jalil
Officers: Matthew Guinchard [1984] Buying & Merchandising Director; Abu Talib Jalil [1965] Director

Flying Trade Group PLC
Incorporated: 25 July 1989 *Employees:* 798
Net Worth: £48,284,344 *Total Assets:* £112,340,544
Registered Office: Europa House, Europa Way, Parkstone, Harwich, Essex, CO12 4PT
Activities: Activities of head offices
Shareholders: Sukhjit Singh Dulai; Kewal Singh Dulai; Chandan Kaur Dulai
Officers: Sukhjit Singh Dulai, Secretary; Adosh Chatrath [1964] Director/Solicitor; Harjit Singh Dulai [1971] Director; Sukhjit Singh Dulai [1966] Director

Flying Trade Limited
Incorporated: 8 August 1988 *Employees:* 205
Net Worth: £17,183,052 *Total Assets:* £50,511,628
Registered Office: Europa House, 4 Europa Way, Parkstone, Harwich, Essex, CO12 4PT
Activities: Other retail sale in non-specialised stores
Parent: Flying Trade Group PLC
Officers: Sukhjit Singh Dulai, Secretary/Director; Harjit Singh Dulai [1971] Director; Sukhjit Singh Dulai [1966] Director

Flynn Pharma (Holdings) Limited
Incorporated: 13 July 2006 *Employees:* 84
Net Worth: £26,636,828 *Total Assets:* £39,612,872
Registered Office: 2nd Floor, Hertlands House, Primett Road, Stevenage, Herts, SG1 3EE
Activities: Activities of head offices
Shareholder: Jos Ensink
Officers: Daniel Timms, Secretary; Dr David William Fakes [1960] Director/Head of R & D; Steven Jonathan Kaye [1965] Director/Businessman; Warren Roiter [1951] Director/Solicitor; Marvin Samson [1941] Director [American]; David Edward Walters [1951] Director/Commercial Manager

Focus Tankers Limited
Incorporated: 28 June 2013
Net Worth: £37,948,716 *Total Assets:* £37,956,832
Registered Office: Portland House, 69-71 Wembley Hill Road, Wembley, Middlesex, HA9 8BU
Activities: Other service activities n.e.c.
Parent: Union Maritime Limited
Officers: Bhupendra Shantilal Kansagra, Secretary; Laurent Elie Cadji [1977] Director/Businessman; Lewis Levy Cadji [1938] Director/Businessman; Bhupendra Shantilal Kansagra [1956] Director/Businessman; Ramesh Shantilal Kansagra [1950] Director/Businessman

Focusrite Audio Engineering Limited
Incorporated: 10 March 1989 *Employees:* 145
Net Worth: £23,693,000 *Total Assets:* £34,002,000
Registered Office: Windsor House, Turnpike Road, High Wycombe, Bucks, HP12 3FX
Activities: Manufacture of consumer electronics
Shareholders: Phillip Dudderidge; Jennifer Anne Dudderidge; Focusrite PLC
Officers: Katie Charlotte Bettison, Secretary; Timothy Paul Carroll [1962] Director [American]; Timothy John Dingley [1981] Operations Director; Philip Stephen Dudderidge [1949] Director; Damian Robert Hawley [1971] Sales Director; Simon Holt [1977] Director; Giles Richard Orford [1977] Director/Marketing; Jeremy Michael Charles Wilson [1966] Finance Director

Focusrite PLC
Incorporated: 14 November 2014 *Employees:* 209
Net Worth: £43,447,000 *Total Assets:* £54,926,000
Registered Office: Windsor House, Turnpike Road, High Wycombe, Bucks, HP12 3FX
Activities: Manufacture of other electrical equipment
Shareholders: Jennifer Anne Dudderidge; Philip Stephen Dudderidge
Officers: Francine Godrich, Secretary; David Charles Bezem [1960] Director; Timothy Paul Carroll [1962] Director [American]; Naomi Wendy Climer [1964] Director; Paul David Dean [1961] Director; Philip Stephen Dudderidge [1949] Director; Jeremy Michael Charles Wilson [1966] Finance Director

Fold Hill Foods Limited
Incorporated: 6 June 1979 *Employees:* 165
Net Worth: £13,206,181 *Total Assets:* £18,500,264
Registered Office: Fold Hill, Old Leake, Boston, Lincs, PE22 9PJ
Activities: Manufacture of prepared pet foods
Parent: J. W. Grant
Officers: James Edward Grant, Secretary; Andrew John Grant [1955] Director/Farmer; James Edward Grant [1953] Director/Farmer

Food Processing Holding Ltd
Incorporated: 13 February 2015
Net Worth: £8,527,226 *Total Assets:* £8,529,726
Registered Office: Gresham House, Pinetrees Business Park, Salhouse Road, Norwich, NR7 9BB
Activities: Activities of head offices
Parent: Middleby Europe SL
Officers: Timothy John FitzGenerald [1969] Director/Vice President and Chief Financial Officer [American]; Martin McKay Lindsay [1964] Director/Corporate Treasurer [American]; Agustin Zufia [1967] Director/Group Controller [Spanish]

Fooks Property Company Limited
Incorporated: 17 January 1884 *Employees:* 3
Net Worth: £11,256,791 *Total Assets:* £11,445,773
Registered Office: The Lodge, 93 Normanston Drive, Oulton Broad, Lowestoft, Suffolk, NR32 2PX
Activities: Other letting and operating of own or leased real estate
Shareholder: Maureen Heather Fooks
Officers: Neil Stephen Cunliffe, Secretary; Jeremy John David Fooks [1965] Director/Chartered Surveyor; Maureen Heather Fooks [1936] Director/Housewife; William James Oliver Fooks [1969] Director; Sarah Giulia Keeling [1960] Director/Human Resources Consultant

Football Association Limited
Incorporated: 23 June 1903 *Employees:* 1,062
Net Worth: £146,243,008 *Total Assets:* £675,270,016
Registered Office: Wembley Stadium, Wembley, Middlesex, HA9 0WS
Activities: Other sports activities
Officers: Richard James McDermott, Secretary; Rupinder Bains [1974] Director/Solicitor; Stacey Cartwright [1963] Director; Gregory Clarke [1957] Director/Chairman Football Association Limited; Robert Malcolm Cotter [1949] Director/Retired; Martin Richard Glenn [1960] Director/Chief Executive Officer; Mervyn Reginald Leggett [1949] Director/Company Secretary; Peter David Godfrey McCormick [1952] Director/Solicitor; John David Pearce [1949] Director/Football Manager; James Richard Rodwell [1970] Director/Chief Executive Officer; Kate Helena Tinsley [1976] Director/Chief Executive Officer

Foray 989 Limited
Incorporated: 31 December 1996 *Employees:* 3
Net Worth: £65,892,000 *Total Assets:* £126,810,000
Registered Office: 1 Park Lane, Hemel Hempstead, Herts, HP2 4YL
Activities: Activities of head offices
Parent: Bourne Leisure Holdings Limited
Officers: Jane Elizabeth Bentall [1970] Director/Accountant; Paul Charles Flaum [1970] Director; Iain Stuart Macmillan [1976] Director

Ford International Liquidity Management Limited
Incorporated: 25 July 2003
Net Worth: £405,825,024 *Total Assets:* £988,768,704
Registered Office: Room 1-447, Eagle Way, Great Warley, Brentwood, Essex, CM13 3BW
Activities: Activities of head offices
Parent: Ford Motor Company Limited
Officers: Monazza Khan, Secretary; David Nicholas Robinson, Secretary; Peter Richard Davies [1970] Director/Treasurer, Ford of Europe; Simon James Domoney [1973] Director/Financial Reporting Manager; Shaun Glanville [1965] Finance Director

Ford JL Limited
Incorporated: 15 October 1982
Net Worth: £20,313,110 *Total Assets:* £20,319,110
Registered Office: Ford Motor Company Central Office, Eagle Way, Brentwood, Essex, CM13 3BW
Activities: Activities of head offices
Parent: Ford Motor Company
Officers: David Nicholas Robinson, Secretary; Peter Richard Davies [1970] Director/Treasurer, Ford of Europe; Simon James Domoney [1973] Director/Financial Reporting Manager; Shaun Glanville [1965] Finance Director

Ford Motor Company Limited
Incorporated: 7 December 1928 *Employees:* 8,893
Net Worth: £2,116,000,000 *Total Assets:* £4,653,000,192
Registered Office: Eagle Way, Brentwood, Essex, CM13 3BW
Activities: Manufacture of motor vehicles
Parent: Blue Oval Holdings
Officers: Monazza Khan, Secretary; David Nicholas Robinson, Secretary; Andrew John Barratt [1963] Chairman and Managing Director; Kieran James Vincent Cahill [1967] Director PTO FOE; Peter Richard Davies [1970] Director/Treasurer, Ford of Europe; John Spencer Gardiner [1962] Executive Director, Communications & PA; Shaun Glanville [1965] Finance Director; Madeleine Rachel Hallward [1977] Director Governmental Affairs; Graham Russell Hoare [1966] Executive Director; Jane Louise Skerry [1969] Executive Director, Human Resources

Ford Retail Limited
Incorporated: 27 July 1923 *Employees:* 3,091
Net Worth: £71,900,000 *Total Assets:* £521,963,008
Registered Office: 2 Charter Court, Newcomen Way, Colchester Business Park, Colchester, Essex, CO4 9YA
Activities: Sale of new cars and light motor vehicles
Parent: Ford Retail Group Ltd
Officers: Michael Peter Darnell, Secretary; Mary Lucy Ransome, Secretary; Stuart Edgar Foulds [1954] Director; Nicholas John Jason [1973] Director [American]; Stuart David Mustoe [1976] Finance Director

Ford VH Limited
Incorporated: 24 November 2009
Net Worth: £1,552,801,536 *Total Assets:* £1,662,572,288
Registered Office: Room 1-447, Eagle Way, Brentwood, Essex, CM13 3BW
Activities: Activities of head offices
Parent: Ford Motor Company
Officers: Monazza Khan, Secretary; David Nicholas Robinson, Secretary; Peter Richard Davies [1970] Director/Treasurer, Ford of Europe; Simon James Domoney [1973] Director/Financial Reporting Manager; David Ainsley Webb [1974] Director/Assistant Treasurer [American]

Forebury Estates Limited
Incorporated: 13 March 1947 *Employees:* 8
Net Worth: £18,225,532 *Total Assets:* £19,652,080
Registered Office: Forebury House, Sawbridgeworth, Herts, CM21 9BD
Activities: Development of building projects
Shareholder: Mary Elizabeth Shipman
Officers: Mary Elizabeth Shipman, Secretary; Anne Christine Buck [1954] Director/Assistant; Ian Michael Shipman [1944] Director/Estate Manager; Mary Elizabeth Shipman [1948] Director/Estate Manager; Nicholas Shipman [1965] Director/Commercial Property Manager

Foregain Limited
Incorporated: 3 September 1999
Net Worth: £11,500,973 *Total Assets:* £14,143,351
Registered Office: Unit 2 Goddard Road, Whitehouse Industrial Estate, Ipswich, Suffolk, IP1 5NP
Activities: Other service activities n.e.c.
Parent: Foregain Holdings Limited
Officers: Melvyn John Walton, Secretary; Simon Edwin Cutting [1966] Contracts Director; Melvyn John Walton [1964] Managing Director

Foreign Currency Direct PLC
Incorporated: 24 March 2004 *Employees:* 34
Net Worth: £2,696,681 *Total Assets:* £34,767,336
Registered Office: Currencies Mews, Badminton Court, Old Amersham, Bucks, HP7 0DD
Activities: Financial intermediation not elsewhere classified
Parent: Currency Holdings Limited
Officers: Phillipa Jane Sherman, Secretary; Martin John Bennett [1969] Director/Chairman; Tracy Anne Bownes [1977] Director; David Robert Dawson [1983] Director; Michael James Peter England [1981] Director; Thomas Richard Higham [1982] Director/Currency Broker; Phillipa Jane Sherman [1964] Finance Director

The Foremost Currency Group Ltd
Incorporated: 24 August 2005 *Employees:* 29
Net Worth: £3,061,234 *Total Assets:* £16,955,046
Registered Office: Sutton Court, Church Yard, Tring, Herts, HP23 5BB
Activities: Other business support service activities n.e.c.
Parent: Currencies Direct Holdings Limited
Officers: Jonathan Matthew Beddell [1978] Director; Adam Melies Bobroff [1984] Director of Foreign Exchange; Neil Cooper [1957] Director; Keith Nigel Hatton [1958] Director; Leonidas Markides [1971] Director

Forest Commercial Services Limited
Incorporated: 18 March 1996 *Employees:* 3
Net Worth: £8,867,916 *Total Assets:* £16,475,931
Registered Office: Holwell, St Paul's Street, Stamford, Lincs, PE9 2BG
Activities: Other professional, scientific and technical activities n.e.c.
Major Shareholder: Simon Robert Smith
Officers: Simon Robert Smith [1964] Director/Road Haulage Manager

Forest Freight Limited
Incorporated: 30 December 1971 *Employees:* 104
Net Worth: £4,977,059 *Total Assets:* £11,339,004
Registered Office: Barlow Way South, Manor Way, Rainham, Essex, RM13 8RH
Activities: Freight transport by road
Major Shareholder: George Malcolm Stuart Fullerton
Officers: Andrew Richard Saltwell, Secretary; George Malcolm Stuart Fullerton [1943] Director; Andrew Richard Saltwell [1958] Director/Accountant; Nicholas Richard Saltwell [1986] Operational Director

Forextra Developments Limited
Incorporated: 22 July 1986 *Employees:* 6
Net Worth: £80,567,624 *Total Assets:* £146,904,336
Registered Office: 8 Highbridge Close, Radlett, Herts, WD7 7GW
Activities: Other letting and operating of own or leased real estate
Parent: Frelene Limited
Officers: Freddy Salem [1941] Director/Buying Agent; Philip Joseph Salem [1981] Director

Forfarmers UK Holdings Limited
Incorporated: 21 March 2012
Previous: Forfarmers UK Limited
Net Worth Deficit: £8,688,000 *Total Assets:* £31,717,000
Registered Office: Horizon House, Fred Castle Way, Rougham Industrial Estate, Rougham, Bury St Edmunds, Suffolk, IP30 9ND
Activities: Manufacture of prepared feeds for farm animals
Officers: Anna Lindsay Stoodley Mortenson, Secretary; Yoram Maurits Knoop [1969] Director/Chief Executive [Dutch]; Steven Richard Read [1963] Director/Chief Operating Officer; Stijn Anton Steendijk [1969] Director [Dutch]; Arnout Engelbert Traas [1959] Director [Dutch]

Forfarmers UK Limited
Incorporated: 8 July 1899 *Employees:* 1,060
Previous: BOCM Pauls Ltd
Net Worth: £86,980,000 *Total Assets:* £262,495,008
Registered Office: Horizon House, Fred Castle Way, Rougham Industrial Estate, Rougham, Bury St Edmunds, Suffolk, IP30 9ND
Activities: Manufacture of prepared feeds for farm animals
Officers: Anna Lindsay Stoodley Mortenson, Secretary; Jonathan David Farnhill [1959] Business Unit Director; Yoram Maurits Knoop [1969] Director/Chief Executive [Dutch]; Nicholas Charles Major [1961] Business Unit Director; Steven Richard Read [1963] Director/Chief Operating Officer; Stijn Anton Steendijk [1969] Director [Dutch]; Arnout Engelbert Traas [1959] Director [Dutch]

Fork Rent Limited
Incorporated: 14 May 2015 *Employees:* 4
Previous: Wren Rollco Limited
Net Worth: £25,332,156 *Total Assets:* £25,332,156
Registered Office: 32 Crown Road, Enfield, Middlesex, EN1 1TH
Activities: Renting and leasing of construction and civil engineering machinery and equipment
Officers: Francois Dekker [1975] Director [Dutch]; Jeremy Peter Fish [1965] Director/Chief Executive Officer; Stuart Russell McMinnies [1968] Investment Director; Julian Alexander O'Neill [1971] Director

Former Reichmann Properties PLC
Incorporated: 21 November 1995
Previous: Reichmann Properties PLC
Net Worth: £3,903,969 *Total Assets:* £17,363,948
Registered Office: 5 Elstree Gate, Elstree Way, Borehamwood, Herts, WD6 1JD
Activities: Other business support service activities n.e.c.
Officers: Dov Reichmann, Secretary; Daniel Reichmann [1988] Director; Dov Reichmann [1930] Director

Formula One Auto Centres Limited
Incorporated: 16 July 1979 *Employees:* 653
Net Worth: £4,678,906 *Total Assets:* £28,280,052
Registered Office: Aston House, Boulton Road, Stevenage, Herts, SG1 4QX
Activities: Maintenance and repair of motor vehicles
Parent: Aston Group Holdings Limited
Officers: Janet Glencross, Secretary; Jonathan Gary Butcher [1966] Director; Janet Glencross [1948] Director/Secretary; Leon Glencross [1972] Director; Philip Stanley Glencross [1949] Director; Steven Lant [1951] Director

Fortem Solutions Limited
Incorporated: 16 January 2003 *Employees:* 852
Previous: Willmott Dixon Partnerships Limited
Net Worth: £2,577,594 *Total Assets:* £21,291,008
Registered Office: Spirella 2, Icknield Way, Letchworth, Herts, SG6 4GY
Activities: Other specialised construction activities n.e.c.
Parent: Wimpole Equity Holdings Limited
Officers: Jonathan Law, Secretary; Wendy Jane McWilliams, Secretary; Graham Mark Dundas [1979] Director/Chartered Accountant; Colin Enticknap [1958] Director/Chartered Surveyor; William George Kay [1965] Commercial Director; Wendy Jane McWilliams [1958] Director/Solicitor; Paul Raymond Smith [1959] Director/Engineer; Michael John Williamson [1966] Director; Richard John Willmott [1963] Director/Chartered Builder

Forth Ports Finance PLC
Incorporated: 16 October 2013
Net Worth: £57,000 *Total Assets:* £395,316,000
Registered Office: Leslie Ford House, Tilbury Freeport, Tilbury, Essex, RM18 7EH
Activities: Activities of other holding companies n.e.c.
Parent: Forth Ports Limited
Officers: Pamela June Smyth, Secretary; Simon Daniel Beer [1980] Director/Asset Manager; Diana Callebaut [1980] Director/Investments [Australian]; Richard Wing-Eng Chang [1971] Director/Investment Professional [British/Australian]; Patrick Charbonneau [1978] Managing Director [Canadian]; Carole Jean Cran [1970] Director/Chief Financial Officer; Simon George Davy [1970] Director/Investment Manager; Charles Graham Hammond [1961] Director; Stephen Kynaston [1978] Director/Investment Manager; Patrick Samson [1971] Director [Canadian]; Lord Robert Smith [1944] Managing Director; Stuart James Wallace [1970] Director/Chief Operating Officer

Fortis Property Investment LLP
Incorporated: 14 April 2005
Net Worth: £3,747,239 *Total Assets:* £10,665,583
Registered Office: 57 High Street, Ingatestone, Essex, CM4 0AT
Officers: Alex Russell Bartlett [1987] Member; Edward George Bartlett [1990] Member; Russell Derek Bartlett [1956] Member

The Forum Trust Limited
Incorporated: 19 November 1997 *Employees:* 83
Net Worth: £30,211,508 *Total Assets:* £30,978,092
Registered Office: The Forum, Millennium Plain, Norwich, NR2 1TF
Activities: Other information service activities n.e.c.
Officers: Sonya Doris Cooper, Secretary; Andrew Jonathan Barnes [1957] Director/Chief Executive; Professor Sarah Elizabeth Barrow [1968] Director/Academic; John Anthony Fry [1957] Director/Business Executive; Susan Elizabeth Guest [1962] Director; Gail Paula Harris [1953] Director/Councillor; Linda Caroline Jarrold [1959] Director/Community Affairs Adviser; Professor Richard John Last [1954] Director/Academic; Christopher Maw [1961] Director/Chartered Accountant; David John Nicholas Merrick [1957] Director; Stephen John Morphew [1952] Director/County Councillor; Corrienne Peasgood [1962] Director/Principal & CEO, City College Norwich

Fotolec Technologies Holdings Limited
Incorporated: 6 June 2014
Net Worth: £2,600,000 *Total Assets:* £8,498,769
Registered Office: The Gables, Old Market Street, Thetford, Norfolk, IP24 2EN
Activities: Activities of other holding companies n.e.c.
Parent: Viribus Holdings Limited
Officers: Michael Graham-Cloete, Secretary; Michael Graham-Cloete [1945] Finance Director; Christopher Leslie Payne [1972] Director; Julie Carol Payne [1972] Director

Foulger Transport Limited
Incorporated: 23 January 1990 *Employees:* 228
Net Worth: £4,369,516 *Total Assets:* £9,592,695
Registered Office: The Circuit, Snetterton, Norfolk, NR16 2JU
Activities: Freight transport by road
Parent: Kinaxia Transport and Warehousing Limited
Officers: Peter Richard Fields [1960] Director; Barry John Germany [1968] Director/Transport Manager; Graham Richard Norfolk [1961] Director

Four CS MAT
Incorporated: 2 August 2010 *Employees:* 350
Previous: Arthur Mellows Village College
Net Worth: £17,003,708 *Total Assets:* £21,109,614
Registered Office: Company Secretary Office, Arthur Mellows Village College, Helpston Road, Glinton, Peterborough, PE6 7JX
Activities: Regulation of health care, education, cultural and other social services, not incl. social security
Officers: Dr Emma Louise Black [1987] Managing Director of Cascade Cash Management; Gary Edward James Dawkins [1955] Director/Retired; Iain Erskine [1954] Director/Co-Principal of The Fulbridge Academy; Dr Mary Kiernan [1960] Director/Academic; David Gilmour McLaren [1944] Director/Retired; Jonathan Stephen Theobalds [1964] Managing Director; David Alan Whiles [1958] Director/Chartered Engineer

Fowler Smith & Jones Trust
Incorporated: 4 June 2009 *Employees:* 1
Net Worth: £9,663,335 *Total Assets:* £10,085,867
Registered Office: Third Floor, Marlborough House, Victoria Road South, Chelmsford, Essex, CM1 1LN
Activities: Other letting and operating of own or leased real estate
Officers: Philip John Tolhurst, Secretary; Nicholas Spencer Charrington [1960] Director/Farmer; Richard Charles Furlonger [1956] Director; George Nicholas Jones [1955] Director/Chartered Surveyor; Philip John Tolhurst [1950] Director/Solicitor

Fox International Group Limited
Incorporated: 12 November 1973 *Employees:* 119
Net Worth: £20,510,980 *Total Assets:* £28,032,884
Registered Office: 1 Myrtle Road, Warley, Brentwood, Essex, CM14 5EG
Activities: Manufacture of sports goods
Parent: MN Sports Bidco Limited
Officers: David Stanley Algar [1961] Director/Chairman; Ian Peter Astley [1965] Director; Shaun Michael McSpadden [1975] Director; Paul Reeves [1975] Director

FPS 1995 Limited
Incorporated: 6 June 1995 *Employees:* 7
Previous: Funeral Planning Services Limited
Net Worth: £26,236,368 *Total Assets:* £67,660,536
Registered Office: Flint House, Ipswich Road, Long Stratton, Norwich, NR15 2TA
Activities: Funeral and related activities
Officers: Richard David Smithies, Secretary/Solicitor; Julian John Austin Mobbs [1943] Director/Chartered Accountant (Retired); Richard David Smithies [1949] Director/Solicitor; Nicholas Vincent Taylor [1950] Director; Graham Peter Williams [1956] Director

Framingham House Investments Limited
Incorporated: 27 November 1985 *Employees:* 119
Net Worth: £17,082,984 *Total Assets:* £26,916,964
Registered Office: Prospect House, Loddon Industrial Park, Loddon, Norwich, NR14 6JD
Activities: Other letting and operating of own or leased real estate
Officers: Jan Louise Baines Burton [1954] Director/Secretary; John Burton [1960] Sales Director; Karen Louise Burton [1967] Director/Secretary; Peter Michael Burton [1965] Director/Sales Manager

Francis Associates (43) LLP
Incorporated: 9 August 2012
Net Worth: £14,105,513 *Total Assets:* £14,355,587
Registered Office: 48 Haseldine Road, London Colney, St Albans, Herts, AL2 1RT
Officers: John Michael Francis [1943] Member; Susan Elizabeth Francis [1952] Member; Ashley John Jamie Francis [1978] LLP Member; Danielle Melissa Francis [1980] LLP Member; India Suzanna Francis [1984] LLP Member; Romani Elizabeth Francis [1991] LLP Member

Franke Coffee Systems UK Limited
Incorporated: 9 January 2007 *Employees:* 99
Net Worth: £7,068,874 *Total Assets:* £13,562,108
Registered Office: 1 Nelson Street, Southend on Sea, Essex, SS1 1EG
Activities: Repair of other equipment
Major Shareholder: James Philip Nicholson
Officers: Daniel Orwin, Secretary; Marga Gyger [1945] Director/CEO Franke Coffee Systems [German]; James Philip Nicholson [1961] Director

Joyce Frankland Academy, Newport
Incorporated: 9 July 2012 *Employees:* 109
Net Worth: £12,410,285 *Total Assets:* £14,777,702
Registered Office: Joyce Frankland Academy, Bury Water Lane, Newport, Saffron Walden, Essex, CB11 3TR
Activities: General secondary education
Officers: Helen Mary Abrahams [1969] Executive Director, Royal Society of Chemistry; Susan Nicola Arnold [1968] Finance Director; Kate Beaumont [1961] Director/Headteacher; Kirsty Brown [1972] Director/Vice Principal; Colleen Cassidy [1971] Director/Retired; Luke Driscoll [1972] Director/Teacher; Stephen Paul Fanthorpe [1960] Director/Headteacher; Malcolm George Jessop [1950] Director/Chartered Accountant; Linda McFarlane [1946] Director; Nigel Poad [1966] Director/Chartered Surveyor; Duncan Roberts [1985] Director/Principal; Samuel Stuthridge [1975] Director/Member of HM British Forces; Lorna Summerfield [1974] Director/Banker; David Watts [1964] Director

S. Franses Limited
Incorporated: 17 August 1959 *Employees:* 11
Net Worth: £5,793,923 *Total Assets:* £10,273,747
Registered Office: York House, Empire Way, Wembley, Middlesex, HA9 0FQ
Activities: Wholesale of household goods (other than musical instruments) n.e.c
Major Shareholder: David Sidney Franses
Officers: Sara Rebecca Franses, Secretary; David Sidney Franses [1926] Director; Sara Rebecca Franses [1962] Director; Simon Franses [1960] Director

Alexander Fraser & Son,Limited
Incorporated: 1 July 1908 *Employees:* 9
Net Worth: £4,034,140 *Total Assets:* £8,030,567
Registered Office: 1 St James Road, Brentwood, Essex, CM14 4LH
Activities: Financial intermediation not elsewhere classified
Officers: Ian David Wilson, Secretary/Director; Billy Steven Faires [1984] Director/Financier; David Mark Ferguson [1973] Director/Attorney [South African]; David Clive Emerson Ferguson [1938] Director/Chartered Accountant [South African]; Ian David Wilson [1956] Director

Fraser Capital Management Limited
Incorporated: 19 February 2004 *Employees:* 418
Net Worth: £19,922,588 *Total Assets:* £29,278,020
Registered Office: Woodlands, Wellpond Green, Standon, Herts, SG11 1NN
Activities: Other amusement and recreation activities n.e.c.
Shareholders: Raymond McKenzie Fraser; Brian Fraser
Officers: Brian Fraser [1958] Director

Fraserfort Limited
Incorporated: 15 March 1956
Net Worth: £8,363,000 *Total Assets:* £8,472,000
Registered Office: Queens Court, 9-17 Eastern Road, Romford, Essex, RM1 3NG
Activities: Non-trading company
Parent: BPH Finance Number 1 Limited
Officers: Jonathan Patrick Braidley [1965] Director/Investment Professional; Christopher Andre Kula [1983] Director/Chartered Accountant [German/Canadian]

Freedom Destinations Limited
Incorporated: 30 May 2001 *Employees:* 54
Net Worth: £3,195,337 *Total Assets:* £11,073,008
Registered Office: Manufactory House, Bell Lane, Hertford, SG14 1BP
Activities: Travel agency activities
Major Shareholder: David Philip Wallis
Officers: Frances Ruth Anne Wallis, Secretary; David Philip Wallis [1953] Director

The Freedom Travel Group Limited
Incorporated: 30 July 1999 *Employees:* 7
Net Worth: £2,387,000 *Total Assets:* £39,729,000
Registered Office: Westpoint, Peterborough Business Park, Lynch Wood, Peterborough, Cambs, PE2 6FZ
Activities: Travel agency activities
Parent: Future Travel Limited
Officers: Shirley Bradley, Secretary; Alan Charles Donald [1963] Director

Freeline Therapeutics Limited
Incorporated: 19 March 2015 *Employees:* 45
Net Worth: £16,479,772 *Total Assets:* £18,233,322
Registered Office: Stevenage Bioscience Catalyst, Gunnels Wood Road, Stevenage, Herts, SG1 2FX
Activities: Research and experimental development on biotechnology
Parent: Syncona Limited
Officers: Martin Andrews [1963] Director; Dr Christopher Hollowood [1974] Director; Dr Amit Chunilal Nathwani [1960] Director/Doctor; Anne Prener [1957] Director [Danish]

Freiberger (UK) Limited
Incorporated: 4 July 1989 *Employees:* 14
Net Worth: £2,968,656 *Total Assets:* £23,464,196
Registered Office: Broadgate House, Westlode Street, Spalding, Lincs, PE11 2AF
Activities: Wholesale of other food, including fish, crustaceans and molluscs
Parent: Suedzucker AG
Officers: Andrew John Thorne, Secretary; Herr Hans Detlev Schulz [1953] Director [German]; Andrew John Thorne [1965] Director/Salesman

Frelene Limited
Incorporated: 7 May 1985
Net Worth: £10,790,866 *Total Assets:* £16,000,356
Registered Office: 8 Highbridge Close, Radlett, Herts, WD7 7GW
Activities: Other letting and operating of own or leased real estate
Parent: Rothschild & Co
Officers: Freddy Salem, Secretary; Freddy Salem [1941] Director/Buying Agent; Philip Joseph Salem [1981] Director

Freman College
Incorporated: 29 June 2011 *Employees:* 123
Net Worth: £9,441,000 *Total Assets:* £10,273,000
Registered Office: Freman College, Bowling Green Lane, Buntingford, Herts, SG9 9BT
Activities: General secondary education
Officers: Samantha Hebditch, Secretary; Dr Sara Aguilar [1968] Director/Teacher [Spanish]; Carole Anne Bennett [1972] Director/Management Consultant; Graham Keith Bonner [1951] Director/Retired; Mark Thomas Burchell [1965] Director/Financial Services; Susan Claire Challans Coote [1965] Procurement Director; Matthew Robert Grimley [1977] Director/Network Manager; Elizabeth Mary Hinton [1955] Director/Headmistress; Dr Paul Michael Jackson [1960] Director/Trade Association Professional; Susan Lankester [1965] Director/Administrator; Helen Jane Littleford [1973] Director/Senior Marketing Manager; Helen Claire Loughran [1966] Director/Headteacher; Jacqueline Margaret Martin [1952] Director/NHS Manager; David Howard Paull Wills [1955] Director/Consultant; Gillian Mary Perkins [1955] Director/Educational Psychologist; Dr Anastasia Vishnivetskaya [1983] Director/Teacher; Jeannette Wright [1968] Director/Administrator

The Fremantle Trust
Incorporated: 8 June 1992 *Employees:* 2,209
Net Worth Deficit: £20,029,000 *Total Assets:* £10,988,000
Registered Office: Woodley House, 64-65 Rabans Close, Aylesbury, Bucks, HP19 8RS
Activities: Residential nursing care facilities
Officers: Elizabeth Mary Turvey, Secretary; Caroline Mary Aston [1939] Director; Andrew David Hall Forrest [1961] Director/Self Employed; Nicholas Francis Barry Heald [1947] Director/Retired Solicitor; Alan John Howard [1950] Director/Self Employed; Charles Alexander Hutchison [1941] Executive Director; Diane Christine Kerwood [1947] Director/Retired MD; Sandra Galbraith Laird [1970] Director/Management Consultant; Ian Philip Shepherd [1949] Director/Retired; Stephen John Wooler [1948] Director/Retired Civil Servant

French & Jupps Limited
Incorporated: 11 March 1920 *Employees:* 23
Net Worth: £13,642,729 *Total Assets:* £14,657,962
Registered Office: The Maltings, Roydon Road, Stanstead Abbotts, Herts, SG12 8HG
Activities: Manufacture of beer
Shareholders: David Holroyd Jupp; Jennifer Jupp
Officers: David Holroyd Jupp [1959] Director/Malster; David Frank Watson [1964] Director

Fresh Linen Limited
Incorporated: 24 December 2009 *Employees:* 267
Net Worth: £3,838,273 *Total Assets:* £10,608,290
Registered Office: Stephenson Road, Gorse Lane Industrial Estate, Clacton on Sea, Essex, CO15 4XA
Activities: Washing and (dry-)cleaning of textile and fur products
Parent: Fresh Linen Holdings Limited
Officers: Antony Charles Moore [1962] Director

Fresh Wharf Estates Limited
Incorporated: 5 October 1928 *Employees:* 9
Net Worth: £15,354,778 *Total Assets:* £20,026,982
Registered Office: Studio F5, The Granary, Abbey Road, Barking, Essex, IG11 7BT
Activities: Other letting and operating of own or leased real estate
Officers: Doctor Christopher Douglas Hewett [1938] Director/Veterinary Surgeon; Julian John Hewett [1954] Director/Analyst; Rodney Muirhead Goodwin Hewett [1941] Director/Civil Engineer; Flavia Penelope Sophia Jokic [1963] Director; Andrew Michael Leahy [1963] Director; Timothy John Muirhead Sanders Hewett [1950] Director

Freshlinc Group Limited
Incorporated: 24 January 2008 *Employees:* 359
Previous: Freshlinc (Spalding) Limited
Net Worth: £4,485,797 *Total Assets:* £29,158,818
Registered Office: Wool Hall Farm, Cross Gate, Wykeham, Spalding, Lincs, PE12 6HW
Activities: Freight transport by road
Shareholder: Robin Hancox
Officers: Aubrey Edward Day, Secretary/Chartered Management Accountant; Aubrey Edward Day [1958] Director/Chartered Management Accountant; Robin Hancox [1956] Director; Martin John Tate [1966] Director

Freshlinc Limited
Incorporated: 2 November 2000 *Employees:* 330
Net Worth: £3,795,428 *Total Assets:* £28,383,608
Registered Office: Wool Hall Farm, Cross Gate, Wykeham, Spalding, Lincs, PE12 6HW
Activities: Freight transport by road
Parent: Freshlinc Group Limited
Officers: Aubrey Edward Day, Secretary/Chartered Management Accountant; Aubrey Edward Day [1958] Director/Chartered Management Accountant; Robin Hancox [1956] Director; Lee Scott Juniper [1972] Operations Director; Stephen John King [1972] Director/Management Accountant; Martin John Tate [1966] Director

Freshtime UK Limited
Incorporated: 16 November 1999 *Employees:* 324
Net Worth: £1,659,736 *Total Assets:* £14,393,080
Registered Office: Riverside Industrial Estate, Marsh Lane, Boston, Lincs, PE21 7RJ
Activities: Manufacture of other food products n.e.c.
Parent: The Bay Group Limited
Officers: Ian Ripley, Secretary; Richard Ian Andrews [1955] Director/Sales Manager; Stephen John Evans [1967] Managing Director; John Curran Mills Richmond [1953] Director; Kathryn Louise Richmond [1986] Director/Barrister; Ian Ripley [1962] Director; Jane Diane Speakman [1966] Director

Friar's Pride Limited
Incorporated: 19 May 1975 *Employees:* 177
Net Worth: £13,383,481 *Total Assets:* £18,178,222
Registered Office: Oxney Road West Industrial Estate, Oxney Road, Peterborough, Cambs, PE1 5YW
Activities: Non-specialised wholesale of food, beverages and tobacco
Shareholder: Rebecca Jane Lord
Officers: Rebecca Jane Lord, Secretary/Managing Director; David Bryn Major Briggs [1946] Director; Josephine Briggs [1944] Director; Rebecca Jane Lord [1973] Managing Director; Louise Marshall [1976] Director; Nigel Swepson [1975] Director; Vincent Willows [1958] Director

Friargate Coventry Development Limited
Incorporated: 24 March 1998 *Employees:* 3
Net Worth Deficit: £16,836,672 *Total Assets:* £20,164,530
Registered Office: Lupins Close, Littleport, Ely, Cambs, CB6 1FN
Activities: Construction of domestic buildings
Parent: Cannon Kirk Limited
Officers: Michael Canon, Secretary; Cathal Canon [1953] Director [Irish]; Michael Canon [1956] Director [Irish]; Owen Kirk [1952] Director [Irish]

Friars 716 Limited
Incorporated: 11 July 2016 *Employees:* 67
Net Worth: £7,053,000 *Total Assets:* £19,001,000
Registered Office: 1 Regal Lane, Soham, Ely, Cambs, CB7 5BA
Activities: Activities of head offices
Shareholders: Martin Bell; Colin Stott; James Alan Fairley Walker
Officers: Martin Bell [1961] Director; David Jonathan Pett [1958] Director/Accountant; Colin Andre Stott [1964] Director; James Alan Fairley Walker [1949] Director

Fricor Limited
Incorporated: 21 February 1996 *Employees:* 129
Net Worth: £2,678,591 *Total Assets:* £9,089,048
Registered Office: Liston House, Liston Gardens, Liston, Sudbury, Suffolk, CO10 7HY
Activities: Freight transport by road
Parent: BNX Holdings Limited
Officers: Allan William Spence Binks, Secretary; Allan William Spence Binks [1941] Director; Thomas Allan Binks [1972] Director/Warehouse Manager; William Andrew Binks [1966] Director/Transport & Warehousing

Frimstone Limited
Incorporated: 3 November 1975 *Employees:* 100
Net Worth: £7,076,191 *Total Assets:* £14,466,948
Registered Office: 6 Lancaster Way, Ermine Business Park, Huntingdon, Cambs, PE29 6XU
Activities: Operation of gravel and sand pits; mining of clays and kaolin
Parent: Mick George Limited
Officers: Karen Farrell, Secretary; Mark Edward Davenport [1967] Director; Michael Alexander George [1984] Managing Director; Michael Eric George [1956] Managing Director; Sharon Colette Spain [1972] Director; Jonathan Paul Stump [1964] Finance Director; Mark Andrew Swan [1967] Commercial Director

Frisco (U.K.) Sales Limited
Incorporated: 20 March 1981 *Employees:* 49
Net Worth: £6,888,001 *Total Assets:* £13,002,582
Registered Office: 14 Pindar Road, Hoddesdon, Herts, EN11 0DE
Activities: Other service activities n.e.c.
Parent: Insignia Investments Limited
Officers: Marc Flynn, Secretary/Chairman; Marc Flynn [1964] Director; Simon Gary Foord [1978] Operations Director; Gary Zubiena [1958] Sales Director

Fristling Hall Farm Limited
Incorporated: 6 January 2005
Net Worth Deficit: £866,984 *Total Assets:* £8,859,298
Registered Office: 144 New London Road, Chelmsford, Essex, CM2 0AW
Activities: Mixed farming
Shareholder: Gary Paul Sharp
Officers: Julie Sharp, Secretary; Gary Paul Sharp [1961] Director

Frith's Flexible Packaging Limited
Incorporated: 25 January 1960
Net Worth: £2,894,637 *Total Assets:* £15,586,405
Registered Office: 1 The Forum, Coopers Way, Temple Farm Industrial Estate, Southend on Sea, Essex, SS2 5TE
Activities: Other manufacturing n.e.c.
Shareholders: David John Watson; Paul Stuart Watson
Officers: David John Barnish, Secretary; David John Watson [1947] Director; Paul Stuart Watson [1983] Director

JW Froehlich UK Limited
Incorporated: 14 May 1975 *Employees:* 95
Net Worth: £10,710,147 *Total Assets:* £15,302,396
Registered Office: Sable Way, Southfields Business Park, Laindon, Essex, SS15 6TU
Activities: Manufacture of other machine tools
Parent: JW Froehlich Maschinenfabrik GmbH
Officers: Karon Jane Fowler, Secretary; Gary Stephen Brinkley [1961] Technical Director; Joseph Wolfgang Froehlich [1935] Director/Chairman [Austrian]; Heinrich Liebgott [1956] Director/Financial Controller [German]; Daniel Ludin [1959] Director [German]; David Keith Wells [1960] Director

Frontier Bidco Limited
Incorporated: 12 November 2013 *Employees:* 4
Net Worth: £96,315,000 *Total Assets:* £343,931,008
Registered Office: Charter Court, 74-78 Victoria Street, St Albans, Herts, AL1 3XH
Activities: Activities of head offices
Parent: Ontario Teachers Pension Plan Board
Officers: Simon Leon Browne [1970] Director; Cleo Yet-Mann Cheung [1986] Director/Senior Principal [Canadian]; Jean-Charles Charles Douin [1978] Director [French]; Nicholas Peter Field [1978] Director

Frontier Developments PLC
Incorporated: 28 January 1994 *Employees:* 345
Net Worth: £55,288,000 *Total Assets:* £65,543,000
Registered Office: 26 Science Park, Milton Road, Cambridge, CB4 0FP
Activities: Publishing of computer games
Shareholder: David John Braben
Officers: Alexander Peter Bevis, Secretary; Alexander Peter Bevis [1975] Director/Chief Financial Officer; David John Braben [1964] Director/Business Executive; Charles William Alfred Cotton [1947] Director; David Ranken Gammon [1961] Director/Consultant; David John Walsh [1964] Director/Software Engineering; Jonathan Francis Watts [1969] Director/Manager

Frontier Holdco Limited
Incorporated: 12 November 2013
Net Worth Deficit: £4,994,000 *Total Assets:* £102,742,000
Registered Office: Charter Court, 74-78 Victoria Street, St Albans, Herts, AL1 3XH
Activities: Activities of head offices
Parent: Ontario Teachers Plan Board
Officers: Simon Leon Browne [1970] Director; Cleo Yet-Mann Cheung [1986] Director/Senior Principal [Canadian]; Jean-Charles Charles Douin [1978] Director [French]; Nicholas Peter Field [1978] Director

Frontier Midco Limited
Incorporated: 12 November 2013 *Employees:* 4
Net Worth: £102,742,000 *Total Assets:* £118,117,000
Registered Office: Charter Court, 74-78 Victoria Street, St Albans, Herts, AL1 3XH
Activities: Activities of head offices
Parent: Ontario Teachers Pension Plan Board
Officers: Simon Leon Browne [1970] Director; Cleo Yet-Mann Cheung [1986] Director/Senior Principal [Canadian]; Jean-Charles Charles Douin [1978] Director [French]; Nicholas Peter Field [1978] Director

Frontline Limited
Incorporated: 8 July 1937 *Employees:* 274
Net Worth Deficit: £279,000 *Total Assets:* £60,731,000
Registered Office: Media House, Peterborough Business Park, Lynch Wood, Peterborough, Cambs, PE2 6EA
Activities: Retail sale of newspapers and stationery in specialised stores
Parent: Bauer Consumer Media Limited
Officers: Thomas Pierre Bureau [1968] Director; Kevin Costello [1964] Director; Brian John Freeman [1964] Director/Accountant; Nicholas Paul Howitt [1967] Director; Paul Anthony Keenan [1963] Director/Publisher; Kevin Donald Langford [1964] Director; Robert James Munro-Hall [1966] Group Managing Director; Frank Carl Straetmans [1971] Managing Director [Belgian]

Fujichem Sonneborn Limited
Incorporated: 25 June 1947 *Employees:* 142
Net Worth: £13,261,350 *Total Assets:* £22,759,570
Registered Office: Jaxa Works, 91-95 Peregrine Road, Hainault, Essex, IG6 3XH
Activities: Manufacture of paints, varnishes and similar coatings, mastics and sealants
Parent: Fujikura Kasei Co. Ltd
Officers: Edward Vincent Cox, Secretary; Edward Vincent Cox [1951] Director and Company Secretary; Hiroya Dejima [1961] Director/Chief Executive Officer [Japanese]; Hisashi Kajiwara [1959] Director [Japanese]; Hiroshi Kawai [1958] Director/Chief Finance Officer [Japanese]; Keith Mannas [1967] Director; Robert Frank Sheppard [1957] Director/Chief Operations Officer

Fujitsu General Air Conditioning (UK) Limited
Incorporated: 12 June 2007 *Employees:* 30
Previous: FG Eurofred Limited
Net Worth: £3,111,000 *Total Assets:* £11,606,000
Registered Office: Unit 150 Centennial Park, Centennial Avenue, Elstree, Herts, WD6 3SG
Activities: Other professional, scientific and technical activities n.e.c.
Officers: Ignacio Franquesa Castrillo [1966] Director [Spanish]; Hirofumi Fuji [1954] Director [Japanese]; Takashi Harada [1970] Director [Japanese]; Marc Sabe Richer [1969] Director/Board Advisor [Spanish]

Fulca Limited
Incorporated: 8 June 2012
Net Worth Deficit: £3,318,941 *Total Assets:* £9,060,190
Registered Office: Hill House, Lowlands Road, Harrow, Middlesex, HA1 3EQ
Activities: Development of building projects
Major Shareholder: Donovan Gijsbertus Wijsmuller
Officers: Brian Martin Comer [1960] Director [Irish]; Luke Andrew Comer [1957] Director [Irish]

Fullfield Limited
Incorporated: 4 November 2008 *Employees:* 347
Net Worth Deficit: £694,195 *Total Assets:* £13,795,072
Registered Office: 25 Hornsby Square, Laindon, Essex, SS15 6SD
Activities: Other business support service activities n.e.c.
Shareholders: David Warren; John Nicholas Hammond; Paul Anthony Cranwell
Officers: Paul Anthony Cranwell [1966] Director; Kevin Finn [1960] Director; John Nicholas Hammond [1968] Sales Director; David Terance Warren [1967] Director

Fulton Central Limited
Incorporated: 20 May 2017
Net Worth: £9,757,355 *Total Assets:* £17,405,402
Registered Office: Portland House, 69-71 Wembley Hill Road, Wembley, Middlesex, HA9 8BU
Activities: Other business support service activities n.e.c.
Parent: Fulton Maritime Holdings Limited
Officers: Bhupendra Shantilal Kansagra, Secretary; Laurent Elie Cadji [1977] Director/Businessman; Lewis Levy Cadji [1938] Director/Businessman; Bhupendra Shantilal Kansagra [1956] Director/Businessman; Ramesh Shantilal Kansagra [1950] Director/Businessman

Fulton Clover Limited
Incorporated: 29 March 2017
Net Worth: £7,511,983 *Total Assets:* £12,850,465
Registered Office: Portland House, 69-71 Wembley Hill Road, Wembley, Middlesex, HA9 8BU
Activities: Other business support service activities n.e.c.
Officers: Bhupendra Shantilal Kansagra, Secretary; Laurent Elie Cadji [1977] Director/Businessman; Lewis Levy Cadji [1938] Director/Businessman; Bhupendra Shantilal Kansagra [1956] Director/Businessman; Ramesh Shantilal Kansagra [1950] Director/Businessman

Fulton Grand Limited
Incorporated: 21 July 2017
Net Worth: £7,696,419 *Total Assets:* £14,022,891
Registered Office: Portland House, 69-71 Wembley Hill Road, Wembley, Middlesex, HA9 8BU
Activities: Other business support service activities n.e.c.
Officers: Bhupendra Shantilal Kansagra, Secretary; Laurent Elie Cadji [1977] Director/Businessman; Lewis Levy Cadji [1938] Director/Businessman; Bhupendra Shantilal Kansagra [1956] Director/Businessman; Ramesh Shantilal Kansagra [1950] Director/Businessman

Fulton Hyde Limited
Incorporated: 29 March 2017
Net Worth: £9,619,591 *Total Assets:* £16,997,012
Registered Office: Portland House, 69-71 Wembley Hill Road, Wembley, Middlesex, HA9 8BU
Activities: Other business support service activities n.e.c.
Officers: Bhupendra Shantilal Kansagra, Secretary; Laurent Elie Cadji [1977] Director/Businessman; Lewis Levy Cadji [1938] Director/Businessman; Bhupendra Shantilal Kansagra [1956] Director/Businessman; Ramesh Shantilal Kansagra [1950] Director/Businessman

Fulton Lincoln Limited
Incorporated: 1 February 2017
Net Worth: £6,434,414 *Total Assets:* £10,182,852
Registered Office: Portland House, 69-71 Wembley Hill Road, Wembley, Middlesex, HA9 8BU
Activities: Other business support service activities n.e.c.
Officers: Bhupendra Shantilal Kansagra, Secretary; Laurent Elie Cadji [1977] Director/Businessman; Lewis Levy Cadji [1938] Director/Businessman; Bhupendra Shantilal Kansagra [1956] Director/Businessman; Ramesh Shantilal Kansagra [1950] Director/Businessman

Fulton Maritime Holdings Limited
Incorporated: 25 October 2016 *Employees:* 3
Net Worth: £50,441,992 *Total Assets:* £87,923,608
Registered Office: Portland House, 69-71 Wembley Hill Road, Wembley, Middlesex, HA9 8BU
Activities: Sea and coastal freight water transport
Parent: Fulton Maritime Limited
Officers: Tristan Frisell, Secretary; Laurent Elie Cadji [1977] Director/Businessman; Lewis Levy Cadji [1938] Director/Businessman; Ramesh Shantilal Kansagra [1950] Director/Businessman

Fulton Maritime Limited
Incorporated: 19 October 2016
Net Worth: £13,392,910 *Total Assets:* £88,097,576
Registered Office: Portland House, 69-71 Wembley Hill Road, Wembley, Middlesex, HA9 8BU
Activities: Sea and coastal freight water transport
Officers: Tristan Frisell, Secretary; Laurent Elie Cadji [1977] Director/Businessman; Lewis Levy Cadji [1938] Director/Businessman; Ramesh Shantilal Kansagra [1950] Director/Businessman

Fulton Regent Limited
Incorporated: 1 February 2017
Net Worth: £6,302,328 *Total Assets:* £10,135,039
Registered Office: Portland House, 69-71 Wembley Hill Road, Wembley, Middlesex, HA9 8BU
Activities: Other business support service activities n.e.c.
Officers: Bhupendra Shantilal Kansagra, Secretary; Laurent Elie Cadji [1977] Director/Businessman; Lewis Levy Cadji [1938] Director/Businessman; Bhupendra Shantilal Kansagra [1956] Director/Businessman; Ramesh Shantilal Kansagra [1950] Director/Businessman

Fulton St James Limited
Incorporated: 13 July 2017
Net Worth: £10,580,521 *Total Assets:* £19,762,148
Registered Office: Portland House, 69-71 Wembley Hill Road, Wembley, Middlesex, HA9 8BU
Activities: Other business support service activities n.e.c.
Officers: Bhupendra Shantilal Kansagra, Secretary; Laurent Elie Cadji [1977] Director/Businessman; Lewis Levy Cadji [1938] Director/Businessman; Bhupendra Shantilal Kansagra [1956] Director/Businessman; Ramesh Shantilal Kansagra [1950] Director/Businessman

Future Travel Limited
Incorporated: 25 November 1996 *Employees:* 7
Net Worth: £716,000 *Total Assets:* £11,843,000
Registered Office: Westpoint, Peterborough Business Park, Lynch Wood, Peterborough, Cambs, PE2 6FZ
Activities: Travel agency activities
Parent: Co-op Group Travel 2 Holdings Limited
Officers: Shirley Bradley, Secretary; Alan Charles Donald [1963] Director; David John Elstob [1944] Director; Paul Russell [1962] Director

Futuresource Holdings Limited
Incorporated: 7 June 2017
Net Worth: £12,572,335 *Total Assets:* £14,223,611
Registered Office: 4 Beaconsfield Road, St Albans, Herts, AL1 3RD
Activities: Other service activities n.e.c.
Parent: Global Data Insights Limited
Officers: Sarah Stewart Carroll [1962] Director; Chris Herwig [1979] Director/Service [American]; Greg Evan Lindberg [1970] Director [American]; Ian Brian Roper [1966] Director

G's Fresh Beetroot Limited
Incorporated: 5 February 1991 *Employees:* 222
Net Worth: £8,998,000 *Total Assets:* £11,755,000
Registered Office: G's Fresh Beetroot Limited, Barway, Ely, Cambs, CB7 5TZ
Activities: Growing of vegetables and melons, roots and tubers
Parent: G's Fresh Limited
Officers: Graham George Forber [1957] Director/Business Manager; James Paul Green [1969] Finance Director; Kuldip Singh Kular [1960] Director

G's Fresh Limited
Incorporated: 29 April 2005 *Employees:* 69
Net Worth: £13,261,000 *Total Assets:* £60,424,000
Registered Office: Barway, Ely, Cambs, CB7 5TZ
Activities: Growing of vegetables and melons, roots and tubers
Parent: G's Group Holdings Limited
Officers: James Paul Green, Secretary; James Paul Green [1969] Finance Director; Kuldip Singh Kular [1960] Director; John Bourne Shropshire [1955] Director

G's Group Holdings Limited
Incorporated: 19 March 1984 *Employees:* 4,688
Net Worth: £74,991,000 *Total Assets:* £278,699,008
Registered Office: Barway Road, Barway, Ely, Cambs, CB7 5TZ
Activities: Growing of vegetables and melons, roots and tubers
Shareholders: John Bourne Shropshire; Davina Helen Harvey; Edward Frank Vivian Perrott
Officers: Julia Wynne Money, Secretary; James Paul Green [1969] Finance Director; John Michael Jack [1946] Director; Guy Peter Shropshire [1957] Director; John Bourne Shropshire [1955] Director

G's Growers Limited
Incorporated: 4 April 1984 *Employees:* 299
Net Worth: £1,771,000 *Total Assets:* £45,887,000
Registered Office: Barway, Ely, Cambs, CB7 5TZ
Activities: Growing of vegetables and melons, roots and tubers
Officers: Fay Karen Colson, Secretary; Rodney Pennington Baker-Bates [1944] Director; Fay Karen Colson [1965] Managing Director; James Railstone Foskett [1957] Director/Farmer; Richard John Hirst [1961] Director/Farmer; Julius John Joel [1961] Managing Director; William Oliver Jolly [1988] Director/Farmer; Alastair Ambrose David Morbey [1982] Director/Farmer; Edward Frank Vivian Perrott [1946] Director; Peter Jeremy Sargeant [1974] Director/Farmer; Guy Peter Shropshire [1957] Director/Farmer; John Bourne Shropshire [1955] Director/Farmer; Richard John Shropshire [1978] Director/Farmer; Timothy Edward Jehu Young [1982] Director/Farmer

G.B.N. Services Limited
Incorporated: 3 November 1986 *Employees:* 233
Net Worth: £15,354,652 *Total Assets:* £35,935,224
Registered Office: Ground Floor, Swift House, 18 Hoffmanns Way, Chelmsford, Essex, CM1 1GU
Activities: Treatment and disposal of non-hazardous waste
Parent: RVL Holdings Limited
Officers: David William Thompson, Secretary; Anthony Eric Dickens [1960] Director/Manager; Garry Martin Hobson [1970] Director/Recycling Manager; David William Thompson [1947] Director; Grant David Thompson [1972] Director

G.K. Holdings No.1 Limited
Incorporated: 20 August 2009
Net Worth: £554,979,968 *Total Assets:* £555,361,984
Registered Office: Westgate Brewery, Bury St Edmunds, Suffolk, IP33 1QT
Activities: Activities of head offices
Parent: Greene King Brewing and Retailing Limited
Officers: Lindsay Anne Keswick, Secretary; Richard Smothers [1967] Director

Gada Limited
Incorporated: 4 October 1993 *Employees:* 5
Net Worth: £12,765,527 *Total Assets:* £12,918,597
Registered Office: 11 Chestnut Avenue, Northwood, Middlesex, HA6 1HR
Activities: Other letting and operating of own or leased real estate
Shareholders: Dipen Hasmukhlal Shah; Sheilina Shah
Officers: Dipen Hasmukhlal Shah, Secretary/Chartered Accountant; Dipen Hasmukhlal Shah [1967] Director/Chartered Accountant; Radhika Shah [1969] Director/Chartered Accountant; Sheilina Shah [1972] Director/Management Accountant

Gade Property Developments Limited
Incorporated: 15 April 1971 *Employees:* 9
Net Worth: £8,457,943 *Total Assets:* £15,730,458
Registered Office: First Floor, Radius House, 51 Clarendon Road, Watford, Herts, WD17 1HP
Activities: Development of building projects
Officers: Sonia Whitehead, Secretary; Anita Jane Dalton [1945] Director; Raymond Charles Russell Dalton [1934] Director; William Raymond Dalton [1985] Director/Property Development

Gago Invest Limited
Incorporated: 5 November 2014 *Employees:* 5
Net Worth: £12,506,046 *Total Assets:* £12,525,304
Registered Office: 5 Elstree Gate, Elstree Way, Borehamwood, Herts, WD6 1JD
Activities: Other service activities n.e.c.
Shareholders: Frederic Gastaldo-Nigra; Francoise Gastaldo-Nigra
Officers: Nathalie Gastaldo-Godeau [1972] Director [French]; Francoise Gastaldo-Nigra [1946] Director [French]; Frederic Gastaldo-Nigra [1977] Director [French]; Philippe Godeau [1961] Director [French]; Sylvain Lagneaux [1957] Director/Lawyer Associate [French]

GAIAE Limited
Incorporated: 25 March 2014
Net Worth: £246,673 *Total Assets:* £11,240,534
Registered Office: 107 Hindes Road, Harrow, Middlesex, HA1 1RU
Activities: Activities of other holding companies n.e.c.
Officers: Manuel Alsoni [1982] Director [Italian]

Gainsborough's House Society
Incorporated: 6 October 2016
Net Worth: £10,101,097 *Total Assets:* £10,136,767
Registered Office: Gainsborough's House, 46 Gainsborough Street, Sudbury, Suffolk, CO10 2EU
Activities: Operation of arts facilities
Officers: Mark Stephen Bills [1963] Museum Executive Director; Dr Nigel Lynn Evans [1954] Director/Company Chairman (Flipper Ltd); Mark Harris [1959] Director/Chartered Accountant; Lowell John Libson [1956] Director/Art Dealer; Suzanne Jane Marriott [1969] Director/Solicitor and Notary Public; Brian James Moody [1943] Director/Retired; Dr Martin Myrone [1971] Director/Curator; John Mark Pendlington [1957] Director/Deputy Lieutenant of Suffolk; Edmund Christian Stewart-Smith [1969] Director; Wilfred John Weeks [1948] Director/Retired

The Gala Film Partners, LLP
Incorporated: 7 May 2003
Net Worth: £112,058,120 *Total Assets:* £112,058,120
Registered Office: 99 Kenton Road, Harrow, Middlesex, HA3 0AN
Officers: Junghwa Aitken [1960] LLP Member; Thomas David Guy Arculus [1946] LLP Member; Lisa Arnold [1962] LLP Member; Niall Richard Bamford [1966] LLP Member; John Edward Gilder Bateson [1948] LLP Member; Abraham Bejerano [1947] LLP Member; Alan Richard Bekhor [1960] LLP Member; Charles Louis Berman [1958] LLP Member; George Boateng [1975] LLP Member; James Everett Burgess [1964] LLP Member; William Patrick Cadogan [1947] LLP Member; Roger William Carey [1944] LLP Member; Steven John Bentley Carr [1961] LLP Member; Stephen Leonard Conn [1946] LLP Member; Nick Criticos [1958] LLP Member; Gael de Boissard [1967] LLP Member; Thomas Dicker [1953] LLP Member; Marcus Benjamin Donn [1973] LLP Member; Derek James Duffy [1954] LLP Member; Ian Keith Fisher [1959] LLP Member; Dr Stephen Garnett [1957] LLP Member; Michael David Goldman [1949] LLP Member; Colin Stewart Grassie [1961] LLP Member; Richard William John Hardie [1948] LLP Member; Robin Leonard Henshall [1959] LLP Member; Francis Paul Henri Pie Herve [1953] LLP Member; Nicola Karina Christina Horlick [1960] LLP Member; Marc Ronald Hotimsky [1956] LLP Member; Yann Le Garrec [1962] LLP Member; Barry Lewis [1954] LLP Member; Susan Jane Livesey [1959] LLP Member; Jonathan Angus MacDonald [1960] LLP Member; Christopher John Mallet [1957] LLP Member; Christopher Mary Masterson [1956] LLP Member; John Anthony McLevy [1949] LLP Member; Andrew McMillan [1965] LLP Member; Pierre Jean Henri Mirat [1965] LLP Member; Patrick Jacques Elkin Mocatta [1949] LLP Member; Kenneth Morton [1942] LLP Member; Michael Murphy [1965] LLP Member; Michael Darren Murphy [1965] LLP Member; Alan Daniel Neilson [1957] LLP Member; David Leslie Newland [1968] LLP Member; Craig Wyndham Orr [1962] LLP Member; Peter Edward Owen [1946] LLP Member; Gillian Mary Payne [1937] LLP Member; Humphrey Richard Percy [1956] LLP Member; Thomas Martin Harwood Reid [1960] LLP Member; Terence Ian Sadler [1948] LLP Member; Rajiv Sharma [1970] LLP Member; Trevor Hugh Silver [1953] LLP Member; Roderick John Sinclair [1944] LLP Member; Colin Spencer Smith [1946] LLP Member; Alison Mary Straszewski [1963] LLP Member; Jonathan William Summers [1971] LLP Member; Rhoderick Martin Swire [1951] LLP Member; Oliver Robert Takacs [1969] LLP Member; Hugh Ian Taylor [1945] LLP Member; Ian John Thacker [1957] LLP Member; Guy Henry Toller [1958] LLP Member; Stanislav Varga [1972] LLP Member; Alan Edward Westall [1947] LLP Member; Manjit Wolstenholme [1964] LLP Member; Alan James Wood [1958] LLP Member; Mark John Lyon Wyllie [1963] LLP Member

Galapagos Biotech Limited
Incorporated: 8 July 1997
Previous: Inpharmatica Limited
Net Worth: £4,832,896 *Total Assets:* £13,221,579
Registered Office: Salisbury House, Station Road, Cambridge, CB1 2LA
Activities: Other professional, scientific and technical activities n.e.c.
Officers: Xavier Maes, Secretary; Walid Michael Abi-Saab [1965] Director [American]; Bart Filius [1970] Director [Dutch]; Xavier Marie Bernard Cecile Maes [1980] Director [Belgian]; Dr Onno Van de Stolpe [1959] Director [Dutch]; Piet Tom B Wigerinck [1964] Director [Belgian]

Galderma (U.K.) Limited
Incorporated: 14 February 1962 *Employees:* 81
Net Worth: £2,385,000 *Total Assets:* £16,943,000
Registered Office: Meridien House, 69-71 Clarendon Road, Watford, Herts, WD17 1DS
Activities: Wholesale of pharmaceutical goods
Officers: Jacques Bodevin [1961] Director/Chief Financial Officer Nestle Skin Health [Swiss]; Can Davut Ongen [1965] Director/Regional VP EMEA [Swiss]; Alexandra Tretyakova [1972] Director/General Manager [Russian]

Galileo Homes Limited
Incorporated: 13 December 2010
Net Worth: £2,182,517 *Total Assets:* £12,817,154
Registered Office: 87a High Street, The Old Town, Hemel Hempstead, Herts, HP1 3AH
Activities: Development of building projects
Shareholders: Antony Carey; Frances Heather Carey
Officers: Frances Heather Carey [1952] Director

Joseph Gallagher Group Limited
Incorporated: 21 June 1999 *Employees:* 231
Net Worth: £15,421,579 *Total Assets:* £41,862,936
Registered Office: Neagron House, Stanford Road, Orsett, Essex, RM16 3BX
Activities: Non-trading company
Shareholders: Joseph Jude Gallagher; Mrs Agnes Teresa Gallagher
Officers: Agnes Theresa Gallagher, Secretary; Agnes Teresa Gallagher [1954] Director; Joseph Jude Gallagher [1945] Director [Irish]; Paul Joseph Gallagher [1981] Director; Steven Keith Harvey [1963] Managing Director

Gallagher Holdings Limited
Incorporated: 12 August 1981
Net Worth: £100,916,920 *Total Assets:* £103,837,488
Registered Office: Pendragon House, 65 London Road, St Albans, Herts, AL1 1LJ
Activities: Activities of construction holding companies
Parent: Gallagher Investments Limited
Officers: Daniel Paul Gallagher, Secretary [Irish]; Brian Joseph Gallagher [1953] Director/Barrister [Irish]; Charles Hubert Gallagher [1959] Director [Irish]; Daniel Paul Gallagher [1964] Sales Director [Irish]; David Andrew Gallagher [1960] Director [Irish]; Ellen Pauline Gallagher [1929] Director [Irish]

Joseph Gallagher Limited
Incorporated: 2 March 1982 *Employees:* 192
Net Worth: £11,078,520 *Total Assets:* £28,537,716
Registered Office: Neagron House, Stanford Road, Orsett, Essex, RM16 3BX
Activities: Construction of bridges and tunnels
Parent: Joseph Gallagher Group Limited
Officers: Agnes Theresa Gallagher, Secretary; Claire Elaine Dale [1983] Director/Quantity Surveyor; Agnes Theresa Gallagher [1946] Director; Joseph Jude Gallagher [1945] Director [Irish]; Paul Joseph Gallagher [1981] Director; Steven Harvey [1963] Director/Civil Engineer; Anthony Andrew Matheson [1968] Group Commercial Director; John Timothy O'Dwyer [1970] Contracts Director; Clive Wigley [1946] Director/Civil Engineer

Charles Gallagher Limited
Incorporated: 21 October 1974
Net Worth: £13,011,553 *Total Assets:* £13,316,507
Registered Office: Pendragon House, 65 London Road, St Albans, Herts, AL1 1LJ
Activities: Construction of domestic buildings
Parent: Matthew Investments Limited
Officers: Daniel Paul Gallagher, Secretary/Sales Director [Irish]; Charles Hubert Gallagher [1959] Director [Irish]; Daniel Paul Gallagher [1964] Sales Director [Irish]; David Andrew Gallagher [1960] Director [Irish]; Ellen Pauline Gallagher [1929] Director [Irish]; Neville William Hutchinson [1941] Director; Peter Michael Jones [1962] Director/Surveyor; Barry Martin Jordan [1967] Land Director

Galldris Construction Limited
Incorporated: 23 March 1998 *Employees:* 4
Previous: Sedo Holdings 2016 Limited
Net Worth: £338,507 *Total Assets:* £12,304,427
Registered Office: 166 College Road, Harrow, Middlesex, HA1 1RA
Activities: Other specialised construction activities n.e.c.
Shareholders: Donal Gallagher; Sean Peter O'Driscoll
Officers: Sean Peter O'Driscoll, Secretary/Civil Engineer [Irish]; Donal Gallagher [1972] Director/Construction Manager [Irish]; Martin McDonough [1958] Health & Safety Director; Sean Peter O'Driscoll [1971] Director/Civil Engineer [Irish]; Jeremy Charles Pasley [1961] Construction Director [Irish]

Galldris Holdings Limited
Incorporated: 15 April 2016 *Employees:* 48
Net Worth: £4,579,660 *Total Assets:* £57,328,408
Registered Office: 166 College Road, Harrow, Middlesex, HA1 1RA
Activities: Activities of other holding companies n.e.c.
Major Shareholder: Donal Gallagher
Officers: Donal Gallagher [1972] Director [Irish]; Sean Peter O'Driscoll [1971] Director [Irish]

Galldris Services Ltd
Incorporated: 24 March 2010 *Employees:* 42
Previous: Galldris Construction Limited
Net Worth: £11,303,958 *Total Assets:* £64,286,348
Registered Office: 166 College Road, Harrow, Middlesex, HA1 1RA
Activities: Activities of head offices
Parent: Galldris Holdings Limited
Officers: Sean O'Driscoll, Secretary; Donal Gallagher [1972] Director [Irish]; Sean Peter O'Driscoll [1971] Director/Civil Engineer [Irish]

Galliard Construction Limited
Incorporated: 7 February 1996
Net Worth: £31,742,446 *Total Assets:* £87,221,768
Registered Office: 3rd Floor, Sterling House, Langston Road, Loughton, Essex, IG10 3TS
Activities: Development of building projects
Parent: Galliard Holdings Limited
Officers: Allan William Porter, Secretary; Victoria Elizabeth Anthony [1977] Group HR Director; John Leslie August [1939] Director/Project Manager; David Edward Conway [1976] Director; Stephen Stuart Solomon Conway [1948] Director; Robin Hawkins [1957] Director/Contracts Manager; Darren Paul Maguire [1970] Construction Director; Donagh O'Sullivan [1968] Construction Director [Irish]; Allan William Porter [1957] Director/Accountant; Michael William Watson [1952] Director/Architectural Technologist

Galliard Developments Limited
Incorporated: 1 August 2014
Net Worth: £66,038,056 *Total Assets:* £153,230,640
Registered Office: 3rd Floor, Sterling House, Langston Road, Loughton, Essex, IG10 3TS
Activities: Other business support service activities n.e.c.
Parent: GDL Holdco Limited
Officers: Allan William Porter, Secretary; John Cole [1971] Director; Stephen Stuart Solomon Conway [1948] Director; Jonathan Simon Goldstein [1966] Director; Donagh O'Sullivan [1968] Director [Irish]

Galliard Group Limited
Incorporated: 13 February 2012 *Employees:* 567
Previous: Galliard (Group) Limited
Net Worth: £239,578,000 *Total Assets:* £741,121,024
Registered Office: 3rd Floor, Sterling House, Langston Road, Loughton, Essex, IG10 3TS
Activities: Activities of other holding companies n.e.c.
Shareholder: Stephen Stuart Solomon Conway
Officers: Allan William Porter, Secretary; Low See Ching [1975] Director/Deputy CEO [Singaporean]; David Edward Conway [1976] Director; Gary Alexander Conway [1973] Director; Richard Matthew Conway [1978] Director; Stephen Stuart Solomon Conway [1948] Director; Paul Laurence Huberman [1961] Director/Chartered Accountant; Luke Oliver Johnson [1962] Director/Restaurateur; Ching Chiat Kwong [1965] Director/Chairman & CEO [Singaporean]; Jonathan Michael Morgan [1978] Director; Donagh O'Sullivan [1968] Construction Director [Irish]; Michael William Watson [1952] Director/Architectural Technologist; Jonathan Paul White [1951] Director

Galliard Holdings Limited
Incorporated: 9 May 1997
Net Worth: £44,670,496 *Total Assets:* £299,718,112
Registered Office: 3rd Floor, Sterling House, Langston Road, Loughton, Essex, IG10 3TS
Activities: Activities of head offices
Parent: Galliard Group Limited
Officers: Allan William Porter, Secretary; David Edward Conway [1976] Director; Stephen Stuart Solomon Conway [1948] Director; Paul Laurence Huberman [1961] Director/Chartered Accountant; Jonathan Michael Morgan [1978] Director; Donagh O'Sullivan [1968] Construction Director [Irish]; Michael William Watson [1952] Director/Architectural Technologist; Jonathan Paul White [1951] Director

Galliard Homes Limited
Incorporated: 28 August 1987 *Employees:* 427
Net Worth: £11,531,404 *Total Assets:* £257,703,344
Registered Office: 3rd Floor, Sterling House, Langston Road, Loughton, Essex, IG10 3TS
Activities: Development of building projects
Parent: Galliard Holdings Limited
Officers: Allan William Porter, Secretary; Victoria Elizabeth Anthony [1977] Group HR Director; David Edward Conway [1976] Director/Property Developer; Stephen Stuart Solomon Conway [1948] Director; Amanda Louise Dijk [1976] Director/Group Financial Controller; David Galman [1963] Sales Director; David Joseph Hirschfield [1985] Director/Solicitor; Paul Laurence Huberman [1961] Director/Chartered Accountant; Jonathan Michael Morgan [1978] Director; Donagh O'Sullivan [1968] Construction Director [Irish]; Allan William Porter [1957] Director/Accountant; Michael John Watson [1974] Architectural & Technical Director; Michael William Watson [1952] Director/Architectural Technologist

Gamit Limited
Incorporated: 10 December 1990
Net Worth: £12,420,595 *Total Assets:* £14,683,744
Registered Office: Buildings 21 & 22, M11 Business Link, Parsonage Lane, Stansted, Essex, CM24 8GF
Activities: Other service activities n.e.c.
Major Shareholder: Kadri Muhiddin
Officers: Veronique Marie Barat-Muhiddin, Secretary; Veronique Marie Barat Muhiddin [1957] Director [French]; Kadri Muhiddin [1956] Director/Chairman [French]; Nadeem Kadri Muhiddin [1985] Director/Project Manager; Tarek Muhiddin [1983] Director/Aircraft Engineer; Waleed Muhiddin [1981] Director/Aviation Marketing Manager

Gannett International Finance LLP
Incorporated: 29 February 2016
Net Worth: £313,151,264 *Total Assets:* £313,151,264
Registered Office: Loudwater Mill, Station Road, High Wycombe, Bucks, HP10 9TY

The Gap Partnership Bidco Limited
Incorporated: 27 April 2016 *Employees:* 4
Net Worth Deficit: £3,845,890 *Total Assets:* £56,270,084
Registered Office: Ashlyns Hall, Chesham Road, Berkhamsted, Herts, HP4 2ST
Activities: Activities of head offices
Parent: The Gap Partnership Group Limited
Officers: Kirsten Anne Gates, Secretary; Graham Botwright [1968] Director/Management Consultant; Stephen Walter Gates [1960] Director/Training Manager; Roger Greenfield [1970] Director/Management Consultant; Nigel Ellis Wolfin [1969] Director

The Gap Partnership Group Limited
Incorporated: 27 April 2016 *Employees:* 195
Net Worth Deficit: £9,398,283 *Total Assets:* £66,720,896
Registered Office: Ashlyns Hall, Chesham Road, Berkhamsted, Herts, HP4 2ST
Activities: Activities of head offices
Officers: Kirsten Anne Gates, Secretary; Graham Botwright [1968] Director/Management Consultant; Donald John Campbell [1963] Director; Stephen Walter Gates [1960] Director/Training Manager; Roger Greenfield [1970] Director/Management Consultant; Paul Price [1955] Director [American]; Nigel Ellis Wolfin [1969] Director

The Gap Partnership Holdings Limited
Incorporated: 16 June 2011 *Employees:* 4
Net Worth: £11,330,455 *Total Assets:* £11,542,918
Registered Office: Ashlyns Hall, Chesham Road, Berkhamsted, Herts, HP4 2ST
Activities: Activities of head offices
Parent: The Gap Partnership Bidco Limited
Officers: Kirsten Anne Gates, Secretary; Graham Botwright [1968] Director/Management Consultant; Stephen Walter Gates [1960] Director/Training Manager; Roger Greenfield [1970] Director/Management Consultant; Nigel Ellis Wolfin [1969] Director

The Gap Partnership Limited
Incorporated: 18 November 1997 *Employees:* 96
Net Worth: £5,549,408 *Total Assets:* £13,806,309
Registered Office: Ashlyns Hall, Chesham Road, Berkhamsted, Herts, HP4 2ST
Activities: Management consultancy activities other than financial management
Parent: The Gap Partnership Holdings Limited
Officers: Kirsten Anne Gates, Secretary; Graham Botwright [1968] Director/Management Consultant; Stephen Walter Gates [1960] Director/Training Manager; Roger Greenfield [1970] Director/Management Consultant; Nigel Ellis Wolfin [1969] Finance Director

Gapsun Properties Limited
Incorporated: 12 February 2014
Net Worth: £31,743,996 *Total Assets:* £36,992,648
Registered Office: Hawke House, Old Station Road, Loughton, Essex, IG10 4PL
Activities: Dormant company
Parent: TRAD Properties LLP
Officers: Doretta Smith, Secretary; Doretta Smith [1943] Director; Hayden Francis Smith [1939] Director

Gardar Property Co Limited
Incorporated: 29 July 2016
Net Worth: £10,579,748 *Total Assets:* £10,927,883
Registered Office: Nuffield Road, Trinity Hall Industrial Estate, Cambridge, CB4 1TS
Activities: Activities of other holding companies n.e.c.
Shareholders: Gardar Holding Co Limited; Gardar Holding Co Limited
Officers: Rachel Elizabeth Anderson [1962] Director/Housewife; Duncan John Elliot Ridgeon [1964] Director/Vicar; Gordon Hugh Elliot Ridgeon [1962] Director/Businessman; Anne Kathleen Sam [1966] Director/Member; Amanda Helen Joan Smith [1969] Director

Garden City (Scotfield) LLP
Incorporated: 20 March 2008
Net Worth: £4,329,767 *Total Assets:* £20,969,870
Registered Office: 1 St Marys Court, Main Street, Hardwick, Cambridge, CB23 7QS
Officers: David Ian Newett [1959] Member; Martin Rapley [1957] Member

Gardiner Real Estate PLC
Incorporated: 5 August 1919 *Employees:* 3
Previous: William Nash P L C
Net Worth: £14,212,000 *Total Assets:* £14,560,000
Registered Office: Nash House, Hackmans Lane, Purleigh, Chelmsford, Essex, CM3 6RP
Activities: Other letting and operating of own or leased real estate
Shareholder: Broadland Properties Limited
Officers: Louise Emily Park, Secretary; John Frederick Hall [1959] Director/Chartered Surveyor; John Leslie MacDonald [1949] Director/Chartered Surveyor; Francis Robert Murphy [1942] Director/Papermaker; Jonathan Smale Nash [1956] Director

Gardline Holdings Limited
Incorporated: 22 December 2014 *Employees:* 692
Net Worth: £53,180,000 *Total Assets:* £88,261,000
Registered Office: Endeavour House, Admiralty Road, Great Yarmouth, Norfolk, NR30 3NG
Activities: Activities of head offices
Parent: Koninklijke Boskalis Westminster N.V.
Officers: Richard Stanley Coward [1974] Director; Christiaan Arie Vermeijden [1973] Director [Dutch]

Gardline Limited
Incorporated: 13 November 2002 *Employees:* 467
Previous: Gardline Geosurvey Limited
Net Worth Deficit: £3,569,057 *Total Assets:* £32,058,864
Registered Office: Endeavour House, Admiralty Road, Great Yarmouth, Norfolk, NR30 3NG
Activities: Other professional, scientific and technical activities n.e.c.
Parent: Gardline Marine Sciences Limited
Officers: Nicholas Mark Bayfield [1965] Director; Richard Stanley Coward [1974] Director; Christiaan Arie Vermeijden [1973] Director [Dutch]

Gardline Marine Sciences Limited
Incorporated: 3 January 1991
Net Worth: £9,741,928 *Total Assets:* £20,774,840
Registered Office: Endeavour House, Admiralty Road, Great Yarmouth, Norfolk, NR30 3NG
Activities: Other professional, scientific and technical activities n.e.c.
Parent: Gardline Shipping Limited
Officers: Richard Stanley Coward [1974] Director; Christiaan Arie Vermeijden [1973] Director [Dutch]

Gardline Maritime Limited
Incorporated: 9 April 2014 *Employees:* 4
Net Worth: £7,453,758 *Total Assets:* £10,143,781
Registered Office: Endeavour House, Admiralty Road, Great Yarmouth, Norfolk, NR30 3NG
Activities: Other professional, scientific and technical activities n.e.c.
Shareholders: Gardline Brasil Limited; Flavio Nogueira Pinheiro de Andrade
Officers: Richard Jenkins [1960] Director; Alan Pillar [1968] Director; Flavio Nogueira Pinheiro de Andrade [1964] Director [Brazilian]; Haroldo Nogueira Solberg [1964] Director [Brazilian]

Gardline Shipping Limited
Incorporated: 14 May 1969 *Employees:* 9
Net Worth: £44,803,000 *Total Assets:* £92,055,000
Registered Office: Endeavour House, Admiralty Road, Great Yarmouth, Norfolk, NR30 3NG
Activities: Activities of head offices
Parent: Gardline Holdings Limited
Officers: Richard Stanley Coward [1974] Director; Christiaan Arie Vermeijden [1973] Director [Dutch]

Garnham Management Services Limited
Incorporated: 9 July 2007 *Employees:* 57
Net Worth: £7,523,710 *Total Assets:* £11,771,305
Registered Office: 1 Claydon Business Park, Great Blakenham, Ipswich, Suffolk, IP6 0NL
Activities: Other business support service activities n.e.c.
Shareholders: Katherine Anna Skerry; Anthony Philip Skerry
Officers: Anthony Philip Skerry, Secretary; Anthony Philip Skerry [1969] Director; Katherine Anna Skerry [1972] Director

Garreg Lwyd Energy Limited
Incorporated: 23 October 2012
Net Worth Deficit: £3,186,000 *Total Assets:* £86,383,000
Registered Office: Beaufort Court, Egg Farm Lane, Kings Langley, Herts, WD4 8LR
Activities: Other business support service activities n.e.c.
Parent: European Wind Investments Group Limited
Officers: Dominic James Hearth, Secretary; Steven William Hughes [1972] Global Support Services Director, UK&I - Commercial; Fraser Stephen Merry [1968] Director/Chartered Surveyor; Mitesh Raj Patel [1982] Director/Group Financial Controller

Garrets Bidco 2 Limited
Incorporated: 17 February 2012
Previous: Garrets (Holdings) Limited
Net Worth: £9,365,943 *Total Assets:* £13,286,820
Registered Office: 3rd Floor, South Wing, St James House, 27-43 Eastern Road, Romford, Essex, RM1 3NH
Activities: Activities of other holding companies n.e.c.
Parent: Garrets Holding Limited
Officers: Robert Steen Kledal [1969] Director/Chief Executive Officer [Danish]; Anders Skipper [1967] Director/Chief Financial Officer [Danish]

Garrets Bidco Limited
Incorporated: 17 February 2012
Net Worth: £18,473,512 *Total Assets:* £18,780,188
Registered Office: 3rd Floor, South Wing, St James House, 27-43 Eastern Road, Romford, Essex, RM1 3NH
Activities: Other service activities n.e.c.
Parent: Garrets Bidco 2 Limited
Officers: Geoffrey Brian Battersby [1960] Director; Robert Steen Kledal [1969] Director/Chief Executive Officer [Danish]; Anders Skipper [1967] Director/Chief Executive Officer [Danish]

Garrets International Limited
Incorporated: 19 May 1993 *Employees:* 52
Net Worth: £4,152,419 *Total Assets:* £16,437,936
Registered Office: 3rd Floor, South Wing, St James House, 27-43 Eastern Road, Romford, Essex, RM1 3NH
Activities: Operation of warehousing and storage facilities for land transport activities
Parent: Garrets Bidco Limited
Officers: Geoffrey Brian Battersby [1960] Director; Soeren Joergensen [1974] Director/Chief Commercial Officer [Danish]; Robert Steen Kledal [1969] Director/Chief Executive Officer [Danish]; Stanley Watt Morrice [1963] Director; Richard Owen Page [1965] Operations Director; Anders Skipper [1967] Director/Chief Financial Officer [Danish]; Niels Mors Snog [1971] Director/Chief Executive Officer [Danish]

Gascoigne Halman Group Limited
Incorporated: 25 September 2015
Net Worth: £9,783,000 *Total Assets:* £10,280,000
Registered Office: Cumbria House, 16-20 Hockliffe Street, Leighton Buzzard, Beds, LU7 1GN
Activities: Activities of other holding companies n.e.c.
Parent: Connells Limited
Officers: Richard Twigg, Secretary; Martin Lee Forrest [1958] Director/Accountant; John Frederick Halman [1952] Director/Estate Agent Chartered Surveyor; Peter John Higham [1963] Director/Estate Agent; David Christopher Livesey [1959] Director; David Kerry Plumtree [1969] Director; Reginald Stephen Shipperley [1958] Director; Richard John Twigg [1965] Director/Chartered Accountant

Gates Group Limited
Incorporated: 4 August 1995 *Employees:* 314
Net Worth: £15,210,762 *Total Assets:* £64,662,576
Registered Office: Gates Corner, Edinburgh Way, Harlow, Essex, CM20 2EG
Activities: Other letting and operating of own or leased real estate
Shareholders: Heath Greenall; Suzanne Greenall
Officers: Martin David Cottenden [1951] Director; Heath Greenall [1967] Director; Suzanne Greenall [1966] Director

Frank G. Gates Limited
Incorporated: 17 February 1930 *Employees:* 312
Net Worth: £16,341,889 *Total Assets:* £48,764,520
Registered Office: Gates Corner, Edinburgh Way, Harlow, Essex, CM20 2EG
Activities: Sale of new cars and light motor vehicles
Parent: Gates Group Limited
Officers: Mohammad Shoaib Ali [1982] Director; John Steven Belton [1974] Director; Philip Lloyd Benson [1975] Director; Peter Brian Bosher [1962] Director; Darren James Cooper [1977] Director; Heath Greenall [1967] Director; Suzanne Greenall [1966] Director; Stuart John Overs [1965] Director

Gatetrade Limited
Incorporated: 25 August 1994
Net Worth: £30,399,414 *Total Assets:* £43,130,088
Registered Office: 27 Beaumont Avenue, St Albans, Herts, AL1 4TL
Activities: Other letting and operating of own or leased real estate
Shareholder: Paul Adam Wilton
Officers: Alison Bernice Wilton, Secretary/Director; Alison Bernice Wilton [1964] Director; Paul Wilton [1961] Director

Gateway Learning Community
Incorporated: 21 June 2006 *Employees:* 512
Net Worth: £36,530,428 *Total Assets:* £47,700,860
Registered Office: The Gateway Academy, Marshfoot Road, Grays, Essex, RM16 4LU
Activities: Primary education
Officers: Joanna Susan Jones, Secretary; Paul Victor Connew [1957] Director/Consultant; Graham Foster [1952] Director/Education Adviser; Lucy Emma Harris [1968] Director/Administrator; Hilary Ruth Hodgson [1960] Charity Director; Victoria Jane Reid [1971] Director/Headteacher; Kevin John Sadler [1961] Director/Headteacher; Margaret Christine Smith [1945] Director/Analytical Chemist (Retired); Peter John Ward [1964] Commercial Director

Gateway Reversions Limited
Incorporated: 12 November 2014 *Employees:* 1
Net Worth Deficit: £1,108 *Total Assets:* £12,789,421
Registered Office: Gateway House, 10 Coopers Way, Southend on Sea, Essex, SS2 5TE
Activities: Activities of other holding companies n.e.c.
Parent: Gateway Securities Limited
Officers: Antony John Dean [1965] Director

M. Gaze & Co. Limited
Incorporated: 9 April 1969 *Employees:* 44
Net Worth: £9,002,644 *Total Assets:* £12,003,954
Registered Office: Crossways Farm, Thurlton, Norwich, NR14 6NZ
Activities: Collection of non-hazardous waste
Officers: Rebekah Ursula Gaze, Secretary; Edmund Mervyn Gaze [1945] Director; Mitchell James Gaze [1977] Director; Rebekah Ursula Gaze [1974] Director/Operations Manager

GB Ingredients Limited
Incorporated: 1 November 1932 *Employees:* 58
Net Worth: £3,825,000 *Total Assets:* £15,319,000
Registered Office: Dock Road, Felixstowe, Suffolk, IP11 3QW
Activities: Manufacture of other food products n.e.c.
Parent: Lallemand UK Limited
Officers: Ainsley Buck, Secretary; Antoine Chagnon [1977] Director/General Manager [Canadian]; Jean Frederic Chagnon [1949] Director/Company President [Canadian]; Dr Ronald Michael Chell [1950] Commercial Director; Francois Leblanc [1959] Director/Vice President of Finance [Canadian]; Victor Moises Martins de Melo [1958] Managing Director [Portuguese]; Johannes Gerhardus Steenkamp [1962] Director/General Manager [South African]

GBST Limited
Incorporated: 18 August 1964 *Employees:* 38
Net Worth: £4,033,024 *Total Assets:* £11,609,151
Registered Office: Building 3, Hatters Lane, Croxley Green Business Park, Watford, Herts, WD18 8YG
Activities: Business and domestic software development
Parent: GBST Holdings Limited
Officers: Jillian Glenda Bannan, Secretary; Robert Dedominicis [1965] Director [Australian]; David Simpson [1969] Director/Business Executive

GDL (Aylesbury) Limited
Incorporated: 27 January 2017
Net Worth Deficit: £2,000 *Total Assets:* £10,556,005
Registered Office: 3rd Floor, Sterling House, Langston Road, Loughton, Essex, IG10 3TS
Activities: Development of building projects
Parent: Galliard Developments Limited
Officers: Allan William Porter, Secretary; Edward Azouz [1949] Director; John Cole [1971] Director; Stephen Stuart Solomon Conway [1948] Director; Scott Matthew Franklin [1966] Director; Jonathan Simon Goldstein [1966] Director; Rory Anthony O'Connor [1959] Director [Irish]; Donagh O'Sullivan [1968] Construction Director [Irish]

GDL (Luton) Developments Limited
Incorporated: 20 January 2016
Net Worth Deficit: £261,245 *Total Assets:* £16,923,480
Registered Office: 3rd Floor, Sterling House, Langston Road, Loughton, Essex, IG10 3TS
Activities: Development of building projects
Parent: Galliard Developments Limited
Officers: Allan William Porter, Secretary; John Cole [1971] Director; Stephen Stuart Solomon Conway [1948] Director; Jonathan Simon Goldstein [1966] Director; Donagh O'Sullivan [1968] Director [Irish]; Sabeeta Thukral [1973] Director

GDL (Millharbour) Limited
Incorporated: 8 October 2014
Net Worth: £41,253,264 *Total Assets:* £162,070,064
Registered Office: 3rd Floor, Sterling House, Langston Road, Loughton, Essex, IG10 3TS
Activities: Development of building projects
Parent: Galliard Developments Limited
Officers: Allan William Porter, Secretary; John Cole [1971] Director; Stephen Stuart Solomon Conway [1948] Director; Jonathan Simon Goldstein [1966] Director; Donagh O'Sullivan [1968] Director [Irish]

GDL (Romford) Limited
Incorporated: 11 June 2016
Net Worth: £349,837 *Total Assets:* £8,516,545
Registered Office: 3rd Floor, Sterling House, Langston Road, Loughton, Essex, IG10 3TS
Activities: Development of building projects
Parent: Galliard Developments Limited
Officers: Allan William Porter, Secretary; John Cole [1971] Director; Stephen Stuart Solomon Conway [1948] Director; Jonathan Simon Goldstein [1966] Director; Donagh O'Sullivan [1968] Director [Irish]

GDL (Slough Developments) Limited
Incorporated: 17 December 2015
Net Worth Deficit: £1,014,053 *Total Assets:* £19,077,416
Registered Office: 3rd Floor, Sterling House, Langston Road, Loughton, Essex, IG10 3TS
Activities: Development of building projects
Parent: Galliard Developments Limited
Officers: Allan William Porter, Secretary; John Cole [1971] Director; Stephen Stuart Solomon Conway [1948] Director; Jonathan Simon Goldstein [1966] Director; Donagh O'Sullivan [1968] Director [Irish]

GDL Holdco Limited
Incorporated: 26 April 2016
Net Worth: £46,763,844 *Total Assets:* £445,380,064
Registered Office: 3rd Floor, Sterling House, Langston Road, Loughton, Essex, IG10 3TS
Activities: Activities of construction holding companies
Shareholders: Galliard (Group) Limited; Todd Boehly
Officers: Alan William Porter, Secretary; John Cole [1971] Director; Stephen Stuart Solomon Conway [1971] Director; Jonathan Simon Goldstein [1966] Director; Donagh O'Sullivan [1968] Director [Irish]

GDSK Limited
Incorporated: 28 March 2014 *Employees:* 291
Net Worth: £113,415,416 *Total Assets:* £166,474,480
Registered Office: Kingfisher House, No 11 Hoffmanns Way, Chelmsford, Essex, CM1 1GU
Activities: Other food services
Officers: Gurprit Dhaliwal [1982] Director; Surinderjit Singh Kandola [1965] Director

GE Bio-Sciences Investments Limited
Incorporated: 21 May 1992
Net Worth: £44,561,000 *Total Assets:* £157,712,000
Registered Office: Pollards Wood, Nightingales Lane, Chalfont St Giles, Bucks, HP8 4SP
Activities: Activities of head offices
Parent: General Electric Company
Officers: Katherine Ann Jones [1976] Director/Financial Controller; Anna Lena Walsh [1976] Director/Accountant [Irish]

GE Healthcare Limited
Incorporated: 16 February 1971 *Employees:* 851
Net Worth: £736,966,976 *Total Assets:* £932,070,016
Registered Office: Amersham Place, Little Chalfont, Bucks, HP7 9NA
Activities: Manufacture of basic pharmaceutical products
Parent: GE Industrial Consolidation Limited
Officers: William Henry Bushill-Matthews, Secretary; Tricia Ann Clark [1976] Director/Executive EHS, GE Healthcare [American]; Ian Alistair Dale [1963] Director/General Manager; Michael Joseph Murphy [1965] Director/General Manager [Irish]; Kevin Michael O'Neill [1968] Director/Accountant

GE Healthcare UK Limited
Incorporated: 17 March 1997 *Employees:* 270
Net Worth: £430,340,000 *Total Assets:* £748,172,032
Registered Office: Amersham Place, Little Chalfont, Bucks, HP7 9NA
Activities: Manufacture of basic pharmaceutical products
Parent: GE Medical Systems Limited
Officers: Judit Kalman, Secretary; Maria de Los Angeles Khoury Gonzalo [1970] Director/Financial Management [American]; Emmanuel Francois Joel Ligner [1970] Director/Management Executive [French]; Kevin Michael O'Neill [1968] Director/Accountant

GE Medical Systems Limited
Incorporated: 8 December 1930 *Employees:* 676
Net Worth: £477,595,008 *Total Assets:* £695,057,984
Registered Office: Amersham Place, Little Chalfont, Bucks, HP7 9NA
Activities: Non-specialised wholesale trade
Parent: GE UK Holdings
Officers: Jane Alison Beastall [1971] Director/Accountant; Karl Gregory William Blight [1963] Director/General Manager

GE Money Home Finance Limited
Incorporated: 4 November 1957
Net Worth: £242,772,912 *Total Assets:* £262,042,608
Registered Office: P O Box 2497, Building 4, Hatters Lane, Watford, Herts, WD18 1YY
Activities: Financial intermediation not elsewhere classified
Parent: GE Money Home Lending Finance Limited
Officers: Samantha Jones [1981] Director; Jonathan Edward Taylor [1980] Director/Risk and Compliance Leader

GE Money Home Lending Holdings Limited
Incorporated: 14 May 2004
Net Worth: £1,547,659,136 *Total Assets:* £1,547,659,136
Registered Office: P O Box 2497, Building 4, Hatters Lane, Watford, Herts, WD18 1YY
Activities: Activities of head offices
Shareholders: GE Capital International 2 Limited; GE Capital International 6 Limited; GE Capital International Holdings Limited
Officers: Paul Kilrain Goudie [1964] Director [American]; Samantha Jones [1981] Director; Jonathan Edward Taylor [1980] Director/Risk and Compliance Leader

GE Money Servicing Limited
Incorporated: 11 October 1999 *Employees:* 95
Net Worth: £265,084,000 *Total Assets:* £359,737,984
Registered Office: P O Box 2497, Building 4, Hatters Lane, Watford, Herts, WD18 1YY
Activities: Other business support service activities n.e.c.
Parent: Igroup8 Limited
Officers: Samantha Jones [1981] Director; Jonathan Edward Taylor [1980] Director/Risk and Compliance Leader

Gearhouse Broadcast Limited
Incorporated: 29 September 1993 *Employees:* 99
Net Worth: £18,893,000 *Total Assets:* £29,481,000
Registered Office: 32-34 Greenhill Crescent, Watford, Herts, WD18 8JU
Activities: Television programming and broadcasting activities
Parent: Gravity Media Group UK Holdings Limited
Officers: Nikki Petken, Secretary; Eamonn MacArten Dowdall [1963] Director; Elliot Saul Kaye [1971] Director; Kevin Moorhouse [1958] Director; John Richard Newton [1963] Director/Chief Executive; Nicholas Peter Newton [1962] Commercial Director

Gee Group Ltd
Incorporated: 21 January 1981 *Employees:* 58
Net Worth: £8,471,416 *Total Assets:* £15,895,332
Registered Office: 11 Argent Court, Sylvan Way, Southfields Business Park, Basildon, Essex, SS15 6TH
Activities: Activities of head offices
Parent: Headcrown Group PLC
Officers: Nigel John Rickman, Secretary; Carl Adrian Brian [1965] Director/Chartered Accountant; John Newby [1939] Director/Builder

GEMS Schools Limited
Incorporated: 27 March 1986 *Employees:* 79
Net Worth: £12,876,681 *Total Assets:* £16,124,856
Registered Office: 100 Hills Road, Cambridge, CB2 1PH
Activities: Primary education
Parent: Gems Spartacus Limited
Officers: Jay Sunny Varkey [1984] Director [Indian]

General Domestic Appliances Holdings Limited
Incorporated: 2 September 1958
Net Worth: £114,043,000 *Total Assets:* £146,974,000
Registered Office: Morley Way, Peterborough, Cambs, PE2 9JB
Activities: Activities of head offices
Parent: Indesit Company UK Holdings Limited
Officers: Tetiana Pidhaina, Secretary; Lucianna Raffaini Carvalho [1973] Director [Italian]; Andrzej Tuleja [1973] Director [Polish]

Generations Multi Academy Trust
Incorporated: 1 September 2011 *Employees:* 196
Previous: Goffs School
Net Worth: £46,114,864 *Total Assets:* £49,084,224
Registered Office: Goffs School, Goffs Lane, Cheshunt, Waltham Cross, Herts, EN7 5QW
Activities: General secondary education
Officers: Ian David Denchfield, Secretary; Andrew Bertram Clarke [1956] Director/Queen's Counsel; Lisa Claire Joanna Clowes [1978] Director/Project Manager; Donna Marie Cooper [1974] Director; Kathy Dunnett [1957] Director/Governance Officer; Ian Peter Fish [1971] Director; Giovanna Formoso [1966] Director; Alison Garner [1965] Director/Headteacher; Francoise Grote [1966] Director/Attendance and Parent Support Officer [French]; Jean Margaret Holt [1955] Director; Martin Peter Jackson [1970] Director/HR Manager; John Joseph O'Sullivan [1943] Director/Human Resources Manager; Toyin Oyelade [1978] Director/Teacher [Nigerian]; Patrick James Philpott [1989] Managing Director; Sandra Skinner [1964] Director/Student Support Officer; Vanessa Wright [1972] Director/Vice President

Generics (U.K.) Limited
Incorporated: 29 April 1981 *Employees:* 262
Net Worth: £45,680,000 *Total Assets:* £85,286,000
Registered Office: Station Close, Potters Bar, Herts, EN6 1TL
Activities: Manufacture of basic pharmaceutical products
Parent: Mylan Group BV
Officers: Caroline Rebecca Louise Dixon, Finance Director; Jean-Yves Brault [1967] Director/Area Head Northern Europe [Canadian]; Jose Javier Cotarelo [1972] Director/Commercial Head of Northern & Western Europe [American]; Caroline Rebecca Louise Dixon [1968] Finance Director; Balwant Singh Heer [1959] Director/Global Head - Product Safety & Risk Management

Genesis Pharmaceuticals Limited
Incorporated: 29 September 1999 *Employees:* 10
Net Worth: £3,607,776 *Total Assets:* £12,483,941
Registered Office: 3rd Floor, Scottish Provident House, 76-80 College Road, Harrow, Middlesex, HA1 1BQ
Activities: Wholesale of pharmaceutical goods
Parent: Genethics Europe Limited
Officers: Nilesh Prataprai Mehta, Secretary/Director; Patrick Anthony Kingsford Chubb [1956] Commercial Director; Bharat Prataprai Mehta [1952] Director; Nilesh Prataprai Mehta [1962] Director; Dr David Louis Charles Solomon [1970] Director

Genie Bidco Limited
Incorporated: 10 February 2016 *Employees:* 11
Net Worth Deficit: £2,318,229 *Total Assets:* £8,712,453
Registered Office: Suite 1, Clare Hall, St Ives Business Park, Parsons Green, St Ives, Cambs, PE27 4WY
Activities: Activities of other holding companies n.e.c.
Parent: Genie Topco Limited
Officers: Lee Andrew Cowles [1969] Director; Simone Ceri Girardeau [1989] Director; Simon Angus Guild [1964] Director; David John Kirby [1985] Director; Robert James Maynard [1974] Finance Director; Paul James Ward [1968] Director

Genie Topco Limited
Incorporated: 10 February 2016 *Employees:* 43
Net Worth Deficit: £3,424,000 *Total Assets:* £16,063,000
Registered Office: Suite 1, Clare Hall, St Ives Business Park, Parsons Green, St Ives, Cambs, PE27 4WY
Activities: Activities of other holding companies n.e.c.
Shareholders: Livingbridge Enterprise LLP; Livingbridge Enterprise GP Limited
Officers: Lee Andrew Cowles [1969] Director; Simone Ceri Girardeau [1989] Director; Simon Angus Guild [1964] Director; David John Kirby [1985] Director; Robert James Maynard [1974] Finance Director; Paul James Ward [1968] Director

Gentec Energy PLC
Incorporated: 12 August 1996 *Employees:* 80
Net Worth: £10,036,925 *Total Assets:* £22,644,030
Registered Office: Unit 7 Chancery Gate Close, Stonefield Way, South Ruislip, Middlesex, HA4 0JS
Activities: Agents involved in the sale of machinery, industrial equipment, ships and aircraft
Officers: Navaratnarajah Navendrha, Secretary; Asha Khilnani [1959] Director; Colin Richard Walker [1951] Managing Director

Gentian (Mid-Essex) Limited
Incorporated: 1 June 2010 *Employees:* 2
Net Worth: £4,636,845 *Total Assets:* £8,497,281
Registered Office: 146 New London Road, Chelmsford, Essex, CM2 0AW
Activities: Other letting and operating of own or leased real estate
Parent: Gentian Investments Limited
Officers: Nicholas Kethro Ekins [1969] Director; Stefan Fitzsimmons [1973] Director

Gentian (Newcastle) Limited
Incorporated: 10 December 2003 *Employees:* 2
Net Worth: £7,648,738 *Total Assets:* £9,885,537
Registered Office: 146 New London Road, Chelmsford, Essex, CM2 0AW
Activities: Other letting and operating of own or leased real estate
Parent: Gentian Partnerships Limited
Officers: Juliette Louise Kerslake Ekins [1972] Director; Nicholas Kethro Ekins [1969] Director/Chartered Surveyor

Gentian Investments Limited
Incorporated: 22 July 2005 *Employees:* 2
Net Worth: £1,244,876 *Total Assets:* £20,633,750
Registered Office: 146 New London Road, Chelmsford, Essex, CM2 0AW
Activities: Activities of head offices
Shareholders: Gentian Partnerships Limited; Hulten Investments Limited
Officers: Nicholas Kethro Ekins [1969] Director/Chartered Surveyor; Stefan Fitzsimmons [1973] Finance Director

Gentian Partnerships Limited
Incorporated: 6 August 2002 *Employees:* 2
Net Worth: £34,434,636 *Total Assets:* £42,814,832
Registered Office: 146 New London Road, Chelmsford, Essex, CM2 0AW
Activities: Activities of head offices
Major Shareholder: Nicholas Kethro Ekins
Officers: Juliette Louise Kerslake Ekins [1972] Director; Nicholas Kethro Ekins [1969] Director/Chartered Surveyor

Genzyme Limited
Incorporated: 21 April 1981 *Employees:* 255
Net Worth: £163,684,000 *Total Assets:* £205,024,992
Registered Office: 37 Hollands Road, Haverhill, Suffolk, CB9 8PU
Activities: Manufacture of basic pharmaceutical products
Parent: Sanofi
Officers: Sara Morrish, Secretary; Francois Xavier Duhalde [1965] Director [French]; James Moretta [1966] Director/Site Head

Geo Management Limited
Incorporated: 25 November 1999 *Employees:* 2
Net Worth: £3,165,746 *Total Assets:* £9,321,333
Registered Office: Ingram House, Meridian Way, Norwich, NR7 0TA
Activities: Other letting and operating of own or leased real estate
Major Shareholder: Daniel John Mills
Officers: Daniel John Mills, Secretary/Professional Footballer; Daniel John Mills [1977] Director; Lisa Michelle Mills [1976] Director

Geodis United Kingdom Limited
Incorporated: 10 May 1985 *Employees:* 301
Previous: Geodis UK Limited
Net Worth: £324,440 *Total Assets:* £18,675,016
Registered Office: Geodis UK Limited, Coronation Road, High Wycombe, Bucks, HP12 3TA
Activities: Freight transport by road
Officers: Robert Huw Cousins, Secretary; Beatrice Charlery de La Masseliere [1958] Finance Director [French]; Olivier Alain Rene Melot [1971] Director/Vice President Groupage and Express Division [French]

Geoghegan Bros. Limited
Incorporated: 21 November 1973
Net Worth: £14,920,291 *Total Assets:* £16,305,339
Registered Office: Niall House, 24-26 Boulton Road, Stevenage, Herts, SG1 4QX
Activities: Construction of commercial buildings
Shareholder: Kathryn Ann Hall
Officers: Kathryn Ann Geoghegan, Secretary; Kathryn Ann Geoghegan [1964] Director/Secretary; Patrick Christopher Geoghegan [1939] Director [Irish]

Mick George Limited
Incorporated: 29 August 1989 *Employees:* 921
Net Worth: £32,593,000 *Total Assets:* £128,930,000
Registered Office: 6 Lancaster Way, Ermine Business Park, Huntingdon, Cambs, PE29 6XU
Activities: Quarrying of ornamental and building stone, limestone, gypsum, chalk and slate
Major Shareholder: Michael Eric George
Officers: Karen Ann Farrell, Secretary; Geoffrey Craven [1964] Logistics Director; Michael Alexander George [1984] Contracts Director; Michael Eric George [1956] Director/Haulage Contractor; Neil Graham Johnson [1971] Technical Waste Director; Peter David Newman [1957] Engineering Director; Jonathan Paul Stump [1964] Finance Director

Gerrard International Limited
Incorporated: 26 February 1992 *Employees:* 117
Net Worth: £10,928,076 *Total Assets:* £12,418,943
Registered Office: 47 Theobald Street, Borehamwood, Herts, WD6 4RT
Activities: Other business support service activities n.e.c.
Shareholders: Ian Gerrard; Susan Angela Gerrard
Officers: Susan Angela Gerrard, Secretary/Director; Amanda Eileen Cook [1958] Director/National Sales Manager; Ian Gerrard [1944] Director; Lisa Gerrard [1967] Director; Susan Angela Gerrard [1945] Director

Getech Limited
Incorporated: 26 October 1989 *Employees:* 77
Net Worth: £6,097,000 *Total Assets:* £11,317,000
Registered Office: Solutions Centre, Knightsdale Road, Ipswich, Suffolk, IP1 4JQ
Activities: Wholesale of computers, computer peripheral equipment and software
Parent: IP Telecom Limited
Officers: Sharon Ann Lough, Secretary; Robert Earl Baker [1963] IT Director; Ian Christopher Little [1964] Director/Chartered Accountant; Sharon Ann Lough [1963] Director/Accountant; Guy Francis Watts [1965] Managing Director

GH London Ground Handling Services Limited
Incorporated: 23 May 2012 *Employees:* 520
Previous: Azzurra Ground Handling Services Limited
Net Worth: £1,800,057 *Total Assets:* £9,162,851
Registered Office: 249 Cranbrook Road, Ilford, Essex, IG1 4TG
Activities: Service activities incidental to air transportation
Officers: Paolo de Ruggiero [1968] Director of Operations [Italian]; Vittorio Mazza [1968] Director [Italian]; Marco Tierno [1971] Director [Italian]; Paolo Zincone [1961] Director [Italian]

GHG 11 (Mount Alvernia Hospital) Limited
Incorporated: 18 April 2006
Net Worth Deficit: £34,798,000 *Total Assets:* £41,477,000
Registered Office: Springfield Lodge, Colchester Road, Springfield, Chelmsford, Essex, CM2 5PW
Activities: Other letting and operating of own or leased real estate
Parent: Hospital Midco S.A R.L.
Officers: David Duggins [1955] Director/Business Executive

GHG 12 (Hampshire Clinic) Limited
Incorporated: 18 April 2006
Net Worth Deficit: £16,868,000 *Total Assets:* £48,009,000
Registered Office: Springfield Lodge, Colchester Road, Springfield, Chelmsford, Essex, CM2 5PW
Activities: Other letting and operating of own or leased real estate
Parent: Hospital Midco S.A R.L.
Officers: David Duggins [1955] Director/Business Executive

GHG 13 (Chaucer Hospital) Limited
Incorporated: 18 April 2006
Net Worth Deficit: £16,895,000 *Total Assets:* £30,781,000
Registered Office: Springfield Lodge, Colchester Road, Springfield, Chelmsford, Essex, CM2 5PW
Activities: Other letting and operating of own or leased real estate
Parent: Hospital Midco S.A R.L.
Officers: David Duggins [1955] Director/Business Executive

GHG 14 (Shirley Oaks Hospital) Limited
Incorporated: 18 April 2006
Net Worth Deficit: £15,555,000 *Total Assets:* £32,080,000
Registered Office: Springfield Lodge, Colchester Road, Springfield, Chelmsford, Essex, CM2 5PW
Activities: Other letting and operating of own or leased real estate
Parent: Hospital Midco S.A R.L.
Officers: David Duggins [1955] Director/Business Executive

GHG 15 (Highfield Hospital) Limited
Incorporated: 18 April 2006
Net Worth Deficit: £13,959,000 *Total Assets:* £32,127,000
Registered Office: Springfield Lodge, Colchester Road, Springfield, Chelmsford, Essex, CM2 5PW
Activities: Other letting and operating of own or leased real estate
Parent: Hospital Midco S.A R.L.
Officers: David Duggins [1955] Director/Business Executive

GHG 16 (Chelsfield Park Hospital) Limited
Incorporated: 18 April 2006
Net Worth Deficit: £10,359,000 *Total Assets:* £31,572,000
Registered Office: Springfield Lodge, Colchester Road, Springfield, Chelmsford, Essex, CM2 5PW
Activities: Other letting and operating of own or leased real estate
Parent: Hospital Midco S.A R.L.
Officers: David Duggins [1955] Director/Business Executive

GHG 17 (Ridgeway Hospital) Limited
Incorporated: 18 April 2006
Net Worth: £1,302,000 *Total Assets:* £46,269,000
Registered Office: Springfield Lodge, Colchester Road, Springfield, Chelmsford, Essex, CM2 5PW
Activities: Other letting and operating of own or leased real estate
Parent: Hospital Midco S.A R.L.
Officers: David Duggins [1955] Director/Business Executive

GHG 18 (Saxon Clinic) Limited
Incorporated: 18 April 2006
Net Worth Deficit: £7,519,000 *Total Assets:* £30,262,000
Registered Office: Springfield Lodge, Colchester Road, Springfield, Chelmsford, Essex, CM2 5PW
Activities: Other letting and operating of own or leased real estate
Parent: Hospital Midco S.A R.L.
Officers: David Duggins [1955] Director/Business Executive

GHG 19 (Albyn Hospital) Limited
Incorporated: 18 April 2006
Net Worth: £659,000 *Total Assets:* £39,160,000
Registered Office: Springfield Lodge, Colchester Road, Springfield, Chelmsford, Essex, CM2 5PW
Activities: Other letting and operating of own or leased real estate
Parent: Hospital Midco S.A R.L.
Officers: David Duggins [1955] Director/Business Executive

GHG 2 (Clementine Churchill Hospital) Limited
Incorporated: 18 April 2006
Net Worth Deficit: £70,037,000 *Total Assets:* £124,077,000
Registered Office: Springfield Lodge, Colchester Road, Springfield, Chelmsford, Essex, CM2 5PW
Activities: Other letting and operating of own or leased real estate
Parent: Hospital Midco S.A R.L.
Officers: David Duggins [1955] Director/Business Executive

GHG 20 (Sarum Road Hospital) Limited
Incorporated: 18 April 2006
Net Worth Deficit: £11,982,000 *Total Assets:* £17,853,000
Registered Office: Springfield Lodge, Colchester Road, Springfield, Chelmsford, Essex, CM2 5PW
Activities: Other letting and operating of own or leased real estate
Parent: Hospital Midco S.A R.L.
Officers: David Duggins [1955] Director/Business Executive

GHG 22 (Garden Hospital) Limited
Incorporated: 18 April 2006
Net Worth Deficit: £3,233,000 *Total Assets:* £13,530,000
Registered Office: Springfield Lodge, Colchester Road, Springfield, Chelmsford, Essex, CM2 5PW
Activities: Other letting and operating of own or leased real estate
Parent: Hospital Midco S.A R.L.
Officers: David Duggins [1955] Director/Business Executive

GHG 24 (Sloane Hospital) Limited
Incorporated: 18 April 2006
Net Worth: £5,002,000 *Total Assets:* £18,675,000
Registered Office: Springfield Lodge, Colchester Road, Springfield, Chelmsford, Essex, CM2 5PW
Activities: Other letting and operating of own or leased real estate
Parent: Hospital Midco S.A R.L.
Officers: David Duggins [1955] Director/Business Executive

GHG 25 (Werndale Hospital) Limited
Incorporated: 18 April 2006
Net Worth Deficit: £1,739,000 *Total Assets:* £9,820,000
Registered Office: Springfield Lodge, Colchester Road, Springfield, Chelmsford, Essex, CM2 5PW
Activities: Other letting and operating of own or leased real estate
Parent: Hospital Midco S.A R.L.
Officers: David Duggins [1955] Director/Business Executive

GHG 26 (Beardwood Hospital) Limited
Incorporated: 18 April 2006
Net Worth: £4,211,000 *Total Assets:* £14,874,000
Registered Office: Springfield Lodge, Colchester Road, Springfield, Chelmsford, Essex, CM2 5PW
Activities: Other letting and operating of own or leased real estate
Parent: Hospital Midco S.A R.L.
Officers: David Duggins [1955] Director/Business Executive

GHG 28 (Manor Hospital) Limited
Incorporated: 18 April 2006
Net Worth Deficit: £549,000 *Total Assets:* £8,315,000
Registered Office: Springfield Lodge, Colchester Road, Springfield, Chelmsford, Essex, CM2 5PW
Activities: Other letting and operating of own or leased real estate
Parent: Hospital Midco S.A R.L.
Officers: David Duggins [1955] Director/Business Executive

GHG 3 (Ross Hall Hospital) Limited
Incorporated: 18 April 2006
Net Worth Deficit: £56,660,000 *Total Assets:* £112,766,000
Registered Office: Springfield Lodge, Colchester Road, Springfield, Chelmsford, Essex, CM2 5PW
Activities: Other letting and operating of own or leased real estate
Parent: Hospital Midco S.A R.L.
Officers: David Duggins [1955] Director/Business Executive

GHG 31 (Blackheath Hospital) Limited
Incorporated: 18 April 2006
Net Worth Deficit: £26,747,000 *Total Assets:* £49,633,000
Registered Office: Springfield Lodge, Colchester Road, Springfield, Chelmsford, Essex, CM2 5PW
Activities: Other letting and operating of own or leased real estate
Parent: Hospital Midco S.A R.L.
Officers: David Duggins [1955] Director/Business Executive

GHG 32 (Goring Hall Hospital) Limited
Incorporated: 18 April 2006
Net Worth Deficit: £2,085,000 *Total Assets:* £29,452,000
Registered Office: Springfield Lodge, Colchester Road, Springfield, Chelmsford, Essex, CM2 5PW
Activities: Other letting and operating of own or leased real estate
Parent: Hospital Midco S.A R.L.
Officers: David Duggins [1955] Director/Business Executive

GHG 33 (Beaumont Hospital) Limited
Incorporated: 18 April 2006
Net Worth: £952,000 *Total Assets:* £17,927,000
Registered Office: Springfield Lodge, Colchester Road, Springfield, Chelmsford, Essex, CM2 5PW
Activities: Other letting and operating of own or leased real estate
Parent: Hospital Midco S.A R.L.
Officers: David Duggins [1955] Director/Business Executive

GHG 34 (Priory Hospital) Limited
Incorporated: 18 April 2006
Net Worth Deficit: £91,888,000 *Total Assets:* £89,559,000
Registered Office: Springfield Lodge, Colchester Road, Springfield, Chelmsford, Essex, CM2 5PW
Activities: Other letting and operating of own or leased real estate
Parent: Hospital Midco S.A R.L.
Officers: David Duggins [1955] Director/Business Executive

GHG 35 (Droitwich Spa Hospital) Limited
Incorporated: 18 April 2006
Net Worth Deficit: £7,510,000 *Total Assets:* £22,101,000
Registered Office: Springfield Lodge, Colchester Road, Springfield, Chelmsford, Essex, CM2 5PW
Activities: Other letting and operating of own or leased real estate
Parent: Hospital Midco S.A R.L.
Officers: David Duggins [1955] Director/Business Executive

GHG 36 (Winterbourne Hospital) Limited
Incorporated: 18 April 2006
Net Worth Deficit: £7,329,000 *Total Assets:* £26,355,000
Registered Office: Springfield Lodge, Colchester Road, Springfield, Chelmsford, Essex, CM2 5PW
Activities: Other letting and operating of own or leased real estate
Parent: Hospital Midco S.A R.L.
Officers: David Duggins [1955] Director/Business Executive

GHG 37 (Alexandra Hospital) Limited
Incorporated: 18 April 2006
Net Worth Deficit: £162,216,000 *Total Assets:* £187,176,992
Registered Office: Springfield Lodge, Colchester Road, Springfield, Chelmsford, Essex, CM2 5PW
Activities: Other letting and operating of own or leased real estate
Parent: Hospital Midco S.A R.L.
Officers: David Duggins [1955] Director/Business Executive

GHG 4 (Princess Margaret Hospital) Limited
Incorporated: 18 April 2006
Net Worth Deficit: £31,115,000 *Total Assets:* £75,675,000
Registered Office: Springfield Lodge, Colchester Road, Springfield, Chelmsford, Essex, CM2 5PW
Activities: Other letting and operating of own or leased real estate
Parent: Hospital Midco S.A R.L.
Officers: David Duggins [1955] Director/Business Executive

GHG 5 (London Independent Hospital) Limited
Incorporated: 18 April 2006
Net Worth Deficit: £16,888,000 *Total Assets:* £70,235,000
Registered Office: Springfield Lodge, Colchester Road, Springfield, Chelmsford, Essex, CM2 5PW
Activities: Other letting and operating of own or leased real estate
Parent: Hospital Midco S.A R.L.
Officers: David Duggins [1955] Director/Business Executive

GHG 6 (Thornbury Hospital) Limited
Incorporated: 18 April 2006
Net Worth Deficit: £47,848,000 *Total Assets:* £48,506,000
Registered Office: Springfield Lodge, Colchester Road, Springfield, Chelmsford, Essex, CM2 5PW
Activities: Other letting and operating of own or leased real estate
Parent: Hospital Midco S.A R.L.
Officers: David Duggins [1955] Director/Business Executive

GHG 7 (Chiltern Hospital) Limited
Incorporated: 18 April 2006
Net Worth Deficit: £28,710,000 *Total Assets:* £76,218,000
Registered Office: Springfield Lodge, Colchester Road, Springfield, Chelmsford, Essex, CM2 5PW
Activities: Other letting and operating of own or leased real estate
Parent: Hospital Midco S.A R.L.
Officers: David Duggins [1955] Director/Business Executive

GHG 8 (Park Hospital) Limited
Incorporated: 18 April 2006
Net Worth Deficit: £39,167,000 *Total Assets:* £63,514,000
Registered Office: Springfield Lodge, Colchester Road, Springfield, Chelmsford, Essex, CM2 5PW
Activities: Other letting and operating of own or leased real estate
Parent: Hospital Midco S.A R.L.
Officers: David Duggins [1955] Director/Business Executive

GHG 9 (Bath Clinic) Limited
Incorporated: 18 April 2006
Net Worth Deficit: £57,212,000 *Total Assets:* £33,564,000
Registered Office: Springfield Lodge, Colchester Road, Springfield, Chelmsford, Essex, CM2 5PW
Activities: Other letting and operating of own or leased real estate
Parent: Hospital Midco S.A R.L.
Officers: David Duggins [1955] Director/Business Executive

GHL (Crescent Lane) Limited
Incorporated: 9 May 2014
Net Worth Deficit: £887,303 *Total Assets:* £9,001,030
Registered Office: 3rd Floor, Sterling House, Langston Road, Loughton, Essex, IG10 3TS
Activities: Development of building projects
Shareholders: Aria Investments Limited; Galliard Holdings Limited
Officers: Allan William Porter, Secretary; David Edward Conway [1976] Director; Stephen Stuart Solomon Conway [1948] Director; Jonathan Michael Morgan [1978] Director

GHL (Kilmorie) Limited
Incorporated: 12 July 2017
Net Worth Deficit: £116,026 *Total Assets:* £11,403,809
Registered Office: 3rd Floor, Sterling House, Langston Road, Loughton, Essex, IG10 3TS
Activities: Development of building projects
Parent: Galliard Holdings Limited
Officers: Allan William Porter, Secretary; David Edward Conway [1976] Director; Stephen Stuart Solomon Conway [1948] Director; Donagh O'Sullivan [1968] Construction Director [Irish]

GHL (Summerstown) Limited
Incorporated: 8 November 2017
Net Worth Deficit: £29,119 *Total Assets:* £10,332,428
Registered Office: 3rd Floor, Sterling House, Langston Road, Loughton, Essex, IG10 3TS
Activities: Development of building projects
Parent: Galliard Holdings Limited
Officers: Allan William Porter, Secretary; Stephen Stuart Solomon Conway [1948] Director; Donagh O'Sullivan [1968] Construction Director [Irish]

Gibbons (Holdings) Limited
Incorporated: 4 January 1996 *Employees:* 6
Net Worth: £26,415,372 *Total Assets:* £27,881,952
Registered Office: Manor Farm, Baston, Peterborough, Cambs, PE6 9PB
Activities: Growing of cereals (except rice), leguminous crops and oil seeds
Major Shareholder: David John Gibbons
Officers: Andrew Colin Eason, Secretary; David John Gibbons [1951] Managing Director

Robert Gibbs (Contracting) Company Limited
Incorporated: 9 December 1986 *Employees:* 61
Net Worth: £10,370,444 *Total Assets:* £13,294,702
Registered Office: Bridge Works, Normandy Way, off Pindar Road, Hoddesdon, Herts, EN11 0EW
Activities: Wholesale of waste and scrap
Shareholders: Barry Albert Elvidge; Howard Victor Jones
Officers: Barry Albert Elvidge, Secretary; Howard Victor Jones, Secretary/Scrap Metal Merchant; David Maskell [1966] Director

Gibbs Denley Holdings Limited
Incorporated: 22 May 2017
Net Worth: £4,659,871 *Total Assets:* £9,069,830
Registered Office: Crystal House, Buckingway Business Park, Swavesey, Cambridge, CB24 4UL
Activities: Activities of financial services holding companies
Major Shareholder: Mark Norman Denley
Officers: Mark Norman Denley [1963] Director/Financial Adviser; David Richard Ellis [1961] Director; Simon Rees [1989] Director

Gibson Bidco Limited
Incorporated: 8 April 2016 *Employees:* 2
Net Worth: £9,807,000 *Total Assets:* £10,194,000
Registered Office: Regal House, Royal Crescent, Ilford, Essex, IG2 7JY
Activities: Activities of other holding companies n.e.c.
Parent: Gibson Topco Limited
Officers: Harnoop Singh Atkar [1986] Director; Daren Dalmedo [1978] Director

Gibson Developments Limited
Incorporated: 30 April 1973 *Employees:* 5
Net Worth: £7,995,845 *Total Assets:* £12,027,817
Registered Office: 341 Hills Road, Cambridge, CB2 0QT
Activities: Development of building projects
Parent: Gibson Holdings Ltd
Officers: Alfred James Griffiths, Secretary; David Richard Gibson [1971] Director/Marketing Consultant; Evelyn Margaret Gibson [1947] Director/Personal Secretary; Peter Alan Gibson [1976] Director/Electrical Design Engineer; Richard Byron Gibson [1946] Director/Heating Engineer; Alfred James Griffiths [1951] Director/Accountant; Alison Lee Ratcliffe [1973] Director; Benjamin John Ratcliffe [1973] Development Director

Thomas Gibson Fine Art Limited
Incorporated: 26 August 1970 *Employees:* 5
Net Worth: £5,626,908 *Total Assets:* £9,049,142
Registered Office: 19 Coombehurst Close, Hadley Wood, Herts, EN4 0JU
Activities: Retail sale in commercial art galleries
Major Shareholder: Benjamin Hugh George Gibson
Officers: Benjamin Hugh George Gibson [1973] Director

Gibson Propco Limited
Incorporated: 15 April 2016 *Employees:* 2
Net Worth: £8,928,000 *Total Assets:* £24,043,000
Registered Office: Regal House, Royal Crescent, Ilford, Essex, IG2 7JY
Activities: Activities of other holding companies n.e.c.
Parent: Gibson Bidco Limited
Officers: Harnoop Singh Atkar [1986] Director; Daren Dalmedo [1978] Director

Gilbertson & Page Limited
Incorporated: 24 January 1898 *Employees:* 85
Previous: Gilbertson & Page,Limited
Net Worth: £9,036,882 *Total Assets:* £16,385,766
Registered Office: 45-55 Brownfields, Welwyn Garden City, Herts, AL7 1AN
Activities: Manufacture of prepared feeds for farm animals
Shareholder: Richard Ivor Wakefield Ware
Officers: Kim Kong Wong, Secretary; Richard Godfrey Battersby [1942] Director; Alexander Joseph Dale [1957] Operations Director; James Andrew Harris [1971] Director; Christopher Arthur Cory Ware [1972] Director; Richard Ivor Wakefield Ware [1939] Director; Kim Kong Wong [1959] Financial Director [Malaysian]

Gilead Sciences International Ltd.
Incorporated: 25 March 1996 *Employees:* 198
Net Worth: £25,787,000 *Total Assets:* £46,055,000
Registered Office: Flowers Building, Granta Park, Abington, Cambridge, CB21 6GT
Activities: Other business support service activities n.e.c.
Parent: Gilead Sciences, Inc.
Officers: Johanna Henry, Secretary; Rudolf Ertl [1960] Director [German]; Gwenaelle Marie Jose Patrick Pemberton [1965] Director [French]; Brett Pletcher [1968] Director [American]; Robin Washington [1962] Director [American]

The Giles Academy
Incorporated: 20 August 2010 *Employees:* 165
Net Worth: £12,988,601 *Total Assets:* £14,631,260
Registered Office: The Giles Academy, Church End, Old Leake, Boston, Lincs, PE22 9LD
Activities: General secondary education
Officers: Diane Patricia Burrell, Secretary; Helen Theresa Banham [1967] Director; Albert Guy Bull [1953] Director; Alan Castley [1959] Director/Teacher; Roy Timothy Cowern [1953] Director/Retired; Sophie Curtis [1996] Director/Sales & Marketing Executive; Maxine Hill [1957] Director/Florist; Geoffrey Martin Prior [1951] Director/Business Manager; David Relton [1957] Director/Teacher of Design Technology; Sarah Anwen Whelbourn [1961] Director; Ian Charles Widdows [1968] Director/Headteacher

T Gilmartin Holdings Limited
Incorporated: 15 September 2016 *Employees:* 144
Net Worth: £4,956,561 *Total Assets:* £9,800,848
Registered Office: c/o Hillier Hopkins LLP, First Floor, Radius House, 51 Clarendon Road, Watford, Herts, WD17 1HP
Activities: Activities of other holding companies n.e.c.
Major Shareholder: Terence Martin Gilmartin
Officers: Terence Martin Gilmartin [1965] Director

Gilmore Jacobs Limited
Incorporated: 13 September 2000
Net Worth: £75,990,832 *Total Assets:* £77,194,880
Registered Office: 7 Nelson Street, Southend on Sea, Essex, SS1 1EH
Activities: Artistic creation
Shareholder: Daniel Jacob Radcliffe
Officers: Marcia Genine Gresham Radcliffe, Secretary; Marcia Genine Gresham Radcliffe [1957] Casting Director; Alan George Radcliffe [1959] Director

Gippeswyk Community Educational Trust
Incorporated: 3 June 2011 *Employees:* 262
Previous: Copleston High School
Net Worth: £15,468,215 *Total Assets:* £17,385,916
Registered Office: Copleston High School, Copleston Road, Ipswich, Suffolk, IP4 5HD
Activities: General secondary education
Officers: Tracey Ann Goodchild, Secretary; Matthew William Capp [1969] Director/Business Analyst; Shaun Common [1962] Director/Headteacher; Valerie Lamond-Mattocks [1958] Director/Senior Audit Services Manager; Willaim Robinson [1946] Director/Retired; Roger Gayford Smith [1938] Director; Robert Brian Wade [1949] Director/Retired; Andrew Charles Wright [1976] Director/Software Engineer

Girls' Education Company,Limited
Incorporated: 21 February 1896 *Employees:* 303
Net Worth: £49,932,000 *Total Assets:* £61,070,000
Registered Office: Wycombe Abbey School, High Wycombe, Bucks, HP11 1PE
Activities: General secondary education
Officers: Niall Thomas Campbell, Secretary; Richard Harrington Ashby [1949] Director & Chartered Surveyor; Jeremy William Bailey [1955] Director/Investment Banker; Sue Carr [1964] Director/Barrister QC; Dr Louise L'estrange Fawcett Posada [1955] Director/Fellow, University Lecturer; Dr Carolyn Jane Godlee [1956] Director/General Practitioner; Simon Charles Henderson [1975] Director/Headmaster; John Patrick Lewis [1965] Director/Retailer; David Peter Lillycrop [1956] Director; Dr Margaret Jane MacDougall [1958] Director/Consultant Gynaecologist; Diana Rose [1955] Director/Headteacher; Lady Sarah Caroline Ray Sassoon [1955] Director/Textile Manufacturer & Consultant; Patrick Philip Sherrington [1951] Director/Solicitor; Alan Thomas Lawrence Wilson [1955] Director/Bishop; Richard Thomas George Winter [1963] Director/Chartered Accountant

Girton Town Charity
Incorporated: 28 May 2009 *Employees:* 2
Net Worth: £35,057,000 *Total Assets:* £35,382,000
Registered Office: Girton Town Charity, 1 Fairway, Girton, Cambs, CB3 0QF
Activities: Other business support service activities n.e.c.
Officers: Marc Alain Bermann [1968] Director/Self Employed [Australian/French]; Rita Ann Bonnett [1952] Director/Design Consultant; Raymond William Gordon [1938] Director/Retired; Vivian Yvonne Higgons [1950] Director/Management Consultant; Dr Charles Robin Hiley [1948] Director/Retired; Jennifer Mary Knights [1951] Director/Retired; Brian Ernest Pycock [1946] Director/Retired; Patricia Jean Smith [1958] Director/Retired; Philippa Temple [1948] Director/Company Secretary

Gita Properties Limited
Incorporated: 5 January 1968 *Employees:* 7
Net Worth: £24,510,924 *Total Assets:* £28,789,296
Registered Office: Treviot House, 186-192 High Road, Ilford, Essex, IG1 1LR
Activities: Buying and selling of own real estate
Shareholders: Joseph Henri Szlezinger; Kathrin Jane Szlezinger
Officers: Kathrine Jane Szlezinger, Secretary; Jason Szlezinger [1970] Director; Joseph Henri Szlezinger [1935] Managing Director; Kathrine Jane Szlezinger [1944] Director/Secretary

Geo. E. Gittus & Sons Limited
Incorporated: 24 February 1958 *Employees:* 29
Net Worth: £5,719,176 *Total Assets:* £16,359,677
Registered Office: Windsor Wood House, Little Saxham, Bury St Edmunds, Suffolk, IP29 5LA
Activities: Growing of cereals (except rice), leguminous crops and oil seeds
Officers: George Frederick Gough Gittus, Secretary/Farmer/Director; Ethne Diana Gittus [1941] Director/Farmer; George Frederick Gough Gittus [1965] Farmer/Director; Richard Alan Gittus [1967] Director; Malcolm Glen McAllister [1947] Director/Management Consultant; Ian Mighell Monks [1960] Director/Chartered Surveyor; Mark James Ben Wells [1973] Director/Farming

GK Foods (UK) Limited
Incorporated: 10 January 2007
Net Worth: £12,909,000 *Total Assets:* £12,909,000
Registered Office: Grace House, Bessemer Road, Welwyn Garden City, Herts, AL7 1HW
Activities: Other food services
Officers: Khine Oo, Secretary; Andrea Denise Lewis-Coy [1970] Director/Chief Executive, Gracekennedy Foods International [Jamaican]; Brian Anthony Mitchell [1983] Director/Chief Financial Officer [Jamaican]

Gladstone Court Developments Limited
Incorporated: 24 April 2012
Net Worth Deficit: £28,421,760 *Total Assets:* £48,541,488
Registered Office: 3rd Floor, Sterling House, Langston Road, Loughton, Essex, IG10 3TS
Activities: Other business support service activities n.e.c.
Parent: Gladstone Holdings Limited
Officers: Allan William Porter, Secretary; David Edward Conway [1976] Director; Stephen Stuart Solomon Conway [1948] Director; Donagh O'Sullivan [1968] Construction Director [Irish]

Glasswells Limited
Incorporated: 3 April 1958 *Employees:* 289
Net Worth: £32,065,304 *Total Assets:* £40,298,344
Registered Office: Glasswells, Newmarket Road, Bury St Edmunds, Suffolk, IP33 3TU
Activities: Retail sale of carpets, rugs, wall and floor coverings in specialised stores
Major Shareholder: Paul Jeremy Glasswell
Officers: Fiona Jane Glasswell [1957] Director/Buyer; Heather June Glasswell [1931] Director/Housewife; Paul Jeremy Glasswell [1958] Director/House Furnisher; Peggy Edith Reardon [1929] Director/Housewife; Kevin William Robertson [1967] Sales Director

Glastry Advisory Partners Limited
Incorporated: 20 November 2012 *Employees:* 1
Net Worth: £16,128,881 *Total Assets:* £16,196,895
Registered Office: 5 Elstree Gate, Elstree Way, Borehamwood, Herts, WD6 1JD
Activities: Management consultancy activities other than financial management
Major Shareholder: Joyce Anne Smyth
Officers: Joyce Anne Smyth [1957] Director/Solicitor

Glazewing Limited
Incorporated: 15 April 1986 *Employees:* 82
Net Worth: £181,901 *Total Assets:* £9,882,679
Registered Office: Glazewing House, Station Road, West Dereham, Kings Lynn, Norfolk, PE33 9RR
Activities: Wholesale of waste and scrap
Parent: Valens Resources Group PLC
Officers: Simon David Miles, Secretary/Chartered Accountant; Jonathan Miles [1963] Director; Simon David Miles [1960] Director/Chartered Accountant; Jason Minns [1976] Director/Accountant

Glazing Vision Limited
Incorporated: 4 November 1994 *Employees:* 142
Net Worth: £4,388,518 *Total Assets:* £8,346,891
Registered Office: Glazing Vision Limited, Saw Mills Road, Diss, Norfolk, IP22 4RG
Activities: Manufacture of doors and windows of metal
Parent: Visiongroup (GB) Limited
Officers: Andrew Rochford, Secretary; Jeremy Paul Dunn [1962] Director/Business Manager; Andrew Rochford [1975] Finance Director; Kevin James Shaw [1958] Director; Jonathan William Shooter [1976] Director/Business Manager; Ian Edward Andrew Wyatt [1951] Director/Chartered Accountant

Glenageary Estates LLP
Incorporated: 26 February 2008
Net Worth: £11,097,579 *Total Assets:* £11,102,064
Registered Office: 4 Elstree Gate, Elstree Way, Borehamwood, Herts, WD6 1JD

Glenchamber Wind Energy Limited
Incorporated: 8 April 2014
Net Worth Deficit: £10,402,000 *Total Assets:* £61,071,000
Registered Office: Beaufort Court, Egg Farm Lane, Kings Langley, Herts, WD4 8LR
Activities: Production of electricity
Parent: Boreas Energy Limited
Officers: Dominic James Heath, Secretary; Peter Edward Dias [1981] Director; Christopher Peter Gaydon [1978] Director [Hungarian]; Paul Stephen Latham [1956] Director; Thomas James Rosser [1985] Director

Gleneden Plant Sales Limited
Incorporated: 7 December 1998 *Employees:* 12
Net Worth: £5,007,289 *Total Assets:* £10,867,942
Registered Office: 46-48 Rothesay Road, Luton, Beds, LU1 1QZ
Activities: Wholesale of other machinery and equipment
Major Shareholder: Raymond Charles Gill
Officers: Sinead Gill, Secretary; Raymond Charles Gill [1964] Director/Sales Manager

Glenmark Pharmaceuticals Europe Limited
Incorporated: 10 February 2004 *Employees:* 83
Net Worth: £12,932,667 *Total Assets:* £50,697,828
Registered Office: Laxmi House, 2B Draycott Avenue, Kenton, Harrow, Middlesex, HA3 0BU
Activities: Wholesale of pharmaceutical goods
Shareholders: Blanche Saldanha; Cherylann Pinto; Glenn Saldanha
Officers: Fiona Hill, Secretary; Oliver Henry Bourne [1980] Director; Achin Gupta [1976] Director [Indian]

Global Chair Components Limited
Incorporated: 21 February 1996 *Employees:* 45
Net Worth: £2,873,910 *Total Assets:* £10,985,535
Registered Office: 1 Global Court, Reydon Business Park, Southwold, Suffolk, IP18 6SY
Activities: Wholesale of office furniture
Parent: Glochair Holdings Ltd
Officers: Justin Peter Renwick Adams [1965] Director; Darryl John Dawson [1950] Director [Irish]; David Darryl Dawson [1978] Director [Irish]; Alex Mark Moller [1975] Director [Danish]; Peter Thomas Small [1953] Technical Sales Director; Ian Andrew Watson [1972] Director; Edward Neil Yeldham [1975] Director

Global Education Management Systems Limited
Incorporated: 23 April 2003 *Employees:* 282
Net Worth Deficit: £82,358,184 *Total Assets:* £48,202,720
Registered Office: 100 Hills Road, Cambridge, CB2 1PH
Activities: Other business support service activities n.e.c.
Officers: Cherusseril Narayanan Nair Radhakrishnan [1956] Executive Director [Indian]; Jay Varkey [1984] Director [Indian]

Global Graphics (UK) Limited
Incorporated: 4 January 1993
Net Worth: £1,232,014 *Total Assets:* £8,673,429
Registered Office: 2nd Floor, Building 2030, Cambourne Business Park, Cambourne, Cambridge, CB23 6DW
Activities: Activities of head offices
Parent: Global Graphics PLC
Officers: Graeme Redgrave Huttley, Secretary; Gary Peter Fry [1968] Director/Chief Executive Officer; Graeme Redgrave Huttley [1972] Director/Chartered Accountant

Global Graphics PLC
Incorporated: 23 December 2013 *Employees:* 112
Net Worth: £16,678,912 *Total Assets:* £23,807,400
Registered Office: 2030 Cambourne Business Park, Cambourne, Cambridge, CB23 6DW
Activities: Activities of head offices
Officers: Graeme Huttley, Secretary; Clare Findlay [1962] Director; Gary Peter Fry [1968] Director; Graeme Redgrave Huttley [1972] Director; Guido Van Der Schueren [1952] Director [Belgian]

Global Graphics Software Limited
Incorporated: 26 August 1986 *Employees:* 61
Net Worth: £23,371,500 *Total Assets:* £24,995,400
Registered Office: 2nd Floor, Building 2030, Cambourne Business Park, Cambourne, Cambridge, CB23 6DW
Activities: Business and domestic software development
Parent: Global Graphics (UK) Ltd
Officers: Graeme Redgrave Huttley, Secretary; Gary Peter Fry [1968] Director/Chief Executive Officer; Graeme Redgrave Huttley [1972] Director/Chartered Accountant

Global Group (UK) Ltd
Incorporated: 25 August 2006 *Employees:* 4
Net Worth: £197,000 *Total Assets:* £12,943,000
Registered Office: 800 The Boulevard, Capability Green, Luton, Beds, LU1 3BA
Activities: Other business support service activities n.e.c.
Parent: Medacs Global Group Limited
Officers: Rebecca Jane Watson, Secretary; Nigel Marsh [1962] Director; Julia Robertson [1958] Director; Rebecca Jane Watson [1969] Director/Solicitor

Global Marine Holdings Limited
Incorporated: 14 January 2002 *Employees:* 413
Previous: Bridgehouse Marine Limited
Net Worth: £197,213,168 *Total Assets:* £315,619,040
Registered Office: Ocean House, 1 Winsford Way, Boreham Interchange, Chelmsford, Essex, CM2 5PD
Activities: Other business support service activities n.e.c.
Parent: Global Marine Holdings LLC
Officers: Jaime Violet Cable, Secretary; Wayne Barr [1964] Director/Business Executive [American]; Dick Helgeson Fagerstal [1960] Director/Business Executive [American/Swedish]; Michael Sena [1973] Director [American]

Global Marine Systems (Vessels) Limited
Incorporated: 18 January 2007
Net Worth: £23,147,492 *Total Assets:* £23,147,494
Registered Office: Ocean House, 1 Winsford Way, Boreham Interchange, Chelmsford, Essex, CM2 5PD
Activities: Sea and coastal freight water transport
Parent: Global Marine Systems Limited
Officers: Jaime Violet Cable, Secretary; Ian David Douglas [1968] Managing Director; Richard Fraser-Smith [1964] Director

Global Marine Systems Limited
Incorporated: 22 March 1983 *Employees:* 413
Net Worth: £210,300,672 *Total Assets:* £322,786,080
Registered Office: Ocean House, 1 Winsford Way, Boreham Interchange, Chelmsford, Essex, CM2 5PD
Activities: Other specialised construction activities n.e.c.
Parent: Global Marine Holdings Limited
Officers: Jaime Violet Cable, Secretary; Ian Peter Bryan [1960] Director; Michael John Daniel [1956] Managing Director; Ian David Douglas [1968] Managing Director; Dick Fagerstal [1960] Director [American]; Richard Fraser-Smith [1964] Director; Bruce James Neilson-Watts [1970] Director

Global Medics Limited
Incorporated: 22 May 2002 *Employees:* 40
Net Worth Deficit: £7,438,000 *Total Assets:* £9,373,000
Registered Office: 800 The Boulevard, Capability Green, Luton, Beds, LU1 3BA
Activities: Temporary employment agency activities
Parent: Global Group (UK) Ltd
Officers: Rebecca Jane Watson, Secretary; Nigel Marsh [1962] Director; Julia Robertson [1958] Director; Rebecca Jane Watson [1969] Director/Solicitor

Global Metcorp Limited
Incorporated: 30 August 2001 *Employees:* 17
Net Worth: £10,149,544 *Total Assets:* £41,590,520
Registered Office: Grove House, 55 Lowlands Road, Harrow on the Hill, Middlesex, HA1 3AW
Activities: Wholesale of waste and scrap
Parent: Greta Investments Limited
Officers: Ritesh Shah, Secretary; Ashish Chaudhari [1979] Director [Indian]; Gaurav Chaudhary [1984] Director [Indian]; Rajan Choudhary [1985] Director [Indian]

Global Resale, Ltd
Incorporated: 17 February 2016 *Employees:* 47
Net Worth: £421,993 *Total Assets:* £14,125,037
Registered Office: Unit 620 Skyline 120, Braintree, Essex, CM77 7AA
Activities: Other information technology service activities
Major Shareholder: Andrew Seth Weinberg
Officers: Ronak Amin [1989] Director/Finance [American]; Christopher Farrell [1979] Director/General Manager; Thomas J. Meredith [1950] Director/Finance (Senior Partner) [American]; Jeffrey Kyle Stouder [1971] Director [American]; Andrew Seth Weinberg [1974] Director/Finance (Managing Partner) [American]; Jeffrey Allan Zeigler [1970] Director/Entrepreneur [American]

Global Resources Investment Trust PLC
Incorporated: 16 October 2012
Net Worth: £8,250,000 *Total Assets:* £8,333,000
Registered Office: Springfield Lodge, Colchester Road, Springfield, Chelmsford, Essex, CM2 5PW
Activities: Activities of investment trusts
Officers: Simon James Farrell [1950] Director [Australian]; Haruko Fukuda OBE [1946] Director; David James Hutchins [1960] Director; David Albert Lloyd Johnston [1956] Director [Australian]; Jonathan Richard Reynolds [1966] Director [Australian]

Global Ridgeway Holdings Limited
Incorporated: 25 October 2011
Net Worth: £8,199,077 *Total Assets:* £8,216,143
Registered Office: Unit B2, Basepoint Business Centre, 110 Butterfield, Great Marlings, Luton, Beds, LU2 8DL
Activities: Activities of head offices
Major Shareholder: Shay Jacob Reches
Officers: Robert John Bygrave [1970] Director/Accountant; Shay Jacob Reches [1955] Director [Israeli]

Global Self Drive Limited
Incorporated: 5 December 1995 *Employees:* 44
Net Worth: £2,890,433 *Total Assets:* £35,909,784
Registered Office: Global House, Saville Road, Peterborough, PE3 7PR
Activities: Renting and leasing of cars and light motor vehicles
Parent: CCW 600 Limited
Officers: Fraser Alexander Winchester Morrison, Secretary/Accountant; Christopher Charles Webb [1971] Director/Manager

Glorious Solutions Limited
Incorporated: 7 May 2009 *Employees:* 43
Net Worth: £3,111,186 *Total Assets:* £20,526,442
Registered Office: Media Park, 40b River Road, Barking, Essex, IG11 0DW
Activities: Activities of other holding companies n.e.c.
Officers: Ofir Mor, Secretary; Ofir Mor [1969] Director/Sales Manager

Go Homes Ltd
Incorporated: 19 September 2006 *Employees:* 9
Net Worth: £1,563,597 *Total Assets:* £16,853,836
Registered Office: Bonks Hill House, Bonks Hill, High Wych Road, Sawbridgeworth, Herts, CM21 9HT
Activities: Development of building projects
Officers: Zeana Instance, Secretary; Oliver Hookway [1970] Finance Director; Nigel Stewart Noel Tedder [1966] Technical Director

Go Interiors Limited
Incorporated: 19 October 2001 *Employees:* 89
Net Worth: £3,563,691 *Total Assets:* £16,250,010
Registered Office: Unit 5 Humphrys Road, Woodside Industrial Estate, Dunstable, Beds, LU5 4TP
Activities: Non-specialised wholesale trade
Parent: Invesco Capita Holdings Limited
Officers: Gerard Aidan Abbott-Drake [1968] Director; Jeremy Anker [1971] Financial Director; Brendan Peter Dunne [1974] Sales Director; John Mark O'Leary [1955] Director

Godstowe Preparatory School Company Limited (The)
Incorporated: 20 December 1900 *Employees:* 123
Net Worth: £9,217,199 *Total Assets:* £11,947,864
Registered Office: Godstowe Preparatory School, Shrubbery Road, High Wycombe, Bucks, HP13 6PR
Activities: Primary education
Shareholder: Kathryn Ann Allner
Officers: Michael John Tebbot, Secretary/Architect; Kathryn Ann Allner [1960] Director; Nichola Amanda Caroline Annable [1963] Director; Martin William Ashworth [1964] Director; Janet Brent [1947] Director/Doctor; Nicola Lee Lindsay Kemp [1960] Director/Parish Councillor; Tara Louise Leaver [1969] Director; Linda Anne Poore [1953] Director; Thomas William Richardson-Bunbury [1965] Director/Headmaster; Michael John Tebbot [1947] Director/Architect; Andrew Mark Wilkinson [1976] Director; Stephanie Christine Forester Young [1985] Director/Solicitor

Gog Magog Partnership LLP
Incorporated: 21 February 2012
Net Worth: £12,528,000 *Total Assets:* £42,817,000
Registered Office: The Power House, Gunpowder Mill, Powdermill Lane, Waltham Abbey, Essex, EN9 1BN

Goldstar Transport Holdings Limited
Incorporated: 9 March 2016
Net Worth: £1,000 *Total Assets:* £43,354,924
Registered Office: Goldstar Transport Holdings Limited, Parker Avenue, Felixstowe, Suffolk, IP11 4HF
Activities: Activities of distribution holding companies
Parent: Turners (Soham) Limited
Officers: Jason Marc Andrews [1971] Director/General Manager; Matthew John Ashworth [1965] Director; Paul Edwin Day [1958] Director; Simon John Day [1970] Director; Winifred Mary Day [1934] Director; Anthony Lewis Stafford [1972] Director/General Manager; Mark John Walsh [1973] Director/General Manager

Goldstar Transport Limited
Incorporated: 27 July 1994 *Employees:* 698
Net Worth: £23,734,224 *Total Assets:* £65,369,708
Registered Office: Goldstar Transport Limited, Parker Avenue, Felixstowe, Suffolk, IP11 4HF
Activities: Freight transport by road
Parent: Goldstar Transport Holdings Limited
Officers: Matthew John Ashworth, Secretary; Matthew John Ashworth [1965] Director; Derek Cawston [1969] Director; Simon John Day [1970] Director; Tony Robert Harman [1966] Director/Road Haulage; Simon David Underwood [1970] Director/Road Haulage

Golf Entertainment International Limited
Incorporated: 22 December 2003
Net Worth: £48,893,816 *Total Assets:* £48,893,816
Registered Office: Kinetic House, Theobold Street, Elstree, Herts, WD6 4PJ
Activities: Operation of sports facilities
Parent: Topgolf UK Holdings Limited Partnership
Officers: Kieren Charles Mildwaters, Secretary; Eldridge Allen Burns [1969] Director/General Counsel [American]; William Barry Davenport [1971] Finance Director [American]

Gonville Hotels Limited
Incorporated: 15 October 1962 *Employees:* 39
Net Worth: £7,882,338 *Total Assets:* £8,806,158
Registered Office: The Gonville Hotel, Cambridge, CB1 1LY
Activities: Hotels and similar accommodation
Parent: The Abington Group Limited
Officers: Hilary Ann Russell, Secretary/Director; Peter Simeon Bradford [1968] Director; David John Harold Chaplin [1963] Director/Finance Manager; Simon Robert Frank Chaplin [1967] Director/Farmer; Hilary Ann Russell [1965] Director

Good for Food Limited
Incorporated: 22 August 2013 *Employees:* 1
Net Worth: £3,884,871 *Total Assets:* £10,715,997
Registered Office: 42 Lytton Road, Barnet, Herts, EN5 5BY
Activities: Other letting and operating of own or leased real estate
Shareholders: Wayne Michael Selt; Lewis Selt
Officers: Lewis Selt [1963] Director; Wayne Michael Selt [1958] Director

Good Harvest Group Limited
Incorporated: 8 July 1996 *Employees:* 4
Net Worth: £32,322,438 *Total Assets:* £49,967,744
Registered Office: Old Barn House, High Road, Eastcote, Pinner, Middlesex, HA5 2EW
Activities: Other letting and operating of own or leased real estate
Officers: Michael Richard Cowen, Secretary; Paul Allan Beer [1948] Director/Chartered Accountant; Michael Richard Cowen [1961] Director/Chief Financial Officer; Anthony Ronald William Parfitt [1952] Director/Chartered Accountant

Good Harvest Properties (Southwark) Limited
Incorporated: 11 August 2004
Net Worth: £9,841,946 *Total Assets:* £14,631,545
Registered Office: Old Barn House, High Road, Eastcote, Pinner, Middlesex, HA5 2EW
Activities: Other letting and operating of own or leased real estate
Parent: Good Harvest Group Limited
Officers: Michael Richard Cowen, Secretary; Paul Allan Beer [1948] Director/Chartered Accountant; Michael Richard Cowen [1961] Director/Chief Financial Officer; Anthony Ronald William Parfitt [1952] Director/Chartered Accountant

The Good Shepherd Catholic Trust
Incorporated: 7 July 2011 *Employees:* 140
Previous: The Palmer Catholic Academy
Net Worth: £11,455,245 *Total Assets:* £12,335,773
Registered Office: The Palmer Catholic Academy, Aldborough Road South, Seven Kings, Ilford, Essex, IG3 8EU
Activities: General secondary education
Officers: Nazmul Islam, Secretary; Thomas Alexander [1967] Director/HR Officer; John Anthony [1949] Director; Joseph Daniel Bau-Mann [1966] Director; Father Sean Connolly [1964] Director/Priest; Michael Corcoran [1974] Director; Gerard Adrian Durcan [1960] Director; Reverend Andrew Michael John Headon [1966] Director/Priest; John Jacobson [1965] Director/Administrator; Marian Leslie-Povoas [1961] Director/Bank Manager [Irish]; Eoin McHugh [1979] Director/Teacher; Roger Melder [1965] Director/Technical Administrator; George Reynolds [1963] Director/Accountant; Natasha Scott [1977] Director/Headteacher

Goodfellow Cambridge Limited
Incorporated: 23 October 1974 *Employees:* 72
Net Worth: £8,410,000 *Total Assets:* £10,748,000
Registered Office: Units C1 and C2, Spitfire Close, Ermine Business Park, Huntingdon, Cambs, PE29 6WR
Activities: Manufacture of other plastic products
Parent: Metals & Materials Limited
Officers: Andrew Watson, Secretary; Stephen Charles Aldersley [1957] Director; Jane Elizabeth Stoner [1961] Director

Goodkind Estates Limited
Incorporated: 27 January 1998 *Employees:* 4
Net Worth: £7,000,048 *Total Assets:* £11,093,533
Registered Office: 1 Brookmans Avenue, Brookmans Park, Herts, AL9 7QH
Activities: Other letting and operating of own or leased real estate
Shareholders: Graham Goodkind; Lisa Goodkind
Officers: Lisa Goodkind, Secretary; Graham Clifford Goodkind [1966] Director/Consultant; Lisa Dannielle Goodkind [1965] Director/Banker

Goodman Family Investments Limited
Incorporated: 2 August 1996 *Employees:* 5,251
Previous: J S A Group Limited
Net Worth: £5,662,656 *Total Assets:* £23,247,308
Registered Office: 4th Floor, Radius House, 51 Clarendon Road, Watford, Herts, WD17 1HP
Activities: Non-trading company
Parent: JSA Newco Limited
Officers: Andrew Graham Goodman [1962] Director/Chairman/Investor; John Hugo Hoskin [1974] Director; Kwasi Martin Missah [1969] Director

Goodmayes Properties Ltd
Incorporated: 15 February 2000
Net Worth: £6,040,538 *Total Assets:* £9,820,061
Registered Office: 148 Cranbrook Road, Ilford, Essex, IG1 4LZ
Activities: Other letting and operating of own or leased real estate
Major Shareholder: Pavneet Kaur Kataria
Officers: Gurvinder Kataria, Secretary; Pavneet Kaur Kataria [1970] Director

Goodwill SIP Limited
Incorporated: 14 April 2004 *Employees:* 5
Net Worth: £4,625,101 *Total Assets:* £29,198,068
Registered Office: 114-116 Goodmayes Road, Ilford, Essex, IG3 9UZ
Activities: Hotels and similar accommodation
Shareholder: Sukhbinder Singh Takhar
Officers: Iqbal Kaur Takhar, Secretary; Iqbal Kaur Takhar [1960] Director; Pirthipal Singh Takhar [1982] Director; Sukhbinder Singh Takhar [1954] Director

The Gorhambury Estates Company Limited
Incorporated: 8 June 1923
Net Worth: £3,403,866 *Total Assets:* £8,167,348
Registered Office: The Estate Office, Gorhambury, St Albans, Herts, AL3 6AH
Activities: Other letting and operating of own or leased real estate
Officers: Patrick Alexander Beddows, Secretary; Patrick Alexander Beddows [1961] Director/Chartered Surveyor; Viscount James Walter Grimston [1978] Director/Investment Banker; Rosanagh Viola Alexandra Grimston [1979] Director/Interior Designer; Lord John Duncan Verulam [1951] Director/Investment Consultant

Gough Hotels Limited
Incorporated: 13 August 1965 *Employees:* 225
Net Worth: £4,097,836 *Total Assets:* £17,352,792
Registered Office: Saxon House, Fornham All Saints, Bury St Edmunds, Suffolk, IP28 6JY
Activities: Hotels and similar accommodation
Shareholder: Robert Charles Gough
Officers: Caroline Bombarde [1961] Director/Executive; Claire Gough [1968] Director/Designer; Mary Frances Gough [1936] Director/Hotelier; Robert Charles Gough [1966] Director/Hotelier

Gower Acres Limited
Incorporated: 11 June 2012 *Employees:* 1
Net Worth: £506,586 *Total Assets:* £8,633,592
Registered Office: St Johns Innovation Centre, Cowley Road, Cambridge, CB4 0WS
Activities: Growing of cereals (except rice), leguminous crops and oil seeds
Major Shareholder: Andrew Christopher Gower
Officers: Andrew Christopher Gower [1978] Director/Software Developer

Gowrie Laxmico Limited
Incorporated: 8 October 1997 *Employees:* 297
Previous: Gowrie Limited
Net Worth: £17,930,260 *Total Assets:* £35,392,188
Registered Office: Unit 4 Bradfield Road, Ruislip, Middlesex, HA4 0NU
Activities: Wholesale of pharmaceutical goods
Officers: Govindji Thakershi Hathi, Secretary; Alpa Hathi [1968] Director/HR; Govindji Thakershi Hathi [1941] Director; Samit Hathi [1967] Director/Chief Executive

Goymour Properties Limited
Incorporated: 4 October 1929 *Employees:* 152
Net Worth: £17,569,048 *Total Assets:* £22,249,016
Registered Office: The Grove, Banham, Norwich, NR16 2HE
Activities: Other letting and operating of own or leased real estate
Officers: Kevin Richard Ward, Secretary; Caroline Goymour [1960] Director/Manager; Charles Adam Goymour [1987] Director/Manager; Kiera Lee Goymour [1984] Director/Manager; Martin Goymour [1950] Property and Leisure Director; Kevin Richard Ward [1962] Director/Accountant

Gozzett Holdings Limited
Incorporated: 20 January 2004 *Employees:* 81
Net Worth: £3,855,613 *Total Assets:* £12,978,038
Registered Office: Quest House, 287 Rayne Road, Braintree, Essex, CM7 2QN
Activities: Activities of head offices
Shareholders: Robin John Gozzett; Martin John Gozzett
Officers: Robin John Gozzett, Secretary/Director; Martin John Gozzett [1962] Director; Robin John Gozzett [1956] Director

GPL Investments Limited
Incorporated: 20 November 2006
Net Worth Deficit: £70,658,264 *Total Assets:* £456,754,112
Registered Office: Energy House, Woolpit Business Park, Woolpit, Bury St Edmunds, Suffolk, IP30 9UP
Activities: Activities of other holding companies n.e.c.
Parent: BUUK Infrastructure No 2 Limited
Officers: Christopher Mumford, Secretary; Graham Collins [1978] Director/Accountant; Darryl John Corney [1960] Director; Paul David Edwards [1974] Director; Clive Eric Linsdell [1962] Director/Manager

GPP Langstone LLP
Incorporated: 8 November 2012
Net Worth: £50,997,724 *Total Assets:* £51,733,540
Registered Office: 2a Chequers Court, Huntingdon, Cambs, PE29 3LJ

GPS Food Group (UK) Limited
Incorporated: 4 June 2008 *Employees:* 43
Net Worth: £6,180,140 *Total Assets:* £29,946,258
Registered Office: Windsor House, Queensgate, Britannia Road, Waltham Cross, Herts, EN8 7NX
Activities: Wholesale of meat and meat products
Parent: GPS Food Group Holdings Limited
Officers: Padraig Anthony McCarthy, Secretary; Padraig McCarthy [1967] Director [Irish]; Brian Perkins [1962] Director; Fergus Quinn-Smith [1965] Director

Grace Foods UK Limited
Incorporated: 19 August 1907
Net Worth: £7,774,000 *Total Assets:* £16,555,000
Registered Office: Grace House, Bessemer Road, Welwyn Garden City, Herts, AL7 1HW
Activities: Non-specialised wholesale of food, beverages and tobacco
Parent: GK Foods (UK) Limited
Officers: Khine Oo, Secretary; Philip David Cross [1960] Managing Director; Joseph Peter Esau [1946] Director/Business Executive [Trinidadian]; Sarath L Lankage [1955] Director [Canadian]; Andrea Denise Lewis-Coy [1970] Director/CEO, Gracekennedy Foods International [Jamaican]; Brian Anthony Mitchell [1983] Director/Chief Financial Officer [Jamaican]; Angella Marie Rainford [1979] Director/Developer; Gordon Valentine Shirley [1956] Commercial Director [Jamaican]; Donald George Wehby [1963] Finance Director [Jamaican]

Gracechurch Sports Management Limited
Incorporated: 17 September 2002
Net Worth: £1,350,267 *Total Assets:* £8,001,742
Registered Office: 2 Linksway, Northwood, Middlesex, HA6 2XB
Activities: Development of building projects
Officers: Donald Owen Scott, Secretary/Chartered Accountant; Michael Charles Grahame Davey [1946] Director/Retired Chartered Surveyor; Manoj Kumar Saluja [1959] Director/Accountant; Reva Saluja [1963] Director/Manager

Gracewell Healthcare Limited
Incorporated: 24 August 2010
Net Worth: £18,540,000 *Total Assets:* £31,813,000
Registered Office: Sunrise House, Post Office Lane, Beaconsfield, Bucks, HP9 1FN
Activities: Other human health activities
Officers: Antony Nigel Brister [1972] Director; Jerry Liang [1984] Finance Director [American]

D.N. Grady & Sons Limited
Incorporated: 28 February 1996 *Employees:* 3
Net Worth: £7,085,249 *Total Assets:* £9,518,366
Registered Office: Bankside, 300 Peachman Way, Broadland Business Park, Norwich, NR7 0LB
Activities: Development of building projects
Shareholder: Dennis Norman Grady
Officers: Justin Andrew Grady, Secretary; Dennis Norman Grady [1945] Director/Master Builder; Justin Andrew Grady [1971] Director/Property Developer; Mark Dennis Grady [1973] Director/Property Developer

Graincorp (Canada) Holdings UK Limited
Incorporated: 29 October 2009
Net Worth: £48,116,000 *Total Assets:* £48,116,000
Registered Office: Station, Maltings, Witham, Essex, CM8 2DU
Activities: Manufacture of malt
Officers: Alistair Garrard Bell [1961] Director/Chief Financial Officer [Australian]; Darren Smith [1968] Director/President [Canadian]; Roger Graham Woodley [1958] Director/Maltster (CEO)

Graincorp UK Limited
Incorporated: 28 October 2009
Net Worth: £84,188,000 *Total Assets:* £129,298,000
Registered Office: Station Maltings, Witham, Essex, CM8 2DU
Activities: Manufacture of malt
Officers: Alistair Garrard Bell [1961] Director/Chief Financial Officer [Australian]; Darren Smith [1968] Director/President [Canadian]; Roger Graham Woodley [1958] Director/Maltster (CEO)

Grange Management (Holdings) Limited
Incorporated: 1 April 1986 *Employees:* 9
Net Worth: £38,870,104 *Total Assets:* £41,500,924
Registered Office: 4 Grange Court, The Limes, Ingatestone, Essex, CM4 0GB
Activities: Activities of head offices
Shareholders: Graham Charles Chambers; Barry Gordon Cuthbert; Zoe Hodge
Officers: Colin Frederick Chambers [1953] Director; Graham Charles Chambers [1947] Director; Victoria Jane Chambers [1995] Director/Business Manager

Grange Renewable Energy Limited
Incorporated: 18 May 2011
Net Worth Deficit: £4,550,000 *Total Assets:* £26,079,000
Registered Office: Beaufort Court, Egg Farm Lane, Kings Langley, Herts, WD4 8LR
Activities: Production of electricity
Parent: Trafalgar Wind Holdings Limited
Officers: Dominic James Hearth, Secretary; Steven William Hughes [1972] Generation & Asset Management Director; Fraser Stephen Merry [1968] Director/Chartered Surveyor; Mitesh Raj Patel [1982] Director/Group Financial Controller

Grangebrook Estates Limited
Incorporated: 2 April 1986
Net Worth: £12,200,491 *Total Assets:* £16,751,529
Registered Office: 4 Grange Court, The Limes, Ingatestone, Essex, CM4 0GB
Activities: Other letting and operating of own or leased real estate
Officers: Colin Frederick Chambers [1953] Director; Graham Charles Chambers [1947] Director; Victoria Jane Chambers [1995] Director/Business Manager

Grangewood Brentwood Limited
Incorporated: 13 December 1999
Net Worth: £9,189,175 *Total Assets:* £11,779,108
Registered Office: 4 Grange Court, The Limes, Ingatestone, Essex, CM4 0GB
Activities: Other letting and operating of own or leased real estate
Parent: Grange Management (Holdings) Ltd
Officers: Colin Frederick Chambers [1953] Director; Graham Charles Chambers [1947] Director; Victoria Jane Chambers [1995] Director/Business Manager

Grangewood Builders Limited
Incorporated: 15 May 1992 *Employees:* 122
Net Worth: £2,097,644 *Total Assets:* £12,724,654
Registered Office: 12-16 Lionel Road, Canvey Island, Essex, SS8 9DE
Activities: Other building completion and finishing
Shareholders: Richard Mark Stevens; Michael Stevens
Officers: Emma Maile, Secretary; Paul Stephen Goddard [1957] Director; Emma Maile [1979] Director/Accounts Manager; Warren Stead [1976] Director/Surveyor; Michael Stevens [1965] Director/Manager; Richard Mark Stevens [1961] Director/Quantity Surveyor; John Peter Thorpe [1949] Director

Granitte Investments (UK) Limited
Incorporated: 30 July 2012
Net Worth: £125,548,904 *Total Assets:* £125,554,400
Registered Office: Ground Floor, Unit 501 Centennial Park, Centennial Avenue, Elstree, Borehamwood, Herts, WD6 3FG
Activities: Activities of other holding companies n.e.c.
Officers: Ying-Chou Yang [1955] Director [Taiwanese]

Grant & Bowman International Limited
Incorporated: 10 March 2016 *Employees:* 10
Net Worth: £1,533,840 *Total Assets:* £19,532,718
Registered Office: 1st Floor, Sheraton House, Lower Road, Chorleywood, Rickmansworth, Herts, WD3 5LH
Activities: Activities of distribution holding companies
Shareholders: Malcolm Bowman; Myles David Jaakko Bowman
Officers: David Alistair Bowman [1957] Director; Malcolm Bowman [1935] Director; Myles David Jaakko Bowman [1973] Director

Grant & Bowman Limited
Incorporated: 18 October 1967 *Employees:* 19
Net Worth: £9,923,470 *Total Assets:* £14,443,814
Registered Office: 1st Floor, Sheraton House, Lower Road, Chorleywood, Herts, WD3 5LH
Activities: Non-specialised wholesale trade
Shareholder: David Alistair Bowman
Officers: Maria Hajineocli, Secretary; David Alistair Bowman [1957] Director; Malcolm Bowman [1935] Director; Myles David Jaakko Bowman [1973] Director; Daniel Barrie Estrin [1971] Director; Raymond Mark Estrin [1946] Director

Grant & Boyd Limited
Incorporated: 9 November 1938 *Employees:* 8
Net Worth: £11,215,276 *Total Assets:* £16,081,908
Registered Office: York House, Empire Way, Wembley, Middlesex, HA9 0FQ
Activities: Other letting and operating of own or leased real estate
Shareholders: Grant Family Holdings Limited; Grant Family Investments Limited
Officers: Roger Lloyd Jamie Grant, Company Secretary; Benjamin Paul Grant [1980] Director; Daniel Scot Grant [1978] Director; Ian Douglas Grant [1953] Director; Roger Lloyd Jamie Grant [1947] Director

R. & I. Grant & Co. Limited
Incorporated: 27 July 1973 *Employees:* 7
Net Worth: £9,161,270 *Total Assets:* £15,115,267
Registered Office: York House, Empire Way, Wembley, Middlesex, HA9 0FQ
Activities: Other letting and operating of own or leased real estate
Shareholders: Grant Family Holdings Limited; Grant Family Investments Limited
Officers: Roger Lloyd Jamie Grant, Secretary/Director; Ian Douglas Grant [1953] Director; Roger Lloyd Jamie Grant [1947] Director; Susan Melanie Grant [1958] Director; Victoria Sharon Grant [1947] Director

Grant & Stone Limited
Incorporated: 10 February 1986 *Employees:* 276
Net Worth: £16,524,640 *Total Assets:* £29,137,628
Registered Office: Unit 2 Mill End Road, High Wycombe, Bucks, HP12 4AX
Activities: Agents involved in the sale of timber and building materials
Officers: Graham Philip Akers, Secretary; Graham Philip Akers [1960] Finance Director; Matthew Bland [1976] Director; Peter Allan Cudd [1966] Commercial Director; Peter Alan Gourd [1948] Director/Accountant; Andrew David Grant [1977] Director; Robert David Grant [1947] Director/Chairman; Susan Margaret Grant [1949] Director; Nicolas Arthur House [1957] Director/Chief Executive; Matthew Miller [1975] Director; Richard Joseph Stone [1948] Director; Susan Stone [1951] Director

J W Grant Co
Incorporated: 8 October 1954 *Employees:* 188
Previous: J.W.Grant
Net Worth: £17,440,776 *Total Assets:* £25,227,008
Registered Office: Fold Hill, Old Leake, Boston, Lincs, PE22 9PJ
Activities: Growing of cereals (except rice), leguminous crops and oil seeds
Shareholders: James Edward Grant Trustee of WE Grant Settlement 1982; James Edward Grant Trustee of WE Grant Settlement 1989
Officers: James Edward Grant, Secretary; Andrew John Grant [1955] Director/Farmer; James Edward Grant [1953] Director/Farmer; John James Grant [1930] Director/Farmer; June Grant [1927] Director/Married Woman

Grant Family Holdings Limited
Incorporated: 25 June 2015
Net Worth: £20,087,692 *Total Assets:* £20,179,292
Registered Office: York House, Empire Way, Wembley, Middlesex, HA9 0FQ
Activities: Activities of head offices
Shareholder: Roger Lloyd Jamie Grant
Officers: Benjamin Paul Grant [1980] Director; Roger Lloyd Jamie Grant [1947] Director; Victoria Sharon Grant [1947] Director

Grant Family Investments Limited
Incorporated: 25 June 2015
Net Worth: £20,087,692 *Total Assets:* £20,179,292
Registered Office: York House, Empire Way, Wembley, Middlesex, HA9 0FQ
Activities: Activities of head offices
Shareholder: Ian Douglas Grant
Officers: Daniel Scot Grant [1978] Director; Ian Douglas Grant [1953] Director; Susan Melanie Grant [1958] Director

Grant Farming Limited
Incorporated: 7 September 2012 *Employees:* 7
Net Worth: £5,133,944 *Total Assets:* £10,220,038
Registered Office: Laburnum House, Main Road, Langrick, Boston, Lincs, PE22 7AN
Activities: Activities of agricultural holding companies
Major Shareholder: Linda May Whatton
Officers: Mark Richard Grant [1967] Director/Farmer; Nicola Jayne Grant [1972] Director; Paul John Grant [1969] Director/Farmer

Granta Design Limited
Incorporated: 6 April 1993 *Employees:* 165
Net Worth: £10,578,496 *Total Assets:* £15,869,667
Registered Office: 300 Rustat House, 62 Clifton Road, Cambridge, CB1 7EG
Activities: Business and domestic software development
Parent: ANSYS, Inc.
Officers: Philippe Antonio [1978] Director [French]; Richard Alan Belcher [1970] Director/Chartered Accountant

Granta Park Estates Limited
Incorporated: 14 November 1990 *Employees:* 3
Net Worth: £32,885,554 *Total Assets:* £44,871,264
Registered Office: Granta Park, Great Abington, Cambridge, CB21 6AL
Activities: Buying and selling of own real estate
Parent: Welding Institute (The)
Officers: Gillian Astrid Leech, Secretary; Aamir Khalid [1964] Director/Chief Executive; Ian Michael Laing [1946] Director; Gillian Astrid Leech [1963] Associate Director

Grantol Investments Limited
Incorporated: 9 February 2006
Net Worth Deficit: £7,120,166 *Total Assets:* £15,415,446
Registered Office: First Floor, Woodgate Studios, 2-8 Games Road, Cockfosters, Barnet, Herts, EN4 9HN
Activities: Other business support service activities n.e.c.
Major Shareholder: Friese Wolfgang Rudiker
Officers: Maria Papaioannou [1979] Director/Employee [Cypriot]

Grants of Shoreditch Limited
Incorporated: 3 December 1992 *Employees:* 92
Net Worth: £12,375,131 *Total Assets:* £15,935,510
Registered Office: Grant House, Prospect Way, Hutton, Brentwood, Essex, CM13 1XD
Activities: Construction of commercial buildings
Major Shareholder: Lee O'Connor
Officers: Michael Denyer [1967] Managing Director; Lee Daniel O'Connor [1969] Director/General Manager; Jason Lee Plumstead [1968] Director/Quantity Surveyor

Gratnells Limited
Incorporated: 22 February 1940 *Employees:* 59
Net Worth: £8,170,671 *Total Assets:* £10,635,009
Registered Office: 8 Howard Way, Harlow, Essex, CM20 2SU
Activities: Manufacture of other plastic products
Officers: Peter Errol Mayo, Secretary; Murray McCrone Hudson [1967] Managing Director; Peter Errol Mayo [1960] Financial Director; Paula Minowa [1966] Director; Nicholas Keith Pearch [1955] Director

Gravity Media Group Holdings Limited
Incorporated: 19 May 2016 *Employees:* 308
Net Worth Deficit: £8,771,000 *Total Assets:* £74,647,000
Registered Office: 32-34 Greenhill Crescent, Watford, Herts, WD18 8JU
Activities: Activities of head offices
Major Shareholder: John Richard Newton
Officers: Nikki Petken, Secretary; David Wayne Checketts [1955] Director/Executive Investor [American]; Paul John Greensmith [1967] Director/Chief Financial Officer; Gordon Andrew Holmes [1969] Managing Director [Irish]; Peter Joseph Lewis [1964] Director [Australian]; Kevin Moorhouse [1958] Director; John Richard Newton [1963] Director

Gravity Media Group Limited
Incorporated: 18 November 1999 *Employees:* 6
Net Worth: £2,022,000 *Total Assets:* £9,672,000
Registered Office: 32-34 Greenhill Crescent, Watford, Herts, WD18 8JU
Activities: Activities of head offices
Parent: Gravity Media Group Holdings Limited
Officers: Nikki Petken, Secretary; Eamonn MacArten Dowdall [1963] Director; Paul John Greensmith [1967] Director/Chief Financial Officer; Elliot Saul Kaye [1971] Finance Director; Kevin Moorhouse [1958] Director; John Richard Newton [1963] Director; Nicholas Peter Newton [1962] Commercial Director

Gray & Sons (Chelmsford) Limited
Incorporated: 17 August 1972 *Employees:* 12
Net Worth: £16,542,927 *Total Assets:* £18,147,604
Registered Office: Rignals Lane, Galleywood, Chelmsford, Essex, CM2 8RE
Activities: Growing of cereals (except rice), leguminous crops and oil seeds
Shareholders: Nicola Jane Kitchiner; Elizabeth Alison Meer; Lindsay Margaret Pendray
Officers: Elizabeth Alison Meer, Secretary; Nicola Jane Kitchiner [1968] Director; Elizabeth Alison Meer [1970] Director

Gray's Inn 10 Limited
Incorporated: 6 November 2007
Net Worth: £442,677 *Total Assets:* £17,638,348
Registered Office: Botanic House, Hills Road, Cambridge, CB2 1PH
Activities: Buying and selling of own real estate
Shareholders: Gray's Inn Holdings Limited; Gray's Inn Capital 2 Limited
Officers: Natalie Chambers, Secretary; Andrea Williams, Secretary; Natalie Chambers [1976] Estates Director; Paul Langford [1971] Finance Director; Michael Anthony Platt [1966] Director/Chartered Accountant

Gray's Inn Capital 2 Limited
Incorporated: 13 April 2016
Previous: Gray's Inn Capital 2 Limited
Net Worth: £1,704,181 *Total Assets:* £58,627,048
Registered Office: Botanic House, Hills Road, Cambridge, CB2 1PH
Activities: Buying and selling of own real estate
Shareholders: Gray's Inn Holdings Limited; Gray's Inn Holdings Limited
Officers: Natalie Chambers, Secretary; Andrea Williams, Secretary; Natalie Chambers [1976] Estates Director; Paul Langford [1971] Finance Director; Michael Anthony Platt [1966] Director/Chartered Accountant

Gray's Inn Capital Limited
Incorporated: 24 January 2011
Net Worth: £5,056,533 *Total Assets:* £55,939,044
Registered Office: Botanic House, Hills Road, Cambridge, CB2 1PH
Activities: Dormant company
Parent: Gray's Inn Holdings Limited
Officers: Natalie Chambers, Secretary; Andrea Williams, Secretary; Natalie Chambers [1976] Estates Director; Paul Langford [1971] Finance Director; Michael Anthony Platt [1966] Director/Chartered Accountant

Gray's of Norwich Limited
Incorporated: 4 July 1997
Net Worth: £8,157,182 *Total Assets:* £8,362,398
Registered Office: Brickyard Farm, Hall Lane, Drayton, Norwich, NR8 6HH
Activities: Development of building projects
Shareholders: Leslie Alan Gray; Margaret Julie Gray
Officers: Leslie Alan Gray, Secretary/Business Proprietor; Leslie Alan Gray [1958] Director/Business Proprietor; Margaret Julie Gray [1959] Director/Business Proprietor

Graysons Hospitality Limited
Incorporated: 11 October 2010 *Employees:* 590
Net Worth: £4,038,000 *Total Assets:* £11,518,000
Registered Office: Devon House, Anchor Street, Chelmsford, Essex, CM2 0GD
Activities: Licenced restaurants
Major Shareholder: Francis Henry MacKay
Officers: Barnaby Watson, Secretary; Ian Daly [1950] Director; Sir Francis Henry MacKay [1944] Director; Barnaby Hugh Cochrane Watson [1972] Director

Greater Peterborough UTC
Incorporated: 12 November 2012 *Employees:* 41
Net Worth: £8,123,864 *Total Assets:* £8,252,830
Registered Office: Peterborough Regional College, Park Crescent, Peterborough, Cambs, PE1 4DZ
Activities: Technical and vocational secondary education
Officers: Peter Neil Walker, Secretary; David Alan Bisley [1978] Director/Acting Principal; Phillip David Brown [1961] Director; Dr Anne Devlin [1958] Director/Deputy Dean; Karl Stephen Hick [1959] Director; David Richard Hiorns [1967] Director/Manufacturing Supervisor; Charlotte Anne Maybank [1991] Director/Teacher/Student Manager; Lisa Tricia Lynne Russell [1975] Director; Peter Neil Walker [1959] Director/Vice Principal; Hou-Fung Yuen [1988] Director/Commercial Manager

Gredley House Investments Limited
Incorporated: 10 January 2001
Net Worth: £14,826,432 *Total Assets:* £25,669,238
Registered Office: Unex House, Church Lane, Stetchworth, Newmarket, Suffolk, CB8 9TN
Activities: Other letting and operating of own or leased real estate
Shareholders: Timothy Casey Oscar Gredley; Pollyana Georgina Gredley
Officers: Andrew John Page, Secretary; Timothy Casey Oscar Gredley [1986] Director; William Jerome Gredley [1933] Director; Andrew John Page [1976] Director/Certified Chartered Accountant

Green Energy Options Ltd
Incorporated: 18 April 2006 *Employees:* 62
Net Worth: £8,262,971 *Total Assets:* £11,850,639
Registered Office: 3 St Marys Court, Main Street, Hardwick, Cambridge, CB23 7QS
Activities: Manufacture of consumer electronics
Officers: Paul David Hebden, Secretary; Simon Bryan Patrick Anderson [1950] Director/Business Consultant; Patrick Caiger-Smith [1961] Director/Engineer; Paul David Hebden [1965] Director Accountant; Nicholas David Jenkins [1967] Director; Anthony Alfred Leigh White [1953] Director

Peter Green Haulage Limited
Incorporated: 27 January 1977 *Employees:* 129
Net Worth: £3,528,432 *Total Assets:* £9,033,584
Registered Office: Naval House, King's Quay Street, Harwich, Essex, CO12 3JJ
Activities: Freight transport by road
Officers: Allan William Spence Binks, Secretary; Allan William Spence Binks [1941] Director; Thomas Allan Binks [1972] Director/Warehouse Manager; William Andrew Binks [1966] Director/Transport & Warehousing; Nicholas John Haggett [1956] Director/Transport Manager

Green Hill Energy Limited
Incorporated: 6 July 2009
Net Worth Deficit: £1,998,000 *Total Assets:* £45,007,000
Registered Office: Beaufort Court, Egg Farm Lane, Kings Langley, Herts, WD4 8LR
Activities: Other business support service activities n.e.c.
Parent: Trafalgar Wind Holdings Limited
Officers: Dominic James Hearth, Secretary; Steven William Hughes [1972] Generation & Asset Management Director; Fraser Stephen Merry [1968] Director/Chartered Surveyor; Mitesh Raj Patel [1982] Director/Group Financial Controller

Green Label Farms LLP
Incorporated: 2 August 2009 *Employees:* 47
Net Worth: £1,803,284 *Total Assets:* £9,714,011
Registered Office: Loomswood Farm, Hasketon, Woodbridge, Suffolk, IP13 6JW
Officers: Geoffrey Maurice Buchanan [1970] Member; Maurice William Buchanan [1938] Member; Miriam Elizabeth Buchanan [1937] Member; William Edwin Buchanan [1968] Member

Green Label Foods Ltd.
Incorporated: 9 April 1999 *Employees:* 454
Net Worth: £13,772,032 *Total Assets:* £46,437,396
Registered Office: Loomswood Farm, Hasketon, Woodbridge, Suffolk, IP13 6JW
Activities: Production of meat and poultry meat products
Shareholders: Geoffrey Maurice Buchanan; William Edwin Buchanan
Officers: Geoffrey Maurice Buchanan, Secretary; Geoffrey Maurice Buchanan [1970] Director/Farmer; William Edwin Buchanan [1968] Director; Stephen Andrew Harley [1963] Director/Chief Financial Officer

Green Label Poultry Limited
Incorporated: 12 February 2014 *Employees:* 101
Net Worth: £5,889,056 *Total Assets:* £21,890,184
Registered Office: Loomswood Farm, Hasketon, Woodbridge, Suffolk, IP13 6JW
Activities: Raising of poultry
Shareholders: Geoffrey Maurice Buchanan; William Edwin Buchanan
Officers: Geoffrey Maurice Buchanan [1970] Director; William Edwin Buchanan [1968] Director; Stephen Andrew Harley [1963] Director/Chief Financial Officer; Martin Edward Alan Newman [1957] Farms Director

Green Mountain Estates Ltd
Incorporated: 25 February 2014
Net Worth: £2,863,998 *Total Assets:* £12,238,257
Registered Office: 5 Elstree Gate, Elstree Way, Borehamwood, Herts, WD6 1JD
Activities: Other business support service activities n.e.c.
Major Shareholder: Marc Shalam
Officers: Marc Shalam [1977] Director/Property Investment [American]

Green Space London Limited
Incorporated: 27 February 2007 *Employees:* 5
Net Worth: £3,843,134 *Total Assets:* £9,016,640
Registered Office: Price Mann and Co, 447 Kenton Road, London, HA3 0XY
Activities: Other business support service activities n.e.c.
Officers: Abbas Mosawi [1985] Director/Hotelier; Ali Reza Mosawi [1992] Director/Hotelier

Green Spark Renewable Energy (UK) Ltd
Incorporated: 16 January 2013 *Employees:* 4
Net Worth: £4,051,501 *Total Assets:* £13,400,612
Registered Office: 820 The Crescent, Colchester Business Park, Colchester, Essex, CO4 9YQ
Activities: Production of electricity
Shareholders: Geoff John Parker; Louise Gail Parker
Officers: Geoffrey John Parker [1974] Director; Louise Gail Parker [1975] Sales Director

Greenbrook Industries Limited
Incorporated: 14 January 1988 *Employees:* 58
Net Worth: £2,443,408 *Total Assets:* £17,893,746
Registered Office: 62 West Road, Harlow, Essex, CM20 2BG
Activities: Manufacture of wiring devices
Shareholders: David Robert Green; Henry Richard Green
Officers: David Robert Green, Secretary; David Robert Green [1951] Director/Electrical Goods Manufacturer; Evelyn Green [1952] Director/Executive [British/German]; Henry Richard Green [1949] Director; Vivien Clere Green [1957] Director/Executive; Richard Darrell Shaw [1957] Managing Director; Diane Tomkins [1952] Finance Director

Greene King Acquisitions No.2 Limited
Incorporated: 25 May 2005
Net Worth: £44,716,000 *Total Assets:* £192,723,008
Registered Office: Westgate Brewery, Bury St Edmunds, Suffolk, IP33 1QT
Activities: Activities of head offices
Parent: Greene King Brewing and Retailing Limited
Officers: Lindsay Anne Keswick, Secretary; Richard Smothers [1967] Director

Greene King Brewing and Retailing Limited
Incorporated: 6 January 1997 *Employees:* 39,168
Net Worth: £1,954,000,000 *Total Assets:* £3,969,999,872
Registered Office: Westgate Brewery, Bury St Edmunds, Suffolk, IP33 1QT
Activities: Manufacture of beer
Parent: Greene King Pubs Limited
Officers: Lindsay Anne Keswick, Secretary; Rooney Anand [1964] Director; Nicholas Robertson Elliot [1966] Director; Richard Lewis [1970] Director; Wayne Shurvinton [1978] Director; Richard Smothers [1967] Director; Matthew Anthony Starbuck [1969] Director; Philip Andrew Thomas [1969] Director

Greene King Developments Limited
Incorporated: 1 November 2010 *Employees:* 6
Net Worth Deficit: £2,988,374 *Total Assets:* £38,514,772
Registered Office: Westgate Brewery, Bury St Edmunds, Suffolk, IP33 1QT
Activities: Development of building projects
Parent: Greene King PLC
Officers: Lindsay Anne Keswick, Secretary; Rooney Anand [1964] Director; Richard Lewis [1970] Director; Richard Smothers [1967] Director

Greene King Investments Limited
Incorporated: 2 November 2010
Net Worth: £719,179,008 *Total Assets:* £719,790,976
Registered Office: Westgate Brewery, Bury St Edmunds, Suffolk, IP33 1QT
Activities: Activities of head offices
Parent: Greene King PLC
Officers: Lindsay Anne Keswick, Secretary; Rooney Anand [1964] Director; Richard Smothers [1967] Director

Greene King Neighbourhood Estate Pubs Limited
Incorporated: 15 March 2004
Net Worth: £485,764,992 *Total Assets:* £487,143,008
Registered Office: Westgate Brewery, Bury St Edmunds, Suffolk, IP33 1QT
Activities: Non-trading company
Parent: G.K. Holdings No. 1 Limited
Officers: Lindsay Anne Keswick, Secretary; Richard Smothers [1967] Director

Greene King PLC
Incorporated: 1 June 1887 *Employees:* 39,168
Net Worth: £2,056,899,968 *Total Assets:* £5,221,199,872
Registered Office: Westgate Brewery, Bury St Edmunds, Suffolk, IP33 1QT
Activities: Activities of head offices
Officers: Lindsay Anne Keswick, Secretary; Rooney Anand [1964] Director; Michael Andrew Coupe [1960] Director; Robert Oscar Rowley [1949] Director; Richard Smothers [1967] Director; Lynne Marie Weedall [1967] Director; Philip Edward Yea [1954] Director

Greene King Properties Limited
Incorporated: 25 February 2011
Net Worth: £38,778,856 *Total Assets:* £83,318,560
Registered Office: Westgate Brewery, Bury St Edmunds, Suffolk, IP33 1QT
Activities: Management of real estate on a fee or contract basis
Parent: Greene King PLC
Officers: Lindsay Anne Keswick, Secretary; Richard Lewis [1970] Director; Richard Smothers [1967] Director

Greene King Pubs Limited
Incorporated: 2 November 2010
Net Worth: £1,495,782,016 *Total Assets:* £1,511,479,040
Registered Office: Westgate Brewery, Bury St Edmunds, Suffolk, IP33 1QT
Activities: Activities of head offices
Shareholders: Greene King Investments Limited; Greene King PLC
Officers: Lindsay Anne Keswick, Secretary; Richard Smothers [1967] Director

Greene King Retailing Limited
Incorporated: 20 October 2004 *Employees:* 15,488
Net Worth Deficit: £190,000,000 *Total Assets:* £2,168,999,936
Registered Office: Westgate Brewery, Bury St Edmunds, Suffolk, IP33 1QT
Activities: Hotels and similar accommodation
Parent: Greene King Retailing Parent Limited
Officers: Lindsay Anne Keswick, Secretary; Rooney Anand [1964] Director; Nicholas Robertson Elliot [1966] Director; Richard Lewis [1970] Director; Wayne Shurvinton [1978] Director; Richard Smothers [1967] Director; Matthew Anthony Starbuck [1969] Director; Philip Andrew Thomas [1969] Director

Greene King Retailing Parent Limited
Incorporated: 20 October 2004 *Employees:* 15,488
Net Worth Deficit: £172,900,000 *Total Assets:* £2,145,500,032
Registered Office: Westgate Brewery, Bury St Edmunds, Suffolk, IP33 1QT
Activities: Activities of head offices
Parent: Greene King PLC
Officers: Lindsay Anne Keswick, Secretary; Rooney Anand [1964] Director; Richard Lewis [1970] Director; Richard Smothers [1967] Director

Greenfields Family Investment Company Limited
Incorporated: 27 July 2012 *Employees:* 5
Net Worth: £9,228,240 *Total Assets:* £11,286,136
Registered Office: Greenfields, Hay Green Lane, Blackmore, Ingatestone, Essex, CM4 0QE
Activities: Security dealing on own account
Officers: Cheryl Jane Patten [1956] Director; Colin Charles Patten [1951] Director; David Patten [1987] Director; Rachel Patten [1989] Director; Steven Alan Patten [1984] Director

Greenheath Farming Company Limited
Incorporated: 12 July 2013 *Employees:* 6
Net Worth: £2,202,112 *Total Assets:* £10,785,384
Registered Office: Toggam Farm, Newfen Gravel Drove, Sedge Fen Gravel Drove, Lakenheath, Suffolk, IP27 9LN
Activities: Growing of cereals (except rice), leguminous crops and oil seeds
Shareholders: Thomas Philip Vincent Clayton; Sophie Julia Clayton
Officers: Sophie Julia Clayton [1986] Director; Thomas Philip Vincent Clayton [1980] Director/Businessman; John Stuart Hughes [1948] Director; Robert James Southgate [1973] Director/Chartered Accountant

Greens Farming Limited
Incorporated: 9 June 1986 *Employees:* 1
Net Worth: £125,908 *Total Assets:* £10,254,904
Registered Office: Beaufort House, 136 High Street, Newmarket, Suffolk, CB8 8JP
Activities: Growing of cereals (except rice), leguminous crops and oil seeds
Parent: Greens of Soham Limited
Officers: James Wesley Planton, Secretary; John Thomas Addams-Williams [1974] Managing Director; Greg Alexander Colebrook [1991] Director; Rachel Natasha Fletcher [1976] Finance Director; Jane Louise Perkins [1980] Finance Director

Greens of Soham Limited
Incorporated: 28 January 2000 *Employees:* 128
Net Worth: £7,469,000 *Total Assets:* £22,175,000
Registered Office: Beaufort House, 136 High Street, Newmarket, Suffolk, CB8 8JP
Activities: Support activities for crop production
Parent: Spearhead International Limited
Officers: James Wesley Planton, Secretary; John Thomas Addams-Williams [1974] Managing Director; Rachel Natasha Fletcher [1976] Finance Director; Jane Louise Perkins [1980] Finance Director

Greenseed International Limited
Incorporated: 31 July 1979
Net Worth: £1,838,109 *Total Assets:* £15,661,782
Registered Office: Beaufort House, 136 High Street, Newmarket, Suffolk, CB8 8JP
Activities: Growing of vegetables and melons, roots and tubers
Parent: Greens of Soham Limited
Officers: James Wesley Planton, Secretary; John Thomas Addams Williams [1974] Director/Farming; Rachel Natasha Fletcher [1976] Finance Director; Jane Louise Perkins [1980] Finance Director

Greenshoots Limited
Incorporated: 30 May 2003 *Employees:* 28
Net Worth: £848,419 *Total Assets:* £10,009,976
Registered Office: Hollyhouse Farm, Horseway, Chatteris, Cambs, PE16 6XQ
Activities: Growing of vegetables and melons, roots and tubers
Officers: Ian David Hall, Secretary; Patrick William Allpress [1964] Director/Farmer; Ian David Hall [1967] Director/General Manager; Christopher Fred Hartley [1950] Director/Farmer; James Harry Hawes [1988] Director/Farmer; Marc Edwin Heading [1965] Director/Farmer; James Frederick Martin [1961] Director/Farmer

Greenstone Oxford Limited
Incorporated: 6 December 2016 *Employees:* 2
Net Worth: £68,572 *Total Assets:* £32,909,552
Registered Office: c/o Hillier Hopkins LLP, First Floor, Radius House, 51 Clarendon Road, Watford, Herts, WD17 1HP
Activities: Other letting and operating of own or leased real estate
Parent: Greenstone Property Holdings Limited
Officers: Stephen Barrow [1956] Director; Simon Richard Hope [1964] Director

Greenswan Consultants Limited
Incorporated: 23 March 1994 *Employees:* 168
Net Worth: £4,399,857 *Total Assets:* £12,355,968
Registered Office: Trinity House, Foxes Parade, Sewardstone Road, Waltham Abbey, Essex, EN9 1PH
Activities: Residential nursing care facilities
Shareholders: Nasreen Begum Raja; Mohammed Moazam Raja
Officers: Nasreen Begum Raja, Secretary/Administration; Mohammed Moazam Raja [1953] Director/Businessman; Nasreen Begum Raja [1953] Director/Administration

Greentech Distribution PLC
Incorporated: 25 February 2010 *Employees:* 31
Previous: Greentech Recycling PLC
Net Worth: £6,673,785 *Total Assets:* £12,112,316
Registered Office: Unit 7 Treadaway Tech Centre, Treadaway Hill, Loudwater, High Wycombe, Bucks, HP10 9RS
Activities: Wholesale of electronic and telecommunications equipment and parts
Parent: Luri Ltd
Officers: Clive Merrick, Secretary; Lucky Anand [1968] Director; Richard Alexander Crawley [1972] Director; Clive Andrew Merrick [1974] Managing Director

Greenvale AP Limited
Incorporated: 23 February 1996 *Employees:* 718
Net Worth: £21,214,000 *Total Assets:* £83,000,000
Registered Office: Greenvale AP, Floods Ferry Road, Doddington, March, Cambs, PE15 0UW
Activities: Growing of vegetables and melons, roots and tubers
Parent: Produce Investments PLC
Officers: Angus Stuart Walton Armstrong [1964] Director; Andrew Clarkson [1977] Retail Commercial Director; Paul Michael Coleman [1965] Director/Technical Manager; Nicholas John Douglas [1974] Director; Andrew Ferguson [1967] HR Director; Leon Mundey [1975] Director; David Campbell Rankin [1972] Director

Greenwich Millennium Village Limited
Incorporated: 12 October 1998
Net Worth: £42,387,308 *Total Assets:* £74,629,264
Registered Office: Countryside House, The Drive, Great Warley, Brentwood, Essex, CM13 3AT
Activities: Development of building projects
Shareholders: Taylor Wimpey Developments Limited; Countryside Properties (UK) Limited
Officers: Tracy Marina Warren, Secretary; Kurt Frederick Adamson [1970] Residential Director; Christopher Richard Bladon [1977] Managing Director - East; Christopher Paul Hearn [1965] Finance Director; Philip Jenkins [1971] Managing Director; Peter Leonard Willis [1969] Director; Richard John Woolsey [1972] Finance Director

Greenyard Flowers UK Ltd
Incorporated: 9 January 1995 *Employees:* 124
Previous: Winchester Growers Limited
Net Worth: £22,736,456 *Total Assets:* £29,020,288
Registered Office: c/o Duncan & Toplis Limited, Enterprise Way, Pinchbeck, Spalding, Lincs, PE11 3YR
Activities: Growing of other non-perennial crops
Shareholder: Hein Valere Maria Deprez
Officers: Giles Anthony Armstrong, Secretary; Giles Anthony Armstrong [1970] Financial Director; Alan Alexander Forrester [1957] Director; Stella Willcox [1959] Human Resources Director

Greenyard Fresh UK Ltd
Incorporated: 8 August 1989 *Employees:* 546
Previous: Univeg Katope UK Ltd
Net Worth: £21,837,072 *Total Assets:* £44,951,624
Registered Office: c/o Duncan & Toplis Limited, Enterprise Way, Pinchbeck, Spalding, Lincs, PE11 3YR
Activities: Wholesale of fruit and vegetables
Shareholder: Hein Valere Maria Deprez
Officers: Giles Anthony Armstrong, Secretary; Giles Anthony Armstrong [1970] Financial Director; Hein Valere Maria Deprez [1961] Director [Belgian]; Veerle Maria Deprez [1960] Director [Belgian]; Alan Alexander Forrester [1957] Director; Karl Jozef Peeters [1957] Director [Belgian]; Stella Willcox [1959] Director

Greenyard Frozen UK Limited
Incorporated: 24 April 2002 *Employees:* 291
Previous: Pinguin Foods UK Limited
Net Worth: £13,599,000 *Total Assets:* £103,519,000
Registered Office: Greenyard Frozen UK Limited, Greenyard Way, Hardwick Industrial Estate, King's Lynn, Norfolk, PE30 4WS
Activities: Other processing and preserving of fruit and vegetables
Shareholder: Hein Valere Maria Deprez
Officers: Arjan Buschman, Secretary; Nigel Stuart Terry [1951] Non-Executive Director Chairman

Gresham Insurance Company Limited
Incorporated: 27 June 1910
Net Worth: £66,000,000 *Total Assets:* £342,000,000
Registered Office: 8 Surrey Street, Norwich, NR1 3NG
Activities: Non-life insurance
Parent: Aviva Insurance Limited
Officers: Robin Barker [1972] Director [South African/Italian]; Thomas James Latter [1977] Director/Accountant; Philip John Sowter [1968] Director; Robert Ian Leyman Townend [1967] Director/Insurance Company Official

Gresham's School
Incorporated: 3 August 2004 *Employees:* 370
Net Worth: £22,420,194 *Total Assets:* £29,330,988
Registered Office: Gresham's School, Cromer Road, Holt, Norfolk, NR25 6EA
Activities: Other education n.e.c.
Officers: Graham George Able [1947] Director; Martin Bailey [1967] Director; Alexander Edward Guinness de Capell Brooke [1968] Director; Anna Maria Dugdale [1966] Director/Chief Executive; Sir James Dyson [1947] Director/Chairman/Founder; James Fforde [1961] Director; Nigel Clark Flower [1955] Director/Retired; Michael Lee Goff [1955] Director/Chartered Accountant; Simon Neville Gorton [1957] Director/Landowner; Edward John Humphrey Gould [1943] Director/Educational Consultant; Virginia Raymonde Graham [1944] Director/Retired; David Christopher Fraser Jones [1959] Director/Investment Management; Paul Harvey Marriage [1971] Director/Fund Manager; James William Maunder Taylor [1972] Director/Chartered Surveyor; Jonathan Meyrick [1952] Director/Bishop of Lynn; James Kenrick Morgan [1970] Director/Solicitor; Stephen Mark Oldfield [1961] Director/Accountant; Dr Susan Penelope-Ann Rubin [1952] Director/Consultant Paediatrician (Retired); Rosamund Jane Walwyn [1953] Director/Retired Headteacher

Greystead Properties Limited
Incorporated: 17 August 1962 *Employees:* 5
Net Worth: £18,178,450 *Total Assets:* £22,134,078
Registered Office: The Old Brickworks, Church Road, Harold Wood, Romford, Essex, RM3 0JA
Activities: Other letting and operating of own or leased real estate
Officers: Irene Yolande Krantz, Secretary; Joshua James Bates [1969] Director; Michael Bates [1936] Director/Building Contractor; Irene Yolande Krantz [1940] Director/Archivist; Jeremy Robert Maurice Krantz [1968] Director/Property Consultant; Dr Allan Robert Salem [1944] Director; Zoe Warren [1963] Director

Griffin Davy Saffron Estates LLP
Incorporated: 26 May 2011
Net Worth: £9,641,391 *Total Assets:* £9,675,555
Registered Office: 10 Wellington Street, Cambridge, CB1 1HW
Officers: Anne Patricia Richer [1937] Member; Mark David Richer [1964] Member

Grigny (UK) Limited
Incorporated: 1 December 1977 *Employees:* 2
Net Worth: £840,275 *Total Assets:* £96,418,048
Registered Office: The Rivers Office Park, Denham Way, Maple Cross, Herts, WD3 9YS
Activities: Other professional, scientific and technical activities n.e.c.
Shareholders: Renault SA; Renault SA
Officers: James Alexander Blendis, Secretary; Cyril Francois Roger Abiteboul [1977] Managing Director [French]; El-Hassan Aitsaid [1964] Finance Director [Belgian]

Grimme (U.K.) Limited
Incorporated: 20 August 1993 *Employees:* 85
Net Worth: £10,572,309 *Total Assets:* £21,413,880
Registered Office: Station Road, Swineshead, Boston, Lincs, PE20 3PS
Activities: Manufacture of agricultural and forestry machinery other than tractors
Shareholders: Christoph Grimme; Philipp Grimme; Franz Josef Bernard Grimme
Officers: Donna Hall, Secretary; Patrick Albert Franz Graf Grote [1990] Managing Director [German]; Donna Hall [1980] Finance Director; Jens Walter [1963] Director/Administrative Manager [German]; Barry Vernon White [1959] Director

Grimsthorpe & Drummond Castle Trust Limited
Incorporated: 9 March 1978 *Employees:* 105
Net Worth: £38,195,548 *Total Assets:* £38,646,920
Registered Office: Grimsthorpe Estate Office, Grimsthorpe, Bourne, Lincs, PE10 0LY
Activities: Silviculture and other forestry activities
Officers: Francis John Fane Marmion Dymoke, Secretary; Richard Edward Ion Calvocoressi [1951] National Museum Director NDPB; Francis John Fane Marmion Dymoke [1955] Director/Land Owner; Sir Mark Ellis Powell Jones [1951] Director/College Warden; David Logan Laird [1937] Director/Retired; Sir John Lucas-Tooth [1932] Director/Banker; Hugh Patrick Matheson [1949] Director/Farmer; Sebastian Miller [1965] Director/Army Officer; Lady Jane Willoughby de Eresby [1934] Director

Grimston Trust Limited
Incorporated: 24 March 1915
Net Worth: £13,766,464 *Total Assets:* £14,012,352
Registered Office: Gorhambury, St Albans, Herts, AL3 6AH
Activities: Activities of head offices
Officers: Victoria Neil, Secretary; Viscount James Walter Grimston [1978] Director/Investment Banker; Rosanagh Viola Alexandra Grimston [1979] Director/Interior Designer; The Right Honourable The Seventh Earl of Verulam [1951] Director

Grindley Biogas Limited
Incorporated: 30 December 2015
Net Worth Deficit: £629,721 *Total Assets:* £10,562,677
Registered Office: Beeston Lodge, Beeston Lane, Spixworth, Norwich, NR10 3TN
Activities: Manufacture of gas
Parent: Yeo Power Limited
Officers: Matthew David Leggett [1977] Director/Chartered Accountant

Gristwood and Toms Limited
Incorporated: 22 November 1991 *Employees:* 155
Net Worth: £6,142,024 *Total Assets:* £8,466,469
Registered Office: c/o Hillier Hopkins LLP, First Floor, Radius House, 51 Clarendon Road, Watford, Herts, WD17 1HP
Activities: Support services to forestry
Shareholders: Andrew Philip Toms; David Charles Gristwood
Officers: Andrew Philip Toms, Secretary/Tree Surgeon; David Charles Gristwood [1953] Director/Tree Surgeon; Andrew Philip Toms [1953] Director/Tree Surgeon

John Grose Group Limited
Incorporated: 17 April 1980 *Employees:* 414
Net Worth: £25,255,000 *Total Assets:* £64,323,000
Registered Office: Whapload Road, Lowestoft, Suffolk, NR32 1NN
Activities: Sale of new cars and light motor vehicles
Shareholder: Ian Robert Twinley
Officers: Peter Smith, Secretary; David John Grose [1957] Director/Manager; Richard Ashley Howard [1967] Director/Sale of Motor Vehicles; Peter Smith [1962] Director; Ian Robert Twinley [1963] Director/Motor Executive; Roger Walton [1948] Director/Chartered Accountant

Grosvenor Park (Harris & Trotter) 2002 Film LLP
Incorporated: 24 October 2001
Net Worth: £22,162,680 *Total Assets:* £22,162,680
Registered Office: 99 Kenton Road, Harrow, Middlesex, HA3 0AN
Officers: David Thomas Bassett [1944] LLP Member; John David Burns [1944] LLP Member; Mark Stephen Butterworth [1958] LLP Member; Guy Antony Chambers [1963] LLP Member; Craig Laurence Feldman [1963] LLP Member; Stephen Michael Garbutta [1949] LLP Member; Andrew Graham Goodman [1961] LLP Member; Andrew Hale [1962] LLP Member; Julio Salomon Harari [1962] LLP Member; Nicholas Piers Killeen [1959] LLP Member; Alexander Justin Krzeczunowicz [1967] LLP Member; Bruce Charles Nicholas Lane [1953] LLP Member; Hugh Michael Lask [1957] LLP Member; Jack David Linton [1955] LLP Member; Ian Alexander MacDonald [1939] LLP Member; Jason Maratos [1959] LLP Member; Ian David Myers [1954] LLP Member; Richard Francis Jackson Park [1948] LLP Member; Patrick Ranger [1959] LLP Member; Ahmet Vedat Ratib [1963] LLP Member; Harold James Redknapp [1947] LLP Member; Jamie Frank Redknapp [1973] LLP Member; David Henry Rosen [1955] LLP Member; Jayant Sanghrajka [1955] LLP Member; Donald Arthur Starr [1948] LLP Member; Giles Storey [1954] LLP Member; Daniel James Breden Taylor [1958] LLP Member; Alan Keith Thomas [1946] LLP Member; John Patrick Thomson [1969] LLP Member; Paul Anthony Tipton [1954] LLP Member; Richard John Waller [1961] LLP Member; Malcolm Webber [1949] LLP Member

Grosvenor Park 2002 Film LLP
Incorporated: 18 October 2001
Net Worth: £50,934,048 *Total Assets:* £50,934,048
Registered Office: 99 Kenton Road, Harrow, Middlesex, HA3 0AN

Grosvenor Park 2004 Film Partnership No.1 LLP
Incorporated: 21 May 2003
Net Worth: £26,292,000 *Total Assets:* £26,292,000
Registered Office: 99 Kenton Road, Harrow, Middlesex, HA3 0AN
Officers: Peter Minshull Armstrong [1949] LLP Member; Brian Atkinson [1951] LLP Member; Richard Andrew Baker [1962] LLP Member; Eric Edmund Barnett [1961] LLP Member; Susanne Barron [1966] LLP Member; Andrew Gratrix Bennison [1959] LLP Member; Jonathan David Berger [1962] LLP Member; David John Bermingham [1962] LLP Member; Anthony John Best [1960] LLP Member; Carolyn Anne Blore Mitchell [1961] LLP Member; Winston Bogarde [1970] LLP Member; Mark Boothright [1964] LLP Member; Patrick Thomas Joseph Brooke [1947] LLP Member; Olivier Brousse [1965] LLP Member; Richard Brown [1953] LLP Member; David Nigel Caplan [1954] LLP Member; Nigel Alexander Carter [1968] LLP Member; Dominic Kern Chambers [1963] LLP Member; Jeremy John Champion [1962] LLP Member; Mark Gerard Clough [1953] LLP Member; Ian Stuart Cohen [1967] LLP Member; Angus Christopher Calvert Collett [1964] LLP Member; Daniel John Cunliffe [1971] LLP Member; Giles Roderick Dealtry [1963] LLP Member; Dr Yogeshkumar Shantilal Desai [1949] LLP Member; Nicolas Dossiter [1966] LLP Member; Anthony Charles Stephen Druttman [1951] LLP Member; Anthony Due [1970] LLP Member; Andrew John Dunlop [1966] LLP Member; Gillian Anne Dunlop [1965] LLP Member; Andrew David Eady [1964] LLP Member; Robert Elliot [1952] LLP Member; Patrick Noel Farrelly [1955] LLP Member; Nigel Andrew Foster [1958] LLP Member; Paul David Friedman [1966] LLP Member; Richard Peter Garnett [1960] LLP Member; Brian Gaunt [1958] LLP Member; Richard Henry George [1954] LLP Member; Raymond Neil Goodman [1955] LLP Member; Charles Richard Gray [1955] LLP Member; Barry Ludlow Green [1943] LLP Member; Robert Alan Hall [1949] LLP Member; Christopher Hancock [1965] LLP Member; Neil Hugh Thomas Hart [1972] LLP Member; Andrew Peter Joseph Edward Hogan [1973] LLP Member; John Charles Hollis [1953] LLP Member; Richard Halliday Jackson [1965] LLP Member; Thomas Stuart Jackson [1937] LLP Member; Philippe Pierre Jacquemard [1971] LLP Member; Robert Terence Johnson [1962] LLP Member; Robert Hylton Jolliffe [1960] LLP Member; Stephen Ransford Jones [1962] LLP Member; Stephen Frederick Joynes [1935] LLP Member; James Christopher Kaberry [1970] LLP Member; Paul George Kirtley [1959] LLP Member; Arno Kitts [1963] LLP Member; Markos Komondouros [1963] LLP Member; Laura Lawrence [1965] LLP Member; Kenneth Charles Leeper [1965] LLP Member; Jack David Linton [1955] LLP Member; Charles Marcus Sykes Longbottom [1969] LLP Member; John Dyer Lumley [1960] LLP Member; Donald James MacKay [1949] LLP Member; Gaurang Majmudar [1960] LLP Member; David Thomas Joseph Mansfield [1976] LLP Member; Ashley Terence Marston [1960] LLP Member; Philip Joseph McLaughlin [1948] LLP Member; John James McPhillips [1957] LLP Member; Tej Bahadur Singh Metha [1953] LLP Member; Emmanuelle Michels [1967] LLP Member; Timothy John Miller [1957] LLP Member; Andrew Robert Mitchell [1954] LLP Member; John Robert Morgan [1943] LLP Member; Tom Mark Harmer Nichols [1974] LLP Member; David Hase Osborne [1957] LLP Member; Christopher Adrian Palmer [1956] LLP Member; Biagino Palmeri [1967] LLP Member; Naishad Patel [1963] LLP Member; Dr Rashmika Patel [1959] LLP Member; Leslie Joseph Phillips [1958] LLP Member; David Riley [1950] LLP Member; Jocelyn Riley [1950] LLP Member; Jeffery Roberts [1961] LLP Member; Mark James Sadie [1969] LLP Member; Timothy Sice [1959] LLP Member; Paul Anthony Smith [1956] LLP Member; Nigel John Stacey [1970] LLP Member; Donald Arthur Starr [1948] LLP Member; Graham Stedman [1956] LLP Member; Mark Paul Stradling [1965] LLP Member; Andrew David Taylor [1956] LLP Member; Daniel James Breden Taylor [1958] LLP Member; Paul Anthony Tipton [1954] LLP Member; Joanna Trollope [1943] LLP Member; Christopher Richard Underwood [1954] LLP Member; Paul Jeffrey Vann [1947] LLP Member; Helen Walker [1966] LLP Member

Grosvenor Park 2005 Film Partnership No.1 LLP
Incorporated: 6 April 2004
Net Worth: £46,802,168 *Total Assets:* £46,802,520
Registered Office: 99 Kenton Road, Harrow, Middlesex, HA3 0AN
Officers: Hani Al Salih [1946] LLP Member; Shiblee Alam [1971] LLP Member; Steven Kenneth Allport [1971] LLP Member; Peter Minshull Armstrong [1949] LLP Member; Nicholas Anthony Athanasou [1953] LLP Member; Vincent Francis Baczor [1956] LLP Member; John Adam Ball [1969] LLP Member; Wendy Ball [1970] LLP Member; Deborah Bangay [1957] LLP Member; Fiona Margaret Anne Barlow [1959] LLP Member; Eric Edmund Barnett [1961] LLP Member; Jonathan David Berger [1962] LLP Member; David John Bermingham [1962] LLP Member; Thomas Bjorn [1971] LLP Member; Roderick James Blackwell [1958] LLP Member; Nicholas Blezard [1944] LLP Member; Andrew John Booth [1964] LLP Member; Mark Boothright [1964] LLP Member; Paul Martin Boston [1967] LLP Member; Simon Laurence Bowen [1966] LLP Member; Richard Brown [1953] LLP Member; John Scott Cameron [1965] LLP Member; David Nigel Caplan [1954] LLP Member; Giovanni Lorenzo Centi Colella [1976] LLP Member; Dominic Kern Chambers [1963] LLP Member; Gillian Kay Christie [1958] LLP Member; Steven Christie [1965] LLP Member; Lee Robert Clark [1972] LLP Member; Kevin Coogan [1951] LLP Member; Peter Thomas Cook [1956] LLP Member; Rodney Wayne Correia [1956] LLP Member; Stephen Hugh Stapleton Cotton [1949] LLP Member; Daniel John Cunliffe [1971] LLP Member; Julien Francois Olivier Dauchez [1972] LLP Member; Antony Charles William Davis [1964] LLP Member; Simon Henry Davis [1966] LLP Member; Giles Roderick Dealtry [1963] LLP Member; Gary John Dillon [1966] LLP Member; William Douglass Dodd [1946] LLP Member; Jonathan Downes [1961] LLP Member; Anthony Due [1970] LLP Member; John Stanley Durham [1939] LLP Member; Tonianne Dwyer [1962] LLP Member; Paul Anthony Stuart Dyke [1951] LLP Member; David Baron Eccleston [1964] LLP Member; Colin Benjamin Ettinger [1952] LLP Member; Roderick Clifford Evans [1964] LLP Member; Craig Laurence Feldman [1963] LLP Member; Daniel John Finestein [1965] LLP Member; Andrew Flounders [1958] LLP Member; Richard Henry George [1954] LLP Member; Thomas George [1960] LLP Member; Robert Malcolm Gilbert [1965] LLP Member; Sean David Gilbert [1964] LLP Member; Bruce Malcolm Gordon [1959] LLP Member; Ian Gray [1960] LLP Member; Barry Ludlow Green [1943] LLP Member; Patrick Green [1947] LLP Member; Massimo Guiati [1972] LLP Member; Pankaj Gupta [1972] LLP Member; David Gerard Heffron [1965] LLP Member; George Heydon [1961] LLP Member; Stuart William Hindle [1955] LLP Member; Alistair James Hollingdale [1970] LLP Member; Stephen Martyn Hopkins [1960] LLP Member; Jennifer Pamela Houghton [1946] LLP Member; Harvinderpal Singh Hungin [1960] LLP Member; Iain Catleugh Hutchinson [1965] LLP Member; Trevor John Immelman [1979] LLP Member; Kevin David Jackson [1956] LLP Member; Richard Halliday Jackson [1965] LLP Member; Prof Howard Saul Jacobs [1938] LLP Member; Philippe Pierre Jacquemard [1971] LLP Member; Rajat Jain [1965] LLP Member; Sean St John James [1965] LLP Member; Nils Eric Johansson [1980] LLP Member; Robert Terence Johnson [1962] LLP Member; Gareth Jones [1951] LLP Member; Ian Martin Jones [1955] LLP Member; Stephen Ransford Jones [1962] LLP Member; Timothy Francis Comyn Jordan [1960] LLP Member; Stephen Frederick Joynes [1935] LLP Member; Sean Gary Kenwrick [1965] LLP Member; David William Kerr [1963] LLP Member; Jodie Elizabeth Kidd [1978] LLP Member; Arno Kitts [1963] LLP Member; Barry Douglas Lane [1960] LLP Member; Andrew John Leake [1957] LLP Member; Bruce Lightbody [1962] LLP Member; David Patrick Lumley [1958] LLP Member; Bruce John MacDonald [1967] LLP Member; Magdalena Maczan [1975] LLP Member; Mark Joseph Massetti [1959] LLP Member; Karita Mattila [1960] LLP Member; Kevin Connal McGeeney [1970] LLP Member; Alister Hugh Mellor [1962] LLP Member

Grosvenor Park 2005 S42 Film LLP
Incorporated: 6 April 2004
Net Worth: £10,430,000 *Total Assets:* £10,430,548
Registered Office: 99 Kenton Road, Harrow, Middlesex, HA3 0AN
Officers: Colin Steven Braid [1966] LLP Member; Ian Anthony Brown [1974] LLP Member; Peter Harry Dunsby [1969] LLP Member; James Leslie Hayman Joyce [1945] LLP Member; Robert Warwick Hetherington [1964] LLP Member; Brian Eric Charles Lynch [1970] LLP Member; Bruce John MacDonald [1967] LLP Member; Mark Jeremy Melville Naylor [1959] LLP Member; Rudolph Jack Paul Alfred Reginiano [1949] LLP Member; Christopher Andrew Stainton [1970] LLP Member

Grosvenor Park 2006 S48 Film LLP
Incorporated: 18 April 2005
Net Worth: £8,726,160 *Total Assets:* £8,726,160
Registered Office: 99 Kenton Road, Harrow, Middlesex, HA3 0AN
Officers: Cecil Ashe [1944] LLP Member; James Neil Bargeron [1964] LLP Member; Matthew George Butcher [1976] LLP Member; Dominic Kern Chambers [1963] LLP Member; John Bernard Clare [1955] LLP Member; Andrew John Clark [1961] LLP Member; Stuart Douglas Cooper [1966] LLP Member; Nicholas Cusworth [1964] LLP Member; David Richard William Good [1948] LLP Member; Colin Walsh Graham [1970] LLP Member; Tessa Christine Hopkins [1952] LLP Member; Stuart Lindsay Isaacs [1952] LLP Member; Prof Howard Saul Jacobs [1938] LLP Member; Harald Torbjorn Gabriel Jakob Kinde [1958] LLP Member; Howard Martin King [1969] LLP Member; Arno Kitts [1963] LLP Member; Michael Angelo Le Houx [1959] LLP Member; Philip George Llewellyn [1961] LLP Member; Stewart Cameron McAndie [1973] LLP Member; Andrew Gwyn Menary [1959] LLP Member; Andrew Robert Mitchell [1954] LLP Member; Martin James Gerard Moore [1953] LLP Member; Andrew Raymond Moorfield [1966] LLP Member; Peter Anthony Parker [1959] LLP Member; Marcus Ewart Ronksley Potts [1960] LLP Member; Philip James Sweetland [1964] LLP Member; Alan Malcolm Thompson [1951] LLP Member; Raymond Clive Tooth [1940] LLP Member; John Alexander Yule [1964] LLP Member

Grosvenor Park 2007 S48 Film LLP
Incorporated: 1 December 2005
Net Worth: £23,177,000 *Total Assets:* £23,177,000
Registered Office: 99 Kenton Road, Harrow, Middlesex, HA3 0AN
Officers: Omar Mohammed Bachir Abdellaoui [1972] LLP Member; Riccardo Branchetti [1966] LLP Member; Vincent David Robin [1963] LLP Member; Filippo de Nicolais [1966] LLP Member; Leif Oveson Hoegh [1963] LLP Member; Morten Westye Hoegh [1973] LLP Member; Thomas Christian Hoegh [1966] LLP Member; Roberto Hoornweg [1968] LLP Member; Dr Christoph Michael Ladanyi [1956] LLP Member; Guy Delemere Lafferty [1954] LLP Member; Anders Larsen [1967] LLP Member; Anthony Henry Alfred Laubi [1965] LLP Member; Philip Lynch [1965] LLP Member; Alexandre Cyrille Araze Mouradian [1970] LLP Member; Emanuele Ravano [1964] LLP Member; Jerome Roussel [1965] LLP Member

Ground Construction Limited
Incorporated: 30 October 1997 *Employees:* 91
Net Worth: £19,330,324 *Total Assets:* £42,434,328
Registered Office: 2-3 Little Burrows, Welwyn Garden City, Herts, AL7 4SP
Activities: Construction of other civil engineering projects n.e.c.
Parent: Ground Construction Holdings Limited
Officers: John Diviney [1971] Commercial Director; Trevor Diviney [1967] Director/Surveyor; John Joe Power [1961] Construction Director [Irish]

Ground Control Holdings Limited
Incorporated: 4 March 2004 *Employees:* 953
Net Worth: £17,883,028 *Total Assets:* £87,304,584
Registered Office: Kingfisher House, Radford Way, Billericay, Essex, CM12 0EQ
Activities: Activities of head offices
Major Shareholder: Simon Hobart Charles Morrish
Officers: Jonathan Coote, Finance Director; Jonathan Coote [1952] Director; Simon Donnell Hughes [1949] Director; Kimberley Anne Morrish [1966] Director/Consultant [American]; Simon Hobart Charles Morrish [1974] Director; Dereka Anne Symes [1962] Director/Chartered Accountant; Dr Marcus John Watson [1972] Director

Ground Control Limited
Incorporated: 27 February 1984 *Employees:* 475
Net Worth: £18,416,374 *Total Assets:* £54,382,528
Registered Office: Kingfisher House, Radford Way, Billericay, Essex, CM12 0EQ
Activities: Landscape service activities
Parent: Ground Control Holdings Limited
Officers: Jonathan Coote, Secretary/Director; Jonathan Coote [1952] Director; Simon Hobart Charles Morrish [1974] Managing Director; Dereka Anne Symes [1962] Director/Chartered Accountant; Dr Marcus John Watson [1972] Managing Director

Group Lotus Limited
Incorporated: 12 June 1958
Previous: Group Lotus PLC
Net Worth: £75,155,000 *Total Assets:* £283,384,000
Registered Office: Potash Lane, Hethel, Norwich, NR14 8EZ
Activities: Activities of head offices
Parent: Lotus Group International Limited
Officers: Dr James Bradley, Secretary; Daniel Li Donghui [1970] Director [Chinese]; Feng Qingfeng [1972] Director [Chinese]; Sharifah Sofia Binti Syed Mokhtar Shah [1993] Director [Malaysian]; Mohamed Sharil Bin Mohamed Tarmizi [1969] Director [Malaysian]; Nathan Ning Yu [1970] Director [American]

Group Tyre Wholesale Limited
Incorporated: 7 October 2010 *Employees:* 113
Net Worth: £2,728,772 *Total Assets:* £12,405,432
Registered Office: Group House, Park Street, Aylesbury, Bucks, HP20 1QN
Activities: Wholesale trade of motor vehicle parts and accessories
Shareholders: Tanvic Group Limited; B A Bush & Sons Limited; S and M Tyres Limited
Officers: Nigel Arthur Bush [1956] Director; Stephen David McCracken [1972] Director; Gary James Oliver [1955] Managing Director; Richard John Whittemore [1961] Director

Grove & Dean (Holdings) Limited
Incorporated: 4 December 2013 *Employees:* 139
Net Worth: £3,560,278 *Total Assets:* £10,878,883
Registered Office: Tollgate House, 96 Market Place, Romford, Essex, RM1 3ER
Activities: Non-life insurance
Shareholder: Damian Paul Collett
Officers: Richard Ernest Brewster [1946] Director; Damian Paul Collett [1970] Managing Director; Matthew Paul Collett [1974] Director; Hannah Louise Thomson [1972] Director

Grove & Dean Limited
Incorporated: 17 April 1974 *Employees:* 138
Net Worth: £3,542,759 *Total Assets:* £10,859,063
Registered Office: Tollgate House, 96 Market Place, Romford, Essex, RM1 3ER
Activities: Non-life insurance
Parent: Grove & Dean (Holdings) Ltd
Officers: Richard Ernest Brewster [1946] Director; Damian Paul Collett [1970] Director/Insurance Consultant; Matthew Paul Collett [1974] Director; Gordon Robert Pratt [1959] Director; Hannah Louise Thomson [1972] Director

Grovemere Property Limited
Incorporated: 11 February 1957 *Employees:* 15
Net Worth: £18,740,596 *Total Assets:* £31,147,182
Registered Office: 112 Lancaster Way Business Park, Ely, Cambs, CB6 3NX
Activities: Buying and selling of own real estate
Parent: Grovemere Holdings Limited
Officers: Harvey Philip Bibby [1972] Director; Anne Elizabeth Brand [1953] Director; David Joseph Brand [1953] Director; Thomas David Joseph Brand [1986] Director; Nicola Charlotte Tuck [1980] Director/Surveyor

Grundfos Pumps Limited
Incorporated: 20 May 1964 *Employees:* 187
Net Worth: £18,264,000 *Total Assets:* £52,742,000
Registered Office: Grovebury Road, Leighton Buzzard, Beds, LU7 4TL
Activities: Manufacture of pumps
Officers: Robert Dalby, Secretary; Angelo Colombo [1963] Regional Service Director [Italian]; Hans Jorgen Hansen [1956] Finance Director [Danish]; Hung Chung Humphrey Lau [1966] Managing Director [Danish]

GS Acquisitions Limited
Incorporated: 17 May 2010
Net Worth Deficit: £248,520,000 *Total Assets:* £102,444,000
Registered Office: Coronation Road, Cressex, High Wycombe, Bucks, HP12 3TZ
Activities: Activities of head offices
Parent: Biffa Group Limited
Officers: Richard Neil Pike [1969] Director/Chief Financial Officer; Michael Robert Mason Topham [1972] Director/Chief Executive Officer

GTC Pipelines Limited
Incorporated: 20 September 1995
Net Worth Deficit: £71,760,400 *Total Assets:* £379,185,600
Registered Office: Energy House, Woolpit Business Park, Woolpit, Bury St Edmunds, Suffolk, IP30 9UP
Activities: Transport via pipeline
Parent: GPL Investments Limited
Officers: Christopher Mumford, Secretary; Susan Lisa Standring, Secretary; Darryl John Corney [1960] Director; Keith Johnston [1959] Director; Clive Eric Linsdell [1962] Managing Director; John Trounson [1966] Director

Guarding UK Ltd
Incorporated: 19 February 2003 *Employees:* 737
Net Worth: £2,070,174 *Total Assets:* £9,113,401
Registered Office: 249 Cranbrook Road, Ilford, Essex, IG1 4TG
Activities: Public order and safety activities
Officers: Michael John Rust [1947] Director

Guia Limited
Incorporated: 1 June 2011
Net Worth: £2,194,044 *Total Assets:* £80,000,096
Registered Office: Tollgate Barn, Tollgate West, Colchester, Essex, CO3 8RJ
Activities: Development of building projects
Shareholders: Carole Ann Watts; Jayne Catherine Gee; Daniel John Watts; Jason James Watts
Officers: Jayne Catherine Gee [1967] Director; Daniel John Watts [1975] Director

The Guild of Construction Workers Limited
Incorporated: 3 April 2001
Net Worth: £77,975 *Total Assets:* £13,253,820
Registered Office: Fifth Floor, 79 College Road, Harrow, Middlesex, HA1 1BD
Activities: Other business support service activities n.e.c.
Parent: Guild Corporate Services Group Limited
Officers: Derek Stephen Reynolds [1959] Managing Director

Gunpowder Mill Developments Limited
Incorporated: 19 November 2002 *Employees:* 1
Net Worth: £6,239,000 *Total Assets:* £12,296,000
Registered Office: The Power House, Gunpowder Mill, Powdermill Lane, Waltham Abbey, Essex, EN9 1BN
Activities: Other letting and operating of own or leased real estate
Major Shareholder: Andrew Richard Hill
Officers: Neil Stuart Williams, Secretary; Andrew Richard Hill [1958] Director

GVS Prepaid Limited
Incorporated: 29 August 2014 *Employees:* 2
Net Worth: £2,265,174 *Total Assets:* £139,968,496
Registered Office: Westside, London Road, Hemel Hempstead, Herts, HP3 9TD
Activities: Non-specialised wholesale trade
Parent: Minister for Communications Climate Action and Environment
Officers: Michelle Josephine Wainhouse, Secretary; Declan Byrne [1961] Director/Business Executive [Irish]

GW Pharma Limited
Incorporated: 29 January 1999 *Employees:* 123
Net Worth: £12,442,472 *Total Assets:* £84,644,096
Registered Office: Sovereign House, Vision Park, Chivers Way, Histon, Cambridge, CB24 9BZ
Activities: Manufacture of pharmaceutical preparations
Parent: GW Pharmaceuticals PLC
Officers: Adam David George, Secretary; Adam David George [1970] Director/Chartered Accountant; Dr Geoffrey William Guy [1954] Director/Doctor; Christopher John Tovey [1965] Director/Chief Operating Officer

GW Pharmaceuticals PLC
Incorporated: 15 February 2001 *Employees:* 533
Net Worth: £278,175,008 *Total Assets:* £332,915,008
Registered Office: Sovereign House, Vision Park, Chivers Way, Histon, Cambridge, CB24 9BZ
Activities: Other human health activities
Officers: Adam David George, Secretary; Cabot Brown [1961] Director [American]; Justin David Gover [1971] Director; Dr Geoffrey William Guy [1954] Director Medical Practitioner; Thomas Gerard Lynch [1956] Director; Catherine Mackey [1955] Director [American]; James Julian Noble [1959] Director; Alicia Secor [1962] Director [American]; Lord William Arthur Waldegrave [1946] Director

GW Research Limited
Incorporated: 28 September 1995 *Employees:* 321
Net Worth Deficit: £328,517,728 *Total Assets:* £35,856,184
Registered Office: Sovereign House, Vision Park, Chivers Way, Histon, Cambridge, CB24 9BZ
Activities: Research and experimental development on biotechnology
Parent: GW Pharmaceuticals PLC
Officers: Adam David George, Secretary; Adam David George [1970] Director/Chartered Accountant; Dr Geoffrey William Guy [1954] Director/Medical Practitioner; Christopher John Tovey [1965] Director/Chief Operating Officer

Gyron Internet Limited
Incorporated: 22 June 2001 *Employees:* 116
Net Worth: £118,587,000 *Total Assets:* £246,318,000
Registered Office: 3 Centro, Boundary Way, Hemel Hempstead, Herts, HP2 7SU
Activities: Data processing, hosting and related activities
Parent: NTT Communications Corporation
Officers: Clive Hamilton [1967] Managing Director; Kiyoshi Maeda [1956] Director/Vice President [Japanese]; Ryuichi Matsuo [1963] Director/Vice President [Japanese]; Rupprecht Felix Rittweger [1970] Director/Chief Executive Officer [German]

H & D Support Services (Holdings) Limited
Incorporated: 8 January 2004
Net Worth Deficit: £5,424,000 *Total Assets:* £20,426,000
Registered Office: Astral House, Imperial Way, Watford, Herts, WD24 4WW
Activities: Activities of head offices
Parent: Infrastructure Investments Holdings Limited
Officers: Ian Hudson, Secretary; David Wyn Davies [1968] Director/Accountant; Hannah Holman [1980] Director

H & D Support Services Limited
Incorporated: 8 January 2004
Net Worth Deficit: £5,424,000 *Total Assets:* £20,426,000
Registered Office: Astral House, Imperial Way, Watford, Herts, WD24 4WW
Activities: Combined facilities support activities
Parent: H & D Support Services (Holdings) Limited
Officers: Ian Hudson, Secretary; David Wyn Davies [1968] Director/Accountant; Hannah Holman [1980] Director

H (Lincs) Limited
Incorporated: 20 October 1978 *Employees:* 44
Net Worth: £19,164,148 *Total Assets:* £34,164,976
Registered Office: Sausthorpe Hall, Sausthorpe, Spilsby, Lincs, PE23 4JN
Activities: Activities of head offices
Officers: Roger William Hawkes, Secretary; Roger William Hawkes [1942] Director/Farmer

H L C (Wood Products) Limited
Incorporated: 24 July 1986 *Employees:* 311
Net Worth: £5,791,849 *Total Assets:* £21,056,724
Registered Office: The Gravel Pit, Needham, Norfolk, IP20 9LB
Activities: Other manufacturing n.e.c.
Parent: Scott Timber Limited
Officers: Norman Scott, Secretary; Alan Gibson [1956] Director; Paul Russell Lewis [1981] Director; Ryan Peter Michael Lewis [1978] Director; Robert William MacLean [1975] Director; Norman Robert Scott [1968] Director; Tracy Jayne Trotter [1975] Director

H. G. Construction (Holdings) Limited
Incorporated: 20 January 2000 *Employees:* 71
Net Worth: £14,913,000 *Total Assets:* £55,033,000
Registered Office: 4 Hunting Gate, Hitchin, Herts, SG4 0TJ
Activities: Activities of head offices
Shareholders: Christoper Furniss Benham; Kevin Joseph Quinn
Officers: Alan Peter Nixon, Secretary; Christopher Furniss Benham [1957] Director; Kevin Joseph Quinn [1958] Director/Chartered Engineer

H. W. Group Ltd.
Incorporated: 5 August 1993 *Employees:* 68
Net Worth: £3,759,479 *Total Assets:* £8,355,054
Registered Office: Piggotts Farm, Albury End, Ware, Herts, SG11 2HS
Activities: Residential care activities for the elderly and disabled
Shareholders: Playle Farms Limited; Whites Limited
Officers: Joan Esther Hockley, Secretary; Joanna Lesley Gavin [1970] Director; Sean Francis Gavin [1962] Director/Accountant; Charles William Hockley [1968] Director/Farmer; Joan Esther Hockley [1931] Director

H.& G.Car Parks Limited
Incorporated: 30 April 1971 *Employees:* 4
Net Worth: £15,499,260 *Total Assets:* £20,502,416
Registered Office: Coopers House, 65a Wingletye Lane, Hornchurch, Essex, RM11 3AT
Activities: Other service activities incidental to land transportation, n.e.c.
Parent: Step Property Group Limited
Officers: Mark William Perkins, Secretary; Gary Perkins [1959] Director

H.L. Foods Limited
Incorporated: 21 November 1990
Net Worth: £182,000,000 *Total Assets:* £915,600,000
Registered Office: Premier House, Centrium Business Park, Griffiths Way, St Albans, Herts, AL1 2RE
Activities: Activities of head offices
Parent: Premier Foods (Holdings) Limited
Officers: Simon Nicholas Wilbraham, Secretary; Duncan Neil Leggett [1979] Director; Simon Alan Rose [1966] Director/Solicitor; Simon Nicholas Wilbraham [1969] Director/Company Secretary

Haag-Streit UK Limited
Incorporated: 21 April 1986 *Employees:* 44
Net Worth: £8,822,848 *Total Assets:* £10,090,963
Registered Office: Unit A, Edinburgh Way, Harlow, Essex, CM20 2TT
Activities: Manufacture of optical precision instruments
Parent: Clement Clarke (Holdings) Limited
Officers: Stephen David Jacobs, Secretary; Peter Demarmels [1977] Director/Head of Corporate Development [Swiss]; Dean Johnson [1968] Managing Director; Rene Ott [1956] Director [Swiss]

Haas 2007 Limited
Incorporated: 28 November 2007 *Employees:* 81
Net Worth: £5,540,649 *Total Assets:* £15,853,689
Registered Office: 2 Convent Road, Norwich, NR2 1PA
Activities: Agents involved in the sale of machinery, industrial equipment, ships and aircraft
Shareholder: Andrew Walter Ward
Officers: Patrick Harry John Fenn, Secretary; Patrick Harry John Fenn [1951] Director; Andrew Walter Ward [1968] Director/Engineer

Haas Automation Limited
Incorporated: 14 October 1980 *Employees:* 81
Net Worth: £5,541,620 *Total Assets:* £15,893,589
Registered Office: 2 Convent Road, Norwich, NR2 1PA
Activities: Agents involved in the sale of machinery, industrial equipment, ships and aircraft
Parent: Haas 2007 Ltd
Officers: Patrick Harry John Fenn, Secretary/Director; Patrick Harry John Fenn [1951] Director; Gregory Stuart Smith [1981] Commercial Director; Andrew Walter Ward [1968] Engineering Director

Habendum Limited
Incorporated: 19 July 1996 *Employees:* 2
Net Worth: £26,679,806 *Total Assets:* £36,671,224
Registered Office: Aquila House, Waterloo Lane, Chelmsford, Essex, CM1 1BN
Activities: Other letting and operating of own or leased real estate
Major Shareholder: Stephen Clarence Hancock
Officers: Edith Lily Hancock [1992] Director/Journalist; Harold Thomas Hancock [1990] Director/HR Manager; Jane Mary Hancock [1956] Director

Hadleigh Bakery Limited
Incorporated: 1 May 1961 *Employees:* 4
Net Worth: £11,194,237 *Total Assets:* £15,772,858
Registered Office: 75 Springfield Road, Chelmsford, Essex, CM2 6JB
Activities: Retail sale of bread, cakes, flour confectionery and sugar confectionery in specialised stores
Shareholders: Guy Judd; Diane Cynthia Judd
Officers: Diane Cynthia Judd, Secretary; Diane Cynthia Judd [1946] Director/Company Secretary; Guy Mathew Judd [1975] Director/Rent Administration

Hadleigh Holdings Limited
Incorporated: 15 February 2005 *Employees:* 235
Net Worth: £17,241,192 *Total Assets:* £25,341,416
Registered Office: 22-26 King Street, King's Lynn, Norfolk, PE30 1HJ
Activities: Non-life insurance
Shareholders: David James Flux; Yvonne Flux
Officers: David James Flux, Secretary; David James Flux [1968] Director/Insurance Broker; Yvonne Flux [1948] Director/Insurance Broker

Hagondale Limited
Incorporated: 11 December 1991 *Employees:* 322
Net Worth: £46,910,480 *Total Assets:* £98,650,648
Registered Office: Enterprise House, Stansted Airport, Stansted, Essex, CM24 1RN
Activities: Activities of other holding companies n.e.c.
Major Shareholder: Gene Hedley Willson
Officers: Esen Fethi, Secretary; Graham Neal Baguley [1964] Director; Joseph Clarence Dennett [1971] Director/Pilot; Stefan Paul Payne [1981] Finance Director; Alastair Mark Willson [1986] Director; Gene Hedley Willson [1950] Director/Pilot

Haileybury Academy Trust
Incorporated: 26 June 2015 *Employees:* 113
Net Worth: £13,946,123 *Total Assets:* £15,172,721
Registered Office: Haileybury, London Road, Hertford Heath, Hertford, SG13 7NU
Activities: General secondary education
Officers: Stephen James Michael Campbell [1985] Director/Deputy Headteacher; Martin Anthony Richard Collier [1963] Director/Headteacher; John Giesen [1950] Director/Housing Association Executive; David John Kilgallon [1960] Director/Education; Russell Leslie Matcham [1958] Director/Teacher; Evelyn Anne Pope [1972] Director/Teaching Assistant; Dr Laura Beth Pugsley [1977] Director/Teacher; Ian Ashley Richardson [1959] Director/Solicitor; Ruth Rissen [1966] Director/Home Help; Neil Michael Taylor [1976] Director/Creative Partner; Stuart Alker Westley [1947] Director/Retired Headteacher/Consultant; Robert Joseph Whitaker [1977] Director/Solicitor

Halamar (Chancery Lane) Limited
Incorporated: 26 June 2015
Net Worth Deficit: £8,827,984 *Total Assets:* £70,298,448
Registered Office: 85-87 Holtspur Lane, Wooburn Green, Bucks, HP10 0AU
Activities: Other building completion and finishing
Shareholders: Amarpreet Singh Randhawa; New End Developments Limited
Officers: Lord Patrick James Earl of Clanwilliam [1960] Director/Business Consultant; Galina Gurinova [1970] Director [Cypriot]; Amarpreet Singh Randhawa [1982] Director

F.H. Hale & Sons (Builders) Limited
Incorporated: 7 April 1959 *Employees:* 5
Net Worth: £12,704,299 *Total Assets:* £14,184,136
Registered Office: First Floor, Radius House, 51 Clarendon Road, Watford, Herts, WD17 1HP
Activities: Buying and selling of own real estate
Shareholders: Alison Featherstone Hale; Sheila Eleanor Gillett
Officers: Alison Featherstone Hale, Secretary; Amanda Dodd [1965] Director/Teacher; Barry Gillett [1950] Director/Retired; Sheila Eleanor Gillett [1930] Director; Alison Featherstone Hale [1939] Director

Richard Hale School
Incorporated: 17 June 2013 *Employees:* 108
Net Worth: £15,805,174 *Total Assets:* £17,787,580
Registered Office: Richard Hale School, Hale Road, Hertford, SG13 8EN
Activities: General secondary education
Officers: Gregor John McLennan Anderson [1963] Director; Hamish Terence Kinnear Brown [1957] Director/Accountant; Thomas Brownlee [1961] Director/Teacher; Roger Stuart Gambles [1963] Director/Company Secretary; Victor Goddard [1968] Director/Chief Executive; Neill Jonathan Hanlon [1974] Director/Solicitor; Ian Harrison Hawkins [1976] Director/Headteacher; Barbara Jane Holm [1953] Director/College Principal; Laura Hosking [1970] Director; Reverend Joan Loveridge [1957] Director/Vicar; Catherine Margaret MacLeod [1952] Director/Media Consultant; Joanne Rita McCallig [1962] Director; Harvey Kleis Moore [1974] Director/Accountant; Louise Eleanor Riley [1971] Director/Consultant; Pippa Louise Simou [1973] Director/ADHD Coach/Trainer; James Douglas Thornton [1947] Director/Civil Engineer; Allan John Tyrer [1963] Finance Director; Karen Jane Webster [1974] Director/Chemistry Technician

Derek Hales (Plumbing Contractors) Limited
Incorporated: 14 June 1974 *Employees:* 10
Net Worth: £9,438,158 *Total Assets:* £9,780,453
Registered Office: 30 Market Place, Swaffham, Norfolk, PE37 7QH
Activities: Construction of domestic buildings
Major Shareholder: Derek Arthur Hales
Officers: Karen Gooch, Secretary; Derek Arthur Hales [1946] Director; Helen Hales [1949] Director; Ian Hales [1972] Director

Hales Group Limited
Incorporated: 21 April 1999 *Employees:* 1,747
Net Worth: £2,982,122 *Total Assets:* £10,724,789
Registered Office: Unit 3b, Flag Business Exchange, Vicarage Farm Road, Peterborough, Cambs, PE1 5TX
Activities: Temporary employment agency activities
Shareholders: Nicola Amanda Fowler; Nigel William Wray
Officers: Jeffrey Fowler [1954] Director; Nicola Jane Mewse [1970] Group Managing Director; Kamal Somchand Shah [1959] Director

Halfen Limited
Incorporated: 27 December 1989 *Employees:* 23
Net Worth: £8,993,000 *Total Assets:* £11,601,000
Registered Office: A1/A2 Portland Close, Houghton Regis, Beds, LU5 5AW
Activities: Other specialised construction activities n.e.c.
Officers: Brian Davis, Secretary; Brian Davis [1959] Director; Mark Jason Smith [1969] Director; Richard Wachter [1961] Managing Director [German]

Hall & Watts Holdings Limited
Incorporated: 20 July 2010 *Employees:* 27
Net Worth: £4,996,124 *Total Assets:* £9,858,509
Registered Office: Unit A3, Merlin Centre, Acrewood Way, St Albans, Herts, AL4 0JY
Activities: Activities of head offices
Shareholders: Arvindkumar Maganlal Thakkar; John Hoskins
Officers: John Hoskins [1938] Director; Arvind Thakkar [1943] Director/Accountant

Hall Contracts (Lakenheath) Limited
Incorporated: 10 July 1998 *Employees:* 11
Net Worth: £8,017,037 *Total Assets:* £10,485,211
Registered Office: 27-29 Old Market, Wisbech, Cambs, PE13 1NE
Activities: Real estate agencies
Major Shareholder: Jeffrey Hall
Officers: Timothy William Stevenson, Secretary; Jeffrey Hall [1964] Director/Builder; Nicola Fiona Hall [1967] Director

Hall of Fame Stud Limited
Incorporated: 20 December 2012
Net Worth Deficit: £1,173,938 *Total Assets:* £9,362,927
Registered Office: Lushington House, 119 High Street, Newmarket, Suffolk, CB8 9AE
Activities: Other professional, scientific and technical activities n.e.c.
Major Shareholder: Sheikh Fahad Al Thani
Officers: Sheikh Fahad Al Thani [1989] Director/Special Adviser [Qatari]; David John Luke Redvers [1970] Director/Bloodstock Agent

Hallam Meat Company Limited
Incorporated: 20 September 1971 *Employees:* 53
Net Worth: £63,774,156 *Total Assets:* £65,665,856
Registered Office: Cheveley Park Stud, Duchess Drive, Newmarket, Suffolk, CB8 9DD
Activities: Wholesale of meat and meat products
Shareholders: David Brian Thompson; Patricia Thompson
Officers: Christopher James Dant, Secretary; Roy Bernard Copus [1959] Director/Chartered Accountant; Christopher James Dant [1969] Director/Chartered Accountant; David Brian Thompson [1936] Director; Patricia Thompson [1940] Director

Hallgarten Wines,Limited
Incorporated: 2 April 1947 *Employees:* 102
Net Worth: £7,799,690 *Total Assets:* £17,434,252
Registered Office: Dallow Road, Luton, Beds, LU1 1UR
Activities: Wholesale of wine, beer, spirits and other alcoholic beverages
Officers: Jayne Elizabeth Foster, Secretary; Andrew Nicholas Bewes [1964] Sales Director; Howard Warren Falk [1963] Finance Director

Hallmark Care Homes (Brighton) Ltd
Incorporated: 19 April 2011 *Employees:* 135
Net Worth: £2,005,194 *Total Assets:* £8,983,063
Registered Office: 2 Kingfisher House, Woodbrook Crescent, Radford Way, Billericay, Essex, CM12 0EQ
Activities: Medical nursing home activities
Parent: Hallmark Care Homes Group Limited
Officers: Ram Krishan Goyal, Secretary; Avnish Mitter Goyal [1966] Director; Ram Krishan Goyal [1962] Director

Hallmark Care Homes Group Holdings Limited
Incorporated: 10 January 2007 *Employees:* 1,832
Net Worth: £40,925,260 *Total Assets:* £115,878,248
Registered Office: 2 Kingfisher House, Woodbrook Crescent, Radford Way, Billericay, Essex, CM12 0EQ
Activities: Activities of head offices
Shareholder: Vidya Bhushan Goyal
Officers: Ram Krishan Goyal, Secretary; Avnish Mitter Goyal [1966] Director; Ram Krishan Goyal [1962] Director; Vidya Bhushan Goyal [1955] Director

Halma Euro Trading Limited
Incorporated: 13 August 2009 *Employees:* 2
Net Worth Deficit: £432,014 *Total Assets:* £87,525,712
Registered Office: Misbourne Court, Rectory Way, Amersham, Bucks, HP7 0DE
Activities: Activities of head offices
Parent: Halma PLC
Officers: Mark Alun Jenkins, Secretary; Marc Arthur Ronchetti [1976] Director/Chartered Accountant; Andrew John Williams [1967] Director

Halma Financing Limited
Incorporated: 26 April 2004 *Employees:* 2
Net Worth: £729,477,184 *Total Assets:* £729,502,336
Registered Office: Misbourne Court, Rectory Way, Amersham, Bucks, HP7 0DE
Activities: Activities of head offices
Parent: Halma Overseas Funding Limited
Officers: Mark Alun Jenkins, Secretary; Marc Arthur Ronchetti [1976] Director/Chartered Accountant; Andrew John Williams [1967] Director

Halma International Limited
Incorporated: 8 April 1975 *Employees:* 67
Net Worth: £236,912,992 *Total Assets:* £884,907,008
Registered Office: Misbourne Court, Rectory Way, Amersham, Bucks, HP7 0DE
Activities: Activities of head offices
Shareholders: Halma PLC; Halma Euro Trading Limited
Officers: Mark Alun Jenkins, Secretary; Marc Arthur Ronchetti [1976] Director/Chartered Accountant; Andrew John Williams [1967] Director

Halma Investment Holdings Limited
Incorporated: 6 May 2004 *Employees:* 2
Net Worth: £608,011,648 *Total Assets:* £621,440,256
Registered Office: Misbourne Court, Rectory Way, Amersham, Bucks, HP7 0DE
Activities: Activities of head offices
Parent: Halma Financing Limited
Officers: Mark Alun Jenkins, Secretary; Marc Arthur Ronchetti [1976] Director/Chartered Accountant; Andrew John Williams [1967] Director

Halma Overseas Funding Limited
Incorporated: 14 February 2008 *Employees:* 2
Net Worth: £773,910,976 *Total Assets:* £817,015,616
Registered Office: Misbourne Court, Rectory Way, Amersham, Bucks, HP7 0DE
Activities: Activities of head offices
Parent: Halma International Limited
Officers: Mark Alun Jenkins, Secretary; Marc Arthur Ronchetti [1976] Director/Chartered Accountant; Andrew John Williams [1967] Director/Chief Executive

Halma Public Limited Company
Incorporated: 13 April 1894 *Employees:* 6,113
Net Worth: £829,024,000 *Total Assets:* £1,446,855,936
Registered Office: Misbourne Court, Rectory Way, Amersham, Bucks, HP7 0DE
Activities: Activities of head offices
Officers: Mark Alun Jenkins, Secretary; Daniela Barone Soares [1970] Director [Brazilian/British]; Carole Cran [1970] Director/Accountant; Jo Nell Harlow [1962] Director [American]; Adam Jay Meyers [1961] Director [American]; William Anthony Rice [1952] Director/Management Accountant; Marc Arthur Ronchetti [1976] Director/Chartered Accountant; Roy Michael Twite [1967] Director; Paul Ashton Walker [1957] Director; Jennifer Suzanne Ward [1973] Director [American]; Andrew John Williams [1967] Director

Halsbury Homes (South East) Limited
Incorporated: 4 February 2015
Net Worth: £321,649 *Total Assets:* £13,795,717
Registered Office: Seymour House, Little Money Road, Loddon, Norwich, NR14 6JD
Activities: Development of building projects
Parent: GBGB2 Ltd
Officers: Benita Louise Neale, Secretary; Karl Roy Dawson [1974] Director; Jason Timothy Green [1970] Director; Patrick Stephen Jeans [1987] Director; Phillip Patrick Jeans [1960] Director; Stephanie Marie Jeans [1989] Sales Director; Shaun Campbell McNamee [1968] Finance Director

Halsbury Strategic Limited
Incorporated: 6 January 2015
Net Worth Deficit: £1,063,794 *Total Assets:* £37,050,132
Registered Office: Seymour House, Little Money Road, Loddon, Norwich, NR14 6JD
Activities: Development of building projects
Parent: GBGB2 Ltd
Officers: Phillip Patrick Jeans, Secretary; Jason Timothy Green [1970] Director; Patrick Stephen Jeans [1987] Director; Phillip Patrick Jeans [1960] Director; Shaun Campbell McNamee [1968] Finance Director

Halstead Securities Limited
Incorporated: 4 September 1985
Net Worth: £2,020,272 *Total Assets:* £12,863,214
Registered Office: 1 Nelson Street, Southend on Sea, Essex, SS1 1EG
Activities: Activities of head offices
Shareholders: Brian Ernest Edward Burrett; Lorna Anne Sara Burrett
Officers: Janet Lord, Secretary; David Christian Wyatt [1951] Director/Sales Manager

Hamamatsu Photonics UK Limited
Incorporated: 9 March 1988 *Employees:* 48
Net Worth: £10,396,682 *Total Assets:* £16,714,114
Registered Office: 2 Howard Court, 10 Tewin Road, Welwyn Garden City, Herts, AL7 1BW
Activities: Wholesale of other intermediate products
Parent: Hamamatsu Photonics Kk
Officers: Chanchal Singh, Secretary; Dr. Peter Johann Eggl [1953] Director [German]; Timothy Stokes [1966] Director; Atsushi Tsujimura [1959] Director/Engineer [Japanese]

Hamden Homes Limited
Incorporated: 14 July 1995 *Employees:* 4
Net Worth: £8,090,396 *Total Assets:* £11,166,515
Registered Office: 3 Manor Courtyard, Hughenden Avenue, High Wycombe, Bucks, HP13 5RE
Activities: Development of building projects
Major Shareholder: Peter John Hatch
Officers: Nicola Joy Hatch, Secretary; Nicola Joy Hatch [1968] Director/Company Administration; Peter John Hatch [1963] Director/Property Developer

Hamelin Brands Limited
Incorporated: 19 January 2006 *Employees:* 52
Net Worth: £14,127,000 *Total Assets:* £21,712,000
Registered Office: Kings Warren Business Park, Red Lodge, Bury St Edmunds, Suffolk, IP28 8WG
Activities: Wholesale of household goods (other than musical instruments) n.e.c
Parent: Holdham SA
Officers: Philip Peter Stafford Beer, Secretary; Philip Peter Stafford Beer [1965] Director; Stephane Hamelin [1961] Director [French]

Hamlin Electronics Europe Limited
Incorporated: 4 May 1961 *Employees:* 10
Net Worth: £9,598,000 *Total Assets:* £10,587,000
Registered Office: Kingfisher House, 1 Gilders Way, off Barrack Street, Norwich, NR3 1UB
Activities: Manufacture of other electrical equipment
Officers: Roger Van Hal, Secretary; Aidas Kucys [1974] Director [Lithuanian]; Jurgen Scheele [1964] Director [German]; Meenal Anil Sethna [1969] Director/Senior Vice President, Finance [American]

A.W. & D. Hammond Limited
Incorporated: 14 September 1970 *Employees:* 262
Net Worth: £7,035,297 *Total Assets:* £14,535,519
Registered Office: Norwich Road, Halesworth, Suffolk, IP19 8BU
Activities: Sale of new cars and light motor vehicles
Shareholders: Derek Roy Hammond; Glen Richard Hammond
Officers: Derek Roy Hammond [1954] Director/Engineer; Glen Richard Hammond [1957] Director/Engineer

John Hampden Grammar School
Incorporated: 18 May 2011 *Employees:* 109
Net Worth: £15,166,162 *Total Assets:* £17,252,404
Registered Office: John Hampden Grammar School, Marlow Hill, High Wycombe, Bucks, HP11 1SZ
Activities: General secondary education
Officers: Katherine Natalia Bailey, Secretary; Rowan Margaret Aylett [1987] Director/Teacher; Faraz Ahmed Baber [1974] Director/Chartered Surveyor; Kate Louise Box [1974] Director/HR Consultant; Dr Anthony Richard Burne [1944] Director; Barry Keith Clarke [1939] Director; Professor Andrew John Timothy George [1963] Director/University Vice Principal; Barbara Rebecca Harrison [1961] Director/Learning Resource Centre Manager; Tracey Elizabeth Hartley [1965] Director/Headteacher; Philip John Maskell [1959] Finance Director; Shivaun Mason [1967] Director/Teacher; Mark Paul Phillips [1959] Director/Barrister; Peter Sangster Phippen [1960] Director/Media Executive; Nicholas Rogers [1977] Director/Teacher; Carl Frank Rycroft [1969] Director/Headmaster; Gregory Nicholas Christopher Stevenson [1962] Director/Chartered Accountant

Hampden Holdings Limited
Incorporated: 13 July 1995 *Employees:* 206
Net Worth: £66,706,440 *Total Assets:* £136,648,496
Registered Office: Hampden House, Great Hampden, Great Missenden, Bucks, HP16 9RD
Activities: Activities of head offices
Shareholders: Alexa Kate Louise Camroux Pearmund; Timothy Patrick Camroux Oliver; James Richard Camroux-Oliver; Charles Guy Camroux-Oliver
Officers: Charles Guy Camroux-Oliver [1970] Director/Solicitor; James Richard Camroux-Oliver [1967] Director; Stephen James Harris [1970] Director/Company Secretary; Timothy Patrick Camroux Oliver [1944] Director/Chairman

Hampden Insurance Holdings Limited
Incorporated: 24 August 1972 *Employees:* 18
Net Worth: £4,352,551 *Total Assets:* £16,417,032
Registered Office: Hampden House, Great Hampden, Great Missenden, Bucks, HP16 9RD
Activities: Activities of head offices
Parent: Hampden Holdings Limited
Officers: Charles Guy Camroux-Oliver [1970] Director/Solicitor; Stephen James Harris [1970] Director/Group Chief Operating Officer; Francis William Johnston [1952] Director/Chartered Accountant; William David Alexander Justice [1939] Director/Chartered Accountant; Timothy Patrick Camroux Oliver [1944] Director/Insurance Broker

Hampton Academies Trust
Incorporated: 14 July 2014 *Employees:* 227
Net Worth: £36,159,132 *Total Assets:* £38,401,788
Registered Office: Hampton College, Eagle Way, Hampton Vale, Peterborough, Cambs, PE7 8BF
Activities: Primary education
Officers: Caroline Angela Behan, Secretary; Laura Rhiannon Cross [1965] Director/Civil Servant; Samantha Olivia East [1973] Director/Solicitor; Arturo Kim Garcia [1952] Director; John Grant [1947] Director/Retired; Alastair John Kingsley [1969] Managing Director; Matthew James Patchett [1979] Director/Office Supervisor; Deborah Pope [1980] Director/Business Development Manager; Helen Elizabeth Price [1966] Director/Headteacher; Tessa Jane Wilson [1969] Director/Office Manager

Hamsard 3352 Limited
Incorporated: 9 October 2014 *Employees:* 177
Net Worth Deficit: £21,065,030 *Total Assets:* £237,866,800
Registered Office: Building 4, Hatters Lane, Croxley Green Business Park, Watford, Herts, WD18 8YF
Activities: Renting and leasing of cars and light motor vehicles
Officers: Laura Catherine Elizabeth Alexander [1979] Director/Chief Financial Officer; Clive Andrew Whistler Baker [1974] Director [British/South African]; Paul Gilshan [1975] Director; David Hosking [1963] Managing Director; Paul Dominic Ian McCreadie [1979] Director; Richard John Prosser [1957] Director/Chairman

Hamsard 3353 Limited
Incorporated: 9 October 2014 *Employees:* 5
Net Worth Deficit: £27,635,996 *Total Assets:* £93,007,432
Registered Office: Building 4, Hatters Lane, Croxley Green Business Park, Watford, Herts, WD18 8YF
Activities: Renting and leasing of cars and light motor vehicles
Parent: Hamsard 3352 Limited
Officers: Laura Catherine Elizabeth Alexander [1979] Director/Chief Financial Officer; Paul Gilshan [1975] Director; Paul Dominic Ian McCreadie [1979] Director

Hamton Environmental Services Limited
Incorporated: 12 July 1973 *Employees:* 599
Net Worth: £11,128,644 *Total Assets:* £17,124,328
Registered Office: 249 Cranbrook Road, Ilford, Essex, IG1 4TG
Activities: Combined facilities support activities
Major Shareholder: Antoinette Carter
Officers: Louise Jane Beenham, Secretary; Jessica Elizabeth Beenham [1981] Director; Antoinette Carter [1955] Director; Michelle Denise Carter [1959] Director; Philip Michael Joslin [1964] Director; Terence Arthur Vincent [1952] Director

Hand Laundry (Bury) Limited (The)
Incorporated: 7 January 1930 *Employees:* 7
Net Worth: £10,090,008 *Total Assets:* £10,466,038
Registered Office: 16 Forbes Business Centre, Kempson Way, Bury St Edmunds, Suffolk, IP32 7AR
Activities: Other letting and operating of own or leased real estate
Officers: Sheila Mary Killingley Bayne, Secretary; Duncan James Bayne [1968] Director; James Warrender Bayne [1938] Director/Chairman; Sheila Mary Killingley Bayne [1938] Director/Company Secretary; Justine Isabella Murray [1963] Managing Director

John Hanlon & Co. Limited
Incorporated: 2 May 1977
Net Worth: £5,266,925 *Total Assets:* £32,050,052
Registered Office: Highlands, Campton, Beds, SG17 5NZ
Activities: Renting and leasing of trucks and other heavy vehicles
Major Shareholder: John Hanlon
Officers: Patrick John Hanlon, Secretary; John Francis Hanlon [1931] Director/Engineer

Hanmere Polythene Limited
Incorporated: 4 April 1966 *Employees:* 100
Net Worth: £5,949,360 *Total Assets:* £10,874,486
Registered Office: Blackhorse Road, Letchworth, Herts, SG6 1HD
Activities: Manufacture of other plastic products
Parent: Trueman Parent A Limited
Officers: Jim Farrell, Secretary; Jim Farrell [1970] Director [Irish]; Martin John Foreman [1946] Director; Mushtaq Khan [1959] Director; David Lennon [1966] Director [Irish]; Glen Raymond Morris [1963] Managing Director

Hanover Housing Developments Limited
Incorporated: 24 March 2009
Net Worth: £68,982,000 *Total Assets:* £70,036,000
Registered Office: Nelson House, Alington Road, Little Barford, St Neots, Cambs, PE19 6RE
Activities: Development of building projects
Parent: Hanover Housing Association
Officers: Michael Douglas Fuller, Secretary; Mary Keane, Secretary; Jane Rachel Ashcroft [1966] Director/Chief Executive; Mark Curran [1959] Director of Development; Mark Charles Greaves [1966] Managing Director of Care Services; Sarah Elizabeth Jones [1968] Director/Chief Financial Officer; Christopher David Munday [1959] Managing Director Housing Operations; Rona Nicholson [1957] Director of Governance and Compliance

Hapag-Lloyd (U.K.) Limited
Incorporated: 15 January 1936 *Employees:* 203
Net Worth: £3,890,553 *Total Assets:* £18,103,140
Registered Office: Hapag Lloyd House, Cambridge Road, Barking, Essex, IG11 8HH
Activities: Other transportation support activities
Parent: Hapag-Lloyd Aktiengesellschaft
Officers: Roberto Falleni, Secretary; Cameron Leslie Bowie [1961] Managing Director; Michael Pradel [1967] Managing Director [German]

Haras Investments Limited
Incorporated: 10 March 1933
Net Worth: £20,148,528 *Total Assets:* £20,151,376
Registered Office: The Balsams Barn, Balsams Lane, Standon, Ware, Herts, SG11 1NS
Activities: Activities of financial services holding companies
Parent: Cadastra Ltd
Officers: John Howard Williamson [1944] Director

Harber Properties Limited
Incorporated: 5 July 1976 *Employees:* 5
Net Worth: £8,244,214 *Total Assets:* £12,842,437
Registered Office: Bankside, 300 Peachman Way, Broadland Business Park, Norwich, NR7 0LB
Activities: Other letting and operating of own or leased real estate
Shareholders: Avril Viola Margaret Grapes; Robert Charles Harber
Officers: Glenys Ann Black, Secretary; Robert Charles Harber [1949] Director; Gary John Nurse [1964] Director/Chartered Accountant

Harbour Club Limited
Incorporated: 28 May 1993 *Employees:* 126
Net Worth: £20,191,000 *Total Assets:* £30,071,000
Registered Office: The Hangar, Mosquito Way, Hatfield Business Park, Hatfield, Herts, AL10 9AX
Activities: Activities of sport clubs
Parent: Next Generation Clubs Limited
Officers: Patrick James Burrows [1967] Director/Chartered Accountant; Donald Glenn Earlam [1965] Director

Harbour Shipping Limited
Incorporated: 28 January 1983 *Employees:* 54
Net Worth: £6,604,998 *Total Assets:* £11,785,648
Registered Office: Star Cargo House, 1 Parkway, Porters Wood, St Albans, Herts, AL3 6PA
Activities: Other transportation support activities
Parent: Star Cargo PLC
Officers: Alexander Robert Russell Hodgkinson, Secretary; Stephen John Applebee [1970] Director/Customer Clearance Manager; Alistair James Caldwell [1969] Commercial Director; Stephen Cummings [1960] Director/General Manager; Alexander Robert Russell Hodgkinson [1982] Director/Chartered Accountant; John Gwynne James [1946] Director; Thomas Gwynne James [1976] Director

Hardall International Limited
Incorporated: 7 October 1987 *Employees:* 49
Net Worth: £8,886,409 *Total Assets:* £10,052,168
Registered Office: Hardall House, Ludun Close, Dunstable, Beds, LU5 4PN
Activities: Manufacture of other fabricated metal products n.e.c.
Officers: Joanna Elizabeth Shields, Secretary; Anthony Charles Bishop [1961] Works Manager/Director; David James Bishop [1965] Works Director; Liam Charles Bishop [1988] Director/Contracts Manager; John David Ledwidge [1969] Director

Hardwicke Investments Limited
Incorporated: 14 December 2007 *Employees:* 3,022
Net Worth: £74,828,000 *Total Assets:* £521,184,992
Registered Office: Spirella, 2 Icknield Way, Letchworth Garden City, Herts, SG6 4GY
Activities: Activities of head offices
Officers: Wendy Jane McWilliams, Secretary; Colin Enticknap [1958] Director/Group Chairman; Christopher Julian Sheridan [1943] Director/Chartered Banker; Richard John Willmott [1963] Director/Chartered Builder

Hardys Farm Limited
Incorporated: 11 August 2015 *Employees:* 11
Net Worth: £8,107,515 *Total Assets:* £9,975,530
Registered Office: Grays Farm, Anchor Lane, Ingoldmells, Skegness, Lincs, PE25 1LZ
Activities: Growing of cereals (except rice), leguminous crops and oil seeds
Parent: Hardys Farm Group Limited
Officers: Geoffrey David Hardy [1960] Director/Farmer; John George Hardy [1956] Director/Farmer; Stuart Dean Hardy [1981] Director/Farmer

Harlequin Direct Limited
Incorporated: 25 September 1996 *Employees:* 1
Net Worth: £8,283,941 *Total Assets:* £11,393,563
Registered Office: 1 Beauchamp Court, Victors Way, Barnet, Herts, EN5 5TZ
Activities: Other business support service activities n.e.c.
Major Shareholder: Garry Michael Brandt
Officers: Suzanne Brandt, Secretary; Garry Michael Brandt [1964] Director/Importer; Suzanne Brandt [1961] Director

Harlow Agricultural Merchants Limited
Incorporated: 7 October 1980 *Employees:* 117
Net Worth: £14,792,279 *Total Assets:* £25,117,320
Registered Office: Latchmore Bank, Little Hallingbury, Bishop's Stortford, Herts, CM22 7PJ
Activities: Agents selling agricultural raw materials, livestock, textile raw materials and semi-finished goods
Officers: Melvin John Trundle, Secretary; Stuart James Attridge [1963] Director/Grain Trader; Darrell Brabant Clark [1967] Director/Seedsman; Christopher Romer Collings [1968] Director; John Adrian Bartley Halliday [1958] Director/Fertiliser Trader; Melvin John Trundle [1961] Director/Administrator

Harlow and District Sports Trust
Incorporated: 10 March 1959 *Employees:* 44
Net Worth: £8,260,434 *Total Assets:* £9,622,407
Registered Office: Harlow Leisurezone, Second Avenue, Harlow, Essex, CM20 3DT
Activities: Operation of sports facilities
Officers: John William Abbott [1956] Director/Retired; Robin Alton [1950] Director/Business Consultant; Louise Frances Clark [1974] Director/Accountant; Charles Richard Cochrane [1950] Director/Trade Union Official; Tony Graham Crisp [1963] Director/Chartered Accountant; Patrick Andrew Hay [1949] Director/Retired; Gabriela Helena Horecka [1959] Director/Charity Worker [British/Polish]; Richard Little [1950] Director/Chartered Surveyor; Lucy Jane Lomas [1979] Director/Fundraising Manager; David Charles Sharp [1938] Director/Retired; John William Wright [1945] Director/Retired

The Harlow Education Trust
Incorporated: 12 August 2010
Net Worth: £10,973,191 *Total Assets:* £10,974,151
Registered Office: The Harlow Study Centre, Netteswellbury Farm, Harlow, Essex, CM18 6BW
Activities: Educational support services
Officers: Christopher John Fluskey, Secretary; Emma Susan Bloomfield [1974] Director/Headteacher; Neil Malcolm Coster [1979] Director/Headteacher; Mary Cleland Evans [1956] Director/Headteacher; Helen Alison Ginger [1969] Director/Headteacher; Victor Godddard [1968] Director/Headteacher; Ian Paul Kendal [1971] Director/Headteacher; Maria Bernadette Miele [1962] Director/Headteacher; Christine Susan Peden [1976] Director/Headteacher; Robert John Smith [1946] Director/Retired; Jonathan Michael Tye [1971] Director/Headteacher

The Harlow Health Centres Trust Limited
Incorporated: 5 August 1994 *Employees:* 1
Net Worth: £22,021,270 *Total Assets:* £31,567,586
Registered Office: The Latton Bush Centre, Southern Way, Harlow, Essex, CM18 7BL
Activities: Other service activities n.e.c.
Officers: Patricia Larkin, Secretary/Retired Teacher; Pamela Heeks [1937] Director/Retired; John James Houston [1964] Director; Byron Jones [1955] Director/Consultant; Patricia Larkin [1938] Director/Teacher; Stephen James Lemay [1961] Director; Arthur Stanley Newens [1930] Director/Retired

Harman Automotive UK Limited
Incorporated: 16 October 2012 *Employees:* 37
Net Worth: £118,480,720 *Total Assets:* £316,307,360
Registered Office: Ground Floor, Westside Two, London Road, Apsley, Hemel Hempstead, Herts, HP3 9TD
Activities: Manufacture of electrical and electronic equipment for motor vehicles and their engines
Parent: Harman International Industries Limited
Officers: Marcus Allen [1973] Director; Roderick Burns [1966] Director; Frank Georg Donald Groth [1961] Director [German]; John Stacey [1965] Director [American]

Harman International Industries Limited
Incorporated: 14 March 1980 *Employees:* 83
Net Worth: £74,333,000 *Total Assets:* £141,404,992
Registered Office: Ground Floor, Westside Two, London Road, Apsley, Hemel Hempstead, Herts, HP3 9TD
Activities: Manufacture of other electrical equipment
Parent: Harman International Industries Incorporated
Officers: Marcus Allen [1973] Director; Roderick Burns [1966] Finance Director; Frank Georg Donald Groth [1961] Director [German]; John Stacey [1965] Director [Canadian]

Harouni Group of Companies Limited
Incorporated: 16 November 2011
Net Worth Deficit: £739,725 *Total Assets:* £16,696,130
Registered Office: 2nd Floor, Unicorn House, Station Close, Potters Bar, Herts, EN6 1TL
Activities: Management of real estate on a fee or contract basis
Major Shareholder: Ester Louise Nassiv
Officers: David Samuel Harouni [1977] Director; Ester Louise Nassiv [1952] Director

Harrington (Properties) Limited
Incorporated: 20 January 1982
Net Worth: £8,123,270 *Total Assets:* £12,405,532
Registered Office: Harrington House, Exhibition Grounds, Fourth Way, Wembley, Middlesex, HA9 0UQ
Activities: Construction of commercial buildings
Shareholders: Cornelius Francis Harrington; Anthony Francis Harrington
Officers: Anthony Francis Harrington, Secretary; Anthony Francis Harrington [1975] Company Secretary/Director; Cornelius Francis Harrington [1940] Director/Building Contractor [Irish]

Harringtons Builders PLC
Incorporated: 18 January 2001 *Employees:* 48
Net Worth: £8,771,173 *Total Assets:* £11,947,578
Registered Office: 27a Maxwell Road, Northwood, Middlesex, HA6 2XY
Activities: Other building completion and finishing
Shareholders: Cornelius Francis Harrington; Anthony Francis Harrington
Officers: Anthony Francis Harrington, Secretary/Director; Gary Fagg [1966] Director; Anthony Francis Harrington [1975] Director; Cornelius Francis Harrington [1940] Director/Building Contractor [Irish]; James Patrick Kavanagh [1969] Director

Harris (Belmont) Charity
Incorporated: 10 September 2012 *Employees:* 18
Net Worth: £44,178,252 *Total Assets:* £44,451,272
Registered Office: Salisbury House, Station Road, Cambridge, CB1 2LA
Activities: Archives activities
Officers: Lord Alastair Colin Leckie Colgrain [1951] Director/Recruitment Consultant; Dominic Michael Del Mar [1972] Director/Consultant; Isabelle Jacqueline Laline Hay [1955] Director/Farmer; Vicki Jessel [1958] Director/Partner in a Farming Business; Alastair Mathewson [1960] Director/Trustee; Andrew John Shirley Ross [1959] Director/Investment Fund Manager

Harris Commercial Repairs Limited
Incorporated: 2 January 1974 *Employees:* 123
Net Worth: £5,663,272 *Total Assets:* £8,581,317
Registered Office: 601 London Road, West Thurrock, Essex, RM20 4AU
Activities: Sale of other motor vehicles
Parent: Harris Holdings (Grays) Limited
Officers: Peter James Harlow, Secretary; Gary John Carpenter [1971] Director/Engineer; Peter Joseph Greenyer [1956] Director/Certified Accountant; Francesca Emma Harlow [1986] Director; Peter James Harlow [1985] Director; Frank Douglas Harris [1964] Director; James Daniel Selway [1989] Director; Danielle Elizabeth Van Der Wiel [1962] Director

Harris Family Finance Company Limited
Incorporated: 17 March 2015
Net Worth: £9,838,712 *Total Assets:* £11,186,659
Registered Office: Lordship House, Lordship Stud, London Road, Newmarket, Suffolk, CB8 0TP
Activities: Activities of financial services holding companies
Major Shareholder: Trevor Frank Harris
Officers: Elizabeth Anne Harris [1959] Director; Trevor Frank Harris [1945] Director

Harris Holdings (Grays) Limited
Incorporated: 23 October 1973 *Employees:* 541
Net Worth: £34,019,276 *Total Assets:* £60,435,548
Registered Office: 601 London Road, West Thurrock, Essex, RM20 4AU
Activities: Activities of head offices
Shareholder: Danielle Elizabeth van der Wiel
Officers: Peter James Harlow, Secretary; Peter Joseph Greenyer [1956] Director/Certified Accountant; Francesca Emma Harlow [1986] Director/Accounts Manager; Peter James Harlow [1985] Director/Chartered Accountant; Frank Douglas Harris [1964] Director; Norman Sydney Harris [1937] Director; James Daniel Selway [1989] Director/Engineer; Danielle Elizabeth Van Der Wiel [1962] Director

Harrod UK Limited
Incorporated: 25 March 1966 *Employees:* 142
Net Worth: £7,152,687 *Total Assets:* £8,149,635
Registered Office: 1-3 Pinbush Road, South Lowestoft Industrial Estate, Lowestoft, Suffolk, NR33 7NL
Activities: Manufacture of sports goods
Shareholders: Christopher Michael Harrod; Stephanie Harrod
Officers: Stephanie Harrod, Secretary/Director; David John Bowling [1961] Director/Manufacturer; Christopher Michael Harrod [1955] Director; Stephanie Harrod [1962] Director

The Harrodian School Limited
Incorporated: 25 January 1993 *Employees:* 219
Net Worth: £27,614,340 *Total Assets:* £46,261,300
Registered Office: c/o Hill Wooldridge & Co, 107 Hindes Road, Harrow, Middlesex, HA1 1RU
Activities: General secondary education
Major Shareholder: Thomas Alford Houstoun-Boswall
Officers: Sir Thomas Alford Houstoun-Boswall [1947] Director; Amber Georgina Moore [1946] Director/House Manager

The Harrogate International Hotel Limited
Incorporated: 8 April 1982 *Employees:* 194
Net Worth: £19,460,000 *Total Assets:* £40,575,000
Registered Office: Queens Court, 9-17 Eastern Road, Romford, Essex, RM1 3NG
Activities: Hotels and similar accommodation
Parent: BPH Finance Number 1 Limited
Officers: Jonathan Patrick Braidley [1965] Director/Investment Professional; Christopher Andre Kula [1983] Director/Chartered Accountant [German/Canadian]

The Harrow Academies Trust
Incorporated: 6 May 2014 *Employees:* 21
Net Worth: £16,600,512 *Total Assets:* £16,948,598
Registered Office: Pinner High School, Beaulieu Drive, Pinner, Middlesex, HA5 1NB
Activities: Primary education
Officers: Dr Andleeb Ahmed [1970] Director/Doctor; David Chappell [1963] Director/Academy Head, Holland Park School; Paul Stuart Gamble [1973] Director/Headteacher; Susan Hammond [1962] Director/Headteacher; Dr Janice Karen Howkins [1955] Director; Susan Mary Maguire [1966] Director/Headteacher; Dr John Reavley [1958] Director; James Andrew Varley [1962] Director/Chartered Accountant; Christopher David Woolf [1977] Director/Headteacher

Harrow High School
Incorporated: 6 July 2011 *Employees:* 110
Net Worth: £11,269,925 *Total Assets:* £13,889,414
Registered Office: Harrow High School, Gayton Road, Harrow, Middlesex, HA1 2JG
Activities: General secondary education
Officers: Pete Bains [1958] Director/Retired; Donna Campbell [1967] Director; Stefan Arthur Clayton [1958] Director/Managing Agent; Andrew Steven Desai [1985] Director/Teacher; Stephen Fisher [1953] Director/Site Supervisor; Paul Stuart Gamble [1973] Director; Josephine Lang [1950] Director/Retired; Kishan Bhimji Patel [1987] Director/Actuarial Trainee; Mavji Patel [1971] Director/Teacher; Nigel William Rowlands [1961] Director/Headteacher Consultant

The Hart Schools Trust Ltd
Incorporated: 29 September 2011 *Employees:* 141
Previous: The North Hertfordshire Studio School Trust
Net Worth: £27,070,000 *Total Assets:* £29,082,856
Registered Office: The Thomas Alleyne Academy, High Street, Stevenage, Herts, SG1 3BE
Activities: Pre-primary education
Officers: Robert Malcolm Dale, Secretary; Dr Geoffrey Cleverdon [1948] Director/Retired; Kit Davies [1974] Director/Principal; Jonathan James Edward Ellam [1964] Director; Mark Christopher John Lewis [1981] Director/Principal; Stephen Marshman [1978] Director/Head of Contracting; Vicky Parsey [1967] Director/Executive Principal; Gary Phillips [1982] Director; Andrew Brian Simmons [1957] Director/Local Authority Employee; Jane Winterbone [1962] Director

Hartismere Family of Schools
Incorporated: 10 August 2010 *Employees:* 231
Previous: Hartismere School
Net Worth: £24,483,692 *Total Assets:* £27,139,760
Registered Office: Hartismere School, Castleton Way, Eye, Suffolk, IP23 7BL
Activities: General secondary education
Officers: Deborah Ann Ebbage, Secretary; Christopher Aldous [1951] Director/Deputy Headteacher (Retired); John Edward Battersby [1964] Director/Doctor; Simon Kenneth Hooton [1956] Director/Local Government Manager; Cleeve Lee MacDonald [1948] Director/Retired [Australian]; James Doherty McAtear [1965] Director/Headmaster; Marion Ravenhill [1949] Director [Irish]; Nicholas Roche [1950] Finance Director

Fred Hartley (Estates) Limited
Incorporated: 15 July 1947 *Employees:* 15
Net Worth: £6,511,300 *Total Assets:* £12,460,526
Registered Office: The Offices, Town Street, Upwell, Wisbech, Cambs, PE14 9DQ
Activities: Growing of cereals (except rice), leguminous crops and oil seeds
Major Shareholder: Christopher Fred Hartley
Officers: Christopher Fred Hartley, Secretary; Christopher Fred Hartley [1950] Director/Farmer

Harvest Investments Solutions Limited
Incorporated: 28 April 2009
Net Worth: £10,801 *Total Assets:* £20,705,364
Registered Office: 13 Clarence Lodge, Taverners Way, Hoddesdon, Herts, EN11 8TH
Activities: Management consultancy activities other than financial management
Major Shareholder: Hartmut Jacob
Officers: Phoebus Papapetrou [1950] Director

Harwich International (Holdings) Limited
Incorporated: 2 July 1997
Net Worth: £6,393,000 *Total Assets:* £74,942,000
Registered Office: Tomline House, The Dock, Felixstowe, Suffolk, IP11 3SY
Activities: Activities of other holding companies n.e.c.
Parent: Hutchison Ports (UK) Limited
Officers: Simon Richard Mullett, Secretary; Clemence Chun Fun Cheng [1958] Director; Sing Chi IP [1953] Director [Chinese]; Edith Shih [1952] Director

Harwich International Port Limited
Incorporated: 28 March 1990 *Employees:* 193
Net Worth: £28,715,000 *Total Assets:* £57,908,000
Registered Office: Tomline House, The Dock, Felixstowe, Suffolk, IP11 3SY
Activities: Sea and coastal passenger water transport
Parent: Harwich International (Holdings) Limited
Officers: Simon Richard Mullett, Secretary; Clemence Chun Fun Cheng [1958] Director; Sing Chi IP [1953] Director [Chinese]; Edith Shih [1952] Director

Harwood Hutton Limited
Incorporated: 22 February 2010 *Employees:* 49
Net Worth: £5,495,803 *Total Assets:* £8,042,977
Registered Office: 22 Wycombe End, Beaconsfield, Bucks, HP9 1NB
Activities: Accounting and auditing activities
Officers: Peter David Agius [1954] Director/Accountant; John Raymond Spencer Brace [1943] Director/Accountant; Margaret El Khalidi [1972] Director/Accountant; David Edward Jones [1963] Director/Accountant; Keir Graham Singleton [1980] Director/Chartered Accountant; Adam James Stronach [1968] Director/Accountant

Hascombe & Valiant Stud Limited
Incorporated: 30 September 2015 *Employees:* 13
Net Worth: £3,345,062 *Total Assets:* £17,552,200
Registered Office: Hascombe Stud, Moulton Road, Cheveley, Newmarket, Suffolk, CB8 9DW
Activities: Raising of horses and other equines
Major Shareholder: Anthony Ernest Oppenheimer
Officers: Fiona McGlone, Secretary; Sophie Clare Lussier [1965] Director; Arabella Elizabeth Morris [1972] Director; Anthony Ernest Oppenheimer [1937] Director; Antoinette Maria Oppenheimer [1947] Director; Emily Victoria Oppenheimer Turner [1968] Director

HaskoningDHV UK Holdings Limited
Incorporated: 23 June 1994
Net Worth: £20,746,128 *Total Assets:* £26,844,944
Registered Office: Rightwell House, Bretton Centre, Peterborough, PE3 8DW
Activities: Activities of head offices
Officers: Jonathan Simon Bull [1974] Director/Chartered Structural Engineer; Craig John Huntbatch [1961] Director/Chartered Civil and Structural Engineer; Mazhar Hussain [1964] Director/Accountant; Johan Theodorus Van Manen [1953] Director/Financial Controller [Dutch]

HaskoningDHV UK Limited
Incorporated: 1 November 1977 *Employees:* 490
Net Worth: £12,385,852 *Total Assets:* £46,037,972
Registered Office: Rightwell House, Bretton Centre, Peterborough, PE3 8DW
Activities: Activities of head offices
Parent: HaskoningDHV UK Holdings Limited
Officers: Jonathan Simon Bull [1974] Director/Chartered Structural Engineer; Craig John Huntbatch [1961] Director; Mazhar Hussain [1964] Director/Accountant; Johan Theodorus Van Manen [1953] Director/Financial Controller [Dutch]

Hatch End High School
Incorporated: 1 July 2011 *Employees:* 178
Net Worth: £21,715,824 *Total Assets:* £26,020,154
Registered Office: Headstone Lane, Harrow, Middlesex, HA3 6NR
Activities: General secondary education
Officers: Maria Abrams [1954] Director/Pastoral Manager; Rebecca Ann Cleary [1986] Director/Teacher; Anton Collyer [1951] Director/Retired; Timothy Matthew Dalton [1979] Director/Teacher; Catherine Mary Deed [1954] Director; Christopher Firth [1985] Director/Pastoral Support Manager; Sayed Hamid [1972] Director/Teacher [Afghan]; Oky Lee [1976] Director/Project Manager; Clement Alexander Lewis [1928] Director/Retired; Susan Mary Maguire [1966] Director; Edwin Solomon [1950] Director; Ketan Chandrakant Varia [1968] Director/Management Consultant; Dr Nandini Varma [1945] Director/Retired Community Paediatrician; Emma Wennington [1985] Director/Brand Marketing; Catherine Garnons Williams [1952] Director

Hatfield Trading Limited
Incorporated: 11 October 2006 *Employees:* 511
Net Worth: £16,563,866 *Total Assets:* £18,215,704
Registered Office: 2 The Parade, St Albans Road East, Hatfield, Herts, AL10 0EY
Activities: Other letting and operating of own or leased real estate
Shareholders: Ian Dennis Matthews; Penelope Anne Matthews
Officers: Penelope Anne Matthews, Secretary/Director; Ian Denis Matthews [1948] Director; Penelope Anne Matthews [1947] Director; Rupert John Matthews [1980] Managing Director

Hats Group Ltd
Incorporated: 8 December 1995 *Employees:* 23
Previous: Olympic (South) Limited
Net Worth: £2,665,846 *Total Assets:* £8,106,915
Registered Office: c/o LSR Management Ltd, Unit C2A Comet Studios, De Havilland Court, Amersham, Bucks, HP7 0PX
Activities: Other passenger land transport
Shareholders: Henry Bilinski; Anthony Howard
Officers: Henry Stanislaw Bilinski [1961] Director

Hauck Heat Treatment Limited
Incorporated: 28 July 1966 *Employees:* 180
Previous: TTI Group Limited
Net Worth: £153,000 *Total Assets:* £10,627,000
Registered Office: 39-43 Bilton Way, Luton, Beds, LU1 1UU
Activities: Treatment and coating of metals
Parent: Aalberts Industries UK Limited
Officers: Denise Coughlan, Secretary; Andrew Nicholas Borg [1967] Director; Marcus Wendel [1966] Managing Director [German]

Haven Leisure Limited
Incorporated: 4 December 1985 *Employees:* 6,123
Net Worth: £227,772,992 *Total Assets:* £818,675,968
Registered Office: No 1 Park Lane, Hemel Hempstead, Herts, HP2 4YL
Activities: Recreational vehicle parks, trailer parks and camping grounds
Parent: Bourne Leisure Limited
Officers: Jane Elizabeth Bentall [1970] Director/Accountant; Paul Charles Flaum [1970] Director; Iain Stuart Macmillan [1976] Director

Havens Christian Hospice
Incorporated: 30 March 1993 *Employees:* 296
Net Worth: £15,014,000 *Total Assets:* £16,029,000
Registered Office: Stuart House, 47 Second Avenue, Westcliff on Sea, Essex, SS0 8HX
Activities: Specialists medical practice activities
Officers: Andrew John Smith, Secretary; Roberto de Cristofano [1966] Director/Investment Banker; Terry Harding [1961] Director/Retired (Accountant); Barry John Linger [1947] Director/Retired; Revd Clive William Pegler [1944] Director/Retired; Richard Blyth Player [1947] Director/Retired Senior Civil Servant; Marion Roberts-Smith [1960] Director/Teaching Assistant; Brian Richard Terry [1945] Director/Senior NHS Manager (Retired); Stewart Edward Turner [1975] Director/Financial Analyst

Hawk Incentives Holdings Limited
Incorporated: 17 May 1983 *Employees:* 20
Previous: The Grass Roots Group Holdings Limited
Net Worth: £10,289,000 *Total Assets:* £44,010,000
Registered Office: Westside, London Road, Hemel Hempstead, Herts, HP3 9TD
Activities: Other business support service activities n.e.c.
Parent: Blackhawk Network Holdings, Inc.
Officers: Michelle Josephine Wainhouse, Secretary; Patrick Philip Gurney [1970] Director/Accountant; Matthew David Howe [1971] Managing Director; Kirsten Ellen Richesson [1969] Director/General Counsel and Secretary [American]

Hawk Incentives Limited
Incorporated: 7 February 2001 *Employees:* 353
Previous: The Grass Roots Group UK Limited
Net Worth: £19,076,000 *Total Assets:* £98,199,000
Registered Office: Westside, London Road, Hemel Hempstead, Herts, HP3 9TD
Activities: Other business support service activities n.e.c.
Parent: Hawk Incentives Holdings Limited
Officers: Michelle Josephine Wainhouse, Secretary; Patrick Philip Gurney [1970] Director/Accountant; Matthew David Howe [1971] Managing Director; Kirsten Ellen Richesson [1969] Director/General Counsel and Secretary [American]

Hawkes Limited
Incorporated: 18 March 1959 *Employees:* 25
Net Worth: £5,821,461 *Total Assets:* £21,351,756
Registered Office: Sausthorpe Hall, Sausthorpe, Spilsby, Lincs, PE23 4JN
Activities: Raising of swine and pigs
Officers: Roger William Hawkes, Secretary; Roger William Hawkes [1942] Director/Farmer; Simon Roger Hawkes [1967] Director/Farmer

Hawkins & Associates Limited
Incorporated: 13 December 1999 *Employees:* 156
Net Worth: £10,606,105 *Total Assets:* £16,970,284
Registered Office: Miller House, 120 Cambridge Science Park, Milton Road, Cambridge, CB4 0FZ
Activities: Engineering related scientific and technical consulting activities
Shareholder: Hawkins & Associates (Trustees) Ltd
Officers: Andrew John Alasdair Muston, Secretary; Dr John Bertram Frank Anderson [1960] Director/Consulting Scientist; Andrew Robert Bryce [1965] Director/Consulting Scientist; Alexander David Chambers [1975] Finance Director; Ian Giddings [1975] Director/Consulting Engineer; Dr Andrew Charles Malcolm Moncriff [1962] Director/Consulting Scientist; Andrew John Alasdair Muston [1963] Director/Consulting Scientist & Engineer; Dr Andrew Christopher Prickett [1975] Director/Consulting Engineer

Hay Farming Limited
Incorporated: 11 February 1982 *Employees:* 22
Net Worth: £7,325,804 *Total Assets:* £8,352,721
Registered Office: Somerset Farm, St Marks Road, Holbeach St Marks, Spalding, Lincs, PE12 8ED
Activities: Growing of cereals (except rice), leguminous crops and oil seeds
Parent: Hay Farming Group Limited
Officers: Helen Fiona Ralling, Secretary; Simon Bartlett [1970] Director/Farm Manager; Julia Margaretha Coulson [1967] Director/Housewife; Maria Margaretha Petronella Hay [1943] Director [Dutch]; Karen Mary Lang [1969] Director/Chartered Surveyor; Helen Fiona Ralling [1973] Director/Sales Manager

Haydon Holdings Limited
Incorporated: 1 November 1988 *Employees:* 77
Net Worth: £8,088,068 *Total Assets:* £10,374,261
Registered Office: Prospect House, Elm Farm Park, Great Green, Thurston, Bury St Edmunds, Suffolk, IP31 3SH
Activities: Development of building projects
Major Shareholder: Duncan Michael Haydon
Officers: Darryl Long, Secretary; Duncan Michael Eric Haydon [1969] Director/Contract Manager; Michael John Haydon [1937] Director/Builder

Haydon School
Incorporated: 9 March 2011 *Employees:* 208
Net Worth: £30,342,600 *Total Assets:* £32,915,100
Registered Office: Haydon School, Wiltshire Lane, Eastcote, Pinner, Middlesex, HA5 2LX
Activities: General secondary education
Officers: Beyhan Ercan-Razvi, Secretary; Claire Louise Barry [1972] Director/Strategy Manager; Stuart John Burnaby [1978] Director/Teacher; Jane Elizabeth Davies [1958] Director/School Pastoral Assistant Leader; Angela Amelda Dennie [1958] Director/Bookkeeper; Steven Edwards [1981] Director/Government; Dr Christopher Hayes [1973] Director/Barrister; Derek Honeygold [1936] Director/Senior University Lecturer (Retired); Dr Tanya Yvonne Huehns [1965] Director/Doctor; Robert William Jones [1967] Director/Headteacher; Carol Anne Katugampola [1968] Director/PCJ Fast Food Limited; Janet Ann Keal [1962] Director/Housewife; Sandeep Kumar [1967] Director/IT Analyst; Giuseppe Schettino [1970] Director/Scientist [Italian]

Hayes Point (Sully) Limited
Incorporated: 5 December 2003
Net Worth Deficit: £34,712,076 *Total Assets:* £32,034,484
Registered Office: 3rd Floor, Sterling House, Langston Road, Loughton, Essex, IG10 3TS
Activities: Other business support service activities n.e.c.
Shareholder: Zestplan Limited
Officers: Allan William Porter, Secretary; Stephen Stuart Solomon Conway [1948] Director; Donagh O'Sullivan [1968] Construction Director [Irish]

Hayman Group Limited
Incorporated: 18 January 1984 *Employees:* 113
Previous: Hayman Limited
Net Worth: £10,682,569 *Total Assets:* £23,930,704
Registered Office: Eastways Park, Witham, Essex, CM8 3YE
Activities: Other manufacturing n.e.c.
Shareholder: Christopher Frank Hayman
Officers: Daryl Weston Birden [1966] Director; Christopher Frank Hayman [1947] Director; James Christopher Barton Hayman [1976] Director; Elizabeth Lown [1969] Director; Miranda Sophie Carin Nevin [1974] Director; Simon Keith Strutt [1969] Director/Accountant

Hayter Holdings Limited
Incorporated: 15 November 2004
Net Worth: £35,180,000 *Total Assets:* £35,180,000
Registered Office: Spellbrook, Bishop's Stortford, Herts, CM23 4BU
Activities: Activities of other holding companies n.e.c.
Parent: The Toro Company
Officers: Bradley Wayne Dolan [1963] Director/MD, Finance Operations [American]; Julie Ann Kerekes [1966] Director/MD, Tax & Treasury [American]; Angela Dawn Snavely [1977] Director [American]

Hayter Limited
Incorporated: 15 November 2004 *Employees:* 134
Net Worth: £12,191,000 *Total Assets:* £19,320,000
Registered Office: Spellbrook, Bishop's Stortford, Herts, CM23 4BU
Activities: Manufacture of other special-purpose machinery n.e.c.
Parent: Hayter Holdings Limited
Officers: Kunjunni Raghunath Das [1952] Operations Director; Bradley Wayne Dolan [1963] Director/MD, Finance Operations [American]; Julie Ann Kerekes [1966] Director/MD, Tax & Treasury [American]

Hayward Tyler Limited
Incorporated: 15 October 1997
Net Worth: £1,481,000 *Total Assets:* £35,148,000
Registered Office: 1 Kimpton Road, Luton, Beds, LU1 3LD
Activities: Manufacture of electric motors, generators and transformers
Parent: Hayward Tyler Group Limited
Officers: Russell Jukes [1969] Director; Stephen Michael King [1966] Director; Stephen McQuillan [1961] Director

Hazlemere Holdings Limited
Incorporated: 19 March 2003 *Employees:* 78
Net Worth: £6,885,053 *Total Assets:* £10,729,429
Registered Office: Wellington Road, Cressex Industrial Estate, High Wycombe, Bucks, HP12 3PR
Activities: Activities of other holding companies n.e.c.
Shareholders: Christopher Howard Green; Sonia Michelle Braham; Stuart James Braham
Officers: Stuart James Braham, Secretary/Director; Mark Jonathan Austin [1962] Director; Anthony Beale [1963] Director; Jason Leonard Bradshaw [1965] Director; Stuart James Braham [1966] Director; Rachel Louise Braham-Hill [1990] Director

HBVB
Incorporated: 20 March 2013 *Employees:* 472
Net Worth Deficit: £147,328,992 *Total Assets:* £810,892,032
Registered Office: Media House, Peterborough Business Park, Lynch Wood, Peterborough, Cambs, PE2 6EA
Activities: Activities of other holding companies n.e.c.
Major Shareholder: Yvonne Saskia Bauer
Officers: Paul Anthony Keenan [1963] Director/Publisher; Sarah Jane Vickery [1963] Finance Director

HCL Insurance BPO Services Limited
Incorporated: 1 December 2004 *Employees:* 366
Net Worth: £5,763,000 *Total Assets:* £13,412,000
Registered Office: HCL House, 28-36 Eastern Road, Romford, Essex, RM1 3PJ
Activities: Other activities auxiliary to insurance and pension funding
Major Shareholder: Sivaprasad Sivasubramaniam Nadar
Officers: Nicholas Adrian Dumonde [1968] Director/Chief Operating Officer; Subramanian Gopalakrishnan [1967] Director [Indian]; Sugata Gupta [1965] Director [Irish]; Vijay Udupi Mallya [1964] Director [Indian]

HCT Portland Limited
Incorporated: 13 January 2017 *Employees:* 4
Net Worth: £3,979,384 *Total Assets:* £73,717,096
Registered Office: Portland House, 69-71 Wembley Hill Road, Wembley, Middlesex, HA9 8BU
Activities: Other business support service activities n.e.c.
Parent: South Central Property Limited
Officers: Bhupendra Shantilal Kansagra, Secretary; Laurent Elie Cadji [1977] Director/Businessman; Lewis Levy Cadji [1938] Director/Businessman; Bhupendra Shantilal Kansagra [1956] Director/Businessman; Ramesh Shantilal Kansagra [1950] Director/Businessman

A. & E. G. Heading Limited
Incorporated: 15 June 1953 *Employees:* 16
Net Worth: £7,698,975 *Total Assets:* £15,581,271
Registered Office: Greenwood House, Greenwood Court, Bury St Edmunds, Suffolk, IP32 7GY
Activities: Growing of cereals (except rice), leguminous crops and oil seeds
Shareholders: John Edwin Heading; Henry James Heading
Officers: John Edwin Heading, Secretary; John Edwin Heading [1940] Director/Farmer; Marc Edwin Heading [1965] Director/Farmer

Healthcare (Barts) Limited
Incorporated: 23 June 2005
Net Worth: £26,630 *Total Assets:* £25,617,806
Registered Office: 2 Hunting Gate, Hitchin, Herts, SG4 0TJ
Activities: Activities of head offices
Shareholders: DIF Infrastructure II UK Limited; Innisfree Secondary Partners 1 LLP
Officers: Louis Javier Falero [1977] Director; Paul William Nash [1967] Director/Fund Manager; Sabrina Sidhu [1979] Investment Director

Healthcare Homes Group Limited
Incorporated: 13 July 2005 *Employees:* 1,442
Net Worth: £6,826,274 *Total Assets:* £17,872,780
Registered Office: The Beeches, Apex 12, Old Ipswich Road, Ardleigh, Colchester, Essex, CO7 7QR
Activities: Residential nursing care facilities
Parent: Healthcare Homes Holdings Limited
Officers: Graham Charles Lomer, Secretary/Director; David John Bates [1954] Director; Gordon Douglas Cochrane [1962] Director; Samantha Caroline Dixon [1969] Director; Helen Gidlow [1967] Director; Mathew James King [1984] Finance Director; Graham Charles Lomer [1957] Director

Healthcare Homes Holdings Limited
Incorporated: 26 March 2008 *Employees:* 3,274
Net Worth: £11,232,614 *Total Assets:* £25,066,880
Registered Office: The Beeches, Apex 12, Old Ipswich Road, Ardleigh, Colchester, Essex, CO7 7QR
Activities: Activities of head offices
Shareholders: Graham Charles Lomer; David John Bates
Officers: Graham Charles Lomer, Secretary/Director; David John Bates [1954] Director; Gordon Douglas Cochrane [1962] Director; Philip William George [1951] Director; Mathew James King [1984] Director; Graham Charles Lomer [1957] Director

Hearing Dogs for Deaf People
Incorporated: 26 November 1985 *Employees:* 192
Net Worth: £18,377,510 *Total Assets:* £19,148,224
Registered Office: The Grange, Wycombe Road, Saunderton, Princes Risborough, Bucks, HP27 9NS
Activities: Social work activities without accommodation for the elderly and disabled
Officers: Paul Richard Hester, Secretary; John Stephen Morton Bower [1942] Director/Veterinary Surgeon; Alan Christopher Bowers [1970] Director/Chartered Accountant; Gary Peter Burchett [1964] Managing Director; Faith Beatrice Clark [1943] Director/Retired; Barry Stephen Downes [1949] Director/Retired; Kathryn Ann England [1977] Director/Head of Commercial; Bruce Fogle [1944] Director/Veterinary Surgeon; Andrew Peter Freeland [1943] Director/Retired Surgeon; Dr Anne Victoria Harrison [1942] Director; David Leslie Hay [1950] Director/Retired Solicitor; Adrian Mark Horsley [1949] Director/Architect; Victoria Augusta Hunt [1968] Director/Information Management Senior Vendor Manager; Christina Margaret Patricia O'Donovan-Rossa [1963] Director/Head of HR; Professor Richard Thomas Ramsden [1944] Director/Retired

Heathland Whitefriars Federation
Incorporated: 2 June 2014 *Employees:* 224
Net Worth: £19,973,672 *Total Assets:* £23,349,020
Registered Office: Healthland School, Eastcote Lane, Harrow, Middlesex, HA2 9AG
Activities: Pre-primary education
Officers: Angela Rosalind Bowd, Secretary; Lucy Emma Caswell [1971] Director/Executive Headteacher; Anup Chalisey [1979] Director/Mechanical Engineer; Roulla Chandarana [1974] Director/Pharmacist; Fiona Ruth Hopkins [1985] Director/Associate Headteacher; Thangavadivelu Jegatheesan [1974] Director; Lynne Malzard [1965] Director/Learning Support Assistant; David Harris Mattison [1948] Director/Retired; Marie-Louise Straub Nolan [1958] Director; Jonathan Robert Watson [1981] Director/Associate Headteacher

Heathpatch Limited
Incorporated: 5 June 1997 *Employees:* 232
Net Worth: £41,216,792 *Total Assets:* £71,413,920
Registered Office: Dairy Farm Office, Semer, Ipswich, Suffolk, IP7 6RA
Activities: Mixed farming
Officers: Penelope Anne Andrews, Secretary; John Baker-Cresswell [1965] Director/Farmer; James Kennedy Buckle [1964] Director/Farmer; Charles Paul Course [1961] Director; James Martin Hutchinson [1965] Director/Chartered Accountant

Heathrow Aviation Engineering UTC
Incorporated: 31 January 2011 *Employees:* 30
Net Worth: £8,821,438 *Total Assets:* £10,451,370
Registered Office: Heathrow Aviation Engineering UTC, Potter Street, Northwood, Middlesex, HA6 1QG
Activities: General secondary education
Officers: Robert John Bush, Secretary; Jennifer Body [1953] Director/Retired; Joanne Stephanie Harper [1970] Director/Teacher; Dr Sarmin Hossain [1971] Director/University Lecturer; Prof Geoffrey John Rodgers [1963] Director/Academic; Dr Rosa Scoble [1961] Director of Planning [Italian]; Paula Stannett [1965] Director/Chief People Officer

HEB Real Estate Limited
Incorporated: 17 September 2014
Net Worth: £18,187,812 *Total Assets:* £57,800,000
Registered Office: 21 Fulton Road, Wembley, Middlesex, HA9 0GA
Activities: Activities of other holding companies n.e.c.
Major Shareholder: Hasibullah Akbary
Officers: Hasibullah Akbary [1965] Director [Canadian]

Hedgemans Limited
Incorporated: 11 December 1984
Net Worth: £11,557,513 *Total Assets:* £13,375,961
Registered Office: 15 Woodlands Avenue, Hornchurch, Essex, RM11 2QT
Activities: Buying and selling of own real estate
Shareholder: Virendra Patel
Officers: Virendra Patel [1958] Director/Pharmacist

Hedingham School and Sixth Form
Incorporated: 13 December 2012 *Employees:* 151
Net Worth: £9,821,493 *Total Assets:* £12,947,634
Registered Office: Hedingham School and Sixth Form, Yeldham Road, Sible Hedingham, Halstead, Essex, CO9 3QH
Activities: General secondary education
Officers: Helena Frances Carter, Secretary; Nicola Barton [1966] Director/Primary School Teacher; Emma Brown [1979] Director/Cover Supervisor; Sarah Ford [1973] Director/Retired Police Officer; Andrew Harvison [1966] Director/Deputy Headteacher; Stuart Jarvis [1978] Director/Network Manager; Julia Mary King [1958] Director/Self Employed; Daniel Robert Lee [1980] Director; Dr Martin Lee [1967] Director/Police Officer; John Antony Panayi [1954] Director/Headteacher; Rebecca Bridgid Poynter [1964] Director/Self Employed/Education Consultant; Stuart Miles Scrivens [1944] Director/Retired Lecturer

Hel Group Limited
Incorporated: 26 October 2017 *Employees:* 6
Net Worth Deficit: £452,099 *Total Assets:* £10,800,524
Registered Office: 9-10 Capital Business Park, Manor Way, Borehamwood, Herts, WD6 1GW
Activities: Non-trading company
Parent: Ensco 1261 Limited
Officers: Andrew Roger Dixey [1950] Director; Luke Edward Matthews [1982] Director; Dr Jasbir Singh [1953] Director; Paul Stuart Sturgeon [1966] Finance Director

Heley Holdings Limited
Incorporated: 27 November 2001 *Employees:* 53
Net Worth: £6,215,829 *Total Assets:* £12,813,648
Registered Office: 712 London Road, West Thurrock, Grays, Essex, RM20 3JT
Activities: Non-trading company
Shareholders: George Heley; George Alexander Frederick Heley
Officers: Michael Schultz, Secretary; George Heley [1957] Director; George Alexander Frederick Heley [1938] Director

Helgor Trading Limited
Incorporated: 20 November 1998 *Employees:* 9
Net Worth: £6,281,509 *Total Assets:* £9,927,330
Registered Office: Swiss House, Beckingham Street, Tolleshunt Major, Essex, CM9 8LZ
Activities: Other letting and operating of own or leased real estate
Shareholders: Free D Limited; Ongar Fifty Two Limited
Officers: Abraham Aharon Dodi, Secretary/Director; Abraham Aharon Dodi [1963] Director; Angelique Glata [1966] Director; John Simon Helfgott [1958] Director; Nir Shamir [1957] Director

Heli Properties LLP
Incorporated: 25 October 2016
Net Worth: £2,849,753 *Total Assets:* £8,140,383
Registered Office: 51 Castle Street, High Wycombe, Bucks, HP13 6RN
Officers: Keith Duncan MacRae [1968] Member; Mairi MacRae [1962] Member

Helmet Integrated Systems Limited
Incorporated: 23 November 1992 *Employees:* 149
Net Worth: £4,786,082 *Total Assets:* £10,302,487
Registered Office: Unit 3, Focus 4, Fourth Avenue, Letchworth, Herts, SG6 2TU
Activities: Other manufacturing n.e.c.
Officers: Morten Bisgaard, Secretary; Heather Acker [1952] Director [American]; Richard Anthony Dellar [1964] Director; Leonard Frieder III [1973] Director [American]

Hemel Snowcentre Limited
Incorporated: 1 August 2007 *Employees:* 232
Net Worth: £13,929,000 *Total Assets:* £23,288,000
Registered Office: The Snow Centre, St Albans Hill, Hemel Hempstead, Herts, HP3 9NH
Activities: Other service activities n.e.c.
Officers: David Ian Brown [1967] Managing Director; Richard John Cook [1972] Director; Thomas Woodstock Harris [1963] Director/Engineer

Hemnall Investments Limited
Incorporated: 31 March 2016 *Employees:* 2
Net Worth Deficit: £18,350 *Total Assets:* £32,862,030
Registered Office: Sealand House, Hemnall Street, Epping, Essex, CM16 4LG
Activities: Development of building projects
Major Shareholder: John Alan Clarke
Officers: John Alan Clarke [1943] Director; Sandra Elaine Clarke [1943] Director

Hemnall Limited
Incorporated: 11 August 2010 *Employees:* 1
Net Worth: £12,937,092 *Total Assets:* £47,236,056
Registered Office: Sealand House, Hemnall Street, Epping, Essex, CM16 4LG
Activities: Development of building projects
Major Shareholder: John Alan Clarke
Officers: John Alan Clarke [1943] Director

Henbrandt Limited
Incorporated: 12 March 1971 *Employees:* 36
Net Worth: £12,224,514 *Total Assets:* £14,219,180
Registered Office: 5 Wentworth Road, Ransomes Europark, Ipswich, Suffolk, IP3 9SW
Activities: Other business support service activities n.e.c.
Shareholders: Julian Mark Starns; Harlequin Direct Limited
Officers: Laurence John Gannon, Secretary; Garry Michael Brandt [1964] Managing Director; Laurence John Gannon [1965] Director; Julian Mark Starns [1964] Director

Hendrie Estates Limited
Incorporated: 22 April 2010 *Employees:* 1
Net Worth: £3,776,393 *Total Assets:* £9,640,564
Registered Office: 7 The Close, Norwich, NR1 4DJ
Activities: Buying and selling of own real estate
Major Shareholder: Martyn Richard Hendrie
Officers: Martyn Richard Hendrie [1972] Director

Henfield Hire Limited
Incorporated: 10 February 2003 *Employees:* 26
Net Worth: £3,399,561 *Total Assets:* £10,114,325
Registered Office: Bankside, 300 Peachman Way, Broadland Business Park, Norwich, NR7 0LB
Activities: Other letting and operating of own or leased real estate
Parent: John Coldham Limited
Officers: Jennifer Elizabeth Crossley, Secretary/Director; Andrew Charles Dawson Crossley [1967] Director; Jennifer Elizabeth Crossley [1939] Director; Thomas Hird Crossley [1937] Director

Henkel Limited
Incorporated: 5 August 1926 *Employees:* 407
Net Worth: £149,992,992 *Total Assets:* £270,438,016
Registered Office: Henkel Limited, Wood Lane End, Hemel Hempstead, Herts, HP2 4RQ
Activities: Manufacture of other chemical products n.e.c.
Parent: Henkel AG & Co. KGaA
Officers: Sutinder Singh Bhandal, Secretary; Sutinder Singh Bhandal [1968] Director/Legal Counsel; Peter David Budden [1963] Director/Accountant; Mark Crane [1958] Director; Eamonn Gallagher [1960] Director/Product Development; Carsten Knobel [1969] Director/Economist [German]

Henley Group Finance Limited
Incorporated: 2 July 2013 *Employees:* 1
Net Worth: £78,859 *Total Assets:* £8,026,161
Registered Office: 28 Church Road, Stanmore, Middlesex, HA7 4XR
Activities: Financial intermediation not elsewhere classified
Parent: Henley Group Holdings Limited
Officers: Julian Mark Miller [1966] Director/Manager

Henley Group Holdings Limited
Incorporated: 13 March 1995 *Employees:* 1
Net Worth: £14,022,806 *Total Assets:* £14,042,932
Registered Office: 28 Church Road, Stanmore, Middlesex, HA7 4XR
Activities: Activities of head offices
Major Shareholder: Peter Gordon Watts
Officers: Julian Mark Miller [1966] Director/Manager

Henlow Church of England Academy
Incorporated: 19 March 2012 *Employees:* 80
Net Worth: £12,392,174 *Total Assets:* £13,097,991
Registered Office: Church Road, Henlow, Beds, SG16 6AN
Activities: General secondary education
Officers: Alison Jane Allen [1969] Director/Charity Adviser; Edwin Sidney Barnes [1970] Director/Construction; Jacqueline Burke [1964] Director/Sales Manager; Mark John Clark [1965] Director/Police Officer; Gavin Andrew Coombs [1979] Director/Facilities Management; Patsy Eva Critchley [1949] Director/Clergy; Caren Earp [1965] Director; Karen Evans [1983] Director/Business Administrator; Sheree Ann Gudgin [1964] Director/Unqualified Teacher; Graham Arthur Paul Hayward [1961] Director/Consulting Engineer; Paul Vernon Hughes [1953] Director/Archdeacon of Bedford; Perry Melvin Huntley [1963] Director/Retail Manager; Susan Jones [1961] Director/Teacher; Tracy Dawn Molyneux [1977] Director/Accountant; Shaun Lawrence Speller [1965] Director/Vicar

I Hennig & Co Limited
Incorporated: 31 December 1959 *Employees:* 34
Net Worth: £8,328,621 *Total Assets:* £11,044,106
Registered Office: 9 Pine Grove, Bricket Wood, St Albans, Herts, AL2 3ST
Activities: Agents specialised in the sale of other particular products
Parent: Hattron Ltd
Officers: Sarah Lindsey Stewart, Secretary; James Daryl Hambro [1949] Director/Investment Banker; Francis John Adrian Howard [1935] Director/Business Consultant; Arie Sela [1962] Director/Diamond Broker [Israeli]; Dani Sheldon Shein [1952] Director/Diamond Broker; Sarah Lindsey Stewart [1970] Finance Director; Grant John Frederick Stubbs [1959] Director/Private Equity [Irish]

John Henry and Sons (Developments) Ltd
Incorporated: 16 July 2013
Net Worth: £23,334,188 *Total Assets:* £31,168,772
Registered Office: The Mount, The Sidings, Station Road, Longstanton, Cambridge, CB24 3DS
Activities: Non-trading company
Parent: Shamrock Bidco Limited
Officers: James Henry [1965] Director; John Gerard Henry [1970] Director

John Henry Group Limited
Incorporated: 9 November 1992 *Employees:* 389
Previous: John Henry & Sons (Civil Engineers) Ltd.
Net Worth: £5,084,371 *Total Assets:* £44,252,884
Registered Office: The Mount, The Sidings, Station Road, Longstanton, Cambridge, CB24 3DS
Activities: Construction of other civil engineering projects n.e.c.
Parent: John Henry & Sons (Holdings) Limited
Officers: James Henry [1965] Director/Contractors; John Gerard Henry [1970] Director/Contractors

Heptares Therapeutics Limited
Incorporated: 4 June 2007 *Employees:* 120
Net Worth: £60,517,356 *Total Assets:* £76,371,416
Registered Office: Granta Park, Great Abington, Cambridge, CB21 6DG
Activities: Research and experimental development on biotechnology
Officers: Andrew Brimblecombe, Secretary; Christopher Robert Cargill [1984] Director [Australian]; Kieran Roy Darren Johnson [1969] Director; Dr Timothy Charles Gadsden Tasker [1953] Director/Chief Medical Officer; Malcolm Weir [1958] Director/Biochemist

Hera Primary Academy Trust
Incorporated: 19 January 2017 *Employees:* 145
Net Worth: £8,498,481 *Total Assets:* £10,347,522
Registered Office: Hera Primary Academy Trust, Lawford Mead Primary School, Trent Road, Chelmsford, Essex, CM1 2JH
Activities: Primary education
Officers: Isabelle Anne Jamesina Bailey [1978] Director/Management Consultant; Dawn Michelle Baker [1963] Director; Malcolm Paul Cummings [1971] Director/Product Manager; Stephanie Goater [1981] Director/Banking Consultant; Andrew Mark Montague [1982] Director/Police Sergeant; Nicola Anne Nunn [1958] Director/Business Manager

Heraeus Noblelight Limited
Incorporated: 5 December 1978 *Employees:* 137
Net Worth: £11,557,000 *Total Assets:* £16,245,000
Registered Office: 161 Cambridge Science Park, Milton Road, Cambridge, CB4 0GQ
Activities: Other manufacturing n.e.c.
Parent: Heraeus Beteiligungsverwaltungsgesellschaft mbH
Officers: Simon Mountford, Secretary; Philipp Gloeggler [1975] Finance Director [German]; Sandra Niedermeier [1979] Director/Lawyer [German]; Deborah Louise Playle [1966] Director; Wolfgang Stang [1957] Director [German]

Heritage Care Limited
Incorporated: 1 April 2010 *Employees:* 1,461
Net Worth: £10,241,000 *Total Assets:* £23,166,000
Registered Office: Connaught House, 112-120 High Road, Loughton, Essex, IG10 4HJ
Activities: Social work activities without accommodation for the elderly and disabled
Officers: Mark Timothy Milton, Secretary; Alan Twan Bates [1979] Director/Barrister; Nigel Owen Fletcher [1976] HR Director; Simon William Paul Griffiths [1961] Director/NHS Manager; Scott Thomas Haldane [1959] Finance Director; Richard James Edward Jones [1961] Director/Business Executive; Margaret Mary Lally [1953] Director/Retired; Jeanette Mitchell [1949] Director/Retired/Sessional Community Support Worker; Iain Francis O'Neil [1974] Director/Civil Servant; Lorraine Reynolds [1954] Director/Consultant [American]; John Peter Schuster [1950] Director/Retired; Richard John Smallwood [1955] Director/Retired

Heritage Developments Limited
Incorporated: 6 August 2003 *Employees:* 14
Net Worth Deficit: £1,415,019 *Total Assets:* £22,887,240
Registered Office: 10th Floor, Norfolk Tower, 48-52 Surrey Street, Norwich, NR1 3PA
Activities: Development of building projects
Shareholders: John Edward Maynard; Matthew Bartram
Officers: Matthew Bartram, Secretary/Director; Toby Ashworth [1977] Director; Matthew Bartram [1967] Director; Paul Feavearyear [1980] Construction Director; John Edward Maynard [1946] Director

Herma UK Limited
Incorporated: 7 February 1991 *Employees:* 103
Net Worth: £6,444,425 *Total Assets:* £16,311,131
Registered Office: 5 The Hollands Centre, Hollands Road, Haverhill, Suffolk, CB9 8PR
Activities: Manufacture of paper and paperboard
Parent: Herma GmbH
Officers: Robert Jenkinson, Secretary; Dr Thomas Baumgaertner [1960] Director [German]; Paul Eggbeer [1963] Divisional Director; Robert Jenkinson [1971] Divisional Director; Martin Kuhl [1966] Director [German]; Mario Zirn [1972] Director [German]

Herts & Essex Multi Academy Trust
Incorporated: 24 September 2013 *Employees:* 229
Previous: The Hertfordshire & Essex High School
Net Worth: £22,676,424 *Total Assets:* £25,844,080
Registered Office: The Hertfordshire & Essex High School, Warwick Road, Bishop's Stortford, Herts, CM23 5NJ
Activities: General secondary education
Officers: Emma Nelson, Secretary; John Robert Barfoot [1954] Director/Owner of Printing Company; Dr Sue Brindley [1951] Director/University Lecturer; Steve John Cox [1966] Director/Assistant Chief Executive - Thurrock Council; Susannah Rosemary Peta Dutton [1970] Director/Solicitor; Robert Arthur Fielden [1951] Director/Technical Consultant; Ann Forbes [1951] Director/Retired; Irene Graham [1937] Director/Retired; Gary David Griffiths [1954] Director/Retired; Paula Jane Harding [1958] Director/Owner of Dog Kennels; Judith Keogh [1960] Director/Teachers; Simon Calvert Loveday [1957] Director/Solicitor; Suman Sandhu [1971] Director/Pharmaceutical Consultancy; Graham Savage [1943] Director/Retired; Catherine Tooze [1966] Director/Headteacher; Samantha Joan Wilks [1965] Director/Accountant

Herts Insurance Consultants Limited
Incorporated: 15 March 1999 *Employees:* 201
Net Worth: £11,858,359 *Total Assets:* £20,964,260
Registered Office: 22-26 King Street, King's Lynn, Norfolk, PE30 1HJ
Activities: Non-life insurance
Parent: Hadleigh Holdings Ltd
Officers: David James Flux, Secretary/Insurance Broker; David James Flux [1968] Director/Insurance Broker; Yvonne Flux [1948] Director/Insurance Broker

Hertswood Academy
Incorporated: 15 March 2012 *Employees:* 154
Net Worth: £39,391,384 *Total Assets:* £43,777,864
Registered Office: Cowley Hill, Borehamwood, Herts, WD6 5LG
Activities: General secondary education
Officers: Joy Linda Wells Cox [1957] Director; Martin Wolfgang Doe [1966] Director/Computer Programmer; Peter Gillett [1970] Director; Fiona Helen Gubb Blackwood [1974] Director/Children's Centre Manager; Ann Muriel Harrison [1946] Director; Richard Arthur Kirk [1942] Director; Elizabeth Longworth [1968] Director/Teacher; Julie Dawn Smith [1966] Director/Sales Programme Support Manager; Christine Wainright [1954] Director/KS3 Co-ordinator

Heulwen Solar Limited
Incorporated: 9 January 2014 *Employees:* 2
Net Worth: £3,926,670 *Total Assets:* £9,544,876
Registered Office: Beeston Lodge, Beeston Lane, Spixworth, Norwich, NR10 3TN
Activities: Production of electricity
Parent: Share Nominees Limited
Officers: George Samuel Krempels [1986] Director; James Ignatius Schwerdt [1990] Director/Portfolio Manager

Hevingham Development Company Limited
Incorporated: 15 March 1961 *Employees:* 14
Net Worth: £7,244,532 *Total Assets:* £9,019,179
Registered Office: The Sawmills, The Street, Felthorpe, Norwich, NR10 4DH
Activities: Development of building projects
Shareholders: Patricia Christine Hinchley; Angela Mary Magnus
Officers: Angela Mary Magnus, Secretary; Patricia Christine Hinchley [1948] Director; Adrian Paul Magnus [1969] Director; Angela Mary Magnus [1943] Director; Julian Thomas Magnus [1974] Director

A.E.Hewison Limited
Incorporated: 24 December 1971 *Employees:* 2
Net Worth: £2,729,699 *Total Assets:* £10,463,817
Registered Office: Ashtree Farm House, Mill Lane, Addlethorpe, Skegness, Lincs, PE25 1HW
Activities: Retail sale in non-specialised stores with food, beverages or tobacco predominating
Major Shareholder: David MacDonald Hewison
Officers: David MacDonald Hewison [1962] Director/Store Manager; Janet Christine Hewison [1956] Director

Hewitsons LLP
Incorporated: 9 February 2008 *Employees:* 233
Net Worth: £5,481,419 *Total Assets:* £11,215,645
Registered Office: Shakespeare House, 42 Newmarket Road, Cambridge, CB5 8EP
Officers: Simon Geoffrey Biggin [1958] Member; David William Browne [1964] Member; Colin David Jones [1965] Member; Timothy Stephen Middleton [1960] Member; Deborah Jane Sharples [1966] Member; Rebecca Austin [1975] LLP Member; Carolyn Marjorie Bagley [1960] LLP Member; Julian John Hugh Bishop [1955] LLP Member; Christine Margaret Bowyer-Jones [1959] LLP Member; Lucinda Louise Jane Brown [1980] LLP Member; Marc Draper Carter [1962] LLP Member; Clare Elizabeth Vivienne Colacicchi [1958] LLP Member; Daniel Joseph Curtis [1972] LLP Member; Nicholas Jameson Hall [1964] LLP Member; Neil Thomas Harpham [1961] LLP Member; Susanne Romose Hinde [1973] LLP Member; Dominic Adrian Hopkins [1964] LLP Member; David John James [1965] LLP Member; Christopher Harrington Knight [1968] LLP Member; Valerie Clare Lambert [1973] LLP Member; James Patrick Lawrence [1961] LLP Member; Clare Ann Martin [1958] LLP Member; Natalie Minott [1980] LLP Member; Benedict Robert Kirwan Moorhead [1958] LLP Member; Yvette Mary Morgan [1961] LLP Member; Bernadette O'Reilly [1967] LLP Member; Andrew David Priest [1965] LLP Member; Timothy John Richards [1959] LLP Member; Emma Jane Shipp [1966] LLP Member; Stuart Anthony Simoes [1968] LLP Member; William Generald Hacon Thatcher [1958] LLP Member; Clare Rebecca Waller [1973] LLP Member; David Gareth John Wells [1974] LLP Member; Edward Charles Lothian Wheen [1958] LLP Member; Denise Wilkinson [1959] LLP Member; Gareth Royston Williams [1973] LLP Member; Jason Anthony Williams [1961] LLP Member

Hexagon Investment Holdings Limited
Incorporated: 11 May 2005 *Employees:* 3,200
Net Worth: £994,190 *Total Assets:* £14,830,570
Registered Office: Interaction House, 43 High Street, Huntingdon, Cambs, PE29 3AQ
Activities: Temporary employment agency activities
Major Shareholder: Andrew Iain Gilchrist
Officers: Geoff Holder, Secretary; David Mark Dickson [1962] Sales Director; Andrew Iain Gilchrist [1962] Director/Chartered Accountant

Hexcel (U.K.) Limited
Incorporated: 29 December 1972
Net Worth: £134,534,640 *Total Assets:* £182,416,512
Registered Office: Ickleton Road, Duxford, Cambridge, CB22 4QB
Activities: Activities of head offices
Parent: Hexcel Holdings (UK) Limited
Officers: Ian Blaydon, Secretary; Timothy Brackin [1964] Director/Accountant; Gail Lehman [1959] Director/General Counsel [American]; Patrick Joseph Winterlich [1969] Director/Accountant

Hexcel Composites Limited
Incorporated: 19 June 1995 *Employees:* 469
Net Worth: £270,641,984 *Total Assets:* £399,604,000
Registered Office: Ickleton Road, Duxford, Cambridge, CB22 4QB
Activities: Other manufacturing n.e.c.
Parent: Hexcel Europe Limited
Officers: Ian Blaydon, Secretary; Timothy John Brackin [1964] Director/Accountant; Gail Lehman [1959] Director/General Counsel [American]; Paul Dominic MacKenzie [1959] Director/Manager; Thierry Philippe Merlot [1960] Director/Manager [French]; Patrick Joseph Winterlich [1969] Director/Accountant

Hexcel Europe Limited
Incorporated: 2 October 2002
Net Worth: £147,875,664 *Total Assets:* £147,885,440
Registered Office: Ickleton Road, Duxford, Cambridge, CB22 4QB
Activities: Activities of other holding companies n.e.c.
Parent: Hexcel Corporation
Officers: Ian Blaydon, Secretary; Timothy Brackin [1964] Director/Accountant; Gail Lehman [1959] Director/General Counsel [American]; Patrick Joseph Winterlich [1969] Director/Accountant

Hexcel Holdings (UK) Limited
Incorporated: 7 November 2000
Net Worth: £259,983,136 *Total Assets:* £260,003,072
Registered Office: Ickleton Road, Duxford, Cambridge, CB22 4QB
Activities: Activities of head offices
Parent: Hexcel Corporation
Officers: Ian Blaydon, Secretary; Timothy John Brackin [1964] Director/Accountant; Gail Lehman [1959] Director/General Counsel [American]; Patrick Joseph Winterlich [1969] Director/Accountant

Hexcel Overseas
Incorporated: 16 February 1999
Net Worth: £20,998,224 *Total Assets:* £21,061,278
Registered Office: Ickleton Road, Duxford, Cambridge, CB22 4QB
Activities: Activities of production holding companies
Shareholders: Hexcel Europe Limited; Hexcel Europe Limited
Officers: Ian Blaydon, Secretary; Timothy John Brackin [1964] Director/Accountant; Gail Lehman [1959] Director/General Counsel [American]; Patrick Joseph Winterlich [1969] Director/Accountant

Heythrop Park Limited
Incorporated: 10 December 1999 *Employees:* 137
Previous: Firoka (Heythrop Park) Limited
Net Worth: £2,442,063 *Total Assets:* £33,644,216
Registered Office: 1 Park Lane, Hemel Hempstead, Herts, HP2 4YL
Activities: Hotels and similar accommodation
Parent: Bourne Leisure Holdings Limited
Officers: Jane Elizabeth Bentall [1970] Director/Accountant; Paul Charles Flaum [1970] Director; Iain Stuart Macmillan [1976] Director; Simon Thompson [1971] Director

HFC Finance Limited
Incorporated: 2 November 2015
Net Worth Deficit: £7,925,097,472 *Total Assets:* £48,204,828,672
Registered Office: Porter Tun House, 500 Capability Green, Luton, Beds, LU1 3LS
Activities: Activities of production holding companies
Parent: AB InBev UK Finance Company Limited
Officers: Yannick Nicolas Bomans [1983] Director/Employee [Belgian]; Gert Boulange [1977] Director/Employee [Belgian]

HFIS PLC
Incorporated: 20 September 1996 *Employees:* 215
Net Worth: £4,381,265 *Total Assets:* £9,232,645
Registered Office: First Floor, Lumiere, Elstree Way, Borehamwood, Herts, WD6 1JH
Activities: Non-life insurance
Major Shareholder: Simon Fox
Officers: David Anthony Jacobs, Secretary; Graham Marshall Coates [1956] Director/Management Consultant; Teresa Anne Dunne [1964] Human Resources Director; Edward William Hooker [1967] Director/Insurance Consultant; David Anthony Jacobs [1958] Director/Accountant; Ben John Terrett [1972] Finance Director

HG Construction Limited
Incorporated: 26 February 1982 *Employees:* 71
Net Worth: £11,253,000 *Total Assets:* £50,590,000
Registered Office: 4 Hunting Gate, Hitchin, Herts, SG4 0TJ
Activities: Construction of commercial buildings
Officers: Alan Peter Nixon, Secretary; Christopher Furniss Benham [1957] Director/Chartered Surveyor; Alan Peter Nixon [1963] Finance Director; Greg Purkiss [1981] Director/Quantity Surveyor; Adam Quinn [1982] Construction Director; Kevin Joseph Quinn [1958] Director/Chartered Engineer; Anthony Conor Rice [1975] Construction Director [Irish]

Hi-Tec Europe Limited
Incorporated: 31 August 2016 *Employees:* 58
Net Worth: £465,245 *Total Assets:* £8,129,508
Registered Office: Unit 1 Colonial Business Park, Colonial Way, Watford, Herts, WD24 4PR
Activities: Other retail sale in non-specialised stores
Major Shareholder: Rajiv Batra
Officers: Rajesh Batra [1955] Director [Indian]; Rajiv Batra [1961] Director; Ian McDonald McLean Cameron [1967] Director; Poopalasingham Rudran [1961] Finance Director

Hi-Tec Sports Public Limited Company
Incorporated: 5 February 1974
Net Worth: £65,311,388 *Total Assets:* £72,359,424
Registered Office: 7 Nelson Street, Southend on Sea, Essex, SS1 1EH
Activities: Wholesale of clothing and footwear
Shareholders: Hi-Tec Sports International Holdings BV; Franklin Van Wezel; Sunningdale Corporation Limited
Officers: Henry Stupp, Secretary; Martinus Christiaan Binnendijk [1964] Director [Dutch]; Kimberly Hope Doyle [1980] Managing Director [American]; Henry Stupp [1963] Director [American]

Hi-Tec Sports UK Limited
Incorporated: 31 October 1988 *Employees:* 1
Net Worth: £5,515,819 *Total Assets:* £8,056,063
Registered Office: 7 Nelson Street, Southend on Sea, Essex, SS1 1EH
Activities: Retail sale of footwear in specialised stores
Parent: Hi-Tec Sports PLC
Officers: Kimberly Hope Doyle [1980] Managing Director [American]; Henry Stupp [1963] Director [American]

Frederick Hiam,Limited
Incorporated: 5 May 1925 *Employees:* 70
Net Worth: £29,730,024 *Total Assets:* £37,692,032
Registered Office: Frederick Hiam Limited, Brandon Fields, Brandon, Suffolk, IP27 0SE
Activities: Growing of cereals (except rice), leguminous crops and oil seeds
Officers: Ashley Paul Malpass, Secretary; Carol Tania Bushnell [1966] Director/Printer; Nicholas John Gilford [1960] Commercial Director; Lindsay Harrison Hargreaves [1956] Managing Director; Ashley Paul Malpass [1974] Director/Chartered Certified Accountant; Christopher James Hiam Wilson [1966] Director/Agriculturist; Sophia Jane Wilson [1966] Director/Agriculturist

HIC Racing (Chiswick) Limited
Incorporated: 25 November 1981
Net Worth: £499,114,144 *Total Assets:* £499,137,952
Registered Office: Maple Court, Central Park, Reeds Crescent, Watford, Herts, WD24 4QQ
Activities: Non-trading company
Parent: Hilton Worldwide Holdings, Inc
Officers: Stuart Beasley [1971] Director/Financial Controller; Richard Geoffrey Beeston [1982] Director/Chartered Accountant; Michelle Momdjian [1976] Director/Attorney; George Christopher Ogle [1974] Director/Attorney; James Owen Percival [1968] Director/Accountant

HIC Treasury Limited
Incorporated: 29 June 1982
Net Worth: £512,404,288 *Total Assets:* £514,079,584
Registered Office: Maple Court, Central Park, Reeds Crescent, Watford, Herts, WD24 4QQ
Activities: Non-trading company
Parent: Hilton Finance (UK) Limited
Officers: Stuart Beasley [1971] Director/Financial Controller; Richard Geoffrey Beeston [1982] Director/Chartered Accountant; Michelle Momdjian [1976] Director/Attorney; George Christopher Ogle [1974] Director/Attorney; James Owen Percival [1968] Director/Accountant

Higgins Construction PLC
Incorporated: 27 February 1961 *Employees:* 306
Net Worth: £31,662,000 *Total Assets:* £120,509,000
Registered Office: One Langston Road, Loughton, Essex, IG10 3SD
Activities: Development of building projects
Parent: Higgins Group PLC
Officers: Mark Kevin Francis, Secretary; Stephen Bailess [1969] Director; Mark William Bradbury [1961] Construction Director; Philip David Burrows [1962] Director; Mark Kevin Francis [1980] Director; Declan Graham Higgins [1992] Director; Richard Graham Higgins [1956] Director; Stephen John Leakey [1969] Director/Construction; Antony Millidge [1961] Construction Director; Sean David Robinson [1975] Commercial Director

Higgins Group PLC
Incorporated: 16 February 1989 *Employees:* 379
Net Worth: £56,196,000 *Total Assets:* £199,340,000
Registered Office: One Langston Road, Loughton, Essex, IG10 3SD
Activities: Activities of head offices
Shareholders: Richard Graham Higgins; Martin James Higgins; Stephen Peter Higgins
Officers: Mark Kevin Francis, Secretary; Mark Kevin Francis [1980] Director; Martin James Higgins [1960] Director; Richard Graham Higgins [1956] Director; Stephen Peter Higgins [1958] Director

Higgins Homes PLC
Incorporated: 29 March 1965 *Employees:* 60
Net Worth: £21,425,000 *Total Assets:* £106,665,000
Registered Office: One Langston Road, Loughton, Essex, IG10 3SD
Activities: Development of building projects
Parent: Higgins Group PLC
Officers: Mark Kevin Francis, Secretary; Stephen James Boreham [1973] Construction Director; Mark Kevin Francis [1980] Director/Accountant; Steven Hancocks [1957] Director/Chartered Surveyor; Martin James Higgins [1960] Director; Richard Graham Higgins [1956] Director; William Michael Higgins [1986] Director; Jeremy Paul Marcus [1964] Sales Director; Christopher Miller [1966] Commercial Director; Malcolm Stuart Wallace [1958] Construction Director

Higgins Investments PLC
Incorporated: 5 December 1989 *Employees:* 3
Net Worth: £3,998,016 *Total Assets:* £13,784,537
Registered Office: One Langston Road, Loughton, Essex, IG10 3SD
Activities: Buying and selling of own real estate
Parent: Higgins Group PLC
Officers: Mark Kevin Francis, Secretary; Mark Kevin Francis [1980] Director/Accountant; Martin James Higgins [1960] Director; Richard Graham Higgins [1956] Director

Highassets Limited
Incorporated: 21 November 2003
Net Worth Deficit: £290,616 *Total Assets:* £8,245,822
Registered Office: c/o S2 Asset Management Ltd, 3rd Floor, Argyle House, Northside, Joel Street, Northwood Hills, Northwood, Middlesex, HA6 1NW
Activities: Buying and selling of own real estate
Parent: Milebank Ltd
Officers: Hardip Singh [1973] Director; Bharat Kumar Hirji Thakrar [1957] Director

The Highcrest Academy
Incorporated: 13 May 2011 *Employees:* 126
Net Worth: £9,023,465 *Total Assets:* £11,119,521
Registered Office: The Highcrest Academy, Hatters Lane, High Wycombe, Bucks, HP13 7NQ
Activities: General secondary education
Officers: Nigel Albert Walker, Secretary; Paul John Basham [1965] Director/Principal Scientist; Glen Darren Burke [1966] Director/Principal; Ben Elliot Croft [1989] Director/Year Manager; Guy John Garden [1968] Director/Teacher; Angela Hay [1967] Director/Project Coordinator; Susan Jollands [1961] Director/Self Employed Consultant; Zara Khan [1977] Director/Vice Chair 6 Counties Kidney Patients Association; Jennifer Lee [1979] Director of Hemar & Advocacy at Janssen [Canadian/Australian]; Alethae Mango [1979] Director/Registered Nurse; Natasha Louise Quelch [1974] Director/Health & Beauty Assistant; Glyn Ian Rowland [1963] Director/Civil Servant; Wendy Thornton [1963] Director

Highfield Park Trust
Incorporated: 2 May 1996 *Employees:* 4
Net Worth: £8,890,551 *Total Assets:* £8,963,462
Registered Office: Highfield Park Visitor Centre, Hill End Lane, St Albans, Herts, AL4 0RA
Activities: Operation of sports facilities
Officers: Richard Andrew Bull, Secretary; Timothy Ian Abbott [1965] Director/Student; Kevin Barnes [1944] Director/Retired; Michael John Curtis [1961] Director/Chartered Accountant; Ian Jamieson Day [1957] Director/Editor; Roger John Owen Thomas [1943] Director/Lecturer

Highrak Limited
Incorporated: 2 November 1988 *Employees:* 7
Net Worth: £4,876,098 *Total Assets:* £8,368,730
Registered Office: Runway House, The Runway, Ruislip, Middlesex, HA4 6SE
Activities: Hotels and similar accommodation
Parent: SME Holdings Ltd
Officers: Aly Mohamed Esmail, Secretary; Sayed Mohamed Esmail, Secretary; Aly Mohamed Esmail [1982] Director; Sayed Mohamed Esmail [1986] Director

Highway Stops Retail Limited
Incorporated: 8 August 2011 *Employees:* 3
Net Worth: £12,992,547 *Total Assets:* £23,157,496
Registered Office: Unit 11 Metro Trading Centre, Second Way, Wembley, Middlesex, HA9 0YJ
Activities: Other business support service activities n.e.c.
Major Shareholder: Sharad Mohanlal Raja
Officers: Anthony David Head [1968] Director; Sharad Mohanlal Raja [1949] Director; Shilan Raja [1986] Director; Shobhana Sharad Raja [1953] Director

Hilands Property Partners LLP
Incorporated: 30 March 2007 *Employees:* 2
Net Worth: £12,183,434 *Total Assets:* £12,190,634
Registered Office: Enterprise House, Eastern Road, Romford, Essex, RM1 3PJ
Officers: Dennis Edward Myers [1950] Member; Patricia Anne Myers [1948] Member

Hilborough Farms Limited
Incorporated: 14 December 1998 *Employees:* 13
Previous: Mossdale Farms Limited
Net Worth: £7,165,969 *Total Assets:* £23,654,136
Registered Office: Hilborough House, Hilborough, Thetford, Norfolk, IP26 5BQ
Activities: Raising of sheep and goats
Officers: William Henry Van Cutsem, Secretary; Edward Bernard Charles Van Cutsem [1973] Director; Emilie Elise Christine Van Cutsem [1946] Director; Hugh Ralph Van Cutsem [1974] Director/Institutional Broker Dealer; Nicholas Pieter Geoffrey Van Cutsem [1977] Director; William Henry Van Cutsem [1979] Director/Student

Hildo Limited
Incorporated: 31 January 2012
Net Worth: £13,342,024 *Total Assets:* £15,655,811
Registered Office: Hill House, Lowlands Road, Harrow, Middlesex, HA1 3EQ
Activities: Development of building projects
Major Shareholder: Donovan Gijsbertus Wijsmuller
Officers: Brian Martin Comer [1960] Director [Irish]; Luke Andrew Comer [1957] Director [Irish]

Hildon House Limited
Incorporated: 19 March 1986 *Employees:* 65
Net Worth: £2,524,351 *Total Assets:* £10,454,791
Registered Office: 2 Crossways Business Centre, Bicester Road, Kingswood, Aylesbury, Bucks, HP18 0RA
Activities: Other service activities n.e.c.
Shareholder: Balaji Ramamoorthy
Officers: Leonard Kevin Chandran Sebastian [1969] Managing Director [Swiss]; Balaji Ramamoorthy [1964] Director/Businessman [American]; Brian Vikram Ramamoorthy [1997] Director/Student [American]

The Hill Company Limited
Incorporated: 11 November 2003 *Employees:* 63
Net Worth: £5,416,503 *Total Assets:* £27,435,568
Registered Office: Solus 31, Motherwell Way, West Thurrock, Essex, RM20 3LB
Activities: Archives activities
Parent: Motherwell Holdings Ltd
Officers: James Douglas Hill, Secretary/Director; Ryan James Brazier [1989] Director; Andrew Douglas Hill [1931] Director; James Douglas Hill [1968] Director; Sarah Jane Hill [1966] Director; David Victor Malempre [1949] Director/Corporate Lawyer; Roger Joseph McGlynn [1957] Director/Company Accountant

Hill Group Services Limited
Incorporated: 14 April 2009 *Employees:* 26
Net Worth: £4,022,000 *Total Assets:* £117,019,000
Registered Office: The Power House, Gunpowder Mill, Powdermill Lane, Waltham Abbey, Essex, EN9 1BN
Activities: Other business support service activities n.e.c.
Parent: Hill Holdings Limited
Officers: Andrew Richard Hill [1958] Director; Gregory James Hill [1986] Director; Kieran Thomas Larkin [1953] Director; Neil Stuart Williams [1961] Finance Director

Hill Holdings Limited
Incorporated: 20 April 2001 *Employees:* 432
Net Worth: £128,543,000 *Total Assets:* £376,777,984
Registered Office: The Power House, Gunpowder Mill, Powdermill Lane, Waltham Abbey, Essex, EN9 1BN
Activities: Activities of construction holding companies
Major Shareholder: Andrew Richard Hill
Officers: Neil Stuart Williams, Secretary; Ernest Stephen Battey [1959] Director; Andrew Richard Hill [1958] Director; Gregory James Hill [1986] Director; Kieran Thomas Larkin [1953] Director; Neil Stuart Williams [1961] Finance Director

Hill of Towie Limited
Incorporated: 6 July 2009
Net Worth Deficit: £16,366,000 *Total Assets:* £64,152,000
Registered Office: Beaufort Court, Egg Farm Lane, Kings Langley, Herts, WD4 8LR
Activities: Other business support service activities n.e.c.
Parent: Trafalgar Wind Holdings Limited
Officers: Dominic James Hearth, Secretary; Steven William Hughes [1972] Generation & Asset Management Director; Fraser Stephen Merry [1968] Director/Chartered Surveyor; Mitesh Raj Patel [1982] Director/Group Financial Controller

Hill Partnerships Limited
Incorporated: 8 April 1991 *Employees:* 319
Net Worth: £35,963,000 *Total Assets:* £224,531,008
Registered Office: The Power House, Gunpowder Mill, Powdermill Lane, Waltham Abbey, Essex, EN9 1BN
Activities: Construction of domestic buildings
Parent: Hill Holdings Limited
Officers: Neil Stuart Williams, Secretary; Andrew Richard Hill [1958] Managing Director; Gregory James Hill [1986] Director; Thomas Hill [1988] Director; Ian Jamie Hunter [1967] Director; Robert Allan Jack [1974] Director; Paul Robert Jordan [1964] Director; Stephen John Kane [1964] Commercial Director; Kieran Thomas Larkin [1953] Director; Simon William Trice [1978] Director; Neil Stuart Williams [1961] Finance Director

Hill Residential Limited
Incorporated: 13 July 2001 *Employees:* 78
Net Worth: £97,007,000 *Total Assets:* £305,825,984
Registered Office: The Power House, Gunpowder Mill, Powdermill Lane, Waltham Abbey, Essex, EN9 1BN
Activities: Buying and selling of own real estate
Parent: Hill Holdings Limited
Officers: Neil Stuart Williams, Secretary; David Stewart Eardley [1968] Director; Robert Hall [1967] Director; Ryan Paul Harris [1982] Director; Andrew Richard Hill [1958] Director; Gregory James Hill [1986] Director; Ian Jamie Hunter [1967] Director; Stephen John Kane [1964] Director; Kieran Thomas Larkin [1953] Director; Amanda Miller [1964] Director/Solicitor; Damian O'Hara [1964] Director; Anthony Charles Parker [1971] Director/Chartered Accountant; Nicholas Parkinson [1960] Design Director; Cain Peters [1972] Director; Jon Thistlethwaite [1969] Director; Neil Stuart Williams [1961] Finance Director; Anthony John Woodman [1960] Director

Hill's Garages (Woodford) Limited
Incorporated: 6 June 1945 *Employees:* 108
Net Worth: £4,302,805 *Total Assets:* £13,312,039
Registered Office: 536-564 High Road, Woodford Green, Essex, IG8 0PR
Activities: Sale of new cars and light motor vehicles
Parent: Hills Group Enterprises Limited
Officers: Rosanna Hill, Secretary; Ashley Boyd Humphries, Secretary; Rosanna Francesca Hill [1988] Director; Ashley Boyd Humphries [1959] Director

Hillary Bidco Limited
Incorporated: 23 March 2012 *Employees:* 661
Net Worth Deficit: £45,515,000 *Total Assets:* £37,972,000
Registered Office: Everest House, Sopers Road, Cuffley, Potters Bar, Herts, EN6 4SG
Activities: Activities of head offices
Major Shareholder: Jonathan Paul Moulton
Officers: Robert Alexander Asplin [1979] Director; Joanne Maria Holland [1960] Director [Australian]; Karl Sean Munns [1970] Director

S.Hille & Co.(Holdings) Limited
Incorporated: 20 October 1964 *Employees:* 5
Net Worth: £11,208,170 *Total Assets:* £12,025,737
Registered Office: 132 St Albans Road, Watford, Herts, WD24 4AE
Activities: Other letting and operating of own or leased real estate
Officers: Ian Scheer, Secretary; Brian Ivan Leaver [1936] Director/Chartered Surveyor; Cherrill Sheila Scheer [1939] Director; Ian Scheer [1933] Director/Printer; Terence Ivan Scheer [1968] Director/Printer

JF Hillebrand UK Limited
Incorporated: 13 January 1982 *Employees:* 133
Net Worth: £5,352,729 *Total Assets:* £26,352,304
Registered Office: Dissegna House, Weston Avenue, West Thurrock, Grays, Essex, RM20 3ZP
Activities: Other transportation support activities
Officers: Joanne Christina Kelly, Secretary; Thorsten Beer [1971] Director/Chief Financial Officer [German]; Gavin Herman [1967] Director/Chief Operating Officer; Joanne Christina Kelly [1979] Finance Director; Cornelis Sigmund Van Gent [1962] Director/Chief Executive [Dutch]

Hills Group Enterprises Limited
Incorporated: 19 November 2002 *Employees:* 108
Net Worth: £7,664,311 *Total Assets:* £16,674,323
Registered Office: 536-564 High Road, Woodford Green, Essex, IG8 0PR
Activities: Activities of head offices
Major Shareholder: Richard Martin Hill
Officers: Rosanna Hill, Secretary; Ashley Boyd Humphries, Secretary; Rosanna Francesca Hill [1988] Director; Ashley Boyd Humphries [1959] Director

Hilton Finance (UK) Limited
Incorporated: 18 November 1999
Net Worth: £1,663,046,016 *Total Assets:* £1,676,255,104
Registered Office: Maple Court, Central Park, Reeds Crescent, Watford, Herts, WD24 4QQ
Activities: Other business support service activities n.e.c.
Parent: Hilton UK Hotels Limited
Officers: Stuart Beasley [1971] Director/Financial Controller; Richard Geoffrey Beeston [1982] Director/Chartered Accountant; Michelle Momdjian [1976] Director/Attorney; George Christopher Ogle [1974] Director/Attorney; James Owen Percival [1968] Director/Accountant

Hilton Food Group PLC
Incorporated: 16 March 2007 *Employees:* 3,545
Net Worth: £158,650,000 *Total Assets:* £433,360,000
Registered Office: 2-8 Interchange, Latham Road, Huntingdon, Cambs, PE29 6YE
Activities: Activities of head offices
Officers: Neil Michael George, Secretary; Christine Cross [1951] Director; Philip John Heffer [1966] Director; Nigel Richard Majewski [1960] Finance Director; Dr Angus James Porter [1957] Director; Robert Andrew Watson [1958] Director/Chief Executive Officer; John Graham Worby [1950] Director

Hilton HHC Limited
Incorporated: 19 January 2006
Net Worth: £1,552,382,464 *Total Assets:* £1,552,382,464
Registered Office: Maple Court, Central Park, Reeds Crescent, Watford, Herts, WD24 4QQ
Activities: Activities of head offices
Parent: Hilton HIH Limited
Officers: Stuart Beasley [1971] Director/Financial Controller; Richard Geoffrey Beeston [1982] Director/Chartered Accountant; Michelle Momdjian [1976] Director/Attorney; George Christopher Ogle [1974] Director/Attorney; Brian McKay Wilson [1962] Director/Company Secretary

Hilton International Hotels (UK) Limited
Incorporated: 12 June 1961
Net Worth: £666,311,040 *Total Assets:* £1,487,772,288
Registered Office: Maple Court, Central Park, Reeds Crescent, Watford, Herts, WD24 4QQ
Activities: Hotels and similar accommodation
Parent: Hilton International IP Holding Limited
Officers: Stuart Beasley [1971] Director/Financial Controller; Richard Geoffrey Beeston [1982] Director/Chartered Accountant; Stephen Patrick Cassidy [1968] Director/SVP Operations UK & Ireland; Michelle Momdjian [1976] Director/Attorney; George Christopher Ogle [1974] Director/Attorney; James Owen Percival [1968] Director/Accountant; Simon Robert Vincent [1963] Director; Brian McKay Wilson [1962] Director/Company Secretary

Hilton International IP Holding 2 Limited
Incorporated: 6 December 2016
Net Worth: £2,394,365,184 *Total Assets:* £2,523,724,800
Registered Office: Maple Court, Central Park, Reeds Crescent, Watford, Herts, WD24 4QQ
Activities: Hotels and similar accommodation
Parent: Hilton International Master Holding Limited
Officers: Stuart Beasley [1971] Director/Financial Controller; Richard Geoffrey Beeston [1982] Director/Chartered Accountant; Stephen Patrick Cassidy [1968] Director/Senior Vice President Operations; Michelle Momdjian [1976] Director/Attorney; George Christopher Ogle [1974] Director/Attorney; James Owen Percival [1968] Director/Accountant; Brian McKay Wilson [1962] Director/Company Secretary

Hilton International IP Holding Limited
Incorporated: 8 July 2016
Net Worth: £2,694,447,104 *Total Assets:* £3,080,324,096
Registered Office: Maple Court, Central Park, Reeds Crescent, Watford, Herts, WD24 4QQ
Activities: Hotels and similar accommodation
Parent: Hilton International IP Holding 2 Limited
Officers: Stuart Beasley [1971] Director/Financial Controller; Richard Geoffrey Beeston [1982] Director/Chartered Accountant; Stephen Patrick Cassidy [1968] Director/Senior Vice President Operations; Michelle Momdjian [1976] Director/Attorney; George Christopher Ogle [1974] Director/Attorney; James Owen Percival [1968] Director/Accountant; Brian McKay Wilson [1962] Director/Company Secretary

Hilton Properties Limited
Incorporated: 12 January 1994 *Employees:* 3
Net Worth: £9,845,918 *Total Assets:* £21,732,836
Registered Office: Unit 2 Raynham Road, Bishop's Stortford, Herts, CM23 5PJ
Activities: Other letting and operating of own or leased real estate
Shareholders: Peter Andrew Hilton; Sarah Ann Hilton
Officers: Peter Andrew Hilton [1963] Director; Sarah Ann Hilton [1965] Director

Hilton UK Hotels Limited
Incorporated: 18 May 1904
Net Worth: £1,272,785,152 *Total Assets:* £1,338,172,928
Registered Office: Maple Court, Central Park, Reeds Crescent, Watford, Herts, WD24 4QQ
Activities: Hotels and similar accommodation
Parent: Hilton Worldwide Holding 2 Limited
Officers: Stuart Beasley [1971] Director/Financial Controller; Richard Geoffrey Beeston [1982] Director/Chartered Accountant; Stephen Patrick Cassidy [1968] Senior Vice President and Managing Director; Michelle Momdjian [1976] Director/Attorney; George Christopher Ogle [1974] Director/Attorney; James Owen Percival [1968] Director/Accountant; Simon Robert Vincent [1963] Director; Brian McKay Wilson [1962] Director/Company Secretary

Hilton UK Manage Limited
Incorporated: 15 October 2007
Net Worth: £28,088,258 *Total Assets:* £36,292,152
Registered Office: Maple Court, Central Park, Reeds Crescent, Watford, Herts, WD24 4QQ
Activities: Hotels and similar accommodation
Parent: Hilton Worldwide Limited
Officers: Stuart Beasley [1971] Director/Financial Controller; Richard Geoffrey Beeston [1982] Director/Chartered Accountant; Michelle Momdjian [1976] Director/Attorney; George Christopher Ogle [1974] Director/Attorney; James Owen Percival [1968] Director/Accountant; Simon Robert Vincent [1963] Director; Brian McKay Wilson [1962] Director/Company Secretary

Hilton Worldwide FS Treasury Limited
Incorporated: 18 February 2014
Net Worth: £9,563,753 *Total Assets:* £986,574,848
Registered Office: Maple Court, Central Park, Reeds Crescent, Watford, Herts, WD24 4QQ
Activities: Other business support service activities n.e.c.
Parent: Hilton Worldwide Manage Limited
Officers: Stuart Beasley [1971] Director/Financial Controller; Richard Geoffrey Beeston [1982] Director/Chartered Accountant; Stephen Patrick Cassidy [1968] Director/Senior Vice President Operations; Michelle Momdjian [1976] Director/Attorney; George Christopher Ogle [1974] Director/Attorney; James Owen Percival [1968] Director/Accountant; Brian McKay Wilson [1962] Director/Attorney

Hilton Worldwide Holding 2 Limited
Incorporated: 12 February 2014
Net Worth: £397,220,800 *Total Assets:* £2,394,284,288
Registered Office: Maple Court, Central Park, Reeds Crescent, Watford, Herts, WD24 4QQ
Activities: Hotels and similar accommodation
Parent: Hilton HHC Limited
Officers: Stuart Beasley [1971] Director/Financial Controller; Richard Geoffrey Beeston [1982] Director/Chartered Accountant; Stephen Patrick Cassidy [1968] Director/Senior Vice President Operations UK & Ireland; Michelle Momdjian [1976] Director/Attorney; George Christopher Ogle [1974] Director/Attorney; James Owen Percival [1968] Director/Accountant; Brian McKay Wilson [1962] Director/Attorney

Hilton Worldwide Holding LLP
Incorporated: 4 April 2014
Net Worth: £2,958,252,800 *Total Assets:* £2,958,253,056
Registered Office: Maple Court, Central Park, Reeds Crescent, Watford, Herts, WD24 4QQ

Hilton Worldwide Manage Limited
Incorporated: 7 December 2010 *Employees:* 32
Net Worth: £1,429,282,432 *Total Assets:* £2,571,142,144
Registered Office: Maple Court, Central Park, Reeds Crescent, Watford, Herts, WD24 4QQ
Activities: Hotels and similar accommodation
Shareholders: Hilton International IP Holding Limited; Hilton International Hotels (UK) Limited
Officers: Stuart Beasley [1971] Director/Financial Controller; Richard Geoffrey Beeston [1982] Director/Chartered Accountant; Stephen Patrick Cassidy [1968] Director/Senior Vice President Operations UK & Ireland; Michelle Momdjian [1976] Director/Attorney; George Christopher Ogle [1974] Director/Attorney; James Owen Percival [1968] Director/Accountant; Brian McKay Wilson [1962] Director/Company Secretary

Himelight Limited
Incorporated: 28 April 1999 *Employees:* 1
Net Worth: £5,583,437 *Total Assets:* £8,014,373
Registered Office: 1 Warner House, Harrovian Business Village, Bessborough Road, Harrow, Middlesex, HA1 3EX
Activities: Renting and operating of Housing Association real estate
Shareholder: Robert Milton Fu
Officers: Robert Milton Fu, Secretary; Robert Milton Fu [1964] Director [Brazilian]

Hincroft Limited
Incorporated: 8 June 2012
Net Worth Deficit: £18,032,442 *Total Assets:* £71,227,072
Registered Office: Hill House, Lowlands Road, Harrow, Middlesex, HA1 3EQ
Activities: Development of building projects
Parent: Mingold Limited
Officers: Brian Martin Comer [1960] Director [Irish]; Luke Andrew Comer [1957] Director [Irish]

Hindu Education Authority Ltd
Incorporated: 25 May 2004 *Employees:* 7
Previous: IFoundation Ltd
Net Worth: £9,811,863 *Total Assets:* £10,800,594
Registered Office: Bhaktivedanta Manor, Dharam Marg, Hilfield Lane, Aldenham, Watford, Herts, WD25 8EZ
Activities: Primary education
Officers: Dhruva-Kusa Shah, Secretary; Dr Sanjiv Kumar Agarwal [1963] Director/Consultant Surgeon; Sulabh Agarwal [1977] Director/Consultant; Dr Kapil Chawla [1976] Director/Doctor; William John Martin Fleming [1954] Director/Businessman; Upendra Kalan [1953] Director/Chartered Accountant; Kartik Rajen Khandwala [1979] Director/Consultant; Shailesh Patel [1958] Director/Priest

F.W. Hipkin Limited
Incorporated: 1 January 1937 *Employees:* 48
Net Worth: £4,082,694 *Total Assets:* £10,233,493
Registered Office: Acorn House, Coppen Road, off Selinas Lane, Chadwell Heath, Dagenham, Essex, RM8 1NU
Activities: Non-specialised wholesale trade
Parent: Hipkin Holdings Limited
Officers: Frank Dulson Lafford [1928] Director; Simon Lafford-Walker [1972] Director; Peter Rolland [1964] Director

Historic House Hotels Limited
Incorporated: 30 July 1979 *Employees:* 233
Net Worth: £18,704,148 *Total Assets:* £20,545,322
Registered Office: Hartwell House, Oxford Road, Hartwell, Aylesbury, Bucks, HP17 8NR
Activities: Hotels and similar accommodation
Officers: Neil James Kenyon, Secretary; Richard Broyd [1948] Director; Lionel Antoine Joseph Chatard [1972] Hotel Director [French]; Chris John Feeney [1963] Director/Accountant; Matthew Anthony Chadwick Johnson [1971] Director/Manager; Jacqueline Emily Jordan [1968] Director; Neil James Kenyon [1974] Finance Director; Elgan Lloyd Roberts [1971] Director/Hotel General Manager; Sarah Elizabeth Staniforth [1953] Historic Properties Director; Peter Jules Maria Vermeulen [1975] Director of Finance

Hitchin Boys' School
Incorporated: 8 November 2012 *Employees:* 125
Net Worth: £20,631,976 *Total Assets:* £22,343,014
Registered Office: Hitchin Boys' School, Grammar School Walk, Hitchin, Herts, SG5 1JB
Activities: Other education n.e.c.
Officers: Deborah Susan Ivory-Webb, Secretary; Philip Robert Addison [1958] Human Resources Director; Emily Jane Brinkley [1991] Director/Teacher; Martin Brown [1963] Director/Headteacher; Dr Helen Mary Corkill [1953] Director/University Manager; Cheryl Jean Grainger [1956] Director/Training Consultant; Stephen Alan Hall [1973] Director/IT Technician; Philip Laws [1964] Director/Senior Project Manager for BT; Christopher David Maylin [1968] Director/Chartered Accountant; Michael Patrick Taylor [1938] Director; Richard Arthur Charles Thake [1942] County & District Councillor - Director; John Simon Turney [1969] Director; Kathryn Sophie White [1989] Director/Teacher; Virginia Brenda Wilson [1961] Director

Hitchin Girls' School
Incorporated: 7 July 2011 *Employees:* 118
Net Worth: £22,392,052 *Total Assets:* £24,518,878
Registered Office: Hitchin Girls' School, Highbury Road, Hitchin, Herts, SG4 9RS
Activities: General secondary education
Officers: Anthony Derek Hankin, Secretary; Charlotte Jayne Astill [1973] Director/Self Employed Construction Consultant; Kieran Myles Balfe [1960] Director/Teacher; Joanne Elizabeth Briggs [1973] Director/Police Officer; Kenneth David Down [1977] Director/Research Chemist; Geoffrey Ian Edwards [1965] Director/Business Executive; Christine Anne Emmings [1967] Director/Data & Examinations Officer; Anthony Richard Fitzakerly [1957] Director/Regulation & Compliance Manager; Christopher John Lomas Hall [1964] Managing Director; Dilys Nesta Job [1948] Director/Manager; Daljit Kaur [1975] Director/Solicitor; Mary Elizabeth King [1956] Director/Teacher; Simon Thomas Gilby Lucas [1983] Director/Headhunter & Business Owner; Frances Catherine Manning [1961] Director/Headteacher; Dr Katherine Sarah Middleton [1977] Director/Psychologist & Church Leader; Steven Mills [1969] Director/Headmaster; Christopher Colin Minton [1938] Director/Retired; Sonia Yvonne Morrison [1962] Director; Katharine Rowe [1967] Director/Teacher; Toby George Mountford Scott [1968] Director/Manager; Mark Wilfred Seaman Hill [1957] Director/Chartered Surveyor; Stuart Alexander Sprawson [1957] Director/Solicitor

Hitchin Property Trust Limited (The)
Incorporated: 23 January 1937 *Employees:* 9
Net Worth: £47,526,400 *Total Assets:* £54,147,968
Registered Office: The Maltings, Bridge Street, Hitchin, Herts, SG5 2DE
Activities: Development of building projects
Officers: Jean Angela Seaton Ray, Secretary; Norman Ewart Livings [1945] Director/Farmer; Jean Angela Seaton Ray [1923] Director; Jean Margaret Ray [1948] Director; John Ray [1950] Director/Quantity Surveyor; Alexandra Melanie Roberton [1977] Director

HJP Media LLP
Incorporated: 17 March 2015 *Employees:* 2
Net Worth: £8,237,433 *Total Assets:* £8,792,276
Registered Office: 166 College Road, Harrow, Middlesex, HA1 1RA
Officers: Paul John Hollywood [1966] Member

HL Display UK Holding Limited
Incorporated: 8 December 2009
Net Worth: £17,175,000 *Total Assets:* £24,489,000
Registered Office: 1-2 Horsecroft Road, Harlow, Essex, CM19 5BH
Activities: Activities of head offices
Parent: HL Display AB
Officers: Duncan Hill, Secretary; Benno Eliasson [1965] Director [Swedish]; Duncan Hill [1959] Director; Nina Katriina Jonsson [1965] Managing Director [Finnish]; Howard Martin Williams [1962] Finance Director

HLT Stakis Operator Limited
Incorporated: 15 October 2007
Net Worth Deficit: £48,437,320 *Total Assets:* £14,441,632
Registered Office: Maple Court, Central Park, Reeds Crescent, Watford, Herts, WD24 4QQ
Activities: Hotels and similar accommodation
Parent: Hilton Worldwide Limited
Officers: Stuart Beasley [1971] Director/Financial Controller; Richard Geoffrey Beeston [1982] Director/Chartered Accountant; Stephen Patrick Cassidy [1968] Director/SVP Operations UK & Ireland; Michelle Momdjian [1976] Director/Attorney; George Christopher Ogle [1974] Director/Attorney; James Owen Percival [1968] Director/Accountant

E. Hobbs (Farms) Limited
Incorporated: 13 March 1958 *Employees:* 13
Net Worth: £31,215,178 *Total Assets:* £39,735,652
Registered Office: Warden House, 37 Manor Road, Colchester, Essex, CO3 3LX
Activities: Growing of cereals (except rice), leguminous crops and oil seeds
Major Shareholder: Malcolm Eric Hobbs
Officers: Sally Ann Blackwell, Secretary; Sally Ann Blackwell [1959] Director; Eric Hobbs [1935] Director/Farmer; Malcolm Eric Hobbs [1960] Director/Farmer; Margaret Gladys Hobbs [1937] Director/Secretary

Hockerill College Academy Trust
Incorporated: 11 January 2011 *Employees:* 172
Net Worth: £29,313,000 *Total Assets:* £37,989,000
Registered Office: Hockerill Anglo-European College, Dunmow Road, Bishop's Stortford, Herts, CM23 5HX
Activities: General secondary education
Officers: Amanda Jane Everett, Secretary; Dr Tareq Abouharb [1968] Director/Doctor; Stephen William Beach [1955] Director/School Bursar; Dr Judith Kate Braeckman [1962] Director/Consultant Financial Assistant; Marie Calnan [1965] Director/Learning Support Assistant; Shamiela Davids [1970] Director/Teacher [British/South African]; Jane Elizabeth Dewhurst [1963] Director/Examinations Officer; Simon James Hutley [1967] Client Services Director; Rachel Claire Lawson [1964] Director; Patrick Lewis [1964] Director/Barrister; Richard Trevelyan Markham [1971] Director/Principal; Branimir Radukic [1966] Director/Civil Engineer; John Stenhouse [1961] Director; James Robert Sutton Tatchell [1969] Director/Financial Consultant; Simon Nicholas Thomas Waring [1963] Director; Jonathan Williams [1956] Director/Chartered Shipbroker; Rebecca Williams [1961] Director/Local Government Lawyer

Hoddesdon Developments Ltd
Incorporated: 27 October 2006 *Employees:* 2
Net Worth: £7,463,800 *Total Assets:* £11,024,788
Registered Office: 57-59 High Street, Hoddesdon, Herts, EN11 8TQ
Activities: Other letting and operating of own or leased real estate
Shareholders: Giuseppe Ricotta; Giuseppina Ricotta
Officers: Joe Ricotta, Secretary/Director; Giuseppina Ricotta [1969] Director; Joe Ricotta [1966] Director

The Hoddesdon School Trust
Incorporated: 8 March 2011 *Employees:* 256
Previous: The John Warner School
Net Worth: £45,248,412 *Total Assets:* £47,362,856
Registered Office: The Hoddesdon School Trust, Stanstead Road, Hoddesdon, Herts, EN11 0QF
Activities: Primary education
Officers: David Andrew Allman, Secretary; Jane Eileen Margaret Carson [1953] Director/Headteacher; Peter Cuffaro [1957] Director/Solicitor; Graeme Alan Dykes [1965] Director/Chartered Accountant; Alison Heal [1963] Director/Retired; Sarah Anne Hurwood [1965] Director/Headteacher; Fiona Louise Ives [1956] Director; David James Patrick Kennedy [1958] Director/Headteacher [Irish]; Anthony Clive Lebaigue [1958] Director; Robert McCarthy [1961] Director/Civil Engineer; Rachel Elizabeth Semark [1967] Director/Headteacher; Adrian Shah-Cundy [1973] Corporate Responsibility Director; Mary Catherine Sykes [1965] Marketing Director [Canadian/British]

Holdcare Limited
Incorporated: 22 October 2008 *Employees:* 125
Net Worth: £2,070,754 *Total Assets:* £8,160,756
Registered Office: 45 Mymms Drive, Brookmans Park, Hatfield, Herts, AL9 7AE
Activities: Other residential care activities n.e.c.
Shareholder: Anil Khosla
Officers: Anil Khosla, Secretary; Anil Khosla [1963] Director/Chartered Accountant; Georgina Seaton [1960] Director/Care Manager

Holden & Holden Limited
Incorporated: 23 August 1978 *Employees:* 113
Net Worth: £5,372,000 *Total Assets:* £18,530,000
Registered Office: 22 Heigham Street, Norwich, NR2 4TF
Activities: Sale of new cars and light motor vehicles
Major Shareholder: Timothy Peter Holden
Officers: Anthony Ernest Holden, Secretary; Anthony Ernest Holden [1939] Director; Timothy Peter Holden [1979] Director; Gavin Croft Wilcock [1948] Director/Solicitor

Holdings U.K. No.3 Limited
Incorporated: 2 March 2011
Previous: GM Holdings U.K. No. 3 Limited
Net Worth: £10,000,000 *Total Assets:* £10,000,000
Registered Office: Griffin House, UK1-101-135 Osborne Road, Luton, Beds, LU1 3YT
Activities: Other business support service activities n.e.c.
Parent: Automotive UK No.1
Officers: Rabiya Nagi, Secretary; James Charles Highnam [1969] Finance Director; Peter Thomas Hope [1966] Director; Stephen Norman [1954] Director [French]; Leanne Charlotte Pratt-Massey [1976] Director

Hollywood Bowl Group PLC
Incorporated: 13 June 2016 *Employees:* 2,044
Net Worth: £94,938,000 *Total Assets:* £153,584,000
Registered Office: Focus 31 West Wing, Cleveland Road, Hemel Hempstead Industrial Estate, Hemel Hempstead, Herts, HP2 7BW
Activities: Other sports activities
Officers: Nicholas Paul Backhouse [1963] Director; Peter Ashley Boddy [1965] Director; Stephen Burns [1976] Director/Chief Executive; Laurence Brian Keen [1976] Finance Director; Ivan Schofield [1967] Director; Claire Tiney [1960] Director

The Holmes Care (Group) Limited
Incorporated: 25 April 2006 *Employees:* 1,192
Net Worth: £24,918,116 *Total Assets:* £65,683,720
Registered Office: 228 St Marys Lane, Upminster, Essex, RM14 3DH
Activities: Activities of head offices
Shareholders: Shiraz Lakhani; Indumati Lakhani
Officers: Indumati Lakhani [1942] Director; Sharifa Lakhani [1987] Managing Director; Shiraz Lakhani [1945] Director

The Holmes Care Limited
Incorporated: 3 November 1994 *Employees:* 72
Net Worth Deficit: £444,843 *Total Assets:* £19,503,908
Registered Office: 228 St Mary's Lane, Upminster, Essex, RM14 3DH
Activities: Other human health activities
Parent: Holmes Care (Group) Limited
Officers: Indumati Lakhani, Secretary; Shiraz Lakhani [1945] Director

Ivor Holmes Limited
Incorporated: 24 December 1959 *Employees:* 89
Net Worth Deficit: £293,489 *Total Assets:* £13,031,888
Registered Office: Arlington Business Park, Gunnells Wood Road, Stevenage, Herts, SG1 2BE
Activities: Sale of new cars and light motor vehicles
Parent: Specialist Cars Holdings Limited
Officers: Clive Michael James, Secretary; Julian Lance Bourne [1960] Director/Dealer Principal; Michael Jacob Donovan [1959] Director; Clive Martin Fletcher [1959] Director; Mr Clive Michael James [1961] Director

Holywells Residential Lettings Limited
Incorporated: 17 August 2016
Previous: Landex Lettings Limited
Net Worth: £135,371 *Total Assets:* £9,588,030
Registered Office: 19 Holywells Road, Ipswich, Suffolk, IP3 0DL
Activities: Other letting and operating of own or leased real estate
Parent: Landex Commercial Property Limited
Officers: Julian Paul Wallace-King, Secretary; Barbara Elizabeth Davies [1947] Director; Daniel James Davies [1977] Director; Thomas Glyn Davies [1949] Director; Julian Paul Wallace-King [1955] Director

Home Counties Estates Limited
Incorporated: 9 August 1973
Net Worth: £5,528,024 *Total Assets:* £16,229,434
Registered Office: Houghton Hall, The Green, Houghton Regis, Dunstable, Beds, LU5 5DY
Activities: Other letting and operating of own or leased real estate
Parent: Chamberlain Holdings PLC
Officers: Vena Chambury, Secretary; Christopher Paul Bugden [1966] Finance Director; John Maxwell Chamberlain [1942] Director; Vena Chambury [1955] Director/Estate Management; Stefan Mucha [1957] Director; Peter Bernard Wayte [1949] Director/Solicitor

Homeguard Properties Limited
Incorporated: 13 January 1998 *Employees:* 3
Net Worth: £10,198,001 *Total Assets:* £19,216,532
Registered Office: 5 Elstree Gate, Elstree Way, Borehamwood, Herts, WD6 1JD
Activities: Other letting and operating of own or leased real estate
Officers: Daniel Naftali Reichmann [1988] Director

Homepines Investments Limited
Incorporated: 12 November 1985 *Employees:* 3
Net Worth: £2,862,807 *Total Assets:* £12,574,484
Registered Office: Suite 105, Viglen House, Alperton Lane, Wembley, Middlesex, HA0 1HD
Activities: Other business support service activities n.e.c.
Major Shareholder: Augusto Montanari
Officers: William Robert Hawes [1945] Director

Honywood Community Science School
Incorporated: 5 April 2011 *Employees:* 181
Net Worth: £9,156,771 *Total Assets:* £12,283,731
Registered Office: Honywood Community Science School, Westfield Drive, Coggeshall, Colchester, Essex, CO6 1PZ
Activities: General secondary education
Officers: Scott Mason Caygill [1987] Staff Director; Tayrina Ferguson [1974] Parent Director; Anela Hall [1961] Director; Alison Dawn Lightly [1966] Director; Dawn Tracey McIntosh [1962] Director; James Ross Munro [1976] Director; James Lawrence Saunders [1975] Director; Timothy Revill John Styles [1962] Director; Angela Jill Ward [1944] Director; Sarah Warren [1966] Director

Hoo Hing Holdings Limited
Incorporated: 6 June 1978 *Employees:* 293
Net Worth: £26,456,588 *Total Assets:* £34,708,916
Registered Office: Hoo Hing House, Freshwater Road, Dagenham, Essex, RM8 1RX
Activities: Non-specialised wholesale trade
Shareholder: Tim Fuk Poon
Officers: Caroline Poon, Secretary; Caroline Poon [1963] Director/Trader; Ken Poon [1964] Director; Tim Fuk Poon [1941] Director/Trader

Hoo Hing Limited
Incorporated: 1 July 1991 *Employees:* 293
Net Worth: £18,786,808 *Total Assets:* £27,048,712
Registered Office: Hoo Hing House, Freshwater Road, Dagenham, Essex, RM8 1RX
Activities: Non-specialised wholesale trade
Parent: Hoo Hing Holdings Ltd
Officers: Caroline Poon, Secretary; Caroline Poon [1963] Director/Trader; Ken Poon [1964] Director/Trader; Tim Fuk Poon [1941] Director/Trader

Hoole Hall Country Club Limited
Incorporated: 22 November 2006 *Employees:* 131
Net Worth: £814,000 *Total Assets:* £41,544,000
Registered Office: Queen Court, 9-17 Eastern Road, Romford, Essex, RM1 3NG
Activities: Hotels and similar accommodation
Officers: Jonathan Patrick Braidley [1965] Director/Real Estate Investment and Finance Professional; Christopher Andre Kula [1983] Director/Chartered Accountant [German/Canadian]

Hoopers Limited
Incorporated: 18 January 1929 *Employees:* 364
Net Worth: £39,896,952 *Total Assets:* £43,706,348
Registered Office: The Office, Cheveley Park Stud, Duchess Drive, Newmarket, Suffolk, CB8 9DD
Activities: Activities of head offices
Shareholders: David Brian Thompson; Patricia Thompson
Officers: Christopher James Dant, Secretary; Debra Angus [1965] Director; Roy Bernard Copus [1959] Director/Chartered Accountant; David Brian Thompson [1936] Director; Patricia Thompson [1940] Director; Katharine Patricia Woodward [1968] Director/Buyer

Hopkins and Moore (Developments) Limited
Incorporated: 8 September 1987 *Employees:* 182
Net Worth: £116,052,000 *Total Assets:* £223,499,008
Registered Office: Melton Park House, Melton, Woodbridge, Suffolk, IP12 1TJ
Activities: Construction of domestic buildings
Shareholders: James Jonathan Hopkins; Jahco Limited
Officers: Robert Edward Whiting, Secretary; Michael John Cox [1958] Finance Director; James Jonathan Hopkins [1960] Director/Developer; Selina Karen Hopkins [1973] Director

Hopkins Homes Limited
Incorporated: 26 November 1993 *Employees:* 174
Net Worth: £107,677,000 *Total Assets:* £206,300,992
Registered Office: Melton Park House, Melton, Woodbridge, Suffolk, IP12 1TJ
Activities: Construction of domestic buildings
Parent: Hopkins Homes Holdings Limited
Officers: Robert Edward Whiting, Secretary/Accountant; Marcus Charles Armitage [1965] Production Director; Martin Bailey [1967] Director/Chartered Surveyor; Lee Carl Barnard [1976] Sales and Marketing Director; Simon Charles Wesley Bryan [1964] Development Director; Michael John Cox [1958] Director/Chartered Accountant; James Jonathan Hopkins [1960] Director/Property Developer; Iain David Jamie [1977] Land Director

Hops Pub Company Limited
Incorporated: 19 December 2007 *Employees:* 894
Net Worth Deficit: £1,571,000 *Total Assets:* £39,525,000
Registered Office: Porter Tun House, 500 Capability Green, Luton, Beds, LU1 3LS
Activities: Public houses and bars
Parent: Town and City Pub Group Limited
Officers: Suzanne Louise Baker [1963] Director; Simon David Longbottom [1971] Director/Chief Executive Officer; David Andrew Ross [1973] Director/Chief Financial Officer

Horizon Discovery Group PLC
Incorporated: 4 March 2014 *Employees:* 288
Net Worth: £171,156,992 *Total Assets:* £193,164,992
Registered Office: Building 8100, Cambridge Research Park, Beach Drive, Waterbeach, Cambridge, CB25 9TL
Activities: Research and experimental development on biotechnology
Officers: Jayesh Pankhania, Secretary; Grahame David Cook [1958] Director; Susan Galbraith [1965] Director/Company Executive; Dr Ian David Gilham [1960] Director; Dr Vishal Kumar Gulati [1970] Director/Venture Capitalist; Margarita Krivitski [1989] Director [American]; Jayesh Pankhania [1970] Director and Company Secretary; Terence William Pizzie [1961] Director/Chief Executive Officer; Susan Jane Searle [1963] Director

Horizon Discovery Limited
Incorporated: 14 February 2005 *Employees:* 174
Net Worth Deficit: £12,901,000 *Total Assets:* £37,828,000
Registered Office: 8100 Cambridge Research Park, Waterbeach, Cambridge, CB25 9TL
Activities: Research and experimental development on biotechnology
Parent: Horizon Discovery Group PLC
Officers: Dr Ian David Gilham [1960] Director; Jayesh Pankhania [1970] Director; Terence William Pizzie [1961] Director

Horizon Land Limited
Incorporated: 29 December 2000
Net Worth: £3,213,165 *Total Assets:* £13,711,959
Registered Office: P O Box 19, Six Hills Way, Stevenage, Herts, SG1 2DA
Activities: Buying and selling of own real estate
Parent: MBDA UK Limited
Officers: Claire Lois Game, Secretary; Peter Heinrich Charles Bols [1965] Director; Christopher Nigel Evans [1958] Director/Head of Legal UK; Iain David West [1970] Finance Director

The Horse Trust
Incorporated: 16 December 1938
Net Worth: £26,224,564 *Total Assets:* £26,617,376
Registered Office: Westcroft Stables, Slad Lane, Lacey Green, Princes Risborough, Bucks, HP27 0PP
Activities: Veterinary activities
Officers: Jeanette Allen, Secretary; Professor Mark Bowen [1973] Director/Veterinary Surgeon; Professor Peter Clegg [1962] Director/Veterinary Surgeon; David Allan Hancock Cook [1946] Director/Retired; Lord Rupert Charles de Mauley [1957] Director/Retired; Bronwen Jones [1963] Director/Solicitor; Christopher James William Marriott [1944] Director/Chartered Surveyor; Professor Bruce Campbell McGorum [1961] Director/Veterinary Surgeon; Rupert Hugh Maxwell Neal [1952] Director/Investment Manager; Professor Julian David Slater [1962] Director/Veterinary Surgeon; Camilla Rose Soames [1960] Director/Farmer

Horsforth Holdings Limited
Incorporated: 21 November 2011 *Employees:* 356
Net Worth: £3,246,000 *Total Assets:* £26,262,000
Registered Office: LDH House, St Ives Business Park, Parsons Green, St Ives, Cambs, PE27 4AA
Activities: Other business support service activities n.e.c.
Officers: Mark Braithwaite [1978] Managing Director [British/South African]; Jonathan Philip Dyson [1964] Director; Keith Hamill [1952] Director; Ian Arthur Hendrie [1970] Director; Julian Frederick Nicholls [1951] Director

Horsham Properties Limited
Incorporated: 29 February 2012 *Employees:* 2
Net Worth: £3,457,735 *Total Assets:* £9,821,486
Registered Office: Larking Gowen LLP, King Street House, 15 Upper King Street, Norwich, NR3 1RB
Activities: Other letting and operating of own or leased real estate
Parent: Joseph King Holdings Limited
Officers: Deborah Gertrude Clipsham [1951] Director; Terence John Gould [1952] Director/Solicitor; Neil Generald Alexander King [1956] Director/QC; Annie Phillips [1951] Director

Horta Properties Limited
Incorporated: 5 September 1986
Net Worth: £19,099,228 *Total Assets:* £19,575,724
Registered Office: Suite 123, Milton Hall, Ely Road, Milton, Cambridge, CB24 6WZ
Activities: Other letting and operating of own or leased real estate
Parent: Horta Investments Limited
Officers: John Dickens [1946] Director; Mark Dujardin [1964] Director; Marios Michaelides [1963] Director/Chief Financial Officer

Hospice of St. Francis (Berkhamsted) Limited
Incorporated: 14 July 1980 *Employees:* 129
Net Worth: £8,378,000 *Total Assets:* £8,838,000
Registered Office: Spring Garden Lane, Northchurch, Berkhamsted, Herts, HP4 3GW
Activities: Residential nursing care facilities
Officers: Julia Marianne Bolsom [1973] PR Director; Sarah Melinda Byrt [1963] Director/Solicitor; Timothy David Curry [1971] Director/Consultant; Matthew John Gorman [1977] Deputy Director of Development; Mark Richard Hampton [1964] Director/Chief Financial Officer; Nicholas Charles Hanling [1963] Director/Consultant; Tracy Jane Moores [1965] Director; Magaret Salmon [1947] Director; Dr Berndine Gesiene Tipple [1960] Director/General Practitioner [Dutch]; David Grey Williams [1951] Director; Alison Clare Woodhams [1956] Finance Director

The Hospital Company (Oxford John Radcliffe) Holdings Limited
Incorporated: 15 August 2003
Net Worth Deficit: £80,998,000 *Total Assets:* £156,732,992
Registered Office: 2 Hunting Gate, Hitchin, Herts, SG4 0TJ
Activities: Hospital activities
Parent: Infrastructure Investments Portsmouth Limited
Officers: Clement David Baptiste Leverd [1986] Director/Investment Executive [French]; Natalia Poupard [1977] Director/Asset Manager; Geoffrey Alan Quaife [1955] Director/Asset Manager

The Hospital Company (Oxford John Radcliffe) Limited
Incorporated: 15 August 2003
Net Worth Deficit: £80,998,000 *Total Assets:* £156,732,992
Registered Office: 2 Hunting Gate, Hitchin, Herts, SG4 0TJ
Activities: Hospital activities
Parent: The Hospital Company (Oxford John Radcliffe) Holdings Limited
Officers: Clement David Baptiste Leverd [1986] Director/Investment Executive [French]; Natalia Poupard [1977] Director/Asset Manager; Geoffrey Alan Quaife [1955] Director/Asset Manager

The Hospital Company (QAH Portsmouth) Holdings Limited
Incorporated: 29 April 2005
Net Worth Deficit: £12,030,000 *Total Assets:* £325,800,000
Registered Office: 2 Hunting Gate, Hitchin, Herts, SG4 0TJ
Activities: Hospital activities
Parent: Infrastructure Investments (Portsmouth) Limited
Officers: David Alexander John Foot [1968] Director; Scott Springett [1968] Director/Asset Manager

The Hospital Company (QAH Portsmouth) Limited
Incorporated: 29 April 2005
Net Worth Deficit: £12,030,000 *Total Assets:* £325,800,000
Registered Office: 2 Hunting Gate, Hitchin, Herts, SG4 0TJ
Activities: Hospital activities
Parent: The Hospital Company (QAH Portsmouth) Holdings Limited
Officers: David Alexander John Foot [1968] Director; Scott Springett [1968] Director/Asset Manager

Hospital Topco Limited
Incorporated: 22 October 2014
Net Worth Deficit: £734,236,032 *Total Assets:* £1,451,212,032
Registered Office: Springfield Lodge, Colchester Road, Chelmsford, Essex, CM2 5PW
Activities: Activities of other holding companies n.e.c.
Shareholders: CCP Credit Acquisition Holdings Luxco SARL; KAM Credit Investors SARL
Officers: David Duggins [1955] Director/Business Executive; Jeremy Michael Jorgen Malherbe Jensen [1959] Director; David Peter Mobbs [1960] Director; Dr Karen Anita Prins [1961] Director/Doctor [South African]; Giorgia Rodigari [1983] Director/Investment Professional [Italian]; Andrew Wollaston [1961] Director/Business Adviser

Hotel Chocolat Group PLC
Incorporated: 16 July 2013 *Employees:* 1,248
Previous: Hotel Chocolat Group Limited
Net Worth: £39,611,420 *Total Assets:* £60,220,024
Registered Office: Mint House, Newark Close, Royston, Herts, SG8 5HL
Activities: Activities of other holding companies n.e.c.
Shareholders: Angus Thirwell; Peter Mark Harris
Officers: Peter Mark Harris, Secretary; Andrew Martin Gerrie [1963] Director; Peter Mark Harris [1955] Director; Brian Gregory Hodder [1952] Director; Matthew Paul Margereson [1970] Director; Matthew Robert Phillip Pritchard [1974] Director; Angus Thirlwell [1963] Director; Sophie Alice Tomkins [1969] Director

Hotel Chocolat Limited
Incorporated: 1 April 1993 *Employees:* 546
Net Worth: £7,314,467 *Total Assets:* £38,670,712
Registered Office: Mint House, Newark Close, Royston, Herts, SG8 5HL
Activities: Manufacture of cocoa and chocolate confectionery
Parent: Hotel Chocolat Group PLC
Officers: Peter Mark Harris, Secretary; Peter Mark Harris [1955] Director; Matthew Paul Margereson [1970] Director; Matthew Robert Phillip Pritchard [1974] Director; Angus Thirlwell [1963] Director

Hotel Chocolat Retail Ltd
Incorporated: 3 April 2009 *Employees:* 538
Net Worth: £13,624,014 *Total Assets:* £31,846,558
Registered Office: Mint House, Newark Close, Royston, Herts, SG8 5HL
Activities: Retail sale of bread, cakes, flour confectionery and sugar confectionery in specialised stores
Parent: HOTC Limited
Officers: Peter Mark Harris, Secretary; Peter Mark Harris [1955] Director; Matthew Paul Margereson [1970] Director; Matthew Robert Phillip Pritchard [1974] Director; Angus Thirlwell [1963] Director

The Hotel Folk Limited
Incorporated: 4 September 1995 *Employees:* 370
Previous: TA Hotel Collection Limited
Net Worth: £3,967,471 *Total Assets:* £25,424,332
Registered Office: Thorpeness Hotel & Golf Club, Lakeside Avenue, Thorpeness, Leiston, Suffolk, IP16 4NH
Activities: Hotels and similar accommodation
Shareholders: Joan Annette Whybrow; James Maynard Dinwiddy; Michael Guy Hilliard Heald
Officers: Andrew Michael Hilliard Heald [1987] Director; Lucinda Jane Fullerton Heald [1953] Director; Michael Guy Hilliard Heald [1950] Director/Banker; Joan Annette Whybrow [1951] Director/Solicitor; Ingo Wiangke [1967] Operations Director [German]; Andrew Charles Wood [1960] Director

Hotels4U.Com Limited
Incorporated: 28 January 2003
Net Worth: £26,947,000 *Total Assets:* £53,600,000
Registered Office: Westpoint, Peterborough Business Park, Lynch Wood, Peterborough, Cambs, PE2 6FZ
Activities: Travel agency activities
Parent: Thomas Cook Retail Limited
Officers: Shirley Bradley, Secretary; Alan Charles Donald [1963] Director

Housing Gateway Limited
Incorporated: 13 March 2014 *Employees:* 2
Net Worth: £8,501,047 *Total Assets:* £128,319,832
Registered Office: Civic Centre, Silver Street, Enfield, Middlesex, EN1 3XA
Activities: Buying and selling of own real estate
Parent: The Mayor and Burgesses of The London Borough of Enfield
Officers: Joanne Drew [1968] Director/Local Government Officer; Joanna Michelle Embling [1949] Director; Timothy Leaver [1966] Director/Chartered Accountant; Sally Ann McTernan [1963] Director/Local Government Officer; Jayne Middleton-Albooye [1963] Director/Solicitor; Peter Chukuaduom Madako Nwosu [1965] Director/Chartered Accountant

Hovis Holdings Limited
Incorporated: 15 January 2014 *Employees:* 3,246
Net Worth: £45,849,000 *Total Assets:* £220,691,008
Registered Office: The Lord Rank Centre, Lincoln Road, High Wycombe, Bucks, HP12 3QS
Activities: Activities of head offices
Shareholder: Premier Foods Group Limited
Officers: Peter Andrew Hill, Secretary; John Paul Danner [1965] Director [American]; Fernando Goni [1973] Director [French]; Nishpank Rameshbabu Kankiwala [1957] Director; Alastair Sholto Neil Murray [1960] Director/Chief Financial Officer

Hovis Limited
Incorporated: 15 January 2014 *Employees:* 2,975
Net Worth: £98,870,000 *Total Assets:* £234,578,000
Registered Office: The Lord Rank Centre, Lincoln Road, High Wycombe, Bucks, HP12 3QS
Activities: Manufacture of bread; manufacture of fresh pastry goods and cakes
Parent: Hovis Holdings Limited
Officers: Peter Andrew Hill, Secretary; Peter Andrew Hill [1980] HR Director; Dr George Idicula [1959] Supply Chain Director; Chad Leembuggen [1972] Director; Lawrence Anthony Watson [1965] Director

Howard Bedford Limited
Incorporated: 19 May 2014
Net Worth: £1,037,643 *Total Assets:* £11,255,967
Registered Office: 93 Regent Street, Cambridge, CB2 1AW
Activities: Other letting and operating of own or leased real estate
Officers: Nicholas Cecil John Bewes [1967] Director; Gavin Edward Oliver Howard [1969] Director; Alun Huw Jones [1961] Finance Director

Howard Cambridge Limited
Incorporated: 6 August 2015
Net Worth: £600,295 *Total Assets:* £13,013,268
Registered Office: 93 Regent Street, Cambridge, CB2 1AW
Activities: Other letting and operating of own or leased real estate
Parent: Howard Residential Limited
Officers: Nicholas Cecil John Bewes [1967] Director; Patrick James Bushnell [1952] Consultant and Funds Director; Gavin Edward Oliver Howard [1969] Director; Alun Huw Jones [1961] Director

Howard Investment Company Limited
Incorporated: 8 September 2005
Net Worth: £71,649,344 *Total Assets:* £116,120,264
Registered Office: 93 Regent Street, Cambridge, CB2 1AW
Activities: Other letting and operating of own or leased real estate
Shareholders: Caroline Laura Elizabeth Margaret Bewes; Gavin Edward Oliver Howard
Officers: Caroline Laura Elizabeth Margaret Bewes, Secretary; Caroline Laura Elizabeth Margaret Bewes [1967] Director; Nicholas Cecil John Bewes [1967] Managing Director; William John Ashworth Bullough [1950] Director; Patrick James Bushnell [1952] Director; Gavin Edward Oliver Howard [1969] Director; Alun Huw Jones [1961] Finance Director; Dominic Joseph Gerard Reilly [1956] Director

Howard Lewisham Limited
Incorporated: 21 December 2000
Net Worth: £16,986,456 *Total Assets:* £36,078,172
Registered Office: 93 Regent Street, Cambridge, CB2 1AW
Activities: Other letting and operating of own or leased real estate
Officers: Nicholas Cecil John Bewes [1967] Director; Gavin Edward Oliver Howard [1969] Director; Alun Huw Jones [1961] Finance Director

P.C. Howard Limited
Incorporated: 1 June 1951 *Employees:* 199
Net Worth: £7,187,709 *Total Assets:* £16,779,960
Registered Office: West Hay, Stamford Road, King's Cliffe, Peterborough, PE8 6XX
Activities: Freight transport by road
Officers: Percival William Howard, Secretary; Andrew Percival Howard [1960] Director/Chartered Accountant; Anthony Frederick Howard [1948] Director/Haulage Contractor & Farmer; Percival William Howard [1943] Director/Haulage Contractor & Farmer; Peter Charles Howard [1960] Director

Howard Sawston Ltd
Incorporated: 17 November 2010
Net Worth: £4,023,458 *Total Assets:* £17,377,340
Registered Office: 93 Regent Street, Cambridge, CB2 1AW
Activities: Other letting and operating of own or leased real estate
Parent: Howard Crescent Limited
Officers: Nicholas Cecil John Bewes [1967] Director; Gavin Edward Oliver Howard [1969] Director; Alun Huw Jones [1961] Finance Director

Howard Stansted Limited
Incorporated: 8 October 2001
Net Worth: £2,218,205 *Total Assets:* £11,574,031
Registered Office: 93 Regent Street, Cambridge, CB2 1AW
Activities: Other letting and operating of own or leased real estate
Parent: Howard Crescent Limited
Officers: Nicholas Cecil John Bewes [1967] Director; Gavin Edward Oliver Howard [1969] Director; Alun Huw Jones [1961] Finance Director

Howard Ventures Limited
Incorporated: 3 August 2006 *Employees:* 17
Net Worth: £14,872,256 *Total Assets:* £26,599,556
Registered Office: 93 Regent Street, Cambridge, CB2 1AW
Activities: Buying and selling of own real estate
Shareholders: Judith Howard; Caroline Laura Elizabeth Margaret Bewes; Gavin Edward Oliver Howard
Officers: Caroline Laura Elizabeth Margaret Bewes, Secretary; Caroline Laura Elizabeth Margaret Bewes [1967] Director; Nicholas Cecil John Bewes [1967] Managing Director; John Bullough [1950] Director/Chartered Surveyor; Patrick James Bushnell [1952] Director; Gavin Edward Oliver Howard [1969] Director; Alun Huw Jones [1961] Finance Director; Dominic Joseph Gerard Reilly [1956] Director

HP Solar Limited
Incorporated: 1 July 2013
Net Worth: £335,737 *Total Assets:* £10,853,181
Registered Office: Cokenach Estate Office, Barkway, Royston, Herts, SG8 8DL
Activities: Production of electricity
Major Shareholder: Niels Holch Povlsen
Officers: Kenneth Grant [1977] Director; Niels Holch Povlsen [1977] Director [Danish]

HPC Healthline UK Limited
Incorporated: 14 March 1986 *Employees:* 132
Net Worth: £11,392,000 *Total Assets:* £36,579,000
Registered Office: Polyco Healthline, South Fen Road, Bourne, Lincs, PE10 0DN
Activities: Wholesale of clothing and footwear
Parent: Polyco Healthline Limited
Officers: Jason Matthew Prichard, Secretary; Neil Antony Wilson, Secretary; David Greenwood [1955] Director; Jason Matthew Prichard [1969] Director; Neil Antony Wilson [1976] Director

HRS Investments Limited
Incorporated: 19 March 1999 *Employees:* 179
Net Worth: £3,747,879 *Total Assets:* £14,872,608
Registered Office: HRS House, 10-12 Caxton Way, Watford Business Park, Watford, Herts, WD18 8JY
Activities: Activities of head offices
Major Shareholder: Steven Edward Pither
Officers: Robert Michael Twydle, Secretary; Francisco Javier Abad Ruiz [1969] Director/Accountant [Spanish]; Linda Amanda Galdes [1964] Director; Catherine Elizabeth Pither [1991] Director; Jack Edward Pither [1994] Director; Steven Edward Pither [1957] Director

HTG Investments Limited
Incorporated: 13 June 2013 *Employees:* 93
Net Worth: £4,582,000 *Total Assets:* £9,121,000
Registered Office: 106 Claydon Business Park, Great Blakenham, Ipswich, Suffolk, IP6 0NL
Activities: Other food services
Shareholders: David McCulloch; David Wrench
Officers: Lisa Jane Jillett, Secretary; Simon Andrew Aspin [1972] Director [Swedish]; Peter John Gray [1974] Director; Lisa Jane Jillett [1968] Director/Accountant; David McCulloch [1947] Director [Canadian]; Martin George Wood [1957] Director; David Wrench [1946] Director [Canadian]

HTG Trading Limited
Incorporated: 28 June 1984 *Employees:* 93
Net Worth: £7,750,000 *Total Assets:* £12,281,000
Registered Office: 106 Claydon Business Park, Great Blakenham, Ipswich, Suffolk, IP6 0NL
Activities: Wholesale of other intermediate products
Parent: Taylor Freezer (UK) Limited
Officers: Lisa Jane Jillett, Secretary; Simon Andrew Aspin [1972] Director [Swedish]; Peter John Gray [1974] Director; Lisa Jane Jillett [1968] Director/Accountant; Martin George Wood [1957] Director/Accountant

HTS Estates Limited
Incorporated: 9 September 1976 *Employees:* 5
Net Worth: £4,658,353 *Total Assets:* £11,861,277
Registered Office: Salisbury House, Station Road, Cambridge, CB1 2LA
Activities: Other letting and operating of own or leased real estate
Officers: Paulette Brown, Secretary; Colin Lawrence Brown [1941] Director; Nicholas Lawrence Brown [1970] Director; Paulette Brown [1943] Director/Company Secretary; Vicki Louise Brown [1968] Director [Australian]; Caroline Margot Hill [1968] Director

Hubbard Products Limited
Incorporated: 18 April 2007 *Employees:* 163
Net Worth Deficit: £5,029,666 *Total Assets:* £8,898,400
Registered Office: 1-7 Bluestem Road, Ransomes Europark, Ipswich, Suffolk, IP3 9RR
Activities: Manufacture of non-domestic cooling and ventilation equipment
Officers: Ilias Katsoulis, Secretary; Ilias Katsoulis [1977] Managing Director [Greek]; Patrick Adrian Maughan [1959] Director; Junji Umamoto [1961] Director [Japanese]

Hudson Almere Limited
Incorporated: 17 January 2017
Net Worth: £699,948 *Total Assets:* £14,802,959
Registered Office: Portland House, 69-71 Wembley Hill Road, Wembley, Middlesex, HA9 8BU
Activities: Other business support service activities n.e.c.
Officers: Bhupendra Shantilal Kansagra, Secretary; Laurent Elie Cadji [1977] Director/Businessman; Lewis Levy Cadji [1938] Director/Businessman; Bhupendra Shantilal Kansagra [1956] Director/Businessman; Ramesh Shantilal Kansagra [1950] Director/Businessman

Hudson Arnhem Limited
Incorporated: 17 January 2017
Net Worth Deficit: £7,979 *Total Assets:* £10,414,724
Registered Office: Portland House, 69-71 Wembley Hill Road, Wembley, Middlesex, HA9 8BU
Activities: Other business support service activities n.e.c.
Officers: Bhupendra Shantilal Kansagra, Secretary; Laurent Elie Cadji [1977] Director/Businessman; Lewis Levy Cadji [1938] Director/Businessman; Bhupendra Shantilal Kansagra [1956] Director/Businessman; Ramesh Shantilal Kansagra [1950] Director/Businessman

Hudson Brent Limited
Incorporated: 17 January 2017
Net Worth: £1,289,010 *Total Assets:* £10,286,558
Registered Office: Portland House, 69-71 Wembley Hill Road, Wembley, Middlesex, HA9 8BU
Activities: Other business support service activities n.e.c.
Officers: Bhupendra Shantilal Kansagra, Secretary; Laurent Elie Cadji [1977] Director/Businessman; Lewis Levy Cadji [1938] Director/Businessman; Bhupendra Shantilal Kansagra [1956] Director/Businessman; Ramesh Shantilal Kansagra [1950] Director/Businessman

Hudson Camden Limited
Incorporated: 17 January 2017
Net Worth: £1,026,544 *Total Assets:* £10,631,425
Registered Office: Portland House, 69-71 Wembley Hill Road, Wembley, Middlesex, HA9 8BU
Activities: Other business support service activities n.e.c.
Officers: Bhupendra Shantilal Kansagra, Secretary; Laurent Elie Cadji [1977] Director/Businessman; Lewis Levy Cadji [1938] Director/Businessman; Bhupendra Shantilal Kansagra [1956] Director/Businessman; Ramesh Shantilal Kansagra [1950] Director/Businessman

Hudson Chemical Tankers Limited
Incorporated: 17 January 2017 *Employees:* 4
Net Worth: £5,307,836 *Total Assets:* £73,716,288
Registered Office: Portland House, 69-71 Wembley Hill Road, Wembley, Middlesex, HA9 8BU
Activities: Other business support service activities n.e.c.
Shareholder: Shipping and Intermodal Investment Fund II LLC
Officers: Bhupendra Shantilal Kansagra, Secretary; Laurent Elie Cadji [1977] Director/Businessman; Edwin Erik Gelbert Jager [1966] Managing Director [Dutch]; Bhupendra Shantilal Kansagra [1956] Director/Businessman; Ramesh Shantilal Kansagra [1950] Director/Businessman

Hudson Kensington Limited
Incorporated: 17 January 2017
Net Worth: £605,679 *Total Assets:* £10,048,801
Registered Office: Portland House, 69-71 Wembley Hill Road, Wembley, Middlesex, HA9 8BU
Activities: Sea and coastal freight water transport
Officers: Bhupendra Shantilal Kansagra, Secretary; Laurent Elie Cadji [1977] Director/Businessman; Lewis Levy Cadji [1938] Director/Businessman; Bhupendra Shantilal Kansagra [1956] Director/Businessman; Ramesh Shantilal Kansagra [1950] Director/Businessman

Hudson Lisse Limited
Incorporated: 17 January 2017
Net Worth: £584,616 *Total Assets:* £15,234,200
Registered Office: Portland House, 69-71 Wembley Hill Road, Wembley, Middlesex, HA9 8BU
Activities: Sea and coastal freight water transport
Officers: Bhupendra Shantilal Kansagra, Secretary; Laurent Elie Cadji [1977] Director/Businessman; Lewis Levy Cadji [1938] Director/Businessman; Bhupendra Shantilal Kansagra [1956] Director/Businessman; Ramesh Shantilal Kansagra [1950] Director/Businessman

Hudson Richmond Limited
Incorporated: 17 January 2017
Net Worth: £798,401 *Total Assets:* £10,457,273
Registered Office: Portland House, 69-71 Wembley Hill Road, Wembley, Middlesex, HA9 8BU
Activities: Sea and coastal freight water transport
Officers: Bhupendra Shantilal Kansagra, Secretary; Laurent Elie Cadji [1977] Director/Businessman; Lewis Levy Cadji [1938] Director/Businessman; Bhupendra Shantilal Kansagra [1956] Director/Businessman; Ramesh Shantilal Kansagra [1950] Director/Businessman

Hughes Electrical Limited
Incorporated: 13 March 1946 *Employees:* 953
Net Worth: £25,815,634 *Total Assets:* £71,319,464
Registered Office: Hughes Electrical, Mobbs Way, Gorleston Road Industrial Estate, Gorleston Road, Lowestoft, Suffolk, NR32 3AL
Activities: Retail sale of electrical household appliances in specialised stores
Shareholder: Phyllis Mary Spratt
Officers: Christopher William Thornton, Secretary; Robert John Hughes [1963] Director/Manager; Lavinia Lawford [1949] Director; Andrew Bryn David Pallant [1958] Sales and Marketing Director; Phyllis Mary Spratt [1921] Director; Christopher William Thornton [1979] Finance Director

Hughes TV and Audio Limited
Incorporated: 15 June 1961 *Employees:* 805
Net Worth: £12,597,154 *Total Assets:* £40,402,320
Registered Office: Hughes Electrical, Mobbs Way, Gorleston Road Industrial Estate, Lowestoft, Suffolk, NR32 3AL
Activities: Retail sale of electrical household appliances in specialised stores
Parent: Hughes Electrical Limited
Officers: Christopher William Thornton, Secretary; Mark Coleby [1966] Service Director; Simon Stuart Charles Cox [1969] Director; Neil Andrew Duncan [1967] Director/Manager; Nicholas Mark Heffer [1960] Director/Manager; Jeremy Charles Hughes [1965] Purchasing Director; Robert John Hughes [1963] Director/Manager; Lavinia Lawford [1949] Director; Andrew Bryn David Pallant [1958] Sales and Marketing Director; Phyllis Mary Spratt [1921] Director; Christopher William Thornton [1979] Director/Chartered Accountant

Hull Holdings Limited
Incorporated: 8 September 2016
Net Worth: £1,763 *Total Assets:* £16,944,852
Registered Office: 27-29 Lumley Avenue, Skegness, Lincs, PE25 2AT
Activities: Dormant company
Parent: Brayford Hotels Holdings Limited
Officers: Leigh Morris Hall [1969] Director; Dean Anthony Wann [1971] Director

Hull Propco Limited
Incorporated: 18 September 2015
Net Worth: £2,147,000 *Total Assets:* £41,279,000
Registered Office: Porter Tun House, 500 Capability Green, Luton, Beds, LU1 3LS
Activities: Other letting and operating of own or leased real estate
Parent: TDR Capital LLP
Officers: Simon David Longbottom [1971] Director/Chief Executive Officer; Brian Jonathan Magnus [1966] Director/Partner, Private Equity; Ian Timothy Payne [1953] Director/Chairman; David Andrew Ross [1973] Director/Accountant

Hunnable Holdings Limited
Incorporated: 13 November 1973 *Employees:* 7
Net Worth: £7,600,726 *Total Assets:* £9,731,600
Registered Office: Hunnable Industrial Estate, Great Yeldham, Essex, CO9 4HD
Activities: Activities of head offices
Officers: Julian Scott Hunnable, Secretary; Christopher William Hunnable [1964] Director; Julian Scott Hunnable [1968] Director; Martyn Thomas Hunnable [1960] Director

Howard Hunt (City) Limited
Incorporated: 28 August 1990 *Employees:* 268
Net Worth: £12,863,000 *Total Assets:* £49,997,000
Registered Office: 3rd Floor, Crown House, 151 High Road, Loughton, Essex, IG10 4LG
Activities: Printing n.e.c.
Shareholders: Martin Albert Pigott; Howard Hunt Mail Limited
Officers: Luke Martin Pigott, Secretary/Managing Director; Daniel Clarke [1981] Sales Director; Paul Kemp [1969] Operations Director; Luke Martin Pigott [1972] Managing Director; Martin Albert Pigott [1944] Director; Keith Edwin Whitehead [1958] Production Director

John F Hunt Group Ltd
Incorporated: 3 May 2006 *Employees:* 403
Previous: John F Hunt Ltd
Net Worth: £22,005,184 *Total Assets:* £44,868,924
Registered Office: Europa Park, London Road, Grays, Essex, RM20 4DB
Activities: Other specialised construction activities n.e.c.
Major Shareholder: John Alan Hall
Officers: Charles Richard Green, Secretary; Janet Hall, Secretary; Ian David Saville, Secretary; John Alan Hall [1949] Director; Ian David Saville [1968] Finance Director

John F Hunt Limited
Incorporated: 9 December 1981 *Employees:* 167
Previous: John F. Hunt Demolition Ltd
Net Worth: £9,993,262 *Total Assets:* £17,978,696
Registered Office: Europa Park, London Road, Grays, Essex, RM20 4DB
Activities: Demolition
Parent: John F Hunt Ltd
Officers: Charles Richard Green, Secretary; Ian David Saville, Secretary; Paul Bland [1972] Managing Director; Michael John Blizzard [1964] Divisional Director; Glen Clark [1967] Managing Director; John Alan Hall [1949] Director; Jason Mark Hill [1970] Commercial Director; Ian David Saville [1968] Finance Director

Howard Hunt Mail Limited
Incorporated: 18 August 2009 *Employees:* 54
Net Worth: £4,312,632 *Total Assets:* £13,418,588
Registered Office: 3rd Floor, Crown House, 151 High Road, Loughton, Essex, IG10 4LG
Activities: Other business support service activities n.e.c.
Shareholders: Martin Albert Pigott; Luke Martin Pigott
Officers: Luke Martin Pigott [1972] Managing Director; Martin Albert Pigott [1944] Director; Catherine Jane Wozencroft [1962] Director

John F Hunt Power Limited
Incorporated: 10 June 2005 *Employees:* 53
Net Worth: £6,761,469 *Total Assets:* £20,003,154
Registered Office: Europa Park, London Road, Grays, Essex, RM20 4DB
Activities: Renting and leasing of construction and civil engineering machinery and equipment
Major Shareholder: John Alan Hall
Officers: Charles Richard Green, Secretary; Janet Hall, Secretary; Ian David Saville, Secretary; Kevin Davies [1957] Director; John Alan Hall [1949] Director; David Paul Hunt [1966] Sales Director; Ian David Saville [1968] Finance Director; Keith Andrew Scott [1963] Director

Domnick Hunter Group Limited
Incorporated: 14 September 1989
Net Worth: £33,531,000 *Total Assets:* £35,116,000
Registered Office: Parker House, 55 Maylands Avenue, Hemel Hempstead Industrial Estate, Hemel Hempstead, Herts, HP2 4SJ
Activities: Activities of head offices
Parent: Parker Hannifin Manufacturing Limited
Officers: Graham Mark Ellinor, Secretary; Graham Mark Ellinor [1964] Director/Accountant; James Alan David Elsey [1970] HR Director

John Huntingdon's Charity
Incorporated: 9 January 2007 *Employees:* 5
Net Worth: £9,987,058 *Total Assets:* £10,110,274
Registered Office: John Huntingdon Centre, 189 High Street, Sawston, Cambridge, CB22 3HJ
Activities: Other service activities n.e.c.
Officers: Jill Mary Hayden, Secretary; David John Baslington [1960] Director/Administrator; Eleanor Brenda Clapp [1978] Director/Basketmaker; Kieran John Lawson Cooper [1967] Director/IT Project Manager; Reginald Charles Cullum [1939] Director/Design Surveyor; Sandra Ann Davidson [1961] Director/Charity Shop Manager; Dr Ruth Margaret Franklin [1969] Director/Retired GP; Christine Mary Ingham [1943] Director/Retired Headteacher; Rev Alan Christopher Partridge [1955] Director/Minister of Religion; Susan Reynolds [1959] Director/Senior Money Matters Adviser; Eileen Patricia Wheatley [1943] Director/Retired Social Worker

Huntleigh Healthcare Limited
Incorporated: 13 November 1968 *Employees:* 151
Net Worth: £19,781,000 *Total Assets:* £38,141,000
Registered Office: ArjoHuntleigh House, Houghton Hall Business Park, Houghton Regis, Dunstable, Beds, LU5 5XF
Activities: Manufacture of medical and dental instruments and supplies
Parent: Huntleigh Luton Limited
Officers: Andrew John Scott-Green, Secretary; Peter Cashin [1956] Director; Khizer Ismail Ibrahim [1973] Director; Paul Gerard Lyon [1962] Director/President Global Sales & Service [Australian]; Andrew John Scott-Green [1967] Finance Director

Huntleigh International Holdings Limited
Incorporated: 3 September 1992
Net Worth: £6,637,993 *Total Assets:* £20,284,438
Registered Office: ArjoHuntleigh House, Houghton Hall Business Park, Houghton Regis, Dunstable, Beds, LU5 5XF
Activities: Activities of head offices
Shareholders: Huntleigh SST Limited; Huntleigh Technology Limited
Officers: Khizer Ismail Ibrahim, Secretary; Sukraj Singh Gill [1984] Finance Director; Khizer Ismail Ibrahim [1973] Director; Geoffrey Alan Nix [1972] Director/Accountant

Huntleigh Technology Limited
Incorporated: 4 March 1985
Net Worth: £40,671,168 *Total Assets:* £418,406,784
Registered Office: ArjoHuntleigh House, Houghton Hall Business Park, Houghton Regis, Dunstable, Beds, LU5 5XF
Activities: Activities of head offices
Officers: Khizer Ismail Ibrahim, Secretary; Sukraj Singh Gill [1984] Finance Director; Khizer Ismail Ibrahim [1973] Director; Geoffrey Alan Nix [1972] Director/Accountant

Hurco Europe Limited
Incorporated: 14 April 1982 *Employees:* 46
Net Worth: £8,301,662 *Total Assets:* £11,422,529
Registered Office: Halifax Road, Cressex Business Park, High Wycombe, Bucks, HP12 3SN
Activities: Manufacture of other machine tools
Officers: Adrian Carl Soden, Secretary; Michael Doar [1955] Director [American]; Sonja McClelland [1971] Director [American]; David Waghorn [1964] Managing Director

Hutchinson Group Limited
Incorporated: 3 February 2003 *Employees:* 442
Net Worth: £80,591,000 *Total Assets:* £114,041,000
Registered Office: Hutchinson Group Limited, Weasenham Lane, Wisbech, Cambs, PE13 2RN
Activities: Support activities for crop production
Shareholders: David Anthony Hutchinson; Michael Leslie Hutchinson
Officers: David Anthony Hutchinson, Secretary/Director; David Anthony Hutchinson [1962] Director; Jean Mary Hutchinson [1924] Director; Melanie Jane Hutchinson [1961] Director; Michael Leslie Hutchinson [1964] Director

H.L. Hutchinson Limited
Incorporated: 15 December 1947 *Employees:* 395
Net Worth: £60,818,000 *Total Assets:* £97,800,000
Registered Office: Hutchinsons, Weasenham Lane, Wisbech, Cambs, PE13 2RN
Activities: Support activities for crop production
Parent: Hutchinson Group Limited
Officers: Richard Keith Johnson, Secretary; David Howell Crossman [1962] Director; John Robert Cawdron Harris [1947] Director; David Anthony Hutchinson [1962] Director/Chartered Accountant; Michael Leslie Hutchinson [1964] Director; Richard Keith Johnson [1966] Finance Director; Andrew McShane [1963] Managing Director; Andrew Richard Orme [1963] Director

Hutchison Ports (UK) Holding Limited
Incorporated: 29 April 1991
Previous: Hutchison Ports (Europe) Limited
Net Worth: £106,606,000 *Total Assets:* £126,277,000
Registered Office: Tomline House, The Dock, Felixstowe, Suffolk, IP11 3SY
Activities: Activities of other holding companies n.e.c.
Parent: Hutchison Ports Europe Limited
Officers: Simon Richard Mullett, Secretary; Clemence Chun Fun Cheng [1958] Director; Sing Chi IP [1953] Director [Chinese]; Dominic Kai Ming Lai [1953] Director; Edith Shih [1952] Director; Frank John Sixt [1951] Director [Canadian]

Hutchison Ports (UK) Limited
Incorporated: 23 December 1997 *Employees:* 2,802
Net Worth: £266,347,008 *Total Assets:* £746,881,984
Registered Office: Tomline House, The Dock, Felixstowe, Suffolk, IP11 3SY
Activities: Activities of head offices
Parent: Hutchison Ports (UK) Holding Limited
Officers: Simon Richard Mullett, Secretary; Clemence Chun Fun Cheng [1958] Director; Sing Chi IP [1953] Director [Chinese]; Edith Shih [1952] Director; David Antonius Yang [1968] Director [Singaporean]

Hutchison Ports Europe Limited
Incorporated: 16 May 1995 *Employees:* 2,818
Previous: Hutchison Westports Limited
Net Worth: £295,096,992 *Total Assets:* £912,062,016
Registered Office: Tomline House, The Dock, Felixstowe, Suffolk, IP11 3SY
Activities: Activities of head offices
Officers: Simon Richard Mullett, Secretary; Clemence Chun Fun Cheng [1958] Director; Sing Chi IP [1953] Director [Chinese]; Dominic Kai Ming Lai [1953] Director; Edith Shih [1952] Director; Frank John Sixt [1951] Director [Canadian]

Hutton Construction Limited
Incorporated: 2 May 1986 *Employees:* 118
Net Worth: £3,832,799 *Total Assets:* £14,502,867
Registered Office: Birch Business Centre, Maldon Road, Birch, Colchester, Essex, CO2 0LT
Activities: Construction of commercial buildings
Parent: Hutton Holdings Limited
Officers: Mathew Julian Smith, Secretary; David Scott Ball [1966] Construction Director; John Anthony Bendelack [1959] Director/Construction Manager; Nicholas David Hughes [1958] Director/Construction Manager; Peter Melvyn Saville [1972] Commercial Director; Mathew Julian Smith [1972] Finance Director; Paul Snoxell [1961] Estimating Director

Hutton East Limited
Incorporated: 13 August 2015 *Employees:* 118
Net Worth: £4,483,970 *Total Assets:* £15,182,505
Registered Office: Birch Business Centre, Maldon Road, Birch, Colchester, Essex, CO2 0LT
Activities: Construction of commercial buildings
Officers: David Scott Ball [1966] Construction Director; John Anthony Bendelack [1959] Director; Nicholas David Hughes [1958] Director; Peter Melvyn Saville [1972] Commercial Director; Mathew Julian Smith [1972] Finance Director; Paul Snoxell [1961] Estimating Director

Huxley Global Limited
Incorporated: 7 September 2017
Net Worth: £27,004 *Total Assets:* £8,538,746
Registered Office: Potland House, 69-71 Wembley Hill Road, Wembley, Middlesex, HA9 8BU
Activities: Non-specialised wholesale trade
Parent: Solai Holdings Limited
Officers: Bhupendra Shantilal Kansagra, Secretary; Bhupendra Shantilal Kansagra [1956] Director; Ramesh Shantilal Kansagra [1950] Director; Rishi Ramesh Kansagra [1981] Director; Ronak Kansagra [1987] Director

Hy-Pro International Limited
Incorporated: 19 June 1992 *Employees:* 45
Net Worth: £7,333,000 *Total Assets:* £11,285,000
Registered Office: Hy-Pro House, Centrus Park, Arenson Way, Dunstable, Beds, LU5 5BN
Activities: Other sports activities
Shareholders: Pareshkumar Shah; Euroblue Investments Ltd
Officers: Muthukrishna Ravindra Rajah, Secretary; Varsha Shah, Secretary; Muthukrishna Ravindra Rajah [1956] Director/Chartered Accountant; Atul Shah [1959] Director; Nigel William Wray [1948] Director

Hydac Limited
Incorporated: 8 April 1991 *Employees:* 1,189
Net Worth: £136,536,192 *Total Assets:* £165,738,576
Registered Office: 55 Station Road, Beaconsfield, Bucks, HP9 1QL
Activities: Activities of head offices
Shareholders: Alexander Dieter; Mathias Dieter
Officers: Renate Huber, Secretary [German]; Dr Werner Heinz Dieter [1929] Director [German]; Otmar Peter Schon [1929] Director [German]

Hydac Technology Limited
Incorporated: 2 June 1976 *Employees:* 128
Net Worth: £16,412,741 *Total Assets:* £19,970,478
Registered Office: 55 Station Road, Beaconsfield, Bucks, HP9 1QL
Activities: Machining
Parent: Hydac Limited
Officers: Kevin George Brownlee [1958] Director; Dr Werner Heinz Dieter [1929] Director [German]; Renate Huber [1940] Director [German]; George Victor Francis Muscat [1947] Director; Otmar Peter Schon [1929] Director [German]; Darren James Wait [1970] Managing Director

Hydraquip Hose & Hydraulics Limited
Incorporated: 20 October 2003 *Employees:* 237
Previous: Universal Hose Limited
Net Worth: £2,577,490 *Total Assets:* £8,871,910
Registered Office: 11 Queens Road, Brentwood, Essex, CM14 4HE
Activities: Non-specialised wholesale trade
Shareholder: Duncan Munro MacBain
Officers: Fintan Cornelius Ennis [1962] Director [Irish]; Duncan Munro MacBain [1961] Director; Jay Luke MacBain [1987] Director

Hypnos Limited
Incorporated: 24 April 1926 *Employees:* 298
Net Worth: £4,440,347 *Total Assets:* £12,696,132
Registered Office: 1 Longwick Road, Princes Risborough, Bucks, HP27 9RT
Activities: Manufacture of mattresses
Officers: Robert Lincoln Eastoe [1961] Director/Accountant; James Peter George Keen [1975] Director; Christopher John Ward [1967] Sales and Marketing Director; Stephen Hedley Ward [1952] Managing Director

Hypro EU Limited
Incorporated: 3 January 1991 *Employees:* 45
Net Worth: £14,914,000 *Total Assets:* £17,574,000
Registered Office: Station Road, Longstanton, Cambridge, CB24 3DS
Activities: Other manufacturing n.e.c.
Parent: Pentair UK Group Limited
Officers: Mark Campbell, Secretary; Mark Campbell [1960] Director; Guillaume Stephane Gousse [1971] Director/Vice President EMEA Operations [French]; Grant William O'Grady [1970] Director/General Counsel [Australian]; Henning Wolfgang Wistorf [1982] Director/Controller [German]

Hyundai Motor UK Limited
Incorporated: 9 May 2005 *Employees:* 217
Net Worth: £66,104,000 *Total Assets:* £566,403,968
Registered Office: 728 London Road, High Wycombe, Bucks, HP11 1HE
Activities: Sale of new cars and light motor vehicles
Officers: Ashley Ward Andrew [1971] Managing Director; Yun Jong Choi [1969] Director [South Korean]; Kyuwan Lim [1976] Director [South Korean]

I & C Holdings Limited
Incorporated: 29 May 2015 *Employees:* 52
Net Worth Deficit: £717,428 *Total Assets:* £13,721,347
Registered Office: Harbour Landing, Fox's Marina, Wherstead, Ipswich, Suffolk, IP2 8NJ
Activities: Activities of head offices
Officers: Kenneth Robert Beaty [1968] Independent Director; Kristen Branford [1977] Commercial Director; Nicholas William Offord [1962] Director; Joanne Richardson [1975] Director/Chartered Management Accountant; Andrew Thomas Wynn [1984] Director/Partner

I & C Limited
Incorporated: 29 May 2015 *Employees:* 52
Net Worth Deficit: £50,714 *Total Assets:* £13,688,336
Registered Office: Harbour Landing, Fox's Marina, Wherstead, Ipswich, Suffolk, IP2 8NJ
Activities: Other specialised construction activities n.e.c.
Parent: I & C Holdings Ltd
Officers: Kenneth Robert Beaty [1968] Independent Director; Kristen Branford [1977] Commercial Director; Nicholas William Offord [1962] Director; Joanne Richardson [1975] Director/Chartered Management Accountant; Andrew Thomas Wynn [1984] Director/Partner

I F E Global Holdings Limited
Incorporated: 8 October 2014 *Employees:* 73
Net Worth: £896,040 *Total Assets:* £9,841,866
Registered Office: 13 Bentalls Business Park, Bentalls, Basildon, Essex, SS14 3BN
Activities: Freight transport by road
Officers: Jamie Andrew Cramer [1976] Director; Stephen Charles Cramer [1952] Director; Tao Jiajie [1972] Director [Chinese]; Kang Jinhong [1971] Director [Chinese]; Dieter Barry Parish [1979] Director; Shen Yan [1969] Director [Chinese]

I Go 4 Ltd.
Incorporated: 5 April 2004 *Employees:* 252
Net Worth Deficit: £5,226,103 *Total Assets:* £21,012,030
Registered Office: IGO4 House, Staniland Way, Peterborough, Cambs, PE4 6JT
Activities: Activities of insurance agents and brokers
Officers: Geoffrey Cornelis Baars [1965] Director [Australian]; Mark Edwin Holmes Bennett [1975] Director; David Nicholas Burns [1960] Director; Christopher Felix Boyce Mays [1962] Director; Matthew Paul Munro [1973] Managing Director; Christian Charles Plumer [1966] Director/Chief Financial Officer; Philip Douglas Burgoyne Zeidler [1968] Director/Chairman

I S & G (Holdings) Limited
Incorporated: 12 September 2007 *Employees:* 79
Net Worth: £6,098,569 *Total Assets:* £10,694,187
Registered Office: Unit 25a Claydon Business Park, Gipping Road, Great Blakenham, Ipswich, Suffolk, IP6 0NL
Activities: Activities of head offices
Shareholder: Anthony Richard Brocas Burrows
Officers: Angela Margaret Burrows, Secretary; Angela Margaret Burrows [1947] Director; Anthony Richard Brocas Burrows [1939] Director/Industrialist; Edward Brocas Burrows [1975] Director; Joanna Molly Anne Cunningham-Reid [1969] Director/Masseuse; Carey Jane English [1968] Director/Artist; Angela Petra Walker [1972] Director/Administrator

I.M.O. Precision Controls Limited
Incorporated: 6 August 1963 *Employees:* 62
Net Worth: £15,114,020 *Total Assets:* £19,038,160
Registered Office: The Interchange, Frobisher Way, Hatfield, Herts, AL10 9TG
Activities: Manufacture of electronic components
Officers: Fausto Furlotti [1963] Director; Richard Mark Hatter [1963] Director/Property Developer

The I.S. Group Limited
Incorporated: 14 May 1979 *Employees:* 73
Net Worth: £6,502,455 *Total Assets:* £10,265,530
Registered Office: Stirling House, Stirling Way, Bretton, Peterborough, Cambs, PE3 8YD
Activities: Agents involved in the sale of a variety of goods
Officers: Sandip Rajbhandari, Secretary; Nigel Richard Douthwaite [1954] Director/Consultant; Peter Vincent Lansdale [1952] Director/Florist; Mario Doroteo Larreta [1953] Managing Director; Neil Anthony Warwick [1963] Director

I4B Holdings Limited
Incorporated: 16 December 2016
Net Worth: £11,301,000 *Total Assets:* £46,464,000
Registered Office: Civic Centre, 9 Engineers Way, Wembley, Middlesex, HA9 0FJ
Activities: Other business support service activities n.e.c.
Parent: London Borough of Brent
Officers: George Crane [1949] Director; Akintoye Mobolaji Durowoju [1969] Director/Chartered Surveyor; Peter Gadsdon [1962] Director; Martin Frank Smith [1960] Director; Gail Elizabeth Tolley [1957] Director

IBC Vehicles Limited
Incorporated: 20 January 1987 *Employees:* 1,418
Net Worth: £90,610,000 *Total Assets:* £188,624,000
Registered Office: Kimpton Road, Luton, Beds, LU2 0JX
Activities: Manufacture of motor vehicles
Parent: Peugeot S.A.
Officers: Rabiya Sultana Nagi, Secretary/Solicitor; Nicholas Paul Barrett [1967] Director/Accountant; David James Connell [1972] Director; James Charles Highnam [1969] Director of Finance; Peter Thomas Hope [1966] Director; Mark Christopher Noble [1964] Director; Stephen Norman [1954] Managing Director [French]; Michael Wright [1963] Director

Icandy World Limited
Incorporated: 18 December 1933 *Employees:* 62
Net Worth: £7,561,902 *Total Assets:* £12,520,670
Registered Office: Icandy World Limited, Montgomery Way, Biggleswade, Beds, SG18 8UB
Activities: Non-specialised wholesale trade
Shareholders: Bradley Appel; Warren Appel
Officers: Bradley Appel, Secretary; Bradley Appel [1960] Director; Debra Stacey Appel [1963] Director/Merchandiser; Nicola Appel [1966] Director/Merchandiser; Warren Appel [1963] Director

Icknield High School
Incorporated: 1 November 2011 *Employees:* 202
Net Worth: £17,255,616 *Total Assets:* £19,599,454
Registered Office: Icknield High School, Riddy Lane, Luton, Beds, LU3 2AH
Activities: General secondary education
Officers: Tina Louise Freeman, Secretary; Khalid Ali [1982] Director/Teacher; Mohammed Sowab Ali [1963] Director; Stephen John Blake [1962] Director; Terri Brooks [1970] Director/Project Administrator; Stephen John Clarke [1962] Director/Police Officer (Retired); Home/Garden Maintenance; Tahir Mahmood [1968] Director/Project Manager; John Noble [1968] Director/Headteacher; Azra Shaheen [1974] Director; Paul Smith [1961] Director/Electrical Engineer

Ideal Shopping Direct Limited
Incorporated: 15 December 1980 *Employees:* 799
Net Worth: £28,518,000 *Total Assets:* £82,227,000
Registered Office: Ideal Home House, Newark Road, Peterborough, Cambs, PE1 5WG
Activities: Retail sale via mail order houses or via Internet
Parent: Aurelius Alpha Limited
Officers: Jamie Brian Morris Martin [1972] Director; Martin Shaun Purcell [1955] Director; Dr Caspaar Friedrich Trautwein [1964] Director [German]

IFCO Systems UK Ltd
Incorporated: 1 December 1994 *Employees:* 37
Net Worth: £9,979,869 *Total Assets:* £21,765,852
Registered Office: Albert House, Queen Victoria Road, High Wycombe, Bucks, HP11 1AG
Activities: Other service activities n.e.c.
Officers: Margit Kendler [1972] Director [Austrian]; Wolfgang Orgeldinger [1957] Director [German]; Christopher Taylor [1967] Managing Director

IGD Services Limited
Incorporated: 22 April 1997
Net Worth: £652,052 *Total Assets:* £12,871,688
Registered Office: Grange Lane, Letchmore Heath, Watford, Herts, WD25 8GD
Activities: Other information service activities n.e.c.
Parent: The Institute of Grocery Distribution
Officers: Julia Clare Bastiman, Secretary; Ann Michelle Bell [1971] People Director, International; Nicolas Paul Michael Angelo Mills-Hicks [1971] Food Commercial Director; Bradley Moore [1972] Grocery Sales Director; Ian Douglas Morley [1966] Group Sales Director; David O'Flynn [1970] Director/Chief Financial Officer [Irish]; Jill Margaret Ross [1973] Director/Vice President, Customer Development; Philip John Tenney [1970] Director/Vice President and CIO; Mark John Webster [1972] Director/Financial Controller

Igroup 8 Limited
Incorporated: 10 December 1999
Net Worth: £1,434,001,024 *Total Assets:* £3,009,617,920
Registered Office: P O Box 2497, Building 4, Hatters Lane, Watford, Herts, WD18 1YY
Activities: Other business support service activities n.e.c.
Parent: GE Money Home Lending Finance Limited
Officers: Samantha Jones [1981] Director; Jonathan Edward Taylor [1980] Director/Risk and Compliance Leader

Ikarim Business Services Ltd
Incorporated: 12 January 2011 *Employees:* 4
Net Worth: £301 *Total Assets:* £12,753,014
Registered Office: The Coach House, Powell Road, Buckhurst Hill, Essex, IG9 5RD
Activities: Other information technology service activities
Major Shareholder: Mohammed Shakeel Mughal
Officers: Mohammed Shakeel Mughal [1965] Director

Ikarus Engineering Limited
Incorporated: 9 January 1997 *Employees:* 5
Net Worth: £3,612,067 *Total Assets:* £12,166,363
Registered Office: George Hay, Brigham House, High Street, Biggleswade, Beds, SG18 0LD
Activities: Other business support service activities n.e.c.
Parent: Ikarus Engineering (Holdings) Ltd
Officers: Laszlo Csiki, Secretary; Laszlo Csiki [1951] Director [Hungarian]

ILB Investments Limited
Incorporated: 3 September 2008 *Employees:* 4
Net Worth: £3,520,188 *Total Assets:* £60,520,232
Registered Office: C P House, Otterspool Way, Watford By-Pass, Watford, Herts, WD25 8JJ
Activities: Other letting and operating of own or leased real estate
Shareholders: Iris Gibbor; Lady Lilly Schreier
Officers: Eric Lewis, Secretary; Iris Gibbor [1951] Director; Mark Gibbor [1988] Director/Accountant; Lady Lilly Schreier [1924] Director

Iliffe Media Limited
Incorporated: 25 January 2016 *Employees:* 357
Net Worth: £10,236,029 *Total Assets:* £21,469,556
Registered Office: Winship Road, Milton, Cambridge, CB24 6PP
Activities: Publishing of newspapers
Major Shareholder: The Honourable Edward Richard Iliffe
Officers: Ricky Allan [1968] Commercial Director; Paul Damon Brackley [1977] Director; David Sidney Fordham [1953] Director; The Honourable Edward Richard Iliffe [1968] Director/Chartered Surveyor; Richard Parkinson [1958] Director; Stephen Paul Sadler [1966] Finance Director; Tracy Alan Wright [1962] Director/Electrical Engineer

Iliffe Print Cambridge Limited
Incorporated: 11 July 1929 *Employees:* 21
Net Worth Deficit: £9,129,000 *Total Assets:* £12,335,000
Registered Office: Winship Road, Milton, Cambridge, CB24 6PP
Activities: Publishing of newspapers
Parent: Iliffe News and Media Limited
Officers: Catherine Elinor Fleming, Secretary; Catherine Elinor Fleming [1961] Director/Chartered Secretary; The Honourable Edward Richard Iliffe [1968] Director/Chartered Surveyor; Stephen Paul Sadler [1966] Finance Director; Tracy Alan Wright [1962] Director/Electrical Engineer

Illumina Cambridge Limited
Incorporated: 2 September 1998 *Employees:* 428
Net Worth: £718,459,520 *Total Assets:* £890,447,296
Registered Office: 19 Granta Park, Great Abington, Cambridge, CB21 6DF
Activities: Research and experimental development on biotechnology
Parent: Illumina Inc
Officers: Charles Dadswell, Secretary; Paula Lynn Dowdy [1965] Director [American]; Rebecca Jane Edwards [1980] Director, HR; Andre Jacques Nel [1972] Finance Director [South African]

Ilot Capital UK Ltd
Incorporated: 29 May 2015
Net Worth: £5,618,447 *Total Assets:* £18,871,134
Registered Office: First Floor, Sheraton House, Lower Road, Chorleywood, Herts, WD3 5LH
Activities: Financial intermediation not elsewhere classified
Parent: Intralot S.A Integrated Lottery Systems and Services
Officers: Evangelos Raptis [1969] Director [Greek]

Ilot Investments UK Ltd
Incorporated: 29 May 2015
Net Worth: £5,543,211 *Total Assets:* £18,942,062
Registered Office: First Floor, Sheraton House, Lower Road, Chorleywood, Herts, WD3 5LH
Activities: Financial intermediation not elsewhere classified
Parent: Intralot S.A Integrated
Officers: Evangelos Raptis [1969] Director [Greek]

Imagination Technologies Group Limited
Incorporated: 18 April 1994 *Employees:* 1,068
Previous: Imagination Technologies Group PLC
Net Worth: £85,375,000 *Total Assets:* £130,912,000
Registered Office: Imagination House, Home Park Estate, Kings Langley, Herts, WD4 8LZ
Activities: Other information service activities n.e.c.
Parent: CBFI Investment Limited
Officers: Ray Bingham [1945] Director [American]; Ronald Douglas Black [1963] Director [American]; John Kao [1969] Director [Chinese]; Peter Kuo [1971] Director [Chinese]

Imagination Technologies Limited
Incorporated: 1 April 1977 *Employees:* 661
Net Worth: £7,923,000 *Total Assets:* £84,409,000
Registered Office: Imagination House, Home Park Estate, Kings Langley, Herts, WD4 8LZ
Activities: Other information technology service activities
Parent: Imagination Technologies Group PLC
Officers: Ronald Douglas Black [1963] Director [American]

IMBOLC Limited
Incorporated: 5 July 2016
Net Worth: £20,299,934 *Total Assets:* £20,299,934
Registered Office: Millennium House, 65 Walton Street, Aylesbury, Bucks, HP21 7QG
Activities: Other information technology service activities
Shareholders: Charles Joseph Kennelly; Stuart Richard Bonthrone
Officers: Stuart Richard Bonthrone [1965] Director; Charles Joseph Kennelly [1965] Director

Imerys Aluminates Limited
Incorporated: 31 December 1985 *Employees:* 63
Previous: Kerneos Limited
Net Worth: £19,779,000 *Total Assets:* £35,623,000
Registered Office: Kerneos, Dolphin Way, Purfleet, Essex, RM19 1NZ
Activities: Manufacture of cement
Parent: Kerneos Holding Northern Europe Limited
Officers: Ian William Adamson, Secretary; Paul Bottomley [1958] Director/Commercial Manager; Patrick Michael Molitor [1967] Director [German]; Tony Vivian Newton [1959] Director/Commercial Manager; Peter Arthur Odendaal [1968] Works Director

Immobiliare Cardi Marmi Limited
Incorporated: 7 December 2016
Net Worth: £82,481,720 *Total Assets:* £82,481,720
Registered Office: Dickens House, Guithavon Street, Witham, Essex, CM8 1BJ
Activities: Buying and selling of own real estate
Parent: Sextant Consolidated Limited
Officers: Vincenzo Bianchi [1958] Director [Italian]; Luigi Cardi [1959] Director/Entrepreneur [Italian]; Philip Lawrence [1953] Director

IMO Car Wash Group Limited
Incorporated: 30 April 2009 *Employees:* 4
Net Worth: £211,848,000 *Total Assets:* £400,265,984
Registered Office: 35-37 Amersham Hill, High Wycombe, Bucks, HP13 6NU
Activities: Activities of head offices
Parent: Rose Midco Ltd
Officers: Jonathan Samuel Booth [1961] Director; Thomas Bruce Mangas [1967] Director/Chief Executive Officer [American]; Nilesh Kundanlal Pandya [1971] Director; Michael Andrew James Smith [1962] Director

Impellam Group PLC
Incorporated: 21 February 2008 *Employees:* 3,267
Net Worth: £260,200,000 *Total Assets:* £1,101,500,032
Registered Office: 800 The Boulevard, Capability Green, Luton, Beds, LU1 3BA
Activities: Temporary employment agency activities
Officers: Rebecca Jane Watson, Secretary; Lord Michael Anthony Ashcroft [1946] Director/Businessman [British/Belizean]; Angela Elizabeth Entwistle [1961] Corporate Communications Director; Mike Ettling [1964] Director [British/South African]; Michael Ivan Laurie [1949] Director; Julia Robertson [1958] Director; Baroness Tina Wendy Stowell [1967] Director

Impellam Holdings Limited
Incorporated: 5 January 1951 *Employees:* 4
Net Worth: £69,328,000 *Total Assets:* £363,576,000
Registered Office: 800 The Boulevard, Capability Green, Luton, Beds, LU1 3BA
Activities: Activities of head offices
Officers: Rebecca Jane Watson, Secretary; Simon Ian Moore [1978] Director/Accountant; Julia Robertson [1958] Director; Rebecca Jane Watson [1969] Director/Solicitor

Impellam UK Limited
Incorporated: 1 May 2009 *Employees:* 114
Net Worth: £36,313,000 *Total Assets:* £254,456,992
Registered Office: 800 The Boulevard, Capability Green, Luton, Beds, LU1 3BA
Activities: Activities of head offices
Parent: Impellam Group PLC
Officers: Rebecca Jane Watson, Secretary; Julia Robertson [1958] Director; Rebecca Jane Watson [1969] Director/Solicitor

Imperial Pharmaceuticals Limited
Incorporated: 14 August 1996 *Employees:* 14
Net Worth: £21,344,456 *Total Assets:* £43,295,732
Registered Office: Unit 4 Imperial Park, Stonefield Way, South Ruislip, Middlesex, HA4 0JW
Activities: Wholesale of perfume and cosmetics
Shareholder: Manisha Thakrar
Officers: Manisha Thakrar, Secretary; Nayan Thakrar [1960] Director; Shivani Thakrar [1987] Director/Dentist

Import Services Limited
Incorporated: 14 June 1991 *Employees:* 101
Net Worth: £6,375,513 *Total Assets:* £12,805,501
Registered Office: 700 Avenue West, Great Notley, Braintree, Essex, CM77 7AA
Activities: Operation of warehousing and storage facilities for land transport activities
Parent: Xpediator PLC
Officers: Stephen William Blyth [1955] Director/Chief Executive; John Sidney Eynon [1943] Director; Stuart John Howard [1971] Director; Roger Vernon Loveless [1960] Director; Christopher Leslie Shrubb [1963] Director/Accountant; Michael Edward Thomas [1959] Director

Inca Digital Printers Limited
Incorporated: 20 March 2000 *Employees:* 213
Net Worth: £18,448,000 *Total Assets:* £31,495,000
Registered Office: 515 Coldhams Lane, Cambridge, CB1 3JS
Activities: Manufacture of other special-purpose machinery n.e.c.
Officers: Matthew Graham Negus, Secretary; Tsuneo Baba [1954] Managing Director [Japanese]; Akira Hayakawa [1962] Director/Deputy CEO [Japanese]; Satoshi Hirose [1973] Director/Manager [Japanese]; Matthew Graham Negus [1982] Director/Chartered Accountant; Yoshinari Otani [1964] Director/Manager [Japanese]; Stephen George Tunnicliffe Wilson [1972] Director of New Product Development

Incodia International Ltd
Incorporated: 19 June 1979 *Employees:* 232
Previous: CPI Card Group - UK Limited
Net Worth: £12,274,000 *Total Assets:* £16,982,000
Registered Office: Graphic House, Telford Way, Severalls Park, Colchester, Essex, CO4 9QF
Activities: Printing n.e.c.
Parent: Sea Fox Bidco Limited
Officers: Nicholas Cahn [1964] Managing Director; Christopher John Huckle [1959] Director; Elliott George Nicholson [1982] Director/Investor; Jonas Rave [1984] Director [German]

Incorporated Bishop's Stortford College Association (The)
Incorporated: 2 June 1904 *Employees:* 310
Net Worth: £31,804,000 *Total Assets:* £41,871,000
Registered Office: 10 Maze Green Road, Bishop's Stortford, Herts, CM23 2PJ
Activities: Primary education
Officers: Paul Michael Stanley, Secretary; Doug Moray Alexander [1962] Finance Director; Guy Ernest Baker [1965] Director/Surveyor; Professor Graeme William Walter Barker [1946] Director/University Professor; Andrew John William Conti [1967] Director/Chartered Accountant; Peter Edmund Dodd [1968] Director/Solicitor; Monica Goitiandia [1961] Director [Spanish]; Dr Philip John Hargrave [1950] Director/Chartered Engineer; Richard Charles Vyvyan Harrison [1967] Director; Sir Stephen James Lander [1947] Director/Consultant; Pauline Mullender [1944] Director/Retired; Dr Suhail Nurbhai [1965] Director/Medical Research; Irene Mary Pearman [1961] Director; Charles Peter Solway [1967] Director/Chartered Quantity Surveyor; David Fraser Thomson [1960] Director/Chartered Accountant

Independent Meters Limited
Incorporated: 11 February 2004
Net Worth: £6,206,331 *Total Assets:* £20,383,076
Registered Office: Energy House, Woolpit Business Park, Windmill Avenue, Woolpit, Bury St Edmunds, Suffolk, IP30 9UP
Activities: Other business support service activities n.e.c.
Parent: Inexus Group (Holdings) Limited
Officers: Christopher Paul Mumford, Secretary; Darryl John Corney [1960] Director; Clive Eric Linsdell [1962] Director

Independent Pipelines Limited
Incorporated: 21 June 1993
Net Worth: £43,702,528 *Total Assets:* £174,732,416
Registered Office: Energy House, Woolpit Business Park, Windmill Avenue, Woolpit, Bury St Edmunds, Suffolk, IP30 9UP
Activities: Distribution of gaseous fuels through mains
Parent: Inexus Group (Holdings) Limited
Officers: Christopher Paul Mumford, Secretary/Legal Adviser; Susan Lisa Standring, Secretary; Graham Collins [1978] Director/Accountant; Darryl John Corney [1960] Director; Keith Johnston [1959] Director; Clive Eric Linsdell [1962] Director; John Trounson [1966] Director

Independent Power Networks Limited
Incorporated: 16 October 2003
Net Worth: £6,904,571 *Total Assets:* £18,686,192
Registered Office: Energy House, Woolpit Business Park, Windmill Avenue, Woolpit, Bury St Edmunds, Suffolk, IP30 9UP
Activities: Distribution of electricity
Parent: Inexus Group Holdings Limited
Officers: Christopher Paul Mumford, Secretary/Legal Adviser; Susan Lisa Standring, Secretary; Darryl John Corney [1960] Director; Clive Eric Linsdell [1962] Director; David Walter Overman [1961] Director; John Trounson [1966] Director

Indesit Company UK Holdings Limited
Incorporated: 13 February 2002
Net Worth Deficit: £72,993,784 *Total Assets:* £291,823,264
Registered Office: Morley Way, Peterborough, Cambs, PE2 9JB
Activities: Activities of other holding companies n.e.c.
Parent: Whirlpool Corporation
Officers: Tetiana Pidhaina, Secretary; Lucianna Raffaini Carvalho [1973] Director [Italian]; Andrzej Tuleja [1973] Director [Polish]

Indo European Foods Limited
Incorporated: 10 November 2000 *Employees:* 45
Net Worth: £2,294,188 *Total Assets:* £18,626,150
Registered Office: Kohinoor House, Langer Road, Felixstowe, Suffolk, IP11 2BW
Activities: Wholesale of other food, including fish, crustaceans and molluscs
Major Shareholder: Satnam Arora
Officers: Gurnam Arora [1950] Director [Indian]; Jugal Kishore Arora [1943] Director [Indian]; Sumit Arora [1978] Director

Industrial and Financial Systems, IFS UK Ltd
Incorporated: 12 November 1996 *Employees:* 262
Net Worth: £13,221,579 *Total Assets:* £57,601,820
Registered Office: Artisan, Hillbottom Road, Sands Industrial Estate, High Wycombe, Bucks, HP12 4HJ
Activities: Business and domestic software development
Officers: Kevin Dennis Fletcher, Secretary; Anders Magnus Lindholm [1979] Director [Swedish]; Mark Soden [1960] Sales Director

Industrial Chemicals Group Limited
Incorporated: 10 March 1976 *Employees:* 511
Net Worth: £48,226,352 *Total Assets:* £121,617,424
Registered Office: Titan Works, Hogg Lane, Grays, Essex, RM17 5DU
Activities: Manufacture of other chemical products n.e.c.
Shareholders: John William Carver; Allen Rodney Carver; Charles Daryl Carver
Officers: Benjamin James Lowthian, Secretary; Allen Rodney Carver [1947] Director; Charles Daryl Carver [1964] Director; John William Carver [1945] Director; Edwin John Strang [1958] Finance Director

Industrial Chemicals Limited
Incorporated: 30 November 1999 *Employees:* 495
Net Worth: £17,625,142 *Total Assets:* £48,816,096
Registered Office: Titan Works, Titan Industrial Estate, Hogg Lane, Grays, Essex, RM17 5DU
Activities: Manufacture of other inorganic basic chemicals
Shareholders: John William Carver; Allen Rodney Carver; Charles Daryl Carver
Officers: Benjamin James Lowthian, Secretary; Allen Rodney Carver [1947] Director; Charles Daryl Carver [1964] Director; John William Carver [1945] Director; Edwin John Strang [1958] Finance Director

Industrial Tool Supplies (London) Limited
Incorporated: 29 August 1979 *Employees:* 116
Net Worth: £12,778,751 *Total Assets:* £17,399,344
Registered Office: DC One, Edinburgh Way, Harlow, Essex, CM20 2BN
Activities: Agents involved in the sale of machinery, industrial equipment, ships and aircraft
Shareholders: John Joseph Wild; Valerie Ann Wild
Officers: Kevin Ray Hubbard, Secretary; Kevin Ray Hubbard [1975] Managing Director; Paul Ernest Alfred Hubbard [1982] Director; John Joseph Wild [1949] Managing Director; Valerie Ann Wild [1951] Director

Industrial Water Jetting Systems Group Limited
Incorporated: 16 August 2010 *Employees:* 411
Net Worth: £3,154,173 *Total Assets:* £27,162,302
Registered Office: Dickens House, Old Stowmarket Road, Woolpit, Bury St Edmunds, Suffolk, IP30 9QS
Activities: Sewerage
Shareholder: Christopher Barry Stewart
Officers: Danielle Anna Ashton, Secretary; Julia Clarfield, Secretary; Max William Simon Ashton [1961] Director/Accountant; Andrew Clarfield [1970] Director/Accountant; Christopher Stewart [1973] Director; Dale James Storrer [1973] Finance Director

Industrial Water Jetting Systems Limited
Incorporated: 10 June 1977 *Employees:* 409
Net Worth: £4,778,352 *Total Assets:* £28,761,624
Registered Office: Dickens House, Old Stowmarket Road, Woolpit, Bury St Edmunds, Suffolk, IP30 9QS
Activities: Sewerage
Parent: Industrial Water Jetting Systems Group Limited
Officers: Max William Simon Ashton [1961] Director/Accountant; Andrew Clarfield [1970] Director/Accountant; Christopher Stewart [1973] Director; Dale James Storrer [1973] Finance Director

Inero Limited
Incorporated: 9 February 2015
Net Worth: £8,936,755 *Total Assets:* £8,936,755
Registered Office: Dickens House, Guithavon Street, Witham, Essex, CM8 1BJ
Activities: Buying and selling of own real estate
Parent: Sextant Consolidated Limited
Officers: Vincenzo Bianchi [1958] Director [Italian]; Philip Lawrence [1953] Director; Ilija Naletilic [1954] Director [Croatian]

Inexus (Services) Limited
Incorporated: 26 November 1993 *Employees:* 10
Net Worth: £10,537,261 *Total Assets:* £11,235,683
Registered Office: Energy House, Woolpit Business Park, Windmill Avenue, Woolpit, Bury St Edmunds, Suffolk, IP30 9UP
Activities: Management consultancy activities other than financial management
Parent: Inexus Group (Holdings) Limited
Officers: Christopher Paul Mumford, Company Secretary; Darryl John Corney [1960] Director; Clive Eric Linsdell [1962] Director

Inexus Connections Limited
Incorporated: 30 June 2005
Net Worth: £200,346,368 *Total Assets:* £670,928,576
Registered Office: Energy House, Woolpit Business Park, Windmill Avenue, Woolpit, Bury St Edmunds, Suffolk, IP30 9UP
Activities: Activities of head offices
Parent: BUUK Infrastructure No 2 Limited
Officers: Christopher Paul Mumford, Secretary; Graham Collins [1978] Director/Accountant; Darryl John Corney [1960] Director; Clive Eric Linsdell [1962] Director

Inexus Group (Holdings) Limited
Incorporated: 24 May 2001
Net Worth: £11,954,967 *Total Assets:* £201,603,168
Registered Office: Energy House, Woolpit Business Park, Windmill Avenue, Woolpit, Bury St Edmunds, Suffolk, IP30 9UP
Activities: Activities of head offices
Parent: Inexus Connections Limited
Officers: Christopher Paul Mumford, Secretary; Graham Collins [1978] Director/Accountant; Darryl John Corney [1960] Director; Clive Eric Linsdell [1962] Director

Inflite Engineering Services Limited
Incorporated: 30 September 1987 *Employees:* 301
Net Worth: £18,773,136 *Total Assets:* £24,626,656
Registered Office: Inflite House, Stanstead Airport, Stanstead, Essex, CM24 1RY
Activities: Manufacture of metal structures and parts of structures
Parent: Swan Investments Group Ltd
Officers: Linda Vera Ellis, Secretary; Pauline May Monksfield [1982] Director/Customer Liaison; Penny Annette Stephens [1952] Director/Customer Liaison Administration; Raymond Aubrey Stephens [1937] Director/Engineer; William Charles Stephens [1985] Director/Purchasing

Ingleby (1884) Limited
Incorporated: 21 March 2012 *Employees:* 150
Net Worth: £5,606,000 *Total Assets:* £15,573,000
Registered Office: Fontana House, Works Road, Letchworth Garden City, Herts, SG6 1LD
Activities: Activities of head offices
Parent: LDC (Nominees) Limited
Officers: Mark Hawkins, Secretary; Jonathan Howard Ford [1962] Director; Mark Hawkins [1974] Financial Director; Robert Schofield [1971] Director; Mark Warren Masters Smith [1959] Director

Ingram Micro Services Holdings Ltd
Incorporated: 24 February 2000
Previous: A Novo Holdings Ltd
Net Worth: £9,824,000 *Total Assets:* £20,903,000
Registered Office: Communications House, Vulcan Road North, Norwich, NR6 6AQ
Activities: Other telecommunications activities
Parent: HNA Group Ltd
Officers: Richard Hammond, Finance Director; Kevin Coleman [1972] Director; Karel Victor Hubert Gabrielle Maria Everaet [1965] Director [Belgian]; Kris Emile Paul Mees [1972] Director/VP Finance Europe [Belgian]

Ingrebourne Valley Holdings Ltd
Incorporated: 17 October 2012 *Employees:* 113
Net Worth: £24,220,574 *Total Assets:* £52,131,416
Registered Office: Cecil House, Foster Street, Harlow, Essex, CM17 9HY
Activities: Activities of other holding companies n.e.c.
Shareholder: Ahern Land Reclamation Limited
Officers: Elsie Louise Rees, Secretary; Patrick Brian Ahern [1947] Director; Andrew Stuart Clark [1960] Director; Paul Delaney [1957] Finance Director; Cecil John Pryor [1947] Director; Roger Generald Pryor [1953] Director; David Pembroke Gilbert Rees [1938] Director; Lilian Beatrice Scott [1948] Director; Peter Ryan Scott [1978] Director

Ingrebourne Valley Limited
Incorporated: 27 August 1993 *Employees:* 75
Net Worth: £22,372,266 *Total Assets:* £49,465,152
Registered Office: Cecil House, Foster Street, Harlow Common, Harlow, Essex, CM17 9HY
Activities: Operation of gravel and sand pits; mining of clays and kaolin
Parent: Ingrebourne Valley Holdings Ltd
Officers: Paul Delaney, Secretary; Patrick Brian Ahern [1947] Director; Andrew Stuart Clark [1960] Director; Paul Delaney [1957] Director/Accountant; Cecil John Pryor [1947] Director; Roger Generald Pryor [1953] Director; Lilian Beatrice Scott [1948] Director; Peter Ryan Scott [1978] Director

Inhealth Group Holdings PLC
Incorporated: 29 September 2005 *Employees:* 1,699
Net Worth: £102,538,000 *Total Assets:* £152,156,992
Registered Office: Beechwood Hall, Kingsmead Road, High Wycombe, Bucks, HP11 1JL
Activities: Activities of head offices
Parent: Inhealth UK Holdings Limited
Officers: Alice Sarah Louise Cummings, Secretary; Ivan Harold Bradbury [1946] Director; Richard James Bradford [1963] Director; Sir Arthur David Chessells [1941] Director; Alice Sarah Louise Cummings [1963] Finance Director

Inhealth Group Limited
Incorporated: 18 December 2002 *Employees:* 169
Net Worth: £107,029,000 *Total Assets:* £156,195,008
Registered Office: Beechwood Hall, Kingsmead Road, High Wycombe, Bucks, HP11 1JL
Activities: Activities of head offices
Parent: Inhealth Group Holdings PLC
Officers: Richard James Bradford [1963] Director; Sir Arthur David Chessells [1941] Director; Alice Sarah Louise Cummings [1963] Finance Director

Inhealth Limited
Incorporated: 27 July 2004 *Employees:* 1,080
Net Worth: £54,489,000 *Total Assets:* £145,763,008
Registered Office: Beechwood Hall, Kingsmead Road, High Wycombe, Bucks, HP11 1JL
Activities: General medical practice activities
Parent: Inhealth Group Limited
Officers: Richard James Bradford [1963] Director; Alice Sarah Louise Cummings [1963] Finance Director

Inhealth Molecular Imaging Limited
Incorporated: 2 March 2007
Net Worth: £11,262,000 *Total Assets:* £14,021,000
Registered Office: Beechwood Hall, Kingsmead Road, High Wycombe, Bucks, HP11 1JL
Activities: Other professional, scientific and technical activities n.e.c.
Parent: Inhealth Limited
Officers: Richard James Bradford [1963] Director; Alice Sarah Louise Cummings [1963] Finance Director

Inhealth Properties Limited
Incorporated: 16 September 2004
Net Worth: £615,000 *Total Assets:* £8,417,000
Registered Office: Beechwood Hall, Kingsmead Road, High Wycombe, Bucks, HP11 1JL
Activities: Buying and selling of own real estate
Parent: Inhealth Group Limited
Officers: Richard James Bradford [1963] Director; Alice Sarah Louise Cummings [1963] Finance Director

Inhealth UK Holdings Limited
Incorporated: 18 August 2009 *Employees:* 1,700
Net Worth: £95,333,000 *Total Assets:* £149,200,992
Registered Office: Beechwood Hall, Kingsmead Road, High Wycombe, Bucks, HP11 1JL
Activities: Activities of head offices
Major Shareholder: Ivan Harold Bradbury
Officers: Ivan Harold Bradbury [1946] Director

The Injured Jockeys Fund
Incorporated: 26 November 2004
Net Worth: £48,887,896 *Total Assets:* £49,120,868
Registered Office: 15 Kings Court, Willie Snaith Road, Newmarket, Suffolk, CB8 7SG
Activities: Other social work activities without accommodation n.e.c.
Officers: Lisa Jeanette Hancock, Secretary; George Edward Norton Baker [1982] Director/Jockeys Agent; Valda Francis Burke [1959] Director; Michael Caulfield [1961] Director; Edward Alan Chamberlin [1974] Director/TV Presenter; Sam Bernard Waley Cohen [1982] Director; Chloe Fairley [1978] Director/Barrister; Michael Anthony Foy [1952] Director/Consultant Orthopaedic and Spinal Surgeon; Guy Henderson [1958] Director; William Norris [1951] Director/Barrister; Hazel Gilchrist Peplinski [1962] Director; Jonathan Frederick Powell [1945] Director/Journalist; John Brough Scott [1942] Director/Journalist; Jeffrey Colin Smith [1945] Director/Executive Chairman; Andrew Thornton [1972] Director/National Hunt Jockey

Inland Finance Ltd
Incorporated: 20 February 2008
Net Worth: £4,832,078 *Total Assets:* £50,457,752
Registered Office: Decimal Place, Chiltern Avenue, Amersham, Bucks, HP6 5FG
Activities: Buying and selling of own real estate
Parent: Inland Homes 2013 Ltd
Officers: Nishith Malde [1958] Director; Gary John Skinner [1968] Managing Director; Stephen Desmond Wicks [1951] Director

Inland Homes (Essex) Limited
Incorporated: 29 December 2011
Net Worth: £366,637 *Total Assets:* £26,959,236
Registered Office: Decimal Place, Chiltern Avenue, Amersham, Bucks, HP6 5FG
Activities: Buying and selling of own real estate
Parent: Inland Ltd
Officers: Nishith Malde, Secretary; Nishith Malde [1958] Director; Gary John Skinner [1968] Managing Director; Stephen Desmond Wicks [1951] Director

Inland Homes 2013 Limited
Incorporated: 14 November 2013
Net Worth: £100 *Total Assets:* £187,183,264
Registered Office: Decimal Place, Chiltern Avenue, Amersham, Bucks, HP6 5FG
Activities: Buying and selling of own real estate
Parent: Inland Homes PLC
Officers: Nishith Malde [1958] Finance Director; Gary John Skinner [1968] Managing Director; Stephen Desmond Wicks [1951] Director

Inland Homes Developments Limited
Incorporated: 15 February 2012
Net Worth: £2,923,825 *Total Assets:* £32,649,186
Registered Office: Decimal Place, Chiltern Avenue, Amersham, Bucks, HP6 5FG
Activities: Buying and selling of own real estate
Parent: Inland Homes 2013 Ltd
Officers: Nishith Malde, Secretary; Nishith Malde [1958] Director; Gary John Skinner [1968] Managing Director; Stephen Desmond Wicks [1951] Director

Inland Homes PLC
Incorporated: 16 June 2005 *Employees:* 93
Net Worth: £142,400,000 *Total Assets:* £299,600,000
Registered Office: Decimal Place, Chiltern Avenue, Amersham, Bucks, HP6 5FG
Activities: Development of building projects
Officers: Nishith Malde, Secretary; Simon Charles Bennett [1958] Director; Laure Duhot [1961] Director [French]; John Brian Hansen Johnson [1961] Director; Nishith Malde [1958] Director; Terry Rene Roydon [1946] Director; Gary John Skinner [1968] Managing Director; Gary John Skinner [1968] Managing Director; Stephen Desmond Wicks [1951] Director

Inland Limited
Incorporated: 16 June 2005 *Employees:* 87
Net Worth: £20,324,876 *Total Assets:* £169,394,176
Registered Office: Decimal Place, Chiltern Avenue, Amersham, Bucks, HP6 5FG
Activities: Development of building projects
Parent: Inland Homes 2013
Officers: Thomas Cuff [1939] Director/Solicitor; Nishith Malde [1958] Director; Gary John Skinner [1968] Director; Desmond Richard Wicks [1989] Land Director; Stephen Desmond Wicks [1951] Director

Inland Property Limited
Incorporated: 4 March 2015
Net Worth: £25,225,228 *Total Assets:* £45,341,128
Registered Office: Decimal Place, Chiltern Avenue, Amersham, Bucks, HP6 5FG
Activities: Buying and selling of own real estate
Parent: Poole Investments Ltd
Officers: Nishith Malde [1958] Director; Gary John Skinner [1968] Managing Director; Stephen Desmond Wicks [1951] Director

John Innes Centre
Incorporated: 25 September 1952 *Employees:* 410
Net Worth: £101,135,000 *Total Assets:* £131,468,000
Registered Office: Norwich Research Park, Colney, Norwich, NR4 7UH
Activities: Other research and experimental development on natural sciences and engineering
Officers: David Foreman, Secretary; John Hugh Innes [1959] Director/Investment Manager; Dr Deborah Jane Keith [1957] Director; Professor Ottoline Leyser [1965] Director; Robert John Maskell [1969] Director of High Performing Computing; Jennifer Kristin Midura [1966] Director/Head of Strategy [British/American]; Professor John Colin Murrell [1957] Director/University Professor; Keith Richard Norman [1959] Technical Director - Arable; Professor Nicholas Jose Talbot [1965] Director/Research Scientist; Dr William Henry Lewarne West [1968] Director/Biotech CEO

John Innes Foundation
Incorporated: 26 September 2005
Net Worth: £43,749,412 *Total Assets:* £44,336,944
Registered Office: St James Mill, Whitefriars, Norwich, NR3 1SH
Activities: Other education n.e.c.
Officers: Dr Tina Lorraine Barsby [1957] CEO & Director; Professor Ian Richard Crute [1949] Research Director; David John McLeavy Hill [1957] Director; Peter David Innes [1952] Director/Recruitment Consultant; Dr David Kenneth Lawrence [1949] Director/Retired; Keith Richard Norman [1959] Technical Director

Innovative Design Systems Limited
Incorporated: 10 May 2000 *Employees:* 86
Net Worth: £5,942,921 *Total Assets:* £10,714,940
Registered Office: 1 Bunkell Road, Rackheath Industrial Estate, Rackheath, Norwich, NR13 6PX
Activities: Glazing
Parent: Hunter Group Holdings Limited
Officers: Elaine Hunter [1975] Director; Richard Stephen Hunter [1966] Director

Inntel Group Limited
Incorporated: 12 December 2011 *Employees:* 134
Net Worth: £3,384,744 *Total Assets:* £13,731,509
Registered Office: Inntel House, Threshelfords Business Park, Inworth Road, Feering, Colchester, Essex, CO5 9SE
Activities: Other reservation service activities n.e.c.
Major Shareholder: Douglas O'Neill
Officers: Mark Jeffrey Wheeler, Secretary; Dolina Isabelle O'Neill [1976] Director; Douglas O'Neill [1970] Director

Inntel Limited
Incorporated: 16 August 1988 *Employees:* 134
Net Worth: £4,252,420 *Total Assets:* £12,639,540
Registered Office: Inntel House, Threshelfords Business Park, Inworth Road, Feering, Essex, CO5 9SE
Activities: Other reservation service activities n.e.c.
Parent: Inntel Group Limited
Officers: Mark Jeffrey Wheeler, Secretary; Dolina Isabelle O'Neill [1976] Director; Douglas O'Neill [1970] Director

Inpra UK Limited
Incorporated: 14 December 2011 *Employees:* 139
Net Worth Deficit: £233,996 *Total Assets:* £12,144,319
Registered Office: 46-48 Rothesay Road, Luton, Beds, LU1 1QZ
Activities: Other service activities n.e.c.
Shareholder: Jeremiah Samson Hope Stephenson
Officers: Dr Fabio Petroni [1960] Director [Italian]; Niccolo Petroni [1997] Director [Italian]

Insignia Investments Limited
Incorporated: 11 October 2007 *Employees:* 52
Net Worth: £6,552,756 *Total Assets:* £14,180,130
Registered Office: 14 Pindar Road, Hoddesdon, Herts, EN11 0DE
Activities: Activities of head offices
Shareholders: Tara Flynn; Marc Flynn
Officers: James Flynn [1941] Director/Retired [Irish]; Marc Flynn [1964] Director; Ian Andrew Wright [1955] Director

Insignis Academy Trust
Incorporated: 3 June 2011 *Employees:* 108
Previous: Sir Henry Floyd Grammar School Academy Trust
Net Worth: £14,586,001 *Total Assets:* £17,393,248
Registered Office: Sir Henry Floyd Grammar School, Oxford Road, Aylesbury, Bucks, HP21 8PE
Activities: General secondary education
Officers: John Robert Huskinson, Secretary; Stephen David Box [1955] Director/Headteacher; Gaynor Bull [1961] Director/Housewife; Dr Nicolette Tamsin Habgood [1965] Director/Academic (Senior Lecturer in H.E. Retired); Mark Glyn Hardy [1953] Director/Company Secretary; Stephen David Louis [1966] Director; Anthony Roy Withells [1952] Director/Teacher

Inspectorate Holdings PLC
Incorporated: 8 June 1992
Net Worth: £12,491,429 *Total Assets:* £28,058,984
Registered Office: 2 Perry Road, Witham, Essex, CM8 3TU
Activities: Non-trading company
Parent: Bureau Veritas SA
Officers: David John Lappage, Secretary; Richard David Bryan [1963] Director/Accountant; David John Lappage [1951] Director

Inspectorate International Limited
Incorporated: 30 September 1959 *Employees:* 467
Net Worth: £40,875,000 *Total Assets:* £59,093,000
Registered Office: 2 Perry Road, Witham, Essex, CM8 3TU
Activities: Activities of head offices
Parent: Inspectorate International Holdings PLC
Officers: David John Lappage, Company Secretary; Richard David Bryan [1963] Director/Accountant; Richard Charles Downs [1963] Business Director; David John Lappage [1951] Director

Inspiration Trust
Incorporated: 14 August 2012 *Employees:* 942
Net Worth: £82,320,616 *Total Assets:* £93,723,832
Registered Office: Weights and Measures Building, 28 Bethel Street, Norwich, NR2 1NR
Activities: Primary education
Officers: Sally Ann Culling, Secretary; Dame Rachel Mary de Souza [1968] Director/Principal; Professor Colin James Diamond [1950] Director/Professor of Educational Leadership; David Robert Earnshaw [1945] Director/Retired; Julian Christopher Hanson-Smith [1962] Director/Private Equity Fund Manager; Helena Christine Mills [1967] Director/Chief Executive Officer; David Charles Tibble [1952] Director

Instalcom Limited
Incorporated: 19 August 1997 *Employees:* 81
Net Worth: £15,067,343 *Total Assets:* £29,624,182
Registered Office: 467 Rayners Lane, Pinner, Middlesex, HA5 5ET
Activities: Other specialised construction activities n.e.c.
Parent: OCU Group Limited
Officers: Timothy Gerard O'Connor, Secretary/Contractor [Irish]; John McVeigh [1964] Managing Director [Irish]; Thomas Joseph O'Connor [1961] Director [Irish]; Timothy Gerard O'Connor [1960] Director [Irish]

Institute of Advanced Motorists Limited (The)
Incorporated: 10 March 1956 *Employees:* 65
Net Worth: £7,947,000 *Total Assets:* £9,621,000
Registered Office: 1 Albany Place, Hyde Way, Welwyn Garden City, Herts, AL7 3BT
Activities: Driving school activities
Officers: Ruth Bridger, Secretary; Georgina Gaye Bromage [1956] Director/Veterinary Surgeon; Elizabeth Marguerite Coyle-Camp [1960] Director/Public Relations Professional; Dr. Charles James Doyle [1959] Director; Dr Peter John Pashley Holden [1955] Director/General Medical Practitioner; Kenneth William Keir [1950] Director; Dr Catherine Ann Lloyd [1962] Director/Legal Administrator; Derek John McMullan [1951] Director/Retired; Professor William Angus Wallace [1948] Director/University Prof of Orthopaedic & Accident Surgery

Institute of Grocery Distribution (The)
Incorporated: 1 November 1909 *Employees:* 149
Net Worth: £9,113,861 *Total Assets:* £16,713,299
Registered Office: Grange Lane, Letchmore Heath, Watford, Herts, WD25 8GD
Activities: Other professional, scientific and technical activities n.e.c.
Officers: Julia Clare Bastiman, Secretary; Ann Michelle Bell [1971] People Director, International; Andrew James Clappen [1965] Corporate Services Director; Bradley Moore [1972] Grocery Sales Director; Ian Douglas Morley [1966] Group Sales Director; David Oflynn [1970] Director/Chief Financial Officer [Irish]; Jill Margaret Ross [1973] Director/Vice President, Customer Development; Philip John Tenney [1970] Director/Vice President and CIO; Mark John Webster [1972] Director/Financial Controller; Christopher Paul Whitfield [1969] Director/Chief Operating Officer

Instrumel Ltd
Incorporated: 31 October 1997 *Employees:* 2
Previous: Plasticard Limited
Net Worth: £3,369,114 *Total Assets:* £12,019,719
Registered Office: 69 Knowl Piece, Wilbury Way, Hitchin, Herts, SG4 0TY
Activities: Management consultancy activities other than financial management
Major Shareholder: Elliot James Lamb
Officers: Elliot James Lamb, Secretary/Director; Susan Patricia Brown [1954] Director; Elliot James Lamb [1962] Director

Integrated Microwave Technology Ltd
Incorporated: 13 December 2016 *Employees:* 94
Net Worth: £5,806,137 *Total Assets:* £13,817,817
Registered Office: Waterside House, Earls Colne Business Park, Colchester, Essex, CO6 2NS
Activities: Manufacture of communication equipment other than telegraph, and telephone apparatus and equipment
Officers: Roger Glenn Branton [1967] Director/Chief Financial Officer [American]; John Bayly Payne IV [1969] Director/President [American]; David Ian Robins [1982] Director/VP of Sales

Intelek Limited
Incorporated: 4 February 1949
Net Worth: £20,265,000 *Total Assets:* £21,614,000
Registered Office: 106 Waterhouse Lane, Chelmsford, Essex, CM1 2QU
Activities: Activities of head offices
Parent: Teledyne Technologies Incorporated
Officers: Nicholas James Wargent, Secretary; Robert Mehrabian [1941] Director/Corporate Executive [American]; Aldo Pichelli [1952] Director [American]; Nicholas James Wargent [1973] Director/Solicitor

Interaction Recruitment PLC
Incorporated: 26 July 1989 *Employees:* 3,200
Net Worth: £5,241,129 *Total Assets:* £14,820,169
Registered Office: Interaction House, 43 High Street, Huntingdon, Cambs, PE29 3AQ
Activities: Temporary employment agency activities
Parent: Hexagon Investment Holdings
Officers: Geoff Holder, Secretary; Benjamin Ambler [1981] Corporate Portfolio Director; Mark Dickson [1962] Sales Director; Andrew Iain Gilchrist [1962] Director/Accountant; Geoffrey George Holder [1972] Finance Director; Jean Lenton [1961] Operations Director; John Vazquez [1982] Director

Interguide Group Limited
Incorporated: 11 April 2007 *Employees:* 1
Net Worth: £6,940,600 *Total Assets:* £14,276,818
Registered Office: New Bury Farm, Mill Road, Slapton, Leighton Buzzard, Beds, LU7 9BT
Activities: Activities of head offices
Major Shareholder: Alan Richard Dugard
Officers: Alan Richard Dugard [1968] Director

Interiors with Art Limited
Incorporated: 15 August 2002 *Employees:* 32
Net Worth: £5,376,193 *Total Assets:* £8,479,317
Registered Office: 505 Pinner Road, Harrow, Middlesex, HA2 6EH
Activities: Other business support service activities n.e.c.
Shareholders: Sanjay Dev Sharma; Shailja Vohora
Officers: Pius Chirayathu Thomas, Secretary; Sanjay Dev Sharma [1968] Director/Consultant [Indian]; Shailja Vohora [1963] Director

Interlink Direct Limited
Incorporated: 2 March 2000 *Employees:* 37
Net Worth: £6,153,980 *Total Assets:* £12,912,190
Registered Office: 402-404 Roding Lane South, Woodford Green, Essex, IG8 8EY
Activities: Agents involved in the sale of food, beverages and tobacco
Major Shareholder: Yin Ha Kwok
Officers: Fu Kit Kwok, Secretary; Fu Kit Kwok [1966] Director/Office Manager; Fu Leung Kwok [1967] Director/Operation Manager; Yin Ha Kwok [1957] Director

Intermay Management Ltd
Incorporated: 23 May 2002
Net Worth: £11,646,867 *Total Assets:* £12,002,911
Registered Office: First Floor, Woodgate Studios, 2-8 Games Road, Cockfosters, Barnet, Herts, EN4 9HN
Activities: Other professional, scientific and technical activities n.e.c.
Major Shareholder: Oksana Marchenko
Officers: Anzelika Pasenidou, Secretary; Andreas Sofocleous [1967] Director [Cypriot]

Intermune Holdings Limited
Incorporated: 18 April 2012
Net Worth: £21,863,888 *Total Assets:* £21,910,400
Registered Office: 6 Falcon Way, Shire Park, Welwyn Garden City, Herts, AL7 1TW
Activities: Research and experimental development on biotechnology
Parent: Intermune, Inc.
Officers: Mandy Elizabeth Robertson, Secretary; Richard William Erwin [1967] Director/General Manager; Padraic Ward [1965] Director [Irish]

International Car Wash Group Financing PLC
Incorporated: 9 June 2014 *Employees:* 4
Previous: Boing Group Financing PLC
Net Worth Deficit: £1,535,000 *Total Assets:* £268,332,992
Registered Office: 35-37 Amersham Hill, High Wycombe, Bucks, HP13 6NU
Activities: Other retail sale of new goods in specialised stores (not commercial art galleries and opticians)
Parent: Boing Acquisitions Limited
Officers: Jessica Rowena Shaffrey, Secretary; Thomas Bruce Mangas [1967] Director/Chief Executive Officer [American]; Nilesh Kundanlal Pandya [1971] Director/Chief Financial Officer; Michael Andrew James Smith [1962] Director

International Car Wash Group Ltd.
Incorporated: 9 June 2014 *Employees:* 6
Previous: Boing Topco Limited
Net Worth: £43,285,000 *Total Assets:* £153,356,000
Registered Office: 35-37 Amersham Hill, High Wycombe, Bucks, HP13 6NU
Activities: Other retail sale in non-specialised stores
Parent: Shine Acquisition Co Limited
Officers: Ezra Field [1969] Director/Investment Professional [American]; Matthew Kaelin [1982] Director/Investment Professional [American]; Thomas Bruce Mangas [1967] Director/Chief Executive Officer [American]; Nilesh Kundanlal Pandya [1971] Director; Michael Scott Sharkey [1985] Director/Investment Professional [American]; Michael Andrew James Smith [1962] Director

International Fertilizer Association Limited
Incorporated: 22 March 1962 *Employees:* 26
Previous: International Fertilizer Industry Association Limited
Net Worth: £7,284,819 *Total Assets:* £9,477,764
Registered Office: Confederation House, East of England Showground, Peterborough, Cambs, PE2 6XE
Activities: Activities of professional membership organisations
Officers: Charlotte Caroline Hebebrand, Secretary; Samir Al Abdrabbuh [1961] Director/Executive Vice President [Saudi Arabian]; Yves Caprara [1956] Director/Chief Executive Officer [Belgian]; Andrey Guryev [1982] Director/Chief Executive Officer [Russian]; Ian Hansen [1961] Director/Divisional Chief Operating Officer [Australian]; Brent Heimann [1960] Director/President and CEO [American]; Alexa Hergenroether [1970] Director/Chief Executive Officer [German]; Svein Tore Holsether [1972] Director [Norwegian]; Munish Jindal [1967] Director/Chief Executive Officer [Indian]; Jeanne Johns [1962] Managing Director & Chief Executive Officer [Australian]; Rakesh Kapur [1954] Joint Managing Director [Indian]; Tariq Khan [1957] Chief Executive & Managing Director [Pakistani]; Dmitry Konyaev [1971] Director/Chief Executive Officer [Russian]; Chuck Magro [1969] Director/President and Chief Executive Officer [Canadian]; Manoj Mishra [1961] Chairman and Managing Director [Indian]; William O'Neill [1945] Director/President [American]; James O'Rourke [1960] Director/Chief Executive Officer [American]; Daniel Pettarin [1957] Director/General Manager [Argentinian]; Mulyono Prawiro [1958] President Director [Indonesian]; Hengde Qin [1970] Director/Chief Executive Officer [Chinese]; Marcos Stelzer [1973] Managing Director [Brazilian]; Mr Takashi Sumi [1963] Director/President and Chief Executive Officer [Japanese]; Mostafa Terrab [1955] Director/CEO/Chairman IFA Finance Committee [Moroccan]; Anthony Will [1965] Director/President and Chief Executive Officer [American]; Jidong Zhai [1964] Director/Executive Vice President [Chinese]

International Flavours & Fragrances (GB) Holdings Limited
Incorporated: 14 December 2000
Net Worth: £613,990,976 *Total Assets:* £627,436,992
Registered Office: Duddery Hill, Haverhill, Suffolk, CB9 8LG
Activities: Activities of head offices
Officers: Keith John Hammond [1958] Finance Director; Jeroen Henricus Maria Van Noorden [1960] Director/Lawyer [Dutch]

International Flavours & Fragrances I.F.F.(Great Britain) Limited
Incorporated: 5 June 1926 *Employees:* 258
Net Worth: £110,712,000 *Total Assets:* £132,164,000
Registered Office: Duddery Hill, Haverhill, Suffolk, CB9 8LG
Activities: Manufacture of other organic basic chemicals
Officers: John Kim Fox [1955] Global Accounts Director; Keith John Hammond [1958] Finance Director; Susanne Jane Olive [1973] Director/HR Manager UK

International Industrial Metals Limited
Incorporated: 11 August 2014 *Employees:* 644
Net Worth: £16,271,306 *Total Assets:* £102,287,560
Registered Office: Faulkner House, Victoria Street, St Albans, Herts, AL1 3SE
Activities: Other business support service activities n.e.c.
Major Shareholder: Maurice Elliot Sherling
Officers: Graham Charles Hudson [1959] Director; Anthony Patrick Mullins [1947] Director [Irish]; Maurice Elliot Sherling [1949] Director [Irish]

International Society for Krishna Consciousness Limited
Incorporated: 15 September 1969 *Employees:* 230
Net Worth: £38,726,092 *Total Assets:* £41,681,696
Registered Office: Oak House, 1 Watford Road, Radlett, Herts, WD7 8LA
Activities: Activities of religious organisations
Officers: Grace Olapoju, Secretary; Terry Michael Anderson [1959] Director/Priest; Anthony William Howchin [1956] Director/Priest Branch Manager; George Thomas McMullan [1963] Director/Voluntary Worker; Paul Patrick Murphy [1961] Director/Restaurateur [Irish]; Kamlesh Kumar Maheshwar Patel [1962] Director/Corporate Financial Advisor

International Tin Association Ltd
Incorporated: 24 November 1994 *Employees:* 21
Previous: ITRI Limited
Net Worth: £2,815,327 *Total Assets:* £8,474,704
Registered Office: Unit 3 Curo Park, Frogmore, St Albans, Herts, AL2 2DD
Activities: Support activities for other mining and quarrying
Officers: Sally Gent, Secretary; Mohd Ajib Bin Haji Anuar [1950] Executive Director [Malaysian]; Andrew John Davies [1969] Managing Director; Inge Emiel Maria Hofkens [1970] Director/Sales Officer [Belgian]; Raveentiran Krishnan [1963] Director/Group Chief Operating Officer, Smelting [Malaysian]; Juan Luis Kruger [1970] Director/Chief Executive [Peruvian]; Gang Li [1970] Director/General Manager of Yunnan Tin Group [Chinese]; Michael Yde Marcussen [1952] Director/Company President [Danish]; Mariano Ignacio Pero [1971] Director/General Manager [Bolivian]; Stephen Daniel Robinson [1965] Director/Executive General Manager [Australian]; Mochtar Riza Pahlevi Tabrani [1968] Director [Indonesian]; Anthony John Yeates Turner [1948] Director; Mian Thong Yong [1953] Director/Chief Executive [Malaysian]

International Transport Limited
Incorporated: 14 November 1991
Net Worth: £99,061,000 *Total Assets:* £519,320,000
Registered Office: Leslie Ford House, Tilbury, Essex, RM18 7EH
Activities: Activities of other holding companies n.e.c.
Parent: Forth Ports Limited
Officers: Pamela June Smyth, Secretary; Carole Jean Cran [1970] Director/Chief Financial Officer; Charles Graham Hammond [1961] Director/Solicitor

Interquest Group (UK) Limited
Incorporated: 5 May 2000 *Employees:* 265
Net Worth: £14,306,818 *Total Assets:* £40,527,684
Registered Office: Castle Chambers, 87a High Street, Berkhamsted, Herts, HP4 2DF
Activities: Other activities of employment placement agencies
Parent: Interquest Group Limited
Officers: Clare Hartnell, Secretary; Gary Peter Ashworth [1960] Director; David Charles Bygrave [1968] Director/Chartered Accountant; Christopher Ernest Eldridge [1973] Director

Intertain (Bars) Limited
Incorporated: 30 September 2009
Net Worth Deficit: £31,058,000 *Total Assets:* £38,221,000
Registered Office: Porter Tun House, Capability Green, Luton, Beds, LU1 3LS
Activities: Public houses and bars
Parent: Intertain Limited
Officers: Simon David Longbottom [1971] Director; Ian Timothy Payne [1953] Director; David Andrew Ross [1973] Director

Intertain Limited
Incorporated: 20 August 2009 *Employees:* 313
Net Worth Deficit: £3,116,000 *Total Assets:* £36,027,000
Registered Office: Porter Tun House, Capability Green, Luton, Beds, LU1 3LS
Activities: Other amusement and recreation activities n.e.c.
Parent: TDR Capital LLP
Officers: Simon David Longbottom [1971] Director; Ian Timothy Payne [1953] Director; David Andrew Ross [1973] Director

Intertek Capital Resources Limited
Incorporated: 3 December 1999
Previous: Moody Int. Trading Limited
Net Worth: £9,926,397 *Total Assets:* £375,728,736
Registered Office: Academy Place, 1-9 Brook Street, Brentwood, Essex, CM14 5NQ
Activities: Financial intermediation not elsewhere classified
Parent: Intertek Testing Services Holdings Limited
Officers: Fiona Maria Evans [1965] Director/Group Company Secretary; Nicholas Anthony Hare [1977] Director/Deputy Group Financial Controller; Ross McCluskey [1980] Director

Intertek Finance No. 2 Ltd
Incorporated: 16 May 2012
Net Worth: £32,798,308 *Total Assets:* £32,798,308
Registered Office: Academy Place, 1-9 Brook Street, Brentwood, Essex, CM14 5NQ
Activities: Financial intermediation not elsewhere classified
Parent: Intertek Holdings Limited
Officers: Fiona Maria Evans [1965] Director/Group Secretary; Nicholas Anthony Hare [1977] Director/Deputy Group Financial Controller; Ross McCluskey [1980] Director

Intertek Finance PLC
Incorporated: 19 July 1996
Net Worth: £253,256,992 *Total Assets:* £1,983,534,976
Registered Office: Academy Place, 1-9 Brook Street, Brentwood, Essex, CM14 5NQ
Activities: Financial intermediation not elsewhere classified
Parent: Intertek Testing Services Holdings Limited
Officers: Fiona Maria Evans [1965] Director/Group Company Secretary; Nicholas Anthony Hare [1977] Director/Deputy Group Financial Controller; Ross McCluskey [1980] Director

Intertek Holdings Limited
Incorporated: 29 November 2002
Net Worth: £406,844,000 *Total Assets:* £529,723,008
Registered Office: Academy Place, 1-9 Brook Street, Brentwood, Essex, CM14 5NQ
Activities: Activities of head offices
Parent: Intertek Group PLC
Officers: Fiona Maria Evans [1965] Director/Group Company Secretary; Nicholas Anthony Hare [1977] Director/Deputy Group Financial Controller; Ross McCluskey [1980] Director

Intertek Inspection Services UK Limited
Incorporated: 23 June 1969 *Employees:* 105
Net Worth: £17,723,000 *Total Assets:* £40,266,000
Registered Office: Academy Place, 1-9 Brook Street, Brentwood, Essex, CM14 5NQ
Activities: Other business support service activities n.e.c.
Parent: RCG-Moody International Limited
Officers: Julian Charles Burge [1973] Director/Accountant; Robert Alan Van Dorp [1977] Director; Jan Henry Henriksen [1965] Director/General Manager [Norwegian]

Intertek International Limited
Incorporated: 14 February 1906 *Employees:* 228
Net Worth: £29,243,000 *Total Assets:* £49,566,000
Registered Office: Academy Place, 1-9 Brook Street, Brentwood, Essex, CM14 5NQ
Activities: Other business support service activities n.e.c.
Parent: Intertek Holdings Limited
Officers: Ian Edward Galloway [1974] Director/Accountant; Darren Hodsoll [1977] Director/Accountant; Thomas Kordick [1963] Director/Senior Vice President [German]; Matthew Paul Skinner [1976] Director

Intertek Nominees Limited
Incorporated: 10 November 2003
Net Worth: £37,574,000 *Total Assets:* £37,580,000
Registered Office: Academy Place, 1-9 Brook Street, Brentwood, Essex, CM14 5NQ
Activities: Activities of head offices
Parent: Moody International (Holdings) Limited
Officers: Thomas Andrew Dunlop [1974] Director/Accountant; Fiona Maria Evans [1965] Director/Group Company Secretary; Ross McCluskey [1980] Director

Intertek Overseas Holdings Limited
Incorporated: 31 March 1952
Net Worth: £100,048,000 *Total Assets:* £145,764,000
Registered Office: Academy Place, 1-9 Brook Street, Brentwood, Essex, CM14 5NQ
Activities: Activities of head offices
Parent: Intertek Holdings Limited
Officers: Fiona Maria Evans [1965] Director/Group Company Secretary; Nicholas Anthony Hare [1977] Director/Deputy Group Financial Controller; Ross McCluskey [1980] Director

Intertek Testing & Certification Limited
Incorporated: 31 October 1996 *Employees:* 141
Net Worth Deficit: £202,000 *Total Assets:* £11,108,000
Registered Office: Academy Place, 1-9 Brook Street, Brentwood, Essex, CM14 5NQ
Activities: Technical testing and analysis
Parent: Intertek UK Holdings Limited
Officers: Julian Charles Burge [1973] Director/Accountant; Ayush Dhital [1981] Director/Business Line Leader - Electrical & Wireless; Robert Alan Van Dorp [1977] Director

Intertek Testing Management Ltd
Incorporated: 17 February 1969 *Employees:* 71
Net Worth Deficit: £63,340,000 *Total Assets:* £51,020,000
Registered Office: Academy Place, 1-9 Brook Street, Brentwood, Essex, CM14 5NQ
Activities: Other business support service activities n.e.c.
Parent: Intertek Holdings Limited
Officers: Fiona Maria Evans [1965] Director/Group Company Secretary; Nicholas Anthony Hare [1977] Director/Deputy Group Financial Controller; Ross McCluskey [1980] Director

Intertek Testing Services Holdings Limited.
Incorporated: 19 July 1996 *Employees:* 2
Net Worth: £683,952,000 *Total Assets:* £1,042,019,968
Registered Office: Academy Place, 1-9 Brook Street, Brentwood, Essex, CM14 5NQ
Activities: Other business support service activities n.e.c.
Parent: Intertek Group PLC
Officers: Fiona Maria Evans [1965] Director/Group Company Secretary; Nicholas Anthony Hare [1977] Director/Deputy Group Financial Controller; Ross McCluskey [1980] Director

Intertek UK Holdings Limited
Incorporated: 18 April 1942
Net Worth Deficit: £22,516,000 *Total Assets:* £79,448,000
Registered Office: Academy Place, 1-9 Brook Street, Brentwood, Essex, CM14 5NQ
Activities: Activities of head offices
Parent: Intertek Holdings Limited
Officers: Fiona Maria Evans [1965] Director/Group Company Secretary; Nicholas Anthony Hare [1977] Director/Deputy Group Financial Controller; Ross McCluskey [1980] Director

Intertek USD Finance Ltd
Incorporated: 11 April 2011
Net Worth: £506,796,736 *Total Assets:* £848,457,408
Registered Office: Academy Place, 1-9 Brook Street, Brentwood, Essex, CM14 5NQ
Activities: Activities of head offices
Parent: Intertek Testing Services Holdings Limited
Officers: Fiona Maria Evans [1965] Director/Group Company Secretary; Nicholas Anthony Hare [1977] Director/Deputy Group Financial Controller; Ross McCluskey [1980] Director

Into UEA LLP
Incorporated: 11 October 2007 *Employees:* 141
Net Worth: £3,000 *Total Assets:* £16,856,000
Registered Office: The Registry, University of East Anglia, Norwich, NR4 7TJ

Intralot Finance UK Limited
Incorporated: 11 December 2007 *Employees:* 2
Previous: Intralot Finance UK PLC
Net Worth Deficit: £4,683,278 *Total Assets:* £618,260,544
Registered Office: 1st Floor, Sheraton House, Lower Road, Chorleywood, Rickmansworth, Herts, WD3 5LH
Activities: Other business support service activities n.e.c.
Parent: Intralot SA Integrated Lottery Systems and Services
Officers: Antonios Kerastaris [1969] Director/Chief Financial Officer [Greek]; Evangelos Raptis [1969] Director/Treasurer [Greek]; Vasileios Vasdaris [1957] Director/Economist [Greek]

Intrasales (Lye Lane) Limited
Incorporated: 18 September 1997
Previous: 03436020 Limited
Net Worth Deficit: £2,574,077 *Total Assets:* £8,022,078
Registered Office: Pattisson House, Addison Road, Chesham, Bucks, HP5 2BD
Activities: Development of building projects
Major Shareholder: George McKenzie
Officers: George McKenzie [1942] Director [American]

Invesco Capita Holdings Limited
Incorporated: 15 June 2004 *Employees:* 165
Net Worth: £4,457,539 *Total Assets:* £23,217,878
Registered Office: Unit 5 Humphrys Road, Woodside Industrial Estate, Dunstable, Beds, LU5 4TP
Activities: Activities of other holding companies n.e.c.
Shareholders: Gerard Aidan Abbott-Drake; John Mark O'Leary
Officers: Gerard Aidan Abbott-Drake [1968] Director; John Mark O'Leary [1955] Director

Investland Limited
Incorporated: 27 June 2008 *Employees:* 8
Net Worth: £100,260 *Total Assets:* £8,706,044
Registered Office: 42 Lytton Road, Barnet, Herts, EN5 5BY
Activities: Other business support service activities n.e.c.
Shareholders: Sassoon Raymond; Suraia Gorjian; Michael Gerrard; Joseph Peter Gerrard
Officers: Joseph Peter Gerrard [1954] Director/Accountant; Michael Gerrard [1957] Director/Textile Merchant

Investment Company PLC (The)
Incorporated: 14 November 1868 *Employees:* 1
Net Worth: £17,334,092 *Total Assets:* £17,451,180
Registered Office: Hamilton Centre, Rodney Way, Chelmsford, Essex, CM1 3BY
Activities: Activities of investment trusts
Officers: Ian Robert Dighe [1955] Director; Timothy Mark Metcalfe [1972] Director; Martin Henry Withers Perrin [1954] Director/Chartered Accountant

Investment Properties (Luton) Limited
Incorporated: 23 April 1948 *Employees:* 10
Net Worth: £13,411,184 *Total Assets:* £14,128,222
Registered Office: First Floor, 8-10 Upper Marlborough Road, St Albans, Herts, AL1 3UR
Activities: Other letting and operating of own or leased real estate
Shareholder: The Leslie Sell Charitable Trust
Officers: Sharon Joan Long, Secretary; John Russell Sell [1944] Director/Architect; Nicholas Jody Sell [1972] Director/Consultant; Emma Jane Simpson [1969] Director/Marketing Consultant; Alice Ruth Taylor [1980] Director/Consultant; Edward John Wiltshire [1976] Director/Horticulturalist; Mary Russell Wiltshire [1946] Director/Retired; Tom Wiltshire [1973] Director/Computer Consultant

The Invicta Film Partnership No. 17, LLP
Incorporated: 1 September 2003
Net Worth: £15,699,488 *Total Assets:* £17,576,724
Registered Office: 99 Kenton Road, Harrow, Middlesex, HA3 0AN
Officers: Paul Anderson [1956] LLP Member; Caroline Susan Bailey [1961] LLP Member; James Edward Baird [1952] LLP Member; John Beare [1953] LLP Member; Mary Catherine Best [1960] LLP Member; Nicholas Charles Birch [1959] LLP Member; Alan James Brydon [1954] LLP Member; James Robert Burgess [1956] LLP Member; Stephen James Burnhope [1956] LLP Member; David John Cameron [1942] LLP Member; Dr Joseph Chandy [1941] LLP Member; Lee Robert Clark [1972] LLP Member; Dr Mark Nathaniel Collins [1952] LLP Member; John Robert Davy [1955] LLP Member; Andrew David Dick [1965] LLP Member; Alexander Charles Duncan [1960] LLP Member; Ralph Godley [1949] LLP Member; Robert David Goffman [1960] LLP Member; Bryan Neil Grainger [1951] LLP Member; Doctor Philip Gerard Guest [1957] LLP Member; Philippa Ryan Hamilton James [1968] LLP Member; Charles Dominic Hazlehurst [1966] LLP Member; Iain Catleugh Hutchinson [1965] LLP Member; Renaud Hugues Edmond Isman [1963] LLP Member; Victoria Reynolds Jenkinson [1962] LLP Member; Seth Art Maurice Johnson [1979] LLP Member; Maria Zofia Kempinska-Davy [1953] LLP Member; Ian David Kennedy [1947] LLP Member; Nicholas John Kirk [1943] LLP Member; Leighton Richard Lloyd [1963] LLP Member; Dr Craig Howard Macmillan [1958] LLP Member; Gaetano William Mammana [1962] LLP Member; Roger Frank Millett [1952] LLP Member; Malcolm Bruce Oastler [1959] LLP Member; Ranjan Madhukar Patwardhan [1959] LLP Member; Dominic Paul Price [1967] LLP Member; Michael David Pryke Smith [1967] LLP Member; Mudalagiri Dasappa Ramakrishna Gupta [1945] LLP Member; David Ernest Henry Robson [1940] LLP Member; Shaun William Sargent [1967] LLP Member; Guduthur Raghavendra Setty [1942] LLP Member; Rajiv Sharma [1970] LLP Member; Adrian Vaughan Shipman Sharpe [1948] LLP Member; Ronald William Southern [1956] LLP Member; Alan Stubbs [1971] LLP Member; Geoffrey Peter Taylor [1956] LLP Member; Manoj Vadhera [1970] LLP Member; Maria Genevieve Vardy [1967] LLP Member; Richard John Ward [1959] LLP Member; Alexandra Patricia Wilson [1955] LLP Member; Stephen John Yarwood [1961] LLP Member

The Invicta Film Partnership No.10, LLP
Incorporated: 20 May 2002
Net Worth: £42,361,056 *Total Assets:* £46,335,496
Registered Office: 99 Kenton Road, Harrow, Middlesex, HA3 0AN
Officers: Adam Paul Apter [1962] LLP Member; Colin Ian McMillan Armstrong Bell [1969] LLP Member; Nicholas Anthony Athanasou [1953] LLP Member; James Edward Baird [1952] LLP Member; John Beare [1953] LLP Member; Primo Bertorelli [1953] LLP Member; Winston Bogarde [1970] LLP Member; Andrew Giles Finlinson Brash [1956] LLP Member; David Richard Brooke [1958] LLP Member; Alan Neil Brown [1957] LLP Member; Alan James Brydon [1954] LLP Member; James Robert Burgess [1956] LLP Member; Stuart Alan Charles Cakebread [1954] LLP Member; Nigel Alexander Carter [1968] LLP Member; Susanne Carter [1966] LLP Member; James Patrick Casiddy [1966] LLP Member; Celine Ann Cassidy [1966] LLP Member; Dr Joseph Chandy [1941] LLP Member; Dr Mark Nathaniel Collins [1952] LLP Member; David Ashley Cook [1944] LLP Member; David Craggs [1955] LLP Member; Jonathan Charles Creagh Coen [1964] LLP Member; Simon Csoka [1968] LLP Member; Adrienne Lesley de Vos [1962] LLP Member; Nicholas Thomas de Winton [1960] LLP Member; Laurent Delorge [1979] LLP Member; Damien Devine [1960] LLP Member; Thomas Dicker [1953] LLP Member; Anthony Charles Stephen Druttman [1951] LLP Member; Alexander Charles Duncan [1960] LLP Member; Peter David Ebdon [1970] LLP Member; Robert Willoughby Elias [1955] LLP Member; Christopher Evangeli [1967] LLP Member; Nicholas Evangeli [1939] LLP Member; Roderick Clifford Evans [1964] LLP Member; Frank Geoffrey Fielding [1947] LLP Member; Michael Lawrence Filer [1960] LLP Member; Malcolm Foulis [1953] LLP Member; Helen Mary Fryer [1963] LLP Member; Roy Anthony Gabbie [1953] LLP Member; David Gibbs [1969] LLP Member; Charles Richard Gray [1955] LLP Member; Matthew Robert Green [1967] LLP Member; Nicholas David Anthony Greenstone [1944] LLP Member; William Robert Griffiths [1948] LLP Member; Alain Leopold Grisay [1954] LLP Member; Doctor Philip Gerard Guest [1957] LLP Member; John Norman Harris [1957] LLP Member; Pamela Mary Harris [1958] LLP Member; Peter Hennell [1947] LLP Member; Gerrard Leslie Henry [1953] LLP Member; Robin Jeremy Charles Higham [1956] LLP Member; Michael Hilton [1970] LLP Member; Stephen Benjamin Howard [1970] LLP Member; Christopher Martin Huggett [1964] LLP Member; Michael Makepeace Eugene Jeffries [1944] LLP Member; Victoria Reynolds Jenkinson [1962] LLP Member; Mohammed Hassan Jiva [1974] LLP Member; Seth Art Maurice Johnson [1979] LLP Member; Geoffrey Arthur Jordan [1946] LLP Member; Georgina Susanne Keene [1971] LLP Member; Gabriel Choon Moi Kow [1948] LLP Member; Karl Nicholas Langhorne [1969] LLP Member; Nadir Sikander Latif [1962] LLP Member; Geoffrey Richard Long [1960] LLP Member; David Charles Longley [1945] LLP Member; Kieran Looney [1967] LLP Member; Timothy Geoffrey Fraser Lord [1953] LLP Member; John Dyer Lumley [1960] LLP Member; Andrew John Magson [1960] LLP Member; Elaine Ann Magson [1955] LLP Member; Sanjiv Mahal [1961] LLP Member; James Bruce McKendrick [1962] LLP Member; James Measures [1931] LLP Member; David Miles Middleton [1935] LLP Member; John Morrison Robert Millar [1962] LLP Member; David Christopher Morris [1925] LLP Member; Ramakrishna Mudadagiri [1945] LLP Member; Alan Stewart Nedas [1938] LLP Member; Patrick Gerard Newton [1957] LLP Member; Nicholas Nicholson [1968] LLP Member; Matthew John Northover [1971] LLP Member; Gerard Anthony O'Brien [1957] LLP Member; Malcolm Bruce Oastler [1959] LLP Member; Edward Martin Burgess Olley [1967] LLP Member; Petra Katherine Osborne Fardon [1969] LLP Member; Rajesh Parkash [1970] LLP Member; Martin George Parker [1952] LLP Member; Prashant Babubhai Patel [1956] LLP Member; Leslie James Patient [1958] LLP Member; Humphrey Richard Percy [1956] LLP Member; David Rhodes [1959] LLP Member; Jonathan Rhodes [1966] LLP Member; David Ernest Henry Robson [1940] LLP Member; Amanda Ross [1962] LLP Member; Simon John Ross [1958] LLP Member; Josephine June Rowley [1938] LLP Member; Kenneth John Rowley [1950] LLP Member

The Invicta Film Partnership No.11, LLP
Incorporated: 28 May 2002
Net Worth: £11,357,982 *Total Assets:* £11,357,982
Registered Office: 99 Kenton Road, Harrow, Middlesex, HA3 0AN
Officers: Trevor Steven Allan [1965] LLP Member; Francoise Ellen Atherton [1947] LLP Member; Dr Peter Granville Atherton [1944] LLP Member; Neville James Buckley [1958] LLP Member; Stephen Leonard Conn [1946] LLP Member; Thomas Dicker [1953] LLP Member; Roger Michael Gabb [1938] LLP Member; David Hall [1951] LLP Member; Julian Alexander Robert Jakobi [1951] LLP Member; Victoria Reynolds Jenkinson [1962] LLP Member; Andrew James McIntyre [1956] LLP Member; Jeremy Nicholas Roff [1959] LLP Member; Joanna Trollope [1943] LLP Member; Giammarco Vela [1968] LLP Member

The Invicta Film Partnership No.12, LLP
Incorporated: 1 August 2002
Net Worth: £8,706,501 *Total Assets:* £9,506,957
Registered Office: 99 Kenton Road, Harrow, Middlesex, HA3 0AN
Officers: Maria Theresa Barlow [1953] LLP Member; Peter George Barlow [1953] LLP Member; Primo Bertorelli [1953] LLP Member; Anthony Mark Biggs [1957] LLP Member; Mark Dominic Dempsey [1963] LLP Member; Marc Joel Duschenes [1975] LLP Member; Alfred Michael Dwan [1959] LLP Member; Christopher Evangeli [1967] LLP Member; Nicholas Evangeli [1939] LLP Member; Sheldon Barry Neil Fagelman [1961] LLP Member; Frank Geoffrey Fielding [1947] LLP Member; Richard Ian Griffiths [1966] LLP Member; Christopher Hancock [1965] LLP Member; David Jonathan Healy [1979] LLP Member; Robin Jeremy Charles Higham [1956] LLP Member; Michael Hilton [1970] LLP Member; Iain Catleugh Hutchinson [1965] LLP Member; Geoffrey Arthur Jordan [1946] LLP Member; Daniel Kerven [1975] LLP Member; Geoffrey Richard Long [1960] LLP Member; John Dyer Lumley [1960] LLP Member; James Bruce McKendrick [1962] LLP Member; Alister Hugh Mellor [1962] LLP Member; Ian George Nicoll [1947] LLP Member; Matthew John Northover [1963] LLP Member; Leslie James Patient [1958] LLP Member; Richard Sheridan [1956] LLP Member; Lee Martin Stenson [1954] LLP Member; Alan Stubbs [1971] LLP Member; Manoj Vadhera [1970] LLP Member; Mark Andrew Woods [1964] LLP Member; Andrew Hylton Young [1962] LLP Member; Dr Antonios Camille Zamar [1965] LLP Member

The Invicta Film Partnership No.13, LLP
Incorporated: 1 August 2002
Net Worth: £21,920,020 *Total Assets:* £24,578,374
Registered Office: 99 Kenton Road, Harrow, Middlesex, HA3 0AN
Officers: Rajesh Kumar Bhardwaj [1969] LLP Member; Ian George Bradley [1959] LLP Member; Valerie Josephine Bradley [1943] LLP Member; Michael Dudley Moran Davies [1957] LLP Member; Anthony Arthur Dove [1946] LLP Member; Rupert Alexander Lendon English [1966] LLP Member; Raymond Charles Eyre [1955] LLP Member; Andrew Jason Fearon [1969] LLP Member; Susan Garrard [1957] LLP Member; Stephen Gutteridge [1954] LLP Member; Andrew Charles Hodson [1966] LLP Member; Ashley John King [1967] LLP Member; John Henry King [1945] LLP Member; Philip Alexander Mastriforte [1965] LLP Member; Paris Moayedi [1938] LLP Member; Mark Stephen Edward Ryan [1965] LLP Member; Steven Paul Sharp [1962] LLP Member; Hugh Ian Taylor [1945] LLP Member; Anthony Oliver Thorold [1945] LLP Member; Paul Augustus Warren [1968] LLP Member; Hugh Mark Warrender [1968] LLP Member; Andrew James Willoughby [1965] LLP Member; Christopher David Winfield [1964] LLP Member; Shaun Michael Wyles [1965] LLP Member

The Invicta Film Partnership No.14, LLP
Incorporated: 1 August 2002
Net Worth: £46,022,276 *Total Assets:* £46,030,152
Registered Office: 99 Kenton Road, Harrow, Middlesex, HA3 0AN
Officers: Sami Al Sayed [1956] LLP Member; Adam Paul Apter [1962] LLP Member; David Banks [1969] LLP Member; Maria Theresa Barlow [1953] LLP Member; David Robert Beaton [1968] LLP Member; Primo Bertolli [1953] LLP Member; Mary Catherine Best [1960] LLP Member; Stephen Best [1957] LLP Member; Anthony Mark Biggs [1957] LLP Member; David Bonner [1959] LLP Member; Olivier Brousse [1965] LLP Member; Peter Alfred Brown [1952] LLP Member; Robert Mark Hartley Camping [1968] LLP Member; Anthony Edwin Carlisle [1947] LLP Member; Joseph Wayne Case [1944] LLP Member; Ailene Margaret Charlton [1962] LLP Member; James Edward Chilcott [1971] LLP Member; Lee Robert Clark [1972] LLP Member; James Coldwell [1964] LLP Member; Terence Shelby Cole [1932] LLP Member; David Paul Couch [1966] LLP Member; Robert James Curson [1951] LLP Member; Nikos Dabizas [1973] LLP Member; Oliver Dacourt [1974] LLP Member; Alok Dhanda [1962] LLP Member; Ivan Richard Dunn [1945] LLP Member; Marcelino Elena Sierra [1971] LLP Member; Nicholas Paul Farrell [1966] LLP Member; Lord Gary Blair Farrow [1955] LLP Member; Andrew Charles Fisher [1961] LLP Member; Christopher David Fishwick [1961] LLP Member; Gordon William Galloway French [1955] LLP Member; Bhupendra Gandhi [1964] LLP Member; Howard Leslie Gant [1961] LLP Member; Keith Howard Garber [1962] LLP Member; Susan Barbara Garrad [1957] LLP Member; Ian William Gibson [1957] LLP Member; Martin James Gilbert [1955] LLP Member; Peter Frank Gosling [1951] LLP Member; Alan Gray [1958] LLP Member; Alain Leopold Grisay [1954] LLP Member; Andrew Marshall Halmer [1958] LLP Member; Anders Hansen [1970] LLP Member; Christopher Richard Scott Hardie [1957] LLP Member; Keith Reginald Harris [1953] LLP Member; Geoffrey Demaine Hill [1947] LLP Member; John Robert Hutt [1967] LLP Member; Wendy Johnston [1962] LLP Member; Paul John Kavanagh [1969] LLP Member; Michael Kelly [1961] LLP Member; Paul Geoffrey Killik [1947] LLP Member; Timothy Anthony Kilroe [1964] LLP Member; George Brian Kirk [1940] LLP Member; Christopher Peter Lane [1948] LLP Member; Henry Norman Lewis [1939] LLP Member; Joan Alison Linney [1955] LLP Member; John Linney [1957] LLP Member; Robert Ross Linney [1971] LLP Member; Gary Lloyd [1961] LLP Member; Andrew Douglas Lloyd-Skinner [1954] LLP Member; Paul Mason [1960] LLP Member; Angus McLanders [1964] LLP Member; Glenn George McCrory [1964] LLP Member; Catherine Lynda McLanders [1963] LLP Member; Stanley Leslie Miller [1961] LLP Member; William Robert Moody [1956] LLP Member; Kenneth John Morris [1961] LLP Member; Michael David Moss [1950] LLP Member; David Charles Moulsdale [1968] LLP Member; Elizabeth Patricia Norton [1954] LLP Member; Grant Notman [1959] LLP Member; Gordon Edward Orr [1949] LLP Member; Martin Orr [1964] LLP Member; Matthew Nicholson Orr [1962] LLP Member; David Hase Osborne [1957] LLP Member; John Michael Osborne [1953] LLP Member; Jonathan William Frederic Peart [1965] LLP Member; Julian Henry Ponsonby [1963] LLP Member; Mark Price [1971] LLP Member; Steven Patrick Ronksley [1958] LLP Member; Mrs Jm Ruddle 1997 Discretionary Settlement [2003] LLP Member; Jonathan Andrew Sadler [1965] LLP Member; James Denis Saunders [1960] LLP Member; David Lee Scorah [1951] LLP Member; Peter Glenn Sellars [1952] LLP Member; Ann Elizabeth Shankland [1950] LLP Member; Adrian Vaughan Shipman Sharpe [1948] LLP Member; Anthony Slimmings [1963] LLP Member; Ronald William Southern [1956] LLP Member; Mark Neil Steinberg [1959] LLP Member; Robert Michael Storey [1960] LLP Member; James Sweeney [1960] LLP Member; Alan Malcolm Thompson [1951] LLP Member; David Hugh Thompson [1950] LLP Member; Martin John Edward Tidd [1960] LLP Member; Stephen William Vaughan [1960] LLP Member; Dr Graham John Walker [1962] LLP Member

The Invicta Film Partnership No.15, LLP
Incorporated: 1 August 2002
Net Worth: £20,950,716 *Total Assets:* £20,950,716
Registered Office: 99 Kenton Road, Harrow, Middlesex, HA3 0AN
Officers: Edward Oscar Belgeonne [1962] LLP Member; Philip Charles Easter [1953] LLP Member; Raymond Charles Eyre [1955] LLP Member; Robert Blackburn Gray [1950] LLP Member; William Robert Griffiths [1948] LLP Member; Dr Eric Yves Leon [1947] LLP Member; Philip Alexander Mastriforte [1965] LLP Member; Humphrey Richard Percy [1956] LLP Member; Roderick John Sinclair [1944] LLP Member; Andrew Nicholas Sutton [1954] LLP Member; Hugh Ian Taylor [1945] LLP Member; Constantine Thanassoulas [1952] LLP Member

The Invicta Film Partnership No.20, LLP
Incorporated: 15 March 2004
Net Worth: £61,241,400 *Total Assets:* £65,264,124
Registered Office: 99 Kenton Road, Harrow, Middlesex, HA3 0AN
Officers: Mark Stephen Adams [1962] LLP Member; Charmian Ali [1954] LLP Member; Stephen Charles Ashworth [1967] LLP Member; Nicholas Anthony Athanasou [1953] LLP Member; Christopher Francis Henry Baker [1955] LLP Member; Nigel Robert James Baker [1942] LLP Member; Richard John Beale [1959] LLP Member; Sanjeev Lalji Bhanderi [1971] LLP Member; Jonathan David Bowes [1966] LLP Member; Edward Leonard Bradley [1957] LLP Member; Peter Lincoln Breitenbach [1954] LLP Member; Duncan Broadbent [1963] LLP Member; Ian Blaine Brook [1949] LLP Member; Richard James Emmett Bryan [1970] LLP Member; Richard James Butland [1971] LLP Member; James Aldo Campanini [1968] LLP Member; Clive Stephen Carpenter [1953] LLP Member; Clive Anderson Carr [1954] LLP Member; Barry Gareth Cashman [1966] LLP Member; Michael Chesterton [1970] LLP Member; Richard Childs [1959] LLP Member; Mark Gerard Clough [1953] LLP Member; Christopher Cole [1968] LLP Member; Stephen Leonard Conn [1946] LLP Member; Peter David Cook [1964] LLP Member; David John Courtley [1957] LLP Member; Ian Curtis [1968] LLP Member; Martin Sinclair Davies [1956] LLP Member; Peter John Day [1966] LLP Member; Paul di Leo [1962] LLP Member; Gary Anthony Dugan [1961] LLP Member; Peter David Ebdon [1970] LLP Member; Neal Errington [1956] LLP Member; Christopher Evangeli [1967] LLP Member; Jonathan Howard Fine [1974] LLP Member; David Martin Fletcher [1963] LLP Member; John Foster [1970] LLP Member; Mark Haakon Gaunt [1961] LLP Member; Andrew Gavan [1960] LLP Member; Charles Philip Gaynor [1961] LLP Member; Brian Grant [1947] LLP Member; Dr Philip Raymond Greene [1948] LLP Member; Bruce John Hanton [1962] LLP Member; Andrew John Harrison [1970] LLP Member; Mark Charles Haswell [1965] LLP Member; Mark Hollister [1962] LLP Member; Ian Horsley [1974] LLP Member; Susan Deborah Howard [1964] LLP Member; Christopher Martin Huggett [1964] LLP Member; Gary Hulme [1975] LLP Member; John Denby Robert Jakeways [1962] LLP Member; Roisin Helen Anne Jordan [1962] LLP Member; Simon William Judd [1964] LLP Member; Harold Kahan [1945] LLP Member; Leo Kane [1950] LLP Member; Peter Kane [1961] LLP Member; Jonathan David Keating [1963] LLP Member; Anil Kumar Khiani [1972] LLP Member; Cyrus Mohan Korat [1972] LLP Member; Graham Richard David Lay [1956] LLP Member; Matthew Robert Layton [1961] LLP Member; Elizabeth Anne Linton [1949] LLP Member; Gary Lloyd [1961] LLP Member; Phillip Stephen Loach [1967] LLP Member; Martin John Lockyer [1967] LLP Member; Jamieson John Logie [1961] LLP Member; Mark Adrian Lubbock [1958] LLP Member; Angus John Elsom MacCormick [1965] LLP Member; Avril Catherine Burns Martindale [1961] LLP Member; Richard Andrew Matthews [1966] LLP Member; Donald Stuart McClumpha [1964] LLP Member; Adrian McDonald [1964] LLP Member; Thomas Wardrope McEwan [1958] LLP Member; Frank McHugh [1958] LLP Member; Brian Patrick Meehan [1967] LLP Member; Symon David Meikle [1972] LLP Member; David John Moore [1958] LLP Member; Dr Timothy Marcus Mulchay [1969] LLP Member; Paul Alexander Murdoch [1947] LLP Member; Guy Timothy Napier [1961] LLP Member; Mark Robert Newall [1966] LLP Member; Mark Brian Nichols [1963] LLP Member; Kathryn Trudy Norris-Grey [1960] LLP Member; Patricia Helen Nuttall [1944] LLP Member; Catherine Lena Peterson [1963] LLP Member; Richard William Philips [1966] LLP Member; Russell James Platts [1975] LLP Member; Adnrew David Raikes [1972] LLP Member; Gavin Robert Duthie Ralston [1960] LLP Member; Howard Reece-Smith [1951] LLP Member; Ron Victor Reeves [1952] LLP Member; Jonathan Richard Reynolds [1954] LLP Member; Ian David Richards [1945] LLP Member; Stephen Mark Rodney [1965] LLP Member; Kenneth James Gordon Harvey Ross [1971] LLP Member; Jeffrey Arron Rubinoff [1965] LLP Member; Simeon Spencer Perrott Rudin [1961] LLP Member

The Invicta Film Partnership No.22, LLP
Incorporated: 15 March 2004
Net Worth: £39,226,080 *Total Assets:* £42,851,436
Registered Office: 99 Kenton Road, Harrow, Middlesex, HA3 0AN
Officers: Steven Kenneth Allport [1971] LLP Member; Dirk Posthumus Anthony [1963] LLP Member; Christopher Francis Henry Baker [1955] LLP Member; Patrick George Barker [1947] LLP Member; Michael Andrew Bradley [1961] LLP Member; Jennifer Bryant [1957] LLP Member; Clive Stephen Carpenter [1953] LLP Member; Nicholas John Chaffey [1969] LLP Member; Simon Charles [1970] LLP Member; Robin Raj Chhabra Chhabra [1970] LLP Member; Richard Childs [1959] LLP Member; Steven Lindsay Cloran [1964] LLP Member; Estelle Conron [1970] LLP Member; David John Courtley [1957] LLP Member; Timothy Eric Cox [1960] LLP Member; James Henry Davey [1962] LLP Member; Giles Roderick Dealtry [1963] LLP Member; Nicholas Dennys [1951] LLP Member; Richard Andrew Fellows [1960] LLP Member; Paul Gregory Franklin [1956] LLP Member; John Gardner [1959] LLP Member; Andrew Gavan [1960] LLP Member; Ian Charles Gibson [1958] LLP Member; John Anthony Goodey [1972] LLP Member; Nicholas Edward Greenwood [1970] LLP Member; Neil Hugh Thomas Hart [1972] LLP Member; Peter Charles Hill [1952] LLP Member; Andrew James Hough [1972] LLP Member; Susan Deborah Howard [1964] LLP Member; Steven Hull [1963] LLP Member; James Anthony Hyde [1962] LLP Member; Nicholas St John Isitt [1964] LLP Member; John Denby Robert Jakeways [1962] LLP Member; Christopher Basil Johnson [1967] LLP Member; Robert Francis Raymond Jolliffe [1968] LLP Member; Gareth Neil Jones [1958] LLP Member; Mark Royce Jones [1969] LLP Member; Peter Francis Kenyon [1953] LLP Member; John Jeremy King [1962] LLP Member; Nicholas John Kirk [1943] LLP Member; John Jekabs Krumins [1964] LLP Member; Richard Guy Rafe Lister [1966] LLP Member; Richard Brian Lowe [1954] LLP Member; Stephen Paul Lundy [1956] LLP Member; Marcus Charles MacKenzie [1965] LLP Member; Christopher Peter Milligan [1970] LLP Member; David Allan Murray [1964] LLP Member; David Anthony Nickson [1971] LLP Member; Paul Robert Norris [1963] LLP Member; Dominic Kevin O'Carroll [1960] LLP Member; Timothy Simon Oldfield [1964] LLP Member; Kevin Bryan Orgill [1962] LLP Member; David Hase Osborne [1957] LLP Member; Sir Michael Parkinson [1935] LLP Member; Gary Senior [1962] LLP Member; Bernard Francis Seymour [1960] LLP Member; David Charles Simpson [1960] LLP Member; David Stanley Spillane [1950] LLP Member; Alasdair Bruce Stewart [1954] LLP Member; Kenneth Paul Tollet [1954] LLP Member; Paul Frederick Tutin [1962] LLP Member; Garry Tibbott Veale [1960] LLP Member; Simon Walker [1964] LLP Member; Richard John Ward [1959] LLP Member; Trevor Ward [1961] LLP Member; Guy Rodney Warrington [1957] LLP Member; Christopher Ian Watson [1957] LLP Member; Andrew Roger Wedderburn-Day [1962] LLP Member; Ross Kirkwood Williams [1974] LLP Member

The Invicta Film Partnership No.23, LLP
Incorporated: 15 March 2004
Net Worth: £89,952,400 *Total Assets:* £99,070,112
Registered Office: 99 Kenton Road, Harrow, Middlesex, HA3 0AN
Officers: Masood Ahmad [1942] LLP Member; Nuzhat Ahmad [1945] LLP Member; Jahangeer Ahmed [1956] LLP Member; Dr Peter Russell Allamby [1958] LLP Member; Claude Edward Ashmore [1974] LLP Member; Joseph Colin Aspinall [1960] LLP Member; Steven Mark Avery Gee [1953] LLP Member; Ruth Bailey [1961] LLP Member; Christopher Bailey-Woods [1971] LLP Member; Niall Richard Bamford [1966] LLP Member; Dr Khalid Barakat [1966] LLP Member; Gary James Barber [1960] LLP Member; Philip John Barnatt [1949] LLP Member; Michael Forsyth Barnett [1970] LLP Member; Peter John Beddis [1952] LLP Member; David Frank Bell [1962] LLP Member; Michael George Bell [1967] LLP Member; Marcus Peter Bemrose [1956] LLP Member; Duncan Howard Blatch [1963] LLP Member; John Alan Booth [1970] LLP Member; Richard James Bowskill [1964] LLP Member; Michael Andrew Bradley [1961] LLP Member; William Angus Bridger [1968] LLP Member; Simon Anthony Briggs [1962] LLP Member; Andrew Christopher Briscoe [1971] LLP Member; Paul Antony Broadhurst [1960] LLP Member; Garry Burden [1958] LLP Member; Alastair Butler [1973] LLP Member; Robert Paul Camping [1973] LLP Member; David Nigel Caplan [1954] LLP Member; Christopher John Chandler [1958] LLP Member; Satnam Singh Chase [1966] LLP Member; Pratim Kumar Chaudhury [1948] LLP Member; Sushma Chopra [1957] LLP Member; Peter Charlton Christie [1951] LLP Member; Patrick Alan Clarke [1965] LLP Member; Carlyle Cyril Clump [1953] LLP Member; Harvey Stewart Cohen [1965] LLP Member; James Winston Collings [1965] LLP Member; Kevin Cooke [1961] LLP Member; John Benedict Leodoghar Cooper [1955] LLP Member; Dr David Richard Cox [1957] LLP Member; Philip John Craven [1958] LLP Member; Cheryl Ann Cribbin [1966] LLP Member; Nicholas Cusworth [1964] LLP Member; Rodney Graeme Dacomb [1955] LLP Member; Miles John Davidson [1963] LLP Member; Ian Charles Davies [1952] LLP Member; Aidan Christopher Goddard Day [1962] LLP Member; Gareth Wyn Derbyshire [1962] LLP Member; Hugh Philip Egerton Dumas [1942] LLP Member; Stuart William Duncan [1948] LLP Member; Steven Peter Eccleston [1964] LLP Member; Richard Jeffrey Ellingworth [1968] LLP Member; Paul Jeremy Epstein [1963] LLP Member; James William Farrand [1947] LLP Member; Oliver Paul Farrer [1963] LLP Member; Gary Michael Finn [1957] LLP Member; Kaye Forsythe [1961] LLP Member; Fiona Claire Foster [1962] LLP Member; Andrew Foxley [1962] LLP Member; Justin Paul Martin Gale [1964] LLP Member; Grant Gardner [1960] LLP Member; Stephen Paul Gelder [1966] LLP Member; Christopher John Gerber [1959] LLP Member; Mark Govan [1972] LLP Member; Paul Richard Greaney [1970] LLP Member; Barry Ludlow Green [1943] LLP Member; Brian Rex Green [1934] LLP Member; Philip Stuart Hanna [1962] LLP Member; Elizabeth Kay Harriman [1956] LLP Member; Andrew John Harvey [1964] LLP Member; Mark Vernon Henderson [1969] LLP Member; Rebecca Jane Hewetson [1974] LLP Member; Paul Joseph Higgins [1955] LLP Member; James Andrew Paul Hines [1960] LLP Member; Kausar Hirani [1967] LLP Member; John Walter Holmes [1958] LLP Member; Nicholas St John Isitt [1964] LLP Member; Michael Makepeace Eugene Jeffries [1944] LLP Member; Thomas Arthur John Jenkins [1972] LLP Member; Eric William Jones [1952] LLP Member; Gareth Wyn Jones [1960] LLP Member; Bruce Douglas King [1955] LLP Member; Paul George Kirtley [1959] LLP Member; Doctor Ormala Krishnan [1969] LLP Member; Nicholas Ronald Lancaster [1948] LLP Member; Graeme Neil Langford [1961] LLP Member; Michael Angelo Le Houx [1959] LLP Member; Amanda Jane Lipman [1962] LLP Member; Matthew Louis Lorenzo [1958] LLP Member; Laurence Bruce Lovat [1962] LLP Member; Andrew Lumley [1953] LLP Member; Stephen Paul Lundy [1956] LLP Member; Denis James Anthony MacDaid [1944] LLP Member; Kirankumar Vardhaman Malde [1954] LLP Member; Rajesh Vardhaman Malde [1959] LLP Member; Sirishkumar Vardhaman Malde [1951] LLP Member

The Invicta Film Partnership No.25, LLP
Incorporated: 18 March 2004
Net Worth: £30,980,424 *Total Assets:* £33,805,844
Registered Office: 99 Kenton Road, Harrow, Middlesex, HA3 0AN
Officers: Georgina Jane Agnew [1949] LLP Member; Niall Richard Bamford [1966] LLP Member; Raymond James Batters [1950] LLP Member; Kirsty Bell [1966] LLP Member; Jonathan David Berger [1962] LLP Member; Mary Catherine Best [1960] LLP Member; Nicholas Charles Birch [1959] LLP Member; Stephen Boylan [1952] LLP Member; Anthony Omer Browne [1950] LLP Member; Robert James Buckland [1968] LLP Member; Dr Joseph Chandy [1941] LLP Member; Shahid Mahmood Choudry [1971] LLP Member; Salvatore Ciullo [1958] LLP Member; Lee Robert Clark [1972] LLP Member; David Paul Couch [1966] LLP Member; Simon Christopher Cowie [1969] LLP Member; Anthony Maurice Cross [1958] LLP Member; Tapan Kumar Datta [1958] LLP Member; Christopher Daw [1970] LLP Member; Alok Dhanda [1962] LLP Member; Dr Simon John Dolin [1952] LLP Member; Christopher William Duffy [1957] LLP Member; Peter David Ebdon [1970] LLP Member; John Brynmor Edwards [1957] LLP Member; Dr Antony Michael Esprey [1950] LLP Member; Christopher Evangel [1967] LLP Member; Nicholas Evangeli [1939] LLP Member; Ian Keith Fisher [1959] LLP Member; James Alistair Fok [1979] LLP Member; Doctor Anton Franckeiss [1956] LLP Member; Susan Garrard [1957] LLP Member; Ian Gray [1960] LLP Member; Nicholas John Hall [1960] LLP Member; Nicola Jane Harris [1969] LLP Member; Michael Heppell [1967] LLP Member; George Heydon [1961] LLP Member; Timothy Charles Hill [1963] LLP Member; Dr Wayne Kevin Hirschowitz [1965] LLP Member; David Edmund Hoggett [1962] LLP Member; Nicholas Hopkin [1955] LLP Member; Steven Hull [1963] LLP Member; Quentin John Hunt [1975] LLP Member; Dr Roy Richard Huson [1973] LLP Member; Keith Martin Jobson [1959] LLP Member; Robert Terence Johnson [1962] LLP Member; Simon Henry Kenner [1962] LLP Member; David Kerr [1963] LLP Member; Adrian Geoffrey Knight [1957] LLP Member; Lisa Gillian Claire Knight [1961] LLP Member; Gabriel Choon Moi Kow [1948] LLP Member; Nadir Sikander Latif [1962] LLP Member; Andrew John Leake [1957] LLP Member; Bruce Lightbody [1962] LLP Member; Robert John Llewellyn [1962] LLP Member; Simon Timothy Lofthouse [1966] LLP Member; Roy Maplesden [1960] LLP Member; Paul Robert Marshall [1954] LLP Member; Andrew Charles Arthur McBride [1960] LLP Member; Spiros Michael [1974] LLP Member; David Miles Middleton [1935] LLP Member; Peter Minshull Armstrong [1949] LLP Member; Andrew Robert Mitchell [1954] LLP Member; Edward David South Morse [1960] LLP Member; David Charles Moulsdale [1968] LLP Member; Philip O'Hagan [1961] LLP Member; Paul Theodore Orchart [1953] LLP Member; Dr Hemant Kumar Patel [1968] LLP Member; Jayantibhai Chimanbhai Patel [1945] LLP Member; Dr Katherine Mary Patel [1968] LLP Member; Kirit Chimanbhai Patel [1949] LLP Member; Jane Ann Peace [1961] LLP Member; Michael Robert Pedder [1949] LLP Member; Pieter Daniel Pienaar [1956] LLP Member; Michael David Prince [1947] LLP Member; Dorothy Rose Purdew [1932] LLP Member; Stephen James Purdew [1959] LLP Member; David Rhodes [1959] LLP Member; Jonathan Rhodes [1968] LLP Member; Eamonn Joseph Rice [1963] LLP Member; Nicholas John Robinson [1956] LLP Member; Christopher Gregory Rodgers [1957] LLP Member; Josephine June Rowley [1938] LLP Member; Kenneth John Rowley [1950] LLP Member; Dominic James Ryder [1968] LLP Member; John Ryder [1955] LLP Member; Martin Paul Sasada [1958] LLP Member; Guduthur Raghavendra Setty [1942] LLP Member; Richard Anthony Sharp [1966] LLP Member; Robert Douglas Shears [1953] LLP Member; Richard Graham Simons [1965] LLP Member; Ian Simpson [1970] LLP Member; Neil James Smith [1965] LLP Member; Jeremy Lewis Charles Spencer [1958] LLP Member; Paul David Robert Spraggs [1963] LLP Member; Graham Stedman [1956] LLP Member; Douglas Mark Stuart [1961] LLP Member; Stephen Lee Sweet [1951] LLP Member; Christine Ann Taylor [1960] LLP Member

The Invicta Film Partnership No.26, LLP
Incorporated: 18 March 2004
Net Worth: £22,715,108 *Total Assets:* £24,924,640
Registered Office: 99 Kenton Road, Harrow, Middlesex, HA3 0AN
Officers: Richard John Julian Addison [1961] LLP Member; Justin Martyn Anim [1968] LLP Member; Niall Richard Bamford [1966] LLP Member; Raymond James Batters [1950] LLP Member; Kirsty Bell [1966] LLP Member; Mark Andrew Binns [1961] LLP Member; Stephen Boylan [1952] LLP Member; William George Bush [1954] LLP Member; David Joseph Chadwick [1944] LLP Member; Gillian Jean Bird Cottam [1956] LLP Member; Gary Steven Cottle [1966] LLP Member; Shaun Christopher Craig Coulson [1963] LLP Member; Anthony Maurice Cross [1958] LLP Member; Alok Dhanda [1962] LLP Member; Paul William Henry Dixon [1943] LLP Member; Simon Timothy Dixon [1966] LLP Member; Dr Simon John Dolin [1952] LLP Member; Peter David Ebdon [1970] LLP Member; John Brynmor Edwards [1957] LLP Member; Dr Antony Michael Esprey [1950] LLP Member; Christopher Evangeli [1967] LLP Member; Nicholas Evangeli [1939] LLP Member; Rodley Evans [1953] LLP Member; Andrew Jason Fearon [1969] LLP Member; Anthony John Blakeley Fogg [1950] LLP Member; Doctor Anton Franckeiss [1956] LLP Member; Christopher Thomas Freeman [1961] LLP Member; Roy Anthony Gabbie [1953] LLP Member; Irena Greaves [1952] LLP Member; Nyasha Gwatidzo [1962] LLP Member; Nicholas John Hall [1960] LLP Member; Nicola Jane Harris [1969] LLP Member; Christopher Alan Harrison [1955] LLP Member; Michael Heppell [1967] LLP Member; Sally Ann Horrox [1967] LLP Member; Steven Hull [1963] LLP Member; Roy Richard Huson [1973] LLP Member; Prof Howard Saul Jacobs [1938] LLP Member; Keith Martin Jobson [1959] LLP Member; Roy Johnson [1952] LLP Member; Robert Frances Raymond Joliffe [1968] LLP Member; Matthew George Justice [1965] LLP Member; Sean Gary Kenwrick [1965] LLP Member; Adrian Geoffrey Knight [1957] LLP Member; Lisa Gillian Claire Knight [1961] LLP Member; William George Lane [1960] LLP Member; Robert John Llewellyn [1962] LLP Member; Leighton Richard Lloyd [1963] LLP Member; Rosalind Loveridge [1972] LLP Member; Spiros Michael [1974] LLP Member; Spiros Michael [1974] LLP Member; Ramakrishna Mudalagiri [1945] LLP Member; Ronald Edward Clayton Myland [1946] LLP Member; Paul NG [1967] LLP Member; Philip O'Hagan [1961] LLP Member; Jayantibhai Chimanbhai Patel [1945] LLP Member; Kirit Chimanbhai Patel [1949] LLP Member; John Richard Peace [1956] LLP Member; Michael Robert Pedder [1949] LLP Member; Michael David Prince [1947] LLP Member; Dorothy Rose Purdew [1932] LLP Member; Stephen James Purdew [1959] LLP Member; Peter Elisa Roos [1953] LLP Member; Magnus Scaddan [1972] LLP Member; Richard Graham Simons [1965] LLP Member; Dr Jacob Francois Smit [1962] LLP Member; Anthony Bernard Solomon [1956] LLP Member; Dr Paul John Rackham Soper [1943] LLP Member; Matteo Stefanel [1975] LLP Member; Dipak Maganlal Thakrar [1966] LLP Member; Rachana Thakrar [1965] LLP Member; Anthony Harold Todd [1947] LLP Member; Paul Harold MacKenzie Turner [1958] LLP Member; Gyles Turrell [1966] LLP Member; Paul Vallance [1946] LLP Member; Diane Walton [1952] LLP Member; Philip George Walton [1949] LLP Member; Peter Lawrence Warne [1968] LLP Member; Peter Gilhespy Willey [1951] LLP Member; Adrian Mark Williamson [1957] LLP Member; Nigel James Yates [1949] LLP Member

The Invicta Film Partnership No.27, LLP
Incorporated: 18 March 2004
Net Worth: £27,615,968 *Total Assets:* £29,141,476
Registered Office: 99 Kenton Road, Harrow, Middlesex, HA3 0AN
Officers: Yvonne Kathleen Agha [1968] LLP Member; David John Allonby [1978] LLP Member; Cecil Ashe [1944] LLP Member; John Adam Ball [1969] LLP Member; Anthony Paul Barnfather [1964] LLP Member; Robert Ashley Barrett [1962] LLP Member; Raymond James Batters [1950] LLP Member; Jonathan Paul Beacon [1946] LLP Member; Charles James Bennett [1962] LLP Member; Charles Jefferis Woodburn Benson [1962] LLP Member; Nicholas Blezard [1944] LLP Member; Stephen Boylan [1952] LLP Member; Ian Alan Bull [1961] LLP Member; Christopher Jordan Carlson [1978] LLP Member; Mr Robert Carlyle [1961] LLP Member; Dr Joseph Chandy [1941] LLP Member; Michael Chesterton [1970] LLP Member; Barry Alan Church [1947] LLP Member; William David Clouston [1946] LLP Member; Peter Cole [1967] LLP Member; Ian Curtis [1968] LLP Member; Nicholas Cusworth [1964] LLP Member; Colin Davies [1959] LLP Member; Simon Downing de Lacy Adams [1961] LLP Member; Alok Dhanda [1962] LLP Member; Dr Alan Joseph Dobkin [1943] LLP Member; Ellis George Downes [1965] LLP Member; Neal Errington [1956] LLP Member; Paul Francis Fraser [1960] LLP Member; Thomas George [1960] LLP Member; Arthur Edward Goddard [1948] LLP Member; David Joseph Goddard [1953] LLP Member; Gaias Gozem [1950] LLP Member; Nicholas Hopkin [1955] LLP Member; Ian Horsley [1974] LLP Member; Keith Jackson [1957] LLP Member; Christopher Basil Johnson [1967] LLP Member; Rachel Daisy Jones [1968] LLP Member; Roy Barry Jones [1962] LLP Member; Rosalind Elisabeth Kendall [1950] LLP Member; Michael Warwick Lawrence [1955] LLP Member; Michael Angelo Le Houx [1959] LLP Member; Michael Phillip David Lording [1958] LLP Member; Gregor Lachlan MacLean [1971] LLP Member; Andrew Charles Arthur McBride [1960] LLP Member; Kevin Connal McGeeney [1970] LLP Member; Jarlath James McHale [1958] LLP Member; Andrew Gwyn Menary [1959] LLP Member; Bryan Edward Mouat [1967] LLP Member; David Charles Moulsdale [1968] LLP Member; Susan Vanessa Noble [1970] LLP Member; Philip O'Hagan [1961] LLP Member; John Patrick O'Sullivan [1937] LLP Member; Giles Martin Oberheim [1970] LLP Member; Peter Anthony Parker [1959] LLP Member; Jayantibhai Chimanbhai Patel [1945] LLP Member; Kirit Chimanbhai Patel [1949] LLP Member; Angus Thien Siang Phang [1961] LLP Member; Dr Julian Mark Potter [1963] LLP Member; Michael David Prince [1947] LLP Member; Dorothy Rose Purdew [1932] LLP Member; Stephen James Purdew [1959] LLP Member; Dr Monica Reinach [1968] LLP Member; Diana Clare Robson [1954] LLP Member; Josephine June Rowley [1938] LLP Member; Kenneth John Rowley [1950] LLP Member; Ian Scarr-Hall [1938] LLP Member; Timothy James Scoble [1957] LLP Member; Mark Anthony Sensier [1966] LLP Member; Richard Anthony Sharp [1966] LLP Member; Robert Douglas Shears [1953] LLP Member; Richard Graham Simons [1965] LLP Member; Richard Charles Smith [1957] LLP Member; Robert Anthony Stiles [1976] LLP Member; Stuart Timmins [1958] LLP Member; Graham Stewart Alexander Walker [1971] LLP Member; Philip Alan Wander [1943] LLP Member; Dr Stuart Charles Webb [1950] LLP Member; Alistair Stevenson Webster [1953] LLP Member; Antony Paul Christopher Williams [1972] LLP Member; Robert Darren Withecombe [1965] LLP Member; Alastair David Wright [1967] LLP Member; Nigel James Yates [1949] LLP Member

The Invicta Film Partnership No.34, LLP
Incorporated: 4 April 2005
Net Worth: £11,915,357 *Total Assets:* £12,911,442
Registered Office: 99 Kenton Road, Harrow, Middlesex, HA3 0AN
Officers: Robert Fredrik Martin Adair [1956] LLP Member; Shiblee Alam [1971] LLP Member; Jean Felix Aniel Quiroga [1968] LLP Member; Charles Jefferis Woodburn Benson [1962] LLP Member; Jean Marc Blankert [1970] LLP Member; Philip Charles Barry Bruce [1949] LLP Member; Alastair Andrew Bertram Cade [1972] LLP Member; Gillian Carrick [1943] LLP Member; William David Clouston [1946] LLP Member; Carlyle Cyril Clump [1953] LLP Member; Roger William Cowell [1972] LLP Member; Steven John Cowling [1960] LLP Member; Alok Dhanda [1962] LLP Member; Robert Stephen Dodds [1952] LLP Member; Brendan Paul Farmer [1965] LLP Member; Robert Steven Fountain [1954] LLP Member; John Gordon [1952] LLP Member; Barry Ludlow Green [1943] LLP Member; Norma Frances Heyman [1937] LLP Member; David Edmund Hoggett [1962] LLP Member; Leonard Simon Horwich [1956] LLP Member; David William Jinks [1966] LLP Member; Andrew Ian Kennedy [1965] LLP Member; Michael Warwick Lawrence [1955] LLP Member; Leighton Richard Lloyd [1963] LLP Member; Esme Charles Harlowe Lowe [1962] LLP Member; David Rugbinder Singh Mattu [1958] LLP Member; Andrew Gwyn Menary [1959] LLP Member; Dr Ramakrishnagupta Dasappagupta Mudalagiri [1945] LLP Member; Susanne Vanessa Noble [1970] LLP Member; Sameer Satish Patel [1976] LLP Member; Dr Julian Mark Potter [1963] LLP Member; Mark Graham Pullen [1963] LLP Member; The Executors of The Estate of David Ernest Henry Robson [1940] LLP Member; Kenneth John Rowley [1950] LLP Member; Ravi Sher Singh [1969] LLP Member; Geoffrey Robert Spiller [1951] LLP Member; Paul David Robert Spraggs [1963] LLP Member; Nicholas John Symons [1969] LLP Member; Raymond Clive Tooth [1940] LLP Member; Karl Brian Vella [1959] LLP Member; Guy Michael Linsley Weaver [1961] LLP Member; James John Wheeler [1965] LLP Member; Kenneth Grant Williamson [1967] LLP Member

The Invicta Film Partnership No.37, LLP
Incorporated: 4 April 2005
Net Worth: £89,910,760 *Total Assets:* £97,431,904
Registered Office: 99 Kenton Road, Harrow, Middlesex, HA3 0AN
Officers: Michael Anthony Acratopulo [1968] LLP Member; Robert Fredrik Martin Adair [1956] LLP Member; Rawle Hamilton Adams [1966] LLP Member; Richard John Julian Addison [1961] LLP Member; Bhikam Chand Agarwal [1952] LLP Member; Dr Sarmid Abdul Karim Al Kamil [1965] LLP Member; Dr Peter Russell Allamby [1958] LLP Member; Charles John Maynard Andrews [1960] LLP Member; Jean Felix Aniel Quiroga [1968] LLP Member; Daniel Andre Arbili [1971] LLP Member; Carol Claire Ashton [1962] LLP Member; Robert John Charles Astley [1979] LLP Member; Edward Samuel Awty [1951] LLP Member; Andrew Baird [1964] LLP Member; David Michael Baker [1960] LLP Member; Philip John Barnatt [1949] LLP Member; Doctor Christopher John Batty [1963] LLP Member; Grant Martin Eugene Beglan [1964] LLP Member; John Charles Bentley [1964] LLP Member; Rajesh Kumar Bhardwaj [1969] LLP Member; Michael Francis Antony Borrelli [1954] LLP Member; Willem Albertus Botha [1964] LLP Member; Giovanni Brighi [1965] LLP Member; Kelvin John Bromley [1955] LLP Member; Paul Andrew Buckland [1965] LLP Member; John Campbell [1960] LLP Member; Lucy Campbell [1959] LLP Member; Dominic Francis John Cheetham [1966] LLP Member; Sven Martin Chipchase [1967] LLP Member; Andrew John Clark [1961] LLP Member; James Anthony Clegg [1966] LLP Member; Graham Richard Cockroft [1959] LLP Member; David Anthony Collins [1965] LLP Member; Dr Yogesh Contractor [1965] LLP Member; John Patrick Costello [1970] LLP Member; Philip John Craven [1958] LLP Member; Nicholas James Cross [1976] LLP Member; Miles John Davidson [1965] LLP Member; Andrew William Dawson [1963] LLP Member; Antony Peter di Lorenzo [1962] LLP Member; Peter Harry Dunsby [1969] LLP Member; Richard Colin Ellis [1969] LLP Member; Stephen Christopher Alesbury Ellis [1959] LLP Member; Pieter Esterhuysen [1967] LLP Member; Raymond Charles Eyre [1955] LLP Member; Brendan Paul Farmer [1965] LLP Member; Sean Thomas Farrell [1973] LLP Member; Kenneth Rodney Ferguson [1963] LLP Member; Gary Michael Finn [1957] LLP Member; Alan Roy Fitzpatrick [1939] LLP Member; Martin Alan Charles Fitzpatrick [1969] LLP Member; Andrew Fraser [1972] LLP Member; Andrew Gavan [1960] LLP Member; Peter James Gerrard [1962] LLP Member; Vijay Narendra Gohil [1976] LLP Member; Christopher Gunning [1944] LLP Member; Simon David Hague [1966] LLP Member; Dr Shiba Hameed [1956] LLP Member; Christopher Hancock [1965] LLP Member; Peter Edward Joseph Hansell [1966] LLP Member; Dr Grant Richard Harris [1968] LLP Member; Keith John Harvey [1966] LLP Member; John Simon Helfgott [1958] LLP Member; Alan James Highton [1957] LLP Member; James Andrew Paul Hines [1960] LLP Member; Wallace Simon Duthie Hinshelwood [1963] LLP Member; Dr Mohammad Altaf Hossain [1941] LLP Member; Laurence Gerrad Howard [1957] LLP Member; Jonathan Richard Jeff [1974] LLP Member; Richard Mark Jones [1968] LLP Member; Timothy Francis Comyn Jordan [1960] LLP Member; Abu Yousuf Fazlul Karim [1944] LLP Member; Geoffrey Arthur Kent [1954] LLP Member; Arno Kitts [1963] LLP Member; Karl Roderick Knipe [1966] LLP Member; Pietro Lamberti [1961] LLP Member; Richard Gwilym Langley [1953] LLP Member; Nadir Sikander Latif [1962] LLP Member; Michael Angelo Le Houx [1959] LLP Member; Mitchel Andrew Lenson [1954] LLP Member; Keith Malcolm Lewin [1957] LLP Member; Sean Richard Ormsby Lindsay [1967] LLP Member; Gordon Ionwy David Llewelyn [1956] LLP Member; Linda Jane Lord [1970] LLP Member; Peter John Lowless [1952] LLP Member; Richard Lucas James [1964] LLP Member; Geoffrey Charles Maddock [1964] LLP Member; Kirankumar Vardhaman Malde [1954] LLP Member; Rajesh Vardhaman Malde [1959] LLP Member; Sirishkumar Vardhaman Malde [1951] LLP Member; Simon Charles Caldwell Marsh [1959] LLP Member; John Russell Mathers [1956] LLP Member; David Scott Meads [1966] LLP Member; Nigel Headley Meredith [1953] LLP Member; Richard John Mitchell [1970] LLP Member; Andrew Raymond Moorfield [1966] LLP Member; Frank Murphy [1941] LLP Member; Dr Philip John Naish [1951] LLP Member

The Invicta Film Partnership No.8, LLP
Incorporated: 19 March 2002
Net Worth: £27,242,708 *Total Assets:* £27,248,724
Registered Office: 99 Kenton Road, Harrow, Middlesex, HA3 0AN
Officers: Fatima Albizua Ureta [1971] LLP Member; Suneel Bakhshi [1958] LLP Member; David Keith Bee [1961] LLP Member; Winston Bogarde [1970] LLP Member; Martin Major Bradford [1942] LLP Member; Graham Maxwell Brown [1958] LLP Member; Trevor Brown [1942] LLP Member; Stewart James Cameron [1969] LLP Member; Duncan Campbell [1952] LLP Member; Neil Robert Chamberlain [1958] LLP Member; Peter Robert Chapman [1943] LLP Member; William Clutterbuck [1959] LLP Member; Wayne Anthony Cook [1966] LLP Member; Martin John Crabtree [1960] LLP Member; Julian Charles Desmond Culhane [1966] LLP Member; Jeremy Jenkin Davies [1963] LLP Member; Mark Andrew Deane [1956] LLP Member; Graeme Ryland Frederick Dell [1964] LLP Member; Martin Jeremy Dyer [1956] LLP Member; Robert Simon Ford [1965] LLP Member; Brian John Forster [1950] LLP Member; Iain Fraser [1965] LLP Member; Brian Gaunt [1958] LLP Member; Helen Green [1961] LLP Member; John Harding [1973] LLP Member; Robert Mark Hartley [1968] LLP Member; Mark Colin Heaney [1967] LLP Member; Peter Hennell [1947] LLP Member; Stephen Benjamin Howard [1970] LLP Member; Harvinderpal Singh Hungin [1960] LLP Member; Richard George Hurdley [1968] LLP Member; John Jekabs Krumins [1964] LLP Member; Gillian Lancaster [1964] LLP Member; Frederick Mark Latham [1959] LLP Member; Philip Anthony Leaper [1965] LLP Member; Stavros Loizou [1964] LLP Member; Graham Jack Longhurst [1957] LLP Member; Angus John Elsom MacCormick [1965] LLP Member; Donald Hugh MacLiver [1956] LLP Member; Donald Robert Mark [1956] LLP Member; Granville Robert May [1947] LLP Member; Mario Dino Patrick Melchiot [1976] LLP Member; Kazuichi Mihara [1946] LLP Member; Timothy John Miller [1957] LLP Member; Deborah Jane Monks [1959] LLP Member; Malcolm Colin Monks [1956] LLP Member; Richard Morgan [1957] LLP Member; Ian Morris [1961] LLP Member; Steven Neat [1961] LLP Member; Colin Vincent Austin Nunn [1963] LLP Member; Malcolm Bruce Oastler [1959] LLP Member; Peter James Palmer [1953] LLP Member; Matthew Richard Peachey [1967] LLP Member; Timothy Hugh Pitcher [1965] LLP Member; John Roden Plimmer [1958] LLP Member; William Jean Marie Pratt [1953] LLP Member; Ahmet Vedat Ratib [1963] LLP Member; Andrew Lawrence Reay [1971] LLP Member; Bennett Riley [1972] LLP Member; Pamela Florence Roberts [1946] LLP Member; Malcolm Murray Robertson [1954] LLP Member; Brian Ralph Shubrook [1950] LLP Member; Calvin Francis Smith [1968] LLP Member; Robert Ian Dickson Strong [1970] LLP Member; Gordon McKenzie Stuart [1963] LLP Member; Hutton Daniel John Swinglehurst [1970] LLP Member; Robert Emile Morley Taussig [1950] LLP Member; Nicholas John Thurlow [1961] LLP Member; Craig Francis Tillotson [1964] LLP Member; Brian John Twigger [1954] LLP Member; Richard Francis Usmar [1946] LLP Member; Peter Edwin Villa [1944] LLP Member; Lewis FitzGenerald Watts [1964] LLP Member; Alistair Stevenson Webster [1953] LLP Member; Barry John Westwood [1951] LLP Member; Peter George Wilson [1953] LLP Member; Andrew Winfield [1958] LLP Member; Curtis Woodhouse [1980] LLP Member

The Invicta Film Partnership No.9, LLP
Incorporated: 20 May 2002
Net Worth: £21,350,728 *Total Assets:* £21,354,288
Registered Office: 99 Kenton Road, Harrow, Middlesex, HA3 0AN
Officers: Michael Adcock [1962] LLP Member; Nicholas Anthony Athanasou [1953] LLP Member; Suneel Bakhshi [1958] LLP Member; David Keith Bee [1961] LLP Member; Nicola Jane Blakemore [1966] LLP Member; Winston Bogarde [1970] LLP Member; David Bonner [1959] LLP Member; Steve John Brigden [1962] LLP Member; Steven Astley Brown [1959] LLP Member; Sally Ann Carre [1961] LLP Member; William Clutterbuck [1959] LLP Member; James Coldwell [1964] LLP Member; Malcolm Alan Cook [1948] LLP Member; Peter David Cook [1964] LLP Member; Trevor John Cook [1958] LLP Member; Martin John Crabtree [1960] LLP Member; Julian Charles Desmond Culhane [1966] LLP Member; Jeremy Jenkin Davies [1963] LLP Member; Michael John Trefor Davies [1960] LLP Member; Bradley James Edward Day [1962] LLP Member; Paul di Leo [1962] LLP Member; Brian Gaunt [1958] LLP Member; Peter John Bradford Gibson [1956] LLP Member; Jonathan Martin Grantham [1962] LLP Member; Richard Haining [1951] LLP Member; Richard John Stephen Hart [1948] LLP Member; Ian Allison Henderson [1957] LLP Member; Stephen Benjamin Howard [1970] LLP Member; Michael Makepeace Eugene Jeffries [1944] LLP Member; Graham Douglas Kendrick [1946] LLP Member; Janis Jekabs Krumins [1964] LLP Member; William George Lane [1960] LLP Member; Frederick Mark Latham [1959] LLP Member; Angus John Elsom MacCormick [1965] LLP Member; Donald Hugh MacLiver [1956] LLP Member; Gaetano William Mammana [1962] LLP Member; David Scott Meads [1966] LLP Member; Mario Dino Patrick Melchiot [1976] LLP Member; Timothy John Miller [1957] LLP Member; Linda Karen Morey Smith [1963] LLP Member; Margaret Morrison [1961] LLP Member; Timothy Paul Murray [1963] LLP Member; Steven Neat [1961] LLP Member; Mark Neil [1954] LLP Member; Guy Jeremy Norgrove [1951] LLP Member; Malcolm Bruce Oastler [1959] LLP Member; Donald Kennedy Pepper [1961] LLP Member; Karl Gregory Pick [1967] LLP Member; John Roden Plimmer [1958] LLP Member; Karen Linda Anne Richardson [1955] LLP Member; Bennett Riley [1972] LLP Member; Pamela Florence Roberts [1946] LLP Member; Malcolm Murray Robertson [1954] LLP Member; Trudi Ometha Ryan Dawes [1960] LLP Member; Daman Marcus Sanders [1964] LLP Member; Adrian Vaughan Shipman Sharpe [1948] LLP Member; Gavin Sinclair [1952] LLP Member; Calvin Francis Smith [1968] LLP Member; Robin Simon Southwell [1960] LLP Member; Mark Neil Steinberg [1959] LLP Member; Robert Emile Morley Taussig [1950] LLP Member; David Taylor [1962] LLP Member; Craig Francis Tillotson [1964] LLP Member; Richard Francis Usmar [1946] LLP Member; John Michael Vickerman [1961] LLP Member; Peter George Wilson [1953] LLP Member; Andrew Winfield [1958] LLP Member; Ian Leslie Zant-Boer [1953] LLP Member

Invordan Britannia Limited
Incorporated: 22 September 2015
Net Worth: £8,929,068 *Total Assets:* £30,445,110
Registered Office: Swiss House, Beckingham Street, Tolleshunt Major, Essex, CM9 8LZ
Activities: Buying and selling of own real estate
Shareholder: Ordan UK Limited
Officers: Abraham Aharon Dodi [1963] Director; Michael Sean Nurtman [1969] Director

Ipeco Holdings Limited
Incorporated: 13 October 1960 *Employees:* 771
Net Worth: £70,715,000 *Total Assets:* £86,283,000
Registered Office: Aviation Way, Southend on Sea, Essex, SS2 6UN
Activities: Manufacture of air and spacecraft and related machinery
Parent: Castledon Ltd
Officers: Bernadette Clare Barber, Secretary; Christopher Johnson [1947] Director/Engineer; Elizabeth Johnson [1947] Director; Steven John Johnson [1969] Director; Sarah Jane Nash [1967] Director/Accountant

Ipswich Borough Assets Limited
Incorporated: 7 April 2016
Net Worth Deficit: £593,623 *Total Assets:* £66,532,344
Registered Office: Grafton House, Russell Road, Ipswich, Suffolk, IP1 2DE
Activities: Other letting and operating of own or leased real estate
Parent: Ipswich Borough Council
Officers: Jennifer Anne Mitchell, Secretary; Ian Paul Blofield [1966] Director/Local Government Officer; James David Fairclough [1970] Director/Local Government Officer; Colin John Kreidewolf [1960] Finance Director; Jane Elizabeth Riley [1963] Director/Solicitor; Russell Stuart Williams [1972] Director/Local Authority Chief Executive

Ipswich Town Finance Company Limited
Incorporated: 27 April 2001
Net Worth: £549,000 *Total Assets:* £39,209,000
Registered Office: Portman Road, Ipswich, Suffolk, IP1 2DA
Activities: Operation of sports facilities
Parent: Marcus Evans Worldwide Holdings (IOM) Limited
Officers: Mark Simon Andrews, Secretary; Mark Simon Andrews [1966] Finance Director; Maarten Van Os [1971] Director [Dutch]

Ipswich Town Football Club Company Limited
Incorporated: 19 June 1936 *Employees:* 884
Net Worth Deficit: £77,452,000 *Total Assets:* £27,443,000
Registered Office: Portman Road, Ipswich, Suffolk, IP1 2DA
Activities: Operation of sports facilities
Parent: Marcus Evans Worldwide Holdings (IOM) Limited
Officers: Mark Simon Andrews, Secretary; Mark Simon Andrews [1966] Finance Director; Maarten Van Os [1971] Director [Dutch]

Ipswich Town Stadium Company Limited
Incorporated: 1 March 2001
Net Worth Deficit: £8,230,000 *Total Assets:* £35,385,000
Registered Office: Portman Road, Ipswich, Suffolk, IP1 2DA
Activities: Operation of sports facilities
Parent: Marcus Evans Worldwide Holdings
Officers: Mark Simon Andrews, Secretary; Mark Simon Andrews [1966] Finance Director; Maarten Van Os [1971] Director [Dutch]

IQGeo Group PLC
Incorporated: 11 October 2005 *Employees:* 139
Previous: Ubisense Group PLC
Net Worth: £11,692,000 *Total Assets:* £24,572,000
Registered Office: CB1 Business Centre, 20 Station Road, Cambridge, CB1 2JD
Activities: Activities of head offices
Officers: Timothy Gingell, Secretary; Timothy Gingell [1967] Director; Ian Edward Kershaw [1964] Director; Riccardo Ettore Petti [1967] Director/Chief Executive Officer; Robert Daniell Sansom [1959] Director/Technology Investor; Oliver Rupert Andrew Scott [1967] Director/Investment Manager; Paul Ronald Taylor [1964] Director/Accountant

Iris Insurance Brokers Limited
Incorporated: 15 September 2000 *Employees:* 50
Net Worth: £1,387,710 *Total Assets:* £22,769,232
Registered Office: The Baxter Building, 80 Baxter Avenue, Southend on Sea, Essex, SS2 6HZ
Activities: Non-life insurance
Major Shareholder: Mark Edward Paul Hutley
Officers: Don Kealon Patrick Cantwell [1961] Director/Reinsurance Broker [Irish]; Margarita Hutley [1976] Director; Mark Edward Paul Hutley [1970] Director/Insurance Broker

Ironmongerydirect Limited
Incorporated: 2 November 1995 *Employees:* 167
Net Worth: £9,603,361 *Total Assets:* £14,691,625
Registered Office: Units 3-4 Courtauld Road, Basildon, Essex, SS13 1ND
Activities: Retail sale via mail order houses or via Internet
Parent: Group Hardware Limited
Officers: Mark Frederick James Norris, Secretary; Brigitte Auffret [1961] Director/Deputy Chief Executive Officer [French]; Monsieur Pierre-Olivier Brial [1973] Director/Deputy Chief Executive Officer [French]; Xavier Emmanuel Guichard [1973] Director/Chief Executive Officer [French]; Wayne Vernon Lysaght-Mason [1958] Managing Director; Mark Frederick James Norris [1970] Finance Director

J. Isaacs Management Limited
Incorporated: 2 October 1958 *Employees:* 6
Net Worth: £9,003,763 *Total Assets:* £9,451,799
Registered Office: Suite 117, Catalyst House, 720 Centennial Court, Centennial Park, Elstree, Herts, WD6 3SY
Activities: Other letting and operating of own or leased real estate
Shareholder: J Isaacs Israel Ltd
Officers: Laurence Joseph Gordon, Secretary; Leah Miriam Besser [1972] Director/Pharmacist; Adam Samuel Isaacs [1971] Director; Nathan David Isaacs [1936] Director/Retired [Israeli]; Michelle Anne Lawrence [1967] Director/Fundraising Property; Jonathan Maurice Paull [1962] Director/Chartered Marketer

Islam Channel Limited
Incorporated: 6 February 2003 *Employees:* 15
Net Worth: £19,919,676 *Total Assets:* £22,683,580
Registered Office: 428-432 Ley Street, Ilford, Essex, IG2 7BS
Activities: Television programming and broadcasting activities
Major Shareholder: Mohamed Ali Harrath
Officers: Mohamed Ali Harrath [1963] Director/Businessman

Island Waste Services Limited
Incorporated: 25 March 1981 *Employees:* 4
Net Worth: £8,838,668 *Total Assets:* £13,078,739
Registered Office: Coronation Road, Cressex, High Wycombe, Bucks, HP12 3TZ
Activities: Collection of non-hazardous waste
Parent: Biffa Holdings Ltd
Officers: Richard Neil Pike [1969] Director/Chief Financial Officer; Michael Robert Mason Topham [1972] Director/Chief Executive Officer

ISN Europe Limited
Incorporated: 18 February 2016 *Employees:* 126
Net Worth: £2,863,672 *Total Assets:* £23,214,898
Registered Office: Unit 5 Lotus Court, Harvard Industrial Estate, Harvard Way, Kimbolton, Huntingdon, Cambs, PE28 0NJ
Activities: Other business support service activities n.e.c.
Officers: James Colin Boon [1972] Director; John Anthony Snowden [1966] Director [American]; Peter Charles Spraggs [1960] Director; David Bruce Weber [1963] Director [American]

Istec Services Limited
Incorporated: 20 January 1989 *Employees:* 33
Net Worth: £9,863,444 *Total Assets:* £10,483,850
Registered Office: 8 Bluecoats Avenue, Hertford, SG14 1PB
Activities: Specialised design activities
Officers: Michael Joseph Coulson [1949] Director/Production Engineer; Anne Quelch [1967] Director/Accountant

Isuzu Truck (UK) Limited
Incorporated: 5 November 2003 *Employees:* 51
Net Worth: £1,410,396 *Total Assets:* £20,784,428
Registered Office: Isuzu House, 164 Great North Road, Hatfield, Herts, AL9 5JN
Activities: Sale of other motor vehicles
Parent: Isuzu Motors Europe NV
Officers: Vijay Patel, Secretary; Peter Murphy [1965] Managing Director; Yasuyuki Niijima [1959] Director/Business Executive [Japanese]; Isao Otsuka [1962] Director of Corporate Planning and Finance [Japanese]

IT Luggage Limited
Incorporated: 3 December 1985 *Employees:* 91
Net Worth: £21,877,992 *Total Assets:* £34,542,608
Registered Office: Luggage House, The Chase, Foxholes Business Park, Hertford, SG13 7NN
Activities: Non-specialised wholesale trade
Shareholder: Sedat Selvi
Officers: Sedat Selvi, Secretary; Mehmet Ali Cetin [1960] Director; Michael John Lanston [1962] Director; Paul Richardson [1971] Director; Sedat Selvi [1959] Director; Anand Mahesh Varu [1984] Director; Nareshkumar Williams [1955] Director

ITAB Holdings UK Ltd
Incorporated: 3 January 2001 *Employees:* 12
Previous: ITAB UK Ltd
Net Worth: £10,620,421 *Total Assets:* £11,539,123
Registered Office: City House, Swallowdale Lane, Hemel Hempstead, Herts, HP2 7EA
Activities: Activities of head offices
Parent: ITAB Shop Concept AB
Officers: Andrew John Tweddle, Secretary; David Anthony Dignam [1977] Director; Roy Timothy French [1965] Director; Mikael Kjell Christer Gustavsson [1964] Director [Swedish]

ITAB Shop Products UK Ltd
Incorporated: 19 May 2006 *Employees:* 39
Net Worth: £4,803,000 *Total Assets:* £8,754,000
Registered Office: ITAB House, Swallowdale Lane, Hemel Hempstead Industrial Estate, Hemel Hempstead, Herts, HP2 7EA
Activities: Wholesale of other machinery and equipment
Parent: ITAB Shop Concept AB
Officers: Andrew John Tweddle, Secretary; David Anthony Dignam [1977] Director; Roy Timothy French [1965] Director; Mikael Kjell Christer Gustavsson [1964] Director/Chief Banking Officer [Swedish]

ITAB UK Ltd
Incorporated: 29 July 1997 *Employees:* 193
Previous: ITAB Shop Concept UK Ltd
Net Worth: £13,275,326 *Total Assets:* £27,955,988
Registered Office: ITAB House, Swallowdale Lane, Hemel Hempstead Industrial Estate, Hemel Hempstead, Herts, HP2 7EA
Activities: Manufacture of other fabricated metal products n.e.c.
Parent: ITAB UK Ltd
Officers: Andrew John Tweddle, Secretary; David Anthony Dignam [1977] Director; Roy Timothy French [1965] Director; Mikael Kjell Christer Gustavsson [1964] Director [Swedish]

ITC Enterprises Limited
Incorporated: 20 September 2010
Net Worth Deficit: £51,373,904 *Total Assets:* £47,797,640
Registered Office: Westpoint, Peterborough Business Park, Lynch Wood, Peterborough, Cambs, PE2 6FZ
Activities: Other business support service activities n.e.c.
Parent: Thomas Cook Continental Holdings Limited
Officers: Litsa Constantinou [1955] Director; Thomas Fridolin Hohn [1965] Director [German]; Marcus Rohricht [1974] Director [German]

Itron Development UK Ltd
Incorporated: 30 March 2007
Net Worth: £26,017,336 *Total Assets:* £222,199,360
Registered Office: Itron Development UK Ltd, Langer Road, Felixstowe, Suffolk, IP11 2ER
Activities: Activities of head offices
Officers: Chantel Margaret Landers, Secretary; Nigel Eric Hughes [1975] Director/General Manager; Joel Vach [1972] Director [American]

Itron Metering Solutions UK Limited
Incorporated: 21 August 2001 *Employees:* 202
Net Worth: £24,442,000 *Total Assets:* £49,543,000
Registered Office: Langer Road, Felixstowe, Suffolk, IP11 2ER
Activities: Manufacture of electronic measuring, testing etc. equipment, not for industrial process control
Officers: Chantel Margaret Landers, Secretary; Nigel Eric Hughes [1975] Director/General Manager; Joel Vach [1972] Director [American]

ITS Testing Services (UK) Limited
Incorporated: 10 January 1979 *Employees:* 1,701
Net Worth: £23,103,000 *Total Assets:* £138,723,008
Registered Office: Academy Place, 1-9 Brook Street, Brentwood, Essex, CM14 5NQ
Activities: Technical testing and analysis
Parent: Intertek UK Holdings Limited
Officers: Julian Charles Burge [1973] Director/Accountant; Robert Alan Van Dorp [1977] Director; Stephen Arthur Harrington [1957] Director

Iveco Holdings Limited
Incorporated: 9 November 1967 *Employees:* 3
Net Worth: £46,155,000 *Total Assets:* £109,994,000
Registered Office: Cranes Farm Road, Basildon, Essex, SS14 3AD
Activities: Activities of distribution holding companies
Parent: CNH Industrial NV
Officers: Simon Marc McCarthy, Secretary/Solicitor; Paul Jeff Hunter [1956] Director; Simon Marc McCarthy [1971] Director/Solicitor [British/Australian]; James Stuart Webster [1961] Director

Iveco Limited
Incorporated: 7 January 1986 *Employees:* 111
Net Worth: £44,622,000 *Total Assets:* £428,003,008
Registered Office: Cranes Farm Road, Basildon, Essex, SS14 3AD
Activities: Wholesale trade of motor vehicle parts and accessories
Parent: Iveco Holdings Limited
Officers: Simon Marc McCarthy, Secretary/Solicitor; Mario Bruni [1974] Director [Italian]; Paul Jeff Hunter [1956] Director; Edmund James Kerley [1974] Human Resources Director; Simon Marc McCarthy [1971] Director/Solicitor [British/Australian]; James Stuart Webster [1961] Director

J & A (International) Holdings Limited
Incorporated: 31 January 2017
Net Worth: £28,684,488 *Total Assets:* £30,188,420
Registered Office: Insignia House, Vale Road, Spilsby, Lincs, PE23 5HE
Activities: Activities of production holding companies
Shareholders: Peter Leslie Cropley; Simon James Fry; Charles Jeremy Fry
Officers: Peter Jeffery Law, Secretary; Randy Carr [1972] Director; Charles Jeremy Fry [1967] Director

J & A (International) Limited
Incorporated: 11 June 1981 *Employees:* 138
Net Worth: £8,041,417 *Total Assets:* £9,419,233
Registered Office: Insignia House, Vale Road, Spilsby, Lincs, PE23 5HE
Activities: Other manufacturing n.e.c.
Parent: J & A (International) Holdings Limited
Officers: Peter Jeffery Law, Secretary; Adrian Peter Apletree [1964] International Sales & Marketing Director; Jamie Carr [1970] Director [American]; Randy Carr [1972] Director [American]; Charles Jeremy Fry [1967] Director/Chief Executive Officer; Simon Dominic Holderness [1966] UK Sales & Service Director; Martin David Kemp [1968] Managing Director

J & J Restaurants Limited
Incorporated: 16 April 2003 *Employees:* 695
Net Worth: £5,613,421 *Total Assets:* £13,098,473
Registered Office: First Floor, Kefco House, Rochford Business Park, Cherry Orchard Way, Rochford, Essex, SS4 1GP
Activities: Activities of head offices
Major Shareholder: William Huw James
Officers: Andrew John Russell Hitch, Secretary/Chartered Accountant; Andrew John Russell Hitch [1966] Director/Chartered Accountant; William Huw James [1957] Director; Lynsey Patricia Johnston [1981] Director; Philip Thomas Johnston [1977] Director; Claire Josephine Owen [1974] Director/Human Resources

J C A Engineering Ltd
Incorporated: 8 May 2002 *Employees:* 132
Net Worth: £4,805,000 *Total Assets:* £23,321,000
Registered Office: Solar House, Stevenage Leisure Park, Kings Way, Stevenage, Herts, SG1 2UA
Activities: Electrical installation
Parent: JCA HQ Group Holdings Ltd.
Officers: Anna Charlotte Stillman, Secretary; Thomas Andrew Absalom [1973] Director/Engineer; Dean Cocklin [1968] Director/Engineer; Ian Coleman [1961] Director; Timothy John Edwins [1971] Director/Engineer; Ian David Hodges Jackson [1969] Director/Engineer; David George Johnson [1968] Director; Leslie Mak [1966] Director/Accountant

J E Investments Limited
Incorporated: 7 December 2004
Net Worth: £5,915,664 *Total Assets:* £9,368,510
Registered Office: 27 Beaumont Avenue, St Albans, Herts, AL1 4TL
Activities: Other letting and operating of own or leased real estate
Shareholder: Paul Adam Wilton
Officers: Alison Bernice Wilton, Secretary; Alison Bernice Wilton [1964] Director; Paul Wilton [1961] Director

J J Food Service Holdings Limited
Incorporated: 4 October 2000
Net Worth: £65,140,624 *Total Assets:* £83,924,080
Registered Office: 7 Solar Way, Innova Park, Enfield, Middlesex, EN3 7XY
Activities: Other letting and operating of own or leased real estate
Major Shareholder: Mustafa Hussein Kiamil
Officers: Mustafa Hussein Kiamil, Secretary; Mustafa Hussein Kiamil [1956] Director; Rifat Kiamil [1983] Director/IT Manager

J P & S Servicess Ltd
Incorporated: 24 March 2004 *Employees:* 55
Net Worth: £1,463,452 *Total Assets:* £8,810,590
Registered Office: Accountancy Solutions, 797 Harrow Road, Sudbury Town, Wembley, Middlesex, HA0 2LP
Activities: Retail sale in non-specialised stores with food, beverages or tobacco predominating
Shareholders: Jeyakumary Yoganathan; Visvanathan Yoganathan
Officers: Jeyakumary Yoganathan, Secretary; Visvanathan Yoganathan [1960] Director/Retail Consultant

J W D Holdings Limited
Incorporated: 14 August 2000 *Employees:* 55
Net Worth: £17,079,732 *Total Assets:* £29,450,662
Registered Office: Holbeach St Johns, Spalding, Lincs, PE12 8SQ
Activities: Activities of head offices
Officers: Graham Collishaw [1958] Director; Charles Graham Doubleday-Collishaw [1987] Director; Ian James Doubleday-Collishaw [1981] Director; Jayne Elizabeth Doubleday-Collishaw [1958] Director; Zoe Spencer [1985] Director

J.A.C. Computer Services Limited
Incorporated: 16 January 1980 *Employees:* 49
Net Worth: £3,989,695 *Total Assets:* £9,504,991
Registered Office: Aurum Court, Sylvan Way, Southfields Business Park, Basildon, Essex, SS15 6TH
Activities: Business and domestic software development
Parent: Project Ruby Ultimate Parent Corp
Officers: Stephen Michael Morgan [1979] Director/Chief Operations Officer [American]; Robert Durham Tysall Blay [1957] Director/Chief Executive; Robert Watkins [1959] Director/Finance and Accounting [American]; Rob Weber [1971] Director [American]

J.L.G.Investments Limited
Incorporated: 11 December 1945 *Employees:* 10
Net Worth: £13,552,504 *Total Assets:* £21,596,648
Registered Office: 3 Claridge Court, Lower Kings Road, Berkhamsted, Herts, HP4 2AE
Activities: Other letting and operating of own or leased real estate
Officers: Audrey Godfrey, Secretary; Elaine Rachel Chester [1976] Director/Engineer; Michael Peter Chester [1945] Director/Structural Engineer; Allan Russell Godfrey [1967] Director/Horticulturalist; Audrey Godfrey [1942] Director; Colin Roger Godfrey [1970] Director; John Stephen Godfrey [1953] Director/Chartered Surveyor; Richard Scott Godfrey [1956] Director; Robert Paul Godfrey [1959] Director; Jane Frances Mowat [1950] Director; Walter Stanton [1929] Director/Accountant

J.S.T. (U.K.) Limited
Incorporated: 25 February 1982 *Employees:* 41
Net Worth: £48,954,076 *Total Assets:* £51,579,028
Registered Office: Blyth Road, Halesworth, Suffolk, IP19 8EW
Activities: Manufacture of electronic components
Major Shareholder: Miyoko Nishimoto
Officers: Michael David Bowen, Secretary; Miyoko Nishimoto [1951] Company Executive-Director [Japanese]; Atsuhiro Takahashi [1976] Director [Japanese]; Masao Yoshimura [1946] Director [Japanese]

Jabac Finances Limited
Incorporated: 31 August 1962 *Employees:* 5
Net Worth: £4,484,334 *Total Assets:* £15,498,803
Registered Office: Lynwood House, 373-375 Station Road, Harrow, Middlesex, HA1 2AW
Activities: Banks
Officers: Adam Craig Newman [1965] Director; Clive Barry Newman [1960] Director; Harold Maurice Newman [1934] Director/Chartered Accountant; Paul Newman [1963] Director/Accounts Administrator

Jacklin Properties Limited
Incorporated: 7 January 2016 *Employees:* 7
Net Worth: £8,279,351 *Total Assets:* £16,981,492
Registered Office: Salisbury House, Station Road, Cambridge, CB1 2LA
Activities: Other letting and operating of own or leased real estate
Shareholders: David John Jacklin; Cecile Anne-Marie Auty-Jacklin
Officers: Cecile Anne-Marie Auty-Jacklin [1964] Director; David John Jacklin [1947] Director

Jackson Civil Engineering Group Limited
Incorporated: 23 December 2008 *Employees:* 288
Net Worth: £5,288,258 *Total Assets:* £38,469,624
Registered Office: 30 White House Road, Ipswich, Suffolk, IP1 5LT
Activities: Construction of roads and motorways
Officers: Trevor Mark Dixon, Secretary; James David Chaplin [1959] Director; Rupert Andrew Chitty [1972] Director; Brian John Crofton [1973] Director [South African]; Trevor Mark Dixon [1974] Finance Director; Richard William Neall [1964] Director/Chief Executive [Australian]; Paul David Stanhope [1974] Director

Jackson Civils Limited
Incorporated: 16 December 2003 *Employees:* 4
Net Worth: £1,508,442 *Total Assets:* £9,965,656
Registered Office: 30 White House Road, Ipswich, Suffolk, IP1 5LT
Activities: Construction of roads and motorways
Officers: Trevor Mark Dixon, Secretary; James David Chaplin [1959] Director; Rupert Andrew Chitty [1972] Director; Brian John Crofton [1973] Director [South African]; Trevor Mark Dixon [1974] Finance Director; Richard William Neall [1964] Managing Director [Australian]; Paul David Stanhope [1974] Director

Jackson Frameworks Limited
Incorporated: 8 March 2007
Net Worth: £1,309,240 *Total Assets:* £23,483,726
Registered Office: 30 White House Road, Ipswich, Suffolk, IP1 5LT
Activities: Construction of roads and motorways
Officers: Trevor Mark Dixon, Secretary; James David Chaplin [1959] Director; Rupert Andrew Chitty [1972] Director; Brian John Crofton [1973] Director [South African]; Trevor Mark Dixon [1974] Finance Director; Richard William Neall [1964] Director/Chief Executive [Australian]; Paul David Stanhope [1974] Director

Jackson Mechanical Services (UK) Limited
Incorporated: 23 February 2000 *Employees:* 64
Net Worth: £4,724,718 *Total Assets:* £19,010,232
Registered Office: 34 Coldharbour Lane, Harpenden, Herts, AL5 4UN
Activities: Renting and leasing of construction and civil engineering machinery and equipment
Major Shareholder: Mark Leroy Jackson
Officers: Mark Leroy Jackson, Secretary; Michael Eric Howells [1981] Director; Mark Leroy Jackson [1971] Director; Justin Lynn [1972] Director

Jagex Limited
Incorporated: 28 April 2000 *Employees:* 307
Net Worth: £36,963,384 *Total Assets:* £77,512,520
Registered Office: 220 Cambridge Science Park, Cambridge, CB4 0WA
Activities: Ready-made interactive leisure and entertainment software development
Parent: Fukong Interactive Entertaining Co,. Ltd
Officers: Yuanhui Huang, Secretary; Zhijia Feng [1985] Director [Chinese]; Yuanhui Huang [1984] Director/Company Secretary; Philip Mansell [1980] Director; Jinyu Pan [1981] Director [Chinese]; Shizong Yuan [1990] Director [Chinese]

Jalaram Limited
Incorporated: 15 August 1974
Net Worth: £6,145,302 *Total Assets:* £8,962,572
Registered Office: 39 South Parade, Mollison Way, Edgware, Middlesex, HA8 5QL
Activities: Dispensing chemist in specialised stores
Officers: Ramesh Manibhai Patel, Secretary; Hement Manibhai Patel [1942] Director; Jayendra Patel [1948] Director; Ramesh Manibhai Patel [1937] Director

Jaltek Holdings Limited
Incorporated: 20 November 2014 *Employees:* 76
Net Worth: £3,830,370 *Total Assets:* £10,027,652
Registered Office: Unit 13 Dencora Way, Sundon Business Park, Luton, Beds, LU3 3HP
Activities: Activities of production holding companies
Officers: John Steven Pittom [1972] Director/Sales & Marketing; Anmol Kumar Sood [1981] Director/Chartered Accountant; Pravin Kumar Sood [1950] Director

Jaltek Systems Limited
Incorporated: 4 November 1988 *Employees:* 72
Net Worth: £6,257,919 *Total Assets:* £12,623,971
Registered Office: Unit 13 Sundon Business Park, Dencora Way, Sundon Park, Luton, Beds, LU3 3HP
Activities: Manufacture of electronic measuring, testing etc. equipment, not for industrial process control
Parent: Jaltek Holdings Limited
Officers: Anmol Kumar Sood, Secretary; John Steven Pittom [1972] Director/Salesperson; Anmol Kumar Sood [1981] Director/Chartered Accountant; Pravin Kumar Sood [1950] Director/Chairman

Stephen James (Automotive) Limited
Incorporated: 18 August 2015 *Employees:* 413
Net Worth: £11,172,000 *Total Assets:* £56,729,000
Registered Office: Unit 1 Martinbridge Estate, Lincoln Road, Enfield, Middlesex, EN1 1SP
Activities: Sale of new cars and light motor vehicles
Parent: DC Management Services Limited
Officers: Benjamin James Collins [1977] Managing Director; Richard Ennis [1975] Director; Peter David Williams [1971] Director/Accountant [Australian]

Jamestown Industries Limited
Incorporated: 8 December 1997 *Employees:* 3
Net Worth: £5,840,827 *Total Assets:* £11,534,398
Registered Office: Faulkner House, Victoria Street, St Albans, Herts, AL1 3SE
Activities: Manufacture of other fabricated metal products n.e.c.
Parent: Envirolead Distribution Limited
Officers: Gerard O'Riordan [1958] Director/Accountant [Irish]; Maurice Elliot Sherling [1949] Director [Irish]

Janssen-Cilag Limited
Incorporated: 19 October 1971 *Employees:* 939
Net Worth: £266,952,000 *Total Assets:* £415,416,992
Registered Office: 50-100 Holmers Farm Way, High Wycombe, Bucks, HP12 4EG
Activities: Manufacture of pharmaceutical preparations
Parent: Johnson & Johnson
Officers: Liesbeth Aerts [1979] Finance Director [Belgian]; Shelagh Mary Anderson [1960] Regulatory Affairs Director; Rozlyn Cooper [1978] Medical Director; Mark Iain Hicken [1971] Director/Business Executive; Nicholas George Hodges [1972] Director/Vice President, Global Clinical Operations; Clare Sicklen [1971] HR Director

Jardine Motors Group UK Limited
Incorporated: 14 February 1990 *Employees:* 3,678
Net Worth: £128,149,000 *Total Assets:* £552,494,976
Registered Office: 770 The Crescent, Colchester Business Park, Colchester, Essex, CO4 9YQ
Activities: Activities of head offices
Officers: Mark Finch, Secretary; Anthony Philip Hawkins [1952] Director; Adam Phillip Charles Keswick [1973] Director; David John Muir [1980] Director; Lord James Meyer Sassoon [1955] Director; David Neil Williamson [1965] Director

Jark Industrial Limited
Incorporated: 18 January 2007 *Employees:* 10
Net Worth: £193,719 *Total Assets:* £12,583,139
Registered Office: 89 High Street, Hadleigh, Ipswich, Suffolk, IP7 5EA
Activities: Other activities of employment placement agencies
Parent: Jark Ventures PLC
Officers: David Simon Jaffrey, Secretary; Paul Mizen [1972] Director

Jark Ventures PLC
Incorporated: 15 July 1996 *Employees:* 157
Previous: Jark PLC
Net Worth: £6,344,511 *Total Assets:* £23,114,560
Registered Office: Beechurst, 8 Commercial Road, Dereham, Norfolk, NR19 1AE
Activities: Activities of head offices
Parent: The Recruit Venture Group Ltd
Officers: David Simon Jaffrey, Secretary/Accountant; Preston James Andrews [1961] Director; Paul Mizen [1972] Director; Neil William Charles Rogers [1976] Director

Jarrold & Sons Limited
Incorporated: 31 October 1902 *Employees:* 478
Net Worth: £68,911,000 *Total Assets:* £103,712,000
Registered Office: Whitefriars, Norwich, NR3 1SH
Activities: Other retail sale in non-specialised stores
Officers: Christopher John Doggett, Secretary; Christopher John Doggett [1960] Finance Director; Michael Findlay [1968] Director; Diana Grace Michelle Jarrold [1962] Director; Bridget Fiona McIntyre [1961] Director; David John McLeavy Hill [1957] Director; Minnie Moll [1961] Director/Chief Executive; Anthony John Cleeves Palmer [1951] Director

Jarrold (St. James) 3 SJC Limited
Incorporated: 27 July 2005 *Employees:* 2
Net Worth: £4,825,197 *Total Assets:* £11,145,356
Registered Office: St James Mill, Whitefriars, Norwich, NR3 1SH
Activities: Other letting and operating of own or leased real estate
Officers: Christopher John Doggett, Secretary/Director; Christopher John Doggett [1960] Director; David John McLeavy Hill [1957] Director

Jarrold (St. James) D1/D2 Limited
Incorporated: 17 October 2006 *Employees:* 2
Net Worth: £4,463,056 *Total Assets:* £23,796,932
Registered Office: St James Mill, Whitefriars, Norwich, NR3 1SH
Activities: Other letting and operating of own or leased real estate
Officers: Christopher John Doggett, Secretary/Director; Christopher John Doggett [1960] Director; David John McLeavy Hill [1957] Director

Jarrold (St. James) Limited
Incorporated: 17 October 2006 *Employees:* 2
Net Worth: £4,359,248 *Total Assets:* £13,168,514
Registered Office: St James Mill, Whitefriars, Norwich, NR3 1SH
Activities: Other letting and operating of own or leased real estate
Officers: Christopher John Doggett, Secretary/Director; Christopher John Doggett [1960] Director; David John McLeavy Hill [1957] Director

Jarvis Commercial Properties Limited
Incorporated: 7 November 2000 *Employees:* 5
Net Worth: £9,981,928 *Total Assets:* £10,925,077
Registered Office: No 1 Waterside, Station Road, Harpenden, Herts, AL5 4US
Activities: Other letting and operating of own or leased real estate
Officers: Samuel John Chandler [1970] Director/Accountant; David Anthony Jump [1946] Director/Quantity Surveyor; Christopher James Lewis [1973] Director/Solicitor; Emma Jane Bridget Parkinson [1961] Director

Jarvis Contracting Limited
Incorporated: 22 March 1990 *Employees:* 93
Net Worth: £3,121,465 *Total Assets:* £16,112,338
Registered Office: No 1 Waterside, Station Road, Harpenden, Herts, AL5 4US
Activities: Construction of commercial buildings
Parent: Jarvis Group Construction Ltd
Officers: Samuel John Chandler [1970] Director/Accountant; Mark Stephen Doyle [1965] Director [Irish]; Emma Jane Bridget Parkinson [1961] Director; Stuart Michael Talbot [1971] Commercial Director

Jarvis Group Limited
Incorporated: 5 February 2001 *Employees:* 187
Net Worth: £17,147,000 *Total Assets:* £39,724,920
Registered Office: No 1 Waterside, Station Road, Harpenden, Herts, AL5 4US
Activities: Development of building projects
Officers: Samuel John Chandler [1970] Director/Accountant; David Anthony Jump [1946] Director/Quantity Surveyor; Christopher James Lewis [1963] Director/Solicitor; Emma Jane Bridget Parkinson [1961] Director/Analyst

Jarvis Homes Limited
Incorporated: 20 April 1971 *Employees:* 20
Net Worth: £8,915,376 *Total Assets:* £19,621,248
Registered Office: No 1 Waterside, Station Road, Harpenden, Herts, AL5 4US
Activities: Construction of commercial buildings
Parent: Jarvis Group Developments Ltd
Officers: Samuel John Chandler [1970] Director/Accountant; Andrew James Driver [1972] Director/Surveyor; Michael Simon Margereson [1961] Director; Emma Jane Bridget Parkinson [1961] Director

Jawaby Property Investment Limited
Incorporated: 10 February 1982 *Employees:* 4
Net Worth: £51,699,608 *Total Assets:* £66,645,216
Registered Office: Cutlers Farmhouse, Marlow Road, Lane End, High Wycombe, Bucks, HP14 3JW
Activities: Other letting and operating of own or leased real estate
Parent: The Government of National Accord of The State of Libya
Officers: Ahmed Mohamed Ahmida Abdalla [1962] Director/Oil Sector Executive [Libyan]; Naim Khalifa Mohamed Gheriani [1958] Director [Libyan]; Ahmed Ibrahim Hasan [1980] Director/Oil Sector Lawyer/Legal Officer [Libyan]; Abdulfetah Salem Shagan [1954] Director/Oil Sector Executive [Libyan]

Jaysam Contractors Limited
Incorporated: 3 July 1986 *Employees:* 56
Net Worth: £18,337,174 *Total Assets:* £37,892,284
Registered Office: 14 Oxford Road, Wealdstone, Middlesex, HA3 7RG
Activities: Construction of domestic buildings
Major Shareholder: Samji Shivji Patel
Officers: Chhaya Gorsia, Secretary; Dhiraj Dabasia [1984] Director/Chartered Surveyor; Sundip Samji Dabasia [1983] Director/Office Manager; Samji Shivji Patel [1956] Director/Carpenter

Jaysam Developments Borehamwood Limited
Incorporated: 17 July 2014
Net Worth Deficit: £719,381 *Total Assets:* £28,973,820
Registered Office: 14 Oxford Road, Wealdstone, Middlesex, HA3 7RG
Activities: Construction of domestic buildings
Officers: Dhiraj Dabasia [1984] Director/Commercial Manager; Hitesh Samji Dabasia [1980] Director/Orthopaedic Surgeon; Sundip Samji Dabasia [1983] Director/Purchasing Manager; Samji Shivji Patel [1956] Director/Businessman; Gaurang Babulal Velani [1973] Director/Development Manager

JBS Global (UK) Limited
Incorporated: 11 September 2001 *Employees:* 24
Net Worth: £28,589,878 *Total Assets:* £54,645,752
Registered Office: 2nd Floor, Building 1, Imperial Place, Maxwell Road, Borehamwood, Herts, WD6 1JN
Activities: Wholesale of meat and meat products
Officers: Ian Geoffrey Kemp, Secretary/Administration Manager; Wesley Mendonca Batista Filho [1991] Director [Brazilian]; Marcus Enda O'Sullivan [1970] Director [Irish]

JCA Head Co Limited
Incorporated: 16 October 2015 *Employees:* 132
Net Worth: £4,398,000 *Total Assets:* £22,464,000
Registered Office: Solar House, Stevenage Leisure Park, Kings Park, Stevenage, Herts, SG1 2UA
Activities: Activities of other holding companies n.e.c.
Major Shareholder: Ian David Hodges Jackson
Officers: Anna Charlotte Stillman, Secretary; Thomas Andrew Absalom [1973] Director; Ian David Hodges Jackson [1969] Director/Engineer

JDM Technology Group Limited
Incorporated: 21 December 2006 *Employees:* 120
Previous: Explorer Group UK Limited
Net Worth: £1,251,131 *Total Assets:* £14,360,296
Registered Office: Breakspear Park, Breakspear Way, Hemel Hempstead, Herts, HP2 4TZ
Activities: Other information technology service activities
Shareholders: James Douglas McFarlane; Judy McFarlane
Officers: James Douglas McFarlane [1950] Director [Canadian]

Jean-Luc Developments Ltd
Incorporated: 3 February 2009 *Employees:* 77
Net Worth: £2,736,749 *Total Assets:* £11,829,471
Registered Office: First Floor, Radius House, 51 Clarendon Road, Watford, Herts, WD17 1HP
Activities: Construction of commercial buildings
Major Shareholder: Nicola Louise Spence
Officers: Russell Jonathan James Spence, Secretary; Andrew Hill [1966] Director; Luke Johnson Spence [1988] Director; Russell Jonathon James Spence [1985] Director

Jeesal Akman Holdings Limited
Incorporated: 18 February 2014 *Employees:* 337
Net Worth: £13,397,124 *Total Assets:* £24,132,036
Registered Office: 16-18 High Street, Dereham, Norfolk, NR19 1DR
Activities: Other letting and operating of own or leased real estate
Officers: Sami Carly Colk, Secretary; Tugay Akman [1967] Director; Sally Anne Subramaniam [1955] Director

Jeesal Holdings Limited
Incorporated: 17 February 2014 *Employees:* 226
Net Worth: £6,324,321 *Total Assets:* £11,152,477
Registered Office: 16-18 High Street, Dereham, Norfolk, NR19 1DR
Activities: Other letting and operating of own or leased real estate
Major Shareholder: Jeevaraj Subramaniam
Officers: Sami Carly Colk, Secretary; Sally Anne Subramaniam [1955] Director

Jelmac (Primary Care) Properties Limited
Incorporated: 24 November 2008 *Employees:* 3
Net Worth: £10,578,965 *Total Assets:* £16,186,455
Registered Office: Jelmac House, 269 High Street, Berkhamsted, Herts, HP4 1AA
Activities: Other letting and operating of own or leased real estate
Shareholders: Alistair Piers Spooner; Mark Jeremy Spooner; Claire Elizabeth Rose
Officers: Frank David George Cattley, Secretary; Claire Elizabeth Rose [1970] Director; Alistair Piers Spooner [1972] Director/Property Consultant; Mark Jeremy Spooner [1972] Director

Jelmac Properties
Incorporated: 11 November 2008
Net Worth: £32,619,098 *Total Assets:* £34,260,152
Registered Office: Jelmac House, 269 High Street, Berkhamsted, Herts, HP4 1AA
Activities: Other letting and operating of own or leased real estate
Shareholder: Elizabeth Jane Burgess
Officers: Frank David George Cattley, Secretary; Claire Elizabeth Rose [1970] Director; Alistair Piers Spooner [1972] Director; Mark Jeremy Spooner [1972] Director

Jenga (UK) Limited
Incorporated: 27 February 2014
Net Worth Deficit: £111,521 *Total Assets:* £9,483,444
Registered Office: 9a The Broadway, Stanmore, Middlesex, HA7 4DA
Activities: Real estate agencies
Shareholders: Hitenkumar Mansukhlal Shah; Mahesh Raojibhai Patel; Navika Hitenkumar Shah; Alpa Mahesh Patel
Officers: Mahesh Raojibhai Patel, Secretary; Alpa Mahesh Patel [1972] Director/Pharmacist; Mahesh Raojibhai Patel [1968] Director/Businessman; Hitenkumar Mansukhlal Shah [1968] Director/Businessman; Navika Hitenkumar Shah [1972] Director/Pharmacist

Jensten Group Limited
Incorporated: 22 November 2012 *Employees:* 179
Previous: CISG Limited
Net Worth: £3,556,652 *Total Assets:* £26,954,544
Registered Office: Coversure House, Vantage Park, Washingley Road, Huntingdon, Cambs, PE29 6SR
Activities: Activities of financial services holding companies
Parent: Cambridge Bidco Limited
Officers: Georgina Elizabeth Bourner, Secretary; Carl Anthony Ashton [1980] Director; Cheryl Dawn Astley [1962] Director; Robert Michael Darling [1963] Director; Sarah Darling [1969] Director; Edward George FitzGenerald Hannan [1978] Director/Chief Financial Officer; Stephen Guy Parker [1965] Director

Jepco Limited
Incorporated: 24 December 1997 *Employees:* 127
Net Worth: £9,459,250 *Total Assets:* £19,430,632
Registered Office: Norfolk House Farm, Gedney Marsh, Spalding, Lincs, PE12 9PB
Activities: Activities of agricultural holding companies
Shareholder: Stuart William Piccaver
Officers: Simon Goddard, Secretary; Simon Goddard [1959] Director/Accountant; Phillip Paul Hubbert [1955] Director/Farm Manager; Stuart William Piccaver [1971] Sales & Marketing Director

Jessica House Developments Limited
Incorporated: 21 December 2015
Net Worth Deficit: £1,136,190 *Total Assets:* £18,121,020
Registered Office: 3rd Floor, Sterling House, Langston Road, Loughton, Essex, IG10 3TS
Activities: Development of building projects
Parent: Galliard Developments Limited
Officers: Allan William Porter, Secretary; John Cole [1971] Director; Stephen Stuart Solomon Conway [1948] Director; Jonathan Simon Goldstein [1966] Director; Donagh O'Sullivan [1968] Director [Irish]

Jet Investments Limited
Incorporated: 24 April 2014 *Employees:* 2
Net Worth Deficit: £487,294 *Total Assets:* £11,420,842
Registered Office: 9 Great Chesterford Court, London Road, Great Chesterford, Essex, CB10 1PF
Activities: Buying and selling of own real estate
Major Shareholder: Shaun Taylor
Officers: Joanna Luan Taylor [1973] Director; David Brian Warburton [1966] Director

Jewers Doors Limited
Incorporated: 31 July 1984 *Employees:* 53
Net Worth: £10,505,333 *Total Assets:* £12,422,484
Registered Office: Normandy Lane, Stratton Business Park, Biggleswade, Beds, SG18 8QB
Activities: Manufacture of doors and windows of metal
Officers: Patricia Gwendoline Jewers, Secretary; Marcus Dudley Allen [1974] Contracts Director; Benjamin Mohan Chowdhary [1978] Director/Engineer; Christopher Nigel Jewers [1967] Managing Director; Jonathan Charles Jewers [1972] Field Director; Mark Oliver Jewers [1969] Sales Director

The Jewish Community Secondary School Trust
Incorporated: 15 December 2004
Net Worth: £39,723,764 *Total Assets:* £40,056,592
Registered Office: JCoSS School, Castlewood Road, Cockfosters, Barnet, Herts, EN4 9GE
Activities: General secondary education
Officers: Jamie Robert Cassell, Secretary; Nicole Julia Ronson Allalouf [1972] Director/CEO Nicron Productions Ltd; Jamie Robert Cassell [1973] Director/Chartered Accountant; Stephen Alan Clayman [1968] Director/Police Superintendent; Joel Anthony Courts [1982] Director/Chartered Accountant; Mark David Freedman [1970] Director/Solicitor; Graham Andrew Harris [1963] Managing Director; Tamara Margaret Isaacs [1967] Director/Civil Servant; Jeremy Paul Kosky [1968] Director/Solicitor; David Mark Kyte [1960] Director; Stephen David Moss [1952] Director

JJ Food Service Limited
Incorporated: 23 December 1988 *Employees:* 823
Net Worth: £34,158,096 *Total Assets:* £50,369,880
Registered Office: 7 Solar Way, Innova Park, Enfield, Middlesex, EN3 7XY
Activities: Non-specialised wholesale of food, beverages and tobacco
Parent: JJ Food Service Holdings Limited
Officers: Mustafa Hussein Kiamil, Secretary; Mustafa Hussein Kiamil [1956] Director; Rifat Kiamil [1983] Director/IT Manager

JMBC Properties Ltd
Incorporated: 28 April 2014
Net Worth: £289,476 *Total Assets:* £14,850,377
Registered Office: Burton Bower, Burton End, Stansted, Essex, CM24 8UE
Activities: Other letting and operating of own or leased real estate
Major Shareholder: Mark Nicholson
Officers: Jacquelynne Maria Nicholson [1963] Director/Manager; Martin Nicholson [1963] Director/Owner Property Company

Jobserve Limited
Incorporated: 23 August 1993 *Employees:* 75
Net Worth: £24,943,756 *Total Assets:* £30,930,700
Registered Office: Tower Business Park, Kelvedon Road, Tiptree, Colchester, Essex, CO5 0LX
Activities: Other business support service activities n.e.c.
Shareholders: Aspire Media Group Limited; Aspire Media Group Limited
Officers: Helen Haworth, Secretary; Robert Arthur Cowling [1960] Managing Director

Jockey Club Estates Limited
Incorporated: 23 December 1968 *Employees:* 59
Net Worth: £32,040,000 *Total Assets:* £42,437,000
Registered Office: Jockey Club Office, 101 High Street, Newmarket, Suffolk, CB8 8JL
Activities: Operation of sports facilities
Officers: Richard Anthony Attwell, Secretary; Andrew Ian Henry Bedford [1962] Director; Nicholas Cheyne [1960] Client Relations Director; Lisa Jeanette Hancock [1971] Director; Alastair Reginald MacDonald-Buchanan [1960] Director/Business Manager; Nicholas Robert Patton [1979] Managing Director; Stuart John Richmond-Watson [1951] Director/Chartered Surveyor; The Honourable Peter Hugh Charles Stanley [1964] Director/Stud Manager; Timothy Dominic James Syder [1958] Director/Chartered Accountant

Johnson & Johnson Innovation Limited
Incorporated: 21 August 2000
Net Worth: £29,083,000 *Total Assets:* £36,677,000
Registered Office: 50-100 Holmers Farm Way, High Wycombe, Bucks, HP12 4UL
Activities: Other letting and operating of own or leased real estate
Parent: Johnson & Johnson Management Limited
Officers: Gemma Storey, Secretary; Harpal Kumar [1965] Director/Innovation Centre Leader; Nerida Scott [1969] Senior Director, Transactions; Gert Vandewaerde [1983] Finance Director [Belgian]

Johnson Care Limited
Incorporated: 15 November 2012 *Employees:* 930
Net Worth: £8,830,697 *Total Assets:* £21,071,216
Registered Office: 57-59 Avenue Road, Westcliff on Sea, Essex, SS0 7PJ
Activities: Other business support service activities n.e.c.
Major Shareholder: Davie Seeiappan Vive-Kananda
Officers: Natalie-Jane Elizabeth Vive-Kananda, Secretary; Davie Seeniappan Vive Kananda [1951] Director; Stuart John Mohan Vive-Kananda [1982] Director

Richard Johnston Limited
Incorporated: 29 December 1980 *Employees:* 59
Net Worth: £16,044,047 *Total Assets:* £17,812,262
Registered Office: Harling Road, Snetterton, Norwich, NR16 2JU
Activities: Growing of cereals (except rice), leguminous crops and oil seeds
Major Shareholder: Richard Bernard Johnston
Officers: Wendy Diane Johnston [1937] Director; Robin Ian McIndoe [1967] Finance Director

Jojo's Mojo Limited
Incorporated: 16 February 2012 *Employees:* 3
Net Worth: £10,152,944 *Total Assets:* £10,268,139
Registered Office: Cambridge House, 16 High Street, Saffron Walden, Essex, CB10 1AX
Activities: Book publishing
Shareholder: Pauline Sara Jo Moyes
Officers: Pauline Sara Jo Moyes [1969] Director/Author

WO & PO Jolly Holdings Limited
Incorporated: 22 June 1994 *Employees:* 9
Net Worth: £71,367,880 *Total Assets:* £75,387,776
Registered Office: Philip House, St William Court, Kesgrave, Ipswich, Suffolk, IP5 2QP
Activities: Activities of other holding companies n.e.c.
Shareholder: Crispin Michael Rope
Officers: Jeremy Philip Winteringham Heal, Secretary/Solicitor; Ellen Mary Jolly [1957] Director/Administrator; Patrick Jolly [1949] Director; Philip Hugh Jolly [1956] Director; Timothy Andrew Jolly [1950] Director/Farmer; Crispin Michael Rope [1930] Director

Leonard F.Jollye (Brookmans Park) Limited
Incorporated: 24 June 1971 *Employees:* 604
Net Worth: £4,396,229 *Total Assets:* £12,799,988
Registered Office: 1 Lea Road, Waltham Abbey, Essex, EN9 1AS
Activities: Retail sale of flowers, plants, seeds, fertilizers, pet animals and pet food in specialised stores
Parent: Leonard F Jollye (Holdings) Limited
Officers: David Leslie Hutchinson [1969] Director; Warwick Richard Thresher [1974] Director; Christian Robert Philip Ward [1972] Director

Leonard F Jollye (Holdings) Limited
Incorporated: 9 September 2005
Net Worth: £8,899,890 *Total Assets:* £8,900,390
Registered Office: 1 Lea Road, Waltham Abbey, Essex, EN9 1AS
Activities: Activities of other holding companies n.e.c.
Parent: Jollyes Group Limited
Officers: David Leslie Hutchinson [1969] Director; Warwick Richard Thresher [1974] Director; Christian Robert Philip Ward [1972] Director

Jollyes Group Limited
Incorporated: 21 December 2007
Net Worth: £21,738,400 *Total Assets:* £26,417,982
Registered Office: 1 Lea Road, Waltham Abbey, Essex, EN9 1AS
Activities: Activities of other holding companies n.e.c.
Parent: Jollyes Retail Group Limited
Officers: David Leslie Hutchinson [1969] Director; Warwick Richard Thresher [1974] Director; Christian Robert Philip Ward [1972] Director

Jollyes Retail Group Limited
Incorporated: 21 June 2011 *Employees:* 604
Net Worth: £19,382,716 *Total Assets:* £37,843,816
Registered Office: 1 Lea Road, Waltham Abbey, Essex, EN9 1AS
Activities: Activities of other holding companies n.e.c.
Parent: Jaguar Bidco Limited
Officers: David Leslie Hutchinson [1969] Director; Warwick Richard Thresher [1974] Director; Christian Robert Philip Ward [1972] Director

JPJ Installations Limited
Incorporated: 27 March 1997 *Employees:* 78
Net Worth: £7,962,825 *Total Assets:* £13,850,398
Registered Office: 7 Bradbury Drive, Braintree, Essex, CM7 2SD
Activities: Manufacture of metal structures and parts of structures
Parent: Ralm Holdings Limited
Officers: John Mark Belton [1970] Director/Shopfitter; Paul Frank Belton [1971] Director/Shopfitter; John Robert Clarke [1970] Director/Shopfitter; Richard MacKenzie [1980] Director

JRL Group Holdings Limited
Incorporated: 16 October 2009 *Employees:* 871
Net Worth: £41,824,040 *Total Assets:* £244,142,128
Registered Office: 4 Elstree Way, Borehamwood, Herts, WD6 1RN
Activities: Activities of construction holding companies
Shareholder: Kevin William Keegan
Officers: Ronan Joseph Gleeson, Secretary [Irish]; Ronan Joseph Gleeson [1976] Director [Irish]; Kevin William Keegan [1963] Director [Irish]; John James Reddington [1972] Director [Irish]

JRL Group Limited
Incorporated: 26 March 2008 *Employees:* 871
Net Worth: £39,052,300 *Total Assets:* £229,338,288
Registered Office: 4 Elstree Way, Borehamwood, Herts, WD6 1RN
Activities: Activities of construction holding companies
Parent: JRL Group Holdings Ltd
Officers: Ronan Joseph Gleeson, Secretary [Irish]; Ronan Joseph Gleeson [1976] Director/Chartered Accountant [Irish]; Kevin William Keegan [1963] Director [Irish]; John James Reddington [1972] Director [Irish]

JRL Plant and Logistics Limited
Incorporated: 17 April 2003 *Employees:* 148
Net Worth: £968,887 *Total Assets:* £62,889,348
Registered Office: 4 Elstree Way, Borehamwood, Herts, WD6 1RN
Activities: Renting and leasing of construction and civil engineering machinery and equipment
Parent: JRL Group Ltd
Officers: Ronan Joseph Gleeson, Secretary/Director [Irish]; Ronan Joseph Gleeson [1976] Director [Irish]; Kevin William Keegan [1963] Director/Estimator [Irish]; John James Reddington [1972] Director/Formwork [Irish]

JRL Property Holdings Limited
Incorporated: 24 February 2017 *Employees:* 3
Net Worth: £4,660,324 *Total Assets:* £29,217,624
Registered Office: 4 Elstree Way, Borehamwood, Herts, WD6 1RN
Activities: Activities of other holding companies n.e.c.
Parent: JRL Group Holdings Limited
Officers: Ronan Gleeson, Secretary; Ronan Joseph Gleeson [1976] Director/Chartered Accountant [Irish]; Kevin William Keegan [1963] Director [Irish]; John James Reddington [1972] Director [Irish]

JSA Services Limited
Incorporated: 24 July 1989 *Employees:* 5,251
Net Worth: £2,865,712 *Total Assets:* £19,393,340
Registered Office: 4th Floor, Radius House, 51 Clarendon Road, Watford, Herts, WD17 1HP
Activities: Accounting and auditing activities
Shareholders: Goodman Family Investments Limited; JSA Newco Limited
Officers: Katherine Mary Rogers, Secretary; Andrew Graham Goodman [1962] Director; John Hugo Hoskin [1974] Director; Kwasi Martin Missah [1969] Legal Director; Katherine Mary Rogers [1953] Director

JSM Construction Limited
Incorporated: 1 July 1998 *Employees:* 191
Net Worth: £8,117,488 *Total Assets:* £16,643,443
Registered Office: Sterling House, Mutton Lane, Potters Bar, Herts, EN6 3AR
Activities: Construction of utility projects for electricity and telecommunications
Parent: JSM Group Holdings Limited
Officers: John Joseph Scanlon, Secretary; John Joseph Scanlon [1968] Director; Mark Vincent Scanlon [1969] Director; Stuart Wiltshire [1965] Director

JSM Group Holdings Limited
Incorporated: 4 September 2015 *Employees:* 191
Net Worth: £8,117,488 *Total Assets:* £16,643,443
Registered Office: c/o Hillier Hopkins LLP, First Floor, Radius House, 51 Clarendon Road, Watford, Herts, WD17 1HP
Activities: Activities of other holding companies n.e.c.
Shareholder: Mark Vincent Scanlon
Officers: John Joseph Scanlon [1968] Director; Mark Vincent Scanlon [1969] Director; Stuart Wiltshire [1965] Director

Juddmonte Farms Limited
Incorporated: 17 August 1983 *Employees:* 99
Net Worth: £19,339,636 *Total Assets:* £90,121,096
Registered Office: Banstead Manor Stud, Cheveley, Newmarket, Suffolk, CB8 9RD
Activities: Raising of horses and other equines
Major Shareholder: Khalid Bin Abdullah
Officers: Michael Stephen Saunders, Secretary; Douglas Vernon Erskine Crum [1949] Director; Michael Stephen Saunders [1966] Director/Chartered Accountant; James William Coffman Swartz [1946] Director/Lawyer [American]

K & R Projects Company Limited
Incorporated: 16 May 2002
Net Worth: £6,019,152 *Total Assets:* £10,329,996
Registered Office: 1 Brewery House, Brook Street, Wivenhoe, Colchester, Essex, CO7 9DS
Activities: Buying and selling of own real estate
Major Shareholder: Raymond Raymond
Officers: Karen Ann Horrocks, Secretary; Jacqueline Ann Raymond [1947] Director; Raymond Raymond [1928] Director

K K Investment Ltd
Incorporated: 6 April 2004
Net Worth: £839,355 *Total Assets:* £12,435,536
Registered Office: 7 The Broadway, Preston Road, Wembley, Middlesex, HA9 8JT
Activities: Development of building projects
Major Shareholder: Khosrow Khosravani
Officers: Khosrow Khosravani Shiri [1962] Director/Building Developer

K L Technologies Limited
Incorporated: 4 June 2007 *Employees:* 316
Net Worth: £7,949,446 *Total Assets:* £20,173,406
Registered Office: Riverside Industrial Estate, Estuary Road, Kings Lynn, Norfolk, PE30 2HS
Activities: Activities of production holding companies
Parent: KL Technologies Holdings Limited
Officers: Mark William Hamilton, Secretary; Geoffrey Paul Davies [1959] Director; Mark William Hamilton [1969] Director; Mark Littlewood [1962] Director

K U H Limited
Incorporated: 16 May 1946
Net Worth: £19,626,304 *Total Assets:* £48,324,208
Registered Office: The Balsams Barn, Balsams Lane, Standon, Ware, Herts, SG11 1NS
Activities: Activities of financial services holding companies
Parent: Leda Investments Ltd
Officers: John Howard Williamson [1944] Director

K.C.Y. Limited
Incorporated: 23 September 1999 *Employees:* 1
Net Worth: £5,649,118 *Total Assets:* £10,596,495
Registered Office: 10 Long Drive, South Ruislip, Middlesex, HA4 0HG
Activities: Other letting and operating of own or leased real estate
Shareholders: Christos Yiannakis; Christos Yiannakis
Officers: Julia Yiannakis, Secretary; Christina Louise Yiannakis [1989] Director; Christos Yiannakis [1951] Director/Restaurateur [Greek]; Katherine Elissa Yiannakis [1987] Director

K.E.M. Property Services Limited
Incorporated: 24 January 2003 *Employees:* 5
Net Worth: £5,706,766 *Total Assets:* £9,165,317
Registered Office: 36a Goodmayes Road, Goodmayes, Essex, IG3 9UR
Activities: Management of real estate on a fee or contract basis
Major Shareholder: Ashley Parker
Officers: Nitan Bafna, Secretary; Ashley Parker [1962] Director/Manager; Edward Charles Parker-Bancroft [1957] Director/Acquisitions Manager

K.M. Packaging Holdings Limited
Incorporated: 5 October 2007 *Employees:* 20
Net Worth: £9,411,593 *Total Assets:* £12,754,119
Registered Office: 44 West Street, Oundle, Northants, PE8 4EF
Activities: Activities of head offices
Shareholder: Charles Smithson
Officers: James Edwin Bruce Close, Secretary; James Edwin Bruce Close [1951] Director; Graham Holding [1960] Commercial Director; Charles Smithson [1964] Director

K.M. Packaging Services Limited
Incorporated: 2 August 1984 *Employees:* 20
Net Worth: £9,882,877 *Total Assets:* £13,225,403
Registered Office: 44 West Street, Oundle, Northants, PE8 4EF
Activities: Manufacture of plastic packing goods
Shareholder: Charles Smithson
Officers: James Edwin Bruce Close, Secretary; James Edwin Bruce Close [1951] Director; Graham Holding [1960] Commercial Director; Charles Smithson [1964] Director

Kailas Hotel Finance Company Limited
Incorporated: 19 November 2012
Net Worth: £1 *Total Assets:* £12,270,350
Registered Office: 505 Pinner Road, Harrow, Middlesex, HA2 6EH
Activities: Other letting and operating of own or leased real estate
Officers: Denise Olival, Secretary; Rishi Ramesh Sachdev [1976] Director; Uday Vyas [1978] Director

Kampa UK Ltd
Incorporated: 12 October 2006 *Employees:* 27
Net Worth: £10,582,919 *Total Assets:* £18,537,160
Registered Office: Little Braxted Hall, Little Braxted, Witham, Essex, CM8 3EU
Activities: Non-specialised wholesale trade
Officers: Jason Charles Wordley, Secretary; Henrik Boggild [1972] Director/Chief Financial Officer [Danish]; Peter Kruk [1968] Director/President EMEA [Swedish]; Myles Salmon [1970] Sales Director; Jason Charles Wordley [1984] Finance Director

Kane Group Limited
Incorporated: 23 September 1991 *Employees:* 204
Net Worth: £2,889,000 *Total Assets:* £11,999,000
Registered Office: Hartfield Place, 40-44 High Street, Northwood, Middlesex, HA6 1BN
Activities: Activities of head offices
Shareholders: Jonathan Stephen Henry Arthur Kane; Grace Ventures LLC
Officers: Robert Christopher Clow [1948] Director/Chartered Accountant; Jonathan Stephen Henry Arthur Kane [1965] Director; Michael John Paul Charles Kane [1960] Director [American]

Kanta Enterprises Limited
Incorporated: 26 January 1982 *Employees:* 34
Net Worth: £9,001,002 *Total Assets:* £23,451,408
Registered Office: Kanta House, Victoria Road, South Ruislip, Middlesex, HA4 0JQ
Activities: Wholesale of pharmaceutical goods
Officers: Satish Jamnadas Chatwani, Secretary; Jawahar Jamnadas Chatwani [1948] Director; Rashmi Jamnadas Chatwani [1954] Director; Satish Jamnadas Chatwani [1953] Director

Kara Designs Ltd
Incorporated: 26 March 1999 *Employees:* 22
Net Worth: £10,195,480 *Total Assets:* £11,538,804
Registered Office: Unit 6 Haslemere Business Centre, Lincoln Way, Enfield, Middlesex, EN1 1TE
Activities: Manufacture of other women's outerwear
Shareholders: Ahmet Karaman; Yee Yoke Karaman; Huseyin Karaman
Officers: Yee Yoke Karaman, Secretary; Ahmet Karaman [1974] Director/Production Manager

Kara Management Ltd
Incorporated: 14 March 2003
Net Worth: £1,879,268 *Total Assets:* £9,607,503
Registered Office: Unit 6 Haslemere Business Centre, Lincoln Way, Enfield, Middlesex, EN1 1TE
Activities: Other letting and operating of own or leased real estate
Shareholders: Ahmet Karaman; Yee Yoke Karaman; Huseyin Karaman
Officers: Yee Yoke Karaman, Secretary; Ahmet Karaman [1974] Director/Dressmaker

Karsten UK Limited
Incorporated: 5 December 2003
Net Worth: £10,361,438 *Total Assets:* £23,012,368
Registered Office: Karsten UK Ltd, Camel Gate, Spalding, Lincs, PE12 6ES
Activities: Support activities for crop production
Officers: Hermanus Gideon Engelbrecht, Secretary [South African]; Hermanus Gideon Engelbrecht [1968] Director/Chartered Accountant [South African]; Belia Hendrika Karsten [1978] Director/Chartered Accountant [South African]; Petrus Abraham Karsten Jr [1975] Director/Fruit Producer Exporter [South African]; Petrus Abraham Karsten [1948] Director/Farmer [South African]

Katrin Properties Limited
Incorporated: 15 January 2003 *Employees:* 5
Net Worth: £13,645,954 *Total Assets:* £26,322,198
Registered Office: 834 Hertford Road, Enfield, Middlesex, EN3 6UE
Activities: Other letting and operating of own or leased real estate
Shareholder: Kerem Yavuzarslan
Officers: Kerem Yavuzarslan [1961] Managing Director

Katsouris Brothers Limited
Incorporated: 22 October 1964 *Employees:* 216
Net Worth: £10,970,954 *Total Assets:* £20,508,800
Registered Office: 98-100 Queensbury Road, Wembley, Middlesex, HA0 1QG
Activities: Non-specialised wholesale trade
Parent: Katsouris Brothers Limited
Officers: Katerina Charalambous, Secretary; Costas Constantinou [1957] Director/Consultant [Cypriot]; Loizos Constantinou [1958] Director; Demos Habeshis [1951] Director/Manager; Alexander Katsouris [1980] Director/Manager; Antonios Prodromou Yerolemou [1942] Director

Kaykem Fast Foods Limited
Incorporated: 4 July 1986 *Employees:* 48
Net Worth: £6,193,785 *Total Assets:* £9,301,802
Registered Office: 11b High Street, Colchester, Essex, CO1 1DA
Activities: Other food services
Shareholder: Kemal Ahmet
Officers: Bilkay Ahmet, Secretary; Bilkay Ahmet [1949] Director; Cengiz Kemal Ahmet [1971] Director; Kemal Ahmet [1948] Director

KCG Holdings Ltd
Incorporated: 9 June 2016
Net Worth: £17,500,100 *Total Assets:* £17,500,100
Registered Office: 4 Brick Knoll Park, Ashley Road, St Albans, Herts, AL1 5UG
Activities: Other letting and operating of own or leased real estate
Parent: Millennium Ladieswear Manufacturers Limited
Officers: Kyriacos Antoniou [1969] Director

KCH (UK) Holdings Limited
Incorporated: 30 September 2014 *Employees:* 417
Net Worth: £2,195,467 *Total Assets:* £43,489,848
Registered Office: Kingsley House, Clapham Road South, Lowestoft, Suffolk, NR32 1QS
Activities: Residential care activities for the elderly and disabled
Officers: Wasantha Darshana [1978] Director; Deborah Ann Edwards [1974] Director; Ian Stuart Jarvis [1966] Director; Sumithra Chandrakanthi Thayanandarajah [1959] Director/Business Executive; Velummayilum Thayanandarajah [1961] Director/Business Executive

KCK Peterborough Devco LLP
Incorporated: 23 November 2016
Net Worth: £7,360,000 *Total Assets:* £9,097,000
Registered Office: Tempsford Hall, Sandy, Beds, SG19 2BD

KDM International Limited
Incorporated: 2 May 1975 *Employees:* 33
Net Worth: £7,004,014 *Total Assets:* £11,253,666
Registered Office: The Havens, Ransomes Europark, Ipswich, Suffolk, IP3 9SJ
Activities: Wholesale of wood, construction materials and sanitary equipment
Parent: KDM Timber Limited
Officers: Mark William Sampson Handley, Secretary; Neville James Greenwood [1957] Director/Timber Trader; Mark William Sampson Handley [1964] Director/Accountant; Stephen Frederick Henry [1956] Director/Timber Trader; Giles Lankester [1977] Operations Director; James Robert Menzies [1973] Director/Timber Trader; Andrew David Walshe [1969] Director/Chairman; Ivan Graham Walshe [1971] Sales Director

KDM Timber Limited
Incorporated: 2 October 2012 *Employees:* 33
Net Worth: £7,105,647 *Total Assets:* £11,752,581
Registered Office: 18 The Havens, Ransomes Europark, Ipswich, Suffolk, IP3 9SJ
Activities: Other business support service activities n.e.c.
Major Shareholder: Andrew David Walshe
Officers: Mark William Sampson Handley, Secretary; Neville James Greenwood [1957] Director/Timber Trader; Stephen Frederick Henry [1956] Director/Timber Trader; Andrew David Walshe [1969] Director; Ivan Graham Walshe [1971] Director/Timber Trader

Kebbell Development Limited
Incorporated: 27 July 1959 *Employees:* 52
Net Worth: £52,042,776 *Total Assets:* £70,591,016
Registered Office: Kebbell House, 21 London End, Beaconsfield, Bucks, HP9 2HN
Activities: Construction of domestic buildings
Officers: Simon Jennaway, Secretary; Richard William Barrett [1959] Finance Director; Fiona Shan Alexandra Binney [1959] Director; Andrea Fawell [1965] Sales Director; Nicolas Rowland MacDonald Kebbell [1951] Managing Director; Dudley John Mills [1965] Director/Land Buyer; Michael Mulligan [1962] Director/Building Manager; Denise Hilary Ann Newport [1954] Director

Kebbell Holdings Limited
Incorporated: 15 March 1963 *Employees:* 52
Net Worth: £53,548,984 *Total Assets:* £71,795,368
Registered Office: Kebbell House, 21 London End, Beaconsfield, Bucks, HP9 2HN
Activities: Other letting and operating of own or leased real estate
Officers: Simon Jennaway, Secretary; Meryl Audrey Kebbell [1924] Director; Nicolas Rowland MacDonald Kebbell [1951] Managing Director

Keech Hospice Care
Incorporated: 3 March 1994 *Employees:* 286
Net Worth: £12,384,000 *Total Assets:* £13,013,000
Registered Office: Keech Hospice Care, Great Bramingham Lane, Streatlley, Luton, Beds, LU3 3NT
Activities: Other human health activities
Officers: Peter Kevin Canon [1958] Director; Maria Margaret Collins [1954] Director; Frank James Dalton [1968] Director/Accountant; Miriam Stone Heyes [1980] Director; Michael Hubbocks [1942] Director/Retired; Clive Edward Medlam [1958] Director/Retired; Patricia Ann Norman [1960] Director; Bronwen May Philpott [1947] Director/HR Consultant; Karen Jane Proctor [1960] Director/Deputy Chief Operating Officer; Sukhdeep Saini [1973] Director/Solicitor

Keelings Fresh International Limited
Incorporated: 8 June 2006 *Employees:* 6
Net Worth: £5,508,752 *Total Assets:* £12,463,365
Registered Office: Sandringham House, Harlow Business Park, Sandringham Avenue, Harlow, Essex, CM19 5QS
Activities: Wholesale of fruit and vegetables
Parent: Keelings International Limited
Officers: Michael Kilduff, Secretary/Director [Irish]; Steven Fagg [1967] Managing Director; Caroline Keeling [1970] Director [Irish]; David Keeling [1973] Director [Irish]; Joseph Edmund Keeling [1944] Director [Irish]; William Keeling [1966] Director [Irish]; Michael Kilduff [1964] Finance Director [Irish]

Keelings UK Group Limited
Incorporated: 25 October 1971
Net Worth Deficit: £363,933 *Total Assets:* £10,465,914
Registered Office: Sandringham House, Harlow Business Park, Sandringham Avenue, Harlow, Essex, CM19 5QS
Activities: Activities of head offices
Parent: Keelings (UK Holdings) Unlimited
Officers: Michael Kilduff, Secretary/Accountant [Irish]; Caroline Keeling [1970] Director; David Keeling [1973] Director [Irish]; Joseph Edmund Keeling [1944] Director/Chairman [Irish]; William Keeling [1966] Managing Director [Irish]

Keen & Toms Holdings Limited
Incorporated: 21 August 2009 *Employees:* 487
Net Worth: £3,257,480 *Total Assets:* £19,667,552
Registered Office: c/o Hypnos Limited, Longwick Road, Princes Risborough, Bucks, HP27 9RT
Activities: Activities of head offices
Shareholder: Peter George Keen
Officers: Robert Lincoln Eastoe [1961] Director; James Peter George Keen [1975] Sales Director; Judith Keen [1944] Director; Peter George Keen [1944] Director/Furniture Manufacturer; Richard Keen [1980] Director; Sarah Keen [1973] Director

Keepstem Limited
Incorporated: 14 November 1997 *Employees:* 161
Net Worth: £3,629,446 *Total Assets:* £30,536,480
Registered Office: Wool Hall Farm, Cross Gate, Wykeham, Spalding, Lincs, PE12 6HW
Activities: Growing of vegetables and melons, roots and tubers
Shareholder: Robin Hancox
Officers: Aubrey Edward Day, Secretary/Chartered Management Accountant; Aubrey Edward Day [1958] Director/Chartered Management Accountant; Robin Hancox [1956] Director; Martin John Tate [1966] Director

Kefco Sales Limited
Incorporated: 23 February 1972 *Employees:* 628
Net Worth: £14,582,538 *Total Assets:* £18,256,392
Registered Office: First Floor, Kefco House, Rochford Business Park, Cherry Orchard Way, Rochford, Essex, SS4 1GP
Activities: Unlicenced restaurants and cafes
Shareholders: William Huw James; J & J Restaurants Limited
Officers: Andrew John Russell Hitch, Secretary; Andrew John Russell Hitch [1966] Director/Chartered Accountant; Jane Anne James [1956] Director; William Huw James [1957] Director; Philip Thomas Johnston [1977] Director; Claire Josephine Owen [1974] Director/Human Resources

Kelling Estate LLP
Incorporated: 10 November 2008 *Employees:* 50
Net Worth: £37,757,808 *Total Assets:* £38,293,188
Registered Office: The Kelling Estate Office, Kelling, Norfolk, NR25 7EW
Officers: Beverley Ann Widdowson [1960] Member; Gary Albert Widdowson [1958] Member

Kelly Comms Limited
Incorporated: 17 April 1998 *Employees:* 257
Net Worth: £2,518,773 *Total Assets:* £27,006,284
Registered Office: Kelly House, Fourth Way, Wembley, Middlesex, HA9 0LH
Activities: Other business support service activities n.e.c.
Parent: Kelly Communications Trading Group Limited
Officers: James Patrick Bradley, Secretary; Timothy Joseph Kelly [1954] Director [Irish]

Kelly Communications Enterprises Limited
Incorporated: 10 October 2012 *Employees:* 1
Net Worth: £1 *Total Assets:* £10,000,001
Registered Office: Kelly House, Fourth Way, Wembley, Middlesex, HA9 0LH
Activities: Non-trading company
Parent: Kelly Communications Group Limited
Officers: Timothy Joseph Kelly [1954] Director [Irish]

Kelly Communications Group Limited
Incorporated: 18 November 1996 *Employees:* 846
Net Worth: £32,972,540 *Total Assets:* £75,496,664
Registered Office: Kelly House, Fourth Way, Wembley, Middlesex, HA9 0LH
Activities: Other specialised construction activities n.e.c.
Major Shareholder: Timothy Kelly
Officers: James Patrick Bradley, Secretary; Timothy Patrick Kelly [2000] Director; Timothy Joseph Kelly [1954] Director [Irish]; Rosita Westropp-Bennett [1965] Finance Director [Irish]

Kelly Communications Limited
Incorporated: 9 June 1988 *Employees:* 364
Net Worth: £2,494,419 *Total Assets:* £38,074,008
Registered Office: Kelly House, Fourth Way, Wembley, Middlesex, HA9 0LH
Activities: Other construction installation
Parent: Kelly Communications Trading Group Limited
Officers: James Patrick Bradley, Secretary; Timothy Joseph Kelly [1954] Director [Irish]

Kelly Fleet Services Limited
Incorporated: 24 June 1996 *Employees:* 62
Net Worth: £1,898,484 *Total Assets:* £23,571,540
Registered Office: Kelly House, Fourth Way, Wembley, Middlesex, HA9 0LH
Activities: Other specialised construction activities n.e.c.
Parent: Kelly Communications Trading Group Limited
Officers: James Patrick Bradley, Secretary; Timothy Joseph Kelly [1954] Director [Irish]; Larry McGrane [1968] Director

Kelly Property Company Limited
Incorporated: 11 July 2003
Net Worth: £5,506,194 *Total Assets:* £27,588,656
Registered Office: Kelly House, Fourth Way, Wembley, Middlesex, HA9 0LH
Activities: Other letting and operating of own or leased real estate
Parent: Kelly Communications Group Limited
Officers: James Patrick Bradley, Secretary; Timothy Joseph Kelly [1954] Director [Irish]

Kelly Rail Group Ltd
Incorporated: 24 January 2011 *Employees:* 65
Previous: Kelly Integrated Ltd
Net Worth: £5,026,420 *Total Assets:* £13,264,636
Registered Office: Kelly House, Fourth Way, Wembley, Middlesex, HA9 0LH
Activities: Other specialised construction activities n.e.c.
Major Shareholder: Timothy Joseph Kelly
Officers: James Patrick Bradley, Secretary; Timothy Patrick Kelly [2000] Director; Timothy Joseph Kelly [1954] Director [Irish]; Rosita Westropp-Bennett [1965] Finance Director [Irish]

Kelly Rail U.K. Ltd
Incorporated: 8 April 2002 *Employees:* 65
Previous: Kelly Integrated Transport Services Ltd
Net Worth: £2,908,631 *Total Assets:* £13,083,854
Registered Office: Kelly House, Fourth Way, Wembley, Middlesex, HA9 0LH
Activities: Construction of commercial buildings
Parent: Kelly Rail UK Services Ltd
Officers: James Patrick Bradley, Secretary; Timothy Joseph Kelly [1954] Director [Irish]

Kelvin Hughes Limited
Incorporated: 8 November 1971 *Employees:* 168
Net Worth: £83,414,000 *Total Assets:* £98,847,000
Registered Office: Voltage, Mollison Avenue, Enfield, Middlesex, EN3 7XQ
Activities: Manufacture of other electrical equipment
Shareholders: KKR & Co Inc; KH Finance Limited
Officers: David John Millard, Secretary; Russell Charles Gould [1963] Director/Chief Executive; David John Millard [1970] Finance Director

Kendallco Limited
Incorporated: 14 August 2014 *Employees:* 5
Net Worth Deficit: £11,876,000 *Total Assets:* £79,369,000
Registered Office: Focus 31 West Wing, Cleveland Road, Hemel Hempstead Industrial Estate, Hemel Hempstead, Herts, HP2 7BW
Activities: Other sports activities
Parent: Kanyeco Limited
Officers: Stephen Burns [1976] Managing Director; Laurence Brian Keen [1976] Finance Director

Kendon Packaging Group Public Limited Company
Incorporated: 21 September 1933 *Employees:* 107
Net Worth: £23,068,222 *Total Assets:* £30,774,174
Registered Office: 7 Innova Way, Innova Park, Enfield, Middlesex, EN3 7FL
Activities: Packaging activities
Shareholders: Alistair John Kendon; Edwin Alexander Kendon
Officers: Alistair John Kendon, Secretary; Alistair John Kendon [1944] Executive Director; Edwin Alexander Kendon [1941] Executive Director; Frazer Alistair John Kendon [1977] Director; John Proctor [1966] Director

Kendric Ash Limited
Incorporated: 18 December 1998
Net Worth: £17,753,196 *Total Assets:* £17,753,196
Registered Office: Peoplebuilding, 2 Peoplebuilding Estate, Maylands Avenue, Hemel Hempstead, Herts, HP2 4NW
Activities: Management consultancy activities other than financial management
Parent: Northgate Public Services (UK) Limited
Officers: Stephen James Callaghan [1960] Director

Kenford Developments Limited
Incorporated: 14 September 1973
Net Worth Deficit: £5,417,746 *Total Assets:* £15,424,357
Registered Office: 1 Nelson Street, Southend on Sea, Essex, SS1 1EG
Activities: Construction of other civil engineering projects n.e.c.
Shareholders: Brian Ernest Edward Burrett; Lorna Anne Sara Burrett
Officers: Janet Lord, Secretary; David Christian Wyatt [1951] Director/Sales Manager

Kenninghall Holdings Limited
Incorporated: 30 March 1998 *Employees:* 3
Net Worth: £65,161,948 *Total Assets:* £75,251,056
Registered Office: The Kelling Estate Office, Kelling, Norfolk, NR25 7EW
Activities: Renting and operating of Housing Association real estate
Shareholders: GWFS Group Limited; Kenninghall Group Limited
Officers: Beverley Ann Widdowson, Secretary; Duncan Alexander Ross [1967] Director; Beverley Ann Widdowson [1960] Director; Gary Albert Widdowson [1958] Managing Director

G.B. Kent & Sons PLC
Incorporated: 2 July 1900 *Employees:* 45
Net Worth: £5,568,743 *Total Assets:* £8,718,532
Registered Office: London Road, Apsley, Hemel Hempstead, Herts, HP3 9SS
Activities: Manufacture of brooms and brushes
Major Shareholder: Alan Hugo Lambert Cosby
Officers: Alan Hugo Lambert Cosby [1948] Managing Director; Benjamin Giles Hugo Cosby [1975] Director; Marcia Rose Cosby [1950] PR Director

Kent Blaxill Group Limited
Incorporated: 6 May 2014 *Employees:* 244
Net Worth: £12,026,394 *Total Assets:* £19,149,880
Registered Office: 129-139 Layer Road, Colchester, Essex, CO2 9JY
Activities: Retail sale of hardware, paints and glass in specialised stores
Shareholder: Simon Christopher Blaxill
Officers: Kevin Geoffrey Pryke, Secretary; John Terry Barnes [1959] Director; Anthony John Blaxill [1927] Director; Hugh Robert Blaxill [1969] Director/Engineer; Simon Christopher Blaxill [1961] Director; Elizabeth Ann Cash [1959] Director; Philip William George [1951] Director; Benjamin Richard Kent [1967] Director/Market Researcher; Kevin Geoffrey Pryke [1981] Finance Director

Kent Leisure Parks Limited
Incorporated: 1 March 2005 *Employees:* 15
Previous: Two Chimneys Limited
Net Worth: £3,711,420 *Total Assets:* £8,439,404
Registered Office: Prospero House, 46-48 Rothesay Road, Luton, Beds, LU1 1QZ
Activities: Other business support service activities n.e.c.
Shareholders: Linda Dorothy Sullivan; Michael Andrew Godden; Andrew Martin Godden
Officers: Linda Dorothy Sullivan, Secretary/Director; Andrew Martin Godden [1962] Director; Michael Andrew Godden [1951] Director; Linda Dorothy Sullivan [1949] Director

The Kent, Surrey and Sussex Community Rehabilitation Company Limited
Incorporated: 4 December 2013 *Employees:* 442
Net Worth: £1,975,000 *Total Assets:* £21,794,000
Registered Office: 75-77 Main Road, Hockley, Essex, SS5 4RG
Activities: Justice and judicial activities
Parent: Seetec Business Technology Centres Ltd
Officers: John Baumback, Secretary; Lesley Barry [1958] Director/Accountant; John Baumback [1968] Director/Senior Manager Welfare and Justice; Alison Jane Bunney [1978] Ireland and Group Business Development Director

Kent,Blaxill & Co,Limited
Incorporated: 22 February 1905 *Employees:* 226
Net Worth: £9,694,764 *Total Assets:* £15,106,639
Registered Office: 129-139 Layer Road, Colchester, Essex, CO2 9JY
Activities: Agents involved in the sale of timber and building materials
Parent: Kent Blaxill Group Ltd
Officers: Kevin Geoffrey Pryke, Secretary; John Terry Barnes [1959] Director/Chartered Accountant; Anthony John Blaxill [1927] Director; Hugh Robert Blaxill [1969] Director/Engineer; Simon Christopher Blaxill [1961] Director; Elizabeth Ann Cash [1959] Director; Philip William George [1951] Director; Benjamin Richard Kent [1967] Director/Market Researcher; Kevin Geoffrey Pryke [1981] Finance Director

Kenwake Limited
Incorporated: 17 January 1980
Net Worth: £17,294,028 *Total Assets:* £69,879,800
Registered Office: OOCL House, Levington Park, Bridge Road, Levington, Suffolk, IP10 0NE
Activities: Other transportation support activities
Parent: China Cosco Shipping Corporation Limited
Officers: Mark Richard Banham [1966] Director/Accountant; Chee Fun Lee [1961] Director/Group Legal Advisor [Malaysian]; Derek Stuart O'Galligan [1966] Director [Irish]

Kenwyn Solar Limited
Incorporated: 16 August 2013
Net Worth: £275,000 *Total Assets:* £8,403,000
Registered Office: Beaufort Court, Egg Farm Lane, Kings Langley, Herts, WD4 8LR
Activities: Production of electricity
Parent: European Investments Solar Holdings 2 Limited
Officers: Dominic James Hearth, Secretary; Steven William Hughes [1972] Global Support Services Director, UK&I - Commercial; Mitesh Raj Patel [1982] Director/Group Financial Controller; Tracy Jane Scott [1976] Director/Delivery Project Manager - New Technologies UK&I; Mark Christopher Wayment [1958] Director

Kerneos Holding Northern Europe Limited
Incorporated: 16 October 2007
Net Worth: £51,310,000 *Total Assets:* £90,405,000
Registered Office: Kerneos Ltd, Dolphin Way, Purfleet, Essex, RM19 1NZ
Activities: Non-trading company
Parent: Kerneos SA
Officers: Ian William Adamson, Secretary; Philippe Guy Pascal Bourg [1967] Director/Senior Vice President [French]

Wm.Kerr (Farms) Limited
Incorporated: 21 June 1954 *Employees:* 25
Net Worth: £2,258,113 *Total Assets:* £9,395,973
Registered Office: Farm Office, Abbey Farm Hoo, Woodbridge, Suffolk, IP13 7QY
Activities: Mixed farming
Major Shareholder: John Kerr
Officers: Bruce William Kerr [1970] Director/Farmer; Fiona Elizabeth Siddall [1971] Director/Events Management

Kershaw Group Limited
Incorporated: 23 September 2003 *Employees:* 201
Net Worth: £4,327,293 *Total Assets:* £17,925,080
Registered Office: Edward Leonard House, Pembroke Avenue, Waterbeach, Cambridge, CB25 9QR
Activities: Activities of head offices
Parent: Kershaw Group Holdings Limited
Officers: Kathleen Elizabeth Smith, Secretary; Andrew Colin Edward Crouch [1977] Finance Director; Geoffrey Paul Davies [1959] Director; Ian Michael Greenstock [1961] Director; Gary David Smith [1963] Director; Kathleen Elizabeth Smith [1970] HR Director [American]

Kesgrave High School
Incorporated: 24 June 2011 *Employees:* 206
Net Worth: £15,295,937 *Total Assets:* £17,379,164
Registered Office: Kesgrave High School, Main Road, Kesgrave, Ipswich, Suffolk, IP5 2PB
Activities: General secondary education
Officers: Julie Elizabeth Garnett, Secretary; Mrs Kelly Abbott [1976] Director/Teacher; Mark Bearn [1970] Director/Businessman; Catherine Beresford [1968] Director/Electrical Engineer; David John Bevan [1949] Director/Retired; Eunice Barbara Emma Brain [1973] Director/Administration; Nigel Paul Burgoyne [1959] Director/Headteacher; Rosalind Coe [1963] Director; Tom Corker [1981] Director/Teacher; Julia Dessaur [1961] Director; Jennifer Ellis [1968] Director/Administrator; Faye Hubbard [1979] Director/Teacher; Lauren Hunwicks [1988] Director/Teacher; Darren Johnson [1968] Director; Jason Logan [1969] Director/IT Consultant; Dr Margaret Rowe [1965] Director/Administration; Stephen Russell Shaw [1973] Director; Melanie Warnes [1962] Director; Susan White [1969] Director

Kestates Limited
Incorporated: 5 November 2015
Net Worth Deficit: £1,129,770 *Total Assets:* £11,154,944
Registered Office: Portland House, 69-71 Wembley Hill Road, Wembley, Middlesex, HA9 8BU
Activities: Other letting and operating of own or leased real estate
Parent: Solai Holdings Limited
Officers: Bhupendra Shantilal Kansagra, Secretary; Bhupendra Shantilal Kansagra [1956] Director; Ramesh Shantilal Kansagra [1950] Director

Kestrel Acquisitions Limited
Incorporated: 25 February 2004
Net Worth Deficit: £395,175,008 *Total Assets:* £75,718,000
Registered Office: Arcadia House, Warley Hill Business Park, The Drive, Great Warley, Brentwood, Essex, CM13 3BE
Activities: Activities of financial services holding companies
Parent: Kestrel Holdings Limited
Officers: Stephen Francis McConnell, Secretary; Amanda Brooks [1965] Director; Andrew Robert Punch [1960] Director

Kestrel Holdings Limited
Incorporated: 25 February 2004 *Employees:* 91
Net Worth Deficit: £339,791,008 *Total Assets:* £182,340,992
Registered Office: Arcadia House, Warley Hill Business Park, The Drive, Great Warley, Brentwood, Essex, CM13 3BE
Activities: Activities of financial services holding companies
Parent: Alchemy Partners LLP
Officers: Stephen Francis McConnell, Secretary; Stephen Graham Bodger [1949] Director/Chartered Accountant; Amanda Brooks [1965] Director; Andrew Robert Punch [1960] Director

Kestrel Loans No. 4 Limited
Incorporated: 2 July 2013
Net Worth: £66,068,000 *Total Assets:* £184,448,000
Registered Office: Arcadia House, Warley Hill Business Park, The Drive, Great Warley, Brentwood, Essex, CM13 3BE
Activities: Financial intermediation not elsewhere classified
Parent: Kestrel No.4 Limited
Officers: Stephen McConnell, Secretary; Amanda Brooks [1965] Director; Andrew Robert Punch [1960] Director

The Keswick Enterprises Group Limited
Incorporated: 23 June 2004 *Employees:* 168
Net Worth: £6,239,616 *Total Assets:* £13,552,875
Registered Office: 19-20 Bourne Court, Southend Road, Woodford Green, Essex, IG8 8HD
Activities: Management consultancy activities other than financial management
Major Shareholder: John Harvey
Officers: Geoffrey Michael Gillo, Secretary/Executive; Geoffrey Michael Gillo [1952] Director/Executive; John Anthony Harvey [1935] Director/Consultant; Michael Wallis [1958] Director; Gavin David Withers [1965] Director/Consultant

Keswick European Holdings Limited
Incorporated: 10 October 2013
Net Worth: £9,794,534 *Total Assets:* £9,794,534
Registered Office: 19-20 Bourne Court, Southend Road, Woodford Green, Essex, IG8 8HD
Activities: Activities of other holding companies n.e.c.
Shareholders: Yusen Logistics Co., Ltd.; Nippon Yusen Kabushiki Kaisha
Officers: Kenichiro Miyamoto [1968] Director [Japanese]; Willem Emiel Pauwels [1955] Director [Belgian]

Kettle Foods Ltd.
Incorporated: 31 March 1988 *Employees:* 477
Net Worth: £40,997,000 *Total Assets:* £73,952,000
Registered Office: 38 Barnard Road, Bowthorpe Employment Area, Norwich, NR5 9JP
Activities: Manufacture of other food products n.e.c.
Parent: DFKA UK Holdings Limited
Officers: Katherine Susan Atkinson, Secretary; Carlos Arturo Abrams-Rivera [1967] Director [American]; Ashley James Hicks [1974] Managing Director; Thomas Smith [1955] Director [American]

Key Developments (Godalming) LLP
Incorporated: 18 March 2013 *Employees:* 2
Net Worth: £18,101,918 *Total Assets:* £19,195,320
Registered Office: Spirella, 2 Icknield Way, Letchworth Garden City, Herts, SG6 4GY

Keymed (Medical & Industrial Equipment) Limited
Incorporated: 21 November 1969 *Employees:* 985
Net Worth: £142,316,992 *Total Assets:* £279,856,992
Registered Office: Keymed House, Stock Road, Southend on Sea, Essex, SS2 5QH
Activities: Manufacture of electronic measuring, testing etc. equipment, not for industrial process control
Parent: Olympus Keymed Group Limited
Officers: John Enmin Rowe, Secretary; Stefan Kaufmann [1968] Director [German]; John Enmin Rowe [1962] Director; Carl Andrew Yallop [1967] Director; Constantin Zangemeister [1971] Managing Director [German]

Keystone 1 Limited
Incorporated: 3 September 2015
Net Worth: £1,667,498 *Total Assets:* £10,738,972
Registered Office: Building 6002, Taylors End, Stansted Airport, Stansted, Essex, CM24 1RL
Activities: Other business support service activities n.e.c.
Parent: Keystone Leasing (UK) Limited
Officers: Stephen William Spencer Norton [1959] Finance Director; Nita Ramesh Savjani [1980] Director

Keystone 2 Limited
Incorporated: 3 September 2015
Net Worth: £3,014,663 *Total Assets:* £19,282,810
Registered Office: Building 6002, Taylors End, Stansted Airport, Stansted, Essex, CM24 1RL
Activities: Other business support service activities n.e.c.
Parent: Keystone Leasing (UK) Limited
Officers: Stephen William Spencer Norton [1959] Finance Director; Nita Ramesh Savjani [1980] Director

Keystone Developments (LG) Limited
Incorporated: 11 September 2001
Net Worth: £2,725,000 *Total Assets:* £20,349,000
Registered Office: Leverett House, Gilbert Drive, Endeavour Park, Boston, Lincs, PE21 7TQ
Activities: Construction of domestic buildings
Officers: Robert Ian Griffiths, Secretary; Patricia Elizabeth Brandum [1955] Director/Consultant; Robert Ian Griffiths [1976] Finance Director; William Alan James Patman [1956] Director/Retired; Robert Gerrard Wilson [1950] Director/Retired

KFG Quickserve Limited
Incorporated: 6 July 2005 *Employees:* 832
Net Worth: £1,635,000 *Total Assets:* £11,356,000
Registered Office: 100-102 High Street, Ruislip, Middlesex, HA4 8LS
Activities: Other retail sale of food in specialised stores
Officers: Abdul-Mohsen Mohsen Al Homaizi [1967] Director [Kuwaiti]; Madam Fadwa Al Homaizi [1957] Director [Kuwaiti]

KFG Restaurants Limited
Incorporated: 3 September 2007 *Employees:* 21
Net Worth Deficit: £3,303,000 *Total Assets:* £9,961,000
Registered Office: 100-102 High Street, Ruislip, Middlesex, HA4 8LS
Activities: Licenced restaurants
Officers: Madam Fadwa Al Homaizi [1957] Director [Kuwaiti]

KFM Holdings Limited
Incorporated: 8 January 2008
Previous: Timbmet Holdings Limited
Net Worth: £8,681,114 *Total Assets:* £10,487,314
Registered Office: Suite 1, Leavesden Park, Hercules Way, Leavesden, Watford, Herts, WD25 7GS
Activities: Wholesale of wood, construction materials and sanitary equipment
Shareholders: Simon Lewis Fineman; Evelyn Frances Kemp; Ashwani Malham
Officers: Simon Lewis Fineman [1959] Operations Director; Dr Evelyn Frances Kemp [1961] Director; Ashwani Malhan [1968] Director; Sunit Malhan [1962] Director

KGM Underwriting Services Limited
Incorporated: 24 January 2017
Net Worth Deficit: £914,559 *Total Assets:* £29,555,680
Registered Office: 2nd Floor, St James House, 27-43 Eastern Road, Romford, Essex, RM1 3NH
Activities: Activities of insurance agents and brokers
Parent: Trafalgar Bidco Limited
Officers: Andrew Galbraith, Secretary; James Maxwell Carruthers [1954] Director; Andrew James Galbraith [1970] Director; Clive Adam Nathan [1965] Director; Matthew James Puttick [1979] Director; Carl Anthony Shuker [1961] Director

KH Finance Limited
Incorporated: 5 October 2007
Net Worth Deficit: £45,944,000 *Total Assets:* £52,648,000
Registered Office: Voltage, Mollison Avenue, Enfield, Middlesex, EN3 7XQ
Activities: Activities of head offices
Shareholders: KKR & Co Inc; KH Finance No.2 Limited
Officers: David John Millard, Secretary; Russell Charles Gould [1963] Director/Chief Executive; David John Millard [1970] Finance Director

KH Finance No.2 Limited
Incorporated: 18 July 2013
Net Worth: £17,962,000 *Total Assets:* £25,071,000
Registered Office: Voltage, Mollison Avenue, Enfield, Middlesex, EN3 7XQ
Activities: Activities of head offices
Shareholders: KKR & Co Inc; KH Holdco Limited
Officers: David John Millard, Secretary; Russell Charles Gould [1963] Director/Chief Executive; David John Millard [1970] Finance Director

KH Holdco Limited
Incorporated: 5 October 2007
Net Worth: £43,257,000 *Total Assets:* £50,366,000
Registered Office: Voltage, Mollison Avenue, Enfield, Middlesex, EN3 7XQ
Activities: Activities of head offices
Officers: David John Millard, Secretary; Russell Charles Gould [1963] Director/Chief Executive; David John Millard [1970] Finance Director; Erwin Manfred Paulus [1961] Director/Head of Radar [German]; Joerg Sigurd Ristow [1957] Director [German]; Christoph Erich Ruffner [1977] Director [German]

Kidde Products Limited
Incorporated: 19 December 2002 *Employees:* 47
Net Worth: £126,710,000 *Total Assets:* £166,066,000
Registered Office: Stokenchurch House, Oxford Road, Stokenchurch, Bucks, HP14 3SX
Activities: Other manufacturing n.e.c.
Parent: Kidde UK
Officers: Craig Alexander Forbes [1963] Finance Director; Vaclav Malimanek [1970] Finance Director [Czech]; John Simpson [1963] Director/General Manager

Kidney Research UK
Incorporated: 12 May 1967 *Employees:* 54
Net Worth: £10,105,000 *Total Assets:* £26,428,000
Registered Office: Nene Hall, Lynch Wood Park, Peterborough, Cambs, PE2 6FZ
Activities: Other human health activities
Officers: Anne Marie McCarthy, Secretary; Adrian Christopher Akers [1952] Director/Retired; Professor Sunil Bhandari [1966] Director/NHS Medical Consultant; Doctor David Hughes [1956] Director/Consultant Paediatric Nephrologist; Professor Jeremy Hughes [1961] Director/Doctor; Dr Deirdre Ellen Jennings [1969] Director [Irish]; Brian Thomas Kelly [1979] Director/Financial Services; Professor Elizabeth Beatrice Lightstone [1959] Director/Medical Practitioner; Julia Dorothy Moross [1962] Director; Dr Jill Tessa Norman [1955] Director/University Faculty; Iain Charles Pearson [1954] Director/Retired; Federica Pizzasegola [1978] Director/Financial Services [Italian]; David Prosser [1959] Director/Retired; Dr Adnan Sharif [1979] Director/Doctor; Dr Charles Richard Vernon Tomson [1956] Director/Doctor

Kier (Newcastle) Investment Ltd
Incorporated: 31 January 2016
Net Worth: £1 *Total Assets:* £12,602,751
Registered Office: Tempsford Hall, Sandy, Beds, SG19 2BD
Activities: Activities of financial services holding companies
Parent: Kier Project Investment Limited
Officers: Bethan Melges, Secretary; Mark Bladon [1972] Director/Banker; Thomas George Gilman [1970] Director; Shivani Goolab [1988] Director/Chartered Accountant [South African]; Lee Howard [1981] Associate Director; Mark Ian Robinson [1976] Director; Hayley Scott [1981] Director/Banker

Kier (NR) Limited
Incorporated: 16 July 2008
Net Worth: £2,663,000 *Total Assets:* £30,405,000
Registered Office: Tempsford Hall, Sandy, Beds, SG19 2BD
Activities: Construction of railways and underground railways
Parent: Kier Commercial Investments Limited
Officers: Bethan Melges, Secretary; Thomas George Gilman [1970] Director; Lee Howard [1981] Director; Andrew Nicholas Cenwulf Storey [1957] Director; Leigh Parry Thomas [1971] Business Space Development Director

Kier Business Services Limited
Incorporated: 7 December 1998 *Employees:* 723
Previous: Mouchel Business Services Limited
Net Worth: £16,676,000 *Total Assets:* £45,610,000
Registered Office: Tempsford Hall, Sandy, Beds, SG19 2BD
Activities: Management consultancy activities other than financial management
Parent: Kier Holdings Limited
Officers: Bethan Melges, Secretary; Lee Howard [1981] Director; Ian Charles Meredith [1963] Director; Leigh Parry Thomas [1971] Director

Kier Commercial Investments Limited
Incorporated: 26 May 2000
Net Worth Deficit: £2,789,000 *Total Assets:* £42,511,000
Registered Office: Tempsford Hall, Sandy, Beds, SG19 2BD
Activities: Development of building projects
Parent: Kier Property Limited
Officers: Bethan Melges, Secretary; Lee Howard [1981] Director; Leigh Parry Thomas [1971] Business Space Development Director

Kier Construction Limited
Incorporated: 12 February 1987 *Employees:* 2,629
Net Worth: £130,322,000 *Total Assets:* £849,164,032
Registered Office: Tempsford Hall, Sandy, Beds, SG19 2BD
Activities: Construction of commercial buildings
Parent: Kier Limited
Officers: Bethan Melges, Secretary; Graham Charles Garvie [1960] Director; David Bernard Hodson [1956] Director/Certified Accountant; Marcus Faughey Jones [1970] Finance Director; Peter Ronald Young [1967] Director

Kier Cross Keys Dev LLP
Incorporated: 19 January 2017
Net Worth: £58,008,000 *Total Assets:* £165,480,000
Registered Office: Tempsford Hall, Sandy, Beds, SG19 2BD

Kier Cross Keys Holdco 1 LLP
Incorporated: 18 January 2017
Net Worth: £57,818,000 *Total Assets:* £57,818,000
Registered Office: Tempsford Hall, Sandy, Beds, SG19 2BD

Kier Developments Limited
Incorporated: 2 April 2002
Net Worth: £104,167,000 *Total Assets:* £124,506,000
Registered Office: Tempsford Hall, Sandy, Beds, SG19 2BD
Activities: Construction of commercial buildings
Parent: Kier Property Limited
Officers: Bethan Melges, Secretary; Thomas George Gilman [1970] Director; Lee Howard [1981] Director; Andrew Nicholas Cenwulf Storey [1957] Director; Leigh Parry Thomas [1971] Business Space Director

Kier Dormant Holdings Limited
Incorporated: 21 January 2000
Previous: Mouchel Dormant Holdings Limited
Net Worth Deficit: £11,825,000 *Total Assets:* £30,826,000
Registered Office: Tempsford Hall, Sandy, Beds, SG19 2BD
Activities: Activities of other holding companies n.e.c.
Parent: MRBL Limited
Officers: Bethan Melges, Secretary; Lee Howard [1981] Director

Kier Facilities Services Limited
Incorporated: 28 June 1991 *Employees:* 1,758
Net Worth: £4,250,000 *Total Assets:* £78,801,000
Registered Office: Tempsford Hall, Sandy, Beds, SG19 2BD
Activities: Combined facilities support activities
Parent: Kier Services Limited
Officers: Bethan Melges, Secretary; Iain Richard Bray [1965] Commercial Director; Marcus Faughey Jones [1970] Finance Director; David Mawson [1961] Regional Managing Director; Clive Thomas [1966] Director/Accountant

Kier Finance & Treasury Holdings Limited
Incorporated: 26 July 2006
Previous: Mouchel Finance & Treasury Holdings Limited
Net Worth: £32,750,000 *Total Assets:* £56,800,000
Registered Office: Tempsford Hall, Sandy, Beds, SG19 2BD
Activities: Activities of other holding companies n.e.c.
Parent: MRBL Limited
Officers: Bethan Melges, Secretary; Mark Stephen Dale [1972] Director

Kier Finance Limited
Incorporated: 26 July 2006
Previous: Mouchel Finance Limited
Net Worth: £54,850,000 *Total Assets:* £193,208,992
Registered Office: Tempsford Hall, Sandy, Beds, SG19 2BD
Activities: Other business support service activities n.e.c.
Parent: Kier Finance & Treasury Holdings Limited
Officers: Bethan Melges, Secretary; Mark Stephen Dale [1972] Director

Kier Fleet Services Limited
Incorporated: 30 April 1987 *Employees:* 37
Net Worth: £35,397,000 *Total Assets:* £65,921,000
Registered Office: Tempsford Hall, Sandy, Beds, SG19 2BD
Activities: Other business support service activities n.e.c.
Parent: Kier Plant Limited
Officers: Bethan Melges, Secretary; Adrian Paul Jones [1972] Director; Anthony Cornelius Donald Parish [1967] Director

Kier Foley Street Holdco 1 LLP
Incorporated: 24 July 2015
Net Worth: £25,034,000 *Total Assets:* £25,034,000
Registered Office: Tempsford Hall, Station Road, Sandy, Beds, SG19 2BD

Kier Group PLC
Incorporated: 21 April 1992 *Employees:* 20,064
Net Worth: £599,400,000 *Total Assets:* £2,809,400,064
Registered Office: Tempsford Hall, Sandy, Beds, SG19 2BD
Activities: Activities of head offices
Officers: Hugh Edward Earle Raven, Secretary; Justin Richard Atkinson [1960] Director; Constance Frederique Baroudel [1974] Director [French]; Ann Kirsty Bashforth [1970] Director/Head of Organisational Effectiveness; Philip Gotsall Cox [1951] Director; Beverley Edward John Dew [1971] Finance Director; Claudio Veritiero [1973] Director; Adam Christopher Walker [1967] Director

Kier Hammersmith Holdco Limited
Incorporated: 19 June 2014
Net Worth: £13,200,000 *Total Assets:* £13,200,000
Registered Office: Tempsford Hall, Sandy, Beds, SG19 2BD
Activities: Buying and selling of own real estate
Shareholders: Kier Property Developments Limited; Investec Bank PLC
Officers: Lee Howard [1981] Director; Leigh Parry Thomas [1971] Director

Kier Hammersmith Limited
Incorporated: 21 November 2013
Net Worth: £18,020,000 *Total Assets:* £42,532,000
Registered Office: Tempsford Hall, Sandy, Beds, SG19 2BD
Activities: Development of building projects
Parent: Kier Hammersmith Holdco Limited
Officers: Ian Chapman, Secretary; Lee Howard [1981] Director; Leigh Parry Thomas [1971] Director

Kier Highways Limited
Incorporated: 28 October 2005 *Employees:* 2,017
Previous: EM Highway Services Limited
Net Worth: £62,628,000 *Total Assets:* £192,764,992
Registered Office: Tempsford Hall, Sandy, Beds, SG19 2BD
Activities: Construction of roads and motorways
Parent: Kier Limited
Officers: Bethan Melges, Secretary; Giuseppe Incutti [1970] Finance Director; Keith Charles Jackson [1953] Director/Civil Engineer; David James Wright [1959] Managing Director

Kier Holdings Limited
Incorporated: 26 July 2006
Previous: Mouchel Holdings Limited
Net Worth: £94,868,000 *Total Assets:* £365,131,008
Registered Office: Temspford Hall, Sandy, Beds, SG19 2BD
Activities: Activities of head offices
Parent: Kier Finance Limited
Officers: Bethan Melges, Secretary; Lee Howard [1981] Director; Leigh Parry Thomas [1971] Director

Kier Homes Caledonia Limited
Incorporated: 11 April 1988
Net Worth Deficit: £42,074,000 *Total Assets:* £41,733,000
Registered Office: Tempsford Hall, Sandy, Beds, SG19 2BD
Activities: Construction of domestic buildings
Parent: Kier Living Limited
Officers: Bethan Melges, Secretary; John Bruce Anderson [1963] Managing Director; Daniel Harry Rate Browne [1972] Land Director; Sarah Jayne Cooper [1973] Finance Director; Nicholas Charles Moore [1968] Commercial Director; Trevor David Thomas [1966] Sales & Marketing Director

Kier Infrastructure and Overseas Limited
Incorporated: 16 January 1974 *Employees:* 989
Net Worth: £10,793,000 *Total Assets:* £190,048,000
Registered Office: Tempsford Hall, Sandy, Beds, SG19 2BD
Activities: Construction of other civil engineering projects n.e.c.
Parent: Kier National Limited
Officers: Bethan Melges, Secretary; Peter Thomas Bimson [1955] Operations Director; Sean David Fenner [1973] Director; Anita Suzanne Harris [1975] Finance Director; Adrian Paul Jones [1972] Director; Mark Russell Pengelly [1964] Director; Nigel Robert Quelch [1962] Commercial Director; Philip Charles Anthony Suter [1984] Director

Kier Integrated Services (Estates) Limited
Incorporated: 7 October 1926
Previous: Kier MG Estates Limited
Net Worth: £12,171,000 *Total Assets:* £13,142,000
Registered Office: Tempsford Hall, Sandy, Beds, SG19 2BD
Activities: Other letting and operating of own or leased real estate
Parent: Kier Integrated Services Group Limited
Officers: Bethan Melges, Secretary; Lee Howard [1981] Director; Marcus Faughey Jones [1970] Finance Director

Kier Integrated Services (Holdings) Limited
Incorporated: 13 November 2001
Previous: Kier MGIS Limited
Net Worth: £14,219,000 *Total Assets:* £24,048,000
Registered Office: Tempsford Hall, Sandy, Beds, SG19 2BD
Activities: Activities of construction holding companies
Parent: Kier Limited
Officers: Bethan Melges, Secretary; Marcus Faughey Jones [1970] Finance Director; David James Wright [1959] Managing Director

Kier Integrated Services Group Limited
Incorporated: 14 April 1989
Previous: Kier MG Group Limited
Net Worth: £7,433,000 *Total Assets:* £16,377,000
Registered Office: Tempsford Hall, Sandy, Beds, SG19 2BD
Activities: Activities of construction holding companies
Parent: Kier Integrated Services (Holdings) Limited
Officers: Bethan Melges, Secretary; Marcus Faughey Jones [1970] Finance Director; David James Wright [1959] Managing Director

Kier Integrated Services Limited
Incorporated: 7 March 1966 *Employees:* 2,759
Previous: Kier MG Limited
Net Worth: £3,894,000 *Total Assets:* £303,859,008
Registered Office: Tempsford Hall, Sandy, Beds, SG19 2BD
Activities: Collection of non-hazardous waste
Parent: Kier Integrated Services Group Limited
Officers: Bethan Melges, Secretary; Marcus Faughey Jones [1970] Finance Director; Barry Stuart McNicholas [1962] Director; Nigel Robert Quelch [1962] Commercial Director; Lee Woodall [1976] Director; David James Wright [1959] Director

Kier International Limited
Incorporated: 26 June 1964 *Employees:* 43
Net Worth Deficit: £173,167,008 *Total Assets:* £130,469,000
Registered Office: Tempsford Hall, Sandy, Beds, SG19 2BD
Activities: Construction of other civil engineering projects n.e.c.
Parent: Kier Infrastructure and Overseas Limited
Officers: Bethan Melges, Secretary; Anita Suzanne Harris [1975] Finance Director; Marcus Faughey Jones [1970] Finance Director

Kier Limited
Incorporated: 3 February 1982 *Employees:* 876
Net Worth: £233,700,000 *Total Assets:* £3,475,500,032
Registered Office: Tempsford Hall, Sandy, Beds, SG19 2BD
Activities: Activities of head offices
Parent: Kier Group PLC
Officers: Hugh Edward Earle Raven, Secretary; Beverley Edward John Dew [1971] Director; Claudio Veritiero [1973] Director

Kier Living Limited
Incorporated: 30 September 1963 *Employees:* 408
Net Worth: £71,061,000 *Total Assets:* £443,208,000
Registered Office: Tempsford Hall, Sandy, Beds, SG19 2BD
Activities: Construction of domestic buildings
Parent: Kier Group PLC
Officers: Bethan Melges, Secretary; John Bruce Anderson [1963] Managing Director; Martin Robert Bessant [1974] Director; Sarah Jayne Cooper [1973] Finance Director; Nicholas Charles Moore [1968] Commercial Director; Susan Warwick [1968] Director

Kier Management Consulting Limited
Incorporated: 11 April 1990 *Employees:* 12
Previous: Mouchel Management Consulting Limited
Net Worth: £5,132,000 *Total Assets:* £9,504,000
Registered Office: Tempsford Hall, Sandy, Beds, SG19 2BD
Activities: Management consultancy activities other than financial management
Parent: Kier Holdings Limited
Officers: Bethan Melges, Secretary; Lee Howard [1981] Director; Ian Charles Meredith [1963] Director; Leigh Parry Thomas [1971] Director

Kier Minerals Limited
Incorporated: 12 February 1987 *Employees:* 83
Net Worth Deficit: £32,120,000 *Total Assets:* £15,247,000
Registered Office: Tempsford Hall, Sandy, Beds, SG19 2BD
Activities: Construction of other civil engineering projects n.e.c.
Parent: Kier Infrastructure and Overseas Limited
Officers: Bethan Melges, Secretary; Derek Mark Harrington [1962] Divisional Director; Mark Russell Pengelly [1964] Director; Philip Charles Anthony Suter [1984] Director

Kier National Limited
Incorporated: 16 February 1987
Net Worth Deficit: £2,312,000 *Total Assets:* £52,719,000
Registered Office: Tempsford Hall, Sandy, Beds, SG19 2BD
Activities: Activities of head offices
Parent: Kier Limited
Officers: Bethan Melges, Secretary; Adrian Paul Jones [1972] Director; Marcus Faughey Jones [1970] Finance Director; Nigel Robert Quelch [1962] Commercial Director

Kier North Tyneside Limited
Incorporated: 8 June 2009 *Employees:* 378
Net Worth: £3,260,000 *Total Assets:* £11,702,000
Registered Office: Tempsford Hall, Sandy, Beds, SG19 2BD
Activities: Combined facilities support activities
Parent: Kier Services Limited
Officers: Michael Richard Bailey, Secretary; Michael Ian Furze [1960] Regional Director; Paul John Leadbitter [1968] Director/Regional Commercial Manager; Matthew Edward Lockett [1969] Commercial Director; Mark Edward Longstaff [1964] Director; David Mawson [1961] Director; Philip Oades [1956] Director

Kier Overseas (Nine) Limited
Incorporated: 28 November 1980 *Employees:* 7
Net Worth Deficit: £6,204,821 *Total Assets:* £67,820,752
Registered Office: Tempsford Hall, Sandy, Beds, SG19 2BD
Activities: Construction of other civil engineering projects n.e.c.
Parent: Kier International Limited
Officers: Bethan Melges, Secretary; Anita Suzanne Harris [1975] Finance Director; Bethan Anne Elizabeth Melges [1975] Director/Chartered Secretary

Kier Overseas (Seventeen) Limited
Incorporated: 20 November 1979 *Employees:* 58
Net Worth Deficit: £33,409,750 *Total Assets:* £22,145,916
Registered Office: Tempsford Hall, Sandy, Beds, SG19 2BD
Activities: Construction of other civil engineering projects n.e.c.
Parent: Kier International Limited
Officers: Bethan Melges, Secretary; Anita Suzanne Harris [1975] Finance Director; Bethan Anne Elizabeth Melges [1975] Director/Chartered Secretary

Kier Overseas (Twenty-Three) Limited
Incorporated: 30 April 1987
Net Worth: £7,796,670 *Total Assets:* £9,036,413
Registered Office: Tempsford Hall, Sandy, Beds, SG19 2BD
Activities: Construction of commercial buildings
Parent: Kier International Limited
Officers: Bethan Melges, Secretary; Anita Suzanne Harris [1975] Finance Director; Bethan Anne Elizabeth Melges [1975] Director/Chartered Secretary

Kier Parkman Servigroup Limited
Incorporated: 28 November 2003
Previous: Mouchel Parkman Servigroup Limited
Net Worth: £31,398,000 *Total Assets:* £33,647,000
Registered Office: Tempsford Hall, Sandy, Beds, SG19 2BD
Activities: Non-trading company
Parent: Kier Dormant Holdings Limited
Officers: Bethan Melges, Secretary; Lee Howard [1981] Director

Kier Partnership Homes Limited
Incorporated: 28 June 2001 *Employees:* 87
Net Worth: £12,346,000 *Total Assets:* £72,971,000
Registered Office: Tempsford Hall, Sandy, Beds, SG19 2BD
Activities: Construction of domestic buildings
Parent: Kier Limited
Officers: Bethan Melges, Secretary; Amerjit Kaur Atwal [1971] Director; Martin Robert Bessant [1974] Director; Sarah Jayne Cooper [1973] Finance Director; Dean Murrell [1976] Director; Paul Kevin Smart [1978] Director

Kier Project Investment Limited
Incorporated: 30 April 1987 *Employees:* 19
Net Worth: £14,480,000 *Total Assets:* £42,445,000
Registered Office: Tempsford Hall, Sandy, Beds, SG19 2BD
Activities: Activities of head offices
Parent: Kier Limited
Officers: Bethan Melges, Secretary; Thomas George Gilman [1970] Director; Lee Howard [1981] Director; Andrew Nicholas Cenwulf Storey [1957] Director; Leigh Parry Thomas [1971] Business Space Development Director

Kier Property Developments Limited
Incorporated: 14 March 1966 *Employees:* 79
Net Worth: £93,210,000 *Total Assets:* £324,087,008
Registered Office: Tempsford Hall, Sandy, Beds, SG19 2BD
Activities: Development of building projects
Parent: Kier Developments Limited
Officers: Bethan Melges, Secretary; Thomas George Gilman [1970] Director; Lee Howard [1981] Director; Andrew Nicholas Cenwulf Storey [1957] Director; Leigh Parry Thomas [1971] Business Space Development Director

Kier Property Limited
Incorporated: 12 June 2002
Net Worth: £652,000 *Total Assets:* £79,416,000
Registered Office: Tempsford Hall, Sandy, Beds, SG19 2BD
Activities: Development of building projects
Parent: Kier Limited
Officers: Bethan Melges, Secretary; Thomas George Gilman [1970] Director; Lee Howard [1981] Director; Andrew Nicholas Cenwulf Storey [1957] Director; Leigh Parry Thomas [1971] Business Space Development Director

Kier Reading Holdco 1 LLP
Incorporated: 1 October 2014
Net Worth: £20,851,000 *Total Assets:* £20,851,000
Registered Office: Tempsford Hall, Station Road, Sandy, Beds, SG19 2BD

Kier Reading LLP
Incorporated: 1 October 2014
Net Worth: £20,852,000 *Total Assets:* £21,832,000
Registered Office: Tempsford Hall, Station Road, Sandy, Beds, SG19 2BD

Kier Services Limited
Incorporated: 7 October 1991 *Employees:* 3,990
Net Worth: £47,641,000 *Total Assets:* £253,762,000
Registered Office: Tempsford Hall, Sandy, Beds, SG19 2BD
Activities: Activities of head offices
Parent: Kier Limited
Officers: Bethan Melges, Secretary; Iain Richard Bray [1965] Commercial Director; Marcus Faughey Jones [1970] Finance Director; David Mawson [1961] Regional Managing Director; Lee Woodall [1976] Director

Kier Stoke Limited
Incorporated: 5 October 2007 *Employees:* 490
Net Worth: £6,468,000 *Total Assets:* £15,945,000
Registered Office: Tempsford Hall, Sandy, Beds, SG19 2BD
Activities: Combined facilities support activities
Parent: Kier Services Limited
Officers: Clive Thomas, Secretary; Matthew Edward Lockett [1969] Commercial Director; David Mawson [1961] Regional Managing Director; Philip Oades [1956] Director; Clive Thomas [1966] Director/Accountant

Kier Trade City Holdco 1 LLP
Incorporated: 11 June 2014
Net Worth: £13,659,000 *Total Assets:* £13,659,000
Registered Office: Tempsford Hall, Station Road, Sandy, Beds, SG19 2BD

Kier Trade City LLP
Incorporated: 11 June 2014
Net Worth: £13,661,000 *Total Assets:* £19,496,000
Registered Office: Tempsford Hall, Station Road, Sandy, Beds, SG19 2BD

Kier Ventures Limited
Incorporated: 26 November 1979
Net Worth: £10,267,000 *Total Assets:* £71,587,000
Registered Office: Tempsford Hall, Sandy, Beds, SG19 2BD
Activities: Development of building projects
Parent: Kier Property Limited
Officers: Bethan Melges, Secretary; Thomas George Gilman [1970] Director; Lee Howard [1981] Director; Andrew Nicholas Cenwulf Storey [1957] Director; Leigh Parry Thomas [1971] Business Space Development Director

Kigass Limited
Incorporated: 3 September 1924 *Employees:* 6
Net Worth: £17,751,934 *Total Assets:* £21,296,502
Registered Office: 72 London Road, St Albans, Herts, AL1 1NS
Activities: Development of building projects
Parent: Kigass Holdings Limited
Officers: Joanne Mary Wardman-Smith, Secretary; Peter Jeffrey Mark Platt [1956] Director; Joanne Mary Wardman-Smith [1970] Managing Director

Killiney UK Limited
Incorporated: 20 October 2005
Net Worth: £4,868,846 *Total Assets:* £9,155,209
Registered Office: Gable Cottage, Village Way, Little Chalfont, Amersham, Bucks, HP7 9PU
Activities: Buying and selling of own real estate
Shareholders: Cathryn Towlson; Hilary Murray
Officers: Neville John Askew, Secretary; Neville John Askew [1962] Director/Chartered Surveyor; Cathryn Towlson [1961] Director/Accountant [Irish]; David John Hough Williams [1964] Director/Solicitor

Kilmorie Investments LLP
Incorporated: 4 December 2006
Net Worth: £1,319,501 *Total Assets:* £8,648,531
Registered Office: 3rd Floor, Sterling House, Langston Road, Loughton, Essex, IG10 3TS

Kiln Park Estates Limited
Incorporated: 30 November 1959 *Employees:* 138
Net Worth: £3,939,000 *Total Assets:* £17,714,000
Registered Office: 1 Park Lane, Hemel Hempstead, Herts, HP2 4YL
Activities: Recreational vehicle parks, trailer parks and camping grounds
Parent: Bourne Leisure Group Limited
Officers: Jane Elizabeth Bentall [1970] Director/Accountant; Paul Charles Flaum [1970] Director; Iain Stuart Macmillan [1976] Director

Kimberley Capital Limited
Incorporated: 23 June 2017
Net Worth: £8,757 *Total Assets:* £9,447,750
Registered Office: Kimberley House, 31 Burnt Oak Broadway, Edgware, Middlesex, HA8 5LD
Activities: Other credit granting n.e.c.
Parent: Deekay Holdings (UK) Limited
Officers: Khimchand Hansraj Chandaria [1935] Director; Bhavik Patel [1984] Director; Neel Mahendra Shah [1974] Director

Kimberley Property Investments Limited
Incorporated: 4 December 2001 *Employees:* 2
Net Worth: £3,143,298 *Total Assets:* £8,743,523
Registered Office: Kimberley House, 31 Burnt Oak Broadway, Edgware, Middlesex, HA8 5LD
Activities: Other letting and operating of own or leased real estate
Officers: Bipin Shah, Secretary; Bipin Mohanlal Shah [1958] Director/Certified Chartered Accountant; Hiren Hasmukh Shah [1979] Director/Accountant

Kimbolton School
Incorporated: 8 April 2003 *Employees:* 300
Net Worth: £38,528,408 *Total Assets:* £45,850,828
Registered Office: Kimbolton School, Kimbolton, Huntingdon, Cambs, PE28 0EA
Activities: Primary education
Officers: Edward Francis Patrick Valletta, Secretary; Peter Richard Frank Dobson Aylott [1965] Director/Chief Operating Officer; Sarah Marion Brereton [1973] Director/Marketing Consultant; John William Bridge [1950] Director; Professor Fiona Broughton Pipkin [1946] Director/University Professor; Joanna Louise Doyle [1965] Director; Sarah Elizabeth Duberly [1945] Director/Married Woman; Peter John Farrar [1952] Director/Retired Headmaster; Jonathan Alexander Gray [1970] Director/Insurance Sales; Debra Ann Hellett [1962] Director/Housewife; Dr Thomas Paul Hynes [1952] Director/University Lecturer; Katherine Lancaster [1968] Director/Solicitor; Bron Ellen Madson [1965] Director/Public Relations/Reputation Management; Simon Frederick Jonathan Page [1964] Director/Sales Manager; Graham Rex Kenworthy Peace [1945] Director/Retired; Joanna Louise Rice [1967] Director; Derek John Suckling [1972] Director/Airline Pilot; George Robb Yeandle [1957] Director/Accountant (Retired)

Ashley King (Developments) Limited
Incorporated: 27 June 2001 *Employees:* 23
Net Worth: £5,978,256 *Total Assets:* £14,858,661
Registered Office: 1 Goodison Road, Lincs Gateway Business Park, Spalding, Lincs, PE12 6FY
Activities: Development of building projects
Parent: Ashley King Group Limited
Officers: Ashley John King [1967] Director/Property Developer; Jane King [1964] Director/Property Developer

Joseph King (Norfolk) Co-ordination Limited
Incorporated: 16 December 1970
Net Worth: £21,942,974 *Total Assets:* £24,650,144
Registered Office: Larking Gowen LLP, King Street House, 15 Upper King Street, Norwich, NR3 1RB
Activities: Financial intermediation not elsewhere classified
Parent: Joseph King Holdings Limited
Officers: Deborah Gertrude Clipsham [1951] Director; Terence John Gould [1952] Director/Solicitor; Michael Alan Jones [1954] Director/Retired; Neil Generald Alexander King [1956] Director/Barrister; Annie Phillips [1951] Director/Company Secretary

Nicholas King Developments PLC
Incorporated: 10 April 2008 *Employees:* 46
Net Worth: £2,597,000 *Total Assets:* £28,041,000
Registered Office: 10 Penn Road, Beaconsfield, Bucks, HP9 2LH
Activities: Construction of domestic buildings
Officers: Nicholas James Philip Bilsland, Secretary; Nicholas James Philip Bilsland [1966] Finance Director; Susan Elizabeth Jacquest [1964] Director; Nicholas Geoffrey King [1951] Director/Chairman; Paul Jeremy Lobatto [1950] Director; Kelly John Speller [1969] Director

The King Edmund School
Incorporated: 13 May 2011 *Employees:* 223
Net Worth: £23,515,652 *Total Assets:* £26,687,660
Registered Office: The King Edmund School, Vaughan Close, Rochford, Essex, SS4 1TL
Activities: General secondary education
Officers: Christine Susan Packer, Secretary; David John Adsett [1947] Director; Katrina Janette Cooper [1977] Director/Teacher; David James Cottis [1944] Director/Retired; Peter Dennis Devaliant [1955] Director/Retired; Lee Robert Emptage [1980] Director/Solicitor; Gary Frost [1958] Director/Inclusion Manager; Karen Gardiner [1963] Director/Civil Servant; Graham Dennis Jackson [1959] Director; Malcolm MacDonald [1973] Director/Retired; Margaret Anne Nimants [1967] Director/Finance Manager; Jonathan Ian Stanley Osborn [1968] Director/Headteacher; Jason Matthew Anthony Roberts [1994] Director/Teacher [Irish]; Dominic Thomas Roche [1959] Director/Senior Contract Manager; Paul James Schofield [1969] Director/Analyst; Ben Sheppard [1978] Director/General Manager; Alan Craig Stanton [1945] Director/Retired; Andrew Keith Stanton [1967] Director/IT Security; Anna Eileen Stokes [1974] Director/Receptionist; Patricia Helen Thorn [1936] Director/Retired; Kenneth Roy Wickham [1947] Managing Director; Beverley Joan Woolley [1962] Director/Pastoral Support Manager

King Edward VI Grammar School, Chelmsford
Incorporated: 14 March 2011 *Employees:* 150
Net Worth: £11,074,000 *Total Assets:* £13,848,000
Registered Office: King Edward VI Grammar School, Broomfield Road, Chelmsford, Essex, CM1 3SX
Activities: General secondary education
Officers: Lorraine Purkiss, Secretary; Adenrele Michael Adewole [1974] Director/Council Employee; Christine Emily Aldridge [1950] Director/Retired; Jill Dorothy Attenborough [1966] Director/Charity Worker; Alison Jane Brock [1966] Director/Chartered Accountant; Thomas Patrick Carter [1968] Director/Headmaster; Matthew Michael Chivers [1972] Director/Accountant; Jane Patricia Corsham [1962] Director/HR Consultant; Andrew Jonathan Cristin [1965] Director/Accountant; Bruce William Forster [1961] Director/School Medical Officer; Andrew Goodwin [1965] Director; David Dominic Hall [1959] Director/Science Teacher; Walter Hall [1946] Director/Retired; Sidra Naeem [1969] Director/Chaplain; Michael Nye [1955] Director/Retired; Hugh Charles Felix Pattenden [1986] Director/Teacher; Laura June Read [1970] Director; John Gurparshad Singh [1957] Director/YISP Co-ordinator; Edward Oliver Turner [1942] Director/Retired; Mary Turner [1951] Director/Teacher; Spencer Wilcox [1951] Director/Retired; Dr Christopher Willis [1963] Director

J H & A J King Farms Limited
Incorporated: 2 June 2015 *Employees:* 2
Net Worth: £6,524,265 *Total Assets:* £20,645,944
Registered Office: 1 Goodison Road, Lincs Gateway Business Park, Spalding, Lincs, PE12 6FY
Activities: Growing of cereals (except rice), leguminous crops and oil seeds
Parent: Ashley King Group Limited
Officers: Ashley John King [1967] Director/Farmer; Jane King [1964] Director/Farmer

Joseph King Holdings Limited
Incorporated: 16 December 1970 *Employees:* 4
Net Worth: £24,480,124 *Total Assets:* £31,143,144
Registered Office: Larking Gowen LLP, King Street House, 15 Upper King Street, Norwich, NR3 1RB
Activities: Activities of head offices
Shareholders: Terence John Gould; Virginia Clare Edgecombe
Officers: Deborah Gertrude Clipsham [1951] Director; Terence John Gould [1952] Director/Solicitor; Neil Generald Alexander King [1956] Director/Barrister; Annie Phillips [1951] Director

Nicholas King Homes PLC
Incorporated: 28 January 1991 *Employees:* 33
Net Worth: £4,022,000 *Total Assets:* £17,183,000
Registered Office: 10 Penn Road, Beaconsfield, Bucks, HP9 2LH
Activities: Construction of domestic buildings
Officers: Nicholas James Philip Bilsland, Secretary; Nicholas Geoffrey King, Secretary/Chairman; Nicholas James Philip Bilsland [1966] Finance Director; Susan Elizabeth Jacquest [1964] Sales Director; Nicholas Geoffrey King [1951] Director/Chairman; Paul Jeremy Lobatto [1950] Group Land Director; Kelly John Speller [1969] Technical Director

W.D.King Limited
Incorporated: 25 February 1935 *Employees:* 4
Net Worth: £6,598,792 *Total Assets:* £13,699,625
Registered Office: 120 High Street, Edgware, Middlesex, HA8 7EL
Activities: Development of building projects
Parent: Kingrose Limited
Officers: Jeffrey Lionel Rosenbaum [1940] Director; Joshua Da Silva Rosenbaum [1986] Director

King Street Manchester Property LLP
Incorporated: 21 October 2015
Net Worth: £8,343,913 *Total Assets:* £18,640,838
Registered Office: Aprirose House, 48a High Street, Edgware, Middlesex, HA8 7EQ

The King's (The Cathedral) School, Peterborough
Incorporated: 8 December 2010 *Employees:* 152
Net Worth: £19,403,846 *Total Assets:* £20,919,308
Registered Office: The King's (The Cathedral) School, Park Road, Peterborough, Cambs, PE1 2UE
Activities: General secondary education
Officers: Martin Robert Blee, Secretary; Sharon Jerusha Abbott [1975] Director/Businesswoman; Tina Jane Allen [1976] Director/Teacher; Hedley Richard Quentin Arnold [1963] Finance Director; Darren Ayling [1965] Director/Headteacher; Martin Derek Bloom [1956] Director; Andrew Peter Boulton [1969] Director; Canon Sarah Romilly Denner Brown [1965] Director/Minister of Religion; Susan Mary Burgess [1972] Director/Chiropodist; Tansy Castledine [1978] Director of Music; Stephen John Crane [1951] Director/Education Adviser; Christopher Charles Dalliston [1956] Director/Dean of The Church of England; Elizabeth Jane Dunmore [1977] Director/Teacher; Reverend Mandy Carol Flaherty [1963] Director/Parish Priest & School Chaplain; Timothy John Hitch [1952] Director; Barbara Susan John [1959] Director/Psychotherapist; Susan Elizabeth Lowe-Lauri [1958] Director; Kevin Stephan Palmer [1957] Director; Christopher Frank Trotman [1945] Director

The King's School, Ely
Incorporated: 6 November 1989 *Employees:* 461
Net Worth: £9,739,648 *Total Assets:* £23,124,940
Registered Office: The Bursar's Office, The Kings School, Ely, Cambs, CB7 4DB
Activities: Pre-primary education
Officers: Dr Roger Leonard Axworthy, Secretary; Gavin John Acheson [1965] Director/Solicitor; Clive Arthur Bairsto [1959] Director/RAF Officer; Mark Philip John Bonney [1957] Director/Priest/Dean; Philip John Simon Cantwell [1960] Director; Graham Frank Chase [1954] Director/Chartered Surveyor; David John Day [1959] Director/Company Chairman; Amanda Hazell East [1963] Director/Retired Engineer/Housewife; Jeffrey Christopher Hayes [1953] Director/Retired Businessman; Anthea Jane Kenna [1952] Director/Headteacher; Mark Edward Myers [1961] Director/Chief Executive; Isobel Philippa Newport-Mangell [1961] Director; Sir James Edward Thornton Paice [1949] Director/M.P; Joseph Anthony Peake [1954] Director/Quality Assurance Officer ISTIP; Professor Michael Richard Edward Proctor [1950] Director/Professor

Kingfisher (EU) Limited
Incorporated: 8 June 2011 *Employees:* 6
Net Worth: £6,224,255 *Total Assets:* £15,549,479
Registered Office: 27 Hornsby Square, Southfields Business Park, Basildon, Essex, SS15 6SD
Activities: Development of building projects
Officers: Ram Krishan Goyal, Secretary; Avnish Mitter Goyal [1966] Director; Ram Krishan Goyal [1962] Director; Vidya Bhushan Goyal [1955] Director/Property Developer

Kings Hedges Investments Limited
Incorporated: 3 June 1997
Net Worth: £2,777,414 *Total Assets:* £9,403,726
Registered Office: Unex House, Church Lane, Stetchworth, Cambs, CB8 9TN
Activities: Buying and selling of own real estate
Shareholders: Timothy Casey Oscar Gredley; Pollyanna Georgina Gredley
Officers: Andrew John Page, Secretary; Timothy Casey Oscar Gredley [1986] Director; William Jerome Gredley [1933] Director; Andrew John Page [1976] Director/Certified Chartered Accountant; Stephen Walsh [1959] Director/Architect

Kings Langley School
Incorporated: 29 October 2012 *Employees:* 163
Net Worth: £24,540,424 *Total Assets:* £26,733,576
Registered Office: Kings Langley School, Love Lane, Kings Langley, Herts, WD4 9HN
Activities: General secondary education
Officers: Diane Marie Bell, Secretary; David Bernard Ash Butler [1966] Bank Director; Graham James Craggs [1965] Director/Chartered Surveyor; Dawn Helfgott [1968] Director/Financial Advisor; Mark John Hutchings [1968] Director; Gary Michael Lewis [1957] Director/Headteacher; Mark Morant [1968] Director/Head of Supply Chain; Joanne Clare O'Sullivan [1974] Director/Customer Service Executive; Simon Matthew Setterfield [1964] Commercial Director; Frances Stickley [1956] Director/Facilities Management; Lisa Welling [1972] Franchise Director; Angela Westlake [1956] Director/Business Support Manager; Simon Christopher Wood [1963] Director/Chartered Surveyor; Helen Young [1985] Director/Solicitor

Kings Leisure Limited
Incorporated: 8 January 1958 *Employees:* 1
Net Worth: £10,637,870 *Total Assets:* £17,175,358
Registered Office: Sutherland House, 1759 London Road, Leigh on Sea, Essex, SS9 2RZ
Activities: Recreational vehicle parks, trailer parks and camping grounds
Major Shareholder: Harold William King
Officers: Holly Ellen King, Secretary; Holly Ellen King [1989] Director; John Michael O'Dell [1952] Health & Safety Director

Kingsgate Community Church
Incorporated: 11 May 2004 *Employees:* 90
Net Worth: £7,013,242 *Total Assets:* £10,217,656
Registered Office: 2 Staplee Way, Parnwell, Peterborough, Cambs, PE1 4YT
Activities: Activities of religious organisations
Officers: Sally Ann Duffy, Secretary; Albert Barry Featherstone [1946] Director; Richard Keith Johnson [1966] Director; Matthew Graham Negus [1982] Director; Norman Paskin [1949] Director; David Andrew Smith [1963] Director/Senior Pastor; Simon Duncan Wilson [1963] Director/Solicitor

Kingshott School Trust Limited
Incorporated: 14 July 1980 *Employees:* 81
Net Worth: £9,741,921 *Total Assets:* £14,414,740
Registered Office: Kingshott School, St Ippolyts, Hitchin, Herts, SG4 7JX
Activities: Primary education
Officers: Judith Anne Ilott, Secretary; James Bentall [1968] Director/Accountant; Peter Thomas Brooks [1955] Director/Doctor - Retired; David Keast [1947] Director/Retired; Harriet Marsh [1988] Director/Marketing Manager; Richard John Midgley [1975] Director/Assistant Headteacher; David Alan Morgan [1959] Director/Retired; Lara Elizabeth Pechard [1976] Director/Teacher; Samantha Selkirk [1966] Director/Teacher; Martin John Sudweeks [1969] Director/Quantity Surveyor

Kingsley Care Homes Limited
Incorporated: 24 May 2002 *Employees:* 291
Net Worth: £12,702,981 *Total Assets:* £26,228,764
Registered Office: Kingsley House, Clapham Road South, Lowestoft, Suffolk, NR32 1QS
Activities: Residential care activities for the elderly and disabled
Officers: Velummayilum Thayanandarajah, Secretary; Wasantha Darshana [1978] Director/Business Executive; Deborah Ann Edwards [1974] Director/Business Executive; Sarah Louise Ferguson [1966] Director/Business Executive; Ian Stuart Jarvis [1966] Director/Business Executive; Cameron Dyer Thayan [1995] Director/Trainee Accountant; Ewan Dyer Thayan [1997] Director/Trainee Accountant; Sumithra Chandrakanthi Thayanandarajah [1959] Director/Business Executive; Velummayilum Thayanandarajah [1961] Director/Company Executive

Kingsmead School
Incorporated: 17 September 2010 *Employees:* 168
Net Worth: £12,429,796 *Total Assets:* £13,411,465
Registered Office: 196 Southbury Road, Enfield, Middlesex, EN1 1YQ
Activities: General secondary education
Officers: Andrea Gajadhar, Secretary; Alok Kumar Agrawal [1945] Director; David Philip Boothroyd [1947] Director/Teacher; Denise Chan [1969] Director/Governor [Malaysian]; Joanne Eaton [1974] Director/Governor; Rhodoulla Flindall [1978] Director/Teacher; Carmien Gharbaoui [1974] Director/Governor; Ken Gregory [1936] Director/Retired; Usman Haroon [1994] Director/Volunteer; Dr Rachel Andromache Harris [1969] Director/Governor; Randolph Hoyte [1972] Director/Teacher; David Medway [1980] Director/Headteacher; Andrew Calder Nicholas [1955] Director; Samantha Ojokor [1967] Director/Governor; Kim Pickering [1958] Director/Retired; Lesley Pitcher [1962] Director/Data Manager; George Rhoden [1961] Director/Retired; Angela Velasco [1988] Director/Teacher; Deborah Ann Watson [1960] Director/Governor

Kingspan Timber Solutions Limited
Incorporated: 25 September 2003 *Employees:* 103
Net Worth: £8,729,014 *Total Assets:* £15,050,853
Registered Office: Eltisley Road, Great Gransden, Sandy, Beds, SG19 3AR
Activities: Manufacture of other products of wood; manufacture of articles of cork, straw and plaiting materials
Parent: Kingspan Holdings (Structural & Offsite) Limited
Officers: Mark Stevenson [1972] Director; Peter Charles Wilson [1956] Director [Irish]

Kingsway Asset Co Limited
Incorporated: 10 September 2014
Net Worth Deficit: £3,769,037 *Total Assets:* £177,003,936
Registered Office: 505 Pinner Road, Harrow, Middlesex, HA2 6EH
Activities: Activities of other holding companies n.e.c.
Officers: Rishi Ramesh Sachdev [1976] Director; Uday Vyas [1978] Director

Kingsway Hall Hotel Limited
Incorporated: 10 September 2001
Net Worth: £51,107,112 *Total Assets:* £51,120,312
Registered Office: 505 Pinner Road, Harrow, Middlesex, HA2 6EH
Activities: Hotels and similar accommodation
Officers: Rishi Ramesh Sachdev [1976] Director; Uday Vyas [1978] Director

Kingsway Mezz Co Limited
Incorporated: 10 September 2014
Net Worth: £1,357,354 *Total Assets:* £54,069,952
Registered Office: 505 Pinner Road, Harrow, Middlesex, HA2 6EH
Activities: Activities of other holding companies n.e.c.
Officers: Rishi Ramesh Sachdev [1976] Director; Uday Vyas [1978] Director

Kingsway Mezz Hold Co Limited
Incorporated: 10 September 2014 *Employees:* 88
Net Worth Deficit: £2,098,473 *Total Assets:* £131,986,816
Registered Office: 505 Pinner Road, Harrow, Middlesex, HA2 6EH
Activities: Activities of other holding companies n.e.c.
Officers: Rishi Ramesh Sachdev [1976] Director; Uday Vyas [1978] Director

Kingsway Senior Hold Co Limited
Incorporated: 10 September 2014
Net Worth Deficit: £23,400 *Total Assets:* £53,024,576
Registered Office: 505 Pinner Road, Harrow, Middlesex, HA2 6EH
Activities: Activities of other holding companies n.e.c.
Officers: Rishi Ramesh Sachdev [1976] Director; Uday Vyas [1978] Director

Kingswood Village Limited
Incorporated: 19 April 2017
Net Worth: £13,125 *Total Assets:* £11,718,365
Registered Office: Crane Court, 302 London Road, Ipswich, Suffolk, IP2 0AJ
Activities: Construction of domestic buildings
Major Shareholder: Michael Hintze
Officers: Dominic Charles David Richards [1966] Director

Kirkmore Capital Limited
Incorporated: 9 September 2016
Net Worth: £83,760 *Total Assets:* £26,217,256
Registered Office: Eden House, Reynolds Road, Beaconsfield, Bucks, HP9 2FL
Activities: Other credit granting n.e.c.
Shareholders: Jason Charles Andrew Berger; Peter Ashley Gropper
Officers: Jason Charles Andrew Berger [1969] Director/Surveyor; Peter Ashley Gropper [1967] Director

Kirkmore HT Limited
Incorporated: 10 May 2017
Net Worth: £1,135 *Total Assets:* £11,742,264
Registered Office: Eden House, Reynolds Road, Beaconsfield, Bucks, HP9 2FL
Activities: Other credit granting n.e.c.
Parent: Kirkmore Capital Limited
Officers: Jason Charles Andrew Berger [1969] Director/Surveyor; Peter Ashley Gropper [1967] Director

Kirkmore Rhino 1 Limited
Incorporated: 26 August 2016
Net Worth: £926 *Total Assets:* £8,115,622
Registered Office: Eden House, Reynolds Road, Beaconsfield, Bucks, HP9 2FL
Activities: Other credit granting n.e.c.
Parent: Kirkmore Capital Limited
Officers: Jason Charles Andrew Berger [1969] Director/Surveyor; Peter Ashley Gropper [1967] Director

Kirly Limited
Incorporated: 14 December 1973 *Employees:* 5
Net Worth: £14,108,443 *Total Assets:* £25,276,404
Registered Office: 11 Luard Road, Cambridge, CB2 8PJ
Activities: Non-life insurance
Shareholder: Marcus Walter Johnson
Officers: Marcus Walter Johnson [1951] Director; Margaret Ann Johnson [1948] Director

Kiss FM Radio Limited
Incorporated: 3 May 1989 *Employees:* 43
Net Worth: £6,158,000 *Total Assets:* £8,056,000
Registered Office: Media House, Peterborough Business Park, Lynch Wood, Peterborough, Cambs, PE2 6EA
Activities: Television programme production activities
Parent: Bauer Radio Limited
Officers: Deidre Ann Ford [1960] Managing Director; Paul Anthony Keenan [1963] Director/Publisher; Sarah Jane Vickery [1963] Finance Director

Kitchen Range Foods Limited
Incorporated: 12 March 1971 *Employees:* 193
Net Worth: £12,511,000 *Total Assets:* £18,533,000
Registered Office: Kingfisher Way, Hinching Brooke Business Park, Huntingdon, Cambs, PE29 6FJ
Activities: Manufacture of rusks and biscuits; manufacture of preserved pastry goods and cakes
Parent: Moy Park (Newco) Limited
Officers: Raymond Gerard McGinley, Secretary; Christopher John Kirke [1970] Director/Company President; Flavio Gomes Malnarcic [1964] Director [Portuguese]; Fabio Sandri [1971] Director [Brazilian]

Kitewood (Creekside) Limited
Incorporated: 15 December 2016
Net Worth Deficit: £2,474,957 *Total Assets:* £15,473,662
Registered Office: 3rd Floor, Sterling House, Langston Road, Loughton, Essex, IG10 3TS
Activities: Buying and selling of own real estate
Parent: GDL (Creekside) Limited
Officers: Allan Porter, Secretary; John Cole [1971] Director; Stephen Stuart Solomon Conway [1948] Director; John Stephen Faith [1948] Director/Chartered Surveyor; Jonathan Goldstein [1971] Director; Philip Owen Van Reyk [1958] Director

Klipspringer Limited
Incorporated: 21 June 2011 *Employees:* 40
Net Worth: £5,256,038 *Total Assets:* £8,082,018
Registered Office: Rynor House, Farthing Road, Ipswich, Suffolk, IP1 5AP
Activities: Wholesale of other machinery and equipment
Shareholders: Jonathan James Carlyon; Timothy Andrew Carlyon
Officers: Elizabeth Jane Carlyon, Secretary; Elizabeth Jane Carlyon [1945] Director; John Michael Carlyon [1944] Director; Jonathan James Carlyon [1966] Director; Timothy Andrew Carlyon [1967] Director

KLM UK Engineering Limited
Incorporated: 18 June 1990 *Employees:* 358
Net Worth Deficit: £8,592,000 *Total Assets:* £14,290,000
Registered Office: Liberator Road, Norwich Airport, Norwich, NR6 6ER
Activities: Service activities incidental to air transportation
Parent: KLM Royal Dutch Airlines N.V.
Officers: Wayne Easlea, Secretary; Wayne Easlea [1974] Operations Director; Mathieu Essenberg [1973] Director/SVP Airframe Operations [Dutch]; Rene Robert Kalmann [1953] Program Director KLM Engineering & Maintenance [Dutch]; Peter Van Der Horst [1960] Managing Director [Dutch]; Gerda Van Der Landen [1967] Director/Financial Controller [Dutch]; Jozef Bernardus Veenstra [1967] Director/VP Finance & Control KLM [Dutch]

Kluman and Balter Holdings Limited
Incorporated: 15 March 2012 *Employees:* 62
Net Worth: £7,834,214 *Total Assets:* £24,322,160
Registered Office: Unit 8 The IO Centre, Lea Road, Waltham Abbey, Essex, EN9 1AS
Activities: Activities of head offices
Shareholder: DK Investments Limited
Officers: Simon Douglas, Secretary; Diana Kluman, Secretary; Omer Tahir, Secretary; Danny Kluman [1975] Director; Jamie Kluman [1978] Director

Klyne Air Limited
Incorporated: 6 September 2007 *Employees:* 4
Net Worth Deficit: £6,550,963 *Total Assets:* £10,311,751
Registered Office: Broadacres, Waveney Hill, Oulton Broad, Lowestoft, Suffolk, NR32 3PR
Activities: Non-scheduled passenger air transport
Parent: Klyne Aviation (Holdings) Limited
Officers: Bridget Claxton Klyne, Secretary; Alexander Paschal Durand [1969] Director; Bridget Claxton Klyne [1942] Director; Roger Kylne [1939] Director; Christopher John Mace [1973] Commercial Director

Klyne Aviation Limited
Incorporated: 4 December 2008 *Employees:* 96
Net Worth: £5,555,508 *Total Assets:* £24,853,164
Registered Office: Broadacres, Waveney Hill, Oulton Road, Lowestoft, Suffolk, NR32 3PR
Activities: Non-scheduled passenger air transport
Shareholders: Roger Klyne; Bridget Claxton Klyne
Officers: Bridget Claxton Klyne, Secretary/Director; Alexander Paschal Durand [1969] Director/Business Executive; Nicholas Paul Hallett [1958] Director/Accountant; Bridget Claxton Klyne [1942] Director; Roger Klyne [1939] Director

KM Estates Limited
Incorporated: 22 October 2015 *Employees:* 2
Net Worth: £10,601,569 *Total Assets:* £13,638,141
Registered Office: Nicholas House, River Front, Enfield, Middlesex, EN1 3FG
Activities: Other letting and operating of own or leased real estate
Shareholders: Aminmohamed Fazal Alidina Pabani; Shabnam Pabani
Officers: Omar Aminmohamed Pabani, Secretary; Amin Fazal Alidina Pabani [1948] Director; Omar Aminmohamed Pabani [1992] Director

KMG Systems Limited
Incorporated: 15 March 1978 *Employees:* 132
Net Worth: £9,548,938 *Total Assets:* £17,691,124
Registered Office: Station Road, Gamlingay, Sandy, Beds, SG19 3HE
Activities: Manufacture of machinery for food, beverage and tobacco processing
Shareholder: Helen Louise Weatherley
Officers: Helen Louise Weatherley, Secretary/Finance; Julia Katherine Maddocks [1969] Director/Resources; Keith Lever Maddocks [1938] Director/Engineer; Helen Louise Weatherley [1967] Director/Finance

Knight Build Limited
Incorporated: 10 May 1994
Net Worth: £9,805,490 *Total Assets:* £14,961,662
Registered Office: Unit 22 Childerditch Industrial Park, Childerditch Hall Drive, Brentwood, Essex, CM13 3HD
Activities: Other specialised construction activities n.e.c.
Major Shareholder: John Edward Knight
Officers: John Edward Knight, Secretary/Director [Irish]; Gerard Martin Cassidy [1973] Director/Surveyor [Irish]; Edward Emmanuel Daize [1967] Director/Accountant; John Edward Knight [1966] Director [Irish]; Bradley Vivian Pearse [1966] Director/Surveyor

Knight Noise Limited
Incorporated: 2 June 2006 *Employees:* 130
Net Worth Deficit: £822,280 *Total Assets:* £11,193,108
Registered Office: Allcures House, Arisdale Avenue, South Ockendon, Essex, RM15 5TT
Activities: Non-trading company
Officers: Jaipal Singh Cheema [1956] Director

Knight Precision Metals Limited
Incorporated: 1 September 2011 *Employees:* 59
Net Worth: £9,063,258 *Total Assets:* £11,088,492
Registered Office: Linkside Summit Road, Cranborne Road, Potters Bar, Herts, EN6 3JL
Activities: Manufacture of metal structures and parts of structures
Officers: Judith Maxine Townsend, Secretary; Sophie Harrieth Blyth [1966] Director; Carolyn Yvette Ferguson [1961] Director; Brien Walter Knight [1929] Director; Darrell Edward Alfred Knight [1963] Director; Christopher Smyth [1941] Director; Judith Maxine Townsend [1964] Director; Emma Louise Wright [1966] Director

Knight Roadworks (2010) Limited
Incorporated: 9 March 2010 *Employees:* 4
Net Worth: £14,635,473 *Total Assets:* £15,670,964
Registered Office: 1 Gainsborough Road, Felixstowe, Suffolk, IP11 7HT
Activities: Activities of head offices
Parent: Chevalier (2015) Ltd
Officers: William Edward Anthony [1955] Director; Guy Barker [1974] Commercial Director; Dean Anthony Braybrook [1971] Managing Director; Christopher Peter Featherstone [1956] Director; Gary James Spicer [1965] Director; Richard James Stannard [1982] Estimating Director

J.L. Knight Roadworks Limited
Incorporated: 5 July 1977 *Employees:* 167
Net Worth: £7,244,126 *Total Assets:* £26,005,224
Registered Office: 1 Gainsborough Road, Felixstowe, Suffolk, IP11 7HT
Activities: Construction of roads and motorways
Parent: Knight Roadworks (2010) Limited
Officers: Gary James Spicer, Secretary; William Edward Anthony [1955] Director; Guy Barker [1974] Commercial Director; Dean Anthony Braybrook [1971] Managing Director; Daniel Peter Burke [1980] Construction Director; Christopher Peter Featherstone [1956] Director; Gary James Spicer [1965] Director; Richard James Stannard [1982] Estimating Director

Knight Strip Metals Limited
Incorporated: 29 September 1943 *Employees:* 54
Net Worth: £9,464,157 *Total Assets:* £11,338,008
Registered Office: Linkside Business Centre, Summit Road, Cranborne Road, Potters Bar, Herts, EN6 3JL
Activities: Manufacture of metal structures and parts of structures
Parent: Knight Precision Metals Limited
Officers: Judith Maxine Townsend, Secretary; Brien Walter Knight [1929] Director; Michael Stephen O'Neill [1961] Director; Christopher Smyth [1941] Director; Martin Ken Wiltshire [1962] Financial Director

Knighton Foods Limited
Incorporated: 24 March 2014 *Employees:* 321
Net Worth Deficit: £18,300,000 *Total Assets:* £21,500,000
Registered Office: Premier House, Centrium Business Park, Griffiths Way, St Albans, Herts, AL1 2RE
Activities: Manufacture of other food products n.e.c.
Parent: Knighton Foods Investments Limited
Officers: Simon Nicholas Wilbraham, Secretary; Mark Rivers Hughes [1960] Director; Richard Matthew Ilsley [1965] Director; Duncan Neil Leggett [1979] Director; David Monk [1957] Director

The Knights Templar School
Incorporated: 4 March 2011 *Employees:* 160
Net Worth: £26,352,928 *Total Assets:* £27,963,070
Registered Office: The Knights Templar School, Park Street, Baldock, Herts, SG7 6DZ
Activities: General secondary education
Officers: Fiona Roper, Secretary; Sarah Barker [1966] Director/Deputy Headteacher; Nicky Bull [1962] Director; Catherine Connolly [1968] Director/Project Manager; Michelle Dudderidge [1976] Director/Social Worker; Christine Gough [1955] Director/Semi-Retired Teacher; Joe Grove [1980] Director/Teacher; Graham Thorp Kingsley [1939] Director/Retired; Timothy Scott Litchfield [1962] Director/Headteacher; Beth Morris [1965] Director; Pauline Poole [1960] Director/Specialist Teacher/FE Manager; Jackie Spinks [1966] Director/Architect; John William Swift [1965] Finance Director; Duncan Robert Wardrop [1953] Director/Geologist; Susan Elizabeth Welch [1965] Director/Civil Servant

KNM Project Services Limited
Incorporated: 7 February 2011
Net Worth: £153,767 *Total Assets:* £13,322,356
Registered Office: Ruthlyn House, 90 Lincoln Road, Peterborough, Cambs, PE1 2SP
Activities: Other specialised construction activities n.e.c.
Parent: KNM Europa BV
Officers: Filippo Molinari [1975] Director/General Manager [Italian]; Flavio Porro [1970] Director [Italian]

Knott Park One LLP
Incorporated: 17 November 2011
Net Worth: £11,939,762 *Total Assets:* £11,944,262
Registered Office: Eaton Court, Maylands Avenue, Hemel Hempstead Industrial Estate, Hemel Hempstead, Herts, HP2 7TR
Officers: Adrian Neil Raeburn McAlpine [1944] Member; Sir Andrew William McAlpine [1960] Member; Cullum McAlpine [1947] Member; The Honourable David Malcolm McAlpine [1946] Member; Douglas James McAlpine [1983] Member; Gavin Malcolm McAlpine [1974] Member; Hector George McAlpine [1980] Member; Ian Malcolm McAlpine [1942] Member; Richard Hugh McAlpine [1958] Member; Robert Edward McAlpine [1978] Member

Knowles (Transport) Limited
Incorporated: 10 December 1947 *Employees:* 234
Net Worth: £24,465,176 *Total Assets:* £35,372,984
Registered Office: New Road, Wimblington, March, Cambs, PE15 0RG
Activities: Freight transport by road
Shareholders: Pamela Ann Knowles; Anthony Roy Knowles
Officers: Marcus Allebone, Secretary; Alexander Anthony Knowles [1990] Director; Anthony Roy Knowles [1945] Director/Haulage Contractor; Pamela Ann Knowles [1958] Director

Knowles (UK) Limited
Incorporated: 22 January 1987 *Employees:* 38
Net Worth: £19,116,126 *Total Assets:* £24,675,106
Registered Office: Hethel Engineering Centre, Chapman Way, Hethel, Norwich, NR14 8FB
Activities: Manufacture of electronic components
Officers: Mark Pacioni, Secretary; Peter Christian Bell [1975] Finance Director [American]; Christopher Burnham Dugan [1965] Director/Business Executive [American]; Stephen John Watts [1967] Director

Kodak Alaris Holdings Limited
Incorporated: 30 May 2013 *Employees:* 2,207
Net Worth: £115,790,560 *Total Assets:* £361,712,192
Registered Office: Hemel One, Boundary Way, Hemel Hempstead, Herts, HP2 7YU
Activities: Activities of other holding companies n.e.c.
Parent: KPP (No.2) Trustees Limited
Officers: John O'Reilly, Secretary; Mark Robert William Alflatt [1966] Director/Chartered Accountant; Patrick Jean-Marie de Smedt [1955] Director [Belgian]; Mark Wynne Elliott [1949] Director/Retired Information Technology and Services Executive [American]; Marc Jourlait [1967] Director/Chief Executive [French]; Brian Paul Larcombe [1953] Director/Investment Banker; Stephen Paul Webster [1952] Director/Chartered Accountant

Kodak Alaris Limited
Incorporated: 31 May 2013 *Employees:* 158
Net Worth: £29,983,392 *Total Assets:* £95,606,152
Registered Office: Hemel One, Boundary Way, Hemel Hempstead, Herts, HP2 7YU
Activities: Manufacture of photographic and cinematographic equipment
Parent: Kodak Alaris Holdings Limited
Officers: John O'Reilly, Secretary; Mark Robert William Alflatt [1966] Director/Chartered Accountant; Dennis Bruce Olbrich [1960] Director/Business President [American]; Nicoletta Assaro Zongrone [1958] Director [American]

Kodak International Finance Limited
Incorporated: 30 March 1983
Net Worth: £56,501,848 *Total Assets:* £408,733,472
Registered Office: Building 8, Croxley Green Business Park, Hatters Lane, Watford, Herts, WD18 8PX
Activities: Financial intermediation not elsewhere classified
Officers: Helen Veronica Griffiths, Secretary; Evelina Latuta [1973] Director/Financial Controller; William George Love [1956] Director/Finance/Treasurer [American]; Manfred Hubert Stegmaier [1957] Director/EAMER Controller [German]

Kodak Limited
Incorporated: 15 November 1898 *Employees:* 205
Net Worth: £95,900,000 *Total Assets:* £255,500,000
Registered Office: Building 8, Croxley Green Business Park, Hatters Lane, Watford, Herts, WD18 8PX
Activities: Other publishing activities
Officers: Helen Veronica Griffiths, Secretary; Helen Veronica Griffiths [1962] Legal Director; John Gerard O'Grady [1964] Director/General Manager WW Sales, Senior Vice President [Irish]; Susan White [1972] HR Director

Koei Tecmo Europe Limited
Incorporated: 8 August 2002 *Employees:* 7
Net Worth: £44,714,812 *Total Assets:* £49,884,272
Registered Office: Unit 209a Spirella Building, Bridge Road, Letchworth Garden City, Herts, SG6 4ET
Activities: Ready-made interactive leisure and entertainment software development
Parent: Koei Tecmo Holdings Co., Ltd
Officers: Hidekiyo Kobayashi, Secretary; Keiko Erikawa [1949] Director [Japanese]; Yoichi Erikawa [1950] Director [Japanese]; Hidekiyo Kobayashi [1965] Director [Japanese]; Hisashi Koinuma [1971] Director [Japanese]

Konica Minolta Business Solutions (UK) Limited
Incorporated: 6 September 1973 *Employees:* 2,386
Net Worth: £56,272,000 *Total Assets:* £126,706,000
Registered Office: Konica House, Miles Gray Road, Basildon, Essex, SS14 3AR
Activities: Other information service activities n.e.c.
Parent: Konica Minolta Incorporated
Officers: Catherine Bland, Secretary; Keiji Okamoto [1963] Director/Business Executive [Japanese]; Martin James Tierney [1967] Director; Kazuyuki Tsukamoto [1967] Director [Japanese]

Konings Juices & Drinks UK Limited
Incorporated: 1 June 2016 *Employees:* 89
Net Worth: £1,385,239 *Total Assets:* £19,725,720
Registered Office: Konings Juices & Drinks UK Ltd, Stoke Road, Boxford, Sudbury, Suffolk, CO10 5AF
Activities: Manufacture of soft drinks; production of mineral waters and other bottled waters
Parent: New-Kon NV
Officers: Dirk Stany Urbain Jozef Ghislain Maris [1964] Director/Chief Executive Officer [Belgian]; Anne Marina Moors [1988] Director [Belgian]; Luc Leon Alfons Nulens [1964] Director/Chief Operating Officer [Belgian]

Korda Developments Limited
Incorporated: 7 December 2001 *Employees:* 67
Net Worth: £13,197,962 *Total Assets:* £18,174,750
Registered Office: Orbital House, 20 Eastern Road, Romford, Essex, RM1 3PJ
Activities: Other retail sale not in stores, stalls or markets
Major Shareholder: Daniel William Fairbrass
Officers: Damian Keith Clarke [1971] Director/Head of Operations; Daniel William Fairbrass [1970] Director/Angling Consultant

Kotecha Ltd
Incorporated: 6 August 2007
Net Worth: £143,506 *Total Assets:* £15,312,185
Registered Office: 70 Bishops Road, Trumpington, Cambridge, CB2 2NH
Activities: Motion picture distribution activities
Shareholder: Rasiklal Haridas Kotecha
Officers: Sharda Kotecha, Secretary; Rasiklal Haridas Kotecha [1951] Director/Accountant

Kout Food Group Restaurants UK Limited
Incorporated: 22 May 2012
Net Worth Deficit: £16,985,000 *Total Assets:* £8,641,000
Registered Office: 100-102 High Street, Ruislip, Middlesex, HA4 8LS
Activities: Activities of other holding companies n.e.c.
Officers: Fadwa Alhomaiz [1957] Director/Chairwoman [Kuwaiti]

KPIT Technologies (UK) Limited
Incorporated: 17 October 1996 *Employees:* 160
Net Worth: £15,863,656 *Total Assets:* £29,745,258
Registered Office: Gautam House, 1-3 Shenley Avenue, Ruislip Manor, Middlesex, HA4 6BP
Activities: Other business support service activities n.e.c.
Parent: KPIT Technologies Limited
Officers: Amit Avinash Bhave, Secretary; Deepak Koshal [1951] Director/Chartered Accountant; Kishore Parshuram Patil [1962] Director/Chartered Accountant [Indian]; Pankaj Sathe [1967] Director/Management Professional [Indian]

Kreutzer Touristik GB Limited
Incorporated: 13 January 2016 *Employees:* 2
Net Worth Deficit: £16,506 *Total Assets:* £84,572,904
Registered Office: Queens Court, 9-17 Eastern Road, Romford, Essex, RM1 3NH
Activities: Other reservation service activities n.e.c.
Major Shareholder: Menachem Shaked
Officers: Anna Dubro [1977] Director [Latvian]

Kristall Real Estate Limited
Incorporated: 4 April 2016
Net Worth: £100 *Total Assets:* £9,415,099
Registered Office: Dickens House, Guithavon Street, Witham, Essex, CM8 1BJ
Activities: Other business support service activities n.e.c.
Parent: Kristall Investment Limited
Officers: Massimo di Fazio [1973] Director [Italian]

Kristall Realty Investments Limited
Incorporated: 23 September 2016
Net Worth: £8,526,193 *Total Assets:* £8,526,193
Registered Office: Dickens House, Guithavon Street, Witham, Essex, CM8 1BJ
Activities: Buying and selling of own real estate
Parent: Sextant Consolidated Limited
Officers: Vincenzo Bianchi [1958] Director [Italian]; Massimo di Fazio [1973] Director [Italian]; Philip Lawrence [1953] Director

Kromachem Holdings Limited
Incorporated: 30 November 1989 *Employees:* 42
Net Worth: £14,218,621 *Total Assets:* £16,031,411
Registered Office: Unit 10 Moor Park Industrial Centre, Tolpits Lane, Watford, Herts, WD18 9ER
Activities: Activities of head offices
Major Shareholder: Ewald Josef Kensbock
Officers: Ewald Josef Kensbock [1939] Director/Industrial Chemist [German]; Margrit Doris Kensbock [1941] Director [German]; Uwe Kensbock [1971] Managing Director [German]

Kromachem Limited
Incorporated: 6 September 1982 *Employees:* 30
Net Worth: £9,631,276 *Total Assets:* £10,286,504
Registered Office: Unit 10 Moor Park Industrial Centre, Tolpits Lane, Watford, Herts, WD18 9ER
Activities: Manufacture of paints, varnishes and similar coatings, mastics and sealants
Parent: Kromachem Holdings Ltd
Officers: Ewald Josef Kensbock [1939] Director/Industrial Chemist [German]; Uwe Kensbock [1971] Managing Director [German]

KSEYE Capital Holdings Limited
Incorporated: 26 April 2016 *Employees:* 2
Net Worth: £609,122 *Total Assets:* £42,678,068
Registered Office: 1 Kenyngton Place, Harrow, Middlesex, HA3 0DW
Activities: Activities of financial services holding companies
Parent: KSEYE Group Limited
Officers: Jitendra Khagram [1971] Director/Business Adviser; Nikes Khagram [1984] Director/Consultant

KSEYE Capital No.1 Limited
Incorporated: 27 April 2016 *Employees:* 2
Net Worth: £269,487 *Total Assets:* £21,745,690
Registered Office: 1 Kenyngton Place, Harrow, Middlesex, HA3 0DW
Activities: Other credit granting n.e.c.
Parent: KSEYE Capital Holdings Limited
Officers: Jitendra Khagram [1971] Director/Business Adviser; Nikes Khagram [1984] Director/Consultant

KSEYE Capital No.2 Limited
Incorporated: 27 April 2016 *Employees:* 2
Net Worth: £325,207 *Total Assets:* £20,979,084
Registered Office: 1 Kenyngton Place, Harrow, Middlesex, HA3 0DW
Activities: Other credit granting n.e.c.
Parent: KSEYE Capital Holdings Limited
Officers: Jitendra Khagram [1971] Director/Business Adviser; Nikes Khagram [1984] Director/Consultant

KSEYE Group Limited
Incorporated: 26 April 2016 *Employees:* 4
Net Worth: £6,187,885 *Total Assets:* £44,022,188
Registered Office: 1 Kenyngton Place, Harrow, Middlesex, HA3 0DW
Activities: Activities of other holding companies n.e.c.
Shareholders: Jitendra Khagram; Nikes Khagram
Officers: Jitendra Khagram [1971] Director/Business Adviser; Nikes Khagram [1984] Director/Consultant

Kubach & Sambrook (Metals) Limited
Incorporated: 28 February 1973 *Employees:* 11
Net Worth: £4,151,229 *Total Assets:* £16,255,821
Registered Office: 57 Manor Park Crescent, Edgware, Middlesex, HA8 7LY
Activities: Manufacture of basic iron and steel and of ferro-alloys
Officers: Pareshkumar Dahyabhai Patel, Secretary; Ajay Arunkant Doshi [1958] Director [Australian]

Kudos Catering (UK) Limited
Incorporated: 17 August 2000 *Employees:* 427
Net Worth: £4,248,051 *Total Assets:* £8,801,063
Registered Office: Crown House, 855 London Road, Grays, Essex, RM20 3LG
Activities: Event catering activities
Parent: Crown Holdings Limited
Officers: Javed Taher, Secretary; Charles Nicholas Beer [1971] Director/Catering Hospitality; Matthew Erich Herter [1972] Director [American]; Nigel Mark Hutson [1958] Managing Director; Deirdre Morgan [1952] Director; Russell Lee Christopher Morgan [1952] Director/Co Chairman; Christopher John Sullivan [1956] Director

Kudos Pharmaceuticals Limited
Incorporated: 12 December 1997
Net Worth: £197,699,008 *Total Assets:* £1,517,933,056
Registered Office: 1 Francis Crick Avenue, Cambridge Biomedical Campus, Cambridge, CB2 0AA
Activities: Other business support service activities n.e.c.
Parent: AstraZeneca UK Limited
Officers: Matthew Ian Conacher, Secretary; Iain Alistair Collins [1970] Director; Katie Louise Jackson-Turner [1966] Director/Solicitor; Adrian Charles Noel Kemp [1966] Director

Kwik-Fit (GB) Limited
Incorporated: 27 April 1971 *Employees:* 4,814
Net Worth: £125,875,000 *Total Assets:* £294,072,000
Registered Office: Etel House, Avenue One, Letchworth Garden City, Herts, SG6 2HU
Activities: Maintenance and repair of motor vehicles
Parent: Kwik Fit Holdings Limited
Officers: Ian Vincent Ellis, Secretary; Paul Boulton [1958] Director; Mark Lynott [1975] Director; Mark Richard Slade [1975] Director

Kwik-Fit (NL) Limited
Incorporated: 13 November 2006
Net Worth Deficit: £27,878,000 *Total Assets:* £69,987,000
Registered Office: Etel House, Avenue One, Letchworth Garden City, Herts, SG6 2HU
Activities: Activities of head offices
Parent: Kwik Fit Euro Limited
Officers: Ian Vincent Ellis, Secretary; Yasuyuki Harada [1959] Director [Japanese]; Mark Lynott [1975] Director

Kwik-Fit Euro Limited
Incorporated: 4 November 1998
Net Worth: £10,146,000 *Total Assets:* £220,903,008
Registered Office: Etel House, Avenue One, Letchworth Garden City, Herts, SG6 2HU
Activities: Activities of head offices
Parent: Kwik Fit Holdings Limited
Officers: Ian Vincent Ellis, Secretary; Yasuyuki Harada [1959] Director [Japanese]; Mark Lynott [1975] Director

Kwik-Fit Finance Limited
Incorporated: 1 July 2002
Net Worth: £5,587,000 *Total Assets:* £142,388,992
Registered Office: Etel House, Avenue One, Letchworth Garden City, Herts, SG6 2HU
Activities: Activities of head offices
Parent: Kwik Fit Group Ltd
Officers: Ian Vincent Ellis, Secretary; Yasuyuki Harada [1959] Director [Japanese]; Mark Lynott [1975] Director

Kwik-Fit Group Limited
Incorporated: 1 July 2002
Net Worth: £111,196,000 *Total Assets:* £364,127,008
Registered Office: Etel House, Avenue One, Letchworth Garden City, Herts, SG6 2HU
Activities: Activities of head offices
Parent: Speedy 1 Limited
Officers: Ian Vincent Ellis, Secretary; Yasuyuki Harada [1959] Director [Japanese]; Mark Lynott [1975] Director

Kwik-Fit Holdings Limited
Incorporated: 12 July 1940
Net Worth: £28,510,000 *Total Assets:* £29,419,000
Registered Office: Etel House, Avenue One, Letchworth Garden City, Herts, SG6 2HU
Activities: Activities of head offices
Parent: Kwik Fit Finance Limited
Officers: Ian Vincent Ellis, Secretary; Yasuyuki Harada [1959] Director [Japanese]; Mark Lynott [1975] Director

KWS UK Limited
Incorporated: 10 August 1981 *Employees:* 79
Net Worth: £13,744,000 *Total Assets:* £16,579,000
Registered Office: 56 Church Street, Thriplow, Royston, Herts, SG8 7RE
Activities: Growing of cereals (except rice), leguminous crops and oil seeds
Parent: KWS Saat SE
Officers: Robert Geoffrey Hunt [1980] Commercial Director; Andrew David Newby [1961] Director/Commercial Manager; Dr Christopher Robert Tapsell [1956] Technical Director

Kymab Group Limited
Incorporated: 6 October 2016 *Employees:* 161
Net Worth: £39,811,000 *Total Assets:* £49,372,000
Registered Office: The Bennet Building (B930), Babraham Research Campus, Cambridge, CB22 3AT
Activities: Other business support service activities n.e.c.
Shareholder: The Wellcome Trust Limited (as Trustee of The Wellcome Trust)
Officers: Anne Hyland, Secretary; Professor Allan Bradley [1960] Scientist and Institute Director; Jean-Michel Yves Sylvain Cossery [1959] Director [French]; Christian Martin Itin [1964] Director/Consultant [Swiss]; Martin Nicklasson [1955] Director [Swedish]; Lisha Nagin Patel [1980] Director/Investment Manager; Dr Timothy James Rink [1946] Consultant Director; Hong Fang Song [1965] Director/Senior Partner [Chinese/Hong Kong]; Li Tan [1964] Director/Vice President [Chinese]; Edward Ian Walker Arnott [1939] Director/Solicitor; Dr Timothy Nigel Carl Wells [1962] Director/Research Scientist

Kymab Limited
Incorporated: 23 September 2009 *Employees:* 159
Net Worth Deficit: £43,770,000 *Total Assets:* £17,714,000
Registered Office: The Bennet Building (B930), Babraham Research Campus, Cambridge, CB22 3AT
Activities: Other professional, scientific and technical activities n.e.c.
Parent: Kymab Group Limited
Officers: Anne Hyland, Secretary; Professor Allan Bradley [1960] Scientist and Institute Director

L & L Inc Limited
Incorporated: 12 April 2002 *Employees:* 174
Net Worth: £17,016,472 *Total Assets:* £41,962,976
Registered Office: Merc Benz of Hertford, John Tate Road, Hertford, SG13 7LB
Activities: Sale of new cars and light motor vehicles
Officers: Ken Glass, Secretary; Kai Hung Michael Leung [1942] Director/Merchant [Canadian]; Brian Man Bun Li [1974] Director/Banker; David Presley [1949] Brand Director; Jim Wang [1957] Director/Management Executive

L & M (Heating) Supplies Limited
Incorporated: 27 April 1970 *Employees:* 40
Net Worth: £11,093,762 *Total Assets:* £17,089,968
Registered Office: 103 Lockfield Avenue, Enfield, Middlesex, EN3 7PY
Activities: Non-specialised wholesale trade
Parent: L & M Holding Limited
Officers: Hasnain Ali [1978] Director; Michael Leonard Louis Jones [1949] Director; Muhammad Ali Makkani [1976] Director [Pakistani]

L & M Holding Ltd
Incorporated: 16 December 2014 *Employees:* 40
Net Worth: £4,894,165 *Total Assets:* £13,660,850
Registered Office: 795 St Albans Road, Watford, Herts, WD25 9LA
Activities: Activities of head offices
Officers: Hasnain Ali [1978] Director; Muhammad Ali Makkani [1976] Director [Pakistani]

L V Shipping Limited
Incorporated: 25 July 1983 *Employees:* 204
Net Worth: £9,188,914 *Total Assets:* £19,670,016
Registered Office: LV House, Walton Avenue, Felixstowe, Suffolk, IP11 3AL
Activities: Other transportation support activities
Officers: Lee Woolams, Secretary; Colin Ainsley [1957] Transport & Warehouse Director; Timothy Collier [1960] Project Director; Adrian Paul French [1959] Director; Christopher John Craig Thomas Lewin [1951] Director; Kevin Walsh [1966] UK Sales Director; Andrew John Willis - Betts [1966] Director/Import/Export Agent; Stuart Young [1971] Director

L.H.D.Limited
Incorporated: 1 December 1943 *Employees:* 64
Net Worth: £18,337,332 *Total Assets:* £54,914,556
Registered Office: Excelsior House, 9 Quay View Business Park, Barnards Way, Lowestoft, Suffolk, NR32 2HD
Activities: Other service activities n.e.c.
Officers: Hazel Jane Henderson, Secretary; Andrew Crossan [1975] Director; Hazel Jane Henderson [1959] Director/Accountant; Richard Harald Simpson [1956] Director; Brian Spence [1969] Director; Charles Gary Spence [1969] Director/Fish Salesman

Labvantage Solutions Limited
Incorporated: 14 March 1997 *Employees:* 22
Net Worth: £2,021,899 *Total Assets:* £19,619,416
Registered Office: Instron House, Coronation Road, High Wycombe, Bucks, HP12 3SY
Activities: Other information technology service activities
Officers: Marc Aronowitz [1963] Director [American]; Swadesh Chatterjee [1947] Director [American]

Laen Limited
Incorporated: 17 December 2002
Net Worth: £10,864,139 *Total Assets:* £11,042,900
Registered Office: c/o Gaswise Services Limited, Horsleys Fields, Hardwick Road, Kings Lynn, Norfolk, PE30 5DD
Activities: Other letting and operating of own or leased real estate
Officers: Susan Barbara Neal, Secretary; Frank Anthony Neal [1949] Director/Engineer; Mark James Neal [1972] Director/Manager; Paul Anthony Neal [1969] Director/Manager; Susan Barbara Neal [1950] Director/Manager

Laindon Holdings Limited
Incorporated: 11 October 1937 *Employees:* 3
Net Worth: £19,486,946 *Total Assets:* £96,455,984
Registered Office: Service House, West Mayne, Basildon, Essex, SS15 6RW
Activities: Management consultancy activities other than financial management
Major Shareholder: Michael John Toomey
Officers: Neil Duncan Rickwood, Secretary; Jonathan Paul Brook [1950] Director; Peter Lewis Gillett [1942] Director/Chartered Accountant; Daniel Trevor Martine [1975] Director; Neil Duncan Rickwood [1974] Director/Chartered Accountant; Michael John Toomey [1938] Director; Timothy Edward Wallace [1949] Director

Laindon Trading LLP
Incorporated: 4 November 2010 *Employees:* 168
Net Worth: £9,837,853 *Total Assets:* £12,315,570
Registered Office: Courtauld House, Courtauld Road, Basildon, Essex, SS13 1RZ
Officers: Graham Joseph Toomey [1961] Member

Lakehouse Contracts Limited
Incorporated: 19 April 1991 *Employees:* 228
Net Worth: £2,469,000 *Total Assets:* £82,165,000
Registered Office: Academy Place, 1-9 Brook Street, Brentwood, Essex, CM14 5NQ
Activities: Development of building projects
Parent: Mapps Group Limited
Officers: Mark Elkington [1967] Group SHEQ Director; Darren Colin Pace [1964] Director

Lakeside Food Group Limited
Incorporated: 15 June 1989 *Employees:* 33
Net Worth: £2,510,994 *Total Assets:* £25,919,416
Registered Office: The Courtyard, Ketteringham Hall, Church Road, Ketteringham, Wymondham, Norfolk, NR18 9RS
Activities: Wholesale of meat and meat products
Parent: Bellfort Limited
Officers: Graham Mark Edwards, Secretary/Director; Adrian James Carr [1962] Director; Graham Mark Edwards [1970] Director; Gary Irvine [1966] Sales Director; Hayley Rebecca Toleman [1984] Finance Director

W Lamb Limited
Incorporated: 20 August 1942 *Employees:* 4
Net Worth: £10,897,947 *Total Assets:* £25,146,604
Registered Office: Painesend Farm, Painesend, Tring, Herts, HP23 6JU
Activities: Operation of warehousing and storage facilities for land transport activities
Parent: W Lamb Holdings Ltd
Officers: Philippa Jane Gill, Secretary; Peter Samuel Vallis [1942] Director

Lamb-Weston/Meijer UK Limited
Incorporated: 14 February 1991 *Employees:* 141
Net Worth: £20,780,262 *Total Assets:* £26,444,370
Registered Office: Wesenham Lane, Wisbech, Cambs, PE13 2RN
Activities: Other business support service activities n.e.c.
Parent: Smith & Holbourne (Holdings) Limited
Officers: Simon Hendrik Peter Van Wouwe, Secretary; Bas Albas [1960] Managing Director [Dutch]; Simon Hendrik Pieter Van Wouwe [1967] Director [Dutch]; Johannes Adriaan Willem Wiskerke [1971] Director [Dutch]

Mervyn Lambert Plant Limited
Incorporated: 1 July 1987 *Employees:* 276
Net Worth: £12,863,685 *Total Assets:* £32,723,292
Registered Office: 89 High Street, Hadleigh, Ipswich, Suffolk, IP7 5EA
Activities: Other specialised construction activities n.e.c.
Major Shareholder: Mervyn Lambert
Officers: Kevin Shepherd, Secretary; Richard John Edmunds [1956] Director/Plant Manager; James Mervyn Lambert [1973] Director/Manager; Mervyn Lambert [1948] Director; Kevin Shepherd [1955] Director/Accountant; Dennis Norman Varley [1968] Director; Peter John West [1979] Director

Lamesta Limited
Incorporated: 31 March 2015
Net Worth: £1,846,918 *Total Assets:* £14,738,456
Registered Office: 516 London Road, Westcliff on Sea, Essex, SS0 9LD
Activities: Other letting and operating of own or leased real estate
Officers: Harvey Shaw, Secretary; Alice Mence [1982] Director; Stuart Mence [1980] Director

CW Lamley & Co Limited
Incorporated: 20 August 2014 *Employees:* 34
Net Worth: £65,382,768 *Total Assets:* £67,733,312
Registered Office: King Street House, 15 Upper King Street, Norwich, NR3 1RB
Activities: Hotels and similar accommodation
Parent: Mansley Group Holdings Limited
Officers: Margaret Ann Fletcher, Secretary; Margaret Ann Fletcher [1950] Director; Sir Richard Charles Rowley [1959] Director; Colin William Stone [1971] Commercial Director

Lanber Nursing Homes LLP
Incorporated: 16 September 2008
Net Worth: £7,634,926 *Total Assets:* £26,723,600
Registered Office: 47 Canons Drive, Edgware, Middlesex, HA8 7RG

Lanber Properties LLP
Incorporated: 16 September 2008
Net Worth: £149,818,208 *Total Assets:* £418,378,048
Registered Office: 47 Canons Drive, Edgware, Middlesex, HA8 7RG

Lancaster Cars Limited
Incorporated: 17 August 1954 *Employees:* 910
Net Worth: £22,504,000 *Total Assets:* £100,647,000
Registered Office: 770 The Crescent, Colchester Business Park, Colchester, Essex, CO4 9YQ
Activities: Sale of new cars and light motor vehicles
Parent: Lancaster PLC
Officers: Mark Finch, Secretary; David John Muir [1980] Director; David Neil Williamson [1965] Director

Lancaster Luxury Vehicles Limited
Incorporated: 18 June 1954 *Employees:* 371
Net Worth: £24,889,000 *Total Assets:* £87,158,000
Registered Office: 770 The Crescent, Colchester Business Park, Colchester, Essex, CO4 9YQ
Activities: Sale of new cars and light motor vehicles
Parent: Lancaster PLC
Officers: Mark Finch, Secretary; David John Muir [1980] Director; David Neil Williamson [1965] Director

Lancaster Motor Company Limited
Incorporated: 15 March 1919 *Employees:* 1,968
Net Worth: £18,103,000 *Total Assets:* £217,504,992
Registered Office: 770 The Crescent, Colchester Business Park, Colchester, Essex, CO4 9YQ
Activities: Sale of new cars and light motor vehicles
Parent: Lancaster PLC
Officers: Mark Finch, Secretary; David John Muir [1980] Director; David Neil Williamson [1965] Director

Lancaster Public Limited Company
Incorporated: 13 January 1981 *Employees:* 3,676
Net Worth: £46,141,000 *Total Assets:* £545,438,976
Registered Office: 770 The Crescent, Colchester Business Park, Colchester, Essex, CO4 9YQ
Activities: Sale of new cars and light motor vehicles
Parent: Jardine Motors Group UK Limited
Officers: Mark Finch, Secretary; David John Muir [1980] Director; David Neil Williamson [1965] Director

Lancaster Specialist Cars Limited
Incorporated: 6 August 1963 *Employees:* 158
Net Worth: £10,632,000 *Total Assets:* £25,487,000
Registered Office: 770 The Crescent, Colchester Business Park, Colchester, Essex, CO4 9YQ
Activities: Sale of new cars and light motor vehicles
Parent: Lancaster PLC
Officers: Mark Finch, Secretary; David John Muir [1980] Director; David Neil Williamson [1965] Director

Lancaster Sports Cars Limited
Incorporated: 19 December 1990 *Employees:* 28
Net Worth: £6,708,000 *Total Assets:* £31,183,000
Registered Office: 770 The Crescent, Colchester Business Park, Colchester, Essex, CO4 9YQ
Activities: Sale of new cars and light motor vehicles
Parent: Lancaster PLC
Officers: Mark Finch, Secretary; David John Muir [1980] Director; David Neil Williamson [1965] Director

Land Charter (Harlow) Ltd
Incorporated: 10 November 2015 *Employees:* 8
Net Worth Deficit: £2,089,530 *Total Assets:* £32,171,076
Registered Office: The Barn, Woods Farm, Grange Road, Pleshey, Chelmsford, Essex, CM3 1HZ
Activities: Development of building projects
Shareholder: Henrik Maurice Darlington
Officers: Michael John Burton [1961] Director; Edward Generald Buttleman [1959] Director; Sheldon Ross Collins [1965] Director; Henrik Maurice Darlington [1961] Director; Michael Joseph Lumanto [1994] Director [Indonesian]

Land Finance & Mortgage Corporation Limited (The)
Incorporated: 29 June 1933 *Employees:* 5
Net Worth: £6,479,620 *Total Assets:* £9,289,210
Registered Office: 84 Market Place, Romford, Essex, RM1 3JE
Activities: Buying and selling of own real estate
Parent: Romford Construction Company Ltd
Officers: Nicholas Hilbery Chaplin, Secretary; Sir Malcolm Hilbery Chaplin [1934] Director/Chartered Surveyor; Nicholas Hilbery Chaplin [1965] Director/Chartered Surveyor; Ruth Mary Chaplin [1966] Director/Chartered Surveyor

The Land Group (Suffolk) Limited
Incorporated: 17 July 2006
Net Worth Deficit: £1,075,277 *Total Assets:* £14,885,395
Registered Office: 1 Quay Point, Station Road, Woodbridge, Suffolk, IP12 4AL
Activities: Other business support service activities n.e.c.
Officers: Andrew George Doyle, Secretary; Andrew George Doyle [1956] Director; Lindsay Stewart Neilson [1948] Director; Nigel Charles Seaton Robson [1963] Director; David Jeremy Winch [1955] Director

Land Management Limited
Incorporated: 29 April 1922
Net Worth: £9,817,464 *Total Assets:* £11,257,629
Registered Office: 43 Market Place, Romford, Essex, RM1 3AB
Activities: Other letting and operating of own or leased real estate
Shareholder: William D'Urban Sunnucks
Officers: Conor O'Mahony, Secretary; Shaun David Barker [1971] Director; William D'Urban Sunnucks [1956] Director/Accountant

Landchief Limited
Incorporated: 9 December 1971
Net Worth: £9,085,763 *Total Assets:* £14,434,618
Registered Office: Houghton Hall, The Green, Houghton Regis, Dunstable, Beds, LU5 5DY
Activities: Other letting and operating of own or leased real estate
Parent: Chamberlain Holdings PLC
Officers: Vena Chambury, Secretary; Christopher Paul Bugden [1966] Finance Director; John Maxwell Chamberlain [1942] Director; Vena Chambury [1955] Director/Estate Management; Stefan Mucha [1957] Director; Peter Bernard Wayte [1949] Director/Solicitor

Landex Commercial Property Limited
Incorporated: 16 August 2016 *Employees:* 4
Net Worth: £8,359,348 *Total Assets:* £8,533,218
Registered Office: 19 Holywells Road, Ipswich, Suffolk, IP3 0DL
Activities: Other letting and operating of own or leased real estate
Shareholders: Daniel James Davies; Barbara Elizabeth Davies; Thomas Glyn Davis
Officers: Julian Paul Wallace-King, Secretary; Barbara Elizabeth Davies [1947] Director; Daniel James Davies [1977] Director; Thomas Glyn Davies [1949] Director; Julian Paul Wallace-King [1955] Director

Landex Holdings Limited
Incorporated: 7 September 2016
Net Worth: £5,799,352 *Total Assets:* £15,324,004
Registered Office: 19 Holywells Road, Ipswich, Suffolk, IP3 0DL
Activities: Activities of other holding companies n.e.c.
Shareholders: Barbara Elizabeth Davies; Daniel James Davies; Thomas Glyn Davies
Officers: Julian Paul Wallace-King, Secretary; Barbara Elizabeth Davies [1947] Director; Daniel James Davies [1977] Director; Thomas Glyn Davies [1949] Director

Landex Limited
Incorporated: 25 April 2006 *Employees:* 20
Net Worth: £11,146,920 *Total Assets:* £20,665,156
Registered Office: 19 Holywells Road, Ipswich, Suffolk, IP3 0DL
Activities: Construction of domestic buildings
Shareholders: Thomas Glyn Davies; Barbara Elizabeth Davies; Daniel James Davies
Officers: Julian Paul Wallace-King, Secretary; Tony James Burrows [1961] Director/Construction; Daniel James Davies [1977] Director; Thomas Glyn Davies [1949] Director; Julian Paul Wallace-King [1955] Director/Chartered Accountant

Landis + Gyr Limited
Incorporated: 4 March 1975 *Employees:* 778
Net Worth Deficit: £47,075,000 *Total Assets:* £79,693,000
Registered Office: 1 Lysander Drive, Northfields Industrial Estate, Market Deeping, Peterborough, PE6 8FB
Activities: Manufacture of electronic components
Parent: Bayard Metering (UK)
Officers: Stephen George Cunningham [1966] Director/Chief Executive Officer UK and Ireland; Adrian Theiler [1972] Director [Swiss]; Charles Philip Walker [1972] Director/Chief Financial Officer

Landlink Ltd
Incorporated: 30 September 1982 *Employees:* 7
Net Worth: £5,228,411 *Total Assets:* £9,908,202
Registered Office: Hardy House, Northbridge Road, Berkhamsted, Herts, HP4 1EF
Activities: Construction of domestic buildings
Shareholders: Simon Keeler; Nicholas Keeler; Kate Marcella Keeler
Officers: Nicholas Keeler, Secretary; Timothy Wainwright, Secretary; Nicholas Keeler [1965] Director/Development Surveyor; Simon Keeler [1963] Director/Chartered Surveyor

Landmark Aviation (UK) Limited
Incorporated: 28 March 2014 *Employees:* 2
Net Worth: £1 *Total Assets:* £10,099,046
Registered Office: Voyager House, 142 Prospect Way, Luton, Beds, LU2 9QH
Activities: Activities of other holding companies n.e.c.
Parent: BBA Overseas Holdings Limited
Officers: Yvette Helen Freeman [1967] Director; Daniel David Ruback [1977] Finance Director

Langley School (1960) Limited
Incorporated: 14 April 1960 *Employees:* 163
Net Worth: £7,311,014 *Total Assets:* £14,387,005
Registered Office: Langley Park, Loddon, Norfolk, NR14 6BJ
Activities: Primary education
Officers: Stephen John Brown [1957] Director/Quantity Surveyor; Brett William Burton [1966] Director/Business Owner; Anthony Steward Harmer [1943] Non-Executive Director Chairman; John Hamilton Miller [1962] Director/Marketing Consultant; Dr Hannah Mary Nearney [1978] Director/Consultant Psychiatrist; Matthew Timothy Newnham [1976] Director/Solicitor; Mark Alexander Nicholas [1976] Director; Sharon Leigh Turner [1957] Director/Accountant; Zak Ashley Virgin [1975] Director/Solicitor; Graham Ernest Watson [1962] Director/Chartered Secretary

Lanswood Limited
Incorporated: 10 June 1999 *Employees:* 20
Net Worth: £2,730,175 *Total Assets:* £11,249,099
Registered Office: Middleborough House, 16 Middleborough, Colchester, Essex, CO1 1QT
Activities: Development of building projects
Major Shareholder: Darin Muthana Shaikly
Officers: Valerie Ruth Shaikly, Secretary; Darin Muthana Shaikly [1966] Director; Valerie Shaikly [1969] Director

Lantern Recovery Specialists PLC
Incorporated: 2 November 1987
Net Worth: £6,534,051 *Total Assets:* £11,841,107
Registered Office: Lantern House, 39-41 High Street, Potters Bar, Herts, EN6 5AJ
Activities: Maintenance and repair of motor vehicles
Parent: Lantern Services (Holdings) Ltd
Officers: Craig Coleman, Secretary; Craig Coleman [1976] Director; Lee Coleman [1977] Director; Raymond Michael Coleman [1956] Director; Ryan Coleman [1982] Director

Lantern Services (Holdings) Ltd
Incorporated: 8 February 2013 *Employees:* 145
Net Worth: £20,017,228 *Total Assets:* £24,863,076
Registered Office: 39-41 High Street, Potters Bar, Herts, EN6 5AJ
Activities: Activities of other holding companies n.e.c.
Shareholder: Raymond Michael Coleman
Officers: Craig Coleman, Secretary; Craig Coleman [1976] Director; Lee Coleman [1977] Director; Raymond Michael Coleman [1956] Director; Ryan Coleman [1982] Director

Lapid Developments Limited
Incorporated: 29 January 1971
Net Worth: £21,827,756 *Total Assets:* £24,292,516
Registered Office: 5 Elstree Gate, Elstree Way, Borehamwood, Herts, WD6 1JD
Activities: Renting and operating of Housing Association real estate
Parent: Meekport Limited
Officers: Eldad Aizenberg, Secretary; Eldad Aizenberg [1957] Managing Director; Naomi Braybrooke [1967] Director/Museum Education; Daniel Cigman [1969] Director; Julie Cigman [1954] Director/Advisory Teacher; Dr Ruth Cigman [1951] Director/University Lecturer

Laridge Investments Limited
Incorporated: 21 November 2002
Net Worth: £62,080,636 *Total Assets:* £62,087,812
Registered Office: First Floor, Woodgate Studios, 2-8 Games Road, Cockfosters, Barnet, Herts, EN4 9HN
Activities: Other business support service activities n.e.c.
Major Shareholder: Oksana Marcheno
Officers: Anna Korelidou, Secretary; Menelaos Sazos [1974] Director/Advocate [Cypriot]

Larkfleet Homes Limited
Incorporated: 27 May 2015 *Employees:* 86
Net Worth: £23,762,122 *Total Assets:* £85,049,576
Registered Office: Larkfleet House, Falcon Way, Southfields Business Park, Bourne, Lincs, PE10 0FF
Activities: Activities of head offices
Shareholders: Karl Stephen Hick; Kingfisher Ventures Limited
Officers: Deborah Brown, Secretary; Helen Hick [1959] Director; Karl Stephen Hick [1959] Director

Larkfleet Limited
Incorporated: 2 March 1998 *Employees:* 79
Net Worth: £23,784,376 *Total Assets:* £76,677,024
Registered Office: Larkfleet House, Falcon Way, Southfields Business Park, Bourne, Lincs, PE10 0FF
Activities: Construction of domestic buildings
Parent: Larkfleet Holdings Limited
Officers: Deborah Brown, Secretary; Daniel Michael Endersby [1986] Director; Helen Hick [1956] Director; Karl Stephen Hick [1959] Director; Daryl Kirkland [1967] Director; Mark Mann [1960] Director; Terry Rene Roydon [1946] Director

Larkspur Investments Limited
Incorporated: 24 July 2012
Net Worth: £7,678 *Total Assets:* £8,533,528
Registered Office: 68 St Margarest Road, Edgware, Middlesex, HA8 9UU
Activities: Buying and selling of own real estate
Major Shareholder: Bina Raju Kishinani
Officers: Bina Kishinani, Secretary; Bina Raju Kishinani [1960] Director

Lasted Limited
Incorporated: 7 September 2011 *Employees:* 3
Net Worth: £8,072,313 *Total Assets:* £22,026,456
Registered Office: Northside House, Mount Pleasant, Barnet, Herts, EN4 9EE
Activities: Other letting and operating of own or leased real estate
Shareholders: Melvyn Frank Cooper; Jason Robert Cooper
Officers: Adam Cooper, Secretary; Adam Cooper [1971] Director; Jason Robert Cooper [1971] Director; Melvyn Frank Cooper [1941] Director

James Latham Public Limited Company
Incorporated: 7 April 1900 *Employees:* 385
Net Worth: £89,789,000 *Total Assets:* £131,763,000
Registered Office: Unit 3 Swallow Park, Finway Road, Hemel Hempstead, Herts, HP2 7QU
Activities: Wholesale of wood, construction materials and sanitary equipment
Officers: David Alan Dunmow, Secretary; David Alan Dunmow [1964] Finance Director; Philip Luke Fabian French [1959] Director; Nicholas Charles Latham [1968] Director; Piers Francis Latham [1971] Director; Christopher David Sutton [1958] Director; Andrew George Wright [1964] Director

Lathams Limited
Incorporated: 1 December 1969 *Employees:* 360
Net Worth: £92,158,000 *Total Assets:* £125,868,000
Registered Office: Unit 3 Swallow Park, Finway Road, Hemel Hempstead, Herts, HP2 7QU
Activities: Wholesale of wood, construction materials and sanitary equipment
Parent: James Latham PLC
Officers: David Alan Dunmow, Finance Director; Andrew Carey Duffin [1962] Director; David Alan Dunmow [1964] Finance Director; Stephen Andrew Frommont [1971] Commercial Director; Nicholas Charles Latham [1968] Director; Piers Francis Latham [1971] Director; Christopher David Sutton [1958] Director; Nicholas James Widlinski [1981] Panel Sales Director; Andrew George Wright [1964] Director

Latif International Limited
Incorporated: 2 September 1998
Net Worth: £975,970 *Total Assets:* £8,841,004
Registered Office: Latif House, First Way, Wembley, Middlesex, HA9 0JD
Activities: Manufacture of woven or tufted carpets and rugs
Major Shareholder: Abdul Abraham Latif
Officers: Latifa Latif [1972] Director

Latimer Hill LLP
Incorporated: 15 February 2017
Net Worth: £8,756,000 *Total Assets:* £14,366,000
Registered Office: The Power House, Gunpowder Mill, Powdermill Lane, Waltham Abbey, Essex, EN9 1BN

R.A. Latta (Farms) Limited
Incorporated: 26 April 1977
Net Worth: £10,330,378 *Total Assets:* £17,036,968
Registered Office: Salisbury House, Station Road, Cambridge, CB1 2LA
Activities: Growing of cereals (except rice), leguminous crops and oil seeds
Shareholders: Hannelore Latta; Mathew Rodger Robert Latta
Officers: Hannelore Latta, Secretary; Hannelore Latta [1943] Director; Mathew Rodger Robert Latta [1974] Director/Farming

Ralph Lauren UK Limited
Incorporated: 17 August 1994
Net Worth: £8,572,470 *Total Assets:* £79,218,344
Registered Office: 46 Clarendon Road, Watford, Herts, WD1 1DR
Activities: Wholesale of clothing and footwear
Parent: RL Retail Services Limited
Officers: Aldo Alex Fleri [1961] Director/Vice President Sales UK; Carmel Ann Pedatella [1974] Director/Business Executive [American]; Robert Patrick Ranftl [1971] Director/Business Executive [American]; Andrew Howard Smith [1971] Director/Business Executive

Laurence Homes (Eastern) Limited
Incorporated: 2 November 1981 *Employees:* 8
Net Worth: £8,736,480 *Total Assets:* £11,456,866
Registered Office: 1 Nelson Street, Southend on Sea, Essex, SS1 1EG
Activities: Construction of domestic buildings
Officers: Barry Hickey, Secretary; Ian John Baker [1958] Building Director; Kenneth Elman [1961] Director/Solicitor

Lawes Agricultural Trust
Incorporated: 19 February 2014
Net Worth: £23,730,634 *Total Assets:* £26,624,868
Registered Office: Rothamsted, Harpenden, Herts, AL5 2JQ
Activities: Support activities for crop production
Officers: Peter Duncan Oxley, Secretary; Dr Tina Lorraine Barsby [1957] Director/Institute CEO; Professor Sir David Charles Baulcombe [1952] Director; Dr Graham John Birch [1960] Director/Farmer; Lord Ewen James Hanning Cameron [1949] Director/Landowner; William Andrew Lindsay Gemmill [1965] Farming Consultant and Senior Director; Professor Hugh Charles Jonathan Godfray [1958] Director/Research Professor; Peter Ashley Kendall [1960] Director/Farmer

Lawford & Sons Limited
Incorporated: 28 April 1910 *Employees:* 2
Net Worth: £8,782,605 *Total Assets:* £9,563,350
Registered Office: The Barn, Green Farm, Bovingdon Green, Hemel Hempstead, Herts, HP3 0LF
Activities: Buying and selling of own real estate
Major Shareholder: Graham Frederick Barrett
Officers: Graham Frederick Barrett, Secretary; Graham Frederick Barrett [1956] Director; Raymond Barrett [1924] Director

Lawson Partners Limited
Incorporated: 4 November 1998 *Employees:* 149
Net Worth: £22,220,182 *Total Assets:* £35,412,956
Registered Office: Hill House Farm, Stradbroke, Eye, Suffolk, IP21 5NB
Activities: Activities of head offices
Shareholders: Robert George Lawson; Adrian Phillip Lawson
Officers: Mark Philip Ledger, Secretary; Adrian Philip Lawson [1958] Director; Robert George Lawson [1959] Director

Lawsons (Whetstone) Limited
Incorporated: 16 February 1993 *Employees:* 431
Net Worth: £22,302,332 *Total Assets:* £33,820,152
Registered Office: Tyttenhanger Farm, Coursers Road, Colney Heath, Herts, AL4 0PG
Activities: Wholesale of wood, construction materials and sanitary equipment
Parent: Lawsons Holdings Limited
Officers: Paul Julian Rushent, Secretary; Paul Walter Benton [1943] Director/Chartered Accountant; Anthony John Elliott [1948] Director/Consultant; Michael Terence Hillier [1966] Director; John Edmund Maltby Lawson [1932] Director; Simon John Lawson [1960] Director/Manager; Jeremy Nicholas Norris [1967] Director/IT Manager; Paul Julian Rushent [1957] Director; Paul William Sexton [1964] Director

Lawsons Holdings Limited
Incorporated: 2 July 2003 *Employees:* 461
Net Worth: £50,308,108 *Total Assets:* £72,056,328
Registered Office: Tyttenhanger Farm, Coursers Road, Colney Heath, Herts, AL4 0PG
Activities: Agents involved in the sale of timber and building materials
Shareholder: John Edmund Maltby Lawson
Officers: Paul Julian Rushent, Secretary; Paul Walter Benton [1943] Director/Chartered Accountant; John Edmund Maltby Lawson [1932] Director; Simon John Lawson [1960] Director/Manager; Jeremy Nicholas Norris [1967] Director; Paul Julian Rushent [1957] Director; Paul William Sexton [1964] Director

Laxkan Holdings Ltd
Incorporated: 30 November 2016
Net Worth: £126,006 *Total Assets:* £15,322,764
Registered Office: Kimberley House, 31 Burnt Oak Broadway, Edgware, Middlesex, HA8 5LD
Activities: Other service activities n.e.c.
Officers: Premchand Kantilal Shah [1937] Director; Vinay Shah [1974] Director

Laxkan Ltd
Incorporated: 30 November 2016
Net Worth: £8,328,111 *Total Assets:* £14,028,788
Registered Office: Kimberley House, 31 Burnt Oak Broadway, Edgware, Middlesex, HA8 5LD
Activities: Other service activities n.e.c.
Parent: Laxkan Holdings Limited
Officers: Premchand Kantilal Shah [1937] Director; Vinay Shah [1974] Director

Laxmi BNS Holdings Limited
Incorporated: 10 February 2010 *Employees:* 646
Net Worth: £22,051,180 *Total Assets:* £109,609,696
Registered Office: Unit 4 Bradfield Road, Ruislip, Middlesex, HA4 0NU
Activities: Manufacture of basic pharmaceutical products
Officers: Govindji Hathi, Secretary; Alpa Hathi [1968] Director/HR; Govindji Thakershi Hathi [1941] Director; Samit Govindji Hathi [1967] Director

Laxmico Limited
Incorporated: 21 April 2009 *Employees:* 234
Net Worth: £3,491,584 *Total Assets:* £75,175,608
Registered Office: Unit 4 Bradfield Road, Ruislip, Middlesex, HA4 0NU
Activities: Wholesale of pharmaceutical goods
Major Shareholder: Samit Govindji Hathi
Officers: Govindji Hathi, Secretary; Alpa Hathi [1968] Director/HR; Govindji Thakershi Hathi [1941] Director; Samit Hathi [1967] Director/Pharmacist

Lay & Wheeler Limited
Incorporated: 6 March 2006 *Employees:* 24
Net Worth: £3,603,000 *Total Assets:* £16,707,000
Registered Office: Majestic House, The Belfry, Colonial Way, Watford, Herts, WD24 4WH
Activities: Wholesale of wine, beer, spirits and other alcoholic beverages
Parent: Majestic Wine Warehouses Limited
Officers: Alex Iapichino, Secretary; James Crawford [1977] Finance Director; Rowan Gormley [1962] Director [Irish]; Kathryn Dibble Andersen Keating [1986] Director/Businesswoman [American]

Layher Limited
Incorporated: 29 June 1987 *Employees:* 26
Net Worth: £2,942,729 *Total Assets:* £29,869,548
Registered Office: Unit 1b, Focus 4, Fourth Avenue, Letchworth Garden City, Herts, SG6 2TU
Activities: Wholesale of wood, construction materials and sanitary equipment
Parent: Layher International GmbH
Officers: Sean Pike, Secretary; Carolin Langer [1965] Director [German]; Georg Layher [1965] Director [German]; Sean Pike [1970] Managing Director

LB Enterprises Limited
Incorporated: 30 March 1998 *Employees:* 117
Net Worth: £12,461,668 *Total Assets:* £22,029,252
Registered Office: 118-126 Ilford Lane, Ilford, Essex, IG1 2LE
Activities: Retail sale in non-specialised stores with food, beverages or tobacco predominating
Shareholders: Arvind Bachubhai Sedani; Vipul Bachubhai Sedani; Pius Bachubhai Sedani
Officers: Arvind Bachubhai Sedani, Secretary; Arvind Bachubhai Sedani [1952] Director/Businessman [Kenyan]; Vipul Bachubhai Sedani [1963] Director/Businessman

LC Bet Limited
Incorporated: 4 May 2000 *Employees:* 2
Net Worth Deficit: £1,487,000 *Total Assets:* £11,133,000
Registered Office: Waterloo House, Unit 27 M11 Business Link, Parsonage Lane, Stansted, Essex, CM24 8GF
Activities: Non-trading company
Parent: The Wastepack Group Limited
Officers: Lynne Anne Cullis, Secretary; Lynne Anne Cullis [1969] Director/Chief Executive; Barry Peter Van Danzig [1948] Director/Entrepreneur

LC Packaging UK Ltd
Incorporated: 24 April 1981 *Employees:* 54
Net Worth: £3,227,389 *Total Assets:* £11,107,196
Registered Office: Bridge Road, Long Sutton, Spalding, Lincs, PE12 9EF
Activities: Non-specialised wholesale trade
Parent: LC Packaging International BV
Officers: Lucas Lammers [1966] Director [Dutch]; Martijn Schrooder [1969] Director [Dutch]

LDC (Boston) Limited
Incorporated: 13 October 1964
Net Worth: £10,716,034 *Total Assets:* £11,046,398
Registered Office: 14a South Parade, Boston, Lincs, PE21 7PL
Activities: Growing of cereals (except rice), leguminous crops and oil seeds
Major Shareholder: Willem Adrianus Den-Hartog
Officers: Adrian Den Hartog, Secretary; Adrian Den Hartog [1969] Director/Manager; Willem Adrianus Den-Hartog [1939] Director [Dutch]; Karen Louise Kirkendall [1968] Director

LDH (La Doria) Limited
Incorporated: 12 December 1996 *Employees:* 73
Net Worth: £58,814,000 *Total Assets:* £116,552,000
Registered Office: LDH House, Parsons Green, St Ives, Cambs, PE27 4AA
Activities: Wholesale of fruit and vegetables
Parent: La Doria S.P.A.
Officers: Enzo Diodato Lamberti, Secretary; Giuseppe di Martino [1970] Director [Italian]; Andrea Ferraioli [1957] Director [Italian]; Antonio Ferraioli [1954] Director [Italian]; Rosa Ferraioli [1951] Director/Manager [Italian]; Alberto Festa [1960] Director of Finance [Italian]; Barry Ivor Fine [1958] Director; David Elias Fine [1952] Director; Sergio Persico [1938] Director/Tax Consultant [Italian]; Paul Gerrard Reenan [1967] Managing Director John West UK Ltd [Irish]; David Sankowicz [1968] Director/Lawyer [French]

Le Bas Investment Trust Limited
Incorporated: 23 October 1930
Net Worth: £1,010,261 *Total Assets:* £18,025,536
Registered Office: Claydon Business Park, Gipping Road, Great Blakenham, Ipswich, Suffolk, IP6 0NL
Activities: Activities of head offices
Parent: Le Bas Limited
Officers: Angela Margaret Burrows, Secretary; Angela Margaret Burrows [1947] Director; Mark Quentin Harrison [1947] Director

Edward Le Bas Limited
Incorporated: 3 January 1962 *Employees:* 5
Net Worth: £16,974,848 *Total Assets:* £18,668,884
Registered Office: Claydon Business Park, Gipping Road, Great Blakenham, Ipswich, Suffolk, IP6 0NL
Activities: Activities of head offices
Parent: Le Bas Investment Trust Limited
Officers: Angela Margaret Burrows, Secretary; Angela Margaret Burrows [1947] Director; Edward Brocas Burrows [1975] Director; Fiona Elizabeth Fenella Burrows [1973] Director/Restoration; Joanna Molly Anne Cunningham-Reid [1969] Director/Masseuse; Carey Jane English [1968] Director/Artist; Angela Petra Walker [1972] Director/Administrator

Edward Le Bas Properties Limited
Incorporated: 13 May 1952
Net Worth: £28,213,576 *Total Assets:* £36,403,928
Registered Office: Claydon Business Park, Gipping Road, Great Blakenham, Ipswich, Suffolk, IP6 0NL
Activities: Other letting and operating of own or leased real estate
Parent: Edward Le Bas Limited
Officers: Angela Margaret Burrows, Secretary; Angela Margaret Burrows [1947] Director; Anthony Richard Brocas Burrows [1939] Director/Industrialist; Edward Brocas Burrows [1975] Director

Le Vack Estates Limited
Incorporated: 3 March 2014
Net Worth Deficit: £387,621 *Total Assets:* £8,053,605
Registered Office: Charter House, 103-105 Leigh Road, Leigh on Sea, Essex, SS9 1JL
Activities: Construction of domestic buildings
Major Shareholder: Robin Levy
Officers: Benjamin George Levy [1986] Director; Robin Levy [1944] Director/Property Developer

Lea Bridge Hill LLP
Incorporated: 1 December 2014
Total Assets: £28,153,000
Registered Office: The Power House, Gunpowder Mill, Powdermill Lane, Waltham Abbey, Essex, EN9 1BN

Learning Pathways Academy
Incorporated: 9 March 2012 *Employees:* 331
Net Worth: £14,475,660 *Total Assets:* £18,359,500
Registered Office: Learning Pathways Academy, Lyons Hall Primary School, Deerleap Way, Braintree, Essex, CM7 9FH
Activities: Primary education
Officers: Helen Davina Boyd [1978] Director/Auditor; Gavin Bradley [1972] Director/Headteacher; Darren Cross [1982] Director/Personnel Manager; Anthony Davenport [1978] Director/Teacher; Alison Ann Fiala [1957] Director/Lead Commissioner Primary Improvement; Lorraine Laudrum [1960] Director/Headteacher; Paul Arthur Lincoln [1946] Director/Retired; John Benedict O'Shea [1972] Director/Shopping Centre Manager; Joanne Olley [1970] Director/Chartered Accountant; Ryan Pearcy [1984] Director/Accountant; Rachel Claire Pritchard [1971] Director/Education; Nicholas Ridley [1973] Owner/Director Communications; Andrew David Smith [1963] Director/Education; Christopher Smith [1957] Director/Head of Education Technology & Business Development; Stephen Whitfield [1967] Director/Educational Psychologist

Leda Investments Limited
Incorporated: 1 October 2001
Net Worth: £1 *Total Assets:* £20,473,632
Registered Office: The Balsams Barn, Balsams Lane, Standon, Ware, Herts, SG11 1NS
Activities: Activities of other holding companies n.e.c.
Parent: Haras Investments Ltd
Officers: John Howard Williamson [1944] Director

C.J.C. Lee (Saxthorpe) Limited
Incorporated: 26 October 1954 *Employees:* 30
Net Worth: £3,058,718 *Total Assets:* £10,471,551
Registered Office: The Great Farm, Saxthorpe, Norfolk, NR11 7BX
Activities: Growing of cereals (except rice), leguminous crops and oil seeds
Major Shareholder: Peter John George Seaman
Officers: Sally Anne Mary Seaman, Secretary; Alexandra Flather [1986] Director/Farm Secretary; Peter John George Seaman [1948] Director/Farmer; Sally-Anne Seaman [1953] Director

Lee Chapel Multi Academy Trust
Incorporated: 17 June 2011 *Employees:* 289
Previous: Lee Chapel Academy Trust
Net Worth: £20,668,000 *Total Assets:* £27,055,000
Registered Office: Lee Chapel Primary School, The Knares, Basildon, Essex, SS16 5RU
Activities: Primary education
Officers: Victoria Louise Carter, Secretary; Michael Stephen Betteridge [1948] Director; Julie Anne Bird [1962] Director/Teacher; Alison Ann Fiala [1957] Director/Education Adviser; Susan Lynda Jackson [1961] Director/Headteacher; Megan Lillian Jenkins [1954] Director/Supports Governing Bodies; Dermot Gerard Kavanagh [1957] Director/Legal Cashier; Craig O'Callaghan [1962] Director/Chief Operating Officer; Grace Ebun Olugbodi [1978] Managing Director; Roderick Charles Graham Pollington [1970] Director/Shipping Planner; Steven Robson [1963] Director/Groundsman; Michael Donald Smith [1944] Director/Retired; Joyce Waylett [1939] Director/Retired

Robert Lee Distribution Limited
Incorporated: 30 April 1984 *Employees:* 200
Net Worth: £9,495,839 *Total Assets:* £17,693,266
Registered Office: Riverside Place, Lea Road, Waltham Abbey, Essex, EN9 1AS
Activities: Wholesale of wood, construction materials and sanitary equipment
Parent: New River Holdings Limited
Officers: Robert Alfred Ellender, Secretary; Barrie Colston Brackstone [1961] Director/Operations Manager; Martin Stewart Earle [1946] Director/Manager; Matthew Richard Earle [1973] Commercial Director; David John Ground [1963] Director; Charles William Valens Smith [1949] Director/Manager; Timothy John Wayman [1960] Managing Director

Leena Plaza Limited
Incorporated: 28 April 2006 *Employees:* 3
Net Worth: £2,590,369 *Total Assets:* £34,866,832
Registered Office: Kirkland House, 11-15 Peterborough Road, Harrow, Middlesex, HA1 2AX
Activities: Hotels and similar accommodation
Officers: Haider Ladhu Jaffer [1940] Director/Businessman; Hassanali Amirali Dawood Suleman [1954] Director/Businessman; Cameron Beresford Sunter [1956] Director/Solicitor

Legra Academy Trust
Incorporated: 11 May 2012 *Employees:* 479
Previous: Belfairs High School
Net Worth: £43,596,600 *Total Assets:* £53,961,176
Registered Office: Belfairs Academy, Highlands Boulevard, Leigh on Sea, Essex, SS9 3TG
Activities: General secondary education
Officers: Fay Evans [1937] Director/Councillor; Claire Louise Hankey [1972] Director/Manager; Chris John Hatton [1975] Director; John Peter Hunt [1971] Director/Deputy CEO; Anthony Robin Marcus [1956] Director/Solicitor; Adam Tregoning [1971] Director/Mayor's Officer; Beverley Ann Williams [1965] Director; Cheryl Janice Woolf [1952] Director/Headteacher

Leica Microsystems (UK) Limited
Incorporated: 30 December 1949 *Employees:* 155
Net Worth: £32,766,000 *Total Assets:* £53,985,000
Registered Office: Lothbury House, Newmarket Road, Cambridge, CB5 8PB
Activities: Other retail sale not in stores, stalls or markets
Parent: Launchchange Operations Ltd
Officers: David Lawrence Edwards, Secretary/Accountant; David Lawrence Edwards [1965] Director/Financial Controller; Andrew John Humes [1972] Director; Markus Rudolf Vornhagen [1970] Director [German]

Leica Microsystems Cambridge Limited
Incorporated: 21 February 1992 *Employees:* 30
Net Worth: £75,511,000 *Total Assets:* £78,326,000
Registered Office: Lothbury House, Newmarket Road, Cambridge, CB5 8PB
Activities: Other professional, scientific and technical activities n.e.c.
Parent: Kaltenbach & Voight Holdings GmbH
Officers: David Lawrence Edwards, Secretary/Accountant; David Lawrence Edwards [1965] Director/Finance Manager; Melanie Hammerschmidt-Broman [1969] Director/Chief Financial Officer [German]; Markus Rudolf Vornhagen [1970] Director [German]

Leicester Citybus Limited
Incorporated: 14 March 1986 *Employees:* 252
Net Worth: £40,761,000 *Total Assets:* £51,021,000
Registered Office: Bus Depot, Westway, Chelmsford, Essex, CM1 3AR
Activities: Other urban, suburban or metropolitan passenger land transport (not underground, metro or similar)
Parent: Firstbus (South) Limited
Officers: Michael Hampson, Secretary; David Brian Alexander [1965] Regional Managing Director; Simon Chadfield [1971] Director/Driver; Nigel Wilfrid Eggleton [1958] Managing Director

Leidos Limited
Incorporated: 25 February 2011 *Employees:* 30
Net Worth: £694,000 *Total Assets:* £59,838,000
Registered Office: Unit G8, Stirling House, Denny End Road, Waterbeach, Cambridge, CB25 9PB
Activities: Other business support service activities n.e.c.
Officers: Brendan Turley, Secretary; Matthew John Gethin Wiles [1961] Managing Director; Loraine Maureen Gregory [1959] Director/Financial Controller; Graham Moore [1964] Director/Financial Executive; James Corbett Reagan [1958] Director/Business Executive [American]

Leisure Parks Real Estate (Holdings) Limited
Incorporated: 7 February 2013 *Employees:* 3
Net Worth: £18,800,268 *Total Assets:* £50,471,672
Registered Office: 166 College Road, Harrow, Middlesex, HA1 1RA
Activities: Activities of other holding companies n.e.c.
Shareholder: Maurice Sines
Officers: Colin Crickmore [1958] Director; James Robert Crickmore [1980] Director; Maurice Sines [1962] Director

Leisure Parks Real Estate Limited
Incorporated: 13 August 2007 *Employees:* 3
Net Worth: £8,169,301 *Total Assets:* £31,056,944
Registered Office: 166 College Road, Harrow, Middlesex, HA1 1RA
Activities: Recreational vehicle parks, trailer parks and camping grounds
Parent: Leisure Parks Real Estate (Holdings) Limited
Officers: James Robert Crickmore, Secretary; Colin Crickmore [1958] Director; James Robert Crickmore [1980] Director; Maurice Sines [1962] Director

Leisuregrow Holdings Limited
Incorporated: 27 November 2000 *Employees:* 123
Net Worth: £9,596,000 *Total Assets:* £18,682,000
Registered Office: Dewmead Farm, New Inn Road, Hinxworth, Baldock, Herts, SG7 5HG
Activities: Activities of distribution holding companies
Parent: RGHV Limited
Officers: Richard Lynch, Secretary; Richard Paul Grimmer [1950] Director; James Travis [1958] Director

Leisuregrow Products Limited
Incorporated: 11 February 1999 *Employees:* 50
Net Worth: £3,020,014 *Total Assets:* £10,058,143
Registered Office: Dewmead Farm, New Inn Road, Hinxworth, Baldock, Herts, SG7 5HG
Activities: Non-specialised wholesale trade
Parent: Broomco (1356) Limited
Officers: Richard Lynch, Secretary/Director; Jody Richard Grimmer [1977] Commercial Director; Richard Paul Grimmer [1950] Director; Frank David Kaminski [1960] Director; James Quigley [1975] Director/Company Executive; James Travis [1958] Director/Commercial Executive

Leitrim Properties Limited
Incorporated: 31 October 1997 *Employees:* 2
Net Worth: £9,142,493 *Total Assets:* £15,569,435
Registered Office: 101 Rowlands Avenue, Hatch End, Pinner, Middlesex, HA5 4AW
Activities: Other letting and operating of own or leased real estate
Parent: Rowlands 2014 Limited
Officers: Noreen O'Hara, Secretary; Michael O'Hara [1947] Director/Public Works Contractor [Irish]

Lemon Groundwork Solutions Ltd
Incorporated: 26 September 1978 *Employees:* 97
Net Worth: £4,141,229 *Total Assets:* £13,436,697
Registered Office: Russell Gardens, Wickford, Essex, SS11 8BH
Activities: Manufacture of metal structures and parts of structures
Parent: CP (WBL) Limited
Officers: Kevin Roy Childs, Secretary; Kevin Roy Childs [1954] Director; Paul Hart [1979] Director/Depot Manager; Paul Pannell [1984] Director/Financial Controller; Colin John Prior [1960] Managing Director

Lenta Properties Limited
Incorporated: 4 March 1981 *Employees:* 55
Net Worth: £54,831,952 *Total Assets:* £70,508,912
Registered Office: CP House, Otterspool Way, Watford, Herts, WD25 8HR
Activities: Other letting and operating of own or leased real estate
Parent: Lenta Business Space Limited
Officers: Eric Lewis, Secretary/Solicitor; Paul Andrew Filer [1957] Director/Chartered Accountant; Ian Leslie Gibbor [1950] Director; Iris Gibbor [1951] Director; Mark Gibbor [1988] Director; Geoffrey Grodner [1961] Director/Chartered Accountant; Eric Lewis [1927] Director/Solicitor; Alexei James Schreier [1976] Director; Sarra Gay Temple [1959] Commercial Director

A.E. Lenton (Holdings) Limited
Incorporated: 8 May 1961 *Employees:* 31
Net Worth: £10,580,934 *Total Assets:* £18,018,910
Registered Office: Church End, Friskney, Boston, Lincs, PE22 8NE
Activities: Activities of agricultural holding companies
Shareholders: Markham Timothy Lenton Burnett; Graham John Shooter
Officers: Markham Timothy Lenton Burnett, Secretary; Markham Timothy Lenton Burnett [1967] Sales Director; Alan Edward Lenton Shooter [1978] Director; Graham John Shooter [1947] Director; Oliver John Lenton Shooter [1980] Farm Director

A.E. Lenton Limited
Incorporated: 6 October 1949 *Employees:* 16
Net Worth: £5,702,028 *Total Assets:* £12,291,994
Registered Office: Church End, Friskney, Lincs, PE22 8NE
Activities: Wholesale of fruit and vegetables
Parent: A.E. Lenton (Holdings) Limited
Officers: Marlene Shooter, Secretary; Markham Timothy Lenton Burnett [1967] Sales Director; Graham John Shooter [1947] Director; Oliver John Lenton Shooter [1980] Farm Director

Leonardo MW Ltd
Incorporated: 25 September 1989 *Employees:* 6,856
Previous: Selex ES Ltd
Net Worth: £1,670,075,008 *Total Assets:* £3,811,793,920
Registered Office: Sigma House, Christopher Martin Road, Basildon, Essex, SS14 3EL
Activities: Manufacture of communication equipment other than telegraph, and telephone apparatus and equipment
Parent: Leonardo S.P.A.
Officers: Kevin Geoffrey Thomsit, Secretary; Norman James Bone [1962] Managing Director; Gian Piero Cutillo [1963] Director [Italian]; Simonetta Iarlori [1962] Director/Chief People, Organisation and Transformation Officer [Italian]; Geoffrey Frank Munday [1955] Director; Andrea Parrella [1966] Director/Group General Counsel [Italian]; Craig Porter [1970] Finance Director

Les Residence Falcon Wharf Limited
Incorporated: 26 March 2007
Net Worth Deficit: £11,194,428 *Total Assets:* £17,120,400
Registered Office: 17 The Old Maltings, Hockerill Street, Bishop's Stortford, Herts, CM23 2ED
Activities: Buying and selling of own real estate
Major Shareholder: Iqbal Latif
Officers: Nasreen Latif, Secretary; Malcolm Roy Bass [1957] Director/Chartered Accountant; Nasreen Latif [1963] Director/Secretary [Pakistani]

Lester Hotels Group Limited
Incorporated: 9 September 1999 *Employees:* 206
Net Worth: £6,255,133 *Total Assets:* £12,769,418
Registered Office: St John House, The Walk, Potters Bar, Herts, EN6 1QQ
Activities: Non-trading company
Major Shareholder: Simon Mark Lester
Officers: Martin Johnstone, Secretary; Linda Lester [1963] Director; Simon Mark Lester [1964] Director

Letchworth Hall Hotel (Trading) Limited
Incorporated: 27 July 1976 *Employees:* 45
Net Worth Deficit: £1,303,751 *Total Assets:* £10,612,703
Registered Office: Kanta House, Victoria Road, South Ruislip, Middlesex, HA4 0JQ
Activities: Hotels and similar accommodation
Officers: Satish Jamnadas Chatwani, Secretary/Director; Jawahar Jamnadas Chatwani [1948] Director; Rashmi Jamnadas Chatwani [1954] Director; Satish Jamnadas Chatwani [1953] Director

Letchworth Housing Investments Limited
Incorporated: 18 January 2010 *Employees:* 2
Net Worth: £10,433,296 *Total Assets:* £11,100,612
Registered Office: P O Box 501, The Nexus Building, Broadway, Letchworth Garden City, Herts, SG6 9BL
Activities: Fund management activities
Officers: Corinna Drury Tabor, Secretary; John Hilditch [1945] Director/Estate Agent; Keith William Middleton [1951] Director/Accountant; Corinna Drury Tabor [1954] Director/Company Secretary Bookkeeper

Letting International Limited
Incorporated: 27 August 1997 *Employees:* 53
Net Worth: £2,520,060 *Total Assets:* £10,095,509
Registered Office: Gabrielle House, 332-336 Perth Road, Ilford, Essex, IG2 6FF
Activities: Management of real estate on a fee or contract basis
Parent: Lint Group Limited
Officers: Tarsaim Chand, Secretary/Director; Tarsaim Chand [1967] Director; Rizwan Patel [1974] Director

Levantera Developments Limited
Incorporated: 29 October 2012
Net Worth: £2,958,140 *Total Assets:* £44,040,472
Registered Office: Beeston Lodge, Beeston Lane, Spixworth, Norwich, NR10 3TN
Activities: Renting and leasing of other machinery, equipment and tangible goods n.e.c.
Parent: Aegletes Holdco Limited
Officers: Steven Disley [1989] Director [Canadian]; Brian Moncik [1975] Director/Business Executive [Canadian]; Alina Osorio [1966] Director/Business Executive [Canadian]; Othman Taleb [1988] Director/Business Executive [Moroccan]

Levolux Limited
Incorporated: 19 July 1984 *Employees:* 103
Net Worth: £9,198,000 *Total Assets:* £14,732,000
Registered Office: 1 Forward Drive, Harrow, Middlesex, HA3 8NT
Activities: Other specialised construction activities n.e.c.
Parent: The Alumasc Group PLC
Officers: Andrew Magson, Secretary; David Patrick Gordon [1953] Sales & Marketing Director; Graham Paul Hooper [1956] Director; Andrew Magson [1966] Director; Stephen James Smith [1965] Finance Director; Katie Stewart [1987] Director/Accountant

Levy Associates Limited
Incorporated: 30 November 1999 *Employees:* 27
Net Worth: £15,271,000 *Total Assets:* £17,654,000
Registered Office: Pilgrims Lodge, Holywell Hill, St Albans, Herts, AL1 1ER
Activities: Other activities of employment placement agencies
Parent: Jemhafin Limited
Officers: Franco Cancelliere [1971] Sales Director [Italian]; Jamie Duke [1974] Sales Director; Matthew James Murphy [1974] Managing Director

Lexitron Limited
Incorporated: 6 March 1975 *Employees:* 2
Net Worth: £10,037,229 *Total Assets:* £16,584,190
Registered Office: Marley Road, St Ives, Huntingdon, Cambs, PE27 3EX
Activities: Other letting and operating of own or leased real estate
Officers: Michael Andrew Smith, Secretary; Michael Andrew Smith [1962] Director; Stephen James Smith [1960] Director

The Leys and St Faith's Schools Foundation
Incorporated: 22 August 2011 *Employees:* 565
Net Worth: £35,545,000 *Total Assets:* £51,478,000
Registered Office: The Leys School, Trumpington Road, Cambridge, CB2 7AD
Activities: Primary education
Officers: Paul Dominic McKeown, Secretary; Alexander Simon Barrett [1966] Director/Financial Adviser; Judith Bell [1992] Director/Leysian Missioner; Sir Anthony Russell Brenton [1950] Director; Martin Brown [1954] Director/Retired; Annabel Margaret Brunner [1949] Director; Thomas Oliver Buchanan [1967] Director/Consultant; Julia Louise Clarke [1970] Director/Primary School Teacher; Mark Andrew Elliott [1964] Managing Director; Patricia Graves [1952] Director/Retired Church Steward; Elizabeth Hooley [1961] Director/Solicitor, Company Secretary; David Charles Humphreys [1961] Director/General Secretary of a Charity; Charles Michael Kidman [1950] Director; Christopher Ian Kirker [1950] Director/Retired; Steven Michael Levy [1962] Director/Theatre Producer/Theatre Owner [British/American]; Stephanie Loft [1962] Director/Voluntary Bursar of a School; Ian McCaig [1966] Director; Richard John Mitchell [1960] Director; Timothy Charles Moore [1957] Director/Landlord; Wendy Nelson-Challen [1954] Director/Retired; Stephen Michael Peak [1965] Director/Chartered Accountant; Rev Julian Pursehouse [1967] Director/Chair of East Anglia Methodist District; Helena Margaret Renfrew-Knight [1968] Director; Ashley Victor Silverton [1960] Director/Investment Manager; Rev Alison Elizabeth Walker [1975] Director/Minister; Dr Robin Douglas Howard Walker [1947] Director/College Fellow; Roger Barry Webster [1953] Director/Chartered Accountant

Leywood Estates Limited
Incorporated: 16 October 1954 *Employees:* 4
Net Worth: £7,160,287 *Total Assets:* £9,588,801
Registered Office: Leywood House, 47 Woodside Road, Amersham, Bucks, HP6 6AA
Activities: Other letting and operating of own or leased real estate
Shareholder: Linda Jane Watson
Officers: Sarah Teresa Simmonds, Secretary; Simon Kennedy Funnell [1960] Director/Chartered Surveyor; Ian Francis Charles Murray [1956] Director; Susan Mary Queenborough [1950] Director/Housewife; Carole Watson [1967] Director; Linda Jane Watson [1948] Director/Housewife; Alfred James Woodley [1952] Managing Director; John Richard Woodley [1964] Director/Farmer

LGS Holdings Limited
Incorporated: 22 August 2016 *Employees:* 97
Net Worth: £2,559,283 *Total Assets:* £12,022,776
Registered Office: Russell Gardens, Wickford, Essex, SS11 8BH
Activities: Activities of other holding companies n.e.c.
Major Shareholder: Kevin Roy Childs
Officers: Kevin Roy Childs [1954] Director; Paul Hart [1979] Director/Depot Manager; Paul Pannell [1984] Director/Financial Controller; Colin John Prior [1960] Managing Director

Libra (Longhurst Group) Treasury PLC
Incorporated: 21 May 2012
Net Worth Deficit: £26,534,000 *Total Assets:* £411,956,992
Registered Office: Leverett House, Gilbert Drive, Endeavour Park, Boston, Lincs, PE21 7TQ
Activities: Renting and operating of Housing Association real estate
Parent: Longhurst Group Limited
Officers: Robert Ian Griffiths, Secretary; Clive Barnett [1957] Director/Business Executive; Daniel James Elkins [1971] Director; Robert Ian Griffiths [1976] Finance Director; Hilary Frances Lindsay [1948] Director/Retired; Angela Morris [1960] Director/Self Employed Health Consultant

Liebherr - Great Britain Limited
Incorporated: 12 December 1960 *Employees:* 359
Net Worth: £28,702,196 *Total Assets:* £100,768,560
Registered Office: Normandy Lane, Stratton Business Park, Biggleswade, Beds, SG18 8QB
Activities: Manufacture of machinery for mining
Officers: Claire Michelle Webber, Secretary; Richard James Everist [1966] Joint Managing Director; Lee Palmer [1974] Director; Claire Michelle Webber [1973] Director

Liebherr-Rental Limited
Incorporated: 8 February 2007 *Employees:* 11
Net Worth: £7,318,676 *Total Assets:* £14,808,942
Registered Office: Normandy Lane, Stratton Business Park, Biggleswade, Beds, SG18 8QB
Activities: Renting and leasing of construction and civil engineering machinery and equipment
Officers: Claire Webber, Secretary; Lee Palmer [1974] Director; Claire Michelle Webber [1973] Director

Life Build Solutions Ltd
Incorporated: 22 February 2005 *Employees:* 41
Net Worth: £3,919,250 *Total Assets:* £13,032,305
Registered Office: Hardy House, Northbridge Road, Berkhamsted, Herts, HP4 1EF
Activities: Construction of commercial buildings
Shareholders: Kenneth Mark Adams; Michael Stuart Wilde
Officers: Michael Stuart Wilde, Secretary; Kenneth Mark Adams [1960] Managing Director; Arthur Leonard Robert Morton [1942] Director/Chartered Accountant; Michael Stuart Wilde [1966] Operations Director; Kenneth George Wilkins [1943] Director

Life Education Trust
Incorporated: 12 June 2012 *Employees:* 211
Previous: The Frances Bardsley Academy for Girls
Net Worth: £27,527,000 *Total Assets:* £29,559,000
Registered Office: The Frances Bardsley Academy for Girls, Brentwood Road, Romford, Essex, RM1 2RR
Activities: General secondary education
Officers: Toni Juanita Burrowes-Cromwell [1965] Director/Management Consultant; Mary Cherry [1967] Director/Bursar; Michael Debens [1946] Director/Retired; Louise Douglas [1967] Director/Consultant; Julian Dutnall [1971] Director/Headteacher; Sophia Malik [1979] Director/Lawyer; David Mansfield [1959] Director/Executive Headteacher; Steve Odart [1968] Director/Founder & VP Sales

Life Fitness (UK) Limited
Incorporated: 14 September 1992 *Employees:* 120
Net Worth: £6,719,471 *Total Assets:* £19,815,374
Registered Office: Queen Adelaide, Ely, Cambs, CB7 4UB
Activities: Wholesale of other machinery and equipment
Parent: Brunswick Corporation
Officers: Jennifer Helen Greenard, Secretary; Florian Koestner [1971] Director/Business Executive [German]; Daniel Peter Oliver [1974] Director/UK Country Manager

Lifehealth Limited
Incorporated: 2 February 1995 *Employees:* 1
Net Worth: £42,174,956 *Total Assets:* £69,330,896
Registered Office: 2nd Floor, Building 3, Abbey View, Everard Close, St Albans, Herts, AL1 2PS
Activities: Other business support service activities n.e.c.
Parent: Lundbeck Group Limited
Officers: Roberto Lapenna, Secretary; Joao Carlos Nunes Rocha [1958] Director [Brazilian]

Lifeplus Europe Limited
Incorporated: 31 July 1996 *Employees:* 334
Net Worth: £12,297,067 *Total Assets:* £25,389,920
Registered Office: Lifeplus House, Little End Road, Eaton Socon, St Neots, Cambs, PE19 8JH
Activities: Retail sale via mail order houses or via Internet
Officers: Robert E Christian, Secretary/Executive [American]; Richard Joseph Cesarski [1964] Director [American]; Robert E Christian [1961] Director/Executive [American]; William J Evans [1969] Director/Executive [American]; Frank Newton III [1940] Director/Executive [American]; Malcolm Vincent [1965] Director

Lighthouse Healthcare Group Limited
Incorporated: 21 March 2014
Net Worth: £11,832,000 *Total Assets:* £45,142,000
Registered Office: 2 Imperial Place, Maxwell Road, Borehamwood, Herts, WD6 1JN
Activities: Activities of head offices
Parent: Elysium Healthcare Holdings 3 Limited
Officers: Sarah Juliette Livingston, Secretary; Lesley Joy Chamberlain [1963] Director/Group Chief Executive; Dr Quazi Shams Mahfooz Haque [1968] Executive Medical Director; Steven John Woolgar [1955] Director of Policy and Regulation

Lignacite Limited
Incorporated: 10 June 1947 *Employees:* 81
Net Worth: £17,800,512 *Total Assets:* £22,220,824
Registered Office: Norfolk House, High Street, Brandon, Suffolk, IP27 0AX
Activities: Manufacture of concrete products for construction purposes
Officers: Beth Edwards, Secretary; Giles Antony Joly de Lotbiniere [1959] Director; Harry Edmond Joly de Lotbiniere [1986] Director; Allan George Fredrick Eastwood [1959] Director; Guy Archibald Innes [1956] Finance Director; Michael Edmond Joly de Lotbiniere [1932] Director; Nicholas Henry Joly de Lotbiniere [1955] Director/Chartered Surveyor; William Nicholas Mason-Jones [1955] Director/Chartered Surveyor; Mark Anthony Pearson [1960] Director

Lima Orthopaedics UK Limited
Incorporated: 23 December 2009 *Employees:* 35
Net Worth: £4,672,742 *Total Assets:* £14,129,957
Registered Office: 2a Chequers Court, Huntingdon, Cambs, PE29 3LJ
Activities: General medical practice activities
Parent: Limacorporate S.P.A
Officers: Luigi Ferrari [1968] Director [Italian]

Lincoln's Farm & Investments Limited
Incorporated: 6 February 2009
Net Worth: £8,474,321 *Total Assets:* £9,085,295
Registered Office: 5 Yeomans Court, Ware Road, Hertford, SG13 7HJ
Activities: Other letting and operating of own or leased real estate
Shareholders: Peter Charles Lincoln; Margaret Rose Lincoln
Officers: Margaret Rose Lincoln, Secretary/Director; Margaret Rose Lincoln [1942] Director; Peter Charles Lincoln [1936] Managing Director; Tony Lincoln [1972] Director/Tyre Fitter

Lincolnshire Field Products Limited
Incorporated: 10 December 1984 *Employees:* 139
Net Worth: £14,126,545 *Total Assets:* £37,033,788
Registered Office: Wool Hall Farm, Cross Gate, Wykeham, Spalding, Lincs, PE12 6HW
Activities: Growing of vegetables and melons, roots and tubers
Parent: Keepstem Limited
Officers: Aubrey Edward Day, Secretary; Aubrey Edward Day [1958] Director/Chartered Management Accountant; Robin Hancox [1956] Director; Martin John Tate [1966] Director

Lindal Holdings Limited
Incorporated: 21 November 1996 *Employees:* 138
Net Worth: £13,900,000 *Total Assets:* £21,799,000
Registered Office: Cherrycourt Way, Stanbridge Road, Leighton Buzzard, Beds, LU7 4UH
Activities: Activities of head offices
Parent: Lindal Group Holding GmbH
Officers: Vicki Jane Marsh, Secretary; Francois-Xavier Gilbert [1966] Director [French]; Jerome Marion [1972] Finance Director [French]

Lindal Valve Company Limited
Incorporated: 1 July 1959 *Employees:* 138
Net Worth: £10,142,000 *Total Assets:* £21,855,000
Registered Office: Cherrycourt Way, Stanbridge Road, Leighton Buzzard, Beds, LU7 4UH
Activities: Manufacture of other plastic products
Parent: Lindal Holdings
Officers: Vicki Jane Potter, Secretary; Paul Dennis Bamford [1960] Operations Director; John William Hopkins [1952] Sales Director; Bjorn Klemp [1966] Managing Director [German]; Phil Lever [1967] Director; Vicki Jane Potter [1965] Finance Director

The Lindsell Train Investment Trust PLC
Incorporated: 29 November 2000
Net Worth: £149,416,000 *Total Assets:* £152,376,000
Registered Office: Hamilton Centre, Rodney Way, Chelmsford, Essex, CM1 3BY
Activities: Activities of investment trusts
Officers: Nicholas Timothy Allan [1958] Director; Charles Julian Cazalet [1947] Director; Richard Stormont Hughes [1957] Director; Rory Buchanan Landman [1961] Director/Senior Bursar; Vivien Mary Lickorish [1957] Director; Michael James Lindsell [1960] Director/Investment Manager

P.F.K. Ling Limited
Incorporated: 13 December 1961 *Employees:* 106
Net Worth: £3,754,574 *Total Assets:* £12,834,476
Registered Office: 55 Mendham Lane, Harleston, Norfolk, IP20 9DW
Activities: Sale of new cars and light motor vehicles
Shareholders: Anne Mabel Jary; David John Jary
Officers: Paul Marshall Charles Barkshire [1962] Operations Director; Matthew James Barwick [1981] Finance Director; Belinda Suzanne Farmer [1971] Director; Anne Mabel Jary [1941] Director; Christopher James Jary [1968] Managing Director; David John Jary [1937] Director

Linkage Community Trust
Incorporated: 14 January 1976 *Employees:* 619
Previous: Linkage Community Trust Limited (The)
Net Worth: £17,905,428 *Total Assets:* £23,459,206
Registered Office: Toynton Hall, Main Road, Toynton All Saints, Spilsby, Lincs, PE23 5AE
Activities: Other education n.e.c.
Officers: Anthony Terence Bake [1955] Director/Retired; Michael Bell [1952] Director/Self Employed; Professor Stephen Frederick Brown [1939] Director/Retired; Reginald Roger Harfoot [1945] Director/Retired; Simon James Hatchman [1972] Finance Director; Clare Jervis [1973] Director/Full Time Mother; Azad Shamcaddin Najmaldin [1950] Director/Paediatrician [Iraqi]; Michael John Oliver [1949] Director/Retired; Stephanie May Simpson [1972] Director/Management Consultant; Samantha Jane Stewart [1966] Director/Schools Effectiveness Adviser

Linkhaven Estates Ltd
Incorporated: 23 April 2004
Net Worth: £4,299,521 *Total Assets:* £8,105,050
Registered Office: 148 Cranbrook Road, Ilford, Essex, IG1 4LZ
Activities: Other letting and operating of own or leased real estate
Major Shareholder: Pavneet Kaur Kataria
Officers: Gurvinder Kataria, Secretary; Pavneet Kaur Kataria [1970] Director/Developer

Lint (Redington Road) Limited
Incorporated: 13 April 2005
Net Worth Deficit: £65,922 *Total Assets:* £10,437,188
Registered Office: Gabrielle House, 332-336 Perth Road, Ilford, Essex, IG2 6FF
Activities: Construction of domestic buildings
Parent: Lint Group Limited
Officers: Tarsaim Chand, Secretary/Director; Tarsaim Chand [1967] Director; Rizwan Patel [1974] Managing Director

Lint Group Limited
Incorporated: 22 April 2005 *Employees:* 57
Net Worth: £2,413,998 *Total Assets:* £18,456,874
Registered Office: Gabrielle House, 332-336 Perth Road, Ilford, Essex, IG2 6FF
Activities: Activities of other holding companies n.e.c.
Shareholders: Tarsaim Chand; Rizwan Patel
Officers: Tarsaim Chand, Director and Secretary; Tarsaim Chand [1967] Director & Secretary; Rizwan Patel [1974] Director

Linx Printing Technologies Limited
Incorporated: 22 October 1986 *Employees:* 218
Net Worth: £107,983,000 *Total Assets:* £124,090,000
Registered Office: Linx House, 8 Stocks Bridge Way, Compass Point Business Park, St Ives, Cambs, PE27 5JL
Activities: Manufacture of other special-purpose machinery n.e.c.
Parent: Launchchange Operations Ltd
Officers: Mark James Cooper [1973] Commercial Director; Harinder Singh Sandhu [1980] Finance Director; Keith Graham Ward [1953] Director

Lipman Properties Limited
Incorporated: 20 November 2003 *Employees:* 3
Net Worth Deficit: £390,987 *Total Assets:* £10,387,718
Registered Office: c/o Forward Financial Accounting Limited, Catalyst House, 720 Centennial Court, Centennial Park, Elstree, Herts, WD6 3SY
Activities: Real estate agencies
Major Shareholder: Steven Roy Lipman
Officers: Miriam Lipman, Secretary; Adam Lipman [1989] Director; Miriam Lipman [1965] Director [Danish]; Steven Roy Lipman [1962] Director

Thomas Lipton Ltd
Incorporated: 22 June 2017
Net Worth Deficit: £551,884 *Total Assets:* £13,378,481
Registered Office: 1st Floor, Woodgate Studios, 2-8 Games Road, Cockfosters, Barnet, Herts, EN4 9HN
Activities: Development of building projects
Major Shareholder: George Philippou
Officers: George Philippou [1965] Director

Lismire LLP
Incorporated: 16 May 2012
Net Worth: £13,920,003 *Total Assets:* £13,944,123
Registered Office: Old Bishops' College, Churchgate, Cheshunt, Herts, EN8 9XP
Officers: Richard John Murphy [1956] Member; Colette Helen Murphy [1989] LLP Member; Daniel Richard Murphy [1987] LLP Member; Siobhan Murphy [1985] LLP Member

Littleberries LLP
Incorporated: 26 May 2016
Net Worth: £2,460,000 *Total Assets:* £16,251,027
Registered Office: Grenville House, 4 Grenville Avenue, Broxbourne, Herts, EN10 7DH

Littlebury Developments Limited
Incorporated: 24 March 2016
Net Worth: £8,567,834 *Total Assets:* £8,567,834
Registered Office: 9 Commerce Road, Lynch Wood, Peterborough, Cambs, PE2 6LR
Activities: Development of building projects
Shareholders: Paul John Allgood; Leonard John Allgood
Officers: Paul John Allgood [1971] Director

Lituanica UK Ltd
Incorporated: 6 November 2003 *Employees:* 144
Net Worth: £13,654,582 *Total Assets:* £21,924,308
Registered Office: 3 Gallions Close, Barking, Essex, IG11 0JD
Activities: Non-specialised wholesale of food, beverages and tobacco
Shareholders: Ruta Sakauskiene; Aurimas Sidlauskas
Officers: Ruta Sakauskiene, Secretary; Rasa Apostol [1968] Director [Lithuanian]; Rolandas Sakauskas [1972] Director [Lithuanian]; Ruta Sakauskiene [1972] Director [Lithuanian]

Livingston Ltd
Incorporated: 22 August 1967 *Employees:* 46
Net Worth: £21,995,000 *Total Assets:* £44,311,000
Registered Office: Unit 1 Waverley Industrial Park, Hailsham Drive, Harrow, Middlesex, HA1 4TR
Activities: Renting and leasing of other machinery, equipment and tangible goods n.e.c.
Officers: Nigel Brown [1957] Director; Masten Gregory Evans [1960] Director; John Joseph Hafferty [1956] Director/Chief Financial Officer [American]; David Whitfield [1959] Director

David Lloyd Clubs Holdings Limited
Incorporated: 16 January 2017 *Employees:* 712
Net Worth Deficit: £10,496,000 *Total Assets:* £95,138,000
Registered Office: The Hangar, Mosquito Way, Hatfield Business Park, Hatfield, Herts, AL10 9AX
Activities: Operation of sports facilities
Parent: David Lloyd Leisure Limited
Officers: Brian Jonathan Magnus [1966] Director/Private Equity Partner; Mark Andrew Stephens [1982] Director/Investment Professional [Irish]

David Lloyd Clubs Limited
Incorporated: 16 January 2017 *Employees:* 713
Net Worth Deficit: £10,496,000 *Total Assets:* £94,857,000
Registered Office: The Hangar, Mosquito Way, Hatfield Business Park, Hatfield, Herts, AL10 9AX
Activities: Operation of sports facilities
Parent: David Lloyd Clubs Holdings Limited
Officers: Patrick James Burrows [1967] Director/Chartered Accountant; Donald Glenn Earlam [1965] Director; Brian Jonathan Magnus [1966] Director/Private Equity Partner; Mark Andrew Stephens [1982] Director/Investment Professional [Irish]

David Lloyd Leisure GR Limited
Incorporated: 27 August 2015
Net Worth Deficit: £3,603,000 *Total Assets:* £489,438,016
Registered Office: The Hangar, Hatfield Business Park, Mosquito Way, Hatfield, Herts, AL10 9AX
Activities: Other service activities n.e.c.
Parent: David Lloyd Leisure Limited
Officers: Patrick James Burrows [1967] Director/Chartered Accountant; Brian Jonathan Magnus [1966] Director/Investment Professional; Mark Andrew Stephens [1982] Director/Investment Professional [Irish]

David Lloyd Leisure Group Limited
Incorporated: 29 May 2007
Net Worth Deficit: £201,670,000 *Total Assets:* £603,902,976
Registered Office: The Hangar, Mosquito Way, Hatfield Business Park, Hatfield, Herts, AL10 9AX
Activities: Activities of head offices
Parent: David Lloyd Leisure Operations Holdings Limited
Officers: Patrick James Burrows [1967] Director/Chartered Accountant; Mark Andrew Stephens [1982] Director/Investment Professional [Irish]

David Lloyd Leisure Limited
Incorporated: 8 September 1980 *Employees:* 3,269
Net Worth: £537,411,008 *Total Assets:* £1,191,868,032
Registered Office: The Hangar, Mosquito Way, Hatfield Business Park, Hatfield, Herts, AL10 9AX
Activities: Activities of sport clubs
Parent: David Lloyd Leisure Group Limited
Officers: Patrick James Burrows [1967] Director/Chartered Accountant; Donald Glenn Earlam [1965] Director

David Lloyd Leisure Operations Holdings Limited
Incorporated: 12 May 2008
Net Worth: £62,829,000 *Total Assets:* £119,509,000
Registered Office: The Hangar, Mosquito Way, Hatfield Business Park, Hatfield, Herts, AL10 9AX
Activities: Activities of head offices
Parent: Deuce Acquisitions Limited
Officers: Patrick James Burrows [1967] Director/Chartered Accountant; Mark Andrew Stephens [1982] Director/Investment Professional [Irish]

David Lloyd Leisure Properties No.1 Limited
Incorporated: 27 July 2007 *Employees:* 3
Net Worth: £34,762,000 *Total Assets:* £48,891,000
Registered Office: The Hangar, Mosquito Way, Hatfield Business Park, Hatfield, Herts, AL10 9AX
Activities: Other letting and operating of own or leased real estate
Parent: Deuce Acquisitions Limited
Officers: Patrick James Burrows [1967] Director/Chartered Accountant; Mark Andrew Stephens [1982] Director/Investment Professional [Irish]

David Lloyd Leisure Properties No.2 Limited
Incorporated: 12 May 2008 *Employees:* 3
Net Worth: £53,939,000 *Total Assets:* £135,176,992
Registered Office: The Hangar, Mosquito Way, Hatfield Business Park, Hatfield, Herts, AL10 9AX
Activities: Other letting and operating of own or leased real estate
Parent: Deuce Acquisitions Limited
Officers: Patrick James Burrows [1967] Director/Chartered Accountant; Mark Andrew Stephens [1982] Director/Investment Professional [Irish]

David Lloyd Leisure Properties No.3 Limited
Incorporated: 12 May 2008
Net Worth: £18,885,000 *Total Assets:* £106,861,000
Registered Office: The Hangar, Mosquito Way, Hatfield Business Park, Hatfield, Herts, AL10 9AX
Activities: Other letting and operating of own or leased real estate
Parent: Deuce Acquisitions Limited
Officers: Patrick James Burrows [1967] Director/Chartered Accountant; Mark Andrew Stephens [1982] Director/Investment Professional [Irish]

David Lloyd Leisure Properties No.4 Limited
Incorporated: 12 May 2008 *Employees:* 3
Net Worth: £23,633,000 *Total Assets:* £123,962,000
Registered Office: The Hangar, Mosquito Way, Hatfield Business Park, Hatfield, Herts, AL10 9AX
Activities: Other letting and operating of own or leased real estate
Parent: Deuce Acquisitions Limited
Officers: Patrick James Burrows [1967] Director/Chartered Accountant; Mark Andrew Stephens [1982] Director/Investment Professional [Irish]

Local Boy'z Group Holding Limited
Incorporated: 11 September 2009 *Employees:* 28
Net Worth: £11,016,244 *Total Assets:* £16,085,824
Registered Office: 1 Beauchamp Court, Victors Way, Barnet, Herts, EN5 5TZ
Activities: Other business support service activities n.e.c.
Major Shareholder: Stephen Mucklow
Officers: Muhammad Naeem, Secretary; Stephen Mucklow [1962] Director

Local Car and Van Rental Limited
Incorporated: 15 May 2006 *Employees:* 29
Net Worth: £9,520,811 *Total Assets:* £79,721,456
Registered Office: 2 Redman Court, Bell Street, Princes Risborough, Bucks, HP27 0AA
Activities: Sale of new cars and light motor vehicles
Shareholders: John Patrick Ryan; Karen Ryan
Officers: Karen Ryan, Secretary; John Lewis Davies [1949] Director; Guy Jonathan Easton [1956] Director; Shaun Parnaby [1968] Director; Owain Ashley Price [1971] Sales and Marketing Director; John Patrick Ryan [1961] Director

Local Generation Limited
Incorporated: 30 May 2008
Net Worth: £5,383,000 *Total Assets:* £13,092,000
Registered Office: 362 Wisbech Road, March, Cambs, PE15 0BA
Activities: Production of electricity
Shareholder: GVO B-1 Limited
Officers: Neil Francis Hunter [1970] Director; Andrew Piers Symons Keeling [1973] Director; Michael Bernd Kuessner [1971] Director [German]

Lochailort Fairfield Limited
Incorporated: 11 March 2016
Net Worth Deficit: £6,914 *Total Assets:* £20,909,460
Registered Office: James Hall, Parsons Green, St Ives, Cambs, PE27 4AA
Activities: Development of building projects
Parent: JCAM Commercial Real Estate Property XVII Ltd
Officers: Hugo Peter Haig [1962] Director; Toby John Markham [1966] Director

Lodwick Homes Limited
Incorporated: 18 February 1997 *Employees:* 2
Net Worth: £11,115,823 *Total Assets:* £14,500,062
Registered Office: 457 Southchurch Road, Southend on Sea, Essex, SS1 2PH
Activities: Development of building projects
Major Shareholder: Paul Simon Althasen
Officers: Erika Justine Althasen [1994] Director; Lisa Debra Althasen [1968] Director; Paul Simon Althasen [1964] Director

London and Hertfordshire Limited
Incorporated: 19 April 2016
Net Worth Deficit: £43,011 *Total Assets:* £17,566,748
Registered Office: The Lodge, Heriots, The Common, Stanmore, Middlesex, HA7 3HG
Activities: Buying and selling of own real estate
Shareholders: TPS Abbeydale St Albans Limited; KIG St Albans Limited
Officers: Marc Simon Franks [1981] Director; Gary Hackner [1982] Director [South African]; Lee Richard Joseph Portnoi [1959] Director

London Care Partnership Limited
Incorporated: 9 January 2007 *Employees:* 207
Net Worth: £14,114,941 *Total Assets:* £26,390,636
Registered Office: c/o Elysium Healthcare, 2 Imperial Place, Maxwell Road, Borehamwood, Herts, WD6 1JN
Activities: Other residential care activities n.e.c.
Parent: Careprogress Limited
Officers: Sarah Juliette Livingston, Secretary; Lesley Joy Chamberlain [1963] Director/Group Chief Executive; Dr Quazi Shams Mahfooz Haque [1968] Executive Medical Director; Steven John Woolgar [1955] Director of Policy and Regulation

London City Bond Limited
Incorporated: 20 April 1988 *Employees:* 367
Net Worth: £2,073,670 *Total Assets:* £17,133,680
Registered Office: Olympus, 91-101 River Road, Barking, Essex, IG11 0EG
Activities: Operation of warehousing and storage facilities for land transport activities
Shareholders: Benjamin Arthur Crawshay Jones; Alexandra Jones
Officers: Alfred John Allington [1960] Director/Warehouse Manager; Brian John Davis [1953] Director/Business Development Manager; David Hogg [1955] Sales Director; Nicholas Andrew Joyce [1958] Finance Director

London Distribution Park LLP
Incorporated: 19 November 2012
Net Worth: £20,208,632 *Total Assets:* £20,301,448
Registered Office: Leslie Ford House, Tilbury Freeport, Tilbury, Essex, RM18 7EH

London Executive Aviation Limited
Incorporated: 24 October 1995 *Employees:* 88
Net Worth Deficit: £2,676,000 *Total Assets:* £15,557,000
Registered Office: Lea Office Building, Stapleford Aerodrome, Stapleford Tawney, Romford, Essex, RM4 1SJ
Activities: Non-scheduled passenger air transport
Parent: Executive Aviation Group Limited
Officers: Anthony George Medlock, Secretary; Aleksei Bazhenov [1973] Director; George Christos Galanopoulos [1963] Director; Patrick Joseph Albert Hansen [1972] Director [Luxembourger]; Patrick Joseph George Margetson-Rushmore [1959] Director; Charlotte Pedersen [1970] Director [Danish]

London Fluid System Technologies Limited
Incorporated: 28 June 2000 *Employees:* 47
Net Worth: £7,413,554 *Total Assets:* £9,684,841
Registered Office: Kingley Park, Station Road, Kings Langley, Herts, WD4 8GW
Activities: Manufacture of other fabricated metal products n.e.c.
Major Shareholder: Adrian Wynne
Officers: Deborah Ann Cridford, Secretary; Adrian Wynne [1961] Managing Director

London Hoist Limited
Incorporated: 28 February 1986 *Employees:* 167
Net Worth: £307,600 *Total Assets:* £9,780,384
Registered Office: 43 London Road, Stanford Rivers, Ongar, Essex, CM5 9PJ
Activities: Installation of industrial machinery and equipment
Officers: Anita Millington [1954] Finance Director; William Fredrick Vonck [1956] Managing Director [Dutch]

London Inn Hotels (Stratford) Limited
Incorporated: 13 July 2001 *Employees:* 51
Net Worth: £28,282,488 *Total Assets:* £52,877,656
Registered Office: 36 Railway Approach, Harrow, Middlesex, HA3 5AA
Activities: Hotels and similar accommodation
Parent: TLC Group Limited
Officers: Gagan Puri, Secretary; William Charles Neal [1986] Director; Paavan Popat [1985] Managing Director; Honourable Shivaan Shillin Popat [1988] Director; Gagan Puri [1978] Finance Director

London Internet Exchange Limited
Incorporated: 14 December 1995 *Employees:* 68
Net Worth: £11,834,525 *Total Assets:* £14,157,472
Registered Office: Trinity Court, Trinity Street, Priestgate, Peterborough, Cambs, PE1 1DA
Activities: Other telecommunications activities
Officers: Howard John Fisher, Secretary; Michael Andrew Blanche [1976] Director/Program Manager; Lee Mark Hetherington [1982] Director/Interconnection Manager; Malcolm Samuel Agar Hutty [1973] Director/Head of Public Affairs; Thomas Sebastien Antero Lahtinen [1979] Director; Kurt Erik Johannes Lindqvist [1974] Director/Chief Marketing Officer [Finnish]; Richard Petrie [1971] Director/Chief Technical Officer; John Bernard Souter [1952] Director/Chief Executive Officer; Simon Paul Woodhead [1974] Director; Steven Wright [1986] Director/Internet Service Provider

London Luton Airport Group Limited
Incorporated: 12 January 1998 *Employees:* 751
Net Worth: £62,408,000 *Total Assets:* £230,424,000
Registered Office: Navigation House, Airport Way, London Luton Airport, Luton, Beds, LU2 9LY
Activities: Other business support service activities n.e.c.
Parent: London Luton Airport Holdings I Limited
Officers: Jose Ignacio Ascacibar [1964] International Business Development Director [Spanish]; Nicholas Barton [1966] Director/Chief Executive Officer; Mariano Domingo Calvo [1966] Director of Infrastructure and Technology [Spanish]; Mercedes Aurora Garcia Sanguino [1973] Director/Lawyer [Spanish]; Rodrigo Marabini Ruiz [1962] Director [Spanish]; Hywel Gwyn Rees [1972] Director

London Luton Airport Holdings I Limited
Incorporated: 12 November 2013 *Employees:* 756
Net Worth: £67,659,000 *Total Assets:* £558,017,984
Registered Office: Navigation House, Airport Way, London Luton Airport, Luton, Beds, LU2 9LY
Activities: Activities of other holding companies n.e.c.
Parent: London Luton Airport Holdings II Limited
Officers: Jose Ignacio Ascacibar [1964] International Business Development Director [Spanish]; Malcolm Brown [1967] Director; Rafael Fernandez Villasante [1970] Operations, Security and Services Director (AENA) [Spanish]; Mercedes Aurora Garcia Sanguino [1973] Director/Lawyer [Spanish]; Rodrigo Marabini Ruiz [1962] Director [Spanish]; Hywel Gwyn Rees [1972] Director

London Luton Airport Holdings II Limited
Incorporated: 12 November 2013
Net Worth: £97,836,000 *Total Assets:* £193,224,992
Registered Office: Navigation House, Airport Way, London Luton Airport, Luton, Beds, LU2 9LY
Activities: Activities of other holding companies n.e.c.
Parent: London Luton Airport Holdings III Limited
Officers: Malcolm Brown [1967] Director; Marta Campomanes Camino [1967] Director/Legal Counsel [Spanish]; Mariano Domingo Calvo [1966] Director of Infrastructure and Technology [Spanish]; Susana Garcia Herradon [1958] Director/Economist [Spanish]; Hywel Gwyn Rees [1972] Director

London Luton Airport Holdings III Limited
Incorporated: 11 November 2013 *Employees:* 758
Net Worth Deficit: £27,363,000 *Total Assets:* £558,387,968
Registered Office: Navigation House, Airport Way, London Luton Airport, Luton, Beds, LU2 9LY
Activities: Activities of other holding companies n.e.c.
Shareholders: AMP Capital Investors Limited; Aena, S.M.E., S.A.
Officers: Jose Ignacio Ascacibar [1964] International Business Development Director [Spanish]; Malcolm Brown [1967] Director; Maria de Los Reyes Escrig Teigeiro [1970] Director/Lawyer [Spanish]; Susana Garcia Herradon [1958] Director/Economist [Spanish]; Rodrigo Marabini Ruiz [1962] Director [Spanish]; Hywel Gwyn Rees [1972] Director

London Luton Airport Limited
Incorporated: 16 May 1986
Net Worth: £466,740,992 *Total Assets:* £611,750,016
Registered Office: Hart House, Business Centre, Kimpton Road, Luton, Beds, LU2 0LA
Activities: Other letting and operating of own or leased real estate
Parent: Luton Borough Council
Officers: David Agbley [1967] Director/Scientist; Waheed Akbar [1961] Director/Councillor; Tahir Khan [1967] Director/Local Government Officer; Andrew David Malcolm [1984] Director/Lecturer; Amy Rose O'Callaghan [1989] Director/Manager; James John Taylor [1989] Director/Logistics; John Victor Young [1946] Director/Retired

London Luton Airport Operations Limited
Incorporated: 12 January 1998 *Employees:* 749
Net Worth: £39,336,000 *Total Assets:* £225,952,992
Registered Office: Navigation House, Airport Way, London Luton Airport, Luton, Beds, LU2 9LY
Activities: Service activities incidental to air transportation
Parent: London Luton Airport Group Limited
Officers: Juan Jose Alvarez-Gallego [1955] Director AENA International [Spanish]; Jose Ignacio Ascacibar [1964] Director/International Business Development [Spanish]; Nicholas Barton [1966] Director/Chief Executive Officer; Malcolm Brown [1967] Director; Marta Campomanes Camino [1967] Legal Counsel (Alternate Director) [Spanish]; Maria de Los Reyes Escrig Teigeiro [1970] Director/Lawyer [Spanish]; Jose Manuel Fernandez Bosch [1968] Commercial Director (AENA) [Spanish]; Barry Robert Hunter [1974] Director/Chief Financial Officer; Jose Leo Vizcaino [1960] Director/CFO AENA [Spanish]; Rodrigo Marabini Ruiz [1962] Director [Spanish]; Bodhisattva Pahari [1962] Director; Hywel Gwyn Rees [1972] Director

The London Outpost Limited
Incorporated: 14 March 1984
Net Worth Deficit: £8,926,094 *Total Assets:* £9,531,085
Registered Office: Unit 2 Capital Business Park, Manor Way, Borehamwood, Herts, WD6 1GW
Activities: Other business support service activities n.e.c.
Parent: Pipestone Properties Limited
Officers: Karen Millie-James, Secretary; Moustapha El Solh [1970] Director [Lebanese]; Marc Thevenoux [1956] Director [French]

London Pharma & Chemicals Group Ltd
Incorporated: 11 February 2003 *Employees:* 9
Net Worth: £10,177,704 *Total Assets:* £16,735,017
Registered Office: Unit 10 Delta Court, Manor Way, Borehamwood, Herts, WD6 1FJ
Activities: Bookkeeping activities
Parent: London Pharma & Chemicals Holdings Ltd
Officers: Alan Edward Eastwood [1955] Director; Christian Leemann [1958] Director/Chief Executive Officer [Swiss]; Jamie Andrew Sandler [1976] Finance Director; Daniel Reuben Straus [1972] Director/Business Manager

London Pharma & Chemicals Holdings Ltd
Incorporated: 18 November 2009 *Employees:* 135
Net Worth: £18,496,670 *Total Assets:* £35,091,484
Registered Office: Unit 10 Delta Court, Manor Way, Borehamwood, Herts, WD6 1FJ
Activities: Activities of head offices
Shareholders: Claire Joanne Sharon Straus; Daniel Reuben Straus
Officers: Claire Joanne Sharon Straus [1969] Director; Daniel Reuben Straus [1972] Director/Business Manager

London School of Theology
Incorporated: 25 June 1943 *Employees:* 64
Net Worth: £11,476,952 *Total Assets:* £13,359,058
Registered Office: Green Lane, Northwood, Middlesex, HA6 2UW
Activities: First-degree level higher education
Officers: Ruwani Christine Gunawardene, Secretary; Rev Bunmi Yemi Adedeji [1961] Director of The One People Commission, Minister; Graham Alan Cray [1947] Director/Minister; Rev Jonathan William Dixon Douglas [1975] Director/Minister; Margaret Marian Doyle [1953] Director/School Tutor; Steve Hughes [1949] Director/Retired; Revd Dr Alex Irving [1987] Director/Minister; Malcolm Douglas Peckham [1946] Director/Retired; Paul Maurice Smith [1945] Director/Consultant Electrical Engineer; Ian Thompson [1968] Director/Banker; Professor Hugh Godfrey Maturin Williamson [1947] Director/Regius Professor

London Tower Crane Hire & Sales Limited
Incorporated: 25 April 2003 *Employees:* 58
Net Worth: £21,214,614 *Total Assets:* £46,363,016
Registered Office: 4 Elstree Way, Borehamwood, Herts, WD6 1RN
Activities: Renting and leasing of construction and civil engineering machinery and equipment
Parent: JRL Group Ltd
Officers: Ronan Joseph Gleeson, Secretary/Director [Irish]; Ronan Joseph Gleeson [1976] Director [Irish]; Martin Harvey [1972] Director/Operations Manager; Kevin William Keegan [1963] Director/Estimator [Irish]; John James Reddington [1972] Director/Formwork [Irish]

Richard Long Group Limited
Incorporated: 25 January 2005 *Employees:* 21
Net Worth: £20,913,752 *Total Assets:* £25,548,540
Registered Office: Whitehall Farm, Crownthorpe, Wymondham, Norfolk, NR18 9EP
Activities: Activities of head offices
Officers: Lorraine June Long, Secretary; Lorraine June Long [1954] Director/Manager; Richard Thomas Long [1953] Director/Farmer

Long Term Reversions (Dulwich) Limited
Incorporated: 19 July 1999
Previous: Ground Rents (Regisport) Limited
Net Worth: £7,563,347 *Total Assets:* £8,180,588
Registered Office: 7 Nelson Street, Southend on Sea, Essex, SS1 1EH
Activities: Buying and selling of own real estate
Parent: Long Term Reversions (Winchester) Limited
Officers: Piers de Vigne [1981] Director; Katharine Morshead [1985] Director/Analyst

Long Term Reversions (Harrogate) Limited
Incorporated: 20 February 1989
Previous: Regisport Limited
Net Worth: £13,825,186 *Total Assets:* £14,875,668
Registered Office: 7 Nelson Street, Southend on Sea, Essex, SS1 1EH
Activities: Buying and selling of own real estate
Parent: Long Term Reversions (Winchester) Limited
Officers: Piers de Vigne [1981] Director; Katharine Morshead [1985] Director/Analyst

Long Term Reversions (Torquay) Limited
Incorporated: 19 July 1999
Previous: Ground Rents (Regis) Limited
Net Worth: £18,757,598 *Total Assets:* £19,960,864
Registered Office: 7 Nelson Street, Southend on Sea, Essex, SS1 1EH
Activities: Buying and selling of own real estate
Parent: Regis Group (Reversions No.1) Limited
Officers: Piers de Vigne [1981] Director; Katharine Morshead [1985] Director/Analyst

Long Term Reversions No 1 Limited
Incorporated: 13 May 2002
Previous: Regis Group No. 1 Limited
Net Worth: £8,974,374 *Total Assets:* £8,974,374
Registered Office: 7 Nelson Street, Southend on Sea, Essex, SS1 1EH
Activities: Buying and selling of own real estate
Parent: Regis Group (Holdings) Limited
Officers: Piers de Vigne [1981] Director; Katharine Morshead [1985] Director/Analyst

Longford Securities & Equities (K & T) Limited
Incorporated: 3 March 2003
Net Worth: £6,045,536 *Total Assets:* £28,351,580
Registered Office: Alton House, 66-68 High Street, Northwood, Middlesex, HA6 1BL
Activities: Development of building projects
Major Shareholder: Barry Attarzadeh
Officers: Peter William Johnson, Secretary; Barry Attarzadeh [1956] Director/Property Developer [Canadian]

Longford Securities & Equities Limited
Incorporated: 17 June 1993
Net Worth Deficit: £712,672 *Total Assets:* £12,183,284
Registered Office: Alton House, 66 High Street, Northwood, Middlesex, HA6 1BL
Activities: Development of building projects
Major Shareholder: Barry Attarzadeh
Officers: Peter William Johnson, Secretary; Barry Attarzadeh [1956] Director/Property Developer [Canadian]; Peter William Johnson [1948] Director/Chartered Quantity Surveyor

Longmill Realty Limited
Incorporated: 31 October 1984 *Employees:* 11
Net Worth: £5,246,337 *Total Assets:* £13,562,213
Registered Office: 5 Elstree Gate, Elstree Way, Borehamwood, Herts, WD6 1JD
Activities: Non-specialised wholesale trade
Major Shareholder: David Yamin-Joseph
Officers: Veerasingham Ganeshan Jeyabavan, Secretary/Director; Veerasingham Ganeshan Jeyabavan [1960] Director; David Yamin-Joseph [1965] Director/Merchant [Italian]

Longmill Rickbost Ltd
Incorporated: 9 January 2012
Net Worth: £451,390 *Total Assets:* £12,921,310
Registered Office: 5 Elstree Gate, Elstree Way, Borehamwood, Herts, WD6 1JD
Activities: Buying and selling of own real estate
Parent: Longmill Realty Limited
Officers: Veerasingham Ganeshan Jeyabavan [1960] Director; David Yamin-Joseph [1965] Director [Italian]

Loose Hall Farm Limited
Incorporated: 18 March 1953 *Employees:* 10
Net Worth: £8,571,425 *Total Assets:* £9,803,768
Registered Office: The Farm Office, Loose Hall Drive, Hitcham, Ipswich, Suffolk, IP7 7LY
Activities: Growing of cereals (except rice), leguminous crops and oil seeds
Shareholders: Andrew Brian Morley; Roger Mark Morley
Officers: Roger Mark Morley, Secretary/Investment Manager; Andrew Brian Morley [1969] Director/Design Engineer; Ella Valerie Morley [1932] Director/Farmer; Roger Mark Morley [1971] Director/Portfolio Manager

Loppingdale Plant Limited
Incorporated: 19 February 1992 *Employees:* 79
Net Worth: £2,938,964 *Total Assets:* £10,049,394
Registered Office: Loppingdales, Gaunts End, Elsenham, Essex, CM22 6DR
Activities: Other specialised construction activities n.e.c.
Major Shareholder: Eugene Brendan Corr
Officers: Rachael Lauraine Corr, Secretary; Brendan Corr [1969] Director/Manager; Kieran John FitzGenerald [1978] Director/Project Manager; Christopher Simon Kirk [1967] Contracts Director

Lord Rayleigh's Farms Limited
Incorporated: 8 October 1930 *Employees:* 39
Net Worth: £11,162,100 *Total Assets:* £12,598,131
Registered Office: Terling Place, Terling, Chelmsford, Essex, CM3 2QW
Activities: Mixed farming
Shareholders: John Gerald Rayleigh; Honourable John Frederick Strutt
Officers: Alexander Martin Dyke, Secretary; Lord John Generald Rayleigh [1960] Director/Farmer; Honourable John Frederick Strutt [1993] Director/Trainee Chartered Surveyor; Neil Richard Taylor [1965] Director/Chartered Surveyor

Lorien Limited
Incorporated: 15 September 2009
Net Worth: £840,000 *Total Assets:* £17,225,000
Registered Office: 800 The Boulevard, Capability Green, Luton, Beds, LU1 3BA
Activities: Temporary employment agency activities
Parent: Impellam Holdings Limited
Officers: Rebecca Jane Watson, Secretary; Julia Robertson [1958] Director; Rebecca Jane Watson [1969] Director/General Counsel & Company Secretary

Lorien Resourcing Limited
Incorporated: 11 October 1977 *Employees:* 227
Net Worth: £35,237,000 *Total Assets:* £110,621,000
Registered Office: 800 The Boulevard, Capability Green, Luton, Beds, LU1 3BA
Activities: Other activities of employment placement agencies
Parent: Lorien Limited
Officers: Rebecca Jane Watson, Secretary; Julia Robertson [1958] Director; Rebecca Jane Watson [1969] Director/General Counsel and Company Secretary

Lorne Stewart PLC
Incorporated: 16 January 1978 *Employees:* 727
Net Worth: £13,031,000 *Total Assets:* £65,703,000
Registered Office: Stewart House, Kenton Road, Harrow, Middlesex, HA3 9TU
Activities: Electrical installation
Parent: LSRM Holdings Ltd
Officers: Inbaraj Rajakumar, Secretary; Tarek Fuad Abuzayyad [1969] Director/Finance; Gary Heitmann [1970] Group Business Development Director; Paul James Hughes [1956] Group Commercial Director; Jacob Kurian [1958] Director/Group Financial Controller [Australian]; Puliyelethu Mathai Mathew [1952] Director/Group Vice Chairman [Indian]; Ramesh Krishna Murthy [1962] Director/Group Chief Financial Officer [Indian]; Simon Roopchand [1973] Director/Group Chief Executive Officer; David Webb [1971] Managing Director - FM; Gary Robert Worrall [1959] Director/CEO - Contracting Division

Lors Homes Limited
Incorporated: 27 March 2012
Net Worth: £1,464,643 *Total Assets:* £9,252,404
Registered Office: Rosewood Offices, Freckenham Road, Chippenham, Ely, Cambs, CB7 5QH
Activities: Development of building projects
Major Shareholder: Wayne Ashley Murfet
Officers: Wayne Murfet, Secretary; Kelly Helen Murfet [1982] Director; Pamela Murfet [1959] Director; Wayne Ashley Murfet [1982] Director

Lotus Cars Limited
Incorporated: 1 January 1967 *Employees:* 771
Net Worth: £65,240,000 *Total Assets:* £377,296,000
Registered Office: Potash Lane, Hethel, Norwich, NR14 8EZ
Activities: Manufacture of motor vehicles
Parent: Group Lotus PLC
Officers: Dr. James Bradley, Secretary; Daniel Li Donghui [1970] Director [Chinese]; Feng Qingfeng [1972] Director [Chinese]

Lotus Group International Limited
Incorporated: 30 June 1993 *Employees:* 843
Net Worth: £24,108,000 *Total Assets:* £145,638,000
Registered Office: Potash Lane, Hethel, Norwich, NR14 8EZ
Activities: Other service activities n.e.c.
Parent: Geely International (Hong Kong) Limited
Officers: Dr James Bradley, Secretary; Daniel Li Donghui [1970] Director [Chinese]; Qingfeng Feng [1972] Director [Chinese]

Loughton Care Centre Limited
Incorporated: 25 November 2011 *Employees:* 63
Net Worth: £3,071,000 *Total Assets:* £10,939,000
Registered Office: Regal House, Royal Crescent, Ilford, Essex, IG2 7JY
Activities: Residential nursing care facilities
Parent: Gibson Propco Limited
Officers: Harnoop Singh Atkar [1986] Director; Daren Dalmedo [1978] Director

Lousin Holdings Limited
Incorporated: 19 November 2012 *Employees:* 18
Net Worth: £10,537,140 *Total Assets:* £25,285,380
Registered Office: Millhouse, 32-38 East Street, Rochford, Essex, SS4 1DB
Activities: Other business support service activities n.e.c.
Shareholder: Andrew Sheridan McCutcheon
Officers: Sara Jane McCutcheon, Secretary; Daniel Fisk [1986] Director; Andrew Sheridan McCutcheon [1965] Director/Media Consultant; Sara Jane McCutcheon [1959] Director; Michael Nissim [1980] Director

Loxford School Trust Limited
Incorporated: 22 October 2013 *Employees:* 776
Net Worth: £78,953,616 *Total Assets:* £88,856,584
Registered Office: Loxford School, Loxford Lane, Ilford, Essex, IG1 2UT
Activities: Other education n.e.c.
Officers: Peter William Ballard [1948] Director; David Francis Hubbard [1948] Director; Anita Johnson [1965] Director; David Anthony Low [1950] Director/Retired; Michael McIntyre [1957] Director/Project Management and Mentoring

LPA Group PLC
Incorporated: 14 March 1961 *Employees:* 181
Net Worth: £10,721,000 *Total Assets:* £18,937,000
Registered Office: Light & Power House, Shire Hill, Saffron Walden, Essex, CB11 3AQ
Activities: Activities of production holding companies
Officers: Christopher James Buckenham, Secretary; Christopher James Buckenham [1971] Company Secretary/Director; Paul Vincent Curtis [1972] Director; Peter Glen Pollock [1946] Director; Leonard Keith Porter [1952] Director; Michael Rusch [1945] Director

LRW Engineering Limited
Incorporated: 17 July 2002 *Employees:* 15
Net Worth: £8,845,206 *Total Assets:* £9,541,693
Registered Office: Victoria House, 50 Alexandra, Street, Southend on Sea, Essex, SS1 1BN
Activities: Other professional, scientific and technical activities n.e.c.
Shareholders: Lawrence Ralph Warr; Sian Loiise Warr
Officers: Michael Charles Warr, Secretary; Lawrence Ralph Warr [1974] Director/Engineer; Sian Warr [1978] Director/Administrator

LSF9 Robin Investments Limited
Incorporated: 10 September 2015
Net Worth: £197,711,008 *Total Assets:* £745,630,976
Registered Office: Vincent House, 4 Grove Lane, Epping, Essex, CM16 4LH
Activities: Activities of head offices
Parent: LSF9 Robin Newco 2 Limited
Officers: William Bahlsen Bannister [1967] Director/Chief Executive Officer; Jeremy Clarke [1963] Managing Director; Simon Paul Lane [1963] Director/Accountant

LSF9 Robin Midco Limited
Incorporated: 10 September 2015
Net Worth: £204,964,992 *Total Assets:* £263,548,992
Registered Office: Vincent House, 4 Grove Lane, Epping, Essex, CM16 4LH
Activities: Activities of head offices
Parent: LSF9 Robin Topco Limited
Officers: William Bahlsen Bannister [1967] Director/Chief Executive Officer; Jeremy Clarke [1963] Managing Director; Simon Paul Lane [1963] Director/Accountant

LSF9 Robin Newco 1 Limited
Incorporated: 22 November 2016
Net Worth: £247,152,992 *Total Assets:* £504,305,984
Registered Office: Vincent House, 4 Grove Lane, Epping, Essex, CM16 4LH
Activities: Activities of head offices
Parent: LSF9 Robin Midco Limited
Officers: William Bahlsen Bannister [1967] Director/Chief Executive Officer; Jeremy Clarke [1963] Managing Director; Simon Paul Lane [1963] Director/Accountant

LSF9 Robin Newco 2 Limited
Incorporated: 29 November 2016
Net Worth: £246,044,000 *Total Assets:* £257,162,000
Registered Office: Vincent House, 4 Grove Lane, Epping, Essex, CM16 4LH
Activities: Activities of head offices
Parent: LSF9 Robin Newco 1 Limited
Officers: William Bahlsen Bannister [1967] Director/Chief Executive Officer; Jeremy Clarke [1963] Managing Director; Simon Paul Lane [1963] Director/Accountant

Lumendi Limited
Incorporated: 24 December 2014 *Employees:* 3
Net Worth: £22,549,908 *Total Assets:* £24,993,696
Registered Office: Abbey Place, 24-28 Easton Street, High Wycombe, Bucks, HP11 1NT
Activities: Manufacture of other special-purpose machinery n.e.c.
Officers: Dr Robert Bider [1947] Director [Swiss]; Dr. Peter Johann [1957] Director [German]; Renzo Zanolari [1974] Director [Swiss]

Lumesse Corporate Limited
Incorporated: 1 October 2001
Net Worth Deficit: £34,458,976 *Total Assets:* £34,194,132
Registered Office: 475 The Boulevard, Capability Green, Luton, Beds, LU1 3LU
Activities: Information technology consultancy activities
Parent: Lumesse Holdings Limited
Officers: Eric John Graham [1971] Director [Canadian]; Shanna Jane Helen Laughton [1973] Director [Canadian]; Michael Stewart [1966] Director [Canadian]

Lumesse Holdings Limited
Incorporated: 20 November 2009 *Employees:* 4
Net Worth Deficit: £146,178,912 *Total Assets:* £82,672,792
Registered Office: 475 The Boulevard, Capability Green, Luton, Beds, LU1 3LU
Activities: Information technology consultancy activities
Parent: Libra Acquireco Limited
Officers: Eric Graham [1971] Director [Canadian]; Shanna Jane Helen Laughton [1973] Director [Canadian]; Michael Stewart [1966] Director [Canadian]

Lumesse Holdings UK Limited
Incorporated: 29 June 2005
Net Worth Deficit: £2,265,022 *Total Assets:* £11,036,322
Registered Office: 475 The Boulevard, Capability Green, Luton, Beds, LU1 3LU
Activities: Information technology consultancy activities
Parent: Lumesse Holdings Limited
Officers: Eric John Graham [1971] Director [Canadian]; Shanna Jane Helen Laughton [1973] Director [Canadian]; Michael Stewart [1966] Director [Canadian]

Lumesse Limited
Incorporated: 12 November 1999 *Employees:* 155
Net Worth Deficit: £3,716,849 *Total Assets:* £40,739,432
Registered Office: 475 The Boulevard, Capability Green, Luton, Beds, LU1 3LU
Activities: Information technology consultancy activities
Parent: Lumesse Holdings UK Limited
Officers: Eric John Graham [1971] Director [Canadian]; Shanna Jane Helen Laughton [1973] Director [Canadian]; Michael Stewart [1966] Director [Canadian]

Luminescence Holdings Ltd
Incorporated: 10 April 2014 *Employees:* 70
Net Worth: £16,976,998 *Total Assets:* £18,707,136
Registered Office: The Fairway, Bush Fair, Harlow, Essex, CM18 6NG
Activities: Activities of other holding companies n.e.c.
Parent: DIC Corporation
Officers: Paul Joseph Cooper [1966] Technical Director; Gregory William Hayes [1962] Director; Martijn Jan Charles Marie Schoonenberg [1977] Director [Dutch]; Gary Silver [1978] Director

Luminescence International Ltd
Incorporated: 18 March 1999 *Employees:* 70
Net Worth: £10,682,995 *Total Assets:* £12,394,648
Registered Office: The Fairway, Bush Fair, Harlow, Essex, CM18 6NG
Activities: Manufacture of printing ink
Parent: Luminescence Holdings Ltd
Officers: Paul Joseph Cooper [1966] Technical Director; Gregory William Hayes [1962] Director; Martijn Jan Charles Marie Schoonenberg [1977] Director [Dutch]; Gary Silver [1978] Director

Luna Estates Limited
Incorporated: 6 February 2015
Net Worth: £5,145,296 *Total Assets:* £11,116,017
Registered Office: 50 Lancaster Road, Enfield, Middlesex, EN2 0BY
Activities: Other letting and operating of own or leased real estate
Shareholders: Richard James Paterson; Janet Margaret Paterson
Officers: Janet Margaret Paterson [1957] Director/Housewife; Richard James Paterson [1957] Director

Lundbeck Group Limited
Incorporated: 26 April 1994 *Employees:* 2
Net Worth: £120,093,208 *Total Assets:* £121,013,320
Registered Office: 2nd Floor, Building 3, Abbey View, Everard Close, St Albans, Herts, AL1 2PS
Activities: Activities of head offices
Parent: H Lundbeck A/S
Officers: Roberto Lapenna, Secretary; Thomas Bo Bjorn Klee [1971] Managing Director [Danish]; Joao Carlos Nunes Rocha [1958] Director/Chairman [Brazilian]

Lundbeck Limited
Incorporated: 1 February 1972 *Employees:* 54
Net Worth: £16,451,111 *Total Assets:* £23,865,264
Registered Office: 2nd Floor, Building 3, Abbey View, Everard Close, St Albans, Herts, AL1 2PS
Activities: Wholesale of pharmaceutical goods
Parent: Lundbeck Group Limited
Officers: Roberto Lapenna, Secretary; Thomas Bo Bjorn Klee [1971] Managing Director [Danish]; Joao Carlos Nunes Rocha [1958] Director/Chairman [Brazilian]

Lundbeck UK LLP
Incorporated: 1 July 2009
Net Worth: £171,134,000 *Total Assets:* £171,163,008
Registered Office: 2nd Floor, Building 3, Abbey View, Everard Close, St Albans, Herts, AL1 2PS

Lupo Limited
Incorporated: 30 June 2004
Net Worth: £190,372,000 *Total Assets:* £381,716,000
Registered Office: Gladstone Place, 36-38 Upper Marlborough Road, St Albans, Herts, AL1 3UU
Activities: Other letting and operating of own or leased real estate
Parent: Malthurst (UK) Limited
Officers: David Hathaway, Secretary; William Bahlsen Bannister [1967] Director/Chief Executive; Jeremy Clarke [1963] Director/Chief Operating Officer; Simon Paul Lane [1963] Director/Chief Financial Officer

Luvata Welwyn Garden Ltd
Incorporated: 12 August 1991 *Employees:* 48
Net Worth: £10,642,000 *Total Assets:* £12,289,000
Registered Office: Centrapark, Bessemer Road, Welwyn Garden City, Herts, AL7 1HT
Activities: Machining
Parent: Luvata Ohio, Inc
Officers: Carla Grispino, Secretary/Accountant [American]; Amanda Dawson [1966] Director/Business Management; Dirk Greywitt [1965] Director/Business Management [American]; Jussi Helavirta [1957] Director/Executive [Finnish]

Luxottica North Europe Limited
Incorporated: 8 February 1984 *Employees:* 223
Net Worth: £8,600,000 *Total Assets:* £70,059,000
Registered Office: Verulam Point, Station Way, St Albans, Herts, AL1 5HE
Activities: Non-specialised wholesale trade
Parent: Luxottica Group SpA
Officers: Paolo Alberti [1962] Director [American]; Franco Ferrante [1978] Director/Country Manager [Italian]; John David Williams [1957] Director/Chartered Accountant

Luxottica Retail UK Ltd
Incorporated: 25 November 1992 *Employees:* 1,105
Net Worth: £39,490,000 *Total Assets:* £66,817,000
Registered Office: Verulam Point, Station Way, St Albans, Herts, AL1 5HE
Activities: Retail sale by opticians
Parent: Luxottica Group SpA
Officers: Sara Francescutto [1974] Director [Italian]; John David Williams [1957] Director/Chartered Accountant

Lymington Precision Engineering (LPE) Limited
Incorporated: 1 February 2011
Net Worth: £26,576,000 *Total Assets:* £26,579,000
Registered Office: 59-61 High Street, Rickmansworth, Herts, WD3 1RH
Activities: Manufacture of other fabricated metal products n.e.c.
Parent: Senior UK Limited
Officers: Andrew John Bodenham, Secretary; Martin John Barnes [1966] Director; Andrew John Bodenham [1966] Director; Bindi Jayantilal Jivraj Foyle [1973] Director

Lymington Precision Engineers Co. Limited
Incorporated: 6 February 1981 *Employees:* 174
Net Worth: £6,019,000 *Total Assets:* £11,594,000
Registered Office: 59-61 High Street, Rickmansworth, Herts, WD3 1RH
Activities: Manufacture of other fabricated metal products n.e.c.
Parent: Lymington Precision Engineering (LPE) Limited
Officers: Andrew John Bodenham, Secretary; Martin John Barnes [1966] Director; Andrew John Bodenham [1966] Director; Bindi Jayantilal Jivraj Foyle [1973] Director

L. Lynch (Holdings) Limited
Incorporated: 14 June 1990 *Employees:* 3
Net Worth: £13,180,713 *Total Assets:* £27,694,116
Registered Office: Boundary Way, Hemel Hempstead, Herts, HP2 7YU
Activities: Renting and leasing of construction and civil engineering machinery and equipment
Major Shareholder: Liam Lynch
Officers: Fabian Swampillai, Secretary; Liam Lynch [1954] Managing Director [Irish]; Merrill Liam Lynch [1979] Director; Robert Martin Lynch [1980] Director

L. Lynch (Plant Hire & Haulage) Limited
Incorporated: 2 August 1993 *Employees:* 124
Net Worth: £13,416,444 *Total Assets:* £55,744,604
Registered Office: Boundary Way, Hemel Hempstead, Herts, HP2 7YU
Activities: Renting and leasing of construction and civil engineering machinery and equipment
Major Shareholder: Liam Lynch
Officers: Fabian Swampillai, Secretary; Liam Lynch [1954] Managing Director [Irish]; Merrill Liam Lynch [1979] Director; Robert Martin Lynch [1980] Director

Lyndon Hurst Limited
Incorporated: 6 June 1988
Net Worth: £3,902,048 *Total Assets:* £8,081,361
Registered Office: 29 High Street, Harston, Cambridge, CB22 7PX
Activities: Other letting and operating of own or leased real estate
Major Shareholder: Glen Martin Frederick Pilgrim
Officers: Lisa Stella Jane Pilgrim, Secretary; Glen Martin Frederick Pilgrim [1962] Director/Construction Manager

Lynton Homes (3) Limited
Incorporated: 26 September 2016 *Employees:* 2
Net Worth: £42,970 *Total Assets:* £12,656,336
Registered Office: 4 & 5 The Cedars, Apex 12, Old Ipswich Road, Colchester, Essex, CO7 7QR
Activities: Other business support service activities n.e.c.
Shareholders: Kathryn de la Garza; Mark Anthony Hughes
Officers: Kathryn de La Garza [1962] Director; Mark Anthony Hughes [1971] Director/Groundwork

Lynxvale Limited
Incorporated: 20 September 1989
Net Worth: £100 *Total Assets:* £17,691,848
Registered Office: The Old Schools, Trinity Lane, Cambridge, CB2 1TS
Activities: Development of building projects
Officers: Emma Rampton, Secretary; Spencer John Moore [1966] Director; Lesley Margaret Thompson [1959] Director; Beverley Weston [1970] Director

Lysander Student Properties Operations Limited
Incorporated: 21 May 2014
Net Worth: £2,228,000 *Total Assets:* £23,441,000
Registered Office: Tempsford Hall, Sandy, Beds, SG19 2BD
Activities: Construction of domestic buildings
Parent: Lysander Student Properties Limited
Officers: Bethan Melges, Secretary; Mark Bladon [1972] Director/Banker; Thomas George Gilman [1970] Director; Shivani Goolab [1988] Director/Banker [South African]; Lee Howard [1981] Director; Mark Ian Robinson [1976] Director; Hayley Scott [1981] Director/Banker

M & D Developments Limited
Incorporated: 13 January 1981 *Employees:* 2
Net Worth: £2,196,398 *Total Assets:* £13,431,778
Registered Office: Hengrave Hall, Hengrave, Bury St Edmunds, Suffolk, IP28 6LZ
Activities: Development of building projects
Major Shareholder: David Hugh Harris
Officers: David Hugh Harris, Secretary; David Hugh Harris [1955] Director/Property Developer; Rodger Issac [1946] Director/Site Manager

M & W Newco Limited
Incorporated: 19 June 2014
Net Worth: £11,919,090 *Total Assets:* £11,919,091
Registered Office: 6 Bridgegate Business Park, Gatehouse Way, Aylesbury, Bucks, HP19 8XN
Activities: Activities of head offices
Officers: Steven Mackintosh [1958] Director

M G 111 Ltd
Incorporated: 22 November 2016
Net Worth Deficit: £43,462 *Total Assets:* £10,195,050
Registered Office: 364-368 Cranbrook Rd, Gants Hill, London, IG2 6HY
Activities: Other business support service activities n.e.c.
Parent: Millennium Cash & Carry Limited
Officers: Rishi Lakhani [1982] Director

M Group Services Limited
Incorporated: 4 July 2016 *Employees:* 7,339
Net Worth: £108,774,000 *Total Assets:* £647,417,984
Registered Office: Abel Smith House, Gunnels Wood Road, Stevenage, Herts, SG1 2ST
Activities: Activities of other holding companies n.e.c.
Parent: Thor Holdco Limited
Officers: Ian Cusden, Secretary; James Michael Arnold [1965] Director/Chief Executive Officer; Martin Geoffrey Beesley [1966] Director/Chief Financial Officer; Ian Vincent Cusden [1957] Director/Chartered Accountant; Artem Silonov [1987] Director; James Robert Winnicott [1968] Director

M L Accessories Limited
Incorporated: 22 January 1998 *Employees:* 91
Net Worth: £15,470,003 *Total Assets:* £26,038,210
Registered Office: Unit E, Chiltern Park, Boscombe Road, Dunstable, Beds, LU5 4LT
Activities: Other service activities n.e.c.
Officers: Ian Gabriel, Secretary/Financial Controller; Jens Marcel Aertgeerts [1968] Director [Belgian]; Catherine Connolly [1968] Director

M-Ship Limited
Incorporated: 14 October 2005 *Employees:* 36
Net Worth: £4,776,215 *Total Assets:* £10,065,852
Registered Office: The Naval House, Kings Quay Street, Harwich, Essex, CO12 3JJ
Activities: Activities of head offices
Parent: BNX Holdings Limited
Officers: Jonathan Paul Ward, Secretary; Allan William Spence Binks [1941] Director; Thomas Allan Binks [1972] Director/Warehouse Manager; William Andrew Binks [1966] Operations Director

M. & J. Engineers Limited
Incorporated: 3 November 1955 *Employees:* 149
Net Worth: £16,382,067 *Total Assets:* £27,153,640
Registered Office: Cashel House, Cadwell Lane, Hitchin, Herts, SG4 0SQ
Activities: Renting and leasing of construction and civil engineering machinery and equipment
Parent: Abbey Group Limited
Officers: Alexander Leon Ford, Secretary; David John Dawson [1964] Director; Alexander Leon Ford [1979] Company Secretary/Director; Charles Hubert Gallagher [1959] Director [Irish]; Peter David James [1965] Director/Accountant [New Zealander]; Robert Neil Kennedy [1953] Director; Stephen Peter Randall [1955] Plant Director

M.J.S. Construction (March) Limited
Incorporated: 23 November 1995 *Employees:* 48
Net Worth: £5,890,212 *Total Assets:* £12,717,433
Registered Office: MJS House, Wisbech Road, Westry, March, Cambs, PE15 0BA
Activities: Construction of commercial buildings
Officers: Judith Anne Saxby, Secretary; Jamie Burton [1981] Director; Ben John Saxby [1988] Director/Construction Manager; Michael John Saxby [1954] Director; Sean Michael Saxby [1992] Construction Director

M.J.S. Holdings (March) Limited
Incorporated: 14 July 2015 *Employees:* 48
Net Worth: £15,889,415 *Total Assets:* £22,720,636
Registered Office: MJS House, Wisbech Road, Westry, March, Cambs, PE15 0BA
Activities: Other specialised construction activities n.e.c.
Shareholders: Ben John Saxby; Sean Michael Saxby
Officers: Ben John Saxby [1988] Director; Sean Michael Saxby [1992] Director

M.P.I. (Herts) Limited
Incorporated: 11 November 2003 *Employees:* 79
Net Worth: £11,004,471 *Total Assets:* £19,687,272
Registered Office: International House, The Chase, Foxholes Business Park, Hertford, SG13 7NN
Activities: Activities of head offices
Officers: Helena Arrandale Hall, Secretary; Mark Hurley [1969] Director/Real Estate Investment [American]; Edward Robert Pearson [1967] Director

M.P.I. Limited
Incorporated: 10 September 1992 *Employees:* 79
Net Worth: £5,882,670 *Total Assets:* £19,684,456
Registered Office: International House, The Chase, Foxholes Business Park, Hertford, SG13 7NN
Activities: Temporary employment agency activities
Officers: David Madell, Secretary; Sarah Jane Grant [1969] Director/Payroll Manageress; Colin Paul Richard Green [1964] Director/Sales; Simon Colin Henser [1977] Director/Sales; John Alan Herbert [1962] Director/Sales Manager; Gemma Louise Newby [1980] Director/Recruitment Consultant; Ellen Jane Swain [1972] Director/Recruitment Consultant; Adam Webb [1966] Director/Sales

MA Securities London Limited
Incorporated: 17 November 2016
Net Worth: £100 *Total Assets:* £16,654,916
Registered Office: 166 College Road, Harrow, Middlesex, HA1 1RA
Activities: Other business support service activities n.e.c.
Major Shareholder: Mark Stuart Allan
Officers: Mark Stuart Allan [1962] Director

Macarthys Laboratories Limited
Incorporated: 30 January 1959 *Employees:* 440
Net Worth: £112,461,000 *Total Assets:* £137,148,992
Registered Office: Bampton Road, Harold Hill, Romford, Essex, RM3 8UG
Activities: Manufacture of basic pharmaceutical products
Parent: Orphea Limited
Officers: Michael Christopher James Harris [1970] Director/Chief Executive; Roseline Georgette Joannesse [1959] Director/Vice President Legal Affairs [French]; Philip Edward Parry [1965] Director/Quality Assurance Professional

MacDonald Humfrey (Automation) Limited
Incorporated: 2 June 1988 *Employees:* 326
Net Worth: £32,610,000 *Total Assets:* £53,419,000
Registered Office: 29-35 Bolton Road, Luton, Beds, LU1 3HY
Activities: Manufacture of other electrical equipment
Parent: L-3 Communications U.K. Ltd.
Officers: Pak-Khong Khong Chin [1972] Director/Business Executive [American]; Ronald Cook [1953] Director; Alan Edward Crawford [1982] Director/Business Executive [Australian]; Michael William James MacDonald [1954] Director [Irish]; Mark Douglas Simon [1958] Director [American]; Arthur Yeager [1956] Director/Business Executive [American]

MacDuffy (Holdings) Limited
Incorporated: 10 August 2016 *Employees:* 202
Net Worth: £3,257,214 *Total Assets:* £9,238,074
Registered Office: 13 & 14 Raynham Road, Bishop's Stortford, Herts, CM23 5PB
Activities: Other business support service activities n.e.c.
Shareholders: Lee McNaughton; Stewart Stephen Duffy
Officers: Stewart Stephen Duffy [1977] Director; Lee McNaughton [1976] Director

MacIntyre Transport Limited
Incorporated: 1 February 2000 *Employees:* 249
Net Worth: £4,453,631 *Total Assets:* £11,687,246
Registered Office: 1 Fordham Road, Newmarket, Suffolk, CB8 7NR
Activities: Freight transport by road
Parent: Turners (Soham) Limited
Officers: Laura Ann Day [1996] Director/Student; Paul Edwin Day [1958] Director; Winifred Mary Day [1934] Director; Paul Miller [1970] Director

Mack-Brooks Exhibitions Limited
Incorporated: 3 December 1969 *Employees:* 90
Net Worth: £25,905,250 *Total Assets:* £41,500,960
Registered Office: Romeland House, Romeland Hill, St Albans, Herts, AL3 4ET
Activities: Activities of exhibition and fair organisers
Parent: Reed Exhibitions Limited
Officers: Jacqueline Mary Poole, Secretary; Alexander David Stuart Bowden [1967] Director/Accountant; Hans-Joachim Erbel [1959] Director [German]; Nicola Hamann [1970] Director [German]; Darren Geoffrey Johnson [1966] Director; Michele Ruth Tiley-Hill [1972] Director

MacKenzie Taylor Holdings Limited
Incorporated: 24 October 2014 *Employees:* 2
Net Worth: £2,677,958 *Total Assets:* £8,928,267
Registered Office: Mead Court, 10 The Mead Business Centre, 176-178 Berkhampstead Road, Chesham, Bucks, HP5 3EE
Activities: Activities of head offices
Parent: National Financial Partners Corp
Officers: Robert Hilzenrath [1966] Director/Finance and Operations Manager [American]; Duncan George Jarrett [1965] Director; Matthew Stephen Pawley [1976] Director

MacLeans (Foils) Limited
Incorporated: 6 April 2000
Net Worth Deficit: £443,959 *Total Assets:* £9,676,976
Registered Office: 1 The Forum, Coopers Way, Temple Farm Industrial Estate, Southend on Sea, Essex, SS2 5TE
Activities: Other manufacturing n.e.c.
Shareholders: David John Watson; Pauk Stuart Watson
Officers: David John Barnish, Secretary; David John Watson [1947] Director; Paul Stuart Watson [1983] Director

Macquarie Corona Energy Holdings Limited
Incorporated: 2 May 2003
Net Worth: £12,107,631 *Total Assets:* £18,975,828
Registered Office: Building 2, Level 2, Croxley Park, Watford, Herts, WD18 8YA
Activities: Activities of head offices
Parent: Macquarie Investments 2 Limited
Officers: Shaheda Begum Thomas, Secretary; Neil Trevor Mitchell [1974] Commercial Director; Philip Morton [1968] Finance Director; Paul Christian Plewman [1972] Director/Banker [Irish]

Macron Safety Systems (UK) Limited
Incorporated: 9 May 1974 *Employees:* 115
Net Worth: £75,330,000 *Total Assets:* £84,565,000
Registered Office: Burlingham House, Hewett Road, Gapton Hall Industrial Estate, Great Yarmouth, Norfolk, NR31 0NN
Activities: Other manufacturing n.e.c.
Parent: Tyco Fire & Integrated Solutions (UK) Limited
Officers: Mark Ayre [1963] Finance Director; John Huxtable [1960] Manufacturing Operations Director

Magdalene Limited
Incorporated: 15 May 1996 *Employees:* 164
Net Worth: £4,792,000 *Total Assets:* £10,484,000
Registered Office: Abel Smith House, Gunnels Wood Road, Stevenage, Herts, SG1 2ST
Activities: Wired telecommunications activities
Parent: Magdalene Holdings Ltd
Officers: Ian Vincent Cusden, Secretary; James Michael Arnold [1965] Director; Martin Geoffrey Beesley [1966] Director; Alain Hubertus Philomena Loosveld [1968] Director [Dutch]; Mark Anthony Turner [1971] Director; James Robert Winnicott [1968] Director

Mainline Communications Group Limited
Incorporated: 13 October 1993
Previous: Mainline Communications Group PLC
Net Worth: £4,503,000 *Total Assets:* £10,042,000
Registered Office: Trident Place, Mosquito Way, Hatfield, Herts, AL10 9BW
Activities: Activities of head offices
Parent: EE Limited
Officers: Steven Paul Rathborne [1967] Director; Mike Tomlinson [1967] Finance Director

Maison Moti Limited
Incorporated: 31 October 1996 *Employees:* 74
Net Worth: £4,408,931 *Total Assets:* £9,041,150
Registered Office: 8a Southbury Road, Enfield, Middlesex, EN1 1YT
Activities: Other service activities n.e.c.
Major Shareholder: Maya Mahtani
Officers: Mostak Ahmed [1971] Managing Director; Maya Mahtani [1946] Director; Vinod Mahtani [1969] Director/Doctor

Majestic Bingo Limited
Incorporated: 10 October 2013 *Employees:* 338
Net Worth: £2,452,000 *Total Assets:* £11,707,000
Registered Office: Regent Bingo Club, Westlode Street, Spalding, Lincs, PE11 2AE
Activities: Gambling and betting activities
Major Shareholder: Luke Oliver Johnson
Officers: Gary Roger Bennett [1973] Director/Chartered Accountant; Mark Edward Jepp [1967] Director/Gaming Consultant; Luke Oliver Johnson [1962] Director/Businessman; Paul Lewis Viner [1970] Director

Majestic Property & Estates Limited
Incorporated: 13 May 1975 *Employees:* 1
Net Worth: £130,005 *Total Assets:* £19,955,034
Registered Office: Sealand House, Hemnall Street, Epping, Essex, CM16 4LG
Activities: Non-trading company
Shareholders: John Alan Clarke; Sandra Elaine Clarke
Officers: Sandra Elaine Clarke, Secretary; John Alan Clarke [1943] Director

Majestic Wine PLC
Incorporated: 28 July 1988 *Employees:* 1,528
Net Worth: £121,761,000 *Total Assets:* £251,967,008
Registered Office: Majestic House, The Belfry, Colonial Way, Watford, Herts, WD24 4WH
Activities: Wholesale of wine, beer, spirits and other alcoholic beverages
Officers: Alex Iapichino, Secretary; Justin James Apthorp [1962] Director/Buyer; James Crawford [1977] Finance Director; Rowan Gormley [1962] Director/Chief Executive Officer [Irish]; Ian Andrew Harding [1964] Director/Company Executive; Brian Gregory Hodder [1952] Director; David Anthony Stead [1958] Director/Auditor

Majestic Wine Warehouses Limited
Incorporated: 30 October 1981 *Employees:* 1,168
Net Worth: £86,652,000 *Total Assets:* £138,679,008
Registered Office: Majestic House, The Belfry, Colonial Way, Watford, Herts, WD24 4WH
Activities: Wholesale of wine, beer, spirits and other alcoholic beverages
Parent: Majestic Wine PLC
Officers: Alex Iapichino, Secretary; James Crawford [1977] Director; Olivia FitzGenerald [1972] Director/Businesswoman; Rowan Gormley [1962] Director/Chief Executive [Irish]; Stuart Christopher Lane [1981] Finance Director; Joshua Benjamin Geoffrey Lincoln-Creese [1984] Managing Director

Make Believe Ideas Ltd
Incorporated: 28 May 2004 *Employees:* 76
Net Worth: £8,681,549 *Total Assets:* £16,366,366
Registered Office: The Wilderness, Berkhamsted, Herts, HP4 2AZ
Activities: Book publishing
Major Shareholder: Joanna Noelle Bicknell
Officers: Joanna Noelle Bicknell, Secretary; Ellie Berger [1959] Director/Publishing [American]; Joanna Noelle Bicknell [1966] Director; Gil Dickoff [1961] Director/Finance/Treasurer [American]; Simon John Walker [1988] Director; Wilfred Wikkerink [1973] Director [Canadian]

Maldon Crystal Salt Company Limited
Incorporated: 19 June 1926 *Employees:* 42
Net Worth: £9,509,000 *Total Assets:* £15,561,000
Registered Office: Wycke Hill Business Park, Maldon, Essex, CM9 6UZ
Activities: Extraction of salt
Officers: David Charles Coubrough, Secretary/Company PLC Chief Executive; David Charles Coubrough [1955] Director/Company PLC Chief Executive; Louise Mary Coubrough [1961] Director/Solicitor; Clive Christopher Osborne [1943] Director/Retired; Steve John Osborne [1974] Managing Director; Sarah Catherine Alison Phillips [1963] Director/Arts Administration; Mark Nicholas Soudah [1965] Director

Maldon Electric Securities,Limited
Incorporated: 27 April 1932
Net Worth: £16,449,317 *Total Assets:* £17,316,856
Registered Office: Princel House, Princel Lane, Dedham, Colchester, Essex, CO7 6HD
Activities: Security dealing on own account
Major Shareholder: Maralyn Jane Jewell
Officers: Maralyn Jane Jewell, Secretary; Maralyn Jane Jewell [1946] Director/Secretary

Mallard Leasing Limited
Incorporated: 2 December 1992 *Employees:* 27
Net Worth: £3,163,380 *Total Assets:* £15,307,777
Registered Office: Hophouse, Maltings Park, West Bergholt, Colchester, Essex, CO6 3TJ
Activities: Financial leasing
Parent: Mallard Consolidated Limited
Officers: Philip Nicholas Amphlett [1948] Director/Banker; Steven Peter Day [1977] Director/Chartered Accountant; Edward Francis Richard Stevenson [1984] Director; Nicholas John Stevenson [1955] Director/Financier

Malt U.K. Holdco Limited
Incorporated: 22 August 2006
Net Worth Deficit: £4,748,000 *Total Assets:* £45,052,000
Registered Office: Station Maltings, Witham, Essex, CM8 2DU
Activities: Other business support service activities n.e.c.
Parent: Graincorp UK Limited
Officers: Brett Alan Weimann, Secretary; Alistair Garrard Bell [1961] Director/Chief Financial Officer [Australian]; Darren Smith [1968] Director/President [Canadian]; Roger Graham Woodley [1958] Director/Maltster (CEO)

Maltco 3 Limited
Incorporated: 11 October 1989
Net Worth: £45,012,000 *Total Assets:* £65,776,000
Registered Office: Station Maltings, Witham, Essex, CM8 2DU
Activities: Financial intermediation not elsewhere classified
Parent: Ulgrave Limited
Officers: Brett Alan Weimann, Secretary; Alistair Garrard Bell [1961] Director/Chief Financial Officer [Australian]; Darren Smith [1968] Director/President [Canadian]; Roger Graham Woodley [1958] Director/Maltster (CEO)

Malthurst (UK) Limited
Incorporated: 28 November 1997
Net Worth: £71,500,000 *Total Assets:* £71,500,000
Registered Office: Gladstone Place, 36-38 Upper Marlborough Road, St Albans, Herts, AL1 3UU
Activities: Activities of head offices
Parent: MRH (GB) Limited
Officers: David Hathaway, Secretary; William Bahlsen Bannister [1967] Director/Chief Executive; Jeremy Clarke [1963] Director/Chief Operating Officer; Simon Paul Lane [1963] Director/Chief Financial Officer

Malthurst Estates Limited
Incorporated: 12 December 2012
Net Worth: £53,380,000 *Total Assets:* £119,496,000
Registered Office: Gladstone Place, 36-38 Upper Marlborough Road, St Albans, Herts, AL1 3UU
Activities: Other letting and operating of own or leased real estate
Parent: Malthurst (UK) Limited
Officers: David Hathaway, Secretary; William Bahlsen Bannister [1967] Director/Chief Executive; Jeremy Clarke [1963] Director/Chief Operating Officer; Simon Paul Lane [1963] Director/Chief Financial Officer

Malthurst Limited
Incorporated: 7 October 1997 *Employees:* 2
Net Worth: £118,159,000 *Total Assets:* £243,398,000
Registered Office: Gladstone Place, 36-38 Upper Marlborough Road, St Albans, Herts, AL1 3UU
Activities: Retail sale of automotive fuel in specialised stores
Parent: Refined Holdings Limited
Officers: David Hathaway, Secretary; William Bahlsen Bannister [1967] Director/Chief Executive; Jeremy Clarke [1963] Director/Chief Operating Officer; Simon Paul Lane [1963] Director/Chief Financial Officer

Malthurst Petroleum Limited
Incorporated: 28 May 1963
Net Worth: £130,467,000 *Total Assets:* £212,475,008
Registered Office: Gladstone Place, 36-38 Upper Marlborough Road, St Albans, Herts, AL1 3UU
Activities: Retail sale of automotive fuel in specialised stores
Parent: Refined Holdings Limited
Officers: David Hathaway, Secretary; William Bahlsen Bannister [1967] Director/Chief Executive; Jeremy Clarke [1963] Director/Chief Operating Officer; Simon Paul Lane [1963] Director/Chief Financial Officer

Malthurst Retail Limited
Incorporated: 31 January 1997 *Employees:* 196
Net Worth: £55,734,000 *Total Assets:* £172,567,008
Registered Office: Gladstone Place, 36-38 Upper Marlborough Road, St Albans, Herts, AL1 3UU
Activities: Other letting and operating of own or leased real estate
Parent: Refined Holdings Limited
Officers: David Hathaway, Secretary; William Bahlsen Bannister [1967] Director/Chief Executive; Jeremy Clarke [1963] Director/Chief Operating Officer; Simon Paul Lane [1963] Director/Chief Financial Officer; Graham Paul Timbers [1959] Managing Director

Malthurst South East Limited
Incorporated: 4 March 2015
Net Worth: £50,086,000 *Total Assets:* £124,077,000
Registered Office: Gladstone Place, 36-38 Upper Marlborough Road, St Albans, Herts, AL1 3UU
Activities: Other letting and operating of own or leased real estate
Parent: Malthurst (UK) Limited
Officers: David Hathaway, Secretary; William Bahlsen Bannister [1967] Director/Chief Executive; Jeremy Clarke [1963] Director/Chief Operating Officer; Simon Paul Lane [1963] Director/Chief Financial Officer

Mando Corporation Limited
Incorporated: 15 September 1977 *Employees:* 18
Net Worth: £9,926,212 *Total Assets:* £12,457,688
Registered Office: 27 Faraday Road, Rabans Lane, Aylesbury, Bucks, HP19 8TY
Activities: Financial intermediation not elsewhere classified
Parent: WPP Group PLC
Officers: Paul Andrew Townsend, Secretary; Clare Louise Jones [1979] Client Services Director; Laurence Mellman [1965] Director; Rebecca Louise Munday [1971] Managing Director; Paul Andrew Townsend [1971] Director/Chartered Accountant

Manford Securities & Investments Limited
Incorporated: 1 June 1988
Net Worth Deficit: £85,778 *Total Assets:* £8,829,439
Registered Office: The Old Star, Church Street, Princes Risborough, Bucks, HP27 9AA
Activities: Credit granting by non-deposit taking finance houses and other specialist consumer credit grantors
Shareholder: Marc Lewis Fox
Officers: Marc Lewis Fox [1962] Director/Financial Underwriter

Manichem Limited
Incorporated: 2 January 2007 *Employees:* 188
Net Worth Deficit: £3,600,441 *Total Assets:* £9,575,481
Registered Office: 109-111 Field End Road, Pinner, Middlesex, HA5 1QG
Activities: Wholesale of pharmaceutical goods
Parent: Merrygood Ltd
Officers: Krishma Vikash Patel [1981] Director/Pharmacist; Niral Narendra Patel [1981] Director; Vikash Patel [1982] Director; Viresh Patel [1985] Director

Manor (2016) Holdings Limited
Incorporated: 31 March 2016 *Employees:* 262
Net Worth: £5,696,324 *Total Assets:* £39,028,252
Registered Office: Suite E2, 2nd Floor, The Octagon, Middleborough, Colchester, Essex, CO1 1TG
Activities: Activities of other holding companies n.e.c.
Parent: Thailand Carpet Manufacturing Public Company Ltd
Officers: Zoe Caroline Dickens [1973] Director; Pimol Srivikorn [1964] Director/Business Owner [Thai]; Taya Teepsuwan [1972] Director/Business Owner [Thai]; Walliwan Varavarn [1957] Director/Employee [Thai]

Manor Crest Construction Limited
Incorporated: 30 May 2001 *Employees:* 7
Previous: Manor Crest (Carline) Ltd
Net Worth: £338,350 *Total Assets:* £9,659,841
Registered Office: 27-29 Lumley Avenue, Skegness, Lincs, PE25 2AT
Activities: Construction of domestic buildings
Parent: Manor Crest Homes Limited
Officers: Leigh Morris Hall, Secretary/Director; Leigh Morris Hall [1969] Director; Dean Anthony Wann [1971] Director

Manor Crest Homes Limited
Incorporated: 24 February 2006 *Employees:* 29
Net Worth: £7,745,280 *Total Assets:* £12,657,548
Registered Office: 27-29 Lumley Avenue, Skegness, Lincs, PE25 2AT
Activities: Construction of domestic buildings
Shareholders: Leigh Morris Hall; Dean Anthony Wann
Officers: Leigh Morris Hall, Secretary; Leigh Morris Hall [1969] Director; Deborah Ledbrook [1964] Director/Operations Manager; Dean Anthony Wann [1971] Director

Manor Farm Solar Limited
Incorporated: 20 April 2011
Net Worth Deficit: £2,867,554 *Total Assets:* £11,456,423
Registered Office: Beaufort Court, Egg Farm Lane, off Station Road, Kings Langley, Herts, WD4 8LR
Activities: Production of electricity
Parent: European Investments (Cornwall) Limited
Officers: Dominic Hearth, Secretary; Steven William Hughes [1972] Global Support Services Director, UK&I - Commercial; Mitesh Raj Patel [1982] Director/Chartered Accountant; Tracy Jane Scott [1976] Director/Delivery Project Manager; Mark Christopher Wayment [1958] Director

Manor Fresh Limited
Incorporated: 18 November 2005 *Employees:* 172
Net Worth: £5,578,542 *Total Assets:* £12,508,413
Registered Office: Manor Farm, Holbeach Hurn, Spalding, Lincs, PE12 8LR
Activities: Wholesale of fruit and vegetables
Shareholders: Fresca Group Limited; A H Worth & Company Limited
Officers: Nigel Roland Baker, Secretary; Nigel Roland Baker [1962] Director; Ian Alexander Craig [1957] Director; Michael David Scott [1966] Director; Brett Geoffrey Sumner [1973] Finance Director; Martin John Taylor [1971] Director; Duncan Richard Worth [1965] Director

Manor Lodge School
Incorporated: 22 June 1993 *Employees:* 87
Net Worth: £6,900,102 *Total Assets:* £10,201,621
Registered Office: Manor Lodge School, Rectory Lane, Ridge Hill, Shenley, Radlett, Herts, WD7 9BG
Activities: Primary education
Officers: Anne-Marie Claire Ridler, Secretary; David Arnold [1939] Director; Graham Thomas Black [1943] Director/Retired Bursar; Trudy Capaldo [1970] Director/Chartered Accountant; Mark Christopher Cherry [1962] Director/Property Development; Sonia Kaya Coventry [1978] Director/Teacher; Helen Marie Gunasekera [1971] Director/Lawyer; Sarah Ann Hollis [1966] Director/Headmistress; Melody Jones [1975] Director/Teacher; Dr Mohammed Shahzad Ahmed Malik [1967] Director/Venture Capitalist; James Adam Segal [1970] Director/Solicitor; Andrew Monro Williams [1966] Director/Teacher; Stephen Wilson [1947] Director/Retired

Manor Service Stations Limited
Incorporated: 14 August 1985 *Employees:* 100
Net Worth: £14,318,000 *Total Assets:* £17,179,000
Registered Office: Gladstone Place, 36-38 Upper Marlborough Road, St Albans, Herts, AL1 3UU
Activities: Retail sale of automotive fuel in specialised stores
Parent: Motor Fuel Limited
Officers: Timothy Edward Douglas Allan [1966] Director; William Bahlsen Bannister [1967] Director/Chief Executive Officer; Thomas McKenzie Biggart [1966] Director/Surveyor; Jeremy Clarke [1963] Managing Director; Simon Lane [1963] Director/Accountant

Manormaker (Nominee No. 1) Limited
Incorporated: 7 December 2015 *Employees:* 3
Net Worth: £14 *Total Assets:* £11,445,329
Registered Office: 11 Black Horse Lane, Ipswich, Suffolk, IP1 2EF
Activities: Other letting and operating of own or leased real estate
Parent: Manormaker Partnership LLP
Officers: Stephen Montague Clark, Secretary; Stephen Montague Clark [1956] Director/Chartered Surveyor; Timothy Michael Hayne [1954] Director/Fund Manager

Manpower Holdings Limited
Incorporated: 11 July 2003 *Employees:* 1
Net Worth: £253,054,000 *Total Assets:* £532,308,992
Registered Office: The Old Dairy, Griffin Farm, Conger Lane, Toddington, Beds, LU5 6BT
Activities: Activities of head offices
Parent: Manpowergroup Inc
Officers: Andrew Lewis Windmill, Secretary; Mark Anthony Cahill [1958] Director; Donald Mondano [1971] Director [American]; Stefano Scabbio [1964] Director [Italian]; Damian Paul Whitham [1967] Director; Andrew Lewis Windmill [1956] Director

Mansley Group Holdings Limited
Incorporated: 3 November 2014 *Employees:* 51
Net Worth: £74,864,264 *Total Assets:* £84,375,952
Registered Office: King Street House, 15 Upper King Street, Norwich, NR3 1RB
Activities: Other accommodation
Shareholders: Richard Charles Rowley; Julian Thomas Burn-Callander; Dowager Lady Astrid Pennington Cleife Rowley
Officers: Margaret Ann Fletcher, Secretary; Margaret Ann Fletcher [1950] Director; Sir Richard Charles Rowley [1959] Director; Colin William Stone [1971] Commercial Director

Manu Ventures LLP
Incorporated: 31 August 2016
Net Worth: £8,606,226 *Total Assets:* £8,611,226
Registered Office: Hedgerley End House, Hedgerley Lane, Beaconsfield, Bucks, HP9 2JR
Officers: Manojkumar Ganapathy [1981] Member; Anudarshini Manojkumar [1984] Member

Manufacturing Services Investment Limited
Incorporated: 30 January 2014 *Employees:* 24
Net Worth: £12,989,897 *Total Assets:* £21,423,330
Registered Office: Cumberland House, 24-28 Baxter Avenue, Southend on Sea, Essex, SS2 6HZ
Activities: Activities of other holding companies n.e.c.
Shareholders: Ian Cressey Homan; Georgina Homan
Officers: Peter Wynne Davies [1949] Director; Robert Michael Henry [1954] Director; Ian Cressey Homan [1967] Director; Jeremy David Kraft [1965] Director; Paul Richard Williams [1964] Director

Map Media Limited
Incorporated: 11 May 2009 *Employees:* 18
Net Worth: £7,084,539 *Total Assets:* £18,166,048
Registered Office: Millhouse, 32-38 East Street, Rochford, Essex, SS4 1DB
Activities: Advertising agencies
Parent: Lousin Holdings Limited
Officers: Andrew Sheridan McCutcheon [1965] Director

Mapeley Columbus II Limited
Incorporated: 25 August 2000
Net Worth Deficit: £63,861,000 *Total Assets:* £15,750,000
Registered Office: Cambridge House, Clarendon Road, Watford, Herts, WD17 1HP
Activities: Other letting and operating of own or leased real estate
Officers: Michael Anthony Wilson, Secretary; Simon David Ainslie Jones [1970] Director/Chief Financial Officer; Mark Julian Smith [1970] Director; Edward Michael Swales [1979] Director; Michael Anthony Wilson [1956] Director/Solicitor

Mapeley Steps Contractor Limited
Incorporated: 12 October 2000
Net Worth Deficit: £73,247,000 *Total Assets:* £46,538,000
Registered Office: Cambridge House, Clarendon Road, Watford, Herts, WD17 1HP
Activities: Other letting and operating of own or leased real estate
Officers: Michael Anthony Wilson, Secretary; Simon David Ainslie Jones [1970] Director/Chief Financial Officer; Mark Julian Smith [1970] Director; Edward Michael Swales [1979] Director; Michael Anthony Wilson [1956] Director/Solicitor

Marblelane Limited
Incorporated: 6 September 2000 *Employees:* 54
Net Worth: £13,057,358 *Total Assets:* £23,281,300
Registered Office: Hainey Farm, Barway Road, Ely, Cambs, CB7 5TZ
Activities: Growing of cereals (except rice), leguminous crops and oil seeds
Officers: David Thompson, Secretary/Accountant; Guy Peter Shropshire [1957] Director; John Bourne Shropshire [1955] Director; David Thompson [1968] Director/Accountant

Marcantonio Foods Limited
Incorporated: 6 April 1945 *Employees:* 153
Previous: Marcantonio Foods.Limited
Net Worth: £1,813,411 *Total Assets:* £10,779,802
Registered Office: 20 Thames Road, Barking, Essex, IG11 0HZ
Activities: Manufacture of other food products n.e.c.
Officers: Nicholas Philip Venditti, Secretary; John Patrick Aalhuizen [1965] Director [Swedish]; Thomas Ernst Bruck [1962] Director [German]; Riccardo Antonio Marcantonio [1980] Director; Nadia Millar [1968] Director; Tor Agner Osmundsen [1978] Director of Subsidiaries [Norwegian]; Bernard Bertram Pooley [1957] Finance Director; Nicholas Philip Venditti [1971] Director/Salesperson; Michael Wodskou [1967] Director [Danish]

Marchanson Limited
Incorporated: 20 November 1972 *Employees:* 4
Net Worth: £7,877,851 *Total Assets:* £13,118,397
Registered Office: York House, Empire Way, Wembley, Middlesex, HA9 0FQ
Activities: Operation of arts facilities
Shareholders: Richard Phillip Marchant; Stuart Julian Marchant
Officers: Stuart Julian Marchant, Secretary; Richard Phillip Marchant [1936] Director/Antique Dealer; Stuart Julian Marchant [1963] Director/Antique Dealer

Marchase Limited
Incorporated: 17 August 2005 *Employees:* 221
Net Worth: £21,805,892 *Total Assets:* £34,260,184
Registered Office: Riverside Place, 1-9 Lea Road, Waltham Abbey, Essex, EN9 1AS
Activities: Activities of distribution holding companies
Shareholder: Charles William Smith
Officers: Martin Stewart Earle, Secretary; Martin Stewart Earle [1946] Director/Manager; Charles William Valens Smith [1949] Director/Manager

Marden Homes Limited
Incorporated: 30 November 1992 *Employees:* 20
Net Worth: £5,345,413 *Total Assets:* £15,226,653
Registered Office: 601 London Road, Westcliff on Sea, Essex, SS0 9PE
Activities: Construction of commercial buildings
Shareholders: Richard Anthony Tappenden; Shaun Rowland Pridmore
Officers: Deborah Anne Murray, Secretary; Shaun Rowland Pridmore [1965] Director/Bookmaker; Richard Anthony Tappenden [1960] Director

Marine Point Property LLP
Incorporated: 22 June 2016
Net Worth: £14,048,415 *Total Assets:* £14,048,415
Registered Office: Aprirose House, 48a High Street, Edgware, Middlesex, HA8 7EQ
Officers: Manish Mansukhlal Gudka [1970] Member; Gareth Jones [1973] Member; Suraj Rashmikant Shah [1982] LLP Member

Maritime Group Limited
Incorporated: 11 July 2001 *Employees:* 2,205
Net Worth: £54,887,000 *Total Assets:* £156,342,000
Registered Office: Maritime House, Clickett Hill Road, Felixstowe, Suffolk, IP11 4AX
Activities: Freight transport by road
Major Shareholder: John Howard Williams
Officers: Alan McNicol, Secretary; John Howard Williams [1959] Director

Maritime Transport Limited
Incorporated: 19 February 1974 *Employees:* 2,025
Net Worth: £30,836,000 *Total Assets:* £143,298,000
Registered Office: Maritime House, Clickett Hill Road, Felixstowe, Suffolk, IP11 4AX
Activities: Freight transport by road
Major Shareholder: John Howard Williams
Officers: Alan McNicol, Secretary; David Stewart Boomer [1967] Director; Derek Paul Keeble [1971] Director - IT; Richard John Lond [1970] Financial Director; Andrew John McNab [1965] Director [Irish]; Alan McNicol [1965] Group Financial Director; Simon Leslie Smart [1966] Director; Stuart Charles Wardlaw [1955] Director - Fleet; John Howard Williams [1959] Director; Thomas Ross Williams [1988] Commercial Director

Maritime Transport Services Limited
Incorporated: 27 June 1989
Net Worth Deficit: £1,695,000 *Total Assets:* £43,561,000
Registered Office: Tomline House, The Dock, Felixstowe, Suffolk, IP11 3SY
Activities: Sea and coastal freight water transport
Parent: MTS (Holdings) Limited
Officers: Simon Richard Mullett, Secretary; Clemence Chun Fun Cheng [1958] Director; Sing Chi IP [1953] Director [Chinese]; Edith Shih [1952] Director

Maritzcx Limited
Incorporated: 9 October 1981 *Employees:* 317
Net Worth: £4,996,471 *Total Assets:* £9,826,336
Registered Office: Artisan, Hillbottom Road, Sands Industrial Estate, High Wycombe, Bucks, HP12 4HJ
Activities: Media representation services
Parent: Maritzcx Holdings (UK) Limited
Officers: Ian Michael Taylorson, Secretary; Richard Thomas Ramos [1962] Director/CFO Group [American]; Stephan Thun [1966] Managing Director [German]

Market Field Learning Community
Incorporated: 23 September 2016 *Employees:* 145
Net Worth: £8,773,934 *Total Assets:* £10,648,381
Registered Office: Market Field School, School Road, Elmstead, Colchester, Essex, CO7 7ET
Activities: Other education n.e.c.
Officers: Jim Addison [1951] Director/Retired; Michael Frank Andrews [1945] Director; Ian David Coleman [1965] Director/Senior Police Officer; Alan Goggin [1947] Director/IFA, Local Councillor and Board Member; Brian Shaw [1957] Director/Retired; Gary Russell Smith [1957] Director/Headteacher

Marlborough Highways Group Limited
Incorporated: 8 April 2013 *Employees:* 204
Previous: Marlborough Surfacing (2013) Limited
Net Worth: £4,004,024 *Total Assets:* £16,001,876
Registered Office: Woolf Building, 7 Eagle Way, Regiment Business Park, Chelmsford, Essex, CM3 3FY
Activities: Construction of roads and motorways
Major Shareholder: Matthew James Revell
Officers: William David Blostone [1980] Director; James Francis Revell [1950] Director; Joseph Anthony Revell [1981] Director; Matthew James Revell [1978] Director; John Woolf [1945] Director

Marlborough Information Services Limited
Incorporated: 6 July 2005 *Employees:* 13
Net Worth Deficit: £965,839 *Total Assets:* £25,400,120
Registered Office: 1st Floor, Unit 1 Kinsbourne Court, 96-100 Luton Road, Harpenden, Herts, AL5 3BL
Activities: Technical and vocational secondary education
Major Shareholder: Eric Norman Wiltsher
Officers: Eric Norman Wiltsher [1954] Director

The Marlborough Science Academy Limited
Incorporated: 23 March 2012
Net Worth: £17,369,276 *Total Assets:* £19,276,802
Registered Office: The Marlborough Science Academy Limited, Watling Street, St Albans, Herts, AL1 2QA
Activities: General secondary education
Officers: Diana Dean, Secretary; Brian Carter [1951] Director/Retired Teacher; Fran Edmunds [1966] Director/Teacher; Ruth Anna Gannon [1967] Director/Solicitor; Jennifer Hill [1975] Director/School Bursar; David Hogan [1988] Director/Teacher [Irish]; Lyndsey Jane Hooper [1974] Director/Social Worker; Armin John Monadi [1974] Director/Risk & Internal Audit Manager; Sue Noon [1965] Director/Sonographer; Sarah Prestridge [1968] Director/Shop Assistant; Mark Ezzard Quamina [1969] Director/Driving Instructor; Michael Smethers [1947] Director/Retired; Emma Smith [1971] Director/Learning & Development Consultant; Richard John Sullivan [1960] Personnel Director; Ryan Brinthan Theivamanoharan [1985] Director/Teacher; Sarah Thompson [1984] Director/HR Manager; Anne Frances Thomson [1964] Director/Headteacher; Jane Helen Walker-Smith [1960] Director; Simon Adrian Robert Walsh [1969] Director/Solicitor; John Whitby [1978] Director

W.& H.Marriage & Sons Limited
Incorporated: 21 April 1961 *Employees:* 166
Net Worth: £9,102,563 *Total Assets:* £18,132,350
Registered Office: Chelmer Mills, Chelmsford, Essex, CM1 1PN
Activities: Grain milling
Shareholders: George David Marriage; Simon Henry Marriage; Sampson Peter Marriage
Officers: Steven Richard Smith, Secretary; George David Marriage [1951] Director/Miller; Hannah Louise Marriage [1984] Director/Marketing Executive; James Henry Marriage [1984] Director/Sales Manager; Sampson James Marriage [1978] Director/Sales Manager; Sampson Peter Marriage [1947] Director/Miller; Simon Henry Marriage [1956] Director/Farmer

Marriott Holdings Limited
Incorporated: 8 August 2000 *Employees:* 473
Net Worth: £10,994,610 *Total Assets:* £58,072,360
Registered Office: Wolsey House, Sproughton Road, Ipswich, Suffolk, IP1 5AN
Activities: Sale of new cars and light motor vehicles
Shareholder: Harley John Barnard
Officers: Paul Generald Barnard, Secretary; Harley John Barnard [1945] Director; Paul Generald Barnard [1978] Director; Steven Anthony Bridges [1966] Director/Accountant

Marriott Motor Group Limited
Incorporated: 25 February 1999 *Employees:* 393
Net Worth: £11,223,634 *Total Assets:* £57,265,016
Registered Office: Wolsey House, Sproughton Road, Ipswich, Suffolk, IP1 5AN
Activities: Retail trade of motor vehicle parts and accessories
Shareholders: Harley John Barnard; Paul Gerald Barnard
Officers: Paul Generald Barnard, Secretary; Harley John Barnard [1945] Director; Paul Generald Barnard [1978] Director; Steven Anthony Bridges [1966] Finance Director; Ian Michael Woodward [1962] Brand Director

Marsdens Caterers of Sheffield Limited
Incorporated: 28 December 1939 *Employees:* 587
Net Worth: £8,579,723 *Total Assets:* £13,265,836
Registered Office: 34-36 London Road, Wembley, Middlesex, HA9 7EX
Activities: Other food services
Parent: Marz Limited
Officers: Mohammed Adil, Secretary; Raja Jameel Adil [1971] Director/Solicitor

Marshall Group Properties Limited
Incorporated: 1 September 1986
Net Worth: £37,648,512 *Total Assets:* £44,776,512
Registered Office: Airport House, The Airport, Cambridge, CB5 8RY
Activities: Other letting and operating of own or leased real estate
Parent: Marshall of Cambridge (Holdings) Ltd
Officers: Sarah Jane Moynihan, Secretary; Sean Vincent Cummins [1962] Director; Richard Harold Howe [1951] Director; Robert David Marshall [1962] Director; Sarah Jane Moynihan [1969] Director

Marshall Land Systems Ltd
Incorporated: 8 November 1991 *Employees:* 186
Net Worth: £7,297,067 *Total Assets:* £15,575,617
Registered Office: Airport House, The Airport, Cambridge, CB5 8RY
Activities: Manufacture of bodies (coachwork) for motor vehicles (except caravans)
Parent: Marshall of Cambridge (Holdings) Ltd
Officers: Sarah Jane Moynihan, Secretary; Raymond David Cutting [1960] Director; Alistair Dickson McPhee [1958] Director; Gary John Scott Moynehan [1979] Director

Marshall Motor Group Limited
Incorporated: 29 December 1934 *Employees:* 1,534
Net Worth: £52,718,000 *Total Assets:* £337,616,992
Registered Office: Airport House, The Airport, Cambridge, CB5 8RY
Activities: Sale of new cars and light motor vehicles
Parent: Marshall Motor Holdings PLC
Officers: Stephen Robert Jones, Secretary; Richard John Blumberger [1975] Director; Helen Annette Burrows [1964] Director; Jamie Hamilton Crowther [1962] Director; Daksh Gupta [1970] Director

Marshall Motor Holdings PLC
Incorporated: 1 September 1986 *Employees:* 3,923
Previous: Marshall Motor Holdings Limited
Net Worth: £191,210,000 *Total Assets:* £765,670,976
Registered Office: Airport House, The Airport, Cambridge, CB5 8RY
Activities: Activities of head offices
Parent: Marshall of Cambridge (Holdings) Limited
Officers: Stephen Robert Jones, Secretary; Richard John Blumberger [1975] Director; Sarah Marie Dickins [1971] Director; Francesca Eva Ecsery [1963] Director; Alan Murray Ferguson [1958] Director; Daksh Gupta [1970] Director; Kathryn Helen Jenkins [1966] Director; Richard Parry-Jones [1951] Director; Christopher Mark Hutton Walkinshaw [1965] Director

Marshall North West Limited
Incorporated: 6 January 1937 *Employees:* 218
Net Worth Deficit: £3,741,000 *Total Assets:* £42,052,000
Registered Office: Airport House, The Airport, Cambridge, CB5 8RY
Activities: Sale of new cars and light motor vehicles
Parent: Marshall Motor Holdings PLC
Officers: Stephen Robert Jones, Secretary; Richard John Blumberger [1975] Director; Daksh Gupta [1970] Director

Marshall of Cambridge (Garage Properties) Limited
Incorporated: 1 September 1986
Net Worth: £14,113,000 *Total Assets:* £48,992,000
Registered Office: Airport House, The Airport, Cambridge, CB5 8RY
Activities: Other letting and operating of own or leased real estate
Parent: Marshall Motor Holdings PLC
Officers: Stephen Robert Jones, Secretary; Richard John Blumberger [1975] Director; Daksh Gupta [1970] Director

Marshall of Cambridge (Holdings) Limited
Incorporated: 1 September 1986 *Employees:* 6,211
Net Worth: £167,384,992 *Total Assets:* £939,100,032
Registered Office: Airport House, The Airport, Cambridge, CB5 8RY
Activities: Activities of head offices
Shareholder: Michael John Marshall
Officers: Sarah Jane Moynihan, Secretary; Julia Margaret Baddeley [1951] Director; Aubrey James Francis Buxton [1956] Director; Sean Vincent Cummins [1962] Director; Alex Moore Dorrian [1946] Director; Robert David Marshall [1962] Director/Chief Executive; Philip Edward Yea [1954] Director

Marshall of Cambridge Aerospace Limited
Incorporated: 13 February 1930 *Employees:* 1,455
Net Worth: £508,000 *Total Assets:* £128,769,000
Registered Office: Airport House, The Airport, Cambridge, CB5 8RY
Activities: Manufacture of air and spacecraft and related machinery
Parent: Marshall of Cambridge (Holdings) Ltd
Officers: Sarah Jane Moynihan, Secretary; Sean Vincent Cummins [1962] Director; Rupert Ashley Dix [1971] Director; Robert David Marshall [1962] Director; Alistair Dickson McPhee [1958] Director; Gary John Scott Moynehan [1979] Director

Marshall of Scunthorpe Limited
Incorporated: 14 June 1974 *Employees:* 84
Net Worth Deficit: £875,000 *Total Assets:* £11,708,000
Registered Office: Airport House, The Airport, Cambridge, CB5 8RY
Activities: Sale of new cars and light motor vehicles
Parent: Marshall Motor Holdings PLC
Officers: Stephen Robert Jones, Secretary; Richard John Blumberger [1975] Director; Daksh Gupta [1970] Director

Marshall of Stevenage Limited
Incorporated: 11 December 2007 *Employees:* 54
Net Worth Deficit: £36,000 *Total Assets:* £8,490,000
Registered Office: Airport House, The Airport, Cambridge, CB5 8RY
Activities: Sale of new cars and light motor vehicles
Parent: Marshall Motor Holdings PLC
Officers: Stephen Robert Jones, Secretary; Richard John Blumberger [1975] Director; Daksh Gupta [1970] Director

Marshall Thermo King Limited
Incorporated: 2 May 1963 *Employees:* 363
Net Worth Deficit: £2,282,202 *Total Assets:* £11,576,450
Registered Office: Aiport House, The Airport, Cambridge, CB5 8RY
Activities: Maintenance and repair of motor vehicles
Parent: Marshall Fleet Solutions Limited
Officers: Sarah Jane Moynihan, Secretary; Mark Nigel Howell [1970] Director; Francis Laud [1970] Director; Robert David Marshall [1962] Director

Martin Audio Limited
Incorporated: 7 July 2003 *Employees:* 56
Net Worth: £2,425,851 *Total Assets:* £8,464,731
Registered Office: Unit 2 Century Point, Halifax Road, Cressex Business Park, High Wycombe, Bucks, HP12 3SL
Activities: Manufacture of other electrical equipment
Parent: Ensco 1287 Limited
Officers: Dominic Harter, Secretary; Philip Geoffrey Hart [1944] Director; Dominic James Andrew Hatfeild Harter [1977] Director; Steven David Miller [1975] Director

Martin Mathew & Co. Limited
Incorporated: 7 August 1973 *Employees:* 40
Net Worth: £14,637,123 *Total Assets:* £23,228,284
Registered Office: 50a St Andrew Street, Hertford, SG14 1JA
Activities: Wholesale of other food, including fish, crustaceans and molluscs
Major Shareholder: James Philip Donnelly
Officers: Martin Spencer Donnelly [1969] Director/Importers and Distributor; Matthew James Donnelly [1972] Director/Importer and Distributor; Malcolm William Smith [1954] Sales Director

Martin-Brower UK Ltd
Incorporated: 2 December 1981 *Employees:* 2,004
Net Worth: £42,531,000 *Total Assets:* £297,467,008
Registered Office: Third Floor, South Wing, One Park Lane, Hemel Hempstead, Herts, HP2 4YJ
Activities: Freight transport by road
Shareholders: Michael Jude Reyes; Joseph Christopher Reyes
Officers: Cynthia Sysol McCauley [1983] Director/General Counsel [American]; Robert McGonigle [1961] Director/Chief Operating Officer [American]

Martlane Limited
Incorporated: 30 January 2001 *Employees:* 98
Net Worth: £14,333,626 *Total Assets:* £16,817,976
Registered Office: 9 Spareleaze Hill, Loughton, Essex, IG10 1BS
Activities: Residential nursing care facilities
Parent: Abbey Total Care Group Ltd
Officers: Devyani Jayanti Patel, Secretary/Director; Devyani Jayanti Patel [1953] Director; Jayanti Mohanlal Patel [1949] Director

Marton Geotechnical Services Limited
Incorporated: 15 March 1990 *Employees:* 76
Net Worth: £4,637,879 *Total Assets:* £10,018,815
Registered Office: Geotechnical Centre, Rougham Industrial Estate, Rougham, Bury St Edmunds, Suffolk, IP30 9ND
Activities: Manufacture of plastic plates, sheets, tubes and profiles
Shareholders: Anthony Malcolm Osborne; Martin Alexander Clegg
Officers: Anthony Malcolm Osborne, Secretary; Martin Alexander Clegg [1954] Director; Anthony Malcolm Osborne [1955] Director

Marwin Securities Limited
Incorporated: 6 October 1955 *Employees:* 10
Net Worth: £16,194,382 *Total Assets:* £19,456,530
Registered Office: 28 Church Road, Stanmore, Middlesex, HA7 4XR
Activities: Development of building projects
Shareholders: Michael Stephen Winkler; Richard Anthony Winkler; Mark Jonathan Winkler
Officers: Michael Stephen Winkler, Secretary; Mark Jonathan Winkler [1955] Director; Michael Stephen Winkler [1949] Director

Marylebone Finco Limited
Incorporated: 5 February 2016
Net Worth: £45,646 *Total Assets:* £61,022,936
Registered Office: Regent House, Allum Gate, Theobald Street, Elstree, Borehamwood, Herts, WD6 4RS
Activities: Other letting and operating of own or leased real estate
Officers: Rishi Ramesh Sachdev [1976] Director; Uday Vyas [1978] Director

Marylebone Square Holdings Ltd
Incorporated: 4 January 2017
Net Worth: £14,836,221 *Total Assets:* £15,528,017
Registered Office: Alpha House, 176a High Street, Barnet, Herts, EN5 5SZ
Activities: Buying and selling of own real estate
Major Shareholder: David Warwicker
Officers: David Warwicker [1949] Director

Marz Limited
Incorporated: 24 October 2005 *Employees:* 587
Net Worth Deficit: £634,860 *Total Assets:* £13,388,672
Registered Office: 34-36 London Road, Wembley, Middlesex, HA9 7EX
Activities: Activities of head offices
Major Shareholder: Raja Jameel Adil
Officers: Mohammed Adil, Secretary; Raja Jameel Adil [1971] Director/Solicitor

MAS (Holdings) Limited
Incorporated: 23 December 2013 *Employees:* 24
Net Worth: £2,416,561 *Total Assets:* £13,536,307
Registered Office: Unit A3, Merlin Centre, Acrewood Way, St Albans, Herts, AL4 0JY
Activities: Activities of head offices
Shareholders: Arvindkumar Maganlal Thakkar; John Hoskins
Officers: John Hoskins [1938] Director; Arvindkumar Maganlal Thakkar [1943] Director/Accountant

R. Maskell (Holdings) Limited
Incorporated: 23 December 2011 *Employees:* 23
Net Worth: £2,824,957 *Total Assets:* £13,072,307
Registered Office: Watergate, Broxhill Road, Havering-atte-Bower, Romford, Essex, RM4 1QH
Activities: Dormant company
Major Shareholder: Richard Henry Maskell
Officers: Nicholas Richard Maskell, Secretary; Lawrence Jefferson Gilbert [1948] Sales Director; Nicholas Richard Maskell [1974] Director/Businessman

R. Maskell Limited
Incorporated: 20 June 1972 *Employees:* 6
Net Worth: £8,758,561 *Total Assets:* £13,745,360
Registered Office: Watergate, Broxhill Road, Havering-atte-Bower, Romford, Essex, RM4 1QH
Activities: Wholesale of household goods (other than musical instruments) n.e.c
Major Shareholder: Richard Henry Maskell
Officers: Nicholas Richard Maskell, Secretary; Justin Simon Gilbert [1975] Director/Businessman; Lawrence Jefferson Gilbert [1948] Sales Director; Nicholas Richard Maskell [1974] Director/Businessman; Richard Henry Maskell [1943] Director

Maurice Mason Limited
Incorporated: 9 October 1947 *Employees:* 19
Net Worth: £5,929,332 *Total Assets:* £11,815,013
Registered Office: Hall Farm, Fincham, Kings Lynn, Norfolk, PE33 9DQ
Activities: Growing of cereals (except rice), leguminous crops and oil seeds
Major Shareholder: Hugh Mason
Officers: Hugh Mason [1964] Director/Farmer

Geoffrey Mason Limited
Incorporated: 20 October 1954 *Employees:* 16
Net Worth: £6,146,493 *Total Assets:* £11,099,426
Registered Office: Great Palgrave Farm, Sporle, King's Lynn, Norfolk, PE32 2EL
Activities: Growing of cereals (except rice), leguminous crops and oil seeds
Shareholders: Jeremy Geoffrey George Mason; Gillian Mason
Officers: Jeremy Geoffrey George Mason, Secretary; Gillian Mason [1963] Director/Housewife; Jeremy Geoffrey George Mason [1960] Director/Farmer

Mason Pearson Bros. Limited
Incorporated: 11 January 1973 *Employees:* 77
Net Worth: £8,554,603 *Total Assets:* £9,241,883
Registered Office: 7 Easter Park, Ferry Lane South, Rainham, Essex, RM13 9BP
Activities: Other manufacturing n.e.c.
Officers: Michael John Pearson, Secretary; Juliette Mary Boulton [1954] Director; Anthony James Jackson [1938] Director; Michael John Pearson [1951] Director

Mass Consultants Limited
Incorporated: 11 March 1983 *Employees:* 301
Net Worth: £24,341,000 *Total Assets:* £31,821,000
Registered Office: Enterprise House, Great North Road, Little Paxton, St Neots, Cambs, PE19 6BN
Activities: Information technology consultancy activities
Parent: Mass Limited
Officers: Sarita Bilkhu, Secretary; Christopher Andrew Stanley [1964] Director; Andrew Stephen Thomis [1964] Director; Simon Robert Walther [1967] Director

Mastercard Prepaid Management Services Limited
Incorporated: 20 April 2005 *Employees:* 166
Previous: Access Prepaid Worldwide Ltd.
Net Worth: £70,805,000 *Total Assets:* £111,878,000
Registered Office: Access House, Cygnet Road, Cygnet Park, Hampton, Peterborough, PE7 8FJ
Activities: Other business support service activities n.e.c.
Parent: Mastercard Incorporated
Officers: Daniel Kim, Secretary; Fabrizio Burlando [1974] Director [Italian]; Joseph Rickard Halprin [1964] Director/Group Head, Lead Global Core Products Counsel [American]; Andrea Scerch [1964] Director [Italian]; Robert Scott Williams [1958] Director [American]

Masterlord Estates Limited
Incorporated: 9 July 2004 *Employees:* 9
Net Worth: £6,254,228 *Total Assets:* £14,780,794
Registered Office: Crane Court, 302 London Road, Ipswich, Suffolk, IP2 0AJ
Activities: Buying and selling of own real estate
Shareholders: Jonathan William Bloomfield; Christopher Hamilton Dawson; Jonathan William Bloomfield
Officers: Jonathan William Bloomfield, Secretary/Chartered Surveyor; Jonathan William Bloomfield [1972] Director/Chartered Surveyor; Christopher Hamilton Dawson [1957] Director/Commercial Surveyor

Masteroast Coffee Co. Limited
Incorporated: 15 August 1983 *Employees:* 106
Net Worth: £6,346,453 *Total Assets:* £11,942,184
Registered Office: Plantation House, Newark Road, Peterborough, Cambs, PE1 5UA
Activities: Production of coffee and coffee substitutes
Parent: Masteroast Holdings Limited
Officers: Yvonne Eileen Victoria Mills, Secretary; Terence Black [1956] Director/Production Manager; Andrew Graham Fawkes [1964] Director; Leslie Graham Mills [1945] Director; Yvonne Eileen Victoria Mills [1951] Director

Masteroast Holdings Limited
Incorporated: 22 January 2008 *Employees:* 109
Net Worth: £6,242,045 *Total Assets:* £14,395,083
Registered Office: 1 The Forum, Minerva Business Park, Lynch Wood, Peterborough, Cambs, PE2 6FT
Activities: Wholesale of coffee, tea, cocoa and spices
Shareholders: Yvonne Eileen Victoria Mills; Leslie Graham Mills
Officers: Yvonne Eileen Victoria Mills, Secretary; Andrew Graham Fawkes [1964] Director; Leslie Graham Mills [1945] Director; Yvonne Eileen Victoria Mills [1951] Director

Masterson Holdings Limited
Incorporated: 29 June 2001 *Employees:* 268
Net Worth: £24,080,776 *Total Assets:* £78,976,696
Registered Office: Atlantic House, 7 Stirling Way, Borehamwood, Herts, WD6 2BT
Activities: Activities of head offices
Shareholder: Michael Masterson
Officers: Michael Masterson, Secretary; Keith Leonard Masterson [1973] Director/Surveyor [Irish]; Margaret Masterson [1976] Director/Accountant [Irish]; Michael Christian Masterson [1980] Director [Irish]; Michael Masterson [1950] Director Construction Company [Irish]; Mona Ann Masterson [1952] Director; Sean Masterson [1977] Director/Construction Manager [Irish]; Nigel Mark Warnes [1955] Construction Director

Matchroom Sport Limited
Incorporated: 23 April 1982 *Employees:* 72
Net Worth: £29,053,460 *Total Assets:* £101,950,608
Registered Office: Mascalls Lane, Great Warley, Brentwood, Essex, CM14 5LJ
Activities: Television programme production activities
Major Shareholder: Barry Maurice William Hearn
Officers: Stephen James Dawson, Secretary; Stephen James Dawson [1959] Director/Financial Accountant; Catherine Louise Godding [1976] Director of Programming; Barry Maurice William Hearn [1948] Director/Chartered Accountant; Edward John Hearn [1979] Director; Matthew Richard Porter [1980] Director/Chief Executive; Frank John Smith [1992] Director

The Mathworks Limited
Incorporated: 29 September 1997 *Employees:* 200
Net Worth: £4,020,219 *Total Assets:* £28,340,612
Registered Office: Matrix House, Cowley Park, Cambridge, CB4 0HH
Activities: Business and domestic software development
Parent: Mathworks Inc
Officers: Joanne Garner, Secretary; Shamim Ahmed [1965] Director/Control Engineer; Jeanne O'Keefe [1953] Director [American]

Matrix Networks Limited
Incorporated: 11 December 2006 *Employees:* 50
Net Worth: £3,834,249 *Total Assets:* £10,998,472
Registered Office: 22-26 King Street, Kings Lynn, Norfolk, PE30 1HJ
Activities: Construction of utility projects for electricity and telecommunications
Parent: Matrix Networks (Holdings) Limited
Officers: Matthew Alexander Sanderson, Secretary; Wendy Andrews [1971] Director; Paul Michael Jeffrey Beck [1965] Director; Christopher James Mann [1967] Director; Matthew Alexander Sanderson [1972] Director; Robert James Sparkes [1974] Managing Director; Neil Walsh [1968] Director; Francis Paul Welsh [1972] Director

Matthew Homes Limited
Incorporated: 29 April 1975 *Employees:* 56
Net Worth: £107,084,936 *Total Assets:* £131,039,160
Registered Office: Pendragon House, 65 London Road, St Albans, Herts, AL1 1LJ
Activities: Construction of domestic buildings
Officers: Daniel Paul Gallagher, Secretary [Irish]; Paul English [1955] Construction Director; Brian Joseph Gallagher [1953] Director/Barrister [Irish]; Charles Hubert Gallagher [1959] Director [Irish]; Daniel Paul Gallagher [1964] Sales Director [Irish]; David Andrew Gallagher [1960] Director [Irish]; Ellen Pauline Gallagher [1929] Director [Irish]; Neville William Hutchinson [1941] Director; Peter Michael Jones [1962] Director/Surveyor; Barry Martin Jordan [1967] Land Director

Matthews International Transport Limited
Incorporated: 25 May 1979 *Employees:* 147
Net Worth: £4,928,704 *Total Assets:* £8,486,223
Registered Office: Lefevre Way, Gapton Hall Industrial Estate, Great Yarmouth, Norfolk, NR31 0NW
Activities: Freight transport by road
Major Shareholder: Trevor Arthur Matthews
Officers: Trevor Arthur Matthews, Secretary; Jonathan Matthews [1988] Director/Mechanic; Linda Matthews [1958] Director/Clerk; Rachael Jean Matthews [1990] Director; Russell Glen Matthews [1959] Director/Road Haulier; Trevor Arthur Matthews [1949] Director/Road Haulier

Maybury Media LLP
Incorporated: 9 May 2003
Net Worth: £11,513,930 *Total Assets:* £11,514,990
Registered Office: 99 Kenton Road, Harrow, Middlesex, HA3 0AN
Officers: Rt Hon Lord Kenneth Wilfred Baker [1934] LLP Member; Anthony John Bethell [1957] LLP Member; Steven Astley Brown [1959] LLP Member; Stuart Andrew Brydson [1966] LLP Member; Panayotis Christoforou [1957] LLP Member; Mark Gerard Clough [1953] LLP Member; Peter David Cook [1964] LLP Member; David John Courtley [1957] LLP Member; Paul Duffy [1959] LLP Member; David Ereira [1956] LLP Member; Roderick Clifford Evans [1964] LLP Member; David Hill [1954] LLP Member; Mark Hollister [1962] LLP Member; Andrew Hough [1971] LLP Member; Paul McPhie Johnston [1972] LLP Member; Bruce Douglas King [1955] LLP Member; Andrew Christopher Lapping [1963] LLP Member; Gary Lloyd [1961] LLP Member; Christopher John Loynes [1947] LLP Member; Angus John Elsom MacCormick [1965] LLP Member; Deborah Jean Marshall [1961] LLP Member; Dominic Kevin O'Carroll [1960] LLP Member; Christopher Hugh Adrian Oakley [1956] LLP Member; Nicholas John Preston [1955] LLP Member; Linda Ann Reid [1942] LLP Member; Peter Eric Reid [1936] LLP Member; Stewart Martin Robertson [1966] LLP Member; Barrie David Sheers [1963] LLP Member; Robin Turner Shelton [1947] LLP Member; Donald Arthur Starr [1948] LLP Member; Jacqueline Stephens [1960] LLP Member; Mark Paul Stradling [1965] LLP Member; Richard Terley [1912] LLP Member; Paul John Trowbridge [1955] LLP Member; Garry Tibbott Veale [1960] LLP Member; Simon John Wilders [1953] LLP Member; Nicholas Ian Wilson [1960] LLP Member; Robert Harold Youngjohns [1951] LLP Member

Mayday Healthcare PLC
Incorporated: 3 December 2003 *Employees:* 78
Net Worth: £18,303,404 *Total Assets:* £21,135,084
Registered Office: Hygeia, 66-68 College Road, Harrow, Middlesex, HA1 1BE
Activities: Temporary employment agency activities
Major Shareholder: Kevin Michael Coyle
Officers: Howard Pepperdine, Secretary; Anna Louise Cooper [1978] Director; Christopher John Coyle [1984] Director; Kevin Michael Coyle [1956] Managing Director; Sean Deslandes [1974] Director; Michael Howard Helleur [1981] Director; Nicolas Poturicich [1978] Director

Mayfair Carpet Gallery Limited
Incorporated: 22 April 1981 *Employees:* 3
Net Worth: £4,799,775 *Total Assets:* £10,941,125
Registered Office: c/o Syedain & Co, 2nd Floor, Heron House, 109 Wembley Hill Road, Wembley, Middlesex, HA9 8DA
Activities: Wholesale of furniture, carpets and lighting equipment
Officers: Mahmood Anwar, Secretary; Ahmed Hassan Khawaja [1946] Director/Carpet Dealer; Ahmen Khawaja [1984] Director; Arfah Khawaja [1985] Director

Mayflower High School
Incorporated: 4 July 2011 *Employees:* 237
Net Worth: £4,964,495 *Total Assets:* £9,965,367
Registered Office: Mayflower High School, Stock Road, Billericay, Essex, CM12 0RT
Activities: General secondary education
Officers: Susan Jennifer Mason, Secretary; Lucy Rebecca Beavon [1982] Director of Marketing and Communications; Lee Brumby [1961] Director/Headteacher; Timothy John Fox [1981] Director/Teacher; David Richard Hayhow [1972] Director/Insurance Broker; Andrew Peter Hunter [1951] Director/Management Consultant; Scott Paul Lister [1971] Director/Chartered Engineer; Nicholas John Morris [1971] Director/Police Officer; Peter John Sharp [1949] Director/Financial Controller (Retired); Elizabeth Jane Whitworth [1964] Director/Housewife; Alan Timothy Wilson [1966] Director/Local Authority School Improvement Adviser; Stephen Peter Wright [1956] Director/Engineer

Geoffrey Mayhew Farms (Holdings) Limited
Incorporated: 5 September 2011 *Employees:* 1
Net Worth: £8,437,602 *Total Assets:* £8,437,602
Registered Office: Pond Farm House, Warren Lane, Erwarton, Ipswich, Suffolk, IP9 1LH
Activities: Activities of head offices
Major Shareholder: Geoffrey Peter Mayhew
Officers: Geoffrey Peter Mayhew [1959] Director; Kim Mayhew [1970] Director/Farm Administrator

Geoffrey Mayhew Farms Limited
Incorporated: 10 December 2010 *Employees:* 2
Net Worth: £740,724 *Total Assets:* £10,099,397
Registered Office: Pond Farm House, Warren Lane, Erwarton, Ipswich, Suffolk, IP9 1LH
Activities: Growing of cereals (except rice), leguminous crops and oil seeds
Major Shareholder: Geoffrey Peter Mayhew
Officers: Geoffrey Peter Mayhew [1959] Director; Kim Mayhew [1970] Director/Farm Administrator

Maylands Green Limited
Incorporated: 22 November 1991 *Employees:* 62
Net Worth: £8,235,202 *Total Assets:* £12,394,912
Registered Office: 84 Market Place, Romford, Essex, RM1 3JE
Activities: Development of building projects
Shareholders: Nicholas Hilbery Chaplin; Paul William Hodge; Malcolm Hilbery Chaplin
Officers: Nicholas Hilbery Chaplin, Secretary; Sir Malcolm Hilbery Chaplin [1934] Director/Chartered Surveyor; Nicholas Hilbery Chaplin [1965] Director/Chartered Surveyor

MBDA UK Limited
Incorporated: 11 January 1996 *Employees:* 3,234
Net Worth: £177,500,000 *Total Assets:* £1,418,300,032
Registered Office: Six Hills Way, Stevenage, Herts, SG1 2DA
Activities: Other manufacturing n.e.c.
Parent: MBDA SAS
Officers: Christopher Nigel Evans, Secretary; Christopher James Allam [1967] Managing Director; Peter Heinrich Charles Bols [1965] Director; Antoine Bouvier [1959] Director [French]; Pasquale di Bartolomeo [1969] Managing Director [Italian]; Keith Murray Garden [1961] Deputy Managing Director; Iain David West [1970] Finance Director

MBH Finco. Limited
Incorporated: 31 October 2013
Net Worth: £58,152 *Total Assets:* £75,860,288
Registered Office: 505 Pinner Road, Harrow, Middlesex, HA2 6EH
Activities: Other letting and operating of own or leased real estate
Officers: Rishi Ramesh Sachdev [1976] Director; Uday Vyas [1978] Director

MBI MBO Limited
Incorporated: 21 August 1975 *Employees:* 3
Net Worth: £15,472,476 *Total Assets:* £27,927,000
Registered Office: Dane End House, Dane End, Ware, Herts, SG12 0LR
Activities: Financial intermediation not elsewhere classified
Major Shareholder: Bryan Scott Alan Duffy
Officers: Christopher Houry, Secretary; Bryan Scott Alan Duffy [1943] Director; Kingsley Scott Bryan Duffy [1971] Director; Louise Duffy [1975] Director

MC Power Limited
Incorporated: 14 December 2011
Net Worth Deficit: £2,921,000 *Total Assets:* £15,195,000
Registered Office: Beaufort Court, Egg Farm Lane, Kings Langley, Herts, WD4 8LR
Activities: Production of electricity
Parent: Trafalgar Wind Holdings Limited
Officers: Dominic James Hearth, Secretary; Steven William Hughes [1972] Generation & Asset Management Director; Fraser Stephen Merry [1968] Director/Chartered Surveyor; Mitesh Raj Patel [1982] Director/Group Financial Controller

MC Treasury Limited
Incorporated: 23 October 2007
Net Worth: £763,508,992 *Total Assets:* £1,086,730,624
Registered Office: Maple Court, Central Park, Reeds Crescent, Watford, Herts, WD24 4QQ
Activities: Other business support service activities n.e.c.
Parent: HIC Treasury Limited
Officers: Stuart Beasley [1971] Director/Financial Controller; Richard Geoffrey Beeston [1982] Director/Chartered Accountant; James Owen Percival [1968] Director/Accountant; Brian McKay Wilson [1962] Director/Company Secretary

Sir Robert McAlpine (A19) Limited
Incorporated: 8 June 2015
Net Worth: £2,039,591 *Total Assets:* £71,256,816
Registered Office: Eaton Court, Maylands Avenue, Hemel Hempstead Industrial Estate, Hemel Hempstead, Herts, HP2 7TR
Activities: Financial intermediation not elsewhere classified
Parent: Robert McAlpine Road Holdings Limited
Officers: Kevin John Pearson, Secretary; David Honeyman [1967] Director/Financial Controller; Robert John William Wotherspoon [1967] Director/Chartered Accountant

Sir Robert McAlpine (Holdings) Limited
Incorporated: 12 October 1992 *Employees:* 2,203
Net Worth: £78,855,000 *Total Assets:* £880,270,976
Registered Office: Eaton Court, Maylands Avenue, Hemel Hempstead Industrial Estate, Hemel Hempstead, Herts, HP2 7TR
Activities: Activities of head offices
Parent: Newarthill Limited
Officers: John Alistair Dempsey, Secretary; Kevin John Pearson, Secretary; Kevin John Pearson, Secretary; Karen Joy Brookes [1962] Director of People & Infrastructure; Paul Christopher Hamer [1969] Director/Chief Executive; Hector George McAlpine [1980] Director; Robert Edward Thomas William McAlpine [1978] Director; Boyd Atkinson McFee [1958] Director/Civil Engineer; James Leighton More [1976] Director/Chief Financial Officer; Martin Clive Pitt [1964] Director

Sir Robert McAlpine Capital Ventures Limited
Incorporated: 9 February 1995
Net Worth: £81,581,632 *Total Assets:* £182,715,392
Registered Office: Eaton Court, Maylands Avenue, Hemel Hempstead Industrial Estate, Hemel Hempstead, Herts, HP2 7TR
Activities: Financial intermediation not elsewhere classified
Parent: Robert McAlpine Enterprises Limited
Officers: Kevin John Pearson, Secretary; David Honeyman [1967] Director/Financial Controller; Robert John William Wotherspoon [1967] Director/Accountant

Sir Robert McAlpine Enterprises Limited
Incorporated: 14 September 1978
Net Worth: £58,972,000 *Total Assets:* £189,664,992
Registered Office: Eaton Court, Maylands Avenue, Hemel Hempstead, Herts, HP2 7TR
Activities: Activities of other holding companies n.e.c.
Parent: Newarthill Limited
Officers: Elizabeth Carol Beard, Secretary; Kevin John Pearson, Secretary; Adrian Neil Raeburn McAlpine [1944] Director/Property Executive; Sir Andrew William McAlpine [1960] Director/Civil Engineering; Cullum McAlpine [1947] Director/Civil Engineering & Building Contractor; The Hon David Malcolm McAlpine [1946] Director/Civil Engineering & Building Contractor; Douglas James McAlpine [1983] Director/Manager, Demand Side Management, Americas; Gavin Malcolm McAlpine [1966] Director; Hector George McAlpine [1980] Director; Ian Malcolm McAlpine [1942] Director/Building & Civil Engineering Contractor; Kenneth McAlpine [1920] Director/Civil Engineering & Building Construction; Richard Hugh McAlpine [1958] Director; Robert Edward Thomas William McAlpine [1978] Director; Robert John William Wotherspoon [1967] Director/Chartered Accountant

Sir Robert McAlpine Limited
Incorporated: 31 May 1956 *Employees:* 2,118
Net Worth: £43,183,000 *Total Assets:* £833,086,016
Registered Office: Eaton Court, Maylands Avenue, Hemel Hempstead Industrial Estate, Hemel Hempstead, Herts, HP2 7TR
Activities: Construction of commercial buildings
Parent: Robert McAlpine (Holdings) Limited
Officers: John Alistair Dempsey, Secretary; Kevin John Pearson, Secretary; Kevin John Pearson, Secretary; Karen Joy Brookes [1962] Director of People & Infrastructure; Paul Christopher Hamer [1969] Director/Chief Executive; Hector George McAlpine [1980] Director; Robert Edward Thomas William McAlpine [1978] Director; Boyd Atkinson McFee [1958] Director/Civil Engineer; James Leighton More [1976] Director/Chief Financial Officer; Martin Clive Pitt [1964] Director

Sir Robert McAlpine Road Holdings Limited
Incorporated: 23 June 2015
Net Worth Deficit: £641,184 *Total Assets:* £77,887,336
Registered Office: Eaton Court, Maylands Avenue, Hemel Hempstead Industrial Estate, Hemel Hempstead, Herts, HP2 7TR
Activities: Activities of other holding companies n.e.c.
Parent: Robert McAlpine Capital Ventures Limited
Officers: Kevin John Pearson, Secretary; David Honeyman [1967] Director/Financial Controller; Robert John William Wotherspoon [1967] Director/Chartered Accountant

McCann Family LLP
Incorporated: 10 August 2006
Net Worth: £3,814,929 *Total Assets:* £8,050,408
Registered Office: 20 Bridge Street, Leighton Buzzard, Beds, LU7 7AL
Officers: Hannah Elizabeth Albertella [1971] Member; Louise Ann Burchell [1977] Member; James Christopher McCann [1973] Member; Jeanette Marie McCann [1948] LLP Member; Terence Patrick McCann [1947] LLP Member

Martin McColl Limited
Incorporated: 28 March 1935 *Employees:* 13,771
Net Worth: £186,239,008 *Total Assets:* £672,665,024
Registered Office: McColl's House, Ashwells Road, Brentwood, Essex, CM15 9ST
Activities: Retail sale of tobacco products in specialised stores
Parent: TM Group Holdings Limited
Officers: David Alexander Archibald [1967] Director; Robbie Ian Bell [1973] Director/Chief Financial Officer; Simon Jeremy Ian Fuller [1977] Director; Steven Green [1981] Director; Simon Jonathan Miller [1963] Director; David Thomas [1960] Director

Martin McColl Retail Limited
Incorporated: 20 April 2005
Net Worth Deficit: £11,683,000 *Total Assets:* £88,414,000
Registered Office: McColl's House, Ashwells Road, Brentwood, Essex, CM15 9ST
Activities: Activities of head offices
Parent: McColl's Retail Group PLC
Officers: Robbie Ian Bell [1973] Director/Chief Financial Officer; Simon Jeremy Ian Fuller [1977] Finance Director; Steven Green [1981] Director; Simon Jonathan Miller [1963] Director; David Thomas [1960] Director

McColl's Retail Group PLC
Incorporated: 20 November 2013 *Employees:* 21,261
Net Worth: £145,908,000 *Total Assets:* £483,860,000
Registered Office: McColl's House, Ashwells Road, Brentwood, Essex, CM15 9ST
Activities: Retail sale in non-specialised stores with food, beverages or tobacco predominating
Officers: Rachel Peat, Secretary; Robbie Ian Bell [1973] Director/Chief Financial Officer; Sharon Mary Brown [1968] Director; Simon Jeremy Ian Fuller [1977] Director/Chief Finance Officer; Georgina Harvey [1964] Director; Jens Tjeerd Hofma [1966] Director/Chief Executive Officer [Dutch]; Simon Jonathan Miller [1963] Director; Dr Angus James Porter [1957] Director; David Phillip Thomas [1960] Director

McCormick Europe Limited
Incorporated: 26 October 1995
Net Worth: £297,451,008 *Total Assets:* £309,884,000
Registered Office: Haddenham Business Park, Pegasus Way, Haddenham, Aylesbury, Bucks, HP17 8LB
Activities: Activities of other holding companies n.e.c.
Parent: McCormick & Company Incorporated
Officers: Laird Everett Creighton [1974] Director [American]; Francois Gouby [1960] Director/VP Operations [French]; Christopher Jinks [1961] Director/Vice President Industrial EMEA; Lawrence Erik Kurzius [1958] Director/President EMEA [American]; Malcolm Stuart Swift [1960] Director/President; Melanie Clare Williams [1964] Director/Vice President HR

McCormick International Holdings
Incorporated: 21 January 2000
Net Worth: £293,673,984 *Total Assets:* £394,406,016
Registered Office: Haddenham Business Park, Pegasus Way, Haddenham, Aylesbury, Bucks, HP17 8LB
Activities: Activities of other holding companies n.e.c.
Parent: McCormick Europe Limited
Officers: Laird Everett Creighton [1974] Director [American]; Christopher Jinks [1961] Director; Lawrence Erik Kurzius [1958] Director/President - EMEA [American]; Malcolm Stuart Swift [1960] Director/President

McCormick Kutas Food Service Limited
Incorporated: 5 January 1996 *Employees:* 156
Net Worth: £16,355,737 *Total Assets:* £33,466,626
Registered Office: Haddenham Business Park, Pegasus Way, Haddenham, Aylesbury, Bucks, HP17 8LB
Activities: Activities of other holding companies n.e.c.
Shareholders: McCormick (UK) Limited; Kutas Tarim Urunleri Dis Tic Ve San AS
Officers: Laird Everett Creighton [1974] Director [American]; Francois Gouby [1960] Director/VP Supply Chain Operations [French]; Ilhan Feyzi Gurel [1942] Director/Industrialist [Turkish]; Kazim Ilter Gurel [1964] Director/Industrialist [Turkish/British]; Christopher Jinks [1961] Director/Vice President Industrial EMEA; Mehmet Gurel Kapani [1972] Director/Industrialist [Turkish]

McCutcheon Norveil Consultancy Limited
Incorporated: 1 October 1997 *Employees:* 18
Net Worth: £3,452,671 *Total Assets:* £16,556,840
Registered Office: Millhouse, 32-38 East Street, Rochford, Essex, SS4 1DB
Activities: Advertising agencies
Parent: Lousin Holdings Limited
Officers: Sara Jane McCutcheon, Secretary; Andrew Sheridan McCutcheon [1965] Director/Media Consultant

Gerald McDonald & Company Limited
Incorporated: 14 September 1931 *Employees:* 44
Net Worth: £8,309,062 *Total Assets:* £14,922,663
Registered Office: Cranes Farm Road, Basildon, Essex, SS14 3GT
Activities: Other food services
Major Shareholder: Gerald Alistair McDonald
Officers: Stephen Derek Crawford [1971] Director/Chartered Accountant; Generald Alistair McDonald [1955] Director; Maria Elena McDonald [1950] Director [Argentinian]; Maxim Generald McDonald [1983] Director/Trader; Andrew Charles Bentham Moss [1964] Director/Trader

MCF Commercial Limited
Incorporated: 13 June 2007 *Employees:* 3
Net Worth: £1,550,036 *Total Assets:* £48,084,928
Registered Office: Lunar House, Wooburn Green, High Wycombe, Bucks, HP10 0HH
Activities: Activities of head offices
Parent: Comland Group Limited
Officers: Christopher Giles Martin, Secretary/Director; Christopher Robert Ayres [1982] Director; Stuart James Crossley [1944] Director; Christopher Giles Martin [1968] Director

McGee Civil Engineering Limited
Incorporated: 6 November 1963 *Employees:* 123
Previous: McGee Group Limited
Net Worth: £6,887,510 *Total Assets:* £16,900,368
Registered Office: 340-342 Athlon Road, Wembley, Middlesex, HA0 1BX
Activities: Construction of commercial buildings
Parent: McGee Group (Holdings) Limited
Officers: John Paul McGee, Secretary; John Joseph Hennessey [1960] Director/Safety Officer; Brian James McGee [1964] Group Managing Director; John Paul McGee [1966] Director - Head of Group Resources; Michael Thomas McGee [1963] Director [Irish]

McGee Group (Holdings) Limited
Incorporated: 13 June 1968 *Employees:* 353
Net Worth: £15,257,771 *Total Assets:* £48,231,040
Registered Office: 340-342 Athlon Road, Wembley, Middlesex, HA0 1BX
Activities: Construction of commercial buildings
Parent: MFCOIL Limited
Officers: Paul Hickey, Secretary; Sebastian Fossey [1981] Director; John Joseph Hennessy [1960] Director/Safety Professional; Paul Hickey [1965] Director/Chartered Accountant [Irish]; Brian James McGee [1964] Group Managing Director; John Paul McGee [1966] Director - Head of Group Resources; Michael Thomas McGee [1963] Director/Plant Manager [Irish]; Nicholas Mark Taylor [1967] Director; Darren Wayne Wickins [1972] Director

McGinley Aviation Holdings Limited
Incorporated: 2 September 2016 *Employees:* 9
Net Worth: £991,772 *Total Assets:* £11,717,253
Registered Office: 56 Clarendon Road, Watford, Herts, WD17 1DA
Activities: Other activities of employment placement agencies
Major Shareholder: Colm John McGinley
Officers: Donnacha Sean Holly [1984] Director [Irish]; Colm John McGinley [1982] Director [Irish]; Seamus Patrick McGinley [1955] Director [Irish]

McGrath Bros. (Environmental) Ltd.
Incorporated: 21 December 2005
Net Worth: £2,262,237 *Total Assets:* £26,192,572
Registered Office: 62 River Road, Barking, Essex, IG11 0DS
Activities: Other letting and operating of own or leased real estate
Parent: McGrath Brothers (Holdings) Ltd
Officers: David Oliver McGrath, Secretary [Irish]; David Oliver McGrath [1952] Director/Builder [Irish]; Michael McGrath [1950] Director/Waste Management Executive [Irish]; Patrick McGrath [1958] Director/Builder [Irish]

McGrath Bros. (Waste Control) Limited
Incorporated: 30 November 1981 *Employees:* 92
Net Worth: £13,550,247 *Total Assets:* £22,663,392
Registered Office: 62 River Road, Barking, Essex, IG11 0DS
Activities: Recovery of sorted materials
Officers: David Oliver McGrath, Secretary [Irish]; Tara Katherine Donaghy [1975] Director/Business Manager; John Martin McDaid [1967] Transport Director; David Gerard McGrath [1978] Director/Plant Manager [Irish]; David Oliver McGrath [1952] Director/Builder [Irish]; Michael McGrath [1950] Director/Builder [Irish]; Patrick McGrath [1958] Director/Builder [Irish]; Stephen McGrath [1981] Director/Manager [Irish]; James Roland Oliver [1966] Director/Accountant; Gerard Edward Vines [1961] Plant Director

McGrath Brothers (Holdings) Limited
Incorporated: 2 July 1982 *Employees:* 101
Net Worth: £38,739,484 *Total Assets:* £54,844,800
Registered Office: 62 River Road, Barking, Essex, IG11 0DS
Activities: Activities of other holding companies n.e.c.
Shareholders: David Oliver McGrath; Michael McGrath
Officers: David Oliver McGrath, Secretary [Irish]; David Oliver McGrath [1952] Director/Builder [Irish]; Michael McGrath [1950] Director/Builder [Irish]; Patrick McGrath [1958] Director/Builder [Irish]; Stephen McGrath [1981] Director/Manager [Irish]

McLaren Construction (London) Limited
Incorporated: 30 October 2015
Net Worth: £12,456,018 *Total Assets:* £55,406,156
Registered Office: McLaren House, 100 Kings Road, Brentwood, Essex, CM14 4EA
Activities: Other business support service activities n.e.c.
Parent: McLaren Construction Limited
Officers: Maurice Archer [1964] Director; Philip James Pringle [1963] Managing Director

McLaren Construction (Midlands & North) Limited
Incorporated: 30 October 2015
Net Worth: £9,325,642 *Total Assets:* £37,570,376
Registered Office: McLaren House, 100 Kings Road, Brentwood, Essex, CM14 4EA
Activities: Other business support service activities n.e.c.
Parent: McLaren Construction Limited
Officers: Maurice Archer [1964] Director; Philip James Pringle [1963] Managing Director

McLaren Construction (South) Limited
Incorporated: 30 October 2015
Net Worth: £14,284,356 *Total Assets:* £50,998,824
Registered Office: McLaren House, 100 Kings Road, Brentwood, Essex, CM14 4EA
Activities: Other business support service activities n.e.c.
Parent: McLaren Construction Limited
Officers: Maurice Archer [1964] Director; Philip James Pringle [1963] Managing Director

McLaren Construction (UK) Limited
Incorporated: 30 January 2001
Previous: McLaren Construction Limited
Net Worth: £6,638,030 *Total Assets:* £31,339,948
Registered Office: McLaren House, 100 Kings Road, Brentwood, Essex, CM14 4EA
Activities: Construction of commercial buildings
Parent: McLaren Construction Limited
Officers: Maurice Archer [1964] Director; Philip James Pringle [1963] Managing Director

McLaren Construction Limited
Incorporated: 28 February 2005 *Employees:* 691
Previous: Verve Construction Limited
Net Worth: £17,508,288 *Total Assets:* £205,860,512
Registered Office: McLaren House, 100 Kings Road, Brentwood, Essex, CM14 4EA
Activities: Construction of commercial buildings
Parent: McLaren Construction Group PLC
Officers: Maurice Archer [1964] Director; Philip James Pringle [1963] Managing Director

McMullen & Sons, Limited
Incorporated: 1 March 1897 *Employees:* 1,129
Net Worth: £150,388,000 *Total Assets:* £171,648,000
Registered Office: 26 Old Cross, Hertford, SG14 1RD
Activities: Manufacture of beer
Officers: Alison Penfold, Secretary; Charles David Brims [1950] Director/Chairman; Steven Gill [1957] Commercial Director; Alexander Brodie McMullen [1981] Director/Chartered Accountant; David Shaun McMullen [1945] Director; Fergus John McMullen [1958] Director; Thomas Peter McMullen [1976] Director; Heydon Mizon [1974] Director; Andrew Wayne Newbury [1955] Property Director; Jenny Strathern [1964] Property Director

McNicholas Construction (Holdings) Limited
Incorporated: 26 March 1971 *Employees:* 1,690
Net Worth Deficit: £31,736,000 *Total Assets:* £53,749,000
Registered Office: Tempsford Hall, Sandy, Beds, SG19 2BD
Activities: Activities of other holding companies n.e.c.
Parent: Kier Limited
Officers: Bethan Anne Elizabeth Melges, Secretary; Thomas Lee Foreman [1976] Director; Marcus Faughey Jones [1970] Director; Barry Stuart McNicholas [1962] Director/Chief Executive

McNicholas Construction Services Limited
Incorporated: 5 August 1980 *Employees:* 1,770
Net Worth Deficit: £15,274,000 *Total Assets:* £64,961,000
Registered Office: Tempsford Hall, Sandy, Beds, SG19 2BD
Activities: Other service activities n.e.c.
Parent: McNicholas Construction (Holdings) Limited
Officers: Bethan Anne Elizabeth Melges, Secretary; Thomas Lee Foreman [1976] Director; Andrew Hornsey [1970] Director; Marcus Faughey Jones [1970] Director; Barry Stuart McNicholas [1962] Director/Chief Executive

MCSA Group Limited
Incorporated: 22 May 1979 *Employees:* 137
Previous: Maindec Computer Solutions Limited
Net Worth Deficit: £569,521 *Total Assets:* £17,531,404
Registered Office: Maindec House, Holtspur Lane, Wooburn Green, Bucks, HP10 0AB
Activities: Information technology consultancy activities
Shareholder: Roger Jeffrey Timms
Officers: Peter Anthony Darraugh, Secretary; Sasha Louise Brooke-Williams [1982] Director; Peter Anthony Darraugh [1964] Director/Accountant; Mark Reginald Hodge [1959] Director; Brenda Joyce Timms [1952] Director/Administration Assistant; Christopher Jeffrey Timms [1980] Director; Paul Roger Timms [1976] Director/Engineer; Roger Jeffrey Timms [1949] Director; Scott Robert Timms [1978] Director

MDM Timber Limited
Incorporated: 16 February 1989 *Employees:* 25
Net Worth: £10,773,477 *Total Assets:* £31,131,984
Registered Office: Howard Chase, Pipps Hill, Basildon, Essex, SS14 3BE
Activities: Wholesale of wood, construction materials and sanitary equipment
Major Shareholder: Malcolm John Allum
Officers: Malcolm John Allum, Secretary; Malcolm John Allum [1951] Finance Director; Mark John Allum [1976] Director/Financial Manager; Mark David Cheriton [1968] Director; Kenneth John Fuller [1957] Purchasing Director; Peter William Holmes [1963] Sales Director

MDS Civil Engineering Limited
Incorporated: 24 May 2000 *Employees:* 178
Net Worth: £3,489,743 *Total Assets:* £10,032,659
Registered Office: Town Wall House, Balkerne Hill, Colchester, Essex, CO3 3AD
Activities: Construction of commercial buildings
Officers: Roy John Marfleet, Secretary; Darren Chaston [1980] Director; Lesley Marfleet [1956] Director; Roy John Marfleet [1957] Director; Richard Pullen [1983] Director

Meadow Holdings Limited
Incorporated: 27 September 1955 *Employees:* 4
Net Worth: £12,678,416 *Total Assets:* £14,514,291
Registered Office: Mercer House, 15 High Street, Redbourn, St Albans, Herts, AL3 7LE
Activities: Other letting and operating of own or leased real estate
Parent: Newmill Holdings Ltd
Officers: Jean Mary Miller, Secretary; Joanne Lisa Binns [1976] Director/Property Manager; Andrew James Miller [1978] Director/Property Manager; Glen Andrew Miller [1950] Director/Accountant; Jean Mary Miller [1951] Director

Medacs Global Group Limited
Incorporated: 13 December 2011 *Employees:* 3
Previous: Impellam Healthcare Holdings Ltd
Net Worth: £2,319,000 *Total Assets:* £28,353,000
Registered Office: 800 The Boulevard, Capability Green, Luton, Beds, LU1 3BA
Activities: Activities of head offices
Parent: Impellam Group PLC
Officers: Rebecca Jane Watson, Secretary; Julia Robertson [1958] Director; Rebecca Jane Watson [1969] Director/Solicitor

Medacs Healthcare PLC
Incorporated: 4 July 1990 *Employees:* 561
Net Worth: £40,141,000 *Total Assets:* £60,833,000
Registered Office: 800 The Boulevard, Capability Green, Luton, Beds, LU1 3BA
Activities: Temporary employment agency activities
Parent: Medacs Global Group Limited
Officers: Rebecca Jane Watson, Secretary; Nigel Philip Marsh [1962] Director; Julia Robertson [1958] Director; Rebecca Jane Watson [1969] Director/Solicitor

Media 10 Holdings Limited
Incorporated: 10 June 2009 *Employees:* 288
Net Worth: £2,136,577 *Total Assets:* £22,715,204
Registered Office: Crown House, 151 High Road, Loughton, Essex, IG10 4LF
Activities: Activities of head offices
Shareholder: Lee Steven Newton
Officers: Jane Louise Musgrove, Secretary; Richard John Morey [1965] Director/Publisher; Daren John Newton [1968] Director/Publisher; Lee Steven Newton [1965] Director; Eric John William Wenham [1950] Director

Media 10 Limited
Incorporated: 12 December 2002 *Employees:* 257
Net Worth: £1,908,944 *Total Assets:* £19,237,392
Registered Office: Crown House, 151 High Road, Loughton, Essex, IG10 4LF
Activities: Publishing of consumer and business journals and periodicals
Parent: Media 10 Holdings Limited
Officers: Jane Louise Musgrove, Secretary; Richard John Morey [1965] Director/Publisher; Daren John Newton [1968] Director/Sales Manager; Lee Steven Newton [1965] Director; Eric John William Wenham [1950] Director/Accountant

Medimmune Limited
Incorporated: 11 December 1989 *Employees:* 523
Net Worth Deficit: £843,352,000 *Total Assets:* £963,582,976
Registered Office: Milstein Building, Granta Park, Cambridge, CB21 6GH
Activities: Other research and experimental development on natural sciences and engineering
Parent: Cambridge Antibody Technology Group Limited
Officers: Matthew Ian Conacher, Secretary; Iain Alistair Collins [1970] Director; Katie Louise Jackson-Turner [1966] Director; Adrian Charles Noel Kemp [1966] Director

Mediterranean Shipping Company (UK) Limited
Incorporated: 21 December 1977 *Employees:* 679
Net Worth: £17,329,000 *Total Assets:* £94,421,000
Registered Office: Medite House, The Havens, Ransomes Europark, Ipswich, Suffolk, IP3 9SJ
Activities: Service activities incidental to water transportation
Shareholders: Gianluigi Aponte; Rafaela Aponte-Diamant
Officers: Anne Maria Gordon, Secretary/Accountant; Maurizio Aponte [1960] Director/Manager [Italian]; Elvio Battista Bourquin [1959] Director/Manager [Swiss]; Jonathan James Burke [1971] Operations Director; Michael Collins [1975] Commercial Director; Daniel Charles Everitt [1967] Director/Shipping Manager; Anne Maria Gordon [1959] Director/Accountant; Lawrence Christopher Frederick Matthews [1951] Director/Manager

Medivet Group Limited
Incorporated: 16 December 1997 *Employees:* 1,298
Net Worth: £17,021,080 *Total Assets:* £128,100,616
Registered Office: 4 Mowat Industrial Estate, Sandown Road, Watford, Herts, WD24 7UY
Activities: Veterinary activities
Parent: Medivet Partnership LLP
Officers: Arnold Stephen Levy, Secretary/Veterinary Surgeon; Dr Guy Richard Carter [1964] Director/Veterinary Surgeon; Arnold Stephen Levy [1959] Director/Veterinary Surgeon; Kevin Lance Morris [1973] Director; John William Hampden Smithers [1963] Director/Veterinary Surgeon

Medivet Partnership LLP
Incorporated: 20 March 2009 *Employees:* 1,297
Net Worth Deficit: £160,000 *Total Assets:* £72,368,000
Registered Office: 4 Mowat Industrial Estate, Sandown Road, Watford, Herts, WD24 7UY
Officers: David Abratt [1973] Member; Yorram Ariel [1966] Member; Dr Guy Richard Carter [1964] Member; Jan Harold Doedens [1966] Member; Erwin Wilhelm Hohn [1959] Member; Matthew James Holgate [1974] Member; Nitzan Kroter [1969] Member; Jeffrey Stephen Langberg [1958] Member; Richard Mary Leonard [1958] Member; Arnold Stephen Levy [1959] Member; Kevin Lance Morris [1973] Member; Adi Nell [1968] Member; Daniel Preter [1967] Member; Gareth Richardson [1970] Member; John William Hampden Smithers [1963] Member

Medlock Electrical Distributors Limited
Incorporated: 27 March 1947 *Employees:* 241
Net Worth: £22,618,216 *Total Assets:* £45,418,612
Registered Office: 109-115 Eleanor Cross Road, Waltham Cross, Herts, EN8 7NT
Activities: Wholesale of radio, television goods & electrical household appliances (other than records, tapes, CDs)
Major Shareholder: Alan Leslie Moore
Officers: Alan Leslie Moore, Secretary/Director [Irish]; Alan Leslie Moore [1950] Director [Irish]; Ben Patrick Moore [1983] Director [Irish]; Christine Leslie Moore [1952] Marketing Director; David Scott Moore [1972] Director [Irish]; Peter Robert Moore [1978] Sales Director [Irish]

Medtronic Limited
Incorporated: 8 September 1972 *Employees:* 763
Net Worth: £31,142,000 *Total Assets:* £212,692,992
Registered Office: Building 9, Croxley Park, Hatters Lane, Watford, Herts, WD18 8WW
Activities: Manufacture of medical and dental instruments and supplies
Parent: Medtronic Public Limited Company
Officers: Philip John Albert [1965] Director/Vice-President of Corporate Tax [American]; Helen Louise Brown [1975] HR Director; Mark Justin Elsey [1967] Finance Director; Jacqueline Fielding [1964] VP & Regional Director, UK/Ireland

Medway Fundco Limited
Incorporated: 28 July 2004
Net Worth Deficit: £8,613,196 *Total Assets:* £23,485,214
Registered Office: 55 Station Road, Beaconsfield, Bucks, HP9 1QL
Activities: Management of real estate on a fee or contract basis
Parent: Medway Community Estates Limited
Officers: Nigel Raymond Dodds, Secretary; Ross William Driver [1981] Finance Director; David Alexander John Foot [1968] Investment Director, Infrastructure; James Christopher Heath [1975] Director; Balasingham Ravi Kumar [1975] Investment Director; Ashley Brendon George West [1944] Director; Adam Iden Wickings [1962] Director/NHS Chief Operating Officer

Meg Trading Limited
Incorporated: 5 January 2011
Net Worth Deficit: £826,612 *Total Assets:* £9,171,223
Registered Office: 12 West Street, Ware, Herts, SG12 9EE
Activities: Buying and selling of own real estate
Shareholder: Lawrence Eaglestone
Officers: Lawrence Eaglestone [1964] Director; Maisie Merner [1990] Director

Megaman (UK) Limited
Incorporated: 26 September 2000 *Employees:* 34
Net Worth Deficit: £7,975,988 *Total Assets:* £9,394,464
Registered Office: Unit 2 Quadrant Park, Mundells, Welwyn Garden City, Herts, AL7 1FS
Activities: Wholesale of electronic and telecommunications equipment and parts
Officers: Diane Margaret Swann, Secretary; Kum Cheong Chan [1976] Director [Singaporean]; Glen Robin Krise [1965] Director; Wing Tak Lee [1963] Director [Chinese]; Diane Margaret Swann [1959] Director

Megnum Limited
Incorporated: 5 March 2003
Net Worth: £3,679,119 *Total Assets:* £10,416,754
Registered Office: 2 Hathaway Close, Stanmore, Middlesex, HA7 3NR
Activities: Buying and selling of own real estate
Major Shareholder: Meena Chotai
Officers: Pradip Khodidas Dhamecha, Secretary/Director; Meena Chotai [1960] Director/Cash Officer Manager; Pradip Khodidas Dhamecha [1958] Director; Shantilal Ratanshi Dhamecha [1931] Director Businessman

MEL Aviation Components Limited
Incorporated: 15 April 2013 *Employees:* 11
Net Worth: £2,386,385 *Total Assets:* £8,746,572
Registered Office: Laurence Walter House, Addison Road, Chilton Industrial Estate, Sudbury, Suffolk, CO10 2YW
Activities: Engineering design activities for industrial process and production
Shareholders: Nicholas Francis Smith; Gary Walter Harvey
Officers: Roger William Blyth Argent, Secretary; Neil James Ackroyd [1974] Director/Consultant; Gary Walter Harvey [1957] Director; Nicholas Gary Harvey [1987] Director; Nicholas Francis Smith [1958] Director

MEL Aviation Limited
Incorporated: 25 September 1968 *Employees:* 172
Net Worth: £21,227,840 *Total Assets:* £30,741,658
Registered Office: Laurence Walter House, 32 Addison Road, Sudbury, Suffolk, CO10 2YW
Activities: Other engineering activities
Major Shareholder: Nicholas Francis Smith
Officers: John Bedford, Secretary; Gary Walter Harvey [1957] Director/Engineer; Nicholas Gary Harvey [1987] Director; Nicholas Francis Smith [1958] Director/Engineer

Melbourn Science Park Limited
Incorporated: 13 December 1999 *Employees:* 2
Net Worth: £25,221,000 *Total Assets:* £26,897,000
Registered Office: c/o TTP Group PLC, Melbourn Science Park, Cambridge Road, Melbourn, Royston, Herts, SG8 6EE
Activities: Renting and operating of Housing Association real estate
Parent: TTP Group PLC
Officers: Keith Alexander Haddow, Secretary; Keith Alexander Haddow [1958] Director/Chartered Accountant; Peter John Taylor [1953] Director/Scientist

Meldire Limited
Incorporated: 21 March 1968
Net Worth: £19,118,908 *Total Assets:* £25,837,640
Registered Office: Unit 10 The Maltings, Millfield, Cottenham, Cambs, CB24 8RE
Activities: Construction of domestic buildings
Officers: Susan Carolyn Death, Secretary; Susan Carolyn Death [1962] Director/Secretary; Margaret Jane Mordey [1960] Director; Andrew Clifford Moss [1964] Director/Building Sub Contractor; Paul Keith Ursell [1953] Director

Meldongreen Limited
Incorporated: 22 May 1979 *Employees:* 141
Net Worth: £3,566,303 *Total Assets:* £8,220,038
Registered Office: 1 Nelson Street, Southend on Sea, Essex, SS1 1EG
Activities: Retail sale of flowers, plants, seeds, fertilizers, pet animals and pet food in specialised stores
Shareholders: Michael Rex Seaby; Diane Rosemary Seaby; Nicholas Paul Seaby
Officers: Michael Rex Seaby, Secretary/Builder; Nicholas Paul Seaby, Secretary; Michael Rex Seaby [1947] Director/Builder; Nicholas Paul Seaby [1975] Director/Manager

Melesey Limited
Incorporated: 9 June 2000 *Employees:* 283
Net Worth: £33,488,000 *Total Assets:* £108,172,000
Registered Office: No 1 Park Lane, Hemel Hempstead, Herts, HP2 4YL
Activities: Activities of head offices
Parent: Bourne Leisure Limited
Officers: Jane Elizabeth Bentall [1970] Director/Accountant; Paul Charles Flaum [1970] Director; Iain Stuart Macmillan [1976] Director

The Meller Educational Trust
Incorporated: 12 June 2009 *Employees:* 284
Net Worth: £48,465,204 *Total Assets:* £50,062,852
Registered Office: The Bushey Academy, London Road, Bushey, Herts, WD23 3AA
Activities: General secondary education
Officers: David Robert Hughes, Secretary; Kate Prudence Bearman [1971] Director; Richard Arthur Elms [1947] Director/Chief Executive; Rita Susan Halbright [1961] Director/School Administrator [British/American]; David Robert Hughes [1970] Director of Finance and Operations; Clive Ashley Ross [1949] Director/Chartered Surveyor; Andrew Jonathan Sheach [1963] Director/Solicitor; Gillian Elizabeth Wiscarson [1954] Director/University Lecturer

Melton House Investments Limited
Incorporated: 7 March 2011 *Employees:* 43
Net Worth: £8,949,815 *Total Assets:* £26,362,588
Registered Office: Melton House, 65-67 Clarendon Road, Watford, Herts, WD17 1DS
Activities: Hotels and similar accommodation
Shareholders: Gursharan Singh Chadha; Jasbir Chadha
Officers: Gursharan Singh Chadha [1960] Director; Vivek Singh Chadha [1988] Director

Memec Group Holdings Limited
Incorporated: 4 May 2000 *Employees:* 2
Net Worth: £357,438,944 *Total Assets:* £1,636,634,240
Registered Office: Avnet House, Rutherford Close, Stevenage, Herts, SG1 2EF
Activities: Activities of head offices
Officers: Mark McKrell [1966] Finance Director; Harvey Woodford [1963] Director/VP Corporate Secretary [American]

Memec Group Limited
Incorporated: 4 May 2000 *Employees:* 2
Net Worth: £172,897,072 *Total Assets:* £173,006,208
Registered Office: Avnet House, Rutherford Close, Stevenage, Herts, SG1 2EF
Activities: Activities of other holding companies n.e.c.
Parent: Avnet Holdings UK Limited
Officers: Mark McKrell [1966] Finance Director; Harvey Woodford [1963] Director/VP Corporate Secretary [American]

Memec Holdings Limited
Incorporated: 29 February 2000 *Employees:* 2
Net Worth: £1,011,198,848 *Total Assets:* £1,025,385,088
Registered Office: Avnet House, Rutherford Close, Stevenage, Herts, SG1 2EF
Activities: Activities of head offices
Parent: Memec Group Holdings Limited
Officers: Mark McKrell [1966] Finance Director; Harvey Woodford [1963] Director/VP Corporate Secretary [American]

Memorial Gardens Limited
Incorporated: 19 August 2015 *Employees:* 1
Net Worth: £7,650,184 *Total Assets:* £12,004,784
Registered Office: 58 Mill Street, St Osyth, Clacton on Sea, Essex, CO16 8EN
Activities: Funeral and related activities
Major Shareholder: Daniel Moretti
Officers: Daniel Moretti [1965] Director

Mentmore Gransden Limited
Incorporated: 5 September 2011
Net Worth Deficit: £288,603 *Total Assets:* £16,466,602
Registered Office: Cambridge House, 16 High Street, Saffron Walden, Essex, CB10 1AX
Activities: Development of building projects
Shareholder: Hugo Octavius Warner
Officers: Hugo Octavius Warner [1969] Director

Mentmore Limited
Incorporated: 23 November 1935 *Employees:* 2
Net Worth: £130,272,000 *Total Assets:* £376,945,984
Registered Office: c/o Safestore Holdings PLC, Brittanic House, Stirling Way, Borehamwood, Herts, WD6 2BT
Activities: Activities of other holding companies n.e.c.
Parent: Safestore Acquisition Limited
Officers: Andrew Brian Jones [1966] Director/Chartered Accountant; Federico Vecchioli [1966] Director [French]

Mercantile Trust Limited
Incorporated: 18 September 2009 *Employees:* 3
Previous: Central Lending Servicing Limited
Net Worth: £7,196,000 *Total Assets:* £17,774,000
Registered Office: St Crispins House, Duke Street, Norwich, NR3 1PD
Activities: Activities of mortgage finance companies
Parent: Norfolk Capital Limited
Officers: Anthony Richardson, Secretary; Debbie Carol Burton [1971] Director/Chief Executive; Paul Joseph Hollander [1980] Director/Chartered Accountant; Warren Anthony Travis [1965] Director/Accountant; Andrew Clive Turner [1958] Director/Accountant

Merchant Taylors' School
Incorporated: 30 July 1997 *Employees:* 355
Net Worth: £33,755,376 *Total Assets:* £39,653,028
Registered Office: Sandy Lodge, Northwood, Middlesex, HA6 2HT
Activities: General secondary education
Officers: Ian Douglas Williams, Secretary; Richard John Brooman [1955] Director/Chartered Accountant; Dr Jonathan Mark Cox [1966] Director/Headmaster; Guy Beetham Maurice Henry Du Parc Braham [1966] Director/Chief Risk Officer; Alan Roy Eastwood [1955] Director/Retired Chartered Accountant; Lynn Barbara Gadd [1953] Director/Principal; Georgina Jayne Gardiner [1985] Director/Assistant Professor; Christopher Peter Hare [1947] Director Lloyds Managing Agent; Deepak Haria [1963] Director/Chartered Accountant; Sarah Angharad Morgan [1978] HR Director; Andrew Graham Moss [1958] Director/Chartered Accountant; Jane Katherine Mary Redman [1957] Director/Solicitor [Irish]; Dipesh Jayantilal Shah [1953] Director; Robert John Temmink [1973] Director/Barrister; Sir Michael John Tomlinson [1942] Director/Retired; James Douglas Robert Twining [1972] Director/Chief Executive

Merck Sharp & Dohme (Holdings) Limited
Incorporated: 29 September 1928
Net Worth: £455,592,992 *Total Assets:* £455,840,992
Registered Office: Hertford Road, Hoddesdon, Herts, EN11 9BU
Activities: Activities of head offices
Parent: Schering-Plough Holdings Limited
Officers: Richard Robinski, Secretary; Louise Jane Houson [1976] Director; Simon Nicholson [1975] Director; Ebru Can Temucin [1972] Director [Turkish]

Merck Sharp & Dohme Finance Europe Limited
Incorporated: 21 October 1993 *Employees:* 3
Net Worth: £324,069,280 *Total Assets:* £1,183,533,696
Registered Office: Hertford Road, Hoddesdon, Herts, EN11 9BU
Activities: Other business support service activities n.e.c.
Parent: Merck & Co., Inc.
Officers: Richard Robinski, Secretary; Michael Hobbs [1960] Director; Richard Robinski [1958] Director/Secretary; Ebru Can Temucin [1972] Director [Turkish]

Merck Sharp & Dohme Limited
Incorporated: 25 September 1964 *Employees:* 1,162
Net Worth: £440,820,992 *Total Assets:* £607,619,008
Registered Office: Hertford Road, Hoddesdon, Herts, EN11 9BU
Activities: Manufacture of basic pharmaceutical products
Parent: Merck Sharp & Dohme (Holdings) Limited
Officers: Richard Robinski, Secretary; Louise Jane Houson [1976] Director; Simon Nicholson [1975] Director; Ebru Can Temucin [1972] Director [Turkish]

Mercury Land Holdings Limited
Incorporated: 18 November 2015 *Employees:* 1
Net Worth: £8,166,816 *Total Assets:* £23,169,784
Registered Office: 2 River Chambers, High Street, Romford, Essex, RM1 1HR
Activities: Other letting and operating of own or leased real estate
Parent: London Borough of Havering
Officers: Keith Oliver, Secretary; Andrew Blake-Herbert [1970] Director; Garry Kevin Green [1955] Director/Chartered Surveyor; Anthony Vincent Huff [1961] Assistant Director; Ian Philip Rhodes [1963] Director

Meridian Audio Limited
Incorporated: 29 April 1992 *Employees:* 75
Net Worth Deficit: £613,868 *Total Assets:* £10,298,243
Registered Office: Latham Road, Huntingdon, Cambs, PE29 6YE
Activities: Manufacture of consumer electronics
Major Shareholder: Donald John Buchanan
Officers: Neil Robson, Secretary; Allen John Boothroyd [1943] Director/Product Design Consultant; Donald John Buchanan [1973] Director; Sean David Jagoe [1951] Director/Investment Banker [Irish]; Sang Woo Park [1965] Director [South Korean]; Neil Robson [1969] Finance Director

Meritcape Limited
Incorporated: 11 May 1988 *Employees:* 18
Net Worth: £169,602,288 *Total Assets:* £300,435,936
Registered Office: Hadley Hurst, Hadley Common, Barnet, Herts, EN5 5QG
Activities: Development of building projects
Parent: Blendhall Limited
Officers: Anna Victoria Kinsman, Secretary; Anthony George Bunker [1944] Director/Tax Consultant; Alexander Mahboubian [1972] Director/Designer; Enid Mahboubian [1943] Director; Farrokh Mahboubian [1932] Director [Iranian]

Merloni Domestic Appliances Limited
Incorporated: 2 March 1959
Net Worth: £44,445,000 *Total Assets:* £53,276,000
Registered Office: Morley Way, Peterborough, Cambs, PE2 9JB
Activities: Wholesale of radio, television goods & electrical household appliances (other than records, tapes, CDs)
Parent: Indesit Company UK Holdings Limited
Officers: Tetiana Pidhaina, Secretary; Lucianna Raffaini Carvalho [1973] Director [Italian]; Andrzej Tuleja [1973] Director [Polish]

Merritts Properties Limited
Incorporated: 2 November 1960 *Employees:* 6
Net Worth: £28,839,952 *Total Assets:* £42,388,588
Registered Office: Merritt House, Hill Avenue, Amersham, Bucks, HP6 5BQ
Activities: Other letting and operating of own or leased real estate
Shareholders: Anthony David Holt; Christina Jane Hitchcock; Timothy James Merritt
Officers: Charles Nicholas Morton, Secretary; Christina Jane Hitchcock [1964] Director/Property Manager; Sandra Ann McGrath [1968] Finance Director [Irish]; Timothy James Merritt [1960] Director; Arthur Leonard Robert Morton [1942] Director/Chartered Accountant; Charles Nicholas Morton [1984] Director; David Maurice Norman [1957] Director/Chartered Surveyor

Mersea Homes Limited
Incorporated: 1 February 1990
Net Worth: £15,605,892 *Total Assets:* £19,774,444
Registered Office: Eagle House, 45 Kingsland Road, West Mersea, Colchester, Essex, CO5 8RA
Activities: Development of building projects
Officers: Stuart Trevor Cock, Secretary; Darren Peter Cock [1970] Director/Builder; Stuart Trevor Cock [1966] Director; Trevor Stephen Cock [1940] Director

Merton Acquisitions Limited
Incorporated: 20 December 2016
Net Worth Deficit: £7,466,808 *Total Assets:* £39,461,368
Registered Office: 3rd Floor, Sterling House, Langston Road, Loughton, Essex, IG10 3TS
Activities: Development of building projects
Shareholders: Luke Oliver Johnson; Galliard Holdings Limited
Officers: Allan William Porter, Secretary; Donagh O'Sullivan [1968] Construction Director [Irish]; Ben John Redmond [1968] Director

Metals & Materials Limited
Incorporated: 27 September 2013
Net Worth: £17,391,000 *Total Assets:* £22,585,000
Registered Office: Units C1 and C2 Spitfire Close, Ermine Business Park, Huntingdon, Cambs, PE29 6WR
Activities: Activities of head offices
Major Shareholder: Stephen Charles Aldersley
Officers: Andrew Watson, Secretary; Stephen Charles Aldersley [1957] Director; Stephen Marcel Grenier [1961] Director; Simon John Kenney [1967] Sales Director; Jane Elizabeth Stoner [1961] Director; Andrew Watson [1986] Finance Director

Metaswitch Networks Ltd
Incorporated: 10 August 1981 *Employees:* 494
Net Worth Deficit: £24,459,660 *Total Assets:* £97,042,192
Registered Office: 100 Church Street, Enfield, Middlesex, EN2 6BQ
Activities: Information technology consultancy activities
Officers: Jason Aaron Brein [1984] Director [American]; Ian Stewart Ferguson [1943] Director; James Goetz [1965] Director/Managing Partner [American]; Hans Martin Nielsen Lund [1968] Director/Business Executive [American]; Graeme MacArthur [1963] Director; Stephen Patrick Mullaney [1963] Director [American]; Deep Shah [1979] Director

Metier Healthcare Limited
Incorporated: 16 January 1997
Net Worth Deficit: £1,223,367 *Total Assets:* £34,452,380
Registered Office: 4 Estates Yard, Wellhouse Lane, Barnet, Herts, EN5 3DG
Activities: Activities of other holding companies n.e.c.
Parent: Metier Holdings Limited
Officers: Mark John Griffiths [1967] Regional Director; Simon Hayman [1966] Director; Mark Geoffrey David Holden [1957] Investment Director; Mark Christopher Wayment [1958] Director; Elena Giorgiana Wegener [1975] Investment Director

Metier Holdings Limited
Incorporated: 24 November 1998
Net Worth Deficit: £1,223,367 *Total Assets:* £34,452,380
Registered Office: 4 Estates Yard, Wellhouse Lane, Barnet, Herts, EN5 3DG
Activities: Hospital activities
Parent: Infrastructure Investments Holdings Limited
Officers: Mark John Griffiths [1967] Regional Director; Simon Hayman [1966] Director; Mark Geoffrey David Holden [1957] Investment Director; Mark Christopher Wayment [1958] Director; Elena Giorgiana Wegener [1975] Investment Director

Metis Homes Limited
Incorporated: 16 November 2007 *Employees:* 18
Previous: Burton Property Ventures Limited
Net Worth: £2,938,310 *Total Assets:* £25,263,516
Registered Office: Graham House, 7 Wyllyotts Place, Potters Bar, Herts, EN6 2JD
Activities: Development of building projects
Parent: RO Trading Limited
Officers: Anthony William Rawes Burton [1961] Director; Alistair Harris [1977] Planning Director; Adam John O'Brien [1980] Director; Rupert Adam Joleyn Price [1960] Director; Edward Thomas Morton Rowlandson [1974] Director; Andrew John Ormiston Sinclair [1968] Director/Property Developer; Richard Woodman-Bailey [1950] Director

Metro Global Holdings Limited
Incorporated: 16 July 2010 *Employees:* 116
Net Worth: £8,787,381 *Total Assets:* £31,833,718
Registered Office: Upminster Court, 133 Hall Lane, Upminster, Essex, RM14 1AL
Activities: Combined office administrative service activities
Officers: Barry George Tuck, Secretary; Paul Carlile [1955] Director; Stephen William George Ireland [1966] Director; Iain Robert Liddell [1963] Director; Andrew White [1965] Director/General Manager

Metro Investments (Stevenage) LLP
Incorporated: 25 July 2016
Net Worth: £1,040,357 *Total Assets:* £8,568,294
Registered Office: Congress House, 14 Lyon Road, Harrow, Middlesex, HA1 2EN
Officers: Amit Kumar Shantilal Dhamecha [1969] Member; Manish Shantilal Dhamecha [1959] Member; Pradip Khodidas Dhamecha [1958] Member; Rupen Shantilal Dhamecha [1967] Member; Ashok Mathuradas Lakhani [1946] Member; Bharat Lakhani [1951] Member

Metro Partners LLP
Incorporated: 1 April 2008 *Employees:* 6
Net Worth: £6,869,295 *Total Assets:* £16,880,308
Registered Office: Congress House, 14 Lyon Road, Harrow, Middlesex, HA1 2EN
Officers: Pradip Khodidas Dhamecha [1958] Member; Ashok Mathuradas Lakhani [1946] Member; Amit Kumar Shantilal Dhamecha [1969] LLP Member; Manish Shantilal Dhamecha [1959] LLP Member; Rupen Shantilal Dhamecha [1967] LLP Member; Bharat Mathuradas Lakhani [1951] LLP Member

Metro Properties Limited
Incorporated: 9 September 1999 *Employees:* 4
Net Worth: £6,046,998 *Total Assets:* £11,234,227
Registered Office: 251 Ilford Lane, Ilford, Essex, IG1 2SB
Activities: Hotels and similar accommodation
Officers: Abdul Wahid, Secretary/Director; Abdul Wahid [1954] Director Chief Executive; Ikram Wahid [1977] Director

Metropolitan Infrastructure Limited
Incorporated: 28 March 2006
Net Worth Deficit: £10,529,767 *Total Assets:* £30,776,924
Registered Office: Energy House, Woolpit Business Park, Windmill Avenue, Woolpit, Bury St Edmunds, Suffolk, IP30 9UP
Activities: Other business support service activities n.e.c.
Parent: Inexus Group (Holdings) Limited
Officers: Christopher Paul Mumford, Secretary/Lawyer; Darryl John Corney [1960] Director; Clive Eric Linsdell [1962] Director; John Graham Marsh [1964] Director

Metrosold Limited
Incorporated: 7 May 1999
Net Worth: £1,797,083 *Total Assets:* £14,919,094
Registered Office: 3rd Floor, Sterling House, Langston Road, Loughton, Essex, IG10 3TS
Activities: Other business support service activities n.e.c.
Parent: Galliard Holdings Limited
Officers: Allan William Porter, Secretary; David Edward Conway [1976] Director; Stephen Stuart Solomon Conway [1948] Director

Metsa Wood UK Limited
Incorporated: 21 June 1995 *Employees:* 446
Net Worth: £37,490,000 *Total Assets:* £66,394,000
Registered Office: Old Golf Course, Fishtoft Road, Boston, Lincs, PE21 0BJ
Activities: Sawmilling and planing of wood
Parent: Metsaliitto Oy
Officers: Alice Olsson, Secretary; Alice Olsson [1978] Finance Director; Henrik Soderstrom [1979] Director/Senior Vice President Timber & Upgrades [Finnish]

Mettler-Toledo Safeline X-Ray Limited
Incorporated: 3 October 2000 *Employees:* 114
Net Worth: £51,361,348 *Total Assets:* £56,543,816
Registered Office: Unit 1 Greenfield, Royston, Herts, SG8 5HN
Activities: Manufacture of other special-purpose machinery n.e.c.
Parent: Mettler-Toledo Holdings LLC
Officers: David Edward Wood, Secretary; Nigel John King [1950] Director; Kristian Laskey [1969] Director

MHE JVCO Limited
Incorporated: 19 June 2013
Net Worth: £102,800,000 *Total Assets:* £105,500,000
Registered Office: Buildings One & Two, Trident Place, Mosquito Way, Hatfield, Herts, AL10 9UL
Activities: Non-trading company
Shareholders: Ocado Operating Limited; Wm Morrison Supermarkets PLC; Ocado Operating Limited; Wm Morrison Supermarkets PLC
Officers: Robert McNeill Cooper, Secretary; Joanna Louise Goff [1978] Finance Director; Mark Antony Richardson [1964] Director; Duncan Eden Tatton-Brown [1965] Director

MHL Holdco Limited
Incorporated: 26 June 2013 *Employees:* 7
Net Worth: £122,357,600 *Total Assets:* £155,523,360
Registered Office: Bradbury House, 830 The Crescent, Colchester Business Park, Colchester, Essex, CO4 9YQ
Activities: Residential nursing care facilities
Parent: Myriad Healthcare Holdings Ltd
Officers: Nigel Bennett Schofield, Secretary; Derek George Cormack [1959] Director/Accountant [Irish]; Iain Anderson Corstorphine [1968] Director; Craig Griffin [1967] Director; Peter Martin Hill [1968] Director; Paul Anthony Keith Jeffery [1966] Director; Helena Jeffrey [1945] Director; Michael Medlicott [1943] Director; Nigel Bennett Schofield [1950] Director

Michell Instruments Limited
Incorporated: 12 September 1974 *Employees:* 136
Net Worth: £10,523,194 *Total Assets:* £13,266,787
Registered Office: 48 Lancaster Way Business Park, Ely, Cambs, CB6 3NW
Activities: Manufacture of electronic industrial process control equipment
Parent: Parametric Investments Limited
Officers: David Paul Leonard, Secretary; Michael Bannister [1957] Director/Chief Executive Officer; David Paul Leonard [1966] Finance Director; Adam Dean Markin [1966] Director/Chairman

Microlease Limited
Incorporated: 28 December 1973 *Employees:* 220
Previous: Microlease PLC
Net Worth: £16,805,000 *Total Assets:* £88,697,000
Registered Office: Unit 1 Waverley Business Park, Hailsham Drive, Harrow, Middlesex, HA1 4TR
Activities: Renting and leasing of other machinery, equipment and tangible goods n.e.c.
Parent: Newmir Limited
Officers: Nigel Brown [1957] Director; John Joseph Hafferty [1956] Director/Chief Financial Officer [American]; Paul Joseph McCloskey [1960] Director; Nigel Rennie [1960] Director; David Whitfield [1959] Director

Microlights Limited
Incorporated: 23 February 1984 *Employees:* 108
Net Worth: £4,373,166 *Total Assets:* £10,337,502
Registered Office: 6 Little Burrow, Welwyn Garden City, Herts, AL7 4SW
Activities: Manufacture of electric lighting equipment
Parent: Microlights Group Limited
Officers: Kevin Bell [1951] Managing Director; Paul Johnson [1956] Director

Micronclean Limited
Incorporated: 31 August 1921 *Employees:* 455
Previous: Fenland Laundries Limited
Net Worth: £14,661,862 *Total Assets:* £21,314,632
Registered Office: Roman Bank, Skegness, Lincs, PE25 1SQ
Activities: Washing and (dry-)cleaning of textile and fur products
Major Shareholder: Simon James Fry
Officers: Michelle Sharon Simpson, Secretary; Philip Cresswell [1963] Sales Director; Clare Margaret Fry [1964] Director; Simon James Fry [1963] Director; Andrew John Kettle [1967] Director; Robert James Parker [1964] Director/Accountant

Micropress Printers Limited
Incorporated: 9 November 1979 *Employees:* 170
Net Worth: £12,730,570 *Total Assets:* £14,605,279
Registered Office: Fountain Way, Reydon Business Park, Reydon, Southwold, Suffolk, IP18 6SZ
Activities: Printing n.e.c.
Major Shareholder: Michael Jimmy Cross
Officers: Shirley Ann Cross, Secretary; Paul William Coby [1979] Director; James Neville Cross [1979] Director; Michael Jimmy Cross [1949] Director; Robert Cross [1983] Director; Shirley Ann Cross [1958] Director

Microsoft Research Limited
Incorporated: 12 May 1997 *Employees:* 147
Net Worth: £36,564,000 *Total Assets:* £51,162,000
Registered Office: 21 Station Road, Cambridge, CB1 2FB
Activities: Other information technology service activities
Officers: Keith Ranger Dolliver [1963] Director/Attorney [American]; Benjamin Owen Orndorff [1971] Director/Attorney [American]

Micross Components Holdings Ltd
Incorporated: 28 February 2006
Net Worth: £2,906,013 *Total Assets:* £9,901,345
Registered Office: 2 Hellesdon Park Road, Drayton High Road, Norwich, NR6 5DR
Activities: Activities of head offices
Parent: Micross UK Solutions Ltd
Officers: Richard Oliver Kingdon [1954] Director; Victor Lance Vescovo [1966] Director/Chief Operating Officer [American]

Micross Components Limited
Incorporated: 27 March 1984 *Employees:* 91
Net Worth: £8,459,052 *Total Assets:* £10,916,706
Registered Office: 2 Hellesdon Park Road, Drayton High Road, Norwich, NR6 5DR
Activities: Manufacture of electronic components
Parent: Micross Components Holdings Ltd
Officers: Neil Davies [1968] Finance Director; Richard William Gibbs [1959] Managing Director; Richard Oliver Kingdon [1954] Director; Michael William Rooney [1967] Director/Chief Finance Officer [American]; Victor Lance Vescovo [1966] Director/Chief Operating Officer [American]

Micross Foods Holdings Limited
Incorporated: 15 November 2012 *Employees:* 108
Net Worth: £1,491,815 *Total Assets:* £22,578,652
Registered Office: Community House, 29-31 Eastways, Witham, Essex, CM8 3YQ
Activities: Non-specialised wholesale trade
Shareholder: Martin Leslie Rome
Officers: David Andrew Gray, Secretary; Martin Leslie Rome [1961] Managing Director

Micross UK Solutions Limited
Incorporated: 7 January 2013 *Employees:* 96
Net Worth Deficit: £7,765,965 *Total Assets:* £23,309,576
Registered Office: 2 Hellesdon Park Road, Drayton High Road, Norwich, NR6 5DR
Activities: Activities of head offices
Parent: Micross USA UK Holdings LLC
Officers: Richard Oliver Kingdon [1954] Director; Victor Lance Vescovo [1966] Director/Chairman [American]

Mid Holding Co UK Limited
Incorporated: 16 May 2014 *Employees:* 1,415
Net Worth: £15,383,396 *Total Assets:* £102,321,984
Registered Office: Hapag-Lloyd House, Cambridge Road, Barking, Essex, IG11 8HH
Activities: Construction of commercial buildings
Major Shareholder: Sahel Majali
Officers: Jacqueline Margaret Diane Adams-Hooker [1969] Director/Accountant; Sahel Majali [1962] Director/Entrepreneur; Shaker Sahel Majali [1988] Director/Architect; Andrew David Shepherd [1978] Director

Mid Norfolk Academy Trust
Incorporated: 1 February 2017 *Employees:* 138
Net Worth: £11,084,040 *Total Assets:* £13,307,961
Registered Office: Mid Norfolk Academy Trust, Dereham Neatherd High School, Norwich Road, Dereham, Norfolk, NR20 3AX
Activities: General secondary education
Officers: Martyn Davey [1967] Director/College Manager; Peter Andrew Devonish [1965] Director/Academy CEO; Steve Frost [1963] Director/Sales & Business Development; Andrew Richard Long [1962] Director/Market Research; Andrew Duncan Rowley [1954] Director/Chartered Accountant; Leda Carol Ann Tarabay [1960] Director/Accountant; Vince Alan Warren [1970] Director/Property Consultant

Midgard Ltd
Incorporated: 22 February 2006 *Employees:* 100
Net Worth: £4,822,688 *Total Assets:* £71,057,872
Registered Office: 4 Elstree Way, Borehamwood, Herts, WD6 1RN
Activities: Construction of commercial buildings
Parent: JRL Group Ltd
Officers: Ronan Joseph Gleeson, Secretary/Director [Irish]; Ronan Joseph Gleeson [1976] Director [Irish]; Kevin William Keegan [1963] Director/Estimator [Irish]; John James Reddington [1972] Director/Formwork [Irish]

Midland Chilled Foods Limited
Incorporated: 26 March 1973 *Employees:* 146
Net Worth: £4,687,084 *Total Assets:* £12,348,820
Registered Office: Brierly Place, New London Road, Chelmsford, Essex, CM2 0AP
Activities: Non-specialised wholesale of food, beverages and tobacco
Parent: Granarolo UK Limited
Officers: Aldo Bosco [1961] Managing Director [Italian]; Anthony Graham Bosco [1984] Import Director; Andrea Dalla Via [1973] Director [Italian]; Filippo Marchi [1967] Director [Italian]; Stefano Palmieri [1968] Director [Italian]

Midwich Group PLC
Incorporated: 27 November 2013 *Employees:* 646
Previous: Midwich Group Limited
Net Worth: £49,979,000 *Total Assets:* £207,031,008
Registered Office: Vinces Road, Diss, Norfolk, IP22 4YT
Activities: Wholesale of computers, computer peripheral equipment and software
Officers: Stephen Lamb, Secretary; Michael Ashley [1967] Director; Stephen Barry Fenby [1963] Director; Andrew Charles Herbert [1960] Director/Chartered Accountant; Stephen Lamb [1973] Finance Director; Hilary Wright [1959] Group HR Director

Midwich Limited
Incorporated: 11 July 1979 *Employees:* 350
Net Worth: £21,214,000 *Total Assets:* £116,061,000
Registered Office: Midwich Limited, Vinces Road, Diss, Norfolk, IP22 4YT
Activities: Non-specialised wholesale trade
Parent: Midwich PLC
Officers: Stephen Barry Fenby, Secretary; Stephen Barry Fenby [1963] Finance Director; Stephen Lamb [1973] Finance Director

Milbank Ventures Limited
Incorporated: 28 February 2012 *Employees:* 232
Net Worth: £5,193,885 *Total Assets:* £19,102,024
Registered Office: Earls Colne Business Park, Earls Colne, Colchester, Essex, CO6 2NS
Activities: Activities of head offices
Major Shareholder: Sean Rickard Milbank
Officers: Anna Mary Gittus Milbank [1969] Director; John Gearon Byford Milbank [1944] Director; Sean Rickard Milbank [1970] Director; Matthew James Sparrow [1980] Director/Accountant

Milburn Productions Limited
Incorporated: 4 April 1973
Net Worth: £23,378,000 *Total Assets:* £26,073,310
Registered Office: 35-37 Amersham Hill, High Wycombe, Bucks, HP13 6NU
Activities: Buying and selling of own real estate
Officers: Peter James Davies [1978] Director; Nazim Ilyas [1982] Finance Director; Tim Neil Walton [1973] Managing Director

Mill Hill Properties Limited
Incorporated: 14 September 1998 *Employees:* 1
Net Worth: £24,507 *Total Assets:* £10,449,145
Registered Office: 105 Viglen House, Alperton Lane, London, HA0 1HD
Activities: Management of real estate on a fee or contract basis
Shareholders: Bijan Sheibani; Azadeh Majlesi
Officers: Azadeh Majlesi, Secretary/Manager [Iranian]; Bijan Sheibani [1947] Director/Manager [Iranian]; Seyed Ahmad Zolfaghari [1946] Director/Businessman

The Mill Hotel Limited
Incorporated: 28 February 1995 *Employees:* 163
Net Worth: £2,406,904 *Total Assets:* £9,555,213
Registered Office: DVS House, Spring Villa Road, Edgware, Middlesex, HA8 7EB
Activities: Hotels and similar accommodation
Parent: Chester Mill Limited
Officers: Julan Shah [1977] Director; Prag Shah [1989] Director; Priyan Dhirajlal Shah [1980] Director

Millennium Cash & Carry Limited
Incorporated: 8 December 1999 *Employees:* 73
Net Worth: £20,582,116 *Total Assets:* £53,710,732
Registered Office: 364-368 Cranbrook Road, Gants Hill, Ilford, Essex, IG2 6HY
Activities: Wholesale of wine, beer, spirits and other alcoholic beverages
Major Shareholder: Panna Mashru
Officers: Rishi Lakhani [1982] Director

Millennium Investments 2000 Ltd
Incorporated: 1 September 1998 *Employees:* 6
Net Worth: £45,154,472 *Total Assets:* £54,958,592
Registered Office: Forest Road House, Forest Road, Colchester, Essex, CO4 3XA
Activities: Renting and operating of Housing Association real estate
Major Shareholder: Cengiz Candan
Officers: Stuart Jason Foster, Secretary; Cengiz Candan [1961] Director; Oznur Candan [1966] Director; Stuart Jason Foster [1975] Director/Accountant

Miller & Miller (Chemicals) Limited
Incorporated: 4 November 1977 *Employees:* 18
Net Worth: £8,437,924 *Total Assets:* £9,843,544
Registered Office: Haslers, Old Station Road, Loughton, Essex, IG10 4PL
Activities: Wholesale of pharmaceutical goods
Shareholder: John Simon Miller
Officers: Natalie Laura Livingston, Secretary; Natalie Laura Livingston [1972] Director; David Miller [1974] Sales Director; John Simon Miller [1943] Director/Chemist

Millharbour Developments Limited
Incorporated: 22 December 2005
Net Worth: £2,227,962 *Total Assets:* £9,549,624
Registered Office: 3rd Floor, Sterling House, Langston Road, Loughton, Essex, IG10 3TS
Activities: Buying and selling of own real estate
Parent: Raceguide Limited
Officers: Allan William Porter, Secretary; Stephen Stuart Solomon Conway [1948] Director; Donagh O'Sullivan [1968] Construction Director [Irish]

Thomas Mills High School
Incorporated: 14 April 2011 *Employees:* 108
Net Worth: £7,188,825 *Total Assets:* £8,433,917
Registered Office: Thomas Mills High School, Saxtead Road, Framlingham, Woodbridge, Suffolk, IP13 9HE
Activities: General secondary education
Officers: Katharine Ross Archer [1974] Director/Home Maker; Janet Margaret Bell [1961] Director; Melanie Chew [1966] Development Director; Adam Lewis Chittock [1984] Director/Teacher; Genevieve Wilhelmina Enid Christie [1965] Director/Publisher; Martin John Morgan Churchill [1967] Director/Travel Agent; Richard Henry Hanley [1962] Director; Duncan Horrocks [1968] Director/Computer Programmer; Barbara Nora Howard [1943] Director; Philip John Hurst [1974] Director/Headteacher; Stephen Paul Lovett [1961] Director/Retired Project Manager; Penelope Jane Marguerite Miller-Williams [1961] Director/Teaching Assistant; Mark Mugliston [1964] Director/Estate Agent; Stephen Martin Peters [1973] Director/Teacher; Susan Jane Preston [1952] Director/Puzzle Designer; Ying Hui Scrivener [1955] Director [Singaporean]; Douglas William Stewart [1947] Director; Sarah Elizabeth Thorne [1950] Director

Milltrust BLA LLP
Incorporated: 22 August 2016
Net Worth: £5,951,664 *Total Assets:* £16,225,272
Registered Office: Ground Floor, 4 Victoria Square, St Albans, Herts, AL1 3TF

Milpharm Limited
Incorporated: 11 April 1997 *Employees:* 31
Net Worth: £12,127,246 *Total Assets:* £27,974,948
Registered Office: Ares Block, Odyssey Business Park, West End Road, South Ruislip, Middlesex, HA4 6QD
Activities: Wholesale of pharmaceutical goods
Parent: Agile Pharma B.V.
Officers: Thomas Broeer [1960] Director [German]; Venugopalan Muralidharan [1955] Director; Gorla Phaneemdra Prasad [1957] Finance Director [Indian]

John Milton Academy Trust
Incorporated: 27 July 2016 *Employees:* 237
Net Worth: £21,162,772 *Total Assets:* £22,886,282
Registered Office: Stowupland High School, Church Road, Stowupland, Stowmarket, Suffolk, IP14 4BQ
Activities: Primary education
Officers: Timothy Gwynne Barker [1940] Director/Retired; Jeffrey Deane [1955] Director; Elizabeth Gibson [1973] HR Director; Eric Leslie Griffiths [1947] Director/Educational Consultant; Karen Diana Lillian Grimes [1960] Director/Headteacher; Allen Martin Mayhew [1972] Director of Human Resources; David Nunn [1954] Director/Farmer; Alan Ridealgh [1956] Director; Phil Thirkettle [1950] Director/Retired

Milton Hall Cambridge Limited
Incorporated: 13 June 2013 *Employees:* 6
Net Worth: £8,299,250 *Total Assets:* £11,575,671
Registered Office: Lawrence House, 5 St Andrews Hill, Norwich, NR2 1AD
Activities: Other service activities n.e.c.
Parent: Milton Hall Holdings Limited
Officers: Anthony Sidney Cheeseman [1942] Director; Isabel Margaret Cheeseman [1947] Director; Sandra Germeney [1968] Director; Nigel Clifford Lubbock [1950] Director/Solicitor; Tanya Price [1977] Director; Anthony John Purnell [1958] Director

Milton Hall Estates Limited
Incorporated: 27 October 1998 *Employees:* 2
Net Worth: £8,694,129 *Total Assets:* £11,910,715
Registered Office: Lawrence House, 5 St Andrews Hill, Norwich, NR2 1AD
Activities: Other letting and operating of own or leased real estate
Parent: Milton Hall Holdings Limited
Officers: Anthony Sidney Cheeseman [1942] Director; Isabel Margaret Cheeseman [1947] Director; Nigel Clifford Lubbock [1950] Director/Solicitor; Alison Shirley Purnell [1967] Director; Anthony John Purnell [1958] Director

Mingold Limited
Incorporated: 31 December 2015
Net Worth: £2 *Total Assets:* £44,881,000
Registered Office: Hill House, Lowlands Road, Harrow, Middlesex, HA1 3EQ
Activities: Buying and selling of own real estate
Parent: Denland Limited
Officers: Brian Martin Comer [1960] Director [Irish]; Luke Andrew Comer [1957] Director [Irish]

Minhoco 20 Limited
Incorporated: 6 September 2012 *Employees:* 2
Net Worth: £17,688,000 *Total Assets:* £17,688,000
Registered Office: Kingfisher House, Radford Way, Billericay, Essex, CM12 0EQ
Activities: Activities of head offices
Parent: Ground Control Holdings Ltd
Officers: Simon Hobart Charles Morrish [1974] Director; Dereka Anne Symes [1962] Director/Chartered Accountant

Minhoco 26 Limited
Incorporated: 8 April 2015 *Employees:* 478
Net Worth: £11,743,106 *Total Assets:* £15,297,341
Registered Office: Kingfisher House, Radford Way, Billericay, Essex, CM12 0EQ
Activities: Activities of other holding companies n.e.c.
Shareholders: Ground Control Holdings Ltd; James Anthony Johnson
Officers: Simon Hobart Charles Morrish [1974] Director; Dereka Anne Symes [1962] Director/Chartered Accountant

Minton Holdings Limited
Incorporated: 19 March 1953 *Employees:* 3
Net Worth: £8,973,836 *Total Assets:* £10,979,686
Registered Office: Treviot House, 186-192 High Road, Ilford, Essex, IG1 1LR
Activities: Development of building projects
Major Shareholder: Ivor Spiro
Officers: Denise Spiro, Secretary/Director; Denise Spiro [1939] Director; Ivor Spiro [1940] Director; Mandy Susan Spiro [1964] Director/Property Manager

Miriad Property Investments Limited
Incorporated: 4 August 2016
Net Worth: £12,647,237 *Total Assets:* £26,427,208
Registered Office: Haslers, Old Station Road, Loughton, Essex, IG10 4PL
Activities: Development of building projects
Officers: Adam Lopez Dias [1973] Director; Mark Iestyn Lewis [1974] Director/Manager; Simon Emanuel Raine [1981] Director/Manager

Mirrorstoke Limited
Incorporated: 3 January 1972
Net Worth: £9,956,109 *Total Assets:* £13,632,225
Registered Office: 290 High Street, Aldeburgh, Suffolk, IP15 5DQ
Activities: Development of building projects
Officers: Vanessa Jean Gorst, Secretary; Julie Buss [1981] Director/Manager; Blake Nicholas Gorst [1945] Director/Chartered Surveyor; Vanessa Jean Gorst [1944] Director/Property Consultant

Mission Therapeutics Limited
Incorporated: 11 May 2011 *Employees:* 45
Net Worth Deficit: £49,176,512 *Total Assets:* £26,634,878
Registered Office: Babraham Hall, Babraham, Cambridge, CB22 3AT
Activities: Research and experimental development on biotechnology
Officers: David Luther, Secretary; Dr Maria Gabriella Camboni [1957] Director [Italian]; Colin Goddard [1959] Director; Dr Deborah Harland [1960] Director/Partner; Prof Stephen Philip Jackson [1962] Director/Professor; Dr Elaine Jones [1955] Director/Venture Capitalist [American]; Dr Anker Lundemose [1961] Director/Chief Executive Officer [Danish]; Dr Michael Moore [1942] Director; Carole Nuechterlein [1961] Director [American]; Graziano Seghezzi [1969] Director/Partner Sofinnova Partners [Italian]

Mistras Group Limited
Incorporated: 17 October 1983 *Employees:* 216
Net Worth: £14,256,000 *Total Assets:* £18,807,000
Registered Office: 1 Dillington, Great Staughton, St Neots, Cambs, PE19 5DH
Activities: Other professional, scientific and technical activities n.e.c.
Parent: Mistras Group Inc.
Officers: Mark Timothy Wilkins, Secretary; Mehdi Batel [1977] Director [French]; Timothy Peter Bradshaw [1976] Director; Kenneth Barclay Bruce [1962] Delivery Director; Nicola Diane McGlynn [1969] Director; Sotirios Vahaviolos [1946] Director/President Physical Acoustics Corporation [American]; Timothy Martin Walsh [1962] Director; Jonathon Richard Watson [1975] Director; Mark Timothy Wilkins [1962] Director/Chartered Accountant

Mitcham Earthmoving Limited
Incorporated: 1 July 1974 *Employees:* 8
Net Worth: £8,214,508 *Total Assets:* £12,266,373
Registered Office: Berkeley House, Burwell, Cambs, CB25 0DY
Activities: Agents involved in the sale of machinery, industrial equipment, ships and aircraft
Officers: Michael Robert Mitcham, Secretary/Director; Marguerite Marie Mitcham [1946] Director; Michael Robert Mitcham [1960] Director

B.P. Mitchell Haulage Contractors Limited
Incorporated: 20 May 1999 *Employees:* 110
Net Worth: £16,713,255 *Total Assets:* £22,840,176
Registered Office: Burnside, Hertford Road, Hatfield, Herts, AL9 5RB
Activities: Other specialised construction activities n.e.c.
Major Shareholder: Brendan Pius Mitchell
Officers: Carol Ann Carter, Secretary; Brendan Pius Mitchell [1967] Director [Irish]

MJC Properties (Essex) Limited
Incorporated: 30 December 1998 *Employees:* 3
Net Worth: £6,196,844 *Total Assets:* £16,813,306
Registered Office: Charter House, 105 Leigh Road, Leigh on Sea, Essex, SS9 1JL
Activities: Other letting and operating of own or leased real estate
Shareholders: Michael Charles Casey; Paul John Casey
Officers: Vivien Casey, Secretary; Michael Charles Casey [1969] Director; Paul John Casey [1971] Director; Vivien Casey [1946] Director

MJT Securities Limited
Incorporated: 18 April 1991 *Employees:* 488
Net Worth: £54,007,628 *Total Assets:* £167,686,224
Registered Office: Service House, West Mayne, Basildon, Essex, SS15 6RW
Activities: Management consultancy activities other than financial management
Major Shareholder: Michael John Toomey
Officers: Neil Duncan Rickwood, Secretary; Jonathan Paul Brook [1950] Director; Peter Lewis Gillett [1942] Director; Daniel Trevor Martine [1975] Director; Neil Duncan Rickwood [1974] Director; Michael John Toomey [1938] Director; Timothy Edward Wallace [1949] Director

ML Accessories Group Limited
Incorporated: 2 September 2015
Net Worth: £8,978,071 *Total Assets:* £29,631,966
Registered Office: Unit 4 Foster Avenue, Woodside Park, Dunstable, Beds, LU5 5TA
Activities: Activities of other holding companies n.e.c.
Parent: SLV Group Holding UK Limited
Officers: Catherine Connolly [1968] Director; Sven Erhardt Schirmer [1972] Director [German]

MLM Consulting Engineers Limited
Incorporated: 16 May 1995 *Employees:* 317
Net Worth: £1,932,499 *Total Assets:* £10,622,410
Registered Office: North Kiln, Felaw Maltings, 46 Felaw Street, Ipswich, Suffolk, IP2 8PN
Activities: Other service activities n.e.c.
Parent: MLM Holdings Ltd
Officers: Iain Thom, Secretary; Nicholas David Ash [1964] Director/Chartered Engineer; Lee Christopher Bowker [1972] Director/Chartered Engineer; Bawden Burrows [1970] Director/Engineer; Steven James Cox [1963] Director/Chartered Engineer; Toby Crayden [1970] Director/Engineer; David Francis Crookes [1962] Director [Irish]; Kevin James Foster [1976] Director; Jason Fox [1971] Director/Chartered Engineer; Benjamin Peter Thomas Freedman [1983] Director/Chartered Civil Engineer; Darren Gill [1969] Director/Chartered Geologist; Shahram Hemmati [1959] Director; Martin Crawford Liddell [1966] Director/Chartered Engineer; Robert Gary Mawson [1964] Director; James Martin William Mayland [1962] Director; Christopher Terry Neeves [1972] Director/Engineer; Stephen James Oliver [1963] Director/Chartered Engineer; Joseph David Palmer [1983] Director; James Nicholas Rudd [1966] Director/Engineer; Mark Peter Scaife [1974] Director/Acoustic Engineer; Matthew Douglas Sealby [1973] Director/Engineer; Robert Miles Seller [1966] Director/Chartered Engineer; Mel Stockwell [1961] Director; Peter Leonard Welham [1955] Director/Incorporated Engineer; Mark Jonathan Winslade [1970] Director; Richard Anthony Wood [1978] Director/Chartered Engineer

MLS (Overseas) Limited
Incorporated: 17 December 1999 *Employees:* 9
Net Worth: £7,603,713 *Total Assets:* £15,935,551
Registered Office: Unit 210 The Courtyard, Skyline 120 Business Park, Avenue West, Great Notley, Braintree, Essex, CM77 7AA
Activities: Other business support service activities n.e.c.
Major Shareholder: Frank Rafaraci
Officers: Dr Anton Micallef, Secretary [Maltese]; Jessica Farhadian [1965] Director/Shipping Agent; Manish Khanna [1969] Director/Shipping Agent; John Frank Mills [1936] Director; Frank Rafaraci [1952] Director [American]; Mario Sennacheribbo Pons [1962] Director/Businessman [Spanish]

MM (UK) Limited
Incorporated: 4 September 2002 *Employees:* 313
Net Worth: £21,561,596 *Total Assets:* £74,536,256
Registered Office: Frans House, Fenton Way, Chatteris, Cambs, PE16 6UP
Activities: Wholesale of fruit and vegetables
Parent: Munoz Group Ltd
Officers: Fernando Juan de Lucas Lopez [1973] Director [Spanish]; David John Haresign [1963] Director; Jonathan Michael Hedge [1964] Director; Ian Duncan MacIntyre [1954] Director; Alvaro Munoz Beraza [1966] Director [Spanish]; Philip Scott Whelan [1974] Director

MM Flowers Limited
Incorporated: 4 February 2006 *Employees:* 146
Net Worth: £917,341 *Total Assets:* £15,242,891
Registered Office: APS Enterprise Campus, Alconbury Weald, Huntingdon, Cambs, PE28 4YA
Activities: Wholesale of flowers and plants
Shareholders: Munoz-Elite Flowers Ltd; Millhouse Limited
Officers: David Michael Johnson [1968] Director; Andrew James Kirkham [1968] Director; Juan Carlos Madrinan [1969] Director [Colombian]; Alonso Paredes [1958] Director/Lawyer [Colombian]; Philip Scott Whelan [1974] Managing Director; Colin Malcolm Williamson [1972] Director

MN Fox Bidco Limited
Incorporated: 3 September 2015 *Employees:* 4
Net Worth Deficit: £10,061,424 *Total Assets:* £53,329,552
Registered Office: 1 Myrtle Road, Brentwood, Essex, CM14 5EG
Activities: Activities of other holding companies n.e.c.
Parent: MN Fox Topco Limited
Officers: David Stanley Algar [1961] Director; Ian Peter Astley [1965] Director; Jonathan Alfred Brod [1974] Director; Kunal Dasgupta [1976] Director/Private Equity Investment Professional; Daniel Sasaki [1963] Director/Private Equity Investment Professional

MN Fox Topco Limited
Incorporated: 3 September 2015 *Employees:* 184
Net Worth Deficit: £9,529,009 *Total Assets:* £61,494,680
Registered Office: 1 Myrtle Road, Brentwood, Essex, CM14 5EG
Activities: Activities of other holding companies n.e.c.
Shareholders: MN Fox Investment Limited; Mayfair Equity Partners Nominees Limited
Officers: David Stanley Algar [1961] Director; Ian Peter Astley [1965] Director; Jonathan Alfred Brod [1974] Director; Kunal Dasgupta [1976] Director/Private Equity Investment Professional; Nicholas Jon Keegan [1975] Director/Marketing Consultant; Bill Ronald [1955] Director; Daniel Sasaki [1963] Director/Private Equity Investment Professional

MN Sports Bidco Limited
Incorporated: 12 June 2014 *Employees:* 4
Net Worth: £8,444,094 *Total Assets:* £32,489,954
Registered Office: 1 Myrtle Road, Warley, Brentwood, Essex, CM14 5EG
Activities: Activities of other holding companies n.e.c.
Parent: MN Sports Holdings Limted
Officers: David Algar [1961] Director; Ian Peter Astley [1965] Director; Shaun Michael McSpadden [1975] Director; Paul Reeves [1975] Director

MN Sports Holdings Limited
Incorporated: 23 May 2014
Net Worth: £18,767,764 *Total Assets:* £18,767,960
Registered Office: 1 Myrtle Road, Warley, Brentwood, Essex, CM14 5EG
Activities: Activities of financial services holding companies
Parent: MN Fox Bidco Limited
Officers: David Stanley Algar [1961] Director; Ian Peter Astley [1965] Director

MNS Care PLC
Incorporated: 11 March 1997 *Employees:* 165
Net Worth: £5,764,783 *Total Assets:* £15,414,494
Registered Office: 116 Headstone Drive, Harrow, Middlesex, HA1 4UH
Activities: Residential nursing care facilities
Parent: SAI Ram Care Limited
Officers: Sandip Ruparelia, Secretary/Care Home Operator; Priti Ruparelia [1963] Director/Care Home Operator; Sandip Ruparelia [1963] Director/Care Home Operator

Molecular Products Limited
Incorporated: 2 June 1992 *Employees:* 84
Net Worth: £11,985,534 *Total Assets:* £15,500,573
Registered Office: Parkway, Harlow Business Park, Harlow, Essex, CM19 5FR
Activities: Manufacture of other chemical products n.e.c.
Parent: Molecular Products Group Limited
Officers: Christopher David Laws, Secretary; Joseph Carloto [1956] Director [American]; Malcolm Little [1983] Director [American]; Peter Michael Manos [1966] Director [American]; John Troy Rhudy [1970] Director [American]

Moller Institute Limited
Incorporated: 7 September 1992 *Employees:* 87
Previous: The Moller Centre for Continuing Education Limited
Net Worth: £6,981,449 *Total Assets:* £11,482,398
Registered Office: Churchill College, Cambridge, CB3 0DS
Activities: Hotels and similar accommodation
Officers: Gillian Mary Secrett, Secretary; Dr Simon Hastings Bittleston [1961] Director/Vice President of Research; Professor Dame Athene Margaret Donald [1953] Director/Academic; Professor Sir Michael John Gregory [1948] Director/Emeritus Professor; Timothy Francis How [1950] Director; Tamsin Melanie James [1977] Director/Bursar; Dr Lisa Jayne Jardine-Wright [1976] Director/Educational Outreach Officer; Dr Christopher Graeme Potts [1956] Director/Executive Chairman; Daniel Ralph [1963] Director/University Academic; Gillian Mary Secrett [1960] Director of Centre

Monarock Limited
Incorporated: 31 December 2001
Net Worth: £11,233,374 *Total Assets:* £16,269,961
Registered Office: 34 West Drive, Harrow Weald, Middlesex, HA3 6TS
Activities: Buying and selling of own real estate
Shareholders: Sheetal Dalia-Patel; Heena Rajiv Sodha
Officers: Chandrabala Dalia, Secretary/Director; Sheetal Dalia-Patel [1972] Director; Heena Rajiv Sodha [1969] Director

Monitor Audio Limited
Incorporated: 5 December 2006 *Employees:* 70
Net Worth: £1,713,354 *Total Assets:* £13,170,543
Registered Office: 24 Brook Road, Rayleigh, Essex, SS6 7XJ
Activities: Manufacture of electric domestic appliances
Parent: Monitor Audio Group Limited
Officers: Robert John Barford, Secretary; Robert John Barford [1980] Finance Director; Hareesh Dhand [1957] Director/Corporate Financier; Andrew Robert Foster Flatt [1968] Managing Director; Diane Elizabeth Flatt [1972] Director

Monk's Walk School
Incorporated: 8 August 2012 *Employees:* 154
Net Worth: £8,196,000 *Total Assets:* £10,784,000
Registered Office: Monk's Walk School, Knightsfield, Welwyn Garden City, Herts, AL8 7NL
Activities: General secondary education
Officers: Tracie Smith, Secretary; Beverley Joy Bevan [1970] Director/Administrator; Sanjay Kumar Bhasin [1966] Finance Director; Alexis Ian Cheshire [1975] IT Director; Amber Cook [1985] Director/Teacher; Elizabeth Haye Eksteen [1957] Director/Administrator; Alex John Felthouse [1973] Director/Chartered Engineer; Adam Raymond Lancaster [1982] Director/Librarian; Sally Jane Mileson [1960] Director/Housewife; Alexander Ferguson Paterson [1963] Director/Estate Manager; Carole Elizabeth Pomfret [1961] Director/Accountant; Kathleen Smith [1962] Director/Headteacher; Colleen Stewart [1967] Director/Reprographics Assistant; Alan Richard Tucker [1946] Director; Clive James Wilson [1967] Director/Education; Katherine Elizabeth Woodhead [1987] Director/Administrator; Zoe Jeannette Wright [1970] Director/Clerical Officer

Mono Holdings Limited
Incorporated: 26 November 1999
Net Worth: £8,449,775 *Total Assets:* £14,510,316
Registered Office: Unit 4 Baird Road, Enfield, Middlesex, EN1 1SJ
Activities: Activities of head offices
Shareholder: Angelo Yianni
Officers: Maria Yianni, Secretary/Director; Andronikki Yianni [1978] Director; Angelo Yianni [1958] Director [Greek]; Maria Yianni [1980] Director

Mono Properties Limited
Incorporated: 3 February 1999
Net Worth: £7,407,436 *Total Assets:* £9,513,597
Registered Office: Unit 4 Baird Road, Enfield, Middlesex, EN1 1SJ
Activities: Development of building projects
Parent: Mono Holdings Limited
Officers: Maria Yianni, Secretary/Director; Andronikki Yianni [1978] Director; Angelo Yianni [1958] Director/Manufacturer [Greek]; Maria Yianni [1980] Director

Monsanto UK Limited
Incorporated: 27 July 2000 *Employees:* 24
Net Worth: £50,749,000 *Total Assets:* £71,629,000
Registered Office: 230 Cambridge Science Park, Milton Road, Cambridge, CB4 0WB
Activities: Growing of cereals (except rice), leguminous crops and oil seeds
Parent: Bayer New UK M3939 LLC
Officers: Natalia Voruz, Secretary; Mark Buckingham [1968] Director/Corporate Affairs Lead; Geoffrey Hall [1965] Director

Montanaro UK Smaller Companies Investment Trust PLC
Incorporated: 21 December 1994
Net Worth: £227,335,008 *Total Assets:* £247,676,992
Registered Office: Hamilton House, Rodney Way, Chelmsford, Essex, CM1 3BY
Activities: Activities of investment trusts
Officers: Katharine Blanche Mary Bolsover [1958] Director; Arthur Tyrer Copple [1954] Director; Roger Edward Cuming [1948] Director/Investment Manager; James Peyton Robinson [1953] Director

Monumart Limited
Incorporated: 21 May 2014 *Employees:* 22
Net Worth: £329,334 *Total Assets:* £11,903,880
Registered Office: Europa House, Europa Way, Ipswich, Suffolk, IP1 5DL
Activities: Retail sale via mail order houses or via Internet
Major Shareholder: Jie Liu
Officers: Colin Louch, Secretary; Jie Liu [1984] Director [Chinese]; Colin Andrew Louch [1955] Director

Monument Group Limited
Incorporated: 29 November 2001 *Employees:* 1
Net Worth: £2,260,291 *Total Assets:* £9,683,589
Registered Office: 7 The Close, Norwich, NR1 4DJ
Activities: Other letting and operating of own or leased real estate
Major Shareholder: Sarah Davies
Officers: Sarah Davies [1976] Director/Chartered Accountant

Moody Homes Limited
Incorporated: 4 October 1993
Net Worth: £21,660,924 *Total Assets:* £22,531,148
Registered Office: Hoe Mill Barns, Manor Road, Woodham Walter, Maldon, Essex, CM9 6GH
Activities: Construction of domestic buildings
Shareholder: Donald Alfred Moody
Officers: Sally Jane Ellis [1959] Director; Alison Elizabeth Ivey [1961] Director; Catherine Ann Moody [1966] Director; Donald Alfred Moody [1929] Director/Property Developer; Jennifer Louise Moody [1961] Managing Director; Shirley Moody [1936] Director

Moody International (Russia) Limited
Incorporated: 16 September 1976
Net Worth: £9,515,534 *Total Assets:* £13,562,750
Registered Office: Academy Place, 1-9 Brook Street, Brentwood, Essex, CM14 5NQ
Activities: Other business support service activities n.e.c.
Parent: RCG-Moody International Limited
Officers: Robert Alan Van Dorp [1977] Director; Thomas Andrew Dunlop [1974] Director/Accountant; Igor Vladimirovich Obodan [1971] Managing Director [Ukrainian]

Donald Moody Investments and Developments Limited
Incorporated: 21 August 1972 *Employees:* 7
Net Worth: £14,418,451 *Total Assets:* £14,824,668
Registered Office: Moody House, 106-108 High Street, Ingatestone, Essex, CM4 0BA
Activities: Other letting and operating of own or leased real estate
Officers: Sally Jane Ellis [1959] Director; Alison Elizabeth Moody [1961] Director/State Registered Nurse; Catherine Ann Moody [1966] Director; Donald Alfred Moody [1929] Managing Director; Jennifer Louise Moody [1961] Director; Shirley Moody [1936] Director

Jenny Moody Properties Limited
Incorporated: 7 May 1985 *Employees:* 10
Net Worth: £9,223,192 *Total Assets:* £9,785,297
Registered Office: Hoe Mill Barns, Manor Road, Woodham Walter, Maldon, Chelmsford, Essex, CM9 6GH
Activities: Construction of domestic buildings
Major Shareholder: Jennifer Louise Lomas
Officers: Jennifer Louise Moody [1961] Managing Director; Shirley Moody [1936] Director; Graham Harold Reeves [1961] Contracts Director

Moody Venture Capital LLP
Incorporated: 3 February 2014 *Employees:* 4
Net Worth: £16,741,754 *Total Assets:* £18,801,380
Registered Office: 106-110 High Street, Ingatestone, Essex, CM4 0BA
Officers: Catherine Ann Moody [1966] Member; Sally Jane Ellis [1959] LLP Member; Alison Elizabeth Ivey [1961] LLP Member; Jennifer Louise Lomas [1961] LLP Member; Thomas John Mines [1942] LLP Member; Donald Alfred Moody [1929] LLP Member; Shirley Moody [1936] LLP Member

Moog Fernau Limited
Incorporated: 22 September 1970 *Employees:* 29
Net Worth: £4,160,637 *Total Assets:* £13,377,836
Registered Office: Airport Executive Park, President Way, Luton, Beds, LU2 9NY
Activities: Manufacture of other special-purpose machinery n.e.c.
Parent: Moog Inc.
Officers: Peter Garrad, Secretary; Richard Eric Burghardt [1958] Director/Group VP Finance [American]; Paul John Dellaneve [1958] Director/Group VP [American]; Paul Anthony Revell [1967] Managing Director; David John Sharples [1960] Finance Director; John Randolph Willey [1954] Director/General Manager [American]

Henry Moore Foundation (The)
Incorporated: 23 April 1976 *Employees:* 84
Net Worth: £118,894,512 *Total Assets:* £119,924,160
Registered Office: Dane Tree House, Perry Green, Much Hadham, Herts, SG10 6EE
Activities: Archives activities
Officers: Ian Glen Parker, Secretary; Charles Arthur Rolls Asprey [1971] Director/Art Dealer; Martin Ronald Barden [1963] Director; Nigel Martyn Carrington [1956] Director/Vice Chancellor; Henry Channon [1970] Director; Celia Olwen Clear [1948] Director/Retired CEO of Tate Enterprises Ltd; William Thomas Edgerley [1956] Director; Anthony Vaughan Griffiths [1951] Director/Retired Museum Curator; Pamela Rose Raynor [1952] Finance Director; Anne Middleton Wagner [1949] Director/Scholar, Teacher and Writer [American]; John Peter Dimitri Wienand [1963] Director/Solicitor

Moorepay Limited
Incorporated: 10 November 1966 *Employees:* 199
Net Worth: £17,472,000 *Total Assets:* £23,245,000
Registered Office: Peoplebuilding 2, Peoplebuilding Estate, Maylands Avenue, Hemel Hempstead Industrial Estate, Hemel Hempstead, Herts, HP2 4NW
Activities: Data processing, hosting and related activities
Parent: Moorepay Group Limited
Officers: Elizabeth Leppard, Secretary; John Richard Martin Petter [1970] Director; Nicholas Paul Wain [1972] Director

Moores Refrigeration Controlled Transport Limited
Incorporated: 13 November 1974 *Employees:* 275
Net Worth: £4,029,448 *Total Assets:* £10,857,401
Registered Office: Potash Lane, Mid Suffolk Business Park, Eye, Suffolk, IP23 7HE
Activities: Freight transport by road
Shareholders: Heather Dawn Britton; Adrian Denis Moore; Graham Keith Moore
Officers: Craig Martin Boardman [1971] Commercial Director; David Christopher Brown [1960] Director; Neil John Goldsmith [1969] Financial Director; Adrian Denis Moore [1956] Director/Business Manager; Darren Paul Moore [1975] Director and Company Secretary; Graham Keith Moore [1950] Director/Business Manager

Moralis Group Limited
Incorporated: 17 January 2014 *Employees:* 282
Previous: RVLGH Limited
Net Worth: £44,670,056 *Total Assets:* £76,208,752
Registered Office: Ground Floor, Swift House, 18 Hoffmanns Way, Chelmsford, Essex, CM1 1GU
Activities: Activities of head offices
Major Shareholder: David William Thompson
Officers: Garry Martin Hobson [1970] Director; Soliman Motala [1980] Director; David William Thompson [1947] Director; Grant David Thompson [1972] Director

Morelli Group Limited
Incorporated: 5 May 1992 *Employees:* 210
Net Worth: £7,778,253 *Total Assets:* £15,901,264
Registered Office: Unit 2 Baird Road, Enfield, Middlesex, EN1 1SJ
Activities: Non-specialised wholesale trade
Officers: Robert Cohen, Secretary; Robert Paul Cohen [1977] Director; Joan Laybourn [1941] Director; Michele Laybourn [1965] Director; Andrew Moring [1967] Director; David Moring [1940] Director; John Moring [1948] Director; Julie Moring [1953] Director; Mark Moring [1973] Director; Phyllis Moring [1940] Director; Ruth Rosina Moring-Beale [1962] Director; Stuart Morning [1965] Director; Graham Robert Parker [1968] Director; Allan John Toms [1947] Financial Director; Linda Toms [1950] Director

The Morley Agricultural Foundation
Incorporated: 26 March 2003 *Employees:* 3
Net Worth: £28,536,340 *Total Assets:* £29,651,606
Registered Office: Morley Business Centre, Deopham Road, Morley St Botolph, Norfolk, NR18 9DF
Activities: Other business support service activities n.e.c.
Officers: Michaela Elizabeth Canham, Secretary; Timothy Simon Evans [1961] Director/Partner; Christine Elizabeth Alexandra Paterson Hill [1952] Director/Farmer; Stephen Rawsthorne [1957] Director/Retired; Philip Edward Richardson [1947] Director/Farmer; Robert John Salmon [1955] Director/Farmer; Nicholas John Steed [1945] Director/Consultant; John Sale Wallace [1949] Director/Farmer; Richard Wilbourn [1960] Director/Farm Manager

Morley Finco Limited
Incorporated: 23 April 2014
Net Worth: £6,428 *Total Assets:* £40,970,660
Registered Office: 505 Pinner Road, Harrow, Middlesex, HA2 6EH
Activities: Other letting and operating of own or leased real estate
Officers: Rishi Ramesh Sachdev [1976] Director; Uday Vyas [1978] Director

Morplan Limited
Incorporated: 1 July 1999 *Employees:* 136
Net Worth: £5,750,751 *Total Assets:* £9,280,863
Registered Office: P O Box 54, Temple Bank, Harlow, Essex, CM20 2TS
Activities: Retail sale via mail order houses or via Internet
Major Shareholder: Daniele Kapel-Marcovici
Officers: Daniel Cohen, Secretary; Daniel Cohen [1950] Director [French]; Daniele Kapel-Marcovici [1946] Director [French]; Vincent Terradot [1960] Managing Director [French]

H. Morrell Property Investments Limited
Incorporated: 18 September 1947 *Employees:* 1
Net Worth: £9,092,096 *Total Assets:* £10,222,718
Registered Office: Strachan House, Dunmow Road, Great Bardfield, Braintree, Essex, CM7 4SD
Activities: Other letting and operating of own or leased real estate
Officers: Mavis Lavinia Hall [1939] Director/Secretary; Hayley Elizabeth Matthews [1983] Director/Businesswoman; Christopher John Morrell [1950] Director; David John Morrell [1950] Director/Accountant; Jamie Paul Smith [1972] Director/Businessman

Morris Education Trust
Incorporated: 5 January 2012 *Employees:* 377
Previous: Impington Village College
Net Worth: £13,608,618 *Total Assets:* £16,478,094
Registered Office: Impington Village College, New Road, Impington, Cambridge, CB24 9LX
Activities: General secondary education
Officers: Jenna Louise Bickley, Secretary; Francis Difranco, Secretary; Robert Campbell [1966] Director/Headteacher; Joanne Garner [1976] Director; David Jenkins [1947] Director/Business Consultant; Martin Paul Rigby [1955] Director; Professor Alan Rodger [1951] Director/Scientist; Victoria Margaret Stubbs [1975] Director; Keith Thomson [1959] Director

Morrison Data Services (Water) Limited
Incorporated: 15 November 2002 *Employees:* 315
Previous: Meter U Limited
Net Worth: £3,612,000 *Total Assets:* £8,523,000
Registered Office: Abel Smith House, Gunnels Wood Road, Stevenage, Herts, SG1 2ST
Activities: Other service activities n.e.c.
Parent: Morrison Data Services Limited
Officers: Ian Vincent Cusden, Secretary; James Michael Arnold [1965] Director; Martin Geoffrey Beesley [1966] Director; Simon Best [1976] Director; Claire Helen Conolly [1975] Director; James Robert Winnicott [1968] Director

Morrison Data Services Limited
Incorporated: 5 July 1995 *Employees:* 1,956
Previous: G4S Utility and Outsourcing Services (UK) Limited
Net Worth: £13,393,000 *Total Assets:* £58,320,000
Registered Office: Abel Smith House, Gunnels Wood Road, Stevenage, Herts, SG1 2ST
Activities: Other professional, scientific and technical activities n.e.c.
Parent: M Group Services Limited
Officers: Ian Vincent Cusden, Secretary; James Michael Arnold [1965] Director; Martin Geoffrey Beesley [1966] Director; Simon Best [1976] Managing Director; Claire Helen Conolly [1975] Finance Director; James Robert Winnicott [1968] Director

Morrison Utility Services Holdings Limited
Incorporated: 19 February 2008
Net Worth Deficit: £124,945,000 *Total Assets:* £189,391,008
Registered Office: Abel Smith House, Gunnels Wood Road, Stevenage, Herts, SG1 2ST
Activities: Activities of head offices
Parent: Morrison Utility Services Investments Limited
Officers: Ian Vincent Cusden, Secretary/Accountant; James Michael Arnold [1965] Director/Chief Executive Officer; Martin Geoffrey Beesley [1966] Director/Accountant; Ian Vincent Cusden [1957] Director/Chartered Accountant; James Robert Winnicott [1968] Director

Morrison Utility Services Investments Limited
Incorporated: 19 February 2008
Net Worth Deficit: £15,891,000 *Total Assets:* £123,531,000
Registered Office: Abel Smith House, Gunnels Wood Road, Stevenage, Herts, SG1 2ST
Activities: Activities of head offices
Parent: Morrison Utility Services Group Limited
Officers: Ian Vincent Cusden, Secretary/Accountant; James Michael Arnold [1965] Director/Chief Executive Officer; Martin Geoffrey Beesley [1966] Director/Accountant; Ian Vincent Cusden [1957] Director/Chartered Accountant; James Robert Winnicott [1968] Director

Morrison Utility Services Limited
Incorporated: 10 September 2002 *Employees:* 4,234
Net Worth: £189,799,008 *Total Assets:* £382,244,000
Registered Office: Abel Smith House, Gunnels Wood Road, Stevenage, Herts, SG1 2ST
Activities: Construction of utility projects for electricity and telecommunications
Parent: Morrison Utility Services Holdings Limited
Officers: Ian Vincent Cusden, Secretary/Accountant; James Michael Arnold [1965] Director/Chief Executive; Martin Geoffrey Beesley [1966] Director/Accountant; Ian Vincent Cusden [1957] Director/Accountant; John Mark Edwards [1966] Executive Director; Adam Piers Gosnold [1963] Director; Jeremy Harrison [1964] Plant Director; Michael William Harrison [1955] Area Director; Trevor Matthew Hoyle [1965] Director; Sean Kelly [1967] Executive Director; Alain Hubertus Philomena Loosveld [1968] Director [Dutch]; Michael Standen [1967] Director/Construction Commercial Management; James Robert Winnicott [1968] Commercial Director

A.J. Morrisroe & Sons Limited
Incorporated: 1 March 1977 *Employees:* 83
Net Worth: £27,699,638 *Total Assets:* £83,417,040
Registered Office: Unit 4 Oaks Court, Warwick Road, Borehamwood, Herts, WD6 1GS
Activities: Construction of commercial buildings
Major Shareholder: Brian Quinlan Morrisroe
Officers: Brian Quinlan Morrisroe, Secretary; Daniel James Bannister [1976] Health & Safety Director; Michael Ioannou [1968] Commercial Director; Gerard Olaivar Marapao [1961] Director/Accountant; Brian Quinlan Morrisroe [1955] Managing Director

Morrisroe Group Limited
Incorporated: 14 November 2006 *Employees:* 208
Net Worth: £43,130,848 *Total Assets:* £108,799,408
Registered Office: Unit 4 Oaks Court, Warwick Road, Borehamwood, Herts, WD6 1GS
Activities: Other professional, scientific and technical activities n.e.c.
Major Shareholder: Brian Quinlan Morrisroe
Officers: Gerard Olaivar Marapao, Secretary/Chartered Accountant; Daniel James Bannister [1976] Health & Safety Director; Michael Ioannou [1968] Commercial Director; Gerard Olaivar Marapao [1961] Director/Certified Chartered Accountant; Brian Quinlan Morrisroe [1955] Managing Director

Mortgage Guarantee Limited
Incorporated: 27 March 1980 *Employees:* 4
Previous: Mortgage Guarantee PLC
Net Worth: £11,218,144 *Total Assets:* £11,380,622
Registered Office: Lynwood House, 373-375 Station Road, Harrow, Middlesex, HA1 2AW
Activities: Activities of mortgage finance companies
Major Shareholder: Kenneth Johnson
Officers: Linda Joyce Perrin, Secretary; Kenneth Johnson [1942] Director/Financier

H.C.Moss (Builders) Limited
Incorporated: 6 December 1965 *Employees:* 11
Net Worth: £10,299,898 *Total Assets:* £11,434,513
Registered Office: Unit 10 The Maltings, Millfield, Cottenham, Cambs, CB24 8RE
Activities: Construction of domestic buildings
Officers: Susan Carolyn Death, Secretary/Accounts Administrator; Susan Carolyn Death [1962] Director/Secretary; Paul Keith Ursell [1953] Director/Building Trade

The Mossbourne Federation
Incorporated: 24 June 2002 *Employees:* 37
Net Worth: £79,728,000 *Total Assets:* £84,459,000
Registered Office: Gardiner House, 6b Hemnall Street, Epping, Essex, CM16 4LW
Activities: General secondary education
Officers: Donald Hayes, Secretary; Lady Joy Hilary Bourne [1946] Director; Robert Leslie Feld [1951] Director/Chartered Accountant; Daniel John Flitterman [1965] Director; Donald Hayes [1934] Director; Geoffrey Norman Levy [1939] Director/Retired; Sylvie Pierce [1948] Director/MD Property Regeneration Company

Mothercare Group Limited (The)
Incorporated: 21 July 1927
Net Worth Deficit: £13,809,000 *Total Assets:* £70,013,000
Registered Office: Cherry Tree Road, Watford, Herts, WD24 6SH
Activities: Activities of head offices
Parent: Mothercare PLC
Officers: Lynne Samantha Medini, Secretary; Taimoor Anwar [1980] Director/Chartered Accountant [Pakistani]; Kirsty Rowena Homer [1974] HR Director

Mothercare PLC.
Incorporated: 26 September 1985 *Employees:* 4,737
Net Worth: £4,600,000 *Total Assets:* £276,700,000
Registered Office: Cherry Tree Road, Watford, Herts, WD24 6SH
Activities: Other retail sale of new goods in specialised stores (not commercial art galleries and opticians)
Officers: Lynne Samantha Medini, Secretary; William Glyn Lawrence Hughes [1976] Director/Chief Financial Officer; Gillian Dawn Celia Kent [1963] Director; Mark Newton-Jones [1967] Director; Nicholas Barry Edward Wharton [1966] Director; Clive Peter Whiley [1960] Director/Executive Chairman

Mothercare UK Limited
Incorporated: 8 May 1954 *Employees:* 2,604
Net Worth Deficit: £183,600,000 *Total Assets:* £231,000,000
Registered Office: Cherry Tree Road, Watford, Herts, WD24 6SH
Activities: Other retail sale of new goods in specialised stores (not commercial art galleries and opticians)
Parent: Mothercare (Holdings) Limited
Officers: Lynne Samantha Medini, Secretary; Kirsty Rowena Homer [1974] HR Director; William Glyn Lawrence Hughes [1976] Director/Chief Financial Officer; Mark Newton-Jones [1967] Director; Kevin Jonathan Rusling [1977] Managing Director, International

Mothers Ltd
Incorporated: 29 July 2005
Net Worth: £8,873,576 *Total Assets:* £18,980,012
Registered Office: 19-20 Bourne Court, Southend Road, Woodford Green, Essex, IG8 8HD
Activities: Buying and selling of own real estate
Parent: Spacious Developments Ltd
Officers: Jacob Schreiber, Secretary/Company Officer; Israel Moskovitz [1964] Director [Canadian]

Motherwell Holdings Limited
Incorporated: 7 November 2003 *Employees:* 63
Net Worth: £15,917,140 *Total Assets:* £24,807,754
Registered Office: Solus 31, Motherwell Way, West Thurrock, Essex, RM20 3LB
Activities: Activities of head offices
Shareholders: Andrew Douglas Hill; James Douglas Hill
Officers: James Douglas Hill, Secretary/Director; Andrew Douglas Hill [1931] Director; James Douglas Hill [1968] Director

Motivair Compressors Limited
Incorporated: 19 October 1967 *Employees:* 120
Net Worth: £3,033,690 *Total Assets:* £8,746,272
Registered Office: Victoria House, Britannia Road, Waltham Cross, Herts, EN8 7NU
Activities: Other manufacturing n.e.c.
Major Shareholder: Julian Paul Leach
Officers: Iain Beadle [1967] Director; Julian Paul Leach [1953] Director; Jon Andrew Victor Sopher [1965] Director/Consultant

Moto Finance PLC
Incorporated: 8 March 2011 *Employees:* 2
Net Worth: £50,000 *Total Assets:* £147,866,000
Registered Office: Toddington Services Area, Junction 11-12 Southbound, Toddington, Beds, LU5 6HR
Activities: Financial intermediation not elsewhere classified
Parent: Moto Ventures Limited
Officers: Julia Elson, Secretary; Kennedy McMeikan [1965] Director/C.E.O; Robert James Prynn [1964] Director/C.F.O

Moto Holdings Limited
Incorporated: 23 March 2006 *Employees:* 5,165
Net Worth: £178,935,008 *Total Assets:* £941,016,000
Registered Office: Toddington Services Area, Junction 11-12 M1 Southbound, Toddington, Beds, LU5 6HR
Activities: Activities of other holding companies n.e.c.
Parent: Universities Superannuation Scheme Limited
Officers: Julia Elson, Secretary; Kennedy McMeikan [1965] Director/C.E.O; Robert James Prynn [1964] Director/C.F.O

Moto Hospitality Limited
Incorporated: 3 September 1962 *Employees:* 5,165
Net Worth Deficit: £345,007,008 *Total Assets:* £915,643,008
Registered Office: Toddington Services Area, Junction 11-12 M1 Southbound, Toddington, Beds, LU5 6HR
Activities: Other retail sale in non-specialised stores
Parent: Moto Investments Limited
Officers: Julia Elson, Secretary; Kennedy McMeikan [1965] Director/C.E.O; Robert James Prynn [1964] Director

Moto Investments Limited
Incorporated: 23 March 2006 *Employees:* 5,165
Net Worth Deficit: £763,091,008 *Total Assets:* £944,910,016
Registered Office: Toddington Services Area, Junction 11-12 M1 Southbound, Toddington, Beds, LU5 6HR
Activities: Activities of other holding companies n.e.c.
Parent: Moto Ventures Limited
Officers: Julia Elson, Secretary; Kennedy McMeikan [1965] Director/C.E.O; Robert James Prynn [1964] Director/C.F.O

Moto Ventures Limited
Incorporated: 28 March 2006 *Employees:* 5,165
Net Worth: £180,580,992 *Total Assets:* £942,611,008
Registered Office: Toddington Services Area, Junction 11-12 M1 Southbound, Toddington, Beds, LU5 6HR
Activities: Activities of other holding companies n.e.c.
Parent: Moto Holdings Limited
Officers: Julia Elson, Secretary; Kennedy McMeikan [1965] Director/C.E.O; Robert James Prynn [1964] Director

Motocaddy Holdings Limited
Incorporated: 16 June 2010 *Employees:* 45
Net Worth: £9,127,681 *Total Assets:* £12,157,212
Registered Office: Stansted Distribution Centre, Start Hill, Great Hallingbury, Herts, CM22 7DG
Activities: Activities of other holding companies n.e.c.
Shareholders: Antony Webb; John David Wells
Officers: Roderick Anthony Brown [1972] Director; John Peter Helas [1968] Director; Neil Robert Parker [1962] Director; Antony Webb [1965] Managing Director; John David Wells [1961] Director

Motocaddy Limited
Incorporated: 16 July 2004 *Employees:* 45
Net Worth: £10,849,447 *Total Assets:* £12,088,785
Registered Office: Units 16-17 Stansted Distribution Centre, Start Hill, Bishop's Stortford, Herts, CM22 7DG
Activities: Manufacture of sports goods
Parent: Motocaddy Holdings Limited
Officers: Roderick Anthony Brown [1972] Director; John Peter Helas [1968] Director; Neil Robert Parker [1962] Sales Director; Paul Straker [1965] Director; Antony Webb [1965] Managing Director; John David Wells [1961] Director/Chairman

Motor Fuel Limited
Incorporated: 16 August 2004 *Employees:* 70
Net Worth: £112,405,000 *Total Assets:* £600,638,016
Registered Office: Gladstone Place, 36-38 Upper Marlborough Road, St Albans, Herts, AL1 3UU
Activities: Retail sale of automotive fuel in specialised stores
Parent: Scimitar Topco Limited
Officers: Timothy Edward Douglas Allan [1966] Director; William Bahlsen Bannister [1967] Director/Development Manager; Thomas McKenzie Biggart [1966] Director/Surveyor; Jeremy Clarke [1963] Managing Director

Motor Parts Direct Limited
Incorporated: 28 July 1998 *Employees:* 1,015
Net Worth: £12,447,331 *Total Assets:* £45,425,640
Registered Office: Unit 7 Optima Business Park, Pindar Road, Hoddesdon, Herts, EN11 0DY
Activities: Maintenance and repair of motor vehicles
Officers: Ninna Shah, Secretary; Darshni Shah [1994] Director; Kiran Zaverchand Shah [1957] Director/Business Manager; Mukesh Zaverchand Shah [1960] Director/Business Partner; Neeta Shah [1980] Director; Ninna Shah [1964] Director and Company Secretary; Priyen Shah [1996] Director; Sagar Shah [1988] Director

Motorclean Group Limited
Incorporated: 1 March 2005
Net Worth: £405,951 *Total Assets:* £13,056,928
Registered Office: 25 Hornsby Square, Southfields Industrial Park, Laindon, Essex, SS15 6SD
Activities: Activities of head offices
Parent: Fullfield Limited
Officers: Paul Anthony Cranwell [1966] Director; John Nicholas Hammond [1968] Sales Director; David Terance Warren [1967] Director

Motorclean Limited
Incorporated: 19 October 1984 *Employees:* 168
Net Worth: £12,701,907 *Total Assets:* £21,524,038
Registered Office: 25 Hornsby Square, Southfields Industrial Park, Laindon, Essex, SS15 6SD
Activities: Other professional, scientific and technical activities n.e.c.
Parent: Motorclean Group Limited
Officers: Paul Anthony Cranwell [1966] Director; John Nicholas Hammond [1968] Sales Director; David Terance Warren [1967] Director

Motus Group (UK) Limited
Incorporated: 23 March 1960 *Employees:* 1,157
Previous: Imperial Commercials Ltd
Net Worth: £23,186,000 *Total Assets:* £105,122,000
Registered Office: Ground Floor, Oakingham House, West Wing, London Road, Loudwater, High Wycombe, Bucks, HP11 1JU
Activities: Sale of other motor vehicles
Parent: Motus Holdings (UK) Ltd
Officers: Andrew Barrie Welch, Finance Director; Osman Suluman Arbee [1959] Director [South African]; Matthew Derek Lawrenson [1970] Divisional Executive Director; Philip Bernard Michaux [1960] Director [South African]; Andrew Barrie Welch [1965] Finance Director

Motus Holdings (UK) Limited
Incorporated: 12 September 2005
Previous: IH Mobility Holdings (UK) Limited
Net Worth: £20,692,748 *Total Assets:* £42,667,856
Registered Office: Ground Floor, Oakingham House, West Wing, London Road, Loudwater, High Wycombe, Bucks, HP11 1JU
Activities: Activities of head offices
Officers: Andrew Barrie Welch, Secretary/Director; Osman Suluman Arbee [1959] Director [South African]; Philip Bernard Michaux [1960] Director [South African]; Andrew Barrie Welch [1965] Director

Moulton Bulb Company Limited
Incorporated: 24 February 1964 *Employees:* 242
Net Worth: £12,595,600 *Total Assets:* £20,634,594
Registered Office: Long Lane, Moulton, Spalding, Lincs, PE12 6PP
Activities: Other processing and preserving of fruit and vegetables
Shareholders: Denis John Grimwood; Robert Henry Oldershaw Snr
Officers: Jane Roberta Ashby Cooke, Secretary; Jane Roberta Ashby Cooke [1949] Director; Alfred Richard Greetham [1962] Director/Packhouse Manager; Denis John Grimwood [1945] Director/Farmers Onion Grower; David William Hodgson [1946] Managing Director; Robert Henry Oldershaw Jnr [1979] Director/Account Manager; Robert Henry Oldershaw Snr [1952] Director/Farmer & Onion Grower; Bridgett Lucy Posey [1958] Director; Christopher Jamie Woodrow [1977] Director

Mount Grace School
Incorporated: 6 July 2011 *Employees:* 108
Net Worth: £11,566,370 *Total Assets:* £12,742,163
Registered Office: Mount Grace School, Church Road, Potters Bar, Herts, EN6 1EZ
Activities: General secondary education
Officers: Paul Seymour, Secretary; Peter Robert Baker [1959] Director/Headteacher; Christopher Cardell-Williams [1946] Director; Janice Diane Couzens [1949] Director/Deputy CEO; Colin Ronald Daniel [1960] Director/Electrical Engineer; Karis Anne Folan [1975] Director; Helen Margaret Frost [1945] Director/Retired; Dawn Gamble [1965] Director/HR Manager; Philip Harding [1960] Finance Director; Sarah Julia Haws [1971] Director/Finance Assistant; Victoria Horne [1983] Director/Teacher; Jean Evelyn Mackie [1949] Director; Paul Michael Pytches [1959] Director/Teacher; David Redington [1952] Director

Mountcharm (S.E.) Limited
Incorporated: 6 October 2000
Net Worth: £9,094,645 *Total Assets:* £11,910,514
Registered Office: Northside House, Mount Pleasant, Barnet, Herts, EN4 9EE
Activities: Buying and selling of own real estate
Shareholder: Melvyn Frank Cooper
Officers: Jason Robert Cooper, Secretary/Director; Adam Cooper [1971] Director; Jason Robert Cooper [1967] Director; Melvyn Frank Cooper [1941] Director

Mountcharm Limited
Incorporated: 12 December 1994 *Employees:* 4
Net Worth: £32,150,532 *Total Assets:* £59,818,216
Registered Office: Northside House, Mount Pleasant, Barnet, Herts, EN4 9EE
Activities: Other service activities n.e.c.
Shareholder: Melvyn Frank Cooper
Officers: Jason Robert Cooper, Secretary/Director; Adam Cooper [1971] Director; Jason Robert Cooper [1967] Director; Melvyn Frank Cooper [1941] Director

Mountfield Group PLC
Incorporated: 18 September 2007 *Employees:* 25
Net Worth: £5,352,877 *Total Assets:* £11,414,190
Registered Office: 3c Sopwith Crescent, Wickford Business Park, Wickford, Essex, SS11 8YU
Activities: Activities of head offices
Shareholder: Graham John Read
Officers: Peter Harry Jay, Secretary; Andrew Collins [1964] Director; Peter Harry Jay [1944] Director/Solicitor; Graham John Read [1956] Director

Mouskos & Sons Co. Limited
Incorporated: 7 February 1969 *Employees:* 3
Net Worth: £8,024,588 *Total Assets:* £9,782,518
Registered Office: 1st Floor, Woodgate Studios, 2-8 Games Road, Cockfosters, Herts, EN4 9HN
Activities: Hotels and similar accommodation
Parent: Mouskos Holdings Limited
Officers: Christopher Mouskos, Secretary; Christopher Mouskos [1961] Director/Businessman; John Mouskos [1964] Director/Businessman

Mouskos Capital Limited
Incorporated: 17 February 2016
Net Worth: £23,987,352 *Total Assets:* £23,990,352
Registered Office: 1st Floor, Woodgate Studios, 2-8 Games Road, Cockfosters, Barnet, Herts, EN4 9HN
Activities: Activities of head offices
Shareholders: Christopher Mouskos; John Michael Mouskos; Geraldina Mouskos
Officers: Generaldina Mouskos, Secretary; Christopher Mouskos [1961] Director; Generaldina Mouskos [1936] Director; John Michael Mouskos [1964] Director

Mouskos Holdings Limited
Incorporated: 17 February 2016
Net Worth: £27,218,164 *Total Assets:* £27,300,036
Registered Office: 1st Floor, Woodgate Studios, 2-8 Games Road, Cockfosters, Barnet, Herts, EN4 9HN
Activities: Activities of head offices
Shareholders: Christopher Mouskos; John Michael Mouskos; Geraldina Mouskos
Officers: Generaldina Mouskos, Secretary; Christopher Mouskos [1961] Director; Generaldina Mouskos [1936] Director; John Michael Mouskos [1964] Director

Mouskos LLP
Incorporated: 12 December 2012
Net Worth: £49,189,968 *Total Assets:* £49,201,652
Registered Office: 1st Floor, Woodgate Studios, 2-8 Games Road, Cockfosters, Herts, EN4 9HN

Movac Group Limited
Incorporated: 30 October 1975 *Employees:* 123
Net Worth: £1,776,431 *Total Assets:* £9,872,440
Registered Office: 11 Portman Road, Ipswich, Suffolk, IP1 2BP
Activities: Retail sale of hardware, paints and glass in specialised stores
Major Shareholder: Mark Clinton Peter Smith
Officers: Robert William Lang, Secretary; Mark Clinton Peter Smith [1959] Director

Movac Holdings Limited
Incorporated: 30 November 2001 *Employees:* 123
Net Worth: £1,348,870 *Total Assets:* £9,444,879
Registered Office: 11 Portman Road, Ipswich, Suffolk, IP1 2BP
Activities: Agents specialised in the sale of other particular products
Major Shareholder: Mark Clinton Peter Smith
Officers: Robert William Lang, Secretary; Mark Clinton Peter Smith [1959] Director

MoveWithUs Conveyancing Limited
Incorporated: 10 July 2001 *Employees:* 60
Net Worth: £23,314,574 *Total Assets:* £34,170,176
Registered Office: Grant Hall, St Ives Business Park, Parsons Green, St Ives, Cambs, PE27 4AA
Activities: Other service activities n.e.c.
Parent: Move with Us Limited
Officers: Robert Matson, Secretary; Benjamin Paul Greco [1979] Director; David Jeremy Grossman [1970] Director; Robert Matson [1970] Director/Chartered Accountant

Mowbray Indigo Limited
Incorporated: 13 February 2008 *Employees:* 2
Net Worth: £4,124,142 *Total Assets:* £9,554,123
Registered Office: 36 Phillips Court, Water Street, Stamford, Lincs, PE9 2EE
Activities: Dental practice activities
Major Shareholder: Christopher George Sprinz
Officers: Christopher George Sprinz [1959] Director

Mr. Fothergill's Seeds Limited
Incorporated: 30 March 1983 *Employees:* 160
Net Worth: £9,746,796 *Total Assets:* £18,125,452
Registered Office: Gazeley Road, Kentford, Newmarket, Suffolk, CB8 7QB
Activities: Other manufacturing n.e.c.
Officers: Phillip James Hurst, Secretary; David Andrew Carey [1970] Sales Director; John Stephen Fothergill [1971] Export Director; Phillip James Hurst [1983] Finance Director; Timothy Christopher Jeffries [1957] Commercial Director; Jeremy Sharp [1971] Production Director

MRB Holdings Ltd
Incorporated: 20 December 2004
Net Worth: £2,232,355 *Total Assets:* £18,909,664
Registered Office: Hunters House, 109 Snakes Lane West, Woodford Green, Essex, IG8 0DY
Activities: Other business support service activities n.e.c.
Major Shareholder: Martin Roderick Brown
Officers: Anne Brown, Secretary; Martin Roderick Brown [1947] Director

MRBL Limited
Incorporated: 13 August 2012
Net Worth: £39,800,000 *Total Assets:* £154,090,000
Registered Office: Tempsford Hall, Sandy, Beds, SG19 2BD
Activities: Activities of other holding companies n.e.c.
Parent: Kier Limited
Officers: Bethan Melges, Secretary; Marcus Faughey Jones [1970] Finance Director; David James Wright [1959] Managing Director

MRH (GB) Limited
Incorporated: 4 September 2007 *Employees:* 747
Net Worth: £737,779,008 *Total Assets:* £1,289,891,968
Registered Office: Gladstone Place, 36-38 Upper Marlborough Road, St Albans, Herts, AL1 3UU
Activities: Activities of head offices
Parent: LSF9 Robin Investments Limited
Officers: David Hathaway, Secretary; William Bahlsen Bannister [1967] Director/Chief Executive; Jeremy Clarke [1963] Director/Chief Operating Officer; Simon Paul Lane [1963] Director/Chief Financial Officer

MSCM Limited
Incorporated: 11 November 1999 *Employees:* 99
Net Worth: £13,115,207 *Total Assets:* £17,119,856
Registered Office: MSCM Subsea Technology & Development Facility, Coronation Road, Cressex Business Park, High Wycombe, Bucks, HP12 3TA
Activities: Manufacture of pumps
Major Shareholder: John Merryfield
Officers: Patrick Joseph Cosgrove, Secretary; Patrick Joseph Cosgrove [1952] Director; Mark Dixon Lowther [1960] Managing Director; Neil Robinson [1963] Director; Kim Irene White [1965] Finance Director

MSHA International Ltd.
Incorporated: 13 September 1991 *Employees:* 930
Net Worth: £10,422,072 *Total Assets:* £35,705,724
Registered Office: The Pavilion, Rosslyn Crescent, Harrow, Middlesex, HA1 2SZ
Activities: Activities of head offices
Parent: MSHA Holdings Ltd
Officers: Hamid Ali [1956] Director

MSX International Limited
Incorporated: 24 September 1985 *Employees:* 652
Net Worth: £42,351,000 *Total Assets:* £334,536,992
Registered Office: The Octagon, Middleborough, Colchester, Essex, CO1 1TG
Activities: Other business support service activities n.e.c.
Parent: MSXI UK Limited
Officers: Sam Richard Del Mar [1974] Director/Chief Financial Officer; Frederick Karl Minturn [1956] Director/VP Controller OEM Auto Operations [American]

MSXI UK Limited
Incorporated: 30 August 2007
Net Worth Deficit: £4,259,000 *Total Assets:* £294,891,008
Registered Office: The Octagon, Middleborough, Colchester, Essex, CO1 1TG
Activities: Activities of other holding companies n.e.c.
Parent: Pacific (BC) Bidco Limited
Officers: Sam Richard Del Mar [1974] Director/Chief Financial Officer; Frederick Karl Minturn [1956] Director/Vice-President Controller [American]

MTALX Limited
Incorporated: 23 February 2010 *Employees:* 8
Previous: Prospero Metals Limited
Net Worth: £7,229,434 *Total Assets:* £28,795,316
Registered Office: Lynwood House, 373-375 Station Road, Harrow, Middlesex, HA1 2AW
Activities: Management consultancy activities other than financial management
Parent: Prospero Global Holdings Limited
Officers: Daniel Harvey Goldberg [1960] Director/Commodity Trader; Isaac Goldberg [1991] Director; Amos Jessurun Wittenberg [1951] Director [Dutch]

MTCE Limited
Incorporated: 13 May 1992 *Employees:* 190
Net Worth: £1,222,681 *Total Assets:* £46,017,740
Registered Office: Shakespeare House, 42 Newmarket Road, Cambridge, CB5 8EP
Activities: Manufacture of motor vehicles
Parent: Multimatic Limited
Officers: Stefan Proniuk, Secretary; Stefan Theodor Proniuk [1958] Director/Barrister and Solicitor [Canadian]; Michael Spence [1973] Director/Chief Financial Officer [Canadian]

MTK Wireless Limited
Incorporated: 13 August 2007 *Employees:* 113
Net Worth: £80,352,632 *Total Assets:* £84,693,952
Registered Office: Building 2010, Cambourne Business Park, Cambourne, Cambridge, CB23 6DW
Activities: Wireless telecommunications activities
Officers: Ku TA-Wei, Secretary; Kou-Hung Loh [1960] Director [Taiwanese]; Ku TA-Wei [1969] Director [Taiwanese]

The MTL Instruments Group Limited
Incorporated: 14 December 1984
Net Worth: £57,973,000 *Total Assets:* £60,413,000
Registered Office: Great Marlings, Butterfield, Luton, Beds, LU2 8DL
Activities: Manufacture of electronic industrial process control equipment
Parent: Eaton Industries (U.K.) Limited
Officers: Philippe Patrick Andre Delsaut [1969] Director/Senior Counsel [Belgian]; Cyril Grandjean [1982] Director/Treasury Manager [Swiss]

MTS (Holdings) Limited
Incorporated: 20 January 1995 *Employees:* 82
Net Worth Deficit: £39,754,000 *Total Assets:* £43,478,000
Registered Office: Tomline House, The Dock, Felixstowe, Suffolk, IP11 3SY
Activities: Activities of other holding companies n.e.c.
Shareholders: London Thamesport Investments Limited; Hutchison Ports (UK) Limited
Officers: Simon Richard Mullett, Secretary; Da-Chih Chang [1963] Director [Taiwanese]; Clemence Chun Fun Cheng [1958] Director; Sing Chi IP [1953] Director [Chinese]; Edith Shih [1952] Director

Mulalley & Co. Limited
Incorporated: 15 December 1980 *Employees:* 507
Net Worth: £61,513,000 *Total Assets:* £107,964,000
Registered Office: Teresa Gavin House, Woodford Avenue, Woodford Green, Essex, IG8 8FA
Activities: Construction of commercial buildings
Parent: Sherrygreen Ltd
Officers: Eamon O'Malley, Secretary; Brendan O'Malley [1954] Director; Eamon O'Malley [1955] Director; Vincent O'Malley [1951] Director; Teresa Taylor [1963] Director

Mulcroft Limited
Incorporated: 31 October 1989 *Employees:* 293
Net Worth: £3,307,172 *Total Assets:* £8,559,722
Registered Office: First Floor, Kirkland House, 11-15 Peterborough Road, Harrow, Middlesex, HA1 2AX
Activities: Unlicenced restaurants and cafes
Parent: Fieldrose Limited
Officers: Maya Bharat Patel, Secretary; Bharat Chandubhai Patel [1964] Director/Businessman; Maya Bharat Patel [1965] Director/Secretary

Multimatic Ltd.
Incorporated: 20 May 1996 *Employees:* 633
Net Worth Deficit: £1,788,790 *Total Assets:* £74,386,488
Registered Office: Shakespeare House, 42 Newmarket Road, Cambridge, CB5 8EP
Activities: Manufacture of other parts and accessories for motor vehicles
Major Shareholder: Peter Czapka
Officers: Stefan Proniuk, Secretary; Stefan Theodor Proniuk [1958] Director/Barrister and Solicitor [Canadian]; Michael Spence [1973] Director/Chief Financial Officer [Canadian]

Multitrust Property Investments Limited
Incorporated: 23 May 1991
Net Worth: £218,791 *Total Assets:* £15,567,156
Registered Office: Unicorn House, Station Close, Potters Bar, Herts, EN6 1TL
Activities: Buying and selling of own real estate
Parent: Panther Securities PLC
Officers: Simon Jeffrey Peters, Secretary; Andrew Stewart Perloff [1944] Director; John Henry Perloff [1968] Director; Simon Jeffrey Peters [1977] Director

Mumford & Wood Limited
Incorporated: 20 July 1961 *Employees:* 102
Net Worth: £5,190,854 *Total Assets:* £9,543,218
Registered Office: Tower Business Park, Kelvedon Road, Tiptree, Essex, CO5 0LX
Activities: Manufacture of other builders' carpentry and joinery
Officers: Richard John Haycocks [1949] Director/Chartered Accountant; Dion Lee Panting [1970] Director; Jay Pengelly [1974] Director; Timothy Roy Wakeman [1946] Director

Mumford's Mill Rentals Limited
Incorporated: 10 March 2005
Net Worth: £1,971,170 *Total Assets:* £10,236,803
Registered Office: Unex House, Bourges Boulevard, Peterborough, Cambs, PE1 1NG
Activities: Other letting and operating of own or leased real estate
Shareholder: Charles John Yarborough
Officers: Lord Charles John Yarborough [1963] Director/Landowner

Mundibiopharma Limited
Incorporated: 21 October 2014 *Employees:* 10
Net Worth Deficit: £19,397,526 *Total Assets:* £75,442,888
Registered Office: Unit 196 Cambridge Science Park, Milton Road, Cambridge, CB4 0AB
Activities: Wholesale of pharmaceutical goods
Shareholders: Hermance Bernadette Monique Schaepman; Jonathan David Sackler; Richard Stephen Sackler
Officers: Stuart David Baker [1935] Director/Lawyer [American]; Bryan George LEA [1961] Director/Lawyer; Alberto Martinez [1972] Director [Spanish]; David Alan Silver [1965] Director/Accountant; Ake Gunnar Wikstrom [1951] Director/Advisor [Swedish]

Mundipharma International Limited
Incorporated: 9 November 1992 *Employees:* 151
Net Worth: £11,108,000 *Total Assets:* £22,263,000
Registered Office: Unit 196 Cambridge Science Park, Milton Road, Cambridge, CB4 0AB
Activities: Management consultancy activities other than financial management
Shareholder: Leslie John Schreyer
Officers: Stuart David Baker [1935] Director/Attorney [American]; Anna Maria Ingemarsdotter Kjellberg [1960] EU Director of People and Business Transformation [Swedish]; Peter James McGowan [1965] Director/Accountant [Australian/British]; David Alan Silver [1965] Director; Christopher Paul Surridge [1979] European Director of Strategy; Ake Gunnar Wikstrom [1951] Director/Advisor [Swedish]

Mundipharma Research Limited
Incorporated: 4 December 2002 *Employees:* 249
Net Worth: £16,725,000 *Total Assets:* £59,977,000
Registered Office: Unit 194 Cambridge Science Park, Milton Road, Cambridge, CB4 0AB
Activities: Other research and experimental development on natural sciences and engineering
Shareholder: Stuart David Baker
Officers: Stuart David Baker [1935] Lawyer & Director [American]; Dr Julie Ducharme [1966] Managing Director [Canadian]; Mohammed Gibril Mansaray [1968] Executive Director of Regulatory Affairs; Ake Gunnar Wikstrom [1951] Director/Advisor [Swedish]

Munnelly Group PLC
Incorporated: 8 June 2005 *Employees:* 108
Previous: Munnelly Group Limited
Net Worth: £6,690,000 *Total Assets:* £22,497,000
Registered Office: Munnelly House, 84-88 Pinner Road, Harrow, Middlesex, HA1 4LP
Activities: Activities of head offices
Major Shareholder: Philip Anthony Munnelly
Officers: Gareth Brewerton, Secretary; Christopher Mark Harrison [1981] Director/Chief Financial Officer; James Philip Munnelly [1983] Director; Paul David Munnelly [1986] Director; Paul Vincent Munnelly [1960] Director/Building Contractor; Philip Anthony Munnelly [1955] Director; William James Walter Noble [1979] Director

Munnelly Support Services Limited
Incorporated: 23 March 1982 *Employees:* 85
Net Worth: £5,791,000 *Total Assets:* £15,170,000
Registered Office: Munnelly House, 84-88 Pinner Road, Harrow, Middlesex, HA1 4LP
Activities: Other specialised construction activities n.e.c.
Parent: Munnelly Group PLC
Officers: Gareth Brewerton, Secretary; Christopher Mark Harrison [1981] Director/Chief Financial Officer; James Philip Munnelly [1983] Commercial Director; Paul David Munnelly [1986] Director/Procurement; Paul Vincent Munnelly [1960] Director/Building Contractor; Philip Anthony Munnelly [1955] Director/Building Contractor; William James Walter Noble [1979] Director/Commercial Executive

Munro Holdings (Cambridge) Limited
Incorporated: 9 February 2015 *Employees:* 75
Net Worth: £4,898,264 *Total Assets:* £10,924,094
Registered Office: 9 Quy Court, Colliers Lane, Stow-Cum-Quy, Cambridge, CB25 9AU
Activities: Activities of head offices
Officers: David John Murdoch Munro [1950] Director; Malcolm Ian Watson [1954] Director

Muntons (Holdings) PLC
Incorporated: 19 June 1979 *Employees:* 315
Net Worth: £36,584,000 *Total Assets:* £84,695,000
Registered Office: Cedars Maltings, Stowmarket, Suffolk, IP14 2AG
Activities: Activities of head offices
Officers: Paul Douglas Chamberlain, Secretary; Dr Nigel Leslie Davies [1960] Director; Steven George Miller [1960] Director; Neil Andrew Pearmain [1964] Director; Andrew John Simpson [1964] Director; Mark William Rawdon Slim [1960] Director/Property Consultant; Timothy John Stonehouse [1960] Director; John Walter Sutcliffe [1950] Director; Mark Robert Tyldesley [1969] Director; Paul Richard Wells [1958] Director

Muntons PLC
Incorporated: 27 September 1921 *Employees:* 315
Net Worth: £35,595,000 *Total Assets:* £83,778,000
Registered Office: Cedars Maltings, Stowmarket, Suffolk, IP14 2AG
Activities: Manufacture of malt
Parent: Muntons (Holdings) PLC
Officers: Paul Douglas Chamberlain, Secretary; Dr Nigel Leslie Davies [1960] Director; Steven George Miller [1960] Director; Neil Andrew Pearmain [1964] Director; Andrew John Simpson [1964] Director; Mark William Rawdon Slim [1960] Director/Property Consultant; Timothy John Stonehouse [1960] Director; John Walter Sutcliffe [1950] Director; Mark Robert Tyldesley [1969] Director; Paul Richard Wells [1958] Director

Muraspec Decorative Solutions Limited
Incorporated: 14 May 1998 *Employees:* 189
Net Worth: £13,639,000 *Total Assets:* £21,036,000
Registered Office: Zodiac 2, Boundary Way, Hemel Hempstead Industrial Estate, Hemel Hempstead, Herts, HP2 7SJ
Activities: Manufacture of wallpaper
Shareholder: Tariq Rashid
Officers: Stephen Luke, Secretary; Said Amin Amiri [1956] Director/Financier; Tariq Rashid [1958] Finance Director

Murfitts Industries Limited
Incorporated: 12 June 2000 *Employees:* 62
Net Worth: £9,756,368 *Total Assets:* £13,456,248
Registered Office: Station Road, Lakenheath, Brandon, Suffolk, IP27 9AD
Activities: Manufacture of other rubber products
Parent: Murfitts Group Limited
Officers: Jayne Clare Phillips, Secretary; Mark James Murfitt [1962] Director; Rebecca Shelly Murfitt [1962] Director; Jayne Clare Phillips [1977] Finance Director

Murkett Brothers (Holdings) Limited
Incorporated: 18 July 2002 *Employees:* 98
Net Worth: £9,135,842 *Total Assets:* £13,016,665
Registered Office: 137 Histon Road, Cambridge, CB4 3JD
Activities: Activities of head offices
Shareholders: Nigel Anthony Murkett; Simon David Murkett
Officers: Nigel Anthony Murkett, Secretary; Alwyn David Murkett [1934] Director/Automobile Engineer; Nigel Anthony Murkett [1955] Director/Automobile Engineer; Simon David Murkett [1965] Director/Automobile Engineer

Murkett Brothers Limited
Incorporated: 12 April 1972 *Employees:* 10
Net Worth: £5,972,332 *Total Assets:* £9,655,599
Registered Office: 137 Histon Road, Cambridge, CB4 3JD
Activities: Maintenance and repair of motor vehicles
Parent: Murkett Brothers Holdings Ltd
Officers: Nigel Anthony Murkett, Secretary; Alwyn David Murkett [1934] Director/Automobile Engineer; Nigel Anthony Murkett [1955] Director/Automobile Engineer; Simon David Murkett [1965] Director/Automobile Engineer

Musco (St Albans Place) Ltd
Incorporated: 25 January 2013
Net Worth Deficit: £2,183,054 *Total Assets:* £12,563,735
Registered Office: Wood Hall Farm Office, Woodhall Lane, Shenley, Herts, WD7 9AA
Activities: Development of building projects
Shareholders: Musco Developments Ltd; Roca Investments Ltd
Officers: Iain Williamson, Secretary; Andrew Lynton Cohen [1953] Director; Walid Wasfi Wasif Musmar [1974] Director; Iain Williamson [1972] Director/Chartered Accountant

Mustard Global Limited
Incorporated: 8 October 2015
Net Worth: £147,797,872 *Total Assets:* £147,909,088
Registered Office: St John's Place, Easton Street, High Wycombe, Bucks, HP11 1NL
Activities: Activities of other holding companies n.e.c.
Parent: Mustard Holdings Limited
Officers: Judith Bean, Secretary; Lisa Agar-Rea [1968] Director; Peter Wynne Davies [1949] Director; Stuart Antony Grant [1975] Director; Kara Eugenie Groves [1969] Director; Elizabeth Claire Houghton [1964] Director; Benjamin Joseph Lewis [1967] Director; Bernard Lewis [1926] Director; Clive Robert Lewis [1956] Director

MVM Holdings Limited
Incorporated: 15 March 1995
Net Worth: £10,723,000 *Total Assets:* £12,993,000
Registered Office: Peoplebuilding 2, Peoplebuilding Estate, Maylands Avenue, Hemel Hempstead Industrial Estate, Hemel Hempstead, Herts, HP2 4NW
Activities: Dormant company
Parent: Northgate Public Services (UK) Limited
Officers: Stephen James Callaghan [1960] Director

MY Construction & Carpentry Limited
Incorporated: 31 January 2005 *Employees:* 38
Net Worth: £5,761,134 *Total Assets:* £18,180,600
Registered Office: 103 High Street, Waltham Cross, Herts, EN8 7AN
Activities: Development of building projects
Shareholder: Yoav Tal
Officers: Yoav Tal [1970] Director/Civil Engineer [Israeli]

Myatt's Field Development LLP
Incorporated: 16 March 2012
Net Worth: £227,968 *Total Assets:* £23,142,160
Registered Office: 1 Langston Road, Loughton, Essex, IG10 3SD

Myddleton London Limited
Incorporated: 20 September 2011 *Employees:* 23
Net Worth: £19,099,908 *Total Assets:* £21,065,404
Registered Office: Francis House, 2 Park Road, High Barnet, Barnet, Herts, EN5 5RN
Activities: Activities of other holding companies n.e.c.
Major Shareholder: Philip Silver
Officers: Debra Silver, Secretary; Philip Silver [1959] Director

Mylan Holdings Acquisition 2 Limited
Incorporated: 22 August 2016
Net Worth: £438,781,632 *Total Assets:* £438,799,488
Registered Office: Trident Place, Building 4, Mosquito Way, Hatfield, Herts, AL10 9UL
Activities: Activities of other holding companies n.e.c.
Parent: Mylan N.V.
Officers: Alan Weiner, Secretary; John Paul Llewellyn Munson [1965] Director/Head of Global Accounts; Alan Weiner [1962] Director [American]

Mylan Holdings Acquisition Limited
Incorporated: 5 August 2016
Net Worth: £3,791,208,704 *Total Assets:* £3,811,553,024
Registered Office: Trident Place, Building 4, Mosquito Way, Hatfield, Herts, AL10 9UL
Activities: Activities of other holding companies n.e.c.
Parent: Mylan N.V.
Officers: Alan Weiner, Secretary; John Paul Llewellyn Munson [1965] Director/Head of Global Accounts; Alan Weiner [1962] Director [American]

Mylan Holdings Ltd.
Incorporated: 9 February 2015
Net Worth: £20,995,215,360 *Total Assets:* £20,996,255,744
Registered Office: Trident Place, Building 4, Mosquito Way, Hatfield, Herts, AL10 9UL
Activities: Activities of other holding companies n.e.c.
Parent: Mylan N.V.
Officers: Alan Weiner, Secretary; John Paul Llewellyn Munson [1965] Director/Mylan VP Global Accounts; Alan Weiner [1962] Director [American]

Mylan Pharma UK Limited
Incorporated: 8 November 2011 *Employees:* 141
Net Worth: £29,811,000 *Total Assets:* £44,497,000
Registered Office: 20 Station Close, Potters Bar, Herts, EN6 1TL
Activities: Other research and experimental development on natural sciences and engineering
Parent: McDermott Laboratories Limited
Officers: Caroline Rebecca Louise Dixon, Secretary; Dr Walter Grant Cook [1967] Managing Director; Caroline Rebecca Louise Dixon [1968] Finance Director

Mylan UK Healthcare Limited
Incorporated: 28 August 2014 *Employees:* 29
Previous: BGP Products Ltd.
Net Worth: £18,299,000 *Total Assets:* £94,587,000
Registered Office: 20 Station Close, Potters Bar, Herts, EN6 1TL
Activities: Wholesale of pharmaceutical goods
Parent: Mylan Holdings Ltd
Officers: Falk Patrick Nuernberger, Secretary; Jean-Yves Brault [1967] Director/General Manager [Canadian]; Caroline Rebecca Louise Dixon [1968] Finance Director

Myriad Capital PLC
Incorporated: 29 November 2013
Net Worth: £196,000 *Total Assets:* £219,074,000
Registered Office: 33 Springfield Lyons Approach, Springfield, Chelmsford, Essex, CM2 5LB
Activities: Financial intermediation not elsewhere classified
Parent: Chelmer Housing Partnership Ltd
Officers: Jeremy John Jacobs, Secretary; Paul Leslie Edwards [1978] Director of Resources; Mary Joyce Gibbons [1973] Director/Chief Executive; Nicola Mary Sawford [1965] Director

Myriad Healthcare Holdings Limited
Incorporated: 27 November 2015 *Employees:* 6,213
Net Worth: £112,692,000 *Total Assets:* £155,879,008
Registered Office: Bradbury House, 830 The Crescent, Colchester Business Park, Colchester, Essex, CO4 9YQ
Activities: Residential nursing care facilities
Major Shareholder: Paul Anthony Keith Jeffery
Officers: Peter Martin Hill [1968] Director; Paul Anthony Keith Jeffrey [1966] Director/Accountant; Nigel Bennett Schofield [1950] Director

Mytravel Group Limited
Incorporated: 3 December 1962
Net Worth: £420,700,000 *Total Assets:* £2,188,100,096
Registered Office: Westpoint, Peterborough Business Park, Lynch Wood, Peterborough, Cambs, PE2 6FZ
Activities: Other business support service activities n.e.c.
Parent: Thomas Cook Investments (2) Limited
Officers: Shirley Bradley, Secretary; Alan Charles Donald [1963] Director

Mytravel North America Limited
Incorporated: 21 March 2001
Net Worth Deficit: £299,224,864 *Total Assets:* £53,028,248
Registered Office: Westpoint, Peterborough Business Park, Lynch Wood, Peterborough, Cambs, PE2 6FZ
Activities: Other business support service activities n.e.c.
Parent: Thomas Cook Group UK Limited
Officers: Shirley Bradley, Secretary; Paul Andrew Hemingway [1971] Director

Mytravel Pioneer Limited
Incorporated: 25 April 2002
Net Worth Deficit: £20,700,000 *Total Assets:* £150,000,000
Registered Office: Westpoint, Peterborough Business Park, Lynch Wood, Peterborough, Cambs, PE2 6FZ
Activities: Non-trading company
Parent: Mytravel Group Limited
Officers: Shirley Bradley, Secretary; Shirley Bradley [1960] Director

N & C Building Products Limited
Incorporated: 30 September 1856 *Employees:* 324
Net Worth: £15,855,892 *Total Assets:* £23,468,466
Registered Office: 41-51 Freshwater Road, Chadwell Heath, Romford, Essex, RM8 1SP
Activities: Wholesale of wood, construction materials and sanitary equipment
Parent: Nicholls & Clarke Limited
Officers: Geraint David Cooper, Secretary; Geraint David Cooper [1958] Director/Accountant; David Ian Forbes [1965] Director; Kenneth Stuart Alexander Forbes [1937] Director; Stephen Andrew Forbes [1963] Director; Gary Kenneth Gingell [1968] Director; Keith David Hall [1965] Director; Richard John Hill [1971] Director

N.E.M. Co. Limited
Incorporated: 11 July 1983 *Employees:* 131
Net Worth: £5,030,537 *Total Assets:* £9,832,953
Registered Office: Wedgewood Way, Stevenage, Herts, SG1 4SX
Activities: Manufacture of computers and peripheral equipment
Shareholders: David Norman Pearce; Angela Barbara Pearce
Officers: Angela Barbara Pearce, Secretary; David Duric [1963] Director; Robert John Parker [1965] Production Director; Angela Barbara Pearce [1950] Director; David Norman Pearce [1949] Director

N.P.K. Holdings Limited
Incorporated: 14 June 1864 *Employees:* 5
Net Worth: £9,355,876 *Total Assets:* £10,719,184
Registered Office: 37 Cambridge Place, Cambridge, CB2 1NS
Activities: Development of building projects
Shareholders: Robert James Morell Keatley; John Rankin MacDonald Keatley
Officers: Robert James Morell Keatley, Secretary; Dr Azucena Maria Keatley [1967] Director [Spanish]; John Rankin MacDonald Keatley [1933] Director/Chairman; Robert James Morell Keatley [1965] Director

N.R.C. Plant Limited
Incorporated: 13 January 1997 *Employees:* 33
Net Worth: £7,642,994 *Total Assets:* £19,035,140
Registered Office: Neagron House, Stanford Road, Orsett, Essex, RM16 3BX
Activities: Renting and leasing of other machinery, equipment and tangible goods n.e.c.
Parent: Joseph Gallagher Limited
Officers: Paul Joseph Gallagher, Secretary; Joseph Jude Gallagher [1945] Managing Director [Irish]; Steven Keith Harvey [1963] Director/Civil Engineer; Anthony Andrew Matheson [1968] Group Commercial Director

Nacropolis (Langley) Ltd
Incorporated: 7 October 2016
Net Worth Deficit: £192,710 *Total Assets:* £8,042,739
Registered Office: Suite 1, Stanmore Towers, 8-14 Church Road, Stanmore, Middlesex, HA7 4AW
Activities: Development of building projects
Shareholders: Bhaman Ltd; Nacropolis Developments Ltd
Officers: Amar Pankhania, Secretary; Amar Pankhania [1989] Director; Ravi Pankhania [1977] Director

Naga UK Bidco Limited
Incorporated: 27 June 2013
Net Worth: £235,443,008 *Total Assets:* £364,713,984
Registered Office: Dagger Lane, Elstree, Herts, WD6 3BX
Activities: Other human health activities
Parent: Naga UK Topco Limited
Officers: Kieu Hoang [1944] Director [American]; Kevin Lane [1961] Director/President [American]; Xu Wu [1967] Director/Businessman [Chinese]

Naga UK Topco Limited
Incorporated: 27 June 2013 *Employees:* 2,893
Net Worth: £157,711,008 *Total Assets:* £409,176,992
Registered Office: Dagger Lane, Elstree, Herts, WD6 3BX
Activities: Other human health activities
Parent: Tiancheng International Investment Limited
Officers: Kieu Hoang [1944] Director [American]; Lars Holmqvist [1959] Director/Senior Advisor [Swedish]; Kevin Patrick Lane [1961] Director/Consultant [American]; Xu Wu [1967] Director/Manager [Hong Kong]; Tan Yang [1972] Director/Business Executive [Chinese]

Naked Wines International Limited
Incorporated: 24 November 2011 *Employees:* 2
Net Worth: £10,049,000 *Total Assets:* £18,161,000
Registered Office: Majestic House, The Belfry, Colonial Way, Watford, Herts, WD24 4WH
Activities: Activities of head offices
Parent: Majestic Wine PLC
Officers: Alex Iapichino, Secretary; James Crawford [1977] Director; Eamon William FitzGenerald [1984] Director/COO, Naked Wines [Irish]

Naked Wines Prepayments Trustee Company Limited
Incorporated: 13 November 2008
Net Worth Deficit: £10,000 *Total Assets:* £13,361,000
Registered Office: Majestic House, The Belfry, Colonial Way, Watford, Herts, WD24 4WH
Activities: Wholesale of wine, beer, spirits and other alcoholic beverages
Parent: www.nakedwines.com Limited
Officers: Alex Iapichino, Secretary; James Crawford [1977] Director; Eamon William FitzGenerald [1984] Director/COO, Naked Wines [Irish]

Namu Limited
Incorporated: 4 December 2012
Net Worth: £936,210 *Total Assets:* £9,363,888
Registered Office: 3 Lowther Close, Elstree, Herts, WD6 3PY
Activities: Other letting and operating of own or leased real estate
Major Shareholder: Nadia Parvez
Officers: Shakeel Ahmed [1959] Director; Nadia Parvez Manzoor [1982] Director

Napp Laboratories Limited
Incorporated: 26 September 1923 *Employees:* 3
Net Worth: £12,968,000 *Total Assets:* £16,254,000
Registered Office: Unit 196 Cambridge Science Park, Milton Road, Cambridge, CB4 0AB
Activities: Wholesale of pharmaceutical goods
Parent: Napp Pharmaceutical Group Limited
Officers: Stuart David Baker [1935] Director/Attorney [American]; Bryan George LEA [1961] Director/Solicitor; Ake Gunnar Wikstrom [1951] Director/Advisor [Swedish]

Napp Pharmaceutical Group Limited
Incorporated: 27 July 1966
Net Worth: £82,254,000 *Total Assets:* £87,942,000
Registered Office: Unit 196 Cambridge Science Park, Milton Road, Cambridge, CB4 0AB
Activities: Manufacture of pharmaceutical preparations
Parent: Napp Pharmaceutical Holdings Limited
Officers: Stuart David Baker [1935] Director/Lawyer [American]; Ake Gunnar Wikstrom [1951] Director/Advisor [Swedish]

Napp Pharmaceutical Holdings Limited
Incorporated: 19 December 1997 *Employees:* 612
Net Worth: £191,744,000 *Total Assets:* £304,665,984
Registered Office: Unit 196 Cambridge Science Park, Milton Road, Cambridge, CB4 0AB
Activities: Manufacture of pharmaceutical preparations
Shareholder: Stuart David Baker
Officers: Stuart David Baker [1935] Director/Lawyer [American]; Ake Gunnar Wikstrom [1951] Director/Advisor [Swedish]

Napp Pharmaceuticals Limited
Incorporated: 22 December 1998 *Employees:* 179
Net Worth: £6,491,000 *Total Assets:* £41,612,000
Registered Office: Unit 196 Cambridge Science Park, Milton Road, Cambridge, CB4 0AB
Activities: Wholesale of pharmaceutical goods
Parent: Napp Pharmaceutical Holdings Limited
Officers: Stuart David Baker [1935] Director/Attorney [American]; Hywel Rhys Day [1974] Managing Director; Bryan George LEA [1961] Director; Dr Julian Paul Schofield [1959] Medical Director; David Alan Silver [1965] Director/Accountant; Ake Gunnar Wikstrom [1951] Director/Advisor [Swedish]

Narada Europe (UK) Ltd
Incorporated: 28 August 2007 *Employees:* 2
Net Worth: £31,983 *Total Assets:* £8,068,727
Registered Office: Gladstone Place, 36-38 Upper Marlborough Road, St Albans, Herts, AL1 3UU
Activities: Wholesale of electronic and telecommunications equipment and parts
Officers: Chen Bo [1968] Director [Chinese]

F.H. Nash Limited
Incorporated: 10 January 1964 *Employees:* 99
Net Worth: £11,730,661 *Total Assets:* £16,339,382
Registered Office: Four Elms Mills, Bardfield Saling, Braintree, Essex, CM7 5EJ
Activities: Manufacture of prepared feeds for farm animals
Shareholders: Adrienne Gay Venner; George Knowles
Officers: Christelle Melamud, Secretary; Elizabeth Anne Bulbrook [1965] Director/Equine Nutritionist; Claire Selene Knowles [1943] Director; George Picton Knowles [1942] Director; Rominta Meriel Knowles [1978] Director; Christelle Melamud [1983] Finance Director; Adrienne Gay Venner [1946] Director; Jolyon Paul Venner [1973] Production Director; Paul Venner [1949] Director

National Adhesives Holding Ltd.
Incorporated: 3 March 2008
Net Worth: £39,505,000 *Total Assets:* £39,540,000
Registered Office: National Adhesives Holding Ltd, Wood Lane End, Hemel Hempstead, Herts, HP2 4RQ
Activities: Other manufacturing n.e.c.
Parent: Henkel AG & Co. KGaA
Officers: Sutinder Bhandal, Secretary; Peter David Budden [1963] Director/Accountant; Csaba Pal Szendrei [1967] Business Director [Hungarian]

National Film and Television School (The)
Incorporated: 11 June 1970 *Employees:* 107
Net Worth: £25,658,344 *Total Assets:* £37,639,464
Registered Office: Beaconsfield Film Studios, Station Road, Beaconsfield, Bucks, HP9 1LG
Activities: Technical and vocational secondary education
Officers: Trevor Hall, Secretary; Riffat Ahmed [1985] Film Director and Visual Artist; Professor Geoffrey Joel Crossick [1946] Director/Retired University Vice-Chancellor; Neil Andrew Forster [1970] Finance Director; Patrick Fuller [1966] Director; Caroline Daniela Kavan Woodford Hollick [1975] Director/Head of Drama at Channel 4; Oliver Richard Hyatt [1979] Director, Chair of Animation; Timothy Kyte [1968] Director/IT Support; Ian Lewis Lewis [1962] Group Director, Sky Cinema; Stephen David Louis [1966] Director/Venture Capitalist; Andrew Imre Flint MacDonald [1966] Director/Producer; Patrick Anthony McKenna [1956] Director/CEO Ingenious Media; Steven William Mertz [1957] Director/Lawyer [American]; Susan Nicola Moffat [1960] Producer & Board Director; Siobhan Margaret Reddy [1979] Studio Director [Irish/Australian]; Raja Adil Rehman [1974] Director/Actor, Writer, Broadcaster; Laurent David Henri Samama [1971] Director - Strategic Relations [French]; Balraj Samra [1966] Commercial Director BBC

National Football Centre Limited
Incorporated: 18 July 1990 *Employees:* 278
Net Worth Deficit: £26,993,000 *Total Assets:* £69,510,000
Registered Office: Wembley Stadium, Wembley, Middlesex, HA9 0WS
Activities: Operation of sports facilities
Parent: The Football Association Limited
Officers: Richard James McDermott, Secretary; Mark Paul Burrows [1969] Director/Chief Financial Officer; Martin Richard Glenn [1960] Director/Chief Executive Officer

National Institute of Agricultural Botany Trust
Incorporated: 26 October 2011
Net Worth: £50,496,000 *Total Assets:* £53,406,000
Registered Office: Huntingdon Road, Cambridge, CB3 0LE
Activities: Research and experimental development on biotechnology
Officers: Richard Charles Butler [1950] Director/Farmer; John Andrew Elliot [1952] Director/Farmer; Dr Helen Ferrier [1977] Director/Chief Science and Regulatory Affairs Adviser; Jeremy Wynn Lewis [1949] Director/Business Consultant and Farmer; Dr Charles William Looker [1950] Director/Farmer; Richard Francis Antony Pemberton [1970] Director/Landowner and Farmer; Andrew Michael Slack [1949] Director

National Pharmacy Association Limited
Incorporated: 14 October 1976 *Employees:* 160
Net Worth: £20,706,000 *Total Assets:* £36,872,000
Registered Office: Mallinson House, 40-42 St Peters Street, St Albans, Herts, AL1 3NP
Activities: Activities of business and employers membership organisations
Officers: Michael Guerin, Secretary; Raj Kumar Aggarwal [1949] Director/Pharmacy; Jan Barend Badenhorst [1976] Director/Pharmacist [British/South African]; Reena Barai [1977] Director/Pharmacist; Dr Ian James Cubbin [1958] Director/Pharmacist; Philip Callaghan Galt [1970] Director/Pharmacist; Michael Francis Guerin [1963] Director/Pharmacist [Irish]; Nicholas Robert Kaye [1975] Director/Pharmacist; Andrew Lane [1959] Director/Pharmacist; Amish Dipakkumar Patel [1985] Director/Pharmacist; Hemant Ramanbhai Patel [1954] Director/Pharmacist; Hiten Kumar Patel [1959] Director/Pharmacy; Rajesh Ramniklal Patel [1964] Director/Pharmacist; Umesh Babubhai Patel Bsc Mrpharms [1950] Director/Pharmacist [Indian]; Olivier Picard [1974] Director [French]; Anil Kumar Sharma [1973] Director/Pharmacist; Nitin Trembaklal Sodha [1955] Director/Pharmacist; Ian Cameron Strachan [1961] Pharmacist Director

Nationwide Metal Recycling Limited
Incorporated: 26 September 2007 *Employees:* 80
Net Worth: £7,736,148 *Total Assets:* £13,915,019
Registered Office: Roundwood Farm, Bentley Lane, Stutton, Ipswich, Suffolk, IP9 2SY
Activities: Recovery of sorted materials
Shareholder: James Edwards
Officers: Douglas Edwards, Secretary; Douglas Edwards [1959] Director; Helen Mary Edwards [1965] Director/Administrator; James Edwards [1964] Director

Natural Balance Foods Limited
Incorporated: 24 March 2004 *Employees:* 55
Net Worth: £8,069,706 *Total Assets:* £14,336,937
Registered Office: 1 Drakes Drive, Long Crendon, Aylesbury, Bucks, HP18 9BA
Activities: Manufacture of other food products n.e.c.
Shareholders: Jamison Christopher Combs; Jan Marcel Mattieu Maria Boone
Officers: John Johnston, Secretary; Jan Marcel Mattieu Maria Boone [1971] Director [Belgian]; Gregory Combs [1962] Director; Jamison Christopher Combs [1971] Director; Isabelle Maes [1974] Director [Belgian]

Natures Menu Limited
Incorporated: 2 March 1981 *Employees:* 208
Net Worth: £2,973,791 *Total Assets:* £14,840,652
Registered Office: 22-26 King Street, King's Lynn, Norfolk, PE30 1HJ
Activities: Manufacture of prepared feeds for farm animals
Parent: Anexhold Limited
Officers: Gonzalo Raspall Coromina, Secretary; Paula Michelle Clatworthy [1970] Director; Gonzalo Raspall Coromina [1972] Director [Spanish]; Ramon Andreu Ferrando [1964] Director [Spanish]; Peter Coventry Roy [1971] Director; Craig Richard Taylor [1966] Director; Francisco Javier Serra Torres [1957] Director/Businessman [Spanish]

Navigator Terminals Midco Limited
Incorporated: 18 November 2015
Net Worth: £76,242,000 *Total Assets:* £209,240,000
Registered Office: Oliver Road, West Thurrock, Grays, Essex, RM20 3ED
Activities: Support activities for petroleum and natural gas mining
Officers: Mark Roy Charles Shaha, Secretary; Michael David Brennan [1969] Director [Irish]; Tamara Gail Earley [1968] Director/Deputy Chief Executive; Roderick John Gadsby [1969] Director/Investment Professional; Robin William Gisby [1956] Director; James McPhillimy [1964] Director/Chartered Engineer/Consultant; Grant Daniel Rayner [1982] Director [Australian]

Navigator Terminals North Tees Limited
Incorporated: 25 November 2015 *Employees:* 29
Net Worth: £17,123,000 *Total Assets:* £32,549,000
Registered Office: Oliver Road, Grays, Essex, RM20 3ED
Activities: Support activities for petroleum and natural gas mining
Parent: Navigator Terminals Limited
Officers: Mark Roy Charles Shaha, Secretary; Jason Ralph Hornsby [1973] Managing Director; Mark Roy Charles Shaha [1979] Director/Chartered Accountant

Navigator Terminals Seal Sands Limited
Incorporated: 27 November 1964 *Employees:* 75
Previous: Vopak Terminal Teesside Limited
Net Worth: £22,345,000 *Total Assets:* £49,185,000
Registered Office: Navigator Terminals Seal Sands Limited, Oliver Road, Grays, Essex, RM20 3ED
Activities: Operation of warehousing and storage facilities for land transport activities
Parent: Navigator Terminals UK Limited
Officers: Mark Roy Charles Shaha, Secretary; Jason Ralph Hornsby [1973] Managing Director; Mark Roy Charles Shaha [1979] Director/Chartered Accountant

Navigator Terminals UK Limited
Incorporated: 25 November 1977 *Employees:* 5
Previous: Vopak Holding Logistics UK Limited
Net Worth: £35,067,000 *Total Assets:* £36,138,000
Registered Office: Oliver Road, West Thurrock, Grays, Essex, RM20 3ED
Activities: Activities of head offices
Parent: Navigator Terminals Limited
Officers: Mark Roy Charles Shaha, Secretary; Jason Ralph Hornsby [1973] Managing Director; Mark Roy Charles Shaha [1979] Director/Chartered Accountant

Navitas Petroleum Limited
Incorporated: 21 February 2013
Net Worth Deficit: £9,301,000 *Total Assets:* £25,953,000
Registered Office: Elm Park House, Elm Park Court, Pinner, Middlesex, HA5 3NN
Activities: Extraction of crude petroleum
Parent: Navitas Petroleum Limited Partnership
Officers: Benjamin Cuby [1975] Director/Business Development Manager; Adrian Gerard John Olivero [1967] Director; Chanan Reichman [1977] Director [Israeli]; Gideon Abraham Tadmor Cohen [1963] Director/Company Executive [Israeli]

NBC Europe Ltd.
Incorporated: 16 November 2011
Net Worth: £8,566,000 *Total Assets:* £14,784,000
Registered Office: 50 Clarendon Road, Watford, Herts, WD17 1TX
Activities: Activities of other holding companies n.e.c.
Parent: TJX Europe Limited
Officers: Susan Beaumont, Secretary; Alicia Colarte Kelly, Secretary; Lisa Schwartz, Secretary; David Lawrence Averill [1967] SVP Corporate Tax Director [American]; John Joseph Klinger [1964] Director/SVP, Corporate Controller [American]; Mary Blier Reynolds [1955] Director/SVP Treasurer [American]

NDC Technologies Limited
Incorporated: 24 June 1959 *Employees:* 328
Net Worth: £38,686,000 *Total Assets:* £46,868,000
Registered Office: Bates Road, Maldon, Essex, CM9 5FA
Activities: Manufacture of electronic industrial process control equipment
Parent: Spectris Group Holdings Limited
Officers: David Wambold, Secretary; David Joseph Atkinson [1955] Director; Ian Beethom Benson [1954] Director; Dave Roland [1959] Director [American]; David Wambold [1957] Director/Accountant [American]

NDEMIC Creations Ltd
Incorporated: 30 January 2012 *Employees:* 8
Net Worth: £14,858,374 *Total Assets:* £15,878,876
Registered Office: First Floor, Healthaid House, Marlborough Hill, Harrow, Middlesex, HA1 1UD
Activities: Business and domestic software development
Major Shareholder: Thomas James Vaughan
Officers: Rosanna Louise Vaughan [1986] Director; Thomas James Vaughan [1987] Director/Consultant

NEC (UK) Ltd.
Incorporated: 19 June 1973 *Employees:* 92
Net Worth Deficit: £32,641,000 *Total Assets:* £40,467,000
Registered Office: Athene Odyssey Business Park, West End Road, South Ruislip, Middlesex, HA4 6QE
Activities: Wholesale of computers, computer peripheral equipment and software
Parent: NEC Europe Ltd
Officers: Hiroshi Komazaki, Secretary; Chris Richard Jackson [1967] Director/IT Professional; Hiroshi Komazaki [1963] Director [Japanese]; Hironobu Kurosaki [1960] Director [Japanese]

NEC Capital (UK) PLC
Incorporated: 17 February 1987 *Employees:* 3
Net Worth: £9,959,000 *Total Assets:* £154,100,000
Registered Office: Athene Odyssey Business Park, West End Road, South Ruislip, Middlesex, HA4 6QE
Activities: Other service activities n.e.c.
Parent: NEC Corporation
Officers: Hiroshi Komazaki, Secretary; Hiroshi Komazaki [1963] Director/Senior Vice President, CFO [Japanese]; Hironobu Kurosaki [1960] Director/President & CEO [Japanese]; Koji Suwahara [1962] Director/General Manager of Finance Division of NEC Corporation [Japanese]

NEC Europe Ltd
Incorporated: 25 June 1993 *Employees:* 248
Net Worth: £18,872,468 *Total Assets:* £151,679,792
Registered Office: Athene Odyssey Business Park, West End Road, South Ruislip, Middlesex, HA4 6QE
Activities: Wholesale of electronic and telecommunications equipment and parts
Parent: NEC Corporation
Officers: Hiroshi Komazaki, Secretary; Yukio Hioki [1968] Director/Deputy General Manager, Corporate Strategy [Japanese]; Hironobu Kurosaki [1960] Director/President & CEO [Japanese]; Toshiya Matsuki [1960] Director/Executive Vice President, NEC Corporation [Japanese]; Sir Richard Francis Needham [1942] Director; Toshiyuki Otake [1963] Director/Deputy Corporate Controller [Japanese]

NEEB Holdings Ltd.
Incorporated: 9 April 1959 *Employees:* 11
Net Worth: £25,430,584 *Total Assets:* £26,273,942
Registered Office: 3 The Cedars, Apex 12, Old Ipswich Road, Ardleigh, Colchester, Essex, CO7 7QR
Activities: Other letting and operating of own or leased real estate
Officers: Julie Anne Eeles, Secretary; Jean Raymond [1950] Director/Administrator; Raymond William Raymond [1954] Director/Property Developer; Roger Charles Raymond [1954] Director/Property Developer; Susan Raymond [1951] Director/Administration; Kay Sadler [1947] Director/Administrator

NeilMed Holding Company Limited
Incorporated: 23 June 2016 *Employees:* 18
Net Worth: £6,346,587 *Total Assets:* £11,773,630
Registered Office: 221 Kenton Lane, Kenton, Harrow, Middlesex, HA3 8RP
Activities: Wholesale of pharmaceutical goods
Major Shareholder: Ketan Chandrakant Mehta
Officers: Dr Ketan Chandrakant Mehta [1956] Director/Physician [American]; Nina Mehta [1961] Director [American]

Nellsar Limited
Incorporated: 6 July 1999 *Employees:* 712
Net Worth: £12,801,256 *Total Assets:* £44,493,512
Registered Office: 147a High Street, Waltham Cross, Herts, EN8 7AP
Activities: Other residential care activities n.e.c.
Shareholders: Arinesarajah Ragumoorthy; Jegathambikai Ragumoorthy
Officers: Jegathambikai Ragumoorthy, Secretary; Arinesarajah Ragumoorthy [1945] Director

Nemo (UK) Holdco, Ltd.
Incorporated: 2 November 2015 *Employees:* 595
Net Worth Deficit: £51,749,000 *Total Assets:* £71,130,000
Registered Office: The Lodge, 92 Uxbridge Road, Harrow Weald, Middlesex, HA3 6DQ
Activities: Activities of other holding companies n.e.c.
Officers: Michael Stephan Haringman, Secretary; James Michael Chu [1958] Director/Managing Partner of Catterton Management Company [American]; Leonard Fluxman [1958] Director/President and Chief Executive Officer [American]; Marc Magliacano [1974] Director/Partner of Catterton Management Company [American]

Nene Park Trust
Incorporated: 23 August 1988 *Employees:* 51
Net Worth: £38,654,000 *Total Assets:* £39,504,000
Registered Office: Ham Farm House, Ham Lane, Peterborough, Cambs, PE2 5UU
Activities: Other amusement and recreation activities n.e.c.
Officers: Philip Hugh Rolfe, Secretary; Simon Frederick Barkham [1983] Director/Salesman; Matthew Anthony Wilson Bradbury [1964] Director/Chief Executive; Councillor Graham Peter Casey [1963] Director/Musician; Martin Brian Chillcott [1956] Director/Marketing Consultant; Thomas Hornby Graham Cooper [1950] Director/Chartered Surveyor; Christine Anne de Ferrars Green [1964] Director/Solicitor; Professor Ian David Hodge [1952] Director/University Professor; Jonathan Clifford Marsden [1959] Director/Local Government Officer; Colin Duncan Prosser [1963] Director/Geologist; Paul Thomas Simmons [1955] Director/Business Coach; Allan Simpson [1984] Director/Town Planner, Utilities; Councillor June Elizabeth Stokes [1942] Director/Councillor

Neopost Technologies Limited
Incorporated: 3 October 1963 *Employees:* 172
Net Worth: £10,885,000 *Total Assets:* £13,761,000
Registered Office: Oakwood Hill Industrial Estate, Oakwood Hill, Loughton, Essex, IG10 3TZ
Activities: Manufacture of office machinery and equipment (except computers and peripheral equipment)
Officers: Danny Westlake, Secretary/Accountant; Emmanuelle de Groote [1971] Director/Business Executive [French]; Jean Francois Labadie [1967] Group Supply Chain Director [French]; Thierry Le Jaoudour [1964] Director/Business Executive [French]; Danny Westlake [1965] Director/Accountant

NET Academies Trust
Incorporated: 19 September 2012 *Employees:* 255
Net Worth: £12,840,000 *Total Assets:* £18,812,000
Registered Office: Latton Green Primary Academy, Riddings Lane, Harlow, Essex, CM18 7HT
Activities: Educational support services
Officers: Professor Derek Bell [1950] Director/Retired; Andrew Johnston Calderwood [1954] Director/Retired; Richard John Carr [1966] Managing Director; Joanne Lisa Coton [1972] Director; Harry Meikle [1958] Director; Luke Pledger [1968] Managing Director; Peter William Shephard [1953] Director/Education Consultant; Charlotte Janet Warmington [1972] Director/HR Manager; Nigel Ralph Wyrely-Birch [1954] Director/Chartered Accountant

Net Pay (EUR) Limited
Incorporated: 29 December 2004 *Employees:* 2
Net Worth: £54,959 *Total Assets:* £35,109,772
Registered Office: 5 Elstree Gate, Elstree Way, Borehamwood, Herts, WD6 1JD
Activities: Information technology consultancy activities
Major Shareholder: Alon Elbaz
Officers: Alon Elbaz [1971] Director/Computer Consultant [Israeli]

Netcall PLC
Incorporated: 1 May 1984 *Employees:* 217
Net Worth: £21,704,000 *Total Assets:* £44,958,000
Registered Office: 1st Floor, Building 2, People Building Estate, Maylands Avenue, Hemel Hempstead Industrial Estate, Hemel Hempstead, Herts, HP2 4NW
Activities: Activities of head offices
Officers: Michael Charles Greensmith, Secretary; Henrik Peter Bang [1958] Director [Danish]; Michael Edward Wilson Jackson [1950] Director; Michael Patrick Neville [1954] Director; James Andrew Ormondroyd [1972] Director

Netcall Telecom Limited
Incorporated: 29 June 1993 *Employees:* 170
Net Worth: £4,571,000 *Total Assets:* £13,866,000
Registered Office: 1st Floor, Building 2, People Building Estate, Maylands Avenue, Hemel Hempstead Industrial Estate, Hemel Hempstead, Herts, HP2 4NW
Activities: Other telecommunications activities
Parent: Netcall PLC
Officers: Michael Charles Greensmith, Secretary; Henrik Peter Bang [1958] Chief Executive Officer/Director [Danish]; Mark David Holmes [1969] Sales Director; Michael Patrick Neville [1954] Director; James Andrew Ormondroyd [1972] Director

Netcracker Technology EMEA Limited
Incorporated: 11 August 1989 *Employees:* 165
Net Worth: £24,278,000 *Total Assets:* £63,528,000
Registered Office: 2010 Cambourne Business Park, Cambourne, Cambs, CB23 6DW
Activities: Information technology consultancy activities
Parent: Netcracker Technology Corporation
Officers: Andrew Michael Feinberg [1970] Director/Chief Executive Officer [American]; Michael Alexander Feinberg [1947] Director/Chief Technology Officer [American]

Netherhall Gardens Ltd
Incorporated: 17 July 2014
Net Worth Deficit: £64,796 *Total Assets:* £37,621,308
Registered Office: Suite 2, Fountain House, 1a Elm Park, Stanmore, Middlesex, HA7 4AU
Activities: Development of building projects
Parent: Netherhall Gardens Hampstead Ltd
Officers: Robert Stephen Godfrey [1954] Director/Clothing Manufacturer; Tal Orly [1963] Director/Property Developer [Israeli]

Netscientific PLC
Incorporated: 12 April 2012 *Employees:* 41
Net Worth: £15,371,000 *Total Assets:* £16,346,000
Registered Office: c/o Wilkins Kennedy LLP, Anglo House, Bell Lane Office Village, Bell Lane, Amersham, Bucks, HP6 6FA
Activities: Other business support service activities n.e.c.
Officers: Ian Postlethwaite, Secretary; Dr Francois-Regis Marie Eugene Martelet [1960] Director/Chief Executive Officer [French]; Ian Postlethwaite [1962] Director/Chief Financial Officer; Dr Stephen Kevin Smith [1951] Director; Sir Richard Brook Sykes [1942] Director; Barry Woodrow Wilson [1944] Director/Global Healthcare Advisor

Netsupport Ltd.
Incorporated: 18 May 1989 *Employees:* 92
Net Worth: £10,353,678 *Total Assets:* £11,369,666
Registered Office: Netsupport House, Towngate East, Market Deeping, Peterborough, Cambs, PE6 8NE
Activities: Business and domestic software development
Parent: 4a Investment (Jersey) Ltd
Officers: Helen Hankinson, Secretary; Andrew John Gibbons [1968] Technical Director; Robert David Hawkins [1968] Development Director; Matthew Jones [1971] Director/Business Development; Alastair John Kingsley [1969] Managing Director; Marcus Rex Kingsley [1973] Marketing Director

Network Homes Investments (Stockwell) Limited
Incorporated: 14 February 2007
Previous: Community Housing Development Ltd
Net Worth Deficit: £187,782 *Total Assets:* £11,853,693
Registered Office: Olympic Office Centre, 8 Fulton Road, Wembley, Middlesex, HA9 0NU
Activities: Buying and selling of own real estate
Officers: Tabitha Kassem, Secretary; Graham Gregg [1975] Director/Head of Accounting Services; Jennifer Ann Hodgkins [1956] Director/Head of Treasury; Colin James Mitchell [1958] Director/Head of Corporate Finance

Network Homes Investments Limited
Incorporated: 14 February 2007
Previous: Network Stadium Investments Limited
Net Worth: £66,928,128 *Total Assets:* £92,629,920
Registered Office: Olympic Office Centre, 8 Fulton Road, Wembley, Middlesex, HA9 0NU
Activities: Buying and selling of own real estate
Officers: Tabitha Kassem, Secretary; David Howard Gooch [1964] Executive Director of Development; Jonathan Michael Gooding [1953] Director/Chartered Surveyor; Graham Gregg [1975] Director/Head of Accounting Services; Jennifer Ann Hodgkins [1956] Director/Head of Treasury; Colin James Mitchell [1958] Director/Head of Corporate Finance

Network New Build Limited
Incorporated: 19 September 2000
Net Worth: £20,224 *Total Assets:* £22,708,172
Registered Office: Olympic Office Centre, 8 Fulton Road, Wembley, Middlesex, HA9 0NU
Activities: Other letting and operating of own or leased real estate
Officers: Tabitha Kassem, Secretary; Graham Gregg [1975] Director/Head of Accounting Services; Jennifer Ann Hodgkins [1956] Director/Head of Treasury; Colin James Mitchell [1958] Director/Head of Corporate Finance

Network Treasury Services Limited
Incorporated: 12 November 2007
Net Worth: £10,005,763 *Total Assets:* £506,721,056
Registered Office: Olympic Office Centre, 8 Fulton Road, Wembley, Middlesex, HA9 0NU
Activities: Financial intermediation not elsewhere classified
Officers: Tabitha Kassem, Secretary; Bernadette Sarah Conroy [1966] Director/Board Member; Helen Elizabeth Evans [1959] Director/Chief Executive Officer; Patricia Anne Turner [1956] Director/Housing Association Chief Operating Officer; Sean Allan West [1977] Director, Treasury [British/Australian]; Philip Williams [1966] Director/Banker

Neville Trust Limited
Incorporated: 11 March 1986 *Employees:* 168
Net Worth: £8,587,527 *Total Assets:* £13,459,802
Registered Office: Neville House, Marsh Road, Leagrave, Luton, Beds, LU3 2RZ
Activities: Activities of other holding companies n.e.c.
Officers: Victoria Mary Louise Trumper, Secretary; Michael Bernard Neville Henman [1934] Director/Builder; Peter John Henman [1937] Director/Builder; Angela Mary Tatum-Hume [1946] Director/Company Executive; Ian Carl Trumper [1964] Director/Chartered Accountant; Victoria Mary Louise Trumper [1964] Director

New Anglia Local Enterprise Partnership Limited
Incorporated: 28 June 2011 *Employees:* 51
Net Worth: £42,390,600 *Total Assets:* £42,756,584
Registered Office: Mills & Reeve LLP, 1 St James Court, Whitefriars, Norwich, NR3 1RU
Activities: Other business support service activities n.e.c.
Officers: David Thomas Ellesmere [1970] Director/Software Developer; Douglas John Field [1972] Director/Chartered Accountant; John Henry Morgan Griffiths [1953] Borough Councillor/Co-owner/Director; Matthew Jonathan Rawle Hicks [1963] Director; Dominic John Keen [1977] Director; William Nunn [1965] Director/Councillor; Stephen James Oliver [1963] Director/Chairman; Andrew James Proctor [1947] Director/Councillor; Johnathan Edward Reynolds [1981] Director; Professor David John Richardson [1964] Director/Vice Chancellor University of East Anglia; Lindsey Claire Rix [1980] Director/Chief Operating Officer; Sandra Louise Ruddock [1967] Director/Business Proprietor; Dr Nikos Savvas [1970] Director/Principal West Suffolk College; Alan Henry Waters [1953] Director/Learning and Development Manager; Jeanette Deborah Wheeler [1970] Director/Solicitor; Dr Timothy John Whitley [1965] Managing Director

New Demipower Limited
Incorporated: 24 May 2002 *Employees:* 1,385
Net Worth: £4,639,528 *Total Assets:* £37,636,804
Registered Office: Jubilee House, 7-9 The Oaks, Ruislip, Middlesex, HA4 7LF
Activities: Activities of head offices
Shareholders: Amirali Hassanali Moledina Janmohamed; Alim Amirali Janmohamed
Officers: Alim Amirali Janmohamed, Secretary; Alim Amirali Janmohamed [1981] Director; Amirali Hassanali Moledina Janmohamed [1952] Director

New Hall School Trust
Incorporated: 6 June 2005 *Employees:* 279
Net Worth: £18,597,540 *Total Assets:* £30,183,080
Registered Office: New Hall School, The Avenue, Boreham, Chelmsford, Essex, CM3 3HS
Activities: Primary education
Officers: Elizabeth Ruth Murphy, Secretary; John Francis Aldridge [1945] Director/Essex County Councillor, Retired; Janis Elizabeth Croom [1951] Director/Retired Business Manager; Malcolm John Day [1966] Director/Banker; Dr Miriam Edelsten [1949] Director/General Practitioner and Senior Partner; Katherine Anne Jeffrey [1970] Director/School Principal; Joseph Anthony Peake [1954] Director/Headmaster & Consultant for Teacher Training; Rachel Marion Skells [1971] Director/Chartered Accountant; Robert Edwin Talbut [1960] Independent Director; Agnes Therese Williams [1954] Director/Retired Headteacher; Pauline Marie Wilson [1951] Director/Headteacher; Philip Robert Andrew Wilson [1971] Charity and Business Director

New Ladderswood LLP
Incorporated: 23 June 2011
Net Worth: £57,338,856 *Total Assets:* £61,847,616
Registered Office: Teresa Gavin House, Woodford Avenue, Woodford Green, Essex, IG8 8FA

New Landmark Investment Limited
Incorporated: 19 April 2013 *Employees:* 2
Net Worth: £999,644 *Total Assets:* £22,262,130
Registered Office: 72 Darlands Drive, Barnet, Herts, EN5 2DF
Activities: Other business support service activities n.e.c.
Major Shareholder: Peter Breier
Officers: Richard Derrick Bridges [1954] Director; Bradley Paul Kramer [1950] Director

New River Holdings Limited
Incorporated: 19 September 1950 *Employees:* 221
Net Worth: £21,697,232 *Total Assets:* £34,151,528
Registered Office: Riverside Place, 1-9 Lea Road, Waltham Abbey, Essex, EN9 1AS
Activities: Activities of distribution holding companies
Parent: Marchase Limited
Officers: Martin Stewart Earle, Secretary; Martin Stewart Earle [1946] Director/Manager; Matthew Richard Earle [1973] Managing Director; Charles William Valens Smith [1949] Director/Manager

New Sparta Film Distribution Limited
Incorporated: 19 September 2013 *Employees:* 2
Net Worth Deficit: £4,714,486 *Total Assets:* £16,922,080
Registered Office: Abbey House, 51 High Street, Saffron Walden, Essex, CB10 1AF
Activities: Motion picture distribution activities
Parent: New Sparta Holdings Limited
Officers: Dr Jerome Paul Booth [1963] Director

New Sparta Holdings Limited
Incorporated: 18 September 2013 *Employees:* 1
Net Worth: £2,930,060 *Total Assets:* £35,658,912
Registered Office: Abbey House, 51 High Street, Saffron Walden, Essex, CB10 1AF
Activities: Activities of other holding companies n.e.c.
Major Shareholder: Jerome Paul Booth
Officers: Dr Jerome Paul Booth [1963] Director

Newarthill Limited
Incorporated: 21 April 1972 *Employees:* 2,209
Net Worth: £71,938,000 *Total Assets:* £781,009,984
Registered Office: Eaton Court, Maylands Avenue, Hemel Hempstead Industrial Estate, Hemel Hempstead, Herts, HP2 7TR
Activities: Activities of head offices
Parent: R H McAlpine, A W McAlpine, G M McAlpine, R E T McAlpine and Others as Trustees of The McAlpine Partnership Trust
Officers: John Alistair Dempsey, Secretary; Kevin John Pearson, Secretary; David Stannard Jenkins [1947] Director; Donald Crawford Joyce [1973] Director; Sir Andrew William McAlpine [1960] Director/Civil Engineering & Building Contractor; Cullum McAlpine [1947] Director/Civil Engineering and Building; The Hon David Malcolm McAlpine [1946] Director/Civil Engineering and Building; Robert John William Wotherspoon [1967] Director/Chartered Accountant

Newcome-Baker Farms Limited
Incorporated: 15 October 1957 *Employees:* 8
Net Worth: £2,206,200 *Total Assets:* £8,925,846
Registered Office: Wethered Manor, Sedgeford, Hunstanton, Norfolk, PE36 5LR
Activities: Growing of cereals (except rice), leguminous crops and oil seeds
Shareholders: Louise Katy Barber; William Geoffrey Newcome Barber
Officers: Charles Alan Whitaker Bsc AG, Secretary/Agricultural Consultant; Abigail Lucy Barber [1991] Director; Louise Katy Barber [1962] Director; Megan Rebecca Barber [1988] Director; William Geoffrey Newcome Barber [1959] Director/Farmer; Charles Alan Whitaker [1962] Director/Agricultural Consultant

Newell Properties Developments Limited
Incorporated: 2 March 2004 *Employees:* 5
Net Worth: £21,294,524 *Total Assets:* £28,293,432
Registered Office: Dickens House, Guithavon Street, Witham, Essex, CM8 1BJ
Activities: Buying and selling of own real estate
Major Shareholder: Douglas John Carroll
Officers: Mandy Carroll, Secretary; Douglas John Carroll [1952] Director/Property Developer

Newell Properties Limited
Incorporated: 11 August 1997
Net Worth: £5,845,580 *Total Assets:* £11,132,191
Registered Office: Dickens House, Guithavon Street, Witham, Essex, CM8 1BJ
Activities: Other letting and operating of own or leased real estate
Shareholders: Douglas John Carroll; Douglas John Carroll
Officers: Douglas John Carroll, Secretary/Property Dealer; Douglas John Carroll [1952] Director/Property Dealer; Mandy Carroll [1963] Director/Property Developer

Newfields Agricultural Holdings Limited
Incorporated: 8 March 2016 *Employees:* 1
Net Worth: £16,858,032 *Total Assets:* £18,242,404
Registered Office: 3 Twyford Court, High Street, Dunmow, Essex, CM6 1AE
Activities: Growing of cereals (except rice), leguminous crops and oil seeds
Major Shareholder: Graham Frederick Peacock
Officers: Adam Thomas Peacock [1983] Director/Consultant; Graham Frederick Peacock [1950] Director; James Christopher Peacock [1980] Director/Actuary

Newhall Land Limited
Incorporated: 1 December 2016
Net Worth: £1 *Total Assets:* £20,760,996
Registered Office: Countryside House, The Drive, Great Warley, Brentwood, Essex, CM13 3AT
Activities: Development of building projects
Parent: Countryside Properties (UK) Limited
Officers: Tracy Marina Warren, Secretary; Graham Stewart Cherry [1959] Director; Peter Williams [1983] Director

Newincco 1270 Limited
Incorporated: 13 November 2013 *Employees:* 4
Net Worth: £61,679,296 *Total Assets:* £123,700,328
Registered Office: 3rd Floor, Premier House, Elstree Way, Borehamwood, Herts, WD6 1JH
Activities: Other business support service activities n.e.c.
Parent: Galene Bidco Limited
Officers: Emily Henrietta Gestetner [1967] Director; Harry Leon Landy [1978] Director; Stephen Bryan Wasserman [1984] Director; Danny Stephen Waters [1984] Director

Newman Street Hotel Limited
Incorporated: 17 February 2016
Net Worth: £48,262,764 *Total Assets:* £48,265,764
Registered Office: 1st Floor, Woodgate Studios, 2-8 Games Road, Cockfosters, Barnet, Herts, EN4 9HN
Activities: Activities of head offices
Parent: Mouskos Capital Limited
Officers: Generaldina Mouskos, Secretary; Christopher Mouskos [1961] Director; Generaldina Mouskos [1936] Director; John Michael Mouskos [1964] Director

Newmarston Ltd
Incorporated: 7 August 2001
Net Worth: £56,703,080 *Total Assets:* £83,866,736
Registered Office: 41 Walsingham Road, Enfield, Middlesex, EN2 6EY
Activities: Other business support service activities n.e.c.
Officers: David Newirth, Secretary; Jacob Adler [1969] Director/Property Manager; Refoel Halpern [1971] Director/Secretary; David Neuwirth [1970] Director; Sir Weis [1981] Director

Newport School Solutions (Holdings) Limited
Incorporated: 3 October 2003
Net Worth Deficit: £3,126,000 *Total Assets:* £14,298,000
Registered Office: Astral House, Imperial Way, Watford, Herts, WD24 4WW
Activities: Activities of head offices
Parent: Infrastructure Investments Holdings Limited
Officers: Ian Hudson, Secretary; David Wyn Davies [1968] Director/Accountant; Hannah Holman [1980] Director

Newport School Solutions Limited
Incorporated: 2 April 2002
Net Worth Deficit: £3,126,000 *Total Assets:* £14,298,000
Registered Office: Astral House, Imperial Way, Watford, Herts, WD24 4WW
Activities: Activities of head offices
Parent: Newport School Solutions (Holdings) Limited
Officers: Ian Hudson, Secretary; David Wyn Davies [1968] Director/Accountant; Hannah Holman [1980] Director

Newsells Park Estates Limited
Incorporated: 16 May 2000
Net Worth: £12,658,000 *Total Assets:* £12,789,000
Registered Office: Newsells Park, Barkway, Royston, Herts, SG8 8DY
Activities: Other letting and operating of own or leased real estate
Officers: David John Whitwood, Secretary; Nicolas Bugler [1974] Director/Accountant [Swiss]; Walter Andreas Jacobs [1963] Director/Entrepreneur [German]; Michael Daniel Tuchschmid [1973] Director [Swiss]

Newsells Park Stud Limited
Incorporated: 26 April 2000 *Employees:* 31
Net Worth: £25,237,000 *Total Assets:* £33,275,000
Registered Office: Estate Office, Newsells Park, Barkway, Royston, Herts, SG8 8DY
Activities: Raising of horses and other equines
Officers: David John Whitwood, Secretary; Nicolas Bugler [1974] Director/Accountant [Swiss]; Walter Andreas Jacobs [1963] Director/Entrepreneur [German]; Michael Daniel Tuchschmid [1973] Director [Swiss]

Newsquest Capital Limited
Incorporated: 31 July 1995
Previous: Newsquest Capital PLC
Net Worth Deficit: £94,232,000 *Total Assets:* £219,000,000
Registered Office: Loudwater Mill, Station Road, High Wycombe, Bucks, HP10 9TY
Activities: Activities of head offices
Parent: Newsquest Limited
Officers: Neil Edward Carpenter, Secretary; Barbara Wartelle Wall, Secretary; Simon Alton Westrop, Secretary; Robert John Dickey [1957] Director [American]; Alison Kaye Engel [1970] Director [American]; Henry Kennedy Faure Walker [1972] Director; Paul Anthony Hunter [1964] Financial Director; Barbara Wartelle Wall [1956] Director/Solicitor [American]

Newsquest Media Group Limited
Incorporated: 9 November 1982 *Employees:* 1,891
Net Worth: £102,287,000 *Total Assets:* £262,886,000
Registered Office: Loudwater Mill, Station Road, High Wycombe, Bucks, HP10 9TY
Activities: Publishing of newspapers
Parent: Newsquest Capital Limited
Officers: Neil Edward Carpenter, Secretary; Barbara Wartelle Wall, Secretary; Simon Alton Westrop, Secretary; Robert John Dickey [1957] Director [American]; Alison Kaye Engel [1970] Director [American]; Henry Kennedy Faure Walker [1972] Director; Paul Anthony Hunter [1964] Financial Director; Barbara Wartelle Wall [1956] Director/Solicitor [American]

Newstraid Benevolent Fund
Incorporated: 20 October 2006 *Employees:* 8
Net Worth: £11,726,713 *Total Assets:* £11,778,210
Registered Office: Suites 1 & 2, Thremhall Estate, Start Hill, Bishop's Stortford, Herts, CM22 7TD
Activities: Activities of other membership organisations n.e.c.
Officers: Helen Ann Ryan, Secretary; Colin Fletcher [1946] Director/Retired; David George Holliday [1945] Director/Publisher; Neil Hilton Jagger [1962] Circulation Director; Ingrid Mary Jones [1951] Director/Business Development Manager [Irish]; Thomas Melvyn Lewis [1947] Managing Director; Tracy O'Sullivan [1967] Director; Ravindra Patel [1954] Director/Independent Retailer; Ronald William Rushbrook [1939] Director/Retired Newsagent; Richard John Webb [1965] Information Systems Director

Next Generation Clubs Limited
Incorporated: 5 November 1996 *Employees:* 757
Net Worth: £19,171,000 *Total Assets:* £77,038,000
Registered Office: The Hangar, Mosquito Way, Hatfield Business Park, Hatfield, Herts, AL10 9AX
Activities: Activities of sport clubs
Parent: David Lloyd Leisure Limited
Officers: Patrick James Burrows [1967] Director/Chartered Accountant; Donald Glenn Earlam [1965] Director

Nexus Infrastructure PLC
Incorporated: 24 November 2005 *Employees:* 823
Previous: Garbol PLC
Net Worth: £17,013,000 *Total Assets:* £76,042,000
Registered Office: 1 Tamdown Way, Braintree, Essex, CM7 2QL
Activities: Other specialised construction activities n.e.c.
Major Shareholder: Michael Thomas Morris
Officers: Dawn Rosina Hillman, Secretary; Geoffrey Howard French [1947] Director/Chairman; Ffion Haf Griffith [1969] HR Director; Richard Anthony Kilner [1956] Director; Alan Christopher Martin [1966] Director; Michael Thomas Morris [1967] Director; Alexander Simon Wiseman [1957] Director/Consultant

NGB Construction Limited
Incorporated: 12 March 2014 *Employees:* 175
Net Worth: £3,514,179 *Total Assets:* £12,472,619
Registered Office: 25 Hampstead Avenue, Mildenhall, Bury St Edmunds, Suffolk, IP28 7AS
Activities: Construction of domestic buildings
Major Shareholder: Stephen Nugent
Officers: Justin Peter Buckingham [1971] Director; Timothy Andrew Grant [1962] Director; Stephen Christopher Nugent [1977] Director

NHS Professionals Limited
Incorporated: 23 September 2008 *Employees:* 17,036
Net Worth: £55,940,000 *Total Assets:* £162,048,992
Registered Office: Breakspear Park, Breakspear Way, Hemel Hempstead, Herts, HP2 4TZ
Activities: Temporary employment agency activities
Parent: Secretary of State for Health
Officers: Colin McCready, Secretary; Oliver Guy Blackaby [1962] Director/Consultant; Anne Challinor [1954] Director; Stephen John Collier [1957] Director; John Flook [1949] Director; Nicholas George Kirkbride [1959] Director/Chief Executive Officer; Colin McCready [1975] Director/Chief Financial Officer; Anne O'Brien [1968] Director of Clinical Governance; Elizabeth Jane Robb [1953] Director/Healthcare Consultant

NHS Shared Business Services Limited
Incorporated: 8 November 2004 *Employees:* 811
Net Worth: £39,046,000 *Total Assets:* £59,393,000
Registered Office: Three Cherry Trees Lane, Hemel Hempstead, Herts, HP2 7AH
Activities: Information technology consultancy activities
Shareholders: Sopra Steria Limited; Secretary of State for Dept of Health
Officers: Peter Atherton Cashmore, Secretary; Davinder Singh Ahluwalia [1952] Director; David Albert Edmonds [1944] Director; Professor Justin Allan Spaven Jewitt [1954] Director; Benjamin Michael Patrick Masterson [1964] Director/Senior Civil Servant; Marcus James Thorman [1972] Director/Accountant; John Powell Torrie [1954] Director

NHV Helicopters Ltd
Incorporated: 3 December 2015 *Employees:* 55
Net Worth Deficit: £3,946,703 *Total Assets:* £15,174,545
Registered Office: Klyne Business Aviation Centre, Buck Courtney Crescent, Norwich, NR6 6JT
Activities: Scheduled passenger air transport
Major Shareholder: Eric Van Hal
Officers: Michael Gislam [1987] Director; Jamie Lee John [1985] Director; Brieuc Spindler [1964] Director/Chief Operating Officer of NHV Group [Belgian]

NIAB.
Incorporated: 1 July 1997 *Employees:* 350
Net Worth Deficit: £12,784,000 *Total Assets:* £14,125,000
Registered Office: Huntingdon Road, Cambridge, CB3 0LE
Activities: Growing of cereals (except rice), leguminous crops and oil seeds
Officers: Dr Tina Lorraine Barsby [1957] Director; Stephen John Ellwood [1957] Director; Kathleen Elizabeth Fidgeon [1958] Director/Chartered Accountant; James Eric Godfrey [1953] Director; Robert Harle [1952] Director/Farmer; Dr Nigel Wells Kerby [1953] Director; Dr Charles Alfred Lang [1936] Director/Retired Computer Specialist; Robert Campbell Lowson [1949] Director Civil Servant; Richard Auld MacDonald [1954] Director; Professor Ian James Puddephat [1963] Research Director; Professor Alison Smith [1956] Director/Plant Scientist

Anthony Nicholas (UK) Limited
Incorporated: 5 July 2007
Net Worth: £16,890,974 *Total Assets:* £58,186,260
Registered Office: 3rd Floor, Premier House, Elstree Way, Borehamwood, Herts, WD6 1JH
Activities: Activities of head offices
Officers: Noel Coyle [1962] Director [Irish]; Mark Naughton-Rumbo [1960] Director; Tony Obernik [1943] Director [Irish]

Nicholls & Clarke Limited
Incorporated: 18 July 1900 *Employees:* 568
Net Worth: £41,292,204 *Total Assets:* £51,268,684
Registered Office: 41-51 Freshwater Road, Chadwell Heath, Romford, Essex, RM8 1SP
Activities: Activities of head offices
Officers: Geraint David Cooper, Secretary; Geraint David Cooper [1958] Director/Accountant; David Ian Forbes [1965] Director; Kenneth Stuart Alexander Forbes [1937] Director; Stephen Andrew Forbes [1963] Director; Gary Kenneth Gingell [1968] Director; Richard John Hill [1971] Director

Nicholls Limited
Incorporated: 23 April 2015 *Employees:* 44
Net Worth: £5,627,103 *Total Assets:* £13,458,243
Registered Office: Sinks Pit, Main Road, Kesgrave, Ipswich, Suffolk, IP5 2PE
Activities: Recovery of sorted materials
Major Shareholder: Guy John Nicholls
Officers: Kieran Caleb Cobb [1977] Finance Director; Anthony Derek Marshall [1975] Sales Director; Guy John Nicholls [1963] Director; Jake Guy Nicholls [1990] Director

Nikon X-Tek Systems Limited
Incorporated: 23 January 1986 *Employees:* 111
Previous: X-Tek Systems Limited
Net Worth Deficit: £1,654,000 *Total Assets:* £32,208,000
Registered Office: Tring Business Centre, Icknield Way, Tring, Herts, HP23 4JX
Activities: Manufacture of electronic industrial process control equipment
Parent: Nikon Metrology UK Limited
Officers: Koenraad Van Der Elst, Secretary; Tadashi Nakayama [1961] Director/Business Manager [Japanese]; Satoru Nishiura [1965] Director [Japanese]; Jeffry Ward Walker [1956] Director [American]

Nine Heathrow Ventures Limited
Incorporated: 11 December 2014 *Employees:* 5
Net Worth Deficit: £1,943,331 *Total Assets:* £19,260,404
Registered Office: Melton House, 65-67 Clarendon Road, Watford, Herts, WD17 1DS
Activities: Development of building projects
Parent: Chadha Capital Investments Limited
Officers: Gursharan Singh Chadha [1960] Director; Vivek Chadha [1988] Director

Nine Reading Hotel Limited
Incorporated: 9 November 2016 *Employees:* 28
Net Worth: £230,298 *Total Assets:* £11,058,695
Registered Office: 65-67 Clarendon Road, Watford, Herts, WD17 1DS
Activities: Hotels and similar accommodation
Parent: Chadha Capital Investments Limited
Officers: Vivek Singh Chadha [1988] Director

NIS Acquisitions Limited
Incorporated: 3 December 2007
Net Worth: £329,867,008 *Total Assets:* £687,932,032
Registered Office: Peoplebuilding 2, Peoplebuilding Estate, Maylands Avenue, Hemel Hempstead Industrial Estate, Hemel Hempstead, Herts, HP2 4NW
Activities: Activities of head offices
Parent: Northgate Information Solutions Limited
Officers: Malcolm Robert Bennett, Secretary; Steven James Chalker [1974] Chief Financial Director; Andrew Phillip Monshaw [1962] Director [American]

NIS Receivables No. 2 Limited
Incorporated: 3 December 2007
Net Worth: £49,100,000 *Total Assets:* £49,100,000
Registered Office: Peoplebuilding 2, Peoplebuilding Estate, Maylands Avenue, Hemel Hempstead Industrial Estate, Hemel Hempstead, Herts, HP2 4NW
Activities: Other business support service activities n.e.c.
Parent: Northgate Information Solutions Holdings Limited
Officers: Malcolm Robert Bennett, Secretary; Steven James Chalker [1974] Chief Financial Director; Andrew Phillip Monshaw [1962] Director [American]

NIS Receivables No.1 Limited
Incorporated: 26 March 2008
Net Worth: £75,000,000 *Total Assets:* £75,000,000
Registered Office: Peoplebuilding 2, Peoplebuilding Estate, Maylands Avenue, Hemel Hempstead Industrial Estate, Hemel Hempstead, Herts, HP2 4NW
Activities: Activities of head offices
Parent: Northgate Information Solutions Holdings Limited
Officers: Malcolm Robert Bennett, Secretary; Steven James Chalker [1974] Chief Financial Director; Andrew Phillip Monshaw [1962] Director [American]

Nissan Motor (GB) Limited
Incorporated: 21 June 1990 *Employees:* 196
Net Worth: £183,110,000 *Total Assets:* £767,649,024
Registered Office: The Rivers Office Park, Denham Way, Maple Cross, Rickmansworth, Herts, WD3 9YS
Activities: Sale of new cars and light motor vehicles
Parent: Nissan Holdings (UK) Limited
Officers: Steven Neil Tiffin, Secretary; Laurent Franck Christian David [1971] Director/Senior Vice President - Administration and Finance [French]; Gareth John Main [1967] Director/General Manager; Kenneth Alexander Ramirez [1968] Director [American]; Alan David Tennant [1954] Director

NMSIM Group Limited
Incorporated: 25 October 2011
Net Worth: £8,107,523 *Total Assets:* £8,127,476
Registered Office: Unit B2, Basepoint Business Centre, 11 Butterfield, Great Marlings, Luton, Beds, LU2 8DL
Activities: Other activities auxiliary to insurance and pension funding
Parent: Global Ridgeway Holdings Limited
Officers: Robert John Bygrave [1970] Finance Director; Shay Jacob Reches [1955] Director [Israeli]

No Climb Products Limited
Incorporated: 2 March 1965 *Employees:* 102
Net Worth: £9,846,844 *Total Assets:* £14,774,944
Registered Office: Edison House, 163 Dixons Hill Road, Welham Green, Herts, AL9 7JE
Activities: Other manufacturing n.e.c.
Parent: Et Ceteris Limited
Officers: Philip Richard Bartlam [1970] Sales Director; Robert Campbell [1967] Director; Alison Kiernan [1975] HR Director; John Stuart Mortimer [1972] Operations Director; Fraser Robertson Redpath [1970] Finance Director; William Jonathan Rossiter [1965] Managing Director

Noahs Ark Chemicals Limited
Incorporated: 19 June 2001 *Employees:* 10
Net Worth: £562,203 *Total Assets:* £9,640,393
Registered Office: 2nd Floor Office, 253-269 High Road, Woodford Green, Essex, IG8 9FB
Activities: Wholesale of chemical products
Major Shareholder: Bharat Bhardwaj
Officers: Rashmi Bhardwaj, Secretary/Chartered Accountant; Dr Bharat Bhardwaj [1968] Director/Chemical Engineer; Rashmi Bhardwaj [1961] Director/Chartered Accountant

Noble Foods (We) Limited
Incorporated: 5 April 1991 *Employees:* 4
Previous: Gubblecote Properties Limited
Net Worth: £2,215,566 *Total Assets:* £12,804,017
Registered Office: Beeches Farm, Icknield Way, Tring, Herts, HP23 4LA
Activities: Production of electricity
Shareholders: Peter Donald Dean; Susan Jane Dean
Officers: Peter Donald Dean, Secretary/Director; Peter Donald Dean [1944] Director; Sarah Lois Dean [1971] Director

Noble Gift Packaging Limited
Incorporated: 26 June 1992 *Employees:* 42
Net Worth: £5,065,652 *Total Assets:* £11,711,019
Registered Office: 73 Lockfield Avenue, Enfield, Middlesex, EN3 7QL
Activities: Other business support service activities n.e.c.
Shareholders: David Stobiecki; Samuel Herzog
Officers: Miriam Stobiecki, Secretary; David Stobiecki [1964] Director/Sales; Peter Weiner [1947] Director/Accountant [Canadian]

Nobo Group Limited
Incorporated: 26 November 1985
Net Worth: £9,000,000 *Total Assets:* £9,000,000
Registered Office: Oxford House, Oxford Road, Aylesbury, Bucks, HP21 8SZ
Activities: Activities of head offices
Officers: Robert Michael Grimes, Secretary; Dr. Walter Joe Thomas [1966] Director/Solicitor

Noodle Properties Limited
Incorporated: 2 March 2015 *Employees:* 2
Net Worth: £461,751 *Total Assets:* £9,237,281
Registered Office: 28 Watersfield Way, Edgware, Middlesex, HA8 6RZ
Activities: Other letting and operating of own or leased real estate
Officers: Adam Kaye [1968] Director; Samantha Sanson [1970] Director

Nordson (U.K.) Limited
Incorporated: 1 June 1972 *Employees:* 52
Net Worth: £12,317,955 *Total Assets:* £26,051,878
Registered Office: 14 Apex Business Centre, Boscombe Road, Dunstable, Beds, LU5 4SB
Activities: Non-specialised wholesale trade
Parent: Nordson Corporation
Officers: Steve Hankin [1966] Director/General Manager; Bernhard Perschke [1957] Director [German]; Gregory Alan Thaxton [1961] Director/Corporate Controller [American]; Axel Wenz [1953] Director [German]

Norfolk Academies
Incorporated: 13 February 2012 *Employees:* 254
Net Worth: £19,680,000 *Total Assets:* £23,246,000
Registered Office: c/o CCN, Ipswich Road, Norwich, NR2 2LJ
Activities: Primary education
Officers: Lauren Frances Dilrew [1986] Director/Chartered Accountant; Dr Anne Mary Fry [1958] Director/Educational Psychologist [British/Canadian]; James Doherty McAtear [1965] Director/Headteacher; Dr Ben Milner [1969] Director/University Associate Dean; Christopher James Randle [1980] Director; Piers Frank Ranger [1954] Director/Retired

Norfolk and Waveney Enterprise Services
Incorporated: 5 May 1982 *Employees:* 85
Net Worth: £1,802,166 *Total Assets:* £14,477,050
Registered Office: Rouen House, Rouen Road, Norwich, NR1 1RB
Activities: Other business support service activities n.e.c.
Officers: Lucy Jane Cannell, Secretary; Joanna Clarke [1961] Deputy Chief Executive/Director; Nicholas William Doyle [1966] Director; James Robert Pinchbeck [1964] Director/Marketing Partner; Philip Roger Watkins [1959] Director; Laurie Wiseman [1959] Director

Norfolk Broads Direct Limited
Incorporated: 22 November 1967 *Employees:* 64
Net Worth: £8,939,638 *Total Assets:* £10,850,555
Registered Office: Loynes House, The Bridge, Wroxham, Norfolk, NR12 8RX
Activities: Repair and maintenance of ships and boats
Parent: Norfolk Broads Holdings Ltd
Officers: Paul Anthony Greasley, Secretary; Barbara Kay Greasley [1962] Director/Teaching Assistant; Paul Anthony Greasley [1962] Director/Accountant

Norfolk Broads Holdings Limited
Incorporated: 5 February 2003 *Employees:* 64
Net Worth: £8,940,638 *Total Assets:* £10,850,552
Registered Office: Loynes House, The Bridge, Wroxham, Norfolk, NR12 8RX
Activities: Activities of head offices
Shareholder: Paul Anthony Greasley
Officers: Paul Anthony Greasley, Secretary; Barbara Kay Greasley [1962] Director; Paul Anthony Greasley [1962] Director/Accountant

Norfolk Capital Group Limited
Incorporated: 4 July 1946
Net Worth: £18,913,000 *Total Assets:* £18,913,000
Registered Office: Queens Court, 9-17 Eastern Road, Romford, Essex, RM1 3NG
Activities: Non-trading company
Parent: BPH Finance Number 1 Limited
Officers: Jonathan Patrick Braidley [1965] Director/Investment Professional; Christopher Andre Kula [1983] Director/Chartered Accountant [German/Canadian]

Norfolk Capital Hotels Limited
Incorporated: 6 October 1927 *Employees:* 14
Net Worth: £10,648,000 *Total Assets:* £10,649,000
Registered Office: Queens Court, 9-17 Eastern Road, Romford, Essex, RM1 3NG
Activities: Hotels and similar accommodation
Parent: Norfolk Capital Group Limited
Officers: Jonathan Patrick Braidley [1965] Director/Investment Professional; Christopher Andre Kula [1983] Director/Chartered Accountant [German/Canadian]

Norfolk Capital Limited
Incorporated: 13 February 2015 *Employees:* 275
Net Worth: £81,122,000 *Total Assets:* £168,826,000
Registered Office: St Crispin's House, Duke Street, Norwich, NR3 1PD
Activities: Activities of financial services holding companies
Major Shareholder: Andrew Clive Turner
Officers: Anthony Richardson, Secretary; Andrew Clive Turner [1958] Director/Accountant; Sharon Leigh Turner [1957] Director

Norfolk Community Foundation
Incorporated: 17 September 2004 *Employees:* 11
Net Worth: £22,715,000 *Total Assets:* £23,163,000
Registered Office: St James Mill, Whitefriars, Norwich, NR3 1TN
Activities: Other information service activities n.e.c.
Officers: Martin Webster, Secretary; Stephen Graham Stafford Allen [1951] Director/Accountant; Henry Greville Cator [1956] Director/Chartered Surveyor; Virginia Clare Edgecombe [1968] Director/Solicitor; Frank Eric Eliel [1946] Director of Signs Express; Lady Karen Jean Fisher [1951] Director; Peter Karl James Franzen [1947] Director; Michael Anthony James Gurney [1954] Director/Farmer, Advertising & Marketing; Charles Iain Hayton Mawson [1955] Director/Partner MA Partners LLP; Caroline McKenzie Money [1963] Director/Local Government Officer; Jonathan Charles Pearson [1962] Director; Nicholas Julian Hedley Pratt [1958] Director/Farmer; Michelle Mai Raper [1967] Director/Accountant; Timothy Robert Seeley [1960] Bank Director

Norfolk Environmental Waste Services Limited
Incorporated: 30 July 1991 *Employees:* 3
Net Worth: £4,018,171 *Total Assets:* £12,326,008
Registered Office: 280 Fifers Lane, Norwich, NR6 6EQ
Activities: Other service activities n.e.c.
Parent: Norse Commercial Services Limited
Officers: Andrew David Jamieson [1956] Director/Corporate Advisor; Fiona McDiarmid [1961] Director; Dean Thorvald Wetteland [1976] Commercial Director

Norfolk Farm Produce Limited
Incorporated: 24 July 1970 *Employees:* 44
Net Worth: £18,234,068 *Total Assets:* £23,956,256
Registered Office: Greenwood House, Greenwood Court, Bury St Edmunds, Suffolk, IP32 7GY
Activities: Growing of cereals (except rice), leguminous crops and oil seeds
Major Shareholder: Christopher Griffin
Officers: Pamela Susann Griffin, Secretary; Christopher Luke Griffin [1979] Director; Pamela Susann Griffin [1946] Director

Norfolk Free Range Limited
Incorporated: 19 December 2003 *Employees:* 106
Net Worth: £11,630,317 *Total Assets:* £31,133,952
Registered Office: Snowre Hall, Main Road, Fordham, Downham Market, Norfolk, PE38 0LN
Activities: Raising of swine and pigs
Shareholders: Steven Hart; Sally Ann Hart
Officers: Sally Ann Hart, Secretary/Farmer; Sally Ann Hart [1969] Director/Farmer; Steven Hart [1960] Director/Farmer

Norfolk Truck & Van Limited
Incorporated: 4 September 1984 *Employees:* 106
Net Worth: £5,319,595 *Total Assets:* £11,625,560
Registered Office: School Lane, Sprowston, Norwich, NR7 8TL
Activities: Sale of other motor vehicles
Parent: Saint Vincent Holdings Limited
Officers: Emma Jane Colby, Secretary; Michael John Sutton, Secretary; Simon William Beckett [1964] Director/Accountant; Peter George Colby [1942] Director

Norfolk Wildlife Trust
Incorporated: 5 November 1926 *Employees:* 66
Net Worth: £19,265,148 *Total Assets:* £20,993,532
Registered Office: Bewick House, 22 Thorpe Road, Norwich, NR1 1RY
Activities: Other service activities n.e.c.
Officers: Pamela Mary Abbott, Secretary; Gregory Nicholas Beeton [1967] Director - International Charity; Jonathan Andrew Humphreys [1960] Director/Banker; Alice Brigham Liddle [1954] Director/Solicitor; Philip Ross Norton [1959] Director/Solicitor; Dr Jeff Price [1959] Director/Senior Researcher [American]; Geoffrey Randall [1948] Director/Retired Architect; Susan Roe [1949] Director/Retired Environmentalist; John Sharpe [1957] Director/Retired; David Thompson [1952] Director/Retired Architect; Michael Patrick Toms [1968] Director/Ornithologist; Heather Jane Tyrrell [1957] Director/Retired

Norish Limited
Incorporated: 28 December 1972 *Employees:* 160
Net Worth: £4,524,766 *Total Assets:* £23,631,248
Registered Office: Northern Industrial Estate, Bury St Edmunds, Suffolk, IP32 6NL
Activities: Operation of warehousing and storage facilities for land transport activities
Parent: Norish (NI) Limited
Officers: Aidan Vincent Hughes, Secretary; Aidan Vincent Hughes [1965] Director/Chartered Accountant [Irish]; Timothy Joseph O'Neill [1951] Director [Irish]

Norpap Property (Telford) Ltd
Incorporated: 31 July 2015
Net Worth: £188,488 *Total Assets:* £9,556,848
Registered Office: 4 Warner House, Bessborough Road, Harrovian Business Village, Harrow, Middlesex, HA1 3EX
Activities: Other letting and operating of own or leased real estate
Shareholder: Paul Fecher
Officers: Paul King, Secretary; Adam Scott Fecher [1974] Director; Marc Darren Fecher [1971] Director; Paul Fecher [1946] Director; Paul Edward King [1974] Director/Accountant

C.John Norris (Cars & Caravans) Limited
Incorporated: 11 January 1939 *Employees:* 43
Net Worth: £10,893,977 *Total Assets:* £15,464,725
Registered Office: Thorney Road, Eye, Peterborough, PE6 7UB
Activities: Sale of new cars and light motor vehicles
Shareholders: Executors of Jonathan Norris; Sally Norris
Officers: Sally Norris, Secretary; Sally Norris [1963] Director/Company Secretary; Anna Spriggs [1963] Director/Solicitor

Norse Care Limited
Incorporated: 19 November 2010 *Employees:* 1,638
Net Worth: £18,431,908 *Total Assets:* £45,711,972
Registered Office: 280 Fifers Lane, Norwich, NR6 6EQ
Activities: Residential care activities for the elderly and disabled
Parent: Norse Group Limited
Officers: Andrew John Merricks, Secretary; Andrew David Jamieson [1956] Director/Corporate Advisor; Karen Elizabeth Knight [1960] Director/Senior Manager; Fiona McDiarmid [1961] Director; Dean Thorvald Wetteland [1976] Commercial Director

Norse Commercial Services Limited
Incorporated: 18 January 1994 *Employees:* 6,195
Net Worth: £20,896,104 *Total Assets:* £78,416,576
Registered Office: 280 Fifers Lane, Norwich, NR6 6EQ
Activities: Combined facilities support activities
Parent: Norse Group Limited
Officers: Andrew John Merricks, Secretary; Andrew David Jamieson [1956] Director/Corporate Advisor; Karen Elizabeth Knight [1960] Director/Senior Manager; Fiona McDiarmid [1961] Director; Dean Thorvald Wetteland [1976] Commercial Director

Norse Eastern Limited
Incorporated: 19 November 2010 *Employees:* 1,653
Net Worth: £1,639,528 *Total Assets:* £9,143,978
Registered Office: 280 Fifers Lane, Norwich, NR6 6EQ
Activities: Combined facilities support activities
Parent: Norse Commercial Services Limited
Officers: Andrew David Jamieson [1956] Director/Corporate Advisor; Karen Elizabeth Knight [1960] Director/Senior Manager; Fiona McDiarmid [1961] Director; Dean Thorvald Wetteland [1976] Commercial Director

Norse Group Limited
Incorporated: 1 February 2006 *Employees:* 9,558
Net Worth: £19,132,000 *Total Assets:* £175,304,000
Registered Office: 280 Fifers Lane, Norwich, NR6 6EQ
Activities: Other service activities n.e.c.
Parent: Norfolk County Council
Officers: Andrew John Merricks, Secretary; Andrew David Jamieson [1956] Director/Corporate Advisor; Karen Elizabeth Knight [1960] Director/Senior Manager; Fiona McDiarmid [1961] Director; Dean Thorvald Wetteland [1976] Commercial Director

North Essex Multi-Academy Trust
Incorporated: 29 June 2011 *Employees:* 294
Net Worth: £18,666,156 *Total Assets:* £25,669,688
Registered Office: Notley High School & Braintree Sixth Form, Notley Road, Braintree, Essex, CM7 1WY
Activities: General secondary education
Officers: Paul Raymond Griffiths, Secretary; Andrew Jason Allocca [1972] Director/New Business & Development Manager; David Conway [1957] Director/Headteacher; David Reginald Gask [1946] Director/Retired Automotive Engineer; Angela Patricia Hicks [1962] Director/School Improvement Partner; Trevor Keith Parrott [1950] Director/Retired Chartered Engineer; Gary Robert Sprawling [1962] Director

North Herts Hospice Care Association
Incorporated: 25 July 1986 *Employees:* 177
Net Worth: £8,673,645 *Total Assets:* £9,472,188
Registered Office: Garden House Hospice, Gillison Close, Letchworth, Herts, SG6 1QU
Activities: Specialists medical practice activities
Officers: Sir Robert James Timothy Wilson, Secretary; Eleanor Clare Cooke [1962] Director/Housewife; Helen Dodd [1958] Director/Retired; Doctor Kenneth Farrington [1948] Director/Consultant Nephrologist; Roger Arthur Gochin [1948] Director/Management Consultant; Susan Greenbank [1964] Director/Self Employed [British/Canadian]; Dr John Machen [1950] Director/Retired General Medical Practitioner; Steve Mellish [1957] Director/Risk and Resilience Professional; Dawn Morrish [1956] Director/Retired; John Procter [1944] Director/Local Government Officer Retired; Rhona Seviour [1948] Director/Consultant; James David Silsby [1974] Associate Director; Sir Robert James Timothy Wilson [1949] Director

The North London Collegiate School
Incorporated: 17 May 1993 *Employees:* 45
Net Worth: £28,371,208 *Total Assets:* £39,737,320
Registered Office: Canons Drive, Edgware, Middlesex, HA8 7RJ
Activities: General secondary education
Officers: Keith Breslauer [1966] Director/Banker [American]; Sophie Christine Carter [1970] Director/School Governor; Elaine Davis [1968] Director; Dr Anton Vignaraj Emmanuel [1965] Director/Doctor; Dr Adam Tobias Fox [1972] Director/Doctor; John Stuart Herlihy [1954] Director; Steven Harold Jaffe [1950] Director/Chartered Accountant; Peter John Nicholas Linthwaite [1956] Director/Investment Manager; Peter David Needleman [1955] Director/Actuary; Eileen Annabelle Raperport [1951] Director/Accountant; Timothy John Suter [1956] Director; Professor Brian Young [1963] Director/University Professor

North Norfolk Academy Trust
Incorporated: 6 October 2011 *Employees:* 172
Net Worth: £14,431,000 *Total Assets:* £15,903,000
Registered Office: Sheringham High School, Holt Road, Sheringham, Norfolk, NR26 8ND
Activities: Pre-primary education
Shareholders: Christine Candlish; Timothy Roderick; Stephen Brenden Foster
Officers: Christine Candlish [1967] Director/Head of Continuous Improvement; Julia Drury [1950] Director/Retired; Gill Pegg [1958] Director/Professional Development Quality; Doctor Andrew Huw Richardson [1967] Director/Headteacher; Constance Tyce [1946] Director; John Bidlake Wollocombe [1960] Director/Community Governor

North West Steel Limited
Incorporated: 22 June 1988 *Employees:* 26
Net Worth: £7,383,586 *Total Assets:* £9,922,967
Registered Office: 1 Fenlake Business Centre, Fengate, Peterborough, Cambs, PE1 5BQ
Activities: Other specialised construction activities n.e.c.
Major Shareholder: John Patrick William Roe
Officers: Jean Robertson [1964] Director; John Patrick William Roe [1958] Director; Clinton John Taylor [1961] Director

Northfield Avenue (Holdings) Limited
Incorporated: 9 July 2004 *Employees:* 2
Net Worth: £6,084,658 *Total Assets:* £18,292,048
Registered Office: First Floor, Radius House, 51 Clarendon Road, Watford, Herts, WD17 1HP
Activities: Development of building projects
Parent: Northfield Avenue Properties Limited
Officers: Richard David Swaine, Secretary; Richard David Swaine [1962] Director; Jonathan James Willoughby [1966] Director

Northgate Information Solutions Holdings Limited
Incorporated: 5 November 1992 *Employees:* 139
Net Worth Deficit: £141,783,008 *Total Assets:* £965,958,016
Registered Office: Peoplebuilding 2, Peoplebuilding Estate, Maylands Avenue, Hemel Hempstead Industrial Estate, Hemel Hempstead, Herts, HP2 4NW
Activities: Activities of head offices
Parent: NIS Acquisitions Limited
Officers: Malcolm Robert Bennett, Secretary; Steven James Chalker [1974] Chief Financial Director; Andrew Phillip Monshaw [1962] Director [American]

Northgate Information Solutions Limited
Incorporated: 3 December 2007 *Employees:* 6,693
Net Worth: £164,100,000 *Total Assets:* £295,300,000
Registered Office: Peoplebuilding 2, Peoplebuilding Estate, Maylands Avenue, Hemel Hempstead Industrial Estate, Hemel Hempstead, Herts, HP2 4NW
Activities: Other business support service activities n.e.c.
Parent: Northgate UK Holdings 4 Limited
Officers: Malcolm Robert Bennett, Secretary; Steven James Chalker [1974] Chief Financial Director; Andrew Phillip Monshaw [1962] Director [American]

Northgate Public Services (UK) Limited
Incorporated: 17 December 1969 *Employees:* 1,228
Previous: Northgate Information Solutions UK Limited
Net Worth: £163,456,000 *Total Assets:* £431,332,000
Registered Office: Peoplebuilding 2, Peoplebuilding Estate, Maylands Avenue, Hemel Hempstead Industrial Estate, Hemel Hempstead, Herts, HP2 4NW
Activities: Manufacture of computers and peripheral equipment
Parent: NPS (Holdings) Limited
Officers: Stephen James Callaghan [1960] Director; Tomonori Hira [1968] Director [Japanese]; Alan George O'Reilly [1961] Director [Irish]

Northgate Public Services Limited
Incorporated: 3 December 2014 *Employees:* 2
Net Worth Deficit: £38,500,000 *Total Assets:* £126,600,000
Registered Office: Peoplebuilding 2, Peoplebuilding Estate, Maylands Avenue, Hemel Hempstead Industrial Estate, Hemel Hempstead, Herts, HP2 4NW
Activities: Other information technology service activities
Officers: Stephen James Callaghan [1960] Director; Alan George O'Reilly [1961] Director [Irish]

Northgate UK Holdings 1 Limited
Incorporated: 3 February 2016
Net Worth Deficit: £40,000,000 *Total Assets:* £232,000,000
Registered Office: Peoplebuilding 2, Peoplebuilding Estate, Maylands Avenue, Hemel Hempstead Industrial Estate, Hemel Hempstead, Herts, HP2 4NW
Activities: Other business support service activities n.e.c.
Officers: Malcolm Robert Bennett, Secretary; Michael John Magee [1991] Director/Investment Professional [Irish]; Andrew Phillip Monshaw [1962] Director [American]; Emilie Railhac [1979] Director/Investment Professional [French]; James Reynolds [1975] Director/Investment Professional [French]; Michael Christopher Small [1973] Director/Partner

Northgate UK Holdings 2 Limited
Incorporated: 3 February 2016
Net Worth: £232,900,000 *Total Assets:* £232,900,000
Registered Office: Peoplebuilding 2, Peoplebuilding Estate, Maylands Avenue, Hemel Hempstead Industrial Estate, Hemel Hempstead, Herts, HP2 4NW
Activities: Other business support service activities n.e.c.
Parent: Northgate UK Holdings 1 Limited
Officers: Malcolm Robert Bennett, Secretary; Michael John Magee [1991] Director/Investment Professional [Irish]; Andrew Phillip Monshaw [1962] Director [American]; Emilie Railhac [1979] Director/Investment Professional [French]; James Reynolds [1975] Director/Investment Professional [French]; Michael Christopher Small [1973] Director/Partner

Northgate UK Holdings 3 Limited
Incorporated: 3 February 2016
Net Worth: £232,000,000 *Total Assets:* £232,000,000
Registered Office: Peoplebuilding 2, Peoplebuilding Estate, Maylands Avenue, Hemel Hempstead Industrial Estate, Hemel Hempstead, Herts, HP2 4NW
Activities: Other business support service activities n.e.c.
Parent: Northgate UK Holdings 2 Limited
Officers: Malcolm Robert Bennett, Secretary; Michael John Magee [1991] Director/Investment Professional [Irish]; Andrew Phillip Monshaw [1962] Director [American]; Emilie Railhac [1979] Director/Investment Professional [French]; James Reynolds [1975] Director/Investment Professional [French]; Michael Christopher Small [1973] Director/Partner

Northgate UK Holdings 4 Limited
Incorporated: 3 February 2016
Net Worth: £168,200,000 *Total Assets:* £790,800,000
Registered Office: Peoplebuilding 2, Peoplebuilding Estate, Maylands Avenue, Hemel Hempstead Industrial Estate, Hemel Hempstead, Herts, HP2 4NW
Activities: Other business support service activities n.e.c.
Parent: Northgate UK Holdings 3 Limited
Officers: Malcolm Robert Bennett, Secretary; Michael John Magee [1991] Director/Investment Professional [Irish]; Andrew Phillip Monshaw [1962] Director [American]; Emilie Railhac [1979] Director/Investment Professional [French]; James Reynolds [1975] Director/Investment Professional [French]; Michael Christopher Small [1973] Director/Partner

Northwood Paper Sales Limited
Incorporated: 15 July 1998 *Employees:* 21
Net Worth: £2,994,494 *Total Assets:* £36,769,968
Registered Office: 4 Warner House, Harrovian Business Village, Bessborough Road, Harrow, Middlesex, HA1 3EX
Activities: Agents specialised in the sale of other particular products
Major Shareholder: Paul Fecher
Officers: Kishor Vekaria, Secretary/Accountant; Adam Scott Fecher [1974] Director/Sales; Paul Fecher [1946] Director

Norton Way Motors Limited
Incorporated: 25 July 1962 *Employees:* 436
Net Worth: £9,297,000 *Total Assets:* £52,995,000
Registered Office: Norton Way North, Letchworth, Herts, SG6 1BL
Activities: Sale of new cars and light motor vehicles
Parent: Marubeni Auto Investment (UK) Limited
Officers: Arran Bangham, Secretary; Tsugutoshi Akano [1974] Director [Japanese]; Arran Bangham [1968] Director; David Grainger [1954] Director; Naonori Ishii [1967] Director [Japanese]; Shuichi Kamizono [1965] Director [Japanese]; Kazuhiro Kondo [1967] Director [Japanese]; Richard Siney [1965] Director

Norwich Airport Limited
Incorporated: 28 November 1986 *Employees:* 272
Net Worth: £27,253,764 *Total Assets:* £40,069,680
Registered Office: Norwich Airport, Norwich, NR6 6JA
Activities: Service activities incidental to air transportation
Parent: Omniport Norwich Limited
Officers: Katherine Georgina Cook, Secretary; Andrew Michael Bell [1979] Director; Richard John Pace [1968] Director/Airport General Manager; Andrew James Proctor [1947] Director/Councillor; Sir Peter Rigby [1943] Director; Alan Henry Waters [1953] Director/City Councillor

Norwich City Football Club PLC
Incorporated: 2 April 1919 *Employees:* 291
Net Worth: £37,752,000 *Total Assets:* £111,391,000
Registered Office: Carrow Road, Norwich, NR1 1JE
Activities: Activities of sport clubs
Shareholders: Edward Michael Spencer Wynn-Jones; Delia Ann Smith
Officers: Benjamin William Dack, Secretary; Michael Martin Foulger [1954] Director; Stephan John Phillips [1955] Director; Delia Ann Smith [1941] Director/Writer; Thomas Owen Bartlett Smith [1981] Director/Business Owner; Edward Michael Spencer Wynn-Jones [1941] Director

Norwich Diocesan Board of Finance Limited (The)
Incorporated: 28 March 1906 *Employees:* 46
Net Worth: £142,528,992 *Total Assets:* £150,900,000
Registered Office: Diocesan House, 109 Dereham Road, Easton, Norwich, NR9 5ES
Activities: Activities of religious organisations
Officers: Michael Richard Butler, Secretary/Chief Executive; Revd Michael Asquith [1960] Director/Vicar; Robin Philip Back [1946] Director; The Venerable Steven James Betts [1964] Director/Minister of Religion; Hugh Murray Charles Coghill [1950] Director of Savills; Michael Anthony James Gurney [1954] Director; Ray Hollands [1935] Director/Retired; William Eric Husselby [1939] Director/Company Chairman; Kandara Rachelle Kammoun [1960] Director/Administrator; Susan Gail Martin [1961] Director/Retired; Patricia Menaul [1938] Director/Retired; Captain Anthony Mervyn Poulter [1946] Director/Retired; Angela Robson [1961] Director/Chartered Accountant; Simon Colin Stokes [1962] Director/Vicar; Julian Taylor [1956] Director/Landowner/Farmer; Revd Canon Sally Margaret Theakston [1962] Director/Clerk in Holy Orders; Revd Timothy Weston [1948] Director/Priest

Norwood Ravenswood
Incorporated: 9 October 1996 *Employees:* 648
Net Worth: £43,448,000 *Total Assets:* £52,817,000
Registered Office: Broadway House, 80-82 The Broadway, Stanmore, Middlesex, HA7 4HB
Activities: Educational support services
Officers: Abiola Yusuf, Secretary; Yonni Leslie Spiero Abramson [1984] Director/Property Developer; Julia Sarah Chain [1957] Director/Solicitor; Tamara Margaret Finkelstein [1967] Director/Civil Servant; Linda Goldberg [1942] Director/Retired; Philip Lee Hertz [1967] Director/Global Head of Restructuring and Insolvency; Angela Hodes [1956] Director/Barrister; Glynnis Joffe [1952] Director/Retired; Neville Kahn [1963] Director/Managing Partner; Mark Pollack [1961] Director; Anthony Leon Philip Rabin [1955] Director; Lady Elaine Sacks [1949] Director; Gary Hilton Sacks [1965] Director; David Mark Smith [1970] Director/Group Head of Tax and Corporate Finance; David Mark Stanton [1969] Board Director and Deputy Chairman

Norwood Schools Ltd.
Incorporated: 9 March 1953 *Employees:* 616
Net Worth: £29,180,000 *Total Assets:* £38,106,000
Registered Office: Broadway House, 80-82 The Broadway, Stanmore, Middlesex, HA7 4HB
Activities: Residential care activities for learning difficulties, mental health and substance abuse
Officers: Abiola Yusuf, Secretary; Neville Kahn [1963] Director/Managing Partner; David Mark Smith [1970] Director/Group Head of Tax and Corporate Finance; David Mark Stanton [1969] Board Director/Deputy Chairman

Notcutts Group Limited
Incorporated: 24 May 2011 *Employees:* 1,337
Net Worth: £35,830,852 *Total Assets:* £78,049,856
Registered Office: The Nursery, Cumberland Street, Woodbridge, Suffolk, IP12 4AF
Activities: Other retail sale in non-specialised stores
Officers: Julian Herbert, Secretary; Nicholas Alan Burrows [1961] Director; Nicola Joy Dulieu [1963] Director; Julian Herbert [1968] Finance Director; Bryan John Laxton [1960] Director; Caroline Jane Notcutt [1965] Director

Notcutts Limited
Incorporated: 10 February 1945 *Employees:* 1,337
Net Worth: £39,164,452 *Total Assets:* £81,382,808
Registered Office: The Nursery, Cumberland Street, Woodbridge, Suffolk, IP12 4AF
Activities: Other retail sale in non-specialised stores
Parent: Notcutts Group Limited
Officers: Julian Herbert, Secretary; Nicholas Alan Burrows [1961] Director; Nicola Joy Dulieu [1963] Director; Julian Herbert [1968] Finance Director; Bryan John Laxton [1960] Director; Caroline Jane Notcutt [1965] Director/Landscape Architect

Novum Holdings UK Limited
Incorporated: 19 April 2007 *Employees:* 56
Net Worth: £3,501,460 *Total Assets:* £10,470,726
Registered Office: 8 Hopper Way, Diss Business Park, Diss, Norfolk, IP22 4GT
Activities: Activities of construction holding companies
Parent: Novum Structures LLC
Officers: Ben Johnsen, Secretary; Alan Roy Bridger [1965] Director; Richard Clayton Brock [1969] Director [American]

Novum Structures UK Limited
Incorporated: 1 March 2007 *Employees:* 56
Net Worth: £5,170,005 *Total Assets:* £10,468,736
Registered Office: 8 Hopper Way, Diss Business Park, Diss, Norfolk, IP22 4GT
Activities: Other specialised construction activities n.e.c.
Parent: Novum Holdings UK Limited
Officers: Thomas Charles Churchyard, Secretary; Alan Roy Bridger [1965] Director; Richard Clayton Brock [1969] Director [American]; Richard Mattocks [1965] Director

Nower Hill High School
Incorporated: 1 July 2011 *Employees:* 189
Net Worth: £22,000,092 *Total Assets:* £25,637,360
Registered Office: George V Avenue, Pinner, Middlesex, HA5 5RP
Activities: General secondary education
Officers: Ian Peter Noutch, Secretary; Janet Beverley Buckingham [1960] Director; Christina Byrne [1969] Director/Community Leadership Manager [Irish]; Adeela Chowdhry [1971] Director/Project Manager; Julie Ann Gardner [1984] Director/Teacher; Janet Herson [1953] Director/Teacher; Abdeslam Ahmed Karmoun [1963] Director/IT Risk Manager [British/Moroccan]; Sukaina Kassam [1975] Director/Housewife; Diana Mary MacLeod La Rue [1951] Director; Andrew Simon Lane [1966] Director; Christopher James Livesey [1964] Director/Headteacher; Roy McKerracher [1956] Director/Accountant; Kala Nair [1967] Director/Teacher [Singaporean]; Asad Omar [1944] Director/Retired; Chandreyi Parkin [1967] Director/Teaching and Learning Assistant; Kevin Mark Ward [1965] Director/Manager; Michelle Weerasekera [1969] Director/Voluntary Sector

NPA Insurance Limited
Incorporated: 23 November 1899 *Employees:* 24
Net Worth: £18,117,924 *Total Assets:* £34,502,848
Registered Office: Mallinson House, 40-42 St Peters Street, St Albans, Herts, AL1 3NP
Activities: Non-life insurance
Parent: National Pharmacy Association Ltd
Officers: Gareth Richards, Secretary; Paul Neville Coleman [1960] Insurance Director; Bernard Mageean [1956] Director/Insurance; Iain Colquhoun McCusker [1952] Director/Chartered Accountant; Rajesh Ramniklal Patel [1964] Director/Pharmacist

NPMA Ltd
Incorporated: 24 January 1989 *Employees:* 46
Net Worth: £10,628,000 *Total Assets:* £12,622,000
Registered Office: Bishop Hall Lane, Chelmsford, Essex, CM1 1SQ
Activities: Buying and selling of own real estate
Parent: Anglia Ruskin Enterprise Ltd
Officers: Paul Wakefield Bogle, Secretary; Paul Wakefield Bogle [1972] Director/Secretary & Clerk; Stuart David Powell [1974] Director/Accountant; James Rolfe [1967] Director/Professional Services in Higher Education

NPS (Holdings) Limited
Incorporated: 5 November 2014
Net Worth: £315,700,000 *Total Assets:* £346,600,000
Registered Office: Peoplebuilding 2, Peoplebuilding Estate, Maylands Avenue, Hemel Hempstead Industrial Estate, Hemel Hempstead, Herts, HP2 4NW
Activities: Other information technology service activities
Parent: Argon NPS Limited
Officers: Stephen James Callaghan [1960] Director; Alan George O'Reilly [1961] Director [Irish]

NPS (UK2) Limited
Incorporated: 7 March 2008
Previous: Northgate Public Sector Holdings Limited
Net Worth: £61,786,000 *Total Assets:* £61,786,000
Registered Office: Peoplebuilding 2, Peoplebuilding Estate, Maylands Avenue, Hemel Hempstead Industrial Estate, Hemel Hempstead, Herts, HP2 4NW
Activities: Information technology consultancy activities
Parent: Northgate Public Services (UK) Limited
Officers: Stephen James Callaghan [1960] Director

NPS (UK4) Limited
Incorporated: 22 July 1987
Previous: Northgate Land and Property Solutions Limited
Net Worth: £36,500,000 *Total Assets:* £36,500,000
Registered Office: Peoplebuilding 2, Peoplebuilding Estate, Maylands Avenue, Hemel Hempstead Industrial Estate, Hemel Hempstead, Herts, HP2 4NW
Activities: Information technology consultancy activities
Parent: MVM Holdings Limited
Officers: Stephen James Callaghan [1960] Director

NPS (UK5) Limited
Incorporated: 14 January 1998
Previous: Northgate Public Sector Limited
Net Worth: £49,887,000 *Total Assets:* £49,887,000
Registered Office: Peoplebuilding 2, Peoplebuilding Estate, Maylands Avenue, Hemel Hempstead Industrial Estate, Hemel Hempstead, Herts, HP2 4NW
Activities: Other information technology service activities
Parent: NPS (UK2) Limited
Officers: Stephen James Callaghan [1960] Director

NPS (UK6) Limited
Incorporated: 20 January 1999
Previous: Northgate Secure Information Solutions Limited
Net Worth: £15,425,000 *Total Assets:* £15,425,000
Registered Office: Peoplebuilding 2, Peoplebuilding Estate, Maylands Avenue, Hemel Hempstead Industrial Estate, Hemel Hempstead, Herts, HP2 4NW
Activities: Information technology consultancy activities
Parent: NPS (UK2) Limited
Officers: Stephen James Callaghan [1960] Director

NPS Property Consultants Limited
Incorporated: 17 January 1994 *Employees:* 1,736
Net Worth Deficit: £19,652,000 *Total Assets:* £56,866,000
Registered Office: 280 Fifers Lane, Norwich, NR6 6EQ
Activities: Architectural activities
Parent: Norse Group Limited
Officers: Andrew John Merricks, Secretary; Andrew David Jamieson [1956] Director/Corporate Advisor; Karen Elizabeth Knight [1960] Director/Senior Manager; Fiona McDiarmid [1961] Director; Dean Thorvald Wetteland [1976] Commercial Director

NQA Certification Limited
Incorporated: 11 December 2014 *Employees:* 101
Net Worth: £1,559,913 *Total Assets:* £15,076,540
Registered Office: Warwick House, Houghton Hall Park, Houghton Regis, Dunstable, Beds, LU5 5ZX
Activities: Activities of head offices
Officers: Lisa Wood, Secretary; Kevin Beard [1959] Director/President NQA USA [American]; Rachel Joshi [1973] Director/Corporate Controller of NTS [American]; Raymond Milchovich [1949] Director [American]; Lisa Wood [1966] Director/Chief Financial Officer [American]; Nicholas Laurence Wright [1986] Managing Director

NVSM Limited
Incorporated: 29 March 2001 *Employees:* 2
Net Worth: £11,677,186 *Total Assets:* £17,151,288
Registered Office: 4th Floor, Metroline House, 118-122 College Road, Harrow, Middlesex, HA1 1BQ
Activities: Buying and selling of own real estate
Major Shareholder: Vasam Shabnem Ibrahim
Officers: Vasam Shabnem Ibrahim [1970] Director/Stockbroker; Sadia Zafar [1976] Director

NW3 Capital Ltd
Incorporated: 26 October 2012 *Employees:* 2
Net Worth: £3,314,826 *Total Assets:* £12,304,672
Registered Office: c/o Jarvis & Co Business Services, 75 Main Road, Gidea Park, Romford, Essex, RM2 5EL
Activities: Construction of domestic buildings
Major Shareholder: Robbi Malandreniotis
Officers: Dimitri Malandreniotis [1977] Director; Robbi Malandreniotis [1977] Director/Property Developer

NWES Property Services Limited
Incorporated: 10 February 2005 *Employees:* 37
Net Worth: £1,332,261 *Total Assets:* £13,028,604
Registered Office: Rouen House, Rouen Road, Norwich, NR1 1RB
Activities: Other business support service activities n.e.c.
Officers: Lucy Jane Cannell, Secretary; Joanna Clarke [1961] Deputy Chief Executive/Director; Nicholas William Doyle [1966] Director; James Robert Pinchbeck [1964] Director/Marketing Partner; Philip Roger Watkins [1959] Director; Laurie Wiseman [1959] Director

O'Brien Waste Recycling Solutions Holdings Limited
Incorporated: 24 April 2015 *Employees:* 171
Net Worth: £5,932,000 *Total Assets:* £15,288,000
Registered Office: Coronation Road, Cressex, High Wycombe, Bucks, HP12 3TZ
Activities: Activities of other holding companies n.e.c.
Officers: Rachael Hambrook, Secretary; Richard Neil Pike [1969] Director/Chief Financial Officer; Michael Robert Mason Topham [1972] Director/Chief Executive Officer

O'Brien Waste Recycling Solutions Ltd
Incorporated: 19 December 2014 *Employees:* 178
Net Worth: £7,219,000 *Total Assets:* £16,987,000
Registered Office: Coronation Road, Cressex, High Wycombe, Bucks, HP12 3TZ
Activities: Collection of non-hazardous waste
Parent: O'Brien Waste Recycling Solutions Holdings Limited
Officers: Rachael Hambrook, Secretary; Richard Neil Pike [1969] Director/Chief Financial Officer; Michael Robert Mason Topham [1972] Director/Chief Executive Officer

O'Hara Property Investment Holding Company Limited
Incorporated: 21 February 1985
Net Worth: £10,962,729 *Total Assets:* £15,568,922
Registered Office: 101 Rowlands Avenue, Hatch End, Middlesex, HA5 4AW
Activities: Other letting and operating of own or leased real estate
Shareholders: Patrick Joseph O'Hara; Michael O'Hara
Officers: Patrick Joseph O'Hara, Secretary; Patrick Joseph O'Hara [1944] Director/Manager [Irish]; Michael O'Hara [1947] Director/Manager [Irish]

O'Malley Haulage Limited
Incorporated: 22 June 2005 *Employees:* 5
Net Worth: £5,635,022 *Total Assets:* £10,745,246
Registered Office: Hilfield Lane, Aldenham, Watford, Herts, WD25 8DT
Activities: Freight transport by road
Parent: New ACH Limited
Officers: Thomas O'Malley [1947] Director [Irish]; Adrian Thomas Omalley [1980] Director

O'Neill Investments Limited
Incorporated: 18 March 2002 *Employees:* 4
Net Worth: £22,025,076 *Total Assets:* £31,838,832
Registered Office: 1 Beauchamp Court, Victors Way, Barnet, Herts, EN5 5TZ
Activities: Other letting and operating of own or leased real estate
Shareholders: Sean James O'Neill; Jean Therese Wheeler
Officers: Sean James O'Neill, Secretary; Sean James O'Neill [1963] Director/Property Investor/Developer; Jean Therese Wheeler [1963] Director/Administrator [Irish]

O-I Glass Limited
Incorporated: 17 December 1953 *Employees:* 717
Previous: O-I Manufacturing UK Limited
Net Worth: £56,516,000 *Total Assets:* £100,909,000
Registered Office: Head Office, Edinburgh Way, Harlow, Essex, CM20 2UG
Activities: Manufacture of hollow glass
Officers: Paul Malcolm Boreham, Secretary; Robert Gachot [1957] Director [French]; Steve Holden [1967] Sales Director; Alan Hunter [1960] Director/Plant Manager; Denise Parker [1966] Director; Jim Rankine [1968] Director; Tracy Simpson [1959] Director

O-I Sales and Distribution UK Limited
Incorporated: 20 February 2006 *Employees:* 17
Net Worth: £13,654,000 *Total Assets:* £23,462,000
Registered Office: Edinburgh Way, Harlow, Essex, CM20 2UG
Activities: Other business support service activities n.e.c.
Officers: Paul Malcolm Boreham, Secretary; Scott Gibb [1968] Director; Paul McLavin [1967] Director; Evan Williams [1967] Director

O.B.C. (Europe) Limited
Incorporated: 20 February 1998 *Employees:* 4
Net Worth: £8,949,323 *Total Assets:* £9,564,465
Registered Office: York House, Empire Way, Wembley, Middlesex, HA9 0FQ
Activities: Other letting and operating of own or leased real estate
Shareholders: Alan Richard Bekhor; Julia Ruth Bekhor
Officers: Julia Ruth Bekhor, Secretary; Alan Richard Bekhor [1960] Director; Julia Ruth Bekhor [1960] Director

OAG Aviation Worldwide Limited
Incorporated: 7 March 2013 *Employees:* 87
Net Worth: £15,868,000 *Total Assets:* £26,871,000
Registered Office: 1 Capability Green, Luton, Beds, LU1 3LU
Activities: Other business support service activities n.e.c.
Parent: OAG Aviation Holdings Limited
Officers: Philip Giles Callow [1972] Director; Matthew Paul Plose [1973] Finance Director

Oak Tree Schools Holdings Limited
Incorporated: 15 March 1995 *Employees:* 270
Net Worth: £7,025,651 *Total Assets:* £14,004,221
Registered Office: 6 Albion Hill, Loughton, Essex, IG10 4RA
Activities: Other business support service activities n.e.c.
Shareholders: Matthew Hagger; Nicholas Osborne Hagger; Madeline Ann Hagger
Officers: Matthew Hagger, Secretary; Madeline Ann Hagger [1950] Director; Matthew Hagger [1974] Director; Nicholas Osborne Hagger [1939] Director

Oakbridge Homes (Group) Ltd
Incorporated: 4 June 1986 *Employees:* 6
Net Worth: £7,746,469 *Total Assets:* £10,227,017
Registered Office: The Priory, High Street, Redbourn, Herts, AL3 7LZ
Activities: Development of building projects
Major Shareholder: Martin David Hemmings
Officers: Martin David Hemmings, Secretary; Anna Hemmings [1972] Director; Ceridwen Rowena Hemmings [1945] Director/Retired; Darren Aiden Hemmings [1975] Director/Advertising Consultant; Martin David Hemmings [1946] Director/Builder

Oakbridge Homes Limited
Incorporated: 2 August 1993 *Employees:* 6
Net Worth: £7,652,904 *Total Assets:* £10,222,191
Registered Office: The Priory, High Street, Redbourn, St Albans, Herts, AL3 7LZ
Activities: Construction of domestic buildings
Major Shareholder: Martin David Hemmings
Officers: Martin David Hemmings, Secretary; Anna Hemmings [1972] Director; Ceridwen Rowena Hemmings [1945] Sales Director; Darren Aiden Hemmings [1975] Director/Advertising Consultant; Martin David Hemmings [1946] Director/Builder

Oakburn European Properties Limited
Incorporated: 23 March 1998
Net Worth: £11,178,230 *Total Assets:* £17,665,056
Registered Office: Riverside House, 1-5 Como Street, Romford, Essex, RM7 7DN
Activities: Development of building projects
Parent: Oakburn Properties Limited
Officers: Simon Ansel Blausten, Secretary/Surveyor; Benjamin Blausten [1986] Director; Deborah Elizabeth Blausten [1990] Director; Douglas Blausten [1951] Director/Chartered Surveyor; Hannah Blausten [1991] Director; Jonathan Andrew Blausten [1992] Director; Samuel Blausten [1991] Director; Simon Ansel Blausten [1956] Director/Chartered Surveyor

Oakburn Properties Limited
Incorporated: 31 July 1959
Net Worth: £6,551,017 *Total Assets:* £13,053,889
Registered Office: Riverside House, 1-5 Como Street, Romford, Essex, RM7 7DN
Activities: Other letting and operating of own or leased real estate
Shareholders: Douglas Blausten; Simon Ansel Blausten
Officers: Simon Ansel Blausten, Secretary/Surveyor; Douglas Blausten [1951] Director/Chartered Surveyor; Simon Ansel Blausten [1956] Director/Chartered Surveyor

M. S. Oakes Securities Limited
Incorporated: 8 June 1973
Net Worth: £5,153,613 *Total Assets:* £8,556,476
Registered Office: Units 1-5 Mobbs Way Business Park, Lowestoft, Suffolk, NR32 3BE
Activities: Other letting and operating of own or leased real estate
Officers: Vivienne Oakes, Secretary; Mark Stanley Oakes [1966] Contracts Director; Vivienne Oakes [1944] Director/Company Secretary

Oakeve Limited
Incorporated: 11 March 2004
Net Worth: £1,294,568 *Total Assets:* £9,666,006
Registered Office: Wildacre, Pollards Park, Nightingales Lane, Chalfont St Giles, Bucks, HP8 4SN
Activities: Construction of domestic buildings
Shareholders: Paul Joseph Newton; Iona Elizabeth Dunlop Newton
Officers: Iona Elizabeth Dunlop Newton, Secretary; Iona Elizabeth Dunlop Newton [1970] Managing Director; Paul Joseph Newton [1966] Finance Director

Oakfield (Foods) Limited
Incorporated: 24 February 1987 *Employees:* 52
Net Worth: £23,582,060 *Total Assets:* £44,994,880
Registered Office: 1st Floor, 3 Elstree Gate, Elstree Way, Borehamwood, Herts, WD6 1JD
Activities: Production of meat and poultry meat products
Officers: David Lee Burr, Secretary; David Lee Burr [1971] Finance Director; Mark David Glass [1967] Sales Director; Thomas Matthew Greaney [1988] Director; Daniel Ian Hargreaves [1981] Technical Director; Harvey Philip Ingram [1947] Director/Solicitor; Alison Levy [1959] Director; Miles Ivor Levy [1956] Sales Director; Darren John Short [1966] Director

Oakman Inns and Restaurants Limited
Incorporated: 22 April 2005 *Employees:* 328
Net Worth: £3,396,272 *Total Assets:* £17,146,456
Registered Office: 9 Akeman Street, Tring, Herts, HP23 6AA
Activities: Public houses and bars
Officers: Joseph Oliver Evans, Secretary; Peter James Borg Neal [1961] Director; Joseph Oliver Evans [1975] Finance Director; Alex Ford [1981] Operations Director; Andrew John Harman [1962] Director; John Stewart Leslie [1959] Director; Mark Radley [1963] Director/Builder; David Mark Sherratt [1967] Director; David George Sidwell [1956] Director/Businessman; Michael John Smith [1960] Director; Keith James Wilson [1961] Director

Oakray Limited
Incorporated: 31 October 1979 *Employees:* 196
Net Worth: £11,856,817 *Total Assets:* £15,224,925
Registered Office: 1 Warner House, The Harrovian Business Village, Bessborough Road, Harrow, Middlesex, HA1 3EX
Activities: Plumbing, heat and air-conditioning installation
Officers: Maureen Franklin, Secretary; Andrew Clark [1962] Director; Wayne John Dejager [1966] Director; Keith Sidney Mottram [1957] Director

OAT 2012 Limited
Incorporated: 2 February 2012 *Employees:* 105
Net Worth: £20,223,028 *Total Assets:* £23,404,640
Registered Office: Washway House Farm, Washway Road, Holbeach, Spalding, Lincs, PE12 7PP
Activities: Growing of cereals (except rice), leguminous crops and oil seeds
Shareholders: John Derek Taylor of Holbeach; Roger David Taylor; Sam Roger Taylor; Sarah Ann Taylor; Lady Julia Aileen Taylor; Brian Dennis Taylor; Hon Adam Edwin John Taylor
Officers: Sam Roger Taylor, Secretary; Hon Adam Edwin John Taylor [1975] Marketing Director; Roger David Taylor [1945] Director/Bulb Wholesaler; Sam Roger Taylor [1977] Agricultural and Horticultural Director

Oblue Limited
Incorporated: 20 March 2012
Net Worth: £6,190,328 *Total Assets:* £8,407,542
Registered Office: Portland House, 69-71 Wembley Hill Road, Wembley, Middlesex, HA9 8BU
Activities: Sea and coastal freight water transport
Parent: Union Maritime Limited
Officers: Bhupendra Shantilal Kansagra, Secretary; Laurent Elie Cadji [1977] Director/Businessman; Lewis Levy Cadji [1938] Director/Businessman; Bhupendra Shantilal Kansagra [1956] Director/Businessman; Ramesh Shantilal Kansagra [1950] Director/Businessman

OBM Properties Limited
Incorporated: 21 November 2006
Net Worth: £7,922,439 *Total Assets:* £11,013,415
Registered Office: 23 Robjohns Road, Widford Industrial Estate, Chelmsford, Essex, CM1 3AG
Activities: Other letting and operating of own or leased real estate
Officers: Julie Higdon [1965] Director/Accountant

Ocado Central Services Limited
Incorporated: 19 May 2014 *Employees:* 12,223
Net Worth: £99,300,000 *Total Assets:* £387,900,000
Registered Office: Buildings One & Two, Trident Place, Mosquito Way, Hatfield, Herts, AL10 9UL
Activities: Activities of head offices
Shareholders: Ocado Holdings Ltd; Ocado Holdings Limited
Officers: Neill Abrams, Secretary; Robert McNeill Cooper, Secretary; Neill Abrams [1964] Director; Luke Giles William Jensen [1966] Director/Chief Executive Officer; Mark Antony Richardson [1964] Director; Timothy Steiner [1969] Director; Duncan Eden Tatton-Brown [1965] Director

Ocado Group PLC
Incorporated: 8 December 2009 *Employees:* 12,233
Net Worth: £270,700,000 *Total Assets:* £894,499,968
Registered Office: Buildings One & Two, Trident Place, Mosquito Way, Hatfield, Herts, AL10 9UL
Activities: Retail sale in non-specialised stores with food, beverages or tobacco predominating
Officers: Neill Abrams, Secretary; Robert McNeill Cooper, Secretary; Neill Abrams [1964] Director/Lawyer; Moreen Ruth Anderson [1953] Director; Andrew John Harrison [1970] Director/Deputy Chief Executive; Luke Giles William Jensen [1966] Director/Chief Executive Officer; Emma Elizabeth Lloyd [1969] Director; Douglas Stuart McCallum [1966] Director/Manager; Jorn Rausing [1960] Director [Swedish]; Mark Antony Richardson [1964] Operations Director; Stuart Rose [1949] Director; Julie Helen Southern [1959] Director; Timothy Steiner [1969] Director; Duncan Eden Tatton-Brown [1965] Finance Director

Ocado Holdings Limited
Incorporated: 5 February 2010 *Employees:* 5
Net Worth: £506,500,000 *Total Assets:* £796,200,000
Registered Office: Buildings One & Two, Trident Place, Mosquito Way, Hatfield, Herts, AL10 9UL
Activities: Activities of head offices
Parent: Ocado Group PLC
Officers: Neill Abrams, Secretary; Robert McNeill Cooper, Secretary; Neill Abrams [1964] Director/Lawyer; Luke Giles William Jensen [1966] Director/Chief Executive Officer; Mark Antony Richardson [1964] Operations Director; Timothy Steiner [1969] Director; Duncan Eden Tatton-Brown [1965] Finance Director

Ocado Innovation Limited
Incorporated: 13 December 2013 *Employees:* 5
Net Worth: £226,200,000 *Total Assets:* £484,800,000
Registered Office: Buildings One & Two, Trident Place, Mosquito Way, Hatfield, Herts, AL10 9UL
Activities: Other information technology service activities
Parent: Ocado Group PLC
Officers: Robert McNeill Cooper, Secretary; Neill Abrams [1964] Director; Luke Giles William Jensen [1966] Director/Chief Executive Officer; Mark Antony Richardson [1964] Director; Timothy Steiner [1969] Director; Duncan Eden Tatton-Brown [1965] Finance Director

Ocado Operating Limited
Incorporated: 19 May 2014
Net Worth: £155,500,000 *Total Assets:* £663,800,000
Registered Office: Buildings One & Two, Trident Place, Mosquito Way, Hatfield, Herts, AL10 9UL
Activities: Other letting and operating of own or leased real estate
Parent: Ocado Holdings Limited
Officers: Neill Abrams, Secretary; Robert McNeill Cooper, Secretary; Neill Abrams [1964] Director; Luke Giles William Jensen [1966] Director/Chief Executive Officer; Mark Antony Richardson [1964] Director; Timothy Steiner [1969] Director; Duncan Eden Tatton-Brown [1965] Director

Ocado Retail Limited
Incorporated: 11 November 1999
Net Worth: £64,500,000 *Total Assets:* £476,100,000
Registered Office: Buildings One & Two, Trident Place, Mosquito Way, Hatfield, Herts, AL10 9UL
Activities: Retail sale in non-specialised stores with food, beverages or tobacco predominating
Shareholders: Ocado Holdings Limited; Ocado Holdings Limited
Officers: Neill Abrams, Secretary/Lawyer; Robert McNeill Cooper, Secretary; Neill Abrams [1964] Director/Lawyer; Luke Giles William Jensen [1966] Director/Chief Executive Officer; Mark Antony Richardson [1964] Operations Director; Timothy Steiner [1969] Director/Chief Executive; Duncan Eden Tatton-Brown [1965] Finance Director

Ocean Gateway LLP
Incorporated: 19 February 2009
Net Worth: £13,218,958 *Total Assets:* £13,291,004
Registered Office: Upminster Court, 133 Hall Lane, Upminster, Essex, RM14 1AL
Officers: Iain Robert Liddell [1963] Member

Ocean Holidays Limited
Incorporated: 18 June 2013 *Employees:* 145
Net Worth: £831,498 *Total Assets:* £25,649,200
Registered Office: Floor 9, North House, St Edwards Way, Romford, Essex, RM1 3AE
Activities: Tour operator activities
Officers: George Hardie Hastings [1977] Director; Harry Rawson Hastings [1983] Director; Daniel James Ox [1979] Director; David John Ox [1978] Director

The Ockendon Academy
Incorporated: 25 November 2010 *Employees:* 185
Net Worth: £22,698,648 *Total Assets:* £25,208,908
Registered Office: Erriff Drive, South Ockendon, Essex, RM15 5AY
Activities: General secondary education
Officers: Jacqueline Insole, Secretary; Kathleen Ann Cooney [1949] Director; Donna Driscoll [1978] Director/Learning Base Supervisor; Lorraine Jean Hodges [1958] Director/Support-Cover Supervisor; Samantha Kahn [1973] Director; James Lepine [1993] Director/Casework Assistant Crown Prosecution Service; Richard Charles Milligan [1954] Director/Retired; Olubunmi Adefunke Bisola Obisesan [1992] Director/Company Secretary; Kifwanakene Pupe [1975] Director/Financial Consultant; Joanne Edgeworth Rainey [1974] Director/Principal; Richard Douglas Haydon Wickens [1990] Director/Technical Specialist - Data - Banking

Ocourage Limited
Incorporated: 5 November 2012
Net Worth: £10,713,758 *Total Assets:* £15,176,342
Registered Office: Portland House, 69-71 Wembley Hill Road, Wembley, Middlesex, HA9 8BU
Activities: Sea and coastal freight water transport
Parent: Union Maritime Limited
Officers: Bhupendra Shantilal Kansagra, Secretary; Laurent Elie Cadji [1977] Director/Businessman; Lewis Levy Cadji [1938] Director/Businessman; Bhupendra Shantilal Kansagra [1956] Director/Businessman; Ramesh Shantilal Kansagra [1950] Director/Businessman

OEC Europe Holdings Limited
Incorporated: 26 April 1948 *Employees:* 29
Previous: Clifford-Thames (Holdings) Limited
Net Worth: £11,734,117 *Total Assets:* £22,444,252
Registered Office: Springfield Lyons House, Chelmsford Business Park, Chelmsford, Essex, CM2 5TH
Activities: Activities of head offices
Parent: OEC International Limited
Officers: Perry Charles [1966] Director/Certified Public Accountant; Scott James Christie [1972] Director/Chief Data Officer; Ronald Philip Coill [1962] Director [American]; Ike Charles Herman [1974] Director/Chief Operating Officer EU and Asia Pacific [American]

OEC International Limited
Incorporated: 4 July 2014 *Employees:* 484
Previous: Clifford Thames (Topco) Limited
Net Worth: £50,072,000 *Total Assets:* £62,348,000
Registered Office: Springfield Lyons House, Chelmsford Business Park, Chelmsford, Essex, CM2 5TH
Activities: Activities of head offices
Officers: Perry Charles [1966] Director/Certified Public Accountant; Scott James Christie [1972] Director; Ronald Philip Coill [1962] Director [American]; Ike Charles Herman [1974] Director/Chief Operating Officer EU and Asia Pacific [American]

OEConnection Limited
Incorporated: 2 March 1989 *Employees:* 106
Previous: Clifford Thames Limited
Net Worth: £12,422,200 *Total Assets:* £25,020,248
Registered Office: Springfield Lyons House, Chelmsford Business Park, Chelmsford, Essex, CM2 5TH
Activities: Other information technology service activities
Parent: OEC Europe Holdings Limited
Officers: Perry Charles [1966] Director/Certified Public Accountant; Scott James Christie [1972] Director/Chief Data Officer; Ronald Philip Coill [1962] Director [American]; Ike Charles Herman [1974] Director/Chief Operating Officer EU and Asia Pacific [American]

Offerco Limited
Incorporated: 18 May 2009
Net Worth: £10,621,678 *Total Assets:* £10,707,692
Registered Office: Grenville House, 4 Grenville Avenue, Broxbourne, Herts, EN10 7DH
Activities: Activities of head offices
Major Shareholder: Peter John Hearn
Officers: Peter John Hearn, Secretary; Peter John Hearn [1953] Director; Simon James Murphy [1964] Director

Offley Chase Estates Limited
Incorporated: 16 May 1989
Net Worth: £12,341,077 *Total Assets:* £17,192,640
Registered Office: Houghton Hall, The Green, Houghton Regis, Beds, LU5 5DY
Activities: Buying and selling of own real estate
Parent: Chamberlain Holdings PLC
Officers: Vena Chambury, Secretary; Christopher Paul Bugden [1966] Finance Director; John Maxwell Chamberlain [1942] Managing Director; Vena Chambury [1955] Director; Stefan Mucha [1957] Director; Peter Bernard Wayte [1949] Director/Solicitor

Offsite Archive Storage and Integrated Services (UK) Limited
Incorporated: 14 January 2008 *Employees:* 54
Net Worth: £9,819,624 *Total Assets:* £17,257,258
Registered Office: Quadrant 1, Homefield Road, Haverhill, Suffolk, CB9 8QP
Activities: Other business support service activities n.e.c.
Shareholders: MPE (General Partner V) Ltd; Montagu Private Equity LLP; Offsite Archive Storage and Integrated Services (Ireland) Limited
Officers: David Manifold, Secretary; Espen Halvorsen [1962] Director/Interim CEO [Norwegian]; David Manifold [1969] Director/Chief Financial Officer [Irish]

Oikos Storage Limited
Incorporated: 16 June 1936 *Employees:* 24
Net Worth: £58,567,076 *Total Assets:* £62,062,652
Registered Office: Hole Haven Wharf, Haven Road, Canvey Island, Essex, SS8 0NR
Activities: Operation of warehousing and storage facilities for water transport activities
Officers: Samuel Stuart Parlour, Secretary; Emil Petar Pahljina [1964] Director/Fund Manager [Australian]; Wessel Remi Schevernels [1971] Divisional Director [Dutch]; Peter Geoffrey Schliebs [1975] Director/Senior Portfolio Manager [Australian]; Vasanthi Smedley [1979] Director/Lawyer [Australian]; Anthony John Woodward [1960] Director/Fuel Storage Manager

Old English Inns Limited
Incorporated: 25 October 1999
Net Worth: £561,401,024 *Total Assets:* £562,993,024
Registered Office: Westgate Brewery, Bury St Edmunds, Suffolk, IP33 1QT
Activities: Non-trading company
Parent: Greene King Brewing and Retailing Limited
Officers: Lindsay Anne Keswick, Secretary; Richard Smothers [1967] Director

Oldeurope Limited
Incorporated: 28 April 2010
Previous: Pitney Bowes Europe Limited
Net Worth: £356,286,016 *Total Assets:* £359,551,008
Registered Office: Building 5, Trident Place, Hatfield Business Park, Mosquito Way, Hatfield, Herts, AL10 9UJ
Activities: Non-trading company
Shareholders: Pitney Bowes Inc; Pitney Bowes Global Ltd
Officers: Ryan John Higginson [1973] Director/Vice President; Gerard Richard Willsher [1967] Director/Lawyer

Oldrid & Co.,Limited
Incorporated: 1 February 1934 *Employees:* 715
Net Worth: £29,004,424 *Total Assets:* £39,196,568
Registered Office: 11 Strait Bargate, Boston, Lincs, PE21 6UF
Activities: Other retail sale in non-specialised stores
Officers: Peter Isaac, Secretary; Richard Keith Broadhead [1969] Managing Director; Steven David Goulder [1960] Director; Kathryn Ann Ingleton [1963] Staff Director; Dawn Marie Isaac [1972] Director/Garden Designer; Martin James Isaac [1961] Director/Retail Manager; Peter Edward Isaac [1977] Director/Chartered Accountant; Marcus Anthony Meadows [1971] Retail Operations Director; Natalie Skins [1979] Staff Director; Ruth Elizabeth Stephenson [1959] Director

Oleoland Hotel Company Limited
Incorporated: 26 October 1990 *Employees:* 1
Net Worth: £10,921,244 *Total Assets:* £12,656,068
Registered Office: 7 Redbridge Lane East, Ilford, Essex, IG4 5ET
Activities: Other accommodation
Officers: Panna Unadkat, Secretary; Panna Unadkat [1954] Director

Olive Business Solutions Limited
Incorporated: 27 January 2003 *Employees:* 125
Net Worth Deficit: £3,524,451 *Total Assets:* £21,160,996
Registered Office: Olive House, Mercury Park, Wooburn Green, High Wycombe, Bucks, HP10 0HH
Activities: Other telecommunications activities
Parent: Olive Communications Solutions Limited
Officers: Martin Dieter Flick [1967] Managing Director; Roger Patrick Flynn [1962] Director/Chief Executive; Mark Geraghty [1975] Sales Director [Australian]

The Olive Tree Limited
Incorporated: 24 September 1991
Net Worth: £5,360,919 *Total Assets:* £14,876,810
Registered Office: Darley Ash, Chipperfield Road, Bovingdon, Herts, HP3 0JN
Activities: Other letting and operating of own or leased real estate
Shareholders: Christine Mary Scacco; Piero Scacco
Officers: Christine Mary Scacco, Secretary; Christine Mary Scacco [1947] Director/Housewife; Piero Scacco [1938] Director/Baker [Italian]

Olivegate Properties Limited
Incorporated: 4 March 2002 *Employees:* 2
Net Worth: £24,097,736 *Total Assets:* £36,333,076
Registered Office: Hadley Hurst, Hadley Common, Barnet, Herts, EN5 5QG
Activities: Other business support service activities n.e.c.
Parent: Blendhall Limited
Officers: Anna Victoria Kinsman, Secretary; Alexander Mahboubian [1972] Director/Developer; Farrokh Mahboubian [1932] Director [Iranian]

Olivewood Limited
Incorporated: 20 March 1995 *Employees:* 20
Net Worth: £3,955,603 *Total Assets:* £8,748,244
Registered Office: Unit B2, Neptune Road, Harrow, Middlesex, HA1 4HX
Activities: Agents involved in the sale of timber and building materials
Shareholders: Laxman Lalji Murji; Sanjay Laxman Murji
Officers: Amratben Laxman Murji [1960] Director; Laxman Lalji Murji [1961] Director; Sanjay Laxman Murji [1984] Director

Olympus Keymed Group Limited
Incorporated: 2 May 1975
Net Worth: £59,692,000 *Total Assets:* £59,692,000
Registered Office: Keymed House, Stock Road, Southend on Sea, Essex, SS2 5QH
Activities: Activities of head offices
Parent: Olympus Europa Holding SE
Officers: Constantin Zangemeister, Secretary; Stefan Kaufmann [1969] Director [German]; Yasuo Takeuchi [1957] Director [Japanese]; Carl Constantin Zangemeister [1971] Director [German]

Omar Group Finance Limited
Incorporated: 28 March 2017 *Employees:* 421
Net Worth Deficit: £1,337,079 *Total Assets:* £64,971,980
Registered Office: 227 London Road, Brandon, Suffolk, IP27 0NE
Activities: Other business support service activities n.e.c.
Parent: Simba Topco Limited
Officers: Derek Geoffrey Chilton [1964] Director; Graeme Craig [1971] Director; Roy Charles Greenacre [1965] Director; David Richard Wardrop [1977] Director; Dean Adrian Westmoreland [1964] Director

Omar Group Holdings Limited
Incorporated: 28 March 2017
Net Worth Deficit: £315,418 *Total Assets:* £64,971,976
Registered Office: 227 London Road, Brandon, Suffolk, IP27 0NE
Activities: Other business support service activities n.e.c.
Shareholders: Rutland III GP LLP; Dean Adrian Westmoreland
Officers: Derek Geoffrey Chilton [1964] Director; Graeme Craig [1971] Director; Roy Charles Greenacre [1965] Director; Terry Joseph Scicluna [1957] Director; David Richard Wardrop [1977] Director; Dean Adrian Westmoreland [1964] Director

Omar Group Investments Limited
Incorporated: 28 March 2017
Net Worth Deficit: £2,685,614 *Total Assets:* £50,569,632
Registered Office: 227 London Road, Brandon, Suffolk, IP27 0NE
Activities: Other business support service activities n.e.c.
Parent: Omar Group Finance Limited
Officers: Derek Geoffrey Chilton [1964] Director; Graeme Craig [1971] Director; Roy Charles Greenacre [1965] Director; David Richard Wardrop [1977] Director; Dean Adrian Westmoreland [1964] Director

Omar Park Homes Limited
Incorporated: 26 March 2009 *Employees:* 421
Net Worth: £16,979,016 *Total Assets:* £31,190,724
Registered Office: London Road, Brandon, Suffolk, IP27 0NE
Activities: Other manufacturing n.e.c.
Parent: Omar Group Limited
Officers: Dean Adrian Westmoreland, Secretary; Derek Geoffrey Chilton [1964] Director; Graeme Craig [1971] Director; Roy Charles Greenacre [1965] Director; Dean Adrian Westmoreland [1964] Director

Omavale Limited
Incorporated: 27 October 1977 *Employees:* 1
Net Worth: £13,624,618 *Total Assets:* £19,027,584
Registered Office: The Coach House, Powell Road, Buckhurst Hill, Essex, IG9 5RD
Activities: Other letting and operating of own or leased real estate
Officers: James Thomas Jordan [1957] Director

Omex Agrifluids Limited
Incorporated: 28 January 1991 *Employees:* 34
Net Worth: £8,279,193 *Total Assets:* £12,278,895
Registered Office: OMEX Agrifluids Ltd, Saddlebow Road, Kings Lynn, Norfolk, PE34 3JA
Activities: Manufacture of fertilizers and nitrogen compounds
Officers: David O'Donnell, Secretary; Manuela Bowyer [1963] Director; Christopher James Gipp [1961] Production Director; David Alan Lowes [1953] Export Director; Marcelo Luiz Marino Santos [1967] Director [Brazilian]; David O'Donnell [1958] Finance Director; Peter Charles Elvy Prentis [1958] Export Director; Nils Alexander Winkler Von Stiernhielm [1985] Director; Olof Joachim Winkler Von Stiernhielm [1949] Director [German]

Omniport Limited
Incorporated: 14 April 2000
Net Worth: £9,399,719 *Total Assets:* £9,472,469
Registered Office: Norwich Airport, Amsterdam Way, Norwich, NR6 6JA
Activities: Activities of other holding companies n.e.c.
Parent: Regional & City Airports Holdings Ltd
Officers: Katherine Georgina Cook, Secretary; Andrew Michael Bell [1979] Director; Katherine Georgina Cook [1979] Director/Certified Chartered Accountant

Omniport Norwich Limited
Incorporated: 10 February 2004
Net Worth Deficit: £7,750,673 *Total Assets:* £14,622,938
Registered Office: Norwich Airport, Amsterdam Way, Norwich, NR6 6JA
Activities: Activities of other holding companies n.e.c.
Parent: Omniport Limited
Officers: Katherine Georgina Cook, Secretary; Andrew Michael Bell [1979] Director; Katherine Georgina Cook [1979] Finance Director

One Broker Limited
Incorporated: 17 June 2009 *Employees:* 102
Net Worth: £1,951,328 *Total Assets:* £12,155,480
Registered Office: Lakeside, 300 Old Chapel Way, Broadland Business Park, Norwich, NR7 0WG
Activities: Activities of head offices
Shareholders: Robin Edward Plaster; Clare Elizabeth Plaster
Officers: Clare Elizabeth Plaster, Secretary; Robin Edward Plaster [1961] Director

One GE Healthcare UK
Incorporated: 21 December 2010
Net Worth: £52,154,000 *Total Assets:* £54,736,000
Registered Office: Pollards Wood, Nightingales Lane, Chalfont St Giles, Bucks, HP8 4SP
Activities: Activities of head offices
Parent: GE UK Group
Officers: Katherine Ann Jones [1976] Director/Financial Controller; Adrian Ashwin Narayan [1973] Director/Accountant

One Group Construction Limited
Incorporated: 9 May 2013 *Employees:* 542
Net Worth: £11,724,951 *Total Assets:* £77,921,280
Registered Office: 30 White House Road, Ipswich, Suffolk, IP1 5LT
Activities: Activities of head offices
Officers: Trevor Mark Dixon, Secretary; Graham Edwin Emmerson [1948] Director/Civil Engineer; Richard William Neall [1964] Director [Australian]

One Stop Private Doctors Limited
Incorporated: 30 January 2014 *Employees:* 5
Net Worth: £22,943,968 *Total Assets:* £24,633,720
Registered Office: Ground Floor, Unit 3 Grovelands, Boundary Way, Hemel Hempstead, Herts, HP2 7TE
Activities: General medical practice activities
Major Shareholder: Peter Woodstock Harris
Officers: Paul Edward Woodstock Harris [1969] Director/Banker; Peter Woodstock Harris [1934] Director; Thomas Woodstock Harris [1963] Director; Alison Mary Swinburn [1965] Director; Hamish Christopher Ward [1975] Finance Director [New Zealander]

Oni PLC
Incorporated: 17 March 1992 *Employees:* 73
Net Worth: £3,386,327 *Total Assets:* £10,183,827
Registered Office: 24 Crawley Green Road, Luton, Beds, LU2 0QX
Activities: Information technology consultancy activities
Shareholders: Mark Ian Collins; Kevin Ross Kivlochan
Officers: Mark Ian Collins, Secretary; Mark Ian Collins [1966] Director; Philip James Cotterill [1972] Sales Director; Kevin Ross Kivlochan [1962] Director; Trevor John Mockett [1963] Director; Richard Clive Smith [1964] Finance Director

Onix Investments UK Ltd
Incorporated: 25 August 2017
Net Worth: £379,004,064 *Total Assets:* £795,908,160
Registered Office: 2nd Floor, Building 1, Imperial Place, Maxwell Road, Borehamwood, Herts, WD6 1JN
Activities: Activities of financial services holding companies
Parent: Pilgrim's Pride Corporation
Officers: Jose Jardim [1975] Director; Fabio Sandri [1971] Director/Chief Financial Officer [Brazilian]

Onslow Inc. Ltd
Incorporated: 13 January 2017 *Employees:* 1
Net Worth Deficit: £71,200 *Total Assets:* £9,831,311
Registered Office: 5 Elstree Gate, Elstree Way, Borehamwood, Herts, WD6 1JD
Activities: Other service activities n.e.c.
Major Shareholder: Sheila Marie Labatt
Officers: Sheila Marie Labatt [1960] Director [Canadian]

Ontex Retail UK Limited
Incorporated: 12 February 1982 *Employees:* 18
Net Worth: £16,203,679 *Total Assets:* £35,052,964
Registered Office: 1st Floor, Unit 5 Grovelands Business Park, Boundary Way, Hemel Hempstead, Herts, HP2 7TE
Activities: Wholesale of pharmaceutical goods
Parent: Ontex Group NV
Officers: Thierry Navarre [1967] Director/Chief Operating Officer [French]; Steven Paul Jules Vandenbogaerde [1970] Finance Director [Belgian]

OOCL (Europe) Limited
Incorporated: 28 July 1995
Net Worth Deficit: £32,599,468 *Total Assets:* £38,896,160
Registered Office: OOCL House, Levington Park, Bridge Road, Levington, Suffolk, IP10 0NE
Activities: Other transportation support activities
Parent: Orient Overseas Container Line (Europe) Limited
Officers: Mark Richard Banham [1966] Director/Accountant; Danny Raymond C Van Den Bosch [1967] Director [Belgian]; Trelawny Robert Cross [1970] Director; John David Knight [1973] Trade Director; Jan Christof Schmahl [1967] Director [German]; Samantha Clare Sherman [1967] Director/Manager; Neil Stringer [1958] Director/Shipping Manager

OOCL Logistics (Europe) Limited
Incorporated: 14 January 1985
Net Worth Deficit: £7,448,000 *Total Assets:* £10,702,000
Registered Office: OOCL House, Levington Park, Bridge Road, Levington, Ipswich, Suffolk, IP10 0NE
Activities: Other transportation support activities
Parent: OOCL (Europe) Limited
Officers: Joern Wilhelm Boeger [1966] Director [German]; Andreas Hendrik Brakel [1968] Director [Dutch]; Jianping Ye [1963] Director [Chinese]

OP UK Bidco Limited
Incorporated: 20 February 2017
Net Worth: £8,441,822 *Total Assets:* £42,779,068
Registered Office: 9 Stock Road, Southend on Sea, Essex, SS2 5QF
Activities: Activities of other holding companies n.e.c.
Parent: Onineprinters Holdings GmbH
Officers: Michael Fries [1968] Managing Director [German]; Dirk Muller [1965] Managing Director [German]

Opal Bay Limited
Incorporated: 11 January 1995 *Employees:* 4
Net Worth: £5,820,055 *Total Assets:* £27,281,920
Registered Office: Rutland House, 90-92 Baxter Avenue, Southend on Sea, Essex, SS2 6HZ
Activities: Development of building projects
Officers: Mark Daniel Rubin, Secretary/Director; Chesney Alan Lewis [1946] Director; Marilyn June Lewis [1947] Director; Anthony Robert Rubin [1953] Director; Mark Daniel Rubin [1951] Director

OPD Group Limited
Incorporated: 21 May 1996
Net Worth: £37,256,848 *Total Assets:* £37,850,904
Registered Office: Grenville House, 4 Grenville Avenue, Broxbourne, Herts, EN10 7DH
Activities: Activities of other holding companies n.e.c.
Shareholders: Offerco Limited; MPM Connect
Officers: Peter Hearn, Secretary; Peter John Hearn [1953] Director/Chartered Accountant; Simon James Murphy [1964] Director

Opecprime Properties Limited
Incorporated: 17 December 1985 *Employees:* 3
Net Worth: £11,356,132 *Total Assets:* £22,600,000
Registered Office: Hill House, Lowlands Road, Harrow, Middlesex, HA1 3EQ
Activities: Development of building projects
Shareholders: Luke Andrew Comer; Brian Martin Comer
Officers: Brian Martin Comer [1960] Director [Irish]; Luke Andrew Comer [1957] Director [Irish]; Thomas Donnellan [1960] Director [Irish]

Open Fibre Networks Limited
Incorporated: 4 April 2005
Previous: Independent Next Generation Networks Limited
Net Worth: £2,541,691 *Total Assets:* £22,853,760
Registered Office: Energy House, Woolpit Business Park, Windmill Avenue, Woolpit, Bury St Edmunds, Suffolk, IP30 9UP
Activities: Wired telecommunications activities
Parent: Inexus Group (Holdings) Limited
Officers: Christopher Paul Mumford, Company Secretary; Susan Lisa Standring, Secretary; Darryl John Corney [1960] Director; Clive Eric Linsdell [1962] Director; Andrew Robinson [1962] Director; Jason John Roissetter [1973] Director

Openarch Estates Limited
Incorporated: 28 September 1999
Previous: Whitfield Estates Ltd
Net Worth: £13,076,217 *Total Assets:* £27,036,236
Registered Office: The Grange, Market Street, Swavesey, Cambridge, CB24 4QG
Activities: Other letting and operating of own or leased real estate
Parent: Openarch Properties Limited
Officers: Jane Alison Bridgeman [1964] Director; Michael John Horan [1972] Director/Chartered Surveyor; Neil Richard Jenkins [1982] Director/Chartered Accountant; Anthony Nicholas Legg [1953] Director/Banker; Jonathan Paul Whitfield [1970] Director/Builder

Openarch Greenside Limited
Incorporated: 26 February 1996
Previous: Greenside (Over) Limited
Net Worth: £13,003,539 *Total Assets:* £19,970,492
Registered Office: The Grange, 20 Market Street, Swavesey, Cambridge, CB24 4QG
Activities: Other letting and operating of own or leased real estate
Parent: Openarch Properties Limited
Officers: Jane Alison Bridgeman [1964] Director; Michael John Horan [1972] Director/Chartered Surveyor; Neil Richard Jenkins [1982] Director/Chartered Accountant; Anthony Nicholas Legg [1953] Director/Banker; Jonathan Paul Whitfield [1970] Director

Openarch Properties Limited
Incorporated: 30 January 2013 *Employees:* 32
Previous: Whitfield (Holdings) Limited
Net Worth: £19,253,116 *Total Assets:* £53,053,384
Registered Office: The Grange, Market Street, Swavesey, Cambridge, CB24 4QG
Activities: Other letting and operating of own or leased real estate
Parent: Openarch Holdings Limited
Officers: Jane Alison Bridgeman [1964] Director; Michael John Horan [1972] Director/Chartered Surveyor; Neil Richard Jenkins [1982] Director/Chartered Accountant; Anthony Nicholas Legg [1953] Director/Banker; Jonathan Paul Whitfield [1970] Director

Openarch Towerview Limited
Incorporated: 28 February 2000
Previous: Tower View Properties Ltd
Net Worth: £8,146,506 *Total Assets:* £30,706,960
Registered Office: The Grange, 20 Market Street, Swavesey, Cambridge, CB24 4QG
Activities: Other letting and operating of own or leased real estate
Parent: Openarch Properties Limited
Officers: Jane Alison Bridgeman [1964] Director; Michael John Horan [1972] Director/Chartered Surveyor; Neil Richard Jenkins [1982] Director/Chartered Accountant; Anthony Nicholas Legg [1953] Director/Banker; Jonathan Paul Whitfield [1970] Director/Builder

Openview Group Limited
Incorporated: 28 April 2004 *Employees:* 307
Net Worth: £8,792,224 *Total Assets:* £22,470,132
Registered Office: Openview House, Chesham Close, Romford, Essex, RM7 7PJ
Activities: Non-trading company
Shareholders: Mark Philip Ingleson; Kevin Charles Hall; Paul Bullen
Officers: Paul Bullen [1969] Director; Kevin Charles Hall [1956] Director; Mark Philip Ingleson [1961] Director

Openview Security Solutions Limited
Incorporated: 27 May 1997 *Employees:* 295
Net Worth: £10,469,136 *Total Assets:* £24,037,484
Registered Office: Openview House, Chesham Close, Romford, Essex, RM7 7PJ
Activities: Electrical installation
Parent: Openview Group Limited
Officers: Paul Bullen [1969] Director; Kevin Charles Hall [1956] Director; Mark Philip Ingleson [1961] Director

Optima Chemical Ltd
Incorporated: 16 August 2012
Net Worth: £1,063,033 *Total Assets:* £19,829,948
Registered Office: 80 Strafford Gate, Potters Bar, Herts, EN6 1PG
Activities: Agents involved in the sale of fuels, ores, metals and industrial chemicals
Major Shareholder: Artur Khikhlya
Officers: Christopher Engeham [1950] Director/Company Consultant; Artur Khikhlya [1964] Director/Business Consultant [Cypriot]; Valery Tayim [1988] Director/Secretary [Cypriot]

Optima Contracting Limited
Incorporated: 15 February 1985 *Employees:* 381
Net Worth: £17,258,238 *Total Assets:* £35,641,144
Registered Office: 57 London Road, High Wycombe, Bucks, HP11 1BS
Activities: Construction of other civil engineering projects n.e.c.
Parent: Optima Investments Limited
Officers: Nicholas William Caley, Secretary; Nicholas William Caley [1962] Financial Director; Sean Dann [1970] Director; Gary Evans [1970] Sales Marketing Director; Andrew Grey [1969] Director/Surveyor; Robert Keith Judd [1957] Director

Optima Investments Limited
Incorporated: 22 December 2008 *Employees:* 381
Net Worth: £17,290,812 *Total Assets:* £35,816,160
Registered Office: 57 London Road, High Wycombe, Bucks, HP11 1BS
Activities: Activities of construction holding companies
Major Shareholder: Robert Keith Judd
Officers: Nicholas William Caley, Secretary; Nicholas William Caley [1962] Financial Director; Gary Evans [1970] Sales Marketing Director; Andrew Grey [1969] Director/Surveyor; Robert Keith Judd [1957] Director

Optimise Media (UK) Limited
Incorporated: 6 June 2002 *Employees:* 57
Previous: OMG Services Limited
Net Worth: £951,650 *Total Assets:* £11,654,392
Registered Office: 8th Floor, Norfolk Tower, Surrey Street, Norwich, NR1 3PA
Activities: Other information technology service activities
Parent: Optimise Media (Europe) Limited
Officers: Emily Harriet Syme, Secretary/Director; Richard Antoni Savelli [1969] Director/Accountant; Robert Paul Starkey [1975] Director; Richard David Syme [1971] Director

Optimise Media Group Limited
Incorporated: 6 August 2001 *Employees:* 179
Previous: Online Media Group Limited
Net Worth: £1,276,514 *Total Assets:* £15,326,013
Registered Office: 8th Floor, Norfolk Tower, Surrey Street, Norwich, NR1 3PA
Activities: Activities of other holding companies n.e.c.
Shareholders: Robert Paul Starkey; Richard David Syme
Officers: Emily Harriet Syme, Secretary; Richard Antoni Savelli [1969] Director/Accountant; Robert Paul Starkey [1975] Director; Richard David Syme [1971] Director

Optimum Group Services PLC
Incorporated: 3 May 1989 *Employees:* 439
Net Worth: £2,656,944 *Total Assets:* £16,675,437
Registered Office: Jebsen House, 53-61 High Street, Ruislip, Middlesex, HA4 7BD
Activities: Other business support service activities n.e.c.
Shareholders: John Francis Crehan; Annette Crehan
Officers: Annette Crehan, Secretary; John Francis Crehan [1961] Director/Air Conditioning; James Edward Moore [1962] Director/Chief Executive

Optionis Group Limited
Incorporated: 2 September 2014 *Employees:* 136
Previous: Arkarius Group Limited
Net Worth Deficit: £26,814,368 *Total Assets:* £25,394,012
Registered Office: KD Tower, Cotterells, Hemel Hempstead, Herts, HP1 1FW
Activities: Activities of head offices
Parent: Optionis Limited
Officers: Ifti Ahmed [1966] Director; Kevin John Budge [1961] Director/Chief Financial Officer; Heather Hayden [1967] Director; Derek Andrew Kelly [1972] Director; Jeremy Steven Newman [1959] Director/Chartered Accountant

Optionis Limited
Incorporated: 2 September 2014 *Employees:* 7,426
Previous: Optionis Holdco Limited
Net Worth Deficit: £66,315,780 *Total Assets:* £148,430,544
Registered Office: KD Tower, Cotterells, Hemel Hempstead, Herts, HP1 1FW
Activities: Activities of other holding companies n.e.c.
Shareholders: Management Opportunities Limited; Sovereign Capital Partners LLP
Officers: Kevin John Budge [1961] Director/Chief Financial Officer; Derek Andrew Kelly [1972] Director; Jeremy Steven Newman [1959] Director/Chartered Accountant

Optoma Europe Ltd
Incorporated: 7 July 1997 *Employees:* 98
Net Worth: £14,382,000 *Total Assets:* £52,228,000
Registered Office: 1 Bourne End Mills, Hemel Hempstead, Herts, HP1 2UJ
Activities: Wholesale of computers, computer peripheral equipment and software
Parent: Optoma Corporation
Officers: Peter Fosh, Secretary; Wei Yi Chang [1953] Director/Merchant [Taiwanese]; Shih Yuan Chen [1961] Director/Merchant [Taiwanese]; Thierry Michel Marius Millet [1963] Managing Director [French]; Hsiu-Hui Wu [1962] Director [Chinese]

Opus Bestpay Limited
Incorporated: 29 December 2010
Net Worth Deficit: £249,074 *Total Assets:* £10,308,810
Registered Office: Suite A, 82 James Carter Road, Mildenhall, Bury St Edmunds, Suffolk, IP28 7DE
Activities: Other business support service activities n.e.c.
Major Shareholder: Morris Adam Quinton Hazell
Officers: Adrian Benedict Sacco [1966] Director

OPW Holdco Limited
Incorporated: 14 May 2010
Net Worth: £45,459,000 *Total Assets:* £305,996,000
Registered Office: Unit 2A Century Mews, 100A Church Road, Tiptree, Essex, CO5 0AB
Activities: Trade of electricity
Parent: OPW Midco Limited
Officers: Neeti Mukundrai Anand [1984] Director; Cornelia Bernadette Maria Van Heijningen [1971] Investment Director Infrastructure [Dutch]

OPW Midco Limited
Incorporated: 10 September 2010
Net Worth: £15,333,000 *Total Assets:* £63,051,000
Registered Office: Unit 2A Century Mews, 100a Church Road, Tiptree, Essex, CO5 0AB
Activities: Activities of other holding companies n.e.c.
Parent: OPW Topco Limited
Officers: Neeti Mukundrai Anand [1984] Director; Cornelia Bernadette Maria Van Hiejningen [1971] Investment Director Infrastructure [Dutch]

OPW Topco Limited
Incorporated: 4 November 2009
Net Worth Deficit: £42,556,000 *Total Assets:* £217,980,000
Registered Office: Unit 2A Century Mews, 100 Church Road, Tiptree, Colchester, Essex, CO5 0AB
Activities: Activities of other holding companies n.e.c.
Officers: Neeti Mukundrai Anand [1984] Director; Cornelia Bernadette Maria Van Heijningen [1971] Investment Director Infrastructure [Dutch]

Oranmore Precast Limited
Incorporated: 21 October 2011
Net Worth: £3,957,684 *Total Assets:* £9,291,420
Registered Office: Oranmore Precast, Mundford Road, Weeting, Norfolk, IP27 0PL
Activities: Other specialised construction activities n.e.c.
Officers: Richard Burke [1969] Director [Irish]; Derek Forde [1981] Director [Irish]; Ross Melville [1982] Director [Irish]

Orbit Investment Securities Services PLC
Incorporated: 4 July 2000 *Employees:* 8
Net Worth: £8,168,637 *Total Assets:* £8,273,677
Registered Office: Suite 2, 5th Floor, Congress House, 14 Lyon Road, Harrow, Middlesex, HA1 2EN
Activities: Security dealing on own account
Officers: Sakshi Shah, Secretary; Brian Page Constant [1937] Director; Jayechund Jingree [1947] Non-Executive Director Chairman [Mauritian]; Sudip Shah [1982] Director/Chief Executive

Orchard Funding Group PLC
Incorporated: 2 June 2015 *Employees:* 18
Net Worth: £14,037,000 *Total Assets:* £32,489,000
Registered Office: 721 Capability Green, Luton, Beds, LU1 3LU
Activities: Activities of financial services holding companies
Officers: Liam Leo McShane, Secretary; Gary Antony Jennison [1957] Director; Liam Leo McShane [1957] Director/Chartered Certified Accountant; Jonathan Paul David Shearman [1970] Director/Consultant; Rabinder Singh Takhar [1965] Director/Solicitor

Orchard Funding Limited
Incorporated: 25 July 2008 *Employees:* 8
Net Worth: £928,121 *Total Assets:* £11,088,239
Registered Office: 721 Capability Green, Luton, Beds, LU1 3LU
Activities: Credit granting by non-deposit taking finance houses and other specialist consumer credit grantors
Parent: Orchard Funding Group PLC
Officers: Liam Leo McShane, Secretary; Tatiana Korenkova [1972] Director/Head of Finance; Emmia Louise Stratford [1982] Director/Head of Operations/Financial Services; Ravi Takhar [1965] Director

Orchid Drinks Limited
Incorporated: 9 January 1992
Net Worth: £12,764,000 *Total Assets:* £14,113,000
Registered Office: Breakspear Park, Breakspear Way, Hemel Hempstead, Herts, HP2 4TZ
Activities: Manufacture of soft drinks; production of mineral waters and other bottled waters
Parent: Britvic Soft Drinks Limited
Officers: Judith Moore, Secretary; Mathew James Dunn [1974] Director/Chief Financial Officer; Peter Simon Litherland [1964] Director/Chief Executive; Alexandra Clare Thomas [1974] Director/General Counsel and Company Secretary

Ordan UK Limited
Incorporated: 17 January 2003
Net Worth: £5,950,583 *Total Assets:* £32,745,952
Registered Office: Swiss House, Beckingham Street, Tolleshunt Major, Essex, CM9 8LZ
Activities: Buying and selling of own real estate
Major Shareholder: Abraham Aharon Dodi
Officers: Limor Dodi-Ezer, Secretary; Abraham Aharon Dodi [1963] Director

Origin Frames Limited
Incorporated: 28 May 2002 *Employees:* 266
Net Worth: £7,693,117 *Total Assets:* £15,283,468
Registered Office: 1st Floor, Bridge House, 25 Fiddle Bridge Lane, Hatfield, Herts, AL10 0SP
Activities: Other manufacturing n.e.c.
Officers: Malcolm John Ginger, Secretary; Victoria Brockelsby [1980] Director; Andrew Leslie Ginger [1949] Director/Salesman; Malcolm John Ginger [1952] Director/Company Secretary; Neil Ginger [1973] Sales Director; Oliver John Ginger [1981] Director; Andrew Graham Halsall [1962] Managing Director

Origin Holdings (UK) Limited
Incorporated: 7 December 2007
Net Worth: £10,054,293 *Total Assets:* £69,451,488
Registered Office: Orchard Road, Royston, Herts, SG8 5HW
Activities: Activities of head offices
Parent: Agrii Holdings (UK) Limited
Officers: Sean Gerard Coyle [1972] Director [Irish]; Peter Michael Dunne [1973] Director/Chartered Accountant [Irish]; Ronan Andrew Hughes [1968] Director/Company Executive [Irish]; Liam Noel Larkin [1956] Director [Irish]; Thomas Joseph O'Mahony [1962] Director [Irish]; James Marshall Rennie [1957] Director

Origin UK Operations Limited
Incorporated: 31 January 1990 *Employees:* 167
Net Worth: £50,678,000 *Total Assets:* £126,524,000
Registered Office: 1-3 Freeman Court, Jarman Way, Orchard Road, Royston, Herts, SG8 5HW
Activities: Manufacture of fertilizers and nitrogen compounds
Parent: Origin Enterprises UK Limited
Officers: Robert Emile Beeney [1976] Director/Accountant; Christopher Clark [1961] Director; Sean Gerard Coyle [1972] Director [Irish]; Peter Michael Dunne [1973] Director/Chartered Accountant [Irish]; Brendan Francis Kent [1968] Director/Company Executive [Irish]; William Noel Larkin [1956] Director/Company Executive [Irish]; Thomas Joseph O'Mahony [1962] Director/Company Executive [Irish]; Michael St John Pater [1962] Sales Director

The Original Bowling Company Limited
Incorporated: 25 June 2004 *Employees:* 1,802
Net Worth: £58,337,000 *Total Assets:* £100,523,000
Registered Office: Focus 31, West Wing, Cleveland Road, Hemel Hempstead Industrial Estate, Hemel Hempstead, Herts, HP2 7BW
Activities: Other sports activities
Parent: Kendallco Limited
Officers: Stephen Burns [1976] Director; Melanie Dickinson [1974] Talent Director; Mathew Hart [1969] Director; Laurence Brian Keen [1976] Finance Director

The Original Cottage Company Limited
Incorporated: 3 July 2009 *Employees:* 234
Net Worth: £6,071,687 *Total Assets:* £27,320,876
Registered Office: Bank House, Market Place, Reepham, Norwich, NR10 4JJ
Activities: Other reservation service activities n.e.c.
Major Shareholder: James Ashley Ellis
Officers: John Nicholas Willmot, Secretary; James Ashley Ellis [1978] Director; Lesley Anne Ellis [1959] Director/Secretary; Richard Marriott Ellis [1955] Director/Accountant; Thomas Marriott Ellis [1983] Director; Sonia Wendy Holman [1981] Director; Christopher David Simpson [1950] Director; Martin Wickham [1969] Director; John Nicholas Willmot [1978] Director

Orion Alloys Limited
Incorporated: 4 March 1998 *Employees:* 37
Net Worth: £6,654,447 *Total Assets:* £11,383,459
Registered Office: 3 Warners Mill, Silks Way, Braintree, Essex, CM7 3GB
Activities: Wholesale of metals and metal ores
Shareholders: John Alfred Halford; Jayne Lea Halford
Officers: Jayne LEA Halford, Secretary; Jeremy Carter [1968] Sales Director; Jayne LEA Halford [1967] Director; John Alfred Halford [1965] Director

Orion Media Limited
Incorporated: 7 May 2009
Net Worth Deficit: £10,185,000 *Total Assets:* £21,853,000
Registered Office: Media House, Peterborough Business Park, Lynch Wood, Peterborough, Cambs, PE2 6EA
Activities: Television programme production activities
Parent: Orion Media Holdings Limited
Officers: Deidre Ann Ford [1960] Managing Director; Paul Anthony Keenan [1963] Director/Publisher; Sarah Jane Vickery [1963] Finance Director

Orley Farm School Trust
Incorporated: 21 May 1959 *Employees:* 108
Net Worth: £11,316,055 *Total Assets:* £15,772,453
Registered Office: South Hill Avenue, Harrow, Middlesex, HA1 3NU
Activities: Primary education
Officers: Trishna Kamal Vaid, Secretary; Michael John Andrews [1958] Chartered Surveyor and Director; Colin John Hayfield [1955] Director/Chartered Accountant; Kim Louise Hill [1964] Director/Headteacher; Philippa Jackson [1950] Director/Company Secretary; Shivani Kothari [1971] Director/Certified Chartered Accountant; Leena Malde [1966] Director/Company Secretary; Dilip Navapurkar [1961] Director/Property Developer; Rajesh Mansukhlal Raithatha [1972] Managing Director; Doctor Mary Elizabeth Short [1958] Director/Headmistress; Alan Nigel Smith [1962] Director/Banker; Anil Sofat [1972] Commercial Director

Orlight Limited
Incorporated: 11 March 1997 *Employees:* 108
Net Worth: £6,894,914 *Total Assets:* £15,203,643
Registered Office: Parkbury, Unit 3 Victor Way, Colney Street, St Albans, Herts, AL2 2FL
Activities: Other business support service activities n.e.c.
Parent: Source To Site Holdings Limited
Officers: Linda Dangoor, Secretary/Director; Thusitha Indika Bandara Basnayake [1974] Finance Director; Ezra Haskell Dangoor [1944] Director; Kelly Dangoor [1978] Director; Linda Dangoor [1953] Director; Michael Dangoor [1984] Director; Situl Jetha [1986] Design Director; Wilson Diogo Mendes-Abreu [1990] Operations Director [Portuguese]

Orthene Holdings Limited
Incorporated: 17 August 2010 *Employees:* 57
Net Worth: £6,638,203 *Total Assets:* £11,594,368
Registered Office: Unit 13 South Harrow Industrial Estate, Brember Road, Harrow, Middlesex, HA2 8UJ
Activities: Manufacture of other chemical products n.e.c.
Major Shareholder: Charles James Ker
Officers: Charles James Ker [1967] Director

Ortona Limited
Incorporated: 5 February 1988 *Employees:* 10
Net Worth: £16,950,676 *Total Assets:* £19,276,264
Registered Office: 55 Colegate, Norwich, NR3 1DD
Activities: Buying and selling of own real estate
Officers: Stephen Graham Stafford Allen, Secretary; Stephen Graham Stafford Allen [1951] Director/Accountant; Edward James Brundle [1980] Director/Engineer; Thomas Henry Jackson Brundle [1977] Director/Accountant; Darran Karl Burch [1977] Director/Property Manager; Alan John Dawson [1981] Director/Commercial Manager; Stephen MacDonald Dawson [1954] Director; David John Hupton [1960] Director; Katherine Jemima Hupton [1986] Director/Public Relations

Ortona Management Limited
Incorporated: 21 March 2012 *Employees:* 10
Net Worth: £14,476,882 *Total Assets:* £15,938,720
Registered Office: 55 Colegate, Norwich, NR3 1DD
Activities: Management of real estate on a fee or contract basis
Parent: Ortona Limited
Officers: Stephen Graham Stafford Allen, Secretary; Stephen Graham Stafford Allen [1951] Director/Accountant; Edward James Brundle [1980] Director/Engineer; Thomas Henry Jackson Brundle [1977] Director/Accountant; Darran Karl Burch [1977] Director/Property Manager; Alan John Dawson [1981] Director/Commercial Manager; Stephen MacDonald Dawson [1954] Director; David John Hupton [1960] Director; Katherine Jemima Hupton [1986] Director/Public Relations

Ortona Properties Limited
Incorporated: 21 March 2012
Net Worth: £3,491,795 *Total Assets:* £17,989,976
Registered Office: 55 Colegate, Norwich, NR3 1DD
Activities: Buying and selling of own real estate
Parent: Ortona Limited
Officers: Stephen Graham Stafford Allen, Secretary; Stephen Graham Stafford Allen [1951] Director/Accountant; Edward James Brundle [1980] Director/Engineer; Darran Karl Burch [1977] Director/Property Manager; Stephen MacDonald Dawson [1954] Director; David John Hupton [1960] Director

ORTU Federation Ltd
Incorporated: 7 June 2011 *Employees:* 349
Previous: The Stanford & Corringham Schools Trust
Net Worth: £20,802,000 *Total Assets:* £28,315,000
Registered Office: Southend Road, Corringham, Stanford-le-Hope, Essex, SS17 8JT
Activities: General secondary education
Officers: Des Shillingford, Secretary; Dr Sophina Asong [1980] Director/Headteacher; Phil Burr [1950] Director/Property Management; Georgina Anne Clark [1952] Director/Public Affairs Adviser; Paul Dale [1950] Director Logistics; Tony Eatherton [1950] Director/Health & Safety Advisor; Philip Leonard Edgar [1947] Director/Forklift Driver; Robb Philip Harman [1964] Managing Director; Carey Anne Jacobs [1973] Director/Solicitor; Steve Nash [1949] Director/Teacher

Orwell Multi Academy Trust
Incorporated: 3 March 2017 *Employees:* 254
Net Worth: £18,802,554 *Total Assets:* £20,423,148
Registered Office: Orwell Multi Academy Trust, Halifax Primary School, Prince of Wales Drive, Ipswich, Suffolk, IP2 8PY
Activities: Primary education
Officers: Jason Mark Addison [1969] Director/Sales Manager; Paul Joseph Carter [1967] Director/Clerk in Holy Orders; Stella Jane Day [1968] Director of HR Consultancy; Sohail Faruqi [1957] Regional Director - Teach First; Roger Edwin Fern [1943] Director/Retired; Maxwell John Harnden [1957] Director/Solicitor; Anna Estelle Hennell James [1963] Director; Jason John Kirk [1969] Director/Accountant; Naomi Smith [1978] Director/Occupation Registered Nurse

Orwell Trucks Limited
Incorporated: 19 April 1991 *Employees:* 235
Net Worth: £4,907,000 *Total Assets:* £30,579,000
Registered Office: Travellers Lane, Welham Green, Hatfield, Herts, AL9 7HN
Activities: Dormant company
Parent: Motus Holdings (UK) Ltd
Officers: William James Davey [1968] Director; Andrew Barrie Welch [1965] Finance Director

Osborne Co-operative Academy Trust
Incorporated: 13 July 2011 *Employees:* 529
Previous: St Clere's Co-operative Academy Trust
Net Worth: £60,453,000 *Total Assets:* £74,568,000
Registered Office: St Clere's School, Butts Lane, Stanford-le-Hope, Essex, SS17 0NW
Activities: Pre-primary education
Officers: Kathryn Elizabeth Draper, Secretary; John Edward Baines [1947] Director/Chartered Civil Engineer; Shelagh Mary Cosgrow [1953] Director/Retired; Ian Robert Duerden [1958] Director/Senior Business Manager; Michael William Fall [1957] Director/Electronics Technician; Lisa Fergus [1974] Assistant Director of Education; Kay Rebecca Goodacre [1963] Director/Accountant; Paul John Griffiths [1957] Director/Chief Executive Officer; Trisha Jaffe [1951] Director/Retired; Dawn Marie Mummery [1975] Director/Nurse; Andrew Stephen Walker [1968] Creative Director

Osem U.K. Limited
Incorporated: 23 September 1959 *Employees:* 34
Net Worth: £11,492,423 *Total Assets:* £15,267,264
Registered Office: 7-8 Hemmells Park, Hemmells, Laindon, Essex, SS15 6GF
Activities: Wholesale of other food, including fish, crustaceans and molluscs
Parent: Nestle S.A
Officers: Avi Ben Assayag [1965] Director/Manager [Israeli]; Bo Bochenek [1963] Director; Michael John Collyer [1948] Director; Pinhas Kimelman [1963] Director/Deputy CEO [Israeli]; Martin Mendoza [1925] Director; Dan Propper [1941] Director [Israeli]; Itzik Saig [1956] Director [Israeli]

OSG U.K. Limited
Incorporated: 2 October 1969 *Employees:* 48
Net Worth: £8,020,962 *Total Assets:* £11,113,925
Registered Office: Shelton House, 5 Bentalls, Pipps Hill Industrial Estate, Basildon, Essex, SS14 3BY
Activities: Manufacture of tools
Officers: David Edward Hettrel Titheradge, Secretary; Tony Brian Cooper [1961] Director/Sales Management; Mitsutoshi Kano [1967] Director/Area Regional Manager [Japanese]; Hideaki Osawa [1974] Director [Japanese]; Nobuaki Osawa [1968] Managing Director [Japanese]; David Edward Hettrel Titheradge [1936] Director/Chartered Accountant

Osprey Acquisitions Limited
Incorporated: 24 August 2006 *Employees:* 4,727
Net Worth: £630,600,000 *Total Assets:* £11,306,300,416
Registered Office: Lancaster House, Lancaster Way, Ermine Business Park, Huntingdon, Cambs, PE29 6XU
Activities: Other business support service activities n.e.c.
Parent: Osprey Holdco Limited
Officers: Claire Tytherleigh Russell, Secretary; Projesh Banerjea [1986] Director/Financier [Indian]; John Richard Barry [1968] Director/Investor; Dr Stephen Robert Billingham [1948] Director; James Alexander Bryce [1974] Director/Senior Principal; Mamoun Jamai [1981] Director/Senior Portfolio Manager [Moroccan]; Scott Robert James Longhurst [1967] Finance Director; Manoj Mehta [1970] Investment Director; Niall Patrick Mills [1968] Director/Chartered Engineer; Robert Stewart Napier [1947] Director/Chief Executive; Alexandros Nassuphis [1969] Director/Investment Professional [German]; Peter John Simpson [1967] Director; Duncan John Symonds [1973] Director/Civil Engineer

Osprey Holdco Limited
Incorporated: 24 August 2006 *Employees:* 4,939
Net Worth: £436,900,000 *Total Assets:* £11,413,799,936
Registered Office: Lancaster House, Lancaster Way, Ermine Business Park, Huntingdon, Cambs, PE29 6XU
Activities: Activities of head offices
Officers: Claire Tytherleigh Russell, Secretary; Projesh Banerjea [1986] Director/Financier [Indian]; John Richard Barry [1968] Director/Investor; Dr Stephen Robert Billingham [1948] Director; James Alexander Bryce [1974] Director/Senior Principal; Mamoun Jamai [1981] Director/Senior Portfolio Manager [Moroccan]; Scott Robert James Longhurst [1967] Finance Director; Manoj Mehta [1970] Investment Director; Niall Patrick Mills [1968] Director/Chartered Engineer; Robert Stewart Napier [1947] Director/Chief Executive; Alexandros Nassuphis [1969] Director/Investment Professional [German]; Peter John Simpson [1967] Director; Duncan John Symonds [1973] Director/Civil Engineer

OTV Birwelco Limited
Incorporated: 1 September 1989
Net Worth: £2,408,000 *Total Assets:* £48,530,000
Registered Office: Windsor Court, Kingsmead Business Park, High Wycombe, Bucks, HP11 1JU
Activities: Activities of other holding companies n.e.c.
Parent: Veolia UK Ltd
Officers: Ian Thomas Heggie, Secretary; Philip Andrew Chattle [1958] Director; Martyn Paul Fisher [1961] Director; Sunil Kumar Lakhenpaul [1961] Director/Accountant

Ovenden Papers Limited
Incorporated: 29 November 1943 *Employees:* 81
Net Worth: £4,044,219 *Total Assets:* £18,115,964
Registered Office: Swordfish House, Unit C, River Way, Harlow, Essex, CM20 2DP
Activities: Wholesale of other intermediate products
Shareholder: Nigel David Ovenden
Officers: Alison Charlotte Edwardson Gilchrist, Secretary; Nicholas Joseph Blackham Hayward [1969] Operations Director; Alison Charlotte Edwardson-Gilchrist [1959] Finance Director; James Michael Ovenden [1977] Joint Managing Director; Nigel David Ovenden [1961] Joint Managing Director

Overture Bidco Limited
Incorporated: 14 October 2016
Net Worth: £83,261,000 *Total Assets:* £129,579,000
Registered Office: Mandeville House, 62 The Broadway, Amersham, Bucks, HP7 0HJ
Activities: Non-trading company
Parent: Overture Midco II lmited
Officers: Steven William James Kent [1962] Director; Richard James Riegel [1963] Director [American]; Jacqueline Susan Veness [1960] Director

Overture Midco II Limited
Incorporated: 14 October 2016
Net Worth: £82,830,000 *Total Assets:* £82,830,000
Registered Office: Mandeville House, 62 The Broadway, Amersham, Bucks, HP7 0HJ
Activities: Non-trading company
Parent: Overture Midco Limited
Officers: Richard James Riegel [1963] Director [American]; Jacqueline Susan Veness [1960] Director

Overture Midco Limited
Incorporated: 14 October 2016 *Employees:* 2
Net Worth: £82,830,000 *Total Assets:* £82,830,000
Registered Office: Mandeville House, 62 The Broadway, Amersham, Bucks, HP7 0HJ
Activities: Non-trading company
Parent: Overture Topco Limited
Officers: Richard James Riegel [1963] Director [American]; Jacqueline Susan Veness [1960] Director

Overture Topco Limited
Incorporated: 14 October 2016 *Employees:* 357
Net Worth Deficit: £16,823,000 *Total Assets:* £122,598,000
Registered Office: Mandeville House, 62 The Broadway, Amersham, Bucks, HP7 0HJ
Activities: Non-trading company
Parent: Vitruvian Partners LLP
Officers: Steven William James Kent [1962] Director/Chairman; Richard James Riegel [1963] Director [American]; Karen Jane Roy [1966] Director; Jacqueline Susan Veness [1960] Director

Oxford Cambridge and RSA Examinations
Incorporated: 16 December 1997 *Employees:* 403
Net Worth: £112,100,000 *Total Assets:* £130,200,000
Registered Office: The Triangle Building, Shaftesbury Road, Cambridge, CB2 8EA
Activities: Other education n.e.c.
Officers: Jennifer Elliot, Secretary; Sir David Charles Maurice Bell [1946] Director/Retired; Christopher James Kennedy [1945] Director/Retired; Saul Edward Nasse [1965] Director/Chief Executive; Anthony Louis Odgers [1967] Director/University Administration; Richard John Partington [1969] Director/Lecturer; Peter Andrew Jestyn Phillips [1962] Director/Chief Executive; Professor Richard William Prager [1962] Director/Academic; David Walter Runciman [1967] Director/University Academic; Michael Nicholas Fraser Temple [1949] Director/Chartered Accountant; Dr Annette Christina Thomas [1965] Director; Professor Graham Virgo [1966] Director/Senior Pro-Vice-Chancellor; John Peter Williams [1953] Director/Accountant

Oxley Wharf Limited
Incorporated: 25 October 2013
Net Worth: £3,432,209 *Total Assets:* £208,570,912
Registered Office: Suite E2, 2nd Floor, The Octagon, Middleborough, Colchester, Essex, CO1 1TG
Activities: Development of building projects
Officers: Chiat Kwong Ching [1965] Director [Singaporean]; See Ching Low [1975] Director [Singaporean]

Oxley Wharf Property 1 Limited
Incorporated: 27 November 2013
Net Worth: £19,003,092 *Total Assets:* £505,461,952
Registered Office: Suite E2, 2nd Floor, The Octagon, Middleborough, Colchester, Essex, CO1 1TG
Activities: Development of building projects
Officers: Chiat Kwong Ching [1965] Director [Singaporean]; See Ching Low [1975] Director [Singaporean]

Oxley Wharf Property 2 Limited
Incorporated: 18 November 2013
Net Worth: £3,577,914 *Total Assets:* £219,689,360
Registered Office: Suite E2, 2nd Floor, The Octagon, Middleborough, Colchester, Essex, CO1 1TG
Activities: Development of building projects
Officers: Chiat Kwong Ching [1965] Director [Singaporean]; See Ching Low [1975] Director [Singaporean]

Oxley Wharf Property 3 Limited
Incorporated: 18 November 2013
Net Worth Deficit: £1,971,332 *Total Assets:* £91,353,488
Registered Office: Suite E2, 2nd Floor, The Octagon, Middleborough, Colchester, Essex, CO1 1TG
Activities: Development of building projects
Officers: Chiat Kwong Ching [1965] Director [Singaporean]; See Ching Low [1975] Director [Singaporean]

OYO Developments Limited
Incorporated: 13 June 2005 *Employees:* 2
Net Worth: £4,377,434 *Total Assets:* £12,816,066
Registered Office: 2 Lambseth Street, Eye, Suffolk, IP23 7AG
Activities: Development of building projects
Parent: Ravenbourne Securities Limited
Officers: Ingrid Ruth Wright, Secretary; Michel Alain Henri [1961] Director/Surveyor; Dr Rachel Tarn Pedder-Smith [1975] Director/Teacher

Oyster Properties Limited
Incorporated: 27 January 2006 *Employees:* 8
Net Worth: £7,447,740 *Total Assets:* £15,145,685
Registered Office: The Pavilion, Fox's Marina, Ipswich, Suffolk, IP2 8NJ
Activities: Development of building projects
Major Shareholder: Richard Burnell Matthews
Officers: Sally Ann Morton, Secretary; Richard Burnell Matthews [1948] Director; Sally Ann Morton [1962] Director/Property Manager

P & O Ferrymasters Holdings Limited
Incorporated: 18 September 2002
Net Worth: £9,872,726 *Total Assets:* £40,558,996
Registered Office: Wherstead Park, Wherstead, Ipswich, Suffolk, IP9 2WG
Activities: Activities of head offices
Officers: Bastiaan Belder, Secretary [Dutch]; Bastiaan Belder [1960] Director/Accountant [Dutch]; Janette Susan Bell [1964] Director; Christopher Neil Cassidy [1970] Finance Director

P G S International Limited
Incorporated: 27 February 2006 *Employees:* 3
Net Worth Deficit: £22,679,598 *Total Assets:* £184,642,336
Registered Office: 2-4 Eastern Road, Romford, Essex, RM1 3PJ
Activities: Other reservation service activities n.e.c.
Parent: PGS Otelcilik Turizm Ticaret A.S.
Officers: Nicola Jane Cheater [1978] Director

P J M Farms Limited
Incorporated: 10 December 2010 *Employees:* 3
Net Worth: £1,535,859 *Total Assets:* £10,187,853
Registered Office: Monkey Lodge, Main Road, Woolverstone, Ipswich, Suffolk, IP9 1AJ
Activities: Growing of cereals (except rice), leguminous crops and oil seeds
Shareholders: Philip John Mayhew; Cornelia Elisabeth Mayhew
Officers: Cornelia Elisabeth Mayhew [1952] Director/Housewife [Dutch]; Philip John Mayhew [1954] Director

P.I.P. Electrics Limited
Incorporated: 18 December 1969 *Employees:* 93
Net Worth: £8,464,396 *Total Assets:* £15,552,661
Registered Office: Fenton House, Fenton Way, Southfields Business Park, Basildon, Essex, SS15 6TD
Activities: Electrical installation
Parent: PIP EOT Limited
Officers: Gary Pascoe, Secretary; Steven Brewer [1964] Director/Electrical Engineer; Gary Pascoe [1960] Director/Electrical Engineer

P2P Mailing Ltd
Incorporated: 19 December 2008 *Employees:* 150
Net Worth: £11,856,160 *Total Assets:* £31,127,270
Registered Office: Dunton Distribution Centre, Christy Way, Basildon, Essex, SS15 6TR
Activities: Licensed carriers
Parent: Fedex Crossborder UK Holdings Limited
Officers: Iii Klank, Secretary; Carl Asmus [1943] Director/Business Executive [American]; Malcolm Barrell [1962] Director; Ian Dowie [1961] Director/Mail; Michael Edward Hagan [1958] Director/Business Executive [American]; Thomas Lawrence Holland [1957] Director/Business Executive [American]; Michael John Owen [1973] Director/Certified Accountant

Pacific (BC) Topco 2 Limited
Incorporated: 10 November 2016
Net Worth: £141,320,560 *Total Assets:* £141,320,560
Registered Office: The Octagon, Middleborough, Colchester, Essex, CO1 1TG
Activities: Non-trading company
Officers: Sam Richard Del Mar [1974] Director/Chief Financial Officer; Frederick Karl Minturn [1956] Director/Chief Executive [American]

Pacific (BC) Topco 3 Limited
Incorporated: 10 November 2016
Net Worth: £137,943,584 *Total Assets:* £203,882,384
Registered Office: The Octagon, Middleborough, Colchester, Essex, CO1 1TG
Activities: Non-trading company
Parent: Pacific (BC) Topco 2 Limited
Officers: Sam Richard Del Mar [1974] Director/Chief Financial Officer; Frederick Karl Minturn [1956] Director/Chief Executive [American]

Pacific (BC) Topco 4 Limited
Incorporated: 3 November 2016
Net Worth: £131,458,304 *Total Assets:* £196,308,000
Registered Office: The Octagon, Middleborough, Colchester, Essex, CO1 1TG
Activities: Non-trading company
Parent: Pacific (BC) Topco 3 Limited
Officers: Sam Richard Del Mar [1974] Director/Chief Financial Officer; Frederick Karl Minturn [1956] Director/Chief Executive [American]

Pacific (BC) Topco 5 Limited
Incorporated: 25 October 2016 *Employees:* 3
Net Worth: £196,555,424 *Total Assets:* £196,817,488
Registered Office: The Octagon, Middleborough, Colchester, Essex, CO1 1TG
Activities: Non-trading company
Parent: Pacific (BC) Topco 4 Limited
Officers: Sam Richard Del Mar [1974] Director/Chief Financial Officer; Frederick Karl Minturn [1956] Director/Chief Executive [American]

The Paddocks Care Home Ltd
Incorporated: 26 September 2000 *Employees:* 109
Net Worth: £8,494,949 *Total Assets:* £14,987,614
Registered Office: Lincoln House, Dereham Road, Swanton Morley, Dereham, Norfolk, NR20 4LT
Activities: Other human health activities
Parent: Castlemeadow Group Holdings Ltd
Officers: Sonya Kaushal, Secretary; Dr Sanjay Kaushal [1967] Director; Sonya Kaushal [1971] Director

S & J Padfield & Partners LLP
Incorporated: 29 January 2013 *Employees:* 15
Net Worth: £7,619,014 *Total Assets:* £9,118,094
Registered Office: Codham Hall, Codham Hall Lane, Great Warley, Brentwood, Essex, CM13 3JT
Officers: Christopher Scott Padfield [1961] Member; Herbert Charles Scott Padfield [1932] Member; Joyce Winifred Padfield [1934] Member

Padfield (Hayleys) Limited
Incorporated: 7 September 1959 *Employees:* 12
Net Worth: £17,505,928 *Total Assets:* £19,640,844
Registered Office: The Estate Office, Hayleys Manor Farm, Upland Raod, Epping Upland, Epping, Essex, CM16 6PQ
Activities: Growing of cereals (except rice), leguminous crops and oil seeds
Shareholders: Ian George Padfield; Peter George Padfield
Officers: Emma Jane Padfield, Secretary; Ian George Padfield [1963] Director/Farmer; Peter George Padfield [1938] Director/Farmer

S & J Padfield Estates LLP
Incorporated: 29 January 2013 *Employees:* 1
Net Worth: £4,137,295 *Total Assets:* £9,619,884
Registered Office: Codham Hall, Codham Hall Lane, Great Warley, Brentwood, Essex, CM13 3JT
Officers: Christopher Scott Padfield [1961] Member; Herbert Charles Scott Padfield [1932] Member; Joyce Winifred Padfield [1934] Member

Padwicks Travel (Wembley) Limited
Incorporated: 21 October 1981 *Employees:* 36
Net Worth: £7,229,062 *Total Assets:* £30,341,244
Registered Office: 523 High Road, Wembley, Middlesex, HA0 2DH
Activities: Travel agency activities
Shareholders: Pramila Patel; Rashmi Chhotabhai Patel
Officers: Pramila Ashok Patel, Secretary; Pramila Ashok Patel [1952] Director/Travel Agent; Rashmi Chhotabhai Patel [1955] Director/Travel Agent

Painesend Farm LLP
Incorporated: 23 November 2005 *Employees:* 3
Net Worth: £15,983,992 *Total Assets:* £17,446,600
Registered Office: Painesend Farm, Painesend, Tring, Herts, HP23 6JU
Officers: Karin Vallis [1951] Member; Peter Samuel Vallis [1942] Member

Pajef Limited
Incorporated: 28 March 1994 *Employees:* 86
Net Worth: £5,977,279 *Total Assets:* £9,752,659
Registered Office: Rhys House, Minerva Business Park, Lynchwood, Peterborough, Cambs, PE2 6FT
Activities: Management consultancy activities other than financial management
Parent: Executors of Janice and Philp Friend
Officers: Ewan Rhys Friend [1982] Director/IT Consultant; Ieuan Rhys Friend [1981] Director/IT Consultant

Palacath Limited
Incorporated: 11 September 1972
Net Worth: £29,606,992 *Total Assets:* £35,614,168
Registered Office: Atlas House, 28 Great Cambridge Road, Enfield, Middlesex, EN1 1UU
Activities: Development of building projects
Officers: Judith Erlich, Secretary; Baruch Erlich [1962] Director/Solicitor; Judith Erlich [1960] Director/Secretary

Palatial Leisure Limited
Incorporated: 1 March 1993 *Employees:* 133
Net Worth: £4,152,345 *Total Assets:* £8,929,539
Registered Office: The Great Yarmouth Palace, Church Plain, Great Yarmouth, Norfolk, NR30 1PL
Activities: Gambling and betting activities
Major Shareholder: Patrick Michael Sarto Duffy
Officers: Chris Pugh, Secretary; Jan Andersen [1967] Director/Air Steward [Danish]; Patrick Michael Sarto Duffy [1954] Director/Bingo Operator [Irish]; Brian Pugh [1937] Director/Manager

Palm Paper Limited
Incorporated: 23 July 1964 *Employees:* 187
Net Worth: £349,697,280 *Total Assets:* £380,070,784
Registered Office: Saddlebow Industrial Estate, Poplar Avenue, Kings Lynn, Norfolk, PE34 3AL
Activities: Manufacture of paper and paperboard
Parent: Hera GmbH
Officers: Jose Antonio Villatoro, Secretary; Wolfgang Palm [1953] Director/Businessman [German]

Palm Recycling Limited
Incorporated: 5 February 2010 *Employees:* 14
Net Worth: £5,198,240 *Total Assets:* £14,946,428
Registered Office: Saddlebow Industrial Estate, Poplar Avenue, Kings Lynn, Norfolk, PE34 3AL
Activities: Recovery of sorted materials
Parent: Palm Paper Limited
Officers: Jose Antonio Villatoro, Secretary; Gero Hempel [1966] Managing Director [German]; Wolfgang Palm [1953] Director/Businessman [German]

W.H.Palmer & Co.(Industries) Limited
Incorporated: 19 June 1962 *Employees:* 56
Net Worth: £17,585,920 *Total Assets:* £22,525,120
Registered Office: Charringtons House, The Causeway, Bishop's Stortford, Herts, CM23 2ER
Activities: Activities of head offices
Officers: Robert Harry Ling, Secretary; Jeremy Alton [1947] Director/Solicitor; Matthew Henry Colling [1955] Director/Self Employed; Richard Charles Evans [1964] Director; Robert Harry Ling [1952] Director/Accountant; Adam John Wallis [1960] Director; Natalie Mary Wallis [1989] Director/Commercial Manager

Palmers (St Albans) Limited
Incorporated: 19 September 1997 *Employees:* 126
Net Worth: £1,448,355 *Total Assets:* £13,698,190
Registered Office: Pennine Way, Redbourn Road, Hemel Hempstead, Herts, HP2 7AZ
Activities: Sale of new cars and light motor vehicles
Parent: Palmers & Sons Holdings Limited
Officers: Christine Palmer [1964] Director/Housewife; Daniel Christopher Palmer [1963] Director

Palmhall Limited
Incorporated: 23 April 1981 *Employees:* 136
Net Worth: £1,745,000 *Total Assets:* £15,091,000
Registered Office: 1 Park Lane, Hemel Hempstead, Herts, HP2 4YL
Activities: Recreational vehicle parks, trailer parks and camping grounds
Parent: Colaingrove Limited
Officers: Jane Elizabeth Bentall [1970] Director/Accountant; Paul Charles Flaum [1970] Director; Iain Stuart Macmillan [1976] Director

Pamina Estates Limited
Incorporated: 6 February 2015
Net Worth: £5,279,249 *Total Assets:* £8,188,296
Registered Office: 50 Lancaster Road, Enfield, Middlesex, EN2 0BY
Activities: Other letting and operating of own or leased real estate
Major Shareholder: Michael Blakey
Officers: Michael Blakey [1963] Director; Paula May Blakey [1963] Director

Pampisford Properties Limited
Incorporated: 11 May 2000 *Employees:* 2
Net Worth: £3,114,727 *Total Assets:* £10,738,799
Registered Office: The Old Mill Workshop, Mill Farm Lane, Pampisford, Cambs, CB2 4EQ
Activities: Other letting and operating of own or leased real estate
Shareholders: Kevin Roy Satchell; Nicholas Leonard Satchell
Officers: Hayley Satchell, Secretary; Kevin Roy Satchell, Secretary; Kevin Roy Satchell [1961] Financial Director; Leonard Roy Satchell [1938] Managing Director; Margaret Eunice Satchell [1938] Director; Nicholas Leonard Satchell [1962] Director

Pangbourne Developments Limited
Incorporated: 21 December 2011
Net Worth: £2,933,000 *Total Assets:* £20,678,000
Registered Office: Gate House, Turnpike Road, High Wycombe, Bucks, HP12 3NR
Activities: Buying and selling of own real estate
Parent: Taylor Wimpey UK Limited
Officers: Katherine Elizabeth Hindmarsh, Secretary; Ingrid Ruth Osborne [1977] Director; Richard Buchanan Smith [1973] Associate Development Director

Pant y Wal Investments Limited
Incorporated: 24 August 2011
Net Worth: £11,646,300 *Total Assets:* £11,646,300
Registered Office: 2 Hunting Gate, Hitchin, Herts, SG4 0TJ
Activities: Other business support service activities n.e.c.
Parent: Ventus Investments Ltd
Officers: Valeria Rosati [1975] Director/Fund Manager [Italian]; Marissa Ann Szczepaniak [1980] Associate Director

Pantheon Hotels and Leisure Limited
Incorporated: 8 June 1981 *Employees:* 124
Net Worth: £10,223,317 *Total Assets:* £17,291,444
Registered Office: The Barn Hotel, West End Road, Ruislip, Middlesex, HA4 6JB
Activities: Hotels and similar accommodation
Parent: SNB Holdings Limited
Officers: Kathirgamathamby Jegeswaran, Secretary/Accountant; Nor Fazlina Bhattessa [1963] Director [Malaysian]; Shalil Nalin Bhattessa [1968] Director/Businessman

Panther (VAT) Properties Limited
Incorporated: 25 June 1996
Net Worth: £14,378,993 *Total Assets:* £55,986,056
Registered Office: Unicorn House, Station Close, Potters Bar, Herts, EN6 1TL
Activities: Buying and selling of own real estate
Parent: Panther Securities PLC
Officers: Simon Jeffrey Peters, Secretary; Andrew Stewart Perloff [1944] Director; John Henry Perloff [1968] Director; Simon Jeffrey Peters [1977] Director

Panther Investment Properties Limited
Incorporated: 9 April 1973
Net Worth: £12,678,165 *Total Assets:* £27,539,376
Registered Office: Unicorn House, Station Close, Potters Bar, Herts, EN6 1TL
Activities: Buying and selling of own real estate
Parent: Panther Securities PLC
Officers: Simon Jeffrey Peters, Secretary; Andrew Stewart Perloff [1944] Director; John Henry Perloff [1968] Director; Simon Jeffrey Peters [1977] Director

Panther Securities P L C
Incorporated: 17 October 1934 *Employees:* 21
Net Worth: £91,212,000 *Total Assets:* £211,962,000
Registered Office: Unicorn House, Station Close, Potters Bar, Herts, EN6 1TL
Activities: Buying and selling of own real estate
Officers: Simon Jeffrey Peters, Secretary/Director; Bryan Richard Galan [1943] Director/Chartered Surveyor; Peter Michael Kellner [1942] Director; Andrew Stewart Perloff [1944] Director; John Henry Perloff [1968] Director; Simon Jeffrey Peters [1977] Director

Panther Trading Limited
Incorporated: 9 July 1974
Net Worth: £8,727,900 *Total Assets:* £16,531,522
Registered Office: Unicorn House, Station Close, Potters Bar, Herts, EN6 1TL
Activities: Buying and selling of own real estate
Parent: Panther Securities PLC
Officers: Simon Jeffrey Peters, Secretary; Andrew Stewart Perloff [1944] Director; John Henry Perloff [1968] Director; Simon Jeffrey Peters [1977] Director

Papa Midco Limited
Incorporated: 23 October 2014 *Employees:* 87
Net Worth Deficit: £63,689,000 *Total Assets:* £133,035,000
Registered Office: Johnston House, 8 Johnston Road, Woodford Green, Essex, IG8 0XA
Activities: Financial management
Parent: Papa Topco Limited
Officers: Michael Douglas Comish [1965] Operations Director [British/Canadian]; Dirk Gustaf Eller [1972] Director/Partner [American]; Peter William James [1983] Director; Karen Elisabeth Dind Jones [1956] Director

Papa Topco Limited
Incorporated: 23 October 2014 *Employees:* 4,311
Net Worth Deficit: £273,806,016 *Total Assets:* £133,039,000
Registered Office: Johnston House, 8 Johnston Road, Woodford Green, Essex, IG8 0XA
Activities: Financial management
Shareholders: David Bonderman; James George Coulter
Officers: Michael Douglas Comish [1965] Operations Director [British/Canadian]; Dirk Gustaf Eller [1972] Director/Partner [American]; Peter William James [1983] Director; Karen Elisabeth Dind Jones [1956] Director

The Papworth Trust
Incorporated: 16 November 1917 *Employees:* 249
Net Worth: £20,987,000 *Total Assets:* £55,098,000
Registered Office: Head Office, Papworth Everard, Cambridge, CB23 3RG
Activities: Construction of domestic buildings
Officers: Mark Colin Blake, Secretary; Peter Lawson Agar [1950] Director of Development and Alumni Relations; David John Atkinson [1970] Director/Retired; Wes Paul Cuell [1947] Director/Social Worker; Robert Charles Hammond [1947] Director; Andrew John Hirst [1961] Director; Patrick John Hughes [1954] Director/Consultant; Richard Michael Norton [1953] Director/Retired; Debbie Martine Sorkin [1960] Director; Vanessa Clare Stanislas [1966] Director

Paradigm Commercial PLC
Incorporated: 13 January 1993
Net Worth: £25,791,000 *Total Assets:* £26,445,000
Registered Office: 1 Glory Park Avenue, Wooburn Green, High Wycombe, Bucks, HP10 0DF
Activities: Development of building projects
Parent: Paradigm Homes Charitable Housing Association Limited
Officers: Richard Archer [1973] Director/Chief Risk Advisor; Julian Charles Corbett Ashby [1947] Director; Matthew Roy Bailes [1970] Director/Chief Executive Officer; Mathew George Bishop [1978] Managing Director; Patricia Elizabeth Brandum [1955] Director/Consultant; John William Cross [1953] Director/Consultant; Eva Cullen [1966] Director/Head of Customer Fulfilment Operations [Irish]; Philippa Simone Lowe [1961] Director; Janet Ogundele [1967] HR Director; Peter Anthony Quinn [1957] Director; Philip Ernest Shepley [1973] Director/Chief Operating Officer; John Nicol Simpson [1947] Director

Paradigm Development Services Limited
Incorporated: 19 January 2009 *Employees:* 4
Net Worth: £494,000 *Total Assets:* £20,196,000
Registered Office: 1 Glory Park Avenue, Wooburn Green, High Wycombe, Bucks, HP10 0DF
Activities: Other business support service activities n.e.c.
Parent: Paradigm Housing Group Ltd
Officers: Matthew Roy Bailes [1970] Director/Chief Executive Officer; Jane Mary Harrison [1962] Director/Accountant

Paradine Holdings Limited
Incorporated: 11 August 2015
Net Worth: £9,499,622 *Total Assets:* £10,175,627
Registered Office: 5 Elstree Gate, Elstree Way, Borehamwood, Herts, WD6 1JD
Activities: Activities of other holding companies n.e.c.
Shareholders: George Frost; Wilfred Paradine Frost
Officers: George Frost [1987] Director; Wilfred Paradine Frost [1985] Director

Paragon Land & Estates Ltd
Incorporated: 13 October 2014 *Employees:* 5
Net Worth: £15,686,333 *Total Assets:* £24,622,824
Registered Office: Foxwood Lodge, Marefen Drove, Littleport, Cambs, CB6 1RH
Activities: Development of building projects
Shareholder: Rick Parisi
Officers: Ricardo Ettore Parisi [1954] Director

Parametric Investments Limited
Incorporated: 18 May 2004 *Employees:* 1
Net Worth: £13,301,155 *Total Assets:* £21,635,436
Registered Office: 48 Lancaster Way Business Park, Ely, Cambs, CB6 3NW
Activities: Manufacture of electronic industrial process control equipment
Parent: Process Sensing Technologies Ltd
Officers: Michael Bannister [1957] Director; David Paul Leonard [1966] Director; Adam Dean Markin [1966] Director/Chairman

Pareto Law Limited
Incorporated: 30 October 1995 *Employees:* 398
Net Worth: £3,388,000 *Total Assets:* £8,516,000
Registered Office: 450 Capability Green, Luton, Beds, LU1 3LU
Activities: Temporary employment agency activities
Parent: Randstad UK Holding Limited
Officers: Robin Fisher, Secretary; David Julian Bruce [1966] Director/Chief Financial Officer; Mark Jonathan Bull [1964] Director; Jonathan Paul Fitchew [1962] Director; Andrew Edgar Sawer [1962] Sales Director

Park Air Systems Limited
Incorporated: 1 October 1985 *Employees:* 136
Net Worth: £31,591,000 *Total Assets:* £48,685,000
Registered Office: Northfields, Market Deeping, Peterborough, Cambs, PE6 8UE
Activities: Wireless telecommunications activities
Parent: NGC UK Limited
Officers: Susie Lee Choung, Secretary; Roger Campbell Wiltshire, Secretary; Peter Beange [1958] Director Commercial Operations Europe; Daniel Milligan [1956] Managing Director; Jeffrey Quentin Palombo [1960] Director/VP Business Development, Mission Systems [American]; Steven David Spiegel [1964] Director [American]; Roger Campbell Wiltshire [1967] Deputy European Legal Director

Park High School
Incorporated: 1 July 2011 *Employees:* 182
Net Worth: £20,294,172 *Total Assets:* £23,561,744
Registered Office: Park High School, Thistlecroft Gardens, Stanmore, Middlesex, HA7 1PL
Activities: Technical and vocational secondary education
Officers: Marilyn Joy Ashton [1953] Director/Planning Consultant; Sean Guiheen [1985] Director/Teacher; Bhupendra Vishram Hirani [1971] Director/Self Employed; Karen Elaine Hogge [1969] Director/Teaching Assistant; David Emlyn Lumley [1958] Director; Sam Methuen [1959] Director/Solicitor; Josephine Muir [1948] Director/Retired; Naresh Patel [1966] Director/Mechanical Engineer; Sangita Hitesh Patel [1965] Director/Accountant; Toral Patel [1968] Director/ICT, Data & Library Manager; Hayley Louise Perren [1988] Director/Teacher; Richard Samuels [1986] Director/Pastoral Support Assistant; Dr John Phillip Wise [1945] Director; John Woodgate [1959] Director/Retired Fire Officer

Park Securities Limited
Incorporated: 6 October 1994 *Employees:* 3
Net Worth: £2,296,449 *Total Assets:* £12,041,426
Registered Office: 15 Park Avenue South, Harpenden, Herts, AL5 2DZ
Activities: Security dealing on own account
Shareholders: John Stewart Wilson; Clare Margaret Wilson
Officers: Susan Elizabeth McGill, Secretary; Henry George Wilson [1952] Director/Consultant

Parkdale Investments Limited
Incorporated: 9 June 1961
Net Worth: £3,838,464 *Total Assets:* £38,207,036
Registered Office: Atlas House, 28 Great Cambridge Road, Enfield, Middlesex, EN1 1UU
Activities: Buying and selling of own real estate
Officers: Judith Erlich, Secretary; Baruch Erlich [1962] Director/Solicitor; Judith Erlich [1960] Director/Secretary

G.H. Parker (North Cotes) Limited
Incorporated: 26 February 1953 *Employees:* 10
Net Worth: £4,711,509 *Total Assets:* £17,146,736
Registered Office: The Farm Office, Pinchbeck Farm, Sea Lane, Wainfleet St Mary, Skegness, Lincs, PE24 4BA
Activities: Growing of cereals (except rice), leguminous crops and oil seeds
Parent: Anne's Settlement
Officers: Anne Elizabeth Hickling, Secretary; Anne Elizabeth Hickling [1955] Director; William Henry Wrisdale [1985] Director/Farm Manager

C.W.Parker (Wainfleet) Limited
Incorporated: 5 April 1951 *Employees:* 10
Net Worth: £4,732,407 *Total Assets:* £10,608,598
Registered Office: The Farm Office, Pinchbeck Farm, Sea Lane, Wainfleet St Mary, Skegness, Lincs, PE24 4BA
Activities: Growing of cereals (except rice), leguminous crops and oil seeds
Shareholders: Anne Elizabeth Hickling; A E Hickling Accum. and Maint.
Officers: Emma Jane Cook, Secretary; Anne Elizabeth Hickling [1955] Director; Craig Jonathan Norwood [1961] Director/Manager

Parker Hannifin (GB) Limited
Incorporated: 17 December 1946
Net Worth: £8,709,000 *Total Assets:* £266,548,992
Registered Office: Parker House, 55 Maylands Avenue, Hemel Hempstead Industrial Estate, Hemel Hempstead, Herts, HP2 4SJ
Activities: Management of real estate on a fee or contract basis
Parent: Alenco (Holdings) Limited
Officers: Graham Mark Ellinor, Secretary; Graham Mark Ellinor [1964] Director/Accountant; James Alan David Elsey [1970] HR Director

Parker Hannifin (Holdings) Limited
Incorporated: 10 February 2000
Net Worth: £22,233,000 *Total Assets:* £22,234,000
Registered Office: Parker House, Maylands Avenue, Hemel Hempstead Industrial Estate, Hemel Hempstead, Herts, HP2 4SJ
Activities: Activities of head offices
Parent: Parker Hannifin Corporation
Officers: Graham Mark Ellinor, Secretary; Graham Mark Ellinor [1964] Director/Accountant; James Alan David Elsey [1970] HR Director

Parker Hannifin 2007 LLP
Incorporated: 23 April 2007
Net Worth: £268,478,016 *Total Assets:* £268,478,016
Registered Office: Parker House, 55 Maylands Avenue, Hemel Hempstead Industrial Estate, Hemel Hempstead, Herts, HP2 4SJ

Parker Hannifin Industries Limited
Incorporated: 23 July 2007
Net Worth: £15,311,000 *Total Assets:* £15,311,000
Registered Office: Parker House, 55 Maylands Avenue, Hemel Hempstead Industrial Estate, Hemel Hempstead, Herts, HP2 4SJ
Activities: Non-trading company
Parent: Parker Hannifin Corporation
Officers: Graham Mark Ellinor, Secretary; Graham Mark Ellinor [1964] Director/Accountant; James Alan David Elsey [1970] HR Director

Parker Hannifin Limited
Incorporated: 7 April 2011 *Employees:* 367
Net Worth: £52,595,000 *Total Assets:* £143,076,000
Registered Office: Parker House, 55 Maylands Avenue, Hemel Hempstead Industrial Estate, Hemel Hempstead, Herts, HP2 4SJ
Activities: Manufacture of fluid power equipment
Parent: Parker Hannifin Corporation
Officers: Graham Mark Ellinor, Secretary; Jane Brogan [1973] Director/Customer Service Manager; Martin Peter Eldridge [1969] Director/General Manager; Graham Mark Ellinor [1964] Director; James Alan David Elsey [1970] HR Director; William Ellard Sheedy [1973] Director/Mechanical Engineer [Irish]

Parker Hannifin Manufacturing (UK) Limited
Incorporated: 3 February 1998 *Employees:* 219
Net Worth: £49,493,000 *Total Assets:* £61,215,000
Registered Office: Parker House, 55 Maylands Avenue, Hemel Hempstead Industrial Estate, Hemel Hempstead, Herts, HP2 4SJ
Activities: Manufacture of fluid power equipment
Parent: Parker Hannifin Industries Limited
Officers: Graham Mark Ellinor, Secretary; Graham Mark Ellinor [1964] Director/Accountant; James Alan David Elsey [1970] HR Director; Harvey Preston [1965] Director/General Manager

Parker Hannifin Manufacturing Limited
Incorporated: 20 June 2003 *Employees:* 1,494
Net Worth: £203,582,000 *Total Assets:* £512,844,000
Registered Office: Parker House, 55 Maylands Avenue, Hemel Hempstead Industrial Estate, Hemel Hempstead, Herts, HP2 4SJ
Activities: Manufacture of fluid power equipment
Parent: Parker Hannifin (GB) Limited
Officers: Graham Mark Ellinor, Secretary; Graham Eric Bielinski-Bradbury [1960] Director/General Manager; Graham Mark Ellinor [1964] Director/Accountant; James Alan David Elsey [1970] HR Director; Kris Robert Holmes [1977] Director/General Manager; Harvey Preston [1965] Director/General Manager; Andrew Spivey [1971] Director/General Manager; Mark Zanna [1975] Director/Group Quality Manager MSGE

The Parkes LLP
Incorporated: 12 June 2003
Net Worth: £11,213,380 *Total Assets:* £17,316,784
Registered Office: Stag House, Old London Road, Hertford, SG13 7LA
Officers: Derek Parkes [1944] Member; Stephen Albert Smith [1947] Member

Parkstone Limited
Incorporated: 14 December 1981 *Employees:* 364
Net Worth: £6,042,569 *Total Assets:* £22,716,966
Registered Office: The Office, Cheveley Park Stud, Duchess Drive, Newmarket, Suffolk, CB8 9DD
Activities: Other retail sale in non-specialised stores
Parent: Hoopers Limited
Officers: Christopher James Dant, Secretary; Debra Angus [1965] Director; Roy Bernard Copus [1959] Director/Chartered Accountant; David Brian Thompson [1936] Director; Patricia Thompson [1940] Director; Katharine Patricia Woodward [1968] Director/Buyer

Parkway Hellas Holdings Limited
Incorporated: 29 October 2004
Net Worth: £27,500,000 *Total Assets:* £28,500,000
Registered Office: Westpoint, Peterborough Business Park, Lynch Wood, Peterborough, Cambs, PE2 6FZ
Activities: Other business support service activities n.e.c.
Parent: Thomas Cook Group Hedging Limited
Officers: Shirley Bradley, Secretary; Alan Charles Donald [1963] Director

Parthings Farm - Management and Promotion Limited
Incorporated: 9 March 2010 *Employees:* 2
Net Worth: £5,156,247 *Total Assets:* £8,586,173
Registered Office: The Estate Office, Dorton Road, Chilton, Aylesbury, Bucks, HP18 9LR
Activities: Buying and selling of own real estate
Officers: Harry Buchanan Aubrey-Fletcher [1982] Director/Property Developer; Sir Henry Egerton Aubrey-Fletcher [1945] Director; Peter Robert Michael Bond [1935] Director/Solicitor

Partners in Property (U.K.) Limited
Incorporated: 13 March 1997 *Employees:* 156
Net Worth: £2,210,775 *Total Assets:* £33,841,200
Registered Office: Grant Hall, Parsons Green, St Ives, Cambs, PE27 4AA
Activities: Buying and selling of own real estate
Parent: Move with Us Ltd
Officers: Robert Matson, Secretary; Benjamin Paul Greco [1979] Director; David Jeremy Grossman [1970] Director; Robert Matson [1970] Director/Chartered Accountant

The Partnership in Care Limited
Incorporated: 21 August 1986 *Employees:* 396
Net Worth: £5,704,702 *Total Assets:* £8,830,949
Registered Office: Risby Hall, Hall Lane, Risby, Bury St Edmunds, Suffolk, IP28 6RS
Activities: Residential care activities for the elderly and disabled
Major Shareholder: Ian Denton Turner
Officers: Elaine Turner, Secretary; Rachel Elizabeth Fitton [1979] Director/Registered Nurse; Emma Claire John [1977] Director/Accountant; Elaine Turner [1949] Director/Registered General Nurse; Ian Denton Turner [1950] Director

Pass J. Holdings Limited
Incorporated: 20 September 1985 *Employees:* 112
Net Worth: £5,007,681 *Total Assets:* £11,181,216
Registered Office: Online House, 240 Freshwater Road, Dagenham, Essex, RM8 1RX
Activities: Freight transport by road
Officers: Pamela Rose Oleary, Secretary; Juanita Dora Oleary [1965] Director/Controller Staff Agency; Pamela Rose Oleary [1940] Director/Office Manager; Steven James Oleary [1961] Director/Transport Operations Manager

The Passmores Co-operative Learning Community
Incorporated: 10 August 2011 *Employees:* 346
Net Worth: £26,496,258 *Total Assets:* £31,966,984
Registered Office: Passmores Academy, Tracyes Road, Harlow, Essex, CM18 6JH
Activities: General secondary education
Officers: Paul Adams [1973] Director/Principal Licensing Officer; Paul Terence Beashel [1945] Director/Education Consultant; Victor Goddard [1968] Director/Headteacher; Christine Anne Kirk [1948] Director/Retired; Neil Baxter Lawson [1961] Director/Education; Francis Richard Woods [1955] Director/Retired

Passportcard Limited
Incorporated: 3 October 2014 *Employees:* 187
Net Worth: £6,156,567 *Total Assets:* £14,473,239
Registered Office: 43 Bushfield Crescent, Edgware, Middlesex, HA8 8XQ
Activities: Other business support service activities n.e.c.
Officers: Eyal Ben Chelouce [1961] Director [Israeli]; Teresa Chia [1981] Director [American]; Alon Ketzef [1967] Director [Israeli]; Robert L Seelig [1968] Director [American]

Pasta Foods Investments Limited
Incorporated: 20 May 2015 *Employees:* 149
Net Worth: £2,719,517 *Total Assets:* £20,813,194
Registered Office: Pasteur Road, Great Yarmouth, Norfolk, NR31 0DW
Activities: Manufacture of macaroni, noodles, couscous and similar farinaceous products
Shareholders: David Lewis; Peter Nigel George Barry; Simon Milton Webber
Officers: Peter Nigel George Barry [1951] Director; David Lewis [1946] Director; Simon Milton Webber [1962] Director

Pasta Foods Limited
Incorporated: 18 May 1956 *Employees:* 149
Net Worth: £10,343,645 *Total Assets:* £28,254,192
Registered Office: Pasteur Road, Great Yarmouth, Norfolk, NR31 0DW
Activities: Manufacture of macaroni, noodles, couscous and similar farinaceous products
Parent: Pretty 1050 Limited
Officers: Peter Nigel George Barry [1951] Director; David Lewis [1946] Director; Simon Milton Webber [1962] Director

Patek Philippe Salon Limited
Incorporated: 25 October 2005 *Employees:* 24
Net Worth: £27,598,504 *Total Assets:* £35,443,052
Registered Office: 55 Station Road, Beaconsfield, Bucks, HP9 1QL
Activities: Other business support service activities n.e.c.
Parent: Rhone Products (UK) Limited
Officers: Andrew Mark Hearn, Secretary; Andrew Mark Hearn [1959] Director; Claude Peny [1951] Director [Belgian]

Pauls Malt Limited
Incorporated: 25 May 1906 *Employees:* 116
Net Worth: £41,261,000 *Total Assets:* £75,864,000
Registered Office: 24-25 Eastern Way, Bury St Edmunds, Suffolk, IP32 7AD
Activities: Manufacture of malt
Parent: Boortmalt UK Limited
Officers: Jean-Francios Loiseau [1961] Director [French]; Yvan Shaepman [1974] Director [Belgian]; Charles Nicholas George Tozer [1971] Director; David Roy Wilkes [1962] Director

Paypoint Collections Limited
Incorporated: 15 June 1998 *Employees:* 21
Net Worth: £11,355,347 *Total Assets:* £148,905,184
Registered Office: 1 The Boulevard, Shire Park, Welwyn Garden City, Herts, AL7 1EL
Activities: Other business support service activities n.e.c.
Parent: Paypoint PLC
Officers: Susan Catherine Court, Secretary; Rachel Elizabeth Kentleton [1969] Finance Director; Dominic Clamor Von Trotha Taylor [1958] Director

Paypoint Network Limited
Incorporated: 3 October 1994 *Employees:* 424
Net Worth: £3,706,643 *Total Assets:* £56,049,036
Registered Office: No 1 The Boulevard, Shire Park, Welwyn Garden City, Herts, AL7 1EL
Activities: Other business support service activities n.e.c.
Parent: Paypoint PLC
Officers: Susan Catherine Court, Secretary; Rachel Elizabeth Kentleton [1969] Finance Director; Dominic Clamor Von Trotha Taylor [1958] Director

Paypoint PLC
Incorporated: 15 June 1998 *Employees:* 638
Net Worth: £61,293,000 *Total Assets:* £262,524,000
Registered Office: 1 The Boulevard, Shire Park, Welwyn Garden City, Herts, AL7 1EL
Activities: Other information technology service activities
Officers: Susan Catherine Court, Secretary; Gillian Carole Barr [1958] Director; Rachel Elizabeth Kentleton [1969] Director; Giles Francis Bertram Kerr [1959] Director; Rakesh Sharma [1961] Director; Dominic Clamor Von Trotha Taylor [1958] Director; Nicholas Winston Brian Wiles [1961] Director

Paypoint Retail Solutions Limited
Incorporated: 3 July 2002 *Employees:* 21
Net Worth: £6,508,788 *Total Assets:* £11,082,752
Registered Office: 1 The Boulevard, Shire Park, Welwyn Garden City, Herts, AL7 1EL
Activities: Other business support service activities n.e.c.
Parent: Paypoint PLC
Officers: Susan Catherine Court, Secretary; Rachel Elizabeth Kentleton [1969] Finance Director; Dominic Clamor Von Trotha Taylor [1958] Director

Paytemp Limited
Incorporated: 10 December 2001
Net Worth: £17,838 *Total Assets:* £12,476,315
Registered Office: 89 High Street, Hadleigh, Ipswich, Suffolk, IP7 5EA
Activities: Other activities of employment placement agencies
Parent: Jark Ventures PLC
Officers: David Simon Jaffrey, Secretary; John Timothy Buckman [1964] Director

PCL Transport Limited
Incorporated: 15 January 2002 *Employees:* 6
Net Worth: £8,333,116 *Total Assets:* £30,098,416
Registered Office: 57-59 High Street, Hoddesdon, Herts, EN11 8TQ
Activities: Freight transport by road
Shareholders: Giuseppe Ricotta; Giuseppina Ricotta
Officers: Joe Ricotta, Secretary; Cristina Ricotta [1995] Director; Giuseppe Ricotta [1966] Director; Giuseppina Ricotta [1969] Director

Peachey Basildon Group Limited (The)
Incorporated: 9 October 1969 *Employees:* 2
Net Worth: £5,756,392 *Total Assets:* £11,475,234
Registered Office: Unit 7 Bentalls Business Park, Bentalls, Basildon, Essex, SS14 3BN
Activities: Activities of head offices
Parent: Peachey Holdings Ltd
Officers: Gary Paul Peachey, Secretary; Gary Paul Peachey [1960] Director; Terence Brian Peachey [1938] Director

Peacock Holdings (2015) Limited
Incorporated: 20 March 2015 *Employees:* 321
Net Worth: £7,914,643 *Total Assets:* £27,645,786
Registered Office: Kingsley House, Clapham Road South, Lowestoft, Suffolk, NR32 1QS
Activities: Activities of other holding companies n.e.c.
Officers: Wasantha Darshana [1978] Director; Deborah Ann Edwards [1974] Director; Ian Stuart Jarvis [1966] Director; Sumithra Chandrakanthi Thayanandarajah [1959] Director/Business Executive; Velummayilum Thayanandarajah [1961] Director/Business Executive

Peak Securities Limited
Incorporated: 25 September 1961 *Employees:* 3
Net Worth: £50,514,408 *Total Assets:* £108,068,072
Registered Office: Russell House, 140 High Street, Edgware, Middlesex, HA8 7LW
Activities: Other letting and operating of own or leased real estate
Parent: Regentsmead Limited
Officers: Lee Robert Mesnick [1968] Director/Accountant; Richard Alan Ross [1942] Director

Pear Tree Mead Academy
Incorporated: 22 July 2014 *Employees:* 87
Net Worth: £6,983,545 *Total Assets:* £8,258,817
Registered Office: Pear Tree Mead Academy, Trotters Road, Harlow, Essex, CM18 7BY
Activities: Primary education
Officers: Wendy Louise Beckett [1971] Director/Civil Servant; Linda Joyce Blackburn [1952] Director/Business Account Manager; Julie Lisa Gallagher [1970] Director/Paramedic; Clive Hawkins [1963] Director/School Caretaker; Charlotte Louise Ling [1986] Director/Teacher; Sarah Jane Martin [1981] Director/Assistant Headteacher; Christine Peden [1976] Director/Headteacher; Mark Graham Sunshine [1968] Director/Training & Development Manager; Stephanie Joan Wise [1967] Director/Business Support Administrator

Pearl Properties Limited
Incorporated: 30 November 1993 *Employees:* 6
Net Worth: £3,591,628 *Total Assets:* £11,731,613
Registered Office: College House, 17 King Edwards Road, Ruislip, Middlesex, HA4 7AE
Activities: Management of real estate on a fee or contract basis
Major Shareholder: Gideon Ian Israel
Officers: Gideon Ian Israel, Secretary/Engineer; Adam Israel [1989] Director/Researcher; Denise Israel [1951] Director/Housewife; Gideon Ian Israel [1948] Director/Engineer; Joanna Israel [1986] Director/Fine Arts Valuer; Rachile Israel [1924] Director/Teacher; Ben Benjamin Kfir [1975] Director/Property Manager; Alexandra Lucie Van Someren [1968] Director/Administrator

G.& J.Peck Limited
Incorporated: 27 July 1916 *Employees:* 134
Net Worth: £5,541,244 *Total Assets:* £12,599,288
Registered Office: 90 Lancaster Way Business Park, Ely, Cambs, CB6 3NX
Activities: Agents involved in the sale of machinery, industrial equipment, ships and aircraft
Shareholders: Judith Mary Loversidge; Ian John Loversidge
Officers: Judith Mary Loversidge, Secretary; Stewart William Barnett [1959] Director/Sales Manager; Ian John Loversidge [1967] Director/Service; Judith Mary Loversidge [1957] Director/Computer Manager; Jonathan Thomas Wareing [1972] Director/Sales Manager

Peerglow Asset Limited
Incorporated: 15 July 2014
Previous: Solarplicity Asset Limited
Net Worth Deficit: £4,522,339 *Total Assets:* £161,026,672
Registered Office: Unit 8 Peerglow Centre, Marsh Lane, Ware, Herts, SG12 9QL
Activities: Production of electricity
Parent: Solarplicity Group Limited
Officers: Julie Anne Clare [1959] Director; David Stuart Elbourne [1964] Director

Peerless Europe Ltd.
Incorporated: 9 July 1991 *Employees:* 353
Net Worth: £3,450,166 *Total Assets:* £8,325,214
Registered Office: 31 St Neots Road, Eaton Ford, St Neots, Cambs, PE19 7BA
Activities: Other manufacturing n.e.c.
Officers: Jennifer Leigh Turner, Secretary; David Andrew Barker [1980] Managing Director; Matthew Kurt Eckl [1980] Director [American]; Mathilda Huessy Padden [1957] Director/Accountant [American]; Dennis Robert Sadlowski [1961] Director/Chairman [American]; Jennifer Leigh Turner [1979] Director [American]

Peli Biothermal Limited
Incorporated: 23 December 2013 *Employees:* 95
Net Worth: £8,964,366 *Total Assets:* £24,329,584
Registered Office: Celsius House, The Stanbridge Building, Stanbridge Road, Leighton Buzzard, Beds, LU7 4QQ
Activities: Other business support service activities n.e.c.
Parent: Peli Biopharma S.L.U.
Officers: Lyndon John Faulkner [1960] Director/Chief Executive Officer [American]; Piero Marigo [1971] Director/General Manager [Italian]

Pemberton Farms (Holdings) Limited
Incorporated: 12 December 2013
Net Worth: £3,972,163 *Total Assets:* £8,081,007
Registered Office: Hall Farm, Woodham Mortimer, Maldon, Essex, CM9 6SN
Activities: Growing of cereals (except rice), leguminous crops and oil seeds
Shareholder: Stephen Ronald Pemberton
Officers: Richard John Pemberton [1937] Director; Stephen Ronald Pemberton [1962] Director/Farmer

Pemberton Farms Limited
Incorporated: 3 April 1964 *Employees:* 10
Net Worth: £11,621,885 *Total Assets:* £13,144,839
Registered Office: Hall Farm, Woodham Mortimer, Maldon, Essex, CM9 6SN
Activities: Growing of cereals (except rice), leguminous crops and oil seeds
Officers: Ian David Pemberton [1958] Director/Farmer; Richard John Pemberton [1937] Director; Simon Michael Pemberton [1960] Director/Consultant; Stephen Ronald Pemberton [1962] Director/Farmer

Pengethley Potatoes Limited
Incorporated: 17 January 1989 *Employees:* 2
Net Worth: £7,637,191 *Total Assets:* £12,938,748
Registered Office: 5 Resolution Close, Endeavour Park, Boston, Lincs, PE21 7TT
Activities: Growing of cereals (except rice), leguminous crops and oil seeds
Shareholders: Stephen James Pugh; Shirley Ann Pugh
Officers: Shirley Ann Pugh, Secretary; Shirley Ann Pugh [1943] Director; Stephen James Pugh [1965] Director

Penlaw & Company Limited
Incorporated: 6 October 1977 *Employees:* 67
Net Worth: £3,906,868 *Total Assets:* £17,231,378
Registered Office: Penlaw House, Robert Way, Wickford, Essex, SS11 8DD
Activities: Other construction installation
Major Shareholder: Richard James Gray
Officers: Mohammed Ahmed [1985] Director; Paul Glackin [1962] Managing Director; Richard James Gray [1948] Director; Brett David Sherwin [1972] Director

Pentagon Limited
Incorporated: 12 November 1984 *Employees:* 393
Net Worth: £23,856,000 *Total Assets:* £91,099,000
Registered Office: Airport House, The Airport, Cambridge, CB5 8RY
Activities: Sale of new cars and light motor vehicles
Parent: Ridgeway Garages (Newbury) Limited
Officers: Stephen Robert Jones, Secretary; Richard John Blumberger [1975] Director; Daksh Gupta [1970] Director

Pepkor UK Retail Limited
Incorporated: 30 October 2014 *Employees:* 283
Net Worth Deficit: £38,717,488 *Total Assets:* £27,856,412
Registered Office: Oak House, Reeds Crescent, Watford, Herts, WD24 4QP
Activities: Other retail sale in non-specialised stores
Parent: Poundland Limited
Officers: Mathew David Ankers, Secretary; Mathew David Ankers [1986] Director/Accountant; Sean Nicholas Nennens Cardinaal [1967] Director/Business Executive; Darren Vernon [1968] Retail Director

E.W.Pepper Limited
Incorporated: 3 December 1949 *Employees:* 107
Net Worth: £34,720,672 *Total Assets:* £45,070,812
Registered Office: Orchard House, Bury Lane Farm, Melbourn, Royston, Herts, SG8 6DF
Activities: Mixed farming
Major Shareholder: Jeremy James Amphlett Clayton
Officers: Jennifer Jean Clayton, Secretary/Director; Jennifer Jean Clayton [1955] Director/Farmer/Secretary; Jeremy James Amphlett Clayton [1956] Director/Farmer; Joscelyne Clayton [1986] Director/Retail Assistant; William Jeremy James Clayton [1983] Director/Teacher; Ian James Larkins [1971] Retail Director; Stehen David Ward [1973] Director/Flower Grower

Peppercorn Investments Limited
Incorporated: 20 December 2004 *Employees:* 2
Net Worth: £4,922,567 *Total Assets:* £11,360,579
Registered Office: c/o Messrs Elliot Woolfe & Rose, Equity House, 128-136 High Street, Edgware, Middlesex, HA8 7TT
Activities: Management of real estate on a fee or contract basis
Parent: Peppercorn Property Investments Ltd
Officers: Elisabeth MacHugh, Secretary; Stephen Melville [1949] Director/Property Consultant; Martin Anthony Nathan [1948] Director/Lawyer

Peppercorn Property Investments Limited
Incorporated: 11 April 1985 *Employees:* 3
Net Worth: £17,702,836 *Total Assets:* £22,478,208
Registered Office: c/o Messrs Elliot Woolfe & Rose, 1st Floor, Equity House, 128-136 High Street, Edgware, Middlesex, HA8 7TT
Activities: Development of building projects
Shareholders: Bedford Square Properties Limited; Woodfield House Properties Limited; Bedford Square Properties Limited
Officers: Elisabeth MacHugh, Secretary; Stephen Melville [1949] Director/Property Consultant; Martin Anthony Nathan [1948] Director/Lawyer

Perfect Practices Group Limited
Incorporated: 6 April 2017 *Employees:* 2
Net Worth Deficit: £631,688 *Total Assets:* £9,160,334
Registered Office: Nicholas House, River Front, Enfield, Middlesex, EN1 3FG
Activities: Dental practice activities
Parent: Dentex Healthcare Group Limited
Officers: Bhavna Doshi [1970] Director; Rahul Rohit Doshi [1968] Director; Barry Koors Lanesman [1959] Director [South African]; Michael Brent Zurowski [1965] Director

Performance Timber Products Group Limited
Incorporated: 2 February 2009 *Employees:* 151
Net Worth: £20,752 *Total Assets:* £10,869,843
Registered Office: Tower Business Park, Kelvedon Road, Tiptree, Essex, CO5 0LX
Activities: Manufacture of other builders' carpentry and joinery
Parent: Graphite Capital General Partner VII LLP
Officers: Richard John Haycocks [1949] Director/Chartered Accountant; Jay Pengelly [1974] Managing Director; Timothy Roy Wakeman [1946] Director

Perkinelmer (UK) Holdings Limited
Incorporated: 23 April 1999
Net Worth: £20,844,000 *Total Assets:* £82,093,000
Registered Office: Chalfont Road, Seer Green, Beaconsfield, Bucks, HP9 2FX
Activities: Activities of head offices
Officers: Andrew John Crook, Secretary; Andrew John Crook [1959] Director/Manager; John Leo Healy [1960] Director/Associate General Counsel [American]

Perkinelmer LAS (UK) Limited
Incorporated: 30 April 1999 *Employees:* 151
Net Worth: £18,978,000 *Total Assets:* £26,261,000
Registered Office: Chalfont Road, Seer Green, Beaconsfield, Bucks, HP9 2FX
Activities: Other professional, scientific and technical activities n.e.c.
Officers: Andrew John Crook, Secretary; Andrew John Crook [1959] Director/Manager; John Leo Healy [1960] Director/Associate General Counsel [American]

Perkinelmer Life Sciences International Holdings
Incorporated: 16 April 2002
Net Worth: £4,085,000 *Total Assets:* £72,018,000
Registered Office: Chalfont Road, Seer Green, Beaconsfield, Bucks, HP9 2FX
Activities: Activities of other holding companies n.e.c.
Officers: Andrew John Crook, Secretary; Andrew John Crook [1959] Director/Manager; John Leo Healy [1960] Director/Associate General Counsel [American]

Perkinelmer Limited
Incorporated: 23 April 1999 *Employees:* 162
Net Worth: £54,425,000 *Total Assets:* £60,081,000
Registered Office: Chalfont Road, Seer Green, Beaconsfield, Bucks, HP9 2FX
Activities: Other manufacturing n.e.c.
Officers: Andrew John Crook, Secretary; Andrew John Crook [1959] Director/Manager; John Leo Healy [1960] Director/Associate General Counsel [American]

Perkins Engines Company Limited
Incorporated: 14 January 1987 *Employees:* 2,306
Net Worth: £356,225,984 *Total Assets:* £748,249,984
Registered Office: Eastfield, Frank Perkins Way, Peterborough, Cambs, PE1 5FQ
Activities: Manufacture of engines and turbines, except aircraft, vehicle and cycle engines
Parent: Caterpillar UK Engines Company Limited
Officers: Johanna Elizabeth Deason, Secretary; Nigel John Burroughs [1964] Director/Tax Accountant; Mark Clinton Albert Dorsett [1962] HR Director; Steven Ferguson [1968] Director/Vice President [American]; Jasbir Singh Gill [1965] Director/General Manager; David John Goldspink [1966] Director/General Manager; Paul David Thompson [1980] Director/Business Resource Manager [American]

Perkins Group Limited
Incorporated: 24 May 1989 *Employees:* 3
Net Worth: £35,440,000 *Total Assets:* £116,042,000
Registered Office: Eastfield, Frank Perkins Way, Peterborough, Cambs, PE1 5FQ
Activities: Manufacture of engines and turbines, except aircraft, vehicle and cycle engines
Parent: Caterpillar International Holding S.A.R.L
Officers: Johanna Elizabeth Deason, Secretary; Nigel John Burroughs [1964] Director/Tax Accountant; David John Goldspink [1966] Director/General Manager; Paul David Thompson [1980] Director/Business Resource Manager [American]

Perkins Holdings Limited
Incorporated: 1 February 1952 *Employees:* 1
Net Worth: £489,863,008 *Total Assets:* £490,375,008
Registered Office: Eastfield, Frank Perkins Way, Peterborough, Cambs, PE1 5FQ
Activities: Activities of head offices
Parent: Perkins International Inc
Officers: Johanna Elizabeth Deason, Secretary; Nigel John Burroughs [1964] Director/Tax Accountant; Steven Ferguson [1968] Director/Vice President [American]; David John Goldspink [1966] Director/General Manager; Paul David Thompson [1980] Director/Business Resource Manager [American]

F. Perkins Limited
Incorporated: 7 June 1932 *Employees:* 3
Net Worth: £178,160,992 *Total Assets:* £241,420,992
Registered Office: Eastfield, Frank Perkins Way, Peterborough, Cambs, PE1 5FQ
Activities: Other letting and operating of own or leased real estate
Parent: Caterpillar International Holding S.A.R.L
Officers: Johanna Elizabeth Deason, Secretary; Nigel John Burroughs [1964] Director/Tax Accountant; David John Goldspink [1966] Director/General Manager; Paul David Thompson [1980] Director/Business Resource Manager [American]

Perkins Small Engines Limited
Incorporated: 12 October 1994 *Employees:* 174
Previous: Perkins Shibaura Engines Limited
Net Worth: £21,288,000 *Total Assets:* £44,683,000
Registered Office: Eastfield, Frank Perkins Way, Peterborough, Cambs, PE1 5FQ
Activities: Manufacture of engines and turbines, except aircraft, vehicle and cycle engines
Officers: Johanna Elizabeth Deason, Secretary; Michael John Casey [1974] Director/Senior Business Resource Manager [American]; Steven Ferguson [1968] Director/Vice President [American]; David John Goldspink [1966] Director/General Manager; Paul David Thompson [1980] Director/Business Resource Manager [American]

Permastore Group Limited
Incorporated: 17 October 2001 *Employees:* 196
Net Worth: £5,992,000 *Total Assets:* £15,304,000
Registered Office: Permastore Ltd, Airfield Industrial Park, Airfield 1, Eye, Suffolk, IP23 7HS
Activities: Activities of head offices
Major Shareholder: Andrew Roger Gare
Officers: Dr Francesco Angelo Cutri [1965] Director; Andrew Roger Gare [1949] Director; David James Gare [1976] Director; Robert John Gare [1978] Director; Stephen Dene Heywood [1966] Director; Elliott Michael Mannis [1961] Director

Permastore Limited
Incorporated: 10 May 1931 *Employees:* 191
Net Worth: £6,097,000 *Total Assets:* £15,293,000
Registered Office: Airfield Industrial Park, Eye, Suffolk, IP23 7HS
Activities: Manufacture of other tanks, reservoirs and containers of metal
Parent: Permastore Holdings Limited
Officers: Saqlain Ali [1977] Director; Johnathon Michael Brook [1975] Director; Dr Francesco Angelo Cutri [1965] Director; Graham Paul Franklin [1968] Director; Andrew Roger Gare [1949] Director; Stephen Dene Heywood [1966] Director

The Pero Investments Limited
Incorporated: 14 October 2004 *Employees:* 1
Net Worth: £2,177,913 *Total Assets:* £8,288,811
Registered Office: Old School House, Fincham Road, Barton Bendish, King's Lynn, Norfolk, PE33 9DL
Activities: Other letting and operating of own or leased real estate
Parent: Albanwise Limited
Officers: Janine Grant, Secretary; Janine Grant [1972] Director/Financial Controller

Perrin Group Holdings Limited
Incorporated: 3 June 1997 *Employees:* 103
Net Worth: £2,316,443 *Total Assets:* £12,789,620
Registered Office: Hemisphere House, 53-65 White House Road, Ipswich, Suffolk, IP1 5PB
Activities: Other transportation support activities
Major Shareholder: Andrew Colin Perrin
Officers: Tracy Jean Perrin, Secretary; Andrew Colin Perrin [1967] Director/Freight Forwarder

Perry Ellis Europe Limited
Incorporated: 4 June 1970 *Employees:* 229
Net Worth Deficit: £6,382,617 *Total Assets:* £28,153,460
Registered Office: Crittall Road, Witham, Essex, CM8 3DJ
Activities: Wholesale of clothing and footwear
Officers: Darren Michael Brown, Secretary; Julie Ann Dow [1981] HR Director; George Feldenkreis [1935] Director/Chairman & CEO [American]; Fanny Feldenkreis Hanono [1961] Director [American]; Jorge Narino [1967] Director/Interim Chief Financial Officer [American]

Perrywood Garden Centre & Nurseries Limited
Incorporated: 8 April 1999 *Employees:* 150
Net Worth: £7,963,398 *Total Assets:* £9,364,987
Registered Office: Perrywood, Kelvedon Road, Inworth, Colchester, Essex, CO5 9SX
Activities: Retail sale of flowers, plants, seeds, fertilizers, pet animals and pet food in specialised stores
Major Shareholder: Alan Leslie Bourne
Officers: Karin Kristina Bourne, Secretary/Director; Alan Leslie Bourne [1951] Director; Karin Kristina Bourne [1955] Director; Simon Charles Bourne [1979] Director; Tristan James Bourne [1981] Director; Hannah Charlotte Powell [1977] Director

The Perse School
Incorporated: 25 October 2006 *Employees:* 360
Net Worth: £46,936,000 *Total Assets:* £57,740,000
Registered Office: The Perse School, Hills Road, Cambridge, CB2 8QF
Activities: Pre-primary education
Officers: Generald Anthony Ellison, Secretary; Dr Helen Bettinson [1963] Development Director; Dr Anita Mary Bunyan [1967] Director of Studies in Modern Languages [Irish]; Katy Alexandra Davies [1982] Director/Head of Finance; William Mark Ransford Dawkins [1956] Director/Business Executive; Ian Geoffrey Galbraith [1949] Director/Retired Headmaster; Stephen William Graves [1957] Director/Chief Executive NHS Trust; Christopher Patrick Hancock [1960] Director/Barrister; Dr Elizabeth Mary Harper [1964] Director/University Lecturer; Simon David Lebus [1957] Director/Chief Executive; Dr Richard Colin St.Helier Mason [1970] Director/Chief Executive; Dr Louise Ann Merrett [1970] Director/University Lecturer; Graeme John Proudfoot [1964] Director; Stephen Cheveley Roberts [1956] Director/Consultant; Jonathan Willoughby Scott [1956] Director/Retired; Diana Miller Shave [1947] Director/HR Coach/Mentor; Brian Phillip Smith [1952] Director/Retired; Sian Louise Steele [1968] Director/Chartered Tax Advisor; Caroline Jane Stenner [1959] Director/Solicitor; Dr Denise Williams [1957] Director/Paediatric Oncologist; Sir David John Wright [1944] Director/Banker

Personnel Holdings Limited
Incorporated: 19 December 2000
Net Worth: £910,000 *Total Assets:* £15,655,000
Registered Office: 99 Bridge Road East, Welwyn Garden City, Herts, AL7 1GL
Activities: Activities of head offices
Parent: Teaching Personnel Holdings Limited
Officers: Jonathan Nicholas Roback, Secretary; Jonathan Nicholas Roback [1969] Finance Director

Pertwee & Back,Limited
Incorporated: 22 February 1929 *Employees:* 37
Net Worth: £4,022,359 *Total Assets:* £8,928,536
Registered Office: Gapton Hall Road, Gapton Hall Industrial Estate, Great Yarmouth, Norfolk, NR31 0NJ
Activities: Sale of new cars and light motor vehicles
Shareholders: Richard Stuart Coller; Nicholas Lempriere Coller
Officers: Stephen Paul Hatton, Secretary; Mervyn Tarrant Coller [1929] Director/Chairman; Nicholas Lempriere Coller [1962] Service Director; Richard Stuart Coller [1959] Managing Director; Thomas Mervyn Coller [1988] Director/HR Manager

Pet and Aquatics Properties Limited
Incorporated: 25 February 2009
Net Worth: £5,606,000 *Total Assets:* £10,580,000
Registered Office: Tropical Marine Centre, Solesbridge Lane, Chorleywood, Herts, WD3 5SX
Activities: Renting and operating of Housing Association real estate
Parent: Tropical Marine Centre (2012) Ltd
Officers: Amanda Kathryn Taylor, Secretary; Amanda Kathryn Taylor [1959] Director and Company Secretary; Christopher John Thomas [1955] Director; Paul Desmond West [1957] Managing Director

Peterborough Diocesan Board of Finance (The)
Incorporated: 4 December 1922 *Employees:* 191
Net Worth: £142,791,952 *Total Assets:* £146,862,800
Registered Office: Diocesan Office, The Palace, Minster Precincts, Peterborough, Cambs, PE1 1YB
Activities: Other business support service activities n.e.c.
Officers: Andrew Roberts, Secretary; The Right Reverend Donald Spargo Allister [1952] Director/Lord Bishop of Peterborough; Robert Frederick Baker [1950] Director; The Revd Jane Elizabeth Baxter [1951] Director/Clerk in Holy Orders; Neil John Bradley [1970] Director/Retired; Dr Paul Vinton Buckingham [1948] Director/Medical Practitioner; Isobel Jane Burbidge [1950] Director/Retired; Dr Hilary Creek [1947] Director/Retired University Administrator; Norman James Critchlow [1948] Director/Retired; Hilary Jane Daniels [1954] Director; Christine Hall [1962] Director; Mr Andrew Clive Hawkins [1958] Director/Retail Assistant Manager; John Hindle [1950] Director/Self Employed; Gerard John Hoare [1942] Director/Farm Consultant; The Right Reverend John Holbrook [1962] Director/Bishop; The Reverend Katrina Hutchins [1962] Director/Clerk in Holy Orders; The Reverend Mark Wesley Lucas [1962] Director/Clerk in Holy Orders; Peter Holtby McKay [1943] Director/Retired; Jeremy Orme [1943] Director/Accountant; Richard Jeremy Ormston [1961] Director/Archdeacon of Northampton; Andrew Kenneth Owst [1956] Finance Director; Robert Purser [1950] Director; Neil Andrew Elsom Robertson [1942] Director; Reverend George Huchinson Rogers [1951] Director/Vicar [Canadian/British]; The Venerable Gordon John Steele [1955] Director/Minster of Religion; Michael John Truman [1942] Director/Certified Accountant Retired

Peterborough Keys Academies Trust
Incorporated: 12 December 2017 *Employees:* 807
Net Worth: £49,097,000 *Total Assets:* £57,105,000
Registered Office: Jack Hunt School, Bradwell Road, Peterborough, PE3 9PY
Activities: Primary education
Officers: Bernard Martin Champness [1950] Director/Clerk to Parish Council; Colin Graham Hammond [1965] Director/Business Development Manager; Tracey Elizabeth Hedges [1981] Director/Accountant; Claire Patricia Higgins [1963] Director/Chief Executive; William Peter Kerry [1985] Director/Accountant; Lisa Dawn Lloyd [1981] Director/Education, Head of House; Adriano Pacitti [1978] Director/Chartered Engineer; Alan Ralph Sadler [1958] Director/Self Employed

Ralph Peters & Sons Limited
Incorporated: 16 June 1988 *Employees:* 106
Net Worth: £5,036,640 *Total Assets:* £13,414,859
Registered Office: Slush Puppie Ltd, Coronation Road, Cressex Business Park, High Wycombe, Bucks, HP12 3TA
Activities: Other business support service activities n.e.c.
Major Shareholder: Mark Jeffrey Peters
Officers: Laura Peters [1988] Director/Stock Controller; Mark Jeffrey Peters [1958] Managing Director; Ralph Peters [1930] Director/Retired

PFE Express Limited
Incorporated: 5 April 1983 *Employees:* 112
Net Worth: £16,153,701 *Total Assets:* £35,138,688
Registered Office: Foremost House, Waterside Business Park, Eastways, Witham, Essex, CM8 3PL
Activities: Other transportation support activities
Shareholders: Adam Julian Collins; Peter Albert Collins
Officers: Doreen Toms, Secretary; Adam Julian Collins [1967] Director/Shipping Manager; Peter Albert Collins [1933] Director; David Girling [1961] Director/General Manager; Aron Mark Newton [1970] Director; Doreen Toms [1943] Director/Accounts Supervisor

PGR Enterprises Ltd
Incorporated: 26 October 2010 *Employees:* 117
Net Worth: £17,143,004 *Total Assets:* £29,564,568
Registered Office: Courtauld House, Courtauld Road, Basildon, Essex, SS13 1RZ
Activities: Other letting and operating of own or leased real estate
Officers: Graham Joseph Toomey [1961] Director

Pharmaceuticals Direct Limited
Incorporated: 25 November 1999 *Employees:* 18
Net Worth: £18,600,224 *Total Assets:* £33,313,492
Registered Office: Old Station Road, Loughton, Essex, IG10 4PL
Activities: Wholesale of pharmaceutical goods
Parent: Pharmadent Holdings lmited
Officers: Hital Patel, Secretary; Bemal Patel [1973] Director; Hital Patel [1974] Director/Company Secretary

Pharmadent Holdings Limited
Incorporated: 15 June 2010 *Employees:* 44
Net Worth: £11,048,828 *Total Assets:* £28,510,594
Registered Office: c/o Haslers, Old Station Road, Loughton, Essex, IG10 4PL
Activities: Activities of head offices
Parent: SIP Trustees Limited
Officers: Hital Patel, Secretary; Bemal Patel [1973] Director

Pharmathen Holding 4 Ltd
Incorporated: 21 April 2015 *Employees:* 824
Net Worth: £197,087,632 *Total Assets:* £572,464,256
Registered Office: Stag House, Old London Road, Hertford, SG13 7LA
Activities: Activities of other holding companies n.e.c.
Officers: Matthew George Evans [1987] Director/Investment Professional; Mark Philip Hersee [1971] Director/Partner; Stylianos Ilia [1981] Director/Investment Executive [Cypriot]; Maximilian Hendrik Kastka [1978] Director/Investment Manager [German]; Vassilios Katsos [1973] Director [Greek]; Eleni Katsou [1965] Director [Greek]; Nikolaos Stathopoulos [1969] Director/Managing Partner

Pheasant Eye Limited
Incorporated: 3 April 2007
Net Worth: £21,844,556 *Total Assets:* £21,962,856
Registered Office: Pine House, Chandlers Way, Southend on Sea, Essex, SS2 5SE
Activities: Activities of open-ended investment companies
Shareholders: Simon Meyrick Browne; Peter Paul Thomson
Officers: Peter Paul Thomson, Secretary; Simon Meyrick Browne [1956] Director/Landowner; Peter Paul Thomson [1965] Director/Chief Executive, Investment Manager

Phelan Construction Limited
Incorporated: 15 July 1987 *Employees:* 147
Net Worth: £5,009,550 *Total Assets:* £23,631,652
Registered Office: 1 Brunel Court, Brunel Road, Clacton-on-Sea, Essex, CO15 4LU
Activities: Development of building projects
Major Shareholder: Kieran William O'Phelan
Officers: Neil Ian Coy [1975] Director/Surveyor; Paul Michael Leppard [1969] Finance Director; Daniel William McGowan [1966] Director/Contracts Manager; Kieran William O'Phelan [1960] Director; Steven Andrew Tucker [1984] Director/Surveyor

PHH 1 Limited
Incorporated: 2 November 2012 *Employees:* 8,038
Net Worth: £22,300,000 *Total Assets:* £87,468,000
Registered Office: Building 1, Imperial Place, Elstree Way, Borehamwood, Herts, WD6 1JN
Activities: Licenced restaurants
Parent: HWS 3 Limited
Officers: Maria Rachael Watkins, Secretary; Jens Tjeerd Hofma [1966] Managing Director [Dutch]; Andrew Mark Platt [1967] Director/Accountant

PHH 2 Limited
Incorporated: 2 November 2012
Net Worth Deficit: £12,585,291 *Total Assets:* £18,859,400
Registered Office: Building 1, Imperial Place, Elstree Way, Borehamwood, Herts, WD6 1JN
Activities: Licenced restaurants
Parent: PHH 1 Limited
Officers: Maria Rachael Watkins, Secretary; Jens Tjeerd Hofma [1966] Managing Director [Dutch]; Andrew Mark Platt [1967] Director/Accountant

David Phillip (Investments) Limited
Incorporated: 20 November 1975 *Employees:* 9
Net Worth: £8,778,957 *Total Assets:* £11,723,731
Registered Office: Bankside, 300 Peachman Way, Broadland Business Park, Norwich, NR7 0LB
Activities: Construction of domestic buildings
Shareholder: David William Barrell
Officers: David William Barrell, Secretary; David William Barrell [1946] Director/Builder; Ian David Barrell [1977] Director/Builder; Thomas Oliver Peart [1988] Director/Builder; Vincent Philip Peart [1980] Director/Builder

J.A. Phillips Holdings Limited
Incorporated: 20 August 1991 *Employees:* 20
Net Worth: £18,046,756 *Total Assets:* £20,419,454
Registered Office: Unit 8 Trafalgar Business Centre, 77-89 River Road, Barking, Essex, IG11 0JU
Activities: Activities of head offices
Major Shareholder: James Albert Phillips
Officers: Emma Margaret Warran, Secretary; James Daniel Phillips [1981] Director; James Albert Phillips [1959] Director; Matthew John Phillips [1988] Director

H.R. Philpot & Son (Barleylands) Limited
Incorporated: 3 April 1964
Net Worth: £22,754,444 *Total Assets:* £28,809,888
Registered Office: Barleylands Farmhouse, Barleylands Road, Billericay, Essex, CM11 2UD
Activities: Mixed farming
Shareholder: Peter John Harold Philpot
Officers: Joanna Christina Westwood Philpot, Secretary; Philip Forbes Burrows [1979] Director; Peter John Hockley [1980] Director; Andrew Peter Thomas Philpot [1971] Director Farmer; Christopher James Harold Philpot [1969] Director; Peter John Harold Philpot [1943] Director; Stuart John Ross Philpot [1975] Director/Farmer

Phlexglobal Limited
Incorporated: 14 April 1998 *Employees:* 180
Net Worth: £17,839,000 *Total Assets:* £22,103,000
Registered Office: Mandeville House, 62 London Road, Amersham, Bucks, HP7 0HJ
Activities: Other professional, scientific and technical activities n.e.c.
Parent: Emerald Bidco Limited
Officers: Richard James Riegel [1963] Director [American]; Karen Jane Roy [1966] Director; Jacqueline Susan Veness [1960] Director

Phoenix Advance Limited
Incorporated: 5 June 2014 *Employees:* 127
Net Worth: £611,000 *Total Assets:* £55,333,000
Registered Office: 1 Victoria Stables, Essex Way, Bourne, Lincs, PE10 9JZ
Activities: Activities of other holding companies n.e.c.
Officers: Paul Christian Lee Knight [1971] Managing Director; Matthew Lloyd Turner [1966] Financial Director; David Michael York [1949] Director/Chairman

Phoenix Datacom Limited
Incorporated: 29 June 1984 *Employees:* 32
Net Worth: £6,634,177 *Total Assets:* £13,216,794
Registered Office: Phoenix House, Smeaton Close, Rabans Lane, Aylesbury, Bucks, HP19 8UW
Activities: Agents involved in the sale of machinery, industrial equipment, ships and aircraft
Major Shareholder: Ian Anthony Farr
Officers: Gareth Chapman, Secretary; John Francis Carson [1962] Director; Gareth Chapman [1953] Director; Richard Eric Sidney Cull [1952] Director; Ian Anthony Farr [1939] Director/Chairman

J.E.Piccaver & Co. (Gedney Marsh)
Incorporated: 28 June 1950 *Employees:* 127
Net Worth: £9,399,683 *Total Assets:* £19,566,324
Registered Office: Norfolk House Farm, Gedney Marsh, Spalding, Lincs, PE12 9PB
Activities: Growing of vegetables and melons, roots and tubers
Parent: Jepco Ltd
Officers: Simon Goddard, Secretary; Simon Goddard [1959] Director/Accountant; Phillip Paul Hubbert [1955] Director/Farm Manager; Anthony Padoan [1964] Managing Director; Stuart William Piccaver [1971] Sales & Marketing Director

Pickering Interfaces Limited
Incorporated: 29 October 1971 *Employees:* 174
Net Worth: £13,627,432 *Total Assets:* £15,112,178
Registered Office: Pickering, Stephenson Road, Clacton on Sea, Essex, CO15 4NL
Activities: Manufacture of telegraph and telephone apparatus and equipment
Major Shareholder: Keith Thomas Moore
Officers: Steven Michael Edwards, Secretary; Ian John Johnston [1966] Director/General Manager; Adam Charles Mitchell [1966] Director/Design Engineer; Keith Thomas Moore [1960] Director

Pico Technology (Holdings) Limited
Incorporated: 15 November 2004 *Employees:* 127
Net Worth: £13,593,981 *Total Assets:* £16,307,159
Registered Office: James House, Colmworth Business Park, Eaton Socon, St Neots, Cambs, PE19 8YP
Activities: Manufacture of electronic measuring, testing etc. equipment, not for industrial process control
Major Shareholder: Alan David Tong
Officers: Jane Ellen Ann Percy, Secretary; Guy Allen Roderick [1939] Director; Alan David Tong [1970] Director; Caroline Tong [1973] Director

PIL Membranes Limited
Incorporated: 8 October 2003 *Employees:* 104
Net Worth: £6,352,330 *Total Assets:* £8,723,631
Registered Office: Riverside Industrial Estate, Estuary Road, King's Lynn, Norfolk, PE30 2HS
Activities: Manufacture of plastic plates, sheets, tubes and profiles
Parent: KL Technologies Limited
Officers: Mark William Hamilton, Secretary/Director; Mark William Hamilton [1969] Director; Mark Littlewood [1962] Director; John Mark Vautier [1964] Director

Pilgrim Foodservice Limited
Incorporated: 3 August 2005 *Employees:* 259
Net Worth: £12,999,264 *Total Assets:* £24,178,890
Registered Office: Marsh Lane, Boston, Lincs, PE21 7SJ
Activities: Non-specialised wholesale of food, beverages and tobacco
Major Shareholder: Peter John Bateman
Officers: Charles John Bateman, Secretary; Charles John Bateman [1987] Director; Peter John Bateman [1959] Director; Philip Parker [1953] Procurement Director

Pineridge Investments Limited
Incorporated: 13 May 1991
Net Worth: £10,748,772 *Total Assets:* £24,892,824
Registered Office: 28 Church Road, Stanmore, Middlesex, HA7 4XR
Activities: Other letting and operating of own or leased real estate
Shareholders: Franco Pietro Giovanni Sidoli; Charterhouse Square Holdings Limited
Officers: Jacqueline Smith, Secretary; Martin Keith Rodwell [1961] Director/Architect; Franco Sidoli [1963] Director/Chartered Surveyor

Pinewood School Academy Trust
Incorporated: 22 July 2014 *Employees:* 76
Net Worth: £9,004,105 *Total Assets:* £10,087,884
Registered Office: Pinewood School, Hoe Lane, Ware, Herts, SG12 9PB
Activities: General secondary education
Officers: Michelina Adams [1964] Director/Teacher; Annette Joye Burns [1955] Director/Teaching Assistant; Robert Martin Cregan [1961] Director; Naomi Laura Divall [1990] Director/Research Scientist; Paul Patrick Dunne [1966] Director; Wendy Jane Eveleigh [1967] Director/Secretary; David John McGachen [1967] Director/Headteacher; Gillian Mary Peck [1959] Director/General Manager

Pinnacle Foods Limited
Incorporated: 2 May 2007 *Employees:* 49
Net Worth: £5,579,996 *Total Assets:* £10,280,604
Registered Office: Windsor House, Britannia Road, Waltham Cross, Herts, EN8 7NX
Activities: Processing and preserving of meat
Parent: GPS Food Group (UK) Limited
Officers: Padraig Anthony McCarthy [1967] Director [Irish]; Fergus Quinn-Smith [1965] Director; Graham Reed [1964] Director; Christopher John Wilson [1961] Director

Pinnacle Insurance PLC
Incorporated: 14 April 1971
Net Worth: £158,516,992 *Total Assets:* £332,326,016
Registered Office: Pinnacle House, A1 Barnet Way, Borehamwood, Herts, WD6 2XX
Activities: Life insurance
Parent: Cardif Pinnacle Insurance Holdings PLC
Officers: Matthew Justin Lorimer, Secretary; Gerard Binet [1953] Development and Strategy Director [French]; Peter John Box [1952] Director; Stanislas Louis Paul Francois Chevalt [1961] Director/Exco Member - Co - BNPPC [French]; Marie Haderer [1979] Director/Actuary [French]; Matthew Justin Lorimer [1967] Director/Solicitor; Nicholas Dutfield Rochez [1954] Director; Andrew Miles Wigg [1972] Director

Pinnacle Schools (Gateshead) Limited
Incorporated: 20 April 2005
Net Worth Deficit: £5,836,056 *Total Assets:* £48,456,844
Registered Office: Eaton Court, Maylands Avenue, Hemel Hempstead Industrial Estate, Hemel Hempstead, Herts, HP2 7TR
Activities: Other business support service activities n.e.c.
Parent: Pinnacle Schools (Gateshead) Holdings Limited
Officers: Kevin John Pearson, Secretary; David Honeyman [1967] Director/Financial Controller

Pioneer DJ Europe Limited
Incorporated: 23 September 2014 *Employees:* 64
Net Worth: £12,357,470 *Total Assets:* £54,872,156
Registered Office: Artemis, Odyssey Business Park, West End Road, South Ruislip, Middlesex, HA4 6QE
Activities: Manufacture of other electrical equipment
Parent: Pioneer DJ Corporation
Officers: Anita Toni Wilkinson, Secretary; Kei Aikawa [1975] Director [Japanese]; Anita Toni Wilkinson [1970] Director/Solicitor

Pioneering Foods Group Limited
Incorporated: 15 March 2002 *Employees:* 20
Net Worth: £3,004,552 *Total Assets:* £8,543,003
Registered Office: Icefresh House, Dunkirk, Aylsham, Norwich, NR11 6RR
Activities: Activities of head offices
Parent: N.V.Poppies International
Officers: Frans Camiel Hector Castelein [1951] Director [Belgian]; Philip John Webster [1975] Sales Director

Pipers Corner School
Incorporated: 1 February 1952 *Employees:* 159
Net Worth: £12,307,564 *Total Assets:* £19,523,812
Registered Office: Pipers Corner School, Pipers Lane, Great Kingshill, Bucks, HP15 6LP
Activities: Primary education
Officers: Colonel Graham Robert Pearce, Secretary; Adrian Canon [1963] Director/Business Consultant; Elizabeth Joy Carrighan [1962] Director/Management Consultant; Marcus Francis Thomas Harborne [1943] Director/Training Manager; Joan Bailey Ingram [1946] Director/Lawyer; Professor Bryan Mogford [1940] Director/Retired; Helen Frances Morton [1952] Director/Retired; Reverend Helen Elizabeth Peters [1967] Director/Associate Minister; Lady Elizabeth Ann Redgrave [1960] Director/Medical Doctor; Hugh Benedict Polmear Roberts [1962] Director/Accountant; Janet Elizabeth Smith [1952] Director/Consultant; Philip Brian Wayne [1966] Director/Headmaster

Pirin Ltd
Incorporated: 7 March 1972
Previous: Pirin PLC
Net Worth: £12,490,393 *Total Assets:* £18,658,932
Registered Office: Sage House, New Ford Business Centre, New Ford Road, Waltham Cross, Herts, EN8 7PG
Activities: Other letting and operating of own or leased real estate
Parent: Pirin Holdings Limited
Officers: Joyce Kathleen Hammond, Secretary; Thea Patricia Buisson [1971] Director/Administrator; Neal Peter Hammond [1973] Director/Builder

Pitchset Limited
Incorporated: 23 June 2010
Net Worth: £6,200,989 *Total Assets:* £10,778,681
Registered Office: Northside House, Mount Pleasant, Barnet, Herts, EN4 9EE
Activities: Other service activities n.e.c.
Shareholders: Melvyn Frank Cooper; Jason Robert Cooper
Officers: Adam Cooper, Secretary; Adam Cooper [1971] Director; Jason Robert Cooper [1967] Director; Melvyn Frank Cooper [1941] Director

Pitney Bowes Finance Limited
Incorporated: 24 September 1964 *Employees:* 18
Net Worth: £55,303,000 *Total Assets:* £59,288,000
Registered Office: Building 5, Trident Place, Hatfield Business Park, Mosquito Way, Hatfield, Herts, AL10 9UJ
Activities: Financial leasing
Parent: Pitney Bowes Holdings Limited
Officers: Gerard Richard Willsher, Secretary; Ryan John Higginson [1973] Director/Vice President; Gerard Richard Willsher [1967] Director/Solicitor

Pitney Bowes Global Ltd.
Incorporated: 8 June 2000
Net Worth: £427,316,000 *Total Assets:* £428,969,984
Registered Office: Building 5, Trident Place, Hatfield Business Park, Mosquito Way, Hatfield, Herts, AL10 9UJ
Activities: Other business support service activities n.e.c.
Parent: Pitney Bowes Inc
Officers: Gerard Richard Willsher, Secretary/Solicitor; Ryan John Higginson [1973] Director/Vice President; Gerard Richard Willsher [1967] Director/Solicitor

Pitney Bowes Holdco Limited
Incorporated: 30 August 2012
Net Worth Deficit: £10,621,000 *Total Assets:* £266,402,000
Registered Office: Building 5, Trident Place, Hatfield Business Park, Mosquito Way, Hatfield, Herts, AL10 9UJ
Activities: Non-trading company
Shareholders: Oldeurope Limited; Pitney Bowes Inc
Officers: Ryan John Higginson [1973] Director/Vice President; Gerard Richard Willsher [1967] Director/Solicitor

Pitney Bowes Holdings Limited
Incorporated: 16 August 1976
Net Worth: £221,423,008 *Total Assets:* £221,423,008
Registered Office: Building 5, Trident Place, Hatfield Business Park, Mosquito Way, Hatfield, Herts, AL10 9UJ
Activities: Activities of head offices
Shareholders: Pitney Bowes Holdco Limited; Pitney Bowes Inc
Officers: Ryan John Higginson [1973] Director/Vice President; Gerard Richard Willsher [1967] Director/Solicitor

Pitney Bowes Limited
Incorporated: 25 May 1922 *Employees:* 802
Net Worth: £29,197,000 *Total Assets:* £190,344,000
Registered Office: Building 5, Trident Place, Hatfield Business Park, Mosquito Way, Hatfield, Herts, AL10 9UJ
Activities: Manufacture of other special-purpose machinery n.e.c.
Shareholders: Pitney Bowes Holdings Limited; Pitney Bowes Inc
Officers: Gerard Richard Willsher, Company Secretary; Ryan John Higginson [1973] Managing Director; Gerard Richard Willsher [1967] Director/Solicitor

Pitney Bowes Software Europe Limited
Incorporated: 14 January 1986 *Employees:* 177
Net Worth: £79,201,000 *Total Assets:* £106,453,000
Registered Office: Building 5, Trident Place, Hatfield Business Park, Mosquito Way, Hatfield, Herts, AL10 9UJ
Activities: Information technology consultancy activities
Parent: Pitney Bowes Software Holdings Limited
Officers: Gerard Richard Willsher, Secretary/Solicitor; Simon John Alderson [1977] Director/Vice President, EMEA; Gerard Richard Willsher [1967] Director/VP Deputy General Counsel

Pitney Bowes Software Holdings Limited
Incorporated: 1 October 1997
Net Worth Deficit: £35,017,000 *Total Assets:* £48,438,000
Registered Office: Building 5, Trident Place, Hatfield Business Park, Mosquito Way, Hatfield, Herts, AL10 9UJ
Activities: Business and domestic software development
Parent: Pitney Bowes Inc
Officers: Gerard Richard Willsher, Secretary/Solicitor; Gerard Richard Willsher [1967] Director/Solicitor

Pizza Gogo Ltd
Incorporated: 21 September 1995 *Employees:* 94
Net Worth: £7,733,404 *Total Assets:* £14,916,840
Registered Office: Unit 6 Teakcroft, Fairview Industrial Park, Marsh Way, Rainham, Essex, RM13 8UH
Activities: Butter and cheese production
Officers: Hamid Haghighat, Secretary/General Manager; Homayoun Aminnia [1963] Director/General Manager; Hamid Haghighat [1960] Director/General Manager

Pizza Hut (U.K.) Limited
Incorporated: 21 September 1972 *Employees:* 8,033
Net Worth: £53,007,000 *Total Assets:* £97,308,000
Registered Office: Building 1, Imperial Place, Elstree Way, Borehamwood, Herts, WD6 1JN
Activities: Licenced restaurants
Parent: PHH 2 Limited
Officers: Maria Rachael Watkins, Secretary; Kathryn Elizabeth Austin [1976] HR Director; Jens Tjeerd Hofma [1966] Director [Dutch]; Susan Marshall [1973] Chief Director for Operations; Andrew Mark Platt [1967] Director/Accountant; Michael William Edward Spencer [1969] Director of Operations - Dine-In

PJG Developments Limited
Incorporated: 23 October 1992
Net Worth: £4,375,199 *Total Assets:* £10,000,778
Registered Office: 11-12 Hallmark Trading Centre, Fourth Way, Wembley, Middlesex, HA9 0LB
Activities: Buying and selling of own real estate
Major Shareholder: Martin Joseph Finnerty
Officers: Martin Joseph Finnerty [1951] Director

PJHP Limited
Incorporated: 3 August 2011 *Employees:* 59
Net Worth: £25,539,912 *Total Assets:* £39,342,392
Registered Office: Barleylands Farm House, Barleylands Road, Billericay, Essex, CM11 2UD
Activities: Mixed farming
Shareholder: Peter John Harold Philpot
Officers: Joanna Christina Westwood Philpot, Secretary; Andrew Peter Thomas Philpot [1971] Director; Christopher James Harold Philpot [1969] Director; Peter John Harold Philpot [1943] Director; Stuart John Ross Philpot [1975] Director

R.& J.M.Place Limited
Incorporated: 1 September 1954 *Employees:* 495
Net Worth: £18,661,580 *Total Assets:* £21,720,984
Registered Office: Church Farm, Tunstead, Norwich, NR12 8RQ
Activities: Activities of agricultural holding companies
Major Shareholder: Timothy Margetson Place
Officers: James Derek Starling, Secretary; William Thomas Noel Patrick Goff [1944] Director/Solicitor; Catrina Anne Harding Place [1964] Director; John Margetson Place [1931] Director; Shirley Anne Place [1936] Director; Timothy Margetson Place [1963] Director

Place UK Limited
Incorporated: 7 February 2001 *Employees:* 492
Net Worth: £992,734 *Total Assets:* £10,255,596
Registered Office: Church Farm, Tunstead, Norwich, NR12 8RQ
Activities: Growing of other tree and bush fruits and nuts
Parent: R & JM Place Limited
Officers: James Derek Starling, Secretary; Noel Frederick Bartram [1952] Director/Accountant; William Thomas Noel Patrick Goff [1944] Director/Solicitor; Timothy Margetson Place [1963] Director; Anthony David James Rose [1985] Operations Director; James Derek Starling [1974] Finance Director; John Walker [1961] Commercial Director

Planshore Limited
Incorporated: 14 October 1988 *Employees:* 73
Net Worth: £11,142,473 *Total Assets:* £12,753,003
Registered Office: 9 Spareleaze Hill, Loughton, Essex, IG10 1BS
Activities: Residential nursing care facilities
Officers: Devyani Jayanti Patel, Secretary; Devyani Jayanti Patel [1953] Director/Administrator; Jayanti Mohanlal Patel [1949] Director/Secretary

Plastic Extruders Limited
Incorporated: 31 December 1962 *Employees:* 77
Net Worth: £6,682,144 *Total Assets:* £10,880,418
Registered Office: Russell Gardens, Wickford, Essex, SS11 8DN
Activities: Manufacture of other plastic products
Shareholders: David Edward O'Sullivan; Peter Laurence O'Sullivan
Officers: David Bevan [1970] Director; David Edward O'Sullivan [1959] Director; Gemma Louise O'Sullivan [1986] Marketing Director; Peter Laurence O'Sullivan [1960] Director; Dawn Linda Tunak [1972] Director

Plastique Holdings Limited
Incorporated: 18 April 2002
Net Worth: £10,158,776 *Total Assets:* £10,158,776
Registered Office: Richmond House, Walkern Road, Stevenage, Herts, SG1 3QP
Activities: Manufacture of plastic packing goods
Parent: Plastique Group Limited
Officers: Mark Dunger [1962] Director [American]; Richard Garretson [1958] Director [American]; Alyson Schlinger Barclay [1959] Director [American]

Platinum Acquisition Limited
Incorporated: 22 August 2016 *Employees:* 3
Net Worth: £70,676,224 *Total Assets:* £149,896,496
Registered Office: Catalyst House, 720 Centennial Court, Centennial Park, Elstree, Herts, WD6 3SY
Activities: Other business support service activities n.e.c.
Parent: Platinum Midco Limited
Officers: Thomas Christopher Barnds [1968] Director [American]; Maurice Andre Hernandez [1981] Director [American]; Jason Michael Klein [1973] Director [American]

Platinum Midco 2 Limited
Incorporated: 1 September 2016 *Employees:* 3
Net Worth: £90,332,704 *Total Assets:* £90,332,704
Registered Office: Catalyst House, 720 Centennial Court, Centennial Park, Elstree, Herts, WD6 3SY
Activities: Other business support service activities n.e.c.
Parent: Platinum Topco Limited
Officers: Thomas Christopher Barnds [1968] Director [American]; Maurice Andre Hernandez [1981] Director [American]; Jason Michael Klein [1973] Director [American]

Platinum Midco Limited
Incorporated: 22 August 2016 *Employees:* 3
Net Worth: £90,332,704 *Total Assets:* £90,332,704
Registered Office: Catalyst House, 720 Centennial Court, Centennial Park, Elstree, Herts, WD6 3SY
Activities: Other business support service activities n.e.c.
Parent: Platinum Midco 2 Limited
Officers: Thomas Christopher Barnds [1968] Director [American]; Maurice Andre Hernandez [1981] Director [American]; Jason Michael Klein [1973] Director [American]

Platinum Newco II Limited
Incorporated: 1 August 2016 *Employees:* 1
Net Worth: £119,901,816 *Total Assets:* £125,000,000
Registered Office: Catalyst House, 720 Centennial Court, Centennial Park, Elstree, Herts, WD6 3SY
Activities: Activities of other holding companies n.e.c.
Parent: Platinum Newco III Limited
Officers: James Brown [1971] Director; Jon Stratford [1970] Director

Platinum Topco Limited
Incorporated: 22 August 2016 *Employees:* 176
Net Worth Deficit: £50,161,772 *Total Assets:* £171,971,168
Registered Office: Catalyst House, 720 Centennial Court, Centennial Park, Elstree, Herts, WD6 3SY
Activities: Other business support service activities n.e.c.
Officers: Thomas Christopher Barnds [1968] Director [American]; James Brown [1971] Director; Maurice Andre Hernandez [1981] Director [American]; Jason Michael Klein [1973] Director [American]; Rachel Spasser [1967] Director/Operating Principal [American]

Plaut International Limited
Incorporated: 20 December 1988 *Employees:* 21
Net Worth: £2,773,238 *Total Assets:* £9,271,291
Registered Office: 8c Bourne Court, Southend Road, Woodford Green, Essex, IG8 8HD
Activities: Agents involved in the sale of timber and building materials
Shareholders: Edward James Lindenberg; Peter Lindenberg
Officers: Dominic Higman, Secretary; Dominic Higman [1977] Finance Director; Edward James Lindenberg [1946] Director/Chairman; James Edward Charles Lindenberg [1971] Director; Peter Karl Lindenberg [1987] Sales Director; Stephen Paul Pinder [1971] Sales Director; John Stephen Yates [1960] Managing Director

Playags UK Limited
Incorporated: 3 June 2015
Net Worth: £7,112,105 *Total Assets:* £9,624,531
Registered Office: 1st Floor, Healthaid House, Marlborough Hill, Harrow, Middlesex, HA1 1UD
Activities: Publishing of computer games
Officers: David Lopez [1973] Director [American]

Playmobil (U.K.) Limited
Incorporated: 23 April 1980 *Employees:* 29
Net Worth: £3,061,775 *Total Assets:* £12,219,283
Registered Office: Regency House, 1 Miles Gray Road, Basildon, Essex, SS14 3RW
Activities: Wholesale of household goods (other than musical instruments) n.e.c
Officers: Philip Graham Dove, Secretary; Rene Feser [1975] Director [German]; Axel Schmitz [1955] Director [German]

Plaza Investments Limited
Incorporated: 12 March 2002 *Employees:* 11
Net Worth: £2,280,817 *Total Assets:* £9,433,733
Registered Office: Bells Amusements, Vickers Point, Anchor Lane, Ingoldmells, Skegness, Lincs, PE25 1LX
Activities: Other amusement and recreation activities n.e.c.
Major Shareholder: Frazer William Bell
Officers: Rachel Scarborough, Secretary; Frazer William Bell [1967] Director; Rachel Elizabeth Scarborough [1987] Director

Pledge Office Chairs Limited
Incorporated: 8 May 1970 *Employees:* 164
Net Worth: £12,096,799 *Total Assets:* £14,494,900
Registered Office: Millstream Works, Mill Road, Leighton Buzzard, Beds, LU7 1BA
Activities: Manufacture of office and shop furniture
Officers: Doreen Ann Carter, Secretary; David Ernest Carter [1938] Director/Office Chair Manufacturer; Doreen Ann Carter [1937] Director; Kaye Ann Carter [1965] Director; Stephen David Carter [1962] Director; Michael Mugford [1957] Technical Director; Stephen John Russell [1966] Director

Pledream Properties Limited
Incorporated: 22 July 1971 *Employees:* 3
Net Worth: £9,729,355 *Total Assets:* £13,850,547
Registered Office: 32 Phipps Hatch Lane, Enfield, Middlesex, EN2 0HN
Activities: Other letting and operating of own or leased real estate
Major Shareholder: Richard Morris Jenkins
Officers: Maureen Matilda Susan Amar, Secretary/Director; Maureen Matilda Susan Amar [1944] Director/Marketing Manager; Richard Morris Jenkins [1944] Director; Michael Samuel Sheridan [1945] Director/Solicitor

Plotplan Limited
Incorporated: 15 October 2007
Net Worth Deficit: £1,790,268 *Total Assets:* £11,041,436
Registered Office: 3rd Floor, Sterling House, Langston Road, Loughton, Essex, IG10 3TS
Activities: Development of building projects
Shareholders: David Edward Conway; Richard Matthew Conway; Gary Alexander Conway
Officers: David Edward Conway, Secretary; David Edward Conway [1976] Director; Gary Alexander Conway [1973] Director

Plumbcity Limited
Incorporated: 4 July 2002 *Employees:* 112
Net Worth: £10,533,585 *Total Assets:* £15,348,757
Registered Office: Unit 7 Commerce Way, Whitehall Industrial Estate, Colchester, Essex, CO2 8HR
Activities: Wholesale of hardware, plumbing and heating equipment and supplies
Parent: Plumbing and Heating Investments Limited
Officers: Douglas Brash Christie [1978] Director; Angus Kenneth Falconer [1969] Director; Roger David Goddard [1953] Director; Douglas Talbot McNair [1947] Director; Steven John Wimbledon [1971] Managing Director; William Sones Woof [1951] Director/Solicitor

Plume School
Incorporated: 16 November 2011 *Employees:* 267
Net Worth: £21,683,944 *Total Assets:* £26,001,436
Registered Office: Fambridge Road, Maldon, Essex, CM9 6AB
Activities: General secondary education
Officers: Joan Mary Binder [1944] Director/Retired; Michael Chaplin [1952] Director/Retired; John Robert Everard [1948] Director/Engineer; Mark Howell [1957] Director/IT Manager; Elliott John Judge [1972] Director/Police Officer; Gillian Mary McKinnell [1961] Director/School Bursar; Paul Douglas Nagle [1969] Director/Local Government Officer; Christopher Roger Pond [1967] Director/Senior Engineering Manager; Adrian Thomas Stead [1968] Director/Finance Manager; Debra Julie Thomas [1960] Managing Director; Carl Andrew Wakefield [1971] Director/Principal; Clare Dawn Whitaker [1971] Director/Manager (Insurance)

Plutus Estates Limited
Incorporated: 14 May 2014
Net Worth: £498,684 *Total Assets:* £10,229,884
Registered Office: 7 St John's Road, Harrow, Middlesex, HA1 2EY
Activities: Other letting and operating of own or leased real estate
Shareholders: Pankaj Keshavlal Rajani; Shailesh Virendra Patel
Officers: Shailesh Virendra Patel [1963] Director/Accountant; Pankaj Keshavlal Rajani [1963] Director/Accountant

Plymouth (Notte Street) Limited
Incorporated: 31 March 2016
Net Worth Deficit: £876,691 *Total Assets:* £17,104,904
Registered Office: 2nd Floor, Unicorn House, Station Close, Potters Bar, Herts, EN6 1TL
Activities: Other letting and operating of own or leased real estate
Parent: Harouni Group of Companies Limited
Officers: David Samuel Harouni [1977] Director; Jeremiah Harouni [1949] Director; Philip James Saunders [1947] Director

PMQUE Limited
Incorporated: 26 November 2012
Net Worth: £685,716 *Total Assets:* £27,638,876
Registered Office: Stour, The Street, East Bergholt, Colchester, Essex, CO7 6TF
Activities: Non-life insurance
Shareholders: Birte Kelly; Paul Kelly
Officers: Dr Birte Kelly [1948] Director [Danish]; Dr Paul Kelly [1943] Director

PMS International Group PLC
Incorporated: 25 July 1979 *Employees:* 265
Net Worth: £17,710,000 *Total Assets:* £31,663,000
Registered Office: International House, Cricketers Way, Basildon, Essex, SS13 1ST
Activities: Wholesale of household goods (other than musical instruments) n.e.c
Officers: Sarah Lawrence, Secretary; Mark John Benson [1961] Director/Accountant; Paul William Beverley [1950] Director; Robert James Crowe [1958] Director; David John Evans [1950] Director/Accountant; Tony Goding [1961] Sales Director; David Charles Topple [1965] Purchasing Director

PMS International Holdings PLC
Incorporated: 5 December 1985 *Employees:* 278
Net Worth: £21,169,000 *Total Assets:* £35,895,000
Registered Office: International House, Cricketers Way, Basildon, Essex, SS13 1ST
Activities: Wholesale of household goods (other than musical instruments) n.e.c
Shareholders: Paul William Beverley; Langtry Trust Co (Channel Islands) Limited
Officers: Mark John Benson, Secretary/Accountant; Mark John Benson [1961] Director/Accountant; Paul William Beverley [1950] Director; Robert James Crowe [1958] Sales Director; Tony Goding [1961] Sales Director

Poggenpohl Group UK Limited
Incorporated: 11 October 1974 *Employees:* 47
Net Worth: £4,533,176 *Total Assets:* £8,996,083
Registered Office: 100 London Road, St Albans, Herts, AL1 1NX
Activities: Retail of furniture, lighting, and similar (not musical instruments or scores) in specialised store
Parent: Poggenpohl Mobelwerke GmbH
Officers: Sharon Wallis, Secretary; Simon John Richmond [1967] Operations Director

Point Pedro Property Holdings Limited
Incorporated: 26 February 2015
Net Worth: £5,681,288 *Total Assets:* £15,288,470
Registered Office: Kingsley House, Clapham Road South, Lowestoft, Suffolk, NR32 1QS
Activities: Residential care activities for the elderly and disabled
Officers: Wasantha Darshana [1978] Director; Deborah Ann Edwards [1974] Director; Ian Stuart Jarvis [1966] Director; Sumithra Chandrakanthi Thayanandarajah [1959] Director/Business Executive; Velummayilum Thayanandarajah [1961] Director/Business Executive

Polar Speed Distribution Limited
Incorporated: 5 February 1996 *Employees:* 288
Net Worth: £6,229,499 *Total Assets:* £85,041,064
Registered Office: 8 Chartmoor Road, Leighton Buzzard, Beds, LU7 4WG
Activities: Freight transport by road
Parent: UPS (UK Holding) Limited
Officers: Boris Dobberstein [1969] Director/Manager [German]; Louis Anthony Rivieccio Jr [1965] Director [American]; Peter Raoul Stewardson [1964] Director/Legal Attorney

Policyfast Limited
Incorporated: 30 September 2005 *Employees:* 67
Net Worth: £2,012,283 *Total Assets:* £11,766,191
Registered Office: Unit 5 Vantage Park, Washingley Road, Huntingdon, Cambs, PE29 6SR
Activities: Activities of insurance agents and brokers
Parent: C I S G Ltd
Officers: Georgina Elizabeth Bourner, Secretary; Carl Anthony Ashton [1980] Risk and Compliance Director; Cheryl Dawn Astley [1962] Director/Chief Technology Officer; Robert Michael Darling [1963] Managing Director; Sarah Darling [1969] Group Sales and Marketing Director; Edward George FitzGenerald Hannan [1978] Director/Chief Financial Officer; Stephen Guy Parker [1965] Managing Director

Polyco (Group) Limited
Incorporated: 5 October 2012
Net Worth: £14,609,000 *Total Assets:* £25,086,000
Registered Office: Polyco Healthline, South Fen Road, Bourne, Lincs, PE10 0DN
Activities: Other manufacturing n.e.c.
Officers: Neil Antony Wilson, Secretary; David Greenwood [1955] Director; Jason Prichard [1969] Director; Neil Antony Wilson [1976] Director/Chief Financial Officer

Polyco Healthline Limited
Incorporated: 8 January 2016 *Employees:* 274
Net Worth Deficit: £12,209,000 *Total Assets:* £99,279,000
Registered Office: Polyco Healthline, South Fen Road, Bourne, Lincs, PE10 0DN
Activities: Other manufacturing n.e.c.
Officers: Neil Wilson, Secretary; Leslie Miles Blustin [1951] Director; David Greenwood [1955] Director; Lesley Jayne Lindberg [1966] Director; Gregory James Murray [1949] Director; Barry Peter Prichard [1943] Director; Jason Prichard [1969] Director; Scott Michael Prichard [1971] Director; Neil Antony Wilson [1976] Director

Polyfield Property Limited
Incorporated: 8 June 1990 *Employees:* 45
Net Worth: £41,948,072 *Total Assets:* £54,363,792
Registered Office: University of Hertfordshire, College Lane, Hatfield, Herts, AL10 9AB
Activities: Development of building projects
Parent: UH Holdings Limited
Officers: Susan Carol Grant, Secretary; Professor Ian Gordon Campbell [1963] Director/Deputy Vice-Chancellor; David Connell [1975] University Director of Sport; Ian Grimes [1972] Director/University Manager; Sharon Harrison-Barker [1965] Director/University Manager; Alistair Moffat [1964] Finance Director

Poole Investments Limited
Incorporated: 29 July 1988
Net Worth: £11,730,062 *Total Assets:* £13,190,435
Registered Office: Decimal Place, Chiltern Avenue, Amersham, Bucks, HP6 5FG
Activities: Renting and operating of Housing Association real estate
Parent: Inland Homes PLC
Officers: Nishith Malde [1958] Director; Gary John Skinner [1968] Managing Director; Stephen Desmond Wicks [1951] Director

Poplars Resource Management Company Limited
Incorporated: 18 July 1991
Net Worth Deficit: £1,948,000 *Total Assets:* £11,928,000
Registered Office: Coronation Road, Cressex, High Wycombe, Bucks, HP12 3TZ
Activities: Collection of non-hazardous waste
Parent: Biffa Holdings Limited
Officers: Richard Neil Pike [1969] Director/Chief Financial Officer; Michael Robert Mason Topham [1972] Director/Chief Executive Officer

Popsoda Limited
Incorporated: 15 October 2003 *Employees:* 25
Net Worth: £9,065,348 *Total Assets:* £9,522,041
Registered Office: 48-50 Fowler Road, Hainault Business Park, Ilford, Essex, IG6 3UT
Activities: Wholesale of clothing and footwear
Parent: Popsoda Holdings Limited
Officers: Shelly Kudhail, Secretary; Balraj Kudhail [1965] Director/Sales Person

Porcelanosa (South East) Limited
Incorporated: 6 December 1995 *Employees:* 162
Net Worth: £8,815,000 *Total Assets:* £19,179,000
Registered Office: Units 1-6 Otterspool Way, Bushey, Watford, Herts, WD25 8HL
Activities: Wholesale of wood, construction materials and sanitary equipment
Parent: Porcelanosa Group Limited
Officers: Deep Shah, Secretary; Silvestre Segarra [1966] Director [Spanish]; Igor Vazquez [1976] Director/Manager [Spanish]

Porcelanosa U.K. Limited
Incorporated: 5 September 1995 *Employees:* 456
Net Worth: £110,485,000 *Total Assets:* £134,772,000
Registered Office: Units 1-6 Otterspool Way, Bushey, Watford, Herts, WD25 8HL
Activities: Leasing of intellectual property and similar products, except copyright works
Shareholder: Asuncion Manzanet
Officers: Deep Shah, Secretary; Manuel Colonques [1942] Director [Spanish]

Port of Boston Limited
Incorporated: 25 November 1987 *Employees:* 69
Net Worth: £12,664,000 *Total Assets:* £20,960,000
Registered Office: The Dock, Boston, Lincs, PE21 6BN
Activities: Cargo handling for water transport activities
Major Shareholder: Mark Alexander Vernon Gatehouse
Officers: David Sydney Martin, Secretary; Mark Alexander Vernon Gatehouse [1949] Director; Andrew Duncan Lawrence [1964] Port Director; David Sydney Martin [1955] Director

Port of Felixstowe Limited
Incorporated: 8 March 1991 *Employees:* 2,527
Net Worth: £303,648,000 *Total Assets:* £542,270,016
Registered Office: Tomline House, The Dock, Felixstowe, Suffolk, IP11 3SY
Activities: Sea and coastal freight water transport
Parent: Hutchison Ports (UK) Limited
Officers: Simon Richard Mullett, Secretary; Clemence Chun Fun Cheng [1958] Director; Sing Chi IP [1953] Director [Chinese]; Dominic Kai Ming Lai [1953] Director; Edith Shih [1952] Director; Frank John Sixt [1951] Director [Canadian]

Port of Tilbury London Limited
Incorporated: 25 October 1991 *Employees:* 641
Net Worth: £119,671,000 *Total Assets:* £711,844,992
Registered Office: Leslie Ford House, Tilbury Freeport, Tilbury, Essex, RM18 7EH
Activities: Service activities incidental to water transportation
Parent: International Transport Limited
Officers: Pamela June Smyth, Secretary; Carole Jean Cran [1970] Director/Chief Financial Officer; Paul Stuart Dale [1971] Asset and Site Director; Charles Graham Hammond [1961] Director/Solicitor; Stuart James Wallace [1970] Director/Chief Operating Officer; Peter John Ward [1964] Commercial Director

Portcrest Limited
Incorporated: 20 February 2008 *Employees:* 232
Net Worth: £10,092,708 *Total Assets:* £41,222,624
Registered Office: 3-5 Fornham Road, Bury St Edmunds, Suffolk, IP32 6AL
Activities: Activities of head offices
Shareholders: Nick Storey; Paula Storey
Officers: Matthew Neil Stockdale, Secretary; Nicholas Storey [1961] Director; Paula Storey [1966] Director

Porter and Makins Limited
Incorporated: 24 June 1957
Net Worth Deficit: £306,831 *Total Assets:* £9,343,976
Registered Office: Pensthorpe, Fakenham Road, Fakenham, Norfolk, NR21 0LN
Activities: Growing of cereals (except rice), leguminous crops and oil seeds
Major Shareholder: William John Jordan
Officers: Martin Ralph Bonynge, Secretary; Deborah Ann Jordan [1957] Director/Shop Manager; William John Jordan [1949] Director/Miller

Portugal Finco Limited
Incorporated: 21 December 2012
Net Worth: £33,403,000 *Total Assets:* £81,490,000
Registered Office: Holland Place, Wardentree Park, Pinchbeck, Spalding, Lincs, PE11 3ZN
Activities: Activities of other holding companies n.e.c.
Officers: Jonathan Pallas [1962] Director; Gary Edward Rehwinkel [1961] Director [American]

Porvair Filtration Group Limited
Incorporated: 28 September 1966 *Employees:* 315
Net Worth: £23,126,000 *Total Assets:* £36,905,000
Registered Office: 7 Regis Place, Bergen Way, King's Lynn, Norfolk, PE30 2JN
Activities: Manufacture of other plastic products
Parent: Porvair Filtration Limited
Officers: Dr Simon Jon Rodgers, Secretary; Ian Stuart Boxall [1963] Technical Director; Thomas Mark Liddell [1975] Sales Director; David Malcolm Mellor [1979] Finance Director; Ian Stirling [1953] Director; Benjamin Denys William Stocks [1962] Director; Christopher Patric Tyler [1962] Finance Director; Stuart Wells [1950] Operations Director

Porvair Filtration Limited
Incorporated: 18 October 1995
Net Worth: £5,291,000 *Total Assets:* £23,997,000
Registered Office: 7 Regis Place, Bergen Way, King's Lynn, Norfolk, PE30 2JN
Activities: Non-trading company
Parent: Porvair PLC
Officers: Dr Simon Jon Rodgers, Secretary; Benjamin Denys William Stocks [1962] Director; Christopher Patric Tyler [1962] Finance Director

Porvair PLC
Incorporated: 3 September 1982 *Employees:* 819
Net Worth: £74,869,000 *Total Assets:* £127,947,000
Registered Office: 7 Regis Place, Bergen Way, Kings Lynn, Norfolk, PE30 2JN
Activities: Manufacture of basic pharmaceutical products
Officers: Christopher Patric Tyler, Finance Director; Paul David Dean [1961] Director; Sarah Jean Martin [1965] Director [Irish]; John Edward Nicholas [1956] Director; Benjamin Denys William Stocks [1962] Director; Christopher Patric Tyler [1962] Finance Director

Positive Entertainment Ltd
Incorporated: 19 November 2013
Net Worth: £8,340,216 *Total Assets:* £10,110,334
Registered Office: 30 Station Lane, Hornchurch, Essex, RM12 6NJ
Activities: Sound recording and music publishing activities
Major Shareholder: Andrew Paul Green
Officers: Andrew Paul Green [1965] Director; Niall Green [1993] Director; Jamie Duncan McGilvray [1983] Director/Business Development Manager; Albert Steven Turner [1970] Director/Accountant

Poste Holdings Limited
Incorporated: 15 July 1994 *Employees:* 174
Net Worth: £7,949,329 *Total Assets:* £19,559,456
Registered Office: The George Hotel, Stamford, Lincs, PE9 2LB
Activities: Hotels and similar accommodation
Shareholders: Lawrence Oliver Hoskins; I.P.M. Trustees Limited
Officers: David Stephen Landry, Finance Director; Lawrence Oliver Hoskins [1940] Director/Hotelier

Poste Hotels Limited
Incorporated: 7 November 1968 *Employees:* 174
Net Worth: £17,002,508 *Total Assets:* £21,733,034
Registered Office: The George Hotel, Stamford, Lincs, PE9 2LB
Activities: Hotels and similar accommodation
Shareholders: Lawrence Oliver Hoskins; Poste Holdings Limited
Officers: David Stephen Landry, Secretary; Emily Jane Casey [1972] Director/Teacher; Andrea Aline Nelia Hoskins [1952] Director/Hotelier; Andrew Martin Hoskins [1972] Director/Hotelier; Lawrence Oliver Hoskins [1940] Director/Hotelier; Mark Oliver Hoskins [1972] Director/Hotelier; David Stephen Landry [1949] Director/Finance; Ivo Vannocci [1938] Director/Hotelier [Italian]

Potter & Moore Innovations Limited
Incorporated: 22 January 2003 *Employees:* 266
Net Worth: £6,439,000 *Total Assets:* £14,846,000
Registered Office: 1210 Lincoln Road, Werrington, Peterborough, Cambs, PE4 6ND
Activities: Manufacture of perfumes and toilet preparations
Parent: Creightons PLC
Officers: Mary Teresa Carney [1953] Director/Tax Consultant; Philippa Clark [1969] Sales & Marketing Director; Paul Forster [1958] Director/Chartered Accountant; William Torrance Glencross [1946] Director/Marketing Consultant; Bernard James Mary Johnson [1945] Director/Management Consultant; William Oliver McIlroy [1945] Director; Nicholas Desmond John O'Shea [1954] Director/Management Consultant; Martin Stevens [1961] Technical Director

Power Adhesives Limited
Incorporated: 9 December 1974 *Employees:* 39
Net Worth: £4,653,814 *Total Assets:* £9,676,196
Registered Office: 1 Lords Way, Basildon, Essex, SS13 1TN
Activities: Manufacture of glues
Shareholder: Stephen James Sweeney
Officers: William David Howlett, Secretary; William David Howlett [1947] Sales Director; Stephen James Sweeney [1959] Managing Director

Power on Connections Ltd
Incorporated: 26 September 2003 *Employees:* 197
Net Worth: £8,124,768 *Total Assets:* £35,199,272
Registered Office: Energy House, Woolpit Business Park, Woolpit, Bury St Edmunds, Suffolk, IP30 9UP
Activities: Electrical installation
Parent: Power On Investments Limited
Officers: Christopher Mumford, Secretary; Darryl John Corney [1960] Director; Neil Gerard Fitzsimons [1978] Director [Irish]; Clive Eric Linsdell [1962] Director; Robert Stephen Theobald [1959] Managing Director

Power On Investments Limited
Incorporated: 24 January 2008
Net Worth Deficit: £4,241,106 *Total Assets:* £24,551,076
Registered Office: Energy House, Woolpit Business Park, Woolpit, Bury St Edmunds, Suffolk, IP30 9UP
Activities: Activities of other holding companies n.e.c.
Parent: BUUK Infrastructure No 2 Limited
Officers: Christopher Mumford, Secretary; Darryl John Corney [1960] Director; Paul David Edwards [1974] Director; Clive Eric Linsdell [1962] Director

Powergas Africa Limited
Incorporated: 10 September 2014 *Employees:* 72
Net Worth: £18,993,298 *Total Assets:* £37,415,864
Registered Office: Unit 7 Chancery Gate Close, Stonefield Way, South Ruislip, Middlesex, HA4 0JS
Activities: Manufacture of gas
Officers: Navaratnarajah Navendrha, Secretary; Riya Grover [1988] Director; Aditya Khilnani [1990] Director; Deepak Khilnani [1959] Director

PPA Group Limited
Incorporated: 27 March 2015 *Employees:* 43
Net Worth: £4,186,332 *Total Assets:* £8,237,172
Registered Office: Falcon House, Primett Road, Stevenage, Herts, SG1 3EE
Activities: Travel agency activities
Major Shareholder: Philip Edmund Cook
Officers: Philip Edmund Cook [1959] Director

PPD CT Investments LLP
Incorporated: 14 December 2009
Net Worth: £212,357,808 *Total Assets:* £212,380,416
Registered Office: Granta Park, Great Abington, Cambridge, CB21 6GQ

PPD Global Ltd
Incorporated: 29 May 1981 *Employees:* 1,508
Net Worth: £198,484,000 *Total Assets:* £777,835,008
Registered Office: Granta Park, Great Abington, Cambridge, CB21 6GQ
Activities: Other research and experimental development on natural sciences and engineering
Parent: PPD UK Holdings Limited
Officers: Christopher David Neild, Secretary/Accountant; Julia Mary James [1974] Director/Solicitor; Christopher David Neild [1962] Director/Accountant; Roger Stephen Newbery [1960] Director/Executive Management

PPD International Investments Limited
Incorporated: 17 April 2012
Net Worth: £735,043,968 *Total Assets:* £789,945,984
Registered Office: PPD, Granta Park, Great Abington, Cambridge, CB21 6GQ
Activities: Non-trading company
Parent: Wildcat Acquisition Holdings (UK) Limited
Officers: Julia Mary James [1974] Director/Legal Counsel; Christopher David Neild [1962] Director; Roger Stephen Newbery [1960] Director

PPD UK Holdings Limited
Incorporated: 20 June 1996
Net Worth: £82,799,000 *Total Assets:* £202,576,000
Registered Office: Granta Park, Great Abington, Cambridge, CB21 6GQ
Activities: Activities of other holding companies n.e.c.
Parent: PPD International Investments Limited
Officers: Christopher David Neild, Secretary; Julia Mary James [1974] Director/Solicitor; Christopher David Neild [1962] Director/Accountant; Roger Stephen Newbery [1960] Director/Executive Management

PPG Holdings (U.K.) Limited
Incorporated: 18 June 1987 *Employees:* 3
Net Worth Deficit: £21,653,000 *Total Assets:* £118,706,000
Registered Office: P O Box 162, Needham Road, Stowmarket, Suffolk, IP14 2ZR
Activities: Activities of head offices
Parent: PPG Industries Inc
Officers: Susan Elaine Clarkson [1971] Finance Director; Paul Richard Dowie [1973] HR Director; Steven Pocock [1962] Director; Ruth Stewart [1976] Finance Director

PPG Industries (UK) Limited
Incorporated: 13 March 1987 *Employees:* 663
Net Worth: £30,302,000 *Total Assets:* £185,780,992
Registered Office: P O Box 162, Needham Road, Stowmarket, Suffolk, IP14 2ZR
Activities: Manufacture of plastics in primary forms
Parent: PPG Holdings (U.K.) Limited
Officers: Susan Elaine Clarkson [1971] Finance Director; Paul Richard Dowie [1973] HR Director; Richard Michael Goode [1967] Director/Market Manager; David Heal [1976] Regional Protective Coatings Director - Western Europe; Ruth Stewart [1976] Finance Director; Charles Raymond Turner [1963] Technical Director; Michael Christopher Walsh [1979] Director/Plant Manager - Refinish Stowmarket

PPG Kansai Automotive Finishes UK LLP
Incorporated: 2 November 2004
Net Worth: £7,132,726 *Total Assets:* £13,543,955
Registered Office: P O Box 162, Needham Road, Stowmarket, Suffolk, IP14 2ZR

PQW Brenley Corner Limited
Incorporated: 29 November 2007
Net Worth Deficit: £227,399 *Total Assets:* £8,399,154
Registered Office: 147a High Street, Waltham Cross, Herts, EN8 7AP
Activities: Residential nursing care facilities
Shareholders: Arinesarajah Ragumoorthy; Jegathambikai Ragumoorthy
Officers: Jegathambikai Ragumoorthy, Secretary; Arinesarajah Ragumoorthy [1945] Director

The Practice (Group) Limited
Incorporated: 24 January 2006 *Employees:* 653
Net Worth: £169,000 *Total Assets:* £20,820,000
Registered Office: Rose House, Bell Lane Office Village, Bell Lane, Little Chalfont, Amersham, Bucks, HP6 6FA
Activities: Activities of head offices
Parent: Centene UK Limited
Officers: Caroline Michelle Bailes [1970] Director/Chief Financial Officer; Samantha Generaldine Jones [1971] Director/Chief Executive; Dr Ajit Gordon Vimalendran Kadirgamar [1963] Director; Dr Jeremy David Rose [1955] Director

The Practice Corporate Management Limited
Incorporated: 13 June 2011 *Employees:* 37
Net Worth: £1,808,000 *Total Assets:* £14,463,000
Registered Office: Rose House, Bell Lane Office Village, Bell Lane, Little Chalfont, Amersham, Bucks, HP6 6FA
Activities: Activities of head offices
Shareholders: Jeremy David Rose; Ajit Gordon Vimalendran Kadirgamar
Officers: Samantha Generaldine Jones [1971] Director/Chief Executive; Dr Jeremy David Rose [1955] Director/GP

The Practice Surgeries Limited
Incorporated: 27 March 2008 *Employees:* 361
Net Worth Deficit: £6,153,000 *Total Assets:* £17,858,000
Registered Office: Rose House, Bell Lane Office Village, Bell Lane, Little Chalfont, Amersham, Bucks, HP6 6FA
Activities: General medical practice activities
Shareholders: Jeremy David Rose; Ajit Gordon Vimalendran Kadirgamar
Officers: Samantha Generaldine Jones [1971] Director/Chief Executive; Dr Jeremy David Rose [1955] Clinical Director

Dr Michael Prager Holdings Limited
Incorporated: 18 November 2011
Net Worth: £7,071,336 *Total Assets:* £11,820,336
Registered Office: 195a Kenton Road, Harrow, Middlesex, HA3 0HD
Activities: Activities of head offices
Major Shareholder: Frank Michael Prager
Officers: Christina Christoforou, Secretary; Dr Frank Michael Prager [1968] Director [German]

Pratt & Whitney Canada (UK) Limited
Incorporated: 26 February 1997 *Employees:* 23
Net Worth: £8,962,868 *Total Assets:* £10,042,931
Registered Office: Unit 13 Bilton Court, Bilton Way, Luton, Beds, LU1 1LX
Activities: Maintenance and repair of motor vehicles
Parent: United Technolgies Holdings Limited
Officers: Jacques Jean Blondeau [1960] Director/General Manager [American]; Nicole Marie Nelson [1974] Senior Director Finance [American]

S H Pratt Group Limited
Incorporated: 23 September 1959 *Employees:* 235
Previous: S.H. Pratt & Co. (Bananas) Limited
Net Worth: £10,748,510 *Total Assets:* £41,329,732
Registered Office: Musca Court, Laporte Way, Luton, Beds, LU4 8EN
Activities: Other processing and preserving of fruit and vegetables
Parent: S H Pratt Holdings Limited
Officers: Shahida Mohamed, Secretary; David Vernon Bateman [1965] Managing Director; Shahida Mohamed [1955] Director; Robert John Wells [1961] Director

S H Pratt Holdings Limited
Incorporated: 19 October 2015 *Employees:* 235
Net Worth: £11,801,228 *Total Assets:* £41,530,084
Registered Office: Musca Court, Laporte Way, Luton, Beds, LU4 8EN
Activities: Wholesale of fruit and vegetables
Major Shareholder: Robert John Wells
Officers: Shahida Mohamed, Secretary; David Vernon Bateman [1965] Managing Director; Shahida Mohamed [1955] Director; Robert John Wells [1961] Director

Precision Printing Co. Limited
Incorporated: 14 December 1979 *Employees:* 167
Net Worth: £1,496,706 *Total Assets:* £15,753,570
Registered Office: Unit 15 Thames Gateway Park, Chequers Lane, Dagenham, Essex, RM9 6PR
Activities: Printing n.e.c.
Shareholders: Clive David Cooper; Gary Ian Peeling
Officers: Margaret Anne Howell, Secretary/Accountant; Clive David Cooper [1947] Director; Gloria Cooper [1953] Director/Marketing Executive; Margaret Anne Howell [1948] Director/Accountant; Paul Brian Mason [1971] Commercial Director; Gary Ian Peeling [1971] Managing Director; Andrew Skarpellis [1973] Director; Edward Allan Steward [1947] Director

Precon Products Ltd
Incorporated: 19 February 2007 *Employees:* 35
Net Worth: £3,490,268 *Total Assets:* £10,461,211
Registered Office: Fitzroy House, Crown Street, Ipswich, Suffolk, IP1 3LG
Activities: Wholesale of metals and metal ores
Shareholders: Julian Matthew Green; Ashleigh Thomas Hawes; Michael David Philpot
Officers: Ashleigh Thomas Hawes, Secretary; Julian Matthew Green [1968] Director/Sales Manager; Ashleigh Thomas Hawes [1984] Director; Lee Kevin O'Sullivan [1974] Sales Director; Michael David Philpot [1971] Director

Prefect Software LLP
Incorporated: 9 December 2004
Net Worth: £21,970,278 *Total Assets:* £43,967,152
Registered Office: 166 College Road, Harrow, Middlesex, HA1 1RA
Officers: Barry Belasco [1940] LLP Member; Helen Belasco [1940] LLP Member; Joseph Gabriel Bowman [1968] LLP Member; Patrick Doherty [1942] LLP Member; Andrea Longhi [1968] LLP Member; Alastair Keith MacKeith [1958] LLP Member; Malik Moiz [1958] LLP Member; Paresh Patel [1977] LLP Member; Richard Derek Platt [1976] LLP Member; Priya Nalin Kantilal Shah [1972] LLP Member

Pregis Europe Limited
Incorporated: 2 February 2016 *Employees:* 72
Net Worth: £7,065,837 *Total Assets:* £31,071,240
Registered Office: Richmond House, Walkern Road, Stevenage, Herts, SG1 3QP
Activities: Activities of other holding companies n.e.c.
Officers: Kevin Baudhuin [1962] Director/President and CEO [American]; Manu Bettegowda [1973] Director/Private Equity [Indian]; David Michael Haddad [1974] Director/Private Equity [American]; Donald Keith Lavanway [1964] Director/President & CFO [American]; Chase Ormond [1982] Director/Private Equity [American]

Pregis Limited
Incorporated: 3 March 1992 *Employees:* 46
Previous: Easypack Limited
Net Worth: £9,800,463 *Total Assets:* £13,380,024
Registered Office: Richmond House, Walkern Road, Stevenage, Herts, SG1 3QP
Activities: Other manufacturing n.e.c.
Parent: Pregis Europe Limited
Officers: Kevin Baudhuin [1962] Director [American]; Jason Cox [1970] Operations Director; Donald Keith Lavanway [1964] Director [American]; George Graham Voice [1990] Director

Premiair Aerospace Limited
Incorporated: 17 December 2013
Net Worth: £14,906,367 *Total Assets:* £16,138,727
Registered Office: Station Cottage, The Street, Nacton, Ipswich, Suffolk, IP10 0HR
Activities: Repair and maintenance of aircraft and spacecraft
Major Shareholder: Graham Avery
Officers: Graham Avery [1945] Director

Premier 1983 Limited
Incorporated: 7 November 2007 *Employees:* 38
Net Worth: £1,716,360 *Total Assets:* £8,213,219
Registered Office: Premier Business Park, Dencora Way, Luton, Beds, LU3 3HP
Activities: Wholesale of computers, computer peripheral equipment and software
Major Shareholder: Hugh Martin Byrne
Officers: Terry Susan Kintas, Secretary; Hugh Martin Byrne [1962] Director; Terry Susan Kintas [1964] Director; Kevan Anthony McCreesh [1963] Director/Chartered Accountant; Karen Jean Ord [1970] Director

Premier Bidco Limited
Incorporated: 21 August 2015 *Employees:* 3
Net Worth Deficit: £2,428,022 *Total Assets:* £23,187,088
Registered Office: The Manorway, Coryton, Stanford-le-Hope, Essex, SS17 9LN
Activities: Non-trading company
Parent: Premier Midco Limited
Officers: Andrew David Willson, Secretary; Nicholas Brian Pye [1974] Director/Chief Executive Officer; Andrew David Willson [1964] Director

Premier Decorations Limited
Incorporated: 4 February 1988 *Employees:* 82
Net Worth: £1,021,388 *Total Assets:* £10,791,078
Registered Office: Premier House, Braintree Road, Ruislip, Middlesex, HA4 0EJ
Activities: Wholesale of household goods (other than musical instruments) n.e.c
Shareholder: Jarnail Singh Athwal
Officers: Michael Geoffrey Sancto, Secretary/Accountant; Jarnail Singh Athwal [1953] Director; Jasmin Athwal [1977] Director/H & S Training; Jason Jaswinder Athwal [1980] Director/IT Manager; Jito Kaur Athwal [1955] Director/Administrator; Heny Lachman Mahtani [1964] Director; Vinod Lachman Mahtani [1961] Director; Pravin Patel [1961] Director/General Manager

Premier Euro Hotels Limited
Incorporated: 23 April 2015 *Employees:* 4
Net Worth: £1,970,074 *Total Assets:* £36,904,408
Registered Office: Kirkland Hose, 11-15 Peterborough Road, Harrow, Middlesex, HA1 2AX
Activities: Hotels and similar accommodation
Officers: Dinesh Gordhandas Bhattessa [1946] Director/Businessman; Haider Ladhu Jaffer [1940] Director; Dr Manoj Raman [1960] Director/Businessman; Hassanali Amirali Dawood Suleman [1954] Director

Premier Financing Limited
Incorporated: 19 February 1999
Net Worth: £1,127,800,064 *Total Assets:* £1,658,599,936
Registered Office: Premier House, Centrium Business Park, Griffiths Way, St Albans, Herts, AL1 2RE
Activities: Activities of head offices
Parent: Premier Foods (Holdings) Limited
Officers: Simon Nicholas Wilbraham, Secretary; Duncan Neil Leggett [1979] Director; Simon Alan Rose [1966] Director/Solicitor; Simon Nicholas Wilbraham [1969] Director/Company Secretary

Premier Foods Finance PLC
Incorporated: 13 February 2014
Net Worth: £200,000 *Total Assets:* £529,000,000
Registered Office: Premier House, Centrium Business Park, Griffiths Way, St Albans, Herts, AL1 2RE
Activities: Activities of head offices
Parent: Premier Foods Investments Limited
Officers: Simon Nicholas Wilbraham, Secretary; Duncan Neil Leggett [1979] Director; Simon Alan Rose [1966] Director/Solicitor; Simon Nicholas Wilbraham [1969] Director/Company Secretary

Premier Foods Group Limited
Incorporated: 17 November 1933 *Employees:* 3,524
Net Worth: £89,100,000 *Total Assets:* £2,759,600,128
Registered Office: Premier House, Centrium Business Park, Griffiths Way, St Albans, Herts, AL1 2RE
Activities: Grain milling
Parent: Premier Foods Group Services Limited
Officers: Simon Nicholas Wilbraham, Secretary; Mark Rivers Hughes [1960] Group Procurement Director; Duncan Neil Leggett [1979] Director; Alastair Sholto Neil Murray [1960] Director/Chief Financial Officer; Simon Alan Rose [1966] Director/Solicitor; Alexander Richard Whitehouse [1969] Director

Premier Foods Group Services Limited
Incorporated: 20 April 2000 *Employees:* 207
Net Worth: £1,769,600,000 *Total Assets:* £2,043,000,064
Registered Office: Premier House, Centrium Business Park, Griffiths Way, St Albans, Herts, AL1 2RE
Activities: Activities of head offices
Parent: RHM Group Three Limited
Officers: Simon Nicholas Wilbraham, Secretary; Mark Rivers Hughes [1960] Group Procurement Director; Duncan Neil Leggett [1979] Director; Alastair Sholto Neil Murray [1960] Director/Chief Financial Officer; Simon Alan Rose [1966] Director/Solicitor; Alexander Richard Whitehouse [1969] Director

Premier Foods Investments Limited
Incorporated: 29 April 2002
Net Worth: £729,000,000 *Total Assets:* £3,851,200,000
Registered Office: Premier House, Centrium Business Park, Griffiths Way, St Albans, Herts, AL1 2RE
Activities: Activities of head offices
Parent: Premier Foods Investments No.1 Limited
Officers: Simon Nicholas Wilbraham, Secretary; Duncan Neil Leggett [1979] Director; Simon Alan Rose [1966] Director/Solicitor; Simon Nicholas Wilbraham [1969] Director/Company Secretary

Premier Foods Investments No.1 Limited
Incorporated: 13 January 2004
Net Worth: £126,700,000 *Total Assets:* £697,100,032
Registered Office: Premier House, Centrium Business Park, Griffiths Way, St Albans, Herts, AL1 2RE
Activities: Activities of head offices
Parent: Premier Foods PLC
Officers: Simon Nicholas Wilbraham, Secretary; Duncan Neil Leggett [1979] Director; Simon Alan Rose [1966] Director/Solicitor; Simon Nicholas Wilbraham [1969] Director/Company Secretary

Premier Foods PLC
Incorporated: 22 June 2004 *Employees:* 4,053
Net Worth: £949,299,968 *Total Assets:* £2,188,499,968
Registered Office: Premier House, Centrium Business Park, Griffiths Way, St Albans, Herts, AL1 2RE
Activities: Activities of head offices
Officers: Simon Alan Rose, Secretary; Simon Anthony Bentley [1955] Director; Keith Hamill [1952] Director; Richard Paul Hodgson [1969] Director; Shinji Honda [1958] Director [Japanese]; Alastair Sholto Neil Murray [1960] Director/Chief Financial Officer; Pamela Powell [1963] Director [American]; Daniel Wosner [1982] Director

Premier Holidays Limited
Incorporated: 14 February 1984 *Employees:* 128
Net Worth: £3,256,677 *Total Assets:* £11,365,323
Registered Office: Building 1020, Cambourne Business Park, Cambourne, Cambridge, CB23 6DW
Activities: Tour operator activities
Shareholders: Renford Laurence Sargent; Peter Spencer Andrews
Officers: Susan Helen Earnshaw, Secretary; Peter Spencer Andrews [1943] Director; Heidi Amanda Blades [1976] Director; Susan Earnshaw [1958] Director; Mark James Godfrey [1980] Director; Deborah Karen Goffin [1969] Director; Renford Laurence Sargent [1945] Director; Nicola Louise Waters [1975] Director

Premier Inn Hotels Limited
Incorporated: 25 May 2004 *Employees:* 2
Net Worth: £948,200,000 *Total Assets:* £1,612,189,056
Registered Office: Whitbread Court, Houghton Hall Business Park, Porz Avenue, Houghton Regis, Dunstable, Beds, LU5 5XE
Activities: Hotels and similar accommodation
Parent: Whitbread Group PLC
Officers: Daren Clive Lowry, Secretary; Simon David Ewins [1969] Director; Simon Edward Jones [1976] Managing Director Premier Inn UK

Premier Inn International Development Limited
Incorporated: 28 August 2014 *Employees:* 10
Net Worth Deficit: £5,876,885 *Total Assets:* £16,714,270
Registered Office: Whitbread Court, Houghton Hall Business Park, Porz Avenue, Houghton Regis, Dunstable, Beds, LU5 5XE
Activities: Hotels and similar accommodation
Parent: WHRI Holding Company Limited
Officers: Daren Clive Lowry, Secretary; Mark Anderson [1971] Director; Nicholas Theodore Cadbury [1966] Director; Christopher David Vaughan [1964] Director; Matthew Yates [1977] Director/Lawyer

Premier Inn Ochre Limited
Incorporated: 16 July 2012 *Employees:* 2
Net Worth: £16,371,000 *Total Assets:* £119,652,000
Registered Office: Whitbread Court, Houghton Hall Business Park, Porz Avenue, Houghton Regis, Dunstable, Beds, LU5 5XE
Activities: Hotels and similar accommodation
Parent: Premier Inn Hotels Limited
Officers: Daren Clive Lowry, Secretary; Simon David Ewins [1969] Director; Simon Edward Jones [1976] Managing Director Premier Inn UK

Premier Lotteries Capital UK Limited
Incorporated: 17 March 2010 *Employees:* 963
Net Worth Deficit: £137,000,000 *Total Assets:* £815,200,000
Registered Office: Tolpits Lane, Watford, Herts, WD18 9RN
Activities: Activities of head offices
Parent: Premier Lotteries Investments UK Limited
Officers: John Edward Michael Dillon, Secretary; John Edward Michael Dillon [1963] Legal Director and Company Secretary; Ilya Kachko [1979] Director/Portfolio Manager [Canadian]; Andrew Jonathan Mark Taylor [1961] Director/Private Equity Investor

Premier Lotteries UK Limited
Incorporated: 17 March 2010 *Employees:* 963
Net Worth Deficit: £19,800,000 *Total Assets:* £814,899,968
Registered Office: Tolpits Lane, Watford, Herts, WD18 9RN
Activities: Non-trading company
Parent: Premier Lotteries Capital UK Limited
Officers: John Edward Michael Dillon, Secretary; John Edward Michael Dillon [1963] Legal Director and Company Secretary; Ilya Kachko [1979] Director/Portfolio Manager [Canadian]; Andrew Jonathan Mark Taylor [1961] Director/Private Equity Investor

Premier Midco Limited
Incorporated: 21 August 2015
Net Worth Deficit: £4,943,876 *Total Assets:* £17,584,038
Registered Office: The Manorway, Coryton, Stanford-le-Hope, Essex, SS17 9LN
Activities: Non-trading company
Parent: Premier Topco Limited
Officers: Andrew David Willson, Secretary; Nicholas Brian Pye [1974] Director/Chief Executive Officer; Andrew David Willson [1964] Director

Premier PLC
Incorporated: 3 February 1988 *Employees:* 82
Net Worth: £7,540,387 *Total Assets:* £14,417,769
Registered Office: Premier House, Braintree Road, Ruislip, Middlesex, HA4 0EJ
Activities: Activities of distribution holding companies
Shareholder: Jarnail Singh Athwal
Officers: Michael Geoffrey Sancto, Secretary/Accountant; Jarnail Singh Athwal [1953] Director; Jito Kaur Athwal [1955] Director; Heny Lachman Mahtani [1964] Director; Vinod Lachman Mahtani [1961] Director

Premier Quilting Company Limited
Incorporated: 6 July 1959 *Employees:* 41
Net Worth: £5,178,334 *Total Assets:* £8,675,334
Registered Office: York House, Empire Way, Wembley, Middlesex, HA9 0FQ
Activities: Wholesale of textiles
Officers: David Lobenstein, Secretary; David Hochhauser [1981] Director; Ronald Edward Hochhauser [1959] Director

Premier Topco Limited
Incorporated: 21 August 2015 *Employees:* 54
Net Worth Deficit: £6,643,098 *Total Assets:* £29,625,332
Registered Office: The Manorway, Coryton, Stanford-le-Hope, Essex, SS17 9LN
Activities: Non-trading company
Officers: Andrew David Willson, Secretary; Craig Lucas Goodfellow [1964] Director; Ian Edward Kershaw [1964] Director; Luke Anthony Kingston [1978] Director; Diane Lenora Lance [1964] Director; Nicholas Brian Pye [1974] Director/Chief Executive Officer; Andrew David Willson [1964] Director

Premonition Analytics Limited
Incorporated: 24 February 2015
Net Worth: £21,600,000 *Total Assets:* £21,600,000
Registered Office: 2 Low Road, Congham, King's Lynn, Norfolk, PE32 1AE
Activities: Other information service activities n.e.c.
Shareholders: Stratagem Ops Limited; Setasi Holdings Limited
Officers: Guy Kurlandski [1968] Director; Roberto Marco Francesco Pola [1955] Director/Chartered Accountant; Toby William Unwin [1973] Director

Prentice Aircraft and Cars Limited
Incorporated: 30 June 1938 *Employees:* 27
Net Worth: £8,057,667 *Total Assets:* £23,539,168
Registered Office: Sinks Pit, Main Road, Kesgrave, Ipswich, Suffolk, IP5 2PE
Activities: Sale of other motor vehicles
Major Shareholder: Guy John Nicholls
Officers: Shirley Nicholls, Secretary; Kieran Caleb Cobb [1977] Finance Director; Anthony Derek Marshall [1975] Sales Director; Guy John Nicholls [1963] Director; Jake Guy Nicholls [1990] Director; Julie Anne Nicholls [1962] Director; Shirley Nicholls [1935] Director/Company Secretary; Trudi Louise Nicholls [1960] Director

Presdales School Academy Trust
Incorporated: 14 March 2012 *Employees:* 181
Net Worth: £11,170,361 *Total Assets:* £13,057,244
Registered Office: Presdales School Academy Trust, Hoe Lane, Ware, Herts, SG12 9NX
Activities: General secondary education
Officers: Paul Stewart Abraham [1976] Regional Director; Kathleen Veronica Belinis [1952] Director/Chief Executive Officer; Oyindamola Temitope Bishi [1974] Director/Marketing Professional; Peter Joseph Dougherty [1946] Director/Retired Building Surveyor; Revd Mark Philip Dunstan [1970] Director/Minister of Religion/Anglican Priest; Patrick Lloyd Edwards [1961] Director/Chief Executive; Howard Leslie Freed [1952] Director/Self Employed Education Consultant; Jacqueline Yvonne Janet Harvey [1964] Director/Homemaker; Geoffrey Raymond Hayter [1966] Director/Local Government Accountancy; Alison Hobson [1970] Director/Marketing Manager; Michael Alan Robinson [1951] Director/Retired; Madeline Anne Waller [1966] Director/Event Manager; Matthew Lee Warren [1973] Director/Headteacher

Preston Manor Academy Trust
Incorporated: 14 January 2013 *Employees:* 251
Net Worth: £27,444,716 *Total Assets:* £31,668,798
Registered Office: Preston Manor School, Carlton Avenue East, Wembley, Middlesex, HA9 8NA
Activities: General secondary education
Officers: Jonathan Richard Bach [1956] Director/Education Consultant; Badrun Nessa Salina Chowdhury [1973] Director; Everton Counsell [1966] Director; Sandra Eismann [1978] Director; Beth Ann Kobel [1971] Director/Headteacher; Susan Estella Lawrence [1963] Director/Headteacher; Vivek Luthra [1971] Director; Shiraz Nasrabadi [1968] Director; Donald Balford Palmer [1962] Director/Lecturer; Kinna Patel [1988] Director/Product Manager; Leela Paul [1990] Director/Teacher; Deborah Margaret Sloan [1988] Director [Irish]

Pretoria Energy Company (Chittering) Limited
Incorporated: 24 February 2012 *Employees:* 7
Previous: Pretoria Energy Company Limited
Net Worth: £3,775,887 *Total Assets:* £30,328,772
Registered Office: Padro House, Chear Fen, Ely Road, Chittering, Cambridge, CB25 9GE
Activities: Production of electricity
Parent: Pretoria Energy Company Holdings Limited
Officers: Steven David Ely Ripley [1968] Director; Andrew Rhead Shaw [1947] Director/Chartered Accountant

Pretoria Energy Company (Mepal) Limited
Incorporated: 27 January 2015 *Employees:* 11
Net Worth: £427,661 *Total Assets:* £61,717,656
Registered Office: Padro House, Chear Fen, Ely Road, Chittering, Cambridge, CB25 9GE
Activities: Production of electricity
Parent: Pretoria Energy Company Holdings Limited
Officers: Steven David Ely Ripley [1968] Director; Andrew Rhead Shaw [1947] Director

PRGX UK Ltd
Incorporated: 8 February 1980 *Employees:* 196
Net Worth: £3,110,030 *Total Assets:* £20,247,620
Registered Office: 731 Capability Green, Luton, Beds, LU1 3LU
Activities: Accounting and auditing activities
Parent: PRGX UK Holdings Ltd
Officers: Tracey Field, Secretary; Ronald Edwin Stewart [1955] Director [American]

Price Bailey Group Limited
Incorporated: 12 December 2002 *Employees:* 362
Net Worth: £3,723,000 *Total Assets:* £16,839,000
Registered Office: Causeway House, Dane Street, Bishop's Stortford, Herts, CM23 3BT
Activities: Activities of other holding companies n.e.c.
Officers: Charles William Olley, Secretary/Chartered Accountant; Martin William Herbert Clapson [1967] Director/Chartered Accountant; Paul Nicholas Cullen [1967] Director/Accountant; Gary William Miller [1955] Director/Chartered Accountant; Charles William Olley [1958] Director/Chartered Accountant; Howard William Sears [1964] Director/Chartered Accountant

Price Bailey LLP
Incorporated: 1 April 2004 *Employees:* 316
Net Worth: £3,707,000 *Total Assets:* £14,421,000
Registered Office: Causeway House, Dane Street, Bishop's Stortford, Herts, CM23 3BT
Officers: Martin William Herbert Clapson [1967] Member; Paul Nicholas Cullen [1967] Member; Gary William Miller [1955] Member; Charles William Olley [1958] Member; Howard William Sears [1964] Member; Simon James Blake [1973] LLP Member; Richard Arthur Day [1958] LLP Member; Jamie Paul Gladstone [1970] LLP Member; Christopher Godsave [1976] LLP Member; Richard James Grimster [1989] LLP Member; Daphne Christine Hemingway [1963] LLP Member; Matthew Robert Howard [1975] LLP Member; Nadia Eileen Khan [1974] LLP Member; James Andrew King [1971] LLP Member; Anthony Clayton Pennison [1970] LLP Member; Paul James Pittman [1965] LLP Member; Stephen Granville Reed [1968] LLP Member; Jayant Sanghrajka [1955] LLP Member; Jitendra Meghji Shah [1950] LLP Member; Trevor James Smith [1959] LLP Member; Stephen Michael Ufland [1954] LLP Member; Richard Leslie Vass [1967] LLP Member; Kirsty Warner [1980] LLP Member; John Spencer Warren [1960] LLP Member; Aaron Widdows [1969] LLP Member; Helena Wilkinson [1967] LLP Member; Catherine Louise Willshire [1974] LLP Member; William Jack Wilson [1978] LLP Member

M.Price Limited
Incorporated: 6 May 1958 *Employees:* 146
Net Worth: £6,959,844 *Total Assets:* £18,238,488
Registered Office: 1 Haslemere Business Centre, Lincoln Way, Enfield, Middlesex, EN1 1DX
Activities: Glazing
Parent: M Price Group Limited
Officers: Colin Frank Chapman, Secretary; Beverley Pauline Chapman [1972] Director; Colin Frank Chapman [1965] Director; Daren Robert Fletcher [1970] Construction Director; Adam Waring [1977] Managing Director

Pride Care Homes Peterborough Limited
Incorporated: 2 March 2016 *Employees:* 49
Net Worth: £4,063,726 *Total Assets:* £10,553,846
Registered Office: 236 Eastfield Road, Peterborough, PE1 4BD
Activities: Residential care activities for the elderly and disabled
Officers: Ajay Majara [1979] Director; Amar Majara [1977] Director; Baldev Singh Majara [1947] Director; Shamshad Bano Majara [1945] Director

Primagraphics Limited
Incorporated: 26 April 1982 *Employees:* 47
Net Worth: £18,513,300 *Total Assets:* £39,947,688
Registered Office: Cambridge House, Number 2 Focus Four, Fourth Avenue, Letchworth Garden City, Herts, SG6 2TU
Activities: Manufacture of computers and peripheral equipment
Parent: Curtiss-Wright Controls (UK) Limited
Officers: Paul Jude Ferdenzi, Secretary; Harry Jakubowitz, Secretary; Marc Sebastian O'Casal, Secretary; Robert Shaw, Secretary [American]; Glenn Edward Tynan, Secretary/Business Executive [American]; Kathryn Rose Barron [1974] Director/Division Controller [Canadian]; Kenneth Evans [1952] Director; Mark Liversidge [1963] Director/General Manager Avionics UK Business, CWC; Kevin Terence Andrew Rooney [1964] Director/General Management; Robert Shaw [1952] Director/Lawyer [American]; Glenn Edward Tynan [1958] Director/Vice President & CFO [American]

Prime Estates Limited
Incorporated: 11 June 1984 *Employees:* 2
Net Worth: £9,551,276 *Total Assets:* £9,864,104
Registered Office: 64 Wilbury Way, Hitchin, Herts, SG4 0TP
Activities: Activities of other holding companies n.e.c.
Shareholders: Regina Emily Louise Bandet; Henry John Harper Bandet; Boyer Investments Limited
Officers: Regina Emily Louise Bandet [1960] Director [American]; Solomon Benjamin Benaim [1955] Director; Isabel Alice Melina Frances Boyer [1961] Director; Jack Byron Boyer [1959] Alternate Director

Prime Place (Millbrook) LLP
Incorporated: 16 October 2015 *Employees:* 2
Net Worth: £13,058,760 *Total Assets:* £36,097,628
Registered Office: Spirella, 2 Icknield Way, Letchworth Garden City, Herts, SG6 4GY

Prime Place (Woking Island Site) LLP
Incorporated: 30 October 2015 *Employees:* 3
Net Worth: £9,718,551 *Total Assets:* £13,387,849
Registered Office: Spirella, 2 Icknield Way, Letchworth Garden City, Herts, SG6 4GY

Princebuild Holdings Limited
Incorporated: 27 November 1985 *Employees:* 201
Net Worth: £12,185,303 *Total Assets:* £23,969,410
Registered Office: Empson Road, Peterborough, Cambs, PE1 5UP
Activities: Development of building projects
Officers: Stuart Stanley Pudney, Secretary; Dale John Asplin [1970] Director/Contracts Manager; Derek John Asplin [1947] Director; Mark Derek Asplin [1966] Director/Contracts Manager; Jonathan Mark Pudney [1969] Director/Contracts Manager; Matthew James Pudney [1972] Director/Contracts Manager; Stuart Stanley Pudney [1944] Director

Princebuild Limited.
Incorporated: 7 October 1971 *Employees:* 196
Net Worth: £7,126,583 *Total Assets:* £21,868,492
Registered Office: Empson Road, Peterborough, Cambs, PE1 5UP
Activities: Development of building projects
Parent: Princebuild Holdings Ltd
Officers: Stuart Stanley Pudney, Secretary; Dale John Asplin [1970] Director; Derek John Asplin [1947] Director; Mark Derek Asplin [1966] Director; Paul Baker [1979] Construction Director; James Manning [1972] Director; Jonathan Mark Pudney [1969] Director; Matthew James Pudney [1972] Director; Stuart Stanley Pudney [1944] Director

Princes Risborough School
Incorporated: 20 July 2011 *Employees:* 143
Net Worth: £11,860,974 *Total Assets:* £15,184,344
Registered Office: Princes Risborough School, Merton Road, Princes Risborough, Bucks, HP27 0DT
Activities: General secondary education
Officers: Nicholas Jonathan Simms, Secretary; Rachel Ann Gray [1972] Director/IT Consultant; Peggy Hulse [1953] Director/Education Consultant; Kate Louise Nicolle [1974] Director/Learning & Training Development Manager; Samantha Marie Owen [1966] Director/Examinations Investigator; Peter John Rowe [1962] Director/Executive Headteacher; Andrew Charles Rysdale [1973] Director/Chartered Surveyor; Barry David Tomkins [1943] Director; Fiona Elizabeth Waterhouse [1968] Director/School Business Manager

Prinhold Limited
Incorporated: 1 August 2011 *Employees:* 1
Net Worth: £3,164,371 *Total Assets:* £23,869,468
Registered Office: c/o Hillier Hopkins LLP, Radius House, 51 Clarendon Road, Watford, Herts, WD17 1HP
Activities: Other letting and operating of own or leased real estate
Major Shareholder: Jonathan Russell Beck
Officers: Jonathan Russell Beck [1967] Director/Investor

Prior Scientific Instruments Limited
Incorporated: 4 February 1946 *Employees:* 99
Net Worth: £10,867,939 *Total Assets:* £13,114,236
Registered Office: Units 3-4 Fielding Industrial Estate, Wilbraham Road, Fulbourn, Cambridge, CB21 5ET
Activities: Manufacture of medical and dental instruments and supplies
Shareholders: Myles John O'Leary Fielding; James Fielding; Fintan Fitzgerald Fielding
Officers: Simon John Smith, Secretary; Fintan FitzGenerald Fielding [1972] Director [Irish]; James Finbar Lockyer Fielding [1970] Director; Myles John O'Leary Fielding [1969] Director [Irish]; Thomas Freda [1960] Director/President of Prior Scientific [American]; Stuart Jarvis [1967] Director/R&D Engineer; Simon John Smith [1967] Director/Accountant

Pro Cam CP Limited
Incorporated: 17 May 1979 *Employees:* 210
Net Worth: £20,610,000 *Total Assets:* £42,218,000
Registered Office: 2020 Cambourne Business Park, Cambourne, Cambridge, CB23 6DW
Activities: Support activities for crop production
Parent: Pro Cam UK Ltd
Officers: Michael John Andrews, Company Secretary; Ian Donald Beswick [1960] Director; John David Bianchi [1958] Commercial Director; Christopher John Butt [1951] Managing Director; Diane Rachel Heath [1973] Managing Director; David John Parish [1964] Director/Chartered Accountant; Anthony John White [1942] Director

Pro Cam Europe Limited
Incorporated: 22 November 2007 *Employees:* 570
Net Worth: £19,462,000 *Total Assets:* £87,089,000
Registered Office: 2020 Cambourne Business Park, Cambourne, Cambridge, CB23 6DW
Activities: Support activities for crop production
Major Shareholder: Anthony John White
Officers: David John Parish, Secretary; Ian Donald Beswick [1960] Director/Chartered Accountant; Christopher John Butt [1951] Director; Anthony John White [1942] Director

Pro Cam UK Limited
Incorporated: 12 April 1989 *Employees:* 30
Net Worth: £4,469,000 *Total Assets:* £11,878,000
Registered Office: 2020 Cambourne Business Park, Cambourne, Cambridge, CB23 6DW
Activities: Activities of agricultural holding companies
Parent: Pro Cam Europe Ltd
Officers: Michael John Andrews, Secretary; Ian Donald Beswick [1960] Director/Chartered Accountant; John David Bianchi [1958] Managing Director; Christopher John Butt [1951] Director; Diane Rachel Heath [1973] Managing Director; David John Parish [1964] Director/Chartered Accountant; Anthony John White [1942] Director

Probe Oil Tools Limited
Incorporated: 26 April 1974 *Employees:* 36
Net Worth: £27,821,000 *Total Assets:* £29,237,000
Registered Office: Ferryside, Ferry Road, Norwich, NR1 1SW
Activities: Other manufacturing n.e.c.
Parent: Acteon Group Limited
Officers: David Brennan [1962] Director; Dr Bernhard Bruggaier [1961] Director [German]

Process Sensing Technologies Ltd.
Incorporated: 14 October 2016 *Employees:* 2
Net Worth: £39,677,968 *Total Assets:* £123,401,472
Registered Office: 48 Lancaster Way Business Park, Ely, Cambs, CB6 3NW
Activities: Other engineering activities
Parent: BV PMT Holdings Ltd.
Officers: Jesse Ross Feldman [1977] Director/Private Equity Investor [American]; Adam Dean Markin [1966] Director/Chairman; Zachary Smotherman [1983] Director/Private Equity Investor [American]

Proctor Bros. (Long Sutton) Limited
Incorporated: 14 March 1949 *Employees:* 35
Net Worth: £4,855,801 *Total Assets:* £11,185,980
Registered Office: c/o Duncan & Toplis Limited, Enterprise Way, Pinchbeck, Spalding, Lincs, PE11 3YR
Activities: Growing of cereals (except rice), leguminous crops and oil seeds
Major Shareholder: Stafford Julian Allin Proctor
Officers: Stafford Julian Allin Proctor, Secretary; Julian Hickman Proctor [1938] Director/Farmer; Rosalind Diana May Proctor [1939] Director; Stafford Julian Allin Proctor [1968] Director/Farm Manager; Sue Emma Proctor [1967] Director/Freelance Journalist

The Produce Connection Limited
Incorporated: 24 November 1995 *Employees:* 21
Net Worth: £4,090,441 *Total Assets:* £11,902,403
Registered Office: Padro House, Ely Road, Chittering, Cambs, CB25 9PZ
Activities: Landscape service activities
Major Shareholder: Steven David Ely Ripley
Officers: Andrew Rhead Shaw, Secretary; Steven David Ely Ripley [1968] Director/Produce Merchant

Produce Investments Limited
Incorporated: 16 November 2005 *Employees:* 1,233
Previous: Produce Investments PLC
Net Worth: £44,146,000 *Total Assets:* £114,788,000
Registered Office: Greenvale AP, Floods Ferry Road, Doddington, March, Cambs, PE15 0UW
Activities: Activities of head offices
Officers: John Clegg, Secretary; Angus Stuart Walton Armstrong [1964] Director; Angus Burt [1984] Director; Michael Burt [1975] Director; Mark Raymond Clarke [1964] Director; John Clegg [1979] Director

Produce World Group Ltd
Incorporated: 23 October 1995 *Employees:* 606
Net Worth: £4,392,000 *Total Assets:* £37,972,000
Registered Office: Stanley's Farm, Great Drove, Yaxley, Peterborough, PE7 3TW
Activities: Wholesale of fruit and vegetables
Parent: Produce World Investments Ltd
Officers: Ian Alexander Anderson [1968] Director; James Edward Barker [1977] Director; David William Ashley Burgess [1968] Director; Geoff Calder [1953] Director

Produce World Investments Ltd
Incorporated: 27 September 1995 *Employees:* 612
Net Worth: £3,618,000 *Total Assets:* £42,609,000
Registered Office: Stanley's Farm, Great Drove, Yaxley, Peterborough, PE7 3TW
Activities: Activities of head offices
Parent: Russell Burgess Ltd
Officers: James Edward Barker [1977] Director; Andrew Stanley Burgess [1965] Director; David William Ashley Burgess [1968] Director; Jason Charles Burgess [1966] Director; David Michael Higgins [1956] Director; Robert Giles Russell Smith [1951] Director/Farming

The Professional Darts Corporation Limited
Incorporated: 28 November 1997 *Employees:* 13
Net Worth: £6,876,134 *Total Assets:* £12,316,423
Registered Office: Mascalls Lane, Great Warley, Brentwood, Essex, CM14 5LJ
Activities: Other sports activities
Shareholder: Matchroom Sport Ltd
Officers: Wendy Frances Barker, Secretary; Rodney Kenneth Harrington [1957] Director/Pro Sportsman; Barry Maurice William Hearn [1948] Director/Chartered Accountant; Edward John Hearn [1979] Director; Edward Robert Charles Lowy [1962] Director; Matthew Richard Porter [1980] Director/Chief Executive; Marcus Craigie Robertson [1956] Director/Chairman; Robert Scott [1953] Director; Oliver Michael Slipper [1976] Director

Progress Rail Services UK Limited
Incorporated: 28 February 2011 *Employees:* 400
Net Worth: £43,466,000 *Total Assets:* £62,417,000
Registered Office: Eastfield, Frank Perkins Way, Peterborough, Cambs, PE1 5FQ
Activities: Construction of railways and underground railways
Parent: Caterpillar Luxembourg S.A.R.L.
Officers: Johanna Elizabeth Deason, Secretary; Nigel John Burroughs [1964] Director/Tax Account; Colin Murphy [1962] Managing Director; Jonathan George Newman [1974] Director/Senior Vice President Corporate Services [American]

Project Helix Holdco Ltd
Incorporated: 19 December 2014 *Employees:* 5
Net Worth Deficit: £14,124 *Total Assets:* £23,940,140
Registered Office: Decimal Place, Chiltern Avenue, Amersham, Bucks, HP6 5FG
Activities: Activities of construction holding companies
Parent: CPC Helix Ltd
Officers: Andrew John Chrysostomou [1984] Director/Chartered Surveyor; Nishith Malde [1958] Director; Gary John Skinner [1968] Managing Director

Prometic Pharma SMT Limited
Incorporated: 11 December 2015 *Employees:* 11
Net Worth: £55,836,120 *Total Assets:* £82,372,512
Registered Office: Prometic Pharma SMT Limited, Horizon Park, Barton Road, Comberton, Cambridge, CB23 7AJ
Activities: Manufacture of basic pharmaceutical products
Parent: Prometic Pharma SMT Holdings Limited
Officers: Prof. Simon Geoffrey Best [1956] Director; Kurt Stefan Victor Clulow [1970] Director [Canadian/British]; Kenneth Harry Galbraith [1962] Director [Canadian]; David John Jeans [1950] Director; Dr John Edward Moran [1945] Director/Chief Medical Officer [American/Canadian]; Bruce Philip Pritchard [1972] Director; Patrick Sartore [1974] Director and Company Secretary [Canadian]; Bruce Jeffrey Wendel [1953] Director [American]

Property & Investment Management Limited
Incorporated: 21 January 1994 *Employees:* 3
Net Worth: £10,487,334 *Total Assets:* £14,908,334
Registered Office: 39 Windsor End, Beaconsfield, Bucks, HP9 2JN
Activities: Buying and selling of own real estate
Shareholders: Ian Benington Trott; Anne Norina Trott
Officers: Philip James Marsh, Secretary/Chartered Surveyor; Philip James Marsh [1960] Director/Chartered Surveyor; Anne Norina Trott [1934] Director; Ian Benington Trott [1932] Director/Accountant

Property and Commercial Enterprises Limited
Incorporated: 25 June 1984 *Employees:* 21
Previous: Property and Commercial Enterprises PLC
Net Worth: £7,750,735 *Total Assets:* £17,964,918
Registered Office: 461-463 Southchurch Road, Southend on Sea, Essex, SS1 2PH
Activities: Buying and selling of own real estate
Major Shareholder: Bernard Jeffery Horwood
Officers: Bernard Jeffrey Horwood, Secretary; Bernard Jeffrey Horwood [1953] Director; Crystal Jayne Horwood [1979] Business Development Director

Property Finance Capital Limited
Incorporated: 21 July 2010 *Employees:* 1
Net Worth: £23,820 *Total Assets:* £60,334,692
Registered Office: 1st Floor, Health Aid House, Marlborough Hill, Harrow, Middlesex, HA1 1UD
Activities: Financial intermediation not elsewhere classified
Parent: Alternative Bridging Corporation Limited
Officers: Robert Jeffrey Piper, Secretary; Giovanni Primo Losi [1948] Director [Italian]; Stephen Daniel Meller [1967] Director/Finance Broker; Melvin Frank Robinson [1956] Director; Brian Leslie Rubins [1939] Director; Jonathan Rubins [1967] Director

Property Finance Nominees (No.3) Limited
Incorporated: 29 May 1996
Net Worth: £100 *Total Assets:* £57,545,068
Registered Office: 1st Floor, Health Aid House, Marlborough Hill, Harrow, Middlesex, HA1 1UD
Activities: Financial intermediation not elsewhere classified
Parent: Alternative Bridging Corporation Limited
Officers: Robert Jeffrey Piper, Secretary; Stephen Daniel Meller [1967] Director/Finance Broker; Brian Leslie Rubins [1939] Director; Jonathan Rubins [1967] Director

Property Recycling Group PLC
Incorporated: 31 March 2005 *Employees:* 3
Net Worth: £15,107,962 *Total Assets:* £23,319,254
Registered Office: Manor Farm, Bridgham, Norwich, NR16 2RX
Activities: Buying and selling of own real estate
Officers: Paul Anthony Rackham Snr [1936] Director; Paul Anthony Rackham Jnr [1965] Director; Stephen Russell Stuteley [1955] Director

The Property Warehouse Limited
Incorporated: 22 October 2003 *Employees:* 1
Net Worth Deficit: £1,183,714 *Total Assets:* £10,018,453
Registered Office: 19-20 Bourne Court, Southend Road, Woodford Green, Essex, IG8 8HD
Activities: Development of building projects
Parent: AVDIME Limited
Officers: Tracey Joanna Aviram, Secretary; David Aviram [1953] Director

Propshop Limited
Incorporated: 14 November 1994 *Employees:* 55
Net Worth: £9,423,196 *Total Assets:* £16,431,915
Registered Office: Building 425, Duxford Airfield, Duxford, Cambridge, CB22 4QR
Activities: Service activities incidental to air transportation
Major Shareholder: John James Romain
Officers: Anna Marie Adriana McDowell, Secretary; John James Romain [1959] Director/Engineer

Proquest European Holdings Limited
Incorporated: 8 May 2013 *Employees:* 430
Net Worth: £44,910,680 *Total Assets:* £61,985,740
Registered Office: The Quorum, Barnwell Road, Cambridge, CB5 8SW
Activities: Other publishing activities
Parent: Proquest LLC
Officers: Justin Paul Jonathan Allen [1972] Director; Patrick Michael Randall [1964] Director [American]; Larisa Avner Trainor [1970] Director [American]

Proquest Information and Learning Limited
Incorporated: 5 February 1973 *Employees:* 401
Net Worth: £10,167,443 *Total Assets:* £32,391,066
Registered Office: The Quorum, Barnwell Road, Cambridge, CB5 8SW
Activities: Other publishing activities
Parent: Proquest UK Holdings Limited
Officers: Justin Paul Jonathan Allen, Secretary/Accountant; Justin Paul Jonathan Allen [1972] Director/Accountant; Larisa Avner Trainor [1970] Director/Informational Services [American]

Proquest UK Holdings Ltd
Incorporated: 21 June 1968 *Employees:* 418
Net Worth: £29,773,760 *Total Assets:* £38,280,296
Registered Office: The Quorum, Barnwell Road, Cambridge, CB5 8SW
Activities: Other information service activities n.e.c.
Parent: Proquest European Holdings Limited
Officers: Larisa Avner Trainor, Secretary/Lawyer [American]; Justin Paul Jonathan Allen [1972] Director/Accountant; Larisa Avner Trainor [1970] Director/Lawyer [American]

Provide Community Interest Company
Incorporated: 20 July 2010 *Employees:* 1,017
Net Worth: £5,264,497 *Total Assets:* £16,994,058
Registered Office: 900 The Crescent, Colchester Business Park, Colchester, Essex, CO4 9YQ
Activities: Other human health activities
Officers: Philip Brian Richards, Secretary; Dr Virginia Craig [1957] Director; Stephanie Dawe [1963] Director/Chief Nurse; Derek Mark Heasman [1964] Director; Derrick Jonathan Louis [1965] Director; John Joseph Niland [1962] Director/Chief Executive [Irish]; Philip Brian Richards [1962] Finance Director; Victoria Frances Ann Waldon [1966] Executive Director Integrated Pathway Hub; Rachael White [1969] Finance Director

Providence Marian Company
Incorporated: 8 April 2009 *Employees:* 5
Net Worth: £22,268,136 *Total Assets:* £25,274,174
Registered Office: Providence House, 4 Melbourn Road, Royston, Herts, SG8 7DB
Activities: Other business support service activities n.e.c.
Officers: Sister Veronica Maguire, Secretary; Sister Margaret Cloghessy [1928] Director/Religious Sister [Irish]; Sister Marthe Marie Dachet [1943] Director/Religious Sister [Belgian]; Sister Genevieve Cecile Defrenne [1941] Director/Religious Sister [Belgian]; Sister Mary Flannigan [1928] Director/Religious Sister [Irish]; Sister Martha Magdalena Geers [1939] Director/Religious Sister [Belgian]; Mary Hannaway [1929] Director/Religious Sister [Irish]; Sister Marie-Jose Herbeuval [1946] Director/Religious Sister [Belgian]; Veronica Maguire [1929] Director/Religious Sister [Irish]; Sister Patricia Ryan [1938] Director/Religious Sister [Irish]

PS Construction Investments Ltd
Incorporated: 21 November 2013
Net Worth: £9,185,047 *Total Assets:* £9,185,047
Registered Office: Dickens House, Guithavon Street, Witham, Essex, CM8 1BJ
Activities: Buying and selling of own real estate
Parent: Sextant Consolidated Limited
Officers: Vincenzo Bianchi [1958] Director [Italian]; Philip Lawrence [1953] Director; Siro Picchio [1957] Director [Italian]

Punjab House Associated Ltd
Incorporated: 13 October 2011 *Employees:* 2
Net Worth: £7,387,622 *Total Assets:* £13,301,499
Registered Office: 232a Northolt Road, Harrow, Middlesex, HA2 8DU
Activities: Other letting and operating of own or leased real estate
Shareholders: Surinder Kaur Chopra; Surinder Kaur Chopra
Officers: Waryam Singh Kakol [1970] Director/Consultant [Dutch]

Purcell School (The)
Incorporated: 30 April 1963 *Employees:* 142
Net Worth: £13,554,334 *Total Assets:* £14,567,751
Registered Office: The Purcell School, Aldenham Road, Bushey, Watford, Herts, WD23 2TS
Activities: General secondary education
Officers: Aideen Catherine McNamara, Secretary; Charles Esmond Beer [1956] Director/Tax Adviser; Professor Timothy James Blinko [1965] Director/Academic; Jonathan Edward Eley [1971] Director/Solicitor; James Christopher Fowler [1962] Director/Headmaster; Janice Graham [1968] Director/Violinist; Sir Roger Tustin Jackling [1943] Director/Retired; Professor Colin James Lawson [1949] Director/Academic; William Rufus Benjamin McDonnell [1973] Director/Group Chief Risk Officer; Dr Rebecca Mooney [1968] Director/Solicitor; Ian Hearle David Odgers [1938] Director/Executive Search; Mark Edmund Racz [1955] Director/Academic [American]; Joanna Van Heyningen [1945] Director/Architect; Kirsty Von Malaise [1974] Director/Headmistress

Pure International Limited
Incorporated: 23 September 2016 *Employees:* 61
Net Worth: £5,263,746 *Total Assets:* £12,681,089
Registered Office: Concept House, Home Park Road, Kings Langley, Herts, WD4 8UD
Activities: Manufacture of consumer electronics
Shareholder: Ing. Christian Trapl
Officers: Johann Hager [1949] Director [Austrian]; Martin Muller [1988] Director [Austrian]; Sir Hossein Yassaie [1956] Director/Chairman

Pure Recycling Warwick Limited
Incorporated: 26 November 2007 *Employees:* 7
Net Worth Deficit: £5,021,000 *Total Assets:* £15,515,000
Registered Office: Tempsford Hall, Sandy, Beds, SG19 2BD
Activities: Treatment and disposal of non-hazardous waste
Parent: Kier Services Limited
Officers: Bethan Melges, Secretary; Nigel Roderick Sheppard [1957] Contracts Director; Lee Woodall [1976] Director

Purebond Limited
Incorporated: 9 July 1991
Net Worth: £8,761,799 *Total Assets:* £9,725,268
Registered Office: Portland House, 69-71 Wembley Hill Road, Wembley, Middlesex, HA9 8BU
Activities: Other service activities n.e.c.
Parent: Solai Holdings Limited
Officers: Bhupendra Shantilal Kansagra, Secretary; Bhupendra Shantilal Kansagra [1956] Director; Ramesh Shantilal Kansagra [1950] Director; Rishi Ramesh Kansagra [1981] Director

Purple Surgical Holdings Limited
Incorporated: 26 April 1973 *Employees:* 143
Net Worth: £5,076,322 *Total Assets:* £12,701,356
Registered Office: York House, Empire Way, Wembley, Middlesex, HA9 0FQ
Activities: Activities of head offices
Major Shareholder: Robert Sharpe
Officers: Philip David Franklin, Secretary; Richard Lampert [1948] Director/Chartered Accountant; Jane Eddy Sharpe [1967] Director/Executive; Robert Sharpe [1963] Director

Purslow Investments Limited
Incorporated: 3 April 2012
Previous: New Malden Golf Centre Limited
Net Worth: £4,433,190 *Total Assets:* £11,433,935
Registered Office: 1st Floor, 5 Century Court, Tolpits Lane, Watford, Herts, WD18 9PX
Activities: Operation of sports facilities
Major Shareholder: Christian Mark Cecil Purslow
Officers: Christian Mark Cecil Purslow [1963] Director; Jayne Elizabeth Purslow [1962] Director

PX Manufacturing Ltd
Incorporated: 19 October 1994 *Employees:* 46
Previous: P X Manufacturing & Distribution Company Limited
Net Worth: £9,952,654 *Total Assets:* £28,387,940
Registered Office: 40 Thorby Avenue, March, Cambs, PE15 0AZ
Activities: Manufacture of electricity distribution and control apparatus
Officers: Elzbieta Tetnowska, Secretary; Dr Pawel Tomil Tetnowski [1970] Director; Rafal Tetnowski [1971] Director; Stanislaw Frank Tetnowski [1943] Director [Polish]

PXP Financial Limited
Incorporated: 22 April 2005 *Employees:* 3
Previous: Kalixa Accept Limited
Net Worth: £10,989,590 *Total Assets:* £77,055,944
Registered Office: The Corn Mill, 1 Roydon Road, Stanstead Abbotts, Herts, SG12 8XL
Activities: Banks
Parent: Kalixa Payments Group Limited
Officers: Jonathan Richard Bell [1972] Director/Chief Financial Officer; Gabriele Anna Griesbacher [1977] Director [Austrian]; Richard Alan Knight [1972] Director/Head of Risk and Compliance; Koen Peter Vanpraet [1968] Director/Chief Executive Officer [Belgian]; Keith James Woodhead [1973] Director/Chartered Accountant

Q Acoustics Limited
Incorporated: 26 June 2014 *Employees:* 92
Net Worth: £72,016 *Total Assets:* £11,336,041
Registered Office: Units 7 & 8 Stortford Hall Industrial Park, Dunmow Road, Bishop's Stortford, Herts, CM23 5GZ
Activities: Activities of distribution holding companies
Shareholder: George Leonard Dexter
Officers: Nicola Ann Spence, Secretary; George Leonard Dexter [1962] Director; Chris William Emerson [1957] Director; Nicola Ann Spence [1962] Director

Q V Foods Limited
Incorporated: 14 June 1988 *Employees:* 379
Net Worth: £10,826,000 *Total Assets:* £29,194,000
Registered Office: Fleet Estate Office, Manor Farm, Holbeach Hurn, Holbeach, Spalding, Lincs, PE12 8LR
Activities: Other processing and preserving of fruit and vegetables
Parent: AHW (Operating) Co Limited
Officers: Mark Richard Henson, Secretary; Martin John Taylor [1971] Group Managing Director; Duncan Richard Worth [1965] Director/Farmer

Q.N. Hotels Limited
Incorporated: 6 September 1993 *Employees:* 120
Net Worth: £11,607,775 *Total Assets:* £19,404,120
Registered Office: QN House, Unit 4 Loughton Business Centre, 5 Langston Road, Loughton, Essex, IG10 3FL
Activities: Hotels and similar accommodation
Officers: Qamar Ahmed, Secretary/Hotelier; Aftab Ahmed [1944] Director/Hotelier; Qamar Ahmed [1973] Director/Hotelier

Qatar Bloodstock Limited
Incorporated: 28 October 2010
Net Worth: £3,479,189 *Total Assets:* £64,815,956
Registered Office: Lushington House, 119 High Street, Newmarket, Suffolk, CB8 9AE
Activities: Other retail sale not in stores, stalls or markets
Parent: QIPCO Holdings
Officers: Sheikh Fahad Bin Abdulla Bin Khalifa Al Thani [1989] Executive Director [Qatari]; Kareem Adeeb Abdallah Altaji [1966] Director of Finance [Jordanian]; David John Luke Redvers [1970] Director/Certified Chartered Accountant

Qatar Racing Limited
Incorporated: 23 March 2012 *Employees:* 4
Net Worth Deficit: £68,835,544 *Total Assets:* £21,275,036
Registered Office: Lushington House, 119 High Street, Newmarket, Suffolk, CB8 9AE
Activities: Activities of racehorse owners
Parent: QIPCO Holdings
Officers: Sheikh Fahad Abdulla Al Thani [1989] Director/Special Adviser [Qatari]; Kareem Adeeb Abdallah Altaji [1966] Director/Accountant [Qatari]; David John Luke Redvers [1970] Director/Stud Farmer

QED (Slough) Limited
Incorporated: 6 October 2005 *Employees:* 3
Net Worth Deficit: £9,022,633 *Total Assets:* £45,413,172
Registered Office: 2 Hunting Gate, Hitchin, Herts, SG4 0TJ
Activities: Construction of other civil engineering projects n.e.c.
Parent: QED (Slough) Holdings Limited
Officers: Alastair William Hopps [1986] Director/Accountant; Alexander Toby Shedden Parry [1976] Director/Chartered Accountant

QED Luton (Challney) Holdings Limited
Incorporated: 24 March 2009
Net Worth Deficit: £6,871,000 *Total Assets:* £30,447,000
Registered Office: 2 Hunting Gate, Hitchin, Herts, SG4 0TJ
Activities: Other business support service activities n.e.c.
Shareholders: Building Schools for The Future Investments LLP; The Council of The Borough of Luton
Officers: Kate Louise Flaherty [1980] Investment Director; Robin Stuart Porter [1973] BSF Programme Director

QED Luton (Challney) Limited
Incorporated: 24 March 2009
Net Worth Deficit: £6,871,000 *Total Assets:* £30,447,000
Registered Office: 2 Hunting Gate, Hitchin, Herts, SG4 0TJ
Activities: Other business support service activities n.e.c.
Parent: Luton Challney (REFICO) Limited
Officers: Kate Louise Flaherty [1980] Investment Director; Robin Stuart Porter [1973] BSF Programme Director

QI Partners
Incorporated: 22 May 2015 *Employees:* 4
Previous: CFH Facilities
Net Worth: £59,307,000 *Total Assets:* £81,193,000
Registered Office: Quadram Institute Bioscience, Colney Lane, Colney, Norwich, NR4 7UA
Activities: Combined facilities support activities
Officers: David Foreman, Secretary; Dr Timothy Brears [1961] Director; Dr Paul Roland Burrows [1960] Executive Director Policy, Strategy and Evidence; Philip Mark Redvers Davies [1958] Director/Chief Executive; Professor David John Richardson [1964] Director/Vice Chancellor

QOTD Film Investment Limited
Incorporated: 11 October 2013
Net Worth Deficit: £134,285 *Total Assets:* £8,769,251
Registered Office: 3rd Floor, Vyman House, 104 College Road, Harrow, Middlesex, HA1 1BQ
Activities: Motion picture production activities
Officers: Michael Benaroya [1981] Director [American]

Quadram Institute Bioscience
Incorporated: 16 January 1995 *Employees:* 140
Previous: The Institute of Food Research
Net Worth: £36,273,000 *Total Assets:* £40,941,000
Registered Office: Norwich Research Park, Colney Lane, Norwich, NR4 7UA
Activities: Other research and experimental development on natural sciences and engineering
Officers: David Foreman, Secretary; Dr Timothy Brears [1961] Director; Dr Celia Ann Caulcott [1957] Director/Vice-Provost (Enterprise) UCL; Professor Gordon Dougan [1952] Director/Scientist; Professor Stephen Michael Feast [1960] Managing Director; Professor Peter John Morgan [1956] Director/Academic Research Professor; Dr Steven James Walker [1960] Director General; Stephen Raymond West [1958] Finance Director

Quadro Epsom Limited
Incorporated: 3 May 2006
Previous: Quadro Design Limited
Net Worth: £8,000 *Total Assets:* £9,785,000
Registered Office: Harston Mill, Royston Road, Harston, Cambridge, CB22 7GG
Activities: Other professional, scientific and technical activities n.e.c.
Parent: Science Group PLC
Officers: Sarah Elizabeth Cole, Secretary; Rebecca Anne Archer [1981] Director; Sarah Elizabeth Cole [1979] Director/Lawyer

Qualcomm Technologies International, Ltd.
Incorporated: 11 November 1998 *Employees:* 658
Previous: Cambridge Silicon Radio Limited
Net Worth: £1,080,325,376 *Total Assets:* £3,480,067,840
Registered Office: Churchill House, Cambridge Business Park, Cowley Road, Cambridge, CB4 0WZ
Activities: Manufacture of electronic components
Parent: Cambridge Silicon Radio Holdings Limited
Officers: Kevin John Cadieux [1961] Director [American]; Gordon Thomas Rowe [1965] Senior Director, Finance [Canadian]

Quanta Consultancy Services Group Ltd
Incorporated: 15 June 2017 *Employees:* 57
Net Worth: £5,429,979 *Total Assets:* £18,037,472
Registered Office: Redwood House, Rectory Lane, Berkhamsted, Herts, HP4 2DH
Activities: Other professional, scientific and technical activities n.e.c.
Shareholders: Stephen John Trigg; David John Broome; Spencer James Trigg
Officers: David John Broome [1976] Director; Spencer James Trigg [1980] Director; Stephen John Trigg [1950] Director

Quanta Consultancy Services Limited
Incorporated: 6 April 1992 *Employees:* 57
Net Worth: £4,469,576 *Total Assets:* £16,980,568
Registered Office: Redwood House, Rectory Lane, Berkhamsted, Herts, HP4 2DH
Activities: Other professional, scientific and technical activities n.e.c.
Parent: Quanta Consultancy Services Group Limited
Officers: David John Broome [1976] Director; Spencer James Trigg [1980] Director; Stephen John Trigg [1950] Director

Quanticate Limited
Incorporated: 30 July 2007 *Employees:* 196
Net Worth: £7,449,886 *Total Assets:* £10,692,478
Registered Office: Bevan House, 9-11 Bancroft Court, Hitchin, Herts, SG5 1LH
Activities: Non-trading company
Major Shareholder: David Douglas Underwood
Officers: Daniel Simon Chapple [1973] Commercial Director; James Richard McDermott [1968] Director; Alan Stuart Morgan [1964] Director/Chief Operating Officer; David Douglas Underwood [1952] Director

Quartix Holdings PLC
Incorporated: 10 October 2007 *Employees:* 128
Net Worth: £19,452,000 *Total Assets:* £25,436,000
Registered Office: 9 Dukes Court, 54-62 Newmarket Road, Cambridge, CB5 8DZ
Activities: Manufacture of other transport equipment n.e.c.
Shareholder: Andrew John Walters
Officers: Daniel Christian Mendis, Secretary; Paul Victor Boughton [1955] Director; Daniel Christian Mendis [1982] Director/Chief Financial Officer; Andrew John Walters [1956] Director; David James Warwick [1965] Director

Quebec Court Freehold Limited
Incorporated: 11 May 2010 *Employees:* 4
Net Worth: £169,318 *Total Assets:* £9,496,658
Registered Office: Kajaine House, 57-67 High Street, Edgware, Middlesex, HA8 7DD
Activities: Other letting and operating of own or leased real estate
Major Shareholder: Tariq Mahmood Chaudhry
Officers: Ali Sattar Chaudri, Secretary; Kalim Ahmad Tahir [1956] Director/Finance Manager

Queen Elizabeth's Girls' School (Barnet)
Incorporated: 8 July 2011 *Employees:* 119
Net Worth: £17,166,906 *Total Assets:* £18,958,656
Registered Office: High Street, Barnet, Herts, EN5 5RR
Activities: General secondary education
Officers: Professor Ashley Braganza [1961] Director/University Professor; Dr Susan Cottam [1967] Director/Clinical Psychologist; Alison Davis [1963] Director/Chief Information Officer; Royden Gothelf [1960] Director/IT Production Manager; Rebecca Eloise Hanley [1967] Director/Broadcast Journalist; Lisa Hartshorn [1979] Director/Deputy Company Secretary; Alan James Jenner [1951] Director/Retired; Deborah Lane [1958] Director/Landscape Gardener; Dr Dewi Lewis [1967] Director/Chemist and Tutor; Bhavin Mistry [1984] Director/Head of Financial Operations; Uzoamaka Joy Nwamuu [1970] Director/Housewife; Rebecca Elizabeth Peer [1975] Director/Housewife; Hannah Ross [1980] Director/Lawyer; Carrie Arboleda Scott [1987] Director/Senior Auditor [American]; Violet Walker [1958] Director/Headteacher

Queen Elizabeth's School Barnet
Incorporated: 19 August 2010 *Employees:* 115
Net Worth: £24,766,726 *Total Assets:* £26,613,764
Registered Office: Queen Elizabeth's School Barnet, Queen's Road, Barnet, Herts, EN5 4DQ
Activities: General secondary education
Officers: Emine Aghdiran, Secretary; Matthew Beard [1968] Director/Public Relations; Anthony Michael Binstock [1983] Director/Self Employed; Martyn Henry Stewart Bradish [1951] Director/Chartered Accountant; David James Burton [1959] Director/Chartered Accountant; Kenneth Reginald Cooper [1931] Director; Roger Anthony Delves [1957] Director; Neil James Dominic Enright [1977] Director/Headmaster; David John Farrer [1943] Director; Jane Elizabeth Ferguson [1950] Director; Reverend Christopher Ferris [1977] Director/Clerk of Holy Orders; Andrew Nicholas Gaskell [1949] Director/Chartered Accountant; Maureen Janet Hooley [1952] Operations Director; Eric Houston [1952] Director; Anne MacDonald [1979] Director/Teacher; Barrie Robert Martin [1934] Director/Chartered Surveyor; Dr Caroline Martin [1969] Director/Science Adviser; Colin William Price [1961] Director/Teacher; Naresh Harsadray Raval [1957] Director/Architect; Patricia Reid [1967] Director/Health Visitor; Dr Voi Shim Wong [1961] Director/Medicine (Specialist) [Malaysian]

Queens' School (Bushey)
Incorporated: 27 May 2011 *Employees:* 175
Net Worth: £39,479,916 *Total Assets:* £41,587,780
Registered Office: Queens' School, Aldenham Road, Bushey, Herts, WD23 2LX
Activities: General secondary education
Officers: Tracy Anne Jenner, Secretary; Catherine Agnihotri [1965] Director/Support Worker (SEND); Lyndsey Rebecca Billinge [1984] Director/Teacher; Keith Burberry Cook [1963] Director/Accountant; Susan Mary Gorton [1960] Director/Examinations Officer; Gillian Sarah Kate Gray [1966] Director/Librarian; David Charles Hall [1944] Director/Retired; Sian Elizabeth Ann Henry [1969] Director/Social Work; Stephen Robert Jakeman [1956] Director/Accountant; Sunil Jobanputra [1989] Director/Civil Servant; Jonathan Morrell [1973] Director/Headteacher; Jayesh Jayantilal Patel [1982] Director/Train Operator; Rakesh Patel [1972] Director/Bank Manager; Julie Raybould [1967] Director/Recruitment Consultant; Clare Jean Rose [1975] Director/Service Delivery Manager; Carole Watson [1952] Director/Retired

Queensgate Finco Ltd
Incorporated: 9 December 2015
Net Worth: £10,434 *Total Assets:* £10,264,102
Registered Office: 505 Pinner Road, Harrow, Middlesex, HA2 6EH
Activities: Other letting and operating of own or leased real estate
Parent: Queensgate Mezz Hold Co Ltd
Officers: Jiten Rameshchandra Kantaria [1973] Director; Rupal Jiten Kantaria [1979] Director; Ramesh Chandra Govindji Sachdev [1945] Director

Queenswood School Limited
Incorporated: 22 February 1894 *Employees:* 176
Net Worth: £19,184,404 *Total Assets:* £23,533,380
Registered Office: Queenswood, Hatfield, Herts, AL9 6NS
Activities: General secondary education
Officers: Ian Williams, Secretary; Ralph Andrew Baines [1957] Director/Management Consultant; Reverend David Michael Chapman [1960] Director/Methodist Minister; Havilland James de Sausmarez [1958] Director/Investments; Timothy Claude Garnham [1956] Director/Chief Executive; Kate Olivia Harvey [1988] Director/Higher Education Regulatory and Governance Work; Dr Oonagh McGuinness [1965] Director/Doctor; Simon Morris [1962] Director/Headmaster; Natalie Penny [1979] Director; Andrew David Poppleton [1968] Director/Technology Consultant; Edmund Mark Sautter [1958] Director/Solicitor; Honourable Nicholas Stamp [1978] Director/Investment Banker; Revd Timothy Andrew Swindell [1960] Director/Chartered Accountant; Patricia May Wrinch [1962] Human Resources Director

Quest Motor Group Limited
Incorporated: 20 January 2004 *Employees:* 77
Net Worth: £1,557,223 *Total Assets:* £9,396,238
Registered Office: Quest House, 287 Rayne Road, Braintree, Essex, CM7 2QN
Activities: Sale of new cars and light motor vehicles
Parent: Gozzett Holdings Limited
Officers: Robin John Gozzett, Secretary; Martin John Gozzett [1962] Director; Robin John Gozzett [1956] Director

Quickdrop Limited
Incorporated: 2 September 2003
Net Worth Deficit: £5,668,109 *Total Assets:* £67,552,240
Registered Office: 3rd Floor, Sterling House, Langston Road, Loughton, Essex, IG10 3TS
Activities: Buying and selling of own real estate
Parent: Galliard Holdings Limited
Officers: Allan William Porter, Secretary; David Edward Conway [1976] Director; Stephen Stuart Solomon Conway [1948] Director; Donagh O'Sullivan [1968] Construction Director [Irish]

Quinn Investment Holdings (London) Limited
Incorporated: 9 December 2013 *Employees:* 115
Net Worth: £6,975,182 *Total Assets:* £19,140,008
Registered Office: Suite D, The Business Centre, Faringdon Avenue, Romford, Essex, RM3 8EN
Activities: Activities of other holding companies n.e.c.
Shareholders: Marian Ann Quinn; Seamus Anthony Quinn
Officers: Marian Ann Quinn [1954] Director; Seamus Anthony Quinn [1958] Director

Quinta Raddison Limited
Incorporated: 9 June 1981 *Employees:* 65
Net Worth: £10,987,159 *Total Assets:* £14,771,891
Registered Office: Stour House, High Lift Road, Langham, Colchester, Essex, CO4 5TD
Activities: Wholesale of other machinery and equipment
Shareholders: Adrian James Muir; Susan Ruth Muir
Officers: Susan Ruth Muir, Secretary; David Stephen Linscott [1967] Director/Manager; Adrian James Muir [1954] Director; Susan Ruth Muir [1953] Director/Secretary; Stephen Paul Urwin [1966] Director/Manager

Quinto Crane & Plant Limited
Incorporated: 25 March 1966 *Employees:* 108
Net Worth: £4,617,364 *Total Assets:* £13,196,822
Registered Office: Anson Road, Norwich Airport, Norwich, NR6 6EH
Activities: Renting and leasing of construction and civil engineering machinery and equipment
Shareholder: Oliver William Arnold
Officers: Oliver William Arnold [1975] Director/Business Owner

Quixant PLC
Incorporated: 5 November 2001 *Employees:* 176
Net Worth: £35,600,752 *Total Assets:* £55,619,584
Registered Office: Aisle Barn, 100 High Street, Balsham, Cambridge, CB21 4EP
Activities: Other information technology service activities
Officers: Louise Emily Park, Secretary; Gaye Anne Yvonne Hudson [1957] Director; Nicholas Charles Leopold Jarmany [1961] Director; Jonathan Francis Jayal [1982] Director/Chief Operating Officer; Chen Tai Lin [1963] Director [Taiwanese]; Guy Leighton Millward [1965] Director; Gary Paul Mullins [1971] Sales Director; Dr Michael John Peagram [1943] Director; Guy Christopher Van Zwanenberg [1954] Director

Quixant UK Limited
Incorporated: 31 January 2013 *Employees:* 12
Net Worth: £17,904,270 *Total Assets:* £19,843,388
Registered Office: Aisle Barn, 100 High Street, Balsham, Cambridge, CB21 4EP
Activities: Other information technology service activities
Parent: Quixant PLC
Officers: Louise Emily Park, Secretary; Stuart Ross Fisher [1982] Director/Chartered Certified Accountant; Nicholas Charles Leopold Jarmany [1961] Director; Jonathan Francis Jayal [1982] Director/Chief Operating Officer; John Colin Albert Malin [1970] Sales Director

R Group Holdings Limited
Incorporated: 21 November 2006
Net Worth Deficit: £506,000 *Total Assets:* £15,374,000
Registered Office: Total Produce, Enterprise Way, Pinchbeck, Spalding, Lincs, PE11 3YR
Activities: Activities of head offices
Parent: TPH (UK) Ltd
Officers: Mark Christopher Owen, Secretary; Jacinta Frances Devine [1972] Director [Irish]; Francis Gerard McKernan [1962] Director [Irish]; Mark Christopher Owen [1965] Director; Denis Leslie Punter [1953] Director

R K Property Investments Ltd.
Incorporated: 13 July 1979 *Employees:* 3
Net Worth: £4,630,944 *Total Assets:* £8,951,534
Registered Office: Unit 10 Loughton Business Centre, Langston Road, Loughton, Essex, IG10 3FL
Activities: Other construction installation
Major Shareholder: Ranjit Singh
Officers: Deepak Rani, Secretary; Inderpal Singh Matharu [1972] Director/Quantity Surveyor; Deepak Rani [1950] Director/Housewife; Ranjit Singh [1939] Director

R O Ventures Limited
Incorporated: 10 October 1963
Net Worth: £28,223,264 *Total Assets:* £91,076,080
Registered Office: Graham House, 7 Wyllyotts Place, Potters Bar, Herts, EN6 2JD
Activities: Activities of head offices
Parent: RO Enterprises Limited
Officers: Edward Thomas Morton Rowlandson [1974] Director; Richard Graham St John Rowlandson [1939] Director/Chartered Accountant

R P Valves Limited
Incorporated: 14 January 1994 *Employees:* 43
Net Worth: £58,855,600 *Total Assets:* £61,078,300
Registered Office: Merlin House, Fred Dannatt Road, Mildenhall, Bury St Edmunds, Suffolk, IP28 7RD
Activities: Wholesale of other machinery and equipment
Major Shareholder: Robert Anthony Charles Palmer
Officers: Kevin Edward Frost, Secretary; Dr Nicholas Richard Amor [1958] Director/Solicitor; Kevin Edward Frost [1969] Director of Finance and Operations; Matthew Robert George [1984] Sales Director; Robert Anthony Charles Palmer [1967] Managing Director; Steven Jay Pooley [1973] Director/Engineer; Steven Peter Withers [1969] Quality Assurance/Quality Control Director

R.B. Securities Limited
Incorporated: 23 August 1985
Net Worth: £2,159,959 *Total Assets:* £12,118,672
Registered Office: 1 Nelson Street, Southend on Sea, Essex, SS1 1EG
Activities: Other service activities n.e.c.
Shareholders: Brian Ernest Edward Burrett; Lorna Anne Sara Burrett
Officers: Brian Ernest Edward Burrett, Secretary; Janet Lord, Secretary; David Christian Wyatt, Secretary/Sales Manager; Brian Ernest Edward Burrett [1939] Director/Solicitor; David Christian Wyatt [1951] Director/Sales Manager

R.B.R. (Crops) Limited
Incorporated: 14 November 1967 *Employees:* 21
Net Worth: £6,194,466 *Total Assets:* £8,446,081
Registered Office: Carlton Farm, Old Yarmouth Road, North Walsham, Norfolk, NR28 9NA
Activities: Growing of cereals (except rice), leguminous crops and oil seeds
Shareholders: Stuart Paul Brighton; Mark Stephen Brighton
Officers: Mark Stephen Brighton [1963] Director/Potato Merchant; Stuart Paul Brighton [1966] Director; David Robert Southwell [1965] Director/Potato Trader

R.D.Trading Limited
Incorporated: 23 March 1992 *Employees:* 301
Net Worth: £21,224,956 *Total Assets:* £27,504,084
Registered Office: Tekhnicon, Springwood, Braintree, Essex, CM7 2YN
Activities: Other information technology service activities
Parent: Arrow Electronics UK Holding Limited
Officers: Marie-Astrid Pointeau [1971] Director [French]; James Anthony Stannard [1978] Director; Christopher David Stansbury [1965] Director [American]; Gregory Paul Tarpinian [1962] Director [American]

R.V.L. Properties Limited
Incorporated: 29 May 1979 *Employees:* 6
Net Worth: £25,249,900 *Total Assets:* £41,608,816
Registered Office: Ground Floor, Swift House, 18 Hoffmanns Way, Chelmsford, Essex, CM1 1GU
Activities: Other letting and operating of own or leased real estate
Parent: RVL Holdings Limited
Officers: David William Thompson, Secretary; David Croger [1952] Director; Richard Harris [1987] Director; Soliman Motala [1980] Director; David William Thompson [1947] Director; Grant David Thompson [1972] Director

R3 Polygon UK Ltd.
Incorporated: 3 January 1946 *Employees:* 350
Net Worth: £12,266,000 *Total Assets:* £21,393,000
Registered Office: Blackstone Road, Stukeley Meadows Industrial Estate, Huntingdon, Cambs, PE29 6EE
Activities: Other specialised construction activities n.e.c.
Parent: Polygon International AB
Officers: Purmpal Singh Taggar, Secretary; Axel Jorg Granitz [1968] Director [German]; Mats Sixten Norberg [1959] Director [Swedish]; Jeremy Anthony Langrove Sykes [1961] Managing Director

RA Securities London Limited
Incorporated: 17 November 2016 *Employees:* 1
Net Worth: £100 *Total Assets:* £13,602,942
Registered Office: 166 College Road, Harrow, Middlesex, HA1 1RA
Activities: Other business support service activities n.e.c.
Major Shareholder: Roy Derek Allan
Officers: Roy Derek Allan [1957] Director

Rabbah Bloodstock Limited
Incorporated: 11 August 1981
Net Worth Deficit: £108,917,896 *Total Assets:* £91,309,224
Registered Office: Dalham Hall Stud, Duchess Drive, Newmarket, Suffolk, CB8 9HE
Activities: Raising of horses and other equines
Officers: Neil Barry Whiteside, Secretary; James Martin Hyland [1969] Director/General Manager [Irish]; Jonathan Edward Mills [1975] Director; William Francis O'Rourke [1961] Director [Irish]; Bruce Hunter Raymond [1943] Director/Racing Manager; Andrew George Cameron Wiles [1973] Director/Group Chief Financial Officer

Racal Acoustics Limited
Incorporated: 19 January 2004 *Employees:* 83
Net Worth: £63,774,000 *Total Assets:* £66,500,000
Registered Office: Waverley Industrial Estate, Hailsham Drive, Harrow, Middlesex, HA1 4TR
Activities: Manufacture of other electrical equipment
Parent: Weston Aerospace Limited
Officers: Dick Heinrich [1962] Director [Dutch]; Stephen Nolan [1969] Director [American]; Curtis Carl Reusser [1960] Director/President and Chief Executive Officer [American]; Albert Scott Yost [1965] Director/Group Vice President [American]

Racing Welfare
Incorporated: 28 November 2000 *Employees:* 30
Net Worth: £30,084,000 *Total Assets:* £30,493,000
Registered Office: 20b Park Lane, Newmarket, Suffolk, CB8 8QD
Activities: Other social work activities without accommodation n.e.c.
Officers: John William Marshall Barlow [1964] Director; Simon William Clarke [1965] Director/Farmer; Jonathan Lancelot Eddis [1960] Director/Banker; Richard Charles Farquhar [1962] Director/Head of Securities Trading; Morag Graham Gray [1962] Director/Corporate Advisor; Nicky Lyon [1961] Director/Chartered Accountant; Gary Middlebrook [1954] Director; Joey Newton [1956] Director/Farmer; Patrick James Russell [1952] Director/Lawyer; Rodney Grant Street [1966] Director/Chief Executive; Venetia Anne Wrigley [1957] Director/Housewife

Paul Rackham Limited
Incorporated: 20 October 1989 *Employees:* 13
Net Worth: £20,104,188 *Total Assets:* £31,795,774
Registered Office: Manor Farm, Bridgham, Norwich, NR16 2RX
Activities: Mixed farming
Parent: Rackham Group Limited
Officers: Stephen Russell Stuteley, Secretary; Sheila Anne Rackham [1940] Director/Company Executive; Paul Anthony Rackham Snr [1936] Director/Company Executive; Paul Anthony Rackham Jnr [1965] Director/Manager; Stephen Russell Stuteley [1955] Director/Administrator

Radia Estates Limited
Incorporated: 13 July 2001 *Employees:* 13
Net Worth: £3,089,788 *Total Assets:* £11,398,139
Registered Office: Rosslyn House, 34 Railway Approach, Harrow, Middlesex, HA3 5AA
Activities: Other letting and operating of own or leased real estate
Major Shareholder: Mukesh Kumar Radia
Officers: Tina Ghelani, Secretary; Mukesh Kumar Radia [1959] Director/Solicitor

Radical Investments Limited
Incorporated: 28 October 2015
Net Worth: £2 *Total Assets:* £17,080,976
Registered Office: 3rd Floor, Sterling House, Langston Road, Loughton, Essex, IG10 3TS
Activities: Financial intermediation not elsewhere classified
Shareholders: Galliard Holdings Limited; Allied Commercial Exporters Limited
Officers: Allan William Porter, Secretary; Edward Azouz [1949] Director; Stephen Stuart Solomon Conway [1948] Director; Michael William Watson [1952] Director

Radical Motorsport Limited
Incorporated: 28 January 1997 *Employees:* 92
Net Worth Deficit: £4,641,265 *Total Assets:* £9,324,192
Registered Office: 24 Ivatt Way, Peterborough, Cambs, PE3 7PG
Activities: Manufacture of motor vehicles
Parent: Radical Sportscars Limited
Officers: Hitesh Katechia, Secretary; Joseph Anwyll [1956] Director; Hitesh Katechia [1966] Director/Chartered Accountant; Jan Martin Osterloh [1971] Director [German]

Radical Sportscars Limited
Incorporated: 14 March 2011 *Employees:* 118
Net Worth: £1,731,436 *Total Assets:* £9,776,224
Registered Office: 24 Ivatt Way, Peterborough, PE3 7PG
Activities: Activities of production holding companies
Shareholders: Andreas Ernst Zielke; Jan Martin Osterloh
Officers: Hitesh Katechia, Secretary; Joseph Anwyll [1956] Director; Hitesh Katechia [1966] Director/Chartered Accountant; Dr Jan Martin Osterloh [1971] Director [German]; Andreas Ernst Zielke [1960] Director/Entrepreneur [German]

Radio Developments Ltd
Incorporated: 13 August 2013 *Employees:* 2
Net Worth: £5,683,140 *Total Assets:* £12,430,948
Registered Office: Haslers, Old Station Road, Loughton, Essex, IG10 4PL
Activities: Other letting and operating of own or leased real estate
Shareholders: Simon Emanuel Raine; Adam Lopez Dias
Officers: Adam Lopez Dias [1973] Director; Simon Emanuel Raine [1981] Director/Manager

Ragleth Limited
Incorporated: 4 July 2005 *Employees:* 359
Net Worth: £89,767,000 *Total Assets:* £170,010,000
Registered Office: Great Ryburgh, Fakenham, Norfolk, NR21 7AS
Activities: Manufacture of other food products n.e.c.
Shareholder: The Honourable Edward Richard Iliffe
Officers: Alan William Clark, Secretary; The Honourable Edward Richard Iliffe [1968] Director/Chartered Surveyor; Christopher Guy Johnson [1964] Director/Property Developer; David George Fossett Thompson [1954] Director/Brewer and Farmer; George Alexander Thompson [1984] Director/Chartered Accountant; Ernest Raymond Anthony Travis [1943] Director/Retired Businessman; Edward John Whitley [1961] Director/Investment Manager

Rainham Industrial Services Limited
Incorporated: 5 November 2002 *Employees:* 554
Net Worth: £583,000 *Total Assets:* £12,320,000
Registered Office: 795 London Road, Grays, Essex, RM20 3LH
Activities: Construction of commercial buildings
Shareholder: Timothy Edward McCarthy
Officers: Tim McCarthy [1960] Director; David Paget [1970] Director/Engineer; Andrew Phillip Pearson [1958] Director; Karen Louise Richards [1964] Director/Financial Controller; Andrew Mark Rynston [1965] Director; Michael Anthony Scaife [1959] Director/Engineer; Nicholas Paul David Winks [1948] Director

Rakon UK Holdings Limited
Incorporated: 30 November 2006
Net Worth: £695,000 *Total Assets:* £13,980,000
Registered Office: Antell House, Windsor Place, Harlow, Essex, CM20 2GQ
Activities: Other research and experimental development on natural sciences and engineering
Parent: Rakon Limited
Officers: Dr. Sinan Altug [1971] Director/Chief Operating Officer [Turkish]; Dr Philip Charles Davies [1962] Director/Business Unit Manager; Brent John Robinson [1959] Managing Director [New Zealander]; Darren Paul Robinson [1961] Marketing Director [New Zealander]

Ramblers Holidays Group Limited
Incorporated: 1 July 2011 *Employees:* 60
Net Worth: £11,265,135 *Total Assets:* £15,583,555
Registered Office: Lemsford Mill, Lemsford Village, Welwyn Garden City, Herts, AL8 7TR
Activities: Tour operator activities
Officers: Anthony Philip Ward, Secretary; Clare Jennifer Bonnick [1961] Director/Compliance Consultant; Annette Kathleen Cotter [1948] Director/Retired; Michael John Duxbury [1947] Director/Legal Consultant; Kevin James O'Regan [1968] Managing Director; Shaun O'Reilly [1944] Director/Retired; Martin Shepley [1945] Director/Retired; Jeffrey Sissons [1963] Director/Consultant; Anthony Philip Ward [1966] Finance Director; Gillian Patricia Ann Welsman [1949] Director/Retired

Ramco (Harlow) Limited
Incorporated: 9 March 1992 *Employees:* 32
Net Worth: £10,931,031 *Total Assets:* £16,202,669
Registered Office: Sixty Six North Quay, Great Yarmouth, Norfolk, NR30 1HE
Activities: Dispensing chemist in specialised stores
Shareholders: Ramesh Rambhai Patel; Sobhana Ramesh Patel
Officers: Sobhana Ramesh Patel, Secretary; Dr Anisha Ramesh Patel [1980] Director/Dentist; Dr Davina Ramesh Patel [1982] Director/Dentist; Dr Rajvi Ramesh Patel [1990] Director/Dentist; Ramesh Rambhai Patel [1948] Director/Pharmacist; Sobhana Ramesh Patel [1952] Director

Rammamere House Limited
Incorporated: 6 January 2017
Net Worth: £17,873 *Total Assets:* £11,334,457
Registered Office: Rammamere House, Stockgrove, Leighton Buzzard, Beds, LU7 0BB
Activities: Other service activities n.e.c.
Shareholders: Michelle Jackson; Andrew Jackson
Officers: Andrew Jackson [1959] Director; Michelle Jackson [1967] Director/Fitness Instructor

Ramon Holdings Limited
Incorporated: 13 September 2006 *Employees:* 97
Net Worth: £6,443,009 *Total Assets:* £11,013,729
Registered Office: Ramon Holdings Limited, Campfield Road, Shoeburyness, Southend on Sea, Essex, SS3 9FL
Activities: Manufacture of other textiles n.e.c.
Parent: Empress Garland Limited
Officers: Gordon Rennie Peters, Secretary; Azor Alinson [1952] Director/Manufacturing Manager; Simon Nicholas Baldock [1959] Sales & Marketing Director; John Yeatman Butler [1956] Director/Logistics Manager; Terence David Dearlove [1945] Director; Gordon Rennie Peters [1953] Director/Accountant; Roger William Walters [1945] Director

Sir William Ramsay School Academy Trust
Incorporated: 7 July 2011 *Employees:* 134
Net Worth: £18,672,470 *Total Assets:* £21,760,852
Registered Office: Sir William Ramsay School, Rose Avenue, Hazlemere, High Wycombe, Bucks, HP15 7UB
Activities: General secondary education
Officers: Elizabeth Walker, Secretary; Clifford William Brown [1952] Director/Charity Worker; Stuart Carter [1976] Director/Business Analyst; Nigel Cole [1953] Director/Accountant; Paul Fleming [1966] Director/Marketing Manager; Kim Brian Frost [1960] University Secretary & Director of Human Resources; Kieran Hughes [1969] Director/Teacher; Julie Irwin [1963] Director, Student Success, Bucks New University; Christine McLintock [1966] Director/Headteacher; Mark Meardon [1973] Director/Minister of Religion (Church of England); Professor Bryan Mogford [1940] Director/Retired; Matt Spooner [1988] Director/Businessman

Ramsgate Development Company Limited
Incorporated: 4 February 2015
Net Worth: £100 *Total Assets:* £9,895,806
Registered Office: Blue House Farm Office, Brentwood Road, West Horndon, Essex, CM13 3LX
Activities: Development of building projects
Shareholder: Colin Hill
Officers: Anthony Albert Hollis [1939] Director

RANC Care Homes Limited
Incorporated: 6 December 1988 *Employees:* 936
Net Worth: £38,889,360 *Total Assets:* £41,548,828
Registered Office: Coopers House, 65a Wingletye Lane, Hornchurch, Essex, RM11 3AT
Activities: Residential nursing care facilities
Parent: RANC Holdings Limited
Officers: Aneet Rai, Secretary; Aneet Rai [1967] Director; Rabinder Singh Rai [1960] Director

RANC Holdings Limited
Incorporated: 27 June 2014
Net Worth: £87,942,552 *Total Assets:* £148,106,368
Registered Office: Coopers House, 65a Wingletye Lane, Hornchurch, Essex, RM11 3AT
Activities: Residential nursing care facilities
Shareholders: Aneet Kaur Rai; Rabinder Singh Rai
Officers: Aneet Rai [1967] Director; Rabinder Singh Rai [1960] Director

Randstad CPE Limited
Incorporated: 27 August 1976 *Employees:* 333
Net Worth: £44,489,000 *Total Assets:* £58,950,000
Registered Office: 450 Capability Green, Luton, Beds, LU1 3LU
Activities: Temporary employment agency activities
Parent: Randstad UK Holding Limited
Officers: Robin Fisher, Secretary; David Julian Bruce [1966] Director/Chief Financial Officer; Mark Jonathan Bull [1964] Director; Owen Neil Goodhead [1970] Managing Director

Randstad Group UK
Incorporated: 20 August 1999
Net Worth: £1,164,034,944 *Total Assets:* £1,516,844,032
Registered Office: 450 Capability Green, Luton, Beds, LU1 3LU
Activities: Temporary employment agency activities
Officers: Robin Fisher, Secretary; David Julian Bruce [1966] Director/Chief Financial Officer; Mark Jonathan Bull [1964] Director; Jacobus Wim Van Den Broek [1960] Director [Dutch]

Randstad HR Solutions Limited
Incorporated: 3 March 1994 *Employees:* 37
Net Worth: £10,372,000 *Total Assets:* £15,021,000
Registered Office: 450 Capability Green, Luton, Beds, LU1 3LU
Activities: Temporary employment agency activities
Parent: Randstad Employment Bureau Ltd
Officers: Robin Fisher, Secretary; David Julian Bruce [1966] Director/Chief Financial Officer; Mark Jonathan Bull [1964] Director

Randstad Luxembourg UK Limited
Incorporated: 20 December 2013
Net Worth: £1,077,890,048 *Total Assets:* £1,077,890,048
Registered Office: 450 Capability Green, Luton, Beds, LU1 3LU
Activities: Temporary employment agency activities
Parent: Randstad Group UK
Officers: Robin Fisher, Secretary; David Julian Bruce [1966] Director/Chief Financial Officer; Mark Jonathan Bull [1964] Director; Jacobus Wim Van Den Broek [1960] Director [Dutch]

Randstad Middle East Limited
Incorporated: 31 August 1990 *Employees:* 32
Net Worth: £8,967,000 *Total Assets:* £9,496,000
Registered Office: 450 Capability Green, Luton, Beds, LU1 3LU
Activities: Management consultancy activities other than financial management
Officers: Robin Fisher, Secretary; David Julian Bruce [1966] Director/Chief Financial Officer; Mark Jonathan Bull [1964] Director

Randstad Solutions Limited
Incorporated: 25 May 1989 *Employees:* 201
Previous: Randstad Employment Bureau Limited
Net Worth: £13,044,000 *Total Assets:* £66,218,000
Registered Office: 450 Capability Green, Luton, Beds, LU1 3LU
Activities: Temporary employment agency activities
Parent: Randstad UK Holding Limited
Officers: Robin Fisher, Secretary; David Julian Bruce [1966] Director/Chief Financial Officer; Mark Jonathan Bull [1964] Director

Randstad Sourceright Limited
Incorporated: 2 November 1999 *Employees:* 210
Previous: Randstad Managed Services Limited
Net Worth Deficit: £10,826,000 *Total Assets:* £36,655,000
Registered Office: 450 Capability Green, Luton, Beds, LU1 3LU
Activities: Temporary employment agency activities
Parent: Randstad UK Holding Limited
Officers: Christine Evans, Secretary; David Julian Bruce [1966] Director/Chief Financial Officer; Michael John Smith [1983] Managing Director [Australian]

Randstad UK Holding Limited
Incorporated: 19 September 1983 *Employees:* 304
Net Worth: £101,867,000 *Total Assets:* £154,052,000
Registered Office: 450 Capability Green, Luton, Beds, LU1 3LU
Activities: Temporary employment agency activities
Parent: Randstad Group UK
Officers: Robin Fisher, Secretary; David Julian Bruce [1966] Director/Chief Financial Officer; Mark Jonathan Bull [1964] Director; Jacobus Wim Van Den Broek [1960] Director [Dutch]

Rangemist Limited
Incorporated: 19 December 2008
Net Worth: £4,282,556 *Total Assets:* £11,854,180
Registered Office: 24 Carfax Road, Hornchurch, Essex, RM12 4BA
Activities: Other letting and operating of own or leased real estate
Major Shareholder: Osman Yusuf
Officers: Osman Yusuf [1970] Director/Developer

Rank Hovis Milling Limited
Incorporated: 12 December 2014 *Employees:* 271
Net Worth: £15,317,000 *Total Assets:* £52,255,000
Registered Office: The Lord Rank Centre, Lincoln Road, High Wycombe, Bucks, HP12 3QS
Activities: Grain milling
Parent: Hovis Limited
Officers: Peter Andrew Hill, Secretary; Peter Andrew Hill [1980] HR Director; Dr George Idicula [1959] Supply Chain Director; Terence Strain [1960] Director; Lawrence Anthony Watson [1965] Director

Rannerlow Limited
Incorporated: 2 January 1992 *Employees:* 1
Net Worth: £10,970,191 *Total Assets:* £16,395,316
Registered Office: Office 10, E-Space South, 26 St Thomas Place, Ely, Cambs, CB7 4EX
Activities: Buying and selling of own real estate
Shareholders: Marilyn Winifred Bateson; Robert Anthony Daniel Bateson
Officers: Marilyn Winifred Bateson, Secretary; James Oliver Daniel Bateson [1982] Director/Property Manager; Marilyn Winifred Bateson [1950] Director; Robert Anthony Daniel Bateson [1949] Director

Rannoch Food Group Limited
Incorporated: 3 April 2002 *Employees:* 1
Net Worth: £7,164,345 *Total Assets:* £15,890,600
Registered Office: Albion House, 32 Pinchbeck Road, Spalding, Lincs, PE11 1QD
Activities: Other business support service activities n.e.c.
Officers: John Edward Dutton [1954] Director; Robert John Williams [1942] Director

Ranplan Holdings Limited
Incorporated: 22 December 2014 *Employees:* 7
Net Worth: £8,423,574 *Total Assets:* £8,437,738
Registered Office: Upper Pendrill Court, Ermine Street North, Papworth Everard, Cambridge, CB23 3UY
Activities: Wireless telecommunications activities
Parent: Ranplan Group AB
Officers: Christopher John Caswell [1951] Director/Chartered Accountant; Alastair Mark Williamson [1964] Director

Ransome's Dock Limited
Incorporated: 30 June 1988 *Employees:* 4
Net Worth: £40,508,220 *Total Assets:* £42,670,700
Registered Office: Cardinal House, St Nicholas Street, Ipswich, Suffolk, IP1 1TT
Activities: Other letting and operating of own or leased real estate
Parent: Ransome's Dock Holding Company Limited
Officers: Katherine Louise Harriet Cooke, Secretary; John Julius Fitzpatrick Cooke [1985] Director/Author; Katherine Louise Harriet Cooke [1955] Director; Paul Neville Rodney Cooke [1947] Director; Clemency Frances Nesbit [1983] Director/Gallery Sales Executive

Ransome's Trading Holding Company Limited
Incorporated: 20 March 2009
Net Worth: £27,824,008 *Total Assets:* £70,168,304
Registered Office: Cardinal House, St Nicholas Street, Ipswich, Suffolk, IP1 1TT
Activities: Activities of head offices
Major Shareholder: Paul Neville Rodney Cooke
Officers: Katherine Louise Harriet Cooke, Secretary/Director; John Julius Fitzpatrick Cooke [1985] Director/Communications and Events Officer; Katherine Louise Harriet Cooke [1955] Director; Paul Neville Rodney Cooke [1947] Director; Clemency Frances Nesbit [1983] Director/Gallery Sales Executive

Ransome's Trading Limited
Incorporated: 14 September 2007
Net Worth: £18,370,248 *Total Assets:* £18,415,952
Registered Office: Cardinal House, St Nicholas Street, Ipswich, Suffolk, IP1 1TT
Activities: Other business support service activities n.e.c.
Parent: Ransome's Trading Holding Company Limited
Officers: Katherine Louise Harriet Cooke, Secretary/Director; Katherine Louise Harriet Cooke [1955] Director; Paul Neville Rodney Cooke [1947] Director

Ransomes Jacobsen Limited
Incorporated: 8 September 1972 *Employees:* 317
Net Worth: £36,603,000 *Total Assets:* £64,194,000
Registered Office: West Road, Ransomes Europark, Ipswich, Suffolk, IP3 9TT
Activities: Manufacture of other special-purpose machinery n.e.c.
Parent: Ransomes Limited
Officers: Alan Martin Prickett [1962] Director

Ransomes Limited
Incorporated: 12 May 1884
Net Worth: £40,049,000 *Total Assets:* £40,062,000
Registered Office: West Road, Ransomes Europark, Ipswich, Suffolk, IP3 9TT
Activities: Activities of head offices
Parent: Textron Limited
Officers: Alan Martin Prickett [1962] Director

Rapid Electronics Holdings Limited
Incorporated: 6 October 2010 *Employees:* 123
Net Worth: £10,907,323 *Total Assets:* £14,298,119
Registered Office: Severalls Hall, Severalls Lane, Colchester, Essex, CO4 5JS
Activities: Activities of distribution holding companies
Officers: James Glen Bates [1977] Managing Director; James Adam Bell [1966] Managing Director

Rapid Electronics Limited
Incorporated: 28 July 1980 *Employees:* 123
Net Worth: £6,604,192 *Total Assets:* £9,654,326
Registered Office: Severalls Hall, Severalls Lane, Colchester, Essex, CO4 5JS
Activities: Wholesale of electronic and telecommunications equipment and parts
Parent: Rapid Electronics Holdings Ltd
Officers: James Glen Bates [1977] Managing Director; James Adam Bell [1966] Managing Director

Rapidrop Global Limited
Incorporated: 8 July 2005 *Employees:* 93
Net Worth: £5,092,387 *Total Assets:* £13,277,743
Registered Office: Unit 1-3 Rutland Business Park, Newark Road, Peterborough, Cambs, PE1 5WA
Activities: Other specialised construction activities n.e.c.
Major Shareholder: Daniel Percy James Gill
Officers: Martyn Alan Curran [1977] Sales Director; Dominic Lawrence Ellicott [1973] Finance Director; Keith Stephen Plater [1964] Director; Mark Smith [1968] Commercial Director; Martyn Peter Willimer [1975] Sales Director

Rapleys Limited Liability Partnership
Incorporated: 15 June 2004 *Employees:* 109
Net Worth: £4,917,682 *Total Assets:* £8,118,729
Registered Office: Falcon Road, Hinching Brooke Business Park, Huntingdon, Cambs, PE29 6FG
Officers: Roderick Ian Bishop [1954] Member; Martin Ian Carey [1966] Member; Ian Robert Clarke [1967] Member; Justin Tuckwell [1974] Member; Paul Adams [1964] LLP Member; Alfred James Bartlett [1966] LLP Member; Philip Jon Blackford [1961] LLP Member; Anthony John Clements [1969] LLP Member; Daniel John Cook [1981] LLP Member; Richard Mark Curry [1962] LLP Member; Jeremy Clive Day [1969] LLP Member; Adam de Acetis [1971] LLP Member; Jonathan Doulton [1980] LLP Member; David Lewis Ensor [1967] LLP Member; Nicholas Fell [1980] LLP Member; Simon James Harbour [1979] LLP Member; Adam Henry Harvey [1975] LLP Member; Timothy Peter Holt [1957] LLP Member; Richard Terry Huteson [1971] LLP Member; Angus Bell Hamilton Irvine [1968] LLP Member; Alun Jones [1964] LLP Member; Neil Jones [1980] LLP Member; Jason Alexander Lowes [1975] LLP Member; William Jonathan Maby [1982] LLP Member; Alexander David Marsh [1982] LLP Member; Simon Matley [1976] LLP Member; Jason Rex Mound [1970] LLP Member; Peter Nicholas [1970] LLP Member; Duncan Neil Parr [1965] LLP Member; James Alexander Porter [1986] LLP Member; Simon Milner Robson [1976] LLP Member; Geoffrey Richard Sayer [1974] LLP Member; Graham William Allan Smith [1960] LLP Member; Rusell Hamlyn Smith [1961] LLP Member; Sarah Ruth Smith [1966] LLP Member; Colin Robert Steele [1960] LLP Member; Stephen Brian Sulston [1963] LLP Member; Daniel Keith Tapscott [1980] LLP Member; Steven John Turner [1971] LLP Member

Raspberry Pi Foundation
Incorporated: 25 November 2008 *Employees:* 97
Net Worth: £22,917,582 *Total Assets:* £26,148,986
Registered Office: 37 Hills Road, Cambridge, CB2 1NT
Activities: Other professional, scientific and technical activities n.e.c.
Officers: Louisa Wood, Secretary; Matilda Phoebe Blyth [1971] Director/Museum Curator; Dr Caroline Anne Brown [1962] Director; David Douglas Cleevely [1953] Director; Sherry Leigh Coutu [1964] Director [Canadian]; Jonathan Ilan Drori [1960] Director/Management Consultant; Peter Barry Lomas [1955] Director/Electronics Engineer; Christopher John Mairs [1957] Director/Technologist

Ratcliff Group Limited (The)
Incorporated: 30 August 1968 *Employees:* 284
Net Worth: £12,114,620 *Total Assets:* £19,052,848
Registered Office: Ratcliff Group, Bessemer Road, Welwyn Garden City, Herts, AL7 1ET
Activities: Activities of head offices
Officers: Mark Christopher David Ivinson, Secretary; Mark Christopher David Ivinson [1964] Director; John Edward Ratcliff [1936] Director; Roger Clive Williams [1950] Director

R.T.Rate Limited
Incorporated: 30 August 1955 *Employees:* 76
Net Worth: £4,899,521 *Total Assets:* £11,092,069
Registered Office: Hogg Lane Service Station, Hogg Lane, Grays, Essex, RM17 5QL
Activities: Sale of new cars and light motor vehicles
Shareholders: Colin John Rate; Catharina Adriana Maria Rate
Officers: Michael Day [1967] Aftermarket Director; Luke Padbury-Clark [1980] Sales Director; Catharina Adriana Maria Rate [1953] Director [Dutch]; Colin John Rate [1946] Managing Director; Sebastiaan John Rate [1980] Director

Rateneed Limited
Incorporated: 12 April 1984 *Employees:* 12
Net Worth: £7,089,853 *Total Assets:* £10,935,814
Registered Office: 5 Imperial Court, Laporte Way, Luton, Beds, LU4 8FE
Activities: Retail sale in non-specialised stores with food, beverages or tobacco predominating
Officers: Anilkumar Premchand Shah, Secretary; Anilkumar Premchand Shah [1948] Director/Retailer

Rational UK Limited
Incorporated: 23 January 1991 *Employees:* 68
Net Worth: £2,759,768 *Total Assets:* £18,518,472
Registered Office: Titan Court, Unit 4 Laporte Way, Luton, Beds, LU4 8EF
Activities: Manufacture of ovens, furnaces and furnace burners
Parent: Rational AG
Officers: Michael James Keeley, Secretary; Simon Martin Lohse [1963] Managing Director; Gotz Sauer [1966] Director/Vice President [German]

Rattlerow Farms Limited
Incorporated: 4 November 1998 *Employees:* 121
Net Worth: £4,448,440 *Total Assets:* £14,265,120
Registered Office: Hill House Farm, Stradbroke, Eye, Suffolk, IP21 5NB
Activities: Growing of cereals (except rice), leguminous crops and oil seeds
Parent: Lawson Partners Limited
Officers: Mark Philip Ledger, Secretary/Accountant; Adrian Philip Lawson [1958] Director; Robert George Lawson [1959] Director

Rattlerow Properties Limited
Incorporated: 4 November 1998 *Employees:* 2
Net Worth: £17,095,256 *Total Assets:* £20,115,896
Registered Office: Hill House Farm, Stradbroke, Eye, Suffolk, IP21 5NB
Activities: Other letting and operating of own or leased real estate
Parent: Lawson Partners Limited
Officers: Mark Philip Ledger, Secretary; Adrian Philip Lawson [1958] Director; Robert George Lawson [1959] Director

Ravensale Limited
Incorporated: 1 February 1980 *Employees:* 8
Net Worth: £32,260,092 *Total Assets:* £53,164,788
Registered Office: 115 Wembley Commercial Centre, East Lane, North Wembley, Middlesex, HA9 7UR
Activities: Activities of head offices
Officers: Sandra Clarissa Jarvis, Secretary; Bruce Darrel Grayston Jarvis [1948] Director; Joseph Richard Jarvis [1974] Director; Sandra Clarissa Jarvis [1950] Director

Rayfern Holdings Limited
Incorporated: 14 June 2012 *Employees:* 153
Net Worth: £6,050,135 *Total Assets:* £10,709,147
Registered Office: Treerange House, Minerva Business Park, Lynch Wood, Peterborough, Cambs, PE2 6QR
Activities: Activities of head offices
Parent: Edwin James Holdings Limited
Officers: John Keith Beeston [1974] Director/Chartered Accountant; Ashley James Maile [1970] Director; Darren John Martin [1970] Director; Ian Roy Morris [1963] Director; Derek Smith [1966] Director/Chief Executive

Rayleigh Schools Trust
Incorporated: 13 February 2013 *Employees:* 246
Previous: The Sweyne Park School
Net Worth: £5,270,089 *Total Assets:* £9,197,546
Registered Office: The Sweyne Park School, Sir Walter Raleigh Drive, Rayleigh, Essex, SS6 9BZ
Activities: General secondary education
Officers: Simon Paul Smith, Secretary; Peter George Hennessy [1953] Director/Accountant; Andrew John Michael Hodgkinson [1971] Director/Headteacher; Keith Henry Hudson [1947] Director/Retired; Ceri Jones [1974] Director/Headteacher; Clare Hellen Laidler [1960] Director/Management Consultant; June Morgan [1955] Director/Retired; Debbie Stokes [1950] Director/Retired

Raynham Farm Company Limited (The)
Incorporated: 25 March 1957 *Employees:* 19
Net Worth: £13,974,125 *Total Assets:* £23,923,140
Registered Office: Estate Office, Hall Farm House, East Raynham, Fakenham, Norfolk, NR21 7EE
Activities: Mixed farming
Major Shareholder: Viscount Thomas Charles Raynham
Officers: Sandy Douglas [1952] Director/Rural Consultant; Holly Jane Lamming [1981] Director/Chartered Accountant; Thomas Charles Raynham [1977] Director/Chartered Surveyor; Lord John Patrick Townshend [1962] Director/Copy Writer

Raytheon Systems Limited
Incorporated: 23 March 1946 *Employees:* 1,703
Net Worth: £557,121,984 *Total Assets:* £1,008,046,016
Registered Office: Kao One, Kao Park, Harlow, Essex, CM17 9NA
Activities: Defence activities
Parent: Raytheon United Kingdom Limited
Officers: John Alan Reilly, Secretary/Solicitor; Roy Azevedo [1960] Director [American]; David John Broadbent [1972] Director [American]; Richard Nicholas Daniel [1960] Director/Business Executive; Paul Bryan Ferraro [1967] Director [American]; John Delanier Harris II [1961] Director [American]; Dr Taylor Walton Lawrence [1963] Director [American]; Sarah Jill Lennard [1956] Director; John Alan Reilly [1960] Director/Business Executive; Sir Nigel Elton Sheinwald [1953] Director; Richard Kevin Smith [1960] Director; Lord Thomas Galloway Dunlop Du Roy de Blicquy Strathclyde [1960] Director; Pamela Ann Wickham [1962] Director [American]

Raytheon United Kingdom Limited
Incorporated: 24 February 1938
Net Worth: £259,303,008 *Total Assets:* £263,128,992
Registered Office: Kao One, Kao Park, Harlow, Essex, CM17 9NA
Activities: Activities of head offices
Parent: Raytheon Company
Officers: John Alan Reilly, Secretary/Solicitor; Richard Nicholas Daniel [1960] Director; John Alan Reilly [1960] Director/Lawyer

RBR Property Investments Limited
Incorporated: 14 June 2006 *Employees:* 3
Net Worth: £1,096,751 *Total Assets:* £8,021,086
Registered Office: 962 Eastern Avenue, Newbury Park, Ilford, Essex, IG2 7JD
Activities: Buying and selling of own real estate
Major Shareholder: Jamil Raja
Officers: Paul Nicholas Boughtwood [1962] Director

RC Bond Holdings Limited
Incorporated: 12 March 2014
Net Worth: £7,000 *Total Assets:* £193,568,992
Registered Office: Future Business Centre, King's Hedges Road, Cambridge, CB4 2HY
Activities: Activities of financial services holding companies
Officers: Ian Coleman [1960] Director; Gordon Patrick D'Silva [1955] Director/Entrepreneur; Alexander James Goodenough [1986] Director; Thomas Ernest Hackett [1945] Director/Bank Official (Retired); Sandra Diana Skeete [1965] Director; John Hartley Tattersall [1952] Director

RCG-Moody International Limited
Incorporated: 25 March 1936 *Employees:* 9
Net Worth: £72,163,000 *Total Assets:* £104,807,000
Registered Office: Academy Place, 1-9 Brook Street, Brentwood, Essex, CM14 5NQ
Activities: Other business support service activities n.e.c.
Parent: Intertek Nominees Limited
Officers: Julian Charles Burge [1973] Director/Accountant; Robert Alan Van Dorp [1977] Director; Thomas Andrew Dunlop [1974] Director/Accountant

RCI Financial Services Limited
Incorporated: 15 January 1997 *Employees:* 268
Net Worth: £304,297,984 *Total Assets:* £5,533,118,976
Registered Office: Rivers Office Park, Denham Way, Maple Cross, Rickmansworth, Herts, WD3 9YS
Activities: Credit granting by non-deposit taking finance houses and other specialist consumer credit grantors
Parent: RCI Banque SA
Officers: Sukhraj Jouhal, Secretary; Jean-Louis Labauge [1968] Managing Director [French]; Peter McEvoy [1978] Finance Director [Irish]; Enrico Rossini [1970] Director [Italian]

RCT Construction Limited
Incorporated: 22 February 1989 *Employees:* 5
Net Worth: £7,753,417 *Total Assets:* £8,681,129
Registered Office: 10 Market Walk, Saffron Walden, Essex, CB10 1JZ
Activities: Development of building projects
Major Shareholder: Richard Charles Tomkins
Officers: Beryl Tomkins, Secretary; Claudette Nicole Ginolfi [1969] Director; Michaela Jane Martindale [1978] Director; Richard Charles Tomkins [1941] Director/Property Developer; Russell Tomkins [1979] Director/Construction

RDL1 Limited
Incorporated: 2 November 2016 *Employees:* 2
Net Worth Deficit: £2,653,296 *Total Assets:* £9,522,393
Registered Office: Batchworth House, Church Street, Rickmansworth, Herts, WD3 1JE
Activities: Development of building projects
Shareholders: Christopher John Leslie Burdge; Alan Francis Springford
Officers: Christopher John Leslie Burdge, Secretary; Christopher John Leslie Burdge [1955] Director/Accountant; Alan Francis Springford [1956] Director

Reach Active Group Limited
Incorporated: 10 June 2005 *Employees:* 159
Net Worth: £2,216,075 *Total Assets:* £8,969,035
Registered Office: Printing House, 66 Lower Road, Harrow, Middlesex, HA2 0DH
Activities: Other specialised construction activities n.e.c.
Shareholders: John Thomas Gallagher; Seamus Andrew Gallagher
Officers: John Thomas Gallagher [1968] Director [Irish]; Seamus Andrew Gallagher [1966] Director [Irish]

Readie Construction Limited
Incorporated: 26 January 2007 *Employees:* 104
Net Worth: £920,742 *Total Assets:* £27,932,864
Registered Office: Unit 18 Falcon Business Centre, Ashton Road, Romford, Essex, RM3 8UR
Activities: Construction of commercial buildings
Parent: Readie Management Limited
Officers: Jessica McCarthy [1978] Finance Director; Glenn Stuart Read [1970] Director/Construction; David Ian Stephens [1982] Director/Construction; Paul Michael Stephens [1979] Construction Director

Reads Property Developments Ltd
Incorporated: 17 August 1982 *Employees:* 15
Net Worth: £9,327,784 *Total Assets:* £17,103,278
Registered Office: Hopper Way, Sandy Lane, Diss, Norfolk, IP22 4GT
Activities: Other letting and operating of own or leased real estate
Shareholders: Joe Read; Carol Susan Read
Officers: Carol Susan Read, Secretary; Carol Susan Read [1956] Director/Secretary; Joseph Read [1955] Director

Reald Europe Limited
Incorporated: 24 October 2008 *Employees:* 14
Net Worth: £15,860,615 *Total Assets:* £21,406,884
Registered Office: Suite C1, Breakspear Park, Breakspear Way, Hemel Hempstead, Herts, HP2 4TZ
Activities: Other business support service activities n.e.c.
Officers: Michael Lewis [1963] Director [American]; Jeffrey Richard Spain [1965] Director/Chief Financial Officer [American]; John Edmund Trafford-Owen [1971] Managing Director

Realpubs II Limited
Incorporated: 23 November 2007
Net Worth: £26,352,000 *Total Assets:* £53,473,000
Registered Office: Westgate Brewery, Bury St Edmunds, Suffolk, IP33 1QT
Activities: Licenced restaurants
Parent: Greene King PLC
Officers: Lindsay Anne Keswick, Secretary; Richard Smothers [1967] Director

Realpubs Limited
Incorporated: 30 March 2002
Net Worth: £12,632,305 *Total Assets:* £12,668,125
Registered Office: Westgate Brewery, Bury St Edmunds, Suffolk, IP33 1QT
Activities: Public houses and bars
Parent: Greene King PLC
Officers: Lindsay Anne Keswick, Secretary; Richard Smothers [1967] Director

RealVNC Limited
Incorporated: 24 May 2002 *Employees:* 95
Net Worth: £6,915,334 *Total Assets:* £11,812,564
Registered Office: Betjeman House, 104 Hills Road, Cambridge, CB2 1LQ
Activities: Business and domestic software development
Officers: Tom McGuire, Secretary/Solicitor; Adam Greenwood-Byrne [1980] Director; Dr Andrew Charles Harter [1961] Director/Chief Executive Officer; Professor Andrew Hopper [1953] Director/Chairman

Rebus Group Limited
Incorporated: 3 October 1995
Net Worth: £53,963,000 *Total Assets:* £53,963,000
Registered Office: Peoplebuilding 2, Peoplebuilding Estate, Maylands Avenue, Hemel Hempstead Industrial Estate, Hemel Hempstead, Herts, HP2 4NW
Activities: Activities of other holding companies n.e.c.
Parent: Rebus HR Holdings Limited
Officers: Malcolm Robert Bennett, Secretary; Steven James Chalker [1974] Chief Financial Director; Andrew Phillip Monshaw [1962] Director [American]

Rebus Holdings Limited
Incorporated: 19 October 1994
Net Worth: £48,950,000 *Total Assets:* £53,017,000
Registered Office: Peoplebuilding 2, Peoplebuilding Estate, Maylands Avenue, Hemel Hempstead Industrial Estate, Hemel Hempstead, Herts, HP2 4NW
Activities: Other professional, scientific and technical activities n.e.c.
Parent: Rebus Group Limited
Officers: Malcolm Robert Bennett, Secretary; Steven James Chalker [1974] Chief Financial Director; Andrew Phillip Monshaw [1962] Director [American]

The Recruit Venture Group Ltd
Incorporated: 5 May 2009 *Employees:* 319
Previous: Jark Holdings Limited
Net Worth: £10,493,873 *Total Assets:* £40,511,532
Registered Office: Beechurst, 8 Commercial Road, Dereham, Norfolk, NR19 1AE
Activities: Activities of head offices
Shareholders: John Timothy Buckman; Preston James Andrews
Officers: David Jaffrey, Secretary; Preston James Andrews [1961] Director; Paul Mizen [1972] Director; Daniel William Parr [1974] Director; Neil William Charles Rogers [1976] Director

Rectory Homes Limited
Incorporated: 18 January 1991 *Employees:* 48
Net Worth: £12,603,720 *Total Assets:* £35,903,320
Registered Office: Rectory House, Thame Road, Haddenham, Aylesbury, Bucks, HP17 8DA
Activities: Construction of domestic buildings
Major Shareholder: Simon Peter Vickers
Officers: Jayne Caroline Blake, Secretary; Robert Davidson [1972] Finance Director; David Ullathorne [1958] Director/Deputy Chief Executive; Sarah Vickers [1961] Director; Simon Peter Vickers [1958] Managing Director

Red Gate Software Limited
Incorporated: 12 October 1999 *Employees:* 216
Net Worth: £4,373,156 *Total Assets:* £37,652,364
Registered Office: Newnham House, Cambridge Business Park, Cambridge, CB4 0WZ
Activities: Business and domestic software development
Parent: Red Gate Software Group Limited
Officers: Simon William Bridgemore Brown [1961] Director/Consultant; Neil Gavin Davidson [1972] Technical Director; Dr Simon David Galbraith [1972] Marketing Director; Anthony John Payne [1970] Director/Chief Operating Officer; Philippa Snare [1973] Marketing Director (Prof)

Red Kite Schools Trust
Incorporated: 7 July 2011 *Employees:* 123
Previous: White Hill Schools Trust
Net Worth: £16,347,917 *Total Assets:* £20,175,320
Registered Office: Chesham Grammar School, White Hill, Chesham, Bucks, HP5 1BA
Activities: Primary education
Officers: Paul Raymond Griffiths, Secretary; Andrew Edward Garnett [1963] Director/Senior Advisor; Annmarie McNaney [1966] Director/Headteacher; Kate Jane Morris [1958] Director/HR; Anthony James Ogden [1944] Director; Michael John Park [1966] Director/Chartered Accountant; Francis Richard Sanger [1945] Director/Computer Programmer; Susan Rachel Walton [1957] Director/Independent Consultant

Red Tree (2004) LLP
Incorporated: 2 November 2004
Net Worth: £21,267,900 *Total Assets:* £21,403,640
Registered Office: c/o Rickaby & Co, 4 Claridge Court, Lower Kings Road, Berkhamsted, Herts, HP4 2AF
Officers: James Koe [1961] Member

Redbridge Produce & Flowers Limited
Incorporated: 17 March 1995 *Employees:* 340
Net Worth: £7,212,000 *Total Assets:* £19,995,000
Registered Office: Total Produce, Enterprise Way, Pinchbeck, Spalding, Lincs, PE11 3YR
Activities: Wholesale of fruit and vegetables
Parent: Saybest Limited
Officers: Mark Christopher Owen, Secretary; Andrew Roger Allmond [1944] Director/Certified Accountant; Jacinta Frances Devine [1972] Director [Irish]; Francis Gerard McKernan [1962] Director [Irish]; Mark Christopher Owen [1965] Director; Denis Leslie Punter [1953] Managing Director

Redbridge Sports Centre Trust Limited
Incorporated: 22 January 1971 *Employees:* 165
Net Worth: £7,706,628 *Total Assets:* £8,929,152
Registered Office: Forest Road, Barkingside, Essex, IG6 3HD
Activities: Activities of sport clubs
Officers: Carolynne Spencer, Secretary; Eric William Brown [1941] Director; Paul Robert Fawssett Clarke [1950] Director/Bank Executive; John Cecil Fortescue [1928] Director/Retired Brewer; Judith Anne Naomi Garfield [1966] Director/Trustee; Rasmita Gohil [1964] Director; Jayna Jogia [1988] Director/Trustee; Jane Kelloe [1952] Director/Solicitor (Non Practising); Martin Lawrence [1965] Director/Badminton Development Officer; Kenneth Stewart Leggate [1962] Director; Councillor Robert Charles Littlewood [1952] Director/Teacher; John Norman [1962] Director; Clive Beverly Rippon [1944] Director; Joyce Ellen Ryan [1941] Director/Teacher; Kartar Singh [1955] Director/Trustee; Carolynne Spencer [1967] Director/Accountant

J. Reddington Ltd
Incorporated: 23 July 1996 *Employees:* 123
Net Worth: £32,858,140 *Total Assets:* £85,098,440
Registered Office: 4 Elstree Way, Borehamwood, Herts, WD6 1RN
Activities: Construction of commercial buildings
Parent: JRL Group Ltd
Officers: Ronan Joseph Gleeson, Secretary/Director [Irish]; Ronan Joseph Gleeson [1976] Director [Irish]; Kevin William Keegan [1963] Director/Estimator [Irish]; John James Reddington [1972] Director/Formwork [Irish]

Redeemed Christian Church of God
Incorporated: 27 October 2000 *Employees:* 47
Net Worth: £11,900,650 *Total Assets:* £12,237,841
Registered Office: Redemption House, Gunnels Wood Park, Gunnels Wood Road, Stevenage, Herts, SG1 2TA
Activities: Activities of religious organisations
Officers: Ajibade Kolawole Bamigbade, Secretary; Andrew Adeleke [1960] Director; Ajibade Kolawole Bamigbade [1956] Director/Clergy; Agu Irukwu [1964] Director/Pastor; Wunmi Oladunjoye [1960] Director/Pastor; Femi Popoola [1958] Director; Adeleke Sanusi [1962] Director/Minister of Religion

Redsky IT (Hemel) Limited
Incorporated: 26 August 1975 *Employees:* 87
Net Worth: £8,521,838 *Total Assets:* £14,391,736
Registered Office: Breakspear Park, Breakspear Way, Hemel Hempstead, Herts, HP2 4TZ
Activities: Other information technology service activities
Parent: Redsky IT Holdings Limited
Officers: James Douglas McFarlane [1950] Director [Canadian]

Redsky IT Holdings Limited
Incorporated: 27 November 1998
Net Worth: £21,569,000 *Total Assets:* £32,542,000
Registered Office: Breakspear Park, Breakspear Way, Hemel Hempstead, Herts, HP2 4TZ
Activities: Other business support service activities n.e.c.
Parent: Explorer Holdings UK Limited
Officers: James Douglas McFarlane [1950] Director [Canadian]

Redwings Horse Sanctuary
Incorporated: 10 March 1998 *Employees:* 236
Net Worth: £35,716,572 *Total Assets:* £36,801,868
Registered Office: Norwich Road, Hapton, Norwich, NR15 1SP
Activities: Raising of horses and other equines
Officers: Lynn Cutress, Secretary; David John Buckton [1947] Director/Retired; Stephen Clark [1954] Director/Technician; Paul John Fileman [1957] Director/Consultant; Andrew Edwin Fryer [1963] Director/Manager; Peter Graham Horrocks [1944] Director/Solicitor; Mark Richard Little [1963] Director/Chartered Surveyor; Ann Georgina Polley [1940] Director/Retired Charity Chief Executive

Reesink Turfcare UK Limited
Incorporated: 27 November 2015 *Employees:* 139
Net Worth: £8,718,239 *Total Assets:* £27,616,120
Registered Office: 1 Station Road, St Neots, Huntingdon, Cambs, PE19 1QH
Activities: Agents involved in the sale of machinery, industrial equipment, ships and aircraft
Officers: David Jonathan Cole [1962] Director; Hieronymus Menzo Hylkema [1954] Director/The Netherlands [Dutch]; Gerrit Van Der Scheer [1960] Director [Dutch]

Refined Holdings Limited
Incorporated: 30 July 2004
Net Worth: £102,347,000 *Total Assets:* £106,678,000
Registered Office: Gladstone Place, 36-38 Upper Marlborough Road, St Albans, Herts, AL1 3UU
Activities: Activities of head offices
Parent: MRH (GB) Limited
Officers: David Hathaway, Secretary; William Bahlsen Bannister [1967] Director/Chief Executive Officer; Jeremy Clarke [1963] Director/Chief Operating Officer; Simon Paul Lane [1963] Director/Chief Financial Officer

Rega Research Limited
Incorporated: 13 June 1973 *Employees:* 110
Net Worth: £7,729,268 *Total Assets:* £9,128,473
Registered Office: 6 Coopers Way, Temple Farm Industrial Estate, Southend on Sea, Essex, SS2 5TE
Activities: Manufacture of other electrical equipment
Major Shareholder: Roy Louis Kenneth Gandy
Officers: Roy Louis Kenneth Gandy [1945] Director/Engineer

Regal Healthcare Holdings Limited
Incorporated: 4 August 2010 *Employees:* 307
Net Worth: £10,032,101 *Total Assets:* £39,255,436
Registered Office: Kingsley House, Clapham Road South, Lowestoft, Suffolk, NR32 1QS
Activities: Residential care activities for the elderly and disabled
Shareholder: Velummayilum Thayanandarajah
Officers: Wasantha Darshana [1978] Director; Ian Stuart Jarvis [1966] Director/Business Executive; Cameron Dyer Thayan [1995] Director/Trainee Accountant; Ewan Dyer Thayan [1997] Director/Trainee Accountant; Sumithra Chandrakanthi Thayanandarajah [1959] Director/Business Executive; Velummayilum Thayanandarajah [1961] Director/Business Executive

Regal Healthcare Properties Limited
Incorporated: 16 May 2003 *Employees:* 149
Net Worth: £6,314,185 *Total Assets:* £15,984,177
Registered Office: Kingsley House, Clapham Road South, Lowestoft, Suffolk, NR32 1QS
Activities: Residential care activities for the elderly and disabled
Officers: Ian Stuart Jarvis, Secretary; Wasantha Darshana [1978] Director/Business Executive; Deborah Ann Edwards [1974] Director/Business Executive; Sarah Louise Ferguson [1966] Director/Business Executive; Ian Stuart Jarvis [1966] Director/Business Executive; Cameron Dyer Thayan [1995] Director/Trainee Accountant; Ewan Dyer Thayan [1997] Director/Trainee Accountant; Sumithra Chandrakanthi Thayanandarajah [1959] Director/Business Executive; Velummayilum Thayanandarajah [1961] Director/Business Executive

Regaltags Global Limited
Incorporated: 5 March 2014 *Employees:* 21
Net Worth: £4,630,587 *Total Assets:* £10,701,417
Registered Office: Fountain Drive, Mead Lane, Hertford, SG13 7UB
Activities: Manufacture of printed labels
Officers: Alan John Lewis [1942] Director/Printer; Anne Kathryn Lewis [1964] Director/Administrative Assistant; Elinor Jane Lewis [1972] Director/Administrative Assistant; Faith Miriam Lewis [1946] Director/Administrative Assistant; Julian Paul Lewis [1967] Director/Printer; Naomi Ruth Lewis [1977] Director/Administrative Assistant; Simon Peter Lewis [1976] Director/Printer; Timothy Edwin Lewis [1970] Director/Printer

Regency Homes Limited
Incorporated: 8 May 2012 *Employees:* 7
Net Worth: £449,111 *Total Assets:* £15,092,611
Registered Office: Manor of Groves Hotel, High Wych, Sawbridgeworth, Herts, CM21 0JU
Activities: Development of building projects
Shareholder: Sebastien Yu Sau Hung
Officers: Isabelle Yu Ying Hung, Secretary; Michelle Hung [1954] Director; Sebastien Yu Sau Hung [1985] Director/Economist; Stephen Bing Sun Hung [1951] Director/Engineer

Regentsmead Limited
Incorporated: 14 October 1991 *Employees:* 12
Net Worth: £51,465,568 *Total Assets:* £63,029,272
Registered Office: Russell House, 140 High Street, Edgware, Middlesex, HA8 7LW
Activities: Financial intermediation not elsewhere classified
Shareholders: Richard Alan Ross; Lee Richard Joseph Portnoi
Officers: Lee Robert Mesnick [1968] Director/Accountant; Richard Alan Ross [1942] Director

Regis 2000 Limited
Incorporated: 13 November 2000 *Employees:* 1
Net Worth: £6,432,728 *Total Assets:* £17,150,980
Registered Office: 28 Watersfield Way, Edgware, Middlesex, HA8 6RZ
Activities: Other letting and operating of own or leased real estate
Major Shareholder: Jonathan Kaye
Officers: Arun Maganlal Bathia, Secretary; Jonathan Samuel Kaye [1978] Director

Regis Group (Barclays) Limited
Incorporated: 29 March 1999
Net Worth: £4,357,362 *Total Assets:* £17,686,348
Registered Office: 7 Nelson Street, Southend on Sea, Essex, SS1 1EH
Activities: Buying and selling of own real estate
Parent: Regis (Barclays) Holdings Limited
Officers: Piers de Vigne [1981] Director; Edward Gould [1993] Director; Katharine Morshead [1985] Director/Analyst

Regis Group (Holdings) Limited
Incorporated: 5 November 2008 *Employees:* 246
Net Worth: £37,489,080 *Total Assets:* £339,087,360
Registered Office: 7 Nelson Street, Southend on Sea, Essex, SS1 1EH
Activities: Activities of head offices
Shareholders: Nicholas Charles Gould; Peter Edward Gould; Keith Edward Bell; The Trustees of The Frank Gould 1998 No 1 Settlement
Officers: Piers de Vigne [1981] Director; Nicholas Charles Gould [1958] Director; Peter Edward Gould [1959] Director; Katharine Morshead [1985] Director/Analyst; Michael Pearson [1972] Director/Company Advisor; Sydney Englebert Taylor [1967] Director/Chief Financial Officer

Regis Group (Nationwide) Limited
Incorporated: 29 March 1999
Net Worth Deficit: £6,050,281 *Total Assets:* £31,826,976
Registered Office: 7 Nelson Street, Southend on Sea, Essex, SS1 1EH
Activities: Buying and selling of own real estate
Parent: Regis (Nationwide) Holdings Limited
Officers: Piers de Vigne [1981] Director; Edward Gould [1993] Director; Katharine Morshead [1985] Director/Analyst

Regis Group (UBK) Limited
Incorporated: 29 March 1999
Net Worth Deficit: £10,576,945 *Total Assets:* £42,504,644
Registered Office: 7 Nelson Street, Southend on Sea, Essex, SS1 1EH
Activities: Buying and selling of own real estate
Parent: Regis (UBK) Holdings Limited
Officers: Piers de Vigne [1981] Director; Edward Gould [1993] Director; Katharine Morshead [1985] Director/Analyst

Regis Group Services Limited
Incorporated: 29 March 1999 *Employees:* 35
Net Worth: £60,645,976 *Total Assets:* £93,702,584
Registered Office: 7 Nelson Street, Southend on Sea, Essex, SS1 1EH
Activities: Buying and selling of own real estate
Parent: Regis Services Holdings Limited
Officers: Piers de Vigne [1981] Director; Edward Gould [1993] Director; Katharine Morshead [1985] Director/Analyst

Registration Transfers Limited
Incorporated: 22 February 2000 *Employees:* 109
Net Worth: £23,103,868 *Total Assets:* £42,187,484
Registered Office: 139 High Street South, Dunstable, Beds, LU6 3SS
Activities: Retail sale via mail order houses or via Internet
Major Shareholder: Tony Barrie Brown
Officers: Paul Brown, Secretary; Tony Barrie Brown [1961] Director

Regulus Bidco Limited
Incorporated: 3 March 2015
Net Worth: £9,964,489 *Total Assets:* £48,721,544
Registered Office: Financial Research Centre, Haddenham Business Park, Pegasus Way, Haddenham, Aylesbury, Bucks, HP17 8LJ
Activities: Activities of financial services holding companies
Parent: Regulus Midco Limited
Officers: Remko Peter Bijtjes [1971] Director [Dutch]; Syed Zahid Hussain Bilgrami [1971] Director; Alastair Colin Gillies Brown [1974] Director; Christopher John Loraine Samuel [1958] Director; Philip Simon Shapiro [1975] Director

Regulus Midco Limited
Incorporated: 3 March 2015 *Employees:* 125
Net Worth Deficit: £6,192,681 *Total Assets:* £26,996,276
Registered Office: Financial Research Centre, Haddenham Business Park, Pegasus Way, Haddenham, Aylesbury, Bucks, HP17 8LJ
Activities: Activities of other holding companies n.e.c.
Parent: Regulus Topco Limited
Officers: Remko Peter Bijtjes [1971] Director [Dutch]; Syed Zahid Hussain Bilgrami [1971] Director; Alastair Colin Gillies Brown [1974] Director

Regulus Topco Limited
Incorporated: 3 March 2015 *Employees:* 125
Net Worth Deficit: £6,065,684 *Total Assets:* £27,001,328
Registered Office: Financial Research Centre, Haddenham Business Park, Pegasus Way, Haddenham, Aylesbury, Bucks, HP17 8LJ
Activities: Activities of other holding companies n.e.c.
Officers: Remko Peter Bijtjes [1971] Director [Dutch]; Syed Zahid Hussain Bilgrami [1971] Director; Alastair Colin Gillies Brown [1974] Director; Christopher John Loraine Samuel [1958] Director; Philip Simon Shapiro [1975] Director

Reichmann Properties PLC
Incorporated: 22 April 1998 *Employees:* 13
Previous: Glenville Investments PLC
Net Worth: £5,063,965 *Total Assets:* £18,139,238
Registered Office: 5 Elstree Gate, Elstree Way, Borehamwood, Herts, WD6 1JD
Activities: Other letting and operating of own or leased real estate
Officers: Dov Reichmann, Secretary; Daniel Naftali Reichmann [1988] Director; Dov Reichmann [1930] Director

Reids of Norwich Limited
Incorporated: 20 November 2006 *Employees:* 16
Net Worth: £3,722,755 *Total Assets:* £10,460,726
Registered Office: Golden Lion House, 15 St John Maddermarket, Norwich, NR2 1DN
Activities: Wholesale of meat and meat products
Officers: Geoffrey Buchanan [1970] Director/Farmer; William Edwin Buchanan [1968] Director; Gareth Charles Long [1980] Finance Director; Philip Richard Mullen [1982] Trading Director; John Michael Reid [1964] Director; Robert John Spence [1971] Export Director

Reilly Concrete Pumping Limited
Incorporated: 11 February 1994 *Employees:* 67
Net Worth: £4,886,831 *Total Assets:* £13,202,001
Registered Office: High Road, Thornwood Common, Epping, Essex, CM16 6LU
Activities: Other specialised construction activities n.e.c.
Parent: Oxford Pumping Holdings Ltd.
Officers: David Anthony Faud [1966] Director

Reliance Entertainment Productions 7 Ltd
Incorporated: 15 December 2011
Net Worth: £6,749,562 *Total Assets:* £13,636,532
Registered Office: 99 Kenton Road, Harrow, Middlesex, HA3 0AN
Activities: Motion picture production activities
Officers: Deepak Nayar [1959] Director/Film Producer [American]; Laure Marie Vaysse [1984] Director/Chief Operating Officer [French]

Reliance Infra Projects (UK) Limited
Incorporated: 12 May 2008
Net Worth: £159,158 *Total Assets:* £118,668,744
Registered Office: Amba House, 4th Floor, Kings Suite, 15 College Road, Harrow, Middlesex, HA1 1BA
Activities: Other business support service activities n.e.c.
Officers: Hussaini Jawadwala [1979] Director/Service [Indian]

Renaissance Global Investment Ltd
Incorporated: 11 September 2014
Net Worth: £8,427,574 *Total Assets:* £8,427,574
Registered Office: Dickens House, Guithavon Street, Witham, Essex, CM8 1BJ
Activities: Buying and selling of own real estate
Parent: Sextant Consolidated Limited
Officers: Vincenzo Bianchi [1958] Director [Italian]; Philip Lawrence [1953] Director; Filippo Tandoi [1960] Director [Italian]

Renault Group U.K. Limited
Incorporated: 18 October 1990
Net Worth: £16,670,781 *Total Assets:* £16,671,500
Registered Office: Renault Group UK Limited, The Rivers Office Park, Denham Way, Maple Cross, Rickmansworth, Herts, WD3 9YS
Activities: Accounting and auditing activities
Parent: Renault SA
Officers: James Alexander Blendis, Secretary; El-Hassan Aitsaid [1964] Finance Director [Belgian]; Thierry Antoine Joseph Cognet [1955] Director [French]

Renault U.K. Limited
Incorporated: 19 December 1904 *Employees:* 230
Net Worth: £26,936,000 *Total Assets:* £300,583,008
Registered Office: The Rivers Office Park, Denham Way, Maple Cross, Rickmansworth, Herts, WD3 9YS
Activities: Sale of new cars and light motor vehicles
Parent: Renault Group UK Limited
Officers: James Alexander Blendis, Secretary; El-Hassan Aitsaid [1964] Finance Director [Belgian]; Mark Alexander Crockett [1967] Director, Services and Quality; Lucy Kate Jones [1976] HR Director; Jean-Louis Labauge [1968] Managing Director [French]; Timothy Peter Mariott [1969] Aftersales Director; Nicholas Roy Tame [1965] Sales Director; Vincent Noel Tourette [1969] Managing Director [French]; Adam Vance Thomas Wood [1983] Marketing Director

Renewable Energy Systems Holdings Limited
Incorporated: 26 September 2003 *Employees:* 1,683
Net Worth: £296,894,016 *Total Assets:* £620,592,000
Registered Office: Beaufort Court, Egg Farm Lane, off Station Road, Kings Langley, Herts, WD4 8LR
Activities: Activities of head offices
Shareholders: Douglas James McAlpine; Richard Hugh McAlpine; Andrew William McAlpine; Gavin Malcolm McAlpine; Robert Edward Thomas William McAlpine; Hector George McAlpine
Officers: Dominic James Hearth, Secretary; Ivor Douglas Catto [1966] Director/Deputy CEO; Donald Crawford Joyce [1973] Director/Chief Financial Officer; Chris Michael Marsh [1963] Director; Douglas James McAlpine [1983] Director; Dr Gavin Malcolm McAlpine [1976] Director; Marco Perona [1967] Director [French]; Graham Matthew Reid [1962] Director/Chief Executive Officer, Americas; Rachel Ruffle [1967] Managing Director, UK & Ireland

Renewable Energy Systems Limited
Incorporated: 8 October 1981 *Employees:* 357
Net Worth: £193,522,000 *Total Assets:* £336,766,016
Registered Office: Beaufort Court, Egg Farm Lane, Station Road, Kings Langley, Herts, WD4 8LR
Activities: Construction of commercial buildings
Parent: Renewable Energy Systems Holdings Limited
Officers: Dominic James Hearth, Secretary; Ivor Douglas Catto [1966] Director/Deputy CEO; Dominic James Hearth [1966] Director/General Counsel; Steven William Hughes [1972] Generation & Asset Management Director; Donald Crawford Joyce [1973] Director/Chief Financial Officer; Chris Michael Marsh [1963] Director; Rachel Ruffle [1967] Projects Director, Western Europe and Deputy MD; Richard Paul Russell [1981] Finance Director

Republic Technologies (UK) Limited
Incorporated: 11 March 1966 *Employees:* 36
Net Worth: £4,450,000 *Total Assets:* £16,375,000
Registered Office: Sword House, Totteridge Road, High Wycombe, Bucks, HP13 6DG
Activities: Manufacture of tobacco products
Parent: Republic Technologies International SAS
Officers: Gary Martin Long, Secretary; John Joseph Catania [1967] Managing Director; Santiago Sanchez Vila [1961] Director [Spanish]

RES UK & Ireland Limited
Incorporated: 26 September 2003
Net Worth: £54,556,000 *Total Assets:* £78,506,000
Registered Office: Beaufort Court, Egg Farm Lane, off Station Road, Kings Langley, Herts, WD4 8LR
Activities: Other business support service activities n.e.c.
Parent: Renewable Energy Systems Limited
Officers: Dominic James Hearth, Secretary; Jasbir Singh Bains [1966] Director/Commercial Manager; Steven William Hughes [1972] Generation & Asset Management Director; Rachel Ruffle [1967] Projects Director, Western Europe and Deputy MD; Richard Paul Russell [1981] Finance Director

Resham PLC
Incorporated: 25 March 1986 *Employees:* 4
Net Worth: £7,336,939 *Total Assets:* £21,289,094
Registered Office: c/o Parker Cavendish, 28 Church Road, Stanmore, Middlesex, HA7 4XR
Activities: Buying and selling of own real estate
Major Shareholder: Davinder Singh Mander
Officers: Pritpal Kaur Mander, Secretary; Balwinder Kaur Mander [1975] Director/Secretary; Dr Davinder Singh Mander [1965] Director/Travel Agent; Harinder Singh Mander [1970] Director/Travel Agent; Pritpal Kaur Mander [1938] Director/Travel Agent

Residential Land Holdings Limited
Incorporated: 24 October 2006 *Employees:* 45
Net Worth: £14,338,465 *Total Assets:* £21,526,836
Registered Office: 19-20 Bourne Court, Southend Road, Woodford Green, Essex, IG8 8HD
Activities: Activities of head offices
Major Shareholder: Bruce Weir Ritchie
Officers: Jonathan Simon David Anthony Rust, Company Secretary; Bruce Weir Ritchie [1965] Director

Residential Land Management 2 Ltd
Incorporated: 16 April 2010
Net Worth: £10,410,065 *Total Assets:* £15,896,826
Registered Office: 19-20 Bourne Court, Southend Road, Woodford Green, Essex, IG8 8HD
Activities: Development of building projects
Parent: Residential Land Holdings Limited
Officers: Bruce Weir Ritchie [1965] Director

Residential Loans Ltd.
Incorporated: 10 August 1998 *Employees:* 1
Net Worth: £5,030,329 *Total Assets:* £9,312,835
Registered Office: c/o Richards Solicitors, 1st Floor, Grosvenor House, 1 High Street, Edgware, Middlesex, HA8 7TA
Activities: Other credit granting n.e.c.
Officers: David Levitus, Secretary; Dorothy Fleming [1956] Director/Administration Manager; David Levitus [1968] Director; Susan Adele Levitus [1968] Director/Administrator; Allan Smith [1981] Director

Residential Management Group Limited
Incorporated: 21 August 1980 *Employees:* 406
Net Worth: £5,594,000 *Total Assets:* £9,818,000
Registered Office: RMG House, Essex Road, Hoddesdon, Herts, EN11 0DR
Activities: Management of real estate on a fee or contract basis
Parent: Places for People Ventures Operations Limited
Officers: Christopher Paul Martin, Secretary; David Cowans [1957] Director; Alan James Inglis [1958] Finance Director; Hugh Jordan McGeever [1960] Director/Manager; Christopher Robin Leslie Phillips [1950] Director/Chairman

Resolute Corporate Holdings Limited
Incorporated: 12 July 2007 *Employees:* 109
Net Worth: £8,745,398 *Total Assets:* £11,478,855
Registered Office: Ingram House, Meridian Way, Norwich, NR7 0TA
Activities: Activities of head offices
Shareholders: Matthew James Doughty; Kate Elizabeth Reeve
Officers: Kate Elizabeth Reeve, Secretary; Ian Stormont Doughty [1951] Director; Matthew James Doughty [1977] Director; Kate Elizabeth Reeve [1979] Director

Respivert Ltd.
Incorporated: 18 December 2006 *Employees:* 1
Net Worth: £6,989,000 *Total Assets:* £11,975,000
Registered Office: 50-100 Holmers Farm Way, High Wycombe, Bucks, HP12 4EG
Activities: Other research and experimental development on natural sciences and engineering
Parent: Johnson & Johnson
Officers: Gemma Storey, Secretary; Liesbeth Aerts [1979] Finance Director [Belgian]; Dr Ian Keith Anderson [1966] Director/Business Executive; Nerida Scott [1969] Senior Director, Transactions

Result Clothing Limited
Incorporated: 17 August 1995 *Employees:* 37
Net Worth: £26,257,088 *Total Assets:* £32,560,452
Registered Office: Clement House, Commerce Way, Colchester, Essex, CO2 8HY
Activities: Wholesale of clothing and footwear
Shareholders: David Sanders-Smith; Pauline Gesina Sanders-Smith
Officers: Richard Garnet Clayton, Secretary; Jane Emma Coverdale [1974] Director; David Sanders-Smith [1947] Managing Director; Pauline Gesina Sanders-Smith [1947] Director; Sara Rachel Sanders-Smith [1968] Director

Retail Charity Bonds PLC
Incorporated: 14 March 2014
Net Worth: £57,000 *Total Assets:* £193,619,008
Registered Office: Future Business Centre, King's Hedges Road, Cambridge, CB4 2HY
Activities: Financial intermediation not elsewhere classified
Parent: RC Bond Holdings Limited
Officers: Philip John Caroe, Secretary; Ian Coleman [1960] Director; Gordon Patrick D'Silva [1955] Director/Entrepreneur; Alexander James Goodenough [1986] Director; Thomas Ernest Hackett [1945] Director/Bank Official (Retired); Timothy Roy Treleaven Jones [1956] Director/Chairman; Sandra Diana Skeete [1965] Interim Project Director; John Hartley Tattersall [1952] Director; Philip Duncan Wright [1953] Director/Accountant

Retreat East Limited
Incorporated: 25 November 2004 *Employees:* 2
Net Worth: £3,827,027 *Total Assets:* £9,539,649
Registered Office: Crane Court, 302 London Road, Ipswich, Suffolk, IP2 0AJ
Activities: Other business support service activities n.e.c.
Major Shareholder: Dominic Charles David Richards
Officers: Dominic Charles David Richards [1966] Director/Developer

Retro Properties Limited
Incorporated: 14 July 2004
Net Worth: £76,123,000 *Total Assets:* £122,175,000
Registered Office: Gladstone Place, 36-38 Upper Marlborough Road, St Albans, Herts, AL1 3UU
Activities: Other letting and operating of own or leased real estate
Parent: Malthurst (UK) Limited
Officers: David Hathaway, Secretary; William Bahlsen Bannister [1967] Director/Chief Executive; Jeremy Clarke [1963] Director/Chief Operating Officer; Simon Paul Lane [1963] Director/Chief Financial Officer

Rex Partners LLP
Incorporated: 20 December 2006
Net Worth: £27,939,492 *Total Assets:* £28,973,348
Registered Office: Harmile House, 54 St Marys Lane, Upminster, Essex, RM14 2QT
Officers: Hilary Ann Williams [1946] Member; Stuart Kenneth Mathieson Williams [1944] Member

Rex Trade Associates Limited
Incorporated: 26 March 2007
Net Worth: £2,330,501 *Total Assets:* £13,606,803
Registered Office: Harmile House, 54 St Mary's Lane, Upminster, Essex, RM14 2QT
Activities: Other business support service activities n.e.c.
Major Shareholder: Stuart Kenneth Mathieson Williams
Officers: Lisa Sheppard, Secretary; Andrew Mathieson Williams [1972] Director/TV Producer; Hilary Ann Williams [1946] Director/Theatre/Theatrical Producer; Stuart Kenneth Mathieson Williams [1944] Director/Property Developer/Retailer

Rex Venture Resources Limited
Incorporated: 2 February 2007
Net Worth: £9,590,554 *Total Assets:* £9,591,554
Registered Office: 54 St Marys Lane, Upminster, Essex, RM14 2QT
Activities: Fund management activities
Major Shareholder: Stuart Kenneth Mathieson Williams
Officers: Lisa Sheppard, Secretary; Andrew Mathieson Williams [1972] Director/Retailer; Hilary Ann Williams [1946] Director/Theatre Producer; Stuart Kenneth Mathieson Williams [1944] Director/Property Developer

Rexam Beverage Can (India Holdings) Limited
Incorporated: 16 May 1995
Net Worth: £49,172,496 *Total Assets:* £146,070,464
Registered Office: 100 Capability Green, Luton, Beds, LU1 3LG
Activities: Non-trading company
Parent: Rexam Limited
Officers: Philip James Hocken [1977] Director/Vice President; Richard John Peachey [1965] Director/Solicitor

Rexam European Holdings Limited
Incorporated: 6 October 1987
Net Worth: £369,886,144 *Total Assets:* £1,055,580,032
Registered Office: 100 Capability Green, Luton, Beds, LU1 3LG
Activities: Activities of head offices
Parent: Rexam Group Holdings Limited
Officers: Philip James Hocken [1977] Director/Vice President; Richard John Peachey [1965] Director/Solicitor

Rexam Finance Company Limited
Incorporated: 8 October 1958
Net Worth: £59,419,040 *Total Assets:* £146,840,592
Registered Office: 100 Capability Green, Luton, Beds, LU1 3LG
Activities: Other business support service activities n.e.c.
Parent: Rexam Group Holdings Limited
Officers: Philip James Hocken [1977] Director/Vice President; Richard John Peachey [1965] Director/Solicitor

Rexam Finance Germany Limited
Incorporated: 6 March 2007
Net Worth: £76,537,568 *Total Assets:* £76,747,352
Registered Office: 100 Capability Green, Luton, Beds, LU1 3LG
Activities: Other business support service activities n.e.c.
Parent: Rexam European Holdings Limited
Officers: Philip James Hocken [1977] Director; Richard John Peachey [1965] Director/Solicitor

Rexam Finance Netherlands Limited
Incorporated: 6 March 2007
Net Worth: £96,402,192 *Total Assets:* £96,665,768
Registered Office: 100 Capability Green, Luton, Beds, LU1 3LG
Activities: Other business support service activities n.e.c.
Parent: Rexam European Holdings Limited
Officers: Philip James Hocken [1977] Director; Richard John Peachey [1965] Director/Solicitor

Rexam Finance Poland Limited
Incorporated: 6 March 2007
Net Worth: £12,469,069 *Total Assets:* £12,503,138
Registered Office: 100 Capability Green, Luton, Beds, LU1 3LG
Activities: Other business support service activities n.e.c.
Parent: Rexam European Holdings Limited
Officers: Philip James Hocken [1977] Director; Richard John Peachey [1965] Director/Solicitor

Rexam Finance Sweden Limited
Incorporated: 6 March 2007
Net Worth: £170,322,752 *Total Assets:* £170,789,856
Registered Office: 100 Capability Green, Luton, Beds, LU1 3LG
Activities: Other business support service activities n.e.c.
Parent: Rexam European Holdings Limited
Officers: Philip James Hocken [1977] Director; Richard John Peachey [1965] Director/Solicitor

Rexam Group Holdings Limited
Incorporated: 7 February 2005 *Employees:* 40
Net Worth: £763,257,536 *Total Assets:* £3,550,648,320
Registered Office: 100 Capability Green, Luton, Beds, LU1 3LG
Activities: Activities of head offices
Parent: Rexam Limited
Officers: Richard David Pallister Hewitson [1961] Director/Accountant; Philip James Hocken [1977] Director/Vice President; Richard John Peachey [1965] Director/Solicitor

Rexam Limited
Incorporated: 13 July 1923 *Employees:* 39
Previous: Rexam PLC
Net Worth: £3,298,401,536 *Total Assets:* £6,200,710,656
Registered Office: 100 Capability Green, Luton, Beds, LU1 3LG
Activities: Activities of head offices
Parent: Ball UK Acquisition Limited
Officers: Charles Ernest Baker [1957] Director/VP, General Counsel and Corporate Secretary [American]; John Arthur Hayes [1965] Director/Chairman, President and CEO [American]; Scott Charles Morrison [1962] Director/Senior Vice President & Chief Financial Officer [American]

Rexam Overseas Holdings Limited
Incorporated: 29 June 1901
Net Worth: £2,694,794,752 *Total Assets:* £2,762,554,112
Registered Office: 100 Capability Green, Luton, Beds, LU1 3LG
Activities: Activities of head offices
Parent: Rexam Group Holdings Limited
Officers: Philip James Hocken [1977] Director/Vice President; Richard John Peachey [1965] Director/Solicitor

Rexam Property Developments Limited
Incorporated: 17 October 1946
Net Worth: £58,441,816 *Total Assets:* £58,462,436
Registered Office: 100 Capability Green, Luton, Beds, LU1 3LG
Activities: Other business support service activities n.e.c.
Parent: Rexam Group Holdings Limited
Officers: Philip James Hocken [1977] Director; Richard John Peachey [1965] Director/Solicitor

Rexam UK Holdings Limited
Incorporated: 19 January 1935
Net Worth: £834,504,448 *Total Assets:* £1,195,672,320
Registered Office: 100 Capability Green, Luton, Beds, LU1 3LG
Activities: Activities of head offices
Parent: Rexam Group Holdings Limited
Officers: Philip James Hocken [1977] Director/Vice President; Richard John Peachey [1965] Director/Solicitor

Reyhold Limited
Incorporated: 30 November 2015 *Employees:* 927
Net Worth: £3,257,000 *Total Assets:* £53,438,000
Registered Office: National Distribution Centre, Britannia Road, Waltham Cross, Herts, EN8 7RQ
Activities: Activities of head offices
Major Shareholder: Antony William Reynolds
Officers: Antony William Reynolds [1964] Director

Reynolds Catering Supplies Limited
Incorporated: 4 August 1994 *Employees:* 927
Net Worth: £5,516,000 *Total Assets:* £53,377,000
Registered Office: National Distribution Centre, Britannia Road, Waltham Cross, Herts, EN8 7RQ
Activities: Wholesale of fruit and vegetables
Parent: Reyhold Limited
Officers: Andrew David Austin [1973] Finance Director; Richard Alexander Calder [1963] IT Director; Paul James Collins [1965] Commercial Director; Stephen David High [1971] Director; Paul Stephen William Pegg [1957] Director; Antony William Reynolds [1964] Director/Caterer; Linda Sarah Simons [1969] Director

RG Reversions 2014 Limited
Incorporated: 22 June 2005
Net Worth: £11,424,373 *Total Assets:* £11,889,146
Registered Office: 7 Nelson Street, Southend on Sea, Essex, SS1 1EH
Activities: Buying and selling of own real estate
Parent: Long Term Reversions (Winchester) Limited
Officers: Piers de Vigne [1981] Director; Katharine Morshead [1985] Director/Analyst

RG Securities (No.2) Limited
Incorporated: 18 March 1988
Net Worth: £26,083,544 *Total Assets:* £26,723,616
Registered Office: 7 Nelson Street, Southend on Sea, Essex, SS1 1EH
Activities: Buying and selling of own real estate
Parent: Ground Rent Partners Ltd
Officers: Piers de Vigne [1981] Director; Katharine Morshead [1985] Director/Analyst

Rhiannon Properties Limited
Incorporated: 26 October 1987 *Employees:* 5
Net Worth: £1,922,335 *Total Assets:* £8,473,616
Registered Office: c/o Fenleys, 1st Floor, 168 High Street, Watford, Herts, WD17 2EG
Activities: Buying and selling of own real estate
Major Shareholder: Malcolm James Ablett
Officers: Rachel Ablett, Secretary/Administrator; Malcolm James Ablett [1952] Director/Property Dealer

RHM Group Holding Limited
Incorporated: 20 May 2005
Net Worth: £36,400,000 *Total Assets:* £1,402,599,936
Registered Office: Premier House, Centrium Business Park, Griffiths Way, St Albans, Herts, AL1 2RE
Activities: Activities of head offices
Parent: RHM Limited
Officers: Simon Nicholas Wilbraham, Secretary; Duncan Neil Leggett [1979] Director; Simon Alan Rose [1966] Director/Solicitor; Simon Nicholas Wilbraham [1969] Director/Company Secretary

Rhodia Holdings Limited
Incorporated: 22 November 1995
Net Worth: £249,571,008 *Total Assets:* £501,308,992
Registered Office: 34 Clarendon Road, Watford, Herts, WD17 1JJ
Activities: Activities of head offices
Officers: Alison Murphy, Secretary; Alexis Michel Brouhns [1955] Director/Manager [Belgian]; Melvin John Dawes [1967] Director/Solicitor; Nathan Mills [1977] Director/Engineer [American]; Alison Murphy [1965] Director/Financial Controller

Rhodia International Holdings Limited
Incorporated: 27 July 1898
Net Worth: £55,610,000 *Total Assets:* £55,991,000
Registered Office: 34 Clarendon Road, Watford, Herts, WD17 1JJ
Activities: Activities of head offices
Parent: Rhodia Holdings Limited
Officers: Alison Murphy, Secretary; Melvin John Dawes [1967] Director/Solicitor; Tom Dutton [1964] Director/Health, Safety & Environment Manager; Alison Murphy [1965] Director/Financial Controller

Rhodia Limited
Incorporated: 6 May 1926
Net Worth: £150,058,000 *Total Assets:* £211,896,000
Registered Office: 34 Clarendon Road, Watford, Herts, WD17 1JJ
Activities: Manufacture of other inorganic basic chemicals
Parent: Rhodia Holdings Limited
Officers: Alison Murphy, Secretary; Tom Dutton [1964] Director/Health, Safety & Environment Manager; John Stuart Moorhouse [1951] Director/Chemical Engineer; Alison Murphy [1965] Director/Financial Controller

Rhone Products (UK) Limited
Incorporated: 10 May 1946 *Employees:* 74
Net Worth: £48,693,332 *Total Assets:* £77,570,408
Registered Office: 55 Station Road, Beaconsfield, Bucks, HP9 1QL
Activities: Wholesale of household goods (other than musical instruments) n.e.c
Major Shareholder: Thierry Henri Stern
Officers: Andrew Mark Hearn, Secretary; Andrew Mark Hearn [1959] Director/Manager; Claude Peny [1951] Director [Belgian]; Thierry Henri Stern [1970] Director [Swiss]

Rican Securities Limited
Incorporated: 4 November 1993 *Employees:* 3
Net Worth: £11,725,455 *Total Assets:* £15,836,983
Registered Office: Ground Floor, rear The Estate House, 201 High Road, Chigwell, Essex, IG7 5BJ
Activities: Other service activities n.e.c.
Major Shareholder: Andrew Paul Klein
Officers: Howard Malcolm Klein, Secretary; Andrew Paul Klein [1966] Director/Businessman; Howard Malcolm Klein [1940] Director

Jack Richards & Son Limited
Incorporated: 8 February 1972 *Employees:* 701
Net Worth: £7,354,539 *Total Assets:* £38,321,272
Registered Office: 2 Garrood Drive Industrial Estate, Fakenham, Norfolk, NR21 8NN
Activities: Freight transport by road
Parent: Jack Richards Holdings Limited
Officers: Katherine Brown, Secretary; Victoria Carine Banks [1974] Finance Director; Peter Ralph Brown [1961] Director; Lisa Victoria Carniel [1982] Director; Anthony John Wilfred Richards [1958] Director/Haulage Contractor; Mark Vincent White [1966] Director

Richards Dry Dock and Engineering Limited
Incorporated: 6 October 1994 *Employees:* 169
Net Worth: £4,512,588 *Total Assets:* £12,390,600
Registered Office: Southtown Road, Great Yarmouth, Norfolk, NR31 0JJ
Activities: Repair and maintenance of ships and boats
Parent: 2SD Limited
Officers: Simon Coote [1973] Director; Stephen Frederick Thacker [1965] Director/Engineering Manager

Jack Richards Holdings Limited
Incorporated: 7 April 2006 *Employees:* 703
Net Worth: £14,414,300 *Total Assets:* £43,423,372
Registered Office: 2 Garrood Drive Industrial Estate, Fakenham, Norfolk, NR21 8NL
Activities: Activities of head offices
Major Shareholder: Anthony John Richards
Officers: Gladys Richards, Secretary; Lisa Victoria Carniel [1982] Director; Anthony John Wilfred Richards [1958] Director; Karen Pamela Richards [1957] Director

Richardson & Cock Limited
Incorporated: 26 March 1955 *Employees:* 12
Net Worth: £9,032,700 *Total Assets:* £9,954,495
Registered Office: Cedar Lodge, Postland, Crowland, Peterborough, Cambs, PE6 0JX
Activities: Growing of cereals (except rice), leguminous crops and oil seeds
Officers: Simon Jonathan James Blake, Secretary; Simon Jonathan James Blake [1981] Director/Farmer; Michael John Cock [1949] Director/Farmer; Robert Harry Richardson [1954] Director/Farmer

Richardsons Leisure Limited
Incorporated: 9 March 1961 *Employees:* 292
Net Worth: £14,708,609 *Total Assets:* £24,743,276
Registered Office: Richardsons Boatyard, The Staithe, Stalham, Norwich, NR12 9BX
Activities: Building of pleasure and sporting boats
Shareholders: Clive James Richardson; Paul Jonathan Richardson; Laura Joan Richardson
Officers: Paul Jonathan Richardson, Secretary; Greg Munford [1966] Director/Chief Executive; Clive James Richardson [1977] Director; Laura Joan Richardson [1973] Director; Paul Jonathan Richardson [1975] Director

Rickmansworth School
Incorporated: 14 March 2011 *Employees:* 143
Net Worth: £16,730,769 *Total Assets:* £18,782,918
Registered Office: Rickmansworth School, Scots Hill, Rickmansworth, Herts, WD3 3AQ
Activities: General secondary education
Officers: David Wilson, Secretary; Jonathon Peter Nicholas James Bowers [1968] Director/Police Officer; Harvey Alan Frederick Collyer [1946] Director/Retired; Geoffrey Cox [1952] Director/Senior HR Consultant; John Andrew de Braux [1950] Director/Recruitment Consultant; Keith Charles Deboice Douglas [1964] Director/Headteacher; Jennifer Ellen Dufton [1969] Director/IT Manager; Mark Fletcher [1968] Director/Bank Officer [Australian]; Peter Harman [1946] Director/Retired; Timothy John Lester Harrison [1954] Director/Chartered Surveyor; Ubaid Hassan [1971] Director/IT and Finance Consultant; Neeshat Hussein [1960] Director; Ashley Lagrange [1952] Director/Teacher [Zimbabwean]; Qasim Latif [1982] Director/Professional Services Consultant; Josanne Leon [1964] Director/Head of Human Resources; Ian Anthony Martin [1963] Director/Teacher; Gillian Robson [1965] Director/School Secretary; Anthony Robert Walker [1958] Director/Company Secretary; Dr David Wellings [1965] Director/Teacher/Researcher; Susan Helen Wilson [1968] Director/Teacher

Ridgeland Properties Limited
Incorporated: 22 December 1997
Net Worth: £30,934,108 *Total Assets:* £73,175,928
Registered Office: Hill House, Lowlands Road, Harrow, Middlesex, HA1 3EQ
Activities: Development of building projects
Major Shareholder: Donovan Gijsbertus Wijsmuller
Officers: Brian Martin Comer [1960] Director [Irish]; Luke Andrew Comer [1957] Director [Irish]

Ridgeon Estate Company Limited
Incorporated: 1 January 1953 *Employees:* 4
Net Worth: £5,243,983 *Total Assets:* £10,986,132
Registered Office: Abington Park Farm, Great Abington, Cambridge, CB21 6AX
Activities: Buying and selling of own real estate
Parent: Ventress Group Limited
Officers: Hilary Ann Russell, Secretary/Director; David John Harold Chaplin [1963] Director; Nathalie Ghislaine Chaplin [1970] Director/Project Manager [French]; Simon Robert Frank Chaplin [1967] Director/Farmer; Hilary Ann Russell [1965] Director

Ridgeon Holdings Limited
Incorporated: 29 July 2016 *Employees:* 851
Net Worth: £69,157,000 *Total Assets:* £98,714,000
Registered Office: c/o Ridgeons Limited, Station Road, Pampisford, Cambs, CB22 3HB
Activities: Activities of other holding companies n.e.c.
Officers: John Paul Frederick Lawes [1969] Director; Dewi Morris [1970] Director; Ian Christopher Anthony Northern [1974] Director; Terence Owen [1962] Director; Elin Sion [1985] Director; Jeremy Paul Slee [1957] Director

Ridgeon Properties Limited
Incorporated: 1 February 1947
Net Worth: £21,874,856 *Total Assets:* £40,472,460
Registered Office: c/o Ridgeons Limited, Station Road, Pampisford, Cambs, CB22 3HB
Activities: Other letting and operating of own or leased real estate
Parent: Ridgeons Support Services Limited
Officers: John Paul Frederick Lawes [1969] Finance Director; Dewi Morris [1970] Director; Ian Christopher Anthony Northern [1974] Director/Chartered Accountant; Terence Owen [1962] Director; Elin Sion [1985] Director; Jeremy Paul Slee [1957] Director

Ridgeons Land LLP
Incorporated: 3 January 2013
Net Worth: £21,630,000 *Total Assets:* £23,332,000
Registered Office: Trinity Hall Industrial Estate, Nuffield Road, Cambridge, CB4 1TS
Officers: Amanda Helen Joan Smith [1969] Member; Hugh Anderson [1997] LLP Member; Peter Alastair Ridgeon Anderson [1994] LLP Member; Rachel Elizabeth Anderson [1962] LLP Member; Daniel Ridgeon [1993] LLP Member; Duncan John Elliot Ridgeon [1964] LLP Member; Gordon Hugh Elliot Ridgeon [1962] LLP Member; Jill Elizabeth Ridgeon [1934] LLP Member; Naomi Rose Ridgeon [1996] LLP Member; Thomas Michael Absalom Ridgeon [1996] LLP Member; William Benjamin Arthur Ridgeon [1998] LLP Member; Anne Kathleen Sam [1966] LLP Member

Ridgeons Limited
Incorporated: 24 August 1989 *Employees:* 839
Net Worth: £40,129,000 *Total Assets:* £76,379,000
Registered Office: c/o Ridgeons Limited, Station Road, Pampisford, Cambs, CB22 3HB
Activities: Agents involved in the sale of timber and building materials
Parent: Ridgeons Support Services Limited
Officers: John Paul Frederick Lawes [1969] Finance Director; Dewi Morris [1970] Director; Ian Christopher Anthony Northern [1974] Director/Chartered Accountant; Terence Owen [1962] Director; Elin Sion [1985] Director; Jeremy Paul Slee [1957] Director

Ridgepoint Homes Limited
Incorporated: 16 August 2006 *Employees:* 21
Net Worth: £3,901,605 *Total Assets:* £8,741,330
Registered Office: Terriers House, Amersham Road, High Wycombe, Bucks, HP13 5AJ
Activities: Development of building projects
Major Shareholder: Nicholas Paul McEntyre
Officers: Nicholas Paul McEntyre [1976] Land Director

Ridgeway Bavarian Limited
Incorporated: 31 January 2012 *Employees:* 214
Net Worth Deficit: £2,100,000 *Total Assets:* £37,651,000
Registered Office: Airport House, The Airport, Cambridge, CB5 8RY
Activities: Sale of new cars and light motor vehicles
Parent: Ridgeway Garages (Newbury) Limited
Officers: Stephen Robert Jones, Secretary; Richard John Blumberger [1975] Director; Daksh Gupta [1970] Director

Ridgeway Garages (Newbury) Limited
Incorporated: 30 December 1996
Net Worth: £36,500,000 *Total Assets:* £157,060,000
Registered Office: Airport House, The Airport, Cambridge, CB5 8RY
Activities: Retail trade of motor vehicle parts and accessories
Parent: Marshall Motor Holdings PLC
Officers: Stephen Robert Jones, Secretary; Richard John Blumberger [1975] Director; Daksh Gupta [1970] Director

Thomas Ridley and Son,Limited
Incorporated: 17 October 1917 *Employees:* 210
Net Worth: £9,054,543 *Total Assets:* £19,910,284
Registered Office: Rougham Industrial Estate, Rougham, Bury St Edmunds, Suffolk, IP30 9ND
Activities: Wholesale of wine, beer, spirits and other alcoholic beverages
Parent: Ridley Godfrey (Holdings) Limited
Officers: Hugh Edward Godfrey, Secretary; Hugh Edward Godfrey [1944] Director/Chartered Accountant; Jennifer Patricia Godfrey [1946] Director; Justin Alexander Godfrey [1975] Director/Chartered Accountant

Ridley Godfrey (Holdings) Limited
Incorporated: 19 July 2013 *Employees:* 210
Net Worth: £16,468,013 *Total Assets:* £29,120,916
Registered Office: Rougham Industrial Estate, Rougham, Bury St Edmunds, Suffolk, IP30 9ND
Activities: Activities of distribution holding companies
Officers: Hugh Edward Godfrey [1944] Director; Jennifer Patricia Godfrey [1946] Director; Justin Alexander Godfrey [1975] Director

Rigby Taylor Limited
Incorporated: 24 July 1919 *Employees:* 78
Net Worth: £6,034,000 *Total Assets:* £14,985,000
Registered Office: 1-3 Freeman Court, Jarman Way, Orchard Road, Royston, Herts, SG8 5HW
Activities: Non-specialised wholesale trade
Parent: Origin Enterprises UK Limited
Officers: Robert Emile Beeney [1976] Director/Accountant; Christopher Clark [1961] Managing Director; Peter Michael Dunne [1973] Director/Chartered Accountant [Irish]; Ronan Andrew Hughes [1968] Director [Irish]

Rigel Capital Partners Limited
Incorporated: 16 July 2014
Net Worth Deficit: £2,698,578 *Total Assets:* £18,180,716
Registered Office: 9 Warley Hill, Brentwood, Essex, CM14 5HT
Activities: Financial intermediation not elsewhere classified
Parent: SOL Capital B.V.
Officers: Michael Sudagar Basi [1980] Director; Saulius Garbaravicius [1984] Director [Lithuanian]

Right Choice Insurance Brokers Limited
Incorporated: 9 November 2007 *Employees:* 306
Net Worth: £8,412,678 *Total Assets:* £18,314,632
Registered Office: St James House, 27-43 Eastern Road, Romford, Essex, RM1 3NH
Activities: Non-life insurance
Parent: Right Choice Holdings Limited
Officers: Michael Paul Joseph, Secretary; Darren Jason Joseph [1969] Director/Operations Manager; Michael Paul Joseph [1971] Director; Robert John Taberner [1957] Director/Chartered Accountant

Rightforsuccess Trust
Incorporated: 6 November 2012 *Employees:* 492
Net Worth: £60,525,120 *Total Assets:* £67,436,608
Registered Office: Sewell Park Academy Right for Success Trust, St Clements Hill, Norwich, NR3 4BX
Activities: Other education n.e.c.
Officers: Neil Bloomfield [1963] Director/Head of Procurement; Patricia Clark [1939] Director/Social Worker (Retired); Don Evans [1966] Director; Gareth Hand [1971] Director/Compliance & Sales Manager; Poppy Jones [1991] Director/Risk & Internal Audit Manager; John Middleton [1961] Director/Mental Health Community Nurse (Retired); David Stewart Pollock [1962] Director/Senior Teacher; Stuart Riseborough [1964] Relationship Director; John Paul William Roche-Kelly [1953] Director/Independent Education Consultant; Geoffrey Sadler [1951] Director/Ministry Cabinet Office (Retired); Susan Stavers [1969] Director/Senior Manager - Housing Association

Rights and Issues Investment Trust Public Limited Company
Incorporated: 2 October 1962 *Employees:* 1
Net Worth: £198,690,000 *Total Assets:* £198,870,000
Registered Office: Hamilton Centre, Rodney Way, Chelmsford, Essex, CM1 3BY
Activities: Activities of investment trusts
Officers: David Martin Best [1958] Director; David Matthew Bramwell [1947] Director; Dr Andrew Joseph Hosty [1965] Director; Simon John Bradley Knott [1958] Director/Fund Manager; Jonathan Burnell Roper [1951] Director

Rijac Properties Limited
Incorporated: 21 November 1977 *Employees:* 2
Net Worth: £7,825,495 *Total Assets:* £9,321,262
Registered Office: York House, Empire Way, Wembley, Middlesex, HA9 0FQ
Activities: Other letting and operating of own or leased real estate
Parent: Lindsay Drive General Investment Company Limited
Officers: Alexander Terence Shields, Secretary; Alexander Terence Shields [1981] Director; Michael George Shields [1943] Director/Chartered Surveyor

Rimex Metals (U.K.) Limited
Incorporated: 18 December 1959 *Employees:* 86
Net Worth: £3,542,555 *Total Assets:* £10,193,596
Registered Office: 17 Aden Road, Enfield, Middlesex, EN3 7SU
Activities: Manufacture of other fabricated metal products n.e.c.
Parent: Rimex Metals Group Ltd
Officers: Barbara Ellen Brandt, Secretary; Nicholas Edward Stanley Barnes [1962] Sales Director; Timothy John Childs [1966] Director; Richard John Watson [1965] Production Director

Ripmax Limited
Incorporated: 7 April 1949 *Employees:* 60
Net Worth: £4,103,665 *Total Assets:* £9,129,936
Registered Office: 241 Green Street, Enfield, Middlesex, EN3 7SJ
Activities: Wholesale of other intermediate products
Parent: Ultimate Model Corporation Limited
Officers: Mark Henley, Secretary; Graham John Hales [1948] Director; Robert Allan Hales [1953] Director; Peter Alan Halman [1945] Director/Engineer; Mark David Henley [1971] Director/Chartered Accountant; Matthew Hull [1981] Commercial Director; Jason Harvey Metcalf [1968] Director/Corporate Financier; Nicholas Julian Moss [1964] Managing Director; Colin Mark Peter Straus [1960] Director/Export Executive; Mark Wood [1957] Purchasing Director

T.Rippon & Sons (Holdings) Limited
Incorporated: 6 May 1955 *Employees:* 8
Net Worth: £12,271,375 *Total Assets:* £13,839,137
Registered Office: Burgundy Court, 64-66 Springfield Road, Chelmsford, Essex, CM2 6JY
Activities: Management consultancy activities other than financial management
Shareholders: Kevin Patrick Thomas; Aidan Albert Julian Royle
Officers: Lesley Carole West, Secretary; Leonard Grose Menhinick [1927] Director; Colin Pardoe [1955] Director/Accountant; David John Porter [1963] Director/Chartered Accountant; Dr Georgina Mary Jane Rippon [1950] Director/University Lecturer; Peter John Rippon [1950] Director/Designer

T. Rippon Estates Limited
Incorporated: 1 October 1957 *Employees:* 5
Net Worth: £9,933,052 *Total Assets:* £15,393,681
Registered Office: Burgundy Court, 64-66 Springfield Road, Chelmsford, Essex, CM2 6JY
Activities: Management consultancy activities other than financial management
Parent: T. Rippon & Sons (Holdings) Limited
Officers: Lesley Carole West, Secretary; Leonard Grose Menhinick [1927] Director; Colin Pardoe [1955] Director/Accountant; David John Porter [1963] Director/Chartered Accountant; Dr Georgina Mary Jane Rippon [1950] Director/University Lecturer; Peter John Rippon [1950] Director/Designer

Ritelite (Systems) Limited
Incorporated: 29 February 1988 *Employees:* 46
Net Worth: £17,752,740 *Total Assets:* £19,349,188
Registered Office: Meadow Park, Bourne Road, Essendine, Stamford, Lincs, PE9 4LT
Activities: Manufacture of electric lighting equipment
Major Shareholder: Marcus John Batty
Officers: Sarah Batty, Secretary; Marcus John Batty [1964] Director

Rittal Holdings Limited
Incorporated: 5 November 1980 *Employees:* 464
Net Worth: £22,394,000 *Total Assets:* £42,555,000
Registered Office: Roy's Barn, North Street, Burnham Market, King's Lynn, Norfolk, PE31 8HG
Activities: Non-trading company
Officers: Dr Stephen Hobbs, Secretary; Christopher Shelley Barker [1932] Director/Retired Solicitor; Dr Stephen Hobbs [1956] Managing Director; Herr Friedhelm Loh [1946] Director [German]

Riva Holdco 1 Limited
Incorporated: 19 July 2016 *Employees:* 139
Net Worth: £21,450,624 *Total Assets:* £75,228,032
Registered Office: Verulam Point, Station Way, St Albans, Herts, AL1 5HE
Activities: Activities of other holding companies n.e.c.
Parent: Riva Midco Limited
Officers: Sebastien Marie Julien Briens [1973] Director/Private Equity Investment Professional [French]; David Ian Issott [1977] Director/Investor

Riva Holdco 2 Limited
Incorporated: 20 July 2016
Net Worth: £24,610,596 *Total Assets:* £28,474,828
Registered Office: Verulam Point, Station Way, St Albans, Herts, AL1 5HE
Activities: Activities of other holding companies n.e.c.
Parent: Riva Holdco 1 Limited
Officers: Sebastien Marie Julien Briens [1973] Director/Private Equity Investment Professional [French]; David Ian Issott [1977] Director/Investor

Riva Topco Limited
Incorporated: 26 February 2016 *Employees:* 139
Net Worth Deficit: £8,707,815 *Total Assets:* £80,563,944
Registered Office: Verulam Point, Station Way, St Albans, Herts, AL1 5HE
Activities: Other information technology service activities
Parent: HG Pooled Management Limited
Officers: Sebastien Marie Julien Briens [1973] Director/Private Equity Investment Professional [French]; David Ian Issott [1977] Director/Investor

Rivers Finance Group PLC
Incorporated: 18 October 2002 *Employees:* 9
Net Worth: £1,090,958 *Total Assets:* £16,517,509
Registered Office: Amba House, 15 College Road, Harrow, Middlesex, HA1 1BA
Activities: Renting and leasing of office machinery and equipment (including computers)
Major Shareholder: Ratankumar Daryani
Officers: John Nicholson, Secretary; Ratankumar Daryani [1960] Director; Michael David Friend [1958] Director

Rivers Leasing PLC
Incorporated: 14 September 2010 *Employees:* 9
Previous: Rivers Leasing Limited
Net Worth: £453,160 *Total Assets:* £16,499,837
Registered Office: Amba House, 15 College Road, Harrow, Middlesex, HA1 1BA
Activities: Renting and leasing of office machinery and equipment (including computers)
Major Shareholder: Ratankumar Daryani
Officers: John Roger Nicholson, Secretary; Stephen Charles Bassett [1953] Director; Ratankumar Daryani [1960] Director; Michael David Friend [1958] Director

Rivers Multi Academy Trust
Incorporated: 7 July 2011 *Employees:* 186
Previous: Leventhorpe Trust
Net Worth: £21,371,668 *Total Assets:* £23,059,332
Registered Office: Leventhorpe, Cambridge Road, Sawbridgeworth, Herts, CM21 9BY
Activities: General secondary education
Officers: Jacqueline Moodie, Secretary; Gary Arthur Austin [1964] Director/Facilitator; Maureen Ann Bray [1965] Director/Global Business Analyst; Dr Anthony John Evans [1955] Director/IT; Raymond John James [1944] Director/Retired; David John Martin [1950] Director/University Lecturer; Peter Anson Westbrook [1966] Director/Solicitor; Malcolm White [1969] Director/Headteacher

Riverstone Europe LLP
Incorporated: 30 April 2007 *Employees:* 14
Net Worth: £8,098,227 *Total Assets:* £9,803,717
Registered Office: 5 Elstree Gate, Elstree Way, Borehamwood, Herts, WD6 1JD
Officers: Robin Joseph Alexander Duggan [1966] LLP Member; Christopher Barton Hunt [1963] LLP Member

Riverstone Pictures (Show Dogs) Limited
Incorporated: 19 May 2016
Net Worth: £87 *Total Assets:* £19,864,386
Registered Office: 99 Kenton Road, Harrow, Middlesex, HA3 0AN
Activities: Motion picture production activities
Parent: Riverstone Pictures Limited
Officers: Nicholas Anthony Crosfield Bower [1975] Director/Film Producer; Deepak Nayar [1959] Director/Film Producer [American]

Riverstone Solutions 2 Limited
Incorporated: 5 May 2016
Net Worth: £636 *Total Assets:* £14,035,968
Registered Office: 99 Kenton Road, Harrow, Middlesex, HA3 0AN
Activities: Motion picture production activities
Parent: Riverstone Pictures Limited
Officers: Nicholas Anthony Crosfield Bower [1975] Director/Film Producer; Deepak Nayar [1959] Director/Film Producer [American]

Riverway Investments Limited
Incorporated: 8 April 2014 *Employees:* 160
Net Worth: £7,929,581 *Total Assets:* £11,138,222
Registered Office: Haslers, Old Station Road, Loughton, Essex, IG10 4PL
Activities: Other letting and operating of own or leased real estate
Parent: Riverway Investments Holdings Limited
Officers: Jon Warren Crosby, Secretary; Jon Warren Crosby [1978] Director; Stephen Douglas Crosby [1974] Director; Stephen Clive Crosby [1950] Director

RJM Metal Consultancy Limited
Incorporated: 5 September 2008
Net Worth: £8,126,797 *Total Assets:* £8,145,859
Registered Office: Suite 1, Bowden Terminal, Luckyn Lane, Basildon, Essex, SS14 3AX
Activities: Wholesale of metals and metal ores
Major Shareholder: William de Fries
Officers: William Francis de Fries [1953] Director/General Manager

RL Retail Services Limited
Incorporated: 23 December 1999 *Employees:* 1,748
Net Worth: £15,512,272 *Total Assets:* £27,429,290
Registered Office: 46 Clarendon Road, Watford, Herts, WD17 1HE
Activities: Other business support service activities n.e.c.
Parent: Ralph Lauren Corporation
Officers: Aldo Alex Fleri [1961] Director/Vice President Sales UK; Carmel Ann Pedatella [1974] Director/Business Executive [American]; Robert Patrick Ranftl [1971] Director/Business Executive [American]; Andrew Howard Smith [1971] Director/Business Executive

RMPA Holdings Limited
Incorporated: 24 October 2003 *Employees:* 11
Net Worth: £7,631,000 *Total Assets:* £492,438,016
Registered Office: Building P05, Merville Barracks, Circular Road South, Colchester, Essex, CO2 7UT
Activities: Activities of head offices
Shareholders: Colne Topco Limited; Corn Investment Limited
Officers: Charles Peter Barrington [1946] Director; Stuart Anthony Carter [1965] Director; Jonathan Nigel Edward Cowdell [1966] Alternate Director; Andrew Julian Frederick Cox [1967] Alternate Director; John McDonagh [1969] Director; Vanessa Claudia Tiziana Menzies [1970] Director/Investment Manager; Hannah O'Gorman [1971] Director, Fund Management Company

RMPA Services PLC
Incorporated: 27 October 2003
Net Worth: £7,631,000 *Total Assets:* £492,438,016
Registered Office: Building P05, Merville Barracks, Circular Road South, Colchester, Essex, CO2 7UT
Activities: Other business support service activities n.e.c.
Parent: RMPA Holdings Limited
Officers: Charles Peter Barrington [1946] Director; Stuart Anthony Carter [1965] Director; Jonathan Nigel Edward Cowdell [1966] Alternate Director; Andrew Julian Frederick Cox [1967] Alternate Director; John McDonagh [1969] Director; Vanessa Claudia Tiziana Menzies [1970] Director/Investment Manager; Hannah O'Gorman [1971] Director, Fund Management Company

RMR Capital Limited
Incorporated: 15 March 2013 *Employees:* 2
Previous: RMR Capital Partners Limited
Net Worth: £18,193,562 *Total Assets:* £24,877,212
Registered Office: Heydon Lodge, Flint Cross, Newmarket Road, Heydon, Royston, Herts, SG8 7PN
Activities: Other business support service activities n.e.c.
Officers: Claire Annabel Randall [1968] Director; Robert Michael Randall [1965] Director

RO Financing Company Limited
Incorporated: 11 February 2011
Net Worth: £46,587,744 *Total Assets:* £46,587,744
Registered Office: Graham House, 7 Wyllyotts Place, Potters Bar, Herts, EN6 2JD
Activities: Non-trading company
Parent: RO Trading Limited
Officers: Edward Thomas Morton Rowlandson [1974] Director

RO Properties Limited
Incorporated: 11 October 2004 *Employees:* 4
Net Worth Deficit: £14,342,000 *Total Assets:* £38,183,000
Registered Office: Graham House, 7 Wyllyotts Place, Potters Bar, Herts, EN6 2JD
Activities: Activities of other holding companies n.e.c.
Shareholders: Richard Graham St John Rowlandson; Edward Thomas Morton Rowlandson; Richard Woodman-Bailey
Officers: David Colin Roberts [1962] Director/Solicitor; Edward Thomas Morton Rowlandson [1974] Director; Richard Graham St John Rowlandson [1939] Director/Chartered Accountant; Richard Woodman-Bailey [1950] Director

RO Property Management Limited
Incorporated: 8 September 1966 *Employees:* 8
Net Worth: £9,884,277 *Total Assets:* £59,752,972
Registered Office: Graham House, 7 Wyllyotts Place, Potters Bar, Herts, EN6 2JD
Activities: Development of building projects
Parent: RO Trading Limited
Officers: Edward Thomas Morton Rowlandson [1974] Director; Richard Graham St John Rowlandson [1939] Director/Chartered Accountant

RO Trading Limited
Incorporated: 19 November 2004 *Employees:* 61
Net Worth: £84,494,000 *Total Assets:* £111,794,000
Registered Office: Graham House, 7 Wyllyotts Place, Potters Bar, Herts, EN6 2JD
Activities: Activities of other holding companies n.e.c.
Shareholders: Richard Graham St John Rowlandson; Edward Thomas Morton Rowlandson; Richard Woodman-Bailey
Officers: David Colin Roberts [1962] Director/Solicitor; Edward Thomas Morton Rowlandson [1974] Director; Richard Graham St John Rowlandson [1939] Director/Chartered Accountant; Richard Woodman-Bailey [1950] Director

Road Tech Computer Systems Limited
Incorporated: 7 May 1986 *Employees:* 64
Net Worth: £5,145,236 *Total Assets:* £8,350,735
Registered Office: First Floor, Radius House, 51 Clarendon Road, Watford, Herts, WD17 1HP
Activities: Other software publishing
Parent: Road Tech Holdings Limited
Officers: Bernadette Beevor, Secretary; Adrian Paul Barrett [1965] Director; Bernadette Beevor [1958] Director; Derek Anthony Beevor [1955] Director; Benjamin Samuel Clewett [1971] Director; Daren Anthony Cole [1967] Director; Diane Alice Dooling [1964] Director; Tony Paul Jeffree [1982] Director; Philip David Thornhill [1982] Director

Road Tech Holdings Limited
Incorporated: 23 February 2016 *Employees:* 64
Net Worth: £5,145,236 *Total Assets:* £8,350,735
Registered Office: c/o Hillier Hopkins LLP, First Floor, Radius House, 51 Clarendon Road, Watford, Herts, WD17 1HP
Activities: Activities of other holding companies n.e.c.
Major Shareholder: Derek Anthony Beevor
Officers: Adrian Paul Barrett [1965] Director; Bernadette Beevor [1958] Director; Derek Anthony Beevor [1955] Director; Benjamin Samuel Clewett [1971] Director; Daren Anthony Cole [1967] Director; Diane Alice Dooling [1964] Director; Tony Paul Jeffree [1982] Director; Philip David Thornhill [1982] Director

Roadside Group Ltd
Incorporated: 12 July 1995
Net Worth: £15,600,000 *Total Assets:* £17,351,000
Registered Office: Gladstone Place, 36-38 Upper Marlborough Road, St Albans, Herts, AL1 3UU
Activities: Retail sale of automotive fuel in specialised stores
Parent: Motor Fuel Limited
Officers: Timothy Edward Douglas Allan [1966] Director; William Bahlsen Bannister [1967] Director/Chief Executive Officer; Thomas McKenzie Biggart [1966] Director/Surveyor; Jeremy Clarke [1963] Managing Director; Simon Lane [1963] Director/Accountant

R.Robinson & Co.(Motor Services) Limited
Incorporated: 15 February 1956 *Employees:* 59
Net Worth: £35,921,084 *Total Assets:* £45,826,848
Registered Office: Heigham Causeway, Heigham Street, Norwich, NR2 4LX
Activities: Activities of head offices
Parent: Robinsons Asset Management Limited
Officers: David John Edward Bonfield, Secretary/Accountant; David John Edward Bonfield [1963] Director/Accountant; Clare Elizabeth Kenvyn [1963] Director/Consultant; Roger Robinson [1943] Director; Thomas Edward Charles Robinson [1974] Director; Martin Brett Wallace [1968] Director

William Robinson Gravetye Charity
Incorporated: 14 April 2009
Net Worth: £9,757,733 *Total Assets:* £9,904,080
Registered Office: 1st Floor, 168 High Street, Watford, Herts, WD17 2EG
Activities: Other letting and operating of own or leased real estate
Officers: Sheila Ann Taylor, Secretary; Dr Mary Margaret Barkham [1961] Director/Environmental Research Consultant; Karen Lesley Dukes [1963] Director/Chartered Accountant; Andrew John Martin [1946] Director/FRICS; Michael Harry Walker Neal [1956] Director/Land and Property Consultant; Gillian Hazel Sandham [1947] Director; Sir Henry William Studholme [1958] Director/Forest Manager/Chartered Accountant

Robinson Young Holdings Limited
Incorporated: 5 March 2008 *Employees:* 69
Net Worth: £1,443,547 *Total Assets:* £12,214,360
Registered Office: Ibson House, Eastern Way, Bury St Edmunds, Suffolk, IP32 7AB
Activities: Activities of head offices
Major Shareholder: Michael Christopher Giles Robinson
Officers: Michael Ian Jones, Finance Director; Michael Ian Jones [1963] Director; Michael Christopher Gyles Robinson [1959] Director; Kevin Andreas Sperling [1960] Director

Robinson Young Limited
Incorporated: 22 August 1972 *Employees:* 69
Net Worth: £4,900,692 *Total Assets:* £15,671,505
Registered Office: Ibson House, Eastern Way, Bury St Edmunds, Suffolk, IP32 7AB
Activities: Wholesale of household goods (other than musical instruments) n.e.c
Parent: Robinson Young Holdings Limited
Officers: Michael Ian Jones, Finance Director; Michael Ian Jones [1963] Finance Director; Michael Christopher Gyles Robinson [1959] Managing Director; Kevin Andreas Sperling [1960] Sales Director

Robinsons (Finance) No.2 Limited
Incorporated: 23 September 2010
Net Worth: £295,417,984 *Total Assets:* £295,481,984
Registered Office: Breakspear Park, Breakspear Way, Hemel Hempstead, Herts, HP2 4TZ
Activities: Manufacture of soft drinks; production of mineral waters and other bottled waters
Officers: Judith Moore, Secretary; Mathew James Dunn [1974] Director/Chief Financial Officer; Peter Simon Litherland [1964] Director/Chief Executive; Alexandra Clare Thomas [1974] Director/General Counsel and Company Secretary

Robinsons Autoservices Limited
Incorporated: 25 August 1941 *Employees:* 361
Net Worth: £5,526,686 *Total Assets:* £53,065,276
Registered Office: Heigham Causeway, Heigham Street, Norwich, NR2 4LX
Activities: Sale of new cars and light motor vehicles
Parent: Robinsons Autoservices Holdings Limited
Officers: David John Edward Bonfield, Secretary/Accountant; David John Edward Bonfield [1963] Director/Accountant; Clare Elizabeth Kenvyn [1963] Director/Consultant; Roger Robinson [1943] Director; Thomas Edward Charles Robinson [1974] Director; Martin Brett Wallace [1968] Director

Robinsons Soft Drinks Limited
Incorporated: 4 November 1994
Net Worth: £205,435,008 *Total Assets:* £371,625,984
Registered Office: Breakspear Park, Breakspear Way, Hemel Hempstead, Herts, HP2 4TZ
Activities: Manufacture of soft drinks; production of mineral waters and other bottled waters
Parent: Britvic Soft Drinks Limited
Officers: Judith Moore, Secretary; Mathew James Dunn [1974] Director/Chief Financial Officer; Peter Simon Litherland [1964] Director/Chief Executive; Alexandra Clare Thomas [1974] Director/General Counsel and Company Secretary

Robsons of Spalding Limited
Incorporated: 14 July 1998 *Employees:* 125
Net Worth: £6,322,701 *Total Assets:* £10,055,982
Registered Office: Fleming Road, South Holland Enterprise Park, Pinchbeck, Spalding, Lincs, PE11 3YR
Activities: Other service activities n.e.c.
Parent: Culina Group Limited
Officers: Nigel Stephen Jury [1950] Director; David Charles Pugh [1981] Director; Timothy Bruce Robson [1960] Director/Chief Executive Officer; Thomas Van Mourik [1963] Director [Dutch]; Steven James Winwood [1968] Director

Robus Multi Academy Trust
Incorporated: 24 June 2011 *Employees:* 199
Net Worth: £8,371,294 *Total Assets:* £11,417,043
Registered Office: Kingston Primary School, Church Road, Thundersley, Benfleet, Essex, SS7 3HG
Activities: Primary education
Officers: Stephen Michael Bish [1975] Director/Partnership Development Manager; Julie Amanda Donnelly [1974] Director/Headteacher; Stephen Robert Golder [1957] Director/Retired; Paul Harrod [1966] Director/Business Analyst; David Frank Mills [1960] Director/Accountant; David William Hugh Norris [1961] Director/Army Officer; Tania Bridget Perry [1960] Director/Headteacher; Adrian Charles Spreadborough [1964] Director; Cheryl Linda Vickers [1964] Director/Senior Education Welfare Officer

Roche Holding (UK) Limited
Incorporated: 13 May 1997
Net Worth: £100,000,000 *Total Assets:* £190,786,000
Registered Office: 6 Falcon Way, Shire Park, Welwyn Garden City, Herts, AL7 1TW
Activities: Other professional, scientific and technical activities n.e.c.
Parent: Roche Holding AG
Officers: Mandy Elizabeth Robertson, Secretary; Richard William Erwin [1967] Director/General Manager; Beat Christoph Kraehenmann [1957] Director/Attorney at Law [Swiss]; Padraic Ward [1965] Director [Irish]

Roche Products Limited
Incorporated: 14 December 1908 *Employees:* 1,460
Net Worth: £247,339,008 *Total Assets:* £474,462,016
Registered Office: 6 Falcon Way, Shire Park, Welwyn Garden City, Herts, AL7 1TW
Activities: Manufacture of pharmaceutical preparations
Parent: Roche Holding (UK) Limited
Officers: Mandy Elizabeth Robertson, Secretary; Richard William Erwin [1967] Director/General Manager; Beat Christoph Kraehenmann [1957] Director/Attorney at Law [Swiss]; Geoffrey John Twist [1971] Managing Director

Rocket Medical Group PLC
Incorporated: 2 February 2016 *Employees:* 162
Net Worth: £11,480,740 *Total Assets:* £13,290,275
Registered Office: Bermer House, Imperial Way, Watford, Herts, WD24 4XX
Activities: Activities of head offices
Officers: Jeffrey Donald Jackson, Secretary; Robert Lee Bernberg [1960] Director; Jeffrey Donald Jackson [1962] Finance Director

Rocket Medical PLC
Incorporated: 11 November 1996 *Employees:* 154
Net Worth: £11,593,395 *Total Assets:* £13,167,504
Registered Office: Bermer House, Imperial Way, Watford, Herts, WD24 4XX
Activities: Manufacture of medical and dental instruments and supplies
Officers: Jeffrey Donald Jackson, Secretary; Robert Lee Bernberg [1960] Director; Stuart Hastings [1957] Marketing Director; Jeffrey Donald Jackson [1962] Finance Director; Leslie John Todd [1962] Operations Director

Rockford Components Limited
Incorporated: 7 August 1984 *Employees:* 265
Net Worth: £5,475,969 *Total Assets:* £8,437,227
Registered Office: Rockford House, Acer Road, Rendlesham, Woodbridge, Suffolk, IP12 2GJ
Activities: Manufacture of other electronic and electric wires and cables
Shareholder: Patricia Ann Marks
Officers: Patricia Ann Marks, Secretary/Director-Electronics; Lee Andrew Betts [1972] Engineering Director; Barrie Steven Hayter [1982] Sales & Marketing Director; Steven Denis Hayter [1957] Finance Director; Peter Anthony Lion [1962] Production Director; Patricia Ann Marks [1942] Director-Electronics

Rockley Dene Homes Limited
Incorporated: 11 March 1987 *Employees:* 302
Net Worth: £53,177,544 *Total Assets:* £88,143,448
Registered Office: 36 Railway Approach, Harrow, Middlesex, HA3 5AA
Activities: Residential nursing care facilities
Parent: TLC Group Limited
Officers: Gagan Puri, Secretary; William Charles Neal [1986] Director; Paavan Popat [1985] Managing Director; Honourable Shivaan Shillin Popat [1988] Director; Gagan Puri [1978] Finance Director

Rockley Sands (Estates) Limited
Incorporated: 17 January 1956 *Employees:* 239
Net Worth: £6,050,000 *Total Assets:* £25,649,000
Registered Office: 1 Park Lane, Hemel Hempstead, Herts, HP2 4YL
Activities: Recreational vehicle parks, trailer parks and camping grounds
Parent: Bourne Leisure Group Limited
Officers: Jane Elizabeth Bentall [1970] Director/Accountant; Paul Charles Flaum [1970] Director; Iain Stuart Macmillan [1976] Director

Roe Bros. & Co Ltd.
Incorporated: 1 June 1981 *Employees:* 149
Net Worth: £13,288,519 *Total Assets:* £27,416,088
Registered Office: 1 Fenlake Business Centre, Fengate, Peterborough, Cambs, PE1 5BQ
Activities: Manufacture of other fabricated metal products n.e.c.
Shareholders: Frank William Randle Roe; John Patrick William Roe; Richard John Clark; Paul Roe
Officers: Jean Robertson [1964] Director; John Patrick William Roe [1958] Director/Chartered Accountant; Clinton John Taylor [1961] Director

Rogers Rental Limited
Incorporated: 14 October 1988 *Employees:* 3
Previous: Summerleys Estates Limited
Net Worth: £4,338,618 *Total Assets:* £10,026,678
Registered Office: 3 Carrera House, Merlin Centre, Gatehouse Close, Aylesbury, Bucks, HP19 8DP
Activities: Construction of commercial buildings
Shareholders: Christopher Rogers; Sheila Rogers
Officers: Shirley Rogers, Secretary; Curtis Frederick Rogers [1989] Director/Property Maintenance

Rogerson Holdings Limited
Incorporated: 28 April 1994 *Employees:* 56
Net Worth: £7,875,760 *Total Assets:* £11,427,661
Registered Office: Church Field House, Church Field Road, Sudbury, Suffolk, CO10 2YA
Activities: Activities of construction holding companies
Major Shareholder: Malcolm John Rogerson
Officers: Alison Jean Rogerson, Secretary; Malcolm John Rogerson [1952] Director; Stuart Geoffrey Rogerson [1983] Director

Rolec Services Limited
Incorporated: 9 September 1988 *Employees:* 95
Net Worth: £11,860,578 *Total Assets:* £13,523,962
Registered Office: Ralphs Lane, Frampton West, Boston, Lincs, PE20 1QU
Activities: Electrical installation
Major Shareholder: Kieron Jeffery Alsop
Officers: Kieron Jeffery Alsop [1961] Managing Director; Holly Toni Brown [1975] Operations Director; Martin Georgeson [1973] Sales Director; Lee Orrey [1978] Director

Rolling Components Limited
Incorporated: 15 March 1984 *Employees:* 28
Net Worth: £5,583,518 *Total Assets:* £10,948,669
Registered Office: 22-25 Paycocke Road, Basildon, Essex, SS14 3DR
Activities: Wholesale trade of motor vehicle parts and accessories
Parent: Rollco Group Holdings Limited
Officers: Gaurav Malhotra [1972] Director; Sudesh Kumar Malhotra [1940] Director; Usha Malhotra [1944] Director

Rollins & Sons (London) Limited
Incorporated: 24 June 1924 *Employees:* 96
Net Worth: £5,732,181 *Total Assets:* £16,373,052
Registered Office: Rollins House, 1 Parkway, Harlow Business Park, Harlow, Essex, CM19 5QF
Activities: Wholesale of hardware, plumbing and heating equipment and supplies
Shareholder: Stuart Charles Elsom
Officers: David Ian Roland Woollard, Secretary; Dominic Edward Elsom [1971] Director; Stuart Charles Elsom [1964] Director; Roger Ronald Partridge [1960] Director; Martin Graham Tompsett [1952] Director; Andrew James White [1949] Director; Edward John White [1987] Sales Director; David Roland Woolard [1965] Director/Accountant

Roman Investments Limited
Incorporated: 6 June 1989
Net Worth: £8,523,546 *Total Assets:* £17,029,512
Registered Office: Lynwood House, 373-375 Station Road, Harrow, Middlesex, HA1 2AW
Activities: Development of building projects
Major Shareholder: David Jonathan Rosenberg
Officers: David Jonathan Rosenberg [1956] Director/Businessman

The Helena Romanes School
Incorporated: 9 March 2012 *Employees:* 141
Net Worth: £15,145,328 *Total Assets:* £18,815,024
Registered Office: The Helena Romanes School, Parsonage Downs, Dunmow, Essex, CM6 2AU
Activities: General secondary education
Officers: Timothy Edward Bousfield [1993] Director; Valerie Margaret Cumming Newell [1959] Director/Teacher; Rebecca Anne Durston [1953] Director/Retired Headteacher; Richard Brian Elliott [1966] Director/Banker; Susan Carol Este [1957] Director/Personnel Officer; Alison Farrell [1963] Director/Police Staff; Marcus James Frost [1969] Director/Marketing; Ian Derek Morley Keast [1947] Director/Travel Consultant; Simon Peter Knight [1960] Director/Headteacher; Donald Stuart Macmillan [1976] Director/Accountant; Joanne Louise Owens [1969] Director/Registered Nurse; Mike Derek Perry [1951] Director/Photographer

Romeo Midco Limited
Incorporated: 14 January 2009
Net Worth: £32,960,000 *Total Assets:* £43,309,000
Registered Office: Third Floor, 29 Broadwater Road, Welwyn Garden City, Herts, AL7 3BQ
Activities: Activities of head offices
Parent: Treehouse Group Limited
Officers: Jim Kelleher [1959] Director [Irish]; Richard Price [1963] Director

Rooff Group Limited (The)
Incorporated: 20 April 1929
Net Worth: £6,997,003 *Total Assets:* £8,047,577
Registered Office: The Granary, 80 Abbey Road, Barking, Essex, IG11 7BT
Activities: Activities of head offices
Parent: Rooff Holdings Limited
Officers: John Anthony Pearson, Secretary; Alan Alfred Horn [1929] Director; Mark Patrick Seebold Horn [1967] Director/Builder; John Anthony Pearson [1954] Finance Director

Rooff Holdings Limited
Incorporated: 2 December 1998 *Employees:* 78
Net Worth: £16,136,072 *Total Assets:* £26,858,154
Registered Office: The Granary, 80 Abbey Road, Barking, Essex, IG11 7BT
Activities: Activities of head offices
Officers: John Anthony Pearson, Secretary; Alan Alfred Horn [1929] Director; Mark Patrick Seebold Horn [1967] Director/Builder; John Anthony Pearson [1954] Finance Director

Rooff Ltd
Incorporated: 20 July 1976 *Employees:* 12
Net Worth: £4,114,240 *Total Assets:* £14,435,934
Registered Office: The Granary, 80 Abbey Road, Barking, Essex, IG11 7BT
Activities: Construction of commercial buildings
Parent: The Rooff Group Limited
Officers: John Anthony Pearson, Secretary; Stephen John Drury [1965] Director/Building & Development; Ghanshyam Hirani [1982] Operations Director; Alan Alfred Horn [1929] Director; Mark Patrick Seebold Horn [1967] Director/Builder; Ronald Nicholls [1959] Commercial Director; Antony Charles Pearce [1963] Construction Director; John Anthony Pearson [1954] Finance Director

Rooff Property LLP
Incorporated: 8 September 2006
Net Worth: £11,513,261 *Total Assets:* £11,712,768
Registered Office: The Granary, 80 Abbey Road, Barking, Essex, IG11 7BT
Officers: Alan Alfred Horn [1929] Member; Mark Patrick Seebold Horn [1967] Member

Roos Energy Limited
Incorporated: 17 May 2011
Net Worth Deficit: £2,740,000 *Total Assets:* £33,296,000
Registered Office: Beaufort Court, Egg Farm Lane, Kings Langley, Herts, WD4 8LR
Activities: Production of electricity
Parent: Trafalgar Wind Holdings Limited
Officers: Dominic James Hearth, Secretary; Steven William Hughes [1972] Generation & Asset Management Director; Fraser Stephen Merry [1968] Director/Chartered Surveyor; Mitesh Raj Patel [1982] Director/Group Financial Controller

Roots Hall Limited
Incorporated: 3 February 1999 *Employees:* 4
Net Worth Deficit: £1,023,939 *Total Assets:* £26,523,532
Registered Office: Verulam Point, Station Way, St Albans, Herts, AL1 5HE
Activities: Buying and selling of own real estate
Officers: Geoffrey King, Secretary; Geoffrey King [1946] Director/Chartered Company Secretary; Jack Leonard Martin [1989] Director/Real Estate Investor; Ronald Martin [1953] Director

Rose Builders Ltd
Incorporated: 27 September 1995 *Employees:* 154
Net Worth: £5,130,076 *Total Assets:* £12,323,222
Registered Office: Riverside House, Riverside Avenue East, Lawford, Manningtree, Essex, CO11 1US
Activities: Development of building projects
Parent: Rose Group Ltd
Officers: Andrew Martin Bowles, Secretary/Chartered Accountant; Anthony Leonard Auger [1951] Director/Construction Estimator/Surveyor; Andrew Martin Bowles [1965] Financial Director; Steven William Jolian Rose [1960] Director/Builder; Jonathan Michael Woods [1956] Director/Building Contractor

Rose Film Partnership LLP
Incorporated: 20 April 2007
Net Worth: £16,761,960 *Total Assets:* £16,761,960
Registered Office: 99 Kenton Road, Harrow, Middlesex, HA3 0AN
Officers: David James Lyndsey Harper [1980] Member; Peter Daniel Arduino [1968] LLP Member; Richard Bernard Charles [1954] LLP Member; Sean Devine [1963] LLP Member; Leslie Gough [1950] LLP Member; Allan Watson Graham [1960] LLP Member; Colin Steuart Grassie [1961] LLP Member; Timothy Charles Robert Henderson [1961] LLP Member; George Heydon [1961] LLP Member; Jamie Hutchin [1975] LLP Member; Jonathan Richard Jeff [1974] LLP Member; Ajitsinh Moahnsinh Kara [1967] LLP Member; Nigel Lindsay Kennedy [1955] LLP Member; John Joseph King [1963] LLP Member; Michael James King [1956] LLP Member; Ian Alexander MacDonald [1939] LLP Member; Calum Neil Forbes MacInnes [1961] LLP Member; Guy Kenneth Peter Marshall [1965] LLP Member; Tom Foulery McGrath [1968] LLP Member; Julian Ralph Stewart Newiss [1953] LLP Member; Adrian Kim Parker [1960] LLP Member; Dr Duncan Fraser Ralston [1962] LLP Member; Alexander George Malcolm Ritchie [1954] LLP Member; Paul Howard Ross [1966] LLP Member; Michael Leslie Says [1960] LLP Member; James Richard Scott [1975] LLP Member; Mark Andrew Wallace [1959] LLP Member; Guy Ian Swinburn Wilson [1972] LLP Member; Christopher Alan Wimhurst [1951] LLP Member

Rose Group Limited
Incorporated: 8 October 2002 *Employees:* 158
Net Worth: £16,179,149 *Total Assets:* £27,264,040
Registered Office: Riverside House, Riverside Avenue East, Lawford, Manningtree, Essex, CO11 1US
Activities: Activities of construction holding companies
Shareholders: Steven William Jolian Rose; Ensors Trustee Company Limited
Officers: Andrew Martin Bowles, Secretary/Chartered Accountant; Andrew Martin Bowles [1965] Financial Director; Jennifer Mary Rose [1964] Director; Steven William Jolian Rose [1960] Director/Builder

Rose Holdco Limited
Incorporated: 30 April 2009 *Employees:* 28
Net Worth: £189,862,000 *Total Assets:* £273,116,992
Registered Office: 35-37 Amersham Hill, High Wycombe, Bucks, HP13 6NU
Activities: Activities of head offices
Parent: Boing Acquisitions Ltd
Officers: Jonathan Samuel Booth [1961] Director; Thomas Bruce Mangas [1967] Director/Chief Executive Officer [American]; Nilesh Kundanlal Pandya [1971] Director; Michael Andrew James Smith [1962] Director

Rose Midco Limited
Incorporated: 30 April 2009 *Employees:* 4
Net Worth: £155,838,000 *Total Assets:* £383,684,992
Registered Office: 35-37 Amersham Hill, High Wycombe, Bucks, HP13 6NU
Activities: Activities of head offices
Parent: Rose Holdco Ltd
Officers: Jonathan Samuel Booth [1961] Director; Thomas Bruce Mangas [1967] Director/Chief Executive Officer [American]; Nilesh Kundanlal Pandya [1971] Director; Michael Andrew James Smith [1962] Director

Roselead (Wattisham) Limited
Incorporated: 14 June 2006
Net Worth Deficit: £1,577,285 *Total Assets:* £15,474,613
Registered Office: Two Station Place, Cambridge, CB1 2FP
Activities: Management of real estate on a fee or contract basis
Parent: Brookgate Ltd
Officers: Jonathan Christian Wooles, Secretary; Sven Jurgen Topel [1966] Director; Jonathan Christian Wooles [1963] Director/Chartered Accountant

Roselead Limited
Incorporated: 29 April 1999
Net Worth: £10,737,920 *Total Assets:* £68,582,288
Registered Office: Two Station Place, Cambridge, CB1 2FP
Activities: Buying and selling of own real estate
Parent: Roselead Holdings Ltd
Officers: Jonathan Christian Wooles, Secretary; Sven Jurgen Topel [1966] Director; Jonathan Christian Wooles [1963] Director/Chartered Accountant

Rosemary & Thyme Limited
Incorporated: 12 June 1996 *Employees:* 58
Net Worth: £7,164,747 *Total Assets:* £14,450,627
Registered Office: Progress Way, Mid Suffolk Business Park, Eye, Suffolk, IP23 7HU
Activities: Other processing and preserving of fruit and vegetables
Parent: Ardo Business Support NV
Officers: Simon Rowland Hurran, Secretary; Ignace Cyriel Marie Haspeslagh [1957] Director [Belgian]; Jan Jozef Maria Haspeslagh [1961] Director [Belgian]; Simon Rowland Hurran [1966] Finance Director

Rosper Estates Limited
Incorporated: 27 March 1998 *Employees:* 4
Net Worth: £10,391,274 *Total Assets:* £15,031,205
Registered Office: Beacon End Farmhouse, London Road, Colchester, Essex, CO3 0NQ
Activities: Other letting and operating of own or leased real estate
Officers: Steven William Jolian Rose, Secretary/Director; Nicholas James Percival [1958] Director; Steven William Jolian Rose [1960] Director

Rotamead Limited
Incorporated: 11 June 1979 *Employees:* 15
Net Worth: £17,546,908 *Total Assets:* £21,396,398
Registered Office: Essex Works, Hawk Lane, Battlesbridge, Essex, SS11 7RL
Activities: Non-specialised wholesale trade
Major Shareholder: Barry George Norfolk
Officers: Grant Barry Norfolk, Secretary; Matthew James Anderson [1971] Director; Robert Jones [1957] Purchasing Director; Barry George Norfolk [1945] Director; Grant Barry Norfolk [1970] Sales Director

Rothamsted Enterprises Limited
Incorporated: 4 March 1999
Previous: Rothamsted Centre for Research and Enterprise Limited
Net Worth Deficit: £737,985 *Total Assets:* £12,768,342
Registered Office: Rothamsted Research, West Common, Harpenden, Herts, AL5 2JQ
Activities: Other business support service activities n.e.c.
Shareholders: Lawes Agricultural Trust; Rothamsted Research Limited
Officers: Louise Ann Warren, Secretary; Derek Thomas Edward Jones [1961] Director; Professor Angela Karp [1957] Director; Peter Duncan Oxley [1976] Director; Zahir Husein Sachak [1962] Director/Civil Servant; Nicole Louise Sadd [1980] Executive Director

Rothamsted Research Limited
Incorporated: 7 June 1989 *Employees:* 410
Net Worth: £69,464,000 *Total Assets:* £81,311,000
Registered Office: Harpenden, Herts, AL5 2JQ
Activities: Other research and experimental development on natural sciences and engineering
Officers: Louise Ann Warren, Secretary; Professor Sir David Charles Baulcombe [1952] Director/Academic; Sir John Rex Beddington [1945] Director/Trustee; Russell Leon Brooks [1972] Director/Lawyer; Dr Oliver Peter Doubleday [1952] Director/Farmer; Professor Hugh Charles Jonathan Godfray [1958] Director/University Professor; Stuart James Jarvis [1969] Director/Asset Management; Dr Alastair Roland Leake [1961] Director/Agricultural Scientist; Sally Ann Smith [1973] Director/Environmental Sustainability Manager; Professor David Michael Winter [1955] Director/University Professor

The Rothschild Foundation
Incorporated: 18 August 2010 *Employees:* 238
Net Worth: £654,974,912 *Total Assets:* £673,321,664
Registered Office: Windmill Hill, Silk Street, Waddesdon, Aylesbury, Bucks, HP18 0JZ
Activities: Activities of extraterritorial organisations and bodies
Officers: The Honourable Janet Francis de Botton [1952] Director; Emily Magda Freeman-Attwood [1967] Director/Farmer; Francesco Jonathan Goedhuis [1982] Director/Principal; Lord David John Ogilvy [1958] Director/Landowner/Musician; The Hon Hannah Mary Rothschild [1962] Director/Film Producer; Lord Nathaniel Charles Jacob Rothschild [1936] Director; Peter John Charles Troughton [1948] Director

Roundwood Park School Academy Trust
Incorporated: 6 July 2011 *Employees:* 223
Net Worth: £12,332,236 *Total Assets:* £13,617,675
Registered Office: Roundwood Park School, Roundwood Park, Harpenden, Herts, AL5 3AE
Activities: General secondary education
Officers: Anthony Kenneth Smith, Secretary; Heather Bayne [1968] Director/Garden Designer; Dr Joanne Clare Betts [1972] Director/Research Scientist; Judith Helen Codling [1965] Director/Pension Scheme Secretary; Sylvia Crowley [1956] Director/Retired; Kevin John Ford [1959] Director/Engineer; Raymond Stephen Fryer [1969] Director/Database Architect; Moira Greta Hart [1959] Director/Teacher; Fiona Ann Haynes [1963] Director/Integration Officer; Alan Charles Henshall [1967] Director; Dean Jamie Inns [1994] Director/Network Manager; Jean-Michel Jacquinot [1969] Director/Teacher [French]; Mark Andrew Jones [1988] Director/Teacher; Sharleen Mortimer [1964] Director/University Lecturer; Christopher Keith Salmon [1968] Director/Central Banking; Benjamin David Donald Turner [1968] Director; Nicholas Velody [1965] Director/Author; Michael Anthony Wells [1953] Director/Retired

Routebuy Limited
Incorporated: 14 March 1996 *Employees:* 3
Net Worth: £3,718,374 *Total Assets:* £14,339,306
Registered Office: Commodity House, Braxted Road, Great Braxted, Witham, Essex, CM8 3EW
Activities: Other letting and operating of own or leased real estate
Officers: Alec Gunn [1953] Director/Property Developer; Andrew Derek Jordan [1983] Finance Director; Dean Warriner [1984] Director

Rowan International Limited
Incorporated: 5 March 1990 *Employees:* 63
Net Worth: £11,532,130 *Total Assets:* £21,866,686
Registered Office: Endeavour House, Endeavour Drive, Festival Leisure Park, Basildon, Essex, SS14 3WF
Activities: Non-specialised wholesale trade
Parent: Lloyds Investments Group Holdings Limited
Officers: Duncan Clive Mastin [1967] Director; David Richard Parry [1959] Director; John Christopher Place [1977] Director

Rowan International Topco Limited
Incorporated: 29 June 2017 *Employees:* 63
Net Worth Deficit: £22,587 *Total Assets:* £15,457,829
Registered Office: Endeavour House, Endeavour Drive, Festival Leisure Park, Basildon, Essex, SS14 3WF
Activities: Non-trading company
Officers: Jonathan Bradley Cleland [1965] Director; Duncan Clive Mastin [1967] Director; David Richard Parry [1959] Director; John Christopher Place [1977] Director; Pascal Adrian Wittet [1981] Director

Rowe Farming Limited
Incorporated: 19 November 2004 *Employees:* 205
Net Worth: £6,650,000 *Total Assets:* £16,421,000
Registered Office: Greenvale AP Limited, Floods Ferry Road, Doddington, March, Cambs, PE15 0UW
Activities: Growing of vegetables and melons, roots and tubers
Parent: Produce Investments PLC
Officers: Angus Stuart Walton Armstrong [1964] Director; Daniel Collins [1980] Director; Caroline Davies [1974] Director; Robert James Keverne Stacey [1974] Director

Rowlands 2014 Limited
Incorporated: 22 August 2014 *Employees:* 61
Net Worth: £15,997,321 *Total Assets:* £22,445,204
Registered Office: 101 Rowlands Avenue, Hatch End, Pinner, Middlesex, HA5 4AW
Activities: Activities of other holding companies n.e.c.
Major Shareholder: Michael O'Hara
Officers: Colin Hambling, Secretary; Michael O'Hara [1947] Director [Irish]

Rowlandson Investments Limited
Incorporated: 3 November 1961 *Employees:* 7
Net Worth Deficit: £10,899,915 *Total Assets:* £25,810,204
Registered Office: Graham House, 7 Wyllyotts Place, Potters Bar, Herts, EN6 2JD
Activities: Financial intermediation not elsewhere classified
Parent: RO Group Property Ventures Limited
Officers: Edward Thomas Morton Rowlandson [1974] Director; Richard Graham St John Rowlandson [1939] Director/Chartered Accountant

The Royal Air Force Central Fund
Incorporated: 4 June 2013 *Employees:* 11
Net Worth: £41,842,520 *Total Assets:* £44,561,656
Registered Office: Hurricane Building, HQ Air Command, Wycombe Road, RAF High Wycombe, High Wycombe, Bucks, HP14 4UE
Activities: Defence activities
Officers: Nicola Graske, Secretary; Sally Bridgeland [1964] Director/Actuary; Jonathan Crossley [1968] Director/RAF Warrant Officer; Alison Farmery [1962] Director/Media Consultant; John Charles Michaelson [1953] Director/Venture Capital [American]; Dr Eamonn Mark Molloy [1971] Director/Professor; Michael Wigston [1968] Director/RAF Officer; Mark Williams [1959] Director/RAF Reserve

Royal Docks Property LLP
Incorporated: 20 October 2016 *Employees:* 27
Net Worth: £49,646,900 *Total Assets:* £71,380,480
Registered Office: Apirose House, 48a High Street, Edgware, Middlesex, HA8 7EQ
Officers: Manish Mansukhlal Gudka [1970] Member; Gareth Jones [1973] Member; Suraj Rashmikant Rashmikant [1982] LLP Member

Roys (Wroxham),Limited
Incorporated: 20 May 1931 *Employees:* 791
Net Worth: £34,349,828 *Total Assets:* £40,307,512
Registered Office: Hoveton, St John, Wroxham, Norfolk, NR12 8DB
Activities: Retail sale in non-specialised stores with food, beverages or tobacco predominating
Shareholders: Katherine Ann Roy; Edward Martin Roy
Officers: Edward Martin Roy, Secretary/Director; Tim How [1950] Director; Alison Jill Levett [1958] Director; Edward Martin Roy [1969] Director; Paul Arnold Roy [1971] Director; John Wheeler [1949] Director

Royston Holdings Limited
Incorporated: 21 June 2016 *Employees:* 210
Net Worth: £2,870,760 *Total Assets:* £34,668,704
Registered Office: Unit B1, Luton Enterprise Park, Sundon Park Road, Luton, Beds, LU3 3GU
Activities: Activities of distribution holding companies
Major Shareholder: Divyesh Mansukhlal Kamdar
Officers: Divyesh Mansukhlal Kamdar, Secretary; Anita Divyesh Kamdar [1962] Director; Divyesh Mansukhlal Kamdar [1961] Director; Ishan Divyesh Kamdar [1988] Director

The Royston Schools Academy Trust
Incorporated: 6 July 2011 *Employees:* 167
Net Worth: £6,828,245 *Total Assets:* £10,436,495
Registered Office: Meridian School, Garden Walk, Royston, Herts, SG8 7JH
Activities: General secondary education
Officers: Alison Merritt, Secretary; Carol Boston [1961] Director/Banker; David Brynjolffssen [1949] Director; Catherine Ann Fage [1967] Director/Administrator; Gordon James Farquhar [1975] Director/Headteacher; David Alan Morgan [1959] Director/Semi Retired; Laura Rawlings [1980] Director/Headteacher; Dennis Edward Webster [1938] Director/Retired

Roythornes Limited
Incorporated: 4 June 2008 *Employees:* 188
Net Worth: £7,756,359 *Total Assets:* £11,299,595
Registered Office: Roythornes Limited, Enterprise Way, Pinchbeck, Spalding, Lincs, PE11 3YR
Activities: Other business support service activities n.e.c.
Officers: Ann Elizabeth Barrasso, Secretary; Peter William Wels Cusick [1965] Director/Solicitor; Thomas Guy Foottit [1961] Director/Solicitor; Nicholas Guy Ingrey [1957] Director/Lawyer; Vember Mortlock [1966] Director/Solicitor; Jarred Thomas Wright [1973] Director/Solicitor

RP2 Holdings Limited
Incorporated: 31 January 2006 *Employees:* 45
Net Worth: £3,243,639 *Total Assets:* £12,601,265
Registered Office: Aquila House, Waterloo Lane, Chelmsford, Essex, CM1 1BN
Activities: Activities of head offices
Shareholders: Victoria Elizabeth Bird; Martin Cole
Officers: Victoria Elizabeth Bird [1977] Director; Martin Cole [1973] Director; Daniel Jones [1971] Director

RP2 Limited
Incorporated: 20 September 1991 *Employees:* 45
Net Worth: £1,860,042 *Total Assets:* £10,700,064
Registered Office: Aquila House, Waterloo Lane, Chelmsford, Essex, CM1 1BN
Activities: Pre-press and pre-media services
Parent: RP2 Holdings Limited
Officers: Victoria Elizabeth Bird [1977] Director/Advertising; Martin Cole [1973] Director; Daniel Jones [1971] Director

RPSD2 Limited
Incorporated: 12 August 2016
Net Worth: £102 *Total Assets:* £15,011,804
Registered Office: 99 Kenton Road, Harrow, Middlesex, HA3 0AN
Activities: Motion picture production activities
Parent: Riverstone Pictures Limited
Officers: Nicholas Anthony Crosfield Bower [1975] Director/Film Producer; Deepak Nayar [1959] Director/Film Producer [American]

RQ Capital Limited
Incorporated: 18 January 2012 *Employees:* 4
Net Worth: £1,753,772 *Total Assets:* £19,815,660
Registered Office: Bawdeswell Hall, Bawdeswell, Dereham, Norfolk, NR20 4SA
Activities: Development of building projects
Shareholder: Robert Edward Quintin Gurney
Officers: Antony Mark Francis [1957] Director; Jonathan Peter Freeland [1976] Director; Robert Edward Quintin Gurney [1969] Director/Property Financier; Edwin Harrell [1965] Director

RQ Capital Loans Limited
Incorporated: 17 May 2017
Net Worth: £537,191 *Total Assets:* £17,963,524
Registered Office: Bawdeswell Hall, Bawdeswell, Dereham, Norfolk, NR20 4SA
Activities: Other business support service activities n.e.c.
Parent: RQ Capital Limited
Officers: Antony Mark Francis [1957] Director; Jonathan Peter Freeland [1976] Director; Robert Edward Quintin Gurney [1969] Director; Edwin Harrell [1965] Director

RRD GDS Limited
Incorporated: 14 April 2005
Net Worth: £11,042,000 *Total Assets:* £11,042,000
Registered Office: Tower Close, Huntingdon, Cambs, PE29 7YD
Activities: Other business support service activities n.e.c.
Parent: RR Donnelley Global Document Solutions Group Limited
Officers: Jonathan Simon Richard Dally, Secretary; John Samuel Farmer [1960] Director; Kevin Trevor Woor [1965] Director/Financial Controller

RSA Island Village Limited
Incorporated: 20 March 1997 *Employees:* 3
Net Worth: £6,932,279 *Total Assets:* £9,314,666
Registered Office: 12 Island Centre Way, Enfield, Middlesex, EN3 6GS
Activities: Other service activities n.e.c.
Officers: Alan Charles Ray, Secretary; Martin Frank Jewell [1944] Director/Planning Consultant; Michael Anthony Polledri [1945] Director/Chartered Accountant; Robert Michael Taylor [1942] Director; Gary John Walker [1948] Director; Roger Philip Weeks [1961] Director/Retired; Michael Frederick Wehrmann [1947] Director/Business Consultant

RSS Jet Centre Limited
Incorporated: 27 December 1961 *Employees:* 41
Net Worth: £6,172,371 *Total Assets:* £20,442,050
Registered Office: Voyager House, 142 Prospect Way, Luton, Beds, LU2 9QH
Activities: Scheduled passenger air transport
Parent: BBA Overseas Holdings Limited
Officers: Yvette Helen Freeman [1967] Director; Daniel David Ruback [1977] Finance Director

Ruislip High School
Incorporated: 3 March 2014 *Employees:* 125
Net Worth: £15,408,638 *Total Assets:* £17,633,988
Registered Office: Ruislip High School, Sidmouth Drive, Ruislip, Middlesex, HA4 0BY
Activities: General secondary education
Officers: Mark Robert Bedwell [1961] Director/Accountant; Emma Flynn [1988] Director/Teacher; John Frederick Garner [1969] Director/Retired; Laura Horton [1990] Director/Teacher; Charles Khan [1972] Director; Edward Francis Lavery [1960] Director/Bank Manager; Martina Anne Bernadette Lecky [1971] Director/Teacher; Anna Leeves [1974] Director/Data Manager; Amarjit Mikulko-Valley [1975] Director/Teacher; Pauline Anne Nixon [1952] Director/Interim Head of Education Borough of Harrow; Maria Penicud [1954] Director/Education Consultant; Dr Mary Richards [1966] Director/University Lecturer; Nicholas Jon Symmons [1956] Director/IT Consultant; Steven Tuckwell [1968] Director/Head of Distribution/Logistics; Joannna Nicola Wagstaffe [1961] Director/Academic Registrar University of Law

Runwood Homes Limited
Incorporated: 30 July 1962 *Employees:* 4,387
Net Worth: £170,137,984 *Total Assets:* £344,548,032
Registered Office: Runwood House, 107 London Road, Hadleigh, Essex, SS7 2QL
Activities: Residential care activities for the elderly and disabled
Major Shareholder: Gordon George Sanders
Officers: Martin James Cooper, Secretary; Kathryn Clark [1975] Director; Martin James Cooper [1979] Director/Certified Chartered Accountant; Muyiwa Ilesanmi [1976] Director of Operations (England); Gavin James O'Hare-Connolly [1982] Group Operations Director; Gordon George Sanders [1946] Director/Chief Executive Officer; Sarah Jane Sanders [1975] HR Director; Thomas Sanders [1966] Building and Construction Director; Sue Smith [1964] Marketing Director

Rusant Limited
Incorporated: 24 March 2006 *Employees:* 23
Net Worth: £2,218,131 *Total Assets:* £9,633,257
Registered Office: 39 Parkside, Cambridge, CB1 1PN
Activities: Other mining and quarrying n.e.c.
Officers: Jocelyn Severyn de Warrene Waller, Secretary; Lord Peter Gilbert Daresbury [1953] Director; Yury Gulko [1950] General Director [Russian]; Alexey Malygi [1985] Director/Financial Analyst [Russian]; Jocelyn Severyn Waller [1943] Director

A Russell (Farmers) Limited
Incorporated: 3 September 1951 *Employees:* 18
Net Worth: £5,385,182 *Total Assets:* £8,393,092
Registered Office: Pentowan Farm, Church Road, Noak Hill, Romford, Essex, RM4 1LD
Activities: Growing of cereals (except rice), leguminous crops and oil seeds
Major Shareholder: David Guy Russell
Officers: David Guy Russell, Secretary; Daniel Russell [1986] Director; David Guy Russell [1959] Director/Farmer; Lloyd David Russell [1983] Director

Hilary Russell Group Ltd
Incorporated: 30 November 2016 *Employees:* 2
Net Worth: £16,865,658 *Total Assets:* £18,810,644
Registered Office: Abington Park Farm, Great Abington, Cambs, CB21 6AX
Activities: Mixed farming
Parent: Chaplin Group Limited
Officers: Hilary Ann Russell [1965] Director; William Anthony Bowater Russell [1965] Director

RWF Health and Community Developers (Tranche 1) Limited
Incorporated: 17 February 2004
Net Worth Deficit: £7,780,078 *Total Assets:* £22,827,822
Registered Office: 55 Station Road, Beaconsfield, Bucks, HP9 1QL
Activities: Other letting and operating of own or leased real estate
Parent: RWF Health and Community Developers Limited
Officers: Nigel Raymond Dodds, Secretary; Jamie Andrews [1970] Director; Ross William Driver [1981] Finance Director; David Alexander John Foot [1968] Investment Director, Infrastructure; James Christopher Heath [1975] Director

RWH Travel Limited
Incorporated: 24 December 1953 *Employees:* 60
Previous: Ramblers Holidays Limited
Net Worth: £10,452,522 *Total Assets:* £15,583,813
Registered Office: Lemsford Mill, Lemsford Village, Welwyn Garden City, Herts, AL8 7TR
Activities: Tour operator activities
Parent: Ramblers Holidays Group Limited
Officers: Anthony Philip Ward, Secretary; Clare Jennifer Bonnick [1961] Compliance Director; Annette Kathleen Cotter [1948] Director/Retired; Michael John Duxbury [1947] Director/Legal Consultant; Kevin James O'Regan [1968] Managing Director; Shaun O'Reilly [1944] Director/Retired; Martin Shepley [1945] Director/Retired; Jeffrey Sissons [1963] Director/Consultant; Anthony Philip Ward [1966] Finance Director; Gillian Patricia Ann Welsman [1949] Director/Retired

Ryan Elizabeth Holdings Public Limited Company
Incorporated: 23 December 1971 *Employees:* 16
Net Worth: £20,166,766 *Total Assets:* £26,457,876
Registered Office: Merchant House, 33 Fore Street, Ipswich, Suffolk, IP4 1JL
Activities: Other letting and operating of own or leased real estate
Parent: Elizabeth Holdings PLC
Officers: Abigail Louise Cattermole Dunnett, Secretary; Philip Thomas Barden [1961] Director/Solicitor; Abigail Louise Cattermole [1977] Director

Sue Ryder
Incorporated: 28 November 1968 *Employees:* 1,312
Net Worth: £55,510,000 *Total Assets:* £67,543,000
Registered Office: Kings House, King Street, Sudbury, Suffolk, CO10 2ED
Activities: Other human health activities
Officers: Helen Organ, Secretary; Michael John Attwood [1961] Director/Trustee; Dr Katherine Louise Buxton [1976] Director/Doctor; Dr Simon Jeremy Stovold Chataway [1965] Director/Consultant Neurologist; Jason Davies [1973] Director/Head of Audit and Risk; Murray Crombie Duncanson [1953] Director; Neil Geoffrey Goulden [1953] Director; Nicola Josephine Hayes [1970] Director; Susan Averil Hopgood [1956] Director/Retired; Stuart James Hudson [1982] Director; Margaret Anne Moore [1959] Director/Lawyer; Kevin Jonathan Rusling [1977] Managing Director; Helen Thomson [1958] Director; John Michael Wythe [1956] Director

Rylston Road Limited
Incorporated: 15 March 2000
Net Worth: £10,977,922 *Total Assets:* £13,203,523
Registered Office: Jubilee House, Jubilee Court, Dersingham, Kings Lynn, Norfolk, PE31 6HH
Activities: Buying and selling of own real estate
Shareholders: Nigel Anthony Knighton; Suzanne Knighton
Officers: Nigel Anthony Knighton [1959] Director/Surveyor; Suzanne Knighton [1960] Director/Investment Manager

Rysa Lodge Residential Properties Limited
Incorporated: 27 January 1993 *Employees:* 5
Net Worth: £10,146,121 *Total Assets:* £11,021,501
Registered Office: RYSA Lodge, School Road, Seething, Norwich, NR15 1DL
Activities: Buying and selling of own real estate
Parent: Otley Investments Limited
Officers: Christine Jill Key [1947] Director/Farmer; Jamie Key [1980] Director; Robin Wesley Key [1944] Director; Sophia Olivia Key [1983] Director/Solicitor; Timothy Key [1989] Director/Marketing Consultant

S & B Commercials Limited
Incorporated: 12 May 1982 *Employees:* 278
Previous: S & B Commercials PLC
Net Worth: £8,420,000 *Total Assets:* £60,623,000
Registered Office: S & B Commercials PLC, Travellers Lane, Welham Green, Hatfield, Herts, AL9 7HN
Activities: Sale of new cars and light motor vehicles
Parent: Motus Holdings (UK) Ltd
Officers: Andrew Barrie Welch, Secretary; William James Davey [1968] Director; Andrew Barrie Welch [1965] Director

S & T Audio Limited
Incorporated: 18 March 1999 *Employees:* 212
Net Worth: £10,511,376 *Total Assets:* £15,651,796
Registered Office: Suite 3, Warren House, 10-20 Main Road, Hockley, Essex, SS5 4QS
Activities: Other retail sale of new goods in specialised stores (not commercial art galleries and opticians)
Shareholders: Simon John Gilson; Terence Allen Hope
Officers: Simon John Gilson, Secretary/Director; Simon John Gilson [1963] Director; Terence Allen Hope [1963] Director

S & W Design & Build (Group) Limited
Incorporated: 3 April 2017
Net Worth: £10,670,398 *Total Assets:* £10,672,160
Registered Office: S & W House, Longhill Road, March, Cambs, PE15 0BL
Activities: Activities of other holding companies n.e.c.
Major Shareholder: Richard Whyles
Officers: Diane Lynn Nunn [1961] Director; Richard Whyles [1980] Director

S A Designer Parfums Limited
Incorporated: 11 April 2001 *Employees:* 58
Net Worth: £9,479,150 *Total Assets:* £38,092,696
Registered Office: Amertrans Park, Bushey Mill Lane, Watford, Herts, WD24 7JG
Activities: Wholesale of perfume and cosmetics
Parent: Shaneel Enterprises Ltd
Officers: Hitesh Bhogilal Mehta, Secretary; Dilesh Bhogilal Mehta [1960] Director; Hitesh Bhogilal Mehta [1956] Director

S and J Investments (Delivery Office Southall) Limited
Incorporated: 5 August 2011 *Employees:* 1
Net Worth: £2,772,253 *Total Assets:* £9,803,563
Registered Office: Melton House, 65-67 Clarendon Road, Watford, Herts, WD17 1DS
Activities: Activities of open-ended investment companies
Shareholder: Gursharan Singh Chadha
Officers: Gursharan Singh Chadha [1960] Finance Director; Vivek Singh Chadha [1988] Director/Businessman

S N B Holdings Limited
Incorporated: 15 March 2002 *Employees:* 167
Net Worth: £11,704,291 *Total Assets:* £18,470,068
Registered Office: The Barn Hotel, West End Road, Ruislip, Middlesex, HA4 6JB
Activities: Non-trading company
Major Shareholder: Shalil Nalin Bhattessa
Officers: Kathirgamathamby Jeggswaran, Secretary; Shalil Nalin Bhattessa [1968] Director/Hotelier

S-P RIL Limited
Incorporated: 14 July 1961
Net Worth: £52,179,000 *Total Assets:* £52,808,000
Registered Office: West Hill, Hertford Road, Hoddesdon, Herts, EN11 9BU
Activities: Non-trading company
Parent: Schering-Plough Holdings Limited
Officers: Richard Robinski, Secretary; Louise Jane Houson [1976] Director; Simon Nicholson [1975] Director; Ebru Can Temucin [1972] Director [Turkish]

S.A. (300) Limited
Incorporated: 7 January 1929
Net Worth: £8,638,000 *Total Assets:* £8,638,000
Registered Office: Yule Catto Building, Temple Fields, Harlow, Essex, CM20 2BH
Activities: Non-trading company
Parent: Synthomer PLC
Officers: Richard Atkinson, Secretary; Richard Atkinson [1962] Director/Company Secretary; Stephen Guy Bennett [1964] Director

S.C.W.S. (Holdings) Limited
Incorporated: 22 February 1966 *Employees:* 114
Net Worth: £8,551,522 *Total Assets:* £12,642,381
Registered Office: Abbotsgate House, Hollow Road, Bury St Edmunds, Suffolk, IP32 7FA
Activities: Activities of head offices
Major Shareholder: Andrew Walter Scales
Officers: Andrew Walter Scales, Secretary; Kate Sarah Mantle [1981] Director; Nicola Anne Murphy [1984] Director; Andrew Walter Scales [1952] Director/Structural Engineer; Emma Lindsey Watson [1977] Director

S.T.C.Plumbing & Heating Merchants Limited
Incorporated: 4 May 1972 *Employees:* 40
Net Worth: £9,488,906 *Total Assets:* £17,098,472
Registered Office: Hopson House, Breakspear Road, Ruislip, Middlesex, HA4 7SE
Activities: Wholesale of hardware, plumbing and heating equipment and supplies
Major Shareholder: Terence John Clyne
Officers: Jason Clyne [1972] Director/Manager; Terence John Clyne [1943] Director/Heating Consultant

SA.GI.MA. Limited
Incorporated: 25 September 2014
Net Worth: £8,068,944 *Total Assets:* £8,068,944
Registered Office: Dickens House, Guithavon Street, Witham, Essex, CM8 1BJ
Activities: Buying and selling of own real estate
Parent: Sextant Consolidated Limited
Officers: Vincenzo Bianchi [1958] Director [Italian]; Sabrina Guariento [1970] Director [Italian]; Philip Lawrence [1953] Director

Saba Infra Cambridgeshire Limited
Incorporated: 9 October 2012
Previous: Indigo Infra Cambridgeshire Limited
Net Worth Deficit: £1,176,686 *Total Assets:* £13,827,983
Registered Office: Oak House, Reeds Crescent, Watford, Herts, WD24 4PH
Activities: Other transportation support activities
Parent: Saba Infra UK Limited
Officers: Gary Charles Pickard, Secretary; Phillip David Herring [1970] Managing Director; Josep Oriol Carreras [1961] Director [Spanish]; Gary Charles Pickard [1965] Director/Chartered Accountant

Saba Infra Cardiff Limited
Incorporated: 2 February 1996
Previous: Indigo Infra Cardiff Limited
Net Worth: £8,628,463 *Total Assets:* £10,321,327
Registered Office: Oak House, Reeds Crescent, Watford, Herts, WD24 4PH
Activities: Other transportation support activities
Parent: Saba Infra Holdings UK Limited
Officers: Gary Charles Pickard, Secretary; Phillip David Herring [1970] Managing Director; Josep Oriol Carreras [1961] Director [Spanish]; Gary Charles Pickard [1965] Finance Director

Saba Infra Gloucestershire Limited
Incorporated: 7 August 2009
Previous: Indigo Infra Gloucestershire Limited
Net Worth: £3,857,069 *Total Assets:* £11,914,174
Registered Office: Oak House, Reeds Crescent, Watford, Herts, WD24 4PH
Activities: Other transportation support activities
Parent: Saba Infra UK Limited
Officers: Gary Charles Pickard, Secretary; Phillip David Herring [1970] Managing Director; Josep Oriol Carreras [1961] Director [Spanish]; Gary Charles Pickard [1965] Finance Director

Saba Infra Hertfordshire Limited
Incorporated: 28 May 2010
Previous: Indigo Infra Hertfordshire Limited
Net Worth: £3,128,728 *Total Assets:* £10,594,414
Registered Office: Oak House, Reeds Crescent, Watford, Herts, WD24 4PH
Activities: Other transportation support activities
Parent: Saba Infra UK Limited
Officers: Gary Charles Pickard, Secretary; Phillip David Herring [1970] Managing Director; Josep Oriol Carreras [1961] Director [Spanish]; Gary Charles Pickard [1965] Finance Director

Saba Infra Holdings UK Limited
Incorporated: 31 October 1991
Previous: Indigo Infra Holdings UK Limited
Net Worth: £14,647,520 *Total Assets:* £28,750,320
Registered Office: Oak House, Reeds Crescent, Watford, Herts, WD24 4PH
Activities: Activities of head offices
Parent: Saba Group UK Limited
Officers: Gary Charles Pickard, Secretary; Phillip David Herring [1970] Managing Director; Josep Oriol Carreras [1961] Director [Spanish]; Gary Charles Pickard [1965] Finance Director

Saba Park Services UK Limited
Incorporated: 17 March 1989 *Employees:* 832
Previous: Indigo Park Services UK Limited
Net Worth: £7,544,901 *Total Assets:* £18,971,592
Registered Office: Oak House, Reeds Crescent, Watford, Herts, WD24 4PH
Activities: Other transportation support activities
Parent: Saba Infra Holdings UK Limited
Officers: Gary Charles Pickard, Secretary; Phillip David Herring [1970] Managing Director; Josep Oriol Carreras [1961] Director [Spanish]; Gary Charles Pickard [1965] Finance Director

Sabre Retail Fashion Limited
Incorporated: 23 January 2012 *Employees:* 817
Net Worth: £28,590,000 *Total Assets:* £50,532,000
Registered Office: St John's Place, Easton Street, High Wycombe, Bucks, HP11 1NL
Activities: Retail sale of clothing in specialised stores
Parent: Mustard Global Limited
Officers: Judith Anne Bean, Secretary; Lisa Agar-Rea [1968] Brand Director; Peter Wynne Davies [1949] Director; Stuart Antony Grant [1975] Director/Chief Operating Officer; Kara Eugenie Groves [1969] Director; Elizabeth Claire Houghton [1964] Director/Chief Executive

Sabres Educational Trust
Incorporated: 8 November 2010 *Employees:* 80
Net Worth: £7,975,709 *Total Assets:* £8,283,485
Registered Office: IES Breckland School, Crown Street, Brandon, Suffolk, IP27 0NJ
Activities: General secondary education
Officers: Linda Dawn Challis [1964] Director/School Caretaker; Natalie Chandler [1973] Director/Nurse; Kate Curtis [1970] Director/Office Manager; Joseph Michael Green [1984] Director/Manager; Penelope Anne Lury [1950] Director/Part Time Exam Invigilator; Robert Pritchard [1963] Director/Charity Manager; Barbara Sparks [1959] Director/Teaching Assistant; Iain Crispin Trafford [1966] Director/Teacher; Ben Willgress [1993] Director/Teacher

S. Sacker (Claydon) Limited
Incorporated: 3 November 1980 *Employees:* 74
Net Worth: £4,964,117 *Total Assets:* £14,481,174
Registered Office: Railway Sidings, Gipping Road, Great Blakenham, Ipswich, Suffolk, IP6 0JB
Activities: Collection of non-hazardous waste
Shareholders: Adrian Alexander Dodds; David Graeme Dodds
Officers: Adrian Alexander Dodds [1960] Director/Metal Reclaimer; Charles Anthony Robert Dodds [1931] Director/Metal Reclaimer; David Graeme Dodds [1962] Director/Metal Reclaimer; Ewan Christopher Cameron Dodds [1959] Director/Surveyor

Safe Computing Limited
Incorporated: 3 March 1975 *Employees:* 144
Net Worth: £19,027,000 *Total Assets:* £25,791,000
Registered Office: The Old School, School Lane, Stratford St Mary, Colchester, Essex, CO7 6LZ
Activities: Other information technology service activities
Parent: Safe Computing Holdings Limited
Officers: Christopher Andrew Armstrong Bayne [1971] Director; Stephen James Blundell [1970] Director; Adam John Witherow Brown [1963] Director/Chief Commercial Officer

Safegold Properties Limited
Incorporated: 19 September 1986 *Employees:* 2
Net Worth: £18,110,116 *Total Assets:* £24,876,724
Registered Office: 5 Chartwell Place, Middle Road, Harrow, Middlesex, HA2 0HE
Activities: Other letting and operating of own or leased real estate
Officers: Kiran Dalia, Secretary; Kiran Dalia [1959] Director/Property Dealer; Rasiklal Chatrabhuj Dalia [1952] Director/Property Dealer

Safestore Acquisition Limited
Incorporated: 16 July 2003 *Employees:* 2
Net Worth: £251,432,992 *Total Assets:* £576,177,024
Registered Office: Brittanic House, Stirling Way, Borehamwood, Herts, WD6 2BT
Activities: Activities of head offices
Parent: Safestore Group Limited
Officers: Andrew Brian Jones [1966] Director/Chartered Accountant; Federico Vecchioli [1966] Director [French]

Safestore Group Limited
Incorporated: 16 July 2003 *Employees:* 2
Net Worth: £8,886,000 *Total Assets:* £543,182,976
Registered Office: Brittanic House, Stirling Way, Borehamwood, Herts, WD6 2BT
Activities: Activities of head offices
Parent: Safestore Investments Limited
Officers: Andrew Brian Jones [1966] Director/Chartered Accountant; Federico Vecchioli [1966] Director [French]

Safestore Holdings PLC
Incorporated: 8 April 2003 *Employees:* 584
Net Worth: £637,699,968 *Total Assets:* £1,156,600,064
Registered Office: Brittanic House, Stirling Way, Borehamwood, Herts, WD6 2BT
Activities: Activities of head offices
Officers: Helen Mary Bramall, Secretary; Claire Balmforth [1967] Director; Andrew Brian Jones [1966] Director/Chartered Accountant; Joanne Louise Kenrick [1966] Director; Ian Stephen Krieger [1952] Director; Alan Stuart Lewis [1952] Director/Investment Banker; William Alder Oliver [1956] Director; Federico Vecchioli [1966] Director [French]

Safestore Investments Limited
Incorporated: 23 November 2006 *Employees:* 2
Net Worth: £1,256,000 *Total Assets:* £150,000,000
Registered Office: Brittanic House, Stirling Way, Borehamwood, Herts, WD6 2BT
Activities: Activities of other holding companies n.e.c.
Parent: Safestore Holdings PLC
Officers: Andrew Brian Jones [1966] Director/Chartered Accountant; Federico Vecchioli [1966] Director [French]

Safestore Limited
Incorporated: 19 July 2005 *Employees:* 453
Net Worth: £156,804,992 *Total Assets:* £447,948,000
Registered Office: Brittanic House, Stirling Way, Borehamwood, Herts, WD6 2BT
Activities: Other letting and operating of own or leased real estate
Parent: Safestore Acquisition Limited
Officers: Andrew Brian Jones [1966] Director/Chartered Accountant; David Roy Penniston [1958] Property Director; Federico Vecchioli [1966] Director [French]

Safestore Properties Limited
Incorporated: 15 January 1996 *Employees:* 3
Net Worth: £126,238,000 *Total Assets:* £223,668,992
Registered Office: Brittanic House, Stirling Way, Borehamwood, Herts, WD6 2BT
Activities: Other letting and operating of own or leased real estate
Parent: Mentmore Limited
Officers: Andrew Brian Jones [1966] Director/Chartered Accountant; David Roy Penniston [1958] Property Director; Federico Vecchioli [1966] Director [French]

Saffie Investments Limited
Incorporated: 15 January 2016 *Employees:* 2
Net Worth: £1,234,559 *Total Assets:* £11,110,722
Registered Office: JPB Harris, Harmile House, 54 St Mary's Street, Upminster, Essex, RM14 2QT
Activities: Activities of investment trusts
Shareholders: Damon Marcus Buffini; Lady Deborah Si Yin Buffini
Officers: Sir Damon Marcus Buffini [1962] Director/Venture Capitalist; Lady Deborah SI Yin Buffini [1962] Director/Solicitor

Saffron Academy Trust
Incorporated: 28 April 2011 *Employees:* 589
Net Worth: £22,303,288 *Total Assets:* £34,285,536
Registered Office: Saffron Walden County High School, Audley End Road, Saffron Walden, Essex, CB11 4UH
Activities: General secondary education
Officers: Paul Douglas Wilson, Secretary; Steven Keith Bancroft [1968] Director/Programme and Account Manager; David Anthony Barrs [1955] Director/Headteacher; Caroline Harriet Derbyshire [1965] Director/Headteacher; Sarah Elizabeth Dignasse [1957] Director/Retired; Mark Philip Hayes [1956] Director; Dr James Henry Keeler [1959] Director/University Lecturer; John David Kerr [1959] Director; Jane Dolores Marshall [1971] Director [Irish]; Ian Andrew Murphy [1958] Director/Business Owner; Paul John Blair Sinnott [1967] Accounts Director; Jacqueline Sweeting [1963] Director/School Business Manager; Linda Godelieve Fabiola Vincent-Van Overloop [1960] Director [Belgian]

Saffron Housing Finance PLC
Incorporated: 6 June 2013
Net Worth: £50,000 *Total Assets:* £128,359,000
Registered Office: Saffron Barn, Swan Lane, Long Stratton, Norwich, NR15 2XP
Activities: Financial intermediation not elsewhere classified
Officers: Ian Paul Hill, Secretary; Anthony Ellis Hall [1961] Director/Chief Executive; Iain Richard Innes [1977] Finance Director; James Joseph Tully [1973] Director/Senior Manager Royal Mail; Robert Vernon Walder [1954] Director/Retired

Saffron Insurance Holdings Limited
Incorporated: 24 July 2009 *Employees:* 125
Net Worth: £2,258,722 *Total Assets:* £8,251,955
Registered Office: 22 High Street, Saffron Walden, Essex, CB10 1AX
Activities: Activities of head offices
Parent: Stamford Investment Holdings Limited
Officers: Colin John Fellows, Secretary; David Charles Beswick [1964] Director; Ian Edward Clark [1960] Director; Colin John Fellows [1966] Director/Accountant; Desmond Joseph O'Connor [1971] Director/Insurance Banker

SAFL British Hotels Limited
Incorporated: 15 March 2017
Net Worth: £9,995,786 *Total Assets:* £9,996,787
Registered Office: Belstead Brook Hotel, Belstead, Ipswich, Suffolk, IP2 9HB
Activities: Hotels and similar accommodation
Officers: Chidambaram Arumugam [1955] Director [Indian]; Ravi Venkatraman [1965] Director/Head of Audit [Singaporean]

Safran Electrical & Power UK Ltd
Incorporated: 14 November 2012 *Employees:* 478
Previous: Safran Power UK Ltd.
Net Worth: £160,408,992 *Total Assets:* £224,582,000
Registered Office: Pitstone Green Business Park, Westfield Road, Pitstone, Leighton Buzzard, Beds, LU7 9GT
Activities: Manufacture of air and spacecraft and related machinery
Parent: Safran
Officers: Gaelle Claire Moss, Secretary; Gildas Bodolec [1978] Director/Power Division Controller [French]; Paul Clifford [1963] Managing Director; Alain Sauret [1958] Director/Chairman and CEO [French]

Sagentia Limited
Incorporated: 9 December 1986 *Employees:* 129
Net Worth: £14,908,000 *Total Assets:* £44,449,000
Registered Office: Harston Mill, Royston Road, Harston, Cambridge, CB22 7GG
Activities: Management consultancy activities other than financial management
Parent: Science Group PLC
Officers: Sarah Elizabeth Cole, Secretary; Rebecca Anne Archer [1981] Director; Sarah Elizabeth Cole [1979] Director/Solicitor

Sahara Care Limited
Incorporated: 28 February 2000 *Employees:* 137
Previous: Sahara Care Homes Limited
Net Worth: £6,628,119 *Total Assets:* £8,354,130
Registered Office: Haslers, Old Station Road, Loughton, Essex, IG10 4PL
Activities: Residential care activities for the elderly and disabled
Shareholders: Terence William Brown; Hurjinder Sharon Kaur
Officers: Darren Scott Turner, Secretary; Terence William Brown [1942] Director; Sharon Lynn Bye [1963] Director/Chief Executive; Hurjinder Sharon Kaur [1967] Director/Manager; Christopher Brian Charles Manhire [1955] Director/Chartered Surveyor; Darren Scott Turner [1969] Director/Certified Accountant

Saint Francis Hospice
Incorporated: 11 May 1978 *Employees:* 296
Net Worth: £12,996,000 *Total Assets:* £13,928,000
Registered Office: The Hall, Broxhill Road, Havering-atte-Bower, Romford, Essex, RM4 1QH
Activities: Hospital activities
Officers: Lynn Bryan, Secretary; Peter Adams [1944] Director/Retired; Peter John Batt [1974] Divisional Managing Director; Peter Desmond Crutchett [1951] Director/Actuary; David Thomas Forster [1948] Director/Retired; Paul Gwinn [1946] Director/Retired; Amanda Camille Hallums [1958] NHS Director (Interim); Linda Ann Huggett [1952] Director/Councillor; Malcolm Paul Miller [1949] Director/Retired; Pauline Margaret Russell [1951] Director/Retired; Dr Gurdev Singh Saini [1947] Director/GP; Dr Robert MacKenzie Weatherstone [1946] Director/Consultant Physician; Colin Robert Wilkins [1981] Director/Account Manager

Saint Vincent Holdings Limited
Incorporated: 13 October 2011 *Employees:* 277
Net Worth: £36,450,000 *Total Assets:* £78,216,000
Registered Office: School Lane, Sprowston, Norwich, NR7 8TL
Activities: Non-trading company
Major Shareholder: Peter George Colby
Officers: Michael John Sutton, Secretary; Simon William Beckett [1964] Director; Peter George Colby [1942] Director

Salavera Trading Limited
Incorporated: 22 March 2012
Net Worth Deficit: £131,562 *Total Assets:* £8,245,438
Registered Office: Office 11, 6-8 Dartford Road, Regent Buildings, March, Cambs, PE15 8AQ
Activities: Other business support service activities n.e.c.
Officers: Jorge Luis Castillo [1971] Director [Belizean]

Salient Investments Ltd.
Incorporated: 19 January 1994
Net Worth: £4,279,515 *Total Assets:* £8,179,708
Registered Office: 2nd Floor, 29-33 Church Road, Stanmore, Middlesex, HA7 4AR
Activities: Buying and selling of own real estate
Officers: Mukesh Kanubhai Patel, Secretary; Minaben Mahesh Patel [1961] Director

Salisbury Holdings Limited
Incorporated: 11 March 2014 *Employees:* 407
Net Worth: £11,356,000 *Total Assets:* £22,835,000
Registered Office: Cambridge House, 47 Clarendon Road, Watford, Herts, WD17 1HP
Activities: Combined facilities support activities
Officers: Michael Anthony Wilson, Secretary; Simon David Ainslie Jones [1970] Director/Chief Financial Officer; Mark Julian Smith [1970] Director; Edward Michael Swales [1979] Director; Michael Anthony Wilson [1956] Director/Solicitor

Salisbury Workplace Services Limited
Incorporated: 6 March 2012 *Employees:* 137
Previous: Salisbury FM Limited
Net Worth: £10,552,000 *Total Assets:* £21,566,000
Registered Office: Cambridge House, Clarendon Road, Watford, Herts, WD17 1HP
Activities: Combined facilities support activities
Parent: Salisbury Holdings Limited
Officers: Michael Anthony Wilson, Secretary; Simon David Ainslie Jones [1970] Director/Chief Financial Officer; Mark Julian Smith [1970] Director; Edward Michael Swales [1979] Director; Michael Anthony Wilson [1956] Director/Solicitor

Salmon Management and Finance Limited
Incorporated: 30 September 1949 *Employees:* 3
Previous: Foumar Properties Limited
Net Worth: £23,117,916 *Total Assets:* £23,369,664
Registered Office: c/o Landmark Chartered Accountants, Leavesden Park, 5 Hurcules Way, Watford, Herts, WD25 7GS
Activities: Other credit granting n.e.c.
Shareholders: Cripps Trust Corporation Limited; Isobel Jean Hunter; Jacqueline Mary Oates; Penelope Jacqueline Warr; Maurice Bertram Gluck
Officers: Maurice Bertram Gluck [1930] Director/Chartered Accountant; Paul Jeremy Roger Newman [1951] Director; Harold Charles Wilson [1955] Director/Accountant

Salperton Park Estate Limited
Incorporated: 16 August 1995 *Employees:* 14
Net Worth: £7,600,824 *Total Assets:* £15,077,502
Registered Office: St John's Court, Easton Street, High Wycombe, Bucks, HP11 1JX
Activities: Growing of cereals (except rice), leguminous crops and oil seeds
Parent: Rysaffe Actionnaires SARL
Officers: Jason Timothy Houghton, Secretary; Jason Timothy Houghton [1969] Director/Company Manager

Samson Materials Handling Limited
Incorporated: 4 April 1975 *Employees:* 36
Net Worth Deficit: £185,465 *Total Assets:* £8,382,472
Registered Office: Gemini House, Cambridgeshire Business Park, 1 Bartholomews Walk, Ely, Cambs, CB7 4EA
Activities: Manufacture of lifting and handling equipment
Major Shareholder: Franz-Walter Aumund
Officers: Franz Walter Aumund [1944] Director [German]; Andreas Christian Klottka [1962] Managing Director [German]; Dale Lockley [1970] Director

Samsung Cambridge Solution Centre Limited
Incorporated: 24 September 2012 *Employees:* 139
Net Worth: £74,480,032 *Total Assets:* £82,883,376
Registered Office: St John's House, St John's Innovation Park, Cowley Road, Cambridge, CB4 0DS
Activities: Wireless telecommunications activities
Officers: Rajinder Singh Gawera [1968] Director/Vice President; Hyunjoon Kang [1980] Director/Employee [South Korean]; Joonsuk Kim [1969] Director [American]; Jungsuk Oh [1970] Managing Director [South Korean]

Sanctuary Personnel Limited
Incorporated: 20 October 2006 *Employees:* 231
Net Worth: £3,612,317 *Total Assets:* £19,584,872
Registered Office: 15 Friars Street, Ipswich, Suffolk, IP1 1TD
Activities: Temporary employment agency activities
Officers: David Anthony Hill [1981] Director/Recruitment; Paula Anne McPherson [1967] Director; James Rook [1974] Director/Recruitment

Sandbrook Overseas Investments Limited
Incorporated: 10 October 2007
Net Worth: £1,459,459,456 *Total Assets:* £1,577,538,688
Registered Office: Westpoint, Peterborough Business Park, Lynch Wood, Peterborough, Cambs, PE2 6FZ
Activities: Activities of head offices
Parent: Thomas Cook Group PLC
Officers: Shirley Bradley, Secretary; Alice Hannah Marsden [1983] Director

D.H.Sanderson and Son Limited
Incorporated: 29 November 1957 *Employees:* 9
Net Worth: £13,980,676 *Total Assets:* £16,384,989
Registered Office: St John's Farm, Beachamwell, King's Lynn, Norfolk, PE37 8BE
Activities: Growing of cereals (except rice), leguminous crops and oil seeds
Shareholders: John Stanley Hamilton Sanderson; Gillian Sanderson
Officers: Gillian Sanderson, Secretary; Caroline Lindsay Sanderson [1967] Director; Gillian Sanderson [1937] Director/Secretary; Hugh Howard Hamilton Sanderson [1966] Director/Purchasing Manager; John Stanley Hamilton Sanderson [1934] Director/Farmer; Thomas Charles Hamilton Sanderson [1964] Director

Sandfields Farms Limited
Incorporated: 20 July 2007 *Employees:* 395
Net Worth: £10,495,063 *Total Assets:* £19,236,968
Registered Office: Hainey Farm, Barway, Ely, Cambs, CB7 5TZ
Activities: Growing of cereals (except rice), leguminous crops and oil seeds
Parent: JB Shropshire & Sons Ltd
Officers: David Thompson, Secretary/Accountant; John Bourne Shropshire [1955] Director; David Thompson [1968] Director/Accountant; William Derek Wilkinson [1966] Director/Vegetable Grower

Sandhill Homes Limited
Incorporated: 25 January 1999
Net Worth: £1,345,958 *Total Assets:* £16,372,683
Registered Office: Unit 5 Charlton Mead Lane, Hoddesdon, Herts, EN11 0DJ
Activities: Construction of domestic buildings
Parent: The Sandhill Homes Corporation Limited
Officers: Nicholas David Cooper, Secretary; David John Cooper [1953] Director; Nicholas David Cooper [1977] Director/Builder

Sandhill Park Limited
Incorporated: 20 November 1991 *Employees:* 6
Net Worth: £7,400,632 *Total Assets:* £8,041,243
Registered Office: York House, Empire Way, Wembley, Middlesex, HA9 0FQ
Activities: Other letting and operating of own or leased real estate
Officers: Sylvia Frances Fineberg, Secretary; David Fineberg [1940] Director/Chartered Surveyor; Paul Francis Fineberg [1963] Director; Simon Vivian Fineberg [1966] Director; Sylvia Frances Fineberg [1942] Director

Saniflo Limited
Incorporated: 21 February 1979 *Employees:* 31
Net Worth: £4,521,623 *Total Assets:* £8,017,655
Registered Office: Howard House, The Runway, South Ruislip, Middlesex, HA4 6SE
Activities: Wholesale of hardware, plumbing and heating equipment and supplies
Major Shareholder: Claude Perdriel
Officers: Arnaud Corbier [1961] Director [French]; Tim Pestell [1957] Managing Director

Sansbury Bailey Holdings Limited
Incorporated: 30 March 2001 *Employees:* 358
Net Worth: £4,725,000 *Total Assets:* £24,553,000
Registered Office: Washway Road, Fosdyke, Spalding, Lincs, PE12 6LQ
Activities: Other service activities n.e.c.
Major Shareholder: Colin Sansbury Bailey
Officers: Lisa Jayne Alcock, Secretary; Lisa Jayne Alcock [1984] Director; Colin Sansbury Bailey [1969] Director; Sarah Bailey [1976] Director; Alexander Boughton [1987] Sales Director; Tim James Fitzsimmons [1976] Operations Director; David Alan Trumble [1980] Finance Director

Santray Limited
Incorporated: 30 October 2007 *Employees:* 3
Net Worth Deficit: £65,765 *Total Assets:* £36,447,964
Registered Office: 2nd Floor, Hygeia House, 66 College Road, Harrow, Middlesex, HA1 1BE
Activities: Other business support service activities n.e.c.
Officers: Leisha Ann Joyce Frett [1987] Director [Guyanese]; Dr Christoph Bernhard Gutmann [1976] Director [Swiss]; Jerome Rubin-Delanchy [1980] Director [French]

Sanwalton Limited
Incorporated: 2 December 1999 *Employees:* 3
Net Worth: £18,363,620 *Total Assets:* £29,112,644
Registered Office: 29 St Neots Road, Sandy, Beds, SG19 1LE
Activities: Activities of head offices
Shareholders: Richard Lewin Banks; Judith Anne Clements
Officers: Gary Leon Carney, Secretary; Richard Lewin Banks [1942] Director; William Lewin Banks [1973] Director/Pilot; Judith Anne Clements [1945] Director; Heather Fiona Spavins [1976] Director/Quality Auditor; Melanie Catherine Tuke-Hastings [1974] Director/Head of Production TV

Sapientia Education Trust
Incorporated: 10 December 2010 *Employees:* 765
Previous: Wymondham College Academy Trust
Net Worth: £53,972,000 *Total Assets:* £62,967,000
Registered Office: Wymondham College, Golf Links Road, Morley, Wymondham, Norfolk, NR18 9SZ
Activities: General secondary education
Officers: Robert William Moorhouse, Secretary; Ian David Baker [1961] Bank Director; Francis Norman Davey [1952] Director/Chartered Surveyor; Richard David Hill [1963] Director/Engineer; Professor John Last [1953] Director/Vice Chancellor Norwich University of The Arts; Roger Patrick Margand [1972] Director/Solicitor; Philip Ross Norton [1959] Director/Solicitor; Peter Jonathan Rout [1953] Director/Farmer; Elizabeth Sally Soule [1949] Director/Retired; Jonathan Stuart Taylor [1971] Director/Principal; Lucy Wayman [1960] Director/Headteacher

Sapphire Food North East No.1 Limited
Incorporated: 2 September 2002
Net Worth: £11,636,365 *Total Assets:* £11,669,363
Registered Office: Westgate Brewery, Bury St Edmunds, Suffolk, IP33 1QT
Activities: Other business support service activities n.e.c.
Parent: Greene King Retailing Limited
Officers: Lindsay Anne Keswick, Secretary; Richard Smothers [1967] Director

Sapphire Food North West No. 3 Limited
Incorporated: 2 September 2002
Net Worth: £10,823,402 *Total Assets:* £10,854,095
Registered Office: Westgate Brewery, Bury St Edmunds, Suffolk, IP33 1QT
Activities: Other business support service activities n.e.c.
Parent: Greene King Retailing Limited
Officers: Lindsay Anne Keswick, Secretary; Richard Smothers [1967] Director

Sapphire Food South East No.4 Limited
Incorporated: 2 September 2002
Net Worth: £15,388,746 *Total Assets:* £15,432,386
Registered Office: Westgate Brewery, Bury St Edmunds, Suffolk, IP33 1QT
Activities: Other business support service activities n.e.c.
Parent: Greene King Retailing Limited
Officers: Lindsay Anne Keswick, Secretary; Richard Smothers [1967] Director

Sapphire Food South West No. 2 Limited
Incorporated: 2 September 2002
Net Worth: £9,405,478 *Total Assets:* £9,432,150
Registered Office: Westgate Brewery, Bury St Edmunds, Suffolk, IP33 1QT
Activities: Other business support service activities n.e.c.
Parent: Greene King Retailing Limited
Officers: Lindsay Anne Keswick, Secretary; Richard Smothers [1967] Director

Sapphire Rural Destination No. 5 Limited
Incorporated: 2 September 2002
Net Worth: £12,776,975 *Total Assets:* £12,813,208
Registered Office: Westgate Brewery, Bury St Edmunds, Suffolk, IP33 1QT
Activities: Other business support service activities n.e.c.
Parent: Greene King Retailing Limited
Officers: Lindsay Anne Keswick, Secretary; Richard Smothers [1967] Director

Sara (London) Limited
Incorporated: 23 May 1984 *Employees:* 3
Net Worth: £5,683,722 *Total Assets:* £11,542,600
Registered Office: First Floor, Kirkland House, 11-15 Peterborough Road, Harrow, Middlesex, HA1 2AX
Activities: Agents specialised in the sale of other particular products
Parent: Eastern Focus Investments Ltd.
Officers: Ashok Ramchand Mohinani [1963] Director/Businessman [Indian]; Ramchand Udharam Mohinani [1935] Director [Indian]

Sardar Properties (U.K.) Limited
Incorporated: 25 May 1993
Net Worth: £21,656,040 *Total Assets:* £23,952,000
Registered Office: 50 Ollards Grove, Loughton, Essex, IG10 4DW
Activities: Other letting and operating of own or leased real estate
Officers: Charanjit Singh, Secretary/Salesman; Balbir Singh Doal [1956] Director/Manufacturer; Sadhu Ram [1953] Director/Manufacturer; Charanjit Singh [1950] Director/Salesman; Diyal Singh [1925] Director/Manufacturer; Harbans Singh [1958] Director/Manufacturer; Tarsem Singh [1947] Director/Manufacturer

Sarena House LLP
Incorporated: 18 November 2014 *Employees:* 2
Net Worth: £1,395,071 *Total Assets:* £58,106,640
Registered Office: 3rd Floor, Sterling House, Langston Road, Loughton, Essex, IG10 3TS

Satco Investments Limited
Incorporated: 25 September 1987
Net Worth: £16,537,554 *Total Assets:* £22,797,708
Registered Office: Aprirose House, 48a High Street, Edgware, Middlesex, HA8 7EQ
Activities: Other letting and operating of own or leased real estate
Parent: Satco Investments Holding Limited
Officers: Mansukhlal Gosar Gudka, Secretary; Kumud Mansukhlal Gudka [1945] Director/Company Secretary; Manish Mansukhlal Gudka [1970] Director; Mansukhlal Gosar Gudka [1941] Director; Parag Mansukhlal Gudka [1971] Director

Satco Plastics Limited
Incorporated: 26 October 2005 *Employees:* 56
Net Worth: £8,038,333 *Total Assets:* £12,255,343
Registered Office: Satco House, Unit 2 Aragon Park, Foster Avenue, Dunstable, Beds, LU5 5GN
Activities: Manufacture of other plastic products
Shareholder: Sultan Asaria
Officers: Farida Asaria, Secretary; Sultan Asaria [1951] Director; Hasnain Karawalli [1978] Director [Kenyan]

Sato UK Limited
Incorporated: 7 May 1958 *Employees:* 109
Net Worth: £1,935,000 *Total Assets:* £13,872,000
Registered Office: Valley Road, Harwich, Essex, CO12 4RR
Activities: Manufacture of other articles of paper and paperboard n.e.c.
Parent: Sato Holdings Corporation
Officers: Tetsushi Kondo [1973] Director/General Manager [Japanese]; Yuji Shimizu [1974] Director/General Manager [Japanese]; Jason Alan Wise [1971] Director/General Manager

John Saul Limited
Incorporated: 6 April 1989 *Employees:* 26
Net Worth: £8,468,932 *Total Assets:* £17,299,194
Registered Office: The Hall, Outgate, Leverton, Boston, Lincs, PE22 0AA
Activities: Growing of cereals (except rice), leguminous crops and oil seeds
Shareholders: Arthur Saul; Graham Clive Holdich Smith; Brian Thomas Borrill; John Saul (Holdings) Limited
Officers: Paul Richard Freeman [1953] Director/Farm Management; Arthur Saul [1955] Director/Farmer; Michele Mary Saul [1955] Director/Farmer; Oliver Saul [1987] Director/Farmer

Saw Property Company Limited
Incorporated: 6 December 2012 *Employees:* 3
Net Worth: £12,798,640 *Total Assets:* £16,162,275
Registered Office: Robin Hood Park, South Road, Chapel St Leonards, Skegness, Lincs, PE24 5TR
Activities: Buying and selling of own real estate
Parent: SAW Property Company Holdings Limited
Officers: Peter Raymond Franciscus Holmes [1948] Director/Certified Accountant; Jonathan Scott Moses [1974] Director/Caravan Park Manager; Sally-Ann Woodward [1967] Director

Sawston Farms (Cambs) Limited
Incorporated: 22 July 1957 *Employees:* 3
Net Worth: £9,061,750 *Total Assets:* £10,839,513
Registered Office: Abington Park Farm, Great Abington, Cambridge, CB21 6AX
Activities: Development of building projects
Shareholders: David John Harold Chaplin; Simon Robert Frank Chaplin; Hilary Ann Russell
Officers: Hilary Ann Russell, Secretary; David John Harold Chaplin [1963] Director; Simon Robert Frank Chaplin [1967] Director/Farmer; Hilary Ann Russell [1965] Director

Saxonchart Limited
Incorporated: 10 September 2007 *Employees:* 2
Net Worth Deficit: £3,336,778 *Total Assets:* £30,768,108
Registered Office: 19-20 Bourne Court, Southend Road, Woodford Green, Essex, IG8 8HD
Activities: Development of building projects
Shareholder: Residential Land Holdings Limited
Officers: Jonathan Simon David Anthony Rust, Company Secretary; Deepak Jalan [1974] Director; Bruce Weir Ritchie [1965] Director

Saxton 4x4 Limited
Incorporated: 21 August 2003 *Employees:* 66
Net Worth: £9,458,792 *Total Assets:* £29,712,520
Registered Office: Widford Industrial Area, Westway, Chelmsford, Essex, CM1 3BH
Activities: Sale of used cars and light motor vehicles
Shareholders: Alan Austin; Janice Catherine Austin
Officers: Janice Catherine Austin, Secretary; Alan Austin [1950] Director; Danny Austin [1975] Director; Glen Austin [1979] Director

Saxton Limited
Incorporated: 10 June 2009 *Employees:* 66
Net Worth: £13,469,662 *Total Assets:* £29,712,904
Registered Office: 249 Cranbrook Road, Ilford, Essex, IG1 4TG
Activities: Other business support service activities n.e.c.
Shareholders: Jane Catherine Austin; SIP Trustees Ltd; Alan Austin
Officers: Alan Austin [1950] Director; Janice Catherine Austin [1952] Director/Secretary

Saybest Limited
Incorporated: 21 February 1995
Net Worth: £12,136,000 *Total Assets:* £21,355,000
Registered Office: Total Produce, Enterprise Way, Pinchbeck, Spalding, Lincs, PE11 3YR
Activities: Activities of head offices
Parent: Redbridge Holdings Limited
Officers: Mark Christopher Owen, Secretary; Andrew Roger Allmond [1944] Director/Certified Accountant; Jacinta Frances Devine [1972] Director [Irish]; Francis Gerard McKernan [1962] Director [Irish]; Mark Christopher Owen [1965] Director; Denis Leslie Punter [1953] Director/Chief Executive

SBG Holding International Ltd
Incorporated: 23 April 2013 *Employees:* 6
Net Worth: £11,473,827 *Total Assets:* £11,611,418
Registered Office: 12 Argent Court, Southfields Business Park, Sylvan Way, Laindon, Essex, SS15 6TH
Activities: Activities of other holding companies n.e.c.
Officers: Barbara Bertani [1975] Director/Manager [Italian]; Silvio Bertani [1944] Director/Entrepreneur [Italian]; Jesus Ciria [1967] Director/General Manager [Spanish]; Italo Scaietta [1960] Director/Manager [Italian]

SBH Gatwick Limited
Incorporated: 23 April 2015 *Employees:* 22
Net Worth Deficit: £1,363,068 *Total Assets:* £21,996,404
Registered Office: Park House, 10 Penn Road, Beaconsfield, Bucks, HP9 2LH
Activities: Hotels and similar accommodation
Officers: Jonathan Andrew Baker [1976] Finance Director; Paul Arthur Callingham [1958] Director/Hotelier; Rivka Niederman [1976] Director/Hotelier; Jacob Schreiber [1974] Director/Hotelier; Miriam Schreiber [1952] Director/Hotelier; Moses Schreiber [1986] Director/Hotelier; Nathan Schreiber [1991] Director/Hotelier

SBH Tamworth Limited
Incorporated: 30 September 2016 *Employees:* 21
Net Worth: £62,145 *Total Assets:* £8,485,613
Registered Office: Park House, 10 Penn Road, Beaconsfield, Bucks, HP9 2LH
Activities: Hotels and similar accommodation
Shareholder: Paul Arthur Callingham
Officers: Rifka Niederman, Secretary; Jonathan Andrew Baker [1976] Finance Director; Paul Arthur Callingham [1958] Director; Jacob Schreiber [1974] Director

SCB Holdings (Sandy) Limited
Incorporated: 19 April 2000 *Employees:* 6
Net Worth: £17,670,716 *Total Assets:* £18,779,712
Registered Office: 29 St Neots Road, Sandy, Beds, SG19 1LE
Activities: Activities of head offices
Shareholders: Richard Lewin Banks; Judith Anne Clements; Sanwalton Limited
Officers: Gary Leon Carney, Secretary; Richard Lewin Banks [1942] Director/Agricultural Merchant; Judith Anne Clements [1945] Director/Farmer

SCCS Survey Equipment Limited
Incorporated: 18 August 2005 *Employees:* 97
Previous: Paul MacArthur Limited
Net Worth: £14,313,000 *Total Assets:* £20,437,000
Registered Office: Alpha House, Alpha Drive, Eaton Socon, St Neots, Cambs, PE19 8JJ
Activities: Other specialised construction activities n.e.c.
Parent: Hexagon AB
Officers: Andrew Paul Young, Secretary; Paul Walker Peter MacArthur [1955] Director

SCH 2014 Limited
Incorporated: 26 September 2014 *Employees:* 3
Net Worth: £3,497,954 *Total Assets:* £15,143,761
Registered Office: The Old School, School Lane, Stratford St Mary, Colchester, Essex, CO7 6LZ
Activities: Non-trading company
Parent: Access UK Ltd
Officers: Christopher Andrew Armstrong Bayne [1971] Director; Stephen James Blundell [1970] Director; Adam John Witherow Brown [1963] Director/Chief Commercial Officer

Schering-Plough Holdings Limited
Incorporated: 15 September 1988
Net Worth: £436,287,008 *Total Assets:* £498,076,992
Registered Office: West Hill, Hertford Road, Hoddesdon, Herts, EN11 9BU
Activities: Activities of head offices
Parent: Merck & Co., Inc.
Officers: Richard Robinski, Secretary; Louise Jane Houson [1976] Director; Simon Nicholson [1975] Director; Ebru Can Temucin [1972] Director [Turkish]

Schneider Electric Software GB Limited
Incorporated: 27 April 1998 *Employees:* 107
Previous: Spiral Software Limited
Net Worth: £9,906,608 *Total Assets:* £21,025,080
Registered Office: 101 Science Park, Milton Road, Cambridge, CB4 0FY
Activities: Business and domestic software development
Parent: Samos Acquisition Company Limited
Officers: Harpreet Singh Gulati [1969] Director/Vice President [French]; Andrew James Shipley [1968] Finance Director; David Mathew Ward [1976] Director

Scholars' Education Trust
Incorporated: 7 July 2011 *Employees:* 423
Previous: Sir John Lawes Academies Trust
Net Worth: £58,164,000 *Total Assets:* £62,194,000
Registered Office: Sir John Lawes School, Manland Way, Harpenden, Herts, AL5 4QP
Activities: Primary education
Officers: Hazel Wale, Secretary; Susan Lucy Archer [1968] Director/Chartered Surveyor; Sanjeevan Bala [1972] Director/Head of Data Science; Amar Barot [1969] Director; Catherine Baxendale [1969] Director/HR Consultant; Stephen John Owen [1960] Director/Head of Human Resources; Geoffrey Donald Stephen Payne [1975] Director/Barrister; Alan Robert Read [1934] Director/Retired; Claire Elizabeth Robins [1967] Director/CEO/Headteacher; Martin John Sidders [1958] Finance Director; Nicholas Andrew Spittal [1965] Director/Banker

Schottlander Limited
Incorporated: 30 July 1991 *Employees:* 54
Net Worth: £12,178,344 *Total Assets:* £14,279,057
Registered Office: Fifth Avenue, Letchworth Garden City, Herts, SG6 2WD
Activities: Activities of head offices
Major Shareholder: Brian Dennis Schottlander
Officers: Mark Seaman, Secretary; Dr Brian Dennis Schottlander [1943] Director; Ian James Schottlander [1974] Director; Susan Ann Schottlander [1947] Director

Science Group PLC
Incorporated: 17 March 2008 *Employees:* 320
Net Worth: £37,739,000 *Total Assets:* £76,609,000
Registered Office: Harston Mill, Royston Road, Harston, Cambridge, CB22 7GG
Activities: Management consultancy activities other than financial management
Shareholder: Martyn Roy Ratcliffe
Officers: Sarah Elizabeth Cole, Secretary; Rebecca Anne Archer [1981] Director; David John Courtley [1957] Director; Michael Julian Lacey-Solymar [1963] Director; Martyn Roy Ratcliffe [1961] Director

Science Recruitment Group Ltd
Incorporated: 27 January 1992 *Employees:* 94
Net Worth: £18,137,000 *Total Assets:* £41,527,000
Registered Office: 800 The Boulevard, Capability Green, Luton, Beds, LU1 3BA
Activities: Temporary employment agency activities
Parent: Impellam UK Limited
Officers: Rebecca Jane Watson, Secretary; Julia Robertson [1958] Director; Rebecca Jane Watson [1969] Director/Solicitor

Science, Engineering and Manufacturing Technologies Alliance
Incorporated: 5 December 1988
Net Worth: £29,402,000 *Total Assets:* £35,358,000
Registered Office: Unit 2 The Orient Centre, Greycaine Road, Watford, Herts, WD24 7GP
Activities: Technical and vocational secondary education
Officers: Andrew Stephen McLachrie, Secretary; Paul Adrian Birt [1961] HR Director; Karen Boswell [1963] Managing Director; Michael James Evans [1963] Managing Director; Dame Judith Elizabeth Hackitt [1954] Director/Chair; Selma Hunter [1964] Director; Jose Luis Martins Dos Santos Lopes [1964] Director/Manager Product Development; Indro Mario Mukerjee [1960] Director/Chief Executive Officer; Sharron Alexandra Pamplin [1969] Director/HR; Sarah Louise Sandle [1969] Director/VP Strategy; Mark Ian Tarry [1971] Director/Accountant; Ian Waddell [1965] Director/National Officer of Unite

Scientific Digital Imaging PLC
Incorporated: 28 September 2007 *Employees:* 121
Net Worth: £12,560,000 *Total Assets:* £17,513,000
Registered Office: Beacon House, Nuffield Road, Cambridge, CB4 1TF
Activities: Non-trading company
Officers: Jonathan Paul Abell, Secretary; Jonathan Paul Abell [1961] Finance Director; Michael John Creedon [1960] Director/Accountant; Eric Kenelm Ford [1949] Director; Isabel Napper [1958] Director; David Frank Tilston [1957] Director

Scimitar Care Hotels PLC
Incorporated: 14 August 1978 *Employees:* 357
Net Worth: £33,259,680 *Total Assets:* £37,530,288
Registered Office: The Lodge, Coopers Lane Road, Potters Bar, Herts, EN6 4AD
Activities: Residential care activities for the elderly and disabled
Officers: Valerie Irene Gerrard, Secretary; Valerie Irene Gerrard [1946] Director of Care; Joanne Maria Mason [1963] Director/Residential Care; Luke Matthew Sargeant [1978] Operations Director; Paul David Sargeant [1966] Finance Director

Scimitar House (Holdings) Limited
Incorporated: 24 June 2016 *Employees:* 2
Net Worth Deficit: £43,215 *Total Assets:* £8,663,172
Registered Office: 166 College Road, Harrow, Middlesex, HA1 1RA
Activities: Development of building projects
Parent: Estates and Lets 2 LLP
Officers: Michael Spencer Docker [1963] Director; Michele Docker [1965] Director

Scimitar Topco Limited
Incorporated: 2 December 2011 *Employees:* 77
Net Worth: £96,913,000 *Total Assets:* £613,473,024
Registered Office: Gladstone Place, 36-38 Upper Marlborough Road, St Albans, Herts, AL1 3UU
Activities: Activities of head offices
Parent: CD & R Firefly Bidco Limited
Officers: Timothy Edward Douglas Allan [1966] Director; Alasdair James Dougall Locke [1953] Director

Scira Offshore Energy Limited
Incorporated: 5 May 2004
Net Worth: £524,152,000 *Total Assets:* £1,154,504,960
Registered Office: Wind Farm Place, Edgar Road, Walsingham, Norfolk, NR22 6EJ
Activities: Production of electricity
Shareholders: Equitix Offshore 5 Limited; Statoil Wind Limited
Officers: Lina Balbuckaite, Secretary; Hugh Barnabas Crossley [1973] Director; Robert John Fradley [1973] Director; Kamala Hajiyeva [1976] Director/Manager, Operations, New Energy Operations [Azerbaijani]; Olav Leivestad [1966] Director/Financial Controller [Norwegian]; Mona Riis [1965] Director/Manager Statoil [Norwegian]; Pablo Saavedra [1978] Associate Director Asset Management [Spanish]; Karl Ben Smith [1977] Director/Fund Manager; Alexis Eduardo Ulens [1967] Director/Fund Manager [Belgian]

Scotline Limited
Incorporated: 27 January 1983 *Employees:* 20
Net Worth: £5,397,575 *Total Assets:* £9,884,397
Registered Office: 75 Main Road, Gidea Park, Romford, Essex, RM2 5EL
Activities: Sea and coastal freight water transport
Shareholder: Peter Thomas Millatt
Officers: Peter Thomas Millatt, Secretary; Marion Terase Frances Osborne, Secretary/Director; Roy John Brooks [1949] Director/Ship Manager; Cindy Lee Crancher [1962] Director/Manager; Peter Thomas Millatt [1949] Director; Marion Terase Frances Osborne [1960] Director

Scotsdale Nursery and Garden Centre Limited
Incorporated: 23 September 1964 *Employees:* 254
Net Worth: £12,583,555 *Total Assets:* £18,003,356
Registered Office: Scotsdale Nusery & Garden Centre Ltd, Cambridge Road, Great Shelford, Cambridge, CB22 5JT
Activities: Retail of furniture, lighting, and similar (not musical instruments or scores) in specialised store
Shareholders: David Anthony Rayner; Caroline Anne Elizabeth Owen; Mills & Reeve Trust Corporation Limited
Officers: Caroline Anne Elizabeth Owen [1956] Director; Benjamin Thomas William Rayner [1969] Director/Accountant; David Anthony Rayner [1928] Director/Farmer

M R Scott Limited
Incorporated: 25 January 2017 *Employees:* 2
Net Worth: £1 *Total Assets:* £10,268,870
Registered Office: Suite 5, Oyster House, Severalls Lane, Colchester, Essex, CO4 9PD
Activities: Development of building projects
Parent: M Scott Property Group Limited
Officers: Martin Robert Scott [1960] Director; Robert John Scott [1990] Director

Screen Subtitling Systems Limited
Incorporated: 25 March 1991 *Employees:* 37
Net Worth: £10,198,334 *Total Assets:* £11,300,446
Registered Office: The Old Rectory, Church Lane, Claydon, Ipswich, Suffolk, IP6 0EQ
Activities: Other information technology service activities
Parent: Broadstream Holdings Limited
Officers: David Edward Bowes, Secretary; David Edward Bowes [1956] Director; Herbert Eduard Johannes Brenninkmeijer [1955] Director [Dutch]

T.E.Scudder Limited
Incorporated: 27 May 1958 *Employees:* 91
Net Worth: £8,946,292 *Total Assets:* £20,308,644
Registered Office: Carey House, Great Central Way, Wembley, Middlesex, HA9 0HR
Activities: Demolition
Parent: Carey Group PLC
Officers: Fiona Mary O'Donnell, Secretary; John Carey [1941] Director [Irish]; Denis Patrick Deacy [1965] Director; Gary Whyton [1961] Director

SD Underwriting Limited
Incorporated: 6 February 2008
Net Worth: £1,560,912 *Total Assets:* £15,501,952
Registered Office: Hampden House, Great Hampden, Great Missenden, Bucks, HP16 9RD
Activities: Non-life insurance
Parent: SDIC Limited
Officers: Mary Elisabeth Dickinson [1945] Director

SDJ Enterprises Limited
Incorporated: 22 December 2009 *Employees:* 155
Net Worth: £9,981,322 *Total Assets:* £14,420,452
Registered Office: Second Floor, Ashdon House, Moon Lane, Barnet, Herts, EN5 5YL
Activities: Activities of financial services holding companies
Shareholders: Joshus Steven Landy; Dewayne Walter Bridges; Stephen Craig Mitchem
Officers: Joshus Steven Landy [1969] Director [American]; Jeremy Dean Shaffer [1971] Director [American]

SDSDAB Limited
Incorporated: 30 March 2012 *Employees:* 443
Net Worth: £1,837,155 *Total Assets:* £13,122,368
Registered Office: c/o A & B Glass, Addison Road, Sudbury, Suffolk, CO10 2YW
Activities: Glazing
Shareholders: David Frank Barrett; Stephen Frank Stone
Officers: David Frank Barrett [1957] Director; Paul Brian McManus [1967] Director; Stephen Derek Stone [1963] Director

SDV 2025 ZDP PLC
Incorporated: 25 October 2017
Net Worth: £13,000 *Total Assets:* £14,413,000
Registered Office: Hamilton Centre, Rodney Way, Chelmsford, Essex, CM1 3BY
Activities: Activities of investment trusts
Parent: Chelverton UK Dividend Trust PLC
Officers: Howard Vivian Peter Myles [1949] Director; William Alexander Van Heesewijk [1959] Director/Investment Trust Management [Dutch]; Andrew Keith Watkins [1952] Director

Seabourne Group Limited
Incorporated: 7 July 1972 *Employees:* 427
Net Worth: £3,297,675 *Total Assets:* £14,315,059
Registered Office: Gardiner House, 6b Hemnall Street, Epping, Essex, CM16 4LW
Activities: Operation of warehousing and storage facilities for land transport activities
Officers: Donald Hayes, Secretary; Lady Joy Hilary Bourne [1946] Director; Daniel John Flitterman [1965] Director/Chief Executive; Donald Hayes [1934] Company Secretary & Director; Nigel Charles Hudson [1963] Finance Director

Seabrook Holdings Limited
Incorporated: 6 November 1989 *Employees:* 132
Net Worth: £8,853,284 *Total Assets:* £33,100,808
Registered Office: Admiral House, 853 London Road, West Thurrock, Essex, RM20 3LG
Activities: Activities of head offices
Major Shareholder: Michael Ronald Seabrook
Officers: Stuart Michael Seabrook, Secretary; Michael Ronald Seabrook [1950] Director/Freight Forwarder; David Lee Tanner [1952] Director/Freight Forwarder

Seabrook Warehousing Limited
Incorporated: 18 April 1995 *Employees:* 88
Net Worth: £4,073,068 *Total Assets:* £10,200,498
Registered Office: Admiral House, 853 London Road, West Thurrock, Essex, RM20 3LG
Activities: Operation of warehousing and storage facilities for water transport activities
Parent: Seabrook Holdings Limited
Officers: Stuart Michael Seabrook, Secretary; Stuart Michael Seabrook [1973] Director; David Lee Tanner [1952] Director

Seachill UK Limited
Incorporated: 20 April 1950 *Employees:* 772
Previous: Icelandic Group UK Limited
Net Worth: £56,612,000 *Total Assets:* £113,339,000
Registered Office: Hilton Food Group PLC, 2-8 The Interchange, Latham Road, Huntingdon, Cambs, PE29 6YE
Activities: Manufacture of prepared meals and dishes
Parent: Hilton Foods Limited
Officers: Neil Michael George, Secretary; Philip John Heffer [1966] Director; Nigel Richard Majewski [1960] Director; Frank McMyler [1969] Director [Irish]; Andrew John Harding Rutherford [1969] Finance Director; Simon John Smith [1962] Director

Seajacks 1 Limited
Incorporated: 27 February 2012
Net Worth: £9,091,818 *Total Assets:* £163,129,808
Registered Office: South Denes Business Park, South Beach Parade, Great Yarmouth, Norfolk, NR30 3QR
Activities: Activities of other holding companies n.e.c.
Parent: Seajacks International Limited
Officers: Thomas Berg [1958] Director/Chief Financial Officer [Norwegian]; Satoru Harada [1967] Director/Management [Japanese]; Satoru Nakagawa [1965] Director [Japanese]; Peter Niklai [1973] Director/Financial Investor [Hungarian]; Ikumori Osuka [1988] Director [Japanese]; Kosuke Tashiro [1976] Director/Management [Japanese]; Tetsuro Toyoda [1962] Director/Private Equity Fund Manager [Japanese]

Seajacks 2 Limited
Incorporated: 24 February 2012
Net Worth: £1,408,028 *Total Assets:* £178,079,824
Registered Office: South Denes Business Park, South Beach Parade, Great Yarmouth, Norfolk, NR30 3QR
Activities: Activities of other holding companies n.e.c.
Parent: Seajacks International Limited
Officers: Thomas Berg [1958] Director/Chief Financial Officer [Norwegian]; Satoru Harada [1967] Director/Management [Japanese]; Satoru Nakagawa [1965] Director [Japanese]; Peter Niklai [1973] Director/Financial Investor [Hungarian]; Ikumori Osuka [1988] Director [Japanese]; Kosuke Tashiro [1976] Director/Management [Japanese]; Tetsuro Toyoda [1962] Director/Private Equity Fund Manager [Japanese]

Seajacks 3 Limited
Incorporated: 24 February 2012
Net Worth: £24,235,620 *Total Assets:* £154,071,056
Registered Office: South Denes Business Park, South Beach Parade, Great Yarmouth, Norfolk, NR30 3QR
Activities: Activities of other holding companies n.e.c.
Parent: Seajacks International Limited
Officers: Thomas Berg [1958] Director/Chief Financial Officer [Norwegian]; Satoru Harada [1967] Director/Management [Japanese]; Satoru Nakagawa [1965] Director [Japanese]; Peter Niklai [1973] Director/Financial Investor [Hungarian]; Ikumori Osuka [1988] Director [Japanese]; Kosuke Tashiro [1976] Director/Management [Japanese]; Tetsuro Toyoda [1962] Director/Private Equity Fund Manager [Japanese]

Seajacks 4 Limited
Incorporated: 16 May 2012
Net Worth: £8,857,275 *Total Assets:* £92,655,336
Registered Office: South Denes Business Park, South Beach Parade, Great Yarmouth, Norfolk, NR30 3QR
Activities: Activities of other holding companies n.e.c.
Parent: Seajacks International Limited
Officers: Thomas Berg [1958] Director/Chief Financial Officer [Norwegian]; Satoru Harada [1967] Director/Management [Japanese]; Satoru Nakagawa [1965] Director [Japanese]; Peter Niklai [1973] Director/Financial Investor [Hungarian]; Ikumori Osuka [1988] Director [Japanese]; Kosuke Tashiro [1976] Director/Management [Japanese]; Tetsuro Toyoda [1962] Director/Private Equity Fund Manager [Japanese]

Seajacks 5 Limited
Incorporated: 8 May 2013
Net Worth: £8,958,782 *Total Assets:* £202,436,176
Registered Office: South Denes Business Park, South Beach Parade, Great Yarmouth, Norfolk, NR30 3QR
Activities: Activities of other holding companies n.e.c.
Parent: Seajacks International Limited
Officers: Thomas Berg [1958] Director/Chief Financial Officer [Norwegian]; Satoru Harada [1967] Director/Management [Japanese]; Satoru Nakagawa [1965] Director [Japanese]; Peter Niklai [1973] Director/Financial Investor [Hungarian]; Ikumori Osuka [1988] Director [Japanese]; Kosuke Tashiro [1976] Director/Management [Japanese]; Tetsuro Toyoda [1962] Director/Private Equity Fund Manager [Japanese]

Seajacks International Limited
Incorporated: 24 February 2012 *Employees:* 239
Net Worth: £503,258,240 *Total Assets:* £842,342,336
Registered Office: South Denes Business Park, South Beach Parade, Great Yarmouth, Norfolk, NR30 3QR
Activities: Activities of other holding companies n.e.c.
Parent: Atlantis Midco Limited
Officers: William Burton Blair Ainslie [1963] Managing Director; Satoru Harada [1967] Director/Management [Japanese]; Satoru Nakagawa [1965] Director [Japanese]; Peter Niklai [1973] Director/Financial Investor [Hungarian]; Ikumori Osuka [1988] Director [Japanese]; Kosuke Tashiro [1976] Director/Management [Japanese]; Tetsuro Toyoda [1962] Director/Private Equity Fund Manager [Japanese]

Seajacks UK Limited
Incorporated: 15 February 2007 *Employees:* 63
Net Worth Deficit: £15,967,395 *Total Assets:* £29,017,994
Registered Office: South Denes Business Park, South Beach Parade, Great Yarmouth, Norfolk, NR30 3QR
Activities: Construction of utility projects for electricity and telecommunications
Parent: Seajacks International Limited
Officers: William Burton Blair Ainslie [1963] Director; Thomas Berg [1958] Director/Chief Financial Officer [Norwegian]; Satoru Harada [1967] Director/Management [Japanese]; Tetsuro Toyoda [1962] Director/Private Equity Fund Manager [Japanese]

Sealed Air Limited
Incorporated: 2 October 1997 *Employees:* 431
Net Worth: £122,594,000 *Total Assets:* £218,580,992
Registered Office: Clifton House, 1 Marston Road, St Neots, Huntingdon, Cambs, PE19 2HN
Activities: Manufacture of plastic packing goods
Parent: Sealed Air B.V.
Officers: Karenjit Kaur Kalirai, Secretary; Karenjit Kaur Kalirai [1975] Director/Global Business Services [British/Canadian]; Chad Louis Keller [1969] Director/Treasurer [American]; William Gregory Stiehl [1961] Director/Controller [American]; Michael Peter Thurland [1956] Director/Global Process Management Partner

Sealey (UK) Limited
Incorporated: 15 March 1990 *Employees:* 357
Net Worth: £66,592,000 *Total Assets:* £75,251,000
Registered Office: 820 The Crescent, Colchester Business Park, Colchester, Essex, CO4 9YQ
Activities: Activities of distribution holding companies
Shareholders: Caroline Jane Stenner; John Llewelyn Sealey; Timothy William Galloway
Officers: Patricia Dorothy Sealey, Secretary; John Llewelyn Sealey [1942] Director; Patricia Dorothy Sealey [1946] Director

Jack Sealey Limited
Incorporated: 8 September 1977 *Employees:* 357
Net Worth: £66,591,000 *Total Assets:* £75,250,000
Registered Office: 820 The Crescent, Colchester Business Park, Colchester, Essex, CO4 9YQ
Activities: Wholesale of other machinery and equipment
Shareholders: John Llewelyn Sealey; Timothy William Galloway; Caroline Jane Stenner
Officers: Patricia Dorothy Sealey, Secretary/Director; Steven Generald Buckle [1970] Marketing Director; David Nicholas Riches [1970] Sales Director; Benjamin Jasper James Sealey [1983] Director; John Llewelyn Sealey [1942] Director; Patricia Dorothy Sealey [1946] Director; Robert John Sealey [1968] Logistics Director; Mark Sweetman [1965] Managing Director; Nigel Christopher Sykes [1950] Non Executive Director; Timothy Richard Thompson [1966] Commercial Director

Searles (Camping Ground) Limited
Incorporated: 14 January 1954 *Employees:* 197
Net Worth: £6,977,921 *Total Assets:* £14,942,513
Registered Office: 3 South Beach Road, Hunstanton, Norfolk, PE36 5BB
Activities: Hotels and similar accommodation
Officers: Victoria Rebecca Searle, Company Secretary; Andrew John Geoffrey Searle [1972] Leisure Resort Director; Paul Richard Searle [1970] Managing Director; William John Searle [1951] Sea Tours Director; Joanna Alice Elizabeth Symonds [1978] Financial Director

Seaside Leisure Parks Limited
Incorporated: 7 August 1978 *Employees:* 16
Net Worth: £12,918,141 *Total Assets:* £20,313,196
Registered Office: 27-29 Lumley Avenue, Skegness, Lincs, PE25 2AT
Activities: Recreational vehicle parks, trailer parks and camping grounds
Shareholders: Reginald Roy Pritchard; Pamela Joan Pritchard
Officers: Pamela Joan Pritchard, Secretary; Andrew Robin Charles Pritchard [1966] Director; Pamela Joan Pritchard [1930] Director; Reginald Roy Pritchard [1928] Director

Seasons Hotels Limited
Incorporated: 30 July 2008 *Employees:* 18
Net Worth: £1,556,072 *Total Assets:* £12,051,679
Registered Office: Lakeview House, 4 Woodbrook Crescent, Billericay, Essex, CM12 0EQ
Activities: Hotels and similar accommodation
Shareholders: Barry Thomas Hurley; Sharon Angela Jeanette Kinsella
Officers: Sharon Angela Jeanette Kinsella, Secretary; Barry Thomas Hurley [1955] Director

Seatrax (U.K.) Limited
Incorporated: 11 November 1994 *Employees:* 39
Net Worth: £9,488,196 *Total Assets:* £10,229,627
Registered Office: Portland Wharf, Southtown Road, Great Yarmouth, Norfolk, NR31 0JJ
Activities: Manufacture of lifting and handling equipment
Major Shareholder: Albert William Gunter
Officers: Michael Ian Cleghorn, Secretary; John Patrick Emrick [1956] Director/General Manager [American]

Seax Trust
Incorporated: 19 August 2011 *Employees:* 246
Previous: Thriftwood School
Net Worth: £23,597,188 *Total Assets:* £28,476,304
Registered Office: Thriftwood College, Fox Crescent, Chelmsford, Essex, CM1 2BN
Activities: Other education n.e.c.
Officers: Catherine Sarah Burnside, Secretary; Stephen Thomas Bennett [1958] Director; Dr Angela Gail Bradding [1957] Director/Private Practitioner; Ann-Marie Briggs [1949] Director; Sally Coode-Bate [1954] Director/Retired; David Charles Cottrell [1948] Director; Anthony Raymond Cox [1950] Director; Sally Davies [1953] Director/Headteacher; Andrew Peter Hunter [1951] Director/Management Consultant; Dr Sally Louise Lockyer [1976] Director

Seckford Education Trust
Incorporated: 21 May 2012 *Employees:* 105
Previous: The Seckford Foundation Free Schools Trust
Net Worth: £22,288,000 *Total Assets:* £23,083,000
Registered Office: Marryott House, Burkitt Road, Woodbridge, Suffolk, IP12 4JJ
Activities: General secondary education
Officers: Simon Matthew James Stafford, Secretary; Graeme Barrie Bruce [1956] Director/Teacher; Samantha Claire Chenery-Morris [1969] Director/Associate Professor; Jude Generald Chin [1956] Director/Consultant; Inga Margaret Amy Grimsey [1952] Director/Retired Non-Executive; William Frederick Stephen Mayne [1951] Director/Company Chairman; Katherine Victoria Measures [1971] Director; Vanessa Rosanna Nicholson [1951] Director; Graham Ernest Watson [1962] Director/Chartered Secretary; James Dermot Wellesley Wesley [1957] Director

The Seckford Foundation
Incorporated: 29 July 2005 *Employees:* 380
Net Worth: £45,780,000 *Total Assets:* £52,260,000
Registered Office: Marryott House, Burkitt Road, Woodbridge, Suffolk, IP12 4JJ
Activities: Primary education
Officers: Graham Ernest Watson, Secretary; Neil John Alderton [1990] Director/Governance Consultant; Jude Generald Chin [1956] Director; Wendy Susan Evans Hendrick [1969] Director of Development; Roger John Finbow [1952] Director/Solicitor; Jill Alison Gibbs [1957] Director; Inga Margaret Amy Grimsey [1952] Director; Geoffrey Edwin Holdcroft [1953] Director; Sarah Jenny Cole Holsgrove [1985] Director; Graham Andrew Kill [1965] Director; Bryan John Laxton [1960] Director; Canon Kevan Sean McCormack [1950] Director/Clerk in Holy Orders; Margaret Charlotte McKenna [1959] Director/Retired; Jeston Nanakhorn [1971] Director/Store Manager Sainsburys; Emily Clare Skinner [1987] Director/Solicitor; Martin Thomas Sylvester [1955] Director; James Dermot Wellesley Wesley [1957] Director/Investment Banker; Professor Jane Elizabeth Anne Wright [1957] Director/Professor of Law

Securon Holdings Limited
Incorporated: 31 August 2017 *Employees:* 120
Net Worth: £10,474,411 *Total Assets:* £12,291,989
Registered Office: Cherry Tree Works, The Hill, Winchmore Hill, Amersham, Bucks, HP7 0NZ
Activities: Activities of other holding companies n.e.c.
Major Shareholder: Amanda Alexandra John
Officers: Amanda Alexandra John [1966] Director [New Zealander]; William David John [1960] Director

Sedum Limited
Incorporated: 19 August 1996 *Employees:* 61
Net Worth: £5,292,388 *Total Assets:* £10,325,868
Registered Office: Pontlands Park Hotel, West Hanningfield Road, Great Baddow, Chelmsford, Essex, CM2 8HR
Activities: Activities of other holding companies n.e.c.
Officers: Julia Kilham, Secretary; Jason Joseph Bartella [1967] Director

Seetec Business Technology Centre Limited
Incorporated: 30 August 1988 *Employees:* 1,405
Net Worth: £39,482,000 *Total Assets:* £72,501,000
Registered Office: 75-77 Main Road, Hockley, Essex, SS5 4RG
Activities: Technical and vocational secondary education
Major Shareholder: Peter Albert Cooper
Officers: John Baumback, Secretary; Lesley Barry [1958] Director/Accountant; John Baumback [1968] IT Director; Alison Jane Bunney [1978] Business Development Director; Alexander Butt [1955] Director/Head of Risk Management; Peter Albert Cooper [1953] Managing Director; David John Reynolds [1947] Director/Accountant

SEH (Property and Administration) Limited
Incorporated: 16 September 1971
Net Worth: £1,945,328 *Total Assets:* £8,350,237
Registered Office: 30 White House Road, Ipswich, Suffolk, IP1 5LT
Activities: Activities of head offices
Officers: Trevor Mark Dixon, Secretary; Graham Edwin Emmerson [1948] Director/Civil Engineer; Richard William Neall [1964] Director [Australian]

SEH Group Limited
Incorporated: 19 March 2008
Net Worth: £17,859,806 *Total Assets:* £26,563,954
Registered Office: 30 White House Road, Ipswich, Suffolk, IP1 5LT
Activities: Activities of construction holding companies
Officers: Trevor Mark Dixon, Secretary; Graham Edwin Emmerson [1948] Director/Civil Engineer; Richard William Neall [1964] Director [Australian]

Selborne Care Limited
Incorporated: 19 July 2005 *Employees:* 534
Net Worth: £8,646,126 *Total Assets:* £14,845,953
Registered Office: 5th Floor, Metropolitan House, 3 Darkes Lane, Potters Bar, Herts, EN6 1AG
Activities: Other human health activities
Parent: Caretech Community Services Limited
Officers: Gareth Dufton, Secretary; Gareth Dufton [1976] Director/Chartered Accountant; John Joseph Ivers [1962] Director; Farouq Rashid Sheikh [1958] Director

The Sele School
Incorporated: 29 June 2012 *Employees:* 54
Net Worth: £8,459,828 *Total Assets:* £9,982,146
Registered Office: The Sele School, Welwyn Road, Hertford, SG14 2DG
Activities: General secondary education
Officers: Peter Simon Beattie [1989] Director/Manager; Natasha Louise Browne [1972] Director/Head of HR Support Services; Lorena Diomidous [1972] Director; Neil Dunn [1972] Director/Headteacher; Linda Louise Gentry [1972] Director; Julia Ann Hays-Bateson [1966] Director; Benjamin William Jay [1970] Director/Accountant; Stephen John McEnally [1950] Director/Retired CEO; Paul John Pickard [1969] Director/Teacher; Sian Lyn Shrimpton-Davies [1965] Recruitment Director; Catherine Jane Sleath [1973] Director/Social Finance Officer; Matthew Roy Smith [1991] Director/Business Planning Analyst; Alison Marie Steaggles [1961] Director/Pastoral Leader; Robert Charles Wilson [1941] Director/Retired

Select Enterprises (Holdings) Limited
Incorporated: 12 January 2011
Net Worth: £5,425,217 *Total Assets:* £14,678,742
Registered Office: Crown House, 227 Aldborough Road South, Ilford, Essex, IG3 8HZ
Activities: Pre-primary education
Shareholders: Savinderjit Singh Kalsi; Balvinder Kalsi
Officers: Balvinder Kalsi, Secretary; Balvinder Kalsi [1967] Director/Chartered Accountant; Sarup Singh Kalsi [1939] Director; Savinderjit Kalsi [1964] Director/Chartered Surveyor

Select Enterprises Limited
Incorporated: 4 April 2005
Net Worth: £1,402,625 *Total Assets:* £13,570,220
Registered Office: Crown House, 227 Aldborough Road South, Ilford, Essex, IG3 8HZ
Activities: Other letting and operating of own or leased real estate
Shareholders: Savinderjit Singh Kalsi; Balvinder Kalsi
Officers: Balvinder Kalsi, Secretary/Director; Balvinder Kalsi [1967] Director; Savinderjit Singh Kalsi [1964] Director

Selecta Holding Limited
Incorporated: 14 June 2007
Net Worth: £14,375,000 *Total Assets:* £18,314,000
Registered Office: Apollo House, West End Road, Odyssey Business Park, Ruislip, Middlesex, HA4 6QD
Activities: Activities of head offices
Parent: KKR & Co.L.P.
Officers: Daniel Henry Abrahams [1973] Director; Jan Marck Vrijlandt [1965] Managing Director [Dutch]

Selecta U.K. Limited
Incorporated: 25 April 1991 *Employees:* 1,088
Previous: Pelican Rouge Coffee Solutions Limited
Net Worth: £9,668,000 *Total Assets:* £73,467,000
Registered Office: Apollo House, Odyssey Business Park, West End Road, Ruislip, Middlesex, HA4 6QD
Activities: Other food services
Parent: Selecta UK Holding Limited
Officers: Daniel Henry Abrahams [1973] Director/Accountant; David Christophe Marc Flochel [1973] Director [French]; Wesley Mulligan [1963] Managing Director [Irish]

Selecta UK Holding Limited
Incorporated: 19 October 1925
Previous: Pelican Rouge Coffee Solutions Group Limited
Net Worth Deficit: £84,711,000 *Total Assets:* £83,043,000
Registered Office: Apollo House, Odyssey Business Park, West End Road, Ruislip, Middlesex, HA4 6QD
Activities: Other food services
Parent: KKR & Co.L.P.
Officers: Daniel Henry Abrahams [1973] Director; David Christophe Marc Flochel [1973] Director [French]; Wesley Mulligan [1963] Managing Director [Irish]; Gabriel Pirona [1970] Director [French]

Selex Elsag Limited
Incorporated: 22 October 1969 *Employees:* 1
Net Worth: £111,179,000 *Total Assets:* £111,179,000
Registered Office: Sigma House, Christopher Martin Road, Basildon, Essex, SS14 3EL
Activities: Wireless telecommunications activities
Parent: Leonardo MW Ltd
Officers: Craig Porter [1970] Finance Director; Kevin Geoffrey Thomsit [1979] Director, Legal, Corporate Affairs and Compliance

Selex ES International Ltd
Incorporated: 22 October 1969
Net Worth: £61,004,000 *Total Assets:* £95,750,000
Registered Office: Sigma House, Christopher Martin Road, Basildon, Essex, SS14 3EL
Activities: Activities of other holding companies n.e.c.
Parent: Leonardo S.P.A.
Officers: Marco Buratti [1958] Director [Italian]; Michael William John Clayforth-Carr [1954] Director/Executive Chairman; Virna Catherine Tomaselli [1977] Director

Sema Lease UK Limited
Incorporated: 5 February 2004 *Employees:* 46
Net Worth: £6,003,663 *Total Assets:* £34,949,944
Registered Office: 2 Fison Way, Thetford, Norfolk, IP24 1HT
Activities: Renting and leasing of cars and light motor vehicles
Major Shareholder: Richard Carey Ames
Officers: Graham John Balaam, Secretary; Richard Carey Ames [1955] Director; Graham John Balaam [1962] Director/Company Accountant

Sembmarine SLP Ltd
Incorporated: 12 July 2010 *Employees:* 201
Net Worth Deficit: £26,587,000 *Total Assets:* £12,219,000
Registered Office: Hamilton Dock, Hamilton Road, Lowestoft, Suffolk, NR32 1XF
Activities: Manufacture of metal structures and parts of structures
Parent: Sembmarine North Sea Ltd
Officers: Colin James Yaxley, Secretary; Lim Chiang Theng [1953] Director/General Manager [Singaporean]; William Khor Boon Goh [1962] Director [Singaporean]; Paul David Thomson [1956] Managing Director; Samuel Wing Wah Wong [1966] Director [Singaporean]; Weng Sun Wong [1962] Director/President & CEO [Singaporean]; Colin James Yaxley [1973] Director/Accountant

Sen Trust Southend
Incorporated: 2 March 2012 *Employees:* 338
Previous: The St Christopher School Academy Trust
Net Worth: £37,429,884 *Total Assets:* £43,739,704
Registered Office: The St Christopher School, Mountdale Gardens, Leigh on Sea, Essex, SS9 4AW
Activities: Pre-primary education
Officers: Helen Grimwade, Secretary; Dorcy Burgess [1958] Director/Retired; Kathryn Brigid Duddridge [1975] Director [Irish]; Nicholas Keith Forrester Hyde [1948] Director/Accountant; Ross Gerrie [1980] Director/Commissioning Manager; Franklin John Hartle [1943] Director/Management Consultant; Barry Philip Levitt [1952] Director/Retired; Jacqueline Rossina Mullan [1957] Director/Headteacher; Dr Jane Caroline Oliver [1957] Director/Educational Consultant; Margaret Ellen Wall [1957] Director/Local Government Officer

Seneca Environmental Solutions Ltd
Incorporated: 16 December 2008 *Employees:* 47
Net Worth: £3,452,341 *Total Assets:* £29,532,112
Registered Office: Carey House, Great Central Way, Wembley, Middlesex, HA9 0HR
Activities: Recovery of sorted materials
Parent: Carey Group PLC
Officers: Fiona Mary O'Donnell, Secretary; John Anthony Carey [1964] Director [Irish]; Patrick Joseph Carey [1945] Director [Irish]; Denis Patrick Deacy [1965] Director; Kenneth Eamon Doran [1978] Director [Irish]

Senior Engineering Investments Limited
Incorporated: 17 September 1968
Net Worth: £669,816,000 *Total Assets:* £1,019,582,976
Registered Office: 59-61 High Street, Rickmansworth, Herts, WD3 1RH
Activities: Activities of head offices
Parent: Senior PLC
Officers: Andrew John Bodenham, Secretary; Andrew John Bodenham [1966] Director and Company Secretary; Bindi Jayantilal Jivraj Foyle [1973] Director; David Hamilton Squires [1963] Director

Senior Finance Four Limited
Incorporated: 12 June 2009
Net Worth: £43,373,000 *Total Assets:* £183,024,992
Registered Office: 59-61 High Street, Rickmansworth, Herts, WD3 1RH
Activities: Activities of head offices
Parent: Senior Engineering Investments Limited
Officers: Andrew John Bodenham, Secretary; Andrew John Bodenham [1966] Director; Bindi Jayantilal Jivraj Foyle [1973] Director

Senior Finance Seven Limited
Incorporated: 13 March 2014
Net Worth: £12,720,575 *Total Assets:* £12,720,575
Registered Office: 59-61 High Street, Rickmansworth, Herts, WD3 1RH
Activities: Activities of head offices
Parent: Senior Engineering Investments Limited
Officers: Andrew John Bodenham, Secretary; Andrew John Bodenham [1966] Director; Bindi Jayantilal Jivraj Foyle [1973] Director

Senior Finance Six Limited
Incorporated: 16 November 2011
Net Worth: £86,993,320 *Total Assets:* £130,925,520
Registered Office: 59-61 High Street, Rickmansworth, Herts, WD3 1RH
Activities: Activities of head offices
Parent: Senior Engineering Investments Limited
Officers: Andrew John Bodenham, Secretary; Andrew John Bodenham [1966] Director; Bindi Jayantilal Jivraj Foyle [1973] Director

Senior Five Limited
Incorporated: 13 September 2011
Net Worth: £283,276,704 *Total Assets:* £570,557,504
Registered Office: 59-61 High Street, Rickmansworth, Herts, WD3 1RH
Activities: Activities of head offices
Parent: Senior US Holdings Inc.
Officers: Andrew John Bodenham, Secretary; Andrew John Bodenham [1966] Director and Company Secretary; Bindi Jayantilal Jivraj Foyle [1973] Director

Senior PLC
Incorporated: 18 December 1933 *Employees:* 7,658
Net Worth: £531,600,000 *Total Assets:* £950,800,000
Registered Office: 59-61 High Street, Rickmansworth, Herts, WD3 1RH
Activities: Activities of head offices
Officers: Andrew John Bodenham, Secretary; Dr Celia Frances Baxter [1958] Director; Susan Brennan [1962] Director [American]; Bindi Jayantilal Jivraj Foyle [1973] Director; Giles Frances Bertram Kerr [1959] Director; Ian Graham King [1956] Director; Rajiv Sharma [1966] Director [Singaporean]; David Hamilton Squires [1963] Director; Mark Edward Vernon [1953] Director [American]

Senior UK Limited
Incorporated: 3 July 1985 *Employees:* 1,299
Net Worth: £66,473,000 *Total Assets:* £149,584,000
Registered Office: 59-61 High Street, Rickmansworth, Herts, WD3 1RH
Activities: Manufacture of other special-purpose machinery n.e.c.
Parent: Senior Engineering Investments Limited
Officers: Andrew John Bodenham, Company Secretary; Andrew John Bodenham [1966] Director and Company Secretary; Bindi Jayantilal Jivraj Foyle [1973] Director; Michael Sheppard [1959] Director/President-APD [American]; David Hamilton Squires [1963] Director

Senju Manufacturing (Europe) Limited
Incorporated: 7 October 1996 *Employees:* 22
Net Worth: £7,221,343 *Total Assets:* £12,698,394
Registered Office: 5 The Gateway Centre, Coronation Road, Cressex Business Park, High Wycombe, Bucks, HP12 3SU
Activities: Other non-ferrous metal production
Officers: Satoru Akita [1969] Director [Japanese]; Eihiko Muramatsu [1962] Director [Japanese]; Tetsuya Okuno [1959] Director [Japanese]

Sensient Colors UK Ltd
Incorporated: 15 November 1962 *Employees:* 68
Net Worth: £4,413,664 *Total Assets:* £10,762,310
Registered Office: Oldmedow Road, Hardwick Industrial Estate, Kings Lynn, Norfolk, PE30 4LA
Activities: Manufacture of dyes and pigments
Parent: Sensient Holdings UK Limited
Officers: Bradley Michael Conners [1977] Director/Senior Attorney [American]; Nicola Claire Laroiya [1974] Director/General Manager; Jeffrey Thomas Makal [1963] Director [American]

Sepura PLC
Incorporated: 16 January 2002 *Employees:* 239
Net Worth: £39,776,088 *Total Assets:* £142,070,320
Registered Office: 9000 Cambridge Research Park, Beach Drive, Waterbeach, Cambridge, CB25 9TL
Activities: Other research and experimental development on natural sciences and engineering
Shareholders: Qingzhou Chen; Project Shortway Limited
Officers: Stephen Paul Barber [1964] Director; Duncan James Crouch [1961] Director; Gordon John Watling [1967] Director

Sequence (UK) Limited
Incorporated: 10 August 2001 *Employees:* 3,145
Net Worth: £18,501,000 *Total Assets:* £43,965,000
Registered Office: Cumbria House, 16-20 Hockliffe Street, Leighton Buzzard, Beds, LU7 1GN
Activities: Activities of insurance agents and brokers
Parent: Connells Limited
Officers: Richard John Twigg, Secretary; David Christopher Livesey [1959] Director; David Kerry Plumtree [1969] Director/Chief Executive; Reginald Stephen Shipperley [1958] Director; Richard John Twigg [1965] Director

Serruys Property Company Limited
Incorporated: 2 October 1973 *Employees:* 12
Net Worth: £26,778,718 *Total Assets:* £27,517,096
Registered Office: SPC House, Atlas Works, Norwich Road, Lenwade, Norfolk, NR9 5SN
Activities: Buying and selling of own real estate
Parent: SPC Holdings Ltd
Officers: Andre Paul Serruys [1956] Director; Leticia Serruys [1975] Director/Translator [British/Cuban]; Sonja Clare Serruys [1960] Director

Services Machinery & Trucks Ltd
Incorporated: 16 June 2017 *Employees:* 438
Net Worth: £21,292,000 *Total Assets:* £85,918,000
Registered Office: Moorfield Road, Duxford, Cambridge, CB22 4QX
Activities: Sale of other motor vehicles
Major Shareholder: Philippe Charles de Moerloose
Officers: Nicholas John Allen [1966] Managing Director; Jerome Francois Henri Barioz [1975] Director [French]; Paul David Humphrey [1979] Commercial Director

Seven Asset Limited
Incorporated: 22 July 1997 *Employees:* 69
Net Worth: £3,617,582 *Total Assets:* £27,036,750
Registered Office: Cardinal Court, 35-37 St Peters Street, Ipswich, Suffolk, IP1 1XF
Activities: Renting and leasing of cars and light motor vehicles
Major Shareholder: Roy Victor Dunnett
Officers: Mark Harman, Secretary; Stephen Terry Cole [1959] Director; Jacqueline Hazel Dunnett [1960] Director; Roy Victor Dunnett [1947] Director; Warwick Richard Dunnett [1974] Director; Timothy Foreman [1961] Director; Michael Forsdyke [1956] Director; Chris Hall [1965] Director; Mark Harman [1964] Director; Anthony Peter John Joy [1957] Director; Marc Mellon [1978] Operations Director; James Smith [1976] Director

Sewells Reservoir Construction Limited
Incorporated: 20 February 1989 *Employees:* 131
Net Worth: £11,895,769 *Total Assets:* £26,855,104
Registered Office: Lodge B, Highwood Quarry, Little Canfield, Great Dunmow, Essex, CM6 1SL
Activities: Other mining and quarrying n.e.c.
Shareholders: Oliver John Rees; Louise Jane Yeates
Officers: Louise Jane Yeates, Secretary; David William Hunter [1958] Director/Site Manager; Clinton Layzell [1988] Sales and Transport Director; Oliver John Rees [1987] Director; Louise Jane Yeates [1962] Director/Secretary

Seymour Distribution Limited
Incorporated: 27 July 1994 *Employees:* 77
Net Worth: £141,000 *Total Assets:* £22,586,000
Registered Office: Media House, Peterborough Business Park, Lynch Wood, Peterborough, Cambs, PE2 6EA
Activities: Retail sale of newspapers and stationery in specialised stores
Parent: Frontline Limited
Officers: Jonathan Mark Lambert [1965] Finance Director; Tracy Frances O'Sullivan [1967] Sales Director; Duncan Shearer [1975] Services Director; Dan Sims [1972] Director; Frank Carl Straetmans [1971] Managing Director [Belgian]

Seymour House Residential Care Homes Limited
Incorporated: 24 February 2003 *Employees:* 74
Net Worth: £3,041,362 *Total Assets:* £8,594,592
Registered Office: Seymour House, 13-17 Rectory Road, Rickmansworth, Herts, WD3 1FH
Activities: Residential care activities for the elderly and disabled
Parent: Seymour House Investments Limited
Officers: Salim Rhemtulla, Secretary; Murad Rhemtulla [1944] Director; Salim Rhemtulla [1977] Director; Yasmin Rhemtulla [1972] Director

Seymour International Limited
Incorporated: 23 June 1994 *Employees:* 20
Net Worth: £811,000 *Total Assets:* £16,707,000
Registered Office: Media House, Peterborough Business Park, Lynch Wood, Peterborough, Cambs, PE2 6EA
Activities: Retail sale of newspapers and stationery in specialised stores
Parent: Frontline Limited
Officers: Jonathan Mark Lambert [1965] Finance Director; Tracy Frances O'Sullivan [1967] Sales Director; Duncan Shearer [1975] Services Director; Dan Sims [1972] Director; Frank Carl Straetmans [1971] Managing Director [Belgian]

SF11 Limited
Incorporated: 5 August 2011
Net Worth: £563,631 *Total Assets:* £23,219,880
Registered Office: Kinetic Business Centre, The Kinetic Centre, Theobald Street, Borehamwood, Herts, WD6 4PJ
Activities: Financial intermediation not elsewhere classified
Parent: Spring Finance Limited
Officers: Moshe Moses, Secretary; George Leo Benninger [1946] Director/Attorney [American]; Martin David Chesler [1973] Director/Accountant; Christopher Charles Chew [1972] Director/Head of Lending; Paul Julian Mann [1968] Investment Director; Graeme Edward Wade [1979] Director/Head of Sales

SFAET Ltd
Incorporated: 1 July 2011 *Employees:* 191
Previous: Success for All Educational Trust
Net Worth: £25,028,000 *Total Assets:* £27,800,000
Registered Office: Redden Court School, Cotswold Road, Harold Wood, Romford, Essex, RM3 0TS
Activities: General secondary education
Officers: Justin Paul Barrett, Secretary; Adam Beddoe [1975] Director/Banker; Parminder Kohli [1971] Director; Quenton Shiel Lennon [1970] Director/Businessman; Anita Stewart [1980] Director/Virtual Headteacher; Joanna Wilkinson [1977] Director; Neil Yeomans [1962] Director/Retired

SG Technologies Group Limited
Incorporated: 1 December 2011 *Employees:* 188
Previous: S G Technologies Group Limited
Net Worth: £3,853,000 *Total Assets:* £14,823,000
Registered Office: 85 Ferry Lane, Rainham, Essex, RM13 9YH
Activities: Other manufacturing n.e.c.
Shareholder: John Stephen Taylor
Officers: Stuart Andrew Hutcheon [1970] Sales Director; Timothy George Robinson [1973] Operation Director; Jonathan Clark Swift [1975] Director/Engineer; John Stephen Taylor [1963] Director; Stephen Thomas Quentin Williams [1951] Director

SG Technologies Limited
Incorporated: 11 September 1987 *Employees:* 187
Previous: S G Technologies Limited
Net Worth: £5,431,000 *Total Assets:* £16,504,000
Registered Office: Tesla House, 85 Ferry Lane, Rainham, Essex, RM13 9YH
Activities: Other manufacturing n.e.c.
Officers: Stuart Andrew Hutcheon [1970] Director/Sales Manager; Timothy George Robinson [1973] Operations Director; Jonathan Clark Swift [1975] Director/Engineer; John Stephen Taylor [1963] Director/Development; Stephen Thomas Quentin Williams [1951] Director

Shakoor Capital Limited
Incorporated: 12 February 1998 *Employees:* 1
Previous: Handsel Limited
Net Worth: £8,887,165 *Total Assets:* £9,465,524
Registered Office: Premier Suite, 4 Churchill Court, 58 Station Road, North Harrow, Middlesex, HA2 7ST
Activities: Security dealing on own account
Major Shareholder: Was Shakoor
Officers: Waseem Shakoor [1967] Director/Management Consultant

Shamir UK Limited
Incorporated: 15 November 1988 *Employees:* 29
Net Worth: £19,484,012 *Total Assets:* £21,544,656
Registered Office: P O Box 76, Bridge House, Saxon Way, Bar Hill, Cambridge, CB23 8SH
Activities: Manufacture of medical and dental instruments and supplies
Officers: Yair di Segni, Secretary; Catherine Johnston-Roussillon [1958] Managing Director Europe [French]; Yagen Moshe [1969] Director/Finance Manager [Israeli]; Lior Regev [1977] Director [Israeli]

Shamrock Bidco Limited
Incorporated: 5 May 2016 *Employees:* 5
Net Worth: £18,648,350 *Total Assets:* £44,416,624
Registered Office: The Mount, The Sidings, Station Road, Longstanton, Cambridge, CB24 3DS
Activities: Other business support service activities n.e.c.
Parent: Shamrock Midco Limited
Officers: Kevin Timothy Collins [1970] Director/Accountant; James Henry [1965] Director; John Gerard Henry [1970] Director; Patrick Henry [1965] Director; Stephen James Henry [1969] Telecommunications Director; Natalie Claire Keogh [1975] Director

Shamrock Midco Limited
Incorporated: 5 May 2016 *Employees:* 4
Net Worth Deficit: £5,254,693 *Total Assets:* £41,308,772
Registered Office: The Mount, The Sidings, Station Road, Longstanton, Cambridge, CB24 3DS
Activities: Other business support service activities n.e.c.
Parent: Shamrock Topco Limited
Officers: James Henry [1965] Director; John Gerard Henry [1970] Director; Patrick Henry [1965] Director

Shamrock Topco Limited
Incorporated: 5 May 2016 *Employees:* 393
Net Worth Deficit: £1,228,050 *Total Assets:* £54,167,856
Registered Office: The Mount, The Sidings, Station Road, Longstanton, Cambridge, CB24 3DS
Activities: Other business support service activities n.e.c.
Shareholders: Growth Capital Partners GP Limited; Growth Capital Partners LLP
Officers: Barry Canfield [1958] Director/Chartered Accountant; James Henry [1965] Director; John Gerard Henry [1970] Director; Patrick Henry [1965] Director; Richard John Penston [1959] Director

Shaneel Enterprises Limited
Incorporated: 30 September 1987 *Employees:* 150
Net Worth: £55,743,016 *Total Assets:* £92,480,160
Registered Office: 78 Wembley Park Drive, Wembley, Middlesex, HA9 8HE
Activities: Wholesale of perfume and cosmetics
Officers: Chetna Dilesh Mehta, Secretary; Dilesh Bhogilal Mehta [1960] Director/Businessman Wholesaler; Hitesh Bhogilal Mehta [1956] Director/Pharmacist

Shanly Homes Limited
Incorporated: 4 January 1993 *Employees:* 173
Net Worth: £183,379,440 *Total Assets:* £213,357,648
Registered Office: Sorbon, Aylesbury End, Beaconsfield, Bucks, HP9 1LW
Activities: Development of building projects
Parent: Sorbon Homes Limited
Officers: Nicholas Mark Trott, Secretary; Tamra Michelle Booth [1974] Director; Robin Nicholas Dorran [1957] Director; Michael James Shanly [1945] Director; Nicholas Mark Trott [1964] Director/Chartered Accountant

Sharan Properties Limited
Incorporated: 24 October 1984 *Employees:* 3
Net Worth: £10,794,672 *Total Assets:* £11,806,635
Registered Office: 106 Sudbury Court Drive, Harrow, Middlesex, HA1 3TG
Activities: Buying and selling of own real estate
Shareholder: Usha Gupta
Officers: Usha Gupta, Secretary; Prashant Gupta [1970] Director; Usha Gupta [1945] Director

The Share Centre Limited
Incorporated: 22 January 1990 *Employees:* 207
Net Worth: £12,077,000 *Total Assets:* £38,213,000
Registered Office: Oxford House, Oxford Road, Aylesbury, Bucks, HP21 8SZ
Activities: Security and commodity contracts dealing activities
Parent: Share PLC
Officers: Giles Pemberton, Secretary; Michael David Birkett [1972] Finance Director; Francesca Eva Ecsery [1963] Director/Businesswoman; Gavin David Redvers Oldham [1949] Director/Member of Stock Exchange; Linda Elizabeth Roberts [1962] Director; John Victor Sargeant [1970] Director; Richard Adam Stollery [1962] Director; Richard William Stone [1973] Finance Director; Gareth Vaughan Thomas [1957] Director; Richard Ian Tolkien [1955] Director/Businessman

Share PLC
Incorporated: 8 September 1994 *Employees:* 207
Net Worth: £18,189,000 *Total Assets:* £45,286,000
Registered Office: Oxford House, Oxford Road, Aylesbury, Bucks, HP21 8SZ
Activities: Activities of head offices
Major Shareholder: Gavin David Redvers Oldham
Officers: Giles Pemberton, Secretary; Michael David Birkett [1972] Finance Director; Francesca Eva Ecsery [1963] Director; Gavin David Redvers Oldham [1949] Director/Member of Stock Exchange; Richard William Stone [1973] Finance Director; Gareth Vaughan Thomas [1957] Director; Richard Ian Tolkien [1955] Director/Businessman

The Shared Learning Trust
Incorporated: 6 October 2006 *Employees:* 485
Previous: Barnfield Academy Trust
Net Worth: £67,961,000 *Total Assets:* £72,919,000
Registered Office: The Chalk Hills Academy, Leagrave High Street, Luton, Beds, LU4 0NE
Activities: Primary education
Officers: Catherine Anne Barr [1968] Director/Chief Executive; David Jerome Forbes [1952] Director/Retired; Robert James Grant [1968] Estates Director; Trefor Lewis Hamer [1945] Director/Retired; Deborah Harris-Ugbomah [1967] Director/Accountant; Sarah Caroline Mortimer [1960] Director/Vice Principal; Tricia Patricia Ethel Penfold [1952] Director/Retired; David Martin Sheridan [1950] Director

Shared Services Connected Ltd
Incorporated: 25 March 2013 *Employees:* 1,466
Net Worth: £39,491,000 *Total Assets:* £150,602,000
Registered Office: Three Cherry Trees Lane, Hemel Hempstead, Herts, HP2 7AH
Activities: Other business support service activities n.e.c.
Parent: Sopra Steria Limited
Officers: Peter Atherton Cashmore, Secretary; Davinder Singh Ahluwalia [1952] Director; Peter Atherton Cashmore [1962] Director/Solicitor [New Zealander]; Peter Atherton Cashmore [1962] Director/Solicitor [New Zealander]; Michael Brian Driver [1961] Director/Chief Financial Officer; Maria Greene [1967] Director/Accountant; John Nairn MacGregor Neilson [1961] Human Resources Director; Mark David Thomson [1962] Director; John Powell Torrie [1954] Director

Sharksfin Holdings Limited
Incorporated: 25 July 1997 *Employees:* 1
Net Worth: £64,107,080 *Total Assets:* £72,016,672
Registered Office: 146 High Street, Billericay, Essex, CM12 9DF
Activities: Activities of head offices
Major Shareholder: Martin Arthur Mills
Officers: Martin Arthur Mills [1952] Director

Shawbrook Bank Limited
Incorporated: 29 June 1944 *Employees:* 671
Net Worth: £615,000,000 *Total Assets:* £5,752,000,000
Registered Office: Lutea House, The Drive, Warley Hill Business Park, Great Warley, Brentwood, Essex, CM13 3BE
Activities: Banks
Parent: Shawbrook Group PLC
Officers: Daniel James Rushbrook, Secretary; Robin James Ashton [1958] Director; John Dalrymple Callender [1950] Director; Ian Cowie [1960] Director; Andrew Didham [1956] Director; Mr Cedric Dubourdieu [1974] Director [French]; Paul Joseph Lawrence [1961] Director; Roger Vincent Lovering [1959] Director; Lindsey Villon McMurray [1971] Director/Investment Professional; Dylan Minto [1980] Director

Shawbrook Group PLC
Incorporated: 30 April 2010 *Employees:* 671
Previous: Shawbrook Group Limited
Net Worth: £623,100,032 *Total Assets:* £5,758,700,032
Registered Office: Lutea House, Warley Hill Business Park, The Drive, Great Warley, Brentwood, Essex, CM13 3BE
Activities: Activities of head offices
Parent: Marlin Bidco Limited
Officers: Daniel James Rushbrook, Secretary; Robin James Ashton [1958] Director; John Dalrymple Callender [1950] Director; Ian Cowie [1960] Director; Andrew Didham [1956] Director; Mr Cedric Dubourdieu [1974] Director [French]; Paul Joseph Lawrence [1961] Director; Roger Vincent Lovering [1959] Director; Lindsey McMurray [1971] Director/Investment Professional; Dylan Minto [1980] Director

Shawcor UK Limited
Incorporated: 13 August 1991 *Employees:* 247
Net Worth: £15,453,000 *Total Assets:* £30,019,000
Registered Office: Shawcor House, Viking Road, Gapton Hall Industrial Estate, Great Yarmouth, Norfolk, NR31 0NU
Activities: Support activities for petroleum and natural gas mining
Officers: Darrell Robert Ewert, Secretary; Simon Laurence Dewey [1972] Director/Business Executive; Darrell Robert Ewert [1956] Director/Business Executive [Canadian]; Stephen Michael Orr [1963] Director/Business Executive [Canadian]; Gaston Alfonso Tano [1969] Director/Business Executive [Canadian]

Shearer Property C Limited
Incorporated: 3 July 2014
Net Worth: £2,698,998 *Total Assets:* £13,824,684
Registered Office: 41 Plantation Road, Amersham, Bucks, HP6 6HL
Activities: Buying and selling of own real estate
Major Shareholder: Guy Edwin Angus Shearer
Officers: Adam Charles Drury Markwell [1959] Director; Paul David Newell [1961] Director; Guy Edwin Angus Shearer [1953] Director

Shedmead Limited
Incorporated: 24 March 1998
Net Worth: £9,825,493 *Total Assets:* £13,875,975
Registered Office: Newney Hall, Newney Green, Writtle, Chelmsford, Essex, CM1 3SE
Activities: Buying and selling of own real estate
Shareholders: Gail Jane Jones; George Nicholas Jones
Officers: George Nicholas Jones, Secretary/Chartered Surveyor; Gail Jane Jones [1955] Director/Retired Chartered Surveyor; George Nicholas Jones [1955] Director

Sheikh Holdings Group (Investments) Limited
Incorporated: 26 May 2011 *Employees:* 63
Net Worth: £26,006,516 *Total Assets:* £51,078,424
Registered Office: 7th Floor, Metropolitan House, 3 Darkes Lane, Potters Bar, Herts, EN6 1AG
Activities: Activities of other holding companies n.e.c.
Shareholders: Haroon Rashid Sheikh; Farouq Rashid Sheikh
Officers: Gareth Dufton, Secretary; Matthew James Davis [1970] Director; Gareth Norman Dufton [1976] Director/Chartered Accountant; Akbar Sheikh [1989] Director; Farouq Rashid Sheikh [1958] Director; Haroon Rashid Sheikh [1956] Non-Executive Director Chairman; Yusuf Rashid Sheikh [1992] Director

Shelbourne Reynolds Engineering Limited
Incorporated: 25 May 1972 *Employees:* 127
Net Worth: £13,677,598 *Total Assets:* £15,986,637
Registered Office: Shepherds Grove Industrial Estate, Stanton, Bury St Edmunds, Suffolk, IP31 2AR
Activities: Manufacture of agricultural and forestry machinery other than tractors
Parent: Stanton Holding Ltd
Officers: Claire Jayne Bloomfield, Secretary; Claire Jayne Bloomfield [1965] Finance Director; Andrey Evguenyevich Budakov [1968] Director/Economist [Russian]; Stephen Victor Fairburn [1955] Director/Partner of C J Jones Solicitors LLP; Nikolay Gorbunov [1970] Director/Businessman [Russian]; Alexander Kuznetsov [1968] Director/Business Consultant [Russian]; Lyudmila Obraztsova [1960] Director/Businesswoman [Russian]; Neil Martyn Smith [1969] Sales Director

Shelfside (Holdings) Limited
Incorporated: 20 December 2000 *Employees:* 93
Net Worth: £7,114,410 *Total Assets:* £37,585,772
Registered Office: 166 College Road, Harrow, Middlesex, HA1 1RA
Activities: Renting and operating of Housing Association real estate
Parent: Best Holdings (UK) Limited
Officers: Ian Michael Farr, Secretary; Alfred William Best [1970] Director; Waseem Hanif [1967] Director

Shelfside Group LLP
Incorporated: 10 August 2016 *Employees:* 2
Net Worth: £38,964,948 *Total Assets:* £50,248,940
Registered Office: 166 College Road, Harrow, Middlesex, HA1 1RA
Officers: Alfred William Best [1970] Member

Shenfield High School
Incorporated: 5 January 2012 *Employees:* 132
Net Worth: £23,265,852 *Total Assets:* £27,761,460
Registered Office: Shenfield High School, Alexander Lane, Shenfield, Brentwood, Essex, CM15 8RY
Activities: General secondary education
Officers: Stuart Roberts, Secretary; Julian Beard [1964] Director/Lawyer; Katharine Boulton [1970] Director/SAHM; Leanne Hedden [1959] Director/Retired Civil Servant; Carole Jean Herman [1963] Director/Headteacher; Graham Peter Herniman [1965] Director/Business Development; Gillian Meriel Jones [1963] Director/Royal Mail Manager; Simon Laurence Murray [1972] Director/Solicitor; Neil Purbrick [1974] Director; Stuart James Roberts [1978] Director/Business Manager; Karuna Shaunak-Hobbs [1980] Director/Teacher; Jane Michelle Swettenham [1965] Director/Non Practising Solicitor; Andrew Williams [1969] Director/Banking; Andrew Graham Worth [1965] Director

Shenley Park Trust
Incorporated: 23 May 1990 *Employees:* 5
Net Worth: £10,191,887 *Total Assets:* £10,235,764
Registered Office: The Bothy, Shenley Park, Radlett Lane, Shenley, Radlett, Herts, WD7 9DW
Activities: Other amusement and recreation activities n.e.c.
Officers: Glyn Stewart Dredge, Secretary; Glyn Stewart Dredge [1966] Park Director; Rosemary Elizabeth Gilligan [1957] Director; Warren Barry Gordon [1968] Director/Solicitor; Steve James Harrington-Smith [1974] Director; Anthony Charles Harris [1976] Director/Solicitor; Neil James Hibbert [1962] Director/Accountant; Seamus Quilty [1951] Director/Councillor; Natalie Rowan [1980] Director; Anthony Philip Spencer [1948] Director; William Susman [1967] Director/Estate Agent; Howard Wand [1955] Director/Printer; Simon Ward [1963] Director/IT Consultant

Sherfield School Limited
Incorporated: 2 September 2003 *Employees:* 128
Net Worth Deficit: £18,353,176 *Total Assets:* £12,436,704
Registered Office: 100 Hills Road, Cambridge, CB2 1PH
Activities: Primary education
Parent: GEMS Schools Finance Limited
Officers: Jay Sunny Varkey [1984] Director [Indian]

George A. Sherriff Limited
Incorporated: 29 November 2007 *Employees:* 306
Net Worth: £21,099,668 *Total Assets:* £39,190,160
Registered Office: Blackwater Place, Blackwater Trading Estate, The Causeway, Maldon, Essex, CM9 4GG
Activities: Wholesale of wood, construction materials and sanitary equipment
Shareholders: Mark Sherriff; George Albert Sherriff
Officers: Richard William Dawkes, Secretary; George Albert Sheriff [1937] Director; Mark Sheriff [1961] Director

Sherrygold No.1 Limited
Incorporated: 5 December 2002
Net Worth: £5,950,404 *Total Assets:* £14,630,546
Registered Office: Jubilee House, 7-9 The Oaks, Ruislip, Middlesex, HA4 7LF
Activities: Other letting and operating of own or leased real estate
Major Shareholder: Amiran Hassan Moledina Janmohamed
Officers: Alim Amirali Janmohamed, Secretary; Alim Amirali Janmohamed [1981] Director; Amirali Hassanali Moledina Janmohamed [1952] Director

Sherrygreen Homes Ltd
Incorporated: 9 February 2006 *Employees:* 10
Net Worth: £6,163,197 *Total Assets:* £26,906,754
Registered Office: Teresa Gavin House, Woodford Avenue, Woodford Green, Essex, IG8 8FA
Activities: Development of building projects
Parent: Sherrygreen Ltd
Officers: Eamon O'Malley, Secretary; Brendon O'Malley [1954] Director; Eamon O'Malley [1955] Director; Martin Taylor [1952] Director/Manager; Teresa Taylor [1963] Director

Sherrygreen Limited
Incorporated: 19 October 1983 *Employees:* 527
Net Worth: £103,762,000 *Total Assets:* £171,018,000
Registered Office: Teresa Gavin House, Woodford Avenue, Woodford Green, Essex, IG8 8FA
Activities: Activities of head offices
Officers: Eamon O'Malley, Secretary; Brendon O'Malley [1954] Managing Director; Eamon O'Malley [1955] Director; Shaun O'Malley [1966] Director; Vincent O'Malley [1951] Director; Teresa Taylor [1963] Director

Shields Environmental Group (Holdings) Ltd.
Incorporated: 14 May 2015 *Employees:* 138
Net Worth Deficit: £4,866,000 *Total Assets:* £20,411,000
Registered Office: Shields Environmental, Kerry Avenue, Aveley, South Ockendon, Essex, RM15 4YE
Activities: Activities of head offices
Shareholder: William Anthony Rice
Officers: David Harry Challis [1962] Director/Chief Financial Officer; Daniel Jones [1982] Director; William Anthony Rice [1952] Director

Shields Environmental Investment (Holdings) Limited
Incorporated: 15 May 2015 *Employees:* 4
Net Worth Deficit: £3,059,000 *Total Assets:* £19,212,000
Registered Office: Shields Environmental, Kerry Avenue, Aveley, South Ockendon, Essex, RM15 4YE
Activities: Activities of head offices
Parent: Shields Environmental Group (Holdings) Ltd
Officers: David Harry Challis [1962] Director; Daniel Jones [1982] Director; William Anthony Rice [1952] Director

Shiva Kingsway Limited
Incorporated: 10 September 2014 *Employees:* 88
Net Worth: £429,304 *Total Assets:* £117,024,896
Registered Office: 505 Pinner Road, Harrow, Middlesex, HA2 6EH
Activities: Hotels and similar accommodation
Officers: Rishi Ramesh Sachdev [1976] Director; Uday Vyas [1978] Director

The Shoe Quarter Limited
Incorporated: 25 August 2015
Net Worth: £31,360 *Total Assets:* £14,008,924
Registered Office: Crane Court, 302 London Road, Ipswich, Suffolk, IP2 0AJ
Activities: Development of building projects
Shareholders: Michael Hintze; Dominic Charles David Richards
Officers: Dominic Charles David Richards [1966] Director

Shogun Finance Limited
Incorporated: 22 November 1985 *Employees:* 12
Net Worth: £5,886,000 *Total Assets:* £227,207,008
Registered Office: 116 Cockfosters Road, Barnet, Herts, EN4 0DY
Activities: Financial intermediation not elsewhere classified
Shareholders: Spitalgate Dealer Services Limited; Black Horse Group Limited
Officers: David Dermot Hennessey, Secretary; Christopher Michael Adams [1982] Director; Paul Andrew Brigden [1966] Director; Masami Ichiki [1968] Director [Japanese]; Richard Andrew Jones [1972] Marketing Director; David William Ramsey [1963] Managing Director; Dr Nagla Thabet [1974] Director

SHOO 802AA Limited
Incorporated: 26 April 2017 *Employees:* 102
Net Worth: £535,000 *Total Assets:* £20,611,000
Registered Office: Burleighfield House, London Road, Loudwater, Bucks, HP10 9RF
Activities: Public relations and communications activities
Officers: Robert John Jozef Apollo [1985] Director; Christian Lewis Bruning [1969] Director; Matthew Robert James Gorham [1976] Director; Dennis Simon O'Brien [1975] Director; Janet Elizabeth Steele [1964] Director; Timothy Hugh Southcombe Trotter [1959] Director/Chairman

SHOO 803AA Limited
Incorporated: 9 May 2017 *Employees:* 10
Net Worth Deficit: £31,000 *Total Assets:* £19,160,000
Registered Office: Burleighfield House, London Road, Loudwater, Bucks, HP10 9RF
Activities: Public relations and communications activities
Shareholders: SHOO 802AA Limited; SHOO 802AA Limited
Officers: Dennis Simon O'Brien [1975] Director; Janet Elizabeth Steele [1964] Director

Shopfittings Direct Limited
Incorporated: 12 June 1998 *Employees:* 74
Net Worth: £3,495,894 *Total Assets:* £10,263,358
Registered Office: 186-192 High Road, Ilford, Essex, IG1 1LR
Activities: Non-specialised wholesale trade
Shareholder: David Neil Brooks
Officers: Paul Martin Brooks, Secretary; Paul Martin Brooks [1963] Director

K.J. Shortis Limited
Incorporated: 26 August 1971 *Employees:* 620
Net Worth: £36,537,000 *Total Assets:* £41,775,000
Registered Office: 186-200 Salhouse Road, Norwich, NR7 9AH
Activities: Activities of head offices
Officers: Stephen Paul Allman, Secretary; Kevin John Shortis [1939] Managing Director; Richard John Shortis [1969] Director; Victoria Constance Shortis [1939] Director

Showcard Print Limited
Incorporated: 21 September 2011 *Employees:* 146
Net Worth: £6,454,000 *Total Assets:* £19,416,000
Registered Office: Fontana House, Works Road, Letchworth Garden City, Herts, SG6 1LD
Activities: Printing n.e.c.
Parent: Ingleby (1884) Limited
Officers: Mark Hawkins, Secretary; Mark Hawkins [1974] Financial Director; Mark Warren Masters Smith [1959] Director

J.B Shropshire & Sons Limited
Incorporated: 25 February 1998 *Employees:* 1,286
Net Worth: £31,216,208 *Total Assets:* £62,983,860
Registered Office: Hainey Farm, Barway, Ely, Cambs, CB7 5TZ
Activities: Growing of cereals (except rice), leguminous crops and oil seeds
Major Shareholder: John Bourne Shropshire
Officers: David Thompson, Secretary; John Bourne Shropshire [1955] Director; David Thompson [1968] Director

G.S. Shropshire & Sons Limited
Incorporated: 7 January 1958 *Employees:* 16
Net Worth: £17,116,508 *Total Assets:* £19,851,734
Registered Office: Hainey Farm, Barway, Ely, Cambs, CB7 5TZ
Activities: Growing of cereals (except rice), leguminous crops and oil seeds
Parent: GS Shropshire Holdings Ltd
Officers: David Thompson, Secretary/Accountant; Guy Peter Shropshire [1957] Director/Farmer; David Thompson [1968] Director

Shropshire Energy (UK) Limited
Incorporated: 2 May 2012 *Employees:* 4
Net Worth: £9,881,822 *Total Assets:* £13,132,561
Registered Office: Hainey Farm, Barway Road, Soham, Cambs, CB7 5TZ
Activities: Production of electricity
Shareholders: Guy Peter Shropshire; JB Shropshire & Sons Ltd
Officers: Frederick James George Clark [1990] Director; Charles Shropshire [1986] Director; David Thompson [1968] Director

G S Shropshire Holdings Limited
Incorporated: 6 April 1994 *Employees:* 16
Net Worth: £40,832,432 *Total Assets:* £43,635,592
Registered Office: Hainey Farm, Barway, Ely, Cambs, CB7 5TZ
Activities: Activities of head offices
Major Shareholder: Guy Peter Shropshire
Officers: David Thompson, Secretary; Guy Peter Shropshire [1957] Director; David Thompson [1968] Director

Shure Europe Holdings Limited
Incorporated: 4 November 2010 *Employees:* 765
Net Worth: £103,405,272 *Total Assets:* £124,386,464
Registered Office: Unit 2 The IO Centre, Lea Road, Waltham Abbey, Essex, EN9 1AS
Activities: Activities of other holding companies n.e.c.
Officers: Paul Lance Applebaum [1963] Director/Executive VP and General Counsel [American]; Christine Marie Schyvinck [1967] Director [American]; Bruce Douglas Skof [1971] Director/Accountant [American]

Richard Shuttleworth Trustees
Incorporated: 1 May 1992 *Employees:* 68
Net Worth: £85,647,000 *Total Assets:* £86,653,000
Registered Office: Old Warden Park, Old Warden, Biggleswade, Beds, SG18 9EP
Activities: Non-trading company
Officers: Andrew Philip Rutt, Secretary; Professor Michael David Alder [1947] Director/Retired Principal; Patrick John Ashley [1957] Director/Landowner; Roger Bailey [1951] Director/Retired; Viscount Christopher Charles Cobham [1947] Director; Edward Andrew Davies [1950] Managing Director; Simon Gardner [1984] Director/Farm Manager; Richard Graf Von Waldburg Wolfegg [1965] Director/Banking [German]; Princess Xenia Hohenlohe [1972] Director/Consultant in Sustainability Issues [German]; Timothy Routsis [1959] Director/Chief Executive Officer; Charles Edward Samuel Whitbread [1963] Director; Edmund Michael Wood [1943] Director/Chartered Accountant

Sick (UK) Ltd.
Incorporated: 27 November 1973 *Employees:* 80
Net Worth: £7,873,000 *Total Assets:* £13,214,000
Registered Office: 39 Hedley Road, St Albans, Herts, AL1 5BN
Activities: Manufacture of optical precision instruments
Parent: Sick AG
Officers: Alan John Reeves, Secretary; Mats Goekstorp [1965] Director/Manager [Swedish]; Alan John Reeves [1964] Director/Accountant; Markus Vatter [1966] Finance Director [German]

Sifcon International PLC
Incorporated: 25 October 1946 *Employees:* 58
Net Worth: £6,634,617 *Total Assets:* £16,430,931
Registered Office: New Ford Road, Brittania Road Industrial Estate, Waltham Cross, Herts, EN8 7PG
Activities: Wholesale of household goods (other than musical instruments) n.e.c
Major Shareholder: Nicholas Stephen Tiffin
Officers: Alan Charles Pimm, Secretary; Alan Charles Pimm [1949] Director; John Pugh [1955] Director/Sales; Tracy Frances Storan [1965] Director/Chartered Accountant; Nicholas Stephen Tiffin [1960] Director; Peter Michael Tuck [1954] Director/Credit Controller

Sigma Imaging (UK) Limited
Incorporated: 27 November 2000 *Employees:* 14
Net Worth: £11,446,016 *Total Assets:* £12,546,896
Registered Office: 13 Little Mundells, Welwyn Garden City, Herts, AL7 1EW
Activities: Manufacture of photographic and cinematographic equipment
Parent: The Sigma Corporation
Officers: Tetsu Kubota, Secretary; Kazuto Yamaki [1968] Director/Chief Executive Officer - Sigma Corporation [Japanese]

Signature Flatbreads (UK) Ltd
Incorporated: 17 December 2014 *Employees:* 1,083
Net Worth: £33,113,000 *Total Assets:* £61,579,000
Registered Office: Unit C, Chiltern Park Industrial Estate, Boscombe Road, Dunstable, Beds, LU5 4LT
Activities: Manufacture of bread; manufacture of fresh pastry goods and cakes
Parent: Bakery Investments Limited
Officers: Charles Samir Eid [1966] Director/Chief Executive; William Samir Eid [1964] Director

Signature Flight Support Limited
Incorporated: 2 July 2003 *Employees:* 3
Net Worth: £89,625,048 *Total Assets:* £89,625,048
Registered Office: Voyager House, 142 Prospect Way, Luton, Beds, LU2 9QH
Activities: Regulation of and contribution to more efficient operation of businesses
Parent: BBA Overseas Holdings Limited
Officers: Shawn Christopher Fallon [1981] Director/Finance [American]; Yvette Helen Freeman [1967] Director; Daniel David Ruback [1977] Finance Director

Signature Flight Support London Luton Limited
Incorporated: 19 August 1988 *Employees:* 144
Net Worth: £82,794,368 *Total Assets:* £94,052,920
Registered Office: Voyager House, 142 Prospect Way, Luton, Beds, LU2 9QH
Activities: Non-scheduled passenger air transport
Parent: Signature Flight Support UK Regions Limited
Officers: Shawn Christopher Fallon [1981] Director/Finance [American]; Yvette Helen Freeman [1967] Director; Daniel David Ruback [1977] Finance Director

Signature Lessee I Limited
Incorporated: 23 November 2016 *Employees:* 3
Net Worth: £5,750,002 *Total Assets:* £12,507,380
Registered Office: Grosvenor House, Horseshoe Crescent, Beaconsfield, Bucks, HP9 1LJ
Activities: Other letting and operating of own or leased real estate
Parent: Signature Senior Lifestyle Finance Limited
Officers: Tom James Ball [1983] Finance Director; Frank Cerrone [1959] Director/Senior Vice President, General Counsel & Secretary [Canadian]; James Hardy [1959] Director/Chief Investment Officer & CEO [Canadian]; Thomas Bruce Newell [1957] Director/Executive Chairman [American]; Aidan Gerard Roche [1966] Managing Director [Irish]

Signature Lessee Limited
Incorporated: 11 December 2012 *Employees:* 3
Net Worth: £1,326,391 *Total Assets:* £12,788,826
Registered Office: Grosvenor House, Horseshoe Crescent, Beaconsfield, Bucks, HP9 1LJ
Activities: Financial intermediation not elsewhere classified
Parent: Signature Senior Lifestyle Finance Limited
Officers: Tom James Ball [1983] Finance Director; Frank Cerrone [1959] Director/Senior Vice President, General Counsel & Secretary [Canadian]; James Hardy [1959] Director/Chief Investment Officer & CFO [Canadian]; Thomas Bruce Newell [1957] Director [American]; Aidan Gerard Roche [1966] Director [Irish]

Signature Senior Lifestyle Finance Limited
Incorporated: 30 November 2005 *Employees:* 3
Net Worth: £45,574,424 *Total Assets:* £63,823,416
Registered Office: Grosvenor House, Horseshoe Crescent, Beaconsfield, Bucks, HP9 1LJ
Activities: Other letting and operating of own or leased real estate
Parent: Signature Senior Lifestyle Holdings Limited
Officers: Tom James Ball, Secretary; Tom James Ball [1983] Finance Director; Frank Cerrone [1959] Director/Senior Vice President, General Counsel & Secretary [Canadian]; James Hardy [1959] Director/Chief Investment Officer & CFO [Canadian]; Thomas Bruce Newell [1957] Director [American]; Aidan Gerard Roche [1966] Director [Irish]

Signet Direct Diamond Sourcing Limited
Incorporated: 12 April 2011
Net Worth: £79,225,376 *Total Assets:* £86,724,216
Registered Office: Imperial Place, 3 Maxwell Road, Borehamwood, Herts, WD6 1JN
Activities: Other business support service activities n.e.c.
Parent: Signet Holdings Limited
Officers: Benjamin Harris [1983] Director/Attorney; Rory O'Donnell [1977] Director/Financial Controller [American]; Michele Santana [1970] Director/Chief Financial Officer [American]

Signet Group Limited
Incorporated: 27 January 1950 *Employees:* 1
Net Worth: £631,923,072 *Total Assets:* £1,798,029,184
Registered Office: Imperial Place, 3 Maxwell Road, Borehamwood, Herts, WD6 1JN
Activities: Activities of head offices
Parent: Signet Jewelers Limited
Officers: Benjamin Harris, Secretary; Marianne Kelly [1974] Director/Head of Finance; Raina Margaret Miles [1962] Director/Chartered Accountant; Michele Santana [1970] Director/Chief Financial Officer [American]

Signet Group Services Limited
Incorporated: 13 May 1999 *Employees:* 7
Net Worth: £3,711,000 *Total Assets:* £17,505,000
Registered Office: Imperial Place, 3 Maxwell Road, Borehamwood, Herts, WD6 1JN
Activities: Other business support service activities n.e.c.
Parent: Signet Holdings Limited
Officers: Benjamin Harris, Secretary; Marianne Kelly [1974] Director/Head of Finance; Raina Margaret Miles [1962] Director/Chartered Accountant; Michele Santana [1970] Director/Chief Financial Officer [American]

Signet Holdings Limited
Incorporated: 13 May 1999
Net Worth: £1,155,329,152 *Total Assets:* £1,202,115,712
Registered Office: Imperial Place, 3 Maxwell Road, Borehamwood, Herts, WD6 1JN
Activities: Non-trading company
Parent: Signet Group Limited
Officers: Benjamin Harris, Secretary; Marianne Kelly [1974] Director/Head of Finance; Raina Margaret Miles [1962] Director/Chartered Accountant; Michele Santana [1970] Director/Chief Financial Officer [American]

Signet Trading Limited
Incorporated: 12 May 1999 *Employees:* 3,255
Net Worth: £290,904,000 *Total Assets:* £369,443,008
Registered Office: Imperial Place, 3 Maxwell Road, Borehamwood, Herts, WD6 1JN
Activities: Other business support service activities n.e.c.
Parent: Signet Holdings Limited
Officers: Benjamin Harris, Secretary; Shaun David Carney [1966] Finance Director; Benjamin Harris [1983] Director/Attorney

Signet UK Finance PLC
Incorporated: 17 April 2014
Net Worth: £4,957,018 *Total Assets:* £306,881,696
Registered Office: Imperial Place, 3 Maxwell Road, Borehamwood, Herts, WD6 1JN
Activities: Other business support service activities n.e.c.
Parent: Signet Group Limited
Officers: Benjamin Harris, Secretary; Marianne Kelly [1974] Director/Head of Finance; Raina Margaret Miles [1962] Director/Chartered Accountant; Michele Santana [1970] Director/Chief Financial Officer [American]

Sika Limited
Incorporated: 23 December 1927 *Employees:* 443
Net Worth: £18,448,768 *Total Assets:* £106,345,200
Registered Office: Watchmead, Welwyn Garden City, Herts, AL7 1BQ
Activities: Manufacture of other inorganic basic chemicals
Parent: Sika AG
Officers: Daniel Emil Lang [1971] Director/Head Finance & Controlling Region EMEA [Swiss]; Paul Schuler [1955] Director/Head of Region EMEA [Swiss]

Silk Industries Limited
Incorporated: 17 February 2003 *Employees:* 147
Net Worth: £1,672,319 *Total Assets:* £8,462,408
Registered Office: Gregory Mills, Weavers Lane, Sudbury, Suffolk, CO10 1BB
Activities: Weaving of textiles
Major Shareholder: David Eric Tooth
Officers: Steven Anthony Oxley, Secretary; Laura Jayn Gore [1977] Sales Director; Tro Steven Manoukian [1977] Director; Stephen Andrew Nixon [1963] Design Director; Steven Anthony Oxley [1955] Director; David Eric Tooth [1949] Director/Company Chairman

M & D Silk Properties Ltd
Incorporated: 10 November 2010
Net Worth: £25,173,256 *Total Assets:* £31,327,848
Registered Office: 2 Fauna Close, Stanmore, Middlesex, HA7 4PX
Activities: Buying and selling of own real estate
Officers: David Christopher Leslie Silk [1961] Director; Lynne Carol Silk [1962] Director

Silnat Holdings Limited
Incorporated: 23 May 2014
Net Worth: £16,285,834 *Total Assets:* £16,500,291
Registered Office: York House, Empire Way, Wembley, Middlesex, HA9 0FQ
Activities: Activities of other holding companies n.e.c.
Shareholders: David Rothman; Harold Rothman
Officers: David Rothman [1959] Director; Harold Rothman [1956] Director

Silver Street Automotive Limited
Incorporated: 1 March 1962 *Employees:* 258
Net Worth: £3,812,000 *Total Assets:* £33,324,000
Registered Office: Airport House, The Airport, Cambridge, CB5 8RY
Activities: Sale of new cars and light motor vehicles
Parent: Marshall Motor Holdings PLC
Officers: Stephen Robert Jones, Secretary; Richard John Blumberger [1975] Director; Daksh Gupta [1970] Director

Silverbridge Properties Limited
Incorporated: 18 March 2002
Net Worth: £3,159,151 *Total Assets:* £15,552,931
Registered Office: Ground Floor, 4 Victoria Square, St Albans, Herts, AL1 3TF
Activities: Buying and selling of own real estate
Major Shareholder: Russell Grahame Baldwin
Officers: Tina Lesley Benjamin, Secretary; Ross Nicholas Albrow [1956] Director; Russell Grahame Baldwin [1959] Property Director; Tina Lesley Benjamin [1949] Director/Bookkeeper

Silverson Machines Holdings Limited
Incorporated: 23 May 2014 *Employees:* 113
Net Worth: £21,838,684 *Total Assets:* £29,534,494
Registered Office: York House, Empire Way, Wembley, Middlesex, HA9 0FQ
Activities: Activities of production holding companies
Shareholders: Harold Rothman; David Rothman
Officers: David Rothman [1959] Director; Harold Rothman [1956] Director

Silverson Machines Limited
Incorporated: 26 July 1946 *Employees:* 113
Net Worth: £14,293,701 *Total Assets:* £16,510,545
Registered Office: York House, Empire Way, Wembley, Middlesex, HA9 0FQ
Activities: Manufacture of other special-purpose machinery n.e.c.
Parent: Silverson Machines Holdings Limited
Officers: David Rothman, Secretary; David Rothman [1959] Director; Harold Rothman [1956] Director

Silverton Property Investments Limited
Incorporated: 25 July 1997 *Employees:* 4
Previous: Silverton Developments Limited
Net Worth: £9,631,691 *Total Assets:* £14,273,929
Registered Office: 9-11 High Beech Road, Loughton, Essex, IG10 4BN
Activities: Other accommodation
Major Shareholder: Mohammed Iqbal Vesamia
Officers: Munira Banu Vesamia, Secretary; Aamir Mohammed Vesamia [1996] Director; Abdul Rehman Vesamia [1944] Director; Fatima Vesamia [1972] Director; Mohammed Iqbal Vesamia [1967] Director; Munira Banu Vesamia [1947] Director; Saniya Vesamia [1997] Director

Silverwell Technology Limited
Incorporated: 13 November 2000
Previous: Camcon Oil Limited
Net Worth Deficit: £10,904,598 *Total Assets:* £22,375,742
Registered Office: St John Innovation Park, Cowley Road, Cambridge, CB4 4WS
Activities: Other research and experimental development on natural sciences and engineering
Shareholders: David Ivor Young of Graffham; Nathan Kirsch
Officers: Daniel Robert Chapchal [1945] Director; Lloyd Dorfman [1952] Director; Darrell Paul Johnson [1964] Director; Nigel Francis Penney [1959] Director/Chartered Accountant; Barry Stiefel [1949] Director [German]; James Munro Murray Sutherland [1954] Director; Frederick Thomas Tilton [1953] Director [American]; Lord David Ivor Young of Graffham [1932] Director

Simarco Holdings Limited
Incorporated: 4 September 2013 *Employees:* 276
Net Worth: £7,757,490 *Total Assets:* £19,120,640
Registered Office: Simarco Holdings, Crittall Road, Witham, Essex, CM8 3DR
Activities: Activities of head offices
Major Shareholder: Simon Anthony Lionel Reed
Officers: Simon Anthony Lionel Reed [1967] Director

Simarco International Limited
Incorporated: 27 March 1997 *Employees:* 276
Net Worth: £6,330,077 *Total Assets:* £17,272,356
Registered Office: Simarco House, Crittall Road, Witham, Essex, CM8 3DR
Activities: Operation of warehousing and storage facilities for land transport activities
Parent: Simarco Holdings Limited
Officers: Christopher William Bentley [1958] Sales Director; David Knowles [1976] European Operations Director; Simon Anthony Lionel Reed [1967] Director; Trevor Scott [1974] Managing Director; Barry Charles Spencer [1959] Warehousing & Distribution Director

Simat Properties Limited
Incorporated: 8 November 1963 *Employees:* 5
Net Worth: £1,735,487 *Total Assets:* £12,479,319
Registered Office: 2nd Floor, Hygeia House, 66 College Road, Harrow, Middlesex, HA1 1BE
Activities: Development of building projects
Shareholders: June Viiolet Beckley; Simon Charles Derek Beckley
Officers: Simon Charles Derek Beckley, Secretary; June Violet Beckley [1931] Director; Simon Charles Derek Beckley [1959] Director

Simm Tronic Limited
Incorporated: 25 September 1992 *Employees:* 104
Net Worth: £5,400,862 *Total Assets:* £8,387,818
Registered Office: Unit 3 Waterside Industrial Estate, Charlton Mead Lane, Hoddesdon, Herts, EN11 0QR
Activities: Manufacture of electric lighting equipment
Officers: Mario Costanzo, Secretary; Mario Costanzo [1963] Director; Steven Terence Goskie [1963] Director; Giacomo Russo [1955] Director; Vincenzo Russo [1959] Director; Raymond Arthur Vos [1964] Director

Simmons (Bakers) Limited
Incorporated: 10 October 1946 *Employees:* 511
Net Worth: £7,890,129 *Total Assets:* £12,178,610
Registered Office: 2 The Parade, St Albans Road East, Hatfield, Herts, AL10 0EY
Activities: Manufacture of bread; manufacture of fresh pastry goods and cakes
Officers: Neal Richard Tuson, Secretary; Gillian Mary Ewing [1965] Director/Regional Sales Manager; Ian Denis Matthews [1948] Director; Penelope Anne Matthews [1947] Director; Rupert John Matthews [1980] Director/Communications Manager; Neal Richard Tuson [1961] Director/Accountant; Peter John Williams [1964] Director/Bakery Manager

J O Sims Holdings (1896) Limited
Incorporated: 9 November 2012 *Employees:* 129
Net Worth: £41,253,292 *Total Assets:* £93,618,784
Registered Office: Pudding Lane, Pinchbeck, Spalding, Lincs, PE11 3TJ
Activities: Activities of head offices
Shareholder: Christopher Oliver Sims
Officers: Andrew Bell, Secretary; Andrew James Bell [1972] Director; Alexander George Oliver Sims [1988] Director; Christopher Oliver Sims [1959] Director; James Victor Oliver Sims [1985] Director

J O Sims Holdings Limited
Incorporated: 1 March 1954 *Employees:* 129
Net Worth: £43,030,904 *Total Assets:* £94,023,232
Registered Office: Pudding Lane, Pinchbeck, Spalding, Lincs, PE11 3TJ
Activities: Wholesale of fruit and vegetables
Parent: J O Sims Holdings (1896) Limited
Officers: Andrew James Bell, Secretary; Andrew James Bell [1972] Director; Christopher Oliver Sims [1959] Director; James Victor Oliver Sims [1985] Director

J O Sims Limited
Incorporated: 15 December 1986 *Employees:* 87
Net Worth: £20,252,266 *Total Assets:* £65,364,976
Registered Office: Pudding Lane, Pinchbeck, Spalding, Lincs, PE11 3TJ
Activities: Wholesale of fruit and vegetables
Parent: J O Sims Holdings Limited
Officers: Andrew James Bell, Secretary; Andrew James Bell [1972] Director; Christopher Oliver Sims [1959] Director; James Victor Oliver Sims [1985] Director

Sinai (Antiques) Limited
Incorporated: 11 July 1977 *Employees:* 7
Net Worth: £2,964,505 *Total Assets:* £9,345,633
Registered Office: Lynwood House, 373-375 Station Road, Harrow, Middlesex, HA1 2AW
Activities: Retail sale of other second-hand goods in stores (not incl. antiques)
Parent: Mount Sinai Holdings Limited
Officers: Sylvia Sinai, Secretary; Elcana Sinai [1947] Director/Antique Dealer [Israeli]

Sinclair International Limited
Incorporated: 16 September 1991 *Employees:* 143
Net Worth: £18,389,000 *Total Assets:* £31,210,000
Registered Office: Jarrold Way, Bowthorpe, Norwich, NR5 9JD
Activities: Manufacture of printed labels
Major Shareholder: Jeremy Flug
Officers: Andrew Paul Crowe, Secretary; Daniel Marco Bejarano [1947] Director; David Charles Burall [1941] Director; Michael Francis Dacey [1944] Director/Business Executive [American]; Jeremy Flug [1961] Director/Business Executive [American]; Geoffrey T Gordon [1939] Director/Business Executive [American]; William Frank Hallier [1945] Director [American]; Erik I Teranchi [1945] Director/Business Executive [American]; Colin Paul Woodward [1962] Director/Chief Executive

Thomas Sinden Limited
Incorporated: 28 January 1997 *Employees:* 107
Net Worth: £5,178,521 *Total Assets:* £20,384,588
Registered Office: 137-145 Church Road, Harold Wood, Romford, Essex, RM3 0SH
Activities: Development of building projects
Shareholders: Desmond Francis Thomas; Graeme Sinden
Officers: Jonathan Neil Taylor, Secretary; Stephen Thomas McMahon [1969] Director; Graeme Sinden [1965] Director; Desmond Francis Thomas [1960] Director

Sinek Global Finance & Trading LLP
Incorporated: 21 July 2008
Net Worth: £20,152,748 *Total Assets:* £30,981,460
Registered Office: First Floor, Healthaid House, Marlborough Hill, Harrow, Middlesex, HA1 1UD

Sines LLP
Incorporated: 13 January 2009 *Employees:* 10
Net Worth: £6,638,991 *Total Assets:* £12,040,737
Registered Office: 166 College Road, Harrow, Middlesex, HA1 1RA
Officers: Elaine Ann Sines [1965] Member; Maurice Sines [1962] Member

Sines Parks (S.E.) Limited
Incorporated: 2 February 2007 *Employees:* 6
Net Worth: £4,183,018 *Total Assets:* £9,846,920
Registered Office: 166 College Road, Harrow, Middlesex, HA1 1RA
Activities: Other business support service activities n.e.c.
Major Shareholder: Maurice Sines
Officers: Elaine Ann Sines, Secretary; Elaine Ann Sines [1965] Director; Maurice Sines [1962] Director

Sines Parks Holdings Limited
Incorporated: 6 December 2012
Net Worth: £6,884,420 *Total Assets:* £18,351,088
Registered Office: 166 College Road, Harrow, Middlesex, HA1 1RA
Activities: Activities of other holding companies n.e.c.
Major Shareholder: Maurice Sines
Officers: Elaine Ann Sines [1965] Director; Maurice Sines [1962] Director

Sines Parks Ltd
Incorporated: 27 January 2003 *Employees:* 2
Net Worth: £2,109,031 *Total Assets:* £20,432,996
Registered Office: 166 College Road, Harrow, Middlesex, HA1 1RA
Activities: Recreational vehicle parks, trailer parks and camping grounds
Parent: Sines Parks Holdings Limited
Officers: Elaine Ann Sines, Secretary; Elaine Ann Sines [1965] Director; Maurice Sines [1962] Director

SintecMedia Global Ltd
Incorporated: 22 December 2000
Net Worth: £18,999,208 *Total Assets:* £19,009,208
Registered Office: Artemis House, Odyssey Business Park, West End Road, Ruislip, Middlesex, HA4 6QE
Activities: Business and domestic software development
Officers: Elad Lustig, Secretary; Lorne Brown [1975] Director [American]; Paul Nicholas Bryan-Harris [1970] Director

SintecMedia LON Ltd
Incorporated: 20 November 2005 *Employees:* 13
Net Worth: £6,116,877 *Total Assets:* £46,466,108
Registered Office: Artemis House, Odyssey Business Park, West End Road, Ruislip, Middlesex, HA4 6QE
Activities: Other professional, scientific and technical activities n.e.c.
Officers: Lorne Brown [1975] Director [American]; Paul Nicholas Bryan-Harris [1970] Director

SintecMedia WEM Ltd
Incorporated: 2 December 1999 *Employees:* 41
Net Worth: £1,731,650 *Total Assets:* £25,215,930
Registered Office: Artemis House, Odyssey Business Park, West End Road, Ruislip, Middlesex, HA4 6QE
Activities: Business and domestic software development
Officers: Elad Lustig, Secretary; Lorne Brown [1975] Director [American]; Paul Nicholas Bryan-Harris [1970] Director

SIP Group Limited
Incorporated: 10 May 2004
Net Worth: £10,713,801 *Total Assets:* £19,897,728
Registered Office: 114-116 Goodmayes Road, Ilford, Essex, IG3 9UZ
Activities: Activities of head offices
Shareholders: Sukhbinder Singh Takhar; Iqbal Kaur Takhar; Pirthipal Singh Takhar
Officers: Iqbal Kaur Takhar, Secretary; Iqbal Kaur Takhar [1960] Director/Company Secretary; Pirthipal Singh Takhar [1982] Director; Sukhbinder Singh Takhar [1954] Director

John Sisk & Son Limited
Incorporated: 20 December 1985 *Employees:* 391
Net Worth Deficit: £4,327,000 *Total Assets:* £92,521,000
Registered Office: 1 Curo Park, Frogmore, St Albans, Herts, AL2 2DD
Activities: Construction of commercial buildings
Parent: Sisk Consolidated Investments Limited
Officers: Maura Toles, Secretary; Stephen Bowcott [1955] Director; Guy Fowler [1973] Director; Mark Joseph McGreevy [1972] Director [Irish]; Ajaz Shafi [1966] Director/Business Executive; Maura Toles [1963] Director/Management Accountant [Irish]

Sisk Consolidated Investments Limited
Incorporated: 30 October 1989 *Employees:* 2
Net Worth: £6,424,446 *Total Assets:* £11,598,033
Registered Office: 1 Curo Park, Frogmore, St Albans, Herts, AL2 2DD
Activities: Construction of commercial buildings
Parent: John Sisk & Son (Holdings) Limited
Officers: Maura Toles, Secretary; Stephen Bowcott [1955] Director; Maura Toles [1963] Director [Irish]

Site Sales Marketing Limited
Incorporated: 19 July 1989 *Employees:* 53
Net Worth: £20,688,224 *Total Assets:* £22,387,996
Registered Office: Haslers, Old Station Road, Loughton, Essex, IG10 4PL
Activities: Real estate agencies
Shareholders: Denise Lorraine Smith; Murray George Smith
Officers: Denise Lorraine Smith, Secretary; Murray George Smith [1963] Director/Estate Agent

Sitecrest Limited
Incorporated: 23 July 1984 *Employees:* 5
Net Worth: £13,801,840 *Total Assets:* £14,391,378
Registered Office: Harmile House, 54 St Mary's Lane, Upminster, Essex, RM14 2QT
Activities: Other letting and operating of own or leased real estate
Major Shareholder: Robert David Hagger
Officers: Tracey Lynn Hagger, Secretary; Robert David Hagger [1959] Director; Tracey Lynn Hagger [1967] Director

SJD Accountancy Limited
Incorporated: 12 June 2007 *Employees:* 170
Net Worth: £22,044,786 *Total Assets:* £24,285,448
Registered Office: KD Tower, Cotterells, Hemel Hempstead, Herts, HP1 1FW
Activities: Other business support service activities n.e.c.
Parent: Arkarius Bidco Limited
Officers: Kevin John Budge [1961] Director; Derek Andrew Kelly [1972] Director

SJO Enterprises Limited
Incorporated: 4 February 2010
Net Worth: £13,645,701 *Total Assets:* £23,605,686
Registered Office: Vantage House, 6-7 Claydons Lane, Rayleigh, Essex, SS6 7UP
Activities: Management consultancy activities other than financial management
Parent: LJ Capital Limited
Officers: David Owen, Secretary; Sandra Jane Owen [1965] Director

SJR Farming Limited
Incorporated: 24 August 2006 *Employees:* 10
Net Worth: £20,705,746 *Total Assets:* £26,053,000
Registered Office: Dollymans Farmhouse, Doublegate Lane, Rawreth, Essex, SS11 8UD
Activities: Growing of cereals (except rice), leguminous crops and oil seeds
Major Shareholder: Stuart John Ross Philpot
Officers: Joanne Ruth Philpot, Secretary; Peter John Harold Philpot [1943] Director; Stuart John Ross Philpot [1975] Director

Skanska Cementation International Holdings Limited
Incorporated: 5 February 1969
Net Worth: £18,565,000 *Total Assets:* £18,610,000
Registered Office: Maple Cross House, Denham Way, Maple Cross, Rickmansworth, Herts, WD3 9SW
Activities: Activities of head offices
Parent: Skanska Construction Holdings UK Limited
Officers: Steven Leven, Secretary; Mark Lawson Galloway [1955] Director/Solicitor; Culdip Kelly Kaur Gangotra [1970] Director/Accountant

Skanska Cementation International Limited
Incorporated: 26 July 1948
Net Worth: £20,569,000 *Total Assets:* £33,210,000
Registered Office: Maple Cross House, Denham Way, Maple Cross, Rickmansworth, Herts, WD3 9SW
Activities: Construction of commercial buildings
Parent: Skanska Construction Holdings UK Limited
Officers: Steven Leven, Secretary; Mark Lawson Galloway [1955] Director/Solicitor; Culdip Kelly Kaur Gangotra [1970] Director/Accountant

Skanska Construction (Regions) Limited
Incorporated: 24 October 1927
Net Worth: £4,604,000 *Total Assets:* £11,881,000
Registered Office: Maple Cross House, Denham Way, Maple Cross, Rickmansworth, Herts, WD3 9SW
Activities: Construction of commercial buildings
Parent: Skanska UK PLC
Officers: Steven Leven, Secretary; David William Kyriacos [1976] Director; Steven Leven [1967] Director/Company Secretary; Steven Edward Lindsay [1975] Director

Skanska Construction Holdings UK Limited
Incorporated: 30 October 2000
Net Worth: £2,960,000 *Total Assets:* £314,691,008
Registered Office: Maple Cross House, Denham Way, Maple Cross, Rickmansworth, Herts, WD3 9SW
Activities: Activities of head offices
Parent: Skanska AB
Officers: Mark Lawson Galloway, Secretary; Gregor Lawrence Craig [1963] Managing Director; Culdip Kelly Kaur Gangotra [1970] Director/Accountant

Skanska Construction UK Limited
Incorporated: 19 July 1923 *Employees:* 5,125
Net Worth: £250,718,000 *Total Assets:* £774,459,008
Registered Office: Maple Cross House, Denham Way, Maple Cross, Rickmansworth, Herts, WD3 9SW
Activities: Construction of commercial buildings
Parent: Skanska UK PLC
Officers: Steven Leven, Secretary; Gregor Lawrence Craig [1963] Managing Director; Katrina Mary Dowding [1970] Director; Thomas Peter Faulkner [1974] Director; Culdip Kelly Kaur Gangotra [1970] Director/Accountant; Martin George Neeson [1968] Director/Manager

Skanska Infrastructure Development UK Limited
Incorporated: 21 February 1995 *Employees:* 39
Net Worth Deficit: £50,734,000 *Total Assets:* £22,338,000
Registered Office: Maple Cross House, Denham Way, Maple Cross, Rickmansworth, Herts, WD3 9SW
Activities: Development of building projects
Parent: Skanska AB
Officers: Steven Leven, Secretary; Paul Alan Bannister [1959] Director; Simon Richard Thorpe Beauchamp [1973] Commercial Director

Skanska Infrastructure Investment UK Limited
Incorporated: 23 December 2002
Net Worth: £71,613,000 *Total Assets:* £91,503,000
Registered Office: Maple Cross House, Denham Way, Maple Cross, Rickmansworth, Herts, WD3 9SW
Activities: Other business support service activities n.e.c.
Parent: Skanska AB
Officers: Steven Leven, Secretary; Paul Alan Bannister [1959] Director; Simon Richard Thorpe Beauchamp [1973] Commercial Director

Skanska J.V. Projects Ltd
Incorporated: 18 December 1998 *Employees:* 30
Net Worth: £46,048,000 *Total Assets:* £97,344,000
Registered Office: Maple Cross House, Denham Way, Maple Cross, Rickmansworth, Herts, WD3 9SW
Activities: Other business support service activities n.e.c.
Parent: Skanska Construction UK Limited
Officers: Steven Leven, Secretary; Katrina Mary Dowding [1970] Director; Thomas Peter Faulkner [1974] Director; Culdip Kelly Kaur Gangotra [1970] Director/Accountant

Skanska Major Projects Limited
Incorporated: 9 November 1970 *Employees:* 8
Net Worth: £13,079,000 *Total Assets:* £22,816,000
Registered Office: Maple Cross House, Denham Way, Maple Cross, Rickmansworth, Herts, WD3 9SW
Activities: Other specialised construction activities n.e.c.
Parent: Skanska Construction UK Limited
Officers: Steven Leven, Secretary; Katrina Mary Dowding [1970] Director; Culdip Kelly Kaur Gangotra [1970] Director/Accountant

Skanska Project Developments Limited
Incorporated: 24 November 2006 *Employees:* 9
Net Worth: £20,098,000 *Total Assets:* £115,084,000
Registered Office: Maple Cross House, Denham Way, Maple Cross, Rickmansworth, Herts, WD3 9SW
Activities: Development of building projects
Parent: Skanska UK PLC
Officers: Steven Leven, Secretary; Culdip Kelly Kaur Gangotra [1970] Director/Accountant; Helen Katherine Martin [1975] Director/Civil Engineer; Martin George Neeson [1968] Director/Manager

Skanska Rashleigh Weatherfoil Limited
Incorporated: 26 March 1964 *Employees:* 1,074
Net Worth: £66,226,000 *Total Assets:* £202,738,000
Registered Office: Maple Cross House, Denham Way, Maple Cross, Rickmansworth, Herts, WD3 9SW
Activities: Electrical installation
Parent: Skanska Construction UK Limited
Officers: Steven Leven, Secretary; Katrina Mary Dowding [1970] Director; Adam Michael McDonald [1983] Director

Skanska TAM Limited
Incorporated: 1 March 2013
Net Worth: £42,658,000 *Total Assets:* £87,536,000
Registered Office: Maple Cross House, Denham Way, Maple Cross, Rickmansworth, Herts, WD3 9SW
Activities: Development of building projects
Parent: Skanska Construction Services Trustee Limited
Officers: Nigel John Pitchers, Secretary; Harvey James Francis [1965] Director; Philippa Jane Smith [1958] Director; David Ian Wills [1962] Director

Skanska UK PLC
Incorporated: 16 December 1963 *Employees:* 5,741
Net Worth: £261,776,000 *Total Assets:* £891,872,000
Registered Office: Maple Cross House, Denham Way, Maple Cross, Rickmansworth, Herts, WD3 9SW
Activities: Construction of commercial buildings
Parent: Skanska Construction Holdings UK Limited
Officers: Mark Lawson Galloway, Secretary; Gregor Lawrence Craig [1963] Managing Director; Katrina Mary Dowding [1970] Director; Thomas Peter Faulkner [1974] Director; Harvey James Francis [1965] Director; Mark Lawson Galloway [1955] Director/Solicitor; Culdip Kelly Kaur Gangotra [1970] Director/Accountant; Martin George Neeson [1968] Director/Manager

Skechers USA Ltd.
Incorporated: 21 August 2000 *Employees:* 477
Net Worth: £7,434,000 *Total Assets:* £35,301,000
Registered Office: CT3 Centrium, Griffiths Way, St Albans, Herts, AL1 2RE
Activities: Wholesale of clothing and footwear
Parent: Skechers USA Inc
Officers: Philip Paccione, Secretary/Business Executive [American]; Michael Greenberg [1963] Director/Business Executive [American]; David Weinberg [1950] Director/Business Executive [American]

Skeltools Limited
Incorporated: 13 December 1951 *Employees:* 4
Net Worth: £8,788,279 *Total Assets:* £10,443,987
Registered Office: Church Farm Accounts Office, Church Road, Slapton, Leighton Buzzard, Beds, LU7 9BX
Activities: Other letting and operating of own or leased real estate
Parent: Storland Limited
Officers: Elizabeth Anne Phipps, Secretary; Elizabeth Anne Phipps [1960] Director; Cicely Margaret Thompson [1959] Director

Skewbald Limited
Incorporated: 14 December 2001 *Employees:* 53
Net Worth: £1,859,663 *Total Assets:* £10,219,899
Registered Office: Redhill Farm, Harlington Road, Toddington, Dunstable, Beds, LU5 6HF
Activities: Other passenger land transport
Shareholders: Nicholas Roach; THL Motorhomes UK Limited
Officers: Nicholas Roach, Secretary; Nicholas Roach [1969] Director; Sarah Roach [1973] Director/Equestrian Marketing; Daniel Schneider [1966] Director [Swiss]; Grant Webster [1972] Director [New Zealander]

SKF (U.K) Limited
Incorporated: 7 February 1910 *Employees:* 911
Net Worth: £106,734,000 *Total Assets:* £219,952,000
Registered Office: Sundon Park Road, Luton, Beds, LU3 3BL
Activities: Manufacture of bearings, gears, gearing and driving elements
Parent: Trelanoak Limited
Officers: Paula Jane Owen, Secretary/Accountant; Michael Roger Crean [1959] Director [New Zealander]; Paula Jane Owen [1973] Director/Accountant; Sharon Linda Smith [1962] Director/Accountant

Nigel Skinner Financial Advisers Limited
Incorporated: 6 November 2009 *Employees:* 1
Previous: Nigel Skinner Independent Financial Advisors Limited
Net Worth: £4,552,293 *Total Assets:* £10,129,492
Registered Office: The Old Vicarage, Church Close, Boston, Lincs, PE21 6NA
Activities: Financial intermediation not elsewhere classified
Major Shareholder: Nigel Darren Skinner
Officers: Nigel Darren Skinner [1962] Director

Roger Skinner Limited
Incorporated: 12 August 1976 *Employees:* 58
Net Worth: £14,552,531 *Total Assets:* £19,635,860
Registered Office: The Mill, Stradbroke, Eye, Suffolk, IP21 5HL
Activities: Manufacture of prepared pet foods
Officers: Wendy Lynn Skinner, Secretary; Clive William Delamore [1974] Sales Director; Gregory James Panter [1948] Managing Director; Matthew Robert Peters [1971] Operations Director; Roger Alfred Stanley Skinner [1949] Director; Wendy Lynn Skinner [1963] Director/Interior Designer; Desmond John Smith [1965] Managing Director

Skylight Investments Limited
Incorporated: 14 June 2011
Net Worth: £100 *Total Assets:* £17,019,638
Registered Office: Flat 201, Ramsey House, Central Square, Wembley, Middlesex, HA9 7AH
Activities: Other professional, scientific and technical activities n.e.c.
Officers: Diane Patricia Sanger [1960] Director

Skylord Travel PLC
Incorporated: 25 November 1988 *Employees:* 28
Net Worth: £2,475,964 *Total Assets:* £9,513,370
Registered Office: 208 Field End Road, Eastcote, Pinner, Middlesex, HA5 1RD
Activities: Travel agency activities
Shareholders: Rajan Kumar Sehgal; Dalip Kumar Kewalramani
Officers: Kartick Kumari Sehgal, Secretary; Dalip Kumar Kewalramani [1969] Director/Travel Agent; Manjinder Seehra [1970] Director/Travel Agent; Kartick Kumari Sehgal [1956] Director/Travel Agent; Rajan Kumar Sehgal [1951] Director/Accountant; Ujjwal Sehgal [1981] Director/Businessman

Slingsby Advanced Composites Limited
Incorporated: 24 December 1982 *Employees:* 118
Net Worth: £6,238,738 *Total Assets:* £12,784,845
Registered Office: Airport House, The Airport, Cambridge, CB5 8RY
Activities: Manufacture of air and spacecraft and related machinery
Parent: Slingsby Holdings Ltd
Officers: Sarah Jane Moynihan, Secretary; Alistair Dickson McPhee [1958] Director; Gary John Scott Moynehan [1979] Director

SLR Consulting Limited
Incorporated: 19 November 1999 *Employees:* 400
Net Worth: £37,028,220 *Total Assets:* £45,580,956
Registered Office: 7 Wornal Park, Menmarsh Road, Worminghall, Aylesbury, Bucks, HP18 9PH
Activities: Environmental consulting activities
Parent: SLR Holdings Limited
Officers: John Martin Green, Secretary; Dr Alan Jonathan Edwards [1967] Director/Environmental Consultant; John Martin Green [1957] Company Secretary/Director; Peter Robert MacKellar [1965] Director; Neil Christopher Penhall [1964] Director

SLR Holdings Limited
Incorporated: 20 May 2004
Net Worth: £11,746,385 *Total Assets:* £18,029,672
Registered Office: 7 Wornal Park, Menmarsh Road, Worminghall, Aylesbury, Bucks, HP18 9PH
Activities: Environmental consulting activities
Parent: SLR Management Limited
Officers: John Martin Green, Secretary; Neil Christopher Penhall [1964] Director

SLR Management Limited
Incorporated: 18 March 2008 *Employees:* 1,184
Net Worth: £40,782,592 *Total Assets:* £101,139,400
Registered Office: 7 Wornal Park, Menmarsh Road, Worminghall, Aylesbury, Bucks, HP18 9PH
Activities: Environmental consulting activities
Shareholder: 3i Group PLC
Officers: John Martin Green, Secretary; Peter Robert MacKellar [1965] Director; Neil Christopher Penhall [1964] Director; Kevin Grant Rattue [1959] Director

Slug and Lettuce Company Limited
Incorporated: 27 June 2007 *Employees:* 1,165
Net Worth: £41,379,000 *Total Assets:* £85,570,000
Registered Office: Porter Tun House, 500 Capability Green, Luton, Beds, LU1 3LS
Activities: Public houses and bars
Parent: Bay Restaurant Group Limited
Officers: Suzanne Louise Baker [1963] Director/Business Executive; Simon David Longbottom [1971] Director/Chief Executive Officer; David Andrew Ross [1973] Director/Chief Financial Officer

Slush Puppie Limited
Incorporated: 16 June 1945 *Employees:* 88
Net Worth: £6,632,496 *Total Assets:* £13,844,823
Registered Office: Slush Puppie Ltd, Coronation Road, Cressex Business Park, High Wycombe, Bucks, HP12 3TA
Activities: Manufacture of soft drinks; production of mineral waters and other bottled waters
Parent: Ralph Peter's and Sons Ltd
Officers: Susanne Treacher, Secretary; Alan Raymond Beaney [1962] Director/Chairman; Laura Peters [1988] Director/Stock Manager; Mark Jeffrey Peters [1958] Director

SLV Group Holding UK Limited
Incorporated: 7 July 2017
Net Worth: £12,592,380 *Total Assets:* £41,304,756
Registered Office: Unit 4 Foster Avenue, Woodside Park, Dunstable, Beds, LU5 5TA
Activities: Activities of other holding companies n.e.c.
Officers: Catherine Connolly [1968] Director; Erhardt Sven Schirmer [1972] Director [German]

Frederic Smart & Son Limited
Incorporated: 24 May 1966 *Employees:* 26
Net Worth: £6,446,305 *Total Assets:* £10,335,910
Registered Office: 7 Papworth Business Park, Stirling Way, Papworth Everard, Cambridge, CB23 3GY
Activities: Wholesale of grain, unmanufactured tobacco, seeds and animal feeds
Major Shareholder: Douglas Norman Smart
Officers: Douglas Norman Smart, Secretary; Douglas Norman Smart [1968] Director/Grain Trader; Frederic Thomas Andrew Smart [1943] Director/Grain and Seed Merchant

Smart Meter Assets 1 Ltd
Incorporated: 27 January 2014
Net Worth: £7,611,300 *Total Assets:* £168,669,520
Registered Office: Energy House, Woolpit Business Park, Windmill Avenue, Woolpit, Bury St Edmunds, Suffolk, IP30 9UP
Activities: Renting and leasing of other machinery, equipment and tangible goods n.e.c.
Parent: BUUK Infrastructure No 2 Limited
Officers: Christopher Paul Mumford, Secretary; Darryl John Corney [1960] Director; Clive Eric Linsdell [1962] Director; Jeff Studholme [1974] Director of Smart Metering

Smartcomms SC Limited
Incorporated: 11 October 2001 *Employees:* 117
Previous: Thunderhead Limited
Net Worth Deficit: £8,505,000 *Total Assets:* £15,767,000
Registered Office: Catalyst House, 720 Centennial Court, Centennial Park, Elstree, Herts, WD6 3SY
Activities: Business and domestic software development
Parent: Platinum Newco I Limited
Officers: James Brown [1971] Director; Jon Stratford [1970] Director

SME Group PLC
Incorporated: 13 April 1988 *Employees:* 1,620
Net Worth: £55,596,000 *Total Assets:* £111,588,000
Registered Office: Runway House, The Runway, Ruislip, Middlesex, HA4 6SE
Activities: Activities of head offices
Officers: Aly Mohamed Esmail, Secretary; Sayed Mohamed Esmail, Secretary; Aly Esmail [1982] Director; Sayed Mohamed Esmail [1986] Director

SME Holdings Limited
Incorporated: 14 December 2001 *Employees:* 1,012
Net Worth: £23,182,824 *Total Assets:* £63,635,392
Registered Office: Runway House, The Runway, Ruislip, Middlesex, HA4 6SE
Activities: Activities of head offices
Officers: Sayed Mohamed Esmail, Secretary; Aly Mohamed Esmail [1982] Director; Sayed Mohamed Esmail [1986] Director

SME Investments Limited
Incorporated: 10 May 2005 *Employees:* 529
Net Worth: £27,143,268 *Total Assets:* £71,963,288
Registered Office: Runway House, The Runway, Ruislip, Middlesex, HA4 6SE
Activities: Activities of head offices
Parent: SME Group PLC
Officers: Aly Mohamed Esmail, Secretary; Sayed Mohamed Esmail, Secretary; Aly Mohamed Esmail [1982] Director; Sayed Mohamed Esmail [1986] Director

SME Properties Limited
Incorporated: 10 March 2005
Net Worth: £3,134,435 *Total Assets:* £16,102,450
Registered Office: Runway House, The Runway, Ruislip, Middlesex, HA4 6SE
Activities: Other accommodation
Officers: Aly Mohamed Esmail, Secretary; Sayed Mohamed Esmail, Secretary; Aly Mohamed Esmail [1982] Director; Sayed Mohamed Esmail [1986] Director

Smile Stores Limited
Incorporated: 4 November 1959 *Employees:* 1,079
Net Worth: £24,329,000 *Total Assets:* £44,032,000
Registered Office: McColl's House, Ashwells Road, Brentwood, Essex, CM15 9ST
Activities: Retail sale in non-specialised stores with food, beverages or tobacco predominating
Parent: Key Food Stores Limited
Officers: Robbie Ian Bell [1973] Director/Chief Financial Officer; Simon Jeremy Ian Fuller [1977] Director; Steven Green [1981] Director; Simon Jonathan Miller [1963] Director

F.P.Smith (Holdings) Limited
Incorporated: 14 March 1940 *Employees:* 147
Net Worth: £11,568,567 *Total Assets:* £19,659,640
Registered Office: Sturrock Way, Bretton Way, Bretton, Peterborough, Cambs, PE3 8YL
Activities: Sale of new cars and light motor vehicles
Major Shareholder: Jane Margaret Wisniewski
Officers: Mark Alan Edwards, Secretary; Mark Alan Edwards [1972] Finance Director; Daniel Fitzjohn [1972] Director; Sarah Jane Fitzjohn [1973] Director; Jane Margaret Wisniewski [1947] Director/Secretary; Matthew George Wisniewski [1976] Director

Smith and Holbourne (Holdings) Limited
Incorporated: 5 September 1941 *Employees:* 141
Net Worth: £24,918,576 *Total Assets:* £30,192,784
Registered Office: Faulkner House, Victoria Street, St Albans, Herts, AL1 3SE
Activities: Activities of head offices
Officers: Simon Hendrik Pieter Van Wouwe, Secretary; Bas Albas [1960] Managing Director [Dutch]; Simon Hendrik Pieter Van Wouwe [1967] Director [Dutch]

Smith Bros Timber (East Anglia) Limited
Incorporated: 3 July 1992 *Employees:* 31
Net Worth: £8,337,715 *Total Assets:* £9,429,034
Registered Office: No 15 Cooke Road, South Lowestoft Industrial Estate, Lowestoft, Suffolk, NR33 7NA
Activities: Non-specialised wholesale trade
Major Shareholder: Roy Gary Smith
Officers: Valerie Ann Langford, Secretary; Timothy James French [1978] Director; Jason Paul Harness [1970] Director; Stephanie Harrod [1962] Director; Roy Gary Smith [1961] Director/Business Manager

Smith Farms (Clacton) Limited
Incorporated: 18 July 1947 *Employees:* 23
Net Worth: £9,407,092 *Total Assets:* £11,322,960
Registered Office: Wigboro Wick, St Osyth, Clacton on Sea, Essex, CO16 8ER
Activities: Growing of cereals (except rice), leguminous crops and oil seeds
Officers: Catherine Joan Parker [1982] Director; Elizabeth Mary Smith [1990] Director; Guy Henry Smith [1959] Director/Farmer; Jean Mary Smith [1931] Director/Housewife; Penelope Jean Smith [1969] Director; Philip David Smith [1956] Director

H. Smith Food Group PLC
Incorporated: 22 January 1990 *Employees:* 33
Net Worth: £4,419,886 *Total Assets:* £17,509,352
Registered Office: 24 Easter Industrial Park, Ferry Lane South, Rainham, Essex, RM13 9BP
Activities: Wholesale of meat and meat products
Major Shareholder: Christopher Jamie Smith
Officers: Phillip Trevor Wheater, Secretary; Daniel Lawrence Fallis [1976] Sales Director; David Keith Howe [1967] Director/Sales; Richard James Murray [1965] Finance Director; Christopher Jamie Smith [1959] Director/Poultry Merchant; Shaun Daniel Smith [1989] Director/Frozen Food Wholesaler

Smithfield Foods Limited
Incorporated: 24 November 1993 *Employees:* 47
Net Worth: £8,738,000 *Total Assets:* £19,888,000
Registered Office: Norfolk Tower, 48-52 Surrey Street, Norwich, NR1 3PA
Activities: Non-specialised wholesale of food, beverages and tobacco
Parent: Smithfield Foods Group Limited
Officers: Ross Michael Ashton [1975] Finance Director; Ian Lindsay [1967] Director; Charles Shane Smith [1973] Director/Finance [American]

Smiths Business Information Services Limited
Incorporated: 24 September 1996 *Employees:* 83
Net Worth: £9,371,000 *Total Assets:* £18,836,000
Registered Office: First Floor, Building 7, Croxley Business Park, Hatters Lane, Watford, Herts, WD18 8PA
Activities: Information technology consultancy activities
Parent: Smiths Group International Holdings Limited
Officers: Vanya Katreece Hughes, Secretary; Martin James Fox [1965] Director/Accountant; Vanya Katreece Hughes [1978] Director/Solicitor

Smiths Detection-Watford Limited
Incorporated: 14 April 1950 *Employees:* 234
Net Worth Deficit: £21,115,000 *Total Assets:* £48,547,000
Registered Office: Century House, Maylands Avenue, Hemel Hempstead Industrial Estate, Hemel Hempstead, Herts, HP2 7DE
Activities: Manufacture of electronic measuring, testing etc. equipment, not for industrial process control
Parent: Smiths Detection Group Limited
Officers: Liam Peter King [1985] Director; Richard Edward Thompson [1969] Commercial Director

Smiths Industries Industrial Group Limited
Incorporated: 31 October 1968 *Employees:* 49
Net Worth: £65,134,000 *Total Assets:* £68,211,000
Registered Office: Unit 130 Centennial Park, Elstree, Herts, WD6 3TJ
Activities: Other service activities n.e.c.
Parent: Smiths Interconnect Group Limited
Officers: Eric Lakin, Secretary; Paul Harris [1957] Director/President Smiths Connectors; Giuseppe Lancella [1961] Managing Director [Italian]

Smiths Interconnect Group Limited
Incorporated: 9 July 2008 *Employees:* 6
Net Worth: £269,216,992 *Total Assets:* £474,943,008
Registered Office: Unit 130 Centennial Park, Elstree, Herts, WD6 3TJ
Activities: Activities of head offices
Parent: Smiths Group International Holdings Limited
Officers: Eric Lakin, Secretary; Karen Maria Bomba [1964] Director/President [American]; Eric Daniel Lakin [1970] Director/Vice President, Finance; Simon James Price [1974] Director

Smiths Metal Centres Limited
Incorporated: 24 December 1997 *Employees:* 270
Net Worth: £24,369,984 *Total Assets:* £43,564,832
Registered Office: Stratton Business Park, London Road, Biggleswade, Beds, SG18 8QB
Activities: Wholesale of metals and metal ores
Parent: Cobham Aluminium & Stainless Holdings Limited
Officers: Morag Hale, Secretary; James Michael Booth [1975] Director; Paul William Hawkins [1959] Sales Director; Stephen Paul Hawkins [1983] Director/Chief Financial Officer

Snap-On Equipment Limited
Incorporated: 29 October 2001
Net Worth: £55,668,520 *Total Assets:* £55,747,728
Registered Office: 17 Denney Road, Hardwick Industrial Estate, King's Lynn, Norfolk, PE30 4HG
Activities: Wholesale of other machinery and equipment
Parent: Snap-On Business Solutions Ltd
Officers: William Bruno [1961] Director/Vice President Sales & Marketing [American]; David Ellingen [1957] Director/President - Mitchell Repair Information Company [American]

Snape Maltings
Incorporated: 21 May 1970 *Employees:* 146
Previous: Aldeburgh Music
Net Worth: £29,430,000 *Total Assets:* £32,713,000
Registered Office: Snape Maltings Concert Hall, Snape, Saxmundham, Suffolk, IP17 1SP
Activities: Performing arts
Officers: Terence Philip Comer, Secretary; Miranda Elizabeth Page Wood [1962] Director; Andrew Garth Pollard [1945] Director/Retired; David Andrew Robbie [1963] Director; Sir Simon Christopher Townsend Robey [1960] Director/Banker; Patricia Ann Swannell [1952] Director/Visual Artist; Alasdair Wilson Robertson Tait [1973] Director/Chief Executive; Roger William Wright [1956] Director/Chief Executive; Sarah Anne Zins [1957] Director/Retired

Snellings Limited
Incorporated: 21 April 2011 *Employees:* 78
Net Worth: £8,369,260 *Total Assets:* £11,360,836
Registered Office: Blofield Corner, Blofield, Norwich, NR13 4SQ
Activities: Activities of head offices
Shareholders: Rowland Andrew Cogman; Nigel Rudolph Savory
Officers: Rowland Andrew Cogman, Secretary; Rowland Andrew Cogman [1955] Director; Stephan John Phillips [1955] Director; Nigel Rudolph Savory [1953] Director

Snowcentres Limited
Incorporated: 1 August 2007 *Employees:* 232
Net Worth: £13,607,000 *Total Assets:* £23,279,000
Registered Office: The Snow Centre, St Albans Hill, Hemel Hempstead, Herts, HP3 9NH
Activities: Operation of sports facilities
Officers: David Ian Brown [1967] Managing Director; Richard John Cook [1972] Director; Thomas Woodstock Harris [1963] Director

Snowmountain Enterprises Limited
Incorporated: 18 February 1964 *Employees:* 93
Net Worth: £32,410,184 *Total Assets:* £39,137,432
Registered Office: 36-38 King Street, Kings Lynn, Norfolk, PE30 1ES
Activities: Buying and selling of own real estate
Officers: John Michael Skoulding, Secretary; Amy Victoria Brown [1987] Director/Retail Manager; Amanda Jane Herring [1967] Director; Benjamin James Skoulding [1981] Director; Eric Peter Skoulding [1988] Director; John Michael Skoulding [1954] Director; Marjorie Joan Skoulding [1931] Director; Robert Frederick Skoulding [1957] Director; Cindy Ann Tufts [1963] Director; John Michael Tufts [1990] Director/Manager

Soda Studios Limited
Incorporated: 2 April 2007
Net Worth: £1 *Total Assets:* £12,020,679
Registered Office: 42 Lytton Road, Barnet, Herts, EN5 5BY
Activities: Development of building projects
Parent: Investland Limited
Officers: Joseph Peter Gerrard [1954] Director/Property Developer; Michael Gerrard [1957] Director/Property Developer

Sofis Limited
Incorporated: 10 April 1985 *Employees:* 45
Previous: Smith Flow Control Limited
Net Worth: £11,075,735 *Total Assets:* £12,364,706
Registered Office: 6 Waterside Business Park, Eastways Industrial Estate, Witham, Essex, CM8 3YQ
Activities: Manufacture of other fabricated metal products n.e.c.
Parent: Halma PLC
Officers: Andrew David James Harbidge [1972] Managing Director; Bryan Clayton Sanderlin [1963] Director/Chairman [American]; Stan Van Oppen [1977] Finance Director [Dutch]

Softbox (Bidco) Limited
Incorporated: 20 June 2014 *Employees:* 3
Net Worth: £262,602 *Total Assets:* £35,043,948
Registered Office: Units 1-2 Ridgeway, Drakes Drive, Long Crendon, Aylesbury, Bucks, HP18 9BF
Activities: Activities of head offices
Parent: Softbox (Midco) Limited
Officers: Richard William Jones [1961] Director; Edwin Francis Tattam [1961] Director/Consultant; Richard Alexander Everingham Wallace [1966] Financial Director

Softbox (Midco) Limited
Incorporated: 20 June 2014 *Employees:* 3
Net Worth Deficit: £2,628,358 *Total Assets:* £33,731,464
Registered Office: Units 1-2 Ridgeway, Drakes Drive, Long Crendon, Aylesbury, Bucks, HP18 9BF
Activities: Activities of head offices
Parent: Softbox (Topco) Limited
Officers: Richard William Jones [1961] Director; Edwin Francis Tattam [1961] Director/Consultant; Richard Alexander Everingham Wallace [1966] Financial Director

Softbox (Topco) Limited
Incorporated: 20 June 2014 *Employees:* 188
Net Worth Deficit: £7,477,199 *Total Assets:* £76,984,640
Registered Office: Units 1-2 Ridgeway, Drakes Drive, Long Crendon, Aylesbury, Bucks, HP18 9BF
Activities: Activities of head offices
Officers: Adam Dolder [1973] Director/Investment Manager [American]; Bernhard Hampl [1949] Director/Consultant [American]; Jeffrey Jay [1958] Director [American]; Richard William Jones [1961] Director; Wayne Langlois [1952] Director/Global Vice-President [American]; Martin Leblanc [1966] Director/President and Chief Executive Officer [Canadian]; Noah Rhodes [1981] Director/Investor [American]; Edwin Francis Tattam [1961] Director/Consultant

Softbox Systems Limited
Incorporated: 12 October 1995 *Employees:* 89
Net Worth: £20,798,046 *Total Assets:* £49,647,188
Registered Office: Unit 1 Ridge Way, Drake's Drive, Long Crendon, Aylesbury, Bucks, HP18 9BF
Activities: Manufacture of plastic packing goods
Parent: Softbox Systems Holdings Limited
Officers: Marc de Rijk [1965] Director/General Manager [Dutch]; Richard William Jones [1961] Director; Edwin Francis Tattam [1961] Director/Consultant; Richard Alexander Everingham Wallace [1966] Financial Director

Sogea Holdings (UK) Limited
Incorporated: 6 May 1997
Net Worth: £166,660,992 *Total Assets:* £186,660,992
Registered Office: Astral House, Imperial Way, Watford, Herts, WD24 4WW
Activities: Activities of head offices
Parent: Vinci Construction SAS
Officers: Bruno Michel Dupety [1956] Director/Engineer [French]; Yann Paul Grolimund [1959] Director/Chief Financial Officer [French]

Soho Loop Limited
Incorporated: 11 May 2017
Net Worth Deficit: £310,160 *Total Assets:* £8,645,959
Registered Office: 3rd Floor, Sterling House, Langston Road, Loughton, Essex, IG10 3TS
Activities: Development of building projects
Shareholders: Galliard Holdings Limited; Apsley House Capital PLC
Officers: Allan William Porter, Secretary; Stephen Stuart Solomon Conway [1948] Director; Gerard Nock [1947] Director/Company Chairman; Carl Robin Norstrom [1984] Director [Swedish]; Donagh O'Sullivan [1968] Construction Director [Irish]

Solai Holdings Limited
Incorporated: 31 January 1985 *Employees:* 328
Net Worth: £211,682,000 *Total Assets:* £745,441,984
Registered Office: Portland House, 69-71 Wembley Hill Road, Wembley, Middlesex, HA9 8BU
Activities: Other service activities n.e.c.
Officers: Bhupendra Shantilal Kansagra, Secretary; Bhupendra Shantilal Kansagra [1956] Director; Rajni Shantilal Kansagra [1942] Director/Engineer; Ramesh Shantilal Kansagra [1950] Director

The Solihull Hotel Company Limited
Incorporated: 4 September 1987 *Employees:* 70
Net Worth: £14,771,000 *Total Assets:* £19,835,000
Registered Office: Queens Court, 9-17 Eastern Road, Romford, Essex, RM1 3NG
Activities: Hotels and similar accommodation
Parent: BPH Finance Number 1 Limited
Officers: Jonathan Patrick Braidley [1965] Director/Investment Professional; Christopher Andre Kula [1983] Director/Chartered Accountant [German/Canadian]

Solo Cup (UK) Limited
Incorporated: 30 May 2000
Net Worth: £12,115,000 *Total Assets:* £41,692,000
Registered Office: 3 Flaxley Road, Kingston Park, Peterborough, Cambs, PE2 9EN
Activities: Activities of head offices
Parent: Solo Cup Finance Limited
Officers: Claire Theresa Dart [1929] Director/Businesswomen [American]; Robert Charles Dart [1958] Director/Businessman [Irish]; Thomas Lynn Jewell [1967] Director/Businessman [American]; James Donald Lammers [1959] Director/Businessman [American]

Solo Cup Finance Limited
Incorporated: 30 November 2010 *Employees:* 496
Net Worth: £67,697,000 *Total Assets:* £77,963,000
Registered Office: 3 Flaxley Road, Kingston Park, Peterborough, Cambs, PE2 9EN
Activities: Non-trading company
Major Shareholder: Robert Charles Dart
Officers: Claire Theresa Dart [1929] Director/Businesswoman [American]; Robert Charles Dart [1958] Director/Businessman [Irish]; Thomas Lynn Jewell [1967] Director/Businessman [American]; James Donald Lammers [1959] Director/Businessman [American]

Solopark Limited
Incorporated: 11 March 1976 *Employees:* 13
Net Worth: £7,044,721 *Total Assets:* £12,082,575
Registered Office: Salisbury House, Station Road, Cambridge, CB1 2LA
Activities: Agents involved in the sale of timber and building materials
Shareholders: Jane Alexandra Parker; Rodney John Bird
Officers: Rodney John Bird, Secretary; Derek Peter Bird [1951] Director/Manager; Rodney John Bird [1944] Director/Builders Merchant; Jane Alexandra Parker [1977] Director/Executive Search

Solus (London) Limited
Incorporated: 12 July 1995 *Employees:* 596
Net Worth: £24,782,000 *Total Assets:* £33,452,000
Registered Office: 8 Surrey Street, Norwich, NR1 3NG
Activities: Maintenance and repair of motor vehicles
Parent: Aviva Insurance Limited
Officers: Alexander Caldwell [1963] Director/Insurance Company Official; Richard Adam Hiscocks [1964] Director of Casualty and Motor Claims; Andrew James Morrish [1968] Director; Stephen Forder Pond [1969] Director/Chartered Accountant; Nigel Rippon [1970] Director/Accountant

Solvay Solutions UK Limited
Incorporated: 15 July 1892 *Employees:* 283
Net Worth Deficit: £536,819,008 *Total Assets:* £207,010,000
Registered Office: 34 Clarendon Road, Watford, Herts, WD17 1JJ
Activities: Manufacture of other chemical products n.e.c.
Parent: Rhodia Holdings Limited
Officers: Alison Murphy, Secretary; Tom Dutton [1964] Director/Health, Safety & Environment Manager; Michael Neil Holland [1971] Market Director HPC EMEA; Nathan Mills [1977] Director/Engineer [American]; Alison Murphy [1965] Director/Financial Controller

SOM Restaurants Ltd
Incorporated: 29 November 2010 *Employees:* 376
Net Worth: £2,380,639 *Total Assets:* £10,267,467
Registered Office: 146 New London Road, Chelmsford, Essex, CM2 0AW
Activities: Unlicenced restaurants and cafes
Major Shareholder: Zulfikar Somji
Officers: Bhavna Somji [1959] Director; Zulfikar Somji [1958] Director

Sonnet Care Homes (Essex) Limited
Incorporated: 29 July 1986 *Employees:* 216
Previous: Anglia Retirement Homes Limited
Net Worth: £1,980,554 *Total Assets:* £10,557,253
Registered Office: The New Deanery, Deanery Hill, Braintree, Essex, CM7 5SR
Activities: Residential care activities for the elderly and disabled
Parent: Sinnet Care Homes Finance Limited
Officers: Julia Mary Clinton [1963] Director; Joanne Moore [1972] Director

Sonnet Care Homes Finance Limited
Incorporated: 24 July 2013 *Employees:* 3
Net Worth Deficit: £4,757,976 *Total Assets:* £23,822,758
Registered Office: The New Deanery, Deanery Hill, Braintree, Essex, CM7 5SR
Activities: Financial management
Parent: Sonet Care Homes Midco Limited
Officers: Catherine Beck [1980] Director; Julia Mary Clinton [1963] Director; Joanne Moore [1972] Director

Sonnet Care Homes Holdco Limited
Incorporated: 23 July 2013 *Employees:* 220
Net Worth: £10,116,715 *Total Assets:* £16,984,258
Registered Office: The New Deanery, Deanery Hill, Braintree, Essex, CM7 5SR
Activities: Activities of head offices
Parent: August Equity LLP
Officers: Catherine Beck [1980] Director; Julia Mary Clinton [1963] Director; Joanne Moore [1972] Director

Sonnet Care Homes Midco Limited
Incorporated: 4 November 2013
Net Worth: £2,084,071 *Total Assets:* £22,779,628
Registered Office: The New Deanery, Deanery Hill, Braintree, Essex, CM7 5SR
Activities: Activities of head offices
Parent: Sonnet Care Homes Holdco Limited
Officers: Catherine Beck [1980] Director; Julia Mary Clinton [1963] Director; Joanne Moore [1972] Director

SOP International Limited
Incorporated: 21 November 1984 *Employees:* 46
Net Worth: £8,266,340 *Total Assets:* £18,958,460
Registered Office: Orland House, Mead Lane, Hertford, SG13 7AT
Activities: Manufacture of oils and fats
Shareholders: Raymond Chattwell; Antony Chattwell; Patricia Chattwell
Officers: Andrew Frederick George Langley, Secretary; Lesley Campbell [1950] Director; David Chattwell [1977] Director; Rafiul Islam Chowdhury [1971] Sales and Operations Director; Antony David Barrie Grainge [1964] Director; Shabir Patel [1958] Director

Sopra Steria Holdings Limited
Incorporated: 7 August 2001
Previous: Steria Holdings Limited
Net Worth: £185,052,000 *Total Assets:* £567,552,000
Registered Office: Three Cherry Trees Lane, Hemel Hempstead, Herts, HP2 7AH
Activities: Other business support service activities n.e.c.
Parent: Sopra Steria Group SA
Officers: Peter Cashmore, Secretary; Davinder Singh Ahluwalia [1952] Director; Kathleen Mary Clark-Bracco [1967] Commercial Director [American]; John Powell Torrie [1954] Director

Sopra Steria Limited
Incorporated: 26 September 2000 *Employees:* 3,444
Previous: Steria Limited
Net Worth: £211,415,008 *Total Assets:* £646,472,000
Registered Office: Three Cherry Trees Lane, Hemel Hempstead, Herts, HP2 7AH
Activities: Information technology consultancy activities
Parent: Sopra Steria Services Limited
Officers: Peter Cashmore, Secretary; Davinder Singh Ahluwalia [1952] Director; Kathleen Mary Clark-Bracco [1967] Commercial Director [American]; Pierre-Yves Commanay [1965] Director [French]; John Joseph Moran [1961] Director Corporate Finance; John Powell Torrie [1954] Director

Sopra Steria Recruitment Limited
Incorporated: 18 July 1979 *Employees:* 38
Previous: Steria Recruitment Limited
Net Worth: £4,927,000 *Total Assets:* £21,681,000
Registered Office: Three Cherry Trees Lane, Hemel Hempstead, Herts, HP2 7AH
Activities: Temporary employment agency activities
Parent: Sopra Steria Limited
Officers: Peter Atherton Cashmore, Secretary; Davinder Singh Ahluwalia [1952] Director; Peter Atherton Cashmore [1962] Director/Solicitor [New Zealander]; Peter James Holliday [1955] Managing Director

Sopra Steria Services Limited
Incorporated: 13 April 1992
Previous: Steria Services Limited
Net Worth: £193,912,000 *Total Assets:* £286,088,000
Registered Office: Three Cherry Trees Lane, Hemel Hempstead, Herts, HP2 7AH
Activities: Other information technology service activities
Parent: Sopra Steria Holdings Ltd
Officers: Peter Cashmore, Secretary; Davinder Singh Ahluwalia [1952] Director; Kathleen Mary Clark-Bracco [1967] Commercial Director [American]; Pierre-Yves Commanay [1965] Director [French]; John Joseph Moran [1961] Director Corporate Finance; John Powell Torrie [1954] Director

Sopress Investments Limited
Incorporated: 5 January 1970
Net Worth: £20,604,000 *Total Assets:* £21,077,000
Registered Office: Loudwater Mill, Station Road, High Wycombe, Bucks, HP10 9TY
Activities: Renting and operating of Housing Association real estate
Officers: Neil Edward Carpenter, Secretary; Simon Alton Westrop, Secretary; Henry Kennedy Faure Walker [1972] Director; Paul Anthony Hunter [1964] Finance Director

Sorbon Estates Limited
Incorporated: 10 August 1973 *Employees:* 37
Net Worth: £72,743,072 *Total Assets:* £175,584,336
Registered Office: Sorbon, Aylesbury End, Beaconsfield, Bucks, HP9 1LW
Activities: Development of building projects
Parent: Sorbon Investments Limited
Officers: Nicholas Mark Trott, Secretary; Tamra Michelle Booth [1974] Director; Michael James Shanly [1945] Director; Nicholas Mark Trott [1964] Director/Accountant

Sorbon Finance Limited
Incorporated: 11 September 2015 *Employees:* 2
Net Worth: £101,864,008 *Total Assets:* £101,949,224
Registered Office: Sorbon, Aylesbury End, Beaconsfield, Bucks, HP9 1LW
Activities: Other credit granting n.e.c.
Parent: Sorbon Homes Limited
Officers: Michael James Shanly [1945] Director; Nicholas Mark Trott [1964] Director/Accountant

Sorbon Homes Limited
Incorporated: 8 October 1998 *Employees:* 178
Net Worth: £281,009,152 *Total Assets:* £362,632,832
Registered Office: Sorbon, Aylesbury End, Beaconsfield, Bucks, HP9 1LW
Activities: Development of building projects
Major Shareholder: Michael James Shanly
Officers: Nicholas Mark Trott, Secretary; Tamra Michelle Booth [1974] Director; Timothy James Potter [1950] Director; Michael James Shanly [1945] Director; Nicholas Mark Trott [1964] Director/Accountant; Donald Anthony Tucker [1954] Director

Sorbon Investments Limited
Incorporated: 8 October 1998 *Employees:* 39
Net Worth: £112,409,920 *Total Assets:* £287,305,344
Registered Office: Sorbon, Aylesbury End, Beaconsfield, Bucks, HP9 1LW
Activities: Development of building projects
Major Shareholder: Michael James Shanly
Officers: Nicholas Mark Trott, Secretary; Tamra Michelle Booth [1974] Director; Timothy James Potter [1950] Director; Michael James Shanly [1945] Director; Nicholas Mark Trott [1964] Director/Accountant; Donald Anthony Tucker [1954] Director/Accountant

Sotherby LLP
Incorporated: 26 October 2015 *Employees:* 2
Net Worth: £9,555,702 *Total Assets:* £18,917,582
Registered Office: 166 College Road, Harrow, Middlesex, HA1 1RA
Officers: Michael Spencer Docker [1963] Member; Michele Docker [1965] Member

Soul Coffee House Limited
Incorporated: 2 January 2015 *Employees:* 1,103
Net Worth Deficit: £2,860,860 *Total Assets:* £27,126,388
Registered Office: 64 Wolsey Road, Moor Park, Northwood, Middlesex, HA6 2EH
Activities: Activities of head offices
Major Shareholder: Aly Hassanali Moleaina Janmohamed
Officers: Aly Hassanali Moleaina Janmohamed [1957] Director; Shehzad Janmohamed [1984] Director

Soul Foods Limited
Incorporated: 26 March 2002 *Employees:* 777
Net Worth: £4,015,281 *Total Assets:* £17,520,264
Registered Office: 64 Wolsey Road, Northwood, Middlesex, HA6 2EH
Activities: Activities of head offices
Major Shareholder: Aly Hassanali Moleaina Janmohamed
Officers: Samirah Janmohamed, Secretary; Aly Hassanali Moleaina Janmohamed [1957] Director; Shehzad Janmohamed [1984] Director

South Bristol (Ashton Park) Limited
Incorporated: 11 September 2012
Net Worth: £144,000 *Total Assets:* £14,666,000
Registered Office: Gate House, Turnpike Road, High Wycombe, Bucks, HP12 3NR
Activities: Development of building projects
Parent: Taylor Wimpey UK Limited
Officers: Michael Andrew Lonnon, Secretary; Colin Richard Clapham [1945] Director/Company Secretary; Gareth Alan Hawke [1974] Director

South Central Property Limited
Incorporated: 25 January 1993 *Employees:* 46
Net Worth: £75,370,016 *Total Assets:* £268,950,304
Registered Office: Portland House, 67-71 Wembley Hill Road, Wembley, Middlesex, HA9 8BU
Activities: Other letting and operating of own or leased real estate
Officers: Monique Francoise Cadji, Company Secretary; Laurent Elie Cadji [1977] Director/Trader; Lewis Levy Cadji [1938] Director; Monique Francoise Cadji [1949] Director/Company Secretary; Sarita Michele Kraljevic [1971] Director/Housewife; Miriam Martine Taylor [1973] Director/Housewife

South Coast Furnishing Company Limited
Incorporated: 13 March 1951 *Employees:* 4
Net Worth: £7,719,439 *Total Assets:* £11,110,070
Registered Office: 15 Station Road, St Ives, Cambs, PE27 5BH
Activities: Development of building projects
Shareholders: M & B Green Limited; DJS Browne Limited
Officers: Fruma Stephany Browne [1947] Director; Michael Green [1946] Director

South East Essex Academy Trust
Incorporated: 11 February 2011 *Employees:* 352
Net Worth: £34,498,316 *Total Assets:* £39,979,948
Registered Office: Westcliff High School for Girls, Kenilworth Gardens, Westcliff on Sea, Essex, SS0 0BS
Activities: Pre-primary education
Officers: Joanna Clarke [1961] Director/Local Government Officer; Murray Stephen Chatterton Foster [1947] Director/Chairman; Dr Paul Brian Hayman [1958] Director/Headteacher; Michael Ian Lambert [1947] Director/Business Consultant; Amanda Solomons [1995] Director; Mona Sood [1973] Director; Michael Douglas Wilson [1942] Director/Computer Consultant; Sonia Worthington [1964] Director/Local Government Officer

South Eastern Leisure UK Limited
Incorporated: 18 December 1998 *Employees:* 2
Net Worth Deficit: £6,416,260 *Total Assets:* £14,738,644
Registered Office: Roots Hall Stadium, Southend on Sea, Essex, SS2 6NQ
Activities: Development of building projects
Shareholder: Martin Dawn PLC
Officers: Geoffrey King, Secretary; Geoffrey King [1946] Director/Chartered Company Secretary; Ronald Martin [1953] Director

South Essex Academy Trust
Incorporated: 24 June 2011 *Employees:* 238
Net Worth: £9,310,141 *Total Assets:* £13,330,038
Registered Office: Westwood Academy, Beresford Close, Hadleigh, Benfleet, Essex, SS7 2SU
Activities: Pre-primary education
Officers: Helen Giles Norbury, Secretary; Tosca Elizabeth Boothman [1958] Director; Dominic James Carver [1965] Director/Headteacher; Julie Penelope Denham [1968] Director/HR Consultant; Simon Phillip Harbrow [1964] Director/Headteacher; Christopher Michael Jones [1963] Director; Michael John Simmonds [1958] Director/Consultant; Vanessa Van Blerk [1975] Director/Facilities Administrator

South Essex Stockholders Limited
Incorporated: 11 July 1975 *Employees:* 209
Net Worth Deficit: £3,317,416 *Total Assets:* £28,336,720
Registered Office: Metalstock House, 5 Vanguard Way, Shoeburyness, Southend on Sea, Essex, SS3 9RE
Activities: Non-specialised wholesale trade
Parent: MBM Group Services Limited
Officers: Richard John Eyre [1949] Director; Ronald Robinson [1946] Director/Chartered Accountant; Michael Desmond Walton [1964] Director/Business Consultant; Michael Anthony Welden [1969] Director/Chartered Accountant

South Lincolnshire Academies Trust
Incorporated: 10 March 2011 *Employees:* 302
Previous: South Lincolnshire Academies Trust Ltd
Net Worth: £24,890,628 *Total Assets:* £30,782,958
Registered Office: Bourne Academy, Edinburgh Crescent, Bourne, Lincs, PE10 9DT
Activities: General secondary education
Officers: Lucy Conley [1969] Director/Deputy Executive Headteacher; Stephen Alan Haigh [1958] Director/Vocational Learning Advisor; Will Hawkins [1967] Director/Business Manager; Robin Lee Immink [1974] Director/Governor; John Alfred Kirkman [1939] Director/Retired; Duncan Anthony Pickering [1965] Director/Solicitor; John Stokes [1958] Director/Head of Procurement

South Mimms Services Limited
Incorporated: 30 August 1951
Net Worth: £9,528,421 *Total Assets:* £9,763,739
Registered Office: Plantagenet House, 4 Plantagenet Road, New Barnet, Herts, EN5 5JQ
Activities: Other letting and operating of own or leased real estate
Major Shareholder: Christopher Edward Scarfe
Officers: Nicholas James Scarfe, Secretary; Nicholas James Scarfe [1992] Director

South Suffolk Learning Trust
Incorporated: 27 June 2011 *Employees:* 337
Previous: East Bergholt High School
Net Worth: £37,138,000 *Total Assets:* £40,066,000
Registered Office: East Bergholt High School, Heath Road, East Bergholt, Colchester, Essex, CO7 6RJ
Activities: Primary education
Officers: Robert Anthony Barnes, Secretary; Kylie Jane Sayer, Secretary; Linda Esther Bamford [1952] Director/Teacher; Stephen James Carr [1954] Director/Retired; Robert Douglas Dool [1952] Director/Education Consultant; David Fox [1960] Director/Retired; Bryony Godfrey [1966] Director/Human Resources Consultant; Diana Lois Porter [1946] Director/Retired; Sarah Skinner [1968] Director; Gareth Richard John Spinner [1961] Director/Civil Engineer; Jonathan Roy Waters [1965] Director/Solicitor; Rosanne Fay Wijnberg [1966] Director/Chief Operating Officer [South African]

South West Essex Community Education Trust Limited
Incorporated: 5 July 2011 *Employees:* 455
Previous: WESCD Community Education Trust Limited
Net Worth: £34,847,000 *Total Assets:* £43,314,000
Registered Office: Stifford Clays Road, Orsett, Grays, Essex, RM16 3NJ
Activities: Pre-primary education
Officers: Peter James Melville, Secretary; Duncan James Gotobed [1970] Director of Training Consultancy; John King [1950] Director/Education Consultant; Raymond John Moore [1957] Senior Bank Manager and Director; Stephen James Munday [1976] Director/Headteacher; David Robert Pavitt [1966] Director/Retired; Christina Louise Pumfrey [1968] Director/Executive Headteacher; Garry Tapsell [1972] Director/Fitness Manager

James Southall & Company Limited
Incorporated: 24 May 1900 *Employees:* 93
Net Worth: £8,609,000 *Total Assets:* £13,560,000
Registered Office: Peachman Way, Broadland Business Park, Thorpe St Andrew, Norwich, NR7 0WF
Activities: Wholesale of clothing and footwear
Officers: Johanna Westaway, Secretary; Peter James Lamble [1961] Director/Chairman; Richard Evelyn Southall [1963] Director; Kate Tansley [1977] Director

Southbank UK Limited
Incorporated: 7 June 2005 *Employees:* 3
Net Worth: £11,959,463 *Total Assets:* £20,554,700
Registered Office: 1 Kimpton Road, Luton, Beds, LU1 3LD
Activities: Activities of head offices
Parent: Hayward Tyler Group PLC
Officers: Stephen Michael King [1966] Director; Stephen McQuillan [1961] Director

Southend East Community Academy Trust
Incorporated: 27 October 2011 *Employees:* 523
Previous: Shoeburyness High School
Net Worth: £33,330,900 *Total Assets:* £41,973,168
Registered Office: SECAT House, Delaware Road, Shoeburyness, Southend on Sea, Essex, SS3 9NP
Activities: General secondary education
Officers: Ruth Mary Brock [1960] Director/Chief Executive; Pamela Joan Dewey [1946] Director/Retired Teacher; Simon Goodall [1951] Director; Robin Knight [1958] Director; Graham Richard Lane [1948] Director/Retired; Peter James Melville [1976] Director/Chief Operating Officer; Michelle Elizabeth Palles-Clark [1972] Director; Graham Reeder [1948] Director; Susan Elizabeth Rollason [1961] Director/Business Manager Children's Safeguarding Board; Brian George Sandford [1942] Director; Maurice Sweeting [1960] Director

Southend High School for Boys Academy Trust
Incorporated: 7 January 2011 *Employees:* 139
Net Worth: £11,533,654 *Total Assets:* £15,065,219
Registered Office: Southend High School for Boys, Prittlewell Chase, Southend on Sea, Essex, SS0 0RG
Activities: General secondary education
Officers: Dr Mukesh Aggarwal [1961] Director/Property Development; Susan Janet Alabaster [1967] Director/HR Manager; Janet Enid Baldwin [1961] Director/Chartered Accountant; Dr Robin Meredith Bevan [1966] Director/Headteacher; Christopher Jon Briggs [1973] Director/Manager; Julie Eizabeth Burns [1958] Director/Learning Support Assistant; Alex Cass [1981] Director/Teacher; Darren Michael Colderwood [1974] Construction Programme Director; Peter Tyson Crow [1971] Director/Teacher; Susan Denise Currington [1961] Director/Homemaker; William John Hendry [1957] Director; Dr Paul Husselbee [1961] Director/General Practitioner; Godfrey Bratherton Mather [1951] Director/Project Manager; Syed Ali Akber Moinuddin [1973] Director/Medical Researcher; Sharon O'Ryan [1962] Director/HR Consultant; Daniel Walden [1991] Director/Certified Accountant; Alan Thomas Watts [1966] Director/Solicitor; Tracey Whittington [1971] Director/Headteacher

Southend High School for Girls Academy Trust
Incorporated: 10 January 2011 *Employees:* 172
Net Worth: £9,678,655 *Total Assets:* £12,739,329
Registered Office: Southend High School for Girls, Southchurch Boulevard, Southend on Sea, Essex, SS2 4UZ
Activities: General secondary education
Officers: Angela Clarke, Secretary; Tim Mark Andrews [1981] Director/Teacher; Alan John Bacon [1954] Director/Solicitor; Fiona Jillian Brierley [1957] Director/Headteacher; Dionne Brown [1975] Director/Finance Manager; Lalini Hiranthi Fernando [1960] Director/Inspector of Higher Education Institutions; Dr Jane Alison Ladner [1951] Director/Retired; Anna Judith Leman [1976] Director/Teacher; James John Perry [1964] Director/IT Consultant; Anita Slotwinska [1982] Director/Housewife [Polish]; Lucy Traynor [1975] Director/Housewife; Alan Edward White [1962] Director/Surgeon

Southern Cement Ltd
Incorporated: 2 November 2001 *Employees:* 8
Net Worth: £13,997,801 *Total Assets:* £18,976,804
Registered Office: No 1 Shed, Cliff Quay, Port of Ipswich, Suffolk, IP3 0BS
Activities: Manufacture of cement
Parent: Premier Cement Limited
Officers: Denise Geddis, Secretary; John Dalton [1971] Sales and Marketing Director [Irish]; Andrew William John Donnan [1969] Finance Director; Gabriel Malone [1975] Finance Director [Irish]; Eamonn Sweeney [1957] Director; John Nathanial Wilson [1962] Director

P J Southgate Limited
Incorporated: 19 April 2002 *Employees:* 19
Net Worth: £3,789,172 *Total Assets:* £9,206,998
Registered Office: 7 The Close, Norwich, NR1 4DJ
Activities: Growing of cereals (except rice), leguminous crops and oil seeds
Shareholders: Dudley James Southgate; Philip James Southgate; Colin David Wright
Officers: Philip James Southgate, Secretary/Farmer; Dudley James Southgate [1971] Director/Farmer; Philip James Southgate [1947] Director/Farmer

Southgate Packaging Limited
Incorporated: 18 August 2006
Net Worth: £5,979,554 *Total Assets:* £13,991,731
Registered Office: Southgate Packaging Ltd, Hamlins Way, Hardwick Narrows Industrial Estate, King's Lynn, Norfolk, PE30 4NG
Activities: Wholesale of other intermediate products
Parent: Arpo Global Limited
Officers: Stephen Richard Turner, Secretary/Purchasing Director; Charles David McIntyre [1974] Commercial Director; Clive Russell Turner [1977] Director/Manager; Craig Turner [1989] Director; Dale Turner [1991] Director; George Turner [1995] Director; Marcus James Turner [1970] Director/Sales Manager; Stephen Richard Turner [1972] Director/Manager

Southwater Property Promotion Limited
Incorporated: 20 November 2014
Net Worth: £30,262,630 *Total Assets:* £31,320,696
Registered Office: The Estate Office, Dorton Road, Chilton, Aylesbury, Bucks, HP18 9LR
Activities: Development of building projects
Officers: Sir Henry Egerton Aubrey-Fletcher [1945] Director; Peter Robert Michael Bond [1935] Director/Solicitor

Sovereign Recovery (UK) Limited
Incorporated: 15 December 2006
Net Worth: £98,400 *Total Assets:* £9,582,107
Registered Office: 6c Ocean House, Bentley Way, New Barnet, Herts, EN5 5FP
Activities: Maintenance and repair of motor vehicles
Officers: Douglas Pope [1964] Director; Edward Pope [1963] Director

Peter Sowerby Foundation
Incorporated: 17 April 2013
Net Worth: £36,778,320 *Total Assets:* £38,917,536
Registered Office: Oxnead Hall, Oxnead, Norwich, NR10 5HP
Activities: Non-trading company
Officers: David Benjamin Harold Aspinall [1957] Director/Financial Planner; Professor Carole Margaret Longson [1961] Director; Sara Paulios [1977] Director [British/American]; Dr David Lindsay Stables [1958] Director

Space Truust UK Ltd
Incorporated: 8 April 2011
Net Worth: £96,942,280 *Total Assets:* £96,950,280
Registered Office: Unit 2 Popin Business Centre, South Way, Wembley, Middlesex, HA9 0HB
Activities: Financial intermediation not elsewhere classified
Officers: Peter Albert Koley [1965] Director/Entrepreneur [Swiss]

Spaces Personal Storage Limited
Incorporated: 12 February 1998 *Employees:* 3
Net Worth: £53,262,000 *Total Assets:* £53,262,000
Registered Office: c/o Safestore Holdings Limited, Brittanic House, Stirling Way, Borehamwood, Herts, WD6 2BT
Activities: Other letting and operating of own or leased real estate
Parent: Safestore Acquisition Limited
Officers: Andrew Brian Jones [1966] Director/Chartered Accountant; David Roy Penniston [1958] Property Director; Federico Vecchioli [1966] Director [French]

Spalding Grammar School
Incorporated: 11 January 2013 *Employees:* 118
Net Worth: £16,499,449 *Total Assets:* £18,386,160
Registered Office: Spalding Grammar School, Priory Lane, Spalding, Lincs, PE11 2XH
Activities: General secondary education
Officers: Keith John Bean [1943] Director/Retired; Philip Callow [1975] Director; Adrian Charles Cunnington [1960] Director/Head of Research; Craig Spencer Delaney [1971] Director/Solicitor; Sonya Yvonne Ely [1971] Director/Headteacher; Alan John Faulkner [1972] Director/Land Agent; Michael Paul John Flindall [1962] Director/School Caretaker; Debra Haslam [1961] Director/Personal Assistant; Anthony John Holdsworth [1942] Director/Retired; Sharon Ann Lynette Hoult [1954] Director/Science Technician; Jane Lutton [1965] Director/Teacher; Jane-Marie Mayne [1973] Director/Student Support Supervisor; Edward John Rees [1967] Director/Commercial Manager; Steve Wilkinson [1973] Director

Spar (UK) Limited
Incorporated: 4 August 1959 *Employees:* 74
Net Worth: £13,187 *Total Assets:* £24,605,934
Registered Office: Hygeia Building, 66-68 College Road, Harrow, Middlesex, HA1 1BE
Activities: Wholesale of wine, beer, spirits and other alcoholic beverages
Officers: Mark Steven Keeley [1962] Director/Retail; Christopher William Lewis [1968] Trading Director; Jacqueline Elizabeth MacKenzie [1967] Director/Chief Information Officer; Deborah Mary Robinson [1965] Director; Ian David Taylor [1965] Retail Director

Spar Food Distributors Limited
Incorporated: 4 April 1975 *Employees:* 74
Net Worth: £13,436 *Total Assets:* £24,605,884
Registered Office: Mezzanine Floor, Hygeia Building, 66-68 College Road, Harrow, Middlesex, HA1 1BE
Activities: Retail sale in non-specialised stores with food, beverages or tobacco predominating
Officers: Martin John Agnew [1962] Director; Mike Boardman [1972] Director; Michael Dominic Wells Hall [1972] Director; Jeremy Charles Marwood [1958] Director; Colin Gibson McLean [1965] Director; Deborah Mary Robinson [1965] Director

Sparquote Limited
Incorporated: 27 October 1982 *Employees:* 3
Net Worth: £15,630,194 *Total Assets:* £19,368,620
Registered Office: Cavendish House, 369 Burnt Oak Broadway, Edgware, Middlesex, HA8 5AW
Activities: Activities of religious organisations
Officers: Anne-Mette Reichmann [1966] Director; David Reichmann [1962] Director; Dov Reichmann [1930] Director

SPC Holdings Limited
Incorporated: 28 March 1994 *Employees:* 37
Net Worth: £27,675,238 *Total Assets:* £28,996,648
Registered Office: SPC House, Atlas Works, Norwich Road, Lenwade, Norwich, NR9 5SN
Activities: Other professional, scientific and technical activities n.e.c.
Major Shareholder: Andre Paul Serruys
Officers: Andre Paul Serruys [1956] Director; Leticia Serruys [1975] Director/Translator [British/Cuban]

SPD Moorgate Limited
Incorporated: 18 November 2014
Net Worth Deficit: £2,356,000 *Total Assets:* £30,092,000
Registered Office: Maple Cross House, Denham Way, Maple Cross, Rickmansworth, Herts, WD3 9SW
Activities: Development of building projects
Parent: Skanska Project Developments Limited
Officers: Steven Leven, Secretary; Culdip Kelly Kaur Gangotra [1970] Director/Accountant; Helen Katherine Martin [1975] Director/Civil Engineer; Martin George Neeson [1968] Director/Manager

Spearhead International Limited
Incorporated: 5 June 1972
Net Worth: £61,193,000 *Total Assets:* £160,636,000
Registered Office: Beaufort House, 136 High Street, Newmarket, Suffolk, CB8 8JP
Activities: Activities of agricultural holding companies
Parent: P & P Spearhead UK Holdings, Ltd
Officers: Charles Delmar Morgan, Secretary; Jane Louise Perkins [1980] Finance Director; Tomasz Jacek Zdziebkowski [1962] Director [Polish]

Specflue Limited
Incorporated: 20 May 1992 *Employees:* 95
Net Worth: £6,679,783 *Total Assets:* £9,269,537
Registered Office: 8 Curzon Road, Chilton Industrial Estate, Sudbury, Suffolk, CO10 2XW
Activities: Non-specialised wholesale trade
Shareholders: Jeremy Fry; Janet Fry; Shirley Elrema Williams
Officers: Janet Fry [1963] Director; Jeremy Fry [1962] Director; Richard Hall-Roberts [1957] Finance Director; Ian James Sams [1964] Commercial Director; Shirley Elrema Williams [1942] Director

Special New Fruit Licensing Limited
Incorporated: 21 June 2004
Net Worth: £23,476,566 *Total Assets:* £37,458,324
Registered Office: Frans House, Fenton Way, Chatteris, Cambs, PE16 6UP
Activities: Other research and experimental development on natural sciences and engineering
Parent: Munoz Group Ltd
Officers: Amalio Fuster, Secretary; Fernando Juan de Lucas Lopez [1973] Director [Spanish]; David John Haresign [1963] Director; Josep Jove Estiarte [1978] Director [Spanish]; Ian Duncan MacIntyre [1954] Director; Alvaro Munoz Beraza [1966] Director/Chief Executive [Spanish]

Specialist Cars Holdings Limited
Incorporated: 10 January 2007 *Employees:* 331
Net Worth: £19,648,732 *Total Assets:* £56,435,476
Registered Office: c/o Specialist Cars Ltd, Arlington Business Park, Gunnels Wood Road, Stevenage, Herts, SG1 2BE
Activities: Activities of head offices
Shareholders: Clive Martin Fletcher; Michael Jacob Donovan
Officers: Clive Michael James, Secretary; Michael Jacob Donovan [1959] Director; Clive Martin Fletcher [1959] Director

Specialist Cars Limited
Incorporated: 23 August 1989 *Employees:* 172
Net Worth: £12,061,928 *Total Assets:* £28,076,506
Registered Office: Arlington Business Park, Gunnels Wood Road, Stevenage, Herts, SG1 2BE
Activities: Sale of new cars and light motor vehicles
Shareholders: Clive Martin Fletcher; Michael Jacob Donovan
Officers: Clive Michael James, Secretary; Julian Lance Bourne [1960] Director/Dealer Principal; Michael Jacob Donovan [1959] After Sales Director; Clive Martin Fletcher [1959] Managing Director; Mr Clive Michael James [1961] Director

Specialist Cars Property (Stevenage) Limited
Incorporated: 15 January 2007 *Employees:* 3
Net Worth: £5,489,492 *Total Assets:* £11,870,000
Registered Office: c/o Specialist Cars Ltd, Arlington Business Park, Gunnels Wood Road, Stevenage, Herts, SG1 2BE
Activities: Other letting and operating of own or leased real estate
Parent: Specialist Cars Holdings Limited
Officers: Clive Michael James, Secretary; Michael Jacob Donovan [1959] Director; Clive Martin Fletcher [1959] Director

Specialist Cars Tring Limited
Incorporated: 21 April 2008 *Employees:* 80
Net Worth: £1,020,339 *Total Assets:* £11,377,725
Registered Office: Gunnels Wood Road, Stevenage, Herts, SG1 2BE
Activities: Sale of new cars and light motor vehicles
Parent: Specialist Cars Holdings Limited
Officers: Clive Michael James, Secretary/Director; Julian Lance Bourne [1960] Director/Dealer Principal; Michael Jacob Donovan [1959] Director; Clive Martin Fletcher [1959] Director; Mr Clive Michael James [1961] Director

Speciality Stores Limited
Incorporated: 1 August 2014
Net Worth Deficit: £11,400,000 *Total Assets:* £29,800,000
Registered Office: Aquarius House, Bessemer Road, Welwyn Garden City, Herts, AL7 1HH
Activities: Retail sale via mail order houses or via Internet
Parent: Ocado Holdings Ltd
Officers: Neill Abrams, Secretary; Robert McNeill Cooper, Secretary; Neill Abrams [1964] Director; Richard Anthony Exact [1964] Director/Accountant; Richard Anthony Locke [1985] Director; Mark Antony Richardson [1964] Director

Speedy 1 Limited
Incorporated: 13 May 2005
Net Worth: £657,400,000 *Total Assets:* £951,678,976
Registered Office: Etel House, Avenue One, Letchworth Garden City, Herts, SG6 2HU
Activities: Activities of head offices
Parent: European Tyre Enterprise Limited
Officers: Ian Vincent Ellis, Secretary; Yasuyuki Harada [1959] Director [Japanese]; Mark Lynott [1975] Director

Spen Hill Developments Limited
Incorporated: 9 July 2003
Net Worth: £109,283,000 *Total Assets:* £177,520,000
Registered Office: Tesco House, Shire Park, Kestrel Way, Welwyn Garden City, Herts, AL7 1GA
Activities: Other business support service activities n.e.c.
Parent: Tesco Holdings Limited
Officers: John Gibney [1967] Assets and Estates Director [Irish]; Amit Soni [1968] Finance Director [Indian]

Spen Hill Regeneration Limited
Incorporated: 5 November 2007
Net Worth: £49,947,008 *Total Assets:* £115,346,424
Registered Office: Tesco House, Shire Park, Kestrel Way, Welwyn Garden City, Herts, AL7 1GA
Activities: Development of building projects
Parent: Tesco Holdings Limited
Officers: John Gibney [1967] Assets and Estates Director [Irish]; Amit Soni [1968] Finance Director [Indian]; Robert John Welch [1966] Director/Company Secretary

Spence Refit Ltd
Incorporated: 15 June 2005 *Employees:* 42
Net Worth: £2,056,924 *Total Assets:* £9,874,049
Registered Office: First Floor, Radius House, 51 Clarendon Road, Watford, Herts, WD17 1HP
Activities: Construction of commercial buildings
Parent: Jean-Luc Developments Limited
Officers: Denise Carr [1960] Financial Director; Andrew Hill [1966] Director; Luke Johnson Spence [1988] Director; Russell Jonathon James Spence [1985] Director

Spencers Property Investments Limited
Incorporated: 12 August 1996 *Employees:* 4
Net Worth: £10,883,390 *Total Assets:* £21,419,826
Registered Office: 249 Cranbrook Road, Ilford, Essex, IG1 4TG
Activities: Other letting and operating of own or leased real estate
Shareholders: Alan Austin Spencer; Roger Ashley Spencer
Officers: Roger Spencer, Secretary/Director; Alan Austin Spencer [1961] Director; Roger Ashley Spencer [1966] Director

Speycrest Limited
Incorporated: 25 March 1975 *Employees:* 24
Net Worth: £14,386,598 *Total Assets:* £17,964,598
Registered Office: Annasbrook House, Gapton Hall Road, Great Yarmouth, Norfolk, NR31 0HX
Activities: Non-trading company
Major Shareholder: Brian David Knappett
Officers: Brian David Knappett [1943] Director/Engineer; Christine Knappett [1949] Director/Retired Teacher

Spicerhaart Corporate Sales Limited
Incorporated: 10 July 2008 *Employees:* 40
Net Worth: £12,156,000 *Total Assets:* £12,634,000
Registered Office: Colwyn House, Sheepen Place, Colchester, Essex, CO3 3LD
Activities: Other business support service activities n.e.c.
Major Shareholder: Paul Alick Smith
Officers: Russell Jervis [1969] Director; Paul Alick Smith [1960] Director

Spicerhaart Group Limited
Incorporated: 2 October 2000 *Employees:* 1,915
Net Worth: £19,335,000 *Total Assets:* £44,756,000
Registered Office: Colwyn House, Sheepen Place, Colchester, Essex, CO3 3LD
Activities: Other business support service activities n.e.c.
Major Shareholder: Paul Alick Smith
Officers: Paul Alick Smith, Secretary; Mark Hurdle [1966] Director/Financial Officer; Russell Jervis [1969] Director; John Matthew Phillips [1963] Financial Services Director; Paul Alick Smith [1960] Director; John Andrew Spence [1951] Director

Spiral Partnership Trust
Incorporated: 12 April 2012 *Employees:* 265
Previous: Fleetville Trust
Net Worth: £27,199,000 *Total Assets:* £30,279,000
Registered Office: 228 Hatfield Road, St Albans, Herts, AL1 4LW
Activities: Primary education
Officers: Rodney Allen [1979] Sales Director Medical Devices; Kathryn Elizabeth Burton [1977] Director/Charities Partner (Accountant); Terence Thomas Robin Douglas OBE [1948] Director/Management Consultant; Julian Richard Earl [1970] Advertising Strategy Director; Benjamin Paul Evans [1973] Director/Headteacher; Deborah Rose Godbold [1959] Director/Education Consultant; Amanda Jane Godfrey [1962] Director/Headteacher; James John Maton [1971] Director/Solicitor; Andrew John Mayo [1944] Director/Professor; Emma-Jayne Murphy [1973] Director/HR Consultant; Androulla Peek [1962] Director/Education/Headteacher; Hannah Louise Witty [1978] Director/Accountant

Spire Bricks and Mortar Limited
Incorporated: 12 October 2015 *Employees:* 4
Net Worth: £14,793,252 *Total Assets:* £31,562,448
Registered Office: Unit 41, 17 Holywell Hill, St Albans, Herts, AL1 1DT
Activities: Buying and selling of own real estate
Shareholders: Kim William Richardson; Kim William Richardson
Officers: Darren Guiver [1968] Director; Kim William Richardson [1956] Director

Spirit (Faith) Limited
Incorporated: 2 March 1999
Net Worth: £19,281,000 *Total Assets:* £28,865,000
Registered Office: Westgate Brewery, Bury St Edmunds, Suffolk, IP33 1QT
Activities: Buying and selling of own real estate
Officers: Lindsay Anne Keswick, Secretary; Richard Lewis [1970] Director; Richard Smothers [1967] Director

Spirit (SGL) Limited
Incorporated: 28 April 2000
Net Worth: £226,208,000 *Total Assets:* £234,996,000
Registered Office: Westgate Brewery, Bury St Edmunds, Suffolk, IP33 1QT
Activities: Public houses and bars
Parent: Spirit Pubs Parent Limited
Officers: Lindsay Anne Keswick, Secretary; Richard Lewis [1970] Director; Richard Smothers [1967] Director

Spirit Group Equity Limited
Incorporated: 16 August 2001
Net Worth: £53,066,000 *Total Assets:* £491,040,000
Registered Office: Westgate Brewery, Bury St Edmunds, Suffolk, IP33 1QT
Activities: Activities of head offices
Parent: Spirit Managed Holdings Limited
Officers: Lindsay Anne Keswick, Secretary; Richard Smothers [1967] Director

Spirit Group Holdings Limited
Incorporated: 20 August 2003
Net Worth Deficit: £15,137,000 *Total Assets:* £78,843,000
Registered Office: Westgate Brewery, Bury St Edmunds, Suffolk, IP33 1QT
Activities: Activities of head offices
Parent: Spirit Pub Company (SGE) Limited
Officers: Lindsay Anne Keswick, Secretary; Richard Smothers [1967] Director

Spirit Group Parent Limited
Incorporated: 20 August 2003
Net Worth: £441,063,008 *Total Assets:* £1,003,294,976
Registered Office: Westgate Brewery, Bury St Edmunds, Suffolk, IP33 1QT
Activities: Activities of head offices
Parent: Spirit Intermediate Holdings Limited
Officers: Lindsay Anne Keswick, Secretary; Richard Smothers [1967] Director

Spirit Group Retail Limited
Incorporated: 24 June 1999
Net Worth: £964,147,968 *Total Assets:* £1,182,068,992
Registered Office: Westgate Brewery, Bury St Edmunds, Suffolk, IP33 1QT
Activities: Licenced restaurants
Parent: Spirit Retail Bidco Limited
Officers: Lindsay Anne Keswick, Secretary; Richard Smothers [1967] Director

Spirit Managed Funding Limited
Incorporated: 21 October 2004
Net Worth: £1,228,118,016 *Total Assets:* £1,595,494,016
Registered Office: Westgate Brewery, Bury St Edmunds, Suffolk, IP33 1QT
Activities: Other business support service activities n.e.c.
Parent: Spirit Pub Company (SGE) Limited
Officers: Lindsay Anne Keswick, Secretary; Richard Smothers [1967] Director

Spirit Managed Holdings Limited
Incorporated: 16 August 2001
Net Worth: £164,412,000 *Total Assets:* £247,378,000
Registered Office: Westgate Brewery, Bury St Edmunds, Suffolk, IP33 1QT
Activities: Activities of head offices
Parent: Spirit Group Parent Limited
Officers: Lindsay Anne Keswick, Secretary; Richard Smothers [1967] Director

Spirit Pub Company (Derwent) Limited
Incorporated: 20 December 2013
Net Worth: £2,439,000 *Total Assets:* £22,410,000
Registered Office: Westgate Brewery, Bury St Edmunds, Suffolk, IP33 1QT
Activities: Other business support service activities n.e.c.
Parent: Spirit Pub Company (SGE) Limited
Officers: Lindsay Anne Keswick, Secretary; Richard Smothers [1967] Director

Spirit Pub Company (Holdco) Limited
Incorporated: 8 June 2011
Net Worth: £403,062,016 *Total Assets:* £408,715,008
Registered Office: Westgate Brewery, Bury St Edmunds, Suffolk, IP33 1QT
Activities: Activities of other holding companies n.e.c.
Parent: Spirit Pub Company Limited
Officers: Lindsay Anne Keswick, Secretary; Richard Smothers [1967] Director

Spirit Pub Company (Investments) Limited
Incorporated: 16 September 2009
Net Worth Deficit: £4,623,000 *Total Assets:* £55,986,000
Registered Office: Westgate Brewery, Bury St Edmunds, Suffolk, IP33 1QT
Activities: Non-trading company
Parent: Spirit Parent Limited
Officers: Lindsay Anne Keswick, Secretary; Richard Smothers [1967] Director

Spirit Pub Company (Leased) Limited
Incorporated: 6 February 2006
Net Worth Deficit: £975,107,968 *Total Assets:* £398,808,000
Registered Office: Westgate Brewery, Bury St Edmunds, Suffolk, IP33 1QT
Activities: Public houses and bars
Parent: Spirit Pubs Parent Limited
Officers: Lindsay Anne Keswick, Secretary; Nicholas Robertson Elliot [1966] Director; Richard Lewis [1970] Director; Wayne Shurvinton [1978] Director; Richard Smothers [1967] Director; Matthew Anthony Starbuck [1969] Director

Spirit Pub Company (Managed) Limited
Incorporated: 25 October 2004
Net Worth Deficit: £94,669,000 *Total Assets:* £1,094,790,016
Registered Office: Westgate Brewery, Bury St Edmunds, Suffolk, IP33 1QT
Activities: Licenced restaurants
Parent: Spirit Pubs Parent Limited
Officers: Lindsay Anne Keswick, Secretary; Nicholas Robertson Elliot [1966] Director; Richard Lewis [1970] Director; Wayne Shurvinton [1978] Director; Richard Smothers [1967] Director; Matthew Anthony Starbuck [1969] Director; Philip Andrew Thomas [1969] Director

Spirit Pub Company (Services) Limited
Incorporated: 21 October 2004
Net Worth Deficit: £119,188,000 *Total Assets:* £148,659,008
Registered Office: Westgate Brewery, Bury St Edmunds, Suffolk, IP33 1QT
Activities: Other business support service activities n.e.c.
Parent: Spirit Group Parent Limited
Officers: Lindsay Anne Keswick, Secretary; Nicholas Robertson Elliot [1966] Director; Richard Lewis [1970] Director; Wayne Shurvinton [1978] Director; Richard Smothers [1967] Director; Matthew Anthony Starbuck [1969] Director

Spirit Pub Company (SGE) Limited
Incorporated: 8 June 2011
Net Worth: £121,068,000 *Total Assets:* £386,057,984
Registered Office: Westgate Brewery, Bury St Edmunds, Suffolk, IP33 1QT
Activities: Activities of other holding companies n.e.c.
Parent: Spirit Pub Company (Holdco) Limited
Officers: Lindsay Anne Keswick, Secretary; Richard Smothers [1967] Director

Spirit Pub Company (Supply) Limited
Incorporated: 18 December 2001
Net Worth Deficit: £886,000 *Total Assets:* £71,181,000
Registered Office: Westgate Brewery, Bury St Edmunds, Suffolk, IP33 1QT
Activities: Other business support service activities n.e.c.
Parent: Spirit Group Parent Limited
Officers: Lindsay Anne Keswick, Secretary; Nicholas Robertson Elliot [1966] Director; Richard Lewis [1970] Director; Wayne Shurvinton [1978] Director; Richard Smothers [1967] Director; Matthew Anthony Starbuck [1969] Director

Spirit Pub Company (Trent) Limited
Incorporated: 16 March 2006
Net Worth Deficit: £271,244,000 *Total Assets:* £103,507,000
Registered Office: Westgate Brewery, Bury St Edmunds, Suffolk, IP33 1QT
Activities: Other business support service activities n.e.c.
Parent: Spirit Pub Company (SGE) Limited
Officers: Lindsay Anne Keswick, Secretary; Nicholas Robertson Elliot [1966] Director; Richard Lewis [1970] Director; Wayne Shurvinton [1978] Director; Richard Smothers [1967] Director; Philip Andrew Thomas [1969] Director

Spirit Pub Company Limited
Incorporated: 8 June 2011
Previous: Spirit Pub Company PLC
Net Worth: £358,235,008 *Total Assets:* £358,660,992
Registered Office: Westgate Brewery, Bury St Edmunds, Suffolk, IP33 1QT
Activities: Public houses and bars
Parent: Greene King PLC
Officers: Lindsay Anne Keswick, Secretary; Rooney Anand [1964] Director; Richard Smothers [1967] Director

Spirit Pubs Debenture Holdings Limited
Incorporated: 21 October 2004
Net Worth Deficit: £464,927,008 *Total Assets:* £2,010,210,048
Registered Office: Westgate Brewery, Bury St Edmunds, Suffolk, IP33 1QT
Activities: Activities of head offices
Parent: Spirit Parent Limited
Officers: Lindsay Anne Keswick, Secretary; Richard Smothers [1967] Director

Spiritualists' National Union (The)
Incorporated: 22 October 1901 *Employees:* 70
Net Worth: £13,450,415 *Total Assets:* £14,015,770
Registered Office: Redwoods, Stansted Hall, Stansted, Essex, CM24 8UD
Activities: Activities of religious organisations
Officers: Julia Almond [1955] Director/Retired; Lynda Bradley [1963] Director/Civil Servant; David Robert Bruton [1960] Director; June Nellie English [1950] Director/Retired; Suznne Gibson Foy [1969] Director/Psychotherapist and Teacher; Adrian Alv Hirst [1970] Director/Community Centre Manager; Alan Rawnsley [1947] Director/Retired; Patricia Seymour [1945] Director; Steven Upton [1956] Director/Minister of Religion

Spitalfields Works Limited
Incorporated: 9 February 2016
Net Worth Deficit: £81,592 *Total Assets:* £9,622,018
Registered Office: Crane Court, 302 London Road, Ipswich, Suffolk, IP2 0AJ
Activities: Other construction installation
Shareholders: Dominic Charles David Richards; Michael Hintze
Officers: Dominic Charles David Richards [1966] Director

Splendid Hospitality Group LLP
Incorporated: 5 October 2007 *Employees:* 805
Previous: Sojourn Hotels LLP
Net Worth: £296,313,312 *Total Assets:* £593,888,832
Registered Office: Haydon House, 296 Joel Street, Pinner, Middlesex, HA5 2PY
Officers: Nadeem Shirazali Boghani [1978] Member; Shiraz Noormohamed Boghani [1950] Member

Spreadex Limited
Incorporated: 25 February 1999 *Employees:* 117
Net Worth: £69,451,608 *Total Assets:* £100,599,856
Registered Office: Churchill House, 26-30 Upper Marlborough Road, St Albans, Herts, AL1 3UU
Activities: Gambling and betting activities
Shareholder: Peter Woodstock Harris
Officers: Colin David Russell Allen [1960] Director; Paul Edward Woodstock Harris [1969] Director; Thomas Woodstock Harris [1963] Director; David Ross MacKenzie [1979] Director; Allan Philip Morley [1979] Director

Spreadex.Com Limited
Incorporated: 8 April 1998 *Employees:* 117
Net Worth: £69,967,608 *Total Assets:* £100,599,856
Registered Office: Churchill House, 26-30 Upper Marlborough Road, St Albans, Herts, AL1 3UU
Activities: Gambling and betting activities
Shareholder: Peter Woodstock Harris
Officers: Colin David Russell Allen [1960] Director; Paul Edward Woodstock Harris [1969] Director; Thomas Woodstock Harris [1963] Director/Businessman

Spring Petroleum Company Ltd
Incorporated: 19 December 2001 *Employees:* 269
Net Worth: £30,819,000 *Total Assets:* £52,695,000
Registered Office: Gladstone Place, 36-38 Upper Marlborough Road, St Albans, Herts, AL1 3UU
Activities: Retail sale of automotive fuel in specialised stores
Parent: MRH (GB) Limited
Officers: David Hathaway, Secretary; William Bahlsen Bannister [1967] Director/Chief Executive; Jeremy Clarke [1963] Director/Chief Operating Officer; Simon Paul Lane [1963] Director/Chief Financial Officer

Springfield Holdings Limited
Incorporated: 18 March 2015 *Employees:* 1
Net Worth: £247,496 *Total Assets:* £8,848,820
Registered Office: 20 Lodwick, Shoeburyness, Essex, SS3 9HW
Activities: Activities of head offices
Officers: Mohammed Azeem Raja [1956] Director

Spurdown Limited
Incorporated: 9 August 1963 *Employees:* 10
Net Worth: £26,444,688 *Total Assets:* £28,823,032
Registered Office: 1 Nelson Street, Southend on Sea, Essex, SS1 1EG
Activities: Buying and selling of own real estate
Major Shareholder: Peter Leonard Anson
Officers: Victoria Ellen Amelia Parker, Secretary; Brenda Vivienne Anson [1944] Director; Helen Jane Elizabeth Anson [1976] Director; Peter Leonard Anson [1942] Director; Simon Richard Neil Parker [1971] Director/Chartered Surveyor; Victoria Ellen Amelia Parker [1972] Director

Squibb Group Limited
Incorporated: 15 June 1972 *Employees:* 232
Net Worth: £16,758,429 *Total Assets:* £43,628,464
Registered Office: Squibb House, Stanhope Industrial Park, Wharf Road, Stanford-le-Hope, Essex, SS17 0EH
Activities: Remediation activities and other waste management services
Major Shareholder: Leslie Jeffrey Squibb
Officers: Leslie John Henry Squibb, Secretary/Demolition Engineer; Phillip Limber [1951] Director/Operations Manager; Leslie John Henry Squibb [1972] Director/Demolition Engineer; Leslie Jeffrey Squibb [1950] Director/Civil Engineer; Westley Jeffery Thomas Squibb [1980] Director/Demolition Manager; John Elliott Symons [1966] Director/Accountant

SRM (Redcar & Cleveland) Limited
Incorporated: 5 December 2007
Net Worth Deficit: £7,462,474 *Total Assets:* £40,153,800
Registered Office: Eaton Court, Maylands Avenue, Hemel Hempstead Industrial Estate, Hemel Hempstead, Herts, HP2 7TR
Activities: Medical nursing home activities
Parent: SRM (Redcar & Cleveland) Holdings Limited
Officers: Kevin John Pearson, Secretary; David Honeyman [1967] Director/Financial Controller

Ssangyong Motor UK Limited
Incorporated: 18 September 2007 *Employees:* 56
Net Worth: £4,733,000 *Total Assets:* £47,100,000
Registered Office: Units D & E, Airport Executive Park, President Way, Luton, Beds, LU2 9NY
Activities: Sale of new cars and light motor vehicles
Major Shareholder: George Alfred Charles Bassadone
Officers: George Alfred Charles Bassadone [1953] Director; Kevin Jones [1962] Director; Nicholas Grant Laird [1966] Managing Director

SSL Group (UK) Limited
Incorporated: 9 January 2015 *Employees:* 1,309
Net Worth: £12,390,701 *Total Assets:* £78,824,912
Registered Office: Grosvenor House, Horseshoe Crescent, Beaconsfield, Bucks, HP9 1LJ
Activities: Other letting and operating of own or leased real estate
Officers: Tom James Ball [1983] Director; Frank Cerrone [1959] Director/Senior Vice President, General Counsel & Secretary [Canadian]; James Hardy [1959] Director/Chief Investment Officer & CFO [Canadian]; Thomas Bruce Newell [1957] Director [American]; Wayne Paul Pryce [1974] Director; Aidan Gerard Roche [1966] Director [Irish]

St Albans Diocesan Property Company Limited
Incorporated: 18 February 2014
Net Worth: £1,497,363 *Total Assets:* £10,625,620
Registered Office: Holywell Lodge, 41 Holywell Hill, St Albans, Herts, AL1 1HE
Activities: Development of building projects
Parent: St Albans Diocesan Board of Finance
Officers: Susan Elizabeth Pope, Secretary; Colin Graham Bird [1949] Director/Chartered Accountant; John Wesley Butler [1951] Director; Colin Bernard Gage [1941] Director/Retired; Henry Thurston Holland-Hibbert [1959] Director/Chartered Surveyor; The Honourable Richard Oakley Pleydell-Bouverie [1947] Director/Farmer and Landowner; The Venerable Jonathan Peter Smith [1955] Director/Archdeacon; John Barrie Watkiss [1937] Director/Retired; Edmund Michael Wood [1943] Director/Chartered Accountant

St Albans Operating Company Limited
Incorporated: 24 July 2014 *Employees:* 4
Net Worth Deficit: £30,467,000 *Total Assets:* £129,475,000
Registered Office: Gladstone Place, 36-38 Upper Marlborough Road, St Albans, Herts, AL1 3UU
Activities: Retail sale of automotive fuel in specialised stores
Parent: Motor Fuel Limited
Officers: William Bahlsen Bannister [1967] Director; Thomas McKenzie Biggart [1966] Director

St Albans School
Incorporated: 21 March 2002 *Employees:* 171
Net Worth: £18,318,000 *Total Assets:* £25,872,000
Registered Office: St Albans School, Abbey Gateway, St Albans, Herts, AL3 4HB
Activities: General secondary education
Officers: Richard John Hepper, Secretary; Lesley Margaret Ainsworth [1957] Director/Panel Member Competition and Markets Authority; Peter Glanfield Brown [1954] Director/Estate Agent; Matthew William Southworth Cawthorne [1962] Director/Consultant; Anthony Lionel Dalwood [1970] Director/Investment Manager; Stephen Patrick Eames [1948] Director/Solicitor; Derek Foster [1963] Director/Chartered Accountant; Sir Roy Alan Gardner [1945] Director; Anne Elizabeth Hurst [1965] Director/Senior HR Manager; Robert Richard Lucas [1962] Director; Professor John Paul Luzio [1947] Director/Retired (Emeritus Professor); Shantanu Joseph Majumdar [1967] Director/Barrister; Chris McIntyre [1954] Director/Dean of Faculty; Nigel Moore [1962] Director/Solicitor; Carole Elizabeth Pomfret [1961] Director/Chartered Accountant; Michael Edward Punt [1970] Director/Headmaster; Alastair Mark Woodgate [1963] Director/Chartered Surveyor

St Andrew's Tutorial Services Limited
Incorporated: 24 July 1984 *Employees:* 78
Net Worth: £7,065,785 *Total Assets:* £10,914,313
Registered Office: 13 Station Road, Cambridge, CB1 2JB
Activities: General secondary education
Shareholders: David Robert Martin; Hanna Ludmila Claydon; Mervyn John Martin
Officers: Mervyn John Martin, Secretary; Wayne Robert Marshall [1960] Director; David Robert Martin [1980] Director/Salesman; Mervyn John Martin [1949] School Director; David Michael McEwan-Cox [1959] Director

St Bede's Inter Church School
Incorporated: 8 February 2012 *Employees:* 128
Net Worth: £18,228,404 *Total Assets:* £20,812,368
Registered Office: St Bede's Inter Church School, Birdwood Road, Cambridge, CB1 3TD
Activities: General secondary education
Officers: Clare Kirk, Secretary; Charlotte Frances Avery [1970] Director/Headteacher; Christine Branch [1942] Director/Retired; Kathleen Collins [1945] Director/Retired; Revd Dr Geoffrey Malcolm Weston Cook [1938] Director/University Teacher/Minister of Religion; Prof James Francis Crilly [1955] Director [Irish]; Alistair Day [1969] Director/Headteacher; Jonathan Peter Glazier [1959] Director (Media); Jane Henry [1957] Director/Education Manager; Helen Hilton [1974] Director/Project Manager; Doreen Houghton [1961] Director/School Administrator; Julia Carol Ient [1971] Director/Manager; Amy Le Scelle [1984] Director/Teacher; Michael McGarvey [1971] Director; Gary Morgan [1965] Director/Charity Worker; Revd Stephen Plant [1964] Director/Rector; Magdalena Syposz [1969] Director/Clerk; Helen Turner [1972] Director/Buyer for John Lewis; Malcolm Ian Watson [1954] Director; Dr James Whitehorn [1978] Director/Doctor; Paula Wolff [1968] Director/Housewife

St Columba's College and Preparatory School
Incorporated: 4 June 2001 *Employees:* 160
Net Worth: £10,663,171 *Total Assets:* £14,891,098
Registered Office: St Columba's College, King Harry Lane, St Albans, Herts, AL3 4AW
Activities: Primary education
Officers: Paul Gavin Daly, Secretary; Edward Joseph Caddle [1961] Director/Accountant; Christopher Cook [1977] Director/Solicitor; Robert Duigan [1964] Director/Headmaster [South African]; Joanne Wendy Goddard [1960] Director; Angela Gray [1966] Director/Chartered Accountant; Jacqueline Mary Harrison [1950] Director/Retired; Ronald Joseph Hingle [1960] Director/Minister of Religion [American]; Bradley Charles Hutchinson [1985] Director/Lawyer; Andrew Robert Johnson [1967] Director/Headteacher; Ivy Le Blanc [1945] Director/Provincial Superior of a Roman Catholic Religious Order [American]; Kevin Gerard McGovern [1958] Director/Chief Executive; Daniel Camille St Jacques [1949] Director/Minister of Religion [American]; Stephen Nicholas Watson [1959] Finance Director

St Edmundsbury and Ipswich Diocesan Multi-Academy Trust
Incorporated: 19 March 2015 *Employees:* 395
Net Worth: £5,554,885 *Total Assets:* £8,829,444
Registered Office: St Nicholas Centre, 4 Cutler Street, Ipswich, Suffolk, IP1 1UQ
Activities: Primary education
Officers: Michelle Tina Roots, Secretary; Andrew Alexander Blit [1957] Director/Retired; Thomas Nugent Brooke [1959] Director/Solicitor; Stephen Harwood Cole [1952] Director/Retired; Alister James Gourlay [1948] Director/Retired; Reverend Robert Charles Hinsley [1977] Director/Rector; Caroline Erica Robinson [1946] Director/Retired School Inspector; Jane Sheat [1964] Diocesan Director of Education

St George Healthcare Limited
Incorporated: 26 July 1999 *Employees:* 124
Net Worth: £57,503 *Total Assets:* £12,615,239
Registered Office: 2 Imperial Place, Maxwell Road, Borehamwood, Herts, WD6 1JN
Activities: Hospital activities
Parent: Elysium Healthcare (Ultimate Care) Limited
Officers: Sarah Juliette Livingston, Secretary; Lesley Joy Chamberlain [1963] Director/Group Chief Executive; Dr Quazi Shams Mahfooz Haque [1968] Executive Medical Director; Steven John Woolgar [1955] Director of Policy and Regulation

St Georges School (Harpenden) Limited
Incorporated: 18 August 1945 *Employees:* 4
Net Worth: £17,069,884 *Total Assets:* £17,096,652
Registered Office: St Georges School (Harpenden) Ltd, Sun Lane, Harpenden, Herts, AL5 4TD
Activities: General secondary education
Officers: Keith Andrews [1959] Director/Chartered Surveyor; Penelope Jane Carey [1965] Director/University Lecturer; Adrian John Clarke [1964] Director/Structural Engineer; James Alexander Douglas [1962] Director/Chartered Accountant; John Philip Houghton Hayward [1954] Director/Quantity Surveyor; Gillian Mary Ingram [1959] Director; Rev Gareth Charles Lewis [1954] Director/Clergyman; Kevin Robert Parsons [1957] Director/Solicitor; Roger Andrew Usher [1948] Director/Management Consultant

St Ivo School
Incorporated: 13 July 2011 *Employees:* 258
Net Worth: £14,854,199 *Total Assets:* £16,058,093
Registered Office: St Ivo School, High Leys, St Ives, Cambs, PE27 6RR
Activities: General secondary education
Officers: Emillie Louise Newell, Secretary; Judith Margaret Barnes [1947] Director/Retired; Daniel Gary Charles Coulson [1978] Director/Site Manager; Carol Anne Darnell [1965] Director/HR Consultant; Charles Walter Glanville [1959] Director/Medical Facilities; Samuel Barnaby Griffin [1972] Director/Headteacher; Claire Anne Lynn [1966] Director/Public Relations; Dr Martin Andrew McMahon [1969] Director/Senior Manager; Mark Ronald Newstead [1971] Executive Group Director - Property Services; Francis Craig Newton [1942] Director/Retired; Richard Carl Potter [1972] Director/Assistant Headteacher; Jonathan Anthony Read [1970] Director/Scientist; Adrian Mark Smith [1971] Director/Media; Philip Richard Speer [1952] Director/Solicitor; Anthony Ward [1985] Director/ICT Manager; Elaine Ruth Warriner [1975] Director/Teacher; Duncan Sidney Woodall [1953] Director/Retired

St James Media LLP
Incorporated: 6 September 2002
Net Worth: £12,236,442 *Total Assets:* £12,236,442
Registered Office: 99 Kenton Road, Harrow, Middlesex, HA3 0AN
Officers: Rt Hon Lord Kenneth Wilfred Baker [1934] LLP Member; Lady Mary Elizabeth Baker [1937] LLP Member; Bernard Samuel Baron [1950] LLP Member; Peter Lincoln Breitenbach [1954] LLP Member; Jonathan MacNee Carswell [1967] LLP Member; Duncan Duckett [1944] LLP Member; Enrico Filiberto Eusebi [1962] LLP Member; David Paul Grant [1961] LLP Member; Peter Brown Grant [1954] LLP Member; Margaret Harrison [1944] LLP Member; Nicholas Lorraine Edmund Hill [1948] LLP Member; Lois Elizabeth Kerrison [1969] LLP Member; Andrew Christopher Lapping [1963] LLP Member; Gary Lloyd [1961] LLP Member; Christopher John Loynes [1947] LLP Member; Michele Luzi [1956] LLP Member; Steven Morgan [1966] LLP Member; John Culverhouse Muncey [1962] LLP Member; Gordon Climson Perry [1955] LLP Member; Paul Charles Hargrave Pheysey [1962] LLP Member; Hugh Alexander Rutherford [1958] LLP Member; Jonathan Darell Seal [1962] LLP Member; Anil Sri Pathmanathan [1958] LLP Member; Jeremy James Swift [1965] LLP Member; Richard Terley [1912] LLP Member; Andrew Robert Thornhill [1943] LLP Member; Joanna Trollope [1943] LLP Member; Simon John Wilders [1953] LLP Member

St Joseph's College Limited
Incorporated: 22 December 1995 *Employees:* 181
Net Worth: £3,306,755 *Total Assets:* £10,724,256
Registered Office: Birkfield, Belstead Road, Ipswich, Suffolk, IP2 9DR
Activities: Pre-primary education
Officers: John Michael Button [1953] Director/Quantity Surveyor; Prof Penny Cavenagh [1955] Director/Dean of Academic Affairs; Renata Angela Karolina Chester [1968] Director/Chartered Accountant; Philip James Dennis [1973] Director/Chartered Surveyor; Vicky Jane Fox [1975] Marketing Director; Perry Dean Glading [1958] Director; Anthony Basset Newman [1946] Director/Retired; Matthew Bryan Potter [1970] Director/Solicitor; Richard Clive Stace [1966] Director/Solicitor

St Mary's CE Academy, Cheshunt
Incorporated: 21 March 2012 *Employees:* 180
Net Worth: £29,748,000 *Total Assets:* £31,793,000
Registered Office: St Mary's CE Academy, Lieutenant Ellis Way, Cheshunt, Herts, EN7 5FB
Activities: General secondary education
Officers: Stephanie Benbow [1963] Director/Headteacher; Maureen Bruce [1949] Director; Debra Ann Chilton [1963] Director/Banker; Paul George Daniel [1959] Director/Health, Safety and Environment Manager; Natasha Shaneen Graham [1977] Director/Business Manager; Sarah Murphy [1972] Director/Headteacher; Rebecca Clare Shah [1985] Director/Teacher; Nicola Jane Smith [1971] Director/Pre School Leader; Steven John Warner [1973] Director/Teacher

The St Neots Learning Partnership
Incorporated: 13 July 2011 *Employees:* 396
Net Worth: £22,958,350 *Total Assets:* £26,849,380
Registered Office: Longsands Road, St Neots, Cambs, PE19 1LQ
Activities: General secondary education
Officers: Helen Bryson [1968] Director/Head Strategy Business Intelligence; Rev Thomas Roger Henthorne [1930] Director/Retired; Robert Alexander Law [1952] Director/Retired; Julie Ann Smith [1966] Director/Accountant; Karl David Wainwright [1964] Director/Business Development Manager; Graham Arthur Wright [1943] Director/Retired

The St Paul's Walden Bury Estate Company Limited
Incorporated: 27 March 1933 *Employees:* 12
Net Worth: £37,056,956 *Total Assets:* £44,783,732
Registered Office: St Pauls Walden Bury, Hitchin, Herts, SG4 8BP
Activities: Growing of cereals (except rice), leguminous crops and oil seeds
Shareholders: Caljer Investments Limited; Talmi Investments Limited
Officers: Sir Simon Alexander Bowes Lyon, Secretary; Dr Caroline Mary Victoria Bowes Lyon [1940] Director; Fergus Alexander Bowes Lyon [1970] Director; Sir Simon Alexander Bowes Lyon [1932] Director/Chartered Accountant

St. Aubyn's (Woodford Green) School Trust
Incorporated: 8 July 1975 *Employees:* 127
Net Worth: £8,080,006 *Total Assets:* £9,000,073
Registered Office: St Aubyn's School, Woodford New Road, Woodford Green, Essex, IG8 9DU
Activities: Primary education
Officers: Maureen Patricia Foakes, Secretary; Abraham Jacobus Botha [1959] Director/Consultant Surgeon; Debra Elaine Davidson-Smith [1963] Director/Magistrate; Susan Evans [1964] Director/Chartered Accountant; Michael Robert Foster [1941] Director/Architect; Rajesh Kalia [1969] Director/Lawyer; Judith Mary Lunn [1957] Director/Teacher; Joanne Elizabeth Ruff [1962] Director/Solicitor; Dilipkumar Shah [1946] Director/Accountant

St. Christopher School (Letchworth) Limited
Incorporated: 16 July 1954 *Employees:* 171
Net Worth: £9,310,387 *Total Assets:* £12,449,324
Registered Office: Barrington Road, Letchworth, Herts, SG6 3JZ
Activities: Pre-primary education
Officers: William Scott Botterill Hawkes, Secretary; Emma-Kate Henry [1973] Director/Headmistress; Sarah Jane Kilcoyne [1965] Director/Accountant; Mark Andrew Michael Stephen Leigh [1946] Director/Solicitor Advocate; Peter McMeekin [1962] IT Director; Dr Dasha Nicholls [1964] Director/Doctor Consultant; Sophie Nolan [1985] Director/Analyst; John Simmonds [1946] Director; Sir Rabinder Singh [1964] Director/Judge; Benjamin Charles Walker [1964] Director/Headmaster

St. Elizabeth Hospice (Suffolk)
Incorporated: 24 February 1984 *Employees:* 223
Net Worth: £15,113,668 *Total Assets:* £16,067,109
Registered Office: 565 Foxhall Road, Ipswich, Suffolk, IP3 8LX
Activities: Other human health activities
Officers: William David Barnes [1955] Director/Accountant; Grainne Cecelia Drummond [1957] Director/Retired [Irish]; Dr Nigel Gibbons [1959] Director/General Medical Practitioner; Ann Nicola Hogarth [1958] Director/Accountant; Terence Dean Hunt [1957] Director/Retired; Dr Anthony David Joseph Nicholl [1952] Director/Hospital Consultant; Mark William Nicholls [1956] Director/Stockbroker; Anita Parkinson [1960] Director/Retired; Ian John Turner [1959] Director

St. Helena Hospice Limited
Incorporated: 11 August 1980 *Employees:* 352
Net Worth: £10,418,129 *Total Assets:* £12,655,362
Registered Office: St Helena Hospice, Myland Hall, Barncroft Close, Colchester, Essex, CO4 9JU
Activities: Other human health activities
Officers: Brian Michael Bolt, Secretary; Kenneth John Aldred [1950] Director/Retired; Joshua Arkley [1983] Director/General Practitioner; Clive Richard Bull [1955] Director/Commercial Procurement Manager; David Cresswell [1977] Director/Architect; Tracey June Dickens [1968] Director/Solicitor; Andrew Paul Dickerson [1963] Director/Management Accountant; John Hawkins [1949] Director/Retired Chief Executive Local Authority; Dr Sarah Maan [1984] Director/Medical Doctor; Juliette Yvonne Maxam [1969] Director/Media Relations Manager; Dr David Robert Marmion Milne [1957] Director/General Medical Practitioner; Gerry Mordaunt [1939] Director/Retired; Mary Northrop [1960] Director/Lecturer; Professor Anthony Nigel Pye [1958] Director/Professor of Business; Kenneth Nigel Rolls [1946] Director/Retired; Roger Eric Sirman [1950] Director/Accountant; Peter Joseph Vergo [1947] Director/University Teacher

St. Luke's Hospice (Harrow & Brent) Ltd.
Incorporated: 22 June 1987 *Employees:* 164
Net Worth: £9,713,000 *Total Assets:* £10,918,000
Registered Office: Kenton Grange, Kenton Road, Harrow, Middlesex, HA3 0YG
Activities: Hospital activities
Officers: Carolyn Bennett [1976] Director/Fundraiser; Rajesh Bhatia [1963] Director/Banker; Norma Susan Brier [1949] Director; Cheryl Jeanette Brodie [1955] Director/Learning & Development Consultant; Professor Robert Samuel Elkeles [1942] Director/Consultant Physician; Christine Mary Glenn [1952] Director/Barrister; Dr Reena Zivia Majus [1954] Director/General Practitioner; Claire Victoria Melia-Tompkins [1978] Director/Head of Stakeholder Communications; Julia Newland [1959] Director/Solicitor; Dr Gillian Ida Schiller [1955] Director/Partner Gateway Consulting Group

St. Margaret's School Bushey
Incorporated: 20 May 1996 *Employees:* 173
Net Worth: £21,346,244 *Total Assets:* £23,384,684
Registered Office: St Margaret's School, Merry Hill Road, Bushey, Herts, WD23 1DT
Activities: Primary education
Officers: Dr Kenneth Victor Young, Secretary/Bursar; Justin Alford [1970] Director/Lawyer; David Clout [1941] Director/Retired; Brian Thomas Coulshed [1950] Director/Retired Headmaster; Judith Elizabeth Fenn [1966] Director/Business Executive; Rev William John Morris Gibbs [1971] Director/Clerk in Holy Orders; Ellen Hill [1952] Director/Retired; Rachel Floretta Hodgson [1969] Director/Marketing Consultant; Malcolm Spooner [1955] Director/Head of Markets

St. Mary's School Cambridge
Incorporated: 13 August 1984 *Employees:* 149
Net Worth: £13,908,561 *Total Assets:* £23,997,420
Registered Office: Bateman Street, Cambridge, CB2 1LY
Activities: Primary education
Officers: Mark Francis Johnstone, Secretary; Raymond George Burch [1962] Director/Quantity Surveyor; Judy Glenys Gould Clements [1958] Director/Adjudicator H M Revenue & Customs; Sarah Ann Dixon [1955] Director/Retired; Judith Louise Driscoll [1966] Director/Scientist; Victoria Ann Espley [1971] Director; Rachel Anne Gleeson [1986] Director; Andrew Robert Grant [1953] Director; Ronald Haynes [1957] Director/University Computer Officer [American]; Colin David Jones [1965] Director/Solicitor; Michael Donald Ledzion [1967] Director; Sister Wendy Frances Orchard [1944] Director/Religious Sister; Marina Pattinson [1976] Director; Jeremy Mark Pyne [1961] Director/Chief Account Manager; Sarah Laetitia Squire [1949] Director; Jo Storey [1967] Director/Teacher; Dr Brigid Nessa Ward [1955] Director/General Practitioner [Irish]; Stuart Alker Westley [1947] Director

St. Nicholas Hospice (Suffolk)
Incorporated: 24 August 1983 *Employees:* 179
Net Worth: £11,304,293 *Total Assets:* £11,863,814
Registered Office: Macmillan Way, Hardwick Lane, Bury St Edmunds, Suffolk, IP33 2QY
Activities: Residential nursing care facilities
Officers: Rachel Louisa Spencer, Secretary; Karen Chandler-Smith [1971] Director/Business Executive; Susan Mary Hayter [1947] Director/Professional Adviser (Nursing); Ann Langdon [1952] Director/Retired HR Professional; Malcolm Arthur Leith [1954] Director/Management Consultant; Michelle Masson [1981] Director/Chartered Accountant; Marion Christine Miles [1951] Director/Retired Headteacher; Christopher James Minett [1947] Director/Retired; Ian Calder Morgan [1948] Director; Charles Haddon McBratney Simpson [1959] Director/Chartered Accountant; Canon Matthew James Vernon [1971] Director/Minister of Religion; Tessa Jane Wright [1958] Director/Chief Executive

St. Vincent's Charitable Trust
Incorporated: 9 June 1992 *Employees:* 78
Previous: St Vincent's Hospital
Net Worth: £9,140,273 *Total Assets:* £10,010,634
Registered Office: St Vincent's Nursing Home, Wiltshire Lane, Eastcote, Pinner, Middlesex, HA5 2NB
Activities: Medical nursing home activities
Officers: Patricia Kathleen Black [1947] Director/Senior Lecturer (Academic Institute & University); Fergal Davern [1966] Director; Revd John Patrick Deehan [1949] Director/Roman Catholic Priest; Alan Joseph Edmondson [1931] Director/Retired; Kathleen Fox [1953] Director; Dr Robert Christopher Richmond Horsburgh [1949] Director; Linda Ann Martin [1963] Director/Florist; Katie Frances O'Brien [1983] Director; William Parisutham [1951] Director; Neville George Ransley [1945] Director/Retired; Jacqueline Ann Redrup [1954] Director; John Charles Steinitz [1950] Director/Retired

St.Albans Diocesan Board of Finance (The)
Incorporated: 3 November 1916 *Employees:* 35
Net Worth: £161,608,000 *Total Assets:* £179,470,000
Registered Office: Holywell Lodge, 41 Holywell Hill, St Albans, Herts, AL1 1HE
Activities: Other business support service activities n.e.c.
Officers: Susan Elizabeth Pope, Secretary; The Revd Canon Peter Michael Ackroyd [1960] Director/Parish Priest; Simon Henry Crews Baynes [1958] Director/Independent Pensions Trustee; Colin Graham Bird [1949] Director/Chartered Accountant; Mary Eryl Butcher [1954] Director/Retired; John Wesley Butler [1951] Director; Graham Robert Cappleman [1956] Director/Retired; Nigel Challis [1946] Director/Chartered Accountant; Dr David William Dallinger [1953] Director/Chartered Engineer; Patricia Elizabeth Easterbrook [1967] Director/Regulator; Dr Mark William Eaton [1950] Director/Retired; Timothy Russell Fleming [1972] Director/Chartered Accountant; Colin Bernard Gage [1941] Director; Martyn John Gates [1951] Director/Architect; Elizabeth Jane Gogarty [1953] Director/Retired; Philip Richard Lindley [1966] Director/Tax Manager; Janet MacKenzie [1962] Director/Clerk in Holy Orders; The Revd Dominic Generald Newstead [1965] Director/Parish Priest; The Honourable Richard Oakley Pleydell-Bouverie [1947] Director/Farmer & Landowner; Michael Readman [1956] Director/Retired; John Henry Robinson [1951] Director; Rt Revd Dr Alan Gregory Clayton Smith [1957] Director/Bishop; The Venerable Jonathan Peter Smith [1955] Director/Clerk in Holy Orders; Kerry Smith [1961] Director/Administrator; Dr Richard Southern [1973] Director/University Lecturer

St.Albans High School for Girls
Incorporated: 14 December 1936 *Employees:* 199
Net Worth: £22,446,000 *Total Assets:* £30,539,000
Registered Office: The High School, 3 Townsend Avenue, St Albans, Herts, AL1 3SJ
Activities: General secondary education
Officers: Archibald Fraser Campbell, Secretary; David Michael Alterman [1960] Director/Market Research; Paul Anthony Brewster [1958] Director/Surveyor; Moira Ellen Darlington [1952] Director/Retired; Eleanor Alice de Galleani [1978] Director/Solicitor; Neil James Dominic Enright [1977] Director/Headmaster; Timothy David Gardam [1956] Director/Chief Executive Officer; Heather Jane Greatrex [1960] Director/Executive Coach; Dorothy Mary Henderson [1960] Director/Solicitor; Jeffrey Philip Hywel John [1953] Director/Cathedral Dean; Kenneth Matthew Keen [1975] Director/Consultant; Bruce Richard Kettle [1943] Director/Chartered Surveyor; Dr Felicia Marie Kirk [1965] Director/Headteacher [American]; Simon Richard Martin [1961] Director/Lawyer; Daniel Mark Roe [1976] Director/Surveyor; John Stewart Thomson [1947] Director/Chartered Accountant; Robert Harvey Ward [1952] Director/Retired

St.Edmundsbury and Ipswich Diocesan Board of Finance
Incorporated: 16 February 1916 *Employees:* 36
Net Worth: £75,373,000 *Total Assets:* £78,526,000
Registered Office: Diocesan Office, St Nicholas Centre, 4 Cutler Street, Ipswich, Suffolk, IP1 1UQ
Activities: Activities of religious organisations
Officers: Anna Hughes, Secretary; Anthony Robert Allwood [1952] Director; David Martin James Ball [1943] Director/Retired; Penny Bird [1946] Director/Retired; David John Chambers [1947] Director/Retired; Cheryl Anne Collins [1962] Director/Clerk in Holy Orders; Reverend Andrew Steward Dotchin [1956] Director/Vicar; The Right Reverend Michael Robert Harrison [1963] Director/Clerk in Holy Orders; The Very Reverend Joseph Patricius Hawes [1965] Director/Dean of St Edmundsbury; Reverend Mark Haworth [1950] Director/Vicar; David Harold Jenkins [1961] Director/Clergyman; David John Lamming [1947] Director/Barrister; The Revd Canon Ian David John Morgan [1957] Director/Minister of Religion; Reverend Malcolm Eric Osborne [1964] Director/Clerk in Holy Orders; Mark Pendlington [1957] Director of Corporate Affairs; Reverend Sharon Jane Potter [1963] Director/Minister of Religion; Martin Alan Seeley [1954] Director/Clerk in The Holy Orders; Stephen Raymond West [1958] Director; Ian Wigston [1955] Director/Management Consultant

St.Helen's School Northwood
Incorporated: 4 October 1946 *Employees:* 330
Net Worth: £20,457,000 *Total Assets:* £24,897,000
Registered Office: Eastbury Road, Northwood, Middlesex, HA6 3AS
Activities: Primary education
Officers: Mark Richard MacKenzie Crooks, Secretary; Monica Bhandari [1980] Director/Senior Lecturer in Law; Nadeem Shirazali Boghani [1978] Director/Vice Chairman; Dr Sara Rhianydd Gordon [1985] Director/Research Assistant; Puneeta Mongia [1973] Assistant Director Strategy; Alison Mary Phillipson [1952] Director/Retired; Dr Susan Mary Pitts [1955] Director/Lecturer; Elizabeth Radice [1951] Director/Retired; Vivek Sapra [1966] Senior Director; Michelle Weerasekera [1969] Director/Voluntary Worker; Suzanne Lindsay Woolfson [1964] Director/Chartered Accountant

St.Lawrence Hall Farms Limited
Incorporated: 30 April 1963 *Employees:* 17
Net Worth: £2,087,124 *Total Assets:* £13,184,902
Registered Office: Ilketshall Hall, Ilketshall Street, Lawrence, Beccles, Suffolk, NR34 8NH
Activities: Mixed farming
Shareholder: Dominic Rory Parker
Officers: Olivia Jane Parker, Secretary; Dominic Rory Parker [1967] Director/Farmer; Hazel Ann Parker [1933] Director

St.Martins' (Northwood) Preparatory School Trust Limited
Incorporated: 28 November 1961 *Employees:* 77
Net Worth: £10,893,608 *Total Assets:* £13,108,400
Registered Office: 40 Moor Park Road, Northwood, Middlesex, HA6 2DJ
Activities: Primary education
Officers: Alison Claire Curran, Secretary; Simon John Everson [1965] Director/Headmaster; James Christopher Fowler [1962] Director/Headteacher; Vernon William Hales [1961] Director/Headmaster; Andrew Simon Harris [1966] Director/Chartered Accountant; Neil Alexander Hinds [1960] Director/Chartered Surveyor; Mark Richard Jordan [1968] Director; Christine Anne Marks [1958] Director/Consultant; Jeremy William Peter Richards [1962] Director/Investment Manager; Christopher Ralph Scott [1959] Director/Consultant; Dr Rabia Yaqoob [1967] Director/General Practitioner - Partner

St.Michael's Manor Limited
Incorporated: 2 June 1965 *Employees:* 59
Net Worth: £6,532,398 *Total Assets:* £8,589,856
Registered Office: 1 Beauchamp Court, 10 Victors Way, Barnet, Herts, EN5 5TZ
Activities: Hotels and similar accommodation
Parent: Avon Lake Holdings Limited
Officers: Devika Gunputh, Secretary; Devika Gunputh [1957] Director [Mauritian]; Munundev Gunputh [1958] Director [Mauritian]

The Stable Lads Welfare Trust Housing Association Limited
Incorporated: 30 January 2008 *Employees:* 4
Net Worth: £11,362,800 *Total Assets:* £11,696,000
Registered Office: 20b Park Lane, Newmarket, Suffolk, CB8 8QD
Activities: Other accommodation
Officers: Simon William Clarke [1965] Director/Farmer; Craig Anthony Glasper [1965] Director/CEO - Social Housing; Simon Richard Hope [1964] Director/Chartered Surveyor; Gary Middlebrook [1954] Director; Joey Newton [1956] Director/Farmer; Patrick James Russell [1952] Director/Lawyer

Stace LLP
Incorporated: 9 April 2005 *Employees:* 154
Net Worth: £4,608,078 *Total Assets:* £9,168,929
Registered Office: 273 High Street, Epping, Essex, CM16 4DA
Officers: Glyn Frederick Crawley [1961] Member; John Timothy Noble [1957] Member; Matthew Allen Whitehead [1963] Member; Mark Ashby [1981] LLP Member; Edward Bain [1974] LLP Member; Ian Robert Clark [1972] LLP Member; Nigel Alexander Cook [1973] LLP Member; James William Bailey Darbyshire [1971] LLP Member; Marc David Eagles [1967] LLP Member; Gary John Fletcher [1954] LLP Member; Malcolm Howting [1972] LLP Member; Simon Richard Hugill [1969] LLP Member; Michael Albert Hutchins [1958] LLP Member; David Wardlaw Lawrie [1955] LLP Member; Stuart Andrew Riley [1969] LLP Member; Gareth Aaron Sinnamon [1975] LLP Member; Stuart Keith Syddell [1973] LLP Member; Glyn Thomas [1962] LLP Member

Stafford House School of English Limited
Incorporated: 12 April 1960 *Employees:* 199
Net Worth: £1,731,000 *Total Assets:* £11,184,000
Registered Office: Kett House, Station Road, Cambridge, CB1 2JH
Activities: Technical and vocational secondary education
Parent: Stafford House Companies Limited
Officers: Michael Ioakimides [1965] Director; Philip Leslie Symes [1962] Director/Chief Financial Officer; Brendan Grant Webb [1969] Director

Stafford House Study Holidays Limited
Incorporated: 14 July 1989 *Employees:* 63
Net Worth: £1,255,000 *Total Assets:* £12,445,000
Registered Office: Kett House, Station Road, Cambridge, CB1 2JH
Activities: Technical and vocational secondary education
Parent: Stafford House Companies Limited
Officers: Michael Ioakimides [1965] Director; Philip Leslie Symes [1962] Director/Chief Financial Officer; Brendan Grant Webb [1969] Director

H.Stain Limited
Incorporated: 14 April 1949 *Employees:* 10
Net Worth: £15,567,278 *Total Assets:* £18,329,352
Registered Office: York House, Empire Way, Wembley, Middlesex, HA9 0FQ
Activities: Retail sale of watches and jewellery in specialised stores
Major Shareholder: Martin Sydney Stain
Officers: Delia Sherry Stain, Secretary; Sara Melanie Joffe [1963] Director; Lynn Susan Kaye [1961] Director; Delia Sherry Stain [1934] Director; Martin Sydney Stain [1934] Director

Stainless Metalcraft (Chatteris) Limited
Incorporated: 29 May 1990 *Employees:* 158
Net Worth: £6,482,008 *Total Assets:* £17,824,544
Registered Office: Chatteris Engineering Works, 15 Honeysome Road, Chatteris, Cambs, PE16 6SA
Activities: Manufacture of metal structures and parts of structures
Parent: Avingtrans PLC
Officers: Christopher Lewis-Jones, Secretary; Austen Mark Adams [1965] Managing Director; Martin Robert Johnson [1969] Business Conformance Director; Stephen Michael King [1966] Director/Accountant; Martin Derrick Lawrence [1970] Customer Development Director

Stamford Property Company Limited
Incorporated: 25 January 1995 *Employees:* 7
Net Worth: £14,658,842 *Total Assets:* £16,482,476
Registered Office: 14 All Saints Street, Stamford, Lincs, PE9 2PA
Activities: Development of building projects
Shareholders: Simon Mark Caunt; Janet Mary Hindmarch; David John Hindmarch; Castlegate Trustees Limited
Officers: Kevin Glyn Williams, Secretary; Hugh Munro Bater Caseley [1960] Director/Chartered Surveyor; Simon Mark Caunt [1964] Director; Geoffrey Ellwood Fearn [1937] Director/Farmer; Peter Gaskell [1943] Director/Civil Engineer; David John Hindmarch [1965] Director; Mark Thomas Hindmarch [1963] Director/Accountant

Stane Park Ltd.
Incorporated: 22 May 2001 *Employees:* 2
Net Worth: £5,993,756 *Total Assets:* £8,807,172
Registered Office: 2 Beacon End Courtyard, London Road, Stanway, Colchester, Essex, CO3 0NU
Activities: Buying and selling of own real estate
Parent: Conejero Investments
Officers: Joshua Warren [1969] Director

Stanley Dock Properties Limited
Incorporated: 6 November 2009 *Employees:* 2
Net Worth Deficit: £2,184,988 *Total Assets:* £15,561,307
Registered Office: Devonshire House, Manor Way, Borehamwood, Herts, WD6 1QQ
Activities: Development of building projects
Officers: Gerard Michael Comaskey [1970] Director/Property Manager [Irish]; Patrick John Power [1973] Director/Surveyor [Irish]

Stanley Tee LLP
Incorporated: 26 April 2007 *Employees:* 227
Net Worth: £5,453,305 *Total Assets:* £8,141,335
Registered Office: Tees House, 95 London Road, Bishop's Stortford, Herts, CM23 3GW
Officers: Graeme Ross Atkinson [1958] Member; Govan Paul Raymond Bramley [1962] Member; Aaron John Cane [1980] Member; Mark Charles Carter [1953] Member; Janine Marcia Collier [1976] Member; Joshua Graham Alastair I'anson Coombe [1973] Member; Timothy Deeming [1978] Member; Susan Ann Dowman [1968] Member; James Hamish Dowson [1968] Member; Anne Nicola Elliss [1973] Member; Lucy Jayne Folley [1969] Member; Ashton Willis Hunt [1968] Member; Catherine Mary Izzard [1964] Member; David Nicholas Jacobs [1956] Member; Louise Margiotta [1971] Member; Caroline Ann Metcalf [1963] Member; David William Miller [1982] Member; Catherine Elizabeth Mowat [1975] Member; Richard James Payne [1965] Member; Darren Perks [1981] Member; David Brian Perry [1970] Member; Clare Pilsworth [1970] Member; Sally Jane Powell [1975] Member; David Ian Redfern [1957] Member; Ian Justin Robinson [1973] Member; Irena Jozefa Spence [1960] Member; Charles Michael Stevens [1978] Member; Robert Joseph Whitaker [1977] Member; Jane Elizabeth Winfield [1966] Member; Allan Stuart Wright [1957] Member

Stanmore Implants Worldwide Limited
Incorporated: 19 February 1996 *Employees:* 98
Net Worth: £3,219,000 *Total Assets:* £8,373,000
Registered Office: Unit 210 Centennial Park, Centennial Avenue, Elstree, Herts, WD6 3SJ
Activities: Manufacture of medical and dental instruments and supplies
Shareholders: Stryker Corporation; SIW Holdings Limited
Officers: Peter Ewart Bradley [1961] Director/Business Executive; Robert Craig Cohen [1961] Director/Business Executive

Stansted Airport Limited
Incorporated: 19 February 1986 *Employees:* 1,765
Net Worth: £799,860,992 *Total Assets:* £1,443,810,048
Registered Office: Enterprise House, Bassingbourn Road, Stansted Airport, Essex, CM24 1QW
Activities: Scheduled passenger air transport
Parent: Manchester Airport Group Finance Limited
Officers: Charles Thomas Cornish [1959] Director/Chief Executive; John Kenneth O'Toole [1974] Director [Irish]; Neil Philip Thompson [1971] Director/Chief Financial Officer

Stantec Europe Limited
Incorporated: 31 October 1989 *Employees:* 1,701
Previous: MWH Europe Limited
Net Worth: £26,719,000 *Total Assets:* £138,834,000
Registered Office: Buckingham Court, Kingsmead Business Park, London Road, High Wycombe, Bucks, HP11 1JU
Activities: Activities of head offices
Parent: Stantec Holding B.V.
Officers: Victoria Hall Sturt, Secretary; Victoria Jayne Hall-Sturt [1973] Director/Lawyer; Catherine Margaret Schefer [1968] Managing Director; David Anthony Smith [1963] Director/Chief Strategy Officer; Andrew Charles Wilson [1971] Director/Vice President of Financial Services [American]

Stantec Treatment Group Limited
Incorporated: 14 January 2003
Previous: MWH Constructors Limited
Net Worth: £15,617,000 *Total Assets:* £27,792,000
Registered Office: Buckingham Court, Kingsmead Business Park, London Road, High Wycombe, Bucks, HP11 1JU
Activities: Construction of water projects
Parent: Stantec Constructors Holding B.V.
Officers: Victoria Hall-Sturt, Secretary; Paul Jeremy David Alpern [1964] Director/Solicitor [Canadian]; Victoria Jayne Hall-Sturt [1973] Director/Managing Counsel; Catherine Margaret Schefer [1968] Director/Executive Vice President

Stantec UK Limited
Incorporated: 22 October 1974 *Employees:* 1,064
Previous: MWH UK Limited
Net Worth: £33,542,000 *Total Assets:* £91,520,000
Registered Office: Buckingham Court, Kingsmead Business Park, London Road, High Wycombe, Bucks, HP11 1JU
Activities: Other engineering activities
Parent: Stantec Europe Limited
Officers: Victoria Hall Sturt, Secretary; Victoria Jayne Hall-Sturt [1973] Director/Lawyer; Ian Andrew Noble [1957] Director/Civil Engineer; Catherine Margaret Schefer [1968] UK Managing Director; David Anthony Smith [1963] Director/Chief Strategy Officer

Stanton Holding Limited
Incorporated: 30 November 2005 *Employees:* 127
Previous: Russian Shelbourne Limited
Net Worth: £15,591,163 *Total Assets:* £18,660,364
Registered Office: 80 Guildhall Street, Bury St Edmunds, Suffolk, IP33 1QB
Activities: Manufacture of agricultural and forestry machinery other than tractors
Shareholders: Stephen Victor Fairburn; Daniel Greenberg; Lyudmila Obraztsova
Officers: Stephen Victor Fairburn [1955] Director/Solicitor; Alexander Kuznetsov [1968] Director/Business Consultant [Russian]; Lyudmila Obraztsova [1960] Director/Businesswoman [Russian]

R Stanton-Gleaves UK Limited
Incorporated: 25 August 2015
Net Worth: £28,472,620 *Total Assets:* £29,330,048
Registered Office: 19-20 Bourne Court, Southend Road, Woodford Green, Essex, IG8 8HD
Activities: Activities of other holding companies n.e.c.
Major Shareholder: Robin James Stanton-Gleaves
Officers: Robin James Stanton-Gleaves [1968] Director

Staples (Vegetables) Limited
Incorporated: 19 February 1952 *Employees:* 1,109
Net Worth: £10,187,764 *Total Assets:* £38,513,044
Registered Office: Station Farm, Station Road, Sibsey, Boston, Lincs, PE22 0SE
Activities: Other processing and preserving of fruit and vegetables
Officers: Vernon Edward Read, Secretary; George Read [1970] Director/Vegetable Merchant and Haulier; Janet Read [1945] Director; Vernon Edward Read [1968] Director/Farm Manager

Staples Brothers Limited
Incorporated: 16 July 1956 *Employees:* 2
Net Worth: £27,432,988 *Total Assets:* £47,718,688
Registered Office: Station Farm, Sibsey, Boston, Lincs, PE22 0SE
Activities: Growing of vegetables and melons, roots and tubers
Officers: George Read, Secretary; George Read [1970] Director/Farm Manager; Vernon Edward Read [1968] Director/Farm Manager

Staples UK Limited
Incorporated: 29 August 1990 *Employees:* 361
Previous: Corporate Express Limited
Net Worth: £13,101,000 *Total Assets:* £38,789,000
Registered Office: Hampden Court, Kingsmead Business Park, Frederick Place, High Wycombe, Bucks, HP11 1JU
Activities: Non-specialised wholesale trade
Parent: Corporate Express (Holdings) Limited
Officers: Steven Mayes, Secretary; Lisa Cole [1976] Human Resources Director; Michael Celina Herman Henckaers [1983] Director [Belgian]; Steven Paul Mayes [1982] Director/Head of FP&A

Stapleton's (Tyre Services) Limited
Incorporated: 30 September 1937 *Employees:* 1,073
Net Worth: £31,352,000 *Total Assets:* £303,412,000
Registered Office: Fourth Avenue, Letchworth, Herts, SG6 2TT
Activities: Wholesale trade of motor vehicle parts and accessories
Parent: European Tyre Enterprise Ltd
Officers: Ian Vincent Ellis, Secretary; Wataru Goroku [1974] Director [Japanese]; Mark Lynott [1975] Director

Staploe Education Trust
Incorporated: 18 February 2011 *Employees:* 340
Net Worth: £37,200,212 *Total Assets:* £40,127,688
Registered Office: Soham Village College, Sand Street, Soham, Ely, Cambs, CB7 5AA
Activities: Pre-primary education
Officers: Lisa Jayne Tomlinson, Secretary; Anne Jeanette Bevan [1956] Director/Retired; Nicola Close [1951] Director/Public Health Manager; Dr James Stuart Humphrey [1970] Director/Editor; Christine Patricia Littlewood [1947] Director/Teacher; Lorraine Lofting [1957] Director/Retired; Ruth Mary McNaughton [1964] Director/Assertive Mentor; Cllr Joshua Maxwell Schumann [1986] Director/Councillor; David Andrew Snashall [1957] Director/Adviser Education; Dr Carin Jane Taylor [1964] Director/Executive Headteacher; Rev Colin William Watkins [1959] Director/Minister; Simon Paul Wright [1971] Director/Transport Manager (Railways)

Star Cargo PLC
Incorporated: 11 December 1984 *Employees:* 227
Net Worth: £15,540,113 *Total Assets:* £31,941,142
Registered Office: Star Cargo House, 1 Parkway, Porters Wood, St Albans, Herts, AL3 6PA
Activities: Activities of head offices
Major Shareholder: John Gwynne James
Officers: Alexander Robert Russell Hodgkinson, Secretary; Alistair James Caldwell [1969] Commercial Director; Alexander Robert Russell Hodgkinson [1982] Director/Chartered Accountant; John Gwynne James [1946] Director; Thomas Gwynne James [1976] Director

Starbones Limited
Incorporated: 6 February 2007
Net Worth Deficit: £2,989,096 *Total Assets:* £16,362,519
Registered Office: 3rd Floor, Sterling House, Langston Road, Loughton, Essex, IG10 3TS
Activities: Development of building projects
Parent: GDL (Chiswick) LLP
Officers: Allan William Porter, Secretary; Edward Azouz [1949] Director/Chartered Accountant; Jeffrey Azouz [1947] Director/Chartered Surveyor; John Cole [1971] Director; Stephen Stuart Solomon Conway [1948] Director; Jonathan Simon Goldstein [1966] Director; Kim Alexander Gottlieb [1957] Director/Surveyor; Donagh O'Sullivan [1968] Construction Director [Irish]

Starbridge Property Investment Limited
Incorporated: 4 July 2016
Net Worth: £2,762,928 *Total Assets:* £35,278,976
Registered Office: 3c Twyford Court, High Street, Dunmow, Essex, CM6 1AE
Activities: Management of real estate on a fee or contract basis
Parent: SGN Limited
Officers: Matthew Simon Copland, Secretary; Graham Frederick Peacock [1950] Director; Susan Margaret Tobbell [1952] Director

Starglade Parks Limited
Incorporated: 20 December 2005 *Employees:* 2
Net Worth: £5,597,123 *Total Assets:* £8,391,390
Registered Office: 2b Highstone House, 165 High Street, Barnet, Herts, EN5 5SU
Activities: Construction of domestic buildings
Major Shareholder: Royston Cooper
Officers: Royston Cooper [1967] Director

Starke Industries Limited
Incorporated: 7 July 2016 *Employees:* 57
Net Worth: £6,927,242 *Total Assets:* £15,439,765
Registered Office: Chestnut Farm, Langton Green, Eye, Suffolk, IP23 7HL
Activities: Wholesale of other food, including fish, crustaceans and molluscs
Major Shareholder: Edward James Bruce Starke
Officers: Tracey Clark [1972] Director; Edward James Bruce Starke [1971] Director

Start-Rite Shoes Limited
Incorporated: 17 June 1915 *Employees:* 68
Net Worth: £8,388,000 *Total Assets:* £14,050,000
Registered Office: Start-Rite Shoes Ltd, Peachman Way, Broadland Business Park, Norwich, NR7 0WF
Activities: Agents involved in the sale of textiles, clothing, fur, footwear and leather goods
Parent: James Southall & Company Limited
Officers: Johanna Westaway, Secretary; Peter James Lamble [1961] Director; Kate Tansley [1977] Director

Startling Music Limited
Incorporated: 15 July 1968 *Employees:* 1
Net Worth: £16,371,089 *Total Assets:* £16,666,777
Registered Office: 5 Elstree Gate, Elstree Way, Borehamwood, Herts, WD6 1JD
Activities: Sound recording and music publishing activities
Parent: Cornwall
Officers: Bruce Victor Grakal [1940] Director [American]; Graham David Hill [1946] Director/Self Employed

Stat Marine Limited
Incorporated: 30 March 1993 *Employees:* 83
Net Worth: £8,499,510 *Total Assets:* £12,380,829
Registered Office: Premier Suite, 4 Churchill Court, 58 Station Road, North Harrow, Middlesex, HA2 7ST
Activities: Other professional, scientific and technical activities n.e.c.
Parent: Stat Holding International Limited
Officers: Darren Michael Love, Secretary; Luc Guy Delclos [1964] Director/Engineer [French]; Guy Rene Facon [1958] Director [French]; Jerome Samson Raffaelli [1962] Director [French]

Station Road Developments (Cambridge) Limited
Incorporated: 25 January 2005
Net Worth Deficit: £1,750,288 *Total Assets:* £34,554,668
Registered Office: The Tamburlaine, 27-29 Station Road, Cambridge, CB1 2FB
Activities: Construction of commercial buildings
Officers: Noel O'Callaghan, Secretary/Accountant [Irish]; Bryan O'Callaghan [1983] Director/Administrator [Irish]; Charles O'Callaghan [1989] Director [Irish]; Noel O'Callaghan [1949] Director/Accountant [Irish]; Paul O'Callaghan [1985] Director [Irish]

Epic Staunton LLP
Incorporated: 17 July 2012
Net Worth: £18,742,140 *Total Assets:* £27,515,298
Registered Office: Ley Farm, Stetchworth Ley, Stetchworth, Newmarket, Suffolk, CB8 9TX

Stebbings Car Centre Limited
Incorporated: 13 January 2003 *Employees:* 57
Net Worth: £6,046,990 *Total Assets:* £10,072,947
Registered Office: 1 Claydon Business Park, Great Blakenham, Ipswich, Suffolk, IP6 0NL
Activities: Sale of used cars and light motor vehicles
Parent: Garnham Management Services Limited
Officers: Derek William Rayner, Secretary; Richard David Brown [1980] Director; Anthony Philip Skerry [1969] Director; Katherine Anna Skerry [1972] Director/Car Retailer

Stefanini International Holdings Ltd
Incorporated: 7 December 2009 *Employees:* 7,271
Net Worth: £41,418,792 *Total Assets:* £134,697,600
Registered Office: Jubilee House, 3 The Drive, Brentwood, Essex, CM13 3FR
Activities: Information technology consultancy activities
Shareholders: Marc Antonio Silva Stefanini; Maria Das Gracas Vuolo Sajovic Stefanini
Officers: Christopher Mourad [1973] Director [American]; Marco Antonio Silva Stefanini [1960] Director/Businessman [Brazilian]; Maria Das Gracas Vuolo Sajovic Stefanini [1959] Director/Businesswomen [Brazilian]

Steiner UK Limited
Incorporated: 24 September 2009 *Employees:* 3
Net Worth Deficit: £6,617,531 *Total Assets:* £9,136,322
Registered Office: The Lodge, 92 Uxbridge Road, Harrow Weald, Middlesex, HA3 6DQ
Activities: Activities of head offices
Parent: Nemo (UK) Holdco, Ltd.
Officers: Robert Boehm, Secretary [American]; Michael Stephan Haringman, Secretary; Michael Stephan Haringman [1944] Director/Solicitor; Marc Magliacano [1974] Director/Investor [American]; Robert Barry John Schaverien [1964] Managing Director

Stellison Limited
Incorporated: 12 December 1962 *Employees:* 109
Net Worth: £5,788,405 *Total Assets:* £8,811,118
Registered Office: 2nd Floor, Boundary House, 4 County Place, Chelmsford, Essex, CM2 0RE
Activities: Retail sale of electrical household appliances in specialised stores
Officers: Brenda Joyce Scogings, Secretary; Brenda Joyce Scogings [1941] Director; Mark Richard Scogings [1963] Director; Steven Anthony Scogings [1972] Joint Managing Director

Stema Shipping (UK) Limited
Incorporated: 11 January 1995 *Employees:* 25
Net Worth: £2,669,259 *Total Assets:* £20,056,992
Registered Office: Alexandra House, Waterfront, Lakeside, Grays, Essex, RM20 1WL
Activities: Other business support service activities n.e.c.
Parent: Stema Shipping A/S
Officers: Martin Berby Johansen, Secretary; Claus Boisen [1981] Director [Danish]; Martin Berby Johansen [1973] Managing Director [Norwegian]

Step 6 Ltd
Incorporated: 20 September 2012
Net Worth: £5,807,950 *Total Assets:* £8,658,125
Registered Office: Hall Farm, Babingley, King's Lynn, Norfolk, PE31 6AW
Activities: Buying and selling of own real estate
Major Shareholder: Raymond Daniel Assirati
Officers: Raymond Daniel Assirati [1944] Director/Property Investor

The Stephen Perse Foundation
Incorporated: 19 February 2007 *Employees:* 215
Net Worth: £13,558,628 *Total Assets:* £35,345,776
Registered Office: The Stephen Perse Foundation, Union Road, Cambridge, CB2 1HF
Activities: General secondary education
Officers: Jennifer Susanne Neild, Secretary; Dr Claire Yvonne Barlow [1954] Director/University Lecturer; Victor Christou [1966] Senior Investment Director; John Tannatt Dix [1961] Director/Bursar; Dr Michelle Ellefson [1973] Director/University Senior Lecturer [American]; Dr Robert David Foale [1970] Director/Veterinary Surgeon; David Edwin Gill [1959] Managing Director; Beryl Gillispie [1957] Director/Head of Older People's Services; Prof Christopher Jiggins [1971] Director/Prof of Evolutionary Biology; Dr Gordon Johnson [1943] Director/Retired Academic; Dr Duncan James Needham [1973] Director/Senior Tutor; Suzanne Marie Oliver [1973] Director/Patent Attorney; Katherine Antonia Ollerenshaw [1971] Director/Lawyer; Alison Margaret Powell [1954] Director/Fund Manager; Dr Hugh Shercliff [1962] Director/Engineer; Dr Jacqueline Tasioulas [1968] Director/University Lecturer; Dr Annette Christina Thomas [1965] Director/Publisher; Sven Jurgen Topel [1966] Director/Chief Executive; Duncan Edward Walker [1968] Director/Solicitor

Stephensons of Essex Limited
Incorporated: 14 May 1984 *Employees:* 2
Net Worth: £7,099,456 *Total Assets:* £11,763,189
Registered Office: Monometer House, Rectory Grove, Leigh on Sea, Essex, SS9 2HN
Activities: Other passenger land transport
Parent: Eastern Transport Holdings Limited
Officers: Gary John Raven, Secretary; William Hiron [1963] Director; Gary John Raven [1967] Director/Chartered Accountant

Steria UK Corporate Limited
Incorporated: 27 January 1971
Net Worth: £181,152,000 *Total Assets:* £222,722,000
Registered Office: Three Cherry Trees Lane, Hemel Hempstead, Herts, HP2 7AH
Activities: Information technology consultancy activities
Parent: Sopra Steria Group SA
Officers: Peter Cashmore, Secretary; Davinder Singh Ahluwalia [1952] Director; John Joseph Moran [1961] Director, Corporate Finance; John Powell Torrie [1954] Director

H.Stern (Jewellery) Limited
Incorporated: 12 May 1964 *Employees:* 9
Net Worth Deficit: £162,468 *Total Assets:* £8,128,656
Registered Office: York House, Empire Way, Wembley, Middlesex, HA9 0FQ
Activities: Retail sale of watches and jewellery in specialised stores
Major Shareholder: Ruth Stern
Officers: Liu Loo Ly de Oliveira, Secretary; Liu Loo Ly de Oliveira [1955] Director [Chinese]; Oscar Luiz Goldemberg [1956] Director [Brazilian]

Sterndale Systems Limited
Incorporated: 17 December 1992 *Employees:* 1
Net Worth: £10,570,879 *Total Assets:* £14,628,791
Registered Office: Batchworth House, Batchworth Place, Church Street, Rickmansworth, Herts, WD3 1JE
Activities: Other letting and operating of own or leased real estate
Major Shareholder: Peter Nicholas Kopik
Officers: John Kopik, Secretary; Peter Nicholas Kopik [1954] Director/Architect [Irish]

Stevenage Bioscience Catalyst
Incorporated: 19 March 2010 *Employees:* 16
Net Worth Deficit: £319,802 *Total Assets:* £29,295,452
Registered Office: Stevenage Bioscience Catalyst, Gunnels Wood Road, Stevenage, Herts, SG1 2FX
Activities: Other business support service activities n.e.c.
Officers: Dave Allen [1959] Director/Senior Vice President and Therapy Area Head; Dr Veronique Anne Bouchet [1959] Founder Director Novudel Associates [French/British]; Dr Sally Ann Forsyth [1962] Director; Ian Michael Tomlinson [1969] Director/Pharmaceuticals Executive

Stevenage Road Residential Developments Limited
Incorporated: 17 November 2011
Net Worth Deficit: £95,397 *Total Assets:* £15,998,236
Registered Office: 87a High Street, The Old Town, Hemel Hempstead, Herts, HP1 3AH
Activities: Development of building projects
Parent: Galileo Homes Limited
Officers: Frances Heather Carey [1952] Director

Stewards Academy Trust
Incorporated: 12 September 2011 *Employees:* 172
Net Worth: £6,127,172 *Total Assets:* £11,041,368
Registered Office: Stewards Academy Trust, Parnall Road, Harlow, Essex, CM18 7NQ
Activities: General secondary education
Officers: Alison Mary Avis, Secretary; Jeannette Sarah Baldwin [1968] Director; Andrew Patrick Bower [1957] Director/Building Control Surveyor; Stephen Robert Dodd [1961] Director/Sales and Marketing; Helen Alison Ginger [1969] Director/Headteacher; Dr David William Guest [1952] Director/Senior Civil Servant; Paul Michael Hickman [1974] Director/Teacher (Secondary); Brian Edward Moldon [1972] Director; Sarah Nelmes [1980] Director/Teacher; Sandra Jayne Oliver [1965] Director/Senior IT Service Manager; Karen Jane Rushbrooke [1970] Director/Personal Assistant; Jeffrey Victor Tarling [1946] Director/Retired Quality Manager

Stirling Civil Engineering Limited
Incorporated: 14 October 1963
Net Worth: £8,468,000 *Total Assets:* £18,700,000
Registered Office: 310 Harrow Road, Wembley, Middlesex, HA9 6LL
Activities: Development of building projects
Parent: Hadden Shipping Limited
Officers: Sudhir Bhatt [1956] Director [Kenyan]; Maurice Mathias de Souza [1943] Director/Contracts Manager [Kenyan]; Gilbert Josiah Mungu [1962] Director [Kenyan]; Pragnesh Jitendra Patel [1970] Director; Jonathan Reading [1962] Director/Artist; Guiseppe Sabatini [1942] Director/Civil Servant [Italian]; Ashu Tosh Sharma [1969] Director; Gennaro Sirgiovanni [1950] Director [Italian]

Stock Finance (Koruna) Limited
Incorporated: 10 October 2013
Net Worth: £28,622,324 *Total Assets:* £28,645,654
Registered Office: Solar House, Mercury Park, Wooburn Green, Bucks, HP10 0HH
Activities: Financial intermediation not elsewhere classified
Parent: Stock Spirits (UK) Limited
Officers: Sally Kenward, Secretary; Raj Paul Singh Bal [1967] Director/Chief Financial Officer; Steven Colin Weatherley [1968] Director/Lawyer

Stock Spirits (UK) Limited
Incorporated: 20 June 2007 *Employees:* 15
Net Worth: £197,630,000 *Total Assets:* £216,776,992
Registered Office: Solar House, Mercury Park, Wooburn Green, Bucks, HP10 0HH
Activities: Activities of other holding companies n.e.c.
Parent: Stock Spirits Group PLC
Officers: Sally Kenward, Secretary; Raj Paul Singh Bal [1967] Director/Chief Financial Officer; Steven Colin Weatherley [1968] Director/Lawyer

Stock Spirits Group PLC
Incorporated: 12 September 2013 *Employees:* 1,003
Net Worth: £307,561,408 *Total Assets:* £548,683,712
Registered Office: Solar House, Mercury Park, Wooburn Green, Bucks, HP10 0HH
Activities: Activities of head offices
Officers: Sally Kenward, Secretary; Helen Catherine Allum [1965] Director; Raj Paul Singh Bal [1967] Director/Chief Financial Officer; Diego Bevilacqua [1953] Director; Tomasz Wojciech Blawat [1966] Director [Polish]; Michael Guy Butterworth [1961] Director; David Ossian Maloney [1955] Director; John Ross Nicolson [1953] Director; Miroslaw Stachowicz [1962] Director/Chief Executive Officer [Polish]

Stockplace Hartford Ltd
Incorporated: 27 February 2014 *Employees:* 5
Net Worth: £905,476 *Total Assets:* £8,451,924
Registered Office: Mill House, Barn Mill Lane, Hartford End, Chelmsford, Essex, CM3 1JZ
Activities: Development of building projects
Shareholders: Barry Norman Mather; Tanya Jane Mather
Officers: Barry Norman Mather [1949] Director; Tanya Jane Mather [1961] Director/Business Manager

Stockplace Investments Limited
Incorporated: 23 February 2004 *Employees:* 29
Net Worth: £17,891,114 *Total Assets:* £30,712,906
Registered Office: Mill House, Barn Mill Lane, Hartford End, Chelmsford, Essex, CM3 1JZ
Activities: Development of building projects
Major Shareholder: Barry Norman Mather
Officers: Tanya Jane Mather, Secretary; Barry Norman Mather [1949] Director/Property Developer

Stockvale Investments Limited
Incorporated: 4 December 2008 *Employees:* 484
Net Worth: £16,271,946 *Total Assets:* £20,948,290
Registered Office: 7 Nelson Street, Southend on Sea, Essex, SS1 1EH
Activities: Activities of other holding companies n.e.c.
Major Shareholder: Philip Aaron Miller
Officers: Maxine Kim Bean [1956] Finance Director; Marc Jonathan Miller [1973] Director/Company Secretary; Philip Aaron Miller [1955] Director

Stockvale Limited
Incorporated: 6 April 1976 *Employees:* 265
Net Worth: £18,273,876 *Total Assets:* £22,371,544
Registered Office: 7 Nelson Street, Southend on Sea, Essex, SS1 1EH
Activities: Activities of amusement parks and theme parks
Parent: Stockvale Investments Limited
Officers: Marc Jonathan Miller, Company Secretary; Maxine Kim Bean [1956] Finance Director; James Miller [1981] Director; Marc Jonathan Miller [1973] Director/Company Secretary; Philip Aaron Miller [1955] Director/Fairground Operator

Stody Estate Limited
Incorporated: 7 November 1941 *Employees:* 23
Net Worth: £6,135,741 *Total Assets:* £8,944,074
Registered Office: Platinum Building, St Johns Innovation Park, Cowley Road, Cambridge, CB4 0DS
Activities: Growing of cereals (except rice), leguminous crops and oil seeds
Officers: Kate Nancy Doone MacNicol, Secretary; Adel Jean MacNicol [1949] Director; Charles Richmond MacNicol [1980] Managing Director

The Stoke By Nayland Club Ltd.
Incorporated: 14 February 1973 *Employees:* 154
Net Worth: £3,903,548 *Total Assets:* £15,482,543
Registered Office: Stoke by Nayland Golf Club Ltd, Keepers Lane, Leavenheath, Colchester, Essex, CO6 4PZ
Activities: Operation of sports facilities
Officers: Jonathan Loshak, Secretary; Andrew William Cracknell [1963] Director/Accountant; Jonathan Loshak [1944] Director; Matthew Gary Manning [1977] Director/Project Manager; Susanna Peake Rendall [1954] Director; Tamara Clare Unwin [1956] Director

Stonebond Properties Limited
Incorporated: 1 April 2005 *Employees:* 6
Net Worth: £6,570,183 *Total Assets:* £16,312,428
Registered Office: Aquila House, Waterloo Lane, Chelmsford, Essex, CM1 1BN
Activities: Other business support service activities n.e.c.
Shareholders: Graham Stewart Cherry; Richard Stephen Cherry
Officers: Graham Stewart Cherry, Secretary; Christophe Weedon, Secretary; Graham Stewart Cherry [1959] Director; Richard Stephen Cherry [1961] Director; Christopher Paul Weedon [1962] Director

Stonegate Pub Company Financing PLC
Incorporated: 19 March 2014
Net Worth: £50,000 *Total Assets:* £595,761,024
Registered Office: Porter Tun House, 500 Capability Green, Luton, Beds, LU1 3LS
Activities: Other business support service activities n.e.c.
Parent: TDR Capital LLP
Officers: Helen Frances Harvey, Secretary; Simon David Longbottom [1971] Director/Chief Executive Officer; Ian Timothy Payne [1953] Director/Company Chairman; David Andrew Ross [1973] Director/Accountant

Stonemanor Limited
Incorporated: 13 September 2002 *Employees:* 238
Net Worth: £7,905,040 *Total Assets:* £15,797,151
Registered Office: Suite 2, Fountain House, 1a Elm Park, Stanmore, Middlesex, HA7 4AU
Activities: Retail sale of clothing in specialised stores
Major Shareholder: Philip Michael Chaimo
Officers: Hugh Kelly, Secretary/Retail; Philip Michael Chaimo [1960] Director/Buyer

Stonewater Capital Limited
Incorporated: 26 June 1997
Previous: Singh Construction Limited
Net Worth: £5,225,241 *Total Assets:* £14,356,649
Registered Office: 10 Station Road, Letchworth Garden City, Herts, SG6 3AU
Activities: Buying and selling of own real estate
Major Shareholder: Kuldip Singh
Officers: Kuldip Singh, Secretary/Construction Supervisor; Kuldip Singh [1966] Director/Construction Supervisor

Stonewater Enterprises Limited
Incorporated: 16 March 2015
Net Worth: £6,818,372 *Total Assets:* £14,599,352
Registered Office: 10 Station Road, Letchworth Garden City, Herts, SG6 3AU
Activities: Activities of other holding companies n.e.c.
Major Shareholder: Kuldip Singh
Officers: Balvinder Kaur, Secretary; Kuldip Singh [1966] Director

Storm Technologies Limited
Incorporated: 22 May 2000 *Employees:* 138
Net Worth: £2,368,221 *Total Assets:* £21,701,044
Registered Office: 2 The Boulevard, Blackmoor Lane, Croxley Business Park, Watford, Herts, WD18 8YW
Activities: Other information technology service activities
Parent: Storm Technologies Group Limited
Officers: Soraya Brooker, Secretary; John Robert Brooker [1967] Director; Randers Manuel Marquis [1970] Director/Accountant; Trevor John Nickolls [1975] Sales Director; Mark Raymond Smith [1973] Operations Director; Nicholas Marc Umney [1979] Software Sales Director

Stortford Interiors (UK) Limited
Incorporated: 5 February 1992 *Employees:* 70
Net Worth: £2,104,033 *Total Assets:* £8,736,838
Registered Office: Stortford House, 231 London Road, Bishop's Stortford, Herts, CM23 3LA
Activities: Other construction installation
Major Shareholder: James Phiroze Nania
Officers: Steven Harvey [1967] Joinery Director; James Phiroze Nania [1954] Managing Director; Scott Francis Shearing [1977] Director; James Joseph Sheehan [1979] Director/Quantity Surveyor [Irish]

Stourgarden Limited
Incorporated: 9 March 1995 *Employees:* 184
Net Worth: £9,705,217 *Total Assets:* £12,150,241
Registered Office: Lodge Farm, Gt Horkesley, Colchester, Essex, CO6 4AP
Activities: Wholesale of fruit and vegetables
Shareholders: John Gordon Rix; William Howard Rix
Officers: Generald Farrow, Secretary; George Peter Rix [1987] Director/Manager; Samuel John Rix [1989] Director/Technologist; William Howard Rix [1960] Director/Farmer

Stratton Education Trust
Incorporated: 5 October 2011 *Employees:* 190
Net Worth: £16,282,318 *Total Assets:* £19,305,306
Registered Office: Stratton Education Trust, Eagle Farm Road, Biggleswade, Beds, SG18 8JB
Activities: Other education n.e.c.
Officers: Dr Christian Gerhard Glenister Boehmer [1978] Director/Associate Professor in Mathematics [German]; Edward John Kane [1964] Director/Accountant; Madeline Ann Russell [1951] Director/Retired; Richard John Westergreen-Thorne [1951] Director/Retired

Stratton Hall Farms Limited
Incorporated: 10 December 2010 *Employees:* 3
Net Worth: £68,180 *Total Assets:* £8,704,966
Registered Office: Stratton Hall, Levington, Ipswich, Suffolk, IP10 0LL
Activities: Growing of cereals (except rice), leguminous crops and oil seeds
Major Shareholder: Christopher George Mayhew
Officers: Christopher George Mayhew [1956] Director; Nicola Anne Mayhew [1958] Director

Strauss Logistics Limited
Incorporated: 16 August 2005 *Employees:* 3
Net Worth: £938,718 *Total Assets:* £15,744,729
Registered Office: 31 Godfrey Crescent, Takeley, Essex, CM22 6FU
Activities: Wholesale of petroleum and petroleum products
Officers: Dipak Pandya, Secretary; Nita Bhagat [1967] Director; Kunjan Pandya [1959] Director

Streamadvice Limited
Incorporated: 20 January 2003 *Employees:* 6
Net Worth: £5,716,006 *Total Assets:* £11,524,590
Registered Office: 46-54 High Street, Ingatestone, Essex, CM4 9DW
Activities: Development of building projects
Shareholders: David Brian Sparks; Sarah Sparks
Officers: Christopher Matthew Lineham, Secretary; Christopher Matthew Lineham [1970] Director; David Brian Sparks [1971] Director

Paul Strickland Scanner Centre
Incorporated: 3 July 1986 *Employees:* 56
Net Worth: £11,655,830 *Total Assets:* £13,635,338
Registered Office: Paul Strickland Scanner Centre, Rickmansworth Road, Northwood, Middlesex, HA6 2RN
Activities: Hospital activities
Officers: Catherine Ruth Williams, Secretary; Dr Roberto Alonzi [1973] Director/Doctor; Patrick John Kelly [1949] Director/Banker [Irish]; Dilip Manek [1953] Director of Finance [Indian]; Daniel Jonathan Ross [1964] Director/Chief Executive; Palvi Shah [1961] Executive Director and Assistant General Council; Catherine Ruth Williams [1959] Director/Retired NHS Manager and Therapy Radiographer; Dr Terence Richard Wright [1945] Director/Self Employed Business Consultant

Strides Arcolab International Ltd
Incorporated: 10 November 2004 *Employees:* 1
Net Worth: £19,537,040 *Total Assets:* £48,504,460
Registered Office: Unit 4 Metro Centre, Tolpits Lane, Watford, Herts, WD18 9SS
Activities: Other business support service activities n.e.c.
Officers: Vikesh Kumar [1984] Director/Service [Indian]; Krishnan Tirucherai Parthasarathy [1971] Director [Indian]; Mohana Kumar Pillai [1956] Director/Service [Indian]; Rajasekar Visvanathan [1961] Director/Service

Strides Pharma Global (UK) Ltd
Incorporated: 29 July 2015 *Employees:* 2
Net Worth: £16,483,671 *Total Assets:* £20,348,244
Registered Office: Unit 4 Metro Centre, Tolpits Lane, Watford, Herts, WD18 9SS
Activities: Wholesale of pharmaceutical goods
Parent: Strides Arcolab International Limited
Officers: Vikesh Kumar [1984] Director/Service [Indian]; Krishnan Tirucherai Parthasarathy [1971] Director [Indian]; Mohana Kumar Pillai [1956] Director [Indian]

Strongholding Limited
Incorporated: 9 March 2016
Net Worth Deficit: £413,016 *Total Assets:* £9,400,342
Registered Office: 2nd Floor, Unicorn House, Station Close, Potters Bar, Herts, EN6 1TL
Activities: Other letting and operating of own or leased real estate
Parent: Apexbrook Limited
Officers: David Samuel Harouni [1977] Director; Jeremiah Harouni [1949] Director

Structural Holdings and Consultancy Limited
Incorporated: 22 March 1993 *Employees:* 3
Net Worth: £4,778,250 *Total Assets:* £8,468,009
Registered Office: 20b Upstairs, Diss Business Park, Hopper Way, Sandy Lane, Diss, Norfolk, IP22 4GT
Activities: Other letting and operating of own or leased real estate
Major Shareholder: Joe Read
Officers: Louise Claire Read, Secretary/Telesales; Joseph Read [1955] Director

Strutt and Parker (Farms),Limited
Incorporated: 8 October 1918 *Employees:* 67
Net Worth: £49,260,000 *Total Assets:* £97,179,000
Registered Office: 1 Whitbreads Business Centre, Whitbreads Farm Lane, Chatham Green, Chelmsford, Essex, CM3 3FE
Activities: Growing of cereals (except rice), leguminous crops and oil seeds
Officers: Peter Richard Wood, Secretary; Aubrey James Francis Buxton [1956] Director/Chartered Surveyor; The Right Honourable Lord de Ramsey [1942] Director/Farmer; Charles Oswald Fillingham [1960] Director/Farmer; Michael Anthony Hughes [1964] Director; Christopher Maton [1966] Director/Accountant; David Anthony Nutting [1944] Director/Farmer; Peter Robert Jolliffe Tritton [1951] Director/Retired; Stuart Richard Wallis [1980] Director/Chartered Accountant; Duncan Richard Worth [1965] Director/Farmer

Stuart Group Limited
Incorporated: 24 March 1987 *Employees:* 91
Net Worth: £6,028,881 *Total Assets:* £14,114,177
Registered Office: King Street House, 15 Upper King Street, Norwich, NR3 1RB
Activities: Other specialised construction activities n.e.c.
Parent: Shropham Holdings Limited
Officers: John David Sayer, Secretary; Nigel Terence Hood [1968] Director/Certified Accountant; Alison Paula Sayer [1965] Director; John David Sayer [1956] Director/Biochemist; Stewart Sayer [1957] Director; Rodney James Tebble [1965] Director/Engineer; Russell Tregent [1961] Rental Fleet Director; David Ralph Wright [1967] Director/Groundwater Engineer

Subex (UK) Limited
Incorporated: 30 March 2001 *Employees:* 47
Net Worth: £2,722,000 *Total Assets:* £12,333,000
Registered Office: First Floor, Rama, 17 St Anns Road, Harrow, Middlesex, HA1 1JU
Activities: Other software publishing
Officers: Anil Chandanmal Singhvi [1959] Director [Indian]; Venkataraman Gopalasamudram Srinivasan [1969] Director [Indian]; Vinod Kumar Padmanabhan [1970] Director/Service [Indian]

Subway Realty Limited
Incorporated: 7 March 2001 *Employees:* 38
Net Worth: £4,337,408 *Total Assets:* £10,713,355
Registered Office: Chaston House, Mill Court, Great Shelford, Cambridge, CB22 5LD
Activities: Activities of head offices
Officers: John Devine, Secretary/President SREC [American]; John Devine [1959] Director/President SREC [American]; Ernest Oliver [1961] Director/Leasing Manager [American]; Matthew Whelan [1958] Director/International Leasing Specialist [American]; David S Worroll [1958] Director/Controller [American]

J.W. Suckling Transport Limited
Incorporated: 30 January 1974 *Employees:* 250
Net Worth: £6,302,614 *Total Assets:* £18,013,616
Registered Office: 12 Argent Court, Sylvan Way, Southfields Business Park, Laindon, Essex, SS15 6TH
Activities: Freight transport by road
Officers: Fabio Gargioni, Secretary; Barbara Bertani [1975] Director/Manager [Italian]; Jesus Ciria [1967] Director/Manager [Spanish]; Danilo Delledonne [1961] Director/Manager [Italian]; Alan Christopher Dodson [1975] Director/Certified Accountant; Fabio Gargioni [1968] Director/Manager [Italian]; Marco Magnani [1978] Director [Italian]

Suez Water Technologies & Solutions Services UK Limited
Incorporated: 13 February 2004
Previous: GE Mobile Water Limited
Net Worth: £17,546,000 *Total Assets:* £18,932,000
Registered Office: Hydrohouse, Newcombe Way, Orton Southgate, Peterborough, Cambs, PE2 6SE
Activities: Water collection, treatment and supply
Parent: Ionics Ventures Limited
Officers: Ana Rita Dias [1980] Director/Engineering Senior Leader [Portuguese]; Simon Gare [1975] Director/Commercial Engineering Leader, Mobile & Outsource; Jon Paul Hunt [1971] Director; Alexander Charles Ian Stewart [1964] Director

Suffolk Academies Trust
Incorporated: 24 July 2015 *Employees:* 218
Net Worth: £28,265,468 *Total Assets:* £32,306,888
Registered Office: West Suffolk College, Out Risbygate, Bury St Edmunds, Suffolk, IP33 3RL
Activities: General secondary education
Officers: Stephen Clarke [1955] Director/Retired; Elton Francis Louis D'Souza [1960] Contract Director; Susan Rose Daley [1956] Director/Retired; Dr James Gazzard [1975] Director; Sarah Rachel Healey Pearce [1974] Director/Chartered Accountant; Professor Christopher Francis Higgins [1955] Director/Retired (Emeritus Professor); Sarah Howard [1967] Director/President Suffolk Chamber of Commerce; Alan John Maltpress [1938] Director/Retired; Karen Wendy Points [1960] Strategic Director; Christopher David Ridgeon [1963] Director/Accountant; Dr Nikos Savvas [1970] Director/Principal; Julia Wakelam [1952] Director/Mayor of St Edmundsbury; Deborah Elizabeth Wildridge [1953] Director/Manager

Suffolk Agricultural Association
Incorporated: 6 December 1983 *Employees:* 53
Net Worth: £11,507,052 *Total Assets:* £12,688,146
Registered Office: Trinity Park, Felixstowe Road, Ipswich, Suffolk, IP3 8UH
Activities: Other education n.e.c.
Officers: Robert James Baker [1963] Director/Farmer; Sally Ann Bendall [1961] Managing Director; Elizabeth Jane Kemball [1968] Director; Jonathan Lawsell Edward Long [1960] Director/Solicitor; Eric Charles Morton [1955] Director; David Nunn [1954] Director/Farmer; Peter David Over [1962] Director/Farmer; Karen Sharpe [1958] Director/Chartered Accountant; Simon Patrick Tucker [1960] Director/Chartered Accountant

Suffolk Community Foundation
Incorporated: 18 February 2005 *Employees:* 14
Net Worth: £14,861,375 *Total Assets:* £15,811,808
Registered Office: The Old Barns, Peninsula Business Centre, Wherstead, Ipswich, Suffolk, IP9 2BB
Activities: Other business support service activities n.e.c.
Officers: Mandy Jane Abdel-Aziz, Secretary; Jonathan George Shelton Agar [1971] Director/Chief Executive; James Kennedy Buckle [1964] Director/Farmer; Susan Valerie Gull [1962] Director/Chartered Accountant; The Hon Selina Hopkins [1973] Director/Entrepreneur/Hypnotherapist; David Edward Hughes [1960] Director; Iain David Jamie [1977] Director; William Bruce Kendall [1961] Director; Peter George Newnham [1950] Director/Business Consultant; Louisa Catherine Pepper [1967] Director/Retired; George Moubray William Vestey [1964] Director/Chief Executive Officer; Neil Roderick Walmsley [1966] Director/Solicitor; Terence Alan Ward [1952] Director/Retired

Suffolk Life Annuities Limited
Incorporated: 19 May 1971 *Employees:* 6
Net Worth: £2,351,000 *Total Assets:* £3,663,960,064
Registered Office: 153 Princes Street, Ipswich, Suffolk, IP1 1QJ
Activities: Life insurance
Parent: Suffolk Life Group Limited
Officers: Renata Angela Karolina Chester, Secretary; Renata Angela Karolina Chester [1968] Director/Chartered Accountant; Greg Kingston [1972] Director; Jane Ann Ridgley [1968] Operations Director; Nigel Trevor Rodgers [1978] Change Director; William Arthur Self [1982] Director; Ian Charles Stone [1976] Director; Paul James Tarran [1956] Director/Chartered Accountant

Suffolk Life Pensions Limited
Incorporated: 14 August 1974 *Employees:* 302
Net Worth: £10,409,000 *Total Assets:* £17,288,000
Registered Office: 153 Princes Street, Ipswich, Suffolk, IP1 1QJ
Activities: Other activities auxiliary to insurance and pension funding
Parent: Suffolk Life Group Limited
Officers: Renata Angela Karolina Chester, Secretary; Renata Angela Karolina Chester [1968] Director/Chartered Accountant; Greg Kingston [1972] Director; Jane Ann Ridgley [1968] Operations Director; Nigel Trevor Rodgers [1978] Change Director; William Arthur Self [1982] Director; Ian Charles Stone [1976] Director; Paul James Tarran [1956] Director/Chartered Accountant

Suffolk Wildlife Trust Limited
Incorporated: 13 June 1961 *Employees:* 73
Net Worth: £16,468,000 *Total Assets:* £17,258,000
Registered Office: Brooke House, The Green, Ashbocking, Ipswich, Suffolk, IP6 9JY
Activities: Botanical and zoological gardens and nature reserves activities
Officers: David Bryony Alborough [1967] Director/Property Manager; James Matthew William Alexander [1969] Director/Consultant; John Cousins [1953] Director/Farmer; Rachel Jane Eburne [1966] Director/Councillor; Nigel Charles Farthing [1955] Director/Solicitor; Philippa Goodwin [1963] Director/Volunteer; Peter Holborn [1952] Director/Head of Environment; Stephanie Rae Jones [1988] Director/Environment Strategy Officer; Philip John Newton [1966] Director; Simon Roberts [1948] Director/Management Consultant/Farmer; Anna Cordelia Saltmarsh [1975] Director/Biodiversity Project Management

Sumatra Copper & Gold PLC
Incorporated: 11 April 2006 *Employees:* 435
Net Worth Deficit: £19,249,718 *Total Assets:* £40,463,276
Registered Office: 39 Parkside, Cambridge, CB1 1PN
Activities: Mining of other non-ferrous metal ores
Officers: Susan Patricia Hunter, Secretary; Gavin Arnold Caudle [1968] Director [Australian]; David Fowler [1966] Director/Accountant [Australian]; Andrew Coyne Robb [1952] Director/Mining Engineer; Adi Adriansyah Sjoekri [1965] Director [Indonesian]; Jocelyn Severyn Waller [1943] Director

Sumitomo Electric Europe Limited
Incorporated: 29 February 1996 *Employees:* 46
Net Worth: £7,014,000 *Total Assets:* £43,287,000
Registered Office: Unit 220 Centennial Avenue, Centennial Park, Elstree Hill South, Elstree, Borehamwood, Herts, WD6 3SL
Activities: Wholesale of electronic and telecommunications equipment and parts
Parent: Sumitomo Electric Industries Limited
Officers: Koji Kimura, Secretary; Koji Kimura [1969] Director [Japanese]; Eizo Mitani [1961] Director/General Manager - Electron Devices [Japanese]; Yasuyuki Shibata [1964] Director [Japanese]; Masakazu Watanabe [1961] Managing Director [Japanese]

Summerhill Birmingham Limited
Incorporated: 11 September 2017
Net Worth Deficit: £36,330 *Total Assets:* £14,644,183
Registered Office: 3rd Floor, Sterling House, Langston Road, Loughton, Essex, IG10 3TS
Activities: Development of building projects
Shareholders: Galliard Holdings Limited; Apsley House Capital PLC
Officers: Allan William Porter, Secretary; Stephen Stuart Solomon Conway [1948] Director; Gerard Nock [1947] Director/Company Chairman; Carl Robin Norstrom [1984] Director [Swedish]; Donagh O'Sullivan [1968] Construction Director [Irish]

Sunlight PV Ltd
Incorporated: 17 October 2007
Net Worth: £26,473,280 *Total Assets:* £29,480,514
Registered Office: 1 Olympic Way, Wembley, Middlesex, HA9 0NP
Activities: Production of electricity
Shareholders: Liberty Venture Limited; LEM Holdings Limited
Officers: Larisa Nikolaos Kolpidou, Secretary; Sergey Kolpidi [1960] Director/Engineer [Russian]; Michail Sergios Kolpidis [1991] Director/Businessman [Greek]

Sunnen Products Limited
Incorporated: 18 January 1994 *Employees:* 95
Net Worth: £7,378,581 *Total Assets:* £20,447,320
Registered Office: Unit 4b Finway Road, Hemel Hempstead Industrial Estate, Hemel Hempstead, Herts, HP2 7PT
Activities: Non-specialised wholesale trade
Parent: Sunnen Products Company
Officers: Julian Bruce Hooper [1958] Director/Tool Maker; Frederick Christopher Miltenberger [1967] Director [American]; Matthew Sunnen Kreider [1954] Director/President [American]

Sunray Estates Limited
Incorporated: 15 March 2004 *Employees:* 4
Net Worth: £8,306,802 *Total Assets:* £15,948,466
Registered Office: 5 Elstree Gate, Elstree Way, Borehamwood, Herts, WD6 1JD
Activities: Development of building projects
Shareholders: Ady Doron; David Azouri; Ronit Azouri
Officers: Ady Doron, Secretary; David Azouri [1961] Director; Tal Azouri [1989] Director; Ady Doron [1956] Director [British/Israeli]; Dana Doron [1989] Director

Sunrise UK Holdco Limited
Incorporated: 7 August 2014
Net Worth: £3,339,000 *Total Assets:* £31,534,000
Registered Office: Sunrise House, Post Office Lane, Beaconsfield, Bucks, HP9 1FN
Activities: Medical nursing home activities
Officers: Antony Nigel Brister [1972] Director; Dr Natalie-Jane MacDonald [1962] Director; Marcus Edwin Roder [1952] Director/Corporate Controller [American]; Wendy Catherine Sekel [1977] Director/VP Tax [American]

Sunrose Property Limited
Incorporated: 24 June 2005
Net Worth: £2,795,607 *Total Assets:* £9,322,711
Registered Office: 616D Green Lane, Ilford, Essex, IG3 9SE
Activities: Buying and selling of own real estate
Officers: Echewodo Lambert Nwawudu, Secretary/Engineer; Dorothy Ihuoma Nwawudu [1963] Director/IT Consultant; Echewodo Lambert Nwawudu [1964] Director/Engineer

Sunsave 12 (Derriton Fields) Ltd
Incorporated: 30 August 2012
Net Worth: £2,900,000 *Total Assets:* £12,917,000
Registered Office: Beaufort Court, Egg Farm Lane, off Station Road, Kings Langley, Herts, WD4 8LR
Activities: Production of electricity
Parent: European Investments Solar Holdings Limited
Officers: Dominic James Hearth, Secretary; Steven William Hughes [1972] Global Support Services Director, UK&I - Commercial; Mitesh Raj Patel [1982] Director/Group Financial Controller; Tracy Jane Scott [1976] Director/Delivery Project Manager - New Technologies UK&I; Mark Christopher Wayment [1958] Director

Sunsave 25 (Wix Lodge Farm) Limited
Incorporated: 24 May 2013
Net Worth: £8,788,000 *Total Assets:* £19,526,000
Registered Office: Beaufort Court, Egg Farm Lane, off Station Road, Kings Langley, Herts, WD4 8LR
Activities: Production of electricity
Parent: European Investments Solar Holdings Limited
Officers: Dominic James Hearth, Secretary; Steven William Hughes [1972] Global Support Services Director, UK&I - Commercial; Mitesh Raj Patel [1982] Director/Group Financial Controller; Tracy Jane Scott [1976] Director/Delivery Project Manager - New Technologies UK&I; Mark Christopher Wayment [1958] Director

Sunwin Services Group (2010) Limited
Incorporated: 3 February 2012 *Employees:* 648
Net Worth: £27,606,000 *Total Assets:* £32,358,000
Registered Office: First Floor, Building 4, Trident Place, Mosquito Way, Hatfield, Herts, AL10 9UL
Activities: Private security activities
Parent: CATM Europe Holdings Limited
Officers: Michael John Pinder [1969] Director; Andrew Dean Shaw [1970] Director/MD Global Operations

Super Toughened Glass Limited
Incorporated: 1 October 1998 *Employees:* 138
Net Worth: £15,008,221 *Total Assets:* £25,631,762
Registered Office: 65-67 Wembley Hill Road, Wembley, Middlesex, HA9 8DP
Activities: Shaping and processing of flat glass
Shareholders: Karsan Kanji Hirani; Dhanbhai Karsan Hirani; Devji Khimji Meghani; Laxmiben Devji Meghani
Officers: Karsan Kanji Hirani, Secretary; Karsan Kanji Hirani [1959] Director; Devji Khimji Meghani [1953] Director; Sanjay Devji Meghani [1976] Director

Supreme Hotels LLP
Incorporated: 20 December 2011 *Employees:* 137
Net Worth: £2,797,612 *Total Assets:* £16,153,491
Registered Office: Haydon House, 296 Joel Street, Pinner, Middlesex, HA5 2PY
Officers: Nadeem Boghani [1978] Member; Shiraz Boghani [1950] Member

Survey Roofing Group Limited
Incorporated: 19 December 2014 *Employees:* 89
Net Worth: £4,818,737 *Total Assets:* £8,273,365
Registered Office: Kingfisher House, Radford Way, Billericay, Essex, CM12 0EQ
Activities: Roofing activities
Officers: Simon Hobart Charles Morrish [1974] Director; Dereka Anne Symes [1962] Director/Chartered Accountant

Surya Hotels Limited
Incorporated: 4 May 2010 *Employees:* 394
Net Worth Deficit: £847,397 *Total Assets:* £14,728,591
Registered Office: Europa House, 4 Europa Way, Parkstone, Harwich, Essex, CO12 4PT
Activities: Hotels and similar accommodation
Parent: Flying Trade Group PLC
Officers: Adosh Chatrath [1964] Director/Solicitor; Harjit Singh Dulai [1971] Director; Sukhjit Singh Dulai [1966] Director

Sussex Gardens Hotels Limited
Incorporated: 2 May 1973 *Employees:* 3
Net Worth: £19,258,724 *Total Assets:* £21,618,956
Registered Office: 1st Floor, Woodgate Studios, 2-8 Games Road, Cockfosters, Herts, EN4 9HN
Activities: Hotels and similar accommodation
Parent: Mouskos Holdings Limited
Officers: Generaldina Mouskos, Secretary; Christopher Mouskos [1961] Director/Businessman; Generaldina Mouskos [1937] Director/Hotelier; John Mouskos [1964] Director/Businessman

SVK Capital Management Limited
Incorporated: 13 December 2013
Net Worth: £177,980 *Total Assets:* £8,336,550
Registered Office: Bank Chambers, 27a Market Place, Market Deeping, Peterborough, Cambs, PE6 8EA
Activities: Administration of financial markets
Officers: Hugh Victor Cochrane [1965] Director; Shane Vincent Kehoe [1976] Director [Irish]

SW1 Management Limited
Incorporated: 16 June 2010 *Employees:* 2
Net Worth: £1,058,588 *Total Assets:* £9,244,449
Registered Office: The Kelling Estate Office, Kelling, Norfolk, NR25 7EW
Activities: Other business support service activities n.e.c.
Major Shareholder: Gary Albert Widdowson
Officers: Duncan Alexander Ross [1967] Director; Gary Albert Widdowson [1958] Director

SW1 Trading Limited
Incorporated: 23 October 2012
Previous: SW1 Consultancy Limited
Net Worth: £139,979 *Total Assets:* £8,460,992
Registered Office: The Kelling Estate Office, Kelling, Norfolk, NR25 7EW
Activities: Other business support service activities n.e.c.
Major Shareholder: Beverley Ann Widdowson
Officers: Beverley Ann Widdowson [1960] Director; Gary Albert Widdowson [1958] Managing Director

Swan Commercial Services Limited
Incorporated: 29 March 2007
Net Worth: £278,000 *Total Assets:* £36,372,000
Registered Office: Pilgrim House, High Street, Billericay, Essex, CM12 9XY
Activities: Development of building projects
Parent: Swan Housing Association Limited
Officers: Susan Lesley McBride, Secretary; Jamie Alexander Smith [1973] Finance Director; John David Synnuck [1950] Director/Chief Executive

Swan Housing Capital PLC
Incorporated: 19 December 2014
Net Worth: £50,000 *Total Assets:* £210,447,008
Registered Office: Pilgrim House, High Street, Billericay, Essex, CM12 9XY
Activities: Financial intermediation not elsewhere classified
Parent: Swan Housing Association Ltd
Officers: Susan Lesley McBride, Secretary; Jamie Alexander Smith [1973] Director/Accountant; John David Synnuck [1950] Director/Chief Executive

Swan Investments Group Limited
Incorporated: 10 March 1982 *Employees:* 518
Net Worth: £73,913,016 *Total Assets:* £84,370,776
Registered Office: Inflite House, Stansted Airport, Stansted, Essex, CM24 1RY
Activities: Activities of head offices
Parent: Swan Investments Group Holdings Limited
Officers: Linda Vera Ellis, Secretary; Pauline May Monksfield [1982] Director/Administrator; Luisa Marie Stephens [1979] Director/Life Style Management; Penny Annette Stephens [1952] Director/Customer Liaison; Raymond Aubrey Stephens [1937] Director/Engineer; William Charles Stephens [1985] Director/Engineering Assistant

Swan New Homes Limited
Incorporated: 17 August 2004 *Employees:* 49
Net Worth: £4,637,000 *Total Assets:* £109,661,000
Registered Office: Pilgrim House, High Street, Billericay, Essex, CM12 9XY
Activities: Development of building projects
Parent: Swan Housing Association Ltd
Officers: Susan Lesley McBride, Secretary; Steve Akinniyi Akeju [1966] Director/Surveyor; Peter Frederick Baynham [1953] Director/Chartered Accountant; Simon Donald Hardon [1956] Director; Koo Chai Young Marie Paule Li Mow Ching [1951] Director; Valerie Ellen Owen [1957] Director; Elizabeth Ann Sipiere [1958] Director; Jamie Alexander Smith [1973] Director/Deputy Chief Executive; John David Synnuck [1950] Director/Chief Executive

Swanbrae Limited
Incorporated: 27 April 1970 *Employees:* 2
Net Worth: £5,483,778 *Total Assets:* £12,828,343
Registered Office: Raffingers, 19-20 Bourne Court, Southend Road, Woodford Green, Essex, IG8 8HD
Activities: Development of building projects
Major Shareholder: James Patrick Tye
Officers: Lauren Rose Tye, Secretary; James Patrick Tye [1953] Director

Swanlea Limited
Incorporated: 5 February 1990
Net Worth: £14,839,733 *Total Assets:* £19,301,774
Registered Office: Unit 5 Charlton Mead Lane, Hoddesdon, Herts, EN11 0DJ
Activities: Other letting and operating of own or leased real estate
Shareholder: David John Cooper
Officers: Susan Jane Cooper, Secretary; David John Cooper [1953] Director; Susan Jane Cooper [1952] Director

Swarco UK Limited
Incorporated: 9 October 1992 *Employees:* 38
Previous: APT Controls Limited
Net Worth: £14,956,000 *Total Assets:* £19,096,000
Registered Office: 1 Maxted Corner, Maxted Road, Hemel Hempstead Industrial Estate, Hemel Hempstead, Herts, HP2 7RA
Activities: Manufacture of other special-purpose machinery n.e.c.
Parent: Swarco AG
Officers: Steffan John Evans, Secretary; Jeremy Peter Cowling [1967] Director; Steffan John Evans [1978] Financial Director; Dermot Generald William Murphy [1953] Director [Irish]

Swift 1st Limited
Incorporated: 20 January 2004 *Employees:* 91
Net Worth: £13,839,000 *Total Assets:* £14,577,000
Registered Office: Arcadia House, Warley Hill Business Park, The Drive, Great Warley, Brentwood, Essex, CM13 3BE
Activities: Credit granting by non-deposit taking finance houses and other specialist consumer credit grantors
Parent: Swift Advances PLC
Officers: Stephen Francis McConnell, Secretary; Amanda Brooks [1965] Director; Andrew Robert Punch [1960] Director

Swift Advances PLC
Incorporated: 15 March 1984 *Employees:* 91
Net Worth: £66,798,000 *Total Assets:* £72,088,000
Registered Office: Arcadia House, Warley Hill Business Park, The Drive, Great Warley, Brentwood, Essex, CM13 3BE
Activities: Credit granting by non-deposit taking finance houses and other specialist consumer credit grantors
Parent: Kestrel Acquistions Limited
Officers: Stephen Francis McConnell, Secretary; Amanda Brooks [1965] Director; Andrew Robert Punch [1960] Director

Swift Brickwork Contractors Limited
Incorporated: 9 January 1992 *Employees:* 193
Net Worth: £17,238,288 *Total Assets:* £24,444,694
Registered Office: Hampton House, 137 Beehive Lane, Chelmsford, Essex, CM2 9RX
Activities: Construction of commercial buildings
Shareholders: Michael Walsh; Neil Anthony Moye
Officers: Lorraine Moye, Secretary; Nora Mary Angela Walsh, Secretary; Tony Fawcett [1972] Commercial Director; Neil Anthony Moye [1965] Director/Brickwork Specialist; Michael Walsh [1965] Director/Quantity Surveyor [Irish]

Swift Group Holdings Limited
Incorporated: 27 May 1994 *Employees:* 58
Net Worth: £10,885,548 *Total Assets:* £22,380,266
Registered Office: Bankside, 300 Peachman Way, Broadland Business Park, Norwich, NR7 0LB
Activities: Activities of other holding companies n.e.c.
Major Shareholder: David Albert Tunnicliffe
Officers: Terence Rush, Secretary; Terence Andrew Rush [1961] Director; David Albert Tunnicliffe [1962] Director

Swift Hotels Limited
Incorporated: 2 December 1896 *Employees:* 2
Net Worth: £284,796,992 *Total Assets:* £287,163,008
Registered Office: Whitbread Court, Houghton Hall Business Park, Porz Avenue, Houghton Regis, Dunstable, Beds, LU5 5XE
Activities: Development of building projects
Parent: Whitbread (Condor) Holdings Limited
Officers: Daren Clive Lowry [1970] Director/Company Secretary; Matthew Yates [1977] Director/Lawyer

The Swiss Laundry,Limited
Incorporated: 26 June 1925 *Employees:* 240
Net Worth: £9,254,562 *Total Assets:* £20,721,048
Registered Office: The Swiss Laundry Ltd, Cherry Hinton Road, Cambridge, CB1 7BY
Activities: Renting and leasing of other machinery, equipment and tangible goods n.e.c.
Major Shareholder: Marina Stanley Turvill-Smith
Officers: Mark Keith Turvill, Secretary; William Stanley Hammill [1949] Director; Guy James Turvill [1963] Director/Chairman; James Lawrence Turvill [1964] Director/Doctor; Mark Keith Turvill [1973] Director; Richard John Turvill [1965] Managing Director; Marina Stanley Turvill-Smith [1940] Director/Deputy Chairman

SWP Group Limited
Incorporated: 7 January 1952 *Employees:* 5
Previous: SWP Group PLC
Net Worth: £14,840,625 *Total Assets:* £17,644,882
Registered Office: Bedford House, 1 Regal Lane, Soham, Ely, Cambs, CB7 5BA
Activities: Activities of head offices
Parent: Friars 716 Limited
Officers: David Jonathan Pett, Secretary/Accountant; Martin Bell [1961] Director; David Jonathan Pett [1958] Director/Accountant; Colin Andre Stott [1964] Director; James Alan Fairley Walker [1949] Director/Chartered Accountant

Symbio Energy Limited
Incorporated: 21 March 2012 *Employees:* 2
Net Worth Deficit: £4,331,773 *Total Assets:* £9,278,916
Registered Office: GPF Lewis House, Olds Approach, Tolpits Lane, Watford, Herts, WD18 9AB
Activities: Production of electricity
Parent: Dispensary Holdings Limited
Officers: Shamir Pravinchandra Budhdeo [1967] Director

Symology Limited
Incorporated: 11 October 1983 *Employees:* 107
Net Worth: £5,750,429 *Total Assets:* £9,155,261
Registered Office: Vanguard House, Cotswold Park, Millfield Lane, Caddington, Beds, LU1 4AJ
Activities: Business and domestic software development
Officers: Kenneth George Hickson, Secretary; Michael James Bartlett [1972] Managing Director; Thomas James Dunn [1988] Director/Software Developer; Kenneth George Hickson [1945] Director/Programmer; Jonathan Panconi [1971] Director/Support Manager; Sacha Louise Whipp [1969] Director/Admin Assistant

Synergy Flavours Limited
Incorporated: 13 December 1989 *Employees:* 97
Previous: Synergy (High Wycombe) Limited
Net Worth: £13,455,478 *Total Assets:* £25,516,324
Registered Office: Synergy House, 2 Hillbottom Road, Sands Industrial Estate, High Wycombe, Bucks, HP12 4HJ
Activities: Manufacture of dyes and pigments
Parent: Carbery UK Ltd
Officers: Nicola Lynne McFadden, Secretary/Finance Manager; Noel Corcoran [1960] Director/Marketing Manager [Irish]; Jason Mathew Hawkins [1972] Director/Chief Executive [Irish]; Daniel John Holland [1962] Director/Food Scientist [Irish]; Colm Anthony Leen [1962] Director [Irish]; Stephen Morgan [1960] Managing Director

Synergy Multi Academy Trust
Incorporated: 3 September 2012 *Employees:* 278
Previous: Reepham High School and College
Net Worth: £21,443,488 *Total Assets:* £24,285,980
Registered Office: Reepham High School and College, Whitwell Road, Reepham, Norwich, NR10 4JT
Activities: Primary education
Officers: Deborah Boldero [1953] Director; Mark Farrar [1958] Director/School Principal; Tracey Caroline Hughes [1963] Director/Solicitors; Bryan Hurst [1962] Director/Training Manager; Dr Natasha Clair Gillian Hutcheson [1971] Director/Freelance; Richard Madle [1951] Director/Accountant; Dr Graham William Pickhaver [1946] Director/Retired; Andrew Paul Savage [1965] Director; Anthony Thomas Williams [1946] County Councillor Director Former Consultant

Syngenta UK Limited
Incorporated: 14 May 1965 *Employees:* 185
Net Worth: £10,953,000 *Total Assets:* £53,780,000
Registered Office: CPC4, Capital Park, Fulbourn, Cambridge, CB21 5XE
Activities: Manufacture of other inorganic basic chemicals
Parent: Syngenta Holdings Limited
Officers: Matthew David Bayliss, Secretary; Dr Aaron Abbott [1975] Director/Manager; Andrew David Johnson [1964] Director/Finance Head; Gary Mills-Thomas [1965] Director/Sales and Marketing Manager

Synthomer (UK) Limited
Incorporated: 24 February 1966 *Employees:* 349
Net Worth: £127,545,000 *Total Assets:* £221,330,000
Registered Office: Temple Fields, Central Road, Harlow, Essex, CM20 2BH
Activities: Manufacture of other chemical products n.e.c.
Parent: Synthomer Holdings Limited
Officers: Richard Atkinson, Secretary; Richard Atkinson [1962] Director/Company Secretary; Stephen Guy Bennett [1964] Director; Timothy John Hughes [1964] Managing Director; Robert Marcus Tupker [1967] Director [Dutch]; Neil Whitley [1964] Director

Synthomer Holdings Limited
Incorporated: 20 September 2002
Net Worth Deficit: £31,604,000 *Total Assets:* £698,342,976
Registered Office: Yule Catto Building, Temple Fields, Harlow, Essex, CM20 2BH
Activities: Activities of head offices
Parent: Synthomer PLC
Officers: Richard Atkinson, Secretary; Richard Atkinson [1962] Director/Company Secretary; Stephen Guy Bennett [1964] Director

Synthomer PLC
Incorporated: 16 June 1908 *Employees:* 2,789
Net Worth: £387,900,000 *Total Assets:* £1,200,700,032
Registered Office: Temple Fields, Harlow, Essex, CM20 2BH
Activities: Activities of head offices
Officers: Richard Atkinson, Secretary; Stephen Guy Bennett [1964] Director; Brendan Wynne Derek Connolly [1956] Director; Holly Van Deursen [1958] Director [American]; Dr Just Jansz [1957] Director [Dutch]; Neil Anthony Johnson [1949] Director; Caroline Ann Johnstone [1960] Director; Hau Hian Lee [1953] Director [Malaysian]; Calum Grigor MacLean [1963] Director

SystemsAccountants Holdings Limited
Incorporated: 3 December 2015 *Employees:* 47
Net Worth: £1,008,840 *Total Assets:* £9,900,127
Registered Office: Perio Mill, Fotheringhay, Peterborough, PE8 5HU
Activities: Activities of other holding companies n.e.c.
Shareholder: James Francis Bradshaw
Officers: Dean Turner, Secretary; James Francis Bradshaw [1971] Director; Luisa Claire Bradshaw [1969] Director/Administration Manager; Dean Alan Turner [1968] Managing Director

T & B (Contractors) Holdings Limited
Incorporated: 2 December 2013 *Employees:* 125
Net Worth: £6,838,571 *Total Assets:* £19,100,484
Registered Office: Riverside House, 1 Place Farm, Wheathampstead, St Albans, Herts, AL4 8SB
Activities: Activities of construction holding companies
Shareholders: Rae Borras; Carol Ann Borras; The Borras Family Trust
Officers: Carol Ann Borras [1954] Director/Company Secretary; Raymond Duncan Borras [1947] Director

T & B (Contractors) Limited
Incorporated: 28 September 1982 *Employees:* 125
Net Worth: £6,838,571 *Total Assets:* £19,100,484
Registered Office: Riverside House, 1 Place Farm, Wheathampstead, St Albans, Herts, AL4 8SB
Activities: Development of building projects
Parent: T & B (Contractors) Holdings Limited
Officers: Carol Ann Borras, Secretary/Company Secretary; Carol Ann Borras [1954] Director/Company Secretary; Raymond Duncan Borras [1947] Director; Mark David Hickson [1963] Director/Building Contractor; Kevin Roy Odell [1964] Director/Surveyor; Andrew Skilton [1968] Director/Building Contractor; Nigel Raymond Stephen [1966] Marketing Director; Robert William Wishart [1978] Director/Building Contractor

T F S Loans Limited
Incorporated: 25 March 2008 *Employees:* 55
Net Worth: £213,109 *Total Assets:* £21,130,558
Registered Office: Broom House, 39-43 London Road, Hadleigh, Benfleet, Essex, SS7 2QL
Activities: Financial intermediation not elsewhere classified
Parent: The Finance Store Limited
Officers: Paul James Auger [1963] Director/Finance Broker; Martin Paul Graham [1962] Director/Administrator; Ranjit Narwal [1962] Director/Finance Broker; Howard Peter Snell [1955] Director/Financial Executive

T. Bro Investment Limited
Incorporated: 20 March 1995
Net Worth: £2,165,003 *Total Assets:* £10,973,910
Registered Office: Argyle House, Northside Level 3, Joel Street, Northwood, Middlesex, HA6 1NW
Activities: Other letting and operating of own or leased real estate
Major Shareholder: Bharat Kumar Hirji Thakrar
Officers: Bharat Kumar Hirji Thakrar [1957] Director/Businessman

T.S.G. Building Services PLC
Incorporated: 18 January 2000 *Employees:* 259
Net Worth: £7,502,118 *Total Assets:* £16,224,464
Registered Office: TSG House, Cranborne Industrial Estate, Cranborne Road, Potters Bar, Herts, EN6 3JN
Activities: Construction of domestic buildings
Shareholder: Adam James Thrussell
Officers: Robert Joseph Glendinning, Secretary; Robert Joseph Glendinning [1969] Director/Chartered Management Accountant; Stephen James Gwynn [1957] Director/Surveyor; John Philip Holloway [1947] Contracts Director; Bryan Lloyd Rees [1968] Construction Director; Adam James Thrussell [1979] Managing Director

Table Bay Services LLP
Incorporated: 3 October 2011
Net Worth: £14,549 *Total Assets:* £8,033,374
Registered Office: Kings Head House, 15 London End, Beaconsfield, Bucks, HP9 2HN
Officers: John David Dryburgh [1959] Member

The Tabor Group Ltd
Incorporated: 10 March 2000 *Employees:* 239
Net Worth: £3,451,602 *Total Assets:* £12,393,842
Registered Office: Regency House, 33 Wood Street, Barnet, Herts, EN5 4BE
Activities: Other business support service activities n.e.c.
Major Shareholder: Edward Tabor
Officers: Georgina Hill, Secretary; Julie Patmore [1958] Director; Edward James Tabor [1948] Director; Katriona Jane Tabor [1966] Director

Takeda Cambridge Limited
Incorporated: 23 June 1998
Net Worth: £43,780,000 *Total Assets:* £57,073,000
Registered Office: 418 Cambridge Science Park, Milton Road, Cambridge, CB4 0PZ
Activities: Other letting and operating of own or leased real estate
Parent: Takeda Pharmaceutical Company Limited
Officers: Bryan Joseph Driscoll, Secretary; Mark Conrad Fowler [1966] Director; David Isaacs [1973] Finance Director; Andrew Raymond Spicer [1958] Director/Head of Operations - Cambridge Site

Takeda UK Limited
Incorporated: 25 April 1997 *Employees:* 192
Net Worth: £33,735,072 *Total Assets:* £91,023,712
Registered Office: Building 3, Glory Park Avenue, Wooburn Green, High Wycombe, Bucks, HP10 0DF
Activities: Wholesale of pharmaceutical goods
Parent: Takeda Pharmaceuticals International AG
Officers: Jon Neal [1971] Director/General Manager; Andrius Varanavicius [1979] Director/Chief Financial Officer EuCAN [Lithuanian]; William Charles Walker [1953] Director/Business Operations Manager

Takely Education Trust
Incorporated: 20 February 2015 *Employees:* 230
Net Worth: £25,468,000 *Total Assets:* £28,520,000
Registered Office: The Appleton School, Croft Road, Benfleet, Essex, SS7 5RN
Activities: General secondary education
Officers: Ian Kenneth Clark, Secretary; Simon Peter Cox [1975] Director/Headteacher; Terry Curtis [1972] Director/Teacher; Jan Fennelly [1960] Director/HR Manager; Olajumoke Temitope George [1981] Director; Jenny Haken [1974] Director/Deputy Headteacher; Karen Kerridge [1963] Director/Headteacher; Peter King [1949] Director; Karen Sandra Lay [1969] Director/Manager; Hilary Anne Luckman [1966] Director/Headteacher; Terry Anthony Reynolds [1947] Director/Retired; Stephanie Jane Rogers [1969] Director/Clinical Support Worker; Jeramie Sutton [1988] Director/Sales Manager

Talbot House Business Centre Limited
Incorporated: 3 March 1999 *Employees:* 6
Net Worth: £9,236,597 *Total Assets:* £15,386,373
Registered Office: Kajaine House, 57-67 High Street, Edgware, Middlesex, HA8 7DD
Activities: Other letting and operating of own or leased real estate
Shareholders: Stephen Michael Glynne; Stephen Michael Cole
Officers: Stephen Michael Glynne, Secretary/Director; Stephen Michael Cole [1952] Director; Stephen Michael Glynne [1951] Director

Taliesin Management Limited
Incorporated: 19 October 2005 *Employees:* 2
Net Worth: £18,622,112 *Total Assets:* £25,825,456
Registered Office: 1st Floor, Bridge House, 25 Fiddlebridge Lane, Hatfield, Herts, AL10 0SP
Activities: Other professional, scientific and technical activities n.e.c.
Officers: Simon David Austin Davies [1976] Managing Director; Panayot Kostadinov Vasilev [1976] Managing Director [French]

Tallentire Energy Limited
Incorporated: 17 January 2012
Net Worth Deficit: £4,980,000 *Total Assets:* £20,532,000
Registered Office: Beaufort Court, Egg Farm Lane, Kings Langley, Herts, WD4 8LR
Activities: Production of electricity
Parent: Trafalgar Wind Holdings Limited
Officers: Dominic James Hearth, Secretary; Steven William Hughes [1972] Generation & Asset Management Director; Fraser Stephen Merry [1968] Director/Chartered Surveyor; Mitesh Raj Patel [1982] Director/Group Financial Controller

Tallington Holdings Limited
Incorporated: 29 June 2004 *Employees:* 1
Net Worth: £6,367,809 *Total Assets:* £9,320,761
Registered Office: Barholm Road, Tallington, Stamford, Lincs, PE9 4RJ
Activities: Activities of head offices
Major Shareholder: Neil Morgan
Officers: Neil Morgan [1962] Director

TAM International North Sea Limited
Incorporated: 12 December 1984 *Employees:* 60
Net Worth: £25,023,962 *Total Assets:* £30,466,048
Registered Office: c/o Mills & Reeve, 1 St James Court, Whitefriars, Norwich, NR3 1RU
Activities: Support activities for petroleum and natural gas mining
Major Shareholder: Lawrence Bentley Sanford
Officers: Lawrence Bentley Sanford [1955] Director [American]; Steven Robert Scott [1961] Director/Area Manager

Tamdown Group Limited
Incorporated: 9 July 1976 *Employees:* 92
Net Worth: £21,048,000 *Total Assets:* £49,973,000
Registered Office: 1 Tamdown Way, Braintree, Essex, CM7 2QL
Activities: Construction of other civil engineering projects n.e.c.
Parent: Nexus Infrastructure PLC
Officers: Dawn Rosina Hillman, Secretary; Jeremy Kendall Brett [1970] Director; Mark Anthony Cain [1971] Director; Sarah Louise Darville-Downs [1981] Finance Director; Robert Lee Kendal [1981] Commercial Director; Alan Christopher Martin [1966] Director; Michael Thomas Morris [1967] Director; Andrew Parton [1968] Commercial Director; Charles Alan Sweeney [1959] Director; Mark Wadsworth [1970] Construction Director

Tangent International Group PLC
Incorporated: 16 March 1987 *Employees:* 75
Net Worth: £4,699,361 *Total Assets:* £12,952,195
Registered Office: 11 Woodbrook Crescent, Billericay, Essex, CM12 0EQ
Activities: Activities of head offices
Shareholders: Walter John Smallbone; Linda Smallbone
Officers: Geoffrey Alan Slyfield [1947] Director; Linda Smallbone [1953] Director; Walter John Smallbone [1947] Director

Tangent International Limited
Incorporated: 23 March 1981 *Employees:* 73
Net Worth: £4,313,185 *Total Assets:* £12,639,202
Registered Office: 11 Woodbrook Crescent, Billericay, Essex, CM12 0EQ
Activities: Human resources provision and management of human resources functions
Parent: Tangent International Group PLC
Officers: Peter John Connor, Secretary; Peter John Connor [1957] Director/Accountant; Simon Dear [1968] Director; Andrew Jonathan Smallbone [1986] Director; Walter John Smallbone [1947] Director

Tanglewood (Lincolnshire) Limited
Incorporated: 7 September 1988 *Employees:* 464
Net Worth: £21,395,156 *Total Assets:* £33,331,404
Registered Office: 2 Endeavour Park, Wyberton, Boston, Lincs, PE21 7TQ
Activities: Medical nursing home activities
Parent: Tanglewood Care Homes Limited
Officers: Jonathan Charles Griffin [1965] Director/Private Client Advisor; Tracy Ann Shelbourn [1959] Director

Tanglewood Care Homes Limited
Incorporated: 18 August 2011 *Employees:* 492
Net Worth: £14,212,713 *Total Assets:* £31,727,570
Registered Office: 2 Endeavour Park, Wyberton, Boston, Lincs, PE21 7TQ
Activities: Activities of head offices
Shareholders: Tracy Ann Shelbourn; Martin Shelbourn
Officers: Jonathan Charles Griffin [1965] Director/Private Client Advisor; Martin Shelbourn [1958] Director; Tracy Ann Shelbourn [1959] Director

George Tanner (Shalford) Limited
Incorporated: 5 February 1987 *Employees:* 8
Net Worth: £15,396,749 *Total Assets:* £22,768,240
Registered Office: Hill House, Shalford, Braintree, Essex, CM7 5HB
Activities: Growing of cereals (except rice), leguminous crops and oil seeds
Parent: George Tanner (Holdings) Limited
Officers: Angela Emily Tanner, Secretary; Alexander George Tanner [1942] Director; Angela Emily Tanner [1943] Director

Tanners Wharf Limited
Incorporated: 29 June 2011 *Employees:* 1
Net Worth: £5,862,408 *Total Assets:* £13,197,287
Registered Office: Roffey Farm, Ongar Road, Great Dunmow, Essex, CM6 1JH
Activities: Development of building projects
Major Shareholder: Emma Jane Harris
Officers: Emma Jane Harris [1979] Director/Property Manager

Tapesilver Limited
Incorporated: 13 August 2004
Net Worth: £45,394,000 *Total Assets:* £82,094,000
Registered Office: Tesco House, Shire Park, Kestrel Way, Welwyn Garden City, Herts, AL7 1GA
Activities: Other business support service activities n.e.c.
Parent: Tesco PLC
Officers: John Gibney [1967] Assets and Estates Director [Irish]; Lynda Jane Heywood [1964] Director/Corporate Treasurer; Robert John Welch [1966] Director/Company Secretary

Tappenden & Co. Limited
Incorporated: 16 February 1990 *Employees:* 234
Net Worth: £13,168,630 *Total Assets:* £25,087,848
Registered Office: The Maltings, 63 High Street, Ware, Herts, SG12 9AD
Activities: Activities of head offices
Officers: Roger Stuart Gambles, Secretary; Andrew John Grisbrooke [1962] Director/Engineer; Alan Charles Hayllar [1959] Director/Engineer; Andrew Peter Morris [1961] Managing Director

Targetfollow (Development) Limited
Incorporated: 20 December 2007
Net Worth: £213,983 *Total Assets:* £22,564,344
Registered Office: Riverside House, 11-13 Riverside Road, Norwich, NR1 1SQ
Activities: Activities of other holding companies n.e.c.
Parent: Targetfollow Group Ltd
Officers: Ardeshir Naghshineh, Secretary; Ardeshir Naghshineh [1952] Director/Property Consultant; Shapoor Naghshineh [1954] Director; Corin Leonard Thoday [1975] Director/Chief Executive

Targetfollow Group Limited
Incorporated: 8 December 2006 *Employees:* 2
Net Worth: £22,400,000 *Total Assets:* £56,629,000
Registered Office: Riverside House, 11-12 Riverside Road, Norwich, NR1 1SQ
Activities: Activities of other holding companies n.e.c.
Major Shareholder: Ardeshir Naghshineh
Officers: Ardeshir Naghshineh, Secretary; Ardeshir Naghshineh [1952] Director; Shapoor Naghshineh [1954] Director; Corin Leonard Thoday [1975] Director/Chief Executive

Tasmar Limited
Incorporated: 28 September 2004 *Employees:* 188
Net Worth: £24,522,588 *Total Assets:* £33,117,756
Registered Office: 55 Station Road, Beaconsfield, Bucks, HP9 1QL
Activities: Activities of head offices
Major Shareholder: Sylvester Christopher Patrick McDonagh
Officers: Paul Martin McDonagh, Secretary; Paul Martin McDonagh [1971] Managing Director; Sylvester Christopher Patrick McDonagh [1947] Director/Consultant [Irish]

Tati Company Limited
Incorporated: 6 March 1914
Net Worth: £395,462,976 *Total Assets:* £407,121,664
Registered Office: York House, Empire Way, Wembley, Middlesex, HA9 0FQ
Activities: Buying and selling of own real estate
Officers: David Alan Nathan [1949] Director/Senior Partner - Grant Thornton Accountants [South African]; Neville Sweidan [1941] Director/Head of Forensic Services - Grant Thornton [South African]; Sifelani Thapelo [1965] Director/Lawyer [Botswanan]

Tattersalls Limited
Incorporated: 7 February 1964 *Employees:* 79
Net Worth: £65,277,000 *Total Assets:* £117,009,000
Registered Office: Terrace House, Newmarket, Suffolk, CB8 9BT
Activities: Wholesale of live animals
Officers: Robert Alexander Skeggs, Secretary; Gavin Kenneth Davies [1971] Bloodstock Director; James Richard Brandon George [1963] Marketing Director; Edmond Conolly Mahony [1960] Director/Bloodstock Auctioneer; Matthew Joseph Mitchell [1955] Director [Irish]; Philip John Morrey [1972] Property Director; Andrew Ian Henry Russell Fifteenth Duke of Bedford [1962] Director; Robert Alexander Skeggs [1967] Director/Chartered Accountant; Patrick Andrew Tristram Watt [1964] Director/Bloodstock Auctioneer [Irish]

Tattershall Lakes Limited
Incorporated: 26 October 2009 *Employees:* 130
Net Worth: £9,463,133 *Total Assets:* £27,634,676
Registered Office: IMEX, 575-599 Maxted Road, Hemel Hempstead, Herts, HP2 7DX
Activities: Holiday centres and villages
Parent: Away Resorts Ltd
Officers: Neill Timothy Ryder, Secretary; Carl Anthony Castledene [1969] Director; Greg Lashley [1964] Director; Neill Timothy Ryder [1976] Director

The Taxassist Direct Group Limited
Incorporated: 2 July 2014
Net Worth: £5,128,532 *Total Assets:* £8,512,037
Registered Office: Second Floor, Bankside, 300 Peachman Way, Broadland Business Park, Norwich, NR7 0WF
Activities: Activities of head offices
Shareholder: Karl John Quinton Sandall
Officers: John Timothy Chambers [1954] Director; Mark Eric Fordham [1962] Director; James John Mattam [1978] Director; Daren Lee Moore [1972] Group Commercial Director; Sarah Robertson [1966] Director/Consultant; Karl John Quinton Sandall [1956] Director; Phillip Steven Sullivan [1958] Director

O.A.Taylor & Sons Bulbs Limited
Incorporated: 2 February 1970 *Employees:* 105
Net Worth: £20,384,308 *Total Assets:* £23,232,678
Registered Office: Washway House Farm, Washway Road, Holbeach, Spalding, Lincs, PE12 7PP
Activities: Growing of cereals (except rice), leguminous crops and oil seeds
Parent: OAT 2012 Limited
Officers: Sam Roger Taylor, Secretary; The Hon Adam Edwin John Taylor [1975] Director; Roger David Taylor [1945] Director; Sam Roger Taylor [1977] Director

John A.Taylor & Sons Limited
Incorporated: 29 December 1955 *Employees:* 7
Net Worth: £2,522,355 *Total Assets:* £8,263,199
Registered Office: 1 Penta Court, Station Road, Borehamwood, Herts, WD6 1SL
Activities: Non-specialised wholesale of food, beverages and tobacco
Major Shareholder: Ron Auerbach
Officers: Roni Auerbach, Secretary; Chantal Auerbach [1960] Director; Roni Auerbach [1955] Director

James Taylor Construction Limited
Incorporated: 16 August 1993 *Employees:* 17
Net Worth: £8,216,814 *Total Assets:* £9,902,033
Registered Office: James Taylor House, St Albans Road East, Hatfield, Herts, AL10 0HE
Activities: Development of building projects
Officers: Michael Coath, Secretary; Michael Coath [1968] Director/Chartered Accountant; Andrew David Sandwith [1971] Director/Quantity Surveyor; Emil Sohrab [1963] Director

James Taylor Group Limited
Incorporated: 3 October 2015 *Employees:* 34
Net Worth: £11,236,019 *Total Assets:* £13,037,748
Registered Office: James Taylor House, St Albans Road East, Hatfield, Herts, AL10 0HE
Activities: Activities of head offices
Major Shareholder: Emil Sohrab
Officers: Michael Coath, Secretary; Michael Coath [1968] Director/Chartered Accountant; Emil Sohrab [1963] Managing Director

James Taylor Homes (Harrow) Limited
Incorporated: 25 July 2014
Net Worth: £44,607 *Total Assets:* £9,704,903
Registered Office: James Taylor House, St Albans Road East, Hatfield, Herts, AL10 0HE
Activities: Development of building projects
Officers: Michael Coath, Secretary; Michael Coath [1968] Director/Chartered Accountant; Emil Sohrab [1963] Managing Director

James Taylor Homes (Lincolns Inn) Limited
Incorporated: 15 October 2014
Net Worth Deficit: £1,134,864 *Total Assets:* £11,783,210
Registered Office: James Taylor House, St Albans Road East, Hatfield, Herts, AL10 0HE
Activities: Buying and selling of own real estate
Officers: Michael Coath, Secretary; Michael Coath [1968] Director/Chartered Accountant; Emil Sohrab [1963] Managing Director

James Taylor Homes Group Limited
Incorporated: 18 October 2016 *Employees:* 4
Net Worth: £173,936 *Total Assets:* £28,359,404
Registered Office: James Taylor House, St Albans Road East, Hatfield, Herts, AL10 0HE
Activities: Activities of head offices
Major Shareholder: Emil Sohrab
Officers: Michael Coath, Secretary; Michael Coath [1968] Director/Chartered Accountant; Emil Sohrab [1963] Managing Director

Taylor Made Holdings UK Limited
Incorporated: 9 June 2004 *Employees:* 171
Net Worth: £1,027,529 *Total Assets:* £13,481,622
Registered Office: Sutton Road, Catfield, Great Yarmouth, Norfolk, NR29 5BG
Activities: Manufacture of other fabricated metal products n.e.c.
Parent: LCI Industries
Officers: Brian Michael Hall, Secretary; John Clark [1964] Finance Director; Brian Michael Hall [1975] Director/Chief Financial Officer [American]; Jason Douglas Lippert [1972] Director/Chief Executive Officer [American]; Andrew Joseph Namenye [1980] Director/Chief Legal Officer [American]

Taylor Made Joinery Interiors Limited
Incorporated: 26 June 1981 *Employees:* 159
Net Worth: £5,027,960 *Total Assets:* £10,550,596
Registered Office: Manor Wood, Ipswich Road, Bildeston, Ipswich, Suffolk, IP7 7BH
Activities: Joinery installation
Major Shareholder: James Gordon Taylor
Officers: Thomas George Burns, Secretary; Thomas George Burns [1975] Finance Director; Andrew Phillip Catchpole [1948] Director; Pat John Coll [1961] Director/Production Management; Peter James Harkin [1961] Projects Director; Martin Charles Holmes [1962] Director/Project Management; Kevin John Hudson [1967] Director/Quantity Surveyor; Sarah Alice Warren [1985] Business Development Director

Taylor Properties Trading Ltd
Incorporated: 29 September 1951 *Employees:* 5
Net Worth: £7,972,044 *Total Assets:* £15,415,743
Registered Office: 19-21 Station Square, Lowestoft, Suffolk, NR32 1BA
Activities: Development of building projects
Shareholder: Brenda Elizabeth Taylor
Officers: Brenda Elizabeth Taylor, Secretary; Brandon Roger Taylor [1966] Managing Director; Brenda Elizabeth Taylor [1939] Director; Jason Edward Taylor [1969] Director

Taylor Wimpey 2007 Limited
Incorporated: 6 December 2007
Net Worth: £118,685,000 *Total Assets:* £118,685,000
Registered Office: Gate House, Turnpike Road, High Wycombe, Bucks, HP12 3NR
Activities: Other business support service activities n.e.c.
Parent: Taylor Wimpey PLC
Officers: Michael Andrew Lonnon, Secretary; Stephen Roy Impey [1957] Director/Group Treasurer; James John Jordan [1961] Director/Chartered Secretary

Taylor Wimpey Developments Limited
Incorporated: 1 December 1959 *Employees:* 8
Net Worth: £1,938,701,952 *Total Assets:* £2,906,313,984
Registered Office: Gate House, Turnpike Road, High Wycombe, Bucks, HP12 3NR
Activities: Development of building projects
Parent: Taylor Wimpey Holdings Limited
Officers: Michael Andrew Lonnon, Secretary; Jennifer Daly [1970] Director; Nigel Holland [1960] Managing Director; James John Jordan [1961] Director/Company Secretary

Taylor Wimpey Holdings Limited
Incorporated: 6 December 1945
Net Worth: £671,195,008 *Total Assets:* £1,941,644,032
Registered Office: Gate House, Turnpike Road, High Wycombe, Bucks, HP12 3NR
Activities: Development of building projects
Parent: Taylor Wimpey PLC
Officers: Katherine Elizabeth Hindmarsh, Secretary; Christopher Carney [1974] Director; Jennifer Daly [1970] Director; James John Jordan [1961] Director/Company Secretary

Taylor Wimpey PLC
Incorporated: 1 February 1935 *Employees:* 4,995
Net Worth: £3,137,299,968 *Total Assets:* £4,966,099,968
Registered Office: Gate House, Turnpike Road, High Wycombe, Bucks, HP12 3NR
Activities: Activities of head offices
Officers: James John Jordan, Secretary; Dame Katharine Mary Barker [1957] Director; Kevin Stanley Beeston [1962] Director; Gwyneth Victoria Burr [1963] Director; Christopher Carney [1974] Director; Jennifer Daly [1970] Director; James John Jordan [1961] Director/Company Secretary; Angela Ann Knight [1950] Director; Peter Timothy Redfern [1970] Director; Humphrey Stewart Morgan Singer [1965] Director

Taylor Wimpey Property Company Limited
Incorporated: 3 June 1964
Net Worth: £33,185,000 *Total Assets:* £119,677,000
Registered Office: Gate House, Turnpike Road, High Wycombe, Bucks, HP12 3NR
Activities: Development of building projects
Parent: Taylor Wimpey PLC
Officers: Michael Andrew Lonnon, Secretary; Colin Richard Clapham [1945] Director/Company Secretary; Alex David Green [1981] Director

Taylor Wimpey SH Capital Limited
Incorporated: 24 January 2013
Net Worth: £12,061,000 *Total Assets:* £116,364,000
Registered Office: Gate House, Turnpike Road, High Wycombe, Bucks, HP12 3NR
Activities: Management of real estate on a fee or contract basis
Parent: Taylor Wimpey UK Limited
Officers: Katherine Elizabeth Hindmarsh, Secretary; Stephen Roy Impey [1957] Director; Barbara Inskip [1968] Director; Michael Andrew Lonnon [1957] Director/Company Secretary

Taylor Wimpey UK Limited
Incorporated: 6 October 1978 *Employees:* 4,893
Net Worth: £2,093,880,960 *Total Assets:* £4,373,367,808
Registered Office: Gate House, Turnpike Road, High Wycombe, Bucks, HP12 3NR
Activities: Development of building projects
Parent: Taylor Wimpey Developments Limited
Officers: James John Jordan, Secretary; Katherine Anne Billson-Ross [1968] Director; Lee Michael Bishop [1965] Director; Christopher Carney [1974] Director; Jennifer Daly [1970] Director; Nigel Holland [1960] Director; James John Jordan [1961] Director/Company Secretary; Daniel Hugh McGowan [1969] Director; Ingrid Ruth Osborne [1977] Director; Peter Timothy Redfern [1970] Director

Taylor Woodrow Construction
Incorporated: 19 June 1996 *Employees:* 154
Net Worth: £84,972,000 *Total Assets:* £132,612,000
Registered Office: Astral House, Imperial Way, Watford, Herts, WD24 4WW
Activities: Development of building projects
Parent: Vinci Construction UK Limited
Officers: Bruno Michel Dupety [1956] Director/Engineer [French]; Julian Paul Gatward [1966] Director/Civil Engineer; Anthony Kennedy Raikes [1964] Director/Chartered Civil Engineer

Taylors Legal Limited
Incorporated: 28 January 2016 *Employees:* 44
Net Worth: £237,828 *Total Assets:* £8,566,699
Registered Office: 184 Manor Road, Chigwell, Essex, IG7 5PZ
Activities: Activities of patent and copyright agents; other legal activities n.e.c.
Shareholders: Nicola Clare Mercer; Elliott Robert Costa
Officers: Elliott Robert Costa [1975] Director; Nicola Daniel [1980] Director; Shamma Kambo [1989] Director; Nicola Clare Mercer [1972] Director

Taylors Service Garages (Boston) Limited
Incorporated: 17 April 1974 *Employees:* 82
Net Worth: £5,757,962 *Total Assets:* £12,896,352
Registered Office: Taylors Peugeot, Ashton Hall Drive, Boston, Lincs, PE21 7TF
Activities: Sale of new cars and light motor vehicles
Shareholders: Nigel John Taylor; Timothy Charles Taylor
Officers: Nicholas Mark Graves, Secretary; Daphne Joyce Taylor [1933] Director; Nigel John Taylor [1958] Director/General Manager; Timothy Charles Taylor [1959] Director/General Manager

Tazaki Foods Limited
Incorporated: 27 July 1978 *Employees:* 84
Net Worth: £10,340,511 *Total Assets:* £15,858,909
Registered Office: 12 Innova Way, Innova Park, Enfield, Middlesex, EN3 7FL
Activities: Wholesale of meat and meat products
Parent: T. Tazaki & Company Limited
Officers: Masumi Uetsuji, Secretary; Chikahiro Furukawa [1961] Director/Food Importer [Japanese]; Kazuyoshi Ito [1961] Director [Japanese]; Masumi Uetsuji [1963] Director [Japanese]

TBS G.B. Telematic & Biomedical Services Limited
Incorporated: 2 March 2004 *Employees:* 225
Net Worth: £4,113,030 *Total Assets:* £11,527,463
Registered Office: Central House, 8 Clifftown Road, Southend on Sea, Essex, SS1 1AB
Activities: Repair of other equipment
Parent: Ital TBS S.P.A
Officers: Paolo Salotto, Secretary; Nicola Pangher [1967] Director [Italian]; David Anthony Rolfe [1972] Director; Paolo Salotto [1967] Director/Chartered Accountant [Italian]

TC Project Management Limited
Incorporated: 13 June 2013 *Employees:* 1
Net Worth: £9,838 *Total Assets:* £9,178,041
Registered Office: Suite 3, The Hamilton Centre, Rodney Way, Chelmsford, Essex, CM1 3BY
Activities: Construction of domestic buildings
Major Shareholder: Anthony William Ernest Coates
Officers: Anthony William Ernest Coates [1958] Director

TCCT Holdings UK Limited
Incorporated: 21 July 2011
Net Worth: £243,995,008 *Total Assets:* £245,396,992
Registered Office: Westpoint, Peterborough Business Park, Lynch Wood, Peterborough, Cambs, PE2 6FZ
Activities: Other business support service activities n.e.c.
Shareholders: Thomas Cook Retail Limited; Co-operative Specialist Businesses Limited
Officers: Shirley Bradley, Secretary; Kathryn Louise Darbandi [1969] Director; Alan Charles Donald [1963] Director

TCCT Retail Limited
Incorporated: 5 October 2010 *Employees:* 4,005
Net Worth Deficit: £473,031,008 *Total Assets:* £247,055,008
Registered Office: Westpoint, Peterborough Business Park, Lynch Wood, Peterborough, Cambs, PE2 6FZ
Activities: Travel agency activities
Parent: TCCT Holdings UK Limited
Officers: Shirley Bradley, Secretary; Alan Charles Donald [1963] Director; Alice Hannah Marsden [1983] Director

TCGH Holdings Limited
Incorporated: 27 June 2013
Net Worth: £400,000,000 *Total Assets:* £400,000,000
Registered Office: Westpoint, Peterborough Business Park, Lynch Wood, Peterborough, Cambs, PE2 6FZ
Activities: Other business support service activities n.e.c.
Parent: Blue Sea Overseas Investments Limited
Officers: Christopher James Corner [1974] Director

TCL Manufacturing Limited
Incorporated: 26 January 1990 *Employees:* 149
Net Worth: £8,647,676 *Total Assets:* £10,205,224
Registered Office: Unit 1 Gateway XIII, Ferry Lane, Rainham, Essex, RM13 9JY
Activities: Manufacture of other fabricated metal products n.e.c.
Parent: Fortune Brands Home & Security, Inc.
Officers: Angela Pla, Secretary; Nicholas Ian Fink [1974] Director/President [American]; Steven James Geary [1966] Director/Business Executive; John D Lee [1972] Director [American]; Ian Ross Walker [1977] Director

TCMC Furniture Limited
Incorporated: 24 February 2015 *Employees:* 261
Net Worth: £4,628,000 *Total Assets:* £25,608,000
Registered Office: Albro Works, Gosbecks Road, Colchester, Essex, CO2 9JU
Activities: Manufacture of other furniture
Parent: Thailand Carpet Manufacturing PCL
Officers: Terence Henry Cramphorn [1956] Director/Accountant; Zoe Caroline Dickens [1973] Director; Philip Grindrod [1953] Director; Andrew Simon Kennaugh [1969] Director; Chaiyut Srivikorn [1966] Director/Business Owner [Thai]; Pimol Srivikorn [1964] Director/Business Owner [Thai]; Walliwan Varavarn [1957] Director/Employee [Thai]

TCR New Limited
Incorporated: 10 February 2017
Net Worth Deficit: £3,480,386 *Total Assets:* £48,970,824
Registered Office: 22 Barn Rise, Wembley, Middlesex, HA9 9NQ
Activities: Other letting and operating of own or leased real estate
Parent: TCR Finance Limited
Officers: Sarah Davies, Secretary; Anthony David Chambers [1955] Director/Property Developer; Sarah Davies [1976] Director/Property Investor

Teaching Personnel Holdings Limited
Incorporated: 20 June 2007
Net Worth: £910,000 *Total Assets:* £15,655,000
Registered Office: 99 Bridge Road East, Welwyn Garden City, Herts, AL7 1GL
Activities: Activities of head offices
Parent: Education Personnel Bidco Limited
Officers: Jonathan Nicholas Roback, Secretary/Director; John Vincent Bowman [1963] Director; Jonathan Nicholas Roback [1969] Director

Teaching Personnel Limited
Incorporated: 16 July 1996 *Employees:* 320
Net Worth: £103,985,000 *Total Assets:* £117,922,000
Registered Office: 99 Bridge Road East, Welwyn Garden City, Herts, AL7 1GL
Activities: Other activities of employment placement agencies
Parent: Personnel Holdings Limited
Officers: Jonathan Nicholas Roback, Finance Director; John Vincent Bowman [1963] Director; Caroline Ann Cheale [1976] Quality Control Director [Irish]; Fiona Jane Crownshaw [1970] Director; Anthony Raymond Lee [1976] Director; Jonathan Nicholas Roback [1969] Finance Director

Team Consulting Limited
Incorporated: 11 November 1986 *Employees:* 101
Net Worth: £4,805,727 *Total Assets:* £8,858,934
Registered Office: Abbey Barns, Duxford Road, Ickleton, Cambs, CB10 1SX
Activities: Other human health activities
Parent: Team Medical Devices Limited
Officers: Dudley Richard Max Dyer Bartlett, Secretary/Accountant; Dudley Richard Max Dyer Bartlett [1957] Director/Accountant; Daniel James Flicos [1964] Director/Manager; Andrew Robert Fry [1951] Director; Colin James Mathews [1962] Director/Manager; Jeremy John Turner [1951] Director/Consultant Engineer

Techaid Facilities Limited
Incorporated: 7 August 1973 *Employees:* 56
Net Worth: £12,539,529 *Total Assets:* £29,912,552
Registered Office: Loudwater House, London Road, Loudwater, High Wycombe, Bucks, HP10 9TL
Activities: Development of building projects
Shareholders: Martin John Francis Gardener; Julie Dawn Sinton
Officers: Martin John Francis Gardener [1964] Director/Estate Manager; Robin Francis Gardener [1996] Director

E.E. & A. Tee Limited
Incorporated: 22 January 1947 *Employees:* 6
Net Worth: £9,644,066 *Total Assets:* £13,828,376
Registered Office: Ground Floor, 4 Victoria Square, St Albans, Herts, AL1 3TF
Activities: Development of building projects
Shareholders: Teresa Lorraine Baldwin; Kim Sarah Dutton
Officers: Tina Lesley Benjamin, Secretary; Ross Nicholas Albrow [1956] Director/Property Management; Russell Grahame Baldwin [1959] Director/Financial Controller; Audrey White [1936] Director; Donald George White [1927] Director/Chartered Surveyor

Teen Spirit Limited
Incorporated: 20 April 1995 *Employees:* 57
Net Worth: £2,056,969 *Total Assets:* £8,143,551
Registered Office: The Tower Cinema, 111 Lumley Road, Skegness, Lincs, PE25 3LZ
Activities: Other amusement and recreation activities n.e.c.
Shareholders: Walter Sheeran; Sally Jane Sheeran
Officers: Sally Jane Sheeran, Company Secretary; Sally Jane Sheeran [1963] Director/Company Secretary; Walter Sheeran [1962] Managing Director

Teknomek Limited
Incorporated: 12 September 1986 *Employees:* 46
Net Worth: £5,852,975 *Total Assets:* £8,500,207
Registered Office: 1 Brunel Way, Sweet Briar Road Industrial Estate, Norwich, NR3 2BD
Activities: Other manufacturing n.e.c.
Officers: Michael John O'Driscoll [1952] Director; Stephen Tom Worth [1967] Director

Teledyne E2V (UK) Limited
Incorporated: 28 March 1947 *Employees:* 945
Previous: E2V Technologies (UK) Limited
Net Worth: £50,537,000 *Total Assets:* £86,287,000
Registered Office: 106 Waterhouse Lane, Chelmsford, Essex, CM1 2QU
Activities: Manufacture of electronic components
Parent: Teledyne E2V Limited
Officers: Nicholas James Wargent, Secretary; Susan Lee Main [1958] Director/Executive Officer [American]; Nicholas James Wargent [1973] Director/Solicitor

Teledyne E2V Limited
Incorporated: 15 May 2002
Previous: Teledyne E2V PLC
Net Worth: £63,981,000 *Total Assets:* £116,781,000
Registered Office: 106 Waterhouse Lane, Chelmsford, Essex, CM1 2QU
Activities: Activities of head offices
Parent: Rhombi Holdings Limited
Officers: Nicholas James Wargent, Secretary; Susan Lee Main [1958] Director/Executive Officer [American]; Aldo Pichelli [1952] Director/Executive Officer [American]; Edwin Roks [1964] Director/Executive Officer [Dutch]; Jason Vanwees [1971] Director/Executive Officer [American]; Nicholas James Wargent [1973] Director/Solicitor

Telegenic Holdings Limited
Incorporated: 14 September 2004 *Employees:* 106
Net Worth: £6,230,670 *Total Assets:* £17,815,356
Registered Office: Unit 8 The Merlin Centre, Lancaster Road, High Wycombe, Bucks, HP12 3QL
Activities: Activities of head offices
Shareholders: Peter Andrew Bates; Terence Peter James
Officers: Peter Andrew Bates, Secretary/Director; Peter Andrew Bates [1963] Director; Terence Peter James [1958] Director; Barry Gibson Johnstone [1945] Director [New Zealander]; Andrew David Maries [1965] Director/Accountant

Telegenic Limited
Incorporated: 18 March 1981 *Employees:* 106
Net Worth: £12,076,206 *Total Assets:* £23,560,308
Registered Office: 8 The Merlin Centre, Lancaster Road, High Wycombe, Bucks, HP12 3QL
Activities: Television programme production activities
Parent: Telegenic Holdings Limited
Officers: Peter Andrew Bates, Secretary/Director; Peter Andrew Bates [1963] Director of Production; Peter John Bowen [1968] Director/Head of Cameras; Eamonn Cornelius Curtin [1975] Commercial Director; Clive Harold Eggs [1963] Finance Director; Terence Peter James [1958] Director of Operations; Sean Patrick Mulhern [1972] Director of Engineering; David John Rowley [1971] Director/Head of Sound

Telensa Holdings Limited
Incorporated: 20 October 2015 *Employees:* 93
Net Worth: £7,918,462 *Total Assets:* £15,431,291
Registered Office: Iconix 3, London Road, Pampisford, Cambridge, CB22 3EG
Activities: Wireless telecommunications activities
Officers: Josephine Angela Stevens, Secretary; William Robert David Franks [1964] Director; William Gibson [1961] Director; Timothy Jackson [1959] Director; Martin Alexander McNair [1959] Director; Patrick Gerard Sheehan [1960] Investor Director

Telensa Ltd
Incorporated: 29 July 2002 *Employees:* 89
Net Worth: £10,352,689 *Total Assets:* £17,741,052
Registered Office: Iconix 3, London Road, Pampisford, Cambridge, CB22 3EG
Activities: Wireless telecommunications activities
Officers: Josephine Angela Stevens, Secretary; William Gibson [1961] Director; Timothy Jackson [1959] Director

Telephonetics Limited
Incorporated: 12 October 2004
Net Worth: £9,360,000 *Total Assets:* £9,387,000
Registered Office: 1st Floor, Building 2, People Building Estate, Maylands Avenue, Hemel Hempstead Industrial Estate, Hemel Hempstead, Herts, HP2 4NW
Activities: Activities of head offices
Parent: Netcall PLC
Officers: Michael Charles Greensmith, Secretary; Henrik Peter Bang [1958] Director [Danish]; James Andrew Ormondroyd [1972] Director

Telespazio Vega UK Limited
Incorporated: 27 October 2010 *Employees:* 90
Net Worth: £15,414,000 *Total Assets:* £23,795,000
Registered Office: 350 Capability Green, Luton, Beds, LU1 3LU
Activities: Other professional, scientific and technical activities n.e.c.
Parent: Telespazio SpA
Officers: Patrick Lacey, Secretary; Giuseppe Aridon [1958] Director/Manager [Italian]; Vittorio Colella Albino [1966] Director/Manager [Italian]; Marco Folino [1959] Director/Engineer [Italian]; Jean-Marc Roland Pierre Gardin [1961] Director [French]; Patrick Albert Thomas Lacey [1965] Director/Accountant

Telford Homes City North Limited
Incorporated: 3 February 2014
Net Worth: £18,768,000 *Total Assets:* £35,179,000
Registered Office: Telford House, Queens Gate, Britannia Road, Waltham Cross, Herts, EN8 7TF
Activities: Development of building projects
Shareholder: Telford Homes Regeneration Developments Holdings Limited
Officers: Monique Chantal Woudberg, Secretary; David Myles Campbell [1965] Group Sales and Marketing Director; Jonathan Graham Di-Stefano [1974] Director/Chief Executive; John Anthony FitzGenerald [1971] Director/Chief Executive; Katie Rogers [1981] Finance Director

Telford Homes PLC
Incorporated: 1 December 2000 *Employees:* 265
Net Worth: £231,091,008 *Total Assets:* £427,688,000
Registered Office: Telford House, Queensgate, Britannia Road, Waltham Cross, Herts, EN8 7TF
Activities: Development of building projects
Officers: Monique Chantal Woudberg, Secretary; David Myles Campbell [1965] Sales and Marketing Director; Jonathan Graham di Stefano [1974] Financial Director Property; Jane Margaret Earl [1957] Director/Charity Chief Executive; John Anthony FitzGenerald [1971] Managing Director Telford Home; Jerome Patrick Geoghegan [1967] Group Land and Planning Director; Katie Rogers [1981] Financial Director; Andrew Graham Wiseman [1956] Director

Telida Limited
Incorporated: 23 May 2013
Net Worth: £1,538,822 *Total Assets:* £8,044,808
Registered Office: Hill House, Lowlands Road, Harrow, Middlesex, HA1 3EQ
Activities: Development of building projects
Major Shareholder: Donovan Gijsbertus Wijsmuller
Officers: Brian Martin Comer [1960] Director [Irish]; Luke Andrew Comer [1957] Director [Irish]

Temple Fields 514 Limited
Incorporated: 20 September 2002
Net Worth: £44,841,000 *Total Assets:* £76,585,000
Registered Office: Yule Catto Building, Temple Fields, Harlow, Essex, CM20 2BH
Activities: Activities of head offices
Parent: Synthomer PLC
Officers: Richard Atkinson, Secretary; Richard Atkinson [1962] Director/Company Secretary; Stephen Guy Bennett [1964] Director

Temple Fields 522 Limited
Incorporated: 25 July 2005
Net Worth Deficit: £165,956,992 *Total Assets:* £51,146,000
Registered Office: Yule Catto Building, Temple Fields, Harlow, Essex, CM20 2BH
Activities: Non-trading company
Parent: Synthomer PLC
Officers: Richard Atkinson, Secretary; Richard Atkinson [1962] Director/Company Secretary; Stephen Guy Bennett [1964] Director

Tendring Farms Limited
Incorporated: 9 December 2002
Net Worth Deficit: £588,168 *Total Assets:* £9,998,594
Registered Office: Bentfield Place, Bentfield Road, Stanstead, Essex, CM24 8HL
Activities: Mixed farming
Officers: Andrew Ian Sargeant, Secretary; Andrew Ian Sargeant [1971] Director; David Richard Sargeant [1967] Director/Property; Jacqueline Sargeant [1946] Director/Retired; Richard Arthur Sargeant [1944] Director/Retired; Timothy Robert Sargeant [1965] Director/Property

Tenmill Limited
Incorporated: 27 September 2012 *Employees:* 5
Net Worth: £3,302,709 *Total Assets:* £17,036,908
Registered Office: The Old Rectory, Brisley, Dereham, Norfolk, NR20 5LJ
Activities: Other credit granting n.e.c.
Major Shareholder: Richard Charles Higham
Officers: Gabrielle Eleanor Higham [1997] Director; Isabelle Julia Higham [1995] Director; Jacqueline Nada Higham [1960] Director; Richard Charles Higham [1958] Director; Graham Richard Woodford [1952] Director/Accountant

Terex Cranes UK Limited
Incorporated: 13 September 1991 *Employees:* 29
Net Worth: £27,695,000 *Total Assets:* £31,691,000
Registered Office: 14 Hikers Way, Crendon Industrial Park, Long Crendon, Bucks, HP18 9RW
Activities: Agents involved in the sale of machinery, industrial equipment, ships and aircraft
Parent: Terex Corporation
Officers: Eric I Cohen, Secretary/Lawyer [American]; Eric I Cohen [1958] Director/Lawyer [American]; Stoyan Filipov [1968] Director/President [American]; John Daniel Sheehan [1960] Director/Chief Financial Officer [American]; Carsten Von Der Geest [1974] Director [Dutch]

TES Enterprise Solutions Ltd
Incorporated: 27 November 2012 *Employees:* 1
Previous: Tectre Enterprise Solutions Ltd
Net Worth: £783,964 *Total Assets:* £28,815,054
Registered Office: 10 Western Road, Romford, Essex, RM1 3JT
Activities: Agents specialised in the sale of other particular products
Major Shareholder: Ronald William James Argent
Officers: Ronald William James Argent [1953] Director; Stephen Southern [1953] Director

Tesco (Overseas) Limited
Incorporated: 5 February 1982
Net Worth: £236,048,992 *Total Assets:* £811,825,024
Registered Office: Tesco House, Shire Park, Kestrel Way, Welwyn Garden City, Herts, AL7 1GA
Activities: Activities of head offices
Parent: Tesco PLC
Officers: Bhavesh Mistry [1972] Director/Deputy CFO; Robert John Welch [1966] Director/Company Secretary

Tesco Blue (3LP) Limited
Incorporated: 15 April 2016
Net Worth: £29,399,260 *Total Assets:* £29,399,260
Registered Office: Tesco House, Shire Park, Kestrel Way, Welwyn Garden City, Herts, AL7 1GA
Activities: Other business support service activities n.e.c.
Parent: Tesco Property Holdings Limited
Officers: John Gibney [1967] Assets and Estates Director [Irish]; Amit Soni [1968] Finance Director [Indian]

Tesco Blue (GP) Limited
Incorporated: 24 February 2006
Net Worth: £753,545 *Total Assets:* £543,312,000
Registered Office: Tesco House, Shire Park, Kestrel Way, Welwyn Garden City, Herts, AL7 1GA
Activities: Other business support service activities n.e.c.
Shareholders: Tesco Pension Trustees Limited; Tesco Property Holdings (No. 2) Limited
Officers: John Gibney [1967] Assets and Estates Director [Irish]; Ruston Arthur Mark Smith [1964] Non-Executive Director Chairman

Tesco Corporate Treasury Services PLC
Incorporated: 30 July 2013
Net Worth: £88,000,000 *Total Assets:* £8,073,999,872
Registered Office: Tesco House, Shire Park, Kestrel Way, Welwyn Garden City, Herts, AL7 1GA
Activities: Financial management
Parent: Tesco PLC
Officers: Sara Thomson, Secretary; Lynda Jane Heywood [1964] Director/Corporate Treasurer; Alan James Stewart [1960] Director

Tesco Distribution Limited
Incorporated: 30 September 1994 *Employees:* 12,655
Net Worth: £548,486,976 *Total Assets:* £813,977,024
Registered Office: Tesco House, Shire Park, Kestrel Way, Welwyn Garden City, Herts, AL7 1GA
Activities: Freight transport by road
Parent: Tesco Distribution Holdings Limited
Officers: Niamh Allison Doyle [1973] Finance Director; Alan James Stewart [1960] Director; Richard Andrew Woolfenden [1969] UK Distribution Director

Tesco Family Dining Limited
Incorporated: 2 May 2013 *Employees:* 1,663
Net Worth Deficit: £31,637,000 *Total Assets:* £31,887,000
Registered Office: Tesco House, Shire Park, Kestrel Way, Welwyn Garden City, Herts, AL7 1GA
Activities: Unlicenced restaurants and cafes
Parent: Tesco Holdings Limited
Officers: Niamh Allison Doyle [1973] Finance Director; Adam Melville Martin [1963] Marketing and Commercial Director; Jonathan Taylor [1979] Managing Director Large Stores

Tesco Food Sourcing Limited
Incorporated: 21 January 2011
Net Worth: £183,212,000 *Total Assets:* £210,518,000
Registered Office: Tesco House, Shire Park, Kestrel Way, Welwyn Garden City, Herts, AL7 1GA
Activities: Other business support service activities n.e.c.
Parent: Tesco Holdings Limited
Officers: David Alexander Reddoch Berry [1972] Director; Amit Soni [1968] Finance Director [Indian]; Stephanie Wood [1983] Commercial Director, Fresh Food and Commodities; Andrew David Yaxley [1967] Director

Tesco Freetime Limited
Incorporated: 24 December 2001
Net Worth: £4,497,000 *Total Assets:* £122,312,000
Registered Office: Tesco House, Shire Park, Kestrel Way, Welwyn Garden City, Herts, AL7 1GA
Activities: Other service activities n.e.c.
Parent: Tesco Holdings Limited
Officers: Amit Soni [1968] Finance Director [Indian]

Tesco Fuchsia (3LP) Limited
Incorporated: 15 April 2016
Net Worth: £28,947,276 *Total Assets:* £28,947,276
Registered Office: Tesco House, Shire Park, Kestrel Way, Welwyn Garden City, Herts, AL7 1GA
Activities: Other business support service activities n.e.c.
Parent: Tesco Property Holdings Limited
Officers: John Gibney [1967] Assets and Estates Director [Irish]; Amit Soni [1968] Finance Director [Indian]

Tesco Holdings Limited
Incorporated: 16 October 1929
Net Worth: £4,621,000,192 *Total Assets:* £14,917,999,616
Registered Office: Tesco House, Shire Park, Kestrel Way, Welwyn Garden City, Herts, AL7 1GA
Activities: Activities of head offices
Parent: Tesco PLC
Officers: David John Lewis [1965] Director/Chief Executive Officer; Adrian Charles Morris [1967] Director/Group General Counsel; Steven Andrew Rigby [1963] Director/Surveyor; Alan James Stewart [1960] Director; Robert John Welch [1966] Director/Company Secretary

Tesco International Internet Retailing Limited
Incorporated: 21 June 1894
Net Worth: £8,334,000 *Total Assets:* £9,651,000
Registered Office: Tesco House, Shire Park, Kestrel Way, Welwyn Garden City, Herts, AL7 1GA
Activities: Other retail sale not in stores, stalls or markets
Parent: Tesco PLC
Officers: Niamh Allison Doyle [1973] Finance Director; Adrian James Letts [1973] Online - Managing Director [Australian]

Tesco International Services Limited
Incorporated: 21 March 1996
Net Worth: £2,460,000 *Total Assets:* £10,698,000
Registered Office: Tesco House, Shire Park, Kestrel Way, Welwyn Garden City, Herts, AL7 1GA
Activities: Other service activities n.e.c.
Parent: Tesco PLC
Officers: Bhavesh Mistry [1972] Director/Deputy CFO; Robert John Welch [1966] Director/Company Secretary

Tesco Maintenance Limited
Incorporated: 20 November 2006 *Employees:* 1,351
Net Worth: £4,064,000 *Total Assets:* £38,186,000
Registered Office: Tesco House, Shire Park, Kestrel Way, Welwyn Garden City, Herts, AL7 1GA
Activities: Other service activities n.e.c.
Parent: Tesco Holdings Limited
Officers: Timothy Robert Golding [1961] Director/Chief Operating Officer; Amit Soni [1968] Finance Director [Indian]

Tesco Mobile Limited
Incorporated: 29 May 2003 *Employees:* 184
Net Worth: £11,969,000 *Total Assets:* £349,728,992
Registered Office: Shire Park, Welwyn Garden City, Herts, AL7 1GA
Activities: Other telecommunications activities
Shareholders: Tesco Mobile Communications Limited; Tesco Mobile Services Limited
Officers: Alessandra Bellini [1964] Director/Chief Customer Officer [Italian]; Mark Evans [1969] Director/Accountant; Mark David Hardman [1975] Director/Accountant; Roger James Keenan [1964] Director; Bhavesh Mistry [1972] Director/Deputy CFO; Oliver James Potter [1981] Director/Telecoms; Claire Alexandra Soper-Lorains [1980] Category Director, Tesco PLC; Jason Mark Tarry [1967] Director/Retailer

Tesco Mobile Services Limited
Incorporated: 29 May 2003
Net Worth Deficit: £556,000 *Total Assets:* £11,001,000
Registered Office: Tesco House, Shire Park, Kestrel Way, Welwyn Garden City, Herts, AL7 1GA
Activities: Activities of head offices
Parent: Tesco Mobile Communications Limited
Officers: Lynda Jane Heywood [1964] Director/Corporate Treasurer; Bruce Marsh [1968] Director; Robert John Welch [1966] Director/Company Secretary

Tesco Overseas Investments Limited
Incorporated: 2 May 1996
Net Worth: £6,108,000,256 *Total Assets:* £7,190,000,128
Registered Office: Tesco House, Shire Park, Kestrel Way, Welwyn Garden City, Herts, AL7 1GA
Activities: Non-trading company
Parent: Tesco PLC
Officers: Adrian Charles Morris [1967] Director/Group General Counsel; Alan James Harris Stewart [1960] Director; Robert John Welch [1966] Director/Company Secretary

Tesco Overseas ULC
Incorporated: 10 December 1998
Net Worth: £3,215,451,904 *Total Assets:* £3,233,027,072
Registered Office: Tesco House, Shire Park, Kestrel Way, Welwyn Garden City, Herts, AL7 1GA
Activities: Other business support service activities n.e.c.
Parent: Tesco Holdings BV
Officers: Lynda Jane Heywood [1964] Director/Corporate Treasurer; Bhavesh Mistry [1972] Director/Deputy CFO; Robert John Welch [1966] Director/Company Secretary

Tesco Pension Investment Limited
Incorporated: 26 August 2011 *Employees:* 46
Total Assets: £14,896,000
Registered Office: Tesco House, Shire Park, Kestrel Way, Welwyn Garden City, Herts, AL7 1GA
Activities: Financial management
Parent: Tesco Pension Trustees Limited
Officers: Steven Michael Daniels [1959] Director/Chief Investment Officer; Danny Firth [1966] Director/Chief Operating Officer; Ruston Arthur Mark Smith [1964] Non-Executive Director Chairman

Tesco PLC
Incorporated: 27 November 1947 *Employees:* 448,988
Net Worth: £10,480,000,000 *Total Assets:* £44,884,000,768
Registered Office: Tesco House, Shire Park, Kestrel Way, Welwyn Garden City, Herts, AL7 1GA
Activities: Retail sale in non-specialised stores with food, beverages or tobacco predominating
Officers: Robert John Welch, Secretary; John Murray Allan [1948] Director/Chairman; Mark Henry Armour [1954] Director; Melissa Bethell [1974] Director; Stewart Charles Gilliland [1957] Director; Stephen William Golsby [1954] Director; Byron Elmer Grote [1948] Director; David John Lewis [1965] Director/Chief Executive Officer; Anders Bertil Mikael Olsson [1957] Director [Swedish]; Deanna Watson Oppenheimer [1958] Director; Simon Iain Patterson [1973] Director; Elizabeth Alison Platt [1962] Director; Lindsey Jane Pownall [1962] Director; Alan James Stewart [1960] Director

Tesco Property Finance 1 PLC
Incorporated: 27 July 2006
Net Worth: £551,517 *Total Assets:* £543,115,200
Registered Office: Tesco House, Shire Park, Kestrel Way, Welwyn Garden City, Herts, AL7 1GA
Activities: Activities of head offices
Parent: Tesco Property Finance 1 Holdco Limited
Officers: Simon Derwood Austen Drewett [1970] Director/Chartered Surveyor; John Gibney [1967] Assets and Estates Director [Irish]; Lynda Jane Heywood [1964] Director/Corporate Treasurer; William Maunder Taylor [1955] Director/Chartered Surveyor

Tesco Property Holdings (No.2) Limited
Incorporated: 27 July 2006
Net Worth: £5,272,696 *Total Assets:* £264,796,080
Registered Office: Tesco House, Shire Park, Kestrel Way, Welwyn Garden City, Herts, AL7 1GA
Activities: Other business support service activities n.e.c.
Parent: Tesco Holdings Limited
Officers: John Gibney [1967] Assets and Estates Director [Irish]; Steven Andrew Rigby [1963] Director/Surveyor; Amit Soni [1968] Finance Director [Indian]; Robert John Welch [1966] Director/Company Secretary

Tesco Property Holdings Limited
Incorporated: 28 February 1989
Net Worth: £693,739,008 *Total Assets:* £6,563,639,808
Registered Office: Tesco House, Shire Park, Kestrel Way, Welwyn Garden City, Herts, AL7 1GA
Activities: Activities of head offices
Parent: Tesco Holdings Limited
Officers: John Gibney [1967] Assets and Estates Director [Irish]; Steven Andrew Rigby [1963] Director/Surveyor; Amit Soni [1968] Finance Director [Indian]; Robert John Welch [1966] Director/Company Secretary

Tesco Property Partner (No.1) Limited
Incorporated: 28 October 2003
Net Worth: £20,301,228 *Total Assets:* £22,106,228
Registered Office: Tesco House, Shire Park, Kestrel Way, Welwyn Garden City, Herts, AL7 1GA
Activities: Other business support service activities n.e.c.
Parent: Tesco PLC
Officers: John Gibney [1967] Assets and Estates Director [Irish]; Robert John Welch [1966] Director/Company Secretary

Tesco Red (3LP) Limited
Incorporated: 15 April 2016
Net Worth: £70,755,168 *Total Assets:* £70,755,168
Registered Office: Tesco House, Shire Park, Kestrel Way, Welwyn Garden City, Herts, AL7 1GA
Activities: Other business support service activities n.e.c.
Parent: Tesco Property Holdings Limited
Officers: John Gibney [1967] Assets and Estates Director [Irish]; Amit Soni [1968] Finance Director [Indian]

Tesco Stores Limited
Incorporated: 9 May 1953 *Employees:* 171,329
Net Worth: £4,562,999,808 *Total Assets:* £26,563,000,320
Registered Office: Tesco House, Shire Park, Kestrel Way, Welwyn Garden City, Herts, AL7 1GA
Activities: Retail sale in non-specialised stores with food, beverages or tobacco predominating
Parent: Tesco Holdings Limited
Officers: Robert John Welch, Secretary; David John Lewis [1965] Director/Chief Executive Officer; Adrian Charles Morris [1967] Director/Group General Counsel; Steven Andrew Rigby [1963] Director/Surveyor; Alan James Stewart [1960] Director; Jason Mark Tarry [1967] Director/Retailer

Tesco TLB Properties Limited
Incorporated: 15 February 1996
Previous: BLT Properties Limited
Net Worth: £92,845,928 *Total Assets:* £241,308,480
Registered Office: Tesco House, Shire Park, Kestrel Way, Welwyn Garden City, Herts, AL7 1GA
Activities: Management of real estate on a fee or contract basis
Parent: Tesco Property Holdings Limited
Officers: Alistair Ewan Clark [1971] Director/Corporate Treasurer; John Gibney [1967] Assets and Estates Director [Irish]

Tesco Treasury Services PLC
Incorporated: 2 June 2011
Net Worth: £10,000,000 *Total Assets:* £852,000,000
Registered Office: Tesco House, Shire Park, Kestrel Way, Welwyn Garden City, Herts, AL7 1GA
Activities: Financial management
Parent: Tesco PLC
Officers: Sara Thomson, Secretary; Lynda Jane Heywood [1964] Director/Corporate Treasurer; Alan James Stewart [1960] Director; Robert John Welch [1966] Director/Company Secretary

Test Equipment Asset Management Limited
Incorporated: 29 March 2006
Net Worth Deficit: £28,093,000 *Total Assets:* £39,761,000
Registered Office: Unit 1 Waverley Industrial Estate, Hailsham Drive, Harrow, Middlesex, HA1 4TR
Activities: Other professional, scientific and technical activities n.e.c.
Officers: Nigel Brown [1957] Director; John Joseph Hafferty [1956] Director/Chief Financial Officer [American]; Paul Joseph McCloskey [1960] Sales Director

Tetra Pak Processing UK Limited
Incorporated: 26 July 2001 *Employees:* 110
Net Worth: £5,612,852 *Total Assets:* £16,092,751
Registered Office: Eagle House, Peregrine Business Park, Gomm Road, High Wycombe, Bucks, HP13 7DL
Activities: Other service activities n.e.c.
Officers: Kim Barkus [1966] Director; Carl Johan Olof Rabe [1969] Director [Swedish]; Goran Lars Soderstrom [1960] Finance Director [Swedish]

Tetworth Farms LLP
Incorporated: 13 August 2008 *Employees:* 2
Net Worth: £11,799,952 *Total Assets:* £12,095,974
Registered Office: Tetworth Hall Estate Office, Drove Road, Tetworth, Sandy, Beds, SG19 2HU
Officers: Richard John Cook [1972] Member; Rosalind Mary Cook [1945] Member; Olivia Catherine Hall [1976] Member; Julia Elizabeth Shaw [1970] Member

Tex Holdings PLC
Incorporated: 8 March 1946
Net Worth: £10,639,000 *Total Assets:* £24,767,000
Registered Office: Claydon Business Park, Gipping Road, Great Blakenham, Ipswich, Suffolk, IP6 0NL
Activities: Activities of head offices
Officers: Christopher Andrew Parker, Secretary; Anthony Richard Brocas Burrows [1939] Director/Industrialist; George Christopher Gray [1944] Director; Christopher David Palmer-Tomkinson [1942] Director; Christopher Andrew Parker [1962] Director; David Redhead [1947] Director; Christopher Thomas Varley [1948] Director

Tex Plastics (Derby) Limited
Incorporated: 15 November 1976 *Employees:* 149
Net Worth: £896,707 *Total Assets:* £8,160,821
Registered Office: Claydon Business Park, Gipping Road, Great Blakenham, Ipswich, Suffolk, IP6 0NL
Activities: Manufacture of other plastic products
Parent: Tex Holdings PLC
Officers: Christopher Andrew Parker, Secretary; Lee Barker [1973] New Business Development Director; Justin John Davies [1967] Director and General Manager; Michael Rhodes-Price [1989] Commercial Director; Guy Richard Sentance [1968] Manufacturing Director

TFX Group Limited
Incorporated: 24 December 1993 *Employees:* 43
Net Worth: £10,514,000 *Total Assets:* £23,063,000
Registered Office: Grosvenor House, Horseshoe Crescent, Beaconsfield, Bucks, HP9 1LJ
Activities: Other manufacturing n.e.c.
Parent: Teleflex Incorporated
Officers: Gerard Daniel McCaffrey, Secretary; Jean-Luc Albert Dianda [1963] Director/Executive [French]; Matthew James [1971] Director/General Manager; Gerard Daniel McCaffrey [1954] Director [Irish]

TGA Industries Limited
Incorporated: 6 December 2006 *Employees:* 500
Previous: Danaher UK Industries Limited
Net Worth: £299,760,000 *Total Assets:* £364,696,992
Registered Office: Gilbarco Veeder-Root, Crompton Close, Basildon, Essex, SS14 3BA
Activities: Manufacture of electronic industrial process control equipment
Parent: TGA UK Finance Ltd
Officers: Nicholas John Charles Blomfield [1980] Site Leader and Director of Finance; Gregor John Mathers [1963] Finance Director; Trevor Mark Sinkinson [1971] Director; Stephan Dominik Sommer [1971] Business Unit Director [German]

TGA UK Alpha Limited
Incorporated: 18 February 2016
Net Worth Deficit: £1,132,000 *Total Assets:* £470,486,016
Registered Office: Crompton Close, Basildon, Essex, SS14 3BA
Activities: Activities of head offices
Parent: Fortive Corporation
Officers: David Alistair James Rodgers [1979] Finance Director; Trevor Mark Sinkinson [1971] Director; Rajesh Singh Yadava [1972] Director/Treasurer [Indian]

TGA UK Finance Limited
Incorporated: 29 February 2016
Net Worth: £176,200,384 *Total Assets:* £380,143,872
Registered Office: Crompton Close, Basildon, Essex, SS14 3BA
Activities: Activities of head offices
Parent: TGA UK Holdings Limited
Officers: David Alistair James Rodgers [1979] Finance Director; Trevor Mark Sinkinson [1971] Director; Rajesh Singh Yadava [1972] Director/Treasurer [Indian]

TGA UK Holdings Limited
Incorporated: 18 February 2016
Net Worth: £117,714,096 *Total Assets:* £117,714,096
Registered Office: Crompton Close, Basildon, Essex, SS14 3BA
Activities: Activities of head offices
Parent: Fortive Corporation
Officers: David Alistair James Rodgers [1979] Finance Director; Trevor Mark Sinkinson [1971] Director; Rajesh Singh Yadava [1972] Director/Treasurer [Indian]

TGA UK Omega Limited
Incorporated: 29 February 2016
Net Worth: £496,558,016 *Total Assets:* £498,702,016
Registered Office: Crompton Close, Basildon, Essex, SS14 3BA
Activities: Activities of head offices
Parent: TGA UK Alpha Limited
Officers: David Alistair James Rodgers [1979] Finance Director; Trevor Mark Sinkinson [1971] Director; Rajesh Singh Yadava [1972] Director/Treasurer [Indian]

Thames Card Technology Limited
Incorporated: 26 July 1994 *Employees:* 175
Net Worth: £2,195,732 *Total Assets:* £8,799,751
Registered Office: Thames House, Arterial Road, Rayleigh, Essex, SS6 7UQ
Activities: Manufacture of other plastic products
Shareholders: Jo Waktins; BGF GP Limited
Officers: Mark Gunnar Bryant [1962] Director; Andrew David Caffyn [1964] Non-Executive Director; Che Colford [1970] Director; Robin David Hilton [1971] Director; Paul Graham Underwood [1963] Managing Director; Matthew Paul Williams [1958] Director

Thames Industrial Estate Limited
Incorporated: 2 January 2001 *Employees:* 2
Net Worth: £2,175,239 *Total Assets:* £14,454,908
Registered Office: 1st Floor, Sheraton House, Lower Road, Chorleywood, Rickmansworth, Herts, WD3 5LH
Activities: Development of building projects
Major Shareholder: Raymond Valentine Mawhood
Officers: Lisa Jane Ashton-Jones, Secretary; Lisa Jane Ashton-Jones [1966] Director/Landlord & Property Developer; Philip Ashton-Jones [1964] Director/Barrister; Raymond Valentine Mawhood [1942] Director

Thames Reinforcements Limited
Incorporated: 14 February 2006 *Employees:* 140
Net Worth: £7,659,173 *Total Assets:* £20,254,036
Registered Office: 4 Elstree Way, Borehamwood, Herts, WD6 1RN
Activities: Other specialised construction activities n.e.c.
Parent: JRL Group Ltd
Officers: Ronan Joseph Gleeson, Secretary/Director [Irish]; Ronan Joseph Gleeson [1976] Director [Irish]; Kevin William Keegan [1963] Director [Irish]; John James Reddington [1972] Director/Builder [Irish]

Thames Valley Air Ambulance
Incorporated: 24 August 2000 *Employees:* 29
Previous: Thames Valley and Chiltern Air Ambulance Trust
Net Worth: £15,634,631 *Total Assets:* £16,635,763
Registered Office: Stokenchurch House, Oxford Road, Stokenchurch, High Wycombe, Bucks, HP14 3SX
Activities: Other human health activities
Officers: Roland Tudor Lawrence, Secretary; Christopher Ian Bannister [1967] Director/Banker; Lesley Boler [1964] Director/Chief Nurse; David Geoffery Davis [1974] Director/Paramedic; Claire Louise Dobbs [1966] Director/Consultant; Dr John Edward Gaffney [1959] Medical Director; Victoria Anne George [1977] Director/Chartered Accountant; Jonathan Mark Kendrew [1973] Director/Surgeon; Roland Tudor Lawrence [1949] Director/Retired Solicitor; Erica Moon [1973] Director/Business Executive; Richard Hugh Pearce [1968] Director; Timothy Hugo Pollock [1958] Director; Amanda Janine Poole [1958] Director/Management Consultant; Sarah Jane Roberts [1959] Director/Retired; Doctor Michael Elliott Ward [1947] Director/Retired Doctor

Tharros Limited
Incorporated: 4 January 1993
Net Worth: £9,043,463 *Total Assets:* £13,336,089
Registered Office: Botanic House, 100 Hills Road, Cambridge, CB2 1PH
Activities: Growing of cereals (except rice), leguminous crops and oil seeds
Officers: Michael John Aubrey, Secretary/Solicitor; Doctor Francesco Saverio Amman [1957] Director [Italian]; Simon Neil Fowler [1967] Director/Land Agent; Christoph Gruninger [1943] Director/Banker [German]

Theatre Royal (Norwich) Trust Limited
Incorporated: 16 December 1970 *Employees:* 197
Net Worth: £8,494,966 *Total Assets:* £15,215,966
Registered Office: The Theatre Royal, Theatre Street, Norwich, NR2 1RL
Activities: Artistic creation
Officers: Tom Burdett, Secretary; Stephen Askew [1963] Director/Farmer; Charlotte Elizabeth Crawley [1953] Director/Art Historian; David Fullman [1952] Director/Retired; Steven Michael Jaggard [1964] Marketing Director; John Nicholas Lloyd [1948] Director; Michael Clive Newey [1963] Director/Chief Executive; Angela Shireen Robson [1961] Finance Director; Timothy Robert Seeley [1960] Bank Director; Tim Joseph Sweeting [1976] Director/Chief Executive; Sharon Louise Wilson [1970] Director/HR & OD Consultant; Han Yang Yap [1966] Director

Thistledove Limited
Incorporated: 14 October 1998
Net Worth: £23,621,000 *Total Assets:* £216,868,000
Registered Office: McColl's House, Ashwells Road, Brentwood, Essex, CM15 9ST
Activities: Activities of head offices
Parent: Martin McColl Retail Limited
Officers: Robbie Ian Bell [1973] Director/Chief Financial Officer; Simon Jeremy Ian Fuller [1977] Director; Steven Green [1981] Director; Simon Jonathan Miller [1963] Director; David Thomas [1960] Director

Thomas,Arthur & Gordon,Limited
Incorporated: 28 February 1946 *Employees:* 4
Net Worth: £4,892,562 *Total Assets:* £8,091,394
Registered Office: Unit 4 Limes Court, Conduit Lane, Hoddesdon, Herts, EN11 8EP
Activities: Renting and operating of Housing Association real estate
Shareholders: Russell Arthur Gordon Thomas; Barry Adrian Southey Thomas; Louise Laurel Barber
Officers: Louise Laurel Barber [1947] Director; Barry Adrian Southey Thomas [1941] Director

Thompson Investments (London) Limited
Incorporated: 13 November 1987 *Employees:* 14
Net Worth: £155,377,840 *Total Assets:* £180,576,736
Registered Office: Cheveley Park Stud, Duchess Drive, Newmarket, Suffolk, CB8 9DD
Activities: Activities of head offices
Major Shareholder: Patricia Thompson
Officers: Christopher James Dant, Secretary; Roy Bernard Copus [1959] Director/Chartered Accountant; Rupert Howard Milton Horner [1962] Director/Chartered Accountant; David Brian Thompson [1936] Director; Patricia Thompson [1940] Director; Richard Charles Thompson [1964] Director; Katharine Patricia Woodward [1968] Director

Thomson Sawmills Holdings Limited
Incorporated: 20 November 2012 *Employees:* 51
Net Worth: £2,789,875 *Total Assets:* £16,677,180
Registered Office: The Sawmill, Shortthorn Road, Stratton Strawless, Norwich, NR10 5NT
Activities: Mixed farming
Shareholders: Brian Thomson; Brian Thomson; Mary Jane Thomson
Officers: Laura Grimwood [1988] Director/Administrator; Carly Jane Reid [1979] Director/Administrator; Brian Thomson [1958] Director/Sawmiller; Jamie Brian Thomson [1980] Director/Sawmiller; Mary Jane Thomson [1958] Director/Personal Assistant; Oliver Thomson [1991] Director/Sawmiller

Thomson Sawmills Limited
Incorporated: 28 March 1996 *Employees:* 51
Net Worth: £2,656,761 *Total Assets:* £15,907,542
Registered Office: The Sawmill, Shortthorn Road, Stratton Strawless, Norwich, NR10 5NT
Activities: Sawmilling and planing of wood
Shareholders: Thomson Sawmills Holdings Limited; Thomson Sawmills Holdings Limited
Officers: Mary Jane Thomson, Secretary; Laura Grimwood [1988] Director; Carly Jane Reid [1979] Director; Brian Thomson [1956] Director/Sawmiller; Jamie Brian Thomson [1980] Director; Mary Jane Thomson [1958] Director; Oliver Thomson [1991] Director/Sawmill Operator

Thomson Travel Group (Holdings) Limited
Incorporated: 19 July 1996
Net Worth: £11,179,000 *Total Assets:* £11,842,000
Registered Office: Wigmore House, Wigmore Lane, Luton, Beds, LU2 9TN
Activities: Activities of head offices
Parent: TUI Northern Europe Limited
Officers: Simon Kenneth Arnold [1977] Director; Robert Coldrake [1978] Director/Chartered Accountant

Thor Holdco Limited
Incorporated: 1 July 2016
Net Worth: £110,299,000 *Total Assets:* £110,385,000
Registered Office: Abel Smith House, Gunnels Wood Road, Stevenage, Herts, SG1 2ST
Activities: Activities of other holding companies n.e.c.
Parent: Thor Midco Limited
Officers: Ian Cusden, Secretary; James Michael Arnold [1965] Director/Chief Executive Officer; Martin Geoffrey Beesley [1966] Director/Chief Financial Officer; Ian Vincent Cusden [1957] Director/Chartered Accountant; James Robert Winnicott [1968] Director

Thor Midco Limited
Incorporated: 19 July 2016
Net Worth Deficit: £9,457,000 *Total Assets:* £110,966,000
Registered Office: Abel Smith House, Gunnels Wood Road, Stevenage, Herts, SG1 2ST
Activities: Activities of other holding companies n.e.c.
Parent: Thor Topco Limited
Officers: Ian Cusden, Secretary; James Michael Arnold [1965] Director/Chief Executive Officer; Martin Geoffrey Beesley [1966] Director/Chief Financial Officer; Ian Vincent Cusden [1957] Director/Chartered Accountant; James Robert Winnicott [1968] Director

Thor Topco Limited
Incorporated: 19 July 2016 *Employees:* 7,339
Net Worth Deficit: £10,678,000 *Total Assets:* £615,545,024
Registered Office: Abel Smith House, Gunnels Wood Road, Stevenage, Herts, SG1 2ST
Activities: Activities of other holding companies n.e.c.
Officers: Ian Cusden, Secretary; James Michael Arnold [1965] Director/Chief Executive Officer; Martin Geoffrey Beesley [1966] Director/Chief Financial Officer; Ian Vincent Cusden [1957] Director/Chartered Accountant; James Robert Winnicott [1968] Director

Thoratec Europe Limited
Incorporated: 22 February 1995
Net Worth: £86,571,504 *Total Assets:* £87,681,592
Registered Office: Burnett House, Lakeview Court, Ermine Business Park, Huntingdon, Cambs, PE29 6UA
Activities: Other human health activities
Officers: Benjamin Edward Oosterbaan [1963] Director/Assistant Treasurer [American]; Karen Peterson [1965] Director/Business Executive [American]; Brian Bernard Yoor [1969] Director/Business Executive [American]

Thorlabs Limited
Incorporated: 23 March 2004 *Employees:* 232
Net Worth: £17,349,132 *Total Assets:* £28,030,180
Registered Office: 1 St Thomas Place, Cambridgeshire Business Park, Ely, Cambs, CB7 4EX
Activities: Manufacture of other fabricated metal products n.e.c.
Major Shareholder: Alex Cable
Officers: Dr Keith Dhese, Secretary; Alex Cable [1957] Director/Executive [American]

Thorney Bay Park Limited
Incorporated: 28 February 2000 *Employees:* 49
Net Worth Deficit: £397,562 *Total Assets:* £12,679,404
Registered Office: Sutherland House, 1759 London Road, Leigh on Sea, Essex, SS9 2RZ
Activities: Recreational vehicle parks, trailer parks and camping grounds
Parent: Pemican Limited
Officers: Holly Ellen King, Secretary; Holly Ellen King [1989] Director/Secretary; John Michael O'Dell [1952] Health & Safety Director

Thorney Leys Developments Limited
Incorporated: 3 May 2017
Net Worth: £176,221 *Total Assets:* £10,282,169
Registered Office: 3rd Floor, Sterling House, Langston Road, Loughton, Essex, IG10 3TS
Activities: Development of building projects
Parent: Galliard Holdings Limited
Officers: Allan William Porter, Secretary; David Edward Conway [1976] Director; Stephen Stuart Solomon Conway [1948] Director; Jonathan Michael Morgan [1978] Director; Donagh O'Sullivan [1968] Construction Director [Irish]

Thornhill Estates Limited
Incorporated: 7 November 1933 *Employees:* 5
Net Worth: £7,735,276 *Total Assets:* £9,829,936
Registered Office: The Granary, 24a The Street, Diddington, St Neots, Cambs, PE19 5XU
Activities: Other letting and operating of own or leased real estate
Major Shareholder: Edmund George William Thornhill
Officers: Kerry Lisa Simpson, Secretary; Kerry Lisa Simpson [1971] Director/Property Manager; Alison Clare Thornhill [1972] Director; Edmund George William Thornhill [1969] Director/Chartered Surveyor; Margaret Daughne Thornhill [1937] Director

P.J. Thory Limited
Incorporated: 5 October 1976 *Employees:* 87
Net Worth: £5,339,257 *Total Assets:* £12,055,756
Registered Office: White Walls, Eldernell Lane, Coates, Whittlesey, Peterborough, PE7 2DD
Activities: Freight transport by road
Shareholders: James Peter Thory; Timothy David Thory
Officers: James Peter Thory [1961] Director/Manager; Timothy David Thory [1962] Director/Manager

THR Number 12 PLC
Incorporated: 11 May 2017
Net Worth: £54,438,000 *Total Assets:* £96,257,000
Registered Office: Springfield Lodge, Colchester Road, Chelmsford, Essex, CM2 5PW
Activities: Activities of real estate investment trusts
Parent: Target Healthcare REIT Limited
Officers: Professor June Andrews [1955] Director/University Professor; Gordon Charles Coull [1953] Director; Thomas Jamieson Hutchison III [1941] Director [American]; Robert Malcolm Naish [1953] Director/Chartered Surveyor

THR Number 5 Limited
Incorporated: 13 February 2004
Previous: Godswell Park Limited
Net Worth: £16,013,681 *Total Assets:* £16,048,269
Registered Office: Springfield Lodge, Colchester Road, Chelmsford, Essex, CM2 5PW
Activities: Activities of real estate investment trusts
Parent: THR Number 12 PLC
Officers: Professor June Andrews [1955] Director/University Professor; Gordon Charles Coull [1953] Director; Thomas J Hutchison III [1941] Director [American]; Robert Malcolm Naish [1953] Director/Chartered Surveyor

THR Number One PLC
Incorporated: 14 April 2014
Net Worth: £94,337,000 *Total Assets:* £127,210,000
Registered Office: Springfield Lodge, Colchester Road, Chelmsford, Essex, CM2 5PW
Activities: Activities of real estate investment trusts
Parent: Target Healthcare REIT Limited
Officers: Professor June Andrews [1955] Director/University Professor; Gordon Charles Coull [1953] Director; Thomas J Hutchison III [1941] Director [American]; Robert Malcolm Naish [1953] Director/Chartered Surveyor

THR Number Two Limited
Incorporated: 16 December 2013
Net Worth: £15,779,000 *Total Assets:* £35,086,000
Registered Office: Springfield Lodge, Colchester Road, Chelmsford, Essex, CM2 5PW
Activities: Activities of real estate investment trusts
Parent: THR Number One PLC
Officers: Professor June Andrews [1955] Director/University Professor; Gordon Charles Coull [1953] Director; Thomas J Hutchison III [1941] Director [American]; Robert Malcolm Naish [1953] Director/Chartered Surveyor

Three Rivers Property Investments Limited
Incorporated: 2 October 1984
Net Worth: £50,024,096 *Total Assets:* £51,317,440
Registered Office: Hawridge Place, Hawridge Common, Hawridge, Chesham, Bucks, HP5 2ZD
Activities: Other letting and operating of own or leased real estate
Parent: Church Cottage Investments Ltd
Officers: Carys Gadsden, Secretary; Carys Gadsden [1950] Director; Eric John Spencer Gadsden [1944] Director

Thrive Homes Finance PLC
Incorporated: 19 February 2014
Net Worth: £50,000 *Total Assets:* £135,878,000
Registered Office: Westside, London Road, Hemel Hempstead, Herts, HP3 9TD
Activities: Security dealing on own account
Officers: Shaun McLean, Secretary; Elspeth MacKenzie [1959] Director/Chief Executive; Shaun McLean [1970] Director and Company Secretary; Graham Leslie Olive [1965] Director/Deputy Chief Executive

The Thrive Partnership Academy Trust
Incorporated: 10 October 2011 *Employees:* 466
Previous: The Philip Morant School and College Academy Trust
Net Worth: £39,004,208 *Total Assets:* £49,335,416
Registered Office: Philip Morant School and College, Rembrandt Way, Colchester, Essex, CO3 4QS
Activities: General secondary education
Officers: Karen Willis, Secretary; Andrew Michael Cooke [1966] Director/Mortgage Specialist; Sarah Elizabeth Dignasse [1957] Director/Education Consultant; Mark Jeffries [1957] Director/Solicitor; Neil Edward Jones [1956] Director; Stephen Charles Richard Munday [1964] Director/Executive Principal and CEO; Dr Margaret Melrose Wilson [1957] Director/CEO/Headteacher

Thule Holding Limited
Incorporated: 18 August 2004 *Employees:* 2
Net Worth: £8,511,809 *Total Assets:* £16,652,151
Registered Office: Units 1-3 Two Counties Estate, Falconer Road, Haverhill, Suffolk, CB9 7XZ
Activities: Activities of head offices
Officers: Lars Johan Hedberg [1966] Director [Swedish]; Per Lennart Mauritzson [1967] Director [Swedish]

Thule Outdoor Limited
Incorporated: 11 June 1996 *Employees:* 35
Net Worth: £6,643,166 *Total Assets:* £13,157,285
Registered Office: Units 1-3 Two Counties Estate, Falconer Road, Haverhill, Suffolk, CB9 7XZ
Activities: Wholesale trade of motor vehicle parts and accessories
Parent: Thule Holding Limited
Officers: Lars Johan Hedberg [1966] Director [Swedish]; Per Lennart Mauritzson [1967] Director [Swedish]

Thumbzup UK Limited
Incorporated: 16 March 2015 *Employees:* 2
Net Worth: £1,272,899 *Total Assets:* £18,839,764
Registered Office: Suite 105, Viglen House, Alperton Lane, Wembley, Middlesex, HA0 1HD
Activities: Other business support service activities n.e.c.
Officers: Aviad Eyal [1970] Director [Israeli]; Saul Jacob Gorin [1965] Director [South African]

George Thurlow and Sons (Holdings) Limited
Incorporated: 27 April 1903 *Employees:* 667
Net Worth: £19,941,000 *Total Assets:* £76,301,000
Registered Office: Wisbech Road, Littleport, Cambs, CB6 1RA
Activities: Activities of distribution holding companies
Officers: Sally Anne Tew, Secretary; Sally Anne Tew [1963] Director; James Robert Thurlow [1971] Sales Director; John Geoffrey Thurlow [1938] Director/Chairman; Margaret Ann Thurlow [1940] Director; Nicola Jayne Titley [1966] Director/Housewife

Thurlow Estate Farms Limited
Incorporated: 2 November 2009 *Employees:* 18
Net Worth: £2,240,471 *Total Assets:* £12,436,883
Registered Office: Estate Office, Great Thurlow, Haverhill, Suffolk, CB9 7LQ
Activities: Growing of cereals (except rice), leguminous crops and oil seeds
Officers: George Moubray William Vestey [1964] Director/Farmer; James Edmund McLean Vestey [1962] Director/Farmer; Robin John Henry Vestey [1968] Director/Farmer; Timothy Ronald Geoffry Vestey [1961] Director/Farmer

Thurlow Nunn (Holdings) Limited
Incorporated: 3 March 1951 *Employees:* 668
Net Worth: £22,721,000 *Total Assets:* £73,166,000
Registered Office: Wisbech Road, Littleport, Cambs, CB6 1RA
Activities: Other letting and operating of own or leased real estate
Parent: George Thurlow and Sons (Holdings) Limited
Officers: Philip Harvey Addinall, Secretary/Financial; Philip Harvey Addinall [1961] Director/Financial; Nicholas Paul Hallett [1958] Director; Sally Anne Tew [1963] Director; William Christopher Tew [1991] Director; James Robert Thurlow [1971] Director/General Manager; John Geoffrey Thurlow [1938] Director/Chairman

Thurlow Nunn Limited
Incorporated: 19 July 2005 *Employees:* 294
Previous: Thurlow Nunn (JV) Ltd
Net Worth: £5,190,000 *Total Assets:* £22,595,000
Registered Office: Wisbech Road, Littleport, Cambs, CB6 1RA
Activities: Sale of new cars and light motor vehicles
Officers: Philip Harvey Addinall, Secretary/Financial Director; Philip Harvey Addinall [1961] Financial Director; Simon Nicholas Grylls [1969] Sales Director; Gary Brian Osborn [1969] Aftersales Director; James Robert Thurlow [1971] Director

Thurlow Nunn Standen Limited
Incorporated: 10 December 2004 *Employees:* 169
Net Worth: £7,733,000 *Total Assets:* £20,765,000
Registered Office: Wisbech Road, Littleport, Cambs, CB6 1RA
Activities: Sale of other motor vehicles
Officers: Philip Harvey Addinall, Secretary/Financial Director; Philip Harvey Addinall [1961] Financial Director; Adrian Hilary Brown [1965] Director; Jeremy Peter Nunn [1959] Contracts Director; Richard Pipe [1954] Parts Director; Christopher Tew [1963] Sales Director; Sally Anne Tew [1963] Personnel Director; James Robert Thurlow [1971] Sales Director

Thurne-Middleby Ltd
Incorporated: 13 February 2015 *Employees:* 70
Net Worth: £11,801,000 *Total Assets:* £14,790,000
Registered Office: Gresham House, Pinetrees Business Park, Salhouse Road, Norwich, NR7 9BB
Activities: Other manufacturing n.e.c.
Parent: Food Processing Holding Limited
Officers: Timothy John FitzGenerald [1969] Director/Vice President and Chief Financial Officer [American]; Martin McKay Lindsay [1964] Director/Corporate Treasurer [American]; Agustin Zufia [1967] Director/Group Controller [Spanish]

Thursford Collection (The)
Incorporated: 28 September 1976 *Employees:* 60
Net Worth: £10,986,719 *Total Assets:* £13,369,253
Registered Office: Laurel Farm, Thursford, Fakenham, Norfolk, NR21 0AG
Activities: Operation of historical sites and buildings and similar visitor attractions
Officers: Andrew Jonathan Barnes [1957] Director/Solicitor; Mark Jonathan Hazell [1962] Marketing Director; Christopher Edward Self [1948] Director/Chartered Surveyor; Andrew Nicholas Wells [1966] Director/Technical Consultant

Thurstable School Sports College and Sixth Form Centre
Incorporated: 5 July 2011 *Employees:* 183
Net Worth: £12,818,742 *Total Assets:* £17,331,808
Registered Office: Thurstable School Sports College and Sixth Form Centre, Maypole Road, Tiptree, Essex, CO5 0EW
Activities: Other education n.e.c.
Officers: Fiona Beck, Secretary; Miles Alexander Saunders Bacon [1964] Director/Headteacher; Colin Frederick Bigg [1945] Director/Retired; Emma Bowdidge [1991] Director/Teacher; Clare Jane Bragg [1966] Director/Accountant; Sharon Doreen Alice Hausrath [1970] Director/Foster Parent; Rebecca Hennahane [1991] Director/Teacher; Alexander Robert Hens [1972] Managing Director; Alan Christopher Lazell [1951] Director; Debra Karen Morgan [1963] Director/Learning Support Assistant; Elizabeth Oldham [1957] Director/Administrative Assistant; Neal David Phillips [1974] Director/Solution Architect; Prof. Lewis Edward Schnurr [1936] Professor and Director; Steven Paul Sheldrick [1970] Director/Banker; Clare Surface [1972] Director/Assistant Network Manager; Crystal Louise Wadsworth [1981] Director/Teacher; Shane David Waughman [1986] Director/Manager; Timothy Weymouth [1986] Director/Insurance Broker

Tican (Chilled) Limited
Incorporated: 26 May 2000 *Employees:* 78
Net Worth: £5,014,000 *Total Assets:* £17,086,000
Registered Office: 3rd Floor, Crown House, 151 High Road, Loughton, Essex, IG10 4LG
Activities: Other business support service activities n.e.c.
Parent: Tican UK Limited
Officers: Matthew McGeough, Secretary/Director; Richard Neil Burke [1956] Director; Simon Robert Halliday [1965] Director; Andrew Jones [1958] Director; Matthew McGeough [1976] Director; Jason Wilkie [1969] Director

Tican (UK) Holdings Limited
Incorporated: 26 September 2007
Net Worth: £6,109,925 *Total Assets:* £8,861,939
Registered Office: Crown House, 151 High Road, Loughton, Essex, IG10 4LG
Activities: Activities of head offices
Shareholders: Clemens Tonnies; Robert Tonnies
Officers: Matthew McGeough, Secretary; Matthew McGeough [1976] Director; Niels Jorgen Villesen [1966] Finance Director [Danish]

Tican Process Holdings Limited
Incorporated: 25 November 1993
Net Worth Deficit: £465,200 *Total Assets:* £18,412,088
Registered Office: Direct Table Foods Ltd, Saxham Business Park, Bury St Edmunds, Suffolk, IP28 6RX
Activities: Renting and operating of Housing Association real estate
Shareholders: Clemens Tonnies; Robert Tonnies
Officers: Anthony Michael Stanton, Secretary/Director; Anthony Michael Stanton [1957] Director; Ove Thejls [1954] Director [Danish]; Niels Jorgen Villesen [1966] Financial Director [Danish]

Ticketgrange Limited
Incorporated: 12 July 1983 *Employees:* 61
Net Worth: £9,156,707 *Total Assets:* £10,623,406
Registered Office: The Downshire, 71 Baldwins Lane, Croxley Green, Rickmansworth, Herts, WD3 3LT
Activities: Gambling and betting activities
Shareholders: John Harris; Richard Harris
Officers: John Harris, Secretary; John Harris [1958] Director/Amusement Caterer; Richard Harris [1954] Director/Amusement Caterer

Tilda Limited
Incorporated: 25 September 1970 *Employees:* 244
Net Worth: £59,872,000 *Total Assets:* £83,850,000
Registered Office: Coldharbour Lane, Rainham, Essex, RM13 9YQ
Activities: Grain milling
Parent: Hain Frozen Foods UK Limited
Officers: Nicholas Keen, Secretary; Robert Bailie [1972] Finance Director; Denise Menikheim Faltischek [1973] Director/General Counsel [American]; James Michael Langrock [1965] Director [American]; Umesh Parmar [1965] Director; Mark Lawrence Schiller [1961] Director/CEO Hain Celestial [American]

Tilia Properties Limited
Incorporated: 27 August 1965
Net Worth: £12,617,108 *Total Assets:* £24,605,560
Registered Office: Wendover Road, Rackheath, Norwich, NR13 6LR
Activities: Construction of commercial buildings
Parent: Tilia Trading Group Limited
Officers: Amanda Hovey, Secretary; Amanda Carol Hovey [1963] Company Secretary/Director; Nicholas Charles Hovey [1960] Director/Property Manager; Benjamin Mackintosh [1956] Director/Boat Builder

Tilia Trading Group Limited
Incorporated: 20 August 2003 *Employees:* 2
Net Worth: £12,617,108 *Total Assets:* £12,617,108
Registered Office: Tilia, Wendover Road, Rackheath Industrial Estate, Norwich, NR13 6LR
Activities: Activities of construction holding companies
Officers: Amanda Hovey, Secretary; Amanda Carol Hovey [1963] Director/Company Secretary; Benjamin Mackintosh [1956] Director

Tillomed Laboratories Limited
Incorporated: 28 September 1990 *Employees:* 37
Net Worth: £8,127,429 *Total Assets:* £17,229,562
Registered Office: 220 Butterfield, Great Marlings, Luton, Beds, LU2 8DL
Activities: Wholesale of pharmaceutical goods
Parent: Emcure Pharma UK Ltd
Officers: Susan Gaynor Hide, Secretary; Zarir Jal Cama [1947] Director; Vineet Kumar Dixit [1979] Director/Accountant [Indian]; Samit Satish Mehta [1980] Director [Indian]; Tajuddin Shaikh [1974] Director/Accountant [Indian]; Ajit Chand Srimal [1958] Director/Chief Executive

Tilsworth Developments Limited
Incorporated: 28 April 2004
Net Worth: £1,692,512 *Total Assets:* £8,370,648
Registered Office: 59 Union Street, Dunstable, Beds, LU6 1EX
Activities: Other building completion and finishing
Shareholders: Peter John Foster; Peter Wright
Officers: Peter John Wright, Secretary; Peter John Foster [1955] Director/Builder; Peter John Wright [1958] Director/Developer

Timber Connection Limited
Incorporated: 10 February 1994 *Employees:* 20
Net Worth: £5,897,017 *Total Assets:* £19,019,700
Registered Office: 2 Crane Mead Business Park, Crane Mead, Ware, Herts, SG12 9PZ
Activities: Wholesale of wood, construction materials and sanitary equipment
Major Shareholder: Danny Catherall
Officers: David William Green, Secretary; Keeley Katherine Baker [1972] Commercial Director; Danny Catherall [1966] Director; David William Green [1964] Director

Timeboard Industrial Properties LLP
Incorporated: 6 August 2013
Net Worth: £10,824,037 *Total Assets:* £15,028,699
Registered Office: 28 Church Road, Stanmore, Middlesex, HA7 4XR

Timeboard Investments LLP
Incorporated: 28 March 2012
Net Worth: £2,011,769 *Total Assets:* £43,800,520
Registered Office: 28 Church Road, Stanmore, Middlesex, HA7 4XR

Timewell Properties Limited
Incorporated: 18 January 1963 *Employees:* 278
Net Worth: £7,767,129 *Total Assets:* £16,060,228
Registered Office: Bankside, 300 Peachman Way, Broadland Business Park, Norwich, NR7 0LB
Activities: Other holiday and other collective accommodation
Officers: David John Bye [1958] Director/Retired; Edna May Timewell [1926] Director; Michael Claude Timewell [1956] Director; Paul Roger Timewell [1949] Director

John Tinney & Co Limited
Incorporated: 9 July 1982 *Employees:* 6
Net Worth: £6,335,783 *Total Assets:* £10,867,970
Registered Office: Matching Hall, Matching, Harlow, Essex, CM17 0QZ
Activities: Growing of cereals (except rice), leguminous crops and oil seeds
Shareholders: David Lawson Tinney; John Frederick Tinney
Officers: David Lawson Tinney, Secretary; David Lawson Tinney [1971] Director/Farmer; John Frederick Tinney [1937] Director/Farmer; Sally Christine Tinney [1971] Director

R C Tinsley 2012 Limited
Incorporated: 23 February 2012
Net Worth: £10,488,498 *Total Assets:* £16,466,076
Registered Office: c/o Duncan & Toplis Limited, Enterprise Way, Pinchbeck, Spalding, Lincs, PE11 3YR
Activities: Activities of agricultural holding companies
Shareholders: Philippa Mary Ball; Annette Ruth White; Richard Paul Tinsley
Officers: Philippa Mary Ball [1956] Director/Farmer; Richard Paul Tinsley [1962] Director/Farmer

R. C. Tinsley Limited
Incorporated: 24 March 1955 *Employees:* 7
Net Worth: £9,781,070 *Total Assets:* £10,482,164
Registered Office: c/o Duncan & Toplis Limited, Enterprise Way, Pinchbeck, Spalding, Lincs, PE11 3YR
Activities: Growing of cereals (except rice), leguminous crops and oil seeds
Parent: R C Tinsley 2012 Limited
Officers: Eileen Theodora Tinsley, Secretary; Philippa Mary Ball [1956] Director/Farmer; Eileen Theodora Tinsley [1924] Director; Jennifer Gay Tinsley [1959] Director/Farmer; Richard Paul Tinsley [1962] Director/Farmer; Richard Cole Tinsley [1924] Director/Farmer; Annette Ruth White [1957] Director

Titan Airways Limited
Incorporated: 20 January 1988 *Employees:* 104
Net Worth: £15,885,283 *Total Assets:* £56,083,504
Registered Office: Enterprise House, Bassingbourn Road, Stansted Airport, Stansted, Essex, CM24 1RN
Activities: Non-scheduled passenger air transport
Major Shareholder: Gene Hedley Willson
Officers: Esen Fethi, Secretary; Graham Neal Baguley [1964] Operations Director; Joseph Clarence Dennett [1971] Director/Pilot; Alastair James Kiernan [1972] Commercial Director; Stefan Paul Payne [1981] Finance Director; Alastair Mark Willson [1986] Director; Gene Hedley Willson [1950] Director/Pilot

Titano Real Estate Limited
Incorporated: 4 June 2014
Net Worth: £10,220,638 *Total Assets:* £10,220,638
Registered Office: Dickens House, Guithavon Street, Witham, Essex, CM8 1BJ
Activities: Buying and selling of own real estate
Parent: Sextant Consolidated Limited
Officers: Vincenzo Bianchi [1958] Director [Italian]; Giuseppe Gandolfo [1959] Director/Businessman [Italian]; Philip Lawrence [1953] Director

Tithe Academy
Incorporated: 29 June 2011 *Employees:* 171
Previous: Rooks Heath College
Net Worth: £16,703,750 *Total Assets:* £21,301,552
Registered Office: Eastcote Lane, South Harrow, Middlesex, HA2 9AH
Activities: General secondary education
Officers: Pauline Ann Hughes [1954] Director; Pinakin Vithalji Katbamna [1962] Director/Science Teacher; Dr John Reavley [1958] Director; Nicola Roger [1963] Director/Administrator; Savvas Savva [1958] Director; Robin Brownrigg Tullo [1950] Director/Retired

G.J.W.Titmuss Limited
Incorporated: 7 March 1958 *Employees:* 47
Net Worth: £7,460,097 *Total Assets:* £9,142,991
Registered Office: New Mill, Lamer Lane, Wheathampstead, St Albans, Herts, AL4 8RG
Activities: Wholesale of grain, unmanufactured tobacco, seeds and animal feeds
Shareholder: John William Titmuss
Officers: Stuart James Titmuss, Secretary; John William Titmuss [1955] Director/General Manager

Titon Hardware Limited
Incorporated: 13 September 1972 *Employees:* 188
Net Worth: £3,092,000 *Total Assets:* £8,925,000
Registered Office: 894 The Crescent, Colchester Business Park, Colchester, Essex, CO4 9YQ
Activities: Manufacture of builders ware of plastic
Parent: Titon Holdings PLC
Officers: David Alan Ruffell, Secretary; John Neil Anderson [1943] Director/Deputy Chairman; Tyson Neil Anderson [1968] Sales and Marketing Director; Paul Steven Cowell [1975] Technical Director; Tony David Gearey [1967] IT Director; Lionel James Holmes [1962] Operations Director; Keith Archibald Ritchie [1959] Director/Chairman; David Alan Ruffell [1958] Director/Chief Executive; Julian Wiseman [1959] Sales Director

Titon Holdings PLC
Incorporated: 17 December 1981 *Employees:* 244
Net Worth: £14,215,000 *Total Assets:* £20,930,000
Registered Office: 894 The Crescent, Colchester Business Park, Colchester, Essex, CO4 9YQ
Activities: Activities of other holding companies n.e.c.
Officers: David Alan Ruffell, Secretary; John Neil Anderson [1943] Director/Deputy Chairman; Tyson Neil Anderson [1968] Sales & Marketing Director; Tony David Gearey [1967] Director; Nicholas Charles Howlett [1961] Director; Keith Archibald Ritchie [1959] Director/Chairman; David Alan Ruffell [1958] Director/Chief Executive; Kevin Sargeant [1957] Director

TJM (London) LLP
Incorporated: 12 February 2007
Net Worth: £9,054,879 *Total Assets:* £9,151,179
Registered Office: Westfield Farm, Royston Lane, Comberton, Cambridge, CB23 7EE
Officers: John Fenttiman [1960] Member; Rosemarie Lorraine Fenttiman [1962] Member

TJX Europe Buying (Deutschland) Limited
Incorporated: 24 February 1995
Net Worth: £222,000 *Total Assets:* £16,075,000
Registered Office: 50 Clarendon Road, Watford, Herts, WD17 1TX
Activities: Agents involved in the sale of a variety of goods
Parent: TJX UK
Officers: Susan Beaumont, Secretary; Alicia Colarte Kelly, Secretary; Lisa Schwartz, Secretary; David Lawrence Averill [1967] SVP, Corporate Tax Director [American]; John Joseph Klinger [1964] Director/SVP, Corporate Controller [American]; Mary Blier Reynolds [1955] Director/SVP, Treasurer [American]

TJX Europe Buying Limited
Incorporated: 24 January 2011
Net Worth: £268,000 *Total Assets:* £55,088,000
Registered Office: 50 Clarendon Road, Watford, Herts, WD17 1TX
Activities: Other business support service activities n.e.c.
Parent: TJX UK
Officers: Alicia Colarte Kelly, Secretary; David Lawrence Averill [1967] SVP Corporate Tax Director [American]; John Joseph Klinger [1964] Director/SVP, Corporate Controller [American]; Mary Blier Reynolds [1955] Director/SVP Treasurer [American]

TJX Europe Limited
Incorporated: 18 August 1995
Net Worth: £207,720,992 *Total Assets:* £643,612,992
Registered Office: 50 Clarendon Road, Watford, Herts, WD17 1TX
Activities: Other retail sale of new goods in specialised stores (not commercial art galleries and opticians)
Parent: The TJX Companies, Inc.
Officers: Susan Beaumont, Secretary; Alicia Colarte Kelly, Secretary; Lisa Schwartz, Secretary; David Lawrence Averill [1967] SVP, Corporate Tax Director [American]; John Joseph Klinger [1964] Director/SVP, Corporate Controller [American]; Mary Blier Reynolds [1955] Director/SVP Treasurer [American]

TJX Germany Ltd.
Incorporated: 25 July 2013
Net Worth: £36,442,000 *Total Assets:* £36,500,000
Registered Office: 50 Clarendon Road, Watford, Herts, WD17 1TX
Activities: Activities of other holding companies n.e.c.
Parent: TJX Europe Limited
Officers: Susan Beaumont, Secretary; Alicia Colarte Kelly, Secretary; Lisa Schwartz, Secretary; David Lawrence Averill [1967] SVP, Corporate Tax Director [American]; John Joseph Klinger [1964] Director/SVP, Corporate Controller [American]; Mary Blier Reynolds [1955] Director/SVP, Treasurer [American]

TJX UK
Incorporated: 18 August 1995 *Employees:* 20,177
Net Worth: £645,600,000 *Total Assets:* £1,234,300,032
Registered Office: 50 Clarendon Road, Watford, Herts, WD17 1TX
Activities: Other retail sale of new goods in specialised stores (not commercial art galleries and opticians)
Parent: TJX Europe Limited
Officers: Susan Beaumont, Secretary; Alicia Colarte Kelly, Secretary; Lisa Schwartz, Secretary; David Lawrence Averill [1967] SVP Corporate Tax Director [American]; John Joseph Klinger [1964] Director/SVP, Corporate Controller [American]; Mary Blier Reynolds [1955] Director/SVP Treasurer [American]

TJX UK Property Limited
Incorporated: 10 November 2015 *Employees:* 3
Net Worth Deficit: £150,000 *Total Assets:* £16,295,000
Registered Office: 50 Clarendon Road, Watford, Herts, WD17 1TX
Activities: Other letting and operating of own or leased real estate
Parent: The TJX Companies, Inc.
Officers: Susan Beaumont, Secretary; Alicia Colarte Kelly, Secretary; Lisa Schwartz, Secretary; David Lawrence Averill [1967] SVP, Corporate Tax Director [American]; John Joseph Klinger [1964] Director/SVP, Corporate Controller [American]; Mary Blier Reynolds [1955] Director/SVP, Treasurer [American]

TK Maxx
Incorporated: 17 December 1992
Net Worth: £4,907,000 *Total Assets:* £11,160,000
Registered Office: 50 Clarendon Road, Watford, Herts, WD17 1TX
Activities: Retail of furniture, lighting, and similar (not musical instruments or scores) in specialised store
Parent: TJX Europe Limited
Officers: Susan Beamont, Secretary; Alicia Colarte Kelly, Secretary; Lisa Schwartz, Secretary; David Lawrence Averill [1967] SVP, Corporate Tax Director [American]; John Joseph Klinger [1964] Director/SVP, Corporate Controller [American]; Mary Blier Reynolds [1955] Director/SVP, Treasurer [American]

TLC Care Homes Limited
Incorporated: 2 May 1996 *Employees:* 391
Net Worth: £5,512,660 *Total Assets:* £13,344,789
Registered Office: Blamsters Farm, Mount Hill, Halstead, Essex, CO9 1LR
Activities: Residential care activities for the elderly and disabled
Parent: TLC Care Bidco Limited
Officers: Ashley Graham Craig Taylor, Secretary; Paul Reuben Hainsworth [1966] Director

TLC Group Limited
Incorporated: 19 February 1999 *Employees:* 784
Net Worth: £120,999,840 *Total Assets:* £203,683,040
Registered Office: 36 Railway Approach, Harrow, Middlesex, HA3 5AA
Activities: Residential nursing care facilities
Major Shareholder: Lady Sandhya Popat
Officers: Gagan Puri, Secretary; William Charles Neal [1986] Director; Paavan Popat [1985] Managing Director; Lady Sandhya Popat [1954] Director; Honourable Shivaan Shillin Popat [1988] Director; Gagan Puri [1978] Finance Director

TM Group Holdings Limited
Incorporated: 7 November 1997
Net Worth: £83,477,000 *Total Assets:* £178,732,000
Registered Office: McColl's House, Ashwells Road, Brentwood, Essex, CM15 9ST
Activities: Other service activities n.e.c.
Parent: Thistledove Limited
Officers: Robbie Ian Bell [1973] Director/Chief Financial Officer; Simon Jeremy Ian Fuller [1977] Director; Steven Green [1981] Director; Simon Jonathan Miller [1963] Director

TM Vending Limited
Incorporated: 18 December 1981
Net Worth: £60,701,000 *Total Assets:* £80,395,000
Registered Office: McColl's House, Ashwells Road, Brentwood, Essex, CM15 9ST
Activities: Retail sale of tobacco products in specialised stores
Parent: TH Group Holdings Ltd
Officers: David Alexander Archibald [1967] Director; Robbie Ian Bell [1973] Director/Chief Financial Officer; Simon Jeremy Ian Fuller [1977] Director; Steven Green [1981] Director; Simon Jonathan Miller [1963] Director

TN (UK) Consultancy Ltd
Incorporated: 2 February 2011
Net Worth: £347,883 *Total Assets:* £8,001,449
Registered Office: 902 Eastern Avenue, Newbury Park, Ilford, Essex, IG2 7HZ
Activities: Development of building projects
Officers: Naresh Kumar Chopra [1959] Director/Property Developer; Tina Chopra [1963] Director/Bookkeeper

Tobar Group Trading Limited
Incorporated: 11 November 2011 *Employees:* 77
Net Worth: £8,336,779 *Total Assets:* £17,817,164
Registered Office: Yare House, 62-64 Thorpe Road, Norwich, NR1 1RY
Activities: Wholesale of household goods (other than musical instruments) n.e.c
Shareholders: Mark Edward Colley; Tobar International Ltd
Officers: David Mordecai, Secretary; Mark Edward Colley [1984] Director; Martin Grossman [1956] Director/Manager; Glyn Loveday [1970] Finance Director; David Jonathan Mordecai [1962] Director/Chief Executive Officer

Tobar International Limited
Incorporated: 21 December 2015 *Employees:* 328
Net Worth: £4,813,574 *Total Assets:* £16,403,248
Registered Office: Yare House, 62-64 Thorpe Road, Norwich, NR1 1RY
Activities: Activities of head offices
Shareholders: Mark Edward Colley; Merino Industries Ltd
Officers: Mark Edward Colley [1984] Director/Investor; Martin Grossman [1956] Director/Manager; Glyn Loveday [1970] Director; David Jonathan Mordecai [1962] Director

Tompsett Burgess Growers Limited
Incorporated: 2 June 2000 *Employees:* 42
Net Worth: £6,020,861 *Total Assets:* £9,506,076
Registered Office: Whitehall Farm, Temple Road, Isleham, Ely, Cambs, CB7 5RF
Activities: Growing of vegetables and melons, roots and tubers
Officers: Sally Jane Green [1960] Director; Ian David Hall [1967] Director/General Manager; Jacqueline Rose Seddon [1962] Director; Clements Harry Tompsett [1934] Director; Mary Ester Tompsett [1934] Director

Tompsett Holdings Limited
Incorporated: 1 August 2002 *Employees:* 42
Net Worth: £11,406,108 *Total Assets:* £14,804,657
Registered Office: Whitehall Farm, Temple Road, Isleham, Ely, Cambs, CB7 5RF
Activities: Support activities for crop production
Shareholders: Clements Harry Tompsett; Mary Ester Tompsett
Officers: Sally Jane Green [1960] Director; Jacqueline Rose Seddon [1962] Director; Clements Harry Tompsett [1934] Director; Mary Ester Tompsett [1934] Director

Toomey Leasing Group Limited
Incorporated: 25 September 1969 *Employees:* 36
Net Worth: £16,640,905 *Total Assets:* £51,202,128
Registered Office: Service House, West Mayne, Basildon, Essex, SS15 6RW
Activities: Renting and leasing of cars and light motor vehicles
Major Shareholder: Michael John Toomey
Officers: Neil Duncan Rickwood, Secretary; Alexander Frederick Butcher [1971] Director; David Houlgrave [1976] Director; Neil Duncan Rickwood [1974] Director/Chartered Accountant; Michael John Toomey [1938] Director; Martin Howsley Wroe [1963] Director

Toomey Motor Group Limited
Incorporated: 1 January 1938 *Employees:* 134
Previous: J Toomey Motors Limited
Net Worth: £8,187,445 *Total Assets:* £12,508,058
Registered Office: Service House, West Mayne, Basildon, Essex, SS15 6RW
Activities: Sale of new cars and light motor vehicles
Major Shareholder: Michael John Toomey
Officers: Neil Duncan Rickwood, Secretary; Steven Joseph Decelis [1962] Director; Neil Duncan Rickwood [1974] Director/Chartered Accountant; Michael John Toomey [1938] Director

Top 100 Limited
Incorporated: 1 September 2006 *Employees:* 47
Net Worth: £2,733,120 *Total Assets:* £10,281,437
Registered Office: Baverstocks Chartered Accountants, Dickens House, 3-7 Guithavon Street, Witham, Essex, CM8 1BJ
Activities: Sale of new cars and light motor vehicles
Major Shareholder: Jason Nevada Westwood
Officers: Andrew William Phillips [1971] Director; Jason Nevada Westwood [1968] Director

Topfib Limited
Incorporated: 6 July 1992
Net Worth: £8,659,864 *Total Assets:* £9,139,298
Registered Office: Coopers House, 65a Wingletye Lane, Hornchurch, Essex, RM11 3AT
Activities: Financial intermediation not elsewhere classified
Major Shareholder: Keith Robert Carnelley
Officers: Marilyn Joy Payne, Secretary; Keith Robert Carnelley [1949] Director/Businessman

Topgolf Limited
Incorporated: 2 March 1999 *Employees:* 518
Net Worth: £51,981,752 *Total Assets:* £63,387,980
Registered Office: Kinetic House, Theobald Street, Elstree, Herts, WD6 4PJ
Activities: Operation of sports facilities
Parent: Topgolf Group Limited
Officers: Kieren Charles Mildwaters, Secretary; Eldridge Allen Burns [1969] Director/General Counsel [American]; William Barry Davenport [1971] Finance Director [American]

R.H.Topham & Sons Limited
Incorporated: 6 September 1960 *Employees:* 4
Net Worth: £15,925,085 *Total Assets:* £29,288,316
Registered Office: Monks Hardwick, Priory Hill, St Neots, Huntingdon, Cambs, PE19 6ED
Activities: Growing of cereals (except rice), leguminous crops and oil seeds
Parent: Meltcrox Limited
Officers: Michael Raymond Topham [1953] Director/Accountant

Toppesfield Limited
Incorporated: 24 February 2004 *Employees:* 210
Net Worth: £4,248,662 *Total Assets:* £39,023,788
Registered Office: Toppesfield House, Unit 12 Hillview Business Park, Old Ipswich Road, Claydon, Ipswich, Suffolk, IP6 0AJ
Activities: Construction of roads and motorways
Shareholders: F M Conway Limited; Matthew James Pryor
Officers: Mark Alan Salmon, Secretary; Craig John Germeney [1979] Operations Director; Andrew Stephen Hansen [1967] Director; George Benjamin Pryor [1990] Director; Matthew James Pryor [1966] Commercial Director; William James Pryor [1992] Director; Matthew Michael Riley [1988] Director; Mark Alan Salmon [1979] Finance Director

Toro Principal Manufacturing Limited
Incorporated: 18 December 2013
Net Worth: £65,414,988 *Total Assets:* £91,008,752
Registered Office: Spellbrook, Bishop's Stortford, Herts, CM23 4BU
Activities: Manufacture of other special-purpose machinery n.e.c.
Parent: Hayter Holdings Limited
Officers: Angela Dawn Snavely, Secretary; Kunjunni Raghunath Das [1952] Operations Director; Bradley Wayne Dolan [1963] Director/MD, Finance Operations [American]; Blake Grams [1967] Director/VP, Operations [American]

Total Produce Holdings (UK) Limited
Incorporated: 9 August 2006
Net Worth: £31,756,000 *Total Assets:* £33,135,000
Registered Office: Total Produce, Enterprise Way, Pinchbeck, Spalding, Lincs, PE11 3YR
Activities: Activities of head offices
Parent: TPH (UK) Limited
Officers: Mark Christopher Owen, Secretary; Jacinta Frances Devine [1972] Director [Irish]; Francis Gerard McKernan [1962] Director; Mark Christopher Owen [1965] Director; Denis Leslie Punter [1953] Director

Total Produce Limited
Incorporated: 2 October 2006 *Employees:* 332
Net Worth: £11,940,000 *Total Assets:* £39,150,000
Registered Office: Total Produce, Enterprise Way, Pinchbeck, Spalding, Lincs, PE11 3YR
Activities: Wholesale of fruit and vegetables
Parent: Total Produce Holdings (UK) Limited
Officers: Mark Christopher Owen, Secretary; Andrew Roger Allmond [1944] Director; Jacinta Frances Devine [1972] Director [Irish]; Francis Gerard McKernan [1962] Director [Irish]; Mark Christopher Owen [1965] Director; Denis Leslie Punter [1953] Director; Stephen Mark Webster [1962] Director

Total Worldfresh Limited
Incorporated: 28 December 1987 *Employees:* 182
Net Worth: £6,463,000 *Total Assets:* £35,346,000
Registered Office: Total Produce, Enterprise Way, Pinchbeck, Spalding, Lincs, PE11 3YR
Activities: Wholesale of fruit and vegetables
Parent: Saybest Limited
Officers: Mark Christopher Owen, Secretary; Francis Gerard McKernan [1962] Director; Mark Christopher Owen [1965] Director; Denis Leslie Punter [1953] Managing Director

Totes Isotoner (UK) Limited
Incorporated: 27 November 1980
Net Worth: £8,466,156 *Total Assets:* £12,056,711
Registered Office: Eastman House, Radford Crescent, Billericay, Essex, CM12 0DN
Activities: Wholesale of clothing and footwear
Parent: Totes Isotoner Corporation
Officers: Karl Bowden, Secretary; Michael Bate [1947] Managing Director; Karl Bowden [1964] Director/Accountant; Daniel Stephen Rajczak [1963] Director [American]

Tour Partner Group Limited
Incorporated: 5 October 2015 *Employees:* 3
Previous: Mayfair Fox Bidco Limited
Net Worth: £136,076 *Total Assets:* £47,284,208
Registered Office: 5th Floor, Hygeia Building, 66-68 College Road, Harrow, Middlesex, HA1 1BE
Activities: Activities of other holding companies n.e.c.
Parent: Mayfair Fox Midco Limited
Officers: Paul John Maine [1965] Director/Chief Executive; Mark David Mayhew [1959] Director; Mark Pharoah [1964] Finance Director

Tour Partner Group Midco Limited
Incorporated: 5 October 2015
Previous: Mayfair Fox Midco Limited
Net Worth Deficit: £6,170,447 *Total Assets:* £66,387,204
Registered Office: 5th Floor, Hygeia Building, 66-68 College Road, Harrow, Middlesex, HA1 1BE
Activities: Activities of other holding companies n.e.c.
Officers: Paul John Maine [1965] Director/Chief Executive; Mark David Mayhew [1959] Director; Mark Pharoah [1964] Finance Director

Toureen Contractors Limited
Incorporated: 3 July 1992 *Employees:* 164
Net Worth: £5,086,975 *Total Assets:* £27,035,496
Registered Office: 25 Cecil Road, Harrow, Middlesex, HA3 5QY
Activities: Construction of commercial buildings
Parent: Toureen Group Ltd
Officers: Daniel Nolan, Secretary/Construction Manager; Daniel Nolan [1971] Director/Construction Manager; Denis Nolan [1962] Director; David Graham Parker [1969] Director/Quantity Surveyor

Toureen Group Limited
Incorporated: 7 August 2006 *Employees:* 219
Net Worth: £12,908,236 *Total Assets:* £38,441,624
Registered Office: 25 Cecil Road, Wealdstone, Harrow, Middlesex, HA3 5QY
Activities: Other business support service activities n.e.c.
Major Shareholder: Denis Nolan
Officers: David Graham Parker, Secretary; Nicholas Mark Gibson [1971] Director/Quantity Surveyor; Mouwafak Asad Kassir [1972] Director; Daniel Nolan [1971] Director/Construction Manager; Denis Nolan [1962] Director; David Graham Parker [1969] Director/Quantity Surveyor

Tower Bridge Homes Care Limited
Incorporated: 20 June 1996 *Employees:* 1,094
Net Worth: £24,133,836 *Total Assets:* £64,816,460
Registered Office: 228 St Mary's Lane, Upminster, Essex, RM14 3DH
Activities: Other business support service activities n.e.c.
Officers: Indumati Lakhani, Company Secretary; Sharifa Lakhani [1987] Managing Director; Shiraz Lakhani [1945] Director

Tower Crane Asset Management Holdings Limited
Incorporated: 7 March 2006
Previous: Falcon Crane Hire Holdings Limited
Net Worth: £4,210,068 *Total Assets:* £34,274,960
Registered Office: Shipdham Airfield Industrial Estate, Shipdham, Thetford, Norfolk, IP25 7SD
Activities: Renting and leasing of construction and civil engineering machinery and equipment
Shareholder: Doug Charles Genge
Officers: Barabra Brown, Secretary; Andrew Brown [1985] Director/Commercial Manager; Barbara Ivy Brown [1957] Director/Company Secretary; Philip Gale [1969] Director/Operations Manager; Ian Gray [1966] Director/Sales Manager; Steve Paxman [1963] Director/Sales Manager

Towers & Co.,Limited
Incorporated: 28 July 1898 *Employees:* 117
Net Worth: £11,352,000 *Total Assets:* £29,375,000
Registered Office: 3-5 Tower House, Amwell Street, Hoddesdon, Herts, EN11 8UR
Activities: Wholesale of meat and meat products
Parent: Towers Thompson Holdings Ltd
Officers: Paul Dolan [1953] Director/Company Secretary; Terry George Goddard [1957] Director/Chartered Accountant

Towers Thompson Holdings Limited
Incorporated: 18 November 1997 *Employees:* 154
Net Worth: £6,057,000 *Total Assets:* £26,248,000
Registered Office: 3-5 Tower House, Amwell Street, Hoddesdon, Herts, EN11 8UR
Activities: Wholesale of meat and meat products
Officers: Paul Dolan [1953] Director/Executive Chairman; Terry George Goddard [1957] Director/Chartered Accountant

Town and City Pub Group Limited
Incorporated: 21 November 2007 *Employees:* 2,039
Net Worth: £2,200,000 *Total Assets:* £106,963,000
Registered Office: Porter Tun House, 500 Capability Green, Luton, Beds, LU1 3LS
Activities: Public houses and bars
Parent: TDR Capital LLP
Officers: Suzanne Louise Baker [1963] Director; Simon David Longbottom [1971] Director/Chief Executive Officer; David Andrew Ross [1973] Director/Chief Financial Officer

Town Close House Educational Trust Limited
Incorporated: 7 October 1968 *Employees:* 129
Net Worth: £7,082,082 *Total Assets:* £10,223,458
Registered Office: Town Close House, 14 Ipswich Road, Norwich, NR2 2LR
Activities: Pre-primary education
Officers: Benita Ogg, Secretary; Sarah Jayne Anthony [1964] Director; David John Hargreaves Bolton [1950] Director/Farm Business Consultant; Dr Simon Michael Carroll [1963] Director/Doctor; Clare Rosina Costello [1964] Director/Solicitor; Alistair John Fish [1964] Director/Chartered Accountant; Susan Jack [1952] Director/Retired; Alec William Sidney Kingham [1988] Director/Banker; Nicola Ovenden [1962] Director/Public Relations; Adrian Marcus Possener [1964] Director/Solicitor; Sarah Waddington [1957] Director/Headmistress

Townhold Limited
Incorporated: 4 June 1999 *Employees:* 2
Net Worth: £19,678,856 *Total Assets:* £25,175,964
Registered Office: Hadley Hurst, Hadley Common, Barnet, Herts, EN5 5QG
Activities: Development of building projects
Parent: Blendhall Limited
Officers: Anna Victoria Kinsman, Secretary; Alexander Mahboubian [1972] Director; Farrokh Mahboubian [1932] Director [Iranian]

Toy Brokers Holdings Limited
Incorporated: 16 February 2009 *Employees:* 40
Net Worth: £18,674,628 *Total Assets:* £35,664,852
Registered Office: Hercules House, Pierson Road, Alconbury Weald, Huntingdon, Cambs, PE28 4YA
Activities: Manufacture of other games and toys, n.e.c.
Officers: Anthony Carson Shepherd, Secretary/Director; David Lytton Kremer [1964] Director; Michael Moody [1953] Director; Simon Richard Pilkington [1967] Managing Director; Anthony Carson Shepherd [1948] Director

TPH (UK) Limited
Incorporated: 6 November 2006
Net Worth: £20,341,000 *Total Assets:* £62,613,000
Registered Office: Total Produce, Enterprise Way, Pinchbeck, Spalding, Lincs, PE11 3YR
Activities: Activities of head offices
Parent: Total Produce PLC
Officers: Mark Christopher Owen, Secretary; Jacinta Frances Devine [1972] Director [Irish]; Francis Gerard McKernan [1962] Director; Seamus Mulvenna [1953] Director [Irish]; Mark Christopher Owen [1965] Director; Denis Leslie Punter [1953] Director

TRAD Properties LLP
Incorporated: 22 December 2011
Net Worth: £13,536,436 *Total Assets:* £26,020,592
Registered Office: Haslers, Old Station Road, Loughton, Essex, IG10 4PL
Officers: Christopher Hayden Smith [1974] Member; Jacqueline Walker [1959] Member

Tradelink Direct Limited
Incorporated: 25 November 1991 *Employees:* 221
Net Worth: £7,370,957 *Total Assets:* £11,133,583
Registered Office: LHG House, Northside, Marwick Road, March, Cambs, PE15 8PH
Activities: Manufacture of other plastic products
Shareholder: Alan Manuel Greenberg
Officers: James William Moody, Secretary; James William Moody [1965] Managing Director; Anthony Charles Morley [1964] Business Director

Tradewise Group of Companies Limited
Incorporated: 22 November 2013 *Employees:* 197
Net Worth: £8,921,113 *Total Assets:* £47,179,276
Registered Office: 300 Southbury Road, Enfield, Middlesex, EN1 1TS
Activities: Activities of financial services holding companies
Shareholders: North Atlantic Value GP 4 Limited; James William Humphreys
Officers: Jennifer Ann Jones, Secretary; Marcus Charles Killick [1962] Director/Chief Executive; Christopher Mills [1952] Director; David John Ratledge [1970] Director/Chartered Certified Accountant; Michael Robert Tyler [1966] Director/Chief Executive

Tradewise Insurance Services Limited
Incorporated: 23 May 2002 *Employees:* 155
Net Worth: £2,320,088 *Total Assets:* £28,386,768
Registered Office: 300 Southbury Road, Enfield, Middlesex, EN1 1TS
Activities: Activities of insurance agents and brokers
Shareholders: North Atlantic Value GP 4 Limited; James William Humphreys; Tradewise Group of Companies Limited
Officers: Jennifer Ann Jones, Secretary; Paul George Bates [1976] Claims Director; Wayne Michael Bradshaw [1958] Sales & Marketing Director; Bernard Wayne Martin [1975] Claims Director; Alison Claire Middleton [1973] Director; David John Ratledge [1970] Director/Accountant; Annette Bridget Tyler [1972] Director; Michael Robert Tyler [1966] Director

Tradex Insurance Company Limited
Incorporated: 27 October 1994 *Employees:* 30
Net Worth: £18,395,000 *Total Assets:* £224,964,000
Registered Office: 7 Eastern Road, Romford, Essex, RM1 3NH
Activities: Non-life insurance
Parent: Tradex Insurance Holdings Limited
Officers: Steven Jonathon Moore, Secretary; Deborah Ann Austin [1967] Director/Underwriter; Stephen Richard Braine [1954] Director/Chief Financial Officer; Garry Michael Fearn [1950] Director; Nicholas John Taylor [1958] Director/Chief Executive Officer; Andrew Peter Whitehouse [1962] Director

Tradex Insurance Holdings Limited
Incorporated: 3 February 2012 *Employees:* 30
Net Worth: £18,410,000 *Total Assets:* £224,988,992
Registered Office: 7 Eastern Road, Romford, Essex, RM1 3NH
Activities: Non-life insurance
Major Shareholder: Royston William Clegg
Officers: Steven Jonathon Moore, Secretary; Deborah Ann Austin [1967] Director/Underwriter; Stephen Richard Braine [1954] Director/Chief Financial Officer; Garry Michael Fearn [1950] Director; Nicholas John Taylor [1958] Director/Chief Executive Officer; Andrew Peter Whitehouse [1962] Director

Traditional Norfolk Poultry Limited
Incorporated: 26 June 2000 *Employees:* 186
Net Worth: £4,202,793 *Total Assets:* £13,132,753
Registered Office: Oak Tree Business Park, Hargham Road, Shropham, Attleborough, Norfolk, NR17 1DS
Activities: Raising of poultry
Shareholders: David Andrew Garner; Mark Richard Gorton
Officers: Mark Richard Gorton, Secretary; David Andrew Garner [1963] Director/Partner in Poultry Processing; Mark Richard Gorton [1968] Director/Partner in Poultry Processing

Trafalgar Leisure Ltd
Incorporated: 2 February 1999 *Employees:* 58
Net Worth: £19,594,476 *Total Assets:* £40,114,984
Registered Office: Lynwood House, 373-375 Station Road, Harrow, Middlesex, HA1 2AW
Activities: Public houses and bars
Major Shareholder: Sameir Talib Hamadi
Officers: Sheila Louise Hamadi, Secretary; Rashied Hamadi [1969] Director; Sameir Talib Hamadi [1970] Director/Jeweller

Trailer Resources Limited
Incorporated: 24 January 1994
Net Worth: £4,007,652 *Total Assets:* £17,652,592
Registered Office: Garton Court, Boundary Way, Hemel Hempstead, Herts, HP2 7RH
Activities: Retail trade of motor vehicle parts and accessories
Parent: Garton Holdings Limited
Officers: Gaynor O'Connor, Secretary; Amanda Jane Jones [1965] Director; Barry Desmond O'Connor [1967] Managing Director; Desmond O'Connor [1942] Director/Chairman; Gaynor O'Connor [1945] Director

Trans-Siberian Gold PLC
Incorporated: 25 August 1972 *Employees:* 693
Net Worth: £58,769,116 *Total Assets:* £82,058,000
Registered Office: 39 Parkside, Cambridge, CB1 1PN
Activities: Other mining and quarrying n.e.c.
Shareholders: UFG Private Equity Fund I LP; Pavel Fedorov
Officers: Simon Viggor Olsen, Secretary/Finance Manager; Stewart James Dickson [1977] Director/Consultant; Alexander Iosifovich Dorogov [1970] Finance Director [Russian]; Florian Wolfgang Fenner [1971] Director/Investment Banker [German]; Ljupco Lou Naumovski [1956] Director [Canadian]; Charles Emmitt Ryan [1967] Director/Investment Banker [American]; Robert Sasson [1964] Director/Banker

Transam Trucking Limited
Incorporated: 28 March 1977 *Employees:* 120
Net Worth: £5,399,918 *Total Assets:* £9,251,935
Registered Office: 7 Trinity Street, Bungay, Suffolk, NR35 1EH
Activities: Other transportation support activities
Shareholders: Sandra Jane Flatt; Anthony Marcus Guterres
Officers: Sandra Jane Flatt, Secretary; Sandra Jane Flatt [1956] Director; Anthony Marcus Guterres [1954] Director; Natasha Jane Highcroft [1986] Director; Martin Charles Palmer [1959] Director

Transeur Properties Limited
Incorporated: 25 February 2002
Net Worth: £9,388,332 *Total Assets:* £26,975,800
Registered Office: Overseas House, 66-68 High Road, Bushey Heath, Herts, WD23 1GG
Activities: Renting and operating of Housing Association real estate
Major Shareholder: Philip Nandwani
Officers: Philip Nandwani, Secretary; Gobind Hemandas Nandwani [1931] Director/Marketing Manager; Philip Nandwani [1963] Director/General Manager

Transforming Education in Norfolk
Incorporated: 16 May 2012 *Employees:* 1,076
Net Worth: £22,788,000 *Total Assets:* £67,895,000
Registered Office: City College Norwich, Ipswich Road, Norwich, NR2 2LJ
Activities: General secondary education
Officers: Andrew Jonathan Barnes [1957] Director/Chief Executive; John Anthony Fry [1957] Director; Steffan Daniel Anderson Griffiths [1972] Director/Headmaster; Susan Elizabeth Guest [1962] Director/Chairman; Jennifer Lucy Leeder [1973] Director/Lawyer; Christopher Maw [1961] Director/Chartered Accountant; Richard Norman Proctor [1960] Director/Chartered Accountant

Transmec Properties Limited
Incorporated: 11 July 2007 *Employees:* 3
Net Worth: £3,952,516 *Total Assets:* £14,407,471
Registered Office: Transmec Building, London Road, West Thurrock, Essex, RM20 3LH
Activities: Other letting and operating of own or leased real estate
Shareholder: Massimo Montecchi
Officers: Mohammed Imran [1978] Director; Danilo Montecchi [1952] Director [Italian]

Transmec UK Limited
Incorporated: 7 August 1990 *Employees:* 174
Net Worth: £4,856,212 *Total Assets:* £11,061,722
Registered Office: Transmec Building, London Road, West Thurrock, Essex, RM20 3LH
Activities: Freight transport by road
Shareholders: Danilo Montecchi; Massimo Montecchi
Officers: Mohammad Imran, Secretary; Danilo Montecchi [1952] Director/Freight Forwarder [Italian]

Transporter Engineering Limited
Incorporated: 13 May 2002 *Employees:* 142
Previous: Hunwick Engineering Limited
Net Worth: £3,852,218 *Total Assets:* £8,114,486
Registered Office: Unit 4-7 The Old Airfield, Gosfield, Halstead, Essex, CO9 1SA
Activities: Manufacture of metal structures and parts of structures
Major Shareholder: Keith Trevor Ripper
Officers: Darren Hills [1973] Director/Accountant; Darrel Mark Hymas [1976] Sales Director; Mark William Knowles [1967] Director/Design Engineer; Barry Tony Poulter [1971] Director; Keith Trevor Ripper [1956] Director

Transporter Sales & Hire Limited
Incorporated: 29 October 2009 *Employees:* 3
Net Worth: £3,364,568 *Total Assets:* £11,049,455
Registered Office: Unit 4-7 The Old Airfield, Gosfield, Halstead, Essex, CO9 1SA
Activities: Sale of other motor vehicles
Major Shareholder: Keith Trevor Ripper
Officers: Darren Hills [1973] Director/Accountant; Darrel Mark Hymas [1976] Director; Keith Trevor Ripper [1956] Director/Farmer; Andrew John Smith [1969] Director

Travel Choice Limited
Incorporated: 9 August 2004
Net Worth: £33,538,700 *Total Assets:* £33,545,954
Registered Office: Wigmore House, Wigmore Lane, Luton, Beds, LU2 9TN
Activities: Non-trading company
Parent: TUI Travel Overseas Holdings Limited
Officers: Paul Robert Lanaway [1987] Director/Accountant; Thomas Lindner [1968] Director [German]

Travelpack Marketing & Leisure Services Limited
Incorporated: 23 July 1985 *Employees:* 36
Net Worth: £598,434 *Total Assets:* £20,189,584
Registered Office: 523 High Road, Wembley, Middlesex, HA0 2DH
Activities: Travel agency activities
Parent: Padwicks Travel (Wembley) Limited
Officers: Ashokkumar Chhotabhai Patel [1949] Director/Travel Agent; Rashmi Chhotabhai Patel [1955] Director/Travel Agent

TRB Technology Group Limited
Incorporated: 4 June 2007 *Employees:* 176
Previous: Amber Valley Holding Company Limited
Net Worth: £5,962,590 *Total Assets:* £12,663,954
Registered Office: 12 Clifton Road, St Peter's Hill, Huntingdon, Cambs, PE29 7EN
Activities: Activities of head offices
Major Shareholder: Jonathan McQueen
Officers: Richard Bernard Holland [1965] Director; Philip Martin [1953] Director/Accountant; Jonathan McQueen [1969] Director [American]

R.C.Treatt & Co.Limited
Incorporated: 4 October 1913 *Employees:* 198
Net Worth: £22,869,000 *Total Assets:* £55,100,000
Registered Office: Northern Way, Bury St Edmunds, Suffolk, IP32 6NL
Activities: Non-specialised wholesale trade
Parent: Treatt PLC
Officers: Anita Steer, Secretary; Richard Andrew Hope [1966] Finance Director; Daemmon Edward James Reeve [1971] Director/Chief Executive Officer

Treatt PLC
Incorporated: 18 June 1981 *Employees:* 360
Net Worth: £81,625,000 *Total Assets:* £124,265,000
Registered Office: Northern Way, Bury St Edmunds, Suffolk, IP32 6NL
Activities: Non-specialised wholesale trade
Officers: Anita Steer, Secretary; Richard Andrew Hope [1966] Finance Director; Jeffrey Michael Iliffe [1962] Finance Director; Richard Illek [1953] Director [German]; Dr David James Johnston [1965] Director/VP Innovation & Design; Timothy Roy Treleaven Jones [1956] Director/Chief Executive; Daemmon Edward James Reeve [1971] Director/Chief Executive Officer

Treebond Limited
Incorporated: 9 January 2003 *Employees:* 5
Net Worth: £7,356,529 *Total Assets:* £15,179,623
Registered Office: First Floor, Radius House, 51 Clarendon Road, Watford, Herts, WD17 1HP
Activities: Buying and selling of own real estate
Parent: JDM Investments Limited
Officers: Eithne Bridget McGowan, Secretary [Irish]; John Denis McGowan [1966] Director/Publican & Property Developer [Irish]

Treehouse Group Limited
Incorporated: 14 January 2009 *Employees:* 587
Net Worth Deficit: £3,814,000 *Total Assets:* £9,920,000
Registered Office: Third Floor, 29 Broadwater Road, Welwyn Garden City, Herts, AL7 3BQ
Activities: Activities of head offices
Parent: Equistone Partners Europe Limited
Officers: Richard Price [1983] Director; Tim Swales [1978] Director

Treelane Limited
Incorporated: 6 October 2000
Total Assets: £9,944,000
Registered Office: Tomline House, The Dock, Felixstowe, Suffolk, IP11 3SY
Activities: Non-trading company
Parent: Hutchison Ports (UK) Limited
Officers: Simon Richard Mullett, Secretary; Clemence Chun Fun Cheng [1958] Director; Sing Chi IP [1953] Director [Chinese]; Edith Shih [1952] Director

Trelanoak Limited
Incorporated: 30 August 1990
Net Worth: £49,582,000 *Total Assets:* £119,140,000
Registered Office: Sundon Park Road, Luton, Beds, LU3 3BL
Activities: Activities of production holding companies
Parent: Aktiebolaget SKF
Officers: Paula Jane Owen, Secretary/Accountant; Michael Roger Crean [1959] Director [New Zealander]; Sharon Linda Smith [1962] Director/Accountant

Trend Machinery & Cutting Tools Limited
Incorporated: 14 November 1977 *Employees:* 76
Net Worth: £4,722,323 *Total Assets:* £10,083,295
Registered Office: Unit 6 Odhams Trading Estate, Watford, Herts, WD24 7TR
Activities: Wholesale of other machinery and equipment
Shareholders: Annette Kelly; Stephen Julius Phillips
Officers: Christopher Robert Lamb, Secretary; Christopher James Carter [1975] Marketing Director; Grant John Davidson [1965] Operations Director; Christopher Robert Lamb [1973] Finance Director; Neil McMillan [1969] Technical Director; Stephen Julius Phillips [1966] Director/Chairman; Alistair Roberts [1968] CEO & Managing Director; Michael Phillip Tideswell [1976] Sales Director

Trend Marine Products Limited
Incorporated: 6 June 1974 *Employees:* 171
Net Worth: £3,045,806 *Total Assets:* £10,098,777
Registered Office: Sutton Road, Catfield, Great Yarmouth, Norfolk, NR29 5BG
Activities: Other manufacturing n.e.c.
Parent: Taylor Made Holdings UK Limited
Officers: Brian Michael Hall, Secretary; John Clark [1964] Finance Director; Brian Michael Hall [1975] Director/Chief Financial Officer [American]; Jason Douglas Lippert [1972] Director/Chief Executive Officer [American]; Andrew Joseph Namenye [1980] Director/Chief Legal Officer [American]

Trentpeak Limited
Incorporated: 18 June 1976 *Employees:* 1
Net Worth: £2,892,372 *Total Assets:* £13,564,798
Registered Office: Garnault, Bulls Cross, Enfield, Middlesex, EN2 9HD
Activities: Buying and selling of own real estate
Major Shareholder: Omiros Marovouniotis
Officers: Seija Heinonen, Secretary; Omiros Mavrovouniotis [1948] Director

Trevester Limited
Incorporated: 8 October 2008 *Employees:* 100
Net Worth: £4,129,290 *Total Assets:* £11,581,366
Registered Office: New Road, Tiptree, Colchester, Essex, CO5 0HQ
Activities: Activities of construction holding companies
Officers: Marie Paveley, Secretary; Mervyn John Denney [1961] Director/Contracts Manager; Alan Michael Evers [1969] Director/Buyer; Stephen Michael Ewers [1965] Director/Contracts Manager

Tri-Continental Limited
Incorporated: 29 September 1987 *Employees:* 23
Net Worth: £7,157,492 *Total Assets:* £17,101,246
Registered Office: Tricon Plaza, Braintree Road, Ruislip, Middlesex, HA4 0EJ
Activities: Other information technology service activities
Shareholder: Israel Lwanga
Officers: Joseph Nsambu Musisi, Secretary [Ugandan]; Edward Katimbo-Mugwanya [1948] Director/Accountant [Ugandan]; Israel Lwanga [1948] Director [Ugandan]; Joy Namuli-Lule Lwanga [1955] Director [Ugandan]; Joseph Nsambu Musisi [1949] Director/Engineer [Ugandan]

Triangle (Funding One) Limited
Incorporated: 12 November 1998
Net Worth: £29,455,950 *Total Assets:* £36,065,204
Registered Office: 1 Bishop Square, St Albans Road West, Hatfield, Herts, AL10 9NE
Activities: Renting and leasing of air passenger transport equipment
Parent: Triangle Aviation (UK) Holdings Limited
Officers: Sarah Louise Mary Dichlian, Secretary; Jonathan Granger Atkeson [1973] Managing Director [American]; Nicholas Paul Fegan [1974] Managing Director; Marc Keith Furstein [1968] Director [American]

Triangle Aviation (UK) Holdings Limited
Incorporated: 23 May 2011 *Employees:* 50
Net Worth: £97,917,592 *Total Assets:* £123,488,112
Registered Office: 1 Bishop Square, St Albans Road West, Hatfield, Herts, AL10 9NE
Activities: Activities of other holding companies n.e.c.
Officers: Sarah Louise Mary Dichlian, Secretary; Jonathan Granger Atkeson [1973] Managing Director [American]; Nicholas Paul Fegan [1974] Managing Director; Marc Keith Furstein [1968] Director [American]

Triangle Regional Aircraft Leasing Limited
Incorporated: 2 October 2001
Net Worth: £93,565,080 *Total Assets:* £99,569,944
Registered Office: 1 Bishop Square, St Albans Road West, Hatfield, Herts, AL10 9NE
Activities: Renting and leasing of air passenger transport equipment
Parent: Triangle Aviation (UK) Holdings Limited
Officers: Sarah Louise Mary Dichlian, Secretary; Jonathan Granger Atkeson [1973] Managing Director [American]; Nicholas Paul Fegan [1974] Managing Director; Marc Keith Furstein [1968] Director [American]

Triconnex Ltd
Incorporated: 10 December 2010 *Employees:* 186
Net Worth: £4,126,000 *Total Assets:* £24,702,000
Registered Office: 4 Tamdown Way, Braintree, Essex, CM7 2QL
Activities: Other construction installation
Parent: Nexus Infrastructure PLC
Officers: Dawn Hilman, Secretary; Christopher Dore [1969] Director; Simon Christie Gallagher [1983] Director/Chartered Surveyor; Richard Martin Harpley [1958] Director; Dawn Rosina Hillman [1968] Director/Accountant; Michael David Hine [1969] Director/Contracts Manager; Alan Christopher Martin [1966] Director; Michael Thomas Morris [1967] Director; Charles Alan Sweeney [1959] Director; David Graham Topping [1970] Director

Trieste Group LLP
Incorporated: 15 March 2012 *Employees:* 91
Net Worth: £8,411,829 *Total Assets:* £13,177,274
Registered Office: Noble House, Eaton Road, Hemel Hempstead Industrial Estate, Hemel Hempstead, Herts, HP2 7UB
Officers: Nicolas Baxter [1971] Member; Charles Hubert Kingston [1955] Member; Russell Charles Kingston [1988] Member; Lucy Rachel Baxter [1980] LLP Member; Alexander Giles Harvey [1980] LLP Member; Jacqui Louise Harvey [1982] LLP Member; Adenne Lara Kingston [1987] LLP Member; Joanne Esther Kingston [1961] LLP Member; Charles Gareth Stedman [1983] LLP Member; Hazel Elizabeth Stedman [1984] LLP Member

Trimble UK Limited
Incorporated: 12 September 2000 *Employees:* 180
Net Worth: £171,000 *Total Assets:* £29,865,000
Registered Office: 1 Bath Street, Ipswich, Suffolk, IP2 8SD
Activities: Information technology consultancy activities
Officers: James Anthony Kirkland, Secretary/General Counsel; John Henry Gale Heelas [1963] Director/Accountant; James Anthony Kirkland [1959] Director/VP, General Counsel and Assistant Secretary [American]; Robbert Hendrik Herman Reeder [1970] European Director of Finance [Dutch]; John Peter Schreiber [1959] Director/Vice President Global Tax [American]

Trinity (D) Limited
Incorporated: 3 January 2002
Net Worth: £53,932,472 *Total Assets:* £54,845,432
Registered Office: Bidwell House, Trumpington Road, Cambridge, CB2 9LD
Activities: Other letting and operating of own or leased real estate
Officers: Robert Coote, Secretary; Dr Jeremy Richard Frederick Fairbrother [1939] Director/Finance Secretary; Rory Buchanan Landman [1961] Director/Bursar

Trinity College (CSP) Limited
Incorporated: 27 June 1997
Net Worth: £18,733,672 *Total Assets:* £30,960,812
Registered Office: Bidwell House, Trumpington Road, Cambridge, CB2 9LD
Activities: Management of real estate on a fee or contract basis
Officers: Robert Coote, Secretary; Dr Jeremy Richard Frederick Fairbrother [1939] Director/Finance Secretary; Rory Buchanan Landman [1961] Director/Bursar

Trinity View Homes Limited
Incorporated: 12 May 2005
Net Worth Deficit: £867,385 *Total Assets:* £10,365,423
Registered Office: Suite 3, First Floor, The Hamilton Centre, Rodney Way, Chelmsford, Essex, CM1 3BY
Activities: Development of building projects
Shareholder: R Shaffer Discretionary Settlement
Officers: Derek Reginald Govey [1962] Director

Triplehigh Limited
Incorporated: 5 December 1990
Net Worth: £10,070,259 *Total Assets:* £13,952,020
Registered Office: 27a Maxwell Road, Northwood, Middlesex, HA6 2XY
Activities: Development of building projects
Major Shareholder: Mary Flannery
Officers: Mary Flannery, Company Secretary [Irish]; Mary Flannery [1953] Director/Company Secretary [Irish]; Patrick Flannery [1950] Director [Irish]

Triplerose Limited
Incorporated: 20 February 1996
Net Worth: £65,902,736 *Total Assets:* £123,471,992
Registered Office: 88 Edgware Way, Edgware, Middlesex, HA8 8JS
Activities: Buying and selling of own real estate
Officers: Chavi Moskovitz, Secretary; Chavi Moskovitz [1964] Director/Housewife; Israel Moskovitz [1964] Director/Property [Canadian]

Tristel PLC
Incorporated: 9 April 2003 *Employees:* 124
Net Worth: £18,420,000 *Total Assets:* £22,540,000
Registered Office: Unit 1b Lynx Business Park, Fordham Road, Snailwell, Newmarket, Cambs, CB8 7NY
Activities: Non-trading company
Officers: Elizabeth Amanda Dixon, Secretary; Paul Martin Barnes [1953] Director; Elizabeth Amanda Dixon [1970] Director/Accountant; Dr Bruno Luc Myriam Holthof [1961] Director [Belgian]; Tom Arther John Jenkins [1972] Director; Bart Leemans [1962] Director [Belgian]; David William Edmund Orr [1959] Director; Paul Christopher Swinney [1957] Director

Tristel Solutions Limited
Incorporated: 27 February 1998 *Employees:* 91
Net Worth: £3,525,000 *Total Assets:* £12,128,000
Registered Office: Unit 1b Lynx Business Park, Fordham Road, Snailwell, Newmarket, Cambs, CB8 7NY
Activities: Manufacture of other chemical products n.e.c.
Parent: Tristel PLC
Officers: Elizabeth Dixon, Secretary; Elizabeth Amanda Dixon [1970] Director/Accountant; Stephen Richard Garrod [1973] Director/Quality Manager; Esther Maria Hubertina Margaretha Jansen [1985] Marketing Director [Dutch]; Danielle Nugent [1976] Sales Director; Jenny O'Callaghan [1968] Director; Paul Gary Oakley [1979] Director/Accountant; Julija Shabanova [1981] Marketing Director [Lithuanian]; Paul Christopher Swinney [1957] Director

Tritton Farming Partnership LLP
Incorporated: 4 September 2013
Net Worth: £18,590,172 *Total Assets:* £18,903,956
Registered Office: Lyons Hall, Great Leighs, Chelmsford, Essex, CM3 1PL
Officers: James David Gwyn Morris [1965] Member; Alan George Tritton [1931] Member; Anneli Clare Tritton [1965] Member; Charles Courtenay Tritton [1965] Member; Diana Spencer Tritton [1940] Member

Trollope & Colls Limited
Incorporated: 30 November 1903
Net Worth: £1,646,000 *Total Assets:* £8,326,000
Registered Office: Maple Cross House, Denham Way, Maple Cross, Rickmansworth, Herts, WD3 9SW
Activities: Construction of commercial buildings
Parent: Skanska UK PLC
Officers: Steven Leven, Secretary; David William Kyriacos [1976] Director; Steven Leven [1967] Director/Company Secretary; Steven Edward Lindsay [1975] Director

Tropical Marine Centre Limited
Incorporated: 28 January 2009 *Employees:* 94
Net Worth: £2,611,000 *Total Assets:* £10,168,000
Registered Office: Tropical Marine Centre, Solesbridge Lane, Chorleywood, Herts, WD3 5SX
Activities: Marine aquaculture
Parent: Pet & Aquatics Properties Ltd
Officers: Amanda Kathryn Taylor, Secretary; Nicholas Grant Bridel [1974] Director; Brian Joao Schaff [1980] Managing Director [Portuguese]; Amanda Kathryn Taylor [1959] Director and Company Secretary; Derek Thomson [1964] Director; Paul Desmond West [1957] Managing Director

Troston Farms Limited
Incorporated: 14 February 1961 *Employees:* 9
Net Worth: £20,481,092 *Total Assets:* £28,381,980
Registered Office: Troston Farms Ltd, Park Farm Drive, Stanton, Bury St Edmunds, Suffolk, IP31 2DL
Activities: Growing of cereals (except rice), leguminous crops and oil seeds
Officers: Clive Edward Last, Secretary/Chief Executive; Herr Helmut Franz Claas [1926] Director/Manufacturer [German]; Cathrina Anneli Claas-Muehlhaeuser [1975] Director [German]; Alastair John Kerr [1973] Director/Farmer; Clive Edward Last [1947] Director/Chief Executive

Trox UK Limited
Incorporated: 25 January 1962 *Employees:* 144
Net Worth: £5,629,000 *Total Assets:* £9,890,000
Registered Office: Caxton Way, Thetford, Norfolk, IP24 3SQ
Activities: Manufacture of other fabricated metal products n.e.c.
Parent: Trox GmbH
Officers: Suzanne Paula Archer, Secretary; Neil Addison [1967] Sales Director; Suzanne Paula Archer [1972] Finance Director; Robert Douglas Fawkner [1965] Production Director; Udo Peter Jung [1966] Technical Director Production [German]; Thomas Mosbacher [1966] Director/Chief Financial Officer [German]

Truck-Lite Europe Limited
Incorporated: 31 January 1924 *Employees:* 313
Net Worth: £9,305,000 *Total Assets:* £28,167,000
Registered Office: Barrows Road, Harlow, Essex, CM19 5FA
Activities: Manufacture of other parts and accessories for motor vehicles
Officers: Zoe Suzanna Saunders, Secretary; Brian Michael Kupchella [1967] Director/President [American]; Adrian Lloyd [1972] Director

Truckeast Limited
Incorporated: 7 December 1992 *Employees:* 356
Net Worth: £6,039,025 *Total Assets:* £34,319,724
Registered Office: Violet Hill Road, Stowmarket, Suffolk, IP14 1NN
Activities: Maintenance and repair of motor vehicles
Shareholders: John Antony William Biggin; Simon Eric Hobson
Officers: Simon Eric Hobson, Secretary; John Antony William Biggin [1961] Director; Graham Stephen Broughton [1956] Regional Aftersales Director; Martyn Charles Clipston [1969] Regional Aftersales Director; Harley Clive Coulson [1975] Sales Director; Simon Eric Hobson [1966] Director

Truman Securities Limited
Incorporated: 20 June 2015
Net Worth: £41,822 *Total Assets:* £17,147,800
Registered Office: Kirkland House, 11-15 Peterborough Road, Harrow, Middlesex, HA1 2AX
Activities: Hotels and similar accommodation
Officers: Haider Ladhu Jaffer [1940] Director; Hassanali Amirali Dawood Suleman [1954] Director

Trumpf Limited
Incorporated: 21 February 1974 *Employees:* 83
Net Worth: £6,666,930 *Total Assets:* £18,550,284
Registered Office: Unit A, President Way, Airport Executive Park, Luton, Beds, LU2 9NL
Activities: Installation of industrial machinery and equipment
Officers: Jurgen Herr, Secretary; Reinhold Gross [1969] Director [German]; Juergen Herr [1972] Finance Director [German]; Generald Joseph Jones [1959] Sales Director; Lee Moakes [1977] Managing Director

Trurating Limited
Incorporated: 12 October 2012 *Employees:* 36
Net Worth: £9,635,919 *Total Assets:* £10,915,411
Registered Office: Pendragon House, 65 London Road, St Albans, Herts, AL1 1LJ
Activities: Data processing, hosting and related activities
Shareholder: Georgina Kate Nelson
Officers: Peter George Edwin Ayliffe [1953] Director/Chief Executive; Christopher Charles Blundell [1977] Director; Christian Andrew Nelson [1980] Director/Consultant; Georgina Kate Nelson [1979] Director/Lawyer

Trust Estates (Clarence Street) Limited
Incorporated: 25 February 2014 *Employees:* 4
Net Worth: £707 *Total Assets:* £13,832,904
Registered Office: 19 King Street, King's Lynn, Norfolk, PE30 1HB
Activities: Other letting and operating of own or leased real estate
Shareholders: Rui Pan; Qinqin Song; Chengrun He
Officers: Honourable William John Cadogan [1973] Director/Chartered Surveyor; Weipeng Gu [1989] Director [Chinese]; Andrew David Jamieson [1956] Director; Rui Pan [1990] Director [Chinese]

Trust Tees Limited
Incorporated: 18 January 2011 *Employees:* 249
Net Worth: £2,276,033 *Total Assets:* £10,165,131
Registered Office: Tees House, 95 London Road, Bishop's Stortford, Herts, CM23 3GW
Activities: Solicitors
Officers: Govan Paul Raymond Bramley, Secretary; Govan Paul Raymond Bramley [1962] Director/Solicitor; Lucy Jayne Folley [1969] Director/Solicitor; Ashton Willis Hunt [1968] Managing Director; Dr Stephen Wallace Mayson [1955] Director/Strategic Adviser; Catherine Elizabeth Mowat [1975] Director; David Ian Redfern [1957] Director/Solicitor; Andrew Thomas Swarbrick [1953] Director/Chartered Accountant

Trustonic Limited
Incorporated: 22 December 2011 *Employees:* 90
Net Worth Deficit: £310,203 *Total Assets:* £14,463,869
Registered Office: 10 Station Road, Cambridge, CB1 2JD
Activities: Business and domestic software development
Shareholders: ARM Limited; Gemalto N.V.
Officers: Adam Neil Christian Bastin [1978] Senior Director, Corporate Development; Benjamin Stephen Cade [1978] Director/Chief Executive Officer; Martin McCourt [1962] Director [Irish]

TSI Instruments Ltd
Incorporated: 15 July 2002 *Employees:* 44
Net Worth: £6,156,108 *Total Assets:* £8,456,275
Registered Office: 373 Stirling Road, Cressex Business Park, High Wycombe, Bucks, HP12 3ST
Activities: Manufacture of electronic measuring, testing etc. equipment, not for industrial process control
Major Shareholder: John Fauth
Officers: Daniel Happe, Secretary; John Fauth [1945] Director/Executive [American]; Thomas E Kennedy [1960] Director/Executive [American]; Mark Schwirtz [1965] Director [American]

TTKW Limited
Incorporated: 21 August 2015 *Employees:* 216
Net Worth: £8,192,353 *Total Assets:* £12,036,129
Registered Office: Northminster House, Northminster, Peterborough, Cambs, PE1 1YN
Activities: Activities of other holding companies n.e.c.
Shareholders: Adrian John George Jaggard; Antony Jaggard
Officers: John Ashley Bryant, Secretary; Simon Jeremy Banfield [1963] Director/Solicitor; Paul Allan Davis [1954] Director/Solicitor; Matthew David Hoe [1979] Director/Solicitor; Adrian John George Jaggard [1976] Director/Solicitor; Antony Jaggard [1978] Director/Solicitor

TTP Group PLC
Incorporated: 30 September 1987 *Employees:* 437
Net Worth: £80,600,000 *Total Assets:* £99,588,000
Registered Office: Melbourn Science Park, Cambridge Road, Melbourn, Royston, Herts, SG8 6EE
Activities: Management consultancy activities other than financial management
Officers: Keith Alexander Haddow, Secretary; Dr James Charles Fox [1951] Director/Consulting Engineer [Australian]; Keith Alexander Haddow [1958] Director/Chartered Accountant; Dr Samuel Charles William Hyde [1972] Director/Physicist; Dr Jaspal Sanghera [1954] Director/Engineer; Peter John Taylor [1953] Director/Scientist; Dr Colin David Wall [1949] Director/Recruitment Consultant

TTP Labtech Limited
Incorporated: 10 January 1997 *Employees:* 131
Net Worth: £8,298,000 *Total Assets:* £14,975,000
Registered Office: Melbourn Science Park, Cambridge Road, Melbourn, Royston, Herts, SG8 6EE
Activities: Manufacture of plastics and rubber machinery
Parent: SPT Acquico Limited
Officers: Andrew Grieve, Secretary; Patrick Bennett [1964] Director [Canadian]; David Allan Newble [1971] Director/Chief Executive

TTP PLC
Incorporated: 15 January 1997 *Employees:* 236
Previous: The Technology Partnership PLC
Net Worth: £24,550,000 *Total Assets:* £34,569,000
Registered Office: Melbourn Science Park, Cambridge Road, Melbourn, Royston, Herts, SG8 6EE
Activities: Other research and experimental development on natural sciences and engineering
Parent: TTP Group PLC
Officers: Keith Alexander Haddow, Secretary; Keith Alexander Haddow [1958] Director/Chartered Accountant; Dr Samuel Charles William Hyde [1972] Director/Physicist; Peter John Taylor [1953] Director/Scientist

P. Tuckwell Limited
Incorporated: 8 November 1974 *Employees:* 173
Net Worth: £9,896,543 *Total Assets:* £29,179,760
Registered Office: P Tuckwell Ltd, Shop Street, Worlingworth, Woodbridge, Suffolk, IP13 7HU
Activities: Wholesale of agricultural machinery, equipment and supplies
Major Shareholder: Paul Anthony Tuckwell
Officers: Paul Anthony Tuckwell, Secretary/Engineer; James Marcus Tuckwell [1976] Director/Engineer; Paul Anthony Tuckwell [1954] Director/Engineer

Tudor Court Primary Academy Trust
Incorporated: 4 June 2014 *Employees:* 150
Net Worth: £7,595,230 *Total Assets:* £9,942,944
Registered Office: Tudor Court Primary School, Bark Burr Road, Grays, Essex, RM16 6PL
Activities: Primary education
Officers: Julia Mary Violet Edmeades [1974] Director/Human Resources Manager; Riham Ahmed Moustafa Moustafa El Maghraby [1975] Director/Classroom Support Assistant; Chinyere Emuche Eruchalu [1984] Director/Project Manager; Philip Brian Peter Kyriacou [1973] Director/Executive Principal; Cheryl Anne Mason [1979] Director/Chartered Accountant; Andrew McLeod [1975] Director/Security Risk Manager; Kim Lorraine Moore [1972] Director/Sports Injury & Massage Therapist; Paul Robert Raymond [1990] Director/Teacher; Keeley Michele Shelton [1972] Director/Bookkeeper; Emily Louise Sheppard [1988] Director; Kelly Ann Stevens [1978] Director/Teacher

George Tufts and Son Limited
Incorporated: 29 November 1999 *Employees:* 21
Net Worth: £11,217,638 *Total Assets:* £11,880,696
Registered Office: The Willows School Road, Bradenham, Thetford, Norfolk, IP25 7QU
Activities: Wholesale of wood, construction materials and sanitary equipment
Parent: Tufts of Bradenham Ltd
Officers: Cindy Ann Tufts, Secretary; John Michael Tufts [1990] Director; Lucy Tufts [1987] Director; Michael John Tufts [1958] Director of Builders Merchants; Tony Valentine [1960] Director of Builders Merchants

TUI Airways Limited
Incorporated: 28 October 1947 *Employees:* 3,859
Previous: Thomson Airways Limited
Net Worth: £839,000,000 *Total Assets:* £2,847,000,064
Registered Office: Wigmore House, Wigmore Lane, Luton, Beds, LU2 9TN
Activities: Scheduled passenger air transport
Parent: TUI UK Limited
Officers: Robert Coldrake [1978] Director/Chartered Accountant; Dawn Allison Wilson [1966] Director

TUI Group Fleet Finance Limited
Incorporated: 24 March 2017
Net Worth: £6,958,428 *Total Assets:* £135,841,088
Registered Office: Wigmore House, Wigmore Place, Wigmore Lane, Luton, Beds, LU2 9TN
Activities: Other business support service activities n.e.c.
Shareholders: TUI Travel Aviation Finance Limited; TUI Travel Aviation Finance Limited
Officers: Thomas Edward Chandler [1974] Director; Alistair Kenton Jarvis [1968] Director

TUI Ireland Limited
Incorporated: 11 February 1988 *Employees:* 43
Previous: Falcon Leisure Group (Overseas) Limited
Net Worth: £15,911,000 *Total Assets:* £80,144,000
Registered Office: Wigmore House, Wigmore Lane, Luton, Beds, LU2 9TN
Activities: Other service activities n.e.c.
Parent: TUI UK Limited
Officers: Simon James Eaton [1971] Director/Head of Ireland; Steven John Hoar [1978] Director/Accountant

TUI Northern Europe Limited
Incorporated: 2 January 1998
Net Worth: £73,000,000 *Total Assets:* £83,000,000
Registered Office: Wigmore House, Wigmore Lane, Luton, Beds, LU2 9TN
Activities: Activities of head offices
Parent: TUI Travel Holdings Limited
Officers: David John Burling [1968] Director; Alistair Kenton Jarvis [1968] Director; Thomas Gerd Pietzka [1964] Director [German]

TUI Travel Aviation Finance Limited
Incorporated: 10 August 2009
Net Worth: £56,449,624 *Total Assets:* £1,479,454,848
Registered Office: Wigmore House, Wigmore Lane, Luton, Beds, LU2 9TN
Activities: Other business support service activities n.e.c.
Parent: TUI Travel Holdings Limited
Officers: Thomas Edward Chandler [1974] Director; Alistair Kenton Jarvis [1968] Director

TUI Travel Group Solutions Limited
Incorporated: 28 September 1999 *Employees:* 81
Net Worth: £95,495,976 *Total Assets:* £138,948,096
Registered Office: Wigmore House, Wigmore Lane, Luton, Beds, LU2 9TN
Activities: Non-trading company
Parent: TUI Travel Holdings Limited
Officers: Matthew Thomas Broomhall [1975] Director; Marc Steven Jennings [1974] Director; Mark Edwin Russell [1968] Director/Accountant

TUI Travel Holdings Limited
Incorporated: 4 July 2008
Net Worth: £564,691,968 *Total Assets:* £1,510,323,968
Registered Office: Wigmore House, Wigmore Lane, Luton, Beds, LU2 9TN
Activities: Activities of head offices
Parent: TUI Travel Limited
Officers: David John Burling [1968] Director; Alistair Kenton Jarvis [1968] Director

TUI Travel Limited
Incorporated: 29 January 2007
Previous: TUI Travel PLC
Net Worth: £298,000,000 *Total Assets:* £560,000,000
Registered Office: Wigmore House, Wigmore Lane, Luton, Beds, LU2 9TN
Activities: Activities of head offices
Parent: TUI AG
Officers: Kim Michele Clear, Secretary; David John Burling [1968] Director; Alistair Kenton Jarvis [1968] Director

TUI Travel Overseas Holdings Limited
Incorporated: 18 December 2003
Net Worth: £93,001,000 *Total Assets:* £131,721,000
Registered Office: Wigmore House, Wigmore Lane, Luton, Beds, LU2 9TN
Activities: Non-trading company
Parent: TUI Travel Limited
Officers: Kim Michele Clear, Secretary; David John Burling [1968] Director; Alistair Kenton Jarvis [1968] Director; Thomas Lindner [1968] Director [German]; Thomas Gerd Pietzka [1964] Director [German]

TUI UK Limited
Incorporated: 24 June 1993 *Employees:* 3,107
Net Worth: £876,000,000 *Total Assets:* £3,931,000,064
Registered Office: Wigmore House, Wigmore Lane, Luton, Beds, LU2 9TN
Activities: Travel agency activities
Parent: TUI Travel Holdings Limited
Officers: Robert Coldrake [1978] Director/Chartered Accountant; Andrew Flintham [1969] Director; Katharine Rachel McAlister [1976] Director/CMO Tui UK & Ireland; Richard Sofer [1978] Commercial Director - UK & Ireland; Dawn Allison Wilson [1966] Director

TUI UK Retail Limited
Incorporated: 23 October 1979 *Employees:* 4,111
Net Worth: £196,000,000 *Total Assets:* £755,000,000
Registered Office: Wigmore House, Wigmore Lane, Luton, Beds, LU2 9TN
Activities: Travel agency activities
Parent: TUI UK Limited
Officers: Robert Coldrake [1978] Director/Chartered Accountant; Andrew Flintham [1969] Director; Katharine Rachel McAlister [1976] Director/CMO Tui UK & Ireland; Jason Mark Smith [1970] Director/Accountant; Belinda Ruth Vazquez [1975] Director

TUI UK Transport Limited
Incorporated: 16 June 1971
Net Worth: £37,832,000 *Total Assets:* £1,414,221,952
Registered Office: Wigmore House, Wigmore Lane, Luton, Beds, LU2 9TN
Activities: Other service activities n.e.c.
Parent: TUI UK Limited
Officers: Robert Coldrake [1978] Director/Chartered Accountant; Andrew Flintham [1969] Director

Tulip Properties & Real Estate Ltd
Incorporated: 21 July 2015
Net Worth: £3,304,673 *Total Assets:* £11,042,356
Registered Office: 35 Gabrielle House, 332-336 Perth Road, Ilford, Essex, IG2 6FF
Activities: Other letting and operating of own or leased real estate
Officers: Varun Chadha [1982] Director; Nikkita Kewal Mahajan [1983] Director

Tun Abdul Razak Research Centre
Incorporated: 27 January 1938 *Employees:* 81
Net Worth: £4,381,760 *Total Assets:* £11,516,181
Registered Office: Brickendonbury, Hertford, SG13 8NL
Activities: Other research and experimental development on natural sciences and engineering
Officers: Dr Stuart Cook [1958] Director Research; Wan Ahmad Asmady Bin Wan MD Din [1975] Director/Ministerial Officer [Malaysian]; Yeaw Kok Kwey [1965] Managing Director [Malaysian]; Dr Zairossani Bin Mohd Nor [1971] Director/Research Scientist [Malaysian]; Dr Fauzi Bin Mohd Som [1968] Director/Chief Executive Officer [Malaysian]

Tunnelcraft Limited
Incorporated: 3 July 1992 *Employees:* 91
Net Worth: £3,236,013 *Total Assets:* £9,319,844
Registered Office: Ground Floor, Sidney House, Christy Close, Southfields Business Park, Basildon, Essex, SS15 6TN
Activities: Construction of bridges and tunnels
Shareholders: Cormac Phillip Hicks; John Patrick Riordan; James Joseph Riordan
Officers: John Patrick Riordan, Secretary/Carpenter; Cormac Phillip Hicks [1953] Director; James Joseph Riordan [1968] Director; John Patrick Riordan [1965] Director/Carpenter

Turner Properties Limited
Incorporated: 28 August 1986 *Employees:* 4
Net Worth: £7,197,425 *Total Assets:* £12,023,430
Registered Office: Tudor House, 185 Kenton Road, Harrow, Middlesex, HA3 0EY
Activities: Buying and selling of own real estate
Shareholders: Ashwin Motichand Shah; Rasila Ashwin Shah
Officers: Sonal Ashar, Secretary; Rasila Ashwin Shah, Secretary; Meera Rupani [1988] Director; Ashwin MoTIchand Shah [1955] Director/Chartered Accountant; Rasila Ashwin Shah [1953] Director

Turners (East Anglia) Limited
Incorporated: 29 April 2005 *Employees:* 66
Net Worth: £5,900,444 *Total Assets:* £10,995,202
Registered Office: Turner Motor Group, Tayfen Road, Bury St Edmunds, Suffolk, IP33 1TB
Activities: Activities of head offices
Shareholders: Ian John Turner; Glen Paul Turner
Officers: Ian John Turner, Secretary; Glen Paul Turner [1962] Director; Ian John Turner [1959] Director; Pauline Edith Turner [1931] Director

Turners (Soham) Holdings Limited
Incorporated: 21 December 2011 *Employees:* 3,402
Net Worth: £271,799,008 *Total Assets:* £350,580,000
Registered Office: Fordham Road, Newmarket, Suffolk, CB8 7NR
Activities: Freight transport by road
Shareholders: Paul Edwin Day; Winifred Mary Day
Officers: Paul Edwin Day [1958] Director; Winifred Mary Day [1934] Director

Turners (Soham) Limited
Incorporated: 25 July 1947 *Employees:* 3,369
Net Worth: £269,596,992 *Total Assets:* £344,785,984
Registered Office: Fordham Road, Newmarket, Suffolk, CB8 7NR
Activities: Freight transport by road
Officers: John Graham Rex Miller, Secretary; Paul Edwin Day [1958] Director; Winifred Mary Day [1934] Director

Turners Britannia Parks Limited
Incorporated: 3 April 2009 *Employees:* 33
Previous: Turners (Britannia Parks) Limited
Net Worth: £5,719,643 *Total Assets:* £46,165,736
Registered Office: Fordham Road, Newmarket, Suffolk, CB8 7NR
Activities: Other business support service activities n.e.c.
Parent: Turners Parks Group Limited
Officers: Paul Edwin Day, Secretary; Paul Edwin Day [1958] Director; Winifred Mary Day [1934] Director

Turners Parks Group Limited
Incorporated: 11 November 2011
Previous: Turners Park Life Limited
Net Worth Deficit: £1,131,171 *Total Assets:* £39,590,648
Registered Office: Fordham Road, Newmarket, Suffolk, CB8 7NR
Activities: Other business support service activities n.e.c.
Parent: Turners (Soham) Holdings Limited
Officers: Paul Edwin Day [1958] Director; Winifred Mary Day [1934] Director

Turners Regency Parks Limited
Incorporated: 10 November 2009 *Employees:* 8
Previous: Regency Park Homes Limited
Net Worth: £147,664 *Total Assets:* £25,354,924
Registered Office: Fordham Road, Newmarket, Suffolk, CB8 7NR
Activities: Other business support service activities n.e.c.
Shareholders: Paul Edwin Day; Turners Parks Group Limited
Officers: Paul Edwin Day [1958] Director

Turnhold Properties Limited
Incorporated: 6 February 1991 *Employees:* 13
Net Worth: £15,579,005 *Total Assets:* £18,473,580
Registered Office: 249 Cranbrook Road, Ilford, Essex, IG1 4TG
Activities: Development of building projects
Shareholder: Garry Jon Simpson
Officers: Michele Suzanne Simpson, Secretary; David Ronald Elliott [1974] Director; Garry Jon Simpson [1967] Director/Commercial Agent; Michele Suzanne Simpson [1968] Director; Elise Ruth Summers [1966] Director

Turnlet Films (JN) Limited
Incorporated: 30 May 2017
Net Worth: £1 *Total Assets:* £9,366,773
Registered Office: 99 Kenton Road, Harrow, Middlesex, HA3 0AN
Activities: Motion picture production activities
Parent: Turnlet Films Limited
Officers: Simon Horsman [1967] Director; Andrea Scarso [1984] Director [Italian]; Simon Robert Williams [1982] Director

Turnstone Estates Limited
Incorporated: 28 February 1989 *Employees:* 2
Net Worth: £8,537,848 *Total Assets:* £11,880,798
Registered Office: The Warehouse, 33 Bridge Street, Cambridge, CB2 1UW
Activities: Other letting and operating of own or leased real estate
Major Shareholder: Christopher William Goldsmith
Officers: Christopher William Goldsmith, Secretary; Timothy John Deacon [1975] Director; Christopher William Goldsmith [1960] Director; Yvette Marie Gregory [1966] Director/Management Accountant

Turpin Distribution Services Limited
Incorporated: 28 September 1977 *Employees:* 58
Net Worth: £3,153,419 *Total Assets:* £12,916,129
Registered Office: Turpin Distribution, Pegasus Drive, Stratton Business Park, Biggleswade, Beds, SG18 8TQ
Activities: Operation of warehousing and storage facilities for air transport activities
Parent: Turpin Holdings Limited
Officers: Richard Ian Stroud, Secretary; Julie Barnes [1964] HR Director; Neil Castle [1965] Operations Director; Michael Anthony Geelan [1954] Director; Lorna Summers [1952] Managing Director

Tuskerdirect Limited
Incorporated: 25 October 1999 *Employees:* 171
Net Worth: £26,149,160 *Total Assets:* £185,849,040
Registered Office: Building 4, Hatters Lane, Croxley Green Business Park, Watford, Herts, WD18 8YF
Activities: Renting and leasing of cars and light motor vehicles
Parent: Hamsard 3353 Limited
Officers: Laura Catherine Elizabeth Alexander [1979] Director/Chief Financial Officer; Clive Andrew Whistler Baker [1974] Director [British/South African]; Simon English [1960] Director; Paul Gilshan [1975] Director

Tustin Properties Ltd
Incorporated: 22 March 2010 *Employees:* 3
Net Worth: £9,658,567 *Total Assets:* £11,390,600
Registered Office: Suite 2, Fountain House, 1a Elm Park, Stanmore, Middlesex, HA7 4AU
Activities: Buying and selling of own real estate
Shareholder: Alexander Charles Tustin
Officers: Catherine Takhtay [1971] Director/Property Consultant; Alexander Charles Tustin [1973] Director/Sales Executive; Brie Kirsty Tustin [1978] Director/Property Consultant; Elsa Tustin [1947] Director/Textile Artist

Tutis Properties Limited
Incorporated: 14 February 2012 *Employees:* 3
Net Worth: £10,047,981 *Total Assets:* £12,140,165
Registered Office: 10 Jesus Lane, Cambridge, CB5 8BA
Activities: Other letting and operating of own or leased real estate
Major Shareholder: Guilo Aldo Marino
Officers: Giulio Aldo Marino [1961] Director [Italian]

Twentieth Century Fox Television Distribution (U.K.), Ltd.
Incorporated: 24 June 2016
Net Worth: £161,836,432 *Total Assets:* £209,570,784
Registered Office: 99 Kenton Road, Harrow, Middlesex, HA3 0AN
Activities: Motion picture distribution activities
Parent: Twentieth Century Fox International Television Inc
Officers: Jonathan Gottlieb [1972] Director/Lawyer [American]; Jane Waxman [1965] Director/Executive Vice President, Twenty-First Century Fox [American]

Twenty 1 Construction Limited
Incorporated: 3 October 2012 *Employees:* 34
Net Worth: £2,812,092 *Total Assets:* £13,219,799
Registered Office: Wellington House, 273-275 High Street, London Colney, Herts, AL2 1HA
Activities: Development of building projects
Parent: Twenty 1 Group Holdings Limited
Officers: Paul Gaughan, Secretary; Keith Ashcroft [1964] Director/Fit Out Contractor; Paul Michael Gaughan [1970] Director/Quantity Surveyor

TWI Limited
Incorporated: 14 October 1999 *Employees:* 523
Net Worth Deficit: £2,802,000 *Total Assets:* £102,772,000
Registered Office: Bevan Braithwaite Building, Granta Park, Great Abington, Cambridge, CB21 6AL
Activities: Management consultancy activities other than financial management
Officers: Gillian Astrid Leech, Secretary; Aamir Khalid [1964] Director/Chief Executive; Gillian Astrid Leech [1963] Finance Director; Michael Jonathan Russell [1974] Director; Paul Woollin [1963] Director

Twilight Real Estate Limited
Incorporated: 2 March 2017
Net Worth Deficit: £3,152 *Total Assets:* £17,772,256
Registered Office: Unit 4 Imperial Park, Stonefield Way, South Ruislip, Middlesex, HA4 0JW
Activities: Buying and selling of own real estate
Shareholder: Nayan Thakrar
Officers: Nayan Thakrar [1960] Director

Twinglobe Limited
Incorporated: 20 June 1983 *Employees:* 4
Net Worth: £3,945,454 *Total Assets:* £10,668,499
Registered Office: 7 Coombehurst Close, Hadley Wood, Herts, EN4 0JU
Activities: Other letting and operating of own or leased real estate
Shareholders: Twinglobe 2008 Ltd; Nineacre Limited
Officers: Mihir Kantilal Thakerar, Secretary/Businessman/Director; Dipak Thakerar [1965] Businessman/Director; Mihir Kantilal Thakerar [1963] Businessman/Director

Twinmar Group Limited
Incorporated: 29 July 2016 *Employees:* 452
Net Worth: £11,420,811 *Total Assets:* £22,460,782
Registered Office: York House, Empire Way, Wembley, Middlesex, HA9 0FQ
Activities: Activities of other holding companies n.e.c.
Officers: David Bordon [1958] Director; Marcel Bordon [1954] Director; Michael Bordon [1958] Director

Twinmar Investments Holdings Limited
Incorporated: 29 July 2016
Net Worth: £19,399,046 *Total Assets:* £19,399,046
Registered Office: York House, Empire Way, Wembley, Middlesex, HA9 0FQ
Activities: Activities of other holding companies n.e.c.
Officers: David Bordon [1958] Director; Marcel Bordon [1954] Director; Michael Bordon [1958] Director

Twinmar Investments Limited
Incorporated: 29 July 2016
Net Worth: £26,820,442 *Total Assets:* £26,985,058
Registered Office: York House, Empire Way, Wembley, Middlesex, HA9 0FQ
Activities: Activities of other holding companies n.e.c.
Parent: Twinmar Investments Holdings Limited
Officers: David Bordon [1958] Director; Marcel Bordon [1954] Director; Michael Bordon [1958] Director

Twinmar Limited
Incorporated: 11 June 1963 *Employees:* 442
Net Worth: £14,983,944 *Total Assets:* £22,381,960
Registered Office: York House, Empire Way, Wembley, Middlesex, HA9 0FQ
Activities: Retail sale of footwear in specialised stores
Parent: Twinmar Holdings Limited
Officers: Lilly Bordon, Secretary; Lilly Bordon [1928] Director; Marcel Bordon [1954] Director

Ubisense Limited
Incorporated: 18 July 2002 *Employees:* 45
Net Worth Deficit: £3,816,000 *Total Assets:* £24,025,000
Registered Office: St Andrew's House, St Andrew's Road, Chesterton, Cambridge, CB4 1DL
Activities: Other research and experimental development on natural sciences and engineering
Parent: Abyssinian Bidco Limited
Officers: Robin Adrian Bryson [1957] Director; Owen Thomas Henry Pagan [1975] Director [Irish]

UCL Frognal Limited
Incorporated: 18 April 2017
Net Worth: £4,467,897 *Total Assets:* £8,496,399
Registered Office: Portland House, 69-71 Wembley Hill Road, Wembley, Middlesex, HA9 8BU
Activities: Other business support service activities n.e.c.
Officers: Bhupendra Shantilal Kansagra, Secretary; Laurent Elie Cadji [1977] Director/Businessman; Lewis Levy Cadji [1938] Director/Businessman; Bhupendra Shantilal Kansagra [1956] Director/Businessman; Ramesh Shantilal Kansagra [1950] Director/Businessman

Ufford Park Limited
Incorporated: 29 April 1991 *Employees:* 134
Net Worth: £5,781,758 *Total Assets:* £10,295,885
Registered Office: Ufford Park Hotel Golf & Spa, Yarmouth Road, Melton, Woodbridge, Suffolk, IP12 1QW
Activities: Hotels and similar accommodation
Shareholder: Colin Victor Aldous
Officers: Simon Patrick Tucker, Secretary; Colin Victor Aldous [1945] Director; Jolyon Richard Aldous [1971] Director/Accountant; Shirley Ann Aldous [1945] Director; John Anthony Goleczka [1958] Director/Business Coach; Stuart Neil Robertson [1969] Director/Business Owner; Tarnia Denise Robertson [1969] Director/Sales Marketing Executive

UH Holdings Limited
Incorporated: 4 October 2007
Net Worth: £56,676,132 *Total Assets:* £57,600,556
Registered Office: University of Hertfordshire, College Lane, Hatfield, Herts, AL10 9AB
Activities: Activities of other holding companies n.e.c.
Parent: University of Hertfordshire
Officers: Alexander Hall, Secretary; Professor Ian Gordon Campbell [1963] Director/Deputy Vice-Chancellor; Susan Carol Grant [1961] Director/University Secretary and Registrar; Prof Quintin Archibald McKellar [1958] Director/University Vice-Chancellor; Alistair Moffat [1964] Finance Director; Professor Damian Robert Ward [1971] Director/Academic Manager

UIDUK Ltd
Incorporated: 9 August 2011
Net Worth: £927,243 *Total Assets:* £12,182,200
Registered Office: 3 Lowther Close, Elstree, Borehamwood, Herts, WD6 3PY
Activities: Development of building projects
Major Shareholder: Kay Manzoor
Officers: Kay Manzoor [1982] Director

UK Credit Limited
Incorporated: 10 June 2009 *Employees:* 63
Net Worth: £13,919,000 *Total Assets:* £31,181,000
Registered Office: St Crispin's House, Duke Street, Norwich, NR3 1PD
Activities: Credit granting by non-deposit taking finance houses and other specialist consumer credit grantors
Parent: Norfolk Capital Limited
Officers: Anthony Richardson, Secretary; Ian William Dawson [1989] Director/Accountant; Graham Charles Eke [1975] Director/Accountant; Paul Joseph Hollander [1980] Director/Accountant; Andrew Clive Turner [1958] Director/Accountant

The UK Holiday Group Limited
Incorporated: 11 May 1984 *Employees:* 247
Net Worth: £6,107,946 *Total Assets:* £14,103,925
Registered Office: The Old Bakery, 113 Queens Road, Norwich, NR1 3PL
Activities: Hotels and similar accommodation
Major Shareholder: Paul William Bennett
Officers: David William Arnold, Secretary; David William Arnold [1948] Director/Accountant; Paul William Bennett [1960] Director/Tour Operator; Harold Andrew Burke [1955] Sales Director; Michael John Thompson [1958] Director/Accountant

UK Livelines Limited
Incorporated: 24 July 2003 *Employees:* 2
Net Worth: £10,751,005 *Total Assets:* £10,769,800
Registered Office: 12 High Street, Stanford-le-Hope, Essex, SS17 0EY
Activities: Other telecommunications activities
Shareholders: Josephine Margaret Jones; Josephine Margaret Jones
Officers: Lauran Jones, Secretary; Josephine Margaret Jones [1963] Director; Lauran Sarah Helen Jones [1986] Director

UK Real Estate Limited
Incorporated: 6 March 1986 *Employees:* 12
Net Worth: £107,743,128 *Total Assets:* £189,299,520
Registered Office: York House, Empire Way, Wembley, Middlesex, HA9 0FQ
Activities: Development of building projects
Major Shareholder: Nicholas John Capstick-Dale
Officers: Jeremy Louis Landau, Secretary; Nicholas John Capstick-Dale [1962] Director

UK Salads Limited
Incorporated: 23 June 2004 *Employees:* 151
Net Worth: £6,002,333 *Total Assets:* £8,729,347
Registered Office: Franca House, Tower Nursery, Netherall Road, Roydon, Essex, CM19 5JP
Activities: Wholesale of fruit and vegetables
Officers: Pasquale Milazzo, Secretary/Director [Italian]; Giovanni Abella [1934] Director [Italian]; Giuseppina Colletti [1963] Director; Vito Colletti [1960] Director [Italian]; Leonora Milazzo [1966] Director; Pasquale Milazzo [1963] Director [Italian]; Franca Schillaci [1970] Director; Giuseppe Schillaci [1969] Director [Italian]

UK Waste Management Limited
Incorporated: 12 April 1978
Net Worth: £151,243,008 *Total Assets:* £198,639,008
Registered Office: Coronation Road, Cressex, High Wycombe, Bucks, HP12 3TZ
Activities: Collection of non-hazardous waste
Parent: UK Waste Management Holdings Limited
Officers: Richard Neil Pike [1969] Director/Chief Financial Officer; Michael Robert Mason Topham [1972] Director/Chief Executive Officer

UKLS Acquisitions Limited
Incorporated: 4 July 2014 *Employees:* 477
Net Worth Deficit: £37,404,000 *Total Assets:* £51,828,000
Registered Office: Grant Hall, Parsons Green, St Ives, Cambs, PE27 4AA
Activities: Other business support service activities n.e.c.
Parent: UKLS Midco Ltd
Officers: Jean Michel Claude Bonnavion [1971] Director/Partner [French]; Gary Michael Pritchard [1970] Director/Chartered Accountant

Ulgrave Limited
Incorporated: 14 February 1996
Net Worth: £71,605,000 *Total Assets:* £73,215,000
Registered Office: Station Maltings, Witham, Essex, CM8 2DU
Activities: Activities of head offices
Parent: Malt U.K. Holdco Limited
Officers: Brett Alan Weimann, Secretary; Alistair Garrard Bell [1961] Director/Chief Financial Officer [Australian]; Darren Smith [1968] Director/President [Canadian]; Roger Graham Woodley [1958] Director/Maltster (CEO)

UME PFI Investments Holding Limited
Incorporated: 27 July 2007 *Employees:* 2
Net Worth: £86,499 *Total Assets:* £8,877,455
Registered Office: 2 Hunting Gate, Hitchin, Herts, SG4 0TJ
Activities: Activities of head offices
Parent: United Medical Enterprises Group LLP
Officers: Paul William Noake, Secretary; Darren Charles Barclay [1969] Director; John Mark Bullough [1977] Director

UML Chiltern Limited
Incorporated: 27 April 2015
Net Worth: £5,129,875 *Total Assets:* £9,020,699
Registered Office: Portland House, 69-71 Wembley Hill Road, Wembley, Middlesex, HA9 8BU
Activities: Sea and coastal freight water transport
Parent: Union Maritime Limited
Officers: Bhupendra Shantilal Kansagra, Secretary; Laurent Elie Cadji [1977] Director/Businessman; Lewis Levy Cadji [1938] Director/Businessman; Bhupendra Shantilal Kansagra [1956] Director/Businessman; Ramesh Shantilal Kansagra [1950] Director/Businessman

UML Eagle Limited
Incorporated: 30 June 2014
Net Worth: £5,421,567 *Total Assets:* £10,039,261
Registered Office: Portland House, 69-71 Wembley Hill Road, Wembley, Middlesex, HA9 8BU
Activities: Sea and coastal freight water transport
Parent: Focus Tankers Ltd
Officers: Bhupendra Shantilal Kansagra, Secretary; Laurent Elie Cadji [1977] Director/Businessman; Lewis Levy Cadji [1938] Director/Businessman; Bhupendra Shantilal Kansagra [1956] Director/Businessman; Ramesh Shantilal Kansagra [1950] Director/Businessman

UML Marylebone Limited
Incorporated: 12 May 2015
Net Worth: £8,332,677 *Total Assets:* £15,011,344
Registered Office: Portland House, 69-71 Wembley Hill Road, Wembley, Middlesex, HA9 8BU
Activities: Sea and coastal freight water transport
Parent: Union Maritime Limited
Officers: Bhupendra Shantilal Kansagra, Secretary; Laurent Elie Cadji [1977] Director/Businessman; Lewis Levy Cadji [1938] Director/Businessman; Bhupendra Shantilal Kansagra [1956] Director/Businessman; Ramesh Shantilal Kansagra [1950] Director/Businessman

UML Mayfair Limited
Incorporated: 25 January 2016
Net Worth: £3,594,846 *Total Assets:* £8,264,092
Registered Office: Portland House, 69-71 Wembley Hill Road, Wembley, Middlesex, HA9 8BU
Activities: Sea and coastal freight water transport
Parent: Union Maritime Limited
Officers: Bhupendra Shantilal Kansagra, Secretary; Laurent Elie Cadji [1977] Director/Businessman; Lewis Levy Cadji [1938] Director/Businessman; Bhupendra Shantilal Kansagra [1956] Director/Businessman; Ramesh Shantilal Kansagra [1950] Director/Businessman

UML Wembley Limited
Incorporated: 22 December 2015
Net Worth: £2,338,520 *Total Assets:* £12,715,205
Registered Office: Portland House, 69-71 Wembley Hill Road, Wembley, Middlesex, HA9 8BU
Activities: Sea and coastal freight water transport
Parent: Focus Tankers Ltd
Officers: Bhupendra Shantilal Kansagra, Secretary; Laurent Elie Cadji [1977] Director/Businessman; Lewis Levy Cadji [1938] Director/Businessman; Bhupendra Shantilal Kansagra [1956] Director/Businessman; Ramesh Shantilal Kansagra [1950] Director/Businessman

UML Westminster Limited
Incorporated: 19 January 2016
Net Worth: £3,068,397 *Total Assets:* £9,067,016
Registered Office: Portland House, 69-71 Wembley Hill Road, Wembley, Middlesex, HA9 8BU
Activities: Sea and coastal freight water transport
Parent: Union Maritime Limited
Officers: Bhupendra Shantilal Kansagra, Secretary; Laurent Elie Cadji [1977] Director/Businessman; Lewis Levy Cadji [1938] Director/Businessman; Bhupendra Shantilal Kansagra [1956] Director/Businessman; Ramesh Shantilal Kansagra [1950] Director/Businessman

UML Wigmore Limited
Incorporated: 19 March 2015
Net Worth: £2,448,032 *Total Assets:* £9,117,172
Registered Office: Portland House, 69-71 Wembley Hill Road, Wembley, Middlesex, HA9 8BU
Activities: Sea and coastal freight water transport
Parent: Union Maritime Limited
Officers: Bhupendra Shantilal Kansagra, Secretary; Laurent Elie Cadji [1977] Director/Businessman; Lewis Levy Cadji [1938] Director/Businessman; Bhupendra Shantilal Kansagra [1956] Director/Businessman; Ramesh Shantilal Kansagra [1950] Director/Businessman

Underwoods Garage (Tiptree) Limited
Incorporated: 12 October 1981 *Employees:* 203
Net Worth: £6,408,648 *Total Assets:* £12,658,231
Registered Office: 5 Church Road, Tiptree, Essex, CO5 0LG
Activities: Sale of new cars and light motor vehicles
Major Shareholder: Gerald Wiggins
Officers: Generald Wiggins, Secretary/Director; Carolyn Ann O'Keeffe [1959] Administration Director; Generald Wiggins [1952] Director

UNEX Corporation Limited
Incorporated: 27 January 1978
Net Worth: £49,896,604 *Total Assets:* £105,272,592
Registered Office: Unex House, Church Lane, Stetchworth, Cambs, CB8 9TN
Activities: Other letting and operating of own or leased real estate
Shareholders: Timothy Casey Oscar Gredley; Pollyanna Georgina Gredley
Officers: Andrew John Page, Secretary; Timothy Casey Oscar Gredley [1986] Director; William Jerome Gredley [1933] Director; Andrew John Page [1976] Director/Certified Chartered Accountant; Stephen Walsh [1959] Director/Architect

UNEX Finance Limited
Incorporated: 30 May 1973
Previous: UNEX European Finance Limited
Net Worth: £1,071,820 *Total Assets:* £147,775,664
Registered Office: Unex House, Church Lane, Stetchworth, Cambs, CB8 9TN
Activities: Other business support service activities n.e.c.
Shareholders: Timothy Casey Oscar Gredley; Pollyanna Georgina Gredley
Officers: Andrew John Page, Secretary; Timothy Casey Oscar Gredley [1986] Director; William Jerome Gredley [1933] Director; Andrew John Page [1976] Director/Certified Chartered Accountant

UNEX Gredley (Holdings) Limited
Incorporated: 30 October 1969
Net Worth: £1,032,185 *Total Assets:* £15,184,085
Registered Office: Unex House, Church Lane, Stetchworth, Cambs, CB8 9TN
Activities: Activities of head offices
Shareholders: Timothy Casey Oscar Gredley; Pollyanna Georgina Gredley
Officers: Andrew John Page, Secretary; Timothy Casey Oscar Gredley [1986] Director; William Jerome Gredley [1933] Director; Andrew John Page [1976] Director/Certified Chartered Accountant

UNEX Group Holdings Limited
Incorporated: 3 August 2004 *Employees:* 48
Net Worth: £225,075,600 *Total Assets:* £263,355,712
Registered Office: Unex House, Church Lane, Stetchworth, Cambs, CB8 9TN
Activities: Activities of head offices
Shareholders: Timothy Casey Oscar Gredley; Pollyanna Georgina Gredley
Officers: Andrew John Page, Secretary; Guy Anthony Alexander Conrad Gredley [1970] Director; Jeremy Vincent Gredley [1962] Director; Pollyanna Georgina Gredley [1987] Director; Timothy Casey Oscar Gredley [1986] Director; William Jerome Gredley [1933] Director/Company Chairman; Andrew John Page [1976] Director/Certified Chartered Accountant; Sarah Margaret Porter [1970] Director/PA; Stephen Walsh [1959] Director/Architect

UNEX Holdings Limited
Incorporated: 16 January 1998
Net Worth: £27,047,824 *Total Assets:* £143,235,408
Registered Office: Unex House, Church Lane, Stetchworth, Cambs, CB8 9TN
Activities: Other letting and operating of own or leased real estate
Shareholders: Timothy Casey Oscar Gredley; Pollyanna Georgina Gredley
Officers: Andrew John Page, Secretary; Timothy Casey Oscar Gredley [1986] Director; William Jerome Gredley [1933] Director/Company Chairman; Andrew John Page [1976] Director/Certified Chartered Accountant; Sarah Margaret Porter [1970] Director/Personal Assistant; Stephen Walsh [1959] Director/Architect

UNEX Investment Properties Limited
Incorporated: 1 May 1973
Net Worth: £76,775,712 *Total Assets:* £143,787,232
Registered Office: Unex House, Church Lane, Stetchworth, Cambs, CB8 9TN
Activities: Other letting and operating of own or leased real estate
Shareholders: Timothy Casey Oscar Gredley; Pollyanna Georgina Gredley
Officers: Andrew John Page, Secretary; Timothy Casey Oscar Gredley [1986] Director; William Jerome Gredley [1933] Director; Andrew John Page [1976] Director/Certified Chartered Accountant; Stephen Walsh [1959] Director/Architect

UNEX Limited
Incorporated: 19 October 2005
Net Worth: £10,336,020 *Total Assets:* £16,878,644
Registered Office: Unex House, Church Lane, Stetchworth, Cambs, CB8 9TN
Activities: Other letting and operating of own or leased real estate
Shareholders: Timothy Casey Oscar Gredley; Pollyana Georgina Gredley
Officers: Andrew John Page, Secretary; Timothy Casey Oscar Gredley [1986] Director; William Jerome Gredley [1933] Director; Andrew John Page [1976] Director/Certified Chartered Accountant

UNEX Smithfield Limited
Incorporated: 25 September 1973
Net Worth: £5,252,532 *Total Assets:* £12,362,361
Registered Office: Unex House, Church Lane, Stetchworth, Cambs, CB8 9TN
Activities: Other professional, scientific and technical activities n.e.c.
Shareholders: Timothy Casey Oscar Gredley; Pollyanna Georgina Gredley
Officers: Andrew John Page, Secretary; Timothy Casey Oscar Gredley [1986] Director; William Jerome Gredley [1933] Director; Andrew John Page [1976] Director/Certified Chartered Accountant

Unicourt Properties Limited
Incorporated: 7 May 1998
Net Worth: £7,902,236 *Total Assets:* £8,332,172
Registered Office: Little Acre, East End Way, Pinner, Middlesex, HA5 3BS
Activities: Buying and selling of own real estate
Major Shareholder: Jonathan Bradley Coren
Officers: Generald Coren, Secretary/Director; Generald Coren [1927] Director; Joel Anthony Coren [1982] Director/Surveyor; Jonathan Bradley Coren [1956] Director/Chartered Surveyor

Unifruit Group Limited
Incorporated: 7 June 2011 *Employees:* 10
Net Worth: £8,675,038 *Total Assets:* £11,405,024
Registered Office: 155 High Street, Rickmansworth, Herts, WD3 1AR
Activities: Activities of other holding companies n.e.c.
Shareholders: Mukesh Dayalal Tolia; Jayshree Mukesh Tolia
Officers: Jayshree Mukesh Tolia [1958] Director; Mukesh Dayalal Tolia [1954] Director

Unifruit Limited
Incorporated: 21 February 1984 *Employees:* 10
Net Worth: £8,690,137 *Total Assets:* £11,420,123
Registered Office: Unifruit House, 155 High Street, Rickmansworth, Herts, WD3 1AR
Activities: Wholesale of fruit and vegetables
Parent: Unifruit Group Limited
Officers: Jayshree Mukesh Tolia, Secretary/Housewife; Jayshree Mukesh Tolia [1958] Director; Mukesh Dayalal Tolia [1954] Director

Union Carriers Limited
Incorporated: 7 June 2016
Net Worth: £17,289,696 *Total Assets:* £22,164,462
Registered Office: Portland House, 69-71 Wembley Hill Road, Wembley, Middlesex, HA9 8BU
Activities: Sea and coastal freight water transport
Shareholders: Solai Holdings Limited; Samilau Limited
Officers: Bhupendra Shantilal Kansagra, Secretary; Laurent Elie Cadji [1977] Director/Businessman; Lewis Levy Cadji [1938] Director/Businessman; Bhupendra Shantilal Kansagra [1956] Director/Businessman; Ramesh Shantilal Kansagra [1950] Director/Businessman

Union Investcorp Limited
Incorporated: 18 April 2008
Net Worth: £27,243,118 *Total Assets:* £30,790,780
Registered Office: Portland House, 69-71 Wembley Hill Road, Wembley, Middlesex, HA9 8BU
Activities: Other business support service activities n.e.c.
Shareholders: Solai Holdings Limited; South Central Property Limited
Officers: Bhupendra Shatilal Kansagra, Secretary; Laurent Elie Cadji [1977] Director/Businessman; Lewis Levy Cadji [1938] Director/Businessman; Bhupendra Shantilal Kansagra [1956] Director/Businessman; Ramesh Shantilal Kansagra [1950] Director/Businessman

Union Maritime Limited
Incorporated: 12 January 2006 *Employees:* 67
Net Worth: £102,587,064 *Total Assets:* £292,708,416
Registered Office: Portland House, 69-71 Wembley Hill Road, Wembley, Middlesex, HA9 8BU
Activities: Sea and coastal freight water transport
Shareholders: Solai Holdings Limited; South Central Property Limited
Officers: Bhupendra Shantilal Kansagra, Secretary; Laurent Elie Cadji [1977] Director/Businessman; Lewis Levy Cadji [1938] Director/Businessman; Bhupendra Shantilal Kansagra [1956] Director/Businessman; Ramesh Shantilal Kansagra [1950] Director/Businessman; Sarita Michele Kraljevic [1971] Director/Housewife

The Union of Evangelical Churches
Incorporated: 8 September 2008 *Employees:* 6
Net Worth: £20,763,000 *Total Assets:* £21,088,468
Registered Office: 36 Eastwood Road, Rayleigh, Essex, SS6 7JQ
Activities: Activities of religious organisations
Officers: Howard Roy Gardner, Secretary; Christopher Neil Banks [1968] Director; Eric George Blowes [1953] Director; Keith Britton [1949] Director; Stephen Paul Budd [1953] Director; Graham Cutmore [1940] Director; Nigel Graham Drew [1971] Director; Stephen James Farrow [1973] Director; Steve John Hensley [1970] Director/Painter and Decorator; Rev Frederick Charles Hintze [1940] Director; William Hoggard [1954] Director; Rev Dennis Eddie Ivey [1946] Director; Kevin Robert Little [1968] Director; Graham Peter Marshall [1978] Director; Leandro Merigio [1978] Director; Rev Mark David Parrott [1963] Director; Richard William Partridge [1955] Director; Malcolm Richards [1946] Director

Union of UEA Students Limited
Incorporated: 30 June 2015 *Employees:* 647
Net Worth: £4,642,000 *Total Assets:* £8,862,000
Registered Office: Union House, University of East Anglia, Norwich, NR4 7TJ
Activities: Activities of other membership organisations n.e.c.
Officers: Anthony James Moore, Secretary; Sophie Atherton [1995] Director/Student Officer; Georgina Burchell [1996] Director/Student Officer; Jenna Chapman [1995] Director/Student Officer; Oli Gray [1997] Director/Student Officer; Martin Marko [1992] Director/Student Officer [Slovak]

Unique Forwarding Limited
Incorporated: 18 October 2001 *Employees:* 37
Net Worth: £6,970,830 *Total Assets:* £8,620,816
Registered Office: Ground Floor, Swift House, 18 Hoffmanns Way, Chelmsford, Essex, CM1 1GU
Activities: Freight transport by road
Shareholders: Steven Stoffer; Ruben Michael Strasser
Officers: Steven Stoffer, Secretary/Director; Steven Stoffer [1969] Director; Ruben Michael Strasser [1965] Director

Uniserve (Air Freight) Limited
Incorporated: 23 March 1988 *Employees:* 47
Net Worth: £24,624,976 *Total Assets:* £33,466,564
Registered Office: Upminster Court, Hall Lane, Upminster, Essex, RM14 1AL
Activities: Freight air transport
Major Shareholder: Iain Robert Liddell
Officers: Barry George Tuck, Secretary; Leighton Bonnett [1967] Director; Iain Robert Liddell [1963] Director

Uniserve (Europe) Limited
Incorporated: 13 June 1985 *Employees:* 15
Net Worth: £7,919,139 *Total Assets:* £9,889,359
Registered Office: Upminster Court, 133 Hall Lane, Upminster, Essex, RM14 1AL
Activities: Freight transport by road
Parent: Uniserve Holdings Limited
Officers: Barry George Tuck, Secretary; Iain Robert Liddell [1963] Director

Uniserve Holdings Limited
Incorporated: 23 March 1988 *Employees:* 684
Net Worth: £74,631,000 *Total Assets:* £116,781,000
Registered Office: Upminster Court, Hall Lane, Upminster, Essex, RM14 1AL
Activities: Activities of distribution holding companies
Major Shareholder: Iain Robert Liddell
Officers: Barry George Tuck, Secretary; Stephen William George Ireland [1966] Director; Iain Robert Liddell [1963] Director; Paul Stone [1958] HR Director

Uniserve Limited
Incorporated: 21 June 1984 *Employees:* 54
Net Worth: £48,612,580 *Total Assets:* £59,599,056
Registered Office: Upminster Court, 133 Hall Lane, Upminster, Essex, RM14 1AL
Activities: Sea and coastal freight water transport
Parent: Uniserve Holdings Limited
Officers: Barry George Tuck, Secretary; Stephen William George Ireland [1966] Director; Iain Robert Liddell [1963] Director

Unisurge International Limited
Incorporated: 26 January 1988 *Employees:* 272
Net Worth: £17,655,000 *Total Assets:* £43,406,000
Registered Office: Farboud Innovation Park, Formula Drive, Newmarket, Suffolk, CB8 0BF
Activities: Manufacture of medical and dental instruments and supplies
Officers: Azizeh Farboud, Secretary; Arash Farboud [1975] Director/Chief Executive; Azizeh Farboud [1946] Director and Company Secretary; Jahangir Farboud [1944] Director/Chairman; Terence Frederick Turner [1959] Director/Chief Operating Officer; Stuart Wilson [1978] Finance Director

Unit Export Limited
Incorporated: 8 July 1977 *Employees:* 11
Net Worth: £2,621,754 *Total Assets:* £9,498,871
Registered Office: Service House, West Mayne, Basildon, Essex, SS15 6RW
Activities: Non-specialised wholesale trade
Major Shareholder: Michael John Toomey
Officers: Neil Duncan Rickwood, Secretary; Christopher William Pearson [1960] Director; Neil Duncan Rickwood [1974] Director/Chartered Accountant; Michael John Toomey [1938] Director

United Church Schools Foundation Ltd
Incorporated: 12 July 1883 *Employees:* 7,739
Net Worth: £532,716,992 *Total Assets:* £739,315,008
Registered Office: Worldwide House, Thorpe Wood, Peterborough, PE3 6SB
Activities: Other letting and operating of own or leased real estate
Officers: Stephen John Whiffen, Secretary; Dr Stephen Richard Critchley [1951] Director/Retired; Richard Colin Neil Davidson [1951] Director; Michael David George [1973] Director; Joseph Benjamin Gordon [1959] Director and Chartered Civil Engineer; Richard Cecil Greenhalgh [1944] Director/Executive; Michael John Litchfield [1949] Director/Architect; Nigel Rhyl Robson [1951] Director/Retired Solicitor

United Church Schools Trust
Incorporated: 18 January 1993 *Employees:* 2,451
Net Worth: £20,535,000 *Total Assets:* £79,497,000
Registered Office: Worldwide House, Thorpe Wood, Peterborough, PE3 6SB
Activities: Primary education
Parent: United Church Schools Foundation Limited
Officers: Stephen John Whiffen, Secretary; Mary Elizabeth Curnock Cook [1958] Director/Educationalist; Dr Rosalind Margaret Given-Wilson [1955] Director/Doctor; Joseph Benjamin Gordon [1959] Director and Chartered Civil Engineer; Richard Cecil Greenhalgh [1944] Director/Executive; Michael John Litchfield [1949] Director/Retired; Sarah Laetitia Squire [1949] Director/University Senior Administrator

The United Healthcare Land Company Limited
Incorporated: 10 November 2004
Net Worth Deficit: £3,056,185 *Total Assets:* £11,263,950
Registered Office: 1 Quay Point, Station Road, Woodbridge, Suffolk, IP12 4AL
Activities: Buying and selling of own real estate
Shareholders: Andrew George Doyle; Lindsay Stewart Neilson; Michael Anthony O'Brien; Nigel Charles Seaton Robson; David Jeremy Winch
Officers: Andrew George Doyle, Secretary/Director; Andrew George Doyle [1956] Director; Lindsay Stewart Neilson [1948] Director/Surveyor; Michael Anthony O'Brien [1950] Director; Nigel Charles Seaton Robson [1963] Director/Chartered Surveyor; David Jeremy Winch [1955] Director/Surveyor

United Learning Trust
Incorporated: 15 May 2002 *Employees:* 5,145
Net Worth: £483,756,992 *Total Assets:* £550,627,968
Registered Office: Worldwide House, Thorpe Wood, Peterborough, PE3 6SB
Activities: Pre-primary education
Parent: United Church Schools Trust
Officers: Stephen John Whiffen, Secretary; Dame Yasmin Bevan [1953] Director/Executive Principal; Jonathan Andrew Coles [1972] Director/Chief Executive; Richard Colin Neil Davidson [1951] Director; Michael David George [1973] Director; Richard Cecil Greenhalgh [1944] Director/Executive; Dame Reena Keeble [1955] Director/Primary Headteacher - Retired; David Barrie Robinson [1966] Director/Chairman; Nigel Rhyl Robson [1951] Director/Retired Solicitor

The United Reformed Church (Eastern Province) Trust
Incorporated: 22 February 1909 *Employees:* 5
Net Worth: £17,612,756 *Total Assets:* £18,281,024
Registered Office: Eastern Synod Office, 36 Duxford Road, Whittlesford, Cambridge, CB22 4ND
Activities: Activities of religious organisations
Officers: Dr David John Smith, Secretary; Andrew Leonard East [1957] Director/Legal Executive; Gilbert Heathcote [1946] Director/Retired; Keir Robert Hounsome [1952] Director/Retired; Clifford Neil Patten [1951] Director/Architect; Professor David Michael Thompson [1942] Director/University Teacher; Rev Dr Janet Elizabeth Tollington [1951] Director/Retired; Reverend Paul Raymond Whittle [1955] Director/Charity

United Therapeutics Europe, Ltd.
Incorporated: 3 March 2000 *Employees:* 15
Net Worth: £23,296,564 *Total Assets:* £26,513,814
Registered Office: The Officers' Mess, Royston Road, Duxford, Cambs, CB22 4QH
Activities: Wholesale of pharmaceutical goods
Parent: United Therapeutics Corporation
Officers: Marc Charles Dalby, Secretary; Michael Ian Benkowitz [1971] Director [American]; James Edgemond [1967] Director [American]; Doctor Edwin Robert Grover [1960] Director; Martine Rothblatt [1954] Director/Biotech Executive [American]

Unity Education Trust
Incorporated: 30 January 2017 *Employees:* 212
Net Worth: £15,941,033 *Total Assets:* £17,476,628
Registered Office: Dereham Sixth Form College, Crown Road, Dereham, Norfolk, NR20 4AG
Activities: Primary education
Officers: Edward Colman [1997] Director/Marketing & PR; Glyn Hambling [1970] Director/Executive Headteacher; Alan Richard Jones [1945] Director/Retired; Gavin Campbell Redwood [1968] Director/Traditional Boatbuilder; Michael James Rose [1953] Director/Retired

Unity Schools Partnership
Incorporated: 7 October 2010 *Employees:* 1,386
Previous: Samuel Ward Academy Trust
Net Worth: £154,408,000 *Total Assets:* £169,808,000
Registered Office: Unity Schools Partnership Offices, Park Road, Haverhill, Suffolk, CB9 7YD
Activities: Primary education
Officers: Dr Timothy John Coulson [1959] Director/Chief Executive; Ian David Jacobs [1970] Director/Civil Servant; Gordon David Spencer Jones [1948] Director/Retired; Michael Robert Parish [1959] Director; Roger Edward Quince [1946] Director; John Frederick Smith [1959] Director/HR Consultant; Dean Patrick Sykes [1963] Operations Director

University of Essex Knowledge Gateway Holdings Limited
Incorporated: 24 December 2001 *Employees:* 7
Net Worth: £15,359,680 *Total Assets:* £32,182,892
Registered Office: Wivenhoe Park, Colchester, Essex, CO4 3SQ
Activities: Activities of other holding companies n.e.c.
Parent: University of Essex
Officers: Marco Albano, Secretary; Paul Barry Excell [1962] Director; William Hornby Gore [1944] Director; Jane Elizabeth Hamilton [1955] Director; Andrew Keeble [1962] Director of Finance; Owen Bryn Morris [1961] Director/Registrar; Vanessa Ruth Plain [1972] Director/University Employee; Philip John Tolhurst [1950] Director/Solicitor

University of Suffolk Ltd
Incorporated: 19 March 2004 *Employees:* 454
Previous: University Campus Suffolk Ltd
Net Worth: £12,942,000 *Total Assets:* £80,952,000
Registered Office: Waterfront Building, Neptune Quay, Ipswich, Suffolk, IP4 1QJ
Activities: First-degree level higher education
Officers: Timothy John Greenacre, Secretary; Christopher John Bally [1971] Local Government Director; Dr Jennifer Chase Barnes [1960] Director/Administrator/Musicologist/Board Member [British/American]; Deborah Ann Cadman [1963] Director/Chief Executive; Professor Mohammad Dastbaz [1958] Director/Deputy Vice-Chancellor; Georgia Tottenham Jade Downs [1997] Director/President, Students' Union; Celia Ann Malcolm Edey [1946] Director; David Stanley Edwards [1943] Director; Vivien Anne Gillespie [1956] Director/FE College Principal; Fiona Catriona Hotston Moore [1965] Director/Chartered Accountant; Professor Helen Eileen Langton [1959] Director/Vice-Chancellor and Chief Executive Officer; Mark Pendlington [1957] Director; Professor William Pope [1955] Director; Martin Alan Seeley [1954] Director/Bishop of St Edmundsbury and Ipswich; Dr Charles William Holt Thomas [1977] Director/Associate Professor; Russell Stuart Williams [1972] Director/Interim Chief Executive; Paul Winter [1950] Director/Chief Executive; Alexander Fraser Woodburn [1951] Director

Upminster Academies Trust
Incorporated: 14 September 2012 *Employees:* 89
Net Worth: £8,481,000 *Total Assets:* £9,326,000
Registered Office: Upminster Infant School, St Mary's Lane, Upminster, London, RM14 3BS
Activities: Primary education
Officers: Dr Deborah Lee Birrell [1977] Director/Medical Advisor; Heidi Clarke [1977] Director/Accountant; Ann Louise Cooke [1962] Director/School Librarian; Alison Edgcombe [1973] Director/Headteacher; Matthew James Pepper [1972] Director/IT Manager; Jane Elizabeth Margaret Phillips [1974] Director/Accountant; Keri Denise Pitt [1973] Director/Accountant; Jackie Theresa Woodgate [1958] Director/Registered Childminder

The Ursuline Academy Ilford
Incorporated: 11 August 2011 *Employees:* 80
Net Worth: £8,628,732 *Total Assets:* £9,295,986
Registered Office: The Ursuline Academy, Morland Road, Ilford, Essex, IG1 4JU
Activities: General secondary education
Officers: Mariano Scotti, Secretary; Joanna Abazari [1976] Director/Bank Clerk [Polish]; John Anthony [1949] Director/Retired; Louise Bath [1989] Director/Chartered Accountant; Father Matthew Bemand-Qureshi [1976] Director/Parish Priest; Sarah Bergin McCarthy [1972] Director/Human Resources; David Burge [1948] Director/Retired; Robert Caldeira [1963] Director/Consultant Business Analyst; Sister Kathleen Colmer [1948] Director/Provincialate; Jacqueline Da Prato [1955] Director/Retired; Ingrid Doves [1972] Director/Civil Servant; Maureen Duncan [1958] Director/Teacher; Lady Deniece Elizabeth Grant [1959] Director/Teacher; Emma Jakob [1990] Director/Banker; Heather Mackie [1988] Director/Teacher; Karen Reilly [1964] Director/Headteacher; Luke Robertson [1970] Director/Teacher; Angela St Ville [1958] Director/Health Professional

Usborne PLC
Incorporated: 16 May 1966
Net Worth: £13,645,000 *Total Assets:* £19,433,000
Registered Office: Cheveley Park Stud, Duchess Drive, Newmarket, Suffolk, CB8 9DD
Activities: Activities of head offices
Parent: Thompson Investments (London) Limited
Officers: Christopher James Dant, Secretary; Roy Bernard Copus [1959] Director/Chartered Accountant; David Brian Thompson [1936] Director; Patricia Thompson [1940] Director; Katharine Patricia Woodward [1968] Director

User Friendly Properties (No. 2) Limited
Incorporated: 15 April 2009
Net Worth: £32,764,772 *Total Assets:* £37,342,124
Registered Office: Unex House, Church Lane, Stetchworth, Newmarket, Suffolk, CB8 9TN
Activities: Other letting and operating of own or leased real estate
Shareholders: Timothy Casey Oscar Gredley; Pollyanna Georgina Gredley
Officers: Andrew John Page, Secretary; Timothy Casey Oscar Gredley [1986] Director; William Jerome Gredley [1933] Director/Company Chairman; Andrew John Page [1976] Director/Certified Chartered Accountant

User Friendly Properties Limited
Incorporated: 31 July 1995
Net Worth: £18,259,236 *Total Assets:* £19,398,370
Registered Office: Unex House, Church Lane, Stetchworth, Newmarket, Suffolk, CB8 9TN
Activities: Buying and selling of own real estate
Shareholders: Timothy Casey Oscar Gredley; Pollyanna Georgina Gredley
Officers: Andrew John Page, Secretary; Timothy Casey Oscar Gredley [1986] Director; William Jerome Gredley [1933] Director; Andrew John Page [1976] Director/Certified Chartered Accountant; Sarah Margaret Porter [1970] Director/Personal Assistant; Margaret Sheila Rolfe [1958] Director/Accountant; Stephen Walsh [1959] Director/Architect

UTM Limited
Incorporated: 8 November 2000 *Employees:* 47
Net Worth: £1,690,223 *Total Assets:* £12,369,484
Registered Office: Hampstead Avenue, Mildenhall, Suffolk, IP28 7AS
Activities: Manufacture of weapons and ammunition
Parent: Lunovi Ltd
Officers: Mark Stewart Isaacson [1964] Director; Parag Mehta [1968] Director/President and CEO [American]

V.B. Investments Limited
Incorporated: 2 July 2003
Net Worth Deficit: £6,584,000 *Total Assets:* £31,251,000
Registered Office: Astral House, Imperial Way, Watford, Herts, WD24 4WW
Activities: Financial management
Parent: Vinci Pensions Limited
Officers: Christopher Carl Brennan [1969] Director/Accountant; Ian David Hudson [1964] Director/Chartered Accountant

V.U.K. Holdings Limited
Incorporated: 25 June 1954
Net Worth: £12,805,941 *Total Assets:* £12,882,639
Registered Office: Hewitsons LLP, Shakespeare House, 42 Newmarket Road, Cambridge, CB5 8EP
Activities: Management of real estate on a fee or contract basis
Officers: Peter Bang [1969] Director [Danish]; Mick Schou Rasmussen [1977] Director [Danish]; Keith Kendall Riddle [1964] Director/Sales Manager

Vahnea Marolda Investments LLP
Incorporated: 15 January 2014
Net Worth: £15,133,396 *Total Assets:* £15,168,396
Registered Office: 3 Valencia Road, Stanmore, Middlesex, HA7 4JL
Officers: Abhay Varma [1971] Member; Lord Philip Esme Howard [1945] LLP Member; Sarah Sophia Howard [1950] LLP Member; Robin Lawther [1961] LLP Member; Alberto Marolda [1961] LLP Member; Jan Stephen Pethick [1947] LLP Member; Vera Reimann-Dubbers [1962] LLP Member

Vale of Aylesbury Housing Trust Limited
Incorporated: 28 April 2005 *Employees:* 248
Net Worth: £153,399,008 *Total Assets:* £310,596,000
Registered Office: Fairfax House, 69 Buckingham Street, Aylesbury, Bucks, HP20 2NJ
Activities: Renting and operating of Housing Association real estate
Officers: Linda Foster, Secretary; John Roland Balshaw [1944] Director/Consultant; Julian Blundell-Thompson [1974] Director/Copywriter; Stephen Michael Bright [1949] Director; Olivia Jane Clymer [1966] Director/Chief Executive Officer; David George Keeling [1954] Director/Housing Consultant; Steven Michael Lambert [1970] Director/District Councillor; Angela Ria Joyce Macpherson [1959] Director; Barbara Ann Richardson [1967] Managing Director; Stephen Edward Spencer Stringer [1957] Director; Kelly Webster [1975] Director

Valens Resources Group PLC
Incorporated: 16 June 2008 *Employees:* 78
Net Worth: £309,153 *Total Assets:* £9,314,632
Registered Office: Station Road, West Dereham, King's Lynn, Norfolk, PE33 9RR
Activities: Collection of non-hazardous waste
Shareholders: Simon Miles; Jonathan Miles
Officers: Jonathan Miles, Secretary/Director; Jonathan Miles [1963] Director; Simon David Miles [1960] Director/Chartered Accountant

Valiant Holdings Limited
Incorporated: 21 April 2008 *Employees:* 41
Net Worth: £9,742,043 *Total Assets:* £12,875,541
Registered Office: First Floor, North Argyle House, Joel Street, Northwood Hills, Northwood, Middlesex, HA6 1LN
Activities: Activities auxiliary to financial intermediation n.e.c.
Shareholders: Prescient Capital Limited; Suvak Holdings Limited
Officers: Kirenjeet Kaur [1972] Director; Ajay Pabari [1959] Managing Director; Bharat Kumar Hirji Thakrar [1957] Director; Sanjay Thakrar [1979] Director

Valley Trucks Holdings Limited
Incorporated: 19 June 2009 *Employees:* 1
Net Worth: £754,021 *Total Assets:* £14,455,042
Registered Office: 57-59 High Street, Hoddesdon, Herts, EN11 8TQ
Activities: Activities of other holding companies n.e.c.
Major Shareholder: Giuseppe Ricotta
Officers: Giuseppe Ricotta [1966] Director

Van Hage & Company (Holdings) Limited
Incorporated: 8 January 1959 *Employees:* 318
Net Worth: £6,946,564 *Total Assets:* £16,836,390
Registered Office: Great Amwell, Ware, Herts, SG12 9RP
Activities: Retail sale of flowers, plants, seeds, fertilizers, pet animals and pet food in specialised stores
Parent: Intertrust N.V.
Officers: Maria Clazina Charnley [1955] Director; Christopher David Roberts [1958] Director

Van Hage & Company Limited
Incorporated: 22 June 1995 *Employees:* 318
Net Worth: £1,638,060 *Total Assets:* £12,901,151
Registered Office: Van Hage Garden Company, Great Amwell, Ware, Herts, SG12 9RP
Activities: Retail sale of flowers, plants, seeds, fertilizers, pet animals and pet food in specialised stores
Parent: Van Hage & Company (Holdings) Limited
Officers: John Stuart MacDonald Carver [1960] Director; Maria Clazina Charnley [1955] Director; Christopher David Roberts [1958] Director; John Cornelius Van Hage [1965] Director; Jennifer Ann Van Stroud [1958] Director

Vanderbilt Development Finance Ltd
Incorporated: 5 July 2013
Net Worth: £17,213,000 *Total Assets:* £50,253,000
Registered Office: Apollo House, Mercury Park, Wooburn Green, High Wycombe, Bucks, HP10 0HH
Activities: Construction of domestic buildings
Parent: Vanderbilt Holdings Limited
Officers: Daniel Kevin Stern, Secretary; Chris Chiles [1969] Director

Vanderbilt Homes Limited
Incorporated: 9 January 2004 *Employees:* 59
Net Worth Deficit: £4,390,000 *Total Assets:* £70,113,000
Registered Office: Apollo House, Mercury Park, Wooburn Green, Bucks, HP10 0HH
Activities: Development of building projects
Parent: Vanderbilt Development Finance Ltd
Officers: Daniel Kevin Stern, Secretary; Christopher Chiles [1969] Director

Vanderbilt Thames Valley Limited
Incorporated: 5 July 2013
Previous: Vanderbilt Beaconsfield Ltd
Net Worth Deficit: £7,583,000 *Total Assets:* £66,667,000
Registered Office: Apollo House, Mercury Park, Wooburn Green, High Wycombe, Bucks, HP10 0HH
Activities: Construction of domestic buildings
Parent: Vanderbilt Homes Limited
Officers: Daniel Kevin Stern, Secretary; Christopher Chiles [1969] Director

Vanderbilt Topco Ltd
Incorporated: 12 May 2014 *Employees:* 60
Net Worth Deficit: £55,787,000 *Total Assets:* £69,853,000
Registered Office: Apollo House, Mercury Park, Wooburn Green, High Wycombe, Bucks, HP10 0HH
Activities: Construction of domestic buildings
Officers: Daniel Kevin Stern, Secretary; Lord Edward Albert Charles Spencer-Churchill [1974] Director

Vandyke Upper School
Incorporated: 11 July 2011 *Employees:* 143
Net Worth: £14,857,721 *Total Assets:* £16,466,549
Registered Office: Vandyke Upper School, Vandyke Road, Leighton Buzzard, Beds, LU7 3DY
Activities: General secondary education
Officers: Helen Louise O'Connell, Secretary; Annabel Josephine Ashwell [1971] Director; Gayle Alexandra Baker [1966] Director/Accountant; Timothy James Carroll [1960] Director/Headteacher; Martin Hilary Feinhols [1948] Sales Director; Ann Gomersall [1942] Director; Catrin Green [1975] Director/Teacher; John Alan Hassall [1945] Director/Retired; Iain Holloway-McLean [1968] Director/Pharmaceuticals; Susan Hester Howley [1950] Director/Retired; Alison Mary Packer [1950] Director/Retired Headteacher; David Alan Packer [1952] Director/Chief Executive Officer; Samantha Jayne Peplow [1980] Director/Teacher; Ruth Faith Samet [1966] Director/School Administrator; Wayne Roger Stiller [1970] Commercial Director; Nicola Mary Tooman [1967] Director/Education; Maxine Jayne Ward [1961] Director & Governance Advisor

Vanneck Residential LLP
Incorporated: 18 July 2014
Net Worth: £8,747,208 *Total Assets:* £15,878,174
Registered Office: Parker Cavendish, 28 Church Road, Stanmore, Middlesex, HA7 4XR
Officers: Alexander Albert Henry Fraser [1984] Member; Heneage John Stevenson [1978] Member

Vantage Volante Limited
Incorporated: 25 November 1999
Net Worth: £7,513,686 *Total Assets:* £13,718,099
Registered Office: Amwell House, 19 Amwell Street, Hoddesdon, Herts, EN11 8TS
Activities: Management of real estate on a fee or contract basis
Shareholders: Carol Williams; Helen Goate
Officers: Carol Williams, Secretary/Director; Helen Elizabeth Goate [1958] Director/Management; Rachel Marion Susan Hahn [1953] Director/Management; Carol Williams [1947] Director; Richard Stewart Williams [1945] Director

Vauxhall Motors Limited
Incorporated: 12 May 1914 *Employees:* 2,793
Previous: General Motors UK Limited
Net Worth Deficit: £571,800,000 *Total Assets:* £839,100,032
Registered Office: Griffin House, UK1-101-135 Osborne Road, Luton, Beds, LU1 3YT
Activities: Manufacture of motor vehicles
Parent: VHC Sub-Holdings (UK)
Officers: Rabiya Sultana Nagi, Secretary; David James Connell [1972] Director; Xavier Francois Claude Duchemin [1966] Director [French]; Patrick Guilhem Fourniol [1971] Director [French/German]; James Charles Highnam [1969] Finance Director; Peter Thomas Hope [1966] Director; Mark Christopher Noble [1964] Director; Stephen Norman [1954] Managing Director [French]; Jeremy Mark Townsend [1962] Director; Michael Wright [1963] Director

Vega Industries Limited
Incorporated: 14 April 1999 *Employees:* 18
Net Worth: £4,958,907 *Total Assets:* £11,210,557
Registered Office: Suite 3, 1st Floor, Concress House, 14 Lyon Road, Harrow, Middlesex, HA1 2EN
Activities: Installation of industrial machinery and equipment
Officers: Paryank Ramesh Shah, Secretary; Rizwan Gilani [1965] Director [Indian]; Himanshu Patel [1966] Director; Bhadresh Shah [1951] Director/Engineer [Indian]; Paryank Ramesh Shah [1956] Director/Chartered Accountant [Indian]

Velfac Limited
Incorporated: 3 January 1989 *Employees:* 110
Net Worth: £5,726,000 *Total Assets:* £16,340,000
Registered Office: The Old Livery, Hildersham, Cambridge, CB21 6DR
Activities: Agents involved in the sale of timber and building materials
Officers: Sharen Bard, Secretary; Jan Boendorf Madsen [1974] Finance Director [Danish]; Nicholas Julian Brown [1965] Director; Finn Jespersen [1971] Managing Director [Danish]

Ventress Group Limited
Incorporated: 11 November 2016 *Employees:* 2
Net Worth: £16,757,461 *Total Assets:* £17,164,816
Registered Office: Abington Park Farm, Great Abington, Cambs, CB21 6AX
Activities: Hotels and similar accommodation
Parent: Chaplin Group Limited
Officers: David John Harold Chaplin [1963] Director/General Manager; Nathalie Ghislaine Chaplin [1970] Director [French]

Ventress Property Developments Limited
Incorporated: 23 October 1958
Net Worth: £7,707,431 *Total Assets:* £9,693,127
Registered Office: Abington Park Farm, Great Abington, Cambridge, CB21 6AX
Activities: Development of building projects
Shareholder: David John Harold Chaplin
Officers: Hilary Ann Russell, Secretary; David John Harold Chaplin [1963] Director/Accountant; Nathalie Ghislaine Chaplin [1970] Director/Project Manager [French]; Simon Robert Frank Chaplin [1967] Director/Farmer; Hilary Ann Russell [1965] Director/Housewife

Venture Lighting Europe Limited
Incorporated: 27 March 1997 *Employees:* 50
Net Worth Deficit: £1,227,123 *Total Assets:* £14,589,358
Registered Office: Trinity Court, Batchworth Island, Church Street, Rickmansworth, Herts, WD3 1RT
Activities: Non-specialised wholesale trade
Parent: Advanced Lighting Technologies Europe Limited
Officers: Philip Colin Croker [1978] Managing Director; Sabu Krishnan [1958] Director/Engineer [American]

Ventureforth 2000 Limited
Incorporated: 22 December 1995 *Employees:* 3
Net Worth: £8,752,532 *Total Assets:* £9,290,629
Registered Office: Ventureforth House, South Denes Road, Great Yarmouth, Norfolk, NR30 3PT
Activities: Other letting and operating of own or leased real estate
Major Shareholder: James William McKinnon Manclark
Officers: Michael David Futter, Secretary/Estates Manager; Michael David Futter [1952] Director/Estates Manager; James William McKinnon Manclark [1939] Director; Rory Michael Stuart Milne [1965] Director/Solicitor

Ventus Investments Limited
Incorporated: 4 December 1997
Previous: NatWest Commercial Services Limited
Net Worth: £38,964,312 *Total Assets:* £183,856,448
Registered Office: 2 Hunting Gate, Hitchin, Herts, SG4 0TJ
Activities: Other service activities n.e.c.
Parent: RBS Pension Trustee Ltd
Officers: Valeria Rosati [1975] Director/Fund Manager [Italian]; Marissa Ann Szczepaniak [1980] Associate Director

Verco Office Furniture Limited
Incorporated: 5 July 1945 *Employees:* 107
Net Worth: £12,888,137 *Total Assets:* £14,057,772
Registered Office: Chapel Lane, Sands, High Wycombe, Bucks, HP12 4BG
Activities: Manufacture of office and shop furniture
Major Shareholder: Derek William Stevens Vere
Officers: Jeff Laurence Roberts, Secretary; Peter Mitchell [1953] Director; Christopher James Francis Riley [1958] Director; Jeff Laurence Roberts [1964] Finance Director; Derek William Stevens Vere [1946] Managing Director

William Vere (Holdings) Limited
Incorporated: 12 January 1982 *Employees:* 108
Net Worth: £13,716,273 *Total Assets:* £14,993,621
Registered Office: Verco Office Furniture Ltd, Chapel Lane, High Wycombe, Bucks, HP12 4BG
Activities: Activities of head offices
Major Shareholder: Derek William Stevens Vere
Officers: Jeff Laurence Roberts, Secretary; Derek William Stevens Vere [1946] Managing Director

Veritas Educational Trust
Incorporated: 1 August 2011 *Employees:* 156
Previous: Bishop Ramsey Church of England Academies Trust
Net Worth: £12,109,699 *Total Assets:* £14,484,234
Registered Office: Bishop Ramsey Church of England School, Hume Way, Ruislip, Middlesex, HA4 8EE
Activities: General secondary education
Officers: Karen Ball [1961] Director/Civil Servant; Jonathan Chu [1993] Director/Management Consultant; Helen Mary Dimmock [1965] Director/Civil Servant; Catherine Patrice Gower [1968] Director/Lecturer; Elizabeth Ann Richardson [1961] Director/Headteacher; Alison Mary Straszewski [1963] Director/Banker; Susan Elizabeth Vale [1958] Director; Andrew John Wilcock [1955] Director/Headteacher

Vernalis (R & D) Limited
Incorporated: 4 February 1986 *Employees:* 85
Net Worth Deficit: £571,603,968 *Total Assets:* £14,107,000
Registered Office: Granta Park, Great Abington, Cambridge, CB21 6GB
Activities: Manufacture of basic pharmaceutical products
Parent: Vernalis PLC
Officers: Susan Jean Wallcraft, Secretary; Charles Stuart Berkman [1968] Director/Corporate Executive [American]; Matthew William Foehr [1972] Director/Corporate Executive [American]; Matthew Edward Korenberg [1975] Director/Corporate Executive [American]

Vernalis Limited
Incorporated: 13 October 1988 *Employees:* 192
Previous: Vernalis PLC
Net Worth: £27,929,000 *Total Assets:* £37,409,000
Registered Office: Granta Park, Great Abington, Cambridge, CB21 6GB
Activities: Activities of head offices
Parent: Ligand Holdings UK Ltd
Officers: Susan Jean Wallcraft, Secretary; Charles Stuart Berkman [1968] Director/Corporate Executive [American]; Matthew William Foehr [1972] Director/Corporate Executive [American]; Matthew Edward Korenberg [1975] Director/Corporate Executive [American]

Vertical Group Limited
Incorporated: 28 April 2015 *Employees:* 72
Net Worth: £3,697,944 *Total Assets:* £9,509,582
Registered Office: 14 Hemmells, Basildon, Essex, SS15 6ED
Activities: Business and domestic software development
Major Shareholder: Peter Leslie Healey
Officers: Peter Leslie Healey [1951] Sales Director

Verulam School
Incorporated: 1 July 2011 *Employees:* 126
Net Worth: £19,624,248 *Total Assets:* £20,791,232
Registered Office: Verulam School, Brampton Road, St Albans, Herts, AL1 4PR
Activities: General secondary education
Officers: Katherine Melissa Locke, Secretary; John Michael Stuart Acton [1964] Director/Management Consultant; Kiranjit Singh Ahluwalia [1969] Director/Project Manager; Tracey Joan Brodrick [1962] Director/School Invigilator; Marion Denise Brown [1958] Director/Volunteer; Ian Caminsky [1967] Director/Chief Executive Officer [Canadian]; Benjamin Clark [1972] Director; Gary John Dunger [1980] Director/Associate Solicitor; Steven George Hiscock [1980] Director/Teacher; Richard David George Kennedy [1959] Director/Sales Manager; Elisabeth Denise Kragbe [1973] Director/Credit Controller [French]; Melanie Jane Merriden [1970] Director/Human Resources; Jonathan Robin Pitkin [1957] Director/Marketing Manager; Mark John Quinton [1969] Director/Manager; Paul Andrew Ramsey [1968] Director/Teacher; Richard Kelvin Springall [1957] Technical Director; Daniel Stewart Tansley [1983] Director/Teacher; Simon David Threadkell [1971] Design Director

Vetex Limited
Incorporated: 1 February 2016 *Employees:* 2
Net Worth Deficit: £1,536,129 *Total Assets:* £15,314,148
Registered Office: 166 College Road, Harrow, Middlesex, HA1 1RA
Activities: Other business support service activities n.e.c.
Officers: Michael Ackenson [1945] Director/Chartered Accountant; David Geoffrey White [1959] Director/Accountant

VGC Group Limited
Incorporated: 14 March 2006 *Employees:* 1,297
Net Worth: £17,196,830 *Total Assets:* £26,583,700
Registered Office: Cardinal House, Bury Street, Ruislip, Middlesex, HA4 7GD
Activities: Activities of head offices
Shareholders: Matthew John Fitzpatrick; Laurence Richard McKidd
Officers: Olivia Fitzpatrick, Secretary; Sinnathamby Balasundaram [1953] Director/Accountant; Stephen Burns [1970] Business Development Director; Sudarshan Deshmukh [1978] IT Director [Indian]; Terence Roy Dutton-Wells [1948] Director; Matthew John Fitzpatrick [1945] Director [Irish]; Jacques Kriel [1980] Director [South African]; Laurence Richard McKidd [1955] Director; Ciara Melanie Pryce [1979] Director; Andrew Rogers [1946] Director/Consultant [Irish]; Christopher Edward Ryan [1979] Director; Robert John Webb [1949] Director

VHC Sub-Holdings (UK)
Incorporated: 20 April 1990
Net Worth: £10,600,000 *Total Assets:* £10,600,000
Registered Office: Griffin House, UK1-101-135 Osborne Road, Luton, Beds, LU1 3YT
Activities: Activities of head offices
Parent: Holdings UK No.3 Limited
Officers: Rabiya Sultana Nagi, Secretary/Solicitor; James Charles Highnam [1969] Finance Director; Peter Thomas Hope [1966] Director; Stephen Norman [1954] Director [French]; Michael Wright [1963] Director

Victoria Docks Hotel Company (Number Two) Limited
Incorporated: 8 August 2006 *Employees:* 4
Net Worth: £48,293,472 *Total Assets:* £54,760,104
Registered Office: Kirkland House, 11-15 Peterborough Road, Harrow, Middlesex, HA1 2AX
Activities: Other letting and operating of own or leased real estate
Officers: Haider Ladhu Jaffer [1940] Director/Businessman; Dr Manoj Raman [1960] Director/Businessman; Hassanali Amirali Dawood Suleman [1954] Director/Businessman; Cameron Beresford Sunter [1956] Director/Solicitor

Victoria Docks Hotel Company Limited
Incorporated: 8 February 2001 *Employees:* 3
Net Worth: £7,481,308 *Total Assets:* £33,074,908
Registered Office: Kirkland House, 11-15 Peterborough Road, Harrow, Middlesex, HA1 2AX
Activities: Hotels and similar accommodation
Officers: Haider Ladhu Jaffer [1940] Director/Businessman; Hassanali Amirali Dawood Suleman [1954] Director/Businessman; Cameron Beresford Sunter [1956] Director/Solicitor

Victory Housing Trust
Incorporated: 2 November 2004 *Employees:* 86
Net Worth: £69,792,000 *Total Assets:* £167,332,992
Registered Office: 31 King Street, Norwich, NR1 1PD
Activities: Buying and selling of own real estate
Officers: Katherine Alexandra Brown, Secretary; Zoe Daniella Austin [1978] Director PFI Lending; Robert Bennett [1955] Director; Stephen Bernard Burke [1960] Director; Philip John Burton [1954] Director/Retired; Keith Dixon [1959] Director/Quality Manager; Philip Evans [1951] Director/Retired; Michael Anthony Gates [1951] Director/Retired; Penelope Susan Holland [1948] Director/Retired; Joseph David Hood [1959] Director/Self Employed; Stephen Charles Udberg [1954] Director/Chartered Surveyor

Vida Wood UK Limited
Incorporated: 15 February 1985 *Employees:* 9
Net Worth: £3,167,710 *Total Assets:* £20,334,064
Registered Office: Union House, 117 High Street, Billericay, Essex, CM12 9AH
Activities: Agents involved in the sale of timber and building materials
Major Shareholder: Santhe Dahl
Officers: Sharon Elizabeth Thick, Secretary; Fredrik Andersson [1967] Director [Swedish]; Santhe Dahl [1954] Director [Swedish]; Ian David Drane [1969] Director; Mans Jonas Johansson [1975] Director/Sales Manager [Swedish]; Sharon Elizabeth Thick [1962] Director/Stock Controller; Stephen Richard Thick [1955] Director

Videojet Technologies Limited
Incorporated: 6 December 2006 *Employees:* 117
Net Worth: £14,278,000 *Total Assets:* £29,508,000
Registered Office: 4 & 5 Ermine Centre, Lancaster Way, Huntingdon, Cambs, PE29 6XX
Activities: Manufacture of other special-purpose machinery n.e.c.
Parent: Launchchange Operations Limited
Officers: Pavan Khanna, Secretary; Ranjana Bhagwakar [1971] Director/VP Finance [American]; Stephen Hayes [1973] Director; Keith Graham Ward [1953] Director

Viewrose Limited
Incorporated: 26 April 2011 *Employees:* 2
Net Worth: £3,549,942 *Total Assets:* £8,103,932
Registered Office: First Floor, Radius House, 51 Clarendon Road, Watford, Herts, WD17 1HP
Activities: Buying and selling of own real estate
Shareholders: Richard Spencer Frank; J F S Estates Limited
Officers: Richard Spencer Frank [1967] Director; Jonathan Floyd Schuman [1969] Director/Surveyor

Vigeland Properties Ltd
Incorporated: 8 December 1995 *Employees:* 1
Net Worth: £241,982 *Total Assets:* £9,391,358
Registered Office: Vaughan Chambers, Vaughan Road, Harpenden, Herts, AL5 4EE
Activities: Buying and selling of own real estate
Officers: Glencoe Charles Harold Wilson [1944] Director

Viglen Limited
Incorporated: 21 April 1975
Net Worth: £10,131 *Total Assets:* £15,187,131
Registered Office: 7 Handley Page Way, Colney Street, St Albans, Herts, AL2 2DQ
Activities: Manufacture of computers and peripheral equipment
Parent: Westcoast (Holdings) Limited
Officers: Tajinder Singh Dhatt, Secretary; Tajinder Singh Dhatt [1974] Finance Director; Leon Hemani [1971] Director; Sunil Jayantilal Madhani [1966] Director

Villa Plus Limited
Incorporated: 22 July 1986 *Employees:* 42
Net Worth: £16,909,832 *Total Assets:* £35,678,952
Registered Office: 16 Adelaide Street, St Albans, Herts, AL3 5BH
Activities: Tour operator activities
Shareholder: Nicholas David Cooper
Officers: Nicholas David Cooper, Secretary; Nicholas David Cooper [1960] Director/Tour Operator; Rajesh Anantray Mavani [1957] Director/Accountant

Villachase Limited
Incorporated: 19 January 1988
Net Worth: £4,714,429 *Total Assets:* £20,990,900
Registered Office: Unit 17 Hallmark Trading Estate, Fourth Way, Wembley, Middlesex, HA9 0LB
Activities: Other letting and operating of own or leased real estate
Officers: Parminder Gupta [1968] Director/Property Management; Ved Parkash Gupta [1937] Director/Property Developer

Vinayak Properties Limited
Incorporated: 17 March 2009 *Employees:* 2
Net Worth: £4,430,484 *Total Assets:* £21,953,264
Registered Office: 98 Pinner Road, Harrow, Middlesex, HA1 4GZ
Activities: Other letting and operating of own or leased real estate
Shareholders: Khushma Dalia; Rushma Dalia; Trushma Dalia
Officers: Khushma Dalia, Secretary; Khushma Dalia [1982] Director/Businesswoman; Rushma Dalia [1983] Director/Businesswoman; Trushma Dalia [1988] Director/Businesswoman

Vinci Construction UK Limited
Incorporated: 13 September 1988 *Employees:* 3,298
Net Worth: £120,806,000 *Total Assets:* £546,112,000
Registered Office: Astral House, Imperial Way, Watford, Herts, WD24 4WW
Activities: Construction of commercial buildings
Parent: Vinci PLC
Officers: Jean-Pierre Bonnet, Secretary; Christopher Carl Brennan [1969] Director/Accountant; Bruno Michel Dupety [1956] Director/Engineer [French]; Julian Paul Gatward [1966] Director/Civil Engineer; Christopher Michael Hamer [1959] Director/Civil Engineer; Anthony Kennedy Raikes [1964] Director/Chartered Civil Engineer

Vinci Environment UK Limited
Incorporated: 15 May 2007
Net Worth: £46,000 *Total Assets:* £14,973,000
Registered Office: Astral House, Imperial Way, Watford, Herts, WD24 4WW
Activities: Other specialised construction activities n.e.c.
Shareholders: Vinci Construction UK Limited; Vinci Environnement
Officers: Bruno Michel Dupety [1956] Director/Engineer [French]; Francois de Gassart [1977] Director of Operations [French]; Julian Paul Gatward [1966] Director/Civil Engineer; Frederic Yves Marie Peigne [1967] Director [French]; Hughes Guy Marie Patrick Seutin [1974] Director [Belgian]; Luc Valaize [1955] Commercial and Offers Director [French]

Vinci Fleet Services Limited
Incorporated: 22 June 1983
Net Worth: £8,660,000 *Total Assets:* £13,580,000
Registered Office: Astral House, Imperial Way, Watford, Herts, WD24 4WW
Activities: Renting and leasing of construction and civil engineering machinery and equipment
Parent: Vinci PLC
Officers: Mark Blanchard [1959] Director/Accountant; Christopher Carl Brennan [1969] Director/Accountant; Ruth Elizabeth Tilbrook [1968] Director/Accountant

Vinci PLC
Incorporated: 5 October 1962 *Employees:* 3,482
Net Worth: £80,003,000 *Total Assets:* £556,436,992
Registered Office: Astral House, Imperial Way, Watford, Herts, WD24 4WW
Activities: Activities of head offices
Parent: Sogea Holdings (UK) Limited
Officers: Ruth Elizabeth Tilbrook, Secretary; Bruno Michel Dupety [1956] Director/Engineer [French]; Richard Michel Rene Francioli [1959] Director/Company Chairman [French]; Yann Paul Grolimund [1959] Director [French]

Vinci UK Developments Limited
Incorporated: 13 January 1960 *Employees:* 5
Previous: Vinci Investments Limited
Net Worth: £14,502,000 *Total Assets:* £58,511,000
Registered Office: Astral House, Imperial Way, Watford, Herts, WD24 4WW
Activities: Activities of head offices
Parent: Vinci Construction UK Limited
Officers: Bruno Michel Dupety [1956] Director/Engineer [French]; Graham Lambert [1969] Director

F. Vindis & Sons (Bedford) Limited
Incorporated: 23 September 1994 *Employees:* 387
Net Worth: £8,838,400 *Total Assets:* £55,199,932
Registered Office: Vindis House, Washingley Road, Huntingdon, Cambs, PE29 6WP
Activities: Sale of new cars and light motor vehicles
Parent: Vindis Group Ltd
Officers: Stephen Geoffrey Fossey, Secretary; Gary Frank Vindis [1945] Director; Jamie Francis Vindis [1976] Managing Director

F. Vindis & Sons (Sawston) Limited
Incorporated: 17 February 1984 *Employees:* 93
Net Worth: £7,417,160 *Total Assets:* £15,575,142
Registered Office: Vindis House, Washingley Road, Huntingdon, Cambs, PE29 6WP
Activities: Sale of new cars and light motor vehicles
Parent: Vindis Group Ltd
Officers: Stephen Geoffrey Fossey, Secretary; Gary Frank Vindis [1945] Director; Jamie Francis Vindis [1976] Managing Director

Vindis Developments Limited
Incorporated: 2 August 1983 *Employees:* 87
Net Worth: £4,144,902 *Total Assets:* £19,585,020
Registered Office: Vindis House, Washingley Road, Huntingdon, Cambs, PE29 6WP
Activities: Sale of new cars and light motor vehicles
Parent: Vindis Group Ltd
Officers: Stephen Geoffrey Fossey, Secretary; Gary Frank Vindis [1945] Director; Jamie Francis Vindis [1976] Managing Director

Vindis Group Limited
Incorporated: 18 January 1985 *Employees:* 887
Net Worth: £21,380,992 *Total Assets:* £111,467,584
Registered Office: Vindis House, Washingley Road, Huntingdon, Cambs, PE29 6WP
Activities: Sale of new cars and light motor vehicles
Shareholders: Gary Frank Vindis; Estate of Nigel Anthony Vindis
Officers: Stephen Geoffrey Fossey, Secretary; Gary Frank Vindis [1945] Director; Jamie Francis Vindis [1976] Managing Director

Vinepost Limited
Incorporated: 16 October 2007
Net Worth: £1,306,152 *Total Assets:* £18,481,164
Registered Office: 3rd Floor, Sterling House, Langston Road, Loughton, Essex, IG10 3TS
Activities: Activities of open-ended investment companies
Shareholders: David Edward Conway; Gary Alexander Conway; Richard Matthew Conway
Officers: David Edward Conway, Secretary; David Edward Conway [1976] Director; Gary Alexander Conway [1973] Director; Richard Matthew Conway [1978] Director

Viners Capital Properties Limited
Incorporated: 8 April 2014 *Employees:* 5
Net Worth: £690,951 *Total Assets:* £15,850,952
Registered Office: 1 Wall Hall Mansion, Wall Hall Drive, Aldenham, Watford, Herts, WD25 8BZ
Activities: Other letting and operating of own or leased real estate
Officers: Ian Alistair McGregor, Secretary; Anthea Rose Novak [1949] Director; Edna Novak [1954] Director; Leon Beverly Novak [1949] Director; Melvyn Ian Novak [1944] Director

Virbac Limited
Incorporated: 5 September 1972 *Employees:* 52
Net Worth: £3,488,437 *Total Assets:* £13,986,033
Registered Office: Woolpit Business Park, Windmill Avenue, Woolpit, Bury St Edmunds, Suffolk, IP30 9UP
Activities: Wholesale of pharmaceutical goods
Parent: Virbac SA
Officers: Kevin Michael Barton, Secretary; David Ellerton [1960] Managing Director; Christian Karst [1958] Director [French]; Hubert Trentesaux [1958] Director [French]

Virgin Wine Online Limited
Incorporated: 5 July 1999 *Employees:* 156
Net Worth: £8,632,000 *Total Assets:* £19,298,000
Registered Office: Floor 4, St James' Mill, Whitefriars, Norwich, NR3 1TN
Activities: Retail sale in non-specialised stores with food, beverages or tobacco predominating
Parent: Virgin Wines Holding Company Limited
Officers: Graeme David Weir, Secretary; Graeme David Weir [1962] Director; Jeremy Simon Wright [1969] Director

T. Visaman & Sons Limited
Incorporated: 24 October 2006 *Employees:* 2
Net Worth: £5,622,532 *Total Assets:* £12,199,468
Registered Office: 616D Green Lane, Ilford, Essex, IG3 9SE
Activities: Dispensing chemist in specialised stores
Officers: Preeti Pattni, Secretary; Pravin Pattani [1957] Director/Chemist

Vision (Office Automation) Limited
Incorporated: 25 April 1985 *Employees:* 43
Net Worth: £2,766,429 *Total Assets:* £11,019,820
Registered Office: Caxton House, Watermark Way, Foxholes Business Park, Hertford, SG13 7TZ
Activities: Other service activities n.e.c.
Parent: Visiontel Europe Limited
Officers: Allen Bond [1949] Director; Philip Roy Bond [1977] Director; John McLoone [1963] Director; Earl Robinson [1961] Director

Vision Group (Holdings) Limited
Incorporated: 18 March 2011 *Employees:* 113
Previous: Vision Group (Holdings) PLC
Net Worth: £3,854,887 *Total Assets:* £12,402,173
Registered Office: Caxton House, Watermark Way, Foxholes Business Park, Hertford, SG13 7TZ
Activities: Activities of other holding companies n.e.c.
Shareholders: Allen Bond; Philip Roy Bond; Earl Robinson
Officers: Allen Bond, Secretary; Allen Bond [1949] Director; Philip Roy Bond [1977] Director; Earl Robinson [1961] Director; James Edward Royston [1972] Director

Visiongroup (GB) Limited
Incorporated: 25 March 2004 *Employees:* 159
Net Worth: £4,032,478 *Total Assets:* £9,065,733
Registered Office: Heath Priory, Staithe Road, Hickling, Norwich, NR12 0YJ
Activities: Activities of head offices
Major Shareholder: Hugh Callacher
Officers: Hugh Callacher [1952] Director/Business Manager

Visteon Engineering Services Limited
Incorporated: 16 April 2007 *Employees:* 203
Net Worth: £3,432,000 *Total Assets:* £28,963,000
Registered Office: 1 Springfield, Lyons Approach, Chelmsford Business Park, Chelmsford, Essex, CM2 5LB
Activities: Engineering design activities for industrial process and production
Officers: Kate Alleyne Holland [1972] Director; Jennifer Lynn Pretzel [1972] Director [American]; Ian Scott [1963] Director; Robert Ian Swanston [1961] Electronics Director; Andrew Wood [1972] Director

Vix Technology UK Limited
Incorporated: 29 March 1995 *Employees:* 171
Previous: Vix Technology Limited
Net Worth Deficit: £1,057,000 *Total Assets:* £21,746,000
Registered Office: 1st Floor, Unit 406 Cambridge Science Park, Milton Road, Cambridge, CB4 0WW
Activities: Other information technology service activities
Shareholders: UIL Limited; Vix Limited
Officers: Simon David Coulthard, Secretary; Adrian Paul Kelly [1967] Director/Global Head of Product [Irish]; Shane Peter Quinn [1965] Director [Australian]; Aaron Ross [1980] Managing Director (EMEA); Grant Andrew Worner [1967] Director/Chief Operating Officer [Australian]

J. Van Vliet London Cash & Carry Limited
Incorporated: 10 November 1994 *Employees:* 331
Net Worth: £2,402,265 *Total Assets:* £11,620,717
Registered Office: Knapdale Nursery, Cattlegate Road, Enfield, Middlesex, EN2 9ED
Activities: Wholesale of flowers and plants
Parent: Esmeralda Limited
Officers: Rahul Patel, Secretary; Jo-Anne Newham [1973] Director [Irish]

VMS (Fleet Management) Limited
Incorporated: 21 May 2002 *Employees:* 86
Net Worth: £4,246,361 *Total Assets:* £66,223,952
Registered Office: Abbotsgate House, Hollow Road, Bury St Edmunds, Suffolk, IP32 7FA
Activities: Maintenance and repair of motor vehicles
Parent: VMS (Holdings) Ltd
Officers: Richard James Horrex, Secretary; Richard James Horrex [1980] Finance Director; Martin Harold James [1963] Director; Gary Colin Prentice [1963] Director

VMS (Holdings) Limited
Incorporated: 18 August 2010 *Employees:* 137
Net Worth: £4,245,700 *Total Assets:* £66,764,032
Registered Office: Abbottsgate House, Hollow Road, Bury St Edmunds, Suffolk, IP32 7FA
Activities: Activities of head offices
Shareholders: Garry Colin Prentice; Martin Harold James
Officers: Richard James Horrex, Secretary; Richard James Horrex [1980] Finance Director; Martin Harold James [1963] Director; Gary Colin Prentice [1963] Director

VNC Group Limited
Incorporated: 19 May 2006 *Employees:* 95
Net Worth: £6,971,858 *Total Assets:* £11,812,564
Registered Office: Betjeman House, 104 Hills Road, Cambridge, CB2 1LQ
Activities: Business and domestic software development
Officers: Tom McGuire, Secretary; Adam Greenwood-Byrne [1980] Director; Dr Andrew Charles Harter [1961] Director; Professor Andrew Hopper [1953] Director

Voicevale Limited
Incorporated: 1 June 1981 *Employees:* 71
Net Worth: £28,011,732 *Total Assets:* £82,394,624
Registered Office: Voicevale House, Spring Villa Park, Edgware, Middlesex, HA8 7EB
Activities: Non-specialised wholesale trade
Major Shareholder: Robert Teddy Danon
Officers: Linda Christine Barrett, Secretary; Linda Christine Barrett [1966] Director/Financial Controller [Irish]; Edward Danon [1984] Director; Naomi Danon [1957] Director/Marketing Consultant; Roby Teddy Danon [1956] Director; Cho Yin Ho [1964] Director/Commodity Trader; Chiaki Onozuka [1970] Director [Japanese]

Vokera Limited
Incorporated: 28 March 1972 *Employees:* 104
Net Worth: £7,990,000 *Total Assets:* £17,788,000
Registered Office: Borderlake House, Unit 7 Riverside Industrial Estate, London Colney, Herts, AL2 1HG
Activities: Wholesale of hardware, plumbing and heating equipment and supplies
Parent: Riello SpA
Officers: Anthony John Power, Secretary; Philip Michael Gregory Adams [1972] Managing Director; Simon Derrick Boniface [1984] Director/Solicitor; Umberto Paolo Ferretti [1957] Director [Italian]

Volac International Limited
Incorporated: 23 January 1991 *Employees:* 409
Net Worth: £88,300,000 *Total Assets:* £206,500,000
Registered Office: 50 Fishers Lane, Orwell, Royston, Herts, SG8 5QX
Activities: Manufacture of other milk products
Parent: Woodford Holdings Ltd
Officers: Alexander William Rippon, Secretary; Paul Frampton [1970] Director/Accountant; William Struan McBride [1963] Director/Chartered Accountant; David Christopher Neville [1969] Director; James Robert Neville [1966] Managing Director; Mark Richard Neville [1975] Director; Dr Christopher Gareth Joseph Richards [1953] Director; Garyth Christopher Stone [1977] Director/Banker

Volac Renewable Energy Limited
Incorporated: 19 September 2014
Net Worth Deficit: £2,900,000 *Total Assets:* £36,200,000
Registered Office: 50 Fishers Lane, Orwell, Royston, Herts, SG8 5QX
Activities: Production of electricity
Parent: Woodford Holdings Ltd
Officers: Alan Richard Armstrong [1955] Supply Chain Director; Paul Frampton [1970] Director/Accountant

VolkerFitzpatrick Limited
Incorporated: 22 May 1989 *Employees:* 998
Net Worth: £57,666,000 *Total Assets:* £179,503,008
Registered Office: Hertford Road, Hoddesdon, Herts, EN11 9BX
Activities: Construction of commercial buildings
Parent: Volkerwessels Limited
Officers: Naomi Anne Connell [1965] Director; John Anthony Cox [1964] Managing Director [Irish]; David John Griffin [1973] Commercial Director; Ceri Suzanne Humphrey [1971] Director; Richard Andrew Offord [1964] Director; Alan Robert Robertson [1962] Director

Volkerhighways Limited
Incorporated: 1 October 1959 *Employees:* 320
Net Worth: £9,604,000 *Total Assets:* £41,902,000
Registered Office: Hertford Road, Hoddesdon, Herts, EN11 9BX
Activities: Other specialised construction activities n.e.c.
Parent: VolkerFitzpatrick Limited
Officers: Naomi Anne Connell [1965] Director; Jonathon Michael Humphries [1967] Director; Alan Robert Robertson [1962] Director

Volkerlaser Ltd
Incorporated: 13 December 1999 *Employees:* 119
Net Worth: £6,492,000 *Total Assets:* £14,555,000
Registered Office: Hertford Road, Hoddesdon, Herts, EN11 9BX
Activities: Other specialised construction activities n.e.c.
Parent: Volkerwessels Limited
Officers: Naomi Anne Connell [1965] Director; Alan Robert Robertson [1962] Director; Michael James Weaver [1962] Director/Quantity Surveyor

Volkerrail Group Limited
Incorporated: 13 October 2003 *Employees:* 794
Net Worth: £22,881,000 *Total Assets:* £106,023,000
Registered Office: Hertford Road, Hoddesdon, Herts, EN11 9BX
Activities: Activities of construction holding companies
Parent: Volkerwessels UK Limited
Officers: Stephen Jeffrey Cocliff [1958] Director; Naomi Anne Connell [1965] Director; Paul Howard Nolan [1966] Director; Alan Robert Robertson [1962] Director; Andrew Michael Wilkins [1964] Director

Volkerrail Limited
Incorporated: 11 April 1996 *Employees:* 342
Net Worth: £10,877,000 *Total Assets:* £84,958,000
Registered Office: Hertford Road, Hoddesdon, Herts, EN11 9BX
Activities: Construction of roads and motorways
Parent: Volkerrail Group Limited
Officers: Stephen Jeffrey Cocliff [1958] Director; Naomi Anne Connell [1965] Director; Paul Howard Nolan [1966] Director; Alan Robert Robertson [1962] Director; Andrew Michael Wilkins [1964] Director

Volkerrail Specialist Businesses Limited
Incorporated: 10 April 2001 *Employees:* 452
Net Worth: £11,852,000 *Total Assets:* £28,070,000
Registered Office: Hertford Road, Hoddesdon, Herts, EN11 9BX
Activities: Other specialised construction activities n.e.c.
Parent: Volkerrail Group Limited
Officers: Stephen Jeffrey Cocliff [1958] Director; Naomi Anne Connell [1965] Director; Paul Howard Nolan [1966] Director; Alan Robert Robertson [1962] Director; Andrew Michael Wilkins [1964] Director

Volkerservices Limited
Incorporated: 22 May 2000 *Employees:* 243
Net Worth: £4,327,000 *Total Assets:* £26,081,000
Registered Office: Hertford Road, Hoddesdon, Herts, EN11 9BX
Activities: Construction of roads and motorways
Parent: Volkerwessels Limited
Officers: Naomi Anne Connell [1965] Director; Ceri Suzanne Humphrey [1971] Director; Richard Andrew Offord [1964] Director; Alan Robert Robertson [1962] Director

Volkerstevin Group Limited
Incorporated: 9 December 2011 *Employees:* 579
Net Worth: £17,715,000 *Total Assets:* £78,214,000
Registered Office: Hertford Road, Hoddesdon, Herts, EN11 9BX
Activities: Construction of other civil engineering projects n.e.c.
Parent: Volkerwessels UK Limited
Officers: Naomi Anne Connell [1965] Director; Robert Damian Coupe [1965] Director; Alan Robert Robertson [1962] Director; Lynsey Taylor [1975] Finance Director; Anthony Richard Towse [1968] Director

Volkerstevin Limited
Incorporated: 24 May 1934 *Employees:* 436
Net Worth: £19,771,000 *Total Assets:* £58,728,000
Registered Office: Hertford Road, Hoddesdon, Herts, EN11 9BX
Activities: Construction of other civil engineering projects n.e.c.
Parent: Volkerstevin Group Limited
Officers: Naomi Anne Connell [1965] Director; Robert Damian Coupe [1965] Director; Alan Robert Robertson [1962] Director; Lynsey Taylor [1975] Finance Director; Anthony Richard Towse [1968] Director

Volkerwessels Limited
Incorporated: 19 March 1986 *Employees:* 1,360
Net Worth: £70,130,000 *Total Assets:* £211,092,992
Registered Office: Hertford Road, Hoddesdon, Herts, EN11 9BX
Activities: Activities of head offices
Parent: Volkerwessels UK Limited
Officers: Naomi Anne Connell [1965] Director; Richard Andrew Offord [1964] Director; Alan Robert Robertson [1962] Director; Michael James Weaver [1962] Director/Quantity Surveyor

Volkerwessels UK Limited
Incorporated: 31 July 1974 *Employees:* 2,733
Net Worth: £88,947,000 *Total Assets:* £351,801,984
Registered Office: Hertford Road, Hoddesdon, Herts, EN11 9BX
Activities: Construction of commercial buildings
Officers: Naomi Anne Connell, Secretary; Stephen Jeffrey Cocliff [1958] Director; Naomi Anne Connell [1965] Director; Robert Damian Coupe [1965] Director; Hendrik Willem Renier August Maria Janssen [1954] Director/General Counsel [Dutch]; Richard Andrew Offord [1964] Director; Alan Robert Robertson [1962] Director; Alfred Vos [1969] Director [Dutch]

VRS Investments Limited
Incorporated: 5 August 2014 *Employees:* 1,915
Net Worth: £29,174,000 *Total Assets:* £65,282,000
Registered Office: Colwyn House, Sheepen Place, Colchester, Essex, CO3 3LD
Activities: Other business support service activities n.e.c.
Major Shareholder: Paul Alick Smith
Officers: Paul Alick Smith [1960] Director

VSL Group Holdings Limited
Incorporated: 18 March 2010
Net Worth: £7,342,860 *Total Assets:* £15,197,883
Registered Office: Endeavour House, Endeavour Drive, Festival Leisure Park, Basildon, Essex, SS14 3WF
Activities: Other business support service activities n.e.c.
Parent: Rowan International Bidco Limited
Officers: Duncan Clive Mastin [1967] Director; David Richard Parry [1959] Director; John Christopher Place [1977] Director

VWS (UK) Ltd
Incorporated: 14 May 1937 *Employees:* 433
Net Worth: £29,956,000 *Total Assets:* £76,190,000
Registered Office: Windsor Court, Kingsmead Business Park, High Wycombe, Bucks, HP11 1JU
Activities: Water collection, treatment and supply
Parent: OTV Birwelco Ltd
Officers: Ian Thomas Heggie, Secretary; Philip Andrew Chattle [1958] HR Director; Mark Dyson [1961] Director; Beverley Michelle Eagle [1958] HR Director; Martyn Paul Fisher [1961] Director; Ian Thomas Heggie [1968] Financial Director; Nora Ikene [1969] Director; Sunil Kumar Lakhenpaul [1961] Director/Accountant; Annabel Marie Odile Dolores Mouquet [1980] Finance Director [French]

W & L Investments LLP
Incorporated: 2 April 2016
Net Worth: £12,073,404 *Total Assets:* £15,752,335
Registered Office: 42 Lytton Road, Barnet, Herts, EN5 5BY
Officers: Julia Selt [1963] Member; Lauren Selt [1960] Member; Lewis Selt [1963] Member; Wayne Michael Selt [1958] Member

Waddesdon Church of England School
Incorporated: 17 August 2011 *Employees:* 122
Net Worth: £13,109,117 *Total Assets:* £15,508,692
Registered Office: School Lane, Waddesdon, Aylesbury, Bucks, HP18 0LQ
Activities: General secondary education
Officers: Valerie Ann Homewood, Secretary; Matthew Abbott [1974] Director/Headteacher; Julian Ball [1969] Director/Commissioned Officer RAF; Ann Coulter [1979] Director; Revd Jacqueline McClintock Dove [1965] Director/Reverend; Benjamin James Eales [1969] Director/Civil Engineer; Andrew Craig Howard [1969] Director; Kathryn Jill Judson [1950] Director/Education Specialist; Jill Lamb [1960] Director/Teaching Assistant; Karen Leonard [1962] Director/Actuary; Paul David McSweeney [1961] Director/IT Manager; Graham John Parker [1943] Director; Jane Ann Plotkin [1939] Director; Duncan Purchase [1972] Director/ICT Systems Manager; Michael Paul Rogers [1974] Director; Christina Anderson Sato [1969] Director; Suzie Snelson [1965] Director; Stephen Starsmore [1973] Director/Local Government Officer; Rex William Stevens [1948] Director/Retired Senior Civil Servant

Wadlow Energy Holdings Limited
Incorporated: 23 June 2011
Net Worth: £1,000 *Total Assets:* £23,460,000
Registered Office: Beaufort Court, Egg Farm Lane, Kings Langley, Herts, WD4 8LR
Activities: Activities of head offices
Parent: DIF Infra 4 UK Limited
Officers: Dominic James Hearth, Secretary; David Lau [1981] Director/Originator [German]; Helen Mary Murphy [1981] Director/Asset Manager [Irish]

Wadlow Energy Limited
Incorporated: 30 November 2010
Net Worth Deficit: £12,638,000 *Total Assets:* £47,619,000
Registered Office: Beaufort Court, Egg Farm Lane, Kings Langley, Herts, WD4 8LR
Activities: Other specialised construction activities n.e.c.
Parent: Wadlow Energy Holdings Limited
Officers: Dominic James Hearth, Secretary; David Lau [1981] Director/Originator [German]; Helen Mary Murphy [1981] Director/Asset Manager [Irish]

Waldersey Farms Limited
Incorporated: 7 March 1980 *Employees:* 31
Net Worth: £5,725,621 *Total Assets:* £13,519,531
Registered Office: Northfield Farm, Lynn Road, Southery, Downham Market, Norfolk, PE38 0HT
Activities: Growing of cereals (except rice), leguminous crops and oil seeds
Parent: South Yorkshire Pensions Authority
Officers: Robert Brian Loxton, Secretary; David Andrew Gardner [1958] Director/CEO - Royal Agricultural Society of England; Pamela Mary Gladwin [1968] Director; John Nicholas Hattersley [1954] Director/Investment Manager; Alastair John Kerr [1973] Director/Farmer; Robert Brian Loxton [1954] Director/Farm Consultant; Cedric William Porter [1967] Director; Stephen Tom Ward [1959] Director/Farmer

J. Walker & Son (Investments) Limited
Incorporated: 1 April 1950 *Employees:* 3
Previous: J. Walker & Son (Farm) Limited
Net Worth: £16,812,988 *Total Assets:* £19,493,572
Registered Office: 17 Parsonage Road, Chalfont St Giles, Bucks, HP8 4JW
Activities: Other letting and operating of own or leased real estate
Officers: William James Walker, Secretary; Charles Edwyn Walker [1971] Director/Pharmacologist; David John Walker [1963] Director/Chartered Surveyor; Eleanor Mary Walker [1934] Director/Secretary; George Patrick Walker [1965] Director/Chartered Surveyor; James William Walker [1934] Director/Farmer & Timber Merchant; William James Walker [1961] Director/Accountant

Wallace Estates Limited
Incorporated: 15 May 2001
Net Worth: £57,999,000 *Total Assets:* £224,355,008
Registered Office: Botanic House, Hills Road, Cambridge, CB2 1PH
Activities: Buying and selling of own real estate
Parent: Wallace Partnership Group Limited
Officers: Natalie Chambers, Secretary; Andrea Williams, Secretary; Natalie Chambers [1976] Director/Company Secretary; Janine Grant [1972] Director/Financial Controller; Paul Langford [1971] Finance Director; Michael Anthony Platt [1966] Director/Chartered Accountant

Wallace Partnership Group Limited
Incorporated: 20 September 2011 *Employees:* 28
Net Worth: £143,288,000 *Total Assets:* £410,841,984
Registered Office: Botanic House, Hills Road, Cambridge, CB2 1PH
Activities: Buying and selling of own real estate
Parent: Albanwise Limited
Officers: Natalie Chambers, Secretary; Paul Langford [1971] Finance Director; Luca Padulli [1955] Director [Italian]; Michael Anthony Platt [1966] Director/Chartered Accountant

Walsingham College Trust Association Limited
Incorporated: 9 September 1936 *Employees:* 136
Net Worth: £20,828,856 *Total Assets:* £23,400,682
Registered Office: The Shrine Office, Common Place, Walsingham, Norfolk, NR22 6EE
Activities: Hotels and similar accommodation
Officers: Dr Brian John Taylor Hanson, Secretary; The Reverend Jonathan Mark Richard Baker [1966] Director/Clergyman; John David Sebastian Booth [1958] Director/Company Chairman; Amanda McIntyre [1964] Charity Director; Philip John North [1966] Director/Suffragan Bishop; Andrew Roberts [1964] Director/Church Administrator; Graeme Charles Rowlands [1953] Director/Parish Priest; The Reverend Howard Charles Stoker [1963] Director/Clerk in Holy Orders; Ruth Suzanne Ward [1966] Director/Solicitor

Walsingham Estate Management Limited
Incorporated: 24 February 2011 *Employees:* 25
Net Worth: £12,378,256 *Total Assets:* £13,362,742
Registered Office: Walsingham Abbey, Sunk Road, Walsingham, Norfolk, NR22 6DQ
Activities: Management consultancy activities other than financial management
Parent: The Walsingham Estate Company
Officers: John Sayer Downing, Secretary; The Honourable Jerome Patrick Burke Mayhew [1970] Director; Priscilla Ann Meath Baker [1937] Director; William John Clovis Meath Baker [1959] Director

Walsingham Estate Properties Limited
Incorporated: 24 February 2011 *Employees:* 3
Net Worth: £10,596,101 *Total Assets:* £23,180,184
Registered Office: Walsingham Abbey, Sunk Road, Walsingham, Norfolk, NR22 6DQ
Activities: Other letting and operating of own or leased real estate
Parent: The Walsingham Estate Company
Officers: John Sayer Downing, Secretary; Priscilla Ann Meath Baker [1937] Director; William John Clovis Meath Baker [1959] Director

Walstead Finance Limited
Incorporated: 22 December 2015
Net Worth Deficit: £10,061,000 *Total Assets:* £47,963,000
Registered Office: 22 Westside Centre, London Road, Colchester, Essex, CO3 8PH
Activities: Activities of head offices
Parent: Walstead Holdings Limited
Officers: Richard Charles Fookes [1968] Director; Oliver John Tudor Jones [1976] Director/Partner; Zoe Repman [1969] Director; Paul Utting [1965] Director

Walstead Group Limited
Incorporated: 22 December 2015 *Employees:* 19
Net Worth Deficit: £984,000 *Total Assets:* £52,118,000
Registered Office: 22 Westside Centre, London Road, Colchester, Essex, CO3 8PH
Activities: Activities of head offices
Parent: Walstead Finance Limited
Officers: Jose Maria Camacho Fernandez [1974] Director [Spanish]; Richard Charles Fookes [1968] Director; Oliver John Tudor Jones [1976] Director/Partner; Roy Ernest Kingston [1958] Director; Ron Marsh [1950] Director; Gerhard Poppe [1962] Director [Austrian]; Debbie Read [1966] Director; Zoe Repman [1969] Director; Mark Scanlon [1962] Director; Paul Utting [1965] Director

Walstead Holdings Limited
Incorporated: 22 December 2015 *Employees:* 2,291
Net Worth: £24,327,596 *Total Assets:* £237,936,160
Registered Office: 22 Westside Centre, London Road, Colchester, Essex, CO3 8PH
Activities: Activities of head offices
Parent: Rutland III GP LLP
Officers: Richard Charles Fookes [1968] Director; Stephen Thomas Hargrave [1955] Director; Oliver John Tudor Jones [1976] Director/Partner; Ron Marsh [1950] Director; Zoe Repman [1969] Director; Mark Scanlon [1962] Director; Paul George Utting [1965] Director

Walstead Peterborough Limited
Incorporated: 25 May 1988 *Employees:* 175
Previous: Wyndeham Peterborough Limited
Net Worth: £16,850,000 *Total Assets:* £23,477,000
Registered Office: 22 Westside Centre, London Road, Colchester, Essex, CO3 8PH
Activities: Printing n.e.c.
Parent: Wyndeham Holdings Limited
Officers: Zoe Repman, Secretary; Roy Ernest Kingston [1958] Director/Chief Operating Officer; Debbie Read [1966] Group Commercial Director; Zoe Repman [1969] Finance Director; Paul George Utting [1965] Director

Walstead Press Group Limited
Incorporated: 7 June 1968 *Employees:* 44
Previous: Wyndeham Press Group Limited
Net Worth Deficit: £368,000 *Total Assets:* £47,717,000
Registered Office: 22 Westside Centre, London Road, Colchester, Essex, CO3 8PH
Activities: Printing n.e.c.
Parent: Walstead UK Limited
Officers: Zoe Repman, Secretary; Roy Ernest Kingston [1958] Director/Chief Operating Officer; Debbie Read [1966] Group Commercial Director; Zoe Repman [1969] Finance Director; Paul George Utting [1965] Director

Walstead Roche Limited
Incorporated: 9 April 1962 *Employees:* 276
Previous: Wyndeham Roche Limited
Net Worth: £24,511,000 *Total Assets:* £36,188,000
Registered Office: 22 Westside Centre, London Road, Colchester, Essex, CO3 8PH
Activities: Printing n.e.c.
Parent: Wyndeham Holdings Limited
Officers: Zoe Repman, Secretary; Roy Ernest Kingston [1958] Director/Chief Operating Officer; Debbie Read [1966] Group Commercial Director; Zoe Repman [1969] Finance Director; Paul George Utting [1965] Director

Walstead Southernprint Limited
Incorporated: 5 December 1972 *Employees:* 166
Previous: Wyndeham Southernprint Limited
Net Worth Deficit: £822,000 *Total Assets:* £9,288,000
Registered Office: 22 Westside Centre, London Road, Colchester, Essex, CO3 8PH
Activities: Printing n.e.c.
Parent: Wyndeham Southernprint (Holdings) Limited
Officers: Zoe Repman, Secretary; Roy Ernest Kingston [1958] Director/Chief Operating Officer; Debbie Read [1966] Group Commercial Director; Zoe Repman [1969] Finance Director; Paul George Utting [1965] Director

Walstead UK Holdings Limited
Incorporated: 23 June 2009
Previous: Wyndeham Holdings Limited
Net Worth: £260,000 *Total Assets:* £25,912,000
Registered Office: 22 Westside Centre, London Road, Colchester, Essex, CO3 8PH
Activities: Activities of other holding companies n.e.c.
Parent: Walstead UK Limited
Officers: Roy Ernest Kingston [1958] Director/Chief Operating Officer; Debbie Read [1966] Group Commercial Director; Zoe Repman [1969] Finance Director; Paul George Utting [1965] Director

Walstead United Kingdom Limited
Incorporated: 17 November 2008
Previous: Walstead UK Limited
Net Worth: £1,763,000 *Total Assets:* £19,717,000
Registered Office: 22 Westside Centre, London Road, Colchester, Essex, CO3 8PH
Activities: Activities of head offices
Parent: Walstead Group Limited
Officers: Roy Ernest Kingston [1958] Director; Debbie Read [1966] Commercial Director; Zoe Repman [1969] Director; Mark Scanlon [1962] Director; Paul George Utting [1965] Director

Walsworth Limited
Incorporated: 13 August 1997
Net Worth: £58,429,972 *Total Assets:* £76,470,080
Registered Office: Spirella 2, Icknield Way, Letchworth, Herts, SG6 4GY
Activities: Activities of head offices
Parent: Hardwicke Investments Limited
Officers: Wendy Jane McWilliams, Secretary; Colin Enticknap [1958] Director/Chartered Surveyor; Richard John Willmott [1963] Director/Chartered Builder

Walters Holdings Limited
Incorporated: 20 June 2003 *Employees:* 110
Net Worth: £10,721,885 *Total Assets:* £12,189,385
Registered Office: Sudbury Silk Mills, Cornard Road, Sudbury, Suffolk, CO10 2XB
Activities: Activities of other holding companies n.e.c.
Parent: Sudbury Silk Mills Limited
Officers: Nicola Jane Currie, Secretary; Tracey Louise Goldsmith [1968] Finance Director; David John Walters [1942] Director; Julius David Benedict Walters [1971] Director

Wandale Limited
Incorporated: 31 January 2012
Net Worth: £89,437 *Total Assets:* £86,751,960
Registered Office: Hill House, Lowlands Road, Harrow, Middlesex, HA1 3EQ
Activities: Development of building projects
Major Shareholder: Donovan Gijsbertus Wijsmuller
Officers: Brian Martin Comer [1960] Director [Irish]; Luke Andrew Comer [1957] Director [Irish]

Ward Farming Limited
Incorporated: 15 February 2007 *Employees:* 16
Net Worth: £7,222,280 *Total Assets:* £15,393,552
Registered Office: Theberton Hall Farm, Theberton, Leiston, Suffolk, IP16 4SE
Activities: Growing of cereals (except rice), leguminous crops and oil seeds
Shareholders: Joseph William Ward; Annabel Louise Ward
Officers: Annabel Louise Ward, Secretary; India Mary Bacon [1982] Director; Nathaniel John Bacon [1978] Director; Annabel Louise Ward [1954] Director; Joseph William Ward [1951] Director; Piers Joseph Ward [1980] Director

Warehouse Express Limited
Incorporated: 8 May 1997 *Employees:* 144
Net Worth: £12,033,000 *Total Assets:* £26,400,000
Registered Office: 13 Frensham Road, Sweet Briar Industrial Estate, Norwich, NR3 2BT
Activities: Retail sale via mail order houses or via Internet
Parent: Aurelius Phi Limited
Officers: Andrew James Morrissey, Secretary; Bernard Charles Hewitt [1952] Director; Andrew James Morrissey [1979] Finance Director; Louis Wahl [1968] Director/Chief Executive

Warners (Midlands) Public Limited Company
Incorporated: 28 July 1927 *Employees:* 240
Net Worth: £23,456,612 *Total Assets:* £29,143,580
Registered Office: The Maltings, Manor Lane, Bourne, Lincs, PE10 9PH
Activities: Printing n.e.c.
Shareholder: Philip Andrew Warner
Officers: Stephen Aquila Warner, Secretary; Jeannette Marie Warner [1965] Director; Philip Andrew Warner [1967] Director; Stephen Aquila Warner [1965] Director

Warners Group Publications PLC
Incorporated: 7 January 1991 *Employees:* 200
Net Worth: £7,218,525 *Total Assets:* £11,162,679
Registered Office: The Maltings, Manor Lane, Bourne, Lincs, PE10 9PH
Activities: Publishing of consumer and business journals and periodicals
Major Shareholder: Stephen Aquila Warner
Officers: Stephen Aquila Warner, Secretary; Lisa Maria Warner [1967] Director; Philip Andrew Warner [1967] Director; Stephen Aquila Warner [1965] Director

Roger Warnes Transport Limited
Incorporated: 23 October 1984 *Employees:* 12
Net Worth: £7,417,074 *Total Assets:* £9,884,686
Registered Office: Great Dunham Hall, Great Dunham, Kings Lynn, Norfolk, PE32 2LQ
Activities: Freight transport by road
Major Shareholder: Roger Guy Warnes
Officers: Anita Mary Warnes, Secretary; Neville Richard Alderton [1953] Director/Transport Manager; Ian Barclay [1960] Operations Director; Anita Mary Warnes [1950] Director/Company Secretary; Benjamin Roger Warnes [1988] Director; Roger Guy Warnes [1941] Director/Haulier; Timothy John Warnes [1982] Director

Warrant Investments PLC
Incorporated: 22 March 1994 *Employees:* 5
Net Worth: £19,620,204 *Total Assets:* £42,415,112
Registered Office: One Wellstones, Watford, Herts, WD17 2AE
Activities: Other business support service activities n.e.c.
Shareholder: Jeremy Laurence Stevens
Officers: Jeremy Laurence Stevens, Secretary; Anthony Ian Fine [1938] Director/Chartered Surveyor; Jeremy Laurence Stevens [1959] Director/Surveyor

Warrant Properties Limited
Incorporated: 23 May 2003 *Employees:* 5
Net Worth: £7,046,807 *Total Assets:* £19,209,212
Registered Office: One Wellstones, Watford, Herts, WD17 2AE
Activities: Other business support service activities n.e.c.
Major Shareholder: Jeremy Laurence Stevens
Officers: Lesley Anne Stevens, Secretary; Jeremy Laurence Stevens [1959] Director/Surveyor; Lesley Anne Stevens [1963] Director/Interior Designer

Washbrook Capital Limited
Incorporated: 30 July 2013 *Employees:* 2
Net Worth: £1,000,003 *Total Assets:* £20,285,024
Registered Office: Grant Hall, Parsons Green, St Ives, Cambs, PE27 4AA
Activities: Other business support service activities n.e.c.
Parent: UKLS Acquisitions Limited
Officers: Robert Matson, Secretary; David Jeremy Grossman [1970] Director; Robert Matson [1970] Director/Chartered Accountant

Waste Recycling Environmental Limited
Incorporated: 9 May 1997 *Employees:* 13
Net Worth: £5,463,517 *Total Assets:* £13,903,600
Registered Office: Unit 1e Snetterton Business Park, Snetterton, Norfolk, NR16 2JU
Activities: Financial intermediation not elsewhere classified
Officers: Gary Allen [1953] Director/Development Worker - Voluntary Action North Lincs; Christopher John Ellis [1966] Director; Julie Anne Fourcade [1969] Director/Head of External Affairs; Susan Andrea Scott [1960] Director/Consultant; Michael John Woods [1947] Director/Chief Officer, Countryside and Conservation

Water Incorporated
Incorporated: 5 July 2006
Net Worth: £40,492 *Total Assets:* £10,041,309
Registered Office: Northside House, Mount Pleasant, Barnet, Herts, EN4 9EE
Activities: Activities of other membership organisations n.e.c.
Officers: Adam Kaoru Herwegh Vonk [1997] Director [Dutch]; Chiara Yuki Herwegh Vonk [1995] Director [Dutch]; Scipio Akira Herwegh Vonk [1999] Director [Dutch]; Peter Lawrence Ulrich [1958] Director/Administrator

Waters Limited
Incorporated: 24 March 1994 *Employees:* 156
Net Worth: £8,637,000 *Total Assets:* £36,251,000
Registered Office: 610 Centennial Park, Centennial Avenue, Elstree, Herts, WD6 3TJ
Activities: Manufacture of electronic measuring, testing etc. equipment, not for industrial process control
Parent: Micromass Limited
Officers: James Hallam [1973] Director/General Manager, Northern Europe; Michael Cornelius Harrington [1960] Director [Irish]; Gary Joseph Murphy [1960] Director [American]; Columbanus Patrick O'Mahony [1964] Director [Irish]

Watford Association Football Club Limited (The)
Incorporated: 22 July 1909 *Employees:* 254
Net Worth: £2,859,090 *Total Assets:* £168,852,896
Registered Office: Vicarage Road Stadium, Vicarage Road, Watford, Herts, WD18 0ER
Activities: Other sports activities
Parent: Hornets Investment Limited
Officers: Peter James Wastall, Secretary; Scott Ian Duxbury [1972] Director; David Bernard Fransen [1951] Director; Professor Stuart Read Timperley [1943] Director

Watford Grammar School for Boys
Incorporated: 17 August 2010 *Employees:* 200
Net Worth: £18,300,976 *Total Assets:* £20,789,344
Registered Office: Watford Grammar School for Boys, Rickmansworth Road, Watford, Herts, WD18 7JF
Activities: General secondary education
Officers: Caroline Brown, Secretary; Milan Bavisi [1971] Director/Telecommunication Manager; Susan Margaret Branch [1942] Director/Retired; Ian Alexander Cooksey [1974] Director/Headmaster; Caroline Cox [1969] Director/Teacher; Rajesh Gordhandas Dawda [1972] Director/Chartered Accountant; Rachel Dunsby [1966] Director/Exams Officer; Stuart David Hart [1972] Director/Financial Planner; Stephen Anthony Nokes [1952] Director/Headmaster; Adam Edouard Parsons [1970] Director/Journalist; Sameena Riaz [1974] Director/Teacher; Rev Anthony William Rindl [1964] Director/Vicar; Professor David Alastair Ritchie [1959] Director/University Professor; Stephanie Emma Rodgers [1975] Director/Teacher; Stephen Shannon [1957] Financial Director; Andrew William Speirs [1965] Director/Investment Banker; Terry John Sweeney [1968] Finance Director; Anne Watson [1963] Director/Learning Support Assistant

Watford Grammar School for Girls
Incorporated: 17 August 2010 *Employees:* 161
Net Worth: £13,673,997 *Total Assets:* £15,644,219
Registered Office: Watford Grammar School for Girls, Lady's Close, Watford, Herts, WD18 0AE
Activities: General secondary education
Officers: Philip Beasley, Secretary; Sylvia Lucy Chong-Tai [1969] Director/Teacher; Dr Nigel Corp [1952] Director/GP; Russell Guy Deane [1959] Director; Harvey Spencer Griffiths [1968] Director/Investment Manager; Prakash Jani [1970] Director/Consultant; Mr Stephen Ernest Johnson [1953] Director; Clare Kirwan [1977] Director/Teacher; Michael Duncan Lewis [1972] Director/Army Officer; Mary Patricia Meerabux [1954] Director/Teacher; Nicholas John Moorhouse [1955] Director; Akintomide Idowu Oyesola [1963] IT Programme Director; Zia Al Rehman [1977] Director/Electronics Engineer; Rev Anthony William Rindl [1964] Director; Fiona Shore [1953] Director/Teacher; Jane Willis [1955] Director; Camilla Woods [1967] Director

Watford Health Campus Partnership LLP
Incorporated: 7 May 2013
Net Worth: £17,866,000 *Total Assets:* £25,073,000
Registered Office: Tempsford Hall, Sandy, Beds, SG19 2BD

The Watford UTC
Incorporated: 5 July 2013 *Employees:* 31
Net Worth: £8,392,721 *Total Assets:* £10,003,247
Registered Office: 18 Colonial Way, Watford, Herts, WD24 4PT
Activities: Technical and vocational secondary education
Officers: Alexander Hall, Secretary; Christopher John Francis Andrews [1961] Director; Kate Prudence Bearman [1971] Director/Communications Consultant; Richard Arthur Elms [1947] Director; Stephen Peter Hunt [1959] Director/University Lecturer; Celeste Jones [1973] Director/University Manager; Sir Leigh Warren Lewis [1951] Director/Part-Time Consultant; Claire Elaine Lish [1973] Director/Head of Human Resources; Emma Jane Loveland [1969] Director/Principal [Irish]; Mohan Deep Raj Luthra [1979] Director; Ashok Shankar Patil [1945] Director/IT Sales Consultant; Ian Smithson [1970] Director/Regional Officer

David Watson Transport Limited
Incorporated: 13 November 2008 *Employees:* 156
Net Worth: £4,792,408 *Total Assets:* £12,450,602
Registered Office: Mundford Road, Weeting, Norfolk, IP27 0PL
Activities: Freight transport by road
Shareholders: David Cresswell Watson; Jayne Watson
Officers: Jayne Watson, Secretary; Russell John Cooper [1961] Operations Director; Stephen Charles Frazer-Brown [1956] H & S Director; David Cresswell Watson [1956] Director; Mark David Watson [1979] Sales Director

Watts Industries UK Limited
Incorporated: 3 September 1991 *Employees:* 44
Net Worth: £5,117,731 *Total Assets:* £11,307,419
Registered Office: Ambuscade Road, Colmworth Business Park, Eaton Socon, St Neots, Cambs, PE19 8YX
Activities: Manufacture of taps and valves
Parent: Watts Industries Europe BV
Officers: Olivier Paul Jean Giverdon, Secretary; Olivier Paul Jean Giverdon [1978] Director [French]; Nigel Paul Wood [1966] Director

Waveney Valley Academies Trust
Incorporated: 24 June 2011 *Employees:* 321
Previous: Sir John Leman High School
Net Worth: £13,059,000 *Total Assets:* £14,782,000
Registered Office: First Floor Offices, 6 St Marys Street, Bungay, Suffolk, NR35 1AX
Activities: General secondary education
Officers: Alison Joy O'Connor, Secretary; Steven Alderson [1961] Director; David Robert Balls [1948] Director/Retired; Jon Brighton [1962] Director/Retired; Douglas Michael Cadman [1949] Director; Stephanie Mary Challinor [1953] Director; Mark Henry Chapman [1970] Director/Finance Manager; Catherine Louise Ford [1968] Director/Teacher; Christopher Michael Harrod [1955] Director/Chief Executive; Leanne Munro [1973] Director/Head of School; Jeremy Bruce Rowe [1965] Director

Waverley House Hotel Limited
Incorporated: 27 November 1995 *Employees:* 48
Net Worth: £42,155,576 *Total Assets:* £69,639,704
Registered Office: Kanta House, Victoria Road, South Ruislip, Middlesex, HA4 0JQ
Activities: Hotels and similar accommodation
Officers: Bhasker Tailor, Secretary/Chairman; Jawahar Jamnadas Chatwani [1948] Director; Rashmi Jamnadas Chatwani [1954] Director; Satish Jamnadas Chatwani [1953] Director

Waystone Limited
Incorporated: 11 December 1989 *Employees:* 23
Net Worth: £3,426,714 *Total Assets:* £13,491,168
Registered Office: CP House, Otterspool Way, Watford Bypass, Watford, Herts, WD25 8JJ
Activities: Construction of commercial buildings
Parent: Waystone (Holdings) Limited
Officers: Eric Lewis, Secretary; Paul Andrew Filer [1957] Director/Chartered Accountant; Iris Gibbor [1951] Director; Philip Hoffbrand [1967] Director; Alistair James McLoughlin [1968] Director/Business Executive; Helen McLoughlin [1964] Director/Business Manager; Stuart McLoughlin [1939] Director/Engineer; Alexei James Schreier [1976] Director

WCM Investments Ltd
Incorporated: 31 March 2016 *Employees:* 152
Net Worth: £7,720,450 *Total Assets:* £22,858,166
Registered Office: Innovation House, One Juniper West, Fenton Way, Basildon, Essex, SS15 6TD
Activities: Activities of production holding companies
Major Shareholder: Karl Nicholas McGee
Officers: Karl McGee, Secretary; Robert Anderson [1965] Director; Karl Nicholas McGee [1966] Director

WD1A Limited
Incorporated: 13 March 2014
Net Worth: £3,214,083 *Total Assets:* £9,054,424
Registered Office: The Hive, Camrose Avenue, London, HA8 6AG
Activities: Buying and selling of own real estate
Parent: Double A Group Ltd
Officers: Mahendra Patel, Secretary; Anthony Andrew Kleanthous [1966] Director

Webb Investments Ltd.
Incorporated: 2 January 1947 *Employees:* 3
Net Worth: £10,966,571 *Total Assets:* £18,380,896
Registered Office: Rickling Hall, Rickling Green, Saffron Walden, Essex, CB11 3YJ
Activities: Buying and selling of own real estate
Major Shareholder: Barrie John Webb
Officers: Darrell John Webb, Secretary; Conrad Mark Harold Webb [1964] Director; Darrell John Webb [1959] Director

Webster Estates Ltd
Incorporated: 2 May 1989
Previous: D W Group Holdings Limited
Net Worth: £10,685,939 *Total Assets:* £14,026,737
Registered Office: 72 London Road, St Albans, Herts, AL1 1NS
Activities: Other letting and operating of own or leased real estate
Officers: Nicolas Fuselli [1960] Director; Nikola Susan Thompson [1962] Director; Thomas Walter David Webster [1961] Director

Andrew Weir & Company Limited
Incorporated: 4 September 1945 *Employees:* 27
Net Worth: £20,162,000 *Total Assets:* £30,743,000
Registered Office: Bridgeways House, Four Acres, Oving, Aylesbury, Bucks, HP22 4FJ
Activities: Activities of head offices
Officers: Iain Donald MacRitchie [1964] Director; Nicholas John Cordeaux Walters [1958] Director; Andrew Peter Weir [1966] Director/Doctor

Weir Waste Services Limited
Incorporated: 26 May 1999 *Employees:* 120
Net Worth: £3,537,820 *Total Assets:* £14,458,736
Registered Office: Coronation Road, Cressex, High Wycombe, Bucks, HP12 3TZ
Activities: Collection of non-hazardous waste
Parent: Biffa Waste Services Limited
Officers: Rachael Hambrook, Secretary; Michael Robert Mason Topham [1972] Director/Chief Financial Officer

WEL (No 1) Ltd
Incorporated: 27 June 2011
Net Worth: £15,157,398 *Total Assets:* £25,577,424
Registered Office: Botanic House, Hills Road, Cambridge, CB2 1PH
Activities: Buying and selling of own real estate
Parent: Wallace Partnership Reversionary Group Holdings Limited
Officers: Natalie Chambers, Secretary; Andrea Williams, Secretary; Natalie Chambers [1976] Director/Estates Manager/Company Secretary; Janine Grant [1972] Director/Financial Controller; Paul Langford [1971] Finance Director; Michael Anthony Platt [1966] Director/Chartered Accountant

Welch's Group Holdings Limited
Incorporated: 6 April 1981 *Employees:* 154
Net Worth: £16,242,229 *Total Assets:* £18,516,196
Registered Office: Welch's Transport Ltd, Moorfield Road, Duxford, Cambridge, CB22 4PS
Activities: Freight transport by road
Shareholders: Antony Gordon Welch; Roger Neville Welch; James Neville Welch
Officers: James Neville Welch, Secretary; James Neville Welch [1959] Director; Roger Neville Welch [1940] Director

Welding Alloys Limited
Incorporated: 26 February 1964 *Employees:* 25
Net Worth Deficit: £150,580 *Total Assets:* £10,761,293
Registered Office: The Way, Fowlmere, Royston, Herts, SG8 7QS
Activities: Manufacture of wire products, chain and springs
Officers: Richard William Baker [1958] Director; Dominic Charles Stekly [1975] Director/Company MD; Fiona Karen Tosh [1978] Director/Accountant [Australian]

Welding Institute (The)
Incorporated: 6 March 1946 *Employees:* 761
Net Worth: £56,790,000 *Total Assets:* £168,782,000
Registered Office: Granta Park, Great Abington, Cambridge, CB21 6AL
Activities: Other research and experimental development on natural sciences and engineering
Officers: Gillian Astrid Leech, Secretary; Dr Stephen Martin Beech [1955] Director/Engineering Consultant; Iain Leyland Boyd [1963] Director/Engineer; Norman Ian Cooper [1959] Director/Engineering Manager; Alan Keith Denney [1947] Director/Metallurgist/Welding Engineer; Jeffrey David Garner [1959] Director/Consulting Welding Engineer; Dr Nigel Knee [1956] Director/Manager; Professor Scott Andrew Lockyer [1966] Director/Technical Head Materials; Dr David John Mallaburn [1971] Director/Engineer; David William Millar [1958] Managing Director; Grahame Richard Nix [1958] Director; Paul Jonathan Tooms [1956] Director/Engineer; Stephen Edward Webster [1947] Director/Retired

Welland Medical Limited
Incorporated: 29 September 1987 *Employees:* 195
Net Worth: £10,302,138 *Total Assets:* £19,405,456
Registered Office: Cavell House, Knaves Beech Way, Loudwater, High Wycombe, Bucks, HP10 9QY
Activities: Manufacture of medical and dental instruments and supplies
Parent: Clinimed (Holdings) Limited
Officers: Suzanne Bryden, Secretary; Sean LEA Farbrother [1967] Director/Group Chief Executive; Samantha Claire Jackson [1966] Sales and Marketing Director; David James Margetts [1955] Director/Operations Manager; Christopher Donald Primett [1965] Director/Accountant; Mathew Daren Wynn [1977] Finance Director

Wellmode Limited
Incorporated: 3 April 2001 *Employees:* 2
Net Worth Deficit: £19,485,876 *Total Assets:* £57,800,000
Registered Office: Hadley Hurst, Hadley Common, Barnet, Herts, EN5 5QG
Activities: Non-trading company
Officers: Anna Victoria Kinsman, Secretary; Anthony George Bunker [1944] Director/Tax Consultant; Alexander Mahboubian [1972] Director/Designer

Welney Farms Property Limited
Incorporated: 10 September 1999
Net Worth: £11,679,861 *Total Assets:* £13,978,730
Registered Office: Hazlewell Court, Lolworth, Cambridge, CB23 8DS
Activities: Other letting and operating of own or leased real estate
Parent: Hazlewell Land Ltd
Officers: Roger William Cowell [1957] Director/Landlord; Rosalie Mary Orriss [1955] Director/Secretary

Wembley Multi Academy Trust
Incorporated: 10 July 2012 *Employees:* 149
Previous: Wembley High Technology College
Net Worth: £33,675,544 *Total Assets:* £35,774,840
Registered Office: Wembley High Technology College, East Lane, Wembley, Middlesex, HA0 3NT
Activities: Primary education
Officers: Harjagbir Kaur Bal [1959] Director/Headteacher; Jennifer Betterton [1987] Director/Solicitor; Christopher John Caulkin [1980] Director/Investment Analyst; Kishor Mistry [1970] Director/Charity Chief Executive; Councillor James Moher [1946] Director/Lecturer [Irish]; Roderic Henry Patrick Rennison [1955] Director; Bhavik Shah [1964] Director/Sales Manager

Wembley National Stadium Limited
Incorporated: 18 June 1997 *Employees:* 112
Net Worth: £161,159,008 *Total Assets:* £589,750,976
Registered Office: Wembley Stadium, Wembley, Middlesex, HA9 0WS
Activities: Operation of sports facilities
Parent: Football Association Limited
Officers: Richard James McDermott, Secretary; Mark Paul Burrows [1969] Director/Chief Financial Officer; Martin Richard Glenn [1960] Director/Chief Executive Officer; Jonathan Robert Sellins [1963] Operations Director

The Wensum Trust
Incorporated: 8 March 2012 *Employees:* 555
Previous: Hellesdon High School
Net Worth: £37,451,000 *Total Assets:* £45,096,384
Registered Office: Middletons Lane, Hellesdon, Norwich, NR6 5SB
Activities: General secondary education
Officers: Linda Christine Mortimer, Secretary; Rev Anne-Louise Alder [1963] Director/Clerk in Holy Orders; Neil Aylott [1977] Director; Gerard Joseph Batty [1961] Director/Headteacher; Carolyn Anne Baxter [1960] Director; Patrick William Gorman [1952] Director/Mining Engineer; Edwin Pearson [1954] Director; Mary Elisabeth Richards [1960] Director/Operations Manager; John David Smith [1958] Director; Daniel Thrower [1969] Director/Headteacher; Jason Richard Tipple [1971] Director/Brewer

Wensum Valley Hotel Golf & Country Club Limited
Incorporated: 8 November 2011
Net Worth: £4,161,316 *Total Assets:* £8,313,706
Registered Office: Wensum Valley Hotel Golf & Country Club, Beech Avenue, Taverham, Norwich, NR8 6HP
Activities: Retail sale of sports goods, fishing gear, camping goods, boats and bicycles
Major Shareholder: Executors Basil Charles Todd (deceased)
Officers: Bridgette Louise Hall [1972] Director/General Manager

Wenta
Incorporated: 8 August 1983 *Employees:* 44
Net Worth: £6,121,330 *Total Assets:* £11,234,375
Registered Office: Colne Way, Watford, Herts, WD24 7ND
Activities: Other information service activities n.e.c.
Officers: Simon Robert Arbon [1954] Director/Chartered Surveyor; Alfred Anthony Bond [1948] Director; Samantha Jane Chaney [1982] Director/Solicitor; Zoe Julie Hancock [1974] Director/Principal; Graham William Lane [1962] Director/IT Consultant; Paul Owen Layte [1980] Director; Peter Duncan Oxley [1976] Director; Helen Webb [1965] Director/Management Consultant

Wenta Business Centres Limited
Incorporated: 9 July 1990 *Employees:* 7
Net Worth: £3,022,185 *Total Assets:* £10,438,055
Registered Office: Colne Way, Watford, Herts, WD24 7ND
Activities: Development of building projects
Parent: Wenta
Officers: Simon Robert Arbon [1954] Director/Chartered Surveyor; Edward Christopher Jordan [1963] Director

Wentworth Holdings Limited
Incorporated: 8 May 2015
Net Worth: £6,000,000 *Total Assets:* £9,013,501
Registered Office: 3 Hutton Road, Shenfield, Brentwood, Essex, CM15 8LA
Activities: Activities of head offices
Major Shareholder: Richard John Hunt
Officers: Andrew Robert Hunt [1972] Director; Nicola Anne Hunt [1977] Director; Richard John Hunt [1942] Director

Wentworth Hotel Limited
Incorporated: 28 April 1947 *Employees:* 45
Net Worth: £8,124,050 *Total Assets:* £8,906,850
Registered Office: The Wentworth Hotel, Aldeburgh, Suffolk, IP15 5BD
Activities: Hotels and similar accommodation
Shareholders: Michael George Ashby Pritt; Jill Mary Graham Fowles
Officers: Michael George Ashby Pritt, Secretary; Jill Mary Graham Fowles [1938] Director; Annabella Valerie Jackman [1944] Director/Housewife; Michael George Ashby Pritt [1947] Director/Hotelier

Werner Access Products UK Holdings Limited
Incorporated: 18 March 2010
Net Worth Deficit: £10,924,000 *Total Assets:* £16,346,000
Registered Office: The Causeway, Maldon, Essex, CM9 4LJ
Activities: Activities of head offices
Parent: Werner International Poc GmbH
Officers: Geoffrey Robert Hartenstein, Secretary; James Timothy Caudill [1967] Director/Chief Executive Officer [American]; Geoffrey Robert Hartenstein [1961] Director [American]; Timothy Keith Lewis [1965] Director/Chief Financial Officer [American]; Nicolas Scott Platt [1962] Director

Werner UK Operations Limited
Incorporated: 10 February 2014 *Employees:* 238
Net Worth: £2,223,000 *Total Assets:* £10,370,000
Registered Office: The Causeway, Maldon, Essex, CM9 4LJ
Activities: Manufacture of other fabricated metal products n.e.c.
Parent: Werner Global Holdings, S.A R.L.
Officers: Geoffrey Robert Hartenstein, Secretary; James Timothy Caudill [1967] Director/Chief Executive Officer [American]; Timothy Keith Lewis [1965] Director/Chief Financial Officer [American]; Nick Platt [1962] Director

Werner UK Sales & Distribution Ltd.
Incorporated: 19 September 1968 *Employees:* 12
Previous: Abru Limited
Net Worth: £9,576,000 *Total Assets:* £20,798,000
Registered Office: The Causeway, Maldon, Essex, CM9 4LJ
Activities: Manufacture of other fabricated metal products n.e.c.
Parent: Werner Access Products UK Holdings, Ltd.
Officers: Geoffrey Hartenstein, Secretary; Paul Anthony Bruton [1957] Director; James Timothy Caudill [1967] Director/Chief Executive [American]; Timothy Keith Lewis [1965] Director/SVP Finance [American]; Nicolas Scott Platt [1962] Director; Robert Rosati, Director [American]

S.Wernick & Sons (Holdings) Limited
Incorporated: 14 December 1961 *Employees:* 34
Net Worth: £12,031,547 *Total Assets:* £57,941,668
Registered Office: Molineux House, Russell Gardens, Wickford, Essex, SS11 8BL
Activities: Activities of head offices
Major Shareholder: David Mark Wernick
Officers: John Joseph Jaggon, Secretary; Simon Mark Francis Doran [1961] Managing Director; John Joseph Jaggon [1968] Finance Director; David Mark Wernick [1957] Managing Director; Jonathan Samuel Wernick [1990] Director; Lionel Rufus Wernick [1928] Director/Chairman

Wernick Buildings Limited
Incorporated: 6 July 1946 *Employees:* 160
Net Worth: £9,252,364 *Total Assets:* £15,053,596
Registered Office: Molineux House, Russell Gardens, Wickford, Essex, SS11 8BL
Activities: Manufacture of other builders' carpentry and joinery
Major Shareholder: David Mark Wernick
Officers: John Joseph Jaggon, Secretary; Simon Mark Francis Doran [1961] Managing Director; John Joseph Jaggon [1968] Finance Director; Andrew Colin King [1967] Sales Director; Benjamin Boyd Wernick [1979] Director; David Mark Wernick [1957] Managing Director; Lionel Rufus Wernick [1928] Director/Chairman; Stuart Wilkie [1965] Managing Director

Wernick Hire Limited
Incorporated: 29 July 1959 *Employees:* 360
Net Worth: £65,317,612 *Total Assets:* £109,399,168
Registered Office: Molineux House, Russell Gardens, Wickford, Essex, SS11 8BL
Activities: Other accommodation
Major Shareholder: David Mark Wernick
Officers: John Joseph Jaggon, Secretary; Darren Paul Brown [1969] Director; Simon Mark Francis Doran [1961] Director/General Manager; John Joseph Jaggon [1968] Finance Director; Michael Thistlethwaite [1971] Regional Director; David Mark Wernick [1957] Managing Director; Jonathan Samuel Wernick [1990] Director; Lionel Rufus Wernick [1928] Director/Chairman

Wesley House, Cambridge
Incorporated: 24 July 2014 *Employees:* 5
Net Worth: £10,892,738 *Total Assets:* £11,038,986
Registered Office: Wesley House, Jesus Lane, Cambridge, CB5 8BJ
Activities: Post-graduate level higher education
Officers: Roger Paul Ashley [1953] Director/Retired; Rev John Charles Allanson Barrett [1943] Director/Minister of Religion; Michael Peter Briggs [1944] Director/Retired; Rev Stephen John Burgess [1949] Director/Minister of Religion; Revd Catherine Dixon [1974] Director/Minister of Religion; Reverend Stuart Jordan [1949] Director/Methodist Minister; Professor Judith Margaret Lieu [1951] Director/Retired; Elizabeth Helen Ovey [1954] Director/Barrister; Rev Julian Pursehouse [1967] Director/Minister and Chair of Methodist District; David Nicolas Scahill [1948] Director/Retired; John Michael Sharpe [1947] Director/Retired; The Revd Colin Arthur Smith [1955] Director/Minister of Religion

West End Homes Limited
Incorporated: 9 October 1990
Net Worth: £15,788,336 *Total Assets:* £32,745,056
Registered Office: 17 The Old Maltings, Hockerill Street, Bishop's Stortford, Herts, CM23 2ED
Activities: Other letting and operating of own or leased real estate
Major Shareholder: Iqbal Latif
Officers: Nasreen Latif, Secretary; Malcolm Roy Bass [1957] Director/Accountant; Nasreen Latif [1963] Director/Secretary [Pakistani]

West Hatch High School Academy Trust
Incorporated: 10 May 2011 *Employees:* 199
Net Worth: £11,230,000 *Total Assets:* £15,242,000
Registered Office: West Hatch High School, High Road, Chigwell, Essex, IG7 5BT
Activities: General secondary education
Officers: Lisa Catherine Barker, Secretary; Kulvarn Atwal [1974] Director/Headteacher; Stephanie Field [1954] Director/Teacher; John William Haley [1948] Director/Chartered Surveyor; Carl Frederick Hansen [1958] Director; Adrian Samuel Harris [1955] Director/Accountant; Sheila Jones [1958] Director/Private Client Administrator; Harpreet Kaur Kahlon [1979] Director/Cover Supervisor; Daniel Leonard [1978] Director/Headteacher; Matthew Armstrong Lopez-Dias [1970] Director/Web Developer Camera Grip; Marcella Lord [1976] Director; Nancy Janet Lycett [1967] Director; Melanie Frances Marsden [1994] Director/Teacher; Julie Ann Pearce [1964] Director/Clerical Officer; Stephen Barry Phillips [1949] Director; Mohammed Siraj Sait [1965] Director/University Reader [Indian]; Leanne Claire Smith [1968] Director/Catering Manager; David Paul Solomons [1955] Director/Teacher; Justin James Van Wijngaarden [1967] Director/Chartered Accountant; Bertrand Pierre Marie Florent Vandermarcq [1981] Director/Technical Officer [French]; Samantha Ann Vandermarcq [1970] Director; Sheila Weeden [1959] Director/Local Government

West Herts Community Free School Trust
Incorporated: 10 December 2012 *Employees:* 86
Net Worth: £10,876,478 *Total Assets:* £11,487,138
Registered Office: Lanchester Community Free School, Hempstead Road, Watford, Herts, WD17 3HD
Activities: Primary education
Officers: Gayle Cook [1966] Director; Angela Olasubomi Daniel [1975] Director/Head of Finance; Leonard David Gelernter [1945] Director/Judge of The Family Court; Martin Glick [1954] Director/Accountant; John Howard Harris [1956] Director/Self Employed Management Consultant; Gregory Holmes [1985] Director/Local Government Officer; Dr Phillip Mason [1987] Director/Lecturer; Isobel Louise Maxwell [1966] Human Resources Director; Kristian Alexander MacArthur North [1981] Business Director; Anne Lucy Punter [1952] Director/Retired; Amandip Sidhu [1976] Director; Randal Peter John Whittaker [1969] Bank Director

R.F. West Limited
Incorporated: 25 March 2008 *Employees:* 9
Net Worth: £7,770,861 *Total Assets:* £15,579,216
Registered Office: Westside Centre, London Road, Stanway, Colchester, Essex, CO3 5PB
Activities: Development of building projects
Shareholders: Daniel Ronald West; Gavin Andrew West
Officers: Jack West, Secretary; Daniel Ronald West [1962] Director; Gavin Andrew West [1964] Director; Jack Daniel West [1987] Director

West Norfolk Academies Trust
Incorporated: 28 February 2011 *Employees:* 825
Net Worth: £52,415,592 *Total Assets:* £59,114,756
Registered Office: Queensway, Gaywood, King's Lynn, Norfolk, PE30 4AW
Activities: General secondary education
Officers: Roger Keeble Allflatt [1941] Director; Amanda Ann Arterton [1959] Director; Kevin Andrew Baldwin [1964] Director/Self Employed Evangelist; Lesley Bambridge [1948] Director/Retired; Paul Bland [1946] Director/Retired; Nicholas John Daubney [1950] Director/Retired; Peter David Harris [1940] Director/Retired; Andrew Michael Johnson [1973] Director/Headteacher; Roger Livesey [1947] Director/Retired Teacher; Susan Lunnun [1954] Director/Retired Headteacher; Anthony Robert Yates [1955] Director/Local Government Officer

West One Technology Ltd
Incorporated: 31 July 1998 *Employees:* 166
Net Worth: £6,050,517 *Total Assets:* £14,308,900
Registered Office: 153 Brooker Road, Waltham Abbey, Essex, EN9 1JH
Activities: Other telecommunications activities
Shareholders: Kern Ronald Judge; Nicola Pauline Judge
Officers: Nicola Pauline Judge, Secretary; Kern Ronald Judge [1965] Director/Electronics Engineer

Westcliff High School for Boys Limited
Incorporated: 17 August 2010 *Employees:* 143
Net Worth: £22,175,968 *Total Assets:* £23,913,304
Registered Office: Kenilworth Gardens, Westcliff on Sea, Essex, SS0 0BP
Activities: General secondary education
Officers: Fiona Colwell, Secretary; Claire Jane Burden [1967] Director/Teaching Assistant/Supervisor; Charles Casey [1949] Director/Retired; Anthony John Cole [1969] Director/Solicitor; Fiona Louise Colwell [1974] Director/Solicitor; Ian Lionel Croxford [1953] Director/Queens Counsel Barrister; Matthew Kennedy Degrove [1971] Director/Chartered Accountant; Robert Dennis Galvin [1969] Director/Consultant; Jonathan Howard Gershinson [1964] Director/Chartered Surveyor; Steven John Johnson [1969] Director; Samuel Joshua Neagus [1992] Director/Teacher; Cllr David Attlee Norman [1943] Director; Michael Anthony Skelly [1971] Director/Headmaster [Irish]; Mark David Solomons [1963] Director/Consultant

Westfield Academy
Incorporated: 13 May 2013 *Employees:* 102
Net Worth: £28,316,524 *Total Assets:* £30,417,196
Registered Office: Westfield Academy, Tolpits Lane, Watford, Herts, WD18 6NS
Activities: General secondary education
Officers: Timothy Body [1967] Director/Teacher; Louise Everett [1969] Director/Retired; Andrew Leslie Farrer [1961] Director/Senior Marketing Manager; Bruce Mallett [1954] Director/Finance; David William Yuill [1960] Director/Civil Servant

Westgate House Developments Limited
Incorporated: 22 March 2016
Net Worth Deficit: £3,758,031 *Total Assets:* £39,558,556
Registered Office: 3rd Floor, Sterling House, Langston Road, Loughton, Essex, IG10 3TS
Activities: Development of building projects
Shareholders: Galliard Developments Limited; C.J.O'Shea and Company Limited
Officers: Allan William Porter, Secretary; Edward Azouz [1949] Director/Chartered Accountant; Stephen Stuart Solomon Conway [1948] Director; Jonathan Simon Goldstein [1966] Director; Rory O'Connor [1959] Director; Donagh O'Sullivan [1968] Construction Director [Irish]

Westlake Estates Limited
Incorporated: 14 January 1998
Net Worth: £10,508,914 *Total Assets:* £16,449,147
Registered Office: 148 Cranbrook Road, Ilford, Essex, IG1 4LZ
Activities: Other letting and operating of own or leased real estate
Major Shareholder: Devinderjit Singh Kataria
Officers: Inderjit Kaur Sethi, Secretary; Devinderjit Singh Kataria [1965] Director

Westleigh Properties Limited
Incorporated: 21 August 1991
Net Worth: £10,644,495 *Total Assets:* £12,320,530
Registered Office: Lion House, 36 Clarence Street, Southend on Sea, Essex, SS1 1BD
Activities: Other service activities n.e.c.
Officers: Georgina Baum, Secretary; Colin Baum [1956] Director; Georgina Baum [1960] Director; Anne Marcus [1956] Director; Anthony Robin Marcus [1956] Director

Weston Group PLC
Incorporated: 14 March 2001 *Employees:* 425
Net Worth: £84,676,000 *Total Assets:* £265,880,992
Registered Office: The Weston Group Business Centre, Parsonage Road, Takeley, Essex, CM22 6PU
Activities: Activities of head offices
Shareholders: Angela Ivy Taylor; Robert Paul Weston
Officers: Robert Paul Weston, Secretary; Michael William Alden [1967] Director; Stephen Paul Bickel [1967] Director; Martin Andrew Chapman [1957] Director; Richard James Downing [1942] Director/Solicitor; Jonathan Richard Lewis [1969] Director; Stephan Arthur Miles-Brown [1953] Director; Jane Elizabeth Stock [1967] Director; Andrew Richard Taylor [1972] Director; Stuart Richard Thomas [1969] Director; Robert Paul Weston [1955] Director/Chairman; James Gordon Young Wood [1960] Director

Weston Homes PLC
Incorporated: 21 May 1987 *Employees:* 378
Net Worth: £80,322,000 *Total Assets:* £270,049,984
Registered Office: The Weston Group Business Centre, Parsonage Road, Takeley, Essex, CM22 6PU
Activities: Construction of domestic buildings
Shareholders: Weston Group PLC; Anne Elizabeth Bickel
Officers: Laurence Nigel Holdcroft, Secretary; Michael William Alden [1967] Commercial Director; James Thomas Anderson [1958] Director; Stephen Paul Bickel [1967] Director; Martin Andrew Chapman [1957] Director; Richard James Downing [1942] Director/Solicitor; Steven Andrew Hatton [1983] Planning & Design Director; Jonathan Richard Lewis [1969] Sales & Marketing Director; Stephan Arthur Miles-Brown [1953] Director; Gary John Newsome [1978] Managing Director; Jane Elizabeth Stock [1967] Organisational Development Director; Stuart Richard Thomas [1969] Finance Director; Leslie Steven Trott [1962] Director; Robert Paul Weston [1955] Director/Chairman; Shaun Martin Weston [1990] Director; James Gordon Young Wood [1960] Director; Dawn Nicola Wylie [1986] Land Director

Westpoint Property Limited
Incorporated: 14 February 2000 *Employees:* 1
Net Worth: £2,901,105 *Total Assets:* £8,798,897
Registered Office: Kingsridge House, 601 London Road, Westcliff on Sea, Essex, SS0 9PE
Activities: Management of real estate on a fee or contract basis
Shareholders: David Edward Neale; Nicholas Patrick Neale
Officers: Nicholas Patrick Neale [1967] Director

Westway Services Holdings (2010) Ltd.
Incorporated: 2 July 2008
Net Worth: £771,939 *Total Assets:* £13,072,953
Registered Office: Artemis Building, Odyssey Business Park, West End Road, South Ruislip, Middlesex, HA4 6QE
Activities: Activities of head offices
Parent: Westway Services Holdings (2014) Ltd
Officers: Mike Bindeman [1958] Director [American]; Colin Andrew Stevenson [1963] Finance Director

J D Wetherspoon PLC
Incorporated: 25 March 1983 *Employees:* 38,384
Net Worth: £286,561,984 *Total Assets:* £1,476,313,984
Registered Office: Wetherspoon House, Reeds Crescent, Watford, Herts, WD24 4QL
Activities: Public houses and bars
Officers: Nigel Connor, Secretary; Sir Richard Gervase Beckett [1944] Director; Susan Alina Cacioppo [1966] Personnel & Legal Director; John David Hutson [1965] Director/Chief Executive Officer; Timothy Randall Martin [1955] Non-Executive Director Chairman; Elizabeth McMeikan [1962] Director; Harry Michael Charles Morley [1965] Director; Debra Van Gene [1954] Director/Executive Research Consultant; Benjamin Newton Whitley [1978] Finance Director

Charles Wharton Limited
Incorporated: 25 November 1954 *Employees:* 7
Net Worth: £10,259,784 *Total Assets:* £13,804,503
Registered Office: Winsford Hall, Stokesby, Great Yarmouth, Norfolk, NR29 3DG
Activities: Growing of cereals (except rice), leguminous crops and oil seeds
Shareholders: Edward Charles Wharton; Pauline Ann Wharton
Officers: Pauline Ann Wharton, Secretary; Edward Charles Wharton [1966] Director/Farmer; Pauline Ann Wharton [1933] Director/Company Secretary; Victoria Kate Wharton [1971] Director/Farmer

Wheat Quarter Limited
Incorporated: 2 December 2016
Net Worth: £9,818,563 *Total Assets:* £49,967,944
Registered Office: No 1 Hyde Way, Welwyn Garden City, Herts, AL7 3BU
Activities: Other letting and operating of own or leased real estate
Shareholders: B3 Living Limited; Fooks Property Company Limited
Officers: Jeremy John David Fooks [1965] Director/Chartered Surveyor; Pankaj Keshavlal Rajani [1963] Director; Alexander Gabriel Shelock [1977] Finance Director

Wheatland Cheese Co. Limited
Incorporated: 19 June 1984 *Employees:* 16
Net Worth: £9,537,600 *Total Assets:* £11,550,367
Registered Office: 3a Livingstone Court, 55 Peel Road, Harrow, Middlesex, HA3 7QT
Activities: Non-specialised wholesale trade
Officers: Jayant Manishanker Upadhyay [1948] Managing Director; Ravindra Manishanker Upadhyay [1950] Director

Wheatley (Buntingford) Limited
Incorporated: 24 July 2014 *Employees:* 6
Net Worth: £3,148,666 *Total Assets:* £25,767,456
Registered Office: Wheatley House, Dunhams Lane, Letchworth Garden City, Herts, SG6 1BE
Activities: Development of building projects
Parent: Wheatley Properties Limited
Officers: Colin Leonard Stewart, Secretary; Harvey William Baker [1950] Director; Martin John Foreman [1946] Director/Solicitor; Colin Leonard Stewart [1964] Director/Accountant; Geoffrey Simon Woods [1966] Director; Jonathan Peter Woods [1971] Director

Wheatley Group Developments Limited
Incorporated: 10 October 1961 *Employees:* 6
Previous: Wheatley Holdings Limited
Net Worth: £5,287,028 *Total Assets:* £25,292,056
Registered Office: Wheatley House, Dunhams Lane, Letchworth Garden City, Herts, SG6 1BE
Activities: Development of building projects
Parent: Wheatley PLC
Officers: Colin Leonard Stewart, Secretary; Harvey William Baker [1950] Director; Martin John Foreman [1946] Director/Solicitor; Colin Leonard Stewart [1964] Director/Accountant; Geoffrey Simon Woods [1966] Sales Director; Jonathan Peter Woods [1971] Construction Director

Wheatley PLC
Incorporated: 8 June 1964 *Employees:* 18
Net Worth: £1,424,765 *Total Assets:* £18,351,416
Registered Office: Wheatley House, Dunhams Lane, Letchworth Garden City, Herts, SG6 1BE
Activities: Buying and selling of own real estate
Parent: Aspenden Trading Limited
Officers: Colin Leonard Stewart, Secretary; Harvey William Baker [1950] Director; Martin John Foreman [1946] Director/Solicitor; Colin Leonard Stewart [1964] Director/Accountant; Geoffrey Simon Woods [1966] Sales Director; Jonathan Peter Woods [1971] Building Contracts Director

Wheatley Properties Limited
Incorporated: 12 April 1960 *Employees:* 6
Net Worth: £4,764,335 *Total Assets:* £12,295,192
Registered Office: Wheatley House, Dunhams Lane, Letchworth Garden City, Herts, SG6 1BE
Activities: Other letting and operating of own or leased real estate
Parent: Wheatley PLC
Officers: Colin Leonard Stewart, Secretary; Harvey William Baker [1950] Director; Martin John Foreman [1946] Director/Solicitor; Colin Leonard Stewart [1964] Director/Accountant; Geoffrey Simon Woods [1966] Sales Director; Jonathan Peter Woods [1971] Construction Director

Whirlpool UK Appliances Limited
Incorporated: 30 December 1909 *Employees:* 2,840
Previous: Indesit Company UK Limited
Net Worth Deficit: £8,816,000 *Total Assets:* £341,740,000
Registered Office: Morley Way, Peterborough, Cambs, PE2 9JB
Activities: Manufacture of electric domestic appliances
Parent: General Domestic Appliances Holdings Limited
Officers: Tetiana Pidhaina, Secretary; Marco Bellinzona [1970] Director [Italian]; Lucianna Raffaini Carvalho [1973] Director [Italian]; Camila Perina [1982] Director [Brazilian]; Tetiana Pidhaina [1981] Director [Ukrainian]; Andrzej Tuleja [1973] Director [Polish]

Whitbread (Condor) Holdings Limited
Incorporated: 9 November 2016
Net Worth: £498,235,008 *Total Assets:* £498,235,008
Registered Office: Whitbread Court, Houghton Hall Business Park, Porz Avenue, Houghton Regis, Dunstable, Beds, LU5 5XE
Activities: Activities of other holding companies n.e.c.
Shareholders: Whitbread Group PLC; Whitbread Guarantee Company Two Limited
Officers: Daren Clive Lowry [1970] Director; Matthew Yates [1977] Director/Lawyer

Whitbread Group PLC
Incorporated: 25 July 1889 *Employees:* 52,705
Net Worth: £2,815,600,128 *Total Assets:* £4,904,000,000
Registered Office: Whitbread Court, Houghton Hall Business Park, Porz Avenue, Houghton Regis, Dunstable, Beds, LU5 5XE
Activities: Hotels and similar accommodation
Parent: Whitbread PLC
Officers: Christopher David Vaughan, Secretary; Mark Anderson [1971] Director; Alison Jane Brittain [1965] Director; Nicholas Theodore Cadbury [1966] Director; Louise Helen Smalley [1967] Human Resources Director

Whitbread Hotel Company Limited
Incorporated: 2 September 1927
Net Worth: £205,334,000 *Total Assets:* £207,151,008
Registered Office: Whitbread Court, Houghton Hall Business Park, Porz Avenue, Houghton Regis, Dunstable, Beds, LU5 5XE
Activities: Hotels and similar accommodation
Parent: Whitbread Group PLC
Officers: Daren Clive Lowry, Secretary; Simon David Ewins [1969] Director; Simon Edward Jones [1976] Managing Director Premier Inn UK

Whitbread PLC
Incorporated: 1 December 2000 *Employees:* 52,705
Net Worth: £2,802,500,096 *Total Assets:* £4,892,400,128
Registered Office: Whitbread Court, Houghton Hall Business Park, Porz Avenue, Houghton Regis, Dunstable, Beds, LU5 5XE
Activities: Activities of head offices
Officers: Christopher David Vaughan, Secretary; David John Atkins [1966] Director; Alison Jane Brittain [1965] Director; Nicholas Theodore Cadbury [1966] Director; Adam Alexander Crozier [1964] Director; Richard Dunnell Gillingwater [1956] Director/Chairman; Christopher John Kennedy [1964] Finance Director; Deanna Oppenheimer [1958] Director [American]; Louise Helen Smalley [1967] Human Resources Director; Susan Taylor-Martin [1963] Director

G.Holmes White (Properties) Limited
Incorporated: 26 June 1942 *Employees:* 2
Net Worth: £2,857,320 *Total Assets:* £11,026,583
Registered Office: Ground Floor, 4 Victoria Square, St Albans, Herts, AL1 3TF
Activities: Development of building projects
Shareholders: Teresa Lorraine Baldwin; Kim Sarah Dutton
Officers: Tina Lesley Benjamin, Secretary; Ross Nicholas Albrow [1956] Director/Property Management; Russell Grahame Baldwin [1959] Property Director; Audrey White [1936] Director; Donald George White [1927] Director/Chartered Surveyor

Arnold White Estates Limited
Incorporated: 1 January 1937 *Employees:* 10
Net Worth: £17,439,820 *Total Assets:* £40,617,808
Registered Office: 4 Vimy Court, Vimy Road, Leighton Buzzard, Beds, LU7 1FG
Activities: Activities of head offices
Parent: Arnold White Group Limited
Officers: Paul Michael Denvir, Secretary/Director; Paul Michael Denvir [1964] Director; Ian James LEA Foll [1965] Director; Katie Groves [1977] Director/Solicitor; Jeremy Mark White [1963] Director; Matthew Charles White [1965] Director; Robert Geoffrey Williams [1949] Director/Chartered Surveyor

Arnold White Group Limited
Incorporated: 28 February 1992 *Employees:* 10
Net Worth: £21,836,396 *Total Assets:* £37,614,328
Registered Office: 4 Vimy Court, Vimy Road, Leighton Buzzard, Beds, LU7 1FG
Activities: Buying and selling of own real estate
Officers: Paul Michael Denvir, Secretary/Director; Paul Michael Denvir [1964] Director; Ian James LEA Foll [1965] Director; Katie Groves [1977] Director/Solicitor; John Slater-Fearn [1963] Director; Jeremy Mark White [1963] Director; Matthew Charles White [1965] Director; Robert Geoffrey Williams [1949] Director/Chartered Surveyor

White Lodge (Norwich) Limited
Incorporated: 12 December 2011 *Employees:* 2
Net Worth: £2,156,206 *Total Assets:* £8,385,525
Registered Office: Larking Gowen LLP, King Street House, 15 Upper King Street, Norwich, NR3 1RB
Activities: Other letting and operating of own or leased real estate
Parent: Joseph King Holdings Limited
Officers: Deborah Gertrude Clipsham [1951] Director; Terence John Gould [1952] Director/Solicitor; Neil Generald Alexander King [1956] Director/QC; Annie Phillips [1951] Director

Whitecliff Bay Holiday Park Limited
Incorporated: 18 March 1954 *Employees:* 84
Net Worth: £8,876,322 *Total Assets:* £15,145,498
Registered Office: IMEX, 575-599 Maxted Road, Hemel Hempstead, Herts, HP2 7DX
Activities: Holiday centres and villages
Parent: Away Resorts Ltd
Officers: Neill Timothy Ryder, Secretary; Carl Anthony Castledine [1969] Director; Greg Lashley [1964] Director; Neill Timothy Ryder [1976] Director

Whitehall Resources Limited
Incorporated: 15 November 2006 *Employees:* 87
Net Worth: £7,211,172 *Total Assets:* £18,607,244
Registered Office: 350 The Crescent, Colchester, Essex, CO4 9AT
Activities: Other information technology service activities
Major Shareholder: Tremayne Hall
Officers: Helen Langford, Secretary; Tremayne Hall [1970] Director/Business Executive; Ricky Knight [1983] Sales Director

Whitehill & Bordon Development Company Phase 1A Ltd
Incorporated: 28 March 2017
Net Worth Deficit: £573,000 *Total Assets:* £20,580,000
Registered Office: Gate House, Turnpike Road, High Wycombe, Bucks, HP12 3NR
Activities: Development of building projects
Parent: Bordon Developments Holdings Limited
Officers: Michael Andrew Lonnon, Secretary; Ian Michael Amdur [1963] Director; Lee Michael Bishop [1965] Director; James Edward Child [1966] Director; David Hill [1964] Managing Director; Raymond Anthony Peacock [1966] Director; Nicholas John Prior-Davis [1978] Director; Gary Silver [1970] Director/Physician; Paul Anthony Silver [1972] Director

Whitehouse Leisure International Holdings Limited
Incorporated: 22 July 2015 *Employees:* 47
Net Worth: £25,053,530 *Total Assets:* £30,991,480
Registered Office: Gloucester House, Bentalls, Basildon, Essex, SS14 3BX
Activities: Activities of head offices
Major Shareholder: Philip Anthony Setter
Officers: Antony Martin Brown [1969] Director; Philip Anthony Setter [1963] Director

Whitehouse Leisure International Limited
Incorporated: 8 September 1998 *Employees:* 3
Previous: Whitehouse Leisure Holdings Limited
Net Worth: £27,514,548 *Total Assets:* £32,217,508
Registered Office: Gloucester House, Bentalls, Basildon, Essex, SS14 3BX
Activities: Activities of head offices
Major Shareholder: Philip Anthony Setter
Officers: Antony Martin Brown [1969] Director; Alan Potter [1969] Buying Director; Philip Anthony Setter [1963] Managing Director; Mark Thomas Titterton [1961] Director; Ian Whittingham [1968] Buying Director

Whitestone Property Services Limited
Incorporated: 25 April 2017 *Employees:* 2
Net Worth: £3,663,985 *Total Assets:* £8,164,258
Registered Office: 74 Shenley Hill, Radlett, Herts, WD7 7BD
Activities: Activities of other holding companies n.e.c.
Shareholders: Pritpal Singh Millan; Rajpreet Millan
Officers: Pritpal Singh Millan [1971] Director; Rajpreet Millan [1972] Director

Whitfield Finance Limited
Incorporated: 11 March 2015
Net Worth: £6,118,800 *Total Assets:* £15,756,673
Registered Office: The Grange, Market Street, Swavesy, Cambridge, CB24 4QG
Activities: Activities of mortgage finance companies
Shareholders: Dennis Keith Whitfield; Susan Elena Whitfield
Officers: Dennis Keith Whitfield [1940] Director/Builder

WHL Investments Limited
Incorporated: 1 September 2016 *Employees:* 4
Net Worth: £2,692,512 *Total Assets:* £10,018,473
Registered Office: Prospero House, 46-48 Rothesay Road, Luton, Beds, LU1 1QZ
Activities: Other letting and operating of own or leased real estate
Major Shareholder: Darren Harrison
Officers: Darren Harrison [1971] Director

Wholesale Welding Supplies Limited
Incorporated: 6 December 1982 *Employees:* 42
Net Worth: £7,605,823 *Total Assets:* £10,329,870
Registered Office: Peters House, Orbital Centre, Icknield Way, Letchworth Garden City, Herts, SG6 1ET
Activities: Wholesale of other machinery and equipment
Shareholders: Adrian Richard Hawkins; Jennifer Angela Hawkins
Officers: Robert John Case, Secretary; Alexis Natashia Suzanne Bond [1983] Director; Robert John Case [1961] Finance Director; Lee Kevin Darton [1960] Projects Director; Adrian Richard Hawkins [1957] Director; Gareth Hawkins [1979] Director; Jennifer Angela Hawkins [1959] Financial Director

WHTC Ltd
Incorporated: 6 September 2012 *Employees:* 138
Net Worth: £3,435,016 *Total Assets:* £10,884,137
Registered Office: North House, St Edwards Way, Romford, Essex, RM1 3PP
Activities: Other business support service activities n.e.c.
Shareholders: Anthony Edward Chapman; William James Hughes
Officers: Anthony Edward Chapman [1962] Director; William James Hughes [1971] Director

Wickford Development Company Limited
Incorporated: 6 December 1963 *Employees:* 9
Net Worth: £41,005,924 *Total Assets:* £41,692,656
Registered Office: Wickford House, Hatfield Peverel, Chelmsford, Essex, CM3 2EH
Activities: Construction of domestic buildings
Major Shareholder: Brian John De'ath
Officers: Paul Andrew Tayler, Secretary/Building Manager; Brian John De'ath [1934] Director/Builder; Valerie Ann Death [1938] Director; Julie Susan Lewin [1968] Director; Caroline Ann Surgeonor [1957] Director

Wickland (Holdings) Limited
Incorporated: 24 December 1981
Net Worth: £14,327,537 *Total Assets:* £19,022,956
Registered Office: Lyon House, Lyon Road, Romford, Essex, RM1 2BG
Activities: Other letting and operating of own or leased real estate
Shareholders: David Michael Collins; David Michael Collins
Officers: David Michael Collins, Secretary; David Michael Collins [1963] Director

Wilcox Commercial Vehicles Limited
Incorporated: 13 November 2000 *Employees:* 121
Net Worth: £5,927,229 *Total Assets:* £9,755,909
Registered Office: Blenheim Way, Market Deeping, Peterborough, Cambs, PE6 8LD
Activities: Manufacture of trailers and semi-trailers
Parent: Wilcox Holdings Limited
Officers: Vito Ronzano, Secretary/Production Director [Italian]; Christopher John Bartlett [1963] Sales Director; Vito Ronzano [1959] Production Director [Italian]

Wilcox Holdings Limited
Incorporated: 15 November 2001 *Employees:* 121
Previous: R & G Wilcox Limited
Net Worth: £7,781,749 *Total Assets:* £12,389,194
Registered Office: c/o Wilcox Commercial Vehicles Limited, Blenheim Way, Market Deeping, Peterborough, Cambs, PE6 8LD
Activities: Other letting and operating of own or leased real estate
Shareholders: Christopher John Bartlett; Vito Ronzano
Officers: Vito Ronzano, Secretary/Production Director [Italian]; Christopher John Bartlett [1963] Engineer/Sales Director; Vito Ronzano [1959] Production Director [Italian]

Wildcat Acquisition Holdings (UK) Limited
Incorporated: 2 November 2011
Net Worth: £632,992,896 *Total Assets:* £2,814,381,056
Registered Office: Granta Park, Great Abington, Cambridge, CB21 6GQ
Activities: Activities of other holding companies n.e.c.
Officers: Glen Michael Donovan [1973] Director/Chief Accounting Officer [American]; Brainard Judd Hartman [1963] Director/Lawyer [American]; William Jacob Sharbaugh [1962] Director/Chief Operating Officer [American]

Ashley Wilde Group Limited
Incorporated: 3 February 1950 *Employees:* 113
Net Worth: £9,913,289 *Total Assets:* £18,226,848
Registered Office: Emmanuel House, Travellers Close, Welham Green, Herts, AL9 7LD
Activities: Wholesale of textiles
Parent: Ashley Wilde Holdings Limited
Officers: Ashley Leon Brodin, Secretary; Charles Bennett [1970] Director; Ashley Leon Brodin [1945] Director; Simon Dean Brodin [1972] Director; Robert Daniel Goldwater [1964] Finance Director; Paul Thoms [1965] Director

The Wildlife Trust for Bedfordshire, Cambridgeshire and Northamptonshire
Incorporated: 24 August 1990 *Employees:* 89
Net Worth: £20,104,810 *Total Assets:* £21,345,990
Registered Office: Tha Manor House, Broad Street, Great Cambourne, Cambridge, CB23 6DH
Activities: Activities of other membership organisations n.e.c.
Officers: Paul Christopher Mark Solon, Secretary; Dr Jennifer Mary Bishop [1961] Director/Lawyer; Anne Maarit Bland [1969] Director/Independent Business Consultant [Finnish]; Dr Samuel Fraser Brockington [1979] Director/University Lecturer and Curator; Dr Sharon Wynne Erzinclioglu [1959] Director/Research Associate; James Henry Dalrymple Fanshawe [1949] Director/Farmer; Sir Graham Holbrook Fry [1949] Director/Retired; Rebecca Jane Jarrett [1977] Director/HR Manager; Christopher Malcolm Lewis [1955] Director/Project Manager; Dr Ananya Mukherjee [1973] Director/Research Professional/Conservationist [British/Indian]; Paul Christopher Mark Solon [1949] Director/Lawyer; Professor William Stephens [1956] Director/Ecological Scientist; Rebecca Louise Stock [1971] Director/Category Purchasing Manager; Doctor Edgar Clive Turner [1979] Director/Researcher; Doctor Matthew Walpole [1971] Director/Conservation Biologist

Wilkin & Sons Limited
Incorporated: 5 April 1888 *Employees:* 590
Net Worth: £28,455,000 *Total Assets:* £39,123,000
Registered Office: Trewlands Farm, Tiptree, Essex, CO5 0RF
Activities: Other processing and preserving of fruit and vegetables
Officers: Roseanne Georgina Offord, Secretary; Scott Prain Goodfellow [1968] Director; Stuart Allan James [1957] Director/Chartered Accountant; Christopher Worth Newenham [1970] Director/Farmer [Irish]; Roseanne Georgina Offord [1978] Director/Certified Chartered Accountant; Walter William Scott [1950] Director; Peter John Wilkin [1940] Director

Wilkinson Sword Limited
Incorporated: 8 July 1889 *Employees:* 84
Net Worth: £49,581,000 *Total Assets:* £73,601,000
Registered Office: Sword House, Totteridge Road, High Wycombe, Bucks, HP13 6DG
Activities: Non-specialised wholesale trade
Parent: Edgewell Personal Care Holdings UK Limited
Officers: David Paul Hatfield [1960] Director/Executive Officer [American]; Colin Anthony Hutchison [1958] Director/Chief Operating Officer; Rod Ryan Little [1969] Director/Chief Financial Officer [American]

William de Ferrers School
Incorporated: 4 March 2011 *Employees:* 199
Net Worth: £5,983,845 *Total Assets:* £10,763,226
Registered Office: William De Ferrers School, Trinity Square, South Woodham Ferrers, Essex, CM3 5JU
Activities: General secondary education
Officers: Susan Newby, Secretary; Lucy Ann Arnold [1981] Director/University Management; Thomas James Attrill [1991] Director/Accountant; Richard Samuel Blott [1987] Director/IT Systems Manager; Paul Anthony Brough [1975] Director/Senior Manager - Banking; Dr. Nicola Jane Campbell [1966] Commercial and Sales Director; Sarah Cooper [1989] Director/Teacher; Ross Davison [1968] Director/Teacher; Derek Michael John Godfrey-Shaw [1966] Director/Retired; Alexander Leslie Johns [1989] Director/Teacher; Colin Marshall [1973] Director/Policeman; Deborah McGrath [1976] Director/First Aid Officer; Nichola Jane Newman [1981] Director/Senior Manager - Essex Police; Sharon Raynor [1974] Director/Teacher; Brenda Stannard [1949] Director/Safeguarding Consultant; Deborah Anne Warman [1962] Director; Scott Wilson [1974] Director/Communications Manager

S.F. Williams (Foils) Limited
Incorporated: 16 December 1957
Net Worth: £1,832,862 *Total Assets:* £11,608,287
Registered Office: 1 The Forum, Coopers Way, Temple Farm Industrial Estate, Southend on Sea, Essex, SS2 5TE
Activities: Other manufacturing n.e.c.
Shareholders: David John Watson; Paul Stuart Watson
Officers: David John Barnish, Secretary; David John Watson [1947] Director; Paul Stuart Watson [1983] Director

Willis Dawson Property Limited
Incorporated: 19 May 2008 *Employees:* 5
Net Worth: £10,965,519 *Total Assets:* £11,433,607
Registered Office: 20 Bridge Street, Leighton Buzzard, Beds, LU7 1AL
Activities: Renting and operating of Housing Association real estate
Shareholders: Nicola Jane Willis; Sarah Anne Willis
Officers: Christopher John Willis, Secretary/Director; Christopher John Willis [1953] Director; Roger Charles Willis [1950] Director; Simon James Willis [1979] Director/Planning Manager

Willis Gambier (UK) Limited
Incorporated: 6 October 2008 *Employees:* 43
Net Worth Deficit: £13,148,470 *Total Assets:* £8,279,756
Registered Office: Kingfisher House, 1 Gilders Way, St James Place, Norwich, NR3 1UB
Activities: Retail of furniture, lighting, and similar (not musical instruments or scores) in specialised store
Officers: Mohamad Aminozzakeri [1961] Executive Director [American]; Shan-Huei Kuo [1955] Director/Chairman CEO [Taiwanese]; Yi-Mei Liu [1957] Director/Vice Chairperson [Taiwanese]

Willmott Dixon Construction Limited
Incorporated: 19 July 1963 *Employees:* 1,341
Net Worth: £25,369,344 *Total Assets:* £275,884,160
Registered Office: Spirella, 2 Icknield Way, Letchworth Garden City, Herts, SG6 4GY
Activities: Construction of commercial buildings
Parent: Willmott Dixon Public & Commercial Ltd
Officers: Wendy Jane McWilliams, Secretary; Anthony William Dillon [1965] Managing Director; Graham Mark Dundas [1979] Director/Chartered Accountant; Colin Enticknap [1958] Director/Chartered Quantity Surveyor; Roger Mark Forsdyke [1962] Director/Chartered Builder; Richard Anthony Lee [1965] Director/Head of Human Resources; Wendy Jane McWilliams [1958] Director/Solicitor; Peter John Owen [1962] Director/Chartered Builder; Richard Nigel Poulter [1966] Director/Chartered Builder; Neal Douglas Stephens [1968] Director/Chartered Builder; Christopher John Tredget [1964] Director/Chartered Builder; John Frederick Waterman [1964] Director/Chartered Builder; Richard John Willmott [1963] Director/Chartered Builder

Willmott Dixon Holdings Limited
Incorporated: 19 May 1924 *Employees:* 2,062
Net Worth: £142,167,008 *Total Assets:* £486,071,008
Registered Office: Spirella, 2 Icknield Way, Letchworth Garden City, Herts, SG6 4GY
Activities: Development of building projects
Shareholders: Hardwicke Investments Limited; Walsworth Limited
Officers: Wendy Jane McWilliams, Secretary; Graham Mark Dundas [1979] Director/Chartered Accountant; Colin Enticknap [1958] Director/Chartered Surveyor; Michael Leonard Hart [1955] Director/Chartered Builder; Wendy Jane McWilliams [1958] Director/Solicitor; Jonathon Espie Porritt [1950] Director/Environmentalist; Christopher Julian Sheridan [1943] Director/Banker; John Frederick Waterman [1964] Director/Chartered Builder; Richard John Willmott [1963] Director/Chartered Builder

Willmott Dixon Interiors Limited
Incorporated: 1 December 2000 *Employees:* 200
Net Worth: £7,607,667 *Total Assets:* £39,203,756
Registered Office: Spirella, 2 Icknield Way, Letchworth Garden City, Herts, SG6 4GY
Activities: Construction of commercial buildings
Parent: Willmott Dixon Public & Commercial Limited
Officers: Wendy Jane McWilliams, Secretary; Graham Mark Dundas [1979] Director/Chartered Accountant; Michael Leonard Hart [1955] Director/Chartered Builder; Wendy Jane McWilliams [1958] Director/Solicitor; Kevin Neil Potts [1969] Director/Chartered Builder; Graham Patrick Shaw [1974] Director/Chartered Builder; Richard John Willmott [1963] Director/Chartered Builder

Willmott Dixon Public & Commercial Limited
Incorporated: 1 September 2006
Previous: Willmott Dixon Capital Works Limited
Net Worth: £24,180,512 *Total Assets:* £60,193,952
Registered Office: Spirella, 2 Icknield Way, Letchworth Garden City, Herts, SG6 4GY
Activities: Development of building projects
Parent: Willmott Dixon Holdings Limited
Officers: Wendy Jane McWilliams, Secretary; Graham Mark Dundas [1979] Director/Chartered Accountant; Colin Enticknap [1958] Director/Chartered Surveyor; Michael Leonard Hart [1955] Director/Chartered Builder; Wendy Jane McWilliams [1958] Director/Group Company Secretary; John Frederick Waterman [1964] Director/Chartered Builder; Richard John Willmott [1963] Director/Chartered Builder

Willmott Partnership Homes Limited
Incorporated: 4 July 1974 *Employees:* 313
Previous: Willmott Dixon Housing Limited
Net Worth Deficit: £10,141,205 *Total Assets:* £43,801,500
Registered Office: Spirella 2, Icknield Way, Letchworth Garden City, Herts, SG6 4GY
Activities: Construction of domestic buildings
Parent: Willmott Dixon Public & Commercial Limited
Officers: Wendy Jane McWilliams, Secretary; Andrew Fookes [1967] Director/Surveyor; Michael Leonard Hart [1955] Director/Chartered Builder; Simon David Leadbeater [1961] Director/Chartered Builder; Wendy Jane McWilliams [1958] Director/Solicitor; Matthew Anthony Organ [1949] Director/Chartered Builder; Richard John Willmott [1963] Director/Chartered Builder

Willoughby (880) Limited
Incorporated: 6 March 2015 *Employees:* 627
Net Worth Deficit: £1,673,000 *Total Assets:* £120,908,000
Registered Office: IMEX, Embassy House, 575-559 Maxted Road, Hemel Hempstead Industrial Estate, Hemel Hempstead, Herts, HP2 7DX
Activities: Management consultancy activities other than financial management
Officers: Carl Anthony Castledine [1969] Director; Gary Padbury Fletcher [1965] Director; Greg Lashley [1964] Director; Neill Timothy Ryder [1976] Director; Michael Edward Smith [1947] Director; Richard Peter Whitwell [1964] Director

Willow Securities Limited
Incorporated: 21 October 1992 *Employees:* 3
Net Worth: £5,017,146 *Total Assets:* £9,007,788
Registered Office: Construction House, Runwell Road, Wickford, Essex, SS11 7HQ
Activities: Other letting and operating of own or leased real estate
Shareholders: Terence Henry Bambridge; Shirley Anne Nicholls; Sarita Rose Martin
Officers: Charles John Bambridge [1993] Director/Property Development; Susan Carol Bambridge [1955] Director/Property Consultant; Terence Henry Bambridge [1935] Director

Wilson Connolly Holdings Limited
Incorporated: 28 December 1964
Net Worth: £138,352,992 *Total Assets:* £173,555,008
Registered Office: Gate House, Turnpike Road, High Wycombe, Bucks, HP12 3NR
Activities: Activities of head offices
Parent: Taylor Wimpey PLC
Officers: Michael Andrew Lonnon, Secretary; Colin Richard Clapham [1945] Director/Company Secretary; Michael Andrew Lonnon [1957] Director/Company Secretary

Wilson Connolly Limited
Incorporated: 2 January 1930
Net Worth: £2,712,000 *Total Assets:* £23,140,000
Registered Office: Gate House, Turnpike Road, High Wycombe, Bucks, HP12 3NR
Activities: Development of building projects
Parent: Wilson Connolly Holdings Limited
Officers: Michael Andrew Lonnon, Secretary; Colin Richard Clapham [1945] Director/Company Secretary; Sarah Judith Thornley [1985] Director

Charles Wilson Engineers Limited
Incorporated: 10 October 1978 *Employees:* 330
Net Worth: £65,606,392 *Total Assets:* £91,267,480
Registered Office: Pendragon House, 65 London Road, St Albans, Herts, AL1 1LJ
Activities: Renting and leasing of construction and civil engineering machinery and equipment
Parent: Matthew Investments Limited
Officers: Stephen Wallace, Secretary; Charles Hubert Gallagher [1959] Director [Irish]; David Andrew Gallagher [1960] Director [Irish]; Ellen Pauline Gallagher [1929] Director [Irish]; Matthew Gerard Gallagher [1968] Director; Graham John Pollard [1959] Director/Depot Manager; David Alfred Wilson [1937] Director; Mark David Dominic Wilson [1966] Director

Wilson James Group Limited
Incorporated: 7 March 2008 *Employees:* 3,031
Net Worth: £25,622,000 *Total Assets:* £51,979,000
Registered Office: Chalkwell Lawns, 648-656 London Road, Westcliff on Sea, Essex, SS0 9HR
Activities: Activities of head offices
Parent: Wilson James Capital Limited
Officers: Mark Hill Abraham, Secretary/Director; Mark Hill Abraham [1966] Director; Mark Robert Dobson [1971] Managing Director; Sean Kelly [1962] Operations Director; Anthony Palombo [1961] Director; Gemma Elizabeth Quirke [1972] Director [Irish]; Gary Sullivan [1959] Director

Wilson Properties (London) Ltd
Incorporated: 6 July 2000 *Employees:* 8
Net Worth: £40,167,744 *Total Assets:* £79,949,496
Registered Office: 8 Parkway, Welwyn Garden City, Herts, AL8 6HG
Activities: Development of building projects
Shareholder: Charlie Jack Wilson
Officers: Gary James Barton [1975] Managing Director; Charlie Jack Wilson [1990] Director; Paul John Wilson [1959] Director

Wilton & Bain Group Limited
Incorporated: 25 May 2017 *Employees:* 59
Net Worth: £1,286,083 *Total Assets:* £12,059,723
Registered Office: c/o Rostrons, Yare House, 62-64 Thorpe Road, Norwich, NR1 1RY
Activities: Activities of other holding companies n.e.c.
Shareholders: Benjamin Richard Latreuille; Jeremy Sinclair Lindsay Mobbs
Officers: David James Heron [1978] Managing Director; Ben Latreuille [1976] Director; Piers Marmion [1959] Director; Jeremy Sinclair Lindsay Mobbs [1975] Director; Oneib Saeed [1974] Finance Director; Warwick Alexander Gunnar Stacey [1973] Director/Headhunter

Wilton House Limited
Incorporated: 10 March 1986 *Employees:* 158
Net Worth: £17,809,914 *Total Assets:* £29,044,988
Registered Office: Wilton House Limited, 171 Adeyfield Road, Hemel Hempstead, Herts, HP2 5JU
Activities: Residential nursing care facilities
Major Shareholder: Nittianund Reekhaye
Officers: Vishwanand Singh Ramoutar [1968] Director/Nurse

Wilton Park Developments Limited
Incorporated: 7 May 2014 *Employees:* 3
Net Worth: £2,942,768 *Total Assets:* £41,221,760
Registered Office: Decimal Place, Chiltern Avenue, Amersham, Bucks, HP6 5FG
Activities: Buying and selling of own real estate
Parent: Bucks Developments Ltd
Officers: Nishith Malde, Secretary; Nishith Malde [1958] Director; Stephen Desmond Wicks [1951] Director

Wimpey Corporate Services Limited
Incorporated: 15 November 1995
Net Worth: £18,079,000 *Total Assets:* £19,428,000
Registered Office: Gate House, Turnpike Road, High Wycombe, Bucks, HP12 3NR
Activities: Activities of head offices
Parent: George Wimpey Limited
Officers: Michael Andrew Lonnon, Secretary; Colin Richard Clapham [1945] Director/Company Secretary; James John Jordan [1961] Director/Company Secretary

Wimpey Dormant Investments Limited
Incorporated: 31 July 1959
Net Worth: £31,245,000 *Total Assets:* £651,478,976
Registered Office: Gate House, Turnpike Road, High Wycombe, Bucks, HP12 3NR
Activities: Non-trading company
Parent: Wimpey Group Services Limited
Officers: Katherine Elizabeth Hindmarsh, Secretary; James John Jordan [1961] Director/Company Secretary; Michael Andrew Lonnon [1957] Director/Company Secretary

George Wimpey Limited
Incorporated: 3 November 1978
Net Worth: £1,073,544,000 *Total Assets:* £2,676,461,056
Registered Office: Gate House, Turnpike Road, High Wycombe, Bucks, HP12 3NR
Activities: Activities of head offices
Parent: Taylor Wimpey PLC
Officers: James John Jordan, Secretary/Solicitor/Company Secretary; Christopher Carney [1974] Director; James John Jordan [1961] Director/Company Secretary; Peter Timothy Redfern [1970] Director/Group Chief Executive

Wimpey Overseas Holdings Limited
Incorporated: 27 February 2001
Net Worth: £714,009,984 *Total Assets:* £719,470,976
Registered Office: Gate House, Turnpike Road, High Wycombe, Bucks, HP12 3NR
Activities: Activities of head offices
Parent: George Wimpey Limited
Officers: Michael Andrew Lonnon, Secretary; Alex David Green [1981] Director; Stephen Roy Impey [1957] Director; James John Jordan [1961] Director/Company Secretary

Wind Farm Holdings Limited
Incorporated: 26 September 2003
Previous: RES Wind Farm Holdings Limited
Net Worth: £9,735,000 *Total Assets:* £39,600,000
Registered Office: Beaufort Court, Egg Farm Lane, off Ststion Road, Kings Langley, Herts, WD4 8LR
Activities: Activities of head offices
Parent: The Renewables Infrastructure Group (UK) Investments Limited
Officers: Dominic James Hearth, Secretary; Caroline Elizabeth Gilpin [1977] Director/PPA Origination Manager; Steven William Hughes [1972] Generation & Asset Management Director; Mitesh Raj Patel [1982] Director/Group Financial Controller

Windcrest (U.K.) Limited
Incorporated: 6 September 1995
Net Worth: £11,685,602 *Total Assets:* £12,035,480
Registered Office: Unit 8 Abbey Industrial Estate, Mount Pleasant, Wembley, Middlesex, HA0 1NR
Activities: Manufacture of other electrical equipment
Officers: Nilima Patel, Secretary; Hansaraj Santuram Patel [1957] Director

Windsor Integrated Services Group Limited
Incorporated: 5 July 2006 *Employees:* 73
Net Worth: £4,192,216 *Total Assets:* £9,963,176
Registered Office: Unit 29 Childerditch Industrial Estate, Childerditch Hall Drive, Little Warley, Brentwood, Essex, CM13 3HD
Activities: Activities of head offices
Shareholders: Anthony Windsor; Katherine Windsor
Officers: Faye Windsor, Secretary; Marcus Geoffrey Brandon Sanders [1971] Director; Anthony Windsor [1971] Director; Faye Windsor [1975] Operations Director

Winfresh (UK) Limited
Incorporated: 16 May 1994 *Employees:* 91
Net Worth: £20,915,744 *Total Assets:* £35,262,428
Registered Office: High Cross Lane East, Little Canfield, Dunmow, Essex, CM6 1TH
Activities: Wholesale of fruit and vegetables
Officers: Martina Edwin, Secretary; Michael Alexander Church [1952] Director/Economist [Grenadian]; Bernard Cornibert [1947] Director/Economist; Montgomery Daniel [1954] Director/Government Minister [Vincentian]; Martina Edwin [1953] Director/Company Executive; Vanoulst Jno Charles [1932] Director/Farmer [Dominican]; Ezechiel Joseph [1956] Director/Government Minister [Saint Lucian]; Cleophas Regobert [1952] Director/Accountant [Saint Lucian]; Renwick Elsworth Adrian Rose [1948] Director/Retired Manager [Vincentian]; Cecil Frank Ryan [1946] Director/HRD Consultant [Vincentian]; Simon Emmanuel Kervin Stiell [1968] Director/Parliamentary Secretary [Grenadian]; Deles Alfred Warrington [1956] Director/Farmer [Dominican]

Winocap Holding Limited
Incorporated: 28 July 2008
Net Worth: £9,051,812 *Total Assets:* £9,055,529
Registered Office: Ground Floor, 4 Victoria Square, St Albans, Herts, AL1 3TF
Activities: Other business support service activities n.e.c.
Shareholders: Catherine Claude Germaine Judet-Roussel; Vincent Judet
Officers: Roberto Rodriguez Bernal, Secretary; Jean de Mestral [1963] Director [Swiss]

Winpost Limited
Incorporated: 21 November 1988 *Employees:* 3
Net Worth: £4,437,844 *Total Assets:* £9,470,990
Registered Office: 105 Ware Road, Hertford, SG13 7EE
Activities: Buying and selling of own real estate
Major Shareholder: Tek Chand Arora
Officers: Ashok Kumar Arora [1971] Director/Property Manager; Veena Kumari Chand [1947] Director/Administration; Tek Chand Arora [1944] Director

Winstanley and York Road Regeneration LLP
Incorporated: 22 June 2017
Net Worth: £16,848,000 *Total Assets:* £18,146,000
Registered Office: Gate House, Turnpike Road, High Wycombe, Bucks, HP12 3NR

Winter & Co. UK Limited
Incorporated: 1 January 1971 *Employees:* 31
Net Worth: £8,300,613 *Total Assets:* £9,825,453
Registered Office: Stonehill, Huntingdon, Cambs, PE29 6ED
Activities: Wholesale of textiles
Major Shareholder: Philippe Winter
Officers: Timothy James Stewart Edwards, Secretary; Christoph Peter Borer [1970] Director [Swiss]; Stephen Geoffrey Burdett [1956] Sales Director; Paul Davinson [1972] Sales Director; Timothy James Stewart Edwards [1964] Director/Accountant; Beat Paul Schreiber [1958] Director/Accountant [Swiss]

Wintertime Properties Limited
Incorporated: 24 March 2004
Net Worth: £2,621,393 *Total Assets:* £10,091,992
Registered Office: The Barn, 1 Watford House Lane, Watford, Herts, WD17 1BJ
Activities: Other letting and operating of own or leased real estate
Shareholder: Manoj Mahendra Raithatha
Officers: Sarojini Raithatha, Secretary; Manoj Mahendra Raithatha [1972] Director

Wisbech Grammar School
Incorporated: 13 June 2001 *Employees:* 129
Net Worth: £9,537,042 *Total Assets:* £11,139,702
Registered Office: Wisbech Grammar School, North Brink, Wisbech, Cambs, PE13 1JX
Activities: Primary education
Officers: Natalie Jane Miller, Secretary; Dr Dennis Barter [1944] Director/Consultant Paediatrician; Judith Alison Bodger [1951] Director/Education; Christopher Mark Stephen Goad [1982] Director/Chartered Accountant; Karina Simonne Albertine Hart [1959] Director/Consultant Community Paediatrician [Belgian]; Ian MacLachlan [1964] Director/Building Surveyor; Catherine Rebecca Mair [1968] Director/Veterinary Surgeon; The Ven Hugh Kyle McCurdy [1958] Director/Church; Elizabeth Christine Morris [1950] Director/Solicitor; Professor James Russell Raven [1959] Director/University Professor; Dr Quintin Kwing Kee Wong [1962] Director/General Medical Practitioner

Wisdom Toothbrushes Limited
Incorporated: 13 December 1993 *Employees:* 32
Net Worth: £7,754,000 *Total Assets:* £13,932,000
Registered Office: The Silk Mill, Haverhill, Suffolk, CB9 8DT
Activities: Wholesale of household goods (other than musical instruments) n.e.c
Shareholders: Julian James Edge-Partington; Stephen John Larder
Officers: Julian James Edge Partington, Secretary; Julian James Edge Partington [1955] Director/Accountant; Yoko Yamashita Edge Partington [1950] Director [Japanese]; Stephen John Larder [1964] Director/Marketeer; Foye Ann Pascoe [1967] Sales Director

Wise Trading Limited
Incorporated: 13 December 1988 *Employees:* 15
Net Worth: £8,364,867 *Total Assets:* £16,904,696
Registered Office: Long Drive, Station Approach, South Ruislip, Middlesex, HA4 0HN
Activities: Wholesale of wine, beer, spirits and other alcoholic beverages
Officers: Iqbal Singh Johal, Secretary; Balkar Singh Johal [1946] Director; Balraj Singh Johal [1948] Director; Iqbal Singh Johal [1954] Director; Jasbir Singh Johal [1953] Director; Sarnpal Singh Johal [1957] Director

Wivenhoe House Hotel Limited
Incorporated: 13 November 2009 *Employees:* 99
Net Worth: £8,783,701 *Total Assets:* £9,388,912
Registered Office: Wivenhoe Park, Colchester, Essex, CO4 3SQ
Activities: Hotels and similar accommodation
Parent: University of Essex
Officers: Alice Suzanna Barnard [1977] Director/Chief Executive; Anthony Stuart Cox [1974] Director/Hotelier; William Nicholas Dickinson [1963] Director/Hotelier; Professor Peter Albert Jones [1946] Director; Andrew Keeble [1962] Finance Director; Dr Dominic Patrick Micklewright [1970] Director/University Lecturer; Owen Bryn Morris [1961] Director/Registrar; Henry Murray [1939] Director/Hotelier; Christopher Peter Alan Oldham [1972] Commercial Director University Sector; Jane Mary Samuels [1964] Director/Project/Operations Manager

WJ Groundwater Limited
Incorporated: 21 September 1981 *Employees:* 149
Net Worth: £10,728,998 *Total Assets:* £15,310,471
Registered Office: Unit 5 Abbotts Business Park, Primrose Hill, Kings Langley, Herts, WD4 8FR
Activities: Test drilling and boring
Officers: Stevyn David Michael Harris, Secretary; Richard Michael Fielden [1964] Director/Civil Engineer; Stevyn David Michael Harris [1976] Director/Accountant; Dr Gary John Holmes [1970] Director/Engineer; Paul David Adinolfi Judge [1960] Director/Engineer; Dr Toby Ouvry Linfield Roberts [1958] Director/Civil Engineer; Paul Francis Turner [1975] Director/Engineering

WJ Management Limited
Incorporated: 14 July 1997 *Employees:* 248
Net Worth: £9,786,126 *Total Assets:* £15,991,835
Registered Office: Unit 5 Abbotts Business Park, Primrose Hill, Kings Langley, Herts, WD4 8FR
Activities: Non-trading company
Officers: Stevyn David Michael Harris, Secretary; Richard Michael Fielden [1964] Director/Civil Engineer; Stevyn David Michael Harris [1976] Director/Accountant; Dr Gary John Holmes [1970] Director/Engineer; Dr Toby Ouvry Linfield Roberts [1958] Director/Civil Engineer; Paul Francis Turner [1975] Director/Engineering

Wood Farm (Stanmore) Limited
Incorporated: 23 June 2011
Net Worth Deficit: £1,365,843 *Total Assets:* £18,215,322
Registered Office: 14 Oxford Road, Wealdstone, Middlesex, HA3 7RG
Activities: Development of building projects
Officers: Kiran Bhudia [1984] Director/London Property Developers; Dhiraj Dabasia [1984] Director/London Property Developers; Samji Shivji Patel [1956] Director/London Property Developers

Wood Green Animal Shelters
Incorporated: 13 November 1986 *Employees:* 208
Net Worth: £26,412,204 *Total Assets:* £27,560,376
Registered Office: Kings Bush Farm, London Road, Godmanchester, Peterborough, Cambs, PE29 2NH
Activities: Activities of other membership organisations n.e.c.
Officers: Colin Peter Alder [1944] Director/Retired; Angela Yin-Chiu Au [1967] Director/Chartered Accountant; Duncan Inglis Canney [1952] Director/Retired; Dr Steven James Carden [1972] Director/Partner; John Maurice Cousins [1945] Director/Retired; Joanne Day [1968] Human Resources Director; Pamela Lesley Gee [1940] Director/Kennel Cattery Proprietor; Dr Joanna Julia Lawton [1971] Director/Trustee; Lynee Povey [1961] Director/Accountant; Janet Mary South [1939] Director/Charity Executive; Jonathan Daniel Younger [1973] Director/Trustee

Wood Green Investments Limited
Incorporated: 3 July 2005 *Employees:* 2
Net Worth: £4,198,212 *Total Assets:* £8,237,548
Registered Office: Treviot House, 186-192 High Road, Ilford, Essex, IG1 1LR
Activities: Buying and selling of own real estate
Shareholder: Leslie Steven Gilbert
Officers: Leslie Steven Gilbert [1964] Director

Wood Hall Investments Limited
Incorporated: 11 August 1999
Net Worth: £1,951,365 *Total Assets:* £18,096,462
Registered Office: Wood Hall Lane, Shenley, Radlett, Herts, WD7 9AA
Activities: Financial management
Major Shareholder: Andrew Lynton Cohen
Officers: Iain Williamson, Secretary/Chartered Accountant; Andrew Lynton Cohen [1953] Director; Wendy Philippa Cohen [1950] Director; Iain Williamson [1972] Director/Chartered Accountant

Wood Hall Land & Properties Limited
Incorporated: 20 July 2012
Net Worth: £4,574,605 *Total Assets:* £28,376,944
Registered Office: Wood Hall Farm Office, Woodhall Lane, Shenley, Herts, WD7 9AA
Activities: Activities of head offices
Major Shareholder: Andrew Lynton Cohen
Officers: Iain Williamson, Secretary; Andrew Lynton Cohen [1953] Director

Wood International Agency Limited
Incorporated: 26 November 1984
Net Worth: £5,420,088 *Total Assets:* £15,587,165
Registered Office: Wood House, 16 King Edward Road, Brentwood, Essex, CM14 4HL
Activities: Agents involved in the sale of timber and building materials
Shareholders: Michael James Lamont; Alan Lamont; Alan Lamont
Officers: Valerie May Lamont, Secretary; Alan Lamont [1971] Director/Salesman; Clare Lamont [1973] Director; Michael James Lamont [1943] Director; Valerie May Lamont [1944] Director; William Peter Lindenberg [1973] Director

Woodford Heating Holdings Limited
Incorporated: 6 September 2013 *Employees:* 130
Net Worth: £8,846,079 *Total Assets:* £17,343,320
Registered Office: First Floor, Oakwood House, Oakwood Industrial Estate, Loughton, Essex, IG10 3TZ
Activities: Activities of construction holding companies
Major Shareholder: Roy Steven Alderslade
Officers: Roy Steven Alderslade [1960] Director

Woodford Holdings Limited
Incorporated: 23 December 1999 *Employees:* 409
Net Worth: £90,400,000 *Total Assets:* £209,200,000
Registered Office: 50 Fishers Lane, Orwell, Royston, Herts, SG8 5QX
Activities: Activities of head offices
Shareholders: Patricia Jane Neville; Mark Richard Neville; James Robert Neville; David Christopher Neville
Officers: Adrian John Peter Wilson, Secretary; William Struan McBride [1963] Director; David Christopher Neville [1969] Director; James Robert Neville [1966] Managing Director; Mark Richard Neville [1975] Director/Manager; Patricia Jane Neville [1943] Director

A & A Woodford Limited
Incorporated: 27 May 1983 *Employees:* 57
Previous: A. & A. Electrical Distributors Limited
Net Worth: £8,887,202 *Total Assets:* £13,066,474
Registered Office: 3rd Floor, Crown House, 151 High Road, Loughton, Essex, IG10 4LG
Activities: Non-specialised wholesale trade
Parent: A. & A. 2000 Limited
Officers: Ann Kathleen Warren, Secretary; Alan Michael Warren [1957] Director/Electrician; Ann Kathleen Warren [1956] Director/Secretary

Woodland Global Ltd
Incorporated: 18 July 1988 *Employees:* 248
Net Worth: £3,384,789 *Total Assets:* £20,482,866
Registered Office: 40-42 High Street, Maldon, Essex, CM9 5PN
Activities: Freight rail transport
Parent: Woodland Group Limited
Officers: John Peter Stubbings, Secretary; Robert Kenneth Snelson [1948] Director; Kevin George Stevens [1963] Director; John Peter Stubbings [1960] Director/Accountant

Woodland Group Limited
Incorporated: 17 May 2005 *Employees:* 499
Net Worth: £20,822,000 *Total Assets:* £53,996,000
Registered Office: 40-42 High Street, Maldon, Essex, CM9 5PN
Activities: Activities of head offices
Major Shareholder: Kevin George Stevens
Officers: Dawn Stevens, Secretary; John Peter Stubbings, Secretary; Kevin George Stevens [1963] Director; John Peter Stubbings [1960] Director

Woodledge Limited
Incorporated: 4 December 1995
Net Worth: £4,014,122 *Total Assets:* £8,275,650
Registered Office: 5 Elstree Gate, Elstree Way, Borehamwood, Herts, WD6 1JD
Activities: Activities of head offices
Officers: Eldad Aizenberg, Secretary; Eldad Aizenberg [1957] Managing Director; Naomi Braybrooke [1967] Director/Day Centre Manager; Daniel Cigman [1969] Director/Designer; Julie Cigman [1954] Director/Teacher/Writer; Dr Ruth Cigman [1951] Director/Writer

Woods Holdings Limited
Incorporated: 9 August 2001
Net Worth: £11,580,000 *Total Assets:* £48,876,000
Registered Office: c/o Flakt Woods Limited, Axial Way, Cuckoo Farm Business Park, Colchester, Essex, CO4 5ZD
Activities: Manufacture of non-domestic cooling and ventilation equipment
Officers: Emile Erasmus, Secretary; David James Pritchard [1966] Director; Gregory Robert Weston [1968] Director/Chartered Accountant

Woolpit Business Parks Limited
Incorporated: 29 February 2012 *Employees:* 7
Net Worth: £18,287,100 *Total Assets:* £24,020,712
Registered Office: Barrack Farm, Woolpit, Bury St Edmunds, Suffolk, IP30 9RT
Activities: Other letting and operating of own or leased real estate
Officers: Patricia Mary Baker, Secretary; Patricia Mary Baker [1946] Director; Robert Joseph Baker [1939] Director; Timothy Matthew Baker [1975] Director

Workout Limited
Incorporated: 19 September 2003 *Employees:* 7
Net Worth: £479,127 *Total Assets:* £13,325,661
Registered Office: 3rd Floor, Sterling House, Langston Road, Loughton, Essex, IG10 3TS
Activities: Other letting and operating of own or leased real estate
Parent: Galliard Homes Limited
Officers: Allan William Porter, Secretary; Keith Alder Barber [1962] Director/Property Buyer; Stephen Stuart Solomon Conway [1948] Director; Donagh O'Sullivan [1968] Construction Director [Irish]

Worldwide Fruit Limited
Incorporated: 25 August 1999 *Employees:* 327
Net Worth: £6,097,000 *Total Assets:* £24,804,000
Registered Office: Worldwide Fruit, Apple Way, Wardentree Lane, Spalding, Lincs, PE11 3BB
Activities: Wholesale of fruit and vegetables
Shareholders: Fruition PO Limited; Enzafruit New Zealand International Limited
Officers: Robert Andrew Hinge [1963] Director/Farmer; Peter Hans Landon-Lane [1957] Director [New Zealander]; Paul Mansfield [1960] Director/Fruit Grower; Lancelot Peter Morrish [1956] Director/Farmer; Bastian Oliver Von Streit [1979] Director [German]

Worstead Farms Limited
Incorporated: 8 October 1952 *Employees:* 8
Net Worth: £6,110,744 *Total Assets:* £9,510,763
Registered Office: Holly House, Smallburgh, Norfolk, NR12 9NB
Activities: Mixed farming
Parent: G A Paterson 1998 Discretionary Settlement
Officers: Alexander Thomas Paterson [1982] Director/Farmer; Bruce Robert Paterson [1985] Director/Farmer; Gavin James Andrew Paterson [1981] Director/Farmer

A H Worth and Company Limited
Incorporated: 17 March 1948 *Employees:* 383
Net Worth: £39,824,000 *Total Assets:* £61,458,000
Registered Office: Fleet Estate Office, Manor Farm, Holbeach Hurn, Holbeach, Spalding, Lincs, PE12 8LR
Activities: Activities of other holding companies n.e.c.
Officers: Mark Richard Henson, Secretary; Thomas Patrick Brennan [1975] Finance Director; Timothy John Cooper-Jones [1951] Director; Stephen John Ellwood [1957] Director; Martin John Taylor [1971] Director; Duncan Richard Worth [1965] Director; Stephen Tom Worth [1967] Director

M.J. Worth Limited
Incorporated: 20 March 1970 *Employees:* 11
Net Worth: £7,489,184 *Total Assets:* £10,008,585
Registered Office: Ivy House, Wainfleet, Lincs, PE24 4HJ
Activities: Growing of cereals (except rice), leguminous crops and oil seeds
Major Shareholder: Michael John Worth
Officers: Graham Scrimshaw, Secretary; Michael John Worth [1937] Director/Farmer

O.W. Wortley & Sons Limited
Incorporated: 17 March 1972 *Employees:* 22
Net Worth: £15,190,250 *Total Assets:* £17,831,720
Registered Office: Holmebrink Farm, 22 Thornham Road, Methwold, Thetford, Norfolk, IP26 4PH
Activities: Growing of cereals (except rice), leguminous crops and oil seeds
Shareholders: Andrew James Wortley; David Owen Wortley
Officers: Carol Butcher [1961] Director/Farm Secretary; Andrew James Wortley [1955] Director/Farmer; David Owen Wortley [1945] Director/Farmer

WPA Support Services Limited
Incorporated: 31 October 2003
Net Worth Deficit: £5,043,000 *Total Assets:* £19,869,000
Registered Office: Astral House, Imperial Way, Watford, Herts, WD24 4WW
Activities: Other specialised construction activities n.e.c.
Parent: WPA Support Services (Holdings) Limited
Officers: Ian David Hudson [1964] Director/Chartered Accountant; Rory John Murphy [1969] Director/Chartered Surveyor

Wren Buyerco Limited
Incorporated: 16 May 2015 *Employees:* 7
Net Worth Deficit: £25,434,450 *Total Assets:* £94,009,480
Registered Office: 32 Crown Road, Enfield, Middlesex, EN1 1TH
Activities: Renting and leasing of construction and civil engineering machinery and equipment
Officers: Francois Dekker [1975] Director [Dutch]; Jeremy Peter Fish [1965] Director/Chief Executive Officer; Greg Paul FitzGenerald [1964] Director/Chairman; Debbie Mantzouridis [1991] Director/Investment Executive; Stuart Russell McMinnies [1968] Investment Director; Julian Alexander O'Neill [1971] Director

Wren Midco Limited
Incorporated: 15 May 2015 *Employees:* 2
Net Worth: £21,730,244 *Total Assets:* £100,600,096
Registered Office: 32 Crown Road, Enfield, Middlesex, EN1 1TH
Activities: Renting and leasing of construction and civil engineering machinery and equipment
Officers: Francois Dekker [1975] Director [Dutch]; Stuart Russell McMinnies [1968] Investment Director

Wren Topco Limited
Incorporated: 14 May 2015 *Employees:* 282
Net Worth Deficit: £28,396,000 *Total Assets:* £200,296,992
Registered Office: 32 Crown Road, Enfield, Middlesex, EN1 1TH
Activities: Renting and leasing of construction and civil engineering machinery and equipment
Officers: Francois Dekker [1975] Director [Dutch]; Jeremy Peter Fish [1965] Chief Executive Director; Greg Paul FitzGenerald [1964] Director/Chairman; Jonathan Laloum [1986] Director/Investment Professional [French]; Debbie Mantzouridis [1991] Director/Investment Executive; Stuart Russell McMinnies [1968] Investment Director; Julian Alexander O'Neill [1971] Director

Wrest Park Limited
Incorporated: 26 August 2008 *Employees:* 14
Net Worth: £7,036,386 *Total Assets:* £22,351,964
Registered Office: 1st Floor, Sheraton House, Lower Road, Chorleywood, Herts, WD3 5LH
Activities: Development of building projects
Major Shareholder: Raymond Valentine Mawhood
Officers: Lisa Jane Ashton Jones, Secretary; Philip Ashton Jones [1964] Director/Barrister; Raymond Valentine Mawhood [1942] Director

A.G.Wright & Son,(Farms) Limited
Incorporated: 8 September 1950 *Employees:* 26
Net Worth: £11,277,492 *Total Assets:* £13,907,674
Registered Office: Badlingham Manor, Badlingham, Chippenham, Ely, Cambs, CB7 5QQ
Activities: Growing of cereals (except rice), leguminous crops and oil seeds
Major Shareholder: Nicholas Richard Wale Wright
Officers: Nicholas Richard Wale Wright, Secretary; Angela Christine Wright [1935] Director; Godfrey Richard Warde Wright [1928] Director; Nicholas Richard Wale Wright [1961] Director

G.R.Wright & Sons Limited
Incorporated: 25 June 1913 *Employees:* 115
Net Worth: £34,885,784 *Total Assets:* £39,198,168
Registered Office: Ponders End Mills, Enfield, Middlesex, EN3 4TG
Activities: Grain milling
Major Shareholder: David Andrew Wright
Officers: Lorraine Joanne Kaye, Secretary; Alan Cave [1958] Director/Flour Miller; Simon Robert Clack [1950] Director/Project Manager; Lorraine Joanne Kaye [1965] Finance Director; Julian Alastair Woodgate [1970] Director/Bakery Technologist; David Andrew Wright [1962] Director/Miller; James Wright [1989] Production Director/Miller

Wright Medical UK Ltd
Incorporated: 9 October 1996 *Employees:* 69
Net Worth: £5,477,221 *Total Assets:* £13,407,556
Registered Office: 18 Amor Way, Letchworth Garden City, Herts, SG6 1UG
Activities: Retail sale of medical and orthopaedic goods in specialised stores (not incl. hearing aids) n.e.c.
Parent: Wright Medical Europe SAS
Officers: Richard James Adams, Secretary; Peter Stuart Cooke, Secretary; Peter Stuart Cooke [1965] Sales Director [Australian]

Richard Wright Music Limited
Incorporated: 15 August 1972 *Employees:* 2
Net Worth: £12,520,923 *Total Assets:* £17,229,790
Registered Office: 5 Elstree Gate, Elstree Way, Borehamwood, Herts, WD6 1JD
Activities: Artistic creation
Parent: Ramogan Limited
Officers: Gala Wright [1970] Director/Designer; Jamie Wright [1971] Director/Property Manager

Wrist Holding UK Limited
Incorporated: 14 April 2011
Previous: Wrist Europe (UK) Limited
Net Worth: £39,997,000 *Total Assets:* £56,484,000
Registered Office: 3rd Floor, South Wing, St James House, 27-43 Eastern Road, Romford, Essex, RM1 3NH
Activities: Activities of other holding companies n.e.c.
Officers: Soeren Juul Joergensen [1974] Director/Vice President [Danish]; Robert Steen Kledal [1969] Director/President [Danish]; Anders Skipper [1967] Director/Executive Vice President and CFO [Danish]

Wryde Croft Wind Farm Limited
Incorporated: 27 September 2004
Net Worth Deficit: £6,705,000 *Total Assets:* £42,107,000
Registered Office: Beaufort Court, Egg Farm Lane, off Station Road, Kings Langley, Herts, WD4 8LR
Activities: Production of electricity
Parent: Notos Energy Limited
Officers: Dominic James Hearth, Secretary; Peter Edward Dias [1981] Director; Christopher Peter Gaydon [1978] Director [Hungarian]; Paul Stephen Latham [1956] Director; Thomas James Rosser [1985] Director

WTS Media Group Limited
Incorporated: 4 December 1995 *Employees:* 43
Previous: Welltrade Services Limited
Net Worth: £7,526,175 *Total Assets:* £25,686,730
Registered Office: 32 Bower Hill Industrial Estate, Epping, Essex, CM16 7BN
Activities: Other manufacturing n.e.c.
Parent: Glorious Solutions Limited
Officers: Susan Mor, Secretary; Ofir Mor [1969] Director/Sales Manager; Susan Mor [1969] Director/Office Manager

WWW Sunoptic Com UK Limited
Incorporated: 16 April 1996 *Employees:* 4
Net Worth: £333,785 *Total Assets:* £21,345,202
Registered Office: Regus Suite, Level 3, 79 College Road, Harrow, Middlesex, HA1 1BD
Activities: Wholesale of other intermediate products
Officers: Alan Roy Kentish [1966] Director/Chartered Accountant

Www.Nakedwines.Com Limited
Incorporated: 13 August 2008 *Employees:* 120
Net Worth: £2,487,000 *Total Assets:* £23,975,000
Registered Office: Majestic House, The Belfry, Colonial Way, Watford, Herts, WD24 4WH
Activities: Retail sale of beverages in specialised stores
Parent: Naked Wines International Limited
Officers: Alex Iapichino, Secretary; James Crawford [1977] Director; Eamon William FitzGenerald [1984] Director/COO, Naked Wines [Irish]

Wycombe High School Academies Trust
Incorporated: 8 April 2011 *Employees:* 249
Net Worth: £30,976,376 *Total Assets:* £35,518,004
Registered Office: Marlow Road, High Wycombe, Bucks, HP11 1TB
Activities: General secondary education
Officers: Dr David John Palmer, Secretary; Sharon Nadine Cromie [1965] Director/Headteacher; Michael Dollin [1942] Director/Retired; Richard Ivor Lloyd Jones [1940] Director/Retired; Stephen Thomas Jordan [1953] Director; James Gerard O'Hagan [1954] Technical Director; Malcolm Douglas Peckham [1946] Director/Retired

Wymondham Property Management Company Limited
Incorporated: 23 June 1998
Net Worth: £6,253,844 *Total Assets:* £15,272,892
Registered Office: The View, 35 School Road, Drayton, Norwich, NR8 6EF
Activities: Other letting and operating of own or leased real estate
Major Shareholder: Christopher Richard Sapey
Officers: Christopher Richard Sapey [1959] Director/Property Developer

Xaar PLC
Incorporated: 19 February 1997 *Employees:* 603
Net Worth: £147,184,000 *Total Assets:* £169,750,000
Registered Office: Science Park, Cambridge, CB4 0XR
Activities: Manufacture of electronic components
Officers: Camila Cottage, Secretary; Douglas James Edwards [1960] Director/Chief Executive; Andrew Charles Herbert [1960] Director; Shomit Ashok Kenkare [1970] Director [Indian]; Christopher William Morgan [1962] Director [American]; Margaret Frances Rice-Jones [1961] Director; Robin George Walton Williams [1957] Director

Xaar Technology Limited
Incorporated: 13 February 1990 *Employees:* 5
Net Worth: £43,650,000 *Total Assets:* £111,631,000
Registered Office: Science Park, Cambridge, CB4 0XR
Activities: Other research and experimental development on natural sciences and engineering
Parent: Xaar PLC
Officers: Camila Cottage, Secretary; Douglas James Edwards [1960] Director; Shomit Ashok Kenkare [1970] Director [Indian]

Xaarjet Limited
Incorporated: 23 May 1997 *Employees:* 453
Net Worth: £28,819,000 *Total Assets:* £151,696,000
Registered Office: Science Park, Cambridge, CB4 0XR
Activities: Manufacture of other electrical equipment
Parent: Xaar PLC
Officers: Camila Cottage, Secretary; Douglas James Edwards [1960] Director; Shomit Ashok Kenkare [1970] Director [Indian]

Xtera Topco Limited
Incorporated: 24 January 2017 *Employees:* 60
Net Worth: £2,004,485 *Total Assets:* £31,366,754
Registered Office: Bates House, Church Road, Harold Wood, Romford, Essex, RM3 0SD
Activities: Activities of other holding companies n.e.c.
Officers: Dr Stuart Robert Barnes [1953] Director/Chairman; Carl Michael Steve Harring [1976] Director [Swedish]; Dr James George Mitchell [1981] Director [Irish]

Yang Ming (UK) Ltd
Incorporated: 29 January 1997 *Employees:* 63
Net Worth Deficit: £71,830,496 *Total Assets:* £169,668,224
Registered Office: 210 South Street, Romford, Essex, RM1 1TR
Activities: Sea and coastal freight water transport
Officers: Simon John Williams, Secretary; Chao-Feng Chang [1964] Director/Shipping Manager [Taiwanese]; Hsien-Chien Chang [1973] Director [Taiwanese]; Yi-TA Wu [1972] Director [Taiwanese]

The Yare Education Trust
Incorporated: 28 July 2016 *Employees:* 472
Net Worth: £38,088,104 *Total Assets:* £43,439,720
Registered Office: Thorpe St Andrew School and Sixth Form, Laundry Lane, Norwich, NR7 0XS
Activities: Primary education
Officers: Angela Lorraine Durrant, Secretary; Ian Christopher Clayton [1957] Director/Headteacher; Anne Bothwell Gibson [1958] Director/Self Employed; Alfonso Joseph Gotts [1962] Director/Banker; Peter John Harwood [1949] Director/Retired; Owen Ventris Jenkins [1978] Director/Civil Servant; Peter James Lamble [1961] Director; Gary Steven Leverett [1957] Director/Solicitor; Dr Linda Evelyn Steynor [1947] Director/Academic/Retired; Paul John Tacon [1964] Director/Retail Stock Management

Yavneh College Academy Trust
Incorporated: 23 May 2011 *Employees:* 131
Previous: Yavneh College
Net Worth: £30,547,060 *Total Assets:* £31,446,916
Registered Office: Hillside Avenue, Borehamwood, Herts, WD6 1HL
Activities: General secondary education
Officers: Hayley Ann Fraser, Secretary; Daniel Iain Album [1963] Director/Fund Manager; Mark Elliot Frazer [1985] Director/PR; Richard Michael Gilbert [1969] Director/Solicitor; Rolanda Gail Hyams [1955] Director/Chartered Accountant; Roz Levin [1950] Director/Retired; Spencer Lewis [1967] Director/Headteacher; Doreen Morris [1946] Director/Academic Standards Manager; Susan Neale [1952] Director/Retired; Susan Annette Nyman [1956] Director/Chartered Accountant; Daniel Paul Summerfield [1969] Director/Investment Manager

Yazaki Europe Limited
Incorporated: 14 April 1980 *Employees:* 2,162
Net Worth: £358,226,112 *Total Assets:* £1,034,148,224
Registered Office: 1 Zodiac, Boundary Way, Hemel Hempstead, Herts, HP2 7SJ
Activities: Wholesale trade of motor vehicle parts and accessories
Officers: Bo Inge Andersson [1955] Director/President [Swedish/American]; Hiroshi Ichikawa [1956] Director/Executive of Business Firm [Japanese]; Masahiro Kanda [1955] Director/Managing Executive Officer [Japanese]; Junichi Kitami [1959] Director [Japanese]; Naoki Sugie [1958] Director/Executive of Business Firm [Japanese]; Munenori Yamada [1958] Director/Managing Executive Officer [Japanese]; Ryosuke Yazaki [1981] Director/Executive Officer [Japanese]

Yelcon Limited
Incorporated: 3 August 1961 *Employees:* 14
Net Worth: £6,036,076 *Total Assets:* £18,109,448
Registered Office: 1 St Mary's Court, Main Street, Hardwick, Cambridge, CB23 7QS
Activities: Buying and selling of own real estate
Shareholders: Scotfield Group Limited; Martin Rapley
Officers: Terence Joseph Padian, Secretary; Stephen Kenneth Holman [1957] Director/Chartered Surveyor; Terence Joseph Padian [1950] Director/Accountant; Martin Rapley [1957] Director

YMCA Trinity Group
Incorporated: 6 May 1998 *Employees:* 195
Previous: YMCA Cambridgeshire & Peterborough
Net Worth: £11,414,481 *Total Assets:* £19,060,000
Registered Office: Queen Anne House, Gonville Place, Cambridge, CB1 1ND
Activities: Activities of religious organisations
Officers: Neil Portor, Secretary; Jordan Bambridge [1994] Director/Student Engagement Manager; Dominic William Bowles [1961] Director/Management Consultant; Reverend Anthony Chandler [1943] Director/Clerk in Holy Orders C of E; Ian Malcolm Dow [1947] Director/Retired; Kay Elizabeth Hoggett [1961] Director/Coach and Counsellor; Julie Ann Horne [1960] Managing Director; Andy Lucas [1967] Director/Business Support Officer; Antonia Karen MacLean [1962] Director/Management Consultant; Simon Pickering [1983] Director/Charity Consultant; Mary Sanders [1946] Director/Self Employed Science Editor; Chris Wilkinson [1960] Director/Health Worker

Yomans (London) Limited
Incorporated: 19 March 1965 *Employees:* 2
Net Worth: £6,645,765 *Total Assets:* £8,925,338
Registered Office: 21 Jesmond Way, Stanmore, Middlesex, HA7 4QR
Activities: Other letting and operating of own or leased real estate
Major Shareholder: Michael Robin Sitton
Officers: Paula Sitton, Secretary; Michael Robin Sitton [1960] Director/Accountant

The Yonder Digital Group Limited
Incorporated: 18 January 2011 *Employees:* 516
Previous: Direct Response Contact Centres Group Limited
Net Worth Deficit: £2,017,496 *Total Assets:* £10,934,350
Registered Office: 2 Melford Court, The Havens, Ransomes Europark, Ipswich, Suffolk, IP3 9SJ
Activities: Activities of call centres
Parent: Hamsard 3515 Limited
Officers: Cyril David Marc Patrick Molitor [1975] Director [French]

York Apartments Limited
Incorporated: 21 May 2001
Net Worth: £5,396,739 *Total Assets:* £10,688,985
Registered Office: 88 Edgware Way, Edgware, Middlesex, HA8 8JS
Activities: Other letting and operating of own or leased real estate
Shareholder: Zeev Zi-Pear
Officers: Vidhur Mehra, Secretary; Anita Mehra [1953] Director; Vidhur Mehra [1975] Director

York House (Meat Products) Limited
Incorporated: 20 October 1970 *Employees:* 86
Net Worth: £12,638,726 *Total Assets:* £20,976,072
Registered Office: Shannon Place, Potton, Sandy, Beds, SG19 2YH
Activities: Processing and preserving of meat
Parent: York House Foods Limited
Officers: Ian James Affleck [1961] Director; Steven Hardy [1964] Operations Director; Duncan Marsh [1971] Commercial Director

Yorkshire Dales Country Park Limited
Incorporated: 31 March 2009 *Employees:* 3
Net Worth: £7,034,984 *Total Assets:* £9,524,737
Registered Office: 166 College Road, Harrow, Middlesex, HA1 1RA
Activities: Other holiday and other collective accommodation
Parent: Leisure Parks Real Estate (Holdings) Limited
Officers: Colin Crickmore [1958] Director/Businessman; James Robert Crickmore [1980] Director/Businessman; Maurice Sines [1962] Director/Businessman

H.Young & Co.,Limited
Incorporated: 12 January 1899 *Employees:* 5
Net Worth: £23,648,732 *Total Assets:* £35,964,352
Registered Office: Ayton Road, Wymondham, Norfolk, NR18 0RD
Activities: Activities of head offices
Major Shareholder: Peter Hildred Buxton
Officers: David Sean Smith, Secretary; Benjamin Anthony Beaugeard [1965] Human Resources Director; Peter Hildred Buxton [1960] Director; Robert Victor Buxton [1964] Development Director; Ian Peachment [1970] Director; David Sean Smith [1971] Financial Director

Youngman Group Limited
Incorporated: 3 May 2005 *Employees:* 25
Net Worth: £6,268,095 *Total Assets:* £13,653,707
Registered Office: The Causeway, Maldon, Essex, CM9 4LJ
Activities: Manufacture of other fabricated metal products n.e.c.
Parent: Werner Access Products UK Holdings, Ltd.
Officers: Geoffrey Robert Hartenstein, Secretary; James Timothy Caudill [1967] Director/Chief Executive [American]; Timothy Keith Lewis [1965] Director/Company Executive [American]; Chris John Owen [1961] Director; Nick Platt [1962] Director

Yours Clothing Limited
Incorporated: 11 January 1994 *Employees:* 1,104
Net Worth: £9,660,510 *Total Assets:* £26,820,168
Registered Office: Newcombe House, Bakewell Road, Orton Southgate, Peterborough, Cambs, PE2 6XU
Activities: Retail sale of clothing in specialised stores
Parent: A K Retail Holdings Limited
Officers: David James Preece, Secretary; Saeed Hatteea [1950] Director; Anna Maria Heather [1965] Director; Andrew Robert Killingsworth [1962] Director; Richard James Thurlow [1955] Director/Chartered Accountant

Yparho Investments Limited
Incorporated: 6 September 2002
Net Worth: £14,660,658 *Total Assets:* £21,981,840
Registered Office: 2nd Floor, Katherine House, 11 Wylyotts Place, Potters Bar, Herts, EN6 2JD
Activities: Activities of open-ended investment companies
Major Shareholder: Antonakis Chrysostomou
Officers: Chrystalla Chrysostomou, Secretary; Antonakis Chrysostomou [1941] Director/Hotelier

Yum! III (UK) Limited
Incorporated: 29 March 2012 *Employees:* 633
Net Worth: £13,050,000 *Total Assets:* £38,921,000
Registered Office: Building 2, Abbey View, Everard Close, St Albans, Herts, AL1 2QU
Activities: Take-away food shops and mobile food stands
Parent: Yum! Restaurant Holdings
Officers: Timothy Michael Colborn, Secretary; Regina Henriette Borda Heiniger [1973] Managing Director [Swiss]; Timothy Michael Colborn [1957] Director/Chartered Accountant; Neil Amber Dev Manhas [1978] Director/Accountant; Katherine Jane Mellor [1979] Director/Chief Capability & Culture Officer; Reese Edward Neumann [1977] Director/Chief Growth Officer [American]

Z Hotel Poland Street Property LLP
Incorporated: 12 July 2016
Net Worth: £15,058,413 *Total Assets:* £15,058,413
Registered Office: Aprirose House, 48a High Street, Edgware, Middlesex, HA8 7EQ
Officers: Manish Mansukhlal Gudka [1970] Member; Gareth Jones [1973] Member; Suraj Rashmikant Shah [1982] LLP Member

Zara UK Midco Limited
Incorporated: 10 September 2015 *Employees:* 4
Net Worth Deficit: £264,000 *Total Assets:* £24,890,000
Registered Office: Flamingo House, Cockerell Close, Stevenage, Herts, SG1 2NB
Activities: Wholesale of flowers and plants
Parent: Zara UK Topco Ltd
Officers: Peter Ronald Barnhoorn [1973] Director [Dutch]; Richard Capaldi [1960] Director/Accountant; Martin John Hudson [1957] Director; Michel Antoine Van Den Bogaard [1972] Director [Dutch]

Zara UK Topco Limited
Incorporated: 29 July 2015 *Employees:* 8,497
Net Worth: £26,195,000 *Total Assets:* £211,290,000
Registered Office: Flamingo House, Cockerell Close, Stevenage, Herts, SG1 2NB
Activities: Wholesale of flowers and plants
Officers: Sergei Spiridonov [1972] Director; Timothy Rupert John Stubbs [1967] Director

Carl Zeiss Ltd
Incorporated: 18 December 1954 *Employees:* 231
Net Worth: £12,744,000 *Total Assets:* £35,221,000
Registered Office: 509 Coldhams Lane, Cambridge, CB1 3JS
Activities: Other professional, scientific and technical activities n.e.c.
Officers: Daniel Spencer, Secretary; Paul Adderley [1965] Managing Director; Fabian Heller [1967] Director [German]; Dr Jochen Peter [1975] Director/Chairman [German]

Carl Zeiss Microscopy Limited
Incorporated: 5 May 1995 *Employees:* 94
Net Worth: £23,943,000 *Total Assets:* £36,463,000
Registered Office: 509 Coldhams Lane, Cambridge, CB1 3JS
Activities: Manufacture of optical precision instruments
Officers: Vincent Paul Lynch, Secretary; Paul Adderley [1965] Director; Michael Albiez [1976] Director [German]; Daniel Aldridge [1977] Director; Allister McBride [1967] Business Development Director

Zellis UK Limited
Incorporated: 25 September 1981 *Employees:* 1,065
Previous: NorthgateArinso UK Limited
Net Worth: £24,510,000 *Total Assets:* £198,071,008
Registered Office: Peoplebuilding 2, Peoplebuilding Estate, Maylands Avenue, Hemel Hempstead Industrial Estate, Hemel Hempstead, Herts, HP2 4NW
Activities: Other software publishing
Parent: Colour Bidco Limited
Officers: Elizabeth Leppard, Secretary; John Richard Martin Petter [1970] Director; Nicholas Paul Wain [1972] Director

Zenith Hygiene Group Limited
Incorporated: 25 September 2008 *Employees:* 504
Previous: Zenith Hygiene Group PLC
Net Worth: £13,743,000 *Total Assets:* £47,140,000
Registered Office: Zenith House, A1(M) Business, Dixons Hill Road, Welham Green, Herts, AL9 7JE
Activities: Manufacture of soap and detergents
Parent: BCPE Diamond UK Holdco Limited
Officers: Alison Pettitt, Secretary; Simon Peter Bower [1964] Director/Accountant; Michael James Chapman [1961] Director; Ringo Daisley Francis [1955] Director; Alexander Arthur MacDonald [1953] Director; Alison Jane Pettitt [1967] Finance Director; John-Paul Surdo [1984] Director [American]

Zenith Hygiene Systems Limited
Incorporated: 15 May 1996 *Employees:* 502
Net Worth: £749,000 *Total Assets:* £32,489,000
Registered Office: Zenith House, A1(M) Business Centre, Dixons Hill Road, Welham Green, Herts, AL9 7JE
Activities: Manufacture of soap and detergents
Parent: Zenith Hygiene Food and Beverage Limited
Officers: Tony Clough [1964] Technical Director; Warren Edmondson [1982] Sales and Marketing Director; Colin Kenneth Fogarty [1958] Director; Ringo Daisley Francis [1955] Director/Chief Executive Officer; Bakhtiar Hanan [1971] Group Purchasing Director; James Duncan Hannaway [1976] Operations Director; Jennifer James [1960] HR Director; Derek John Lafbery [1968] Director; Rakesh Patel [1971] IT Director; Alison Jane Pettitt [1967] Finance Director

Zenith Multi Academy Trust
Incorporated: 10 March 2011 *Employees:* 376
Previous: The KJS Academy Trust
Net Worth: £25,647,812 *Total Assets:* £32,310,996
Registered Office: c/o The King John School, Shipwrights Drive, Thundersley, Benfleet, Essex, SS7 1RQ
Activities: General secondary education
Officers: Sarah Hanmore, Secretary; Greg David Barsby [1972] Director/Contract Manager; Jamie Bell [1975] Director/Headteacher; Dr Katrina Elizabeth Bentley [1949] Director/Retired; Alan Evan Davies [1961] Director/Risk Manager; Sarah Foster [1967] Director/Regulator; John Marchant [1953] Director/Retired; Stewart Victor Taylor [1964] Director/Self Employed; Dr Margaret Melrose Wilson [1957] Director/Headteacher

Zest Living Limited
Incorporated: 1 October 1982 *Employees:* 3
Net Worth: £3,765,521 *Total Assets:* £20,862,288
Registered Office: 4 Elstree Gate, Elstree Way, Borehamwood, Herts, WD6 1JD
Activities: Other letting and operating of own or leased real estate
Officers: Ronan Patrick Murphy, Secretary; Daniel Gerard Durkan [1964] Director [Irish]; Ronan Patrick Murphy [1969] Director/Chartered Accountant [Irish]

Zian Hi-Tech (U.K.) Limited
Incorporated: 22 June 1998
Net Worth Deficit: £17,155 *Total Assets:* £13,352,515
Registered Office: Mulberry Cottage, Clamp Hill, Stanmore, Middlesex, HA7 3JQ
Activities: Wholesale of textiles
Major Shareholder: Haian Ma
Officers: Jianhua Huang, Secretary; Haian Ma [1966] Director/Importer and Exporter

Ziegler UK Limited
Incorporated: 25 November 2005 *Employees:* 105
Net Worth: £3,829,453 *Total Assets:* £16,594,064
Registered Office: 609 London Road, Grays, Essex, RM20 3BJ
Activities: Other service activities incidental to land transportation, n.e.c.
Parent: Eaglets Limited
Officers: William Geoffrey Craig, Secretary; William Geoffrey Craig [1963] Director/Chartered Management Accountant; Diane Govaerts [1984] Director [Belgian]; Lee James Marshall [1969] Director; Alain Robert Ziegler [1956] Director [Swiss]

Ziji Productions Limited
Incorporated: 18 July 2000 *Employees:* 2
Net Worth: £9,331,060 *Total Assets:* £11,230,180
Registered Office: 5 Elstree Gate, Elstree Way, Borehamwood, Herts, WD6 1JD
Activities: Other service activities n.e.c.
Shareholders: Leila Ansari; Francis George Roddam
Officers: Samantha Hill, Secretary; Leila Ansari [1973] Director [German]; Francis George Roddam [1946] Director

Zip Heaters (UK) Ltd
Incorporated: 24 September 1991 *Employees:* 196
Net Worth: £13,581,660 *Total Assets:* £21,717,238
Registered Office: 14-15 Bertie Ward Way, Dereham, Norfolk, NR19 1TE
Activities: Other manufacturing n.e.c.
Parent: Al Aqua Zip UK Limited
Officers: Jamie Christian Kent, Secretary; Tracey Ann Bamber [1969] Managing Director; Stephen Paul Dolahenty [1970] Director [Australian]; John Anthony Doumani [1957] Director [Australian]; Sarah Anne Williams [1974] HR Director

This page is intentionally left blank

Standard Industrial Classification

01110 Growing of cereals (except rice), leguminous crops and oil seeds [108]

Abbots Ripton Farming Co Ltd
Abbotsley Farms Limited
Abington Farms Limited
Agreserves Limited
Albanwise Limited
J Alston & Sons Limited
Angloflora Farms Limited
Antas Limited
L.C.F.Arthey & Sons Limited
Ascott Farms Limited
J.L. Ashby & Co Ltd
M.Baker Produce Limited
Benacre Company
Bithia Limited
R. Bratley (Quadring) Limited
Burrough Court Estate Limited
C. J. H. Farming Limited
Camfield Estate Co Ltd
C.W. & J. Cargill Limited
R.G. Carter Farms Limited
Caudwell Farms
Chaldean Estate Limited
Chilton Home Farms Ltd
Chivers Farms Limited
Cokenach Limited
E.D. & A.D. Cooke, Bourne (Farms)
Hugh Crane Limited
Maurice Crouch (Growers) Ltd
G.W. Daniels and Son Limited
C.E. Davidson Farms Ltd.
Dawe Estates Limited
Dry Drayton Estate Limited
P.J. Duffy & Son (Farms) Ltd
F.H.Easton Limited
Ellis Bros (Contractors) Ltd
Exagris Limited
A.E. & W.A.Farr Limited
D.J.Fisher (Farms) Limited
Gibbons (Holdings) Limited
Geo. E. Gittus & Sons Limited
Gower Acres Limited
J W Grant Co
Gray & Sons (Chelmsford) Ltd
Greenheath Farming Co Ltd
Greens Farming Limited
Hardys Farm Limited
Fred Hartley (Estates) Ltd
Hay Farming Limited
A. & E. G. Heading Limited
Frederick Hiam,Limited
E. Hobbs (Farms) Limited
Richard Johnston Limited
KWS UK Limited
J H & A J King Farms Limited
LDC (Boston) Limited
R.A. Latta (Farms) Limited
C.J.C. Lee (Saxthorpe) Ltd
Loose Hall Farm Limited
Marblelane Limited
Geoffrey Mason Limited
Maurice Mason Limited
Geoffrey Mayhew Farms Limited
Monsanto UK Limited
NIAB.
Newcome-Baker Farms Limited
Newfields Agricultural Holdings Ltd
Norfolk Farm Produce Limited
OAT 2012 Limited
P J M Farms Limited
Padfield (Hayleys) Limited
G.H. Parker (North Cotes) Ltd
C.W.Parker (Wainfleet) Ltd
Pemberton Farms (Holdings) Ltd
Pemberton Farms Limited
Pengethley Potatoes Limited
Porter and Makins Limited
Proctor Bros. (Long Sutton) Ltd
R.B.R. (Crops) Limited
Rattlerow Farms Limited
Richardson & Cock Limited
A Russell (Farmers) Limited
SJR Farming Limited
Salperton Park Estate Limited
D.H.Sanderson and Son Limited
Sandfields Farms Limited
John Saul Limited
G.S. Shropshire & Sons Ltd
J.B Shropshire & Sons Limited
Smith Farms (Clacton) Limited
P J Southgate Limited
St Paul's Walden Bury Estate Co Ltd
Stody Estate Limited
Stratton Hall Farms Limited
Strutt and Parker (Farms),Limited
George Tanner (Shalford) Ltd
O.A.Taylor & Sons Bulbs Ltd
Tharros Limited
Thurlow Estate Farms Limited
John Tinney & Co Limited
R. C. Tinsley Limited
R.H.Topham & Sons Limited
Troston Farms Limited
Waldersey Farms Limited
Ward Farming Limited
Charles Wharton Limited
M.J. Worth Limited
O.W. Wortley & Sons Limited
A.G.Wright & Son,(Farms) Ltd

01130 Growing of vegetables and melons, roots and tubers [31]

Abbots Ripton Farming Co Ltd
Abington Farms Limited
Allpress Farms Limited
Angloflora Farms Limited
Alan Bartlett & Sons (Chatteris)
R.G. Carter Farms Limited
T.H.Clements & Son Limited
Maurice Crouch (Growers) Ltd
Emmett UK Limited
G's Fresh Beetroot Limited
G's Fresh Limited
G's Group Holdings Limited
G's Growers Limited
Gower Acres Limited
Greens Farming Limited
Greenseed International Ltd
Greenshoots Limited
Greenvale AP Limited
Frederick Hiam,Limited
Keepstem Limited
Lincolnshire Field Products Ltd
OAT 2012 Limited
J.E.Piccaver & Co. (Gedney Marsh)
Proctor Bros. (Long Sutton) Ltd
R.B.R. (Crops) Limited
Rowe Farming Limited
John Saul Limited
Staples Brothers Limited
Stody Estate Limited
O.A.Taylor & Sons Bulbs Ltd
Tompsett Burgess Growers Ltd

01140 Growing of sugar cane

Angloflora Farms Limited
Gower Acres Limited

01190 Growing of other non-perennial crops

Abbey View Produce Limited
Greenyard Flowers UK Ltd

01240 Growing of pome fruits and stone fruits

Boxford (Suffolk) Farms Ltd

01250 Growing of other tree and bush fruits and nuts

Place UK Limited

01290 Growing of other perennial crops

Greenyard Flowers UK Ltd
Place UK Limited

01300 Plant propagation

Greenseed International Ltd

01410 Raising of dairy cattle

Bowes Farms Limited
Chilton Home Farms Ltd
Smith Farms (Clacton) Limited

01420 Raising of other cattle and buffaloes

Abington Farms Limited
Chilton Home Farms Ltd

01430 Raising of horses and other equines

Cheveley Park Stud Limited
Essafinaat UK Limited
Hascombe & Valiant Stud Ltd
Juddmonte Farms Limited
Newsells Park Stud Limited
Rabbah Bloodstock Limited
Redwings Horse Sanctuary

01450 Raising of sheep and goats

Hilborough Farms Limited
R. C. Tinsley Limited

01460 Raising of swine and pigs

Geo. E. Gittus & Sons Limited
Hawkes Limited
Norfolk Free Range Limited
Rattlerow Farms Limited

01470 Raising of poultry

R.G. Boyce Limited
Cobb Europe Limited
A.E. & W.A.Farr Limited
Green Label Poultry Limited
Newcome-Baker Farms Limited
Traditional Norfolk Poultry Ltd

01490 Raising of other animals

Bioline Agrosciences Limited

01500 Mixed farming [29]

Abington Group Limited
Alterra Farms Limited
Averys (Radnage) Limited
The C. Alma Baker Trust
Beckhithe Farms Limited
David Black & Son Limited
Bondgrip Limited
S Chaplin Holdings Limited
Chilton Home Farms Ltd
Countryside Restoration Trust
A.R. Craven Farms Limited
Maurice Crouch (Growers) Ltd
Elveden Farms Limited
Farcet Fen Limited
Fristling Hall Farm Limited
Heathpatch Limited
Wm.Kerr (Farms) Limited
Lord Rayleigh's Farms Limited
PJHP Limited
E.W.Pepper Limited
H.R. Philpot & Son (Barleylands)
Paul Rackham Limited
Raynham Farm Co Ltd
Hilary Russell Group Ltd
Smith Farms (Clacton) Limited
St.Lawrence Hall Farms Limited
Tendring Farms Limited
Thomson Sawmills Holdings Ltd
Worstead Farms Limited

01610 Support activities for crop production [15]

A. F. Machinery Limited
COFCO International UK Ltd
G's Growers Limited
Geo. E. Gittus & Sons Limited
Greens Farming Limited
Greens of Soham Limited
Greenseed International Ltd
Hutchinson Group Limited
H.L. Hutchinson Limited
Karsten UK Limited
Lawes Agricultural Trust
NIAB.
Pro Cam CP Limited
Pro Cam Europe Limited
Tompsett Holdings Limited

01629 Support activities for animal production (other than farm animal boarding)

Lawes Agricultural Trust

01630 Post-harvest crop activities

Greenvale AP Limited
Greenyard Flowers UK Ltd
Smith Farms (Clacton) Limited

01700 Hunting, trapping and related service activities

R.G. Carter Farms Limited

02100 Silviculture and other forestry activities

Benacre Company
Countryside Restoration Trust
Elveden Farms Limited
Grimsthorpe & Drummond Castle Trust

02400 Support services to forestry

Gristwood and Toms Limited

03210 Marine aquaculture

Tropical Marine Centre Limited

06100 Extraction of crude petroleum

Navitas Petroleum Limited

06200 Extraction of natural gas

Navitas Petroleum Limited

07290 Mining of other non-ferrous metal ores

Sumatra Copper & Gold PLC

08110 Quarrying of ornamental and building stone, limestone, gypsum, chalk and slate

Mick George Limited

08120 Operation of gravel and sand pits; mining of clays and kaolin

Frimstone Limited
Ingrebourne Valley Limited

08930 Extraction of salt

Maldon Crystal Salt Co Ltd

08990 Other mining and quarrying n.e.c.

Rusant Limited
Sewells Reservoir Construction Ltd
Trans-Siberian Gold PLC

09100 Support activities for petroleum and natural gas mining

Basetek Limited
Claxton Engineering Services Ltd
E.V. Offshore Limited
Navigator Terminals Midco Ltd
Navigator Terminals North Tees Ltd
Shawcor UK Limited
TAM International North Sea Ltd

09900 Support activities for other mining and quarrying

Basetek Limited
International Tin Association Ltd

10110 Processing and preserving of meat

A 1 Bacon Co Ltd
Direct Table Foods Limited
Pinnacle Foods Limited
York House (Meat Products) Ltd

10130 Production of meat and poultry meat products

Jack Brand Limited
Cheale Meats Limited
Green Label Foods Ltd.
Oakfield (Foods) Limited
Traditional Norfolk Poultry Ltd

10200 Processing and preserving of fish, crustaceans and molluscs

Big Prawn Co. Ltd.

10310 Processing and preserving of potatoes

Greenvale AP Limited

10390 Other processing and preserving of fruit and vegetables [11]

CH Old Co Limited
Camstar Herbs Limited
Chelmer Foods Limited
Greenyard Frozen UK Limited
Moulton Bulb Co Ltd
Place UK Limited
S H Pratt Group Limited
Q V Foods Limited
Rosemary & Thyme Limited
Staples (Vegetables) Limited
Wilkin & Sons Limited

10410 Manufacture of oils and fats

SOP International Limited

10512 Butter and cheese production

Pizza Gogo Ltd

10519 Manufacture of other milk products

Volac International Limited

10611 Grain milling

W.& H.Marriage & Sons Limited
Premier Foods Group Limited
Rank Hovis Milling Limited
Tilda Limited
G.R.Wright & Sons Limited

10710 Manufacture of bread; manufacture of fresh pastry goods and cakes

Aryzta Bakeries UK Ltd
Hovis Limited
Premier Foods Group Limited
Signature Flatbreads (UK) Ltd
Simmons (Bakers) Limited

10720 Manufacture of rusks and biscuits; manufacture of preserved pastry goods and cakes

Burton's Foods Limited
Kitchen Range Foods Limited
Wilkin & Sons Limited

10730 Manufacture of macaroni, noodles, couscous and similar farinaceous products

Pasta Foods Investments Ltd
Pasta Foods Limited
Premier Foods Group Limited

10821 Manufacture of cocoa and chocolate confectionery

Burton's Foods Limited
Hotel Chocolat Limited

10832 Production of coffee and coffee substitutes

Coffeeheaven International Ltd
Costa Limited
Fine Foods International (Manufacturing)
Masteroast Coffee Co. Limited

10850 Manufacture of prepared meals and dishes

Seachill UK Limited

10890 Manufacture of other food products n.e.c. [12]

Anglia Maltings (Holdings) Ltd
Appetite Holdings Limited
Bowman Ingredients Limited
Freshtime UK Limited
GB Ingredients Limited
Kettle Foods Ltd.
Knighton Foods Limited
Marcantonio Foods Limited
Natural Balance Foods Limited
Premier Foods Group Limited
Ragleth Limited
Seachill UK Limited

10910 Manufacture of prepared feeds for farm animals

Agricola Group Limited
Agricola Holdings Limited
Forfarmers UK Holdings Limited
Forfarmers UK Limited
Gilbertson & Page Limited
W.& H.Marriage & Sons Limited
F.H. Nash Limited
Natures Menu Limited
Volac International Limited

10920 Manufacture of prepared pet foods

Fold Hill Foods Limited
Gilbertson & Page Limited
Natures Menu Limited
Roger Skinner Limited
Tropical Marine Centre Limited

11010 Distilling, rectifying and blending of spirits

Adnams PLC
Alcohols Limited

11020 Manufacture of wine from grape

Broadland Wineries Limited

11030 Manufacture of cider and other fruit wines

Broadland Wineries Limited

11050 Manufacture of beer

AB InBev UK Limited
Adnams PLC
George Bateman & Son Limited
French & Jupps Limited
Greene King Brewing and Retailing
McMullen & Sons, Limited

11060 Manufacture of malt

Bairds Malt Limited
Graincorp (Canada) Holdings UK Ltd
Graincorp UK Limited
Muntons PLC
Pauls Malt Limited

11070 Manufacture of soft drinks; production of mineral waters and other bottled waters [13]

Britannia Soft Drinks Limited
Britvic Asset Company No.2 Ltd
Britvic EMEA Limited
Britvic International Investments
Britvic Overseas Limited
Britvic PLC
Britvic Soft Drinks Limited
Dayla Holdings Limited
Konings Juices & Drinks UK Ltd
Orchid Drinks Limited
Robinsons (Finance) No.2 Ltd
Robinsons Soft Drinks Limited
Slush Puppie Limited

12000 Manufacture of tobacco products

Republic Technologies (UK) Ltd

13200 Weaving of textiles

Silk Industries Limited

13931 Manufacture of woven or tufted carpets and rugs

Latif International Limited

13990 Manufacture of other textiles n.e.c.

Ramon Holdings Limited

14132 Manufacture of other women's outerwear

Kara Designs Ltd

14310 Manufacture of knitted and crocheted hosiery

Covidien UK Limited

16100 Sawmilling and planing of wood

Crendon Timber Engineering Ltd
Ellis Timber (Holdings) Ltd
Metsa Wood UK Limited
Thomson Sawmills Limited

16230 Manufacture of other builders' carpentry and joinery

Mumford & Wood Limited
Performance Timber Products Group
Wernick Buildings Limited

16290 Manufacture of other products of wood; manufacture of articles of cork, straw and plaiting materials

Dagless Limited
Kingspan Timber Solutions Ltd

17120 Manufacture of paper and paperboard

Essity Operations Manchester Ltd
Essity UK Limited
Firstan Limited
Herma UK Limited
Palm Paper Limited

17219 Manufacture of other paper and paperboard containers

Caps Cases Limited
Firstan Holdings Limited

17220 Manufacture of household and sanitary goods and of toilet requisites

Essity Operations Manchester Ltd
Essity UK Limited

17230 Manufacture of paper stationery

Acco UK Limited

17240 Manufacture of wallpaper

Muraspec Decorative Solutions Ltd

17290 Manufacture of other articles of paper and paperboard n.e.c.

Avery Dennison U.K. Limited
Sato UK Limited

18121 Manufacture of printed labels

Regaltags Global Limited
Sinclair International Limited

18129 Printing n.e.c. [15]

Ancient House Press PLC
Ancient House Printing Group Ltd
Stephen Austin & Sons Limited
Clays Ltd.
Coveris Flexibles UK Limited
Howard Hunt (City) Limited
Incodia International Ltd
Micropress Printers Limited
Precision Printing Co. Limited
Showcard Print Limited
Walstead Peterborough Limited
Walstead Press Group Limited
Walstead Roche Limited
Walstead Southernprint Limited
Warners (Midlands) PLC

18130 Pre-press and pre-media services

Company of Biologists, Limited
Micropress Printers Limited
RP2 Limited

18140 Binding and related services

Clays Ltd.
Micropress Printers Limited

18203 Reproduction of computer media

Company of Biologists, Limited

19209 Other treatment of petroleum products (excluding petrochemicals manufacture)

Coryton Advanced Fuels Limited

20120 Manufacture of dyes and pigments

Sensient Colors UK Ltd
Synergy Flavours Limited

20130 Manufacture of other inorganic basic chemicals

William Blythe Limited
Climax Molybdenum U.K. Limited
Dow Agrosciences Limited
Industrial Chemicals Limited
Rhodia Limited
Sika Limited
Syngenta UK Limited

20140 Manufacture of other organic basic chemicals

International Flavours & Fragrances
I.F.F.(Great Britain)

20150 Manufacture of fertilizers and nitrogen compounds

Omex Agrifluids Limited
Origin UK Operations Limited

20160 Manufacture of plastics in primary forms

Deltech Europe Limited
Du Pont (U.K.) Limited
Dynamic Cassette International Ltd
PPG Industries (UK) Limited

20301 Manufacture of paints, varnishes and similar coatings, mastics and sealants

Ardex UK Limited
Axalta Coating Systems UK Ltd
Axalta Powder Coating Systems UK Ltd
Brown Brothers Distribution Ltd
Dynamic Cassette International Ltd
Fujichem Sonneborn Limited
Kromachem Limited
PPG Industries (UK) Limited

20302 Manufacture of printing ink

Luminescence International Ltd

20411 Manufacture of soap and detergents

Dimex Limited
Industrial Chemicals Limited
Zenith Hygiene Group Limited
Zenith Hygiene Systems Limited

20420 Manufacture of perfumes and toilet preparations

Creightons PLC
Potter & Moore Innovations Ltd

20520 Manufacture of glues

Power Adhesives Limited

20590 Manufacture of other chemical products n.e.c. [20]

Aeropak (Chemical Products) Ltd
Alcohols Limited
Altro Limited
Antec International Limited
Apatech Limited
Armored Auto UK Limited
Clark-Drain Limited
Deltech Europe Limited
Easy Cleaning Solutions Ltd
Everbuild Building Products Ltd
Farecla Products Limited
Henkel Limited
Industrial Chemicals Group Ltd
Industrial Chemicals Limited
Molecular Products Limited
Orthene Holdings Limited
Solvay Solutions UK Limited
Syngenta UK Limited
Synthomer (UK) Limited
Tristel Solutions Limited

21100 Manufacture of basic pharmaceutical products [23]

A1 Pharmaceuticals Holdings Ltd
Aesica BC Limited
Aesica Holdco Limited
Aesica M1 Limited
Aesica M2 Limited
Aesica Pharmaceuticals Limited
Aesica Queenborough Limited
Astrazeneca PLC
Baxter Healthcare Limited
Bespak Europe Limited
D.D.D. Limited
Diomed Developments Limited
Eisai Manufacturing Limited
GE Healthcare Limited
GE Healthcare UK Limited
Generics (U.K.) Limited
Genzyme Limited
Laxmi BNS Holdings Limited
Macarthys Laboratories Limited
Merck Sharp & Dohme Limited
Porvair PLC
Prometic Pharma SMT Limited
Vernalis (R & D) Limited

21200 Manufacture of pharmaceutical preparations [11]

Accord Healthcare Limited
Amneal Pharma UK Holdings Ltd
Astrazeneca PLC
Bard Pharmaceuticals Limited
Dermal Laboratories Limited
GW Pharma Limited
Janssen-Cilag Limited
Napp Pharmaceutical Group Ltd
Napp Pharmaceutical Holdings Ltd
Roche Products Limited
Vernalis (R & D) Limited

22190 Manufacture of other rubber products

Murfitts Industries Limited

22210 Manufacture of plastic plates, sheets, tubes and profiles

Camvac Limited
Marton Geotechnical Services Ltd
PIL Membranes Limited

22220 Manufacture of plastic packing goods

Albea UK Limited
Betts International Limited
Betts Limited
Coveris Flexibles (Gainsborough) UK
K.M. Packaging Services Ltd
Plastique Holdings Limited
Sealed Air Limited
Softbox Systems Limited

22230 Manufacture of builders ware of plastic

Altro Limited
Titon Hardware Limited

22290 Manufacture of other plastic products [21]

Ammeraal Beltech Limited
Betts Limited
Blowplast Limited
British Gaskets Limited
Centurion Safety Products Ltd
Contamac Limited
Dalebrook Supplies Limited
Dart Products Europe Ltd.
Dynamic Cassette International Ltd
Faerch Plast UK Limited
Fluorocarbon Co Ltd
Goodfellow Cambridge Limited
Gratnells Limited
Hanmere Polythene Limited
Lindal Valve Co Ltd
Plastic Extruders Limited
Porvair Filtration Group Ltd
Satco Plastics Limited
Tex Plastics (Derby) Limited
Thames Card Technology Limited
Tradelink Direct Limited

23120 Shaping and processing of flat glass

Euroview Manufacturing Limited
Super Toughened Glass Limited

23130 Manufacture of hollow glass

O-I Glass Limited

23440 Manufacture of other technical ceramic products

Goodfellow Cambridge Limited
Porvair PLC

23510 Manufacture of cement

Imerys Aluminates Limited
Southern Cement Ltd

23610 Manufacture of concrete products for construction purposes

Lignacite Limited

23690 Manufacture of other articles of concrete, plaster and cement

ACO Technologies PLC

23990 Manufacture of other non-metallic mineral products n.e.c.

Ballast Phoenix Limited

24100 Manufacture of basic iron and steel and of ferro-alloys

Abbey Cross Trading Limited
Kubach & Sambrook (Metals) Ltd

24450 Other non-ferrous metal production

Senju Manufacturing (Europe) Ltd

25110 Manufacture of metal structures and parts of structures

Inflite Engineering Services Ltd
JPJ Installations Limited
Knight Precision Metals Ltd
Knight Strip Metals Limited
Lemon Groundwork Solutions Ltd
Sembmarine SLP Ltd
Stainless Metalcraft (Chatteris) Ltd
Transporter Engineering Ltd
Wernick Buildings Limited

25120 Manufacture of doors and windows of metal

Glazing Vision Limited
JPJ Installations Limited
Jewers Doors Limited
Tradelink Direct Limited

25290 Manufacture of other tanks, reservoirs and containers of metal

Permastore Limited
Stainless Metalcraft (Chatteris) Ltd

25400 Manufacture of weapons and ammunition

UTM Limited

25610 Treatment and coating of metals

Hauck Heat Treatment Limited
Knight Precision Metals Ltd
Knight Strip Metals Limited

25620 Machining

Albon Engineering and Manufacturing PLC
D.H. Industries Limited
Hydac Technology Limited
Luvata Welwyn Garden Ltd
Stainless Metalcraft (Chatteris) Ltd

25730 Manufacture of tools

OSG U.K. Limited

25910 Manufacture of steel drums and similar containers

Stainless Metalcraft (Chatteris) Ltd

25920 Manufacture of light metal packaging

Ball Beverage Packaging UK Ltd

25930 Manufacture of wire products, chain and springs

Welding Alloys Limited

25990 Manufacture of other fabricated metal products n.e.c. [26]

F. Brazil Reinforcements Ltd
Bunting Magnetics Europe Ltd
Clarksteel Holdings Limited
East Anglian Installations Ltd
Eastern Attachments Limited
Goodfellow Cambridge Limited
Gratnells Limited
Hardall International Limited
ITAB UK Ltd
Jamestown Industries Limited
London Fluid System Technologies Ltd
Lymington Precision Engineering (LPE)
Lymington Precision Engineers Co.
Porvair PLC
Rimex Metals (U.K.) Limited
Roe Bros. & Co Ltd.
Sofis Limited
TCL Manufacturing Limited
Taylor Made Holdings UK Ltd
Thorlabs Limited
Titon Hardware Limited
Trox UK Limited
Welding Alloys Limited
Werner UK Operations Limited
Werner UK Sales & Distribution Ltd.
Youngman Group Limited

26110 Manufacture of electronic components [13]

API Microelectronics Limited
API Microwave Limited
Apical Limited
CML Microsystems PLC
Elektron Technology UK Limited
I.M.O. Precision Controls Ltd
J.S.T. (U.K.) Limited
Knowles (UK) Limited
Landis + Gyr Limited
Micross Components Limited
Qualcomm Technologies International, Ltd.
Teledyne E2V (UK) Limited
Xaar PLC

26120 Manufacture of loaded electronic boards

Concurrent Technologies PLC

26200 Manufacture of computers and peripheral equipment

N.E.M. Co. Limited
Northgate Public Services (UK) Ltd
Primagraphics Limited
Viglen Limited

26301 Manufacture of telegraph and telephone apparatus and equipment

CML Microcircuits (UK) Limited
Pickering Interfaces Limited

26309 Manufacture of communication equipment other than telegraph, and telephone apparatus and equipment

Aveva Group PLC
Connectix Limited
Integrated Microwave Technology Ltd
Leonardo MW Ltd

26400 Manufacture of consumer electronics

Azuri Technologies Ltd
Focusrite Audio Engineering Ltd
Green Energy Options Ltd
Meridian Audio Limited
Pure International Limited

26511 Manufacture of electronic measuring, testing etc. equipment, not for industrial process control [11]

Aeroflex Limited
Alphasense Limited
Fluke Precision Measurement Ltd
Itron Metering Solutions UK Ltd
Jaltek Systems Limited
Keymed (Medical & Industrial Equipment)
Leonardo MW Ltd
Pico Technology (Holdings) Ltd
Smiths Detection-Watford Ltd
TSI Instruments Ltd
Waters Limited

26512 Manufacture of electronic industrial process control equipment

D.H. Industries Limited
MTL Instruments Group Limited
Michell Instruments Limited
NDC Technologies Limited
Nikon X-Tek Systems Limited
Parametric Investments Limited
TGA Industries Limited

26513 Manufacture of non-electronic measuring, testing etc. equipment, not for industrial process control

Itron Metering Solutions UK Ltd

26701 Manufacture of optical precision instruments

Avocet Capital Limited
Haag-Streit UK Limited
Nikon X-Tek Systems Limited
Porvair PLC
Sick (UK) Ltd.
Carl Zeiss Microscopy Limited

26702 Manufacture of photographic and cinematographic equipment

Kodak Alaris Limited
Sigma Imaging (UK) Limited

27110 Manufacture of electric motors, generators and transformers

ATB Group UK Limited
Cummins Generator Technologies Ltd
EBM - Papst UK Limited
Hayward Tyler Limited
Nikon X-Tek Systems Limited

27120 Manufacture of electricity distribution and control apparatus

PX Manufacturing Ltd

27320 Manufacture of other electronic and electric wires and cables

PX Manufacturing Ltd
Rockford Components Limited

27330 Manufacture of wiring devices

Greenbrook Industries Limited

27400 Manufacture of electric lighting equipment

Aurora Distribution Limited
Aurora Limited
Automotive Lighting UK Limited
Microlights Limited
Ritelite (Systems) Limited
Simm Tronic Limited

27510 Manufacture of electric domestic appliances

Beko PLC
Electrolux PLC
Monitor Audio Limited
Whirlpool UK Appliances Ltd

27900 Manufacture of other electrical equipment [21]

Airflow Developments Limited
Apem Components Limited
Bosch Lawn and Garden Limited
Datapaq Limited
Domino UK Limited
Electrolux Professional Ltd
Exheat Limited
Focusrite PLC
Hamlin Electronics Europe Ltd
Harman International Industries Ltd
Kelvin Hughes Limited
Keymed (Medical & Industrial Equipment)
MacDonald Humfrey (Automation) Ltd
Martin Audio Limited
Pioneer DJ Europe Limited
Racal Acoustics Limited
Rega Research Limited
Thorlabs Limited
Welding Alloys Limited
Windcrest (U.K.) Limited
Xaarjet Limited

28110 Manufacture of engines and turbines, except aircraft, vehicle and cycle engines

Peter Brotherhood Limited
Perkins Engines Co Ltd
Perkins Group Limited
Perkins Small Engines Limited

28120 Manufacture of fluid power equipment

Parker Hannifin Limited
Parker Hannifin Manufacturing (UK)
Parker Hannifin Manufacturing Ltd

28131 Manufacture of pumps

Aquatronic Group Management PLC
Grundfos Pumps Limited
Hayward Tyler Limited
MSCM Limited

28132 Manufacture of compressors

Hayward Tyler Limited
MSCM Limited

28140 Manufacture of taps and valves

Crane Limited
Hayward Tyler Limited
Watts Industries UK Limited

28150 Manufacture of bearings, gears, gearing and driving elements

Cooper Roller Bearings Co Ltd
SKF (U.K) Limited

28210 Manufacture of ovens, furnaces and furnace burners

Rational UK Limited

28220 Manufacture of lifting and handling equipment

Anglia Autoflow Limited
Didsbury Engineering Co.Limited
Eastern Attachments Limited
Samson Materials Handling Ltd
Seatrax (U.K.) Limited

28230 Manufacture of office machinery and equipment (except computers and peripheral equipment)

Acco UK Limited
Neopost Technologies Limited

28250 Manufacture of non-domestic cooling and ventilation equipment

Flakt Woods Limited
Hubbard Products Limited
Woods Holdings Limited

28290 Manufacture of other general-purpose machinery n.e.c.

Domino Printing Sciences PLC
Itron Metering Solutions UK Ltd
Titon Hardware Limited

28302 Manufacture of agricultural and forestry machinery other than tractors

Grimme (U.K.) Limited
Shelbourne Reynolds Engineering Ltd
Stanton Holding Limited

28490 Manufacture of other machine tools

Aixtron Limited
JW Froehlich UK Limited
Hurco Europe Limited

28921 Manufacture of machinery for mining

Aquaterra Energy Limited
Liebherr - Great Britain Ltd

28922 Manufacture of earthmoving equipment

Liebherr - Great Britain Ltd

28930 Manufacture of machinery for food, beverage and tobacco processing

Baker Perkins Limited
Flo-Mech. Limited
KMG Systems Limited
Sinclair International Limited

28960 Manufacture of plastics and rubber machinery

TTP Labtech Limited

28990 Manufacture of other special-purpose machinery n.e.c. [25]

APT-Skidata Limited
Altair (UK) Ltd
Aquasium Technology Limited
Bosch Rexroth Limited
Bruel & Kjaer VTS Limited
Cambustion Limited
Eastern Attachments Limited
Hayter Limited
Herma UK Limited
Inca Digital Printers Limited
Liebherr - Great Britain Ltd
Linx Printing Technologies Ltd
Lumendi Limited
MSCM Limited
Mettler-Toledo Safeline X-Ray Ltd
Moog Fernau Limited
Nikon X-Tek Systems Limited
Pitney Bowes Limited
Porvair Filtration Group Ltd
Ransomes Jacobsen Limited
Senior UK Limited
Silverson Machines Limited
Swarco UK Limited
Toro Principal Manufacturing Ltd
Videojet Technologies Limited

29100 Manufacture of motor vehicles

Ford Motor Co Ltd
IBC Vehicles Limited
Lotus Cars Limited
MTCE Limited
Radical Motorsport Limited
Vauxhall Motors Limited

29201 Manufacture of bodies (coachwork) for motor vehicles (except caravans)

Marshall Land Systems Ltd

29202 Manufacture of trailers and semi-trailers

Boss Cabins Limited
Transporter Engineering Ltd
Wilcox Commercial Vehicles Ltd

29310 Manufacture of electrical and electronic equipment for motor vehicles and their engines

Harman Automotive UK Limited

29320 Manufacture of other parts and accessories for motor vehicles

BWI UK Limited
Ford Motor Co Ltd
MTCE Limited
Multimatic Ltd.
Truck-Lite Europe Limited

30110 Building of ships and floating structures

Alicat Workboats Limited

30120 Building of pleasure and sporting boats

Fairline Yachts Limited
Richardsons Leisure Limited

30300 Manufacture of air and spacecraft and related machinery

Ipeco Holdings Limited
Leonardo MW Ltd
Marshall of Cambridge Aerospace Ltd
Safran Electrical & Power UK Ltd
Slingsby Advanced Composites Ltd

30990 Manufacture of other transport equipment n.e.c.

Boniface Engineering Limited
Chargemaster Limited
Dhollandia U.K. Limited
Quartix Holdings PLC
Wilcox Commercial Vehicles Ltd

31010 Manufacture of office and shop furniture

Pledge Office Chairs Limited
Verco Office Furniture Limited

31020 Manufacture of kitchen furniture
Commodore Kitchens Limited

31030 Manufacture of mattresses
Hypnos Limited

31090 Manufacture of other furniture
Alstons (Upholstery) Limited
Barlow Tyrie Limited
Ercol Furniture Limited
TCMC Furniture Limited

32300 Manufacture of sports goods
Acushnet Europe Ltd
Fox International Group Ltd
Harrod UK Limited
Motocaddy Limited

32409 Manufacture of other games and toys, n.e.c.
Toy Brokers Holdings Limited

32500 Manufacture of medical and dental instruments and supplies [15]
Arjo UK Limited
Carestream Dental Technology Topco
Carestream Health UK, Limited
Consort Medical PLC
De Soutter Medical Limited
Haag-Streit UK Limited
Huntleigh Healthcare Limited
Keymed (Medical & Industrial Equipment)
Medtronic Limited
Prior Scientific Instruments Ltd
Rocket Medical PLC
Shamir UK Limited
Stanmore Implants Worldwide Ltd
Unisurge International Limited
Welland Medical Limited

32910 Manufacture of brooms and brushes
G.B. Kent & Sons PLC

32990 Other manufacturing n.e.c. [68]
AFE Group Limited
Airbus Defence and Space Ltd
Ardex Holdings UK Limited
Automation Partnership (Cambridge)
Avery Dennison U.K. Limited
B.M. Polyco Limited
Baldwin Filters Limited
Beamglow Limited
Biochrom Limited
British Gaskets Limited
Cremer (UK) Manufacturing Co. Ltd
Crystal Group Limited
Crystal Home Improvements Group Ltd
Crystal Home Improvements Holdings
Crystal Windows & Doors Ltd
Dage Precision Industries Ltd
J.E. & V.M. Dalton Limited
Danfoss Limited
Daylighting Power Limited
Dengie Crops Limited
Du Pont (U.K.) Industrial Ltd
E - Leather Limited
E.G.L. Homecare Limited
Elliott Group Limited
Empress Garland Limited
Encocam Limited
European Flavours & Fragrances PLC
Exaclair Limited
FFEI Holdings Limited
Fibron BX Limited
Flamingo Plants Group Ltd
Flamingo Plants Ltd
Flo-Mech. Limited
Frith's Flexible Packaging Ltd
H L C (Wood Products) Limited
Hayman Group Limited
Helmet Integrated Systems Ltd
Heraeus Noblelight Limited
Hexcel Composites Limited
Hydac Technology Limited
Hypro EU Limited
J & A (International) Limited
Kidde Products Limited
MBDA UK Limited
MacLeans (Foils) Limited
Macron Safety Systems (UK) Ltd
Mason Pearson Bros. Limited
Motivair Compressors Limited
Mr. Fothergill's Seeds Limited
National Adhesives Holding Ltd.
No Climb Products Limited
Omar Park Homes Limited
Origin Frames Limited
Peerless Europe Ltd.
Perkinelmer Limited
Polyco (Group) Limited
Polyco Healthline Limited
Pregis Limited
Probe Oil Tools Limited
SG Technologies Group Limited
SG Technologies Limited
TFX Group Limited
Teknomek Limited
Thurne-Middleby Ltd
Trend Marine Products Limited
WTS Media Group Limited
S.F. Williams (Foils) Limited
Zip Heaters (UK) Ltd

33120 Repair of machinery
TGA Industries Limited

33140 Repair of electrical equipment
Dron & Dickson Limited

33150 Repair and maintenance of ships and boats
Norfolk Broads Direct Limited
Richards Dry Dock and Engineering

33160 Repair and maintenance of aircraft and spacecraft
Air Livery Limited
Anglia Aircraft Restorations Ltd
Leonardo MW Ltd
Premiair Aerospace Limited

33190 Repair of other equipment
Adcock Refrigeration and Air Conditioning
Aquatronic Group Management PLC
Derrick Services (UK) Limited
Draeger Medical UK Limited
Franke Coffee Systems UK Ltd
Kelvin Hughes Limited
TBS G.B. Telematic & Biomedical Services

33200 Installation of industrial machinery and equipment
Arthenella Limited
Flo-Mech. Limited
London Hoist Limited
Trumpf Limited
Vega Industries Limited

35110 Production of electricity [34]
AMP GM 003 Limited
AMP GM001 Limited
AMP GM006 Limited
AMP GM007 Limited
Barking Power Limited
Carraig Gheal Wind Farm Ltd
Churchtown Farm Solar Limited
Cummins Cogeneration Limited
Earlseat Wind Farm Ltd
East Langford Solar Limited
Exagris Limited
Glenchamber Wind Energy Ltd
Grange Renewable Energy Ltd
Green Spark Renewable Energy (UK) Ltd
HP Solar Limited
Heulwen Solar Limited
Kenwyn Solar Limited
Local Generation Limited
MC Power Limited
Manor Farm Solar Limited
Noble Foods (We) Limited
Peerglow Asset Limited
Pretoria Energy Company (Chittering)
Pretoria Energy Company (Mepal) Ltd
Roos Energy Limited
Scira Offshore Energy Limited
Shropshire Energy (UK) Limited
Sunlight PV Ltd
Sunsave 12 (Derriton Fields) Ltd
Sunsave 25 (Wix Lodge Farm) Ltd
Symbio Energy Limited
Tallentire Energy Limited
Volac Renewable Energy Limited
Wryde Croft Wind Farm Limited

35120 Transmission of electricity
Electricity Network Co Ltd

35130 Distribution of electricity
Independent Power Networks Ltd

35140 Trade of electricity
Corona Energy Retail 4 Limited
Cummins ESB Nigeria Limited
F & S Energy Limited
OPW Holdco Limited

35210 Manufacture of gas
Euston Biogas Limited
Grindley Biogas Limited
Powergas Africa Limited
Pretoria Energy Company (Chittering)
Pretoria Energy Company (Mepal) Ltd

35220 Distribution of gaseous fuels through mains
Corona Energy Retail 4 Limited
Independent Pipelines Limited

35230 Trade of gas through mains
Corona Energy Retail 1 Limited

35300 Steam and air conditioning supply

A.M.P. Air Conditioning Ltd
Volac Renewable Energy Limited

36000 Water collection, treatment and supply

Affinity Water Limited
Anglian Water Services Limited
Suez Water Technologies & Solutions Services UK
VWS (UK) Ltd

37000 Sewerage

Anglian Water Services Limited
Biomarsh Environmental Ltd
Industrial Water Jetting Systems Group
Industrial Water Jetting Systems Ltd

38110 Collection of non-hazardous waste [20]

Biffa Corporate Holdings Ltd
Biffa Environmental Municipal Services
Biffa GS UK Holdings Limited
Biffa Holdings Limited
Biffa Leicester Limited
Biffa Municipal Limited
Biffa Waste Management Limited
Biffa Waste Services Limited
F & R Cawley Limited
Ellgia Recycling Ltd
M. Gaze & Co. Limited
Mick George Limited
Island Waste Services Limited
Kier Integrated Services Ltd
O'Brien Waste Recycling Solutions Ltd
Poplars Resource Management Co Ltd
S. Sacker (Claydon) Limited
UK Waste Management Limited
Valens Resources Group PLC
Weir Waste Services Limited

38120 Collection of hazardous waste

Biffa Corporate Holdings Ltd
Biffa Environmental Municipal Services
Biffa Holdings Limited
Biffa Leicester Limited
Biffa Waste Services Limited
M. Gaze & Co. Limited
Island Waste Services Limited
S. Sacker (Claydon) Limited
UK Waste Management Limited

38210 Treatment and disposal of non-hazardous waste [14]

Ballast Phoenix Limited
Biffa Corporate Holdings Ltd
Biffa GS UK Holdings Limited
Biffa Holdings Limited
Biffa Leicester Limited
Biffa Waste Management Limited
Biffa Waste Services Limited
G.B.N. Services Limited
M. Gaze & Co. Limited
Island Waste Services Limited
O'Brien Waste Recycling Solutions Ltd
Pure Recycling Warwick Limited
UK Waste Management Limited
Weir Waste Services Limited

38220 Treatment and disposal of hazardous waste

Biffa Corporate Holdings Ltd
Biffa Holdings Limited
Biffa Leicester Limited
Biffa Waste Services Limited
M. Gaze & Co. Limited
Island Waste Services Limited
UK Waste Management Limited

38320 Recovery of sorted materials [15]

ASM Metal Recycling Ltd.
Biffa Environmental Municipal Services
Biffa Polymers Limited
F.J. Church & Sons Limited
Mick George Limited
McGrath Bros. (Waste Control) Ltd
Murfitts Industries Limited
Nationwide Metal Recycling Ltd
Nicholls Limited
Palm Recycling Limited
Pure Recycling Warwick Limited
S. Sacker (Claydon) Limited
Seneca Environmental Solutions Ltd
Valens Resources Group PLC
Weir Waste Services Limited

39000 Remediation activities and other waste management services

Aspect Contracts Limited
Ballast Phoenix Limited
FJC Topco Limited
S. Sacker (Claydon) Limited
Squibb Group Limited
Valens Resources Group PLC

41100 Development of building projects [310]

2020 Developments (Luton) Ltd
66 Queen Square Limited
Abbey Properties Cambridgeshire Ltd
Acacia Homes Limited
Alfreds Way Investments (No. 2) Ltd
Ambury Developments Limited
M. Anderson Construction Ltd
Andgrove Property Investments Ltd
Apollo Property Investment Ltd
Archaylen Property Limited
Artillery Properties Limited
Ashe Group Holdings Limited
Ashley House PLC.
Asino Limited
Astonpalm Limited
Avocado Developments Limited
R. S. Baker & Sons Limited
Balcraft Properties Limited
Balvraid Properties Limited
Barnes Group Limited
Bath Road Properties Limited
Be Living Group Limited
Be Living Holdings Ltd
Beaufort House Limited
Beechfield Estates Limited
Belgrave Land (Perth) Limited
Bennett PLC
Betcrown Limited
Big Sky Developments Ltd
Blessville Limited
Blitzfair Limited
Boulters Meadow Limited
Bourne Court Properties Ltd
Bourne Holidays Limited
Bridge Road Southall Limited
Broadgate Homes Limited
Brookstream Properties Limited
Michael Broughton Limited
Bucknalls Developments Limited
Bucks Developments Limited
Bugler Developments Limited
Bugler Group Limited
Buildvantage Limited
A.E.Bullock Limited
Burgess Properties Limited
CMS Developments Limited
CRU Sturton Street Limited
Callcott Holdings Limited
Cambridge Medipark Limited
Cambridgeshire Industrial Properties
Camden Development Co Ltd
Cannon Kirk Property Limited
Cantay Estates Limited
Careys New Homes Limited
Carrain Limited
Carter and Ward of Wickford Ltd
Castlestone Investments Ltd
Cathedral Holdings Limited
Central Developments (UK) Ltd
Charlie Properties Limited
Charter Projects (Developments) Ltd
Chelsteen Homes Limited
Cheshunt Lakeside Developments Ltd
Chesside Homes Limited
City & Country Bristol Limited
City & Country Residential Ltd
City & Westminster Developments Ltd
Clarence Estates (London) Ltd
Clearview Homes Limited
Cocksedge Building Contractors Ltd
Commercial Freeholds & Investments Ltd
Conamar Building Services Ltd
Construct Reason Limited
Corporate Investments Limited
Countryside 26 Limited
Countryside Annington (Mill Hill)
Countryside Four Limited
Countryside Maritime Limited
Countryside Properties (Springhead)
Countryside Properties (UK) Ltd
Countryside Properties (Uberior) Ltd
Countryside Properties (WGL) Ltd
Countryside Properties (WHL) Ltd
Countryside Properties (WPL) Ltd
Countryside Sigma Limited
Cricklewood Developments Ltd
Ivor Crowson Developments (Stamford)
Cygnet Street Developments Ltd
Dalin Limited
Delbanco Meyer & Co Ltd
Denecroft Estates Limited
Denland Limited
Dock and Let Limited
Doncaster School Solutions Ltd
Duoview Properties Limited
Durkan Estates Limited
Durkan Holdings Limited
Durkan Limited
Earl Estates Limited
East Anglian Property Limited
Ellis Bros (Contractors) Ltd
Enterprise Residential Development
Eversleigh Investment and Property Co
Fairview Enfield Limited

Fairview Homes Limited
Fairview New Homes (Charlton) Ltd
Fairview New Homes (Chase Road) Ltd
Fairview New Homes (Colindale) Ltd
Fairview New Homes (Developments)
Fairview New Homes (Properties) Ltd
Fairview New Homes (South East) Ltd
Fairview New Homes (Willow Way) Ltd
Fairview Ventures Limited
Falkland Islands Co Ltd
Filross Securities Limited
Fitzjohns Avenue Ltd
Forebury Estates Limited
French & Jupps Limited
Fulca Limited
GDL (Aylesbury) Limited
GDL (Luton) Developments Ltd
GDL (Millharbour) Limited
GDL (Romford) Limited
GDL (Slough Developments) Ltd
GHL (Crescent Lane) Limited
GHL (Kilmorie) Limited
GHL (Summerstown) Limited
Gade Property Developments Ltd
Galileo Homes Limited
Galliard Construction Limited
Galliard Homes Limited
Gibson Developments Limited
Go Homes Ltd
Gracechurch Sports Management Ltd
D.N. Grady & Sons Limited
Gray's of Norwich Limited
Greene King Developments Ltd
Greenwich Millennium Village Ltd
Guia Limited
Halsbury Homes (South East) Ltd
Halsbury Strategic Limited
Hamden Homes Limited
Hanover Housing Developments Ltd
Haydon Holdings Limited
Hemnall Investments Limited
Hemnall Limited
Heritage Developments Limited
Hevingham Development Co Ltd
Higgins Construction PLC
Higgins Homes PLC
Hildo Limited
Hincroft Limited
Hitchin Property Trust Limited
Inland Homes PLC
Inland Limited
Intrasales (Lye Lane) Limited
Jarvis Group Limited
Jessica House Developments Ltd
K K Investment Ltd
Kier Commercial Investments Ltd
Kier Hammersmith Limited
Kier Property Developments Ltd
Kier Property Limited
Kier Ventures Limited
Kigass Limited
Ashley King (Developments) Ltd
W.D.King Limited
Kingfisher (EU) Limited
Lakehouse Contracts Limited
Land Charter (Harlow) Ltd
Lanswood Limited
Thomas Lipton Ltd
Littlebury Developments Ltd
Lochailort Fairfield Limited
Lodwick Homes Limited
Longford Securities & Equities (K & T)
Longford Securities & Equities Ltd
Lors Homes Limited
Lynxvale Limited
M & D Developments Limited
MY Construction & Carpentry Ltd
Marwin Securities Limited
Maylands Green Limited
Mentmore Gransden Limited
Meritcape Limited
Mersea Homes Limited
Merton Acquisitions Limited
Metis Homes Limited
Minton Holdings Limited
Miriad Property Investments Ltd
Mirrorstoke Limited
Mono Properties Limited
Musco (St Albans Place) Ltd
N.P.K. Holdings Limited
Nacropolis (Langley) Ltd
Netherhall Gardens Ltd
Newhall Land Limited
Nine Heathrow Ventures Limited
Noble Foods (We) Limited
Northfield Avenue (Holdings) Ltd
OYO Developments Limited
Oakbridge Homes (Group) Ltd
Oakburn European Properties Ltd
Opal Bay Limited
Opecprime Properties Limited
Oxley Wharf Limited
Oxley Wharf Property 1 Limited
Oxley Wharf Property 2 Limited
Oxley Wharf Property 3 Limited
Oyster Properties Limited
Palacath Limited
Paradigm Commercial PLC
Paragon Land & Estates Ltd
Peppercorn Property Investments Ltd
Phelan Construction Limited
Plotplan Limited
Polyfield Property Limited
Princebuild Holdings Limited
Princebuild Limited.
Property Warehouse Limited
RCT Construction Limited
RDL1 Limited
RO Property Management Limited
RQ Capital Limited
Ramsgate Development Co Ltd
Regency Homes Limited
Residential Land Management 2 Ltd
Ridgeland Properties Limited
Ridgepoint Homes Limited
Roman Investments Limited
Rose Builders Ltd
SPD Moorgate Limited
Sawston Farms (Cambs) Limited
Saxonchart Limited
Scimitar House (Holdings) Ltd
M R Scott Limited
Shanly Homes Limited
Sherrygreen Homes Ltd
Shoe Quarter Limited
Simat Properties Limited
Thomas Sinden Limited
Skanska Infrastructure Development UK
Skanska Project Developments Ltd
Skanska TAM Limited
Soda Studios Limited
Soho Loop Limited
Sorbon Estates Limited
Sorbon Homes Limited
Sorbon Investments Limited
South Bristol (Ashton Park) Ltd
South Coast Furnishing Co Ltd
South Eastern Leisure UK Ltd
Southwater Property Promotion Ltd
Spen Hill Regeneration Limited
St Albans Diocesan Property Co Ltd
Stamford Property Co Ltd
Stanley Dock Properties Ltd
Starbones Limited
Stevenage Road Residential Developments
Stirling Civil Engineering Ltd
Stockplace Hartford Ltd
Stockplace Investments Limited
Streamadvice Limited
Summerhill Birmingham Limited
Sunray Estates Limited
Swan Commercial Services Ltd
Swan New Homes Limited
Swanbrae Limited
Swift Hotels Limited
T & B (Contractors) Limited
TN (UK) Consultancy Ltd
Tanners Wharf Limited
James Taylor Construction Ltd
James Taylor Homes (Harrow) Ltd
Taylor Properties Trading Ltd
Taylor Wimpey Developments Ltd
Taylor Wimpey Holdings Limited
Taylor Wimpey Property Co Ltd
Taylor Wimpey UK Limited
Taylor Woodrow Construction
Techaid Facilities Limited
E.E. & A. Tee Limited
Telford Homes City North Ltd
Telford Homes PLC
Telida Limited
Thames Industrial Estate Ltd
Thorney Leys Developments Ltd
Townhold Limited
Trinity View Homes Limited
Triplehigh Limited
Turnhold Properties Limited
Twenty 1 Construction Limited
UIDUK Ltd
UK Real Estate Limited
Vanderbilt Homes Limited
Ventress Property Developments Ltd
Wandale Limited
Wenta Business Centres Limited
R.F. West Limited
Westgate House Developments Ltd
Wheatley (Buntingford) Limited
Wheatley Group Developments Ltd
G.Holmes White (Properties) Ltd
Whitehill & Bordon Development Company
Phase 1A
Willmott Dixon Holdings Ltd
Willmott Dixon Public & Commercial
Wilson Connolly Limited
Wilson Properties (London) Ltd
Wood Farm (Stanmore) Limited
Wrest Park Limited

41201 Construction of commercial buildings [93]

ARJ Construction Limited
Aspin Group Limited
Aura (Newcastle) Project Co Ltd
Austin (GB) Limited
Autolink Concessionaires (M6) PLC
BAM Construct UK Limited

BAM Construction Limited
BDL Group PLC
Barnes Group Limited
Bauer Technologies Limited
Beeson Wright Limited
Big Sky Developments Ltd
Borras Construction Ltd.
M.& R.Bowman Limited
Brogan Group Ltd
John Burgess & Co. Limited
C.M. Cadman Group Limited
Camfaud Concrete Pumps Limited
Cardiff Gate Business Park Ltd
P.J. Carey (Contractors) Ltd
R.G. Carter Cambridge Limited
R.G. Carter Construction Ltd
R.G. Carter Limited
R.G. Carter Projects Limited
Cementation Skanska Limited
Chalcroft Limited
E.M.Chamberlain Limited
V.G.Clements (Contractors) Ltd
Cocksedge Building Contractors Ltd
Conamar Building Services Ltd
Crispin & Borst Limited
Cunningham Holdings (London) Ltd
Dalton Resources Limited
T.J.Evers Limited
Geoghegan Bros. Limited
Grants of Shoreditch Limited
HG Construction Limited
Harrington (Properties) Ltd
Hutton Construction Limited
Hutton East Limited
Jarvis Contracting Limited
Jarvis Homes Limited
Jean-Luc Developments Ltd
Kelly Rail U.K. Ltd
Kier Construction Limited
Kier Developments Limited
Kier Overseas (Twenty-Three) Ltd
Lakehouse Contracts Limited
Life Build Solutions Ltd
M.J.S. Construction (March) Ltd
MDS Civil Engineering Limited
Marden Homes Limited
Sir Robert McAlpine Limited
McGee Civil Engineering Ltd
McGee Group (Holdings) Limited
McLaren Construction (UK) Ltd
McLaren Construction Limited
Mid Holding Co UK Limited
Midgard Ltd
A.J. Morrisroe & Sons Limited
Mulalley & Co. Limited
Phelan Construction Limited
RCT Construction Limited
Rainham Industrial Services Ltd
Readie Construction Limited
J. Reddington Ltd
Renewable Energy Systems Ltd
Rogers Rental Limited
Rooff Ltd
Rose Builders Ltd
Sherrygreen Homes Ltd
Thomas Sinden Limited
John Sisk & Son Limited
Sisk Consolidated Investments Ltd
Skanska Cementation International
Skanska Construction (Regions) Ltd
Skanska Construction UK Ltd
Skanska UK PLC
Spence Refit Ltd
Station Road Developments (Cambridge)
Swift Brickwork Contractors Ltd
James Taylor Construction Ltd
Tilia Properties Limited
Toureen Contractors Limited
Trollope & Colls Limited
Vinci Construction UK Limited
VolkerFitzpatrick Limited
Volkerwessels UK Limited
Waystone Limited
Wernick Buildings Limited
R.F. West Limited
Willmott Dixon Construction Ltd
Willmott Dixon Interiors Ltd

41202 Construction of domestic buildings [97]

Abbey Developments Limited
Abel Homes Limited
Alfred Homes Limited
Aquinna Homes PLC
Badger Building (E.Anglia) Ltd
Belsize Garages Project Ltd
Bennett PLC
Big Sky Developments Ltd
W.E.Black Limited
Breyer Group PLC
Broadgate Builders (Spalding) Ltd
Broadgate Homes Limited
Cannon Kirk (UK) Limited
P.J. Carey (Contractors) Ltd
Careys New Homes Limited
R.G. Carter Cambridge Limited
R.G. Carter Construction Ltd
R.G. Carter Limited
R.G. Carter Projects Limited
Chartridge Developments Ltd
Chartridge PLC
Chase (Palace Wharf) Limited
Chipperfield Land Co Ltd
Cocksedge Building Contractors Ltd
Conamar Building Services Ltd
Connolly Homes PLC
Countryside 28 Limited
Countryside Sigma Limited
Cripps Developments Limited
Crown House Homes (North Station)
Environ Freshford Mill Limited
Fairview Estates (Housing) Ltd
Friargate Coventry Development Ltd
Galileo Homes Limited
Charles Gallagher Limited
Derek Hales (Plumbing Contractors)
Hill Partnerships Limited
Hopkins Homes Limited
Hopkins and Moore (Developments) Ltd
Jarvis Homes Limited
Jaysam Contractors Limited
Jaysam Developments Borehamwood Ltd
Kebbell Development Limited
Keystone Developments (LG) Ltd
Kier Homes Caledonia Limited
Kier Living Limited
Kier Partnership Homes Limited
Nicholas King Developments PLC
Nicholas King Homes PLC
Kingswood Village Limited
Lakehouse Contracts Limited
Landex Limited
Landlink Ltd
Larkfleet Limited
Laurence Homes (Eastern) Ltd
Le Vack Estates Limited
Life Build Solutions Ltd
Lint (Redington Road) Limited
Lysander Student Properties Operations
Manor Crest Construction Ltd
Manor Crest Homes Limited
Matthew Homes Limited
McGee Civil Engineering Ltd
McGee Group (Holdings) Limited
Meldire Limited
Midgard Ltd
Moody Homes Limited
Jenny Moody Properties Ltd
H.C.Moss (Builders) Limited
Mulalley & Co. Limited
NGB Construction Limited
NW3 Capital Ltd
Oakbridge Homes Limited
Oakeve Limited
Papworth Trust
Phelan Construction Limited
David Phillip (Investments) Ltd
Rectory Homes Limited
J. Reddington Ltd
Rooff Ltd
Rose Builders Ltd
Sandhill Homes Limited
Thomas Sinden Limited
John Sisk & Son Limited
Sisk Consolidated Investments Ltd
Starglade Parks Limited
Swift Brickwork Contractors Ltd
T.S.G. Building Services PLC
TC Project Management Limited
George Tanner (Shalford) Ltd
James Taylor Construction Ltd
Vanderbilt Development Finance Ltd
Vanderbilt Thames Valley Ltd
Vanderbilt Topco Ltd
Weston Homes PLC
Wickford Development Co Ltd
Willmott Partnership Homes Ltd

42110 Construction of roads and motorways [18]

Autolink Concessionaires (A19) Ltd
Autolink Concessionaires (M6) PLC
Autolink Holdings (M6) Ltd
Bondgrip Limited
P.J. Carey (Contractors) Ltd
Connect Plus (M25) Limited
Jackson Civil Engineering Group Ltd
Jackson Civils Limited
Jackson Frameworks Limited
Kier Highways Limited
Kier Integrated Services Ltd
J.L. Knight Roadworks Limited
Marlborough Highways Group Ltd
John Sisk & Son Limited
Sisk Consolidated Investments Ltd
Toppesfield Limited
Volkerrail Limited
Volkerservices Limited

42120 Construction of railways and underground railways

Kier (NR) Limited
Progress Rail Services UK Ltd

42130 Construction of bridges and tunnels

Joseph Gallagher Limited
Jackson Civils Limited
Jackson Frameworks Limited
Kier Construction Limited
Tunnelcraft Limited

42210 Construction of utility projects for fluids

Kier Integrated Services Ltd

42220 Construction of utility projects for electricity and telecommunications

P.J. Carey (Contractors) Ltd
JSM Construction Limited
Kier Integrated Services Ltd
Matrix Networks Limited
Morrison Utility Services Ltd
Seajacks UK Limited

42910 Construction of water projects

J.Browne Construction Co Ltd
Jackson Civils Limited
Jackson Frameworks Limited
Morrison Utility Services Ltd
Stantec Treatment Group Ltd

42990 Construction of other civil engineering projects n.e.c. [32]

Agetur (U.K.) Limited
Ashe Construction Limited
Badger Building (E.Anglia) Ltd
A D Bly Construction Limited
Michael Broughton Limited
Durkin and Sons Limited
Dyer & Butler 2014 Limited
Dyer & Butler Holdings Limited
Dyer and Butler Limited
Etcetera Construction Services Ltd
Ground Construction Limited
John Henry Group Limited
Jackson Civils Limited
Jackson Frameworks Limited
Jarvis Group Limited
Kenford Developments Limited
Kier Construction Limited
Kier Infrastructure and Overseas Ltd
Kier International Limited
Kier Minerals Limited
Kier Overseas (Nine) Limited
Kier Overseas (Seventeen) Ltd
Morrison Utility Services Ltd
Optima Contracting Limited
QED (Slough) Limited
Squibb Group Limited
Tamdown Group Limited
Taylor Woodrow Construction
Toureen Contractors Limited
Vinci Construction UK Limited
Volkerstevin Group Limited
Volkerstevin Limited

43110 Demolition

John F Hunt Limited
McGee Civil Engineering Ltd
T.E.Scudder Limited
Squibb Group Limited
Toureen Contractors Limited

43120 Site preparation

Aitch Demolition Co. Ltd
Mick George Limited
McGee Civil Engineering Ltd
McGee Group (Holdings) Limited
Squibb Group Limited
Toureen Contractors Limited

43130 Test drilling and boring

WJ Groundwater Limited

43210 Electrical installation [14]

Barnes Group Limited
R B Emerson Limited
Emico Limited
Essex Group Holdings International
Essex Group Holdings Limited
Essex Services Group Limited
J C A Engineering Ltd
Lorne Stewart PLC
Openview Security Solutions Ltd
P.I.P. Electrics Limited
Power on Connections Ltd
Rainham Industrial Services Ltd
Rolec Services Limited
Skanska Rashleigh Weatherfoil Ltd

43220 Plumbing, heat and air-conditioning installation

Aston Heating Limited
Barnes Group Limited
Derek Hales (Plumbing Contractors)
J C A Engineering Ltd
Lorne Stewart PLC
Oakray Limited
T.S.G. Building Services PLC

43290 Other construction installation [16]

Breheny Civil Engineering Ltd
Breyer Group PLC
Michael Broughton Limited
Ecotherm Insulation (UK) Ltd
English Architectural Glazing Ltd
Jewers Doors Limited
Kelly Communications Limited
Penlaw & Co Ltd
R K Property Investments Ltd.
Rainham Industrial Services Ltd
Sembmarine SLP Ltd
Spence Refit Ltd
Spitalfields Works Limited
Stortford Interiors (UK) Ltd
Triconnex Ltd
Twenty 1 Construction Limited

43320 Joinery installation

Brown & Carroll (London) Ltd
Jaysam Contractors Limited
Stortford Interiors (UK) Ltd
Taylor Made Joinery Interiors Ltd

43330 Floor and wall covering

DMC Contracts Limited

43341 Painting

Air Works Empire UK Limited
Air Works UK Engineering Ltd

43342 Glazing

A. & B. Glass Co Ltd
Anglian Windows Limited
Everest Limited
Innovative Design Systems Ltd
M.Price Limited
SDSDAB Limited

43390 Other building completion and finishing

Bullen Developments Limited
Clark Construction (South East) Ltd
Dorma UK Limited
Grangewood Builders Limited
Halamar (Chancery Lane) Ltd
Harringtons Builders PLC
Spence Refit Ltd
Tilsworth Developments Limited

43910 Roofing activities

Breyer Group PLC
Survey Roofing Group Limited

43991 Scaffold erection

Brogan Group Ltd
Connect Access Group Ltd
Connect Scaffolding Limited

43999 Other specialised construction activities n.e.c. [63]

Abbey Properties Cambridgeshire Ltd
Access Platform Sales Limited
Tom Blackwell (Contractors & Plant Hire)
Boral (UK) Limited
Bouygues E & S Infrastructure UK Ltd
Breheny Group Limited
Breyer Group PLC
J.Browne Construction Co Ltd
C. U. Lighting Limited
Cavity Insulation Guarantee Agency
City Lifting Limited
J. Coffey Construction Ltd
Crowland Cranes Limited
D & B Scaffolding Limited
DBD Distribution Limited
Derrick Services (UK) Limited
Drayton Building Services Ltd
Falcon Tower Crane Services Ltd
Fastglobe (Mastics) Limited
P. Flannery Plant Hire (Oval) Ltd
Fortem Solutions Limited
Galldris Construction Limited
Global Marine Systems Limited
Halfen Limited
John F Hunt Group Ltd
I & C Limited
Instalcom Limited
KNM Project Services Limited
Kelly Communications Group Ltd
Kelly Communications Limited
Kelly Fleet Services Limited
Kelly Rail Group Ltd
Knight Build Limited
Mervyn Lambert Plant Limited
Levolux Limited
Loppingdale Plant Limited
M.J.S. Holdings (March) Ltd
McGrath Bros. (Waste Control) Ltd
McLaren Construction (UK) Ltd
McLaren Construction Limited

B.P. Mitchell Haulage Contractors
Munnelly Support Services Ltd
Nexus Infrastructure PLC
North West Steel Limited
Novum Structures UK Limited
Oranmore Precast Limited
R3 Polygon UK Ltd.
Rapidrop Global Limited
Reach Active Group Limited
Reilly Concrete Pumping Ltd
SCCS Survey Equipment Limited
Skanska Major Projects Limited
Spence Refit Ltd
Stuart Group Limited
Thames Reinforcements Limited
Twenty 1 Construction Limited
Vinci Environment UK Limited
Volkerhighways Limited
Volkerlaser Ltd
Volkerrail Specialist Businesses Ltd
WJ Groundwater Limited
WPA Support Services Limited
Wadlow Energy Limited

45111 Sale of new cars and light motor vehicles [64]

Altomart Limited
Aprite (GB) Limited
Astle Limited
John Banks Limited
Brayleys Cars Limited
Bussey & Sabberton Bros.Limited
Citygate Automotive Limited
Desira Group PLC
Desira Holdings PLC
Duff Morgan & Vermont Limited
EMG Anglia Limited
Essex Motor Co Ltd
Fairfield Garage (Leigh-on-Sea) Ltd
Falkland Islands Co Ltd
Ford Motor Co Ltd
Ford Retail Limited
Frank G. Gates Limited
John Grose Group Limited
A.W. & D. Hammond Limited
Hill's Garages (Woodford) Ltd
Holden & Holden Limited
Ivor Holmes Limited
Hyundai Motor UK Limited
Stephen James (Automotive) Ltd
L & L Inc Limited
Lancaster Cars Limited
Lancaster Luxury Vehicles Ltd
Lancaster Motor Co Ltd
Lancaster PLC
Lancaster Specialist Cars Ltd
Lancaster Sports Cars Limited
P.F.K. Ling Limited
Local Car and Van Rental Ltd
Marriott Holdings Limited
Marshall Motor Group Limited
Marshall North West Limited
Marshall of Scunthorpe Limited
Marshall of Stevenage Limited
Nissan Motor (GB) Limited
C.John Norris (Cars & Caravans) Ltd
Norton Way Motors Limited
Palmers (St Albans) Limited
Pentagon Limited
Pertwee & Back,Limited
Quest Motor Group Limited
R.T.Rate Limited
Renault U.K. Limited
Ridgeway Bavarian Limited
Robinsons Autoservices Limited
S & B Commercials Limited
Silver Street Automotive Ltd
F.P.Smith (Holdings) Limited
Specialist Cars Limited
Specialist Cars Tring Limited
Ssangyong Motor UK Limited
Taylors Service Garages (Boston) Ltd
Thurlow Nunn Limited
Toomey Motor Group Limited
Top 100 Limited
Underwoods Garage (Tiptree) Ltd
F. Vindis & Sons (Bedford) Ltd
F. Vindis & Sons (Sawston) Ltd
Vindis Developments Limited
Vindis Group Limited

45112 Sale of used cars and light motor vehicles [38]

ABVR Holdings Limited
Aprite (GB) Limited
Aston Barclay Holdings Group Ltd
Aston Barclay Holdings Limited
Aston Barclay Limited
John Banks Limited
Bussey & Sabberton Bros.Limited
Car World (Cambs) Ltd
Citygate Automotive Limited
EMG Anglia Limited
Fairfield Garage (Leigh-on-Sea) Ltd
Frank G. Gates Limited
John Grose Group Limited
A.W. & D. Hammond Limited
Hill's Garages (Woodford) Ltd
Holden & Holden Limited
L & L Inc Limited
P.F.K. Ling Limited
Local Car and Van Rental Ltd
Marshall Motor Group Limited
Marshall North West Limited
Marshall of Scunthorpe Limited
Marshall of Stevenage Limited
Palmers (St Albans) Limited
Pertwee & Back,Limited
R.T.Rate Limited
Robinsons Autoservices Limited
Saxton 4x4 Limited
Silver Street Automotive Ltd
Specialist Cars Tring Limited
Stebbings Car Centre Limited
Taylors Service Garages (Boston) Ltd
Thurlow Nunn Limited
Underwoods Garage (Tiptree) Ltd
F. Vindis & Sons (Bedford) Ltd
F. Vindis & Sons (Sawston) Ltd
Vindis Developments Limited
Vindis Group Limited

45190 Sale of other motor vehicles [12]

Aebi Schmidt UK Limited
Chassis-Cab Limited
Ernest Doe & Sons Limited
Harris Commercial Repairs Ltd
Isuzu Truck (UK) Limited
Motus Group (UK) Limited
Norfolk Truck & Van Limited
Prentice Aircraft and Cars Ltd
S & B Commercials Limited
Services Machinery & Trucks Ltd
Thurlow Nunn Standen Limited
Transporter Sales & Hire Ltd

45200 Maintenance and repair of motor vehicles [54]

Aebi Schmidt UK Limited
Aprite (GB) Limited
BHW Automotive Limited
John Banks Limited
Brayleys Cars Limited
Bussey & Sabberton Bros.Limited
Central Tyre (Commercial) Ltd
Chassis-Cab Limited
Citygate Automotive Limited
Ernest Doe & Sons Limited
EMG Anglia Limited
Electro-Motive Diesel Limited
Fairfield Garage (Leigh-on-Sea) Ltd
Falkland Islands Co Ltd
Ford Retail Limited
Formula One Auto Centres Ltd
Frank G. Gates Limited
John Grose Group Limited
A.W. & D. Hammond Limited
Hill's Garages (Woodford) Ltd
Holden & Holden Limited
Hyundai Motor UK Limited
Kwik-Fit (GB) Limited
L & L Inc Limited
Lantern Recovery Specialists PLC
Marshall Motor Group Limited
Marshall North West Limited
Marshall Thermo King Limited
Marshall of Scunthorpe Limited
Marshall of Stevenage Limited
Motor Parts Direct Limited
Motus Group (UK) Limited
Murkett Brothers Limited
Norfolk Truck & Van Limited
Palmers (St Albans) Limited
Pertwee & Back,Limited
Pratt & Whitney Canada (UK) Ltd
Quest Motor Group Limited
Robinsons Autoservices Limited
S & B Commercials Limited
Services Machinery & Trucks Ltd
Silver Street Automotive Ltd
Solus (London) Limited
Sovereign Recovery (UK) Ltd
Specialist Cars Tring Limited
Taylors Service Garages (Boston) Ltd
Thurlow Nunn Limited
Truckeast Limited
Underwoods Garage (Tiptree) Ltd
VMS (Fleet Management) Limited
F. Vindis & Sons (Bedford) Ltd
F. Vindis & Sons (Sawston) Ltd
Vindis Developments Limited
Vindis Group Limited

45310 Wholesale trade of motor vehicle parts and accessories [23]

Aprite (GB) Limited
L Bennett & Son Holdings Ltd
Brayleys Cars Limited
Caterpillar Logistics (UK) Ltd
R.H.Claydon Limited
Comline Auto Parts Limited
Commercial Body Fittings Ltd
Denso Automotive UK Ltd.
Durite Limited

EMS-FP & S Limited
FAI Automotive PLC
Ford Retail Limited
John Grose Group Limited
Group Tyre Wholesale Limited
A.W. & D. Hammond Limited
Hyundai Motor UK Limited
Iveco Limited
Quest Motor Group Limited
Rolling Components Limited
Ssangyong Motor UK Limited
Stapleton's (Tyre Services) Ltd
Thule Outdoor Limited
Yazaki Europe Limited

45320 Retail trade of motor vehicle parts and accessories [30]

John Banks Limited
Bussey & Sabberton Bros.Limited
Chassis-Cab Limited
Citygate Automotive Limited
Fairfield Garage (Leigh-on-Sea) Ltd
Frank G. Gates Limited
Harris Commercial Repairs Ltd
Holden & Holden Limited
L & L Inc Limited
Marriott Motor Group Limited
Marshall North West Limited
Marshall of Scunthorpe Limited
Marshall of Stevenage Limited
Motor Parts Direct Limited
Motus Group (UK) Limited
Pertwee & Back,Limited
Ridgeway Garages (Newbury) Ltd
Robinsons Autoservices Limited
S & B Commercials Limited
Services Machinery & Trucks Ltd
Silver Street Automotive Ltd
Specialist Cars Tring Limited
Taylors Service Garages (Boston) Ltd
Thurlow Nunn Limited
Trailer Resources Limited
Underwoods Garage (Tiptree) Ltd
F. Vindis & Sons (Bedford) Ltd
F. Vindis & Sons (Sawston) Ltd
Vindis Developments Limited
Vindis Group Limited

45400 Sale, maintenance and repair of motorcycles and related parts and accessories

Palmers (St Albans) Limited

46110 Agents selling agricultural raw materials, livestock, textile raw materials and semi-finished goods

Agricultural Central Trading Ltd
Askew & Barrett (Pulses) Ltd
Elsoms (Spalding) Limited
Elsoms Seeds Limited
Fengrain Limited
Harlow Agricultural Merchants Ltd

46120 Agents involved in the sale of fuels, ores, metals and industrial chemicals

Agricultural Central Trading Ltd
CGN Global Uranium Limited
Optima Chemical Ltd

46130 Agents involved in the sale of timber and building materials [18]

Anglo-Norden Forest Products Ltd
Bauder Limited
Brooks Bros. (UK) Limited
H. Butterfield Limited
CED Limited
Danzer UK Limited
Davroc Limited
Grant & Stone Limited
Kent,Blaxill & Co Ltd
Lawsons Holdings Limited
McGrath Bros. (Waste Control) Ltd
Olivewood Limited
Plaut International Limited
Ridgeons Limited
Solopark Limited
Velfac Limited
Vida Wood UK Limited
Wood International Agency Ltd

46140 Agents involved in the sale of machinery, industrial equipment, ships and aircraft [17]

Air Works Empire UK Limited
Air Works UK Engineering Ltd
George Browns Limited
Burdens Group Limited
Citizen Machinery UK Ltd
Claas UK Limited
Ernest Doe & Sons Limited
Gentec Energy PLC
Haas 2007 Limited
Haas Automation Limited
Industrial Tool Supplies (London)
Mitcham Earthmoving Limited
G.& J.Peck Limited
Phoenix Datacom Limited
Reesink Turfcare UK Limited
Services Machinery & Trucks Ltd
Terex Cranes UK Limited

46160 Agents involved in the sale of textiles, clothing, fur, footwear and leather goods

Branded Stocks (UK) Ltd
Start-Rite Shoes Limited

46170 Agents involved in the sale of food, beverages and tobacco

G's Growers Limited
Interlink Direct Limited

46180 Agents specialised in the sale of other particular products [14]

AOC (UK) Ltd
Aprirose Trading Limited
Basetek Limited
A. T. Cross Limited
Dron & Dickson Limited
H. Erben Holdings Limited
Franke Coffee Systems UK Ltd
I Hennig & Co Limited
Movac Holdings Limited
Northwood Paper Sales Limited
Sara (London) Limited
TES Enterprise Solutions Ltd
Thorlabs Limited
Vega Industries Limited

46190 Agents involved in the sale of a variety of goods

Days of Your Life Limited
H.Erben Limited
Farsound Aviation Limited
I.S. Group Limited
TJX Europe Buying (Deutschland) Ltd

46210 Wholesale of grain, unmanufactured tobacco, seeds and animal feeds

ADM Arkady Limited
Fengrain (Services) Limited
Frederic Smart & Son Limited
G.J.W.Titmuss Limited

46220 Wholesale of flowers and plants [11]

Flamingo Flowers Ltd.
Flamingo Holdings Limited
Flamingo Horticulture Investments
Flamingo Horticulture Ltd
Greenyard Flowers UK Ltd
MM Flowers Limited
OAT 2012 Limited
O.A.Taylor & Sons Bulbs Ltd
J. Van Vliet London Cash & Carry
Zara UK Midco Limited
Zara UK Topco Limited

46230 Wholesale of live animals

Tattersalls Limited

46310 Wholesale of fruit and vegetables [30]

AMT Fruit Limited
Bristol Fruit Sales (Market) Ltd
Capespan International Limited
Crop's Foods Ltd.
Fesa (UK) Limited
Flamingo Holdings Limited
Flamingo Horticulture Investments
Flamingo Produce Ltd.
Greenyard Fresh UK Ltd
Keelings Fresh International Ltd
LDH (La Doria) Limited
A.E. Lenton Limited
MM (UK) Limited
Manor Fresh Limited
Place UK Limited
S H Pratt Holdings Limited
Produce World Group Ltd
Redbridge Produce & Flowers Ltd
Reynolds Catering Supplies Ltd
A Russell (Farmers) Limited
J O Sims Holdings Limited
J O Sims Limited
Stourgarden Limited
Total Produce Limited
Total Worldfresh Limited
UK Salads Limited
Unifruit Limited
Winfresh (UK) Limited
Worldwide Fruit Limited
Zara UK Midco Limited

46320 Wholesale of meat and meat products [15]

ASG2 Limited
Anzco Foods UK Limited
Autumn Foods Holdings Limited
C & K Meats Limited
Cook's Delights Limited
GPS Food Group (UK) Limited
Hallam Meat Co Ltd
Interlink Direct Limited
JBS Global (UK) Limited
Lakeside Food Group Limited
Reids of Norwich Limited
H. Smith Food Group PLC
Tazaki Foods Limited
Towers & Co.,Limited
Towers Thompson Holdings Ltd

46330 Wholesale of dairy products, eggs and edible oils and fats

P J Southgate Limited

46341 Wholesale of fruit and vegetable juices, mineral water and soft drinks

Crop's Foods Ltd.

46342 Wholesale of wine, beer, spirits and other alcoholic beverages [13]

Adnams PLC
Blue Tree Limited
Dhamecha Foods Limited
John E.Fells & Sons Limited
Hallgarten Wines,Limited
Lay & Wheeler Limited
Majestic Wine PLC
Majestic Wine Warehouses Ltd
Millennium Cash & Carry Ltd
Naked Wines Prepayments Trustee Co Ltd
Thomas Ridley and Son,Limited
Spar (UK) Limited
Wise Trading Limited

46370 Wholesale of coffee, tea, cocoa and spices

Masteroast Coffee Co. Limited
Masteroast Holdings Limited

46380 Wholesale of other food, including fish, crustaceans and molluscs

Cook's Delights Limited
Crop's Foods Ltd.
Freiberger (UK) Limited
Indo European Foods Limited
Interlink Direct Limited
Martin Mathew & Co. Limited
Osem U.K. Limited
Starke Industries Limited

46390 Non-specialised wholesale of food, beverages and tobacco [21]

Barnack Estates UK Limited
Velji Bhovan & Sons (Trading) Ltd
Britannia Soft Drinks Limited
Britvic EMEA Limited
Britvic International Investments
Britvic Soft Drinks Limited
Dayla Holdings Limited
Dhamecha Foods Limited
Donatantonio Limited
Friar's Pride Limited
Grace Foods UK Limited
JJ Food Service Limited
Lituanica UK Ltd
Midland Chilled Foods Limited
Pilgrim Foodservice Limited
Thomas Ridley and Son,Limited
Robinsons Soft Drinks Limited
SOP International Limited
Smithfield Foods Limited
John A.Taylor & Sons Limited
Tazaki Foods Limited

46410 Wholesale of textiles

Alami International Limited
Premier Quilting Co Ltd
Ashley Wilde Group Limited
Winter & Co. UK Limited
Zian Hi-Tech (U.K.) Limited

46420 Wholesale of clothing and footwear [13]

Brand Machine Limited
Direct Boot and Shoe Supplies Ltd
E. Feldman Limited
Flyers CNV Limited
HPC Healthline UK Limited
Hi-Tec Sports PLC
Ralph Lauren UK Limited
Perry Ellis Europe Limited
Popsoda Limited
Result Clothing Limited
Skechers USA Ltd.
James Southall & Co Ltd
Totes Isotoner (UK) Limited

46431 Wholesale of audio tapes, records, CDs and video tapes and the equipment on which these are played

Pioneer DJ Europe Limited

46439 Wholesale of radio, television goods & electrical household appliances (other than records, tapes, CDs)

Abbey Cross Trading Limited
Alba Broadcasting Corporation Ltd
Alpha 3 Manufacturing Limited
Armour Home Electronics Ltd
Astro Lighting Limited
Liebherr - Great Britain Ltd
Medlock Electrical Distributors Ltd
Merloni Domestic Appliances Ltd

46440 Wholesale of china and glassware and cleaning materials

E.F.G. Housewares Limited

46450 Wholesale of perfume and cosmetics

Beauty Wholesale Limited
Benefit Cosmetics Limited
Bluestar Enterprise Limited
Imperial Pharmaceuticals Ltd
S A Designer Parfums Limited
Shaneel Enterprises Limited

46460 Wholesale of pharmaceutical goods [43]

A1 Pharmaceuticals Holdings Ltd
A1 Pharmaceuticals PLC
Accord Healthcare Limited
Astrazeneca PLC
BR Pharma International Ltd
Beta Pharmaceuticals Limited
Bracco UK Limited
Bristol Laboratories Limited
Chemilines Group Holdings Ltd
Chemilines Limited
Clinimed Limited
Creo Pharma Limited
Dallas Burston Ashbourne Holdings
Davis and Dann Limited
EUSA Pharma (UK) Limited
Eisai Limited
Emcure Pharma UK Ltd
Ethypharm UK Limited
Galderma (U.K.) Limited
Genesis Pharmaceuticals Ltd
Glenmark Pharmaceuticals Europe Ltd
Gowrie Laxmico Limited
Kanta Enterprises Limited
Laxmi BNS Holdings Limited
Laxmico Limited
Lundbeck Limited
Manichem Limited
Miller & Miller (Chemicals) Ltd
Milpharm Limited
Mundibiopharma Limited
Mylan UK Healthcare Limited
Napp Laboratories Limited
Napp Pharmaceutical Group Ltd
Napp Pharmaceutical Holdings Ltd
Napp Pharmaceuticals Limited
NeilMed Holding Co Ltd
Ontex Retail UK Limited
Pharmaceuticals Direct Limited
Strides Pharma Global (UK) Ltd
Takeda UK Limited
Tillomed Laboratories Limited
United Therapeutics Europe, Ltd.
Virbac Limited

46470 Wholesale of furniture, carpets and lighting equipment

Abbey Cross Trading Limited
Mayfair Carpet Gallery Limited
Medlock Electrical Distributors Ltd

46499 Wholesale of household goods (other than musical instruments) n.e.c [16]

Countrywide Electrical Distributors
DBD Distribution Limited
Deben Group Industries Limited
George East (Housewares) Ltd
S. Franses Limited
Hamelin Brands Limited
R. Maskell Limited
PMS International Group PLC
PMS International Holdings PLC
Playmobil (U.K.) Limited
Premier Decorations Limited
Rhone Products (UK) Limited
Robinson Young Limited
Sifcon International PLC
Tobar Group Trading Limited
Wisdom Toothbrushes Limited

46510 Wholesale of computers, computer peripheral equipment and software

Direktek Ltd
Epson (U.K.) Limited
Getech Limited
Midwich Group PLC
NEC (UK) Ltd.
Optoma Europe Ltd
Premier 1983 Limited
Viglen Limited

46520 Wholesale of electronic and telecommunications equipment and parts [15]

Anglia Components Limited
Arrow Electronics (UK) Limited
Astute Electronics Limited
Connectix Limited
Dron & Dickson Limited
Fluke (UK) Limited
Greentech Distribution PLC
Megaman (UK) Limited
Movac Holdings Limited
NEC (UK) Ltd.
NEC Europe Ltd
Narada Europe (UK) Ltd
Pioneer DJ Europe Limited
Rapid Electronics Limited
Sumitomo Electric Europe Ltd

46610 Wholesale of agricultural machinery, equipment and supplies

Agri-Chemicals Limited
Ernest Doe & Sons Limited
John W. Doubleday Limited
Sunlight PV Ltd
P. Tuckwell Limited

46650 Wholesale of office furniture

Global Chair Components Ltd

46660 Wholesale of other office machinery and equipment

Hamelin Brands Limited

46690 Wholesale of other machinery and equipment [16]

3D Systems Europe Limited
Abbey Cross Trading Limited
Agrifac UK Ltd
Draeger Medical UK Limited
Eastern Attachments Limited
Gleneden Plant Sales Limited
ITAB Shop Products UK Ltd
Klipspringer Limited
Life Fitness (UK) Limited
Medlock Electrical Distributors Ltd
Quinta Raddison Limited
R P Valves Limited
Jack Sealey Limited
Snap-On Equipment Limited
Trend Machinery & Cutting Tools Ltd
Wholesale Welding Supplies Ltd

46711 Wholesale of petroleum and petroleum products

AMI Corporations Ltd
Strauss Logistics Limited

46719 Wholesale of other fuels and related products

Agri-Chemicals Limited
Corona Gas Management Limited

46720 Wholesale of metals and metal ores

A.J.N. Steelstock Ltd.
Associated Lead Mills Ltd.
Orion Alloys Limited
Precon Products Ltd
RJM Metal Consultancy Limited
Smiths Metal Centres Limited

46730 Wholesale of wood, construction materials and sanitary equipment [19]

Brooks Bros. (UK) Limited
C P Timber Limited
Distribution Supplies Limited
KDM International Limited
KFM Holdings Limited
James Latham PLC
Lathams Limited
Lawsons (Whetstone) Limited
Layher Limited
Robert Lee Distribution Ltd
MDM Timber Limited
Movac Holdings Limited
N & C Building Products Ltd
Penlaw & Co Ltd
Porcelanosa (South East) Ltd
Precon Products Ltd
George A. Sherriff Limited
Timber Connection Limited
George Tufts and Son Limited

46740 Wholesale of hardware, plumbing and heating equipment and supplies [10]

A P P Wholesale PLC
Blanco UK Limited
Carl F Groupco Limited
Robert Lee Distribution Ltd
Plumbcity Limited
Rollins & Sons (London) Ltd
S.T.C.Plumbing & Heating Merchants
Saniflo Limited
George Tufts and Son Limited
Vokera Limited

46750 Wholesale of chemical products

Aprirose Trading Limited
Azelis UK Life Sciences Ltd
Bayer Cropscience Limited
Belchim Crop Protection Ltd
Cambridge Commodities Limited
Cornelius Group PLC
De Sangosse Ltd.
Noahs Ark Chemicals Limited
Orthene Holdings Limited

46760 Wholesale of other intermediate products

Arpo Global Limited
Dron & Dickson Limited
HTG Trading Limited
Hamamatsu Photonics UK Limited
Ovenden Papers Limited
Ripmax Limited
Southgate Packaging Limited
WWW Sunoptic Com UK Limited

46770 Wholesale of waste and scrap

Aprirose Trading Limited
Robert Gibbs (Contracting) Co Ltd
Glazewing Limited
Global Metcorp Limited
Solopark Limited

46900 Non-specialised wholesale trade [75]

A.C. Entertainment Technologies Ltd
John Adams Leisure Limited
Ardex Holdings UK Limited
Ariston Thermo UK Ltd
Avnet EMG Ltd.
B.M. Polyco Limited
BEW Electrical Distributors Ltd
BRT (Wisbech) Limited
Ball. Roller & Transmission Bearings
Balton CP Limited
Beckman Coulter United Kingdom Ltd
M.W. Beer & Co. Limited
Bertram Trading Limited
Besana UK Limited
Bio-Rad Laboratories Limited
Bracco UK Limited
British Gaskets Limited
Brown Brothers Distribution Ltd
Buffaload Logistics Limited
Chartco Limited
Coloplast Limited
Community Foods Limited
Costco UK Holdings Limited
Costco Wholesale UK Limited
Dalebrook Supplies Limited
Dawson Books Limited
Displayplan Limited
Dorma UK Limited
Elite Mobile Limited
Festool UK Limited
GE Medical Systems Limited
GVS Prepaid Limited
Go Interiors Limited
Grant & Bowman Limited
F.W. Hipkin Limited
Hoo Hing Holdings Limited
Hoo Hing Limited
Huxley Global Limited
Hydraquip Hose & Hydraulics Ltd
I.S. Group Limited
IT Luggage Limited
Icandy World Limited
Kampa UK Ltd
Katsouris Brothers Limited
Keymed (Medical & Industrial Equipment)
L & M (Heating) Supplies Ltd
LC Packaging UK Ltd
Leisuregrow Products Limited
Longmill Realty Limited
Luxottica North Europe Limited
Micross Foods Holdings Limited
Midwich Limited
Morelli Group Limited
Nordson (U.K.) Limited
PX Manufacturing Ltd
Regaltags Global Limited
Rigby Taylor Limited
Rotamead Limited
Rowan International Limited
Shopfittings Direct Limited
Smith Bros Timber (East Anglia) Ltd
South Essex Stockholders Ltd

Specflue Limited
Staples UK Limited
Stuart Group Limited
Sunnen Products Limited
Syngenta UK Limited
R.C.Treatt & Co.Limited
Treatt PLC
Unit Export Limited
Venture Lighting Europe Ltd
Voicevale Limited
Wheatland Cheese Co. Limited
Wilkinson Sword Limited
A & A Woodford Limited

47110 Retail sale in non-specialised stores with food, beverages or tobacco predominating [18]

C.T. Baker Limited
Crop's Foods Ltd.
Esin Cash & Carry Limited
Falkland Islands Co Ltd
A.E.Hewison Limited
J P & S Servicess Ltd
LB Enterprises Limited
McColl's Retail Group PLC
Ocado Group PLC
Ocado Retail Limited
Rateneed Limited
Roys (Wroxham),Limited
Smile Stores Limited
Spar Food Distributors Limited
Tazaki Foods Limited
Tesco PLC
Tesco Stores Limited
Virgin Wine Online Limited

47190 Other retail sale in non-specialised stores [17]

Velji Bhovan & Sons (Trading) Ltd
Boing Acquisitions Limited
Boing Midco Limited
Clarke International Limited
Clarke Property Partner Ltd
Flying Trade Limited
Hi-Tec Europe Limited
International Car Wash Group Ltd.
Jarrold & Sons Limited
LC Packaging UK Ltd
Moto Hospitality Limited
Notcutts Group Limited
Notcutts Limited
Oldrid & Co.,Limited
Parkstone Limited
Pepkor UK Retail Limited
Roys (Wroxham),Limited

47210 Retail sale of fruit and vegetables in specialised stores

LB Enterprises Limited
Spar (UK) Limited

47220 Retail sale of meat and meat products in specialised stores

Spar Food Distributors Limited

47230 Retail sale of fish, crustaceans and molluscs in specialised stores

Spar Food Distributors Limited

47240 Retail sale of bread, cakes, flour confectionery and sugar confectionery in specialised stores

Hadleigh Bakery Limited
Hotel Chocolat Retail Ltd

47250 Retail sale of beverages in specialised stores

Adnams PLC
C.T. Baker Limited
Greene King Brewing and Retailing
Www.Nakedwines.Com Limited

47260 Retail sale of tobacco products in specialised stores

Dillons Stores Limited
Martin McColl Limited
Smile Stores Limited
Spar (UK) Limited
TM Vending Limited

47290 Other retail sale of food in specialised stores

KFG Quickserve Limited
Spar (UK) Limited
Spar Food Distributors Limited
Tesco Stores Limited

47300 Retail sale of automotive fuel in specialised stores [13]

AS24 Fuel Card Ltd
Chartman Limited
Duff Morgan & Vermont Limited
J P & S Servicess Ltd
Malthurst Limited
Malthurst Petroleum Limited
Manor Service Stations Limited
Moto Hospitality Limited
Motor Fuel Limited
Murkett Brothers Limited
Roadside Group Ltd
Spring Petroleum Co Ltd
St Albans Operating Co Ltd

47410 Retail sale of computers, peripheral units and software in specialised stores

Elegant Electronics Limited

47430 Retail sale of audio and video equipment in specialised stores

Brighthouse Group Limited
Brighthouse Holdings Limited

47510 Retail sale of textiles in specialised stores

Asiatic Carpets Holdings Ltd

47520 Retail sale of hardware, paints and glass in specialised stores

Thomas Brooker & Sons Limited
Kent Blaxill Group Limited
Movac Group Limited

47530 Retail sale of carpets, rugs, wall and floor coverings in specialised stores

Glasswells Limited
Mayfair Carpet Gallery Limited

47540 Retail sale of electrical household appliances in specialised stores

Brighthouse Group Limited
Brighthouse Holdings Limited
Brighthouse Limited
Caversham Finance Limited
Caversham Trading Limited
Hughes Electrical Limited
Hughes TV and Audio Limited
Stellison Limited

47599 Retail of furniture, lighting, and similar (not musical instruments or scores) in specialised store [15]

Anglia Home Furnishings Holdings Ltd
C.T. Baker Limited
Brighthouse Limited
Caversham Finance Limited
Caversham Trading Limited
Chard Properties (UK) Limited
Choice Discount Stores Limited
Dreams Limited
Fishpools Limited
Glasswells Limited
Medlock Electrical Distributors Ltd
Poggenpohl Group UK Limited
Scotsdale Nursery and Garden Centre
TK Maxx
Willis Gambier (UK) Limited

47620 Retail sale of newspapers and stationery in specialised stores

Frontline Limited
Seymour Distribution Limited
Seymour International Limited

47640 Retail sale of sports goods, fishing gear, camping goods, boats and bicycles

Wensum Valley Hotel Golf & Country Club

47650 Retail sale of games and toys in specialised stores

Alex Brands Rocket Holdings Ltd
Entertainer (Amersham) Limited
Tobar Group Trading Limited

47710 Retail sale of clothing in specialised stores [10]

AK Retail Holdings Limited
Choice Discount Stores Limited
W.D. Coe Limited
Ralph Lauren UK Limited
Perry Ellis Europe Limited
Sabre Retail Fashion Limited
Stonemanor Limited
TK Maxx
Tesco Stores Limited
Yours Clothing Limited

47721 Retail sale of footwear in specialised stores

Direct Boot and Shoe Supplies Ltd
Hi-Tec Sports UK Limited
Sabre Retail Fashion Limited
Skechers USA Ltd.
Twinmar Limited

47722 Retail sale of leather goods in specialised stores

Direct Boot and Shoe Supplies Ltd
Sabre Retail Fashion Limited

47730 Dispensing chemist in specialised stores

Borno Chemists Limited
Elgon (Enfield) Limited
Jalaram Limited
Manichem Limited
Ramco (Harlow) Limited
T. Visaman & Sons Limited

47749 Retail sale of medical and orthopaedic goods in specialised stores (not incl. hearing aids) n.e.c.

Wright Medical UK Ltd

47750 Retail sale of cosmetic and toilet articles in specialised stores

Tesco Stores Limited

47760 Retail sale of flowers, plants, seeds, fertilizers, pet animals and pet food in specialised stores

Leonard F.Jollye (Brookmans Park)
Meldongreen Limited
Perrywood Garden Centre & Nurseries
Scotsdale Nursery and Garden Centre
Van Hage & Company (Holdings) Ltd
Van Hage & Co Ltd

47770 Retail sale of watches and jewellery in specialised stores

D.C.K. Concessions Limited
H.Stain Limited
H.Stern (Jewellery) Limited

47781 Retail sale in commercial art galleries

Thomas Gibson Fine Art Ltd

47782 Retail sale by opticians

Luxottica Retail UK Ltd

47789 Other retail sale of new goods in specialised stores (not commercial art galleries and opticians) [11]

AG Retail Cards Limited
Bathstore Group Limited
Bathstore.Com Limited
Early Learning Centre Limited
International Car Wash Group Financing
Mothercare PLC.
Mothercare UK Limited
S & T Audio Limited
TJX Europe Limited
TJX UK
G.J.W.Titmuss Limited

47799 Retail sale of other second-hand goods in stores (not incl. antiques)

Capital Cash Limited
Thomas Dane Limited
Sinai (Antiques) Limited

47910 Retail sale via mail order houses or via Internet [13]

Activity Superstore Limited
Buyagift PLC
Chocolate Tasting Club PLC
Ideal Shopping Direct Limited
Ironmongerydirect Limited
Lifeplus Europe Limited
Monumart Limited
Morplan Limited
Mothercare UK Limited
Registration Transfers Limited
Sabre Retail Fashion Limited
Speciality Stores Limited
Warehouse Express Limited

47990 Other retail sale not in stores, stalls or markets [12]

Astro Lighting Holdings Ltd
Beko PLC
Claas Eastern Ltd
Claas Manns Ltd
Claas Western Ltd
Ideal Shopping Direct Limited
Korda Developments Limited
Leica Microsystems (UK) Ltd
Lifeplus Europe Limited
Olivewood Limited
Qatar Bloodstock Limited
Tesco International Internet Retailing

49200 Freight rail transport

Woodland Global Ltd

49319 Other urban, suburban or metropolitan passenger land transport (not underground, metro or similar)

First Eastern Counties Buses Ltd
First Essex Buses Limited
First Midland Red Buses Ltd
First Potteries Limited
Leicester Citybus Limited

49320 Taxi operation

Colts Cabs Limited

49390 Other passenger land transport

Ensign Bus Co Ltd
Hats Group Ltd
Leicester Citybus Limited
Skewbald Limited
Stephensons of Essex Limited

49410 Freight transport by road [46]

Agri Business Limited
Bartrum's Road Services Ltd
Bartrums Haulage and Storage Ltd
Buffaload Logistics Limited
Carlson Vehicle Transfer Ltd
DSV Road Limited
Delamode PLC
Ebrex Business Solutions Ltd
Express Freight Services (U.K.) Ltd
Fitzmaurice Holdings Limited
Forest Freight Limited
Foulger Transport Limited
Freshlinc Group Limited
Freshlinc Limited
Fricor Limited
Geodis United Kingdom Limited
Goldstar Transport Limited
Peter Green Haulage Limited
P.C. Howard Limited
I F E Global Holdings Limited
Industrial Chemicals Limited
Knowles (Transport) Limited
MacIntyre Transport Limited
Maritime Group Limited
Maritime Transport Limited
Martin-Brower UK Ltd
Matthews International Transport Ltd
Moores Refrigeration Controlled Transport
O'Malley Haulage Limited
PCL Transport Limited
Pass J. Holdings Limited
Polar Speed Distribution Ltd
R.B.R. (Crops) Limited
Jack Richards & Son Limited
Staples (Vegetables) Limited
J.W. Suckling Transport Ltd
Tesco Distribution Limited
P.J. Thory Limited
Transmec UK Limited
Turners (Soham) Holdings Ltd
Turners (Soham) Limited
Unique Forwarding Limited
Uniserve (Europe) Limited
Roger Warnes Transport Ltd
David Watson Transport Ltd
Welch's Group Holdings Limited

49500 Transport via pipeline

British Pipeline Agency Ltd
GTC Pipelines Limited

50100 Sea and coastal passenger water transport

Harwich International Port Ltd

50200 Sea and coastal freight water transport [31]

Alcedo Shipping Limited
B Crystal Limited
B Emerald Limited
Cosco Maritime (UK) Limited
Cosco Shipping Lines (UK) Ltd
Damco UK Limited
Fulton Maritime Holdings Ltd
Fulton Maritime Limited
Geodis United Kingdom Limited
Global Marine Systems (Vessels) Ltd
Harwich International Port Ltd
Hudson Kensington Limited
Hudson Lisse Limited
Hudson Richmond Limited
Maritime Transport Services Ltd
Oblue Limited
Ocourage Limited
Port of Felixstowe Limited
Scotline Limited
UML Chiltern Limited
UML Eagle Limited
UML Marylebone Limited
UML Mayfair Limited
UML Wembley Limited
UML Westminster Limited
UML Wigmore Limited
Union Carriers Limited
Union Maritime Limited
Uniserve Limited

Woodland Global Ltd
Yang Ming (UK) Ltd

50300 Inland passenger water transport

Norfolk Broads Direct Limited

51101 Scheduled passenger air transport

Thomas Cook Airlines Limited
Easyjet Airline Co Ltd
NHV Helicopters Ltd
RSS Jet Centre Limited
Stansted Airport Limited
TUI Airways Limited

51102 Non-scheduled passenger air transport [10]

Amsair Aircraft Limited
First Choice Holidays Limited
Klyne Air Limited
Klyne Aviation Limited
London Executive Aviation Ltd
NHV Helicopters Ltd
Premiair Aerospace Limited
RSS Jet Centre Limited
Signature Flight Support London Luton
Titan Airways Limited

51210 Freight air transport

NHV Helicopters Ltd
Titan Airways Limited
Uniserve (Air Freight) Limited
Woodland Global Ltd

52101 Operation of warehousing and storage facilities for water transport activities

ASCO (DC2) Limited
ASCO (DC4) Limited
Maritime Transport Services Ltd
Oikos Storage Limited
Port of Felixstowe Limited
Seabrook Warehousing Limited

52102 Operation of warehousing and storage facilities for air transport activities

Oikos Storage Limited
Seabrook Warehousing Limited
Turpin Distribution Services Ltd

52103 Operation of warehousing and storage facilities for land transport activities [25]

ASCO (DC2) Limited
ASCO (DC4) Limited
Bowler Group Limited
Chiltern Cold Storage Group Ltd
Delamode PLC
Fitzmaurice Holdings Limited
Garrets International Limited
Geodis United Kingdom Limited
Peter Green Haulage Limited
P.C. Howard Limited
Import Services Limited
Richard Johnston Limited
W Lamb Limited
London City Bond Limited
Martin-Brower UK Ltd
Navigator Terminals Seal Sands Ltd
Norish Limited
Oikos Storage Limited
Seabourne Group Limited
Seabrook Warehousing Limited
Simarco International Limited
Frederic Smart & Son Limited
Transmec UK Limited
Turners (Soham) Holdings Ltd
Turpin Distribution Services Ltd

52211 Operation of rail freight terminals

Maritime Transport Services Ltd
Port of Felixstowe Limited

52219 Other service activities incidental to land transportation, n.e.c.

Balgores Motors (1982) Limited
Bucci Freight Services Limited
Geodis United Kingdom Limited
H.& G.Car Parks Limited
Simarco International Limited
Ziegler UK Limited

52220 Service activities incidental to water transportation

Mediterranean Shipping Company (UK)
Port of Tilbury London Limited
Ziegler UK Limited

52230 Service activities incidental to air transportation

Aerospares 2000 Limited
Air Works Empire UK Limited
Air Works UK Engineering Ltd
GH London Ground Handling Services
KLM UK Engineering Limited
London Luton Airport Operations Ltd
Norwich Airport Limited
Propshop Limited
Ziegler UK Limited

52241 Cargo handling for water transport activities

Harwich International Port Ltd
Maritime Transport Services Ltd
Port of Boston Limited
Port of Felixstowe Limited

52243 Cargo handling for land transport activities

Seabourne Group Limited
Simarco International Limited

52290 Other transportation support activities [29]

ASCO (DC2) Limited
ASCO (DC4) Limited
Alpi UK Limited
M.W. Beer & Co. Limited
Roberto Bucci (U.K.) Limited
Cosco Shipping (UK) Co Ltd
DSV Air & Sea Limited
DSV Road Holding Limited
DSV Solutions Limited
East Midlands Training Limited
Hapag-Lloyd (U.K.) Limited
Harbour Shipping Limited
JF Hillebrand UK Limited
Kenwake Limited
L V Shipping Limited
Movac Group Limited
OOCL (Europe) Limited
OOCL Logistics (Europe) Ltd
PFE Express Limited
Perrin Group Holdings Limited
Saba Infra Cambridgeshire Ltd
Saba Infra Cardiff Limited
Saba Infra Gloucestershire Ltd
Saba Infra Hertfordshire Ltd
Saba Park Services UK Limited
Seabourne Group Limited
Transam Trucking Limited
Woodland Global Ltd
Ziegler UK Limited

53201 Licensed carriers

P2P Mailing Ltd

53202 Unlicensed carriers

Air Business Limited

55100 Hotels and similar accommodation [85]

Abacus Hotels Limited
Abington Group Limited
Ace Investments Limited
Adda Hotels
Agellus Hotels Limited
Alterra Farms Limited
Ariyan Hotels Limited
Beale's Hotels Limited
Beale's Limited
Bryant Park Hospitality UK Ltd
Buckingham Hotels Group Ltd
Butlins Operations Limited
CP Regents Park Two Limited
CQK Limited
Carnarvon Hotels Limited
Castle Green Kendal Limited
Chartridge Conference Co Ltd
Chester International Hotel Ltd
Derbyshire Hotel Derby Limited
FIC Grand Plaza Ltd
Fairview Hotels Limited
Five Star Inns Limited
Gonville Hotels Limited
Goodwill SIP Limited
Gough Hotels Limited
Greene King Retailing Limited
HLT Stakis Operator Limited
Harrogate International Hotel Ltd
Hevingham Development Co Ltd
Heythrop Park Limited
Highrak Limited
Hilton International Hotels (UK) Ltd
Hilton International IP Holding 2
Hilton International IP Holding Ltd
Hilton UK Hotels Limited
Hilton UK Manage Limited
Hilton Worldwide Holding 2 Ltd
Hilton Worldwide Manage Ltd
Historic House Hotels Limited
Hoole Hall Country Club Ltd
Hotel Folk Limited
Kingsway Hall Hotel Limited
CW Lamley & Co Limited
Leena Plaza Limited
Letchworth Hall Hotel (Trading) Ltd
London Inn Hotels (Stratford) Ltd
Melton House Investments Ltd

Metro Properties Limited
Mill Hotel Limited
Moller Institute Limited
Moto Hospitality Limited
Mouskos & Sons Co. Limited
Nine Heathrow Ventures Limited
Nine Reading Hotel Limited
Norfolk Capital Hotels Limited
Pantheon Hotels and Leisure Ltd
Poste Holdings Limited
Poste Hotels Limited
Premier Euro Hotels Limited
Premier Inn Hotels Limited
Premier Inn International Development
Premier Inn Ochre Limited
Q.N. Hotels Limited
SAFL British Hotels Limited
SBH Gatwick Limited
SBH Tamworth Limited
Searles (Camping Ground) Ltd
Seasons Hotels Limited
Shiva Kingsway Limited
Solihull Hotel Co Ltd
St.Michael's Manor Limited
Surya Hotels Limited
Sussex Gardens Hotels Limited
Truman Securities Limited
UK Holiday Group Limited
Ufford Park Limited
Ventress Group Limited
Victoria Docks Hotel Co Ltd
Walsingham College Trust Association
Waverley House Hotel Limited
Wensum Valley Hotel Golf & Country Club
Wentworth Hotel Limited
Whitbread Group PLC
Whitbread Hotel Co Ltd
Wivenhoe House Hotel Limited

55201 Holiday centres and villages

Away Resorts Limited
Sandy Balls Estate Limited
Walter John Cook and Sons Ltd
Flamborough Holidays Limited
Richardsons Leisure Limited
Searles (Camping Ground) Ltd
Tattershall Lakes Limited
Whitecliff Bay Holiday Park Ltd

55209 Other holiday and other collective accommodation

Timewell Properties Limited
Yorkshire Dales Country Park Ltd

55300 Recreational vehicle parks, trailer parks and camping grounds [21]

Birch's Park Homes Limited
Blue Anchor Leisure Limited
Bourne Leisure (Hopton) Ltd
Bourne Leisure Group Limited
Bourne Leisure Holdings Ltd
Bourne Leisure Limited
Butlins Skyline Limited
Coastfields Leisure Limited
Hardys Farm Limited
Haven Leisure Limited
A.E.Hewison Limited
Kiln Park Estates Limited
Kings Leisure Limited
Leisure Parks Real Estate Ltd
Palmhall Limited
Rockley Sands (Estates) Ltd
Searles (Camping Ground) Ltd
Seaside Leisure Parks Limited
Sines Parks Ltd
Thorney Bay Park Limited
Timewell Properties Limited

55900 Other accommodation

CKH Developments Limited
Richard Johnston Limited
Mansley Group Holdings Limited
Oleoland Hotel Co Ltd
SME Properties Limited
Silverton Property Investments Ltd
Stable Lads Welfare Trust Housing Association
Wernick Hire Limited

56101 Licenced restaurants [20]

Anglia Restaurants Ltd
Big Easy Restaurants Limited
Caskade Caterers Limited
Coffeeheaven International Ltd
Costa Limited
Graysons Hospitality Limited
Historic House Hotels Limited
KFG Restaurants Limited
PHH 1 Limited
PHH 2 Limited
Perrywood Garden Centre & Nurseries
Pizza Hut (U.K.) Limited
Poste Holdings Limited
Poste Hotels Limited
Realpubs II Limited
Spirit Group Retail Limited
Spirit Pub Company (Managed) Ltd
Timewell Properties Limited
Wensum Valley Hotel Golf & Country Club
Whitbread Group PLC

56102 Unlicenced restaurants and cafes [15]

Adil Catering Limited
Alderforce Limited
Alderforce North Limited
Arisen Chef Ltd
Chicken Cabins Limited
Demipower (1991) Limited
Demipower Limited
Fieldrose Limited
Graysons Hospitality Limited
Kefco Sales Limited
Moto Hospitality Limited
Mulcroft Limited
Pizza Hut (U.K.) Limited
SOM Restaurants Ltd
Tesco Family Dining Limited

56103 Take-away food shops and mobile food stands

Adil Catering Limited
DOT100 Limited
Yum! III (UK) Limited

56210 Event catering activities

Graysons Hospitality Limited
Heythrop Park Limited
Kudos Catering (UK) Limited
Pizza Gogo Ltd

56290 Other food services [13]

Atalian Servest Food Co Ltd
Chartridge Conference Co Ltd
Enco Products Limited
European Independent Purchasing Co Ltd
Express Vending Limited
GDSK Limited
GK Foods (UK) Limited
HTG Investments Limited
Kaykem Fast Foods Limited
Marsdens Caterers of Sheffield Ltd
Gerald McDonald & Co Ltd
Selecta U.K. Limited
Selecta UK Holding Limited

56302 Public houses and bars [28]

Barley Pub Co Ltd
Bay Restaurant Group Limited
Be at One Holdings Limited
Be at One Limited
Bellcoin Holdings Limited
Capital Pub Co Ltd
Capital Pub Company Trading Ltd
Chestnut Inns Limited
Dominion Pubs and Bars Limited
Gray & Sons (Chelmsford) Ltd
Greene King Brewing and Retailing
Greene King Retailing Limited
Hops Pub Co Ltd
Intertain (Bars) Limited
McMullen & Sons, Limited
Oakman Inns and Restaurants Ltd
Realpubs Limited
Richardsons Leisure Limited
Slug and Lettuce Co Ltd
Spirit (SGL) Limited
Spirit Group Retail Limited
Spirit Pub Company (Leased) Ltd
Spirit Pub Company (Managed) Ltd
Spirit Pub Co Ltd
Town and City Pub Group Ltd
Trafalgar Leisure Ltd
J D Wetherspoon PLC
Whitbread Hotel Co Ltd

58110 Book publishing

Anness Publishing Limited
Jojo's Mojo Limited
Make Believe Ideas Ltd

58130 Publishing of newspapers

Archant Community Media Holdings Ltd
Archant Community Media Ltd
Iliffe Media Limited
Iliffe Print Cambridge Limited
Newsquest Media Group Limited

58141 Publishing of learned journals

Company of Biologists, Limited
Federation of European Biochemical Societies

58142 Publishing of consumer and business journals and periodicals

Media 10 Limited
Warners Group Publications PLC

58190 Other publishing activities

Archant Community Media Ltd
Company of Biologists, Limited
Simon Elvin Limited
Kodak Limited
Micropress Printers Limited
Proquest European Holdings Ltd
Proquest Information and Learning

58210 Publishing of computer games

Frontier Developments PLC
Playags UK Limited

58290 Other software publishing

Aveva Solutions Limited
Road Tech Computer Systems Ltd
Subex (UK) Limited
Zellis UK Limited

59111 Motion picture production activities

QOTD Film Investment Limited
RPSD2 Limited
Reliance Entertainment Productions 7 Ltd
Riverstone Pictures (Show Dogs) Ltd
Riverstone Solutions 2 Limited
Turnlet Films (JN) Limited

59112 Video production activities

Baby Network Limited

59113 Television programme production activities

BBC Studioworks Limited
Bauer Digital Radio Limited
CTV Outside Broadcasts Limited
Kiss FM Radio Limited
Matchroom Sport Limited
Orion Media Limited
Reliance Entertainment Productions 7 Ltd
Telegenic Limited

59131 Motion picture distribution activities

Kotecha Ltd
New Sparta Film Distribution Ltd
Twentieth Century Fox Television Distribution (U.K.), Ltd.

59133 Television programme distribution activities

Baby Network Limited

59200 Sound recording and music publishing activities

Audio Network Limited
Positive Entertainment Ltd
Startling Music Limited

60100 Radio broadcasting

Absolute Radio Limited
Bauer AR Holdings Limited
Celador Radio Broadcasting Ltd

60200 Television programming and broadcasting activities

Al Jazeera International Ltd
Amino Communications Limited
Amino Holdings Limited
Amino Technologies PLC
BBC Studioworks Limited
Gearhouse Broadcast Limited
Ideal Shopping Direct Limited
Islam Channel Limited

61100 Wired telecommunications activities

Comtec Cable Accessories Ltd
Comtec Group (International) Ltd
Getech Limited
Magdalene Limited
Open Fibre Networks Limited

61200 Wireless telecommunications activities

Cyanconnode Holdings PLC
MTK Wireless Limited
Magdalene Limited
Park Air Systems Limited
Ranplan Holdings Limited
Samsung Cambridge Solution Centre
Selex Elsag Limited
Telensa Holdings Limited
Telensa Ltd

61300 Satellite telecommunications activities

Applied Satellite Technology Ltd
Com Dev Europe Limited
Selex Elsag Limited

61900 Other telecommunications activities [23]

Alcatel IP Networks Limited
Bango PLC
Bango. Net Limited
Blancco Technology Group PLC
Business & Communications Ltd
Cambridge Broadband Networks Ltd
Chartco Limited
DB Broadcast Ltd
Deutsche Telekom (UK) Limited
EE Limited
Eckoh PLC
Eckoh UK Limited
Epay Limited
Global Marine Systems Limited
Ingram Micro Services Holdings Ltd
London Internet Exchange Ltd
NEC (UK) Ltd.
Netcall Telecom Limited
Olive Business Solutions Ltd
Subex (UK) Limited
Tesco Mobile Limited
UK Livelines Limited
West One Technology Ltd

62011 Ready-made interactive leisure and entertainment software development

Jagex Limited
Koei Tecmo Europe Limited

62012 Business and domestic software development [27]

ACI Global Limited
Apical Limited
Aveva Finance Limited
Cyberscience PLC
Darktrace Limited
ESRI (UK) Limited
Eurobase Systems Limited
Excitech Limited
GBST Limited
Global Graphics Software Ltd
Granta Design Limited
Industrial and Financial Systems, IFS UK
J.A.C. Computer Services Ltd
Mathworks Limited
NDEMIC Creations Ltd
Netsupport Ltd.
Pitney Bowes Software Holdings Ltd
RealVNC Limited
Red Gate Software Limited
Schneider Electric Software GB Ltd
SintecMedia Global Ltd
SintecMedia WEM Ltd
Smartcomms SC Limited
Symology Limited
Trustonic Limited
VNC Group Limited
Vertical Group Limited

62020 Information technology consultancy activities [44]

1spatial Group Limited
ACI Worldwide (EMEA) Limited
Amino Communications Limited
Amino Holdings Limited
Amino Technologies PLC
Apical Limited
Arinso People Services Limited
Business Control Solutions Group Ltd
Business Control Solutions PLC
Business Management Software Ltd
Comparex UK Limited
Computacenter (UK) Limited
Corbus Europe Limited
Cyberscience PLC
ESRI (UK) Limited
Eurobase Systems Limited
Excelredstone Converged Solutions
Excitech Limited
Getech Limited
J.A.C. Computer Services Ltd
Lumesse Corporate Limited
Lumesse Holdings Limited
Lumesse Holdings UK Limited
Lumesse Limited
MCSA Group Limited
Mass Consultants Limited
Metaswitch Networks Ltd
NHS Shared Business Services Ltd
NPS (UK2) Limited
NPS (UK4) Limited
NPS (UK6) Limited
Net Pay (EUR) Limited
Netcracker Technology EMEA Ltd
Oni PLC
Pitney Bowes Software Europe Ltd
Premier 1983 Limited
Smiths Business Information Services
Sopra Steria Limited
Stefanini International Holdings Ltd

Steria UK Corporate Limited
Subex (UK) Limited
TES Enterprise Solutions Ltd
Trimble UK Limited
Viglen Limited

62030 Computer facilities management activities

Excelredstone Converged Solutions
Excitech Limited
MCSA Group Limited
Oni PLC
Smiths Business Information Services

62090 Other information technology service activities [58]

1spatial PLC
Access UK Ltd
Amino Communications Limited
Amino Holdings Limited
Amino Technologies PLC
Annodata Limited
Apertio Limited
Argon NPS Limited
Arinso People Services Limited
Arinso UK Limited
Bango PLC
Blue 8 Technologies Limited
Boston Limited
CAE Technology Services Ltd
Computacenter (UK) Limited
Contechs Consulting Limited
Cyberscience PLC
D-Link (Europe) Limited
DST Financial Services International
EVI Technologies Limited
Excelredstone Converged Solutions
Excelredstone Services Limited
Excitech Limited
Explorer Holdings UK Limited
Global Resale, Ltd
IMBOLC Limited
Ikarim Business Services Ltd
Imagination Technologies Ltd
J.A.C. Computer Services Ltd
JDM Technology Group Limited
Labvantage Solutions Limited
MCSA Group Limited
Microsoft Research Limited
NEC (UK) Ltd.
NPS (Holdings) Limited
NPS (UK5) Limited
Netcall Telecom Limited
Northgate Public Services Ltd
OEConnection Limited
Ocado Innovation Limited
Oni PLC
Optimise Media (UK) Limited
Paypoint PLC
Quixant PLC
Quixant UK Limited
R.D.Trading Limited
Redsky IT (Hemel) Limited
Riva Topco Limited
Safe Computing Limited
Screen Subtitling Systems Ltd
Smartcomms SC Limited
Smiths Business Information Services
Sopra Steria Services Limited
Storm Technologies Limited
TES Enterprise Solutions Ltd
Tri-Continental Limited
Vix Technology UK Limited
Whitehall Resources Limited

63110 Data processing, hosting and related activities [12]

1spatial Group Limited
Brandbank Limited
DST Financial Services International
Epay Limited
Green Energy Options Ltd
Gyron Internet Limited
Moorepay Limited
Oni PLC
Smiths Business Information Services
Subex (UK) Limited
Trurating Limited
Zellis UK Limited

63990 Other information service activities n.e.c. [11]

Chartco Limited
Forum Trust Limited
IGD Services Limited
Imagination Technologies Group Ltd
Konica Minolta Business Solutions (UK)
Norfolk Community Foundation
Papworth Trust
Premonition Analytics Limited
Proquest UK Holdings Ltd
Quartix Holdings PLC
Wenta

64191 Banks

Aldermore Bank PLC
Enterprise Finance Limited
Jabac Finances Limited
PXP Financial Limited
RQ Capital Limited
Shawbrook Bank Limited

64201 Activities of agricultural holding companies

Farmwealth Limited
Grant Farming Limited
Jepco Limited
A.E. Lenton (Holdings) Ltd
R.& J.M.Place Limited
Pro Cam UK Limited
Spearhead International Ltd
R C Tinsley 2012 Limited

64202 Activities of production holding companies [25]

Ammeraal Beltech UK Holding Ltd
Anexhold Limited
Stephen Austin (Holdings) Ltd
BFC Finance Limited
Baker Perkins Holdings Limited
P.H. Betts (Holdings) Limited
Blackbuck Acquisitions Limited
Blackbuck Midco Limited
Blackbuck Topco Limited
Cardel Group Limited
Domino Investments Limited
Elektron Technology PLC
Euro-Matic (Brazil) Limited
Fidion Limited
HFC Finance Limited
Hexcel Overseas
J & A (International) Holdings Ltd
Jaltek Holdings Limited
K L Technologies Limited
LPA Group PLC
Radical Sportscars Limited
Silverson Machines Holdings Ltd
Thomson Sawmills Holdings Ltd
Trelanoak Limited
WCM Investments Ltd

64203 Activities of construction holding companies [34]

ARJ Construction Holdings Ltd
Alboro Holdings Limited
BAM Construct UK Limited
Barconn Group Limited
Borras Group Holdings Limited
Breyer Holdings Limited
R. G. Carter Holdings Limited
Central Park Enterprises Ltd
Chalcroft Holdings Limited
City North (Telford Homes) Ltd
Connect Plus (M25) Holdings Ltd
Countryside Properties (Holdings)
Countryside Properties (Joint Ventures)
Durman Stearn Holdings Limited
Fairview Holdings Limited
Fairview New Homes Limited
GDL Holdco Limited
Gallagher Holdings Limited
Hill Holdings Limited
JRL Group Holdings Limited
JRL Group Limited
Kier Integrated Services (Holdings)
Kier Integrated Services Group Ltd
Novum Holdings UK Limited
Optima Investments Limited
Project Helix Holdco Ltd
Rogerson Holdings Limited
Rose Group Limited
SEH Group Limited
T & B (Contractors) Holdings Ltd
Tilia Trading Group Limited
Trevester Limited
Volkerrail Group Limited
Woodford Heating Holdings Ltd

64204 Activities of distribution holding companies [16]

Calumet Wex International Ltd
Comline Holdings Limited
Goldstar Transport Holdings Ltd
Grant & Bowman International Ltd
Iveco Holdings Limited
Leisuregrow Holdings Limited
Marchase Limited
New River Holdings Limited
Premier PLC
Q Acoustics Limited
Rapid Electronics Holdings Ltd
Ridley Godfrey (Holdings) Ltd
Royston Holdings Limited
Sealey (UK) Limited
George Thurlow and Sons (Holdings)
Uniserve Holdings Limited

64205 Activities of financial services holding companies [28]

3DS Financial Services EMEA Ltd
3DS Financial Services Ltd
Alterium Limited
BFSL Limited
BGL (Holdings) Limited
BGL Group Limited
Bluestone APAC Holdings Ltd
Bluestone Consolidated Holdings Ltd
Bluestone Mortgage Holdings Ltd
Cadastra Limited
Digital House Group Ltd
Gibbs Denley Holdings Limited
Haras Investments Limited
Harris Family Finance Co Ltd
Jensten Group Limited
K U H Limited
KSEYE Capital Holdings Limited
Kestrel Acquisitions Limited
Kestrel Holdings Limited
Kier (Newcastle) Investment Ltd
MN Sports Holdings Limited
Norfolk Capital Limited
Onix Investments UK Ltd
Orchard Funding Group PLC
RC Bond Holdings Limited
Regulus Bidco Limited
SDJ Enterprises Limited
Tradewise Group of Companies Ltd

64209 Activities of other holding companies n.e.c. [281]

1LMS (Holdings) Limited
2020 Holdings (England) Ltd
8x8 UK Investments Limited
ABVR Finance Limited
ABVR Group Limited
ADB Construction Limited
AER Rents Limited
ARM UK Holdings Limited
ASCO Acquisitions Limited
ASCO Group Limited
Abzena Holdings Limited
Affinity Water Acquisitions (Holdco)
Affinity Water Acquisitions (Investments)
Affinity Water Acquisitions (Midco)
Affinity Water Acquisitions Ltd
Affinity Water Capital Funds Ltd
Affinity Water East Limited
Affinity Water Holdco Finance Ltd
Affinity Water Holdings Ltd
Air Works Empire UK Limited
Air Works UK Engineering Ltd
Alto (UK) Ltd
Amshold Securities Limited
Aquaterra Energy Group Limited
Aquatronic Group Management PLC
Aquila MB2 Limited
Aquila MB3 Limited
Arrow Electronics UK Holding Ltd
Ascend Global Holdings, Ltd.
Ascend Global Intermediate Holdings, Ltd.
Ashcoe Holdings Limited
Atlantis Equityco Limited
Atlantis Investorco Limited
Atlantis Midco Limited
Audbern Limited
Aurora Group Holdings (UK) Ltd
Axalta Coating Systems U.K. (2) Ltd
Axalta Coating Systems UK Holding
BHL (UK) Holdings Ltd
BUUK Infrastructure Limited
BV PMT Holdings Ltd
Bakkavor Estates Limited
David Barke (Holdings) Ltd
Basetek (Holdings) Limited
Bespoke Foods Holding Limited
Best Holdings (UK) Limited
Biffa PLC
Blancco (Software) Services Ltd
Bloom Engineering Holdings Ltd
Russell Burgess Limited
CAE Technology Holdings Ltd
CATM Africa Holdings Limited
CATM Australasia Holdings Ltd
CATM North America Holdings Ltd
CSR Limited
Cambridge Innovation Capital PLC
Cambridge Silicon Radio Holdings Ltd
Cambridge University Press (Holdings)
Camelot Holdco Limited
Camelot Interco Limited
Camelot Midco Limited
Camelot Topco Limited
Camfaud Group Limited
Care UK Health & Social Care PLC
Carpetright of London Limited
Chamberlain Holdings PLC
Chaplin Group Limited
Chard Robinson Usten Ltd
Chesterford Group Limited
Cloud Possibilities Limited
Cokenach Property Limited
Combat Medical Holdings Ltd
Commodity Centre (Group) Ltd
Cornwall
Country Court Care Homes 3 MB Ltd
Country Court Care Homes 3 SB Holdco
Country Court Care Homes 3 SB Ltd
Countryside Properties PLC
Coveris Flexibles Holdings UK Ltd
Hugh Crane Holdings Limited
D & B Scaffolding Holdings Ltd
DJM 88 Limited
Daiwater Investment Limited
Direct Consolidated Limited
Displayplan Holdings Limited
Don Construction Holdings Ltd
Donatantonio Group Limited
Dreams Topco Limited
ESCO UK Holding Company I Ltd
Education Management Corporation Ltd
Elite Mobile (Holdings) Ltd
Environmental Group Limited
Erba Diagnostics UK Limited
European Coffee Corporation Ltd
Fairview Hotels Limited
Fluxys Interconnector Limited
Fluxys UK Limited
Forth Ports Finance PLC
Fotolec Technologies Holdings Ltd
GAIAE Limited
GPL Investments Limited
Galldris Holdings Limited
Galliard Group Limited
Gardar Property Co Limited
Garrets Bidco 2 Limited
Gascoigne Halman Group Limited
Gateway Reversions Limited
Genie Bidco Limited
Genie Topco Limited
Gibson Bidco Limited
Gibson Propco Limited
T Gilmartin Holdings Limited
Glorious Solutions Limited
Granitte Investments (UK) Ltd
HBVB
HEB Real Estate Limited
Hagondale Limited
Harwich International (Holdings) Ltd
Hayter Holdings Limited
Hazlemere Holdings Limited
Hexcel Europe Limited
Hospital Topco Limited
Hotel Chocolat Group PLC
Hutchison Ports (UK) Holding Ltd
Indesit Company UK Holdings Ltd
Ingrebourne Valley Holdings Ltd
International Transport Ltd
Invesco Capita Holdings Ltd
JCA Head Co Limited
JRL Property Holdings Limited
JSM Group Holdings Limited
WO & PO Jolly Holdings Ltd
Leonard F Jollye (Holdings) Ltd
Jollyes Group Limited
Jollyes Retail Group Limited
KSEYE Group Limited
Kanta Enterprises Limited
Keswick European Holdings Ltd
Kier Dormant Holdings Limited
Kier Finance & Treasury Holdings Ltd
Kingsway Asset Co Limited
Kingsway Mezz Co Limited
Kingsway Mezz Hold Co Limited
Kingsway Senior Hold Co Ltd
Kodak Alaris Holdings Limited
Kout Food Group Restaurants UK Ltd
LGS Holdings Limited
Landex Holdings Limited
Landmark Aviation (UK) Limited
Lantern Services (Holdings) Ltd
Leda Investments Limited
Leisure Parks Real Estate (Holdings)
Lint Group Limited
London Luton Airport Holdings I Ltd
London Luton Airport Holdings II Ltd
London Luton Airport Holdings III
Luminescence Holdings Ltd
M Group Services Limited
ML Accessories Group Limited
MN Fox Bidco Limited
MN Fox Topco Limited
MN Sports Bidco Limited
MRBL Limited
MSXI UK Limited
MTS (Holdings) Limited
Manor (2016) Holdings Limited
Manufacturing Services Investment
Sir Robert McAlpine Enterprises Ltd
Sir Robert McAlpine Road Holdings
McColl's Retail Group PLC
McCormick Europe Limited
McCormick International Holdings
McCormick Kutas Food Service Ltd
McGrath Brothers (Holdings) Ltd
McNicholas Construction (Holdings)
Memec Group Limited
Mentmore Limited
Metier Healthcare Limited
Minhoco 26 Limited
Moto Holdings Limited
Moto Investments Limited
Moto Ventures Limited

Motocaddy Holdings Limited
Mustard Global Limited
Myddleton London Limited
Mylan Holdings Acquisition 2 Ltd
Mylan Holdings Acquisition Ltd
Mylan Holdings Ltd.
NBC Europe Ltd.
Nemo (UK) Holdco, Ltd.
Neville Trust Limited
New Sparta Holdings Limited
O'Brien Waste Recycling Solutions Holdings
OP UK Bidco Limited
OPD Group Limited
OPW Midco Limited
OPW Topco Limited
OTV Birwelco Limited
Omniport Limited
Omniport Norwich Limited
Onix Investments UK Ltd
Optimise Media Group Limited
Optionis Limited
PPD UK Holdings Limited
Paradine Holdings Limited
Peacock Holdings (2015) Ltd
Perkinelmer Life Sciences International Holdings
Pharmathen Holding 4 Ltd
Phoenix Advance Limited
Platinum Newco II Limited
Portugal Finco Limited
Power On Investments Limited
Pregis Europe Limited
Price Bailey Group Limited
Prime Estates Limited
Quinn Investment Holdings (London)
RO Properties Limited
RO Trading Limited
Rebus Group Limited
Regulus Midco Limited
Regulus Topco Limited
Ridgeon Holdings Limited
Riva Holdco 1 Limited
Riva Holdco 2 Limited
Road Tech Holdings Limited
Rowlands 2014 Limited
S & W Design & Build (Group) Ltd
SAFL British Hotels Limited
SBG Holding International Ltd
SLV Group Holding UK Limited
Safestore Investments Limited
Seajacks 1 Limited
Seajacks 2 Limited
Seajacks 3 Limited
Seajacks 4 Limited
Seajacks 5 Limited
Seajacks International Limited
Securon Holdings Limited
Sedum Limited
Selex ES International Ltd
Sheikh Holdings Group (Investments)
Shure Europe Holdings Limited
Silnat Holdings Limited
Sines Parks Holdings Limited
Spirit Pub Company (Holdco) Ltd
Spirit Pub Company (SGE) Ltd
R Stanton-Gleaves UK Limited
Stock Spirits (UK) Limited
Stockvale Investments Limited
Stonewater Enterprises Limited
Swift Group Holdings Limited
SystemsAccountants Holdings Ltd
TJX Germany Ltd.
TTKW Limited
Targetfollow (Development) Ltd
Targetfollow Group Limited
Thor Holdco Limited
Thor Midco Limited
Thor Topco Limited
Titon Holdings PLC
Tour Partner Group Limited
Tour Partner Group Midco Ltd
Triangle Aviation (UK) Holdings Ltd
Twinmar Group Limited
Twinmar Investments Holdings Ltd
Twinmar Investments Limited
UH Holdings Limited
Unifruit Group Limited
University of Essex Knowledge Gateway Holdings
Valens Resources Group PLC
Valley Trucks Holdings Limited
Vision Group (Holdings) Ltd
Walstead UK Holdings Limited
Walters Holdings Limited
Whitbread (Condor) Holdings Ltd
Whitestone Property Services Ltd
Wildcat Acquisition Holdings (UK)
Wilton & Bain Group Limited
A H Worth and Co Ltd
Wrist Holding UK Limited
Xtera Topco Limited

64301 Activities of investment trusts [11]

Albendan Limited
CQS Natural Resources Growth and Income
Chelverton UK Dividend Trust PLC
Downing Strategic Micro-Cap Investment Trust
Global Resources Investment Trust PLC
Investment Company PLC
Lindsell Train Investment Trust PLC
Montanaro UK Smaller Companies Investment Trust
Rights and Issues Investment Trust PLC
SDV 2025 ZDP PLC
Saffie Investments Limited

64303 Activities of venture and development capital companies

Amadeus Capital Partners Ltd
Amadeus Partners Limited

64304 Activities of open-ended investment companies

Amersham (Holdings) Ltd.
Bespoke Foods Group Limited
Elvin Investments Limited
Pheasant Eye Limited
S and J Investments (Delivery Office Southall)
Vinepost Limited
Yparho Investments Limited

64306 Activities of real estate investment trusts

Fairview Hotels Investments (2) Ltd
THR Number 12 PLC
THR Number 5 Limited
THR Number One PLC
THR Number Two Limited

64910 Financial leasing [11]

Akira Financial Limited
Brighthouse Group Limited
Brighthouse Holdings Limited
Brighthouse Limited
CNH Industrial Capital Europe Ltd
Caversham Finance Limited
De Lage Landen Leasing Limited
Eastern Credit Limited
FCE Bank PLC
Mallard Leasing Limited
Pitney Bowes Finance Limited

64921 Credit granting by non-deposit taking finance houses and other specialist consumer credit grantors [13]

Assetbridge Finance Limited
Aura Finance (Holdco) Limited
Bexhill UK Limited
Bluestar Enterprise Limited
E.G.T. Bridging Finance Ltd
Fleximize Capital Limited
Fleximize Limited
Manford Securities & Investments Ltd
Orchard Funding Limited
RCI Financial Services Limited
Swift 1st Limited
Swift Advances PLC
UK Credit Limited

64922 Activities of mortgage finance companies [11]

Aura Finance (Holdco) Limited
Basinghall Mortgage Finance No.1 Ltd
Bluestone Mortgage Finance No.2 Ltd
Central Lending Funding Number One
Central Trust Limited
Central Trust Syndicate Number One
FBSE Finance Limited
Mercantile Trust Limited
Mortgage Guarantee Limited
TN (UK) Consultancy Ltd
Whitfield Finance Limited

64929 Other credit granting n.e.c. [18]

CRK Finance Limited
Cambridge Colleges Funding II PLC
Cambridge Colleges Funding PLC
E.G.T. Finance Limited
Eastern Credit Limited
FCE Bank PLC
KSEYE Capital No.1 Limited
KSEYE Capital No.2 Limited
Kimberley Capital Limited
Kirkmore Capital Limited
Kirkmore HT Limited
Kirkmore Rhino 1 Limited
Mallard Leasing Limited
Norfolk Community Foundation
Residential Loans Ltd.
Salmon Management and Finance Ltd
Sorbon Finance Limited
Tenmill Limited

64991 Security dealing on own account

Greenfields Family Investment Co Ltd
Maldon Electric Securities,Limited
Orbit Investment Securities Services PLC
Park Securities Limited
Shakoor Capital Limited
Thrive Homes Finance PLC

64999 Financial intermediation not elsewhere classified [69]

AGCO Finance Limited
Affinity Water Finance (2004) PLC
Agria Pet Insurance Limited
Allandale Investments Limited
Alternative Bridging (UK 1) Ltd
Alternative Bridging (UK 2) Ltd
Alternative Bridging Corporation Ltd
Balanus Limited
M.W. Beer & Co. Limited
Blumarble Capital Limited
Canada Life Finance (U.K.) Ltd
Cashflows Europe Limited
Connect Plus (M25) Intermediate Ltd
Consort Medical Finance 2010 Ltd
Consort Medical Finance Ltd
Corporate Associates Limited
Countrywide Group PLC
Crocus Home Loans Limited
DST Financial Services Europe Ltd
Diligenta Limited
Ebberod Capital Ltd
European Investments (Cornwall) Holdings
Evelyn Trust
Evergreen Finance Limited
FDR U.K. Limited
Finance Store Limited
First Choice Holidays Finance Ltd
First Data Europe Limited
Foreign Currency Direct PLC
Alexander Fraser & Son,Limited
GE Money Home Finance Limited
GVS Prepaid Limited
Henley Group Finance Limited
Ilot Capital UK Ltd
Ilot Investments UK Ltd
Intertek Capital Resources Ltd
Intertek Finance No. 2 Ltd
Intertek Finance PLC
Kestrel Loans No. 4 Limited
Joseph King (Norfolk) Co-ordination
Kodak International Finance Ltd
Lindsell Train Investment Trust PLC
MBI MBO Limited
Maltco 3 Limited
Mando Corporation Limited
Sir Robert McAlpine (A19) Ltd
Sir Robert McAlpine Capital Ventures
Moto Finance PLC
Myriad Capital PLC
Network Treasury Services Ltd
Orbit Investment Securities Services PLC
Property Finance Capital Ltd
Property Finance Nominees (No.3) Ltd
Radical Investments Limited
Regentsmead Limited
Retail Charity Bonds PLC
Rigel Capital Partners Limited
Rowlandson Investments Limited
SF11 Limited
Saffron Housing Finance PLC
Shogun Finance Limited
Signature Lessee Limited
Nigel Skinner Financial Advisers
Space Truust UK Ltd
Stock Finance (Koruna) Limited
Swan Housing Capital PLC
T F S Loans Limited
Topfib Limited
Waste Recycling Environmental Ltd

65110 Life insurance

Canada Life Limited
Cardif Pinnacle Insurance Holdings PLC
Equitable Life Assurance Society,(The)
Pinnacle Insurance PLC
Suffolk Life Annuities Limited

65120 Non-life insurance [18]

BICL Limited
Community Reinsurance Corporation
Direct Insurance Group PLC
Gresham Insurance Co Ltd
Grove & Dean (Holdings) Ltd
Grove & Dean Limited
HFIS PLC
Hadleigh Holdings Limited
Herts Insurance Consultants Ltd
Iris Insurance Brokers Limited
Kirly Limited
NPA Insurance Limited
PMQUE Limited
Pinnacle Insurance PLC
Right Choice Insurance Brokers Ltd
SD Underwriting Limited
Tradex Insurance Co Ltd
Tradex Insurance Holdings Ltd

65202 Non-life reinsurance

Community Reinsurance Corporation
Direct Insurance Group PLC
Iris Insurance Brokers Limited
PMQUE Limited
SD Underwriting Limited

66110 Administration of financial markets

Aviva Health UK Limited
Bamrose Enterprises Limited
SVK Capital Management Limited
TN (UK) Consultancy Ltd

66120 Security and commodity contracts dealing activities

Canada Life Asset Management Ltd
Five Arrows Investments Ltd
Share Centre Limited

66190 Activities auxiliary to financial intermediation n.e.c.

Bondmason Client Ltd
DST Financial Services Europe Ltd
Kirly Limited
Onix Investments UK Ltd
Valiant Holdings Limited

66220 Activities of insurance agents and brokers [11]

Autoprotect (MBI) Ltd
Alan Boswell Insurance Brokers Ltd
Connells Residential
Coversure Insurance Services Ltd
Daly Holdings Limited
Devitt Insurance Services Ltd
I Go 4 Ltd.
KGM Underwriting Services Ltd
Policyfast Limited
Sequence (UK) Limited
Tradewise Insurance Services Ltd

66290 Other activities auxiliary to insurance and pension funding

Direct Insurance Group PLC
HCL Insurance BPO Services Ltd
NMSIM Group Limited
Suffolk Life Pensions Limited

66300 Fund management activities

Amadeus IG Limited
Birchwood Capital Limited
DBCN Limited
Facet Capital Limited
Letchworth Housing Investments Ltd
Rex Venture Resources Limited

68100 Buying and selling of own real estate [239]

41/43 Maddox St. Limited
Abbey Mills Properties Ltd
Abrahams Consolidated Limited
Alfred Homes Limited
Altomart Limited
Amalgamated Berkshire Holdings Ltd
Amshold Group Limited
Amshold International Limited
Amsik Limited
Amsprop Bishopsgate Limited
Amsprop Central Limited
Amsprop City Properties Ltd
Amsprop Estates Limited
Amsprop Investments Limited
Amsprop London Limited
Amsprop Portland Limited
Anacreonte Properties Limited
Anderson Design & Build Ltd
Anglia Ruskin Development Ltd
Archway Apartments Limited
Ares Properties Ltd
Arugula Spruce Limited
Ashworth Homes Limited
Aula Limited
Aurient Investments Limited
Avocado Developments Limited
BAM Glory Mill Limited
BAM Monk Bridge Limited
BAM Properties Limited
David Barke (Holdings) Ltd
Thomas Bates & Son Limited
Be Living Limited
Benchmark Leisure Limited
Berwen Limited
Birch's Park Homes Limited
W.E.Black Limited
Blue Anchor Leisure Holdings Ltd
Brookgate Property Limited
Brooklands Helix Developments Ltd
Buildvantage Limited
Bullen Properties Limited
CSSC Properties Limited
Cambridge Medipark Limited
Cambridge Realty Limited
Camstead Limited
Cantay Estates Limited
Caskade Properties Limited
Cavenham Estates Limited
Cergold Limited
Chaldean Properties Limited
Chappell Estates Limited
Chesterhill Investments Ltd
Churchmanor Estates Company PLC
Churchmanor Holdings Limited

Classic Management Services Ltd
Cleanland Limited
Clearview Homes (Western Avenue) Ltd
Colwyn Developments Limited
Constable Homes Limited
Countryside 26 Limited
Countryside 28 Limited
Countryside Four Limited
Countryside Properties (Bicester)
Countryside Properties (Springhead)
Countryside Properties (UK) Ltd
Countryside Properties (Uberior) Ltd
Countrywide Developments (UK) PLC
Cranfield Technology Park Investments
DSJ Homes Limited
Martin Dawn PLC
Delbanco Meyer & Co Ltd
Denbourne Investments Limited
Dencora 2000 Limited
Desilu Group Limited
Dow Properties Limited
Dunward Properties Limited
Duoview Properties Limited
Eastleaf Ltd
Ellesmere Property Investment Co Ltd
Enfield Innovations Ltd
Eurocity Properties (Central) Ltd
Eversleigh Investment and Property Co
Farmland Reserve UK Limited
Fishnet Properties Limited
Gita Properties Limited
Granta Park Estates Limited
Gray's Inn 10 Limited
Gray's Inn Capital 2 Limited
Greenwich Millennium Village Ltd
Grovemere Property Limited
F.H. Hale & Sons (Builders) Ltd
Hanover Housing Developments Ltd
Hedgemans Limited
Hendrie Estates Limited
Higgins Investments PLC
Highassets Limited
Hill Residential Limited
Horizon Land Limited
Housing Gateway Limited
Howard Ventures Limited
Immobiliare Cardi Marmi Ltd
Inero Limited
Inhealth Properties Limited
Inland Finance Ltd
Inland Homes (Essex) Limited
Inland Homes 2013 Limited
Inland Homes Developments Ltd
Inland Property Limited
Invordan Britannia Limited
Jet Investments Limited
K & R Projects Co Ltd
Kier Hammersmith Holdco Ltd
Killiney UK Limited
Kings Hedges Investments Ltd
Kitewood (Creekside) Limited
Kristall Realty Investments Ltd
Lancaster PLC
Lancaster Sports Cars Limited
Land Finance & Mortgage Corporation
Larkspur Investments Limited
Lawford & Sons Limited
Les Residence Falcon Wharf Ltd
London and Hertfordshire Ltd
Long Term Reversions (Dulwich) Ltd
Long Term Reversions (Harrogate) Ltd
Long Term Reversions (Torquay) Ltd
Long Term Reversions No 1 Ltd
Longmill Rickbost Ltd
Marwin Securities Limited
Marylebone Square Holdings Ltd
Masterlord Estates Limited
Meg Trading Limited
Megnum Limited
Melton House Investments Ltd
Milburn Productions Limited
Millharbour Developments Ltd
Mingold Limited
Mirrorstoke Limited
Monarock Limited
Mothers Ltd
Mountcharm (S.E.) Limited
Multitrust Property Investments Ltd
NPMA Ltd
NVSM Limited
Network Homes Investments (Stockwell)
Network Homes Investments Ltd
Newell Properties Developments Ltd
Oakburn European Properties Ltd
Offley Chase Estates Limited
Ordan UK Limited
Ortona Limited
Ortona Properties Limited
PJG Developments Limited
PS Construction Investments Ltd
Pangbourne Developments Ltd
Panther (VAT) Properties Ltd
Panther Investment Properties Ltd
Panther Securities P L C
Panther Trading Limited
Paradigm Commercial PLC
Parkdale Investments Limited
Parthings Farm - Management and Promotion
Partners in Property (U.K.) Ltd
Polyfield Property Limited
Prime Estates Limited
Property & Investment Management Ltd
Property Recycling Group PLC
Property and Commercial Enterprises
Quickdrop Limited
RBR Property Investments Ltd
RG Reversions 2014 Limited
RG Securities (No.2) Limited
Paul Rackham Limited
Rannerlow Limited
Regis Group (Barclays) Limited
Regis Group (Nationwide) Ltd
Regis Group (UBK) Limited
Regis Group Services Limited
Renaissance Global Investment Ltd
Resham PLC
Rhiannon Properties Limited
Ridgeon Estate Co Ltd
Roots Hall Limited
Roselead Limited
Rylston Road Limited
Rysa Lodge Residential Properties
SA.GI.MA. Limited
Salient Investments Ltd.
Saw Property Co Ltd
Sawston Farms (Cambs) Limited
Serruys Property Co Ltd
Sharan Properties Limited
Shearer Property C Limited
Shedmead Limited
M & D Silk Properties Ltd
Silverbridge Properties Ltd
Snowmountain Enterprises Ltd
Sorbon Estates Limited
Sorbon Investments Limited
Space Truust UK Ltd
Spire Bricks and Mortar Ltd
Spirit (Faith) Limited
Spurdown Limited
Stamford Property Co Ltd
Stane Park Ltd.
Step 6 Ltd
Stonewater Capital Limited
Sunrose Property Limited
TN (UK) Consultancy Ltd
Tanners Wharf Limited
Tati Co Ltd
James Taylor Homes (Harrow) Ltd
James Taylor Homes (Lincolns Inn)
Titano Real Estate Limited
Treebond Limited
Trentpeak Limited
Triplerose Limited
Turner Properties Limited
Tustin Properties Ltd
Twilight Real Estate Limited
Unicourt Properties Limited
United Healthcare Land Co Ltd
User Friendly Properties Ltd
Ventress Property Developments Ltd
Victory Housing Trust
Viewrose Limited
Vigeland Properties Ltd
WD1A Limited
WEL (No 1) Ltd
Wallace Estates Limited
Wallace Partnership Group Ltd
Webb Investments Ltd.
Wheatley PLC
Arnold White Group Limited
Wilson Properties (London) Ltd
Wilton Park Developments Ltd
Winpost Limited
Wood Green Investments Limited
Yelcon Limited

68201 Renting and operating of Housing Association real estate [33]

Charlie Properties Limited
Chelmer Housing Partnership Ltd
Cottis House Limited
Craft & Sons Limited
Dhamecha Property Limited
E & J Properties Limited
A.A.Fisher (Properties) Ltd
D.N. Grady & Sons Limited
Highassets Limited
Himelight Limited
Jarrold & Sons Limited
Kenninghall Holdings Limited
Lancaster PLC
Lancaster Sports Cars Limited
Lapid Developments Limited
Libra (Longhurst Group) Treasury PLC
Megnum Limited
Melbourn Science Park Limited
Millennium Investments 2000 Ltd
PJG Developments Limited
Pet and Aquatics Properties Ltd
Poole Investments Limited
Shelfside (Holdings) Limited
Sopress Investments Limited
South Coast Furnishing Co Ltd
Streamadvice Limited
Thomas,Arthur & Gordon,Limited

Tican Process Holdings Limited
Transeur Properties Limited
Treebond Limited
Vale of Aylesbury Housing Trust Ltd
Victory Housing Trust
Willis Dawson Property Limited

68202 Letting and operating of conference and exhibition centres

Babraham Bioscience Technologies Ltd
Brandon House Limited
Forum Trust Limited

68209 Other letting and operating of own or leased real estate [517]

1 Big Data Management Limited
41/43 Maddox St. Limited
ABSL1 Limited
ACR Investments Limited
AWG Land Holdings Limited
Abbey Investments Limited
Abbey Mills Properties Ltd
Abrahams Consolidated Limited
Acteon Group Properties Ltd
Adil Property Investment Ltd
Adilsons Properties Limited
Albanwise Limited
Alboro Developments Limited
Alconbury Packing Solutions Ltd
Allaway Group Limited
Altenmark Limited
Amalgamated Berkshire Estates Ltd
Amalgamated Berkshire Holdings Ltd
Amalgamated Berkshire Properties Ltd
Anacreonte Properties Limited
C.F.Anderson & Son Limited
Angel Property Investments Ltd
Angelica Estates Limited
Antoniou Investments Limited
Apperly Estates Limited
Aquila BTE 1 Limited
Aquila Chelmsford Limited
Aquila EHS Limited
Aquila Estates Limited
Arcese Real Estate UK Limited
Archaylen Property Limited
Arihant Limited
Ascott Properties Limited
Ashe Group Holdings Limited
Aspire (CRP) Limited
Astor Lodge Holdings Limited
Astwood Securities Limited
Aula Limited
Aurient Investments Limited
Aurient Investments N16 Ltd
Avon Freeholds Limited
B.A.T.S. Ilford Limited
Babraham Bioscience Technologies Ltd
Badger BC Investments Limited
E.W.Ballard Holdings Limited
Bamrose Enterprises Limited
Banks Mills Limited
Barsham Securities Limited
Baruch Holdings Limited
Thomas Bates & Son Limited
Beacon (Mimms) Limited
Belgrave Land (Sheffield) Ltd
Benacre Investments Limited
Benacre Properties Company
Berwen Limited
Birch's Park Homes Limited
Blenheim Estates Limited
Blenheim Property Management Ltd
Bowler Group Limited
M.& R.Bowman Limited
Brandon House Limited
Brent Housing Ltd
Brianco Services Limited
Brick Projects (Marland) Ltd
Broadrich Limited
Buckingham Hotels Group Ltd
Bullen Properties Limited
Burghley House Preservation Trust
Burrough Court Estate Limited
A.J. Bush Limited
C.I. Industries Limited
CEG Properties Limited
CQK Limited
C.M. Cadman Group Limited
Cambridge Construction Limited
Camflats Limited
Canfield House Limited
Caretech Estates (No 2) Ltd
Caretech Estates (No 3) Ltd
Caretech Estates (No 7) Ltd
Caretech Estates (No. 5) Ltd
Caretech Estates (No.4) Ltd
Caretech Estates Limited
Carmelite House (Jarrold) Ltd
Carpetright of London Limited
Casemasters Limited
Cathard Investments Limited
Cathedral Holdings Limited
Cavenham Estates Limited
Central Developments (UK) Ltd
Central Property Investments Ltd
Centre for Engineering and Manufacturing Excellence
Chaldean Properties Limited
E.M. Chamberlain Estates Ltd
E.M. Chamberlain Group Ltd
Chamberlain Holdings PLC
E.M.Chamberlain Limited
Chappell Estates Limited
Charterhouse Simon Limited
Cheergrey Properties Limited
Chelmsford Cars and Commercials Ltd
Chelsea Portfolio Limited
Chicken Villas Limited
Churchmanor Limited
Churchtown Estates Limited
Churton Property Developments Ltd
Citygate Developments 2005 Ltd
Claydon Securities Limited
Clerks Well Properties Limited
Cloverton Property Ltd
Coastfields Leisure Limited
Cokenach Property Limited
Peter Colby Commercials Ltd
Conduit Street Holdings Ltd
Consolidated Equities Limited
Coopers Investments Limited
F. Copson Limited
Corporate Investments Limited
Cossam Investment Co Ltd
Costco Limited
Country Court Care Homes 3 Propco
Countrywide Developments (UK) PLC
Coward Asset Limited
Crane Investments Ltd
Cranfield Technology Park Investments
Cresta Estates Limited
Culham Limited
Curtis Medical Investments Ltd
DC Management Services Limited
DSJ Homes Limited
S. Dad Limited
C.E. Davidson Farms Ltd.
Deanplan Limited
Robert Deards Limited
Deards Services Limited
Deekay Investments Limited
Dencora 2000 Limited
Dencora Estates Limited
Denny Bros Holdings Limited
Desiman Limited
Devantier Properties Limited
Dialgreen Estates Limited
Diamond Corporation Limited
Dilawar Property Ltd.
Dow Properties Limited
Dry Drayton Estate Limited
Dunsfold Airport Limited
Duoview Properties Limited
Eagle 456 Limited
Elizabeth Estates (NWB) Ltd
Elizabeth Holdings PLC
Ellis Bros (Contractors) Ltd
Enfield Innovations Ltd
Epoch RJK Limited
Erindale Limited
Etcetera Construction Services Ltd
Eternit UK Limited
Eurocity Properties (Central) Ltd
Eurosalamis Enterprises Ltd.
Everguard Limited
Eversleigh Investment and Property Co
Fairview Hotels Investments (2) Ltd
Fifty Six Investments Limited
Finer Limited
Flahive Developments Limited
Fooks Property Co Ltd
Forextra Developments Limited
Forum Trust Limited
Fowler Smith & Jones Trust
Framingham House Investments Ltd
Frelene Limited
Fresh Wharf Estates Limited
GHG 11 (Mount Alvernia Hospital) Ltd
GHG 12 (Hampshire Clinic) Ltd
GHG 13 (Chaucer Hospital) Ltd
GHG 14 (Shirley Oaks Hospital) Ltd
GHG 15 (Highfield Hospital) Ltd
GHG 16 (Chelsfield Park Hospital)
GHG 17 (Ridgeway Hospital) Ltd
GHG 18 (Saxon Clinic) Limited
GHG 19 (Albyn Hospital) Ltd
GHG 2 (Clementine Churchill Hospital)
GHG 20 (Sarum Road Hospital) Ltd
GHG 22 (Garden Hospital) Ltd
GHG 24 (Sloane Hospital) Ltd
GHG 25 (Werndale Hospital) Ltd
GHG 26 (Beardwood Hospital) Ltd
GHG 28 (Manor Hospital) Ltd
GHG 3 (Ross Hall Hospital) Ltd
GHG 31 (Blackheath Hospital) Ltd
GHG 32 (Goring Hall Hospital) Ltd
GHG 33 (Beaumont Hospital) Ltd
GHG 34 (Priory Hospital) Ltd
GHG 35 (Droitwich Spa Hospital) Ltd
GHG 36 (Winterbourne Hospital) Ltd
GHG 37 (Alexandra Hospital) Ltd
GHG 4 (Princess Margaret Hospital)
GHG 5 (London Independent Hospital)
GHG 6 (Thornbury Hospital) Ltd

GHG 7 (Chiltern Hospital) Ltd
GHG 8 (Park Hospital) Limited
GHG 9 (Bath Clinic) Limited
Gada Limited
Gallagher Holdings Limited
Gardiner Real Estate PLC
Gates Group Limited
Gatetrade Limited
Gentian (Mid-Essex) Limited
Gentian (Newcastle) Limited
Geo Management Limited
Geoghegan Bros. Limited
Gibbons (Holdings) Limited
Gita Properties Limited
Geo. E. Gittus & Sons Limited
Good Harvest Group Limited
Good Harvest Properties (Southwark)
Good for Food Limited
Goodkind Estates Limited
Goodmayes Properties Ltd
Gorhambury Estates Co Ltd
Goymour Properties Limited
Grangebrook Estates Limited
Grangewood Brentwood Limited
Grant & Boyd Limited
R. & I. Grant & Co. Limited
Gray's of Norwich Limited
Gredley House Investments Ltd
Greenbrook Industries Limited
Greene King Brewing and Retailing
Greenstone Oxford Limited
Greystead Properties Limited
Grimsthorpe & Drummond Castle Trust
Grovemere Property Limited
Guia Limited
Gunpowder Mill Developments Ltd
HTS Estates Limited
Habendum Limited
Hadleigh Bakery Limited
F.H. Hale & Sons (Builders) Ltd
Hand Laundry (Bury) Limited
Harber Properties Limited
Hatfield Trading Limited
Hedgemans Limited
Helgor Trading Limited
Hendrie Estates Limited
Henfield Hire Limited
S.Hille & Co.(Holdings) Ltd
Hilton Properties Limited
E. Hobbs (Farms) Limited
Hoddesdon Developments Ltd
Holywells Residential Lettings Ltd
Home Counties Estates Limited
Homeguard Properties Limited
Horsham Properties Limited
Horta Properties Limited
Housing Gateway Limited
Howard Bedford Limited
Howard Cambridge Limited
Howard Investment Co Ltd
Howard Lewisham Limited
Howard Sawston Ltd
Howard Stansted Limited
Hull Propco Limited
ILB Investments Limited
Investment Properties (Luton) Ltd
Ipswich Borough Assets Limited
J. Isaacs Management Limited
J E Investments Limited
J J Food Service Holdings Ltd
J.L.G.Investments Limited
JMBC Properties Ltd
Jacklin Properties Limited
Jarrold (St. James) 3 SJC Ltd
Jarrold (St. James) D1/D2 Ltd
Jarrold (St. James) Limited
Jarvis Commercial Properties Ltd
Jawaby Property Investment Ltd
Jeesal Akman Holdings Limited
Jeesal Holdings Limited
Jelmac (Primary Care) Properties Ltd
Jelmac Properties
Johnson & Johnson Innovation Ltd
K.C.Y. Limited
KCG Holdings Ltd
KM Estates Limited
Kailas Hotel Finance Co Ltd
Kara Management Ltd
Katrin Properties Limited
Kebbell Holdings Limited
Kelly Property Co Ltd
Kestates Limited
Keystone Developments (LG) Ltd
Kier Integrated Services (Estates)
Kigass Limited
Killiney UK Limited
Kimberley Property Investments Ltd
Kingfisher (EU) Limited
Klyne Aviation Limited
Kotecha Ltd
Laen Limited
Lamesta Limited
Land Management Limited
Landchief Limited
Landex Commercial Property Ltd
Landex Holdings Limited
Lanswood Limited
Lasted Limited
Lawford & Sons Limited
Edward Le Bas Properties Ltd
Leitrim Properties Limited
Lenta Properties Limited
Les Residence Falcon Wharf Ltd
Lexitron Limited
Leywood Estates Limited
Lincoln's Farm & Investments Ltd
Linkhaven Estates Ltd
David Lloyd Leisure Properties No.1
David Lloyd Leisure Properties No.2
David Lloyd Leisure Properties No.3
David Lloyd Leisure Properties No.4
London Luton Airport Limited
Luna Estates Limited
Lupo Limited
Lyndon Hurst Limited
MBH Finco. Limited
MJC Properties (Essex) Limited
Malthurst Estates Limited
Malthurst Retail Limited
Malthurst South East Limited
Manormaker (Nominee No. 1) Ltd
Mapeley Columbus II Limited
Mapeley Steps Contractor Ltd
Marshall Group Properties Ltd
Marshall of Cambridge (Garage Properties)
Marylebone Finco Limited
McGrath Bros. (Environmental) Ltd.
Meadow Holdings Limited
Mercury Land Holdings Limited
Merritts Properties Limited
Milton Hall Estates Limited
Monarock Limited
Monument Group Limited
Donald Moody Investments and
Developments
Morley Finco Limited
H. Morrell Property Investments Ltd
Mothers Ltd
Mountcharm (S.E.) Limited
Multitrust Property Investments Ltd
Mumford's Mill Rentals Limited
NEEB Holdings Ltd.
Namu Limited
Network Homes Investments Ltd
Network New Build Limited
Neville Trust Limited
Newell Properties Limited
Newsells Park Estates Limited
Noodle Properties Limited
Norpap Property (Telford) Ltd
O'Hara Property Investment Holding Co
O'Neill Investments Limited
O.B.C. (Europe) Limited
OBM Properties Limited
Oakburn European Properties Ltd
Oakburn Properties Limited
M. S. Oakes Securities Ltd
Ocado Operating Limited
Offley Chase Estates Limited
Olive Tree Limited
Omavale Limited
Openarch Estates Limited
Openarch Greenside Limited
Openarch Properties Limited
Openarch Towerview Limited
PGR Enterprises Ltd
Palacath Limited
Pamina Estates Limited
Pampisford Properties Limited
Pangbourne Developments Ltd
Panther (VAT) Properties Ltd
Panther Securities P L C
Park Securities Limited
Parkdale Investments Limited
Peak Securities Limited
F. Perkins Limited
Pero Investments Limited
David Phillip (Investments) Ltd
Pineridge Investments Limited
Pirin Ltd
Pledream Properties Limited
Plutus Estates Limited
Plymouth (Notte Street) Ltd
Polyfield Property Limited
Prime Estates Limited
Prinhold Limited
Property & Investment Management Ltd
Property and Commercial Enterprises
Punjab House Associated Ltd
Quebec Court Freehold Limited
Queensgate Finco Ltd
Quickdrop Limited
R.V.L. Properties Limited
RBR Property Investments Ltd
RWF Health and Community Developers
(Tranche 1)
Radia Estates Limited
Radio Developments Ltd
Ramco (Harlow) Limited
Rangemist Limited
Rannerlow Limited
Ransome's Dock Limited
Rattlerow Properties Limited
Reads Property Developments Ltd
Regis 2000 Limited
Reichmann Properties PLC

Retro Properties Limited
Rex Venture Resources Limited
Rhiannon Properties Limited
Ridgeon Estate Co Ltd
Ridgeon Properties Limited
Rijac Properties Limited
Riverway Investments Limited
William Robinson Gravetye Charity
Rosper Estates Limited
Routebuy Limited
Hilary Russell Group Ltd
Ryan Elizabeth Holdings PLC
SSL Group (UK) Limited
Safegold Properties Limited
Safestore Limited
Safestore Properties Limited
Sandhill Park Limited
Sardar Properties (U.K.) Ltd
Satco Investments Limited
Sawston Farms (Cambs) Limited
Select Enterprises Limited
Sharan Properties Limited
Shedmead Limited
Sherrygold No.1 Limited
Signature Lessee I Limited
Signature Senior Lifestyle Finance
Silverson Machines Holdings Ltd
Sitecrest Limited
Skeltools Limited
Sorbon Estates Limited
Sorbon Homes Limited
Sorbon Investments Limited
South Central Property Limited
South Mimms Services Limited
Spaces Personal Storage Ltd
Specialist Cars Property (Stevenage)
Spencers Property Investments Ltd
Spire Bricks and Mortar Ltd
Stamford Property Co Ltd
Step 6 Ltd
Sterndale Systems Limited
Stonewater Capital Limited
Strongholding Limited
Structural Holdings and Consultancy
Swanlea Limited
T. Bro Investment Limited
TCR New Limited
TJX UK Property Limited
Takeda Cambridge Limited
Talbot House Business Centre Ltd
Tanners Wharf Limited
Taylor Properties Trading Ltd
Techaid Facilities Limited
Tendring Farms Limited
Thornhill Estates Limited
Three Rivers Property Investments
Thurlow Nunn (Holdings) Ltd
George Thurlow and Sons (Holdings)
Transmec Properties Limited
Trinity (D) Limited
Triplerose Limited
Trust Estates (Clarence Street) Ltd
Tulip Properties & Real Estate Ltd
Turner Properties Limited
Turners (Soham) Holdings Ltd
Turnstone Estates Limited
Tustin Properties Ltd
Tutis Properties Limited
Twinglobe Limited
UNEX Corporation Limited
UNEX Holdings Limited
UNEX Investment Properties Ltd
UNEX Limited
United Church Schools Foundation Ltd
User Friendly Properties (No. 2) Ltd
Ventress Property Developments Ltd
Ventureforth 2000 Limited
Victoria Docks Hotel Company (Number Two)
Victory Housing Trust
Vigeland Properties Ltd
Villachase Limited
Vinayak Properties Limited
Viners Capital Properties Ltd
WHL Investments Limited
J. Walker & Son (Investments) Ltd
Walsingham Estate Properties Ltd
Webster Estates Ltd
Welney Farms Property Limited
West End Homes Limited
Westlake Estates Limited
Wheat Quarter Limited
Wheatley Properties Limited
White Lodge (Norwich) Limited
Wickland (Holdings) Limited
Wilcox Holdings Limited
Willow Securities Limited
Winpost Limited
Wintertime Properties Limited
Woolpit Business Parks Limited
Workout Limited
Wymondham Property Management Co Ltd
Yomans (London) Limited
York Apartments Limited
Zest Living Limited

68310 Real estate agencies

Connells Residential
Countrywide Estate Agents
Dow Properties Limited
Hall Contracts (Lakenheath) Ltd
Jenga (UK) Limited
Lipman Properties Limited
Property and Commercial Enterprises
Sequence (UK) Limited
Site Sales Marketing Limited

68320 Management of real estate on a fee or contract basis [46]

Abbey Properties Cambridgeshire Ltd
Applepeach Limited
Arcus FM Limited
Beechfield Estates Limited
Bentwaters Parks Limited
Blenheim Consultancy Services Ltd
Bow Village Limited
Brookgate Property Limited
Carlton Group Developments Ltd
Childs Property Limited
Comland Commercial Limited
Countrywide Estate Agents
Dow Properties Limited
Elliot Leigh Property Investments 2 Ltd
First Wave Housing Limited
Greene King Properties Limited
Harouni Group of Companies Ltd
Howard Ventures Limited
K.E.M. Property Services Ltd
Lawford & Sons Limited
Letting International Limited
Mapeley Steps Contractor Ltd
Medway Fundco Limited
Mill Hill Properties Limited
Ortona Management Limited
Parker Hannifin (GB) Limited
Pearl Properties Limited
Peppercorn Investments Limited
Property and Commercial Enterprises
RBR Property Investments Ltd
Residential Management Group Ltd
Roselead (Wattisham) Limited
Roselead Limited
Salmon Management and Finance Ltd
Shedmead Limited
Space Truust UK Ltd
Starbridge Property Investment Ltd
TK Maxx
Taylor Wimpey SH Capital Ltd
Tesco TLB Properties Limited
Trinity College (CSP) Limited
Tulip Properties & Real Estate Ltd
V.U.K. Holdings Limited
Vantage Volante Limited
Vigeland Properties Ltd
Westpoint Property Limited

69102 Solicitors

BC Legal Limited
Duncan Lewis Solicitors Ltd
Trust Tees Limited

69109 Activities of patent and copyright agents; other legal activities n.e.c.

Taylors Legal Limited

69201 Accounting and auditing activities

Bakkavor Central Finance Ltd
Bakkavor Finance Limited
Fiat Chrysler Automobiles Services UK
Harwood Hutton Limited
JSA Services Limited
PRGX UK Ltd
Renault Group U.K. Limited

69202 Bookkeeping activities

London Pharma & Chemicals Group Ltd

69203 Tax consultancy

Bluecastle Enterprises Limited

70100 Activities of head offices [704]

3D European Holdings Limited
3VS UK Limited
4 BG Group Ltd
A-Roads Investments Limited
A. & A. 2000 Limited
A.C. Lighting (Holdings) Ltd
AAG UK Parent Limited
ACI Worldwide (EMEA) Limited
ASL Technology Holdings Ltd.
AST Group Holdings Limited
AWG Group Limited
AWG Parent Co Limited
Abacus Group Limited
Abbey Group Cambridgeshire Ltd
Abbey Group Limited
Abbey Total Care Group Limited
Access Technology Group Ltd
Acco Brands Europe Limited
Acco Europe Limited
Acco-Rexel Group Services Ltd
Accolade Midco Limited
Accolade Topco Limited
Acteon Group Limited
Advanced Lighting Technologies Europe
Agriturf Holdings Limited
Agrofarm London Limited

P.F. Ahern & Sons Limited
Akhter Group Limited
Alchemie GRP Limited
Allaway Group Limited
Altro Group PLC
American Can Holdings (U.K.) Ltd
Amersham Biosciences
Amshold Trading Limited
Anglian Home Improvements Group Ltd
Anglian Venture Holdings Ltd
Anglian Water Services Holdings Ltd
Anglian Water Services Limited
Appleyard Group Limited
Archant Limited
Architectural Glazing Limited
Arcus Solutions (Holdings) Ltd
Arkarius Bidco Limited
Arrhenius Holdings Limited
Arthur Midco 1 Limited
Arthur Midco 2 Limited
Arthur Pikco Limited
Arthur Topco Limited
Artisan (UK) PLC
Aspin Construction Group Ltd
Aspire Media Group Limited
Assetsteady Limited
Astrazeneca Treasury Limited
Astrazeneca UK Limited
Athena Care Homes (UK) Limited
Atlantic Healthcare PLC
Atlas Copco UK Holdings Ltd
Aura (Newcastle) Holding Co Ltd
Aura (Newcastle) Project Company Phase 2
Aura Holdings (Newcastle) Ltd
Avingtrans PLC
Avnet (Holdings) Ltd
B & M Care Group Limited
BAM Construct UK Limited
BBA Aviation Lynton Group Ltd
BMS Limited
BPH Finance Number 1 Limited
BUUK Infrastructure Holdings Ltd
BUUK Infrastructure Issuer PLC
BUUK Infrastructure No 1 Ltd
BUUK Infrastructure No 2 Ltd
Bafin Holdings
Baik Agency Limited
Balanus Limited
Ball Beverage Packaging Holdings UK
Ball UK Holdco Limited
Barstone Limited
Bartrum Group Limited
Baruch Investments Limited
Bauer Consumer Media Limited
Bauer Golden Square Limited
Bauer Radio Limited
Bayard Metering (UK)
Bespak Holdings Limited
Biffa Group Holdings (UK) Ltd
Biffa Group Limited
Biofocus DPI (Holdings) Ltd
Blancco Technology Group PLC
Blue Arrow Holdings Limited
Boortmalt UK Limited
Alan Boswell Group Limited
C J Bourne (Asset Management) Ltd
Bourne Leisure Group Limited
Bourne Leisure Holdings Ltd
Bourne Leisure Limited
Boxford (Suffolk) Holdings Ltd
Boxford Group Ltd.
Brayford Hotels Holdings Ltd
Britvic International Investments
Britvic PLC
Brogan Group Holdings Ltd
George Brown's Implements (Holdings)
Bush Boake Allen Enterprises Ltd
Bush Boake Allen Holdings (U.K.) Ltd
Bush Boake Allen Limited
C.U. Phosco Limited
CD & R Firefly Bidco Limited
CDK U.K. Limited
CN Group Limited
CNH Industrial Capital Limited
CP Holdings Limited
CSS Computer Security Solutions Ltd
Cadena AM Limited
C.M. Cadman Group Limited
Cambridge Education Group Ltd
Camelot Bidco Limited
Canada Life (U.K.) Limited
Carbery (UK) Limited
Cardif Pinnacle Insurance Holdings PLC
Care UK Health & Social Care Finance
Care UK Health & Social Care Holdings
Care UK Health & Social Care Investments
Care UK Limited
Carestream Dental Technology Parent
Caretech Holdings PLC
Carlisle Group Limited
Carter Accommodation Holdings Ltd
RG Carter Group Limited
R. G. Carter Holdings Limited
Castledon Ltd
Caterpillar UK Engines Co Ltd
Caterpillar UK Group Limited
Celador Radio Broadcasting Ltd
Cheale Group Limited
Chelsea Stores Holdings Ltd
Chemtest Holdings Limited
Chevalier (2015) Ltd
Chiltern Distribution Ltd
Chivgate Limited
Churchgate Estates Limited
City & Country Group PLC
City & Country Residential Ltd
City Brewery Limited
City Link (Cardiff) Holdings Ltd
City Link (Cardiff) Limited
Citygate Holdings Limited
Clearsprings (Management) Ltd
Clement Clarke (Holdings) Ltd
Cliffords Limited
Clinimed (Holdings) Limited
Cogels Investments Ltd
Peter Colby Commercials Ltd
Comland Commercial Limited
Comland Group Limited
Computacenter PLC
Consort Medical PLC
Contact Technologies UK Ltd
Contamac Holdings Limited
Contechs Holdings Limited
Thomas Cook Group UK Limited
Copthorn Holdings Limited
Corona Energy Limited
Corporate Express UK Holding Ltd
Costa Express Holdings Limited
Coulson Group Limited
Countrywide Group PLC
Countrywide PLC
Cousins Holdings Limited
Crossco (820) Limited
Crown Holdings Limited
Crownfield Holdings Limited
DC Management Services Limited
DCI Group Limited
DCK Group Limited
DDD Investments Limited
DDW Holdings Limited
DFKA Intermediate Limited
DFKA Ltd
DFKA UK Holdings Limited
DPA Support Services Limited
Dage Holdings Limited
Dagless Holdings Limited
Dashtag
Davroc Limited
Dayla Holdings Limited
De Lage Landen Limited
Defaqto Group Limited
Denny Bros Holdings Limited
Densitron Technologies Limited
Derby School Solutions (Holdings)
Dernford Holdings Limited
Descram Holdings Limited
Deuce Acquisitions Limited
Deuce Holdco Limited
Devantier Group Limited
Dhamecha Group Limited
Dhamecha Holdings Limited
Digica Group Finance Limited
Dippy Ridge Limited
Doe Holdings Limited
Doncaster School Solutions (Holdings)
Druid Group Limited
Duff Morgan & Vermont (Holdings) Ltd
EMG Holdings Limited
EV Finco Limited
EV Holdings Limited
Easyjet PLC
Education Personnel Bidco Ltd
Eisai Europe Limited
Electrolux Investments
Electron House (Overseas) Ltd
Simon Elvin Holdings Limited
S Elvin Limited
Elysium Healthcare (Lighthouse) Ltd
Emerald Bidco Limited
Emerald Midco 1 Limited
Emerald Midco 2 Limited
Emerald Topco Limited
Enfield Fancy Goods Limited
Ensign Holdco 1 Limited
Ensign Holdco 3 Limited
Ensign Holdco 4 Limited
Ercol (Holdings) Limited
Esselte Holdings Limited
Esselte Limited
Essity Holding UK Limited
European Tyre Enterprise Ltd
Exheat Group Limited
Express Vending Group Limited
FIH Group PLC
Fairacres Group Limited
Fairfield Limited
Fishpools Holdings Limited
Flocklynn Limited
Fluorocarbon Group Limited
Flying Trade Group PLC
Flynn Pharma (Holdings) Ltd
Food Processing Holding Ltd
Foray 989 Limited
Ford International Liquidity Management
Ford JL Limited
Ford VH Limited

Friars 716 Limited
Frontier Bidco Limited
Frontier Holdco Limited
Frontier Midco Limited
G.K. Holdings No.1 Limited
GE Bio-Sciences Investments Ltd
GE Money Home Lending Holdings Ltd
GS Acquisitions Limited
Gada Limited
Galldris Services Ltd
Galliard Holdings Limited
Gap Partnership Bidco Limited
Gap Partnership Group Limited
Gap Partnership Holdings Ltd
Gardline Holdings Limited
Gardline Shipping Limited
Gee Group Ltd
General Domestic Appliances Holdings
Gentian Investments Limited
Gentian Partnerships Limited
Global Graphics (UK) Limited
Global Graphics PLC
Global Ridgeway Holdings Ltd
Goymour Properties Limited
Gozzett Holdings Limited
Grange Management (Holdings) Ltd
Grant Family Holdings Limited
Grant Family Investments Ltd
Gravity Media Group Holdings Ltd
Gravity Media Group Limited
Greene King Acquisitions No.2 Ltd
Greene King Investments Ltd
Greene King PLC
Greene King Pubs Limited
Greene King Retailing Parent Ltd
Greens of Soham Limited
Grimston Trust Limited
Ground Control Holdings Ltd
Group Lotus Limited
H & D Support Services (Holdings)
H (Lincs) Limited
H. G. Construction (Holdings) Ltd
H.L. Foods Limited
HBVB
HL Display UK Holding Limited
HRS Investments Limited
Hall & Watts Holdings Limited
Hallam Meat Co Ltd
Hallmark Care Homes Group Holdings
Halma Euro Trading Limited
Halma Financing Limited
Halma International Limited
Halma Investment Holdings Ltd
Halma Overseas Funding Limited
Halma PLC
Halstead Securities Limited
Hampden Holdings Limited
Hampden Insurance Holdings Ltd
Hardwicke Investments Limited
Harris Holdings (Grays) Ltd
HaskoningDHV UK Holdings Ltd
HaskoningDHV UK Limited
Healthcare (Barts) Limited
Healthcare Homes Holdings Ltd
Henley Group Holdings Limited
Hexcel (U.K.) Limited
Hexcel Holdings (UK) Limited
Higgins Group PLC
Hillary Bidco Limited
Hills Group Enterprises Ltd
Hilton Food Group PLC
Hilton HHC Limited
Holmes Care (Group) Limited
Hoopers Limited
Hovis Holdings Limited
Hughes Electrical Limited
Hunnable Holdings Limited
Domnick Hunter Group Limited
Huntleigh International Holdings Ltd
Huntleigh Technology Limited
Hutchison Ports (UK) Limited
Hutchison Ports Europe Limited
Hydac Limited
I & C Holdings Limited
I S & G (Holdings) Limited
IMO Car Wash Group Limited
IQGeo Group PLC
ITAB Holdings UK Ltd
Impellam Holdings Limited
Impellam UK Limited
Inexus Connections Limited
Inexus Group (Holdings) Ltd
Ingleby (1884) Limited
Inhealth Group Holdings PLC
Inhealth Group Limited
Inhealth UK Holdings Limited
Insignia Investments Limited
Inspectorate International Ltd
Intelek Limited
Interguide Group Limited
International Flavours & Fragrances (GB) Holdings
Intertek Holdings Limited
Intertek Nominees Limited
Intertek Overseas Holdings Ltd
Intertek UK Holdings Limited
Intertek USD Finance Ltd
Itron Development UK Ltd
J & J Restaurants Limited
J W D Holdings Limited
Jardine Motors Group UK Ltd
Jark Ventures PLC
K.M. Packaging Holdings Ltd
KH Finance Limited
KH Finance No.2 Limited
KH Holdco Limited
Kane Group Limited
Kebbell Holdings Limited
Keelings UK Group Limited
Keen & Toms Holdings Limited
Kershaw Group Limited
Kestrel Acquisitions Limited
Kestrel Holdings Limited
Kier Group PLC
Kier Holdings Limited
Kier Limited
Kier National Limited
Kier Project Investment Ltd
Kier Services Limited
Joseph King Holdings Limited
Kluman and Balter Holdings Ltd
Knight Roadworks (2010) Ltd
Kromachem Holdings Limited
Kwik-Fit (NL) Limited
Kwik-Fit Euro Limited
Kwik-Fit Finance Limited
Kwik-Fit Group Limited
Kwik-Fit Holdings Limited
L & M Holding Ltd
LSF9 Robin Investments Limited
LSF9 Robin Midco Limited
LSF9 Robin Newco 1 Limited
LSF9 Robin Newco 2 Limited
Lancaster PLC
Lapid Developments Limited
Larkfleet Homes Limited
Lawson Partners Limited
Le Bas Investment Trust Ltd
Edward Le Bas Limited
Lighthouse Healthcare Group Ltd
Lindal Holdings Limited
David Lloyd Leisure Group Ltd
David Lloyd Leisure Operations Holdings
London Pharma & Chemicals Group Ltd
London Pharma & Chemicals Holdings Ltd
Richard Long Group Limited
Lundbeck Group Limited
M & W Newco Limited
M-Ship Limited
M.P.I. (Herts) Limited
MAS (Holdings) Limited
MCF Commercial Limited
MRH (GB) Limited
MSHA International Ltd.
MacKenzie Taylor Holdings Ltd
Macquarie Corona Energy Holdings Ltd
Mainline Communications Group Ltd
Malthurst (UK) Limited
Manpower Holdings Limited
Marshall Motor Holdings PLC
Marshall of Cambridge (Holdings) Ltd
Marz Limited
Masterson Holdings Limited
Geoffrey Mayhew Farms (Holdings)
Sir Robert McAlpine (Holdings) Ltd
Martin McColl Retail Limited
McGee Group (Holdings) Limited
McGrath Brothers (Holdings) Ltd
Medacs Global Group Limited
Media 10 Holdings Limited
Melesey Limited
Memec Group Holdings Limited
Memec Holdings Limited
Merck Sharp & Dohme (Holdings) Ltd
Metals & Materials Limited
Micross Components Holdings Ltd
Micross UK Solutions Limited
Milbank Ventures Limited
Minhoco 20 Limited
Mono Holdings Limited
Moralis Group Limited
Morrison Utility Services Holdings
Morrison Utility Services Investments
Mothercare Group Limited
Motherwell Holdings Limited
Motorclean Group Limited
Motus Holdings (UK) Limited
Mountfield Group PLC
Mouskos Capital Limited
Mouskos Holdings Limited
Munnelly Group PLC
Munro Holdings (Cambridge) Ltd
Muntons (Holdings) PLC
Murkett Brothers (Holdings) Ltd
Murkett Brothers Limited
NIS Acquisitions Limited
NIS Receivables No.1 Limited
NQA Certification Limited
Naked Wines International Ltd
Navigator Terminals UK Limited
Netcall PLC
New Demipower Limited
Newarthill Limited
Newman Street Hotel Limited
Newport School Solutions (Holdings)
Newport School Solutions Ltd

Newsquest Capital Limited
Anthony Nicholas (UK) Limited
Nicholls & Clarke Limited
Nobo Group Limited
Norfolk Broads Holdings Ltd
Northgate Information Solutions Holdings
OEC Europe Holdings Limited
OEC International Limited
OOCL (Europe) Limited
Ocado Central Services Limited
Ocado Holdings Limited
Offerco Limited
Olympus Keymed Group Limited
One Broker Limited
One GE Healthcare UK
One Group Construction Limited
Optionis Group Limited
Origin Holdings (UK) Limited
Osprey Holdco Limited
P & O Ferrymasters Holdings Ltd
PPG Holdings (U.K.) Limited
W.H.Palmer & Co.(Industries) Ltd
Parker Hannifin (Holdings) Ltd
Peachey Basildon Group Limited
Perkinelmer (UK) Holdings Ltd
Perkins Holdings Limited
Permastore Group Limited
Personnel Holdings Limited
Pharmadent Holdings Limited
J.A. Phillips Holdings Ltd
Pioneering Foods Group Limited
Pitney Bowes Holdings Limited
Poole Investments Limited
Portcrest Limited
Practice (Group) Limited
Practice Corporate Management Ltd
Dr Michael Prager Holdings Ltd
Premier Financing Limited
Premier Foods Finance PLC
Premier Foods Group Services Ltd
Premier Foods Investments Ltd
Premier Foods Investments No.1 Ltd
Premier Foods PLC
Premier Lotteries Capital UK Ltd
Produce Investments Limited
Produce World Investments Ltd
Purple Surgical Holdings Ltd
R Group Holdings Limited
R O Ventures Limited
RHM Group Holding Limited
RMPA Holdings Limited
RP2 Holdings Limited
Ransome's Trading Holding Co Ltd
Ransomes Limited
Ratcliff Group Limited
Ravensale Limited
Rayfern Holdings Limited
Raytheon United Kingdom Ltd
Recruit Venture Group Ltd
Refined Holdings Limited
Regis Group (Holdings) Limited
Renewable Energy Systems Holdings
Residential Land Holdings Ltd
Resolute Corporate Holdings Ltd
Rexam European Holdings Ltd
Rexam Group Holdings Limited
Rexam Limited
Rexam Overseas Holdings Ltd
Rexam UK Holdings Limited
Reyhold Limited
Rhodia Holdings Limited
Rhodia International Holdings Ltd
Jack Richards Holdings Ltd
Riverway Investments Limited
R.Robinson & Co.(Motor Services)
Robinson Young Holdings Ltd
Rocket Medical Group PLC
Romeo Midco Limited
Rooff Group Limited
Rooff Holdings Limited
Rose Group Limited
Rose Holdco Limited
Rose Midco Limited
Rowlandson Investments Limited
S.C.W.S. (Holdings) Limited
SCB Holdings (Sandy) Limited
SEH (Property and Administration)
SIP Group Limited
SME Group PLC
SME Holdings Limited
SME Investments Limited
SWP Group Limited
Saba Infra Holdings UK Limited
Safestore Acquisition Limited
Safestore Group Limited
Safestore Holdings PLC
Saffron Insurance Holdings Ltd
Sandbrook Overseas Investments Ltd
Sanwalton Limited
Saybest Limited
Schering-Plough Holdings Ltd
Schottlander Limited
Scimitar Topco Limited
Seabrook Holdings Limited
Selecta Holding Limited
Senior Engineering Investments Ltd
Senior Finance Four Limited
Senior Finance Seven Limited
Senior Finance Six Limited
Senior Five Limited
Senior PLC
Share PLC
Sharksfin Holdings Limited
Shawbrook Group PLC
Sherrygreen Limited
Shields Environmental Group (Holdings) Ltd.
Shields Environmental Investment (Holdings)
K.J. Shortis Limited
G S Shropshire Holdings Ltd
Signet Group Limited
Simarco Holdings Limited
Simmons (Bakers) Limited
J O Sims Holdings (1896) Ltd
Skanska Cementation International Holdings
Skanska Construction Holdings UK Ltd
Smith and Holbourne (Holdings) Ltd
Smiths Interconnect Group Ltd
Snellings Limited
Softbox (Bidco) Limited
Softbox (Midco) Limited
Softbox (Topco) Limited
Sogea Holdings (UK) Limited
Solo Cup (UK) Limited
Sonnet Care Homes Holdco Ltd
Sonnet Care Homes Midco Ltd
Soul Coffee House Limited
Soul Foods Limited
Southbank UK Limited
Specialist Cars Holdings Ltd
Speedy 1 Limited
Spirit Group Equity Limited
Spirit Group Holdings Limited
Spirit Group Parent Limited
Spirit Managed Holdings Ltd
Spirit Pubs Debenture Holdings Ltd
Springfield Holdings Limited
Stantec Europe Limited
Star Cargo PLC
Steiner UK Limited
Stock Spirits Group PLC
Subway Realty Limited
Swan Investments Group Limited
Synthomer Holdings Limited
Synthomer PLC
TFX Group Limited
TGA Industries Limited
TGA UK Alpha Limited
TGA UK Finance Limited
TGA UK Holdings Limited
TGA UK Omega Limited
TPH (UK) Limited
TRB Technology Group Limited
TUI Northern Europe Limited
TUI Travel Holdings Limited
TUI Travel Limited
Tallington Holdings Limited
Tangent International Group PLC
Tanglewood Care Homes Limited
Tappenden & Co. Limited
Tasmar Limited
Taxassist Direct Group Limited
James Taylor Group Limited
James Taylor Homes Group Ltd
Taylor Wimpey PLC
Teaching Personnel Holdings Ltd
Teledyne E2V Limited
Telegenic Holdings Limited
Telephonetics Limited
Temple Fields 514 Limited
Tesco (Overseas) Limited
Tesco Holdings Limited
Tesco Mobile Services Limited
Tesco Property Finance 1 PLC
Tesco Property Holdings Ltd
Tex Holdings PLC
Thistledove Limited
Thompson Investments (London) Ltd
Thomson Travel Group (Holdings) Ltd
Thule Holding Limited
Thurlow Nunn (Holdings) Ltd
Tican (UK) Holdings Limited
Tobar International Limited
Total Produce Holdings (UK) Ltd
Treehouse Group Limited
Turners (East Anglia) Limited
UH Holdings Limited
UME PFI Investments Holding Ltd
UNEX Corporation Limited
UNEX Gredley (Holdings) Ltd
UNEX Group Holdings Limited
UNEX Holdings Limited
Ulgrave Limited
Usborne PLC
V.U.K. Holdings Limited
VGC Group Limited
VHC Sub-Holdings (UK)
VMS (Holdings) Limited
William Vere (Holdings) Ltd
Vernalis Limited
Vinci PLC
Vinci UK Developments Limited
Visiongroup (GB) Limited
Volkerrail Group Limited
Volkerwessels Limited
Volkerwessels UK Limited
Wadlow Energy Holdings Limited

Walstead Finance Limited
Walstead Group Limited
Walstead Holdings Limited
Walstead Press Group Limited
Walstead United Kingdom Ltd
Walsworth Limited
Andrew Weir & Co Ltd
Wentworth Holdings Limited
Werner Access Products UK Holdings
S.Wernick & Sons (Holdings) Ltd
Weston Group PLC
Westway Services Holdings (2010) Ltd.
Wheatley PLC
Whitbread PLC
Arnold White Estates Limited
Whitehouse Leisure International Holdings
Whitehouse Leisure International Ltd
Willmott Dixon Holdings Ltd
Wilson Connolly Holdings Ltd
Wilson James Group Limited
Wimpey Corporate Services Ltd
George Wimpey Limited
Wimpey Overseas Holdings Ltd
Wind Farm Holdings Limited
Windsor Integrated Services Group
Wood Hall Land & Properties Ltd
Woodford Holdings Limited
Woodland Group Limited
Woodledge Limited
Woods Holdings Limited
H.Young & Co.,Limited

70210 Public relations and communications activities

Parthings Farm - Management and Promotion
SHOO 802AA Limited
SHOO 803AA Limited

70221 Financial management [16]

Anglian Group (Investments) Ltd
Aspire Media Group Limited
Clarucci Industry Limited
EE Finance PLC
Hampden Insurance Holdings Ltd
London Pharma & Chemicals Group Ltd
Papa Midco Limited
Papa Topco Limited
Sonnet Care Homes Finance Ltd
Tesco Corporate Treasury Services PLC
Tesco Pension Investment Ltd
Tesco Treasury Services PLC
Thrive Homes Finance PLC
V.B. Investments Limited
Werner Access Products UK Holdings
Wood Hall Investments Limited

70229 Management consultancy activities other than financial management [46]

APM Group Limited
Anderson Construction Limited
Ashley House PLC.
Axcorp Limited
Blenheim Consultancy Services Ltd
Business Control Solutions PLC
Cambridge Enterprise Limited
Campion Willcocks Limited
Cogels Investments Ltd
Comensura Limited
Dai Europe Ltd
Denny Bros Holdings Limited
Dominion Hospitality Limited
EUSA Pharma Holdco 1 (UK) Ltd
EUSA Pharma Holdco 2 (UK) Ltd
Gap Partnership Limited
Gibbons (Holdings) Limited
Glastry Advisory Partners Ltd
HCL Insurance BPO Services Ltd
HTS Estates Limited
Harvest Investments Solutions Ltd
Inexus (Services) Limited
Instrumel Ltd
Kendric Ash Limited
Keswick Enterprises Group Ltd
Kier Business Services Limited
Kier Management Consulting Ltd
Laindon Holdings Limited
MJT Securities Limited
MTALX Limited
Mundipharma International Ltd
Noble Foods (We) Limited
Pajef Limited
RJM Metal Consultancy Limited
Randstad Middle East Limited
T.Rippon & Sons (Holdings) Ltd
T. Rippon Estates Limited
Riverway Investments Limited
SJO Enterprises Limited
Sagentia Limited
Science Group PLC
TTP Group PLC
TWI Limited
T. Visaman & Sons Limited
Walsingham Estate Management Ltd
Willoughby (880) Limited

71111 Architectural activities

Ashley House PLC.
Austin (GB) Limited
NPS Property Consultants Ltd
T.S.G. Building Services PLC

71112 Urban planning and landscape architectural activities

Southwater Property Promotion Ltd

71121 Engineering design activities for industrial process and production

Bucyrus Europe Limited
Bucyrus UK Limited
D.H. Industries Limited
MEL Aviation Components Ltd
Visteon Engineering Services Ltd

71122 Engineering related scientific and technical consulting activities

AVL Powertrain UK Limited
Element Energy Limited
Hawkins & Associates Limited
Science Group PLC

71129 Other engineering activities [10]

Aston Heating Limited
Continental Datagraphics Ltd
Lawrence David Limited
Element Energy Limited
Exploration Electronics Ltd
HaskoningDHV UK Limited
MEL Aviation Limited
MTCE Limited
Process Sensing Technologies Ltd.
Stantec UK Limited

71200 Technical testing and analysis

BRE Global Limited
Hawkins & Associates Limited
ITS Testing Services (UK) Ltd
Intertek Testing & Certification Ltd
Klipspringer Limited
MTCE Limited

72110 Research and experimental development on biotechnology [21]

Abzena (UK) Limited
Abzena Limited
Amgen Limited
Astex Therapeutics Limited
Astrazeneca PLC
Bluegnome Limited
Calchan Holdings Limited
Charles River Discovery Research Services UK
EUSA Pharma (UK) Limited
F-Star Alpha Limited
Freeline Therapeutics Limited
GW Research Limited
Heptares Therapeutics Limited
Horizon Discovery Group PLC
Horizon Discovery Limited
Illumina Cambridge Limited
Intermune Holdings Limited
Mission Therapeutics Limited
National Institute of Agricultural Botany Trust
Prometic Pharma SMT Limited
Vernalis (R & D) Limited

72190 Other research and experimental development on natural sciences and engineering [46]

Apical Limited
BRE Trust
Babraham Institute
Beko PLC
Bespak Europe Limited
Building Research Establishment Ltd
CASP
Cambridge Antibody Technology Group
Cambridge Consultants Limited
Cambridge Display Technology Ltd
Centre for Engineering and Manufacturing Excellence
Dassault Systemes Biovia Ltd
Displaylink (UK) Limited
E - Leather Limited
Earlham Institute
Eisai Limited
Element Energy Limited
Envigo CRS Limited
John Innes Centre
Medimmune Limited
Mundipharma Research Limited
Mylan Pharma UK Limited
NIAB.
National Institute of Agricultural Botany Trust
PPD Global Ltd
Quadram Institute Bioscience
Rakon UK Holdings Limited
Respivert Ltd.
Rothamsted Research Limited
Sagentia Limited
Science Group PLC
Sepura PLC
Silverwell Technology Limited
Special New Fruit Licensing Ltd
Sunlight PV Ltd

TTP Group PLC
TTP Labtech Limited
TTP PLC
TWI Limited
Tun Abdul Razak Research Centre
Ubisense Limited
United Therapeutics Europe, Ltd.
Welding Institute
Xaar PLC
Xaar Technology Limited
Xaarjet Limited

72200 Research and experimental development on social sciences and humanities

Cambridge Pharma Limited

73110 Advertising agencies

Blue Square Marketing Limited
Cambridge University Press (Holdings)
Mando Corporation Limited
Map Media Limited
McCutcheon Norveil Consultancy Ltd
Optimise Media (UK) Limited

73120 Media representation services

Maritzcx Limited
Optimise Media (UK) Limited

73200 Market research and public opinion polling

Cambridge University Press (Holdings)
Defaqto Ltd

74100 Specialised design activities

Istec Services Limited
J C A Engineering Ltd
WJ Groundwater Limited

74901 Environmental consulting activities

SLR Consulting Limited
SLR Holdings Limited
SLR Management Limited

74902 Quantity surveying activities

T.S.G. Building Services PLC

74909 Other professional, scientific and technical activities n.e.c. [65]

AMI Corporations Ltd
Allway Connections Limited
Amazon Spring Waters Investment Ltd
Birdlife International
Blackhawk Network (UK) Ltd.
Bounty (UK) Limited
British Board of Agrement
British Pipeline Agency Ltd
CDT Holdings Limited
CSR Imaging UK Ltd.
Cambridge Consultants Limited
Cambridge Crystallographic Data Centre
Cantel Medical (UK) Limited
Chemtest Limited
Coherent (UK) Limited
Connells Survey & Valuation Ltd
EResearchTechnology Limited
Edstrom UK Holdings PLC
Eisai Europe Limited
Elastomer Trading Limited
Envigo International Limited
Et Ceteris Limited
Five Arrows Limited
Forest Commercial Services Ltd
Fujitsu General Air Conditioning (UK)
Galapagos Biotech Limited
Gardline Limited
Gardline Marine Sciences Ltd
Gardline Maritime Limited
Grigny (UK) Limited
Hall of Fame Stud Limited
Hawkins & Associates Limited
Inhealth Molecular Imaging Ltd
Institute of Grocery Distribution
Intermay Management Ltd
Johnson & Johnson Innovation Ltd
Kromachem Holdings Limited
Kymab Limited
LRW Engineering Limited
Leica Microsystems Cambridge Ltd
Mistras Group Limited
Morrison Data Services Limited
Morrisroe Group Limited
Motorclean Limited
NQA Certification Limited
Perkinelmer LAS (UK) Limited
Phlexglobal Limited
Quadro Epsom Limited
Quanta Consultancy Services Group Ltd
Quanta Consultancy Services Ltd
RJM Metal Consultancy Limited
Raspberry Pi Foundation
Rebus Holdings Limited
Roche Holding (UK) Limited
SPC Holdings Limited
Sagentia Limited
Science Group PLC
SintecMedia LON Ltd
Skylight Investments Limited
Stat Marine Limited
Taliesin Management Limited
Telespazio Vega UK Limited
Test Equipment Asset Management Ltd
UNEX Smithfield Limited
Carl Zeiss Ltd

74990 Non-trading company [112]

1LMS (Holdings) Limited
ABL (Holding) Limited
ADC Holdings Limited
AMPY Holdings Limited
Acheson Industries (Europe) Ltd
Acteon Group Limited
Adonia Medical Group Limited
Affinity Water Southeast Ltd
Alenco (Holdings) Limited
Anglian Group Limited
Anglian Water Facilities Management Holdings (UK)
Ardex Investments UK Limited
Arnold Family Holdings Limited
Aspect Ventures Limited
Avnet Bidco Limited
B & M Care Group Limited
Ball Company
Ball Europe Limited
Ball UK Holdings, Ltd
Beckman Holdings Limited
Burghley House Preservation Trust
R.G. Carter Engineering Ltd
Ceragon (UK) Limited
Charis Trust
Coherent (UK) Holdings Limited
Comland Holdings Limited
Computerlinks (UK) Limited
Costa China Holdings Limited
Costa International Limited
DBD Enterprises Limited
Dhamecha Group Limited
EC English Cambridge Limited
EResearchTechnology UK 1 Ltd
EResearchTechnology UK 2 Ltd
Early Learning Holdings Ltd
Edgewell Personal Care Holdings UK Ltd.
Edgewell Personal Care Investments UK Ltd.
Edgewell Personal Care UK Ltd
Elysium Healthcare Holdings 2 Ltd
Elysium Healthcare Holdings 3 Ltd
Elysium Healthcare LC Limited
Fraserfort Limited
Joseph Gallagher Group Ltd
Goodman Family Investments Ltd
Greene King Neighbourhood Estate Pubs
Greene King Retailing Parent Ltd
HIC Racing (Chiswick) Limited
HIC Treasury Limited
Hel Group Limited
Heley Holdings Limited
John Henry and Sons (Developments) Ltd
Inspectorate Holdings PLC
Kelly Communications Enterprises Ltd
Kerneos Holding Northern Europe Ltd
Kier Dormant Holdings Limited
Kier Parkman Servigroup Ltd
Knight Noise Limited
LC Bet Limited
Lawson Partners Limited
Lester Hotels Group Limited
MHE JVCO Limited
Majestic Property & Estates Ltd
Mytravel Pioneer Limited
Norfolk Capital Group Limited
Old English Inns Limited
Oldeurope Limited
Openview Group Limited
Overture Bidco Limited
Overture Midco II Limited
Overture Midco Limited
Overture Topco Limited
P & O Ferrymasters Holdings Ltd
PPD International Investments Ltd
Pacific (BC) Topco 2 Limited
Pacific (BC) Topco 3 Limited
Pacific (BC) Topco 4 Limited
Pacific (BC) Topco 5 Limited
Parker Hannifin Industries Ltd
Pitney Bowes Holdco Limited
Porvair Filtration Limited
Premier Bidco Limited
Premier Lotteries UK Limited
Premier Midco Limited
Premier Topco Limited
Quanticate Limited
RO Financing Co Ltd
Ransome's Trading Holding Co Ltd
Rexam Beverage Can (India Holdings)
Rittal Holdings Limited
Rowan International Topco Ltd
S N B Holdings Limited
S-P RIL Limited
S.A. (300) Limited
SCH 2014 Limited
Saint Vincent Holdings Limited

Scientific Digital Imaging PLC
Richard Shuttleworth Trustees
Signet Holdings Limited
Solo Cup Finance Limited
Peter Sowerby Foundation
Speycrest Limited
Spirit Pub Company (Investments) Ltd
TUI Travel Group Solutions Ltd
TUI Travel Overseas Holdings Ltd
Temple Fields 522 Limited
Tesco Overseas Investments Ltd
Travel Choice Limited
Treelane Limited
Tristel PLC
WJ Management Limited
Wellmode Limited
Wimpey Dormant Investments Ltd

75000 Veterinary activities

CEVA Animal Health Limited
CVS (UK) Limited
CVS Group PLC
Horse Trust
Medivet Group Limited

77110 Renting and leasing of cars and light motor vehicles [13]

CCW 600 Limited
P.J. Carey Plant Hire (Oval) Ltd
Cargobull Finance Limited
Global Self Drive Limited
Hamsard 3352 Limited
Hamsard 3353 Limited
Henfield Hire Limited
Local Car and Van Rental Ltd
Sema Lease UK Limited
Seven Asset Limited
Toomey Leasing Group Limited
Tuskerdirect Limited
VMS (Fleet Management) Limited

77120 Renting and leasing of trucks and other heavy vehicles

Cargobull Finance Limited
Collease Truck and Trailer Rentals
John Hanlon & Co. Limited
Henfield Hire Limited
Transporter Sales & Hire Ltd
VMS (Fleet Management) Limited

77299 Renting and leasing of other personal and household goods

Hughes Electrical Limited
Hughes TV and Audio Limited

77310 Renting and leasing of agricultural machinery and equipment

Sunlight PV Ltd

77320 Renting and leasing of construction and civil engineering machinery and equipment [20]

P.J. Carey Plant Hire (Oval) Ltd
Emerson Crane Hire Limited
Fork Rent Limited
Hall Contracts (Lakenheath) Ltd
John F Hunt Power Limited
JRL Plant and Logistics Ltd
Jackson Mechanical Services (UK) Ltd
Liebherr-Rental Limited
London Tower Crane Hire & Sales Ltd
L. Lynch (Holdings) Limited
L. Lynch (Plant Hire & Haulage) Ltd
M. & J. Engineers Limited
Prentice Aircraft and Cars Ltd
Quinto Crane & Plant Limited
Tower Crane Asset Management Holdings
Vinci Fleet Services Limited
Charles Wilson Engineers Ltd
Wren Buyerco Limited
Wren Midco Limited
Wren Topco Limited

77330 Renting and leasing of office machinery and equipment (including computers)

Rivers Finance Group PLC
Rivers Leasing PLC

77351 Renting and leasing of air passenger transport equipment

Hagondale Limited
Triangle (Funding One) Limited
Triangle Regional Aircraft Leasing

77390 Renting and leasing of other machinery, equipment and tangible goods n.e.c. [21]

Acclaim Handling Limited
Advante Limited
Amazon Acquisitions Limited
Arjo UK Limited
Carter Accommodation Holdings Ltd
Central Park Enterprises Ltd
Chartco Limited
Elliott Group Holdings (UK) Ltd
Elliott Group Limited
Fiveways Municipal Vehicle Hire Ltd
Gardline Maritime Limited
John Hanlon & Co. Limited
Levantera Developments Limited
Livingston Ltd
M. & J. Engineers Limited
Microlease Limited
N.R.C. Plant Limited
Seven Asset Limited
Smart Meter Assets 1 Ltd
Swiss Laundry,Limited
Charles Wilson Engineers Ltd

77400 Leasing of intellectual property and similar products, except copyright works

Porcelanosa U.K. Limited

78109 Other activities of employment placement agencies [11]

Carbon60 Limited
Day Webster Limited
Eurobase Systems Limited
Interquest Group (UK) Limited
Jark Industrial Limited
Levy Associates Limited
Lorien Resourcing Limited
McGinley Aviation Holdings Ltd
Papworth Trust
Paytemp Limited
Teaching Personnel Limited

78200 Temporary employment agency activities [38]

BS Project Services Limited
Berry Recruitment Limited
Blue Arrow Holdings Limited
Blue Arrow Ltd.
Brook Street (UK) Limited
Carbon60 Limited
Career Teachers Limited
Carlisle Staffing PLC
Carlisle Staffing Services Holdings
Carlisle Staffing Services Ltd
Coyle Personnel PLC
Doctors on Call Limited
Global Medics Limited
Hales Group Limited
Hexagon Investment Holdings Ltd
Impellam Group PLC
Interaction Recruitment PLC
Levy Associates Limited
Lorien Limited
Lumesse Holdings UK Limited
M.P.I. Limited
Mayday Healthcare PLC
Medacs Healthcare PLC
NHS Professionals Limited
Pareto Law Limited
Randstad CPE Limited
Randstad Group UK
Randstad HR Solutions Limited
Randstad Luxembourg UK Limited
Randstad Middle East Limited
Randstad Solutions Limited
Randstad Sourceright Limited
Randstad UK Holding Limited
Sanctuary Personnel Limited
Science Recruitment Group Ltd
Sopra Steria Recruitment Ltd
Teaching Personnel Limited
Whitehall Resources Limited

78300 Human resources provision and management of human resources functions

Levy Associates Limited
Tangent International Limited

79110 Travel agency activities [20]

Australian Pacific Touring (U.K.)
Beds with Ease Limited
Broadway Travel Service (Wimbledon)
CWT Holdco Limited
Carlson Wagonlit New Holdco Ltd
Carlson Wagonlit UK Ltd
Thomas Cook Retail Limited
Thomas Cook Tour Operations Ltd
Freedom Destinations Limited
Freedom Travel Group Limited
Future Travel Limited
Hotels4U.Com Limited
PPA Group Limited
Padwicks Travel (Wembley) Ltd
Skylord Travel PLC
TCCT Retail Limited
TUI UK Limited
TUI UK Retail Limited
Travelpack Marketing & Leisure Services
Vertical Group Limited

79120 Tour operator activities

Broadway Travel Service (Wimbledon)
Ocean Holidays Limited
Premier Holidays Limited
RWH Travel Limited
Ramblers Holidays Group Ltd
Travelpack Marketing & Leisure Services
UK Holiday Group Limited
Villa Plus Limited

79909 Other reservation service activities n.e.c.

Inntel Group Limited
Inntel Limited
Kreutzer Touristik GB Limited
Norfolk Broads Direct Limited
Original Cottage Co Ltd
P G S International Limited

80100 Private security activities

Atalian Servest Security Ltd
Sunwin Services Group (2010) Ltd

80200 Security systems service activities

Openview Security Solutions Ltd

81100 Combined facilities support activities [20]

Aquatronic Group Management PLC
Atalian Servest Group Limited
Atalian Servest Limited
Babraham Bioscience Technologies Ltd
Churchill Contract Services Group Holdings
CloudFM Group Limited
CloudFM Integrated Services Ltd
Derby School Solutions Limited
H & D Support Services Limited
Hamton Environmental Services Ltd
J C A Engineering Ltd
Kier Facilities Services Ltd
Kier North Tyneside Limited
Kier Stoke Limited
Mapeley Steps Contractor Ltd
Norse Commercial Services Ltd
Norse Eastern Limited
QI Partners
Salisbury Holdings Limited
Salisbury Workplace Services Ltd

81210 General cleaning of buildings

Exclusive Contract Services Ltd
Hamton Environmental Services Ltd
Rainham Industrial Services Ltd

81299 Other cleaning services

Churchill Contract Services Ltd

81300 Landscape service activities

Ground Control Limited
Produce Connection Limited

82110 Combined office administrative service activities

Metro Global Holdings Limited

82190 Photocopying, document preparation and other specialised office support activities

Automated Systems Group Ltd
Kodak Alaris Limited

82200 Activities of call centres

Turpin Distribution Services Ltd
Yonder Digital Group Limited

82301 Activities of exhibition and fair organisers

Brooks Events Limited
Mack-Brooks Exhibitions Ltd
Media 10 Limited

82920 Packaging activities

Kendon Packaging Group PLC

82990 Other business support service activities n.e.c. [394]

ACM ULR Limited
AFP 2015-1 Limited
ARM Limited
ASCO (DC3) Limited
AZENCO4 Limited
Acteon Middle East and Far East Investments
Acteon UK Financing II (NOK) Ltd
Acteon UK Financing III (EUR) Ltd
Acteon UK Financing Limited
Acteon US Financing Limited
Acteon US Holdings Limited
Ad Meliora Academy Trust
Aequitas Estates (Poyle) Ltd
P.F. Ahern & Sons Limited
Alliance Asset Management Ltd
R.H.Amar & Co Limited
Amshold Securities Limited
Anglian Water (Osprey) Financing PLC
Anglian Water Services Financing PLC
Archigen Biotech Limited
Arinso People Services Limited
Aston Heating Limited
Astrazeneca Intermediate Holdings
Astrazeneca Sweden Investments Ltd
Astrazeneca US Investments Ltd
Atalian Servest Group Holdings Ltd
Atlas Copco Limited
Aura Finance Limited
Automotive UK No.1
Aviva Consumer Products UK Ltd
Avnet Holdings UK Limited
Azurie Blue Limited
BAM Construct UK Limited
BISL Limited
BPC Interiors Limited
BWP (Cambridge) Limited
Babraham Bioscience Technologies Ltd
Bio Products Laboratory Ltd
Blue Sea Overseas Investments Ltd
Bold-Rock Management and Investments Ltd
Booking.Com Customer Service Center (UK)
Booking.Com Limited
Arthur Branwell & Co. Limited
Bricks St Property Group Ltd
Brookgate Limited
N W Brown Group Limited
J.Browne Construction Co Ltd
Burney Realty Limited
Buzzard Leisure Limited
CATM Europe Holdings Limited
CLFIS (U.K.) Limited
CNH Industrial Oldco Capital Ltd
C.M. Cadman Group Limited
Calpri Ltd
Cambridge University Press (Holdings)
Cambrionix Holdings Limited
Canada Life Group (U.K.) Ltd
Cappagh Browne Utilities Ltd
Cardif Pinnacle Insurance Management Services
Cardpoint Limited
Cardtronics Creative UK Ltd
Cardtronics Holdings Limited
Cardtronics PLC
Cardtronics UK Limited
Care UK Health & Social Care PLC
Carlisle Security Services Ltd
Caterpillar Overseas Limited
Central G H Trust
Centus Biotherapeutics Limited
Chapman Ventilation Group Ltd
Churchgate Estates Limited
Co-op Group Travel 2 Holdings Ltd
Colchester Zoo Holdings Ltd
Compare The Market Limited
Connect Utilities Limited
Kathleen and Michael Connolly Foundation (UK)
Construction Workers Guild Ltd
Contracting Made Easy Ltd
Thomas Cook Aircraft Engineering
Thomas Cook Continental Holdings
Thomas Cook Finance PLC
Thomas Cook Group Hedging Ltd
Thomas Cook Group Treasury Ltd
Thomas Cook Investments (2) Ltd
Thomas Cook UK Limited
Thomas Cook UK Travel Limited
Thomas Cook West Investments Ltd
Corbus Europe Limited
Corporate Express (Holdings) Ltd
Costa Express Limited
Country House Weddings Limited
Countrywide Estate Agents
Countrywide Surveyors Limited
Creative Car Park Ltd
Cwind Ltd
DB Investments Limited
DW Windsor Group Limited
Diaverum Facilities Management Ltd
Digital Copier Systems Eastern Ltd
RR Donnelley UK Limited
ENRA Group Limited
ESRI Holdings Limited
Eisai Europe Limited
Energypro Asset Management Ltd
Enterprise Department Limited
Envirowales Limited
European Investments (Cornwall) Ltd
European Investments (Crook Hill)
European Investments (Earlseat) Ltd
European Investments (Lancashire 2)
European Investments (Lancashire)
European Investments (Reaps Moss)
European Investments (SCEL) Ltd
Europlants (UK) Limited
Exlservice (UK) Limited
Ezra Attia Limited
F-Star Alpha Limited
F-Star Delta Limited

Finecare Homes (Stevenage) Ltd
Flo-Mech Holdings Limited
Foremost Currency Group Ltd
Former Reichmann Properties PLC
Fullfield Limited
Fulton Central Limited
Fulton Clover Limited
Fulton Grand Limited
Fulton Hyde Limited
Fulton Lincoln Limited
Fulton Regent Limited
Fulton St James Limited
GDL (Luton) Developments Ltd
GE Money Servicing Limited
GVS Prepaid Limited
Galliard Developments Limited
Garnham Management Services Ltd
Garreg Lwyd Energy Limited
Gerrard International Limited
Gilead Sciences International Ltd.
Girton Town Charity
Gladstone Court Developments Ltd
Global Education Management Systems
Global Group (UK) Ltd
Global Marine Holdings Limited
Grantol Investments Limited
Green Hill Energy Limited
Green Mountain Estates Ltd
Green Space London Limited
Guild of Construction Workers Ltd
HCL Insurance BPO Services Ltd
HCT Portland Limited
Harlequin Direct Limited
Hawk Incentives Holdings Ltd
Hawk Incentives Limited
Hayes Point (Sully) Limited
Henbrandt Limited
Highway Stops Retail Limited
Hill Group Services Limited
Hill of Towie Limited
Hilton Finance (UK) Limited
Hilton Worldwide FS Treasury Ltd
Holdings U.K. No.3 Limited
Holmes Care (Group) Limited
Homepines Investments Limited
Horsforth Holdings Limited
Hudson Almere Limited
Hudson Arnhem Limited
Hudson Brent Limited
Hudson Camden Limited
Hudson Chemical Tankers Ltd
Howard Hunt Mail Limited
I4B Holdings Limited
ISN Europe Limited
ITC Enterprises Limited
Igroup 8 Limited
Ikarus Engineering Limited
Independent Meters Limited
Interiors with Art Limited
International Industrial Metals Ltd
Intertek Inspection Services UK Ltd
Intertek International Limited
Intertek Testing Management Ltd
Intertek Testing Services Holdings Limited.
Intralot Finance UK Limited
Investland Limited
Jobserve Limited
Johnson Care Limited
K.E.M. Property Services Ltd
KDM Timber Limited
KPIT Technologies (UK) Limited
Kelly Comms Limited
Kent Leisure Parks Limited
Keystone 1 Limited
Keystone 2 Limited
Kier Business Services Limited
Kier Finance Limited
Kier Fleet Services Limited
Kier Services Limited
Kristall Real Estate Limited
Kudos Pharmaceuticals Limited
Kymab Group Limited
Lamb-Weston/Meijer UK Limited
Land Group (Suffolk) Limited
Laridge Investments Limited
Leidos Limited
Lifehealth Limited
Local Boy'z Group Holding Ltd
London Luton Airport Group Ltd
London Outpost Limited
Lousin Holdings Limited
Lynton Homes (3) Limited
M G 111 Ltd
MA Securities London Limited
MC Treasury Limited
MLS (Overseas) Limited
MRB Holdings Ltd
MSX International Limited
MacDuffy (Holdings) Limited
Malt U.K. Holdco Limited
Malthurst Retail Limited
Manufacturing Services Investment
Mastercard Prepaid Management Services
Masterson Holdings Limited
McLaren Construction (London) Ltd
McLaren Construction (Midlands & North)
McLaren Construction (South) Ltd
Merck Sharp & Dohme Finance Europe
Merton Acquisitions Limited
Metropolitan Infrastructure Ltd
Metrosold Limited
Mitcham Earthmoving Limited
Moody International (Russia) Ltd
Morley Agricultural Foundation
Mytravel Group Limited
Mytravel North America Limited
N.P.K. Holdings Limited
NIS Receivables No. 2 Limited
NWES Property Services Limited
Navigator Terminals Midco Ltd
Netcall PLC
Netscientific PLC
New Anglia Local Enterprise Partnership
New Landmark Investment Ltd
Newincco 1270 Limited
Newmarston Ltd
Noble Gift Packaging Limited
Norfolk Community Foundation
Norfolk and Waveney Enterprise Services
Northgate Information Solutions Ltd
Northgate UK Holdings 1 Ltd
Northgate UK Holdings 2 Ltd
Northgate UK Holdings 3 Ltd
Northgate UK Holdings 4 Ltd
O-I Sales and Distribution UK Ltd
OAG Aviation Worldwide Limited
Oak Tree Schools Holdings Ltd
Offsite Archive Storage and Integrated
Services (UK)
Olivegate Properties Limited
Omar Group Finance Limited
Omar Group Holdings Limited
Omar Group Investments Limited
Optimum Group Services PLC
Opus Bestpay Limited
Orlight Limited
Osprey Acquisitions Limited
Pant y Wal Investments Limited
Paradigm Development Services Ltd
Parkway Hellas Holdings Ltd
Passportcard Limited
Patek Philippe Salon Limited
Paypoint Collections Limited
Paypoint Network Limited
Paypoint PLC
Paypoint Retail Solutions Ltd
Peli Biothermal Limited
Peterborough Diocesan Board of Finance
Ralph Peters & Sons Limited
Pinnacle Schools (Gateshead) Ltd
Pitney Bowes Global Ltd.
Platinum Acquisition Limited
Platinum Midco 2 Limited
Platinum Midco Limited
Platinum Topco Limited
Providence Marian Company
QED Luton (Challney) Holdings Ltd
QED Luton (Challney) Limited
Quadro Epsom Limited
RA Securities London Limited
RCG-Moody International Ltd
RES UK & Ireland Limited
RL Retail Services Limited
RMPA Services PLC
RMR Capital Limited
RQ Capital Loans Limited
RRD GDS Limited
Rannoch Food Group Limited
Ransome's Dock Limited
Ransome's Trading Limited
Reald Europe Limited
Redsky IT Holdings Limited
Reliance Infra Projects (UK) Ltd
Retreat East Limited
Rex Trade Associates Limited
Rexam Finance Co Ltd
Rexam Finance Germany Limited
Rexam Finance Netherlands Ltd
Rexam Finance Poland Limited
Rexam Finance Sweden Limited
Rexam Property Developments Ltd
Ridgepoint Homes Limited
Rothamsted Enterprises Limited
Roythornes Limited
S A Designer Parfums Limited
SJD Accountancy Limited
SW1 Management Limited
SW1 Trading Limited
Salavera Trading Limited
Santray Limited
Sapphire Food North East No.1 Ltd
Sapphire Food North West No. 3 Ltd
Sapphire Food South East No.4 Ltd
Sapphire Food South West No. 2 Ltd
Sapphire Rural Destination No. 5 Ltd
Saxton Limited
Shamrock Bidco Limited
Shamrock Midco Limited
Shamrock Topco Limited
Shared Services Connected Ltd
Signet Direct Diamond Sourcing Ltd
Signet Group Services Limited
Signet Trading Limited
Signet UK Finance PLC
Sines Parks (S.E.) Limited
Skanska Infrastructure Investment UK

Skanska J.V. Projects Ltd
Solo Cup (UK) Limited
Sopra Steria Holdings Limited
South Central Property Limited
Spen Hill Developments Limited
Spicerhaart Corporate Sales Ltd
Spicerhaart Group Limited
Spirit Managed Funding Limited
Spirit Pub Company (Derwent) Ltd
Spirit Pub Company (Services) Ltd
Spirit Pub Company (Supply) Ltd
Spirit Pub Company (Trent) Ltd
St.Albans Diocesan Board of Finance
Stema Shipping (UK) Limited
Stevenage Bioscience Catalyst
Stonebond Properties Limited
Stonegate Pub Company Financing PLC
Strides Arcolab International Ltd
Suffolk Community Foundation
TCCT Holdings UK Limited
TCGH Holdings Limited
TJX Europe Buying (Deutschland) Ltd
TJX Europe Buying Limited
TTP Group PLC
TUI Group Fleet Finance Ltd
TUI Travel Aviation Finance Ltd
Tabor Group Ltd
Tapesilver Limited
Taylor Wimpey 2007 Limited
Tesco Blue (3LP) Limited
Tesco Blue (GP) Limited
Tesco Food Sourcing Limited
Tesco Fuchsia (3LP) Limited
Tesco Overseas ULC
Tesco Property Holdings (No.2) Ltd
Tesco Property Partner (No.1) Ltd
Tesco Red (3LP) Limited
Thumbzup UK Limited
Tican (Chilled) Limited
Toureen Group Limited
Tower Bridge Homes Care Ltd
Turners Britannia Parks Ltd
Turners Parks Group Limited
Turners Regency Parks Limited
Turpin Distribution Services Ltd
UCL Frognal Limited
UKLS Acquisitions Limited
UNEX Finance Limited
Ubisense Limited
Union Investcorp Limited
VRS Investments Limited
VSL Group Holdings Limited
Vetex Limited
WHTC Ltd
Walsingham Estate Management Ltd
Warrant Investments PLC
Warrant Properties Limited
Washbrook Capital Limited
Welding Institute
Winocap Holding Limited
Woodledge Limited

84110 General public administration activities

NHS Professionals Limited

84120 Regulation of health care, education, cultural and other social services, not incl. social security

Four CS MAT

84130 Regulation of and contribution to more efficient operation of businesses

Signature Flight Support Ltd

84220 Defence activities

Raytheon Systems Limited
Royal Air Force Central Fund

84230 Justice and judicial activities

Kent, Surrey and Sussex Community Rehabilitation Co

84240 Public order and safety activities

Guarding UK Ltd

85100 Pre-primary education [27]

Abbot's Hill Limited
Active Learning Trust Limited
Aldenham Foundation
Atlas Multi Academy Trust
Avanti Schools Trust
Bentley Wood Trust
Berkhamsted Schools Group
Boston Witham Academies Federation
Cambridge Meridian Academies Trust
Claxton Trust
Thomas Deacon Education Trust
Hart Schools Trust Ltd
Heathland Whitefriars Federation
King's School, Ely
North Norfolk Academy Trust
Osborne Co-operative Academy Trust
Perse School
Select Enterprises (Holdings) Ltd
Sen Trust Southend
South East Essex Academy Trust
South Essex Academy Trust
South West Essex Community Education Trust
St Joseph's College Limited
St. Christopher School (Letchworth)
Staploe Education Trust
Town Close House Educational Trust
United Learning Trust

85200 Primary education [108]

Abbot's Hill Limited
Active Education Academy Trust
Active Learning Trust Limited
Aldenham Foundation
Aldwickbury School Trust Ltd
Alpha Schools (Holdings) Ltd
Aspire Academies Trust
Asset Education
Atlas Multi Academy Trust
Autism Anglia
Avanti Schools Trust
Avocet Academy Trust
Bancroft's School
Barnardiston Hall Preparatory School
Beacon Educational Trust Ltd
Beaconsfield Educational Trust Ltd
Bedfordshire Schools Trust Ltd
Beechwood Park School Limited
Bentley Wood Trust
Berkhamsted Schools Group
Berlesduna Academy Trust
Boston Witham Academies Federation
Broadfields Academy Trust
Bushey St James Trust
Cam Academy Trust
Cambridge Meridian Academies Trust
Cambridge Primary Education Trust
Change Schools Partnership
Charles Kalms, Henry Ronson Immanuel College
Chigwell School
Chilford Hundred Education Trust
Claxton Trust
Connected Learning
Thomas Deacon Education Trust
Diamond Learning Partnership Trust
Diocese of Norwich Education and Academies Trust
Drapers' Multi-Academy Trust
Eastern Multi-Academy Trust
Eden Academy
Edmonton Academy Trust
Enrich Learning Trust
Evolution Academy Trust
Excellence in Education Trust
GEMS Schools Limited
Gateway Learning Community
Godstowe Preparatory School Co Ltd
Hampton Academies Trust
Harrow Academies Trust
Hart Schools Trust Ltd
Heathland Whitefriars Federation
Hera Primary Academy Trust
Hindu Education Authority Ltd
Hoddesdon School Trust
Incorporated Bishop's Stortford College Association
Inspiration Trust
Kimbolton School
King's School, Ely
Kingshott School Trust Limited
Langley School (1960) Limited
Learning Pathways Academy
Lee Chapel Multi Academy Trust
Leys and St Faith's Schools Foundation
Manor Lodge School
John Milton Academy Trust
New Hall School Trust
Norfolk Academies
North Norfolk Academy Trust
Orley Farm School Trust
Orwell Multi Academy Trust
Osborne Co-operative Academy Trust
Pear Tree Mead Academy
Perse School
Peterborough Keys Academies Trust
Pipers Corner School
Red Kite Schools Trust
Robus Multi Academy Trust
Scholars' Education Trust
Seckford Foundation
Sen Trust Southend
Shared Learning Trust
Sherfield School Limited
South East Essex Academy Trust
South Essex Academy Trust
South Suffolk Learning Trust
South West Essex Community Education Trust
Spiral Partnership Trust
St Columba's College and Preparatory School
St Edmundsbury and Ipswich Diocesan Multi-Academy Trust
St Joseph's College Limited

St. Aubyn's (Woodford Green) School Trust
St. Christopher School (Letchworth)
St. Margaret's School Bushey
St. Mary's School Cambridge
St.Helen's School Northwood
St.Martins' (Northwood) Preparatory School Trust
Staploe Education Trust
Synergy Multi Academy Trust
Town Close House Educational Trust
Tudor Court Primary Academy Trust
United Church Schools Trust
United Learning Trust
Unity Education Trust
Unity Schools Partnership
Upminster Academies Trust
Wembley Multi Academy Trust
West Herts Community Free School Trust
Wisbech Grammar School
Yare Education Trust

85310 General secondary education [253]

ACES Academies Trust
AES Tring Park School Trust
Abbey College, Ramsey
Abbot's Hill Limited
Active Learning Trust Limited
Aim Academies Trust
Alban Academies Trust
Aldenham Foundation
Alperton Community School
Alpha Trust
Amersham School
Anglian Learning
Anglo European Academy Trust
Aspire Learning Trust (Whittlesey)
Aspire Schools
Atlas Multi Academy Trust
Avanti Schools Trust
Aylesbury Grammar School
Aylesbury High School
Simon Balle Academies Trust
Bancroft's School
Barnardiston Hall Preparatory School
Beacon Multi-Academy Trust Ltd
Beaconsfield High School
Beaconsfield School
Beaumont School
Bedfordshire Schools Trust Ltd
Benfleet Schools Trust
Bentley Wood Trust
Berkhamsted Schools Group
Birchwood High School
Bishop's Hatfield Girls' School
Boston Witham Academies Federation
Bourne Grammar School
Brentwood Academies Trust
Bridge Academy Trust
Bungay High School
Burnt Mill Academy Trust
Bury St Edmunds Academy Trust
Bushey St James Trust
CASP
CATS Canterbury Limited
CATS College London Limited
CEG Administrative Services Ltd
Cam Academy Trust
Cambridge Academic Partnership
Cambridge Arts & Sciences Ltd
Cambridge Centre for Sixth Form Studies
Cambridge Meridian Academies Trust
Cambridgeshire Educational Trust
Canons High School
Casterton College Rutland
Castle View School Academy Trust
Chadwell Heath Academy
Charles Kalms, Henry Ronson Immanuel College
Chauncy School
Chelmer Valley High School
Chelmsford County High School for Girls
Chelmsford Learning Partnership
Chigwell School
Chilford Hundred Education Trust
Chiltern Learning Trust
Chiltern Way Academy Trust
Chrysalis Multi Academy Trust
Clarion Academy Trust
Claxton Trust
Colchester Royal Grammar School
Compass Education Trust Ltd
Cornelius Vermuyden School
Cromwell Community College
Dame Alice Owen's School
Danes Educational Trust
Thomas Deacon Education Trust
Diocese of Norwich Education and Academies Trust
Diss High School
Dr Challoner's Grammar School
Dr Challoner's High School
Drapers' Multi-Academy Trust
East Barnet School
Eastern Multi-Academy Trust
Eastwood Park Academy Trust
Eden Academy
Edmonton Academy Trust
Elstree UTC
Emerson Park Academy
Empower Learning Academy Trust
Enrich Learning Trust
Farlingaye High School
Fitzwimarc School Academy Trust
Flegg Education Academy Trust
Four CS MAT
Joyce Frankland Academy, Newport
Freman College
GEMS Schools Limited
Gateway Learning Community
Generations Multi Academy Trust
Giles Academy
Gippeswyk Community Educational Trust
Girls' Education Co Ltd
Good Shepherd Catholic Trust
Haileybury Academy Trust
Richard Hale School
John Hampden Grammar School
Hampton Academies Trust
Harrodian School Limited
Harrow Academies Trust
Harrow High School
Hart Schools Trust Ltd
Hartismere Family of Schools
Hatch End High School
Haydon School
Heathland Whitefriars Federation
Heathrow Aviation Engineering UTC
Hedingham School and Sixth Form
Henlow Church of England Academy
Herts & Essex Multi Academy Trust
Hertswood Academy
Highcrest Academy
Hindu Education Authority Ltd
Hitchin Girls' School
Hockerill College Academy Trust
Hoddesdon School Trust
Honywood Community Science School
Icknield High School
Incorporated Bishop's Stortford College Association
Insignis Academy Trust
Inspiration Trust
Jewish Community Secondary School Trust
Kesgrave High School
Kimbolton School
King Edmund School
King Edward VI Grammar School, Chelmsford
King's (The Cathedral) School, Peterborough
King's School, Ely
Kings Langley School
Kingsmead School
Knights Templar School
Langley School (1960) Limited
Legra Academy Trust
Leys and St Faith's Schools Foundation
Life Education Trust
Marlborough Science Academy Ltd
Mayflower High School
Meller Educational Trust
Merchant Taylors' School
Mid Norfolk Academy Trust
Thomas Mills High School
John Milton Academy Trust
Monk's Walk School
Morris Education Trust
Mossbourne Federation
Mount Grace School
New Hall School Trust
Norfolk Academies
North Essex Multi-Academy Trust
North London Collegiate School
North Norfolk Academy Trust
Nower Hill High School
ORTU Federation Ltd
Ockendon Academy
Orley Farm School Trust
Osborne Co-operative Academy Trust
Passmores Co-operative Learning Community
Perse School
Peterborough Keys Academies Trust
Pinewood School Academy Trust
Pipers Corner School
Plume School
Presdales School Academy Trust
Preston Manor Academy Trust
Princes Risborough School
Purcell School
Queen Elizabeth's Girls' School (Barnet)
Queen Elizabeth's School Barnet
Queens' School (Bushey)
Queenswood School Limited
Sir William Ramsay School Academy Trust
Rayleigh Schools Trust
Red Kite Schools Trust
Rickmansworth School
Rivers Multi Academy Trust
The Helena Romanes School
Roundwood Park School Academy Trust
Royston Schools Academy Trust
Ruislip High School
SFAET Ltd
Sabres Educational Trust
Saffron Academy Trust
Sapientia Education Trust

Scholars' Education Trust
Seckford Education Trust
Seckford Foundation
Sele School
Sen Trust Southend
Shared Learning Trust
Shenfield High School
Sherfield School Limited
South East Essex Academy Trust
South Lincolnshire Academies Trust
South Suffolk Learning Trust
South West Essex Community Education Trust
Southend East Community Academy Trust
Southend High School for Boys Academy Trust
Southend High School for Girls Academy Trust
Spalding Grammar School
St Albans School
St Andrew's Tutorial Services Ltd
St Bede's Inter Church School
St Columba's College and Preparatory School
St Georges School (Harpenden) Ltd
St Ivo School
St Joseph's College Limited
St Mary's CE Academy, Cheshunt
St Neots Learning Partnership
St. Aubyn's (Woodford Green) School Trust
St. Christopher School (Letchworth)
St. Margaret's School Bushey
St. Mary's School Cambridge
St.Albans High School for Girls
St.Helen's School Northwood
Staploe Education Trust
Stephen Perse Foundation
Stewards Academy Trust
Suffolk Academies Trust
Synergy Multi Academy Trust
Takely Education Trust
Thrive Partnership Academy Trust
Tithe Academy
Transforming Education in Norfolk
United Church Schools Trust
United Learning Trust
Unity Schools Partnership
Ursuline Academy Ilford
Vandyke Upper School
Veritas Educational Trust
Verulam School
Waddesdon Church of England School
Watford Grammar School for Boys
Watford Grammar School for Girls
Waveney Valley Academies Trust
Welding Institute
Wembley Multi Academy Trust
Wensum Trust
West Hatch High School Academy Trust
West Norfolk Academies Trust
Westcliff High School for Boys Ltd
Westfield Academy
William de Ferrers School
Wisbech Grammar School
Wycombe High School Academies Trust
Yare Education Trust
Yavneh College Academy Trust
Zenith Multi Academy Trust

85320 Technical and vocational secondary education [22]

AES Tring Park School Trust
Alperton Community School
Bedfordshire Schools Trust Ltd
Buckinghamshire UTC.
Centre for Engineering and Manufacturing Excellence
EC English London Limited
Elstree UTC
Greater Peterborough UTC
Hart Schools Trust Ltd
Heathrow Aviation Engineering UTC
Langley School (1960) Limited
Marlborough Information Services Ltd
National Film and Television School
Norfolk Academies
Park High School
Science, Engineering and Manufacturing Technologies Alliance
Seetec Business Technology Centre
Stafford House School of English Ltd
Stafford House Study Holidays Ltd
TWI Limited
Transforming Education in Norfolk
Watford UTC

85410 Post-secondary non-tertiary education

Avanti Schools Trust
Cam Academy Trust
North Norfolk Academy Trust
Osborne Co-operative Academy Trust
Veritas Educational Trust

85421 First-degree level higher education

Coventry Foundationcampus Ltd
London School of Theology
Transforming Education in Norfolk
University of Suffolk Ltd

85422 Post-graduate level higher education

Babraham Institute
Federation of European Biochemical Societies
London School of Theology
University of Suffolk Ltd
Wesley House, Cambridge

85510 Sports and recreation education

Cambridge Meridian Academies Trust

85520 Cultural education

Association for Cultural Exchange
Cambridge Union Society

85530 Driving school activities

Institute of Advanced Motorists Ltd

85590 Other education n.e.c. [25]

Anglia Ruskin Enterprise Ltd
The John Apthorp Charity
Autism Anglia
Bell Educational Trust Limited
Brickfields Trust
Castledon School Academy Trust
Countryside Restoration Trust
Gresham's School
Hitchin Boys' School
John Innes Foundation
Institute of Grocery Distribution
Linkage Community Trust
Loxford School Trust Limited
Market Field Learning Community
Marlborough Information Services Ltd
Moller Institute Limited
Oxford Cambridge and RSA Examinations
Rightforsuccess Trust
Seax Trust
Sen Trust Southend
St. Mary's School Cambridge
Stratton Education Trust
Suffolk Agricultural Association
Thurstable School Sports College and Sixth Form Centre
Yare Education Trust

85600 Educational support services

Active Learning Trust Limited
EC English Cambridge Limited
Greenbrook Industries Limited
Harlow Education Trust
NET Academies Trust
Norwood Ravenswood
South East Essex Academy Trust

86101 Hospital activities [15]

Anglian Community Enterprise (ACE) CIC
East Coast Community Healthcare C.I.C.
Elysium Healthcare (St Mary's) Ltd
Elysium Healthcare No. 2 Ltd
Elysium Healthcare Property 2 Ltd
Elysium Healthcare Property 3 Ltd
Hospital Company (Oxford John Radcliffe) Holdings
Hospital Company (Oxford John Radcliffe)
Hospital Company (QAH Portsmouth) Holdings
Hospital Company (QAH Portsmouth)
Metier Holdings Limited
Saint Francis Hospice
St George Healthcare Limited
St. Luke's Hospice (Harrow & Brent) Ltd.
Paul Strickland Scanner Centre

86102 Medical nursing home activities

Hallmark Care Homes (Brighton) Ltd
SRM (Redcar & Cleveland) Ltd
St. Vincent's Charitable Trust
Sunrise UK Holdco Limited
Tanglewood (Lincolnshire) Ltd

86210 General medical practice activities

Anglian Community Enterprise (ACE) CIC
Care UK (Urgent Care) Limited
East Coast Community Healthcare C.I.C.
Inhealth Limited
Lima Orthopaedics UK Limited
One Stop Private Doctors Ltd
Practice Surgeries Limited

86220 Specialists medical practice activities

Bourn Bioscience Limited
Bourn Hall Limited
Elysium Healthcare (Acorn Care) Ltd
Elysium Healthcare (Healthlinc) Ltd
Havens Christian Hospice
North Herts Hospice Care Association
One Stop Private Doctors Ltd

86230 Dental practice activities

Anglian Community Enterprise (ACE) CIC
Davis Schottlander & Davis Ltd
Dentex Healthcare Group Ltd
Mowbray Indigo Limited
Perfect Practices Group Ltd

86900 Other human health activities [42]

Aesthetic Medical Corporation Ltd
Against Malaria Foundation
Alzheimer's Research UK
Anglian Community Enterprise (ACE) CIC
Bio Products Laboratory Holdings Ltd
Care UK Clinical Services Ltd
Care UK Health & Rehabilitation Services
Care UK Healthcare Holdings Ltd
Caretech Community Services (No.2)
Caretech Community Services Ltd
Chai-Lifeline Cancer Care
Cloud Topco Limited
Colchester Catalyst Charity
Cygnet Care Limited
Cytocell Limited
East Anglia's Childrens Hospices
East Anglian Air Ambulance
East Coast Community Healthcare C.I.C.
Elysium Healthcare (Farndon) Ltd
Elysium Healthcare (Ultimate Care)
Elysium Healthcare No. 3 Ltd
Elysium Healthcare No. 4 Ltd
Essex & Herts Air Ambulance Trust
Falck UK Limited
Farleigh Hospice
GW Pharmaceuticals PLC
Gracewell Healthcare Limited
Holmes Care Limited
Keech Hospice Care
Kidney Research UK
Medtronic Limited
Naga UK Bidco Limited
Naga UK Topco Limited
Paddocks Care Home Ltd
Provide CIC
Sue Ryder
Selborne Care Limited
St. Elizabeth Hospice (Suffolk)
St. Helena Hospice Limited
Team Consulting Limited
Thames Valley Air Ambulance
Thoratec Europe Limited

87100 Residential nursing care facilities [33]

A.G.E. Nursing Homes Limited
AMS Care Limited
Abbey Ravenscroft Park Limited
Angel Care (Orchid Care Homes) Ltd
Angel Care PLC
Askham Village Community Ltd
Caring Homes Healthcare Group Ltd
Clavering Care Limited
Colleycare Limited
Consensus Holdco Limited
Cooperscroft Care Home Limited
Country Court Care Homes 2 Ltd
Country Court Care Homes Ltd
County Care Homes Limited
Edwardian Care Homes Limited
Farrington Care Homes Limited
Fremantle Trust
Greenswan Consultants Limited
Healthcare Homes Group Limited
Hospice of St. Francis (Berkhamsted)
Loughton Care Centre Limited
MHL Holdco Limited
MNS Care PLC
Martlane Limited
Myriad Healthcare Holdings Ltd
PQW Brenley Corner Limited
Planshore Limited
RANC Care Homes Limited
RANC Holdings Limited
Rockley Dene Homes Limited
St. Nicholas Hospice (Suffolk)
TLC Group Limited
Wilton House Limited

87200 Residential care activities for learning difficulties, mental health and substance abuse

Norwood Ravenswood
Norwood Schools Ltd.

87300 Residential care activities for the elderly and disabled [35]

ADR Care Homes Limited
AMS Care Wiltshire Limited
Abbey Ravenscroft Park Limited
Abbeyfield Society
Althea Healthcare (Holdings) Ltd
Black Swan International Ltd
Broadham Care Limited
Brownlow Enterprises Limited
Care UK Community Partnerships Ltd
Careprogress Limited
Consensus Support Services Ltd
Country Court Care Homes 2 Ltd
Country Court Care Homes Ltd
Country Retirement & Nursing Homes Ltd
Denville Hall 2012
Essex County Care Limited
Fremantle Trust
H. W. Group Ltd.
Hallmark Care Homes (Brighton) Ltd
KCH (UK) Holdings Limited
Kingsley Care Homes Limited
Martlane Limited
Norse Care Limited
Partnership in Care Limited
Planshore Limited
Point Pedro Property Holdings Ltd
Pride Care Homes Peterborough Ltd
Regal Healthcare Holdings Ltd
Regal Healthcare Properties Ltd
Runwood Homes Limited
Sahara Care Limited
Scimitar Care Hotels PLC
Seymour House Residential Care Homes
Sonnet Care Homes (Essex) Ltd
TLC Care Homes Limited

87900 Other residential care activities n.e.c. [10]

Action for Children Services Ltd
Autism Anglia
Care Providers Recruitment Ltd
Caretech Community Services (No.2)
Caretech Community Services Ltd
Holdcare Limited
Linkage Community Trust
London Care Partnership Ltd
Nellsar Limited
Seckford Foundation

88100 Social work activities without accommodation for the elderly and disabled

Autism Anglia
Fremantle Trust
Hearing Dogs for Deaf People
Heritage Care Limited
Papworth Trust

88910 Child day-care activities

Action for Children
Action for Children Services Ltd
Norwood Schools Ltd.

88990 Other social work activities without accommodation n.e.c. [12]

Barnardo's
Country Court Care Homes Ltd
Essex Cares Limited
Essex Community Foundation
Injured Jockeys Fund
Norwood Ravenswood
Norwood Schools Ltd.
Paradigm Commercial PLC
Racing Welfare
Saint Francis Hospice
St. Luke's Hospice (Harrow & Brent) Ltd.
St. Nicholas Hospice (Suffolk)

90010 Performing arts

Snape Maltings

90030 Artistic creation

Fifty Shades Ltd
Gilmore Jacobs Limited
Snape Maltings
Theatre Royal (Norwich) Trust Ltd
Richard Wright Music Limited

90040 Operation of arts facilities

Gainsborough's House Society
Latif International Limited
Marchanson Limited
Snape Maltings

91011 Library activities

Fitzwilliam Information Services Trust

91012 Archives activities

Britten-Pears Foundation
Harris (Belmont) Charity
Hill Co Ltd
Henry Moore Foundation

91020 Museums activities

Gainsborough's House Society
Harris (Belmont) Charity
Henry Moore Foundation

91030 Operation of historical sites and buildings and similar visitor attractions

Britten-Pears Foundation
Burghley House Preservation Trust
Grimsthorpe & Drummond Castle Trust
Harris (Belmont) Charity
Henry Moore Foundation
Thursford Collection

91040 Botanical and zoological gardens and nature reserves activities

Colchester Zoo Limited
William Robinson Gravetye Charity
Suffolk Wildlife Trust Limited

92000 Gambling and betting activities [10]

Bellcoin Holdings Limited
Betting Shop Services Limited
Camelot Business Solutions Ltd
Camelot Global Lottery Solutions Ltd
Camelot UK Lotteries Limited
Majestic Bingo Limited
Palatial Leisure Limited
Spreadex Limited
Spreadex.Com Limited
Ticketgrange Limited

93110 Operation of sports facilities [18]

1LIFE Management Solutions Ltd
Double A Group Services Ltd
Golf Entertainment International Ltd
Harlow and District Sports Trust
Highfield Park Trust
Ipswich Town Finance Co Ltd
Ipswich Town Football Club Co Ltd
Ipswich Town Stadium Co Ltd
Jockey Club Estates Limited
David Lloyd Clubs Holdings Ltd
David Lloyd Clubs Limited
National Football Centre Ltd
Purslow Investments Limited
Snowcentres Limited
St. Margaret's School Bushey
Stoke By Nayland Club Ltd.
Topgolf Limited
Wembley National Stadium Ltd

93120 Activities of sport clubs

Harbour Club Limited
David Lloyd Leisure Limited
Next Generation Clubs Limited
Norwich City Football Club PLC
Purslow Investments Limited
Redbridge Sports Centre Trust Ltd
Salperton Park Estate Limited

93130 Fitness facilities

1LIFE Management Solutions Ltd
Harlow and District Sports Trust
National Football Centre Ltd

93191 Activities of racehorse owners

Al Asayl Bloodstock Ltd
Qatar Racing Limited
Rabbah Bloodstock Limited

93199 Other sports activities [14]

Arena Event Services Group Ltd
Bowlplex Limited
Double A Group Services Ltd
Football Association Limited
Harlow and District Sports Trust
Harrod UK Limited
Hollywood Bowl Group PLC
Hy-Pro International Limited
Kendallco Limited
Matchroom Sport Limited
National Football Centre Ltd
Original Bowling Co Ltd
Professional Darts Corporation Ltd
Watford Association Football Club

93210 Activities of amusement parks and theme parks

Blue Anchor Leisure Limited
Stockvale Limited

93290 Other amusement and recreation activities n.e.c. [19]

1LIFE Management Solutions Ltd
Adventure Forest Group Limited
Adventure Forest Limited
Bowlplex Limited
Coaching Inn Group Ltd
Ellis Bros (Contractors) Ltd
Family Amusements Limited
Forum Trust Limited
Fraser Capital Management Ltd
Harlow and District Sports Trust
Highfield Park Trust
Hollywood Bowl Group PLC
Intertain Limited
Nene Park Trust
Plaza Investments Limited
Richardsons Leisure Limited
Shenley Park Trust
Teen Spirit Limited
Trafalgar Leisure Ltd

94110 Activities of business and employers membership organisations

National Pharmacy Association Ltd
Norfolk Community Foundation

94120 Activities of professional membership organisations

International Fertilizer Association
Welding Institute

94910 Activities of religious organisations [19]

BW Foundation
Chelmsford Diocesan Board of Finance
Church of God in Christ (Calvary)
Church of Pentecost - UK
Ely Diocesan Board of Finance
Erinastar Limited
Farmland Reserve UK Limited
International Society for Krishna Consciousness
Kingsgate Community Church
Norwich Diocesan Board of Finance
Redeemed Christian Church of God
Sparquote Limited
Spiritualists' National Union
St.Albans Diocesan Board of Finance
St.Edmundsbury and Ipswich Diocesan Board of Finance
Union of Evangelical Churches
United Reformed Church (Eastern Province) Trust
Walsingham College Trust Association
YMCA Trinity Group

94990 Activities of other membership organisations n.e.c. [13]

Birdlife International
British Limbless Ex-Service Men's Association
Cambridge Union Society
Dispute Service Limited
East of England Agricultural Society
Fauna & Flora International
Institute of Advanced Motorists Ltd
Newstraid Benevolent Fund
Union of UEA Students Limited
Water Incorporated
Wensum Valley Hotel Golf & Country Club
Wildlife Trust for Bedfordshire, Cambridgeshire and Northamptonshire
Wood Green Animal Shelters

95110 Repair of computers and peripheral equipment

Computacenter (UK) Limited
Getech Limited

96010 Washing and (dry-)cleaning of textile and fur products

Eastern Counties Laundries Ltd
Fresh Linen Limited
Micronclean Limited

96030 Funeral and related activities

FPS 1995 Limited
Memorial Gardens Limited

96090 Other service activities n.e.c. [88]

ABM Technical Solutions Ltd
Acclaim DMW Holdings Limited
Anduff Car Wash Limited
Anritsu EMEA Limited
Arjo UK Limited
Aviva Central Services UK Ltd
B/E Aerospace (UK) Limited
BP INV2 Holdco Ltd
BP INV2 Pledgeco Ltd
BW Foundation
Ball Beverage Packaging Europe Ltd
Bellman Property Group Limited
Blancco Technology Group PLC
Book Trade Charity (BTBS)
T F Bowman & Son Limited
Butchers and Drovers Charitable Institution
Buyanovsky Property Management Ltd
Care UK Clinical Services Ltd
Care UK Healthcare Holdings Ltd
Castle Point Gas & Heating Co. Ltd
Chart Forte Holdings Ltd
Childwick Trust
Community Health Services Ltd
Construct Holdings Limited
Dupont (UK) Electronic Materials Ltd
Edwardian Care Homes Limited
Evangelical Lutheran Church of England Trust
Falck EMS UK Limited
Fineraid Limited
First Choice Holidays Limited
Flightsafety International U.K. Ltd
Focus Tankers Limited
Foregain Limited
Frisco (U.K.) Sales Limited
Futuresource Holdings Limited
GE Medical Systems Limited
Gago Invest Limited
Gamit Limited
Garrets Bidco Limited
Harlow Health Centres Trust Ltd
Hemel Snowcentre Limited
Hildon House Limited
John Huntingdon's Charity
IFCO Systems UK Ltd
Inpra UK Limited
L.H.D.Limited
Laxkan Holdings Ltd
Laxkan Ltd
David Lloyd Leisure GR Ltd
Lotus Group International Ltd
M L Accessories Limited
MLM Consulting Engineers Ltd
Maison Moti Limited
Marz Limited
McNicholas Construction Services Ltd
Milton Hall Cambridge Limited
Morrison Data Services (Water) Ltd
Mountcharm Limited
MoveWithUs Conveyancing Ltd
NEC Capital (UK) PLC
Norfolk Environmental Waste Services
Norfolk Wildlife Trust
Norse Group Limited
Onslow Inc. Ltd
Openview Security Solutions Ltd
David Phillip (Investments) Ltd
Pitchset Limited
Produce Connection Limited
Purebond Limited
R.B. Securities Limited
RSA Island Village Limited
Rammamere House Limited
Rican Securities Limited
Robsons of Spalding Limited
Sansbury Bailey Holdings Ltd
Smiths Industries Industrial Group
Solai Holdings Limited
TM Group Holdings Limited
TUI Ireland Limited
TUI UK Transport Limited
Tesco Freetime Limited
Tesco International Services Ltd
Tesco Maintenance Limited
Tetra Pak Processing UK Ltd
Ventus Investments Limited
Vision (Office Automation) Ltd
Westleigh Properties Limited
Ziji Productions Limited

97000 Activities of households as employers of domestic personnel

Burghley House Preservation Trust

98000 Residents property management

Chelmer Housing Partnership Ltd
City & Country Residential Ltd
Close Homes Limited
Mirrorstoke Limited
Sherrygreen Limited
Webb Investments Ltd.

99000 Activities of extraterritorial organisations and bodies

Camfed International
Rothschild Foundation

99999 Dormant company [18]

Anglo-Dutch Property (UK) Holding
Archant Holdings Limited
Blackwater Partners Limited
Bowlplex Limited
Burton's Foods (Holdings) Ltd
CATMJ Limited
Carter Accommodation Group Ltd
Dominion Hospitality Midco Ltd
Dominion Hospitality Topco Ltd
Ellgia Holdings Limited
Ethypharm Holdings UK Ltd
Eurobase International Limited
Gapsun Properties Limited
Gray's Inn Capital Limited
Hull Holdings Limited
MVM Holdings Limited
R. Maskell (Holdings) Limited
Orwell Trucks Limited

This page is intentionally left blank

Printed in 8pt Nimbus Sans L

Designed by URW++ Design and Development GmbH

Dellam Publishing Limited

2 Heath Drive, Sutton, Surrey, SM2 5RP

Fax: 020 8770 7478 email: enquiries@dellam.com

SAN: 0177881 EAN/GLN: 5030670177882

www.ingramcontent.com/pod-product-compliance
Lightning Source LLC
LaVergne TN
LVHW082005200926
848481LV00010B/2809